MW00856833

"Gary Schnittjer has provided interpreters and students of Scripture with an extensively researched, ground-breaking study that will enhance our understanding of the relationship between texts within the Old Testament. In a volume that offers both breadth and depth of coverage, the author carefully outlines and defends his method before marching book-by-book through the Old Testament and identifying literary links and their significance. This monumental work is well-suited as a text for courses in hermeneutics and biblical theology."

Robert B. Chisholm Jr., Chair and Senior Professor,
Old Testament Studies, Dallas Theological Seminary

"One of the most fascinating features of the Old Testament is how the various books of the Old Testament allude to and interpret other books. In *Old Testament Use of Old Testament* Gary Schnittjer provides an insightful and detailed guide to how this phenomenon furthers progressive revelation and the coherence of Scripture. From now on Schnittjer's book will be the starting point for all future study on this important topic. I enthusiastically recommend that all serious students of Scripture have this significant reference book in their library."

Tremper Longman III, Distinguished Scholar and Professor
Emeritus of Biblical Studies, Westmont College

"In *Old Testament Use of Old Testament* Gary Schnittjer has made a major contribution to the study of how the Bible uses the Bible, and this massive tome will, no doubt, quickly become one of the most important works in this field. Everyone writing or teaching in this area of biblical studies will need to consult with and interact with this book. Kudos to Schnittjer for giving us such a helpful tool and for significantly advancing the scholarship in this field of study."

J. Daniel Hays, Professor of Biblical Studies, Ouachita Baptist University

"Though the New Testament's use of the Old Testament is a well-established field of study, the Old Testament's use of itself has been less well served. That gap is handsomely filled here in a work that is thorough and accessible. Gary Schnittjer has produced an important work that opens up this important field of study and which should be a standard point of reference for years to come."

David G. Firth, Lecturer in Old Testament and Academic Dean,
Trinity College Bristol

"This monumental project offers a unique and much-needed resource for students of Scripture. Schnittjer's work is methodologically rigorous and easy to navigate, including a glossary as well as illuminating diagrams to depict prominent networks of exegetical allusions. His focus on exegetical use of Scripture in the Old Testament advances the conversation about both the New Testament and Old Testament use of the Old Testament. I expect it will be an indispensable tool for years to come."

Carmen Joy Imes, Associate Professor of Old Testament, Prairie College

"As an Old Testament professor with a strong preference for exegesis as the starting point for biblical theology, I heartily welcome this combination of hermeneutical introduction to and book-by-book survey of scriptural exegesis within Israel's Scriptures. Schnittjer has done an encyclopedic job in defining and describing where and how such exegesis takes place and why it should be considered a vehicle of God's progressive revelation and a display of the human authors' canonical consciousness. Though it everywhere investigates verbal parallels on the basis of the Hebrew text, it is nonetheless designed for English Bible readers. For that reason, as the co-planter and lead elder of Copenhagener Evangelical Lutheran Church, I consider Schnittjer's survey an important companion for our pastors, preachers, and teachers, since it facilitates a fuller understanding—and preaching—of the gospel. Furthermore, readers with a visual learning style will greatly benefit from the many graphic presentations of the findings. My best recommendations!"

Jens Bruun Kofoed, Professor of Old Testament,
Fjellhaug International University College, Oslo and Copenhagen

"The advances of recent decades in reading the Old Testament in the New are finally matched by this substantial study of the Old Testament's use of its own texts. Schnittjer offers a fascinating exploration of the ways Old Testament books read and interpret each other. With this book, students of Scripture will learn to hear and make sense of the delightfully rich conversations occurring within the Old Testament that also extend into the New. Students, pastors, and teachers will find themselves reaching often for Schnittjer's book."

Matthew Lynch, Assistant Professor of Old Testament, Regent College

"Gary Schnittjer is to be commended for his colossal labors on this extraordinarily useful reference work, which unveils the coherence and beauty of Scripture's organic growth through inspired exegesis. *Old Testament Use of Old Testament* fills a long-standing need for such a foundational work, incorporating a balanced approach to all aspects of scriptural exegesis of Scripture, including judicious evaluations on detecting purposeful allusions and in determining direction of dependence. Accomplishing much of the spade work necessary for studying the use of Scripture in every book of the Hebrew canon, *Old Testament Use of Old Testament* is highly recommended for all exegetes—for pastors, scholars, and students—and will surely become a standard reference tool for Bible study. Biblical and theological libraries will be incomplete without this excellent resource!"

L. Michael Morales, Professor of Biblical Studies,
Greenville Presbyterian Theological Seminary

"Schnittjer's book is a welcome resource in biblical studies. Students and pastors alike will benefit from Gary's careful guidance, helpful analysis, and invitation to evaluate for themselves how the text we love interprets itself. His introduction alone is a 'must read' for any student and pastor thinking about connections between biblical texts, and it also provides an indispensable roadmap for navigating the wealth of information that follows. This is a reference book I will return to again and again."

Wendy L. Widder, Author of *Daniel*, Story of God Bible Commentary

"In this encyclopedic volume, Gary Schnittjer comprehensively summarizes in a book-by-book manner how the authors of the Hebrew Bible exegete Scripture, thereby carrying forward the progressive revelation of God. While the use of the Old Testament by the New is a well-trodden field in biblical studies, this inductive overview of the Old Testament use of the Old is unique and innovative, a helpful guidebook that should be kept within arm's reach of every exegete of Scripture."

Mark L. Strauss, University Professor of New Testament,
Bethel Seminary

"An important aspect of understanding how the Bible fits together is studying how the biblical authors use previous Scripture. While this normally takes the form of studying the New Testament authors' use of the Old Testament, the way that the Old Testament authors use Scripture has often been neglected. No longer! Gary Schnittjer has produced what is now the definitive resource on the subject. Not only does he work book by book through the Old Testament studying key examples, he provides valuable synthesis that demonstrates how the New Testament authors followed their Old Testament predecessors in the ways they use Scripture. This book is a must-have resource for students, pastors, professors, and all who want a deeper grasp of God's Word. I cannot recommend it highly enough!"

Matthew S. Harmon, Professor of New Testament Studies,
Grace College and Theological Seminary

"Schnittjer has offered both Old Testament and New Testament students a guide for reading the Hebrew Bible that includes exegesis, thematic structural and literary features, hermeneutical considerations, revelation and fulfillment, and analysis of every part of the Old Testament. Virtually nothing is overlooked in his approach. The church has awaited a resource that would provide a method of discerning true Old Testament interconnections and echoes from alleged ones not meeting textual criteria for a faithful allusion. Old Testament and New Testament scholars for the church will find this work to be invaluable. There are a great many surprising connections between texts displayed in this volume! I will reach for it on every occasion that I study a passage in the Old Testament."

Eric C. Redmond, Professor of Bible, Moody Bible Institute

"It is exceedingly rare to come across a new volume destined to become a standard research text for pastors, professors, and students of the Bible for a generation to come. This is one such book. It is meticulously researched, carefully presented, and immediately accessible to those who care to use it. I find it hard to come up with appropriate superlatives to describe it, but I can say without hesitation that this is the book I've been waiting for as I seek to understand and to proclaim the Old Testament Scriptures to God's people."

Jonathan L. Master, President, Greenville Presbyterian Theological Seminary

"In biblical studies, the field of intertextuality or inner-biblical interpretation is a confusing maze of competing definitions, methodologies, and inner-canonical connections, especially when it comes to the Old Testament use of the Old Testament! Gary Schnittjer has provided students and scholars of the Hebrew Scriptures with a masterful book-by-book guide through the maze. Encyclopedic in its scope and depth, Schnittjer's contribution to this burgeoning field in biblical studies will serve the church and academy for decades to come. This book will become a set text in my classes."

Jonathan Gibson, Associate Professor of Old Testament,
Westminster Theological Seminary, Philadelphia

"Unparalleled in its scope and culminating decades of biblical-theological inquiry, this remarkably thorough study evaluates leading examples of biblical exegesis of Scripture case by case and book by book through the entire Old Testament. Schnittjer approaches the Hebrew Scriptures as God's revelation and considers the interpretive significance and potential direction of dependence of hundreds of intentional, verifiable parallels within Jesus's only Bible. This exceptional reference tool uses the Old Testament's natural interconnectivity to aid Christian biblical interpretation for students and ministers alike."

Jason S. DeRouchie, Research Professor of Old Testament and
Biblical Theology, Midwestern Baptist Theological Seminary

"Professor Gary Schnittjer's *Old Testament Use of Old Testament* is an outstanding tool. Those who have worked with inner-biblical exegesis and intertextuality have dreamed of a work such as this. It is thorough, insightful, and beautifully arranged. This book is important not only for exegesis but for an appreciation of the development of biblical theology. Highly recommended."

Craig A. Evans, John Bisagno Distinguished Professor of
Christian Origins, Houston Baptist University

OLD TESTAMENT USE *of* OLD TESTAMENT

A Book-by-Book Guide

GARY EDWARD SCHNITTJER

ZONDERVAN ACADEMIC

Old Testament Use of Old Testament

Requests for information should be addressed to:
Zondervan, *3900 Sparks Dr. SE, Grand Rapids, Michigan 49546*

Zondervan titles may be purchased in bulk for educational, business, fundraising, or sales promotional use.
For information, please email SpecialMarkets@Zondervan.com.

ISBN 978-0-310-57110-0 (hardcover)

ISBN 978-0-310-57112-4 (ebook)

Cover Design: Darren Welch Design
Interior Design: Kait Lamphere

Printed in the United States of America

21 22 23 24 25 26 27 28 29 30 31 32 33 34 /TRM/ 18 17 16 15 14 13 12 11 10 9 8 7 6 5 4 3 2 1

To

Nick

קרוב יהוה לכל קראיו

Jess

שומר יהוה את כל אהביו

CONTENTS

Symbols and Abbreviations ... xi
Introduction ... xvii
Bibliographic Note on Lists of Potential Parallels ... xlvii
A Note to Professors ... li

1. Genesis ... 1
2. Exodus ... 14
3. Leviticus ... 37
4. Numbers ... 56
5. Deuteronomy ... 74
6. Joshua ... 154
7. Judges ... 165
8. Samuel ... 175
9. Kings ... 186
10. Isaiah ... 213
11. Jeremiah ... 259
12. Ezekiel ... 312
13. Hosea ... 358
14. Joel ... 373
15. Amos ... 385
16. Obadiah ... 398
17. Jonah ... 403
18. Micah ... 409
19. Nahum ... 420
20. Habakkuk ... 426
21. Zephaniah ... 433
22. Haggai ... 437
23. Zechariah ... 443
24. Malachi ... 460
25. Psalms ... 471
26. Job ... 550
27. Proverbs ... 556
28. Ruth ... 578
29. Song of Songs ... 591
30. Ecclesiastes ... 595
31. Lamentations ... 604
32. Esther ... 613
33. Daniel ... 617
34. Ezra-Nehemiah ... 630
35. Chronicles ... 693
36. Toward the New Testament ... 847
37. Networks ... 873

Scripture Index of Networks ... 885
Glossary ... 889
Bibliography ... 905
Acknowledgments ... 937
Index of Tables, Figures, Maps ... 941
Scripture and Ancient Literature Index ... 943
Subject Index ... 1019
Author Index ... 1047

SYMBOLS AND ABBREVIATIONS

//	Parallel texts with verbal parallel of at least three Hebrew roots plus other factors that together signal A-level confidence of relationship of some sort unless stated otherwise (see A below)
/~/	Synoptic parallel of contexts signaling A-level confidence of relationship of some sort unless stated otherwise (see A below)
~	Similar. Appears with B, C, or D to signal relative level of confidence of potential relationship (see A below)
+	Interpretive blend by which receptor context interprets one donor scriptural tradition in the light of another
>/<	More or less similar but normally filtered out because similarity fails to meet criteria of interpretive use of Scripture (see explanation of Filters in Introduction)
*	Marks passages that appear in Networks near end of volume
†	NIV has been mildly modified to reflect verbal parallel in the original language (see Introduction)
[ ]	Enclose Hebrew verse references when different from English
{ }	Enclose Scripture references out of sequence
=, –, - - -	Used in Networks near end of volume with double line referring to A-level intentional relationships, single line B-level, and broken line C-level confidence of an intentional interpretive relationship (see A below)
A	High confidence of intentional interpretive relationship—whether direct or indirect—with verbal parallel of at least three shared Hebrew roots in nouns, verbs, or other substantial terms plus other syntactic and contextual indicators. Pronouns, pronominal suffixes, prepositions, and other common grammatical and syntactical particles are not counted as parallel terms even though they may contribute to syntactical and/or contextual relations. The following scale relates to the preceding criteria along with subjective judgment: A, highly likely; B, probably, including at least one shared Hebrew root and other criteria; C, possibly, usually with one or more shared Hebrew roots and other criteria; D, probably not, even with shared Hebrew roots and other criteria. Filters exclude non-exegetical similarities. Unless noted explicitly, direction of dependence is not presupposed for any level. See Introduction for further explanation.
AB	Anchor Bible

ABD *Anchor Bible Dictionary*. Edited by David Noel Freedman. 6 vols. New York: Doubleday, 1992

ANEP *The Ancient Near East in Pictures Relating to the Old Testament*. Edited by James B. Pritchard. 2nd ed. Princeton: Princeton University Press, 1969

ANET *Ancient Near Eastern Texts Relating to the Old Testament*. Edited by James B. Pritchard. 3rd ed. Princeton: Princeton University Press, 1969

ARAB *Ancient Records of Assyria and Babylonia*. Daniel David Luckenbill. 2 vols. Chicago: University of Chicago Press, 1926–1927. Repr., London: Histories & Mysteries of Man, 1989

ArBib *The Aramaic Bible*

ARI *Assyrian Royal Inscriptions*. Albert Kirk Grayson. 2 vols. Weisbaden: Harrasowitz, 1972–1976

AYB Anchor Yale Bible

AYBRL Anchor Yale Bible Reference Library

B Probably (see A above)

b. Babylonian Talmud

BabL *The Babylonian Laws*. G. R. Driver and John C. Miles. 2 vols. Oxford: Clarendon, 1952, 1955

BBR *Bulletin for Biblical Research*

BCOTWP Baker Commentary on the Old Testament Wisdom and Psalms

BDAG Danker, Frederick W., Walter Bauer, William Arndt, and F. Wilbur Gingrich. *Greek-English Lexicon of the New Testament and Other Early Christian Literature*. 3rd ed. Chicago: University of Chicago Press, 2000

BDB Brown, Francis S., S. R. Driver, and Charles A. Briggs. *A Hebrew and English Lexicon of the Old Testament*

BH Biblical Hebrew

BHHB Baylor Handbook on the Hebrew Bible

BHK *Biblia Hebraica*. Edited by R. Kittel. Stuttgart: Bibelanstalt, 1951

BHQ *Biblia Hebraica Quinta*. Edited by Adrian Schenker et al. Stuttgart: Deutsche Bibelgesellschaft, 2004–; *Genesis*. Edited by Abraham Tal, 2015; *Deuteronomy*. Edited by Carmel McCarthy, 2007; *Judges*. Edited by Natalio Fernández Marcos, 2012; *Minor Prophets*. Edited by Anthony Gelston, 2010; *Proverbs*. Edited by Jan de Waard, 2008; *General Introduction and Megilloth*. Edited by Jan de Waard, et al., 2004; *Ezra and Nehemiah*. Edited by David Marcus, 2006

BHS *Biblia Hebraica Stuttgartensia*. Edited by Karl Elliger, Wilhelm Rudolph, et al. 5th ed. Stuttgart: Deutsche Bibelgesellschaft, 1997

BibInt *Biblical Interpretation*

Bibl. Aram. Biblical Aramaic

BSac *Bibliotheca Sacra*

BQS *The Biblical Qumran Scrolls*. Eugene Ulrich. 3 vols. Leiden/Boston: Brill, 2012

BZAR *Beihefte zur Zeitschrift für Altorientalische und Biblische Rechtsgeschichte*

BZAW *Beihefte zur Zeitschrift für die alttestamentliche Wissenschaft*

C Possibly (see A above)

CBQ *Catholic Biblical Quarterly*

CBSC Cambridge Bible for Schools and Colleges

CD Cairo Genizah copy of the Damascus Document (collated with 4Q266–4Q270 in *DSSSE* 1:550–627)

CDCH *The Concise Dictionary of Classical Hebrew*. Edited by David J. A. Clines. Sheffield: Sheffield Phoenix, 2009

CH Law Collection of Hammurabi (ca. 1750 BCE) in Roth, *Law Collections*

CLLBH *A Concise Lexicon of Late Biblical Hebrew: Linguistic Innovations in the Writings of the Second Temple Period*. Edited by Avi Hurvitz, et al. Leiden: Brill, 2014

COS *The Context of Scripture*. Edited by William W. Hallo. 3 vols. Leiden: Brill, 2003. Vol. 1, *Canonical Compositions from the Biblical World*; Vol. 2, *Monumental Inscriptions from the Biblical World*; Vol. 3, *Archival Documents from the Biblical World*

CTR *Criswell Theological Review*

CurBR *Currents of Biblical Research*

D Probably not (see A above)

DCHR *Dictionary of Classical Hebrew Revised*. Edited by David J. A. Clines. Sheffield: Sheffield Phoenix Press, 2018–

DM Daʿat Mikra [Hebrew]

DNTUOT *Dictionary of the New Testament Use of the Old Testament*. Edited by G. K. Beale, D. A. Carson, Benjamin D. Gladd, and Andrew D. Naselli. Grand Rapids: Baker Academic, forthcoming

DSSSE *The Dead Sea Scrolls Study Edition*. Edited by Florentino García Martínez and Eibert J. C. Tigchelaar. 2 vols. Leiden: Brill; Grand Rapids: Eerdmans, 1997, 1998

EBC *Expositors Bible Commentary*. Edited by Tremper Longman III and David E. Garland. Rev. ed. Grand Rapids: Zondervan, 2010–2012

EJ *Encyclopedia Judaica*. Edited by F. Skolnik. 22 vols. 2nd ed. Farmington Hills, MI: Thomson Gale, 2007

ESV English Standard Version

ETL *Ephemerides Theologicae Lovanienses*

Even-Shoshan Even-Shoshan, Abraham, ed. *A New Concordance of the Bible*. Jerusalem: Kiryath Sepher, 1990 [Hebrew]

FAT Forschungen zum Alten Testament

GBHS *A Guide to Biblical Hebrew Syntax*. Bill T. Arnold and John H. Choi. Cambridge: Cambridge University Press, 2003

GKC *Gesenius' Hebrew Grammar*. Edited by Emil Kautzsch. Translated by Arthur E. Cowley. 2nd ed. Oxford: Clarendon, 1910

HALOT *The Hebrew and Aramaic Lexicon of the Old Testament*. Ludwig Koehler, Walter Baumgartner, and Johann J. Stamm. 2 vols. Leiden: Brill, 2001

HAR *Hebrew Annual Review*
HBAI *Hebrew Bible and Ancient Israel*
HL Hittite Laws (ca. 1500 BCE) in Roth, *Law Collections*
HSM Harvard Semitic Monographs
HT Hebrew Text
HTR *Harvard Theological Review*
HUCA *Hebrew Union College Annual*
IBC Interpretation: A Bible Commentary for Preaching and Teaching
IBHS *An Introduction to Biblical Hebrew Syntax*. Bruce K. Waltke and Michael O'Connor. Winona Lake, IN: Eisenbrauns, 1990
ICC International Critical Commentary
IDB *The Interpreter's Dictionary of the Bible*. Edited by George A. Buttrick. 4 vols. New York: Abingdon, 1962
IDBSup *Interpreter's Dictionary of the Bible: Supplementary Volume*. Edited by Keith Crim. Nashville: Abingdon, 1976
ISBE *International Standard Bible Encyclopedia*. Edited by Geoffrey W. Bromiley. 4 vols. Grand Rapid: Eerdmans, 1979–1989
JAJ *Journal of Ancient Judaism*
JAOS *Journal of the American Oriental Society*
JBL *Journal of Biblical Literature*
JBTS *Journal of Biblical and Theological Studies*
JETS *Journal of the Evangelical Theological Society*
JHebS *Journal of Hebrew Scriptures*
JNES *Journal of Near Eastern Studies*
Joüon Joüon, Paul. *A Grammar of Biblical Hebrew*. Translated and revised by T. Muraoka. 2nd ed. with corrections. Rome: Pontifical Biblical Institute, 2011
JPSB Jewish Publication Society Bible
JPSC Jewish Publication Society Bible Commentary
JPSTC Jewish Publication Society Torah Commentary
JSNTSup Journal for the Study of the New Testament Supplement Series
JSOT *Journal for the Study of the Old Testament*
JSOTSup Journal for the Study of the Old Testament Supplement Series
JSS *Journal of Semitic Studies*
JTS *Journal of Theological Studies*
ketiv "That which is written" in the Masoretic Text itself versus *qere*/"that which is read" aloud in the synagogue and written in the side margin (masorah parva)
KJV King James Version
LBH Late Biblical Hebrew (syntax and grammar of Esther, Daniel, Ezra-Nehemiah, and Chronicles)
LCL Loeb Classical Library

LE	Laws of Eshnunna (ca. 1770 BCE) in Roth, *Law Collections*
LEH	Lust, Johan, Erik Eynikel, and Katrin Hauspie. *A Greek-English Lexicon of the Septuagint.* 3rd ed. Stuttgart: Deutsche Bibelges, 2015
LHBOTS	Library of Hebrew Bible/Old Testament Studies
lit.	Literal translation mine
LU	Laws of Ur-Namma (ca. 2100 BCE) in Roth, *Law Collections*
LXX	Septuagint. Unless stated otherwise: English translation from NETS; Greek translation from LXX Göttingen for Genesis–Deuteronomy, Jeremiah, Ezra-Nehemiah, and 1 Esdras, and elsewhere from Rahlfs
LXX Cambridge	*The Old Testament in Greek.* Edited by Alan England Brooke, et al. 8 vols. Cambridge: Cambridge University Press, 1906–1935
LXX Göttingen	*Septuaginta, Vetus Testamentum Graecum.* Göttingen: Vandenhoeck and Ruprecht, 1931–
LXX Rahlfs	*Septuaginta.* Edited by Alfred Rahlfs. Rev. ed. Robert Hanhart. Stuttgart: Deusche Bibelgesellschaft, 1935, 2006
m.	*The Mishnah.* Edited and translated by Herbert Danby. New York: Oxford University Press, 1933
MAL	Middle Assyrian Laws (ca. 1200 BCE) in Roth, *Law Collections*
minus	Elements of Samuel/Kings excluded from use in Chronicles (see plus)
MT	Masoretic Text
NA^{28}	*Nestle-Aland Novum Testamentum Graece.* 28th ed. Editors Holger Strutwolf et al. Stuttgart: Deutsche Bibelgesellschaft, 2012
NAC	New American Commentary
NEB	New English Bible
NET	New English Translation
NETS	*A New English Translation of the Septuagint, and Other Greek Translations Traditionally Included under that Title.* Edited by Albert Pietersma and Benjamin G. Wright. New York: Oxford University Press, 2007
NICOT	New International Commentary on the Old Testament
NIDOTTE	*New International Dictionary of Old Testament Theology and Exegesis.* Edited by Willem A. VanGemeren. 5 vols. Grand Rapids: Zondervan, 1997
NIV	New International Version
NIVAC	NIV Application Commentary
NRSV	New Revised Standard Version
NTS	*New Testament Studies*
OTE	*Old Testament Essays*
OTL	Old Testament Library
passim	Subject occurs frequently in that section or writing
plus	Non-synoptic contexts of Chronicles (see minus)
qere	See *ketiv* above

Rashi	*The Metsudah Chumash/Rashi*. 2nd ed. Edited by Avrohom Davis. 5 vols. New York: Ktav, 1996
RB	*Revue Biblique*
REB	Revised English Bible
SBH	Standard Biblical Hebrew (syntax and grammar of Genesis through Kings)
SJOT	*Scandinavian Journal of the Old Testament*
SP	(Samaritan Pentateuch) *Der hebräische Pentateuch der Samaritaner*. Edited by August Freiherrn von Gall. 5 vols. Giessen: Töpelmann, 1914–1918
TDOT	*Theological Dictionary of the Old Testament*. Edited by G. Johannes Botterweck, et al. Translated by John T. Willis, et al. 16 vols. Grand Rapids: Eerdmans, 1974–2018
TOTC	Tyndale Old Testament Commentaries
TWOT	*Theological Wordbook of the Old Testament*. Edited by R. Laird Harris, Gleason Archer Jr., and Bruce K. Waltke. 2 vols. Chicago: Moody, 1980
TynBul	*Tyndale Bulletin*
UBS[5]	*The Greek New Testament*, United Bible Societies, 5th ed. corrected. Edited by Barbara Aland, et al. Stuttgart: Deutsche Bibelgesellschaft, 2019
Vulg.	Vulgate
VT	*Vetus Testamentum*
VTSup	Supplements to Vetus Testamentum
WBC	Word Biblical Commentary
Williams	Williams, Ronald J. *Williams' Hebrew Syntax*. 3rd ed. Revised and expanded by John C. Beckman. Toronto: University of Toronto Press, 2007
WTJ	*Westminster Theological Journal*
ZAW	*Zeitschrift für die alttestamentliche Wissenschaft*
ZECOT	Zondervan Exegetical Commentary on the Old Testament

Standard Hebrew and Aramaic grammatical abbreviations are used. Pronominal suffixes begin with hyphen, such as -1cs.

Q	*qal*	inf. const.	infinitive construct	m	masculine
Nif	*niphal*	p, pf.	perfect (*qatal*)	f	feminine
Piel	*piel*	ptc.	participle	c	common
Pual	*pual*	wci	*vav* consecutive imperfect (*vayyiqtol*)	s	singular
Hith	*hithpael*			p	plural
Hif	*hiphil*	wcp	*vav* consecutive perfect (*veqatal*)	DDO	אֵת, accusative marker/definite direct object marker
Hof	*hophal*				
i, impf.	imperfect (*yiqtol*)	1	first person		
impv.	imperative	2	second person	*	hypothetical form unattested in Scripture
inf. abs.	infinitive absolute	3	third person		

INTRODUCTION

Scriptural exegesis of Scripture is an engine of progressive revelation. To be sure, God's revelation comes in many forms and in many ways. A small subset of his revelation takes the form of exegetical advances within Scripture. The present study evaluates the exegesis of Scripture within Israel's Scriptures.

The commonplace motto of interpreting Scripture by Scripture stands alongside a growing awareness of many perplexing issues in the New Testament's use of Scripture. But it does not start there. The New Testament uses Scripture in many of the same ways that Israel's Scriptures use Scripture.

This reference work provides guidance for students and ministers of the word to study scriptural exegesis within Israel's Scriptures. The study goes book by book, one exegetical passage at a time.

OVERVIEW OF THIS INTRODUCTORY CHAPTER

Sharp debate surrounds nearly every aspect of studying the scriptural use of Scripture. Responsible interpretation of scriptural exegesis within Scripture requires navigating several challenges. This introduction can help users make the most of this book-by-book study resource.

The beginning and ending sections of the introduction offer basic orientation to the scriptural use of Scripture and the leading features of this study. The definitions of scriptural exegesis, allusion, and kindred elements focus on how they fit within progressive revelation. The several middle sections of this introductory chapter get at lightning rod issues. Here is an outline of the sections of this introduction.

Overview of This Introductory Chapter
Starting Points and Basic Definitions
Detecting Allusion
Direction of Dependence
Diachronic versus Synchronic
Models for the Study of the Scriptural Use of Scripture
How to Use This Book

Detecting allusion needs to be discussed because of wildly different and competing claims. Many studies distinguish between quotation, allusion, and echo—but that is not usually the problem. How can students tell the difference between real and imagined allusions? The present study focuses on an even narrower kind of allusion that features interpretive interventions. Detecting real exegetical allusions stands at the start, not the end, of the process of evaluating these allusions.

Evaluating exegetical allusions invites attention to the direction of dependence. The nature of scriptural allusions and the challenges of dating many parts of the Hebrew Scriptures contribute to the difficulties of sorting out which parallel biblical context uses its counterpart.

Both steps—detecting allusion and determining direction of dependence—can be approached by means of diachronic or synchronic studies. Diachronic (literally, through time) studies focus on the author and the text (production). Synchronic (literally, together at one time) studies consider the text and its readership (reception). The choice between the two in most studies does not include spelling out the underlying goals of these approaches. Since underlying goals vary radically, not all diachronic or synchronic approaches are created equal. Connecting aims to diachronic and/or synchronic studies offers a way forward.

Pausing to observe a few of the leading approaches can be of enormous value even after clarifying genuine allusions, direction of dependence, and the goals of diachronic versus synchronic studies. Intense research has been poured into the scriptural use of Scripture in the past fifty-plus years. Examining the broad contours of the work of a few major scholars can help refine a viable approach even further.

All of these things require patience. Nearly every aspect of the scriptural use of Scripture remains contested. The present chapter does not try to settle these contests. Instead, it merely seeks to introduce how the present study evaluates the evidence. Besides the present introductory chapter, a reader new to these matters may find useful the Glossary near the end of the volume.

STARTING POINTS AND BASIC DEFINITIONS

Scriptural **revelation** cannot be confined to divine pronouncements like laws and prophetic oracles. All of Scripture comes to be understood as revelation in the view of Scripture itself.[1] Scripture's inclusive sense of revelation applies to scriptural exegesis of Scripture. "The Bible contains besides the simple record of direct revelations, *the further interpretation* of these immediate disclosures of God by inspired prophets and apostles."[2]

Progressive revelation has long been used to refer to the internal organic growth of

1. See Deut 4:13–14; 2 Sam 23:2; Ezra 7:6; Neh 9:30; Mark 12:36; 2 Tim 3:14–16; Heb 1:1–2; 1 Pet 1:10.
2. Vos, "Inaugural Address," 33, emphasis mine.

teachings within Scripture. In Scripture "the advance of revelation" extends from the beginning through "all expansions of the original message of salvation" in many stages.[3]

An organic versus a mechanical view of revelation rejects attempts to detach biblical authors "from their personality" and lift them "out of the history of their time" so that they can "function only as mindless, inanimate instruments in the hand of the Holy Spirit."[4] God has been pleased to reveal his will by the authors of Scripture, sometimes by immediate direct revelation and sometimes by scriptural exegesis of Scripture.

Exegesis may be used in the narrow sense of explain or in a broader sense of explain, enhance, expand, connect, adjust, and the like.[5] The present study refers to the exegetical use of Scripture in the broader sense. Identifying exegesis within Scripture is not the point. Identification of scriptural interpretation of Scripture only serves as a beginning since exegetical outcomes need to be evaluated on a case-by-case basis.

The inherent challenge of exegesis within authoritative Scripture sometimes leads to a mingling of categories: "Paradoxically, this very idea of authority and immutability itself engenders change."[6] It is easy to agree that scriptural interpretations of divine revelation give pause. How can circumstance necessitate reinterpretation, even slight modifications, to what God has said? But this mixes up who God is with how he relates to his people. God has been pleased to reveal his will incrementally, advancing revelation to facilitate his covenantal relationship with his wayward people.[7] Scripture embodies the enduring word of God. "Scripture clearly teaches that this revelation" of God himself "bears a historical character and unfolds its content only gradually over the course of many centuries."[8] Advancements of revelation by exegesis do not set aside previous scriptural revelation. They unfold from it.

A book-by-book reference study like this one leans on a commitment to an inductive approach.[9] An inductive approach across Scripture can enrich express statements of revelation. But the evidence needs to be evaluated in every case. One of the closing chapters of this book moves toward the New Testament and puts together many of the implications decided along the way. A study like this can help those working on specific parts of Scripture to attend to scriptural exegesis therein even while it also provides evidence to evaluate overarching issues.

Before working out issues related to allusion, the usage of **torah/Torah** as an English loanword should be clarified. The term "Torah" refers to the first five books of the Bible. Meanwhile, "torah" connotes instruction or teaching. The term carries a native

---

3. Ibid., 16–17; and see 21–23.

4. Bavinck, *Reformed Dogmatics*, 1:431. Also see Barrett, *God's Word*, 229–30; idem, *Canon*, 18–20; Vos, *Biblical Theology*, 187–88; Frame, *Systematic*, 595–96; Gamble, *Whole Counsel*, 2:71–72.

5. See Tigay, "Early Technique," 170, n. 3.

6. Sarna, "Psalm 89," 34.

7. On "installments" of progressive revelation see Vos, *Biblical Theology*, 6–7; Kim and Trimm, *OT Theology*, 23, n. 64.

8. Bavinck, *Reformed Dogmatics*, 1:343.

9. As suggested by Johnson, *OT in the New*, 26.

educational sense and only a secondary legal sense because of instruction concerning a large number of legal standards in Torah. Thus, all of Torah is torah in the sense that the Torah is an authoritative instructional narrative. The capital "T" in Torah especially gets at authority or an emerging canonical consciousness within the Hebrew Scriptures. This study uses torah for instruction and Torah to refer to a written scroll of Moses even when it has not yet reached its final form. An example is the Torah of Moses referred to as a scroll in Josh 1:7–8 set before the conquest and establishment of kings in Israel that are referred to in the past within Torah.[10] In any specific instance, whether Scripture is referring to torah or Torah requires critical evaluation before a determination can be made.

DETECTING ALLUSION

Quotation, paraphrase, and allusion are intentional. This study does not need to say "intentional allusion" because if it is not author intended, it is not considered an allusion. Echoes may be accidental or, if purposeful, so subtle as to eliminate readerly certainty. The focus for the moment will remain on allusions inclusive of quotation and paraphrase.

This reference study is designed for English Bible readers even while it everywhere investigates **verbal parallels based on the Hebrew Text** of Scripture. When this study mentions "verbal parallels" and the like, it refers to shared language in Hebrew unless stated otherwise.

One of the early steps in the research included close comparison of any potential parallels in Hebrew. Study notes that highlight parallel language facilitate this comparison. Though the research notes are color-coded, here is an approximation to illustrate (bold emphasis corresponds to grayed-out Hebrew).

I will set him over my **house** and my **kingdom forever**; his **throne will be established forever**.	Your **house** and your **kingdom** will endure **forever** before me; your **throne will be established forever**.	וְהַעֲמַדְתִּיהוּ בְּבֵיתִי וּבְמַלְכוּתִי עַד־הָעוֹלָם וְכִסְאוֹ יִהְיֶה נָכוֹן עַד־עוֹלָם׃	וְנֶאְמַן בֵּיתְךָ וּמַמְלַכְתְּךָ עַד־עוֹלָם לְפָנֶיךָ כִּסְאֲךָ יִהְיֶה נָכוֹן עַד־עוֹלָם׃
(1 Chr 17:14)	(2 Sam 7:16)[a]	(1 Chr 17:14)	(2 Sam 7:16)

[a] The NIV of 2 Sam 7:16 follows LXX and few Hebrew manuscripts with "before me" (לְפָנָי) versus "before you" (לְפָנֶיךָ) in MT (see *BHK/BHS* apparatus n. a).

A color-coded version of the research comparing hundreds of exegetical allusions of the present study in English and Hebrew will be released by Zondervan Academic as an e-resource as well as within select digital Bible study platforms. This e-resource entitled *Old Testament Use of Old Testament in Parallel Layout* serves as a companion to supplement the present work for those who wish to do additional study.

10. See Gen 36:31; Deut 2:12.

The present focus on detecting allusion within Israel's Scriptures gets at how to sort out real from imagined cases of interpretive allusion.

It would be nice to say the present study is objective, but working with exegetical allusion is always subjective.[11] Detecting allusions creates tension between art and science. Some approaches get too mechanical which does not work well when dealing with highly literary Scriptures. Other approaches wind up being too intuitive and rest everything on speculative preferences. Though detecting allusion is more art than science, empirical controls put checks in place to strengthen outcomes. To control subjectivity the present work takes measures to offer verifiable and transparent introduction.

Verifiable introduction especially applies to identifying parallel texts. Critics and friends of comparative Scripture study complain that many alleged scriptural allusions are too subtle. Some wonder if the modern scholarly enterprise of identifying allusions has nothing in common with illiterate and underprivileged constituencies of the earliest Christian communities. Ben Witherington III says,

> The Gospel story may be told in arcane language and may occasionally quote arcane texts but that language and those texts are now part of a new story, a new discourse, and must make sense *without scurrying back to the OT again and again to get the full gist of the story* because probably only a tiny minority of the audience ... are learned enough and sophisticated enough to catch and then probe the allusions or echoes, or even for that matter to know where to look for the quotations.[12]

This complaint has much merit. Does attention to scriptural allusions obstruct the simple gospel? It could, but that is not the point. The Scriptures, like anything else, can be understood in an initial manner without encyclopedic knowledge of backstory and context. Followers of the Messiah need to start somewhere. At the same time, Scripture consistently advocates a life of meditating upon, studying, teaching, and obeying the Scriptures. The initial testimony of the Scriptures provides an on-ramp to a fuller understanding which necessarily includes interpreting exegesis within Scripture. First-time reading of Scripture offers much even while the Scriptures themselves welcome and invite close study including scriptural allusions by subtle devices.

The most widely cited set of criteria for identifying real versus imagined echoes in Scripture comes from Richard Hays: (1) availability of source to author; (2) volume determined by repetition of words and syntax; (3) recurrence to same context by author; (4) thematic coherence between source text and argument of alluding context; (5) historical plausibility that author would have intended it and readership could have understood it; (6) history of interpretation has identified the same echoes; (7) satisfaction refers to degree

11. Sommer rightly says weighing evidence of allusions "is an art, not a science" (*A Prophet Reads Scripture*, 35).

12. Witherington, review of *Echoes of Scripture in the Gospels* (by Hays), emphasis mine. For a similar complaint against scholars expecting ancients to have on hand BDB, *ABD*, or Even-Shoshan, see Baden, "Literary Allusions," 115.

to which proposed echo makes sense.[13] Hays's criteria 2, 3, 4, and 6 can be applied in this study, but 1, 5, and 7 do not relate to verifiable evidence and fall outside the present approach. These criteria work especially well in a New Testament environment. Working with passages of Israel's Scriptures, standing within an unfinished process of becoming Scripture over the course of a thousand years, requires an approach suitable to them.

Allusions are more than the use of the same words. Richard Schultz rightly argues that verbal correspondence needs to be accompanied by syntactical and contextual corroboration. This gets at formal characteristics. But there is more. Schultz speaks of "purposeful reuse."[14] The priority on the function of allusions offers an improvement over merely identifying allusions.

A related perennial problem is how to distinguish purposeful allusions from coincidental stock phrases, common expressions, and figures of speech. Coincidental verbal correspondence must be sorted out from interpretive citation. Michael Fishbane insists that "it makes all the difference—*all* and not some" to discern interpretive reuse versus common idioms or coincidence.[15] Besides stock phrases there remains many non-exegetical broad allusions. The present work uses filters to screen out false positives. Part of the efforts to enhance verifiability means displaying non-exegetical parallels that get filtered out.

Every main chapter ends with a section entitled **Filters** that includes a substantial representation of non-exegetical parallels. Passages that seem parallel, often sharing verbal parallels in Hebrew, are filtered out for factors like:

- broad allusion without interpretation;
- stock phrases and/or common themes;
- literary connections within the same scriptural book.

Filters are not one size fits all but vary genre to genre and book by book. Because of the wide variety of situations encountered, the filters need to be explained on a case-by-case basis.

Transparency comes by means of a rating system, A through F, loosely based on letter grades in a classic American academic grading scale. Every potential exegetical allusion will be rated as more or less likely. The use of rating provides transparency of subjective judgment but also indicates empirical benchmarks.

Level A refers to parallels that interpreters can have great confidence are instances of interpretive scriptural allusion. To achieve level A the parallel passages must share a minimum of three Hebrew roots along with syntactical and contextual considerations.[16]

---

13. Paraphrased from Hays, *Echoes Paul*, 29–32.
14. See Schultz, *Search for Quotation*, 222–24, quotation here from page 222 does not use emphasis as in original.
15. Fishbane, *Biblical Interpretation*, 13, emphasis original. Also see Schultz, "Was Qohelet?," 205.
16. Other approaches use the criterion of two, three, or four terms, but most do not eliminate common terms like

The shared Hebrew roots must be substantial terms like nouns and verbs—prepositions, pronouns, and other minor syntactical particles do not count even though they may contribute to syntactical and/or contextual relations. Level A also includes synoptic parallel passages. Even a modest amount of verbal correspondence in synoptic parallels virtually guarantees a relationship, whether direct or indirect. Synoptic passages are typically laid out in parallel columns by references due to limitations of space. Still, key exegetical issues are discussed more closely.

Level B parallels must share at least one Hebrew root as well as syntactical and contextual indicators—though they almost always have more than one parallel term. The shared roots need to be substantive terms like verbs or nouns. While prepositions, pronouns, and particles are not sufficient of themselves for probability of allusion, they may corroborate syntactic and contextual relations. Level B rating refers to passages that are *probably* cases of exegetical scriptural allusion. It may seem disappointing to have such a low threshold of evidence: one term. Unfortunately, there are a few cases that require this. The allusion to the law of devoting by the delegates from Gibeon in Josh 9:6–7 shares only one common term "distance" with Deut 20:15 yet interpreters widely regard these contexts as intentionally related. The overwhelming majority of B ratings in the present study include more than one parallel term, but the few cases with minimal verifiable evidence will be noted.

Level C means *possibly* the parallel passages represent interpretive allusion. Level C normally has at least one shared Hebrew root, except in extraordinary cases, as well as other syntactical and contextual indicators. The poetic description of the dividing of the nations in Deut 32:8 may relate to the narrative of dividing the nations by languages in Gen 11:1–9 despite the lack of verbal correspondence. In the vast majority of cases, level-C possible parallels feature more than the minimums listed here.

Level D means *probably not*. Because of space limitations examples of level D will not appear too frequently. Typically level D notes explain why a passage should not be considered as intentionally parallel even though one or more scholars have identified it as such.

Level F refers to potential parallels that have been *filtered out* and may be found in the Filters at the end of every main chapter. Non-exegetical parallel Scriptures counted in level F remain just as important as Scriptures in any other level. They simply do not represent exegetical allusions. In certain respects the non-exegetical parallels housed in the Filters throughout the present project may point most strongly to continuity within and between the scrolls of Israel's Scriptures. Pursuing these ends falls outside the present study. The bases of this rating system should not be construed as bearing any relationship to the importance of this or that Scripture.

The rating system only pertains to the relative likelihood of exegetical allusion based on the combination of primarily subjective judgment and secondarily empirical indicators

---

prepositions. During the research phase of the present project different numbers of terms were tested until arriving at a minimum of three words. For other approaches that require three terms to count as parallel, see Beale, *Handbook*, 31; Lee, *Intertextual*, 24.

described above. This is a tool of transparency to help students calibrate the kind of effort and confidence that should be invested in given cases of possible, probable, or likely exegetical allusions.

Verifiability of evidence and transparency of judgment, along with empirical benchmarks, help because verbal, syntactical, and contextual evidence, in cases of potential parallels, varies dramatically. Decisions of intentional parallels must be made on a case by case basis amid seemingly unlimited variables. These realities eliminate creating a definitive list of rules or criteria for detecting interpretive allusions. Even still, it seems useful to offer **a few examples here of the kinds of verbal, syntactical, and contextual evidence that help** determine authentic cases of intentional parallels.[17]

The kinds of evidence in the following challenging examples—challenging in terms of detecting allusion—that make allusion more likely include—*verbal*: distinctive terms and/or rare terms; a set of terms used in ironic manner; *contextual*: common terms and phrases used in distinctive ways or in distinct combinations; *syntactical*: ungrammatical elements in the receptor context because of adapting the donor context with its syntax and vice versa.

The appearance of rare terms can help in detecting allusion. The rare term "mixture" or "woven together" only appears in Lev 19:19 and Deut 22:11 helping confirm a likely allusion (emphases mark verbal parallels).[18]

> Keep my decrees. Do not mate different kinds of animals. <u>Do not plant your</u> field <u>with two kinds of seed</u>. Do not wear clothing **woven together** [שַׁעַטְנֵז] of two kinds of material. (Lev 19:19†)

> <u>Do not plant two kinds of seed in your</u> vineyard, otherwise the produce will be holy, both the seed you have sown and the produce of the vineyard. Do not plow with an ox and a donkey yoked together. Do not wear clothes of wool and linen **woven together** [שַׁעַטְנֵז]. (Deut 22:9–11, v. 9 lit.)

Without the shared rare term "woven together," the substantial differences in these contexts would raise questions about an intentional relationship in spite of several verbal and thematic similarities.

Care must be taken not to merely count uses of a term. Patterns of distribution and other factors need to be evaluated. Though the term "ark" (תֵּבָה) appears more than twenty times, all but one occurrence appears in Genesis 6–9 making a broad non-exegetical allusion in Exodus 2:3 highly likely.[19]

---

17. The discussion and examples here relate only to detecting intentional parallels. See notes on respective contexts for evaluation of exegetical allusions.

18. See "שַׁעַטְנֵז," *HALOT* 2:1610–11.

19. See note on Exod 2:3 in Exodus Filters. For a similar situation with "flood" (מַבּוּל) see note on Ps 29:10 in Psalms Filters.

The contextual use of even commonplace terms can, at times, suggest intentional parallel. The appearance of three common terms—"fame," "praise," and "honor"—as a set used satirically in Jer 13:11 suggests that they have been drawn as a set from Deut 26:19. While the set of terms describes Israel as Yahweh's "treasured people" in Deut 26, Jeremiah uses these terms to shame his audience as Yahweh's dirty loincloth (bold signifies verbal parallels and broken underlining signifies inverted imagery).[20]

> He has declared that he will set you in **praise, fame** and **honor** high above all the nations he has made and that you will be a people holy to Yahweh your God, as he promised. (Deut 26:19)

> "For as a loincloth is bound around the waist, so I bound all the people of Israel and all the people of Judah to me," declares Yahweh, "to be my people for my **fame** and **praise** and **honor**. But they have not listened." (Jer 13:11 lit.)

The inversion of sequence from "praise" and "fame" to "fame" and "praise" reflects a commonplace ancient scribal practice in citations known as Seidel's theory (see Glossary). In addition, Jeremiah makes very heavy use of Deuteronomy. These general tendencies along with the contextual considerations of satire provide moderate evidence of allusion even of common terms.

An unusual use of a term, even a common term, can indicate intentional parallel. The term "pour out" appears many times with the negative sense of pouring out wrath or the like in Ezekiel.[21] When Ezekiel speaks of the spirit, he usually uses the term "give."[22] The only exceptions for these common terms appear in Ezek 39:29. The distinctive phrase in Ezekiel can be compared to the same phrase in Joel (bold signifies verbal parallels).

> I will no longer hide my face from them, for **I will pour out my Spirit** on the people of Israel, declares the Sovereign Yahweh. (Ezek 39:29)

> And afterward, **I will pour out my Spirit** on all people. Your sons and daughters will prophesy, your old men will dream dreams, your young men will see visions. Even on my servants, both men and women, **I will pour out my Spirit** in those days. (Joel 2:28–29 [3:1–2])

The unusual positive use of "pour out" with a common object of "my Spirit" in Ezek 39 and Joel 2[3] suggests intentional parallel. Deciding which prophet used the other or

20. See Holladay, *Jeremiah 2*, 58; "תִּפְאֶרֶת," 5.e *HALOT* 2:1773.

21. See "pour out" (שׁפך) of negative elements in Ezek 4:2; 7:8; 9:8; 14:19; 16:15, 36, 38; 17:17; 18:10; 20:8, 13, 21, 33–34; 21:22, 31[27, 36]; 22:3–4, 6, 9, 12, 22, 27, 31; 23:8, 45; 24:7; 26:8; 30:15; 33:25; 36:18; 39:29.

22. See Ezek 11:19; 36:26, 27; 37:14.

whether they worked from a common source, along with many other challenges in this case, needs to be set aside here.

Although stock phrases normally get filtered out, additional contextual elements, can indicate intentional parallel in some cases. The oft used legal motive clause "for you were residing foreigners in Egypt" would need something else to count as part of an intentional parallel. The verb "mistreat" (ינה) only appears five times with residing foreigner as object.[23] Notice the way this verb and object are used in only two scriptural contexts that feature the motive clause mentioned above (emphases signify verbal parallels).

> **Do not mistreat** or oppress **a residing foreigner,** *for you were residing foreigners in* the land of *Egypt*. (Exod 22:21[20] lit.)

> When a **residing foreigner** resides among you in your land, **do not mistreat** them. The residing foreigner residing among you must be treated as your native-born. Love them as yourself, *for you were residing foreigners in Egypt*. I am Yahweh your God. (Lev 19:33–34 lit.)

In spite of the commonness of this stock phrase and many of the terms in Exod 22:21[20] and Lev 19:33–34, the combination of them together in only two places diminishes the possibility of coincidence and supports the likelihood of allusion.

Consider the syntactical situation in a key part of Jer 34. Notice how Jer 34:14a awkwardly shifts from second person masculine plural to singular, presumably to accommodate the language of a legal donor context from Deut 15 (bold signifies syntactical alignment, underlining signifies syntactical misalignment, and italics signify other verbal parallels).[24]

> If any of your people—*Hebrew* men or women—*sell themselves to* ***you*** [-2ms, לְךָ] and serve you six years, in the *seventh year* **you** [2ms, תְּשַׁלְּחֶנּוּ] *must let* them *go free*. (Deut 15:12)

> Every *seventh year* each of <u>you</u> [2mp, תְּשַׁלְּחוּ] *must free* any fellow *Hebrews* who have *sold themselves to* ***you*** [-2ms, לְךָ]. (Jer 34:14a)

The shift from second person plural to second person singular causes in Jer 34:14a an ungrammaticality that strongly suggests intentional allusion to the legal standard in Deut 15:12.

---

23. In three cases, the term occurs with the commonplace triad of protected classes: widow, orphan, and residing foreigner (Jer 22:3; Ezek 22:7, 29). See "ינה," *HALOT* 1:416; Even-Shoshan, 473.

24. As observed by Fishbane, *Haftarot*, 116.

The opposite syntactical situation of a surprising grammatic congruence within a grammatically incongruent context can also signal intentional parallel. Ezek 36 repeatedly uses grammatically masculine verbs with the grammatically feminine noun "land" (as well as other ungrammatical elements). But at one point in speaking to the personified land, the prophet uses the correct grammatical verb form where it corresponds exactly to the bad report of the ten scouts (bold signifies verbatim parallel and underlining signifies ungrammaticality).

> [Ten scouts say:] "The land we explored **devours** (fs, ptc.) those living in it." (Num 13:32b)

> [Direct address to the land:] I will cause people, my people Israel, to live on <u>you</u> (mp). They will possess <u>you</u> (ms), and <u>you</u> (ms) will be their inheritance; <u>you</u> (ms) will never again deprive them of their children. . . . Because some say to <u>you</u> (mp), "**You devour** (fs, ptc.) people and deprive your nation of its children." (Ezek 36:12–13b)

In spite of the limitation of the parallel to one word, the grammatical anomaly—in this case sudden grammatical congruity—along with a shared thematic element—personification of the land—makes an allusion probable. It also helps that Ezekiel alludes to the wilderness narratives in several places elsewhere.[25]

Syntactical rhythm combined with other contextual factors can also suggest intentional parallels even in cases using common words. Ezekiel frequently alludes to elements in his favorite chapter, Lev 26. He also cites the law of individual responsibility in civil court cases in a couple of places.[26] These tendencies help when evaluating a dark parody featuring an interpretive blend—a receptor text that interprets one donor text in the light of another donor text (see Glossary)—of these contexts (bold and italics signify verbal parallels, and broken underlining signifies parallel imperfect verb forms).[27]

> You *will eat* the flesh of your *sons* and the flesh of your daughters. (Lev 26:29)

> **Parents** are not to <u>be put to death</u> for their *children*, nor *children* <u>put to death</u> for their **parents**; each will die for their own sin. (Deut 24:16)

25. See, e.g., Ezek 7:10; 20:10–21; 44:5–16.

26. Ezek 18:4, 20; cf. Deut 24:16.

27. The syntactical observation here relates to the use of impf. verb forms in the parallel constructions of Deut 24:16ab and Ezek 5:10a. The former context features Hof stems characteristic of death penalties. The verb form "you will eat" in Lev 26:29 is wcp which, though parallel in sense with "will eat" impf. in Ezek 5:10a, features a different grammatical construction than the verb marked with broken underlining in Deut 24:16 and Ezek 5:10a. At the same time, Ezek 5:10 features the verb "eat" that appears in Lev 26:29, with both contexts speaking about cannibalism. See Greenberg, *Ezekiel 1–20*, 113–14.

> Therefore in your midst **parents will eat** their *children*, and *children* **will eat** their **parents**. (Ezek 5:10a)

Ezekiel's parody of equality makes good, if upsetting, use of the syntax and vocabulary from two very different contexts. The confluence of tendencies along with syntactical similarity and thematic parallels—cannibalism and individuality between parents and children—confirm the likelihood of blended allusion.

In sum of this point, the extremely wide range of variables in the scriptural use of Scripture eliminates a definitive list of rules for detecting allusion. The situations of potential allusion vary dramatically from one biblical scroll to the next as well as significant variations within individual scrolls. Every case must be evaluated on its own merits. Decisions on more or less probability of allusion are necessarily subjective because of the literary artistry of the Hebrew Scriptures. At the same time more reliable judgments can be calibrated as more or less likely based on evaluation of the evidence. The most important evidence is verbal parallels. The present study uses empirical benchmarks of minimum verbal parallels. The verbal parallels need to be evaluated in relation to contextual and syntactical evidence. Many kinds of verbal, contextual, and syntactical evidence contribute to greater and lesser likelihood of intentional parallel. Finally, the use of filters to exclude false positives also greatly increases the reliability of detecting actual versus imagined allusions.

Readers will likely disagree with many of the judgments in this study. Disagreement based on different interpretation of the evidence is welcome and expected. Verifiable evidence and transparency of judgment together merely offer a starting point. The rating system described above helps to clarify the overall judgment amid many complicated and sometimes complex sets of evidence that need to be evaluated along the way. Verifiability and transparency do not remove subjectivity. Every case requires critical discernment.

DIRECTION OF DEPENDENCE

After deciding on intentional parallels comes a consideration of the direction of dependence. Studies of the New Testament use of Scripture offer no help here since they simply presume direction of dependence. The situation with Israel's Scriptures gets complicated by a long gestation period in the production of many of its books. Even traditional approaches recognize that Gen 36:31 refers to establishing Israel's kings at some distance in the past; Deut 2:12 looks back upon the bygone days of the settlement of the land; the Psalter features editorial indicators in the headings; Hezekiah's men edit some of Solomon's proverbs as noted in Prov 25:1; editors add headings on the prophetic scrolls, and other cases.[28] In simple terms great care needs to be taken regarding direction of dependence of intentionally parallel passages.

---

28. See Grisanti, "Inspiration," 577–98; Grubbs and Drumm, "What Does Theology Have to Do with the Bible?" 65–79.

Terms like direction of influence and direction of dependence seem clear enough when stated casually even if they do not say the right things. Influence may be real but does not leave behind the kind of evidence that can be quantified in a meaningful way.[29] Dependence rightly speaks to the mechanics of cited elements recycled in a citing context. Yet scriptural exegesis embodies a measure of freedom to advance revelation. The convenience of the term dependence to speak of the mechanics of citation outweighs its dangers. More targeted terms like donor and receptor contexts usually can do the trick without the baggage of the term dependence. Throughout this study **donor text** refers to the cited scriptural tradition and **receptor text** the citing scriptural context.

A large number of scriptural cases that feature probable or almost certain relationships, whether direct or indirect, lack the evidence necessary to determine direction of dependence. Several factors—verbal, syntactical, contextual—point to some kind of relationship between the simile of the blessed person "like a tree planted by the water" in Jer 17:7–8 and Ps 1:2–3. But the contexts lack the evidence necessary to decide which one borrowed from the other or if the relationship has been indirectly mediated by common or related sources now lost. Other shared elements in the two contexts favor some kind of relationship, not simply shared culture.[30] The differences between the two contexts remain exegetically relevant but can only be explained by comparison in the final form of Scripture, not in terms of direction of dependence. Cases like this can be handled in general terms only.

This study presumes no direction of dependence unless stated otherwise. This stems from a commitment to an evidence-based approach. Such limitations naturally raise the value of cases that offer the evidence necessary to confidently determine direction of dependence. It needs to be stressed that quantity of evidence has nothing to do with it.

One of the more helpful approaches to direction of dependence comes from Schultz. He advocates both diachronic and synchronic approaches but warns of diachronic subjectivity which often becomes a "dating game."[31] Schultz emphasizes that synchronic study of scriptural citations needs to respect the context of biblical books, discern different functions of parallels within books versus between books, focus on the effect of citations, distinguish between refrains or formulas versus citation, and compare parallels within their respective contexts.[32]

More recently Schultz pushes back against unreliable approaches to direction of dependence, noting that many of the same criteria are often applied to support opposite conclusions. He complains of little objectivity for diachronic evaluation of interpretive

29. Likewise, oral traditions and/or shared written sources now lost may account for an indirect relationship between some contexts.

30. See note on Ps 1:2–3.

31. See Schultz, *Search for Quotation*, 227–32, citation on 231.

32. See ibid., 232–37. For the more substantive versions of Schultz's sensible approach to direction of dependence and scriptural interpretation of Scripture, see ibid., 222–39; idem, "Ties that Bind," 28–33; idem, "Isaianic Intertextuality," 34–63. Also see idem, "Intertextuality," 20–31; idem, "Job and Ecclesiastes," 191–92; idem, "Fear God," 327–29; idem, "Qohelet," 58–59; idem, "Was Qohelet?," 199–214; idem, "Reuse," 120–21. Other helpful approaches include those by Michael Lyons (see citations in chapter on Ezekiel) and by Will Kynes (see esp. citations in chapter on Job).

evidence.[33] Schultz's warnings underline the tentative and slippery nature of studying the direction of dependence between shared elements. The present approach benefits from the work of Schultz and others, even while framing these matters a little differently.

Detecting direction of dependence, when possible, relates to a single criterion: **interpretive intervention with the right kind of evidence**. At a purely mechanical level, interpretive interventions that may or may not have the necessary evidence include: interpretive blends, inverted citations (Seidel's theory), splitting and developing, interpretive expansions, and others (see Glossary). These interpretive interventions do not themselves point in a direction of dependence. Something about an interpretive intervention or something related to it needs to be available to identify receptor versus donor contexts. The nature of the evidence associated with interpretive interventions needs to be calibrated as more likely and less likely from one case to the next. A few examples may help but one more element needs to be introduced first.

Sometimes scriptural allusions are overtly **marked**. Marking refers to making explicit use of a donor context. One of the versions of the fourth commandment features marking which could refer to an oral or written context (broken underlining denotes marking).

> Remember the Sabbath day by keeping it holy. (Exod 20:8)

> Observe the Sabbath day by keeping it holy, as Yahweh your God has commanded you. (Deut 5:12)

Marking establishes self-consciousness of citation for author and constituents. Often marking accents the authority of the donor text. In the case of the Ten Commandments in Deuteronomy, two of the three revised commandments include marking that strongly suggests it as receptor context.[34]

The phrase "according to what is written" or "as it is written" is one of the more common citation markers. In many cases the citation itself does not follow verbatim the version of the donor text known in the final form of Scripture. Citation formulas with non-verbatim citations create enormous discussion centering on whether the author's copy of the donor text differs from the final form. This debate often ignores the sense of the citation formula. The preposition "as" ranges from "replica" through "like" and "similar" to "after the manner of" and "according to." The preposition connotes agreement whether in quality or kind.[35] As such, an interpretive paraphrase may be "according to what is written." The reason for marking interpretive paraphrases, like the new version of the fourth commandment cited above, includes canonical consciousness. The author

33. See Schultz, "Isaianic Intertextuality," 38–39. For a more detailed complaint along the same lines, see Vang, "When a Prophet Quotes Moses," 278–82.

34. For details, see note on Deut 5.

35. On the sense of the preposition as "agreement" (כְּ), see *IBHS* §11.2.9a, b; also see GKC §118s.

intentionally draws comparative attention to note the accord between the authoritative donor text and the interpretive advancement in the paraphrastic receptor text.

An example from a narrative dialogue offers analogous evidence of how citations may feature interpretative enhancements even while corresponding with the sense of the donor text (italics refer to verbal parallels in Hebrew, bold to interpretive intervention, and broken underlining to overt marking).

> [The brothers say] "*If any* of your servants *is found to have it* [the lord's goblet], *he will* **die**; and the rest of us *will become* **my lord's slaves**." "Very well, then," he [steward of the lord] said, "let it be as you say. *Whoever is found to have it will become* **my slave**; the rest of you *will be* **free from blame.**" (Gen 44:9–10)

The authority figure overtly affirms "as you say," literally "according to your words," even while revising the level of judgment. The preposition "as" or "according to" here demonstrates an agreement in culpability even while downgrading the severity of the punishment. This exchange illustrates by analogy how citations marked by "as it is written" may feature exegetical paraphrases. The sense of "according to your words" as stated by the authority figure connotes real continuity with the accountability offered by the brotherhood even while using authoritative prerogative to commute the sentence.[36]

Evaluation of evidence as it may bear on direction of dependence gets discussed on a case-by-case basis in the present study. Nonetheless, it seems useful to provide here a few abbreviated examples of the evidence necessary to deduce probable direction of dependence. In these samples italics signify verbal parallels in Hebrew, bold signifies interpretive interventions, and broken underlining signifies overt marking of citation when applicable:

> And Yahweh God commanded the man, "*You* are free to *eat from any tree in the garden*; *but you must not eat from the tree* of the knowledge of good and evil, for when you eat from it *you will* certainly *die*." (Gen 2:16–17 lit.)

> Now the serpent . . . said to the woman, "Did God really say, '*You* must **not** *eat from any tree in the garden*'?" The woman said to the serpent . . . "God did say, '*You must not eat* fruit *from the tree* that is in the middle of the garden, **and you must not touch it**, or *you will die*.'" (3:1–2a, 3 lit.)

The serpent and the woman each use interpretive paraphrase. The availability of two exegetical allusions helps clarify the agenda of each. The serpent uses a rhetorical negation,

36. For detailed interaction with the debates on citation formulas, see Hermeneutical Profile of the Use of Scripture in Ezra-Nehemiah.

which amounts to literary signals of a sarcastic tone. The woman adds an interpretive adjustment—whether her own or the man's since he apparently relayed the command to her off stage. Both of these kinds of interpretive elements mildly suggest them as receptor texts but do not offer quite enough evidence of themselves to have high confidence. Since both the serpent and the woman overtly mark their respective interpretive allusions by an oral citation formula, it confirms direction of dependence.

The term "euphemism" refers to figures of speech that soften connotations for a variety of reasons. As an analogy to euphemism in scriptural exegesis of Scripture, notice the euphemistic shift in Isaac's allusion.

> When the men of that place asked him about his wife, he said, "*She is my sister,*" because he was afraid to say, "She is my wife." He thought, "**The men of this place might kill me** *on account of* Rebekah, because she is beautiful." . . . So Abimelek summoned Isaac and said, "She is really your wife! Why did you say, '*She is my sister*'?" Isaac answered him, "Because I thought **I might lose my life** *on account of* her." (Gen 26:7, 9)

Abimelek quotes Isaac's lie verbatim using overt marking as a literary signal of shrill tone: "Why did you say?!" Isaac answers by an interpretive allusion to his own thoughts overtly marked by "I thought."[37] While in his thoughts Isaac targets the men as subjects of killing him, when he cites his thoughts he makes himself the subject of dying, in line with the practice of using the diplomatic deferential language of circumlocution—not speaking directly to or about superiors. He thought "they might kill me" but says more politely "I thought I might die," focusing more on his fear and less on their power that caused the fear. Euphemism strongly suggests direction of dependence since it would only appear in receptor contexts. In this case the citations also include overt marking that makes explicit donor and receptor contexts.

Much debate surrounds the relationship between the holiness collection in Lev 17–26 and Ezekiel. Here is one of many cases that provide the evidence necessary to determine direction of dependence.

> "You shall not *rule over* him *with harshness.*" (Lev 25:43; cf. vv. 46, 53)

> "**With strength** you *ruled over* them, and *with harshness.*" (Ezek 34:4)

The rare term "harshness" appears only in these two contexts and in Exod 1, where it refers to Israel's enslavement. The rarity of the term makes allusion highly likely. Ezekiel

37. The literary signals "saying" (לֵאמֹר) in Gen 26:7 and "I said" (אָמַרְתִּי) in 26:9 are short for "said to his heart," which NIV helpfully renders "thought." The context makes clear Isaac did not say this aloud as observed in "אמר," no. 2 BDB 56. On biblical idioms of internal speech, see Carasik, *Theologies*, 104–24; also see Steiner, "'He Said, He Said,'" 485–91.

apparently explains the rare term by a more common one—"with strength"—making it likely that the tradition in Lev 25 is the donor and Ezek 34:4 the receptor context.[38] Receptor contexts tend to disambiguate and clarify difficulties.

The postexilic restoration assembly sometimes studies Scripture and applies it. This includes memorable cases of mass divorce. While fuller analysis can be found in the note on Neh 13:1–3, the present concern only gets at direction of dependence.

> *An Ammonite or a Moabite shall not enter the assembly of* **Yahweh, even to the tenth generation**, their descendants shall *not enter the assembly of* **Yahweh**. . . . You shall not seek their welfare or their good **all of your days forever.** (Deut 23:3, 6 lit.[4, 7])

> On that day the scroll of Moses was read in the ears of the people and in it was found written that *an Ammonite or a Moabite shall not* **ever** *enter the assembly of* **God. . . .** When the people heard the Torah, they separated from Israel all those of mixed ancestry. (Neh 13:1, 3 lit.)

Nehemiah 13:1 includes two examples of the evidence necessary to determine direction of dependence. Whereas Deut 23:3[4] refers to "even to the tenth generation," which is somewhat vague, Neh 13:1 interprets it as "ever." The interpretation in this case comes from Deut 23:6[7], which clarifies the duration of exclusion as "forever." The abbreviated interpretive paraphrase in Neh 13:1 inserts "ever" in place of the idiomatic expression "even to the tenth generation."[39] Also, Neh 13:1 features overt marking by referring to a written passage found in the scroll of Moses. Both of these lines of evidence strongly suggest the law of the assembly in Deuteronomy is the donor context and the interpretive abridgment in the opening of Neh 13 is the receptor context.

Other situations that often provide the evidence necessary to determine direction of dependence include interpretive blends. An interpretive blend refers to a receptor context that alludes to two or more scriptural donor contexts, often interpreting one scriptural tradition in the light of another (see Glossary). When three texts come together by verifiable intentional parallels, the results frequently include evidence to suggest donor and/or receptor contexts. The kind of overlapping evidence in the case of Joel's and Jonah's use of the attribute formula of Exod 34:6–7 allows for triangulation, which sets all three passages in a particular sequence of dependence.[40]

These few examples merely suggest the kinds of evidence that need to be evaluated on a case-by-case basis to determine direction of dependence. Sometimes a global decision

---

38. See "פֶּרֶךְ," *HALOT* 2:968. This example comes from Milgrom, *Leviticus 23–27*, 2356–57. For many other examples of Ezekiel's dependence on the holiness collection of Leviticus, see 2348–63; and see Hermeneutical Profile of the Use of Scripture in Ezekiel.

39. Deuteronomy 23:6[7] uses "all of your days to forever" (lit., כָּל־יָמֶיךָ לְעוֹלָם), which Neh 13:1 paraphrases as "to forever" (lit., עַד־עוֹלָם).

40. See notes on Joel 2:13–14 and Jonah 4:2.

can be made about entire books. Chronicles is quite late in its present form, no sooner than at least six generations after Zerubbabel, who dates from the early postexilic period, indicating that it serves as receptor context of its version of Kings, which dates from early exilic period. Ezra-Nehemiah in its present form includes lists of people that seem to run down to the time of Alexander the Great's conquest and so can be regarded as the receptor context.[41]

The Torah is an important exception in the present study. This study approaches Torah's use of Torah according to the order of its five books. Excavative study of the legal collections of Torah that dominates diachronic scholarship has not attended to legal exegesis as presented by the text itself.[42] This gap needs attention. The introductory purposes of the present study fit well with taking the necessary first step of studying the Torah's own presentation of its legal exegesis.[43] This exception brings up the question of diachronic and synchronic approaches.

DIACHRONIC VERSUS SYNCHRONIC

The present study uses diachronic and synchronic approaches, both limited to textual aims, to evaluate scriptural exegesis of Scripture. For the broad point here an oversimplification of diachronic and synchronic studies can help, since the terms are generalizations anyway. It has become customary for studies of the scriptural use of Scripture to situate themselves as synchronic or diachronic.[44] One of the problems that plagues studies of scriptural use of Scripture is the failure to connect aims to diachronic or synchronic research programs.

The biblical studies enterprise borrows the terms diachronic and synchronic from linguistic studies to describe different kinds of approaches. **Diachronic** (through time) studies pursue the text and its authorship—production—while **synchronic** (at one time) studies focus on texts and their readers—reception. The unwieldiness of these umbrella terms stems in part from not bothering to identify goals. The outcome has been to lump together somewhat incompatible research programs under the same umbrella terms, virtually eliminating the kind of meaningful generalizations to which the terms should point. Though many complain about the bad fit, the umbrella terms get thrown around without giving attention to underlying agendas.

Aims need to be connected to these approaches. Diachronic studies defined by the

---

41. For detailed discussion of the evidence and dates of Chronicles and Ezra-Nehemiah, see note on 2 Chr 36:22–23.

42. Alter uses the term "excavative" to get at the agendas of many diachronic scholars to disassemble biblical texts to recover theoretical sources, theoretical editorial layers, and the like (*Narrative*, 14).

43. For details of the approach to legal exegesis in Torah, see esp. Hermeneutical Profile of the Use of Torah in Exodus and Hermeneutical Profile of the Use of Torah in Deuteronomy.

44. Overviews of diachronic and synchronic approaches to the study of the scriptural interpretation of Scripture are legion. The most widely cited overview, and possibly the most useful, is Miller, "Intertextuality," 283–309. Lester's overview essay, while reductionistic in terms of labeling scholars, includes an annotated bibliography of about three dozen titles ("Inner-Biblical Interpretation," 444–53; also covering some of the same ground, idem, "Inner-Biblical Allusion," 89–93). Also see Schniedewind, "Innerbiblical Exegesis," 502–9; Kynes, *My Psalm*, 17–60; Levinson, *Legal Revision*, 95–181.

authorship-text dialectic broadly may be driven by excavative aims or textual aims. The term "excavative" aptly gets at study agendas that start with the text in search of something else (see below and see Glossary). Synchronic studies defined by the readership-text dialectic broadly may employ readerly aims or textual aims. Identifying competing agendas within diachronic and synchronic studies offers a small step toward disambiguation (see Figure 1).

FIGURE 1: COMPETING AIMS OF DIACHRONIC AND SYNCHRONIC STUDIES

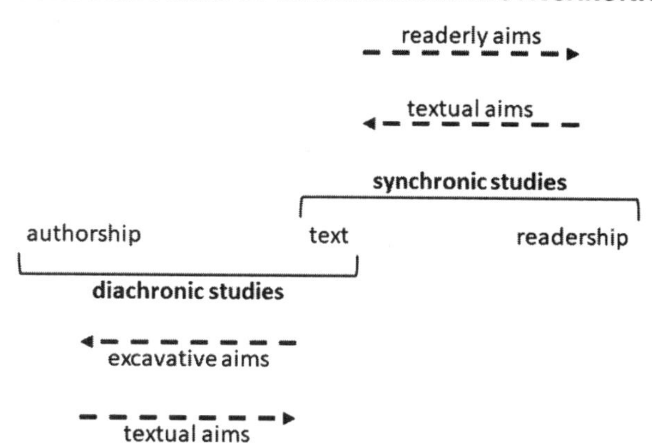

Many diachronic scholars pursue excavative goals. Excavative goals move away from the biblical texts to explain authorial elements like the historical context of authorship. This may include detecting theoretical sources, theoretical editorial layers, and theoretical life-settings of redactors and scribal cultures, as well as dating each of these according to theoretical reconstructions. The importance of authorship-oriented excavative goals is not in question. Others research historical contexts and use empirical models from parallel ancient Near Eastern literatures directed toward the canonical texts of the Hebrew Bible. One set of aims takes apart and the other focuses on what the author has put together. Diachronic excavative goals and diachronic textual goals run in different directions even while working with the same sets of evidence.

Some synchronic scholarship pursues readerly goals. Readerly goals in some cases use the biblical text as a sounding board for experimental comparisons to other texts or modern advocacy reading positions. A readerly study could put queen Esther into conversation with the provincial governor Nehemiah without any intentional parallels between Esther and Ezra-Nehemiah. For theological soundings, Lady Jerusalem of Lamentations might be put into conversation with Lady Wisdom of Proverbs or the psalmist of Ps 2 or Ps 122. Others pursue the final form of the Hebrew Bible synchronically from the vantage point of the New Testament's use of Scripture. When studying scriptural exegesis of Scripture, the Chronicler may be investigated as a reader of his versions of Kings, Psalms, and Torah. A study of the scriptural use of Scripture may employ synchronic textual aims based on the final form of the text without regard for modern or ancient Second Temple

Judaic readerly concerns. A study of scriptural interpretations performed by Jeremiah, Zechariah, and the psalmists gets at the dialectics between these ancient readers and what were scriptural traditions to them. In synchronic studies readerly versus textual aims describe two very different directions among many kinds of research programs.

When studying a case of scriptural interpretation of Scripture, the author of the receptor text is both a "reader" of a scriptural tradition represented by a passage in the final form of Scripture and an "author" of another passage represented in the final form of Scripture. This suggests that adequate research on the scriptural use of Scripture can be conceived as working with elements of both diachronic and synchronic approaches.

To a lesser extent the present study works with select *textual aims* of a synchronic approach. Specifically, evaluating scriptural exegetes as readers needs to be limited to verifiable evidence. This means that the donor text that the scriptural exegete uses, in certain cases needs to be referred to as a scriptural tradition in recognition that the donor text may not be identical to the final canonical form. At the same time, the final canonical form needs to be used as evidence of the donor context to evaluate the scriptural exegesis. There is usually no other evidence.[45]

To a greater extent the present study employs select *textual aims* of a diachronic approach. Evaluating scriptural exegesis in this way means thinking with the author according to available evidence. Authorial concerns in the case of textual aims all focus on the exegetical outcomes found in the scriptural receptor text.

The limitations of the present project do not allow consideration of readerly oriented synchronic approaches or excavative-oriented diachronic approaches. The introductory purposes of the present study along with its wide scriptural focus exclude all other concerns. For those who wish to pursue these other concerns, many valuable studies focused on more advanced diachronic approaches with excavative aims and synchronic approaches with readerly aims can be found in the footnotes.

In sum of the preceding three sections of this introduction, a few points may be noted with regard to detecting allusion, direction of dependence, and diachronic versus synchronic approaches. The present study seeks verifiable outcomes that include transparency of judgment. Because of the nature of the study of scriptural interpretation of Scripture, many elements pivot more on art than science. Objective and verifiable evidence can serve subjective judgments of detecting interpretive allusions by means of checks, standards, and empirical benchmarks. Determining direction of dependence requires careful investigation of the details case by case. In this study textual aims drive a focus on scriptural interpreters as readers and even more so as authors. The overriding theme of the preceding three sections of this introduction is a commitment to evaluating evidence, particularly scriptural evidence.

45. One kind of additional evidence is textual variations. Text critical evaluations are often technical and are usually handled in footnotes in the present study.

MODELS FOR THE STUDY OF THE SCRIPTURAL USE OF SCRIPTURE

Substantial work has been done on scriptural interpretation of Scripture, especially in the last few decades. The starting point of a study of scriptural exegesis of Scripture can be compared to the work of four scholars: Richard Hays, Gerhard von Rad, James Kugel, and Michael Fishbane. These offer models of working backwards versus forwards, Christian versus Judaic outlooks, and how to frame Scripture.

Hays works backwards from Christ and the New Testament to Israel's Scriptures. Hays focuses on the function of "echoes" moving dialectically between Christ and the church and Israel's Scriptures. He demonstrates Paul's "ecclesiocentric hermeneutic" or better "ecclesiotelic reading" by which Israel's "past narratives find their meaning in the present reality of Paul's churches."[46] Hays explains the Gospels as establishing the identity of Christ and his mission by means of Israel's Scriptures.[47] For the present purpose, it is sufficient to take note of his book-by-book, backwards-looking interpretive viewpoint. Hays shows how Paul and the evangelists start with the resurrected Christ and seek out how the Scriptures bear witness to Christ and his people. Hays's approach makes use of biblical books as context in the case of the New Testament, which helpfully provides empirically verifiable controls in contrast to the fuzzy edges of thematic approaches.

Although von Rad acknowledges the viability of reading backwards, his own project turns on reading Scripture forward in historical context. He says:

> Attempts have often been made to understand the Old Testament in light of the New, and they are still legitimate. But the opposite course must also be undertaken, that of outlining *the way from the Old Testament to the New*. It is true that the New Testament saving event was the "guideline" by which the first Christian communities attempted to come to terms with the Old Testament and by which they were led to a completely new perspective on it. But the reverse is equally true: *The Old Testament saving history and the Old Testament revelation of God was a guideline* that enabled them to understand and preach the Christ event, as can be seen say, from the account of the Passion with its many references back to the Old Testament in the theological argument of many of the apostolic letters. The two Testaments legitimate each other. The first principle—that the Old Testament is to be interpreted in the light of Christ—does not seem to be disputed as much today as the second, that we need to read the Old Testament to understand Christ. But is it really the case that we know who Jesus Christ is so well that

46. Hays, "On the Rebound," 94. Also see Hays's full-length study, *Echoes Paul*.

47. See Hays, "Canonical Matrix," 53–75. Also see Hays's two full-length works, *Reading Backwards* and *Echoes of Scripture in the Gospels*.

> we only have a secondary problem to solve, that of finding the relationship between the Old Testament and this Christ whom we already know?[48]

Von Rad's commitment to historical context dominates his theological interpretation of Scripture. His treatment of the prophets provides a most important example. Von Rad works through the prophetic writings according to what he regards as their historical order, based on critical reconstructions, seeking to identify and explain innovations and new aspects at each stage. He sees the prophetic tradition as a general continuity which develops in relation to great historical events. Older Scriptures are "actualized" when they are applied to new contexts whether typologically or otherwise. Von Rad regards the word of God as activating salvation within history: "Jaweh's word, once uttered, reaches its goal under all circumstances in history by virtue of the power inherent in it."[49]

Von Rad's view of a growing prophetic tradition constantly reworking earlier scriptural traditions could be called "cascading actualization."[50] The historical traditions serve as counterparts to the prophetic messages even while von Rad offers sustained attention to the hope of "Israel's anointed."[51] Von Rad often works with biblical books but only as this coincides with his real focus on authorship and critical reconstruction of sources and oral traditions.[52]

Kugel uses "reverse engineering" to trace back from biblical and Second Temple interpretations to Torah contexts. To reverse engineer is an analogy meaning "to recreate the thinking that lies behind each and every one of its [an alluding text's] components."[53] Kugel's *Traditions of the Bible* houses hundreds of ancient interpretations organized by thematic motifs, each related to a particular Torah passage. The thematically arranged interpretations seem to project outward from Torah in every direction, but individual interpretations actually connect backward to specific Torah contexts. Kugel summarizes four assumptions regarding how ancients interpret Scripture. He says ancient interpreters regard Scripture as *cryptic*, with hidden and subtle meaning; *relevant*, written primarily for the sake of instruction (at all places and for all times); *perfect and harmonious*, thus contexts from different parts of the Hebrew Scriptures can be read together and apparent inconsistencies can be harmonized; *divinely inspired*, while explicit in prophetic contexts ("thus says the Lord") this principle came to be applied to all scriptural writings.[54]

For Kugel the vast majority of biblical and ancient Judaic interpretations are in response to difficulties and obscurities *within* the biblical text itself, rather than from

48. Von Rad, *Message of the Prophets*, 284, emphasis mine.

49. Von Rad, *Studies in Deuteronomy*, 78.

50. See Driver, *Childs*, 132.

51. See von Rad, *OT Theology*, 1:306–54. And see Kim and Trimm, *OT Theology*, 45–46, 48.

52. The table of contents of von Rad's *OT Theology* makes evident how his historical approach combined with his critical conclusions results in his breaking up some biblical books even while considering others together.

53. Kugel, *In Potiphar's House*, 251; and see 251–53.

54. See Kugel, *Traditions of the Bible*, 14–19. And see nine theses in idem, *In Potiphar's House*, 247–70; idem, "Beginnings," 13–15.

historical contexts of ancient interpreters.[55] Kugel explains textual and contextual factors within Torah that give rise to interpretive tendencies, then he presents an associated series of interpretations beginning with scriptural interpretations of Torah and continuing through Second Temple Judaic literature, among which he counts the New Testament. While Kugel's work sometimes interacts with interpretations of laws, it is dominated by interpretations of narrative. Because each of these interpretive motifs begin with Torah, everything else is relativized to it. This approach effectively defines all biblical and Second Temple Judaic texts by a twofold division: Torah and its many interpretations. In this sense Kugel's project displays an array of Jewish interpretive traditions, with the New Testament standing among the many commentators on Torah.

Fishbane reads forward, demonstrating scriptural exegesis of Scripture. Fishbane isolates many examples where legal revelation through Moses is developed, adjusted, or reversed by later biblical authors. He repeatedly wonders at the claims of scriptural interpreters since, for him, Torah retains a higher authority than derivative Scriptures. An irony is that Fishbane insists upon innovation for an allusion to qualify as exegesis but then sometimes disparages innovations of Torah as presumptuous. The effect of repeatedly identifying exegetical innovations and then affirming the authority of Torah over and against exegetical traditions effectively sweeps away a place for progressive revelation. Even so, Fishbane frequently pauses to note that derivative scriptural interpretations later become authoritative themselves. A good example is Fishbane's incredulity with Jer 17:19–27, which he sees as innovating Sabbath laws beyond Sinaitic regulations and then claiming revelatory status for these interpretations with "thus says YHWH."

> [S]uch a revelation by the Deity which *presumptively* cites regulations hitherto unrecorded as known and ancient is most remarkable. It points, at the very least, to the *need in ancient Israel to camouflage and legitimate its exegetical innovations*. . . . Indeed, innerbiblical legal exegesis contains many other instances whereby the old revelation is *misrepresented* to one degree or another; but there is none like Jer. 17:21–2 where exegetical innovations are so *brazenly* represented as a citation of the old revelation by YHWH himself.[56]

Fishbane organizes his study around four kinds of exegesis: scribal corrections, haggadic, mantological (oracular), and, most importantly, legal exegesis. The organization of his study into legal, haggadic, and other sorts of exegesis helps demonstrate his claim that early postbiblical rabbinic interpretive traditions—*midrash halakah* and *midrash haggadah*—are extensions of exegetical trajectories within the Scriptures themselves. One reviewer noted that these categories were derived by "working backwards" from rabbinic

55. See Kugel, *Traditions of the Bible*, 19–22.
56. Fishbane, *Biblical Interpretation*, 134, emphasis mine.

interpretation. He suggests that Fishbane uses the scribal comments and corrections category to collect examples that do not fit well so as "to preserve the integrity of the two central modes of halakah and haggadah."[57] In spite of serious criticism to aspects of his argument, Fishbane's work on the scriptural exegesis of Scripture, especially legal exegesis, continues to have wide acclaim.

Though full critique does not suit the present purpose, the differences in these four models of scriptural interpretation of Scripture can situate the field of inquiry. Two of the important elements of these approaches—Judaic versus Christian framework, backwards versus forwards explanation of exegetical phenomena—can be summarized graphically (see Figure 2).

FIGURE 2: FOUR MODELS FOR SCRIPTURAL INTERPRETATION OF SCRIPTURE

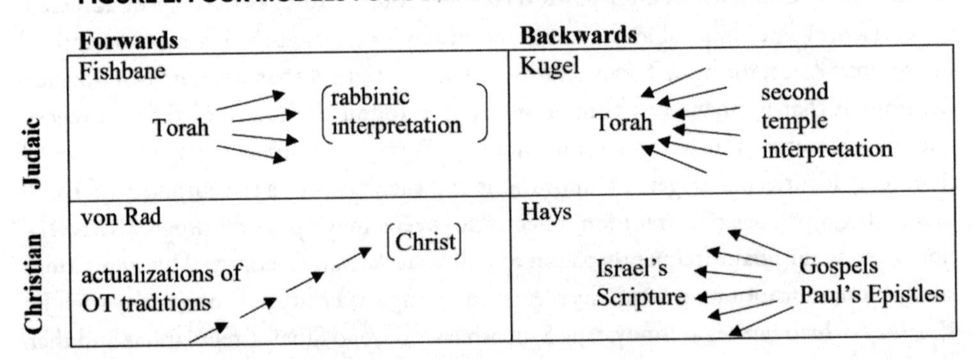

These Judaic/Christian and backwards/forwards differences refer not merely to the analytical outlook of these studies and others, but to exegesis so identified within the Scriptures themselves. While Fishbane and von Rad operate as though they are explaining the "natural" direction that emerging biblical traditions unfold, each moves invariably toward concrete goals: rabbinic exegesis and gospel of Christ in the New Testament, respectively. This is not to deny continuity, at some level, between Tanak/Old Testament and the Judaic and Christian traditions that lay claim to these Scriptures. Rather, there is no need to wink and "objectively" trace the emerging biblical interpretive traditions to their predetermined rabbinic or Christian ends.

Reading forward is not step one but step two. It seems better to take as a starting point "retrospective prospectivity." For the present purposes this might be said more conventionally as reading the Hebrew Bible as Christian Scripture. The New Testament intimates that the revelation of the resurrected Lord activates by God's Spirit new eyes by which to apprehend the Scriptures testifying to the gospel.[58] The present study works forward through the first part of the Christian Bible.

57. Kugel, review of *Biblical Interpretation in Ancient Israel* (by Fishbane), 275.

58. See esp. John 14:25–26; 16:12–14 with 2:17, 22; 12:16; 20:9, 22; cf. Mark 9:32; Luke 24:27, 44–45.

The respective approaches of Kugel and Hays put Torah and Christ and the church on center stage with all the Scriptures treated as a function of these. In Kugel's approach there is Torah and everything else. This approach flattens out differences between texts relative to authority or canonical consciousness. All texts that comment on Torah are considered together without discrimination. Authoritative Scriptures of prophet, psalmist, and (for Christians) New Testament without distinction stand alongside the array of Second Temple Judaic literature from colorful spurious narratives and visions to sectarian propaganda. Isaiah, Psalms, and Romans are no more or less useful to illustrating Torah readings than the Testaments of the Twelve Patriarchs, Rule of the Community (1QS), or the Samaritan Pentateuch.[59] This approach does well to illustrate trends within Second Temple interpretive motifs. A glaring problem is that not all Second Temple texts are created equal.

Though Hays limits his attention almost exclusively to Scripture, isolated passages of Israel's Scripture function apart from their larger contexts with special attention to their use in the Gospels and New Testament epistles. Positively, Hays frames his approach according to New Testament biblical books. There is nothing wrong with projects dedicated to New Testament christological and ecclesiotelic use of Israel's Scripture. A need remains for considering Old Testament use of Old Testament in its own right as Christian Scripture.

The starting point for study of scriptural interpretation within Israel's Scriptures just described—**reading the Hebrew Bible as Christian Scripture**—is not a method, technique, or interpretive approach. It is a starting point. To this may be added major concerns of the present study, namely, a book-by-book approach and progressive revelation.

The present study moves along **book by book**. Other options like the exegetical tendencies of rabbinic interpretation or the reconstructed historical contexts for reconstructed proto-textual traditions like those argued by Fishbane and von Rad offer much insight. But the biblical scrolls house the scriptural use of Scripture. What works in one book may operate differently in another.

The appearance of consistency with the study of interpretation going book by book one passage at a time should not be confused with the shape of progressive revelation itself. Israel's collective identity shifted drastically and repeatedly during the thousand years when the Hebrew Scriptures were written. Messy details surround the people who went from slaves to wanderers to competing kingdoms to captives to those who return to provincial life in their ancestors' homeland. God condescends to reveal his will to his wayward people at many times across many ancient Mediterranean and Mesopotamian lands.

An organic view of revelation does not imply steady, predictable progress that goes in a straight line. On one hand, progressive revelation corresponds to the many crushing

59. For a study of biblical reception sensitive to Christian and Judaic readings, see Levine and Brettler, *Bible With and Without Jesus.*

problems and dramatic shifts in Israel's identity. On the other hand, revelation itself sometimes gives rise to further revelation. That is, some scriptural exegetical advances respond to Israel's crises while others result from bringing together two previous scriptural contexts in a way that the interpretive sum is greater than the two donor texts considered individually. These realities require attention to the contextual situation of every biblical scroll as it bears on the scriptural use of Scripture.

The argument for interpreters to take seriously "the multiformity" of revelation at the level of legal, prophetic, and poetic genres gets it right.[60] The present study builds on this argument because whatever kindred tendencies the prophets share in their exegesis of scriptural traditions, there remains a need to make sense of exegetical tendencies unique to Amos and Isaiah and Ezekiel and Malachi.

The book-by-book, passage-by-passage approach of this study ultimately shines a light on the coherence of progressive revelation by exegesis within Israel's Scriptures. The coherence and continuity of advances of revelation activated by scriptural exegesis stems from Yahweh's covenantal faithfulness. The Scriptures mediate the divine redemptive will to the people of God amid their many messy problems. Interpreters should expect surprising exegetical advances within scriptural revelation. Interpreters should also expect to find familiar patterns of revelation that advance by exegesis.

Scriptural revelation that goes before remains living and active precisely because of the exegetically activated advances of scriptural revelation that come after. Scriptural receptor texts do not replace scriptural donor texts by means of clever exegesis. Scriptural exegesis of Scripture not only honors the donor context but also strengthens its authority.

Responsible interpretation of scriptural exegesis within Scripture means, in part, allowing the shape of exegetical outcomes to be what they are. The interpreter's appetite for symmetry should not lead. Responsible interpretation follows the evidence of exegetical connections within Scripture to discover the ways revelation advances.

The chapters that follow each begin with a brief survey of the **hermeneutical profile of the scriptural use of Scripture within a given biblical book**. The point being that a global description of scriptural exegesis within Israel's Scriptures does not adequately speak to the local hermeneutical situation within this or that scroll. The bulk of the main chapters will be taken up by a **study of scriptural exegesis case by case.**

The term "progressive revelation" gets thrown around pretty casually sometimes. The present study has something much more specific in mind. Exegesis within Scripture represents one way that revelation advances. Each case offers a concrete glimpse of the advancement of revelation. This study takes notice of the ways **scriptural exegesis advances revelation**. This is an incremental and ultimately cumulative concern. One of the final chapters that moves toward the New Testament will attend to some of the

60. See Vos, "Inaugural Address," 21. Also see 22–24.

highlights of studying exegetically activated revelatory advancements. However, the chapter that draws several observations together toward the New Testament is not the point of this study. The purpose of this study is to evaluate scriptural exegesis of Scripture case by case, scroll by scroll through Israel's Scriptures.

HOW TO USE THIS BOOK

Every main chapter includes a short list of **symbols** to make things easier. A fuller set of symbols appears at the beginning of this study to offer a little more detail as needed.

Each main chapter focuses on a particular biblical book and begins with a **set of lists** of scriptural interpretation of Scripture associated with that book. All of the lists include very short informal captions describing the contents of the receptor texts in very broad terms. These short captions have been included so that the set of lists can be studied to identify broad patterns and tendencies of both exegetical donor and receptor scriptural contexts. The set of lists also serves as broad orientation to the exegetical use of Scripture associated with each book of Scripture.

The **first main list** refers to a series of notes on exegesis that can be found in that chapter. This overview list can help users determine the biblical author's go-to scriptural donor contexts as well as distribution of donor and receptor contexts and the like. The **second list** catalogues notes on other texts elsewhere in the Hebrew Bible that feature potential exegetical allusions to the present biblical book. This list can help identify donor contexts in the present book that helped shape scriptural receptor contexts. This second list includes all A-level and B-level notes and nearly all C-level notes. D-level notes have not been cross-listed, nor have a few C-level notes without sufficient detail to warrant cross-referencing. The Scripture Index at the end of this volume covers all notes. The **third list** refers to places in the New Testament that quote or make substantive allusions to the present biblical book. This list serves Old Testament and New Testament studies by showing next steps for investigating how donor texts in the present biblical book contribute to the New Testament. This list also illustrates at a glance locations and clustering among receptor and donor contexts.

A **Bibliographic Note on Lists of Potential Parallels** appears immediately after the present introductory chapter. The bibliographic note explains the sources of the sets of lists featured at the beginning of each main chapter.

Certain scriptural contexts turn out to be favorites and serve as donor texts for many exegetical receptor texts. The repeated exegesis of the same texts sometimes creates interpretive **networks**. A chapter near the end of this volume houses a series of networks laid out graphically. The graphic network summaries are not an end but point back to other scriptural contexts that also may bear on the target context. Passages in networks are noted in the lists along the way in order to make it easy to compare receptor texts that interpret the same donor contexts.

The **glossary** appearing near the end of this volume can help with the necessary array of specialized terminology that often gets used in studies of scriptural use of Scripture. In many cases, discussions of scriptural exegesis of Scripture have been **cross-referenced** to other notes in this study—e.g., "see note on X"—to help users and to avoid undue repetition. An **index of tables, figures, and maps** is located near the end of this book. The comprehensive **Scripture and ancient literature index** as well as the **subject index** and **author index** can help users find related discussions.

This book is **not** a commentary, technical monograph, survey of scholarship, detailed theoretical study, or treatment of theories about the scriptural interpretation of Scripture. This study makes no effort to compile or consider scriptural cross-references. The bar is set at the level of exegesis within Scripture. Because of the wide scope of this study, it only gets into backgrounds, historical contexts, ancient Near Eastern parallels, archaeological evidence, linguistic issues, overview of biblical books, and summary of the research on biblical books if and when these matters bear directly on exegesis within Scripture. The present work does not compete with any of these other critical aspects of study but rather means to narrowly focus on the scriptural use of Scripture as another help among those needed for responsible exegesis. The scope and goals of this work create real limits with difficult choices of what to exclude on nearly every page.

This study introduces **scriptural exegesis within every book of Israel's Scriptures**. While anyone is welcome to read this book, it is designed as a reference study for students and ministers of the word. Although this study features accessible student introduction, sometimes scriptural interpretation of Scripture involves extremely subtle, complicated, and difficult issues. A commitment to student introduction does not mean brushing aside complexities but attempting to provide a starting point for further investigation.

The main text is accessible and introductory relative to students and ministers of the word. **Hebrew** is used only as necessary and in parentheses in the main text with everything translated. **English** Bible readers can skip everything in Hebrew without missing anything. These details appear as needed to help those who study the biblical languages, so they know what they need to look up. When technical issues must be handled, like textual issues, they normally appear in footnotes.

Footnotes feature resources in English whenever possible. Secondary sources are cited by short reference. One can consult the bibliography for fuller detail. Page numbers are included when referring to print editions. When citing commentaries in e-book format scriptural references are provided. For citation of other e-publications, chapter number and/or section heading is/are provided whenever possible. Reference works listed in full in the Abbreviations are not repeated in the Bibliography.

This work uses **default translations for quotation of Scripture and other selected ancient literature.**

Unless otherwise stated, translation of Scripture comes from the NIV. In places the NIV has been mildly modified to reflect verbal parallels in the original language—these cases are marked by †. Other unmarked modifications include Yahweh for "the LORD," Torah or torah as an English loanword for "Law" or "law," and Messiah for "Christ." Translations marked as "lit." (literal) are mine.

Unless stated otherwise: citations of Hebrew Bible from *Biblia Hebraica*, LXX from Göttingen in most cases (see list in Abbreviations) otherwise from Rahlfs, New Testament from NA[28], Qumran biblical contexts from *BQS*, Qumran sectarian texts from *DSSSE*, translation of LXX from NETS, Vulgate from Douay-Rheims, Apocrypha from NRSV, and Targums from *ArBib*.

Filters at end of the main chapters provide representative examples of non-exegetical and/or non-allusive parallels with short literal English glosses rather than NIV. These phrases in the Filters often appear with unpointed Hebrew in parentheses in cases that can benefit users who have studied Hebrew. The unvocalized/unpointed Hebrew text shows the shared language at the level of roots as it appears in stock phrases, figures of speech, and other non-exegetical parallels that have been filtered out. Phrases without quotation marks are summaries rather than direct quotations.

Verse references refer to the English Bible with Hebrew Bible references supplied in **square brackets** [ ] when different. Only English Bible references are used for Exod 20 and Deut 5 because of some double masoretic accents therein.[61]

Stylized brackets { } enclose Scripture references arranged out of sequence when comparing parallel texts side by side. The stylized brackets merely serve to draw attention to intentional re-arrangement of donor texts by receptor texts.

The student will do well to have a copy, or better two, of the Scriptures open to compare the passages under consideration along with their contexts. While every needful passage has been cited, contextual matters everywhere clamor for attention.

The main chapters as listed in the **Contents** follow an older sequence of the Old Testament books (Torah, Prophets, and Writings) found in the standard Hebrew Bible (*BHS/BHQ*) familiar to students who have had a chance to study biblical Hebrew. The decision to use the Hebrew Bible arrangement, which follows the synagogue arrangement of scrolls, helps remind students both that all parallels in this study are based on Hebrew and that biblical scrolls primarily belonged to local congregations collectively at the time of the birth of Christianity.[62] The arrangement of the biblical scrolls, whether like the synagogue and Hebrew Bible or like the English Bible, does not affect the study of scriptural exegesis within Scripture.

---

61. The double accents in Exod 20 and Deut 5 (so-called "upper" and "lower" cantillation) create versing difficulties since *BHS* uses some of each. For a case where the upper and lower cantillation are separated into two sets, see Dotan, *Leningradensia*, 109, 266 (lower cantillation), 1227–28 (upper cantillation). For an overview of manifold ways of handling the double accents of Exod 20 and Deut 5 in *Biblia Hebraica* and other major editions, see Tov, *Textual Criticism*, 6.

62. Scripture only mentions two individuals who have parts of the Scriptures: the eunuch of Ethiopia (Acts 8:28) and Paul (2 Tim 4:13). They represent affluent exceptions—one a royal courtier and the other someone who studied abroad with a leading scholar (Acts 22:3).

An **e-resource companion** to the present work featuring color-coded parallel layouts of hundreds of Scripture parallels examined herein is being released by Zondervan Academic, as noted earlier in this introduction.

A Note to Professors appears near the beginning of this book. The note explains supplementary resources available at no cost.

Is this reference study **comprehensive? No and yes.** The answer is no in that a comprehensive study of all uses of Scripture in Israel's Scriptures is impossible.[63] The authors of Scripture, to varying degrees, invested in scriptural study and communicated by means of sophisticated and subtle literary expression. Scriptural allusion appears everywhere in Scripture. The answer is yes in that the present study makes an effort to evaluate leading uses of Scripture in every book of the Hebrew Bible. Even chapters addressing the few books that do not seem to feature exegetical uses of Scripture have Filters that sort out non-exegetical uses of Scripture.

Study of the scriptural interpretation of Scripture is not the first step or the only step of responsible interpretation. Attending to exegesis within Scripture is an essential part of biblical study. Careful study of the entire Bible personally, within informal or semi-formal contexts, or in an academic program is a significant accomplishment. But it is incomplete without attention to scriptural exegesis of Scripture.

Studying Scripture backwards and forwards by means of Scripture's own interpretive interventions offers promise for stronger and more coherent Christian theology. The challenges facing modern-day Christians call for jettisoning inherently faulty thinking. For example, conceding an Old Testament God of hate in the name of making more attractive a New Testament Christ of love introduces an illegitimate disjunction into divine revelation. The breeding ground for this kind of commonplace dismemberment of scriptural doctrine starts with the practice of working with the Scriptures in a disjointed and isolated manner.

There is no such thing as Messiah or gospel without the Scriptures of Israel. In 1 Cor 15:3–4, Paul and Sosthenes summarize the gospel: "Messiah died for our sins *according to the Scriptures*, that he was buried, that he was raised on the third day *according to the Scriptures*" (emphasis mine). Messiah and the apostles preached repentance, mercy, and righteousness from the Scriptures contextually. God's grace and power in Torah are not something opposed to the uncompromising demands of the prophets and the sometimes shocking forthrightness of the psalmists. Old Testament exegesis of Scripture points the way for interpreting the Christian Bible by means of its natural interconnectivity.

63. Contra Zevit, "Afterword," 242–44, esp. 244. Zevit suggests generating a standardized comprehensive list of "back-referencing" (citations, allusions, and the like) in all 929 chapters of the Hebrew Bible is a straightforward matter of getting scholars to agree on standardized terminology and standardized methods, and then getting them to vote on parallels and direction of dependence. Predictably, basic disagreements on these matters appear even within the book of essays that houses Zevit's claims.

BIBLIOGRAPHIC NOTE ON LISTS OF POTENTIAL PARALLELS

The following paragraphs and list of references explain the sources of the lists of potentially parallel Scriptures in the beginning of each main chapter.

The vast majority of potential parallels come from lists I have developed over the last two decades for students to use in selecting topics for research papers. These lists in turn come out of preparation for several courses I teach. The courses that provide the most important input toward the present project are an upper-level graduate seminar on Old Testament Use of Old Testament and an upper-level graduate elective on New Testament Use of Old Testament.

The research for this project itself included a reexamination of the Hebrew Scriptures by means of a straightforward question: How does this verse, paragraph, chapter, and/or book use Scripture? This research added a good number of potential parallels not previously considered, as well as eliminating others that lacked sufficient evidence.

A mechanical step was added to test and supplement the research noted above. The entire Old Testament was run through an "originality detection" program (the euphemistic name of widely used plagiarism scanning programs). The program is called iThenticate. It needs to be run in a separate quarantined "node" to compare the originality of each part of the Old Testament to only the Old Testament. Each part of the Old Testament, in some cases books but often parts of books, need to be scanned in many small files, unit by unit in comparison to the rest of the Old Testament. The somewhat unorthodox use of a separate node is necessary to eliminate the internet as a comparison set. (The internet is the normal comparison set for using originality detection programs to analyze student assignments.) The New American Standard Bible was chosen for this comparison based on its rigid literalness. The massive results of undifferentiated potential cases of un-originality in the Old Testament needed to be evaluated case by case. It took months to work through the results and identify approximately five pages of additional potential parallels not previously considered to be integrated into the research process. Gratitude for funding and help with the work that went into this arduous task is expressed in the Acknowledgements.

In addition to the research described above, several traditional lists as well as other studies were consulted. In some cases, these provided additional potential parallels that were collated into the research process. The following is a list of resources consulted regarding parallel Scriptures.

Entire Old Testament: Bendavid, *Parallels in the Bible*, 169–219 [Hebrew]; Coogan, *New Oxford Annotated Bible*; Eichorn, *Introduction*, 239–42; Fishbane, *Biblical Interpretation*; Girdlestone, *Deuterographs*; Kent, *Student's Old Testament* series (1904, 1907, 1910, 1914, 1927); Kugel, *Traditions of the Bible*; Lang, "Old Testament Parallels"; *Olive Tree Cross References*; Owen, *Critica Sacra*; Shepherd, *Text in the Middle*, 7–166.

Torah: Block, "Tradition," 137–52; Bolle, *Leviticus*, 2:1–114 (appendix) [Hebrew]; Diewert, "Judah's Argument," 61–74; Driver, *Deuteronomy*, iii–xix, lxxvii–xcv; idem, *Introduction*, 73–75; Hakham, *Exodus*, 2:5–57 (appendix) [Hebrew]; Jericke, "Exodus Material," 137–56; Kiel, *Genesis*, 3:89–174 (appendix) [Hebrew]; Lasserre, *Synopse*, 1–155; Mirsky, *Deuteronomy*, 3–170 (appendix) [Hebrew]; Nelson, *Deuteronomy*, 4–5; Oswald, "Genesis Material," 157–70; Pleins, *Social Visions*, 55; von Rad, *Deuteronomy*, 13; Schnittjer, *Torah Story*, passim; idem, *Torah Story Video Lectures*, passim; idem, "Blessing of Judah," 15–39; idem, "Kadesh Infidelity," 95–120; Weinfeld, *Deuteronomic School*, 320–70.

Former Prophets: Bergen, *1, 2 Kings*, 46–47; Driver, *Introduction*, 105–16, 163; Elitzur, *Judges*, 28–40 [Hebrew]; Harvey, *Retelling the Torah*, 79–81, 101–2; Hays, "1 and 2 Samuel, Books of," *DNTUOT*, forthcoming; Kiel, *Joshua*, 35–53 [Hebrew]; idem, *Samuel*, 1:144–50 [Hebrew]; O'Connell, *Rhetoric*, passim; Ross, "People Heeds Not Scripture," 373–94.

Isaiah: Cheyne, "Critical Study of Parallel Passages," 2:241–58; Childs, *Isaiah*, passim; Hays, *Origins*, 217–50; Schultz, *Search for Quotation*, 339–41; idem, "Isaianic Intertextuality," 57; Sommer, *A Prophet Reads Scripture*, passim.

Jeremiah: Bergren, *Prophets*, 182–83; Bright, "Prose Sermons," 30–35; Carroll, "Intertextuality and Jeremiah," 70–72; Driver, *Introduction*, 277; Holladay, *Jeremiah 2*, 53–63, 86–87; Parke-Taylor, *Formation*, 1–292; Richards, "Influence," 132–36; Weinfeld, *Deuteronomic School*, 320–61.

Ezekiel: Bergsma, "Relevance," 229–35; Bolle, *Leviticus*, 2:69–78 (appendix) [Hebrew]; Driver, *Introduction*, 147; Gile, "Deuteronomic Influence," 152–90, et passim; Greenberg, "Influence," 29–37; Hays, "Ezekiel, Book of," *DNTUOT*, forthcoming; Levitt Kohn, *New Heart*, 31–75, 86–93; Lyons, "Extension,"138–52; idem, *Law to Prophecy*, esp. 162–86; idem, "Marking," 245–50; idem, "Persuasion," 79–86; idem, "Transformation," 1–32; Milgrom, *Leviticus 23–27*, 2348–63; Rooker, "Use of OT Ezekiel," 46–49; Tooman, "Transformation," 50–91.

Hosea: Bass, "Hosea's Use of Scripture," 104–271; Brueggemann, *Tradition for Crisis*, 13–51; Cassuto, *Biblical*, 1:79–100; Ginsberg, "Hosea, Book of," *EJ*, 9:557; Mirsky, Meltzer, and Kiel, *Twelve*, 1:33–47 [Hebrew]; Rooker, "Use of OT Hosea," 51–66; Vang, "When a Prophet Quotes Moses," 288–302.

Joel: Assis, "Date and Meaning," 166–67; Coggins, "Innerbiblical Quotations," 76–81; Driver, *Joel and Amos,* 19–22; Gray, "Parallel Passages," 214–25; Nogalski, *Redactional Processes* 290–91; Redditt, "Book of Joel," 236; Strazicich, *Joel's Use of Scripture,* 59–252.

Amos: Bergren, *Prophets and the Law,* 182–83; Bramer, "Literary Genre," 46–48; Driver, *Joel and Amos,* 113–15; Paul, *Amos,* 4.

Obadiah: Block, *Obadiah,* 40–41; Childs, *Introduction,* 412; Mirsky, Meltzer, and Kiel, *Twelve,* 1:11–13 [Hebrew]; Parke-Taylor, *Formation,* 147–51.

Jonah: Bewer, *Jonah,* 23–24, 44–49; Dell, "Reinventing," 88–99; Driver, *Introduction,* 322–23; Hunter, "Jonah," 144–50; Simon, *Jonah,* xxxvi–xxxix.

Micah: Anderson and Freedman, *Micah,* 27; Bergren, *Prophets and the Law,* 182–83; Cheyne, *Micah,* 12; Driver, *Introduction,* 334, n.; Schultz, *Search for Quotation,* 306.

Nahum: Armerding, "Nahum," 8:560–63; Cathcart, "Nahum, Book of," *ABD* 4:1000; Mirsky, Meltzer, and Kiel, *Twelve,* 2:9 [Hebrew]; Nysse, "Keeping Company," 217–18.

Habakkuk: Anderson, *Habakkuk,* passim; Banister, "Theophanies," 184–91; Chisholm, "Exegetical and Theological Study," 142–204; idem, "Habakkuk, Book of," *DNTUOT,* forthcoming; idem, *Handbook Prophets,* 433–43; idem, "Minor Prophets," 415; Driver, *Introduction,* 337–40; Mirsky, Meltzer, and Kiel, *Twelve,* 2:8–9 [Hebrew]; Ward, *Habakkuk,* 6.

Zephaniah: Berlin, *Zephaniah,* 13–17; Davidson, *Zephaniah,* 104; Keil and Delitzsch, *Zephaniah,* 118; Kselman, "Zephaniah, Book of," *ABD* 6:1077–80.

Haggai: Hill, *Haggai,* 25.

Zechariah: Boda, *Zechariah,* passim; idem, *Exploring,* 2:174–77, 184–89; idem and Floyd, *Bringing Out the Treasure,* 7–200 (Mason), 324–32 (Redditt), and 262 (Tigchelaar); Lee, *Intertextual,* 241; Meyers and Meyers, *Zechariah 9–14,* 40–43; Nurmela, "Growth," 249–58; Stead, *Intertextuality,* 31–36, et passim.

Malachi: Berry, "Malachi's Dual Design," 270–72; Gibson, *Covenant,* 49–69, 85–114, 125–54, 165–81, 187–98, 205–12, 232 (table), 235–56; Hill, *Malachi,* 401–412; Mirsky, Meltzer, and Kiel, *Twelve,* 2:11–13 [Hebrew]; Weyde, *Prophecy,* passim.

Psalms: Brodersen, *The End,* 35–41, 93–98, 137–42, 179–86, 234–41; Cheyne, *Origins,* 461–84; Elliott, "Excurses upon Psalms XCI—C," 506–12; Ḥakham, *Psalms,* 1:XXXVIII–XL; Kirkpatrick, *Psalms Book I,* passim; idem, *Psalms Books II and III,* passim; idem, *Psalms Books IV and V,* passim; Kohlenberger, *Comparative Psalter,* passim.

Job: Cheyne, *Job and Solomon,* 84–88; Ḥakham, *Job,* XVIII–XXXIII; Hartley, *Job,* 11–15; Kwon, *Scribal Culture,* 71–105; Kynes, *Obituary for "Wisdom Literature,"* 161–65, 173; Pfeiffer, "Dual Origin," 202–5; Pyeon, *You Have Not,* 34–40, 84–93, 111–16, 135–38, 150–52, 170–73, 186–88, 204–6.

Proverbs: Ansberry, "Proverbs, Book of," *DNTUOT,* forthcoming; Crenshaw, "Proverbs, Book of" in *ABD* 5:519; essays in Dell and Kynes, *Reading Proverbs Intertextually;*

Kynes, *Obituary for "Wisdom Literature,"* 230–31, 235, 237; Weinfeld, *Deuteronomic School*, 362–63. Also, for parallels within Proverbs, Snell, *Twice-Told Proverbs*, 35–59.

Ruth: Beattie, "Ruth," 251–67; Berlin, "Legal Fiction," 3–18; Berman, "Ancient Hermeneutics," 22–38; Braulik, "Ruth," 1–20; Chan and Venter, "Midrash," 1–6; Chavel, *Oracular Law*, 250–56; Embry, "Legalities," 31–44; Fischer, "Ruth," 140–49; Goulder, "Ruth," 307–19; Jackson, "Ruth," 75–111; Jones, *Reading Ruth*, 65–114; Kelly, "Ethics," 155–66.

Song of Songs: Campbell, "Song of David's Son," 26–32; Carr, *Formation*, 435–38; Davis, *Proverbs*, 245, 255; Fishbane, *Song*, xxix; Kingsmill, "Song," 315–17, 332; Murphy, *Song*, 67–69; Schellenberg, "'May Her Breasts Satisfy,'" 256–61; Strollo, "Value," 196–201, esp. table, 197.

Ecclesiastes: Kynes, *Obituary for "Wisdom Literature,"* 194–203; Schoors, "(Mis)use of Intertextuality," 45–59.

Lamentations: Berlin, *Lamentations*, passim; Bezzel, "Man of Constant Sorrow," 257–58; Gottwald, *Studies*, 44–46; Holladay, *Jeremiah 2*, 84–84; Sommer, *A Prophet Reads Scripture*, 127–30, 271–72, n. 55; Willey, *Remember*, 125–32.

Esther: Berlin, *Esther*, xxxvi–xli; Firth, "When Samuel Met Esther," 15–28; Grossman, "Dynamic Analogies," 394–414; Schellekens, "Accession Days," 120, 127.

Daniel: Henze, "Use of Scripture," 279–307; Lester, *Daniel Evokes Isaiah*, 31–59, et passim; Scheetz, *Concept*, 129–46.

Ezra-Nehemiah: Eskenazi, *In an Age of Prose*, passim; Klein, "Ezra & Nehemiah," passim; Murawski, "Study the Law," passim; Schnittjer, "Bad Ending," 39, 42–44; Slotki, *Daniel, Ezra, Nehemiah*, passim; Smith, "Influence," 345–64; and esp. Schnittjer, *Ezra-Nehemiah*, forthcoming.

Chronicles: Bendavid, *Parallels in the Bible*, 14–164 [Hebrew]; Delitzsch, *Isaiah*, 17–18; Endres, Millar, and Burns, *Chronicles and Its Synoptic Parallels*; Curtis and Madsen, *Chronicles*, 17–19; Driver, *Introduction*, 519–25; von Rad, "Levitical Sermon," in *From Genesis*, 235, 237, n. 5, 265; Schnittjer, "Individual versus Collective," 118–29.

New Testament: Archer and Chirichigno, *OT Quotations in NT*; Gough, *NT Quotations*; NIV; Turpie, *OT in the New*; UBS[5], 857–60. With few exceptions, New Testament parallels are limited to the more explicit ones in these sources. A small number of additional parallels have been added at the suggestion of the blind peer reviewers. Septuagint (LXX) is listed when evidence suggests. For more expansive lists including lesser allusions and possible echoes see NA[28], 836–69; UBS[5], 864–83.

A NOTE TO PROFESSORS

Professors may wish to consider using this study reference as a supplementary textbook to help students think with the authors of Scripture. Working on scriptural exegesis found within the Scriptures themselves can enrich biblical study and strengthen student outcomes. Supplementing individual courses or a series of courses with attention to exegetical interconnections within Scripture offers far-reaching benefits to students. To get **professor helps at no cost**, refer to ZondervanAcademic.com to create an instructor account. From there you can access TextbookPlus Instructor Resources, including the following aids:

- Study and discussion questions with suggested readings to supplement various courses on the Old Testament and Hermeneutics
- Visual aids
- Quiz and exam questions
- Suggested syllabus for a course on Old Testament Use of Old Testament
- Suggested readings as well as study and discussion questions to serve as a supplement for courses on New Testament Use of Old Testament
- Study and discussion questions with suggested readings to supplement various courses on the New Testament

Chapter 1

GENESIS

SYMBOLS[1]

- // verbal parallels (A level)
- /~/ synoptic parallel (A level)
- ~ B, probable interpretive allusion; C, possible; D, probably not
- + interpretive blend
- >/< more or less similar (see Filters)
- * part of interpretive network (see Networks)

USE OF GENESIS CONTEXTS BY OTHER GENESIS CONTEXTS[2]

3:1–5~2:16, 17 (A) (exegetical contest in the garden)

5:1–3~1:26–28 (A)+2:4 (B) (commentary on creation of humans)

9:1–7~1:26, 28–29 (B) (renewal of the human mandate)

49:8, 10*~27:29 (B)+37:5–11 (C) (blessing of Judah) (* see Judah-king network)

OLD TESTAMENT USE OF GENESIS (SEE RESPECTIVE NOTES)

1~Ps 104 (B) (hymn of creation)

1:1~Isa 65:17–18 (B) (new heaven and new earth endure)

1:2~Deut 32:10–11 (B) (like a mother eagle)

1:3–25~Jer 4:23–28 (B) (anti-creation)

1:16, 26, 28~Ps 8:3–8[4–9] (B) (What are mortals?)

1:16~Ps 136:7–9 (B) (maker of great lights in covenantal loyalty retrospective)

1:20–28~Zeph 1:2–3 (B) (anti-creation)

1:26; 3:22; 11:7~Isa 6:8 (C) (divine plural pronouns)

2:2~Exod 40:33 (C) (tabernacle finished)

2:2, 3*~Exod 16:30* (B); ~Exod 20:8–11* (B) (Sabbath) (* see Sabbath network)

2:7~Zech 12:1 (C) (creator of heaven, earth, and the human spirit)

2:7~Ps 103:14 (B) (attribute formula)

2:7; 3:19~Eccl 3:20–21; 12:7 (B) (return dust to the earth and spirit to God)

3:14–15~Isa 25:10b–12 (C) (trampling Moab to the dust)

3:14~Isa 65:25 (B) (curse removed with the exception of upon the serpent)

3:14~Mic 7:17 (B) (lick dust like a snake)

4:1, 2~Zech 13:5 (B) (denying prophetic vocation)

5:3–32+10:2–4, 6–8, 13–18, 22–29+11:10–29~1 Chr 1:1–27 (B) (genealogies Adam to Abraham)

6:4~Num 13:33 (C) (Nephilim)

9:8–17~Isa 54:9 (B) (like the days of Noah)

9:16~Isa 24:5 (C) (everlasting covenant)

10:2, 3, 6~Ezek 38:2, 6 (C) (identity of Gog and his militia)

10:4, 7~Ps 72:10–11 (C) (all kings bring tribute and serve)

10:5~Zeph 2:11 (C) (islands of the nations)

11:7~Deut 32:8 (C) (dividing the nations)

11:27–32~Josh 24:2 (C) (Joshua's panoramic retrospective at Shechem)

12:3*; **18:18***; **22:18***~Ps 72:17* (B) (nations bless him) (* see Abrahamic covenant network)

12:3*; **27:29***//Num 24:9* (expected king) (* see Abrahamic covenant network)

1. For explanation of symbols, see Symbols and Abbreviations and Introduction. For other help, see Glossary.
2. See Bibliographic Note on Lists of Potential Parallels.

12:4~Neh 9:7–8 (C) (covenant with Abraham in panoramic retrospective)
12:10+18:18~Deut 26:5–10 (B) (firstfruits liturgy)
13:17~Deut 19:1–13 (B) (motivation for law of asylum)
14:18–20~Ps 110:4 (B) (priest in the order of Melchizedek)
15:6~Ps 106:29–31 (A) (credited it to him as righteousness)
15:6, 18~Neh 9:7–8 (B) (covenant with Abraham in panoramic retrospective)
17*~Lev 26:40–42 (B) (humble uncircumcised hearts) (* see Abrahamic covenant network)
17:8~Ps 105:11 (B) (land promise in poetic retrospective)
19:5*~Judg 19:22* (B) (bring out the men) (* see cities of the plain network)
20:6–7~Ps 105:15 (B) (protecting messiahs and prophets in poetic retrospective)
22:2~2 Chr 3:1–2 (B) (building the temple in Solomon's fourth year)
25:12–18~1 Chr 1:28–33 (B) (families of Ishmael and Keturah's sons)
25:8~2 Chr 24:15 (C) (Jehoiada was old and full of years)
25:22, 23, 26~Hos 12:3[4] (B) (Jacob wrestles in womb)
26:5~Ps 105:44–45 (B) (commands, precepts, and torah in poetic retrospective)
28:13–19; 35:11–15~Hos 12:5[6] (C) (Yahweh is his memorial)
32:24, 28[25, 29]; 35:15~Hos 12:4[5] (B) (Jacob wrestles with a man)
35:18–19~Mic 5:2[1] (B) (ruler from Bethlehem Ephrathah)
35:21~Mic 4:8 (C) (tower of the flock)
35:22–26~1 Chr 2:1–2 (B) (sons of Israel)
36:1–43~1 Chr 1:34–54 (B) (genealogies and kings of ancient Edom)
38:1–7, 29–30+46:12~1 Chr 2:1–17 (B) (genealogies of Judah through family of David)
41:25, 28, 32~Dan 2:28–29 (B) (divine revelation by dreams)
46:8–9~1 Chr 5:3 (C) (sons of Reuben)
46:10~1 Chr 4:24–31 (C) (early tribe of Simeon)
46:11~1 Chr 6:1–4[5:27–30] (C) (line of Levi)
49:3–4+48:13–20+49:8–12*~1 Chr 5:1–2 (B/C) (Reuben's incest) (* see Judah-king network)
49:8–12*~1 Chr 28:4–6* (B) (election of Solomon based on choosing Judah) (* see Judah-king network)
49:8–9*~Mic 5:8–9[7–8] (C) (like a lion) (* see Judah-king network)
49:9*//Num 24:9* (expected king) (* see Judah-king network)
49:10*~2 Sam 7:14–15* (B) (covenant loyalty shall not depart) (* see Judah-king and place networks)
49:10*~Ezek 21:27*[32] (C) (to whom it belongs shall come) (* see Judah-king network)
49:10*~Ps 2:8–9 (C) (scepter against the nations) (* see Judah-king network)
49:11*~Zech 9:9* (B) (king riding into Jerusalem) (* see Judah-king network)

NEW TESTAMENT USE OF GENESIS

1:3~2 Cor 4:6 (let light shine)
1:27//5:2//Matt 19:4; Mark 10:6 (male and female)
2:2//Heb 4:4 (God rested)
2:7//1 Cor 15:45 (became living being)
2:24//Matt 19:5; Mark 10:7–8; 1 Cor 6:16; Eph 5:31 (one flesh)
5:24 LXX~Heb 11:5 (Enoch taken)
12:1//Acts 7:3 (go to land)
12:3; 18:18; 22:18//Gal 3:8 (nations blessed through you)
12:7; 13:15; 24:7//Gal 3:16 (to your offspring)
12:7//Heb 6:14 (many descendants)
14:18–20~Heb 7:1–2 (priest in the order of Melchizedek)
15:5//Rom 4:18 (so shall offspring be)
15:6//Rom 4:3, 9, 22; Gal 3:6; Jas 2:23 (believed God)
15:13, 14//Acts 7:6–7 (will come out from slavery)
17:5//Rom 4:17, 18 (father of many nations)
17:8~Acts 7:5 (land as promised possession)
18:10, 14//Rom 9:9 (Sarah will have a son)
21:10//Gal 4:30 (get rid of slave woman)
21:12//Rom 9:7; Heb 11:18 (through Isaac)
22:16–17//Heb 6:13–14 (promise of blessing)
22:18//Acts 3:25 (Abraham's offspring)
25:23//Rom 9:12 (older will serve younger)
26:4//Acts 3:25 (Abraham's offspring)
28:12//John 1:51 (Jacob's ladder)
47:31 LXX~Heb 11:21 (leaned on his staff)

HERMENEUTICAL PROFILE OF THE USE OF GENESIS CONTEXTS IN OTHER GENESIS CONTEXTS

Genesis brims full of parallels and interconnections within itself of many kinds. The majority of these interrelated elements exhibit literary functions that contribute to the unity and cohesion of the narrative. All elements within a story contribute to it and get interpreted in relation to all other parts.

Literary relations by allusion—repetitions, *inclusios*, extended echo-effect, and the like—share several common characteristics with exegetical allusions but differ in their purpose. Narrative literary relations serve the needs of the story in terms of cohesion, unity, irony, and so forth. When identifying exegesis, literary relations need to be filtered out as much as possible. These are judgment calls. The present approach seeks to err on the side of filtering out borderline cases in order to focus on scriptural exegesis (see Filters).

Since scriptural exegetical use of Scripture typically refers to interpretive allusions between books, only a few examples appear in Genesis. In each case the receptor context re-presents and re-purposes or enhances donor context(s) by means of interpretive outcomes. The exegetical contest between the serpent and the woman puts a variety of interpretive maneuvers on display and includes overt marking of allusions. The exegetical contest in the garden offers a warning against the dangers of bad exegesis. It also illustrates that just because interpretation appears in the Bible, it may not advance revelation. Much depends on who presents the interpretive allusions along with contextual factors.

The other cases of exegetical allusion within Genesis each feature interpretive elements that go beyond literary coherence. The narrator interpretively blends two donor contexts from the creation days at the head of the "generations of Adam" (Gen 5:1–3). God exegetically expands the human mandate when he renews it with Noah (9:1–7). And Jacob interpretively alludes to events appearing earlier in Genesis when he gives his blessing to Judah (49:8, 10). These cases each involve allusions—intentional reference to other contexts with verbal, syntactic, and/or contextual parallels—and interpretation.

USE OF GENESIS CONTEXTS BY OTHER GENESIS CONTEXTS

3:1–5~2:16, 17 (A) (exegetical contest in the garden). The serpent and the woman engage in a legal exegetical debate concerning the single authoritative prohibition for life in the garden (Gen 3:1–5). After comparing the competing interpretive allusions, each can be evaluated briefly (bold and italics signify verbal parallels at the level of roots, underlining signifies marking, and broken underlining signifies interpretive expansions):

> And Yahweh God commanded the man, "**You** are free to **eat from any tree in the garden**; [17] but from the tree of *the knowledge of good and evil, you must not eat from it*, for when you eat from it *you will certainly die*." (Gen 2:16, 17 lit.)

> Now the serpent was more crafty than any of the wild animals Yahweh God had made. He said to the woman, "Did God really say, '**You** must not **eat from any tree in the garden**'?" [2] The woman said to the serpent, "We may **eat fruit from the trees in the garden,** [3] but from the tree that is in the middle of the garden God did say, '*You must not eat from it,* and you must not touch it, or *you will die*.'" [4] "*You will* not *certainly die*," the serpent said to the woman. [5] "For God knows that when *you eat from it* your eyes will be opened, and you will be like God, *knowing good and evil*." [6] When the woman saw that the fruit of the tree was good for food and pleasing to the eye, and also desirable for gaining wisdom, she took some and ate it. She also gave some to her husband, who was with her, and he ate it. (3:1–6, v. 3 lit.)

The syntax of both parts of the serpent's initial interpretive allusion require care to translate. The phrase "you must not eat from any" in Gen 3:1 can be read as an absolute negation.[3] But the preceding emphatic construction of "Did God really say?" infers a question, captured well by the NIV.[4] The emphatic literary signals suggest that the serpent speaks sarcastically, or better, with an incredulous tone. The serpent effectively suggests an incongruity between free access to all the trees except one. Reading backwards from 3:6, the wide-angle view that reveals the man standing there also, draws attention to the serpent directing his interpretive question "to the woman." She did not directly hear the prohibition.

The woman affirms both the freedom and the exception by direct citation (3:2, 3). Along the way she exegetically embellishes the prohibition by an additional prohibition against touching it (3:3).[5] Since she was not available to hear the utterance, it raises the issue of whether the exegetical embellishment—"and you must not touch it"—is her own or the man's when he told her the rules of the garden. The mediation of the rules happens offstage to provoke readers to wonder about whose exegetical adjustment appears in Gen 3:3. But reading backward from 3:6 with the man standing right there suggests the woman's interpretive allusion fits with the spirit of the man's explanation of the prohibition to her.

The serpent's persuasive second allusion includes interpreting the punishment against the sense of the citation with a bold misreading: "you will not certainly die" (3:4; cf. 2:17). Then the serpent exegetically extrapolates from the name of the tree that eating brings knowledge of good and evil (3:5). The serpent's proposal that eating the fruit would make her "like God" loads heavy irony on the entire exegetical debate within the larger framework of Genesis. The story of the creation days spells out the signature human feature as

---

3. See GKC §152b. The serpent and woman also shift second-person singulars to plurals (as observed by Chapman, "Breath," 253).

4. The emphatic "indeed!" (אַף) in combination with a conditional particle as here (אַף כִּי) connotes an incredulous question—"Really?!" (see "I אַף," no. 5 *HALOT* 1:76). 4QGen[k]/4Q10 adds the interrogative particle in Gen 3:1 to make the question explicit (האף) (*BQS* 1:7). Some other ancient versions make similar adjustments. MT (and SP) preferred (so Tal, *BHQ*, 84*).

5. Post-biblical traditions might call interpretations like this a fence around the law (cf. m. 'Aboth 1:1).

being in the likeness and image of God. The serpent tells the in-likeness-of-God being that she needs to transgress the single prohibition to become like God. Yet transgressing the word of God brings death, remaking the humans as contradictions of themselves. Fallen humans live as contradictions of themselves by being in the very image of God while ever exercising their propensity to rebel against the word of God. They are like-God and unlike God at one time.

In sum, both the serpent and the woman verbally allude to authoritative instructions. Both also interject exegetical enhancements. The interpretive expansion of not touching it, deduced or cited by the woman, proves an ineffective extra measure against crafty serpents. The serpent's subtle interpretive distortions strengthen his bold misreading and carry the day.

5:1–3~1:26–28 (A)+2:4 (B) (commentary on creation of humans). The narrator opens the "generations of Adam" with an interpretive allusion to the story of the creation days. In Gen 5:1–3 the narrator economically recycles and deduces a number of social and theological implications from parallels with Gen 1:26–28 and 2:4.

The term "human being"/"humankind" continues to function both as a collective singular of the human race as a whole (Gen 5:1) and also as a plural inclusive of the diversity of humans as male and female (5:2). The term "human" in Gen 5:2, transliterated as *adam* (אָדָם), does not denote Adam's name but the human race collectively—"he created *them* . . . he named *them* human" (5:2 lit.).[6] Like Gen 1, the commentary in 5:1–2 uses the terms "create" and "make" with an identical sense but preserves the use of "create" for special acts.[7] Notice how the commentary in Gen 5:1–2 features an interpretive blend of 1:27–28 and 2:4 (emphases signify verbal parallels):

> So God *created mankind* in his own image, *in* the image *of God* he created *them*; male and female he created them. God blessed them and said to them, "Be fruitful and increase in number; fill the earth and subdue it. Rule over the fish in the sea and the birds in the sky and over every living creature that moves on the ground." (Gen 1:27–28)

> This is the **account** of the heavens and the earth when they were created, **when** Yahweh **God** made the earth and the heavens. (2:4)

> This is the written **account** of Adam's family line. **When God** created mankind, he made *them in* the likeness *of God.* He created them male and female and blessed them. And he named them "*Mankind*" when *they were created.* (5:1–2)

6. In spite of the twice repeated plural pronoun "of them" the Septuagint translates *'adam* (אָדָם) as "Adam"—"He named their name 'Adam'" (Gen 5:2 LXX). See Tal, *BHQ*, 90*–91* (on 5:1); Wevers, *Notes on Genesis*, 69; Bandstra, *Genesis 1–11*, 287, 289–90.

7. The term "create" appears seven times in the narrative of the creation days, three times in summary statements (Gen 1:1; 2:3, 4), once for the sea serpents (1:21), and three times of creating human beings (1:27 [3x]). In Scripture God is always the subject of the verb "create" in Q (see "I ברא," *DCHR* 2:261; *HALOT* 1:153).

The expression "when" or "in the day" (lit.) continues to denote "at that time," whether of the sixth day or of the entire sequence of creating days (2:4; 5:1).

The terms "image" and "likeness" connote the kind of relationship between biological father and son (5:3), which by backreading speaks to the kind of relationship humans enjoy with the creator (1:26).[8] The commentary in Gen 5:3 affirms that human beings remain in the image of God after the fall as one of its major interpretive outcomes (bold signifies verbal parallels).

> Then God said, "Let us make mankind in our **image**, in our **likeness**, so that they may rule over the fish in the sea and the birds in the sky, over the livestock and all the wild animals, and over all the creatures that move along the ground." (1:26)

> When Adam had lived 130 years, he had a son in his own **likeness**, in his own **image**; and he named him Seth. (5:3)

Parents name the children they conceive (5:3). This suggests the creator's parental role to all of his manifold creations which he names—day, night, heavens, land, seas (1:5, 8, 10). But humans as lords over creation bear a parental responsibility as seen in their naming of the creatures (2:19–20). The close figural association between creator and parent in Gen 5:1–3 underlies many theological connotations concerning God's character developed elsewhere in Scripture. Humans in like manner bear much responsibility as lords of creation in the creator's own image.

In sum, the commentary in Gen 5:1–3 uses an interpretive blend of select elements of the story of the creation days to explain the nature of the relationship between God and humans. The commentary also infers the ongoing reality of humans in the image of God after their rebellion.

9:1–7~1:26, 28–29 (B) (renewal of the human mandate). The post-flood version of the human mandate verbally parallels the mandate to the first humans, establishing continuity with figural patterning between Adam and Noah. The similarities invite consideration of the advancement of revelation, some of which includes exegetical allusion (italics signify verbal parallels).

> *God blessed* them *and said* to them, "*Be fruitful and increase in number; fill the earth* and subdue it." (Gen 1:28)

> Then *God blessed* Noah and his sons, *saying* to them, "*Be fruitful and increase in number and fill the earth*. . . . As for you, *be fruitful and increase in number*; multiply on *the earth and increase* upon it." (9:1, 7)

8. Contra Tigay, who argues that in the likeness of parents refers to no major birth defects ("'He Begot,'" 140, 147).

The term in Gen 9:7 that the NIV translates as "multiply" is the same term from 1:20, 21 translated "teem," as in "let the waters *teem* with living creatures." The expression for manifold aquatic life strengthens the sense of the blessing to Noah's family to fill the earth. The framing of the mandate to Noah by the paraphrase of the same to the first humans invites comparison of several adjustments in the post-flood way of life that appear within the interpretive frame (9:1, 7).

First, while the human dietary limits open beyond vegetation to include animals, consuming blood is prohibited (9:3; cf. 1:29). The rationale turns entirely on the function of blood as signifying life (9:4). Later Torah prohibitions likewise exclude consuming blood based on its function for atoning value in worship (Lev 17:11). The symbolic function of blood as the "life" of flesh drives these several prohibitions (Gen 9:4; Lev 17:14; Deut 12:23). Humans live in a world encoded with theological instruction that speaks every time they dine on meat.

Second, the value of human life extends even to protect it from animals as later law develops more fully (Gen 9:5; Exod 21:28–32).

Third, capital punishment stems from the value of human life created in the image of God (Gen 9:6). The logic needs to be distinguished from an "eye for an eye" limitation that undergirds other biblical laws (Exod 21:24–25). Taking human life remains the prerogative of the creator who gives life. The divine prerogative to take life as punishment is entrusted to human justice in Gen 9:6 because of the value of the life taken. Human life retains mortal value because of the divine image in humans. This same principle of human value because of the likeness of God gets developed further by prohibition against wrongful speech in Jas 3:9–10.

In sum, the similar refrain for the first humans and Noah's family to fill the earth invites comparison to what has changed. God's word to Noah advances revelation by means of interpretive allusion to his word to the first humans. Nearly all the advancements—eating meat, capital punishment—expand on the implications of creation and the residual image of God in humans.

49:8, 10*~27:29 (B)+37:5–11 (C) (blessing of Judah) (* see Judah-king network). Israel's deathbed testament to his first four sons interpretively alludes to elements in the previous narrative. Jacob pronounces words of judgment against Reuben for his incestuous relations with his stepmother (Gen 49:4; cf. 35:22). He speaks judgment against Simeon and Levi because of their bloody vengeance against the people of Shechem (49:7; cf. 34). In these cases, Jacob's testaments do not share verbal parallels with the donor contexts. As such these need to be considered literary, not exegetical. In the case of Jacob's blessing of Judah, he makes interpretive allusions with sufficient verbal parallels to evaluate exegetical agenda.

Jacob's blessing upon Judah makes him ruler over his brothers and his enemies (49:8). He also applies symbolic language of royalty, especially "scepter" (49:10; cf. 35:11). The blessing seems to be in response to Judah's arrangement with Jacob during a time of crisis whereby he honored his word and returned the beloved son to his father (43:8–9;

46:28–30).[9] Jacob uses language from the blessing he stole from Esau and echoes the imagery of response to Joseph's dreams. The brothers who had lived to bow before Joseph may consider Joseph's rule a prototype for the expected Judah-king (italics signify verbal parallels, and broken underlining signifies similar imagery):

> May nations serve you and peoples bow down to you. Be lord over *your brothers*, and *may the sons* of your mother *bow down to you*. May those who curse you be cursed and those who bless you be blessed. (27:29)

> When he told his father as well as his brothers, his father rebuked him and said, "What is this dream you had? Will your mother and I and *your brothers* actually come and *bow down* to the ground before you?" (37:10; cf. v. 8)

> Judah, *your brothers* will praise you; your hand will be on the neck of your enemies; your father's *sons will bow down to you*. . . . The scepter will not depart from Judah, nor the ruler's staff from between his feet, until he to whom it belongs shall come and the obedience of the nations shall be his. (49:8, 10)

The revelatory force of the blessing of Judah has been widely recognized by scriptural writers. Scriptural prophets and narrators return to the blessing of Judah many times. The rich, textured, and ambiguous imagery generates a large number of interpretations. Later scriptural interpretations do not exhaust but increase the generative capabilities of an expectational donor context like the blessing of Judah. Scriptural expectations and their fulfillments tend to invite additional scriptural expectations based on the very same donor texts (see Judah-king network).[10]

But should Jacob's words be granted authority to shape expectations? The authoritative revelation by Jacob has nothing to do with his (un)reliability or tendency to deceive. When Isaac put his word of blessing for rulership upon Jacob, it did not matter that it was under false pretenses. It cannot be changed or taken back (27:37). The ancestral word of blessing within the covenantal framework of Genesis carries an irrevocable or binding authority. In this way Jacob can serve as a vehicle for the advancement of revelation in the blessing of Judah.

FILTERS

Genesis exhibits extensive literary cohesion of several sorts. Mirror imaging or chiastic structures within episodes or by entire ancestral cycles of episodes function as literary parallels rather than exegetical connections.

9. See Schnittjer, *Torah Story*, 166–68; Giffone, "'Israel's' Only Son?" 966–69.

10. For a detailed study of textual issues in Gen 49:8–12 and the interpretive network associated with it, see Schnittjer, "Blessing of Judah," 15–39.

Genesis also features numerous examples of extended echo-effect, with shared verbal and thematic elements, causing them to sound alike and have a familiar feel. These sorts of intentional literary relations function as part of the cohesion and unity of narratives. Literary interconnections that join together elements as a cohesive narrative need to be filtered out from among exegetical allusions.

The highly literary nature of Genesis means that interconnections abound. The following filters include only representative examples of non-exegetical literary parallels within Genesis.[11] These lists are not comprehensive or complete.

Connections within Genesis

Type-scenes refer to common scenarios in literature like a would-be mother with infertility issues or younger siblings trying to overcome their older counterparts. Observing these broad scenarios can be helpful as far as they go, especially for general literary observations. Comparisons of similarities in specific episodes offer more substantial outcomes for scriptural interpretation.

Genesis features many episodes modeled on previous ones. The similarities create an extended echo-effect whereby the earlier story projects connotations on the subsequent one (see Glossary). It can help to lay out similarities and differences in parallel columns. But even without a diagram anyone can hear the sounds of the earlier story in the later one.[12]

When Yahweh personifies sin to Cain and warns that "it *desires* to have you, but you *must rule over* it" (Gen 4:7), it recalls the curse of the woman "your *desire* will be for your husband, and he *will rule over* you" (3:16, emphases signify verbal parallels). The similarities invite comparison of the differences. Many additional similarities between the sin of the parents and Cain load interpretive connotations onto the story of the first murderous brother (3:16–24>/<4:7–16).

The similarities between the human fall and Noah's drunkenness provide connotative effects on the episode (2:8–3:14>/<9:20–25). Remarkably, the similarities between the first humans' sin and Noah's drunkenness are different than those between the sins of the humans in the garden and the sin of Cain. The natural flexibility of narrative partially explains the ongoing connections generated between the beginning of Genesis and its episodes, its ending, the ending of Torah, and the ending of the New Testament.

Other extended echo-effect episodes in Genesis include: the drunkenness of Noah and drunkenness of Lot: they knew/did not know what son/daughters had done (9:21, 24>/<19:32–35); the expansive augmenting of the Abrahamic covenant (>/<12:1–3; 13:14–17; 15:5, 18–20; 17:9–14; 22:15–18; 26:2–6; 28:13–15; 35:9–12; 48:3–4,

11. For potential parallels between Genesis and elsewhere in Scripture see Kiel, *Genesis*, 3:89–174 (appendix) [Hebrew]. Much of Kiel's list presents short phrases with broad similarities to their scriptural counterparts that often seem more like stock phrases than potential parallels.

12. For a side-by-side layout of the similarities of the sin of the parents and Cain, see Schnittjer, *Torah Story*, 84; for the fall and Noah's drunkenness, see 105; and for several other examples mentioned here, see ad loc; Postell, "Abram as Israel," 16–31.

see Table G1 below); the "she's my sister" stories of the Hebrew ancestors (12:10–20> /<20:1–18>/ <26:6–11); Laban's search for the household idols Rachel stole and the Egyptian official's search for the goblet of sorcery in Benjamin's goods (31:19–35>/ <44:1–13).[13] Many, many other episodes in Genesis share connecting similarities.

The ongoing pattern of extended echo-effect stories trains readers to expect that children will act like their parents and God will act again as he has acted. In this way Abraham's sojourn in Egypt, including plagues against the pharaoh and his people, anticipates the story of exodus (12:17–20>/<Gen 45–Exod 14).[14]

Other kinds of embedded literary allusions include the blessings of Israel upon his sons on his deathbed that are framed as poetry. The blessings naturally look backward at the lives of the sons and forward to his word for them (Gen 49:1–28). Torah houses four other long poems that likewise interpretively look backward and forward: the Song of the Sea (Exod 15:1–18); Balaam's oracles (Num 24:3–9, 15–24); the Song of Moses (Deut 32:1–43); and Moses's blessing of the tribes (33:1–29). The Deuteronomistic narrative (Joshua-Judges-Samuel-Kings) also makes use of occasionally embedded poems, though not always as far reaching with their expectations: song of Deborah (Judg 5); prayer of Hannah (1 Sam 2:1–10); song of the bow borrowed from the book of Jashar (2 Sam 1:19–27); song of David (2 Sam 22); David's last words (23:1–7); and Isaiah's taunt against Sennacherib (2 Kgs 19:21–28).

Sometimes forward-looking expectations naturally set up later associated elements, like the word of God to Abraham concerning the nations of Canaan (Gen 15:16; Lev 18:24–30; Deut 7:1–5; 9:4) and burying Joseph in the land of tribal inheritance (Gen 50:24–26; Josh 24:32). Other narrative elements only get activated as expectational types later, like the destruction of the cities of the plain (Gen 19; Deut 29:23[22]).[15]

Synoptic Narratives

Synoptic narratives between books constitute interpretive use of Scripture. Though synoptic narratives within an individual book rightly may be considered interpretive, they have been filtered out as representing literary development rather than exegesis. Genesis features several synoptic episodes with verbal parallels.

Genesis 24 presents the servant of Abraham securing a wife for Isaac. The episode features numerous repetitions of the details: by the narrator, in a prayer, and multiple retellings by the servant to Rebekah and to Laban.[16] The servant's review to Laban includes substantial verbal parallels with the previous accounts. Note a synoptic comparison of securing a wife for Isaac:

---

13. For several parallels between Rachel with the household gods and Benjamin with the sorcery goblet, see Zakovitch, "Through the Looking Glass," 141–43.

14. For a side-by-side presentation of numerous thematic and a few verbal parallels between Abraham's and Israel's sojourns in Egypt, see Sailhamer, *Pentateuch*, 142. Also see Morales, *Exodus* 22–23; Jericke, "Exodus Material," 141–43.

15. See typological patterns in Glossary.

16. See Savran, "Character as Narrator," 3–6.

	Gen 24 narrated	Gen 24 recounted to Laban
Abraham commissions his servant	1–9	34–41
prayer of the servant	12–14	42–44
Rebekah at the well	15a, 1–21, {15b}	45–48

Genesis 41 tells the story of the pharaoh's dreams with verbal repetitions of the details by the pharaoh and by Joseph. Note a synoptic comparison of the pharaoh's dreams:

	Gen 41, narrator	Gen 41, pharaoh	Gen 41, Joseph
dream of fourteen cows	1–4	17–21	25–27
dream of fourteen heads of grain	5–8	22–24	"

Genesis 44 houses Judah's speech to the lord of Egypt. Along the way Judah rehearses and reshapes with manifold verbal parallels a series of events that spanned over a year's time in chs. 42–43. The events Judah compiles include multiple synoptic relations between them. Note a synoptic comparison of Judah's speech (stylized brackets signify rearranged sequence of verses in chart):[17]

	Egypt	Canaan	Egypt again	Judah's speech
first interview with lord of Egypt	42:7–17	42:29–31	—	44:19–21
second interview with lord of Egypt	42:18–20	42:32–34; {43:1–7}	—	44:23–26
rehearsal of loss of brother(s)	42:21, 23–24	—	—	—
Reuben's response	42:22	42:37	—	—
Jacob on losing his sons	—	42:36, 38	—	{44:22}, 27–29[a]
returning silver with grain	42:25–28	{42:35}	43:18–23; 44:8	—
Judah's guarantee	—	43:8–10	—	{44:32–34}
Jacob consents to send Benjamin	—	43:13–14	—	44:30–31

[a] In Gen 44:27–29 Judah blends language from Jacob's grief over losing Joseph from Gen 37:33, 35 with his own projection of what would happen if he loses Benjamin.

17. The synoptic layout here relates to verbal correspondence between multiple accounts. For a series of two-column comparisons between the narrator's versus Judah's presentations, focusing on Judah's wise speech, see Diewert, "Judah's Argument," 65–70. Also see Savran, "Character as Narrator," 6–10.

Judah's boldest interpretive allusion comes when he blends together in Gen 44:27–31 Jacob's grief from losing Joseph (37:33, 35; 42:36, 38) with his reluctant agreement to send Benjamin (43:13, 14). Judah leverages these blended statements to deduce a perpetual state of mourning for all of Jacob's days (44:29, 31).

Abrahamic Promise

Genesis presents a series of theophanies by which God's promise to Abraham gets revealed in stages (Table G1). The later stages expand but do not cite the earlier promises as donor context, and so do not classify as exegetical. Clines organizes the three main elements of the promise as land, descendants, and relationship.[18] The set of promises expands several times advancing revelation, and together stands at the headwaters of scriptural allusions to the covenant to the Hebrew ancestors (see Abrahamic covenant network).

TABLE G1: EXPANSIONS OF THE ABRAHAMIC COVENANT

Genesis	land	descendants	relationship
12:1–3	land deity will show	great nation	families of the earth will be blessed
13:14–18	all the land Abraham can see forever	like dust of the earth	—
15:16–21	return when Amorite iniquity complete; from wadi of Egypt to Euphrates	—	—
17:1–16	land of Canaan	re-named Abraham; sign of circumcision; forever	multitudes of nations; kings
22:16–18	—	like the sand	all nations of the earth shall be blessed

Stock Phrases and Other Similarities

Note: >/<2:4; 5:1; 6:9; 10:1; 11:10, 27; 25:12, 19; 36:1, 9; 37:2, "generations" (תּוֹלְדוֹת); >/<2:9; 3:6, "every tree that is desirable to look at and good for food/the tree is good for food . . . and desirable to make wise" (כל־עץ נחמד למראה וטוב למאכל/טוב העץ למאכל . . . ונחמד העץ להשׂכיל);[19] >/<7:16; 19:10, shut door; >/<11:5; 18:21, came down to see; >/<12:1; 22:2, "go you" and threefold structure; >/<13:6; 36:7, land could not support; >/<16:2; 17:17; 18:12; 25:21; 29:31; 30:2, infertility of Hebrew matriarchs; >/<17:17; 18:12–15; 21:6, 9, laughter/play (cf. 26:8); >/<25:7–8; 35:28–29, ancestral lives full of years (versus 47:9); >/<27:1; 48:10, eyes dim at time of blessing; >/<27:16; 37:31,

18. Clines, *Theme*, 32. For a complete listing of references related to the Abrahamic promise in Torah, see 32–47. On development of the covenant from Gen 12–22, see Won, *Remembering*, 143–52.

19. Thank you to Barbara Arnold who pointed out this potential case of Seidel's theory.

goat to deceive; >/<30:2; 50:19, "am I in the place of God?"; >/<31:32; 44:9, oath on life regarding claim of not stealing; >/<42:25–28, 35; 43:20–22; 44:1–5, silver returned to sacks; >/<23:19–20; 49:29–32; 50:12–14, burying Jacob in ancestral cave.

In Jacob's blessing of Joseph, he personifies the heavens and depths as the breasts and womb of a woman (49:25).[20] This appears to be a coincidental similarity to the human formed out of the dust of the ground (2:7).

20. On the consonance of the Hebrew terms for "heavens" (שָׁמַיִם) and "breasts" (שָׁדַיִם) as well as "deep" (תְּהוֹם) and "womb" (רֶחֶם) in Gen 49:25, see Wenham, *Genesis 16–50*, 487.

Chapter 2

EXODUS

SYMBOLS[1]

// verbal parallels (A level)
/~/ synoptic parallel (A level)
~ B, probable interpretive allusion; C, possible; D, probably not
+ interpretive blend
>/< more or less similar (see Filters)
* part of interpretive network (see Networks)

USE OF TORAH IN EXODUS[2]

16:30*~Gen 2:2–3* (B) (rest on Sabbath day) (* see Sabbath network)
20:8–11*~Gen 2:2–3* (B) (making Sabbath holy) (* see Sabbath network)
31:12–17*~20:8–11* (B) (capital punishment for Sabbath breaking) (* see Sabbath network)
34:6–7*~20:5–6* (A) (attribute formula) (* see attribute formula network)
34:11–16*~20:5+23:23–33* (B) (prohibition against apostasy marriage) (* see assembly, attribute formula, and devoting networks)
34:18–20//23:15+13:12–13 (Passover standards)
34:21*//23:12* (clarifying Sabbath rest in the fields) (* see Sabbath network)
34:22–24*~23:14–17 (A)+23:23–31* (C) (worship travel anticipated in land) (* see attribute formula, devoting, new exodus, and place networks)
35:2–3*//31:15* (clarifying Sabbath rest at home) (* see Sabbath network)
40:33~Gen 2:2 (C) (tabernacle finished)

OLD TESTAMENT USE OF EXODUS (SEE RESPECTIVE NOTES)

2:24*; 6:5~Lev 26:40–42* (B) (humble uncircumcised hearts) (* see Abrahamic covenant, collective confession, and seventy years networks)
3:7~Neh 9:9 (B) (crying out at the sea in panoramic retrospective)
3:8, 17~Num 16:13 (C) (Egypt is the land of milk and honey)
4:10–12~Jer 1:6–9 (C) (prophet deflects commissioning based on poor speech)
4:10~Ezek 3:5–6 (B) (people heavy of tongue)
4:23~Hos 11:1 (C) (Israel my son)
6:16–25~1 Chr 6:1–4[5:27–30] (C) (line of Levi)
7–12~Ps 78:44–51 (B) (seven cosmic terrors against Egyptians in poetic retrospective)
7–12~Ps 105:26–36 (B) (eight cosmic terrors against Egyptians in poetic retrospective)
12:8, 10, 18, 46, 48–49~Num 9:1–14 (B) (alternate time for Passover)
12:9~2 Chr 35:13 (B) (Passover meal fire roasted and boiled)
12:12~Ps 135:8 (B) (smiting firstborn in poetic retrospective)
12:29~Ps 136:10 (B) (smiting firstborn in covenantal loyalty retrospective)

1. For explanation of symbols, see Symbols and Abbreviations and Introduction. For other help, see Glossary.
2. See Bibliographic Note on Lists of Potential Parallels.

12:35, 36~Ezra 1:4, 6 (C) (contributions from neighbors)
12:48~Lev 19:18b, 33–34 (B) (love the residing foreigner)
13:2, 12//Num 3:11–13//8:16–18 (substitution for firstborn of Israel)
13:12–13~Num 18:15–18 (B) (firstborn male of all ritually impure animals)
13:12–13~Neh 10:36[37] (B) (solemn oath of restoration assembly)
14:13~2 Chr 20:15, 17 (B) (divine victory)
14:16~Isa 10:26 (C) (judgment like Midian at rock of Oreb and staff over the sea)
14:21~Hag 2:6 (C) (shake the heavens and dry land)
15–18~Num 10–12 (C) (wilderness temptations all over again)
15:1~Mic 7:18–19 (C) (God who pardons)
15:15, 16~Josh 2:9 (B) (inhabitants of Canaan melt)
15:17~Ps 78:54, 68–69 (C) (mountain and sanctuary in poetic retrospective)
17:7~Ps 95:8–11 (B) (rebellion at Meribah and Massah)
18:13–27~Deut 1:9–18 (C) (appointing judges)
19–20/~/Deut 4:5–5:33 (revelation at the mountain)
19:4~Deut 32:10–11 (B) (like a mother eagle)
19:6~Num 16:3 (C) (the entire congregation is holy)
19:6~Isa 61:5–7 (C) (priests as rulers over people)
19:6~Isa 6:13 (C) (holy seed)
20:1–17//Deut 5:6–21 (Ten Commandments)
20:4a, 5a~Ps 78:58–59 (B) (false image in poetic retrospective)
20:4b//Ps 135:6 (over all creation in poetic retrospective)
20:5–6*~Deut 7:9–10 (B) (a faithful God) (* see attribute formula network)
20:5*~Nah 1:2–3* (C) (a jealous and avenging God) (* see attribute formula network)
20:5~Ps 109:9–15 (C) (request for transgenerational judgment)
20:12~Mal 1:6 (B) (son honors father)
20:13, 14, 15, 16~Jer 7:5–6, 9 (B) (entry prophetic indictment)
20:16~Deut 19:18–21 (B) (measure-for-measure punishment for false witnesses)
20:19*~Deut 18:15–18* (A) (prophet like Moses) (* see prophet like Moses network)
20:24*~Deut 12:2–28* (B) (seek the place Yahweh will choose to put his name) (* see place network)
20:24–25*~Lev 17:3–9* (C) (sacrifices exclusively at tent of meeting) (* see place network)
20:25~1 Kgs 6:7 (C) (building with stones finished offsite)
20:26~Ezek 43:17 (C) (steps of altar)
21:1–11*~Deut 15:12–18* (B) (debt slaves) (* see release statute network)
21:2–6*~Lev 25:35–43* (C) (debt, service, and Jubilee) (* see release statute network)
21:10~Isa 4:1 (C) (passing up standard support of concubine)
21:12–14~Deut 19:1–13 (C) (motivation for law of asylum)
21:13~Num 35:9–34 (B) (cities of asylum)
21:15, 17~Deut 21:18–21 (C) (rebellious son)
21:22~Deut 25:11–12 (B) (if two men fight)
21:24~Deut 19:18–21 (B) (measure-for-measure punishment for false witnesses)
22:7–8[6–7]~Deut 17:2–7, 8–13 (D) (cases elevated from local judges to temple personnel)
22:8, 9[7, 8]~Ps 82:1–6 (C) (confronting bad judges)
22:16–17[15–16]~Deut 22:28–29 (B) (rape)
22:16[15]~Jer 20:7, 8 (B) (seduced, seized, and crying out)
22:20[19]~Deut 13:15–17[16–18] (C) (devoting spoils of worshipers of false gods)
22:21[20]~Lev 19:18b, 33–34 (B) (love the residing foreigner)
22:25*[24]~Deut 23:19–20* (B) (prohibition against charging interest to Israelites) (* see release statute network)
22:25–27*[24–26]~Lev 25:35–43 (B) (debt, service, and Jubilee) (* see release statute network)
22:25–27*[24–26]~Neh 5:1, 4, 7, 8, 11* (C) (reforming predatory loans) (* see release statute network)
22:26–27*[25–26]~Deut 24:6, 10–13*, 17b (B) (loan collateral regulated) (* see release statute network)
22:26*[25]~Amos 2:8 (C) (fornication on the cloak of the needy) (* see release statute network)
22:28[27]~Lev 24:10–23 (B) (precedent by the case of the blasphemer)
22:29–30[28–29]~Deut 15:19–23 (B) (firstlings to Yahweh)

22:31[30]~Lev 17:15; 22:8 (B) (standard for eating animals that die on their own)[3]

23:4–5~Deut 22:1–4 (B) (tending to the animal of your fellow)

23:6~Ps 82:1–6 (C) (confronting bad judges)

23:8~Deut 16:18–20 (B) (standards for local judges)

23:10–11+22:25[24]~Deut 15:1–11* (B) (year of canceling debts) (* see release statute network)

23:11~Neh 10:31[32] (B) (solemn oath of restoration assembly)

23:14–17~Deut 16:16–17* (B) (three mandated pilgrimage festivals) (* see place network)

23:19a~Neh 10:35[36] (B) (solemn oath of restoration assembly)

23:19a; 34:22~Num 15:18–21 (B) (first of processed goods)

23:19b//34:26b//Deut 14:21c (prohibition against boiling a young goat in its mother's milk)

23:20–21*~Isa 11:15–16* (C)~40:3–4 (B) (highway in the wilderness) (* see new exodus network)

23:20*~Isa 63:9 (B) (divine presence with his people) (* see new exodus network)

23:20*~Mal 3:1* (B) (sending delegate to prepare the way) (* see new exodus network)

23:20*~Ps 91:11 (B) (guarding messengers) (* see new exodus network)

23:28~Josh 24:12 (B) (Joshua's panoramic retrospective at Shechem)

25:2~1 Chr 29:6 (C) (free will contribution to the shrine)

25:9; 40~1 Chr 28:19 (B) (the plan of the temple revealed)

26:1, 31; 28:6, 15~Deut 22:9–11 (C) (mixing makes it holy)

32; 34/~/Deut 9:8–10:11 (rebellion of Horeb/Sinai)

32:4//1 Kgs 12:28–29 (two golden calves)

32:4~Neh 9:18 (B) (rebellion in wilderness in panoramic retrospective)

32:10–13* (B)+**34:6–7*** (A)~Num 14:12–19 (intercession at Kadesh) (* see Abrahamic covenant and attribute formula networks)

32:12, 14~Jonah 3:9, 10 (B) (Yahweh relents)

33:11~Deut 34:10–12 (B) (prophet like Moses) (* see prophet like Moses network)

33:13~Ps 103:7–8*, 14 (B) (attribute formula) (* see attribute formula network)

33:21–22*~1 Kgs 19:11–13 (B) (personal theophany on the mountain) (* see prophet like Moses network)

34:6–7*~Mic 7:18–19* (C) (God who pardons) (* see attribute formula network)

34:6–7*~Nah 1:2–3* (B) (a jealous and avenging God) (* see attribute formula network)

34:6*//Jonah 4:2* (anger and the attribute formula) (* see attribute formula network)

34:6*~Ps 86:15–17* (C) (covenant fidelity and grace for the psalmist) (* see attribute formula network)

34:6*~Ps 103:7–8* (A) (attribute formula) (* see attribute formula network)

34:6*~Lam 3:22–23* (B) (new every morning) (* see attribute formula network)

34:6*~Neh 9:16–17 (B) (rebellion in wilderness in panoramic retrospective) (* see attribute formula network)

34:11–16*~Deut 7:1–5* (B) (law of devoting nations of Canaan and prohibition against intermarriage) (* see assembly, attribute formula, and devoting networks)

34:11~Ezra 9:1–2* (B) (mingling the holy seed) (* see assembly network)

34:15–16*~1 Kgs 11:2–4* (B) (turning Solomon's heart away) (* see devoting and assembly networks)

34:16*~Ezra 10:10–11, 19 (C) (reparation offering and mass divorce) (* see assembly network)

34:16~2 Chr 21:13 (C) (Jehoram causes Judah to whore after other gods)

34:24*~Deut 12:2–28* (B) (seek the place Yahweh will choose to put his name) (* see place network)

35:2–3~Num 15:32–36 (B) (the Sabbath breaker) (* see Sabbath network)

40:34–35~1 Kgs 8:10 (B) (glory fills the temple)

40:34–35~2 Chr 7:1–3 (B) (glory)

3. Also see discussion of Exod 22:31[30] in note on Deut 14:21.

NEW TESTAMENT USE OF EXODUS

1:8//Acts 7:18 (new king did not know Joseph)
2:14//Acts 7:27–28, 35 (Did you kill an Egyptian?)
3:5–10//Acts 7:33–34 (holy ground)
3:6//Matt 22:32; Mark 12:26; Luke 20:37; Acts 7:32 (I am the God of Abraham)
3:12//Acts 7:7 (you will worship me here)
3:15//Matt 22:32; Mark 12:26; Acts 3:13 (God of ancestors)
9:16//Rom 9:17 (raised up for this purpose)
12:46//John 19:36 (no bones broken)
13:2, 12//Luke 2:23 (firstborn males consecrated)
16:4~John 6:31 (bread from heaven)
16:18//2 Cor 8:15 (who gathered much)
19:6 LXX~1 Pet 2:9 (royal priesthood)
19:12, 13~Heb 12:20 (if animal touches mountain)
20:12//Matt 15:4; 19:19; Mark 7:10; 10:19; Luke 18:20; Eph 6:2–3 (honor parents)
20:13//Matt 5:21; 19:18; Mark 10:19; Luke 18:20; Rom 13:9; Jas 2:11 (no murder)
20:14//Matt 5:27; 19:18; Mark 10:19; Luke 18:20; Rom 13:9; Jas 2:11 (no adultery)
20:15//Matt 19:18; Mark 10:19; Luke 18:20; Rom 13:9 (not steal)
20:16//Matt 19:18; Mark 10:19; Luke 18:20 (no false witness)
20:17//Rom 7:7; 13:9 (not covet)
21:17//Matt 15:4; Mark 7:10 (not curse parents)
21:24//Matt 5:38 (eye for eye)
22:28[27]//Acts 23:5 (do not speak evil of ruler)
24:8//Heb 9:20 (blood of covenant)
25:40//Heb 8:5 (pattern on mountain)
32:1//Acts 7:40 (make us a calf)
32:6//1 Cor 10:7 (sat to eat and drink)
32:23//Acts 7:40 (make us gods)
33:19//Rom 9:15 (mercy on whom I have mercy)

HERMENEUTICAL PROFILE OF THE USE OF TORAH IN EXODUS

Exodus includes extensive, broad, non-exegetical allusions to Torah in every part—narrative, legal instructions, and instructions for the tabernacle. Internal allusions and internal cross-referencing stand as signature characteristics of Torah style, setting the standard for much of the Scriptures.

Exodus tends to engage and re-engage legal standards in multiple contexts. This naturally puts a certain kind of demand upon those who study God's covenantal will. The renewal of revelation about particular requirements in multiple contexts pushes hard against both casual and rigid readerly attitudes.

The use of scriptural traditions in Exodus centers around legal exegesis. To get at legal exegesis in Exodus requires brief attention to several general areas, namely, collections of legal standards, general outlook, advancements of authoritative legal standards, and frame narratives. After noting each of these general areas, two lightning rods for exegetical intervention within Exodus can be introduced—Sabbath and the transgenerational threat against those who worship images.

First, Exodus itself houses three substantial legal collections: Ten Words (Exod 20), covenant collection (21–23), and a covenant renewal collection (34:11–26). Additional commands appear outside these main collections, especially embedded within the Passover narrative (12–13), giving of manna (16), and instructions for the tabernacle

(25–31). The covenant collection seems to have more overlap with law collections of other ancient Near Eastern cultures than anywhere else in Torah. As more ancient trial records have come to light, the nature and purpose of ancient legal collections have been increasingly disputed.[4] These critically important debates cannot be taken up here because of the limits of this study.[5]

Second, the general outlook of the legal collections in Exodus differs from those in Leviticus and Deuteronomy. Some scholars have argued for certain social outlooks for the main legal collections. Knight considers the covenant collection within village culture, the priestly regulations of Leviticus and Numbers within cultic culture, and Deuteronomy's laws within urban culture.[6] Morrow works from these and sees the covenant collection of Exod 21–23 within a village assembly, the priestly law of Leviticus focused on the courts of the Lord, and the legal collection in Deut 12–26 in an urban setting.[7]

Social outlooks help but the focus needs to be on the settings of legal collections within Torah to get at the exegetical issues. As a general outlook for assessing legal exegesis in Exodus, the focus needs to remain at the mountain where Yahweh reveals his redemptive will for his people. The people rebel at the mountain. Yahweh renews the covenant by an extraordinary self-revelation at the mountain. Once the tabernacle is finished, legal exegesis in Leviticus speaks toward priests and laity with respect to how all of life functions in relation to coming into the courts of Yahweh. Legal exegesis in Deuteronomy pivots on the implications of the pending settlement in the land of promise. These different settings within Torah activate additional regulations and exegetical advancements on many of the same laws.

Third, the reality of legal exegesis in Exodus interrelates with advancements of revelation embodied in law. The Torah knows of no such thing as divine law spoken once. Biblical law does not say: "That is it. No changes." In ancient memories of the Persian court there is talk of the unchangeable law of the Medes and Persians (Esth 1:19; 8:8; Dan 6:8). The humorous problem of unchangeable Persian law traps impotent, hapless sovereigns (Dan 6:14–15). Yahweh and his law operate differently.

The "problem" of legal exegesis seems to be something imported into Torah by modern agendas. The interpretive re-presentation of commands within Leviticus, Numbers, and Deuteronomy overtly puts legal exegesis on display. But even Exodus exhibits interpretive re-presentations of some of its legal standards. In Torah the norm is legal standards with divinely ordained exegetical advances.

Legal exegesis does not stop at the outer boundaries of Torah. Prophets and other divinely appointed authors and spokespersons maintain continuity with Torah by reinterpreting and reapplying legal standards. The divinely given law retains a privileged

4. See Roth, *Law Collections*, 4–5.

5. For an overview of several issues, see Bartor, "Legal Texts," 160–81.

6. See Knight, *Law*, 4.

7. See Morrow, *Introduction*, 11, 253.

place throughout the advancing revelation of God's will in the Scriptures. Study of legal exegesis as presented in Torah can provide help with interpretive allusions to covenantal standards throughout Scripture.

Fourth, adequate evaluation of legal exegesis within Torah requires handling the givens of the frame narratives. The meaning and function of legal exegesis gets bound up together with its narrative situation. Even more, frame narratives control the way legal standards work. Sternberg observes that "the framing of an element within a text entails a communicative subordination of the part to the whole that encloses it."[8] The necessity of the frame narrative suggests that interpretation of legal exegesis within its canonical setting should precede other ventures like diachronic studies with excavative agendas. The limits of the present study only allow for evaluation of legal exegesis within the frame narratives of Scripture.

Having taken note of four general areas of concern for evaluating legal exegesis within Torah, two particular areas of the use of scriptural traditions in Exodus can be introduced. Nearly all of the interpretations of laws in Exodus appear in or near the covenant renewal collection or deal with the Sabbath. At least five interpretative interventions in Exodus concern the Sabbath. Unlike most scriptural laws, the Sabbath is unique to Israel.[9]

The central Sabbath command is rest. The fourth commandment grounds rest in the divine pattern from earth's first weekend (Exod 20:8–11). Sabbath does not function merely as a religious practice. Sabbath violation gets treated as a criminal act punishable by death (31:12–17; 35:2). The most difficult matter of Sabbath regulation concerns what it means to rest. Sabbath rest comprehensively includes entire households—children, slaves, animals (20:10). The interpretive expansions of Sabbath rest show that even during the most pressing times of planting and harvest the Sabbath remains the priority (34:21). And at home even basic necessities like kindling a fire are not appropriate on the Sabbath (35:2–3).

The importance of the Sabbath relates to how it functions as a sign of Israel's everlasting covenant before God (31:12–17). Keeping the Sabbath holy becomes ingrained in Israel's basic identity as the people of God. Every week moves toward Sabbath, and this routine holy day prompts repeated need for advancements in revelation by means of exegesis.

The many interpretive adjustments and expansions of Sabbath-keeping demonstrate both its inherent challenges to ancient life and its importance to Israel's identity. After the first Hebrew commonwealth collapsed, Sabbath-keeping endured as one of the premier symbols of Judaic identity in the empire. The exegetical concerns with the Sabbath in Exodus range from a creational rationale to defining its criminal punishment for disobedience and beginning to work out the slippery idea of what constitutes Sabbath rest.

8. See Sternberg, "Quotation-Land," 108. Also see Averbeck, "Framing," 165.
9. See Wells, "Exodus," 232–33.

The covenant renewal collection (34:11–26) re-presents exegetically enhanced versions of legal standards especially from the covenant collection (21–23). The manner in which Yahweh signifies his commitment to forgive and remain with his people comes in the form of covenant renewal along with interpretive reuse of many commands. The attribute formula asserted by Yahweh himself in a profound revelation to Moses immediately precedes and introduces the covenant renewal collection (34:6–7). The attribute formula gets reinterpreted as much as any other context of the Hebrew Bible. Yet it too reinterprets the transgenerational threat of the image commandment.

The attribute formula's interpretation of the transgenerational threat for worshiping images interrelates with other interpretations of the same in the genetically related prohibitions against intermarriage (34:11–16; Deut 7:1–6). For now, only the reinterpretations of the transgenerational threat in Exodus need to be noted. These interpretations build around divine character (emphases mine).

I, Yahweh your God, am *a jealous God.* (Exod 20:5//Deut 5:9)

Yahweh, Yahweh, *a compassionate and gracious God.* (Exod 34:6†)

Yahweh whose name is Jealous, he is *a jealous God.* (34:14)

What matters is who God is. The interpretations of the transgenerational threat in the attribute formula and the prohibition against apostasy marriage build around programmatic statements of divine character.

In sum, the exegetical agenda of Exodus targets two important and difficult laws from the Ten Commandments—the transgenerational threat of the prohibition against worshiping images and keeping the Sabbath holy. Neither set of exegetical interventions gets finally put to rest in Exodus. Instead these same commandments and their exegetical advancements will undergo further interpretation by Deuteronomy, the prophets, the psalmists, and the restoration assembly (see attribute formula and Sabbath networks). Legal exegesis may solve challenges but it also invites further interpretative advancement.

USE OF TORAH IN EXODUS

16:30*~Gen 2:2–3* (B) (rest on Sabbath day) (* see Sabbath network). The regulations for gathering manna on the sixth day and not the seventh include examples of non-compliance (Exod 16:22–29). The concluding note has parallel language with the narrative of the seventh day of creation, including the word "rest" in its verb form (italics signify verbal parallels; underlining signifies marking; and broken underlining signifies shared roots):

> By the seventh day God had finished the work he had been doing; so *on the seventh day he rested* from all his work. Then God blessed *the seventh day* and *made* it *holy*, because on it *he rested* from all the work of creating that he had done. (Gen 2:2–3)

> He said to them, "This is what Yahweh commanded: 'Tomorrow is to be a day of sabbath rest, a *holy* sabbath to Yahweh.'" . . . So the people *rested on the seventh day.* (Exod 16:23a, 30)

Moses explains that the Sabbath rest from collecting manna is due to the fact that the Sabbath day is "holy" to Yahweh (16:23). The narration of the people's obedience alludes to the rest of God on the seventh creation day (Gen 2:2, 3). Moses uses a citation formula to refer to revelation of the command as the basis for the manna standards (Exod 16:23). The proclaiming of Sabbath rest comes prior to the revelation at the mountain. Elsewhere Genesis and Exodus include inferences of customs that do not get spelled out formally until later, such as: levirate marriage (Gen 38:8; cf. Deut 25:5–10) and remaining chaste temporarily for ritual purity (Exod 19:15; cf. Lev 15:18).

20:8–11*~Gen 2:2–3* (B) (making Sabbath holy) (* see Sabbath network). The fourth commandment closes with a theological rationale based on Yahweh's own work as creator. This interpretive intervention effectively aligns the creation of the heavens and the earth with the weekly human cycle of work and rest. The creator becomes a model to those created in his own image (bold signifies verbal parallels).

> By the seventh day God had finished the work he had been doing; so **on the seventh day** he rested from all his work. Then God **blessed the seventh day and made it holy**, because on it he rested from all the work of creating that he had done. (Gen 2:2–3)

> Remember the Sabbath day by keeping it holy. [9] Six days you shall labor and do all your work, [10] but the seventh day is a sabbath to Yahweh your God. On it you shall not do any work, neither you, nor your son or daughter, nor your male or female servant, nor your animals, nor any foreigner residing in your towns. [11] For in six days Yahweh made the heavens and the earth, the sea, and all that is in them, but he rested **on the seventh day**. Therefore Yahweh **blessed the Sabbath day and made it holy.** (Exod 20:8–11)

The rationales and motivations on laws point to a kind of divine authority in legal instructions that goes beyond "do it because I said it, and do not ask questions." The rationale includes Yahweh's work as creator functioning as a self-conscious model for human life. Yahweh's own actions provide the basis for him to "make holy" the time at the end of each week. While many narratives in Genesis relate to themes in the Ten Commandments—marital fidelity (Gen 2:24), murder (4:8), and so on—only Sabbath-keeping gets explicitly connected to an older rationale.

The explanation in Deuteronomy's version of the Sabbath command displaces the creational with a redemptive rationale but still retains the holiness of the Sabbath now detached from the creational donor context (see note on Deut 5:6–21). Basing the holiness of the Sabbath on the seventh creation day only gets directly mediated in Exod 16:23, 20:11, and 31:17. Other contexts in the Sabbath network of interpretive allusions retain the holiness of Sabbath, though now mediated indirectly by the law of the Sabbath (Exod 20:11; 31:17; cf. 35:2; Deut 5:12). The inferred direction of dependence of the holiness of Sabbath as described in Torah is: Gen 2:3 ← Exod 16:23; 20:11; 31:17 ← 35:2; Deut 5:12. Added confirmation comes from the marking of allusion in Deuteronomy's version of the Ten Commandments, suggesting it as a receptor context—"as Yahweh your God commanded you" (Deut 5:12).

In sum, the creational basis for the holiness of the Sabbath gets mediated to other advancements in Sabbath regulations by the fourth commandment in Exod 20:8–11.

31:12–17*~20:8–11* (B) (capital punishment for Sabbath breaking) (* see Sabbath network). Exodus 31:12–17 reworks Sabbath standards based on the fourth commandment in Exod 20:8–11. Substantial verbal parallels shared between only these two Sabbath commands makes a relationship highly likely (Exod 20:11//31:17) (italics refer to verbal parallels, and broken underlining refers to key interpretive interventions).

> Remember *the Sabbath* day by keeping it *holy*. [9] *Six days* you shall labor and *do* all your *work*, [10] but the seventh day is a sabbath to Yahweh your God. On it you shall not do any work, neither you, nor your son or daughter, nor your male or female servant, nor your animals, nor any foreigner residing in your towns. [11] *For in six days Yahweh made the heavens and the earth*, the sea, and all that is in them, *and* he rested *on the seventh day*. Therefore Yahweh blessed the Sabbath day and made it holy. (Exod 20:8–11)

> Then Yahweh said to Moses, [13] "Say to the Israelites, 'You must observe my Sabbaths. This will be a sign between me and you for the generations to come, so you may know that I am Yahweh, who makes you holy. [14] Observe *the Sabbath*, because it is *holy* to you. Anyone who desecrates it is to be put to death; those who do any work on that day must be cut off from their people. [15] For *six days work is to be done*, but the seventh day is a day of sabbath rest, holy to Yahweh. Whoever does any work on the Sabbath day is to be put to death. [16] The Israelites are to observe the Sabbath, celebrating it for the generations to come as a lasting covenant. [17] It will be a sign between me and the Israelites forever, *for in six days Yahweh made the heavens and the earth, and on the seventh day* he rested and was refreshed.'" (31:12–17†)

The death penalty stands out among other enhancements in this version of the Sabbath command (31:14, 15). The two contexts that get at capital punishment for Sabbath violation in Exodus stand at the end of the instructions for the tabernacle and beginning of the construction of the tabernacle respectively (tabernacle instructions, 25:1–31:11; Sabbath, 31:12–27; Sabbath, 35:1–3; tabernacle construction, 35:4–40:33). The five other examples of capital punishment in Exodus using the passive expression "to be put to death" include murder (21:12), attacking parents (21:15), kidnapping (21:16), cursing parents (21:17), and bestiality (22:19[18]). The use of the passive signals death carried out by persons, while active use refers to death by God (e.g., 22:23[24]).[10]

The importance of Sabbath-keeping while building the tabernacle has often been noted as the reason for the placement of two death penalty passages in Exod 31:12–17 and 35:1–3.[11] This may be part of it, but the deadly serious nature of Yahweh's sanctified time and his holy space may be a greater reason. Just as wrongful entry into holy space brings death (Lev 10:6, 7, 8), so too desecration of holy time (Exod 31:15, 17; 35:2; Num 15:35–36). The collective responsibility of maintaining the Sabbath as a sign and a covenant begins to explain why this law becomes part of criminal law (Exod 31:13, 16, 17). Even when Sabbath-keeping no longer functions within criminal law, it remains an enduring sign of Israel's covenantal responsibilities before God (see note on Neh 13:15–18).

34:6–7*~20:5–6* (A) (attribute formula) (* see attribute formula network). The attribute formula in the stunning theophany to Moses testifies to Yahweh's mercy (Exod 34:6–7). He forgives his people and agrees to continue his presence with them after their rebellion with the calf (32–33). A couple of the key features of the attribute formula emerge by reshaping the second commandment. The substantial verbal, syntactic, and contextual parallels make an intentional relationship almost certain. In addition to the parallel with the transgenerational threat, the attribute formula swaps the single mention of the covenantal name "Yahweh" and double mention of "God" in the image command to highlight its central interpretive advancement.[12] The second commandment uses both the longer and shorter terms for deity (*elohim* אֱלֹהִים and *el* אֵל), but the attribute formula only retains the short form with its shift from "a jealous God" to "a compassionate and gracious God" (20:5; 34:6). Notice the extraordinary way the attribute formula develops the second commandment (emphases signify verbal parallels):

> You shall not make for yourself an image. . . . [5] You shall not bow down to them or serve them; for I, **Yahweh** your God, am **a** jealous **God**, punishing the iniquity of the parents upon the children to the third and fourth generation of those who hate me, [6] but showing *loyalty to thousands* of those who love me and keep my commandments. (Exod 20:4a, 5–6 lit.)

10. See Hamilton, *Exodus*, 523.

11. See ibid., 524; and based on taking the negative particle in Exod 31:13 as "nevertheless" (אַךְ) (Propp, *Exodus 19–40*, 491; Sarna, *Exodus*, 201). But the particle could as likely connote "above all" ("אַךְ," *HALOT* 1:54). Although the LXX of Exodus usually translates the particle *'ak* (אַךְ) with a contrastive "but" (δὲ) (12:15; 21:21), in Exod 31:13 it uses an emphatic "see! even" (ὁρᾶτε καὶ) with the sense of "See to it that even (my Sabbaths)" (so Wevers, *Notes on Exodus*, 512). This affirms the emphatic gloss suggested by *HALOT* (see above in this footnote).

12. The doubling of the name Yahweh in Exod 34:6 occurs nowhere else in Scripture. See Bauckham, *Who?* 67.

> And he passed in front of Moses, calling out, "**Yahweh**, Yahweh, **a God** compassionate and gracious, slow to anger, abounding in loyalty and faithfulness, [7] maintaining *loyalty to thousands*, and forgiving iniquity, transgression, and sin. Yet he does not leave the guilty unpunished; punishing the iniquity of the parents upon the children and upon the grandchildren to the third and fourth generation." (34:6–7 lit.)

The importance of casting Yahweh's character in light of the image commandment provides a dramatic testament to his forgiveness. Israel had made an image and worshiped it (32:1–6). The attribute formula builds off the structure of the prohibition against worshiping images to underline divine forgiveness.

The exchange from "jealous" to "compassionate and gracious" forcefully asserts the basis of the forgiveness of Israel. That is what kind of God he is.

The revelation of divine character in the attribute formula does not erase the teeth of Yahweh's wrath. The attribute formula actually strengthens the force of the transgenerational threat by spelling out "and upon the grandchildren" (34:7). Within the larger context the prohibition against apostasy marriage picks up these threads. The prohibition reasserts Yahweh's jealousy even more strongly than the image commandment (see 34:14).

The attribute formula stands as one of three exegetical advancements provoked by the transgenerational threat in Torah. The prohibition against apostasy marriage at the head of the covenant renewal collection and the context of the parallel prohibition against intermarriage in Deuteronomy also develop it (34:11–16; Deut 7:1–6). The series of exegetical advancements stem from who God is (emphases mine).

> I, Yahweh your God, am *a jealous God.* (Exod 20:5//Deut 5:9)

> Yahweh, Yahweh, *a compassionate and gracious God.* (Exod 34:6†)

> Yahweh whose name is Jealous, he is *a jealous God.* (34:14)

> Yahweh your God, he is God, *the faithful God.* (Deut 7:9 lit.)

The prohibition against worshiping images and its transgenerational threat does not go away. The Ten Commandments in Deuteronomy reassert it nearly verbatim. The transgression of the prohibition displays Yahweh's jealous character. The exact same terrible reality provides a context to reveal Yahweh's compassion and his fidelity.

In sum, the dynamic realities of Yahweh's relationship with his rebellious people provide opportunities to advance revelation of who he is. The attribute formula speaks to forgiveness by a compassionate and gracious God.

34:11–16*~20:5+23:23–33* (B) (prohibition against apostasy marriage) (* see assembly, attribute formula, and devoting networks). The covenant renewal collection begins with a prohibition against apostasy marriage (Exod 34:11–16). Since the would-be spouse continues to worship her people's gods, it would be "marrying out" from the point of view of Israel. The prohibition does not start from scratch, but interprets part of the second commandment against worshiping images as well as parts of the mission to settle in the land of promise (20:5; 23:23–33). The verbal parallels with the image commandment include the phrase "a jealous God," an expression that appears only in Torah (Exod 20:5//Deut 5:9; Exod 34:14; Deut 4:24; 6:15) and is spelled differently twice elsewhere (Josh 24:19; Nah 1:2).[13] The verbal parallels with the mission to settle the land of promise are extensive enough to suggest a probable intentional relationship, whether direct or indirect (emphases signify verbal parallels):

> **You shall not bow down to** them or serve them; **for** I, **Yahweh** your God, am a **jealous God**, punishing the iniquity of the parents upon the children to the third and fourth generation of those who hate me. (Exod 20:5 lit.)

> My angel will go *ahead of you* and bring you into the land of the *Amorites, Hittites, Perizzites, Canaanites, Hivites and Jebusites*, and I will wipe them out. [24] Do not bow down before their gods or serve them or follow their practices. You must demolish them and break their sacred stones to pieces. . . . [28] I will send the hornet ahead of you *to drive the Hivites, Canaanites and Hittites out before you.* [29] But *I will* not *drive* them *out* in a single year, because the land would become desolate and the wild animals too numerous for you. [30] Little by little *I will drive* them *out before you*. . . . [32] Do not make a covenant with them or with their gods. [33] Do not let them live in your *land, otherwise* they will cause you to sin against me, because the worship of their gods will certainly be *a snare* to *you.* (23:23–24, 28–30a, 32–33 lit.)

> Obey what I command you today. *I will drive out before you the Amorites, Canaanites, Hittites, Perizzites, Hivites and Jebusites.* [12] Be careful not to make a covenant with *those who live* in *the land* where you are going, *otherwise* they will be a *snare* among *you.* [13] Break down their altars, break their sacred stones and cut down their Asherah poles. [14] **You shall not bow down to** another god, for **Yahweh**, whose name is Jealous, he is a **jealous God.** [15] Be careful not to make a covenant with those who live in the land; for when they prostitute themselves to their gods and sacrifice to them, they will invite you and you will eat their sacrifices. [16] And when you choose some of their daughters as wives for your sons and those daughters prostitute themselves to their gods, they will lead your sons to prostitute themselves to their gods. (34:11–16 lit.)[14]

---

13. See "קַנָּא," "קַנּוֹא," *HALOT* 2:1110, 1114.

14. The Septuagint adds a phrase to make the prohibition coed: "and you should take from their daughters for your sons *and from your daughters you should give to their sons*" (Exod 34:16 LXX, emphasis marks addition). The addition seems to collate Exod 34:16 with the parallel coed context in Deut 7:3 (see Wevers, *Notes on Exodus*, 563).

The major interpretive advance of the mission to settle the land of promise relates to the shift of the prohibition against a covenant with the locals from a collective political treaty to an individual treaty based on marriages between families (23:32; 34:12, 15). The warning against interrelation with the nations of Canaan does not end once the people have taken up residence. The strong temptation to seek treaty marriages with the established peoples will be an ongoing danger for individual families. Ancient people wanted to help their children by getting them into advantageous marriages with more-established families. Such marriages could provide children with many economic and social benefits.

The prohibition against apostasy marriages spells out where such arrangements go by means of unusual syntax to express the resulting humiliation. The unsavory term "prostitute themselves" features the causative stem to show the outcome of apostasy marriages for hapless sons. This inverts the hopes of the parents who seek treaty marriages among the others. It does not help their sons but amounts to arranging for sons to be placed in the hands of madam-wives who lead their prostitute-husbands to prostitute themselves after her gods (34:16).

The prohibition against apostasy marriage exegetically alludes to the image commandment by affirming and strengthening its reference to Yahweh as "a jealous God" (20:5). The prohibition claims his "name is Jealous" (34:14). Sarna's strained attempt to argue for the connotation of "impassioned" versus "jealous" does not adequately take into account the marital infidelity inferences of the husband prostituting himself to other gods, which activates the jealousy.[15]

The more important interpretive advances come in the form of the explanation of how apostasy marriage fleshes out the transgenerational threat of the image commandment. Those who worship other gods bring judgment upon the third and fourth generation (20:5). The prohibition against apostasy marriages suggests one way this works. Parents who arrange apostasy marriages effectively turn their sons into prostitutes to the gods of their foreign wives. Such marriages lead to grandchildren who grow up under parents who both prostitute themselves after other gods. The problem of treaty marriages demonstrates how the sins of the parents activate the transgenerational wrath of Yahweh. In this case parents and the next generation(s) actively cultivate culpability. The sins of parents in apostasy marriages naturally invite wrath upon their children who themselves deserve it.

34:18–20//23:15+13:12–13 (Passover standards). The Passover regulations appear within the covenant renewal collection of legal instructions (Exod 34:18–20). The covenant renewal collection interpretively advances many commands appearing earlier in Exodus. The legal collection signals the continuing relationship of Yahweh with his people after their sin with the golden calf. Table E1 summarizes both parallels with earlier contexts in the narrative as well as provides a preview of later contexts that develop these regulations.

15. For Sarna's view, see *Exodus*, 110. For a linguistic study that concludes Scripture uses the term for human and divine "jealousy" (קנא), see Schlimm, "Jealousy," 513–28.

TABLE E1: COVENANT RENEWAL COLLECTION AND PARALLEL LEGAL INSTRUCTIONS‡

previous regulations	covenant renewal collection	later regulations
Exod 20:5; 23:23–24, 32–33	34:11–16, prohibition against covenant and intermarriages with nations of Canaan	**Deut 7:1–6**
Exod 20:4–6; cf. 32:4, 8	34:17, no idols	
Exod 12:10–20; 13:3–13; **23:15**	34:18–20, regulations concerning passover	Lev 23:5–8; Num 9:1–14; 28:16–25; Deut 16:1–8
Exod 20:8–11; **23:12**; 31:12–17; 35:1–3	34:21, Sabbath rest[a]	Deut 5:12–15
Exod 23:14–17	34:22–24, pilgrimage festivals[b]	**Deut 12:20–21; 16:16–17**
Exod 23:18	34:25, regulations concerning leaven and fat of sacrifice	
Exod 23:19a	34:26a, firstfruits	Lev 23:9–14
Exod 23:19b	34:26b, prohibition against boiling young goat in its mother's milk	**Deut 14:21b**

‡ Bold in columns one and three signifies substantial verbal parallels with standards in middle column. Table based on research for current project and collated with information in Schnittjer, *Torah Story*, 353.

[a] See Sabbath network for addition references.

[b] Festival of weeks (Pentecost), Exod 23:16; 34:22; Lev 23:15–21; Num 28:26–31; Deut 16:9–12. Festival of tabernacles (ingathering), Exod 23:16; 34:22; Lev 23:33–43; Num 29:12–34; Deut 16:13–15; Zech 14:16–19; Ezra 3:4; Neh 8:14–18; John 7–8.

The interpretive blend of Passover regulations within the covenant renewal collection includes nearly verbatim citations from the laws interspersed with the Passover story (Exod 12–13) and from the covenant collection (Exod 21–23). Notice how the command from the covenant collection becomes an envelope around the mildly enhanced command concerning redeeming firstborn males from Yahweh (italics, bold, and underlining refer to verbal parallels; broken underlining refers to similar terms).

> You are to give over to Yahweh **the first offspring of every womb. All the firstborn males** of your livestock **belong to** Yahweh. [13] **Redeem with a lamb** every **firstborn donkey, but if you do not redeem it, break its neck**. Redeem every firstborn man among your sons. (Exod 13:12–13, v. 13 lit.)

> *Celebrate the Festival of Unleavened Bread; for seven days eat bread made without yeast, as I commanded you. Do this at the appointed time in the month of Aviv, for in the month of Aviv you came out of Egypt. No one is to appear before me empty-handed.* (23:15 lit.)

> *Celebrate the Festival of Unleavened Bread. For seven days eat bread made without yeast, as I commanded you. Do this at the appointed time in the month of Aviv, for in it you came out of Egypt.* [19] **The first offspring of every womb belongs to** me, including **all the**

> **firstborn males** of your livestock, whether from herd or flock. [20] **Redeem the firstborn donkey with a lamb, but if you do not redeem it, break its neck.** Redeem all your firstborn sons. *No one is to appear before me empty-handed.* (34:18–20, v. 18 lit.)

In place of the more generic terms for domesticated cattle in Exod 13:12, the covenant renewal spells out more clearly that this includes all sorts of domesticated flocks and herds (34:19). The other adjustment seems more mechanical. In the Passover itself in Egypt the term for grown "man" refers to all firstborn sons of any age (13:13). In the covenant renewal collection the law only needs to refer to sons since they are redeemed as children along the way (34:20).

34:22–24*~23:14–17 (A)+23:23–31* (C) (worship travel anticipated in land) (* see attribute formula, devoting, new exodus, and place networks). The instructions for the three pilgrimage festivals in the covenant renewal collection (Exod 34:11–26) feature an interpretive blend in anticipation of Israel spread out in the land of promise. The allusion to the pilgrimages in the covenant collection (21–23) includes extensive verbal parallels. The potential allusion to the mission to take the land at the end of the covenant collection seems likely in the context of Exodus even though Exod 34:24 uses a new term for "dispossess." Notice the interpretive blend (italics and bold mark verbal parallels and broken underlining similar connotations).

> **Three** times **a year** you are to celebrate a festival to me. . . . [16] Celebrate *the Festival* of Harvest *with the firstfruits* of the crops you sow in your field. Celebrate *the Festival of Ingathering* at the end *of the year,* when you gather in your crops from the field. [17] **Three times a year all the men are to appear before Sovereign Yahweh.** (23:14, 16–17)

> My angel will go ahead of you and bring you into the land of the Amorites, Hittites, Perizzites, Canaanites, Hivites and Jebusites, and I will wipe them out. . . . [28] I will send the hornet ahead of you to drive the Hivites, Canaanites and Hittites out of your way. [29] But I will not drive them out in a single year, because the land would become desolate and the wild animals too numerous for you. [30] Little by little I will drive them out before you, until you have increased enough to take possession of the land. [31] I will establish your borders from the Red Sea to the Mediterranean Sea, and from the desert to the Euphrates River. I will give into your hands the people who live in the land, and you will drive them out before you. (23:23, 28–31)

> Celebrate *the Festival* of Weeks *with the firstfruits* of the wheat harvest, and *the Festival of Ingathering* at the turn *of the year.* [23] **Three times a year all the men are to appear before Sovereign Yahweh**, the God of Israel. [24] I will dispossess nations before you and enlarge your territory, and no one will covet your land when you go up **three times each year to appear before Yahweh** your God. (34:22–24, vv. 23–24†)

The term "dispossess" (ירשׁ) in Exod 34:24 features Yahweh as subject but is a different verb than Yahweh "wipes out" (כחד) in 23:23, Yahweh "sends" a hornet "to drive out" (גרשׁ) in 23:28, Yahweh "will drive out" (גרשׁ) in 23:29–30, or Yahweh "gives" them into Israel's hand and Israel "drives out" (גרשׁ) in 23:31. In spite of the different verbs, the similarity in subject matter in 23:23–31 and 34:24 gives good reason to suspect that the need for pilgrimages created by enlarged territory (34:24) is due to Yahweh driving out the nations of Canaan (23:23–31).

In any case, the covenant renewal collection makes two related exegetical points in Exod 34:24. First, pilgrimages to worship at the shrine—"appear before Yahweh"—are a natural outcome of inheriting the expansive land promised to the Hebrew ancestors. Second, the worship pilgrimages of the Hebrew males should not cause anxiety about leaving their property in a vulnerable situation while they worship. Since Yahweh will dispossess the nations from the land, there will be no one to covet Israel's property. Both of these exegetical advances provide an anticipated context for worship within the fulfillment of Yahweh's promise.

In sum, the instructions for the pilgrimage feasts in the covenant renewal collection present exegetical advances for worship in a new context of living in the land of promise. The new situation for worship in the land sets the stage for numerous additional exegetical advances in Deuteronomy (see note on Deut 12:2–28 and place network).

34:21*//23:12* (clarifying Sabbath rest in the fields) (* see Sabbath network).

35:2–3*//31:15* (clarifying Sabbath rest at home) (* see Sabbath network). Only two Torah contexts explain what it means to rest on the Sabbath (Exod 34:21; 35:2–3). In spite of this shared function, Exod 34:21 reworks the Sabbath command from the covenant collection (23:12) and 35:2–5 recycles part of the Sabbath command on capital punishment, which stands as its structural counterpart in Exodus (31:15).

As mentioned in the note on Exod 31:12–17, the two capital punishment Sabbath commands appear immediately after the tabernacle instructions and before the tabernacle construction. In this way holy space and holy time form a double bracket around the rebellion with the golden calf and the covenant renewal—tabernacle instructions (25:1–31:11), capital punishment for Sabbath violation (31:12–17), rebellion and revelation (32–34), capital punishment for Sabbath violation (35:1–3), tabernacle construction (35:4–40:33).

Notice how Exod 23:12 reworks the fourth commandment and then serves as donor context to 34:21 while 31:15 serves as donor context to 35:2–3 (bold, underlining, and broken underlining signify verbal parallels; and italics signify interpretive advances):

> Remember the Sabbath day by keeping it holy. [9] Six days you shall labor and do all your work, [10] but the seventh day is a sabbath to Yahweh your God. (Exod 20:8–10a)

Six days do your work, but on the seventh day you shall rest, so that your ox and your donkey may rest, and so that the slave born in your household and the foreigner living among you may be refreshed. (23:12)

Six days work is to be done, but the seventh day is a day of sabbath rest, holy to Yahweh. Whoever does any work on the Sabbath day is surely to be put to death. (31:15 lit.)

Six days you shall labor, **but on the seventh day you shall rest**; *even during the plowing season and harvest* **you must rest.** (34:21)

Six days **do your work**, but the seventh day shall be your holy day, a day of sabbath rest to Yahweh. Whoever does any work on it is to be put to death. *Do not light a fire in any of your dwellings* on the Sabbath day. (35:2–3†)

The minimalist approach to explaining the nature of Sabbath rest eventually led to other enhancements (see Amos 8:5; Jer 17:19–27; Neh 10:31[32]; 13:15, 19). Even the importance of harvest does not provide an exception to observing the Sabbath in the workplace (Exod 34:21). Likewise, even something as essential as making fire may not hinder Sabbath rest in domestic contexts (35:2–3). Such general definitions about a command basic to the identity of Israel begin to explain why the early proto-rabbinic lay scholars known as Pharisees help people get a better sense of the importance of the Sabbath by developing forty examples of prohibited work in the space of one paragraph (m. Shab. 7:2). The much-contested Sabbath regulations repeatedly brought Messiah into conflict with rival scholars (see references in Sabbath network note d).

In sum, Exod 34:21 and 35:2–3 form counterpart exegetical advances by defining prohibited Sabbath work in the field and at home. Exodus 35:2–3 simultaneously serves as a structural counterpart with the other Sabbath instruction featuring capital punishment for violators in 31:12–17.

40:33~Gen 2:2 (C) (tabernacle finished). Many scholars have suggested a resemblance between creation and/or the garden and the tabernacle (and temple).[16] The fourth creation day uses the term "lights" instead of "sun" and "moon," which matches the use of the "light" in the tabernacle (Gen 1:14, 15, 16; Exod 25:6; 27:20; 35:8, 14, 28; 39:37). But this may simply reflect a desire to avoid naming the sun and moon as a silent polemic against ancients who worshiped these celestial bodies.

One of the few verbal parallels between the creation story and the tabernacle comes when the two tasks are completed. Since the shared language includes only common

---

16. See, e.g., Morales, *Who Will Ascend?* 40–42, including his table with shared terms and short phrases (42); Weinfeld, "Sabbath, Temple," 501–12; Walton, "Genesis," 1:22, 24.

terms allusion can be no more than a possibility. The brief parallels include very close syntactical parallels (bold indicates verbal parallels).[17]

> **And so** God **finished** on the seventh day his **work** that he had been doing. So on the seventh day he rested from all his work. (Gen 2:3 lit.)

> **And so** Moses **finished** the **work.** (Exod 40:33b)

The work on creation and the tabernacle may be related. If so, Exodus contents itself with subtle hints of similarity. In either case, the finishing of the tabernacle forms an *inclusio* of sorts around Genesis and Exodus. Genesis begins with the deity making a home for the humans and Exodus ends with Israel making a tent for their God.

FILTERS

Exodus contains many non-exegetical uses of scriptural traditions like broad allusions and extensive synoptic parallels within the book itself. These need to be filtered out since this study only targets the exegetical use of Scripture. Filters help reduce false positives by explicitly noting other functions for non-exegetical allusions and general parallels. The following illustrative lists are not comprehensive or complete.[18]

Non-Exegetical Broad Allusions and Shared Themes

Narrative: **1:1–6**>/<Gen 46, the sons of Israel who came to Egypt; **1:7**>/<Gen 1:28; 9:1, 7, they were fruitful and multiplied; **1:8**>/<Gen 41, did not know Joseph; **1:11–14**>/<Gen 15:13, slavery and oppression of people; **2:2**>/<Gen 1, the account of the birth of Moses mentions his mother's response, namely, "and she saw him that he was good" (וַתֵּרֶא אֹתוֹ כִּי־טוֹב הוּא) (Exod 2:2) which echoes the common phrasing of the creation days, "and God saw the light that it was good" (וַיַּרְא אֱלֹהִים אֶת־הָאוֹר כִּי־טוֹב) (Gen 1:4), "and he saw X . . . that it was good" (וַיַּרְא . . . כִּי־טוֹב) (1:10, 12, 18, 21, 25), and "and God saw all that he had made, and behold, it was very good" (וַיַּרְא אֱלֹהִים אֶת־כָּל־אֲשֶׁר עָשָׂה וְהִנֵּה־טוֹב מְאֹד) (1:31); **2:3**>/<Gen 6–9, "ark" (תבה) only appears in Exod 2:3 and 26x in the flood narrative;[19] **2:22**>/<Gen 15:13, Gershom named for Moses being a "residing foreigner" in a foreign "land" somewhat similar to Abraham as a "residing foreigner" in a strange "land" (גר . . . בארץ);

17. Compare: "and so God finished . . . his work" (וַיְכַל אֱלֹהִים . . . מְלַאכְתּוֹ) (Gen 2:2 lit.) with "and so Moses finished the work" (וַיְכַל מֹשֶׁה אֶת־הַמְּלָאכָה) (Exod 40:33). Since Gen 2:3 says "from *all* his work" (מִכָּל־מְלַאכְתּוֹ) (lit., emphasis mine), it may influence SP, LXX, and Vulg. to add "all" to "the work" (Exod 40:33). MT without "all" is preferred (see *BHS* apparatus).

18. For additional parallels, see Hakham, *Exodus*, 2:5–57 (appendix) [Hebrew], though much of Hakham's list presents very short phrases with similarities akin to cross references or stock phrases; Jericke, "Exodus Material," 137–56; Oswald, "Genesis Material," 157–70. Also see Bibliographic Note on Lists of Potential Parallels.

19. See "תֵּבָה," *HALOT* 2:1678.

2:24>/<Gen 15:18; 17 (13x), God remembers "the covenant" with the Hebrew ancestors (cf. Exod 6:5); **3:4**>/<Gen 22:11; 46:2, twofold calling out and response "'Moses, Moses,' and he said, 'Here I am'" evokes "'Abraham, Abraham,' and he said 'Here I am'" and "'Jacob, Jacob,' and he said 'Here I am'"—the pattern of twofold naming appears over a dozen times in Scripture; **3:6**>/<Gen 26:24, "and he said I am the God of your father" (ויאמר אנכי אלהי אביך); **3:8–10**>/<Gen 15:13–14, granting land of Canaan to descendants; **3:13–16**>/<Gen 12–50, God of your ancestors; **4:24–26**>/<Gen 17, circumcision; **6:2–3**>/<Gen 12–35, divine appearances to Abraham, Isaac, and Jacob; **6:7**>/<Gen 17:7, 8, covenant formula (see Table J1 in Jeremiah); **6:8; 13:11**>/<Gen 12:1; 13:14–18; 15:18–20; 17:8, land of promise; **13:19**>/<Gen 50:24–26, carrying out the bones of Joseph; **14:16, 22, 29; 15:19**>/<Gen 1:9, 10, divide waters for "dry ground" (terms for "divide" differ; see note on Isa 43); **29:45**>/<Gen 17:7, 8, covenant formula (see Table J1 in Jeremiah); **32:13**>/<Gen 12:1–3, "remember" promise to Abraham as basis of forgiveness (cf. Exod 2:23–25).

The advice of Moses's father-in-law to teach the instructions and appoint judges to adjudicate them (18:20–21) appears in a dischronological episode set at the mountain (18:5) before they get to the mountain (19:1–2) (see dischronologized in Glossary). The arrangement uses thematic versus chronological sequence.

The elliptical statement in Exod 19:5 explains that all the earth belongs to Yahweh. Ownership infers creation, thus a broad elliptical allusion to the tradition in Gen 1–2.

Legal instructions: The **covenant collection** brings together judgments (21:1–22:17[16]), additional legal standards (22:18[17]–23:19), and the mission to settle in the land of promise (23:20–33). Though only a few of these develop laws treated previously, many legal instructions later in Torah take up these same laws (see Table E2).

TABLE E2: COVENANT COLLECTION AND PARALLEL LEGAL INSTRUCTIONS

Bold references in right hand column signify more significant verbal parallels.

previous regulations	covenant collection	later regulations
	Exod 21:2–6, 7–11, Hebrew slave regulations	Lev 25:39–46, 47–55; Deut 15:12–18
	21:12–14, manslaughter regulation	Lev 24:17, 21; Num 35:9–28; Deut 4:41–43; 19:1–13; cf. Josh 20
	21:15, not attacking parents	Lev 20:9; Deut 21:18–21
	21:16, not kidnapping	**Deut 24:7**
	21:17, not cursing parents	Lev 20:9; cf. Deut 21:18–21
	21:18–19, assault regulated	
	21:20–21, limitation on beating slave	
	21:22–27, regulations on compensation for injury or damage	**Lev 24:19–20; Deut 19:21**

previous regulations	covenant collection	later regulations
cf. Gen 9:5	21:28–32, 35–36, goring ox	
	21:33–34, responsibility for open pit	cf. Deut 22:8
	22:1–4[21:37–22:3], punishment regulations for stealing	Lev 24:18, 21
	22:5–15[4–14], regulations for property restitution	
	22:16–17[15–18], compensation for seduction of virgin	Deut 22:28–29
	22:18[17], executing sorceress	Lev 20:6–7, 27, cf. 19:31; Deut 18:9–14
	22:19 [18], no bestiality	Lev 18:23; 20:15–16; Deut 27:21
Exod 20:3	22:20[19], no sacrifices to other gods or violator devoted	cf. "devote" Deut 13:15, 17[16, 18]
	22:21–24[20–23], not oppressing socially challenged	Exod 23:9; Lev 19:33–34; Deut 10:18–19; 24:17a, 18
	22:25–27[24–26], lending regulations	Deut 15:1–11; **23:19–20[20–21]**; 24:6, **10–13**; 17b
	22:28[27], do not curse civil rulers	Lev 24:15
Exod 13:12	22:29–30[28–29], prohibition against withholding firstlings	Exod 34:19–20; Lev 27:26; Num 3:13; 8:17; 18:17–18; Deut 15:19–23; cf. 26:1–11
	22:31[30], prohibition against eating meat of mortally wounded animal	Lev 11:40; **17:15–16**; 22:8; **Deut 14:21**
Exod 20:16	23:1–3, standards for legal rulings	Exod 23:6–8; Lev 19:12, 15; Deut 16:18–20; 17:2–7, 8–13; 19:15–20; 24:16 cf. 1:9–18
	23:4–5, showing kindness to livestock of an enemy	Deut 22:1–4
	23:6–8, prohibition against injustice	
Exod 22:21–24 [20–23]	23:9, protected social classes	Lev 19:33–34; **Deut 24:17–18**
	23:10–11, fallow year	Lev 25:1–7; Deut 15:1–11
Exod 20:8–11	23:12, Sabbath rest extended to cattle, slaves, and foreigners[a]	Exod 16:22–30; 31:12–17; **34:21**; 35:2–3; Lev 19:3b, 30; 23:3; 26:2; Num 15:32–36; 28:9–10; Deut 5:12–15
	23:13, not swearing by other gods	

(cont.)

previous regulations	**covenant collection**	**later regulations**
	23:14–17, pilgrimage festivals[b]	**Exod 34:18, 22–24**; **Deut 16:16–17**; 31:12–13
Exod 12:10	23:18, regulations concerning yeast and fat of sacrifice	**Exod 34:25**
	23:19a, firstfruits	**Exod 34:26a**; Lev 23:9–14
	23:19b, prohibition against boiling young goat in its mother's milk	**Exod 34:26b; Deut 14:21b**
	23:21, obey God's delegate during conquest	
	23:24–25, not worship gods of Canaanite nations	**Exod 34:12–13**; Num 33:52; **Deut 7:5**, 24–26; **12:3, 20**
	23:32–33, prohibition against covenants with or residing with nations of Canaan	Exod 34:11–16

[a] See Sabbath network for additional references.

[b] Unleavened bread/passover, Exod 12:10–20; 13:3–13; 23:15; 34:18–20; Lev 23:5–8; Num 9:1–14; 28:16–25; Deut 16:1–8. Festival of weeks (Pentecost), Exod 23:16; 34:22; Lev 23:15–21; Num 28:26–31; Deut 16:9–12. Festival of tabernacles (ingathering), Exod 23:16; 34:22; Lev 23:33–43; Num 29:12–34; Deut 16:13–15; Zech 14:16–19; Ezra 3:4; Neh 8:13–18; John 7–8.

The covenant collection attaches punishments to some of the Ten Commandments. The Ten Commandments do not explain punishments for stealing (Exod 20:15). The financial penalties for stealing are spelled out at varying rates from paying double to five times the value of the animals stolen, depending on circumstances (22:1–3, 7[21:37–22:2, 6]). The verbal parallel between the contexts is the verb "steal."

The first use of the term "devote" (*hrm* חרם) in Scripture appears in Exod 22:20[19]. The meaning of devote to destruction connotes the offender under divine wrath in a special way, not merely a civil case of capital punishment (Lev 27:29). The term "devote" elsewhere gets associated with holy war. The thematic similarities between the first commandment and the punishment is "no other gods before me" (Exod 20:3) and "except Yahweh alone" (22:20[19]).

The covenant collection also elaborates at length judicial standards (23:1–3, 6–8) beyond not bearing false witness (20:16).

The animal that kills a person needs to be held accountable (Gen 9:5). Though the regulations regarding the goring ox are related broadly, they focus on the responsibility of the owner (Exod 21:28–32).[20] While the standards of the goring ox partially overlap

20. On the connection with Genesis, see Paul, *Studies*, 79.

with Gen 9:5, they share close parallels with ancient Near Eastern laws (CH §250, 251; LE §§53–55).[21]

The law for the Sabbath (23:20) follows the fourth commandment with rest for domestic animals, slaves, and residing foreigners (20:10).

The mission to settle the land loosely echoes the boundaries from the promise to Abraham (23:31; cf. Gen 15:18–21).

The **covenant renewal collection** includes numerous recycled commands from earlier in Exodus (see Table E1). Most of the parallels have been repurposed by interpretive enhancements (see notes on Exod 34:11–16; 34:18–20; 34:21). A few of the parallels feature only mild interpretive adjustments: regulations concerning leaven and the fat of sacrifice (23:18//34:25), firstfruits (23:19a//34:26a), and the prohibition against boiling a young goat in its mother's milk (23:19b//34:26b).

Tabernacle

The instructions for and construction of the tabernacle feature extensive synoptic parallels. Normally synoptic parallels between books function exegetically while those within books may be exegetical or literary. The nature and function of the synoptic parallels of the tabernacle instructions and its construction primarily within Exodus, as well as a few parallels in Leviticus and Numbers, seem to serve literary coherence not exegesis. Large segments of the synoptic contexts include verbatim parallels and lightly edited similarities. The differences include the mention of the pattern Moses saw on the mountain (Exod 25:9, 40; 26:30), references to the role of Aaron and his sons (28:1–4, 12, 29–30; 30:19–21), and the one-time redemption payment (30:11–16). A few of the instructions get repeated in Leviticus and Numbers as instructions or narrative, as noted below. The choice to repeat about six chapters of detailed instructions points to the importance of the dwelling for the glory of God. Note a synoptic comparison of the tabernacle (stylized brackets signify out of sequence items):[22]

	instructions	**construction**
offerings for the dwelling	Exod 25:1–8	35:4–9
plan of the dwelling[a]	25:9	—
ark	25:10–22	37:1–9
table	25:23–30	37:10–16
lampstand	25:31–39	37:17–24
plan of the furnishings[a]	25:40	—

(cont.)

21. Ancient legal parallels listed in Childs, *Exodus*, 462–63; Wells, "Interpretation," 238.

22. Synoptic parallels are based on a different presentation in Schnittjer, *Torah Story*, 261; also compare with Bendavid, *Parallels*, 172–81 [Hebrew].

	instructions	construction
dwelling		
• curtains	26:1–6	{36:8–13}
• tent	26:7–14	{36:14–19}
• frames	26:15–25	{36:20–30}
• crossbars	26:26–29	{36:31–34}
• plan of the dwelling[a]	26:30	—
• curtain	26:31–35	{36:35–36; 40:21}
• entrance to the tent	26:36–37	{36:37–38}
altar of burnt offering	27:1–8	38:1–7
courtyard of the dwelling	27:9–19	38:9–20
oil for the lampstand[b]	27:20–21	{Lev 24:1–3}
priestly garments		
• Aaron and his sons	28:1–4	—
• ephod	28:5–14	Exod 39:2–7
• breastplate	28:15–30	39:8–21
• robe	28:31–35	39:22–26
• gold plate	28:36–38	{39:30–31}
• tunic, turban, sash	28:39–41	39:27–28a
• undergarments	28:42–43	39:28b, 29
consecration of the priests[c]	29:1–37	{Lev 8:1–36}
daily offerings[d]	29:38–46	{Num 28:3–8}
altar of incense	30:1–10	{Exod 37:25–28}
atonement money	30:11–16	—
basin for washing	30:17–21	{38:8}
anointing oil	30:22–33	{37:29a}
incense	30:34–38	{37:29b}
appointing Bezalel and Oholiab	31:1–6	{35:30–36:1}
work of appointed craftspersons	31:7–11	{35:10–19//39:33–42}

[a] The pattern of the dwelling Moses saw on the mountain not repeated in construction narrative (Exod 25:9, 40; 26:30).

[b] The command for oil for light is repeated not narrated (Exod 27:20–21//Lev 24:2–3).

[c] The instructions for consecration of the priests (Exod 29:1–37) are re-voiced as narrative (Lev 8:1–36). See illustration of re-voicing in Lev Filters.

[d] An abridged version of the command for daily offerings is repeated (Exod 29:38–46//Num 28:3–8).

Chapter 3

LEVITICUS

SYMBOLS[1]

- // verbal parallels (A level)
- /~/ synoptic parallel (A level)
- ~ B, probable interpretive allusion; C, possible; D, probably not
- + interpretive blend
- >/< more or less similar (see Filters)
- * part of interpretive network (see Networks)

USE OF TORAH IN LEVITICUS[2]

17:3–9*~Exod 20:24–25* (C) (sacrifices exclusively at tent of meeting) (* see place network)

17:15;* 22:8~Exod 22:31[30] (B) (standard for eating animals that die on their own) (* see place network)

19:18b, 33–34~Exod 12:48 (B)+22:21[20] (B) (love the residing foreigner)

24:10–23~Exod 22:28[27] (B) (precedent by the case of the blasphemer)

25:35–43*~Exod 22:25–27*[24–26] (B)+21:2–6* (C) (debt, service, and Jubilee) (* see release statute network)

26:40–42*~Gen 17*+Exod 2:24*; 6:5 (B) (humble uncircumcised hearts) (* see Abrahamic covenant, collective confession, and seventy years networks)

OLD TESTAMENT USE OF LEVITICUS (SEE RESPECTIVE NOTES)

1–6>/<Ps 40:6[7] (C) (sacrifice and offering you do not desire)

1:4~Ps 51:16–17[18–19] (B) (you do not delight in sacrifice)

1:5~2 Chr 30:16 (C) (Levites bring blood from slaughter and priests transport blood to inner sanctuary for worship)

2:11; 7:13~Amos 4:5 (B) (taunt of offering leavened/unleavened bread)

3:3–5, 9–11, 14–16~2 Chr 35:12 (C) (set aside Yahweh's portion of the sacrifices)

3:16–17~1 Sam 2:15–17 (B) (taking the fat of offerings)

5:1–6:7[5:1–26]>/<Ps 51:16–17[18–19] (C) (you do not delight in sacrifice)

5:14–6:7[5:14–26]~Isa 53:10 (B) (servant as guilt offering)

5:15~Ezra 10:10–11, 19 (B) (reparation offering and mass divorce)

6:12–13[5–6]~Neh 10:34[35] (C) (solemn oath of restoration assembly)

9:24~1 Chr 21:26 (B) (fire from Yahweh)

9:24~2 Chr 7:1–3 (B) (fire falls from heaven)

10:1, 10–11*~2 Chr 26:18 (C) (priestly instruction on holy versus common) (* see teachers network)

10:9*~Ezek 44:21* (C) (priests sober when in inner court) (* see teachers network)

10:10–11*~1 Sam 21:4*[5] (B) (bread of the presence for David) (* see teachers network)

10:10–11*~Ezek 44:23* (B) (priest instructs on ritual purity) (* see teachers network)

1. For explanation of symbols, see Symbols and Abbreviations and Introduction. For other help, see Glossary.
2. See Bibliographic Note on Lists of Potential Parallels.

10:10–11*~Hag 2:11–14* (B) (priestly ruling on holy and unclean) (* see teachers network)

10:10–11*~Mal 2:7* (C) (instruction of priests) (* see teachers network)

10:10*~Ezek 22:26* (B) (priests do violence against Torah) (* see teachers network)

11–15~Num 5:1–4 (B) (relocating ritually impure persons outside the encampment)

11:1–28/~/Deut 14:3–21 (dietary regulations)

11:39–40; 17:15+7:18; 19:7~Ezek 4:14 (B) (avoiding ritually impure diet)

13–14~Deut 24:8–9 (B) (skin conditions)

15:16~Deut 23:9–14[10–15] (B) (ritual purity in time of battle)

17*>/<Ezek 14:1–11 (B) (heart idolatry) (* see place network)

17:1–9*+17:10–14*~Deut 12:2–28* (B) (seek the place Yahweh will choose to put his name) (* see place network)

17:7*~2 Chr 11:15 (C) (Jeroboam's aberrant renegade worship) (* see place network)

17:13*~Ezek 24:7–8 (B) (pouring out blood) (* see place network)

18:5~Ezek 20:11, 13, 21, 25 (B) (decrees and ordinances to live)

18:5~Neh 9:29 (B) (cycles of rebellion and deliverance in panoramic retrospective)

18:24–30~Ezek 36:12–19 (C) (defiled land)

18:27~Ezra 9:11–12 (C) (pollution by intermarriage with the other)

19:9–10*~Ruth 2:8* (B) (Moabitess granted residing foreigner gleaning privileges) (* see assembly network)

19:13b~Deut 24:14–15 (C) (wages regulated)

19:15~Ps 82:1–6 (C) (confronting bad judges)

19:19//Deut 22:9–11 (A) (mixing makes it holy)

19:34; 25:10, 45~Ezek 47:22–23 (B/C) (remapping the social identity of residing foreigners)

20:9~Deut 21:18–21 (C) (rebellious son)

21:1–3~Ezek 44:24–27 (B) (standards of worship and ritual purity for priests)

21:5~Ezek 44:20 (B) (priests not shave head or grow hair long)

21:7, 13–15~Ezek 44:22 (B) (requirements for wives of priest)

22:17–25~Mal 1:6–2:9 (B) (reversal of priestly blessing)

22:20, 22~Deut 15:19–23 (B) (firstlings to Yahweh)

23:5~Num 9:1–14 (B) (alternate time for Passover)

23:10–11~Num 15:18–21 (B) (first of processed goods)

23:40~Neh 8:14–16 (B) (making temporary shelters for Tabernacles)

24:1–4~2 Chr 29:7 (B) (lamps of house of Yahweh)

24:5–9*~1 Sam 21:4*[5] (B) (bread of the presence for David) (* see Sabbath and teachers networks)

24:5–9*~2 Chr 29:18 (B) (table and rows of bread in temple) (* see Sabbath network)

24:20~Deut 19:18–21 (B) (measure-for-measure punishment for false witnesses)

25:10~Isa 61:1, 2 (C) (year of release)

25:10, 35–46*~Jer 34:14* (C) (releasing slaves) (* see release statute network)

25:23–26*~Ruth 4:5–6 (B) (legal blend of law of responsibility of near-relative, etc.) (* see release statute network)

25:25–28~Ezek 7:12–13 (C) (sellers shall not return to what is theirs)

25:42, 46*~Neh 5:1, 4, 7, 8, 11* (C) (reforming predatory loans)

26:4–6, 13~Ezek 34:23–31 (B) (Davidic shepherd)

26:29~Ezek 5:10* (B) (multigenerational cannibalism) (* see personal responsibility network)

26:30–31~Ezek 6:4–7 (B) (judgment upon cities and high places)

26:34–35~2 Chr 36:21* (B) (enforced Sabbath years for land) (* see seventy years network)

26:39~Ezek 24:23; 33:10 (B) (rot in iniquity)

26:39~Lam 5:7 (B) (bearing the ancestors' iniquities)

26:40*~Neh 1:8–9* (C) (Yahweh scatters his unfaithful people) (* see collective confession network)

26:40–41*~Dan 9:4–19* (B) (collective confession of sin) (* see collective confession network)

26:40a, 45~Ps 106:44–46 (B) (remembering the covenant in poetic retrospective)

26:41~2 Chr 7:11–22 (B) (second revelation to Solomon)

27:1–25~Num 30:1–16[2–17] (C) (vows by females)

27:30–33~Num 18:21–24 (B) (tithes to Levites)

27:30~Deut 14:22–29 (C) (tithes)

NEW TESTAMENT USE OF LEVITICUS

12:8//Luke 2:24 (purification offering of poor)
18:5//Rom 10:5; Gal 3:12 (who does these lives by them)
19:2//1 Pet 1:16; cf. Lev 11:44, 45 (be holy)
19:18//Matt 5:43; 19:19; 22:39; Mark 12:31, 33; Luke 10:27; Rom 13:9; Gal 5:14; Jas 2:8 (love your neighbor)
20:9//Matt 15:4; Mark 7:10 (not curse parents)
23:29~Acts 3:23 (destroyed from the people)
24:20//Matt 5:38 (eye for eye)
26:12//2 Cor 6:16 (I will walk among them)

HERMENEUTICAL PROFILE OF THE USE OF TORAH IN LEVITICUS

Leviticus interprets scriptural traditions within its story of Yahweh's instructions from the tent and at the mountain. If the legal instructions of Exodus at the mountain define aspects of the redemptive relationship of Israel and Yahweh, and if the laws of Deuteronomy look to the settlement of Israel in the land, then Leviticus works from a different vantage point. The laws of Leviticus consider just about everything as it relates to the courts of Yahweh.

Limited legal exegesis appears in the second half of Leviticus. Priestly concerns dominate the first half of the book. The frame narrative opens with, "Yahweh called to Moses and spoke to him from the tent of meeting. He said, 'Speak to the Israelites and say to them'" (Lev 1:1–2a). Nearly all the chapters following continue with brief kindred literary signals of divine revelation of priestly concerns of sacrifices, establishment of the priesthood, ritual purity standards, and the annual Day of Atonement of the tented shrine of Yahweh (1–7, 8–10, 11–15, 16). Holiness dominates the second half which wraps up with: "These are the decrees, the laws and the regulations that Yahweh established at Mount Sinai between himself and the Israelites through Moses" (26:46). The word of Yahweh for the priests from the tent and for laity and priests at the mountain situates the instructions after Exodus.

Exodus ends by establishing the problem that dominates Leviticus: the holiness of Yahweh's presence. When Israel rebelled with the golden calf, Yahweh decided to take away his presence to avoid his wrath breaking out upon Israel (Exod 33:1–3). Moses persuaded Yahweh to remain with his people, leading to his glory coming into the tabernacle (40:34). The problem, or at least the reality, of the divine holiness is the game changer that necessitates the teachings of holiness for Israel and the attendant exegetical enhancements of several scriptural traditions.

Unlike the legal collections in Exodus and Deuteronomy, Leviticus speaks to Israel—priests and laity—pertaining to coming into the courts of Yahweh. Personal, social, and economic concerns need to be explained in terms of how these could damage and/or help Israel as a tabernacle-going people. Leviticus views all of life relative to its effects on worship. This undercurrent affects everything in Leviticus, including its legal exegesis.

Since the legal exegesis of Leviticus appears in the holiness collection of Lev 17–26, a couple of its features need to be noted. The personification of the land runs throughout the holiness collection.[3] The importance of the land stems from the divine promise of it and the expectation of the tabernacle coming into it. The personified land became nauseous from accumulated ritual contamination from the iniquity of its nations and vomited them out (Lev 18:25). Israel needs to obey the holiness standards or they too shall be vomited out (18:28). The personification of the land includes the need to "circumcise" its fruit trees (19:23–25).[4] Like anyone else, the land needs Sabbath rest (25:4). If Israel fails to obey the instructions, the land will enjoy its Sabbath years while Israel goes into captivity (26:34–35, 43). The running personification of the land helps unify all of life in the land according to the need for holiness.

The legal exegesis of the holiness collection in many respects pivots on viewing all of Israel's life from the vantage point of the holiness of Yahweh's courts. The priests' role in bearing the burden of holiness cannot stem the tide of ritual impurity generated by lifestyles of infidelity. Israel must "be holy" (19:2). But the implications of the holiness of the courts of Yahweh go further. Holiness places demands upon Israel for the "residing foreigners" among them and upon the residing foreigners themselves. Residing foreigners denote included others—versus excluded others—who take the sign of circumcision and live among Israel without land. Their lack of land and lack of full citizenship among the tribes accounts for their social challenges—widows, orphans, and residing foreigners.[5] Residing foreigners participated in Passover (Exod 12:43–49) and may have been among the "mixed multitude" who left Egypt with Israel (12:38). Divine holiness affects everyone and everything.

Evaluating Israel in relation to the courts of Yahweh affects what Israel eats, how they treat neighbors and residing foreigners, and the responsibility to the law by native-born and residing foreigner alike. Each of these laws houses interpretive upgrades according to the demands of holiness.

The presence of divine holiness raises the standards in specific ways that initiates legal adjustments. The legal exegesis in Leviticus advances revelation in light of the requirements of coming into the dwelling place of Yahweh's holy presence.

In sum, the two sides of holiness as dangerous and vulnerable get at the dominant rationale for legal exegesis in Leviticus. The presence of divine glory with Israel triggers a reassessment of Israel's responsibilities. Leviticus makes adjustments on legal standards in the light of Israel as worshipers who need to ever prepare to come before Yahweh.

---

3. See Schnittjer, *Torah Story*, 344–47.

4. For the first three years of entering the land Israel may not eat of fruit trees. They must "regard as foreskin its foreskin, its fruit (וַעֲרַלְתֶּם עָרְלָתוֹ אֶת־פִּרְיוֹ)" (Lev 19:23 lit.). The very unusual comparison of the fruit of trees to foreskin takes its connotation from circumcising male children as a sign of the covenant. It is as though the personified land itself must be circumcised.

5. See "גֵּר," *HALOT* 1:201; *NIDOTTE* 1:837 (no. 2).

USE OF TORAH IN LEVITICUS

17:3–9*~Exod 20:24–25* (C) (sacrifices exclusively at tent of meeting) (* see place network). Leviticus calls for an end to individuals sacrificing anywhere but at the tent of meeting (Lev 17:3–9). The context does not quote or paraphrase Exod 20:24–25, though it shares a few key terms like "altar," "sacrifice," and "burnt offering." Although these two laws serve different agendas, they are the only laws in Torah up to this point that prohibit ritual slaughter elsewhere. The law in Lev 17:3–9 concerns sacrifices of well-being that provide food for worshipers. Exodus 20:24–25 calls for earthen altars of unhewn stone for their sacrifices. Leviticus bans the use of independent altars for fear of people worshiping goat demons (Lev 17:7). The laity continue to do the slaughtering themselves at the tent of meeting with the worship personnel to help them follow sacrificial regulations (1:2–6; 3:1–5). The law in Lev 17:3–9 puts an end to non-ritual slaughter of domesticated animals.[6] The law against blood consumption allows only for non-ritual slaughter of game animals (17:13).

In this context the law of the altar from Exod 20:24–25 provided a temporary measure during the nine months of constructing the tabernacle. Yet Deuteronomy, in spite of its dominant concerns for central worship and decentralized Israel, makes allowance for the limited function of the altar of unhewn stones (Deut 27:6; Exod 20:25). The laws of the altar in Exod 20:24–25, exclusive sacrifice at the tent of meeting in Lev 17:3–9, and centralization of ritual sacrifice and restitution of non-sacred slaughter in Deut 12 have always been difficult for interpreters.[7] See extended discussion in the note on Deut 12.

In sum, the centralization of all sacrifice at the tent of meeting in Lev 17:3–9 eliminates ritual slaughter in the wilderness. All Israel must come to the courts of Yahweh to slaughter domestic animals.

17:15;* 22:8~Exod 22:31[30] (B) (standard for eating animals that die on their own) (* see place network). The verbal parallels between Exod 22:31[30] and Lev 17:15 and 22:8 include only two words. The rare term "animal torn by wild beasts" used in parallel laws makes allusion likely.[8] In Exodus, the prohibition against eating animals that have died in nature is based on the holiness of the people (Exod 22:31[30]). With the erection of the tabernacle, the priests are called to bear the burden of holiness (Lev 8:12;

---

6. Contra Hess who argues that the law of slaughter in Lev 17:2–4 only applies to sacrifices and allows profane slaughter by laity. He says the laws of slaughter in Lev 17 and Deut 12 agree in giving "permission to slaughter nonsacrificial animals outside a sanctuary" ("Leviticus," 1:732). Hess fails to observe that the dietary regulations in Lev 11 do not enumerate sacrificial animals but Deut 14:4–5 does (Bendavid, *Parallels*, 184 [Hebrew]; Driver, *Deuteronomy*, 157). Deut 14:4–5 lists ox, sheep, and goat (cf. Lev 17:3) with the game animals because this law has advanced the legal standards to allow for profane slaughter after Israel is decentralized in the land (Deut 12:15, 20–21). See Table D6, n. a in note on Deut 14:3–21 and see Rüterswörden, "Concerning Deut 14," 98–99; Milgrom, *Leviticus 1–16*, 10.

7. See Levine, *Leviticus*, 112–13.

8. See "טְרֵפָה," *HALOT* 1:380. Besides Exod 22:31[30], Lev 17:15 and its parallels in Lev 22:8 and Ezek 4:14; 44:31 (cf. Lev 7:24), the term only appears three times (Gen 31:39; Exod 22:13[12]; Nah 2:13[14]).

cf. Num 18:1–7). At this point Leviticus makes a distinction between a less holy standard for laity but retains the prohibition for priests (emphases signify verbal parallels):

> You are to be my holy people. So do not *eat* the meat of an animal *torn by wild animals*; throw it to the dogs. (Exod 22:31†[30])

> Anyone, whether native-born or foreigner, who *eats* anything found dead or *torn by wild animals* must wash their clothes and bathe with water, and they will be ceremonially unclean till evening; then they will be clean. (Lev 17:15)

> He [descendant of Aaron] must not *eat* anything found dead or *torn by wild animals*, and so become unclean through it. I am Yahweh. (22:8)

The loosening of the standard for laity to eat meat from animals that had not been slaughtered at the tabernacle but were killed in nature came with the condition of protocol for purification from ritual impurity. Also, the standard for maintaining regulations for ritual purification needs to apply to Israel and residing foreigners alike (17:15). The reason for broad application of ritual purification standards, even to residing foreigners, stems from the need to keep the encampment free from ritual impurity now that the glory of Yahweh indwells the tabernacle. The legal exegesis works out the implications of the people before the courts of Yahweh. When Israel prepares to enter the land, this same regulation on eating animals that died in nature gets reinterpreted again (see detailed discussion in note on Deut 14:21a).

19:18b, 33–34~Exod 12:48 (B)+22:21[20] (B) (love the residing foreigner). The covenant collection calls for protections for the well-known triad of widow, orphan, and residing foreigner (Exod 22:21–24[20–23]) and again for residing foreigners (23:9). Leviticus 19:33–34 shares substantial verbal correspondence with Exod 22:21[20]. The themes of the protected classes themselves become somewhat commonplace. But only three times elsewhere does the verb "mistreat" get used with residing foreigner—probably as a stock phrase in these cases (Jer 22:3; Ezek 22:7, 29).[9] These three uses do not include the analogy of Israel as residing foreigners in Egypt. Only Exod 22:21[20] and Lev 19:33–34 use together "do not mistreat" the residing foreigner with the analogy of Israel's Egyptian sojourn, making allusion likely. The allusion seems to breed a counterpart based on the binary pair of residing foreigner and neighbor. "Neighbors" refers to fellow Israelites when juxtaposed with others like "residing foreigners." The use of the simile "as native-born" in Lev 19:34 suggests that the logic of the simile "as yourself" in "love the residing foreigner as yourself" is derived from the instructions for Passover. The term "native-born" appears fourteen times in Exodus, Leviticus, and Numbers and

---

9. See "ינה," *HALOT* 1:416; Even-Shoshan, 473.

only twice elsewhere. The use of the term in Exod 12 holds the native-born and the circumcised residing foreigner to the same standards for Passover (Exod 12:19, 48, 49; cf. Num 9:14).[10] The exegetical deduction in Lev 19:33–34 goes something like: If the residing foreigner is held to the same Passover standards as native-born citizens of Israel, then native-born citizens should treat residing foreigners like any native-born person. The relationship of the simile "as a native-born" (כְּאֶזְרָח) in Exod 12:48 and Lev 19:34 is likely since the conditional phrase "when a residing foreigner resides among you" (וְכִי־יָגוּר אִתְּךָ גֵּר) only appears in this exact configuration in the Exod 12:48 and Lev 19:33 (lit.).[11] This two-step exegetical advancement needs to be observed and explained (underlining, bold, and broken underlining signify verbal and syntactic parallels):

> When a residing foreigner residing among you wants to celebrate Passover to Yahweh he must have all the males in his household circumcised; then he may take part as a native-born of the land. No uncircumcised male may eat it. (Exod 12:48 lit.)

> **Do not mistreat** or oppress **a residing foreigner, for you were residing foreigners** in the land of **Egypt**. (22:21[20] lit.)

> When a residing foreigner resides among you in your land, **do not mistreat** them. The residing foreigner residing among you must be treated as your native-born. Love them as yourself, **for you were residing foreigners in Egypt**. I am Yahweh your God. (Lev 19:33–34 lit.)

> Love your neighbor as yourself. I am Yahweh. (Lev 19:18b lit.)

The exegetical advances in Leviticus can be taken in two sequential steps. First, Leviticus starts with the prohibition against mistreating residing foreigners and extends it to its positive counterpart—love the residing foreigner as yourself.[12] The logic of this move starts with what may be called the "golden rule" motive clause. To paraphrase the logic: protect sojourners because you know what it is like to be mistreated.[13] Since Israel lived through mistreatment in their Egyptian sojourn, they have the experiential fund for caring for residing foreigners among them. The command to love the residing foreigner is quoted in a summary catechism section of Deuteronomy without further interpretation.

---

10. See Even-Shoshan, 32; "אֶזְרָח," *HALOT* 1:28 ; sec. 1, coll. *DCHR* 1:228. Leviticus and Numbers consistently use the term to refer to legal standards that apply to the native-born but not the residing foreigner (Lev 23:42) or of standards that apply to both the native-born and the residing foreigner (Lev 16:29; 17:15; 18:26; 24:16, 22; Num 15:13–14, 29, 30).

11. See Even-Shoshan, 231 (גור nos. 60, 62). The derivative phrase "When a residing foreigner residing among you (וְכִי־יָגוּר אִתְּכֶם גֵּר)" in Num 9:14 (lit.) comes very close as well as similar phrases in Lev 17:8 and Num 15:14 (ibid., nos. 61, 63, 64).

12. Contra the view that Lev 19:33–34 is an extrapolation from Lev 19:18 as suggested by Akiyama, *Love of Neighbor*, 43, 65; Bosman, "Loving," 581. Akiyama and Bosman fail to observe the dependence of Lev 19:33–34 on Exod 22:21[20].

13. The golden rule logic is from Kelly, "Ethics," 162–63.

"Love the **residing foreigner, for you were foreigners in Egypt**" (Deut 10:19 lit., emphases marks verbal and syntactic parallels with Lev 19:33–34 above).

Second, based on the initial positive counterpart interpretation, Leviticus uses the logic of lesser to greater to deduce a paired command. If Israel must treat residing foreigners like themselves, then Israel must certainly treat fellow Israelites at the same level. The only two places in Leviticus that use the preposition "like" with the second-person singular pronominal suffix are Lev 19:18b and 19:34. And both use an identical verb with identical rare syntax. Typically, the verb "love" (אהב) takes the accusative marker (אֵת) as in the parallel passage—"You shall love the residing foreigner" (וַאֲהַבְתֶּם אֶת־הַגֵּר) (Deut 10:19 lit.). Only in three places does the finite verb "love" use the preposition *le-* (לְ) to mark the direct object (Lev 19:18, 34; 2 Chr 19:2).[14]

Notice that love the residing foreigner and love thy neighbor do not start with humanistic impulse. This pair of commands grows out of Yahweh's redemption of Israel from oppression (Lev 19:34). Redemption motivates love of the other. Love of the other demands love of neighbor.

In sum, two sequential exegetical advances in Lev 19:33–34 and 18b both work something like reverse engineering deductions. The positive counterpart of not mistreating is love. The counterpart of loving the other like oneself is loving one's associates like oneself. This seems to be a case in which legal exegesis generates legal exegesis.

24:10–23~Exod 22:28[27] (B) (precedent by the case of the blasphemer). The exegetical advancement in the case of the blasphemer needs to be compared to its counterpart precedent-setting laws in Torah. The kindred relationship between these five laws has been observed since antiquity. Philo begins his treatment of the laws of Moses with the first four of the five precedent-setting legal narratives that include divine decisions and/or legal amendments—the case of the blasphemer (Lev 24:10–23), an alternate date for Passover (Num 9:1–14), the Sabbath breaker (15:32–36), inheritance and Zelophehad's daughters (27:1–11), and amending female inheritance in the case of Zelophehad's daughters (36:1–12).[15] The cases of the blasphemer and Sabbath breaker share similar structure and relate to divine revelation for sentencing: setting (Lev 24:10; Num 15:32a); problem (Lev 24:11a; Num 15:32b); approach (Lev 24:11b; Num 15:33); oracular inquiry (Lev 24:12–13; Num 15:34–35a); divine case ruling (Lev 24:14; Num 15:35b); statutory law (Lev 24:15–22; Num 15 n/a); fulfillment (Lev 24:23; Num 15:36).[16]

---

14. Bertholet, *Leviticus Erklärt*, 68. Contra Even-Shoshan, 19 (see first collocation) only listing Lev 19:18, 34 (cf. nos. 40, 41, 163). On the preposition *le-* (לְ) to mark the direct object, see GKC §117n; Joüon §125k; *IBHS* §11.2.10g. Brug also includes a use of "love" (ptc) with le- (לְ) in 1 Kgs 5:1[15] but it has an indirect sense ("Show," 295). The conventional DDO with "love" in Deut 10:19 fits with the tendency of receptor texts to disambiguate.

15. See Philo, *Moses II*, §192–245. Also see Targum Neofiti and Targum Pseudo-Jonathan at Lev 24:12; Num 9:8; 15:34; 27:5. Many modern scholars also treat as a set these narratives of divine decision of precedent and/or amendment, though often not mentioning Philo, e.g., Hayes, *What's Divine?*, 17.

16. Adapted from structural comparative chart in Chavel, *Oracular Law*, 6.

The importance of the five episodes with divine rulings goes beyond the cases themselves. These narratives demonstrate a personal interactive relationship between Yahweh and his people. The law and its consequences for criminals are not mechanical or perfunctory but are given within a dynamic covenantal relationship.

The narrative in Lev 24 includes a verbal parallel to Exod 22:28[27], making allusion likely. The case of the blasphemer gets at both the capital punishment for the crime and also the applicability to all members of the community including residing foreigners (Lev 24:15, 16, 22). The application of the law to residing foreigners makes the offender's background important (24:10–11). Notice the relationship between the scenario in the frame narrative and the divine legal revelation (bold signifies verbal parallels; italics signify the divine legal revelation; and broken underlining signifies the ruling):

> Do not **blaspheme** God or curse the ruler of your people. (Exod 22:28[27])

> Now the son of an Israelite mother and an Egyptian father went out among the Israelites, and a fight broke out in the camp between him and an Israelite. [11] The son of the Israelite woman **blasphemed** the Name with a curse; so they brought him to Moses. (His mother's name was Shelomith, the daughter of Dibri the Danite.) [12] They put him in custody until the will of Yahweh should be made clear to them. [13] Then Yahweh said to Moses: [14] *"Take the blasphemer outside the camp. All those who heard him are to lay their hands on his head, and the entire assembly is to stone him.* [15] *Say to the Israelites: 'Anyone who curses their God will be held responsible;* [16] *anyone who blasphemes the name of Yahweh is to be put to death. The entire assembly must stone them. Whether foreigner or native-born, when they blaspheme the Name they are to be put to death. . . .* [22] *You are to have the same law for the foreigner and the native-born. I am Yahweh your God.'"* [23] Then Moses spoke to the Israelites, and they took the blasphemer outside the camp and stoned him. The Israelites did as Yahweh commanded Moses. (Lev 24:10–16, 22–23)

The decision suggests an overlap between criminal and religious legal standards. In addition, the participation of the entire community in the execution shows something of the collective solidarity in legal standards bearing on their relationship with Yahweh. And, most importantly, covenantal legal standards apply to Israel and residing foreigners alike.[17]

In the above citation, note the ellipsis for Lev 24:17–21. These verses collate three other previous regulations and punishments, the first two of which get repeated in a mirror image format: The outer bracket reaffirms capital punishment for murder (Lev 24:17, 21b; cf. Exod 21:12), the inner bracket reaffirms restitution for killing someone's domestic animal (Lev 24:18, 21a; cf. Exod 22:1, 4[21:37; 22:3]), and the central element reaffirms

17. Contra Chavel, who considers the repeated references to the residing foreigner unrelated to the reasons for the ruling (ibid., 35–48, esp. 48). See Fuad, "Curious," 57, 64–67.

the measure-for-measure limitation of judgment (Lev 24:19–20; cf. Exod 21:23–25; Deut 19:21).[18] All three laws seem to be bound together to demonstrate a common principle even while distinguishing between human life and economic interests. The third regulation gets at the underlying principle of limiting punishments and liabilities according to the crime (verbal parallels signified by italics and bold, and underlying principle signified by broken underlining):[19]

> Anyone who takes the life of *a human being is to be put to death.* [18] **whoever kills** someone's **animal must make restitution**—life for life. [19] Anyone who injures their neighbor is to be injured in the same manner: [20] fracture for fracture, eye for eye, tooth for tooth. The one who has inflicted the injury must suffer the same injury. [21] **Whoever kills an animal must make restitution**, but whoever kills *a human being is to be put to death.* (Lev 24:17–21†)

None of the three cited laws features interpretive elements of themselves. They simply loosely paraphrase the gist as they appear in the covenant collection. The interpretive function of these kindred legal standards bears on the divine ruling in the case of the blasphemer. Blaspheming the name cannot be compensated like the death of an animal or a personal injury. It stands as a capital offense like murder for bringing the entire worshiping community under threat of Yahweh's deadly wrath. The narrative does not illustrate the law of measure for measure, but the measure-for-measure limitation on judgment illustrates why the death penalty needs to be meted out on any criminal—native-born or residing foreigner—who blasphemes the name.[20]

25:35–43*~Exod 22:25–27*[24–26] (B)+21:2–6* (C) (debt, service, and Jubilee) (* see release statute network). The legal standards for lending and release from service get treated separately in Exodus and Deuteronomy but together in Leviticus under the Jubilee instructions. The interrelations between these laws remain much contested. Excavative diachronic studies include scholars who see the lending and slave release laws in Deuteronomy as derivative of Exodus and Leviticus versus those who see Leviticus as derivative of Exodus and Deuteronomy.[21] Some approaches frame Lev 25 as "ideal" versus real, which softens the need to compare it with related legal standards in Torah.[22] Other basic issues remain unresolved. Among the most difficult relate to release after

18. On this chiastic structure, see Milgrom, *Leviticus 23–27*, 2129. Milgrom sees the entire episode of the blasphemer (Lev 24:13–23) and the second half of the Sabbath breaker (Num 15:35–36) in chiastic arrangement (2128–30).

19. On whether measure for measure in Scripture requires maiming for personal injuries or alternate compensation, see ibid., 2133–36; Levine, *Leviticus*, 268–70. In spite of one case of maiming a wartime captive (Judg 1:7), legal standards suggest non-maiming alternate compensation (Exod 21:26) (see Wenham, *Leviticus*, 312).

20. See Milgrom, *Leviticus 23–27*, 2106, 2132.

21. See, e.g., ibid., 2251–57, especially 2255–56; Levinson, "Birth," 620–25, 636.

22. See Stackert, *Rewriting*, 113–65, esp. 164; Leuchter, "Manumission," 639–40; Kawashima, "Jubilee," 388–89. However, references to "Jubilee" in other laws (Lev 27:16–25; Num 36:4) suggests it is not a mere utopian ideal (see van Selms, "Jubilee, year of," *IBDSup* 497).

seven years of service in Exodus and Deuteronomy but fifty years in Leviticus. These differences naturally relate to whether newer versions of laws in Torah replace, complement, or advance previous versions.

The present approach focuses on legal exegesis as presented by Torah. The frame narrative places the Jubilee standards of Leviticus at the mountain and those of Deuteronomy as Moses's explanation of torah on the plains of Moab. Prior to deciding if these laws replace, complement, or advance previous versions of the regulations, stands a need to determine if they each speak to the same situations.

Leviticus 25:8–55 deals with two areas—land (Lev 25:8–24) and service (25:25–55) —connected by debt. The regulations of both areas fall under Yahweh's sovereignty. The land standards work from Yahweh's ownership: "*because* the land is mine" (25:23, emphasis mine). The service limitations start from Yahweh's lordship: "*because* they are my servants" (25:42 lit., emphasis mine). The land and the people belong to Yahweh. All limitations and standards on debts pivot on Yahweh's will for his land and his people.

At Jubilee, the land returns to those to whom Yahweh grants it. This standard does not come in the form of case law. The reverting of the land perpetually to those to whom Yahweh grants it converts the real estate system from ownership to virtual leasing.

The limitations on service for debt relate to a series of case laws based on increasing severity of debt from one to the next. Notice the mounting hardship in the four cases (emphases mine):

> *If one of your fellow Israelites becomes poor and sells some of their property*, their nearest relative is to come and redeem what they have sold. . . . (25:25)
>
> *If any of your fellow Israelites become poor and are unable to support themselves among you*, help them as you would a foreigner and stranger. . . . (25:35)
>
> *If any of your fellow Israelites become poor and sell themselves to you*, do not make them work as slaves. . . . (25:39)
>
> *If a foreigner residing among you becomes rich and any of your fellow Israelites become poor and sell themselves to the foreigner or to a member of the foreigner's clan*. . . . (25:47)

The added dimension in each of the four cases in comparison to debt and debt slavery laws in the covenant collection relates to the priority of redemption or financial assistance by extended family (25:25, 29, 48). Other differences also set these laws apart. The focus of comparison between Exodus and Leviticus relates to the second and third cases above, namely, how an Israelite treats impoverished fellow Israelites.

Leviticus 25 does not speak about debt slavery in the way Exod 21:2–11 does. Actually, Lev 25 does not deal with the issue of Hebrew female slaves, so the comparison for the moment needs to be restricted to Exod 21:2–6 and Lev 25:35–38 and 25:39–46. The two main comparisons regarding the second and third cases above need attention.

First, Lev 25:35 does not have the term "like/as" in spite of its being added in by nearly all modern committee translations (bold signifies verbal parallels; broken underlining signifies similarities; and underlining signifies terms not in Hebrew).

> If you lend money to one of my people **among you** who is needy, do not treat it like a business deal; charge no **interest.** (Exod 22:25[24])

> If any of your fellow Israelites become poor and are unable to support themselves **among you**, help them as you would a foreigner and stranger, so they can continue to live among you. [36] Do not take **interest** or any profit from them, but fear your God, so that they may continue to live among you. (Lev 25:35–36)

The lack of simile in Hebrew could signal a legal distinction: Not merely treating the impoverished landed fellow Israelite "like" a residing foreigner, but that they legally become temporary residing foreigners within Israel until Jubilee.[23] Wells refers to this legal status change as the fellow Israelite becoming a "quasi-residing foreigner."[24] Wells examines different kinds of ancient debt scenarios and provides evidence to suggest this accords with an "antichretic pledge." The difference with debt service by an antichretic pledge means the person may not be resold as in an ordinary debt slavery arrangement.[25] This distinction helps explain the shift proposed in lending.

Second, the sense of the verb "sell" in Lev 25:39 requires attention. The verb appears in a stem (Nif) that can function passively as "to be sold"—that is, a person treated like property—or reflexively "to sell oneself"—that is, a person going into debt situation by choice. Milgrom claims that all uses of "sell" in this stem require the passive sense.[26] The problems with Milgrom's claim relate to both the ambiguity of many cases that could be translated passively or reflexively in Scripture and who is selling the person.[27] The repeated use of the second person singular pronoun in vv. 39a and 39b means the creditor and the buyer are one and the same person—"if any of your fellows becomes indebted to *you*" and "he is sold/he sells himself to *you*" (25:39a, 39b lit., emphasis mine).[28] The seller cannot be

23. See Schenker, "Biblical Legislation," 30.

24. See Wells, "Quasi-Alien," 136. Wells says "quasi-alien" but because of the baggage with "alien" the terms "residing foreigner" and "residing foreigner-like" will be used here.

25. Ibid., 147, and see 143–47. Wells goes on to explain that this arrangement may favor the one who helps out their fellow by retaining their profits for service as opposed to mere interest (153). This latter conclusion in part stems from Wells's excavative concerns reading Leviticus as a reaction against Deuteronomy.

26. See Milgrom, *Leviticus 23–27*, 2219–20. For a more complicated argument of the parallel Nif of "sell" in Deut 15:12, see Japhet, "Relationship," 72–73. Levinson refutes the view of Japhet, demonstrating the reflexive use of Nif stem verbs in casuistic protases (Exod 21:22), see "Birth," 633, n. 52. Levinson's larger argument is different from the one pursued here. On the reflexive sense of Nif, see GKC §51c; *IBHS* §23.4b.

27. See Lev 25:47, 48, 50; Deut 15:12; Jer 34:14, listed in Wells, "Quasi-Alien," 139.

28. Ibid.

another creditor because landowners sold into debt service cannot be re-sold (25:42). This means the seller must be the debtor who "sells himself." This evidence argues that the verb be translated in its reflexive sense as in NIV, NRSV, JPSB, and others. Therefore, this is a different case than the debt slavery of Exod 21:2–6 wherein male debt slaves may be re-sold (versus prohibition against re-selling female debt slaves, Exod 21:8). Notice that Exod 21:2 allows for the seller to be the debtor himself or another creditor whereas the debtor and seller in Lev 25:39 must be the same person (broken underlining marks differences).[29]

> If you buy a Hebrew servant, he is to serve you for six years. But in the seventh year, he shall go free, without paying anything. (Exod 21:2)

> If any of your fellow Israelites become poor and sell themselves to you, do not make them work as slaves. They are to be treated as hired workers or temporary residents among you; they are to work for you until the Year of Jubilee. (Lev 25:39–40)

These two laws deal with two different persons in similar but distinct legal scenarios. The debt slave of Exod 21:2–7 apparently does not own land (whether a city dweller or otherwise) versus the indebted landowner of Lev 25:39 who sells himself after selling his land as well as selling his family into debt service, all of whom get released at Jubilee (25:41). Poverty can come upon landowners and landless alike, and they each need laws to protect them.[30]

In sum, the basis of the Jubilee standards of Lev 25 starts from Yahweh as owner of the land and as owner of Israel as his servants (25:23, 42). Within Torah's presentation Lev 25 provides for situations different from the covenant collection. Exodus 22:25[24] protects the poor and Exod 21:2–6 the landless debtor. The legal provisions of Lev 25 offer protections for impoverished landowners. To take advantage of the restoration of family lands requires debt service across the Jubilee cycle. Additional protections include the "free choice" to sell oneself as well as freedom of family and land restoration at Jubilee. In this case, the law does not replace or even complement but supplements the covenant collection.

The overlap between the debt and service laws of Exodus, Leviticus, and Deuteronomy raises many difficult challenges. Though many cannot be solved because of limited evidence, taking stock of common denominators and distinctions among these three can help with difficulties in the sets of laws (Table L1).

---

29. On the minor verbal overlap between Exod 21:2–6 and Lev 25:39–43, see Lasserre, *Synopse*, §3 (p. 10).

30. The view here does not start with "Hebrew" in Exod 21:2 as derived from the Akkadian term *ḫapiru/ḫabiru* or its Semitic parallels inferring landless persons, but from biblical use of the term Hebrew (see Greenberg, *Ḫab/piru*, 92–93; Na'aman, "Ḫabiru," 286–87; Freedman, Willoughby, "עִבְרִי," *TDOT* 10:437–44; contra Wright, "What?" 195–96; idem, "Sabbath Year," *ABD* 5:860). Most biblical uses carry a stigma and refer to the Hebrews from the perspective of Egyptians, Philistines, or Jonah to the sailors (Even-Shoshan, 828). The exceptions are the legal contexts in question that seem to use the term with the connotation of disadvantaged kinspersons of Israel in a sense that is both social and ethnic (Exod 21:2; Deut 15:12; Jer 34:9, 14). For a different approach with similar outcomes, see Averbeck, "Exodus," 47.

TABLE L1: COLLATION OF DEBT AND SERVICE RELEASE STANDARDS OF TORAH

Debt Standards	Exodus 22:25–27 [24–26]	Leviticus 25:35–38	Deuteronomy 15:1–11; 23:19–20 [20–21]; 24:10–13
admonitions	—	• assist a needy fellow Israelite[a] as a residing foreigner (25:35)	• when seven years ends, cancel debts of a neighbor (15:1) • require payment of debt from foreigners (15:3) • be generous lending to neighbor or fellow Israelite[a] (15:8, 10) • charge interest to foreigners (23:20[21]) • remain outside when debtor brings pledge out of house (24:10, 11)
prohibitions	• charge no interest of God's people (22:25[24]) • do not take pledge from neighbor to create hardship (22:26[25])	• take no interest from fellow Israelite[a] (25:36, 37), and do not sell food at profit (25:37)	• do not press claims against neighbor or fellow Israelite[a] (15:2) • do not be hard-hearted or tight-fisted toward neighbor or fellow Israelite[a] in hardship (15:7) • do not charge interest to fellow Israelite[a] (23:19[20]) • do not take pledge to create hardship (24:6, 12)
motives	• God will hear if oppressed debtor cries out (22:27 [26])	• fear your God so fellow Israelite[a] may live with you (25:36) • I am God who brought you out of Egypt to give you Canaan (25:38)	• for Yahweh's canceling is proclaimed (15:1) • Yahweh shall bless (15:6; 23:20[21]) • oppressed may appeal to Yahweh against sinful oppressor (15:9) • giving debtor use of pledge to avoid hardship is righteous before Yahweh (24:13)

[a] Fellow Israelite lit. "brother" (אָח).

Release from Service Standards	Exodus 21:2–6, 7–11	Leviticus 25:39–46	Deuteronomy 15:12–18
admonitions	• Hebrew male goes free in seventh year (21:2) with the pre-existing family of the debt-slave (21:4) • unsatisfactory female debt-slave may be redeemed but not sold (21:8) • female debt-slave acquired for marriage must be granted rights of a daughter (21:9)	• treat a needy fellow Israelite[a] as a hired day-laborer (25:40) • release fellow Israelite and children at Jubilee (25:40, 41) • buy male and female slaves from surrounding nations, or residing sojourners; no release (25:44, 45, 46)	• send out male and female debt servants free in the seventh year (15:12) • generously provide for Hebrew debt servants when they are released (15:14)

Release from Service Standards	Exodus 21:2–6, 7–11	Leviticus 25:39–46	Deuteronomy 15:12–18
prohibitions	• do not set female debt-slave free (21:7) • do not reduce necessities, standard of living, or conjugal rights of female acquired through debt if another wife is taken (21:10) or she is released free (21:11)	• do not make fellow Israelite[a] serve as slave (25:39) • do not rule over any serving persons harshly (25:43, 46)	• do not send out Hebrew debt servants with empty hand (15:13)
motives	—	• God's slaves whom he brought out of Egypt may not be sold as slaves (25:42) • fear your God (25:43)	• auditors were slaves in Egypt when Yahweh redeemed (15:15) • Hebrew debt servants have greater value versus hired workers, and Yahweh will bless (15:18)

[a] Fellow Israelite lit. "brother" (אָח).

The details of Table L1 need to be summarized. First, with respect to debt protections, common denominators across Torah include:

- greater protection for fellow Israelites than others;
- welfare of the impoverished takes priority above profitability or security on loans;
- divine context for standards and adherence.

Differences between debt protections include:

- Leviticus affirms the ideal of early redemption by extended family;
- Deuteronomy accents charitable character of lender and makes explicit the safeguards against predatory loans.

Second, with respect to release from service standards, common denominators across Torah include:

- debt servitude for Hebrew males is not permanent;
- protection for debt servitude of females is explicit and pervasive;
- welfare of Hebrews in servitude is explicit.

Differences between release from service standards include:

- Exodus regulates protective measures for females associated with their reproductive capacities;
- Leviticus excludes debt slavery for Israelites who sell themselves into resident foreigner-like service;
- Deuteronomy further recasts Hebrew debt servitude in the shape of employment.

26:40–42*~Gen 17*+Exod 2:24*; 6:5 (B) (humble uncircumcised hearts) (* see Abrahamic covenant, collective confession, and seventy years networks). Twice Leviticus uses "foreskin" metaphorically: of fruit trees that need to be circumcised when Israel enters the land (Lev 19:23) and of the hearts of Israel in exile (26:41). The challenging imagery in the first use can be noted in passing. When Israel enters the land they must "regard as foreskin its foreskin, its fruit" (19:23 lit.).[31] This unusual imagery combines the personification of the land with circumcision as a sign of the covenant. The second use stands at the pivot point of the expected exile in the covenantal preview of Lev 26. Outside of Leviticus in Torah the key term "foreskin" only appears in Gen 17:14 and Exod 12:48 in contexts of physical circumcision and in Exod 6:12, 30 of Moses's speech impediment (see note on Ezek 3:5–6). The function of removing heart foreskin to activate the covenant in Lev 26:41 suggests an allusion to Gen 17.

The key term "remember," with Yahweh as subject remembering his people who call out to him, appears in Exod 2:24 and 6:5. Elsewhere the loaded term "remember" speaks of the activation of Yahweh to deliver Noah (Gen 8:1), not to destroy humans by flood (9:15, 16), and to open Rachel's womb (30:22). Moses uses this term when he calls upon Yahweh not to destroy his rebellious people but to remember his covenant with the Hebrew ancestors (Exod 32:13). The use of remember in Lev 26:42 seems to allude to the related contexts of Exod 2:24 and 6:5 that likewise refer to remembering the covenant with the Hebrew ancestors when the people are in trouble.[32]

The dramatic interpretive advancement comes when self-humbling gets identified as the trigger to activate Yahweh to remember the ancestral covenant (emphases mark verbal parallels).

> Whether born in your household or bought with your money, they must be circumcised. My covenant in your flesh is to be an everlasting covenant. Any **uncircumcised** male, who has not been circumcised in the flesh, will be cut off from his people; he has broken my covenant. (Gen 17:13–14)

---

31. Note that the literal sense of "regard as foreskin its foreskin, its fruit (וַעֲרַלְתֶּם עָרְלָתוֹ אֶת־פִּרְיוֹ)" (Lev 19:23 lit.) is set aside in modern committee translations—"When you enter the land and plant any kind of fruit tree, *regard its fruit as forbidden*" (19:23a NIV, emphasis marks phrase in question; cf. NRSV, JPSB, etc.).

32. Stackert suggests Lev 26:45 alludes to Exod 2:24; 6:5 in the sense of the precedent for the ancestral promise activating redemption from Egypt ("Distinguishing," 379).

> God heard their groaning and he *remembered* his *covenant with Abraham, with Isaac* and with *Jacob*. (Exod 2:24)

> Moreover, I have heard the groaning of the Israelites, whom the Egyptians are enslaving, and I have *remembered my covenant*. (6:5)

> But if they will confess their sins and the sins of their ancestors—their unfaithfulness and their hostility toward me, which made me hostile toward them so that I sent them into the land of their enemies—then when their **uncircumcised** hearts are humbled and they pay for their sin, I will *remember* my covenant with *Jacob* and *my covenant with Isaac and my covenant with Abraham*, and I will remember the land. (Lev 26:40–42)

The significance of the passive or reflexive verb stem of *humble* (Nif) should probably be understood reflexively as "humble itself" since it corresponds to a reflexive stem verb "they will confess" (Hith) in Lev 26:40.[33] The context promotes collective transgenerational responsibility (26:39). Many prayers in exile follow the shape of Lev 26:40–41 (e.g., Neh 1:5–10; Dan 9:4–19).

FILTERS

Leviticus presents numerous broadly related instructions from elsewhere in Torah. Many of these have non-exegetical similarities even while maintaining the priestly and holiness styles.[34] The following filters include representative examples for the sake of illustration. The lists are not comprehensive or complete.

Non-Exegetical Broad Allusions and Shared Themes

Narratives: The story of anointing Aaron and the establishment of the priesthood in **Lev 8** has a synoptic relationship with the instructions in Exod 29 (see synoptic chart in Exodus Filters). The genetically related chapters include extensive verbal parallels. Across much of the chapter the instructional verbs and shape in Exod 29 get revoiced as third-person narration. Leviticus 8 repeats "as Yahweh commanded Moses" and the like many times (Lev 8:4, 9, 13, 17, 21, 29, 34; cf. vv. 5, 31).[35] Note an example of the instruction and

33. See Schnittjer, "Bad Ending," 47–48.

34. For a list of short phrases with similarities and potential parallels between Leviticus and other Scriptures laid out side by side in Hebrew see Bolle, *Leviticus*, 2:1–114 (appendix) [Hebrew]. For a list of holiness stock expressions of Lev 17–26, see Driver, *Introduction*, 49–50; Milgrom, *Leviticus 17–22*, 1325–26; cf. 1327–28.

35. The phrase "as Yahweh has commanded" (כַּאֲשֶׁר צִוָּה יהוה) that appears seven times in Lev 8 also appears seven times each in the account of making the priestly garments in Exod 39 and assembling the tabernacle in Exod 40 (see Milgrom, "Consecration," 273). Thus, Exod 39, 40, and Lev 8 place a strong emphasis on narrative enactment or actualization of the instructions to emphasize the fulfillment of the instructions for the priests and tabernacle.

its counterpart narrative (italics signify verbal parallels with syntax changes; and broken underlining signifies overt marking of relationship):

> After you *take the breast of the ram* for Aaron's *ordination, wave it before Yahweh as a wave offering, and it will be* your *share.* (Exod 29:26)

> Moses also *took the breast of the ordination ram, and waved it before Yahweh as a wave offering, which was* his *share,* as Yahweh commanded Moses. (Lev 8:29†)

In Lev 10:1–2 fire from Yahweh's presence strikes down Nadab and Abihu. The citation formula in **Lev 10:3** may set up a loose paraphrase of part of Exod 29:43–44 (not used in the synoptic parallel of Lev 8). If so, the sense of "make holy by my glory" speaks to the burden of holiness that the priests had been chosen to bear.

Legal instructions: Within the instruction for ceremonial impurity that accompanies childbirth, male circumcision is noted. Outside of the command to Abraham it is the only legal context on physical circumcision in Torah (**Lev 12:3**; Gen 17; cf. Gen 34:13–29; Exod 4:24–26; 12:44, 48).

The prohibition against consuming blood broadly parallels part of the mandate to Noah (**Lev 17:10–14**; Gen 9:4).

In some cases Leviticus affirms the capital punishment set out by the covenant collection for crimes such as bestiality (**Lev 18:23; 20:15–16**; cf. Exod 22:19[18]). In other cases Leviticus affirms a commandment and adds the punishment, like capital offense for adultery (**Lev 18:20; 20:10**; Exod 20:14) and capital punishment for cursing parents (**Lev 20:9**; Exod 21:17; cf. v. 15).

The verbal parallels between Gen 15:16; Exod 23:27, 28 and **Lev 18:24–25** consist of only two common terms, "iniquity" and "drive out"—one in each—but they share similar themes. Yahweh told Abraham that his descendants would not return to inhabit the land until the iniquities of the Amorites reached their full measure. He told Moses and the people his terror and his hornet would drive out the nations of Canaan. Leviticus 18:24–25 personifies the land and speaks of its ritual impurity and the iniquity that causes it to vomit out its inhabitants whose actions parallel those of "the nations that I am going to drive out" (Lev 18:24).

Leviticus reaffirms commands: to honor parents (**Lev 19:3a**; Exod 20:12; cf. Lev 19:32), honor the Sabbath (**Lev 19:3b, 30; 23:3; 26:2**; Exod 20:8–11; 23:12; 31:12–18), prohibition against false worship (**Lev 19:4; 26:1**; Exod 20:2–6; 20:23; 22:20[19]; 23:24–25; 34:17), do not steal or lie (**Lev 19:11**; Exod 20:15–16), perverting justice (**Lev 19:15**; Exod 23:1–13, 6–8), prohibition against spiritists (**Lev 19:31**; Exod 22:17).

The holiness calendar in **Lev 23** spells out the schedule according to the concerns of individual laity and farmers rather than worship personnel, for the celebration of Unleavened Bread and Passover (Lev 23:4–8; cf. Exod 12:10–20; 13:3–13; 23:15;

34:18–20), Firstfruits (Lev 23:9–14; cf. Exod 34:26), Festival of Weeks (Pentecost) (Lev 23:15–21; cf. Exod 23:16; 34:22), Day of Atonement (Lev 23:26–32; cf. 16:1–34), and Festival of Tabernacles (ingathering) (Lev 23:33–43; cf. Exod 23:16; 34:22).

Leviticus 23:42 refers to Israel living in tabernacles when God brought them out of Egypt; a regulation not referred to in these terms elsewhere in Scripture (cf. note on Neh 8:15–17).

The command to provide oil for perpetual lights before Yahweh is repeated from Exodus (**Lev 24:1–3**//Exod 27:20–21). The regulations for the weekly bread of the presence alludes to the instructions in Exodus (**Lev 24:5–9**; cf. Exod 25:30; 40:23). The phrase "everlasting covenant" (עוֹלָם בְּרִית) in **Lev 24:8** seems to explain that the bread of the presence is put before Yahweh "continually" (תָּמִיד) in Exod 25:30 by its replacement every Sabbath (Lev 24:8).

The narrative of the blasphemer includes two pairs of framing elements/*inclusios* in a legal chiastic insert, with the outer bracket reaffirming the death penalty for murder (**Lev 24:17, 21b**; cf. Exod 21:12) and the inner bracket reaffirming restitution for killing someone's domestic animal (**Lev 24:18, 21a**; cf. Exod 22:1, 4[21:37; 22:3]). See note on Lev 24:10–23.

Leviticus 25:1–7 extensively expands upon the law of the fallow year once every seven years (cf. Exod 23:10–11). The major adjustment relates to the ongoing personification of the land in Leviticus—the fallow year provides Sabbath rest for the land (Lev 25:4).

Leviticus's Non-exegetical Use of Leviticus

Substantial parts of the detailed sacrificial instructions get repeated. The repetitions represent literary connections within the same book rather than exegetical interventions. Examples of verbal repetition include details of the burnt offering (Lev 1:3, 5, 7–9// 1:10–13), grain offering (2:2–3//6:15–16), well-being offering (3:1–5//3:6–11//3:12–16), purification offering (4:22–26//4:27–31//4:32–35), and priestly instructions for vows and freewill offerings (7:16–18//22:29–30; cf. similarities with well-being offering, 19:5–8).[36]

Other verbal repetitions of instructions include prohibitions against handling and eating animal carcasses (11:24–25//11:27b–28//11:39–40), skin conditions (13:3–6// 13:20–23//13:25–28), and the call to be holy (11:44//19:2//20:7–8).[37]

36. For color-coded side-by-side layout of these, see Bendavid, *Parallels*, 182–84 [Hebrew].
37. See ibid., 185–86.

Chapter 4

NUMBERS

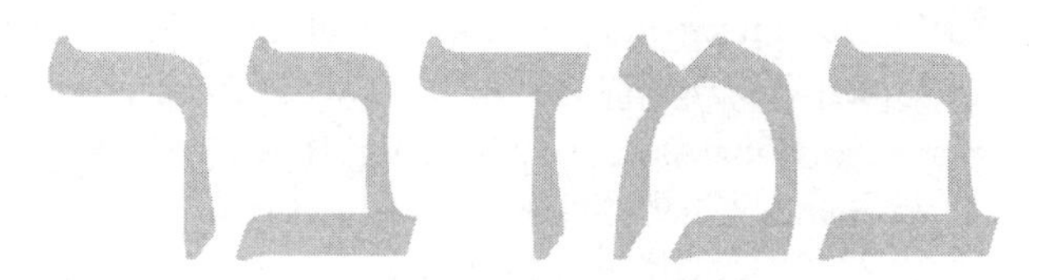

SYMBOLS[1]

// verbal parallels (A level)
/~/ synoptic parallel (A level)
~ B, probable interpretive allusion; C, possible; D, probably not
+ interpretive blend
>/< more or less similar (see Filters)
* part of interpretive network (see Networks)

USE OF TORAH IN NUMBERS[2]

3:11–13//8:16–18//Exod 13:2, 12 (substitution for firstborn of Israel)

5:1–4~Lev 11–15 (B)+Num 2:1–34; 3:21–39 (C) (relocating ritually impure persons outside the encampment)

9:1–14~Exod 12:18; Lev 23:5+Num 5:2+Exod 12:8, 10, 46, 48–49 (B) (alternate time for Passover)

10–12~Exod 15–18 (C) (wilderness temptations all over again)

13:33~Gen 6:4 (C) (Nephilim)

14:12–19*~Exod 32:10–13* (B)+34:6–7* (A) (intercession at Kadesh) (* see Abrahamic covenant and attribute formula networks)

15:18–21~Exod 23:19; 34:22; Lev 23:10–11 (B) (first of processed goods)

15:32–36*~Exod 35:2–3* (B) (the Sabbath breaker) (* see Sabbath network)

16:3~Exod 19:6 (C) (the entire congregation is holy)

16:13~Exod 3:8, 17 (C) (Egypt is the land of milk and honey)

18:15–18~Exod 13:12–13 (B) (firstborn male of all ritually impure animals)

18:21–24~Lev 27:30–33 (B) (tithes to Levites)

24:9*//Gen 12:3*; 27:29*+49:9* (A) (expected king) (* see Abrahamic covenant and Judah-king networks)

30:1–16[2–17]~Lev 27:1–25 (C) (vows by females)

35:9–34~Exod 21:13 (B) (cities of asylum)

36:1–12~26:55 (B)+27:1–11 (A)+Lev 25:8–24 (B) (amendment to law of female inheritance)

OLD TESTAMENT USE OF NUMBERS (SEE RESPECTIVE NOTES)

3:17–20~1 Chr 6:16–19[1–4] (C) (lines of Gershon, Kohath, and Merari of Levi)

4:4–15; 7:9~1 Chr 15:13–15 (B) (Levites carry the ark on their shoulders)

6:2~Amos 2:12 (C) (frustrating Nazirites)

6:23–27~Mal 1:6–2:9 (B) (reversal of priestly blessing)

9:9–11~2 Chr 30:2–3 (B) (shifting Passover observance to second month)

9:10~2 Chr 30:18–20 (C) (unlawful Passover participants forgiven)

10:35–36~Ps 132:8* (B) (ark to the resting place) (* see place network)

11:10–30~Deut 1:9–18 (C) (appointing judges)

11:17, 25~Isa 63:11 (B) (spirit of God upon leaders)

12:10–15~Deut 24:8–9 (B) (skin conditions)

13–14/~/Deut 1:19–45 (rebellion at Kadesh)

13:32~Ezek 36:12–19 (B) (defiled land)

1. For explanation of symbols, see Symbols and Abbreviations and Introduction. For other help, see Glossary.
2. See Bibliographic Note on Lists of Potential Parallels.

14:4~Neh 9:17 (B) (return to slavery in panoramic retrospective)
14:29, 30a, 31b, 32~Ps 106:24–26 (B) (death in wilderness in poetic retrospective)
15:39~Eccl 11:9 (C) (following the ways of heart and eyes)
17:5, 8[20, 23]~Ezek 7:10 (B) (budding staff)
18:1–7~Ezek 44:9–16 (B) (sanctity of the temple)
18:1–7~2 Chr 29:11 (C) (divine election of priests and Levites)
18:1–7~2 Chr 30:16 (C) (Levites bring blood from slaughter and priests transport blood to inner sanctuary for worship)
18:3–4, 6~2 Chr 35:5–6, 11 (C) (Levites perform sacrifices with laity in outer court)
18:19~2 Chr 13:5 (B) (Abijah affirms permanent Davidic rule over Israel)
18:20~Lam 3:22–23 (C) (new every morning)
18:21–24~Deut 14:22–29 (C) (tithes)
20:12~Ps 106:32–33 (C) (sin of Moses)
20:15–16~Deut 26:5–10 (B) (firstfruits liturgy)
21:10–26/~/Judg 11:15–27 (Jephthah's letter)
21:21–35/~/Deut 2:24–3:20 (conquest of Transjordan)
21:28–29~Jer 48:45–46 (A) (oracles against Moab)
22–24/~/Deut 23:4–5*[5–6] (Balaam's curse) (* see assembly network)
22:31~1 Chr 21:16 (C) (inciting David)
24:17*~Isa 25:10b–12 (C) (trampling Moab to the dust) (* see Davidic covenant and Judah-king networks)
24:17*~Jer 48:5, 28–47 (A) (oracles against Moab) (* see Davidic covenant and Judah-king networks)
24:17–19*~Ps 2:8–9* (C) (the scepter against the nations) (* see Davidic covenant and Judah-king networks)
25:11, 13~Ps 106:29–31 (B) (Phinehas blessed in poetic retrospective)
25:12–13~Mal 2:4–5, 8 (C) (covenant with Levi)
27:4, 7~Ruth 4:5–6 (B) (legal blend of laws of inheritance, etc.)
27:14a~Ps 106:32–33 (C) (sin of Moses)
28:16–25~2 Chr 35:16 (C) (Josiah prescribed Passover sacrifices)
32:8, 14~Neh 13:15, 17–18* (B) (Sabbath breaking by merchandizing) (* see Sabbath network)
35:9–34~Deut 19:1–13 (B) (motivation for law of asylum)
35:12~Josh 20:4–6 (B) (explain accidental death to elders for asylum)
35:30~Deut 19:15 (B) (two or three witnesses)
36:4~Ruth 4:5–6 (B) (legal blend of laws of inheritance, etc.)

NEW TESTAMENT USE OF NUMBERS

9:12//John 19:36 (no bones broken)
12:7//Heb 3:5 (Moses was faithful)
16:5~2 Tim 2:19 (the Lord knows who are his)
30:2[3]~Matt 5:33 (perform vows)

HERMENEUTICAL PROFILE OF THE USE OF TORAH IN NUMBERS

Numbers provides many examples of what may be called situational exegesis. The circumstances in the narrative give rise to the occasion for and often the rationale for interpretive allusions to scriptural traditions. The majority of interpretive interventions in Numbers can be described as legal exegesis, but on several different bases. Narrative, expectational, and intercessory exegesis in Numbers are mostly one-offs. These can be introduced first.

Several interpretive allusions enhance tendencies of their donor contexts. The sections of narrative proper in Numbers that move the Torah story forward mostly relate to travel and camp. Many episodes seem to be modeled on the grumbling stories in Exodus. The extensive Exodus-shaped episodes do more than provide continuity. The shared patterns demonstrate the hardened rebellion of Israel as well as the extent of divine patience and mercy.

Yahweh threatens to exterminate Israel and start over with Moses at Kadesh as he had with the golden calf. Moses responds with intercessory prayer closely following his earlier successful prayer on the mountain (Num 14:13–19). This time Moses's prayer does not work.

The wretched prophet Balaam gets forced to speak divine blessing upon Israel time and again. The oracles include far-reaching expectations based on promises in Genesis associated with the Hebrew ancestors.

A few interpretations go against the grain of the scriptural donor traditions to which they allude. The ten scouts seem to use the obscure Nephilim as part of their intentional distortion of the land of promise (13:33). Later the leaders of the revolt against the priesthood misconstrue Yahweh's teachings and promises as part of their sarcastic defiance (16:3, 13).

Many cases of legal exegesis in Numbers get triggered in response to situations that arise along the way. The tabernacle moving into the encampment prompts temporary evacuation of ritually impure persons to avoid ritual pollution of the tented shrine (5:1–4).

Four cases in Numbers make up a set along with the case of the blasphemer in Lev 24. Yahweh directly intervenes and provides new revelation, setting precedents and/or amending legal standards in a series of associated narratives. All told, Yahweh himself makes alternate provisions for those unable to participate in Passover by reason of ritual impurity or travel, sets the precedent to execute the Sabbath breaker, makes a ruling on female inheritance, and later amends the ruling on female inheritance (9:1–14; 15:32–36; 27:1–11; 36:1–12). These precedent-setting and legal-amendment stories provide especially important insight into progressive revelation.

Yahweh's decision to take the tribe of Levi in place of the firstborn of Israel sets up a chain reaction of derivative legal adjustments. The related legal adjustments especially concern providing for the Levites through tithes and offerings over and against provisions for the priests. Many of the adjustments of how the offerings provide for priests and Levites have been collected together in Num 18 immediately following the disastrous revolt against the priesthood in Num 16–17.

Other legal changes amount to interpretive revisions by supplement. These extensions of previous laws include case laws related to female vows and cities of asylum for accidental killing (30; 35).

The many different sorts of interpretation of scriptural traditions in Numbers appear throughout the extended wilderness travels. The sense of situational scriptural interpretation in the shape of the narrative reinforces the provisional effects of many cases. The life of Israel finds its way according to divine revelation. Numbers illustrates repeatedly that sometimes new circumstances lead to exegetical and/or revelatory exegetical outcomes. In Numbers revelation and revelatory exegesis serve the needs of Yahweh's covenantal relationship with his people.

Exegesis increasingly becomes a way for Yahweh to advance revelation. Yahweh continues to provide new revelation for his people. But his enduring will embodied in previous revelation sometimes needs supplement, expansion, adjustment, or other interpretive enhancements. Numbers sets a standard for regarding authorized exegesis of scriptural traditions as advancement of revelation. Yahweh initiates advancement of revelation by means of exegesis of scriptural traditions by his personal interpretive interventions. This establishes the precedent for advancement of revelation by exegesis to be taken up by authorized delegates.

The exegetical advancements in Numbers represent a transition from advancements by new revelation toward advancements by interpretation of scriptural traditions. In many ways Deuteronomy carries this tendency forward and will epitomize a major stream of progressive revelation by authorized exegesis.

USE OF TORAH IN NUMBERS

3:11–13//8:16–18//Exod 13:2, 12 (substitution for firstborn of Israel). Numbers 3:11–13// 8:16–18 interpretively re-present Exod 13:2, 12, switching out the firstborn of every family for the Levites. Elsewhere, Yahweh in turn gives the Levities to the priests to serve in the tabernacle (Num 18:2–5; cf. 3:6–9; 8:19). When Yahweh killed every firstborn of Egypt, he rightfully took possession of every firstborn of Israel. The extensive verbal parallels represent an interpretive quotation (emphases signify verbal parallels):

> **Consecrate to me every firstborn male.** *The first offspring of every womb among the Israelites* belongs to me, whether human or animal. (Exod 13:2; cf. v. 12)

> I have taken the Levites from among the Israelites in place of *the first offspring of every womb among the Israelites.* The Levites are mine, for all the firstborn are mine. When I struck down all the firstborn in Egypt, **I consecrated for myself every firstborn male** in Israel, whether human or animal. They are to be mine. I am Yahweh. (Num 3:12–13†; cf. 8:16–18)

Yahweh took the Levites as a one-time exchange for the firstborn of Israel, humans and animals (3:44–51; Deut 18:5).

Even with the tribe of Levi taken by Yahweh, the firstborn humans and animals of Israel continue to belong to Yahweh (Exod 34:19). Israelites redeem the firstborn males and ritually impure animals according to the set value of five shekels (Num 3:40–41; 18:15–16; Exod 34:20; Lev 27:6). Firstborn ritually pure animals could not be redeemed; they are Yahweh's for the priests—just like devoted things (Lev 27:26; 28–29; Num 18:14, 17–19).

5:1–4~Lev 11–15 (B)+Num 2:1–34; 3:21–39 (C) (relocating ritually impure persons outside the encampment). Numbers 5:1–2 enumerates many of the situations which cause ritual impairment from Lev 11–15: skin conditions, those with discharges, and contact with corpses. The reason for temporarily expelling them from the camp relates directly to the new arrangement of the tribes around the tabernacle (Num 2:1–34; 3:21–39). Now that the tabernacle has been moved into the encampment, its holiness became vulnerable to ritual pollution (5:3; 19:13; cf. 12:15). The list of ritual impairments may represent all ritual impurity or only severe ritual pollution which required more complicated steps toward purification. In this latter case, lesser pollutions like menstruation and childbirth could remain confined within the camp.[3]

9:1–14~Exod 12:18; Lev 23:5+Num 5:2+Exod 12:8, 10, 46, 48–49 (B) (alternate time for Passover). Numbers 9:1–14 features one of the five legal narratives that include an oracle from Yahweh to amend a law or set a precedent—precedent of punishing blasphemer (Lev 24:10–23), amending Passover (Num 9:1–14), precedent of punishing the Sabbath breaker (15:32–36), precedent of female inheritance (27:1–11), and amending female inheritance (36:1–12).[4] Among these five the alternate date for Passover and the inheritance of Zelophehad's daughters share very similar structures: approach (Num 9:6; 27:1–2); claim (9:7; 27:3–4); oracular inquiry (9:8–9; 27:5–6); divine case ruling (n/a; 27:7); statutory law (9:10–14; 27:8–11a); fulfillment (n/a; 27:11b).[5]

In Num 9:1–5 Yahweh reaffirms that the Passover celebration begins on the fourteenth day of the first month (Exod 12:18; Lev 23:5; cf. Exod 13:4; 23:15; 34:18). A contingent of persons approach Moses to inquire why they must be excluded from Passover because of ceremonial impurity from touching a corpse (Num 9:6–7). The problem of corpse defilement was applied to the congregation when the tabernacle moved inside the encampment (5:2; cf. 19:11–20). Elsewhere the prohibition against corpse defilement applies to the priests (Lev 21:1, 11). Moses brings the matter before Yahweh (Num 9:8). Yahweh does not respond directly to the case as he does with Zelophehad's daughters but gives a new alternative standard (9:9–14). The amendment to the date of Passover to the fourteenth day of the second month includes cases of ritual impairment and travel. The exception for travel does not appear in the present situation or any earlier regulations. The amendment draws together several elements of the standards for Passover observance (bold and italics signify verbal parallels, and broken underlining signifies amended standards):[6]

> That same night they are to eat the meat roasted over the fire, *together with bitter herbs, and bread made without yeast*. . . . **Do not** leave **any of it till morning**; if some is left till morning, you must burn it. . . . In the first month you are to eat bread made without yeast, from **twilight** of **the fourteenth day** until the evening of the twenty-first day. . . . It must be eaten inside the house; take none of the meat outside the house. *Do not break any of the bones*. (Exod 12:8†, 10, 18†, 46)

3. So Milgrom, *Numbers*, 33.
4. See Philo, *Moses II*, 192–245.
5. Adapted from structural comparative chart in Chavel, *Oracular Law*, 7.
6. The parallel between Exod 12:8, 10, 46 and Num 9:11, 12 is observed by Chavel, ibid., 122.

> Tell the Israelites: "When any of you or your descendants are unclean because of a dead body or are away on a journey, they are still to celebrate Yahweh's Passover, but they are to do it on **the fourteenth day** of the second month at **twilight**. They are to eat the lamb, *together with unleavened bread and bitter herbs*. They **must not** leave **any of it till morning** or *break any of its bones*. When they celebrate the Passover, they must follow all the regulations." (Num 9:10–12)

Yahweh's Passover amendment goes on to reinforce the inclusive requirement for Israel and resident foreigners by alluding to Exod 12:48–49. This reinforcement of the older standards includes overt marking of legal allusion with "in accordance with its rules and regulations," which refers at least to circumcision (9:14). The citation inverts native-born and residing foreigner in line with Seidel's theory. Compare the inclusive standard in the Passover regulations and the amendment (bold and italics signify verbal parallels, and broken underlining signifies overt marking of allusion):[7]

> **A foreigner residing among you is also to celebrate Yahweh's Passover** must have all the males in his household circumcised; then he may take part like one born in the land. No uncircumcised male may eat it. *The same* torah applies *both to the native-born and to the foreigner* residing among you. (Exod 12:48–49†)

> **A foreigner residing among you is also to celebrate Yahweh's Passover** in accordance with its rules and regulations. You must have *the same* regulations for *both the foreigner and the native-born*. (Num 9:14)

Yahweh's amendment to the Passover celebration date includes several inferences relative to progressive revelation. The inception for this adjustment does not start with Yahweh but with his people. Yahweh advances revelation in response to a request. The basis of the new ruling then rests partially on interpretive reasoning. The adjustment also signifies that legal standards for worship serve the covenantal relationship not the reverse. Laws do not repel but invite interactive appeal to the deity. The advancement of revelation in this case extends opportunity for faithful devotion and worship.

10–12~Exod 15–18 (C) (wilderness temptations all over again). Numbers shapes the wilderness travels of the first and second generation after the wilderness travels from Egypt to the mountain in Exodus. The similarities in Num 10–12 may represent the most pronounced part of the shaping of the travels and encampments after previous kindred events in Torah. Table N1 presents the basic similarities between Exodus and Numbers.

7. The parallel between Exod 12:48–49 and Num 9:14 is observed by ibid., 111.

TABLE N1: RECURRING ELEMENTS IN THE WILDERNESS‡

Journeys	**Red Sea to Sinai**	**Sinai to Kadesh**	**Kadesh to Moab**
Led by cloud	Exod 13:21	Num 10:11	—
Victory over Egypt	14	—	Num 21:21–35
Victory song	15:1–18	10:35–36	21:14–15
Miriam	15:20–21	12	20:1
People complain	15:23–24	11:1	21:5
Moses's intercession	15:25	11:2	21:7
Well	15:27	—	21:16
Manna and quail	16	11:4–35	—
Water from rock	17:1–7	—	20:2–13
Victory over Amalek	17:8–16	—	21:1–3
Moses's father-in-law	18:1–2	10:29–32	—
Encampments	**Sinai**	**Kadesh**	**Moab**
Divine promises	Exod 19:5–6; 23:23–33	Num 13:2	Num 22–24
Forty days	24:18	13:25	—
Rebellion	32:1–8	14:1–10	25:1–3
Moses's intercession	32:11–13	14:13–19	—
Judgment	32:34	14:20–35	25:4
Plague	32:35	14:37	25:8–9
Laws of sacrifice	34:18–26; Lev 1–7	15:1–31	28–29
Trial	Lev 24:10–23	15:32–36	27:1–11
Judgment against priests or Levites	10:1–3	16:1–35	—
Atonement through priests or Levites	Exod 32:26–29	16:36–50	25:7–13
Priestly prerogatives	Lev 6–7; 22	17–18	31:28–30; 35:1–8
Impurity rules	11–16	19	31; 35:9–34
Census	Num 1–4	—	26

‡ This table is adapted from Wenham, *Numbers*, 16–17.

The narrative of Numbers presents the wilderness travels and encampments in many ways that echo Exodus. Many of the elements and often the sequence include similarities. The point of shaping the wilderness struggles according to the earlier narratives seems to have less to do with comparing particular elements and more to do with the overall desired inferences. The first generation in Numbers does not do as well as they had in Exodus. The death of Aaron in the fortieth year in Num 20 helps date the third travel and camp narratives to the second generation (Num 20:24–29; 33:38–39). The similarities between the third travel and encampment narratives indicate the next generation looks exactly like their parents, except maybe a little worse. Moses makes the negative comparison between the two generations explicit in the case of the Transjordanian tribes (32:8, 14).[8] Figure N2 notes the overall recurring pattern in relation to the older and younger generations.

FIGURE N2: SHAPING NUMBERS AFTER EXODUS‡

Sea to Mountain	**Mountain**	**Mountain to Kadesh**	**Kadesh**	**Kadesh to Moab**	**Plains of Moab**
Exod 13–19	Exod 19–Num 10	Num 10–12	Num 13–19	Num 20–21	Num 22–Deut 34

First generation	First generation	Second generation
First travel and camp narrative	**Second travel and camp narrative** sounds like first set of narratives	**Third travel and camp narrative** sounds like first and second sets of narratives

‡ Figure adapted from Schnittjer, *Torah Story Videos*, 20.3.

In sum, the large-scale repetitions in the major travel and encampment narrative cycles in Numbers connote the tendencies of the two generations toward rebellion in the face of God's ongoing mercies.

13:33~Gen 6:4 (C) (Nephilim). The reference to *Nephilim* in Gen 6:4 does not say anything about their size but describes them as "mighty persons of old, persons of name" (lit.). The bad report of the scouts claims the large-size Anakites had descended from the *Nephilim* (Num 13:33). Perhaps on this basis the Septuagintal translators glossed *Nephilim* as "giants" (*gigantes* γίγαντες) in both Gen 6:4 and Num 13:33.[9]

The narrator says the ten scouts spread a "bad report"—a term that could mean a report about bad things or a distorted report (Num 13:32).[10] The only other uses of the term in Torah appear in the present context (14:36, 37) and when Joseph gave a "bad report" to his father about some of his step brothers (Gen 37:2). Whether Joseph distorted

8. See Schnittjer, "Kadesh Infidelity," 108.

9. Aquila renders *Nephilim* as "fallen ones" in Gen 6:4 (Wevers, *Notes on Genesis*, 77, n. 7; Gen 6:4 LXX Cambridge lower apparatus).

10. See "דִּבָּה," *HALOT* 1:208; *DCHR* 2: 454–55.

the facts need not be decided here. The scouts, however, changed their report after Caleb's advice to move forward with the invasion (Num 13:30). The circumstances make it most natural to see "bad report" as referring to the scouts' intentional distortions to sway the people against Caleb's plan. In short, the identification of the *Nephilim* as large in size originates from a purposeful misrepresentation of the Anakites as *Nephilim*.

Whether the *Nephilim* of Gen 6:4 should be identified as large sized as a basis for the scouts' bad report requires more evidence.[11] In either case, the ancient prediluvian *Nephilim* do not have a genealogical relationship to the Anakites in Torah. They died in the flood.

14:12–19*~Exod 32:10–13* (B)+34:6–7* (A) (intercession at Kadesh) (* see Abrahamic covenant and attribute formula networks). When Yahweh threatens to destroy Israel and start over with Moses, he responds by pleading at the mountain and at Kadesh. The brief verbal parallels between Exod 32:10–12 and Num 14:12–14 get complemented by a very similar prayer structure. In both cases Moses warns Yahweh of the public relations disaster that would come from destroying his people.

The two prayers of intercession also differ. At the mountain, Moses rehearses the ancestral covenant (Exod 32:13). At Kadesh, Moses does not refer back to the ancestral covenant but refers to Yahweh's mighty acts in Egypt and the wilderness (Num 14:14). Moses goes on to cite the revelation on the mountain at some length, since Yahweh uttered it when he forgave Israel and renewed the covenant (14:18//Exod 34:6b–7). Overall, the shared intercessory structure differs from the earlier prayer by emphasizing forgiveness rather than covenant (bold and italics signify verbal parallels, broken underlining signifies explicit marking of citation, and underlining signifies omission):[12]

> [Yahweh] "Now leave me alone so that my anger may burn against them and that I may destroy them. Then *I will make you into a great nation*." But Moses sought the favor of Yahweh his God. "Yahweh," he said, "why should your anger burn against your people, whom you brought out of Egypt with great power and a mighty hand? Why should *the Egyptians say*, 'It was with evil intent that he brought them out, to kill them in the mountains and to wipe them off the face of the earth'? Turn from your fierce anger; relent and do not bring disaster on your people. <u>Remember your servants Abraham, Isaac and Israel, to whom you swore by your own self: 'I will make your descendants as numerous as the stars in the sky and I will give your descendants all this land I promised them, and it will be their inheritance forever.</u>'" (Exod 32:10–13)

> And he passed in front of Moses, proclaiming, "**Yahweh**, Yahweh, the compassionate and gracious God, **slow to anger, abounding in love** and faithfulness, [7] maintaining love to thousands, and **forgiving iniquity, rebellion** and sin. **Yet he does not leave the**

11. See discussion in Walton, "Genesis," 45–46.
12. Compare synoptic prayer at the mountain in Deut 9:26–29; cf. synoptic table ad loc.

> **guilty unpunished; he punishes the children** and their children **for the sin of the parents to the third and fourth generation.**" (34:6–7†)

> [Yahweh] "I will strike them down with a plague and destroy them, but *I will make you into a nation greater* and stronger than they." Moses said to Yahweh, "Then *the Egyptians* will hear about it! By your power you brought these people up from among them. And they *will tell* the inhabitants of this land about it. They have already heard that you, Yahweh, are with these people and that you, Yahweh, have been seen face to face, that your cloud stays over them, and that you go before them in a pillar of cloud by day and a pillar of fire by night. If you put all these people to death, leaving none alive, the nations who have heard this report about you will say, 'Yahweh was not able to bring these people into the land he promised them on oath, so he slaughtered them in the wilderness.' Now may the Lord's strength be displayed, just as you have declared: '**Yahweh** is **slow to anger, abounding in love** and **forgiving iniquity** and **rebellion. Yet he does not leave the guilty unpunished; he punishes the children for the sin of the parents to the third and fourth generation.**' In accordance with your great love, forgive the sin of these people, just as you have pardoned them from the time they left Egypt until now." (Num 14:12–19†)

The outcomes of the two prayers contrast sharply—forgiveness and renewal versus forgiveness and judgment (Exod 32:14; Num 14:20–23). The problem in Num 14:13–19 does not seem to be a deficiency in the prayer. Specifically, if Moses again had recalled the ancestral covenant, the outcome likely would remain the same. Little more can be deduced since determining the divine will requires revelation.

One of the important results in Num 14 relates to the limitations of the divine attribute formula in the face of persistent rebellion. Since the divine attribute formula continues to be cited regularly in the prophets and psalms, the narrative of the judgment at Kadesh establishes limits on the deferral of judgment based upon Yahweh as "slow to anger" and "abounding in love" (Exod 34:6; Num 14:18). As Yahweh says, he does forgive even when he brings judgment (Num 14:20).

15:18–21~Exod 23:19; 34:22; Lev 23:10–11 (B) (first of processed goods). The required firstfruits offerings could be interpreted as applying to farmers (Exod 23:19; 34:22; Lev 23:10–11). The term "first" establishes its relationship with the statute in Num 15:18–21. The legal standard in Num 15:18–21 expands this to include processed grain and refers to the first of the dough (cf. Ezek 44:30). This extends the required offering to all the people not just farmers. The requirement gets repeated in Num 18:12–13 and defined as "from the threshing floor," inferring it has been processed by separation from the chaff, not simply the first sheath (cf. 2 Kgs 4:42).[13]

13. See Milgrom, *Numbers*, 121, 428. Thank you to Barbara Arnold for pointing out 2 Kgs 4:42.

15:32–36*~Exod 35:2–3* (B) (the Sabbath breaker) (* see Sabbath network). The narrative of the Sabbath breaker stands as one of the five precedent-setting and amendment legal narratives with direct divine intervention in Torah (Lev 24:10–23; Num 9:1–14; 15:32–36; 27:1–11; 36:1–12).[14] The structure of Num 15:32–36 runs very close to the story of the blasphemer (for comparison see note on Lev 24:10–23, first paragraph).

The legal standard in Exod 35:2–3 offers the second of only two examples in Torah of what activities do not fit with rest—"Whoever does any work on it is to be put to death. *Do not light a fire in any of your dwellings* on the Sabbath day" (Exod 35:2b, 3, emphasis mine). The man did not get caught lighting a fire but "collecting wood" (Num 15:32). That the terms for "gather" (referring to manna) in Exod 16:26 and "gather" (referring to wood) in Num 15:32 differ does not seem to be the point.[15] The issue appears to be whether the example of not lighting fire on the Sabbath applies to all kindred domestic efforts or strictly to making fire. Yahweh's judgment to execute the Sabbath breaker signifies that any kindred domestic work violates the standard for Sabbath rest.[16]

16:3~Exod 19:6 (C) (the entire congregation is holy).

16:13~Exod 3:8, 17 (C) (Egypt is the land of milk and honey). The intentional sarcastic interpretive distortions by rebel leaders can be treated together. Korah, Dathan, Abiram, and On led a revolt against the priesthood. They claimed Aaron's family had no right to act as priests since Yahweh had declared all Israel holy (bold signifies parallel):

> [Yahweh] You will be for me a kingdom of priests and a **holy** nation. (Exod 19:6a)

> They [rebels] came as a group to oppose Moses and Aaron and said to them, "You have gone too far! The whole community is **holy**, every one of them, and Yahweh is with them. Why then do you set yourselves above Yahweh's assembly?" (Num 16:3)

They never mention the term "priest," though Israel as a "kingdom of priests" seems to echo in the background—a trace, perhaps (Exod 19:6). Moses suggests that their true motives include seizing the "priesthood" (Num 16:10). The basis of the rebels' claim gains ground in the light of the command to the laity to "be holy" (Lev 19:2). Once the tabernacle moves into the encampment, all Israel needs to follow holiness standards including some regulations that had previously been associated only with priests, such as avoiding contact with corpses (Num 5:1–4; cf. Lev 21:1–4, 11). The rebels leverage the requirement for holiness as an accusation against the role of Aaron's family. The actual source of bitterness for Korah and the Levitical rebels likely stems from Yahweh's directing the Levites to serve under the order of the priests as porters and in the tabernacle

---

14. The first four are treated as a set at least as early as Philo (*Moses II*, 192–245).

15. On "gather" (לקט) in Exod 16:26 versus "gather" (קשׁשׁ) in Num 15:32, see Chavel, *Oracular Law*, 174–78.

16. The legal exegesis in Num 15:32–36 roughly aligns with what is called type x in the discussion associated with Table EN2 in Hermeneutical Profile of the Use of Scripture in Ezra-Nehemiah.

(Num 3:6–9; 8:19; 16:9, reaffirmed in the aftermath of the rebellions in 18:6). The revolt has a larger following, including others from among the laity (16:1).

The stock phrase "land of milk and honey" eliminates identifying a specific donor context of the interpretive distortion of the rebels in Num 16:13–14. The phrase appears at least seven times referring to the land of promise prior to the rebellion.[17] For the present purposes Exod 3:17 can stand for the group since it offers the most obvious sense of what they seek to contradict (bold signifies verbal parallels):

> [Yahweh] And I have promised to bring you up out of your misery in Egypt into the land of the Canaanites, Hittites, Amorites, Perizzites, Hivites and Jebusites—**a land flowing with milk and honey.** (Exod 3:17)

> [rebels] Isn't it enough that you have brought us up out of **a land flowing with milk and honey** to kill us in the wilderness? And now you also want to lord it over us! Moreover, you haven't brought us into **a land flowing with milk and honey** or given us an inheritance of fields and vineyards. Do you want to treat these men like slaves? No, we will not come! (Num 16:13–14)

In sum, during the revolt Korah and company take revealed expressions and exegetically distort them to attack the priestly establishment. The half-truth argument of the holiness of the laity demonstrates the importance of contextual interpretation to prevent false theology.

18:15–18~Exod 13:12–13 (B) (firstborn male of all ritually impure animals). Because Yahweh redeemed Israel by killing the firstborn of Egypt, his people forever owe him their firstborn male humans and animals. While they give over to the tabernacle the firstborn ritually pure animals, they need to redeem their sons and their ritually impure animals (cf. Lev 27). The ruling in Exod 13:12–13 distinguishes between animals and donkeys, which are ritually impure. This could be narrowly interpreted that the firstborn males of other ritually impure animals do not need to be redeemed. The allusion in Num 18:15 augments a narrow interpretation, making explicit that all male firstborn ritually impure animals need to be redeemed (bold signifies verbal parallels, and broken underlining signifies interpretive advancement).

> You are to give over to Yahweh the first offspring of every womb. All the firstborn males of your livestock belong to Yahweh. Redeem with a lamb every firstborn donkey, but if you do not redeem it, break its neck. **Redeem every firstborn male human** among your sons. (Exod 13:12–13)

17. See Exod 3:8, 17; 13:5; 33:3; Lev 20:24; Num 13:27; 14:8.

The first offspring of every womb, both human and animal, that is offered to Yahweh is yours [family of Aaron]. But **you must redeem the firstborn male human** and every firstborn male of unclean animals. (Num 18:15)

Fishbane suggests that Num 18:15 uses "however" (NIV uses "but" here) to mark the exegetical clarification that includes all male firstborn ritually impure animals.[18]

18:21–24~Lev 27:30–33 (B) (tithes to Levites). Leviticus 27:30–33 affirms that all tithes are holy to Yahweh. In Num 18 after enumerating the other holy offerings, firstfruits, firstborn males, and/or redemptions that Yahweh gives to Aaron's family, he tells Aaron that the tithes go to the Levites. This modification seems to go with the gifting of the Levites to Aaron's family in perpetuity for tabernacle service (Num 3:6–9; 8:19; 16:9; 18:6). Numbers 18 reaffirms and strengthens the role of Aaron's family as priests who must bear the burden of holiness (18:1) and the role of the Levites (18:2–5) in response to the rebellion in Num 16–17. This reaffirmation triggers the need for Aaron's family to see that the Levites get the tithe (18:21–24), who in turn must give a tithe of the tithe to the priests (18:25–30).[19]

24:9*//Gen 12:3*; 27:29*+49:9* (A) (expected king) (* see Abrahamic covenant and Judah-king networks). The third oracle of Balaam includes citations of part of the blessing of Judah spliced together with the ancestral covenant given to Abraham by Yahweh and accidentally by Isaac to Jacob. While most of the language and syntax is nearly identical, the oracle of Balaam uses synonyms for "curse" and "lie down" in comparison with the counterparts in Genesis (emphases signify verbal parallels):

I *will bless those who bless you*, and whoever curses [קלל] you I *will curse* [ארר]; and all peoples on earth will be blessed through you. (Gen 12:3)

May those who curse [ארר] *you be cursed* [ארר] *and those who bless you be blessed.* (27:29b)

You are a lion's cub, Judah; you return from the prey, my son. **Like a lion he crouches** and lies down [רבץ], **like a lioness—who dares to rouse him**? (49:9)

Like a lion he crouches and lies down [שכב], **like a lioness—who dares to rouse him**? *May those who bless you be blessed* and *those who curse* [ארר] *you be cursed* [ארר]! (Num 24:9 lit.)

By blending the Abrahamic promise and the blessing of Judah, Balaam identifies the two together. The correspondence of the fulfillment of the Abrahamic covenant by the expected Davidic ruler finds its fullest expression in Ps 72 (see note on Ps 72:17).[20]

18. See Fishbane, *Biblical Interpretation*, 197. The term "however" or "but" often functions in the restrictive sense as in Num 18:15 ("אַךְ," no. 2 *HALOT* 1:45).

19. See Milgrom, *Numbers*, 155.

20. On other possible expectational elements in Balaam's oracles, see Schnittjer, "Blessing of Judah," 21–24. Also see Postell, "OT in the OT," 96.

30:1–16[2–17]~Lev 27:1–25 (C) (vows by females). Vows include conditional promises of offerings and/or gifts to Yahweh.[21] Meeting the conditions (e.g., safe journey, Gen 28:20–21; victory in battle, Judg 11:30–31; etc.) requires payment of the vow to the shrine. Leviticus 27:1–25 spells out the redemption values of humans, animals, houses, and lands.

Numbers 30 interpretively expands upon the standards for vows and explains the conditions for validating vows made by females. The vow of a daughter must be approved by her father and of a wife by her husband to be valid. If the father or husband does not speak up "on the day" he hears of it, he silently affirms it (Num 30:5[6]). If he says nothing and later nullifies it, he stands guilty (30:15[16]). When a widow or a divorced woman makes a vow, she is bound by it like any man (30:9[10]). The common denominator for confirming female vows amounts to head-of-household validation.

Hannah's vow (1 Sam 1:11) needed to be affirmed by Elkanah (1:21, 23). Vows became commonplace in the Second Temple period and led to four bases for annulment in proto-rabbinic traditions (m. Ned. 3:1; also see note on Eccl 5:4–6[3–5]). Paul and Sosthenes modified vows of temporary abstinence of conjugal relations as requiring consent from the wife for the husband and vice versa—conditionality for male and female vows in this case (1 Cor 7:5).

35:9–34~Exod 21:13 (B) (cities of asylum). The legal instructions concerning cities of asylum for accidental death are developed successively in several contexts and most fully in Num 35:9–34 (Exod 21:13; Deut 4:41–43; 19:1–13; Josh 20:1–9). This context features three significant exegetical expansions in comparison to Exod 21:13. First, the claimant who caused the accidental death shall be protected from the avenger until a trial before the congregation rather than civil or priestly judges (Num 35:12, 24). Second, the person who causes accidental death remains confined to the city of asylum until the death of the high priest (35:25, 28, 32). The remission of the accidental death by the death of the priest fits with the government organizations before and after Israel had a king. Greenberg suggests the death of the high priest symbolizes remission for accidental death since he bears on his person the iniquity of the people (Exod 28:38; cf. Num 18:1).[22] Third, the evidence required for capital punishment of a murderer must exceed the testimony of a single witness. For other developments see notes on Deut 19:13 and Josh 20:4.

36:1–12~26:55 (B)+27:1–11 (A)+Lev 25:8–24 (B) (amendment to law of female inheritance). Numbers 36 houses the last of five precedent-setting and/or amendment legal narratives with direct divine revelation.[23] The context explicitly refers to the ruling

---

21. On the differences between oaths (unconditional assertions or promises), vows (conditional promises), and dedications (unconditional and immediate, like "devoting"/*herem*), see Milgrom, *Numbers*, 488–90.

22. See Greenberg, "Asylum," 130.

23. Compare the precedent of punishing a blasphemer (Lev 24:10–23), amending the date of the Passover (Num 9:1–14), the precedent of punishing a Sabbath breaker (15:32–36), the precedent of female inheritance (27:1–11), and amending female inheritance law (36:1–12).

associated with Zelophehad's daughters and the law of Jubilee, making blended allusion almost certain (Num 36:2, 4; cf. 27:1–11; Lev 25:8–24).

The heads of the ancestral families of the Transjordanian division of Manasseh approach Moses to complain of the problem with granting land inheritance to females. If Zelophehad's daughters marry into another tribe, then at Jubilee the land will be taken from Manasseh and added to the husbands' tribal lands (Num 36:2–4). Moses transmits a divine amendment to the ruling of female inheritance, requiring marriage within the father's tribe to eliminate transfer of land to other tribes (36:5–9). Notice the blended allusions in the complaint (emphases signify verbal parallels):

> In this Year of Jubilee everyone is to return to their own property. (Lev 25:13)

> Be sure that *the land is distributed by lot*. What each group *inherits* will be according to the names for its ancestral tribe. (Num 26:55)

> What **Zelophehad's daughters** are saying is right. You must certainly **give** them property as an **inheritance** among their father's relatives and give their father's inheritance to them. (27:7)

> The family heads of the clan of Gilead son of Makir, the son of Manasseh, who were from the clans of the descendants of Joseph, came and spoke before Moses and the leaders, the heads of the Israelite families. [2] They said, "When Yahweh commanded my lord to give *the land as an inheritance* to the Israelites *by lot*, he ordered you to **give the inheritance** of our brother **Zelophehad** to his **daughters.** [3] Now suppose they marry men from other Israelite tribes; then their inheritance will be taken from our ancestral inheritance and added to that of the tribe they marry into. And so part of the inheritance allotted to us will be taken away. [4] When the Year of Jubilee for the Israelites comes, their inheritance will be added to that of the tribe into which they marry, and their property will be taken from the tribal inheritance of our ancestors." (36:1–4)[24]

Both legal adjustments by divine authority begin with human petitions. Yahweh affirms the complaint of Zelophehad's daughters and then provides a new ruling (27:7). Later he affirms the complaint of the Transjordanian heads of families of Manasseh and amends the new ruling (36:5). Yahweh's affirmation uses the particle "thus" which functions something like "rightly" they have spoken.[25] Notice the similar bases for new rulings (italics signify verbal parallels):

---

24. Numbers 36:1 of 4QNum^{b} (4Q27) and LXX includes "and before Eleazar the priest" (*BQS* 1:170–71; Num 36:1 *BHS* n. c). Since MT and SP lack the phrase, it seems to be a gloss based on the use of the phrase in Num 27:2. MT preferred. See additional considerations in Chavel, *Oracular Law*, 245, n. 137.

25. The sense of the particle (כֵּן) is "the foregoing being the case, therefore" (*IBHS* §39.3.4e).

> And Yahweh said to him, "*What* Zelophehad's daughters *are saying is right*. You must certainly give them property as an inheritance among their father's relatives and give their father's inheritance to them." (27:6–7)

> Then at Yahweh's command Moses gave this order to the Israelites: "*What* the tribe of the descendants of Joseph *is saying is right*." (36:5)

The amendment to the ruling on female inheritance provides important insight into progressive revelation. The amendment in Num 36:5–9 amounts to a divine legal adjustment of an earlier divine legal adjustment—both initiated by human complainants. Views of scriptural legal instruction that do not allow for the dynamics of revelatory advancement misconstrue the nature and function of biblical law. Divinely revealed law should not be treated as inert fossilized data.

Divine law makes demands upon Israel. The divinely authorized advancements of revealed legal instructions demonstrate that law serves covenantal relationship, not the other way around. In essence, Yahweh himself sets the standard, namely, in certain cases, divine legal instruction morphs according to the divine will as need arises. While Yahweh alone can advance revealed legal instruction, he shows his willingness to do so repeatedly, even with respect to previously adjusted standards. Elsewhere in Scripture, Yahweh advances revelation, including legal standards, within many genres—prophetic, lyrical, wisdom—through authorized delegates. The five narratives of legal precedent and amendment by divine intervention in Torah establish exegetical advancement as one norm of progressive revelation.

FILTERS

Numbers often continues or fleshes out elements mentioned earlier. Many of these references make broad and/or non-exegetical allusions. The cross-referencing style of Torah becomes heightened in Numbers. Numbers maintains an especially close relationship with Exodus and Leviticus in terms of style. The purpose of the filters here amounts to identifying non-exegetical similarities to avoid false positives. The following illustrative lists are not comprehensive or complete.

Non-Exegetical Broad Allusions and Shared Themes

The notation on Aaron's family in the censuses of the first and second generations includes an explanation of the death of Nadab and Abihu for offering "strange fire" (אֵשׁ זָרָה) (Num 3:4; 26:61//Lev 10:1; cf. 16:1).[26]

26. The LXX of Lev 16:1 says "when they brought near strange fire" (ἐν τῷ προσάγειν αὐτοὺς πῦρ ἀλλότριον) for which the *BHK* suggests a parent text with a modified verb plus the object "when they brought near strange fire" (בְּהַקְרִיבָם אֵשׁ זָרָה) versus the MT "when they drew near" (בְּקָרְבָתָם) (upper apparatus). By contrast Wevers suggests the LXX translator clarified the statement by giving a fuller explanation (*Notes Leviticus*, 240). Wevers suggestion seems correct since this phrase in 16:1 LXX does not match verbatim Num 3:4 or 26:61 LXX (different verb forms). Wevers

The temporary Nazirite vow required persons to follow some of the high priestly regulations for avoiding ritual impairment from corpses even when close family members die (**Num 6:6–7**; Lev 21:11; for ordinary priests cf. vv. 1–4).

Numbers 7 narrates the public twelve-day dedication of the tabernacle. The heading connects with Exod 40 by mentioning when Moses had finished setting up the tabernacle, namely, on the first day of the first month of the second year (**Num 7:1**; Exod 40:17).

Yahweh reveals his will to Moses in a very direct way in the tent of meeting, echoing similar sentiments elsewhere (**Num 7:89**; Exod 33:11; cf. 25:22; Num 12:8; Deut 34:10).

The cloud leads Israel in the wilderness (**Num 9:15–23**; cf. Exod 13:21–22; 40:36–38).

The divine fire comes out from Yahweh's presence and consumes the sons of Aaron and the rebels (**Num 16:35**; cf. 3:4; 26:61; Lev 10:2; 16:1).

Many elements of **Num 18** review previous contexts regarding the priestly privileges and responsibilities: sacred portions eaten in the sacred area by priests only (Num 18:8–10>/<Lev 2:3; 6:16, 26; 7:6; 10:13, 17; 24:9); consecration of priestly portions by ritual elevation (Num 18:11>/<Exod 29:27–28; Lev 7:30; 10:14–15; 23:20; Num 6:20; 8:13); priestly families may eat holy offerings except the most holy offerings by priests only (Num 18:11–20>/<Lev 10:14–15; 22:10–14); firstfruits (Num 18:13>/<Exod 22:29[28]; 23:19; 34:26; Lev 2:14; Num 15:17–20; Deut 18:4; cf. Lev 19:24); the devoted things (*herem*/devoted thing חֵרֶם) Yahweh gives to the priests (18:14>/<Lev 27:28; Num 21:2; Josh 6:17–21; 8:26; 10:1, 28; cf. Exod 22:20; Deut 13:15); covenant of salt (Num 18:19>/<Lev 2:13; 2 Chr 13:5; cf. Ezra 4:14).

The red heifer purification rituals include several elements used in the ritual purification of persons with skin conditions, namely, cedar wood, hyssop and scarlet wool (**Num 19:6**; cf. Lev 14:4). This helps identify skin conditions and contact with corpses as more severe kinds of ritual pollution.

In a message to the king of Edom (**Num 20:15–16**), Moses alludes to the long Egyptian sojourn (Gen 46–50), crying out to Yahweh (Exod 2:23–25; 6:5), and deliverance by a celestial delegate (14:19).

In Balaam's first oracle he refers to innumerable "dust" of Jacob which echoes the promise (**Num 23:10**; cf. Gen 13:16; also see Table G1 in Genesis Filters).

The holy calendar of **Num 28–29** focuses on additional sacrifices for the festivals and includes a shared framework with the holy calendar in Leviticus, Passover (Lev 23:7–8// Num 28:18–19, 25),[27] Trumpets (Lev 23:23–25//Num 29:1–2), Day of Atonement (Lev 23:26–28//Num 29:7–8), and Tabernacles (Lev 23:34–36//Num 29:12–13,

demonstrates the translation of "bring near" (קרב Hif) with "bring near" (προσφέρω) 52x and "bring near" (προσάγω) 37x merely for the sake of variety (*Notes Leviticus*, xi). This lexical interchangeability by the LXX translator erodes confidence in backtranslation to alternate Hebrew parent texts based on these differences in Lev 10:1; 16:1; Num 3:4; 26:61 LXX. Awabdy affirms Milgrom's reconstruction of "strange fire" in support of his own detailed proposal that 11Q1/11QpaleoLev[a] at Lev 16:1 could be reconstructed like MT or like the parent text of the LXX ("Old Greek," 586–87, 589–91). The evidence in 11Q1/11QpaleoLev[a] is limited to a single letter (ב) of the phrase in question which is not enough for these proposals (see Lev 16:1 *BQS* 1:121). In sum, evidence supports the MT of Lev 16:1 as the more likely original reading especially considering the harmonistic tendencies of the LXX.

27. For a detailed comparison of Lev 23:5–8 and Num 28:16–25 with an excavative agenda, see Müller, Pakkala, and Romeny, *Evidence of Editing*, 27–33.

35–36).[28] The details of the sacrifice for several festivals feature verbal repetitions: new moon, Passover, Weeks, Trumpets, Day of Atonement (Num 28:11–15//28:19–23//28:27–31//29:2–6//29:8–11).[29] The details of a vow of a daughter and a wife get repeated (30:3–5//30:6–8//30:10–12).[30] Also, the instructions for the daily offering repeat and expand upon the same commands elsewhere (Num 28:3–8//Exod 29:38–41).

The itinerary in **Num 33** features brief parallels to several events: striking down the firstborn of Egypt (Num 33:3–4; cf. Exod 12:29–39), lack of water at Rephidim (Num 33:14; cf. Exod 17:1), death of Aaron (Num 33:38–39; cf. 20:23–29), king of Arad (33:40; cf. 21:1–3).

Numbers 33:50–56 sets out standards for conquest and apportioning the land using several stock phrases from Exodus, Leviticus, and Numbers.[31]

Numbers' Non-Exegetical Use of Numbers

Contexts of Numbers frequently interact with other parts of Numbers. These interconnections need to be regarded as literary coherence common to any scroll unless overt signs of exegetical connections indicate otherwise.

After the rebellion of the priestly families and other families in Num 16, the instructions of Num 18 reiterate that the Levites have been given to the priests to serve at the tabernacle (Num 18:2–5; cf. 3:6–9; 8:19).

Moving the tabernacle into the middle of the encampment triggers the need for ritually impure persons to go outside of the camp (5:1–4). One of the ritual impairments that had not been previously explained in terms of ritual purification procedures is ritual contamination from human corpses (5:2). Numbers 19:10–20 spells out the complex procedure for reacquiring a state of ritual purity after ritual contamination from dead bodies to rejoin the camp.

The backwards-looking second oracle of Balaam speaks of redemption from Egypt with imagery akin to the forward-looking third oracle (23:22//24:8). The second and third oracles of Balaam also share imagery of the people who rise like a lioness and the king who will rise like a lioness (23:24; 24:9).

When Moses interrogates his hapless military officers, he notes that the conspiracy for temptation by fornication and false worship recounted in Num 25:1–9 was concocted by Balaam (31:16), apparently after failing to curse Israel.

The census of the second generation makes notations on the families of those who died in the uprising (26:9–10; cf. 16:1) and Zelophehad's daughters (26:3–34; cf. 27:1–11; 36:1–12).

Moses accuses the two and a half Transjordanian tribes of infidelity akin to the rebellion of Kadesh (32:6–15; cf. chs. 13–14).

The land granted to the two and half Transjordanian tribes had been seized during the defeat of kings Sihon and Og (32:33; cf. 21:21–35).

---

28. For color-coded side-by-side layout of these, see Bendavid, *Parallels*, 187 [Hebrew].
29. See ibid., 189–90.
30. See ibid., 190.
31. See parallels discussed by Knoppers, "Establishing," 141–43.

Chapter 5

DEUTERONOMY

דברים

SYMBOLS[1]

- // verbal parallels (A level)
- /~/ synoptic parallel (A level)
- ~ B, probable interpretive allusion; C, possible; D, probably not
- + interpretive blend
- >/< more or less similar (see Filters)
- * part of interpretive network (see Networks)

USE OF TORAH IN DEUTERONOMY[2]

1:9–18~Exod 18:13–27 (C); Num 11:10–30 (C) (appointing judges)

1:19–45/~/Num 13–14 (rebellion at Kadesh)

1:46–2:23/~/Num 21 (not warring against Edom, Moab, and Ammon)

2:24–3:20/~/Num 21:21–35 (conquest of Transjordan)

3:26~Num 20:12 (C) (Moses blames the people)

4:21–22~Num 20:12 (C) (Moses blames the people)

4:5–5:33/~/Exod 19–20 (revelation at the mountain)

5:6–21//Exod 20:1–17 (Ten Commandments)

7:1–5*~Exod 34:11–16* (B) (law of devoting nations of Canaan and prohibition against intermarriage) (* see assembly, attribute formula, and devoting networks)

7:9–10*~5:9–10*//Exod 20:5–6* (B) (a faithful God) (* see attribute formula network)

9:8–10:11/~/Exod 32; 34 (rebellion of Horeb/Sinai)

12:2–28*~Exod 20:24*+Lev 17:1–9*+17:10–14* (B) (seek the place Yahweh will choose to put his name) (* see place network)

13:15–17[16–18]~Exod 22:20[19] (C) (devoting spoils of worshipers of false gods)

14:3–21/~/Lev 11:1–28 (dietary regulations)

14:21b//7:6//14:2 (holy to Yahweh)

14:21c//Exod 23:19b//34:26b (prohibition against boiling a young goat in its mother's milk)

14:22–29*~Lev 27:30; Num 18:21–24 (C) (tithes) (* see place network)

15:1–11*~Exod 23:10–11+22:25*[24] (B) (year of canceling debts) (* see release statute network)

15:12–18*~Exod 21:1–11* (B) (debt slaves) (* see release statute network)

15:19–23*~Exod 22:29–30[28–29] (B)+Lev 22:20, 22 (B) (firstlings to Yahweh) (* see place network)

16:16–17*~Exod 23:14–17 (B) (three mandated pilgrimage festivals) (* see place network)

16:18–20*~1:15+Exod 23:8 (B) (standards for local judges) (* see place network)

17:2–7, 8–13~Exod 22:7–8[6–7] (D) (cases elevated from local judges to temple personnel)

18:15–18*~5:25, 27–28* (A)/~/Exod 20:19* (prophet like Moses) (* see prophet like Moses network)

19:1–13*~Exod 21:12–14 (C); Num 35:9–34 (B) (motivation for law of asylum) (* see place network)

19:15//17:6~Num 35:30 (B) (two or three witnesses)

19:18–21~Exod 20:16 (C)+Exod 21:24; Lev 24:20 (B) (measure-for-measure punishment for false witnesses)

20:16–18*~7:1–2* (B) (law of devoting nations of Canaan) (* see devoting network)

21:18–21~Exod 21:15, 17; Lev 20:9 (C) (rebellious son)

---

1. For explanation of symbols, see Symbols and Abbreviations and Introduction. For other help, see Glossary.
2. See Bibliographic Note on Lists of Potential Parallels.

22:1–4~Exod 23:4–5 (B) (tending to the animal of one's fellow)

22:9–11//Lev 19:19 (A)+Exod 26:1, 31; 28:6, 15 (C) (mixing makes it holy)

22:28–29~Exod 22:16–17[15–16] (B) (rape)

23:4–5*[5–6]/~/Num 22–24 (Balaam's curse) (* see assembly network)

23:9–14[10–15]~Lev 15:16 (B) (ritual purity in time of battle)

23:19–20*~Exod 22:25*[24] (B) (prohibition against charging interest to Israelites) (* see release statute network)

24:6, 10–13*, 17b~Exod 22:26–27*[25–26] (B) (loan collateral regulated) (* see release statute network)

24:8–9~Lev 13–14+Num 12:10–15 (B) (skin conditions)

24:14–15~Lev 19:13b (C) (wages regulated)

25:11–12~Exod 21:22 (B) (if two men fight)

26:5–10*~Num 20:15–16+Gen 12:10+18:18 (B) (firstfruits liturgy) (* see place network)

32:8~Gen 11:7 (C) (dividing the nations)

32:10–11~Gen 1:2+Exod 19:4 (B) (like a mother eagle)

34:10–12*~4:34+18:15–22*+Exod 33:11 (B) (prophet like Moses) (* see prophet like Moses network)

OLD TESTAMENT USE OF DEUTERONOMY (SEE RESPECTIVE NOTES)

1:17~2 Chr 19:5–7, 8–11 (C) (judges accountable to Yahweh in lower and upper courts)

1:27, 32~Ps 106:24–26 (B) (rebellion in wilderness in poetic retrospective)

1:37~Ps 106:32–33 (C) (sin of Moses)

2:3–4, 8, 13, 24, 26, 30–33, 36–37/~/Judg 11:15–27 (Jephthah's letter)

2:33; 3:3~Ps 135:10, 11 (B) (smiting Sihon and Og in poetic retrospective)

3:36~Ps 106:32–33 (C) (sin of Moses)

4:2~Prov 30:5–6 (C) (do not add to his words)

4:21~Ps 106:32–33 (C) (sin of Moses)

4:34~Ps 136:12 (B) (mighty hand and outstretched arm in covenantal loyalty retrospective)

4:38~Ps 135:12 (B) (giving their land as an inheritance in poetic retrospective)

4:39//Josh 2:11 (God of heaven above)

5:6, 7, 9~Ps 81:9–10[10–11] (B) (no other gods)

5:8a, 9a~Ps 78:58–59 (B) (false image in poetic retrospective)

5:9*~Nah 1:2–3* (C) (a jealous and avenging God) (* see attribute formula network)

5:9*~Ps 109:9–15 (C) (request for transgenerational judgment) (* see attribute formula network)

5:9*~Job 21:19 (B) (transgenerational retribution) (* see attribute formula network)

5:12–15*~Jer 17:19–27* (B) (extending implications of Sabbath rest) (* see Sabbath network)

5:16~Mal 1:6 (B) (son honors father)

5:17, 18, 19, 20~Jer 7:5–6, 9 (B) (entry prophetic indictment)

5:32//28:14+29:9[8]+31:5–6~Josh 1:5–9 (B) (obey Torah)

6:6–9*~Prov 3:1–3, 21–24; 6:20–23; 7:1–3 (B) (instructing the next generation)

6:7*~Ps 1:1 (C) (walk, stand, sit)

6:10–11~Josh 24:13 (B) (Joshua's panoramic retrospective at Shechem)

6:11~Neh 9:24, 25 (B) (conquest of Canaan in panoramic retrospective)

6:16~Isa 7:12 (B) (not testing Yahweh)

7:1–2*+20:11*~1 Kgs 9:20–21 (B) (enslaving the remaining peoples of the nations of Canaan) (* see devoting network)

7:1*~Ezra 9:1–2* (B) (mingling the holy seed) (* see assembly network)

7:2*~Josh 6:17 (B) (exception to devoting the nations of Canaan) (* see devoting network)

7:2*~Josh 11:20* (B) (harden hearts of nations of Canaan)

7:3–4*~1 Kgs 11:2–4* (B) (turning Solomon's heart away) (* see devoting network)

7:3*~Ezra 9:11–12 (C) (pollution by intermarriage with the other) (* see devoting network)

7:3*~Ezra 10:10–11, 19 (C) (reparation offering and mass divorce) (* see devoting network)

7:3*~Neh 10:30[31] (B) (solemn oath of restoration assembly) (* see devoting network)

7:6~Isa 6:13 (C) (holy seed)

7:6~Ps 135:4 (B) (election of people in poetic retrospective)

7:8; 10:15~Mal 1:2–3 (C) (love Israel, hate Esau)

7:9*//Dan 9:4* (covenantal fidelity) (* see attribute formula network)

7:10*~Job 21:19* (B) (transgenerational retribution) (* see attribute formula network)

8:2~2 Chr 32:24–26, 31 (B) (Hezekiah's illness and receiving Babylonian representatives)

8:7–8>/<2 Kgs 18:32 (good land)

8:12–14~Hos 13:6 (B) (satisfied, proud, forget)

8:15~Ps 114:3, 5, 8 (B) (sea/river crossing remix)

9:3~Neh 9:24, 25 (B) (conquest of Canaan in panoramic retrospective)

10:17~Ps 136:2, 3 (B) (God of gods in covenantal loyalty retrospective)

11:6~Ps 106:17 (B) (earth swallows in poetic retrospective)

11:7~Judg 2:6–9 (B) (the generation of Joshua)

12:2~Hos 4:13 (C) (upon hills and under trees)

12:5*~1 Kgs 8:15–21* (A) (choosing a place and choosing David) (* see place network)

12:5*~2 Chr 7:11–22* (B) (second revelation to Solomon) (* see place network)

12:5*~1 Chr 16:7–36* (B) (psalm of worship) (* see Abrahamic covenant and place networks)

12:5, 11, 14, 18, 21, 26*~1 Chr 15:1, 3* (C) (place for the ark) (* see place network)

12:8~Judg 17:6//21:25 (B) (right in one's own eyes)

12:9~Ps 95:8–11 (B) (rebellion at Meribah and Massah)

12:9*~Ps 132:8, 13* (C) (ark to the resting place) (* see place network)

12:16, 23–25; 15:23~2 Sam 23:16–17 (C) (water represents the blood of life)

12:16, 23–25; 15:23~1 Chr 11:18–19 (C) (water represents the blood of life)

14:28; 26:12~Amos 4:4 (B) (taunt of sacrifice every morning and tithe every three days)

15:1, 2~Neh 10:31[32] (B) (solemn oath of restoration assembly)

15:1, 12*~Jer 34:14* (B) (releasing slaves) (* see release statute network)

15:21~Mal 1:8, 13 (B) (defective sacrifices)

16:16~Ps 24:3–4* (C) (who may stand in his holy place?) (* see assembly network)

16:7~2 Chr 35:13 (B) (Passover meal fire roasted and boiled)

16:16–17~2 Chr 31:3 (C) (bring offerings to temple for all worship)

16:16~2 Chr 8:12–15 (B) (Solomon's worship)

16:18–19~Amos 5:10, 12 (C) (satire of opposing justice at the gate)

16:18–19; 17:8–11~2 Chr 19:5–7, 8–11 (C) (judges accountable to Yahweh in lower and upper courts)

17:16–17~1 Kgs 10:26–29 (B) (international horse trade)[3]

17:17~1 Sam 8:5 (B) (a king like the nations)

17:17~1 Kgs 11:2–4* (B) (turning Solomon's heart away) (* see devoting network)

18:11~1 Chr 10:1–14 (C) (death of Saul)

18:18~Jer 1:6–9 (B) (prophet deflects commissioning based on poor speech)

19:14~Hos 5:10 (C) (displace boundary marker)

20:15*~Josh 9:6, 14* (B) (obedience to letter of law inadequate) (* see devoting network)

22:25, 27~Jer 20:7, 8 (B) (seduced, seized, and crying out)

23:1–8*[2–9]~Isa 56:1–8* (B) (eunuchs and foreigners in Yahweh's house) (* see assembly network)

23:3–8*[4–9]~Ezra 9:1–2* (B) (mingling the holy seed) (* see assembly network)

23:3–6*[4–7]~Isa 52:1b (uncircumcised and defiled will not enter you again)

23:3–6*[4–7]~Ruth 2:8 (B) (Moabitess granted residing foreigner gleaning privileges) (* see assembly network)

23:3–6*[4–7]~Ruth 4:17, 22 (B) (Moabitess matriarch of David) (* see assembly network)

23:3–6*[4–7]//Neh 13:1–3* (responding to the law of the assembly) (* see assembly network)

23:3*[4]~Lam 1:10* (B) (enemy entering into Lady Jerusalem's holy place) (* see assembly network)

23:3*[4]~Neh 13:23–27* (B) (confronting apostasy husbands) (* see assembly network)

23:3, 7*[4, 8]~1 Kgs 11:1* (B) (women of Egypt and Edom as well as Ammon and Moab) (* see assembly network)

23:6*[7]~Ezra 9:11–12 (B) (pollution by intermarriage with the other) (* see assembly network)

23:10–11*[11–12]~1 Sam 21:4*[5] (C) (bread of the presence for David) (* see Sabbath network)

3. Also see note on 2 Chr 1:14–17 and Table C8 with its associated discussion on cloning vignettes.

23:18[19]~Isa 23:17–18 (C) (wages of Tyre's prostitution sanctified to Yahweh)

23:21–23[22–24]~Eccl 5:4–6[3–5] (B) (on vows)

24:1~Mal 2:16 (B) (if he hates and sends away)

24:1–4~Jer 3:1 (B) (divorce and remarriage eliminate reconciliation)

24:10*~Neh 5:1, 4, 7, 8, 11* (C) (reforming predatory loans) (* see release statute network)

24:16*//2 Kgs 14:6 (each dies for own sins) (* see personal responsibility network)

24:16*~Jer 31:30* (B) (proverb of sour grapes) (* see personal responsibility network)

24:16*~Ezek 5:10* (B) (multigenerational cannibalism) (* see personal responsibility network)

24:16*~Ezek 18:1–4* (B) (proverb of sour grapes) (* see personal responsibility network)

24:16*//2 Chr 25:4* (each dies for own sins) (* see personal responsibility network)

24:17~Amos 2:8 (C) (fornication on the cloak of the needy)

24:19*~Ruth 2:8* (B) (Moabitess granted residing foreigner gleaning privileges) (* see assembly network)

25:5–10~Ruth 4:5–6 (B) (legal blend of laws of levirate marriage, etc.)

26:2, 12~Neh 10:35–37 (B) (solemn oath of restoration assembly)

26:19~Jer 13:11 (B) (people as Yahweh's renown, praise, and honor)

28:49~Hab 1:8 (B) (like an eagle from afar)

29:1–4*[28:69–29:3]~Jer 31:31–34* (B) (new covenant) (* see concealing revelation network)

29:2–4*[1–3]~Isa 6:9–10* (B) (obstructing eyes, ears, hearts) (* see concealing network)

29:20–21[19–20]~Dan 9:11, 13 (B) (curses written in Torah)

29:23*[22]>/<Isa 1:10* (destruction of cities of the plain) (* see cities of the plain network)

29:23*[22]~Ezek 16:53–57* (restoration of Sodom) (* see cities of the plain network)

29:23*[22]~Hos 11:8* (C) (like Admah and Zeboyim) (* see cities of the plain network)

30:3*~Neh 1:8–9* (C) (Yahweh scatters his unfaithful people)

31:6, 8~Ps 22:1[2] (C) (Why have you forsaken me?)

31:11–13~Neh 8:1–3 (C) (pre-Tabernacles Torah reading)

32:1~Isa 1:2 (B) (hear heavens, listen earth)

32:4~Jer 2:5 (C) (pushing back against infidelity)

32:12, 16~Ps 81:9–10[10–11] (B) (no other gods)

32:13, 14~Ps 81:16[17] (B) (provisions in the wilderness)

32:17~Jer 2:11 (C) (gods are not gods)

32:20~Jer 12:4 (C) (reversal—he will not see)

32:51~Ps 106:32–33 (C) (sin of Moses)

33:10*~Mal 2:6* (B) (instruction of Levi) (* see teachers network)

33:10*~Neh 8:7, 8* (C) (Levitical instruction) (* see teachers network)

NEW TESTAMENT USE OF DEUTERONOMY

4:24~Heb 12:29 (consuming fire)

4:35~Mark 12:32 (no other)

5:16//Matt 15:4; 19:19; Mark 7:10; 10:19; Luke 18:20; Eph 6:3 (honor parents)

5:17//Matt 5:21; 19:18; Mark 10:19; Luke 18:20; Rom 13:9; Jas 2:11 (no murder)

5:18//Matt 5:27; 19:18; Mark 10:19; Luke 18:20; Rom 13:9; Jas 2:11 (no adultery)

5:19//Matt 19:18; Mark 10:19; Luke 18:20; Rom 13:9 (not steal)

5:20//Matt 19:18; Mark 10:19; Luke 18:20 (no false witness)

5:21//Rom 7:7; 13:9 (not covet)

6:4//Mark 12:29, 32 (the Lord is one)

6:5//Matt 22:37; Mark 12:30, 33; Luke 10:27 (love God)

6:13//Matt 4:10; Luke 4:8 (worship the Lord only)

6:16//Matt 4:7; Luke 4:12 (not test the Lord)

8:3//Matt 4:4; Luke 4:4 (not bread alone)

9:4~Rom 10:6 (not say in your heart)

9:19~Heb 12:21 (Moses in fear)

13:5[6]; 17:7; 19:19; 21:21; 22:21, 24; 24:7~1 Cor 5:13 (expel the wicked)

15:11~Matt 26:11; Mark 14:7; John 12:8 (always have poor)

18:15//Acts 7:37; cf. 3:22 (prophet like Moses)

18:19~Acts 3:23 (any who do not listen)

19:15//Matt 18:16; 2 Cor 13:1; cf. John 8:17 (two or three witnesses)

19:21//Matt 5:38 (eye for eye)

21:23//Gal 3:13 (cursed who hangs on a tree)

24:1//Matt 5:31; 19:7; Mark 10:4 (divorce)
25:4//1 Cor 9:9; 1 Tim 5:18 (do not muzzle ox)
25:5, 7~Matt 22:24; Mark 12:19; Luke 20:28 (levirate marriage)
27:26 LXX//Gal 3:10 (cursed who does not do all)
29:4[3]//Rom 11:8 (eyes not see)
30:12//Rom 10:6 (Who will ascend?)
30:13//Rom 10:7 (Who will descend?)
30:14~Rom 10:8 (near you)
31:6, 8//Heb 13:5 (never leave you)
32:5//Phil 2:15 (crooked generation)
32:21//Rom 10:19 (make you envious)
32:35//Rom 12:19; Heb 10:30 (mine to avenge)
32:35, 36~Heb 10:30 (judge his people)
32:43~Rom 15:10 (rejoice)
32:43 LXX~Heb 1:6 (celestial messengers worship)

HERMENEUTICAL PROFILE OF THE USE OF TORAH IN DEUTERONOMY

The present discussion identifies four elements of the hermeneutical profile of Deuteronomy's exegetical use of scriptural traditions that can help with many of its individual cases of scriptural exegesis treated in the notes below, namely, Deuteronomy as Torah explained, the authoritative advancement of covenant in Deuteronomy, motivation in Deuteronomy, and exegesis and revelation.

Torah Explained

The narrator announces Deuteronomy as Torah explained. The book spans the last day of Moses's life, housing a series of his final speeches to Israel. As such, Deuteronomy gets the last word of Torah. Moses did not use his last words to say something out of entirely new cloth. Nor does the book offer sentimental nostalgia. Moses retells Torah with extra motivation for obedience.

Moses "explains" Torah (Deut 1:5).[4] Some commentators regard the Torah in Deut 1:5 as referring only to the legal materials of chs. 12–26. Working backward, however, Deut 6:1 heads the motivation section (chs. 6–11)[5] and Deut 4:44 heads the major middle section of the book as: "now, this is the torah," in which Moses encourages Israel to "learn" and obey (5:1), setting laws within narrative (ch. 5). In much the same way Deut 1:5 speaks of Moses explaining Torah in the heading of the book, which begins with numerous narratives interspersed with exhortations (1:6–4:40).[6]

4. The LXX understands the term *be'er* (בֵּאֵר) as "explaining" or "clarifying" (διασαφέω) (see LEH 144; BDAG 236).

5. The characteristic motivational advice and exhortation of Deuteronomy is often called "parenesis" (esp. of Deut 6–11). The present study speaks of "motivation" to refer to the parenetic qualities of Deuteronomy. See discussion below.

6. See Schnittjer, "Kadesh Infidelity," 104, n. 35. For commentators who regard torah in 1:5 as referring only to legal instruction esp. in Deut 12–28, see Nelson, *Deuteronomy*, 17; Craigie, *Deuteronomy*, 92; for those who regard it as referring comprehensively to legal, parenetic, and narrative instruction, see Weinfeld, *Deuteronomy 1–11*, 129; Woods, *Deuteronomy*, 79; and as referring to law of Deut 12–28, exhortation of 5–11, and "perhaps also to the didactic narrative and exhortations of 1:6–4:40" (Tigay, *Deuteronomy*, 5). Wevers deduces that the LXX of Deut 1:5 refers to

The function of torah in Deut 1:5; 4:44; and 6:1 within the framework of the book as context seems inclusive of narrative and legal reinterpretation. Deuteronomy 6:1 heads a major section with the purpose defined as what "Yahweh your God has commanded me *to teach* you" (6:1, emphasis mine). And Deut 12:1 picks up exactly where 6:1 leaves off, calling for Israel's obedience—"This is the commandment, *the decrees and the judgments*" (6:1 lit.) and "these are *the decrees and the judgments*" (12:1 lit., emphases signify verbal parallels).

Moses's explanation of Torah constitutes the frame narrative of Deuteronomy. Nearly the entire book counts itself as interpretation. The self-conscious recycling and enhancing of scriptural traditions signifies that thinking of scriptural revelation as once and done badly misunderstands the scriptural testimony to God's redeeming work.

Deuteronomy calls for what it models: continual Torah study of commands by families (6:5–9); explanation of narratives by parents (6:20–25); the word of Yahweh by prophets (18:18–20; cf. 13:1–5); Torah study by civil rulers (17:18–19); Torah recitation in historic ceremony and monuments (27:1–8, 9–14); public readings of Torah at national assemblies (31:10–13); Torah as a written testimony against rebellion (31:24–27); and repetition at corporate gatherings (31:28–30). Deuteronomy encourages omnipresent scriptural study in Israel. Moses summarizes: "Take to heart all the words I have solemnly declared to you this day, *so that you may command your children to obey carefully all the words of this torah.* They are not just idle words for you—they are your life. By them you will live long in the land you are crossing the Jordan to possess" (32:46–47, emphasis mine). The call to study Torah's teachings and narratives by people at every level of society every day effectively makes Deuteronomy as reinterpreted Torah a paradigm for God's people.

As noted in the introduction, the present study approaches Torah according to its own presentation of the use of scriptural traditions. The present chapter evaluates Deuteronomy's exegesis of donor contexts that can be identified based on verbal, syntactical, and contextual parallels. This includes more than half a dozen retold stories (see Table D1).

TABLE D1: NARRATIVES RETOLD IN DEUTERONOMY‡

1:6–18 appointing judges (Exod 18; Num 11)	**3:21–29 (31:1–8, 14–15, 23)** commission of Joshua (Num 27:12–23)[b]
1:19–45 rebellion at Kadesh (Num 13–14)[a]	**5:1–33** revelation at Horeb (Exod 19–20)
1:46–2:23 not warring against Edom, Moab, and Ammon (Num 21)	**9:7–10:11** rebellion at Horeb (Exod 32)
2:24–3:20 conquest of Transjordan (Num 21)	**23:3–6** Balaam and Moabites (Num 22–24)

‡ Table adapted from Schnittjer, "Kadesh Infidelity," 96.

[a] Also see allusion to rebellion at Kadesh in Deut 9:2, 23.

[b] Additional allusions to the commission of Joshua appear in Deut 32:44–47; 34:9; Josh 1:1–9.

all of 1:6–28:69 by repeating "in the land of Moab" in 29:1[28:69 LXX/MT], thus "law" (νόμος) in a broad inclusive sense (*Notes on Deuteronomy*, 4–5).

At several places in his *Poetics* (ca. 335 BCE), Aristotle considers how narratives on the same events function. The ancient observations on synoptic narratives can help interpretation over and against modern expectations. Although Aristotle mainly deals with fiction, he thinks that historical narratives operate in the same way. "[T]he poet should be more a maker of plots than of verses . . . even should his poetry concern actual events, he is no less a poet for that" (*Poetics*, 1451b, 27–30).[7] The present discussion needs to be restrained to three observations.

First, Aristotle notes that authors decide what to include and what to exclude (1456a, 6–9). This provides an important comparative advantage in synoptic contexts since an ancient author's choices with one-off stories cannot be evaluated.

Second, Aristotle considers arrangement of narrative units as one of the author's choices. The author decides if the story focuses on a person's life, a theme, an event, and so on (1459a, 32–34). Decisions for chronological sequence, dischronological sequence (including previews or flashbacks), and other matters of arrangement make up an important part of what ancient authors do.

Third, Aristotle considers the author's choices for how to voice narratives. He points out that even one different word could change the significance of the story (1458b, 18–21). Voicing includes narration versus characters' speeches, action versus embedded discourses, and even first- versus third-person point of view.

Aristotle's sensible observations for evaluating synoptic narratives provide a helpful starting point. The synoptic narratives in Deuteronomy stand at the headwaters of this commonplace scriptural exegetical activity.[8]

In addition to narratives, Deuteronomy houses an extensive collection of laws. Many of these laws relate to others in Torah. This requires thinking through the relationship between the several legal collections in Torah.

Several competing models for explaining how the legal instructions in Deuteronomy relate to their counterparts elsewhere in Torah fall short. The excavative diachronic views of replacement, complement, and amendment each, in their own ways, frame the differences between parallel laws in Exodus and Deuteronomy as inconsistent and/or contradictory.[9] While this helps draw attention to the specific details of the

---

7. The discussion of Aristotle and the synoptic interpretation here is condensed from Schnittjer, "Kadesh Infidelity," 104.

8. Synoptic narratives include: Gen 1:26–28; 2:4//5:1–2; 24:12–21//24:42–48; 42:7–38; 43:1–8//44:18–34; Exod 25–31//35–40; Josh 14:13–15//15:13–14//Judg 1:10, 20; Josh 15:15–19, 63//Judg 1:11–15, 21; Josh 1:10; 16:10//Judg 1:27, 29; Josh 24:29–31//Judg 2:7–9; 2 Sam 5–24//1 Chr 11–21; 1 Kgs 3–11//2 Chr 1–9; 1 Kgs 12–2 Kgs 25//2 Chr 10–36; 2 Kgs 18–20//Isa 36–39; 2 Kgs 25//Jer 52 (cf. Jer 39); Ezra 1:1–4//2 Chr 36:22–23 (cf. Ezra 5:13–15; 6:3–5); Ezra 2//Neh 7; Acts 9:1–18//22:3–17//26:4–20; 10:1–6//10:30–33//11:13–14 (cf. 10:22); 10:9–16//11:5–14 (cf. 10:28; 15:7–11); and numerous synoptic contexts in Matthew, Mark, and Luke, and a few in John (ibid., 96, n. 2). For synoptic narratives in Deuteronomy, see Table D1.

9. For examples of replacement, see Levinson, *Deuteronomy*, 3–6, 144–50, et passim; of complement, see Berman,

related laws, it does not adequately take into account the function of Torah's frame narrative. The Torah's own presentation of its several legal collections could be thought of more like situational supplementation and advancement. Exodus offers instructions at the mountain, Leviticus reconsiders the need for holiness by laity and priests in light of coming into the courts of Yahweh, and Deuteronomy develops a series of laws based on the challenges of distance from the central sanctuary when Israel enters into its far-flung land. The present approach follows Torah's own presentation of its several legal collections as progressive revelation of the will of Yahweh. Within Deuteronomy's framework the interpretive interventions of previous laws of Torah function as exegetical advances.

Deuteronomy self-identifies as Torah explained to encourage Israel to obey Yahweh in a new situation (1:5; 4:44; 5:1; 6:1; see above). Deuteronomy does not conceive of itself as a revision or new instruction in competition to other laws of Torah. Deuteronomy 29:1[28:69] speaks of the instructions at Moab as a covenant standing alongside—"in addition to"—the Horeb covenant.[10] The idea of explanation in Deut 1:5 means both the enduring validity of the authoritative donor instructions and the advancement of the same. All of this suggests that Deuteronomy's primary forms of legal exegesis are interpretative advancements by expansion and adjustment.

Some of Deuteronomy's interpretive supplements put the corresponding command in a whole new light. Other exegetical interventions seem much more reserved and subtle. But since all of this has been explicitly cast as explaining, setting out, and teaching Torah, Deuteronomy's legal exegesis overtly affirms the enduring authority of previous legal instructions in Torah.

The torah collection refers to the large body of laws in Deut 12–26. Many of these legal instructions have parallels and/or similarities to laws in Exodus, Leviticus, and Numbers. Table D2 offers an overview of the legal instructions in the torah collection. Not every law in the torah collection with parallels to other legal standards in Torah features exegetical allusion. Some share only broad parallels, and others do not advance legal standards. While Table D2 offers a fairly comprehensive list, some of the parallel laws appear in the exegetical notes of this chapter and others in the Filters at the end of the chapter, depending on the way they relate to their counterpart scriptural legal standards.

Inconsistency, esp. 107–98; idem, *Ani Maamin*, 129–57; and of amendment, see Mattison, *Rewriting*, 19–27. Each of these approaches begins by identifying contradictions in Torah. For a comparative overview of these approaches, see Mattison, *Rewriting*, 7–18; for criticism of aspects of these single-solution approaches, see Wells, "Interpretation," 264–65.

10. The expression "in addition to" in Deut 29:1[28:69] comes from a composite term (מִן + לְ + בַּד = מִלְּבַד). Elsewhere in Deuteronomy, the noun "except, beside" (*bad* בַּד) with the same preposition (*le-* לְ) carries the sense of "in addition to" (3:5) and with a negative "not only" (8:3; 29:13[12]).

TABLE D2: TORAH COLLECTION OF DEUTERONOMY 12–26 AND SIMILAR INSTRUCTIONS OF TORAH‡

Bold in right-hand column signifies substantial verbal parallels with corresponding law in Deuteronomy.

torah collection	topically parallel legal standards
12:2–4, demolish worship icons of the other	**Exod 23:24; 34:13**; Num 33:52; **Deut 7:5, 24–26**
12:5–28, central worship	
12:5–14, 17–19, 26–28, tithes and offerings only at place of Yahweh's choosing	**Exod 20:24**, 25 (cf. Deut 27:5, 6); Lev 17:1–9
12:15, 20–22, common slaughter elsewhere	**Exod 34:24** (enlarge territory, cf. Deut 12:20); cf. Lev 17:13 (game)
12:16, 23–25, do not consume blood	Gen 9:4; **Lev 17:10–14**; 19:26a
12:29–31, do not be snared by false worship	Exod 22:20[19]; 23:33; 34:12
12:32[13:1], obedience formula	Deut 4:2
13:1–5, 6–11, 12–18[13:2–6, 7–12, 13–19], prohibition against seduction to idolatry by false prophets, friends and family, a local town	Exod 22:20[19] (cf. "devote" Deut 13:15, 17[16, 18])
14:1–2, prohibition against disfiguring mourning rites	Lev 19:27–28; 21:5
14:3–20, dietary regulations	**Lev 11:1–47**
14:21a, prohibition against eating animals that die on their own	**Exod 22:31[30]**; Lev 11:40; **17:15–16**; 22:8
14:21b, do not boil a young goat in its mother's milk	**Exod 23:19b; 34:26b**
14:22–29, tithes	Lev 27:30–33; Num 18:21–24; cf. Neh 10:37[38]
15:1–11, year of release	Exod 23:10–11 (cf. "remission" 23:11; Deut 15:1); Lev 25:1–7
15:12–18, Hebrew slaves	Exod 21:2–6, 7–11; Lev 25:39–55
15:19–23, firstlings	Exod 13:12; **22:29–30[28–29]**; 34:19; **Lev 22:20–22**; cf. Lev 27:26; Num 3:13; 8:17; 18:17–18
16:1–8, Passover	Exod 12:10–20; 13:3–13; 23:15; 34:18–20; Lev 23:5–8; Num 9:1–14; 28:16–25
16:9–12, Weeks	Exod 23:16; 34:22; Lev 23:15–21; Num 28:26–31
16:13–15, Tabernacles	Exod 23:16; 34:22; Lev 23:33–43; Num 29:12–34
16:16–17, pilgrimage festivals	**Exod 23:14–17**; cf. 34:18, 20b, 22–23
16:18, appointment of judges	—
16:19–20, impartial judgments	Exod 23:1–3, 6–8; Lev 19:15; cf. Deut 1:16–18
16:21–22, prohibition against sacred poles and pillars	Lev 26:1; cf. Exod 23:24; 34:13

torah collection	topically parallel legal standards
17:1, sacrifices without defects	Lev 22:17–24 (cf. "defect" Lev 22:20, 21, 23; Deut 17:1); cf. Deut 15:21
17:2–7, two or three witnesses necessary for capital cases at local tribunal	Num 35:30; cf. Deut 19:15
17:8–13, high court at the place Yahweh chooses	cf. Exod 22:8[7]
17:14–20, law of the king	—
18:1–8, Levitical priestly portion	cf. Levites, Num 18:21–24, 30–32; priests, Lev 7:32–34; Num 18:8–20, 25–29
18:9–14, prohibition against divination and child sacrifice	Exod 22:18[17]; Lev 18:21; 19:31; 20:2–5, 27; cf. Deut 12:31
18:15–22, law of the prophet	**Deut 5:25–28**; Exod 20:19; cf. Deut 34:10–12
19:1–13, asylum for manslaughter	Exod 21:12–14; Lev 24:17, 21; **Num 35:9–28**; Deut 4:41–43; cf. Josh 20
19:14, prohibition against moving boundary marker	cf. Deut 27:17; Prov 22:28; 23:10–11
19:15–21, law of witnesses	**Exod 20:16; 21:23–24; 23:1; Lev 24:20; Deut 17:6**; cf. Exod 23:1–3, 6–8; Num 35:30
20:1–20, law of warfare	Deut 7:1–2; cf. Exod 23:23, 28–31
21:1–9, atonement for unsolved murder	—
21:10–14, protections for female captives	—
21:15–17, protection of rights of firstborn in household with multiple wives	—
21:18–21, judgment for rebellious children	Exod 21:15, 17; Lev 20:9
21:22–23, regulations for corpse of executed person	—
22:1–4, standards for neighbor's stray domestic animal	**Exod 23:4, 5**; cf. Lev 19:18
22:5, prohibition against gender crossdressing	—
22:6–7, limitations on bird's nest	—
22:8, standard for liability without roof guard	cf. Exod 21:33–34
22:9–11, prohibition against mixing seeds or fabrics	**Lev 19:19**
22:12, law of tassels	Num 15:37–41 (cf. "corners")
22:13–21, accusation against newly married bride	—
22:22–27, adultery	Exod 20:14//Deut 5:18; Lev 18:20; 19:20–22; 20:10
22:28–29, rape	Exod 22:16–17[15–16]
22:30[23:1], prohibition against marrying stepmother	Lev 18:8; 20:11; Deut 28:20

(cont.)

torah collection	topically parallel legal standards
23:1–8[2–9], law of the assembly	cf. Num 22–24
23:9–14[10–15], standards for ritual purity during warfare	**Lev 15:16**; cf. Num 5:1–4; 10:35–36
23:15–16[16–17], asylum for escaped slaves	—
23:17–18[18–19], prohibitions against cultic prostitution	Lev 19:29; 21:9
23:19–20[20–21], regulations on charging interest	**Exod 22:25[24]**; Lev 25:35–37
23:21–23[22–24], vows	Lev 27:2; Num 30:2; cf. Eccl 5:4–6[3–5]
23:24–25[25–26], limitations on eating produce in a neighbor's field	—
24:1–4, divorce	—
24:5, newlywed temporary release from military service	—
24:6, 10–13, 17b, limitations on pledges	**Exod 22:26–27[25–26]**
24:7, kidnapping	**Exod 21:16**
24:8–9, skin condition	Lev 13–14; Num 12:10–15
24:14–15, standards for paying needy workers	Lev 19:13b
24:16, individual liability in criminal cases	—
24:17–18, protected social classes	**Exod 22:21–22[20–21]; 23:9**; Lev 19:33–34
24:19–22, regulations on harvest gleanings	Lev 19:9–10; 23:22; cf. Exod 23:11
25:1–3, limitations on punishment	—
25:4, prohibition against muzzling threshing ox	—
25:5–10, levirate marriage	cf. Lev 18:16; 20:21; Num 27:1–11 (esp. "name" 27:4; Deut 25:6, 7)
25:11–12, prohibition against harming reproductive capacity	**Exod 21:22**
25:13–16, prohibition against fraudulent measures	**Lev 19:35–36**
25:17–19, blotting out Amalek	**Exod 17:14**
26:1–11, firstfruits liturgy	firstfruits, Exod 22:29a[28a]; 23:19a; 34:26a; Num 18:12–13; Deut 14:22–23; 18:4; liturgy, **Num 20:15–16; Gen 12:10; 18:18**
26:12–15, tithe liturgy	Deut 14:28–29

‡ Table based primarily on research for the current study and collated with a few details from Driver, *Deuteronomy*, iv–vii; idem, *Introduction*, 73–75; Lasserre, *Synopse*, 1–155; Pleins, *Social Visions*, 55. For consideration of what laws Deuteronomy leaves out from the covenant collection (Exod 21–23) as well as unique laws in Deuteronomy, see Pleins, *Social Visions*, 56–61.

Authoritative Advancement of Covenant

As noted in the preceding section, the most important uses of scriptural traditions in Deuteronomy are retelling narratives and retelling laws (see Tables D1 and D2). Understanding how these work can offer broad insight into the purpose of Deuteronomy's use of scriptural traditions. Redundancy may clarify underlying concerns: Deuteronomy retells authoritative narratives and reissues authoritative commands whereby all donor contexts remain authoritative alongside their authoritative receptor contexts in Deuteronomy.

Divinely authorized revelation is not deleted. It is supplemented, developed, and advanced step by step. Deuteronomy never claims to be Torah unto itself. As noted above, Deuteronomy refers to itself as an explanation of Torah (Deut 1:5), requiring it to stand alongside (29:1[28:69]) the Torah it both explains and completes. That is the point and that is what needs to be explained. Deuteronomy's retold narratives and retold laws function according to covenantal identity and covenantal relationship.

First, the covenantal identity of God's people is founded upon the redeeming acts of God, themselves requiring constant retelling. Instructions for celebrating and annually memorializing the exodus from Egypt are routinely interspersed in the story itself (Exod 12:1–20, 42–49; 13:1–16). The original event itself needs to be celebrated as a historic event wherein each succeeding generation joins together with their ancestors, grounding their identity in the redeeming work of God. The memorialization of the Passover intentionally provokes youthful questions about its meaning (13:14). The answer to such questions includes narrative-shaped acts of Yahweh and the identity of his people (Deut 6:20–25). Deuteronomy does not stop at recasting major revelatory events like the giving of law at the mountain but includes new versions of old sins. The people of Yahweh need instruction which comes in part from manifold and ongoing retelling of the stories of sin, salvation, and revelation.

The past divine acts and instructions are not museum pieces on display for antiquarian interest. Yahweh's past workings remain relevant in part based on the collective identity of his people across time. The most extreme example might be when the directly addressed "you" includes Moses's immediate auditors as their own ancestors within the same context.

> When all these blessings and curses *I have set before you* come on you and you take them to heart wherever Yahweh your God disperses you among the nations, and when you and your children return to Yahweh your God and obey him with all your heart and with all your soul according to everything I command you today, then Yahweh your God will restore your fortunes and have compassion *on you and gather you again from all the nations where he scattered you*. Even if you have been banished to the most distant land under the heavens, from there Yahweh your God will gather you and bring you back.

> *He will bring you to the land that belonged to your ancestors*, and you will take possession of it. *He will make you more prosperous and numerous than your ancestors.* (Deut 30:1–5, emphasis mine)

Those standing before Moses become ancestors, remembered for something they had yet to do. The constant interchange between second-person singular and plural pronouns throughout Deuteronomy, however else it is explained, signifies both personal responsibility and collective identity across time.

Covenantal identity starts with what Yahweh has done. While personal responsibility is ever present, covenantal identity transcends individuality. Yahweh's people together continuously celebrate and interpret his redeeming mercy across the generations. For these reasons every generation needs to retell Yahweh's story and teach his commands every day.

Second, scriptural revelation needs to be re-presented because the covenantal relationship between God and his people is inherently dynamic. His commands are not for robots who need to take their rightful places in a mechanized system. Laws have all the give and take expected of personal relationships within diverse situations. Among the most striking examples of the dynamic nature of divine revelation in Leviticus and Numbers are the series of laws wherein Yahweh makes adjustments based on human appeals, even willing to readjust his own previous adjustments (see notes on Lev 24:10–23; Num 9:1–14; 15:32–36; 36:1–12; cf. 27:1–11). These legal narratives do not depict divine law as static. It is a function of a sovereign God's dynamic relationship with his people and their messy lives.

The give and take of the series of precedent-setting and amendment laws provides paradigmatic insight into the many retold laws of Deuteronomy. Moses retells the commands with manifold adjustments to help Israel make the shift from wilderness encampment to life in the land of promise. The same kinds of questions, suggestions, and complaints that triggered divine rulings in these precedent-setting cases are also brought to light in the retold stories of Deuteronomy. Important examples include the people's request for sending scouts into the land—unstated in the earlier version of the story (Deut 1:22)—and Yahweh's affirming the people's request for a mediator—also previously unstated (5:28).

The divinely sanctioned legal upgrades strengthen the revelation of Yahweh's sovereign power and will. Sometimes Yahweh agrees to appeals made to him: judges to assist Moses (1:9–14; cf. Num 11:11–17) and a prophet like Moses (Deut 5:23–29; 18:16–17). At other times Yahweh does not respond according to people's desires (3:23–28). These answered, unanswered, and rejected complaints and petitions stand at the heart of covenant relations.

The crucial point is that interpreting Deuteronomy's new version of laws and narratives turns on adequately explaining newly revealed elements. Explaining new elements begins with identifying these through comparative study.

Motivation

Legal and narrative retellings within Deuteronomy are infused with motivation. Motivation is not absent in earlier versions of legal standards but is often occasional in small amounts. Motivation dominates Deuteronomy.[11] The torah collection (Deut 12–26) in places reads like preached legal prescriptions with law and motivation interspersed.

Deuteronomy's motivation generally comes in I-you style (first person from Yahweh and Moses intertwined) with singular and plural "you" constantly intermixed, along with smaller portions of impersonal third person lacking direct motivation. Certain cases use motivation clauses in the third person, like instructions for the king (17:20).

Some scholars distinguish between parenesis and motivation within legal discourse. Parenetic discourse advises, counsels, and exhorts persons in a "very general way."[12] Often, parenetic units stand independently, such as those in Deut 6–11. By contrast, motive clauses of legal prescriptions refer to dependent phrases explaining the laws themselves. If parenetic statements call people to obedience, motive clauses explain the reasons and benefits of the law.[13] In spite of the difference in many cases, dependent parenetic statements within legal standards sometimes motivate and thus "fall within the scope of the legal motive clause."[14] Even approaches that differentiate parenetic statements from motive clauses in legal collections at times transgress their own standards.[15] The present study does not distinguish between motivating parenetic phrases *within* legal standards and legal motive clauses. Both motivating parenetic phrases and legal motive clauses can be referred to as motivation, or the like, within motivated legal prescriptions for the broad points under consideration in this study.

Motive clauses get introduced by a variety of literary signals like "for," "so that," "otherwise," "that," and other subordinate clause constructions.[16] Detecting motivational emphases of legal instruction goes a long way toward explaining the use of scriptural traditions in Deuteronomy. A convenient list of legal motive clauses in Deuteronomy may

---

11. The percentage of laws with motivation clauses in the covenant collection is: 16 percent; covenant renewal collection: 13 percent; priestly collection: 20 percent; holiness collection: 51 percent; and torah collection of Deut 12–26: 50 percent (Sonsino, *Motive Clauses*, 102). However, if parenetic exhortation gets added, like the units in Deut 6–11, then none of the other legal collections in Torah come close to Deuteronomy.

12. Von Rad, "Deuteronomy," *IDB* 1:835.

13. See Sonsino, *Motive Clauses*, 66–69; Tiffany, "Parenesis," 20–21, 310; DeRouchie, *Call*, 15–18, 82.

14. See Sonsino, *Motive Clauses*, 69.

15. Sonsino takes "you shall remember . . ." as parenetic in Deut 16:12 (ibid., 251); however, elsewhere he takes "remember . . ." clauses as motive—15:15; 24:9, 18, 22; 25:17–18 (250, 252, 253, 257, 265, 266). Sonsino regards "you must purge . . ." in 19:13 as parenetic (251), but elsewhere he counts "you must purge . . ." as motive—21:21; 22:22 (262, 263). It is possible identifying 19:13 as parenetic is an oversight or typo, since the verse opens with "show not pity," which Sonsino tends to regard as parenetic, e.g., 19:21a; 25:12b (68, 69, 251, 252). The point here is not to be critical of Sonsino's extremely helpful study but to observe that within legal standards parenetic phrases and motive clauses overlap somewhat.

16. Motive clause indicators include: "for" (כִּי), "so that" (לְמַעַן), "otherwise" (פֶּן), "that" (אֲשֶׁר, וְ), and other subordinate grammatical particles. See full list and annotations in ibid., 70–74.

be found elsewhere.[17] For the present purposes motive will often be discussed in relation to exegetical allusions. Notice different characteristic motive clauses of the same law from the holiness and torah collections (bold signifies motive clauses):[18]

> Do not go over your vineyard a second time or pick up the grapes that have fallen. Leave them for the poor and the foreigner. **I am Yahweh your God.** (Lev 19:10)

> When you harvest the grapes in your vineyard, do not go over the vines again. Leave what remains for the foreigner, the fatherless and the widow. **Remember that you were slaves in Egypt. That is why I command you to do this.** (Deut 24:21–22)

The retelling of scriptural stories in Deuteronomy likewise points to motivation of devotion to Yahweh as its signature tendency.

Exegesis and Revelation

Scriptural exegesis in Deuteronomy affects scriptural revelation in general. Legal exegesis in Deuteronomy provides piecemeal, incremental supplements and adjustments in light of the transition from wilderness encampment to residence in the land of promise. Legal exegesis advances revelation step by step. The legal exegesis of Deuteronomy, with all of its motivation, becomes programmatic for the prophetic exposition of Torah.

The use of scriptural traditions in Deuteronomy points to an embryonic canonical consciousness. The self-identity of Deuteronomy as Torah explained invites reading the donor and receptor contexts of scriptural exegesis together. The sense of Deuteronomy as explanation of Torah signals an expectation for continuity between the several parts of Torah. This naturally leads to prophets, psalmists, and narrators who read together various parts of Torah. Deuteronomy's self-conscious exegetical program promotes a sense of continuity and coherence even by its boldest interpretive advancements.

In sum of the four subsections of this hermeneutical profile, Deuteronomy does not start from scratch but constantly instructs by explaining scriptural traditions, often adding motivation. Moses applies the authority of the scriptural traditions to forming a covenant-shaped people according to Yahweh's ongoing interactive will. The people's persistent rebellions and ongoing need for hope naturally invite motivation. Deuteronomy's exegetical use of scripture becomes programmatic for scriptural exegesis throughout the Hebrew Scriptures and emblematic of an emerging canon consciousness.

---

17. The present study generally follows the list of motive clauses (and motivating parenetic phrases) in ibid., 250–68. Minor disagreements include motive clauses in Deut 16:12; 19:13; 20:19 (and see inconsistencies in note above). The present study concurs with Sonsino's suggestion that 22:30b[23:1b] is a motive clause on the analogy of 27:20b (267–68, n. 12). For a summary of the function of legal motive clauses in Torah, including comparison to ancient Near Eastern law collections, based in large part on Soncino's work but applied to current debates on biblical law, see Todd, "That You May Do Them," forthcoming.

18. As identified by Sonsino, *Motive Clauses*, 237, 242, 252, 265.

USE OF TORAH IN DEUTERONOMY

1:9–18~Exod 18:13–27 (C); Num 11:10–30 (C) (appointing judges). Moses begins with a broad retrospective reference to a time when he requested that tribes appoint judges (1:13, 15–16, 18). Parts of his rationale sound like the appointing of judges in Exod 18 and parts like Num 11. The exact relationship of the present retrospective to the narrative presentation of one or both of these is unclear. In all three contexts Moses needs help and all three include affirmations of a need for assistant judges: Jethro suggests, Moses affirms (Exod 18:17–23, 24–26), Moses complains, God provides (Num 11:14, 16–17, 25), and Moses initiates, people affirm (Deut 1:9–13, 14–16).[19]

The motivational reasons in Deut 1 include appointed judges' representation of God's own judgment (1:17; cf. Exod 18:21). Additionally, Moses's rehearsal introduces the first of a series of pluses—new details—relating to affirmation of the ostensive events: selecting judges, scouts, mediator—irrespective of whether this context refers to the events narrated in Exod 18 and/or Num 11 and/or another unrecorded incident (emphases mine).

> You [tribes of Israel] answered me, "What you propose to do is **good.**" (Deut 1:14)

> [Moses said] "The idea **seemed good** to me, so I selected twelve of you, one man from each tribe." (1:23)

> Yahweh said to me, "I have heard what this people said to you. Everything they said **was good.**" (5:28)

The system for justice designed to protect the socially vulnerable was not forced upon Israel; they willingly embraced it (1:14). Justice for all citizens and residing foreigners is a matter of both shared responsibility and representative identity of God and his people (1:16–17).

1:19–45/~/Num 13–14 (rebellion at Kadesh). Deuteronomy 1:19–45 features a synoptic version of the rebellion at Kadesh in Num 13–14. Extensive treatment of the parallels appears elsewhere, so the present comparisons can focus on key elements.[20]

One of the most contested differences between these synoptic parallels concerns Joshua and Caleb. A comparison of how the two contexts handle Joshua and Caleb can be observed before getting at more important distinctions.

---

19. See fuller discussion in Schnittjer, *Torah Story*, 465–68.

20. See Schnittjer, "Kadesh Infidelity," 105–15. Other approaches often predicate their views of Deut 1 on its contradictions, real or apparent, of its counterparts in Torah (e.g., Berman, *Ani Maamin*, 78–79). For critical interaction with such approaches, see Schnittjer, "Kadesh Infidelity," 95–120 (regarding Berman, see 100–1, 105, n. 37, 115–16). The present discussion indebted to 105–15.

	Numbers	Deuteronomy
Caleb's minority report	13:30	—
Joshua and Caleb try to dissuade rebellion	14:6–9	—
private exemption of Caleb	14:24	1:36
public declaration of sparing Joshua and Caleb	14:30	1:38 (Joshua only)
Joshua and Caleb spared judgment of scouts	14:38	—

Numbers and Deuteronomy each handle Joshua and Caleb at Kadesh according to their own symmetrical designs. Numbers presents Caleb's minority report (Num 13:30) and his exemption from judgment in a private divine consultation with Moses (14:24), and Joshua and Caleb together seek to dissuade Israel from rebellion (14:6–9) and are together publicly exempted from judgment of the older generation (14:30) and together are spared from the plague against the scouts (14:38). Thus, Num 13–14 refers to Caleb alone for what he did alone and Caleb and Joshua together for what they did together.

Deuteronomy 1 handles Caleb and Joshua separately according to its own symmetrical logic. In Numbers, Caleb calls the people to invade the land in response to the scouts' report, whereas in Deuteronomy Moses credits himself with urging invasion even prior to the scouts' report (Num 13:30; Deut 1:20–21). In Numbers, Joshua and Caleb seek to persuade the people to turn from rebellion, whereas Moses again gives himself credit in Deuteronomy (Num 14:7–9; Deut 1:29–33). Deuteronomy 1 offers a first-person account from Moses, who focuses more on his own role in the events and less on the two dissenting scouts. In Deut 1:36 and 1:38 Moses treats Joshua and Caleb separately as part of his enumeration of those who may and may not enter the land and why—the evil generation of the Kadesh rebellion may not enter (Deut 1:35), Caleb may enter because of his faith (1:36), Moses may not (1:37), Joshua may enter because of his role in the conquest (1:38), and the little ones of Israel may enter (1:39).

To summarize this point, both Numbers and Deuteronomy handle Joshua and Caleb according to their own narrative agendas.

Ancient narrators decide what elements to include and exclude, what sequence should be used, and how to voice the story in terms of surface agency (see Hermeneutical Profile of the Use of Torah in Deuteronomy). A comparative overview suggests that Deut 1 offers an abbreviated version of the events.[21] Both versions follow the same sequence. Note a comparative summary of the synoptic parallels.[22]

21. Numbers 13:33b SP includes a long insertion basically presenting details from Deut 1:27–33 MT.

22. Table adapted from Schnittjer, "Kadesh Infidelity," 108–9.

	Numbers	Deuteronomy
Moses's call to invasion	—	1:19–21
plan to send scouts	13:1–3	1:22–23
list of scouts	13:4–16	—
commission of expedition	13:17–20	—
scouting expedition	13:21–24	1:24–25a
official report	13:25–29	1:25b
Caleb's recommendation of invasion	13:30	—
second bad report of ten scouts	13:31–33	—
private reminiscence and rebellion	14:1; {13:28}	1:26–28
Israel's collective revolt	14:2–4	—
Moses and Aaron prostrate themselves	14:5	—
advice to not be afraid	14:6–10	1:29–33 (Moses)
Moses advocates to Yahweh	14:11–19	—
Yahweh's judgment presented to Moses	14:20–25	1:34–36
Yahweh's judgment presented to Israel	14:26–35	—
Moses prevented from entering land	—	1:37
younger generation spared	14:31	1:39
remain in the desert	14:34–35	1:40
plague against the ten scouts	14:36–38	—
the people's ill-advised invasion	14:39–45	1:41–46

The major difference between the two versions turns on Num 13–14 emphasizing public, collective failure and Deut 1 private, personal rebellion. Many of the major interpretive differences between the versions of rebellion at Kadesh in Numbers and Deuteronomy pivot on the use of private versus public space. In certain respects the rebellion at Kadesh in Num 13–14 functions as an apologetic for its corporate condemnation. In Numbers the rebellion of the people takes place in public—readers listen to the scouts along with Israel. But in Deuteronomy they reach the decision in the privacy of their own tents—auditors and readers hear the scouts' reports refracted through grumbling individuals (Deut 1:27–28). Where Numbers offers an accelerated presentation of the rebellion, Deuteronomy unfolds the people's systematic investigation, private personal deliberation, and defiant lack of faith.

Some of the most significant interpretive interventions in the re-presentation of the Kadesh infidelity in Deut 1 can be grouped under shifts in agency, but these shifts occur within a revoicing. Moses transitions from a character within a third-person narrative in Num 13–14 to a first-person narrative reminiscer in Deut 1. Though the narrator of Deuteronomy frames Moses's recollections with occasional updates, the only character to speak in Deut 1–11 is Moses. All other embedded discourses, whether Yahweh's or Israel's, are mediated within Moses's reporting voice.[23]

Within Moses's first-person version of the Kadesh rebellion in Deut 1, he speaks directly to the congregation of Israel before him in the second person.[24] The direct communication between Moses and Israel heightens the intensity of accusation and responsibility without need for background narrator commentary. Table D3 summarizes the differences of expressed agency in the surface of the synoptic narratives of rebellion.

TABLE D3: EXPRESSED AGENCY IN SYNOPTIC VERSIONS OF INFIDELITY AT KADESH‡

	Numbers 13–14	**Deuteronomy 1**
idea for reconnaissance	Yahweh (13:1–2)	Israel (1:22)
approval of scouting report initiative	—	Moses (1:23)
encouragement to military action	Caleb (13:30)	Moses (1:20–21)
attempt to dissuade Israel from infidelity	Joshua and Caleb (14:6–9)	Moses (1:29–33)
attempt to dissuade Yahweh from wrath	Moses (14:13–19)	—
responsible for judgment of Moses	Moses (20:12)[a]	Israel (1:37)[b]
attempt to dissuade Israel from unsanctioned invasion	Moses (14:41–43)	Yahweh (1:42)

‡ Table adapted from Schnittjer, "Kadesh Infidelity," 111.

a The narrators of Numbers and Deuteronomy repeatedly cite Yahweh's condemnation of Moses's sin as the reason for disallowing him entrance into the land of promise (Num 20:12; 27:14; Deut 32:51–52; cf. 34:4).

b Three times Moses blames Israel for Yahweh's disallowing him entry into the land of promise (Deut 1:37; 3:26; 4:21).

It seems tempting to think Israel's desire for reconnaissance of the land in Deut 1:22 may be a way for them to find an excuse to back out. If the people already had "mutinous intent," the language—"You (plural) came to me"—runs identical to their approach to Moses after hearing the divine pronouncement of the Ten Words that God affirmed as

23. See Robson, *Deuteronomy 1–11*, 4.

24. The present approach follows the norm of treating the frequent shifts between second-person plural and singular in Deuteronomy as literary emphases to underscore personal responsibility and collective identity. Nelson suggests the alternations only help diachronic concerns in Deut 4 and 12 (*Deuteronomy*, 5–6). The present study does note units of Deut 12 based on the mostly consistent criterion of singular/plural second-person focus (see ad loc.). For a summary of views on this issue, see Grisanti, "Deuteronomy," 2:486. With respect to similar grammatical fluctuations in Ezek 43–48, Greenberg notes ancient evidence (Temple Scroll, Hittite, ancient Aramaic documents) that demonstrates grammatical interchange by the same author, including vacillation between second-person singular and plural ("Design," 185–89).

"good" (5:23, 28; cf. 1:23).[25] Thus, the context of Deuteronomy itself does not condemn the people's initiative.

Moses affirms the solidarity of his congregation and the previous generation with a first-person plural narrative verb: "We set out from Horeb" (1:19).[26] Then Moses reverts to second-person address: "You saw" (1:19).[27] He lays the responsibility upon Israel standing before him: "You were not willing to go up and you rebelled against the word of Yahweh your God" (1:26 lit.). Moses brings his auditors (and the readership) into the tents of the rebels and explains to them what they themselves had said in private: "You grumbled in your tents and you said, '*Because Yahweh hates us* he brought us out of the land of Egypt to give us into the hand of the Amorites'" (1:27 lit., emphasis mine). In private the people categorically reverse Moses's teaching on Yahweh's motivation for covenantal fidelity (7:8)—hatred versus love.[28] Moses further invades Israel's personal space by giving voice to their private fears and motives that they express in their own tents: "Our fellows [scouts] have caused our hearts to melt, saying, 'The people are greater and more numerous than us, with cities large and fortified to the heavens'" (1:28 lit.; cf. note on Josh 2:9). With respect to responsibility, Moses eliminates blaming collective decisions made in public.

Moses goes on to blame the people for his own punishment. This surprising claim stands apart from the various narrative moves discussed above as a special case. Moses did not slip up. He made the same claim three times—and it is not a grammatical issue since he says it in three different ways. Even after Yahweh told him never to speak of it again to him, Moses continues to repeat it to his hapless congregation (italics signify similar syntactic structure even with lexical differences):[29]

> Even *against me Yahweh became angry because of you*, saying "Even you shall not enter there." (Deut 1:37 lit.)
>
> *Yahweh became angry against me because of you*, and he refused to listen to me, and Yahweh said to me, "Enough from you. Do not again speak to me concerning this matter." (3:26 lit.)
>
> *Yahweh was angry against me on your account.* (4:21 lit.)

25. See Weinfeld, *Deuteronomy 1–11*, 143.

26. See Robson, *Deuteronomy 1–11*, 38.

27. See Nelson, *Deuteronomy*, 26.

28. See Carpenter, "Literary Structure," 81.

29. Although the English translation of Moses's blaming Israel in Deut 1:37; 3:26; 4:21 looks very similar in most modern versions, they are worded differently. In Deut 3:26, *HALOT* regards II עבר as a rare root for "anger" (2:781). Since I עבר literally means "cross over," Robson puns, "Yahweh was very cross with me" (*Deuteronomy 1–11*, 122).

Moses's claims push up against the viewpoint of the narrator. The controlling frame-narrative of Deuteronomy repeats the twofold judgment of Yahweh in Numbers against Moses.

> Yahweh said to Moses and Aaron, "Because you did not trust me . . . you shall not bring this congregation to the land." (Num 20:12 lit.)
>
> [Yahweh says] "You [Moses and Aaron] contended against me." (27:14 lit.)
>
> [Yahweh says] "Because you acted unfaithfully against me . . . you shall not enter the land." (Deut 32:51–52 lit.)

Moses's threefold blaming of Israel for his own breach of faith creates a difficult irony. This context features Moses strenuously trying to assign responsibility to his congregants personally, noting the birthing of rebellion in their own tents. Amid such a context Moses shirks his own guilt, blaming his congregants. This forces readers to recognize that while Moses is special—there is no other prophet like him (Num 12:6–8)—he stands under divine judgment for his rebellion like anyone else. If Moses pushes on Israel to take personal responsibility for rebellion, readers realize Moses should do the same thing. Moses's hypocrisy does not undermine his point so much as amaze readers by demonstrating the susceptibility of anyone to make excuses, even someone like Moses. The inclusion of Moses's deflection of responsibility within his lengthy condemnation of Israel deepens the irony and increases the attention such a claim requires from readers.[30]

In sum, whereas Num 13–14 offers a strong case against the collective guilt of Israel, aptly justifying the forty-year death sentence in the wilderness, Deut 1 frames the rebellion in terms of personal responsibility. Deuteronomy lets readers listen in on Moses's condemnation of the congregation as they prepare to enter the land of promise. Like the congregation, Deuteronomy's readers need to be warned of the danger of lingering over rebellious thoughts that lead to unfaithfulness.

1:46–2:23/~/Num 21 (not warring against Edom, Moab, and Ammon). The synoptic text of Deut 1 includes little shared material with its counterpart in Numbers. Note a synoptic comparison of Israel's travels in the Transjordanian wilderness:

	Numbers	**Deuteronomy**
encampment in Kadesh	20:1	1:46
Yahweh's suggestion to travel around Edom	—	2:1–7
request to pass through Edom met with hostility	20:14–21	—

30. On the psalmist's handling of Moses's deflection of blame in Ps 106:33, see note on Ps 106.

	Numbers	Deuteronomy
leaving behind Ezion Geber[a]	—	2:8a
Aaron's death and burial at Mount Hor	20:22–29	—
captivity but then victory over Arad	21:1–3	—
traveling around Edom	21:4	—
snake infestation	21:5–9	—
camp at Oboth and Iye Abarim	21:10–11	—
Yahweh's warning not to harass Moab	—	2:8b–12[b]
crossing wadi Zered	21:12	2:13–16
Yahweh's warning not to harass Ammon	—	2:17–23[b]
travels and poems on the way to Pisgah	21:13–20	—

[a] Ezion Geber (not mentioned in Num 20) precedes Kadesh/Zin and Mount Hor in Num 33:35–36.

[b] Note the narrator's updates in Deut 2:10–12, 20–23.

The substantial expanded materials in Deuteronomy affirm Yahweh's will in granting the respective lands to Edom, Moab, and Ammon (Deut 2:5, 9, 19). Yahweh's warnings to Moses reveal his international interests.

To these revelatory pluses, the narrator of Deuteronomy added additional pluses.[31] The main import of the narrator's pluses are updates to help later readers assimilate the details of the people groups. The updates look back some distance to the days of Joshua's conquest (2:12). The most startling updates are the comparisons of the giant peoples akin to the Anakites driven out of the respective lands of Moabites, Ammonites, and Edomites. "They were a people strong and numerous, and *as tall as the Anakites. Yahweh destroyed them from before* the Ammonites, who drove them out and settled in their place" (2:21, emphasis mine; cf. 2:11–12, 22). These brief notices regarding Yahweh's assistance to Israel's own rivals, giving victory over the very same kinds of Canaanites before whom Israel cowered (cf. 1:26–28), put Israel's rebellion in an even more negative light.

In sum, the barest of details regarding itineraries of battles that never happened provide a framework for extensive interpretive additions, accenting both Yahweh's international sovereign interests and putting Israel's embarrassing failure into sharp relief.

2:24–3:20/~/Num 21:21–35 (conquest of Transjordan). The version of Transjordan conquest in Deuteronomy offers substantial differences from the synoptic counterpart in Numbers. Note a synoptic comparison of the conquest of the kingdoms of Sihon and Og:

31. Narrator updates are typically put in parentheses by translations like the NIV and NRSV (see Deut 2:10–12, 20–23). For a full list of narrator update passages and discussion of related issues, see Schnittjer, *Torah Story*, 459.

	Numbers	Deuteronomy
Yahweh's plan to take possession of Sihon's realm	—	2:24–25
message to Sihon to pass by peacefully[a]	21:21–22	2:26–29
Sihon refuses passage for Israel	21:23a	2:30a
Yahweh hardens Sihon's spirit	—	2:30b–31
Sihon battles Israel at Jabez	21:23b	2:32
Israel devotes Sihon's towns to destruction	—	2:33–35
summary of towns conquered	21:24–26	2:36–37
remembering the ballad singers' taunt songs	21:27–32	—
battle against Og with Yahweh's encouragement	21:33–35	3:1–3
Israel devotes Og's towns to destruction	—	3:4–7
Moses grants the Transjordan to Reuben, Gad and the half-tribe of Manasseh[bc]	—	3:8–20

[a] Note the similarities between the request to pass through Sihon's kingdom (Num 21:22–23; Deut 2:26–29) and the request to pass through Edom (Num 20:17).

[b] Note the narrator's updates in Deut 3:9, 11, 13b–14.

[c] Note similarities on Jair in Deut 3:14 and Num 32:41; cf. Judg 10:3. Also cf. Deut 3:15 and Num 32:39.

The major exegetical adjustments in Deuteronomy appear in the pluses (details not included in Numbers). First, the enmity of Edom and Moab against Israel is softened, or put to political euphemism, in a request for safe passage past the kingdom of Sihon. "Only let us pass through on foot—*as the descendants of Esau, who live in Seir, and the Moabites, who live in Ar, did for us*—until we cross the Jordan into the land Yahweh our God is giving us" (Deut 2:28b–29, emphasis mine). The diplomatic message makes no mention of the large armed forces of Edom that threatened Israel (Num 20:18, 20–21) or Moab's attempts to curse Israel (chs. 22–24).[32] This dramatic expansion emphasizing Israel's efforts at diplomatic solution further accents Sihon as instigator of the battle. This helps soften other new emphases introduced in Deuteronomy's account.

Second, Yahweh hardened the spirit of Sihon, described with language reminiscent of the divine acts of judgment upon the pharaoh's heart. The only two uses of this verb for "harden" in the causative stem (Hif) with Yahweh as subject in Scripture appear in Exod 7:3 and Deut 2:30.[33]

Third, a series of pluses makes explicit the divine will in "giving over" Sihon (Deut 2:33, 36), even emphasizing the strength of the fortified cities (3:5) and the giant size of Og (3:11, narrator's plus). The new details together correspond to some of the reasons for Israel's rebellion at Kadesh rehearsed earlier (1:26–28).

32. Glatt-Gilad suggests ways that Deuteronomy 2 theologically recasts Israel's wilderness encounter with Edom ("Re-Interpretation," 448–52).

33. See the Hif of "harden" (קשה) in Even-Shoshan, 1038, nos. 11, 19.

Fourth, the most striking pluses in Deuteronomy in contrast to Numbers are the uses of the term "to devote" (*hrm* חרם). Deuteronomy includes this holy warfare language in the account of the conquest of the cities of Sihon and Og, explicitly mentioning the killing of all civilians (2:34; 3:6). These pluses seem all the more striking when added to the detail that Israel kept the plunder, including cattle (2:35; 3:7), which is forbidden in the law of devoting (20:16). Michael Fishbane suggests these details of *herem* warfare were intended to align the Transjordanian battles with the laws of devoting in Deuteronomy (see note on 7:1–5).[34]

Also important are the pluses emphasizing further the diplomacy reflected in the accounts of Numbers (2:26–29; cf. Num 21:22). Devoting the towns of the Transjordan is plan B, enacted after diplomacy failed and hurried along as an initially defensive war against the king whose heart had been hardened much like the pharaoh's. In short, the new account of Transjordanian conquest and the law of devoting the nations of Canaan mutually inform each other.

In sum, the narrative of the conquest of the Transjordan in Deuteronomy features many exegetical enhancements. The expansions emphasize the theological rationale for the battles and align the descriptions with the new version of the warfare law in Deut 7.

3:26; 4:21–22~Num 20:12 (C) (Moses blames the people). See notes on Deut 1:19–45; Ps 106:32–33.

4:5–5:33/~/Exod 19–20 (revelation at the mountain). Deuteronomy reproduces the Ten Commandments mostly verbatim. The present note treats the frame narrative and the next note the differences in the Ten Commandments of Deuteronomy. The narrative frame of the revelation at the mountain features extensive expansion in Moses's first-person discourse. The new elements brim full with motivation. Note a synoptic comparison of the revelation at the mountain (the italicized elements signify scriptural allusions, and those marked with ▲ denote revelation at the mountain):

		Deuteronomy
preparations for the revelation	Exod 19	—
exhortation concerning revelation with brief allusions	—	4:5–40
revelation at the mountain ▲	*19:7–24*	*4:10–12, 15*
Ten Commandments ▲	*20:1–17*	*4:13*
book of the covenant ▲	*21–23*	*4:14*
creation	*Gen 1–2*	*4:32*
revelation at the mountain ▲	*Exod 19–20*	*4:33*
deliverance from Egypt	*6–15*	*4:34–35*
revelation at the mountain ▲	*19–20*	*4:36*
deliverance from Egypt	*6–15*	*4:37*
defeat of Transjordanian kingdoms	*Num 21*	*4:38*
Transjordanian cities of refuge	—	4:41–43

(cont.)

34. See Fishbane, *Biblical Interpretation*, 207–8.

		Deuteronomy
revelation not to them but to you here today	—	5:1–5
Ten Commandments	*Exod 20:1–17*	*5:6–21*
Moses selected as mediator for the people	*20:18–21*	*5:22–33*
altar law[a]	20:22–26	—

[a] Deuteronomy may treat the altar law of Exod 20:24–25 as a prologue to the covenant collection; see note on Deut 12.

Moses infuses the exhortation regarding revelation at the mountain in Deut 4 with a series of broad and/or stereotypical allusions to God's great redemptive acts (see italicized elements in the synoptic comparison above). The retrospective series of allusions to redemptive events are at once impressive and, for the most part, ancillary to the point of the context. The exception appears to be the references to the theophany at the mountain (see items marked by ▲ in the synoptic comparison above). By intersplicing the revelation at the mountain with other works of Yahweh, Moses aligns the revelation with the mighty acts of creation, redemption, and conquest of the land of promise.

Moses's long exhortation intermixes motivation and retrospective allusions (Deut 4:5–40). Table D4 distinguishes quantity of motivation versus allusion in the exhortation.

TABLE D4: RETROSPECTIVE ALLUSIONS VERSUS MOTIVATION IN DEUTERONOMY 4

12 verses:	Retrospective allusions to Yahweh's mighty works	Deut 4:10–12, 13, 14, 15, 32, 33, 34–35, 36, 37, 38
21 verses:	Sermonic motivation	Deut 4:5–9, 16–31, 39–40

The imbalance of motivation versus retrospective summary aptly signals the exegetical significance of the use of scriptural traditions in this context. These mostly stereotypical broad allusions together serve the motivational goals of Moses's exhortation. A path forward toward righteous obedience begins by remembering the great works God has done for his people.

The bold, counterintuitive claims of Moses in the beginning of Deut 5 rightly give readers pause. He refers to the Ten Commandments as "this covenant." Moses uses five-fold repetition for clarity (marked by commas and period):

Not with our ancestors did Yahweh cut this covenant,
  but with us,
  us,
  these here today,
  all of us alive (5:3 lit.).[35]

35. Note the Masoretic disjunctive accents on the non-grayed out words which have been marked as commas in translation above (לֹ֣א אֶת־אֲבֹתֵ֔ינוּ כָּרַ֥ת יְהוָ֖ה אֶת־הַבְּרִ֣ית **הַזֹּ֑את** כִּ֣י **אִתָּ֔נוּ** **אֲנַ֨חְנוּ** אֵ֥לֶּה פֹ֛ה **הַיּ֖וֹם** כֻּלָּ֥נוּ חַיִּֽים׃, Deut 5:3).

The multiple repetitions might be something like all caps, which should stifle auditors' desire to say "What?!" Auditors might want to explain that most of them were born within the forty years after the revelation of the Ten Commandments at the mountain. And those over forty were too young and were not held accountable for the community's treachery against their God which is why they are not buried in the wilderness with the rebellious generation.

But Moses pushes forward. The direct theophany Moses has in mind is captured in his next statement: "*Face to face* Yahweh spoke *with you* at the mountain from the midst of the fire" (5:4 lit., emphasis mine).[36] The use of "fire" provides an important connection to the long description of the significance of the revelation Moses had just delivered (4:12; cf. 4:15, 33, 36). While it may be impossible to do justice to this profound point expressed strongly, a few observations relative to the implications for scriptural exegesis will need to suffice here.

First, and most important, the unmistakably direct language for an arguably indirect experience signifies the enduring reality of the covenant at the mountain with the congregation standing before Moses at the river. Excusing themselves by claiming the covenant was with their parents is eliminated.

Second, the direct revelatory experience mediated indirectly, in this case through the witness of Moses and presumably their parents, provides an analog for their own mediatorial role in instructing the next generation. "Only be careful, and watch yourselves closely so that you do not forget the things your eyes have seen or let them fade from your heart as long as you live. *Teach them to your children* and to their children after them" (4:9, emphasis mine; cf. 6:6–9, 20–25; 11:18–21). Later readers are likewise directly responsible based upon the revelatory implications mediated indirectly through the now written word of Torah and the testimony of the older generation.

Third, the importance of the testimony of Yahweh's mighty works to the present generation requires their devotion to his covenantal will because they saw with their own eyes (11:7) what their children have not seen (11:2), namely, terrors against Egypt (11:2–3), deliverance at the sea (11:4), and provision and rebellion in the wilderness (11:5–6). Deuteronomy, it seems, plays it both ways. The mediated revelation counts as direct revelation for the purposes of covenantal responsibility (5:1–4), and the absence of direct experience by the next generation also bears on their responsibility to teach (11:2, 7). Though logical and/or literary issues linger in Deuteronomy's stunning exegesis of scriptural traditions, the implications at every turn drive home covenantal responsibility upon the congregation.

The narrative following the Ten Commandments has been significantly expanded in Deuteronomy's version (cf. Exod 20:18–21; Deut 6:22–33). One new section of narrative uncovers the motives of the people when they suggested that Moses become the

36. The "face to face" (פָּנִים בְּפָנִים) language is nearly identical to the description of Moses's revelatory experiences referred to in Deut 34:10 with a synonymous preposition "to" (פָּנִים אֶל־פָּנִים). Other important examples of theophany using this language include Jacob (Gen 32:30) and Moses (Exod 33:11). In one place an even more intimate statement "mouth to mouth" (פֶּה אֶל־פֶּה) is used to denote the higher revelation of God to Moses than to lesser prophets (Num 12:8). See also Num 7:89; Judg 6:22; and Ezek 20:35.

permanent mediator to prevent further direct address from the divine revelation at the mountain. Moses frames it:

> And you said, "Yahweh our God has shown us his glory and his majesty, and we have heard his voice from the fire. *Today we have seen that a person can live even if God speaks with them*. But now, *why should we die?* This great fire will consume us, and we will die if we hear the voice of Yahweh our God any longer. For what mortal has ever heard the voice of the living God speaking out of fire, as we have, and survived?" (5:24–26, emphasis mine)

The irrational fear of the congregation is captured by the contradiction between their recognition that they have survived the revelation and their desire to avoid dying by revelation. Moses does not explain whether these competing ideas are from different parts of the community.[37] More importantly, the desire to escape targets the unique element of their relationship with God (cf. 4:33, 36).

Yahweh affirms their request. Moses said, "Yahweh heard you when you spoke to me, and Yahweh said to me, 'I have heard what this people said to you. *Everything they said was good*'" (5:28, emphasis mine). This divine response stands in a line of relational affirmations (1:14, 23; 5:28). The dynamic covenantal relationship, especially Yahweh's willingness to make adjustments at the people's request, runs across the retelling of narratives in Deuteronomy. The present case is especially important, for it establishes the historic revelatory event at the mountain as the impetus for the expectation for a prophet like Moses (see notes on 18:15–18; 34:10–12).

In sum, the manifold allusions in the frame narrative of Deuteronomy's version of the Ten Commandments press motivation beyond the normal limits of logic. Yahweh also adjusts his revelatory approach based on the request of his people. These important exegetical interventions underscore how the covenantal relationship triggers advancement of revelation. The overriding interpretive goals of the frame narrative in Deut 4–5 include motivation to obey and motivation to teach.

5:6–21//Exod 20:1–17 (Ten Commandments). The presentation of the Ten Commandments in Deuteronomy differs from the version in Exodus in the case of commandments four, five, and ten. The differences themselves sometimes trouble interpreters. The revelation of the Ten Commandments at the mountain is unique, unprecedented, and unparalleled, as Moses has been explaining at some length in Deut 4 and 5 (see previous note). Of all God's revelations, it is remarkable that the Ten Commandments get adjusted.

The variations in the two versions of the Ten Commandments themselves testify to the realities of progressive revelation. The repetition of the Ten Commandments points to the enduring authority of Yahweh's commanding will. The variations therein simultaneously signify Yahweh's sovereignty over his dynamic covenantal relationship with his people.

---

37. Though Torah typically treats all of Israel together, occasionally subsegments are isolated (see, e.g., Num 11:4).

The **fourth commandment** in Exodus includes a rationale clause based on the creational paradigm. Yahweh made the Sabbath holy for Israel because he rested after creating the heavens and the earth (Gen 2:2–3; Exod 20:11). Deuteronomy re-presents the Sabbath command, retaining "keep it holy" (Exod 20:8//Deut 5:12) and filling out the application from the covenant collection and other adjustments (Exod 23:12; 31:12–17; Deut 5:14) but switching out the rationale. The necessity of granting rest to working animals and slaves provides a weekly memorial of Yahweh's mercy in redeeming Israel (Deut 5:15). Notice the twofold overt marking of "as Yahweh your God has commanded you" signaling the interpretive interventions in Deuteronomy as receptor context (italics and underlining signify verbal parallels, broken underlining signifies overt marking of allusion, and bold signifies new elements):[38]

> *Remember the Sabbath day by keeping it holy.* [9] *Six days you shall labor and do all your work,* [10] *but the seventh day is a sabbath to Yahweh your God. On it you shall not do any work, neither you, nor your son or daughter, nor your male or female servant, nor your animals, nor any foreigner residing in your towns.* [11] For in six days Yahweh made the heavens and the earth, the sea, and all that is in them, but he rested on the seventh day. Therefore Yahweh blessed the Sabbath day and made it holy. (Exod 20:8–11)

> Six days do your work, but on the seventh day do not work, so that your ox and your donkey may rest, and so that the slave born in your household and the foreigner living among you may rest and be refreshed. (23:12 lit.)

> Observe the Sabbath, because it is holy to you. Anyone who desecrates it is to be put to death; those who do any work on that day must be cut off from their people. . . . The Israelites are to observe the Sabbath. (31:14, 16a)

> Observe *the Sabbath day by keeping it holy,* as Yahweh your God has commanded you. [13] *Six days you shall labor and do all your work,* [14] *but the seventh day is a sabbath to Yahweh your God. On it you shall not do any work, neither you, nor your son or daughter, nor your male or female servant,* **nor your ox, your donkey** *or* **any** of *your animals, nor any foreigner residing in your towns,* so that **your male and female servants** may rest, **as you do.** [15] *Remember* **that you were slaves in Egypt and that Yahweh your God brought you out of there with a mighty hand and an outstretched arm.** Therefore Yahweh your God has commanded you to observe *the Sabbath day.* (Deut 5:12–15)

Achenbach makes an excavative argument that the version of the fourth commandment in Exod 20:8–11 combines part of the version from Deut 5:1–15 with the creational

38. Also see Sabbath network.

rationale from Gen 2:2–3.[39] Achenbauch does not explain the parallels between "so that . . . may rest" (Exod 23:12//Deut 5:14) or "observe" and/or "to observe" (Exod 31:14, 16//Deut 12, 15). It is highly unlikely that the fourth commandment from Deut 5:12–15 was imported into Exod 20:8–11 except for the wording that just happened to migrate into 23:12 and 31:14, 16. The reverse makes much better sense of the evidence for direction of dependence, namely, that the fourth commandment of Exodus served as donor context for Deut 5:12–15 and was augmented by elements from other commands regarding the Sabbath. In addition, and even more importantly, the version of the fourth commandment in Deuteronomy features two overt markings of allusion, strongly indicating it is the receptor context (Deut 5:12, 15).

Deuteronomy's version of the **fifth commandment** features added motive clauses. In this case the motive clauses are added to motivation within the Exodus version of the commandment (italics signify verbatim parallels, underlining signifies added motivation, and broken underlining signifies overt marking of citation):

> *Honor your father and your mother, so that you may live long in the land Yahweh your God is giving you.* (Exod 20:12)

> *Honor your father and your mother,* as Yahweh your God has commanded you, *so that you may live long* and that it may go well with you *in the land Yahweh your God is giving you.* (Deut 5:16)

The **tenth commandment** includes three minor adjustments: rearrangement with the neighbor's spouse set off to head the list, change of the verb for the rest of the list, and the addition of land (italics signify verbatim parallels, underlining signifies an addition, and broken underlining signifies a change in wording).

> You shall not covet *your neighbor's house. You shall not covet your neighbor's wife, or his male or female servant, his ox or donkey, or anything that belongs to your neighbor.* (Exod 20:17)

> *You shall not covet your neighbor's wife.* You shall not set your desire on *your neighbor's house* or land, *his male or female servant, his ox or donkey, or anything that belongs to your neighbor.* (Deut 5:21)

The first two changes effectively set apart internal dispositions regarding a neighbor's spouse versus property. These changes have not been explained adequately. The following speculative suggestion seeks to explain why Deuteronomy sets apart and emphasizes not coveting a neighbor's spouse from other coveting. Perhaps this can be explained in terms

39. See Achenbach, "Sermon," 874–75.

of the difference in criminal penalties. Adultery merits capital punishment but theft lesser penalties. A comparative analogy between scriptural criminal punishments versus those in ancient counterparts may indirectly support this suggestion.

Israel's law stands apart from other ancient legal collections in terms of inverted human versus economic priorities. In Mesopotamian law collections, breaking and entering and theft are capital crimes (e.g., CH §§6, 22). Conversely, crimes against property in the Scriptures are not punishable by death (though killing intruders in self-defense is permitted, Exod 22:2[1]). Also, note the contrast between the relative leniency of cutting off a child's hand who strikes the child's father (CH §195; cf. §193) versus the death penalty (Exod 21:15; cf. 21:17; Deut 21:18–21). The leniency relative to property cases and severity in cases involving human life in Scripture and vice versa in other ancient legal collections signify different values. Table D5 summarizes economic versus human valuation in scriptural and other ancient Near Eastern legal collections (brackets help highlight contrasts).

TABLE D5: ECONOMIC VERSUS HUMAN VALUE IN SCRIPTURAL LAW VERSUS ANCIENT COUNTERPARTS‡

Legal Collection	Financial Penalty	Death Penalty	Other
Hittite Law	homicide, assault/battery causing miscarriage	[theft, bestiality]	no punishment for justified homicide
Middle Assyrian Law	homicide	[theft]	literal corporal punishment; legalized violence, multiple punishment
Law Collection of Hammurabi	bodily injury, accidental homicide	[theft/cheating, adultery (choice of offended party)]	literal punishment; equal measure (*talion*) only for social equals[a]
Torah	[property crimes]	intentional homicide; sexual crimes; and religious crimes against God	no literal punishment (financial equivalent); equal measure (*talion*) for all free persons (not for slaves)[b]

‡ Table adapted from Christine Hayes, https://youtu.be/iJ5qYM24vUA (25:39) (accessed 3.1.15). Hayes discusses many details elsewhere without the diagram (see *Introduction*, 135–46, esp. 145–46). Also see Greenberg, "Some Postulates," 31–33.

[a] For literal measure for measure see CH §§196, 197, 200. For financial equivalents see LE §42; LU §§18, 19.

[b] See Exod 21:23–25, 26–27; Lev 24:19–20; Deut 19:21.

The different values between human life and personal property in Scripture versus other ancient legal collections may offer an indirect analogy to the rationale an exegetical intervention in the tenth commandment of Deuteronomy. The perceived incongruity of listing coveting someone else's spouse along with other possessions in the tenth commandment in Exodus could give rise to the change in Deuteronomy. While Exodus does not spell out the punishment for adultery, Leviticus and Deuteronomy call for capital punishment

(Lev 20:10; Deut 22:22). The version of the tenth commandment in Deuteronomy may set apart coveting a neighbor's spouse since acting on this longing is a categorically greater crime than acting on lesser coveting (coveting a neighbor's spouse/adultery > coveting neighbor's belongings/stealing). Whether this speculation is so or not, the new version of the tenth commandment strengthens emphasis upon the fidelity required of the marriage covenant.

7:1–5*~Exod 34:11–16* (B) (law of devoting nations of Canaan and prohibition against intermarriage) (* see assembly, attribute formula, and devoting networks). Torah's two prohibitions against intermarriage share stock phrases and common words (like the list of the nations of Canaan) that may be set aside relative to determining a relationship. The verbal parallels of destroying the idolatrous icons in this configuration are distinct to these two contexts even with shared locutions elsewhere in Deuteronomy (Exod 34:13; Deut 7:5).[40] The verbal and syntactical parallels between "make (no) covenant" in terms of marital arrangements for sons and daughters, though common terms, suggest an intentional relationship given the subject matter and manifold contextual similarities (Exod 34:12, 15//Deut 7:2; Exod 34:16//Deut 7:3). Note the series of shared elements (emphases signify verbal parallels):

Exodus 34	Deuteronomy 7
[11] Obey what I command you today. I will drive out before you the Amorites, Canaanites, Hittites, Perizzites, Hivites and Jebusites. [12] Be careful lest you **make a covenant** with those who live in the land[a] where you are going, otherwise they will be a snare among you.[b] [13] Break down their altars, break their sacred stones and cut down their Asherah poles. [14] Do not bow down before any other god, for Yahweh, whose name is Jealous, is a jealous God. [15] "Be careful lest you **make a covenant** with those who live in the land; for when they prostitute themselves to their gods and sacrifice to them, they will invite you and you will eat their sacrifices. [16] And when you take some of their daughters for your sons and those daughters prostitute themselves to their gods, they will lead your sons to prostitute themselves to their gods (lit.).	[1] When Yahweh your God brings you into the land you are entering to possess[c] and drives out before you many nations—the Hittites, Girgashites, Amorites, Canaanites, Perizzites, Hivites and Jebusites, seven nations larger and stronger than you—[2] and when Yahweh your God has delivered them over to you and you have defeated them, then you must destroy them totally. **Make no covenant** with them, and show them no mercy. [3] Do not intermarry with them. Do not give your daughters to their sons or take their daughters for your sons, [4] for they will turn your children away from following me to serve other gods, and Yahweh's anger will burn against you and will quickly destroy you. [5] This is what you are to do to them: Break down their altars, break their sacred stones, cut down their Asherah poles and burn their idols in the fire (lit.).

[a] Note the exact duplication of "lest you make a covenant with those who live in the land" in Exod 34:12, 15.

[b] Note the shared language between "otherwise they will be a snare among you" (Exod 34:12 lit.) and "otherwise you be ensnared by it" (Deut 7:25 lit.). This parallel suggests a more complex relationship.

[c] Note the exact duplication of "When Yahweh your God brings you into the land you are entering to possess" in Deut 7:1; 11:29; cf. 6:10.

40. The complex relationship between Deut 7:5, 7:24–26, and 12:3 stands at a literary level and cannot be decided based on interpretive intervention. Compare (emphases refer to verbal parallels): "This is what you are to do to them:

The frame narrative of Deuteronomy overall as well as this section presents Moses as "explaining" and "teaching" Torah (Deut 1:5; 4:44; 6:1). The new version of the instructions regarding settlement of the land makes three significant adjustments. After looking at these, the prohibition against intermarriage will be considered.

First, for the first time "devoting" the nations of Canaan gets added into the legal standards for settling the land.[41] The idea initially comes from Israel. When the king of Arad took some of the Israelites captive, the people made a vow to devote the people of Canaan if Yahweh granted victory, which he did (Num 21:2–3). While the vow of devoting could refer to that specific instance, it winds up being applied much more broadly. The people's vow set a precedent, and Yahweh integrates it into the standards for settling the land (Deut 7:2).[42]

The meaning of the disputed terms "devote" and "what has been devoted" refers to removal from common use and dedicated exclusively to the deity. In the case of goods, they are given over to Yahweh (Lev 27:28; Mic 4:13). In the case of persons in warfare, they are removed from common use as slaves and concubines by death. The killing of all inhabitants of some cities (Josh 10:28, 35, 37, 39) affirms the standard translation in those contexts as "devote to destruction."[43]

The Mesha inscription (ca. 830 BCE) uses the equivalent term *ḥrm* in Moabite, a language corresponding to Hebrew in many respects.

> Then Chemosh said to me [king Mesha], "Go, seize Nebo from Israel." So I went by night and I waged war against it from the break of dawn until midday. I seized it and I killed everyone—seven thousand m[e]n and boys and g[ir]ls and young women of marriageable age—because *I had devoted it* (*ḥḥrmth*) to Ashtar-Chemosh. Then I took from there th[e ves]sels of Yahweh and I dragged them before Chemosh. (14b–18a)[44]

The phrase "because I had devoted it" in the inscription does not denote the killing itself but offers a comment about it.[45] The reason Mesha killed everyone stems from his devoting the city to his god. Mesha's "devoting" is akin to the vow Israel made against the

---

Break down their altars, break their sacred stones, hew down their Asherah poles and *burn their images in the fire*" (Deut 7:5 lit.). "**Break down their altars, break their sacred stones** and burn their Asherah poles in the fire; hew down the images of their gods and wipe out their names from those places" (12:3 lit.). "He will give their kings into your hand, and you will wipe out their names from under the heavens. No one will be able to stand up against you, until you destroy them. [25] *The images of their* gods *you are to burn in the fire*" (7:24–25a lit.).

41. The use of "to devote" (חרם) in Exod 22:20[19] applies to false worship, and those in Lev 27:21, 27, 28, 29; Num 18:14 refer to cultic situations.

42. For a similar storyline on "devoting" the nations of Canaan in Scripture, see Greenberg, "Ḥerem" *EJ* 9:11–12. Also see Fishbane, *Biblical Interpretation*, 204–8. The present discussion is indebted to both of these.

43. The standard Hebrew dictionaries define *ḥrm* (חרם) as "devote to destruction" in reference to warfare contexts and "dedicate to" in contexts where the term is collocated with "to Yahweh" (חרם ליהוה), see "חרם," *CDCH* 133; *HALOT* 1:353–54; BDB 355–56; *TWOT* 1:324–25; *TDOT* 5:180–99; *NIDOTTE* 2:276–77. Contra Walton and Walton, *Lost Conquest*, 168–70. And see Grisanti, *Review*, 257–60, esp. 259.

44. Translation from Green, *Great Works*, 104–5. Ashtar is the male counterpart of Ashtarte/Ishtar here combined with the patron deity Chemosh (Smelik, *COS* 2.23:138, n. 16).

45. See Lohfink, "חרם," *TDOT* 5:189–90.

people of Canaan: "Israel vowed a vow to Yahweh, 'If you indeed deliver this people [of Canaan] into our hands then *we shall devote* their cities'" (Num 21:2 lit., emphasis mine).

The crucial issue for the legal exegesis in the law of devoting in Deut 7:1–2 is that the people initiated devoting the nations of Canaan, not Yahweh (Num 21:2). In the mission spelled out in Exodus, Yahweh promised to "wipe out" and "drive out" (used synonymously) the Canaanite nations (Exod 23:23, 29, 30, 31; 34:11).[46] After Israel's vow to devote the Canaanites, Yahweh holds them to it by including it in the instruction of Deut 7:2 and 20:17.

Second, the legal standard for devoting the nations of Canaan does not stand for all time. It only applies to the time when Israel invades the land. The lead in, "When Yahweh your God brings you into the land," includes a near future expiration date (7:1).[47]

Third, the basis for devoting the nations of Canaan does not relate to ethnicity or genealogical identity but to the protection of Israel from temptation. Moses worries that failing to devote the nations would give them opportunity to teach Israel to serve false gods (7:4; 20:18).

While the temporary standard to devote the nations of Canaan expires after Israel had entered the land (7:1), the prohibition against intermarriage endures (7:3). The version of the law against apostasy marriages in the covenant renewal collection only explicitly speaks against Israel's sons marrying their daughters (Exod 34:16). Though it may be reasonable to think this prohibition applies to males and females alike, Moses spells it out in Deuteronomy (italics signify verbal parallels, and bold signifies additions).

> When *you take* some of their daughters *for your sons* and those daughters. (34:16a lit.)
>
> Do not give **your daughters** to their sons or *take* **their daughters** *for your sons.* (Deut 7:3 lit.)

The inclusive scope of this prohibition gets repeated often in the restoration when the people had a tendency to "marry out" (Ezra 9:12; Neh 10:30[31]; 13:25).

In sum, the legal standard on settling in the land for the first time adds the clause on

---

46. Note: "wipe out" (כחד) (Exod 23:23); "drive out" (גרשׁ) (23:28, 29, 30, 31; 34:11).

47. The issue is not merely the syntactic function of "when" (כִּי) with an impf form which could refer to "beginning at the time" of something ongoing or repeated (e.g., *IBHS* §38.7a, no. 2) or could refer to "at the time" of something that is not ongoing (e.g., *IBHS* §31.1.6b, no. 3). The ongoing versus limited sense of "when" depends on how its associated phrase functions. The exact phrase "when Yahweh (your God) brings you into the land" (כִּי יְבִיאֲךָ יהוה [אֱלֹהֶיךָ] אֶל־הָאָרֶץ) appears five times in Scripture all in Torah (Even-Shoshan, 159, nos. 2398–2402; cf. similar Deut 12:29; 17:14; 19:1; 26:3). Exodus 13:5 refers to an ongoing need to celebrate Passover "*From the time when* Yahweh brings you into the land" (lit., emphasis mine; cf. Exod 13:11). Deuteronomy 6:10 refers to the situation of seizing houses, cisterns, vineyards, etc., that only applies to initial entry: "*When* Yahweh your God *initially* brings you into the land" (lit., emphasis mine). Deuteronomy 11:29 refers to a one-time ceremony: "*At the time when* Yahweh your God brings you into the land" (lit., emphasis mine). The function of this phrase in Deut 7:2 fits with the uses in 6:10 and 11:29 referring to the initial entry into the land, as the following verses demonstrate. The presumed failure of Israel to obey the command in Deut 7:2 is handled in 7:3–4 (following after Exod 34:15–16) by forbidding apostasy marriages. If Israel would have devoted the nations of Canaan to destruction (plan A) there would be no need to prohibit intermarrying with them (plan B).

devoting the nations of Canaan in line with Israel's precedent-setting vow. The temporary standard to devote the nations of Canaan only applies to the time when Israel comes into the land. The purpose of the law does not relate to genealogical purity but protection against infidelity against Yahweh. The prohibition against intermarriage makes explicit the gender inclusive application of the standard.

7:9–10*~5:9–10*//Exod 20:5–6* (B) (a faithful God) (* see attribute formula network). Deuteronomy 7:9–10 shares substantial verbal and syntactic elements with the transgenerational threat of the second commandment, which makes a relationship highly likely (emphases signify verbal parallels):

> You shall not make for yourself an image in the form of anything in heaven above or on the earth beneath or in the waters below. You shall not bow down to them or serve them; **for** I, **Yahweh your God**, am a jealous **God**, punishing the iniquity of the parents upon the children to the third and fourth generation of <u>those who hate</u> me, but showing *loyalty to thousands of those who love* me *and keep* my *commandments.* (Exod 20:4–6// Deut 5:8–10 lit.)[48]

> Know therefore **that Yahweh your God** he is God; a faithful **God**, keeping the covenant and *loyalty to those who love* him *and who keep* his *commandments to a thousand* generations. But repaying <u>those who hate</u> him to their face by destruction; he will not be slow to repay to their face <u>those who hate</u> him. (Deut 7:9–10 lit.)

The transgenerational threat against those who worship images initiated a couple interpretive interventions in Exodus. The attribute formula uses "Yahweh, Yahweh, *a compassionate and gracious God*" (Exod 34:6†, emphasis mine) to play off "I, Yahweh your God, am *a jealous God*" (20:5, emphasis mine). The prohibition against apostasy marriage in the covenant renewal collection picks up and strengthens the language from the transgenerational threat "Yahweh whose name is Jealous, he is *a jealous God*" (34:14, emphasis mine). In the context of its own version of the prohibition against intermarriage, Deuteronomy says, "Yahweh your God, he is God; *a faithful God*" (Deut 7:9, emphasis mine). Each context builds its interpretive allusions on the character of Yahweh himself.

The term "faithful" when used of humans gets at integrity (1 Sam 2:35). Yahweh's own fidelity in the present context means both "keeping the covenant loyally" to Yahweh-lovers and that someone else does not pay for a person's disobedience of his commands (Deut 7:9, 10). He pays back Yahweh-haters to their faces. The reason for the chiastic

48. Three differences: (1) Exod 20:4 has a conjunctive *vav* not in Deut 5:8, namely, "you shall not make for yourself an image *or* (וְ) any likeness" (Exod 20:4 lit.) versus "you shall not make for yourself an image of any likeness" (Deut 5:8 lit.). (2) Deut 5:9 has a conjunctive *vav* not in Exod 20:5, namely, "upon the children *and* (וְ) upon the third and fourth generation" (Deut 5:9 lit.) versus "upon the children, upon the third and fourth generation" (Exod 20:5 lit.). (3) *Ketiv* of Deut 5:10 says "his commandments" but *qere* has "my commandments" matching Exod 20:6.

shape of Deut 7:10 seems to be a way to twice say the main exegetical point: "(a) repaying (b) those who hate him to their face, by destruction he will not be slow, (b) to those who hate him to their face (a) he will repay him" (7:10 lit., in Hebrew word order).

Yahweh's faithfulness to punish those who hate him does not replace his jealousy in the transgenerational threat. Interpretation in Deuteronomy works by supplement and advancement, not replacement. Deuteronomy repeatedly affirms that Yahweh is jealous (4:24; 5:9; 6:15). The burden of the exegetical advancement in Deut 7:9 turns on explaining that Yahweh punishes those who deserve it.

9:8–10:11/~/Exod 32; 34 (rebellion of Horeb/Sinai). The frame narrative of Deut 9–10 sets the people on the plains of Moab with Moses explaining and teaching Torah (Deut 9:1; cf. 1:5; 4:44; 6:1). Moses tells them of the rebellion at the mountain with some dischronologized elements along the way. Note a synoptic comparison of the rebellion at Horeb strictly following the account in Deuteronomy (underlining signifies dischronologized previews, and stylized brackets signify references out of sequence):

		Deuteronomy
preview of Yahweh's wrath	—	9:8
forty days to get two tablets of the covenant	Exod 24:15–18; 31:18	9:9–11
Yahweh threatens to blot out Israel	32:7–10	9:12–14
Moses goes down and breaks the tablets	32:15–19	9:15–17
Moses repents for second forty days	{34:8, 28}	9:18–20
turning the calf to dust in the steam	32:20	9:21
rebellion at Massah, and elsewhere[a]	{17:1–7}	9:22
rebellion at Kadesh[b]	{Num 13–14}	9:23–24
prayer of repentance during second forty days	{Exod 32:11–14; 34:9[d]}	9:25–29[d]
second tablets with Ten Words	34:1–4, 27–28	10:1–5
death of Aaron	{Num 20:22–29}	10:6–7
setting apart Levites[c]	{3:11–13//8:16–18}	10:8–9
Moses repents during second forty days	{Exod 32:11–14; 34:9[d]}	10:10–11[d]

[a] On the rebellion at Massah also see Deut 6:16. Exodus 17:7 says Meribah and Massah; cf. Meribah in Num 20:13. The difficulties include the terms *meribah* meaning "contend" and *massah* "test"—key terms in these contexts.

[b] On Kadesh infidelity also see Deut 1:19–45; cf. Num 26:65; 32:8–14; Deut 2:14–15; 8:2.

[c] Setting apart the Levites is confirmed in Num 18:2–6.

[d] Exodus 32:11–14 features a prayer of repentance apparently before Moses came down with the first set of tablets during the first forty days on the mountain, 32:31–32 sometime later, and 34:9 when Moses was on the mountain with the second set of tablets during the second forty days. It is unclear if the prayer in Deut 9:25–29 (and/or 10:10–11) is a flashback to the prayer of the first forty days, the prayer after the first forty days, or of the second forty days (Deut 9:25–29 = Exod 32:11–14 or 32:31–32 or 34:9?). Deuteronomy 9–10 does not mention a prayer during the first forty days, but many elements are not chronologically arranged in Moses's reminiscence.

Christine Hayes makes a detailed comparison of Exod 32 and Deut 9–10 that offers a convenient point of reference for the present purposes.[49] While it is easy to agree with most of Hayes's analysis, a few differences will be noted along the way. She analyzes Exod 32 and finds it coherent and unified over and against many counterclaims (49–71). Hayes regards Deut 9–10 as dependent on Exod 32 in its present form (72). She argues that the differences in Deuteronomy's presentation of the details stem from its goal to discredit Israel, whose incorrigible arrogance has required "Moses' strenuous intercession and God's grace" (73). The summary of Israel's misguided attitude that needs correction can be found in Deut 9:4–5. Driver worries over the mix-up of the language in the prayer in Deut 9:25–29 and that the prayer appears out of sequence compared to Exod 32.[50] Hayes rightly pushes back that the sequence and interpretive adjustments in Deut 9–10 serve its purposes in context (77–78). The evidence in the synoptic table above affirms Hayes's view that chronological sequence fell outside the purposes of Deut 9–10.

Hayes goes on to explain several of the oddities of Deut 9–10 as interpretive solutions motivated by difficulties in Exod 32. She rightly notes that Moses prays for Aaron to soothe Yahweh's wrath in Deut 9:20 to answer the ambivalent treatment of Aaron's role in the golden calf incident in Exod 32 (80).

Hayes takes the next step to explain the seemingly misplaced notations by the narrator in Deut 10:6–9. Modern translations like NIV and NRSV rightly put verses 6–9 in parentheses to indicate that this comment by the narrator in the third person is inserted into Moses's first-person homily. Hayes claims the note on Aaron's death in 10:6 indicates "just punishment for his role in the golden calf incident" (82). This does not work since elsewhere the narrator of Deuteronomy says that Aaron's death and burial on Mount Hor resulted from his sin at Meribah (Deut 32:50–51). That is, the narrator of Deuteronomy agrees with the narrator of Numbers (Num 20:12).

The narrator's comment goes on in Deut 10:8–9 to use the ambiguous marker "at that time" to explain that Yahweh set apart the Levites to minister to him. Hayes suggests that this helps explain how the role of the Levites in the aftermath of the incident with the golden calf set them apart for Yahweh's service in Exod 32:29 (83–84). This suggestion seems to fill in part of the backstory for setting apart the Levites in Num 3:11–13//8:16–18 and 18:2–6.

Hayes suggests that uses of the ancestral promise in the prayers of Exod 32:11–13 and Deut 9:25–29 function differently (77). For Hayes, the prayer of Deut 9:25–29 corresponds better to the chronological place of the prayer in Exod 32:31–32 (78). Perhaps this suggestion comes out of Hayes's limitation to Exod 32. The situation is more complex than her proposal allows. The second set of forty days overlaps with the second set of tablets and its forty days in Exod 34:1–4, 28. It seems better to stick with

49. See Hayes, "Golden Calf Stories," 45–93. References to page numbers hereafter will be parenthetical.

50. See Driver, *Deuteronomy*, 116. See note d in the synoptic parallel above.

the dischronologized format of the discourse in Deut 9–10, especially since the second set of forty days gets mentioned intermittently in 9:18–20, 25–29; 10:10–11 (see stylized brackets which indicate this in the synoptic table and note d above). More importantly, the content of the prayer in Deut 9:25–29 seems much more of a composite representation than Hayes allows for.[51]

Deuteronomy telescopes the details of the two new tablets upon which the Ten Words are re-written "as before" (10:4)—compare the differences in the version in Deut 5 (see note on Deut 5:6–21). Moses makes the ark and places the second set of tablets in it (10:3, 5). The change in agency and dischronologization in comparison to Exod 37:1–9 are typical of synoptic re-presentations for a different purpose (see Hermeneutical Profile of the Use of Torah in Deuteronomy; Table D3). Later Moses puts a scroll with additional torah beside the ark (31:26).

Moses spent at least eighty days on the mountain and a good amount of this time interceding for Israel and Aaron. In addition, Deut 9–10, as Hayes has helpfully demonstrated, loosely engages the thirty-nine-year-old incidents for the purposes of knocking down Israel's pride. The stylized prayer in Deut 9:25–29 pulls from more than one intercessory tradition as well as Moses's own reminiscences of Israel's treachery recounted in Deut 1. Compare several shared locutions in Moses's interpretive representation of his intercession on the mountain (emphases signify verbal parallels):

> But Moses sought the favor of Yahweh his God. "*Yahweh,*" he said, "why should your anger burn against **your people, whom you brought out of Egypt with great power and a mighty hand?** [12] Why should the Egyptians say, 'It was with evil intent that he brought them out, to kill them in the mountains and to wipe them off the face of the earth'? Turn from your fierce anger; relent and do not bring disaster on your people. [13] **Remember your servants Abraham, Isaac and Israel,** to whom you swore by your own self: 'I will make your descendants as numerous as the stars in the sky and I will give your descendants all this land I promised them, and it will be their inheritance forever.'" (Exod 32:11–13)

> [Moses prayed] If you *put* all these people *to death,* leaving none alive, the nations who have heard this report about you will say "*Yahweh was not able to bring* these people *into the land* he promised them on oath, so he slaughtered them *in the wilderness.*" (Num 14:15–16)

> [Moses said] You grumbled in your tents and said, "Yahweh <u>hates</u> us; so <u>he brought</u> us <u>out</u> of Egypt to deliver us into the hands of the Amorites to destroy us." (Deut 1:27)

51. The language from Num 14:16 in Deut 9:28 is one of Driver's concerns (see ibid.).

> I [Moses] prayed to Yahweh and said, "Sovereign *Yahweh*, do not destroy **your people**, your own inheritance that you redeemed by your **great power and brought out of Egypt with a mighty hand.** [27] **Remember your servants Abraham, Isaac and Jacob.** Overlook the stubbornness of this people, their wickedness and their sin. [28] Otherwise, the country from which you brought us will say, 'Because *Yahweh was not able to bring* them *into the land* of which he had told them, and because he hated them, he brought them out *to put them to death in the wilderness.*' [29] But they are your people, your inheritance that you brought out by your great power and your outstretched arm." (9:26–29, v. 28 lit.)

Though it does not show up in English, the inverted word order of "Remember your servants Abraham, Isaac, and Israel/Jacob" suggests a case of Seidel's theory (Exod 32:13//Deut 9:27). Still, the interpretive moves Moses makes in Deut 9:25–29 should not be missed because of the granular connections to two different but related prayers at Horeb and at Kadesh (Exod 32:11–13; Num 14:13–19). Moses's prayer also puts Israel's own words into the mouth of the Egyptians: Yahweh brought out the people because he "hates" them (Deut 1:27; 9:28). This interpretive representation of one small part of Moses's prayers on the mountain helps draw attention to Israel's own embarrassing failures. That is the point. Israel has not interpreted what Yahweh is doing any better than the Egyptians of Moses's prayer life. And the entire purpose of the retrospective in Deut 9–10 is to push back against Israel's self-entitled conceit. They think they are too righteous (9:4–6). Moses's interpretive representation of his intercessions means to help them gain perspective.

In sum, the nonsequential and interpretively stylized retrospective in Deut 9–10 seeks to check Israel's self-indulgent pride. Along the way Moses and the narrator offer a few interpretive helps to perplexing issues in the golden calf incident, like Aaron's sin and setting apart the Levites.

12:2–28*~Exod 20:24*+34:24*+Lev 17:1–9*+17:10–14* (B) (seek the place Yahweh will choose to put his name) (* see place network). The law of the altar immediately precedes the covenant collection in Exod 21–23 (Exod 20:24–25). The instruction for all ritual slaughter at the tent of meeting stands at the head of the holiness collection in Lev 17–26 (Lev 17:1–9). The law of sacrifice at the place Yahweh chooses heads the torah collection in Deut 12–26 (Deut 12:2–28). The legal exegesis in Deut 12 works out the implications of distance when Israel enters the land. The exegetical adjustments turn on the decentralization of Israel in the land of promise more commonly referred to as central worship.

The present study of legal exegesis as presented by Torah evaluates how Deuteronomy begins its major legal collection in relation to the counterparts in Exodus and Leviticus. In this case the direction of dependence is affirmed by two citation formulas, namely, "as I have promised you" (12:20) and "as I have commanded you" (12:21).[52] The first citation formula in verse 20 includes a near verbatim quotation of a phrase from the covenant collection (Exod 34:24; cf. note ad loc.). The reference to Yahweh enlarging Israel's territory highlights the logic of the exegetical advances in Deut 12—the implications of distance to the central shrine. The problem of distance to the shrine in Exod 34:24 gets at the need for being at rest from enemies in order to go on pilgrimages to worship.[53] The problem of distance in Deut 12:20 focuses on the need for profane slaughter when Israel lives far from the place of worship. Notice the first citation formula (bold refers to verbal parallels and broken underlining to marking):

> I will drive out nations before you and **enlarge your territory**, and no one will covet your land when you go up three times each year to appear before Yahweh your God. (Exod 34:24)

> When Yahweh your God **has enlarged your territory** as he promised you, and you crave meat and say, "I would like some meat," then you may eat as much of it as you want. (Deut 12:20)

The next citation formula in verse 21 seems to broadly refer to the altar law by "the place" (Exod 20:24) in relation to slaughter of domestic animals (Lev 17:3). This pair of explicitly marked allusions provides strong evidence for direction of dependence with the laws of the altar and slaughter appearing in Exodus and Leviticus as donor contexts and the law of central worship in Deut 12 as receptor context.

The differences between the altar law of Exod 20:24–26 and the law of centralized worship in Deut 12 serve as an illustrative starting point for Wellhausen's famous documentary hypothesis of the Pentateuch. Wellhausen claims "they differ materially," with the newer law "permitting what had been forbidden, and prohibiting what had been allowed."[54] However, the evidence does not support these claims by Wellhausen.

Deuteronomy does not eliminate the altar law. When making plans for a special ceremony upon entry into the land of promise, Deuteronomy uses the altar law as the starting point (emphases signify verbal parallels):[55]

---

52. As observed by Kilchör, "Sacred," 465 and Mattison, *Rewriting*, 66–67, respectively. For a helpful study of all citation formulas in Deut with a special focus on Deut 12 see Milgrom, "Profane Slaughter," 1–7. While this study shares Milgrom's view that the citation formula establishes Deut 12 as receptor context, his other conclusions go another direction than the present study (Milgrom does not note the use of Exod 34:24 in Deut 12:20).

53. Pitkänen, *Central Sanctuary*, 100–1.

54. Wellhausen, *Prolegomena*, 32, 33.

55. The distinctive verb "wield" to note its absence in using undressed stones for altar making only appears in this sense in Exod 20:25, Deut 27:5, and its counterpart in Josh 8:31 (see "I נוף," *HALOT* 1:682). For a summary of difficulties in Deut 27, see Tigay, *Deuteronomy*, 247, 488–89.

> If you make *an altar of stones* for me, do not build it with hewn stones, for you will defile it if you *wield* a tool on it. (Exod 20:25 lit.)

> Build there *an altar* to Yahweh your God, *an altar of stones.* Do not *wield* any iron tool on them. *Build the altar* of Yahweh your God of unhewn stones and offer burnt offerings on it to Yahweh your God. (Deut 27:5–6 lit.)

The altar of stones spoken of in Deut 27:5–6 cannot be identified with the tabernacle's altar (cf. construction details Exod 27:1–2; 38:1–2).[56] The central worship law of Deut 12 does not entirely get rid of the altar law. Deuteronomy retains the use of the altar law at least on a limited basis.[57]

Still, the central worship instructions of Deut 12 institute substantial changes. The far-reaching effects of central worship and decentralized Israel have a domino effect that requires adjustments in numerous other laws (see place nework).[58] This reality illustrates the enduring authority and relevance of older legal standards within the purview of Deuteronomy. If Deuteronomy retains a place for the altar law even with its critical concern for central worship, then other adjusted laws of Deuteronomy likewise retain the enduring relevance, albeit adjusted, of their scriptural donor legal instructions. This accords with Deuteronomy's self-testimonies as explaining, setting out, and teaching torah (Deut 1:5; 4:4; 6:1; 12:1), as well as posturing itself "in addition to" the Horeb covenant (29:1[28:69]).[59]

Before getting to the exegetical allusions of Deut 12, an alternative reading of the older altar law needs to be considered since it bears directly on the exegetical interventions in Deut 12. Kilchör argues that Exod 20:24 does not speak about local altars. He claims the sense is not "*in every place* where I will cause my name to be honored" but "*for the whole place* where I will cause my name to be honored" (Exod 20:24 lit., emphases mine). Kilchör's argument includes many moving parts: • garden of Eden and burning bush narratives as typological patterns of tabernacle (Gen 1–3; Exod 3); • typological identification of Mount Sinai and tabernacle—"the tabernacle is designated as a movable Sinai"; • rejecting the distributive sense of "all/every" (כָּל) in Exod 20:24; • the replacement of the earthen altar with the tabernacle's altar; • and (especially) all of the preceding to deny

56. Wellhausen does not interact with Deut 27:5–6 in *Prolegomena*. The impossibility of identifying the tabernacle altar with the earthen altar of Exod 20:24–25 undermines Vogt's attempt to argue that Exod 20:24–25 and Deut 12 are saying the same thing (see Vogt, "Centralization," 122–23; as pointed out by Averbeck, "Cult," 247).

57. Others have made this observation, e.g., Niehaus, "Central," 9–10; Foreman, "Sacrifice," 17–19; Block, "What?" 29–31. Excavative diachronic scholarship unhelpfully brackets out evidence that does not fit by claiming the altar of Deuteronomy should be removed either as predeuteronomic or postdeuteronomic (Pitkänen, *Central Sanctuary*, 159–60, n. 222).

58. Many of the legal instructions that change in light of centralized worship are housed in Deut 12–19. Von Rad lists several "centralizing laws": Deut 12; 14:22–29; 15:19–23; 16; 17:8–13; 18:1–8; 19:1–3; cf. 26:12–15 (*Deuteronomy*, 89). Kratz's list includes even more adjusted laws: 12:1–28; 14:22–29; 15:1–18, 19–23; 16:1–18, 18–20; 17:8–13; 18:1–11; 19:1–13, 15–21; 21:1–9; 26:1–16 ("Peg," 253, n. 10). For related laws treated herein, see place network.

59. See extended discussion of this point in Hermeneutical Profile of the Use of Scripture in Deuteronomy.

centralization in Deut 12.[60] The present focus only allows for interaction with two of Kilchör's claims: the sense of "whole" versus "every" in Exod 20:24 and the replacement of the earthen altar with the tabernacle's altar.

First, Kilchör suggests a non-distributive reading of "in the whole place" versus "in every place" in Exod 20:24.[61] Joosten notes that focus cannot be narrowly on the term "all/every" (כָּל) but must include the syntax of its phrase. At issue in this case is "all" + definite noun + relative clause (אֲשֶׁר) with imperfect verb as in "in every/all the place where I will cause my name to be honored (impf)" (בְּכָל־הַמָּקוֹר אֲשֶׁר אַזְכִּיר אֶת־שְׁמִי) (20:24 lit.). When the verb is perfect form in this construction it more likely has the sense of "whole," but the imperfect syntax gets at something hypothetical because it has not happened yet and naturally infers a distributive sense.[62] Consider the parallel syntax of a phrase with an imperfect verb: "At *every place* where we will come (impf) to there, say 'He is my brother'" (Gen 20:13b lit., emphasis mine).[63] Kilchör says he "basically" agrees with this syntactical point but still thinks the distributive does not necessarily apply to Exod 20:24.[64]

Kilchör goes on to a sort of both/and argument, namely, if *kol* (כָּל) is distributive and means "every place," then it should be understood serially referring to a "succession of places," meaning one place at a time.[65] He does not explain how the earthen altar can be erected in a "succession of places" if it is only used once at Sinai and then replaced by, according to Kilchör, the tabernacle's movable replica altar (see below).

Though Kilchör acknowledges that the Septuagint reads Exod 20:24 in a distributive sense—"in every place"—he contends that the Samaritan Pentateuch supports a singular place with "at the place."[66] Kilchör does not acknowledge that the reading in the Samaritan Pentateuch is part of the late layer of sectarian ideology focused on the single shrine at Shechem.[67] In this light the evidence of the Samaritan Pentateuch points in the opposite direction. The Samaritan sectarian scribes needed to "correct" the text of Exod 20:24 since they knew it spoke of an earthen altar "at every place." This evidence favors the

60. See Kilchör, "Sacred," 455–67. Kilchör's excavative diachronic agenda concerning Deut 12 cannot be taken up here.

61. See ibid., 460.

62. See Joosten, "Syntax," 4–6. For a less detailed review of some of the same evidence see Childs, *Exodus*, 447. Both Childs and Joosten reject Gesenius's proposal that the article of "*the* place" of Exod 20:24 was a later scribal addition to neutralize the distributive sense (GKC §127e).

63. Note: "At every place where we will come to there, say 'He is my brother'" (אֶל כָּל־הַמָּקוֹם אֲשֶׁר נָבוֹא שָׁמָּה אִמְרִי־לִי אָחִי הוּא) (Gen 20:13b).

64. See Kilchör, "Sacred," 460.

65. See ibid., 461.

66. See ibid., 460, n. 9. Note: "in every place" (ἐν παντὶ τόπῳ) (Exod 20:24 LXX) and "at the place" (במקום, 20:24 SP). Kilchör does not note that "at every place" in LXX modifies "sacrifice" (θύσετε) in Exod 20:24a rather than "there where I pronounce my name" (οὗ ἐὰν ἐπονομάσω τὸ ὄνομά μου ἐκει) 20:24b as in MT (so Wevers, *Notes on Exodus*, 319).

67. See Knoppers, *Jews and Samaritans*, 207–9; Tigay, "Conflation," 76, and chart, 73; idem, "Empirical," 341. Note that the ancient sectarian emended text "in the place" (במקום) of Exod 20:24 SP accords with "in the place" (בַּמָּקוֹם) of Deut 12:14, 18 MT/SP. For four additional ways the SP of Exod 20:24 was reshaped to conform to elements of Deut 12 see Chavel, "Kingdom," 176. n. 15.

proto-Masoretic Text of Exod 20:24 as the parent text before the scribes of the Septuagint and Samaritan Pentateuch who both understood it in the sense of "at every place."

Second, Kilchör claims the tabernacle's altar replaces the earthen altar. He calls the altar of the tabernacle "a transportable replica" of the earthen altar of Exod 20:24.[68] Kilchör does not acknowledge the lingering reality of the altar law in Deut 27:5–6. The tabernacle's movable altar does not replace the need for special occasional use of earthen altars.

In sum on this point, the evidence affirms the traditional reading of the altar law as referring to making an altar "in every place I cause my name to be honored" (Exod 20:24 lit.).

The central worship law of Deut 12 features interpretive allusions to the altar law of Exod 20:24 and the instructions in Lev 17. In addition, the central worship law of Deut 12 sets out a prerequisite for the temple picked up in the Davidic covenant. Each of these exegetical interventions requires brief attention.

In addition to placement at the head of a law collection, the central worship law of Deuteronomy includes verbal parallels with the altar law, making allusion likely (emphases signify verbal parallels):

> Make an altar of earth for me and sacrifice on it **your burnt offerings** and fellowship offerings, your sheep and goats and your cattle. In every **place** I cause my **name** to be honored, I will come to you and bless you. (Exod 20:24†)

> But you are to seek **the place** Yahweh your God will choose from among all your tribes to put his **Name** there for his dwelling. To that place you must go. . . . Then to **the place** Yahweh your God will choose as a dwelling for his **Name**—there you are to bring everything I command you: **your burnt offerings** and sacrifices, your tithes and special gifts, and all the choice possessions you have vowed to Yahweh. (Deut 12:5, 11)

Whereas the law in Exodus specifies how altars should be built, the counterpart in Deuteronomy emphasizes the altar's location.[69] Deuteronomy retains continuity with the altar law by insisting that sacrifices take place where Yahweh's name dwells. In contrast with the altar law, Deuteronomy envisions a time when Yahweh would choose a specific place for worship.[70]

Deuteronomy 12 often gets divided into four main units—verses 2–7, 8–12, 13–19, and 20–28—with a shift to second-person singular auditors occurring at verse 13.[71] The first three units begin with contrasts (i.e., not *a*, but *b*):

---

68. See Kilchör, "Sacred," 462.

69. See Mattison, *Rewriting*, 40.

70. For detailed interaction with so-called name theology see note on 1 Kgs 8:15–21.

71. See von Rad, *Deuteronomy*, 89, 92; Levinson, *Deuteronomy*, 25–26. Levinson's proposed chiastic structure helps with some of the repetitions: (a) Deut 12:2–7, (b) 12:8–12, (c) 12:13–19, (b) 12:20–28, (a) 12:29–31.

displace the false worship places of the land (12:2–4)
    sacrifice and worship feasts at the place of Yahweh's choosing (12:5–7)
stop your acting according to what is right in your own eyes (12:8–9)
    sacrifice and worship feasts at the place of Yahweh's choosing (12:10–12)
do not offer sacrifices wherever you want (12:13)
    offer all sacrifices at the place Yahweh chooses (12:14)

These contrasts help strengthen the problem of worshiping "anywhere you please" (12:13; cf. vv. 8–9) by aligning it rhetorically with false worship of the other nations that need to be displaced (12:2–4). Though the nations of Canaan may not be worse sinners than other peoples, their proximity to Israel makes them more dangerous (7:4; 9:4–5; 20:18).[72] The third and fourth units (verses 13–19 and 20–28) share a threefold repetition of the same themes (a-b-c, a-b-c):

domestic slaughter of animals decentralized (12:15)[73]
    prohibition against consuming blood (12:16)
        tithes and offerings may only be eaten at place of Yahweh's choosing (12:17–19)
domestic slaughter of animals localized (12:20–22)
    prohibition against consuming blood (12:23–25)
        present sacred donations at place of Yahweh's choosing (12:26–27)

While each of these three broadly overlap with legal standards elsewhere in Torah (see Table D2), the exegetical adjustments in the first two repetitions need brief attention.

Leviticus 17 calls for all slaughter to occur at the tabernacle with the exception of game (Lev 17:13).[74] But even in that case the blood must not be eaten, which accords with the Noahic mandate (Gen 9:4). The blood of game must be "poured out" on the ground, which allows for a parallel with the non-cultic or profane slaughter of domestic animals in Deut 12 (emphases refer to verbal parallels; Lev 17:13–14 here also represents vv. 10–12 with many of the same themes):

> Any Israelite or any foreigner residing among you who hunts any animal or bird that may be eaten must **pour out** the blood and cover it with earth, because *the life* of all *flesh* is its blood. That is why I have said to the Israelites, "***You must not eat the blood*** of any creature, *because the life* of all *flesh is its blood*; anyone who eats it must be cut off." (Lev 17:13–14†)

---

72. See Ford, "Challenge of the Canaanites," 166–69.

73. On the limitation of slaughtering domestic animals at tabernacle see Table D6, n. a in note on Deut 14:3–21 and see first footnote in note on Lev 17:3–9.

74. See previous footnote.

> **But you must not eat the blood**; **pour** it **out** on the ground like water. . . . But be sure you *do not eat the blood, because the blood is the life*, and you must not eat *the life* with *the flesh*. **You must not eat** it; **pour** it **out** on the ground like water. (Deut 12:16, 23–24†; cf. 15:23)

The second-person singular auditors of Deut 12:13–31 remain consistent except for one case. Deuteronomy 12:16 says "you shall not eat" with a plural subject, which matches the second-person plural negative use in Lev 17:14.[75] Within Torah, Deuteronomy seems to use the exception of the game in Lev 17:13 as an analogy for decentralized domestic slaughter. Deuteronomy also retains the mandate to pour out the blood of all animal flesh before consumption, as with the decentralized allowance of game in Leviticus. Deuteronomy's interpretative advances include using the verb for "sacrifice" also of non-sacred slaughter.[76] The minimal effect of this special use of "slaughter" in Deut 12:15, 21 of non-sacred slaughter connotes the legal requirements for pouring out the blood.

Fishbane suggests the provision for non-cultic slaughter sites cannot hide the "blatant contradiction" between the older altar law and the law of centralized worship in Deut 12.[77] Levinson says the reuse of language from the altar law—"In every place" (Deut 12:13; cf. Exod 20:24)—"*camouflages*" Deuteronomy's abrogation of the law. Levinson identifies Deuteronomy's technique as "lemmatic transformation" whereby the language of the altar law has been decontextualized and "atomistically" repurposed (see lemmatic exegesis and atomization in Glossary).[78] Averbeck pushes back, saying, "[t]here is no 'camouflage' here." Averbeck suggests the use of the language of the altar law in Deut 12 does the "opposite" of hiding. "[T]he use of the same lemmas with variants would only highlight the innovations and make the reader fully aware that the author of Deut 12:13–15 was repealing the law of Exod 20:24."[79] While these scholars disagree on the author's intentions for using the language of the older law—cannot hide differences (Fishbane), trying to hide changes (Levinson), trying to draw attention to changes (Averbeck)—they agree that the central worship law does not leave room for the altar law. But from the standpoint of Deuteronomy an adjustment is needed.

Deuteronomy 12 seems to allude to the altar law as part of its proposal of a new reality when Yahweh chooses a place for his name. The centralized place of worship seeks to put

---

75. While Fishbane does not comment on the second-person singular/plural, he notes several other possible interpretive adjustments of Lev 17 in Deut 12 (see *Biblical Interpretation*, 533–34, n. 13). Also see Kilchör, "Wellhausen's," 105–6.

76. See Averbeck, "זבח," OT no. 2 *NIDOTTE* 1:1069; idem, "מִזְבֵּחַ," OT nos. 4, 7, 10, 12, 13, 18 *NIDOTTE* 2:890–97.

77. See Fishbane, *Biblical Interpretation*, 252.

78. See Levinson, *Deuteronomy*, 31 (emphasis original), 33, 34.

79. Averbeck, "Cult," 246.

an end to multiplying worship sites based on personal preferences (Deut 12:8, 13). This still leaves the way open for sanctioned use of earthen altars as taken up elsewhere in Deuteronomy. As noted above, Deut 27:5–6 calls for use of an earthen altar, even alluding to the altar law in Exod 20:25. Whether Deuteronomy envisions using the altar law as a one-time event, an additional option for sanctioned special events, or remaining in effect to supplement the tabernacle until Yahweh chooses the place for his name does not need to be decided here. The point is simply that Deuteronomy's legal exegesis acknowledges the residual authority of its donor scriptural tradition. Deut 12 exegetically advances the legal standards for worship, though Deut 27:5–6 affirms the enduring relevance, albeit modified, for the altar law.

The law of central worship in Deuteronomy does not take effect immediately.[80] The need to stop doing as "we do here today" implies that with the settlement of the Transjordan, Israel is already slaughtering elsewhere than the tabernacle (12:8). The timing for the centralized worship to take place relates to "rest" from enemies which points back to the false worship sites that need to be blotted out in Deut 12:2–4. The Deuteronomistic narrator and Nathan each connect the Davidic promise to the command for centralized worship in Deut 12 (emphases signify verbal parallels):

> You are not to do as we do here today, everyone doing as they see fit, [9] since you have not yet reached the resting place and the inheritance Yahweh your God is giving you. [10] But you will cross the Jordan and settle in the land Yahweh your God is giving you as an inheritance, and he *will give* you *rest from all* your *enemies around* you so that you will live in safety. (Deut 12:8–10)

> After the king was settled in his palace and Yahweh *had given* him *rest from all* his *enemies around* him . . . (2 Sam 7:1)

> I *will* also *give* you *rest from all* your *enemies.* Yahweh declares to you that Yahweh himself will establish a house for you: [12] When your days are over and you rest with your ancestors, I will raise up your offspring to succeed you, your own flesh and blood, and I will establish his kingdom. [13] He is the one who will build a house for my Name, and I will establish the throne of his kingdom forever. (7:11b–13)

When David establishes rest by defeating the neighboring peoples, it opens the way for Solomon to build a temple. Yet, the Chronicler removes the uses of the term "rest" from

80. For a similar discussion, but with excavative goals, developed independently, see Mattison, *Rewriting*, 45–47, 76–81.

his version of the Davidic promise to associate rest with Solomon (see notes on 1 Kgs 5:1–5[15–19]; 1 Chr 17:1–15; 22:5–19; and first point in note on 28:2–3).

In sum, Deut 12 begins the torah collection with central worship and decentralized Israel built upon exegetical allusions to the altar law in Exod 20:24. The requirements for central worship need to be supplemented with a new regulation for non-cultic slaughter by which Deut 12 exegetically advances regulations from counterpart legal standards in Lev 17. The advancement of revelation in Deut 12 creates a ripple effect. The central worship law stands at the headwaters of numerous other legal adjustments in the torah collection of Deuteronomy as well as ongoing reinterpretation in other Scriptures, especially related to the temple (see place network).

13:15–17[16–18]~Exod 22:20[19] (C) (devoting spoils of worshipers of false gods). Much debate continues to surround the possibilities of Deut 13 and 28 as dependent on Neo-Assyrian and/or Hittite treaties.[81] Irrespective of the potential treaty parallels, Deut 13 advances instructions against enticements to worship other gods, whether that enticement comes from false prophets, family members, or the people of local towns. If people of any local town say, "let us go and worship other gods" (Deut 13:13[14]), that town needs to be "devoted" (13:15[16]). This seems to allude to the law of the covenant collection: "Whoever sacrifices to any god other than Yahweh *must be devoted*" (Exod 22:20[19] lit., emphasis mine). The interpretive allusion in Deuteronomy includes two important adjustments: a command to burn everything (13:16[17]) and a warning not to let any devoted spoils "stick to your hand" (13:17[18] NRSV). These measures help eliminate false accusations based on greed, even for priests who would normally benefit by devoted spoils (Lev 27:28; Num 18:14).

14:3–21/~/Lev 11:1–28 (dietary regulations).
14:21b//7:6//14:2 (holy to Yahweh).
14:21c//Exod 23:19b//34:26b (prohibition against boiling a young goat in its mother's milk). The dietary regulations in Deut 14:3–21 share extensive verbal parallels with Lev 11:1–28. Both lists distinguish between animals that are ritually pure/permitted to be eaten versus animals that are ritually impure/forbidden to be eaten. Since the terms for "clean" and "unclean" do not relate to dirt or good health the present discussion speaks of ritual impurity in the sense of worship disability versus ritual purity.

If the dietary regulations in Lev 11 cause every meal to become part of preparing to come before Yahweh in worship, then the version in Deut 14 emphasizes Israel as a holy people in contrast to other peoples. Instead of looking from the dinner table to

81. See, e.g., Weinfeld, *Deuteronomic School*, 59–129; Dillard, "Review," 263–69; Berman, "Hittite Provenance," 25–44; Levinson and Stackert, "Between," 123–40; Zehnder, "Building on Stone? (Part 1)," 341–74; idem, "(Part 2)," 511–35; idem, "Leviticus 26 and Deuteronomy 28," 141–47.

the tabernacle as in Leviticus, Deuteronomy contrasts the animals eaten by Israel versus other peoples in their local residences. Deuteronomy "is not concerned with the altar but with the kitchen table."[82] While a few of these differences come from the contents of Lev 11 and Deut 14 (see Table D6), many differences in function relate to differences of contexts.

TABLE D6: COMPARING DIETARY REGULATIONS IN LEVITICUS 11 AND DEUTERONOMY 14‡

summary—significant differences signified by italics

Leviticus 11	**Deuteronomy 14**
REGULATIONS CONCERNING **LIVING CREATURES**	REGULATIONS CONCERNING **LIVING CREATURES**
—	• general prohibition stated (3)
• permitted land animals defined (1–3)	• ten permitted land animals *enumerated* and defined (4–6)[a]
• prohibited land animals (4–8)	• prohibited land animals (7–8)
• allowed and prohibited water animals defined in detail (9–12)	• allowed and prohibited water animals defined (9–10)
—	• general allowance for ritually pure flying animals (11)
• prohibited flying animals enumerated (13–19)	• prohibited flying animals enumerated (13–18)[b]
• *distinctions between prohibited and allowed flying insects* (20–23)	• blanket prohibition against flying insects (19)
—	• general allowance for ritually pure flying animals (20)
REGULATIONS CONCERNING **DEAD ANIMALS** AND GROUND ANIMALS	REGULATIONS CONCERNING **DEAD ANIMALS**
• *prohibition against contact with ritually impure animal carcasses* (24–28) • *eight ritually impure animals enumerated* (29–31) • *contamination by contact with ritually impure animal carcasses* (32–40) • *prohibition against swarming ground animals with rationale for holiness* (41–45)	• *prohibited for Israel, allowed as gift for residing foreigner* (גֵּר), *and allowed for sale to outside foreigner* (נָכְרִי) (21a) • *rationale for stricter standard for Israel—a people holy to Yahweh* (21b)
General principle for distinction summarized (46–47)	—
—	*Prohibition against cooking a young goat in its mother's milk* (21c)

82. Rüterswörden, "Concerning Deut 14," 101.

Leviticus 11	**Deuteronomy 14**

Key Differences Summarized

LEVITICUS 11

- distinction between prohibited ritually impure (טָמֵא) land animals and ritually impure (שֶׁקֶץ) flying and swimming animals
- distinctions between prohibited and allowed flying insects enumerated (20–23)
- extensive detail for prohibition against contact with carcasses and ground animals (24–45)
- general principle for distinctions summarized (46–47)

DEUTERONOMY 14

- umbrella statements on prohibited land animals (3) and allowed flying animals (11, 20)
- clean land animals enumerated (4–5)
- umbrella term for all ritually impure land, flying, and swimming animals (טָמֵא)
- umbrella prohibition against flying insects (19)
- different standards for Israel, residing foreigners, and outsiders (21)
- prohibition against cooking a young goat in its mother's milk (21c)

‡ Comparison of Lev 11 and Deut 14 developed from Schnittjer, *Torah Story*, 326 (Table 18-C); additional details collated from Driver, *Deuteronomy*, 157–61; Bendavid, *Parallels*, 184–85 [Hebrew]; Lasserre, *Synopse*, 101–3 (§64); Levine, *Leviticus*, 64–65; Nihan, "Laws," 405–6. Also see Friedberg and Hoppe, "Deuteronomy 14," 431–33.

[a] The ritually pure animals, including sacrificial animals, are listed in Deut 14:4–5 but not in Lev 11. In Lev 17:3 ox, sheep, and goat must be slaughtered at the tabernacle for consumption as via well-being offerings (cf. Lev 7:15–20). Deut 14:4–5 includes ox, sheep, and goat with the game animals because this law augments legal standards to allow for profane slaughter of domestic animals. The profane slaughter of ox, sheep, and goat along with game animals in decentralized Israel will be detached from sacrifice at the shrine when the people enter the land (Deut 12:15, 20–21). Comparing the verbal parallels of Lev 11:2–3 and Deut 14:4–5 along with the pluses in the latter (including the domestic animals: ox, sheep, and goat) illustrates how the exegetically expanded dietary regulations of Deut 14 augment the exegetical advancement of revelation of central worship and decentralized Israel in Deut 12 (Bendavid, *Parallels*, 184 [Hebrew]; Lasserre, *Synopse*, 101 (§65); Driver, *Deuteronomy*, 157). Milgrom observes the same pattern with the two birds allowed at the altar (turtledove and pigeon): "Thus, the common denominator of all of the animals listed in [Lev] chap. 11 is that they are not eligible for the altar and, hence, if permitted as food, they are slaughtered profanely, as game" (*Leviticus 1–16*, 647). For an alternate view see first footnote in note on Lev 17:3–9. This evidence is corroborated by the disambiguation of the "divided hooves" (וְשֹׁסַעַת שֶׁסַע פְּרָסֹת) (Lev 11:3 lit.) into "divided hooves into two parts" (וְשֹׁסַעַת שֶׁסַע שְׁתֵּי פְרָסוֹת) (Deut 14:6 lit.) as observed by Friedberg and Hoppe ("Deuteronomy 14," 439). Receptor texts tend to disambiguate.

[b] The approach here is based on the verbal parallel of twenty of twenty-one prohibited birds in Lev 11:16–19 (twenty) and Deut 14:13–18 (twenty-one). Moran's impressive observations regarding ten prohibited birds with accusative markers (אֵת) and ten without in Deut 14:13–18 as coming from two sources, namely, ten without accusative markers from a common source and ten from Lev 11 with accusative markers does not work ("Literary Connection," 276). Moran's argument requires emending the MT with the SP and LXX at Deut 14:13 to get twenty instead of twenty-one (276, n. 24). Also, Moran does not adequately account for the use of "kind" (מִין) with "any *kind of* heron" with no accusative marker in Lev 11:19//Deut 14:18 when this is the only prohibited bird lacking accusative marker in Lev 11:16–19. It makes little sense for Deut 14:18 to adhere to the lack of accusative marker based on Lev 11:19 (contra 276–77), when eleven of twenty-one parallel prohibited birds in Deut 14:13–18 lack the accusative marker versus their counterparts with accusative markers in Lev 11:16–19. This evidence makes a common source not only unnecessary, but something that is more difficult to explain than one list based on the other.

As pointed out in Table D6, Lev 11 and Deut 14 share much in common regarding dietary regulations. Many of the differences turn out to be elements with no parallel in the counterpart instruction. The contextual settings in the priestly instructions and torah collection respectively establish the main differences in how these teachings function.

Broadly, the first sixteen chapters of Leviticus offer instruction for worship: sacrifice (1–7), tabernacle (8–10), ritual purity (11–15), Day of Atonement (16). Whereas Lev 1–10 and 16 largely relate to priestly instructions for worship, chs. 11–15 explain instructions for ritual purity which apply to priests and laity.[83] The ritual purity regulations of Leviticus democratize readiness to worship to all Israel all the time.

Many regulations in Deut 12–26 have been grouped together based on common themes and logical progression. The dietary regulations further define laws of eating meat from decentralized non-sacred slaughter in Deut 12 and complement restrictions for ritual mourning to help Israel avoid practices of the nations of Canaan (Deut 14:1–2).[84] Sacred slaughter will be in the place Yahweh chooses for his name to dwell (12:5, 14, 18). Common slaughter of ritually pure and impure animals will take place in local communities (12:15, 21–22). The dietary regulations of Deut 14 spell out the differences between ritually pure and impure animals for consumption. Deuteronomy 14:4–5 includes together a list of domestic and game animals for consumption, carrying over the decentralization of non-sacrificial slaughter from 12:15. No such list appears in the counterpart of Lev 11:2–3 (see Table D6, note a).[85] But there is more.

Avoiding unfaithfulness to Yahweh stands as one of the leading concerns in the torah collection of Deut 12–26. Disfiguring mourning rites need to be avoided because Yahweh has chosen Israel as his treasured possession (14:1–2). The dietary regulations build on these teachings and continue the theme of faithfulness to Yahweh in marked contrast to the other peoples. Similar motive clauses reveal the similar function of prohibitions against disfiguring mourning rituals and dietary regulations as an *inclusio* (14:2, 21). The motive clause near the end of the dietary regulations also connects it with the broader identity of the people as distinct from other peoples in Deut 7:6 (emphases signify verbal parallels):

> **For you are a people holy to Yahweh your God.** Yahweh your God has chosen you out of all the peoples on the face of the earth to be his people, his treasured possession. (Deut 7:6)
>
> **For you are a people holy to Yahweh your God.** Out of all the peoples on the face of the earth, Yahweh has chosen you to be his treasured possession. (14:2)
>
> **For you are a people holy to Yahweh your God.** (14:21†)

Leviticus also grounds the dietary regulations on Israel's call to holiness (Lev 11:44–45; 20:24–26). The regulations themselves in Lev 11, however, are housed within the standards for worship in Lev 1–16. The point of the dietary regulations in Deuteronomy, by contrast, turns on what sets Israel apart from the nations.

---

83. The ritual purity standards of Lev 11–15 fit well between the resumptive repetition or *inclusio* of the death of Aaron's sons in Lev 10:1–2 and 16:1.

84. See Tigay, *Deuteronomy*, 136, 452.

85. So observed by Rüterswörden, "Concerning Deut 14," 98–99.

In one place, the dietary relations of Deuteronomy make distinctions between standards that seem to be quite different from those in Leviticus but with some overlap with the covenant collection in Exodus (bold and italics signify verbal parallels, and broken underlining signifies syntactical similarity):

> You are to be my **holy** people. So *do not eat* the meat of an animal torn by wild beasts; throw it to the dogs. (Exod 22:31[30])

> Anyone, whether native-born or **residing foreigner** [גֵּר], who *eats* anything *found dead* or torn by wild animals must wash their clothes and bathe with water, and they will be ceremonially impure till evening; then they will be ceremonially pure. (Lev 17:15†)

> *Do not eat* anything you find *already dead*. You may give it to the **residing foreigner** [גֵּר] in any of your towns, and they may eat it, or you may sell it to any other foreigner [נָכְרִי]. But you are a people **holy** to Yahweh your God. Do not cook a young goat in its mother's milk. (Deut 14:21†)[86]

The shared ideals between Exod 22:31[30] and Deut 14:21 make the interpretive intervention of the latter stand out. Meat fit for dogs may be gifted to residing foreigners or sold to other foreigners. The gap between Israel and residing foreigners at this point in Deuteronomy seems especially striking. Understanding what is going on with residing foreigners here requires careful consideration.

Since the priestly regulations seek to protect the tabernacle from pollutions, many contexts emphasize common standards for Israel and residing foreigners: observing Day of Atonement (Lev 16:29); sacrifice (17:8; Num 15:14–16); the prohibition against consuming blood (Lev 17:10, 12, 13); the prohibition against incest, Molech worship, and the like (18:26; 20:2); the death penalty for blasphemy (24:22); celebrating Passover (Num 9:14); the purification offering for unintentional infraction (15:29); defilement by a corpse (19:10, 11); protective asylum for manslaughter (35:11). The prohibition against consuming blood, also appearing in Deut 12:16, 23–24, needs to be detangled from the covenantal instructions since it applies to all humans (Gen 9:4) and is reinforced for gentile Christians by James and the Jerusalem council (Acts 15:20, 29; 21:25).

What is the extent of the distinction between Israel versus residing foreigners versus other foreigners in Deut 14:21? Some use this passage as a prooftext that, for the author of Deuteronomy, gentiles may convert but can never have more than a partial standing

86. While the parallels between Deut 7:6, 14:2, and 14:21 are nearly identical, the wording of Exod 22:31[30] differs somewhat: "for you are a holy people to Yahweh (כִּי עַם קָדוֹשׁ אַתָּה לַיהוה)" (Deut 14:21 lit.) versus "You shall be men holy to me (וְאַנְשֵׁי־קֹדֶשׁ תִּהְיוּן לִי)" (Exod 22:31[31] lit.). Nihan notes the use of the prohibition against boiling a young goat in its mother's milk in Deut 14:21 strengthens the potential relationship to the covenant collection that features this law in Exod 23:19 and 34:26 (see "Laws," 421, n. 42).

in Israel.[87] The inadequacy of such an approach stems from viewing "residing foreigner" (גֵּר) as having a religious versus social connotation. Deuteronomy 14:21 seems to speak to a social distinction between residing foreigners and other foreigners, both of whom in this context are excluded from the assembly of Yahweh, as neither need to worry about ritual contamination. But this cannot be applied indiscriminately to all residing foreigners in Deuteronomy. Elsewhere residing foreigners are treated as "holy" and may participate in the feast funded by tithes every third year like any Levite or Hebrew widow or orphan:

> Then say to Yahweh your God: "I have removed from my house *the sacred portion* [הַקֹּדֶשׁ] and have given it to the Levite, *the foreigner* [גֵּר], the fatherless and the widow, according to all you commanded. I have not turned aside from your commands nor have I forgotten any of them." (Deut 26:13, emphasis mine; cf. 14:29)

The participation of residing foreigners with holy offerings alongside Levites and other protected classes of Israelites in Deut 14:29 and 26:13 demonstrates that the distinction in 14:21 does not dissociate residing foreigners based on ethnicity per se. One side of the difference needs to be understood socially. Residing foreigners receive charity in Deut 14:21 because of social challenges (cf. 14:29; 24:14, 17, 19, 20, 21; 26:12, 13) versus other foreigners who can afford to pay (14:21).[88] The other side of the distinction between residing foreigners and Israel in Deut 14:21 cannot be globalized to all residing foreigners but only those excluded from the assembly of Yahweh. Elsewhere residing foreigners within the worshiping community participate in the pilgrimage festivals (16:11, 14; 26:11; 31:12) and enter the covenant alongside Israel (29:11[10]).[89]

Lastly, the injunction "Do not cook a young goat in its mother's milk" in Deut 14:21 is identical to injunctions in the covenant collection and the renewal of the covenant (Exod 23:19; 34:26). The motivation behind this prohibition is contested (humanitarian versus avoidance of pagan ritual). In any case, the citation in the torah collection of Deuteronomy does not modify the prohibition but places it in a different context. In Exod 23:19 and 34:26 this prohibition appears with instructions for worship pilgrimages. In Deut 14 the command appears with day-to-day dietary regulations for maintaining holiness in local residences.

14:22–29*~Lev 27:30; Num 18:21–24 (C) (tithes) (* see place network). Central worship and decentralized Israel in Deut 12 created a need for a mechanism to regulate tithing. Originally tithes went to the priests (Lev 27:30). When Yahweh took the Levites in place of Israel's firstborn to serve at the temple, the tithes went to the Levites

---

87. See Weinfeld, *Deuteronomic School*, 230–31; Mattison, *Rewriting*, 113. Also see Glanville, *Adopting the Stranger*, 95–96; but see 198; idem, "The *Gēr*," 615, 615, 617, and esp. 620.

88. On the social distinction of charity versus payment in Deut 14:21, see Tigay, *Deuteronomy*, 140; Tigay disagrees with the larger point being made here.

89. In Exodus the distinction between those others who must participate in Passover versus those others who may not participate pivots on the circumcision of the former (Exod 12:43–49). Block also concludes that the residing foreigner (גֵּר) of Deut 14:21 must be uncircumcised ("Sojourner; Alien; Stranger," *ISBE* 4:562, left column).

(Num 18:21–24), and the Levites tithed their tithe to the priests (18:25–29). Central worship in the land means that the tithe was no longer needed to support the Levites and could be eaten by worshipers during pilgrimage festivals at the place of Yahweh's choosing (Deut 12:17–18; 14:22–23).[90] With decentralized life in the land, tithes can be converted to silver (14:24–25) then converted to goods during the pilgrimage festivals (14:25–26). Since the Levites do not have a land allotment, they are classed with the other socially protected classes—widows, orphans, residing foreigners, Levites (12:19; 14:29; 26:13). As such, the tithe of every third year gets allocated locally to the Levites and other socially protected classes (14:28; 26:12).

15:1–11*~Exod 23:10–11+22:25*[24] (B) (year of canceling debts) (* see release statute network).

15:12–18*~Exod 21:1–11* (B) (debt slaves) (* see release statute network). Debts and debt slavery become interrelated in many ways. The case of debts and selling oneself into debt by landowners treats a related but separate set of issues associated with Jubilee, once every seven Sabbath years, when land gets restored and non-redeemed indebted landowners and their families are released (Lev 25). In the discussion of Jubilee in the note on Lev 25, Table L1 compares the details of Deut 15:1–18 and related passages of Deuteronomy. As such, the present note only deals with the ways Deut 15:1–11, 12–18 supplements in a different way debt-slavery laws of the covenant collection (Exod 21–23) and institute regular debt remission.

In the covenant collection the term "let it rest" speaks of letting the field lie fallow every seven years (Exod 23:11). Deuteronomy uses the same root many times with the sense of "remit" debt in the seventh year (Deut 15:1, 2, 3, 9).[91] The remission of debt every seven years gets set on Tabernacles (31:10). Though very concise, with different language, the solemn oath of the restoration, three days after Tabernacles is celebrated, seems to blend the fallow year and debt remission (Neh 10:31b[32b]).

Deuteronomy also advances revelation by eliminating charging interest upon fellow Israelites and allowing interest upon foreigners (Deut 15:3; cf. 23:19–20[20–21]).[92] This expands upon a law in the covenant collection, which only prevented taking interest from poor Israelites (Exod 22:25[24]).

The law of the debt slave in Deut 15:12–18 includes several upgrades from the counterpart in Exod 21:2–6, 7–11. The instruction regarding a female debt slave is more complicated and needs to be treated separately after summarizing modifications to the male debt-slave situation. The covenant collection provides protections and regulations for the male debt slave and owner in Exod 21:2–6. These standards apply to non-landed Hebrew slaves (Exod 21:2), with standards for cases of landed heads of household, residing foreigners, and foreigners spelled out in Lev 25:35–38, 39–46. Deuteronomy does

---

90. For a discussion of the details of the changes with tithes in Deut 12 and 14, presuming centralization as shutting down regional shrines, see Milgrom, *Leviticus 23–27*, 2424–26.

91. See "שמט," "שְׁמִטָּה," *HALOT* 2:1557–58.

92. But see the closely argued study by Issler who takes *nokri* (נָכְרִי) as "trader" not foreigner ("Lending," 777–79).

not speak of "buying" or "acquiring" the Hebrew debt slave as in Exod 21:2. Instead, Deut 15:12 refers to the Hebrew man or woman "selling themselves" into service. This is similar to the landed head of household "selling himself" in Lev 25:39.[93] Whereas the landed head of household who sells himself is not a slave but is like a residing foreigner (Lev 25:40), the Hebrew male or female sells themselves into debt slavery in Deut 15:12. Although this change in language has been called a "legal fiction" it gets at a material change in attitude and identity in Lev 25 and Deut 15.[94] The other big difference in the torah collection is sending out the Hebrew debt slave with gifts (Deut 15:13–14). Deuteronomy retains the option for the debt slave who so desires to become a permanent slave (15:16–17; cf. Exod 21:5–6).

The complications regarding the female debt slave relate to protections because of her sexual and reproductive capacities. Deuteronomy makes explicit that the free woman who sells herself into debt slavery gets freed after seven years like any man (Deut 15:12, 17). The female debt-slave regulations of Exod 21:7–11 retain their place with protections for the female sold into concubinage. An ancient Near Eastern female could not be a slave and wife to the same person (see Deut 21:10–14).[95] But a free person could enter concubinage or be sold into it. And polygamy adds to the complex social dynamics. The protections for the female sold into concubinage include: the option of redemption if she does not please her master; prohibition against reselling her to foreign people; stipulation that if she has been acquired for a son, she shall be treated like a daughter; and stipulation that if her master takes an additional wife, she shall retain full food, clothing, and conjugal relations, or she shall be released (Exod 21:7–11).[96] Deuteronomy stresses that the female slave sold into service, but not concubinage, goes free after seven years like anyone else.[97] Thus, Deut 15:12, 18 supplements the covenant collection law of female debt slavery.

Motivation constitutes the major interpretive tendency of Deut 15:1–11, 12–18. Only eight verses of law (vv. 1–3, 12–14, 16–17) and two verses of unenforceable law (vv. 7–8) stand amid eight verses of motivation (vv. 4–6, 9–11, 15, 18–19). Generosity to fellow Israelites in need is the theme of the heavy-handed motivation. The legal standards on debt and debt slavery do not compel by mere command; they represent Deuteronomy's encouragements and appeal to reason.[98]

---

93. This is based on the reflexive sense of "sell oneself" (Nif of מכר) in Lev 25:39 and Deut 15:12. For details, see note on Lev 25:39.

94. On "selling oneself" as a "legal fiction," see Wells, "Quasi-Alien," 140, n. 18.

95. See Westbrook and Wells, *Everyday Law*, 55; Westbrook, "Female Slave," in *Law*, 2:170–71. An enslaved female could be wife to someone other than her owner whether her husband is free or enslaved (cf. Exod 21:4). Examples include Bilhah and Zilpah.

96. For further details and parallels in ancient Near Eastern legal collections, see Westbrook, "Female Slave," in *Law*, 2:154–55, 172–73. Though the standard view takes the *hapax legomenon* in Exod 21:10 as "conjugal relations" (עֹנָה) (*HALOT* 1:855; NIV; NRSV; etc.), Paul suggests "oil" based on possible cognate parallels, and compares the triad "bread," "clothes," and "oil" in Eccl 9:7–9 (*Studies*, 59–61).

97. Other ancient legal collections speak of three years of debt service (CH §117; see Greengus, *Laws*, 90).

98. These observations come from Tigay, "Deuteronomy 4," 261.

In sum, Deut 15:1–11, 12–18 features legal exegesis for standards of debt and debt slavery over and against counterpart standards in the covenant collection. A few of the interpretive interventions expand or enhance previous legal standards, such as remitting debt every seven years, reconceptualizing debt slavery of Hebrews as persons selling themselves rather than being bought and sold, and giving goods to debt slaves who finish their service. Other adjustments take the form of interpretive supplement, like a prohibition against charging interest to fellow Israelites and making explicit that free females who sell themselves into debt service go free after seven years like any male. The new legal standards for debt slavery do not remove the protections for females sold into concubinage in the covenant collection.

15:19–23*~Exod 22:29–30[28–29] (B)+Lev 22:20, 22 (B) (firstlings to Yahweh) (* see place network). When Yahweh redeemed Israel he laid claim to their firstborn males and firstborn males of their ritually pure animals for perpetuity.[99] Central worship and decentralized Israel in Deut 12 caused several adjustments in the legal standards for the firstlings (bold and italics signify verbal parallels, and broken underlining signifies advancements):

> Do not delay to offer from your granaries or your vats. You must give me the firstborn of your sons. Do the same with **your herd** and **your flock**. Let them stay with their mothers for seven days, but give them to me on the eighth day. (Exod 22:29–30†[28a-29], v. 29a lit.)

> Do not bring anything with a *defect*, because it will not be accepted on your behalf. . . . It must be without *any defect* or blemish to be acceptable. Do not offer to Yahweh the *blind*, the injured or the maimed, or anything with warts or festering or running sores. Do not place any of these on the altar as a food offering presented to Yahweh. (Lev 22:20, 21b–22†)

> Set apart for Yahweh your God every firstborn male of your herds and **flocks**. Do not put the firstborn of **your herd** to work, and do not shear the firstborn of your sheep. Each year you and your family are to eat them in the presence of Yahweh your God at the place he will choose. If an animal has a *defect*, is lame or *blind*, or has *any* serious *defect*, you must not sacrifice it to Yahweh your God. (Deut 15:19–21†)

While the covenant collection insisted on giving the firstling to Yahweh on the eighth day (Exod 22:30[29]), when Israel enters the land the firstlings should be retained until the next pilgrimage festival (Deut 15:20). And, based on central worship and decentralized Israel, the firstling should be part of the family's food during the pilgrimage festivals

99. See Exod 13:12; 34:19; cf. Lev 27:26; Num 3:13; 8:17; 18:17–18.

rather than a gift to the shrine personnel. Presumably, the other priestly portions would sustain the worship personnel in the wake of centralization, and the tithes and firstlings could feed families during their three annual pilgrimage festivals. In the meantime, Israel should not profit by holding on to the firstlings until the next festival (15:19). The torah collection also adds the standard of wholeness for all gifts to Yahweh as in the holiness regulations for vows and offerings (15:21; Lev 22:20–22). Offering blemished and disfigured animals to Yahweh shows great disrespect (Mal 1:6–8).

16:16–17*~Exod 23:14–17 (B) (three mandated pilgrimage festivals) (* see place network). The main interpretive enhancement of the festivals of Passover/Unleavened Bread (Deut 16:1–8), Weeks (16:9–12), and Tabernacles (16:13–15) is the repeated emphasis on celebrating "at the place Yahweh will choose as a dwelling for his name" (16:2, 6, 7, 11, 15).

The torah collection also reworks the overall command for the three annual pilgrimage festivals (Deut 16:16–17). In the covenant collection the command to bring an offering stated in the negative—"Do not appear empty-handed" (Exod 23:15; cf. 34:20b)—could be interpreted as only applying to Passover. Deuteronomy reformats the commands to make it clear that offerings are expected at each of the pilgrimages (bold signifies verbal parallels, italics signify incidental adjustments, and standard and dashed underlining signify primary and secondary interpretive advances):

> Three times a year you are to celebrate a festival to me. [15] Celebrate **the Festival of Unleavened Bread**; for seven days eat bread made without yeast, as I commanded you. Do this at the appointed time in the month of Aviv, for in that month you came out of Egypt. **No one should appear before** *me* **empty-handed.** [16] Celebrate *the Festival of Harvest* with the firstfruits of the crops you sow in your field. Celebrate *the Festival of Ingathering* at the end of the year, when you gather in your crops from the field [17] **Three times a year all the men are to appear before** *Sovereign* **Yahweh**. (Exod 23:14–17†)

> **Three times a year all your men must appear before Yahweh** *your God* at the place he will choose: at **the Festival of Unleavened Bread**, *the Festival of Weeks* and *the Festival of Tabernacles*. **No one should appear before** *Yahweh* **empty-handed.** [17] Each of you must bring a gift in proportion to the way Yahweh your God has blessed you. (Deut 16:16–17)

The covenant collection included the prohibition against appearing empty-handed at the Festival of Unleavened Bread (Exod 23:15), perhaps presuming that the festivals of Harvest/Weeks and Ingathering/Tabernacles naturally infer gifts of firstfruits and tithes (23:16). But firstfruits and tithes could be over-literalized to be understood to include only farmers. Central worship and decentralized Israel correlates with the economic diversification that comes with urbanization (cf. note on Num 15:18–21). Firstfruits and tithes of the farmer symbolically represent the other kinds of income generated by ranching; production of clothing, pottery and other goods; work of smiths; merchandizing; and so forth. By relocating the prohibition against worship without offering, the torah collection clarifies the expected cost of adoration (Deut 16:16). The relocation of the prohibition inclusive of all pilgrimage worship sets up an expanded clarification of the principle of proportional giving according to all forms of income (16:17).

16:18–20*~1:15+Exod 23:8 (B) (standards for local judges) (* see place network). The regional tribal civil court system of ancient Israel stands as one part of the larger interpretive advancement regarding the central place of worship in Deut 12. The establishment of the local court system includes an interpretive blend to emphasize standards of justice (emphases signify verbal parallels):

> **Do not accept** a bribe, **for a bribe blinds** those who see **and twists the words of the innocent.** (Exod 23:8)
>
> So I took the leading men of your *tribes*, wise and respected men, and appointed them to have authority over you—as commanders of thousands, of hundreds, of fifties and of tens and as tribal officials. [16] And I charged your judges at that time, "Hear the disputes between your people and *judge fairly*, whether the case is between two Israelites or between an Israelite and a foreigner residing among you. [17] *Do not show partiality* in judging; hear both small and great alike. Do not be afraid of anyone, for judgment belongs to God. Bring me any case too hard for you, and I will hear it." (Deut 1:15–17)
>
> Appoint judges and officials for each of your *tribes* in every town Yahweh your God is giving you, and *they shall judge* the people *fairly.* [19] *Do not* pervert justice or *show partiality.* **Do not accept** a bribe, **for a bribe blinds** the eyes of the wise **and twists the words of the innocent.** [20] Follow justice and justice alone, so that you may live and possess the land Yahweh your God is giving you. (16:18–20)

The context of the retrospective donor text for the tribal judges anticipates another interpretive advance. Whereas in the wilderness the cases too difficult for tribal judges were brought to Moses—"I will hear it" (1:17)—when the people enter the land, the higher court will be at the place Yahweh chooses for the shrine.

17:2–7, 8–13~Exod 22:7–8[6–7] (D) (cases elevated from local judges to temple personnel). The potential relationship between a case going before the *elohim* in Exod 22:8, 9[7, 8] and to the place Yahweh will choose in Deut 17:8–17 is quite subtle and depends on at least two elements.

First, the twofold structure of Exod 22:7–8[6–7] and Deut 17:2–7, 8–13 needs to be established. Levinson points out that the legal discourse structure of case laws in the covenant collection uses the higher-level hypothetical marker "if" *ki* (כִּי), and for sub-cases the lower-level hypothetical marker "if" *im* (אִם).[100] In this way Exod 22:7a[6a] sets out the general case: "If [כִּי] anyone gives a neighbor silver or goods for safekeeping and they are stolen from the neighbor's house . . ." Then 22:7b, 8[6b, 7] presents the two sub-cases: one with sufficient evidence—"The thief, if [אִם] caught, must pay back double" (22:7b[6b])—and the other that requires adjudication: "If [אִם] the thief is not found then the owner of the house must appear before *elohim*" (22:8[7] lit.). In a similar manner, Deuteronomy provides two cases marked by its use of "if" *ki* (כִּי) for each one (Deut 17:2, 8). The first case gets decided based on evidence—"Two or three witnesses" (17:6). The second case does not have sufficient evidence to convict and comes before the worship personnel at the central shrine (17:9).[101] The twofold structure of both contexts is evidenced by the presence of these syntactical markers.

Second, the relationship of the laws in Exod 22:7–8[6–7] and Deut 2–7, 8–13 pivots on the referent of *elohim* in the former. The identity of the *elohim* in Exod 22:8, 9[7, 8] can better be explained as "judges" than "God." The plural verb "they declare guilty" in Exod 22:9[8] provides the most important evidence that *elohim* in this context refers to judges who represent God's will. It is very unlikely the term would refer to God with a plural verb.[102] This evidence drastically reduces the likelihood of exegetical allusion since the more difficult case in Exod 22:8[7] goes before civil judges, not before functionaries of a local shrine.

In sum, both laws share a broad similarity of a case with sufficient evidence to convict and another case with insufficient evidence requiring adjudication by judges (Exod 22:8[7]) or at the central shrine (Deut 17:8–13). The evidence does not support an exegetical relationship.

18:15–18*~5:25, 27–28* (A)/~/Exod 20:19* (prophet like Moses) (* see prophet like Moses network). The expectation for a prophet like Moses in Deut 18 shares extensive verbal, syntactic, and contextual parallels with the narrative of the revelation at the mountain, making allusion nearly certain. The narrative of the revelation in Deut 5 stands in synoptic relationship to the counterpart narrative in Exod 19–20—the most impressive feature being the re-presentation of the Ten Commandments.

Deuteronomy 5 extensively expands the people's response after the revelation at the mountain. The detailed narrative explains the people's reasons for asking Moses to serve as intermediary and Yahweh's affirmation of their request. The torah collection works through a series of institutional adjustments based on central worship and decentralized

100. See Levinson, *Deuteronomy*, 115–16.

101. See ibid., 98–109.

102. Here following the results of Vannoy, "Use of *hāʾelōhîm*," 225–41. Exod 22:9[8] SP converts the verb to singular with a 3ms pronominal suffix "he found him guilty" (ירשיענו) to treat *elohim* (אלהים) as "God." MT represents the more difficult reading and is preferred, rightly translated by NIV as "the judges declare guilty" (יַרְשִׁיעֻן אֱלֹהִים) (Exod 22:9[8]) (note: MT uses הָאֱלֹהִים in 22:8[7] and אֱלֹהִים in 22:9[8] while SP uses האלהים in both verses). For evidence in support of priestly oracular rulings at cultic centers, see Levinson, *Deuteronomy*, 111–13. Levinson discusses the plural verb in Exod 22:9[8] in 112, n. 37 and 113–14, n. 43 coming to the opposite conclusion as here.

Israel and other social and political developments upon coming into the land (Deut 12–17). Moses warns Israel to avoid any form of divination after the manner of the people of the land (18:9–14). In contrast to the divination practiced by other nations, Moses claims Yahweh will raise up "a prophet like me" (18:15). Moses goes on to explain that the basis for the prophetic institution comes out of the events during the revelation at the mountain. Notice the connections between these contexts (emphases signify verbal parallels):

> [The people] said to Moses, "*You tell us* and *we will listen*. But do not have God speak to us or *we will die*." (Exod 20:19†)
>
> [The people said] "But now, why should we die? **This great fire** will consume us, and *we* ***will die*** if we **hear the voice of Yahweh** our **God any longer. . . .** Go near and listen to all that Yahweh our God says. Then *you tell us* whatever Yahweh our God tells you. *We will listen* and obey." Yahweh heard you when you spoke to me, and Yahweh said to me, "I have heard what this people said to you. **What they said was good.**" (Deut 5:25, 27–28†)
>
> [Moses said] Yahweh your God will raise up for you a prophet like me from among you, from your fellows. You must listen to him. [16] For this is what you asked of Yahweh your God at Horeb on the day of the assembly when you said, "**Let** me not **hear the voice of Yahweh** my **God** nor see **this great fire anymore**, or I **will die**." [17] Yahweh said to me: "All **that they say is good.** [18] I will raise up for them a prophet like you from among their fellows, and I will put my words in his mouth. He will tell them everything I command him." (18:15–18 lit.)

The expectation for a Moses-like prophet, initially stated in the singular, includes overt language of simile with the preposition "like/as" (18:15). The figural expectation naturally projects connotations based on Moses as a model. The narrator's closing of Deuteronomy focuses on key aspects of Moses's ministry, effectively narrowing the forward-looking type to certain characteristics (34:10–12; see note ad loc).

In the present context the expected prophet like Moses refers to a series of prophets (18:20). Moses goes on to explain a sign of false and true prophets. Namely, any prophet who tells of something that does not come to pass is a false prophet. Yahweh's prophets speak in accord with reality (18:22).

19:1–13*~Exod 21:12–14 (C); Num 35:9–34 (B)+Gen 13:17 (B) (motivation for law of asylum) (* see place network). The law of the cities of asylum for accidental homicide in Deut 19 shares little verbal overlap with Exod 21:12–14, amounting to a few common terms: "smite" (Exod 21:12; Deut 19:4, 6, 11); "death/die" (Exod 21:12, 14; Deut 19:5, 6, 11, 12); "take" (Exod 21:14; Deut 19:12); "his neighbor" (Exod 21:14; Deut 19:4,

5, 11).[103] But the shared circumstance, sequence, and thematic similarity offers good reason to think they might share intentional parallels.[104] Numbers 35:9–34 maintains substantial overlap with Deut 19:1–13, with both speaking of six cities of refuge, suggesting a likely relationship (cf. Deut 4:41–43; Josh 20). Those who believe that Numbers uses Deuteronomy on excavative diachronic grounds think that it adds the Levites. This contrasts with those who believe that Deuteronomy uses Numbers and deletes the Levites (Num 35:6). The logic of the latter view often gets thought of as "secularization" of the cities of asylum.[105] Part of the rationale for not including the Levites in Deuteronomy would come from inviting them to move and join the priests in service at the central sanctuary (Deut 18:6–8).

The present approach evaluates legal exegesis as presented by Torah, thus reading Deuteronomy after Exodus and Numbers. In this case the legal standard includes explicit marking that seems to refer to a promise to Abraham. Gen 13:17 is the only ancestral land promise to use "breadth" from the same root as "enlarge" in Deut 19:8 (but see Gen 26:22). These two verses share two additional very common terms: "give" and "the land." One matter complicates the marking of this potential allusion, namely, the use of a near verbatim marked allusion in Deut 12:20 that refers to a statement in the covenant renewal collection in Exod 34:24 (see note on Deut 12:2–28). Though this complication rules out too much confidence of identifying the donor context, marking an allusion provides evidence of direction of dependence to regard the law asylum in Deuteronomy as the receptor context. The overlapping language seems to recycle the citation formula of Deut 12:20 now repurposed to mark an allusion to the promise in Gen 13:17. Notice the marking in Deut 19:8 in relation to its potential donor context (bold refers to verbal and syntactic parallels, italics refer to verbal parallels at the level of shared roots, and broken underlining marking).

> [Yahweh to Abraham] Go, walk through the length and *breadth* [רחב] of *the land*, for I am *giving* it to you. (Gen 13:17)

> I will drive out nations before you and **enlarge** [רחב] **your territory**, and no one will covet your land when you go up three times each year to appear before Yahweh your God. (Exod 34:24)

> When Yahweh your God **has enlarged** [רחב] **your territory** as he promised you, and you crave meat and say, "I would like some meat," then you may eat as much of it as you want. (Deut 12:20)

103. See parallel layout in Stackert, "Why Does Deuteronomy," 33–34.
104. See ibid., 34–38.
105. See Greenberg, "Asylum," 131.

> If Yahweh your God ***enlarges*** [רחב] **your territory**, as he promised on oath to your ancestors, and *gives* you *the* whole *land* he promised them . . . (19:8)

The logic of the marked promise needs to be noted. The basis for the exegetical enhancements to the law of asylum stem from Israel being spread out in the land. The issue of distance accords with ongoing concerns so often associated with central worship in Deut 12 and the implications of distance as this bears on many laws when Israel is spread out in the land of promise. In that sense the interpretive intervention with the law of asylum fits with the many exegetical advances based on central worship and decentralized Israel in Deuteronomy's torah collection (see place network).

The function of the instructions for the asylum cities in Deut 19 relates to the implications of a central sanctuary (Deut 12). In contrast to asylum at the altar in Exod 21:14, the six cities provide regional places of refuge for those far from the central sanctuary. The use of the altar for temporary asylum stands in the background of 1 Kgs 1:50 and 2:28, though Neh 6:10 looks like something else. The instructions for protecting those who commit accidental homicide in both Numbers and Deuteronomy relate to measures against polluting the land with blood (Num 35:33; Deut 19:10).

The version of the legal instruction regarding cities of asylum in Deuteronomy's torah collection introduces a new element (cf. Exod 21:13; Num 35:9–34; Deut 4:41–43; 19:1–13; Josh 20:1–9). In Num 35:25 a congregational trial finding the death accidental causes the complainant to be sent back to the city of asylum. Conversely, Deut 19:12 requires the culprit of intentional death to be sent back to the city of the victim's avenger. Since the context does not explain the process of adjudication, it must be known from elsewhere.[106] Within the context of Torah, the judicial process includes judgment by the congregation (Num 35:24–25). Deuteronomy urges Israel not to allow the murderer to enjoy immunity.[107] Deuteronomy includes motivation: "so that it may go well with you" (Deut 19:13). Also see notes on Num 35:9–34 and Josh 20:4.

19:15//17:6~Num 35:30 (B) (two or three witnesses). Previous regulations had prevented capital cases from being decided on the basis of one witness. This eliminates wrongful executions in she said/she said and he said/he said cases (Num 35:30; Deut 17:6). Deuteronomy 19:15 expands upon this ideal and requires the same standard of evidence for rulings in all civil court cases. Cases that are not dismissed for lack of evidence can be sent for adjudication to the place Yahweh chooses (see Deut 17:8–13). The call for cases requiring more than a single witness provides an upgrade within scriptural legal collections (17:6; 19:15; cf. Num 35:30) and is similar to the

---

106. Wells suggests a collaborative judicial process between officials of the city of the victim's avenger and the city of asylum based on a somewhat parallel Neo-Babylonian case ("Law or Religion?" 297–99).

107. See Greenberg, "City of Refuge," *IDB* 1:639.

conditional verdicts that emerged within Neo-Babylonian court cases in the sixth and fifth centuries BCE.[108]

19:18–21~Exod 20:16 (C)+Exod 21:24; Lev 24:20 (B) (measure-for-measure punishment for false witnesses). The only two places in Torah where the exact phrase "false witness" appears is in the Ten Commandments in Exod 20:16 and the law in Deut 19:18.[109] The use of "malicious witness" in Exod 23:1 and Deut 19:16 and similar themes on justice in trials in Exod 23:1–3, 6–8 make a specific donor context for allusion uncertain. The shared language of eye for eye, tooth for tooth, etc., in Exod 21:24–25, Lev 24:20, and Deut 19:21 makes allusion likely.

The interpretive intervention in Deut 19:18–21 designates the false witness as culpable for whatever punishment would have gone to the defendant. This measure-for-measure accountability complements the standard for two or three witnesses in 19:15. These legal standards make up an important part of Deuteronomy's strong push for justice in trials.

20:16–18*~7:1–2* (B) (law of devoting nations of Canaan) (* see devoting network). The law of devoting the nations of the land in Deut 20:16–18 uses overt marking of allusion, "as Yahweh your God has commanded you" (Deut 20:17), suggesting Deut 7:1–2 as donor context. Several narratives of devoting the nations of Canaan in Joshua repeat the marking "as Yahweh has commanded" (Josh 10:40) and "as Yahweh had commanded Moses" (11:12, 20). In comparison to Deut 7, the law of devoting in Deut 20 makes explicit killing everything that breathes, not just adult males, as opposed to taking these as plunder during warfare elsewhere (Deut 20:16; cf. v. 14).

21:18–21~Exod 21:15, 17; Lev 20:9 (C) (rebellious son). The punishment for striking or cursing parents in Exodus and Leviticus is death (Exod 21:15, 17; Lev 20:9).[110] Deuteronomy 21:18–21 only shares the terms "father" and "mother" with the laws in Exodus and Leviticus. In Deuteronomy the standards are raised because the parents can bring a capital case against their rebellious son who refuses to listen or to accept discipline and may be a glutton and drunkard (Deut 21:18–21). The motivation in Deuteronomy goes beyond purging evil and includes the benefit of bringing fear to all who hear of the punishment (21:21). This motivation clause signals that the punishment has been made purposely harsh.

22:1–4~Exod 23:4–5 (B) (tending to the animal of one's fellow). Deuteronomy 22:1–4 shares verbal, syntactic, and contextual elements with Exod 23:4–5 suggesting allusion. Compare the expansions (emphases signify verbal and syntactic parallels):

---

108. See Wells, "Law or Religion?" 289–92. For a detailed review of Neo-Babylonian cases with conditional sentences pending further evidence or additional witnesses, see Wells, *Law of Testimony*, 110–16, 118–22.

109. Exodus 20:16 says "false testimony" (עֵד שָׁקֶר) and Deut 5:20 says the same thing with a synonym (עֵד שָׁוְא).

110. By contrast the law collection of Hammurabi punishes similar crimes more moderately by cutting off the child's hand or plucking out his eye (CH §§193, 195).

> If you come across your enemy's **ox** or **donkey** wandering off, **be sure to take it back.** *If you see the donkey* of someone who hates you fallen down under its load, do not leave it there; be sure you *help* them *with it.* (Exod 23:4–5†)

> If you see your fellow Israelite's **ox** or sheep straying, do not ignore it but **be sure to take it back** to its owner. [2] If they do not live near you or if you do not know who owns it, take it home with you and keep it until they come looking for it. Then give it back. [3] Do the same if you find their **donkey** or cloak or anything else they have lost. Do not ignore it. [4] *If you see* your fellow Israelite's *donkey* or ox fallen on the road, do not ignore it. *Help* the owner get *it* to its feet. (Deut 22:1–4)[111]

The law of the enemy's lost ox "interrupts" the legal standards for justice in court cases with "legal dispute" or "lawsuit" serving as a resumptive repetition in Exod 23:3, 6.[112] Neither law provides the logic of returning the animal like other ancient legal collections that explain the stray animal needs to be taken back to its owner to avoid charges of theft (LE §50; HL §§45, 71, 79).[113] Neither law in Torah offers any motivation or penalty.

Whereas the covenant collection identifies the lost or struggling animal's owner as one's "enemy" or "one who hates you" (Exod 23:4, 5), the torah collection speaks only of one's fellow citizen, literally "your brother" (Deut 22:1, 2, 4). The logic between the two can be summarized: "[I]f you are under a duty to assist 'someone who hates you,' you are certainly obligated to aid someone who is indifferent to you or who loves you."[114] In this way Deut 22:1–4 works from the lesser to the greater (cf. similar logic in notes on Lev 19:18b; Joel 2:13–14). The view espoused here regards the legal standard in Deut 22:1–4 as interpretation by supplement, not replacement—the responsibility to tend to an enemy's animal in trouble remains (cf. Prov 24:17; 25:21–22; Matt 5:44; Rom 12:17–21). The expansive version of the law in Deuteronomy offers many alternate scenarios, demonstrating the breadth of the principle of the command.

22:9–11//Lev 19:19 (A)+Exod 26:1, 31; 28:6, 15 (C) (mixing makes it holy). Torah legislation against mixing two kinds of seed in planting or two kinds of fabric in garments baffles interpreters, and, sometimes, opens the legal standards of Torah to ridicule from Christians who read the regulations and shake their heads. The exegetical intervention in Deut 22:9 may offer an explanation of why mixing animals, seeds, and fabrics is forbidden.

The exact verbal parallels between Lev 19:19 and Deut 22:9–11 make allusion almost certain, especially in light of the rare term "mixture" only used in these two contexts.[115]

111. The literal phrase "with him" (עִמּוֹ) in both Exod 23:5 and Deut 22:4 is made explicit in the NIV by adding "help."

112. See Paul, *Studies*, 110, n. 1.

113. See Propp, *Exodus 19–40*, 275; Greengus, *Laws*, 233.

114. Huffmon, "Exodus 23:4–5," 276.

115. See "שַׁעַטְנֵז," *HALOT* 2:1610–11. Also see Noonan's convincing etymological proposal ("Unraveling," 95–101).

The other possible connections to mixing fabrics are thematic not verbal and thus can be no more than a possibility. It may be that the mixing of fabrics in the tabernacle curtains and the priestly garments made mixing fabrics off limits for the laity to honor Yahweh's holiness. The exclusion against mixing fabrics may then be applied to mixing other things like seeds and animals. This provides a rationale for why Deut 22:9 explains that the produce of mixed seed is "holy," that is, property of the sanctuary and the priesthood. Notice the possible thematic parallels alongside the evident verbal parallels (underlining signifies verbal parallels, broken underlining possible thematic parallels, and bold an exegetical advance).[116]

> Make the tabernacle with ten curtains of finely twisted linen and blue, purple and scarlet yarn, with cherubim woven into them by a skilled worker. (Exod 26:1; cf. v. 31)

> Make the ephod of gold, and of blue, purple and scarlet yarn, and of finely twisted linen—the work of skilled hands. (28:6; cf. v. 15)

> Keep my decrees. Do not mate different kinds of animals. Do not plant your field with two kinds of seed. Do not wear clothing woven together [שַׁעַטְנֵז] of two kinds of material. (Lev 19:19†)

> Do not plant two kinds of seed in your vineyard, **otherwise the produce will be holy** [פֶּן־תִּקְדַּשׁ], both the seed you have sown and the produce of the vineyard. [10] Do not plow with an ox and a donkey yoked together. [11] Do not wear clothes of wool and linen woven together [שַׁעַטְנֵז]. (Deut 22:9–11, v. 9 lit.)

The added phrase "otherwise it will be holy" in Deut 22:9 provides a crucial interpretive advancement. Whether "clothes of wool and linen" in verse 11 is representative of any fabric mixture or a limitation allowing for other fabric mixtures needs to be set aside here. The phrase "otherwise it will be holy [פֶּן־תִּקְדַּשׁ]" in v. 9 is rendered as "will be defiled" in the NIV and nearly all modern committee translations. The NIV text note on v. 9 explains the sense of defiled as "be forfeited to the sanctuary." If the produce becomes holy it automatically becomes property of the tabernacle, which Yahweh grants to the priests (Lev 27:9, 21; Num 18:9, 19).

The pretext of mixing makes holy seems to be that the mixing of fabrics was preserved exclusively for the tabernacle curtains and priestly garments. As a way for laity to ever

116. For parallels between Lev 19:19 and Deut 22:9–11, see Driver, *Deuteronomy*, 252. On the mixing of sanctuary and priestly fabrics being forbidden to Israel, see Milgrom, *Leviticus 1–16*, 548–49. This association can be corroborated by Erickson's observation that the materials prescribed for the priestly garments are those used for the deity's dwelling—gold, blue, purple, scarlet yarn, and fine linen (Exod 26:1; 28:5). Priests must wear the "housing of the deity" to approach the deity in worship. See Erickson, "Dressing Up."

prepare to enter the courts of Yahweh, they were forbidden to mix seeds, animals, and clothing. This potential interpretation must be held loosely because of lack of verbal connection to the tabernacle and priestly fabrics. One contextual factor that strengthens the possibility of mixing fabrics as exclusive to the sanctuary and its personnel is the heavy use of analogical relations between the mountain of revelation and tabernacle and animal sacrifice and priest running through much of Leviticus.[117]

In sum, the interpretive advancement of Deut 22:9 is that mixing seeds makes the produce holy. Deut 22:9 explains the prohibition against mixing seeds, animals, and fabrics as a practical mechanism for honoring Yahweh's holiness in the everyday life of ancient Israel. Rather than scorning the legal standards of ancient Israel, Christians can gain insight into what it means to take seriously Paul and Sosthenes's statement "all for the glory of God" (1 Cor 10:31).

22:28–29~Exod 22:16–17[15–16] (B) (rape). The brief verbal and syntactic parallels along with contextual similarities suggest that the law of rape in Deut 22:28–29 alludes to the law of seduction in Exod 22:16–17[15–16]. The two cases and the penalties need close consideration (bold signifies verbal parallels):

> **If a man** seduces a virgin **who is not pledged to be married** and sleeps with her, he must pay the bride-price, and she **shall be his wife.** If her father absolutely refuses to give her to him, he must still pay the bride-price for virgins. (Exod 22:16–17[15–16])
>
> **If a man** happens to meet a virgin **who is not pledged to be married** and rapes her and they are discovered, he shall pay her father fifty shekels of silver. **He must marry** the young woman, for he has violated her. He can never divorce her as long as he lives. (Deut 22:28–29)

The traditional rabbinic reading infers that the law of rape supplements the law of seduction. Thus, the father (and his daughter) receives the bride price from the rapist but retains the right to refuse the marriage as in the case of the seducer (b. Ketub. 39b). Neither the seducer nor the rapist has the right to refuse the marriage if that is what the father (and his daughter) decides. The seducer retains his right to divorce, but the rapist does not.[118] The interpretive intervention in Deut 22:28–29 shocks modern readers—marry her rapist?!—and, along with its donor context, needs to be aligned with other ancient legal conventions. Other ancient Near Eastern legal standards likewise deny the rapist the right of any decisions and he must pay triple the bridal price whether the father decides they should marry or not (MAL §A55).[119]

---

117. See Schnittjer, *Torah Story*, 303, 306–9, 350–51.

118. The Temple Scroll denies the seducer the right of divorce, adding the phrase from Deut 22:29 to its version of the law of the seducer (Exod 22:16–17[15–16]): "because he violated her he may not divorce her all of his life" (תחת אשר ענה לוא יוכל לשלחה כול ימיו) (11Q19 46, 8–11 lit., *DSSSE* 2:1288).

119. See Greengus, *Laws*, 64, 67; Tigay, *Deuteronomy*, 208–9; Paul, *Studies*, 97. The married rapist faces additional

In sum, the law of rape in Deut 22:28–29 augments the law of seduction in Exod 22:16–17[15–16]. The father (and his daughter) retains all rights to accept the bride price and accept or refuse marriage, while rapists have less rights than seducers.

23:4–5*[5–6]/~/Num 22–24 (Balaam's curse) (* see assembly network). The abridgement of the Balaam narrative in Deut 23:4–5[6–7] functions as a selective quasi-synoptic narrative. Elsewhere in Torah, a single feature of another event gets pulled out as a narrative abridgement to make a point (Num 32:6–15; cf. chs. 13–14).[120] The purpose-directed abridgment in Deut 23:4–5[5–6] contains substantial verbal parallels, making allusion highly likely.

The law of the assembly in Deut 23 includes within it a long explanation of why the Ammonites and Moabites have been perpetually excluded from the assembly of Yahweh. It does not relate to their ancestors' illegitimate births (Deut 23:2[3]; cf. Gen 19:30–37). Instead, they have been permanently excluded from the assembly of Yahweh because of their treachery against Israel in the wilderness. Specifically, instead of showing Israel hospitality by bringing bread and water, they hired the wicked prophet Balaam to curse Israel. Note some highlights from the Balaam narratives with verbal parallels to the abridgment in Deut 23 (bold signifies verbal parallels, italics signify synonyms, and broken underlining signifies paraphrase):

> [Balak] sent messengers to summon **Balaam son of Beor**, who was at **Pethor**, near the Euphrates River, in his native land. Balak said: "A people **has come out of Egypt**; they cover the face of the land and have settled next to me. [6] Now come and *put a curse* on these people. . . . For I know that whoever you **bless is blessed**, and whoever you *curse* is *cursed*. . . ." [12] But God said to Balaam, "Do not go with them. You must not put a curse on those people, because they **are blessed**. . . ." [9] "Like a lion they crouch and lie down, like a lioness—who dares to rouse them? May those who bless you be blessed and those who curse you be cursed!" (Num 22:5–6, 12; 24:9)

> For they did not come to meet you with bread and water on your way when you **came out of Egypt**, and they hired **Balaam son of Beor** from **Pethor** in Aram Naharaim *to pronounce a curse* on you. [5] However, Yahweh your God would not listen to Balaam but turned the curse into a **blessing** for you, because Yahweh your God loves you. (Deut 23:4–5[5–6])

The claim that the Moabites did not provide water creates tension with the diplomatic message to Sihon: "*Sell us food to eat and water to drink* for their price in silver. Only let

punishments in the form of his handing over his wife to be raped (MAL §A55). MAL §A56 overlaps the standards in the law of the seducer (Exod 22:16–17[15–16]).

120. See Schnittjer, "Kadesh Infidelity," 108.

us pass through on foot—*as* the descendants of Esau, who live in Seir, *and the Moabites*, who live in Ar, *did for us*" (2:28–29, emphasis mine). The sale of food and water by the Edomites and Moabites does not appear elsewhere. Numbers only records hostilities by each of these peoples to Israel. In any case, Deut 23:4–5[5–6] pairs the lack of hospitality by Ammon and Moab with the hiring of Balaam to damn Israel. This serves as the rationale for the legal standard permanently excluding them from the assembly of Yahweh.

Elsewhere in Scripture the two excluded and two included peoples of the law of the assembly get lumped together with the people of Judah. "'The days are coming,' declares Yahweh, 'when I will punish *all who are circumcised only in the flesh—Egypt*, Judah, *Edom, Ammon, Moab*, and all those who cut the hair of their temples short and live in the desert. For all these nations are really uncircumcised, and even the whole house of Israel is uncircumcised in heart'" (Jer 9:25–26[24–25], v. 26 lit., emphasis mine). Because physical circumcision of itself does not provide adequate evidence of entry into the assembly of Yahweh, the law of the assembly spells out the bases of exclusion and potential inclusion into the assembly for peoples who practiced non-covenantal circumcision.[121] Although Jeremiah speaks of the non-covenantal circumcision of these peoples, Second Temple Judaic traditions still think of circumcision as the way Ammonites would assimilate into Israel (Judith 14:10).

Though the legal standard against the Ammonites and Moabites gets grounded in a historical event, this law is consistently interpreted symbolically rather than literally elsewhere in Scripture. The narrative rationale—those who would damn the people of God—seems to function as the basis of the law over and against genealogical or ethnic identity. See notes on 1 Kgs 11:1; Isa 52:1b; 56:1–8; Ruth 2:8; 4:17, 22; Lam 1:10; Ezra 9:1–2; Neh 13:1–3.

23:9–14[10–15]~Lev 15:16 (B) (ritual purity in time of battle). Deuteronomy 23:11[12] shares ritual purification language with Lev 15:16 regarding an emission. The parallel language and contextual issues suggest allusion.

Deuteronomy 23:9–14[10–15] raises the standards for ritual purity during warfare. That said, it seems that Deuteronomy goes out of its way to avoid the normal language of ritual purity in the priestly regulations. Specifically, Deuteronomy does not use the standard priestly terms for ritual impurity but opens with "keep away from everything bad" (lit.) and closes with Yahweh not seeing anything "indecent" (Deut 23:9, 14[10, 15]).[122] In between are rare terms for "emission" and "excrement" (23:10, 13[11, 14]).[123] This evidence suggests Deuteronomy intentionally uses new language without theological baggage to set out a standard for holiness in the wartime encampment. The one exception is the allusion

---

121. See Orian, "Numbers," 114–15.

122. "Bad" (רַע) is a common generic term meaning evil or the like (Deut 23:9[10]). "Indecent" literally "nakedness" (עֶרְוָה) only appears two times in Deuteronomy, here and with reference to "something objectionable" in the wife leading to divorce (23:14[15]; 24:1).

123. "Emission" is a *hapax legomenon* (Deut 23:10[11]), and "excrement" only appears twice (23:13[14]; Ezek 4:12) ("*קָרֶה," "*צֵאָה," *HALOT* 2:992, 1138).

to standard procedures for regaining ritual purity after an emission (bold signifies verbal parallel, and broken underlining signifies the underlying rationale for the new standard):

> When a man has an emission of semen, **he must bathe** his whole body **with water**, and he will be unclean till **evening.** (Lev 15:16)

> When you are encamped against your enemies, keep away from everything impure. [10] If one of your men is unclean because of a nocturnal emission, he is to go outside the camp and stay there. [11] But as **evening** approaches **he is to bathe himself with water**, and at sunset he may return to the camp. [12] Designate a place outside the camp where you can go to relieve yourself. [13] As part of your equipment have something to dig with, and when you relieve yourself, dig a hole and cover up your excrement. [14] For Yahweh your God moves about in your camp to protect you and to deliver your enemies to you. Your camp must be holy, so that he will not see among you anything indecent and turn away from you. (Deut 23:9–14†[10–15])

Elsewhere when the tabernacle came into the civilian camp all ritually impure persons needed to get out (Num 5:1–4). The ark goes with Israel's military, requiring ritual purity in the encampment (10:35–36; 1 Sam 21:4–5[5–6]). Deuteronomy does not mention the ark. Instead the camp must be holy because Yahweh himself walks around in the camp (Deut 23:14; cf. 7:21; 20:4; 31:6, 8). The presence of Yahweh requires both ritual purity and a level of modesty about the very mundane concern of excrement (23:10, 13[11, 14]). Even the case of nocturnal/accidental emission includes within it refraining from intentional relations when going to battle (23:10[11]). These standards are framed representatively to include anything kindred—"Anything bad" and "an indecent thing" (23:9, 14 lit.[10, 15]).[124]

In sum, the advancement of revelation within the law of military encampment raises the standards for holiness to its highest plain. Everything, even accidental or mundane, requires intentional care in light of Yahweh's presence. The extremes of wartime do not provide exemptions but demand higher standards.

23:19–20*~Exod 22:25*[24] (B) (prohibition against charging interest to Israelites) (* see release statute network). See note on Deut 15:1–11.

24:6, 10–13*, 17b~Exod 22:26–27*[25–26] (B) (loan collateral regulated) (* see release statute network). The covenant collection prevents holding pledges overnight, such as a cloak that the impoverished person needs (Exod 22:26–27[25–26]). Deuteronomy 24:12–13 loosely paraphrases this law, making allusion likely. Deuteronomy goes further by insisting that taking cloaks as pledges from widows is categorically banned (Deut 24:17b). Likewise, millstones cannot be held as collateral for debt since they are needed

124. "[T]he principle is more comprehensive than the two examples cited" (Tigay, *Deuteronomy*, 213).

for earnings (24:6). Finally, those making loans may not enter the household of debtors while they get the collateral (24:10–11). All of these elements advance the protections for those who need to borrow.

24:8–9~Lev 13–14+Num 12:10–15 (B) (skin conditions). Deuteronomy 24:8–9 broadly alludes to the instructions housed in Lev 13–14 using the characteristic priestly expression "outbreak of skin diseases." Deuteronomy also overtly marks this allusion by "according to what I have commanded them," strongly suggesting the priestly scriptural tradition as donor context (Deut 24:8). For motivation, Deuteronomy alludes to Miriam's week of skin disease appearing in Num 12:10–15. Notice the interpretive blending emphasizing motivation (italics signify allusions, and broken underlining signifies overt marking of citation):

> In cases of *defiling skin diseases*, be very careful to do exactly as the Levitical priests instruct you. You must follow carefully what I have commanded them. Remember *what Yahweh your God did to Miriam* along the way after you came out of Egypt. (Deut 24:8–9)

24:14–15~Lev 19:13b (C) (wages regulated). Deuteronomy 24:14–15 seems to loosely paraphrase the holiness regulation on paying day laborers (Lev 19:13b). Deuteronomy adds multiple motivations, including the benefit to the workers and warning that they may "call out against you to Yahweh" (Deut 24:15 lit.). The language differs, but the sentiment runs along the lines of Yahweh listening to the socially disadvantaged who "cry out" in the covenant collection (Exod 22:23, 27[22, 26]). While the holiness standard says not to hold the wages "until morning" (Lev 19:13 lit.), Deuteronomy insists payment before sunset (bold signifies verbal parallel, italics signify paraphrase, and broken underlining signifies motivation).

> Do not hold back the wages of **a hired worker** *overnight.* (Lev 19:13b)

> Do not take advantage of **a hired worker** who is poor and needy, whether that worker is a fellow Israelite or a foreigner residing in one of your towns. Pay them their wages each day *before sunset*, because they are poor and are counting on it. Otherwise they may cry to Yahweh against you, and you will be guilty of sin. (Deut 24:14–15)

25:11–12~Exod 21:22 (B) (if two men fight). The legal cases of two men fighting in Exodus 21:22 and Deuteronomy 25:11–12 include evidence to interpret them in direct interpretive relationship. The case in the covenant collection goes on to a sub-case of limitation of judgment in the event of an injury to a bystander—"eye for an eye" (Exod 21:24). The interpretive intervention in Deuteronomy focuses only on expanding the main case itself. Both cases relate to men "fighting," using a word only appearing seven times in Scripture. While the two Hifil uses refer to conflicts between collectives, the five Nifal uses refer to physical altercations between two individuals.[125] The exact phrase "If men are fighting" (כִּי־יִנָּצוּ אֲנָשִׁים) only appears in the two case laws under consideration here.[126]

The version of the law in Deuteronomy expands protections to include both genders which matches similar legal moves elsewhere (see Deut 7:3 and note ad loc). Compare the protections for human reproduction for her and for him in these two laws (bold signifies verbatim parallel, broken underlining signifies interpretive intervention, and underlining signifies a potentially related parallel).

> **If men are fighting** and hit a pregnant woman and she gives birth prematurely but there is no serious injury, the offender must be fined whatever the woman's husband demands and the court allows. [23] But if there is serious injury, you are to take life for life, [24] eye for eye, tooth for tooth, hand for hand, foot for foot, [25] burn for burn, wound for wound, bruise for bruise. (Exod 21:22–25; v. 22†)

> **If men are fighting** each other and the wife of one of them comes to rescue her husband from his assailant, and she reaches out and seizes him by his private parts, you shall cut off her hand. Show her no pity. (Deut 25:11–12†)

The present discussion does not need to untangle the contested interpretations of "and her children come out" (Exod 21:22 lit.) rendered by the NIV as "she gives birth prematurely." However that phrase is handled, the legal protection applies to the woman's unborn child. The legal standard in Deuteronomy 25:11 extends protection to the reproductive capacity of the males fighting. As elsewhere, Deuteronomy shows an interest in making explicit by exegetical expansion the gender inclusive force of the legal protections.

The legal limitation of punishment "an eye for an eye," etc. is generally interpreted to speak of equivalency of financial penalties not physical maiming. But the penalty of the woman who intentionally damages a man's reproductive capacity, no matter how well intentioned she is, may have been liable to a rare physical maiming because of the severity of the crime.[127] This interpretation corresponds to an ancient Mesopotamian law from the eleventh century BCE: "If a woman should crush a man's testicle during a quarrel, they shall cut off one of her fingers . . . or if she should crush the second testicle during the quarrel—they shall gouge out both her [. . .]s" (MAL §8; last word missing).

---

125. See "נצה," *NIDOTTE* 3:137.

126. See Even-Shoshan, 777; "I נצה," *HALOT* 1:715; cf. other Nif uses of "fight" (נצה) Exod 2:13; Lev 24:10; 2 Sam 14:6; Sir 8:3.

127. See detailed discussion of competing interpretations in Tigay, *Deuteronomy*, 484–86.

26:5–10*~Num 20:15–16+Gen 12:10+18:18 (B) (firstfruits liturgy) (* see place network). Deuteronomy 26 presents two liturgies: an annual firstfruits liturgy when the people bring the best portion of their firstfruits to the priests during the pilgrimage Festival of Weeks (Deut 26:1–11; cf. 14:22–27; 16:9–12; 18:4), and a solemn declaration every third year regarding tithes, presumably at Tabernacles so the tithe can be calculated from the harvest (26:12–15; cf. 14:28–29). The entire firstfruits section in verses 1–11 shows marked emphasis on the divine name (14x), the verb "give" (7x), and various forms of "enter/bring" (6x)—the worshiper "brings" the firstfruits because Yahweh "brought" them to the land.[128] The leading phrase of the liturgy "my father was a wandering Aramean" features strong assonance for easy memory, *arami oved avi* (אֲרַמִּי אֹבֵד אָבִי). The term "wandering" seems to carry a rich ancient Near Eastern cultural sense of "political refugee" and "social misfit" in the liturgy referring to Jacob.[129] The use of first-person singular in vv. 3 and 10 makes it sound like a one-time event, but the reference in v. 3 to the priest in office "at that time" infers an annual liturgy. The sense of shared identity fits with other memorial events like Passover.

The firstfruits liturgy seems to use part of the message to the Edomite king as a skeleton, repeating at least five verbs in identical sequence: "went down . . . mistreated . . . cried out . . . heard . . . brought out" (Num 20:15–16; Deut 26:5–8). The shared sequence makes allusion very likely. This framework gets fleshed out by language from the Abrahamic narratives (Gen 12:10; 18:18; Deut 26:5) and manifold Deuteronomic stock phrases (emphases signify verbal parallels):[130]

> Now there was a famine in the land, and Abram went down to Egypt to live there for a while because the famine was severe. (Gen 12:10)
>
> Abraham will surely become a great and powerful nation. (18:18a)
>
> [message to king of Edom] Our **ancestors went down into Egypt**, and we lived there many years. **The Egyptians mistreated us** and our ancestors, but when **we cried out to Yahweh**, he **heard our cry** and sent an angel and **brought us out of Egypt**. "Now we are here at Kadesh, a town on the edge of your territory." (Num 20:15–16)
>
> Then you shall declare before Yahweh your God: "My **ancestor** was a wandering Aramean, and he **went down into Egypt** with a few people and lived there and became a great nation, powerful and numerous. [6] But **the Egyptians mistreated us** and made

128. See ibid, 238.

129. See the review of the scholarly interaction with cognate parallels in Millard, "Wandering Aramean," 153–55.

130. These observations on parallels follow Nelson, *Deuteronomy*, 309. The stock phrases Nelson points out include Yahweh's "hand" and "arm" (Deut 4:34; 5:15; 7:19; 11:2), "great terror" (4:34; 34:12; cf. Exod 14:24; 15:14–16), and "signs and wonders" (Deut 6:22; 28:46; 34:11; cf. Exod 4:21).

us suffer, subjecting us to harsh labor. [7] Then **we cried out to Yahweh**, the God of our ancestors, and Yahweh **heard our cry** and saw our misery, toil and oppression. [8] So Yahweh **brought us out of Egypt** with a mighty hand and an outstretched arm, with great terror and with signs and wonders. [9] He brought us to this place and gave us this land, a land flowing with milk and honey; [10] and now I bring the firstfruits of the soil that you, Yahweh, have given me." Place the basket before Yahweh your God and bow down before him. (Deut 26:5–10†)

Von Rad both drew attention to the lack of reference to revelation at the mountain in the liturgy and proposed that the narrative provides the seed that grew into the great Torah storyline eventually fleshed out by the giving of the law.[131] This influential thesis appears in many studies, though subsequent research suggests von Rad had it backwards, namely, the liturgy is a later summary of the storyline.[132] In any case, the evidence of interpretive allusion noted above points to adaptation of scriptural traditions for an annual confession.

In sum, the remarkable first-person annual firstfruits liturgical confession calls worshipers to adopt and proclaim the covenantal identity of Yahweh's salvation from the Hebrew ancestors in gratitude of the annual bounty in the land of promise.

32:8~Gen 11:7 (C) (dividing the nations). The Septuagint and Masoretic Text feature differences in Deut 32. The language of Deut 32:8 and 32:43 both seem to represent euphemistic scribal intervention in the masoretic version.[133] The discovery of fragments of Deut 32:8 at Qumran confirms the preferability of the Septuagintal version (4QDeut[j/4Q37]). The primary textual witnesses can be compared and briefly discussed.[134]

When the Most High apportioned the nations, when he separated humans, he set the boundaries of the peoples, according to the number **of the Israelites.** (Deut 32:8 MT/SP lit.)

When the Most High was apportioning nations, as he scattered Adam's sons, he fixed boundaries of nations according to the number **of the divine sons.** (32:8 LXX)

---

131. See von Rad, "Problem of the Hexateuch," in *From Genesis*, 1–58, esp. 5–6.

132. See Childs, "Deuteronomic Formula," 30–39, esp. 39; Hyatt, "Historical Credo," 152–70; Durham, "Credo," *IBDSup* 198–99.

133. The present discussion needs to be restricted to the evidence for Deut 32:8. For a helpful overview with diagram of the very difficult textual issues in Deut 32:43, see Tigay, *Deuteronomy*, 516–18.

134. The last phrase reads: "sons of Israel" (בְּנֵי יִשְׂרָאֵל) (MT) and (בני ישראל) (SP), "sons of God" (υἱῶν θεοῦ) (LXX Göttingen), "celestial delegates of God" (ἀγγέλων θεοῦ) (LXX Cambridge/Vaticanus), "sons of God" (בני אלוהים) (4QDeut[j/4Q37] in *BQS* 1:240). The original working out of 4QDeut[j/4Q37] came in two steps since the short form of God *el* of the initial fragment led to a proposal "sons of El" (בני אל), then the rest of the fragment confirmed "sons of God" (בני אלוהים), see Freedman's editorial comment in Hummel, "Enclitic *Mem*," 101, n. 101; Skehan, "Qumran," 21–22.

> When . . . apportioned . . . **of the sons of God.** (32:8 4QDeut[j/4Q37] lit.; the rest missing)

The last phrase in the critical eclectic Septuagintal version is "sons of God" (32:8 lit. LXX Göttingen; rendered as "divine sons" by NETS above) based on the early witness 848 (first century BCE) making this reading "assured."[135] Wevers explains, "The change to 'angels' was clearly a later attempt to avoid any notion of lesser deities in favor of God's messengers."[136] The scribal change in the proto-masoretic Hebrew text of Deut 32:8, apparently during the Hasmonean period or in the first century CE, suggests the same euphemistic logic.[137]

In sum of the textual difficulties, the evidence strongly suggests the older better reading of Deut 32:8 refers to the Most High dividing the nations according to the number of the sons of God. The exegetical point to be discussed presently works either way; it simply makes more sense in light of the original reading.

The Song of Moses in Deut 32:8 appears to offer an exegetical explanation of the dividing of the peoples known in Genesis by the narrative of the tower of Babel. The poetic allusion refers to the same event, though the lack of verbal correspondence means the relationship needs to be considered a possibility. The Song of Moses provides the rationale of the divine comments, including its use of first-person plural verbs in speaking to the celestial court (emphases mine).

> [Yahweh said] "Come, let us go down and let us confuse their language so they will not understand each other." So Yahweh scattered them from there over all the earth, and they stopped building the city. (Gen 11:7–8, v. 7 lit.)

> When the Most High apportioned the nations, When he separated humans, He set the boundaries of the peoples, According to the number of the sons of God. (Deut 32:8 lit.)

According to the Song of Moses, Yahweh addresses the celestial court and calls upon them to go down to confuse the language of the peoples in order to frustrate the project of the tower builders. The seventy peoples listed in the table of nations in Gen 10 suggests the "number of the sons of God" as seventy in the Song of Moses.[138] Other local cultures also thought in terms of seventy sons of deity.[139]

---

135. Wevers, *Notes on Deuteronomy*, 513.

136. Ibid.

137. See McCarthy, *BHQ*, 140*–41*.

138. The change in Deut 32:8 proto-MT to "sons of Israel" required additional changes to make the number of the sons of Jacob going into Egypt be seventy in Gen 46:20, 21, 22, 27; Exod 1:5 (ibid.). Tal notes the textual issue but does not make the connection (*BHQ*, 189* [on Gen 46:27]).

139. See Palace of Baal, 4.vi.46 (Gibson, *Canaanite Myths*, 63; Coogan and Smith, *Stories*, 135).

In sum, the poetic interpretation of the division of humans offers a reason for the seventy nations that appear in Gen 10, namely, one for each of the sons of God in the celestial court.

32:10–11~Gen 1:2+Exod 19:4 (B) (like a mother eagle). The term *tohu* (תֹּהוּ) only appears twice in Torah. It has the sense of "formless" in Gen 1:2 and "barren" in Deut 32:10. Elsewhere the term shows up eighteen times, including once in an anti-creational judgment context (Jer 4:23). The rare term for "hover" occurs only three times, making allusion likely (Gen 1:2; Deut 32:11; and with a different sense Jer 23:3).[140] The likelihood of an allusion to Gen 1:2 gets strengthened by use of general creational imagery for establishing Israel in Deut 32:6. Scripture only uses "eagle" in a maternal sense in Exod 19:4 and Deut 32:11, suggesting intentional parallel.[141] Note the blending of this imagery associated with creation and redemption in the Song of Moses (emphases signify verbal parallels):

> Now the earth was **formless** [תֹּהוּ] and empty, darkness was over the surface of the deep, and the Spirit of God **was hovering** over the waters. (Gen 1:2)
>
> You yourselves have seen what I did to Egypt, and how I carried you on *eagles' wings* and brought you to myself. (Exod 19:4)
>
> In a desert land he found him, in a **barren** [תֹּהוּ] and howling waste. He shielded him and cared for him; he guarded him as the apple of his eye, like an *eagle* that stirs up its nest and **hovers** over its young, that spreads its *wings* to catch them and carries them aloft. (Deut 32:10–11)

The Song of Moses brings together imagery from creation and redemption to describe Yahweh's relationship with Israel. In one sense this reflects the oneness of God spoken of elsewhere in Deuteronomy (6:4). Since he is one, his great works naturally function on analogy with one another. This means creation is redemption shaped and redemption is creation shaped. Isaiah picks up on the same interconnectivity when he brings together creation and sea-crossing imagery (see note on Isa 43).

34:10–12*~4:34+18:15–22*+Exod 33:11 (B) (prophet like Moses) (* see prophet like Moses network). The narrator closes Deuteronomy by reflecting back to the time of Moses and noting that no prophet like Moses has since risen in Israel (Deut 34:10). If the same person acted as narrator for all the updates in the book, they could be written no

---

140. On "formless/barren," see "תֹּהוּ" and on "hover," see "רחף" in *HALOT* 2:1219–20, 1689–90.

141. Elsewhere Torah prohibits eating eagles (Lev 11:13//Deut 14:12) and uses eagles metaphorically as a bird of prey (Deut 28:49). Outside of Torah eagles often function as similes of swiftness, high nests, even baldness, and so on, but only maternally in Exod 19:4 and Deut 32:11 ("נֶשֶׁר," *HALOT* 1:731).

sooner than sometime after the settlement of the land (2:12). But since the narrator needs to explain so many things for readers (e.g., 2:10–11, 20), it could be much later.

Even though Deut 34:10 only shares a common noun ("prophet") and a common verb ("risen") with 18:15, the use of the preposition "like" to create a simile makes allusion highly likely. The strong revelatory relationship of Yahweh with Moses appears in other contexts using different language, such as that which refers to Yahweh as speaking to Moses "mouth to mouth" (Num 12:8 lit.). Another context says, "When Moses entered the tent of meeting to speak with Yahweh, *he heard the voice speaking to him* from between the two cherubim above the atonement cover on the ark of the covenant law. In this way Yahweh spoke to him" (7:89, emphasis mine). The only two contexts that use the expression "face to face" of Yahweh and Moses are Exod 33:11 and Deut 34:10, suggesting a relationship. Most of the imagery in Deut 34:11–12 amounts to common stock phrases. The only contexts in Torah to use "great fear-inspiring acts," or as NIV puts it, "awesome deeds," are Deut 4:34, 26:8, and 32:12.[142] Of these, Deut 4:34 and 34:12 share many expressions not appearing in the firstfruits liturgy in ch. 26. In sum on this point, the evidence suggests a likely exegetical blended allusion by the narrator of the following contexts (emphases signify verbal parallels):

> <u>Yahweh</u> would speak to Moses <u>face to face</u>, as one speaks to a friend. (Exod 33:11a)

> Has any god ever tried to take for himself one nation out of another nation, by testings, by *signs and wonders*, by war, by a *mighty hand* and an outstretched arm, or by *awesome deeds*, like all the things Yahweh your God *did* for you *in Egypt before* your very *eyes*? (Deut 4:34†)

> Yahweh your God **will raise up** for you a **prophet like** me from among you, from your fellow Israelites. You must listen to him. (18:15)

> Since then, no **prophet has risen** in Israel **like** Moses, whom <u>Yahweh</u> knew <u>face to face</u>, who did all those *signs and wonders* Yahweh sent him *to do in Egypt*—to Pharaoh and to all his officials and to his whole land. For no one has ever shown the *mighty hand* or performed the *awesome deeds* that Moses did *before the eyes of* all Israel. (34:10–12†)

Moses himself and Yahweh speak of a prophet singular (18:15, 18), but it functions as a distributive since Yahweh, explicitly mediated by Moses, expected many such prophets (18:19–22).[143] The narrator of Deuteronomy expands the sense of the prophetic

---

142. The only other place in Scripture that collocates "great" (גָּדוֹל) and "fear-inspiring" (מוֹרָא) is Jer 32:21 ("מוֹרָא," *HALOT* 1:560), but that entire context is clearly derivative (see discussion of Jer 32 in Jeremiah Filters).

143. See Driver, *Deuteronomy*, 227; Knoppers, "'To Him You Must Listen,'" 162, n. 1.

expectation by adding the fear-inspiring terrors that Moses announced to the pharaoh (34:11–12). In this way the narrator exegetically advances the expectation to something more than simply the prophetic role of Moses, but a prophet like Moses inclusive of both mediator of revelation and fear-inspiring redemptive power.

The sense of "there has not arisen again" often gets interpreted as "never since" (34:12 NRSV) or "never again" (JPSB). Knoppers observes that the construction functions like the three incomparable descriptions in Kings—none discerning like Solomon; faithful like Hezekiah; and turning to Yahweh with all his heart, soul, and strength like Josiah (1 Kgs 3:12; 2 Kgs 18:5; 23:25).[144] This comparison helps as far as it goes. One difference relates to each of these three comparisons to all kings "before him" and "after him." Since Kings includes all the kings until the fall of Jerusalem, the incompatibility can be complete. By contrast, Ahab did more evil "than all who went before him" (1 Kgs 16:30 lit.). This invites the question if any northern Israelite king after him might be worse? Menahem seems like a contender (2 Kgs 15:16–21). Whether Ahab holds the title does not matter so much as how backwards-only comparisons work. They leave the question open for afterwards. The backwards-only comparison of Deut 34:10–12 works in the same way.

The narrator of Deuteronomy's expanded expectation creates ongoing opportunity to evaluate later Moses-like prophets. Many of those who met the Lord wondered about the expectation for such a prophet (John 1:21, 45; 6:14; 7:40). His early followers seem to take the point of departure from the narrator in Deut 34:10 and reread 18:15 as an expectation for a particular prophet like Moses (Acts 3:22–24; 7:37).

In sum, the narrator of Deuteronomy exegetically advances revelation by inferring that the Moses-like prophet has not yet arisen and by adding redemptive signs and wonders to the revelatory profile of the expected one.

FILTERS

Filtering elements helps prevent false positives in the study of exegetical use of Scripture. Lists of Deuteronomy's idioms, stock phrases, and characteristic expressions can be found elsewhere.[145] The following illustrative filtered elements are not comprehensive or complete.[146]

---

144. See Knoppers, "'To Him You Must Listen,'" 172, n. 23; idem, "'There Was None Like Him,'" 431.

145. See Weinfeld, *Deuteronomic School*, 332–59; Driver, *Introduction*, 99–102; idem, *Deuteronomy*, lxxviii–lxxxiv; Grisanti, "Josiah," 123, 128–29.

146. For a list of allusions to Torah narratives in Deuteronomy, see Driver, *Deuteronomy*, xv. For shared verbal parallels between the narratives in Deuteronomy and their counterparts in Torah, see idem, *Introduction*, 80. For dozens of verbal and thematic parallels between Deuteronomy and Genesis, see Block, "Tradition," 137–52. For an extensive list of similar phrases and potential parallels between Deuteronomy and the Latter Prophets and Writings see Mirsky, *Deuteronomy*, 3–170 (appendix) [Hebrew].

Non-Exegetical Broad Allusions and Shared Themes

Narratives: **4:16–19**>/<Gen 1, listed in nearly reverse order: male or female, animal, bird, creature that moves along the ground, fish, sun and moon, stars, and heavens;[147] **4:32**>/<Gen 1–2, creation of humans; **1:7–8, 10–11; 4:37a; 6:10–11, 18, 23; 7:12; 9:5; 10:15, 22b; 11:9; 26:5a; 30:5**>/<Gen 12; 15; 22; 27; 28, covenant with ancestors; **11:24; 34:1–4**>/<Gen 15:18, extent of land of promise; **2:4–5, 9, 19**>/<Gen 36; 19:33–38, relatives of ancestors—Edom, Ammon, Moab; **29:23[22]**>/<Gen 19, destruction of cities of plain (cf. 32:32); **33:13**>/<Gen 49:25, blessing Joseph from heavens and deeps; **33:16**>/<Gen 49:26, Joseph blessed as prince among brothers; **10:19, 22a; 11:10; 26:5b**>/<Gen 46–50, asylum in Egypt; **4:34–35, 37b; 6:12, 21–22; 7:18–19; 8:14; 10:21; 11:2–4; 26:6–8; 29:2–3[1–2]**>/<Exod 5–15, redemption from Egyptian bondage; **32:6**>/<Exod 4:22, fatherhood of God to Israel signified in the redemption; **25:17–19**>/<Exod 17:14, blotting out remembrance of Amalekites; **4:10–12, 32–33, 36; 18:16; 33:4**>/<Exod 19:7–24, revelation at the mountain; **6:13; 10:20; 13:4[5]**>/<Exod 23:13, monotheistic devotion; **33:8**>/<Exod 28:30, Levi granted Thummim and Urim; **33:9**>/<Exod 32:27, Levi serving God even against family (cf. Deut 13:6–7); **33:10**>/<Lev 10:10–11, Levi teaches Israel torah; **1:6**>/<Num 10:11, journey from Horeb; **1:2**>/<Num 10:11–12:16, travel from Horeb to Kadesh; **2:6; 8:2–4, 15–16; 11:5; 29:5–6; 32:13–14**>/<Exod 16–Num 34, wilderness provisions; **2:14–16; 6:16; 9:7, 22**>/<Exod 17:7; Num 11:1–3, 34, wilderness rebellions; **33:8**>/<Exod 17:7; Num 20:13, testing (Levi) at Massah and Meribah; **32:17**>/<Lev 17:7, sacrificing to demons; **11:6**>/<Num 16:20–34, Sheol swallows rebels; **1:3**>/<Num 14:34, forty years in the wilderness; **9:1–2**>/<Num 13:28, 33, fortified cities of Canaan and Anakites (Deut 1:28); **8:15**>/<Num 21:6–9, fiery snakes (נחש שרף); **1:4; 3:21a; 4:3, 38, 45–46; 29:7[6]; 31:4**>/<Num 20–21; 31, defeat of Transjordanian kingdoms; **32:50**>/<Num 20:22–29, death of Aaron on Mount Hor; **4:13, 14; 6:24–25**>/<Exod 20; 21–24; Deut 1–34, instruction at Horeb/Sinai and/or on plains of Moab; **32:49–50**>/<Num 27:12, Moses to ascend Mount Abarim to see but not enter the land; **3:21b–22; 4:47–49; 7:16; 8:20; 9:1, 3–6; 11:23–25; 26:1, 9; 31:3, 5**>/<Exod 23:20–33, promise to drive out nations from land of promise; **32:30**>/<Lev 26:6, few defeating many; **10:16; 30:6**>/<Lev 26:41, heart circumcision.

Legal standards: **10:19**>/<Lev 19:34, love the residing foreigners; **12:29–31**>/<Exod 22:20[19]; 23:33; 34:12, warning against following other gods of the peoples of the land; **14:1–2**>/<Lev 19:27–28; 21:5, prohibition against disfiguring mourning rites; **17:1**>/<Lev 22:17–24, sacrifices could not have defects (cf. Deut 15:21); **18:1–8**>/<Num 18:8–20, Levitical priestly portion if they migrate to central sanctuary they now share in priestly portions (cf. Levites, Num 18:21–24, 30–32; priests, Lev 7:32–34; Num 18:8–20,

147. See Fishbane, "Varia Deuteronomica," 349.

25–29);[148] **18:9–14**>/<Exod 22:18[17]; Lev 18:21; 19:31; 20:2–5, 27, prohibition against divination and child sacrifice (cf. Deut 12:31); **19:16**>/<Exod 23:1, against the "malicious witness"; **22:8**>/<Exod 21:33–34, putting up a roof guard suggests liability akin to leaving an open pit; **22:12**>/<Num 15:37–41, tassels on four corners of garment—without rationale in Deuteronomy; **23:17–18[18–19]**>/<Lev 19:29, prohibition against cultic prostitution; **24:7**>/<Exod 21:16, prohibition against kidnapping in Deuteronomy emphasizes not doing so to fellow Israelites; **24:17–18**>/<Exod 22:21–22[20–21]; 23:9; Lev 19:33–34, triad of protected classes—widow, orphan, residing foreigner (elsewhere Deuteronomy frequently includes Levites with the protected classes, Deut 12:18–19; 14:27, 29; 26:11, 12, 13); **24:19, 21–22**>/<Lev 19:9–10, regulations for gleaning field and vineyard, and Deut 24:20 adds olive grove to demonstrate the pervasive need to use part of earnings to help protected classes; **25:13–16**>/<Lev 19:35–36, prohibition against fraudulent measures (cf. Prov 20:10); **26:14**>/<Ps 106:28 with Num 25:2, prohibition against offering food to the dead.

The three pilgrimage festivals each mention celebrating them at the place Yahweh chooses (Deut 16:2, 6, 7, 11, 15). The treatment in the torah collection is more developed than the covenant collection and covenant renewal collection but without all the details of the sacrifices in Num 28–29. Note: **Unleavened Bread/Passover**, Deut 16:1–8; cf. Exod 12:10–20; 13:3–13; 23:15; 34:18–20; Lev 23:5–8; Num 9:1–14; 28:16–25; **Weeks** (Pentecost), Deut 16:9–12; cf. Exod 23:16; 34:22; Lev 23:15–21; Num 28:26–31; **Tabernacles** (Ingathering), Deut 16:13–15; cf. Exod 23:16; 34:22; Lev 23:33–43; Num 29:12–34; Zech 14:16–19; Ezra 3:4; Neh 8:13–18; John 7–8.

Note the priestly portion according to Leviticus: "From the fellowship offerings of the Israelites, I have taken *the breast that is waved and the thigh* that is presented and have given them to Aaron the priest and his sons as their perpetual share from the Israelites" (Lev 7:34, emphasis mine; cf. vv. 32–33). The Levitical priests in Deut 18:1 refers to all Levites who are said to get a different portion: "This is the share due the priests from the people who sacrifice a bull or a sheep: *the shoulder, the internal organs and the meat from the head*" (**Deut 18:3**, emphasis mine). Since this refers to sacrifices it may presume those Levites who go to the central place of worship to serve (18:6). The differences cause great challenges and get harmonized differently in traditional approaches—for example, the Levitical portion refers to non-sacred slaughter in towns (but the term for slaughter implies sacred).[149]

The protections for the inheritance of the **"hated wife"** in Deut 21:15–17 may be based on "hated wife" as a legal status. Elsewhere this is only used of accusing the new bride (Deut 22:13) and the wife divorced without cause (24:3). Based on comparative

---

148. For extensive discussion of the differences in the priestly portions including ancient Near Eastern comparisons, see Greer, "'Priestly Portion,'" 263–84.

149. See m. Hul. 10:1. And see discussion in Tigay, *Deuteronomy*, 169–71; Greer, "'Priestly Portion,'" 263–84.

legal evidence from other ancient cultures, Wells suggests that the wife demoted without cause may get protections for the inheritance of her firstborn son (21:15–17).[150] The law in Deut 21:15–17 often gets compared with Leah's situation as a "hated wife" in Gen 29:31.

The limitation against taking mother bird and eggs (**22:6–7**) may be humanitarian protection similar to prohibitions against muzzling an ox while threshing (25:4), slaughtering an animal and its young on the same day (Lev 22:28), or cooking a young goat in its mother's milk (Deut 14:21b//Exod 23:19b//34:26b). Also see limitations in Exod 22:30[29]; Lev 22:27; Deut 20:19.

The Ten Commandments and the holiness collection prohibit adultery, and the latter spells out capital punishment (Exod 20:14//Deut 5:18; Lev 18:20; 20:10). Only one case law works out contingencies of fornication with a betrothed slave that does not require the death penalty because she is not free (Lev 19:20–22). **Deuteronomy 22:22–27** takes up three cases: one of adultery with a wife of another and two of relations with betrothed young women, one in the city and the other in the open country. The penalties get calibrated depending on circumstances (cf. HL §197).

The only prohibition against incest in the torah collection itself is marrying one's stepmother (**Deut 22:30[23:1]**)—though several other incestuous relations appear in the curses (27:20, 22, 23). The language runs somewhat differently than the counterpart in Leviticus. Compare "The nakedness of the wife of your father you shall not uncover. She is the nakedness of your father" (Lev 18:8 lit.) and "A man shall not take the wife of his father, so that he does not uncover the robe of his father" (Deut 22:30 lit.[23:1]).[151]

The prohibition against entry of a person with a crushed or cut off male organ into the assembly of Yahweh (**23:1[2]**) often gets compared to the prohibition of priests from service for several physical defects, including crushed testicles (Lev 21:20).

The law on vows in **Deut 23:21–23[22–24]** goes a somewhat different direction than the regulations concerning equivalencies for persons (Lev 27:2) or doing according to one's vow (Num 30:6). Deuteronomy 23:21[22] encourages that payment "not be slow," echoing the call for offering in the covenant collection (Exod 22:29[28]). At the same time Deut 23:22[23] notes that refraining from vows carries no sinfulness.

The regulation for suggested, but not required, levirate marriage in **Deut 25:5–10** shares concerns over preserving the name of the dead with the law of female inheritance (Num 27:4; cf. Deut 25:6, 7). On the surface it appears that the levirate-marriage provision supplements the prohibition against marriage between brother-in-law and sister-in-law (Lev 18:16; 20:21). If so, the exception comes in the case of the death of the brother whose widow is childless (Deut 25:5). The purpose of the marriage is to have children

150. Wells, "Hated Wife," 135–45; idem, "Law or Religion?" 302–4.

151. The term "robe" is literally "wing" (כָּנָף) (Deut 22:30[23:1]) as though marrying the stepmother is exposing the father. Compare uses of covering with the robe in association with marriage more positively in Ezek 16:8; Ruth 3:9.

(25:6). The holiness "threat clause" for marriage between brother-in-law and sister-in-law, ironically, is that the couple "will be childless" (Lev 20:21).

Recurring Traditions

The commissioning of Joshua appears repeatedly in Numbers, Deuteronomy, and Joshua (Num 27:12–23; Deut 3:21–29; 31:1–8, 14–15, 23; Josh 1:1–9; cf. Deut 32:44–47; 34:9). The basic details get repeated and expanded several times. In Deuteronomy the primary emphasis seems to fall on replacing Moses. For the connection with the mission in Exod 23 see note on Ps 22:1[2].

The obedience formula appears twice. The twofold charge gets at obedience to the law rather than the wording of the law. The verb combination in the first is "do not add . . . or subtract, *but keep*" (Deut 4:2 lit., emphasis mine) and the other "*you shall keep to do*" (12:32[13:1] lit., emphasis mine). The two warnings could secondarily speak to preserving the message of Torah. They do not stand in the way of additional divine revelation in accord with Torah.[152] An important example is the new version of the Ten Commandments in Deut 5 with several differences. At the same time Deut 10:4 says the Ten Words were written on the tablets "as before." Though Deut 10:4 refers back to the second set of stone tablets, Deut 5 houses an interpretive version of the Ten Commandments (see note on Deut 5:6–21).

Love Yahweh and teach the next generation appears at the beginning and end of the motivation section, Deut 6–11 (6:5–9//11:13, 18–20; cf. 30:6).

A similar lead-in appears in Deut 12:29; 17:14; 19:1; and 26:1; for example, "*When you have entered the land Yahweh your God is giving you* as an inheritance and have taken possession of it and settled in it . . ." (26:1, emphasis mine).

The expectations for reciting blessings and curses from Mount Gerizim and Mount Ebal appear at the end of the motivation (Deut 6–11) and the torah collection (12–28) (11:29–30; 27:4, 11–13; cf. Josh 8:30–35). The building of an earthen altar is associated with this ceremony (Deut 27:5; cf. Exod 20:25; Josh 8:31). The reference to blessings and curses fits the same pattern (Deut 11:26–28; 27:15–28:68). The language of "See, I am setting before you today" in Deut 11:26 and 30:15 helps bind together the rhetorical function of Deuteronomy.

The curses of Deut 27:15–26 echo elements earlier in Torah. Cursed be one who: • makes an idol (27:15; cf. 4:15–16; Exod 20:4; Lev 19:4); • dishonors parents (Deut 27:16; cf. 5:16//Exod 20:12; 21:17; Lev 19:3); • moves neighbor's boundary marker (Deut 27:17; cf. 19:14); • misleads blind person (27:18; cf. Lev 19:14); • deprives residing foreigner, orphan, or widow of justice (Deut 27:19; cf. 10:18; 24:17; Exod 22:21[20]); • has relations with stepmother (Deut 27:20; cf. 22:30[23:1]; Lev 18:8); • commits

---

152. See Tigay, "Significance," 138, 141–42; and Grisanti, "Deuteronomy," 2:516–17.

bestiality (Deut 27:21; cf. Exod 22:19[18]; Lev 18:23; 20:15); • has relations with sister or stepsister (Deut 27:22; cf. Lev 18:9; 20:17); • has relations with mother-in-law (Deut 27:23; cf. Lev 18:17; 20:14), • strikes down neighbor in secret (Deut 27:24; cf. Exod 21:12); • takes bribe to shed innocent blood (Deut 27:25; cf. 10:17; Exod 23:8); • does not obey this torah (Deut 27:26; cf. 28:15).[153]

The heavens and the earth serve as witnesses against Israel (4:26; 31:28; 32:1). The theme establishes a point of reference for prophetic charges against Israel (Isa 1:2).

153. For additional parallels of Deut 27:15–26, see Driver, *Deuteronomy*, 299.

Chapter 6

JOSHUA

SYMBOLS[1]

// verbal parallels (A level)
/~/ synoptic parallel (A level)
~ B, probable interpretive allusion; C, possible; D, probably not
+ interpretive blend
>/< more or less similar (see Filters)
* part of interpretive network (see Networks)

USE OF SCRIPTURE IN JOSHUA[2]

1:5–9~Deut 5:32//28:14+29:9[8]+31:5–6 (B) (obey Torah)
2:9~Exod 15:15, 16 (B) (inhabitants of Canaan melt)
6:17*~Deut 7:2* (B) (exception to devoting the nations of Canaan) (* see devoting network)
9:6, 14*~Deut 20:15* (B) (obedience to letter of law inadequate) (* see devoting network)
11:20*~Exod 4:21, etc.+Deut 7:2* (B) (harden hearts of nations of Canaan) (* see devoting network)
20:4–6~Num 35:12 (B) (explain accidental death to elders for asylum)
24:1–15~Torah compilation (B, C) (Joshua's panoramic retrospective at Shechem)

OLD TESTAMENT USE OF JOSHUA (SEE RESPECTIVE NOTES)

1:5–9~1 Kgs 2:1–4 (C) (David commissions Solomon)
1:8~Ps 1:2–3 (B) (like a tree by water)
3:7; 4:14~1 Chr 29:25 (C) (Yahweh exalts Solomon)
4:23~Ps 114:3, 5, 8 (C) (sea/river crossing remix)
7:1~1 Chr 2:3–17 (B) (genealogies of Judah through family of David)
10:10~Isa 28:21 (C) (reversal of divine intervention at Mount Perazim and Gibeon)
13:2–3/~/Judg 1:18–19 (Judah and Philistines)
15:14–19/~/Judg 1:10–15 (account of Aksah)
15:20–34~Neh 11:25–30 (B) (ideal restoration of villages of Judah)
17:12–13/~/Judg 1:27–28 (Manasseh's failure)
19:1–5~1 Chr 4:24–31 (C) (early tribe of Simeon)
21:1–4, 10–19~1 Chr 6:54–60[39–45] (B) (Levitical cities)
21:5–9~1 Chr 6:61–65[46–50] (B) (Levitical cities)
21:20–39~1 Chr 6:66–81[51–66] (B) (Levitical cities)
24:28–31/~/Judg 2:6–9 (the generation of Joshua)

NEW TESTAMENT USE OF JOSHUA

6:17~Heb 11:31; Jas 2:25, (faith of Rahab)

1. For explanation of symbols, see Symbols and Abbreviations and Introduction. For other help, see Glossary.
2. See Bibliographic Note on Lists of Potential Parallels.

HERMENEUTICAL PROFILE OF THE USE OF SCRIPTURE IN JOSHUA

Joshua begins with conscious attention to written Torah as an object of constant recitation. This canonical consciousness translates into frequent marked allusions along with other unmarked uses of narrative and legal traditions of Torah. In most cases Joshua features broad, non-exegetical scriptural allusions (see Filters). The remainder of the present discussion relates to Joshua's exegetical use of scriptural traditions.

Joshua draws on narrative and legal traditions from across Torah: Genesis, Exodus, Numbers, and Deuteronomy. While Joshua favors Deuteronomy, use of priestly and other contexts accord with the cited contexts. Joshua's most pushy interpretations adjust Deuteronomy, or better, push against overly literal readings of selected Deuteronomic traditions.

The most important interpretive agenda in Joshua relates to Deuteronomy's legal instruction on devoting the nations of Canaan to destruction. Even before the first battle, the narrative presents an exception to the law of devoting for the faithful prostitute. Joshua explicitly excludes Rahab's family from devoting along with a rationale and narrative commentary (see note on Josh 7:16). The exegetical parade example of Rahab demonstrates the sense of the law of devoting. It has nothing at all to do with ethnic or genealogical identity. The basis of devoting the nations of Canaan turns on their worship of false gods and the danger of these polytheistic and syncretistic practices for Israel (Deut 7:4–5). The account of Rahab shows that one's birth does not determine one's destiny so much as how one lives before the God of Israel.

Amid numerous accounts of devoting cities of the nations of Canaan to destruction, the narrative returns both to the legal standards for far away peoples of Deut 20 and a theological rationale for devoting the people of the land according to Deut 7.[3] While Joshua shows the same level of interest in the difficult legal instructions on devoting the nations of Canaan as moderns, the interpretive outcomes go a different direction.

The debacle with the Gibeonites challenges the idea of the adequacy of obedience to the letter of law. Covenantal obedience needs to unfold as part of a relationship of constant dependence on Yahweh. The typology of hardening the pharaoh's heart serves to explain the divine role in the warfare of devoting the nations of Canaan. Again, obeying laws are not the end but serve a function within Yahweh's relationship with his people.

The closing scene of Joshua includes the first long panoramic retrospective outside of Torah. Joshua boldly interprets scriptural traditions in light of other traditions not included in Torah. Joshua's speech brings to the fore the instructional function of Torah's narrative traditions. For Joshua, the saving acts of Yahweh motivate obedience to his covenantal will.

---

3. Wenham notes that each battle story ends with a comment on devoting the people ("Deuteronomic," 143).

USE OF SCRIPTURE

1:5–9~Deut 5:32//28:14+7:24+29:9[8]+31:5–6 (B) (obey Torah). Moses commissioned Joshua, calling him to be strong and promising Yahweh's presence with him. Moses told him to fight against the peoples of Canaan according to the commands, apparently referring to the law of devoting in Deut 7:1–6 (Deut 31:5–6; cf. vv. 7–8, 23; and see note on 1 Chr 22:5–19). The narrator reframes the commission as direct discourse from Yahweh (Josh 1:1). The commission of Joshua fleshes out the commands in terms of the written Torah and broadens the outcomes in terms of success by means of an interpretive blend. The broader terms of success correspond with the blessings in Deut 28:1–14 the last part of which runs parallel to 5:32 and Josh 1:7.[4] The most important exegetical intervention relates to prioritizing Torah in a pervasive fashion (1:7–8; cf. 23:6) (italics, bold, and underlining signify verbal parallels, and broken underlining signifies interpretive intervention):[5]

> **So be careful to do** what Yahweh your God has commanded you; **do not turn aside to the right or to the left.** (Deut 5:32; cf. 28:14)
>
> He will give their kings into your hand, and you will wipe out their names from under heaven. *No one will be able to stand up against you*; you will destroy them. (7:24; cf. 11:25)[6]
>
> Carefully follow the terms of this covenant, so that you may be successful in everything you do. (29:9†[8])
>
> Yahweh will deliver them [the nations of Canaan] to you, and you must do to them all that I have commanded you. *Be strong and courageous. Do not be* terrified or *afraid* because of them, *for Yahweh your God goes with you*; he *will never leave you nor forsake you.* (Deut 31:5–6†)
>
> *No one will be able to stand against you* all the days of your life. As I was with Moses, so I will be *with you*; I *will never leave you nor forsake you. . . . Be strong and* very *courageous.* **Be careful to obey** all the torah my servant Moses gave you; **do not turn from it to the right or to the left,** that you may be successful wherever you go. Keep this book of the Torah always on your lips; meditate on it day and night, **so that you may be careful to do** everything written in it. Then you will be prosperous and successful. Have I not

4. See entry on "left" (שמאל), esp. "right and left," in Even-Shoshan, 1166.

5. The purpose of the chiastic structure in Josh 1:5–9 seems to be to repeat the main elements for emphasis: Yahweh with you (Josh 1:5, 9), strong and courageous (1:6, 7, 8), do/obey Torah (1:7, 8), success (1:7, 8).

6. On the parallel of Deut 7:24; 11:25; Josh 1:8 indebted to Firth, *Stranger*, 18.

commanded you? *Be strong and courageous. Do not be afraid*; do not be discouraged, *for Yahweh your God will be with you* wherever you *go*. (Josh 1:5, 7–9)

If Deut 6:6–9 envisions domestic life infused with God's commands, the commission of Joshua applies the same ideals more broadly. The emphasis on Torah as a written scroll signifies canonical consciousness.

2:9~Exod 15:15, 16 (B) (inhabitants of Canaan melt). Rahab testifies to the works of Yahweh at the sea and the victories in the Transjordan (Josh 2:10). She refers to Yahweh as the "God of heaven above and the earth below" (2:11//Deut 4:29). Within this testimony of faith Rahab repeats the very words from a couple of lines of the Song of the Sea (italics signify parallels):

> The chiefs of Edom will be terrified, the leaders of Moab will be seized with trembling, *all who are living in* Canaan *will melt away*; *terror* and dread *will fall on* them. (Exod 15:15–16a†)

> [Rahab] said to them, "I know that Yahweh has given you this land and that a great *terror* of you *has fallen on* us, so that *all who live in* this country *are melting* in fear because of you." (Josh 2:9†)

The importance of Rahab's faith goes beyond deliverance for her and her family. The narrative of Rahab's faith in Josh 2 plays a part in the interpretation of the law of devoting the nations of Canaan in Josh 6 (see note on 6:17).

6:17*~Deut 7:2* (B) (exception to devoting the nations of Canaan) (* see devoting network). The purpose of the law of devoting the nations of Canaan has nothing to do with ethnicity. The law provides protection against Israel turning away from Yahweh (Deut 7:4; 20:18; see note on 7:1–5).[7] The critical concern for providing exegetical application of this law explains why this episode stands at the front end of the Deuteronomistic narrative. Before Israel cuts down one person of Canaan, they make an exception for the prostitute and her family. Rahab delivers the two scouts and confesses her faith (Josh 2:4–7, 9–11).[8] The purpose of the account of Rahab often gets associated with challenging "Deuteronomic dogmatism" by providing a way for acceptance of gentiles, thus "relativizing" the law of devoting.[9] These observations are fine as far as they go, but they need to be tied into the scriptural exegesis within the account itself.

Normally persons who have been devoted may not be redeemed (Lev 27:29). The vow of the scouts affirms the prostitute and her household as exceptions because of her faithful

7. For the function of the nations of Canaan in Scripture, see Ford, "Challenge of the Canaanites," 161–84.
8. Firth says the Rahab story gets fronted in Joshua to get at who can belong the Israel (*Stranger*, 22).
9. See Davis, "Critical Traditioning," 743; Robinson, "Rahab of Canaan," 273.

actions (Josh 2:12–14; 6:22). This episode offers a narrative exegetical advancement of one of the limitations of these standards. The law of devoting does not apply to people of Canaan who worship the God of Israel. If not all descended from Israel are Israel, as the apostle says (Rom 9:6), then not all who descend from the nations of Canaan are Canaanites.[10]

The narrative does not offer an extensive quotation, just one shared verbal root, "devote/what is devoted" (*hrm* חרם); but Joshua makes the connection to the law explicit (Josh 6:17). The account goes on to make clear that every other living thing in Jericho was devoted to destruction (6:21). That Josh 6:17 houses an exception to the law suggests it as receptor context. Notice Joshua's overt interpretation of the exception to the law (italics signify verbal parallel at the level of root, and broken underlining signifies interpretive rationale):

> When Yahweh your God brings you into the land you are entering to possess and drives out before you many nations—the Hittites, Girgashites, Amorites, Canaanites, Perizzites, Hivites and Jebusites, seven nations larger and stronger than you—and when Yahweh your God has delivered them over to you and you have defeated them, then you must *devote them to destruction*. Make no treaty with them, and show them no mercy. (Deut 7:1–2†)

> [Joshua said] The city and all that is in it *are to be devoted* to Yahweh. Only Rahab the prostitute and all who are with her in her house shall be spared, because she hid the spies we sent. (Josh 6:17)

Joshua's rationale for the exception of Rahab and her household from the law of devoting does not depend on the vow of the scouts but "because she hid the spies we sent" (6:17). Rahab hid the scouts before they made the vow (2:2–7; cf. vv. 12–14). Rahab's actions signify faith in Yahweh (2:9–11).

The narrator provides an additional paragraph to explain what happened to the prostitute and her extended family. First they lived "outside" the camp of Israel (6:23). Then they "lived *in the midst of* Israel, to this day" (6:25, emphasis mine). According to a genealogy of the tribe of Judah, her family fully assimilated into the tribe and lived in Bethlehem—her descendants include Boaz, Jesse, David, and Joseph the husband of Mary (Matt 1:5).

The New Testament alludes to the legal decision in Josh 6:17 based on actions prior to the vow: "was not even Rahab the prostitute considered righteous *for what she did when she gave lodging to the spies* and sent them off in a different direction?"

---

10. See Schnittjer, *Torah Story*, 505–6.

(Jas 2:25, emphasis mine; cf. Heb 11:31). It is worth noting that, in James, Rahab's act of faith appears directly after Abraham's near sacrifice of Isaac (Jas 2:21–24; cf. Gen 22:1–14).

9:6, 14*~Deut 20:15* (B) (obedience to letter of law inadequate) (* see devoting network). The Hivites of Gibeon's quartet of towns deceived Israel by pretending to be from a "distant" land (Josh 9:6, 9). The Israelites knew the law prohibited covenants with people nearby (9:7; Deut 20:10–15). They were deliberate enough in adhering to the regulation to sample the spoiled food, but they did not seek Yahweh (Josh 9:16). By adding the phrase "but did not inquire of Yahweh," the narrator exegetically deduces the inadequacy of adhering to the letter of the law without turning to God. Though the parallel includes only one word, the surrounding details make an interpretive allusion probable. Also, the behavior of the Israelites suggests Josh 6 is the receptor context (italics signify verbal parallel, and broken underlining signifies exegetical intervention):

> This is how you are to treat all the cities that are at a *distance* [רְחֹקֹת] from you and do not belong to the nations nearby. However, in the cities of the nations Yahweh your God is giving you as an inheritance, do not leave alive anything that breathes. (Deut 20:15–16)

> Then they went to Joshua in the camp at Gilgal and said to him and the Israelites, "We have come from a *distant* [רְחוֹקָה] country; make a treaty with us." The Israelites said to the Hivites, "But perhaps you live near us, so how can we make a treaty with you? . . ." The Israelites sampled their provisions but did not inquire of Yahweh. (Josh 9:6–7, 14)

In sum, the narrator deduces from Israel's failure that true obedience signifies a relational reality beyond mere compliance.

11:20*~Exod 4:21, etc.+Deut 7:2* (B) (harden hearts of nations of Canaan) (* see devoting network). The narrator appropriates the mantra of the Exodus narrative ("harden the heart" of the pharaoh) to explain a theological dimension of the conquest against the nations of Canaan. Exodus 4:21 here represents the set of contexts with this language (italics and bold signify verbal parallels, and underlining signifies marking):[11]

> Yahweh said to Moses, "When you return to Egypt, see that you perform before Pharaoh all the wonders I have given you the power to do. But I **will harden** his **heart** so that he will not let the people go." (Exod 4:21)

11. For "harden" (חזק) the heart of the pharaoh, see Exod 4:21; 7:13, 22; 8:19[15]; 9:12, 35; 10:20, 27; 11:10; 14:4, 8, 17. Also note that "harden" (קשה) 7:3 and "make heavy" (כבד) 8:15[11]; 10:1 function synonymously. Thank you to Matthew Wilson for helpful observations.

> And when Yahweh your God has delivered them over to you and you have defeated them, then you *must destroy them totally*. Make no treaty with them, and show them no *mercy*. (Deut 7:2)

> For it was Yahweh himself who **hardened** their **hearts** to wage war against Israel, so that *he might destroy them totally*, exterminating them without *mercy*, <u>as Yahweh had commanded Moses.</u> (Josh 11:20)

Just as the account of Rahab focuses on exceptions to the law of devoting, so too Josh 11:20 affirms the divine dimension of a war of devoting (see note on Josh 6:17). The narrative here reveals that the destruction of Canaan is not based on cultural or ethnic hatred but on a judgment by Yahweh.

20:4–6~Num 35:12 (B) (explain accidental death to elders for asylum). Torah explains cities of asylum for accidental death (Exod 21:13; Num 35:9–34; Deut 4:41–43; 19:1–13). The six cities of asylum are Levitical cities, three on each side of the Jordan (Josh 20:7–9; 21:13, 21, 27, 32, 36, 38).[12] The explanation in Joshua largely concurs with the instructions in Deut 19 and especially Num 35 by mentioning the trial before the congregation and release from manslaughter charges upon the death of the high priest (Num 35:12, 25, 28; Josh 20:6). Joshua 20:4 adds an element to the law, namely, entry into the city of asylum of the one who caused accidental death by explaining the case to the elders at the gate of a city of asylum. This exegetical expansion helps grant temporary asylum until the trial before the congregation (Num 35:12; Josh 20:6; see note on Num 35:9–34).

24:1–15~Torah compilation (B, C) (Joshua's panoramic retrospective at Shechem).[13] Joshua gathers Israel in Shechem situated between Mounts Ebal and Gerizim—a setting exuding the covenant because of the blessings and curses associated with the mountains (Josh 24:1; 8:30–35; cf. Deut 11:29–30; 27:1–14). Just as Deuteronomy closes Torah by providing Moses's interpretive challenge to Israel, so too Josh 23 and 24 interpret the conquest in the preceding narrative. Joshua presents an interpretive panoramic retrospective in order to challenge the congregation to turn from idolatry (Josh 24:14–15). Joshua's speech represents the first such long retrospective outside Torah. Joshua does not focus on creation or revelation at the mountain but does allude to many of the major traditions often found in scriptural retrospectives (see Table Josh1).

---

12. See Spencer, "Refuge, Cities of," *ABD* 5:657–58.

13. Joshua's retrospective includes many broad allusions, such as to the Hebrew ancestors in Mesopotamia, Josh 24:2; cf. Gen 11:27–32 and the divine deliverance from Balaam and the Moabites, Josh 24:9–10; cf. Num 22–24. Joshua's speech also features more specific verbal parallels suggesting interpretive allusion, such as the divinely sent hornet in Josh 24:12; cf. Exod 23:28; Deut 7:20; divine gifting of towns Israel did not build and the like Josh 24:13; cf. Deut 6:10–11.

TABLE JOSH1: NARRATIVE TRADITIONS IN LONG SCRIPTURAL RETROSPECTIVES‡

	creation	Hebrew ancestors	redemption from salvery	revelation	wilderness	Transjordan conquest	conquest/ settlement	judges (slavery in land)	kingdom	exile (slavery)
Joshua 24		2–4	5–7[ab]		7b	8–10	11–13			
1 Samuel 12			6–8					9–11		
Jeremiah 32	17–19[c]		20–21				22–23			24–25
Ezekiel 16					3–14				15–34	35–43
Ezekiel 20			4–10	11–12	13–26		27–29			33–35
Ezekiel 23									5–8, 11–21	9–10, 22–35
Psalm 78			12–13[b] 42–53[ab]		14–41		54–55	56–66	67–72	
Psalm 89	5–18								19–37	38–45
Psalm 105		5–22	37–38[a]		39–43		44–45			
Psalm 106			7–12[b]		13–33[d]			34–46		
Psalm 135	5–7		8–9[a]			11	10, 12			
Psalm 136	5–9		10–15[ab]		16	19–20	18, 22			
Nehemiah 9	6	7–8	9–11[b]	13–14	12, 15–21[de]	22	23–25	26–31[e]	32–35	36–37
Acts 7		2–16	17–36[b]	38	37, 39–44[d]		45		46–50	
Acts 13			17		18		19	20	21–23	

‡ Based in part on less developed comparisons in Bautch, *Developments*, 112; Duggan, *Covenant Renewal*, 226. Besides the retrospectives collated in the table are historical surveys in Deut 6:20–25; 26:5–9; 29; 32:1–22; Isa 63:7–14 (see House, "Examining the Narratives," 231; Boda, *Praying the Tradition*, 83); also see 1 Kgs 8:31–53.

[a] Includes plagues; [b] Includes sea crossing; [c] Alludes to retribution formula of second commandment (Exod 20:5–6//Deut 5:9–10); [d] Includes rebellion with golden calf; [e] Alludes to divine attribute formula (Exod 34:6–7).

Joshua's speech at Shechem blends together a series of traditions found in Torah and the Joshua narratives along with a couple traditions that do not appear elsewhere in Scripture (see Table Josh1). The present purpose needs to be limited to four of the most important exegetical advances in the retrospective versus the storylines in Torah and Joshua.

First, Joshua reveals that the Hebrew ancestors served false gods in Mesopotamia (Josh 24:2; cf. Gen 11:27–32). Terah's sojourn and the call of Abraham in Genesis do not refer to turning from idolatry. Rachel imports Laban's false worship (Gen 31:34–35). Jacob purged his household of their idols and buried them under the oak at Shechem, the site of Joshua's sermon (35:2, 4).[14] When Joshua calls his auditors to turn from their gods, they do not bury them at the oak (Josh 24:23).

Second, Joshua connects the events of his own day with those in Torah as one continuous story (24:10–11). The retrospective makes no distinction between the narrative traditions found in Torah and those in Joshua. Joshua regards the congregation before him as in the same story. This continuity of identity—standing in the continuation of the Torah story—is especially significant in the light of the written Torah scroll in the Joshua narrative (1:7, 8; 23:6). Although the Torah scroll in the Joshua narrative may be thought to only contain legal instructions, the marked contexts across the Joshua narrative often include legal narratives, such as that regarding Zelophehad's daughters, but also narratives like the inheritance of Caleb (see Marked Broad Allusions in Filters). In short, Joshua's direct identification of Israel's settlement of the land as continuation of Torah's narrative sets a precedent for readers to identify themselves within the same storyline.

Third, Joshua uses traditions found in Torah to characterize the events of the conquest. The military campaigns can be summarized by allusion to the seven nations of Canaan (24:11; Deut 7:1). The work of God against the Amorites can be referred to as the hornet he sent ahead of them (Josh 24:12; Exod 23:28; Deut 7:20).[15] The people did not destroy all of the towns, dwellings, vineyards, and orchards but acquired them by divine promise (Josh 24:13; Deut 6:10–11).

Fourth, Joshua reveals that their parents worshiped other gods in Egypt (Josh 24:14; cf. Ezek 20:7–8). The Exodus narratives do not include this tradition.

In sum, Joshua reinterpreted the redeeming work of Yahweh in order to call his constituents away from false worship. The retrospective's most surprising advances in revelation fill in the backstory regarding the polytheistic tendencies of the Hebrew ancestors in Mesopotamia and Israel in Egypt. In spite of their immediate affirmative response, Joshua, like Moses, voices strong skepticism about Israel's commitment (24:19–21; cf. Deut 31:26–27). Scriptural narrative makes demands for obedience to the will of God since Israel stands within its story.

FILTERS

Joshua makes many broad non-exegetical allusions to Torah. Some of these reflect self-consciousness by being marked in different ways. The following representative lists are not comprehensive or complete.[16]

---

14. See Maclear, *Joshua*, 203.

15. The only other use of "hornet" is Gen 42:21 SP, and see upper apparatus SP ad loc. ("צִרְעָה," *HALOT* 2:1056–57).

16. For additional parallels, esp. of phrases, style, and the thematic similarities between Joshua and the Torah, see Driver, *Introduction*, 105–16; for an extensive list of parallel stock phrases and other parallel language between Joshua and other Scriptures, esp. Torah and Judges, see Kiel, *Joshua*, 35–53 [Hebrew].

Marked Broad Allusions

Marked and quasi-marked allusions refer to scriptural legal standards as well as nonlegal traditions: • "as I promised Moses" **marks** "I will give you every place where you set your foot, *as I promised Moses*. Your territory will extend from the desert to Lebanon, and from the great river, the Euphrates . . . to the Mediterranean Sea in the west" (**Josh 1:3–4**>/<Deut 11:24; cf. Gen 15:18, "unto the great river, the Euphrates" [עד הנהר הגדול נהר פרת]); • "Remember the command that Moses the servant of Yahweh gave you after he said" **marks** "Yahweh your God will give you rest by giving you this land/until Yahweh gives rest to your fellow Israelites as he has to you" (יהוה אלהיכם מניח לכם ונתן לכם את הארץ הזאת/עד אשר יניח יהוה לאחיכם ככם) (**Josh 1:13**>/<Deut 3:20); • "as Moses the servant of Yahweh had commanded the Israelites, as it is written in the scroll of the Torah of Moses" **marks** "an altar of uncut stones, on which no iron tool had been used" (מזבח אבנים שלמות [אשר] לא הניף עליהן ברזל) (**Josh 8:31**>/<Deut 27:5); • "as Moses the servant of Yahweh had commanded the Israelites. He built it according to *what is written* in the book of the Torah of Moses. . . . Moses the servant of Yahweh had formerly commanded when he gave instructions to bless the people of Israel" (**Josh 8:31, 33**, emphasis mine) **marks** the blessings and curses covenant ceremony on Mounts Ebal and Gerizim (**8:30–35** alluding to Deut 11:29–30; 27:1–14). • "But be very careful to keep the commandment and the law that Moses the servant of Yahweh gave you" **marks** "to love Yahweh your God, to walk in obedience to him, to keep his commands, to hold fast to him and to serve him with all your heart and with all your soul" (**Josh 22:5**, broadly alludes to Deut 10:12; cf. 4:4, 29; 6:5; 11:13, 22).[17]

The account of land allotment refers to fulfillment of Moses's instructions proportionately more than other sections of the narrative:[18] • "So on that day Moses swore to me [Caleb]" **marks** "The land on which your feet have walked will be your inheritance and that of your children forever, because you have followed Yahweh my God wholeheartedly" (**Josh 14:9**, alludes to Num 14:24; Deut 1:36; cf. Josh 14:14); • "Now Zelophehad son of Hepher, the son of Gilead, the son of Makir, the son of Manasseh, had no sons but only daughters, whose names were Mahlah, Noah, Hoglah, Milkah and Tirzah. They went to Eleazar the priest, Joshua son of Nun, and the leaders and said, 'Yahweh commanded Moses to give us an inheritance among our relatives'" **marks** "So Joshua gave them an inheritance along with the brothers of their father, according to Yahweh's command/You must certainly give them property as an inheritance among their father's relatives" (לתת לנו נחלה בתוך אחינו/נתן תתן להם אחזת נחלה בתוך אחי אביהם) (**Josh 17:3–4**>/<Num 27:7); • "as Yahweh had commanded" **marks** "They gave him [Joshua] the town he asked for—Timnath Serah in the hill country of Ephraim. And he built up the town and settled there" (**Josh 19:50,** alludes to Num 14:30; Deut 1:38);[19] • [Tribal leaders of Levi:] "Yahweh

17. See Hess, *Joshua*, 290; Maclear, *Joshua*, 192.

18. See Mann, *Former Prophets*, 42.

19. The marked allotments of Caleb (Josh 14:9) and Joshua (19:50) frame the land allotments (Hess, *Joshua*, 303–4).

commanded through Moses that you give us towns to live in, with pasturelands for our livestock" **marks** "So, as Yahweh had commanded, the Israelites gave the Levites the following towns and pasturelands out of their own inheritance"/"Command the Israelites to give the Levites towns to live in from the inheritance the Israelites will possess. And give them pasturelands around the towns" (**Josh 21:3**>/<Num 35:2).

Unmarked Broad Allusions

While most unmarked broad allusions refer to narrative traditions of Torah, others relate to legal standards: **3:13, 16**>/<Exod 15:8, waters stand and "pile up" (נד) (Ps 78:13); **4:23**>/<Exod 14–15, drying Jordan like the reed sea ("dry up" only used of reed sea in Josh 4:23); **5:15**>/<Exod 3:5, "Take off your sandals, for the place where you are standing is holy/holy ground" (של נעלך מעל רגלך כי המקום אשר אתה עמד עליו קדש/אדמת קדש הוא); **7:1**>/<Lev 27:28; Deut 13:17, taking devoted things (חרם); **7:6**>/<Num 14:5; 16:4, 22; 16:45[17:10]; 20:6, Joshua/Moses/Moses and Aaron "fell on his/their face/s" (נפל על פניו/פניהם); **8:29; 10:26**>/<Deut 21:23, hang "on a tree/s" until evening (על העץ/עצים); **9:10; 12:5–6; 13:21, 27, 30**>/<Num 21:21–35, defeat of Transjordanian kingdoms of Sihon and Og (cf. Deut 2:36; 3:10 and Josh 13:9, 11, 16); **11:21; 14:12; 15:14**>/<Num 13:28, 33, Joshua and Caleb and their associates credited with defeating the Anakim; **13:22**>/<Num 31:8, killing Balaam; **13:14, 33; 14:4; 18:7**>/<Deut 10:9; 18:1–2, no inheritance for Levi; **14:6**>/<Gen 36:15, 42, Caleb a Kenizzite, possibly of Kenaz an Edomite ancestor; **22:17**>/<Num 25:1–5, iniquity of Peor; **23:12–13**>/<Exod 34:12, 15–16; Deut 7:3–4, 16, warning against intermarriage for the nations of Canaan shall be a "snare"; **24:32**>/<Gen 33:19; 50:24–25; Exod 13:19, Joseph's bones buried in the plot Jacob bought from the children of Hamor.

Shared Stock Phrases and Other Similarities

Note a sampling: >/<**2:11; 5:1; 7:5**; Deut 1:28, "hearts melted" (מסס לבב) (this is a different term than the people "will melt" [מוג] in Exod 15:15; Josh 2:9, 24); >/<**2:18, 21**; Song 4:3, "scarlet thread/cord" (חוט/תקות השני), Gen 38:28, 30, "scarlet" (שני); >/<**4:6, 21**; Exod 13:14; Deut 6:20, "when your children ask" (ישאלון בניכם); Deut 13:17, "ruin forever" (תל עולם); >/<**9:21, 27**; Deut 29:11, "woodcutters and water carriers" (חטב עצים שאב מים); >/<**10:24**; 1 Kgs 5:3[17]; Ps 110:1, subject under "feet" (רגלים).

Note a few examples of the use of Joshua contexts by other Joshua contexts: resumptive repetition/*inclusio*, Joshua is "old and advanced in years" (Josh 13:1; 23:1, 2); the accusers of the Transjordanian tribes compare their sin to the iniquity of Peor (Num 25:1–5; Josh 22:17) and the infidelity of Achan (Josh 7:1; 22:20);[20] Joshua's first concluding speech refers to Yahweh fighting for Israel (23:3, 9–10) which alludes in broad terms to many events in the narrative (cf. 8:1; 10:14, 25, 42).

---

20. Others note broad thematic similarities between Josh 22 and the rebellions in Num 13–14 and Num 32 (see Wray Beal, "Past," 463–71).

Chapter 7

JUDGES

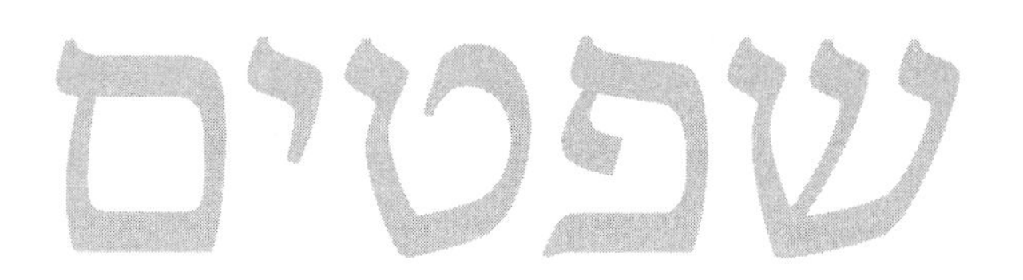

SYMBOLS[1]

- // verbal parallels (A level)
- /~/ synoptic parallel (A level)
- ~ B, probable interpretive allusion; C, possible; D, probably not
- + interpretive blend
- >/< more or less similar (see Filters)
- * part of interpretive network (see Networks)

USE OF SCRIPTURE IN JUDGES[2]

1:10–36/~/Joshua selected texts (incomplete conquest)

2:6–9/~/Josh 24:28–31 (A)+Deut 11:7 (B) (the generation of Joshua)

11:15–27/~/Num 21:10–26+Deut 2:3–4, 8, 13, 24, 26, 30–33, 36–37 (Jephthah's letter)

17:6//21:25~Deut 12:8 (B) (right in one's own eyes)

19:22*~Gen 19:5* (B) (bring out the men) (* see cities of the plain network)

OLD TESTAMENT USE OF JUDGES (SEE RESPECTIVE NOTES)

7:25~Isa 10:26 (C) (judgment like Midian at rock of Oreb and staff over the sea)

9:53–54~2 Sam 11:21 (B) (a woman kills Abimelek)

NEW TESTAMENT USE OF JUDGES

n/a

HERMENEUTICAL PROFILE OF THE USE OF SCRIPTURE IN JUDGES

There seems to be nothing straightforward about the use of scriptural traditions in Judges. The constant ironic non-exegetical echoes and allusions (see Filters) along with the few extended exegetical allusions invite readerly response. The main purpose seems to be pedagogical even if the ironies are often pushy. The use of scriptural traditions in Judges may be described as ironic theological instruction.

The few exegetical uses of scriptural traditions in Judges differ from one to the next. The so-called first and second introductions to Judges (Judg 1:1–2:5; 2:6–3:6) and

1. For explanation of symbols, see Symbols and Abbreviations and Introduction. For other help, see Glossary.
2. See Bibliographic Note on Lists of Potential Parallels.

Jephthah's letter (11:15–27) each feature synoptic parallels, wherein the widely scattered cited materials have been drawn together. The verbal parallels of these synoptic contexts require a relationship, whether direct or indirect. Whereas the first introduction of Judges builds an ominous case for an incomplete conquest and the second introduction uses the passing of Joshua's generation as a point of departure, Jephthah's letter rehearses ancient historical military actions with some ambivalence. The function of his letter may have been (false) diplomacy before the king of Ammon, but it serves a different end within Judges. The letter invites readers to retrace Israel's journeys from Kadesh to the plains of Moab, sorting out the details in Numbers and Deuteronomy. Jephthah's diminishment of Yahweh's role in international affairs baits learners to repair his stunted theology.

The overnight visit of the Levite and his Bethlehemite concubine in Gibeah exudes dark, ironic scriptural echoes. These allusions seem to have an ideological agenda against the hometown of Israel's first king. The borrowed phrase "everyone did as they saw fit" from Deut 12:8 carries inherently negative connotation in Judg 17:6 and 21:25. The phrase from Deuteronomy put the kingless days of tribal life in a bad light. The heavy-handed imagery from the narrative of destroying cities of the plain in Gen 19 serves to tarnish the reputation of the hometown of Saul. The use of scriptural traditions in the smear campaign against Gibeah of Judg 19 stands in sharp contrast to the use of scriptural traditions in Ruth's equally ironic but more upbeat story of widows in Bethlehem, the hometown of David.

The exegetical and non-exegetical uses of scriptural traditions alike use pushy irony apparently to provoke constituents to push back. In short, the use of scriptural traditions in Judges suggests a pedagogical purpose.

USE OF SCRIPTURE

1:10–36/~/Joshua selected texts (incomplete conquest). The better part of Judg 1 corresponds to selected contexts of the land allotment section of Joshua. The patterning of the account of Zebulun, Asher, and Naphtali after Manasseh and Ephraim suggests Joshua as donor and Judges as receptor context (Judg 1:27–29, 30–33; cf. Josh 16:10; 17:12–13).[3] Note a synoptic comparison of the events of Judg 1:10–36:[4]

	Joshua	Judges
defeating Sheshai, Ahiman, and Talmai	15:13, 14	1:10[a]
Othniel's valor wins Aksah	15:15–17	1:11–13
Aksah requests and gets springs	15:18–19	1:14–15
resettlement of Hobab's family with Amalekites	—	1:16

3. See side by side layout of Judg 1:27–28, 29, 30, 31–32, 33, 34–35 in O'Connell, *Rhetoric*, 68.

4. See detailed layout of Judg 1 in ibid., 385–87.

	Joshua	Judges
Simeon inherits within Judah	{19:9}	1:17 (cf. 1:3)
Philistine lands partially under Judah's control	{13:2–3}	1:18–19
Caleb's inheritance	{15:13, 14}	1:20[a]
Benjamin did not drive out Jebusites	—	1:21
house of Joseph conquers Bethel	—	1:22–26[b]
Manasseh does not drive out inhabitants from its territory	17:12–13	1:27–28
Ephraim does not drive out inhabitants of Gezer	{16:10}	1:29
Zebulun does not drive out inhabitants from its territory	—	1:30
Asher does not drive out inhabitants from its territory	—	1:31–32
Naphtali does not drive out inhabitants from its territory	—	1:33
Dan does not drive out inhabitants from its territory	19:47a	1:34–36
Dan migrates and takes possession of Leshem/Laish	19:47b	{18:27–29}

[a] Judges 1:10 and 1:20 appear to refer to Caleb inheriting Hebron as a resumptive repetition enclosing Judah's inheritance (based on Josh 15:13, 14).

[b] Judges 1:22–26 use extended echo-effect to structure its account after Josh 2:1–21; 6:1–27 (Webb, *Judges*, 96–97 as cited in O'Connell, *Rhetoric*, 66).

If Joshua emphasizes Yahweh's fidelity to fulfill his word, Judges focuses on the failure of the tribes (see esp. the extensive use of "all" in Josh 10:40–42; 11:23; 21:43–45; 23:1, 9, 14–15). The narrator of Joshua does not hide the incomplete conquest (13:1–7; 15:63; 16:10; 17:12–13; 18:3; 23:12–13), but the author of Judg 1 compiles and expands the incomplete parts of the conquest. In this way the compiled account of the remnant of the nations of Canaan in Judg 1 sets up the lingering problem of the entire book.

The repurposed accounts of the tribal lands in Judg 1 may also show some mild pro-Judah ideology. One example is the replacement of Caleb with Judah in the account of defeating persons from Hebron (Judg 1:10; cf. Josh 15:13–14).[5] This change projects the victory to Judah more generally. By contrast, the use of scriptural traditions of the other tribes tends to place them in a negative light (see synoptic parallels above). The potential pro-Judah light editing of the donor texts accords with the strong pro-Judah tendency of the frame narrative (Judg 1:1–2).

2:6–9/~/Josh 24:28–31 (A)+Deut 11:7 (B) (the generation of Joshua). The concluding narrative of Josh 24:28–31 serves as a synoptic parallel segue narrative in Judg 2:6–9. The parallel material has been mildly rearranged and edited. The blending of language from Deut 11:7 and Josh 24:31 in Judg 2:7 suggests the latter as receptor context.[6] To suggest

5. For this and numerous other pro-Judah uses of Joshua in Judges 1, see Murawski, "Who?"

6. On the similarities and differences of Deut 11:7; Josh 24:31; and Judg 2:7, see Frevel, "Untying," 288–89.

Deut 11:7 borrows a partial phrase from Judg 2:7 requires too many interpretive gymnastics based on the differences of their contexts combined with their shared parallels to Josh 24:31.

The contexts of the donor and receptor texts need to be quoted somewhat fully to illustrate exegetical recontextualization. Examining the surrounding contexts of these three passages at greater length can shed more light on what the narrator of Judges has in mind. Note especially how the language of Deut 11:7 within Judg 2:7 juxtaposes divine-redemptive events of the wilderness travels against the pending decline in the next generation(s) (emphases signify verbal parallels):

> It was not your children who saw what he did for you in the wilderness until you arrived at this place, [6] and what he did to Dathan and Abiram, sons of Eliab the Reubenite, when the earth opened its mouth right in the middle of all Israel and swallowed them up with their households, their tents and every living thing that belonged to them. [7] But it was your own eyes that **saw** all **these great things** Yahweh has done. (Deut 11:5–7)

> *Then Joshua dismissed the people, each to their own inheritance.* [29] After these things, *Joshua son of Nun, the servant of Yahweh, died at the age of a hundred and ten.* [30] *And they buried him in the land of his inheritance, at Timnath Serah* which is *in the hill country of Ephraim, north of Mount Gaash.* [31] Israel served Yahweh throughout the lifetime of Joshua and of the elders who outlived him and who had experienced all Yahweh had done for Israel. (Josh 24:28–31†)

> After *Joshua had dismissed the Israelites,* they went to take possession of the land, *each to their own inheritance.* [7] The people served Yahweh throughout the lifetime of Joshua and of the elders who outlived him and who **had seen** all **the great things** Yahweh had done for Israel. [8] *Joshua son of Nun, the servant of Yahweh, died at the age of a hundred and ten.* [9] *And they buried him in the land of his inheritance, at Timnath Heres in the hill country of Ephraim, north of Mount Gaash.* [10] After that whole generation had been gathered to their ancestors, another generation grew up who knew neither Yahweh nor what he had done for Israel. (Judg 2:6–10)

The redeployment of the passing of the generation of Joshua serves as a point of departure for Judges. While Joshua in many places notes that much of the land of promise had not been secured, the frame narrative emphasizes Yahweh's fidelity in the conquest.[7] Judges begins with the troubles that emanate from Israel's attraction to the gods of the peoples of the nations of Canaan among whom they live. The blame for the next gener-

---

7. Compare the complete faithfulness of Yahweh in the conquest (Josh 10:40–42; 11:23; 21:43–45; 23:1, 9, 14–15) with the land that still needed to be taken by the tribes (e.g., 13:1–7; 15:63; 16:10; 17:12–13; 18:3; 23:12–13).

ation not knowing of Yahweh's redeeming works falls on parents and their descendants (2:10; cf. Deut 6:7–9, 20–25; 11:19–21).

11:15–27/~/Num 21:10–26+Deut 2:3–4, 8, 9, 13, 19, 24, 26, 30–33, 36–37 (Jephthah's letter). Jephthah's letter creates challenges because of its disconnect (Judg 11:15–27). He sends a diplomatic communication to the ruler of the Ammonites but mostly addresses issues associated with Edom, Moab, and king Sihon, all in the southern Transjordanian region. Note a synoptic comparison of Jephthah's letter (bold signifies contexts with some verbal parallels):

	Numbers	Deuteronomy 2	Judges 11
not taking the lands of Ammon and Moab	—	9, 19	15–16
request to pass through Edom and Moab[a]	20:14–17	—	17
itinerary in Transjordan[b]	21:10	{13, 24}	—
passing by Edom[c] and Moab	**21:11b**	3–4, 8	**18a**
camping on the other side of the Arnon	21:13–15	—	18b
request to pass through Amorite lands	**21:21–22**	26	**19**
Sihon refused	**21:23a**	**30–31**	**20a**
Sihon attacked Israel	**21:23b**	**32**	**20b**
defeat of Sihon	21:24a	**33–36a**	**21a**
occupying land from Arnon to Jabbok	**21:24b–26**	{37}	**21b–22**
Yahweh granted Amorite land to Israel	—	{33, 36b}	23
accepting lands from own gods	—	—	24
no battle against Balak	—	—	25
three hundred years of occupying the Transjordan	—	—	26–27

[a] Request to pass through Moab in Judg 11:17 only.
[b] Compare the itinerary in Num 21:10–11a//33:43–44; cf. Deut 2:8.
[c] See the account of not going through Edom in Num 20:14–21.

The difficulties of Israel's Transjordanian itinerary lead several scholars to suggest the details in Num 21 depend upon and seek to harmonize Num 33, Deut 2, and Judg 11.[8] In spite of the merits of such suggestions, they merely trade off against reasons to see Jephthah's letter indebted to details in Num 21 (esp. Num 21:29; Judg 11:24). More significantly, if the reference to going by Edom in Deut 2:8 refers to a "seemingly different occasion" than Num 21:10–11, then the major alleged element to be harmonized in

8. See, e.g., Sumner, "Encounters," 216–28; Davies, "Itineraries," 1–13; and Miller, "Journey," 577–95.

Numbers goes away.[9] Aside from the geographical details without sufficient evidence to decide definitively, the important elements in the letter turn on Jephthah's theology and diplomacy or lack thereof.

If Jephthah's letter accommodates the theology of the king of Ammon, he demotes Yahweh to a patron deity of Israel. In spite of speaking of giving Sihon into the hand of Israel in Judg 11:21, he views Yahweh on the level of Chemosh. In this respect Jephthah's theological outlook runs along the lines of the ancient poets (emphases mine):

> [Poets] Woe to you, Moab! You are destroyed, people of Chemosh! *He has given up* his sons as fugitives and his daughters as captives to Sihon king of the Amorites. (Num 21:29)

> [Jephthah] Will you not possess what your god Chemosh *gives you to possess*? Likewise, whatever Yahweh our God has given us to possess, we will possess. (Judg 11:24 lit.)

The poets and Jephthah use active verbs "he has given" (נָתַן Q) and "he gives you to possess" (יוֹרִישְׁךָ Hif). Jeremiah "corrects" the aberrant theology of the ancient poets by using a passive verb "your sons *are taken* [לֻקְּחוּ Q pass.] into exile and your daughters into captivity" (Jer 48:46 MT [not in LXX], emphasis mine; see note ad loc.).[10] The urge to dissociate Chemosh from "the one who has given" the sons and daughters also can be seen in Rashi's comments on Num 21:29.[11] Both Jeremiah and Rashi make these adjustments to fit with the viewpoint of Deuteronomy: "Yahweh said to me, 'Do not harass the Moabites. . . . *I have given* [נתן Q] Ar to the descendants of Lot as a possession'" (Deut 2:9, emphasis mine). But Jephthah's theological adjustment works against the outlook of Deuteronomy regarding Yahweh as a local patron deity with interests limited to his people Israel.

It is also possible that Jephthah makes a mistake since the patron deity of Ammon is Molek, not Chemosh the god of the Moabites (Judg 11:24).[12] The narrative of Jephthah leaves space for readers to wonder if he is ignorant or if he intentionally distorts the ideology of his opponent. Of course ignorance and bullying are not mutually exclusive.

---

9. See Tigay, *Deuteronomy*, 25 (also see 424–25 comparing harmonistic and critical approaches). If the itinerary of Num 33 is older, then "they camped at Iye Abarim on the border of Moab [בִּגְבוּל מוֹאָב]" (33:44 lit.) may be read broadly as the basis of "pass through" Moab (Deut 2:27, 29) yet specifically as "they camped at Iye Abarim in the wilderness opposite Moab [עַל־פְּנֵי מוֹאָב] toward the sunrise" (Num 21:11 lit.). See Schnittjer, *Torah Story*, 439 and table on 440–41.

10. Thank you to the blind peer reviewer for pointing out that passive verbs need not signify diminishment but could denote a divine passive in the style of circumlocution. This is correct. However, this suggestion does not align with the evidence in this case. Jer 48:46 does not use the passive (Nif) of "give" (נתן) even though that is one of Jeremiah's normal ways to refer "to be given" into captivity (e.g., Jer 21:10; 32:4, 24; 34:3; 38:3; 39:17). Instead, Jer 48:46 changes the term from "he gave" (נָתַן) to the Q passive of "take" (לֻקְּחוּ) removing Chemosh as related to the verb altogether, whether active or passive. According to Jeremiah Chemosh did not give his people nor were they given by him; they were taken by someone else. The intentionality of this exegetical adjustment is confirmed by the relatively rare use of "be taken" in this sense—5x total and only here in Jeremiah ("I לקח," Pual no. 2 *HALOT* 1:535). ("They were taken" [לֻקְּחוּ] should probably be seen as Q pass with Joüon §§58a, 72j, rather than Pual.)

11. See Rashi, 4:293 (on Num 21:29); also see Milgrom, *Numbers*, 182.

12. See "The Inscription of King Mesha" (*COS* 2.23:137–38; *ANET*, 320–21).

Whether Jephthah's "diplomacy" meant to soothe relations or instigate a battle need not be decided here.

17:6//21:25~Deut 12:8 (B) (right in one's own eyes). Mottos frame the two epilogues of Judges: "In those days Israel had no king" (Judg 17:6//18:1//19:1//21:25) and "In those days Israel had no king; everyone did as they saw fit" (17:6//21:25). Commentators debate whether the narrator espouses a pro- or antimonarchic ideology.[13] Did the narrator of Judges think Israel's theocracy should have a human king or not? If the added phrase "everyone did as they saw fit" alludes to Deut 12:8, it would support a promonarchic angle (bold signifies verbal parallels):[14]

> You are not to do as we do here today, **everyone doing as they see fit**, since you have not yet reached the resting place and the inheritance Yahweh your God is giving you. (Deut 12:8–9)

> In those days Israel had no king; **everyone did as they saw fit.** (Judg 17:6//21:25)

The repetition of this important phrase in contexts trying to characterize Israel in wayward situations makes an interpretive allusion probable. Though direction of dependence could go either way when focused on the parallel language itself, the shared language of Deuteronomy and Judges elsewhere favors Judges as the receptor context (see note on 2:6–9).

Deuteronomy 12:8–9 speaks negatively of decentralized worship at many altars in contrast to the central worship at the place Yahweh will choose for his name to dwell. The interpretive intervention by the narrator of Judges exegetically advances the problem. The lack of a central place of worship gets linked to the lack of the Davidic monarchy and its royal patronage of the temple.[15] The exegetical allusion to Deut 12 in Judg 17:6//21:25 strongly favors a promonarchic perspective of Judges.

19:22*~Gen 19:5* (B) (bring out the men) (* see cities of the plain network). Judges frequently makes broad, possible allusions to scriptural persons, legal instructions, and events to create ironic situations in its narrative vignettes (see Filters). The most pronounced connotes an exegetical function by casting Gibeah after the ancient cities of the plain. Many of the ironic effects in Judg 19 only work based on allusion to Gen 19. The nature of irony suggests Gen 19 as donor context.[16] Anyone who hears the old man

13. For a view of everyone doing what is right before Yahweh in Judg 21:25 meaning without human monarchy to get in the way, see Boling, *Judges*, 293. For a view that without a king like David disorder takes over, see Cundall and Morris, *Judges*, 203–4.

14. The shared language differs only with a different form of "do" (עשׂה)—ptc. in Deut 12:8 and impf. in Judg 17:6//21:25 with both forms inferring continuous activity (GKC §§107e, 116f)—and the use of "all" (כָּל) for emphasis (GKC §127b, c) in "everyone [doing] as they saw fit" (עֹשִׂים . . . אִישׁ כָּל־הַיָּשָׁר בְּעֵינָיו) (Deut 12:8) versus "everyone doing as they saw fit" (אִישׁ הַיָּשָׁר בְּעֵינָיו יַעֲשֶׂה) (Judg 17:6//21:25 lit.).

15. See Boda, "Recycling Heaven's Words," 56–57.

16. Contra Niditch, who bases her opposite judgment on the more difficult sense, as she sees it, of the narrative in

urging the younger couple to leave the square and enter his home can remember Lot doing the same (Gen 19:1–3; Judg 19:18–20).[17] The most notable parallel comes from the requests of the men of the towns (italics signify verbal parallels):

> They called to Lot, "Where are the men who came to you tonight? *Bring* them *out* to us *so that we can have sex with* them." (Gen 19:5)

> While they were enjoying themselves, some of the wicked men of the city surrounded the house. Pounding on the door, they shouted to the old man who owned the house, "*Bring out* the man who came to your house *so we can have sex with* him." (Judg 19:22)

Lot invites the people of the town to take his daughters (Gen 19:8), and the homeowner suggests giving his virgin daughter and his guest's concubine (Judg 19:24). Instead of guests who can blind the men and close the door (Gen 19:11), one of the men—the text does not clarify the homeowner or the visitor—pushes the concubine outside (Judg 19:25).[18]

The exegetical significance of the elaborate extended echo-effect amounts to using the renowned wickedness of the cities of the plain to connote the character of Saul's hometown, Gibeah of Benjamin (Judg 19:14; 1 Sam 10:26). The Levite's act of chopping his concubine's corpse into twelve pieces to send to all the tribes of Israel evokes the incident when Saul chopped his oxen into pieces and sent them throughout the land (Judg 19:29; 1 Sam 11:7).[19] The contrast with Jebus (before it becomes the city of David) and its indigenous inhabitants heightens the dark irony (Judg 19:12). Hosea apparently refers to the terrible events of Judg 19 by the simile "like the days of Gibeah" (Hos 9:9; 10:9).

FILTERS

Judges includes many uses of scriptural traditions that may be filtered out as non-exegetical broad allusions and shared themes. The following filters and their associated lists illustrate but do not exhaust non-exegetical similarities.[20]

Judg 19 ("'Sodomite,'" 375–78). Whether the "more difficult" (*lectio difficilior*) text-critical principle reliably applies to narratives as Niditch claims (376–77) is less relevant than the fact that parody requires a pretext for the parody to work (see discussion of Kynes's argument in Hermeneutical Profile of the Use of Scripture in Job). On the extent of "inverted world" shaping of Judg 19 as a tragic comedy, see Lasine, "Guest," 43–48.

17. For numerous other verbal and thematic parallels between Gen 19 and Judg 19, see the side-by-side layout in Block, "Echo," 328–31; O'Connell, *Rhetoric*, 250–52; Shepherd, *Text in the Middle*, 19–20. Block sees these parallels as the climax of the "Canaanization" of Israel ("Echo," 336). For a list of parallels between Judg 19 and other Scriptures see Gardner, "Hidden," 60–62.

18. See Boling, *Judges*, 276.

19. Gardner lists Judg 19:12–16, 22, 29 as promoting anti-Saul/anti-Benjamin agenda ("Hidden," 69).

20. For a list of parallels between Judg 1 and Joshua, see Driver, *Introduction*, 163, and for an extensive list of parallel stock phrases and other shared language between Judges and other Scriptures, esp. Torah and Joshua, see Elitzur, *Judges*, 28–40 [Hebrew].

Non-Exegetical Broad Allusions and Shared Themes

From the first half of the book note: **1:3, 17**>/<Josh 19:9, conjoining of Simeon and Judah; **1:5**>/<Josh 10:1, battling against Adoni-bezek/Adoni-zedek;[21] **1:8, 21**>/<Josh 15:63, the reference to Judah burning Jerusalem and killing the inhabitants anticipates 2 Kgs 25:9 but is unclear in light of statements of Jerusalem under Jebusite control until the time of David (cf. Judg 19:10–12; 2 Sam 5:6–10); **2:1**>/<Exodus, Joshua passim, "I brought you up from Egypt and into the land"; **2:2**>/<Exod 23:24, 33; 34:12–13; Deut 7:2, 5, prohibition against making covenants with people of the land and command to destroy their worship icons; **2:3**>/<Exod 23:33; 34:12; Deut 7:16; Josh 23:13, their gods shall be a snare (compare parallels in Judg 2:2; cf. 8:27); **2:4; 20:26; 21:2**>/<Gen 35:8, weeping in Bokim/Bethel; **2:12**>/<Exod 1–15, God who brought them out of Egypt; **3:6**>/<Deut 7:3, "They took their daughters in marriage and gave their own daughters to their sons/ Do not give your daughters to their sons or take their daughters for your sons" (ויקחו את בנותיהם להם לנשים ואת בנותיהם נתנו לבניהם/בתך לא תתן לבנו ובתו לא תקח לבנך) (cf. Exod 34:16; Josh 23:12); **4:14**>/<Isa 26:21; Mic 1:3, "Yahweh goes out before you/from his place" (יהוה יצא לפניך/ממקומו); **5:4**>/<Deut 33:2, "Yahweh when you went out from Seir/Yahweh came from Sinai and dawned from Seir" (יהוה בצאתך משׂעיר/יהוה מסיני בא וזרח משׂעיר); **6:8**>/<Exod 13:14; 20:2//Deut 5:6; 6:12; 8:14; 13:5, 10[6, 11]; Josh 24:17; Jer 34:13, "brought up/out from Egypt . . . out of the house of slavery" (עלה/יצא ממצרים . . . מבית עבדים); **6:10**>/<Josh 24:15, "gods of the Amorites" (אלהי האמרי);[22] **6:13**>/<Deut 6:20–24; Pss 44:1[2]; 78:5–6, ancestors tell the next generation of divine acts of redemption.

Ironic Broad Allusions and Echoes

The second half of Judges features several ironic possible allusions and echoes. For example, Jephthah's vow provokes auditors to wonder why no one seems to know about "rash vows" (Lev 5:4; Judg 11:30, 35; cf. Num 30:8). Jephthah's vow in certain respects anticipates Saul's and David's foolish oaths overturned by their constituents (1 Sam 14:24, 45; 25:22, 33–34). In much the same way, dismembering the concubine of Bethlehem foreshadows Saul dismembering oxen (Judg 19:29–30; 1 Sam 11:7). Readers may notice that the messenger of Yahweh does not stop Jephthah from sacrificing his only daughter in a dark counterpoint to Abraham's faith (Gen 22:11; Judg 11:39). There are no messengers to blind the men of the city and shut the door (Gen 19:11; Judg 19:25). These possible allusions, reversing Torah episodes and anticipating Saul, gain momentum by the debacle of Gibeah, which includes enough evidence to constitute an exegetical allusion (see note on Judg 19:22).

Nazirite allusions in the Samson story provide an ironic organizing theme (Num 6:1–22;

---

21. *BHK* proposes that Adoni-bezek (אֲדֹנִי בֶזֶק) in Judg 1:5 be emended to Adoni-zedek (אדֹנִי צֶדֶק) in Josh 10:1, but this suggestion is not followed by *BHS*/*BHQ*. Marcos notes that all extant witnesses support MT (*BHQ*, 41*).

22. Judges 6:7–10 does not appear in 4QJudg[a/4Q49] (*BQS* 1:255), indicating it may be a later insertion (see Marcos, *BHQ*, 65*–66*). This could account for using slightly different stereotypical scriptural allusions, but there is not enough evidence to draw conclusions.

Judg 13:5, 7). While Nazirites may not touch dead bodies, Samson eats honey from a lion carcass and makes riddles about it, and he uses a piece of a dead donkey as a weapon and makes a poem about it (Num 6:6; Judg 14:8–9, 14; 15:15–16). Samson's haircut stands out most prominently (Num 6:5; Judg 16:17, 19). The narrative of Samson does not build on legal instruction so much as uses his situation as a bad Nazirite to connote his failure as a deliverer from the Philistines.

Micah's mother saying "I solemnly consecrate my silver to Yahweh for my son to make a molten image [עשׂה פסל ומסכה]" (Judg 17:3 lit.) ironically inverts "Cursed is anyone who makes a molten image [עשׂה פסל ומסכה]—a thing detestable to Yahweh" (Deut 27:15 lit.). The narrative goes on to flagrantly subvert Torah by making a Levite into a private priest hoping for prosperity from Yahweh (Judg 17:12, 13). The phony priest blesses a mission of the Danites to forsake the land of their inheritance in the name of Yahweh (18:6). The scouts of the Danites in Judg 18:1–10 may serve as an extended echo of similar events in Numbers 13.[23]

The family of the grandson of Moses oversees a shrine to false worship in Dan (18:31).[24] Phinehas serves as high priest at the tabernacle in Bethel (20:27). The references to the grandsons of Moses and Aaron in these two notorious episodes signal that they are dischronological flashbacks. The worst rebellions of Israel happening immediately. The symmetry of worship centers in both Dan and Bethel also evokes with the locations that Jeroboam will erect two golden calves. This connection is strengthened since the narrative looks back from after exile, at least of the Northern Kingdom (18:30).

The tribal judgment upon Gibeah (Judg 20) sometimes gets compared to the required judgment against a city that worships false gods (Deut 13:12–18[13–19]). The two contexts have many partial thematic similarities as well as a few verbal parallels: "wicked men" (בני בליעל) (Deut 13:13[14]; Judg 19:22; 20:13); "purge" (בער) (Deut 13:5[6]; Judg 20:13); "smite with the edge of the sword" (נכה לפי הרב) (Deut 13:15[16]; Judg 20:48); and burn plunder "with fire" (באשׁ) (Deut 13:16[17]; Judg 20:48).[25] Neither the crime nor the judgment line up completely.[26] If this is an intentional allusion, then it may accord with many other ironic allusions depicting a distortion of what life according to Torah should look like in the second half of Judges. At the same time, lack of key terms like "devote" (Deut 13:15, 17[16, 18]) and mismatch of crimes as well as the shared terms being commonplace prevents confidence in allusion.

In sum, Judges often uses scriptural traditions for ironic narrative functions without exegetical development concerning the cited contexts per se.

---

23. See a list of ten comparisons in Milgrom, *Numbers*, 390–91. Also see side by side comparison of Num 13; Deut 1; and Judg 18 in O'Connell, *Rhetoric*, 236.

24. The copyists retain the raised *nun* in *m"sh* (מ׳שה) of Judg 18:31 MT, virtually assuring the original reading as "Moses" (משה) versus "Manasseh" (מנשה). See Marcos, *BHQ: Judges*, 104*–5*.

25. See Ross, "People Heeds Not Scripture," 315–24; O'Connell, *Rhetoric*, 256–57. Also indebted to Kim, "Crime of Gibeah."

26. See Edenburg, "What?" 449–51.

Chapter 8

SAMUEL

שמואל

SYMBOLS[1]

// verbal parallels (A level)
/~/ synoptic parallel (A level)
~ B, probable interpretive allusion; C, possible; D, probably not
\+ interpretive blend
>/< more or less similar (see Filters)
* part of interpretive network (see Networks)

USE OF SCRIPTURE IN SAMUEL[2]

1 Sam 2:15–17~Lev 3:16–17 (B) (taking the fat of offerings)
8:5~Deut 17:17 (B) (a king like the nations)
12:6–17~Torah and judges compilation (C) (Samuel's panoramic retrospective to initiate monarchy)
16:14~Ps 51:11[13] (C) (spirit departs from Saul)
21:4*[5]~Lev 10:10–11* (B)+24:5–9* (B)+Deut 23:10–11*[11–12] (C) (bread of the presence for David) (* see Sabbath and teachers networks)
2 Sam 7:14–15*~Gen 49:10* (B) (covenant loyalty shall not depart) (* see Davidic covenant, Judah-king, and place networks)
11:21~Judg 9:53–54 (B) (a woman kills Abimelek)
24:1~Exod 30:11–16 (D)/Num 1:2–3 (D) (sin of the census)

OLD TESTAMENT USE OF SAMUEL (SEE RESPECTIVE NOTES)

1 Sam 1:1; 8:1~1 Chr 6:27–28[12–13] (C) (Elkanah, Samuel, and his sons in the line of Kohath)
6:1–2~Ps 132:6–7 (C) (his footstool in the fields of Jaar)
9:21; 16:1, 11~Mic 5:2*[1] (C) (ruler from Bethlehem Ephrathah) (* see Davidic covenant network)
17:47~2 Chr 20:15, 17 (B) (divine victory)
28:3–25; 31:1–13/~/1 Chr 10:1–14 (B) (death of Saul)
2 Sam 2:18+17:27~1 Chr 2:3–17 (B) (genealogies of Judah through family of David)
3:2–5+5:5, 13–16+11:3; 12:24~1 Chr 3:1–9 (B) (sons born to David in Jerusalem)
5:1–3/~/1 Chr 11:1–3 (David made king over all Israel)
5:6–10/~/1 Chr 11:4–9 (David captures Jerusalem)
5:6~Isa 29:1, 3 (C) (besieging Ariel)
5:11–12/~/1 Chr 14:1–2 (Hiram acknowledges David)
5:11~1 Kgs 5:1–5 [15–19]* (C) (Solomon's message to Hiram) (* see Davidic covenant network)
5:13–16/~/1 Chr 14:3–7 (sons of David born at Jerusalem)
5:17–25/~/1 Chr 14:8–17 (David defeats Philistines)
5:20~Isa 28:21 (C) (reversal of divine intervention at Mount Perazim and Gibeon)
6:1–11/~/1 Chr 13:5–14 (failed attempt to bring ark to Jerusalem)
6:12–19/~/1 Chr 15:25–16:6 (David and all Israel accompany the Levites in bringing the ark)
6:19–20a/~/1 Chr 16:43 (returning home and David's blessing)
7:1, 11–13*~1 Kgs 5:1–5[15–19]* (A) (Solomon's message to Hiram) (* see Davidic covenant and place networks)

1. For explanation of symbols, see Symbols and Abbreviations and Introduction. For other help, see Glossary.
2. See Bibliographic Note on Lists of Potential Parallels.

7:1–17*, 18–29/~/1 Chr 17:1–15*, 16–27 (Davidic covenant and David's prayer) (* see Davidic covenant, Judah-king, and place networks)
7:8, 13*~1 Kgs 8:15–21* (A) (choosing a place and choosing David) (* see place network)
7:11–16*~Ps 89:3–4, 19–37*[4–5, 20–38] (B) (Davidic covenant) (* see Davidic covenant and place networks)
7:12–15*~Ps 132:11–12* (oath to David) (* see Davidic covenant, Judah-king, and place networks)
7:12*, 27~Amos 9:11–12* (B) (Davidic shelter restored) (* see Davidic covenant and place networks)
7:14–15*~Ps 2:6–7* (B) (divine begetting of the king) (* see Davidic covenant, Judah-king, and place networks)
7:14–15*~1 Chr 28:7 (B) (irrevocable Davidic covenant and its obligations) (* see Davidic covenant and place networks)
8:1–14*/~/1 Chr 18:1–13 (David establishes a regional empire) (* see Judah-king network)
8:1–14*; 12:26–30~Amos 1:3–2:16 (C) (indictment against regional rivals) (* see Judah-king network)
8:12b–13~Ps 60 superscription[60:2] (B) (striking down an enemy in the valley of salt)
8:15–18/~/1 Chr 18:14–17 (David's leading officers)
10:1–19/~/1 Chr 19:1–19 (defeat of Ammonites and Arameans)
11:1; 12:26a, 30–31/~/1 Chr 20:1–3 (defeat of Rabbah)
20:23–26/~/1 Chr 18:14–17 (David's leading officers)
21:18–22/~/1 Chr 20:4–8 (killing the giants of Gath)
22:33–34~Hab 3:19 (B) (treading upon the heights)
23:8–39/~/1 Chr 11:10–47 (David's mighty men)
23:16–17~1 Chr 11:18–19 (water represents the blood of life)
24:1–25/~/1 Chr 21:1–30 (David's sin of the census)

NEW TESTAMENT USE OF SAMUEL

1 Sam 13:14~Acts 13:22 (heart like my own)
21:4–6~Luke 6:3 (David ate holy bread)
2 Sam 7:14~2 Cor 6:18; Heb 1:5 (I will be father)
22:50//Rom 15:9 (praise among gentiles)

HERMENEUTICAL PROFILE OF THE USE OF SCRIPTURE IN SAMUEL

Samuel houses occasional allusions to scriptural traditions. In most cases these amount to brief non-exegetical references. The casual occurrence of many of these allusions and echoes suggests that scriptural narrative traditions and legal standards simply constitute part of the culture of biblical Israel. A general sense of the scripturally allusive outlook can be seen in the representative non-exegetical allusions collected in the Filters.

Several of the interpretive scriptural allusions in Samuel relate to the downfall of Eli and the institution of the Hebrew kingdom. Just as juxtaposition is a leading feature of the narrative in general, so too is the use of scriptural traditions. The sharp contrasts between Hannah and Eli, similarities between Samuel and Eli as fathers, and differences between Saul and David all characterize the narrative settings and the uses of scriptural traditions therein.

The brief allusions to Hophni and Phinehas taking Yahweh's sacrificial fat and David receiving the bread of the presence provide helpful offsetting differences to avoid wrongful stereotyping of scriptural interpretation in Samuel. When Eli's sons take Yahweh's fat, the narrator uses this legal violation as something of an ironic theme culminating in the death of the high priest and his wicked sons on the same day. At the opposite extreme, Ahimelek the priest uses his rightful role to distinguish between holy versus common and ritual purity versus ritual impurity to exegetically advance revelation. In these cases, the reprehensible and virtuous character tendencies of the priests accord with contrasting associated scriptural interpretations.

The people ask for a king to be like the nations right from Deuteronomy's law of the king (1 Sam 8:5; cf. Deut 17:14). If the people use the right words, they signify the wrong reasons. Over Samuel's objections, Yahweh grants their request. To mark the transition, Samuel, like Joshua, frames the turning point as part of a scriptural retrospective (Josh 24:1–15; 1 Sam 12:6–17). Samuel's possible use of scriptural traditions calls for obedience even while once more warning of the dangers of the institution of the monarchy.

Nathan's interpretive allusion to the blessing of Judah does not gloss over royal broken obligations to Yahweh in days to come (2 Sam 7:14–15). Yet within the context of Yahweh punishing the Davidic king as his own son, Nathan sets out a sharp contrast to Saul. Yahweh's punishment will not remove his covenantal loyalty from the Davidic ruler as he did from Saul. This important exegetical advancement makes use of the narrative's signature contrastive juxtaposition.

Nathan's exegetical allusion to the blessing of Judah stands at a watershed of scriptural revelation. The interpretive allusion grounds the Davidic covenant in the ancient Hebrew ancestral expectations for Judah's dominion. Evoking Judah-king expectations from the blessing of Judah sets the Davidic ruler and his temple patronage at the nexus of the larger redemptive work of Yahweh.

In sum, the use of scriptural traditions in Samuel aligns with and strengthens the pervasive tendency toward contrastive juxtaposition in the narrative.

USE OF SCRIPTURE

1 Sam 2:15–17~Lev 3:16–17 (B) (taking the fat of offerings). The hard fat that encases the kidneys and lobe of the liver in animal sacrifices belongs exclusively to Yahweh. Leviticus spells out the standards for sacrifices, but not the reasons.[3] Whatever the reason, Hophni and Phinehas insist on taking the fat of offering for themselves. Though the parallels concern only a single word, the nature of the contexts makes allusion probable. Leviticus frequently explains what to do with the kidneys, the lobe of the liver, and the fat around them (e.g., Lev 3:3, 4, 9, 10, 14, 15, etc.) but only rarely mentions that they belong to Yahweh (3:16, 17; 7:25). Taking the fat that belongs to Yahweh typifies the disdain of the priests (italics signify verbal parallels, and broken underlining signifies interpretive deduction):

> The priest shall burn them on the altar as a food offering, a pleasing aroma. All *the fat* is Yahweh's. This is a lasting ordinance for the generations to come, wherever you live: You must not eat any *fat* or any blood. (Lev 3:16–17)

3. For a reason, see Schnittjer, *Torah Story*, 307.

> But even before *the fat* was burned, the priest's servant would come and say to the person who was sacrificing, "Give the priest some meat to roast; he won't accept boiled meat from you, but only raw." If the person said to him, "Let *the fat* be burned first, and then take whatever you want," the servant would answer, "No, hand it over now; if you don't, I'll take it by force." This sin of the young men was very great in Yahweh's sight, for they were treating Yahweh's offering with contempt. (1 Sam 2:15–17)

The verb translated "treat with contempt" in the intensive stem appears about a dozen times in Scripture, including its use in parallel with "do not believe," to describe the wilderness rebels (Num 14:11).

Although the misdeeds of Hophni and Phinehas included having relations with the women who served at the entrance of the tent of meeting (1 Sam 2:22), their taking the fat set up the metaphorical use of judgment synonyms. The unnamed man of God indicts: "Why do you scorn my sacrifice and offering that I prescribed for my dwelling? Why do you honor your sons more than me *by fattening yourselves* on the choice parts of every offering made by my people Israel?" (2:29, emphasis mine).[4] Their grave sin leads Yahweh to take away the priesthood from Eli's line (2:27–28, 30). The word is fulfilled in stages: a massacre of the priests (22:18–19), and then the banishment of Abiathar (1 Kgs 2:26–27).[5] But other wordplays bring judgment in the near context. The man of God accuses Eli of "honoring" (כבד Piel) his sons above Yahweh (1 Sam 2:29; cf. v. 30). Eli does not fall backward when he hears of the death of his sons but of the loss of the ark; and he died because he was old and "fat" (כבד) (4:18). The same sequence includes the naming of Eli's grandson Ichabod to commemorate the tragedy. Ichabod means "Where is the glory?" (אִי־כָבוֹד); and the new mother says, "Exiled is the glory [כָּבוֹד] of Israel" (4:21).[6]

In sum, the narrator uses a slight but concrete allusion to the prohibition against taking Yahweh's fat to tie together the downfall of the house of Eli.

8:5~Deut 17:17 (B) (a king like the nations). Samuel did not want a king. Many interpreters agree with Samuel that Israel should not have an "earthly king."[7] Others note the ancient expectations for a king in Torah (Gen 17:6, 16; 27:29; 35:11; 49:8; Num 24:7, 17–19; Deut 17:14–20; see note on 1 Chr 28:4–6). On this reading the problem is not that Israel wants a king, but why. They give two reasons (italics signify verbal parallels, and broken underlining signifies the people's stated reasons):

> When you enter the land Yahweh your God is giving you and have taken possession of it and settled in it, and you say, "*Let* me *appoint a king over* me *like all the nations* around us." (Deut 17:14†)

---

4. See "II ברא," *HALOT* 1:154.

5. See McCarter, *I Samuel*, 92.

6. Translation from Fox, *Early Prophets*, 299 ("exiled" here renders גָּלָה).

7. See Weinfeld, "בְּרִית," *TDOT* 2:275. This view often suggests promonarchic, 1 Sam 8:1–22; 10:17–27; 12:1–25; interspersed with antimonarchic contexts, 9:1–10:16; 11:1–15, see Wellhausen, *Bücher Samuelis*, ix, 67, 77. Also see Childs, *Introduction*, 277–78.

> They said to him [Samuel], "You are old, and your sons do not follow your ways; now *appoint a king* to lead us, *like all the nations....*" "Then we will be *like all the nations*, with a king to lead us and to go out before us and fight our battles." (1 Sam 8:5, 20†)

Yahweh frames it differently: "It is not you [Samuel] they have rejected, but *they have rejected me* as their king" (8:7, emphasis mine). The narrative identifies the motivation of the people to be at odds with the will of Yahweh regarding the law of the king.

12:6–17~Torah and judges compilation (C) (Samuel's panoramic retrospective to initiate monarchy). Samuel recounts selected acts of divine deliverance including redemption from Egypt and deliverance by judges (1 Sam 12:6, 8, 9–11; see Table Josh1). The purpose of the narrative framing pivots both on encouraging the people to covenant faithfulness (12:14) and on condemning their evil request for a king (12:17). Samuel presents the sequence of the judges differently than Judges—Jerubbaal (Gideon), Bedan (Barak LXX), Jephthah, Samuel (Samson LXX variants) (12:11).[8] The author of Hebrews uses yet a different sequence—Gideon, Barak, Samson, Jephthah (Heb 11:32). The variations in sequence combined with the dischronologization in the last two stories of Judges underline the general chronological difficulties of the days of the judges (see discussion of Judg 18:31; 20:27 in Judges Filters). In any case, Samuel highlights the incongruity of the repeated deliverances by judges and the people's desire for a king when faced with Nahash of the Ammonites (1 Sam 12:12).

16:14~Ps 51:11[13] (C) (spirit departs from Saul). The anointing of David marks the narrative turning point for the rise of David and the decline of Saul. The narrator captures the moment by referring to "the Spirit of Yahweh departing from Saul" (1 Sam 16:14). The cause-effect linkage helps clarify that the loss of the Spirit, in this case, relates to the loss of dynastic continuation. Popular versions of Christian theology sometimes struggle with the loss of the Spirit. The difficulty tends to come from a confusion of categories regarding the function of the Spirit.

The heading of Ps 51 invites association of the psalm with David's confession for his sins of murder and adultery or rape (2 Sam 12:13). The psalmist calls upon God to not take away the Spirit. The cause-effect of great sin and loss/potential loss of the Spirit suggests that the psalmist or editor of the psalm's superscription may have had the narrative tradition of David's anointing in mind. Though possible, it is more economical, and thus more likely, for the narrator of Samuel to have used the tradition in Ps 51 to explain what happened when Samuel anointed David (emphases signify verbal parallels):

> Do not cast me from your presence or take your Holy *Spirit from* me. (Ps 51:11[13])

> Now the *Spirit* of Yahweh had departed *from* Saul, and an evil spirit from Yahweh tormented him. (1 Sam 16:14)

---

8. See *BHS* apparatus for other variations in ancient witnesses to 1 Sam 12:11.

The possible interpretive relationship between Ps 51:11[13] and 1 Sam 16:14 pivots on the loss of the Spirit as loss of dynastic promise, not loss of salvation. The Spirit left Saul when David was anointed the next king. The psalmist's angst turns on the possibility of the Spirit's departure after a great sin.

21:4*[5]~Lev 10:10–11* (B)+24:5–9* (B)+Deut 23:10–11*[11–12] (C) (bread of the presence for David) (* see Sabbath and teachers networks). The story of David and the bread of the presence houses legal exegesis with several moving parts. The interpretive blend works with three interrelated teachings from Torah: the regulations regarding the bread of the presence (Exod 25:30; 40:23; Lev 24:5–9); the ceremonial purity on the battlefield and associated teachings (Deut 23:9–10; Lev 15:15–16, 18); and the priests' role in distinguishing the ceremonially pure from the ceremonially impure and what is holy from what is profane (Lev 10:10–11). Of these, this narrative relates most directly to the regulation of the bread of the presence, but as interpreted in light of these other legal contexts.

The priest alludes to changing of the bread of the presence every Sabbath (1 Sam 21:6[7]; Lev 24:8). Ahimelek's theological extrapolation, though presented economically in 1 Sam 21:4[5], relies upon several contexts that may be compared before explaining (italics and bold signify verbal parallels, and broken underlining signifies interpretive inferences):

> So that you [Aaron] can distinguish between the *holy* and the common, between the **unclean** and the **clean**, and so you can teach the Israelites all the decrees Yahweh has given them through Moses. (Lev 10:10–11)
>
> When a man has sexual relations with **a woman** and there is an emission of semen, both of them must bathe with water, and they will be **unclean** till evening. (15:18)
>
> This *bread* is to be set out before Yahweh regularly, Sabbath after Sabbath, on behalf of the Israelites, as a lasting covenant. It belongs to Aaron and his sons, who are to eat it in the sanctuary area, because it is a most *holy* part of their perpetual share of the food offerings presented to Yahweh. (24:8–9; NIV supplies "bread" from v. 7)
>
> When you are encamped against your enemies.... If one of your men is not **clean** because of a nocturnal emission .... (Deut 23:9a, 10†[10a, 11])
>
> But the priest answered David, "I don't have any ordinary *bread* on hand; however, there is some *holy bread* here—provided the men have kept themselves from **women**." David replied, "Indeed **women** have been kept from us, as usual whenever I set out. The men's bodies are *holy* even on missions that are not *holy*. How much more so today!" So the priest gave him the *holy bread*, since there was no *bread* there except *the bread* of the Presence that had been removed from before Yahweh and replaced by hot *bread* on the day it was taken away. (1 Sam 21:4–6†[5–7])

Ahimelek's legal exegesis requires the overlapping logics of several legal standards. First, as the priest, Ahimelek held the rightful position to distinguish between holy versus common and ritually pure versus ritually impure (Lev 10:10). Second, standards for ritual purity remain even during times of warfare (Deut 23:9[10]). Third, Ahimelek needed to clarify that David and his men had not become temporarily ritually impure by sexual relations, which David affirms (Lev 18:15; 1 Sam 21:4, 5[5, 6]). Fourth, the bread of the presence is extremely holy and must be consumed by the priests in the holy area after it has been replaced on the Sabbath (Lev 24:8, 9; cf. Exod 35:13; 39:36). The burden of Yahweh's deadly holiness had been placed upon the priests as their exclusive burden even in contrast to the Levites (Num 18:1, 5). Finally, it needs to be remembered that ritual purity/impurity and holy/common are different kinds of things, though both interrelate as prerequisites of tabernacle worship.[9] All of these factors play into Ahimelek's exegetical deduction which takes advantage of the overlap in purity/impurity and holy/common worship prerequisites.

Ahimelek recognizes that the right kind of circumstances can grant qualified latitude. But his concern over the ritual purity of David and his men reveals the limits of his interpretive advances (cf. irony of Saul thinking David is ceremonially impure in 1 Sam 20:26). Ahimelek would not give the holy bread to ritually impure persons. Ritual purity plus pressing circumstances allowed him to use his priestly role to determine that David and his men could have the previous week's bread of the presence (1 Sam 21:4, 6[5, 7]).

The importance of Ahimelek's exegetical advancement relates to the broader context of progressive revelation. For example, Paul deduces that certain days do not connote holiness of themselves from the Lord's new torah that nothing is ritually impure in itself (Rom 14:5, 14; cf. Mark 7:19). Messiah himself explains, in accord with Ahimelek's decision, that moral and social good legally transcend his opponents' prohibitions against work, perhaps akin to the emerging Mishnaic outlook (Luke 6:1–5; cf. m. Shab. 7:2; m. Yoma 8:6).

In sum, only reckless interpretation can see Ahimelek's decision as relaxing all legal standards regarding the burden of holiness. Ahimelek's exegetical decision represents an incremental advancement of revelation based on his sanctioned role as priest to distinguish between holy versus common and ritually pure versus ritually impure.

2 Sam 7:14–15*~Gen 49:10* (B) (covenant loyalty shall not depart) (* see Davidic covenant, Judah-king, and place networks). The high point of the Davidic covenant shares language with the blessing of Judah. Though Nathan uses the common term "scepter" in a different manner, he uses the expression "shall not turn" in an identical verbal, syntactical, and contextual manner to underpin the promise (Gen 49:10; 2 Sam 7:14, 15). Nathan goes on to repeat the same term twice, with a different emphasis, with reference to David's predecessor. Whereas Yahweh promises that his covenantal loyalty shall not

9. See Schnittjer, *Torah Story*, 329–30.

"depart" (סור Q) as he had "removed" (סור Hif) it from Saul whom he "removed" (סור Hif) before David. This evidence makes interpretive allusion probable (cf. second point in note on 1 Chr 28:4–6).[10] The primary force of the scriptural allusion relates to the irrevocability of the Davidic covenant. Note the shared language (emphases in bold and italics signify verbal parallels at the level of roots, and broken underlining signifies interpretive advancement):

> *The scepter* [שֵׁבֶט] **shall not depart** [סור Q] from Judah, nor the ruler's staff from between his feet, until that which belongs to him comes, and the obedience of the peoples is his. (Gen 49:10 lit.)

> I will be a father to him and he will be a son to me, when he does wrong I will punish him [יכח Hif] with *the rod* [שֵׁבֶט] of mortals and with wounds inflicted by humans. But my covenantal loyalty **shall not depart** [סור Q] from him, as **I removed it** [סור Hif] from Saul whom **I removed** [סור Hif] before you. (2 Sam 7:14–15 lit.)

In the broader context of the Davidic covenant, Nathan uses a well-known wordplay on "house" (בַּיִת) as *temple* for Yahweh and *dynasty* for David (7:5, 6, 7, 11, 13, 16, 18, 19, 25, 26, 27, 29[2x]; cf. 7:1, 2). In like manner Nathan shifts the sense from "scepter" (שֵׁבֶט) of rule in the blessing of Judah to "rod" (שֵׁבֶט) of punishment in the Davidic covenant (Gen 49:10; 2 Sam 7:14). This interpretive intervention establishes a surprising continuity. According to Nathan, Yahweh's "covenantal loyalty" shall not depart from David's/Yahweh's son. Thus, the rod of punishment accords with Yahweh's covenantal loyalty. Elsewhere correction/punishment definitively signifies Yahweh's fatherhood of Israel (Deut 8:5). The sage claims, "Yahweh punishes [יכח Hif] the one he loves, as a father the son in whom he delights" (Prov 3:12 lit.; cf. 3:11; Heb 12:5–11).[11] The rod of punishment does not transform the blessing into a curse.[12] Instead Yahweh's paternal devotion naturally uses the rod to punish the royal son he loves.

In sum, Nathan's exegetical advancement of the blessing of Judah situates the promise in contrast to the situation with Saul. In the case of the son of David/son of Yahweh, paternal love may take the form of punishment but will not result in removal of his covenantal loyalty. According to Nathan, the Davidic covenant is irrevocable and includes obligations.[13]

10. The present argument is indebted to Steiner for the basic observation of Nathan's use of the blessing of Judah ("Four Inner-Biblical Interpretations," 43–47). For interaction and disagreement with many of Steiner's subtle associated suggestions, see Schnittjer, "Blessing of Judah," 16, n. 2; 24–26.

11. The verb for "punish" (יסר) in Deut 8:5 differs from "punish" (יכח) in 2 Sam 7:14, but the latter term is often used of fatherly correction in wisdom contexts (Prov 9:8; 15:12; 19:25; see Hif no. 2 of "יכח," *HALOT* 1:410). Prov 3:11 uses nouns related to these two roots as pair words for punishment, glossed as discipline/reproof in NRSV (מוּסָר, תּוֹכַחַת).

12. Contra Steiner, "Four Inner-Biblical Interpretations," 47.

13. I am indebted to Gordon Johnston for this observation, see Schnittjer, "Blessing of Judah," 25–26, n. 22.

11:21~Judg 9:53–54 (B) (a woman kills Abimelek). Joab likely did not think David had poor historical memory. Probably no one but Abimelek thought that hastening his death by his servant's help could remove the shame of being killed by a woman (italics signify verbal parallel, and broken underlining signifies interpretive adjustment).

> *A woman dropped an upper millstone on* his head and cracked his skull. Hurriedly he [Abimelek] called to his armor-bearer, "Draw your sword and kill me, so that they can't say, 'A woman killed him.'" So his servant ran him through, and he died. (Judg 9:53–54)

> [Joab explains what David may say in anger] "Who killed Abimelek son of Jerub-Besheth? Didn't *a woman drop an upper millstone on* him from the wall, so that he died in Thebez? Why did you get so close to the wall?" (2 Sam 11:21)

24:1~Exod 30:11–16 (D)/Num 1:2–3 (D) (sin of the census). In anger for an unknown reason, Yahweh incited David to take a census (2 Sam 24:1). The upshot of the census amounted to numbering those eligible for military service (24:2, 9; cf. Num 1:2–3). But how would that translate into David's sin (2 Sam 24:10)? One suggestion hinges on the difficult-to-maintain requirement for ritual purity by active military (Deut 23:10–11[11–12]).[14] Another possibility is that the census relates to providing funds for a national shrine (Exod 30:11–16). The census for the tabernacle required Israel to give a ransom as a substitute for each life to avoid a plague (30:12).[15] Although the messenger struck Israel with a plague (2 Sam 24:21, 25), this was choice C of punishments (24:13). In short, the nature of David's sin and how it relates to the census is unknown.

FILTERS

Samuel features a modest amount of possible allusions to scriptural traditions. The following lists illustrate but do not exhaust non-exegetical similarities.

Non-Exegetical Broad Allusions and Shared Themes

Hannah's story evokes the barren wife type-scene/character: 1 Sam 1:2–11>/<Gen 16:1–12; 17:15–19 (Sarah); 25:21 (Rebekah); 30:1–8 (Rachel); Judg 13:2–5 (the wife of Manoah); Luke 1:7, 13–20 (Elizabeth).

Note: **1 Sam 1:11**>/<Judg 13:5; 16:17, "no razor will be used on his/my head" (ומורה לא יעלה על ראשו/י); **1:13 4QSam**$^{a/4Q51}$>/<Judg 13:7, "a Nazirite until forever all of the days of..." (נזיר עד עולם כול ימי) (1 Sam 1:13 4QSam$^{a/4Q51}$ "a Nazirite of God... until the day of his death" [נזיר אלהים . . . עד יום מותו]) (Judg 13:7);[16] **1:19–20**>/<Gen

14. See McCarter, *II Samuel*, 514.

15. On the sense of "ransom for his life" (כֹּפֶר נַפְשׁוֹ), see Milgrom, "Atonement in the OT," *IDBSup*, 80.

16. First Samuel 1:13 MT preferred as more original than 1:13 in 4QSam^{a}/4Q51 (see *BQS* 1:260).

30:22, "Yahweh remembered her/God remembered Rachel" and she conceived (ויזכרה יהוה/ויזכר אלהים את רחל);[17] **1:23**>/<Num 30:6–8, Elkanah affirms Hannah's vow; **2:25+3:13**>/<Exod 20:12//Deut 5:16, dishonoring father; **2:25**>/<Judg 13:23, "for Yahweh was resolved to kill them/if Yahweh had meant to kill us" (כי חפץ יהוה להמיתם/לו חפץ יהוה להמיתנו); **4:8**>/<Exod 7–12, striking the Egyptians with terrors in the wilderness (Philistine viewpoint); **6:6**>/<Exod 4:21; 7:13, 22; 8:19[15]; 9:12; 9:35; 10:20, 27; 11:10; 14:4, 8, 17, "harden the heart" of the pharaoh and the Egyptians; however, while Exodus usually speaks of "strengthening the heart" (חזק לבב), the Philistines use the rare expression "make heavy the heart" (כבד לבב), again skewing the tradition;[18] **9:21**>/<Judg 6:15, smallest tribe, "least" clan/weakest clan, "least" in family (צעיר); **11:7**>/<Judg 19:29–30, dismembering oxen/corpse and sending to twelve tribes; **12:3**>/<Num 16:15, "Whose donkey have I taken?/I have not taken from them a single donkey" (וחמור מי לקחתי/לא חמור אחד מהם נשׂאתי); **14:32**>/<Lev 3:17; 17:10–13; Deut 12:16, 23, 27, consuming blood; **15:2**>/<Exod 17:14, punishing the Amalekites for the ancient attacks against Israel in the wilderness; **15:22**>/<see Table A3 in Amos Filters, "to obey is better than sacrifice"; **17:4**>/<Josh 11:22, David's opponent, the large champion from Gath/Joshua and Caleb defeat (large) Anakim who only remain in Gaza, Gath, and Ashdod; **17:40, 49**>/<Judg 20:16, David kills the large champion from Gath using a sling, the Benjamite weapon of choice—this polemic works because if David had killed him any other way it would be less embarrassing for Saul the large Benjamite king (1 Sam 9:2; 10:23); **19:13, 16**>/<Gen 27:16; 37:31, deceive with "goat" hair/skin/blood (עז); **20:26**>/<Lev 11–15, Saul imagining David in ritually impure state; **24:17[18]**>/<Gen 38:26, "you are/she is more righteous than I" (צדיק אתה ממני/צדקה ממני); **28:3**>/<Lev 19:31; 20:6, 27; Deut 18:11, "mediums and spiritists" (אוב וידעני).

The narrative of the battle against Amalek in **1 Sam 15** uses language which echoes elements from Balaam's oracles: "God is not human, that he should lie, not a human being, that he should change his mind. Does he speak and then not act? Does he promise and not fulfill?" (Num 23:19; cf. 1 Sam 15:19) and Agag (Num 24:7; cf. 1 Sam 15:8, 9, 20, 32, 33).

Also note: **2 Sam 1:18**>/<Josh 10:13, "as it is written in the book of Jashar/the upright" (כתובה על ספר הישר); **7:23**>/<Exodus; Joshua passim; **8:2**>/<Num 24:17, Moabites on ground/smash border or skull of Moab (cf. Isa 25:1–12; Jer 48:45);[19] **11:4**>/<Lev 15:28, "she was purifying herself of her ritual impurity/when she is ritually pure from her discharge" (היא מתקדשת מטמאתה/אם טהרה מזובה); **12:6**>/<Exod 22:1[21:37], "he must pay for the lamb four times over/he must pay back . . . four sheep for the sheep" (ואת

17. Based esp. on this parallel, Mollo proposes extensive relationships between the Samson and Hannah/Eli narratives ("Did It Please God?" 100–1). Though most of the possible parallels are too general, it is worth noting the abstinence from wine in the cases of the wife of Manoah and Hannah (Judg 13:4, 7, 14; 1 Sam 1:14, 15) (see 96–98).

18. Twice "make heavy" (כבד) is used of pharaoh's heart (Exod 8:15[11]; 10:1). See first footnote in note on Josh 11:20; cf. "make heavy the ears" (אזנים הכבד) and "fatten the heart" (שמן לב) in Isa 6:10.

19. See Rashi, 4:338 (on Num 24:17).

הכבשה ישלם ארבעתים/ישלם . . . ארבע צאן תחת השה); **15:7**>/<Deut 23:21[22], “pay the vow which I vowed to Yahweh/if you vow a vow to Yahweh your God do not be slow to pay it” (אשלם את־נדרי אשר נדרתי ליהוה/כי תדר נדר ליהוה אלהיך לא תאחר לשלמו).

The suggestion that David’s lust and affair with/crime against Uriah’s wife casts David after Potiphar’s wife is based almost entirely on commonplace phrases like “laid with her” (2 Sam 11:4; cf. Gen 39:7), “house of your lord/his lord” (2 Sam 12:8; Gen 39:2), and the like.[20] The overlap seems more like similar type-scenes than an exegetical allusion. On the song of David in **2 Sam 22** see note on Ps 18 in Doublets in Psalms Filters.

Shared Stock Phrases and Other Similarities

Note:[21] >/<**1 Sam 1:23; 14:36, 40; 2 Sam 19:27, 38[28, 39]**; Gen 16:6; Judg 10:15; 2 Kgs 10:5, “do what is good in your eyes” (עשה הטוב בעיניך); >/< **2:2**; Exod 8:6; Deut 4:7; Ps 113:5, “like Yahweh” (כיהוה); >/<**2:2; 2 Sam 22:32**//Ps 18:31[32]; Deut 32:18, 37; Isa 44:8; Hab 1:12, Yahweh as “rock” (צור); >/<**3:17; 2 Sam 19:14**; 1 Kgs 2:23, “thus may God do to you/me and more” (כה יעשה לך/לי אלהים וכה יוסיף); >/<**3:20; 2 Sam 3:10; 17:11; 24:2, 15**; 1 Kgs 4:25[5:5], “from Dan to Beersheba” (מדן ועד באר שבע); >/<**4:4; 2 Sam 6:2**; 2 Kgs 19:15; Isa 37:16, “Yahweh of hosts/God of Israel who is enthroned above the cherubim” (יהוה צבאות/אלהי ישראל ישב הכרבים); >/<**4:10; 13:2; 2 Sam 19:8[9]; 20:1, 22**; 2 Chr 25:22, “each to his tent” (איש לאהליו); >/<**9:2; 16:12**; Gen 39:6; Exod 2:2, “handsome” (טוב); >/<**9:16**; Exod 22:23[22], “their cry has come to me/I will surely hear their cry” (כי באה צעקתו אלי/שמע אשמע צעקו); >/<**12:22**; Ps 94:14, “for Yahweh will not reject his people” (כי לא יטש יהוה עמו); >/<**12:22; 2 Sam 7:23**; Deut 29:13[12], “as his people” (לו לעם), note variations “as a people of his inheritance” (Deut 4:20), “as his people, a treasured possession” (7:6; 14:2; 26:18), “as his holy people” (28:9); >/<**29:9; 2 Sam 14:17; 19:27[28]**; Zech 12:8, “like the angel of God/Yahweh” (כמלאך אלהים/האלהים/יהוה); >/<**31:4, 5; 2 Sam 17:23**; 1 Kgs 16:18; Matt 27:5, killing oneself.

Also note: >/<**2 Sam 5:6, 8**; Lev 21:18, “blind, lame” (פסח, עור); >/<**12:22**; Joel 2:14; Jonah 3:9, “Who knows? Yahweh may be gracious to me/he may turn and relent” (מי יודע יחנני יהוה/ישוב ונחם); >/<**16:12**; 1 Kgs 2:32, 44, “that Yahweh might repay” (והשיב יהוה); >/<**17:11**; 1 Kgs 4:20, “as numerous as the sand of the sea” (כחול אשר על הים לרב); >/<**18:13**; Hos 5:3; Ps 69:5[6]; 139:15, “not hidden” from the king/from you/from me (לא נכחד); **19:12, 13[13, 14]**; Gen 29:14, “my/your bone and my/your flesh” (עצמי ובשרי/עצמך ובשרך/עצמכם ובשרכם); >/<**21:17**; 1 Kgs 11:36; Ps 132:17, David ruler as “lamp” (נר).[22]

---

20. See Postell, “Potiphar’s Wife,” 107–11.

21. For a list of expressions in Samuel shared with Deuteronomy, Joshua, and Judges, see Driver, *Introduction*, 177. For a list of characteristic expressions of Samuel, see 184–85. For other loose parallels and stock phrases shared between Samuel and other Scriptures, see Bergen, *1, 2 Samuel*, 46–47; Kiel, *Samuel*, 1:144–50 [Hebrew]. For a survey of scriptural parallels associated with Samuel, see Hays, “1 and 2 Samuel,” *DNTUOT*, forthcoming.

22. See “נֵר,” *HALOT* 1:723.

Chapter 9

KINGS

SYMBOLS[1]

- // verbal parallels (A level)
- /~/ synoptic parallel (A level)
- ~ B, probable interpretive allusion; C, possible; D, probably not
- + interpretive blend
- >/< more or less similar (see Filters)
- * part of interpretive network (see Networks)

USE OF SCRIPTURE IN KINGS[2]

1 Kgs 2:1–4~Josh 1:5–9 (C)+2 Sam 7:14, 29 (C) (David commissions Solomon)

4:25[5:5]~Mic 4:4 (C) (sit under vine and fig tree)

5:1–5[15–19]*~2 Sam 5:11 (C)+7:1, 11–13* (A) (Solomon's message to Hiram) (* see Davidic covenant and place networks)

6:7~Exod 20:25; Deut 27:5 (C) (building with stones finished offsite)

8:10~Exod 40:34–35 (B) (glory fills the temple)

8:15–21*~Deut 12:5*+2 Sam 7:8, 13* (A) (choosing a place and choosing David) (* see Davidic covenant and place networks)

9:20–21*~Deut 7:1–2*+20:11* (B) (enslaving the remaining peoples of the nations of Canaan) (* see devoting network)

10:26–29~Deut 17:16–17 (B) (international horse trade)

11:1*~Deut 23:3, 7*[4, 8] (B) (women of Egypt and Edom as well as Ammon and Moab) (* see assembly network)

11:2–4*~Exod 34:15–16*+Deut 7:3–4*+17:17 (B) (turning Solomon's heart away) (* see devoting network)

12:28–29//Exod 32:4 (two golden calves)

19:11–13~Exod 33:21–22* (B) (personal theophany on the mountain) (* see prophet like Moses network)

2 Kgs 14:6*//Deut 24:16* (each dies for own sins) (* see personal responsibility network)

18:5~18:30; 19:10; cf. 18:19, 20, 21, 22, 24 (B) (Hezekiah's faith)

18:21~Isa 30:2 (C) (depending on Egypt)

18:23–24~Isa 31:3 (C) (depending on horses)

18:30, 32, 35~Isa 31:4–5 (C) (Yahweh shall deliver Jerusalem)

18:31~Mic 4:4 (C) (under one's own vine and fig tree)

18:32>/<Deut 8:7–8 (good land)

23:26~Jer 15:4 (C) (because of Manasseh)

24:13*~Jer 27:16–22* (C) (removal of temple vessels with captivity of Jehoiachin) (* see temple vessels network)

OLD TESTAMENT USE OF KINGS (SEE RESPECTIVE NOTES)

1 Kgs 2:10–11/~/1 Chr 29:27–30 (death of David)

2:12/~/1 Chr 29:23 (C) (Solomon sits upon throne)

3:1–15; 4:1a/~/2 Chr 1:1–13 (revelation to Solomon at Gibeon)

3:4~1 Chr 16:39–40 (B) (sacrifices at tabernacle at Gibeon)

3:4~2 Chr 1:3–5 (B) (tabernacle at Gibeon and ark at Kiriath Jearim)

1. For explanation of symbols, see Symbols and Abbreviations and Introduction. For other help, see Glossary.
2. See Bibliographic Note on Lists of Potential Parallels.

4:21*[5:1]~Ps 72:10–11 (B) (all kings bring tribute and serve) (* see Abrahamic covenant network)
4:31[5:11]~1 Chr 2:3–17 (B) (genealogies of Judah through family of David)
5:1–18[5:15–32]; 7:13–14; 8:27; 10:9/~/2 Chr 2:1–18 [1:18–2:17] (Solomon's treaty with Hiram)
5:3, 5[17, 19]*~Ps 110:1 (C) (enemies under feet of Davidic son) (* see Davidic covenant network)
6:1/~/2 Chr 3:1–2 (building the temple in Solomon's fourth year)
6:2–38~2 Chr 3:3–14 (C) (Solomon builds the temple)
6:15~Hag 1:4 (B) (paneled houses)
7:15–51/~/2 Chr 3:15–5:1 (Hiram-abi's work on temple accessories)
8:1–11/~/2 Chr 5:2–14 (Solomon brings the ark into the temple)
8:12–53*/~/2 Chr 6:1–42* (dedication of temple) (* see Davidic covenant and place networks)
8:28b, 47, 50b~Ps 106:44–46 (B) (remembering the covenant in poetic retrospective)
8:29~Neh 1:8–9 (C) (Yahweh scatters his unfaithful people)
8:62–66/~/2 Chr 7:4–10 (dedicate altar and celebrate Tabernacles)
9:1–9//2 Chr 7:11–22 (second revelation to Solomon)
9:10–24, 26–27/~/2 Chr 8:1–11, 17–18 (other settlements, projects, and treaties)
9:25/~/2 Chr 8:12–15 (Solomon's worship)
10:1–13/~/2 Chr 9:1–12 (queen of Sheba visits Solomon)
10:14–29/~/2 Chr 9:13–24 (prosperity of Solomon)
10:26–29//2 Chr 1:14–17 (Solomon's international horse trade)
10:26–29/~/2 Chr 9:25–28 (Solomon's international horse trade)
11:1–4*~Neh 13:23–27* (B) (confronting apostasy husbands) (* see assembly network)
11:15–16~Ps 60 superscription[60:2] (B) (striking down an enemy in the valley of salt)
11:41–43/~/2 Chr 9:29–31 (death of Solomon)
12:1–24/~/2 Chr 10:1–11:4 (Rehoboam's folly and the revolt)
12:28–33~2 Chr 11:15 (B) (Jeroboam's aberrant renegade worship)
14:21–31/~/2 Chr 12:1–16 (Shishak attacks Jerusalem)
15:1–8/~/2 Chr 13:1–23 (rule of Abijah)
15:9–24/~/2 Chr 14:1–16:14 (rule of Asa)
22:2–40/~/2 Chr 18:1–19:3 (alliance of Jehoshaphat and Ahab against Aram)
22:41–51/~/2 Chr 20:31–21:1 (rule of Jehoshaphat)
2 Kgs 3:4~Isa 16:1 (C) (Moab sends tribute of sheep)
8:16–24/~/2 Chr 21:2–20 (rule of Jehoram of Judah)
8:25–29/~/2 Chr 22:1–6 (rule of Ahaziah of Judah)
9:27–29/~/2 Chr 22:7–9 (Jehu kills Ahaziah)
11:1–20/~/2 Chr 22:10–23:21 (Athaliah usurps rule)
12:1–22/~/2 Chr 24:1–27 (rule of Joash of Judah)
14:1–22/~/2 Chr 25:1–26:2 (rule of Amaziah)
15:1–7/~/2 Chr 26:3–23 (rule of Uzziah/Azariah)
15:32–38/~/2 Chr 27:1–9 (rule of Jotham)
16:1–20/~/2 Chr 28:1–27 (rule of Ahaz)
16:5//Isa 7:1 (B) (collaborative opposition of Rezin of Damascus and Pekah of Israel)
18–20/~/Isa 36–39 (siege of Jerusalem and Hezekiah's pride)
18:1–8/~/2 Chr 29:1–2 (opening frame of rule of Hezekiah)
18:13–19:37~2 Chr 32:1–23 (A) (Sennacherib invades Judah)
20:1–11, 12–19~2 Chr 32:24–26, 31 (C) (Hezekiah's illness and receiving Babylonian representatives)
20:7–8/~/Isa 38:21–22 (topical application of figs)
20:20–21/~/2 Chr 32:32–33 (death of Hezekiah)
21:1–18/~/2 Chr 33:1–20 (rule of Manasseh)
21:3–5/~/2 Chr 33:21–25 (revival of Manasseh's cultic rebellion)
21:19–26/~/2 Chr 33:21–25 (rule of Amon)
22:1–23:30/~/2 Chr 34:1–35:27 (rule of Josiah)
22:11~Jer 36:24 (B) (tearing clothes)
22:3–23:3/~/2 Chr 34:8–19 (Torah discovered in temple)
23:4–20/~/2 Chr 34:3–7, 33 (cultic reforms of Jerusalem)
23:21–23/~/2 Chr 35:1–19 (Josiah keeps the Passover)
23:22~2 Chr 30:26 (C) (nearly unprecedented Passover)
23:28–30/~/2 Chr 35:20–27 (death of Josiah)
23:31–35/~/2 Chr 36:1–4 (rule of Jehoahaz)
23:36–24:7/~/2 Chr 36:5–8 (rule of Jehoiakim)
24:13*~2 Chr 36:7, 10* (B) (removal of temple vessels) (* see temple vessels network)

24:8–17/~/2 Chr 36:9–10 (Jehoiachin and Babylonian captivity)
24:18–25:26/~/Jer 52:1–34 (fall of Jerusalem)
24:18–20/~/2 Chr 36:11–17 (rule of Zedekiah)
25:7~2 Chr 33:1–20 (C) (rule of Manasseh)
25:8–21/~/2 Chr 36:18–20 (exile of Judah)

NEW TESTAMENT USE OF KINGS

1 Kgs 19:10, 14//Rom 11:3 (I alone am left)
19:18//Rom 11:4 (seven thousand who have not bowed)

HERMENEUTICAL PROFILE OF THE USE OF SCRIPTURE IN KINGS

Exegetical Conventions in Kings

The exegetical use of scriptural traditions in Kings in certain respects overlaps with the Deuteronomistic narrative at large—the Deuteronomistic serial narrative housed in Joshua-Judges-Samuel-Kings—and stands apart in other ways (for lesser uses of scriptural traditions in Kings see Filters). For the present purposes more attention needs to be given to scriptural exegesis in Kings itself with only brief comparative observations of how this relates to the Deuteronomistic narrative. Most of the use of scriptural traditions in Kings falls into one of five categories: the Davidic promise, residual concerns about the legal instructions regarding the other, the relevance of the events at the mountain, the Assyrian field commander's taunts as they evoke Isaiah, and Jeremiah on the decline and fall of Jerusalem.

First, the middle part of the account of Solomon in Kings makes interpretive allusions to the Davidic promises mediated by Nathan. Solomon's message to Hiram pivots on his interpretation of the "rest" the land needs to build the temple (see note on 1 Kgs 5:1–5[15–19]). Solomon's blessing of the people at the dedication of the temple exegetically blends Yahweh's promised selection of a place for his name with his election of David (8:15–21).

Second, Kings engages several related scriptural legal instructions concerning the other in the account of Solomon. The law of devoting the peoples of the nations of Canaan came with an expiration date: "when Yahweh brings you into the land" (Deut 7:1). The ambiguity of this temporal limitation is definitively concluded by the exegetical explanation of Solomon's permanent enslavement of the remaining peoples of Canaan in the course of his building projects (see note on 1 Kgs 9:20–21). If Solomon's relationship with Hiram king of Tyre and with the queen of Sheba displays the blessings of Yahweh, his relationships with other kingdoms by means of many treaty marriages point to the danger of disobeying Torah prohibitions concerning the other (see notes on 11:1–4).

Third, in three very different contexts Kings figurally engages narrative traditions of

Israel at the mountain that appear in Exodus. The glory filling the temple typologically echoes the glory filling the tabernacle (see note on 8:10). The original sin of Israel with the golden calf provides strong figural undercurrents for Jeroboam's calves and continues to reverberate as the Northern Kingdom's signature rebellion (see note on 12:28–29). Elijah's revelatory experience on Mount Horeb connects Yahweh's enduring ministry to the Northern Kingdom of Israel (see note on 19:11–13). These several figural uses of different narrative traditions at the mountain demonstrate the necessity of making sense of the Hebrew kingdoms by analogy to the great works of Yahweh housed in Torah.

Fourth, the Assyrian field commander's taunt against Jerusalem seems pregnant with allusions to the preaching of some of Judah's contemporary prophets, especially Micah and Isaiah. The narrator of Kings appears to have noticed the similarities between the field commander's ridicule and Isaiah. The arrogant taunts themselves may have served as a guide for how the narrator of Kings applies Isaiah and Micah in his interpretation of Hezekiah (see several notes on 2 Kgs 18).

Fifth, beginning with Josiah, Kings repeatedly seems to use Jeremiah to interpret the events of the last days of Jerusalem (see notes on 2 Kgs 22, 23, 24).

To summarize, the different parts of Kings tend to exegetically use different scriptural traditions

Both Joshua and Kings repeatedly engage the same legal instructions concerning what to do and not to do about the peoples of the nations of Canaan (see notes on Josh 6:17; 9:6, 14; 11:10; 1 Kgs 9:20–21; 11:1–4). Joshua excludes ethnic/biological interpretation of the law of devoting the nations of Canaan. Kings shares the view that the legal standards relate to the religious outlook of the other.

One final comparative observation relates to the use of scriptural traditions in the several programmatic retrospective and prospective speeches that punctuate the Deuteronomistic narrative: the last words of Joshua (Josh 24), the blessing tempered by warning of the monarchy by Samuel (1 Sam 12), Nathan's covenant with the house of David (2 Sam 7), Solomon's prayer of dedication regarding the temple (1 Kgs 8), and the Deuteronomistic narrator's interpretation of the reasons for the fall of the Northern Kingdom of Israel (2 Kgs 17).[3] The speeches in Joshua and Samuel make allusions slightly more specific to scriptural traditions that may be considered "exegetical." The two programmatic interpretations in Kings, by Solomon and the narrator respectively, are very interpretive but allude to scriptural traditions more broadly, especially by use of stereotypical Deuteronomistic expressions (see Filters). When taken together, the several programmatic speeches of the Deuteronomistic narrative make broad yet determinative use of primarily scriptural narrative traditions to interpret the meaning of the rise and fall of the Hebrew kingdoms.

---

3. See Noth, *Deuteronomistic History*, 4–11. But Noth fails to include the programmatic Davidic covenant (see McCarthy, "II Samuel 7," 131–38).

Implications of Scriptural Exegesis in Kings

Each sector of the Kings narrative interprets the meaning of the Hebrew kingdoms at key points by means of scriptural exegesis. The Solomon story deals with the other especially by means of exegetical interventions with legal instructions about intermarriage. One of the more important exegetical blends appears subtly enough by treating the law of the assembly as part and parcel with the prohibitions against intermarriage (1 Kgs 11:1–4). Interpreting the law of the assembly in Deut 23 with the prohibitions against intermarriage in Exod 34 and Deut 7 goes a long way toward making progress on the challenging repeated exegetical interactions with these contexts in the restoration narratives of Ezra-Nehemiah. Kings provides an essential step in the incremental advancement of progressive revelation regarding the people of God and the other.

The various uses of scriptural traditions in Kings demonstrate an emerging canonical consciousness, especially in a few cases where the narrator marks allusions. The narrative does not simply describe the situation of the other during Solomon's rule. The allusions to scriptural legal standards on the other both interpret and move revelation forward incrementally. The figural allusions to the scriptural accounts of events at the mountain do more than provide a point of departure for narrating the institution of the temple, the sin of Jeroboam, and the commission of Elijah for further ministry. The figural allusions to scriptural traditions provide something like an authoritative standard to connote theological significance. The difficult problem of explaining the fall of Jerusalem within the framework of an irrevocable and enduring Davidic covenant naturally triggers the Deuteronomist to turn to prophets like Micah, Isaiah, and Jeremiah. The emerging authoritative place of the prophetic traditions offer the narrator the exegetical leverage to narrate key aspects of the fall of Jerusalem. In sum, canonical consciousness in Kings goes beyond the occasional explicit citation of scriptural traditions. It includes the authoritative substance of scriptural instructions, narratives, and prophecies that explain Israel's standing before Yahweh in the Hebrew kingdoms.

USE OF SCRIPTURE

2:1–4~Josh 1:5–9 (C)+2 Sam 7:14, 29 (C) (David commissions Solomon). David's last words in Kings evoke the commission of Joshua blended with themes from the Davidic covenant (see notes on Josh 1:5–9; 2 Sam 7:14–15; 1 Chr 22:5–19). The verbal parallels to Josh 1 are limited but distinctive with no verbal parallels to Nathan's covenant. The version of the Davidic covenant housed in Ps 132 paraphrases David's commission of Solomon in 1 Kgs 2, affirming the identity of David's loose paraphrase of Nathan (emphases signify verbal parallels; 2 Sam 7:14, 29 included as a point of reference for thematic overlap):

> *Be strong* and very courageous. Be careful to obey all the law my servant Moses gave you; do not turn from it to the right or to the left, ***that you may be successful*** wherever you go. Keep this book of *the Torah* always on your lips; meditate on it day and night, so that you may be careful to do everything *written in* it. Then *you will be* prosperous and *successful*. (Josh 1:7–8)

> [Nathan] "I will be his father, and he will be my son. When he does wrong, I will punish him with a rod wielded by men, with floggings inflicted by human hands." . . . [David] "Now be pleased to bless the house of your servant, that it may continue forever in your sight; for you, Sovereign Yahweh, have spoken, and with your blessing the house of your servant will be blessed forever." (2 Sam 7:14, 29; cf. "throne" in v. 13)

> If your sons keep my covenant
> and the statutes I teach them,
> then their sons will sit
> on your throne for ever and ever. (Ps 132:12)

> "I am about to go the way of all the earth," he said. "So *be strong*, act like a man, and observe what Yahweh your God requires: Walk in obedience to him, and keep his decrees and commands, his laws and regulations, as *written in the Torah* of Moses. Do this *so that you may be successful* in all you do and wherever you go and that Yahweh may keep his promise to me: 'If your descendants watch how they live, and if they walk faithfully before me with all their heart and soul, you will never fail to have a successor on the throne of Israel.'" (1 Kgs 2:2–4†)

David's paraphrase of the covenant obligations uses commonplace Deuteronomy language—"With all their heart and their soul" (2 Kgs 2:4; cf. Deut 4:29; 6:5; 10:12; 11:13; 13:3; 26:16; 30:2, 10; Josh 22:5).

In sum, David's last words to Solomon resemble the commission of Joshua adjusted according to the Davidic covenant. David lays heavy emphasis on Torah obedience which broadly accords with the law of the king (Deut 17:19).

4:25[5:5]~Mic 4:4 (C) (sit under vine and fig tree). See note on 2 Kgs 18:31.

5:1–5[15–19]*~2 Sam 5:11 (C)+7:1, 11–13* (A) (Solomon's message to Hiram) (* see Davidic covenant and place networks). The verbal, syntactic, and contextual parallels between the promise to David mediated by Nathan and Solomon's diplomatic communication to Hiram offer strong evidence of interpretive allusion. The explicit marking of the Davidic promise provides evidence of direction of dependence with Solomon's communication as receptor context. The use of the verb "rest" in the causative stem requires close attention in this context (bold and underlining signify verbal parallels, italics and wavy underlining signify interpretive paraphrase, and broken underlining signifies marking).

> *Now Hiram king of Tyre sent envoys to David, along with cedar logs and carpenters and stonemasons, and they built a palace for David.* (2 Sam 5:11)[4]

> After the king was settled in his palace and Yahweh **had given** him **rest** from all his enemies **on all sides** of him . . . "I have been with you wherever you have gone, and I have cut off all your enemies from before you. Now I will make your name great, like the names of the greatest men on earth. [10] And I will provide a place for my people Israel and will plant them so that they can have a home of their own and no longer be disturbed. Wicked people will not oppress them anymore, as they did at the beginning [11] and have done ever since the time I appointed leaders over my people Israel. I **will** also **give you rest** from all your enemies." Yahweh declares to you that Yahweh himself will establish a house for you: [12] "When your days are over and you rest with your ancestors, I will raise up your offspring to succeed you, your own flesh and blood, and I will establish his kingdom. [13] He is the one who will build a house for my Name, and I will establish the throne of his kingdom forever." (7:1†, 9–13)

> When Hiram king of Tyre heard that Solomon had been anointed king to succeed his father David, he sent his envoys to Solomon, *because he had always been on friendly terms with David.* [2] Solomon sent back this message to Hiram: [3] "You know that because of the wars waged against my father David from **all sides**, he could not build a house for the Name of Yahweh his God until Yahweh put his enemies under his feet. [4] But now Yahweh my God **has given** me **rest** on **every side**, and there is no adversary or disaster. [5] I intend, therefore, to build a house for the Name of Yahweh my God, as Yahweh told my father David, when he said, 'Your son whom I will put on the throne in your place will build the house for my Name.'" (1 Kgs 5:1–5†[15–19])[5]

The communication of Solomon to Hiram builds on the good relations between David and Hiram that could be a loose allusion to the tradition in 2 Sam 5:11. The end of this vignette characterizes Solomon and Hiram's political relationship as peaceful (1 Kgs 5:12[26]).

The two statements about "rest" in the context of the Davidic promise—Yahweh "had given rest" (2 Sam 7:1 [narrator]) and Yahweh "will give rest" (7:11 [Nathan]; cf. vv. 9–10)—need to be considered in a larger context.[6] The same kind of already and not-yet relative to divinely given rest can be seen elsewhere in the Deuteronomistic narrative

---

4. On Solomon's extension of political relations with Hiram compare 1 Kgs 5:1[15] and 5:12[26].

5. NIV supplies "enemies" in 1 Kgs 5:3[17] inferred by a pronoun "them" (so too NRSV, JPSB, etc.). NIV and other modern committee translations follow *ketiv* "under his feet" versus *qere* "under my feet" (see *BHS*).

6. Note: Yahweh is subject of both "had caused to rest" (הֵנִיחַ, נוח Hif pf 3ms) (1 Sam 7:1) and "will cause to rest" (וַהֲנִיחֹתִי, נוח Hif wcp 1cs) (7:11). Hays pushes back against Solomon's characterization of David's warring in 1 Kgs 5 based on the use of "rest" in 2 Sam 7:1 (*Temple*, 192, n. 5; idem, "Has the Narrator?" 166–67). Hays does not take note of the absence of "rest" in 2 Sam 7:11 or the agreement of Chronistic David and the Chronicler with Solomon's characterization in 1 Kgs 5:3 (1 Chr 22:8; 28:3; cf. removal of "rest" 17:1 vs. 2 Sam 7:1). In spite of this problem, it is easy to agree with Hays on the irony in Solomon's securing cedar for a temple (1 Kgs 5:6) in light of Yahweh specifically saying he had not asked for a house of cedar (2 Sam 7:7).

such as the *inclusio* and/or resumptive repetition in the second half of Joshua (italics mark verbal parallels and bold causative stem of "rest").

> *When Joshua had grown old,* Yahweh said to him, "You are now very old, and there are still very large areas of land to be taken over." (Josh 13:1)

> After a long time had passed and Yahweh **had given** Israel **rest** from all their enemies around them, *when Joshua had grown old,* summoned all Israel—their elders, leaders, judges and officials—and said to them: "I *have grown old.*" (23:1–2 lit.)

The book of Judges famously takes up the gap between Israel's divinely given rest from all enemies and the large areas of unconquered territory emphasized in Joshua (see note on Judg 1:10–36 and other references listed there). This same kind of already a beneficiary of divinely given rest and not-yet a beneficiary of divinely given rest appears in the Davidic promise delivered by Nathan (2 Sam 7:1, 11).

The timing for Yahweh to choose a place for his name to dwell corresponds to divinely given rest characterized by "safety."[7] The narrator of Kings makes this point explicitly in the panoramic leading up to Solomon's communication with Hiram (underlining marks verbal parallel and bold causative stem of "rest").

> But you will cross the Jordan and settle in the land Yahweh your God is giving you as an inheritance, and he **will give** you **rest** from all your enemies around you so that you will live in safety. Then to the place Yahweh your God will choose as a dwelling for his Name. . . . (Deut 12:10–11a)

> During Solomon's lifetime Judah and Israel, from Dan to Beersheba, lived in safety, everyone under their own vine and under their own fig tree. (1 Kgs 4:25[5:5])

The only other uses of "safety" with this sense in Deuteronomy and the Deuteronomistic narrative appear in the blessing of Moses (Deut 33:28) and in Samuel's characterization of the days of the judges.[8] Samuel says, "Then Yahweh sent Jerub-Baal, Barak, Jephthah and Samuel, and he delivered you from the hands of your enemies all around you, so that you lived in safety" (1 Sam 12:11, emphasis mine). Samuel speaks of "safety" as something like the already kind of divinely given rest in Josh 23:1 and 2 Sam 7:1 versus the not-yet kind of divinely given rest of Deut 12:10 and 2 Sam 7:11 and the proximate fulfillment in 1 Kgs 4:25[5:5].

When Solomon says "now Yahweh my God **has given** me **rest** on **every side**" he interpretively alludes to Nathan's promise (1 Kgs 5:4[18], emphasis mine; cf. 2 Sam 7:11 in

---

7. For a discussion of a transitional time between settlement and the "ideal" safety to go on pilgrimages to worship in Deut 12, see Pitkänen, *Central Sanctuary*, 103.

8. See "בֶּטַח," *HALOT* 1:120–21; and note the use of "safety" in a different sort of context in Judg 8:11.

comparative layout above). The narrator has set this communication within the context of Solomon's kingdom "living in safety" (1 Kgs 4:25[5:5]) echoing or softly alluding to Deut 12:10. This important allusive undercurrent gets spelled out explicitly in a public statement by Solomon a few years later when he completes the temple (see note on 1 Kgs 8:16–21). Solomon confirms the realization of the promised rest in his blessing: "Praise be to Yahweh, who *has given rest* to his people Israel *just as he promised*. Not one word has failed of all the good promises he gave through his servant Moses" (8:56, emphasis mine).[9]

Solomon's exegetical advance in his communication to Hiram is his identification of David's constant warfare as the basis for Yahweh preventing him from building the temple.[10] This exegetical outcome seems like a deduction based on implicit statements in Nathan's oracle (see phrase with wavy underlining in comparative layout of 5:3[17] above). The Chronicler cites David's exegetical paraphrase of his inability to build the temple along the same lines: "because you are a warrior and have shed blood" (1 Chr 28:3; see note ad loc.; cf. 22:8).

In sum, Solomon interprets the impediment that disallowed David from building the temple as his constant warfare. Since Yahweh has given Solomon rest he can build the temple David had desired to build.

6:7~Exod 20:25; Deut 27:5 (C) (building with stones finished offsite). The legal standards for building altars of unfinished stones seem to stand behind the practice of finishing stones for the temple offsite (Exod 20:25; Deut 27:5). The term "dressed stone" (Exod 20:25) does not appear in 1 Kgs 6:7 but is used in 6:36. The use of dressed stone, but finished offsite, builds on the older standard for altars.

8:10~Exod 40:34–35 (B) (glory fills the temple). Although Moses could withstand Yahweh's presence more than others (Exod 33:7–11; 34:5), even he could not enter the tabernacle when the glory descended upon it (40:34–35). In like manner, when the glory filled the temple the priests were driven out (1 Kgs 8:10–11). The figural correspondence of the dedication of the tabernacle and temple establishes a continuity between the great redeeming works of Yahweh (italics signify verbal parallels):

> Then the *cloud* covered the tent of meeting, and *the glory* of Yahweh *filled* the tabernacle. Moses could not enter the tent of meeting because *the cloud* had settled on it, and *the glory of Yahweh filled* the tabernacle. (Exod 40:34–35)

> When the priests withdrew from the Holy Place, *the cloud filled* the temple of Yahweh. And the priests could not perform their service because of *the cloud*, for *the glory of Yahweh filled* his temple. (1 Kgs 8:10–11)

---

9. See von Rad, "There Remains Still a Rest," in *From Genesis*, 82–85; Knoppers, "Prayer," 244–45.

10. For a similar reading see Cogan, *I Kings*, 226; Gray, *I & II Kings*, 151; Keil and Delitzsch, *Commentary on the OT*, 58–59 (on 1 Kgs 5:4[18]).

It is worth pausing for a moment to observe that the typological fulfillment in 1 Kgs 8:10 is exclusively backwards-looking. That is, the narrative of the tabernacle itself is not expectational. Nathan makes this explicit when he cites Yahweh: "*[D]id I ever say* to any of their rulers whom I commanded to shepherd my people Israel, 'Why have you not built me a house of cedar?'" (2 Sam 7:7, emphasis mine). Apparently building on the typological fulfillment of the glory entering Solomon's temple, the Chronicler unmasks several other backwards-looking typological fulfillments (see Table C10 and Figure C17).

8:15–21*~Deut 12:5*+2 Sam 7:8, 13* (A) (choosing a place and choosing David) (* see Davidic covenant and place networks). At the dedication of the temple Solomon explains its significance to the assembly of Israel. The verbatim citation and close paraphrasing of Deut 12:5 and 2 Sam 7:6, 8, 13 makes a relationship nearly certain. The twofold marking by an oral citation formula in 1 Kgs 8:15 and 18 provides strong evidence that it is the receptor text, and the legal instruction of the place for the name of Yahweh to dwell and the Davidic promise are donor contexts.

Solomon's interpretive blend joins together the divine election of the place of worship and the divine election of Davidic rule.[11] The completion of the temple simultaneously signals the proximate fulfillment of two great divine promises. Notice the way Solomon's exegetical blend interconnects Davidic rule and worship of Yahweh (bold, italics, and underlining refer to verbal parallels and broken underlining marking).

> But you are to seek the place Yahweh your God **will choose from among all** your **tribes** *to set* his **Name** *there* for his dwelling. (Deut 12:5†)

> I have not dwelt in a house from the day I brought the Israelites up out of Egypt to this day. I have been moving from place to place with a tent as my dwelling. [7] Wherever I have moved with all the Israelites, did I ever say to any of their rulers whom I commanded to shepherd my people Israel, "Why have you not built me a house of cedar?" [8] Now then, tell my servant David, "This is what Yahweh Almighty says: I took you from the pasture, from tending the flock, to be ruler over my people Israel. . . . He [David's seed] is the one who will build a house for my Name, and I will establish the throne of his kingdom forever." (2 Sam 7:6–8, 13; v. 7†)

> Then he [Solomon] said: "Praise be to Yahweh, the God of Israel, who with his own hand has fulfilled what he promised with his own mouth to my father David. For he said, [16] 'From the day I brought my people Israel out of Egypt, I **have** not **chosen** a city **from among all the tribes of Israel** to have a house built so that my **Name** might be there, but I have chosen David to be over my people Israel.' [17] My father David had it in

11. Indebted to Richter, *Deuteronomistic History*, 86–89, 251. For others who notice the scriptural parallels see, e.g., Burney, *Notes*, 115.

> his heart to build a house for the Name of Yahweh, the God of Israel. [18] But Yahweh said to my father David, 'You did well to have it in your heart to build a house for my Name. [19] Nevertheless, you are not the one to build the house, but your son, your own flesh and blood—he is the one who will build the house for my Name.' [20] "Yahweh has kept the promise he made: I have succeeded David my father and now I sit on the throne of Israel, just as Yahweh promised, and I have built the house for the Name of Yahweh, the God of Israel. [21] I *have set up a place there* for the ark, in which is the covenant of Yahweh that he made with our ancestors when he brought them out of Egypt." (1 Kgs 8:15–21†)

The sense of Solomon's use of Yahweh's name needs to be distinguished from so-called "name theology." Von Rad's influential treatment of name theology will be adequate to represent this viewpoint for present purposes. Von Rad argues that to correct the older idea of Yahweh himself indwelling the shrine, the author of Deuteronomy speaks of only the presence of his name. For von Rad this use of "the name" runs close to "a hypostasis" as an "almost material presence of the name at the shrine." Von Rad associates the shift from a manifestation of glory to the name as part of the larger move to "demythologize" and to "rationalize" worship ideology.[12] The major problems with name theology turn on a failure to appreciate the linguistic function of the language in its ancient setting.

Richter evaluates the uses of the associated phrases within the Hebrew Bible and then similar language in ancient Near Eastern Akkadian and Aramaic monumental and building texts. She finds evidence that the scriptural authors borrowed the common language from counterpart cultures. Richter thinks the phrase "to cause his name to dwell" within the Hebrew Bible would function somewhat woodenly since it has a well attested idiomatic sense. Ancient Near Eastern shrines included inscriptions naming the deities that rulers honored by patronage to the shrines. In contrast to name theology, Richter argues that the language of "'to place the name' . . . had nothing to do with hypostatized deities and everything to do with the kingly act of installing an inscription."[13] Richter's presentation of the linguistic evidence is convincing.[14]

Besides use of the idiomatic phrase "to cause his name to dwell" to denote an inscription at a shrine in Deut 12, the term "name" carries several other connotations in 2 Sam 7 and 1 Kgs 8. In 2 Sam 7:9, 13, 23 "name" connotes a sense of reputation.[15] Much turns on the wordplay on "house." The "name" of David's house = dynasty in 2 Sam 7:9 speaks to its reputation or fame in a way that could also apply to Yahweh's house = temple for "name" in 7:13 and Yahweh's power, character, and actions for "name" in 7:23.

---

12. Von Rad, *Studies in Deuteronomy*, 38–40; and see idem, *OT Theology*, 1:184. See Richter's discussion of the broad dissemination of von Rad's views (*Deuteronomistic History*, 26–29).

13. Richter, "Placing the Name," 70.

14. For summaries of Richter's argument see ibid., 65–73; idem, "The Place," 343–44; Hundley, 541–43, et passim, and for a full presentation see Richter, *Deuteronomistic History*. Richter's evaluation of the linguistic evidence has merit even if her excavative diachronic agenda is set aside (i.e., double redaction theory of Deuteronomistic History).

15. See Richter, *Deuteronomistic History*, 70.

First Kings 8 alludes to the Davidic promise six times by the phrase "to build a house for the name of Yahweh" with "name" referring to reputation (1 Kgs 8:17, 18, 19, 20, 44, 48; 2 Sam 7:13). In addition, the term "name" refers to acknowledging Yahweh (1 Kgs 8:33, 35), fame (vv. 41, 42, 43), ownership (v. 43).[16] Twice Solomon uses a phrase: "that my name might be there" (לִהְיוֹת שְׁמִי שָׁם) (vv. 16, 29; cf. 2 Kgs 23:27; 2 Chr 7:16; 33:4). In the case of 1 Kings 8:16, the "to be" language appears to derive from Solomon's close verbal and syntactical parallel in the interpretive blend of choosing a place and choosing David (emphases mark verbal parallels): "I *have* not *chosen* [Q pf of בחר] a city from among any tribe of Israel to have a house built so that my Name **might be** [לִהְיוֹת, Q inf. const. of היה] there, but I *have chosen* [Q wci of בחר] David **to be** [לִהְיוֹת, Q inf. const. of היה] over my people Israel" (1 Kgs 8:16).

Close attention to Deut 12:5 can help demonstrate the significance of Solomon's interpretive blend. Following the Masoretic Text, the verse establishes a sharp contrast over and against the local worship shrines spread through the land.[17] The key contrast is between "you shall erase their [gods'] names from that place" (Deut 12:3 lit.) and "you shall seek . . . the place where Yahweh your God will choose . . . to set his name there" (12:5 lit.). Notice the threefold emphasis on the location as a place (marked in bold): "But to **the place where** Yahweh your God will choose from among all the tribes to set his name **there**, you (p) shall seek his residence, and to **there** you (s) shall go" (12:5 lit). As elsewhere, Deuteronomy interchanges second person singular and plural verbs to emphasize the concord between collective and individual responsibility to obey Yahweh.

The completion of the temple stands as the culmination of Yahweh choosing a place for his name. The context of Deut 12:2–4 and 12:5 and following reveals that it takes more than simply setting up his tabernacle in the land. First the names of the deities in their many local shrines need to be erased. But Solomon shifts the focus to Yahweh's election of David. The point that Solomon makes when he addresses the people is that the election of the place comes in tandem with the election of David. Notice how the

---

16. This summary based on ibid., 76–90.

17. Richter says Deut 12:5 helps define the phrase "to cause his name to dwell" (lit.) (לְשַׁכֵּן שְׁמוֹ שָׁם) used nine times in Scripture (Deut 12:11; 14:23; 16:2, 6, 11; 26:2; Jer 7:12; Ezra 6:12; Neh 1:9; cf. Deut 12:21; 14:24; 16:2, 6, 11)—but her solution requires re-vocalizing the Hebrew text. Richter says the more difficult phrase "to set his name there" (לָשׂוּם שְׁמוֹ שָׁם) glossed by "his residence" (לְשִׁכְנוֹ) in the MT of 12:5 should be taken as a Piel (לְשַׁכְּנוֹ) as in SP, LXX, and the targums (ibid., 47, 207; so also *BHK* n. a; *BHS* n. c). This emendation to Piel would read: "to cause to dwell." Richter follows Tov who regards the masoretic "his residence" (לְשִׁכְנוֹ) as "exegesis" of the supposed original vocalization "to make dwell" (לְשַׁכְּנוֹ, Piel inf. const. of שכן plus -3ms pronominal suffix) (Tov, *Textual Criticism*, 2nd ed., 42; Tov deletes discussion of Deut 12:5 from the 3rd ed. of *Textual Criticism*). Others suggest that even though the Hebrew term "residence" (שֵׁכֶן) is not attested elsewhere in the Hebrew Bible, its parallel with "there" (שָׁם) in Deut 12:5 favors retaining the more difficult MT reading (see NET nt.). McCarthy sorts through the ancient textual witnesses in some detail and determines that they (LXX and targum) reflect the proto-MT as their parent text (*BHQ*, 85*; on LXX so also Wevers, *Notes on Deuteronomy*, 209). Kartveit suggests that "his residence" (לְשִׁכְנוֹ) "condenses the full phrase ['to cause his name to dwell there'] לְשַׁכֵּן שְׁמוֹ שָׁם into one word" but without re-vocalizing the text ("Place," 206). This efficiently makes sense of the evidence, namely, that the unique occurrence of "his residence" (לְשִׁכְנוֹ) in Deut 12:5 provides a shorthand for "to cause his name to dwell there" (לְשַׁכֵּן שְׁמוֹ שָׁם) that appears in 12:11; 14:23; 16:2, 6, 11; 26:2. The present discussion likewise follows the MT.

proximate fulfillment of both the choice of the place and the choice of David pivots on Solomon's building of the temple.

> Then he [Solomon] said: "Praise be to Yahweh, the God of Israel, who with his own hand *has fulfilled what he promised with his own mouth to my father David*. For he said, [16] 'From the day I brought my people Israel out of Egypt, I have not chosen a city from among any tribe of Israel to have a house built so that my Name might be there, but I have chosen David to be over my people Israel' . . . "*Yahweh has kept the promise he made*: I have succeeded David my father and now I sit on the throne of Israel, *just as Yahweh promised*, and I have built the house for the Name of Yahweh, the God of Israel." (1 Kgs 8:15–16, 20†, emphasis mine)

By way of wrapping up, two other contexts that bear on the choosing of a place to set Yahweh's name can be noted. First, Solomon enjoying peace with the surrounding nations sealed with many royal treaty marriages comes with the price of reinstalling worship centers to false gods all around Jerusalem and its temple for Yahweh's name (11:1–8). Second, the Chronicler takes the divine choosing of a place for his name in Deut 12 as a key context around which to organize his narrative in several stages from retrieving the ark (1 Chr 15:1–3) step by step until culminating in the glory coming into the temple and the second theophany to Solomon (2 Chr 7:11–22).[18]

9:20–21~Deut 7:1–2*+20:11* (B) (enslaving the remaining peoples of the nations of Canaan) (* see devoting network). Kings carefully notes that Solomon did not make "slaves" (עֶבֶד) of any Israelites (1 Kgs 9:22). This suggests broad use of another term: "conscripted laborers" (מַס) from Israel (5:13[27]) versus "slave labor" (מַס) from the peoples of the former nations of Canaan (9:21).[19] Yet the heavy labor of Solomon's building projects (12:4) led to the revolutionary stoning of Adoniram, the supervisor of Israelite "conscripted labor" (12:18). The issue in 1 Kgs 9:20–21 pivots on an exegetical intervention concerning a new permanent status as "slave labor" for residual peoples of the nations of Canaan.

Deuteronomy features two different legal standards for others who worshiped other gods. Deuteronomy 7:1–2 houses the law of devoting the nations of Canaan, and 20:10–14 the law for treatment of "distant" peoples (Deut 20:15). The legal standard for distant people includes plan A: if they surrender, "subject them to slave labor" (מַס) (20:11), and plan B: if they do not surrender, kill all the men and confiscate all their belongings (20:12–14). The legal standard to "devote to destruction" (*hrm hrm* הַחֲרֵם תַּחֲרִים) all the nations of Canaan came with an expiration date since it only applies to "when Yahweh your God brings you into the land you are entering to possess" (7:1, see

18. See many allusions to Deut 12 in notes on 1 Chr 15 through 2 Chr 7.

19. See "מַס," *HALOT* 1:603–4; *NIDOTTE* 2:992–94; *TDOT* 8:429–30. Also see Gray, *I & II Kings*, 251–52.

note ad loc.). Solomon's conversion of the residual peoples of the nations of Canaan to slave labor, as though they were from far away, during his building projects demonstrates that the time span had expired for the law of devoting the nations of Canaan—or that Solomon was disobedient. Solomon's action gets explained by an interpretive blend of the narrator (emphases signify verbal parallels):

> When Yahweh your God brings you into the land you are entering to possess and drives out before you many nations—*the Hittites*, Girgashites, Amorites, Canaanites, *Perizzites, Hivites and Jebusites*, seven nations larger and stronger than you—and when Yahweh your God has delivered them over to you and you have defeated them, then you **must destroy them totally** [חרם]. Make no treaty with them, and show them no mercy. (Deut 7:1–2)

> If they accept and open their gates, all the people in it shall be subject <u>to slave labor and shall serve</u> you [לָמַס וַעֲבָדוּךָ]. (20:11†)

> There were still people left from the Amorites, *Hittites, Perizzites, Hivites and Jebusites* (these peoples were not Israelites). Solomon conscripted the descendants of all these peoples remaining in the land—whom the Israelites could not **destroy** [חרם]—<u>to serve as slave labor</u> [לְמַס־עֹבֵד], as it is to this day. (1 Kgs 9:20–21†)

Of course, some of the tribes had long ago treated peoples of the nations of Canaan as though they were from distant lands by subjecting them to slave labor (Josh 16:10; 17:13; Judg 1:28, 30, 33, 35). In any case, the permanent subjection of the remaining nations of Canaan to slave labor continued into the postexilic restoration (Ezra 2:58// Neh 7:60; cf. Neh 11:3).[20]

10:26–29~Deut 17:16–17 (B) (international horse trade). The narrative description of Solomon presents details of his wealth and fame at length. With great subtlety the narrator infuses the descriptions with elements forbidden to the king of Israel, namely, too many horses, especially from Egypt, too many wives, and too much wealth (Deut 17:16–17; see note on 2 Chr 1:14–17). The Deuteronomist includes the first and third of these in what seems like a continuation of recounting the glories of Solomon's rule (1 Kgs 10:26–29). Hays suggests the narrator is "winking" at readers by "praising" Solomon with allusions to Deuteronomy's law of the king in 1 Kgs 10:26–29.[21] The narrator finally gets to the matter of too many wives and he reveals that Solomon has flagrantly violated God's standards (see notes on 11:1–4). When readers realize Solomon's excessive treaty marriages violate lawful standards, they can reverse back through the description of

20. The "given ones" or *nethinim* (Ezra 2:58//Neh 7:60 KJV) may refer to the Gibeonites (see Josh 9:7–8, 15).
21. See Hays, "Narrator," 154–57.

opulence to see where things went awry (emphases signify thematic parallels with a few verbal parallels):[22]

> The king, moreover, must not acquire *great numbers of horses* for himself or make the people **return to Egypt to get more of them**, for Yahweh has told you, "You are not to go back that way again." He must not take many wives, or his heart will be led astray. He must not accumulate large amounts of silver and gold. (Deut 17:16–17)

> Solomon accumulated chariots and *horses*; he had fourteen hundred chariots and *twelve thousand horses*, which he kept in the chariot cities and also with him in Jerusalem. The king made silver as common in Jerusalem as stones, and cedar as plentiful as sycamore-fig trees in the foothills. Solomon's **horses were imported from Egypt** and from Kue—the royal merchants purchased them from Kue at the current price. They imported a chariot from Egypt for six hundred shekels of silver, and a horse for a hundred and fifty. They also exported them to all the kings of the Hittites and of the Arameans. . . . He had seven hundred wives of royal birth. (1 Kgs 10:26–29; 11:3a)

By merging Solomon's wealth as a gift from Yahweh and his wrongful accumulation of horses, silver, and treaty wives, the narrator brilliantly demonstrates the easy slide from affluence to rebellion.

11:1*~Deut 23:3, 7*[4, 8] (B) (women of Egypt and Edom as well as Ammon and Moab) (* see assembly network).

11:2–4*~Exod 34:15–16*+Deut 7:3–4*+17:17 (B) (turning Solomon's heart away) (* see devoting network). The law of the assembly distinguishes two kinds of others: those who can never enter the assembly of Yahweh, represented by the Ammonites and Moabites, and those who can enter after three generations, represented by Edomites and Egyptians (Deut 23:3, 7[4, 8]). The Deuteronomist alludes to the law of the assembly by beginning the list of Solomon's treaty wives with these four. By alluding to the law of the assembly the Deuteronomist establishes that this legal standard naturally overlaps with the prohibitions against intermarriage in Exod 34 and Deut 7. The same kind of overlap between these legal standards continues into the postexilic restoration (see notes on Ezra 9:1–2; Neh 13:23–27).

The narrator marks with a quasi-citation formula an interpretive blend alluding to the genetically related prohibitions against intermarriage of Exod 34 and Deut 7, signaling 1 Kgs 11:1–4 as receptor context. Each of the three contexts use different verbs for marriage, rendered literally: "take" (לקח, Exod 34:16), "intermarry" (חתן, Deut 7:3), and "come into" (בוא, 1 Kgs 11:2). The most significant allusion stands at the level of syntax, connecting the causative stem verb "they will cause (your sons) to whore" (וְהִזְנוּ Hif, Exod

22. For a similar independent suggestion, see Jeon, "Retroactive Re-evaluation," 28.

34:16 lit.)/"they will turn aside" (יָסִיר Hif, Deut 7:4 lit.) and "they will cause to turn away (his heart)" (יַטּוּ Hif, 1 Kgs 11:2 lit.). In this way the narrator simultaneously blames the wives of the apostasy marriages and emphasizes the unfaithfulness of the husband/Solomon. The only two places Solomon is the subject of the verb "love" shows his transition from "Solomon loved *Yahweh*" to "Solomon loved *many foreign women*" (3:3; 11:1 lit., emphasis mine).[23] Note the interpretive blend (bold signifies verbal parallels, italics signify similarities, broken underlining signifies shared syntax, and underlining signifies marking):

> And when you take some of their daughters as wives for your sons and those daughters prostitute themselves to their gods, they will cause your sons to prostitute themselves **after their gods.** (Exod 34:16 lit.)

> Do not intermarry with them [people of the nations of Canaan]. Do not give your daughters to their sons or take their daughters for your sons, for they will turn your children away **from following after** me to serve **other gods**, and Yahweh's anger will burn against you and will quickly destroy you. (Deut 7:3–4†)

> He [the king] must not take *many wives*, or his heart will be led astray. (17:17a)

> No **Ammonite** or **Moabite** or any of their descendants may enter the assembly of Yahweh, not even in the tenth generation. . . . Do not despise an **Edomite**, for the Edomites are related to you. Do not despise an *Egyptian*, because you resided as foreigners in their country. (Deut 23:3, 7[4, 8])

> King Solomon, however, loved *many* foreign *women* besides *Pharaoh's daughter*—**Moabites, Ammonites, Edomites**, Sidonians and Hittites. [2] They were from nations about which Yahweh had told the Israelites, "You must not intermarry with them, because they will surely turn your heart **after their gods**." Nevertheless, Solomon held fast to them in love. [3] He had *seven hundred wives* of royal birth and three hundred concubines, and his wives led him astray. [4] As Solomon grew old, his wives turned his heart **after other gods**, and his heart was not fully devoted to Yahweh his God, as the heart of David his father had been. (1 Kgs 11:1–4)[24]

Elsewhere Scripture uses other round numbers of Solomon's harem—"Sixty queens and eighty concubines" (Song 6:8). Whether 140 or 1,000, readers hope the numbers

23. As observed by Wray Beal, *1 & 2 Kings*, 169–70.

24. The LXX of 1 Kgs 11 varies significantly from the MT with omissions and rearrangement. See Knoppers, *Two Nations*, 1:140–43; Talshir, "1 Kings and 3 Kingdoms," 85–87, et passim; Joosten, "Sample Edition," 375–63. The textual difficulties of 1 Kgs 11:1–4 do not relate to the wording of the potential exegetical allusions themselves. The present investigation uses the MT without emendation.

represent literary hyperbole. Yet ancient sources report much larger harems.[25] Solomon's treaty marriages are apostasy marriages since the wives continue to worship the patron deities of their homelands (1 Kgs 11:8). The apostasy marriages began before David died, suggesting arranged treaty-marriage alliances. This can be deduced since Solomon ruled forty years (11:42), and Rehoboam, son of an Ammonitess, was forty-one when he began to rule (14:21), Solomon's marriage to the queen mother occurred before David died earlier by enough to already have a one-year-old heir. Because David was disqualified on the battlefield to build the temple, it makes sense to start Solomon on a strategy of peace in the bedroom (5:3–5). The cost of peace by means of marriage treaties resulted in shrines to every regional god surrounding the temple of Yahweh (11:7).

Two other implications of the list of treaty wives in 1 Kgs 11:1 need to be spelled out. First, the only one of the forbidden Canaanite nations included in the list is the Hittites (1 Kgs 11:1; Deut 7:1). The use of the Hittites as the only one of the seven nations of Canaan in the list of treaty wives makes sense because their lands were more distant. Solomon had already put the proximate peoples of the nations of Canaan into forced labor, including any Hittites in the lands under Solomon's control, eliminating any royalty the nearby former nations of Canaan may have had as well as any need for treaties with them (see note on 1 Kgs 9:20–21). The presence of Hittites with Ammonites, Moabites, Egyptians, and Edomites in the same list of forbidden others in 1 Kgs 11:1 demonstrates that the law of the assembly (Deut 23:3–8[4–9]) and the prohibition against intermarrying with the nations of Canaan (7:1–4; cf. Exod 34:11–16) are mutually enriching counterparts.

Second, the narrator includes Phoenicians among the forbidden others, demonstrating that those people listed as forbidden in the prohibitions against intermarriage and the law of the assembly are merely representative (1 Kgs 11:1; cf. Exod 34:11; Deut 7:1; 23:3[4]). In like manner, the use of Edomites and Egyptians as excluded demonstrates that even expressly included others may be excluded if they do not seek assimilation by covenantal fidelity (1 Kgs 11:1; cf. Deut 23:7[8]).

12:28–29//Exod 32:4 (two golden calves). Jeroboam established two shrines to the God of Israel outfitted with golden calves to keep his religious constituents from reverting to the king of Jerusalem (1 Kgs 12:26–27). The locations of the shrines in Bethel and Dan had been associated with previous shrines since the early days of Israel entering the land (Judg 18:31; 20:27). Jeroboam's proclamation about the calves serves as a most remarkable verbatim parallel to the golden calf in the wilderness.[26] For Aaron the calf symbolized Yahweh (Exod 32:5), and for Jeroboam the calves represented the ancestral God who delivered them from Egypt (1 Kgs 12:28–29).[27] The reference to the "calf" (singular) as "your gods [plural] who

25. See Montgomery, *Kings*, 234–35.

26. For other parallels, see Aberbach and Smolar, "Aaron, Jeroboam," 129–40.

27. Others suggest the calves serve as a pedestal for God as sort of a counterpart to the cherubim in the temple (Friedman, *Who Wrote?*, 47, 72–73). Having pedestals in Bethel and Dan, the northern and southernmost reaches of Israel, would imply that God was enthroned above the entire Northern Kingdom.

brought you up" seems strange in the account of the sin at the mountain (Exod 32:4). The oddity of the plural in the account of Israel's original sin in Exodus fits exactly with the original sin of the Northern Kingdom in Kings (emphases signify verbal parallels):

> He [Aaron] took what they handed him and made it into an idol cast in the shape of a **calf**, fashioning it with a tool. Then they said, "These *are your gods, Israel, who brought you up out of Egypt.*" (Exod 32:4)

> After seeking advice, the king made two golden **calves**. He [Jeroboam] said to the people, "It is too much for you to go up to Jerusalem. Here *are your gods, Israel, who brought you up out of Egypt.*" One he set up in Bethel, and the other in Dan. (1 Kgs 12:28–29)

The Deuteronomist places much of the blame for the downfall of the Northern Kingdom of Israel on the sustained royal patronage of the shrines to Israel's God in Bethel and Dan established by Jeroboam (1 Kgs 14:15–16; 2 Kgs 17:16, 21–23). Although Israel saw the rise and fall of kings from eight houses, the narrator condemns each one who served long enough to offer royal patronage to the calf shrines as sinning after the manner of Jeroboam son of Nebat.[28]

19:11–13~Exod 33:21–22* (B) (personal theophany on the mountain) (* see prophet like Moses network). The story of Elijah and the theophany on Mount Horeb features several echoes of revelation to Moses on the same mountain. The echoes begin when Elijah has "forty days and forty nights" to go to Horeb (1 Kgs 19:8; cf. Exod 34:28; Deut 9:9, 11, 18; 10:10). The revelation itself does not come in the wind, quake, or fire, broadly reminiscent of the public theophany at the mountain (1 Kgs 19:11–12; cf. Exod 19:16). The rare term for silence or whisper provides a memorable counterpart to the attribute formula proclaimed to Moses (1 Kgs 19:12; Exod 34:6–7). Note the similarities and differences (italics signify verbal parallels, and broken underlining signifies broad similarities without verbal parallels):

> Then Yahweh said, "There is a place near me where you may stand on a rock. When my glory *passes by*, I will put you in a cleft in the rock and cover you with my hand until I have *passed by*." (Exod 33:21–22)

> Yahweh said, "Go out and stand on the mountain in the presence of Yahweh, for Yahweh is about to *pass by*." Then a great and powerful wind tore the mountains apart and

28. Nearly every king of Israel is condemned for following the sin of Jeroboam son of Nebat: Nadab (1 Kgs 15:26); Baasha (15:34; 16:2, 7); Elah (16:13); Zimri (16:19); Tibni (not applicable because a splinter faction not able to sponsor shrines); Omri (16:25–26); Ahab (16:31); Ahaziah (22:52[53]); Jehoram/Joram (2 Kgs 3:3); Jehu (10:29, 31); Jehoahaz (13:2); Jehoash/Joash (13:11); Jeroboam II (14:24); Zechariah (15:9); Shallum (not applicable because reign too short to sponsor shrines); Menahem (15:18); Pekahiah (15:24); and Pekah (15:28).

> shattered the rocks before Yahweh, but Yahweh was not in the wind. After the wind there was an earthquake, but Yahweh was not in the earthquake. After the earthquake came a fire, but Yahweh was not in the fire. And after the fire came a gentle whisper. When Elijah heard it, he pulled his cloak over his face and went out and stood at the mouth of the cave. Then a voice said to him, "What are you doing here, Elijah?" (1 Kgs 19:11–13)

The narrative function of the theophany to Elijah stands apart in many respects from the forgiveness and covenant renewal after the golden calf in the wilderness. The striking retrospective figural parallels establish a kind of continuity of divine presence. New Testament allusions to this passage include the transfiguration with Moses and Elijah present and Paul's emphasis on an elect remnant of the people of God (Mark 9:2–7; Rom 11:2–3).

2 Kgs 14:6*//Deut 24:16* (each dies for own sins) (* see personal responsibility network). The narrator marks a nearly verbatim citation of Deut 24:16 as from "the scroll of the Torah of Moses" to describe the rationale for limits of vengeance (2 Kgs 14:6//2 Chr 25:4). Amaziah killed the assassins of his father but did not kill their children as "vicarious punishment" because, according to the narrator, he honored the limitation on punishing only the guilty individuals in civil and criminal cases.[29]

18:5~18:30; 19:10; cf. 18:19, 20, 21, 22, 24 (B) (Hezekiah's faith). The Assyrian field commander builds his taunting speeches around the leading words "trust" and "deliver" (2 Kgs 18:19–25, 28–35; 19:10–13).[30] He challenges the people of Judah to avoid being persuaded by Hezekiah's faith (18:30). The Deuteronomist repurposes the field commander's taunt for his theological evaluation of Hezekiah. The inverted reuse of the field commander's taunt suggests extra irony since the field commander appears to echo the oracles of some of Judah's prophets as a taunt (see notes on 2 Kgs 18:21–32). The exegetical transformation of ridicule used for commendation includes marrying it to a stock phrase of Deuteronomy—holding fast to Yahweh by obeying his commands (Deut 4:4; 10:20; 11:22; etc.; italics signify verbal parallel):

> Hezekiah *trusted* in Yahweh, the God of Israel. There was no one like him among all the kings of Judah, either before him or after him. He held fast to Yahweh and did not stop following him; he kept the commands Yahweh had given Moses. (2 Kgs 18:5–6)

> [Assyrian field commander] Say to Hezekiah king of Judah: "Do not let the god you *trust* deceive you when he says, 'Jerusalem will not be given into the hands of the king of Assyria.'" (19:10†; cf. 18:30)

---

29. See Greenberg, "Avenger of Blood," *IDB* 1:321; Cogan and Tadmor, *II Kings*, 155. In spite of the legal standard for individual responsibility in civil and criminal cases in Deut 24:6, often collectives were punished in the Deuteronomistic narrative, see Judg 21:10–11; 1 Sam 22:18–19; 2 Sam 21:8–9; 2 Kgs 9:26; cf. Josh 7:22–24 (Weinfeld, "Jeremiah," 37, 39).

30. See Childs, *Isaiah and the Assyrian Crisis*, 85.

18:21~Isa 30:2 (C) (depending on Egypt).

18:23–24~Isa 31:3 (C) (depending on horses).

18:30, 32, 35~Isa 31:4–5 (C) (Yahweh shall deliver Jerusalem).

18:31~Mic 4:4 (C) (under one's own vine and fig tree).

18:32>/<Deut 8:7–8 (good land). The Assyrian field commander's taunts against Jerusalem refer to numerous themes that appear in the contemporary prophets of Judah (2 Kgs 18:19–25, 28–35; cf. 19:10–13). He mocks: "Who of all the gods of these countries has been able to save his land from me? How then can Yahweh deliver Jerusalem from my hand?" (18:35). Isaiah warns against trusting in Egypt or horses because Yahweh will deliver Jerusalem (Isa 30:2; 31:3–5; cf. 29:5–8; 31:8–9; 37:35). The field commander presses the same issues upon the hapless Judeans (2 Kgs 18:21, 23–24). The prophetic hopes used to ridicule the people strengthen the vitality of the prophetic messages when Yahweh rescues the city. The field commander's speech in 2 Kgs 18–20 gets imported into Isaiah nearly unedited, which strengthens the likelihood of the field commander's derisive use of the prophets (see note on Isa 36–39, esp. Table I2 in Isaiah). The combination of the vine and fig tree of themselves reflect a commonplace figure of speech (2 Kgs 18:31; cf. 18:32; Deut 8:7–8).[31] But Mic 4:4 and 1 Kgs 4:25[5:5] both use "sit" and "under" in a way that suggests a possible relationship, whether direct or indirect. Elsewhere the Deuteronomist may repurpose this theme from the field commander's speech and/or Mic 4:4 to characterize Solomon's idyllic kingdom in 1 Kgs 4:25[5:5]. The field commander's provision to allow the besieged to come out to their vine and fig trees until forcibly migrated to an equally luxurious land seems like a sarcastic-literal use of Micah's expectational metaphor repurposed to coerce surrender.

23:26~Jer 15:4 (C) (because of Manasseh). The narrator of Kings dramatically juxtaposes the judgment of Judah because of the iniquity of Manasseh directly after the sweeping reformations of Josiah (2 Kgs 23:26; cf. 21:16; 24:3–4; Deut 19:10). The culmination of the account of Josiah echoes the great commandment followed by "nevertheless" to good rhetorical effect: "Neither before nor after Josiah was there a king like him who turned to Yahweh as he did—*with all his heart and with all his soul and with all his strength*, in accordance with all the Torah of Moses. *Nevertheless* . . ." (23:25, 26a, emphasis mine; cf. Deut 6:5). Although the verbal parallel includes only one word, the name Manasseh, the stunning prophetic oracle of Jer 15 seems to supply the basis for the interpretation of the decline and fall of Jerusalem after Josiah (verbal parallel emphasized):

> I will make them abhorrent to all the kingdoms of the earth because of what *Manasseh* son of Hezekiah king of Judah did in Jerusalem. (Jer 15:4)

31. See Num 20:5; Deut 8:8; Isa 34:4; Jer 5:17; 8:13; Hos 2:12[14]; 9:10; Joel 1:7, 12; 2:22; Amos 4:9; Hab 2:17; Hag 2:19; Ps 105:33; Prov 27:18; Song 2:13 (see "תְּאֵנָה," *HALOT* 2:1675).

> Nevertheless, Yahweh did not turn away from the heat of his fierce anger, which burned against Judah because of all that *Manasseh* had done to arouse his anger. (2 Kgs 23:26)

24:13*~Jer 27:16–22* (C) (removal of temple vessels with captivity of Jehoiachin) (* see temple vessels network). The temple vessels get carried into captivity in stages, two of which are recorded in Kings (2 Kgs 24:13; 25:14–15//Jer 52:18–20; cf. Jer 27:16–22). See discussion of these contexts in note on 2 Chr 36:7, 10.

FILTERS

Kings frequently makes broad allusions to scriptural traditions, especially those housed in Deuteronomy, as well as manifold stereotypical Deuteronomistic expressions. Numerous lists of stock phrases and stereotypical expressions of Kings can be found elsewhere and are not included herein.[32] To get a sense of how Deuteronomistic stock phrases appear within prose contexts, see the Jer 7 example in Jeremiah Filters. The use of such stock phrases is similar, but to a lesser extent, in Kings.

The following filters include non-exegetical broad allusions and similarities to scriptural traditions in Kings. In addition, the recurring formulas that frame the rules of the kings have been collated below and can help comparisons with the exegetical developments of Kings in Chronicles. The following representative lists are not comprehensive or complete.

Programmatic Interpretations

Kings features two extensive paraphrastic allusion clusters in the prayer of Solomon and the explanation of the fall of Samaria (1 Kgs 8; 2 Kgs 17). These broadly allude to scriptural traditions by means of Deuteronomistic stock phrases.

The prayer of Solomon uses a sweeping programmatic prospective prayer to situate the meaning and function of the temple (1 Kgs 8:22–53). The speeches of Joshua and Samuel, Nathan's covenant, and the prayer of Solomon each put to words dramatic turning points in Yahweh's relationship with his people (Josh 24:1–15; 1 Sam 12:6–17; 2 Sam 7:1–17; 1 Kgs 8:22–53). Solomon's prayer begins by paraphrasing David's prayer, praising Yahweh for his unique goodness (2 Sam 7:22; 1 Kgs 8:23). He goes on to broadly paraphrase obligations of the Davidic covenant (2 Sam 7:14–15; 1 Kgs 8:24–26). Then Solomon remarkably distinguishes the universal rule of Yahweh over

---

32. For a list of Deuteronomic expressions in Kings, see Burney, *Notes*, xiii–xv; Driver, *Introduction*, 200–202; Weinfeld, *Deuteronomic School*, 320–59. For similar expressions in 2 Kgs 17:13–20; 21:11–15; 22:16–19 and Jeremiah, see Driver, *Introduction*, 203. For a list of connections between Joshua, Judges, Samuel, and Kings, see Grisanti, "Impact," 246, and for similarities between Deut 4 and 1 Kgs 8, see 241, 249; for similarities between 2 Kgs 22–23 and Deuteronomy, Joshua, Judges, Samuel, Kings, see idem, "Josiah," 123, 128–29. For potential parallels between the prophets Samuel and Elisha, see Nobel, "Cultic Prophecy," 56–58.

and against the special dwelling of his glory in the temple (1 Kgs 8:27, 30). The major prospective part of his prayer loosely reworks judgment and restoration themes found in Lev 26:14–45 and Deut 29–30. Solomon's sweeping prospective includes expectations for Yahweh to judge his people by drought and exile (8:37, 46). But he also speaks of the temple as a place where Yahweh will listen to the prayers of foreigners (נָכְרִי, 8:41–43). The central emphasis of Solomon's prayer calls upon Yahweh to forgive when his people turn back to him and confess their transgression (Lev 26:40–41; Deut 30:2; 1 Kgs 8:33, 35, 47, 48). Solomon's prayer differs from Lev 26:41–45 and Deut 30:3–6 by merely asking for divine mercy from captors rather than return from exile (1 Kgs 8:50). Solomon closes by aligning the request for Yahweh's forgiveness with his great works of redemption from Egypt and taking Israel as his own heritage (8:51, 53). The most enduring elements of the prayer of Solomon come to the fore when Nehemiah and the Chronicler reuse some of its ideals (see notes on Neh 1:5–11; 2 Chr 7:11–22). In a real sense Solomon's prayer embodies central hopes of the restoration by the forgiveness of Yahweh.

The narrator of Kings provides an interpretive retrospective to explain the reasons for the fall of Israel (2 Kgs 17:7–21). The retrospective opens with a series of broad allusions: Yahweh brought the people up from Egypt (17:7); Israel followed the practices of the nations Yahweh drove out of the land (Deut 7:4; 2 Kgs 17:8–9); they practiced false worship on every high hill, under every green tree (Deut 12:2; 2 Kgs 17:10); they served prohibited idols (Deut 5:7–8; 2 Kgs 17:12); and they refused to listen to Yahweh's prophets (Deut 18:18–19; 2 Kgs 17:13–14). Having established the background of broken Torah, the narrator summarizes the idolatry and syncretism of the Northern Kingdom in Kings, especially the two golden calves in Bethel and Dan (2 Kgs 17:15–18; cf. 1 Kgs 12:26–33; and list in footnote in note on 1 Kgs 12:28–29). The summary of unfaithful worship includes elements not introduced previously in Kings, namely, worship of the stellar lights and passing their children through fire, which anticipate false worship in Jerusalem under Manasseh (2 Kgs 17:16–17; 21:3–6; cf. 16:3). The intermixing of the infidelity of Israel and the coming unfaithfulness of Judah sets up the major pivot point of the explanation. The narrator of Kings blames Judah for all of the same things: "and even Judah did not keep the commands of Yahweh their God. *They followed the practices Israel had introduced*" (17:19, emphasis mine). The use of the sins of Israel as an analogy for the rebellion of Judah here looks very similar to the updates of Hosea the prophet to Israel to include "and also Judah" and the like (Hos 1:7, 11; 4:15; 5:5, 10, 14; 6:4, 11; 8:14; 10:11; 12:2[3]; cf. 3:5). The retrospective condemnation closes by rehearsing one more time the royal patronage of the two golden calves in Dan and Bethel introduced by Jeroboam (2 Kgs 17:21–23). In sum, the retrospective interpretation of the reasons for the fall of Israel in 2 Kgs 17 features and applies to Judah broad allusions to scriptural traditions, especially by means of Deuteronomistic stock phrases.

Non-Exegetical Broad Allusions and Shared Themes

Note: **1 Kgs 1:33, 38, 44**>/<Gen 49:11; Zech 9:9, Solomon on a "mule" (פִּרְדָּה) is unrelated to the specialized terms for donkey elsewhere (see note on Zech 9:9); **2:5**>/<2 Sam 3:27–30; 20:9–10, Joab's misdeeds; **2:7**>/<2 Sam 17:27–29, Barzillai's loyalty (cf. 2 Sam 19:31–39); **2:8**>/<2 Sam 16:5–14; 19:16–23, Shimei's treachery; **3:1**>/<Exod 34:15–16; Deut 7:3–4, treaty marriage to Egyptian (cf. 1 Kgs 11:1–4); **3:8**>/<Gen 15:5; 22:17, numerous people of God; **4:21[5:1]**>/<Gen 15:18, Solomon rules over land from the Euphrates to the border of Egypt (see note on 2 Chr 1:14–17); **4:32[5:12]**>/<Prov 1:1, 6, three thousand "proverbs" (משל); **5:1[15]**>/<2 Sam 5:11, Hiram king of Tyre, friend of David; **5:3[17]**>/<2 Sam 7:5, David could not make a house for the name of Yahweh; **6:1**>/<Exod 6–15, four hundred and eightieth year after coming out of Egypt; **6:12**>/<2 Sam 7:13–14, obligation for obedience associated with the Davidic covenant (see note on 1 Kgs 2:1–4); **8:2**>/<Lev 23:34, dedicate temple at the Festival of Tabernacles in seventh month; **8:9**>/<Exod 34:28–29; Deut 31:26, two stone tablets from Horeb in the ark; **9:4–5**>/<2 Sam 7:14–16, obligations of the Davidic covenant; **9:9**>/<Deut 29:24–26[23–25], their deduction of sinful cause based on divine judgment; **11:6, 33; 2 Kgs 14:3; 16:2**>/<1, 2 Samuel, not like David (כדוד); **11:13, 32, 34, 36; 15:4**>/<2 Sam 7:15, not completely removing the kingdom from Davidic rulers; **11:15**>/<2 Sam 8:13–14, expansion of when David defeated Edom (see note on Ps 60 superscription); **11:24**>/<2 Sam 8:3, filling in details of David's defeat of Zobah; **14:9**>/<Deut 5:8–10, serving other gods; **14:23**>/<Deut 12:2, false worship under every tree and on every hill; **15:5**>/<2 Sam 11–12, David's sin with Uriah the Hittite; **15:11**>/<1, 2 Samuel, like David (כדוד); **18:31**>/<Gen 32:28; 35:10, twelves tribes for Jacob renamed Israel; **21:3**>/<Num 36:7, permanent allotment of "ancestral inheritance" (נחלת אב); **21:10**>/<Deut 5:20, false witnesses.

Also note: **2 Kgs 2:8**>/<Exod 14:21; Josh 3:17; 4:18, parting water and crossing on "dry ground" (חרבה); **4:42**>/<Lev 23:17, does Elijah appropriate the bread of firstfruits?;[33] **5:27**>/Exod 4:6; Num 12:10, "leprous white as snow" (מצרע כשלג); **6:28–29**>/<Lev 26:29; Deut 28:53–57, siege induced cannibalism; **7:3**>/<Lev 13:46, lepers outside the community; **12:4[5]**>/<Lev 27:1–8, silver value of vow (cf. Exod 30:11–16; Deut 14:25; 2 Chr 24:9); **12:16[17]**>/<Lev 5:1–6:7[5:1–28], commuting purification and reparation offering to silver;[34] **14:25**>/<Jonah 1–4, domestic ministry of Jonah; **15:5**>/<Lev 13:46, separation of leper (Azariah/Uzziah); **16:3; 17:31**>/<Deut 18:10, child sacrifice (cf. Lev 18:21; 20:2, 3; 2 Kgs 16:3; 21:6; Jer 7:31; 19:5; 32:35); **16:3; 17:8**>/<Deut 7:1, the nations Yahweh "drove out" before Israel (ירש); **16:5**>/<Isa 7:1, Rezin of Aram and Pekah of

33. See Gray, *Kings*, 501.

34. Milgrom notes that commuting offerings into silver is not part of sacrificial legislation. He goes on to deduce that the priests use the silver to maintain their stockyard where the animals could be used for the purification and reparation offerings (*Leviticus 1–16*, 287–88). The logic of commuting tithes and vows to silver fits with Lev 27:1–8 and Deut 14:25.

Israel "went up" against Jerusalem (עלה); **16:9**>/<Amos 9:7, Assyrian forced migration of the people of Damascus to their homeland of origin; **17:7**>/<Exod 6–15, redemption from Egypt; **17:10–12**>/<Deut 12:3–4, false worship on every high hill and under every green tree; **17:13**>/<Jer 25:3–4, warned by the prophets to turn away from rebellion; **17:28, 33**>/<Deut 5:7, 8–10, tutor in aberrant worship; **17:35–39**>/<Exod 20:5//Deut 5:9; Exod 6:6; 20:23; Deut 4:34, compilation of stereotypical Deuteronomistic language;[35] **18:4**>/<Deut 7:5, 24–26; 12:3, break down pillars, etc.; **18:4**>/<Num 21:8–9, broke to pieces the bronze serpent lifted up in wilderness; **19:15**//Isa 37:16>/<1 Sam 4:4; 2 Sam 6:2, "Yahweh God of Israel/of hosts who is enthroned above the cherubim" (יהוה אלהי ישראל/צבאות ישב הכרבים); **19:15**//Isa 37:16>/<Jer 32:17, "you have made the heavens and the earth" (עשית את השמים ואת הארץ) (cf. Gen 1; Isa 40:12; 42:5; 44:24; 45:12, 18; 48:13; 51:13);**19:25**//Isa 37:26>/<Isa 40:21, 28; 48:6, 7, 8, "have you not heard?" (לא שמעת/הלא שמעת/תשמעו); **19:35**>/<Exod 12:29, "that night the messenger of Yahweh smote/at midnight Yahweh smote" (בלילה ההוא . . . מלאך יהוה ויך/בחצי הלילה ויהוה הכה); **21:2**>/<Deut 18:9, "detestable practice of the nations" (כתועבת הגוים); **21:3, 7**>/<Deut 16:21, Asherah pole by altar; **21:6**>/<Deut 18:10, "divination and interpreting omens" (ענן ונחש); **21:12**>/<Jer 19:3, "I am going to bring such disaster on Jerusalem and Judah/this place that the ears of everyone who hears of it will tingle" (הנני מביא רעה על ירושלם ויהודה/המקום הזה אשר כל שמעה תצלנה אזניו/שתי אזניו) (cf. 1 Sam 3:11);[36] **21:13**>/<Amos 7:7–9, measuring line of Samaria over Jerusalem (cf. Lam 2:8); **21:16**>/<Deut 19:10, "shed innocent blood" (דם נקי שפך); **23:10**>/<Deut 18:10; Jer 7:31; 19:5; 32:35, defiling Topheth to prevent child sacrifice (cf. Lev 18:21; 20:2, 3; 2 Kgs 16:3; 21:6); **23:21**>/<Deut 16:1–8, keeping Passover; **23:25**>/<Deut 6:5, "with all his/your heart and all his/your soul and all his/your strength" (בכל לבבו/ך ובכל נפשו/ך ובכל מאדו/ך); **24:7**>/<Gen 15:18, "from the river/wadi of Egypt to the great river/the Euphrates river" (מנהר/מנחל מצרים עד נהר הגדל/נהר פרת).

Fulfillments

The Deuteronomistic narrative records numerous fulfillments. Many of these relate to predictions by prophets within Kings itself, which will not be listed here.[37] The following are fulfillments of earlier scriptural expectations fulfilled in Kings: Eli's priestly line banished (1 Kgs 2:26–27, 35; cf. 1 Sam 2:30, 35; 3:13); people as numerous as sand of the sea, plus they controlled kingdoms from Euphrates to border of Egypt (1 Kgs 4:20–21[4:20–5:1]; cf. Gen 22:17+15:18); "rest" from enemies/on every side (נוח, 1 Kgs 5:4[18]; cf. Deut 12:10; 2 Sam 7:11); "he shall build a house for my name" (הוא יבנה בית לשמי, 1 Kgs 5:5[19]) and "Yahweh has kept the promise he made . . . and I have built the

35. See Keil and Delitzsch, *Kings*, 427 (on 2 Kgs 17:34–41).

36. See Parke-Taylor, *Formation*, 219.

37. See list in von Rad, "Deuteronomic Theology," in *From Genesis*, 157–59.

temple for the Name of Yahweh, the God of Israel" (ויקם יהוה את דברו אשר דבר . . . ואבנה הבית לשם יהוה אלהי ישׂראל, 1 Kgs 8:20; cf. 2 Sam 7:13); rebuilder of Jericho loses two sons (1 Kgs 16:34; cf. Josh 6:26).

Royal Formulaic Devices

Kings uses a set of fairly consistent formulas to situate the reigns of the Hebrew kings. The importance of the recurring formulas extends to the reformatting of the kings of Judah in Chronicles' use of Kings (see Table C11 in Chronicles).[38]

Summary of rule: "all which he did/what he did" (כל אשר עשׂה/אשר עשׂה, 1 Kgs 11:41; 14:29; 15:7, 23, 31; 16:5, 14, 27; 22:39, 45[46]; 2 Kgs 1:18; 8:23; 10:34; 12:19[20]; 13:8, 12; 14:28; 15:6, 21, 26, 31; 20:20; 21:17; 23:28; 24:5).

Evaluation—good kings of Judah with good fathers: "and he walked in all the way of his father" (וילך בכל דרך אביו, 1 Kgs 22:43[44]); "according to all which his father had done" (בכל אשר עשׂה אביו, 2 Kgs 14:3; 15:3, 34); **good king with evil fathers:** "he did what was right in the eyes of Yahweh/as David his father/but not as David his father/according to all which David his father had done/and he walked in all the way of David his father and he did not turn aside to the right or left" (ויעשׂ . . . הישר בעיני יהוה/כדוד אביו/רק לא כדוד אביו/ככל אשר עשׂה דוד אביו/וילך בכל דרך דוד אביו ולא סר ימין ושמאול, 1 Kgs 15:11; 2 Kgs 14:3; 18:3; 22:2).[39]

Death and burial of kings of Israel (see Table K1)—**peaceful:** "and X rested with his ancestors/he was buried/they buried him/in Samaria/with the kings of Israel" (וישכב עם אבתיו/ויקבר/ויקברו/בשמרון/עם מלכי ישראל, 1 Kgs 14:20; 16:6, 28; 22:37, 40; 2 Kgs 10:35; 13:9, 13; 14:16, 29; 15:22); **violent:** "he died/and they killed him/smote/smote and killed him" (וימת/וימיתהו/ויד/ויכהו וימתהו, 1 Kgs 15:27–28; 16:10; 2 Kgs 1:17; 9:24; 15:10, 14, 25, 30); "he died and he was brought to Samaria and they buried him in Samaria"(וימת ויבוא שמרון ויקברו בשמרון, 1 Kgs 22:37).

Death and burial of kings of Judah (see Table K1)—**peaceful:** "and X rested with his ancestors and was buried/they buried him/with his ancestors/in the city of David/his father/in the garden of Uzza" (וישכבוישכב X עם אבתיו ויקבר/ויקברו אתו/עם אבתיו/בעיר דוד/בגן עזא, 1 Kgs 2:10; 11:43; 14:31; 15:8, 24; 22:51; 2 Kgs 8:24; 15:7, 38; 16:20; 20:21; 21:18; 24:6); **violent:** "he died/they killed him/he was put to death/they buried him/he was buried/with his ancestors/in the city of David/in the garden of Uzza" (וימת/וימתהו/ותומת/ויקברו/ויקבר אתו/עם אבתיו/בעיר דוד/בגן עזא, 2 Kgs 9:27–28; 11:16; 12:21–22; 14:19–20; 21:23, 26; 23:29–30).

---

38. For death and burial formulas, I am indebted to Halpern and Vanderhooft, "Editions of Kings," 189–90; and evaluation formulas, 205. For the queen mothers of Judah not listed here, see 198.

39. For a list of comparisons to David in Kings, see von Rad "Deuteronomistic Theology," in *From Genesis*, 163.

TABLE K1: SEQUENTIAL COMPARISON OF THE DEATHS OF THE KINGS OF ISRAEL AND JUDAH IN KINGS‡

peaceful death and burial of kings of Judah	violent deaths of kings of Judah	peaceful death and burial of kings of Israel	violent deaths of kings of Israel
1 Kgs 2:10, David			
11:43, Solomon			
		14:20, Jeroboam	
14:31, Rehoboam			
15:8, Abijam			
15:24, Asa			
			15:27–28, Nadab
		16:6, Baasha	
			16:10, Elah
			(16:18, Zimri)
			(16:22, Tibni)
		16:28, Omri	
			22:35, 37, 40, Ahab
22:50[51], Jehoshaphat			
			2 Kgs 1:17, Ahaziah
2 Kgs 8:24, Joram			
			9:24, Jehoram
	2 Kgs 9:27–28, Ahaziah		
		2 Kgs 10:35, Jehu	
	11:16, Athaliah		
	12:21–22, Joash		
		13:9, Jehoahaz	
		13:13; 14:16, Jehoash/ Joash	
	14:19–20, Amaziah		
		14:29, Jeroboam (II)	
15:7, Azariah/Uzziah			
			15:10, Zechariah

(cont.)

peaceful death and burial of kings of Judah	violent deaths of kings of Judah	peaceful death and burial of kings of Israel	violent deaths of kings of Israel
			15:14, Shallum
		15:22, Menahem	
			15:25, Pekahiah
			15:30, Pekah
15:38, Jotham			
16:20, Ahaz			
			(17:4, Hoshea[a])
20:21, Hezekiah			
21:18, Manasseh			
	21:23, 26, Amon		
	23:29–30, Josiah		
	(23:34, Jehoahaz[b])		
24:6, Jehoiakim			
	(24:15, Jehoiachin[c])		
	(25:7, Zedekiah[c])		

‡ Indebted to Halpern and Vanderhooft, "Editions of Kings," 189–90 (except death of Jehu 2 Kgs 10:25[*sic*]).

[a] No death and burial report for Hoshea (2 Kgs 17:4).

[b] No burial report for Jehoahaz (23:34).

[c] No death and burial report for Jehoiachin (24:15), or Zedekiah (25:7).

Source citations of Judah's rulers: "Are they not written in the scroll of the events of the kings of Judah?" (הלא הם/המה כתובים על ספר דברי הימים למלכי יהודה, 1 Kgs 14:29; 15:7, 23; 22:45[46]; 2 Kgs 8:23; 12:19[20]; 14:18; 15:6, 36; 16:19; 20:20; 21:17, 25; 23:28; 24:5; cf. 1 Kgs 11:41).

Succession: "and X his son ruled in his place" (וימלך . . . בנו תחתיו, 1 Kgs 11:43; 14:20, 31; 15:8, 24; 16:6, 28; 22:40, 50[51]; 2 Kgs 8:24; 10:35; 12:21[22]; 13:9, 24; 14:16, 29; 15:7, 22, 38; 16:20; 19:37; 20:21; 21:18, 26; 24:6; cf. 14:21; 21:24; 23:30).

Chapter 10

ISAIAH

SYMBOLS[1]

// verbal parallels (A level)
/~/ synoptic parallel (A level)
~ B, probable interpretive allusion; C, possible; D, probably not
+ interpretive blend
>/< more or less similar (see Filters)
* part of interpretive network (see Networks)

USE OF SCRIPTURE IN ISAIAH[2]

1:2~Deut 32:1 (B) (hear heavens, listen earth)
1:10*>/<Deut 29:23*[22]+32:1 (C) (destruction of cities of the plain) (* see cities of the plain network)
2:1–5//Mic 4:1–5 (mountain of Yahweh)
4:1~Exod 21:10 (C) (passing up standard support of concubine)
6:8~Gen 1:26; 3:22; 11:7 (C) (divine plural pronouns)
6:9–10*~Deut 29:2–4*[1–3] (B) (obstructing eyes, ears, hearts) (* see concealing network)
6:13~Exod 19:6; Deut 7:6 (C) (holy seed)
7:1//2 Kgs 16:5 (B) (collaborative opposition of Rezin of Damascus and Pekah of Israel)
7:12~Deut 6:16 (B) (not testing Yahweh)
10:26~Judg 7:25+Exod 14:16 (C) (judgment like Midian at rock of Oreb and staff over the sea)
11:15–16*~Exod 23:20* (C) (return highway like exodus) (* see new exodus network)
16:1~2 Kgs 3:4 (C) (Moab sends tribute of sheep)
16:13–14~15:1–16:12 (B) (downsizing hopes of Moab)
19:23~11:16 (B) (highway between Assyria and Egypt)
23:17–18~Deut 23:18[19] (C) (wages of Tyre's prostitution sanctified to Yahweh)
24:2~Hos 4:9 (C) (as people so priest)
24:5~Gen 9:16 (C) (everlasting covenant)
25:6~Exod 24:11 (D); ~Deut 14:26 (D); ~Ps 22:26[27] (D) (eating before Yahweh on the mountain)
25:10b–12~Num 24:17*+Gen 3:14–15 (C) (trampling Moab to the dust) (* see Davidic covenant and Judah-king networks)
28:13//28:10+8:15 (B) (strange speech and judgment)
28:21~2 Sam 5:20+Josh 10:10 (C) (reversal of divine intervention at Mount Perazim and Gibeon)
29:1, 3~2 Sam 5:6 (C) (besieging Ariel)
36–39/~/2 Kgs 18–20 (siege of Jerusalem and Hezekiah's pride)
38:21–22/~/2 Kgs 20:7–8 (topical application of figs)
40:1~Lam 1:2, 9, 16, 17, 21 (B) (comfort Jerusalem)
40:3–4*~11:15–16* (B)+26:7–8 (C)+Exod 23:20–21* (B) (highway in the wilderness) (* see new exodus network)
43:1–2, 7, 14–17, 19–20, 21~Gen 1+2:7+Exod 14–15 (B) (Israel's creator, redeemer, and provider)
51:9–11~27:1+30:7+(>/<43:2, etc.) (C) (calling for ancient redemption once again)
52:1a>/<51:9 (Awake! Awake!)
52:1b*~Lam 1:10* (B)+Deut 23:3–6*[4–7] (B) (uncircumcised and defiled will not enter you again) (* see assembly network)
52:2~Lam 2:10 (C) (down in dust)
52:11–12*~Lam 4:15 (B)+Exod 12:11 (B)+14:19 (C)+Lev 13:45 (B) (Depart! Depart! Do not touch!) (* see temple vessels network)

1. For explanation of symbols, see Symbols and Abbreviations and Introduction. For other help, see Glossary.
2. See Bibliographic Note on Lists of Potential Parallels.

53:10~53:5 (B)+Lev 5:14–6:7[5:14–26] (B) (servant as guilt offering)
54:6~Hos 2:14–15[16–17] (C) (restoration like the wife of youth)
54:9~Gen 9:8–17 (B) (like the days of Noah)
55:3–5*~Ps 89:28, 49*[29, 50] (C) (Davidic covenant extended to the nations) (* see Davidic covenant network)
56:1–8*~Deut 23:1–8*[2–9] (B) (eunuchs and foreigners in Yahweh's house) (* see assembly network)
57:14–21~53:5, 10 (B) (restoration of the contrite)
61:1, 2~Lev 25:10 (C) (year of release)
61:5–7~Exod 19:6 (C) (priests as rulers over people)
63:9~Exod 23:20* (B)+Deut 1:31 (C) (divine presence with his people) (* see new exodus network)
63:10~Ps 78:40 (C) (rebelled and grieved him)
63:11~Num 11:17, 25 (B) (spirit of God upon leaders)
63:12>/<Exod 14:16, 21; Ps 78:13 (divided the sea)
63:13>/<Exod 15:5, 8; Isa 51:10; Ps 106:9 (led them through the depths)
63:14~Ps 78:52 (C) (led his people)
65:17–18~Gen 1:1 (B) (new heavens and new earth)
65:25//11:6–9+Gen 3:14 (B) (curse removed with the exception of the serpent)
66:22~Gen 1:1 (C) (new heaven and new earth endure)

OLD TESTAMENT USE OF ISAIAH (SEE RESPECTIVE NOTES)

2:1–5//Mic 4:1–5//Joel 3:10[4:10] (swords and plowshares)
4:2*~Jer 23:5* (C) (righteous branch) (* see branch network)
6:3~Hab 2:14 (B) (earth filled with glory)
7:9~2 Chr 20:20–21 (B) (faith)
11:9~Hab 2:14 (A) (earth filled with glory)
13:13~Hag 2:6 (C) (shake the heavens and dry land)
14:7~Zech 1:11 (B) (the whole earth at rest)
16:6, 7~Jer 48:5, 29–47 (B) (oracles against Moab)
26:19~Dan 12:2 (B) (those who sleep in the dust awake)
28:16~Ps 118:22 (C) (the rejected cornerstone)
30:2~2 Kgs 18:21 (C) (depending on Egypt)
31:3~2 Kgs 18:23–24 (C) (depending on horses)
38:1–20; 39:1–8~2 Chr 32:24–26, 31 (C) (Hezekiah's illness and receiving Babylonian representatives)
40:4*~Zech 4:7 (C) (mountain becomes level) (* see branch network)
41:15–16; 51:1~Dan 2:34–35, 45 (C) (hewn rock destroys empires and becomes mighty kingdom)
42:5~Zech 12:1 (C) (creator of heaven, earth, and the human spirit)
44:28–45:1, 13~2 Chr 36:22–23 (B) (his anointed one Cyrus to commission rebuilding of temple)
44:28*~Zech 4:9 (C) (Zerubbabel lays temple foundation) (* see seventy years network)
45:9~Job 9:12 (C) (What are you doing?)
49:23>/<Ps 72:9 (lick the dust)
52:7~Nah 1:15[2:1] (B) (the feet of one who brings good news)
52:13~Dan 12:3 (C) (lead many to righteousness)
53:7–8~Jer 11:19 (C) (lamb to slaughter)
53:11~Dan 12:3 (B) (lead many to righteousness)
55:3~2 Chr 6:1–42 (C) (dedication of temple)
66:24~Dan 12:2 (B) (those who sleep in the dust awake)

NEW TESTAMENT USE OF ISAIAH

1:9 LXX//Rom 9:29 (like Sodom)
6:3~Rev 4:5, 6 (holy, holy, holy)
6:9–10 LXX//Matt 13:13–15; Mark 4:12; Luke 8:10; John 12:40; Acts 28:26–27 (not seeing, not hearing)
7:14+8:8, 10 LXX//Matt 1:23 (Immanuel)
8:12~1 Pet 3:14 (do not be frightened)
8:14~Rom 9:33; 1 Pet 2:8 (stone makes them stumble)
8:17, 18//Heb 2:13 (put my trust in him)
9:1–2[8:23–9:1]//Matt 4:15–16 (light has dawned)
10:22–23 LXX//Rom 9:27–28 (sentence against them)
11:10 LXX//Rom 15:12 (root of Jesse)
13:10//Matt 24:29; Mark 13:24 (sun dark)
21:9~Rev 14:8; 18:2 (Babylon is fallen)
22:13//1 Cor 15:32 (tomorrow we die)
25:8//1 Cor 15:54 (death swallowed up)
25:8b~Rev 7:17; 21:4 (wipe away tears)
26:20~Heb 10:37 (coming soon)
27:9 LXX~Rom 11:27b (take away sin)
28:11, 12//1 Cor 14:21 (other tongues)

28:16 LXX~Rom 9:33; 10:11; 1 Pet 2:6 (stone in Zion)
29:10~Rom 11:8 (spirit of stupor)
29:13 LXX//Matt 15:8–9; Mark 7:6–7 (honor with lips)
29:14 LXX//1 Cor 1:19 (wisdom of the wise)
29:16~Rom 9:20 (Shall it say to potter?)
34:4//Matt 24:29; Mark 13:25; cf. Luke 21:26 (stars fall)
40:3 LXX//Matt 3:3; Mark 1:2–3; John 1:23 (voice in wilderness)
40:3–5 LXX//Luke 3:4–6 (voice in wilderness)
40:6–8//1 Pet 1:24–25 (people are grass)
40:13 LXX~Rom 11:34; 1 Cor 2:16 (Who has been his counselor?)
42:1–4//Matt 12:18–21 (servant)
42:1~John 1:34 (God's chosen one)
43:20, 21 LXX~1 Pet 2:9 (chosen people)
44:28~Acts 13:22 (he will do everything I want)
45:9~Rom 9:20 (Shall it say to potter?)
45:21~Mark 12:32 (no other)
45:23 LXX//Rom 14:11; cf. Phil 2:10–11 (every knee will bow)
47:7, 8~Rev 18:7 (not a widow)
49:6//Acts 13:47 (light to gentiles)
49:8//2 Cor 6:2 (day of salvation)
49:10~Rev 7:16, 17 (not hunger)
52:5 LXX~Rom 2:24 (name is blasphemed)
52:7//Rom 10:15 (feet that bring good news)
52:11//2 Cor 6:17 (touch no unclean thing)
52:15 LXX//Rom 15:21 (those not told will see)
53:1 LXX//John 12:38; Rom 10:16 (Who has believed?)
53:4, 5, 6 LXX~1 Pet 2:24, 25 (like sheep)
53:4//Matt 8:17 (took our infirmities)
53:7–8 LXX//Acts 8:32–33 (like a sheep to slaughter)
53:9//1 Pet 2:22 (no deceit in mouth)
53:12//Luke 22:37 (numbered with transgressors)
54:1//Gal 4:27 (be glad barren woman)
54:13//John 6:45 (taught by God)
55:3 LXX//Acts 13:34 (blessing to David)
56:7//Matt 21:13; Mark 11:17; Luke 19:46 (house of prayer)
58:6~Luke 4:19 (oppressed go free)
59:7, 8//Rom 3:15–17 (swift to shed blood)
59:20, 21+27:9 LXX//Rom 11:26–27; cf. Jer 31:33, 34 (Zion redeemer)
61:1, 2 LXX//Luke 4:18–19 (Spirit of the Lord is on me)
61:6~1 Pet 2:9 (called to be priests)
62:11~Matt 21:5 (say to daughter Zion)
64:4//1 Cor 2:9 (no eye has seen)
65:1 LXX//Rom 10:20 (found those who did not seek)
65:2 LXX//Rom 10:21 (held out hands)
65:17~Rev 21:1 (new heavens and new earth)
66:1, 2//Acts 7:49–50 (heaven as throne)
66:24//Mark 9:48 (fire not quenched)

HERMENEUTICAL PROFILE OF THE USE OF SCRIPTURE IN ISAIAH

Exegetical Conventions in Isaiah

Isaiah's engagement of scriptural traditions seems omnipresent. The degree of allusive interaction with Israel's scriptural traditions may be unmatched. If Jeremiah, Zechariah, Luke, parts of Romans, Hebrews, the Apocalypse, and some of the psalms come close, they do so in their own ways. The difference comes from repeated internal allusive reworking of Isaiah's own earlier oracles as well as allusions to scriptural traditions external to the book. Spelling out in general terms the superabundant allusive program of Isaiah offers leverage for studying his use of scriptural traditions.

The present discussion notes five aspects of Isaiah's allusive use of scriptural traditions: lyrical packaging, lyrical diffusion, the internal development of Isaiah's own traditions, the use of external scriptural traditions, and the dynamic interweaving of Isaiah's message. Each of these needs to be approached in general and non-technical ways in light of the purpose of this broad hermeneutical profile.

First, the lyrical qualities of Isaiah and the prophetic tradition in general profoundly affect the use of scriptural traditions. The dominant prophetic idiom is poetry. The prophets' enduring gifts include housing their messages in stunning poetic literature.

The point at hand does not relate to how the mechanics of poetry affect the use of scriptural traditions. The dynamics between the A line and B line, eliminating superfluous words, ignoring the normal rules of grammar and syntax for the sake of poetic expression, and more, make a difference. But these features come out of a lyrical way of thinking, preaching, singing, and interpreting scriptural traditions.

When Isaiah says "holy seed," does he allude to the expressions "holy priesthood" and/or "holy people" that appear in Torah (Isa 6:13)? If so, why frame it in a lyrically refracted manner (practically) untethered from its donor context? Column after column of the resultant scroll features lyrical suggestion. The suggestive lyrical interpretation of scriptural traditions constitutes one important reason that the prophets transcend their moment and speak across the generations.

Realistic expectations for evaluating and explaining the use of scriptural traditions in the prophets requires elevating readerly attitudes. Hebrew poetry operates at a higher register. Isaiah interprets scriptural traditions lyrically. This puts special demands on readers to approach Isaiah according to his lyrical presentation of revelation.

Second, emerging poetic scriptural traditions of ancient Israel contribute to what may be thought of as lyrical diffusion. Public dissemination of scriptural psalms and prophecies can dislodge traditions from their original contexts. The manifold recycling and repurposing of the most popular lyrical expressions of scriptural traditions may come from the lyrical diffusion. The point at hand relates to how the receptor context relates to the "context" of the scriptural donor tradition.

A couple studies trying to pin down donor contexts for the allusions in the prayer of Neh 9 offer help for a broader model of widely disseminated scriptural traditions. Carl Anderson sifts through the prayer line by line, often detecting stereotypical expressions, prayer jargon, stock phrases, and the like. He speculates that the use of psalms and other scriptural traditions in temple worship rippled out into a deeply invested religious culture. Anderson speaks of an "unconscious storehouse of religious idiom" that contributes to a "vast treasury of general religious language."[3] Judith Newman wrestles with the difficulty of deciding what to make of the use of widely distributed refrains, stock phrases, and biblicisms. She seeks to draw a distinction between widespread "liturgical idiom" versus scriptural traditions within their donor contexts.[4] The general idea of poetic traditions widely broadcast through lyrical use gets at the problem of detecting donor context(s).

3. See Anderson, "Formation," 140–42, 257–67; the two cited phrases from 259. Also see Zevit, "Echoes," 8–10.

4. See Newman, *Praying by the Book*, 90–91, 103–7.

Lack of available evidence rules out any formal model of lyrical dissemination. But the widespread use of refrains and stock phrases in Scripture provides empirical warnings against importing the wrong donor contexts into receptor contexts.

In this study lyrical diffusion refers to expressions, refrains, stock phrases, and the like appearing in the Scriptures. Lyrical diffusion serves as something of an umbrella term for poetic stock phrases in prophetic, liturgical, and wisdom scriptural contexts. The empirically verifiable evidence of lyrical diffusion in Scripture can be evaluated, even if explaining the causes must remain guesswork. The point of taking lyrical diffusion seriously relates directly to scriptural exegesis. By filtering out stock phrases, focus can be directed toward scriptural traditions purposefully reused by Isaiah.

Third, the book of Isaiah houses extensive recycling and reworking of its own themes. The prophet's use of other contexts in Isaiah requires careful consideration. This may be true of any "book" to some degree. Even speaking of a scroll or book infers coherence and closure, not simply "untidy" collections of literary materials.[5] But the use of Isaiah contexts in other Isaiah contexts often resembles interpretive allusion.

The dominant scholarly approach to Isaiah's use of scriptural traditions focuses on quotations, allusions, and echoes *within* Isaiah. In many cases this relates to ongoing debates about the collaborative authorship of Isaiah over time.[6] Studies of collaborative authorship can help by identifying interconnectivity across every part of Isaiah.

The use of contexts of Isaiah elsewhere in Isaiah makes up an important part of the present investigation. At the same time the subtle lyrical presentation of Isaiah's message and excessive use of lyrical stock phrases from within Isaiah often do not point to exegetical intervention. Many cases of incremental development suggest a particular prophetic style. Representative non-exegetical allusions within Isaiah have been collected in the filters at the end of the chapter. Whether these should be considered "allusions" versus thematic development does not need to be decided here.

Fourth, Isaiah makes heavy use of the scriptural traditions of Torah and shares many elements with the prophets and psalms. Each section of Isaiah features interpretative allusions from various parts of Torah. Interactions with the priestly traditions of Torah are somewhat rare in the prophets outside of Ezekiel.[7] Isaiah includes a few important exegetical interventions of priestly traditions in watershed contexts (see notes on Isa 52:11; 53:10; 61:1–2).

Isaiah interprets scriptural traditions from its place within the prophetic traditions of ancient Israel and Judah. Isaiah shares much with the early prophets. A few highlights can show Isaiah's exegetical tendencies in relation to them. Hosea and Isaiah both use

5. Contra Barton, "What Is a Book?" 14.

6. Many excavative studies continue to speak of First, Second, and Third Isaiah as eighth century BCE, exilic, and postexilic (Isaiah 1–39, 40–55, 56–66 respectively). Others approach the book as though it was under constant scribal intervention from Isaiah's own day until well into the Persian Empire. These issues are important but fall outside the present study.

7. On priestly versus prophetic lexicons of repentance, for example, see Milgrom, *Cult and Conscience*, 121–23.

children as signs and use similes of scriptural traditions, though these are more pronounced in Hosea (Hos 1:4–8, 10; 9:9; 10:9; 11:8; Isa 7:3; 8:3; 10:9, 26).

Like Amos, Isaiah castigates social evils of temple-goers (Amos 5:21–24; Isa 1:10–17; 3:16–4:1). If Amos invents oracles against the nations, Isaiah expands their use beyond the regional kingdoms once under David's own rule (Amos 1–2; Isa 13–23). If Amos focuses on the implications of the Davidic covenant according to the template of the regional Davidic empire (Amos 9:11–12) because Yahweh roars from Zion (1:2), then Isaiah extrapolates the Davidic rule over the great empires and all peoples by means of the prophetic word (Isa 10:12; 37:22–35; cf. 20:1–6). Isaiah even offers hope for the empires along with Israel (19:23–25).

In form and theme Isaiah and Micah stand as counterparts. Isaiah and Micah both envision a temple/David-centered hope, yet Isaiah goes beyond Micah in characterizing theocratic rule over all nations (Isa 2:3–4 versus Mic 4:4–5; Isa 11:10 versus Mic 5:2–5[1–4]). If Micah focuses on human sinfulness as the core problem (Mic 7:18–20), then Isaiah accents the righteousness and justice of Yahweh by his salvation (Isa 56:1).

Fifth, Isaiah's style of thematic development bears heavily on the use of scriptural traditions. The rolling development of the prophetic messages requires readers to work backward and forward.

Commentators sometimes speak of "prophetic narrative" or "storyline" to get at the unity evident within Isaiah.[8] It is easy to affirm the cohesion and interconnectedness evidenced by narrative. But the term narrative does not adequately capture the dynamic interchange of the same themes. Qualifications like "non-linear experimental narrative" ruin the force of the "storyline of Isaiah" metaphor. While thinking in terms of a classical symphony may better catch coherent dynamic progress, the point at hand has nothing to do with labels.

Isaiah 40–55 houses dynamic interweaving of prophetic themes progressing through a new exodus. The individual strands cannot be taken out and strung together into several mini-stories or mini-symphonies without violating their integrity. Each intermittent running theme closely and intentionally clicks together with the other themes to which it is juxtaposed. Table I1 offers a non-technical illustration of representative interweaved themes in the new exodus.

TABLE I1: SELECTED INTERWEAVED RUNNING THEMES IN ISAIAH 40–55‡

creator of the cosmos, 40:12, 21–22, 26, 28; 41:20; 42:5; 44:24; 45:7–10, 12, 18; 48:13; 51:13–14, 16; 54:16
creator of Israel, 43:1–2, 7, 15–17, 21; 44:2, 21, 24; 45:11; 51:9–11; 54:5
enduring word of God, 40:8, 21; 41:4, 26–27; 42:9; 44:26; 45:19, 21, 23; 46:10; 48:3, 16; 52:6; 55:11
incomparable God, 40:25; 44:6–8; 45:5–6, 14, 22; 46:5, 9 (cf. contra 47:8, 10)

8. See Childs, *Isaiah*, 382, 385, et passim.

restoration of Jerusalem, 40:2, 9; 44:26–28; 46:12–13; 48:1–2; 49:14–18, 22, 25; 51:3, 11, 16, 17–20; 52:1–10	
"servant songs,"[a] 42:1–4; 49:1–6; 50:4–9; 52:13–53:12; also see brief reference to servant(s), 41:8–9; 42:18–21; 43:10; 44:1–2, 21, 26; 45:4; 48:20; 49:7; 50:10; 54:17	
setting free prisoners and leading them, 42:6–7, 16; 43:5–6, 19; 49:9–11, 22; 51:9–11, 14; 52:1–2, 11–12	
taunt against idolatry, 40:18–20; 41:7, 22–24, 28–29; 42:17; 43:9; 44:9–20; 45:16, 20; 46:1–2, 6–7; 48:5, 14	

‡ Adapted from Schnittjer, "Idolatry in Isaiah," sec. on evidence. This essay argues for the native fit of the polemic against idolatry which on the surface seems like an independent composition.

[a] The much-contested identification of "servant songs," among other references to the servant(s), overlaps genre discussion more than simply listing theological themes such as those assembled in this table. For a list of recurring and interweaved literary genre components identified in Isa 40–55 (oracle of salvation; proclamation of salvation; trial speech; disputation), see de Waard, "Isaiah," *IDBSup*, 460.

Isaiah's exegesis of scriptural traditions takes place within its dynamic interweaved progression (see Table I1). Within the progression of interweaved themes, the building up of figural exegesis one on top of another is even more important. When Isaiah compares the return from exile to creation and to the ancient exodus from Egypt, he does not view these as two separate comparisons. Isaiah uses these together as though creation itself stands as a type of the exodus. Deciding if the figural relations between creation and the exodus are superimposed from the outside or are interconnected from the inside relates as much to how these themes relate in Torah as in Isaiah. Though Isaiah may project external figural relations at times, the linguistic similarities between Gen 1–2 and Exod 14–15 seem compelling even if readers need Isaiah to point them out first (see note on Isa 43). When Isaiah continues to stack figural patterns—creation, exodus, new exodus, new creation—they start to seem like cascading figural relations.

In sum, Isaiah features an allusive style that constantly engages authoritative scriptural traditions from within itself as well as from many other scriptural contexts. Several features of Isaiah affect its use of scriptural traditions, including lyrical expression and interweaving of themes. Isaiah takes good advantage of the native interconnections of Torah.

Implications of Scriptural Exegesis in Isaiah

The use of scriptural traditions in Isaiah plays an important role in the advancement of revelation of God's redemptive will. Isaiah and the other prophets of the days of the Assyrian crisis use scriptural traditions to explain the transition between regional rivalries and the dawn of oppression from Mesopotamian empires. Hosea, Amos, and Micah define doom and hope from Israel and Judah's covenantal standing before Yahweh. Isaiah works from the same basic covenantal standpoint, but his vision extends further, past the regional to the universal and past the more proximate toward the last days. These differences are only in degree not kind.

Isaiah and the writing prophets of the time of the Assyrian crisis provide authoritative donor traditions which later prophets draw upon liberally in the days of the

Neo-Babylonian crisis and rise of Persian dominion. For New Testament authors, Isaiah is frequently the go-to representative of the entire prophetic tradition.

Many of Isaiah's watershed exegetical advances explain what makes it a favorite of later scriptural authors. Haggai and Zechariah use loaded terms to speak of the rebuilding of the temple, echoing Isaiah (Isa 44:28; Hag 2:18; Zech 4:7–9). Ezra 1 narrates a new exodus by allusion to Torah without citing Isaiah in what could be considered a trace of the prophet's recurring new exodus figural expectations. All of the gospel writers explicitly align their narratives with Isaiah's new exodus in some way. One of the contexts in Isaiah featuring exegetical allusion, namely, Isa 6:9–10 appears many times in the New Testament, especially with the riddle-like scenarios Messiah uses in his teaching. Isaiah's allusion to Genesis by referring to the new heavens and new earth provides an enduring image to the Apocalypse. Though Paul and his coauthors use Isaiah frequently, they tend to cite passages other than those featuring exegetical intervention.[9]

Isaiah's pair of exegetical interventions on who may and who may not enter the new temple typify the significance of Isaiah's advances in scriptural revelation (Isa 52:1; 56:1–8). Although Isaiah's conception of two kinds of others matches the conventions in Torah, Ezekiel, and the restoration narratives, Isaiah offers decisive interpretation. Isaiah demonstrates that the difference between the two kinds of others does not relate to identity from birth or social standing but to commitment to Yahweh (see Table I4). The use of "house of prayer for all nations" from Isa 56:7 in an interpretive blend with Jer 7 becomes emblematic of Messiah's disputations with his opponents (Matt 21:13; Mark 11:17; Luke 19:46).

In sum, Isaiah's exegetical advances play a significant part in progressive revelation. The interpretive allusions themselves embody extensions and expansions of the prophetic word. Progressive revelation in Isaiah's ministry goes far beyond his use of scriptural traditions. Yet, the legacy of Isaiah's exegetical advances provides enduring testimony to the continuity of revelation between Torah, prophets, and gospel.

USE OF SCRIPTURE

1:2~Deut 32:1 (B) (hear heavens, listen earth). Moses calls upon the heavens and earth to stand as witnesses against Israel as he expects them to rebel (Deut 31:28). The personified heavens and earth join the Torah (31:26) to serve as two or three witnesses for Israel's anticipated crimes against Yahweh (17:6; 19:15; cf. Num 35:30). The broad inference at the beginning of the scroll turns on the recruitment of Isaiah to bring Yahweh's case against Israel (Isa 6:8–10; cf. 1:18). In this context Israel stands as a rebellious child, similar thematically but not verbally to the capital offense of the rebellious child (Deut 21:18–21). The fronting of the calling of cosmic witnesses enhances the function of

9. See list of use of Isaiah in Moyise, *Paul and Scripture*, 126–30.

Isaiah's prophecies to indict Israel. This location invites comparison to another allusion to the heaven and the earth, with a very different kind of function, from the beginning of Torah standing at the end of Isaiah (Gen 1:1; Isa 65:17; 66:22). The function of Isa 1:2 as a heading affects the entire book (cf. Mic 1:2). If Isaiah alludes to the Song of Moses, the verbs in the paraphrase have been inverted according to Seidel's theory (emphases signify verbal parallels):

> **Listen** [אזן], you heavens, and I will speak; *hear* [שׁמע], you earth, the words of my mouth. (Deut 32:1)

> *Hear* [שׁמע] me, you heavens! **Listen** [אזן], earth! For Yahweh has spoken: "I reared children and brought them up, but they have rebelled against me." (Isa 1:2)

Though the commonness of the shared language would normally restrict allusion to a possibility, the root for the legal term "bear witness" (Deut 31:28) in the context of the song of Moses intersects with Isaiah indicting Israel which makes allusion probable (Isa 1:18).[10]

1:10*>/<Deut 29:23*[22]+32:1 (C) (destruction of cities of the plain) (* see cities of the plain network). The juxtaposition of the prophetic stock phrase referring to Judah as though a condemned city of the plain within the opening indictment of Isaiah suggests an intentional rhetorical condemnation. The new covenant of Deut 29–30 uses the cities of the plain as a simile of condemnation, a figure that quickly became a favorite prophetic stock phrase (Deut 29:23; cf. Gen 19).[11] Compare the interpretive stock phrase of Isa 1:10 to 1:2 cited above (verbal parallels signified by bold and italics, and allusive interpretation signified by broken underlining):

> *Hear* [שׁמע] the word of Yahweh, you rulers of Sodom; **listen** [אזן] to the instruction of our God, you people of Gomorrah! (Isa 1:10)

2:1–5//Mic 4:1–5 (mountain of Yahweh). Isaiah's vision of the mountain shares non-exegetical similar themes with the so-called songs of Zion: Mount Zion is lofty and God "establishes" (כון) the city of Yahweh forever (Ps 48:2, 8[3, 9]; Isa 2:2; cf. Ps 87:5); the pilgrims say "let us go to the house of Yahweh" and the tribes of Yahweh "go up" (Ps 122:1, 4; Isa 2:3); and "He makes wars cease to the ends of the earth. He breaks the bow and shatters the spear; he burns the shields with fire" (Ps 46:9[10]; cf. Isa 2:4; Ps 76:3[4]).[12] Also note that Jeremiah speaks against Babylon, saying nations shall no longer "stream"

10. For a discussion of extensive single word parallels and thematic similarities between Deut 32 and Isa 1 as a whole, see Bergey, "Song," 39–42, 48. Bergey's conclusions overreach based on the thinness of the evidence.

11. See Isa 1:9–10; 3:9; 13:19; Jer 23:14; 49:18; 50:40; Ezek 16:53 (ironically!); Hos 11:8; Amos 4:11; Zeph 2:9; cf. Gen 19:1–29; Lam 4:6. Also see note on Hos 11:8.

12. See Wildberger, "Die Völkerwallfahrt zum Zion," 73–75; Allen, *Micah*, 323; Roberts, "Zion Tradition," in *IDBSup*, 985–86; von Rad, "City on the Hill," in *From Genesis*, 115–22.

(נהר) to it (Jer 51:44; cf. Isa 2:2). Isaiah's vision of the temple on the mountain and the parallel in Micah offer important perspectives on the place of Jacob and the nations in the eschatological mountain.

The extensive shared verbal and syntactical elements of the oracle of the mountain of Yahweh found in two contemporary prophets in Isa 2 and Mic 4 strongly suggest relationship even though the direction of dependence, or if they drew on a common source, cannot be determined from the shared locutions themselves (but see note on Joel 3:9).[13] Two clues suggest that Micah uses Isaiah: the vision superscription in Isa 2:1 and the quasi-marking in Mic 4:4—"For Yahweh Almighty has spoken."[14] Differences need to be noted in both contexts (no emphasis signifies verbatim parallels, italics signify adjustment, bold signifies unparalleled variations, underlining signifies parallel variations, broken underlining signifies an example of Seidel's theory, and wavy underlining signifies marking):

> In the last days the mountain of Yahweh's temple will be established as the highest of the mountains; it will be exalted above the hills, and peoples will stream to it. [2] Many *nations* will come and say, "Come, let us go up to the mountain of Yahweh, to the temple of the God of Jacob. He will teach us his ways, so that we may walk in his paths." The law will go out from Zion, the word of Yahweh from Jerusalem. [3] He will judge between *many peoples and will settle disputes for strong nations far and wide.* They will beat their swords into plowshares and their spears into pruning hooks. Nation will not take up sword against nation, nor will they train for war anymore. [4] **Everyone will sit under their own vine and under their own fig tree, and no one will make them afraid,** for Yahweh Almighty has spoken. [5] All the nations may walk in the name of their gods, but we will walk in the name of Yahweh our God for ever and ever. (Mic 4:1–5)

> **This is what Isaiah son of Amoz saw concerning Judah and Jerusalem**: [2] In the last days the mountain of Yahweh's temple will be established as the highest of the mountains; it will be exalted above the hills, and all nations will stream to it. [3] Many *peoples* will come and say, "Come, let us go up to the mountain of Yahweh, to the temple of the God of Jacob. He will teach us his ways, so that we may walk in his paths." The law will go out from Zion, the word of Yahweh from Jerusalem. [4] He will judge between *the nations and will settle disputes for many peoples.* They will beat their swords into plowshares and their spears into pruning hooks. Nation will not take up sword against nation, nor will they train for war anymore. [5] Come, descendants of Jacob, let us walk in the light of Yahweh. (Isa 2:1–5)

13. See Byargeon, "Relationship," 14–20; Schultz, *Search for Quotation*, 290–307.

14. See Schultz, *Search for Quotation*, 293, 304. The formula "for the mouth of Yahweh/Yahweh Almighty has spoken" (כִּי פִּי יהוה/יהוה צְבָאוֹת דִּבֵּר) only appears in Mic 4:4; Isa 1:20; 40:5; 58:14.

Micah speaks of prosperity for all peoples everywhere but within a sustained polytheistic international context (see note on Mic 4:1–5). The lack of a prosperity clause (Mic 4:4) and the lack of contrast between the faith of the congregation and the nations (4:5) completely shift the sense of Isaiah's treatment of the nations. The most important differences stem from the parallel cadence of the self-invitations in Isa 2:3 and 2:5. The "many peoples" of 2:3 seem to include both "the nations" in 2:4 and "Jacob" in 2:5 (bold signifies verbal parallels, and italics signify similar syntax and consonance):

> Many peoples will come and say, "**Come**, let us go up to the mountain of Yahweh, to the temple of the God of Jacob. He will teach us his ways, **so that we may walk** *in his paths.*" (Isa 2:3)

> "**Come**, descendants of Jacob, **let us walk** *in the light of Yahweh.*" (2:5)

The identical language of the main verbs of the self-invitations—"Come . . . so that we may walk/let us walk" (לְכוּ . . . וְנֵלְכָה)—identify the overlap between the intentions of "many peoples" (2:3) and "Jacob" (2:5), even if "many peoples" does not include Jacob. This sets up striking oral consonance between the respective objects of their intentions, "in his paths" (*be'orehotav,* בְּאֹרְחֹתָיו) and "in the light" (*be'or,* בְּאוֹר). By this close identification Isaiah uses the vision of the temple-going and Torah-obeying diverse international congregation of the last days and applies it to his own congregation: "Come, descendants of Jacob, let us walk in the light of Yahweh" (2:5). Future hopes speak to present needs. The theological focus of the vision of the mountain in Isaiah as donor context needs to be kept in mind when evaluating its reuse in Micah.

4:1~Exod 21:10 (C) (passing up standard support of concubine). Isaiah condemns the proud daughters of Zion (Isa 3:16). He spells out the loss of their excessive luxuries and affliction and humiliation (3:17–24). The final humiliation comes with a shortage of eligible males through the losses of war (3:25–26). These once-haughty society women now need to share men in a seven-to-one ratio, even giving up the required standards of food and clothing for arranged marriages of female debt slaves (4:1; Exod 21:10). Amos's condemnation of the affluent women of Samaria humiliates them as cows of Bashan (Amos 4:1–3). Isaiah takes a similar tactic, shifting from arrogant outstretched necks to bartering away debt-slave rights just to have an opportunity to bear a child (Isa 3:16; 4:1). The relationship between the law and the prophetic oracle is mostly thematic.

6:8~Gen 1:26; 3:22; 11:7 (C) (divine plural pronouns). Yahweh's use of first-person plural pronouns appears in Gen 1:26; 3:22; 11:7; and Isa 6:8. Within the broader scriptural context, all four cases include celestial figures.[15] In any case, the deity's use of first-

---

15. Compare first-person plural pronouns in Gen 1:26 with sons of God at creation in Job 38:7; first-person plural pronouns in Gen 3:22 with guardian and sword in 3:24; first-person plural pronouns in Gen 11:7 with sons of God by

person plural address in Isaiah's vision, and possibly in the comment "born to us" in Isa 9:6[5], may relate to the accounts of divine use of first-person plural discourse in Genesis.

6:9–10*~Deut 29:2–4*[1–3] (B) (obstructing eyes, ears, hearts) (* see concealing network). The shocking goal of Isaiah's ministry to obstruct his constituents stands at the headwaters of a running theme in Isaiah.[16] The divine commission of Isaiah adapts and strengthens the tradition of obstruction appearing at the beginning of Torah's new covenant (Deut 29:2–4[1–3]).[17] Paul further develops the connection to this Torah tradition (Rom 11:8//Deut 29:4[3]+Isa 29:10). The language for making the heart "fat" (lit.; cf. "calloused" NIV) differs from the language of hardening the pharaoh's heart between each plague, even if the broader concept of divinely sponsored obstruction overlaps.[18] The running theme of the divine obstruction of Israel likewise requires a divine solution (see note on Jer 31:31–34). In the present context note the strengthening of the obstruction in the call of Isaiah (bold and underlining signify verbal parallels, italics signify thematic similarity, and broken underlining signifies irony):

> Moses summoned all the Israelites and said to them: **Your eyes have seen** all that Yahweh did in Egypt to Pharaoh, to all his officials and to all his land. With **your own eyes you saw** those great trials, those signs and great wonders. But to this day Yahweh has not given you a **heart** that *understands* or **eyes that see** or **ears that hear.** (Deut 29:2–4†[1–3])

> He said, "Go and tell this people: "'Be ever **hearing**, but never *understanding*; be ever **seeing**, but never perceiving.' Make the **heart** of this people calloused; make **their ears** dull and close their **eyes**. Otherwise **they might see with their eyes, hear with their ears,** *understand with* **their hearts,** and turn and be healed." (Isa 6:9–10)

6:13~Exod 19:6; Deut 7:6 (C) (holy seed). After the work of the prophet that chops down the forest of Israel, the only thing left is the "holy seed" that is its stump (Isa 6:13). The expression "holy seed" seems to be based on "holy nation" (Exod 19:6) and "holy people" (Deut 7:6), which accents Israel as belonging to Yahweh as his own treasure. In Isaiah's use the possible interpretive expression pivots on the holy seed's place within the deforested wasteland that was Israel. The expressions "shoot" and "root" coming up from (the stump of) Jesse speak of the renewed hope based on Yahweh's enduring fidelity to his covenant (Isa 11:1, 10).

---

whom to divide the peoples in Deut 32:8 LXX/4QDeut^j/4Q37; and first-person plural pronouns in Isa 6:8 with seraphim in 6:2–3. See note on Ps 8:3–8[4–9].

16. On obstruction of eyes, ears, heart, and reversals, see Isa 6:9–10; 29:10; 30:20; 32:3–4; 35:5; 42:18–20; 48:8; 63:17; cf. 30:9–10. Also see McLaughlin, "Use of Isaiah 6, 9–10," 1–25.

17. The trio of "heart," "eyes," and "ears" appears in Deut 29:4[3]; Isa 6:10; 32:3–4; Jer 5:21 (Tigay, *Deuteronomy*, 398, n. 4).

18. The use of "make heavy" (כבד Hif) in Exod 8:15[11]; 10:1 comes closest to "make fat" (שמן Hif) in Isa 6:10. See footnote in note on Josh 11:20 for a list of synonyms in harden pharaoh's heart contexts.

7:1//2 Kgs 16:5 (B) (collaborative opposition of Rezin of Damascus and Pekah of Israel). The opening of Isa 7 mostly matches verbatim the lead-in of the narrative of Ahaz's self-initiated vassalage to Tiglath-pileser (2 Kgs 16:5–9). Elsewhere the evidence suggests Isa 36–39 was adapted from 2 Kgs 18–20 or a source virtually identical to it (see notes on Isa 36–39; 38:21–22). This suggests that Isa 7:1 should be considered a candidate for verbal coordination with the narrative of Ahaz's vassalage in 2 Kgs 16. Irrespective of the direct versus indirect relationship and direction of dependence, the parallel invites mutual crossover interpretation (Isa 7:1//2 Kgs 16:5).

7:12~Deut 6:16 (B) (not testing Yahweh). The prophet urges Ahaz to ask for a sign of assurance to strengthen him to trust the word of protection during the conflict (Isa 7:11). Ahaz refuses with a pious-sounding answer apparently alluding to a tradition that appears in Deut 6:16. The prohibition against testing Yahweh stems from Israel's incessant failures to trust him in the wilderness (italics signify verbal parallels):[19]

> *Do not put Yahweh* your God *to the test* as you did at Massah. (Deut 6:16)

> But Ahaz said, "I will not ask; *I will not put Yahweh to the test.*" (Isa 7:12)

The reader aware of the backstory of vassalage to Tiglath-pileser referenced in Isa 7:1//2 Kgs 16:5 recognizes Ahaz's phony piety. All this talk of a sign sets up a contrast in Isaiah between Ahaz and Hezekiah (see note on Isa 36–39).[20] In addition, the devastating arrogance of Ahaz stands at a major turning point in the prophetic tradition. Unlike the earliest prophets who spoke of punishment from Yahweh himself, now beginning with Isaiah and Micah, Yahweh uses the Mesopotamian empires and siege warfare to punish Israel.[21]

10:26~Judg 7:25+Exod 14:16 (C) (judgment like Midian at rock of Oreb and staff over the sea). Isaiah uses two ancient traditions of military divine intervention as a simile for the beating that Yahweh gives Assyria: the defeat of Midianite leaders during Gideon's campaign and the use of a staff at the sea (Isa 10:26; Judg 7:25; Exod 14:16; cf. Ps 83:9, 11[10, 12]).

11:15–16*~Exod 23:20* (C) (return highway like exodus) (* see new exodus network). Isaiah uses the exodus from Egypt as an expectational type of the return from Mesopotamian exile. The literary signal of an explicit type requires the use of "like," "as," or "according to" (in this case, כַּאֲשֶׁר). Isaiah applies the language of simile to "highway" (מְסִלָּה) in the desert (Isa 11:16). This imagery taps into Yahweh's provision of a delegate to guide Israel on the "way" (דֶּרֶךְ) to the land of promise (Exod 23:20). This forward-looking

19. See Exod 15:25; 17:2, 7; Num 14:22; Deut 33:8; Ps 78:18, 41, 56; 95:9; 106:14.

20. Also compare the reverse use of Deut 6:16 in Matt 4:7//Luke 4:12.

21. See Bloch-Smith, "Impact," 25. Note the use of climactic stages of wrath under desperation of siege warfare turned to cannibalism, see Isa 9:20[19]; Mic 3:2–3; cf. Lev 26:29; Deut 28:53–57.

type stands at the headwaters of the major theme of new exodus in Isaiah.[22] Isaiah's new exodus serves as a rich basis for reuse in the oracles against the nations (Isa 19:23), the postexilic prophets (Zech 4:7; Mal 3;1) and each of the four Gospels (e.g., Mark 1:2–3).

16:1~2 Kgs 3:4 (C) (Moab sends tribute of sheep). If Isa 16:1 plays off the memory of the tribute of sheep from Moab under Mesha (2 Kgs 3:4), it does so by shifting the historical beneficiary from Samaria to Zion. Such a Jerusalem-centered view matches the lingering authority of the long-past regional empire of David in Amos and Micah (see notes on Amos 9:11–12; Mic 5:2[1]).

16:13–14~15:1–16:12 (B) (downsizing hopes of Moab). The opening of Isa 16:12—"And it will be when" (lit.)—makes it sound like this first brief notice offers an update to the preceding oracle. The short notice signals the incongruity between Moab's seeking help at the people's shrines and the preceding hope for Moab grounded in the restored tent of David (Isa 16:5). Then, a second update has been appended, explicitly adjusting the previous oracle.

> *This is the word Yahweh has already spoken concerning Moab. But now Yahweh says*: "Within three years, as a servant bound by contract would count them, Moab's splendor and all her many people will be despised, and her survivors will be very few and feeble." (16:13–14, emphasis mine)

While this adjustment seems to delimit the extent of Moab's hope, that hope nevertheless remains. This adjustment does not change Moab's anticipated refuge for justice and righteousness under the tent of David. But the scope of Moab's hope has been reduced. The juxtaposition of the two appended updates raises the possibility that Moab's sustained prayers to her own gods in Isa 16:12 may somehow relate to her downsized survival in 16:13–14. Alternatively, the signal event of treading down Moab to the dust in 25:10–12 may have been a factor giving rise to the second update in 16:13–14. In any case, the limited remnant spoken of in the second update sets up Jeremiah's remarkable expectation for the reversal of Moab's fortunes (Jer 48:47).

19:23~11:16 (B) (highway between Assyria and Egypt). Like Moab in Isa 15:5; 16:4–5, the surprising imagery of hope for Judah is extended to Egypt and Assyria.

23:17–18~Deut 23:18[19] (C) (wages of Tyre's prostitution sanctified to Yahweh). The imagery of Isa 23:17–18 shocks readers. Torah rejects prostitutes' wages for the temple, which eliminates sacred prostitution often associated with fertility shrines (Deut 23:18[19]). Elsewhere the prophets affirm this principle and refuse financial gain for God's people from the wages of prostitutes (Mic 1:7; cf. Hos 9:1). The surprising interpretive moves of Isaiah include the restoration of Tyre as a prostitute and one who supports Yahweh (Isa 23:16–18).[23] One difference should be registered. Whereas the wages of

---

22. See Isa 11:16; 35:8; 40:3; 42:16; 43:16, 19; 48:17; 49:11; 62:10; cf. 19:23; 51:10; 52:11–12; 58:14; Jer 31:9, 21.
23. See NET note on Isa 23:18.

actual sacred prostitution are rejected in Mic 1:7, the imagery of Tyre as a prostitute serves as a taunting simile for her commercial merchandizing in Isa 23:18.

24:2~Hos 4:9 (C) (as people so priest). Hosea and Isaiah use an identical phrase not appearing elsewhere in Scripture, "as people so priest," to get at comprehensive judgment (Isa 24:2; Hos 4:9 lit). If Isaiah relies on this idea he expands its all-inclusiveness with "as master so servant, as mistress so maidservant," and so on (Isa 24:2 lit.).

24:5~Gen 9:16 (C) (everlasting covenant). The phrase "everlasting covenant" appears occasionally in Scripture, especially in reference to the Noahic, Abrahamic, Davidic, and new covenants, as well as the Sabbath. Proposals for the identity of the broken "everlasting covenant" include the Mosaic or a bundling of Noahic-Abrahamic-Sabbath together, but do not adequately connect to the broad stereotypical language and intentional universal scope of Isa 24–27.[24] The context of global devastation in Gen 6–9 and Isa 24 includes thematic similarities and limited verbal correspondence of the phrases "the windows of the heavens/heights are opened" and "everlasting covenant" (Gen 7:11; 9:16; Isa 24:5, 18). If the prophet has this context in mind, he offers a twofold, deeply ironic interpretation: the nations have broken the covenant God said he would not break, and whereas the flood brought a new beginning, Isaiah threatens an end.[25] The lack of verbal agreement cautions against making deductions.

25:6~Exod 24:11 (D); ~Deut 14:26 (D); ~Ps 22:26[27] (D) (eating before Yahweh on the mountain). The powerful imagery of feasting before Yahweh on the mountain has been identified with several contexts, like the feast during worship pilgrimages and the needy who join the congregation, but without compelling evidence of allusion (Deut 14:26; Ps 22:26[27]).[26]

25:10b–12~Num 24:17*+Gen 3:14–15 (C) (trampling Moab to the dust) (* see Davidic covenant and Judah-king networks). If the textual issue in Num 24:17 should be resolved as "crush the foreheads of Moab," as preferred by most modern committee translations, then it seems Isaiah may be interpreting Balaam's oracle together with the curse against the serpent.[27] Whether a quotation or interpretive paraphrase, Jeremiah reads it as "foreheads" of Moab (Jer 48:45 lit.).[28] The potential interpretive connection between crushing the forehead of Moab and the serpent is strengthened here by Moab being cast down to the "dust"—the serpent diet before a head crushing (Isa 25:12; cf. Gen 3:14–15). The prophetic serpent/Moab imagery uses the humiliation of Moab as a symbolic parallel for the defeat of the original enemy in the garden. Isaiah takes the imagery further by developing a quasi-taunt of Moab trodden down and swimming in a dung heap (Isa 25:10).

24. See Polaski, "Reflections of a Mosaic Covenant," 61; Hibbard, "Isaiah 24–27 and Trito-Isaiah," 195–97.

25. See Seitz, *Isaiah 1–39*, 181–82; Childs, *Isaiah*, 179; Chisholm, "Everlasting Covenant," 249. For a view similar to the one presented here independently, see Hays, *Origins*, 234–37.

26. Contra Delitzsch, *Isaiah*, 439; Childs, *Isaiah*, 184.

27. The evidence favors "crush the forehead [קדקד] of Moab" (SP) versus "crush the borderlands [קרקר] of Moab" (Num 24:17 MT). See Schnittjer, "Blessing of Judah," 23–24.

28. Jeremiah 48:45 is part of a MT plus (not included in LXX).

28:13//28:10+8:15 (B) (strange speech and judgment). Isaiah twice repeats a rhythmic pair of phrases lacking meaningful words: "*tsav latsav tsav latsav, qav laqav qav laqav*" (צַו לָצָו צַו לָצָו קַו לָקָו קַו לָקָו) (28:10, 13). Whether the phrase mimics a meaningless childhood chant that features two adjacent letters of the Hebrew alphabet (like an ABC song) or incoherent drunken mumbling need not be decided here (see 28:7–8, 9b).[29] In any case, if they (the Northern Kingdom) want their leaders to utter meaningless noise (28:10), then Yahweh shall speak to them with the meaningless noise they crave (28:13) by means of "foreign lips and strange tongues" (28:11; cf. 33:19; Jer 5:15). The prophet splices a recycled phrase onto Yahweh's meaningless noise which hints at who comes with strange tongues, namely, the Assyrians (emphases signify verbal parallels):

> Many of them **will stumble**; they will fall **and be broken, they will be snared and captured** [by the Assyrians]. (Isa 8:15; cf. 8:7)
>
> [Drunken priests and prophets say,] "*Blah blah blah. Yak yak yak. A little here, a little here*..." So then, the word of Yahweh to them shall become "*Blah blah blah. Yak yak yak. A little here, a little here*" in order that as **they stumble** backward; **they will be broken and snared and captured** (28:10, 13 lit.).

The prophet immediately pivots with "Therefore hear the word of Yahweh, you scoffers who rule this people in Jerusalem" (28:14). The entire satirical condemnation of the nonsense-cravers of the Northern Kingdom serves as an elaborate rhetorical opening act to condemn the prophet's constituents among Jerusalem's elite.

28:21~2 Sam 5:20+Josh 10:10 (C) (reversal of divine intervention at Mount Perazim and Gibeon).

29:1, 3~2 Sam 5:6 (C) (besieging Ariel). Isaiah reverses a pair of ancient military divine interventions to demonstrate the shift in Yahweh's posture toward Israel. He uses the preposition "like" or "as" to refashion as simile historic moments of salvation—"like Mount Perazin" and "like the Valley of Gibeon" (Isa 28:21 lit.). The use of historical elements as simile by adding prepositions appears frequently in Hosea. Isaiah's brief exegetical interventions invert deliverance at Perazim and Gibeon as symbols of impending doom (2 Sam 5:20; Josh 10:10). The choice of Perazim may have additional subtleties. The name Perazim recalls when Yahweh "broke out like waters" (2 Sam 5:20 lit.). Isaiah has been emphasizing the flood-like decimation of the military attack in line with typical contemporary royal Assyrian propaganda (Isa 8:7–8; 28:15; 30:28).[30] Isaiah switches out

---

29. Elsewhere Isaiah referred to Egypt as a place of "strange speech" using a similar term (18:2, 7). The meaning of "*qav qav*" (קָו־קָו) is disputed. The NIV's "strange speech" and JPSB's "gibber and chatter" in Isa 18:2, 7 follow "II קַו" versus "I קַו," BDB 875, 876.

30. The flood imagery is something of a stock phrase of military destruction in the contemporary royal annals of Tiglath-pileser III (744–727 BCE) (e.g., *ARAB* 1:284, §§790, 791). Also see Jer 47:2; Ps 124:4–5.

"breaking out" and replaces it with "rise up," which thematically matches the recurring overwhelming flood imagery (28:21). Isaiah goes even further by using David's besieging of Jerusalem, here repeatedly referred to as Ariel, as a symbol of the city's impending doom (29:1). In a brilliant twist of prophetic imagery, he uses Jerusalem's first Hebrew king as a simile of the David-like siege of divine wrath (29:3).

36–39/~/2 Kgs 18–20 (siege of Jerusalem and Hezekiah's pride). The dischronologized rearrangement of the healing procedure from after Yahweh's promise in Kings to after the sign of the shadow and Hezekiah's psalm in Isaiah, as well as its attendant syntactical adjustments, suggests that the editors of the book of Isaiah rely on Kings.[31] The present investigation treats the account in Isa 36–39 as an interpretive revision of its parent tradition housed in 2 Kgs 18–20 (regarding direction of dependence see note on 38:20–21). Note a synoptic comparison of Hezekiah's crises:[32]

	2 Kings	**Isaiah**
opening frame[a]	18:1–2	—
evaluation formula[a]	18:3	—
reforms, activities, and theological evaluation	18:4–8	—
synchronization with fall of Samaria	18:9–12	—
invasion of Judah introduced[b]	18:13	36:1
Hezekiah pays tribute to Sennacherib[c]	18:14–16	—
Sennacherib invades Judah[d]	18:17–19:37	36:2–37:38
Hezekiah's illness	20:1–6	38:1–6
topical application of figs	20:7–8	—
sign of reversed shadow	20:9–11	38:7–8
song of Hezekiah	—	38:9–20
topical application of figs	—	38:20–21
visitation of Babylonian envoys	20:12–19	39:1–8
death of Hezekiah	20:20–21	—

[a] On standard royal formulas in Kings, see Table C11 in Chronicles.

[b] As with Isaiah, the Chronistic parallels also begin with Sennacherib's invasion (2 Kgs 18:13//Isa 36:1//2 Chr 32:1).

[c] The submission of Hezekiah and tribute (2 Kgs 18:14–16) broadly correspond to the royal annals of Sennacherib (*ANET*, 288a).

[d] For a later note on the assassination of Sennacherib (681 BCE) in the royal chronicles of Nabonidus (555–539), see *ANET*, 309a.

---

31. See Cogan and Tadmor, *II Kings*, 256–57; Williamson, "Hezekiah," 51–52. Also see note on Isa 38:21–22.

32. Also see Chronistic parallels in note on 2 Chr 32:1–23. In this study "Chronistic" refers to the Chronicles but not Ezra-Nehemiah (see Glossry).

If available to them, the editors of Isaiah chose not to include the executive summary of Hezekiah's unmatched faithfulness or Hezekiah's submission and payment of tribute to Sennacherib (2 Kgs 18:5–6, 14–16). This appears to be a conscious edit since Isaiah includes the heading (18:13//Isa 36:1; see the synoptic comparison above). The Deuteronomist's characterization of Hezekiah adopted the leading word the Assyrian field commander used of him (2 Kgs 18:5; see note ad loc.). The field commander spoke of Hezekiah's trust/faith (בטח) six times in his first speech and two more times in follow-up correspondence, all of which have been retained in Isaiah (18:19, 20, 21[2x], 22, 24, 30; 19:10; Isa 36:4, 5, 6[2x], 7, 9, 15; 37:10).[33] Without the interpretive preamble, the narrative shows rather than tells. This move effectively redirects the field commander's taunts from Hezekiah's response to Isaiah's message (see Table I2).

By opening the Hezekiah narrative at the aqueduct of the upper pool, readers can contrast Ahaz and Hezekiah for themselves (italics signify verbal parallel):

> Then the king of Assyria sent his field commander with a large army from Lachish to King Hezekiah at Jerusalem. When the commander stopped *at the aqueduct of the Upper Pool, on the road to the Launderer's Field*. . . .(Isa 36:2)

> Then Yahweh said to Isaiah, "Go out, you and your son Shear-Jashub, to meet Ahaz at the end of *the aqueduct of the Upper Pool, on the road to the Launderer's Field*." (7:3)

Readers should keep in mind the difference in the situation between Isaiah's offering a sign to Ahaz at the aqueduct versus the Assyrian field commander's ridiculing the faith of Hezekiah. The editors of Isa 36–39 make few changes, but one relates to the sign Hezekiah requests beyond the previous sign Isaiah had granted (37:30; 38:7). The exegetical intervention in Isa 38:22 requires more attention (see separate note below), but for the moment it can show in broad terms how importing the narratives of 2 Kgs 18–20// Isa 36–39 makes Hezekiah a counterpoint to Ahaz (emphasis signifies verbal parallel).

> "Ask Yahweh your God for *a sign*, whether in the deepest depths or in the highest heights." But Ahaz said, "I will not ask; I will not put Yahweh to the test." (7:11–12)

> Hezekiah asked, "What will be *the sign* that I will go up to the temple of Yahweh?" (38:22†)

The similarities and differences between Ahaz and Hezekiah in the narratives of Isa 7 and 36–39 provide guidance to properly evaluate the oracles associated with their

33. See Childs, *Isaiah and the Assyrian Crisis*, 85.

troubles in 8–12 and 28–35 respectively (with the oracles against the nations and universal judgment in between, 13–23, 24–27). But there is more.

The speeches of the arrogant Assyrian field commander provide mocking counterparts to Isaiah's oracles. Just as situation comedy benefits from a "straight man," the taunts of the field commander strengthen the force of the prophet's message. Importing Hezekiah's narrative nearly "as is" with the field commander's speeches retained in full exegetically clarifies Isaiah's message (see Table I2).

TABLE I2: THEMATIC PARALLELS IN THE FIELD COMMANDER'S TAUNTS AND ISAIAH'S MESSAGES‡

	field commander	Isaiah
worthlessness of Egypt as ally	36:6	30:2
futility of Judah trusting horses	36:8–9	31:3
Assyrian domination over peoples and gods	36:19–20	10:9–11
Yahweh shall deliver Jerusalem	36:15, 18, 20	29:5–8; 31:4–5, 8–9; cf. 37:35

‡ See Childs, *Isaiah*, 84; Blenkinsopp, *Isaiah 1–39*, 472.

The Deuteronomistic Hezekiah narratives end with Isaiah warning the king that the treasures of Jerusalem and royal descendants would be taken captive to Babylon (2 Kgs 20:17–18). Hezekiah interprets this as a distant threat as he blesses himself for peace in his own days (20:19). In Kings this leads directly into Manasseh's rebellion which reinforces Hezekiah's shortsightedness. By importing the Hezekiah narratives into Isaiah, the same episode, with only very light edits, takes on a dramatic new function. Isaiah's warning of eventual captivity jump cuts to prophetic consolation of Jerusalem whose people suffer exile in Babylon (Isa 39:7–8; 40:1). Isaiah's warning to Hezekiah in Isa 39:6–7 now serves as a point of reference for the message of the new exodus and restoration (40–55; 56–66). The exegetical repurposing of the same Hezekiah narratives comes by means of a new home among Isaiah's oracles. The timing of this editorial move and other edits of Isaiah do not need to be worked out for the broad interpretive points discussed here. It is enough to note that Sennacherib's death dates two decades after the siege of Jerusalem in 681 BCE (37:38).

In sum, integrating a lightly edited version of the Hezekiah narratives into Isaiah initiates mutual exegetical interconnections between it and the lyrical prophecies (e.g., Table I2). Beginning at the aqueduct (36:2) and retaining the field commander's ridicule (36:4–10, 13–20; 37:10–13) creates the necessary interpretive framework to guide readerly theological apprehension of the first half of Isaiah. Likewise, Isaiah's warning to Hezekiah provides a point of reference for the second half of Isaiah. This represents exegesis by arrangement (see Figure I3).

FIGURE I3: EXEGETICAL EFFECT OF HEZEKIAH NARRATIVES ON ISAIAH 7 AND 28–35

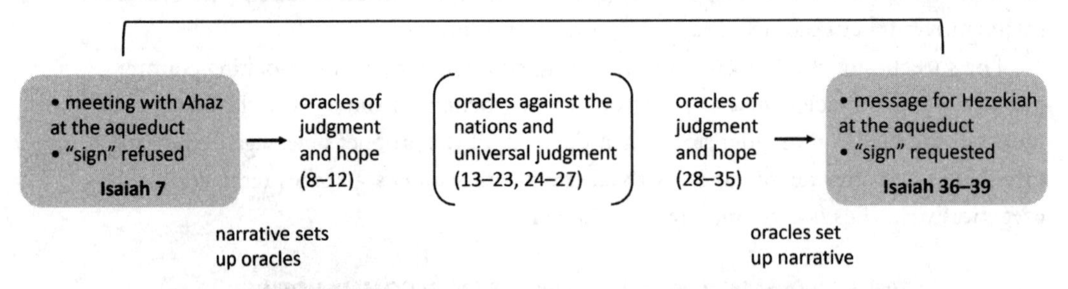

38:21–22/~/2 Kgs 20:7–8 (topical application of figs). The short exchange between Isaiah and Hezekiah concerning a topical application of figs to a boil gets adjusted and relocated (2 Kgs 20:7–8//Isa 38:21–22; see dotted line in synoptic table in note on Isa 36–39). This interpretive intervention contains the evidence necessary to detect direction of dependence. The nature of the set of changes works for Isaiah using Kings or a source exactly like it, but not the other way around. A synopsis of the sequences of the exchange can simplify the discussion here (shaded element relocated in Isaiah).

2 Kgs 20:1–5a	(a)	Isaiah tells Hezekiah that Yahweh has heard his prayer for healing	(A)	Isa 38:1–5a
20:5b	(b)	Promise to heal Hezekiah in three days to go to temple	—	
20:6	(c)	Promise to add fifteen years to Hezekiah and deliver the city from the Assyrians	(C)	38:5b–6
20:7	(d)	Isaiah diagnoses topical application of figs, attendants apply it, Hezekiah **recovered**	—	
20:8	(e)	Hezekiah asks for a sign of healing and going up to the temple	—	
20:9–11	(f)	Isaiah gives the sign of shadow going backwards	(F)	38:7–8
	—	Hezekiah writes a psalm of thanks after he is healed	(G)	38:9–20
	—	Isaiah diagnoses topical application of figs, attendants apply it, so that Hezekiah **will recover**	(D)	38:21
	—	Hezekiah asks for a sign of going up to the temple	(E)	38:22
20:12–13	(h)	Hezekiah receives representatives of Marduk-baladan	(H)	39:1–2

To summarize the sequences: **(a/A, b)** In Kings, Isaiah sends word to Hezekiah that he would be healed and "on the third day go up to the temple" which needs to be deleted in Isaiah since it does not get discussed until later (2 Kgs 20:5a//Isa 38:5). **(c/C)** Then in both accounts Yahweh promises to add fifteen years to Hezekiah's life and deliver the city from Assyria (2 Kgs 20:6//Isa 38:5b–6). This means that the entire episode, in both accounts, is a flashback or dischronologized narrative set at some point before the siege and deliverance of Jerusalem in the previous chapters. **(d)** In Kings, Isaiah instructs the king's attendants to use a topical application of figs on Hezekiah's boil; they do and then he recovered (2 Kgs 20:7). **(e)** Next, Hezekiah asks for a sign of healing (20:8). **(f/F)** In Kings, Isaiah offers a sign as Hezekiah requested (20:9–11), but in Isaiah after the promise (Isa 38:5b–6) Isaiah continues and offers a sign without being asked (38:7). **(h)** Then in Kings, Hezekiah receives Babylonian representatives (2 Kgs 20:12–13). **(G, D, E, H)** But in Isaiah, after the sign, Hezekiah writes a psalm of praise for his healing (Isa 38:9–20). This seems to look back to the near-death illness and the promise of fifteen years (38:1, 5b, 7–8). Then after Isaiah prescribes a topical application of figs for a boil (38:21), Hezekiah responds by asking for a sign that he would go up to the temple (38:22). Based on this comparison, it is now possible to handle three issues related to the exegetical intervention in Isa 38:21–22.

First, the exchange about the topical application of figs and the sign have been mildly edited in terms of verb form (regular font signifies verbatim parallels, underlining signifies stylistic change of synonym, italics signify changes in verb form, and bold signifies deletion):

> Then Isaiah said, "<u>Take</u> a poultice of figs." **They did so** and applied it to the boil, *and he recovered.* Hezekiah asked **Isaiah,** "What will be the sign that **Yahweh will heal me and that** I will go up to the temple of Yahweh **on the third day from now**?" (2 Kgs 20:7–8†)

> Isaiah had said, "<u>Take up</u> a poultice of figs and apply it to the boil, *and he will recover.*" Hezekiah asked, "What will be the sign that I will go up to the temple of Yahweh?" (Isa 38:21–22†)

The past tense verb form of "recovered" (wci) in 2 Kgs 20:7 gets changed to "will recover" (impf.) in Isa 38:21 to match the opening: "you will not recover" becomes "he will recover" (38:1, 21).[34]

Second, the exchange has been streamlined. The tightening by deletion apparently means to focus exclusively on the boil as potential ritual impairment versus a life-threatening condition. The boil (שְׁחִין), even when it heals, requires examination by the priest to determine if the post-boil skin irregularity causes ritual impurity (Lev 13:18–23).[35]

34. See Williamson, "Hezekiah," 50. The difference between "and he recovered" (וַיֶּחִי, wci) (2 Kgs 20:7) and "and he will recover" (וְיֶחִי, *vav* + impf.) (Isa 38:21) involves only vowel pointing not consonantal change. Note LXX of 2 Kgs 20:7 reads "it shall cure him" (ὑγιάσει, corresponding to וְיֶחִי) with Isa 38:21 (see Burney, *Notes*, 348; *BHS* of 2 Kgs 20:7 n. e).

35. See Hoffer, "Exegesis of Isaiah 38.21," 77–78.

This prompts Hezekiah's question not about healing but about a sign to go up to the temple (Isa 38:22). The revised version of the exchange pivots exclusively on questions of ritual ability to participate in temple worship.

Third, the relocation of the exchange has created difficulties for modern interpreters. The NEB and REB "repair" the context by relocating Isa 38:21–22 between 38:6 and 7, where they think it belongs. The NIV, NRSV, ESV, KJV, and others avoid the apparent difficulty by translating the standard dialogue verb form "then Hezekiah said" (וַיֹּאמֶר wci, lit.) as though it were pluperfect "Hezekiah had said."[36] These strategies focus on how to revert the flashback away from its new placement—they read against the sense of the text and effectively undo Isaiah's exegetical advancement. But 38:21–22 needs to be where it is, immediately after the ending of Hezekiah's psalm. The shift from first-person singular to first-person plural in the final lines of Hezekiah's psalm invites the king's constituents to regard the king's healing as a typological trigger for community worship at the temple:[37]

> Yahweh will save **me**, and **we** will sing with stringed instruments all the days of **our** lives in the temple of Yahweh. (38:20, emphasis mine)

The exegetical enhancements function pedagogically. Hezekiah's healing does not merely signal his own personal physical welfare for fifteen more years to show off to the Babylonians. Hezekiah's shortened question about a sign now deals exclusively with going to the temple.[38] His "salvation" activates a lifetime of worship for the congregation.

In sum, the exegetical intervention in Isa 38:21–22 includes paraphrasing and streamlining to focus on salvation of the king as time for the congregation to worship. This shifts the function of the dialogue about the topical application of figs to the more profound need of returning to the temple. This effectively anticipates the consolation of Jerusalem in Isa 40–66.

40:1~Lam 1:2, 9, 16, 17, 21 (B) (comfort of Jerusalem).[39] The poet of Lamentations personifies Jerusalem in her misery with no one to comfort her. The extensive lament captures the moment of the city's desolation. Narratives contextualize the fall of Jerusalem in their forward motion, and prophetic messages situate the city's destruction and exile between kingdom and return. Not so with Lamentations. The lament forever embodies "durational time," turning the city's grief over and over perpetually without before or after.[40]

---

36. See ibid., 69.

37. See Williamson, "Hezekiah," 52.

38. See Raabe, "King Hezekiah," 73.

39. No direction of dependence is presumed here. The discussion follows the inferred "storyline" from absence of comfort (Lam 1:16, etc.) to comfort (Isa 40:1).

40. See Balentine, "Poetry of Exile," 346; Berlin, *Lamentations*, 1.

The opening of the second half of Isaiah answers the anguish and establishes its overarching purpose (italics signify verbal parallels):[41]

> [Jerusalem weeps] "No one is near to *comfort* me, no one to restore my spirit." Zion stretches out her hands, but there is no one to *comfort* her. (Lam 1:16, 17; cf. 1:2, 9, 21)

> *Comfort, comfort* my people, says your God. (Isa 40:1)

40:3–4*~11:15–16* (B)+26:7–8 (C)+Exod 23:20–21* (B) (highway in the wilderness) (* see new exodus network). Isaiah brings together several scriptural expectations in an interpretive blend that fronts the extended treatment of the consolation of Israel (Isa 40–55). Yahweh promised Israel that he would send his delegate with them, in addition to later agreeing to keep his own presence with them (Exod 23:20; 33:17; 34:9). Isaiah extends this ancient promise into an explicit forward-looking typological expectation of a new exodus from Mesopotamian exile using "as" (Isa 11:15–16). Isaiah seems to heighten the divine presence in the return from exile by means of the righteous who wait upon "your name" (26:6–7). The presence of Yahweh himself shall lead the return through the wilderness (40:3).[42] Isaiah's brilliant recycling and intensification of the ancient Torah expectation becomes a lightning rod for explaining the culmination of redemption.[43] Note the progression (bold, underlining, and italics signify verbal parallels at the level of roots; and wavy underlining signifies thematic similarity):

> See, I am sending an angel ahead of you to guard you along **the way** and to bring you to the place I have prepared. . . . my Name is in him. (Exod 23:20, 21b)

> Yahweh will dry up the gulf of the Egyptian sea; with a scorching wind he will sweep his hand over the Euphrates River. He will break it up into seven streams so that anyone can cross over in sandals. There will be a highway for the remnant of his people that is left from Assyria, as [כַּאֲשֶׁר] there was for Israel when they came up from Egypt. (Isa 11:15–16)

> The path of the righteous is *straight*; you, the Upright One, make the way of the righteous smooth. Yes, Yahweh, walking in the way of your laws, we wait for you; your name and renown are the desire of our hearts. (26:7–8)

---

41. On consolation, see Isa 40:1; 49:13; 51:3, 12, 19; 52:9; 54:11; 61:2; 66:13; and no more weeping 25:8; 30:19; 65:19.
42. See intermittent development of this theme: Isa 35:8; 42:16; 43:16, 19; 48:17; 49:11; 51:10; 52:11–12; 58:14.
43. See Zech 4:7, 9; Matt 3:3; Mark 1:2–3; Luke 3:4–6; John 1:23.

> A voice of one calling: "In the wilderness prepare **the way** for Yahweh; *make straight* in the desert a highway for our God. Every valley shall be raised up, every mountain and hill made low; the rough ground shall become level, the rugged places a plain." (40:3–4)

43:1–2, 7, 14–17, 19–20, 21~Gen 1+2:7+Exod 14–15 (B) (Israel's creator, redeemer, and wilderness provider).[44] Isaiah uses several connotation-laden terms that appear also in prominent Torah contexts on creation, redemption, and wilderness provision and applies these to Israel. Yahweh is Israel's creator and redeemer by virtue of the return from Babylonian exile.[45] The loaded terms include "create" (ברא) and "make" (עשׂה) of Gen 1, "form" (יצר) of Gen 2:7, and "redeem" (גאל) of Exod 15. But it would be a mistake to think Isaiah projected relations between Yahweh as creator and redeemer onto unrelated scriptural traditions. The magnetic relationship between creation and redemption stands out in Torah:

- "Spirit/wind" (רוּחַ) over the waters (Gen 1:2; Exod 14:21; 15:8, 10);
- "separating" the waters with two different but synonymous terms (בדל) (Gen 1:4, 6, 7, 14, 18) and (בקע) (Exod 14:16, 21, 29; 15:19);
- "dry ground" for life (יַבָּשָׁה) (Gen 1:9, 10; Exod 14:22, 29; 15:19); and other connections (see note on Deut 32:10–11).

Isaiah started with scriptural traditions already related at a fundamental level and redeployed them together to capture the spirit of the return.[46]

The translucent typological overlays of creation, redemption, and return invite mutually enriching interpretive connections. Isaiah frequently blends creation and redemption scriptural traditions in highly lyrical ways.

51:9–11~27:1+30:7+(>/<43:2, etc.) (C) (calling for ancient redemption once again). Elsewhere Isaiah polemically recasts imaginative religious traditions from competing cultures: personified Death who swallows the living into the underworld is itself swallowed

---

44. The set of exegetical allusions in Isa 43 stands for the running themes of creation and redemption in Isaiah.
Creation:
- >/<Isa 40:26, 28; 41:20; 42:5; 44:24; 45:7, 8, 9, 12, 18; 48:7; 54:16; 57:16, 19; 65:17, 18; 66:2, 22, create (creator)/form/make (maker) (ברא/יצר/עשׂה);
- >/<43:1, 7, 15, 21; 44:2, 21, 24; 45:11, creator/one who forms of Jacob/Israel/his creator/his maker (ברא/יצר יַעֲקֹב/יִשְׂרָאֵל/בראתיו/יצרו);
- 46:11, I formulated (יָצַרְתִּי);
- >/<44:2; 46:4; 49:5; 51:13; 54:5; 64:7, who made you/who formed me/us (עשׂך/יצרי/נו) (cf. 48:13, 16).

Redemption:
- >/<41:14; 43:1, 14; 44:6, 22, 23, 24; 47:4; 48:17, 20; 49:7, 26; 52:9; 54:5, 8; 59:20; 60:16; 63:9, 16, redeem; your(s.)/your(pl.)/his/our redeemer (גאל/ך/כם/ו/נו) (cf. Exod 6:6; 15:3; Mic 4:10; Ps 74:2; 77:15[16]; 78:35; 106:10);
- >/<Isa 51:10; 52:3; 62:12, the redeemed, be redeemed (cf. Ps 107:2).

45. See Anderson, "Exodus Typology," 185.
46. See Schnittjer, *Torah Story Video Lectures*, 11.2.

(Isa 25:8); Yahweh kills Leviathan, the nemesis sea serpent (27:1); and calling Egypt's sea serpent mascot-avatar Rahab the Do-Nothing (30:7; cf. Ps 89:9–10[10–11]).[47] Isaiah brings together elements from running taunt themes to once again call for a new exodus. In that sense the prophetic petition of Isa 51:9–11 does not exegete a particular individual new exodus tradition but a running tradition here represented by 43:2 (emphases signify verbal parallels):[48]

> In that day, Yahweh will punish with his sword—his fierce, great and powerful sword—Leviathan the gliding serpent, Leviathan the coiling serpent; he will slay the **monster** of the sea. (27:1)

> To Egypt, whose help is utterly useless. Therefore I call her <u>Rahab</u> the Do-Nothing. (30:7)

> When *you pass through the waters*, I will be with you; and when *you pass through* the rivers, they will not sweep over you. (43:2a)

> Awake, awake, arm of Yahweh, clothe yourself with strength! Awake, as in days gone by, as in generations of old. Was it not you who cut <u>Rahab</u> to pieces, who pierced that **monster** through? Was it not you who dried up the sea, *the waters* of the great deep, who made a road in the depths of the sea so that the redeemed *might pass through*? (51:9–10†)

The relative function of this typological call for redemption plays an important role in the sequence of Isaiah's new exodus. The lyrical prayer of Isa 51:9–11 opens with one of several twofold imperatives of the new exodus—e.g., "Comfort! Comfort!" (40:1); "Awake! Awake!" (51:9; 52:1); "Build up! Build up!" (57:14); "Cross through! Cross through! . . . Build up! Build up!" (62:10). The more immediate context includes a threefold use of pairs from the same verbal root imploring Yahweh, "Awake! Awake!" to redeem once again (51:9), before calling upon Jerusalem, "Wake yourself! Wake yourself!" (51:17 lit.), and again to Zion, "Awake! Awake!" (52:1).[49] The reinterpretation of the new exodus themes in Isa 51:9–11 returns again with explicit forward-looking typological literary signals, "as [כְּ] in generations of old," much like the programmatic forward-looking typological statement in Isa 11:15–16.

---

47. On Death, see "The Baʿlu Myth," *COS*, 1.86:266; Lotan the seven-headed sea serpent, see 1.86:265 (cf. multi-headed Leviathan Ps 74:14).

48. Isaiah 43:2 here represents Isaiah's running themes: drying the depths to make a path to cross over (Isa 11:15–16; 63:12–13; cf. Exod 15:8) and pathway to return to Zion (Isa 40:3; 43:2, 4, 16, 19). Morales demonstrates how creational echoes serve as undercurrents in Isa 51:9–10 and in other biblical dragon-slaying contexts (*Exodus*, 56–57).

49. The verb for "wake up" (עור) is used in imperative pairs as Q in Isa 51:9; 52:1; and as Hith in 51:17.

52:1a>/<51:9 (Awake! Awake!).

52:1b*~Lam 1:10* (B)+Deut 23:3–6*[4–7] (B) (uncircumcised and defiled will not enter you again) (* see assembly network).

52:2~Lam 2:10 (C) (down in dust). The repetition of imperatives to Zion in Isa 52:1 takes the next step from 51:9–11, 17. The lyrical typology of the new exodus of return to Zion develops along the lines of enduring security of the city. Lady Zion cried out in her slavery after she had been violently raped (Lam 1:1–2, 10). The prophet says get up and get dressed up (Isa 52:1). Her elders sit silently with dust on their heads (Lam 2:10). The prophet calls her to shake off the dust and get up (Isa 52:2; cf. 25:12; 26:5; 47:1). In the larger context the prophet voices Yahweh's message by double commands (italics and bold signify verbal parallels):[50]

> Comfort! comfort! . . . **Awake! Awake!** arm of Yahweh *clothe yourself with strength!* . . . **Wake yourself! Wake yourself! Get up Jerusalem!** . . . **Awake! Awake!** Zion *clothe yourself with strength!* (Isa 40:1; 51:9, 17; 52:1 lit.)

The poet personified Jerusalem as Yahweh's woman and the temple euphemistically as her "treasures" (Lam 1:10, see note ad loc.). The enemies who molested and raped Lady Jerusalem are the very ones who had been forbidden to "come into" the assembly—in an interpretive allusion of the law of the assembly (1:10; Deut 23:3–6[4–7]). The prophecy of Isaiah engages Lam 1:10 in light of its embedded or vertical context in the law of the assembly. The prophet interprets the identity of the military "enemy" who had been "forbidden to come into your assembly" as "uncircumcised" and "defiled," meaning ritually impaired. Notice the way Isa 52:1 activates the horizontal and vertical contexts of Lam 1:10 (bold signifies verbal parallels, and italics and broken underlining signify interpretation; on horizontal and vertical contexts see Figure NT1 and Glossary):

> No *Ammonite or Moabite or any of their descendants* may **enter the assembly of** *Yahweh* [לֹא־יָבֹא . . . בִּקְהַל יהוה], not even in the tenth generation. . . . Do not seek a treaty of friendship with them as long as you live. (Deut 23:3, 6[4, 7])

> The *enemy* laid hands on all her treasures; she saw *nations* **enter** [בָּאוּ] her sanctuary—*those you had forbidden* **to enter** ***your*** **assembly** [לֹא־יָבֹאוּ בַקָּהָל לָךְ]. (Lam 1:10†)

> Awake, awake, Zion, clothe yourself with strength! Put on your garments of splendor, Jerusalem, the holy city. The *uncircumcised* and *defiled* **will not enter** ***you*** again [לֹא יוֹסִיף יָבֹא־בָךְ]. (Isa 52:1)

50. No direction of dependence is presumed here. The discussion follows the inferred "storyline" of law (Deut 23), rape (Lam 1:10), renewed splendor (Isa 52:1).

Torah speaks of two kinds of others in different ways, but it consistently denotes two different kinds. One kind can never enter the assembly of Yahweh because they tried to damn Israel (Deut 23:3–6[4–7]). But the power of God's word foiled this plan, for "whoever curses you I will curse" (Gen 12:3; Num 24:9; Deut 23:5[6]). The other kind of foreigner may enter and in the third generation enjoys standing in the assembly of Yahweh (Deut 23:7–8[8–9]). Elsewhere Torah refers to those who must participate in Passover versus those who may not—circumcised and uncircumcised (Exod 12:43–51).[51] The same distinctions characterize the early Second Temple assembly. They banished some outsiders and welcomed others. Even the newly welcomed others excluded additional others based on whether they had "separated themselves" from ritual pollution unto the Torah of God (Ezra 6:21; Neh 9:2; 10:28[29]). Recognizing the two different kinds of others in Torah and the restoration helps to understand the twofold interpretation in Isa 52:1 versus Isa 56:1–8.

The prophet calls Zion to awaken from her humiliation and assures her of safety from violation by the uncircumcised and ritually polluted (Isa 52:1). Then, with no sleight of hand, he can speak of foreigners and eunuchs who join themselves to Yahweh in faithfulness to his covenant (56:1–8, this context also features interpretive allusion of Deut 23:1–8[2–9]). The issue does not turn on the specific terminology since both contexts use pairs of terms that would traditionally denote excluded others and/or states of exclusion—"Uncircumcised and ritually impaired" (עָרֵל וְטָמֵא) in Isa 52:1 (lit.) and "foreigner" and "eunuch" (בֶּן־הַנֵּכָר, סָרִיס) in 56:3.

Isaiah identifies the excluded pair of others and included pair of others using functional terms which makes all the difference (Isa 52:1; 56:3–7). Torah speaks of inclusion/exclusion with social and functional identities in play. The connotation of "foreigner" (בֶּן־נֵכָר) as excluded versus "residing foreigner" (גֵּר) as included stems from their juxtaposition in the standards for Passover (Exod 12:43–49). By covenantal function the foreigner is uncircumcised (12:43) while the residing foreigner is circumcised (12:48). Similarly, Ammonites and Moabites are not excluded by birth or ethnicity but as a class of people who refused hospitality to Israel even while seeking the condemnation of Israel by Israel's own God (Deut 23:3–6[4–7]). Isaiah maintains full continuity with the covenantal and ritual standings of the included/excluded of Torah but demonstrates that social function may be detached and rearranged. Neither the foreignness of the foreigner nor the ethnicity of the Ammonite relate to their exclusion. The exclusion/inclusion of classes of people relates to covenantal affiliation and fidelity and lack thereof. Table I4 summarizes the social versus functional identities and how these relate to inclusion/exclusion.[52]

---

51. See notes on Isa 56:1–8 and Ezek 44:9–16 and Table Ezk6.

52. The approach to two kinds of others in Tables I4, Ezk6, and kindred discussions here developed independently. For somewhat similar views, see Trimm, "Did Yhwh?" 534–35; Kaminsky, *Yet I Loved Jacob*, 107–36; Awabdy, "Yhwh Exegetes," 697.

TABLE I4: IDENTITY MARKERS OF COVENANTAL EXCLUSION AND INCLUSION

	social identity[a]	functional identity of exclusion[b]	functional identity of inclusion[c]
Exod 12:43–48 (out)	foreigner, sojourner, hired worker	uncircumcised	—
Exod 12:43–48 (in)	slave, residing foreigner	—	circumcision
Deut 23:3–6[4–7] (out)	Ammonites, Moabites	absence of hospitality; attempted cursing	—
Deut 23:7–8[8–9] (in)	Edomites (brothers), Egyptians (residing foreigners)	—	(unstated)
Isa 52:1 (out)	(unstated[d])	uncircumcised, ritually defiled	—
Isa 56:3–7 (in)	eunuch, foreigner	—	bind self to Yahweh; keep the Sabbath; hold fast to covenant; minister to Yahweh; love name of Yahweh; not profane the Sabbath

[a] Lexicon of social identity: "foreigner" (בֶּן נֵכָר ,נֵכָר); "sojourner" (תּוֹשָׁב); "hired worker" (שָׂכִיר); "residing foreigner" (גֵּר); "native born" (אֶזְרָח); "adversary" (צָר); "nations" (גּוֹיִם).

[b] Lexicon of covenantal exclusion: "uncircumcised" (עָרֵל); "curse" (קָלַל); "ritually defiled" (טָמֵא).

[c] Lexicon of covenantal inclusion: "circumcise" (מול); "bind oneself" (לוה Nif); "keep" (שמר); "hold fast" (חזק); "minister" (שרת); "love" (אהב).

[d] The reference to the functional identity in Isa 52:1 as "ritually defiled" implies the social identity of the Neo-Babylonians based on the prohibition against touching that which is "ritually defiled" when going out (Isa 52:11). The parallel of Lam 1:10 and Isa 52:1 confirms this by the functional identity of the excluded class(es) as "adversaries" from the "nations."

As noted in Table I4, Isaiah does not challenge the covenantal basis of the inclusion or exclusion of the other according to Torah. Isaiah 52:1 does not bother with social class because exclusion relates entirely to uncircumcision and ritual defilement as signs of the absence of covenant fidelity.[53] Isaiah 56:3–7 does not relax covenantal standards. The temple-going foreigner bound to Yahweh keeps the Sabbath (holy) and does not profane it. That could only be true of a circumcised and ritually pure other.[54] Isaiah ignores the social signifiers of otherness even while strenuously reiterating the covenantal signifiers of temple-going others. The exegetical development of exclusion boundaries in Isa 52:1 takes a large step in exegetical advancement of the identity of the redeemed community (also see 35:8).

53. The relative rarity of "ritually defiled" outside of Leviticus, Numbers, and Ezekiel (approximately eighty percent of uses appear in these three) highlights Isaiah's intentionality. See "טמא," "טָמֵא," "טֻמְאָה," *HALOT* 1:375–76; *TWOT* 1:349–51; *NIDOTTE* 2:365 (no. 1); Wright, "Unclean and Clean," *ABD* 6:729–41.

54. See Wright, "Holiness (OT)," *ABD* 3:245–46; Hasel, "Sabbath," *ABD* 5:851–52.

In sum, Isaiah spells out two kinds of others in the same way as Torah laws and restoration narratives. In that sense Isaiah maintains continuity with other Scriptures forbidding some others and welcoming different others. As elsewhere, the differences do not stem from genealogical identity or ethnicity but enmity against the people of God versus faithful devotion to Yahweh's covenantal will. In Isa 52:1–2, Isaiah encourages Zion to get dressed up and assures her that she has nothing to fear from the uncircumcised or ritually defiled. While these others are permanently excluded from entry, different others who join themselves to Yahweh are always welcome (see note on 56:1–8). Both of Isaiah's interpretive advances ground these expectations in Yahweh's sovereign word.

52:11–12*~Lam 4:15 (B)+Exod 12:11 (B)+14:19 (C)+Lev 13:45 (B) (Depart! Depart! Do not touch!) (* see temple vessels network). Lamentations and the consolation of Jerusalem in Isaiah continue to share much imagery (see notes on Isa 40:1; 52:1, 2). The only two scriptural contexts to repeat the imperatives, "Depart! Depart!" (סוּרוּ סוּרוּ), are Isa 52:11 and Lam 4:15, which alone suggests some kind of relationship.[55] These intentional parallels rest on a shared allusion to the cry associated with the person with a skin disease in Torah—"Ritually impaired! Ritually impaired!" (Lev 13:45 lit.).[56] Other parallel lexical and syntactical relations between these contexts make intentional interpretation likely. Isaiah also uses elements associated with the exodus in a retrospective typological manner—perhaps based on the forward-looking typology in Isa 11:15–16. The rare term "haste" makes a relationship between Exod 12:11 and Isa 52:12 likely.[57] Because the scriptural tradition of Yahweh and/or his delegate going before Israel is common, one should exercise caution in deciding on a specific donor context in this case. The concept of Yahweh as Israel's "rear guard" also appears elsewhere in Isaiah (Isa 58:8). Still, both the delegate of Yahweh and rear guard appearing in Exod 14:19, along with probable use of 12:11, makes it more likely to regard Exodus as donor context in both cases. The term "articles of Yahweh" likely refers to the plundered temple vessels mentioned frequently elsewhere, but Isa 52:11–12 lacks evidence of intentional parallels (this is why this context has been set apart in the temple vessels network diagram). Notice the way figural echoes of the exodus activate connotations on the hope of new exodus (bold, italics, and underlining signify verbal parallels; broken underlining signifies similar concepts):

> This is how you are to eat it: with your cloak tucked into your belt, your sandals on your feet and your staff in your hand. Eat it in <u>haste</u>; it is Yahweh's Passover. (Exod 12:11)

---

55. No direction of dependence is presumed. The discussion here follows the "storyline" from exile (Lam 4:15) to return (Isa 52:11–12).

56. See Berlin, *Lamentations*, 111.

57. The term "haste" only appears elsewhere in Deut 16:3 (see "חִפָּזוֹן," *HALOT* 1:339).

> Then the angel of God, who had been traveling in front of Israel's army, withdrew and went behind them. The pillar of cloud also moved from in front and stood behind them. (14:19)

> Anyone with such a defiling disease must wear torn clothes, let their hair be unkempt, cover the lower part of their face and cry out, *"Ritually impure! Ritually impure!"* (Lev 13:45 lit.)

> "**Go away!** You are *ritually impure!*" people cry to them. "**Go away! Go away!** *Don't touch!*" When they flee and wander about, people among the nations say, "They can stay here no longer." (Lam 4:15 lit.)

> **Go away! Go away!** Go out from there! *Touch no ritually impure thing!* Come out from it and be pure, you who carry the articles of Yahweh. But you will not leave in haste or go in flight; for Yahweh will go before you, the God of Israel will be your rear guard. (Isa 52:11–12 lit.)

The context of Isa 52:7–10 rehearses and builds upon new exodus themes repeated throughout this entire section of the book (Isa 40–52), but especially reworking the opening section (40:1–11). Part of the point of the review seems to be closure, but the recapitulation also sets up the dramatic departure in 52:11–12. The twofold imperative "Go away! Go away!" in 52:11 reverses the same twofold interjection for Jerusalem to get away like a person with a ritually impure skin disease in Lam 4:15 (Lev 13:45). The prophet takes advantage of the semantic range of the language to infer that the people need to get out of the ritually impure land of captivity.[58] The ritual impurity of the place of captivity may connote the lack of adherence to covenantal ritual purity standards by their captors (Isa 52:11; Ezek 4:13; Hos 9:3; Amos 7:17).

The reversals continue when, unlike the exodus from Egypt, the new exodus excludes the need for leaving in haste, perhaps underlining the confident tone (Isa 52:11 versus Exod 12:11; Deut 16:13). The people have nothing to fear and need not take flight. The most dramatic interpretive intervention waits until last. Isaiah continues to avoid the circumlocution, euphemism, or reality of Israel's new exodus in the hands of a celestial delegate (Exod 23:20, 23, 27, 28; 33:1–2). Elsewhere Isaiah speaks of Yahweh our God, rather than the delegate of Yahweh, going through the wilderness to Zion (Isa 40:3, 9–10; 52:7–8). The presence of Yahweh himself explains part of the reasons for the people to go out and touch no ritually impure thing (52:11). But the situation goes deeper.

Isaiah 52:1 does not draw exclusionary boundaries by traditional ethnic and social terms like "foreigner" or "Moabite." The prophet speaks functionally of banishing the

58. See Sommer, *A Prophet Reads Scripture*, 272, n. 55.

"uncircumcised" and "ritually impure" from the holy city. Israel needs to leave behind the ritually impure or be banished. The comprehensive need for ritual purity covers both the new exodus in order to carry Yahweh's vessels and also the return to Jerusalem because the ritually defiled shall not enter there again (52:1, 11).

53:10~53:5 (B)+Lev 5:14–6:7[5:14–26] (B) (servant as guilt offering). Yahweh delights to crush his servant for a "guilt offering," which loads his suffering with connotations (Isa 53:10; Lev 5:14–6:7[5:14–26]). The set of terms for "guilt offering" overlap between the person's guilt, the payment for guilt, and the guilt offering.[59] An additional complication stems from the language of "guilt/guilt offering" being used to describe the sacrifices for the purification offering (traditionally sin offering, Lev 4:1–5:13) and the reparation offering (traditionally guilt offering, 6:1–7[5:20–26]). The purification offering atones for ritual impurities and unintentional transgressions by priest, collective, or lay person for touching ritually impure things, childbirth, male emission, and menstruation (4:3, 13, 27; 5:1–6; 12:6; 15:15, 30). Ritual impurity obstructs the relationship between the people and their God. The reparation offering functions for unintentional and intentional offenses against fellow citizens including lying, stealing, and sexual relations with a slave promised to another (6:2–3[5:21–22]; 19:20–22). The prerequisites for reparation offerings make things right between persons, and the sacrifice itself serves as a vehicle to seek forgiveness from God.[60]

The function of the servant as reparation offering begins to get explained by the parallel use of "crush" in Isa 53 verses 5 and 10. The servant was crushed for "our transgressions" and "our iniquities" as well as effecting "healing" to the first-person collective ("we," "us"). These terms can be used of actions that damage relations with Yahweh associated with the purification offering. Although Yahweh does not "delight" in the sacrifices of his rebellious people, he "delights" to crush his servant (1:11; 53:10; see note on Ps 40:5[7]). This allows the term "guilt offering" in Isa 53:10 to function broadly to mean that which restores broken relations with others and God. For the present purposes, a short excerpt from the instruction on the reparation offering stands for the many uses of these terms in Lev 5–6 (see below).

Isaiah's major exegetical advancement is associating the suffering of the servant figure with the guilt offering. The effects relate to the iniquity of "us" on him; many are made righteous, and the sin and transgression of many are "lifted up" (Isa 53:6, 11, 12). Elsewhere the causal stem for "make righteous" in a legal sense—acquit—appears six times and seems like the best fit here (Exod 23:7; Deut 25:1; 1 Kgs 8:32//2 Chr 6:23; Prov 17:15; Isa 5:23). This sense functions somewhat oddly here, since the subject would more naturally be Yahweh as judge than his servant.[61] If the term does take the legal sense then the servant functions more like the instrument of divine acquittal. Instead of

59. See "אשם," "אָשָׁם," "אָשֵׁם," and "אַשְׁמָה," *HALOT* 1:95–96.
60. See Milgrom, *Cult and Conscience*, 127–28; Schnittjer, *Torah Story*, 311–14.
61. See Chisholm, "Forgiveness and Salvation," 201–2. Also see Childs, *Isaiah*, 417–18.

the term "forgiveness," the poetical context speaks of him "bearing/lifting up" (using two synonyms) sin and transgressions (53:11, 12). The only other context to collocate "lift up" (סבל) and "iniquity" (עון) does so with a similar sense of transfer of collective culpability: "Our ancestors sinned and are no more, and *we bear* [סבל] *their iniquities* [עון]" (Lam 5:7†, emphasis mine).[62] The focus on the servant bearing the iniquity and transgressions of the many likewise shifts attention from the divine judge to the instrument of forgiveness.

The difficult problem of identifying him, us, and them in Isa 53 is well known.[63] The point at hand only concerns whether the "us" beneficiaries of his suffering in 53:5 relate to "the many" beneficiaries of 53:10. "He," in both cases understood as the servant (52:13), fits a simile of a lamb/full-grown ewe at slaughter/shearing, which seems something of a common figure for undeserved exilic suffering, though muteness intensifies the imagery (53:7; Ps 44:11, 22[12, 23]; but see Jer 12:3).[64] The closely related simile of "us" like wandering sheep in Isa 53:6 suggests he may be one from among "us." The servant bearing the iniquities of "them" in 53:11, and thus being numbered with the transgressors in 53:12, does not necessarily identify the us and the many. For the present purposes it will suffice to note how Isa 57:14–21 interprets the themes introduced in Isa 53 verses 5 and 10, identifying these contexts as two views of the selfsame act for the selfsame beneficiaries.[65] Compare how Isa 53:10 uses the reparation offering and the relationship between 53:10 and 57:14–21 (bold, italics, and underlining signify verbal parallels; and stylized underlining signifies interpretive connectors):

> And as **a penalty for guilt** [אָשָׁם] they must bring to the priest, that is, to Yahweh, their **guilt offering** [אָשָׁם], a ram from the flock, one without defect and of the proper value. In this way the priest will make atonement for them before Yahweh, and they will be forgiven for any of the things they did that made them **guilty** [אַשְׁמָה]. (Lev 6:6–7[5:25–26])

> "There is no peace," says Yahweh, "for the wicked." (Isa 48:22)

> But he was pierced *for our transgressions* [פשע], he was crushed [דכא Pual] *for our iniquities* [עון]; the punishment that brought us peace was on him, and by his wounds we are healed [רפא]. (53:5)

62. See Chisholm, "Forgiveness and Salvation," 199–201.

63. See Clines, *I, He, We, and They*, 25–49.

64. See Baumgartner, *Jeremiah's Poems*, 43. Also see note on Jer 11:19.

65. For a discussion of broader development from "individual" servant in Isa 40–55 to "collective" servants in Isa 54; 56–66, see Lyons, "Psalm 22" 648–50. Lyons' larger objective turns on thematic comparisons to a similar individual/collective shift within Ps 22.

Yet it was Yahweh's will to crush him [דכא Piel] and cause him to suffer, and though Yahweh makes his life **a guilt offering** [אָשָׁם], he will see his offspring and prolong his days, and the will of Yahweh will prosper in his hand. (53:10†)

And it will be said: "Build up, build up, prepare the road! Remove the obstacles out of the way of my people." [15] For this is what the high and exalted One says—he who lives forever, whose name is holy: "I live in a high and holy place, but also with the one who is contrite [דכא] and lowly in spirit, to revive the spirit of the lowly and to revive the heart of the contrite [דכא Nif]. [16] I will not accuse them forever, nor will I always be angry, for then they would faint away because of me—the very people I have made [עשׂה]. [17] I was enraged by *the iniquity* [עון] of their greed; I punished them, and hid my face in anger, yet they kept on in their willful ways. [18] I have seen their ways, but I will heal them [רפא]; I will guide them and restore comfort to Israel's mourners, [19] creating [ברא] praise on their lips. Peace, peace, to those far and near," says Yahweh. "And I will heal them [רפא]." [20] But the wicked are like the tossing sea, which cannot rest, whose waves cast up mire and mud. [21] "There is no peace," says my God, "for the wicked." (57:14–21†)

Every line of Isa 57:14–19 makes allusion to recurring themes treated elsewhere in Isaiah.[66] The twofold use of the roots "contrite" and "heal" combined with development of contextual themes suggest intentional allusion to Isa 53:5, 10 in 57:15, 19. If so, *the one who was crushed* (דכא Pual) by Yahweh's *will to crush* (דכא Piel) provides in this very act a prototype of *contrite* (דכא Nif) attitudes of *contrite persons* (דכא) of divine restoration (53:5, 10; 57:15).[67] The identity of the servant in his suffering itself anticipates the citizens of restoration for whom his crushing provides healing (53:5; 57:18, 19). The "us" who are healed and "the many" whose iniquities he bore are none other than the restored people he "made" (53:5, 11, 12; 57:16). The moral iniquities in the foreground here—greed (57:17)—emphasize the servant's sacrifice in terms of the guilt offering of Lev 6:6–7[5:25–26] (see above).

The expectations of restoration for contrite citizens, marked by wavy underlining above, interconnect with other contexts: return on the new exodus roadway (57:14 with 40:1–11), the pathway that leads to comfort (57:18 with 40:1), and those he "made" by an ancient exodus from Egypt become instruments of "creating praise" in the anticipated new Jerusalem and new heavens and earth (57:19 with 43:7; 44:2; 46:4; 51:13; 54:4 and 65:18; 66:22).[68]

66. The use of the twofold imperative "Build up! Build up!" in 57:14 signifies a self-conscious attempt to situate this lyrical expectation with the others like it (40:1; 51:9, 17; 52:1; 57:14; 62:10). However, the function of Isa 48:22//57:21 seems more like a literary refrain at transitions rather than an exegetical link (see Delitzsch, *Isaiah*, 128; as noted by Schultz, *Search for Quotation*, 233–34, n. 68; but see Blenkinsopp, *Isaiah 40–55*, 296).

67. Though thematically similar, Isa 66:2 uses different language of the humble who enjoy divine favor.

68. Elsewhere the prophecies of Isaiah use synonymously "make" (עשׂה), "create" (ברא), and "form" (יצר), broadly alluding to the terms also used in Gen 1 and 2 (Isa 43:1, 7; 44:2).

In sum, the prophet exegetically advances revelation by identifying the servant's suffering with the guilt offering (53:10). The very crushing of the servant as guilt offering serves as the instrument of forgiveness. Interpretations of the servant's suffering include viewing it as a prototype for contrite citizens of restoration (57:15). His suffering models how redeemed ones should live. This use of the servant's suffering places it as something of a pivot to provide healing and to activate the new exodus and new creation.

54:6~Hos 2:14–15[16–17] (C) (restoration like the wife of youth). Hosea's powerful imagery of restoring wayward Israel to her husband like the days of her "youth" provide opportunity for reuse and development. Isaiah speaks of Yahweh restoring his banished wife like the bride of one's "youth" who will "forget" her shame, which may reverse-echo the rekindling of love lacking since the days of a youthful bride in Hosea (Isa 54:4, 6; Hos 2:13–15[15–17]). However, Isaiah's language also shares similar themes with the conclusion of Lamentations, which asks if Yahweh had "forgotten," "forsaken," and "rejected" and yet hopes for restoration to days of old (Lam 5:20–22; Isa 54:4, 6). Isaiah may be drawing on a rich, widely diffused tradition but not directly alluding to Hosea.

54:9~Gen 9:8–17 (B) (like the days of Noah). The shared language suggests an intentional relationship between the scriptural traditions in Gen 9:8–17 and Isa 54:9. Isaiah uses the days of Noah to refer to Yahweh's oath never again to destroy the earth by flood as a simile for the security of the promise of restoration. Isaiah narrowly refers to the promise after the flood as an enduring covenant of peace (Isa 54:10). The term "covenant of peace" functions as a prophetic stock phrase for restoration hope (Isa 54:10; Ezek 34:25; 37:26). Whereas Isaiah refers to the days after the flood, Messiah uses the days of Noah as a simile for those who will be swept away by wrath like the coming of the flood. Unlike the indiscriminate killing of everything in the flood, the wrath to come targets one but not the other (Matt 24:37–41).

55:3–5*~Ps 89:28, 49*[29, 50] (C) (Davidic covenant extended to the nations) (* see Davidic covenant network).[69] If the exilic psalmist asks, "How long?!" and "Where is your faithful devotion?!" and calls upon Yahweh to "Remember!" then the opening of Isa 55 sounds like a divine answer (Ps 89:46, 49, 50[47, 50, 51]). Psalm 89 uses language of the Davidic covenant and adds the loaded terms "confirmed," "forever" (cf. 2 Sam 23:5), and "faithful devotion" (*hesed* חֶסֶד) (Ps 89:28, 49[29, 50]).[70] But the answer also includes a surprising advancement of revelation concerning the nations (italics and bold signify verbal parallels):[71]

69. No direction of dependence presumed here. This note follows the "storyline" of question (Ps 89:49[50]) and answer (Isa 55:3).

70. See Sarna, "Psalm 89," 38; also see 31–32.

71. The comparison of Isa 55:3 and Ps 89:28, 49[29, 50] is indebted to Willgren, *"Antwort Gottes,"* 108, and see 105–12.

If my [David] house were not right with God, surely he would not have made with me an *everlasting covenant.* (2 Sam 23:5a)

I will maintain my **faithful devotion** to him *forever*, and my *covenant* with him **will be confirmed**. . . . Lord, where is your former **faithful devotion**, which in **your confirmation** you swore **to David**? (Ps 89:28, 49†[29, 50])

I will make an *everlasting covenant* with you, my **faithful devotion confirmed to David**. . . . Surely you will summon nations you know not, and nations you do not know will come running to you, because of Yahweh your God, the Holy One of Israel, for he has endowed you with splendor. (Isa 55:3b, 5†)

Isaiah looks to the restoration of the Davidic covenant in a striking manner. The prophet calls upon the nations to join Israel because of Yahweh's faithful devotion to David in a way that overlaps the oracles of the mountain and the house of prayer (55:5; cf. 2:2; 56:7).[72] Isaiah's bold vision for the nations coming together by the testimony of the everlasting Davidic covenant provides a sequel to restored Israel under David as a testimony to the nations (see note on Ezek 37:28). The invitation to the nations that Israel does not know joining together with them goes beyond the restoration of the local nations once under the shelter of David's regional empire (see note on Amos 9:11–12).

56:1–8*~Deut 23:1–8*[2–9] (B) (eunuchs and foreigners in Yahweh's house) (* see assembly network). The striking lyrical pronouncement at the opening of the last major unit of Isaiah is widely regarded as making an extended allusion to the law of the assembly in Deut 23:1–7[2–8], though verbal parallels are few.[73] The leading word of the law of the assembly "come into" (בוא Q) only appears in allusion to the law with Yahweh as subject of "bring" (בוא Hif) in Isa 56:7. The term in the law of the assembly to describe the person whose male organ "has been cut off" is used as something of a punchline—the faithful eunuch in the new temple "shall not be cut off" (Deut 23:1[2]; Isa 56:5 lit.). The wordplay of this allusion only works with Deut 23:1[2] as donor and Isa 56:5 as receptor context.

The two stereotypical categories of excluded others in Isa 56:1–7, eunuchs and foreigners, correspond to the person with a damaged male organ and Ammonites and Moabites in the law of the assembly in Deut 23. Isaiah's intentional use of "foreigner" (בֶּן־הַנֵּכָר) in 56:3, 6 serves as an inclusive term for excluded others. This symbolic reading of Ammonites and Moabites matches how other Scriptures interpret the law of the assembly (Lam 1:10; Neh 13:3).

The use of Sabbath-keeping as the symbol for faithful eunuchs and foreigners in the new temple seems natural (Isa 56:2, 4, 6). The only one of the Ten Commandments

72. The reading here is objective genitive: "covenantal loyalties to David" (חַסְדֵי דָוִד) (Isa 55:3 lit.). For discussion of the debate, see note on 2 Chr 6:1–42.

73. See Wright and Chan, "King," 100–2.

mentioned by the Levitical intercessors is Sabbath-keeping (Neh 9:14). The restoration assembly includes Sabbath-keeping in their oath and Nehemiah compares Sabbath-breaking to ancient infidelities of Israel (10:31[32]; 13:15–22). Keeping the Sabbath stands with circumcision, dietary regulations, and regular Scripture reading as setting apart "practicing" Second Temple Jews from gentiles.

Isaiah 56:1–8 exegetically advances the law of the assembly in Deut 23 by defining the basis for inclusion and exclusion as fidelity to the covenant rather than anything physical, ethnic, or genealogical. The context speaks of foreigners "joining themselves," using the reflexive stem of the verb (Nif). The use of reflexive stem verbs (Nif) is the norm to describe others who join the assembly. Those who join based on covenant fidelity cannot be excluded. Isaiah's lyrical pronouncement broadly fits the ideals found elsewhere. Others who turn from ritual impurity to Torah in Ezra-Nehemiah are welcome to join the Yahwistic Judeans who have returned from exile. Zechariah also looks ahead eagerly to the ideal of many nations joining the people of Yahweh. Notice how Isa 56 interprets the law of the assembly compared to kindred contexts of entry in Zechariah and Ezra-Nehemiah (all marked fonts signify verbal parallels except broken underlining which signifies use of the reflexive stem [Nif]):

> No one who has been emasculated by crushing or **cutting may enter** [בוא Q] the assembly of Yahweh. . . . No Ammonite or Moabite or any of their descendants **may enter** [בוא Q] the assembly of Yahweh, not even in the tenth generation. (Deut 23;1, 3[2, 4])

> Let no foreigner [בן־נכר] who is bound to Yahweh say, "Yahweh will **surely exclude** [בדל Hif] me from his people." And let no eunuch complain, "I am only a dry tree . . ." I will give them an everlasting name that will not be **cut off**. And foreigners [בְּנֵי הַנֵּכָר] *who bind themselves* [לוה Nif] to Yahweh to minister to him, to love the name of Yahweh, and to be his servants, all who keep the Sabbath without desecrating it and who hold fast to my covenant—these **I will bring** [בוא Hif] to my holy mountain and give them joy in my house of prayer. Their burnt offerings and sacrifices will be accepted on my altar; for my house will be called a house of prayer for all peoples [עַמִּים]. Sovereign Yahweh declares—he who gathers the exiles of Israel: "I will gather still others to them besides those already gathered." (Isa 56:3, 5b–8†)

> Many nations [גוֹיִם] *will bind themselves* [לוה Nif] to Yahweh in that day and will become my people. I will live among you and you will know that Yahweh Almighty has sent me to you. (Zech 2:11†[15])

> So the Israelites who had returned from the exile ate it, together with all who had **separated themselves** [בדל Nif] from the unclean practices of the neighboring nations [גוֹיִם] in order to seek Yahweh, the God of Israel. (Ezra 6:21†)

> Those of Israelite descent [זֶרַע יִשְׂרָאֵל] had **separated themselves** [בדל Nif] from all foreigners [בְּנֵי נֵכָר]. They stood in their places and confessed their sins and the sins of their ancestors. (Neh 9:2)

> The rest of the people—priests, Levites, gatekeepers, musicians, temple servants and all **who separated themselves** [בדל Nif] from the neighboring peoples [עַמֵּי הָאֲרָצוֹת] for the sake of the Torah of God, together with their wives and all their sons and daughters who are able to understand. (10:28†[29])

A most remarkable element of some of the contexts cited here is the use of "ethnic" labels in symbolic ways. The persons referred to by the strong term "seed of Israel" (9:2) are those who signed on the same narrative day the solemn oath including the others who separated themselves to join Israel (10:28[29]). These very same others went on to swear they would not arrange marriages for their children with the "peoples of the land" (10:30[31], see note ad loc.).

The larger framework of religious identity, for lack of a better term, in the Hebrew Scriptures needs to be acknowledged. Torah, prophets, and narratives speak of two kinds of others in many different ways but with a generally shared ideology. In Isaiah, included others worship Yahweh with Israel and excluded others may not (Isa 52:1; 56:1–7). In spite of the array of terms for the two kinds of others—included others and excluded others—this common ideology can be identified in Exodus, Deuteronomy, Isaiah, Ezekiel, and Ezra-Nehemiah (see Table I4 in note on Isa 52:1 and Table Ezk6 in note on Ezek 44:9–16).[74]

The exegetical advancements of Isa 56:1–8 include, first, the powerful lyrical expression itself. Messiah uses the shorthand "house of prayer for all nations" in a way that seems to carry with it the entire horizontal and vertical contexts of the larger assembly interpretive network as he clears the court of the gentiles (Mark 11:17; cf. Matt 21:13; Luke 19:46; John 2:13–17). Second, the others who join themselves to Yahweh and his covenant enjoy a place better than sons and daughters not by their commitment but by Yahweh's fidelity. Yahweh says, "I shall give them a name," "I shall bring them to my holy mountain," and "I shall gather others" (Isa 56:5, 7, 8 lit.). Isaiah's exegetical advances, then, include the theocentric emphasis on sovereign election of the other who embraces

74. Contra Fishbane who identifies contradictions between Deut 23:3–6[4–7], Ezek 44, Isa 56, Ezra-Nehemiah by isolating either included or excluded others from each context and contrasting these to the opposite of other contexts (*Biblical Interpretation*, 138–43). Fishbane generalizes that in Isa 56:7 Yahweh brings "the foreigners and the uncircumcised" into the temple for sacrifices (143, n. 98). But he does not work with Isa 52:1, which uses the very words of the law of the assembly in Deut 23 to banish the "uncircumcised" forever. The need to explain Isa 52:1 in the light of 56:1–7 is not diminished but enhanced by views of collaborative authorship of Isaiah. Fishbane's view resembles a commonplace assessment of Isa 56:1–7 as a direct rebuttal to Ezek 44:6–16, see, e.g., Nihan, "Ethnicity and Identity," 73, 77–78 (but note qualifications, 93–94); Schaper, "Rereading the Law," 133–35; Tuell, "Priesthood of the 'Foreigner,'" 195–204; Haarmann, "'Their Burnt Offerings,'" 160–64; or Isa 56:1–7 as opposing Ezra-Nehemiah's use of Deut 23:1–8[2–9] (e.g., Ezra 9:1–2; Neh 13:1–3, 23–27), so Sommer, *A Prophet Reads Scripture*, 147.

his covenant.[75] Third, the sense of "minister" (שׁרת) often connotes tabernacle and temple service by Levites and priests, which seems a provocative term to include in Isa 56:6.[76] The context does not explain this ministry formally but only refers to normal responsibilities of laity, such as Sabbath-keeping, obedience of covenant, and bringing sacrifices to the house of prayer (cf. Lev 22:18; Num 15:14–16; 1 Kgs 8:41–43).[77] Elsewhere Isaiah uses the same language with Israel's laity serving as priests to the nations, but in a sense that is not analogous (Isa 61:5–7, see note ad loc.).

In sum, whereas Isa 52:1 interpretively alludes to the law of the assembly in Deut 23:1–8[2–9] in accord with Lam 1:10 to affirm permanently excluded others, Isa 56:1–7 exegetically advances the included others from the same law. The new temple prevents entry by the uncircumcised and ritually defiled others but welcomes others who bind themselves to Yahweh according to his covenant.

57:14–21~53:5, 10 (B) (restoration of the contrite). See note on Isa 53:10.

61:1, 2~Lev 25:10 (C) (year of release). The first-person, Spirit-endowed figure proclaims release, echoing two key terms from the instruction on Jubilee (Isa 61:1, 2; cf. קרא, דְּרוֹר, Lev 25:10). The highly lyrical message seems to use the language of release to provide connotative significance to the liberty of captives to rebuild the homeland (61:4). The Jubilee would typically be a once-or-twice-in-a-lifetime event—in theory, however, since there is no evidence of its practice. This once-or-twice-in-a-lifetime release and restoration of rightful inheritance offers poetic force to the captives, though they now dwell in the homeland (61:3). Elsewhere the returned exiles of the restoration speak of themselves as "slaves" in their homeland in reference to the oppressive empire (Ezra 9:8; Neh 9:36). The use of Jubilee imagery builds upon the intermittent hope of release from captivity (Isa 42:7; 49:9).

61:5–7~Exod 19:6 (C) (priests as rulers over people). The prophet may lightly allude to the ancient imagery of Israel as priests but repurposes the connotation (Isa 61:6). Yahweh explains Israel's election as "a kingdom of priests" (Exod 19:6). The imagery evokes their value to Yahweh (19:5; Deut 7:6). The meaning of Israel as royal priesthood implies their service and representation of the kingdoms before Yahweh. Isaiah uses the same imagery but as something of a simile of Israel's enjoying the wealth earned by the strangers and foreigners who raise crops and tend flocks (Isa 61:5). The priestly allotment of Israel amounts to a double portion (cf. Job 42:10). Less clear is a double allotment based on Jerusalem's double payment for her sins in exile since the language differs (Isa 40:2).

---

75. Note the catchwords: "name," "everlasting," and "not cut off" in Isa 55:13; 56:5 in light of the force of 55:11.

76. See Knoppers, "Who or What Is Israel?" 158, n. 25. The phrase "to minister to him" is absent from Isa 56:6 1QIsa[a] perhaps because it offended the scribes (see *BQS* 2:440; Nihan, "Ethnicity and Identity," 77).

77. See Haarmann, "'Their Burnt Offerings,'" 161.

63:9~Exod 23:20* (B)+Deut 1:31 (C) (divine presence with his people) (* see new exodus network).
63:10~Ps 78:40 (C) (rebelled and grieved him).
63:11~Num 11:17, 25 (B) (spirit of God upon leaders).
63:12>/<Exod 14:16, 21; Ps 78:13 (divided the sea).
63:13>/<Ex 15:5, 8; Isa 51:10; Ps 106:9 (led them through the depths).
63:14~Ps 78:52 (C) (led his people). Isaiah 63:7–14 presents a broad lyrical retrospective of Yahweh's redemption of Israel. The poetic presentation corresponds to Ps 78 in several ways (Isa 63:10, 12, 14; Ps 78:13, 40, 52). Elsewhere Isaiah speaks of smiting, hewing, and passing through the sea (Isa 11:15; 51:9; 43:2, 16), but here he employs the common idiom of "cleaving" the sea (63:12; Exod 14:16, 21; Ps 78:13). Two more distinctive figures from Torah seem like intentional allusions.

First, the oracle blends the scriptural traditions of the celestial delegate that goes before the people with Yahweh himself carrying his people (emphases signify verbal parallels):

> See, I am sending **an angel** [מַלְאָךְ] ahead of you to guard you along the way and to bring you to the place I have prepared. (Exod 23:20; cf. 14:19; 23:23, 27, 28)

> There you saw how Yahweh your God *carried* [נשׂא] you, as a father carries his son, all the way you went until you reached this place. (Deut 1:31)

> **[T]he angel** [מַלְאָךְ] of his presence saved them. In his love and mercy he redeemed them; he lifted them up and *carried* [נשׂא] them all the days of old. (Isa 63:9)

After the rebellion with the calf, Yahweh threatened to leave the people with his delegate as an act of mercy to avoid destroying them in their stubbornness (Exod 33:1–3). Moses convinced Yahweh to go with the people (33:14; 34:9). Moses later interpreted the divine mercy in the wilderness as carrying his people after the simile of a father carrying a son (Deut 1:31). This goes a long way to affirming the need for Yahweh's own mercy.

Second, the threefold mention of the Spirit in Isa 63:10, 11, 14 includes a reference to the incident whereby the Spirit was distributed to the elders of Israel (63:11; Num 11:17, 25). The lead-in to the allusion refers to the people grieving the Spirit, perhaps in the land (63:10). This sets up the heart of the retrospective's purpose: "*Then his people recalled the days of old, the days of Moses and his people*—Where is he who brought them through the sea, with the shepherds of his flock? Where is he who set his Holy Spirit among them?" (63:11†, emphasis mine).

The people in the time of rebellion looked back to "the days of old" and wondered "Where is he?" The days of old were defined as the time when "he carried them" (63:9). The ancient people longed for the days of the exodus: at the sea, giving the Spirit to the shepherds, marching with Moses, and dividing the waters (63:11–12). Yahweh was the one who carried them in the exodus (63:9). All of this evokes the shepherd simile, when Yahweh carries his lambs in the new exodus (40:11).

In sum, the Torah retrospective activates the ancient question "Where is he?" The ancient question presumably serves as an analogy for the people of the failing restoration who need to look back to the new exodus and ask the same question. The one whose presence went with his people gave them "rest" (63:14; Exod 33:14). The series of prayers in first-person plural seek the same divine presence again in time of distress (Isa 63:15–19). Isaiah 63:17 evokes themes of divinely hardened hearts (6:9–10), wandering people (53:6), and the need to fear Yahweh recalling the outcomes of the Spirit-filled shoot of Jesse (11:1–5).

65:17–18~Gen 1:1 (B) (new heavens and new earth). The prophet has repeatedly invoked Yahweh's acts of creation to speak of his power and to provide a translucent figural overlay for his work of creating and forming Israel by the exodus—types of the new creation and new exodus (see Table I1 and note on Isa 43; cf. Isa 43:18–19; 66:22). The prophet looks ahead to the creator's new work (bold signifies verbal parallels, and italics signify advancements):

> In the beginning God **created the heavens and the earth.** (Gen 1:1)
>
> See, I will **create** *new* **heavens and** a *new* **earth.** The former things will not be remembered, nor will they come to mind. But be glad and rejoice forever in what I will **create,** for I will **create** *Jerusalem to be a delight and its people a joy.* (Isa 65:17–18)

Isaiah follows up the striking expectation of the new heavens and new earth by reference to creating a new Jerusalem and its joyful people. The new beginning goes back before the revelation at the mountain, before exodus from bondage, before election of Israel, to God's signature act of creation itself. The prophetic interpretation emphasizes the divine power to bring about an entirely new beginning.

65:25//11:6–9+Gen 3:14 (B) (curse removed with the exception of the serpent). Isaiah 11:1–10 and 65:25 each stand in the penultimate positions of their respective units. Isaiah 11 verses 1 and 10 speak of the shoot/root of Jesse and frame the idyllic imagery of the removal of the ancient curse of Eden. All of this could be seen as superfluous imagery of promised salvation from the Assyrian crisis upon Ahaz and Hezekiah "on my holy mountain" (Isa 11:9). Isaiah 65:25 abbreviates the oracle of messianic salvation by verbatim excerpts and blends it with an allusive snippet of the garden tradition. The effect of the exegetical blend recasts and advances the expectation beyond its setting in the Assyrian crisis (emphases signify verbal parallels):[78]

---

78. See Schultz, *Search for Quotation*, 240–56, esp. 255–56; idem, "Understanding," 34.

> So Yahweh God said to the serpent, "Because you have done this, "Cursed are you above all livestock and all wild animals! You will crawl on your belly and you will eat dust all the days of your life." (Gen 3:14)

> **The wolf** will live with **the lamb**, the leopard will lie down with the goat, the calf and the lion and the yearling together; and a little child will lead them. [7] The cow will feed with the bear, their young will lie down together, *and the lion will eat straw like the ox.* [8] The infant will play near the cobra's den, the young child will put its hand into the viper's nest. [9] They will neither harm nor destroy on all my holy mountain, for the earth will be filled with the knowledge of Yahweh as the waters cover the sea. (Isa 11:6–9)

> **The wolf** and **the lamb** will feed together, *and the lion will eat straw like the ox*, and dust will be the serpent's food. They will neither harm nor destroy on all my holy mountain," says Yahweh. (65:25)

The imagery of infants and children playing near cobras and vipers reinforces the point of restoring creational peace and harmony (11:8).[79] Isaiah 65:25 removes this and inserts an allusion to the serpent remaining under its curse even while all the rest of creation has been restored to its Edenic state. This exegetical move corresponds to the dust-eating nations of Isa 49:9, Mic 7:17, and Ps 72:9.[80] It also generally aligns with the Moabites being trampled to the mire and "dust" (Isa 25:10–12).

Isaiah 65:25 has been interpreted as looking for a near fulfillment of the new creation and restoration to Edenic peace in the postexilic restoration, but this depends on the function of the verbal form of "creating" (ptc.) in Isa 65:18.[81] Such a reading may find support in 66:7–9 implying rapid delivery by Zion. This is fine as far as it goes but does not adequately account for the other indexing of proximate versus eschatological fulfillment here. The imagery of "the sound of weeping and of crying will be heard in it no more" in 65:19 aligns with "Sovereign Yahweh will wipe away the tears from all faces; he will remove his people's disgrace from all the earth" in 25:8. It will be when youth dying in Jerusalem is virtually unheard of (65:20). Or, more pointedly, when "he will swallow up death forever" (25:8). These images evoke eschatological expectations. The proximate fulfillment of restoration for Jerusalem did not erase simultaneous eschatological hopes for Zechariah (Zech 8:1–8). The same kind of proximate fulfillment alongside greater eschatological expectations seems natural from the constant repurposing of elements from the earlier part of Isaiah in its last section.

66:22~Gen 1:1 (C) (new heaven and new earth endure). See note on Isa 65:17–18.

---

79. Schultz notes that Isa 65:21–23 reverses the curses of Lev 26:20 and Deut 28:11 ("Understanding," 33).

80. See Schultz, *Search for Quotation*, 254; indebted to Schultz here except Mic 7:7 [*sic*].

81. See Fishbane, *Biblical Interpretation*, 497; Schultz, *Search for Quotation*, 255–56.

FILTERS

The excessively allusive style of Isaiah creates special challenges for interpretation. For the present study, filtering out a legion of broad and noninterpretive allusions, echoes, and coincidental parallels makes possible identifying exegetical uses of scriptural traditions.

That elements are filtered out does not say anything about their relative significance. As noted elsewhere, non-exegetical allusions are the stuff of literary coherence. These literary connectors go a long way toward explaining the rich-textured qualities of Isaiah. The filters and the texts they divert relate only to the challenges of determining real versus imagined interpretive allusions.

The sampling of noninterpretive parallels between Isaiah and *external* counterparts in the prophets and psalms represents lyrical diffusion. The widespread use of common stock phrases, poetic expressions, and closely related thematic developments shows how the lyrical diffusion connects Scripture. Although evidence for the life settings of the interrelations is not available, the lyrical diffusion in Scripture is its empirical effects.[82]

There is a fine line between interpretive allusion to prophetic oracles *within* Isaiah and the literary connectors that bring coherence and closure to a book. Figuring out the difference between exegetical allusion versus literary connection within Isaiah, when it is possible, is an important part of the ongoing debates on dating and authorship. The present approach seeks to err on the side of filtering out borderline cases as literary connectors to concentrate on exegetical interventions.

Phrases without quotation marks represent thematic similarities not direct quotations. The following lists are not complete, comprehensive, or exhaustive. The examples merely illustrate the kinds of parallels filtered out by the criteria of this study.

Non-Exegetical Broad Allusions and Shared Themes

The majority of Isaiah's noninterpretive broad allusions refer to narrative and legal traditions of Torah: **6:5**>/<Exod 24:11; 33:10, mortal danger of seeing divine presence; **9:4**>/<Judg 7:15–25, simile of day of Midian; **10:22; 48:19**>/<Gen 22:17, offspring numerous like sand; **11:6–9**>/<Gen 6–9, undoing the curse of creation;[83] **14:21**>/<Deut 24:16, children pay for sins of parents; **17:9**>/<Exod 23:23; Deut 7:1, like the deserted place of Hivites and Amorites (cf. Num 21:21–35; Deut 2:24–3:11);[84] **19:2**>/<1 Sam 14:20; 2 Chr 20:23, panic of enemy to fight themselves (cf. Exod 23:27; Lev 26:6–7; Judg

82. For further discussion on lyrical diffusion in Scripture, see Hermeneutical Profile of the Use of Scripture in Isaiah and Hermeneutical Profile of the Use of Scripture in Psalms.

83. The suggestion that Isa 11:9 alludes to Noah's flood is unconvincing since it addresses something else. The suggested parallel is based on a few common terms: "evil" (רעע), "corrupt" (שחת), "fill" (מלא), "earth" (ארץ), "water" (מים), and "cover" (כסה), see Jindo, "Reflections," 144–45.

84. Isaiah 17:9 as "wooded heights of the Amorites" with NET versus "wooded heights of the hilltops" (ESV) or "Hivites and Amorites" (LXX) (see *BHS*; 1QIsa[a] col. XIV [17:9] in *BQS* 2:363) shows scribal update of supralinear *vav*, inferring that "and" (ו) likely was not in the parent text of the LXX but supplied later to correct it in accordance with a text resembling proto-MT tradition.

7:22); **19:25; 47:6**>/<Deut 4:20; 9:26, 29; 32:9; 1 Sam 10:1; 26:19; 2 Sam 14:16; 20:19; 21:3; 1 Kgs 8:51; Ps 78:71, "inheritance of Yahweh/God/mine/his" (נַחֲלַת יהוה/אֱלֹהִים/י/לוֹ); **29:22**>/<Gen 12:10–20, redeemer of Abraham; **30:17**>/<Deut 32:30, a thousand flee before one (cf. Lev 26:36–37); **31:1**>/<Deut 17:16; 1 Kgs 10:26–29, trusting Egypt's horses for help; **34:16; 40:8; 55:11**>/<Deut 18:22, word of Yahweh shall come to pass; **34:9–10**>/<Gen 19:24, 28; Deut 29:23, judgment by sulfur with smoke rising; **40:2**>/<Exod 22:4[3], punished double for sin; **41:8; 51:2; 63:16 (ironic)**>/<Gen 12:1–3, blessing of Abraham; **52:4**>/<Gen 46–50, Israel going down to Egypt; **63:1**>/<Deut 33:2; Judg 5:4–5; cf. Hab 3:3, 7, coming up from Edom;[85] **64:1–4**>/<Exod 19:16–18, recalling theophany at the mountain (cf. Deut 4:32–36); **65:2**>/<Deut 21:18–21, God's "rebellious" (סרר) people could imply the fatherhood of God but lacks the criminal context of a court case, which Isa 1:2 features but without verbal connection (cf. Isa 1:2, 23).

Shared Stock Phrases and Other Similarities with Prophetic Contexts

The following sampling of stock phrases and shared themes in Isaiah points to lyrical diffusion of prophetic traditions. Many noninterpretive shared prophetic themes relate to the prophets in the days of the Assyrian crisis (Hosea, Amos, Isaiah, Micah), and, significantly, the same traditions reappear among other prophets like those who ministered in the days of the Neo-Babylonian crisis (Jeremiah, Ezekiel, Habakkuk, Zephaniah) or in the restoration (Haggai, Zechariah).

Prophetic vocation: >/<6:1–4; Exod 24:10; Ezek 1:4–28; Rev 4:1–11, vision of celestial court; >/<21:2–4; Jer 4:19; Hab 3:16, physical convulsions accompanying divine revelation; >/<21:6–12; 56:10 (ironic); Jer 6:17 (ironic); Ezek 3:16–21 (ironic); 33:1–9; Hab 2:1, prophet as sentinel (cf. Isa 52:8); >/<44:2, 24; 49:1, 5; Jer 1:5, formed in womb for service.

Prophetic similes and metaphors: >/<1:8; 3:14; 5:1–7; 27:2–6; Jer 2:21; Hos 10:1; Ps 80:8–16, people of God as vineyard; >/<1:30; Jer 17:8//Ps 1:3, like a tree; >/<7:3; 8:3; Hos 1:4–8, children of prophet with sign names; >/<11:9b; Hab 2:14, as waters cover the sea; >/<13:8; Mic 4:9, 10, like a woman in labor (cf. Hos 13:13; Isa 26:17); >/<47:2–3; Hos 2:10; Ezek 16:37, 39; 23:26, 29, simile of humiliation by uncovering nakedness; >/<51:3; Ezek 36:35, make wilderness like Eden (cf. Isa 35:1).

Warning against the nations (Isaiah's oracles against the nations): >/<14:9–11; Ezek 31:15–18, tyrant entering Sheol (cf. Isa 5:14); >/<16:7; Hos 3:1, cultic raisin cakes (cf. Jer 7:18; 44:19; but see 2 Sam 6:19//1 Chr 16:3; Song 2:5); >/<17:10; 43:12; Deut 32:16; Pss 44:20[21]; 81:9[10], strange god (cf. Hos 8:12);[86] >/<23:13; Ezek 26:7–14, Chaldeans lay siege to Tyre (cf. 29:17–20); >/<23:15, 17; Jer 25:11, 12; 29:10, seventy years of judgment (cf. 27:7).[87]

---

85. See Lynch, "Zion's Warrior," 257–59.

86. See "זָר," no. 4, *HALOT* 1:279.

87. See "Esarhaddon," *COS* 2.120:306. Also see Schnittjer, "Individual versus Collective," 126–28.

Condemnations of the people of God: >/<1:11; Hos 6:6; Pss 40:6–8; 51:18–19, not delight in sacrifice but doing good; >/<1:23; 5:23; 33:15; Amos 5:10, 12; Mic 3:9, 11, bribes instead of justice (cf. Exod 23:8; Deut 16:19); >/<1:17, 23; 3:14–15; 10:2; Amos 2:6–8; 5:11; 8:4–6; Mic 2:1–3; 3:1–4, 9–11, oppression of needy; >/<3:16; Amos 4:1–3, condemnation of affluent women; >/<5:8; Mic 2:2, excessive acquisition of property; >/<29:21; Amos 5:10, injustice at the gate; >/<57:5; Deut 12:2; 1 Kgs 14:23; 2 Kgs 16:4//2 Chr 28:4; 2 Kgs 17:10; Jer 2:20; 3:6, 13; 17:2; Ezek 6:13, spreading tree associated with infidelity in false worship;[88] >/<57:10; Jer 2:25; 18:12, infidelity saying "It is hopeless";[89] >/<58:1; Mic 3:8, "transgression" of my people/Jacob, "sin" of Jacob/Israel; >/<58:1–14; Zech 7:1–7; 8:18–19, superficial versus genuine fasting.

Warnings and threats against the people of God: >/<1:15; Jer 7:16; 11:14; 14:11; Mic 3:4, deity not listening to prayers; >/<5:10; 65:21; Deut 28:30, 39; Amos 5:11; Ezek 19:10–12, minimally yielding vineyards; >/<5:17; 13:19–22; 14:23; 17:2–3; 18:6; 25:2; 27:10–11; 32:13–14; 34:8–15; Jer 9:11; Lam 5:18, reverting to undeveloped wild state; >/<10:9; Amos 6:2, fall of Calno and Hamath as warning; >/<13:7; 19:1; Josh 2:11; 5:1; 7:5; Ezek 21:7[12]; Nah 2:10[11]; Ps 22:14[15], hearts melt (מסס לב); >/<13:10; Joel 2:2, 10, darkening of celestial lights; >/<32:9, 11; Amos 4:1, women of ease (cf. Isa 3:16).

Promises and blessings: >/<2:2; 10:12, 32; 11:9; 16:1; 25:6–7; 29:8; 30:29; 40:9; 57:13; 65:25; Ezek 20:40; 40:2; Ps 48:2, Jerusalem/Zion as chosen mountain; >/<2:3; 45:14; 60:3; Zech 14:16–19, nations pilgrimage to Jerusalem; >/<11:10; Deut 12:9; 1 Kgs 8:56, resting place for people (מְנוּחָה) and Isa 66:1; Ps 132:8, 14; 1 Chr 28:2, resting place for God (מְנוּחָה) (cf. 22:9); >/<14:2; 60:10–14; 61:5–7, oppressors become slaves; >/<19:18; Jer 2:16; 43:7, 13; 44:1, five cities of Egypt established for Judean diaspora; >/<34:3; 66:24; Jer 7:32–33, valley of Hinnom south of Jerusalem as place of slaughter of oppressors (cf. Isa 37:36); >/<49:23; Mic 7:17; Ps 72:9, lick dust (cf. Gen 3:14); >/<52:13; Jer 23:5, both use "act wisely" (שׂכל) and synonyms for "lift up" but in inverted order.

Shared Stock Phrases and Other Similarities with Non-Prophetic Contexts

Liturgical stock phrases and general thematic similarities: >/<6:11; Pss 74:10; 79:5; 89:46; 94:3, how long? (cf. Lam 5:20); >/<9:6[5]; Ps 2:7, "birth" of royal son; >/<9:6–7[5–6]; Ps 72:1–2, royal son rules with righteousness and justice; >/<19:1; Deut 33:26; 2 Sam 22:10–11//Pss 18:9–10; 68:4[5], God as celestial rider; >/<25:1; Ps 31:14[15], "you are my God" (אלהי אתה); >/<26:2; Ps 118:19, "open the gates that the righteous nation may enter/open for me the gates of the righteous" (פתחו שערים ויבא גוי צדיק/פתחו לי

88. See "רַעֲנָן," 1.a, *HALOT* 2:1269. Some of these contexts include extensive parabolic accusation of lust and debauchery (Isa 57:3–13; Jer 2:20–28; Ezek 16).

89. The Nif ptc. "it is hopeless" is an interjection akin to damn!, see "יאשׁ," *HALOT* 1:382.

שערי צדק) (cf. 24:7–10; 100:4); >/<27:1; Ps 74:13–14, killing Leviathan; >/<31:1; Pss 20:7; 33:17, trust in horses and chariots.[90]

Note the cluster of noninterpretive parallels near the end of an important unit of Isaiah: 12:4//Ps 105:1, "Give praise to Yahweh, proclaim his name; make known among the nations what he has done"; 12:5~Exod 15:1, "Sing to Yahweh, for he has done glorious things"; 12:6//Zeph 3:14–15; Zech 2:10[14]; 9:9, "Shout aloud and sing for joy, people of Zion."

Stock phrases and similar imagery with **restoration narratives and wisdom**: >/<22:23, 25; Ezra 9:8, peg in secure/his holy place (יָתֵד בִּמְקוֹם נֶאֱמָן/קָדְשׁוֹ); >/<66:2, 5; Ezra 9:4; 10:3, trembled at word/commands; >/<55:1–2; Prov 9:1–6, invitation to feast on bread and wine.

Connections within Isaiah

Doublets. Isaiah, Jeremiah, Proverbs, and elsewhere feature the same or nearly identical verses in two remote contexts. Deciding if these represent scribal markers, editorial adjustments, connectors, or the like is not easy. Some commentators see the following doublet as a section divider: **48:22//57:21**, "There is no peace," says Yahweh/my God, "for the wicked."[91] The following doublets have been filtered out as non-exegetical literary parallels: **2:9–11//5:15**, humbling the proud; **10:23//28:22**, "the Lord, Yahweh Almighty, will carry out the destruction decreed upon the whole land"; **35:10//51:11**, "Those Yahweh has rescued will return. They will enter Zion with singing; everlasting joy will crown their heads. Gladness and joy will overtake them, and sorrow and sighing will flee away"; **40:10b//62:11b**, "See, his reward is with him, and his recompense accompanies him"; **49:18a//60:4a**, "Lift up your eyes and look around; all your children gather and come to you"; **49:26//60:16**, "Then all mankind/you will know that I, Yahweh, am your Savior, your Redeemer, the Mighty One of Jacob"; **51:5b~60:9a**, "the islands wait upon me"; **55:5b//60:9b**, "Yahweh your God, the Holy One of Israel, for he has endowed you with splendor"; **58:12a//61:4a**, "they will rebuild ancient ruins"; **59:16//63:5**, no one to help so salvation my own.[92]

Structuring devices within and between sections. Many literary parallels used as structural markers in authoring scrolls look and function similar to catchwords and constellations of edited and/or arranged scriptural contexts. The major differences turn on authorial shaping of a scroll (connections within a book) versus citing external scriptural traditions (connections between books). The following are usually regarded as subheadings: >/<5:8, 11, 18, 20, 21, 22; 28:1; 29:1, 15; 30:1; 31:1; 33:1, "woe!" (הוֹי, cf. Amos 5:18; 6:1, 4; Hab 2:6, 9, 12, 15, 19); >/<5:25; 9:12, 17, 21; 10:4; cf. 14:26, 27; 19:16, "his anger is not turned away, his hand is stretched out still"; >/<24:21; 25:9; 26:1; 27:1, 2, 12, 13,

90. For a list of other parallels between Isa 40–55 and Psalms, see Willgren, "*Antwort Gottes*," 111–13.

91. See Keil and Delitzsch, *Isaiah 28–66*, 129; Blenkinsopp, *Isaiah 56–66*, 172–73.

92. For a list of other doublets, see Schultz, *Search for Quotation*, 339–41; idem, "Isaianic Intertextuality," 57.

"on that day" (ביום ההוא). The following may frame a unit: >/<40:7–8; 55:11, the assured accomplishments of the word of Yahweh. There are many links between the oracles of the nations (Isa 13–23) and the universal judgment (24–27). Here are a couple of examples: >/<14:12–15; 24:21, hosts of heaven to the pit; >/<17:6; 24:13, "gleanings remain in it as when olive tree is beaten/as olive tree is beaten as with gleanings" (ונשאר־בו עוללת כנקף זית/כנקף זית כעוללת, Seidel's theory). Other similarities (verbal and/or thematic) within sections are too numerous and peripheral to the aims of the present study to include here.[93]

For the present purpose the sections of Isaiah may be considered Isa 1–12, 13–27, 28–35, 40–55, and 56–66. The following represent a small fraction of potential verbal and thematic literary parallels between sections: >/<1:4; 5:19, 24; 10:17, 20; 12:6; 17:7; 29:19, 23; 30:11–12, 15; 31:1; 37:23; 40:25; 41:14, 16, 20; 43:3, 14, 15; 45:11; 47:4; 48:17; 49:7[2x]; 54:5; 55:5; 60:9, 14, his/your/holy one/of Israel/Jacob (קְדוֹשׁ/וֹ/כֶם/יִשְׂרָאֵל/יַעֲקֹב) (cf. 57:15); >/<1:27; 5:7, 16, 23; 9:7[6]; 28:17; 32:16; 33:5; 58:2; 59:9, 14; cf. 33:15, righteousness (צדקה) and justice (משפט); >/<45:8, 22–23; 46:13; 51:6, 8; 59:16; 61:10–11; 63:1; 64:4–5, righteousness (צדקה) and save/salvation (ישע/ישועה); 56:1, righteousness (צדקה), justice (משפט), salvation (ישועה) (cf. 59:15–17);[94] >/<2:20; 31:6–7, throw away idols; >/<6:9a; 40:6a, reapplying prophetic commission;[95] >/<6:13; 11:1, 10; 60:21, root/shoot of Jesse from a stump; >/<7:14; 8:8, 10, "Immanuel"; >/<8:14, 15; 28:13, a snare/to snare (מוקש/יקש) (cf. Exod 23:33; 34:12; Deut 7:16; Josh 23:13; Judg 2:3; 8:27; Ps 106:36);[96] >/<11:2; 42:1; 44:3; 48:16; 59:21; 61:1, spirit upon his chosen one; >/<11:12–13; 56:7, "gathering the exiles of Israel" (cf. 66:18–21); >/<25:8; 30:19; 65:19, wipe away tears/no more mourning; >/<29:16; 45:9; 64:8[9], potter as sovereign over pottery (cf. Jer 18:1–6; Rom 9:20);[97] >/<30:26; 60:19–20, moon and sun enhanced brightness; >/<40:5; 66:18, glory of Yahweh revealed; >/<40:9; 41:27; 52:7–10; 61:1, bringing good news to Zion (cf. Ps 98:1–4); >/<41:10, 13, 14; 44:2; 49:8; 50:7, 9; 63:5, I help/he will help you/he helps me/none to help (יעזר/עזרתי/ד/יעזר לי/אֵין עֹזֵר); >/<50:2; 59:1, the arm of Yahweh/my arm not "too short"; >/<51:16; 59:21, my words in your mouth (cf. 49:2); >/<52:12; 58:8, your righteousness/Yahweh "will go before" and the glory of Yahweh/God of Israel your "rear guard"; >/<53:6; 56:11, "all turn in their own way."

93. For lists of allusions within Isaiah, see Cheyne, "Critical Study of Parallel Passages," 2:241–58; Childs, *Isaiah*, 446–47; Driver, *Introduction*, 238–40; Hays, *Origins*, 239–50; Hibbard, "Isaiah 24–27 and Trito-Isaiah," 188; Kratz, "Rewriting Isaiah," 253–59. For prophetic formulas including Isaiah, see Girdlestone, *Grammar of Prophecy*, 54–65.

94. For the last three sets of parallels, see Rendtorff, *Canon and Theology*, 184.

95. See Childs, *Isaiah*, 296–97.

96. The natural relationship of Isa 8:14, 15 and 28:13 by means of verbal similarity ("snare") and the proximity of 28:13 and 28:16 may partially relate to the choice of stringing together in 1 Pet 2:6–8 by thematic catchword Isa 28:16, Ps 118:22, and Isa 8:14. That is, Isa 8:14 and 28:16 relate by both catchword and contextual similarities.

97. Potter/pottery imagery seems to play off the root "form" (יצר) used in "creation of Israel" contexts, e.g., Isa 43:1.

Chapter 11

JEREMIAH

SYMBOLS[1]

// verbal parallels (A level)
/~/ synoptic parallel (A level)
~ B, probable interpretive allusion; C, possible; D, probably not
+ interpretive blend
>/< more or less similar (see Filters)
* part of interpretive network (see Networks)

USE OF SCRIPTURE IN JEREMIAH[2]

1:6–9~Exod 4:10–12 (C)+Deut 18:18 (B) (prophet deflects commissioning based on poor speech)
2:2~Hos 2:14–15[16–17] (B) (Israel as youthful bride in the wilderness)
2:5~Deut 32:4 (C) (pushing back against infidelity)
2:11~Deut 32:17+Hos 4:7 (C) (gods are not gods)
2:23~Num 5:11–31 (D) (suspected adulteress denying defilement)
3:1~Deut 24:1–4 (B) (divorce and remarriage eliminate reconciliation)
4:23–28~Gen 1:3–25 (B) (anti-creation)
7:1–2//26:1–2 (temple sermon heading)
7:5–6, 9~Deuteronomic legal instructions (D)+Ten Commandments (B) (entry prophetic indictment)
10:23–25~Prov 20:24+Ps 79:6–7 (B) (request for sovereign Yahweh to pour wrath on nations)
11:19~Isa 53:7–8 (C) (lamb to slaughter)
12:4~Deut 32:20 (C) (reversal—he will not see)
13:11~Deut 26:19 (B) (people as Yahweh's renown, praise, and honor)
14:10//Hos 8:13 (Yahweh remembers their wickedness)
17:19–27*~Deut 5:12–15* (B) (extending implications of Sabbath rest) (* see Sabbath network)
20:7, 8~Exod 22:16[15]+Deut 22:25, 27 (B) (seduced, seized, and crying out)
23:5*~Isa 4:2* (C) (righteous branch) (* see branch network)
25:30~Amos 1:2a//Joel 3:16[4:16] (C) (Yahweh roars)
26:18//Mic 3:12 (Micah's prophecy against Jerusalem)
27:7*~25:11–12*; 29:10–12* (B) (seventy years) (* see seventy years network)
29:16–20>/<24:8–10 (trouble for the bad figs)
30:9*~Hos 3:5 (C) (renewal of Davidic rule) (* see Davidic covenant network)
31:30*~Deut 24:16* (B) (proverb of sour grapes) (* see personal responsibility network)
31:31–34*~Deut 29:1–4*[28:69–29:3] (B)+6:6–7* (C) (new covenant) (* see concealing revelation network)
33:14–22*~23:5–6*+1 Kgs 8:25*+Deut 18:5*+Jer 31:35–37 (B) (righteous branch and Levitical priest) (* see branch and Davidic covenant networks)
34:14*~Deut 15:1+15:12* (B)+Lev 25:10, 35–46* (C) (releasing slaves) (* see release statute network)
36:24~2 Kgs 22:11 (B) (not tearing clothes)
46–51~25:15–26 (C) (oracles against the nations)
48:5, 29–47~Isa 15–16, 24 (B)+Num 21:28–29; 24:17* (A) (oracles against Moab) (* see Davidic covenant and Judah-king networks)

1. For explanation of symbols, see Symbols and Abbreviations and Introduction. For other help, see Glossary.
2. See Bibliographic Note on Lists of Potential Parallels.

49:7, 9–10, 12–13, 14–16, 19–21~Obad 7–8, 5–6+Jer 25:17+Obad 1–4+Jer 50:43–46+48:40–41 (A) (oracle against Edom)

51:44b–50 MT~51:44a LXX+Isa 2:2 (C) (escape from Babylon)

52:1–34/~/2 Kgs 24:18–25:26 (fall of Jerusalem)

OLD TESTAMENT USE OF JEREMIAH (SEE RESPECTIVE NOTES)

10:13~Ps 135:7 (B) (weather maker in poetic retrospective)

14:20~Lam 5:7 (B) (bearing the ancestors' iniquities)

15:4~2 Kgs 23:26 (C) (because of Manasseh)

17:7–8~Ps 1:3 (B) (like a tree by water)

17:21–27*~Neh 13:15, 17–18* (B) (Sabbath breaking by merchandizing) (* see Sabbath network)

18:23~Neh 4:5[3:37] (B) (do not forgive them)

19:5–6~2 Chr 28:3; 33:6 (B) (child sacrifice in the Valley of Ben Hinnom)

22:24~Hag 2:23 (B) (Yahweh's signet ring)

23:1–6~Ezek 34:23–31 (C) (Davidic shepherd)

23:5–6*~Zech 3:8* (B) (branch) (* see branch and Davidic covenant networks)

25:5~Zech 1:4 (B) (message of the former prophets)

25:11, 12; 29:10*~Hag 1:2 (C) (time has not come) (* see seventy years network)

25:11, 12; 29:10*~Zech 1:12* (B) (seventy years) (* see seventy years network)

25:11, 12; 29:10*~Zech 7:5–6* (B) (fasts for seventy years) (* see seventy years network)

25:11, 12; 29:10*~Dan 9:2* (B) (seventy years) (* see seventy years network)

25:11, 12; 29:10*~2 Chr 36:21* (B) (Jeremiah's seventy years) (* see seventy years network)

25:11, 12; 29:10*~2 Chr 36:22–23 (B) (edict of Cyrus) (* see seventy years network)

27:16–22*~2 Kgs 24:13* (C) (removal of temple vessels with captivity of Jehoiachin) (* see temple vessels network)

27:16–22*~2 Chr 36:7–10* (B) (removal of temple vessels) (* see temple vessels network)

27:22*~Ezra 1:7, 11* (B) (vessels of temple returned) (* see temple vessels network)

31:33*~Ezek 36:26–27* (B) (new heart) (* see concealing network)

33:14–18*~Zech 6:11–14* (B) (civil and priestly rulers) (* see branch and Davidic covenant networks)

33:21~Mal 2:4–5, 8 (C) (covenant with Levi)

36:24~2 Kgs 22:11 (B) (tearing clothes)

49:7, 9–10, 12–13, 14–16, 19–21~Obad 7–8, 5–6 (B) (oracle against Edom)

NEW TESTAMENT USE OF JEREMIAH

5:21~Mark 8:18 (eyes but do not see)

7:11//Matt 21:13; Mark 11:17; Luke 19:46 (den of robbers)

9:24[23]//1 Cor 1:31; 2 Cor 10:17 (him who boasts)

10:7~Rev 15:4 (Who would not fear?)

15:2~Rev 13:10 (captivity and sword)

31:15//Matt 2:18 (voice in Ramah)

31:31–34//Heb 8:8–12; 10:16, 17 (new covenant)

51:45~Rev 18:4 (come out of her)

HERMENEUTICAL PROFILE OF THE USE OF SCRIPTURE IN JEREMIAH

Jeremiah uses scriptural traditions extensively. Though the same can be said for Isaiah, the situation of Jeremiah differs dramatically. The widespread use of Jeremiah contexts by other Jeremiah contexts runs along a spectrum from literary to exegetical, as well as including numerous examples of scribal enhancements. The similarities of diction and expression with Deuteronomy, the Deuteronomistic narrative (Joshua, Judges, Samuel, Kings), and scriptural prophetic traditions require special attention.

An array of interpretive challenges and scribal situations bear on Jeremiah's use of scriptural traditions. The present discussion introduces several complex issues in broad terms only insofar as they bear on Jeremiah's exegetical use of scriptural traditions. The filters at the end of the chapter pick up a number of these issues as they relate to Jeremiah's constant use of scriptural traditions in literary, stylistic, and other non-exegetical ways.

Exegetical Conventions in Jeremiah

The use of Jeremiah contexts within the book of Jeremiah presents a difficult set of issues. The bulk of these cases represent literary, not exegetical agendas. Finding a way between exegetical versus literary interrelations does not come easy.

One perennial difficulty involves Jeremiah's constant use of stock phrases, many unique to Jeremiah's prose discourses and others shared in the poetic and prose discourses. Another challenge involves prose developments of poetic messages. The vast majority of these have been bracketed out as non-exegetical literary parallels (see Filters). Still, Jeremiah's use of other contexts in Jeremiah comes up frequently in the notes on uses of other scriptural traditions.

Jeremiah's relationship to and use of Deuteronomy and the Deuteronomistic narrative involve a special set of difficulties and enjoy their own set of secondary literature. While both poetic and prose discourses share language with Deuteronomy and the Deuteronomistic narrative, the prose discourses practically overflow with shared stock phrases.

Jeremiah frequently affirms his unoriginality referring to a long line of prophets who deliver the same basic message:[3]

> For twenty-three years—from the thirteenth year of Josiah son of Amon king of Judah until this very day—the word of Yahweh has come to me and *I have spoken to you again and again*, but you have not listened. [4] And though Yahweh has sent all his servants *the prophets to you again and again*, you have not listened or paid any attention. [5] *They said*, "Turn now, each of you, from your evil ways and your evil practices, and you can stay in the land Yahweh gave to you and your ancestors for ever and ever. [6] Do not follow other gods to serve and worship them; do not arouse my anger with what your hands have made. Then I will not harm you." [7] But you did not listen to me. (Jer 25:3–7a, emphasis mine)[4]

In many places Jeremiah develops elements that appear in earlier prophets, especially Hosea and Isaiah. In some cases these advances stem from interpretive blends of prophets with Torah, usually Deuteronomy. Jeremiah's use of prophetic oracles against the nations from Torah and Isaiah are especially challenging (see notes on 48:5, 29–47). All of this

3. See Jer 7:13, 25; 11:7; 25:3, 4; 26:5; 29:19; 32:33; 35:14, 15; 44:4; also see Schnittjer, "Individual versus Collective," 119–20.

4. While Jer 25:4 MT features first-person narrative from Jeremiah, 25:4 LXX offers the same storyline in first person from the Lord.

takes place in the context of Jeremiah's frequent attacks on false prophets. Jeremiah aligns his own message with the prophets who have left behind written collections with emerging authority and stands against contemporary peace prophets.

Some of Jeremiah's use of Torah and prophets may be thought of as contemporizing. This applies both to many allusions in his poetic and prose oracles against Judah, but especially to his oracles against the nations. Jeremiah repackages oracles against Moab from Torah and Isaiah in a manner that sounds like it applies exactly the same in his own day. The prophetic collapsing of past and present in judgment oracles cautions against simplistic historicizing tendencies common in modern interpretation of Scripture.

One of the difficulties with the use of Jeremiah contexts elsewhere in Jeremiah amounts to his using the same condemnation oracle but switching the objects of Yahweh's wrath. The same oracles in different locations of Jeremiah may condemn Judah versus Babylon or Moab versus Edom (see note on 49:7–21). It is difficult to know how to interpret the details of a boilerplate condemnation that simply removes people X and inserts people Y. Although similar in certain respects to Isaiah's oracles against the individual nations sharing parallels with the universal condemnation (Isa 13–23, 24–27), Jeremiah's recycling of the same oracles with new objects pushes the interchangeability of peoples further. Should the interchangeability of poetical imagery be regarded as generic? Do these mix-and-match oracles represent specific cases of a general attitude that poetic judgment oracles can be appropriated to others? Although these issues cannot be finally decided, exegetical uses as well as non-exegetical cases of boilerplate oracles discussed in the Filters give pause to overreading historical contexts encoded within poetical details.

Jeremiah uses legal standards in highly ironic ways to press his message. He compares Yahweh to a faithful husband with unfaithful ex-wives. The prophet insists that Yahweh's loyalty to his ex-wives includes taking them back after they have been with others even though that violates law (Jer 3:1). Jeremiah's "private" use of scriptural traditions in his prayer life insinuates Yahweh has been treating him after the manner of a sexual predator (20:7–8). These bold rhetorical, not literal, uses of scriptural traditions reveal a prophet under pressure.

Jeremiah excels at interpretive and theological inversion (the latter of which are housed in the Filters). He uses scriptural allusion to reverse creation and divine omniscience and to make even the most famous intercessors ineffective (4:23–28; 12:4; 15:1). Jeremiah contrasts several lesser past symbols of divine power and mercy with greater expectations. Many of these inverted expectations are introduced by "they shall no longer say." But by inserting the greatest symbols of grace as lesser elements in the equations, he virtually hyperbolizes expectations. No one will even remember the ark of the covenant when Jerusalem itself becomes Yahweh's throne and the nations gather before him (3:17–18). Nobody will bother to make oaths by the God who brought his people out of Egypt after he brings them back from land of the north (16:14–15//23:7–8).

Perhaps the most enduring inversion relates to the covenant itself. The new covenant shall not be like the one with the ancestors. Instead of the older generation perpetually instructing the younger generation, Yahweh himself again will write Torah but not on tablets of stone. He will write his covenantal word directly on their hearts. The soul of his people shall be covenant-shaped: "I will be their God, and they will be my people" (31:33). Jeremiah even inverts Yahweh's memory. If captives wait for their God to remember, he says he will not remember their sins (31:34). But Jeremiah does not propose these exegetical advancements of revelation out of thin air. They unfold quite naturally from Torah: "But to this day Yahweh has not given you a mind that understands or eyes that see or ears that hear" (Deut 29:4[3]). Jeremiah's new covenant expects a day that will grant the new mind spoken of by Moses.

In sum, Jeremiah's manifold scriptural allusions include many exegetical advancements. The boldest of these invert, reverse, or ironically commandeer Torah and prophetic traditions to condemn his constituents with ever-fading hopes that they might repent. In all of this, Jeremiah makes no claims of originality. He says that he stands within a long-running chain of Yahweh's servants vainly calling the people to repent. When Jeremiah speaks of hope, he often frames his messages in terms of opposition to the past, but usually the "new" expectation provides an enhanced and upgraded version of its traditional counterpart.

Ancient Versions of Jeremiah

The student new to Old Testament studies may wish to skip this section and return as needed at a later time.

Anyone who reads a modern committee translation of Jeremiah, such as the NIV, can see a range of poetry and prose. Some public discourses feature all poetry or prose while others interchange between the two. The book also features private prayers and personal revelations to the prophet intermittently in Jer 11–20, also in poetry and prose. Besides the public and private discourses in poetry and prose, the book features many third-person prose narratives about Jeremiah. Each of these affects the use of scriptural traditions both in exegetical and non-exegetical ways.

Part of the reason for the variety may relate to the collaborative role of Baruch, Jeremiah's scribe. At one point when an earlier prophetic scroll of Jeremiah had been destroyed, the narrator explains: "So Jeremiah took another scroll and gave it to the scribe Baruch son of Neriah, and as Jeremiah dictated, Baruch wrote on it all the words of the scroll that Jehoiakim king of Judah had burned in the fire. *And many similar words were added to them*" (Jer 36:32, emphasis mine). This note regarding authorized collaboration of Jeremiah and his scribe represents the only explicit evidence of the process of producing prophetic scrolls in Scripture. Though the context would imply Baruch as the subject, Leuchter observes that the statement emphasized above does not state who or when the similar words were added.[5] The use of the "incomplete passive" construction of the phrase

5. See Leuchter, "Personal Missives," 276.

does not specify the agents.[6] Authorized collaboration helps explain some of the different approaches to the use of scriptural traditions in Jeremiah.

The references to more than one scroll—both scrolls authorized and neither scroll defective, even though one represented a fuller prophetic presentation with similar words added—help set precedent for multiple ancient versions of Jeremiah (36:32).[7] The Septuagint bears witness as a translation of a shorter Hebrew version of Jeremiah confirmed by the fragments akin to it among the Qumran manuscripts (4QJer[bd/4Q71, 72a]). The masoretic version features approximately 14 percent more text, including many minor clarifications as well as several longer developments. Three preliminary issues need to be noted to make sense of how the scriptural use of Scripture relates to multiple ancient Hebrew editions of Jeremiah. The complex issues of identifying the older versus the younger edition, how much older and younger, and reckoning with more than one edition in ancient circulation need to be oversimplified for the broad points made in this study.[8] The cited items offer next steps for further study. The point at hand does not relate to any of the theories that conjecture authorship or other excavative goals. The issues relate to available evidence bearing on exegesis in Jeremiah.

First, the normal view regards Septuagintal Jeremiah as an older edition and masoretic Jeremiah as an updated edition.[9] Important objections have been voiced. The most extensive argument that the Septuagintal version is riddled with accidental deletions appears in Lundbom's commentary, featuring long lists of unintentionally skipped passages.[10] Lundbom does not blame the Septuagintal translators but "careless and inattentive" scribes of the Hebrew parent text in Egypt for hundreds of accidents accumulating a loss of 1,715 words, by his count.[11]

Vroom's reevaluation of ancient scribal practices based on cognitive theory takes into account step by step how scribal omissions occur. The key observations relate to short-term "working memory," "phonological loop," and "visuospatial sketchpad." The scribe's working memory does not relate to remembering a series of single letters because people read words not letters. And the working memory means scribes did not need to reread an entire column of text to find where they left off but looked back to approximately

6. See *IBHS* §23.2.2e.

7. Sharp observes that "Jer. xxxvi preserves the literary memory of a shorter (but neither deficient nor secondarily abbreviated) earlier scroll and a longer (but neither corrupted nor secondarily expanded) later scroll" ("'Take Another Scroll,'" 508).

8. Though 4QJer[bd/4Q71, 72a] represent a Hebrew version of Jeremiah more like the parent text of the Septuagint, the present discussion relates only to the full book of Jeremiah in the Septuagintal and masoretic versions. In addition, the limitations of the present study do not allow taking up any proposals for how oral traditions may or may not have contributed to the newer edition of Jeremiah.

9. See Tov, "Literary History," 211–31; for examples in poetic and prose sections, see 212, 221, 223, 227. Also see Tov, *Textual Criticism*, 286–94.

10. See Lundbom, *Jeremiah 1–20*, 885–87; idem, *Jeremiah 37–52*, 549–63; idem, "Haplography," 309–20. Also see more generally, Gentry, "Septuagint," 217–18, n. 66; idem, "Text," 43–44, n. 84.

11. See Lundbom, "Haplography," 306.

the right place in the column.[12] Provisional semicontrolled testing of Vroom's thesis in a simulated ancient scriptorium on graduated samples basically affirms his theoretical discussion. Vroom's list of steps in the ancient copying process does not include re-inking the pen, which, though second nature to working scribes, does mildly adjust what scribes need to do within their working memories.[13] Setting aside the technicalities, anyone can see the general points of Vroom's argument by handwriting a less familiar biblical passage while looking back and forth at the donor and receptor texts. Vroom pushes back against Lundbom's extravagant list of omissions in the Hebrew parent text of Septuagintal Jeremiah. Vroom notes the disconnect with Ludbom's claims that vast omissions were made by mostly "single letter" repetitions (over 80 percent). Word recognition versus reading letters or skipping columns of text by looking at the entirely wrong place on the donor scroll simply does not relate to how people read or copy, even substandard ancient working scribes.[14] By eliminating most of the evidence for excessive accidental deletions, the case for the masoretic version of Jeremiah as the earlier version becomes nearly impossible at an accidental mechanical level. The point at hand relates to treating masoretic Jeremiah as a revised edition of something akin to the Hebrew parent text of the Septuagint relative to the scriptural use of Scripture. In sum of this point, the evidence supports the majority view that the Hebrew parent text of Septuagintal Jeremiah represents an older edition and the proto-masoretic version of Jeremiah an updated edition.

Second, how much older and younger are the Septuagintal and masoretic versions of Jeremiah? The evidence from diachronic studies of ancient Hebrew suggests possible answers. Diachronic studies find that both versions of Jeremiah feature Transitional Biblical Hebrew.[15] Transitional Biblical Hebrew falls between and overlaps both Standard Biblical Hebrew, which refers to the linguistic evidence in Torah and Former Prophets, and Late Biblical Hebrew, which denotes the same in Chronicles, Ezra-Nehemiah, Daniel, and Esther.[16] Much greater weight comes from syntactical versus lexical evidence.[17]

---

12. See Vroom, "Cognitive Approach," esp. 269–76. Reading words not letters is part of "phonological loop." The internal speech of readers, in this case ancient scribes, is comprised of words not individual letters (271). And "visuospatial sketchpad" refers to the spatial orientation, in this case, of scribes looking back to the parent text to approximately the same place from where they left off (272). Both elements are subsumed under the normal working memory of ancient scribes.

13. See ibid., 267. These observations are indebted to vigorous discussions with my students in an upper-level graduate seminar on the Great Isaiah Scroll who participated in an ancient scribal experiment in approximated scriptorium conditions to test Vroom's thesis.

14. See ibid., 275, 278.

15. See Hornkohl, *Ancient Hebrew Periodization*. These findings apply to both the Hebrew parent text of the LXX and the MT, with slight diachronic differences (366–67).

16. See Hornkohl, "Transitional Biblical Hebrew," 31–42; Hendel and Joosten, *How Old?*, 73–84.

17. The reuse of older cherished biblical terms in later texts reduces, but does not eliminate, the value of lexical contrasts *per se*. But later Aramaisms and other control elements offer stronger evidence of Late versus Standard Biblical Hebrew. On diachronic studies of ancient Hebrew, see, e.g., Hendel and Joosten, *How Old?*; Schniedewind, *A Social History of Hebrew;* Garr and Fassberg, *Handbook*; Hurvitz et al., *Concise Lexicon*; Miller-Naudé and Zevit, *Diachrony in Biblical Hebrew*. For short overviews, see Hornkohl, "Biblical Hebrew: Periodization," 1:315–25; Noonan, *Advances*, 223–44; Rooker, "Diachronic," 135–44. For opposing views, see Rezetko and Young, *Historical Linguistics;* Young and

The kind of grammatical and syntactic differences between the 1611 KJV and the 2011 NIV, in certain respects, illustrates what anyone can see by reading the narratives of Genesis and Nehemiah in Hebrew, or Jeremiah in between. The differences should be thought of as approximate since language development interrelates to major crises, like national captivity, as well as slow-moving developments, like provincial agrarian life in economically depressed regions of the empire. The dramatic linguistic changes caused by the exile accelerated the effects upon "Biblical Hebrew" within the thousand-year period during which the Scriptures were produced. In sum of this point, the linguistic evidence supports seeing both versions of Jeremiah in close succession during the "transitional" (exilic) period of development of Biblical Hebrew. These provisional conclusions require caution because dating changes in languages can only be approximations by the nature of language changes, even while the evidence upon which the conclusions are based is empirically verifiable.

Third, how do multiple versions of Jeremiah in ancient circulation bear on authority?[18] With respect to textual criticism of Jeremiah, Tov argues that "both the MT and LXX could reflect an original reading."[19] As such, the differences should be considered literary rather than text-critical concerns.[20] The circulation of two versions of Jeremiah infers a similar situation relative to authority.[21] In the case of intentional variations between the Septuagintal and masoretic versions, most function as literary versus exegetical upgrades. That is, the evidence suggests proto-masoretic Jeremiah is an authorized update of an authorized Hebrew parent text akin to Septuagintal Jeremiah.

The present discussion applies only to the evidence related to the Septuagintal and masoretic versions of Jeremiah. This evidence does not say anything about any other part of the Hebrew Scriptures, Septuagintal translations, or their parent texts.

In sum, complete copies survive of two ancient versions of Jeremiah that circulated simultaneously. The evidence points to the masoretic version as an intentional authorized

---

Rezetko, *Linguistic Dating*; for a critical evaluation of opposing views, see Joosten, review of *Linguistic Dating*; Hendel and Joosten, *How Old?*, 135–44. Schmid admits the value of many aspects of Hornkhol's approach to a diachronic analysis of Jeremiah as "Transitional Biblical Hebrew" (see previous footnotes above). Schmid seeks to add "theological profile" to re-date parts of Jeremiah later ("How to Date Jeremiah," 453–59). For a criticism that shows why Schmid's "theological profile" approach (460–62) does not work see Rom-Shiloni, "From Prophetic Words," 577–80.

18. For a close evaluation of the evidence concluding that the grandson of Ben Sira used written copies of both the Old Greek version of Jeremiah and a proto/semi-Masoretic version of Jermeiah, see Lange, "Book of Jeremiah," 160.

19. Tov, "Hebrew Scripture Editions," 298.

20. See Tov, "Literary History," 237. Contra Giffone, "Can Theological Interpretation?" 153–78. In relation to Jeremiah, Giffone claims that Protestants might be "wrong" about the canon and infers the same about Christianity in general by asking if "the Church was using the wrong Old Testament" (170, 176, et passim). However, Giffone acknowledges that his proposal is not based on a careful comparison of the evidence (176). Giffone does not interact with the diachronic linguistic evidence (in the present work, see the second point of Ancient Versions of Jeremiah above and footnotes therein) or the evidence from the biblical texts discovered in the Judean desert (in the present work, see Figure NT2 and associated discussion including footnotes in chapter on Toward the New Testament). This evidence points in the opposite direction of Giffone's bold claims. The evidence suggests that the issues associated with the ancient versions of Jeremiah are literary not text-critical issues.

21. On "inspiration" and "original autograph," see Hays, "Jeremiah,"134–48.

update of something akin to an authorized Hebrew parent text of the Septuagint. The provisional evaluation of the linguistic evidence suggests exilic dating for both versions.[22] These provisional starting points bear on an evaluation of Jeremiah's use of scriptural traditions.

The present approach attends to the masoretic version of Jeremiah with only the most important Septuagintal differences noted along the way. Several long pluses in the masoretic version of Jeremiah are evaluated with an eye to exegetical versus literary developments (see notes on Jer 7:1–2; 25:30; 27:7; 29:16–20; 33:14–22; 46–51; 51:44b–50; and 39:4–13 explained in note on 52:1–34).[23] Hereafter the translation of the Hebrew parent text of the Septuagintal version of Jeremiah will be abbreviated as LXX and the proto-masoretic version as MT.

USE OF SCRIPTURE

1:6–9~Exod 4:10–12 (C)+Deut 18:18 (B) (prophet deflects commissioning based on poor speech). In spite of few verbal parallels, the call of Moses and Jeremiah may be related merely as type-scenes, especially the similar complaint about poor speaking (Exod 4:10; Jer 1:6). If the call of Jeremiah has been intentionally crafted after the call of Moses, the implication may relate to Jeremiah as a prophet like Moses in a general sense (Deut 18:15). The shared language "I put my words in his/your mouth" strengthens the possibility of an interpretive blend (18:18//Jer 1:9 lit.).

2:2~Hos 2:14–15[16–17] (B) (Israel as youthful bride in the wilderness). Jeremiah seems to broadly allude to Hosea's parabolic treatment of Israel as Yahweh's youthful bride in the wilderness using the distinctive term "youth." Hosea portrays Yahweh trying to rekindle a stale relationship by leading his bride back into the wilderness. Jeremiah extends the theme by giving voice to Yahweh's fond reminiscences of long-gone days of "devotion" (חֶסֶד) that once motivated his youthful bride to follow her God based on love (bold signifies verbal parallels, and italics signify reversals):

> [Yahweh says] "Therefore I am now going to allure her; I will lead her into the **wilderness** and speak tenderly to her. There I will give her back her vineyards, and will make the Valley of Achor a door of hope. There she will respond as in the days of her **youth**, as in the day she came up out of Egypt." (Hos 2:14–15[16–17])

> Go and proclaim in the hearing of Jerusalem: "This is what Yahweh says: 'I remember the devotion [חֶסֶד] of your **youth**, how as a bride *you loved me* and followed me

22. Although I would register differences, Goldingay's accessible description—his shorter work after completing his NICOT volume on Jeremiah—of assembling the Jeremiah scroll in exile offers helpful insight (*Theology of Jeremiah*, 8–9).

23. Additional masoretic pluses which do not seem to reflect exegetical but literary concerns of various sorts include: Jer 10:6–8 (see Filters); 11:7–8; 17:1–5a (doublet, 15:13–14//17:3–4, see Filters); 25:26b (cf. parallel with 51:41).

> through the **wilderness**, through a land not sown. Israel was holy to Yahweh, *the firstfruits of his harvest*; all who *devoured her* were held guilty, and disaster overtook them,'" declares Yahweh. (Jer 2:2–3†)

After Yahweh's walk down memory lane (2:2), Jeremiah shifts to third person and reverses the imagery of love, sanctification, and protection: he speaks of the bride's love in place of that of Yahweh (2:2; cf. Deut 7:8); Yahweh setting apart Israel as his firstfruits versus firstfruits set apart to Yahweh (Jer 2:3; cf. Deut 26:1–5; cf. Exod 23:19; 34:26; Num 28:26); and they devour her versus Israel devouring the nations (Jer 2:3; cf. Num 24:7–8).[24] All of this builds to a punchline that stands in sharp contrast to Hosea, who had spoken of taking his wife back to the wilderness to rekindle their relationship. Jeremiah reminds his congregation of the safety Israel once enjoyed as a young devoted bride. Jeremiah flips the application of the newlywed analogy to bring into clear relief why Jerusalem now found herself surrounded by danger. She had forgotten her youthful days as a devoted bride (cf. Isa 50:1; 54:4–8). In those days her new husband treasured her and protected her from predatory nations.

2:5~Deut 32:4 (C) (pushing back against infidelity). The prophet contends for Yahweh: "What *fault* [עָוֶל] did your ancestors find in me, that they strayed so far from me?" (Jer 2:5). This may allude to the claim that he is "a faithful God and without *fault* [עָוֶל]" (Deut 32:4).[25]

2:11~Deut 32:17+Hos 4:7 (C) (gods are not gods). Continuing the themes from Hosea and the Song of Moses, Jeremiah accuses Israel of "exchanging their glory" for "no god" (Jer 2:11). This combines echoes of "exchanging their glory" (Hos 4:7) for "no god" (Deut 32:17). Though the shared language is limited, the other possible allusions to both of these contexts in Jer 2 increases the possibility of allusion (see notes on Jer 2:2, 5 and Filters; cf. Ps 106:20; Rom 1:23).

2:23~Num 5:11–31 (D) (suspected adulteress denying defilement). The denial "I am not defiled [לֹא נִטְמֵאתִי]" (Jer 2:23) has been compared to the repetition of the potential "defilement" (טָמֵא) of the suspected adulteress (Num 5:13, 14, 20, 27, 28, 29). The evidence is unconvincing.[26]

3:1~Deut 24:1–4 (B) (divorce and remarriage eliminate reconciliation). Jeremiah paraphrases and abridges the law of divorce to set up a lengthy parabolic judgment, featuring several loosely related poetic and prose oracles collated together. Hosea's relationship with Gomer as covenantal metaphor lingers in the background but without concrete parallels. The point at hand relates to the use of the legal instruction (verbal parallels signified by bold, similar concepts signified by italics):

---

24. In Num 24:7–8, Balaam may be broadly alluding to scriptural traditions in Exod 17:8–15; Num 21:1–3, 21–35; 22–24.

25. See Holladay, *Jeremiah 2*, 56.

26. Contra Rom-Shiloni, "How can you say?" 757–75, esp. 769–70.

> If a **man** marries a **woman** who becomes displeasing to him because he finds something indecent about her, and he writes her a certificate of divorce, gives it to her and **sends** her from his house, and if after **she leaves** his house **she becomes the wife of another man**, and her second husband dislikes her and writes her a certificate of divorce, gives it to her and sends her from his house, or if he dies, then her first husband, who divorced her, is not allowed **to return** to marry her again after she has been defiled. That would be detestable in the eyes of Yahweh. *Do not bring sin upon the* ***land*** Yahweh your God is giving you as an inheritance. (Deut 24:1–4)

> If a **man sends** his **wife** and **she leaves** him and **she becomes the wife of another man**, should he **return** to her again? *Would not the* ***land*** *be completely defiled?* But you have lived as a prostitute with many lovers—would you now **return** to me? declares Yahweh. (Jer 3:1 lit.)

Like the law in Deut 24:4, the prophet focuses upon metaphorically polluting the land Yahweh had given. This picks up his concern in Jer 2:7. But in Jer 3:1, 2, 9 he uses a different nonstandard, less ritual term for defiling (חנף) of the land.[27] The term Jeremiah uses elsewhere associates false worship with polluting the land (Ps 106:38). In another context Jeremiah speaks of false prophets as "ungodly" (חנף) for prophesying by Baal (Jer 23:11, 13).[28] The emphasis on false worship, and all that means, fits with the extended parable of infidelity in Jer 3. The exegetical intervention does not relate so much to deritualizing the pollution but to violation of the law by Yahweh to take back his wives. The interpretive inferences only make sense with the law as donor and Jeremiah's oracle as receptor context. Although the covenantal metaphors shift between Yahweh as husband and father, he remains committed to his wives, Rebel Israel and Faithless Judah, calling them to return (3:11–12 JPSB). The allusion to the law that Yahweh needs to "break" to reunite with his wives after they have united themselves to other lovers heightens the sense of his enduring covenantal faithfulness to his people.[29]

4:23–28~Gen 1:3–25 (B) (anti-creation). Both Jeremiah and his contemporary Zephaniah in different ways rewind the narrative tradition regarding the days of creation (see note on Zeph 1:2–3).[30] The direct verbal relationship and reversed storyline by these two prophets suggest they know of the narrative in the opening of Genesis. The purpose of Jeremiah's vivid inversion seems to fall on the slim margin for turning to Yahweh between two divine deliberations "I will not destroy it completely. . . . I have spoken and will not relent" (Jer 4:27, 28). The oracle does not follow a strict sequence but generally moves backward through the creation days (bold signifies terms in Gen 1, and italics signify prophetic language):[31]

---

27. Compare the standard language for defiling (טמא) the land in Lev 18:25–29; Deut 24:1 and Jer 2:7.
28. See "I חנף," *HALOT* 1:335.
29. See Fishbane, *Biblical Interpretation*, 310.
30. Also see broad creational allusions, Jer 10:11–16//51:15–19; 14:22; 32:17, 27; 31:35–37; cf. 33:20, 22, 25.
31. See Fishbane, "Jeremiah IV 23–26 and Job III 3–13," 152; though Fishbane's approach is different than the one here since he emphasizes Jer 4:23–26 strictly following the order of the creation days in Genesis.

> I looked at the earth, and it was **formless and empty** [before day one]; and at **the heavens** [day two], and their **light** was gone [day one]. [24] I looked at the mountains, and they were quaking; all the hills were swaying. [25] I looked, and there were **no people** [אָדָם] [day six]; **every bird** in the sky had flown away [day five]. [26] I looked, and *the fruitful land* was a desert [day three]; all its towns lay in *ruins* before Yahweh, before his fierce anger. [27] This is what Yahweh says: "The whole *land will be ruined*, though I will not destroy it completely. [28] Therefore the earth will mourn and the heavens above *grow dark* [day one], because I have spoken and will not relent, I have decided and will not turn back." (Jer 4:23–28)

After using a series of creation words (4:23–25), Jeremiah switches to his judgment of Judah lexicon: "fruitful land" (4:26; 2:7); "ruins" (4:26; 1:10; 31:28); "ruined" (4:27; 6:8; 9:10; 10:22; 12:10; 32:43; 34:22; 44:6), "dark" (4:28).[32] The jarring threat ends with an ironic determination against reversal—not relent and not turn back. The narrator of Genesis voices Yahweh's self-deliberating regrets (נחם) for creating humans when he decides to destroy by flood (Gen 6:6–7). Jeremiah voices Yahweh's determination not to relent (נחם) from judgment (Jer 4:28).

7:1–2 MT//26:1–2 (temple sermon heading) (on LXX and MT Jeremiah, see Hermeneutical Profile of the Use of Scripture in Jeremiah). The Septuagintal witness to the opening of the temple sermon says, "Hear the word of the Lord, all Judea" (Jer 7:2 LXX). Based on the similarity with the abbreviated version of the message of Jer 7:3–15 in 26:4–6, the setting from 26:1–2 has been adapted to: "This is the word that came to Jeremiah from Yahweh: "*Stand at the gate of Yahweh's house and there proclaim this message:* 'Hear the word of Yahweh, all *you people of* Judah *who come through these gates to worship Yahweh*'" (7:1–2 MT, emphasis signifies plus).[33] This masoretic plus is part of literary coherence, not exegesis.

7:5–6, 9~Deuteronomic legal instructions (D)+Ten Commandments (B) (entry prophetic indictment). The entrance liturgies ask who may enter Yahweh's courts to worship and answer by alluding to Torah righteousness (Pss 15:1; 24:3). Whether gatekeepers called these out to temple-goers, Jeremiah's temple sermon offers a powerful prophetic counterpart.[34] Perhaps the psalmist captures the spirit of Jeremiah's message: "Open for me the gates of the righteous; I will enter and give thanks to Yahweh" (118:19).[35] Jeremiah's prose discourses are styled after Deuteronomy and the Deuteronomistic narrative even while they relate to his poetic oracles (see Filters). The temple sermon brims

32. See "I כַּרְמֶל," "נתץ," "שְׁמָמָה," "קדר," *HALOT* 1:499, 736; 2:1072, 1556. Cf. "mourning" in judgment contexts, Jer 8:21; 14:2.

33. A fragment of 4QJer[a/4Q70] matches Jer 7:1 MT (see *BQS* 2:558). For variants to "correct" 7:1 to MT, see LXX Göttingen apparatus.

34. See von Rad, *Old Testament Theology*, 1:375–76.

35. See McKane, *Jeremiah*, 1:159.

full of characteristic language: "*I spoke to you again and again*, but you did not listen" and "if you do not listen to the words of my servants the prophets, whom *I have sent to you again and again*" (Jer 7:13; 26:5, emphasis signifies a favorite Jeremiah stock phrase). The claim of unoriginality in proclamation corresponds to the five positive and six negative standards of righteousness (italics signify Deuteronomistic and/or Jeremiah's prose idiom, and bold signifies Ten Commandments):

> If you really change your ways and your actions and deal with each other justly, if you do not oppress *the foreigner, the fatherless or the widow* and *do not shed innocent blood* in this place, and *if you do not follow other gods* to your own harm . . .
>
> Will you **steal** and **murder, commit adultery** and **perjury**, *burn incense to Baal* and *follow other gods you have not known*? (7:5–6, 9†)[36]

Jeremiah's confrontation does not turn on a creative use of Torah but on undercutting the people's bogus sense of covenantal safety. First, Jeremiah appropriates the promise of "the place I gave to you and your ancestors" (7:14), referring to the land, and applies it to the temple (7:3, 7; cf. v. 6), on the analogy of "the place" where the temple in Shiloh used to stand (7:12; 26:6; cf. Ps 78:60). Jeremiah's shift in reference for "place" corresponds to his taunt against the "deceptive words" (Jer 7:4, 8) of the people, namely, "This is the temple of Yahweh" (7:4, 14). Second, Jeremiah denies that the temple can function like a "den of thieves," a denial that builds on the covenantal demands for righteousness (7:11). Though David could hide in a "den" during his revolt against the king of Israel (1 Sam 22:1), the temple could never work as a covenantal safe place. Jeremiah's point is that Yahweh's fidelity to the covenant makes the temple the most dangerous place for covenant-breakers to hide out.

10:23–25~Prov 20:24+Ps 79:6–7 (B) (request for sovereign Yahweh to pour wrath on nations). The prophet's prayer features a paraphrase of a wisdom sentence on divine control over humans (Jer 10:23; Prov 20:24) blended with loose quotation for divine wrath upon oppressive nations (Jer 10:25//Ps 79:6–7). The combination evokes mild irony. The prophet uses a wisdom tradition that speaks of divine control of humans but then calls upon Yahweh to bring his wrath upon the nations who did his bidding.[37]

---

36. Jeremiah alludes to the Ten Commandments by means of inf. abs.'s: steal (Exod 20:15//Deut 5:19); murder (Exod 20:13//Deut 5:17); adultery (Exod 20:14//Deut 5:18); and by paraphrase: perjury (Exod 20:16//Deut 5:20). Note the phrases of Jer 7 that run parallel to Deuteronomy: "foreigner, the fatherless, or the widow" (Deut 10:18; 14:29; 16:11, 14; 24:17, 19, 20, 21; 26:12, 13; 27:19); "shed innocent blood" (19:10; 21:8; 27:25; 2 Kgs 21:16; 24:4); "follow after foreign gods" (Deut 6:14; 8:19; 11:28; 13:2[3]; 28:14); "gods you have not known" (11:28; 13:2, 6, 13[3, 7, 14]; 28:64; 29:26[25]; cf. 32:17); and note prose discourse stock phrase of Jeremiah: "burn incense to Baal" (Jer 7:9; 11:13, 17; 19:13; 32:29) (see Weinfeld, *Deuteronomic School*, 320, 322, 324, 356). But the phrase "you really change your ways and your action" only appears in the two versions of the temple sermon (7:3, 5; 26:13) and seems more like a sermon theme than a cliché (contra Weinfeld, 352). See Filters for more details on Deuteronomy and Jeremiah.

37. For a summary of several views of Jer 10:25, none of which satisfies, see Parke-Taylor, *Formation*, 218.

11:19~Isa 53:7–8 (C) (lamb to slaughter). The first of Jeremiah's confessions shares language with the last of Isaiah's servant songs. The most prominent parallel occurs in a simile of the suffering figure as an animal to be slaughtered. If these contexts are related, then the exegetical relation is reversal. Whereas Jeremiah struggled mightily in prayer, calling for retribution against his oppressors (Jer 11:20; cf. 18:23), the servant accepts trouble silently (Isa 53:7; cf. 50:5–7). The commonplace use of the imagery of the animal led to slaughter reduces confidence in a relationship among any of the uses including the expression in Jer 12:3.[38] Evidence is lacking for the direction of dependence, with intentional parallel as only a possibility (emphases signify verbal parallels):

> He was oppressed and afflicted, yet he did not open his mouth; **he was led** like a lamb **to the slaughter** [לַטֶּבַח יוּבָל], and as a sheep before its shearers is silent, so he did not open his mouth. By oppression and judgment he was taken away. Yet who of his generation protested? For he was cut off *from the land of the living* [מֵאֶרֶץ חַיִּים]; for the transgression of my people he was punished. (Isa 53:7–8)

> I had been like a gentle lamb **led to the slaughter** [יוּבַל לִטְבוֹחַ]; I did not realize that they had plotted against me, saying, "Let us destroy the tree and its fruit; let us cut him off *from the land of the living* [מֵאֶרֶץ חַיִּים], that his name be remembered no more." (Jer 11:19)

12:4~Deut 32:20 (C) (reversal—he will not see). Jeremiah gives voice to the rebellious attitude of the people by possibly inverting a line from the Song of Moses. Yahweh said, "I *will see* what *their end will be* [אֶרְאֶה מָה אַחֲרִיתָם]; for they are a perverse generation, children who are unfaithful" (Deut 32:20). Jeremiah reverses the sentiment, "the people are saying, 'He *will not see our end* [לֹא יִרְאֶה אֶת־אַחֲרִיתֵנוּ]'" (Jer 12:4†; cf. 16:17). Jeremiah's inversion aptly captures the people's unfaithfulness. The many parallels of the Song of Moses in Jeremiah increase the possibility of allusion.[39]

13:11~Deut 26:19 (B) (people as Yahweh's renown, praise, and honor). The threefold use of "praise," "fame," and "honor" (תִּפְאֶרֶת ,שֵׁם ,תְּהִלָּה) in Deut 26:19, Jer 13:11, and 33:9 suggest intentional use here.[40] Deuteronomy uses the threefold commendation in the context of referring to Israel as Yahweh's "treasured people" (Deut 26:18). Jeremiah employs the phrase ironically—signifying it as the receptor—as something of a punchline at the end of a long sign involving a filthy loincloth (Jer 13:1–11). Elsewhere he uses the threefold description positively of restoration (33:9). The inversion of the first two terms in Jer 13:11 likely reflects Seidel's theory (see Glossary; emphases signify verbal parallels):

---

38. For this parallel and many single terms in the two contexts, see Sommer, *A Prophet Reads Scripture*, 64–66. For a less confident view of relationship since these are stock phrases, see Baumgartner, *Jeremiah's Poems*, 43. Compare: Isa 53:7; Jer 11:19; 12:3; Ps 44:11, 22[12, 23], like a lamb to slaughter.

39. See Holladay, *Jeremiah 2*, 53–56.

40. See ibid., 58; "תִּפְאֶרֶת," 5.e *HALOT* 2:1773.

> He has declared that he will set you in **praise, fame** and **honor** high above all the nations he has made and that you will be a people holy to Yahweh your God, as he promised. (Deut 26:9)

> "For as a loincloth is bound around the waist, so I bound all the people of Israel and all the people of Judah to me," declares Yahweh, "to be my people for my **fame** and **praise** and **honor**. But they have not listened." (Jer 13:11 lit.)

14:10//Hos 8:13 (Yahweh remembers their wickedness). Jeremiah 14:10 recontextualizes a phrase from Hos 8:13 at the end of a poetic unit. A first-person prose private exchange between Jeremiah and Yahweh has been juxtaposed immediately after the citation. The prose segment thematically restores the context of the futile burnt offerings of the people. Yahweh also prohibits Jeremiah from his prophetic role as advocate on behalf of the damned (Jer 14:11; contra Gen 20:7; Amos 7:2, 5). The prohibition against praying for the people appears repeatedly in the larger context (Jer 7:16; 11:14; 14:11; cf. 15:1). Hosea rebukes his congregation for using worship for personal benefit and threatens doom (Hos 8:11, 14). In Jeremiah, Yahweh heightens his determination for judgment by an unwillingness to hear further prophetic petitions for the people (italics signify verbatim parallel, and broken underlining signifies catchwords).[41]

> Though they offer sacrifices as gifts to me, and though they eat the meat, *Yahweh does not accept with them. Now he will remember their wickedness and punish their sins*: They will return to Egypt. (Hos 8:13†)

> Although our iniquities testify against us, do something, Yahweh, for the sake of your name. For we have often rebelled; we have sinned against you. . . . [10] This is what Yahweh says about this people: "They greatly love to wander; they do not restrain their feet. So *Yahweh does not accept them; he will now remember their iniquity and punish them for their sins*." [11] Then Yahweh said to me, "Do not pray for the well-being of this people. [12] Although they fast, I will not listen to their cry; though they offer burnt offerings and grain offerings, I will not accept them. Instead, I will destroy them with the sword, famine and plague." (Jer 14:7, 10–12†)

17:19–27*~Deut 5:12–15* (B) (extending implications of Sabbath rest) (* see Sabbath network). Torah speaks of the Sabbath in many places but only twice clarifies the nature of prohibited work—in the fields even during harvest in Exod 34:21 and domestically even for making fire in 35:3 (see notes on Exod 31:12–17 and 34:21). The minimalist approach to spelling out this prohibition naturally leads to the kinds of enhancements

41. This observation on catchwords is indebted to Parke-Taylor, *Formation*, 214.

intimated in Amos 8:5 and made in Jer 17:19–27. During the restoration, many Yahwistic Judeans signed an oath to adhere to the prophetically enhanced standards (Neh 10:31[32]; 13:15–22). Everything about Jeremiah's enhancements of the Sabbath standards creates challenges, such as the nature of the burdens the people carried in and out of the gates.[42]

Fishbane argues that Jeremiah "presumptively" adds new prohibitions—not carrying burdens from houses or through gates (Jer 17:21–22, 24, 27)—seeking to legitimize these additions by a "pseudo-citation": "as I commanded your ancestors" (17:22). He says Jeremiah "brazenly" misrepresents his novelties by claiming Sinaitic revelatory status.[43] Fishbane is correct to note Jeremiah's heavy-handed emphasis on the authority of the exegetical advances as he warns of the burning of Jerusalem (17:27). Still, a couple of clarifications are needed. Less importantly, Deuteronomy's presentation of the fourth commandment itself includes a citation formula, "Observe the Sabbath day by keeping it holy *as Yahweh your God has commanded you*" (Deut 5:12, emphasis mine), which fits with what Jeremiah said, namely, "but keep the Sabbath day holy, *as I [Yahweh] commanded your ancestors*" (Jer 17:22, emphasis mine).[44] The citation formula of Deuteronomy should not be taken as a pseudo-citation because of the alternative rationale and interpretive blending in its version of the fourth commandment (see note on Deut 5:6–21 on vv. 12–15). More importantly, Torah includes two clarifications of what it means not to work, which set a precedent for prophets like Amos and Jeremiah to condemn kindred Sabbath violations by divine authorization.

The intent of the command, "Do not add to it or take away from it," is not to fossilize a static Torah (Deut 12:32[13:1]; cf. 4:2). The immediate context defines the intended meaning to be prophets preaching in accord with Torah (13:1–5[2–6]). In a larger context, Moses's role as mediator includes "do not turn aside to the right or left" (5:32). The point of the warnings is obedience. The compound verb in the first is "do not add . . . or subtract, *but keep*" (4:2 lit., emphasis mine) and the other "*you shall keep to do*" (12:32[13:1] lit., emphasis mine).[45] An example directly relevant here is the new version of several of the Ten Commandments in Deut 5 including the Sabbath commandment (see note on Deut 5:6–21).

In the present case, if Torah clarified Sabbath rest in the workplace (Exod 34:21) and at home (35:3), then the prophets speak to prohibitions of the marketplace (Amos 8:5; Jer 17:21–22, 24, 27). The Sabbath regulation from the covenant collection may be compared since it provides part of the blend for Deuteronomy's version of the fourth command (bold and italics signify verbal parallels, underlining signifies marking, and broken underlining signifies motivation):

42. See Achenbach, "Sermon," 877–81.

43. See Fishbane, *Biblical Interpretation*, 132–34.

44. Compare: "as Yahweh your God has commanded you" (כַּאֲשֶׁר צִוְּךָ יהוה אֱלֹהֶיךָ) (Deut 5:12) and "as I [Yahweh] commanded your ancestors" (כַּאֲשֶׁר צִוִּיתִי אֶת־אֲבוֹתֵיכֶם) (Jer 17:22).

45. See Tigay, "Significance," 138, 141–42; Grisanti, "Deuteronomy," 2:516–17.

> Six days do your work, but on the seventh day *you shall rest*, so that *your ox and your donkey may rest*, and so that the slave born in your household and the foreigner living among you may be refreshed. (Exod 23:12)

> Observe **the Sabbath day by keeping it holy,** as Yahweh your God **has commanded you**. [13] Six days you shall labor and do all your work, [14] but the seventh day is a sabbath to Yahweh your God. On it **you shall not do any work**, neither you, nor your son or daughter, nor your male or female servant, *nor your ox, your donkey* or any of your animals, nor any foreigner residing in your towns, so that your male and female servants *may rest, as you do*. (Deut 5:12–14)

> Judah and everyone living in Jerusalem who come through these gates. This is what Yahweh says: Be careful not to carry a load on the Sabbath day or bring it through the gates of Jerusalem. Do not bring a load out of your houses or **do any work** on the Sabbath, but **keep the Sabbath day holy, as I commanded your** ancestors. Yet they did not listen or pay attention; they were stiff-necked and would not listen or respond to discipline. . . . But if you do not obey me **to keep the Sabbath day holy** by not carrying any load as you come through the gates of Jerusalem on the Sabbath day, then I will kindle an unquenchable fire in the gates of Jerusalem that will consume her fortresses. (Jer 17:21–23, 27; cf. 17:24)[46]

20:7, 8~Exod 22:16[15]+Deut 22:25, 27 (B) (seduced, seized, and crying out). Jeremiah's final confession in the series escalates with rhetoric that can be construed as accusing Yahweh as though he were a sexual predator. Jeremiah pushes back against the pressure to preach a message he does not approve of to a people who oppress him for it. The strong language may allude to legal instructions. The use of the term "to talk into something" (פתה) can be rendered "deceive" (Jer 20:7 NIV) or in another context "seduce" (Exod 22:16[15] NIV).[47] Clines and Gunn claim that taking the sexual exploitation sense from the law against the seducer into Jeremiah's lament commits the error of "illegitimate totality transfer."[48] Though that seems correct at first, Jeremiah goes on to use additional language from the counterpart legal instruction in Deuteronomy (not observed by Clines and Gunn), namely, "seize" (חזק) and "cry out" (זעק) (Deut 22:25, 27). Others suggest Jeremiah's deep sense of betrayal and bitterness stand behind the prophet's accusation, using the legal vocabulary of seduction and rape.[49] Baumgartner explains: "Using these bold, but incomparably vivid images, the prophet depicts how he has, half willingly, half under coercion, placed himself in Yahweh's service. . . . But now,

---

46. The inf. const. "to make holy" connects to the negative particle (בִּלְתִּי) by the use of the attached "by" (לְ) in "*to make holy . . . by not* carrying a load" (לְקַדֵּשׁ . . . וּלְבִלְתִּי, Jer 17:27 lit.; see GKC §114s).

47. See Baumgartner, *Jeremiah's Poems*, 74. Also note use of "entice" (פתה) and "prevail over" (יכל) in Jer 20:10.

48. See Clines and Gunn, "'You Tried,'" 21; referring to Barr, *Semantics*, 218.

49. See McKane, Jeremiah 1:468–70; Holladay, *Jeremiah 2*, 57.

like a girl stranded in shame, full of bitterness he must lament: 'Oh, if only I had not let myself be led astray!'"[50] But that stops too soon with seduction. Jeremiah "screams" as one seized only to be mocked. The following retain the NIV's contextual glosses but emphasize verbal parallels.

> If a man *seduces* [פתה Piel] a virgin who is not pledged to be married and sleeps with her, he must pay the bride-price, and she shall be his wife. (Exod 22:16[15])

> But if out in the country a man happens to meet a young woman pledged to be married and **rapes** [חזק Hif] her, only the man who has done this shall die . . . for the man found the young woman out in the country, and though the betrothed woman <u>screamed</u> [זעק], there was no one to rescue her. (Deut 22:25, 27)

> You *deceived* [פתה Piel] me, Yahweh, and I was *deceived* [פתה Nif]; you **overpowered** [חזק Qal] me and prevailed. I am ridiculed all day long; everyone mocks me. Whenever I speak, I <u>cry out</u> [זעק] proclaiming violence and destruction. So the word of Yahweh has brought me insult and reproach all day long. (Jer 20:7–8)

Yates makes the point that Jeremiah does not condone a view of God as rapist, nor do prophetic metaphorical uses of strong language legitimize acts.[51] Coarse thematic imagery only works by standing in condemnation of the imagery. The abrasive language, in this case, comes from a prophet under pressure.

23:5*~Isa 4:2* (C) (righteous branch) (* see branch network). The term "branch" (צֶמַח) of Yahweh appears in an eschatological context of Isa 4:2. Jeremiah may be alluding to Isaiah's cluster of thematically similar figures using synonyms for a "root" and "shoot" to grow up from the stump of Jesse (Isa 11:1, 10). Jeremiah speaks of the "branch of righteousness" somewhat ironically as "Yahweh our righteousness [*zdq* צדק]", likely a taunt against Zedekiah—literally "Yah my righteous [*zidqiyahu* צִדְקִיָּהוּ]." The expectation for Yahweh to raise up a royal branch for David in the twilight of the First Commonwealth constitutes a significant advancement of the irrevocability of the Davidic covenant. Yahweh's fidelity to David endures even in the absence of Davidic rule (also see note on Jer 33:14–18).

25:30 MT (=32:16 LXX)~Amos 1:2a//Joel 3:16[4:16] (C) (Yahweh roars) (on LXX and MT Jeremiah see Hermeneutical Profile of the Use of Scripture in Jeremiah). The old image of Yahweh roaring from Zion heads the oracles against the nations in Amos. The Hebrew parent text of the older LXX version of Jeremiah uses a similar phrase after his oracles against the nations and the summation in the section on the cup of wrath; this juxtaposition is not retained in the MT revision (on rearrangement see note on Jer 46–51; emphasis signifies parallels):

50. Baumgartner, *Jeremiah's Poems*, 74.
51. See Yates, "Jeremiah's Message," 155, n. 42.

Amos	Jeremiah LXX	Jeremiah MT
	Oracles against the nations (Jer 25–31 LXX)	
	Cup of wrath against Jerusalem, Judah, and the nations (32:1–15 LXX)	Cup of wrath against Jerusalem, Judah, and the nations (Jer 25:15–29 MT)
Yahweh roars from Zion and thunders from Jerusalem (Amos 1:2)	The Lord will give an oracle from on high; from his holy place give forth his voice; he will give a word as an oracle over his place (32:16 LXX)	Yahweh will roar from on high; he will thunder from his holy dwelling and roar mightily against his land (25:30 MT)
Oracles against the nations, including Judah and Israel (1:3–2:15)		
		[Oracles against the nations moved elsewhere, 46–51 MT]

The shift from divine judgment coming from Zion in Amos 1:2 to coming from "on high" in Jer 32:16 LXX/25:30 MT does not change the prophet as a vehicle for divine judgment (Amos 3:8–9; Jer 32:14 LXX/25:28 MT; cf. "lair" [*סֹךְ] Jer 25:38 MT; "shelter" [סֻכָּה] Amos 9:11). The shift from Zion to on high signals, for Jeremiah's readership, the fall of Jerusalem. Amos 1:2 as donor context for Jeremiah is less certain in light of Joel's matching statement, "*Yahweh will roar from Zion and thunder from Jerusalem*; the earth and the heavens will tremble. But Yahweh will be a refuge for his people, a stronghold for the people of Israel" (Joel 3:16a[4:16a], emphasis mine). Joel's use of the saying affirms refuge for Jerusalem in Joel 3:16b[4:16b]—something not present in the parallel context of Jeremiah. Although the donor context for Jer 32:16 LXX/25:30 MT is not clear, the relocation of the prophetic motif of roaring emanating from on high rather than Zion remains a striking development in light of the fall of Jerusalem.

26:18//Mic 3:12 (Micah's prophecy against Jerusalem). Jeremiah faced a death sentence for preaching a sermon against the temple (Jer 26:4–6; cf. 7:1–15). The elders defend his message by citing Micah's message of doom against Jerusalem in the days of Hezekiah (italics signify verbatim citation with one term spelled differently, bold signifies verbal parallels, and broken underlining signifies marking):

> [Micah said] Then I said . . . "**This is what Yahweh says** . . . 'Therefore because of you, *Zion will be plowed like a field, Jerusalem will become a heap of rubble, the temple hill a mound overgrown with thickets.*'" (Mic 3:1a, 5a, 12)

> [The elders said] Micah of Moresheth prophesied in the days of Hezekiah king of Judah. He told all the people of Judah, "**This is what Yahweh** Almighty **says**: '*Zion will be*

plowed like a field, Jerusalem will become a heap of rubble, the temple hill a mound overgrown with thickets.'" (Jer 26:18)

Micah blames the establishment of Jerusalem for its imminent doom at the end of a horrific oracle. Micah uses ironic language of the temple mount becoming an "overgrown high place" (בָּמוֹת יָעַר), using a term which connotes false worship (Mic 3:12). This may build on "What is Judah's high place [בָּמוֹת]? Is it not Jerusalem?" (1:5) as well as set up a simile wordplay of the hope of Jacob like a lion among "beasts of the forest" (בְּהֵמוֹת יַעַר) (5:8[7]).[52] The important issue for the elders trying to clear Jeremiah turns on the absence of the fulfillment of Micah's threat of judgment. The standard of prophetic messages' accordance with reality stands in the background (Deut 18:22) as does the ever-present exception clause "unless they turn back" (Jer 26:3).[53] The success of prophetic threats ironically results in avoidance of the judgment they threaten (26:19). The narrative of the death of the prophet Uriah for his Jeremiah-like message against the city reinforces the theme of a constituency refusing to listen (26:20–23). As the next narratives continue emphasizing true versus false prophecies, Jeremiah states an important principle to Hananiah: "From early times the prophets who preceded you and me have prophesied war, disaster and plague against many countries and great kingdoms. *But the prophet who prophesies peace will be recognized as one truly sent by Yahweh only if his prediction comes true*" (28:8–9, emphasis mine).

27:7*~25:11–12*; 29:10–12* (B) (seventy years) (* see seventy years network). In Jeremiah's prose message to Zedekiah's court in relation to hosting representatives from several regional nations (Jer 27:1, 3), Jeremiah makes reference to the duration of the rule of Babylon. Earlier in a prose message during Jehoiakim's tenure, Jeremiah spoke of a seventy-year dominion of an enemy "from the north"/"king of Babylon" (25:11–12 LXX/MT). Jeremiah 27 includes a plus in the masoretic version that interprets the prediction as a round number, referring to the Neo-Babylonian dynasty rather than a set amount of time: "All nations will serve him [Nebuchadnezzar] and his son and his grandson until the time for his land comes; then many nations and great kings will subjugate him" (27:7 MT [not in LXX], on LXX and MT Jeremiah see Hermeneutical Profile of the Use of Scripture in Jeremiah). The basic chronology of neo-Babylonian rule runs a little more than sixty years: Nebuchadnezzar II (605–562 BCE), his son Evil-merodach/Amel-Marduk (561–560), Nebuchadezzar's son-in-law Neriglissar (559–556), Neriglissar's son Labashi-Marduk (556), and unrelated usurper Nabonidus (555–539), whose son Bel-shar-usur/Belshazzar is mentioned in Dan 5.[54] Other ancient contexts use seventy years to refer to the judgment against Tyre in Isa 23:15–17 and regarding Babylon in the Esarhaddon

52. On the wordplay of Mic 3:12 and 5:8[7], see Ben Zvi, "Ancient Readers," 89. See parallel judgments between Samaria and Jerusalem as "a heap of rubble" (עִי) and as a "field" (Mic 1:6; 3:12). Also see note on Jer 26:18 NET.

53. See Chisholm, "When Prophecy," 566–68; Sandy, *Plowshares & Pruning Hooks*, 129–94.

54. See Kuhrt, *Ancient Near East*, 2:592, 597.

inscription (ca. 679 BCE).[55] Whereas Jer 25:11–12 speaks of seventy years of the land's ruin, the letter to the Jehoiachin exiles of 597 speaks of Babylon's seventy years in relation to the return of the remnant (29:10–11). The plus in Jer 27:7 MT continues to focus on Babylonian rule but without using a numerical quantification.[56]

29:16–20 MT>/<24:8–10 LXX/MT (trouble for the bad figs). The long plus in the masoretic version of the letter to those who were exiled with Jehoiachin in 597, in Jer 29:16–20 (not in LXX), does not present exegetical development but literary connection to the message against the bad figs in 24:8–10 (LXX/MT). The plus also includes several other stock phrases (see Filters).

30:9*~Hos 3:5 (C) (renewal of Davidic rule) (* see Davidic covenant network). Hosea 3:5 appears to be one of the updates reflecting a later Judean perspective, much like the "and also Judah" passages running through the prophecies against the Northern Kingdom of Israel.[57] These authorized updates in the "republication" of an Israelite prophet offer its message to an analogously doomed Judean kingdom. The idea that prophetic messages transcend their historical contexts becomes more explicit as canonical consciousness grows (2 Kgs 17:19; Zech 1:4–6; 7:12–13). In any case, the difficulty of dating an inserted update rules out deciding on direction of dependence. In contexts speaking of captivity, the expectations for a restored Davidic king pivot on renewed submission to Yahweh in both Hosea and Jeremiah (emphasis signifies verbatim parallel):

> Afterward the Israelites will return and seek **Yahweh their God and David their king**. They will come trembling to Yahweh and to his blessings in the last days. (Hos 3:5)

> Instead, they will serve **Yahweh their God and David their king**, whom I will raise up for them. (Jer 30:9)

The expectations for a renewed Davidic rule stand among the great prophetic advances of revelation (see notes on Jer 23:5; 33:14–22 MT; Ezek 34:23–24; 37:24–28).

31:30*~Deut 24:16* (B) (proverb of sour grapes) (* see personal responsibility network). Both Jeremiah and his exiled contemporary Ezekiel refer to a complaint proverb regarding the injustice of the forced migrations. Neither prophet denies the claim or softens the implications of exile as divine judgment. Both prophets set up a contrast between a day when "people say" this proverb versus a coming day that will have no room for such claims. In each case the applied commentary of the prophet draws on the restoration of justice using legal instruction from Deuteronomy for individual liability in human courts. It would seem that neither prophet uses the other but both leverage the proverb

55. See "Esarhaddon," *COS* 2.120:306.

56. On the seventy years in Scripture, see Schnittjer, "Individual versus Collective," 126–28.

57. See Hos 1:7, 11[2:2]; 4:15; 5:5, 10, 14; 6:4, 11; 8:14; 10:11; 12:2 (Childs, *Introduction*, 378–79).

against the same legal standard (bold signifies identical language, and italics signify similar constructions):

> **Parents** are not to be put to death for their **children**, nor **children** put to death for their **parents**; *each will die for their own sin.* (Deut 24:16)

> The word of Yahweh came to me: "What do you people mean by quoting this proverb about the land of Israel: '**The parents** *eat* **sour grapes, and the children's teeth are set on edge**'? As surely as I live, declares Sovereign Yahweh, you will no longer quote this proverb in Israel. For everyone belongs to me, **the parent** as well as **the child**—both alike belong to me. *The one who sins is the one who will die.*" (Ezek 18:1–4)

> In those days people will no longer say, "**The parents** *have eaten* **sour grapes, and the children's teeth are set on edge.**" Instead, *each will die for their own iniquity*; whoever eats sour grapes—their own teeth will be set on edge. (Jer 31:29–30 lit.)

The syntactical structure of Jer 31:30 offers a close allusion to the law limiting capital punishment to individuals at fault housed in Deut 24:16.[58] Jeremiah's complainants focus on the problem of deferred judgment. Because Yahweh has been patient allowing opportunity for repentance, the judgment of many generations falls upon those forcibly migrated by the Neo-Babylonians.

The proverbial complaint runs along the lines of a statement in Lamentations: "Our parents sinned and are no more, and we bear their iniquities" (Lam 5:7 lit.). The claim of paying for ancestral sins speaks in terms of a "vertical" generational collective. The proverbial complaint overlaps but differs from that of Ps 44. The psalmists claim they have been faithful to the covenant in spirit and in truth (Ps 44:17–18, 20–21[18–19, 21–22]). They rehearse that they had not forgotten the name of their God, though they nowhere use it in their psalm (44:20[21]; on the so-called Elohistic Psalter, see Psalms Filters). Nonetheless they have been exiled "like sheep to be slaughtered" (44:11, 22[12, 23]). The narratives of Kings and Chronicles as well as the preexilic prophets do not speak directly of a righteous remnant akin to the psalmists. The psalmists claim to be a righteous remnant within rebellious Israel. They do not suffer for their parents' sin—"vertical" collective—but for those of their contemporaries—"horizontal" collective.[59]

The shared grievance in all these cases boils down to paying for the sins of someone else. While the psalmists beg their unnamed divine Lord to remember them, Jeremiah speaks of days to come in which deferred judgment will be replaced by immediate

---

58. The context of the law in Deut 24:16 is dominated by protections for an array of socially challenged persons. Deuteronomy 24:10–11 and 24:12–13 stipulate protections for debtors, 24:14–15 for impoverished employees, and 24:17–22 against injustice and predatory financial practices for protected classes—residing foreigners, orphans, and widows.

59. The concept of "horizontal" versus "vertical" collectives comes from Greenberg, *Ezekiel 1–20*, 339.

accountability (44:23[24]; Jer 31:30). Jeremiah's comments may or may not hold hints of irony. Ezekiel expands upon the issue at length with scenarios, commentary, and a biting ironic conclusion (see note on Ezek 18:1–4).

Although Jeremiah does not challenge the complainants' charge of injustice in this context, elsewhere he speaks as though he does not share their outlook.[60] In poetry, Jeremiah argues a reciprocal relationship between the greedy and their punishment: "Therefore I will give their wives to other men and their fields to new owners. From the least to the greatest, *all are greedy for gain*; prophets and priests alike, *all practice deceit*" (Jer 8:10, emphasis mine; cf. 6:12–13). Jeremiah also preaches in prose that temple-goers need to turn from their own unjust practices or they will be exiled. "*If you really change your ways and your actions* and deal with each other justly, if you do not oppress the foreigner, the fatherless or the widow and do not shed innocent blood in this place, and if you do not follow other gods to your own harm, *then I will let you live in this place*, in the land I gave your ancestors for ever and ever" (7:5–7, emphasis mine). In contrast to the claims of divine injustice in the proverb cited in 31:29 implying innocence, Jeremiah promotes just punishment in his own days, in continuity with Torah, and in the days to come (Deut 24:16; 31:29).[61] The presence of contingent judgment—unless you repent—throughout Jeremiah also places responsibility for deferring judgment on the present generation (see note on Jer 26:18).

31:31–34*~Deut 29:1–4*[28:69–29:3] (B)+6:6–7* (C) (new covenant) (* see concealing revelation network). In many cases Jeremiah projects a future hope in terms of contrast to the great redeeming works of Yahweh: "at that time . . . they will no longer say" with reference to the ark of the covenant (Jer 3:16–17); "the days are coming . . . when it will no longer be said" regarding the exodus from Egypt (16:14//23:7); "in those days they will no longer say" concerning the unfairness of collective judgment (31:29); and "the days are coming . . . it will not be like the covenant I made with their ancestors . . . no longer will they teach their neighbor" in relation to the new covenant (31:31–34).[62] The contrast plays off the lesser to greater but uses something great as the lesser element to virtually hyperbolize the expected greater element, in this case a new covenant.

Jeremiah's use of the new covenant does not replace but renews the Torah. The new covenant of Jeremiah showcases the full covenant formula and offers expansive interpretative advances. The covenant formula in Jer 31:33 shares verbatim parallel with Ezek 37:27—"I will be their God, and they will be my people." Ezekiel refers to an "everlasting covenant," speaking of David, and Jeremiah to a "new covenant" relative to the Mosaic covenant. Both of these prophets frequently use the formula which appears elsewhere often in lightning rod contexts (Table J1).

60. See Domeris, "Jeremiah and the Poor," 52–56.
61. See Greenberg, *Ezekiel 1–20*, 340.
62. See Weinfeld, "Jeremiah," 17–19.

TABLE J1: COVENANT FORMULA‡

Formula **A**, Yahweh being Israel's God[a]; Formula **B**, Israel being God's people[b]; Formula **C**, combined A and B.

Tetrateuch	Deuteronomy	Deuteronomistic Narrative	Prophets[c]	
A, Gen 17:7, 8			C, Jer 7:23	C, Ezek 11:20
C, Exod 6:7	B, Deut 4:20		C, Jer 11:4	C, Ezek 14:11
A, Exod 29:45	B, Deut 7:6		B, Jer 13:11	A, Ezek 34:24
A, Lev 11:45	B, Deut 14:2	B, 1 Sam 12:22	C, Jer 24:7	C, Ezek 34:30[d]
A, Lev 22:33	C, Deut 26:17, 19	C, 2 Sam 7:24	C, Jer 30:22	C, Ezek 36:28
A, Lev 25:38	B, Deut 27:9	B, 2 Kgs 11:17	C, Jer 31:1	C, Ezek 37:23
C, Lev 26:12	B, Deut 28:9		C, Jer 31:33	C, Ezek 37:27
A, Lev 26:45	C, Deut 29:13[12]		C, Jer 32:38	C, Zech 8:8
A, Num 15:41				

‡ Data in table collated from Rendtorff, *Covenant Formula*, 13–14, 93–94 (except Ezek 34:30, see note d).

[a] Literally: "to be for you a God; I am/will be your/their God" (להיות לך לאלהים; והייתי לכם/להם לאלהים), and variations.

[b] Literally: "to be for me a people; to be for him the people of his inheritance" (להיות לי לעם; להיות לו לעם נחלה), and variations.

[c] The covenant formula serves as a pretext for biting prophetic judgments, such as Hosea's son named Not-My-People "for you are not my people and I am not yours" (Hos 1:9 lit.). Most modern committee translations emend the text with "your God" as the last words following LXX, Vulg., *BHK*, and *BHS* apparatus, but the evidence favors a parent text like the MT (see Gelston, *BHQ*, 55*).

[d] The covenant formula in Ezek 34:30 "I, Yahweh their God . . . they are my people" has been split and expanded by a reassurance formula in the MT, thus: "Then they will know that I, Yahweh their God, *am with them* [אִתָּם] and that they are my people, the house of Israel, declares Sovereign Yahweh" (Ezek 34:30†). The emphasized phrase appears in MT but not LXX (see *BHS* apparatus). This observation is made by Lyons, "Extension," 146, n. 43.

The significance of the covenant formula extends to the covenantal relationship as a whole and God's sovereign election of Israel grounded upon the covenant. Most of the uses of the covenant formula in Jeremiah can be characterized as broad allusion or stock phrases (Table J1). The revelation of the new covenant features intentional interpretive advances of contexts of covenant renewal in Torah. The most important likely exegetical allusions include "in addition to" by "new" covenant (Deut 29:1[28:69]; Jer 31:31) and the absence versus divine infusion of "heart knowing" (Deut 29:4[3]; Jer 31:31, 33, 34). Calibrating between possible and probable allusion remains difficult because of the commonness of terms and ideals as well as loose referencing by Jeremiah. The extent of the verbal and contextual parallels between Deut 29:1–4[28:69–29:3] and Jer 31:31–34 suggests a probable parallel. The ironic reversal of Yahweh's not remembering (see below) suggests Jeremiah's new covenant as receptor context.

Attention needs to be restricted to the four most important exegetical advances in Jeremiah's new covenant, namely, a new kind of renewal of a broken covenant, divine internalization of Torah, the role of forgiveness in covenant renewal, and the permanence of the new covenant. Though many scriptural contexts bear on this major prophetic announcement, discussion of these four advances can benefit by comparison here to representative covenant renewal passages in Exodus, Leviticus, and Deuteronomy—yet the parallels with Deut 6:6–7 are possible, and with 29:1–4[28:69–29:3] probable, allusions (the following marked contexts share similar themes and/or shared terms but different syntax in the main):

> "Lord," he said, "if I have found favor in your eyes, then *let the Lord go with us*. Although this is a stiff-necked people, forgive our wickedness and our sin, and take us as your inheritance." Then Yahweh said: **"I am making a covenant with you**. Before all your people I will do wonders never before done in any nation in all the world. The people you live among will see how awesome is the work that I, Yahweh, will do for you." (Exod 34:9–10)

> I will walk among you and *be your God, and you will be my people*. I am Yahweh your God, who brought you out of Egypt.... Yet in spite of this, when they are in the land of their enemies, I will not reject them or abhor them so as to destroy them completely, breaking my covenant with them. I am Yahweh their God. But for their sake I will remember the covenant with the ancients whom I brought out of Egypt in the sight of the nations *to be their God*. I am Yahweh. (Lev 26:12–13a, 44–45, v. 45 lit.)

> [T]he things your eyes have seen or let them fade from your heart as long as you live. Make them known [ידע Hif] to your children and to their children after them. [10] Remember... at Horeb, when he [Yahweh] said to me, "Assemble the people before me to hear my words so that they may learn [למד Q] to revere me as long as they live in the land and may teach [למד Piel] them to their children." (Deut 4:9b–10†)

> These commandments that I give you today are to be on your hearts [לְבָבֶךָ]. Impress them on your children. Talk about them when you sit at home and when you walk along the road, when you lie down and when you get up. (6:6–7)

> Fix these words of mine in your hearts.... Teach [למד Piel] them to your children, talking about them when you sit at home and when you walk along the road, when you lie down and when you get up. (11:18a, 19a)

> These are the terms of **the covenant** Yahweh commanded Moses to make with the Israelites in Moab, **in addition to** the covenant he had made with them at Horeb.... But to this day Yahweh has not given you a heart that knows [לֵב לָדַעַת] or eyes that see or ears that hear.... You are standing here in order to enter into **a covenant with Yahweh your God, a covenant Yahweh is making with you** this day and sealing with an oath, to confirm you this day *as his people, that he may be your God* as he promised you and as he swore to your fathers, Abraham, Isaac and Jacob. (29:1, 4, 12–13[28:69; 29:3, 11–12], v. 4 lit.)

> "The days are coming," declares Yahweh, "**when I will make a new covenant** with the people of Israel and with the people of Judah. [32] It will not be like the covenant I made with their ancestors when I took them by the hand to bring them out of Egypt, because they broke my covenant, though I was a husband to them," declares Yahweh. [33] "This is the covenant I will make with the people of Israel after that time," declares Yahweh. "I will put my torah in their minds and write it on their hearts [לִבָּם]. *I will be their God, and they will be my people.* [34] No longer will they teach [למד Piel] their neighbor, or say to one another, 'Know [דְּעוּ] Yahweh,' because they will all know [יֵדְעוּ] me, from the least of them to the greatest," declares Yahweh. "For I will forgive their wickedness and will remember their sins no more." (Jer 31:31–34, v. 32 lit.)

First, Jeremiah gives voice to Yahweh's new kind of covenant renewal. The term "new" (חָדָשׁ) does not connote uniquely novel and without precedent. Akin to the way the phrase "new song" heads some psalms that recycle and repurpose older songs (Pss 96:1; 98:1), so too the new covenant builds on the Mosaic covenant. Jeremiah does not invent the idea of a new covenant *ex nihlo*, but speaks in a new way regarding the renewal of the covenant spoken of several times in Torah. After the people had broken the covenant by worshiping the golden calf, Yahweh said he would not go with the people but would send a delegate (Exod 33:1–3). Moses begged Yahweh for his presence to remain with the people, and Yahweh responded by renewing the covenant (34:9–10). The same pattern underlies Jeremiah's new covenant for Yahweh to be their God and they to be his people.[63]

Fulfillments breed expectations. Torah anticipates that the people would "break" (פרר) the covenant (Lev 26:15; cf. Deut 31:16, 20). If they break it Yahweh would not (Lev 26:44). The fulfillment of a "broken" (פרר) covenant generates the expectation for a new kind of covenant (Jer 31:32).

Expectations breed expectations. Even before the end of Moses's last earthly day in which he had spoken at length of the Horeb covenant (Deut 5–28), he could already speak of the need for another covenant. The next words from his mouth refer to a covenant "in addition to" the Horeb covenant (29:1[28:69]).[64] Moses and Jeremiah stand in accord. Moses previews another covenant that includes Yahweh himself changing the heart of his people (Deut 29–30; esp. 30:6, 14). Jeremiah calls this additional covenant "the new covenant" (Jer 31:31).

Second, Jeremiah expects a new kind of interior inscribing of Torah. Moses explains the reason for an additional covenant: because "Yahweh has not given you a heart that knows or eyes that see or ears that hear" (Deut 29:4[3] lit.). The absence of knowledge implanted in the heart by Yahweh gets at the basis for the failure of the older covenant

63. See Rendtorff, *Covenant Formula*, 72; idem, "What Is New?," in *Canon*, 198.

64. The idea of "in addition to" derives especially from the partitive function of "*out of* a larger class" (מִן) in the composite term (מִן + לְ + בַּד = מִלְּבַד) in Deut 29:1[28:69] (see GKC §119w, n. 2). The composite term has a similar force in Deut 4:35.

(Jer 4:4; 5:21; 6:10, 17, 19). Against the perennial heart impediment of the people, Jeremiah voices Yahweh's decree: "I will put my torah in their minds and write it on their hearts. I will be their God, and they will be my people" (31:33; cf. 24:7; 32:39). The bold imagery ironically replaces the need to teach in the great commandment. To get the commands "into the hearts" of the next generation called for constant instruction (Deut 4:9–10; 6:6–9; 11:19–20).[65]

Jeremiah's language has often been thought of as if Torah would be downloaded like a program onto the mental hard drive of Neo in *The Matrix*. But to regard Torah written on the heart as mere knowledge overly literalizes the figurative language: "No longer will they teach their neighbor, or say to one another, 'Know Yahweh'" (Jer 31:34). Reducing knowledge of Yahweh to inert cognitive data badly misses the dynamic function of covenantal knowledge. When Yahweh speaks his word, it comes to pass (28:9; cf. Deut 18:22). As Isaiah says, "My word . . . will not return to me empty" (Isa 55:11). When Yahweh writes Torah on the heart, the Torah-shaped soul will produce Torah-compliant lives. The need to embed Torah upon hearts remains the same in Mosaic covenant and new covenant while the teacher and method are new.

The covenantal formula epitomizes the covenantal relationship newly incarnated in Torah-shaped hearts, namely, "I will be their God, and they will be my people" (Jer 31:33).

Third, Jeremiah includes forgiveness of sin within covenant renewal.[66] Moses begs, "forgive our wickedness and our sin, and take us as your inheritance," and Yahweh responds with covenant renewal (Exod 34:9–10). Self-humiliation and confession of sin by the exiles activates Yahweh *to remember* his covenant (Lev 26:40–41, 45). Jeremiah's oracle advances revelation at this very point. He speaks of what Yahweh will *not remember*—their sin (Jer 31:34). New emphasis on forgiveness of sin as signaling covenant renewal enhances a standard prophetic emphasis (Isa 33:24; Mic 7:18).[67] The necessity of forgiveness of sin as the basis of covenant renewal becomes a central function of the new covenant in further advancements of the New Testament (see Luke 22:20; 1 Cor 11:25; 2 Cor 3–4; Heb 8:6, 8–12; 10:12–18).[68]

Fourth, Jeremiah uses the permanence of creational structures to signify the enduring covenantal election of God's people. "This is what Yahweh says, he who appoints the sun to shine by day, who decrees the moon and stars to shine by night. . . . 'Only if these decrees vanish from my sight,' declares Yahweh, 'will Israel ever cease being a nation before me'" (Jer 31:35–36).[69] David likewise uses dependable cosmic events to speak of the fidelity of God to uphold his covenantal word (2 Sam 23:3–5). So too the psalmist

65. See Weinfeld, "Jeremiah," 29–30.

66. See Rendtorff, *Covenant Formula*, 86.

67. See Weinfeld, "Jeremiah," 32.

68. Psalm 40:8b[9b] in the LXX speaks of desiring to do God's will "and your law within my belly" (NETS). This conceptually connects 40:6–8a cited in Heb 10:5–8 with Jer 31:33–34 in Heb 10:16–17. See Guthrie, "Hebrews," 977.

69. Although these verses are rearranged between the two versions of Jeremiah they both house parallel materials (Jer 38:35, 36, 37 LXX = 31:37, 35, 36 MT, with minor adjustments).

prays regarding the Davidic covenant's fulfillment of the Abrahamic covenant: "May his name endure forever; may it continue as long as the sun. Then all nations will be blessed through him, and they will call him blessed" (Ps 72:17).

In sum, Jeremiah's new covenant reverses the concealment of revelation referred to in the so-called "another covenant" of Deut 29:4[3]. The new covenant enhances transmission of Torah from instructing the younger generation in the great commandment to divine inscription of Torah directly upon hearts. The relationship between Yahweh and the people of covenant renewal turns on his not remembering their sin. Yahweh's new-covenant faithfulness to Israel endures in the same way the sun rises every day. In all of these ways Jeremiah's new covenant promotes definitive exegetical advancements of revelation.

33:14–22 MT*~23:5–6*+1 Kgs 8:25*+Deut 18:5*+Jer 31:35–37 (B) (righteous branch and Levitical priest) (* see branch and Davidic covenant networks) (on LXX and MT Jeremiah, see Hermeneutical Profile of the Use of Scripture in Jeremiah). The long addition in the masoretic version of Jer 33:14–18 (not in LXX) features an interpretive blend of Jeremiah's branch expectation (Jer 23:5–6) and other Davidic and Levitical traditions (1 Kgs 8:25; Deut 18:5). The evidence, especially of the revised version of Jeremiah, strongly suggests Jer 33:14–22 as receptor text. This interpretive blend houses a significant development of royal expectations within Jeremiah (italics, bold, and underlining signify verbal parallels; wavy underlining signifies potential verbal parallel; and broken underlining signifies citation marking):[70]

> Levitical priests . . . for Yahweh your God has chosen them and their descendants out of all your tribes to stand and minister in Yahweh's name always [כָּל־הַיָּמִים]. (Deut 18:1a, 5)

> [Solomon prays] Now **Yahweh**, the God of Israel, keep for your servant **David** my father the promises you made to him when you **said**, "You **shall never fail to have a successor to sit** before me **on the throne of Israel**, if only your descendants are careful in all they do to walk before me faithfully as you have done." (1 Kgs 8:25)

> *"The days are coming," declares Yahweh, "when I will raise up for David a righteous Branch,* a King who will reign wisely *and do what is just and right in the land. In* his *days Judah will be saved and* Israel *will live in safety. This is* the name *by which he will be called: Yahweh Our Righteous Savior."* (Jer 23:5–6)

> *"The days are coming," declares Yahweh, "when I will raise up* the good promise I made to the people of Israel and Judah. [15] In those days and at that time I will make to sprout

70. Indebted to Sjöberg, "Inner-Biblical Interpretation," 176–77, 180–81.

> *for David a righteous Branch; he will do what is just and right in the land.* [16] *In* those *days Judah will be saved and* Jerusalem *will live in safety. This is by which it will be called: Yahweh Our Righteous Savior.*" [17] For this is what **Yahweh says: "David will never fail to have a successor to sit on the throne of Israel,** [18] nor will the Levitical priests ever fail to have a man to stand before me always [כָּל־הַיָּמִים] to offer burnt offerings, to burn grain offerings and to present sacrifices." (33:14–18†)

The masoretic plus at Jer 33:14 marks the use of 23:5–6 with "*the good promise* [הַדָּבָר הַטּוֹב] I made to the people of Israel and Judah," a phrase similar to one used elsewhere: "When seventy years are completed for Babylon, I will come to you and fulfill *my good promise* [דְּבָרִי הַטּוֹב] to bring you back to this place" (29:10 MT).[71] The split pattern of retaining the verb "to raise up" but with a different object—"A righteous branch" (23:5) versus "the good promise" (33:14)—appears at times in expanded receptor contexts.[72] The masoretic expansion makes explicit the sense of "raising up a righteous branch from 23:5–6 by blending it with Solomon's intercessory affirmation of the covenant: "David will never fail to have a successor to sit on the throne of Israel" (33:17; cf. 1 Kgs 8:25). But the obligation has not been carried over, namely, "if only your descendants are careful in all they do to walk before me faithfully as you have done" (1 Kgs 8:25). Jeremiah 33:18–22 is the only place the book refers to Levitical priests and Levites. The allusion affirms the expectation for the enduring worship function of Levitical priests (Deut 18:5).[73]

The plus continues with a second oracle in Jer 33:19–22 adapted from 31:35–37.[74] Jeremiah 31:35–37 features a brief poetic affirmation of the permanence of Yahweh's commitment to Israel akin to the cosmic order. The semi-ungrammatical use of "daily" (יוֹמָם) as "daytime" in Jer 31:35 and 33:20, 25 confirms the likelihood of the relationship of these contexts that share numerous other terms.[75] The reuse of the perpetual cosmic order imagery in Jer 33:19–22 advances revelation by affirming the irrevocability of the promise for the Davidic covenant and the Levites within an exilic context where these institutions are not functioning.[76]

In sum, the long masoretic plus in Jer 33:14–22 builds on the expectation for a Davidic branch in older traditions in Jer 23:5–6. The expansion advances revelation by including anticipation for enduring worship ministry of Levitical priests. The importance of these expectations after the fall of Jerusalem turns on the surprising sense of continuity for

---

71. See ibid., 178. The word "good" is lacking in Jer 29:10 LXX; Sjöberg speculates it was added at the same time as the plus in 33:14–18 MT (179). For a similar observation see Schmid, "How to Date Jeremiah," 456.

72. See Sommer, *A Prophet Reads Scripture*, 238, n. 115 (noted by Sjöberg, "Inner-Biblical Interpretation," 176, n. 5).

73. Sjöberg notes the phrase "all of the days" fits other Deuteronomistic and Jeremiah expectations in 1 Sam 2:35 and Jer 35:19 ("Inner-Biblical Interpretation," 183). The allusion to Zadokite priests in 1 Sam 2:25 versus Eli's line who move to Anathoth is worth noting (1 Kgs 2:26; Jer 1:1).

74. On Jer 31:35–37, see footnote in fourth point of note on 31:31–34.

75. See Sjöberg, "Inner-Biblical Interpretation," 184.

76. Compare David's use of cosmic order and the verb "sprout up" (צמח) relative to the covenant in 2 Sam 23:4–5.

irrevocable, permanent covenant fidelity even in the face of a reality without a Davidic ruler. Even a kingless Jerusalem does not speak against Yahweh's faithfulness to David.

34:14*~Deut 15:1+15:12* (B)+Lev 25:10, 35–46* (C) (releasing slaves) (* see release statute network). The prophecy itself, housed in Jer 34, seems clear enough. But constant debate surrounds the legal allusion that serves as the point of departure for the prophetic indictment. Jeremiah uses characteristic "eye for eye" logic to say that the retraction of "release" of slaves merits Yahweh's "release to sword, pestilence, and famine" (Jer 34:17).[77]

Numerous competing views concern the relative dependency of Lev 25:35–46, Deut 15:12–18, Jer 34:8–22, and Neh 5:1–11, though most agree that Exod 21:2–11 predates the other contexts. The present discussion only addresses the most likely allusions in Jer 34:8–9, 14–15, and how these would function.

The use of "proclaim freedom" (דְּרוֹר) in Jer 34:8, 15, and 17 suggests a potential parallel with Lev 25:10 and the debt service laws there (Lev 25:35–46). Though Lev 25:39–46 speaks against enslaving fellow Israelites, literally "brothers," only Deut 15:12 speaks of releasing male and female Hebrew slaves, which aligns with Jer 34:9, 10, 11, 16. The use of "Hebrew slaves, male and female" and "seventh year" suggests a parallel with the slave release laws of Deut 15:12–18. More significantly, the ungrammatical shift in Jer 34:14a from a plural verb "*you* must send free" (2mp) to singular indirect object "sold themselves to *you*" (2ms) confirms the latter as allusion to "sell themselves to *you*" (2ms) from Deut 15:12.[78] This ungrammatical shift is the right kind of evidence to see Jer 34:14a as receptor context (emphases signify verbal parallels):

> At the end of every seven years you must cancel debts. . . . If any of your **fellows—Hebrew** men or women—sell themselves to you and *serve you six years*, in the seventh year *you must let them go free*. (Deut 15:1, 12†)

> [Yahweh said] "'At the end of every seventh year each of you must free any **fellow Hebrews** who have sold themselves to you. After *they have served you six years, you must let them go free*.' Your ancestors, however, did not listen to me or pay attention to me." (Jer 34:14)

The strong parallels between Deut 15:12 and Jer 34:14 do not sweep away lingering issues. The law of release in Deut 15 seems to refer to seven years on an individual basis between slaves and masters, not a universal time of release.[79] Leuchter notes the universal release at the Festival of Tabernacles every seven years (Deut 31:9–11), but this may have more traction in Neh 10:31[32], set three days after Tabernacles (Neh 8:17–18). Still,

77. Compare Jeremiah "sank" in the mud and the message that Zedekiah's feet are "sunk" in the mire (Jer 38:6, 22).
78. This grammatical observation of dependence from Fishbane, *Haftarot*, 116.
79. See Sarna, "Zedekiah's Emancipation," 147.

Leuchter's suggestion enjoys the merits of explaining the difficult "at the end of seven years" (מִקֵּץ שֶׁבַע שָׁנִים) in Jer 34:14 and Deut 31:10 versus after six years of service in Deut 15:12.[80] The proclamation of release "at the end of seven years" in Deut 31:9–11 may relate to the use of "at the end of seven years" in 15:1 blended with 15:12 in Jer 34:14, as suggested by Levinson.[81] Still, the implied relationship between special act of release, a formal covenant ceremony, and the siege lifted suggest a special circumstance in Jer 34.[82]

In sum, Jer 34:14 seems to allude to the law of release in Deut 15:12. The use of "proclaim freedom" (דְּרוֹר) associated with Jubilee in Lev 25, appearing three times in Jer 34, provides good reason for caution, as well as other irregularities. In spite of these and other difficulties with the allusion, the prophetic reverse use of "release" to judgment makes a clear point of Yahweh "releasing" the rebels to sword, pestilence, and famine (Jer 34:17).

36:24~2 Kgs 22:11 (B) (not tearing clothes). The dramatic response of King Josiah to hearing the newly discovered Torah gets reversed by his son Jehoiakim when he hears the scroll of Jeremiah. Josiah tore his clothes and initiated sweeping covenantal reforms (2 Kgs 22:11). Jehoiakim and his courtiers scorn the prophetic message, reading and burning it to pass the time in the winter quarters (Jer 36:24). Note the verbal parallels signified by emphases.

> When *the king* [Josiah] *heard the words* of the book of the Torah, he **tore his clothes.** (2 Kgs 22:11†)
>
> *The king* [Jehoiakim] and all his attendants *who heard* all these *words* showed no fear, nor did they **tear their clothes.** (Jer 36:24)

The nature of this parallel only works with the narrative of Josiah in 2 Kgs 22 as donor context and the narrative of Jehoiakim in Jer 36 as receptor context. If a narrator draws attention to something they do not do, it only signifies when lined up against what they could have done.[83] If Josiah's tearing of his clothes typifies humbling himself (2 Kgs 22:19), not tearing clothes signals hardened arrogance.[84] The fourfold repetition of burning the scroll (Jer 36:23, 25, 27, 32) may also subtly invite consideration of the transition to repeated threats against Zedekiah to burn the city (21:10; 32:29; 34:22; 37:10; 38:17–18, 23; 39:8; 52:13; cf. 17:27).[85]

---

80. See Leuchter, "Manumission Laws," 642–44.

81. See Levinson, "Zedekiah's Release," 320.

82. On the complexities of a royal edict and a blended allusion, see Bergland, "Jeremiah 34," 200.

83. Thank you to Brian J. Musser for this observation. The implications for theories of authorship or complex authorial relationship based on this direction of dependence, in light of potential for parts of Kings alluding to traditions in Jeremiah, cannot be taken up here (see notes on 2 Kgs 23:26 and 24:13).

84. See Nicholson, *Preaching to the Exiles*, 42–45.

85. See Scalise, "Baruch," 294. Scalise also suggests the burning scroll may evoke the kindling of Yahweh's wrath (Jer 4:4; 15:14; 17:4, 27; 21:12, 14; cf. 11:16).

46–51 MT~25:15–26 (C) (oracles against the nations) (on LXX and MT Jeremiah see Hermeneutical Profile of the Use of Scripture in Jeremiah). Properly speaking, the rearrangement and relocation of the oracles against the nations in the masoretic version of Jeremiah may reflect literary versus exegetical concerns. But since these adjustments may shed light on the long additions to the masoretic version of Jeremiah, the exegetical significance needs to be briefly summarized.

In the Septuagintal version, the oracles are located between Jer 25:13 and 32:1 but were relocated to the end of the book in the proto-masoretic edition (Jer 46–51). One effect of this relocation concerns placing the oracles against Babylon at the end of the book. At the same time, the framework of the oracles did not go with the oracles it was originally designed to house. The effect of moving the oracles against the nations but leaving their framework in the middle of the book amounts to creating an *inclusio* by Jer 25 and 46–51. The preexisting relationship between the headings of the book and Jer 25 effectively creates a "scaffolding" effect for the masoretic version of Jeremiah (1:3; 25:3). Jeremiah 1, 25, and 50–51 go a long way to framing the resultant book, an effect somewhat obscured by the addition of Jer 52 (see 51:64).[86]

The reorganization of the oracles against the nations themselves (in addition to their relocation) reveals potential moves toward symmetry as well as literary-theological concerns. The rearrangement in the proto-masoretic version moves from west to east, in the main, from Egypt (46) to Babylon (50–51).[87] Though the eastward movement does not work completely, the possible geographical concerns in the sequence of the oracles in Amos 1–2 could motivate similar concerns in Jeremiah (see Scripture references in Maps J2).

MAPS J2: SEQUENCE OF JEREMIAH'S ORACLES AGAINST THE NATIONS AND GEOGRAPHY

Septuagintal sequence of oracles against the nations

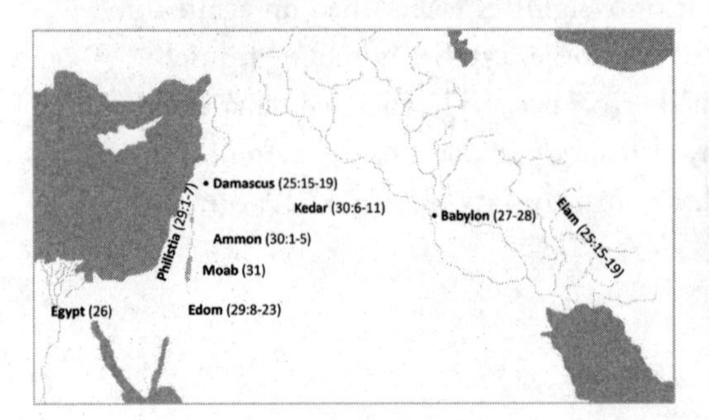

Masoretic sequence of oracles against the nations

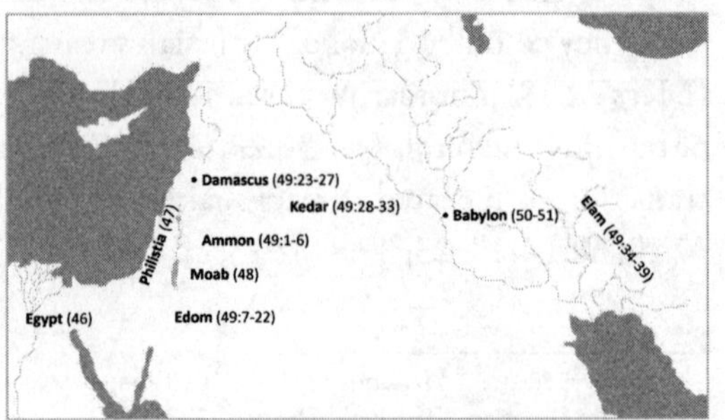

86. See Kessler, "Scaffolding," 57–66; Smelik, "Junction of Jeremiah 50 and 51," 94–98.

87. See Lundbom, "Jeremiah, Book of," *ABD* 3:708.

The new arrangement also aligns more closely the order of the list in the original frame narrative now located in 25:15–26 MT (=32:1–12 LXX) (see Table J3). The rearrangement could reflect concerns toward symmetry.

TABLE J3: SEQUENCE OF JEREMIAH'S ORACLES AGAINST THE NATIONS AND LIST IN JEREMIAH 25[‡]

Septuagintal	Oracles Against the Nations	Masoretic	Oracles Against the Nations	Frame narrative of those who drink the cup (MT references)	
				25:18	Jerusalem, Judah
25:15–19	Elam	46	Egypt	25:19	Egypt
26	Egypt	47	Philistia	25:20	Uz, Philistines
27–28	Babylon	48	Moab	25:21	Edom
29:1–7	Philistia	49:1–6	Ammon	25:21	Moab
29:8–23	Edom	49:7–22	Edom	25:21	Ammon
30:1–5	Ammon	49:23–27	Damascus	25:22	Tyre, Sidon
30:6–11	Kedar	49:28–33	Kedar	25:23–24	Dedan, Tema, Buz, Arabia
30:12–16	Damascus	49:34–39	Elam	25:25	Zimri, Elam, Media
31	Moab	50–51	Babylon	25:26	Sheshak (Babylon)

‡ Indebted to Watts, "Text and Redaction," 439.

The lack of sufficient evidence eliminates confidence. Whatever the logic for the new sequence of the oracles against the nations, the most important outcome stems from placing Babylon climactically at the end of the reorganized oracles against the nations and, simultaneously, placing the oracles at the end of the book.

48:5, 29–47~Isa 15–16, 24 (B)+Num 21:28–29, 24:17* (A) (oracles against Moab) (* see Davidic covenant and Judah-king networks). The oracles against Moab in Jeremiah demonstrate an especially high rate of recycling older oracles concerning Moab from Torah and Isaiah. The nature of the parallels in several cases makes it easy to explain Jeremiah as receptor and Isaiah and Numbers as donor contexts but nearly impossible to explain many of the details in the other direction.[88] Table J4 presents an overview of the likely scriptural allusions.

88. Following Müller, Pakkala, and Romeny, *Evidence of Editing*, 143–57.

TABLE J4: ALLUSIONS TO ISAIAH AND TORAH IN JEREMIAH'S ORACLES AGAINST MOAB‡

Jeremiah 48

5	Isa 15:5	they go up weeping	poetry
29–30	16:6	pride of Moab	"
31	16:7	wail for Moab	"
32	16:8–9	weeping for vineyard	"
33	16:10	joy, rejoicing, and wine cease	"
34	15:4–6	cry from Heshbon	prose
36	16:11	heart moans for Moab	"
36	15:7	riches perish	"
37–38	15:2–3	lamentation of Moab	"
40	Jer 49:22; Deut 28:49	swoop down upon like an eagle	poetry
41	Jer 50:43	seized, like the heart of a woman	"
43–44	Isa 24:17–18	from terror to pit to snare	"
45a	Num 21:28	fire from Heshbon	"
45b	24:17	upon the head of Moab	
46	21:29	people of Chemosh perish	"
47	Jer 49:6, 39	restore fortunes of Moab	"

‡ Indebted to Müller, Pakkala, and Romeny, *Evidence of Editing*, 143–57; Schultz, *Search for Quotation*, 308–28.

A few general scribal issues should be noted. A close examination of the poetic texts revised, adjusted, and supplemented do not show seams or bumps, including adjustments in "poetic parallel" elements. The seamless poetic remix hides the footprints of the editors. Detecting donor texts requires knowledge of them.[89] The prose section in Jer 48:34–38 begins by reusing Isa 15:4–6, perhaps a continuation of Jer 48:5 already based on Isa 15:5. Many of the historical aspects referred to in the donor contexts were already very ancient in Jeremiah's day. For this reason, evaluation requires much caution. A few representative examples can illustrate some of Jeremiah's exegetical concerns.

The relationship between Isa 16:6 and Jer 48:29–30 works more smoothly with the latter including interpretative additions than the former as an abbreviation. The expansion in Jeremiah includes revoicing the second part to create a poetic dialogue, or at least consultation, whereby the people affirm Yahweh's indictment of Moab's vain words and deeds (emphases signify verbal parallels):[90]

89. See detailed evaluation in ibid., 150–51, 157.

90. See ibid., 145–46.

> *We have heard of Moab's pride—how great is her arrogance!—of her conceit, her pride* and **her insolence; but her boasts are empty.** (Isa 16:6)

> "*We have heard of Moab's pride—how great is her arrogance!—of her conceit, her pride,* her arrogance and the haughtiness of her heart. [30] I know **her insolence but her boasts are empty,**" declares Yahweh, "and her deeds accomplish nothing." (Jer 48:29–30†)

Isaiah 16:7a speaks of the Moabites wailing for Moab, perhaps because her boast had come to nothing (Isa 16:6). The second half of the verse refers to the object of her grief as the raisin cakes of Kir Hareseth. The term for "raisin cakes" (אֲשִׁישׁ) is also used in Hos 3:1 and has often been associated with fertility rituals.[91] Jeremiah 48:31 continues to revoice the oracle as first-person divine discourse and, apparently, replaces the obscure raisin cakes with "people of." This change provides evidence to suggest Isaiah as donor context since scribal interventions do not tend to make concepts more difficult (emphases signify verbal parallel even with syntactical differences because of shift of subject):[92]

> *Therefore* the Moabites *wail,* they *all* wail *for Moab.* Lament and *moan* for the raisin cakes *of Kir Hareseth.* (Isa 16:7†)

> *Therefore* I *wail* over Moab, *for all Moab* I cry out, I *moan* for the people *of Kir Hareseth.* (Jer 48:31)[93]

Jeremiah 48:45–46 features a masoretic plus not in the Septuagint. The addition blends two different ancient poems embedded in Numbers not attributed to prophets of Israel. The taunt in Num 21:27–30 comes from "the poets" and serves a similar purpose relative to Israel's own Transjordan conquest narrative. Numbers 24:17 houses part of Balaam's fourth oracle. In short, the use of this blend of ancient non-Israelite taunts against Moab serve a nearly identical purpose in Jeremiah even while the theology gets "corrected" (bold, italics, and underlining signify verbal parallels at the root level; and broken underlining signifies a key exegetical advancement):

> [The poets say] *Fire went out from Heshbon, a blaze from* the city of *Sihon. It consumed* Ar of Moab, the citizens of Arnon's heights. [29] Woe to you, Moab! You are destroyed, people of Chemosh! He has given up his sons as fugitives and his daughters as captives to Sihon king of the Amorites. (Num 21:28–29)

---

91. Alternatively, the term has been seen as "men of" based on the "parallel" in Jer 48:31 ("*אֲשִׁישׁ," *HALOT* 1:95).

92. See Müller, Pakkala, and Romeny, *Evidence of Editing,* 147. For a different explanation, still with Jeremiah as receptor context, see Parke-Taylor, *Formation,* 133.

93. Jeremiah 48:31 MT lit. "he moans" (יֶהְגֶּה) also 2QJer/2Q13 (*BQS* 2:582). Nearly all modern committee translations follow emendation to "I moan" with one MT MS (see *BHS* apparatus).

> [Balaam says] I see him but not now, I behold him but not near, a star will come out from Jacob, and a scepter will rise from Israel, and it will crush **the foreheads of Moab, and the skulls of** all the people of Sheth. (24:17 lit.)[94]

> In the shadow of Heshbon the fugitives stand helpless, for *a fire has gone out from Heshbon, a blaze from* the midst of *Sihon*; *it consumes* **the foreheads of Moab, and the skulls of the** noisy boasters. [46] Woe to you, Moab! The people of Chemosh are destroyed; your sons are taken captive and your daughters into captivity. (Jer 48:45–46†)[95]

Jephthah's alternative viewpoint highlights the significance of Jeremiah's theological adjustment. Whether based on ignorance or as part of intentional distortion to escalate the bad relations to warfare, Jephthah says, "Will you not take *what your god Chemosh gives you?* Likewise, whatever Yahweh our God has given us, we will possess" (Judg 11:24, emphasis mine). The "mistake" is referring to Chemosh the patron deity of Moab instead of Molek the god of Ammon (see note on Judg 11:17–27). The theological error amounts to giving credit to other gods for what Yahweh has done (see Deut 2:9, 19, 21; 32:8). Jeremiah corrects the aberrant theology of the ancient poets, whether or not he had Jephthah in view, by removing the active verb "*he* [Chemosh] *gave* [נָתַן]" and replacing it with a different passive verb "*they* [people of Chemosh] *were taken* [לֻקְּחוּ]" (Num 21:29; Jer 48:46).[96]

Jeremiah adjusts, intermixes, and adapts his prophetic sources (see Table J5). Numbers allowed the poets' oracle to offer credit to Chemosh as a quasi-typological reuse of the oracle to represent Israel's Transjordanian victories. The use of the ancient poets and Balaam in Torah traditions apparently invited Jeremiah to use them alongside prophetic traditions like Isaiah, but he materially adjusts the theology of ancient poets but not necessarily of Balaam (see textual issue in footnote on Num 24:17 cited above).

TABLE J5: CITED SOURCES AND AUTHORITIES FOR PRONOUNCEMENTS ON POSSESSION OF TRANSJORDAN

	source	authority	genre	
Num 21:27–30	poets	Chemosh	taunt song	Amorites seized Transjordan and Moabites exiled
Num 24:17	Balaam	Yahweh	oracle of judgment	star of Jacob/scepter of Israel shall crush borders of Moab

94. The majority of modern committee translations follow the Samaritan Pentateuch "skulls" (קדקד) versus "borders" (קרקר) in the D line of Num 24:17. The somewhat common use of "smash the skull (*qdqd*)" in Ugaritic myths (fifteenth century BCE) also supports this emendation (see, e.g., Baal and Yam, II.iv.25; Baal's Palace, III.v.32; IV.vii.4; see Gibson, *Canaanite Myths*, 44, 53, 64). If this emendation is incorrect, then Jeremiah gets credit for adjusting it by using "skulls" (קדקד). For further detail on the textual issue in Num 24:17, see Schnittjer, "Blessing of Judah," 23–24.

95. Parke-Taylor suggests the modification to "noisy boasters" [lit. "sons of tumult" (בְּנֵי שָׁאוֹן)] may reflect influence from Moab dying amid "tumult" (שָׁאוֹן) in Amos 2:2 (*Formation*, 142).

96. See discussion of Judg 11:24 in note on Judg 11:15–27.

	source	authority	genre	
Deut 2:9, 19, 30–31, 37	Moses	Yahweh	commentary on military actions	seizing of lands limited to Transjordan excluding territory of Ammon and Moab
Judg 11:21–24[a]	Jephthah	Chemosh and Yahweh	diplomatic letter	Yahweh granted Israel to possess Transjordan from Amorites and Chemosh granted Ammon to possess their territory
Isa 15–16	unstated (unknown)	Yahweh	oracle of judgment	defeat of Moab and exile from Moabite territory
Jer 48:34–46	unstated (Isaiah, Balaam, and ancient poets)	Yahweh	oracle of judgment	defeat of Moab modeled on the typology of Amorite and Israelites seizing of Transjordan at different times

[a] Jeremiah 48 does not use Deut 2 or Jephthah's letter. They are included in table for comparison.

The expectation of a restoration of Moab's fortunes fits with such sentiments elsewhere (Jer 48:47; cf. Isa 16:3–5). As with so much else in Jeremiah, the stereotypical hopeful expression runs parallel to hope for Ammon and even Elam (Jer 49:6, 39). In a prose section Jeremiah explains the same kind of umbrella situation for all other nations who oppose Judah: Yahweh shall uproot them and then have compassion and restore them (12:14–15). The broad interchangeability of oracles against the nations, even with oracles to Judah, does not erase the fundamental covenantal place of God's people (12:14, 16).[97]

In sum, Jeremiah recycles many older prophetic traditions, especially those that had gained authority through emerging canonical consciousness. Jeremiah's own prophetic ministry authorized reinterpretation of these prophetic traditions. While much of the historical context remains obscure, the theological tendencies of Jeremiah include: condemning Moab's arrogance, enhancing Yahweh's compassion and mercy for Moab, and eliminating assistance from rival deities. If Moses insists on Yahweh's sovereign establishment of Moab's inheritance, and if Isaiah anticipates Yahweh's mercy for Moab, Jeremiah strengthens these ideologies by recasting traditional prophetic materials.

49:7, 9–10, 12–13, 14–16, 19–21~Obad 7–8, 5–6+Jer 25:17+Obad 1–4+Jer 50:43–46+48:40–41 (A) (oracle against Edom). Jeremiah's oracle against Edom shares verbatim, loosely paraphrased, and close thematic relationship with several contexts in Obadiah and elsewhere in Jeremiah (see Table J6).

The direction of dependence, as well as dating of the materials shared with Obadiah, lacks adequate evidence to draw conclusions. The seamless reworking of Isaiah's poetic oracles against Moab illustrates the problem (see note on Jer 48:5, 29–47). For a comparison of the parallels between Jer 49 and Obadiah see notes on Obadiah.

97. See discussion of boilerplates in Jeremiah Filters.

TABLE J6: PARALLELS WITH OBADIAH IN JEREMIAH'S ORACLES AGAINST EDOM

Jeremiah 49			
7	Obad 7–8	wisdom in Edom	poetry
9–10	5–6	a vulnerable vineyard	"
12–13	Jer 25:17, 21	drink of wrath for Edom	prose
14–16	Obad 1–4	humbling arrogant Edom	poetry
19–21a	Jer 50:44–46a	lion attacking a flock	prose
22a	48:40–41a	an eagle's prey	"
22b	48:41b//50:43b	like a woman in labor	"

The present analysis limits itself to a couple of observations on the parallels within Jeremiah noted in Table J6 (also see discussion in subsection on Exegetical Conventions in Jeremiah in the Hermeneutical Profile of the Use of Scripture in Jeremiah and Doublets in Filters).

First, the parallel materials between Jeremiah's oracle against Edom and oracles elsewhere in Jeremiah only appear in prose (Table J6). Second, the simile of "a woman in labor," though worded differently in Jer 50:43, may have attracted the parallel with 50:44–46a and 49:19–21a as a metaphorical catch-phrase. Compare side by side a prose section of the oracle against Edom in Jer 49:19–22 and its counterparts in the oracles against Babylon and Moab (italics, underlining, and bold signify verbal parallels; double underlining signifies thematic similarity; and wavy underlining signifies differences):

Jer 49:19–22	Jer 50:43–46; 48:40–41
Like a lion coming up from Jordan's thickets to a rich pastureland, I will chase him [Edom] *from its land in an instant. Who is the chosen one I will appoint for this? Who is like me and who can challenge me? And what shepherd can stand against me?"* [20] *Therefore, hear what Yahweh has planned against* Edom, *what he has purposed against* those who live in Teman: The young of the flock will be dragged away; their pasture will be appalled at their fate. [21] At the sound of their fall the earth will tremble; their cry will resound to the Red Sea. [22] **Look! An eagle will soar and swoop down, spreading its wings** over Bozrah. **In that day the hearts of** Edom's **warriors will be like the heart of a woman in labor** (49:19–22†).	The king of Babylon has heard reports about them, and his hands hang limp. Anguish has gripped him, pain like that of a woman in labor. [44] *Like a lion coming up from Jordan's thickets to a rich pastureland, I will chase* them [Babylon] *from their land in an instant. Who is the chosen one I will appoint for this? Who is like me and who can challenge me? And what shepherd can stand against me?"* [45] *Therefore, hear what Yahweh has planned against* Babylon, *what he has purposed against* the land of the Babylonians: The young of the flock will be dragged away; their pasture will be appalled at their fate. [46] At the sound of Babylon's capture the earth will tremble; its cry will resound among the nations (Jer 50:43–46†). This is what Yahweh says: "**Look! An eagle is swooping down, spreading its wings** toward Moab. [41] Kerioth will be captured and the strongholds taken. **In that day the hearts of** Moab's **warriors will be like the heart of a woman in labor** (Jer 48:40–41†)

Explaining the abundant scriptural parallels in Jeremiah's oracles against Edom proves difficult especially without a sense of direction of dependence. Unlike Moab, Ammon, and Elam, Jeremiah's oracles against Edom do not include a statement on restoration of fortunes (cf. 48:47; 49:6, 39). The general theme of unrelenting judgment runs across Jeremiah's oracle against Edom, much like Ezek 25:11–14; 35:1–5; Obadiah; Mal 1:2–5; and Ps 137:7. The one exception stands as a direct address from Yahweh to Edom: "Leave your fatherless children; I will keep them alive. Your widows too can depend on me" (Jer 49:11). If it is literal, it seems as remarkable as Ezekiel's (ironic?!) word of hope for Sodom's restoration (Ezek 16:53, 55). Since there are no variants, nearly all modern committee translations simply render Jer 49:11 akin to the NIV above and leave it to the commentators, who often take it as a sarcastic taunt.[98] With a mild emendation it can be rendered as a sarcastic question: "Am I to keep alive your fatherless children? Are you widows to depend on me?" (Jer 49:11 REB).[99] But without evidence this needs to be left an open question.

In sum, the evidence for the parallels themselves is very strong. Lack of sufficient evidence excludes conclusions about the significance of the scriptural parallels in Jeremiah's oracles against Edom.

51:44b–50 MT~51:44a LXX+Isa 2:2 (C) (escape from Babylon) (on LXX and MT Jeremiah see Hermeneutical Profile of the Use of Scripture in Jeremiah). If the long masoretic plus at Jer 51:44b–49a expands upon the context (versus an accidental omission from the parent text of LXX), then it may offer a kind of response to 51:44a LXX/MT. The context gets set up by the simile of Nebuchadnezzar as sea serpent swallowing Judah:

> *Nebuchadnezzar king of Babylon has devoured us,* he has thrown us into confusion, he has made us an empty jar. *Like a serpent* [תַּנִּין] *he has swallowed us* and filled his stomach with our delicacies, and *then has spewed us out.* (Jer 51:34, emphasis mine)[100]

Jeremiah 51:44a picks up this thread and seems to add an allusion to Isa 2:2. These are the only two contexts which use the verb "stream" (נהר) with nations as a subject.[101] Instead of Nebuchadnezzar like a serpent swallowing (Jer 51:34), now the god Bel swallows (identified with Marduk in 50:2). The nations stream to Zion and Babylon for very different reasons (emphasis signifies verbal parallel):

---

98. See Calvin, *Jeremiah*, 5:71–72 (on 49:11); McKane, *Jeremiah*, 2:1219–20.

99. Also see NEB; and for explanation of the emendation options, see McKane, *Jeremiah*, 2:1230.

100. Jeremiah 51:34 is very difficult due to the pronominal suffixes of five *ketiv* (1cp 5x) versus *qere* (1cs 5x) and the referent of the pronouns relative to 51:35 (see *BHS*). NIV follows *ketiv*: devoured *us*, thrown *us* into confusion, made *us* an empty jar, swallowed *us*, spewed *us* out, versus most other modern committee translations, which follow *qere*: devour *me*, etc. NIV is preferred as following the more difficult reading in 51:34, but not 51:35. The point at hand does not hinge on this textual issue.

101. Even Mic 4:1 says "and *peoples* [עַמִּים] will stream to it" (emphasis mine).

In the last days the mountain of Yahweh's temple will be established as the highest of the mountains; it will be exalted above the hills, and all **nations will stream to it.** (Isa 2:2)

I will punish Bel in Babylon and make him spew out what he has swallowed. **The nations will** no longer **stream to him.** (Jer 51:44a)

At this point the masoretic version inserts a long plus (51:44b–49, and see plus in 51:50). The plus is closely related to Jer 51:49b–53 and may have been developed from this latter context (51:44b//49b, 45//50, 46//51, 47//52, 48//53).[102] The following citation from Jer 51:44b–48 fits in the ellipsis between 28:44, 49 LXX (=51:44, 49 MT; LXX does not have anything for vv. 45–48 but is versed in relation to the MT). The symbols ⌜⌝ signify where the pluses fit in the LXX, which as noted above does not include verses 44b–48, underlining and stylized underlining signify potential donor text in the Hebrew parent text of the LXX, and italics signify masoretic pluses:

[44] I will take vengeance on Babylon and bring out from her mouth what she has swallowed. And the nations shall no longer gather to her ⌜—⌝ [49] ⌜—⌝ And in Babylon slain of all the earth will fall. [50] Since you are survivors of the land, go, and do not stop! ⌜—⌝ [51] We were put to shame, because we have heard our insult; dishonor has covered our face; aliens have entered into our holy places, into the Lord's house. [52] Therefore behold, days are coming, says the Lord, and I will take vengeance on her carved images, and in all her land wounded shall fall, [53] because, if Babylon should mount up like the sky, and because, if she should fortify the height of her strength, from me those who destroy utterly will come upon her, says the Lord. (28:44, 49–53 LXX[= 51:44, 49–53 MT])

[44] I will punish Bel in Babylon and make him spew out what he has swallowed. The nations will no longer stream to him ⌜*And the wall of Babylon will fall.* [45] *Come out of her, my people! Run for your lives! Run from the fierce anger of Yahweh.* [46] *Do not lose heart or be afraid when rumors are heard in the land; one rumor comes this year, another the next, rumors of violence in the land and of ruler against ruler.* [47] *For the time will surely come when I will punish the idols of Babylon; her whole land will be disgraced and her slain will all lie fallen within her.* [48] *Then heaven and earth and all that is in them will shout for joy over Babylon, for out of the north destroyers will attack her," declares Yahweh.*⌝ [49] ⌜*Babylon must fall because of Israel's slain,*⌝ just as the slain in all the earth have fallen because of Babylon. [50] You who have escaped the sword, leave and do not linger! ⌜*Remember Yahweh in a distant land, and call to mind Jerusalem*⌝. (51:44b–50 MT)

102. See McKane, *Jeremiah*, 2:1335.

In light of the manifold moving parts here, the key exegetical interventions can only be noted. First, the relief afforded to all the devoured peoples by the fall of Babylon necessarily follows from the slain of Israel (51:49). Second, this oracle means to direct captives to Yahweh and Jerusalem (51:50).

52:1–34//2 Kgs 24:18–25:26 (fall of Jerusalem). The masoretic version of Jer 51 concludes with a scribal note, "The words of Jeremiah end here" (Jer 51:64).[103] This note separates Jer 52 as an appendix. The situation is somewhat similar to the note of closure in Lev 26:46. Jeremiah 52 (LXX and MT) closely follows 2 Kgs 25. These versions stand much closer together than the other three synoptic versions (Jer 46 LXX; 39 MT; 2 Chr 36). The following synoptic comparison can serve as an overview to distinguish functions of Jer 46 LXX, 39 MT, and 52 MT/LXX over and against 2 Kgs 25 (stylized brackets signify variation of narrative sequence):[104]

	Jeremiah 46–51 LXX	Jeremiah 39–44 MT	Jeremiah 52 LXX	Jeremiah 52 MT	2 Kings 24–25	2 Chronicles 36
opening frame of Zedekiah[a]	—	—	1	1	24:18	11
evaluation formula	—	—	—[c]	2	19	12a
rebellion against Jeremiah and prophets	—	—	—	—	—	12b–16
divine causality of Babylonian invasion	—	—	—[c]	3	20	17
siege of Jerusalem in Zedekiah's ninth year	46:1	39:1	4–5	4–5	25:1–2	—
famine in fourth month ninth day	—	—	6	6	3	—
wall breached	46:2	39:2	7a	7a	4a	—
Babylonian officials sit in middle gate	46:3	39:3	—	—	—	—
Zedekiah and company flight and capture	—[b]	39:4–6	7b–10	7b–10	4b–7	—
Zedekiah blinded and bound to Babylon	—[b]	39:7	11	11	—	—

(cont.)

103. The oracles against the nations appear in the middle of the LXX (Jer 25–31) and conclude with Moab (31:1–44 LXX=48:1–44 MT). The ending of the LXX oracle against Moab is not clear since 48:45–47 MT is a plus (which interestingly includes a closing line: "Here ends the judgment on Moab" [48:47 MT]). Jer 51:35 LXX (=45:5 MT) does not include a closing notation.

104. On the function of 2 Chr 36, see notes ad loc. For a detailed comparison of Jer 52 and 2 Chr 36 see Warhurst, "Merging," 179–208.

	Jeremiah 46–51 LXX	Jeremiah 39–44 MT	Jeremiah 52 LXX	Jeremiah 52 MT	2 Kings 24–25	2 Chronicles 36
Nebuzaradan enters Jerusalem	—	—	12	12	8	—
Jerusalem burned	—[b]	39:8a	13	13	9	{19}
walls broken down[d]	—[b]	39:8b	14	14	10	—
people of Jerusalem exiled	—[b]	39:9	—[c]	15	11	{20}
poorest people left behind	—[b]	39:10	16	16	12	—
Nebuchadnezzar says to free Jeremiah	—[b]	39:11–13	—	—	—	—
inventory of temple plunder	—	—	17–23	17–23	13–17	{18}
remaining priests and officials executed	—	—	24–27	24–27	18–21	—
Gedaliah appointed governor	—	—	—	—	22	—
Jeremiah freed into care of Gedaliah	46:14	39:14	—	—	—	—
oracle concerning Ebed-melech	46:15–18	39:15–18	—	—	—	—
Jeremiah joins Gedaliah in Mizpah	47:1–6	40:1–6	—	—	—	—
Gedaliah offers peace to Judean military	47:7–10	40:7–10	—	—	23–24	—
regional scattered remnant returns to Judah	47:11–12	40:11–12	—	—	—	—
Ishmael assassinates Gedaliah and his court	47:13–48:3	40:12–41:3	—	—	25	—
overthrow of Ishmael's revolt	48:4–18	41:4–18	—	—	—	—
Jeremiah speaks against going to Egypt	49:1–22	42:1–22	—	—	—	—
remnant migrates to Egypt	50:1–7	43:1–7	—	—	26	—
oracle of Babylon's dominion over Egypt	50:8–13	43:8–13	—	—	—	—
remnant rejects Jeremiah's warning	51:1–30	44:1–30	—	—	—	—

	Jeremiah 46–51 LXX	Jeremiah 39–44 MT	Jeremiah 52 LXX	Jeremiah 52 MT	2 Kings 24–25	2 Chronicles 36
total captives of three exiles (597, 586, 582)	—	—	—[c]	28–30[e]	—	—
Jehoiachin released from prison (561)	—	—	31–34	31–34	27–30	—
seventy Sabbath years	—	—	—	—	—	21
edict of Cyrus (539)	—	—	—	—	—	22–23

[a] For standard opening frames see Table C11 in Chronicles.

[b] Jeremiah 46 LXX = Jer 39 MT. Jeremiah 46 LXX skips verses 4–13.

[c] Jeremiah 52 LXX skips verses 2, 3, 15, 28–30.

[d] Codex Vaticanus lacks most of 2 Kgs 25:10 (missing: "The whole Babylonian army . . . broke down the walls around Jerusalem" MT) (see LXX Cambridge). Based upon this lacking phrase in Codex Vaticanus, 25:9, 11 in singular and 25:10 MT in plural, and a few related considerations, Müller, Pakkala, and Romney suggest that the Babylonians may not have broken down the walls of Jerusalem (*Evidence of Editing*, 110–14). The evidence is not sufficient to sustain 25:10 Codex Vaticanus as preserving the original reading or to deduce this historical point. The authors go on to investigate part of the plus in Jer 39:4–13 MT; namely, their agenda limits them to 39:8–9 MT. They speak of this as an intentional "omission" in Jer 46 LXX (=39 MT) (118–19), but this unlikely suggestion misses the whole point of the narrative about Jeremiah in Jer 46 LXX (see below).

[e] It is not clear how the ten thousand captives of 2 Kgs 24:14 relate to the three thousand of Jer 52:28 or the forced migration of 2 Kgs 25:11//Jer 52:15.

Second Kings 25 closes the loop of the Deuteronomistic narrative. The tribe of Judah had burned Jebus early in the conquest even as the Babylonians burned the city at the end of the First Commonwealth (see Judg 1:8; 2 Kgs 25:9; cf. Judg 1:21). Zedekiah is captured in Jericho, the place where Joshua's conquest began, before watching his sons and court slaughtered and then being blinded (see 2 Kgs 25:5–7). The rulers and leading citizens are taken captive, leaving only the poor to tend to Jerusalem and Judah, an event that occurs successively to the elite of Jehoiakim's/Jehoiachin's and Zedekiah's Jerusalem (24:14; 25:11–12). The final notice in the book relates the release of Jehoiachin from prison and his improved situation in Babylon.[105]

Jeremiah 52 serves as an appendix of the book of Jeremiah (Jer 51:64b). This appended narrative bears witness to the fulfillment of Jeremiah's prophecies. Both the Septuagint and masoretic versions of Jeremiah feature the narrative, though only the masoretic version includes the note on the three forced migrations (52:28–30 MT). The third forced migration, known only from this context, may have been in response to the assignation of Gedaliah.

105. For Jehoiachin's oil rations in Babylon, see *ANET*, 308b.

Jeremiah 46 LXX (= 39 MT) briefly mentions the breach of the city. When the Babylonians broke through the walls of Jerusalem, several of the officials sat in the middle gate (46:3 LXX[=39:3 MT]). Then Jeremiah is brought from prison and his storyline continues (46:14 LXX[=39:14 MT]).[106] More to the point, the original version of the fall of Jerusalem in Jer 46 LXX is actually about the prophet Jeremiah, with the fall of Jerusalem narrated tangentially to his situation.[107]

Jeremiah 39 MT (=46 LXX) "repairs" the deficiencies by collating some of the details of the fall of Jerusalem from 2 Kgs 25//Jer 52 (Jer 39:4–10 MT). The masoretic plus steals the show in Jer 39. An unparalleled account of Nebuchadnezzar himself attending to Jeremiah's freedom is also inserted into the narrative (39:11–12 MT). The insert is marked by naming Babylonian officials in a resumptive repetition (39:3, 13).[108] Thus, Jer 39 MT both obscures Jeremiah's storyline by importing details of the fall of Jerusalem but also distinguishes the prophet as a personal concern of the emperor.

FILTERS

The majority of Jeremiah's use of scriptural traditions have been filtered out in order to focus on his exegetical use of scriptural traditions in the notes above. The following filters can only illustrate by representative examples the vast non-exegetical use of scriptural traditions in Jeremiah. The lists are not comprehensive or complete. Many more extensive lists can be found elsewhere.[109] The filtered lists below come from research for the present study unless noted otherwise.

Jeremiah's Non-Exegetical Use of Jeremiah

Boilerplate refers to the reuse of an identical or slightly modified oracle directed toward different peoples. The name of one people is replaced by another. The following are nearly verbatim parallels, with minor spelling and grammatical differences in Hebrew, with alternate elements underlined.

> Look! An eagle ... swoop down, spreading its wings.... In that day the hearts of <u>Moab's/Edom's</u> warriors will be like the heart of a woman in labor. (48:40//49:22; cf. Deut 28:49)

---

106. Jeremiah 46 LXX skips verses 4–13.

107. On the originality of Jer 46 LXX versus 39 MT, see McKane, *Jeremiah*, 2:977–78. The insertion of Jer 39:4–13 causes 39:14–18 to become a flashback (Allen, *Jeremiah*, 418).

108. On the textual difficulties in Jer 39:3, 13, see McKane, *Jeremiah*, 2:973–76; NET note on 39:3.

109. See, e.g., Bergren, *Prophets*, 182–83; Bright, "Prose Sermons," 30–35; Carroll, "Intertextuality and Jeremiah," 70–72; Driver, *Introduction*, 275–77; idem, *Deuteronomy*, xciii; Holladay, *Jeremiah 2*, 53–63; Parke-Taylor, *Formation*, 1–292; Richards, "Influence," 132–36; Thompson, *Jeremiah*, 81–85; Weinfeld, *Deuteronomic School*, 27–32, 320–63 (also see items on Entire OT in Bibliographic Note on Lists of Potential Parallels).

> Like a lion coming up from Jordan's thickets to a rich pastureland, I will chase Edom/Babylon from its land in an instant. Who is the chosen one I will appoint for this? Who is like me and who can challenge me? And what shepherd can stand against me? Therefore, hear what Yahweh has planned against Edom/Babylon, what he has purposed against those who live in Teman/the land of the Babylonians: The young of the flock will be dragged away; their pasture will be appalled at their fate. (49:19–21//50:44–46)

> "Surely, her [Damascus/Babylon] young men will fall in the streets; all her soldiers will be silenced in that day," declares Yahweh Almighty/Yahweh. (49:26//50:30†)

> "Look, an army is coming from ... the north; a great nation ... is/are being stirred up from the ends of the earth. They are armed with bow and spear; they are cruel and show no mercy. They sound like the roaring sea as they ride on their horses; they come like men in battle formation to attack you, Daughter Zion/Babylon." We have/The king of Babylon has heard reports about it/them, and our/his hands hang limp. Anguish has gripped us/him, pain like that of a woman in labor. (6:22b–24//50:41–43)

The boilerplate oracles recycled and applied to other peoples seem somewhat disconcerting from the perspective of interpreters who evaluate the historical significance of the imagery. "How can the same material serve such different purposes?"[110] Even if the question of excessive relevance of revealed oracles pushes things too far, easy interchangeability raises lesser questions. Do boilerplate oracles overlap with the kinds of relationships often observed between judgments against individual nations in Isa 13–23 and the universal judgments in 24–27? Does the interchangeability of oracles reflect a fundamental commitment to the shared human condition? Is the reuse of boilerplate oracles from within Jeremiah exactly the same as Jeremiah using oracles from Isaiah or other prophetic traditions (see note on Jer 48:29–47)? Ironic reversal of judgment may explain some cases, like a people from the north conquering Babylon in the way Babylon of the north once conquered Jerusalem (6:22b–24//50:41–43). Perhaps that provides one reason for the frequent use of boilerplate oracles against Babylon, who once conquered all others.

Whether it can be fully explained or not, Jeremiah's repackaging of the same oracles for other uses minimally points to some sense of transcendent applicability of divine judgments. The inclusion of "and also Judah" and the like throughout Hosea points to the analogous relevance of divine judgment against Israel to another people with similar but different rebellions (Hos 1:7, 11; 4:15; 5:5, 10, 14; 6:4, 11; 8:14; 10:11; 12:2).[111] Zechariah's comments to the restored community regarding the relevance of the preexilic prophets

110. Carroll, "Intertextuality," 72.
111. See Childs, *Introduction*, 378–79.

also overlap (Zech 1:4–6; 7:12–13). The broad application of authoritative prophetic oracles seems to point in the right direction, even if boilerplate oracles resist satisfactory explanation.

Other examples of boilerplate contexts, some with more paraphrasing than others, include: "I am against you. . . . I will kindle a fire" (of house of David/Babylon [Jer 21:13–14//50:13–14]); "'As God overthrew Sodom and Gomorrah/As Sodom and Gomorrah were overthrown, along with their neighboring towns,' says Yahweh, 'so no one will live there; no people will dwell in it'" (of Edom/Babylon [49:18†//50:40]); "everyone who passes by shall be appalled and hiss" (of Jerusalem/Edom/Babylon [19:8//49:17//50:13b]); and "their day has come, the time of their punishment" (of Egypt/land of Chaldeans [46:21b//50:27b]).

Doublets. Jeremiah features many verbatim doublets and a large number of partial and paraphrased quasi-doublets in poetic and prose sections. Theories include marginal notations during an editorial stage migrating into the text and intentional cross-referencing to make literary connections between contexts.[112] Much effort has been expended to investigate what these doublets might show about the development of Jeremiah. These important excavative diachronic questions fall outside the present study.

The present study operates by a view that not all doublets function in the same way. Although some doublets within Jeremiah reflect exegetical modification (see notes) and others work like boilerplates (see Filters above), many seem to provide literary connecting functions even while the purpose of others is not clear.[113] The following representative non-exegetical doublets within Jeremiah illustrate the broader phenomenon: **1:18, 19//15:20**, divine promise to strengthen Jeremiah as a bronze wall against trouble; **5:9//5:29**, "'Should I not punish them for this?' declares Yahweh. 'Should I not avenge myself on such a nation as this?'"; **6:13–15//8:10–12**, against peace prophets; **6:22–24//50:41–43**, "from the north, a great nation . . . are being stirred up from the ends of the earth," and so on; **7:16//11:14//14:11**, "do not pray for the people"; **7:32//19:6**, calling Valley of Ben Hinnom Valley of Slaughter (also 7:30//32:34 and 7:31//19:5//32:35);[114] **7:34//16:9**, sound of gladness banished; **8:15//14:19b**, "We hoped for peace but no good has come, for a time of healing but there is only terror"; **9:15[14]//23:15**, "Therefore this is what Yahweh Almighty says: "'I will make them eat bitter food and drink poisoned water'"; **10:12–16//51:15–19**, "He made the earth by his power . . . including the people

112. See Parke-Taylor, *Formation*, 293–94.

113. For a much longer list of doublets within Jeremiah than what is presented here, see ibid., 325–27. Parke-Taylor's study offers extensive comparative notes on the doublets and discussion of possible direction of dependence (he often acknowledges the speculative nature of the suggestions) (1–212), and brief comments on doublets between Jeremiah and other scriptural contexts (213–42). Parke-Taylor applies his findings to how the doublets may explain the growth of Jeremiah (293–306). Also see the review by McKane that offers fifteen adjustments to Parke-Taylor's analysis of doublets within Jeremiah (review of *Formation*, 326–27).

114. Jer 15:14>/<Deut 32:22, "for a fire is kindled by my anger" (כי אש קדחה באפי); see Holladay, *Jeremiah 2*, 55.

of his inheritance" (cf. Jer 10:13//51:16//Ps 135:7); **11:20//20:12**, calling for Yahweh to judge the heart and bring vengeance; **15:13–14//17:3–4**, treasures given away as plunder because of deity's wrath (loose quotation); **16:14–15//23:7–8**, return from north to eclipse return from Egypt; **49:18//50:40**, "'As Sodom and Gomorrah were overthrown/ I overthrew, along with their neighboring towns,' says Yahweh, 'so no one will live there; no people will dwell in it.'"

Although doublets themselves within Jeremiah tend to be non-exegetical, they can take on new literary-thematic functions based on placements. An example of the difficulties in making deductions is **30:10–11//46:27–28**, which features a promise to limit judgment upon Jacob. The second counterpart of the doublet appears between the oracles of judgment against Egypt and Babylonia in the Septuagintal version (Jer 26:27–28 LXX=46:27–28 MT/English Bible). This placement effectively offers a word of encouragement on the limitation of judgment upon Jacob immediately before the oracle against Babylonia (Jer 27–28 LXX=50–51 MT). The short word of limitation is more difficult to assimilate in the masoretic version because oracles against the nations have been rearranged and it now stands between oracles against Egypt and Philistia (46:27–28) (on rearrangement see note on Jer 46–51). The doublet occurs only in the masoretic version since 30:10–11 is a plus (not in LXX). Thus, the literary function of the limitation in the Septuagintal version apparently has nothing to do with doublets.[115]

Favorite Expressions. Jeremiah uses a large number of stock phrases—some his own and others from Deuteronomistic traditions—in both poetry and prose discourses. Jeremiah often reuses six favorite terms in different combinations: >/<1:10; 31:28, "uproot" (נתשׁ), "tear down" (נתץ), "destroy" (אבד), "overthrow" (הרס), "build" (בנה), "plant" (נטע); 18:7, uproot and pull down/destroy (לִנְתוֹשׁ וְלִנְתוֹץ/ואבד); 12:14[2x], 15, 17[2x]; 31:40; 45:4, uproot/not uproot (נתשׁ/לא נתשׁ); 2:21; 11:17; 12:2; 31:5; 32:41; cf. 29:5, plant (נטע); 1:10; 18:9; 31:28; cf. 29:28; 35:7, to build and to plant (לִבְנוֹת שֶׁלִנְטוֹעַ); 24:6; 42:10; cf. Amos 9:14, 15, build . . . and not tear down . . . plant . . . and not uproot (בנה . . . ולא הרס . . . נטע . . . ולא נתשׁ).

Only a few other important examples of Jeremiah's widespread use of favorite expressions can be included here: >/<1:13, 14, 15; 3:12, 18; 4:6; 6:1, 22; 10:22; 13:20; 15:12; 16:15; 25:9, 26; 46:10, 20, 24; 47:2, north/from the north/from the land of the north (צָפוֹן/מִצָּפוֹן/מֵאֶרֶץ צָפוֹן), 16:15; 23:8; 31:8, Israel (will return) . . . from land of north (יִשְׂרָאֵל . . . מֵאֶרֶץ צָפוֹן), 4:15; 8:16, similarly "sound" (קוֹל), "from Dan" (מִדָּן), and ironically a people from the north against Babylon the former people of the north, 50:3, 9, 41; 51:48; >/<7:13, 25//25:4; 11:7; 25:3; 26:5; 29:19; 32:33; 35:14, 15; 44:4, sending/

115. Parke-Taylor lists six other cases of doublets in MT but not LXX: 6:13–15//8:10b–12; 15:13–14//17:3–4; 39:1–10//52:4–16; 48:40–41//49:22 (*Formation*, 6). He also lists 23:5–6//33:14–16 but 33:14–16 is part of an exegetical expansion (see note on 33:14–22) and 39:1–10//52:4–16 but 39:4–13 is a synoptic expansion (see note on 52:1–34).

speaking/warning/teaching again and again (שלח/דבר/שכם/למד ועור) (cf. 2 Kgs 17:13; 2 Chr 36:15; Mark 12:1–10);[116] >/<25:26; 51:41, Sheshak (Babylon) (cf. 51:1).[117]

Deuteronomy, Jeremiah, and Prose Discourses

Form-critical studies label the three main genres of Jeremiah A, B, and C, with A referring to first-person poetry, B third-person narratives, and C prose discourses. Mowinckel lists B, Baruch's biographical narratives of Jeremiah, with qualifications, as Jer 19:1–2, 10–11a, 14–20:6; 26; 28; 29:24–32; 36; 37:1–10, 11–16, 17–21; 38:1–13, 14–28a, 28b; 39:3, 14; 40:2–12, 13–43:7, 8–13; 44:15–19, 24–30. The prose discourses share much with the style of Deuteronomy and the Deuteronomistic narrative (Joshua, Judges, Samuel, Kings), even while having their own set of distinct stock phrases. Mowinckel lists C, Deuteronomistic prose sermons as, 7:1–8:3; 11:1–5, 9–14; 18:1–12; 21:1–10; 25:1–11a; 32:1–2, 6–16, 26–44; 34:1–7, 8–22; 35:1–19; 44:1–14, along with several other discourse and narrative contexts without the characteristic heading, 3:6–13; 22:1–5; 27:1–22; 29:1–23; 39:15–18; 45:1–5.[118]

These stylistic tendencies can be seen by anyone reading through Jeremiah in a modern translation, like the NIV, that distinguishes prose and poetry in the typesetting. The point at hand does not relate to identifying Jeremiah, Baruch, or other authorial collaborators.

The present study filters out stock phrases and stereotypical expressions to focus on the exegetical use of scriptural traditions. The so-called Deuteronomistic style in Jeremiah is widespread and has been listed by others.[119] Instead of producing another such list, the following presentation of the temple sermon marks stock phrases to illustrate noninterpretive allusive style in Jeremiah's prose discourses. The example of the marked temple sermon demonstrates the profuse non-exegetical use of scriptural allusion running through most of Jeremiah (bold phrases signify characteristic language found in Deuteronomy and/or the Deuteronomistic narrative and the prose discourses of Jeremiah; and italics signify stock phrases of the prose discourses of Jeremiah and/or occasionally other prophets, but not Deuteronomy):[120]

---

116. See Even-Shoshan, 1143. The phrase is literally "rising early and X" (X + שכם) with the sense of "all day long" but metaphorically denoting constant, repeated, and persistent—NIV uses "again and again" and NRSV "persistently." The term "rises early" (שכם Hif inf. abs.) functions as an auxiliary verb emphasizing acts that have already taken place and are still constantly recurring (see *IBHS* §27.4b; 35.3.2c; GKC §§106k, 112dd; *HALOT* 2:1493–4). God is the subject of the constant sending, and the like, in first person or third person. See Schnittjer, "Individual versus Collective Retribution," 119–20.

117. The coded name Sheshak refers to Babylon on the principle of Atbash in which the first letter of the Hebrew alphabet is used for the last, the second for the second-to-last, and so on. In English it would be a=z, b=y, and so on, and in Hebrew *bet=shin* and *kaph=lamed*, thus *sh-sh-k = b-b-l* (ששך = בבל) Babylon. By the same principle *Leb Qamay = Kasdim*, that is, Chaldea (see Jer 51:1 NIV text note).

118. See Mowinckel, *Komposition*, 24, 31, 40; of the latter group he says, "Although they do not bear the characteristic heading, I do not doubt that they belong to Source C" (*Obgleich sie nicht die charakteristische Überschrift tragen, ist es meines Erachtens kaum zweifelhaft, dass sie der Quelle C angehören* [40]). He later decided C was not a source but a tradition (*Spirit*, 136, n. 11).

119. See Parke-Taylor, *Formation*, 248–55, 267–92; and see next footnote.

120. Phrases are marked based on lists in Weinfeld, *Deuteronomic School*, 320–61; Bright, "Prose Sermons," 30–35.

This is the word that came to Jeremiah from Yahweh: [2] "Stand at the gate of Yahweh's house and there proclaim this message:

'Hear the word of Yahweh, all you people of Judah who *come through these gates* to worship Yahweh. [3] This is what Yahweh Almighty, the God of Israel, says:

'*Reform your ways and your actions*, and I will let you live in this place. [4] Do not *trust in deceptive words* and say, "This is the temple of Yahweh, the temple of Yahweh, the temple of Yahweh!" [5] If *you really change your ways and your actions* and deal with each other justly, [6] if you do not oppress the **foreigner, the fatherless or the widow** and do not **shed innocent blood** in this place, and if you do not **follow other gods** *to your own harm*, [7] then I will let you live in this place, in **the land I gave your ancestors** for ever and ever. [8] But look, you are *trusting in deceptive words* that are worthless. [9] Will you steal and murder, commit adultery and perjury, *burn incense to Baal* and **follow other gods you have not known**, [10] and then come and stand before me in **this house, which bears my Name**, and say, 'We are safe'—safe to do all these detestable things? [11] Has **this house, which bears my Name**, become a den of robbers to you? But I have been watching! declares Yahweh.

[12] "'Go now to the place in Shiloh where I first **made a dwelling for my Name**, and see what I did to it because of the wickedness of my people Israel. [13] While you were doing all these things, declares Yahweh, *I spoke to you again and again*, but you did not listen; I called you, but you did not answer. [14] Therefore, what I did to Shiloh I will now do to **the house that bears my Name**, the temple you trust in, **the place I gave to you and your ancestors**. [15] **I will thrust you from my presence**, just as I did all your fellow Israelites, the people of Ephraim.'

[16] "So do not pray for this people nor offer any **plea or petition** for them; do not plead with me, for I will not listen to you. [17] Do you not see what they are doing in *the towns of Judah and in the streets of Jerusalem*? [18] The children gather wood, the fathers light the fire, and the women knead the dough and make cakes to offer to the Queen of Heaven. *They pour out drink offerings to other gods* **to arouse my anger**. [19] But am I **the one they are provoking**? declares Yahweh. Are they not rather harming themselves, to their own shame?

[20] "Therefore this is what Sovereign Yahweh says: '**My anger and my wrath will be poured out** on this place—on **man and beast**, on the trees of the field and on the crops of your land—and it will burn and not be quenched. [21] This is what Yahweh Almighty, the God of Israel, says: Go ahead, add your burnt offerings to your other sacrifices and eat the meat yourselves! [22] For when **I brought your ancestors out of Egypt** and spoke to them, I did not *just give them commands* about burnt offerings and sacrifices, [23] but I gave them this command: **Obey me**, and I will be your God and **you will be my people**. **Walk in obedience** to all I command you, **that it may go well with you**. [24] But *they did not listen or pay attention*; instead, they followed the **stubborn inclinations of their** evil **hearts**. *They went backward and not forward*. [25] **From the time your ancestors left Egypt until now**, day after day, *again and again I sent* you **my servants the prophets**.

> [26] But *they did not listen to me or pay attention*. They **were stiff-necked** and did more evil than their ancestors.'
>
> [27] "When you tell them all this, they will not listen to you; when you call to them, they will not answer. [28] Therefore say to them, 'This is the nation that **has not obeyed** Yahweh its God or *responded to correction*. Truth has perished; it has vanished from their lips.' [29] Cut off your hair and throw it away; take up a lament on the barren heights, for Yahweh has rejected and abandoned this generation that is under his wrath. [30] The people of Judah **have done evil in my eyes**, declares Yahweh. They have set up their **detestable idols** in **the house that bears my Name** and have defiled it. [31] They *have built the high places of Topheth* in the Valley of Ben Hinnom **to burn their sons and daughters in the fire**—*something I did not command, nor did it enter my mind*. [32] So beware, **the days are coming**, declares Yahweh, when people will no longer call it Topheth or the Valley of Ben Hinnom, but the Valley of Slaughter, for they will bury the dead in Topheth until there is no more room. [33] **Then the carcasses of this people will become food for the birds and the wild animals**, and there will be no one to frighten them away. [34] I will bring an end to *the sounds of joy and gladness and to the voices of bride and bridegroom* in *the towns of Judah and the streets of Jerusalem*, for the land will become desolate.
>
> [8:1] "'At that time, declares Yahweh, the bones of the kings and officials of Judah, the bones of the priests and prophets, and the bones of the people of Jerusalem will be removed from their graves. [2] They will be exposed to the sun and the moon and all the stars of the heavens, which they have loved and served and which they have followed and consulted and worshiped. *They will not be gathered up or buried*, but will be *like dung lying on the ground*. [3] **Wherever I banish them**, all the survivors of this evil nation will prefer death to life, declares Yahweh Almighty.'" (Jer 7:1–8:3)

The present study, limited to the scriptural use of scriptural traditions, confirms that no sharp line can be drawn between the poetic and prose discourses of Jeremiah (as others have observed while pursuing excavative goals). The notes on Jeremiah's use of scriptural traditions illustrate a shared hermeneutical profile for use of scriptural traditions in Jeremiah's poetry and prose. At the same time, attending to Jeremiah's stylistic tendencies offers much help to detect how style bears on exegesis.

Non-Exegetical Broad Allusions and Shared Themes

The following representative broad allusions include both verbal parallels and/or thematic similarities: **2:7b**>/<Lev 18:25, 28–29, defiling land by abominations; **2:9**>/<Exod 20:5; 34:7, accuse children's children; **2:27**>/<Deut 32:18, deserting the rock for wood and stone;[121] **2:28**>/<Deut 32:37, taunt: "Where are your/their gods?";[122]

121. See Holladay, *Jeremiah 2*, 55.
122. See ibid.

3:16–17>/<1 Sam 4:4; 2 Sam 6:2, ark of covenant no longer remembered because of Jerusalem as throne; **4:4**>/<Deut 10:16, circumcise your hearts (cf. Jer 9:25–26[24–25]); **5:19; 9:12–14; 16:10–13; 22:8–9**>/<Deut 29:24–28[23–27], Why has Yahweh done this?; **5:24**>/<Deut 16:9–10, weeks of harvest; **5:28**>/<Deut 32:15, they grow fat and sleek (only two uses of Qal שׁמן);[123] **6:9**>/<Lev 19:10; Deut 24:21, violate the law of gleaning;[124] **6:10**>/<Lev 26:40–41; Deut 10:16; 30:6, uncircumcised ears (cf. Jer 4:4; 9:25–26[24–25]); **7:32**>/<Deut 12:5–6, (ironic) no more "place";[125] **7:33**>/<Deut 28:26, corpses food for birds; **8:17**>/<Num 21:6, sending snakes; **10:11**>/<Gen 1:1, (Aramaic) allusion to creation of heavens and earth; **10:12**>/<Prov 8:22–31, founded world by wisdom; **11:7–8**>/<Deut 29:20[19], covenant warning to ancestors;[126] **14:13–16**>/<Deut 18:20–22, judgment against false prophets; **15:1**>/<Moses as intercessor (Exod 32:11–13; 33:12–16; Num 14:5; 16:4, 22, 45) and Samuel as intercessor (1 Sam 7:8–9; 12:18–19, 23); **16:14–15//23:7–8**>/<Exod 6–15, exodus from Egypt (as inadequate); **19:7, 9**>/<Deut 28:26, 53, becoming food for birds, wild animals, and eating their own children (cf. Lev 26:29); **21:8**>/<Deut 30:15, "setting before you life and death" (cf. 11:26); **22:8–9**>/<Deut 29:23–25, "nations will ask why Yahweh has done this, and they will say because they abandoned the covenant of Yahweh their God/God of their ancestors"; **28:10, 11, 12**>/<Lev 26:13, Hananiah "breaks yoke" (cf. Ezek 34:27); **28:14**>/<Deut 28:48, "iron yoke"; **29:13–14**>/<Deut 4:29–30; 30:3, paraphrase: seek Yahweh and he will regather you; **31:9**>/<Exod 4:22, "my firstborn" (בְּכֹרִי) (cf. Jer 31:20; Hos 11:1, 3); **31:18**>/<Hos 10:11, "Ephraim as untrained calf/trained heifer" (אֶפְרַיִם כְּעֵגֶל לֹא לֻמָּד/עֶגְלָה מְלֻמָּדָה); **32:7**>/<Lev 25:25–28, purchase of field by right of redemption; **43:1–7**>/<Exod 6–13, reversal of exodus from Egypt;[127] **51:25**>/<Gen 11:3, make Babylon "a burned-out mountain" (הַר שְׂרֵפָה)/ "let us bake baked" (וְנִשְׂרְפָה לִשְׂרֵפָה) bricks to make tower of Babylon.

Jeremiah polemically derides the nations that make cultic images (Jer 10:1–16). Differences with Isaiah's taunt include contrasts between Yahweh and the idols to emphasize Yahweh's power as creator and the election of Israel *within* the taunt itself. Isaiah, conversely, *intermittently interweaves* taunts as mutually enriching counterparts for the new exodus (see Table I1 in Isaiah; cf. Ps 115:9–11//135:15–18).[128] Specific thematic similarities include: >/<**10:4**; Isa 40:19–20; 41:6–7, gild images and fasten them so they will not fall; >/<**10:5**; Isa 46:7, they carry images; >/<**10:6–7**; Isa 40:18, none like Yahweh (cf. Ps 115:3–8).[129] Cassuto closely compares Jer 10:3–5, 8–9, 12–15 with

123. See ibid., 54.

124. A negative military connotation for the verb usually translated "glean" could be "picked off" (Judg 20:45 JPSB). See Allen, *Jeremiah*, 86, n. 49. On difficulties surrounding Jer 6:9, see McKane, *Jeremiah*, 1:144–45.

125. See Holladay, *Jeremiah 2*, 58.

126. Jeremiah 11:7–8 is a plus in MT (not in LXX) using stereotypical language ("warned them again and again" הַשְׁכֵּם וְהָעֵד). Also see 2 Kgs 17:13–15.

127. For far-reaching comparisons based on broad thematic inversions, see Yates, "New Exodus," 1–22.

128. See Schnittjer, "Idolatry in Isaiah," sec. on evidence. Also see Lynch, "Mapping Monotheism," 53.

129. For discussion of specific language in Jer 10:1–16 and Isaiah's taunts, see Holladay, *Jeremiah 2*, 87.

the taunts in Isa 40:19–22; 41:6–7; 44:9–14; 46:6–7 (which amount to about half of the taunts in Isaiah). Cassuto detects several single-word verbal parallels: some unimpressive like "silver" and "gold" and others impressive, especially the use of "tool" (מַעֲצָד), only appearing in Jer 10:3 and Isa 44:12. Cassuto considers these parallels strong evidence of "direct connection" with Jer 10 dependent on Isaiah, over and against contrary views. In spite of the weight of these observations, Cassuto does not adequately explain the masoretic plus in Jer 10:6–8, 10 (not in LXX), which, as Cassuto notes, sustains literary parallels with other thematically related passages in Jeremiah (2:5; 8:19; 16:19, etc.).[130] In short, the textual difficulties prevent confidence in deciding direction of dependence for these broad thematic parallels.

The prose retrospective in **Jer 32** makes extensive use of broad allusions and non-exegetical allusions to scriptural traditions. In that sense this retrospective stands apart from other scriptural retrospectives that typically include exegesis (e.g., Josh 24, Ps 78, Neh 9). The broad point of the context offers hope for restoration (see third point below). Note the following intentional broad allusions: 32:16–23>/<creation + retribution formula (Exod 20:5–6//Deut 5:9–10) + redemption + land + rebellion. Jeremiah's retrospective prayer especially moves forward by means of stock phrases from Deuteronomy, the Deuteronomistic narrative, and prose discourses in Jeremiah (see discussion above in Jeremiah Filters). Three elements distinguish themselves. First, the use of the retribution formula of the second commandment to connect creation and redemption traditions stands apart from all other long biblical retrospectives (Jer 32:18; Exod 20:5–6//Deut 5:9–10; for comparison see Table Josh1). Second, specific siege warfare language appears within the retrospective (Jer 32:24). Third, the historical retrospective explains the significance of Jeremiah's purchase of land (32:25; cf. 32:15, 43–44).

Shared Stock Phrases and Other Similarities

Figures of speech: >/<2:20; 3:6, 13; 17:2; Deut 12:2; 1 Kgs 14:23; 2 Kgs 16:4//2 Chr 28:4; 2 Kgs 17:10; Isa 57:5; Ezek 6:13; Hos 4:13, "under every spreading tree" (תחת כל עץ רענן), elsewhere "spreading, flourishing" (רַעֲנָן) with positive connotation (cf. Jer 11:16; 17:8; Hos 14:8[9]; Pss 37:35; 52:8[10]; 92:10, 14[11, 15]; Song 1:16); >/<4:3; Hos 10:12, "break up your unplowed ground"; >/<4:7; Isa 31:4; Amos 3:12; Mic 5:8; Nah 2:11–12, simile of lion for military threat; >/<4:31; 48:41; 49:22; 50:43; Isa 13:8; 26:17; Mic 4:9, 10, like woman in labor (cf. Gen 35:16–18); >/<6:17; Ezek 3:17; Hos 9:8, simile of prophets as sentinels (cf. Jer 6:1; 31:6); >/<6:26; Amos 8:10; Zech 12:10, like mourning for an only child; >/<6:27–30; Isa 48:10; Zech 13:9; Mal 3:2–3, prophet as refiner (cf. Jer 9:7[6]); >/<10:13b//Ps 135:7b, "he sends lightning with the rain and brings out the wind from his storehouses" (cf. Deut 28:12; Ps 33:7; Job 38:22); >/<15:10; 20:14; Job 3:3,

130. See Cassuto, *Biblical*, 1:143–48 (Cassuto prefers MT for Jer 10:1–16). Also see "מַעֲצָד," *HALOT* 1:615.

regret day of birth; >/<15:16; Ezek 2:8–3:3, eat the deity's words (to different effects) (cf. Jer 1:9); >/<48:40; 49:22; Deut 28:49, like an eagle swooping upon.

Condemnation: >/<1:16; 2:13, 17, 19; 5:7, 19; 12:7; Isa 1:4, 28; Hos 4:10, abandoning God (עזב);[131] >/<2:30; 26:2–23; 1 Kgs 18:4; 19:10; 2 Kgs 21:16; Neh 9:26; 2 Chr 24:20–22; 36:16; Matt 23:35–37; Luke 11:47–51; Acts 7:52, killing the prophets; >/<5:21; 6:10, 17, 19; Deut 29:4[3]; Isa 6:9–10, eyes but not see, ears but not hear (also see note on Isa 6:9–10); >/<5:28; Exod 22:21–24; 23:6–9; Deut 24:17–18; Isa 1:17; Mic 3:1–3; Zech 7:10, not defending the socially challenged (cf. Deut 1:16–17; 16:19); >/<7:21–23; Amos 5:25, sarcastic "denial" of wilderness sacrifices; >/<7:31; 19:5–6; 32:35; 2 Kgs 16:3; 21:6//2 Chr 28:3; 33:6, child sacrifice in valley of ben Hinnom (see note on 2 Chr 28:3); >/<9:4[3]; Gen 25:26; 27:36; Hos 12:3, "supplant" as pun on "Jacob" [יַעֲקֹב]) in Jer 9:4[3], "every brother is a deceiver" (כָּל־אָח עָקוֹב יַעְקֹב).

Doom: >/<3:3; Lev 26:19; Amos 4:7; Hag 1:10–11, rain withheld (cf. Deut 11:14); >/<6:11; 10:25; Hos 5:10; Zeph 3:8; Ps 69:24; Lam 4:11, liquid wrath; >/<6:21; Ezek 3:20; 7:19; 14:3–4; 44:12, "stumbling block" (cf. Lev 19:14; Isa 28:13; 57:14; Ps 119:165); >/<7:16; 11:14; 14:11; 15:1; Isa 1:15; Mic 3:4, deity not listening to prayers; >/<13:22, 26; Isa 47:2, 3; Ezek 16:37, 39; Lam 1:8, 10, simile of exposure and rape (including exposure of rebel by deity, Jer 13:26; Ezek 16:37); >/<15:8; Gen 22:17; 32:12[13]; 41:49, (ironic) like the sand of the sea; >/<16:16; Isa 37:29; Ezek 29:4; Amos 4:2; Hab 1:14–15, people hunted like fish and game (cf. Lam 4:18–19); >/<25:11, 12; 29:10; Zech 1:12; 7:5; Dan 9:2; 2 Chr 36:21 (seventy years of exile); 27:7 MT (seventy years as three generations); Isa 23:15 (period of judgment); Ps 90:10; Job 42:16 (seventy years as a lifetime); 49:27//Amos 1:4, "it will consume the fortresses of Ben-Hadad" (ואכלה ארמנות בן הדד); 51:58//Hab 2:13, "the people exhaust themselves for nothing . . . for fire/for fire . . . for nothing" (of Babylon);[132] >/<48:44; Isa 24:18, climbs out of a pit to be caught in snare (העולה מתוך הפחת ילכד בפה) (cf. Amos 5:18–19).

Hope: >/<10:16; 51:19; Lam 3:24; reversal Deut 32:9; Mic 2:4, Yahweh is their portion (cf. Num 18:20; Deut 10:9); >/<23:6//33:16; Deut 33:12; Ps 16:9; Prov 1:33 "live in safety" (שכן לבטח);[133] >/<29:14; 30:3, 18; 31:23; 33:7, 11, 26; Ezek 29:14; 39:25; Hos 6:11; Joel 3:1[4:1]; Amos 9:14; Zeph 2:7; 3:20; Pss 14:7; 53:6[7]; 85:1[2]; 126:4; Job 42:10, "restore the fortunes" (שוב . . . שבות)—most importantly, Deut 30:3; also Jer 48:47; 49:6, 39, "restore the fortunes of. . . ." Moab/Ammon/Elam/Samaria (שוב שבות . . . מואב/בני עמון/עלם/שמרון); and Ezek 16:53, ironically, of "restore the fortunes of Sodom"; >/<31:4; Exod 15:20; 2 Sam 6:5; Ps 149:3, tambourines with dancing and merrymaking (תף במחול שחק) (cf. Jer 31:13).

---

131. See Macy, "Sources of Chronicles," 54.

132. The inversion of "for nothing" and "for fire" by Jeremiah or Habakkuk reflects Seidel's theory, contra Parke-Taylor, *Formation*, 182.

133. See Holladay, *Jeremiah 2*, 53.

Chapter 12

EZEKIEL

SYMBOLS[1]

- // verbal parallels (A level)
- /~/ synoptic parallel (A level)
- ~ B, probable interpretive allusion; C, possible; D, probably not
- + interpretive blend
- >/< more or less similar (see Filters)
- * part of interpretive network (see Networks)

USE OF SCRIPTURE IN EZEKIEL[2]

3:5–6~Exod 4:10 (B) (people heavy of tongue)

4:14~Lev 11:39–40; 17:15+7:18; 19:7 (B) (avoiding ritually impure diet)

5:10*~Lev 26:29+Deut 24:16* (B) (multigenerational cannibalism) (* see personal responsibility network)

6:4–7~Lev 26:30–31 (B) (judgment upon cities and high places)

7:2, 3, 6~Amos 8:2 (C) (the end)

7:10~Num 17:5, 8[20, 23] (B) (budding staff)

7:12–13~Lev 25:25–28 (C) (sellers shall not return to what is theirs)

7:19~Zeph 1:18 (C) (silver and gold cannot deliver)

14:1–11*>/<Lev 17 (B) (heart idolatry) (* see place network)

14:14, 20~Gen 6–9; Job 1–42 (C) (even if Noah, Danel, and Job were in the land)

16:53–57*~Deut 29:23*[22] (C) (restoration of Sodom) (* see cities of the plain network)

18:1–4*~Deut 24:16* (B) (proverb of sour grapes) (* see personal responsibility network)

20:1–31>/<Exodus, Numbers (three rebellion retrospectives)

20:11, 13, 21, 25~Lev 18:5 (B) (decrees and ordinances to live)

21:27*[32]~Gen 49:10* (C) (to whom it belongs shall come) (* see Judah-king network)

22:26*~Lev 10:10*+Zeph 3:4 (B) (priests do violence against Torah) (* see teachers network)

24:7–8~Lev 17:13* (B) (pouring out blood) (* see place network)

24:23; 33:10~Lev 26:39 (B) (rot in iniquity)

29:17–20~26:7–14 (B) (shift payment for Nebuchadnezzar)

34:23–31*~Lev 26:4–6, 13 (B)+Jer 23:1–6* (C)+Ezek 37:24–28* (B) (Davidic shepherd) (* see branch and Davidic covenant networks)

36:12–19~Lev 18:24–30 (C)+Num 13:32 (B) (defiled land)

36:26–27*~11:19–20 (B)+Jer 31:33* (B) (new heart) (* see concealing network)

37:24–28*>/<2 Sam 7:11–17*; 23:5*; Lev 26 (D) (restoration of Davidic king/prince) (* see Davidic covenant and place networks)

38–39>/<Ezek 1–37 and other contexts (oracles against Gog)

38:2, 6~Num 24:7 (D)+Ezek 27:10, 14 (C)+Gen 10:2, 3, 6 (C) (identity of Gog and his militia)

39:11, 15>/<Valley of Hinnom (C) (Valley of Hamon Gog)

---

1. For explanation of symbols, see Symbols and Abbreviations and Introduction. For other help, see Glossary.
2. See Bibliographic Note on Lists of Potential Parallels.

39:28–29~Joel 2:27–28[2:27–3:1] (B) (pour out my spirit)
40–48>/<1 Kgs 6; 8 (C) (temple vision)
44:9–16~Num 18:1–7 (B) (sanctity of the temple)
44:17–19~Exod 28:39–43; 39:27–28, 41; Lev 19:19; Deut 22:11 (C) (standards for garments of priests)
44:20~Lev 21:5 (B) (priests not shave head or grow hair long)
44:21*~Lev 10:9* (C) (priests sober when in inner court) (* see teachers network)
44:22~Lev 21:7, 13–15 (B) (requirements for wives of priests)
44:23*~Lev 10:10–11* (B) (priest instructs on ritual purity) (* see teachers network)
44:24–27~Lev 21:1–3 (B) (standards of worship and ritual purity for priests)
45:21–24, 25~Exod 23:15; Lev 23:4–8; Deut 16:1–8 (C) (Passover); Exod 23:16; Lev 23:33–36; Num 29:12–38; Deut 16:13–17 (C) (Tabernacles)
47:22–23~Lev 19:34+25:10, 45 (C) (remapping the social identity of residing foreigners)
47:13–48:35~Josh 13–19 (C) (idealized apportioning of the land)

OLD TESTAMENT USE OF EZEKIEL (SEE RESPECTIVE NOTES)

20:9~Ps 106:8 (B) (redemption for name's sake in poetic retrospective)
34:1–31*~Zech 11:4–16 (C) (breaking the staff and appointing a bad shepherd) (* see Davidic covenant network)
36:23–24~Ps 106:47 (B) (regathering people in poetic retrospective)
37:15–28*~Zech 11:4–16 (C) (breaking the staff and appointing a bad shepherd) (* see Davidic covenant network)
39:29~Joel 2:28–29[3:1–2] (B) (pour out my spirit)
40:3~Zech 2:1[5] (B) (a man to measure)
44:11–12~2 Chr 35:5–6, 11 (C) (Levites perform sacrifices with laity in outer court)

NEW TESTAMENT USE OF EZEKIEL

3:3~Rev 10:9 (eat the scroll)
20:34, 41~2 Cor 6:17 (come out from them)
36:20, 22~Rom 2:24 (profaned among gentiles)

HERMENEUTICAL PROFILE OF THE USE OF SCRIPTURE IN EZEKIEL

Exegetical and Non-Exegetical Use of Scripture

Ezekiel houses allusions to vast numbers of scriptural traditions defined broadly. Everywhere Ezekiel seems to use scriptural expressions and stock phrases in non-exegetical ways. In a much smaller number of cases Ezekiel features exegesis of scriptural traditions. Both of these tendencies require attention.

Ezekiel's heavy dependence upon scriptural traditions helps to construct and flavor an array of sign, allegorical, visionary, and parabolic scenarios. Yet, dependence on scriptural traditions does not restrain intermittent shocking messages.

Ezekiel's tendency to invert and reverse scriptural traditions requires close attention. He does not stand against Torah. Ezekiel's persistent use of irony to condemn his hardened constituents requires the authoritative scriptural standards for exegetical irony to work.

Ezekiel often transcends the temporal bounds between past and present.[3] Perhaps it makes more sense to think of collapsing the past and present into images of judgment. In the scathing scenarios of the unfaithful foundling in Ezek 16 and wayward sister wives of Ezek 23, the entire history of the people collapses into the lifetime of the female character. Ezekiel 20 schematizes two ancient generations in the wilderness to condemn the present generation. The vision of the temple uses the rebellion of Korah in Ezek 44 as a baseline to explain the enhanced holiness standards for worship. In all of these and many other cases, Ezekiel brings together past and present and everything in between as though bearing on the guilt of his constituents. At the same time, Ezekiel gives no ground to complaints about deferred judgment coming upon the present generation in Ezek 18 and 33. He refuses to allow grievances against divine justice to become an excuse for rebellion. He gets at culpability by allusions to scriptural commands.

When Ezekiel turns to hope he often does so by means of exegesis of scriptural traditions. The prophet expects a Davidic shepherd and ruler to right civil and social wrongs according to covenantal standards in Ezek 34 and 37. If Jeremiah speaks of the internalization of Torah (Jer 31:33), Ezekiel emphasizes the spirit to make a new heart (Ezek 36:26).

Study of Ezekiel's non-exegetical use of scriptural traditions enjoys a welcome uptick of late. Certain controls in analyzing potential parallels among recent scholars strengthens confidence in the results. The study of stock phrases and elements that seem like matters of style have been leveraged into hermeneutical deductions. Many non-exegetical uses of scriptural traditions appear in the Filters.

Ezekiel and Torah

In both exegetical and non-exegetical use of scriptural traditions Ezekiel favors the holiness teaching found in Lev 17–26. In broad terms Ezekiel's use of the holiness collection and Jeremiah's use of the teachings of Deuteronomy set their styles apart. But these generalizations should not be overinterpreted. Close reading of Ezekiel demonstrates other scriptural allusions.

The direction of dependence between Ezekiel and Torah has been much disputed. For the moment, focus can be restricted to the most important evidence. Ezekiel and Torah, especially the holiness collection, share much in common, suggesting some kind of relationship. The mechanical evidence and ideological tendencies supports a view that Ezekiel uses the scriptural traditions of Leviticus but not the other way around.

Examining mechanical evidence of verbal and syntactical parallels between Ezekiel and Torah suggests the prophet as receptor, not donor, in a large number of cases. The inversion and abbreviation of elements in a citation by the receptor context does not prove but helps provide the kind of evidence that suggests direction of dependence. An example like the apparent reversal and streamlining of prohibitions against marital relations during

---

3. See Childs, *Introduction*, 361, 363.

a woman's menstruation and ritual defilement by relations with a neighbor's wife points to the prophet's use of holiness instructions (Lev 18:19–20; Ezek 18:6).[4] Ezekiel appears to split the phrase "*I will scatter you* **among the nations**" (Lev 26:33) and redistribute its mildly adjusted elements as "I will disperse you **among the nations** and *scatter you* through the countries" (Ezek 22:15).[5] Another example is when Ezekiel cites a difficult term, "You shall not *rule over* him *with harshness*" (Lev 25:43; cf. 46, 53) and explains it, "<u>With strength</u> you *ruled over* them, and *with harshness*" (Ezek 34:4). The rare term "harshness" (פֶּרֶךְ) makes allusion likely. Ezekiel apparently glossed the rare term by a more common one—"with strength," marked by underlining—which strongly suggests that the tradition in Lev 25 is the donor and Ezek 34 the receptor context.[6] The kind of adjustments in these scriptural uses shows direction of dependence. A large number of mostly non-exegetical cases like these contribute to identifying Ezekiel as receptor context.[7] Based on the evidence mentioned here and summarized in the Filters, Ezekiel will be treated as dependent on scriptural traditions in Torah as the default in this chapter. This provisional conclusion based on mechanical evidence can be collated with ideological tendencies.

Ezekiel's extremely critical ideological use of priestly imagery of Torah reveals his reshaping tendencies. He treats the land of exile as the land of promise, which does not easily work in the other direction, if at all. Ezekiel speaks of captivity as the "land of sojourning" versus Torah, which regards the land of covenant as the land of the Hebrew ancestors' sojourning.[8] Ezekiel's use of "pleasing odor" signifies "impiety and irreverence" of pagan practices versus sacrifices to Yahweh.[9] These and many other inversions and reversals examined in the notes and Filters can be explained by a critical prophet condemning Israel by dark ironies. The ironic stance requires standard baselines in donor contexts to function as irony.

In sum, the mechanical aspects of many uses of scriptural traditions can be explained with Ezekiel using the scriptural traditions of Leviticus, but not the other way around. The ironic inversion of holiness legal imagery can be explained with Ezekiel as the receptor context but not in the other direction, except by using too much ingenuity. The issues at hand do not relate to dating the final form of Ezekiel, Leviticus, and/or Torah, merely to their direction of dependence. The provisional approach here works with a starting point of Ezekiel dependent upon Torah traditions.

---

4. See Lyons, "Marking Innerbiblical Allusion," 247. See Seidel's theory in Glossary.

5. See ibid., 248. In this example emphases mark verbal parallels.

6. See "פֶּרֶךְ," *HALOT* 2:968. This example from Milgrom, *Leviticus 23–27*, 2356–57.

7. For many other examples of Ezekiel depending on holiness traditions, see ibid., 2352–63; idem, "Leviticus 26 and Ezekiel," 57–62; Zehnder, "Leviticus 26," 157–59. For six examples of Ezekiel's dependence on passages of Leviticus and Deuteronomy, sometimes blended, see Bergsma, "Relevance," 229–35.

8. The expression "land of sojourning" (אֶרֶץ מְגוּר) refers to captivity (Ezek 20:38) versus the land of promise (Gen 17:8; 28:4; 36:7; 37:1; Exod 6:4) ("II *מָגוֹר," *HALOT* 1:544). This observation is from Levitt Kohn, "Prophet Like Moses?," 240.

9. The expression "pleasing aroma" (רֵיחַ נִחֹחַ) collocated with "to Yahweh/me" (ליהוה/לי) appears many times in Torah (Gen 8:20, 21; Exod 29:18, 25, 41; Lev 1:9, 13, 17; 2:2, 9, 12; 3:5, 16; 4:31; 6:8, 14[15, 21]; 8:21, 28; 17:6; 23:13, 18; Num 15:3, 7, 10, 13, 14, 24; 18:17; 28:2, 6, 8, 13, 24, 27; 29:2, 6, 8, 13, 36; also see Lev 26:31) versus "pleasing aroma," ironically collocated with "idols" (גִּלּוּל) (Ezek 6:13), "images" (צֶלֶם) (16:19), false worship on high hills and under leafy trees (20:28), and as Yahweh accepting Israel as a "pleasing aroma" (20:41) (see Even-Shoshan, 759). This observation is from Levitt Kohn, "Prophet Like Moses?," 241, 244 (she includes most of the Scripture references cited in this note, see 241, n. 28).

Exegetical Conventions in Ezekiel

Ezekiel's exegetical use of scriptural traditions stands apart in many ways from other scriptural collections of the prophets. For the present purposes attention will be limited to four tendencies of exegetical interventions in Ezekiel. These do not include Ezekiel's massive non-exegetical use of scriptural traditions (see Filters).

First, Ezekiel's own voice dominates even in contexts filled with scriptural allusion. Ezekiel does not mark citations.[10] He constantly acknowledges divine inspiration in ways that sound like immediate revelation even when alluding to scriptural traditions. Lyons comments, "The locutions from Lev 17–26 are depicted as Yhwh's speech to his prophet, not as a text upon which Ezekiel meditates."[11] The importance of this observation may extend beyond Ezekiel's style. When prophets say "Thus says Yahweh," it may include the divine authority of scriptural instruction. Sometimes Ezekiel may use the language of scriptural traditions to express what Yahweh has revealed.[12] Care must be taken not to impose a false distinction upon the prophets between revelation mediated by scriptural traditions versus immediate revelation to the prophet. They stand together in Ezekiel.

Second, Ezekiel's frequent use of scenarios and imagery tends to control the flow of discourse. Since he does not overtly cite scriptural traditions or point out allusion, only those "in the know" get it. Though Ezekiel exercises considerable freedom with allusion, the scriptural traditions leave their mark on his teachings. The heavy use of holiness instruction tends to "cloak his message in forensic terminology."[13] Ezekiel's scripturally allusive expression keeps focus on his vivid scenarios.

Third, Ezekiel's tendency to categorical description combined with extreme imagery requires cautious interpretation. Ezekiel has often been pitted against Isaiah concerning foreigners and the new temple. Placing Isaiah's leniency for anyone (Isa 56:1–7) against Ezekiel's exclusion of foreigners (Ezek 44:9) can distort both prophets. Isaiah and Ezekiel both share with Torah a view of two kinds of others—those who are welcome to worship versus excluded others (see notes on Isa 52:1 and Ezek 14:1–11). Yet even when basic continuities are accounted for, Ezekiel envisions land allotments for residing foreigners with children among Israel in a way that virtually erases their social and economic identity as residing foreigners (see note on Ezek 47:22–23).

Some of Ezekiel's extreme inverted imagery shocks, but works. Ezekiel blends the Deuteronomy prohibition against multigenerational guilt in civil and criminal cases with the Leviticus threat of cannibalism during siege warfare wherein parents eat children and children eat parents (see note on 5:10). Other extreme imagery puzzles. Ezekiel ties the restoration of Jerusalem together with the restoration of her less wayward sisters Samaria and Sodom. Can one sister be literal and the other a figure of speech in the very same

---

10. Also observed by Rooker, "Use of OT Ezekiel," 49; Hays, "Ezekiel," *DNTUOT*, forthcoming.

11. Lyons, *Law to Prophecy*, 159.

12. See helpful discussion on this point in Hays, "Ezekiel," *DNTUOT*, forthcoming. For discussion of a similar situation in Revelation, see Beale and McDonough, "Revelation," 1084–85 (Hays draws attention to this discussion).

13. Childs, *Introduction*, 362.

parabolic scenario? The difficult parable does not hinder the intended shame Ezekiel piles upon his constituents (see note on 16:53–57).

One of the most challenging concepts comes when Ezekiel locates the temple outside the city, or better, the city outside the temple (see note on Ezek 47:13–48:35). Ezekiel's strenuous measures to handle the burden of holiness physically separate civil and religious spheres. The fact that he does not name the city as Jerusalem escalates interpretive difficulty. And all of the separation seems undone when the name of the city is revealed—"Yahweh Is There" (48:35). Even resolving the dichotomy between literal and nonliteral (ideal, symbolic, divine perspective) in any exegetical direction still leaves lingering interpretive space (see note on Zech 2:1[5]).

Fourth, Ezekiel's use of scriptural traditions affirms many old expectations in new ways. Ezekiel expects a Davidic ruler—at one time familiar and different. Ezekiel's new David is a king, but especially a prince. The everlasting covenant of peace associated with David is only one of the worship-oriented new elements Ezekiel expects (see notes on Ezek 34:23–31; 37:24–28). One of Ezekiel's most enduring images may be the new heart and new spirit. Even here the exegetical advances include strengthening sovereign activity upon the heart transplant recipients (see note on 36:26–27). Ezekiel's new covenant expectations have familiar qualities even as they advance revelation.

In sum, Ezekiel's different style of scriptural exegesis naturally corresponds to his alternative prophetic style. The kind of patience Ezekiel requires for responsible interpretation extends to understanding his use of scriptural traditions.

USE OF SCRIPTURE

3:5–6~Exod 4:10 (B) (people heavy of tongue). Yahweh charges Ezekiel with an ironic allusion to the call of Moses. Moses proposed that he has a speech impediment, including a description, literally "heavy of tongue" or "slow of tongue" (Exod 4:10).[14] If Yahweh refuted Moses because he had created talking beings, he likewise assures Ezekiel that his constituents shall understand him (Ezek 3:5–6). The problem with the people has nothing to do with communication but with rebellion. The shared imagery with the call of Moses brings out the ironic expected failure of Ezekiel's prophetic work. Yahweh even makes a contrast assuring Ezekiel that a slow-tongued people would respond more readily than his people (bold signifies verbal parallel, though translated differently because of contextual issues):

> Moses said to Yahweh, "Pardon your servant, Lord. I have never been eloquent, neither in the past nor since you have spoken to your servant. I am **slow of** speech and **tongue** [כְּבַד לָשׁוֹן]." (Exod 4:10)

14. See Tigay, "'Heavy of Mouth,'" 58. The ancient Near East comparative evidence makes certain that "heavy" of mouth and tongue refer to a speech impediment (58–60). Still, some interpreters see the language as a "hyperbolic metaphor" for lack of eloquence, while others suggest, with offsetting evidence, Moses may not know how to speak Hebrew (Exod 4:1, 29–31) or Egyptian (6:12, 30). See detailed discussion in Propp, *Exodus 1–18*, 210–11.

> You are not being sent to a people of obscure speech and **strange language** [כִּבְדֵי לָשׁוֹן], but to the people of Israel—not to many peoples of obscure speech and **strange language** [כִּבְדֵי לָשׁוֹן], whose words you cannot understand. Surely if I had sent you to them, they would have listened to you. (Ezek 3:5–6)

4:14~Lev 11:39–40; 17:15+7:18; 19:7 (B) (avoiding ritually impure diet). Priestly dietary regulations allow laity to eat an animal that dies or is torn, resulting in their temporary ritual defilement (Lev 11:39–40; 17:15; cf. 7:24; and compare other legal standards in note on Deut 14:3–21). Priests, like Ezekiel, are held to a higher standard and forbidden to eat animals that have died or were torn (Lev 22:8). A well-being offering may be eaten for two days, but then the meat becomes "impure" (פִּגּוּל) on the third day (7:18; 19:7). This term for "impure" is only used in the two contexts of Leviticus cited here, by Ezekiel on this occasion, and once of rebels who eat swine and "impure meat" soup (Isa 65:4). In short, Ezekiel claims lifelong fidelity to ritual dietary standards inclusive of avoiding cases in which acceptable meat causes ritual defilement because of circumstances (Ezek 4:14). Yahweh responds by allowing the prophet to cook his sign-bread over cow dung instead of human excrement (4:15).

5:10*~Lev 26:29+Deut 24:16* (B) (multigenerational cannibalism) (* see personal responsibility network). Ezekiel prophesies a dark irony using an interpretive blend of sorts. The threat of famine during siege warfare in antiquity reduced victims to cannibalism, as threatened in Torah (Lev 26:29; Deut 28:53–57). Ezekiel takes the basic syntax and diction of the prohibition limiting judgments in civil and criminal cases as a template—a passage he cites elsewhere (Deut 24:16; cf. Ezek 18:4, 20). He removes the negative particle and replaces the verbs of siege-induced cannibalism (Ezek 5:10).[15] The judgment continues with a combination of language drawn from Leviticus, "scatter" (Lev 26:33), and from Deuteronomy, "eye will not have pity" (Deut 7:16; 13:8[9]; 19:13 cf. 19:21; 25:12) and "not spare" (13:8[9]).[16] Also, the term for "vile things" (שִׁקּוּץ) refers to ritually impure dietary standards in Leviticus, but Ezekiel uses the term for idols as it functions in Deuteronomy and the Deuteronomistic narrative (29:17[16]; cf. 1 Kgs 11:5, 7; 2 Kgs 23:13).[17] Ezekiel's darkly ironic interpretive blend and its context freely draw on both the holiness and Deuteronomic traditions found in Torah (bold and italics signify verbal parallels, wavy underlining signifies language of Leviticus, and broken underlining signifies language of Deuteronomy):

> You *will eat* the flesh of your *sons* and the flesh of your daughters. (Lev 26:29)

---

15. See Greenberg, *Ezekiel 1–20*, 113–14.
16. See "I זרה," "חוס," "חמל," *HALOT* 1:280, 298, 328.
17. See Levitt Kohn, *New Heart*, 89–90, 91. Also see "שִׁקּוּץ," *HALOT* 2:1640.

> **Parents** are not to be put to death for their *children*, nor *children* put to death for their **parents**; each will die for their own sin. (Deut 24:16)

> Therefore in your midst **parents** *will eat* their *children*, and *children will eat* their **parents**. I will inflict punishment on you and will scatter [זרה] all your survivors to the winds. Therefore as surely as I live, declares Sovereign Yahweh, because you have defiled my sanctuary with all your vile things [שִׁקּוּץ] and detestable practices, I myself will shave you; I will not look on you with pity [חוס] or spare you [חמל]. (Ezek 5:10–11†)

6:4–7~Lev 26:30–31 (B) (judgment upon cities and high places). Ezekiel uses a cluster of terms from the threats against covenant violation in Lev 26 to call for imminent fulfillment of divine wrath (Ezek 6:4–7). Lyons notes an incongruity between addressing the "mountains of Israel" but then speaking of "wherever you live" (6:3, 6). For Lyons this confirms direction of dependence.[18] This seems like good reasoning, even factoring in metonymy when compared to the address against the mountain of Israel elsewhere (36:1–12). Compare threat and pending fulfillment (bold signifies verbal parallels, and italics signify parallels at the level of shared roots):

> I will destroy **your high places**, cut down **your incense altars** and pile your dead bodies on the lifeless forms of **your idols**, and I will abhor you. I will turn your *cities into ruins* and *lay waste* your sanctuaries, and I will take no delight in the pleasing aroma of your offerings. (Lev 26:30–31)

> Your altars will be demolished and **your incense altars** will be smashed; and I will slay your people in front of **your idols**. I will lay the dead bodies of the Israelites in front of their idols, and I will scatter your bones around your altars. Wherever you live, *the towns will be ruined* and **your high places** demolished, so that your altars *will be laid waste* and devastated, your idols smashed and ruined, your incense altars broken down, and what you have made wiped out. Your people will fall slain among you, and you will know that I am Yahweh. (Ezek 6:4–7†)

7:2, 3, 6~Amos 8:2 (C) (the end)
7:10~Num 17:5, 8[20, 23] (B) (budding staff)
7:12–13~Lev 25:25–28 (C) (sellers shall not return to what is theirs). Ezekiel opens a traumatic oracle of judgment speaking of "the end," only appearing with the article in this form in Amos's short vision of the summer fruit and in Ezek 7:2, 3, 6 (cf. Amos 8:2).[19]

18. See Lyons, "Transformation of Law," 8–9.
19. See Zimmerli, *Ezekiel 1*, 203.

If the vison of the end of the Northern Kingdom concludes with the command "Silence!," Ezekiel's parody builds up to a loud trumpet (Amos 8:3; Ezek 7:14). The judgment moves forward using "the end" repeatedly but nothing else from Amos's vision sequence, along with other repetitions like the stock phrase from Deuteronomy often used in Ezekiel, "my eye shall not spare" (Ezek 7:4, 9; see Filters). The climactic elements of Ezekiel's parody invert Aaron's staff and frustrate the conventions of the Jubilee. The phrase "staff buds" (מַטֶּה פָּרַח) only appears when Yahweh affirms Aaron's election after rebellion and in this oracle of Ezekiel.[20] Ezekiel alludes to the rebellion elsewhere (Ezek 44:10, 15). Ezekiel capsizes the ancient image meant to prevent further backbiting (bold signifies verbal parallel):

> "The staff belonging to the man I choose will sprout, and I will rid myself of this constant grumbling against you by the Israelites." . . . Aaron's **staff**, which represented the tribe of Levi, had not only sprouted but **had budded**, blossomed and produced almonds. (Num 17:5, 8[20, 23])

> See, the day! See, it comes! Doom has burst forth, **the staff has budded**, arrogance has blossomed. (Ezek 7:10†)[21]

The instruction on the Jubilee and Ezekiel's oracle share several terms including "something sold," only found in two other contexts but not with the other shared terms (Lev 25:25, 27, 28, 29; Ezek 7:13; cf. Deut 18:8; Neh 13:20).[22] Ezekiel seems to be purposefully using the term in a broader sense than the legal idiom in the Jubilee instruction.[23] Ezekiel presents a situation in which the economy is being terminated altogether, eliminating any reason for buyer or seller emotion (emphases signify verbal parallels):

> If one of your fellow Israelites becomes poor and *sells* some of their property, their nearest relative is to come and redeem **what they have sold.** If . . . later on they prosper and acquire sufficient means to redeem it themselves, they are to determine the value for the years since they sold it and refund the balance to the one to *whom they sold it*; they can then go back to their own property. But if they do not acquire the means to repay, what was sold will remain in the possession of *the buyer* until the Year of Jubilee. It will be returned in the Jubilee, and they can then go back to their property. (Lev 25:25–28)

> The time has come! The day has arrived! Let not *the buyer* rejoice nor *the seller* grieve, for my wrath is on the whole crowd. *The seller* will not get back **what was sold**—as

20. See Levitt Kohn, *New Heart*, 70.

21. Allen deletes the continuation of the "rod to punish the wicked"/"rod of wickedness" in Ezek 7:11 as a gloss (*Ezekiel 1–19*, 101), though others retain it in spite of LXX difficulties (Block, *Ezekiel 1–24*, 254–55).

22. See "מִמְכָּר," *HALOT* 1:595.

23. See Dijkstra, "Legal Irrevocability," 111. And see Block, *Ezekiel 1–24*, 259–60; Lyons, "Transforming Visions," 10.

> long as both *buyer* and *seller* live. For the vision concerning the whole crowd will not be reversed. Because of their sins, not one of them will preserve their life. (Ezek 7:12–13a†)

The need to sound the trumpet for the Jubilee has ended. Ezekiel speaks of blowing a trumpet with a different term only used here in Scripture. The trumpet blasts a call to battle because of divine wrath (7:14). In sum, Ezekiel echoes numerous scriptural traditions in a dismal parody, looking to the end of the economic basis undergirding the Jubilee redemption.

7:19~Zeph 1:18 (C) (silver and gold cannot deliver). Ezekiel and slightly earlier contemporary Zephaniah share a parallel saying. Ezekiel develops it—whether from Zephaniah or a common source—by cloning, splitting, and redistributing parts of the saying with his own distinctive language (on cloning see Glossary). Ezekiel typically uses the term "unclean thing" of menstrual impurity (Ezek 7:20; 18:6; 22:10; 36:17) and "stumbling into sin" of idolatry (14:3, 4, 7) (italics signify verbal parallels, and broken underlining signifies expansive developments):

> Neither *their silver* nor *their gold will be able to save them on the day of Yahweh's wrath.* In the fire of his jealousy the whole earth will be consumed, for he will make a sudden end of all who live on the earth. (Zeph 1:18)

> They will throw *their silver* into the streets, *and their gold* will be treated as a thing unclean. *Their silver and gold will not be able to deliver them in the day of Yahweh's wrath.* It will not satisfy their hunger or fill their stomachs, for it has caused them to stumble into sin. (Ezek 7:19)

14:1–11*>/<Lev 17 (B) (heart idolatry) (* see place network). Ezekiel adapts his oracle against idolatrous hearts according to a threefold third-person holiness legal casuistic form of Leviticus. Instead of second-person "if you . . ." case laws, Leviticus and Numbers sometimes use third-person forms. Outside of Leviticus and Numbers, only Ezek 14:4 uses "any persons" (אִישׁ אִישׁ) in a quasi-legal sense (cf. the only other use in Exod 36:4). In this case, Ezekiel especially adapts the legal framework of Lev 17 but does not deal with all domestic and religious slaughter at the shrine nor prohibitions against consuming blood (Lev 17:1–16). This context stands in the borderline between exegetical use of a scriptural tradition versus adaptation of a form, in which case it might fit better with the Filters. The likelihood of so many uses of elements from Lev 17 makes it seem slightly more like exegesis. Ezekiel accuses Israel to the elders of Israel gathered before him, in half-steps, of: case one, keeping idols in their hearts (Ezek 14:4–5); case two, keeping idols in their hearts and seeking prophets (14:6–8); and, case three, prophets deceiving inquirers who wish to be deceived (14:8–11). In this way Ezekiel reformats the holiness impersonal legal case form as part of his indictment against Israel (see Table Ezk1).

TABLE EZK1: HOLINESS LEGAL CASUISTIC FORMULA IN EZEKIEL 14:1–11‡

	Leviticus 17	Ezekiel 14 case one	case two	case three
"Speak to X and say to them"	2	14:4		
"If any from the house/sons of Israel"	3, 8, 10, 13	14:4	14:7	
"and the foreigner residing in Israel/ your midst"	8		14:7	
"in order to"/"in order that never again"	5	14:5		14:11
"I will set my face against"	10		14:8	
"to cut off from his/my people"	4, 9		14:8	
"to bear their iniquity"	16			14:10
"I am Yahweh"[a]		14:4	14:7	14:9

‡ Data in table collated from Block, *Ezekiel 1–24*, 423–24. Also see Zimmerli, *Ezekiel 1*, 302–5.

[a] "I am Yahweh" appears: • Leviticus 52x with 50 of these in Lev 18–26 • Ezekiel 84x • in all other Scriptures combined 59x.

Ezekiel speaks incidentally in this context of "residing foreigners" (גֵּר) sojourning in Israel as being responsible to obey legal standards (Ezek 14:7). Less importantly, this suggests a preexilic setting—which corresponds to the stated dates of Ezek 1–33—since in exile Israel itself would be residing foreigners (Lev 19:34). More importantly, Ezekiel does not innovate but broadly accepts the legal standing of residing foreigners espoused in the holiness collection of Leviticus. Here he affirms residing foreigners as functioning within worshiping Israel (Ezek 14:7). Thus, when Ezekiel excludes "foreigners" (בֶּן־נֵכָר) uncircumcised in heart and flesh it has nothing to do with ethnicity or genealogy, since residing foreigners retain their place in worshiping Israel (see note on 44:9–16). Israel as inclusive of residing foreigners continues into the postexilic period but with an upgrade including their own land allotment (see note on 47:22–23).

14:14, 20~Gen 6–9; Job 1–42 (C) (even if Noah, Danel, and Job were in the land). Ezekiel speaks of three exemplars whose "righteousness" could not forestall judgment if they were in the land. The scriptural traditions of Noah and Job make explicit their "righteousness" (Gen 6:9), or at least their characterization as "blameless, upright, God-fearing, and turning from evil" (Job 1:1, 8; 2;3). In their cases, Noah's righteousness did not stop the flood and Job's integrity served as an indirect cause of the trauma upon his first set of children. The identity of Danel (דָּנִאֵל *ketiv*) versus Daniel (דָּנִיֵּאל *qere*) attracts much attention. Elsewhere Ezekiel refers to Danel (*ketiv*)/Daniel (*qere*) relative to his wisdom rather than his righteousness (Ezek 28:3). If Ezekiel had in mind the Judean Daniel of exile, it would fit with Noah and Job since Daniel's righteousness and wisdom did not deliver him from captivity. If Ezekiel refers to Danel, a non-Israelite of antiquity like the other two, known from the Canaanite legend Aqhat, he may have in mind something like justice for the rights of the socially challenged: "Danel . . . got up and sat at the entrance to the gate, among the leaders on the threshing floor. He judged the cases of widows, presided over orphans' hearings."[24]

16:53–57*~Deut 29:23*[22] (C) (restoration of Sodom) (* see cities of the plain network). Just when it seems like Ezekiel's shocking retrospective allegorical accusation can go no further, he speaks of the restoration of Sodom (on Ezek 16 see Filters). The destruction of the cities of the plain had long stood as a symbol of condemnation (Deut 29:23[22]; Hos 11:8). Ezekiel's surprises include identifying Sodom's sin as pride and not caring for the needy (Ezek 16:49). This suggestion only partially overlaps with a contrast between the citizens of Sodom's lack of hospitality versus Abraham's hospitality and Lot tending to celestial delegates posing as strangers (Gen 18:2–8; 19:1–3; cf. Heb 13:2). The main interpretive question turns on whether Ezekiel uses sister Sodom as part of the rhetorical irony of the accusation or if he literally has in mind some kind of restoration (Ezek 16:53–57). In either case, the humiliation of Jerusalem's restoration hinging on that of sister Samaria and sister Sodom strengthens the larger endgame of covering the shame of the accused prostitute (16:63). For other uses of Sodom with "greater than" logic, see Lam 4:6 and Matt 10:15; 11:23–24.

18:1–4*~Deut 24:16* (B) (proverb of sour grapes) (* see personal responsibility network). Jeremiah and Ezekiel both use a complaint proverb as a point of departure for exegesis of the legal standard concerning individual accountability in Deuteronomy. It seems neither prophet uses the other even while they each leverage the proverb against the same scriptural legal standard to different ends (see note on Jer 31:30). Ezekiel does not deny the proverb directly and immediately but broadly alludes to a pending situation in which the complainants shall be unable to use the proverb. All of this serves as a basis for the prophet's extended scenario of a righteous grandfather, rebellious father, and righteous son (Ezek 18:5–9, 10–13, 14–17). After the three-generation scenario Ezekiel requotes the legal instruction and offers an ironic solution. Note the rearrangement of elements in Ezek 18:20 according to Seidel's theory (see Glossary; bold, italics, and underlining signify similar constructions with some verbal parallels; and broken underlining signifies the proverb shared with Jer 31:30):[25]

> <u>Parents are not to be put to death for their children</u>, **nor children put to death for their parents**; *each will die for their own sin.* (Deut 24:16)

> The word of Yahweh came to me: What do you people mean by quoting this proverb about the land of Israel: "<u>The parents eat sour grapes, and the children's teeth are set on edge</u>"? As surely as I live, declares Sovereign Yahweh, you will no longer quote this

24. Aqhat, I.v.6–8 from Coogan and Smith, *Stories*, 39; cf. III.i.23–25 (p. 47); *ANET*, 151, 153. Also see Jub. 4:20.
25. See Greenberg, *Ezekiel 1–20*, 333.

> proverb in Israel. For everyone belongs to me, the parent as well as the child—both alike belong to me. *The one who sins is the one who will die.* (Ezek 18:1–4)

> The one who sins is the one who will die. **The child will not share the guilt of the parent,** *nor will the parent share the guilt of the child.* The righteousness of the righteous will be credited to them, and the wickedness of the wicked will be charged against them. (18:20)

Ezekiel's exegetical advancement relates to the manner in which the catastrophic judgment against Jerusalem stands in continuity with Torah's standard of individual culpability in the courtroom. The prophet does not disagree with collective responsibility—he denies the self-righteousness of those who quote the proverb.[26] Ezekiel's constituents cannot use a doctrine of "corporate responsibility . . . that absolves them of personal responsibility."[27] Ezekiel condemns the generation of the exile according to their own sin even while Yahweh waits for an opportunity to forgive:

> Yet the Israelites say, "The way of the Lord is not just." Are my ways unjust, people of Israel? Is it not your ways that are unjust? Therefore, you Israelites, *I will judge each of you according to your own ways,* declares Sovereign Yahweh. Repent! Turn away from all your offenses; then sin will not be your downfall. *Rid yourselves of all the offenses you have committed,* and get a new heart and a new spirit. Why will you die, people of Israel? For I take no pleasure in the death of anyone, declares Sovereign Yahweh. *Repent and live!* (18:29–32 emphasis mine)

20:1–31>/<Exodus, Numbers (three rebellion retrospectives).
20:11, 13, 21, 25~Lev 18:5 (B) (decrees and ordinances to live). The threefold rebellion retrospectives of Ezek 20 come to a difficult penultimate conclusion with "I even gave decrees that were not good and ordinances by which they could not live" (Ezek 20:25 lit.). The exact structure of the message continues to be debated primarily because of many uneven repetitions (some elements repeated multiple times). The following threefold structure can serve the present purposes, though explaining exegetical allusions does not require this particular view of the structure (see Table Ezk2).[28]

The tradition of the people's idolatry in Egypt does not appear in Exodus, but, like Ezekiel, Joshua includes it in his speech at Shechem (Ezek 20:7–8; Josh 24:14). In contrast to lists elsewhere (Ezek 18:6–9, 18), Ezekiel here places heavy emphasis on the Sabbath as representative of the "decrees and ordinances" as a whole (20:12, 13, 16, 20, 21, 24).

---

26. See Greenberg, *Ezekiel 1–20*, 340.
27. Block, *Ezekiel 1–24*, 589. Also see Schnittjer, "Individual versus Collective Retribution," 116, n. 17; von Rad, *OT Theology*, 1:394.
28. On other approaches focused more on general parallels between Ezek 20 and Exod 6:1–9, see Sim, "Organization," 120–21 ; Evans, *You Shall Know*, 129–32.

TABLE EZK2: THREEFOLD RETROSPECTIVES OF REBELLION IN EZEKIEL 20‡

Egypt	wilderness first generation	wilderness second generation
• covenant in Egypt (5–6)	• ordinances for life (11)[d] • command: Sabbath to sanctify (12)[b]	• warning and decrees to younger generation (18–19)[a] • command: hallow the Sabbath (20)[b]
• idolatry (7–8)[a]	• profaning the Sabbath (13a)[cd]	• rebellion against ordinances to live by and profane the Sabbath (21a)[cd]
• wrathful intentions restrained (8–9)	• wrathful intentions restrained (13b–14)	• wrathful intentions restrained (21b–22)
• exodus (10)	• forbidden to enter land because people profane the Sabbath, idolatry (15–17)[ac]	• diaspora threatened because people profane the Sabbath and desired ancestors' idolatry (23–24)[ac]
		• not good decrees, not live by (25)[d] • child sacrifice (26)[a]

‡ Table developed independently. For other approaches see Hahn and Bergsma, Ezek 20:5–9, 10–17, 18–26 ("What Laws?" 203); Zimmerli, 20:5–9, 10–16, 17–26 (*Ezekiel 1*, 407); Greenberg, 20:5–10, 11–17, 18–26 (*Ezekiel 1–20*, 377–78); Block, 20:5–9, 10–17, 18–26 (*Ezekiel 1–24*, 622–23); Allen, 20:5–9, 10–14, 15–17, 18–22, 23–26, 30–31 ("Structuring," 452–58). Allen regards 20:27–29 as a later insert (461) that shifts a pre-existing chiastic structure, 20:3//31, 4//30, 6//28, *7a//27*, 7b//26, 8–11//21b–25, 12–13//20–21a, 16//18b, 17//18b (459–60; the italicized element lacks verbal parallel and undermines the suggestion).

[a] Idolatry practiced Ezek 20:7–8, 16, 18, 24, 26, 28, 30–31.

[b] Sabbath laws given 20:12, 20.

[c] Sabbath laws broken 20:13, 16, 21, 24.

[d] Allusion to Lev 18:5.

This broadly corresponds to the Levitical intercessors' postexilic prayer that only specifically mentions the Sabbath as representative of the Ten Commandments at the mountain (Neh 9:14). This correspondence may be coincidental since Ezekiel often emphasizes priestly concerns like holiness, which would include the Sabbath, while the postexilic community commits to those practices that would strengthen the restoration, including Sabbath-keeping (10:31[32], 30–39[31–40]). Ezekiel's brief reference to the wilderness rebellion of the first generation without naming Kadesh does not echo the account in Deut 1 but Num 14 by the use of the people "reject" (מאס), and ironic reversal of Yahweh "lifting up the hand"—not to promise the land but to swear they will not get in (Num 14:30, 31; Ezek 20:15–16).[29] Ezekiel does not seem concerned to refer to the rebellion of Baal Peor (Num 25) but simply accuses the younger generation of Sabbath breaking twice and of idolatry once (Ezek 20:21, 24).[30] Ezekiel's broad allusions to threefold rebellion—in Egypt and by both wilderness generations—serve as a setting to emphasize

29. See Schnittjer, "Kadesh Infidelity," 118. Note Ps 106:26 uses "lift up the hand" against the first generation of rebels in a similar manner as Ezek 20:15.

30. Contra Hahn and Bergsma, "What Laws?," 204. The second generation turned to their parents' idolatry (Ezek 20:18, 24) referring to their Egyptian and/or wilderness infidelities (20:7–8, 16).

profaning the Sabbath and turning to idolatry. These covenant violations begin to get at the three-plus-one set of allusions to Lev 18:5 (Ezek 20:11, 13, 21, 25).

Interpretations vary widely regarding the "not good" statutes Yahweh gave (20:25). Some regard the "not good" laws as including child sacrifice to Yahweh in a legal tradition familiar to Ezekiel (20:26).[31] The major problem with this claim comes from Ezekiel's repeated condemnation of child sacrifice (16:20, 21, 36; 20:31; 23:37, 39). Hahn and Bergsma propose the "not good" decrees refer to the Deuteronomic instruction given to the second generation. They state that Ezekiel regarded the "laws of Deuteronomy as clearly inferior or even offensive."[32] In this view, Ezekiel opposes provision for local profane slaughter (Deut 12:15–25) versus the preferred slaughter at the shrine (Lev 17:1–9), and opposes allowance for the conversion of firstlings to substitutes during annual pilgrimages (Deut 14:24–25) versus the preferred firstlings themselves belonging to Yahweh (Lev 27:26). Yahweh gives defective Deuteronomic laws, according to Hahn and Bergsma, to "defile" (טמא Piel) Israel (Ezek 20:26).[33] For this to work the phrase "sacrifice every firstborn" in Ezek 20:26 cannot refer to child sacrifice but animal firstlings.[34] But this does not fit the evidence of the connected warning to Ezekiel's constituents against "defiling yourselves" (טמא Nif) by "sacrifice of your children in fire" (20:31). Other common views include: a negative view of Mosaic law to bring judgment or allow disobedience; framing it as a rhetorical question ("Did I give them decrees that were not good?"); relocation of 20:25–26 after 20:27 so it seems like a quotation of blasphemy by the ancestors; and the most common view taken up in the second point below.[35]

Ezekiel's extremely difficult reference to "not good" ordinances can be tentatively addressed by two observations: one grammatical and the other based on his repeated use of the saying that appears in Lev 18:5.[36] First, five times in this context Ezekiel refers to "my decrees and my ordinances"—both terms with the first-person possessive suffix (חֻקּוֹתַי, מִשְׁפָּטַי) and "my decrees" in its feminine plural form (20:11, 13, 16, 19, 21, 24). But when he gets to the not good/not live punchline in 20:25 he changes to "decrees" (חֻקִּים) and "ordinances" (מִשְׁפָּטִים) without the attached first-person pronoun and "decrees" in its masculine form to match the warning against following the "decrees of your ancestors" in its masculine form and "their ordinances" in 20:18.[37] In this way the "not good" decrees of Yahweh refer to those transmitted by their parents (bold signifies verbal agreement, and broken underlining signifies verbal but not grammatical parallel):

31. See Patton, "'I Myself Gave,'" 78–79; she refers to Exod 22:29[28].

32. Hahn and Bergsma, "What Laws?" 208.

33. See ibid., 210, 213–15, 218.

34. Against Ezek 20:26 referring to child sacrifice to Molech, see ibid., 211–13. Gile counters that not all child sacrifice in Scripture is associated with Molech (see "Deuteronomic Influence," 130–31). See note on 2 Chr 28:3.

35. List summarized from Friebel, "Decrees," 23–26.

36. Also note allusions to Lev 18:5 in Ezek 18:9, 17, 19, 21 (Sprinkle, "Law and Life," 283–84).

37. See Friebel, "Decrees," 28–29.

> I said to their children in the wilderness, "Do not follow the **decrees** [חֻקִּים mp] of your parents or keep their **ordinances** or defile yourselves [טמא Hith] with their idols." (20:18†)

> So I gave them other **decrees** [חֻקִּים mp] that were not good and **ordinances** through which they could not live. I defiled [טמא Piel] them through their gifts—the sacrifice of every firstborn—that I might fill them with horror so they would know that I am Yahweh. (20:25–26†)

This shift in grammar does not erase the awkwardness of inferring that Yahweh sovereignly takes responsibility for giving the "not good" statutes and "defiling" through their parents.

Second, the most common interpretation of the phrase "not good" decrees regards it as the negative results of Ezek 20:11, 13, 21 because the people misconstrued good laws in not good ways.[38] Leviticus 18:5 uses "my decrees" (חֻקֹּתַי fp) and "my ordinances" (מִשְׁפָּטַי) both with attached first-person pronouns in order to "live" (חיה) (italics, bold, and underlining signify verbal and syntactical parallels; and broken underlining signifies verbal but not grammatical parallels):

> Keep *my decrees* and *my ordinances*, **which the person who obeys them will live by them**. I am Yahweh. (Lev 18:5 lit.)

> I gave them *my decrees* and made known to them *my ordinances*, **which the person who obeys them will live by them.** (Ezek 20:11 lit.)

> Yet the people of Israel rebelled against me in the wilderness. They did not follow *my decrees* but rejected *my ordinances*—**which the person who obeys them will live by them**—and they greatly profaned my Sabbaths. (20:13a lit.)

> But the children rebelled against me. They did not follow *my decrees*, they were not careful to keep *my ordinances*, for **the person who obeys them will live by them** and they profaned my Sabbaths. (20:21†)

> So I gave them decrees that were not good and ordinances, they could not **live by them.** (20:25 lit.)

Yahweh "gave" his decrees and his ordinances to the parents (20:11) but warned the next generation not to follow their parents' decrees and ordinances or risk defiling

38. See ibid., 22. Friebel's view of Ezek 20:25–26 as a commentary on 20:23–24 (30–36) differs from the view here.

themselves (20:18). When the next generation followed their parents' decrees and ordinances against Yahweh's warning, he surprisingly takes responsibility with active verbs "I gave" not good decrees and "I defiled" (20:25–26). The real difficulty pivots on the active verbs by which Yahweh credits his active giving and defiling even though he had tried to prevent this very outcome. The sovereign claim of responsibility in Ezek 20:25 remains perplexing even after considering potential theological "solutions."

The context of Lev 18:5, cited three times positively and then climactically reversed in Ezek 20, offers additional insight. Yahweh warns, "You must *not do as they do in Egypt*, where you used to live, and you must *not do as they do in the land of Canaan*, where I am bringing you. Do not follow their practices" (Lev 18:3, emphases mine). This wilderness-bracketing warning reveals the central themes of Ezekiel's rebellion retrospectives. Both wilderness generations practiced the idolatry of Egypt, and the younger generation settled into Canaanite-like syncretism, establishing continuity of rebellion in the land (Ezek 20:7–8, 28) even child sacrifice "to this very day" (20:31 lit.). By forsaking Yahweh's decrees and ordinances for the ways of Egypt and Canaan, the people reversed from "live by them" to "not live by them." Ezekiel puts these words into his constituents' mouths: "You say, 'We shall be like the nations, like the families of the earth'" (20:32 lit.).

In sum, the extremely difficult saying on the "not good" laws may be resolved, to some degree, from attention to grammatical and syntactical shifts in close reading and especially by attention to the context of Lev 18:5, the donor text cited repeatedly in Ezek 20. First, the grammatical structure shows that Yahweh gave his life-giving decrees and his ordinances to the older wilderness generation (20:11) but warned the younger generation not to follow the decrees and ordinances of the older generation (20:18). In this way the life-giving decrees and ordinances of Yahweh became not-good and not-life-giving when mediated through the older generation (20:25). Second, the context of the repeatedly cited donor text of Lev 18:5 demonstrates why the laws became not-life-giving.[39] Namely, just as the wilderness generations lived like people of Egypt and Canaan (Lev 18:3; Ezek 20:21), so too Ezekiel's constituents defile themselves in the same ways "to this very day" (Ezek 20:31 lit.).

21:27*[32]~Gen 49:10* (C) (to whom it belongs shall come) (* see Judah-king network). Interpreters suggest Ezek 21:27[32] presents a "sinister reinterpretation" of part of the blessing of Judah.[40] The difficult phrase would be taken in the sense of "until it comes to whom it belongs" referring to tribute and glory given to the Judah-king (Gen 49:10). In a dark parody Ezekiel transforms the "it" of the phrase into "ruin"—"Until it [ruin] comes to whom it belongs" (Ezek 21:27[32] lit.). This possible allusive inversion merits consideration in light of Ezekiel's extensive inversion of the blessing of Judah in a satirical

39. As noted above, Ezek 20 verses 11, 13, 21, and 25 each allude to Lev 18:5.

40. See Block, *Ezekiel 25–48*, 692–93; Moran, "Gen 49,10 and Its Use in Ez 21,32," 416–25.

lament (19:1–14). The extreme textual difficulties in Gen 49:10 exclude accepting this as more than a possibility.[41]

22:26*~Lev 10:10*+Zeph 3:4 (B) (priests do violence against Torah) (* see teachers network). Ezekiel 22:26 and Zeph 3:4 are the only biblical texts to use the verb "do violence" (חמס) with "torah" as its object making allusion highly likely.[42] By all appearances Ezekiel blends a tradition from Zephaniah, or a common source, with instructions for priests in Torah. Other common elements in the context of Zeph 3:1–4 appear in the context of Ezek 22:26, such as "wolves" and "lions" (Ezek 22:25, 27; Zeph 3:3).[43] Ezekiel seems likely the receptor context because of inverting both the citations of Lev 10:10 and of Zeph 3:4—a double example of Seidel's theory.[44] Since Ezek 22:26 inverts the elements of Lev 10:10 it follows that Ezek 22:26 would also invert the elements of Zech 3:4. If so, Ezekiel appropriates Zephaniah's summary condemnation, explains it by use of an interpretive blend with an instructional charge to Aaron, and leverages this into the priests' profaning Yahweh by a sin of intentional omission. The interpretive blend complements Ezekiel's use of the same priestly tradition elsewhere (see note on Ezek 44:23) (emphases signify verbal parallels):

> So that you [Aaron and his sons] can <u>distinguish between</u> **the holy and the common, between the unclean and the clean**, and so you can teach the Israelites all the decrees Yahweh has given them through Moses. (Lev 10:10–11)

> Her prophets are unprincipled; they are treacherous people. *Her priests profane what is holy and do violence to the torah.* (Zeph 3:4†)

> *Her priests do violence to* my *torah and profane* my *holy things*; **between the holy and the common** <u>they do</u> not <u>distinguish</u>; **and between the unclean and the clean** they do not make known; and they shut their eyes to the keeping of my Sabbaths, so that I am profaned among them. (Ezek 22:26 lit.)

24:7–8~Lev 17:13* (B) (pouring out blood) (* see place network). The instruction for slaughter of game mandates "pouring out the blood and covering it with dust" (Lev 17:13). Ezekiel appropriates these details as part of his imagery of indictment against wrongful innocent bloodshed in Jerusalem: "She did not pour it upon the earth to cover it with dust" (24:7 lit.; cf. v. 8).[45]

---

41. For detailed discussion of textual issues in Gen 49:10, see Schnittjer, "Blessing of Judah," 16–17, nn. 2, 3.
42. Rooker, "Use of OT Ezekiel," 48.
43. See Kselman, "Zephaniah, Book of," *ABD* 6:1079. Also see "pour out upon them my wrath" (אֶשְׁפֹּךְ/לִשְׁפֹּךְ עֲלֵיהֶם זַעְמִי) (Ezek 22:31//Zeph 3:8).
44. Beentjes observes the inverted use of Zeph 3:4b in Ezek 22:26 but not Lev 10:10 ("Discovering a New Path," 38).
45. See Lyons, "Transformation of Law," 11, n. 27.

24:23; 33:10~Lev 26:39 (B) (rot in iniquity). The culmination of judgment in Lev 26 comes with exile described as "rotting in their iniquities . . . and also because of the iniquities of their ancestors they shall rot" (Lev 26:39 lit.).[46] This somewhat rare term only appears elsewhere in this sense in Ezekiel. The prophet adopts this language of exile in the context of not mourning for the delight of the eyes—Ezekiel's wife/Jerusalem—but rotting in iniquity (Ezek 24:23). And, significantly, he uses the language to emphasize judgment of the individual generation not for divine pleasure but to evoke repentance (33:10; cf. 4:17). The purpose of exile to bring repentance shows continuity between Lev 26:39–40 and Ezek 33:10–11. But the parallels between Ezek 33:10–20 and 18:21–32 accent punishment of the present generation while Lev 26:39 underlines both rotting for personal iniquity and shared culpability with ancestors. The prophet persistently refuses to let the people excuse their own lack of repentance by their ancestors' rebellion.

29:17–20~26:7–14 (B) (shift payment for Nebuchadnezzar). Ezekiel pronounces an oracle (587 BCE) of destruction against Tyre at the hands of Nebuchadnezzar (Ezek 26:7–14). Though Tyre was defeated on the mainland, Nebuchadnezzar besieged the city for thirteen years unsuccessfully (Tyre later fell to Alexander the Great in 332). Sixteen years after the oracle against Tyre, Ezekiel delivered an oracle against Egypt at the hands of Nebuchadnezzar (29:17–20). Since Nebuchadnezzar had done so much work against Tyre at Yahweh's bidding without adequate plunder, Yahweh gave him Egypt as payment (29:20). The need for Ezekiel to explicitly offer an alternative to the unfulfilled oracle illustrates the silent non-echo (trace) but real force of Deuteronomy's standard for the prophetic word to accord with reality (Deut 18:22).[47] In sum, it seems as though the need for a prophet's word to come to pass (18:22) may have prompted an explanation in terms of an alternate fulfillment (Ezek 29:17–20). As with all potential traces, it can be no more than a possibility.

34:23–31*~Lev 26:4–6, 13 (B)+Jer 23:1–6* (C)+Ezek 37:24–28* (B) (Davidic shepherd) (* see branch and Davidic covenant networks). The oracle against the shepherds offers important evidence of Ezek 34 as receptor context of this interpretive blend. Evidence for direction of dependence can be gauged as mild for Ezek 37:24–28, moderate for Jer 23:1–6, and very strong for Lev 26 (see notes a, c, e, f, g, h below).[48] Now that Jerusalem has fallen, Ezekiel looks ahead to Yahweh's covenant of peace mediated by a single shepherd, David, in contrast to the self-serving shepherds. To reduce complexities, the following comparative annotations mainly focus on the important ending of the oracle against the shepherds in Ezek 34 with the main parallels to Lev 26 (bold, italics, and

46. On "rot in iniquity" (מקק בעון), see "מקק," *HALOT* 1:628–29.

47. See discussion in Chisholm, "When Prophecy," 570–72.

48. Other important evidence in this context includes the phrase "do not rule over him harshly" (רדה בפרך) of Lev 25:43, 46, 53 which gets expanded to "*With strength* you have ruled them harshly" (וּבְחָזְקָה רְדִיתֶם אֹתָם וּבְפָרֶךְ) in Ezek 34:4† (emphasis mine). The interpretive addition "with strength" clarifies a rare term and shows direction of dependence (Lyons, "Extension," 144; idem, "Transformation of Law," 6–7). The only other uses of "harshly" are Exod 1:13, 14 (see "פֶּרֶךְ," *HALOT* 1:968).

double underlining signify verbal parallels; underlining signifies textual issues; and wavy underlining signifies interpretive expansions):

> I will send you **showers in its season**, and **the ground will yield its crops and the trees of the field their fruit.** [5] Your threshing will continue until grape harvest and the grape harvest will continue until planting, and you will eat all the food you want and **live *in safety* in your land.** [6] I will grant **peace** in the land, and you will lie down and **no one will make you afraid.** I will **remove wild beasts** from the land, and the sword will not pass through your country. . . . [13] I am Yahweh your God, who brought you out of Egypt so that you would no longer be slaves to the Egyptians; I **broke the bars of your yoke** and enabled you to walk with heads held high. (Lev 26:4–6, 13; vv. 4†, 6†)

> "Woe to the shepherds who are destroying and scattering *the sheep of my pasture*!" declares Yahweh. . . . [4] *"I will raise up over them shepherds* who will tend them, and they will no longer be afraid or terrified, nor will any be missing," declares Yahweh. [5] "The days are coming," declares Yahweh, "when *I will raise up* for David a righteous Branch, a King who will reign wisely and do what is just and right in the land. [6] In his days Judah will be saved and Israel will live *in safety*. This is the name by which he will be called: Yahweh Our Righteous Savior." (Jer 23:1, 4–6; v. 4†)[a]

> My servant David will be king over them, and they will all have one shepherd. They will follow my laws and be careful to keep my decrees. [25] They will live in the land I gave to my servant Jacob, the land where your ancestors lived. They and their children and their children's children will live there forever, and David my servant will be their prince forever. [26] I will make a covenant of peace with them; it will be an everlasting covenant. I will establish them and increase their numbers,[b] and I will put my sanctuary among them forever. [27] My dwelling place will be with them; I will be their God, and they will be my people. [28] Then the nations will know that I Yahweh make Israel holy, when my sanctuary is among them forever. (Ezek 37:24–28)

> *I will raise up over them* one shepherd, my servant David,[c] and he will tend them;[b] he will tend them and be one shepherd[c] to them. [24] I Yahweh will be their God, and my servant David[c] will be prince among them. I Yahweh have spoken. [25] I will make a covenant of peace with them and **rid the land of savage beasts**[d] so that they may live in the wilderness and sleep in the forests *in safety*. [26] I will make them and the places surrounding my hill a blessing. I will send down **showers in season**; there will be showers of blessing.[e] [27] **The trees of the field will yield their fruit and the ground will yield its crops;**[f] the people will be *secure* in their land. They will know that I am Yahweh, **when I break the bars of their yoke**[g] and rescue them from the hands of those who enslaved them. [28] They will no longer be plundered by the nations, nor will wild animals devour them.

> They ***will live in safety,***[h] **and no one will make them afraid.**[i] [30] Then they will know that I, Yahweh their God, am with them and that they are my people,[j] the house of Israel, declares Sovereign Yahweh. [31] You are my sheep, *the sheep of my pasture*, and I am your God, declares Sovereign Yahweh. (Ezek 34:23–28, 30–31; vv. 23†, 27†; 30†)

[a] The large number of verbal, syntactic, and thematic parallels between Jer 23:1–6 and Ezek 34:1–31 make it likely that Ezekiel is developing an expansive allegorical scenario based on the opening of Jer 23. For several other examples of this sort of thing in Ezekiel, see Filters, section on Parabolic/Allegorical/Visionary Scenarios. The parallels here have been drawn from a much longer list of the entire context of Ezek 34:1–31 detailed in Block, *Ezekiel 25–48*, 275–76, n. 17. Also see Goswell, "Davidic Restoration," 353–55.

[b] The phrase "I will establish them and increase their numbers" (וּנְתַתִּים וְהִרְבֵּיתִי אוֹתָם) in Ezek 37:26 appears in MT but not LXX (see *BHS* apparatus). The phrase is similar to the MT plus (not in LXX) in Ezek 36:11 "and they will become numerous and be fruitful" (וְרָבוּ וּפָרוּ) (*BHS* apparatus). This evidence suggests these phrases are later scribal additions. This observation is based on Nihan, "Ezekiel 34–37," 160. Also, the phrase "it is he who will tend them" in Ezek 34:23 is missing in the main LXX witnesses, and thus may be an MT gloss (see 172, n. 70).

[c] A couple of factors mildly suggest that Ezek 34:24–28 is dependent on 37:24–28 as one of its donor contexts: David is referred to as "king over" and "prince" in Ezek 37:24–28 but only as "prince among" in 34:24–28, with a mild downgrade easier to explain in a receptor text (see ibid., 172); and the composite nature of 34:1–31 draws on other contexts esp. Lev 26 and Jer 23. The only dated oracle in Ezek 33–39 is at 33:21. The oracles may be arranged for reasons other than chronology.

[d] Compare: "I will rid the land of savage beasts" (וְהִשְׁבַּתִּי חַיָּה־רָעָה מִן־הָאָרֶץ) (Lev 26:6//Ezek 34:25) (Lyons, "Extension," 143, 146, n. 37; idem, "Marking," 246).

[e] The use of the phrase "your rains in their season" (גִשְׁמֵיכֶם בְּעִתָּם) from Lev 26:4 includes a mildly ungrammatical sequence in Ezekiel's interpretative expansion. He first speaks of "rain" singular but then switches to rain plural to match the donor context: "I will send down the rain [sing] in its season, there will be showers [plural] of blessing" (וְהוֹרַדְתִּי הַגֶּשֶׁם בְּעִתּוֹ גִּשְׁמֵי בְרָכָה יִהְיוּ) (Ezek 34:26 lit.) (see Milgrom, *Leviticus 23–27*, 2349; Lyons, *From Law to Prophecy*, 125; idem, "Extension," 145, 146, n. 39; idem, "Transformation of Law," 9–10). This clarification offers strong evidence of Lev 26 as donor and Ezek 34 as receptor contexts, respectively.

[f] The phrase "the ground will yield its crops and the trees of the field will yield their fruit" from Lev 26:4 is an inverted quotation in Ezek 34:27 (Seidel's theory) (Beentjes, "Discovering a New Path," 37; Lyons, "Extension," 146, n. 40; idem, "Marking," 246).

[g] The phrase "I broke the bars of your yoke" from Lev 26:13 uses a more complex explanation in Ezek 34:27, suggesting the former as donor text (Nihan, "Ezekiel 34–37," 171; Lyons, "Extension," 146, n. 41).

[h] Compare: "Live in safety" (וִישַׁבְתֶּם/וְיָשְׁבוּ לָבֶטַח) Lev 26:5//Ezek 34:28 (Lyons, "Extension," 146, n. 38). Also note "in safety" (לָבֶטַח) seems to be an important catchword to link Lev 26 with these shepherding contexts (Lev 26:5; Jer 23:6; Ezek 34:25, 27, 28).

[i] Compare: "and no one will make you afraid" (וְאֵין מַחֲרִיד) (Lev 26:6//Ezek 34:28) (Lyons, "Extension," 146, n. 42).

[j] On the covenant formula "I, Yahweh their God . . . they are my people" with a reassurance formula insert, see Table J1 in Jeremiah, note d. The modified covenant formula in Ezek 34:30 need not be based on Lev 26:12 since it is widespread as noted in Table J1 (contra Lyons, "Extension," 146, though he partially walks this back, 146, n. 43).

The oracle in Ezek 34 appropriates considerable covenant language from Leviticus and uses it for a different purpose. Lyons suggests that Ezekiel uses this language "as a reversal" of the covenant retribution that culminates in exile in Lev 26:14–39.[49] Ezekiel escalates the imagery from peace in the "land" (Lev 26:5) to peace in the "wilderness" (Ezek 34:25).[50] In sum, the ideals of covenantal expectations or demands become a paradigm for mapping the fulfillment of Yahweh's covenantal fidelity.

49. See Lyons, "Extension," 146.
50. See ibid., 147.

36:12–19~Lev 18:24–30 (C)+Num 13:32 (B) (defiled land). Leviticus personifies the land as a recurring image: ritual defilement causes nausea and vomiting (Lev 18:24–30; 20; 22), the fruit trees need to be circumcised (19:23–25), and it needs Sabbath years (25:1–7; 26:34, 43).[51] The figural logic stems from divine rights over the land in which Israel actually lives as residing foreigners enjoying asylum (25:23). Ezekiel intermittently takes advantage of this land-personification imagery relative to exile. Yahweh speaks to the land in direct address, at one point apparently evoking the mythic distortion of the ten scouts—"The land we explored *devours* those living in it" (Num 13:32b)—saying, "I will cause people, my people Israel, to live on you. They will possess you, and you will be their inheritance; you will never again deprive them of their children . . . Because some say to you, 'You *devour* people and deprive your nation of its children'" (Ezek 36:12–13, emphasis signifies verbal parallel). Although the parallel with Num 13:32 is only a single word, it causes a grammatical anomaly in this context of Ezekiel, which suggests likely dependence on the scouts' saying.[52]

Leviticus speaks of contamination of the land that leads to exile using a term for "ritual impurity" (טמא) within a context listing ritual, social, and moral prohibitions (Lev 18:25). The causes of ritual pollution here are necessarily inclusive of antisocial and immoral actions. The land's "ritual pollution" applies to both Israel and the nations of Canaan, even though the latter were not subject to standards for ritual purity—"It will vomit you out as [כַּאֲשֶׁר] it vomited out the nations that were before you" (18:25). Though Ezekiel often focuses on idolatry and ritual contamination, in this context he uses his stock phrase "shed blood upon the land," denoting social and moral oppression of the innocent and ceremonial defilement (Ezek 36:18). Ezekiel ties these images together by using the simile of a menstruating woman for Israel who defiles the land in her state of ritual impurity (36:17). Notice how Ezekiel uses the simile of a menstruous woman to symbolize the misdeeds of the people.[53]

> Mortal, when the house of Israel lived on their own soil, they defiled it with *their ways and their deeds*; their conduct in my sight was *like the uncleanness of a woman in her menstrual period*. (Ezek. 36:17 NRSV, emphasis mine)

---

51. See Schnittjer, *Torah Story*, 344–47. On the image of circumcising fruit trees in Lev 19:23–25, see footnote in Hermeneutical Profile of the Use of Torah in Leviticus.

52. The address to the land in Ezek 36:12, 13 shifts between masculine plural and singular: "on you" (עֲלֵיכֶם, 2mp), "possess you" (וִירֵשׁוּךָ, 2ms), "you will be" (וְהָיִיתָ, wcp 2ms), "you will not again" (וְלֹא־תוֹסִף, impf. 2ms), "to you" (לָכֶם, 2mp). This is odd because "land" is a feminine noun. But then in 36:13, in an embedded discourse, it switches over to addressing the land in feminine singular including "(she) devours" (אֹכֶלֶת, Q ptc. fs)—an exact parallel with Num 13:32, in Ezek 36:13 complemented by "your nation" (גּוֹיֵךְ, 2fs, *ketiv*). The oddity, then, is a brief switch to more correct grammar when quasi-citing what they say in Num 13:32—the oddness of correct grammar stands out within the context's ungrammaticality. For *ketiv*/*qere* and adjustments in the ancient versions, see *BHS* apparatus.

53. The term "misdeeds" (עֲלִילָה) in Ezek 36:17 (cf. v. 19) may broadly refer to ritual and immoral actions as in 20:43, 44 looking back in the preceding context to idolatry, Sabbath-breaking, child sacrifice, and so on. Ezekiel's contemporary also uses the term of immoral deeds in contrast to humility and truthfulness (Zeph 3:7, 11; cf. vv. 12–13). See "עֲלִילָה," *HALOT* 1:833.

The simile may evoke the instruction of menstrual ritual impurity in Lev 15:19–24. But the ritual purification shifts to "sprinkle" with ritually pure water, using a verb associated with more serious ritual impurity for touching corpses, not menstruation (Ezek 36:25; Num 19:13, 20 negatively, and positively with a different term 19:18, 19).

In sum, Ezekiel's exegesis works with the personification of the land that runs through the holiness instructions of Leviticus. He even includes the colorful characterization of the land devouring people in the bad report of the ten scouts. Ezekiel uses the figural personification of the land to indict the people for ritual defilement and immorality, adding the simile of a menstruating woman who needs a strong ritual purification (Ezek 36:25) and, more importantly, a new spirit (36:26–27).

36:26–27*~11:19–20 (B)+Jer 31:33* (B) (new heart) (* see concealing network). Ezekiel returns to the expectation of a new heart and expands upon it, as he does with many other oracles (see subsection on Recapitulation in Filters). In the earlier context Ezekiel emphasizes unity by means of "one heart" versus doubling "new spirit" in the later context, whether from his earlier oracle or a catchword with Jeremiah (Ezek 11:19; 36:26; Jer 31:31). Part of the expansion appears to be a close approximation of a key line from Jeremiah's new covenant—"I will put my torah in their inner parts" (Jer 31:33, lit.) (נָתַתִּי אֶת־תּוֹרָתִי בְּקִרְבָּם) and "I will put my spirit in your inner parts" (Ezek 36:27, lit. second-person plural) (וְאֶת־רוּחִי אֶתֵּן בְּקִרְבְּכֶם).[54] Both Jeremiah and Ezekiel use the full covenant formula (see Table J1 in note on Jer 31:31–34; emphases signify verbal parallels):

> "The days are coming," declares Yahweh, "when I will make a **new** covenant with the people of Israel and with the people of Judah . . . This is the covenant I will make with the people of Israel after that time," declares Yahweh. "**I will put my** torah **in their minds** and write it on their hearts. I will be their God, and they will be my people." (Jer 31:31, 33)

> *I will give* them an undivided *heart and put a* ***new*** *spirit in* them; *I will remove from* them their *heart of stone and give* them *a heart of flesh.* Then *they will follow my decrees and be careful to keep my laws.* They will be my people, and I will be their God. (Ezek 11:19–20)

> For I will take you out of the nations; I will gather you from all the countries and bring you back into your own land. [25] I will sprinkle clean water on you, and you will be clean; I will cleanse you from all your impurities and from all your idols. [26] *I will give* you *a* **new** *heart and put a new spirit in* you; *I will remove from* you your *heart of stone and give* you *a heart of flesh.* [27] **And I will put my** Spirit **in you** and move you *to follow my decrees and be careful to keep my laws.* [28] Then you will live in the land I gave your ancestors; you will be my people, and I will be your God. (36:24–28)

54. The parallel of Jer 31:33 and Ezek 36:27–28 is observed by Block, "Prophet," 39; idem, *Ezekiel 25–48*, 356–57, n. 97.

In the earlier oracle Ezekiel describes the effects of a new heart of flesh as "they will do" (וְעָשׂוּ) my decrees and laws, while in the later oracle he uses the same verb but with Yahweh as the subject "I will make" (וְעָשִׂיתִי) (11:20; 36:27).[55] This shift can be interpreted as "move you" (NIV), "make you" (NRSV), "I will cause you" (JPSB), "make you conform to my statutes" (REB), and as "divine coercion" or even being "forced" to obey.[56] These suggestions all get at the need for the Spirit to break the long addiction to rebellion.

Compelled involuntary obedience seems oxymoronic. And these suggestions do not adequately emphasize the ending of the compound sentence. Setting aside the awkward syntax in the beginning of the phrase that softens the force of the verb, the sentence goes on to use the same verb with the people as subject: "*I will make it* [וְעָשִׂיתִי] so that in my statutes you will walk and my laws you will keep and *you will do* [וַעֲשִׂיתֶם]" (36:27 lit., emphasis mine). Zimmerli splits the difference, noting Ezekiel's reference to the Spirit goes beyond Jeremiah's reference to interior torah, and this "allows Yahweh to participate directly in man's new obedience."[57] The overemphasis on forced obedience also does not adequately account for the imagery itself. Ezekiel speaks of replacing the "inflexible" heart of stone "with a heart of flesh [that] will enable them to work as they ought to."[58]

In sum, care should be taken not to overexplain the divine workings on human hearts. Ezekiel offers a much-needed word of hope for Spirit-enabled obedience.

37:24–28*>/<2 Sam 7:11–17*; 23:5*; Lev 26 (D) (restoration of Davidic king/prince) (* see Davidic covenant and place networks). The parabolic prophecy of the two sticks rejoined—Judah and Joseph—concludes with David ruling over all Israel (Ezek 37:24–28). The restored rule of David gets combined with numerous broad expectations: promised land (37:25), everlasting covenant of peace (37:26), and tabernacle (37:27). The cluster of fulfillments signify God's fidelity to his covenant using the full formula: "I will be their God, and they will be my people" (37:27). The "covenant of peace" as an "everlasting covenant" suggests allusion to the Davidic covenant (37:26; 2 Sam 7:13, 16; 23:5).[59]

Though Ezek 37:24–28 often gets compared to Lev 26, the general stock phrases do not offer evidence beyond broad similarities.[60] The only notable similarity is the commonplace covenant formula, but this provides no reason to view Lev 26 as donor context (see Table J1 in note on Jer 31:31–34). However, Ezek 34 redeploys some of the elements of 37:24–28 blended together with overt dependence on Lev 26 (see note on Ezek 34:23–31).

---

55. The phrase in Ezek 36:27 uses awkward syntax: verb + accusative marker + relative clause + verb, literally "and I will do that which in my statutes you will walk" (וְעָשִׂיתִי אֵת אֲשֶׁר־בְּחֻקַּי תֵּלֵכוּ) (Ezek 36:27 NET note; cf. Eccl 3:14).

56. Block says "divine coercion" (*Ezekiel 25–48*, 356) and Lyons "forced" ("Extension," 147). Elsewhere Lyons' alternative version of these comments uses similar but less coercive language ("Transformation of Law," 27–28).

57. Zimmerli, *Ezekiel 2*, 249.

58. Carasik, *Theologies*, 110.

59. Also see "my covenant of peace" which is a "covenant of priesthood forever" with Phinehas in Num 25:12, 13.

60. See Nihan, "Ezekiel 34–37," 159, 164.

38–39>/<Ezek 1–37 and other contexts (oracles against Gog).
38:2, 6~Num 24:7 (D)+Ezek 27:10, 14 (C)+Gen 10:2, 3, 6 (C) (identity of Gog and his militia).
39:11, 15>/<Valley of Hinnom (C) (Valley of Hamon Gog).
39:28–29~Joel 2:27–28[2:27–3:1] (B) (pour out my spirit). Only a small fraction of the extensive shared scriptural locutions in the oracles against Gog in Ezek 38–39 features potential exegetical intervention. Tooman demonstrates a large number of shared locutions and motifs in Ezek 38–39 and 1–37 along with a number of other contexts in Torah, prophets, and Psalms. He sets aside Ezekiel's stereotypical expressions and stock phrases. The majority of the other shared locutions amount to short snippets that broadly connect contexts by thematic similarity but not exegetical development. Tooman proposes these shared locutions have been "mined" from Ezek 1–37 and elsewhere. He refers to the outcome as a "textual mosaic" or "pastiche" that was "composed by combining bits and pieces of preexisting texts." The major purpose of the Gog oracles, for Tooman, is to bring closure and harmony to Ezekiel.[61]

The chief menace of Ezek 38–39, Gog could be based on Balaam's oracle, "Their king [Israel] will be greater than Agag" (Num 24:7), also set in the "last days" (24:14; Ezek 38:16). The name Agag (אֲגָג) in the Masoretic Text appears as Gog (גוג) in the Samaritan Pentateuch, Septuagint (Γωγ), and related ancient old Greek witnesses (Aquila, Symmachus, Theodotion).[62] In spite of the strong testimonies to Gog, this Septuagintal context features numerous reinterpretations that reduce its value as witness to its parent text and may reflect intentional connection to Ezek 38–39.[63] The potential allusion to Num 24 lacks adequate evidence.

Gog's confederate militia includes several little-known peoples appearing as Tyre's economic partners in Ezek 27 or as descendants of Japhet and Ham in the table of nations (underlining signifies peoples referred to in Ezek 27:10, 14; and italics signify those referred to in Gen 10:2, 3, 6):

> Son of man, set your face against Gog, of the land of *Magog*, the chief prince of *Meshek* and *Tubal*; prophesy against him. . . . Persia, *Cush* and *Put* will be with them, all with shields and helmets . . . also *Gomer* with all its troops, and Beth *Togarmah* from the far north with all its troops—the many nations with you. (Ezek 38:2, 6)[64]

---

61. See Tooman, "Transformation," 50–110, here citing 50, 80, 92. The appendix to Tooman's study collates the shared locutions verse by verse proposing scriptural parallels for every one of the fifty-two verses in Ezek 38–39. Tooman's excavative agenda cannot be pursued here. For sharp criticism of Tooman's thesis esp. regarding dating the oracle, see Strine, "Compositional," 595–601; Hossfeld, "Gog Oracles," 194–95; Schultz, "Isaianic Intertextuality," 39–40.

62. See Num 24:7 SP, LXX Göttingen, and *BHS* apparatus.

63. See Wevers, *Notes on Numbers*, 405–6.

64. Instead of "chief prince" the LXX transliterates the word for "chief" as a proper name *Rosh* (רֹאשׁ, Ρως) (Ezek 38:2 LXX). Popular evangelical end-times teachers of the twentieth century sensationalized the transliteration by mistakenly identifying *Rosh* with Russia. See explanation in Block, *Ezekiel 25–48*, 434–35.

These peoples do not represent standard enemies of Israel but, except for Persia, "far-flung nations of rumor."[65] The scenario suggests distant peoples gather together against the people of Yahweh in the "center of the earth" (38:12). Tooman notes the sign-oracle of the razor may suggest the scenario, "This is Jerusalem, which I have set in the center of the nations, with countries all around her" (5:5).[66]

Other options for interpreting this much-contested context include Gog as referring to the dynasty of Gyges of Lydia (seventh century BCE).[67] In this view the references to some of the names of peoples who trade with Tyre in Ezek 27 get commandeered to support Gog.[68]

Many difficulties attach themselves to each moving part of this possible allusion to the table of nations. Elsewhere Ezekiel's frequent expanded recapitulations of elements presented in his earlier oracles as well as his penchant for building parabolic, allegorical, and visionary scenarios on scriptural allusions (see Filters) could corroborate the cast of characters in the Gog oracle as based on Ezek 27 and Gen 10.

Gog's burial place could be translated "Valley of Gog's Multitude" (39:11, 15 JPSB). Or it may be a wordplay on Valley of Hinnom using consonance, Valley of Hamon Gog.[69]

When Ezekiel speaks of "giving the spirit" positively elsewhere, he uses the verb "give" (נתן) (Ezek 11:19; 36:26, 27; 37:14). Ezekiel only uses the term "pour out" with a negative connotation, such as pouring out wrath or the like, except in Ezek 39:29.[70] Tooman suggests that Ezek 39:29 cites Joel's expectation of pouring out the spirit of prophecy to interpretively align the promise of a new spirit in Ezekiel.[71] But the direction of dependence is based on dating Joel, which is uncertain, and dating Ezek 38–39, which is Tooman's primary objective. Although the evidence suggests a relationship between the pouring out of the Spirit in Joel and Ezekiel, similar imagery appears elsewhere with a different verb for pour out (Isa 44:3) or the same verb (Zech 12:10). As such, the "surprising twist" of using "pour out my Spirit" inverts the imagery in Ezekiel but does not require Joel.[72] The evidence in Joel suggests Ezek 39:29 as donor context of Joel 2:28–29[3:1–2] (see note ad loc.).

40–48>/<1 Kgs 6; 8 (C) (temple vision). Ezekiel's vision of a temple includes several differences when considered against the tabernacle and Solomon's temple (Ezek 40–48; cf. Exod 25–31; 35–40; 1 Kgs 6; 8). Ezekiel's identity as a priest strengthens the sense of importance of a new temple. The tabernacle and Solomon's temple featured

65. Tooman, "Transformation," 65. Tooman notes that the three nations who witness the invasion (Sheba, Dedan, and Tarshish) appear in Ezek 27:12, 15, 22–23, and Gen 10:4, 7, 28 (65, n. 36).

66. See ibid., 65, n. 38.

67. See reference to Gyges in the royal annals of Assurbanipal, *ARAB* 2:351 (§909); noted by Block, *Ezekiel 25–48*, 433, n. 32.

68. See helpful discussion in Block, *Ezekiel 25–48*, 433–36.

69. See Zimmerli, *Ezekiel 2*, 317; compare Hinnom (הִנֹּם) and Hamon (הָמוֹן).

70. "Pour out" (שׁפך), with different senses, appears throughout this book: Ezek 4:2; 7:8; 9:8; 14:19; 16:15, 36, 38; 17:17; 18:10; 20:8, 13, 21, 33–34; 21:22, 31[27, 36]; 22:3–4, 6, 9, 12, 22, 27, 31; 23:8, 45; 24:7; 26:8; 30:15; 33:25; 36:18; 39:29.

71. See Tooman, "Transformation," 78–79.

72. See Block's helpful discussion of Ezek 39:29 (*Ezekiel 25–48*, 488), though he is not parsing out a potential relationship with Joel.

FIGURE EZK3: RELATIVE SIZES OF THE TABERNACLE, SOLOMON'S TEMPLE, AND EZEKIEL'S TEMPLE[a]

- 10 x 30 cubits,[b] tabernacle (Exod 26)
- 50 x 100 cubits,[c] tabernacle with courtyard (Exod 27:9–19)
- 20 x 60 cubits, Solomon's temple (1 Kgs 6:2)
- 60 x 100 royal cubits,[b] Ezekiel's temple (Ezek 41:10, 13)
- 500 x 500 royal cubits, Ezekiel's temple with courtyard (Ezek 42:20; 45:2)

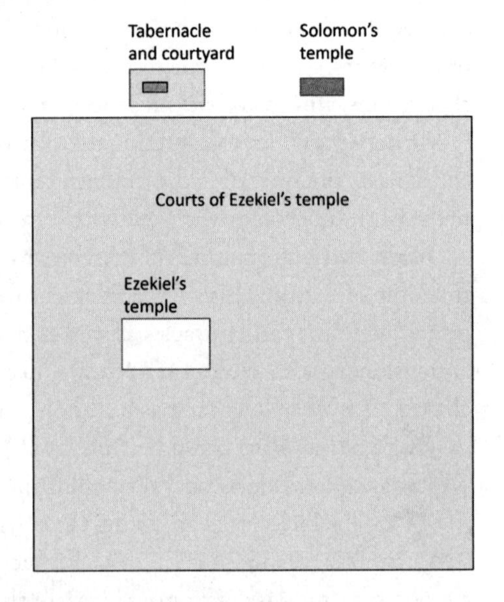

[a] The areas of the diagrams of the tabernacle and its court, Solomon's temple, and Ezekiel's temple and its courts are approximate relative proportions.

[b] The area of tabernacle, its court, and Solomon's temple based on cubits (ca. 18 inches) versus Ezekiel's temple and courts which are based on royal cubits (ca. 21 inches). See Zimmerli, *Ezekiel 2*, 349 (his millimeter measurements have been converted to inches here).

[c] For modern comparison: the courtyard of the tabernacle is exactly half the length and breadth and one-quarter the area of an American football field.

FIGURE EZK4: EZEKIEL'S TEMPLE[a]

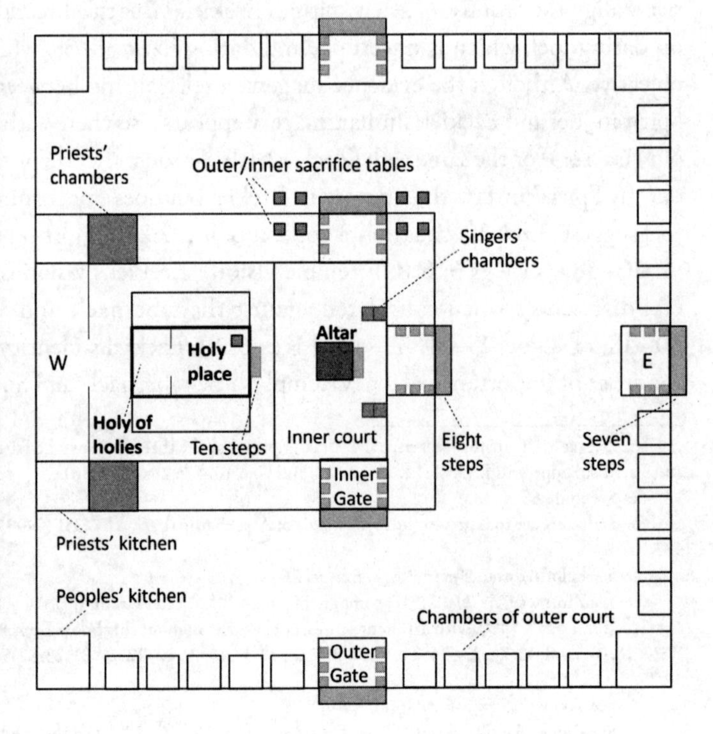

[a] Vertical ascension is not shown, but note seven, eight, and ten steps signifying increasing elevations. Though originally altars to Israel's God could not have steps because of exposing the sacrificer's nakedness (Exod 20:26), the required priestly undergarments covered their nakedness (28:42) allowing for elevations within Ezekiel's temple including steps for the altar (Ezek 43:17). Diagram is not to scale, but simply presents items listed in the text, namely, east outer gate, Ezek 40:6–16; 43:1–5; 44:1–3; north outer gate, 40:20–23; south outer gate, 40:24–27; south inner gate, 40:28–31; east inner gate, 40:32–34; north inner gate 40:35–37; thirty chambers in outer court, 40:17; seven steps going up to outer court, 40:22; eight steps going up to elevated inner court, 40:31, 34; four outer and four inner sacrificial tables, 40:38–43; chambers for singers in inner court, 40:44; altar, 40:47; 43:13–27; ten steps leading up to elevated temple, 40:49 (so LXX); holy place, 41:1–2; holy of holies, 41:3–4; wall decorations—palm trees and guardian cherubim, 41:18–20, 25–26; table of presence, 41:22; priests' chambers, 42:1–14; priests' kitchens, 46:19–20; people's kitchens, 46:21–24.

graduated holiness, increasing with closer proximity to the holy of holies. Likewise, Ezekiel's temple includes ever increasing elevated terraces with stairs and incrementally increasing holy space. These basic continuities between tabernacle, Solomon's temple, and Ezekiel's temple serve as a backdrop to the concerns and innovations of Ezekiel's temple. The spatial observations in Figures Ezk3 and Ezk4 provide context for several of the following notes on specific interpretive allusions in Ezekiel's temple vision.

44:9–16~Num 18:1–7 (B) (sanctity of the temple). Ezekiel's presentation of the sanctity of the temple grows out of his exegetical intervention with the reaffirmation of the election of Aaron's family (Ezek 44:15–16; Num 18:1–7). The reaffirmation of the priestly election in the aftermath of the uprising in the wilderness gives rise to major adjustments to worship at the sanctuary. Ezekiel spells out some of the exegetical implications of this reaffirmation of priestly election for excluded others, laity, Levites, and priests in Ezek 44:9–14, 17–31. The present note deals with the problem of the temple's graduated holiness as it bears on excluded others, laity, and Levites, all stemming from the reaffirmation of the election of Aaron's family. The next set of notes on Ezek 44 gets at some of Ezekiel's exegetical enhancements of the priestly instructions.

Ezekiel develops some of the rationale for two levels of worship leaders—Levites and priests—from interpretive application of Torah (see note on 2 Chr 30:16). The uprising of Korah and company led to Yahweh's reaffirmation of the election of Aaron and his line as priests (Num 16–17). The narrative of the uprising naturally precedes instructions for Levites in maintaining the holiness of the sanctuary (Num 18:2–7, 23). The implied demotion of the Levites to serve under the Aaronic priests in a subordinate role in the tabernacle provides one of Ezekiel's points of departure.

Ezekiel's temple everywhere maintains a strong separation between the Levites who assist laity with slaughtering in the outer courts versus the priests who perform sacrifices and bear divine holiness in the inner courts (see Figure Ezk4; note on 2 Chr 35:5–6; cf. 2 Chr 29:34). Though the responsibilities of Levites and priests may share close wording at times, they serve in different levels of the graduated holy space of Ezekiel's temple. Priestly guards serve in the gatehouses of the inner court and Levitical guards the gatehouses of the outer court (Ezek 40:45–46; 44:14). This corresponds to the twofold holiness of tabernacle service divided between Levite and priest (see Num 18:3, 5).[73] Laity slaughter their own sacrifices at the tabernacle and priests dash the blood (Lev 1:5; 17:6). Ezekiel's temple expands the Levites' role by slaughtering sacrifices for the laity (Ezek 44:11–12), which complements their guarding against intrusions. Most of Ezekiel's uses of Num 18 sustain it without adjustment. Ezekiel's temple does not "slavishly imitate" the worship instructions of Torah but makes adjustments relative to the agenda of his vision (see Table Ezk5).[74]

73. This discussion indebted to Milgrom, "Ezekiel and the Levites," 5.
74. Ibid., 9.

TABLE EZK5: COMPARING EZEKIEL 44 AND NUMBERS 18‡

Continuities

	Ezekiel 44	**with Numbers 18**
• Levites bear their own punishment for not maintaining the sanctity of the shrine[a]	10, 12	23
• Twofold division between priests and Levites	13	3, 5
• Levitical guard duty	11, 14	3–4
• Priests guard the inner court	15–16 (cf. 40:45–46)	7
• Banning excluded persons	9	4

Advancements

	Ezekiel 44	**versus Numbers 18**
• Priests and Levites both have guard duty	14 (cf. 40:44–45)	3
• Levites perform sacrifices once done by laity	11	8–9; cf. Lev 1–6
• Priests and Levites inherit land like other tribes	cf. 48:13–14	cf. 20, 24

‡ Based on Milgrom, "Ezekiel and the Levites," 8–11.

[a] "Bear their own punishment" (נשא עון) is a stock phrase (Exod 28:38, 43; Lev 5:1, 6, 17; 7:18; 10:17; 17:16; 19:8, 17; 20:17, 19; Num 5:31; 14:34; 18:1, 23; 30:15; Isa 33:24; Ezek 4:4, 5, 6; 14:10; 24:23; 44:10, 12; Hos 4:8).

Ezekiel's central concern with the holiness of the temple drives his biting interpretive advance to exclude all foreigners uncircumcised in heart and flesh (Ezek 44:9). As a Zadokite priest, Ezekiel in his prophecy blamed the Levites for allowing uncircumcised foreigners into the temple. Whom did they let in? Options include Solomon's slaves of Canaan with the Gibeonites (1 Kgs 9:20; Josh 9:27), the "given ones" (*nethinim* נְתִינִים) (Ezra 2:43–54// Neh 7:47–56), or Carites who served as royal mercenary guards (2 Kgs 11:4).[75]

Although many interpreters treat Ezek 44:9 as a proof text of a racial exclusion, allowing only for ethnic Israel to enter the new temple, this badly misses Ezekiel's continuity with the scriptural norm. Torah, prophets including Ezekiel, and the narratives of the restoration speak of two kinds of others—those included and those excluded from Israel (see notes on Isa 52:1; 56:1–7; Neh 10:30–39[31–40], esp. on 10:30[31]). Elsewhere Ezekiel not only condemns residing foreigners along with Israelites, who ironically "dedicate themselves away from" Yahweh, but also looks ahead to granting residing foreigners full land rights like any other Israelite (see notes on 14:1–11; 47:22–23). The kind of foreigners Ezekiel excludes from temple worship are those who are uncircumcised; that is, those who do not seek a relationship with Israel's God. Table Ezk6 collates Ezekiel with other scriptural contexts that speak of two kinds of others.

75. See ibid., 7.

TABLE EZK6: TWO KINDS OF OTHERS IN SCRIPTURE‡

excluded others	included others
• Uncircumcised temporary resident or hired worker (Exod 12:45)	• Circumcised residing foreigners (Exod 12:48–49)
• Ammonites and Moabites because of their historical anti-covenantal enmity (Deut 23:3–6[4–7])	• Edomites and Egyptians in the third generation (Deut 23:7–8[8–9])
• Uncircumcised and ritually defiled persons (Isa 52:1)	• Eunuchs and foreigners who bind themselves to Yahweh (Isa 56:1–7)
• Foreigners uncircumcised in heart and uncircumcised in flesh (Ezek 44:9)	• Residing foreigners (Ezek 14:7; 47:22–23)
• "Enemies of Judah and Benjamin . . . people of the land" (Ezra 4:1, 4); "the peoples of the land" (Neh 10:30[31])	• "The ones who separated themselves from the ritual impurities of the nations of the land" (Ezra 6:21 lit.); "all who separated themselves from the peoples of the lands to the Torah of God" (Neh 10:28[29] lit.)

‡ Many terms denoting others are used with moderate consistency in Scripture, but there is overlap and fluidity. The terms used here are: "residing foreigner" (גֵּר), "temporary resident" (תּוֹשָׁר), "hired worker" (שָׂכִיר), "uncircumcised" (עָרֵל), "ritually defiled" (טָמֵא), "foreigner" (בֶּן־נֵכָר), "foreigner uncircumcised in heart and uncircumcised in flesh" (בֶּן־נֵכָר עֶרֶל לֵב וְעֶרֶל בָּשָׂר), and "the ones who separated from" (הַנִּבְדָּל מִן). Also see Table I4 in note on Isa 52:1.

Ezekiel's strong drive to protect the holiness of the temple seems to motivate his reinforcing of many continuities with Torah and prophets. Figure Ezk7 summarizes the kinds of persons distinguished in Ezek 40–48.

FIGURE EZK7: A TYPOLOGY OF PERSONS IN EZEKIEL'S TEMPLE VISION‡

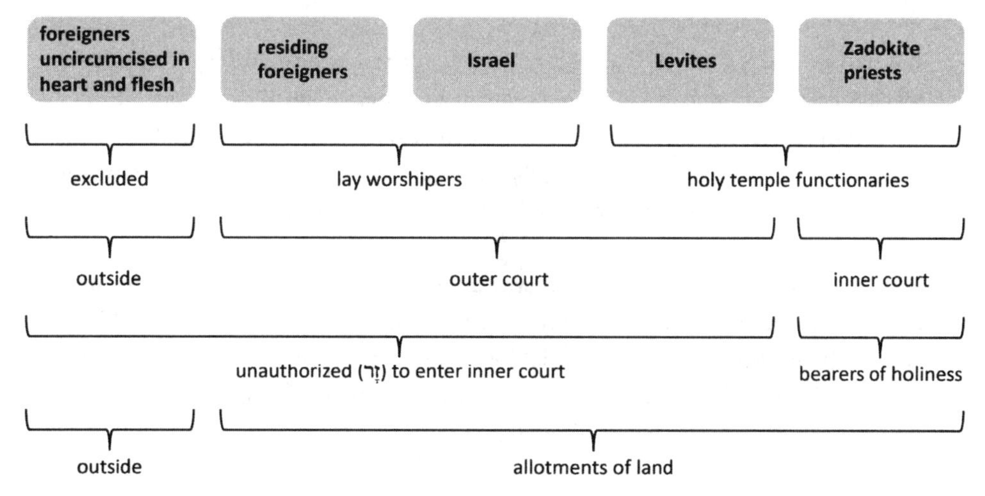

‡ The term "unauthorized person" (זָר) does not appear in Ezek 40–48 but is used of laity and Levites in Num 18:4, 7 who are excluded from the inner shrine areas reserved for priests alone (see Block, "Sojourner; Alien; Stranger" *ISBE* 4:563, left column; Milgrom, *Studies*, 32; Warren, "Sin," 318–19). The term is included here to show how Ezekiel's temple coordinates with Num 18 which it leans on often (see Table Ezk5).

Ezekiel uses the reaffirmation of the election of Aaron as the basis for the election of Zadok. Moses anointed Aaron as priest (Lev 8:12). Yahweh confirmed his selection of Aaron by casting Korah and his family and associates into Sheol and incinerating 250 others who were offering incense during the rebellion (Num 16:31–35). Yahweh made a permanent selection of the line of Aaron from among the Levites to serve as priests (17:8–11[17:23–26]; 18:7). Yahweh selected Eleazar from among Aaron's sons to help with ritual purification in the aftermath of the judgment of Korah and the rebels (16:36–40[17:1–5]).

Korah and his rebel associates put to words the very problem Ezekiel seeks to fix: "You have gone too far! The whole community is holy, every one of them, and Yahweh is with them" (16:3, see note ad loc.; cf. "you have gone too far!" Ezek 44:6 lit.).[76] The uprising of Korah and company and the related instructions that adjust the role of Levite and priests in Num 18:1–7 provide the major pretext for Ezekiel's set of exegetical advances relative to the Levites and the graduated holiness of the new temple (see Table Ezk5).[77]

For his boldest exegetical advancement Ezekiel seems to tap into the outcomes of the uprising in the wilderness as determinative of Yahweh's permanent election of Zadok's line (bold signifies verbal parallels, and broken underlining signifies interpretive advancement).

> Yahweh said to Aaron, "You, your sons and your family are to bear the responsibility for offenses connected with the sanctuary, and you and your sons alone are to bear the responsibility for offenses connected with the priesthood. [2] Bring your fellow Levites from your ancestral tribe to join you and assist you when you and your sons **minister** before the tent of the covenant law . . . You [Aaron and sons] **shall serve as guards** of the **sanctuary** and **as guards** of the altar, so that my wrath will not fall on the Israelites again." (Num 18:1–2, 5, v. 5 lit.)

> But the Levitical priests, who are descendants of Zadok and **who guarded** my **sanctuary** when the Israelites went astray from me, are to come near **to minister** before me; they are to stand before me to offer sacrifices of fat and blood, declares Sovereign Yahweh. [16] They alone are to enter my **sanctuary**; they alone are to come near my table **to minister** before me and **serve** me **as guards**. (Ezek 44:15–16; cf. 40:46; 43:19)

Zadok stood in Eleazar's line and was appointed by Solomon as replacement of Abiathar, whose family was banished to Anathoth (1 Kgs 2:26). The fidelity of Eleazar, and especially his function as role model for exclusivity of priesthood, may explain why Ezekiel went back to this signature moment in the ancestry of Zadok to point toward the ideal in the new temple (see Num 16:40[17:5]).

---

76. See Cook, "Innerbiblical Interpretation," 197–203. Cook notes the parallel reverse use of "You have gone far enough!? (רַב־לָכֶם) in Num 16:7 (versus 16:3) and Ezek 44:6 (197).

77. On the instructions of Num 18 as remedy after the debacle, see Milgrom, "Encroachment," *IDBSup*, 265.

In sum, Ezekiel's several exegetical advances for applying the graduated holiness of the sanctuary to excluded others, laity, Levites, and priests build upon the watershed moment of the divine reaffirmation of the election of the family of Aaron in the wake of the wilderness uprising. Ezekiel explains the election of the Zadokite priestly line as stemming from the reaffirmation of the election of Aaron's family.

44:17–19~Exod 28:39–43; 39:27–28, 41; Lev 19:19; Deut 22:11 (C) (standards for garments of priests).
44:20~Lev 21:5 (B) (priests not shave head or grow hair long).
44:21*~Lev 10:9* (C) (priests sober when in inner court) (* see teachers network).
44:22~Lev 21:7, 13–15 (B) (requirements for wives of priests).
44:23*~Lev 10:10–11* (B) (priest instructs on ritual purity) (* see teachers network).
44:24–27~Lev 21:1–3 (B) (standards of worship and ritual purity for priests).[78]

Ezekiel 44:17–27 brings together many scriptural traditions concerning the standards for priestly service. After Yahweh had struck down Nadab and Abihu for offering unauthorized fire, he gave the priests a series of instructions to avoid being killed (Lev 10:1–2; cf. 16:1). Moses spells out the purpose of those instructions in an overarching statement: "Among those who approach me I will be proved holy; in the sight of all the people I will be honored" (10:3). Those instructions include not ripping clothing, not messing up hair for grief, and sobriety during priestly service (10:6, 9). Ezekiel's regulations for the priests include instructions for garments, hair, and sobriety, but for different reasons. In the aftermath of the death of Aaron's sons, the prohibition against torn clothing and messed-up hair stopped them from ancient mourning rites. The purpose of sobriety relates to the priestly responsibility to instruct Israel by discerning between ritual impurity and purity and between profane and holy (10:9–11). Ezekiel expects priests to be sober during their service, and he expects them to teach holiness, but these regulations are not tied directly together—they stand among a series of other similar regulations (Ezek 44:21, 23; cf. 22:26). By rearranging the standards, Ezekiel detaches enforced sobriety from responsibility to teach, thus requiring sobriety in its own right while serving (emphases signify verbal parallels):

> You and your sons are *not to drink wine* or other fermented drink *whenever you go into* the tent of meeting, or you will die. This is a lasting ordinance for the generations to come, so that you can distinguish **between the holy and the common, between the unclean and the clean**, and so you can <u>teach</u> the Israelites all the decrees Yahweh has given them through Moses. (Lev 10:9–11)[79]

78. A few of the verbal parallels between Leviticus and Ezek 44 are laid out in Bendavid, *Parallels*, 184, 186–87 [Hebrew].

79. The sense of the preposition "for" (לְ) with the inf. constr. as "in reference to" is captured well by the NIV "*so that* you can distinguish . . . *and so* you can teach" (Lev 10:10, 11). See GKC §114p, and see 119u, 143e; cf. Lev 10:10–11 JPSB.

> *No* priest is to *drink wine when he goes into* the inner court. They must not marry widows or divorced women; they may marry only virgins of Israelite descent or widows of priests. They are to teach my people the difference **between the holy and the common** and show them how to distinguish **between the unclean and the clean.** (Ezek 44:21–23†)

Ezekiel outlines a series of priestly regulations designed to protect the temple from ritual defilement and to preserve holiness. He also tries to protect the nonpriestly temple constituents from having the priest's holiness transmitted to them (Ezek 42:14; 44:19; 46:20; cf. Lev 6:27).

Ezekiel's vision collects together many of the standards for priestly holiness of Torah: maintaining hair and beard at appropriate length (Lev 21:5; Ezek 44:20); being sober when serving (Lev 10:9; Ezek 44:21); and instructing Israel in ritual purity and holiness (Lev 10:10–11; Ezek 44:23; see note on Ezek 22:26). In a couple of places Ezekiel raises the standards of priests to that of the high priest: being limited in ritual contamination to burial only of close family members but not parents (Lev 21:11; Ezek 44:25; versus Lev 21:2–4); and limiting marriage for priests to virgins from Israel, in accordance with the standards for a high priest (Lev 21:13–15; Ezek 44:22), but mildly adjusts his adjustment by allowing marriage to a widow of a priest (44:22b).

In sum, there is strong continuity between the requirements of priests in the tabernacle in Leviticus and priests in Ezekiel's temple. In the case of differences, Ezekiel strengthens measures to preserve the holiness of the temple. This may not be identical to erecting torah around torah, but it seems to have the same kind of preservationist logic.

45:21–24, 25~Exod 23:15; Lev 23:4–8; Deut 16:1–8 (C) (Passover); Exod 23:16; Lev 23:33–36; Num 29:12–38; Deut 16:13–17 (C) (Tabernacles). Ezekiel briefly mentions celebrating Passover and Tabernacles. The vision's view of the celebrations themselves basically maintains the status quo.[80] Ezekiel's expansions focus on the prince's role in providing sacrifices for himself and representing the people of the land (Ezek 45:22, 24, 25). This emphasis on the prince stands at the end of a string of elements concerning the princes at the new temple: they no longer oppress people (45:8–9), they have set portions in addition to the priests' portions designed for worship (45:13–17), and they will make regular offerings (46:1–18). Ezekiel both prohibits the prince from oppressing the people and from desecrating the temple's holiness. In that sense Ezekiel's vision does not work out a new polity but targets historically problematic areas.

47:22–23~Lev 19:34 (B)+25:10, 45 (C) (remapping the social identity of residing foreigners). Torah frequently uses the threefold stereotypical list of socially challenged persons: widow, orphan, and residing foreigner (cf. also Ezek 22:7, 29). The common denominator of these three perennial outcasts relates to patriarchal social contexts where only landowning adult males enjoy the full rights and privileges of citizenship and

80. On the Passover sacrifices, see Block, *Ezekiel, 25–48*, 665–66.

worship. In this context widows, orphans, and residing foreigners are without provider or full rights, vulnerable, and often impoverished. Since they lack a provider, Yahweh is their provider insisting that Israel does not prey upon those under his protection (Exod 22:21–24[20–23]; Deut 24:17–18).

In the restoration, Ezekiel's vision adjusts the status of residing foreigners with children from landless sojourners to inheriting land like any Israelite (Ezek 47:22–23). This creates a radical shift, since the enhanced status of landowning residing foreigners virtually erases the social difference which had made them residing foreigners. The difference can be most clearly seen in how Ezekiel transforms the situation of residing foreigners in the year of release. In Leviticus, residing foreigners were not freed like Israelites since they had no land to which they could return. Instead, poverty, which escalated to debt slavery, converted residing sojourners into chattel slaves passed down from one generation to the next (Lev 25:45–46). Since Ezekiel's return includes land allotment for the residing foreigners with children, like any Israelite, they now enjoy the same economic rights as land-holding citizens (bold signifies verbal parallels, and italics signify thematic reversal):[81]

> **The foreigner residing** among you must be treated **as your native-born**. Love them as yourself, for you were foreigners in Egypt. I am Yahweh your God. (Lev 19:34)

> It shall be a Jubilee for you; each of you is to return to your family property and to your own clan. . . . You may also buy some of the sojourners **residing** among you and members of their clans born in your country, and *they will become your property. You can bequeath them to your children* as inherited property and can make them slaves for life, but you must not rule over your fellow Israelites ruthlessly. (25:10b, 45–46†)[82]

> You are to allot it as an inheritance for yourselves and for **the foreigners residing** among you and who have children. You are to consider them **as native-born** Israelites; along with you *they are to be allotted an inheritance* among the tribes of Israel. [23] In whatever tribe a foreigner resides, there you are to *give them their inheritance*, declares Sovereign Yahweh. (Ezek 47:22–23; cf. Lev 25:10; Ezek 46:17)

Outside of Torah, Ezek 47:22 is one of only two places that uses the term "native-born." Among the several uses of the simile "as the native-born" in Torah, only Lev 19:34 fits with the level of benefits depicted in Ezek 44:22–23.[83] Ezekiel essentially works out the implications of love the residing foreigners as yourself. In Ezekiel's vision, treating

81. On comparison between Lev 19:34 and Ezek 47:22 (not Lev 25), see Milgrom, *Leviticus 23–27*, 2355. On transformation of status of residing foreigners, see Allen, *Ezekiel*, 808–9.

82. Note different language: "residing foreigner residing" (הַגֵּר הַגָּר) (Lev 19:34; Ezek 47:22 lit.) and "sojourners residing" (הַתּוֹשָׁבִים הַגָּרִים) (Lev 25:45 lit.).

83. See Even-Shoshan, 32, nos. 8, 9; cf. 11, 12, 16. On Ps 37:35 see *BHS* n. b and "אֶזְרָח," *HALOT* 1:28—both favor LXX.

residing foreigners as native-born extends even to land allotments which, in effect, eliminates the differences between the residing foreigner and the native-born altogether.

47:13–48:35~Josh 13–19 (C) (idealized apportioning of the land). After describing the temple and detailing the role of priests and Levites, Ezekiel's vision goes into extensive detail explaining the tribal apportionment of the land and the plan of the holy district. In broad terms Ezekiel's vision offers dramatic reconfiguration relative to the traditional tribal allotment in Josh 13–19. Ezekiel's use of the term for "tribal portion" connects his redistribution of the land with the allotment in Joshua.[84]

Ezekiel's vision maintains continuity in that he continues to expect Israel to be represented by all twelve tribes (see Tribal Redistribution in Map Ezk8). Elsewhere Ezekiel presents Jerusalem as sibling to Samaria and Sodom (Ezek 16:46). He goes so far as to picture the three sisters—Jerusalem, Samaria, and Sodom (!)—as restored to their former states (see note on 16:53–57). Ezekiel also depicts the former kingdoms of Israel and Judah restored under a Davidic ruler (37:15–28). These somewhat diverse expectations would need more work to assimilate together if they were each regarded as literal versus ideal or allegorical. Childs counters that "idealization" does not quite get it. He says Ezekiel works from a "divine perspective" rather than contextualized particularity.[85] This suggestion sounds good on paper but leaves several interpretive loose ends in the case of Ezekiel's temple. However the literal versus nonliteral referentiality gets decided, Ezekiel's vision anticipates all Israel along with residing foreigners enjoying land inheritance around the holy district.

The most extreme expectation in Ezekiel's vision can be identified as the dissociation of the temple from the city (see Plan of the Holy District in Map Ezk8; 48:10, 15). The city remains a central place for civic commerce especially associated with the pilgrimage feasts for all twelve tribes (45:18–25; 48:15–20). The separation of the temple from the city as a civil community seems especially radical because of the identification of Yahweh electing the place for his name to dwell and its fulfillment by David and Solomon across Deuteronomistic and priestly flavored contexts (Deut 12; 1 Chr 16; 21; 2 Chr 3). The physical separation of temple and city, while radical, aligns with the extensive buffer zone and regulations designed to protect the sanctity of Ezekiel's temple (Ezek 40–44). Since elsewhere Ezekiel speaks freely of the restoration of the Davidic kingdom, the separation of city and temple could point toward the temple vision as ideal versus literal (34:23; 37:24–28). Nowhere in Ezek 40–48 does he use the word "Jerusalem."[86] Instead Ezekiel says the name of the city is "Yahweh Is There," which emphasizes the covenantal goal of the envisioned restoration (48:35). If "Yahweh Is There" in the city, then it becomes difficult to see why the temple needs to be separated from the city. In any case, the covenantal identity of the city should eliminate a secular versus sacred approach to Ezekiel's separation of

84. See Block, *Ezekiel 25–48*, 727–28; "II חֵלֶק," *HALOT* 1:323.

85. Childs, *Introduction*, 362.

86. For a study that pushes the implications of not naming Jerusalem in Ezek 40–48, see Guillaume, "Chronological Limits," 188–94.

the temple and the city. Zechariah's first and third visions affirm the temple in Jerusalem and the glory on Jerusalem, which, in light of his allusion to Ezekiel's temple vision, may support the idea of Ezekiel's temple vision as symbolic (see note on Zech 2:1[5]).

MAP EZK8: APPORTIONING OF LAND AND SITUATION OF TEMPLE IN EZEKIEL 45–48

Tribal Redistribution[a][b]

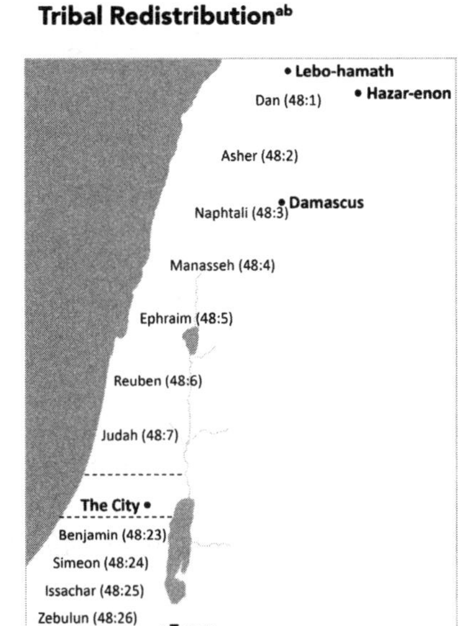

Plan of the Holy District[a][c]

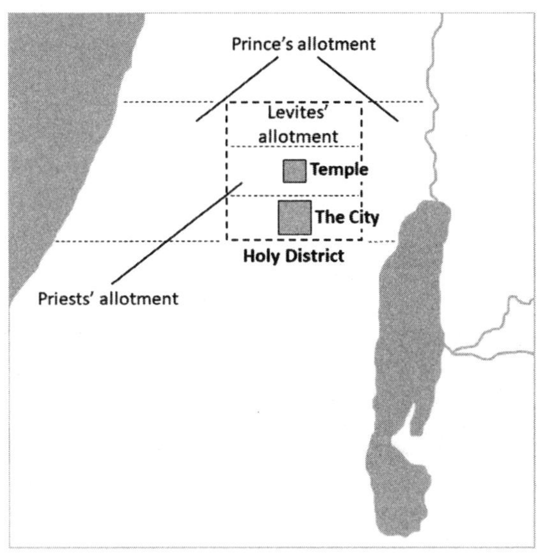

[a] Layouts are not to scale. They present basic graphic placement based on the text.

[b] Boundaries of the land and tribal redistribution are listed in Ezek 45:1–9; 47:13–48:35.

[c] Plan of holy district based on Ezek 45:1–9; 48:8–22. Temple centered with "in the midst of it" (48:10; see Zimmerli, *Ezekiel 2*, 534) and city outside of temple area (48:15). For an alternate view see Block, *Ezekiel 25–48*, 732–33.

In sum of Ezekiel's vision, the temple, priesthood, and Levites take a central role driven by the need to protect and maintain the holiness of Yahweh's dwelling forever.

What is the point of the new temple? Ezekiel's basic concerns include separation between the common and the holy (42:20). Ezekiel's temple requires more space between royal civil leaders and the holy based on the ritually impure implications of close physical proximity. The temple of Ezekiel rectifies the defilement of infidelity and even the burial of kings too close to the temple (43:7–9; cf. 22:26; 23:30). As a prophetic priest, Ezekiel is tasked with teaching the torah of the temple, namely, the entire temple precinct must be holy (Ezek 44:23; Lev 10:10–11). Ezekiel's temple protects holiness and seeks to correct shameful iniquities.

FILTERS

Ezekiel houses extensive non-exegetical use of scriptural traditions. The extent of scriptural allusion and echo in Ezekiel over and against Isaiah and Jeremiah can remain an open question. Ezekiel may seem to use less scriptural traditions because of his prophetic style, or maybe it is less. In any case, the majority of Ezekiel's use of scriptural traditions is non-exegetical.

The line remains fuzzy between Ezekiel's non-exegetical, scripturally allusive idiom versus what may be regarded as a matter of style. Several scholars argue that pervasive echoing of scriptural traditions deeply affects interpretation of Ezekiel (see filters below). Though not all examples are equally compelling, the increased attention to Ezekiel's non-exegetical use of scriptural traditions makes a viable case for taking it seriously.

The filters below correspond to Ezekiel. Many of these filters have helped collect some of the things Ezekiel does with scriptural traditions. The same filters applied to other Scriptures would come up empty.

Many lists of Ezekiel's use of scriptural phrases are more extensive than those included here. Some have produced lists of Ezekiel's stereotypical expressions and stock phrases.[87] Several studies recognize Ezekiel's extensive exegetical and non-exegetical use of scriptural locutions and focus on linguistic dependence to the holiness collection (Lev 17–26) and/or lesser dependence on Deuteronomy. The most helpful are those lists based on criteria like unique and/or rare terms, syntactic congruity/incongruity, distribution to eliminate or at least reduce false positives, and shared locutions of two or more words.[88]

The following lists do not seek to be comprehensive or complete. They simply offer examples of substantial non-exegetical uses of scriptural traditions. More than elsewhere, many of the cases included in Ezekiel Filters could arguably be considered exegetical. Like everything else in the study of the scriptural use of Scripture, decisions on what counts as exegesis is debatable. The present study seeks to err on the side of excluding borderline cases, though disagreements on both sides of this fuzzy boundary are inevitable. In any case, the filters below provide abbreviated rationale for exclusion.

Parabolic/Allegorical/Visionary Scenarios

Ezekiel presents many scenarios that make heavy use of scriptural traditions and themes. These tend not to offer exegetical outcomes but use the scriptural traditions as points of departure for the prophet's far-flung elaborate scenarios. The scenarios include both visions of the celestial realm and vivid parabolic and allegorical scenes and storylines.

Ezekiel 1:4–3:27 presents a multistage celestial scenario related to the call of the prophet. The prophetic descriptions of the scene often use the preposition "like" (כְּ) to

---

87. See Driver, *Introduction*, 297–98; Boadt, "Ezekiel, Book of," *ABD* 2:718; Tooman, "Transformation," 52–53.

88. On shared locutions of Ezekiel and the holiness collection, see Milgrom, *Leviticus 17–22*, 1362; idem, *Leviticus 23–27*, 2348–63; Lyons, *Law to Prophecy*, 166–86; idem, "Persuasion," 79–86; on Ezekiel and Lev 26, see Driver, *Introduction*, 147; Rooker, "Use of OT Ezekiel," 46; on Ezekiel and Leviticus, see appendix in Bolle, *Leviticus*, 2:69–78 [Hebrew]; on Ezekiel and Deuteronomy and Leviticus, Levitt Kohn, *New Heart*, 31–75, 86–93; on Ezekiel and Deuteronomy, Gile, "Deuteronomic Influence," 152–90, et passim; and on shared scriptural locutions in Ezek 38–39, see Tooman, "Transformation," 93–105. Also see Greenberg, "Influence," 29–37; Hays, "Ezekiel," in *DNTUOT*, forthcoming; and items on Entire OT in Bibliographic Note on Lists of Potential Parallels.

clarify surrealistic versus realistic representation.[89] As opposed to other common prepositions, "like, as" does not identify location and does not conjoin in verbal constructions. It functions to express more and/or less similitude or resemblance—from exactly like to something like.[90] The prophet's stylized celestial scenes make use of scriptural themes and imagery as descriptive starting points: 1:4–14>/<Exod 19:16, 18–20; 24:17–18; 2 Sam 22:8–14//Ps 18:7–13, theophany; 1:15–21>/<2 Sam 22:11; Ps 68:17–18, mobile living chariot/thrones (referred to as cherubim/winged-sphinxes in Ezek 10:15, 20);[91] 1:22, 26>/<Exod 24:10, translucent vault of "sapphire, lapis-lazuli" (ספיר); 1:22–28>/<1 Kgs 22:19; Isa 6:1–4, celestial court; 1:28; 3:12, 23>/<10:4 (2x), 18; 11:23; 43:5; 44:4, "glory of Yahweh" (כבוד יהוה) (cf. Exod 24:16, 17; Lev 9:6, 23; 1 Kgs 8:11; 2 Chr 5:14; 7:2); 2:8–3:3>/<Jer 15:16, eat scroll.

Ezekiel 5:1–4, 12 initiates a series of parabolic judgments against Jerusalem loosely revolving around the triad of punishments of Lev 26:25–26.[92] Ezekiel 5:12 uses three terms, namely, "sword" (חֶרֶב), "plague" (דֶּבֶר) and "famine" (רָעָב) to signify the dire outcomes of the hair he shaved off (Ezek 5:1–4).[93] Two of these terms appear in Leviticus as well as the concept of starvation.

> And I will bring the **sword** [חֶרֶב] on you to avenge the breaking of the covenant. When you withdraw into your cities, I will send a **plague** [דֶּבֶר] among you, and you will be given into enemy hands. [26] *When I cut off your supply of bread*, ten women will be able to bake your bread in one oven, and they will dole out the bread by weight. You will eat, but you will not be satisfied (Lev 26:25–26, emphases mine).

Ezekiel 6:11–12 uses the same triad of terms—"sword" (חֶרֶב), "plague" (דֶּבֶר) and "famine" (רָעָב)—to speak of the judgment against those who flee to the mountains. **Ezekiel 7:15–16** repeats the same three terms of the wrath of Yahweh that will come on Israel. **Ezekiel 12:14–16** reuses the same triad of judgment terms against the prince and people of Jerusalem. **Ezekiel 14:21–23** presents four judgments against Jerusalem, the same set of three plus wild beasts. Lyons interprets this set of terminal judgments from Lev 26 as applied by Ezekiel against the captives of 586 BCE to bear witness to the earlier 597 BCE captives. In this reading, the Jerusalem elite of the 597 forced migration to captivity have

---

89. E.g. (each uses *k-* [כְּ] for "like" unless stated otherwise): "like glowing metal" (Ezek 1:4), "like the sole of a calf's foot" (v. 7 lit.), "like burnished bronze" (v. 7), "like burning coals of fire" (v. 13), "like torches" (v. 13), "like flashes of lightning" (v. 14), "like topaz" (v. 16), "like [כַּאֲשֶׁר] a wheel within a wheel" (v. 16), "like a vault" (v. 22), "the sound of their wings, like the roar of rushing waters, like the voice of the Almighty, like the tumult of an army" (v. 24), "like [כְּ] sapphire in the likeness of [דְּמוּת] a throne" (v. 26 lit.), "a form like the appearance of a human" (דְּמוּת כְּמַרְאֵה אָדָם) (v. 26 lit.), etc.

90. See Joüon §133g.

91. Cherubim are composite celestial creatures of different sorts, but all have wings to signify mobility (Meyer, "Cherubim," *ABD* 1:899–900).

92. The set of comparative observations in this discussion come from Lyons, "Out," 605–23, esp. 614–16. Also see idem, "Transformation of Law," 12, n. 34; idem, *Law to Prophecy*, 181–2.

93. For a survey of interpretive options on the hair, see Lyons, "Out," 605–12.

hope, but not so for those of the forced migration in 586.[94] Lyons's impressive observations need to be considered in light of other contemporary similarities. The reading of judgment of the 586 exiles for the sake of the 597 exiles can be broadly collated with the good figs (597 exiles) and bad figs (586 exiles) in Jer 24. The triad of terms (sword, plague, famine) is also commonplace in Jeremiah (Jer 14:12; 21:7, 9; 24:10; 27:8, 13; 29:17, 18; 32:24, 36; 34:17; 38:2; 42:17, 22; 44:13).[95] The use of two of these terms and the theme of the third from Lev 26:25–26 in Ezek 5, 6, 7, 12, and 14 as noted above may owe their origin to Lev 26. But the widespread use of this set of judgment terms in Jeremiah and Ezekiel looks like a prophetic stock phrase against the doomed Jerusalem elite of 597 in the eve of the fall of city.

Ezekiel 8–11 intermittently features imagery that echoes Ezek 1, mostly in reverse order, >/<1:27; 8:2, luminous figure; >/<1:26; 10:1, throne; >/<1:24; 10:5, sounds of wings; >/<1:15–18; 10:9–13, wheels; >/<1:10; 10:14, faces; >/<1:19–21; 10:16–17, coordinated motion.[96]

Ezekiel 16 narrates the scenario of a female foundling turned whore, which loosely offers an allegorical retrospective on Israel's infidelity. The basic storyline very broadly corresponds to wilderness (16:3–14), infidelities of kingdom in vassalage (15–34), and exile (35–43) (see Table Josh1). Important contentions stemming from modern advocacy readings fall outside the present focus on potential uses of scriptural traditions. The key issues turn on form and function. Block regards the preambles of Ezek 16, 20, 22, and 23 as dispute speech (*riv* ריב) between "two parties."[97] The retrospective elements, according to Block, are "shockingly revisionistic"—"Intentionally skewing and distorting their sacred traditions."[98] But the condemned prostitute does not speak and has no legal advocate. That makes it seem less like a court case as a whole and more like legal "charges" or "accusations" (הדוע, Ezek 16:2).[99] The issue of a "bilateral" case versus "unilateral" disclosure seems too specific for the evidence—her complaints are inferred by the long-range outcome of eliminating reasons for the accused prostitute to open her mouth again about her shame (16:63).[100] The broad legal allusion sets up an indictment meant to condemn the accused. Calling it a purposeful distortion does not adequately make room for the selective nature of an accusation.[101] In that sense the retrospective housed in Ezek 16 provides highly stylized and extremely selective allegations pointing to the guilt of the accused prostitute.

---

94. See ibid., 622–23.

95. See "I דָּבָר," *HALOT* 1:212 ; cf. sec. on prep. בְּ *DCHR* 2:478.

96. See Greenberg, *Ezekiel 1–20*, 198.

97. See table on parallel preambles (>/<16:1–2//20:2–4//22:1–12//23:1, 36) in Block, *Ezekiel 1–24*, 461.

98. Ibid., 462.

99. See Haag, Llewelyn, and Tsonis, "Ezekiel 16," 205–6; and see 207–9; Zimmerli, *Ezekiel 1*, 335–36; Greenberg, *Ezekiel 1–20*, 273. On "accusation" lit. "make known" (הוֹדַע, Hif from ידע) in Ezek 16:2; 20:4, 11; 22:2; cf. 43:11, see "ידע," Hif no. 1 *HALOT* 1:392.

100. Modified "bilateral" case, so Block (*Ezekiel 1–24*, 460), versus "unilateral" disclosure, so Haag, Llewelyn, and Tsonis ("Ezekiel 16," 209–10).

101. *Contra*, Block, *Ezekiel 1–24*, 462. For a discussion of the purpose of the negative retrospectives of Ezek 16, 20, and 23, see Peterson, "Ezekiel's Perspective," 296–99.

What scriptural traditions do the retrospective elements of Ezek 16 draw upon? Gile's detailed study of Ezek 16 points to thematic and structural elements that may echo the Song of Moses. Though Gile speaks of literary dependence, the broad echoes or thematic similarities within similar plotlines often seem more like possible points of departure: Yahweh discovers a male/female foundling (Deut 32:10; Ezek 16:6, without shared language); eagle "spread" (פרשׂ) "wings" (כנף)/Yahweh "spread" (פרשׂ) "corner" (כנף) of garment (Deut 32:11; Ezek 16:8);[102] making Yahweh jealous with "strange (gods)" (זרים)/adultery with "strangers" (זרים) (Deut 32:16; Ezek 16:32); anger (Deut 32:16, 21; Ezek 16:26); atones (כפר) (Deut 32:43; Ezek 16:63).[103] The most impressive similarity switches metaphors from foundling to maternal zoomorphic mother eagle "hovering" over her young (Deut 32:11; cf. Gen 1:2; Exod 19:4). But this stands conceptually at a distance from marrying the foundling come of age (Ezek 16:8) and contradicts the central "like mother like daughter" logic of the accusation (16:3, 44, 45). Granting similarity between foundlings in the wilderness and shared broad language does not get directly at the prophetic traditions of finding Israel in the wilderness, leading up to transgression at Baal Peor (Hos 9:10). The prophetic tradition of the wayward wife from her youth seems to explain a point of departure for Ezekiel's dark impressionistic accusation (Hos 2:14–15[16–17]; Isa 1:21; Jer 2:2; 3:1–3, 6–10, 25).[104] None of this gets at the "considerable obscurity" of the retrospective elements themselves (but see note on Ezek 16:53–57).[105] Terms like "transformation," "recontextualization," and "actualization" help to draw attention to donor traditions.[106] But free extrapolation, not dependence, speaks to what the prophet does in allegories like Ezek 16 or 19. The difficulty of identifying "historical referents" of promiscuous imagery suggests that something else is the point, namely, the endgame of covering the shame of Ezekiel's constituents (16:63). The foreground scenario dominates the accusation. The allegorical indictment seems more mercenary than exegetical, even if there are specific scriptural donor contexts which it eclipses.

Ezekiel 17:22–23 may echo prophetic branch and/or root/shoot imagery as a point of departure for the allegorical scenario of the eagles and the twig (Isa 4:2; 11:1, 10; cf. Jer 23:5–6).

Ezekiel 19 seems to borrow language from the blessing of Judah (Gen 49:8–12) as a point of departure for an allegorical scenario of the lioness and her cubs and a comparison of them to a vine that became a scepter—"cub" (גּוּר), "lion" (אַרְיֵה), "prey" (טֶרֶף), "rise" (עלה), "crouch" (רבץ), "lioness" (לָבִיא), "scepter" (שֵׁבֶט), "vine" (גֶּפֶן), and "blood" (דַּם).[107] The parable functions neither as fulfillment nor expectation but lament (Ezek 19:1, 14).[108]

---

102. For "uncovering the wing" as conjugal relations, see Deut 22:30[23:1].

103. See Gile, "Ezekiel 16," 89–96.

104. See Greenberg, "Influence," 33–34; Zimmerli, *Ezekiel 1*, 336.

105. See ibid., 337; cf. Tg Ezek 16:1–13, which identifies scriptural referents as noted by Greenberg, *Ezekiel 1–20*, 302.

106. See Gile, "Ezekiel 16," 108.

107. List from Greenberg, *Ezekiel 1–20*, 357. He lists "nations" (גּוֹיִם) but Gen 49:8, 10 says "enemies" (אֹיֵב) and "peoples" (עַמִּים). Also see idem, "Influence," 30–32 mentioning similarities with Nah 2:12–13[13–14]; Zeph 3:3.

108. See further interaction in Schnittjer, "Blessing of Judah," 26–27.

Ezekiel 23 develops an elaborate allegorical scenario of Yahweh's two unfaithful sister wives Oholah/Samaria and Oholibah/Jerusalem—not with scriptural echoes but with broad retrospectives of rebellion. The basic scenario of unfaithful sister wives also appears in Jer 3:6–10 (see Ezek 16 in Filters above for a similar prophetic tradition).[109] The scenario in Ezek 23 runs through a similar retrospective for both unfaithful sister wives with many parallels between them. The promiscuities and punishment correspond to kingdom and exile (for comparisons see Table Josh1).

- Oholah's promiscuity/kingdom of Samaria (23:5–8), exile (vv. 9–10)
- Oholibah's promiscuity/kingdom of Jerusalem (vv. 11–21), exile (vv. 22–25)

The use of drinking from the cup of divine wrath reflects Ezekiel's imagery even if it is broadly similar to a common prophetic theme (>/<23:31–34; Isa 51:17; Jer 25:15–16, 28; 51:7; Obad 16; Hab 2:15–16; Ps 75:8[9]).

Ezekiel 31 spells out an allegorical scenario of Assyria as the greatest "tree" in the garden of Eden among the other trees/nations. The most extraordinary image is when all the trees of the garden are cast into the underworld, paradise in hell so to speak (Ezek 31:15–18). The point of the allegorical scenario is to speak judgment against the pharaoh (31:18). The expansive allegory may echo Isaiah's short poetic judgment of Yahweh chopping down Assyria, including several similarities (Isa 10:33–34; cf. Dan 4:10–17).

Ezekiel 37:1–14 shares a conceptual similarity with Isa 26:19. The lines: (a) "Your dead shall live" (Isa 26:19a), (b) "as a corpse they shall rise" (19b), and (c) "Awake! Shout for joy you who dwell in the dust" (19c)[110] broadly correspond to: (a) bones to live again (37:3), (b1) bones and flesh reconstituted but not yet alive (7–8), and (b2) re-vivified by the spirit (9–10). The same sequence is abbreviated to: (a) bring up from graves (37:13), and (b2) spirit to re-vivify (14). In this sense the addition of the spirit represents an advancement. Lack of verbal correspondence limits this to thematic similarity.

Ezekiel 38–39 seems to use, according to Tooman, three passages as paradigmatic templates to shape major themes in the oracles against Gog, namely, Ezek 6:1–4, 28:25–26, and Ps 79:1–4.[111] For example, the themes of regathering Israel as visible testimony to the nations and judging the nations in Ezek 28:25–26 serve as something of an outline with many verbal parallels mostly in the same order: "when I gather the house of Israel from the peoples" (28:25//38:9), "then I will be sanctified in the sight of the nations" (28:25//38:23; 39:27), "and they will dwell in the land that . . . Jacob" (28:25//39:25, 26), "and they will dwell upon it securely . . . and they will dwell securely" (28:26//39:26), "when I have executed judgments" (28:26//39:21), "I am Yahweh their

109. For a similar observation on Ezek 23 based on Jer 23:6–10, see Zimmerli, "Message," 144.

110. Taking the *yod* on "as a corpse" (נְבֵלָתִי) as a somewhat unusual adverbial gentilic of state (see *IBHS* §5.7; Schmitz, "Grammar of Resurrection," 147). For the similar sequence of Isa 26:19 and Ezek 37:1–4, see Schmitz, 148.

111. See Tooman, "Transformation," 60–63.

God" (28:26//39:22, 28).[112] Besides these three contexts that seem to help shape the thematic storyline, Ezek 38–39 makes heavy use of shared locutions with Ezek 1–37 and several other scriptural contexts. Almost all of these connect themes and imagery, but not in exegetical ways (for the exceptions with potential exegetical interventions see notes ad loc.).[113]

Ezekiel 40–48 tells of a new temple with many allusions to scriptural traditions. In some cases Ezekiel includes exegetical interventions (see notes on Ezek 40–48). Aside from striking new measures to guard holiness, Ezekiel's temple reaffirms continuity with many worship standards, such as: >/<40:2; Isa 2:2//Mic 4:1, temple on high mountain; >/<40:16, 26; 41:18–20, 25–26; Exod 26:31; 36:8; 1 Kgs 6:29, 35, decorated with palm trees and cherubim; >/<41:3–4; Exod 26:33–34; 1 Kgs 6:16; 7:50; 8:6, holy of holies (as a priest Ezekiel enters the holy place but not holy of holies; but compare vision of chariots 1:4–21); >/<41:22; Exod 25:23–30; 37:10–16, table of presence (cf. Lev 24:5–9); >/<43:4; Exod 40:34–35; 1 Kgs 8:10, glory returned to temple from east (cf. departure and return of glory as literary connection: >/<Ezek 1:20–21; 10:18–19; 11:22–23; 44:2); >/<43:18–27; Exod 29:35–37; 40:10; Lev 8:14–15, dedication of altar (with different rites than tabernacle); >/<44:28; Num 18:20, no inheritance for priests—they shall live in Yahweh's land (cf. 3:11–13; 18:20–24; Ezek 45:1–5); >/<44:29–30; Num 18:8–19, priests eat offerings, and devoted things and tithes belong to priests (cf. Lev 2:3; 6:16, 26[9, 19]; 7:6–7, 34); >/<44:31; Lev 7:24; 22:8; prohibition against priests eating anything which died.

Even some apparent differences turn out to be non-issues. Ezekiel's temple calls for steps leading up to the altar (Ezek 43:17). The prohibition of an elevated altar prevented the priest from being exposed from below his robe (Exod 20:26). However, the temporary measure of no steps was resolved by priestly undergarments (28:42–43; 39:28b–29).[114] Ezekiel's temple features many stairs and elevated terraces to spatially signify graduated holiness.

Ezekiel's Non-Exegetical Use of Ezekiel

Recapitulation. Several passages in Ezekiel re-present similar materials often expanding earlier messages. Sometimes these recapitulations occur within a particular message and sometimes between more-remote messages. Examples of recapitulation within a message include: >/<6:1–10; 36:1–15, reversal of the judgment against the mountains of Israel, like the repopulation of 36:10 (also see 38:8; 39:4, 17);[115] >/<14:13–14//14:15–16//14:17–18//14:19–20, three righteous persons inadequate;[116] >/<13:2–16~13:17–23, false prophets/

112. From ibid., 60.

113. See list in ibid., 94–105.

114. On the rarity of undergarments for ancient priests, see Imes, "Between," 36, n. 33.

115. See Tooman, "Transformation," 61–62. On parallels between Ezek 35–36, see McKenzie, "Edom's Desolation," 96–99.

116. See table in Block, *Ezekiel 1–24*, 444–45.

false prophetesses.[117] In some cases a later message develops imagery introduced in an earlier message: >/<11:3, 7, 11; 24:3–14, pot and meat/filthy pot; >/<11:4–6; 19:1–7; 22:1–12, killing in pot/by lion cubs/by city that sheds blood; >/<18:21–32; 33:10–20, reprise of people's complaint of the Lord's injustice and Ezekiel's that the righteousness of the righteous shall not save them from their wickedness, and so on; >/<Ezek 20; 36:16–38, the latter context speaks of sweeping reversals with a large number of inverting echoes from scattering that brings defilement to regathering and sprinkling with clean water;[118] >/<25:12–14; 35:1–15; 36:5, judgment against Edom; >/<26:20; 31:15–17; 32:17–32, ever-expanding imagery of the underworld—Tyre, Eden, Egypt among the "uncircumcised";[119] >/<29:1–7; 32:1–16, the pharaoh as a dragon defeated by Yahweh; >/<40:47; 43:13–27, altar; >/<45:1–9; 47:13–48:35, land allotment (but see note on 47:22–23).

Ezekiel 28 opens with an oracle against the prince of Tyre (Ezek 28:1–10) and lament over the king of Tyre (28:11–19). These oracles share much imagery with the lament for the city of Tyre (ch. 27) and other contexts. The extravagant imagery, which sometimes features celestial connotations, is used of humans in other scriptural contexts. The use of imagery with human referents can offer caution against overemphasis of proposed mythical and/or celestial functions.

prince/king of Tyre (Ezekiel 28)	**Tyre (27)**	**Other**
"I am God, sitting as God" (2)		king of Babylon like Most High (Isa 14:13, 14)
seated "in heart of the seas" (2)	4, 27	
death "in the heart of the seas" (8)	27	
full of wisdom, perfect in beauty (12, 17)	3, 4, 11	Jerusalem (Ezek 16:14; Lam 2:15)
Eden, the garden of God (13)		Assyria (Ezek 31:9, 16); Egypt (31:18); Israel (36:35); Zion (Isa 51:3)
covered with precious stones (13)		parallel stones in priest's breastplate (Exod 28:17–20//39:10–13)[a]
cast to the ground (17)		princes of Israel (Ezek 19:12); daughter Zion (Lam 2:1)

[a] See chart of breastplate parallels in Block, *Ezekiel 25–48*, 107. Some propose the oracle originally attacked the high priest, see Tuell, "Ezekiel," 74–76; for counterpoints see Block, 111–12.

Stock Phrases and Thematic Parallels. One of Ezekiel's distinct stock phrases is his own designation from divine perspective: >/<2:1, etc., 93x (versus 6x outside Ezekiel), "mortal" lit. "son of a human" versus a celestial being (בן־אדם).

117. See table in Greenberg, *Ezekiel, 1–20*, 242.

118. See Barter, "Reuse of Ezekiel 20," 120–37.

119. On the circumcision of Egyptians, which shames them all the more for underworld dwellings with the uncircumcised, see Greenberg, *Ezekiel 21–37*, 661–62.

Only a few of Ezekiel's literary and connecting uses of themes, imagery, and stock phrases can be included here: >/<3:17, 25–27; 24:27; 33:7, mute sentinel; >/<3:12; 10:9–22; 11:22–25; 43:1–5, chariots and glory lifted up (3:12), to temple threshold (10:19), mountain east of city (11:23), glory reenters temple from east (43:4); >/<8:12; 9:9, "They say, 'Yahweh does not see us; Yahweh has forsaken the land'"/"They say, 'Yahweh has forsaken the land; Yahweh does not see'" (Seidel's theory);[120] >/<16:60; 37:23, 26; Num 25:12–13, everlasting covenant; >/<20:32; 25:8, like the nations (ironically).

Transformation of Torah's Idiom

Lyons presents a series of contexts in Ezekiel that make use of shared and similar locutions in the holiness collection (Lev 17–26) and related contexts of Torah. Lyons contends that Ezekiel adapts and transforms the shared elements in several ways: accusation, judgment, instruction, apologetic for God's reputation, and hope.[121] These methods produce impressive cumulative results. Many of the contexts in which Lyons detects shared locutions fit the profile of non-exegetical uses of scriptural traditions in the present study—shared style and thematic similarities. Though these cases do not function as exegesis of particular contexts, regarding them as examples of "dependence" on donor contexts needs to be qualified. The several passages in Ezekiel bearing marks of heavy use of holiness instructions demonstrate the prophet's calling to advance revelation as much as reliance on Torah. Lyons rightly interprets the effect of the shared locutions as prophet "transforming law"—but this needs to be seen in a literary rather than an exegetical sense.

Ezekiel 22:7–12 offers a representative example of how the prophet transforms shared locutions with holiness instructions of Torah, especially Lev 18–20 (see Lyons's studies for many other kindred case studies). The following example consolidates Lyons's summary and makes a few adjustments for the present purposes (italicized phrases are paired with notes a to h, while broken underlining signifies additional subtler echoes discussed by Lyons):[122]

> In you they *have treated father and mother with contempt;*[a] in you they have oppressed the foreigner and mistreated the fatherless and the widow. [8] You have *despised my holy things*[b] and desecrated *my Sabbaths.*[c] [9] In you are slanderers who are bent on shedding blood; in you are those who eat at the mountain shrines and *commit lewd acts.*[d] [10] In you *a person uncovers the father's nakedness*[e] in you they violate *women during menstruation when they are ritually impure.*[f] [11] In you one man commits a detestable offense with his neighbor's wife, another with *lewdness*[d] defiles his daughter-in-law, and another violates his sister, his own father's daughter. [12] In you are people who accept bribes to shed blood; *you take interest and make a profit*[g] from the poor. You secure unjust gain from *your neighbors by extortion.*[h] And you have forgotten me, declares Sovereign Yahweh. (Ezek 22:7–12†; v. 10 lit.)

120. See Beentjes, "Discovering a New Path," 36.

121. See Lyons, "Transformation of Law," 13–26.

122. Notes a through h adapted and modified from ibid., 13–16.

[a] For "treat with contempt" (קלל) collocated with "father and mother," see Exod 21:17; Lev 20:9; Prov 20:20; 30:11; cf. Deut 27:16 (מַקְלֶה) (see "קלל," *HALOT* 2:1104). But perhaps "treat mother and father with contempt" in Ezek 22:7 inverts "respect mother and father" (Lev 19:3) (see note c).

[b] Thematic similarity between: "desecrate" (חלל) "holy X" in Lev 19:8; 22:2, 15; Num 18:32; Ezek 22:26a//Zeph 3:4b (Seidel's theory) and "despise" (בזה) "holy things" in Ezek 22:8a (note use of "desecrate" in 22:8b).

[c] For "my Sabbaths" see Exod 31:13; Lev 19:3, 30; 26:2; Isa 56:4; Ezek 20:12, 13, 16, 20, 21, 24; 22:8; 23:38; 44:24. Lyons suggests the command to respect mother and father and keep Sabbath in Lev 19:3 may stand behind the series of reversals in Ezekiel here ("Transformation of Law," 15).

[d] The majority of cases in which "lewdness" carries shameful connotations occur in holiness instructions (Lev 18:17; 19:29; 20:14) and Ezekiel (Ezek 16:27, 43, 58; 22:9, 11; 23:21, 27, 29, 35, 44) (see "זִמָּה," *HALOT* 1:272).

[e] The verb "uncover" (גלה) is collocated with "the nakedness of a father" (ערות אב) in Lev 18:7; 20:11; Ezek 22:10; cf. Gen 9:22, 23 for see and cover father's nakedness. More generally, the majority of euphemistic uses of "nakedness" occur in Lev 18, 20, and Ezek 16, 22, 23.

[f] The references to sexual relations with a woman during her menstruation, which causes ritual impurity in Ezek 18:6; 22:10, likely relates to the prohibition in Lev 18:19, where the same roots are collocated (cf. Lev 15:26).

[g] The term "interest" (נֶשֶׁךְ) is collocated with "profit, usury" (תַּרְבִּית) in Lev 25:36, 37; Ezek 18:8, 13, 17; 22:12; Prov 28:8 (see "נֶשֶׁךְ," "תַּרְבִּית," *HALOT* 1:729–30; 2:1787). Lyons excludes Lev 25:37 and Prov 28:8 because they do not use the verb "take" (לקח) interest ("Transformation of Law," 16). Adding in a criterion of collocation with a commonplace term to delimit parallels in contexts only generally related by shared style and similar themes seems unnecessary. Adding unnecessary criteria to enhance uniqueness of parallels weakens results.

[h] The term "extort, extortion" (עשק) is only used with "neighbor" (רֵעַ) in Lev 19:13 and Ezek 22:12, though the prophet uses extort/extortion similarly elsewhere, 18:18; 22:7, 29 ("עֹשֶׁק," *HALOT* 1:897).

By close comparison of locutions in holiness instruction and Ezekiel, Lyons succeeds in demonstrating how the prophet transforms holiness idiom into accusation.[123] The prophet's indebtedness to holiness instruction and literary adaptation of its style needs to be taken seriously. The theology of Ezekiel may be described as within the broad orbit of Torah holiness, even considering his manifold advancements, sometimes extreme, in his scroll as a whole.

Scriptural Stock Phrases and Shared Themes

The following are a few of Ezekiel's non-exegetical uses of imagery, themes, stock phrases, and stereotypical expressions from elsewhere in Scripture: >/<**4:12–13**; Deut 23:13[14], "human excrement" (*צאה) as indirect cause of profaning and/or defilement (only used these two times in Scripture); >/<**4:16**; Lev 26:26, "food supply" lit. "staff of bread" (מטה לחם); >/<**8:16–18**; Deut 4:19; 17:3; 2 Kgs 23:5, 11, sun worship; >/<**13:10, 16**; Jer 6:1; 8:11; 23:17, "'Peace,' when there is no peace" (cf. 29:7–9); >/<**15:1–8**; Isa 5:1–10; Jer 2:21; Hos 10:1; Ps 80:10–16[11–17], worthless vine; >/<**16:20, 21, 36; 20:26, 31; 23:37, 39**, child sacrifice; >/<**16:38; 18:10; 22:3, 6, 9, 27; 23:45; 33:25; 36:18**;

123. Lyons observes and explains many other instances of Ezekiel's dependence on the holiness collection. For example, Ezek 14:13–21 builds a judgment upon many stock phrases and shared language, especially from Lev 26:22–33 (see ibid., 16–19). Evans takes a similar approach, albeit with less controls, and shows Ezekiel as "broadly dependent" on Exodus (*You Shall Know*, 31). Evans's most detailed comparison shows similar commonplace language, stock phrases, and thematic similarities between Exod 6:3–9 and Ezek 20, with special focus on verses 33–42 (128–31). Evans does not show identifiable cases of exegetical outcomes in Ezekiel based on specific donor texts in Exodus, but cumulative non-exegetical Exodus-like idioms in Ezekiel's condemnation of his constituents (160–61).

Num 35:33–34, shedding blood defiles; >/<**25:12; 35:5, 15; 36:5**; Obad 10–14; Ps 137:7, treachery of Edom; >/<**28:22**; Exod 14:17–18, "I will be honored . . . X will know that I am Yahweh"; >/<**28:26**; Lev 25:18, 19, "live upon land in safety"; >/<**35:9**; Jer 49:18; Obad 16, 18; Mal 1:2–5, Edom as permanently destroyed; >/<**29:13–14**; Isa 19:23–24, restore the fortunes of Egypt (but on very different scales); >/<**29:21**; Ps 132:17, "I will make a horn grow" (cf. Lam 2:3); >/<**33:24**; Gen 12–25, Abraham as an individual inherited the entire land now claimed by remnant in the land.

Ezekiel's priestly background likely informs his presentation of straying worship leaders: >/<**8:11**; Num 16:7, 17, 18, 35, 40[17:5], rebel leaders with censer for "incense"; >/<**44:10**; Num 16:2, 22, 41[17:6]; 18:23, Levite rebellion in the wilderness.

Ezekiel uses stereotypical formulas to refer to exile. Some of them seem to be drawn from the **holiness collection**, like "I shall scatter . . . I shall draw the sword after them" (Lev 26:33; Ezek 5:2, 12; 12:14). Ezekiel also repeatedly combines priestly exile language like "scatter" (זרה) with **Deuteronomy** language like "disperse" (פוץ Hif) (Lev 26:33; Deut 30:3; Ezek 12:15; 20:23; 22:15; 29:12; 20:23; 30:26; 36:19).[124]

Ezekiel presents several vice lists with a variety of allusions especially to priestly instructions but also to some in Deuteronomy. These lists share much in common with each other, >/<18:6–8, 11–13, 15–18; 22:6–12, 29; 33:25–26.[125]

Ezekiel uses a number of **stock phrases from Deuteronomy**: >/<5:11; 7:4, 9; 8:18; 9:5; 20:17; Deut 7:16; 13:8[9]; 19:13, 21; 25:12, "eye shall not pity" (לא חוס עין) (cf. Ezek 24:14); >/<6:13; Deut 12:2, "under every spreading tree" (תחת כל עץ רענן) (cf. 1 Kgs 14:23; 2 Kgs 16:4//2 Chr 28:4; 2 Kgs 17:10; Isa 57:5; Jer 2:20; 3:6, 13; 17:2; Hos 4:13); >/<8:10; Deut 4:16–18, idolatrous images of "creeping" animals, but Ezekiel adds "detestable" which is used often in the priestly dietary standards (Lev 7:21; 11:10–13, 20, 23).

Ezekiel uses a number of **Deuteronomy terms for idolatry**: >/<8:3, 5; Deut 4:16, "statue" (סמל); >/<8:10; Deut 4:16, 17, 18, "likeness" (תבנית); >/<5:11; 7:20; 11:18, 21; 20:7, 8, 30; 37:23, "detestable things" (שקוצים); >/<20:32; Deut 4:28; 28:36, 64; 29:17 "wood and stone" (עץ ואבן); >/<20:31; Deut 18:10, "pass children through fire" (העברת הבנים באש). He also uses **priestly terms for idolatry**: >/<8:12; Lev 26:1; Num 33:52, "carved image" (משׂכית); >/<6:4, 6; etc. 39x; Lev 26:30, altar, idolatry (גללים, חמן); >/<7:20; 16:17; 23:14; Num 33:52, images (צלם).[126] Based on this evidence, Ganzel concludes that Ezekiel freely interchanges and "makes no distinction" between priestly and Deuteronomic lexicons of idolatry.[127]

124. See Gile, "Deuteronomy and Ezekiel's Theology," 289–91; also see "I זרה," "פוץ," *HALOT* 1:280; 2:918–19.

125. On Ezekiel using legal instructions from Leviticus, Numbers, and Deuteronomy, see Levitt Kohn, *New Heart*, 78–79, 94.

126. For list of Deuteronomic idolatry language, see Ganzel, "Transformation," 36; idolatry language in Leviticus and Numbers, 43–44; see further discussion of lists, 37–43, 44–45. Also see "מַשְׂכִּית," "חמן," "גִּלּוּלִים," "צלם," *HALOT* 1:192, 329, 641; 2:1028.

127. Ibid., 44.

Chapter 13

HOSEA

SYMBOLS[1]

// verbal parallels (A level)
/~/ synoptic parallel (A level)
~ B, probable interpretive allusion; C, possible; D, probably not
+ interpretive blend
>/< more or less similar (see Filters)
* part of interpretive network (see Networks)

USE OF SCRIPTURE IN HOSEA[2]

4:13~Deut 12:2 (C) (upon hills and under trees)
5:10~Deut 19:14 (C) (displace boundary marker)
11:1~Exod 4:23 (C) (Israel my son)
11:8*~Deut 29:23*[22] (B) (like Admah and Zeboyim) (* see cities of the plain network)
12:3[4]~Gen 25:22, 23, 26 (B) (Jacob wrestles in womb)
12:4[5]~Gen 32:24, 28[25, 29] (B)+35:15 (C) (Jacob wrestles with a man)
12:5[6]~Gen 28:13–19+35:11–15 (C) (Yahweh is his memorial)
13:6~Deut 8:12–14 (B) (satisfied, proud, forget)

OLD TESTAMENT USE OF HOSEA (SEE RESPECTIVE NOTES)

2:14–15[16–17]~Isa 54:6 (C) (restoration like the wife of youth)
2:14–15[16–17]~Jer 2:2 (B) (Israel as youthful bride in the wilderness)
3:5~Jer 30:9 (C) (renewal of Davidic rule)
4:7~Jer 2:11 (C) (gods are not gods)
4:9~Isa 24:2 (C) (as people so priest)
8:13//Jer 14:10 (Yahweh remembers their wickedness)

NEW TESTAMENT USE OF HOSEA

1:10[2:1]//Rom 9:26 (children of living God)
2:23[25]//Rom 9:25 (my people)
3:1~Jas 4:4 (adulterous people)
6:2~Matt 16:21; Mark 8:31 (third day raise us)[3]
6:6//Matt 9:13; 12:7 (mercy not sacrifice)
10:8//Luke 23:30; cf. Rev 6:16 (mountains fall on us)
11:1//Matt 2:15 (out of Egypt)
13:14 LXX//1 Cor 15:55 (Where death is your sting?)

HERMENEUTICAL PROFILE OF THE USE OF SCRIPTURE IN HOSEA

The collection of prophetic narratives and oracles in Hosea offers crucial testimony to the early prophetic use of scriptural traditions in the Northern Kingdom of Israel. Though

1. For explanation of symbols, see Symbols and Abbreviations and Introduction. For other help, see Glossary.
2. See Bibliographic Note on Lists of Potential Parallels.
3. Hosea 6:2 Tg makes resurrection explicit (see Evans, "Jesus," 100–1).

Amos preaches to the Northern Kingdom, he is from Judah. The prophets appearing in numerous colorful narratives of the Northern Kingdom in Kings did not leave behind collections of preaching. Even the book of Jonah is a story and not related to his ministry in Ephraim (2 Kgs 14:25). All of this heightens the value of Hosea.

The potential scriptural allusions to Genesis and Deuteronomy in Hosea attract sharp debate in diachronic studies with predictable contradictory interpretive decisions.[4] Although excavative approaches go beyond the basic goals of the present study, a few details of what is at stake may help with the textual goals here. The main contentions relate to Genesis, Deuteronomy, and Hosea.

From a fully synchronic outlook Genesis could not have reached its known form until sometime after the beginning of royalty in Israel (Gen 36:31). The context does not indicate how long ago a kingship was established in Israel. The narrative frame of Deuteronomy looks back upon settlement of the land at some temporal distance (Deut 2:12). The timespan between the elements in Deuteronomy and the narrative frame are long enough to create the need for numerous explanatory updates, sometimes with the tagline "to this day" (e.g., 2:22; 3:14). The known book of Hosea seems like it has been reissued for analogous use in Judah. In numerous places phrases, like "also Judah," look like add-ons.[5] The book of Hosea fits with a view that prophetic messages transcend their initial contexts and speak to the people of God in other circumstances (e.g., Zech 1:4). According to the testimony of Genesis, Deuteronomy, and Hosea, each seems to feature editorial intervention at some distance from the materials therein. These books enjoy canonical authority in their updated formats. The point at hand turns on the temporal uncertainty that comes with speaking of the form of scriptural traditions known to Hosea and his constituents.

The evidence suggests that Hosea uses scriptural traditions that appear in Genesis and Deuteronomy. The literary signals in each of these writings caution against leaping to conclusions. On the question of direction of dependence, very little offers help. The most suggestive element is the euphemistic use of "delegate" in Hos 12:4[5]. Tendency to euphemism when speaking of the divine points to the receptor, not donor. In spite of no textual evidence, many modern interpreters have been quick to judge such elements as the work of scribes in the transmission process. But euphemistic treatment of the divine extends back into the biblical period (see note on Ps 96:7–8). On the basis of this very limited evidence, the traditions that appear in Genesis seem to be donor and Hosea the receptor context.

More broadly, Hosea seems to casually presuppose his audience knows of legal and narrative traditions that appear in Deuteronomy. Hosea uses an inverted form of these instructions to condemn his audience for rebellion against the covenant. Hosea never

---

4. See summary in Vang, "When a Prophet Quotes Moses," 279–82. Vang finds diachronic decisions about Hosea's potential use of Deuteronomy or vice versa get decided for reasons outside the parallels in question.

5. See Hos 1:1, 7, 11[2:2]; 4:15; 5:5, 10, 12–14; 6:4, 11; 8:14; 10:11; 11:12[12:1]; 12:2. Also see Childs, *Introduction*, 378–79.

treats covenantal standards as impersonal. Hosea's use of scriptural traditions accords with his vivid metaphors of Israel's whorish infidelity juxtaposed against Yahweh's loyalty and love.

Hosea speaks of written torah. The prophet voices Yahweh's message to Ephraim: "*I wrote for them the many things of my torah*, but they regarded them as something foreign" (Hos 8:12, emphasis mine). Though Hosea speaks of written torah, neither he nor the other prophets tend to formally cite it. The prophets' use of torah typically comes up indirectly as they advocate divine messages of doom upon their rebellious audiences.[6] Still, scriptural narrative characterizes at least the northern prophets as advocating torah: "Yahweh warned Israel and Judah *through all his prophets and seers*: 'Turn from your evil ways. *Observe my commands and decrees, in accordance with the entire Torah* that I commanded your ancestors to obey and that I delivered to you *through my servants the prophets*" (2 Kgs 17:13, emphases mine). If Hosea interacts with written Torah, he does so primarily by means of loose allusion. When Hosea's message echoes Torah traditions, it reframes and applies them to his constituents.

Hosea affords an opportunity to investigate the early use of scriptural traditions. The trendsetting work of Hosea and Amos becomes apparent quickly within the scriptural prophetic traditions. The nature of the evidence of scriptural interpretation in Hosea requires due patience and a willingness to leave some questions unanswered.

Only a handful of contexts in Hosea house potential exegetical uses of scriptural traditions based on the criteria of the present study. Representative examples of a large number of other potential non-exegetical scriptural allusions and broad thematic similarities have been collated into the filters below.

USE OF SCRIPTURE

4:13~Deut 12:2 (C) (upon hills and under trees). Hosea 4:13 and Deut 12:2 share memorable and much-repeated imagery that gets connotatively bound up together with the infidelity it describes. The tops of high hills and leafy trees may play off ancient cultic worship and/or prostitution imagery.[7] But even if they refer to shrines of the God of Israel, this multiplicity is exactly what the altar law of Deut 12 seeks to eliminate.[8] In Hosea whorish infidelity serves as a running double entendre for covenantal unfaithfulness (bold signifies verbal parallels, and italics signify similar imagery):

> Destroy completely all the places **on the** high **mountains, on the hills and under** *every spreading tree*, where the nations you are dispossessing worship their gods. (Deut 12:2)

6. See Tucker, "Law," 201–16; Renz, "Torah in the Minor Prophets," 73–94.
7. See Wolff, *Hosea*, 86–87.
8. See Vang, "When a Prophet Quotes Moses," 300.

> They sacrifice **on the mountaintops** and burn offerings **on the hills, under** *oak, poplar and terebinth*, where the shade is pleasant. Therefore your daughters turn to prostitution and your daughters-in-law to adultery. (Hos 4:13)

The use of this imagery of infidelity in Deut 12:2 and/or Hos 4:13 stands at the headwaters of this common prophetic tradition—"On every high hill/hill and under every spreading tree" (1 Kgs 14:23; 2 Kgs 16:4//2 Chr 28:4; 2 Kgs 17:10; Jer 2:20; 3:6, 13; Ezek 6:13) and similar (see stock phrases in Jeremiah Filters). The commonness of the language only permits the possibility of an intentional relationship between Deuteronomy and Hosea.

5:10~Deut 19:14 (C) (displace boundary marker). The causative stem of "displace" is collocated with "boundary marker" in only a few places in Scripture (Deut 19:14; 27:17; Hos 5:10; Prov 22:28; 23:10; Job 24:2).[9] Hosea 5:10 uses this crime as a simile against Judah. The context refers to mustering troops in three of Israel's cities—Gibeah, Ramah, and Beth Aven—and seeking alliance with Assyria (Hos 5:8, 13).[10] These details suggest Judah had seized some of Israel's land beyond reclaiming Benjamite territory previously seized by Israel. Anderson and Freedman favor the conflict between Shallum and Menahem as the setting (2 Kgs 15:13–14) that involved seeking out Pul/Tiglath-pileser III (744–727 BCE) (2 Kgs 15:19; cf. Hos 5:13) rather than the Syria-Israelite confederation (2 Kgs 16:5–6; 2 Chr 28:5–8).[11] The crime of moving a boundary marker could be a general legal reference, yet the context of the law in Deuteronomy provides a rationale for Hosea's indictment. The land granted to tribes falls within the authority of Yahweh's giving of the land (emphasis signifies verbal parallels):

> *Do not move* your neighbor's *boundary stone* set up by your predecessors in the inheritance you receive in the land Yahweh your God is giving you to possess. (Deut 19:14)

> Judah's leaders are like *those who move boundary stones*. I will pour out my wrath on them like a flood of water. (Hos 5:10)[12]

11:1~Exod 4:23 (C) (Israel my son). Hosea 11:1 and Exod 4:23 share the striking statement of Yahweh concerning Israel as "my son" (בְּנִי).[13] The counterpart term in the A line

9. See "סוג," *HALOT* 1:745 (entry cites wrong reference Pss 22:28; 23:10 [*sic*]; see Prov 22:28; 23:10).

10. Beth Aven/House of Wickedness is Hosea's intentional polemic distortion of Bethel/House of God (Hos 4:15; 5:8; 10:5). The smear appears to refer to the calf shrine established by Jeroboam (10:5). Also note its use in Josh 7:2; 18:12; 1 Sam 13:5; 14:23.

11. See Anderson and Freedman, *Amos*, 403–4.

12. On flood as metaphor for military destruction, see the annals of Tiglath-pileser III (e.g., *ARAB* 1:284, §§790, 791).

13. Hosea 11:1 LXX uses "his children" (τὰ τέκνα αὐτοῦ) while Matt 2:15 uses "my son" (τὸν υἱόν μου). Thus, Matt 2:15 follows the Hebrew or a Greek text with a reading like Aquila (see Turpie, *OT in the New*, 22). Hays says Matthew "evokes" Exod 4:21–23 by his use of Hos 11:1 in Matt 2:15 (see Hays, *Reading Backwards*, 40). Also see Estelle, *Echoes of Exodus*, 226–32.

of Hos 11:1 is "child." Exodus 4 sets up killing the pharaoh's son to recover Yahweh's son (Exod 4:21–23; cf. Deut 1:31; 8:5). Hosea 11:1–4 picks up the theme of youthful Israel as an analogy for training up Ephraim. The term "child" (נַעַר) in 11:1 thematically develops the imagery of the "youthful" (נְעוּרִים) bride of 2:15[17] in a similar direction. Hosea reinforces Yahweh's love and devotion to Israel from the beginning as a foil for Israel's infidelity. In any case, the different treatments of the imagery reduce the likelihood of a connection between Exod 4:23 and Hos 11:1 to a possibility.

11:8*~Deut 29:23*[22] (B) (like Admah and Zeboyim) (* see cities of the plain network). Deuteronomy 29:23[22] lists the quartet of cities of the plain destroyed by Yahweh's wrath. Though most other prophets use Sodom or Sodom and Gomorrah as a figure of doom, Hosea alone uses the simile of the two lesser-known destroyed cities, Admah and Zeboyim (Hos 11:8). The only other places they are mentioned are in the table of nations (Gen 10:19) and the narrative of Abraham rescuing Lot and the captives from the cities of the plain (14:8). Zoar is included with them in battle, making it seem like a quintet of cities, but Zoar does not get destroyed (19:22–23). Hosea appears to refer to the tradition in Deut 29:23[22]. Unlike Deut 29:23[22], which speaks of Yahweh "overturning" (הפך) the cities of the plain, the prophet depicts Yahweh as having second thoughts, literally his heart is "overturning" (הפך Nif).[14] Hosea voices Yahweh's inner turmoil: "How can I give you up, Ephraim? How can I hand you over, Israel? How can I treat you *like Admah*? How can I make you *like Zeboyim*? My heart is *changed* [נֶהְפַּךְ] within me; all my compassion is aroused" (Hos 11:8, emphasis mine). The use of "overturn" for Yahweh's inner deliberations over destroying Israel suggests a likely exegetical advance regarding divine judgment. When Yahweh judges the condemned cities of the plain, he overturns them. When Yahweh judges his own people, his heart is overturned.

12:3[4]~Gen 25:22, 23, 26 (B) (Jacob wrestles in womb).

12:4[5]~Gen 32:24, 28[25, 29] (B)+35:15 (C) (Jacob wrestles with a man).

12:5[6]~Gen 28:13–19+35:11–15 (C) (Yahweh is his memorial). In addition to the references to Jacob in Hos 12:3–4[4–5] that bear some resemblance to traditions in Genesis, Hosea speaks of him as fleeing to Aram and serving for a wife (Hos 12:12[13]). Hosea's references to Jacob draw heavy debate both with plentiful proposals for textual emendations as well as all manner of suggestions for how the allusions to Jacob may relate to Genesis, if they do. Before getting at the details relevant to interpretive allusions, textual issues and tricky grammatical difficulties need to be clarified.

Many commentators and other scholars seek to peel off the surface layer and recover Hosea's preredacted poetry. The present approach goes the opposite direction. The scriptural version of Hosea includes the "and also Judah" updates.[15] These scriptural updates feature authorized interpretive interventions to reissue Hosea. Thus, the typical "removal"

---

14. See Wolff, *Hosea*, 201.

15. Judah is emphasized in Hos 1:7, 11; 4:15; 5:5, 10, 14; 6:4, 11; 8:14; 10:11; 12:2[3]; cf. 3:5.

of updates distorts the scriptural version of the scroll. Accordingly, typical approaches suggest the A line and B line of Hos 12:2[3] originally paired Israel and Jacob, both because the context plays on names and the fact that Hosea ministered in Israel.[16] These are both important points. The A line speaks of Yahweh's legal "charge" (רִיב) which fits well with renaming Jacob (יַעֲקֹב) as Israel since he "wrestled" (אבק), a term having consonance with Jacob (Gen 32:26). Yet, with no evidence to the contrary, the A line fits well with Hosea reissued to Judeans. Next, 12:4[5] says "delegate" or "messenger" (מַלְאָךְ), typically rendered by a Greek loanword "angel" (ἄγγελος), also meaning messenger. Although lacking external evidence, commentators often replace the term "delegate" with "God" (אֵל).[17] The more difficult masoretic reading is preferred—"delegate." The masoretic version of 12:4[5] ends with "and there he spoke with us" (lit.), which many modern committee translations emend to third-person singular "him" to keep the focus on Jacob rather than turning to Hosea's constituents.[18] This should be read as "with us" as in the Masoretic Text.

Two grammatical and syntactical difficulties concern how to render the C line of Hos 12:4[5]. First, the verbs of verses 3[4] and 4[5] shift from narrative forms ("he grasped . . . he struggled . . . he struggled . . . he overcame, he wept and begged") to imperfect forms, literally, "he will find . . . he will speak."[19] Second, the pronominal suffix on the end of the verb "find" could be "him" or "us" since they are spelled the same way.[20] In light of these two factors, the suggested reading of the C line of 12:4[5] is "he will find us at Bethel and there he will speak with us" (lit.).[21] Many modern committee translations and commentators retain the focus on Jacob and so render the C line of 12:4[5] as continuing the past tense about "him." However, though Hosea usually derides Bethel (lit. "House of God") as Beth Aven ("House of Iniquity") (4:15; 5:8; 10:5) because of the golden calf, in two places, including the present context, he uses Bethel (10:15; 12:4[5]). All of these elements align and suggest a shift in the C line.

In sum, the present study will work with the Masoretic Text without emendation and follow standard modern committee translations except in Hos 12:4[5] line C, where the prophet shifts to imperfect verbs and first-person plural pronouns.

---

16. *BHS* follows *BHK* and calls for emending "Judah" to "Israel" in Hos 12:2[3] without any external evidence (cf. *BHQ*).

17. So Wolff, *Hosea*, 206; *BHS* apparatus of Hos 12:4[5]. *BHS* also suggests emending "to" (אֶל) to "with" (אֶת) both to smooth out the grammar and to match "with God" (אֶת־אֱלֹהִים) in 12:3[4]. With no external evidence the more difficult reading of the MT is preferred.

18. See Hos 12:4[5] *BHS* apparatus; cf. e.g., NIV, NRSV. The LXX, much like modern committee translations, apparently tries to smooth things out with "to him" (πρὸς αὐτόν) (*BHQ* apparatus). Gelston regards the parent text of the LXX as identical to the proto-MT (*BHQ*, 69*). The present approach prefers the more difficult MT.

19. The shift goes from *qatal* (pf.) and *vayyiqtol* (wci) forms in Hos 12:3[4] through the B line of 12:4[5], then to *yiqtol* (impf.) forms in the C line of 12:4[5].

20. In Hos 12:4[5] the term "he will find him/us" (יִמְצָאֶנּוּ) depends on whether the *dagesh* in the energic *nun* represents *heh*, thus 3ms "him" (הוּ + ןֶ-), or *nun*, thus 1cp "us" (נוּ + ןֶ-) (GKC §58j). Gesenius prefers 3ms "him" in Hos 12:4[5] contra the suggestion here (§58k). McKenzie proposes this grammatical form is "deliberately ambiguous" ("Jacob Tradition," 317).

21. Literal translation based on MT without emendation (בֵּית־אֵל יִמְצָאֶנּוּ וְשָׁם יְדַבֵּר עִמָּנוּ) (Hos 12:4[5]).

The allusions to the Jacob narrative traditions in Hos 12:3–4[4–5] stand within Yahweh's legal accusation against Judah and Jacob, which concludes with an opportunity for response (italics signify verbal parallels, bold signifies parallels at the level of roots, broken underlining signifies oral sound play, and wavy underlining signifies potential interpretive intervention):

> The babies jostled each other within her. . . . [23] Yahweh said to her, "Two nations are *in* your *womb*. . . ." [26] After this, *his brother* came out, with his hand grasping Esau's **heel** [עָקֵב]; so he was named Jacob [יַעֲקֹב]. (Gen 25:22a, 23a, 26a)
>
> So Jacob was left alone, and a man wrestled [אבק] with him till daybreak. . . . [28] Then the man said, "Your name will no longer be Jacob, but Israel, because you ***have struggled*** [שׂרה] with *God* and with humans and *have overcome*." (32:24, 28[25, 29])
>
> Jacob set up a stone pillar at the place where God *had spoken* with him, and he poured out a drink offering on it; he also poured oil on it. [15] Jacob called the place where God *had spoken* with him *there Bethel*. (35:14–15†)
>
> Yahweh has a charge to bring against Judah; he will punish Jacob according to his ways and repay him according to his deeds. [3] *In* the *womb* he **grasped** *his brother's* **heel** [עקב]; as a man he *struggled* [שׂרה] with *God*. [4] He **struggled** [שׂור] with the angel and *overcame* him; he wept and begged for his favor. He will find us at *Bethel* and *will speak* with us *there*. (Hos 12:2–4[3–5], 12:4c lit.)

Hosea 12:3[4] collates the thematically related prenatal and nocturnal struggle traditions that appear in remote contexts of the Jacob cycle in Genesis (Gen 25:2–26; 32:24–28[25–29]). Genesis and Hosea share verbal agreements, which include sound plays, strongly suggesting some kind of relationship. In addition to the sound play between the noun and verb forms of "heel" (עָקֵב), "grasp by the heel" (עקב), "wrestle" (אבק), note the consonance of Jabbok (יַבֹּק) and Jacob (יַעֲקֹב) (25:26; 32:22, 24[23, 25]; Hos 12:3[4]; cf. Gen 27:36).

Hosea 12:4[5] line A uses a term for "wrestle" related to the rare terms for "wrestle" in Gen 32:28[29] and Hos 12:3[4].[22] The second half of the A line in Hos 12:4[5] uses "delegate" or "angel" as a pair to God versus the man/God interplay in Genesis—"A man wrestled. . . . You have struggled with God and humans. . . . 'I saw God face to face'" (Gen 32:24, 28, 30[25, 29, 31]). The euphemistic use of "delegate" in Hos 12:4[5] suggests it as the receptor text.

Enslinger emends the A line of Hos 12:4[5] from "to" (אֶל) to "God" (אֵל) and reads it,

22. See "שׂרה," "I שׂור," *HALOT* 2:1313, 1354.

"But God ruled, and the messenger prevailed."[23] According to Enslinger, Hosea completely reverses the tradition as seen in Genesis because if Jacob exercised "dominion" over his fellows, Hosea's audience should not. In Hosea's alleged revision God/angel defeated Jacob, so too Hosea's audience should repent. McKenzie conjectures that Hos 12:4–5[5–6] may be a quotation of or parody of a worship poem used at Bethel.[24] Chalmers combines these proposals as a starting point and, with additional textual emendations, explains that in Hosea's liturgical satire when El defeated Jacob he cried out for mercy.[25] Without evidence, these emendations and proposals against the sense of the text lack explanatory merit.

Hosea 12:4[5] lines B and C attract much speculation. Though the roots of "weep" and "favor" appear elsewhere in the Jacob stories of Genesis, none fit what Hosea is doing.[26] If the C line plays off the theophany at Bethel in Gen 35, a big if, then Hosea could be filling an applicational gap for his audience in the B line. Did Hosea intend for his audience to see in the B line—"He wept and begged for his favor"—an allusion to one of the other narratives in Genesis, such as Jacob's household putting away idolatry at Bethel (Gen 35:2–4), Jacob's reference at Bethel of divine answer to his distress (35:3), Jacob's offering at Bethel (35:7), the divine revelation at Bethel (35:9–13), or even Jacob's ceremonial commemorative acts at Bethel (35:14)? None seem quite right. Hosea could also have had in mind a tradition known to his audience that is not preserved in Genesis.

Whatever the B line means, Hosea's shift to imperfect verbs and first-person plural pronouns in the C line calls his audience to go to Bethel to seek divine revelation. Cassuto and Kaiser make similar observations relative to these verb forms and pronouns even while their agendas differ from the present approach.[27] Hosea's invitation seems remarkable in light of his running taunts against Bethel as Beth Aven/House of Iniquity (Hos 4:15; 5:8; 10:5). The revelation he speaks of seems especially suggestive in light of the two revelations to Jacob at Bethel in Genesis. In the second theophany at Bethel he said to Jacob, "I am God Almighty" (Gen 35:11), but at the first he had said, "I am Yahweh" (28:13). These may be brought together within an interpretive blend of the revelation Hosea calls upon his audience to seek (emphases signify verbal parallels):[28]

> There above it stood **Yahweh**, and he said: "I am **Yahweh**, the *God* of your father Abraham and the *God* of Isaac. . . ." When Jacob awoke from his sleep, he thought,

---

23. See Enslinger, "Hos 12:5a," 93–94. Part of his logic is to "restore" a chiastic structure in the Hebrew.

24. See McKenzie, "Jacob Tradition," 319–20.

25. See Chalmers, "Who Is the Real El?" 623–29.

26. See Gen 33:4, 5, 11. Also see Esau weeping and begging for a blessing from Isaac (27:38).

27. See Cassuto, *Biblical*, 1:85; Kaiser, "Inner Biblical Exegesis," 42–43. Cassuto sees Hosea as filling in gaps in the narrative. Kaiser's agenda includes a proposal for each phrase of Hos 12:4–5, 13[5–6, 14] aligning with seven events from Jacob's life in Genesis (43, n. 49).

28. Compare: "I am Yahweh" (אֲנִי יהוה) (Gen 28:13), "I am God Almighty" (אֲנִי אֵל שַׁדַּי) (35:11), and "Yahweh God Almighty, Yahweh is his memorial" (וַיהוה אֱלֹהֵי הַצְּבָאוֹת יהוה זִכְרוֹ) (Hos 12:5[6] lit.).

> "Surely **Yahweh** is in this place, and I was not aware of it." He was afraid and said, "How awesome is this place! This is none other than the house of God [בֵּית אֱלֹהִים]; this is the gate of heaven. . . ." He called that place Bethel [בֵּית־אֵל]. (Gen 28:13a, 16–17, 19a)

> And *God* said to him, "I am *God* Almighty. . . ." Jacob called the place where *God* had spoken with him Bethel [בֵּית־אֵל]. (35:11, 15†)

> He will find us at Bethel and will speak with us there—**Yahweh** *God* Almighty, **Yahweh** is his memorial. (Hos 12:4c–5[5c–6] lit.)

This possible interpretive blend in Hos 12:5[6] may extend what the prophet says elsewhere: "I will remove the names of the Baals from her lips; no longer will their names be remembered [זכר]" (2:17†[19]). Hosea 12:5[6] may apply the same idea to worshiping Yahweh by his name as "memorial" (זֵכֶר) as a replacement of the calf image at Bethel. If Hos 12:5[6] interpretively blends the two revelations to Jacob at Bethel that appear in Genesis, the nature of the interpretive intervention would suggest it as receptor context; this agrees with the euphemism in 12:4[5] noted above.

In sum, if the masoretic version is accepted, Hosea seems to exegetically allude to the Jacob traditions known in Genesis. Hosea uses these to call his audience to seek Yahweh himself at Bethel—no calf—by his name.

13:6~Deut 8:12–14 (B) (satisfied, proud, forget). The terms "satisfy," "heart becomes proud," and "forget" only appear together in Deut 8 and Hos 13, suggesting an allusion.[29] The evidence in the interpretive intervention itself does not support direction of dependence. The verb "satisfy" (שׂבע) in Deuteronomy stands in hendiadys, "eat and satisfy," in all but one case. Vang suggests Hosea may modify the tradition with "graze and be satisfied."[30] If Hosea modifies this tradition, he may use "graze" to connect with his running metaphor of Israel/Ephraim as heifer (Hos 4:16; 10:11). The use of bovine imagery for rebellion accords with the Song of Moses—Jeshurun ate, then kicked, then forgot (Deut 32:15, 18). The parallel verbal and thematic imagery in these contexts strengthens the probability of relationship between them (bold signifies verbal parallels, and italics signify similar concepts):

> Otherwise, when you *eat* and **are satisfied**, when you build fine houses and settle down, [13] and when your herds and flocks grow large and your silver and gold increase and all you have is multiplied, [14] then your **heart will become proud** and you **will forget** Yahweh your God, who brought you out of Egypt, out of the land of slavery. (Deut 8:12–14)

29. See Ginsberg, "Hosea, Book of," *EJ*, 9:557; Vang, "When a Prophet Quotes Moses," 289.

30. See Deut 6:11; 8:10, 12; 11:15; 14:29; 23:24[25]; 26:12; 31:20, but not 33:23 (see Vang, "When a Prophet Quotes Moses," 289; Vang does not separate out 33:23).

When they *grazed*, they **were satisfied**; when they were **satisfied**, their **heart became proud**; then they **forgot** me. (Hos 13:6 lit.)

FILTERS

Hosea features many suggestive elements that may or may not allude to scriptural traditions. He uses simile especially often.[31] Many similes suggest scriptural traditions such as "like the days of Gibeah" (Hos 9:9; 10:9) and "like Admah" and "like Zeboyim" (11:8). Hosea also frequently uses geopolitical names to infer historical rebellions and/or other symbolic functions. These and other thematic similarities to Torah and the historical events of ancient Israel enrich Hosea's textured messages. They also often fall below the threshold of exegetical use of scriptural traditions.

There are several long lists of broad parallels between Hosea and Torah available elsewhere. If the lists sometimes house genuine subtle echoes of scriptural traditions, they also seem to contain mostly mere coincidences. Many of the available lists amount to short, commonplace phrases, broad imagery, similar themes, and verses with one or more shared common terms.[32]

The following filters house representative non-exegetical similarities between Hosea and other scriptural contexts. These lists are not complete or comprehensive. They offer a sense of the prophet's non-exegetical use of scriptural traditions.

Non-Exegetical Broad Allusions and Shared Themes

Thematic similarities between Hosea and scriptural traditions found elsewhere sometimes reveal the prophet's distinctive tendencies. The following are a few non-exegetical parallels and possible allusions. The first few are annotated because of their nature and stand for the longer list below.

2:8[10]>/<Deut 8:13; 17:16–17 (multiply silver and gold). The phrase "multiply silver and gold" in this sequence only appears in Deut 8:13, 17:16–17, and Hos 2:8[10]. Vang suggests the phrase has been split and expanded.[33] But silver is not paired with a new element. More to the point, the poetic lines feature a tragic reversal of imagery.

And silver — I have multiplied — for her,
and gold — they used — for Baal (Hos 2:8[10] lit.).

31. Also observed by Wolff, *Hosea*, xxiv.

32. See Bass, "Hosea's Use of Scripture," 104–271; Brueggemann, *Tradition for Crisis*, 13–51; Cassuto, *Biblical*, 1:79–100; Ginsberg, "Hosea, Book of," *EJ*, 9:557; Mirsky, Meltzer, and Kiel, *Twelve*, 33–47 [Hebrew]; Rooker, "Use of OT Hosea," 51–66 (also see items on Entire OT in Bibliographic Note on Lists of Potential Parallels). The longest lists of Bass, Rooker, and Mirsky, Meltzer, and Kiel may be the least useful since they catalogue many minor elements that usually seem like coincidence, as well as stock phrases (see critical evaluation in Vang, "When a Prophet Quotes Moses," 281–82).

33. See Vang, "When a Prophet Quotes Moses," 294–95.

The hendiadys "silver and gold" is exceedingly common in Scripture and so does not favor an interpretive relationship.[34] The shared language appears to be either coincidence or broad non-exegetical use.

3:1; 9:15; 11:1, 4; 14:4[5]>/<Deut 4:37; 7:8, 13; 10:15; 23:5[6] (covenantal love).[35] Ten of eighteen times that God is the subject and Israel is the object of the verb and noun uses of "love" in Scripture appear in Deuteronomy and Hosea. This thematic similarity, along with Israel's love of other gods, is suggestive of a possible relationship regarding covenantal (in)fidelity.

8:4>/<2 Kgs 15–17 (making kings without Yahweh). Hosea said, "They set up kings *without my consent*; they choose princes *without my approval*" (8:4, emphasis mine). Royal houses of Israel were divinely sanctioned up to Jehu, including establishment (except in Omri's case) and termination in each case by word from one of God's prophets: Jeroboam (1 Kgs 11:29–40; 12:15; 14:6–16; 15:9); Baasha (16:1–4, 7, 12); Omri (21:19; 22:38; 2 Kgs 9:36); Jehu (2 Kgs 9:1–3), and four subsequent generations of Jehu—Jehoahaz, Jehoash, Jeroboam II, Zechariah (10:30; 15:12). The series of rulers thereafter without narrative acknowledgment of divine sanction include: Shallum, Menahem, Pekahiah, Pekah, and Hoshea (15:10–12, 13–16, 17–22, 23–26, 27–31; 17:1–6).[36] The break between sanctioned and unsanctioned kings occurs during the ministry of Hosea which corresponds broadly with Hos 8:4 (see Hos 1:1; cf. final mention of prophetic sanction, 2 Kgs 15:12).

9:10>/<Num 25:1–5; Deut 4:3 (shameful thing at Baal Peor). Hosea makes a brief allusion to apostasy at Baal Peor (Hos 9:10; Num 25:1–5; Deut 4:3). The allusion is too fleeting to tie it to a specific scriptural context. Yet Hosea accuses Israel of becoming as vile as the shameful thing they love. The use of the simile to become "like what they love" reverses the same simile in Hos 3:1, where Yahweh instructs Hosea to love his unfaithful wife as Yahweh loves Israel. The irony of becoming what one loves at Baal Peor in ancient times provides an important image for the waywardness of Israel, whose glory flies away like a bird (Hos 9:11).

13:10, 11>/<1 Sam 8:5, 6, 22 (divine appointment of a king in anger). Yahweh appointed Saul as a king even while he considered the people's request a problem. The motives of the people to have a king like other nations runs parallel in law and narrative (Deut 17:14; 1 Sam 8:5, 20). Hosea may broadly allude to this tradition with "So in my anger I gave you a king, and in my wrath I took him away" (Hos 13:11). If Hosea alludes to this tradition, he does so by collapsing the appointment of Saul and the present king. The prophet taunts his audience, "Where is your king, that he may save you?" (13:10). Zechariah, Shallum, or Menahem may be the referent (2 Kgs 15:10, 13–14, 19–20).[37]

---

34. Even-Shoshan, 555, see early entry in n. ג.

35. See "אהב," "אַהֲבָה," *HALOT* 1:17–18. Indebted to Vang, "God's Love," 174, n. 3. See detailed discussion, 174–94.

36. McKenzie notes that each of the "royal houses" in the Northern Kingdom of Israel are "appointed then rejected by a prophet" ("Divided Kingdom," 139). This is a helpful observation and works up to and includes Zechariah in 2 Kgs 15:12. Thereafter, the narrator does not bother with reference to divine endorsement.

37. See Anderson and Freedman, *Hosea*, 635.

13:16[14:1]>/<2 Kgs 15:16 ("Samaria must bear their guilt . . . their pregnant women ripped open"). This appalling ancient standard figure of speech for military excess appears in the narrative of only one Israelite king, Menahem, a contemporary of Hosea (cf. Amos 1:13). Note that 2 Kgs 15:16 appears outside the royal opening formula, so it may apply to Menahem's acts as a military commander before becoming king (on formula see Kings Filters).

Simile format of possible non-exegetical allusions: **1:10**>/<Gen 22:17; 32:12; cf. 15:5; 16:10; 1 Kgs 3:8, people of Israel like sand of sea; **6:7**>/<Gen 3, possible simile "like Adam," otherwise a broad figure of speech "like a human" (Adam's name means human being); **9:9*; 10:9***>/<Judg 19:22–25*, like the days of Gibeah (* see cities of the plain network).

Note several other non-exegetical allusions and/or broad thematic similarities: **1:4**>/<2 Kgs 10:11, blood of Jezreel; **1:9**>/<covenant formula, Not-Mine "for you are not my people and I am not yours" (lit.) (see Table J1 in Jeremiah);[38] **2:15[17]**>/<Josh 7:25, Achor means "trouble" (עכר) used two times in Josh 7:25 (see note on 1 Chr 2:7); **2:15[17]; 11:1; 12:9[10]; 13:4**>/<Exodus–Joshua, out of Egypt (cf. Hos 11:11);[39] **2:18[20]**>/<Lev 26:5, 6, lie down in security amid tamed beasts and warfare abolished; **3:5**>/<2 Sam 7; Amos 9:11–12, return of David (many possible allusions pivot on whether this is part of the apparent "Judah" update elements of Hosea); **4:2**>/<Exod 20:13, 14, 15//Deut 5:17, 18, 19, murder, stealing, adultery with verbal parallel to three of the Ten Commandments, and swearing and lying likely alluding to two more; **4:14**>/<Lev 19:29, men responsible concerning prostituting daughters; **6:8; 12:11[12]**>/<2 Kgs 15:25, possible allusion to conspirators of Gilead; **8:13; 9:3; 11:5**>/<Num 14:3, 4; cf. Deut 17:16; 28:68, return to Egypt; **12:12[13]**>/<Gen 29:1–30, Jacob in Aram; **12:13[14]**>/<Deut 18:15, 18; cf. 34:10, by a prophet Yahweh brought Israel up from Egypt; **13:5 LXX**>/<Deut 8:2, "I *tended* (ποιμαίνω = רְעִיתִיךָ) to you in the wilderness" but MT "I knew you in the wilderness" (MT preferred).[40]

Shared Stock Phrases and Other Similarities

Torah-like stock phrases: >/<3:1; Deut 31:18, "turn to other gods" (פנים אל אלהים אחרים);[41] >/<5:11; Deut 28:33, "oppressed and crushed"; >/<12:7[8]; Amos 8:5; Prov 11:1; 20:23, "dishonest scales" (מֹאזְנֵי מִרְמָה) (cf. righteous scales in Lev 19:36; wicked scales in Mic 6:11); >/<13:4; Deut 5:7, you will know none except me/no other gods before me.[42]

---

38. See Rooker, "Use of OT Hosea," 56.

39. On Hosea's use of "brought up" (עלה) versus "brought out" (יצא) in Deuteronomy, as polemic against the calf at Bethel because Jeroboam said "brought you up" (1 Kgs 12:28), see Hwang, "'I Am,'" 249.

40. Though many modern committee translations follow Hos 13:5 LXX, Gelston suggests the shepherding imagery is a Septuagintal translational innovation (*BHQ*, 71*).

41. The phrase "other gods" (אלהים אחרים) is very common in Deuteronomy and the Former Prophets (Even-Shoshan, 40).

42. Though the wording is different, some suggest similarity between Hos 13:4 and the first commandment (Tucker "Law," 210; Cassuto, *Biblical*, 1:91–92; Cassuto says xiii 14 [*sic*] but he means 13:4 as his citations demonstrate).

Similes: >/<7:16; Ps 78:57, "like a faulty bow" (בקשת רמיה); >/<9:10; Isa 28:4; Mic 7:1; Jer 24:2, like figs ripe before harvest; >/<14:6[7]; Ps 52:8[10]; Job 15:33, "like an olive tree."

Hosea's Non-Exegetical Use of Hosea

Literary thematic connections involving names: >/<1:3; 3:1, Gomer daughter of Two Figs and raisin cakes (cf. Isa 16:7; Jer 7:18; 44:19); >/<1:4, 6, 9; 2:22, 23[24, 25], divine sowing, Jezreel/God Sows, divine pity on Lo-Ruhamah/No Pity, and divine claiming "You are my people" to Lo-Ammi/Not My People; >/<4:15; 5:8; 9:15; indictment against Gilgal, Beth Aven/Bethel (cf. Amos 4:4; 5:5); >/<8:5–6; 10:5, 8, calf of Beth Aven/House-of-Iniquity (ridiculing Bethel) (cf. 1 Kgs 13:1–3; Amos 3:14; 5:5; 9:1); >/<4:16; 10:11–13, Ephraim as heifer (cf. 10:5).

Selected notable running themes:[43] >/<4:1, 4; 12:2[3], legal dispute, controversy (ריב) (cf. Jer 2:9; Mic 4:3); >/<4:1, 6; 8:2; knowledge/no knowledge; >/<2:7[9]; 3:5; 5:4, 15; 6:1, 11; 7:10, 16; 12:6[7]; 14:2, 4, 7[3, 5, 8], return (שוב) (ironically, 8:13; 9:3; 11:5); >/<4:7; 9:11; 10:5, their glory; >/<8:7–9; 12:1, kinship with Assyria like the wind (cf. 2 Kgs 15:19–20; 16:7–9; 17:3; Hos 7:11); >/<6:1–3; 11:9–11; 14:1–9[2–10], invitations to return.

The **doublet** in the A line of 5:5//7:10—"Israel's arrogance testifies against him"—connects with different functions of their B lines.

Parallels within the Book of the Twelve

Deciding the issue of the twelve prophets as "one book" (i.e., the Book of the Twelve) versus "twelve books" falls outside the present study. Still, the ways this debate relates to the scriptural use of Scripture need to be registered, if only briefly. The present study treats most cases of parallels within books as literary rather than exegetical. The unresolved status of the twelve prophets raises several questions regarding how to handle the same kinds of phenomena in it(them). A few examples can help make the concerns concrete.

First, those who regard the twelve prophets as a single book consider the interrelations between them as intentionally unifying.[44] The shared elements in Hosea and Malachi function to frame the entire "book." The important running themes of how marital "love" can connote aspects of Yahweh's relationship with Israel in Hosea and Yahweh's covenantal "love" for Jacob and "hate" of Esau can be regarded as offering a sense of relationship in the Twelve Prophets.

Other theological themes like the day of Yahweh running through many of the Twelve Prophets may share more of an intentional relationship.[45] These kinds of connections may

---

43. The list here comes from research for this project. For another longer list of characteristic language, expressions, and phrases of Hosea, see Harper, *Amos and Hosea*, clxxii–clxxiii.

44. Nogalski discusses how quotations, allusions, catchwords, shared themes and motifs, and framing devices unify the twelve prophets ("Intertextuality," 102–24).

45. See Rendtorf, "How to Read," 75–87; Nogalski, "The Day(s) of YHWH," 192–213.

help contribute to the coherence of the Twelve Prophets, but they operate more like variations on stock phrases and common prophetic traditions and not as interpretive allusions.

Other, less pervasive parallels need to be considered individually. For example, should "silent" before Yahweh in Hab 2:20, Zeph 1:7, and Zech 2:13[17] be regarded as literary connections to conjoin the Twelve Prophets or as variations developing prophetic traditions more generally?

Many suggest Joel 3:16 shares part of Amos 1:4 to "link" these adjacent prophetic collections in the Book of the Twelve (emphasis signifies verbal parallel):[46]

> *Yahweh will roar from Zion and thunder from Jerusalem*; the earth and the heavens will tremble. But Yahweh will be a refuge for his people, a stronghold for the people of Israel. (Joel 3:16[4:16])

> He said: "*Yahweh roars from Zion and thunders from Jerusalem*; the pastures of the shepherds dry up, and the top of Carmel withers." (Amos 1:2)

Even if the connecting function within the Book of the Twelve is true, the parallel does more than this. Overemphasizing the conjoining function somewhat obscures the interpretive blend of Amos 1:2 and Obad 17 within Joel 3:16–17[4:16–17] (see note ad loc.). In addition, the function of Carmel in Amos 1:2 and 9:3 relates to a dynamic within Amos. This evidence within Joel and within Amos suggests that a "connection" between them functions more like catchphrase juxtaposition than literary development.

In individual contexts, Amos 9:12 and Obad 21 appear to be getting at two different things, but they are in adjacent prophets of the Book of the Twelve (italics signify broad similarity):

> "In that day I will restore David's fallen shelter—I will repair its broken walls and restore its ruins—and will rebuild it as it used to be, *so that they may possess the remnant of Edom* and all the nations that bear my name," declares Yahweh, who will do these things. (Amos 9:11–12)

> Deliverers will go up on Mount Zion *to govern the mountains of Esau*. And the kingdom will be Yahweh's. (Obad 21)

Does the proximity of Amos and Obadiah create a relationship between these different ideas—whether the connecting part derives from placement or editorial intervention of the collection? If so, it would relate to themes within the Book of the Twelve but not exegetical development.

46. See Nogalski, "Joel as 'Literary Anchor,'" 99–100. Also see Eng, "Semitic Catchwords," 256–58.

Second, what does it mean for the use of Scripture in situations where an outside Scripture also shares a common element of two or more prophets within the Book of the Twelve? The case of plowshares and pruninghooks in Isa 2:4, Mic 4:3, and Joel 3:10[4:10] raises this issue. The evidence favors Micah using Isaiah or developing a common tradition and Joel using Micah (see notes ad loc.). How can Joel 3:10 be treated like a literary development within the Book of the Twelve if Mic 4:3 and Joel 3:10[4:10] exegetically advance a scriptural tradition in Isa 2?

Exegetical allusions to the attribute formula of Exod 34:6–7 may serve dual functions by connecting the prophecies in the Book of the Twelve while also advancing a scriptural teaching (Joel 2:12–14, 18; Jonah 3:9; 4:2; Nah 1:3; cf. Mic 7:18–19). In this case the possible connecting relations within the Book of the Twelve may coexist with the interpretive allusions without materially affecting the exegetical outcomes in any individual uses of scriptural traditions.

Third, if the Book of the Twelve is a unified and coherent scroll, how do the twelve prophetic headings shift its(their) function(s) relative to the use of Scripture? House says that "Obadiah 10–14 describes Jonah's attitude perfectly."[47] When House makes this point, he is not saying that "You should not gloat over your brother in the day of his misfortune" in Obad 12 offers exegetical allusion to Jonah or vice versa. Instead, if I understand correctly, House observes the kinds of thematic and literary comparisons that naturally come up when investigating elements within any "book."

The three kinds of examples above can be multiplied. But they all get at the same basic issue of the kind of unity and coherence operating within the Book of the Twelve.

Catchphrases and other connectors created by placing the prophets together in the single scroll of the Book of the Twelve produce something more like a constellation than a network. A constellation of stars does not speak to any actual internal relationship between stellar lights. A constellation of stars refers to a relationship between stars imposed upon them from the viewing vantage point of the earth. There is nothing wrong with this. Many interpretive constellations appear in Scripture, such as the five "praise Yah" psalms at the end of the Psalter and the catchword constellation in Rom 9:25–29. Networks of interrelated Scriptures speak to author-intended connections within scriptural contexts themselves, while constellations speak to relationships imposed from outside (see Constellation in Glossary).

In sum, treating the Twelve Prophets as a single book raises several yet-to-be-solved issues that intersect with the scriptural use of Scripture among them. All of these relate to the relative unifying force of the Twelve Prophets within one scroll. The nature of the unity within the Book of the Twelve may be thought of as more like a constellation. If it is a book, it is a different kind of book.

---

47. House, *Unity*, 83.

Chapter 14

JOEL

SYMBOLS[1]

// verbal parallels (A level)
/~/ synoptic parallel (A level)
~ B, probable interpretive allusion; C, possible; D, probably not
\+ interpretive blend
>/< more or less similar (see Filters)
* part of interpretive network (see Networks)

USE OF SCRIPTURE IN JOEL[2]

2:13–14*//Jonah 4:2* (attribute formula) (* see attribute formula network)
2:28–29[3:1–2]~Ezek 39:29 (B) (pour out my spirit)
2:32[3:5]~Obad 17 (B) (those who escape)
3:10[4:10]~Isa 2:4//Mic 4:3 (B) (plowshares into swords)
3:16, 17[4:16, 17]~Amos 1:2+Obad 17 (B) (Yahweh roars from Zion)

OLD TESTAMENT USE OF JOEL

n/a

NEW TESTAMENT USE OF JOEL

1:6~Rev 9:7–8 (locust like lion's teeth)
2:4~Rev 9:7 (locust like horses)
2:11~Rev 6:17 (Who can endure his judgment?)
2:28–32[3:1–5] LXX//Acts 2:17–21 (pouring out of the spirit)
2:31[3:4]~Mark 13:24//Matt 24:29 (cf. Isa 13:10); Rev 6:12 (contrary celestial light events)
2:32[3:5]//Rom 10:13 (all who call upon the name shall be saved)

HERMENEUTICAL PROFILE OF THE USE OF SCRIPTURE IN JOEL

Exegetical Conventions in Joel

Joel features many verbal parallels with other prophets. Among the prophets who often make use of common prophetic traditions, Joel and Zechariah stand out as the most pronounced. While most of these parallels can be found in the Filters, the present discussion focuses on the handful of exegetical allusions.

1. For explanation of symbols, see Symbols and Abbreviations and Introduction. For other help, see Glossary.
2. See Bibliographic Note on Lists of Potential Parallels.

The present study focuses exclusively on the scriptural use of Scripture. In several cases Joel's contexts with verbal parallels to other prophets include interpretive interventions with the evidence necessary to surmise direction of dependence. The cases with the necessary evidence each suggest Joel as receptor and the parallel counterparts as donor contexts. If these interpretive allusions support direction of dependence, even in most cases, it does not translate to dating Joel. This evidence merely signals the relative sequence of Joel and several donor contexts. The important issue for this study relates to how Joel uses scriptural traditions and what this contributes to progressive revelation.

Joel provides little in the way of interacting with legal or narrative traditions of Torah. Even in the few cases in which Joel refers to elements that may come from Torah, like Eden or locusts, they have typically been mediated through prophetic use of these traditions. Joel exhibits extensive interaction with the prophetic traditions of Israel. Joel is a prophet's prophet.

Joel also features substantial internal cross-referencing. Many have noted the reversals in Joel, Zephaniah, and elsewhere in the prophets. But Joel also often reuses verbal parallels, only one time each, for reasons other than reversal. Marcus calls these repetitions "nonrecurring doublets."[3] Joel's nonrecurring doublets do not work on analogy to doublets in Jeremiah (see Jeremiah Filters). Joel reuses elements of Joel as a basic part of his literary-theological strategy. The doublets are so pervasive and predictable that they seem to indicate an intentional multifunctional device. Marcus emphasizes how the nonrecurring doublets help with certain text-critical and diachronic challenges. The present study makes use of Joel's tendency toward doublets to assist with evaluating his use of other prophetic traditions. For more on Joel's nonrecurring doublets see Filters.

Implications of Scriptural Exegesis in Joel

Joel's exegetical use of the prophets offers modest but important insight into the scriptural use of Scripture. The nature of Joel's prophetic allusion-happy tendencies suggests deducing measured conclusions. Even with much caution, Joel offers helpful gains for direction of dependence and prophetic authority.

Interpreting the potential directions of dependence of the parallel contexts based on external historical reference points proves difficult. The superscription of Joel does not situate his ministry to a time period. As such Joel has been assigned to wildly different dates by his interpreters. Joel's several references to the temple suggest he writes before the destruction of Solomon's temple or during the Second Temple period (see Joel 1:9, 14, 16; 2:17; 3:18[4:18]).[4] But this hardly narrows things down. The sharply contested dating of Joel naturally invites competing views of direction of dependence from one commentator to the next based on decisions external to the interpretive interventions themselves.

---

3. See Marcus, "Nonrecurring Doublets," 59–67.

4. Assis, "Date," 165.

The internal evidence of Joel's use of scriptural traditions offers help. Five interpretive interventions in Joel provide the evidence necessary to deduce direction of dependence. Joel appears to use Isaiah or Micah, the ending of the Gog oracles in Ezekiel, Amos, Obadiah, and Jonah.[5] Allowing for a margin of error still suggests helpful perspective on the prophets' use of the prophets more generally. The nature of Joel's use of the prophets seems to work at the level of prophets as written scrolls. Study of the prophets seems to be part of Joel's prophetic ministry.

Joel explicitly ascribes and implicitly signals the authoritative place of the prophets. Joel's quasi-citation formula for one of his uses of Obadiah provides the most substantial example (see note on Joel 2:32[3:5]). Joel deduces theological inferences from Jonah's use of Torah. Since the evidence supports Joel working from Jonah, whether or not he consulted traditions appearing in Exodus, points to the authority of exegetical interventions in Jonah. The authoritative function of Jonah seems even more striking because the exegetical advances are not housed in prophetic oracles but narrative and embedded discourses—even of an unnamed Ninevite ruler.

The evidence of authoritative prophetic interpretation of Torah embodies a significant step in the incremental advancement of divine revelation. The authoritative function of the prophets in Joel helps explain the decisive role of prophets and other Hebrew Scriptures, in addition to Torah, in the New Testament.

USE OF SCRIPTURE

2:13–14*//Jonah 4:2* (attribute formula) (* see attribute formula network). The citation of the attribute formula from Exod 34:6 and related allusions in Jonah 4:2 offer the evidence necessary to suggest Exodus as donor context to Jonah which in turn stands as donor context to Joel. Whereas the allusion in Jonah 4:2 inverts elements of the citation in line with Seidel's theory, Joel follows Jonah (see Table Joel1). The evidence of relationship between the three contexts is very strong and the kind of interpretive intervention that provides evidence of probable direction of dependence as explained below and in more detail in the note on Jonah 4:2.

TABLE JOEL1: DIVINE ATTRIBUTE FORMULA IN SCRIPTURE‡

Exod 34:6	a God	compassionate	and gracious	slow to anger	and abounding in covenantal fidelity	and faithfulness
Num 14:18				Yahweh is slow to anger	and abounding in covenantal fidelity	

(cont.)

5. See notes on Joel 2:13–14; 2:28–29, 32[2:1–2, 5]; 3:10[4:10], and 3:16, 17[4:16–17].

Joel 2:13		for gracious	and compassionate is he		slow to anger	and abounding in covenantal fidelity	
Jonah 4:2	a God	gracious	and compassionate		slow to anger	and abounding in covenantal fidelity	
Ps 86:15	a God		compassionate	and gracious	slow to anger	and abounding in covenantal fidelity	and faithfulness
Ps 103:8			compassionate	and gracious is Yahweh	slow to anger	and abounding in covenantal fidelity	
Ps 145:8		gracious	and compassionate is Yahweh		slow to anger	and great in covenantal fidelity	
Neh 9:17		gracious	and compassionate		slow to anger	and abounding in covenantal fidelity	

‡ Table based on research for this project. Information in table has been compared with Bendavid, *Parallels*, 182–83 [Hebrew]; also see Duggan, *Covenant Renewal*, 211, nn. 95, 96. For a different more detailed diagram see Kelly, "Joel, Jonah," 807. For a list of scriptural echoes of the attribute formula in addition to the interpretive network, see note with attribute formula network.

Although the attribute formula functions as a veritable stock formula of lyrical diffusion, the elements unique to the versions in Jonah and Joel make a relationship probable (emphases signify verbal parallels):

> [Moses said] "*Turn from your fierce anger and relent* concerning the destructions upon your people. . . ." And he passed in front of Moses, proclaiming, "Yahweh, Yahweh, the compassionate and gracious God, slow to anger, abounding in love and faithfulness." (Exod 32:12b lit; 34:6)
>
> [The king of Nineveh proclaimed] "**Who knows?** God *may turn and relent from his fierce anger* so that we will not perish. . . ." He [Jonah] prayed to Yahweh, "Isn't this what I said, Yahweh, when I was still at home? That is what I tried to forestall by fleeing to Tarshish. I knew that you are a gracious and compassionate God, slow to anger and abounding in love, **who relents from sending calamity.**" (Jonah 3:9; 4:2†)
>
> Yahweh thunders at the head of his army; his forces are beyond number, and mighty is the army that obeys his command. The day of Yahweh is great; it is dreadful. Who can endure it? [12] "Even now," declares Yahweh, "return to me with all your heart, with fasting and weeping and mourning." [13] Rend your heart and not your garments. Return to Yahweh your God, for he is gracious and compassionate, slow to anger and abounding in love, **who relents from sending calamity.** [14] **Who knows?** He *may turn and relent* and leave behind a blessing—grain offerings and drink offerings for Yahweh your God. (Joel 2:11–14†)

The exact phrase "and relents from sending calamity" (וְנִחָם עַל־הָרָעָה) appears only in Joel 2:13 and Jonah 4:2, with both cases qualifying the attribute formula.[6] In addition, the hopeful question on the lips of the king of Nineveh "Who knows?" also appears in Joel (Jonah 3:9; Joel 2:14). These verbal parallels support an intentional relationship between these two prophetic contexts. But Joel lacks "from your/his fierce anger" (מֵחֲרוֹן אַפְּךָ/אַפּוֹ), which points to Jonah as borrowing from Exodus (Exod 32:12; Jonah 3:9). In sum, the interpretive interventions provide the evidence necessary to triangulate and deduce the likely direction of dependence between all three.[7]

If Jonah mediates the attribute formula, then Joel does not work directly from the "more exclusive context of Israel" in the covenant renewal at the mountain.[8] The hopeful question—"Who knows?"—of the king of Nineveh invites Joel to turn the attribute formula around again for the doomed of Zion. If Nineveh could repent and turn away Yahweh's wrath, so too Joel's audience has hope. The use of lesser to greater logic appears elsewhere in scriptural exegesis (see notes on Lev 19:18b; Deut 22:1–4). Joel's allusion simultaneously affirms the validity of the exegetical advancement in Jonah—the attribute formula offers opportunity for anyone to repent, even Nineveh—and its offer of enduring hope for the people of Jerusalem to seek mercy in their time of peril. Joel advances further by proclaiming the attribute formula to his doomed audience as part of a call to return to Yahweh. For Joel, the prophetic word, like Jonah's to Nineveh, activates potential for repentance.[9]

Joel's language of "rend your heart not your garments" accents the need for interior realities of humility akin to heart circumcision (Joel 2:13; cf. Lev 26:40; Deut 10:16; Jer 4:4). The sense seems to imply an extra word "rend your hearts and not *only* your garments."[10] Heart rending does not replace acts of remorse. Joel emphasizes that fasting and weeping can symbolize interior realities (Joel 2:12, 13).

2:28–29[3:1–2]~Ezek 39:29 (B) (pour out my spirit).

2:32[3:5]~Obad 17 (B) (those who escape). The shared language in Joel 2:28–29, 32[3:1–2, 5] needs to be taken together since it stands as part of a related message. The integrity of this context enjoys strong support from the presence of seven nonrecurring doublets.[11]

The unusual positive use of the term "pour out" (שׁפך), relative to the twice-used phrase "pour out my spirit," makes a relationship between Ezek 39:29 and Joel 2:28, 29 probable; typically the term is used of judgment with Yahweh as subject (see list of

6. See Gray, "Parallel Passages," 217; Driver, *Joel and Amos*, 23; Lane, "Exodus 34:6–7," 108, n. 55.

7. These deductions are based on Kelly, "Joel, Jonah," 813–14. See note on Jonah 4:2 for other references.

8. Contra Dozeman, "Inner-Biblical Interpretation," 222. Dozeman reads both Joel 2 and Jonah 3–4 each directly against Exod 32–34 in what he calls a "mutual relationship" (222–23).

9. See Wolff, *Joel and Amos*, 49–50.

10. Ibid., 49, emphasis original.

11. See shared locutions in Joel 2:27//3:17[4:17]; 2:28[3:1]//2:29[3:2]; 2:28[3:1]//3:8[4:8]; 2:29[3:2]//3:1[4:1]; 2:30[3:3]//3:16[4:16]; 3:2[4:2]//3:12[4:12]; and 3:4[4:4]//3:7[4:7] (Marcus, "Nonrecurring Doublets," 67). The function of nonrecurring doublets is explained in Filters with examples.

references in footnote of note on Ezek 39:29). If either Ezekiel or Joel coined this surprising phrase, it may be based on "I will pour (יצק) my Spirit upon your descendants" (Isa 44:3) with a more conventional verb. The only other positive use of "pour out [שפך] . . . a spirit of grace and supplication" (Zech 12:10) may be based on these parallels. Tooman wonders if Moses's desire for widespread giving of the spirit of prophecy suggested Joel's framing of his expectation (bold signifies verbal parallels likely due to allusion, and broken underlining signifies parallels at the level of shared roots):[12]

> But Moses replied, "Are you jealous for my sake? I wish that all Yahweh's people were prophets and that Yahweh would put his Spirit on them!" (Num 11:29)

> I will no longer hide my face from them, for **I will pour out my Spirit** on the people of Israel, declares Sovereign Yahweh. (Ezek 39:29)

> And afterward, **I will pour out my Spirit** on all people. Your sons and daughters will prophesy, your old men will dream dreams, your young men will see visions. Even on my servants, both men and women, **I will pour out my Spirit** in those days. (Joel 2:28–29[3:1–2])

The association of the giving of the Spirit to initial widespread prophesying in Num 11:29 and Joel 2:28–29[3:1–2], though suggestive, does not provide adequate evidence to determine an intentional relationship or direction of dependence. The parallel between pouring out my Spirit in Ezekiel and Joel relates to parallels between Joel and Obadiah that need to be introduced before making judgment.

Joel shares verbal parallels with Obad 17 in two places. The twofold set of parallels increases the likelihood of intentionality (italics and bold signify verbal parallels, and broken underlining signifies quasi-marking):

> But *on Mount **Zion** will be deliverance*; it **will be holy**, and Jacob will possess his inheritance. (Obad 17)

> And everyone who calls on the name of Yahweh will be saved; for *on Mount **Zion*** and in Jerusalem *there will be deliverance*, as Yahweh has said, even among the survivors whom Yahweh calls. (Joel 2:32[3:5])

> Then you will know that I, Yahweh your God, dwell in **Zion**, my holy hill. Jerusalem **will be holy**; never again will foreigners invade her. (3:17[4:17])

12. See Tooman, "Transformation," 79, n. 64. Tooman argues for Ezekiel's dependence on Joel, but see Schultz's criticism of Tooman's approach ("Isaianic Intertextuality," 39–40; also see Hossfeld, "Gog Oracles," 194–95; Strine, "Compositional," 595–60).

The shared language of Obad 17 and Joel 3:17[4:17] will be taken up in the note on Joel 3:16, 17[4:16, 17]. The point at hand relates to the similarity between Joel's parallels with Ezek 39:29 and Obad 17. Ezekiel speaks of pouring out the Spirit upon *Israel* and Obadiah looks to deliverance for *Jacob* (Ezek 39:29; Obad 17). Joel refers to pouring out the Spirit upon "*all flesh*" and deliverance on Zion for "*all* who call upon the name of Yahweh" (Joel 2:28, 32[3:1, 5], emphases mine). The parallel universalizing interpretive interventions make it much more likely that Ezekiel and Obadiah are donor contexts and Joel the receptor. In addition, the parallel with Obad 17 is quasi-marked (Joel 2:32[3:5]). The exact phrase "as he has said" (כַּאֲשֶׁר אָמַר) appears seven times in narratives to refer back to something said earlier.[13] Joel's use of this oral-citation formula suggests a conscious use of the prophetic tradition.[14] These factors together all point to the likelihood of Joel as receptor context which, in turn, offers insight into Joel's interpretive agenda.

Joel 2:32[3:5] uses the reciprocal "call upon the name of Yahweh" and "whom Yahweh calls." The former only appears three times of salvation and the latter appears frequently in the new exodus section of Isaiah.[15] In this way Joel affirms both the faith dimension of those whom Yahweh delivers and Yahweh's election upon the remnant of his day of wrath. Joel's inclusive view of the divine works of prophecy and deliverance does not stand against but with Yahweh's sustained fidelity to Jerusalem. Joel envisions Yahweh's eschatological acts of mercy for all of those who call upon his name from among all people.[16] This interpretive expansion broadens the constituency that looks to Jerusalem as a symbol of Yahweh's faithful salvation.

Elsewhere Joel sees in the king of Nineveh's hopeful question "Who knows?" room for Joel's own constituency to seek mercy by repentance (see note on Joel 2:13–14). In the present context Joel applies the same reciprocal logic in the other direction. For Joel, Yahweh's fidelity to Jerusalem undergirds expectation for the spirit of prophecy to all flesh and salvation to all who call upon the name of Yahweh (2:28–29, 32[3:1–2, 32]).

3:10[4:10]~Isa 2:4//Mic 4:3 (B) (plowshares into swords). Joel 3:10[4:10] shares verbal parallels with the well-known imagery of peace by beating swords into plowshares from Isaiah and Micah (see notes on Isa 2:1–5; Mic 4:1–5). The shared imagery is reversed (emphases signify verbal parallels):

> They *will beat* their *swords into plowshares* **and** their spears [חֲנִית] **into pruning hooks.** (Isa 2:4//Mic 4:3)

13. See Gen 21:1; 41:54; 43:17; Exod 17:10; Num 23:30; Josh 11:9; 2 Kgs 8:19.

14. See Wolff, *Joel and Amos*, 68; Driver, *Joel and Amos*, 23. For other reasons for seeing Ezek 39:29 as donor and Joel 2:28–29[3:1–2] as receptor text, see Strine, "Compositional," 596.

15. The collocation "to call upon the name of Yahweh" for salvation appears in Joel 2:32[3:5]; Zeph 3:9; Ps 116:4; cf. ancients in worship, Gen 4:26; 12:8; 13:4; 21:33; 26:25 (see Even-Shoshan, 1026–28, nos. 9, 24, 257, 303, 366, 367, 369, 373). Yahweh is subject of the verb "call" frequently in the new exodus section of Isaiah, see Isa 41:9; 42:6; 45:3, 4; 49:1; 51:2; 54:6 ("קרא," A.3.a, A.4 *HALOT* 2:1129).

16. On potentially universal salvation limited to Yahweh worshipers, see Strazicich, *Joel's Use of Scripture*, 209.

> *Beat* your *plowshares into swords* **and** your **pruning hooks** into spears [רְמָח]. Let the weakling say, "I am strong!" (Joel 3:10[4:10])

Typically, reversals like this could go either way. Though many interpreters suggest Joel reversed the imagery, the opposite logic works equally well.[17] The alternative term for "spear" (רְמָח), however, is a quasi-Aramaism appearing in two older contexts with northern affinities (Judg 5:8; 1 Kgs 18:28), but otherwise only in Num 25:7 or in numerous exilic and postexilic contexts.[18] This evidence suggests Joel updated the language he borrowed and reversed the terms.

By evoking and reversing olden prophetic symbols of peace, Joel heightens the sense of an international pilgrimage to make war against Zion.[19] Joel voices Yahweh's invitation to come up to the valley of Jehoshaphat, a name meaning "Yahweh judges," where he will judge the nations (Joel 3:12[4:12]). Then with tremendous irony relative to the beating of swords into plowshares, Yahweh commands his harvesters to reap the armies with a sickle and tread them in wine presses (3:13[4:13]).

3:16, 17[4:16, 17]~Amos 1:2+Obad 17 (B) (Yahweh roars from Zion). Joel's nonrecurring doublets include the recognition formulas in Joel 2:27 and 3:17[4:17].[20] In the former case the shame-ending blessings lead to recognition: "Then you will know that I am in Israel, that I am Yahweh your God, and that there is no other; never again will my people be shamed" (Joel 2:27, broken underlining marks locutions shared with 3:17[4:17]). In the context under consideration the recognition of formula relates to two poetical allusions.

The shared use of "Yahweh roars from Zion" near the end of Joel and beginning of Amos serves as one of the connecting catchphrases in the Book of the Twelve (see discussion at end of Hosea Filters). The A line of Amos 1:2 relates to the eighth and ninth of the prophet's series of nine rhetorical questions elsewhere: "*The lion has roared*—who will not fear? *Sovereign Yahweh has spoken*—who can but prophesy?" (Amos 3:8, emphasis mine). Amos's climactic point of the series pivots on the "irresistible" need to prophesy in 3:8.[21] The B line of Amos 1:2 refers to Mount Carmel, which elsewhere functions as a symbol of a remote locale: "Though they hide themselves *on the top of Carmel*, there I will hunt them down and seize them. Though they hide from my eyes *at the bottom of the sea*, there I will command the serpent to bite them" (9:3, emphasis mine). Joel pairs the same A line as Amos 1:2 but with a very different B line.

Elsewhere Joel uses a different phrase from Obad 17 as a quasi-marked citation. The citation formula, along with other evidence, suggests Obadiah as donor and Joel as receptor context (see note on Joel 2:32[3:5]). The short verbal parallel with a different part of

---

17. See Schultz, "Isaianic Intertextuality," 37.

18. See Driver, *Joel and Amos*, 22, 73; "רְמָח," BDB 942; "רְמָח," *HALOT* 2:1243; also see Jer 46:4; Ezek. 39:9; 2 Chr 11:12; 14:8[7]; 25:5; 26:14; Neh 4:13, 16, 21[7, 10, 15].

19. On the mocking polemic, see Strazicich, *Joel's Use of Scripture*, 234, with a largely excavative agenda.

20. See Marcus, "Nonrecurring Doublets," 67; also see discussion in Filters.

21. See Paul, *Amos*, 105, 113.

the same context likewise suggests Joel as receptor context here (italics and bold signify verbal parallels, and broken underlining signifies the recognition formula shared with Joel 2:27):

> He said: "*Yahweh roars from Zion and thunders from Jerusalem*; the pastures of the shepherds dry up, and the top of Carmel withers." (Amos 1:2)

> But on Mount **Zion** will be deliverance; it **will be holy**, and Jacob will possess his inheritance. (Obad 17)

> *Yahweh will roar from Zion and thunder from Jerusalem*; the earth and the heavens will tremble. But Yahweh will be a refuge for his people, a stronghold for the people of Israel. "Then you will know that I, Yahweh your God, dwell in **Zion**, my holy hill. Jerusalem **will be holy**; never again will foreigners invade her." (Joel 3:16–17[4:16–17])

In contrast to Amos, Joel uses the imagery of Yahweh's roaring to cause cosmic repercussions. The nonrecurring doublet "the heavens tremble" first appears in Joel 2:10 when locusts come against Judah with Yahweh thundering at the head of the host (2:11) and, in the present context, with Yahweh thundering when the enemy attacks (3:16[4:16]).[22] Whereas Amos uses Yahweh's roar to signal his fear-inspiring word against rebels, Joel repurposes the imagery to give confidence to Israel, who seeks refuge in Yahweh (Amos 1:2; Joel 3:16[4:16]).

Joel's interpretive allusion that Jerusalem "will be holy" extends beyond Zion as a place for Jacob to find safety in Obad 17. Joel goes on to say, "strangers will no longer pass through it" (Joel 3:17[4:17] lit. cf. NIV above). Translations may make this interpretive advancement seem at odds with the inclusive perspective of the spirit of prophecy upon "all flesh" and Jerusalem as sanctuary for "everyone who calls upon the name of Yahweh" (see notes on 2:28–29, 32[3:1–2, 5]). However, the term "stranger" (זָר) plays off the restriction of Jerusalem as "holy" (3:17[4:17]). The burden of inner-temple holiness is restricted to priests. In that context ordinary Israelites are referred to as "strangers" (זָר): "*The lay person* [זָר] shall not eat of anything holy" (Lev 22:10 lit.). The term "stranger" (זָר) has a relative function in the incremental "holiness" of laity, Levite, priest, and high priest. The closer to Yahweh's holy dwelling, the more persons become "strangers" (see Num 18:4, 7; Figure Ezk7). Joel takes advantage of Jerusalem as holy to speak of the exclusion of strangers, something akin to what Isaiah does (see note on Isa 52:1). Yahweh appropriates all of Jerusalem, making it holy, which simultaneously makes the city a safe haven for his covenantal people.[23]

---

22. See Marcus, "Nonrecurring Doublets," 62; and see Filters.
23. See Wolff, *Joel and Amos*, 82.

In sum, Joel 3:16–17[4:16–17] makes interpretive allusions to Amos 1:2 and Obad 17 to spell out the eschatological hope of Israel. Yahweh's roar signifies safe sanctuary in Zion. Jerusalem shall be made holy to the exclusion of religious outsiders.

FILTERS

Joel includes many verbal parallels with other prophets. Longer lists of verbal and thematic parallels between Joel and Scripture can be found in other studies. The majority of these other lists promote competing excavative theories.[24] The following lists are not comprehensive or complete. They provide representative non-exegetical locutions of Joel shared by other Scriptures.

Shared Stock Phrases and Other Similarities

Shared elements between Joel and other Scriptures often do not include an exegetical dimension:[25] **1:3**>/<Ps 78:3–4, telling from generation to generation—"They recount to your children/to us . . . to their children . . . to another generation" (ספרו לבניכם/ספרו לנו . . . לבניהם . . . לדור אחר/אחרון); **1:12**>/<Hag 2:19, languishing of "vine, fig tree, and pomegranate" (רמון, תאנה, גפן); **1:15**>/<Isa 13:6, "for the day of Yahweh is near; it will come like destruction from the Almighty" (כי קרוב יום יהוה [ו]כשד משדי יבוא) (not against Babylon or Egypt but Jerusalem) (cf. Ezek 30:2–3; Obad 15; Zeph 1:7); **2:1b, 2**>/<Zeph 1:14a, 15, "the day of Yahweh is coming, it is near/the great day of Yahweh is near . . . a day of darkness and gloom, a day of clouds and blackness" (בא יום יהוה כי קרוב/קרוב יום יהוה הגדול . . . יום חשך ואפלה יום ענן וערפל); **2:3**>/<Ezek 36:35, reversal of "like the garden of Eden" (כגן עדן) (cf. Isa 51:3); **2:6**>/<Nah 2:10[11], "every face turns pale" (כל פנים/פני כלם קבצו פארור); **2:10**>/<Isa 13:13+13:10, "earth shakes heavens tremble/heavens will shake and earth will shake" (רגזה ארץ רעמים שמים/שמים ארגיז ותרעש הארץ) (Seidel's theory) and cease to shine "sun, moon, stars" (כוכבים, ירח, שמש); 2:11>/<Mal 3:1; 4:5[3:23], "Great is the day of Yahweh and dreadful. . . . Who can endure it?/Who can endure? . . . the great and dreadful day of Yahweh" (גדול יום יהוה ונורא . . . מי כול/מי כול . . . יום יהוה הגדול והנורא); **2:17**>/<Ps 79:10; 115:2, "Why should they say among the peoples/the nations say, 'Where is their God?'" (למה יאמרו בעמים/הגוים איה אלהים) (cf. Mic 7:10; Ps 42:3, 10[4, 11]); **2:23b**>/<Isa 30:20b, "for he gives the teacher of righteousness to you/your teacher(s) will not be hidden any longer, but your eyes will

24. See Assis, "Date and Meaning," 166–67; Coggins, "Innerbiblical Quotations," 76–81; Driver, *Joel and Amos*, 19–22; Gray, "Parallel Passages," 214–25; Nogalski, *Redactional Processes*, 290–91; Redditt, "Book of Joel," 236; Strazicich, *Joel's Use of Scripture*, 59–252; Wolff, *Joel and Amos*, 10–11 (also see items on Entire OT in Bibliographic Note on Lists of Potential Parallels). These lists are uneven. Nogalski's long list of "allusions" are largely shared common terms or broadly similar imagery, most of which seem coincidental (for specific interaction with Nogaliski's list, see Coggins, "Innerbiblical Quotations," 76–78). For a short list of distinctive style within Joel, see Driver, *Joel and Amos*, 24.

25. Many of these examples come from Driver, *Joel and Amos*, 19–22; Gray, "Parallel Passages," 214–25; Wolff, *Joel and Amos*, 10–11.

see your teacher(s)" (כי נתן לכם את המורה לצדקה/ולא יכנף עוד מוריך והיו עיניך ראות את מוריך) (cf. Hos 10:12);[26] **3:1[4:1]**>/<Jer 33:15; 50:4, 20, "In those days and at that time" (בימים ההמה ובעת ההיא) (only in these contexts); **3:2[4:2]**>/<Ezek 38:22, "I shall enter into judgment with them there/by pestilence and bloodshed" (ונשפטתי עמם שם/אתו בדבר ובדם); **3:3[4:3]**>/<Obad 11; Nah 3:10, "for my people/Jerusalem/her nobles they cast lots" (ואל עמי/ועל ירושלם/ועל נכבדיה ידו גורל); **3:4[4:4]**>/<Obad 15, "I will return your deeds/your deeds will return upon your head" (אשיב גמלכם/גמלך ישוב בראשכם); **3:18[4:18]**>/<Amos 9:13, "mountains drip new wine" (נטף ההרים עסיס); **3:19[4:19]**>/<Ezek 29:12, "Egypt desolate" (מצרים שממה); **3:19[4:19]**>/<Obad 10, "because of violence done to people of Judah/to your brother" (מחמס בני יהודה/אחיך) (said to Edom).

Beyond verbal parallels, Joel's leading image of a locust plague also takes advantage of common imagery in Scripture and other ancient parallels: e.g., **1:4; 2:25**>/<Exod 10:12–25; Amos 4:9; Pss 78:46; 105:34–35, locust as agent of divine judgment; **1:6–7**>/<Judg 6:5; Isa 33:4; Nah 3:15–16, simile of locust for military actions.[27] The striking depiction of a fountain emanating from Yahweh's house shares similar imagery with eschatological visions of other prophets: **3:18[4:18]**>/<Ezek 47:1–12; Zech 14:8.

Nonrecurring Doublets

Nonrecurring doublets refer to identical or nearly identical phrases that occur only two times in Joel. Marcus explains three functions of the nonrecurring doublets: emphasizing complementary ideas, reversals, and connecting allusions.[28]

Emphasis: "elders . . . all who live in the land" (זקנים . . . כל ישבי הארץ) (1:2, 14); "call a holy fast, call a sacred assembly" (קדשו צום קראו עצרה) and "Blow the trumpet in Zion" (תקעו שופר בציון) (1:14; 2:1, 15); "Surely he/Yahweh has done great things" (כי הגדיל יהוה לעשות/כי הגדיל לעשות) (2:20, 21); "I will pour out my Spirit" (אשפוך את רוחי) (2:28, 29[3:1, 2]); "valley of decision" (בעמק החרוץ) (3:14[4:14] 2x); "to the valley of Jehoshaphat"—Marcus notes the pun on Jehoshaphat/Yahweh-judges (אל עמק יהושפט) (3:2, 12[4:2, 12]).

Reversal: "For the day of Yahweh is near" (כי קרוב יום יהוה) for Judah (1:15), for the nations (3:14[4:14]; cf. 2:1); "the day of Yahweh is coming" (בא יום יהוה) (2:1, 31[3:4]); "the heavens tremble" (רעשו שמים) when locusts come against Judah (2:10), when the nations attack (3:16[4:16]); "the day of Yahweh is great and dreadful/very dreadful" (גדול יום יהוה ונורא מאד/יום יהוה הגדול והנורא) against Israel (2:11), against the enemies of Israel (2:31[3:4]); "Yahweh thunders" (יהוה נתן קולו) against Israel (2:11), from Zion

26. See Rydelnik, "Teacher of Righteousness," 170–72.

27. For similarity between kinds of locust in a prayer on behalf of Sargon II (721–705) and Joel 1:4; 2:25, see Hurowitz, "Joel's Locust Plague," 597–603.

28. See Marcus, "Nonrecurring Doublets," 60. Marcus defines the phenomenon (59–60), explains three functions with illustrations (61–63), offers examples of how these help with text-critical and diachronic issues (64–65), and includes a list of forty-seven examples in Joel (66–67). The list and categorization here come from Marcus's work (61–63).

(3:16[4:16]); "the sun and moon are darkened, and the stars no longer shine" (שמש וירח קדרו וכוכבים אספו נגהם) when the day comes upon Israel (2:10), when the day comes upon the nations (3:15[4:15]); "Do not make your inheritance an object of scorn . . . among the nations/never again will I make you an object of scorn to the nations" (ואל תתן נחלתך לחרפה . . . בם גוים/לא אין אתכם עוד חרפה בגוים) as a prayer (2:17), as an answer (2:19).

Connections: "wearing sackcloth" (חגר שק) as a personified young widow (1:8), by priests (1:13); threshing floor/winepress "filled . . . the vats overflow/will overflow" (מלא . . . שוק יקב) after relief from locusts (2:24), of enemy ripe for harvest (3:13[4:13]).

One doublet is the recognition formula "then you will know that . . . I am Yahweh your God" (וִידַעְתֶּם כִּי . . . אֲנִי יהוה אֱלֹהֵיכֶם) that appears in Joel 2:27//3:17[4:17]. Regarding the first case, the exceedingly common recognition formula—"You shall know," "they shall know"—is only paired with "there is no other" in divine self-identification in Isa 45:5–6 and Joel 2:27. Variations on "I am Yahweh your God and there is no other" (Joel 2:27) appear in Isa 45:5, 6, 14, 18, 21, 22; 46:9.[29] Other reasons to think Joel may have had the context of Isa 45 in mind include the thematic relationships between "I will pour my Spirit upon your descendants" (Isa 44:3; cf. Joel 2:28, 29) and "you will not be put to shame . . . ever again" (Isa 45:17) with "and my people will not be put to shame ever again" (Joel 2:27).[30] The counterpart recognition formula appears in Joel 3:17[4:17] (see note ad loc.).

---

29. Wolff suggests the divine self-identification in Joel 2:27 is indebted to Isa 45:5, 6, 18, 22; 46:9 (*Joel and Amos*, 10). The phrase "they may know that I am Yahweh their God" occurs many times in Ezekiel (e.g., Ezek 6:7). See similar third-person phrases like "for Yahweh he is God, there is no other" (Deut 4:35, 39; 1 Kgs 8:60). For a comprehensive list of recognition formulas—using "know" (ידע) and "that I am Yahweh" (כי אני יהוה)—in Ezekiel and elsewhere in Scripture, including all manner of variations, see Evans, *You Shall Know*, 93–97, 119–26.

30. Compare: "you will not be put to shame . . . ever again" (לֹא תֵבֹשׁוּ . . . עַד עוֹלְמֵי עַד) (Isa 45:17) with "and my people will not be put to shame ever again" (וְלֹא־יֵבֹשׁוּ עַמִּי לְעוֹלָם) (Joel 2:27).

Chapter 15

AMOS

SYMBOLS[1]

//	verbal parallels (A level)	+	interpretive blend
/~/	synoptic parallel (A level)	>/<	more or less similar (see Filters)
~	B, probable interpretive allusion; C, possible; D, probably not	*	part of interpretive network (see Networks)

USE OF SCRIPTURE IN AMOS[2]

1:3–2:16~2 Sam 8:1–14*; 12:26–30 (C) (indictment against regional rivals) (* see Judah-king network)

2:7~Lev 18:7–8; 20:11 (C) (father and son with same female)

2:8~Exod 22:26*[25]; Deut 24:17 (C) (fornication on the cloak of the needy) (* see release statute network)

2:12~Num 6:2 (C) (frustrating Nazirites)

4:4~Deut 14:28; 26:12 (B) (taunt of sacrifice every morning and tithe every three days)

4:5~Lev 2:11 or 7:13 (B) (taunt of offering leavened/unleavened bread)

5:10, 12~Deut 16:18–19 (C) (satire of opposing justice at the gate)

9:11–12*~2 Sam 7:12*, 27 (B) (Davidic shelter restored) (* see branch, Davidic covenant, and place networks)

OLD TESTAMENT USE OF AMOS (SEE RESPECTIVE NOTES)

1:2~Jer 25:30 (C) (Yahweh roars)

1:2~Joel 3:16, 17[4:16, 17] (B) (Yahweh roars from Zion)

7:14~Zech 13:5 (B) (denying prophetic vocation)

8:2~Ezek 7:2, 3, 6 (C) (the end)

NEW TESTAMENT USE OF AMOS

5:25–27 LXX//Acts 7:42–43 (Sacrifices in wilderness?)

9:11, 12 LXX[3]//Acts 15:16–17 (David's fallen tent)

HERMENEUTICAL PROFILE OF THE USE OF SCRIPTURE IN AMOS

Amos contains many broad allusions to scriptural traditions but few exegetical interventions. The filters at the end of this chapter demonstrate the wide familiarity of the prophet and his constituency with many scriptural narrative and legal traditions.

1. For explanation of symbols, see Symbols and Abbreviations and Introduction. For other help, see Glossary.
2. See Bibliographic Note on Lists of Potential Parallels.
3. Though Acts 15:16–17 is something like Amos 9:11, 12 LXX, there are difficult textual issues.

Amos's exegetical use of scriptural traditions tends to be more indirect or allusive rather than based on lengthy quotations. Amos's exegetical advances relate to his view of the kingdom at the time of David and Solomon as a fixed standard. Amos seems to expect the neighboring rival nations to submit to Yahweh's will as though they were still client peoples under David and Solomon more than two hundred years earlier. Amos uses scriptural legal instructions as prophetic rhetorical weapons against his hapless constituents.

As many have noted, Amos's oracles against the nations and the expectation for a restored shelter of David share some common traits at the beginning and ending of the book. If Amos invented the literary form of oracles against the nations, he did so with an eye on regional rivals once allied with or client states under David and Solomon. Amos uses repetitious stereotypical language to condemn the regional rivals of Israel for crimes against humanity. When he gets to Judah and Israel, the prophet transitions to condemnation according to the standards of the covenant.

One of the clues to explain the authoritative basis for the oracles against the nations comes from Amos's reference to restoring the shelter of David "as in the days of old" (Amos 9:11). Amos speaks of taking possession of the remnant of Edom and all the nations that bear Yahweh's name (9:12). Comparing this ideal to the list of nations on the wrong end of the prophet's oracles in chs. 1–2 suggests Amos looks back to the peoples subjected to the throne in David's own regional empire. Amos does not spell this out so much as manifest his ideology by his use of scriptural traditions. The prophet condemns from a retro-perspective more than two centuries in the past. And, when he looks ahead, he pictures restoration according to the same ideal retro-perspective.

Amos seems well-informed of Torah standards, covenantal instructions, narrative traditions, and the ways his constituents used all of these in lives marked by greed, self-indulgence, and callous disregard for the socially challenged. Amos simply presupposes his constituents share a broad understanding of scriptural legal and narrative traditions.

Amos makes several fleeting allusions to scriptural legal instructions. He never seems concerned to explain or engage the details. Instead, he uses legal standards to mercilessly mock the religious zeal and social disgraces of the affluent class of Israelites. Amos taunts his shrine-going audience for their worthless, over-the-top religious devotion by exaggerating scriptural standards of worship. He also shames them by overstating their callous disregard for the legal protections of the poor.

Amos tells readers little about the law itself. He often uses the law to make fun of elitist phonies. In that sense Amos embodies the prophetic relationship to Torah as motivational.

USE OF SCRIPTURE

1:3–2:16~2 Sam 8:1–14*; 12:26–30 (C) (indictment against regional rivals) (* see Judah-king network). Most agree that the indictments against the nations lead up to Israel in the climactic position, 3+4+1 (on the literary pattern see Filters). Some may agree that the oracles move from "foreign" neighboring cities (Damascus, cities of Philistines, Tyre) to neighboring "relative" peoples (Edom, Ammon, Moab, Judah) to Israel itself.[4] But the question relating to Amos's possible use of scriptural traditions is: Why these nations? The better views relate to Yahweh's sovereignty over all nations and nations within the former regional "empire" of David.

In one view the prophet speaks against foreign nations, presupposing Yahweh's right to condemn them for their crimes against humanity as a prelude to his judgment against Israel for breaking his covenant. The oracles against the nations may extend the Most High's rights as the one who established and founded the seventy nations. The explanation of the Most High's apportioning lands to all nations appears in the Song of Moses, which alludes to confusing the language of the tower builders and to the seventy peoples in the table of nations (see note on Deut 32:8):

> When the Most High *granted the nations inheritance*, when he divided humankind, he established borders for peoples, according to the number of the sons of God. (Deut 32:8 lit., emphasis mine; cf. Gen 11:7–9)

Torah alludes to an even more intimate relationship between Yahweh and the relative trio Edom, Ammon, and Moab, on analogy of his relationship with Israel. The parallel imagery between lands gifted to the trio of regional neighbors and Israel by Yahweh finds a broad parallel elsewhere in Amos. The exodus of Israel from Egypt gets relativized as analogous to Yahweh's providential sponsoring of migration of the Philistines and Arameans (emphases mine):

> Do not provoke them to war, for I will not give you any of their land, not even enough to put your foot on. *I have given* Esau the hill country of Seir as his own. (Deut 2:5)

> Then Yahweh said to me, "Do not harass the Moabites or provoke them to war, for I will not give you any part of their land. *I have given* Ar to the descendants of Lot as a possession." (2:9)

> "When you come to the Ammonites, do not harass them or provoke them to war, for I will not give you possession of any land belonging to the Ammonites. *I have given it* as a possession to the descendants of Lot." . . . They [Rephaites] were a people strong and numerous, and as tall as the Anakites. *Yahweh destroyed them* from before the Ammonites, who drove them out and settled in their place. *Yahweh had done the same* for the descendants of Esau, who lived in Seir, when *he destroyed* the Horites from before them. They drove them out and have lived in their place to this day. (2:19, 21–22)

4. For other possibilities, see Steinmann, "Order," 683–89; Paul, *Amos*, 11–15.

"Are not you Israelites *the same to me* as the Cushites?" declares Yahweh. "Did I not bring Israel up from Egypt, the Philistines from Caphtor and the Arameans from Kir?" (Amos 9:7)

The basis for Yahweh's condemnation of the regional neighbors of Israel, in this view, stems from Yahweh's prerogatives as divine benefactor and sovereign. Table A1 summarizes the scriptural testimony which supports Yahweh's role as judge of all peoples.

TABLE A1: YAHWEH'S ESTABLISHMENT OF THE NATIONS

Regional	Edom	Deut 2:5 (cf. Gen 36:8)
	Moab	Deut 2:9 (cf. Gen 13:10–11; Jer 48:47)
	Ammon[a]	Deut 2:19 (cf. Gen 13:10–11; Jer 49:6)
	Philistia	Amos 9:7 (cf. Gen 10:14; Jer 47:4)
	Aram	Amos 9:7 (cf. 1 Kgs 19:15; 2 Kgs 8:12–13)
Worldwide	seventy nations (Gen 10)	Deut 32:8 (cf. Gen 10:25; 11:8–9; Ps 96:10)

[a] Some of Jephthah's historical survey accords with other biblical accounts (Judg 11:14–23; cf. Num 21:10–35; Deut 2:1–3:11). Other comments betray Jephthah's mistaken views: Chemosh is the patron deity of Moab not Ammon, and Yahweh gave Ammon and Moab their lands, not Chemosh (Judg 11:24; Deut 2:9, 19; cf. Jer 48:46 clarifying Num 21:29; and see note ad loc.). It is also difficult to align his comments about Balak with his antagonism against Israel (Judg 11:25; Num 22–24; cf. 31:16 with 25:1).

In sum, elsewhere Amos espouses a view of Yahweh's sovereignty over the nations and his relationship with them by way of analogy to Israel. Yahweh's prerogatives as sovereign benefactor give him the right to condemn the nations for crimes against humanity and Judah and Israel for covenantal infidelity. In this view, the peoples selected for Amos's oracles against the nations represent all nations.

In another view, Amos speaks against nations which were subjugated under David—Damascus, Philistia, Edom, Ammon, Moab, and all Israel (2 Sam 8:1–14; 12:26–30; see evidence in Table A2). Tyre does not fit with the others, since David did not rule over it. But Amos refers to "the covenant of kinship" of days gone by but that "they do not remember" (Amos 1:9). Amos may be alluding to the covenant between Solomon and Hiram that continued David's own relations with Tyre (1 Kgs 5:12[26]). The Deuteronomist commented that Hiram "had always been on friendly terms with [lit. "loved"] David" (1 Kgs 5:1[15]; cf. 9:13; 2 Sam 5:11). This approach accords with the shape of the restoration of "all nations that bear my name" under the shelter of David (Amos 9:11–12). The collection of Amos's prophetic messages exhibits the shape of the classic Hebrew prophets—judgment then restoration—not only for Israel but for all of nations who find refuge under Davidic rule (see note on 9:11–12).

TABLE A2: DAVIDIC KINGDOM SUBJECTION OF AND ALLIANCES WITH REGIONAL RIVALS

Tyre	2 Sam 5:11 (cf. Solomon,[a] 1 Kgs 5:1, 12[15, 26])	alliance
Philistia	2 Sam 8:1 (cf. 5:17–25)	subjection
Moab	2 Sam 8:2	subjection
Zobah	2 Sam 8:3–4	subjection
Damascus/Aram	2 Sam 8:5–8 (cf. revolt 1 Kgs 11:23–25)	subjection
Hamath	2 Sam 8:9–11	tribute
Edom	2 Sam 8:14	subjection
Ammon	2 Sam 12:26–30 (cf. 2 Kgs 14:25)	subjection
(Egypt)	(cf. Solomon,[a] 1 Kgs 3:1; 9:16, 24)	alliance
Canaanite nations	1 Chr 22:2, 15–16 (cf. Solomon,[a] 1 Kgs 9:20–21)	enslavement

[a] Many of Solomon's political alliances and strategies may have been planned and/or initiated under David's rule. Important examples include Solomon's marriage to Namah the Ammonitess (1 Kgs 14:21, 31) and David's amassing materials and making preparation for the temple (1 Chr 22:5, 15–16; 28:11–19). Much of the wealth and materials for Solomon's Jerusalem building projects may have come from David's plundering regional rivals and their vassal tribute to David (1 Chr 18:8; cf. 22:3–4, 14; 29:2–5).

The audacity of Amos in the second view needs to be noted. Amos ministered over two centuries after the days of David and Solomon (Amos 1:1). The dominion of David by military force and the peaceful relations sealed by Solomon's treaty-wives had long since ceased to maintain Israel's place over its regional rivals. Amos's condemnation based on historical political rule in long gone days would be the approximate equivalent of present-day British prophetic condemnation of the United States based on its former sovereign rule over the thirteen colonies. Amos's bold and politically unrealistic condemnation by means of Yahweh's roaring from Zion signals the covenantal basis of his prophetic authority (1:2). In this view, Amos condemns by the authority of the God of Israel nations once allied with or under Davidic rule. It is as though the days of David's little empire define the scope of Amos's prophetic judgment and blessing.

Both views have merit.[5] The view that the nations mentioned by Amos are representative of all nations gets snagged on the related passage in Amos 9:11–12. Amos does not speak of restoration for "all nations" but for "all the nations that bear my name" (9:12).[6] This suggests a more specific rationale than divine sovereignty over all nations, namely, "the nations that bear my name" will find refuge under the restored shelter of David.

---

5. See Anderson and Freedman, *Amos*, 232–33.

6. For an extensive defense of the nations in Amos 1–2 as representative of all nations as opposed to David's regional empire, see Goswell, "David," 243–57. Goswell does not adequately deal with the identification in Amos 9:12 ("all the nations that bear my name"). He simply says that the phrase "does not need to be limited to former national constituents of the Davidic empire" (257). Goswell's acknowledgement—that the nations could be "limited to the former national constituents of the Davidic empire"—is helpful and the main strength of the opposing view.

The point at hand relates to the possible scriptural basis for the nations selected in the oracles. In either of the views above Amos applies scriptural traditions of Yahweh's authority over Israel's rivals—whether as divine benefactor or Davidic rule (see Tables A1 and A2). If Amos invents the genre of oracles against the nations based on allusion to a scriptural rationale, other prophets expand and redeploy this prophetic form in several new directions (see Isa 13–23; Jer 46–51; Ezek 25–32).

2:7~Lev 18:7–8; 20:11 (C) (father and son with same female).

2:8~Exod 22:26*[25]; Deut 24:17 (C) (fornication on the cloak of the needy) (* see release statute network).

2:12~Num 6:2 (C) (frustrating Nazirites). Amos does not quote, explain, or draw upon scriptural laws as a basis of prophetic authority. Yet he presupposes his audience's extensive familiarity with them.[7] In the main Amos draws upon legal traditions appearing in Torah as part of his blistering satires against his hapless audience. He repeatedly taunts the affluent class of Israelite worshipers for flagrant violations of scriptural standards of justice.

In Amos's condemnation of Israel he makes passing allusions to a series of covenantal violations. Amos does not simply speak of social unrighteousness in abstract terms but accuses of selling socially challenged persons for sandals (Amos 2:6) and elsewhere buying them for a pair of sandals (8:6). This kind of shameful accusation does not evoke particular laws but generally pushes against many scriptural legal protections of the poor.

In some cases Amos also uses specific legal standards in similar ironic ways to exaggerate the social and religious incongruity of the shrine-going Israelites. He accuses Israel of immoral conduct (2:7), oppressive immorality at places of worship (2:8), and frustrating Nazirites (2:12) by alluding to egregious and senseless legal violations. Compare the broad inverted overlap between law and accusation (emphases signify verbal parallels):

> Do not have sexual relations with your *father's* wife; that would dishonor your father. . . . Do not have sexual relations with your daughter-in-law. She is your *son's* wife; do not have relations with her. (Lev 18:8, 15)

> If you take your neighbor's cloak as a **pledge**, return it by sunset, because that cloak is the only covering your neighbor has. What else can they sleep in? (Exod 22:26, 27[25, 26])

> Speak to the Israelites and say to them: "If a man or woman wants to make a special vow, a vow of dedication to Yahweh as a <u>Nazirite</u>, they must abstain from <u>wine</u> and other fermented drink and must not <u>drink</u> vinegar made from wine or other fermented drink." (Num 6:2, 3a)

7. See Tucker, "Law," 203–6.

> They trample on the heads of the poor as on the dust of the ground and deny justice to the oppressed. *Father* and son use the same girl and so profane my holy name. They lie down beside every altar on garments taken in **pledge**. In the house of their god they drink wine taken as fines. . . . But you made the Nazirites drink wine and commanded the prophets not to prophesy. (Amos 2:7, 8, 12)

The nature of Amos's allusions does not lend itself to close verbal parallels. The reference to a father and son having relations with the same "young woman" (נַעֲרָה, not "cultic prostitute" קְדֵשָׁה) may refer to incestuous adultery as in Lev 18:8, 15.[8]

Amos uses the law to shame his audience in the case of misusing pledges for personal luxury. The accusation of inciting Nazirites to violate their vows uses the legal tradition as a rhetorical weapon. The indictment of 2:6–16 may serve a summary collation of the prophet's repeated taunts of Israel, whose worship and social lives stand in immoral contradiction (4:1–5; 5:10–12, 18–23; 6:4–7; 8:4–6).

4:4~Deut 14:28; 26:12 (B) (taunt of sacrifice every morning and tithe every three days).

4:5~Lev 2:11 or 7:13 (B) (taunt of offering leavened/unleavened bread). Amos taunts worshipers by exaggerating their worship to the nth degree. He alludes to selected laws of worship in a misshapen way to mock misguided religious zeal. Amos speaks of the ridiculous idea of sacrificing every day and of tithing every three days instead of every three years (Amos 4:4; cf. Deut 14:28; 26:12). Amos may be scorning them for offering leavened not unleavened bread (Amos 4:5; cf. Lev 2:11).[9] Or, if he has in mind the leavened cakes of Lev 7:13, which are offered but cannot be burned on the altar because of leaven, then he is exaggerating their devotion.[10] This latter possibility fits well with tithing every three days. In either case, Amos parodies and exaggerates the useless religious zeal of the shrine-goers (see Table A3 in Filters).

5:10, 12~Deut 16:18–19 (C) (satire of opposing justice at the gate). Amos 5:10–12 offers another round of biting ridicule against affluent Israelites (see 2:6–16; 4:1–5). The present context flatly accuses Amos's audience of hating justice and walking all over the underprivileged. The catchword "gate" in 5:10 and 12 creates an *inclusio* around the indictment of unjust oppression of the needy.[11] These unflattering accusations overturn scriptural legal traditions demanding justice at "the gate" (Deut 16:18–19; cf. 1:16; Exod 23:6). Amos again and again mines legal standards only to distort the contexts in order to ridicule the hapless rebels he accuses.

9:11–12*~2 Sam 7:12*, 27 (B) (Davidic shelter restored) (* see branch, Davidic covenant, and place networks). Amos looks ahead to the day when the fallen shelter of David

8. Paul suggests it merely refers to immoral conduct (*Amos*, 81–82).
9. See Milgrom, *Leviticus 1–16*, 188–89; 414–15.
10. See Paul, *Amos*, 141.
11. See ibid., 170.

will be raised up (Amos 9:11). Amos's expectation builds upon the expression he coins, "shelter of David," and appears to make an interpretive allusion to the Davidic covenant. The verbal parallels only include "I will raise up" (קום Hif) and "I will build" (בנה) (2 Sam 7:12, 27; Amos 9:11). Though common terms, the specific references to David and "as in the days of old" give good reason to think he has the Davidic promise in mind. The restored shelter of David refers to one that includes the remnant of Edom and "all nations *that bear my name*" (Amos 9:11, 12, emphasis mine). The restriction to the people "that bear my name" from among all nations seems to refer to the regional peoples over whom David ruled "as in days of old." David's regional empire includes alliance with or rule over those whom the prophet pronounced oracles against in Amos 1–2 (see Table A2).

The majority of modern committee translations like NIV and NRSV follow the Septuagint's consistency in the use of prepositions rather than the masoretic version of Amos 9:11. Since "shelter" is a feminine singular noun, the Septuagint's pronouns refer to it, but only one of the masoretic pronouns grammatically refers to it:

> On that day I will raise up the tent of David that is fallen and rebuild *its* [fs] ruins and raise up *its* [fs] destruction, and rebuild *it* [fs] as the days of old. (Amos 9:11 LXX)

> On that day I will raise up the shelter of David that is fallen, and I will repair *their* [fp] breaches, and raise up *its* [ms] ruins, and rebuild *it* [fs] as in days of old. (9:11 lit. MT)

Though the Septuagint offers the attraction of simplicity, the variations in the other ancient versions (e.g., Vulg.) do not support this emendation.[12] The more difficult reading of the masoretic witness is preferred.

Since the Davidic kingdom still remained in Amos's day, the reference to its being "fallen" is frequently interpreted as implying an exilic or postexilic update. This suggestion does not adequately account for the context. In Amos's day the Davidic kingdom did not function as in "days of old" (יְמֵי עוֹלָם), including ruling over "all nations that bear my name" (9:11, 12). The fallen shelter of David needed to be raised up in Amos's day, making later dating for this oracle unnecessary. Near contemporary prophets likewise looked back to David's time as "days of old" (יְמֵי עוֹלָם) (Mic 5:2[1]; 7:14). In both of these contexts Micah mentions restoring peoples and lands no longer under the rule of the Davidic kingdom—"The rest of his brothers return" and "let them feed in Bashan and Gilead" (5:3[2]; 7:14).[13] The counterpart to possessing the nations that bear Yahweh's name (Amos 9:12) may be peoples like Moab finding "shelter" (סֵתֶר) when a ruler is established in the "tent [אֹהֶל] of David" (Isa 16:4, 5)—similar imagery, different terms.

12. *BHK* and *BHS* suggest emending Amos 9:11 to follow LXX, but Gelston points out the lack of agreement among the ancient versions (see *BHQ*, 88*). This evidence favors the originality of the more difficult MT. For a table comparing pronominal suffixes in the ancient versions of Amos 9:11, see Nogalski, "Problematic Suffixes," 414.

13. For a detailed explanation of reading Amos 9:11–12 in the context of Amos's day, see Paul, *Amos*, 290–92.

Moreover, cities and peoples under David's rule such as those listed in Table A2 were delivered up by Yahweh (2 Sam 8:6, 14) and conquered in David's name (12:28).

Based on the masoretic pronominal suffix "I will repair *their* [fp] breaches" (פִּרְצֵיהֶן) (Amos 9:11), Nogalski suggests the pronoun refers to the "ruined cities" (fp) that need to be rebuilt (9:14) and thus sets the expectation in exilic or postexilic times.[14] This suggestion makes a helpful attempt to identify the pronoun's reference but does not take adequate account of evidence concerning the said rebuilding. The restoration in Amos 9:14 uses the same four verbs in the same sequence to undo the judgment pronounced against Israel for hating justice and oppressing the poor in 5:11 (emphases signify verbal parallels):[15]

> Therefore, though you *have built* [בנה] stone mansions, you *will* not *live* [ישב] in them; though you *have planted* [נטע] lush vineyards, you *will* not *drink* [שתה] their wine. (5:11b)
>
> They *will rebuild* [בנה] the ruined cities and *live* [ישב] in them. They *will plant* [נטע] vineyards and *drink* [שתה] their wine. (9:14b)

That Amos spoke of exile for Israel fits both Amos's word and Amaziah's interpretation of it (7:11, 17).[16] This rebuilding in reference to the Northern Kingdom of Israel, however, does not align with David's fallen tent. The contextual evidence suggests Amos 9:11–12 gets at the peoples of the Davidic empire in days of old like those listed in Amos 1–2. Meanwhile, Amos 9:14 clicks together with Amos's judgment against the Northern Kingdom of Israel in Amos 5:11.

In sum, conjectures for regarding the hope to restore the shelter of David as exilic or postexilic only work well by lifting the imagery out of its context. The need to rebuild after the impending destruction (9:14) and to restore under Davidic rule all nations called by Yahweh's name as in days of old (9:11, 12) match Amos's preaching elsewhere in

---

14. See Nogalski, "Problematic Suffixes," 416–17. For another scholar who builds interpretations on Nogalski's error, see Timmer, "Possessing Edom," 469–70. Timmer goes on to use Amos 9:13–15 of "traditional Israel" inclusive of Judah in a way that does not relate to the time of the prophet Amos (477). This move helps Timmer take the phrase "all the nations called by my name" in Amos 9:12 out of the context of the book of Amos so it refers to any nation rather than the client and ally regional nations under David's rule like those listed in Amos 1–2. By contrast, the view argued here is based on Amos 9:11–12 making sense as a promise in the days of the prophet Amos and his constituents. For a convincing explanation of the meaning of the nations "over whom my name is proclaimed" (אֲשֶׁר־נִקְרָא שְׁמִי עֲלֵיהֶם) as "ownership" in Scripture and in Amos 9:12, see Imes, *Bearing YHWH's Name*, 49–61, esp. 60–61.

15. This observation from Paul, *Amos*, 173–74, n. 141; 294.

16. Others argue that the "shelter of David" does not refer to a restoration with a Davidic ruler but the restoration of Jerusalem as the place of the temple (Goswell, "David," 250–57; idem and Abernethy, *God's Messiah*, 145–49), or that it indicates the shelter of David is the temple (Dunne, "David's Tent," 363–74). Setting aside problems with the series of necessary sub-hypotheses for these proposals, they do not work in Amos's day or the Second Temple context. It is hard to make sense of James's reference to restoring the temple unless it is being projected back from a post-70 CE perspective (contra Dunne, 373). Finally, the central place of royal patronage for the temple within the Davidic covenant (2 Sam 7) makes it difficult to excise David from the shelter of David (as proposed for different reasons by Goswell, 257 and Dunne, 367).

this book. The indictments against the nations of the Davidic empire in Amos 1:3–2:16 suggest that their obedience to the divine roaring from Zion will characterize their subjection under the protection of the restored Davidic shelter as in days of old in 9:11–12.

The term "shelter" (סֻכָּה) suggests other possible connections with scriptural traditions. The Qumran sectarian writings splice several Scriptures together:

> "I will raise up your seed after you and I will establish the throne of his kingdom [forev] er. I will be a father to him and he will be a son to me" [2 Sam 7:14]. This is the "branch [צמח] of David," who will arise with the interpreter of the law who [will rise up] in Zi[on in] the [l]ast days, as it is written: *"I will raise up the shelter* [סוכת] *of David which has fallen"* [Amos 9:11]. This is "the shelter [סוכת] of David that has fall[en," w]hich he will raise up to deliver Israel. (4Q174/4QFlor 1.10–13 lit., following *DSSSE* 1:352–53, emphasis mine)[17]

The author of 4Q174 regards Amos's restored shelter of David as referring to the Davidic covenant and corresponding to the branch of David. Isaiah refers to the "branch [צֶמַח] of Yahweh" in a context leading up to the cloud of smoke over Zion, reminiscent of the wilderness cloud, as a "shelter" (סֻכָּה) (Is 4:2, 6). However, the image of the branch may have easily come from Jer 23:5–6 or more likely Zech 3:8 and/or 6:12 since 4Q174 also speaks of two messiahs, one civil ruler and one priestly. The larger context of 4Q174 expands the law of the assembly in Deut 23:2–6[3–7] to exclude from the temple not only Ammonites, Moabites, and those born of a forbidden marriage but also foreigners (בן נכר) and even residing foreigners (גר) (4Q174 1.4).

The restored shelter of David over the nations of his empire provides exactly the right kind of imagery to get at the new realities of Jews and gentiles brought together by the gospel of Messiah. James's paraphrastic use of the Septuagint or an interpretative use of Amos 9:11–12 in Acts 15:16–17 continues to draw lively debate. The term "Edom" (אדם) is spelled with the same consonants as "human race" (אדם). The parallel word pair in Amos 9:12 between Edom (אֱדוֹם, here in plene) and "nations" (גּוֹיִם) could invite revocalizing the term as human race (אָדָם, ἄνθρωπος) in the parent text of the Septuagint or by James, along with other interpretive adjustments.[18] James uses the restored shelter of David to refer to a place for "all the gentiles who bear my name," in sharp contrast to 4Q174, which uses the shelter of David in a context more restrictive than Torah, excluding even proselytes. James's interpretive advancement makes use of the contextual reference to the other whose identity stems from the name of the Lord. In any case, these early readings demonstrate both the continuity of Amos's expectation with the Davidic covenant and the importance of how prophetic expectations guide early Christian scriptural exegesis.

---

17. Also see 4Q266/CD 7:16. On Amos 9:11 in 4Q174 1.17 versus 4Q266/CD 7:16 see Brooke, *Exegesis at Qumran*, 139.

18. See Johnson, *Septuagintal Midrash*, 17–18.

FILTERS

Amos and Hosea stand at the headwaters of the traditions of the writing prophets. Many elements in Amos become stock phrases and common prophetic imagery in later prophets. Uses of Amos's imagery cannot be listed here.[19]

Amos makes many broad references to narrative and legal traditions of Torah. Though broad allusions tend to be non-exegetical, they offer important perspectives on the kinds of traditions familiar to Amos's audience. The following lists are representative.[20]

Non-Exegetical Broad Allusions and Shared Themes

Amos makes broad allusion to numerous narrative traditions of Torah: Edom as brother (Amos 1:11); "overthrow" Sodom and Gomorrah (4:11; cf. Gen 19:21, 25, 29; Deut 29:23[22]); plagues in Egypt (Amos 4:10); brought Israel up from Egypt (עלה Hif, not יצא) (2:10; 3:1; 9:7);[21] forty years in wilderness (2:10; 5:25); conquest and defeat of gigantic Amorites (2:9, 10; cf. Num 13:32–33).

In one place Amos refers to rarely paralleled providential migration of the Philistines and Arameans (cf. Gen 10:14; Jer 47:4) by which Amos makes analogy to the exodus of Israel from Egypt (Amos 9:7; cf. 1:5).[22] The theological basis runs akin to Yahweh granting lands to Moab and Ammon (Deut 2:9, 19). The language of granting inheritance to Moab and Ammon also includes resonances of Yahweh's provision for Israel. To some extent this line of thought fits under the rubric of the Most High assigning lands to all peoples (Deut 32:8; cf. Gen 11:7–9).

In several series of taunts Amos ridicules his resistant Israelite audience for their unjust practices: keeping a pledge overnight (2:8; cf. Exod 22:26–27[25–26]) and commercial dishonesty (Amos 8:5–6; cf. Lev 19:35–36).

Amos broadly refers to several ritual standards found in Torah: tithes, pilgrimages, and various offerings (Amos 4:4, 5; 5:21, 22, 25). Amos alludes to a negative attitude among his audience regarding limitations against commercial dealings on new moons and the Sabbath (8:5). Torah does not speak directly against selling on the Sabbath. Standards against carrying loads through the gates and merchandizing on the Sabbath appear in later prophetic and restoration literature (see Jer 17:21–27; Neh 10:31[32]; 13:15–22).

Amos makes a distinction between ritually clean and unclean (Amos 7:17), though "ritually unclean ground" (אֲדָמָה טְמֵאָה) may simply denote foreign lands. Yet Hosea also

---

19. For a short list of phrases in Amos shared with other prophets, see Driver, *Joel and Amos*, 122. For a list of characteristic language, expressions, and phrases of Amos, see Harper, *Amos and Hosea*, clxx–clxxi. Also see Parallels within the Book of the Twelve in Hosea Filters.

20. The lists here are primarily based on research for the present project and have been compared against and supplemented by Bergren, *Prophets and the Law*, 182–83; Bramer, "Literary Genre," 46–48; Driver, *Joel and Amos*, 113–15; Paul, *Amos*, 4 (also see items on Entire OT in Bibliographic Note on Lists of Potential Parallels).

21. See Dearman, "Some Observations," 256–64.

22. On diminishing of the uniqueness of the exodus in Amos 9:7, see ibid., 262–63.

connected Assyrian exile with eating ritually unclean food (Hos 9:3; cf. Josh 22:19; Ezek 4:13).[23] Though the allusion is very broad, it at least points in the direction of the kind of dietary regulations housed in Lev 11 and Deut 14.

The fivefold structure of the oracles of judgment against Bethel in Amos 4:6, 7–8, 9, 10, 11 broadly align with the fivefold covenantal judgments of Lev 26:14, 18, 21, 23, 27. In Leviticus, the culminating fifth level of judgment centers on exile (Lev 26:33), and in Amos they shall share the fate of the cities of the plain (4:11; cf. Deut 29:23[22]). Wolff notes broadly thematic similarities in many judgments with some verbal parallels in Lev 26, Deut 28, 1 Kgs 8, and Amos 4.[24]

Amos refers to David as musician (6:5; cf. 1 Sam 16:23; Neh 12:36; 1 Chr 23:5).

Many have observed the similarities between Amos's use of "for three sins . . . even for four" (see stock phrases below) and the 7+1 structure of the oracles against the nations and numerical wisdom sayings (cf. Prov 30:15, 18, 21, 29).[25]

The supposed dependence of Amos on wisdom based on shared themes has been denied on several grounds such as the same elements in legal and other prophetic scriptural traditions.[26]

At several junctures Amos makes use of creational themes (Amos 4:13; 5:8–9; 9:5–6). These passages emphasize Yahweh as sovereign creator of the cosmic elements that daily do his bidding. Amos's use of creational themes offers testimony in an early prophetic writing to the broad relationship between Yahweh's sovereignty over all things and his covenantal relationship to his people.

Shared Stock Phrases and Other Similarities

Amos's oracles against the nations repeat a refrain: >/<1:4, 7, 10, 12, 14; 2:2, 5, "I will send fire [אֵשׁ] . . . and it will consume [אָכְלָה]."[27] While the imagery could denote actual fire from military attacks, it may also be a metaphorical way to speak of divine judgment more generally. The same kind of imagery was used by ancient poets cited in Torah: "That is why the poets say: . . . '*Fire* [אֵשׁ] went out from Heshbon, a blaze from the city of Sihon. *It consumed* [אָכְלָה] Ar of Moab, the citizens of Arnon's heights'" (Num 21:27–28, emphasis mine). While the ancient poets speak of "fire" as the subject "going out" and "consuming," Amos refers to Yahweh as subject, speaking in first person, with the fire as an object. This judgment language is used seven times in Amos to speak against the seven other nations, along with "for three sins . . . even for four" used eight times to bind together Israel with the seven other nations indicted by Yahweh's roaring (1:3, 6, 9, 11, 13; 2:1, 4, 6).

23. See Paul, *Amos*, 251.

24. See four-column layout in Wolff, *Joel and Amos*, 213.

25. For additional wisdom-flavored elements in Amos, see Terrien, "Amos and Wisdom," 108–15.

26. See McLaughlin, "Amos," 281-303.

27. The verb "I will send" (שׁלח, 6x) is replaced by "I will kindle" (יצת, 1x) in Amos 1:14 for Rabbah. The same term "kindle" is used of burning Rabbah in Jer 49:2.

Other shared imagery in Amos: >/<1:13; 2 Kgs 8:12; 15:16; Hos 13:16[14:1], rip open pregnant women; >/<3:14; 7:10, 13; 9:1; Hos 8:5–6; 10:5, 8, against the shrine at Bethel (cf. 1 Kgs 13:1–3); >/<3:14; 5:6; Hos 5:8, against Bethel; >/<4:4; 5:5; Hos 4:15; 9:15, against Bethel and Gilgal (Amos also includes Beersheba in 5:5); >/<4:1; Ps 22:12, cattle of Bashan; >/<4:13; Deut 32:13, treads the heights of the earth; >/<7:9; Lev 26:30; Hos 10:8, high places desolate; >/<9:10; Deut 29:19; Jer 7:4, 8, taunt against those who say divine election will save; >/<9:13; Joel 3:18, mountains drip sweet wine.

Amos stands at the root of prophetic condemnations of phony worship (see esp. Amos 5:21–23). The condemnation of bogus worship by two near contemporaries in Amos 5:21–23 and Isa 1:1–17 share about seven terms ("I hate," "assembly," "burnt offerings," "grain offerings," "fatted animals," "remove from me," and "I will not listen") along with several related themes (feasts/festivals, not look/close eyes, and not accept/not pleased).[28] For all this, neither of these two prophets seem directly dependent upon the other but appear to be working within a rich, diverse, and extensive prophetic tradition condemning fake worship. The long and varied criticism against worthless worship does not support even indirect relationship, but an ongoing theological tradition. Table A3 summarizes leading themes from about thirty scriptural contexts criticizing hypocrisy of worship.

TABLE A3: SCRIPTURAL CRITICISM OF FAITHLESS WORSHIP‡

idol worship	Isa 66:3; Jer 7:8–10, 17–18; Ezek 20:39; Hos 2:13–15[15–17]; 13:2
unsolicited offerings	Jer 6:19–20; 14:12; Amos 4:4–5
sacrifice as mere obedience	Isa 29:13
unacceptable offerings because of evil deeds	Isa 43:24; Hos 8:13; Amos 5:21–24; Mic 3:4; Zech 7:13; Mal 1:10; 2:3; 3:5
Yahweh's alternate preferences of X versus what is offered	1 Sam 15:22; Isa 1:10–17; 58:6; Jer 7:21–23; Hos 6:4–6; Mic 6:6–8; Ps 40:6[7]; 50:7–15; 51:18–19[20–21]; Zech 7:10; Prov 15:8, 29; 21:3, 27; 28:9; Eccl 5:7[6]

‡ Data in table are based on Lafferty, *The Prophetic Critique*, 3–4, with additional items collated herein. Also see Shepherd, *Text in the Middle*, 120–22.

28. See Lafferty, *The Prophetic Critique*, 82.

Chapter 16

OBADIAH

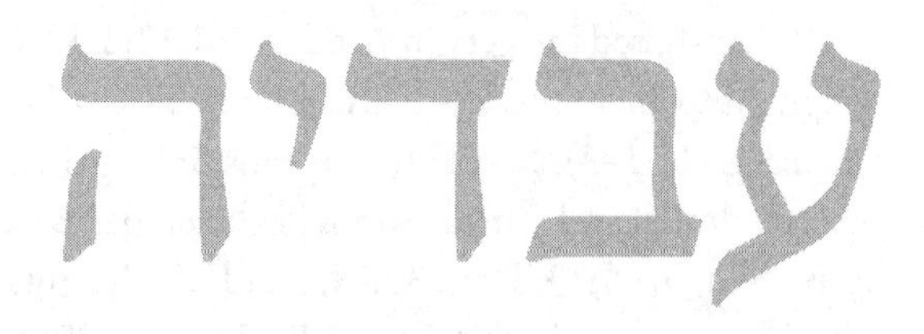

SYMBOLS[1]

- // verbal parallels (A level)
- /~/ synoptic parallel (A level)
- ~ B, probable interpretive allusion; C, possible; D, probably not
- + interpretive blend
- >/< more or less similar (see Filters)
- * part of interpretive network (see Networks)

USE OF SCRIPTURE IN OBADIAH[2]

1–4//Jer 49:14–16 (bringing down the pride of Edom)

5–8//Jer 49:7, 9–10 (destruction of Esau)

OLD TESTAMENT USE OF OBADIAH (SEE RESPECTIVE NOTES)

17~Joel 2:32[3:5] (B) (those who escape)

17~Joel 3:17[4:17] (B) (Zion shall be holy)

NEW TESTAMENT USE OF OBADIAH

n/a

HERMENEUTICAL PROFILE OF THE USE OF SCRIPTURE IN OBADIAH

Almost half of Obadiah shares verbal parallels with other prophetic scriptural contexts—approximately nine of twenty-one verses. Many other elements in Obadiah feature broad thematic parallels and stock phrases from the prophetic tradition (see Filters).

The extensive parallels between Jer 49 and the opening of Obadiah provide strong evidence of relationship. The direction of dependence, or whether Jeremiah and Obadiah draw from a common source, remains sharply contested.[3] The interpretive intervention in Obad 4//Jer 49:16 mildly suggests Jeremiah as donor and Obadiah as receptor context.

One of the two shared locutions between Obad 17 and Joel features an interpretive intervention with fairly strong evidence of Obadiah as donor and Joel as receptor context (see note on Joel 2:32[3:5]). In both interpretive allusions Joel recontextualizes elements from Obad 17.

1. For explanation of symbols, see Symbols and Abbreviations and Introduction. For other help, see Glossary.
2. See Bibliographic Note on Lists of Potential Parallels.
3. See Childs, *Introduction*, 412–13.

Obadiah features strong anti-Edom ideology much in line with other sentiments in other prophetic books. If Obadiah re-presents poetic oracles from the traditions housed in Jer 49, he mildly revises and strengthens them. He also pluralizes the quasi-marking device from "I" to "we" in "We have heard from Yahweh," including his audience with the prophet as receiving the oracles from Jeremiah or his source (Obad 1).

Obadiah strengthens the imagery of Edom's arrogance, hyperbolizing their safe home among the celestial lights (v. 4). Obadiah also excludes the modicum of (sarcastic?) mercy for the war widows and orphans of Edom (v. 7 versus Jer 49:11).

Obadiah's use of scriptural traditions are manifested in his proclamation of well-deserved judgment on Edom. The people of Edom used their mountain cities as veritable hideouts for their long-time slave trade of vulnerable peoples (Amos 1:6, 9). But they made a wrong move by preying on the defenseless of Jerusalem on the day of its judgment (Obad 11–14). There is no place for Edom to hide from the wrath of Yahweh.

USE OF SCRIPTURE

1–4//Jer 49:14–16 (bringing down the pride of Edom).[4] The extensive set of verbal parallels between the oracles against Edom by Obadiah and Jeremiah points to a relationship, whether one borrowed from the other or both drew from a common source. The oracles against Edom in Jer 49 work back and forth between poetry and prose. All of Jeremiah's poetic oracles against Edom run parallel to Obadiah (see Table J6 in Jeremiah). The interpretive interventions between Obadiah and Jer 49 slightly favor the former as receptor context based on the strengthening of imagery (cf. Obad 4//Jer 49:16b); although suggestive, caution and drawing out contrasts are in order (italics, bold, underlining, and double underlining signify verbal parallels; and broken underlining signifies interpretive paraphrase):

Obadiah	**Jeremiah 49**
[1] The vision of Obadiah. This is what my Lord Yahweh says about Edom—We have heard a message from Yahweh: *An envoy was sent to the nations to say, "Rise, let us go against her for battle"*—[2] See, **I will make you small among the nations; you will be utterly despised**. [3] The pride of your heart has deceived you, you who live in the clefts of the rocks and make your home on the heights, you who say to yourself, "Who can bring me down to the ground?" [4] Though you soar like the eagle and make your nest among the stars, from there I will bring you down, declares Yahweh.	[14] I have heard a message from Yahweh; *an envoy was sent to the nations to say,* "Assemble yourselves to attack it! *Rise up for battle!*" [15] Now **I will make you small among the nations, despised** by mankind. [16] The terror you inspire and the pride of your heart have deceived you, you who live in the clefts of the rocks, who occupy the heights of the hill. Though you build your nest as high as the eagle's, from there I will bring you down," declares Yahweh.

4. Also cf. Obad 1 with Isa 40:9; Obad 3 with Isa 2:19–21; Obad 4 with Jer 49:22.

In the parallel between Jer 49:14–16 and Obad 1–4, the former accents international despising of Edom and Edom's famous vindictive terrorism as grounds for their pride. Obadiah goes a slightly different direction, targeting Edom's arrogance itself. Obadiah gives voice to Edom's naïve interior monologue reassuring themselves of their own safety from the kind of terrors they inflict upon other peoples (Obad 3). Block suggests that the use of embedded discourse in Obad 3 strengthens the rhetorical force of the utterance he has brought over from Jeremiah.[5] Edom's pride relates to the relative security of several of its fortress cities against military attack: Sela (see wordplay on "rock" [סֶלַע] v. 3 NET n.), a generic reference to Mount Esau used parallel to Teman (location unknown [8, 9]), and Bozrah (Jer 49:13). Isaiah 2:19–21 warns the house of Jacob to hide in caves and rocks (סֶלַע) from the judgment of Yahweh, while Obadiah and Jeremiah use this stock imagery as a taunt that Edom cannot hide in the clefts of the rock/Sela.[6] Obadiah piles up hyperbole, saying that Edom makes their inaccessible eagle's nest among the celestial lights themselves (Obad 4). The attention to Edom's ego and their protection in the heights further underlines the dramatic judgment of Yahweh to bring them down (4).

Both Jeremiah and Obadiah preserve common theological priorities. The condemnation of Edom for their arrogance comes by the authority of the word of Yahweh (Jer 49:14//Obad 1). Obadiah includes the reception formula in first-person plural.[7] To say "We have heard a message from Yahweh" seems to include Obadiah's audience together with him. This quasi-marking device may further strengthen the very mild indicators of Obadiah as receptor context.

5–8//Jer 49:7, 9–10 (destruction of Esau). The extensive verbal parallels between Obad 5–8 and Jer 49:7–10 feature different arrangements. This section of the respective oracles against Edom end or begin with a taunt against the wisdom of Edom (Obad 8; Jer 49:7). The most significant difference relates to Jeremiah's word of comfort for the war orphans and widows of Edom. Obadiah does not include these sentiments of mercy for Edom.

The question of whether Jer 49:10b should be read literally or as a sarcastic taunt needs to be set aside here (see note on Jer 49:10). Whichever the case, in sharp contrast Obadiah focuses only on the deception and defeat of the Edomites by their own allies (Obad 6–7).[8] In both parts of the book of Obadiah, the prophet emphasizes the definitive and final judgment upon the Edomites (10, 16). This categorical judgment turns on equitable repayment for what Edom has done to Judah (15). The harsh condemnation of Edom also aligns with their long tradition of slave-trade profiteering at the expense of

5. See Block, *Obadiah*, 63.

6. See "I סֶלַע," "II סֶלַע," BDB 700–1.

7. Obadiah 1 LXX uses "I have heard" (ἤκουσα), apparently based on assimilation from singular in Jer 49:14 (so Obad 1 in *BHQ* apparatus; contra Parke-Taylor, *Formation*, 149), thus MT "we have heard" (שָׁמַעְנוּ) is preferred.

8. See Block, *Obadiah*, 67–68.

the most vulnerable (Amos 1:6, 9; Obad 14). The finality of Yahweh's judgment against Edom (Obad 18) gets picked up in Malachi (see note on Mal 1:2–3) (underlining and bold signify verbal parallels; and broken underlining signifies potential interpretive allusion):

Obadiah	Jeremiah 49
[5] If thieves came to you, if robbers in the night—oh, what a disaster awaits you!—would they not steal only as much as they wanted? **If grape pickers came to you, would they not leave a few grapes?** [6] But how **Esau** will be ransacked,[a] his hidden treasures pillaged! [7] All your allies will force you to the border; your friends will deceive and overpower you; those who eat your bread will set a trap for you, but you will not detect it. [8] "In that day," declares Yahweh, "will I not destroy the wise men of Edom, those of understanding in the mountains of Esau?"	[9] **If grape pickers came to you, would they not leave a few grapes?** If thieves came during the night, would they not steal only as much as they wanted? [10] But I will strip **Esau** bare; I will uncover his hiding places, so that he cannot conceal himself. His armed men are destroyed, also his allies and neighbors, so there is no one to say "Leave your fatherless children; I will keep them alive. Your widows too can depend on me." [(7)] Concerning Edom: This is what Yahweh Almighty says: "Is there no longer wisdom in Teman? Has counsel perished from the prudent? Has their wisdom decayed?"

[a] The term "ransack" (חפשׂ) in Obad 6 inverts the *sin* and *pe* of "strip off" (חשׂף) in Jer 49:10 or their common source (Obad 6 in *BHS* apparatus; also see Parke-Taylor, *Formation*, 148). Block suggests Obad 6 is a commentary on the phrase "so that he cannot conceal himself" (Jer 49:10), but he does not take into account the switch from "strip off" (חשׂף, Jer 49:10) to "ransack" (חפשׂ, Obad 6) which points in a different direction (*Obadiah*, 67; 66, n. 29).

FILTERS

Obadiah tends to share broad thematic parallels with other prophetic traditions more so than with Torah. The following representative parallels are not comprehensive or complete.[9] Many shared themes relate to strong anti-Edom ideology.

Non-Exegetical Broad Allusions and Shared Themes

Broad allusions: **5**>/<Lev 23:22, produce left for gleaning (cf. 19:9–10; Deut 24:21; Jer 6:9); **6, 18**>/<Gen 25:30; 36:1, 9, Esau as the ancestor of Edom; **21**>/<Num 24:18, taking possession of Edom.

Obadiah and Zephaniah each feature a tenfold use of "day" (יוֹם). Zephaniah's use of "day" focuses on the day of Yahweh (Zeph 1:14–18), while Obadiah seems to look back on the day Edom took delight in the downfall of Jerusalem (**Obad 11–14**). The perspective of Obadiah's focus on the day is quite challenging. In Obad 12–14 the syntax takes a (warning against future potentiality) jussive prohibition format, literally "you shall not..." (אַל + impf.), eight times. But Obad 11 and 15 frame these with past actions (Obad 11, inf. const. + pf.; 15, pf.). Nogalski summarizes the awkward construction:

9. For longer lists of parallels between Obadiah and many scriptural contexts, see Block, *Obadiah*, 40–41; Mirsky, Meltzer, and Kiel, *Twelve*, 1:11–13 [Hebrew].

"Obad 11 and 15 demonstrate knowledge that Edom *has already* done what vv. 12–14 say not to do."[10]

In addition to the extensive verbal parallels between Obad 1–8 and Jer 49 (see notes on Obad 1–4, 5–8), there is another lesser verbal parallel: >/<**13** (3x); Jer 39:8, "day of disaster/disaster of Esau" (יום איד/איד עשׂו).[11]

Shared Stock Phrases and Other Similarities

Compare: >/<**11**; Joel 3:3[4:3], cast lots at plunder of Jerusalem (cf. Nah 3:10); >/<**14**; Amos 1:6, 9, Edomites as slave traders (cf. Lam 4:19); >/<**18**; Amos 1:12, fire as simile for military defeat of Edom (see stock phrases in Amos Filters).

Anti-Edom themes: **11**>/<Ezek 25:12–14; 35:5; Ps 137:7, participated in and/or celebrated the downfall of Jerusalem (cf. Ezek 36:5); **16**>/<Jer 25:15, 21; 49:12, Edom drinks judgment from Yahweh; **18**>/<Isa 34:5–7; Ezek 35:1–15; Mal 1:3–4; Lam 4:21–22, utter destruction of Edom. Shared themes naturally come from oracles against Edom in other prophets: Isa 21:11–12; 34; Jer 49:7–22; Ezek 35; Amos 1:11–12; Mal 1:3–4.

Amos 9:12 speaks of the people of the restored shelter of David taking possession of the remnant of Edom. The parallel B line refers to taking possession of all the nations that bear the name of Yahweh. Thus, it is not clear whether the sense of possessing the remainder of Edom refers to territory not yet under Israel's control or a political rule similar to the B line. In any case, after Obadiah speaks of "no survivors" of Esau, the sense of **Obad 21** seems to be taking possession of the territory of Edom.[12]

10. Nogalski, "The Day(s)," 208, emphasis original.
11. See Parke-Taylor, *Formation*, 147.
12. For a detailed comparison of Amos 9 and Obadiah, see Nogalski, "Seventy Years," 253–55.

Chapter 17

JONAH

SYMBOLS[1]

- // verbal parallels (A level)
- /~/ synoptic parallel (A level)
- ~ B, probable interpretive allusion; C, possible; D, probably not
- + interpretive blend
- >/< more or less similar (see Filters)
- * part of interpretive network (see Networks near end of volume)

USE OF SCRIPTURE IN JONAH[2]

3:9, 10~Exod 32:12, 14 (B) (Yahweh relents)
4:2*//Exod 34:6* (anger and the attribute formula)
(* see attribute formula network)

OLD TESTAMENT USE OF JONAH (SEE RESPECTIVE NOTES)

4:2*//Joel 2:13–14* (attribute formula) (* see attribute formula network)

NEW TESTAMENT USE OF JONAH

1:17[2:1]~Matt 12:40 (three days in fish)

HERMENEUTICAL PROFILE OF THE USE OF SCRIPTURE IN JONAH

The narrative and prayer of Jonah suggestively evoke many scriptural contexts. The vast majority should be regarded as stock phrases or the like with mere similarity to various scriptural contexts. These manifold echoes demonstrate a narrator well-versed in Israel's scriptural traditions. Many examples of shared imagery and non-exegetical uses of scriptural traditions have been collected in the Filters.

The cluster of interpretive allusions in Jonah stem from Israel's rebellion in Exodus. In Jonah's angry prayer he vents against divine grace. The verbal allusion to the attribute formula in Yahweh's revelation to Moses stands as the centerpiece of the most significant allusion (Exod 34:6). Although the attribute formula is a stock phrase within the lyrical

1. For explanation of symbols, see Symbols and Abbreviations and Introduction. For other help, see Glossary.
2. See Bibliographic Note on Lists of Potential Parallels.

diffusion of Scripture, there are distinctive elements in Jonah's use that demonstrate it has dependence on the narrative traditions of Exodus and is not simply a stock phrase.[3] Joel includes the same allusion with distinctions only shared by Joel and Jonah. These interpretive interventions require close attention because they provide evidence to determine direction of dependence. In short, the evidence suggests Exodus as donor and Jonah as receptor context, and Jonah as donor and Joel as receptor context.

The allusion to the attribute formula should be considered an epicenter for other more subtle allusive uses of Exodus in Jonah. If Moses intercedes to seek forgiveness for Israel, Jonah vents at Yahweh for extending forgiveness to the people of Nineveh. The angry prophet makes clear he had known of the problem of divine mercy for others from the moment he received the first call. The colorful, ironic, satirical account turns around many of the central theological themes from Exodus. Jonah's angst stems from his fear that Yahweh may be too merciful.

The king of Nineveh put to words the same kind of contingency for escaping condemnation ever implied in the warnings of the Hebrew prophets. If "unless his people repent" seems ever present in prophetic indictments against Israel, the king of Nineveh "accidentally" alludes to the attribute formula itself—"Who knows? God may turn and show compassion" (Jonah 3:9 lit.). But it does not end here.

The several interpretive interventions on the attribute formula in Jonah and Joel provide evidence to show, with some level of probability, that Joel applies the theological deductions in Jonah within his own prophetic message. This sequence demonstrates that even a highly stylized ironic narrative like Jonah authoritatively advances revelation. The gentile king's insightful question, "Who knows?," opens the way for Joel to offer the same hope to Zion at a time of terrible threat (see note on Joel 2:13–14). Interpretive advances sometimes come from unlikely exegetes like the king of Nineveh.

USE OF SCRIPTURE

3:9, 10~Exod 32:12, 14 (B) (Yahweh relents).
4:2*//Exod 34:6* (anger and the attribute formula) (* see attribute formula network).
Jonah narrates the repentance of Nineveh and the deity relenting from judgment with the language of Moses pleading for Yahweh to spare the people for the golden calf rebellion (emphases signify verbal parallels):[4]

> [Moses said] "*Turn from your fierce anger and relent* concerning the destructions upon your people. . . ." Then Yahweh *relented concerning the destruction he had threatened.* (Exod 32:12b, 14 lit.)

3. See list of scriptural echoes in note with attribute formula network.

4. These parallels have been noted by others (see Gray, "Parallel Passages," 217; Driver, *Joel and Amos*, 23; Kelly, "Joel, Jonah," 808, 826). However, none of these three include Exod 32:14//Jonah 3:10.

> [The king of Nineveh proclaimed] "Who knows? God *may turn and relent from his fierce anger* so that we will not perish." When God saw what they did and how they turned from their evil ways, he *relented concerning the destruction he had threatened,* and he did not do it. (Jonah 3:9, 10 lit.)

The prophetic narrative goes on to present Jonah's angry prayer based on the language of the attribute formula:

> And he passed in front of Moses, proclaiming, "Yahweh, Yahweh, *the compassionate and gracious God, slow to anger, abounding in love* and faithfulness." (Exod 34:6; cf. Num 14:18)

> He prayed to Yahweh, "Isn't this what I said, Yahweh, when I was still at home? That is what I tried to forestall by fleeing to Tarshish. I knew that you are a *gracious and compassionate God, slow to anger and abounding in love,* a God who relents from sending calamity." (Jonah 4:2)

The attribute formula appears frequently in Scripture (see attribute formula network). Still, the evidence supports a relationship between the attribute formula known in Exodus and Jonah because of verbal parallels distributed between narration and prayers. The inversion of "compassionate and gracious" exhibits an ancient scribal technique for marking quotations known as Seidel's theory, further strengthening evidence of intentional relationship. The evidence suggests the author of the Jonah narrative used the attribute formula within its narrative setting in Exodus because it works off both narrative and attribute formula. The shared language in Joel needs to be evaluated to determine if the relationship between Exodus and Jonah is immediate or mediated by Joel.

The parallels between Jonah 3:9; 4:2 and Joel 2:13–14 contain the evidence necessary to deduce direction of dependence. Both Jonah 4:2 and Joel 2:13 feature the same continuation of the attribute formula "who relents from sending calamity" (וְנִחָם עַל־הָרָעָה). This parallel, appended directly after the attribute formula and appearing only in these two versions of the attribute formula, nearly requires that one of the two uses the other (see the layout in the note on Joel 2:13–14). The parallels in all three contexts allows for triangulation to show Exodus as donor to Jonah and Joel as receptor from Jonah (emphases signify verbal parallels):

> [Moses said] "*Turn from your fierce anger and relent* concerning the destructions upon your people." (Exod 32:12b lit.)

> [The king of Nineveh proclaimed] "**Who knows?** God *may turn and relent from his fierce anger* so that we will not perish." (Jonah 3:9 lit.)

> **Who knows?** He *may turn and relent* and leave behind a blessing. (Joel 2:14)

Jonah could not be borrowing from Joel since the king of Nineveh continues to allude to the prayer of Moses in Exodus with "from your fierce anger," which does not appear in Joel (Exod 32:12; Jonah 3:9). And, Joel could not be borrowing directly from Exodus when he borrows from the king of Nineveh asking, "Who knows?" which does not appear in Exodus (Jonah 3:9; Joel 2:14).[5] The evidence of relationship and direction of dependence provides a basis to observe Jonah's exegetical advances.

Jonah's prayer offers decisive insight into its larger narrative and the overall theological function of the book. Jonah's prayer voices his motives for fleeing toward Tarshish. He fled because of the angst of proclaiming Yahweh's mercy to Nineveh (Jonah 4:2). Jonah knew divine forgiveness could be extended to the Ninevites from Exod 32 and 34. The attribute formula with its divine forgiveness at the head of the covenant renewal in Exod 34 points to a much broader opportunity for forgiveness. If Yahweh could forgive Israel's rebellion with the golden calf, he can forgive Nineveh. For this reason, the narrator identifies Jonah's underlying motives for his prayer. The mercy of Yahweh makes Jonah angry (4:1). More than that, Jonah would rather die than transmit a message that could trigger divine mercy (1:12) or bear witness to forgiveness (4:3). The narrator goes on to ridicule Jonah's tendency to seek death (4:9).

Kelly suggests that the language of Jonah's prayer may further echo Exodus (emphases signify verbal parallels):[6]

> [Israel] "*Isn't this what we said* to you in Egypt, 'Leave us alone; let us serve the Egyptians'? **It would have been better** for us to serve the Egyptians **than to die** in the desert!" (Exod 14:12)

> He [Jonah] prayed to Yahweh, "*Isn't this what I said*, Yahweh, when I was still at home? . . . Now, Yahweh, take away my life, **for it is better for me to die** than to live." (Jonah 4:2, 3)

The potential parallel relates to rather common words. The similarity with Elijah's desire to die cautions against hasty overreading (see Filters). But the other parallels to Moses's prayer and the attribute formula may invite observing other lesser echoes in Jonah's prayer. If Jonah intentionally echoes Israel at the sea, the comparison requires thought. They would rather be slaves than die but he would rather die than see the tyrants delivered. Neither Israel nor Jonah get what they want. Yahweh delivers Israel from slavery and he forgives Nineveh.

The larger significance of Jonah's ministry stems from the prophet's place in the

---

5. These deductions follow Kelly, "Joel, Jonah," 813–14. Lane comes to the opposite conclusion, but based on thematic deduction rather than evidence from interpretive interventions (see "Exodus 34:6–7," 117). For a concise summary of various views on dependence both ways, see Barker, "From Where?" 709, n. 51.

6. This comparison is based on Kelly, "Joel, Jonah," 820; Simon, *Jonah*, 36–37.

Kings narrative (2 Kgs 14:25). Less than two generations after Jonah preached judgment, effecting Nineveh's repentance, king Menahem placed himself under vassalage to Assyria (15:19).[7] In retrospect, vassalage to Assyria marked the twilight of the Northern Kingdom before its exile. If Jonah had succeeded in preventing forgiveness from coming to Nineveh, the doom of Israel in the hands of the empire could have been thwarted. The perspective of readers takes into account the reasons for Jonah's angst over divine mercy. Jonah fails. Mercy prevails. The tyrannical empire continues.

In sum, the interpretive interventions in Jonah provide the evidence necessary to triangulate Exodus as donor context to Jonah and Joel as receptor context from Jonah. Jonah's exegetical advance of the attribute formula pivots on the prophet's detection of divine mercy for any who repent, including Nineveh.

FILTERS

The narrative portions of Jonah share language, themes, and broad imagery with several scriptural contexts. The poetic section of Jonah shares stock phrases, common expressions, and a few potential non-exegetical broad allusions with several scriptural poetic contexts. The lists here are representative.[8]

Shared Stock Phrases and Other Similarities

Shared imagery: >/<**1:3**; Ezek 27:25–29, ships of Tarshish; >/<**1:4–16**; Ps 107:28–32, storm at sea; >/<**2:10[11]**; Job 20:15, Yahweh/God causing vomit.

Shared loaded terms of the sea crossing and Jonah:[9] >/<**1:9, 13; 2:10[11]**; Exod 14:16, 22, 29; 15:19, "dry land" (יַבָּשָׁה); >/<**2:5[6]**; Exod 15:4, 22, "seaweed/reed sea" (סוּף/יַם־סוּף); 2:3[4]; Exod 15:5, "deep waters" (מְצוֹלָה); >/<**2:5[6]**; Exod 15:5, 8, "depths" (תְּהוֹם).

The similarities between Jonah and other scriptural prophetic narratives do not classify as typology since they do not seem to be projecting connotation, unless in ironic ways. They also do not seem like type-scenes, since they are more like one-offs than genre forms. Though it is not clear what to make of them, notice several similarities: • "He [Elijah] himself went a day's journey into the wilderness. He came to a broom bush, sat down under it and prayed that he might die. 'I have had enough, Yahweh,' he said. 'Take my life; I am no better than my ancestors'" (1 Kgs 19:4) compared to "Now, Yahweh, take away my life, for it is better for me to die than to live.... Then Yahweh God provided a leafy plant and made it grow up over Jonah to give shade for his head to ease his discomfort, and Jonah was very happy about the plant" (Jonah 4:3, 6); divine double questions

7. Others have noted the timing also, see e.g., Kelly, "Joel, Jonah," 822–23.

8. For longer lists to which the present study is indebted, see Mitchell, Smith, and Bewer, *Jonah*, 23–24, 44–49; Dell, "Reinventing," 88–99; Driver, *Introduction*, 322–23; Hunter, "Jonah," 144–50; Simon, *Jonah*, xxxvi–xxxix. Also see items on Entire OT in Bibliographic Note on Lists of Potential Parallels.

9. These comparisons come from Hunter, "Jonah," 147–49.

(1 Kgs 19:9, 13 and Jonah 4:4, 9); • Yahweh changing his mind about judgment based on repentance (Jer 18:7–8; 26:3; Jonah 3:9, 10); • complaining prophets (Num 11:10–15; Jer 20:7–8; Jonah 4:1–3); • divine use of animals to manipulate prophet (Num 22:28–30; Jonah 1:17; 2:10[2:1, 11]; 4:7; cf. 3:7, 8; 4:11).

The prayer in Jonah 2 includes many poetic stock phrases and similar expressions from Israel's lyrical diffusion, of which the following are representative:[10] **2:2, 7[8]**>/<Ps 18:6[7], "my prayer rose to you, to your holy temple"/"from his temple he heard my voice, my cry came before him" (cf. Ps 5:7[8]); **2:2, 3b[3, 4b]**>/<Ps 42:7[8], "From deep in the realm of the dead I called for help . . . the currents swirled about me; all your waves and breakers swept over me"/"Deep calls to deep in the roar of your waterfalls; all your waves and breakers have swept over me" (cf. Ps 69:1b, 2, 15[2b, 3, 16]); **2:4[5]**>/<Ps 31:22[23] "I said, 'I have been banished from your sight; yet I will look again toward your holy temple'"/"In my alarm I said, 'I am cut off from your sight!' Yet you heard my cry for mercy when I called to you for help"; **2:5[6]**>/<Ps 18:4–5a[5–6a], "The engulfing waters threatened me, the deep surrounded me; seaweed was wrapped around my head. The cords of the grave coiled around me"/"The cords of death entangled me; the torrents of destruction overwhelmed me. The cords of the grave coiled around me"; **2:6[7]**>/<Ps 30:3[4], "But you, Yahweh my God, brought my life up from the pit"/"You, Yahweh, brought me up from the realm of the dead; you spared me from going down to the pit"; **2:7a[8a]**>/<Ps 142:3a[4a]//143:4a, "when my soul/spirit grows faint"; **2:8a[9a]**>/<Ps 31:6[7], "Those who cling to worthless idols"/"I hate those who cling to worthless idols"; **2:9[10]**>/<Ps 50:14, "But I, with shouts of grateful praise, will sacrifice to you. What I have vowed I will make good. I will say, 'Salvation comes from Yahweh'"/"Sacrifice thank offerings to God, fulfill your vows to the Most High" (cf. Ps 50:23b). Also note similar imagery in Job 14:13; 26:6; 30:22.

Jonah's Non-Exegetical Use of Jonah

The short book of Jonah contains many repetitions. The repetitious style lends itself to numerous proposals for paralleling (Jonah 1 and 3, etc.) as well as competing suggested chiastic structures. One feature called "the growing phrase" refers to expanded repetitions, such as: "a great storm upon the sea" (Jonah 1:4) to "the sea was growing more and more stormy" (1:11) to "the sea was growing more and more stormy about them" (1:13); "the sailors were afraid" (1:5) to "the men feared greatly" (1:10) to "the men feared Yahweh greatly" (1:16); "Is it right for you to be angry?" (4:4) to "Is it right for you to be angry about the plant" (4:9).[11]

10. For a large number of illustrative similarities, see Sasson, *Jonah*, 168–201.
11. See list of "growing phrases" in Simon, *Jonah*, xxxi.

Chapter 18

MICAH

SYMBOLS[1]

// verbal parallels (A level)
/~/ synoptic parallel (A level)
~ B, probable interpretive allusion; C, possible; D, probably not
\+ interpretive blend
>/< more or less similar (see Filters)
* part of interpretive network (see Networks near end of volume)

USE OF SCRIPTURE IN MICAH[2]

4:1–3//Isa 2:1–4 (mountain of Yahweh)
4:4//1 Kgs 4:25[5:5]//Zech 3:10 (under own vine and fig tree)
4:5~Isa 2:5 (B) (walk before Yahweh)
4:8~Gen 35:21 (C) (tower of the flock)
5:2*[1]~Gen 35:18–19 (B)+1 Sam 9:21+16:1, 11 (C) (ruler from Bethlehem Ephrathah) (* see Davidic covenant network)
5:8–9[7–8]~Gen 49:8–9* (C) (like a lion) (* see Judah-king network)
7:17~Gen 3:14 (B) (lick dust like a snake)
7:18–19*~Exod 15:1 (C)+34:6, 7* (C) (God who pardons) (* see attribute formula network)

OLD TESTAMENT USE OF MICAH (SEE RESPECTIVE NOTES)

3:12//Jer 26:18 (Zion plowed)
4:2–3~Zech 8:21–22 (B) (international pilgrimage to Jerusalem)
4:3//Joel 3:10[4:10] (ironically) (swords and plowshares)
4:4~Zech 3:10 (C) (under one's own vine and fig tree)
7:17>/<Ps 72:9 (lick the dust)

NEW TESTAMENT USE OF MICAH

5:2, 4[1, 3]//Matt 2:6; cf. John 7:42 (ruler from Bethlehem)
7:6//Matt 10:35–36 (man against father)

HERMENEUTICAL PROFILE OF THE USE OF SCRIPTURE IN MICAH

Micah tends toward suggestion to evoke scriptural traditions. He uses wordplays and brief lyrical expressions to sketch rich connotations of judgment and hope for his constituency.

1. For explanation of symbols, see Symbols and Abbreviations and Introduction. For other help, see Glossary.
2. See Bibliographic Note on Lists of Potential Parallels.

For this reason many broad scriptural allusions and thematic similarities have been collected into the Filters.

The nature of Micah's style does not normally include verbatim quotation. The single exception is the vision of the mountain in Isa 2:1–5 and Mic 4:1–5, if Isaiah or a shared source is the donor context. The striking differences between the nations that stream to the mountain in Mic 4 versus Isa 2 require pause. If Isaiah emphasizes a common shared commitment to Yahweh's torah, Micah underlines the residual otherness of the nations.

Micah seems to engage the ironic function of Bethlehem Ephrathah in the scriptural traditions of the Davidic ruler coming from the place known by its association with the birth of Benjamin. However the ironic undercurrents play out, Micah emphasizes the ancient hope for a ruler to come out of little Bethlehem Ephrathah.

The rich poetic expectation of vindication from shame over the enemies of God's people in Micah 7:8–20 seems to suggest scriptural traditions from lyrical diffusion in every line. In the closing lines Micah evokes the commonly used attribute formula but blends it with exodus-like imagery. The real enemy turns out to be much closer to home than Egypt or Mesopotamia. Micah personifies sin as a military foe that God will subdue and throw into the sea like any other enemy. By identifying sinfulness as the true enemy, Micah significantly advances revelation.

Micah excels at appropriating and applying fleeting lyrical traditions and poetic stock phrases. He employs these creatively to indict Samaria and especially Judah for rebelling against God's will. Amos, Hosea, and Micah overlap in many ways, but with different angles. Hosea emphasizes historical episodes as similes and lists place names to evoke historical allusions. Amos mocks devout, affluent, shrine-going Israelites with sarcastic, distorted legal references. Micah employs a profusion of traditional lyrical images that suggest rather than spell out manifold allusions to communicate his message of judgment and expectation. Micah's style puts demands upon his audience for patient and connective study of his oracles.

USE OF SCRIPTURE

4:1–3//Isa 2:1–4 (mountain of Yahweh).

4:4//1 Kgs 4:25[5:5]//Zech 3:10 (under own vine and fig tree).

4:5~Isa 2:5 (B) (walk before Yahweh). The extensive verbal and syntactical parallels between Isa 2:1–5 and Mic 4:1–5 require some kind of relationship, whether direct or indirect (also see note on Joel 3:10). Though the shared locutions themselves do not provide evidence of direction of dependence, the frameworks suggest Isa 2:1–5 as donor and Mic 4:1–5 as receptor context. Isaiah's version includes the formal vision superscription, "This is what Isaiah son of Amoz saw concerning Judah and Jerusalem" (Isa 2:1), and Micah's version includes a quasi-marking formula, "for Yahweh Almighty has spoken"

(Mic 4:4).[3] The present context will spell out a few of the exegetical advances in Micah's use of the mountain of Yahweh (no emphasis signifies verbatim parallels, italics signify adjustments, bold signifies unparalleled variations, underlining signifies parallel variations, double underlining signifies quasi-marking, and broken underlining signifies an example of Seidel's theory):

> **This is what Isaiah son of Amoz saw concerning Judah and Jerusalem:** [2] In the last days the mountain of Yahweh's temple will be established as the highest of the mountains; it will be exalted above the hills, and all nations will stream to it. [3] Many *peoples* will come and say, "Come, let us go up to the mountain of Yahweh, to the temple of the God of Jacob. He will teach us his ways, so that we may walk in his paths." The law will go out from Zion, the word of Yahweh from Jerusalem. [4] He will judge between *the nations and will settle disputes for many peoples.* They will beat their swords into plowshares and their spears into pruning hooks. Nation will not take up sword against nation, nor will they train for war anymore. [5] Come, descendants of Jacob, let us walk in the light of Yahweh. (Isa 2:1–5)

> In the last days the mountain of Yahweh's temple will be established as the highest of the mountains; it will be exalted above the hills, and peoples will stream to it. [2] Many *nations* will come and say, "Come, let us go up to the mountain of Yahweh, to the temple of the God of Jacob. He will teach us his ways, so that we may walk in his paths." The law will go out from Zion, the word of Yahweh from Jerusalem. [3] He will judge between *many peoples and will settle disputes for strong nations far and wide.* They will beat their swords into plowshares and their spears into pruning hooks. Nation will not take up sword against nation, nor will they train for war anymore. [4] **Everyone will sit under their own vine and under their own fig tree, and no one will make them afraid,** for Yahweh Almighty has spoken. [5] All the nations may walk in the name of their gods, but we will walk in the name of Yahweh our God for ever and ever. (Mic 4:1–5)

In Isaiah's version the nations and Jacob each "come" to the mountain to walk in the light (Isa 2:3, 5). If the nations come to gain instruction from Yahweh, then when Jacob walks in the light it carries a similar sense (see note on Isa 2:1–5). In sharp contrast, Micah speaks of the nations' coming to learn from Yahweh's instruction, but then they return to worship their own gods (Mic 4:3, 5). Micah's version features an uncomfortable incongruity in the nations coming to learn Yahweh's commands and being committed to obeying his torah (4:2) yet returning to their respective homelands to serve their own gods (4:5). Micah does not explain how the nations can both seek to walk in the path of Yahweh's instruction and yet ignore the demand for exclusive worship of Yahweh (4:5).

---

3. This observation from Schultz, *Search for Quotation*, 293, 304.

This difficult incongruity in Micah's version distinguishes between the people of God and the nations. If Micah did use Isaiah's vison of the mountain as the quasi-marking tentatively suggests, why did he draw a sharp contrast between the walk of Jacob versus the walk of the nations (Isa 2:5; Mic 4:5)? It seems Micah's version of the expectation for fidelity to Yahweh alone corresponds exactly to his present concern which turns on the infidelity of Jerusalem (Mic 3:1–12). In contrast to the present rebellion, Micah uses Isaiah's vision of the mountain to underscore the need for the people of Yahweh to walk in accord with his instruction.

The other significant interpretive advance in Micah's version of the vision of the mountain comes in Mic 4:4. The combination of vine and fig tree reflects a commonplace figure of speech.[4] But the close resemblance of Mic 4:4 and 1 Kgs 4:25[5:5], set apart from related expressions by using both of the common terms "sit" and "under," may suggest some kind of relationship, whether direct or indirect (also similarly in Zech 3:10). Perhaps the Deuteronomist uses the idealistic prophetic imagery of Mic 4:4 to capture the idyllic luxury of Solomon's empire. The use of the same imagery in the taunts of the Assyrian field commander against Jerusalem fits with his other uses of prophetic imagery from Judah's prophets (see Table I2 in Isaiah; note on 1 Kgs 18:31). In any case, the use of the imagery of prosperity in terms of each person under their own vine and fig tree extends beyond the absence of war to prosperity and peace.

In sum, the evidence tentatively suggests Mic 4:1–5 as an exegetical allusion to Isaiah's vision of the mountain of Yahweh. Micah elaborates on personal benefits but also sharply distinguishes between Jacob and "them" in the last days.

4:8~Gen 35:21 (C) (tower of the flock).

5:2*[1]~Gen 35:18–19 (B)+1 Sam 9:21+16:1, 11 (C) (ruler from Bethlehem Ephrathah) (* see Davidic covenant network). Mays suspects the shared themes in Mic 4:8; 5:2, 4[1, 3] indicate that they come from a common source.[5] Whether they do or not, the connectedness of Micah's development of this theme includes the simile of the daughter of Zion/daughter Zion in difficult labor in 4:9, 10, and 5:3[2]. The "watchtower of the flock" appears only in Gen 35:21 and Mic 4:8.[6] Most of the modern committee translations obscure the parallel by transliterating it as a proper name, Migdal Eder (מִגְדַּל־עֵדֶר) in Gen 35:21 but "watchtower of the flock" (מִגְדַּל־עֵדֶר) or the like in Mic 4:8 (NIV, NRSV, etc.). The watchtower seems to be near Ephrath or Bethlehem, where Rachel died after hard labor giving birth to Benjamin (Gen 35:16–21).[7] The strong irony of David

4. See Num 20:5; Deut 8:8; Isa 34:4; Jer 5:17; 8:13; Hos 2:14; 9:10; Joel 1:7, 12; 2:22; Amos 4:9; Hab 2:19; Hag 2:19; Ps 105:33; Prov 27:8; Song 2:13 ("תְּאֵנָה," *HALOT* 2:1675).

5. See Mays, *Micah*, 113. The discussion of Gen 35:21; Mic 4:8; 5:2[1] is indebted to Doolittle, "On the Way to Ephrath," passim, though this study reaches different conclusions.

6. See "II מִגְדָּל," no. 3 *HALOT* 1:544.

7. The location of Ephrath/Ephrathah may be somewhere near the Judah/Benjamin border since one tradition assigns it to Benjamin (1 Sam 10:2) while others identify it with Jaar (Ps 132:6), apparently Kiriath Jearim (1 Sam 7:1) and Bethlehem (Gen 35:19; Ruth 4:11). Chronicles refers to Ephrathah son of Caleb as grandfather of Kiriath Jearim and Bethlehem (1 Chr 2:50–51). This identification is indebted to Sarna, *Genesis*, 407–8.

of Judah hailing from Bethlehem to replace Saul the Benjamite king plays out in the undercurrents of these potential interpretive allusions in Micah. The use of "going out" (יצא) to Babylon, resolving the daughter Zion's labor in Mic 4:10, anticipates reversal by the ruler who "goes out" (יצא) from Bethlehem Ephrathah, whose "going out" (יצא) originates from of old in 5:2[1].

The linkage between Mic 4:8 and 5:2[1] includes "former dominion" and "from of old, from ancient times."[8] Although daughter Zion serves as the subject of the running simile of a woman in labor (Mic 5:9, 10 and 5:3[2]), the ruler will come forth from "you" (ms) Bethlehem Ephrathah (5:2[1]). The imagery of Bethlehem Ephrathah as "small" seems to play off both Saul and David traditions appearing in Samuel (italics, bold, and underlining signify verbal parallels; and broken underlining signifies synonyms):[9]

> As she breathed her last—for she was dying—she named her son Ben-Oni. But his father named him Benjamin. So Rachel died and was buried on the way to **Ephrathah** (that is, **Bethlehem**). . . . Israel moved on again and pitched his tent beyond *tower of the flock* [מִגְדַּל־עֵדֶר]. (Gen 35:18–19, 21†)

> Saul answered, "But am I not a Benjamite, from the smallest tribe of Israel, and is not my clan the least [צְעִיר] of all the clans of the tribe of Benjamin? Why do you say such a thing to me?" (1 Sam 9:21; cf. Ps 68:27[28])

> Yahweh said to Samuel, "How long will you mourn for Saul, since I have rejected him as king over Israel? Fill your horn with oil and be on your way; I am sending you to Jesse of **Bethlehem**. I have chosen one of his sons to be king." . . . So he asked Jesse, "Are these all the sons you have?" "There is still the youngest [קָטָן]," Jesse answered. "He is tending the sheep." Samuel said, "Send for him; we will not sit down until he arrives." (1 Sam 16:1, 11; cf. 17:12)

> As for you, *watchtower of the flock* [מִגְדַּל־עֵדֶר], stronghold of Daughter Zion, the former dominion will be restored to you; kingship will come to Daughter Jerusalem. . . . But you, **Bethlehem Ephrathah**, though you are small [צָעִיר] among the clans of Judah, out of you will come for me one who will be ruler over Israel, whose origins are from of old, from ancient times. (Mic 4:8; 5:2[1])

Micah seems to take advantage of the ironies of David an Ephrathite (1 Sam 17:12) coming from Bethlehem, associated with the birth of Benjamin, to get at ancient

8. Hillers identifies "former dominion" (הַמֶּמְשָׁלָה הָרִאשֹׁנָה) (Mic 4:8) with "from of old, from ancient times" (מִקֶּדֶם מִימֵי עוֹלָם) (5:2[1]) (*Micah*, 56).

9. On the possible associations of "small" (צָעִיר) and "small" (קָטָן) with Saul and David and Micah's oracle, see Mays, *Micah*, 116.

expectations for the Davidic ruler (Mic 5:2[1]). The reference to Bethlehem Ephrathah as small may further draw on the Saul and David traditions by evoking the sense of Saul's small family in a small tribe and David's youth. The same irony attaches to small Bethlehem Ephrathah, once again as an unlikely source of renewal. Micah addresses the town directly and suggestively mentions the ancient expectations as key to future hope.[10] He goes on to speak of the ruler in terms of a shepherd bringing security and peace (5:4–5[3–4]). The shepherding imagery, whether it looks back to Joshua or to David (Num 27:17; 2 Sam 7:7, 8) or is simply a common idea, leans forward to a renewal of the days of old in Mic 7:14.

5:8–9[7–8]~Gen 49:8–9* (C) (like a lion) (* see Judah-king network). Micah uses the simile of a lion to describe the rule of the remnant of Israel (Mic 5:8–9[7–8]). The oracle shares some imagery with the blessing of Judah but not enough to suggest more than a possible allusion (emphases signify verbal parallels at the level of roots):

> Judah, your brothers will praise you; **your hand** will be on the neck of **your enemies**; your father's sons will bow down to you. You are a lion's cub, Judah; you return from *the prey* [טֶרֶף], my son. **Like a lion** he crouches and lies down, like a lioness—who dares to rouse him? (Gen 49:8–9)

> The remnant of Jacob will be among the nations, in the midst of many peoples, **like a lion** among the beasts of the forest, like a young lion among flocks of sheep, which mauls and *mangles* [טרף] as it goes, and no one can rescue. **Your hand** will be lifted up in triumph over your foes, and all **your enemies** will be destroyed. (Mic 5:8–9†[7–8])

7:17~Gen 3:14 (B) (lick dust like a snake). The parallels of "dust" (עָפָר) and "snake" (נָחָשׁ) suggest Mic 7:17 adapts the scriptural tradition that appears in Gen 3:14. Elsewhere the psalmist refers to enemies "licking the dust" as they bow before God's righteous king but without the term snake (Ps 72:9). Micah's use of this imagery serves as a climax of references to enemies trampled down in the mire (Mic 7:10). Micah advances the ancient curse by using it as a description of the enemies of Yahweh's people.

7:18–19*~Exod 15:1 (C)+34:6, 7* (C) (God who pardons) (* see attribute formula network). Micah's use of the language of the attribute formula may not stem directly from the scriptural tradition known in Exod 34:6–7. The imagery enjoyed wide currency in the lyrical diffusion (see list with attribute formula network). Without deciding on direct dependence, the attribute formula of Exodus will be used here for convenience (emphases denote verbal parallels at the level of shared roots):

---

10. Micah's earlier contemporary Amos spoke of the Davidic shelter "in days of old" (כִּימֵי עוֹלָם) (see note on Amos 9:11).

> And he passed in front of Moses, proclaiming, "Yahweh, Yahweh, the **compassionate** and gracious God, slow to anger, abounding in **mercy** and faithfulness, maintaining love to thousands, and *pardons iniquity, transgression*, and sin. . . ." [Moses said,] "forgive our *iniquity* and our sin, and take us as your <u>inheritance</u>." (Exod 34:6–7a, 9b†)

> Who is a God like you, who *pardons iniquity* and forgives *the transgression* of the remnant of his <u>inheritance</u>? You do not stay angry forever but delight to **show mercy**. You will again have **compassion** on us. (Mic 7:18–19a†)

Micah's most significant exegetical advancement pivots on personifying sin as enemy of the people of God. By this personification Micah speaks of subduing iniquity and throwing sin into the depths of the sea (Mic 7:19). Micah's A line refers to divine compassion and the B line to the concept of "subjection," which can be used in non-military contexts like the dominion of humans (Gen 1:28) or in warfare contexts like this one.[11] Micah shifts from long attention to human enemies in Mic 7:8–17 to the military-like subjection of iniquity as enemy.

The C line of Mic 7:19 seems to evoke the Song of the Sea. The verbal evidence only includes the term "depths" but the imagery of casting military is very suggestive. DiFransico builds her case for an allusion by noting numerous shared terms between Mic 7 and the Song of the Sea.[12] Many of these common terms do not make a convincing case. Two factors can be noted about this comparison. First, the Song of the Sea uses archaic language. Second, Micah's standard practice tends to be fleeting poetic suggestions, often in his own style, rather than verbatim quotation. That is, expecting more than poetic suggestion does not fit the nature of the case. The limited evidence fits with "maybe/maybe not" in this study, though many commentators more confidently see an allusion to the Song of the Sea in Mic 7:19.[13] Allen frames the shared imagery well by asking if the Song of the Sea has influenced the oracle again.[14] The advance in Mic 7:19 does not turn on explaining what happened at the sea, but to use exodus-like imagery to depict the defeat of the true enemy of the people of God. Micah uses the abstract concept of sin and virtually personifies it in its losing battle with God himself.[15] The juxtaposition between the forgiveness of the attribute formula and an exodus-like defeat in Mic 7:18–19

11. On biblical uses of "subjugate" see "כבשׁ," *HALOT* 1:460.

12. The shared terms include: "my salvation" (ויהי לישועה/ישעי) (Exod 15:2; Mic 7:7); "cover" them (כפר) (Exod 15:5; Mic 7:10); "your inheritance" (נחלתך) (Exod 15:17; Mic 7:14); "wonders" (פלא) (Exod 15:11; Mic 7:15); "tremble" (רגז) (Exod 15:14; Mic 7:17); "loyalty" or "mercy" (חסד) (Exod 15:13; Mic 7:18)—though this more likely evokes Exod 34:6 as noted above; "Who is like you?" (מי כמכה/מי . . . כמוך) (Exod 15:11; Mic 7:18); as well as a few lesser suggested similarities. See DiFransico, "'He Will Cast,'" 192–93. For a detailed discussion of verbal and thematic parallels between Mic 7:8–20 and many scriptural contexts, see Banister, "Theophanies," 99–120.

13. Anderson and Freedman, *Micah*, 599; Mays, *Micah*, 167–68.

14. See Allen, *Micah*, 402.

15. See Banister, "Theophanies," 120; DiFransico, "'He Will Cast,'" 189–90.

highlight the profound problem of human sinfulness that serves as the pretext for the entire prophetic tradition.

The Song of the Sea and Miriam's refrain are the only two uses in Scripture of this term for "throw" (רמה) with this sense (Exod 15:1, 21).[16] The term for "throw" (ירה) in Exod 15:4 typically refers to shooting arrows but denotes throwing in at least a couple of other cases.[17] Micah 7:19 uses the more normal term for "throw" (שלך), used, e.g., when the pharaoh commands his people to "throw" (שלך) Hebrew male infants into the river (Exod 1:22). Four of twelve uses of the term for "depths" (מְצוֹלָה) in Scripture refer to the Egyptians or Jonah or sin being thrown to the depths (Exod 15:5; Jonah 2:3[4]; Mic 7:19; Neh 9:11).[18] Compare the Song of the Sea and the ending of Micah (bold signifies verbal parallels, and italics signify similarities):

> Then Moses and the Israelites sang this song to Yahweh: "I will sing to Yahweh, for he is highly exalted. Both horse and driver he *has hurled* [רמה] **into the sea.**" (Exod 15:1)

> Pharaoh's chariots and his army he *has hurled* [ירה] **into the sea.** The best of Pharaoh's officers are drowned in the Red **Sea.** The deep waters have covered them; they sank to **the depths** like a stone. (15:4–5)

> Miriam sang to them: "Sing to Yahweh, for he is highly exalted. Both horse and driver he *has hurled* [רמה] **into the sea.**" (15:21)

> He will again have compassion on us; he will subdue our iniquities and you *hurl* [שלך] all their sins **into the depths of the sea.** (Mic 7:19 lit.)

The troubles of the prophet's audience might include political and military crises from empire aggression. But these are not the real problems. They are symptomatic of something deeper. Yahweh takes responsibility for the national crises resulting from Assyria's invasion as divine judgment for rebellion (Mic 3:12). Yahweh will be faithful to grind the enemies of his people into the mire (7:10) and into dust like the serpent of old (7:17). But the prophet flips the tables at this point, exposing the people's own rebellion against God's definitive redemptive work. Micah uses ancient redemptive imagery known in Exodus to speak of defeating the true enemy within the people, namely, their own sinfulness (7:18–20). For Christians, Micah's use of scriptural imagery sounds like it belongs in the New Testament. But that gets it backwards. Micah retrojects his scriptural

---

16. See "I רמה," *HALOT* 2:1239.

17. See "I ירה," *HALOT* 1:436.

18. See "מְצוֹלָה," *HALOT* 1:623. The other uses refer to the depths of the sea, a ravine, floodwaters, or the deity's wonders (Pss 68:22[23]; 69:2, 15[3, 16]; Job 41:31[23]; Zech 1:8) or of the Nile or some unspecified deep place (Zech 10:11; Ps 88:7).

interpretations of good news of victory over sin back into the redemptive traditions of Torah. In this manner God's redemptive plan to vanquish sin unfolds from the forgiveness at the mountain and advances through the prophets of Judah. The New Testament applies this progressive revelation of divine mercy in the gospel of Messiah.

FILTERS

Micah shares many verbal-parallel and thematically similar elements with other Scriptures that do not constitute exegetical allusion. The lists below offer illustrations from the filters applied to Micah in the present study. Other lists elsewhere include additional potential verbal and thematic parallels between Micah and other Scriptures.[19] The following representative lists are not comprehensive or complete.

Non-Exegetical Broad Allusions and Shared Themes

As part of a disputation (ריב), **Mic 6:4–5** presents a short retrospective leading up to a recognition formula—"That you may know the righteous acts of Yahweh" (לְמַעַן דַּעַת צִדְקוֹת יהוה) (Mic 6:5). The retrospective includes "I brought you up" (עלה Hif) from Egypt, sending Moses, Aaron, and Miriam, the plot of Balak and Balaam, and, apparently, the crossing of the Jordan between Shittim and Gilgal (6:4–5). The outline loosely refers to events narrated from Exodus through the opening of Joshua. This is the only reference to Miriam outside Torah except 1 Chr 6:3[5:29] (on the other Miriam see note on 1 Chr 4:17).[20] The characterization of these as "righteous acts" fits the context of a disputation (Mic 5:1).[21] Joosten observes that Samuel's disputation with Israel shares a few locutions with this context in Micah: "Testify against me!" (ענה בי) (1 Sam 12:3; Mic 6:3); reference to sending Moses and Aaron (1 Sam 12:8; Mic 6:4; the pair without the verb elsewhere outside Torah only in Josh 24:5); and "righteous acts of Yahweh" (צדקות יהוה) (1 Sam 12:7; Mic 6:5; elsewhere only in Judg 5:11).[22] These parallels may indicate some kind of relationship, whether direct or indirect, between these two contexts. The general nature of these similarities does not suggest exegetical intervention. In sum: 6:4>/<Exod 4:29–30; 15:20–21, Moses, Aaron, and Miriam; 6:5a>/<Num 22–24, conspiracy of Balak and Balaam; 6:5b>/<Josh 3:1; 4:19, crossing Jordan from Shittim to Gilgal.

Micah 6:6–7 strings together over-the-top hyperbolic offerings to ridicule zealous but hypocritical worshipers and draw a contrast between empty worship and Yahweh's

---

19. See Anderson and Freedman, *Micah*, 27; Bergren, *Prophets and the Law*, 182–83; Cheyne, *Micah*, 12; Driver, *Introduction*, 334, n.; Schultz, *Search for Quotation*, 306 (also see on Entire OT in Bibliographic Note on Lists of Potential Parallels).

20. The speculative emendation from "*My people* remember . . ." (עַמִּי) to open Mic 6:5 to "and Miriam *with him*" (עִמּוֹ) to close 6:4 in *BHS* is without evidence (see *BHQ*; contra Mays, *Micah*, 128, who suggests emendation improves parallelism). MT is preferred.

21. See Dearman, "Observations," 265; Mays, *Micah*, 12, 135–36.

22. See Joosten, "YHWH's Farewell," 453.

demands for justice and humble devotion in 6:8. Micah's memorable conclusion—"And what does Yahweh require of you? To act justly and to love mercy and to walk humbly with your God" (Mic 6:8)—accords with numerous prophetic traditions calling for social righteousness and morality with true worship. See other kindred traditions in Table A3 in Amos Filters.

Other broad non-exegetical allusions: **1:7**>/<Deut 7:5, 24–26; 12:3, destroy idolatry (wages of prostitute, cf. 23:18[19]); **5:6[5]**>/<Gen 10:8–11, land of Nimrod; **5:12[11]**>/<Lev 19:26; Deut 18:10, 14, sorcery; **7:6**>/<Exod 20:12; 21:15, 17; Deut 27:16, (dis)honor parents; **7:15**>/<Exod 6–15, show wonders like the days of coming out from Egypt.

Shared Stock Phrases and Other Similarities

The **opening of Micah** resembles the opening of Isaiah, which, in turn, may allude to the opening of the Song of Moses (Deut 32:1; see note on Isa 1:2). "*Hear* [שמע], you peoples, all of you, listen [קשב], earth and all who live in it" (Mic 1:2), and "*Hear* [שמע] me, you heavens! Listen [אזן], earth!" (Isa 1:2). The similarities in Micah, if more than coincidence, adapt the language in new ways.

Other stock phrases and broad similarities: >/<**1:2**; Hab 2:20, "The Lord from his holy temple/Yahweh in his holy temple" (אדני מהיכל קדשו/יהוה בהיכל קדשו); >/<**1:3**; Amos 4:13, "he treads on high places" (דרך במתי ארץ) (cf. Judg 5:4; Ps 68:7[8]; Deut 33:2); >/<**1:4**; Ps 97:5, mountains melt; >/<**1:8**; Isa 13:21; 34:13; 43:20; Jer 50:39; Job 30:29, howl of jackal and ostriches; >/<**1:16**; Isa 15:2; Jer 7:29; 16:6; Amos 8:10, make bald in mourning; >/<**2:1**; Ps 36:4[5], plot evil "upon bed" (עַל־מִשְׁכָּב); >/<**2:2**; Isa 5:8, seizing fields and houses; >/<**2:11**; Isa 28:7, teachers of wine and intoxication; >/<**2:13**; Exod 19:22, 24; 2 Sam 5:20; 6:8; Ps 106:29; 1 Chr 14:11; 15:13, "break out" (פרץ);[23] >/<**2:13**; Isa 52:12, Yahweh will pass through/go before; >/<**3:2**; Isa 5:20; Amos 5:15, hate good and love evil; >/<**3:5**; Jer 6:14//8:11; 23:17; Ezek 13:10, false "peace" prophets; >/<**3:8**; Isa 58:1, "declare transgression . . . and sin" (נגד . . . פשע . . . חטאת); >/<**3:11; 7:3**; Isa 1:23, ruler and judges accept gifts and bribes; >/<**4:1**; Ps 48:2[3], Zion highest mountain; >/<**4:7**; Zeph 3:19, remnant/salvation of "the lame" (צלע); >/<**4:9**; Isa 13:8, "seizes like a woman in labor" (חזק חיל כילדה) (cf. 21:3; 26:17; Jer 4:31; 48:41; 49:22); >/<**4:10**; Isa 39:6–7//2 Kgs 20:17–18, exile to Babylon; >/<**4:13**; Hos 10:11, simile of threshing work animal; >/<**5:5[4]**; Isa 9:6[5], "he will be our peace" (שלום)/"prince of peace" (שלום); >/<**5:8[7]**; Amos 3:4, 12; 5:19, like a lion (cf. Ps 91:13); >/<**5:13[12]**; Exod 23:24; 34:13; Deut 7:5; 12:3; 16:22, "sacred stones" (מצבה); >/<**5:13[12]**; Isa 2:8, "you will no longer bow down to the work of your hands/to the work of their hands they bow down" (לא תשתחוה עוד למעשה ידיך/למעשה ידיו ישתחוו); >/<**6:11**, "wicked scales" (מאזני רשע), Lev 19:36, "righteous scales" (מאזני צדק), Hos 12:7[8]; Amos 8:5; Prov

23. See "I פרץ," *HALOT* 2:971–72.

11:1; 20:23, "dishonest scales" (מאזני מרמה); >/<**6:16** (ironic); Jer 19:8; 25:9, 18; 51:37; Zeph 2:15; Lam 2:15, 16; 2 Chr 29:8, object of hissing/hiss at; >/<**7:2**; Prov 1:11, lie in wait for blood (ארב לדמים); >/<**7:10a**; Ezek 7:18; Obad 10; Ps 89:45[46], covered with shame (כסה בּוֹשָׁה); >/<**7:10b**; Isa 5:5; 10:6; 28:18; Zech 9:3; 10:5, trod down like mire (cf. 2 Sam 22:43//Ps 18:43); >/<**7:12**; Isa 11:11, regathering remnant from Assyria and Egypt; >/<**7:17**; Isa 49:23, "they will lick the dust" (ילחכו עפר).

Micah's Non-Exegetical Use of Micah

Micah features numerous internal literary connections, such as: **1:5>/<3:12**, "overgrown high place" (בָּמוֹת יָעַר)/"What is Judah's high place?" (בָּמוֹת), cf. wordplay in 5:8[7], "beasts of the forest" (בַּהֲמוֹת יַעַר);[24] **5:4[3]>/<7:14**, tend to his flock (רעה); **1:2>/<6:1–2; 7:9**, listen peoples/mountains/earth! (שׁמע), plead case (ריב).[25]

24. See Ben Zvi, "Ancient Readers," 89.
25. Also see Anderson and Freedman, *Micah*, 28.

Chapter 19

NAHUM

SYMBOLS[1]

// verbal parallels (A level)
/~/ synoptic parallel (A level)
~ B, probable interpretive allusion; C, possible; D, probably not
+ interpretive blend
>/< more or less similar (see Filters)
* part of interpretive network (see Networks)

USE OF SCRIPTURE IN NAHUM[2]

1:2–3*~Exod 20:5*//Deut 5:9* (C)+Exod 34:6–7* (B) (a jealous and avenging God) (* see attribute formula network)

1:15[2:1]~Isa 52:7 (B) (the feet of one who brings good news)

OLD TESTAMENT USE OF NAHUM

n/a

NEW TESTAMENT USE OF NAHUM

1:15~Rom 10:15 (beautiful feet bring good news)
3:4~Rev 17:2 (her promiscuities)

HERMENEUTICAL PROFILE OF THE USE OF SCRIPTURE IN NAHUM

Nahum shares much in terms of outlook and expressions with the scriptural prophetic traditions. But he only uses exegetical intervention with scriptural traditions in a limited way.

Nahum's singular focus on the doom of Nineveh starts with an exegetical use of scriptural traditions. Nahum first speaks of Yahweh as a jealous and avenging God as an on-ramp to empire-ending judgments against Nineveh's longtime domination. Yet, because Nineveh's doom starts with Yahweh's covenantal character, Nahum's oracles offer good news to God's people intertwined with an ironic challenge. Yahweh's avenging character applies to those who transgress his jealous demand for exclusive fidelity. In this way, the good news of Nineveh's doom carries a warning to remain devoted to Yahweh alone.

1. For explanation of symbols, see Symbols and Abbreviations and Introduction. For other help, see Glossary.
2. See Bibliographic Note on Lists of Potential Parallels.

The interpretive intervention in Nah 1:2–3 offers the evidence necessary to deduce that it is the receptor to a blend of donor contexts, namely, the attribute formula (Exod 34:6–7) and the second commandment or a derivative use of it in the covenant renewal (20:5; 34:14).

Several prophets exegetically engage the attribute formula of Exod 34:6–7 toward different agendas. Yahweh frustrates Jonah's angry complaints of extending forgiveness to Nineveh (see note on Jonah 4:2). Joel finds the king of Nineveh's question "Who knows?" an entry point to call Jerusalem to turn to Yahweh in the day of their desperate trouble (see note on Joel 2:13–14). Nahum works on the other side of the attribute formula. Yahweh's jealous character activates his avenging wrath against Nineveh. The doom of Nineveh is good news for his people as they remain faithful to Yahweh alone.

USE OF SCRIPTURE

1:2–3*~Exod 20:5*//Deut 5:9* (C)+Exod 34:6–7* (B) (a jealous and avenging God) (* see attribute formula network). The attribute formula of Exod 34:6–7 explains the divine character based on the second commandment as it applies to covenant renewal. The powerful attribute formula attracts many interpretations in Scripture. In Torah both Exod 34:14–16 and Deut 7:9–10 offer interpretations of the difficult idea of transgenerational punishment (see notes ad loc.). The former of these relates to Nah 1:2 since it identifies Yahweh as "a jealous God" whose very name is Jealous (Exod 34:14). Nahum 1:2 likewise borrows the idea of "a jealous God" from the second commandment but pairs it with "avenging" (Exod 20:5//Deut 5:9; Nah 1:2). Outside of Exod 34:14–16, Deut 7:9–10, and Nah 1:3 all of the many other uses of the attribute formula work out divine mercy, compassion, and covenantal loyalty (see Table Joel1). Jonah and Joel, respectively, feature interpretive applications of the attribute formula to gentiles and Zion in trouble (see notes on Joel 2:13–14; Jonah 4:2). Nahum alone of the prophets exegetically advances the attribute formula with respect to the vengeful outcomes of provoking Yahweh's jealousy.[3]

Nahum 1:2–3 includes evidence of relationship with the attribute formula itself, not the derivative or stock uses, since it uniquely includes verbal correspondence to judgment upon the guilty. The verbal parallels with the attribute formula include the phrases "slow to anger" and "by no means acquit the guilty" (וְנַקֵּה לֹא יְנַקֶּה) (Exod 34:7//Nah 1:3 lit.; cf. Num 14:18), while the third commandment merely says "will not acquit" (לֹא יְנַקֶּה) (Exod 20:7//Deut 5:11 lit.).[4]

The verbal relationship between the second commandment and the attribute formula in Exod 20:5–6 and 34:6–7 strongly suggests the second commandment as donor and the attribute formula as receptor context (see note ad loc.). The interpretive intervention in

3. See Fishbane, "Torah and Tradition," 280–81; idem, *Biblical Interpretation*, 347.

4. The phrase "slow to anger" (אֶרֶךְ אַפַּיִם) appears in Exod 34:6; Num 14:18; Joel 2:13; Jonah 4:2; Nah 1:3; Pss 86:15; 103:8; 145:8; Neh 9:17, and twice not directly related to the attribute formula in Prov 14:29; 16:32.

Exod 34:7 clarifies punishing grandchildren. Its associated prohibition against apostasy marriages in 34:14–16 helps explain how the transgenerational judgment comes out of intermarital idolatry (see note ad loc.). The transgenerational threat evokes interpretive interventions to explain it, not the other way around. Since the attribute formula shares locutions with the second commandment and Nah 1:3, it would be very awkward, almost impossible, to start with Nah 1:2 as donor context for the second commandment in the light of Nahum's word to Nineveh in 1:14. This evidence points to Nah 1:2–3 as receptor context.

The judgment of Nah 1:14 addresses a second-person singular subject that commentators suggest refers to the king of Nineveh.[5] When Yahweh "commands" him concerning the "graven image" (פֶּסֶל), he declares the king shall have no descendants—literally as a passive assertion "no more of your seed shall be sown," or as a reflexive command "you shall not produce seed for yourself to continue your name" (Nah 1:14).[6] In the Rassam cylinder inscription of Assurbanipal (668–626 BCE), the king looks forward to one of his sons honoring his own memorial and the inscription of his name.[7] The second commandment spells out a divine transgenerational threat which does not follow from the interpretive blend of Nah 1:2–3. The command of 1:14 certifies instant terminal judgment rather than something passed down to descendants. An interpretive blend of the second commandment and the attribute formula in Nah 1:2–3 makes sense of Yahweh as jealous and avenging in the context of "slow to anger," even in the light of the terminal command of 1:14. In sum, the triangulation of evidence from the interpretive interventions in the attribute formula and in Nah 1:2–3 suggests direction of dependence. Namely, the second commandment serves as donor context to the attribute formula, and both of these as donor contexts to Nahum's interpretive blend as receptor context.

The phrase "a jealous God" (אֵל קַנָּא) appears only in Torah (Exod 20:5//Deut 5:9; Exod 34:14; Deut 4:24; 6:15) and spelled slightly differently (אֵל קַנּוֹא) twice elsewhere (Josh 24:19; Nah 1:2). The different spelling of the word "jealous" adds a small confirmation to Nah 1:2 as receptor context. Nahum may either have been interacting with the second commandment or the phrase "Yahweh, whose name is Jealous, is a jealous God" in Exod 34:14, itself derivative of the second commandment. Nahum's unique expanded phrase "a jealous and avenging God" seems like a terrible counterpart to "a compassionate and gracious God" (Exod 34:6; Nah 1:2).

Of thirty-five uses of the verb and forty-four uses of noun conjugations of "avenge/vengeance" in Scripture, only Deut 32:41, 43; Jer 46:10; and Nah 1:2 use it with God as subject and enemies (צַר) as object (cf. Isa 59:17, 18).[8] Only Nah 1:2 uses "avenging" three

5. See Robertson, *Nahum*, 68–69; Smith, *Micah–Malachi*, 311–12; Armerding, "Nahum," 8:577.

6. The Nif stem of "produce seed" (זרע) appears twice in Scripture relative to humans (Num 5:28; Nah 1:14).

7. See *ARAB* 2:323, §838.

8. For the present purposes the uses of the verb and noun conjugations of "avenge/vengeance" (נקם) in Scripture may be categorized in three ways: of human vengeance (which is set aside here); of God's vengeance against sinful Israel (Lev 26:25; 2 Kgs 9:7; Isa 1:24; 61:2; Jer 5:9; 29; 9:8; Ezek 24:8; Ps 99:8), against the wicked generically (Pss 58:10[11];

times in such rapid succession with the several uses in Deut 32:35, 41, and 43 coming close.[9] In the immediate context the threefold use of "avenging" in Nah 1:2 may pair with three terms in 1:7—"His indignation," "his fierce anger," and "his wrath"—likewise followed by a statement of divine mercy.[10] Nahum's interpretive expansion of Yahweh as an avenging God sets the theme for his entire book (italics and bold signify verbal parallels, and broken underlining signifies uses of "avenge"):

> You shall not bow down to them or worship them; for I, Yahweh your God, am **a jealous God**, punishing the children for the sin of the parents to the third and fourth generation of those who hate me, [6/10] but showing love to a thousand generations of those who love me and keep my commandments. (Exod 20:5–6//Deut 5:9–10)

> And he passed in front of Moses, proclaiming, "Yahweh, Yahweh, the compassionate and gracious God, *slow to anger*, abounding in love and faithfulness, [7] maintaining love to thousands, and forgiving wickedness, rebellion and sin. Yet he *does not leave the guilty unpunished*; he punishes the children and their children for the sin of the parents to the third and fourth generation." (Exod 34:6–7)

> Yahweh is **a jealous** and avenging **God**; Yahweh takes vengeance and is filled with wrath. Yahweh takes vengeance on his foes and vents his wrath against his enemies. [3] Yahweh is *slow to anger* but great in power; Yahweh *will not leave the guilty unpunished*. His way is in the whirlwind and the storm, and clouds are the dust of his feet. (Nah 1:2–3)

Sarna prefers "impassioned" instead of "jealous." He notes that the term in Scripture is reserved for God, not humans, and should be thought of as "qualitatively" different than a human emotion.[11] Sarna's point relies on the particular form of the term used only in Torah (see list of references above). Other terms from the same root (קנא) refer to human jealousy regarding one's spouse (e.g., Num 5:14), human zeal (e.g., Ps 69:9[10]), or divine zeal (e.g., Deut 29:20[19]).[12] Even the case of Yahweh being a jealous God whose name is Jealous (Exod 34:14) appears as part of the motivation for a prohibition against intermarriage, which leads to infidelity with other gods (34:15–16). Human jealousy seems to well get at the danger of infidelity of worshiping images in the second commandment. For Nahum, Yahweh's avenging wrath naturally pairs with his character as a jealous God.

94:1), or an oath/prayer for divine vengeance (1 Sam 24:12; 2 Sam 22:48//Ps 18:47[48]; Jer 11:20; 20:12; Ps 79:10); of God's vengeance upon enemies of Israel (Deut 32:35, 41, 43; Isa 34:8; 35:4; 47:3; 59:17; Jer 46:10; 50:15, 28; 51:6, 11, 36; Mic 5:15[14]; Nah 1:2; Ps 149:7), or his vengeance upon enemies via Israel (Num 31:2, 3); and in one way whose categorization is unclear (Isa 63:4). See Even-Shoshan, 780.

9. Though spread out more, Jeremiah uses cognates of divine "vengeance" many times in the oracle against Babylon in Jer 50–51 (see references in previous footnote).

10. See Zalcman, "Intertextuality," 614.

11. See Sarna, *Exodus*, 110.

12. The same kinds of human/divine uses fit with the verb also, see "קנא," "קִנְאָה," *HALOT* 2:1110–11.

Nahum's interpretive blend of the second commandment and the attribute formula appears within the most disputed part of the book. Sharp debate concerning an alleged partial acrostic in Nah 1:2–8 has long dominated studies.[13] *Biblia Hebraica* proposes three emendations with no evidence, lists the first half of the Hebrew alphabet in the margin, and re-lines Nah 1:3 and 1:8 to "help."[14] Without emendations, the Masoretic Text features two or three pairs of lines with adjacent letters of the Hebrew alphabet—vv. 3b, 4a, *bet, dalet* (ב, ד), v. 5a, b, *he, vav* (ה, ו), and vv. 6b, 7a, *khet, tet* (ח, ט).[15] The evidence stacks up against several clever attempts to make the partial acrostic work.[16] However, for the sake of argument if, as Ross concludes, Nah 1 houses a hymn "that is *nearly* an acrostic," this would have no bearing on the interpretive blend in Nah 1:2–3.[17] But the interpretive blend beginning with *aleph* (א)—"A God (אֵל) jealous and avenging is Yahweh" (1:2a)—fits in nicely with the unlikely conjectured partial acrostic.

In sum, Nahum grounds the wrath of Yahweh against Nineveh on the character of God. Yahweh takes vengeance upon his enemies because that is who he is. Nahum uses the attribute formula to signify that Yahweh's vengeance does not come from quick-tempered, irrational anger. Yahweh's vengeance and wrath come after he has been slow to anger.

1:15[2:1]~Isa 52:7 (B) (the feet of one who brings good news). Nahum 1:15a[2:1a] and Isa 52:7a share a verbatim parallel. The extent of the parallel requires a direct or an indirect relationship. The verbal parallel does not offer evidence of direction of dependence.

After extensive description of Yahweh's vengeance upon Nineveh, Nah 1:15[2:1] pauses to define the message of doom as good news. The declaration of good news unveils the function of the prophetic message for Judah. The oracles against the nations are not *about* who they are *to*. The prophetic oracles against the nations serve a function for the Hebrew audience. Nahum explains the good news of peace resulting from Yahweh's condemnation of Nineveh. The B and C lines of Nah 1:15[2:1] feature a somewhat ironic message when considered from a later vantage point. Nahum calls his audience to celebrate festivals and fulfill vows. He says that the wicked shall never again invade you. Nahum's prophecy is true relative to the Assyrian Empire against whom he preaches. The irony then does not stem from the immediate referents of Yahweh's vengeance or Nahum's Hebrew audience. The irony comes from the more sinister threat of the Chaldeans who defeat Nineveh. Habakkuk 1 picks up this new, even worse, problem.

Isaiah uses the same line as Nahum but with an entirely different point of reference. Isaiah 52:7 addresses the people in Babylonian exile. In Isaiah the good news relates to the return to Jerusalem. The recontextualization of the shared imagery—whichever

---

13. Popularized by Delitzsch's passing mention (*Psalms*, introduction to Ps 9 [p. 161 in 1892 ed.]).

14. See *BHS* apparatus on Nah 1:4 n. b, 1:6 n. a, and 1:7 n. b, which propose emendations to "repair" the *dalet* (ד), *zayin* (ז), and *yod* (י) lines (making explicit the acrostic rationale for these emendations already appearing in *BHK*). *BHQ* ignores the alleged acrostic since there is no evidence to support it.

15. Line B of Nah 1:3 beginning with bet (ב) follows LXX versus *atnakh* in MT (see *BHS*, LXX).

16. See Floyd, "Chimerical Acrostic," 421–37; Ross, "Text-Critical Question Begging," 459–74.

17. Ross, "Text-Critical Question Begging," 473, emphasis original.

direction—demonstrates the redemptive function of Yahweh toward his people in very different circumstances (emphasis signifies verbal parallel):

> How beautiful *on the mountains are the feet of those who bring good news, who proclaim peace*, who bring good tidings, who proclaim salvation, who say to Zion, "Your God reigns!" (Isa 52:7; cf. Isa 40:9)

> Look, there *on the mountains, the feet of those who bring good news, who proclaim peace!* Celebrate your festivals, Judah, and fulfill your vows. No more will the wicked invade you; they will be completely destroyed. (Nah 1:15†[2:1])

The same powerful descriptive line underscores the good news of the downfall of Nineveh and the hope of return from exile.

FILTERS

Nahum uses language, expressions, and themes which align him broadly with scriptural prophetic traditions.[18] A few examples can illustrate the larger point.

Nahum and the prophets sometimes issue the very same pronouncements against Judah and the nations: >/<**2:13[14]**; **3:5**; Jer 21:13; 50:31; 51:25; Ezek 5:8; 21:3[8]; 26:3; 28:22; 29:3, 10; 35:3; 38:3; 39:1, "I am against you" (הנני אליך/עליך); >/<**3:5**; Jer 13:26, "I will lift up/pull up your skirts over your face to show . . . your shame" (גליתי/חשפתי שוליך על פניך הראיתי/נראה . . . קלונך) (cf. Jer 13:22; Lam 1:9); >/<**3:10**; Isa 13:16; Hos 13:16[14:1], "infants dashed to pieces" (עלל רטש) (cf. Hos 10:14; Ps 137:8).

The kinds of taunts Nahum speaks against Nineveh could almost be reversed for suffering Jerusalem: >/<**3:7**; Lam 2:13, "Where can I find anyone to comfort you?/To what can I liken you, that I may comfort you?" (מאין אבקש מנחמים לך/מה אשוה לך ואנחמך).

Nahum's condemnation of Nineveh echoes Jehu's disparaging comments on Jezebel with three parallel terms at the level of roots: "'How can there be peace,' Jehu replied, 'as long as all the harlotries [זנה] and witchcraft [כשף] of your mother Jezebel abound [רב]?'" (2 Kgs 9:22b lit.) and "all because of the wanton [רב] lust [זנה] of a prostitute [זנה], alluring, the mistress of sorceries [כשף], who enslaved nations by her prostitution [זנה] and peoples by her witchcraft [כשף]" (Nah 3:4). These Jezebel-like similarities have been applied to the female *persona* Nahum attacks, whether she is Nineveh, Ishtar, or Sennacherib's queen Naqia.[19]

---

18. For a list of day of Yahweh similarities in Nahum, see Cathcart, "Nahum, Book of," *ABD* 4:1000. For a list of possible parallels between Nahum and Isaiah 51–52, see Armerding, "Nahum," 8:560–63. For a list of about a dozen phrases in Nahum with loose parallels elsewhere in Scripture, see Mirsky, Meltzer, and Kiel, *Twelve*, 2:9 [Hebrew]. Also see Nysse, "Keeping Company," 217–18; and see on Entire OT in Bibliographic Note on Lists of Potential Parallels.

19. Cook, "Naqia," 899.

Chapter 20

HABAKKUK

SYMBOLS[1]

// verbal parallels (A level)
/~/ synoptic parallel (A level)
~ B, probably interpretive allusion; C, possible; D, probably not
+ interpretive blend
>/< more or less similar (see Filters)

USE OF SCRIPTURE IN HABAKKUK[2]

1:8~Deut 28:49 (B) (like an eagle from afar)
2:14~Isa 6:3+11:9 (B) (earth filled with glory)
3:19~2 Sam 22:33–34//Ps 18:32–33[33–34] (B) (treading upon the heights)

OLD TESTAMENT USE OF HABAKKUK

n/a

NEW TESTAMENT USE OF HABAKKUK

1:5 LXX//Acts 13:41 (look you scoffers)
2:3–4 LXX~Heb 10:37–38 (coming soon)
2:4//Rom 1:17; Gal 3:11 (righteous will live by faith)

HERMENEUTICAL PROFILE OF THE USE OF SCRIPTURE IN HABAKKUK

The fifty-six verses of Habakkuk's dialogical prophetic collection house numerous scriptural allusions. Habakkuk shares language with Deuteronomy, the Former Prophets, select prophets (esp. Isaiah, Micah, Jeremiah, and Zephaniah), and Psalms.

The vast majority of scriptural parallels in Habakkuk are single words and short phrases. These scriptural echoes are significant for the message of Habakkuk even while they do not rise to the level of exegetical allusions. See Filters below for a brief discussion of these echoes.

In three cases Habakkuk makes allusions to specific scriptural contexts in ways that include exegetical outcomes. These three more concrete interpretive allusions invite

1. For explanation of symbols, see Symbols and Abbreviations and Introduction. For other help, see Glossary.
2. See Bibliographic Note on Lists of Potential Parallels.

Habakkuk's constituents to interpret the prophet's message in the light of older scriptural traditions.

Habakkuk's interpretive allusion to the curses of Deut 28 signals the Chaldean threat as judgment upon God's people for breaking the covenant (Hab 1:8). Habakkuk's interpretive blend of Isa 6:3 and 11:9 demonstrates that Yahweh's sovereign justice extends to the wicked Chaldeans (2:14). The reuse of imagery of salvation from the song of David in the closing words of Habakkuk's prayer underline the prophet's faith in Yahweh based upon his historic mighty actions (3:19). In each of these cases Habakkuk advances revelation by exegetical application of scriptural traditions to the unprecedented threat against Judah from the Chaldeans.

When the wicked were rising up to swallow those more righteous than themselves it triggered a theological crisis for the prophet (Hab 1:13). The divine answers to this crisis of perspective arise from scriptural traditions promising judgment and celebrating salvation. Though the Chaldean threat seems like something new, the scriptural traditions of old call the prophet and his constituents to faith and quiet before Yahweh (3:16). Though the prophet thinks Yahweh is silent (1:13), it is all the earth that must be silent before Yahweh (2:20).

USE OF SCRIPTURE

1:8~Deut 28:49 (B) (like an eagle from afar). Only two biblical contexts speak of an enemy "from afar" using the simile of an eagle, namely, Deut 28:49 and Hab 1:8, which of itself makes allusion possible.[3] This possibility gains momentum toward probability because of explicit mention of siege warfare in both contexts (Deut 28:52; Hab 1:10) (bold signifies verbal parallels).

> Yahweh will bring a nation against you **from far away**, from the ends of the earth, like **an eagle** swooping down, a nation whose language you will not understand. (Deut 28:49)

> Their horses are swifter than leopards, fiercer than wolves at dusk. Their cavalry gallops headlong; their horsemen come **from afar**. They fly like **an eagle** swooping to devour. (Hab 1:8)

The context of Deut 28 deals with curses that will come upon rebellious Israel. The eagle-like enemy will pillage and lay siege to the cities (Deut 28:49–52). Yahweh uses this imagery to show that the rise of the Chaldean menace against Judah in Habakkuk's day fulfills the threatened doom for covenant breaking (Hab 1:5–11; cf. v. 4).[4]

---

3. See Chisholm, "Habakkuk, Book of," *DNTUOT*, forthcoming.
4. On similarities between Hab 1:8 and Jer 4:13 see Keil and Delitzsch, *Minor Prophets*, 2:60–61.

2:14~Isa 6:3 (B)+11:9 (A) (earth filled with glory). Habakkuk 2:14 quotes Isa 11:9 at some length making allusion almost certain. Habakkuk takes advantage of the use of overlapping language in Isa 6:3 and 11:9 to splice these contexts together in an elegant interpretive blend. Compare the shared language (bold signifies near verbatim parallels and italics, broken underlining, and underlining signify verbal parallels).

> And they were calling to one another: "*Holy, holy, holy* is Yahweh Almighty; the whole earth is full of his glory [מְלֹא כָל־הָאָרֶץ כְּבוֹדוֹ]." (Isa 6:3)

> They will neither harm nor destroy on all my *holy* mountain, **for the earth will be filled with the knowledge of Yahweh** [כִּי־מָלְאָה הָאָרֶץ דֵּעָה אֶת־יהוה] **as the waters cover the sea.** (11:9)

> **For the earth will be filled with the knowledge of** the glory of **Yahweh** [כִּי תִּמָּלֵא הָאָרֶץ לָדַעַת אֶת־כְּבוֹד יהוה] **as the waters cover the sea.** (Hab 2:14)

This blended interpretive allusion allows Habakkuk to advance revelation by applying the prophetic imagery in a new way even while maintaining continuity with Isaiah.[5] On the surface there seems to be a large gap between the peace and safety of the day of the root of Jesse (Isa 11:1–10) and the five woes against the wicked Chaldeans (Hab 2:6–19).

The continuity stems from the overlapping imagery from the revelation in Isaiah 6 embedded within the citation from Isa 11. The seraphim testify to the holiness of Yahweh and his glory filling the earth even as he seeks a messenger of doom to pour out his wrath upon his own people (Isa 6:1–13). Habakkuk takes advantage of a catchword "holy" and catchphrase "earth filled with X of Yahweh" (6:3; 11:9). Just as the glory of Yahweh fills the earth when he brings judgment upon his own people, so too when he brings his wrath upon the arrogant Chaldeans (Hab 2:12–14).

The manifestation of Yahweh's glory in bringing judgment against Judah in Isaiah 6 and against the Chaldeans in Hab 2 may explain the profound conclusion of the five woes. Habakkuk announces that Yahweh is in his holy temple and calls all the earth to be silent before him (2:20). Those under judgment turn to mute idols (2:18), but all the earth shall be silent before Yahweh in his temple (2:20). In an even more dramatic manner, after Paul starts with Hab 2:4 he concludes with the whole world, Jew and gentile alike, silenced by the Torah (Rom 1:17; 3:9, 19–20).

In sum, Habakkuk's interpretive blend of Isa 6:3 and 11:9 demonstrates the continuity of the holiness and glory of Yahweh. The judgment of the wicked and the peace of the rule of the root of Jesse both put the glory of Yahweh on display.

5. See Chisholm, "Habakkuk, Book of," *DNTUOT*, forthcoming. Conversely, Delitzsch stresses discontinuity between Isa 11:9 and Hab 2:14 (Keil and Delitzsch, *Minor Prophets*, 2:86), and Schultz says the imagery is applied in a "radically different" way (*Search for Quotation*, 328). Delitzsch and Schultz do not observe the connection with Isa 6:3.

3:19~2 Sam 22:33–34//Ps 18:32–33[33–34] (B) (treading upon the heights). Several biblical poems evoke similar imagery of treading upon the heights (Deut 32:13; 33:29; 2 Sam 22:34//Ps 18:33[34]), making it seem more like a stock phrase than an interpretive allusion in Habakkuk 3:19. However, in both the song of David and the prayer of Habakkuk this imagery follows directly after attributing strength to Israel's God (2 Sam 22:33//Ps 18:32[33]; Hab 3:19). Further, the poems of David and Habakkuk both use the simile "like the feet of a deer" which does not appear in the poems of Deuteronomy. Of approximately nine uses of "doe" in Scripture—always in poetry—only 2 Sam 22:34// Ps 18:33[34] and Hab 3:19 use the term in a simile of standing securely.[6] This sequence of poetic elements makes it likely that the conclusion of Habakkuk's prayer alludes to David's song. Compare the shared elements (bold signifies verbal parallels).

> It is God who arms me with **strength** and keeps my way secure. He makes **my feet like the feet of a deer**; he causes me to stand **on the heights**. (2 Sam 22:33–34//Ps 18:32–33[33–34]; cf. 2 Sam 22:33–34)

> Sovereign **Yahweh** is my **strength**; he makes **my feet like the feet of a deer**, he enables me to tread **on the heights**. For the director of music. On my stringed instruments. (Hab 3:19)

The song of David celebrates victory he already enjoys in the deliverance from his enemies. Not so within the framework of the dialogical prophetic collection of Habakkuk. Habakkuk opens with his angst over the Chaldean threat. Yahweh reveals to and through Habakkuk his intention to judge Judah by the Chaldeans (1:5–11) and then to bring judgment upon the Chaldeans (2:5–19). The prayer of Habakkuk presents the prophet's response based upon what Yahweh has revealed. The impressionistic presentation of salvation imagery in Hab 3:3–15 suggests that Yahweh shall act again as he has intervened in past mighty acts (see Filters). The prayer ends with Habakkuk giving voice to divine enablement and security by reusing lyrics from the song of David. The past mighty acts of Yahweh give confidence for salvation even when the enemy threat remains real. Habakkuk's confidence is grounded upon scriptural testimony to the power of Yahweh.

FILTERS

Habakkuk shares much with other Scriptures in terms of form, themes, and even a number of verbal parallels of some length.[7] Most of the shared materials do not seem to include exegetical use of scriptural traditions. The parts of Habakkuk each function differently

---

6. See "אַיֶּלֶת ,אַיָּלָה," *HALOT* 1:40.

7. Timmer makes a general comparison between Job and Habakkuk since each begins with complaint and ends with theophany as well as broad thematic similarities ("Where?" 156–58).

with parallel scriptural traditions—disputation (Hab 1:1–2:5), woe oracles (2:6–20), and psalm (3:1–19). The following are merely representative of the kinds of non-exegetical parallels in Habakkuk.[8]

Non-Exegetical Broad Allusions and Shared Themes

Habakkuk shares several long verbal parallels with earlier and contemporary prophets: **2:5**>/<Isa 5:14, insatiable appetite of Sheol (שאול); **2:12**>/<Mic 3:10, "builds . . . with bloodshed" (בנה . . . בדמים);[9] **2:13**>/<Jer 51:58, "the people's labor is only fuel for the fire, that the nations exhaust themselves for nothing/the peoples exhaust themselves for nothing, the nations' labor is only fuel for the flames" (וייגעו עמים בדי אש ולאמים בדי ריק יעפו/ויגעו עמים בדי ריק ולאמים בדי אש ויעפו); **3:18**>/<Mic 7:7, "I will be joyful in/I wait for God my savior" (אגילה/אוחילה ב/לאלהי ישעי).

Habakkuk 3:10, 11, 15 share a number of terms with Ps 77:16–19[17–20], including: **3:10**>/<Ps 77:16[17] "writhe" (חול), "deep" (תהום); **3:11**>/<77:17[18] "arrows go" (חץ הלך); **3:15**>/<77:19[20] "great waters" (מים רבים), "you tread on/your path in the sea" (דרכת/דרכך בים). In spite of many similarities, these contexts seem to be merely expressing parallel imagery.[10]

Shared Stock Phrases and Other Similarities

Compare: >/<**1:2**; Ps 13:1, 2[2, 3], "How long?" (עד אנה); >/<**1:3**; Jer 20:8, destruction and violence/violence and destruction (שד וחמס/חמס ושד); >/<**1:4**; Isa 59:14; Jer 12:1, justice does not prevail; >/<**1:8**; Jer 4:13, "their horses are swifter than leopards/his horses are swifter than eagles" (קלו מנמרים סוסיו/קלו מנשרים סוסיו); >/<**1:12**; Ps 74:12, "are you not from of old/God is my king from of old" (הלוא אתה מקדם/אלהים מלכי מקדם) (cf. Isa 51:9; Pss 44:1[2]; 77:11[12]); >/<**1:12**; Deut 32:4, 18, 31; 1 Sam 2:2; 2 Sam 22:3, 47//Ps 18:2, 46[3, 47]; Isa 44:8; Ps 19:14[15]; 28:1; 62:2, 7[3, 7]; 92:15[16]; 144:1, Yahweh as "Rock" (צור);[11] >/<**1:13**; Ps 5:4–6[5–7], God does not tolerate the wicked; >/<**2:1**; Isa 21:8; Ezek 3:17; 33:7; Hos 9:8, prophet as sentinel; >/<**2:9**; Jer 6:13, wrongful "gain" (בצע); >/<**2:18–19**; Isa 40:18–20; 41:7, 22–24, 28–29; 42:17; 43:9; 44:9–20; 45:16, 20; 46:1–2, 6–7; 48:5, 14; Jer 10:1–10, taunt against idols; >/<**2:20a**; Ps 11:4, "Yahweh is in his holy temple" (יהוה בהיכל קדשו); >/<**2:20b**; Zeph 1:7; Zech 2:13[17], "be silent before him/the Lord Yahweh/Yahweh" (הס מפניו/אדני יהוה/יהוה); >/<**3:13**;

---

8. For other lists, see Anderson, *Habakkuk*, passim; Banister, "Theophanies," 184–91; Chisholm, "Habakkuk, Book of," *DNTUOT*, forthcoming; Driver, *Introduction*, 337–40; Mirsky, Meltzer, and Kiel, *Twelve*, 2:8–9 [Hebrew]; Smith, Ward, and Bewer, *Habakkuk*, 6 (also see on Entire OT in Bibliographic Note on Lists of Potential Parallels).

9. See Chisholm, "Habakkuk, Book of," *DNTUOT*, forthcoming.

10. See Anderson, *Habakkuk*, 328–29.

11. Chisholm notes that "my Holy One" and "Rock" only appear together in Scripture in Hannah's song (1 Sam 2:2) and Habakkuk's prophetic dialogue (Hab 1:12) (see "Habakkuk, Book of," *DNTUOT*, forthcoming). This important observation is offset by several uses of "rock" applied to Israel's God elsewhere in Scripture (see "I צוּר, צָר," no. 4, *HALOT* 2:1017). Chisholm goes on to make several helpful observations on the similar themes developed in Deut 32; 1 Sam 2; and Hab 1.

Ps 68:21[22], "crush the head of the house of the wicked/crush the head of his enemies" (מחצת ראש מבית רשע/ימחץ ראש איביו).

Theophany Imagery

Habakkuk 3:3–15 features theophanic language that often gets compared to other theophanies in Scripture as well as similar imagery in ancient parallels like Ugaritic mountain and storm traditions. Biblical theophanic imagery is often set at mountains (Paran, Sier, Sinai), depicts natural phenomena (storm, lightning, thunder), and presents Yahweh as warrior.[12] Chisholm argues that theophanic poems in Scripture start with divine saving acts like exodus and revelation at the mountain. These saving acts serve as a basis for "poetic descriptions of providential deliverance." In the case of the psalm of David, Chisholm notes that "the theophanic language reflects the psalmist's deep awareness of Yahweh's sovereign control of circumstances during his time of distress."[13] The depictions of Yahweh's judgment as a theophany in Hab 3:3–15 set it among a constellation of kindred poems in Scripture.

The imagery in Hab 3:3–15 does not make sustained allusions to specific narrative and poetic presentations of saving acts of Yahweh. The prayer draws many fleeting elements from a variety of scriptural contexts of Yahweh's intervention in a way that can be called "a poetic montage."[14] The imagery comes from the exodus, the conquest, Deborah and Barak's defeat of Canaanite forces, and David's victories over regional rivals.[15] For this reason the powerful clusters of broad similarities offer impressionistic testimony to Yahweh's salvation rather than exegetical outcomes based on targeted allusions.

Habakkuk presents Yahweh as coming from southern mountains as in older scriptural poems. Compare: "God came from Teman, the Holy One from Mount Paran" (Hab 3:3) with "Yahweh came from Sinai . . . from Seir . . . from Mount Paran" (Deut 33:2) and "When you, Yahweh, went out from Seir, when you marched from the land of Edom. The mountains quaked before Yahweh, the One of Sinai, before Yahweh, the God of Israel" (Judg 5:4–5).[16] When Habakkuk says "The sun and moon stood still" the imagery echoes Yahweh's victory over the Amorites from the scroll of Jashar (Hab 3:11; Josh 10:12–14). Yahweh as warrior wielding storms reminds of the song of David (Hab 3:8–15; 2 Sam 22:8–16//Ps 18:7–15[8–16]).[17]

---

12. See Hiebert, "Theophany in the OT," *ABD*, 6:505–11.

13. See Chisholm, "Exegetical Study," 115–18, quotations from 117 and 115; also see idem, "Exegetical and Theological Study," 156–57, 204–5, 306–11.

14. Chisholm, *Handbook Prophets*, 434.

15. See Chisholm, "Habakkuk, Book of," *DNTUOT*, forthcoming.

16. Other contexts speak of "the mountain" (Exod 15:17) or Sinai (Ps 68:7–8, 17–18[8–9, 18–19]).

17. Parallels in this paragraph indebted to Chisholm, "Exegetical and Theological Study," 142–204 (Chisholm interacts with similar ancient Mesopotamian, Ugaritic, and Egyptian imagery throughout his discussion of theophanic language in 2 Sam 22//Ps 18 and similar biblical contexts, cf. 313–47); idem, "Habakkuk, Book of," *DNTUOT*, forthcoming; idem, "Minor Prophets," 415.

Habakkuk 3:3–15 uses a mixture of verb forms mostly complete or past aspect.[18] These verb forms lead to rendering it in past tense by NIV and NRSV. But the poem may be seen as describing a coming judgment in terms of past saving acts.[19] As such the JPSB and NET translate the theophany in present tense.

Habakkuk draws on rich theophanic traditions with several scriptural echoes. These echoes invite faith based on the continuity of Yahweh's acts of deliverance.

Connections within Habakkuk

The five woes: >/<2:6, 9, 12, 15, 19, "Woe!" (הוי).

Habakkuk accuses Yahweh of being "silent" (חרש) while the wicked prey on the righteous (1:13); the five woes lead to a call for silence, "Yahweh is in his holy temple; let all the earth be silent [הס] before him" (2:20); as he winds down his psalm he responds anew, "I will wait quietly [אנוח]" (3:16).

18. NET nt. on Hab 3:3–15 lists eleven impf., sixteen pf., and three wci verb forms.

19. Indebted to Chisholm, *Handbook Prophets*, 434; idem, "Minor Prophets," 415.

Chapter 21

ZEPHANIAH

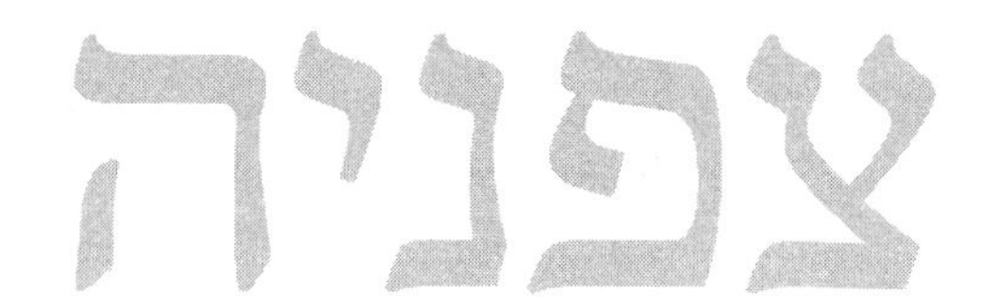

SYMBOLS[1]

// verbal parallels (A level)
/~/ synoptic parallel (A level)
~ B, probable interpretive allusion; C, possible; D, probably not
+ interpretive blend
>/< more or less similar (see Filters)
* part of interpretive network (see Networks)

USE OF SCRIPTURE IN ZEPHANIAH[2]

1:2–3~Gen 1:20–28 (B) (anti-creation)
2:11~Gen 10:5 (C) (islands of the nations)

OLD TESTAMENT USE OF ZEPHANIAH (SEE RESPECTIVE NOTES)

1:18~Ezek 7:19 (C) (silver and gold cannot deliver)
3:4~Ezek 22:26* (B) (priests do violence against Torah) (* see teachers network)

NEW TESTAMENT USE OF ZEPHANIAH

n/a

HERMENEUTICAL PROFILE OF THE USE OF SCRIPTURE IN ZEPHANIAH

Zephaniah's strong imagery and striking language include many elements shared with other Scriptures. The vast majority of the scriptural traditions used in Zephaniah comes in the form of short snippets (see Filters).

Zephaniah opens by applying anti-creational judgment imagery drawn from the traditions housed in Gen 1. The prophet deploys this tradition to condemn the idolatrous worship of Jerusalem. Some of the judgment imagery intersects with false worship from the days of Manasseh according to Kings. Zephaniah's message is especially significant as it is set in the time of Josiah and his reforms (Zeph 1:1). In this way Zephaniah uses the creational power of Yahweh to threaten Judah for serving cosmic elements and false gods.

Based on the probability that Zeph 1:2–3 draws upon the creational imagery known

1. For explanation of symbols, see Symbols and Abbreviations and Introduction. For other help, see Glossary.
2. See Bibliographic Note on Lists of Potential Parallels.

in Gen 1, his other prophecies may also more subtly allude to elements from Gen 1–11. Possible echoes include the oracles against the nations as mildly shaped according to the table of nations in Gen 10 and a reversal of the judgment by languages in Gen 11 (2:11; 3:9, 13). Many interpreters will find these possible echoes too subtle.

USE OF SCRIPTURE

1:2–3~Gen 1:20–28 (B) (anti-creation). Like his contemporary Jeremiah, Zephaniah uses terrifying reversal of creation imagery which echoes the creation tradition of Gen 1 (see note on Jer 4:23–28). Zephaniah voices Yahweh's intentions akin to the wiping away of living creatures of the land and the sky "from the face of the ground" in Genesis (Gen 6:7; 7:4//Zeph 1:2, 3).[3] But Zephaniah's oracle uses different language and goes beyond a great flood even sweeping away fish. The prophet's extreme rhetoric situates divine wrath as a stylistic reversal of the creation days tradition. Zephaniah does not use "swarming" water creatures found in the fifth day (Gen 1:20, 21) but "fish of the sea," like the psalmist (Ps 8:8[9]) and Deuteronomy (Deut 4:18). Zephaniah's oracle makes its point only relative to the later creation days in which water, heavens, and land are filled with light and life (bold signifies verbal parallels with Gen 1, italics signify creational imagery from elsewhere, and broken underlining signifies other possibly related interpretive elements):

> "I will sweep away everything from the face of *the ground* [אֲדָמָה]," declares Yahweh. [3] "I will sweep away both **human** [אָדָם] **and animal** [day six]; I will sweep away the **birds in the sky** *and the fish in the sea* [day five] and that which causes the wicked to stumble. When I destroy all **humans** [אָדָם] on the face of *the ground* [אֲדָמָה]" declares Yahweh, "I will stretch out my hand against Judah and against all who live in Jerusalem. [4] I will destroy every remnant of Baal worship in this place, the very names of the idolatrous priests [5] those who bow down on the roofs to worship the starry host, those who bow down and swear by Yahweh and who also swear by Molek." (Zeph 1:2–5 lit.)[4]

Elsewhere Zephaniah uses the standard term "land" (אֶרֶץ) to speak of comprehensive divine judgment and blessing (1:18; 2:11; 3:8, 19, 20). Zephaniah's use of "ground" in an anti-creational context (1:2, 3) subtly evokes by assonance the much more personal creation of the human [*adam* אָדָם] from the ground [*adamah* אֲדָמָה] (Gen 2:7).

In the days of Zephaniah, "idolatrous priests" were associated with various forms of

3. Elsewhere the phrase "from the face of the ground" (מֵעַל פְּנֵי הָאֲדָמָה) refers to judgment (Gen 4:14; 8:8; Exod 32:12; Deut 6:15; 1 Sam 20:15; 1 Kgs 9:7; 13:34; Jer 28:16; Amos 9:8). Sweeney does not find convincing the possible parallels between the Genesis flood or Deut 4:16–18 because many of these terms can be found elsewhere in Scripture (*Zephaniah*, 63–65). Part of Sweeney's argument rests on excavative dating of the traditions (63).

4. The phrase "and that which causes the wicked to stumble" follows MT. Gelston suggests LXX may omit it because it is difficult to understand (*BHQ*, 126*). The term "stumbling" or "heap of ruins" appears only in Isa 3:6 and Zeph 1:3 ("מַכְשֵׁלָה," *HALOT* 1:582).

syncretism, including worshiping "the starry host" (2 Kgs 23:5). Speaking against the rooftop worshipers of celestial lights in Zeph 1:5 may suggest what he has in mind by the obscure phrase "and that which causes the wicked to stumble" in 1:3, at the very place his audience expect day four—the celestial lights (see broken underline phrase above).[5] Zephaniah's oracle runs along the lines of the prohibitions against making images of humans, animals, birds, creatures of the ground, fish, or the celestial lights (Deut 4:16–19).

In sum, Zephaniah's terrifying anti-creation envisions sweeping away the very objects of Judah's deviant devotion. The prophet's exegesis clarifies that the creator who made the lesser objects of devotion may just as easily sweep away all things creaturely.

2:11~Gen 10:5 (C) (islands of the nations). The term "islands" in the prophets sometimes connotes distant peoples (e.g., Isa 41:1, 5; 42:4, 10). But the phrase "islands of the nations" only appears twice in Scripture: in the table of nations and in Zephaniah's oracle (Gen 10:5; Zeph 2:11). In the context of the table of nations "islands of the nations" refers to maritime peoples, islanders, and those who live along the shores among the descendants of Japhet.[6] Berlin suggests that this parallel functions as an allusion that helps explain Zephaniah's references to several peoples in relation to Gen 10. To make this work, Berlin needs to count Ammon and Moab as Canaanites instead of Shemites.[7] Berlin finds the same kind of theme hinted at in the phrase "I will turn over to peoples of pure speech" (Zeph 3:9), along with emphasis on correct speech (3:13); these subtly allude to uniting all peoples as opposed to the division by languages in Gen 11:7–9.[8] The suggestion that the table of nations paradigmatically shapes Zephaniah's oracles against the nations is a slim possibility. At the same time, the verbal parallel "islands of the nations" hardly provides the basis for an allusion (Gen 10:5; Zeph 2:11).

FILTERS

Zephaniah shares common expressions and imagery with many Scriptures, especially the prophets. The lists below are not comprehensive or complete. The following filters feature representative examples of non-exegetical parallels in Zephaniah.[9]

Shared Stock Phrases and Other Similarities

Compare: >/<**1:2**; Jer 8:13, "I will sweep away" (אסף סוף); >/<1:7; Isa 34:6; Jer 46:10, "for Yahweh has prepared a sacrifice/for Yahweh/Lord Yahweh has a sacrifice" (כי הכין

5. On rooftop worship, also see 2 Kgs 23:12; Jer 19:13; 32:29 (Kselman, "Zephaniah, Book of," *ABD* 6:1077).

6. See Oded, "Table of Nations," 29; Wenham, *Genesis 1–15*, 219.

7. See Berlin, *Zephaniah*, 111, 120–21.

8. See ibid., 14.

9. For other lists of scriptural parallels with Zephaniah, see Berlin, *Zephaniah*, 13–17; Davidson, *Zephaniah*, 104; Keil and Delitzsch, *Zephaniah*, 118; Kselman, "Zephaniah, Book of," *ABD* 6:1077–80. For over sixty single-word similarities between Isa 24–27 and Zephaniah, see Hays, *Origins*, 229–31. Also see on Entire OT in Bibliographic Note on Lists of Potential Parallels. The most significant of these are Berlin's lists, to which the examples in Zephaniah Filters are especially indebted.

יהוה זבח/כי זבח ליהוה/לאדני יהוה); >/<**1:9**; 1 Sam 5:4–5, do not step on threshold superstition; >/<**1:13**; Deut 28:30, "Though they build houses, they will not live in them; though they plant vineyards, they will not drink the wine/You will build a house, but you will not live in it. You will plant a vineyard, but you will not even begin to enjoy its fruit" (בנו בתים ולא ישבו ונטעו כרמים ולא ישתו את יינם/בית תבנה ולא תשב בו כרם תטע ולא תחללנו) (cf. Amos 5:11; Jer 29:5); >/<**1:15**; Joel 2:2, "a day of darkness and gloom, a day of clouds and blackness" (יום חשך ואפלה יום ענן וערפל); >/<**2:2**; Isa 17:13, "like chaff" (כמץ); >/<**2:3**; Mic 6:8, "seek righteousness, seek humility/love loyalty and walk humbly" (בקשו צדק בקשו ענוה/אהבת חסד והצנע לכת); >/<**3:3**; Hab 1:8, "evening wolves" (זאבי ערב); >/<**3:8**; Ezek 22:31, "I will/to pour out upon them my wrath" (אֶשְׁפֹּךְ/לִשְׁפֹּךְ עֲלֵיהֶם זַעְמִי) (see note on Ezek 22:26); >/<**3:10**; Isa 18:7, gifts from Cush; >/<**3:11**; Isa 13:3, "your exultant boasters/exultant in my triumph" (עליזי גאותך/עליזי גאותי); >/<**3:17**; Deut 30:9, "Yahweh ... will delight over you/Yahweh delights over you" (יהוה . . . ישיש עליך/יהוה לשוש עליך); >/<**3:19**; Mic 4:6, 7, restore "lame, exiles" (צלע, נדחה).

The tenfold use of "day" (יום) in **Zeph 1:14–18** should be compared to the tenfold use of day in Obad 11–14. Whereas Zephaniah refers to the day of Yahweh, Obadiah seems to refer to the fall of Jerusalem (see Obadiah Filters for oddities in verbal forms there).

The closing of Zephaniah uses the language of Deuteronomy to offer hope to his audience. The language of "gathering" and "restore your fortunes" connects with the expectation of return from exile in Deuteronomy (Deut 30:3; **Zeph 3:20**). Zephaniah also includes imagery of the people's "fame" (lit. "name") and "praise," which echoes language elsewhere in Deuteronomy (Zeph 3:20; Deut 26:19).[10]

Zephaniah uses terms common to psalms and wisdom but uncommon in prophets: >/<**2:3**; Isa 11:4; Amos 8:4; Pss 37:11; 76:9[10]; 147:6, "humble of the land" (ענוי ארץ); >/<**3:5, 13**; Isa 59:3; 61:8; Ezek 28:15; Hos 10:13; Mic 3:10; Hab 2:12; Mal 2:6; Job 5:16; 6:29–30; 11:14; 13:7; 15:16; 22:23; 24:20; 27:4; 36:23; Pss 37:1; 43:1; 58:2[3]; 64:6[7]; 89:22[23]; 92:15[16]; 107:42; 119:3; 125:3; Prov 22:8, "wrong" (עולה).[11]

Quasi-Boilerplates

Sometimes the prophets reuse the same stock judgments upon different peoples as something like boilerplate judgments:[12] >/<**2:9***, "Moab will become like Sodom, the Ammonites like Gomorrah" (כי מואב כסדם תהיה ובני עמון כעמרה) (* see cities of the plain network); >/<**2:13**; Isa 13:21–22; 34:13–15, return to natural state; >/<**2:15a**; Isa 23:7, "This is/Is this the exultant city/exultant (city)" (זאת/הזאת לכם העיר העליזה) (sarcastically of Nineveh and Tyre); >/<**2:15b**; Isa 47:8, "living in security and saying in her heart, 'I am, and there is no other'" (היושבת לבטח האמרה בלבבה אני ואפסי עוד) (of Nineveh and Babylon); >/<**2:15c**; Jer 19:8, "all who pass by her hiss" (כל עובר עליה ישרק) (of Nineveh, Jerusalem, Edom, Babylon).

10. See Berlin, *Zephaniah*, 14–15.

11. See ibid., 16–17.

12. See discussion of boilerplates in Jeremiah Filters.

Chapter 22

HAGGAI

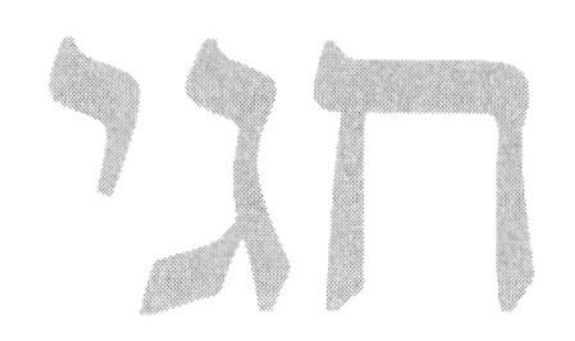

SYMBOLS[1]

//	verbal parallels (A level)	+	interpretive blend
/~/	synoptic parallel (A level)	>/<	more or less similar (see Filters)
~	B, probable interpretive allusion; C, possible; D, probably not	*	part of interpretive network (see Networks)

USE OF SCRIPTURE IN HAGGAI[2]

1:2~Jer 25:11, 12; 29:10* (C) (the time has not come) (* see seventy years network)
1:4~1 Kgs 6:15 (B) (paneled houses)
2:6~Isa 13:13 (C)+Exod 14:21 (C) (shake the heavens and dry land)
2:11–14*~Lev 10:10–11* (B) (priestly ruling on holy and unclean) (* see teachers network)
2:23~Jer 22:24 (B) (Yahweh's signet ring)

OLD TESTAMENT USE OF HAGGAI (SEE RESPECTIVE NOTE)

1:14~Ezra 1:5 (B) (stir up the spirit)

NEW TESTAMENT USE OF HAGGAI

2:6, 21 LXX~Heb 12:26 (shake heaven)

HERMENEUTICAL PROFILE OF THE USE OF SCRIPTURE IN HAGGAI

Haggai everywhere seems to presuppose the covenant in his use of scriptural traditions. It is not as though the exile never happened but that it does not have the power to disrupt covenantal responsibilities. The most striking non-exegetical allusion affirms continuity of the covenant: "*This is what I covenanted with you* when you came out of Egypt. And my Spirit remains among you. Do not fear" (2:5). The ancient covenant seems to be in the air in every case of Haggai's use of scriptural traditions.

For a prophetic collection of less than forty total verses, Haggai features a number of exegetical interventions. The probable interpretive allusions draw on traditions that

1. For explanation of symbols, see Symbols and Abbreviations and Introduction. For other help, see Glossary.
2. See Bibliographic Note on Lists of Potential Parallels.

appear in Leviticus, Kings, and Jeremiah. The nature of these allusions seems to expect familiarity by his audience, especially the cases involving the use of rare scriptural terms. Though Haggai's condemnation of his audience is not subtle, some of his scriptural interpretations provoke enduring debate.

Evaluation of Haggai's use of scriptural traditions does not solve all the interpretive difficulties. But it does add a pervasive canonical consciousness to the ever-present sense of covenant in Haggai's messages. Haggai projects a covenantal identity upon his audience that remains tethered to Israel's scriptural traditions. Haggai's pervasive use of scriptural traditions establishes the defining authority of the identity and destiny of the postexilic congregation.

USE OF SCRIPTURE

1:2~Jer 25:11, 12; 29:10* (C) (the time has not come) (* see seventy years network). Haggai accuses his audience of neglecting to rebuild the temple based on their rationale: "These people say, '*The time has not yet come* to rebuild Yahweh's house'" (Hag 1:2, emphasis mine). It is possible the people claim to be waiting to rebuild the temple until the full seventy years of Jeremiah's prophecy have expired (Jer 25:11, 12; 29:10). In this reading they have not rebuilt the house of Yahweh to honor the prophetic word. Support for the people's preoccupation with the seventy-year prophecy coming to an end can be seen in an exchange between certain representatives and Zechariah two years after Haggai's accusation (see note on Zech 7:5–6). If the people try to use Jeremiah's prophecy to excuse their responsibilities, Haggai is not impressed.

1:4~1 Kgs 6:15 (B) (paneled houses). Haggai accuses his audience of neglecting the house of Yahweh while they live in "paneled houses" (Hag 1:4). The description seems especially incongruent with the severe economic depression throughout the rest of the context (1:6, 10). Elsewhere the poverty of Judah extends for an extremely long time in the postexilic situation (Neh 7:4). The situation in Jerusalem gets so bad that in Nehemiah's time they use a lottery to force "winners" to move into the city of Jerusalem itself (11:1–2; cf. 5:1–5).[3]

Haggai's use of the rare term "paneled" seems to be an intentional allusion to the materials used to build Solomon's temple (1 Kgs 6:15; cf. 6:9). Elsewhere the term only appears to describe the cedar paneling for two of Solomon's other lavish building projects (7:3, 7) and one unrelated context (Jer 22:14).[4] An argument can be made that the exiles' willingness to return to their impoverished homeland represents their faithfulness. They could

3. On poverty in Judah in Haggai's days (520 BCE), see Hag 1:5–6; Isa 64:10; cf. longing for better days in Zech 8:4–6; Isa 63:11–14. Economic depression in Judah continued for many lifetimes, including the days of Nehemiah (445), see Neh 5:1–5.

4. See "ספן," *HALOT* 1:764–65.

even claim that the troubles of economic depression (Hag 1:6, 9) or the trouble from local enemies (Ezra 4:4, 23–24) stood in the way of rebuilding the temple. These real problems get pushed to the side as the prophet castigates his audience (Hag 1:4). The surprising and economically incongruous use of "paneled houses" effectively evokes the use of this rare term in the Deuteronomistic account of Solomon's temple. Haggai accuses the people of living in temple-like houses while the temple remains in ruins.

2:6~Isa 13:13 (C)+Exod 14:21 (C) (shake the heavens and dry land). Haggai uses the term "shake," which appears in Isaiah's threat of doom upon Babylon: "Therefore I will make the heavens tremble; and the earth *will shake* from its place at the wrath of Yahweh Almighty" (Isa 13:13). Elsewhere the verb "shake" is collocated with heavens in a number of contexts, but only Isa 13:13 fits with the sense of Haggai's oracle.[5]

Haggai 2:6 uses a rare, seemingly loaded term, "dry land" (חָרָבָה), elsewhere used of the flood (Gen 7:22), crossing the sea (Exod 14:21), crossing the river (Josh 3:17; 4:18), and Elijah crossing the river (2 Kgs 2:8), with only one other use (Ezek 30:12). The possible allusion to Exod 14:21 imagery is slight and requires a subtle typological sense of second exodus. Haggai speaks of a great act of Yahweh to bring splendor to the Second Temple: "In a little while I will once more *shake* the heavens and the earth, the sea and *the dry land*" (Hag 2:6, emphasis mine; cf. 2:21). The evidence only allows a possible allusion.

2:11–14*~Lev 10:10–11* (B) (priestly ruling on holy and unclean) (* see teachers network). Torah commands priests not to drink wine when they serve, in order for them to teach (Lev 10:9). The law establishes priests as responsible to teach worship standards (10:10–11). Haggai asks the priests questions about scenarios involving potential transfer of holiness and ritual impurity by contact to set up his message (Hag 2:11–14). Though direct contact with a purification offering or its blood causes what it touches to become holy, the priests determine indirect contact of a garment holding holy meat would not transfer holiness. The priests determine that ritual impurity, however, can be transferred indirectly. These different standards stem from holiness versus commonness and ritual purity versus ritual impurity as different sorts of things (bold signifies verbal parallels, and italics and underlining signify thematic similarities):

> So that you can distinguish between the **holy** and the common, between the **ritually impure** and the ritually pure, and so you can teach the Israelites all the decrees Yahweh has given them through Moses. (Lev 10:10–11 lit.)

> <u>Whatever touches any of the flesh [of the purification offering] will become **holy**</u>, and if any of the blood is spattered on a garment, you must wash it in the holy area. (6:27[30]†)

5. See Judg 5:4; 2 Sam 22:8//Ps 18:7[8]; Isa 14:16; 24:18; Jer 8:16; 10:10; 49:21; 50:46; 51:29; Ezek 31:16; 38:20; Joel 2:10; 3:16[4:16]; Nah 1:5; Pss 60:2[4]; 68:8[9]; 77:18[19]. Though the parallels in Joel seem close, it appears to be set at a later time (see note on Joel 3:16, 17[4:16, 17]).

> Anyone from descendants of Aaron who has a skin disease or a bodily discharge, he may not eat the holy offerings until he is made ritually pure. *Whoever touches anything* ***ritually impure*** *by* ***a corpse*** or by anyone who has an emission of semen. (22:4 lit.)

> "Thus says Yahweh Almighty: 'Ask the priests what Torah says: [12] If someone carries **holy** meat in the fold of their garment, and that fold touches some bread or stew, some wine, oil or other food, does it become **holy**?' The priests answered, "No." [13] Then Haggai said, *"If a person* ***ritually impure*** *by contact with* ***a corpse*** *touches one of these things*, does it become **ritually impure**?" "Yes," the priests replied, "it becomes **ritually impure**." [14] Then Haggai said, "'So it is with this people and this nation in my sight,' says Yahweh. 'Whatever they do and whatever they offer there is **ritually impure** " (Hag 2:11–14 lit.)

Haggai applies the priestly ruling to his audience. Normal interpretations include a wrong attitude by the people (1:4); ritual impurity in light of rebuilding the temple (2:15); and the "Samaritans" or different others outside the assembly (Ezra 4:1–2).[6] None of these is especially helpful. The second view could work if the ruling were applied literally.[7] But the threefold use of "so" (כֵּן) in Hag 2:14 seems like the second half of an "as . . . so" sequence, in which case the "so" phrase speaks to analogy, not identity.[8] Since the prophet's audience is like what is ritually impure, they contaminate everything they do and make it unfit for worship. This sense fits with the notion of ritually impure by exile and the need to touch no ritually impure thing when returning to worship (Isa 52:11).

2:23~Jer 22:24 (B) (Yahweh's signet ring). Jeremiah uses distinct language to speak of Jehoiachin's identity at the end of his short-lived rule. The term "signet ring" of the deity's right hand refers to the king as the earthly representative of Yahweh (Jer 22:24).[9] Haggai reverses imagery of Jehoiachin being ripped off and hurled away to speak to the importance of his grandson Zerubbabel's role:

> "As surely as I live," declares Yahweh, "even if you, Jehoiachin son of Jehoiakim king of Judah, were a **signet ring** on my right hand, I would still pull you off." (Jer 22:24)

> "On that day," declares Yahweh Almighty, "I will take you, my servant Zerubbabel son of Shealtiel," declares Yahweh, "and I will make you like my **signet ring**, for I have chosen you," declares Yahweh Almighty." (Hag 2:23)

---

6. See summary and list of proponents for each in Hill, *Haggai*, 88.
7. See Petersen, *Haggai and Zechariah 1–8*, 85.
8. See *IBHS* §38.5.a; Williams §264.
9. See "I חוֹתָם," *HALOT* 1:300; Petersen, *Haggai*, 104.

The striking language of a Davidic heir in 520 BCE during a time of great unrest in the empire after Darius's coronation under questionable circumstances may suggest messianic hopes were in the air. The record of Zerubbabel's importance does not go beyond his role in rebuilding the Second Temple (last mentioned in Ezra 5:2). The remarkable things spoken of at the end of Haggai and elsewhere have been difficult to square with hearing nothing more about him (see note on Zech 4:6–9).[10]

The canonical story of Zerubbabel's celebrated colleague Joshua the high priest ends in a more disappointing way, in spite of the numerous references in Haggai and Zechariah (Hag 1:1, 12; 2:2; Zech 3; 6). Joshua's family stands as first in the list of those involved in apostasy marriages (Ezra 10:18). Joshua's spectacular failure hints at the disappointments of the days of Zerubbabel.

Haggai's oracle dates exactly two months before Zechariah's series of night visions (2:20; Zech 1:7). Although Haggai does not use explicit typological language of Zerubbabel, his contemporary Zechariah refers to Joshua's associates as "signs" or "symbolic of things to come" of Yahweh's servant branch.[11] "Listen, High Priest Joshua, you and your associates seated before you, who are men *symbolic of things to come*: I am going to bring my servant, the Branch" (Zech 3:8, emphasis mine). Whether Haggai considered Zerubbabel a type needs to remain an open question.[12]

In sum, Zerubbabel plays a significant role in rebuilding the temple while Yahweh prepares to "shake the heavens and the earth" (Hag 2:21). In exact reversal of Yahweh tearing off Jehoiachin, he chose his grandson Zerubbabel as signet ring (Jer 22:24; Hag 2:23). The disappointing declension of the restoration may suggest Zerubbabel as a type of a Davidic ruler to come.

FILTERS

Haggai makes non-exegetical use of scriptural traditions, especially from the prophets. The following filters and their associated lists illustrate but do not exhaust non-exegetical similarities.[13]

Non-Exegetical Broad Allusions and Shared Themes

Haggai 2:5 makes an allusion to the Mosaic covenant, saying, "This is what I covenanted with you when you came out of Egypt. And my Spirit remains among you. Do not

---

10. The colorful fictional story of Zerubbabel in 1 Esd 3:1–5:3 underlines the point.

11. Elsewhere the term "sign, symbol" is used of God's cosmic judgments against the pharaoh (Exod 4:21; Deut 4:34; 7:19; 29:3[2]) and prophetic parabolic actions (Isa 8:18; 20:3; Ezek 12:6, 11; 24:24, 27) (see "מוֹפֵת," *HALOT* 1:559).

12. For other eschatological features in Haggai, see Childs, *Introduction*, 469–71.

13. For a longer list of possible allusions, see Hill, *Haggai*, 25 (also see on Entire OT in Bibliographic Note on Lists of Potential Parallels). For shared language and themes between Haggai and Zech 1–8, see Meyers and Meyers, *Haggai, Zechariah 1–8*, xlix, liv.

fear" (Hag 2:5). The verbal parallel to Moses's assurance after the Ten Commandments "do not fear" (אל תיראו) (Hag 2:5//Exod 20:20) can be aligned with other references to cutting the covenant (cf. Exod 24:8; 34:10, 27). Haggai's point is that the returned exiles remain under the same covenant.

Zechariah refers to the prophets present on the day the temple foundation was laid, which fits with Haggai's oracle "from this day" (Hag 2:18–19>/<Zech 8:9).

Shared Stock Phrases and Other Similarities

Compare: >/<1:6, 10; Lev 26:19–20, economic depression; >/<1:11; Deut 7:13; 11:14; 28:51; Hos 2:8[10]; Joel 1:10, "grain, new wine, oil" (דגן, תירוש, יצהר); >/<2:4 (2x); Deut 31:7, 23; Josh 1:6, 7, 9, 18; 1 Chr 22:13; 28:10, 20, "be strong" (חזק); >/<2:17; Deut 28:22; 1 Kgs 8:37//2 Chr 6:28; Amos 4:9, "with blight and with mildew" (בשדפון ובירקון).

Connections within Haggai

Note: >/<1:5, 7; 2:18 "consider" (שימו לבבכם); >/<1:13; 2:4, "I am with you" (אני אתכם); >/<2:6, 21, "I will shake heaven and earth" (אני מרעיש את השמים ואת הארץ); >/<2:18, 19, "from this day" (מן היום הזה).

Chapter 23

ZECHARIAH

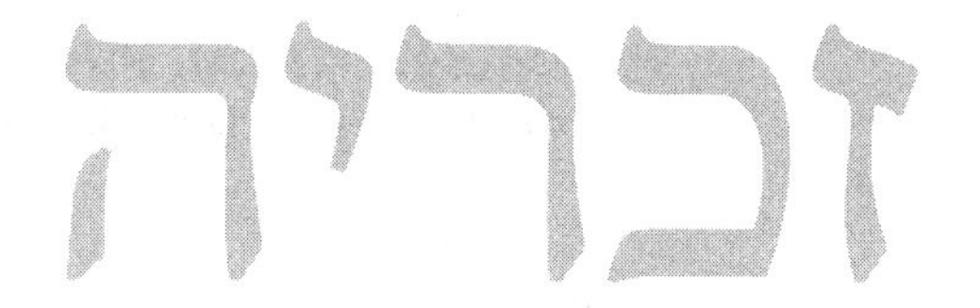

SYMBOLS[1]

- // verbal parallels (A level)
- /~/ synoptic parallel (A level)
- ~ B, probable interpretive allusion; C, possible; D, probably not
- + interpretive blend
- >/< more or less similar (see Filters)
- * part of interpretive network (see Networks)

USE OF SCRIPTURE IN ZECHARIAH[2]

1:4~Jer 25:4–5 (B) (message of the former prophets)
1:11~Isa 14:7 (B) (the whole earth at rest)
1:12*~Jer 25:11, 12; 29:10* (B)+Isa 51:3 (C) (seventy years) (* see seventy years network)
2:1[5]~Ezek 40:3 (B) (a man to measure)
2:11[15]~Isa 56:1–8 (B) (nations joined to Yahweh)
3:8*~Jer 23:5–6* (B) (branch) (* see branch and Davidic covenant networks)
3:10~Mic 4:4 (C) (under one's own vine and fig tree)
4:7*~Isa 40:4* (C) (mountain becomes level) (* see branch, new exodus, and seventy years networks)
4:9*~Isa 44:28* (C) (Zerubbabel lays temple foundation) (* see branch, new exodus, and seventy years networks)
6:11–14*~Jer 33:14–18* (B) (civil and priestly rulers) (* see branch and Davidic covenant networks)
7:5–6*~Jer 25:11, 12; 29:10* (B) (fasts for seventy years) (* see seventy years network)
8:21–22~Mic 4:2–3 (B) (international pilgrimage to Jerusalem)
9:9*~Gen 49:11* (B) (king riding into Jerusalem) (* see Judah-king network)
11:4–16~Ezek 34:1–31*+37:15–28* (C) (breaking the staff and appointing a bad shepherd) (* see Davidic covenant network)
12:1~Gen 2:7+Isa 42:5 (C) (creator of heaven, earth, and the human spirit)
13:5~Amos 7:14+Gen 4:1, 2 (B) (denying prophetic vocation)

OLD TESTAMENT USE OF ZECHARIAH (SEE RESPECTIVE NOTES)

4:7~Ps 118:22 (C) (the rejected cornerstone)
9:10~Ps 72:8* (B) (rule to ends of the earth) (* see Davidic covenant network)

NEW TESTAMENT USE OF ZECHARIAH

4:3, 11, 14~Rev 11:4 (two olive trees)
8:16 LXX~Eph 4:25 (speak truth)
9:9//Matt 21:5; John 12:15; cf. Mark 11:1–8; Luke 19:29–36 (on a donkey)
11:12, 13~Matt 27:10 (thirty pieces of silver)
12:10//John 19:37; Rev 1:7 (whom they pierced)
13:7//Matt 26:31; Mark 14:27 (strike the shepherd)

1. For explanation of symbols, see Symbols and Abbreviations and Introduction. For other help, see Glossary.
2. See Bibliographic Note on Lists of Potential Parallels.

HERMENEUTICAL PROFILE OF THE USE OF SCRIPTURE IN ZECHARIAH

Zechariah features many scriptural allusions, standing on par with Isaiah and Jeremiah. A significant difference in degree relates to more explicit canonical consciousness.[3]

Zechariah opens with a reference to the former prophets (Zech 1:4; cf. 7:12). The self-awareness of authoritative prophetic traditions signals a need to carefully consider Zechariah's persistent allusive style. In several places Zechariah alludes in order to both establish continuity and to extend and/or adjust scriptural prophetic traditions.

Zechariah's intentional advancement of prophetic traditions broadly gets at his transitional role in the twilight of the writing prophets. If Isaiah promises hope after judgment, Zechariah applies these expectations in concrete and ironic ways. If Jeremiah forecasts seventy years, Zechariah repurposes his audience's expectations. If Ezekiel places the temple of his vision outside "the city," Zechariah uses Ezekiel's temple vision imagery to locate the Second Temple construction in Jerusalem. In these and many other cases, Zechariah positions his message on the prophetic traditions, even as his oracles incrementally advance revelation for the new situation of Jerusalem, a city of the empire.

Importantly, Zechariah can summarize the enduring moral and social failures of his own audience by direct application of the earlier prophets. Zechariah starts as though the rebellious ways of the Hebrew ancestors and his audience exactly align. And, even with near fulfillment of the Second Temple, Zechariah looks ahead to that day to come for judgment and salvation in accord with the earlier prophets. In crude terms, Zechariah can speak of concrete actualizations of the Second Temple and restoration but maintains a context of the present threat and future divine intervention akin to the earlier prophets.

Zechariah's "prequel" to the blessing of Judah may be his most enduring exegetical advancement. Zechariah presents the expectation of what comes before the Judah-king enters his vineyard on his mount. Zechariah's exegetical advances—the king coming to Jerusalem on a humble mount—provide a paradigm for a turning point in the Gospel narratives. Zechariah did not so much "fill a gap" as reveal the prequel. This advancement of the blessing of Judah suggests a model for Mark to extend the prequel into a sequel. But there is more. Zechariah also adds theological depth by deducing humility from details of the expected king's mount. The expected humble king in Zechariah both advances revelation and provides a framework for additional advancements.

The exegetical advances of Zechariah, in certain respects, represent a culmination and a transitional pivot within progressive revelation as embodied within prophetic scriptural exegesis. Zechariah demonstrates that both expectations and their proximate fulfillments generate fuller, richer expectations.

Zechariah alludes to Torah traditions of Genesis and Leviticus. Yet Boda points

---

3. See Barrett, *Canon*, 79–82.

out that the prophets and Deuteronomy play greater roles in shaping the theology of Zechariah.[4] Though Zechariah does not include citations or overt exegetical allusions to Deuteronomy, its strong currents are often mediated through prophetic traditions. This reality gives due pause not to underestimate non-exegetical use of scriptural traditions in Zechariah (see Filters).

USE OF SCRIPTURE

1:4~Jer 25:4–5 (B) (message of the former prophets). The language of Zech 1:4 stands close to Jer 25:5, 7, with parallels to 35:15. This fits the many doublets and near doublets in Jeremiah (see Jeremiah Filters). The parallel with Jer 25 becomes more likely since elsewhere in Zech 1 he mentions the seventy years (Jer 25:11, 12; Zech 1:12). Zechariah opens by referring to the preaching of the earlier prophets. Ironically, he even draws this reference from an earlier prophet. In an oracle set in the fourth year of Jehoiakim, that is, the first year of Nebuchadnezzar (605 BCE), Jeremiah looks back and summarizes the long line of prophets preaching essentially the same message (Jer 25:1). Upon return from exile, in the second year of Darius (520), Zechariah summarizes the earlier prophets by citing Jeremiah (emphases denote verbal parallel):

> And though Yahweh has sent all his servants the *prophets* to you again and again, you have not listened or paid any attention. They said, "**Turn now**, each of you, **from** your **evil ways and your evil practices**. . . . But you *did not listen to me*," *declares Yahweh*. (Jer 25:4, 5a, 7a)[5]

> Do not be like your ancestors, to whom the earlier *prophets* proclaimed: This is what Yahweh Almighty says: "**Turn now from** your **evil ways and your evil practices**." But they *would not listen* or pay attention *to me*, *declares Yahweh*. (Zech 1:4†)

The lead-in "to whom the earlier prophets proclaimed" functions as quasi-marking, which, along with the repetition of "declares Yahweh," strongly suggests Zechariah as receptor context (1:4).[6] All of this points to canonical consciousness in terms of the emerging authority of prophetic traditions. Neither Jeremiah nor Zechariah claim to be original. Zechariah loosely paraphrases Jeremiah in a way that ironically embodies the message of prophetic continuity itself. Both prophets cast a wide net and summarize the long prophetic tradition as a futile attempt to try to persuade their audience to turn from evil.

4. See Boda, *Exploring*, 2:194–95 (cf., e.g., 109); Mason, "Echoes," 222, 227.

5. Note that Jer 25:4, 5 LXX is set up as Yahweh's own retrospective: "I would send you my slaves the prophets . . . when I was saying 'Do turn, everyone from his evil way.'" (Jer 25:4, 5 LXX) versus MT as Jeremiah narrating a retrospective: "Yahweh has sent all his servants the prophets. . . . They said, 'Turn now, each of you, from your evil ways.'" (25:4, 5 MT). On LXX and MT versions of Jeremiah, see Hermeneutical Profile of the Use of Scripture in Jeremiah.

6. See Stead, *Intertextuality*, 31–32.

1:11~Isa 14:7 (B) (the whole earth at rest). Isaiah's oracle against the king of Babylon includes the resultant peace and joy of the lands. The language of "all the earth" with "peace" (שקט) only appears together in Isa 14:7 and Zech 1:11, making allusion likely (emphases signify verbal parallels):

> *All the lands* are at rest and *at peace*; they break into singing. (Isa 14:7)

> And they reported to the angel of Yahweh who was standing among the myrtle trees, "We have gone throughout the earth and found *all the lands* at rest and *at peace.*" (Zech 1:11†)

The interpretation in Zechariah's first vision turns on the reversal of the function of the imagery.[7] Whereas the peace in Isa 14 fulfilled Yahweh's will and benefitted Israel, the peace of Zech 1 incites his wrath. The people of God are in a shameful exilic situation, causing the peaceful ease of all the lands to be unacceptable. This general theme may suggest a secondary allusive reversal of Jeremiah's consolation: "Jacob will again have *peace* [שקט] and **security** [שאן], and no one will make him afraid" (Jer 30:10//46:27). In the vision Yahweh says: "I am very angry with the nations that feel **secure** [שאן]. I was only a little angry, but they went too far with the punishment" (Zech 1:15). The catchword peace (שקט) between Isa 14:7 and Jer 30:10//46:27 may have recommended the connection for Zechariah's vision.[8] On this reading the downfall of Babylon did not lead to peace and security for Israel but for the nations. The vision of Zechariah renews hope for consolation and applies it to the temple rebuilding (1:16).

1:12*~Jer 25:11, 12; 29:10* (B)+Isa 51:3 (C) (seventy years) (* see seventy years network). Many Scriptures recycle Jeremiah's seventy years, including Zechariah twice (see note on Zech 7:5). Although a concept like seventy years seems straightforward, it proves flexible enough for numerous scriptural interpretations.[9] Jeremiah himself had not tagged the timing directly on exile or temple but on the domination of the Neo-Babylonians (Jer 25:11–12). Jeremiah treats the seventy years like a symbolic round number when he redefines it as three generations of Neo-Babylonian rule (27:7).[10] Since seventy years of Babylon's rule also appear in a letter to the first wave of exiles of Jerusalem, those taken captive in 597 BCE, it becomes a little more awkward to ground its original function as rebuilding of the temple which has yet to be destroyed (29:10). Both of Jeremiah's traditions that mention seventy years can be compared with Zechariah's allusion (italics signify verbal parallels, and broken underlining signifies a parallel with Zech 1:16 [see below]):

---

7. See Seufert, "Zechariah 1.11," 249, 260; Boda, *Zechariah*, 132–33.

8. See Seufert, "Zechariah 1.11," 259. Seufert discusses this possible allusion in relation to the context of Jer 30:10 but does not interact with the absence of Jer 30:10–11 LXX. On Jer 30:10–11//46:27–28 see doublets in Jeremiah Filters.

9. See Schnittjer, "Individual versus Collective Retribution," 126–29. Also see note on Hag 1:2.

10. The three-generation period appears in a plus in Jer 27:7 MT (lacking in LXX).

> This whole country will become a desolate wasteland, and these nations will serve the king of Babylon *seventy years*. But when the *seventy years* are fulfilled, I will punish the king of Babylon and his nation, the land of the Babylonians, for their guilt, declares Yahweh, and will make it desolate forever. (Jer 25:11, 12)

> This is what Yahweh says: "When *seventy years* are completed for Babylon, I will come to you and fulfill my good promise to bring you back to this place." (29:10)

> Then the angel of Yahweh said, "Yahweh Almighty, how long will you withhold mercy [רחם] from Jerusalem and from the towns of Judah, which you have been angry with these *seventy years*?" (Zech 1:12)

While the prophecy of seventy years in Jer 25 focuses on the judgment of the nations and Judah, the letter in Jer 29 looks forward to restoring the Judean exiles. Zechariah 1:12 in certain respects works off both contexts by speaking of Yahweh withholding "mercy" (רחם). Then Yahweh replied to the celestial messenger with "comforting" (נִחֻמִים) words in a way which may echo Isaiah (italics signify verbal parallels at the level of roots, and broken underlining signifies a parallel with 1:12, see above):

> Yahweh will surely *comfort* [נחם] *Zion* and will look with *compassion* [נחם] on all her ruins. (Isa 51:3a; cf. 40:1)

> So Yahweh spoke kind and *comforting* [נִחֻמִים] words to the angel who talked with me.... "Therefore this is what Yahweh says: 'I will return to Jerusalem with mercy [רַחֲמִים] and there my house will be rebuilt....' Proclaim further: This is what Yahweh Almighty says: 'My towns will again overflow with prosperity, and Yahweh will again *comfort* [נחם] *Zion* and choose Jerusalem.'" (Zech 1:13, 16a, 17)

By means of the celestial delegate and Yahweh's question-and-answer before the prophet, the prophecy supplies the counterpart of the seventy years of desolation in the "comfort" of Zion. This context makes the comfort of Zion concrete in terms of rebuilding the temple. In this way the destruction and rebuilding of the temple relate to the seventy years in Zech 1 as an advancement of revelation.

2:1[5]~Ezek 40:3 (B) (a man to measure). The word of hope to rebuild the temple in Zech 1:16 includes "a measuring line" over Jerusalem. Similar imagery reappears in Zechariah's third vision in a manner that alludes to Ezekiel's temple vision (emphases signify verbal parallels):

> He took me there, *and behold a man* whose appearance was like bronze; he was standing in the gateway with a linen cord and a *measuring* rod *in his hand*. (Ezek 40:3)

Then I looked up, *and behold a man* with a *measuring* line *in his hand.* (Zech 2:1[5])

The vision of Zechariah reaffirms an expectation for renewal and the coming of the glory of Yahweh (Ezek 43:5; Zech 2:5[9]). The sense of "no walls" for Jerusalem in the vision may connote both too much prosperity to be contained and protection by fire and the glory of Yahweh (2:4–5[8–9]).[11] Zechariah's visions affirm the temple to be located in Jerusalem (1:16) and the glory within Jerusalem (2:5[9]). Zechariah's visionary affirmations using imagery from Ezekiel's vision may suggest that Ezekiel's vision of the temple outside of the city should be taken as symbolic of the burden of holiness rather than a literal expectation (see note on Ezek 47:13–48:35).[12]

Based on the probability of a parallel, the direction of dependence makes most sense from Ezekiel to Zechariah. Zechariah uses Ezekiel toward exegetical outcomes but the logic does not work the other direction. In specific, while Ezekiel describes "the city" (unnamed) outside the temple, Zechariah associates the temple with the Second Temple building project in Jerusalem.

2:11[15]~Isa 56:1–8 (B) (nations joined to Yahweh). See notes on Zech 8:21–22 and Isa 56:1–8.

3:8*~Jer 23:5–6* (B) (branch) (* see branch, Davidic covenant network). Jeremiah uses the branch imagery mentioned in Isa 4:2 to develop expectations for a Davidic ruler (see note on Jer 23:5). The masoretic version of Jeremiah includes an expansion of the branch theme (see note on 33:14–22). In Zechariah's fourth vision the delegate of Yahweh says to Joshua the high priest: "Listen, High Priest Joshua, you and your associates seated before you, who are men *symbolic of things to come*: I am going to bring my servant, *the Branch*" (Zech 3:8, emphasis mine). The use of the term "sign" or "symbol" emphasizes the typological function of the eschatological branch.[13] On the contested issue of branch and Zerubbabel see note on Zech 6:11–14.

3:10~Mic 4:4 (C) (under one's own vine and fig tree). See note on Zech 8:21–22.

4:7*~Isa 40:4* (C) (mountain becomes level) (* see branch, new exodus, and seventy years networks).

4:9*~Isa 44:28* (C) (Zerubbabel lays temple foundation) (* see branch, new exodus, and seventy years networks). The celestial delegate's word to Zechariah in the vision of the lampstand may evoke imagery from Isaiah's new exodus (Isa 40–55). While the common term "mountain" does not help, "level ground" only appears in this sense in Isa 40:4, 42:16, and Zech 4:7.[14] In the present context the level area may function as the place to build the temple.[15] The possibility of Zechariah using imagery from Isaiah's new

11. See Boda, *Haggai, Zechariah*, 223–24. On no walls, see Ezek 38:11.
12. Contra overstating Zechariah's vision as a "parody" on Ezekiel's vision (Tuell, "Haggai-Zechariah," 285).
13. See "מוֹפֵת," OT no. 4 *NIDOTTE* 2:881.
14. See "מִישׁוֹר," no. 2 *HALOT* 1:578.
15. See Meyers and Meyers, *Haggai, Zechariah 1–8*, 246.

exodus is strengthened by the reference to Zerubbabel laying the foundation (יסד) of the temple in Zech 4:9, which matches the use of this loaded term in Isa 44:28 (see Ezra 3:8, 10). Zechariah's possible reference to Zerubbabel's role in the Second Temple rebuilding provides reasons to associate Isaiah's new exodus with the restoration (emphases signify verbal parallels):

> Every valley shall be raised up, every *mountain* and hill made low; the rough ground shall become *level*, the rugged places a plain. (Isa 40:4)

> What are you, mighty *mountain*? Before Zerubbabel you will become *level ground*. Then he will bring out the capstone to shouts of "God bless it! God bless it!" (Zech 4:7)

6:11–14*~Jer 33:14–18* (B) (civil and priestly rulers) (* see branch and Davidic covenant networks). In the fourth vision, the delegate of Yahweh told Joshua the high priest to expect the coming of Yahweh's servant branch (Zech 3:8). The eighth vision returns to the theme of two persons and addresses Joshua and branch. The plural of "crowns" (MT, LXX, KJV, JPSB) may correspond to two rulers, Joshua (6:11) and Branch (6:13).[16] The emphasis on a royal ruler named Branch and a priestly ruler corresponds broadly to the expectation for a Davidic branch and Levitical priests in Jer 33:14–18.[17]

Though there is strong reason to see a relationship, based on the use of "branch" and priestly figures, the direction of dependence has challenges.[18] Jeremiah 33:14–26 is a masoretic plus not in the Septuagintal version. The Transitional Biblical Hebrew profile of masoretic Jeremiah suggests the revision of Jeremiah to be exilic and available to Zechariah in 520 BCE when the night visions are dated (1:7; for details, see Hermeneutical Profile of the Use of Scripture in Jeremiah). The nature of diachronic Hebrew evidence, while based on empirical data, can only offer broad dating. One additional factor should be considered. The use of the expression "the good promise" appearing in Jeremiah only in masoretic pluses (not in LXX) in Jer 29:10 and 33:14 suggests they are part of the same update.[19] While so many variables require caution, the combination of evidence discussed in this paragraph strengthens the possibility of Jer 33:14–18 as donor context.

---

16. The plural "crowns" (עֲטָרוֹת) in Zech 6:11 MT is glossed as a "singular of majesty" in the targum, some LXX manuscripts, and Syriac (*BHQ* apparatus). The same term is in singular in 6:14 LXX, which matches the singular verb there (Gelston, *BHQ*, 140*). But plural nouns may be the subject of feminine singular verbs (GKC §145k). Redditt observes that "it is difficult to account for the plural form [of crowns] if it was not original" ("Zerubbabel, Joshua," 252). This seems a case where interpretive issues led to scribal adjustments in the ancient versions (LXX, Syriac, Tg). The two crowns could as easily be explained by one on Joshua (6:11) and the other for Branch (6:13). The MT 6:11, 14 and LXX 6:11 retain the more difficult reading "crowns" followed by a few translations (KJV, JPSB) which is preferred as more original here. Also see Boda, "Oil, Crowns," 4.3.3.

17. The word "branch" (צמח) functioned as a name outside the Scriptures at least as early as the second half of the eighth century BCE (see Arad Ostraca 49.4.1 in Aḥituv, *Echoes*, 147).

18. See Boda, *Exploring*, 2:69, n. 31.

19. Compare "the good promise" (אֶת־דִּבְרֵי הַטּוֹב) (Jer 29:10) with "the good promise" (אֶת־הַדָּבָר הַטּוֹב) (33:14). Elsewhere this phrase appears only in Josh 21:45; 23:15. The speculation that the additions of Jer 29:10 MT and 33:14–18

A case for identifying Branch in Zech 6:12 with Zerubbabel pivots on both figures associated with building the temple (4:9; 6:12, 13). The use of Branch without naming Zerubbabel in 3:8 and 6:12 has provoked manifold speculations.[20] Without evidence excavative conjectures offer little help.

In sum, evidence for an interpretive allusion between Jer 33:14–18 and Zech 6:12 is strong, but everything else is sketchy. The provisional soft deductions here are based on "crowns" in the Masoretic Text of Zech 6:11, 14 without emendation, diachronic Hebrew studies of Jeremiah, the use of "the good promise" in Jer 29:10 and 33:14, and "branch" in the Masoretic Text of Zech 6:12. The evidence favors tentatively identifying Branch in 6:12 as Zechariah's use of the tradition found in Jer 33:14–18. On this reading, Zech 6:11–13 anticipates restoration of Davidic rule with collaboration of a priestly ruler.

7:5–6*~Jer 25:11, 12; 29:10* (B) (fasts for seventy years) (* see seventy years network). A delegation from Bethel asks the priests and prophets if they should continue exilic fasts (Zech 7:2–3).[21] Zechariah offers a sharp response featuring incredulous rhetorical questions (italics signify allusion to Jer 25:11, 12; 29:10; and broken underlining signifies interpretative incredulity):

> Ask all the people of the land and the priests, "When you fasted and mourned in the fifth and seventh months for the past *seventy years*, was it really for me that you fasted? And when you were eating and drinking, were you not just feasting for yourselves?" (7:5–6)

When Haggai and Zechariah oppose their audience, they each sweep aside timing as irrelevant to (dis)obedience (see note on Hag 1:2). While the first vision of Zechariah associates the seventy years with the temple rebuilding, he does not refer to that when responding to the question of fasting (see note on Zech 1:12). The point at hand does not require solution but merely a basis for an ambivalent attitude by Haggai and Zechariah toward their audience's counting off a literal seventy years. More specifically, both Haggai and Zechariah blast their audience for trying to use prophetic timing as an excuse for self-serving ways.

Zechariah does come back around to the exilic fasts that will be converted to feasts: "This is what Yahweh Almighty says: 'The fasts of the fourth, fifth, seventh and tenth months *will become joyful and glad occasions and happy festivals* for Judah. Therefore love truth and peace'" (Zech 8:19). This expected reversal, including the fast of the fifth month, which the delegation originally asked about (7:3), confirms the prophet's

---

MT were made at the same time by the same person, see Sjöberg, "Inner-Biblical Interpretation," 179; Schmid, "How to Date Jeremiah," 456. These studies make different deductions about this evidence than the approach taken here.

20. Speculations include later editors replacing "Zerubbabel" with Joshua and/or "branch." Conjectural emendations of Zech 6:12 are not based on evidence (see *BHK*, *BHS*, *BHQ* apparatus)—contra the "clumsy attempt, by an anxious scribe, to bring the prophet into harmony with history" (Mitchell, Smith, and Bewer, *Zechariah*, 186).

21. The fast of the fifth month marked the burning of the temple (2 Kgs 25:8–10//Jer 52:12–14). On the four exilic fasts (Zech 8:19), see Schnittjer, "Individual versus Collective," 127, n. 62.

condemnation of their bogus religious practices. The timing of the conversion of fasts to feasts may be eschatological, not attached to the building of the temple, in line with the far-flung expectations for restoration of Jerusalem. While in Jerusalem with returned exiles, Zechariah looks forward to a greater return (8:4–8).

8:21–22~Mic 4:2–3 (B) (international pilgrimage to Jerusalem). Isaiah 2:1–5 and Mic 4:1–5 contain an extensive verbal parallel (see notes ad loc.). Zechariah 8:21–22 seems to make allusion to Micah's version based on three reasons: shared imagery between Mic 4:4//Zech 3:10 ("sit under vine and fig tree"; but see note on Mic 4:4 regarding other parallels); the use of "many peoples" in Mic 4:2//Zech 8:22; and most importantly the use of "powerful nations" in Mic 4:3//Zech 8:22 but not in Isa 2:4.[22] In addition to the verbal parallels, note the similar elements Zechariah presents differently (italics and bold signify verbal parallels, and broken underlining signifies similarity):

> Many nations *will come and say*, "*Come, let us* go up to the mountain of Yahweh, to the temple of the God of Jacob. He will teach us his ways, so that we may walk in his paths." The law will go out from Zion, the word of Yahweh from Jerusalem. He will judge between **many peoples** and will settle disputes for **strong nations** far and wide. (Mic 4:2–3a)

> And the inhabitants of one city *will come* to another *and say*, "*Come let us* go at once to entreat Yahweh and seek Yahweh Almighty. I myself am going." And **many peoples** and **powerful nations** will come to Jerusalem to seek Yahweh Almighty and to entreat him. (Zech 8:21–22†)

Zechariah may have selected to reinterpret Micah's version to emphasize the nations as part of the worshiping people of Yahweh. Unlike Isa 2:5, Mic 4:5 maintains that the nations continue to walk in the names of their own gods. The pilgrimage of the nations appears as something of a running theme in Zechariah. Like Isaiah, but with even stronger covenantal language, Zechariah emphasizes that many nations will "join themselves" to Yahweh, using the reflexive (Nif) (see note on Isa 56:1–8) (italics signify verbal parallel, and broken underlining signifies thematic similarity):[23]

---

22. Micah 4:2 begins with "many nations" but Isa 2:3 "many peoples." In a case of Seidel's theory, Isa 2:4 says "He will judge between *the nations* and will settle disputes for many peoples," while Mic 4:3 says "He will judge between many peoples and will settle disputes for strong *nations*." This suggests nations/people function in an interchangeable manner in the parallel. Stead suggests that Zech 8:21–22 alludes to Isa 2:3 but does not discuss the evidence cited in the text above (*Intertextuality*, 34, n. 41). Nurmela discusses some of the evidence presented above but still decides Zech 8:20–23 alludes to Isa 2:2–4 ("Growth," 252–53).

23. Nif can represent passive or reflexive (GKC §51c–f; *IBHS* §23.4.b). The counterpart to "joining oneself" is also used of the other "separating oneself" to join the worshiping assembly: "separating themselves" (בדל Nif) *from* ritual impurity *to* seek Yahweh (Ezra 6:21) and "separating themselves" *from* the other *to* Torah (Neh 10:28[29]). The point here is simply to take note of the common use of Nif when the other joins the worshiping assembly in Scripture. Contra Nurmela, who suggests Zech 2:11[15] alludes to Isa 14:1; but that context does not say "to Yahweh" it says, "the foreigners will join themselves *to them [Israel/Jacob]*" (emphasis mine) ("Growth," 249).

> Let no foreigner who *joins himself* [לוה Nif] *to Yahweh* say, "Yahweh will surely exclude me from his people. . . ." "To them I will give within my temple and its walls a memorial and a name better than sons and daughters; I will give them an everlasting name that will endure forever." (Isa 56:3†, 5)

> Many nations will *join themselves* [לוה Nif] *to Yahweh* in that day and will become my people. I will live among you and you will know that Yahweh Almighty has sent me to you. (Zech 2:11†[15])

In like manner, Zech 14:16–19 depicts the eschatological mandatory international pilgrimage to Jerusalem to participate in the Festival of Tabernacles.

In sum, Zech 8:21–22 may re-present Mic 4:2 in order to emphasize the place of the other among the worshiping assembly as an advancement of the other retaining identity with their own gods (Mic 4:5). In any case, Zechariah presents the ideal worshiping assembly as inclusive of the nations who seek Yahweh.

9:9*~Gen 49:11* (B) (king riding into Jerusalem) (* see Judah-king network). Zechariah looks to the coming of a king on a humble mount (9:9). The distinctive language—"a purebred jack"—makes an interpretive allusion to the blessing of Judah in Gen 49:11 very likely.[24] Zechariah extrapolates from the mount of the expected Judah-king that the coming righteous and saved king exhibits humility.

The royal figure of the blessing of Judah rides into a luxurious vineyard. The superabundant vineyards of Judah require the royal figure to tie his mount to a choice vine and wash his garments in wine. Zechariah widens the event by revealing what comes before the ruler enters upon a donkey. Notice Zechariah' s prequel (bold signifies verbal parallel, and italics signify similarity):[25]

> He binds his *jack* [עִיר] to the vine, **his purebred** [בְּנִי אֲתֹן] to a choice vine, he washes his garment in wine, and his robe in the blood of grapes. (Gen 49:11 lit.)

> Rejoice greatly, Daughter Zion! Shout, Daughter Jerusalem! See, your king comes to you, righteous and saved, humble and riding on a donkey [חֲמוֹר], on *a jack* [עַיִר], **a purebred** [בֶּן־אֲתֹנוֹת]. (Zech 9:9 lit.)

Whatever else Zechariah may have had in mind, his exegetical allusion provides opportunity for connections between suffering-figure themes as integral to the coming of the humble and saved king.[26] Mark takes the next step and builds the narrative of

24. See Way, "Donkey Domain," 105–14.

25. Discussion here based on Schnittjer, "Blessing of Judah," 27–30.

26. Postell suggests that overlapping language in Ps 45 and Gen 49 may explain the use of "humility" (Ps 45:4[5]; Zech 9:9) to characterize the one who rides on a donkey ("Literary," 161–62).

Messiah's entry into Jerusalem around Zech 9:9, but replaces what comes after with a sequel (see Table Z1).

TABLE Z1: ZECHARIAH 9:9 AS PREQUEL AND MARK 11:1–10 AS SET-UP TO IRONIC SEQUEL‡

(**Prequel** Humble king comes riding on a donkey (Zech 9:9))	**Blessing of Judah** Judah-king enters his vineyard with his donkey (Gen 49:11)
Triumphal entry Messiah comes riding on a donkey (Mark 11:1–10)[a]	(**Sequel** Son of vineyard owner executed as king of the Jews (Mark 12:1–11; 15:26))

‡ Table adapted from Schnittjer, "Blessing of Judah," 29–30.

[a] Cf. Matt 21:5; Luke 19:28–36; John 12:15.

11:4–16~Ezek 34:1–31*+37:15–28* (C) (breaking the staff and appointing a bad shepherd) (* see Davidic covenant network). Verbal agreement is scarce between the sign-acts in Zech 11:4–16 and the extended metaphor of the shepherds and sheep in Ezekiel 34 and non-existent between the sign-acts of Ezekiel joining two sticks into one and Zechariah breaking two staffs (Ezek 37:15–27; Zech 11:4–16). A little syntactical similarity may be seen between sheep as objects of actions by evil shepherds in Ezek 34:4 and Zech 11:16.[27] The possible relationship seems to require Zechariah blending Ezekiel's metaphor of the shepherds and sheep and his sign-act joining the staffs. The direction of dependence cannot be deduced from the evidence here but would need to be derived from Zechariah's use of Ezekiel elsewhere (see note on Zech 2:1[5]). In spite of the thin evidence it is possible that Zechariah's sign-act is based on the prophetic traditions in Ezek 34 and 37. Take note of the verbal parallels and broad thematic similarities (bold and underlining refer to verbal parallels and italics to thematic similarity).

> Son of man, prophesy against the shepherds of Israel; prophesy and say to them: "This is what Sovereign Yahweh says: Woe to you shepherds of Israel who only take care of yourselves! Should not shepherds take care of the flock? [3] You **eat** the curds, clothe yourselves with the wool and slaughter the **choice** [בָּרִיא] animals, but you do not take care of the flock. [4] You have not strengthened the weak or **healed** [רפא] the sick or bound up the injured. You have not brought back the strays or **searched** for the lost. You have ruled them harshly and brutally. . . . [10] This is what Sovereign Yahweh says: I am against the shepherds and will hold them accountable for my flock. I will remove them from tending the flock so that the shepherds can no longer feed themselves. I will rescue my flock from their mouths, and it will no longer be food for them." . . . Therefore this

27. See Boda, *Zechariah*, 650–51.

> is what Sovereign Yahweh says to them: See, I myself will judge between the **fat** [בָּרִיא] sheep and the lean sheep. . . .[23] I will place [קום] over them one shepherd, my servant David, and he will tend them; he will tend them and be their shepherd. (Ezek 34:2–4, 10, 20, 23)

> Son of man, take a stick of wood and write on it, "Belonging to Judah and the Israelites associated with him." Then take another stick of wood, and write on it, "Belonging to Joseph (that is, to Ephraim) and all the Israelites associated with him." [17] *Join them together into one stick* so that they will become one in your hand. . . . [24] "My servant David will be king over them, and they will all have one shepherd. They will follow my laws and be careful to keep my decrees." (37:16–17, 24)

> Then I *broke my second staff* called Union, breaking the family bond between Judah and Israel. [15] Then Yahweh said to me, "Take again the equipment of a foolish shepherd. [16] For I am going to raise up [קום] a shepherd over the land who will not care for the lost, or **seek** the young, or **heal** [רפא] the injured, or feed the healthy, but will **eat** the meat of the **choice** [בָּרִיא] sheep, tearing off their hooves." (Zech 11:14–16)

If Zech 11:4–16 makes an interpretive intervention with the expectations in Ezek 34 and 37, then Zechariah's oracle "reverses" the expectations.[28] This would effectively be a postexilic judgment based on the rebellion of the restoration assembly.

One of several major complications springs from identifying the good shepherds. In Ezek 34 Yahweh himself and then David will shepherd the wandering and vulnerable sheep (Ezek 34:10, 23). It is awkward to identify the shepherd in Zech 11:7–14 with Zerubbabel or some other unknown Davidic ruler in the restoration because of the first-person narration. By all accounts the shepherd is the prophet who enacts the sign and breaks the staff—"And I shepherded the sheep . . ." (Zech 11:7). After identifying the shepherd as Zerubbabel in an overview of Zech 11:4–16, Boda identifies the shepherd as Zechariah in his comments on these verses.[29] This leads Boda to deduce that Zechariah is playing a "dramatic" role.[30] This forced creativity seems to strain the interpretation. Ezekiel and Zechariah appear to be playing the role of prophetic delegates when they join sticks and break staffs respectively (Ezek 37:19; Zech 11:10–11, 14). To be clear, Zech 11:4–16 is very difficult with or without an interpretive blend to Ezek 34:1–31 and 37:15–28.[31]

In sum, the difficult sign-acts of Zech 11:4–16 may interpretively blend in order to reverse hopeful expectations for a Davidic shepherd and unity of restored Israel in Ezek

28. See ibid., 651.
29. See ibid., 651–54 contra 655, 659.
30. See ibid., 659–60.
31. For interaction with a different proposed interpretive intervention in Zech 11:4–17 see Filters.

34:1–31 and 37:15–28. The evidence of allusions is not strong. The interpretive outcomes of an allusion are not clear.

12:1~Gen 2:7+Isa 42:5 (C) (creator of heaven, earth, and the human spirit). The opening of Zechariah's last set of oracles introduces Yahweh in a manner akin to the stereotype of old Persian royal inscriptions. These inscriptions refer to Ahuramazda as the one who established the earth, heavens, humans, and peace.[32] The similar form of Zech 12:1 leads to the different purpose of bringing judgment. Although the creational language is common in Scripture, the language including "stretch" heavens, along with other literary elements, only appears in this sequence in Isa 42:5 and Zech 12:1.[33] Zechariah 12:1 also uses the verb "forms" which echoes the creation of the human in Gen 2:7 (italics signify shared language with Isa 42:5, and bold signifies shared language with Gen 2:7):

> A prophecy: The word of Yahweh concerning Israel. Yahweh, who *stretches out the heavens*, who lays the foundation of the earth, and who **forms** the human spirit within a person, declares. (Zech 12:1)

13:5~Amos 7:14+Gen 4:1, 2 (B) (denying prophetic vocation). Zechariah vividly describes a day of shame for false prophets using direct discourse to give voice to a denial about their calling (13:5). Zechariah seems to employ an interpretive blend to highlight their humiliation. Amos claimed he was not a vocational prophet seeking a payday and went on to speak of his ranch and orchards (Amos 7:14). The humbled false prophet begins identically, "I am not a prophet," but goes on to describe himself as something of an indentured servant-farmer echoing language about Cain (Zech 13:5). The phrase "a man who works the soil" only appears twice in Scripture (Gen 4:2; Zech 13:5). The other shared element with the birth of Cain strengthens the likelihood of allusion but is difficult to interpret. The only use of the verb translated "bring forth" (קנה Q) in this sense occurs in Gen 4:1, and the only use of the causal stem of the same verb "sold me" or "hired me out" (קנה Hif) occurs in Zech 13:5.[34] The rarity of occurrences makes both challenging. Zechariah's interpretive use of Amos's famous claim followed by a bad version of Cain's vocation, whatever its precise sense, underscores the shameful destiny of false prophets (bold and italics signify verbal parallels, and broken underlining signifies parallel at the level of root):

> Eve . . . gave birth to Cain. She said, "With the help of Yahweh I have brought forth [קנה Q] a man" . . . and Cain **worked the soil.** (Gen 4:1, 2)

32. See Mitchell, "Creation Formula," 305–6, and inscription cited therein.

33. See ibid., 307. Mitchell takes the verb in Isa 42:6 as "I will form" (אֶצָּרְךָ from יצר) though most modern committee translations take it as "I will keep" (אֶצָּרְךָ from נצר). On the assimilation of *yod* into a middle sibilant in פ״י verbs see GKC §71.

34. See "קנה," Q no. 4, Hif *HALOT* 2:1112–13.

> Amos answered Amaziah, "*I am not a prophet* nor the son of a prophet, but I was a shepherd, and I also took care of sycamore-fig trees." (Amos 7:14†)

> Each will say, "*I am not a prophet*. I am a man who **works the soil**; for a man hired me out [קנה Hif] since my youth." (Zech 13:5, lit.)[35]

FILTERS

Zechariah features a large number of non-exegetical scriptural echoes and allusions. The present purpose includes annotating representative examples and listing others.[36] The following lists are not comprehensive or complete.

Non-Exegetical Broad Allusions and Shared Themes

Zechariah uses traditional prophetic refrains (italics signify parallels): "Shout aloud and *sing* for joy, people of *Zion*, for great is the Holy One of Israel *among you*" (Isa 12:6); "*Sing*, Daughter *Zion*; shout aloud, Israel! *Be glad* and rejoice with all your heart, Daughter Jerusalem! . . . Yahweh is *among you*; never again will you fear any harm" (Zeph 3:14–15†); "'*Sing* and *be glad*, Daughter *Zion*. For I am coming, and I will live *among you*,' declares Yahweh" (**Zech 2:10†[14]**).

Compare (italics signify parallels): "Yahweh is in *his holy* temple; let all the earth *be silent* [הס] *before* him" (Hab 2:20); "*Be silent* [הס] *before* Sovereign Yahweh, for the day of Yahweh is near" (Zeph 1:7); "*Be still* [הס] *before* Yahweh, all mankind, because he has roused himself from *his holy* dwelling" (**Zech 2:13**).

The accusation of the *satan* in the celestial court in **Zech 3:1–5** shares thematic similarity with the celestial court scenes in Job 1–2. The shared imagery functions more like a type-scene than exegetical allusion, irrespective of direction of dependence.[37] Also note: **Zech 1:10**>/<Job 1:7; 2:2, "to go about upon the earth/from roaming upon the earth and going about upon it" (להתהלך בארץ/משוט בארץ ומהתהלך בה).

Zechariah 7:10 summarizes the social indifference against which the "former prophets" spoke (7:12). Zechariah regards the former prophets as speaking in accord with Torah—"They made their hearts as hard as flint and would not listen to *the torah* or to the words that Yahweh Almighty had sent by his Spirit *through the earlier prophets*"

---

35. The translation "hired me out" follows Boda, *Zechariah*, 721. The observations on the use of Gen 4:1, 2 in Zech 13:5 are indebted to Boda, 731–32; idem, *Exploring*, 2:187.

36. For other lists with many additional examples of possible echoes and allusions, see Boda, *Zechariah*, passim; idem, *Exploring*, 2:174–77, 184–89; Boda and Floyd, *Bringing Out the Treasure*, 7–200 (Mason), 324–32 (Redditt), and 262 (Tigchelaar); Lee, *Intertextual*, 241; Meyers and Meyers, *Zechariah 9–14*, 40–43; Nurmela, "Growth," 249–58; Stead, *Intertextuality*, 31–36, et passim. Also see discussion of scriptural genres in Zechariah drawn from scriptural templates in Boda, *Zechariah*, 40; idem, *Exploring*, 2:86–94 (also see on Entire OT in Bibliographic Note on Lists of Potential Parallels).

37. For use of this type-scene in the Second Temple period, see, e.g., Jub. 17:16.

(**Zech 7:12**, emphasis mine). Zechariah summarizes the message of the former prophets: "Do not oppress the widow or the fatherless, the foreigner or the poor. Do not plot evil against each other" (7:10; cf. Table A3 in Amos Filters).

Zechariah 8:9 refers to the prophets present on the day the temple foundation was laid, which fits with Haggai's oracle "from this day" (Hag 2:18–19; Zech 8:9).

Zechariah 8:12 features an inverted citation of Haggai: "heavens have withheld their dew and the earth its crops" (כלאו שמים מטל והארץ כלאה יבולה) (Hag 1:10) and "the earth will produce its crops, and the heavens will drop their dew" (והארץ תתן את יבולה והשמים יתנו טלם) (Zech 8:12).[38]

Zechariah 9:7 speaks of blood taken from the Philistine diet. This accords with the general human prohibition against consuming blood, repeated for Israel and gentile converts to Messiah (Gen 9:4; Lev 17:10–14; Acts 15:20, 29; 21:25). Zechariah goes on to speak of removing "detestable things," which may be an allusion to covenantal dietary regulations (Lev 11; Deut 14:3–21), or the broader language may refer to an end to their idolatrous worship meals (Isa 65:4; 66:3, 17).[39] Surprisingly, Zechariah says that the Philistines shall become a remnant for God within Judah like unto the Jebusites. The positive comparison to the Jebusites being absorbed into Judah may look to those who lived peaceably like Ornan (2 Sam 24:16; 1 Chr 21:18) or their remnant put into slave labor (Josh 15:63; 1 Kgs 9:20–21; 1 Chr 22:2, 15–16).

Stead suggests that the shepherd allegory in **Zech 11:4–17** should be interpreted in light of Jeremiah based on the similarities between "Hear the cry [קול] of the shepherds [רעה], the wailing [יללה] of the leaders [אדיר] of the flock, for Yahweh is destroying [שדד] their pasture" (Jer 25:36) and "Listen [קול] to the wail [יללה] of the shepherds [רעה]; their rich pastures [אדרת, lit. glories] are destroyed [שדד]" (Zech 11:3). Stead sees the three shepherds Yahweh got rid of in one month referring to the time span between the ninth day of the fourth month (Jer 52:6) and the tenth day of the fifth month (52:12) when the temple was burned and the king's sons and many leaders were killed. Based upon these starting points, Stead finds a large number of contexts with similar words in Jeremiah as a whole and Zech 11:4–17.[40] Many of the similarities are based on common terms distributed widely in Jeremiah, making for very general suggested parallels. The more conventional view of the shepherds as unspecified leaders, based on shepherding and the staff thematic similarities between Zech 11:4–17 and Ezek 34:1–31 and 37:15–28, offers more promise along with other difficulties (see note on Zech 11:4–16).

Zechariah 13:7 and Jer 50 share sword language (Jer 50:35–37) and a lion who goes up against the shepherd (50:44) to drag away the "little ones [צערים] of the flock"

38. For this example of Seidel's theory, see Beentjes, "Discovering a New Path," 38.

39. The term for "forbidden food" (NIV) or "detestable things" (JPS) in Zech 9:7 connotes disgusting pagan worship in Hos 9:10 (see "שִׁקּוּץ," I.C, II.C *HALOT* 2:1640–41).

40. See Stead, "Three Shepherds," 149–65.

(only in 50:45; Zech 13:5). Scattering of the sheep may be drawn from elsewhere (e.g., Jer 23:1, 2; Ezek 34:5, 6, 12, 21).[41]

The nations surrounding Jerusalem only to be saved by Yahweh himself in **Zech 14:1–5** broadly aligns with Ezek 38:18–39:6. These contexts depict something like the Chaldean siege of Jerusalem (2 Kgs 25:1) but with a different ending, something more like the failure of Sennacherib (19:35–36).

The term "split" (בקע) is often used of the sea crossing and wilderness acts (Exod 14:16; Ps 78:13, 15; Isa 48:21), which may be connoted by splitting the Mount of Olives (**Zech 14:4**) both as a way of escape for the remnant (**14:5**) combined with flowing water (**14:8**).[42]

Zechariah 14:8 speaks of living waters coming out of Jerusalem by a possible allusion to the waters that will flow from Ezekiel's temple (Ezek 47:12). Whereas Ezekiel's vision forecasts a river flowing to the east, Zechariah speaks of rivers flowing east and west from Jerusalem (cf. Joel 3:18[4:18]). Also note the fountain with ritual purification for those in Jerusalem (Zech 13:1).

Zechariah 14:11 says of Jerusalem, "It will be inhabited; never again will it be destroyed [*herem* חֵרֶם]." The term for "what is destroyed" or "what is devoted" may make a broad allusion to Deut 7:1–2, when the Jebusites were one of the peoples devoted (but see Zech 9:7). The sense in Zech 14:11 may be that devoting the others more generally has been permanently repealed since the nations are required to celebrate Tabernacles (14:16–19).[43]

Zechariah 14:20 anticipates inscribing bells on horses as "holy to Yahweh," which is surprising because horses are included among the ritually impure animals (Lev 11:1–8; Deut 14:3–7). This move goes beyond ritually impure to pure and is now treated as holy—a different category.[44]

Other possible non-exegetical allusions: **4:2**>/<Exod 25:31, 32, "gold lampstand" with seven branches (מנורת זהב); **5:2**>/<1 Kgs 6:3, size of flying scroll and porch of Solomon's temple "twenty cubits length and ten cubits width" (ארך עשׂרים באמה ורחב עשׂר באמה); **5:11**>/<Gen 10:10; 11:2, "Shinar" (=Babylon) (שׁנער); **7:11**>/<Isa 6:10, "close ears" (אזנים כבד);[45] **9:6**>/<Deut 23:2[3], "one of a forbidden union" (ממזר) here associated with Ashdod (cf. Neh 13:23, 24).

Shared Stock Phrases and Other Similarities

Zechariah and prophetic traditions: >/<**1:20**; Isa 54:16; Ezek 21:31[36], judgment by "smiths" (חרשים); >/<**3:2**; Amos 4:11, "brand snatched from the fire" (/אוד מצל מאשׁ

41. These observations indebted to Boda, *Zechariah*, 735–36.
42. Schellenberg, "One," 112; Boda, *Zechariah*, 756.
43. See Boda, *Zechariah*, 770.
44. See ibid., 779.
45. See Nurmela, "Growth," 250.

משׂרפה); >/<**8:2**; Joel 2:18, "I am jealous for Zion with great jealousy/Yahweh was jealous for his land" (קנאתי לציון קנאה גדולה/ויקנא יהוה לארצו); >/<**8:3**; Isa 1:21, 26, "faithful city" (עיר אמת/קריה נאמנה); >/<**8:3**; Isa 11:9; Jer 31:23, Zion as "holy mountain" (הר הקדשׁ); >/<**9:4**; Amos 1:10, "fire to consume" (אשׁ אכל) Tyre (cf. Amos Filters); >/<**9:11**; Isa 42:7; 49:9; 61:1, free prisoners; >/<**9:12**; Isa 61:7; cf. 40:2; Job 42:10, double portion (מִשְׁנֶה); >/<**9:14**; Hab 3:11, theophany storm "like his/your arrow(s) of lightning" (כברק חצו/חציך . . . ברק); >/<**9:14**; Isa 29:6; 40:24; 41:16; Jer 23:19; Ezek 1:4; 13:11, 13, "storm winds" (סערה); >/<**9:16; 10:2**; Num 27:17; 1 Kgs 22:17; Isa 53:6; Jer 12:3; Pss 44:11, 22[12, 23]; 49:14[15]; 77:20[21]; 78:52; 80:1[2]; 107:41; 2 Chr 18:16, "like sheep" (כצאן) (cf. Ezek 36:37; Mic 2:12); >/<**10:8** reverse of Isa 5:26; 7:18, Yahweh "whistles" (שׁקר); >/<**10:10**; Hos 11:11, return from Egypt and Assyria (cf. Deut 30:1–5); >/<**10:11**; Isa 11:15–16, pass though sea to return from Assyria (cf. 43:16); >/<**10:12**; Mic 4:5, "in his name they will walk/we shall walk in the name of Yahweh our God" (ובשׁמו יתהלכו/ואנחנו נלך בשׁם יהוה אלהינו); >/<**11:1–2**; Isa 2:13, "cedar of Lebanon; oaks of Bashan" (לבנון . . . ארז; אלוני בשׁן/ארזי הלבנון . . . אלוני הבשׁן); >/<**12:10**; Ezek 39:29; Joel 2:28[3:1], "pour out spirit" (שׁפך רוח).

Zechariah and other Scriptures: >/<**2:8**; Deut 32:10; Ps 17:8, "apple/pupil of eye" (בבת/אישׁון עין); >/<**6:15**; Exod 15:26; Deut 15:5; 28:1, "if you diligently obey the voice of Yahweh your God" (אם שׁמוע תשׁמעון/ישׁמע בקול יהוה אלהיכם/אלהיך);[46] >/< **9:10**; Ps 46:9[10]; 76:3[4], "bow broken" (כרת/שׁבר קשׁת); >/<**9:10**; Ps 72:8, "rule from sea to sea and from the river to the ends of the earth" (משׁל/רדה מים עד ים ומנהר עד אפסי ארץ) (cf. 1 Kgs 4:24[5:4]); >/<**9:11**; Exod 24:8, "blood of covenant with you" (דם־בריתך/ דם־הברִית . . . עמכם); >/<**9:14**; Exod 19:16, 19; 20:18, theophany with "trumpet" (שׁופר); >/<**11:12**; Exod 21:32; Lev 27:4, price of slave or female "thirty pieces of silver/shekels" (שׁלשׁים כסף/שׁקל).[47]

Connections within Zechariah

Note: >/<1:6; 10:9, exiles turn (וישׁובו/ושׁבו); >/<8:2, 3, 4, 6, 7, 9, 14, 19, 20, 23, "thus says Yahweh" (10x); >/<9:1; 12:1, "a burden, the word of Yahweh" (מַשָּׂא דְבַר־יהוה) (cf. Mal 1:1).[48]

46. On the view that Zech 6:15 alludes to Deut 28:1, see Stead, *Intertextuality*, 33.

47. One shekel per month is based on the wages of hired workers in CH §273 as calculated in *BabL* 1:471. Many difficulties adhere to this legal context.

48. For parallels within Zechariah see Meyers and Meyers, *Haggai, Zechariah 1–8*, lii, liii, lviii; idem, *Zechariah 9–14*, 36–37.

Chapter 24

MALACHI

SYMBOLS[1]

// verbal parallels (A level)
/~/ synoptic parallel (A level)
~ B, probable interpretive allusion; C, possible; D, probably not
+ interpretive blend
>/< more or less similar (see Filters)
* part of interpretive network (see Networks)

USE OF SCRIPTURE IN MALACHI[2]

1:2–3~Gen 25–36+Deut 7:8; 10:15 (C) (love Israel, hate Esau)
1:6–2:9~Num 6:23–27+Lev 22:17–25 (B) (reversal of priestly blessing)
1:6~Exod 20:12//Deut 5:16 (B) (son honors father)
1:8, 13~Deut 15:21 (B) (defective sacrifices)
2:4–5, 8~Num 25:12–13; Jer 33:21 (C) (covenant with Levi)
2:6*~Deut 33:10* (B) (instruction of Levi) (* see teachers network)
2:7*~Lev 10:10–11* (C) (instruction of priests) (* see teachers network)
2:16~Deut 24:1 (B) (if he hates and sends away)
3:1*~Exod 23:20* (B)+Isa 40:3* (C) (sending delegate to prepare the way) (* see new exodus network)

OLD TESTAMENT USE OF MALACHI

n/a

NEW TESTAMENT USE OF MALACHI

1:2, 3//Rom 9:13 (Jacob loved, Esau hated)
3:1//Matt 11:10; Mark 1:2; Luke 7:27 (my messenger)
4:5[3:23]~Matt 17:10–11 (Elijah comes first)

HERMENEUTICAL PROFILE OF THE USE OF SCRIPTURE IN MALACHI

Malachi's use of scriptural traditions stands firmly in the prophetic tradition, but he more often makes allusion to Torah (e.g., versus Joel who uses prophets). In that sense Malachi abounds with prophetic allusions to Torah. Based upon Malachi's setting sometime within the first half of the Second Temple period, the default will be to regard it as

1. For explanation of symbols, see Symbols and Abbreviations and Introduction. For other help, see Glossary.
2. See Bibliographic Note on Lists of Potential Parallels.

the receptor context of intentional parallels. The present focus includes only Malachi's exegetical use of scriptural traditions (for other uses see Filters).

Malachi's use of scriptural traditions functions along the lines of his disputation style. The book presents a series of arguments between Malachi and his increasingly hostile audience. Within several of these disputes he uses scriptural traditions sharply against their rude questions. The main interpretive interventions include counterpoints and reversals.

Malachi uses scriptural traditions as a counterpoint answer to the question to Yahweh, "How have you loved us?" He does not spell out the evidence of Yahweh's mercy. Instead, he explains how Yahweh hates Esau. Though it may not feel like an answer, it is.

Malachi accesses the beloved priestly blessing but reverses it into a curse. The extensive anti-blessing includes several brief allusions to scriptural traditions to shine a light on the failures of the worship establishment and their more affluent congregants.

Malachi makes use of exodus and new exodus traditions but mostly in terms of a warning. In this case Malachi focuses on a counterpoint latent within the scriptural traditions. The coming of the messenger will be a problem for those who do not live like they fear Yahweh. The endgame remains redemptive but by means of a refining fire.

Malachi's tendency to turn cherished scriptural traditions against his audience magnifies the deep trouble of the restoration. The exile did not rid Israel of its rebellion. The people are back, but it is like they never left. Such a situation requires the kind of exegetical applications at which Malachi excels.

In sum, if Malachi's audience finds his message unwelcome, he turns their favorite scriptural contexts against their arrogance. Messages based on scriptural teachings of Yahweh's love, blessing, and redemption can hurt. Malachi features interpretive allusions with an attitude, so to speak.

USE OF SCRIPTURE

1:2–3~Gen 25–36+Deut 7:8; 10:15 (C) (love Israel, hate Esau). The covenantal antonyms "love" and "hate" can be used of humans—those who obey Yahweh's commands love him and those who disobey hate him (Deut 7:9, 10)—or of God. In fear, Israel perversely imagined that he had delivered them from Egypt because "Yahweh hates us" (1:27). While Exodus presents Moses's intercessory imagination as: the Egyptians shall say, "It was *with evil intent* that he brought them out," Deuteronomy paraphrases, "*because he hated them*, he brought them out" (Exod 32:12; Deut 9:28, emphases mine). Malachi uses these loaded antithetical covenantal terms to answer his rude hecklers' question: "'I have loved you,' says Yahweh. But you ask, 'How have you loved us?'" (Mal 1:2).

Malachi frames the answer as half a contrast between two brothers: Esau representing Edom and Jacob representing Israel (Gen 25:25–26, etc.). The vivid use of the names of the ancestral brothers for the nations fits within prophetic traditions.[3] Instead of annotating evidence of divine love, Malachi provides the counterpoint of Esau, the object of divine elective hatred (italics signify verbal parallels, and broken underlining signifies interpretive deduction):

> But it was because Yahweh *loved you* and kept the oath he swore to your ancestors that he brought you out with a mighty hand and redeemed you from the land of slavery. (Deut 7:8)

> Yet Yahweh set his affection on your ancestors and *loved* them, and he chose you, their descendants, above all the nations—as it is today. (10:15)

> "I *have loved you*," says Yahweh. "But you ask, 'How have you *loved* us?' "Was not Esau Jacob's brother?" declares Yahweh. "Yet I *have loved* Jacob, but Esau I have hated, and I have turned his hill country into a wasteland and left his inheritance to the desert jackals." (Mal 1:2–3)

Malachi goes on to reinforce the terminal disaster Yahweh will bring upon Edom if they try to recover (1:4–5). The historical outcomes accord with Malachi's word for later generations of readers (see table M1).

TABLE M1: SELECTED TIMELINE OF EDOM‡

597 BCE, Edom regains control of Negev in wake of Neo-Babylonian campaigns against Judea (1 Esdr 4:50)
586, Edom watches Neo-Babylonians in sacking of Jerusalem, and their profiteers capture fleeing Judeans seeking refuge (Obad 11–14; Ps 137:7)
552, Nabonidus destroys Edom
5th century, Arab tribes overrun region even while Edomite remnant subsists
312, Nabateans take over Edomite region and make Petra their capital while remaining Edomites assimilate or flee to Idumea

‡ Table based on Hill, "Malachi," 5:236.

In sum, Malachi responds to his pretentious audience not with evidence of covenantal love but with the counterpoint of covenantal hate against Edom. Malachi makes room for his audience to align their own opposite realities over and against Edom. They ask: "How have you loved us?" Malachi says Yahweh hates Esau. That is the answer.

3. For prophetic traditions against Edom, see Isa 34:5–15; 63:1–6; Jer 49:7–22; Ezek 25:12–14; Amos 1:11–12; Obad 1–9, 15–21. For extensive attention to shared terms and syntax with Mal 1:2–5, see Gibson, *Covenant*, 49–68.

1:6–2:9~Num 6:23–27+Lev 22:17–25 (B) (reversal of priestly blessing).
1:6~Exod 20:12//Deut 5:16 (B) (son honors father).
1:8, 13~Deut 15:21 (B) (defective sacrifices).
2:4–5, 8~Num 25:12–13; Jer 33:21 (C) (covenant with Levi).
2:6*~Deut 33:10* (B) (instruction of Levi) (* see teachers network).
2:7*~Lev 10:10–11* (C) (instruction of priests) (* see teachers network). Malachi's second disputation primarily against the priests and Levites makes heavy use of scriptural traditions (Mal 1:6–2:9). Malachi 1:12–14 focuses on congregants who bring defective offerings and thus recapitulates 1:7–11 which attacks priests for disgracing the altar with unacceptable sacrifices.[4] The entire disputation, as noted by Fishbane, plays upon the priestly blessing in an ironic way.[5] Along the way Malachi interpretively alludes to several other scriptural contexts that need to be noted before returning to the inversion of the priestly blessing.

Malachi makes broad allusion to the fifth commandment, that children honor parents (Exod 20:12//Deut 5:16; Mal 1:6), as part of a shame tactic against the priestly establishment in the crosshairs of his judgment.

Malachi accuses the priests of offering up unlawful, defective sacrifices, primarily alluding to the language of the prohibition in Deut 15:21 (Mal 1:8). In his recapitulation of the accusation he also condemns congregants for offering defective offerings (1:13–14). The language of the counterpart prohibition in Lev 22:17–25 against defective offerings provides a lesser running echo (1:7–14, esp. "vow" Lev 22:18, 21, 23; Mal 1:14 and "deformed" Lev 22:25; Mal 1:14).[6]

Detecting the reference of Malachi's broad allusion to a covenant with Levi attracts much debate (Mal 2:4, 8). Leading proposals include the covenant of "peace" with Phinehas featuring the same language in Num 25:12–13 as well as Moses's word to Levi in Deut 33:10. But neither of these is exactly a covenant with Levi. Similar to Malachi, Jer 33:21 refers to "my covenant with the Levites who are priests ministering before me" (MT only, not in LXX; see note on Jer 33:14–22). Nehemiah, from the same general timeframe as Malachi, also refers to a covenant with the priests and Levites (Neh 13:29). These passages point to a common view of a covenant with worship personnel but do not help to identify a cited scriptural context. Assis suggests Malachi may be using the phrase generally for rhetorical purposes.[7]

The Levites and priests each have responsibilities to instruct Israel that somewhat overlap (see teachers network). The prophet alludes to the Levites as teachers in Mal 2:6 (cf. Deut 33:10) and priests as those from whom the people seek instruction in 2:7

4. See helpful side by side chart in Assis, "Reproach," 277.
5. See Fishbane, "Form," 118–19; idem, *Biblical Interpretation*, 332–34; idem, *Haftarot*, 36.
6. See Weyde, *Prophecy*, 118–22, esp. parallel tables on 119, 120. Also see Milgrom, *Leviticus 17–22*, 1875, 1882.
7. See Assis, "Reproach," 283. On weighing the options, see Hill, *Malachi*, 206; Gibson, *Covenant*, 101–5.

(cf. Lev 10:10–11). Malachi blasts Levites and priests together for turning people aside by their corrupt instruction (Mal 2:8).

Malachi's condemnation of all these rebellions—dishonor by defective sacrifices and corrupt teaching—have been peppered with a damning anti-priestly blessing. Malachi condemns the priests by making a series of ironic antithetical allusions to the high priestly blessing, playing off many of its key terms—blessing, face, grace, peace, and name. As usual the starting point is a contentious question: "You ask, 'How have we shown contempt for your name?'" (1:6).

Malachi does not speak of blessing but of curse (1:14). Yahweh does not shine his face, bringing grace, but threatens to smear animal excrement on the priests' faces (2:3). This act does not merely humiliate the priests but would "desacralize" them, making them unfit for temple service.[8] This shocking transformation of the priestly blessing into a curse upon the priesthood speaks of the depth of the prophetic angst against the corrupt Second Temple establishment.

The nature of Malachi's interpretive allusion requires a lengthy quotation to illustrate the anti-priestly blessing undercurrents. Malachi deploys antonyms and terms with assonance and consonance to invert the priestly blessing (bold signifies verbal parallels related to the priestly blessing, italics signify verbal parallels regarding defective sacrifice, and broken underlining signifies exegetical inversions):[9]

> Tell Aaron and his sons, "This is how you are to **bless** the Israelites. Say to them: 'Yahweh **bless** you and **keep** you; Yahweh make his **face** shine on you and be **gracious** to you; Yahweh **lift up** his **face** toward you and give you peace.'" So they will put **my name** on the Israelites, and I will **bless** them. (Num 6:23–27†)

> If an animal has a defect, is *lame* or *blind*, or has any serious flaw, you must not *sacrifice* it to Yahweh your God. (Deut 15:21)

> [1:6] "A son honors his father, and a slave his master. If I am a father, where is the honor due me? If I am a master, where is the respect due me?" says Yahweh Almighty. "It is you priests who show contempt for **my name.** "But you ask, 'How have we shown contempt for your **name**?' [7] "By offering defiled food on my altar. "But you ask, 'How have we defiled you?' "By saying that Yahweh's table is contemptible. [8] When you offer *blind* animals for *sacrifice*, is that not wrong? When you sacrifice *lame* or diseased animals,

8. See Fishbane, "Form," 119. The sacrificial regulations called for the "excrement"—which NIV glosses euphemistically as "intestines" in Leviticus—to be disposed of outside the encampment (Lev 4:11; 8:17; 16:27). See "I פֶּרֶשׁ," *HALOT* 2:977.

9. Priestly blessing terms of Num 6:23–27 appear in Mal 1:6–2:9, "blessing" (ברך) 1x, "face" (פָּנֶה) 6x, "grace" (חנן) 1x, "peace" (שָׁלוֹם) 2x, and "name" (שֵׁם) 6x. Note reversals: instead of "shine" (אוּר) and "be gracious" (חנן) in Num 6:25, "do not light" (לֹא אוּר) and "useless" (חִנָּם) in Mal 1:10; instead of "bless" in Num 6:23, 24, "curse" (ארר 3x; מְאֵרָה 1x) in Mal 1:14; 2:2. Also note contrastive use of "great" in Mal 1:11, 14 and "fear" in 1:14; 2:5.

is that not wrong? Try offering them to your governor! Would he be pleased with you? Would he **lift up** your **face**?" says Yahweh Almighty. [9] "Now seek the **face** of God to be **gracious** to us. With such offerings from your hands, will he **lift up** your **faces?**"—says Yahweh Almighty. [10] "Oh, that one of you would shut the temple doors, so that you would not light useless fires on my altar! I am not pleased with you," says Yahweh Almighty, "and I will accept no offering from your hands. [11] **My name** will be great among the nations, from where the sun rises to where it sets. In every place incense and pure offerings will be brought to **my name**, because **my name** will be great among the nations," says Yahweh Almighty. [12] "But you profane it by saying, 'The Lord's table is defiled,' and, 'Its food is contemptible.' [13] And you say, 'What a burden!' and you sniff at it contemptuously," says Yahweh Almighty. "When you bring injured, *lame* or diseased animals and offer them as sacrifices, should I accept them from your hands?" says Yahweh. [14] "Cursed is the cheat who has an acceptable male in his flock and vows to give it, but then sacrifices a blemished animal to the Lord. For I am a great king," says Yahweh Almighty, "and **my name** is to be feared among the nations. [2:1] And now, you priests, this warning is for you. [2] If you do not listen, and if you do not resolve to honor **my name**," says Yahweh Almighty, "I will send a curse on you, and I will curse your **blessings**. Yes, I have already cursed them, because you have not resolved to honor me. [3] Because of you I will rebuke your descendants; I will smear on your **faces** the dung from your festival sacrifices, and you will be carried off with it. [4] And you will know that I have sent you this warning so that my covenant with Levi may continue," says Yahweh Almighty. [5] "My covenant was with him, a covenant of life and **peace**, and I gave them to him; this called for reverence and he revered me and stood in awe of **my name**. [6] True instruction was in his mouth and nothing false was found on his lips. He walked with me in **peace** and uprightness, and turned many from sin. [7] For the lips of a priest ought to **keep** knowledge, because he is the messenger of Yahweh Almighty and people seek instruction from his mouth. [8] But you have turned from the way and by your teaching have caused many to stumble; you have violated the covenant with Levi," says Yahweh Almighty. [9] "So I have caused you to be despised and humiliated before all the people, because you have not **kept** my ways but have shown partiality [lit. lift face] in matters of the Torah." (Mal 1:6–2:9†)

Malachi proclaims that congregants do not offer Yahweh the sacrifices and vows he is due but rather pass off substandard offerings and hold back the better animals (1:13–14). As such, they, like the priesthood, treat Yahweh below the standard of a civil ruler (1:8). In the middle of the judgment of the worship leaders, Malachi makes the embarrassing contrast of worship of Yahweh by the nations (1:11). Though exactly who and what Malachi has in mind remains elusive, the humiliating contrast with the Second Temple leadership lacks subtlety (1:14; 2:5).

In sum, Malachi transforms the priestly blessing by exegetical intervention. Malachi's terrible ironic reversal flips the priestly blessing on its head—cursing the corrupt and self-seeking worship establishment.

2:16~Deut 24:1 (B) (if he hates and sends away). Every line of Mal 2:10–16 attracts sustained debate. Disputed issues include the meaning of "one father" (Mal 2:10), "marrying the daughter of a foreign god" (2:11 lit.), weeping at the altar (2:13), "has he not made one, and the remaining spirit in him?" (2:15 lit.). Many of these difficulties have been matched with possible scriptural contexts that they may echo.[10] The present purposes restrict interaction to only issues directly related to the possible allusion to Deuteronomy divorce passages in Mal 2:16.

The difficulty of Mal 2:16 begins with identifying the subject of the verb "hates." A comparison of several conventional translations can highlight the issue.

> But if, since you hate her, you should send her away (Mal 2:16 LXX/NETS).
> But if you hate her divorce (2:16 4QXII[a] lit.).[11]
> But *if you hate her, divorce her* (2:16 Targum, emphasis original).[12]
> When thou shalt hate her put her away (2:16 Vulg.).
> For . . . he hateth putting away (2:16 KJV).
> For I hate divorce (2:16 *BHK/BHS* emendation lit.).[13]
> The man who hates and divorces his wife (2:16 NIV).
> For I hate divorce (2:16 NRSV).
> For the man who does not love his wife but divorces her (2:16 ESV).
> For/if [no independent subject listed] hates/hating sends/sending away [no object listed] (2:16 MT lit.).[14]

As these ancient and modern translations show, Mal 2:16 has always caused difficulties. The ancient versions (LXX, 4QXII[a], Targum, Vulg.) all understand Mal 2:16 as referring to the law in Deut 24:1 and so "repaired" the apparent difficulty between the contexts.[15] However the translational issues get sorted out, the present concern relates to the possibility of an interpretive allusion to a law about divorce. Modern translations tend to be split between viewing the subject of the verb "he" as a husband or Yahweh (in which case many emend the text to "I"). The problem stands even when retaining the masoretic third-person

---

10. See Hill, *Malachi*, 224–49, 255–58; Gibson, *Covenant*, 125–40.

11. Compare: כִּי־שָׂנֵא שַׁלַּח (Mal 2:16 MT) versus כי אם שנתה שלח (2:16 4QXII[a], *BQS* 3:624).

12. Cathcart and Gordon regard this as a case of "converse translation . . . by which MT is made to say the opposite of what is intended" (*ArBib*, 14:235). See Klein, "Converse Translation," 515–37.

13. HT reads שנא and *BHK/BHS* apparatus emends to שָׂנֵאתִי.

14. Variables: כִּי conditionally as "if" (GKC §159aa; *IBHS* §38.2e) or emphatic as "indeed" (*IBHS* §39.3.4e); "he hates" (שָׂנֵא) as Q pf. 3ms or repointed as "hating" (שֹׂנֵא) Q ptc. m, which would allow the verb to take "I" or "you" as implied subject. The various translations above all render merely three words in Hebrew (כִּי־שָׂנֵא שַׁלַּח).

15. See Gelston, *BHQ*, 151*; Rendtorff, *Canonical Hebrew Bible*, 311.

verb "he hates" by treating it as indirect versus direct discourse. Notice how the King James Version uses an indirect discourse format "For the LORD, the God of Israel, *saith that* he hateth putting away" (2:16 KJV, emphasis mine; cf. Vulg.) versus a direct discourse format "'The man who hates and divorces his wife,' *says Yahweh*, the God of Israel" (2:16 NIV, emphasis mine). The King James Version can treat the first part of the verse as indirect discourse to have Yahweh as the subject of the verb but needs to revert to using a human as subject of the next third-person verb "he covers"—"For the LORD, the God of Israel, saith that he hateth putting away: for *one covereth* violence with his garment, saith the LORD of hosts: therefore take heed to your spirit, that ye deal not treacherously" (2:16 KJV, emphasis mine). The inherent challenges of Mal 2:16 require cautious and provisional decisions.

The present approach works with the Masoretic Text without modification, thus "he hates." Who is he? Since nearly all uses of "says Yahweh" in Malachi should be taken as direct discourse, the same is applied to Mal 2:16 without literary markers to indicate otherwise.[16] Thus, Yahweh is talking about the husband who hates and divorces as per NIV and ESV in the examples above.

In cases dealing with "divorce," literally "sending away" a spouse, Deuteronomy uses several terms for the husband's negative state of mind toward his wife. Compare, for example, "if you are not pleased with her" (Deut 21:14), "he hates her" (22:13, 16; 24:3), and "she does not find favor in his eyes" (24:1). The use of "she does not find favor in his eyes" in Deut 24:1 and "he hates her" in 24:3 demonstrate the relative interchangeability of the terms within the same case law. Malachi may use the stronger term "he hates" in line with his tendency for striking rhetoric (italics signify verbal parallels, and broken underlining signifies a broadly synonymous idea):

> If a man marries a woman who becomes displeasing to him because he finds something indecent about her, and he writes her a certificate of divorce, gives it to her and *sends* [שׁלח] her from his house . . . and her second husband *hates* [שׂנא] her and writes her a certificate of divorce (24:1, 3†).

> "The man who *hates* [שׂנא] and *divorces* [שׁלח] his wife," says Yahweh, the God of Israel, "does violence to the one he should protect," says Yahweh Almighty. So be on your guard, and do not be unfaithful. (Mal 2:16)

The actual allusion in Hebrew very concisely relates to two terms: "he hates" and "sends." Malachi's exegetical intervention does not so much relate to the somewhat opaque language of the remainder of the verse. It is enough, for the present purposes,

16. See examples of "Yahweh says" (אָמַר יהוה) as marking direct discourse in which if the deity refers to himself, he does so in first person (Mal 1:2, 4, 6, 8, 10, 11, 13; 2:2, 4, 8; 3:5, 7, 10, 11, 12, 13, 17, 19[4:1], 21[4:3]) versus examples that mark discourse referring to the deity in third person (1:9) versus cases in which the deity refers to himself both in first and third person (1:14; 3:1).

to see that the prophet expresses divine displeasure for the husband's treachery. The interpretive advance comes in the form of circumscribing what sorts of things a husband should not "hate" about his wife. If compared to the restoration habit of mass divorces in Ezra-Nehemiah (Ezra 10; Neh 9:2; 13:3), the scenario here would be a species of the worst kind. Malachi does not simply get at arranged apostasy marriages for children to "marry up" by "marrying out." He seems to attack the especially detestable husband who divorces the Yahwistic "wife of his youth" to marry "the daughter of a foreign god" (Mal 2:11, 14). Whether this gets at it or not, the prophet's interpretation relates to the challenging elements of Mal 2:10–15, however they are sorted out.

3:1*~Exod 23:20* (B)+Isa 40:3* (C) (sending delegate to prepare the way) (* see new exodus network). Yahweh promised to send his delegate before Israel variously referred to as "messenger," "terror," and "hornet" (Exod 23:20, 23, 27, 28). Isaiah used the exodus as a forward-looking type with the term "as" or "like" to refer to a new exodus as a highway (Isa 11:16). But Isaiah went further, declaring the highway is for Yahweh himself (40:3). The exchange between Yahweh and Moses after the rebellion at the mountain gets at the difference. Yahweh said he would send a "messenger," but he would "not go up" to avoid pouring out his wrath upon the rebellious people (Exod 33:2, 3). Moses famously talked Yahweh out of this decision (33:15–17). In any case, Malachi's exegetical intervention starts with an interpretive blend of the messenger preparing the way for Yahweh (italics signify verbal parallels, and bold signifies alternate references to God):

> See, I am sending a *messenger* ahead of you to guard you along *the way* and to bring you to the place I have prepared. (Exod 23:20†)

> A voice of one calling: "In the wilderness prepare the way for **Yahweh**; make straight in the desert a highway for **our God**." (Isa 40:3)

> "I will send my *messenger*, who will prepare *the way* before **me**. Then suddenly **the Lord** you are seeking will come to his temple; *the messenger* of the covenant, whom you desire, will come," says Yahweh Almighty. But who can endure the day of his coming? Who can stand when he appears? For he will be like a refiner's fire or a launderer's soap. (Mal 3:1–2)

Malachi uses new exodus imagery as something of a threat. He speaks of the "day of his coming" and uses traditional prophetic imagery of judgment: refining metals (Isa 1:25; Jer 6:29; 9:7; Zech 13:9) and "launderer's soap" (Jer 2:22). This imagery of judgment harks back to Amos's ironic turn: "Woe to you who long for the day of Yahweh! Why do you long for the day of Yahweh? That day will be darkness, not light" (Amos 5:18).

Malachi's association of judgment with the new exodus follows precedent within the cited contexts:

> Pay attention to him [the messenger who goes before] and listen to what he says. Do not rebel against him; *he will not forgive your rebellion*, since my Name is in him. (Exod 23:21, emphasis mine)

> See, Sovereign Yahweh comes with power, and he rules with a mighty arm. See, his reward is with him, and *his recompense accompanies him*. (Isa 40:10, emphasis mine)

The language in Exod 23:21 carries a dire threat to rebels. The term appropriately rendered "recompense" carries a positive connotation when paired with "reward" in Isa 40:10 (cf. 62:11). But the term speaks of judgment in kind and is used of punishment in Isa 65:7.[17] Malachi takes advantage of Yahweh's judgment, inclusive of worship infractions, immorality, and social injustice (Mal 3:3, 5). The metaphors of soap and metal refining help emphasize the redemptive outcomes of Yahweh's coming (3:4). Mark takes good advantage of the warning when he alludes to Mal 3:1 by noting John's and Messiah's message of repentance and highlighting undercurrents of judgment imagery with fishing for people (Mark 1:2, 4, 15, 17; cf. Jer 16:16; Ezek 28:4; Amos 4:4; Hab 1:14–15; Matt 11:10; Luke 7:27).

In sum, Malachi extends new-exodus imagery by blending together key expectations from Torah and Isaiah. Malachi underscores the danger of Yahweh's coming for rebels but highlights the redemptive ends of divine judgment.

FILTERS

In addition to Malachi's exegetical scriptural allusions are many lesser allusions and echoes.[18] The following filters and their associated lists illustrate but do not exhaust non-exegetical similarities.

Non-Exegetical Broad Allusions and Shared Themes

Malachi 3:10 sometimes gets cited as an allusion of "windows of the heavens" from the flood story (Gen 7:11; 8:2). If it is, then Malachi could be credited with transforming an image of judgment to one of blessing.[19] However, similar positive expressions like "windows in the heavens" and "showers of blessing" appear elsewhere (2 Kgs 7:2, 19; Ezek 34:26; cf. Gen 49:25).[20]

---

17. See "פְּעֻלָּה," *HALOT* 2:951.

18. For lists of possible scriptural parallels in Malachi, see Berry, "Malachi's Dual Design," 270–72; Gibson, *Covenant*, 49–69, 85–114, 125–54, 165–81, 187–98, 205–12, 232 (summary table), 235–56; Hill, *Malachi*, 401–12; Mirsky, Meltzer, and Kiel, *Twelve*, 2:11–13 [Hebrew]; Weyde, *Prophecy*, passim (also see on Entire OT in Bibliographic Note on Lists of Potential Parallels). For brief criticism of the lists by Berry and Hill, see Schultz, "Ties That Bind," 29–30.

19. Weyde, *Prophecy*, 335–38; Gibson, *Covenant*, 196.

20. Gibson contends the allusion to flood imagery rests on a different syntactical structure in 2 Kgs 7:2, 19, "windows *in* the heavens" (אֲרֻבּוֹת בַּשָּׁמַיִם) versus "windows *of* the heavens" (אֲרֻבֹּת הַשָּׁמַיִם) in Gen 7:11; 8:2 (*Covenant*, 196, n. 138; cf. Weyde, *Prophecy*, 335, n. 42). That slices too thin for the broad point being made here.

Other: **1:2–3**>/<Gen 25:21–26, Jacob and Esau as brothers; **1:6**>/<Exod 20:12, "a son honors father/honor your father" (בן יכבד אב/כבד את אביך); **2:2**>/<Deut 28:20, "I shall send upon you the curse/Yahweh shall send upon you the curse" (שלחתי בכם את המארה/ישלח יהוה בך את המארה); **2:10**>/<Gen 1:26–28; 2:8; 5:1–2; Deut 8:5; 32:6; Jer 31:9, 18, 20, fatherhood of creator; **3:5**>/<Torah violations, such as sorcery (כשף) Deut 18:10, and see similar lists in Table A3 in Amos Filters; **3:8**>/<Num 18:26; Deut 12:6, 11, "tithes and offerings" (מעשׂר ותרומה) (cf. Neh 10:38; 2 Chr 31:12); **3:17**>/<Exod 19:5; Deut 7:6; 14:2; 26:18, "they will be mine . . . treasured possession/you will be my treasured possession/a people for his treasured possession" (והיו לי . . . סגלה/והייתם לי סגלה/לעם סגלה); **4:4[3:22]**>/<Exod 20//Deut 5, remember Torah of Moses at Horeb; **4:5[3:23]**>/<1 Kgs 17–2 Kgs 2, Elijah (Elijah before the day of Yahweh is often connected with the "messenger" before the day of his coming, Mal 3:1, 2); **4:6[3:24]**>/<1 Kgs 18:37, "he will turn the hearts of the parents to their children, and the hearts of the children to their parents"/ Elijah said "you [Yahweh] are turning their hearts back again" (והשיב לב אבות על בנים ולב בנים על אבותם/ואתה הסבת את לבם אחרנית) (cf. Sir 48:10).[21]

Shared Stock Phrases and Other Similarities[22]

Note: >/<**1:1**; Zech 9:1; 12:1, "a burden, the word of Yahweh" (מַשָּׂא דְּבַר־יהוה); >/<**1:3**; Isa 34:5–15; 63:1–6; Jer 49:7–22; Ezek 25:12–14; Amos 1:11–12; Obad 1–9, 15–21, against Edom; >/<**1:11**; Isa 45:6; Pss 50:1; 113:3, "from the rising of the sun to its setting/and from the west" (ממזרח שמש ועד מבואו/וממערבה);[23] >/<**1:14**; Pss 47:2; 95:3, "great king" (מלך גדול); >/<**2:13**; Joel 2:12; Zech 7:3–5, "weeping" as religious devotion (בכה); >/<**2:14, 15**; Isa 54:6; Prov 5:18, "wife of youth/your youth" (אשה נעורים/נעוריך); >/<**3:2; 4:5**[**3:23**]; Joel 2:11, "Who can endure? . . . the great and dreadful day of Yahweh/great is the day of Yahweh and dreadful . . . Who can endure it?" (מי כול . . . יום יהוה הגדול והנורא/גדול יום יהוה ונורא . . . מי כול); >/<**3:2**; Isa 1:25; Jer 6:29; 9:7; Zech 13:9, "refiner's" fire (צרף) (cf. Ezek 22:17–22); >/<**3:7**; Zech 1:3, "return to me and I will return to you" (שובו אלי ואשובה אליכם).

---

21. Chapman, *Law and Prophets*, 142, cited in Gibson, *Covenant*, 243.
22. Also see Parallels within the Book of the Twelve in Hosea Filters.
23. See Hill, *Malachi*, 402.

Chapter 25

PSALMS

SYMBOLS[1]

// verbal parallels (A level)
/~/ synoptic parallel (A level)
~ B, probable interpretive allusion; C, possible; D, probably not
\+ interpretive blend
>/< more or less similar (see Filters)
* part of interpretive network (see Networks near end of volume)

USE OF SCRIPTURE IN PSALMS[2]

1:1~Deut 6:7* (C) (walk, stand, sit) (* see concealing revelation network)

1:2–3~Josh 1:8 (B)+Jer 17:7–8 (B) (like a tree by water)

2:6–7*~2 Sam 7:14–15* (B) (divine begetting of the king) (* see Davidic covenant and place networks)

2:8–9*~Gen 49:10* (C)+Num 24:17–19* (C) (the scepter against the nations) (* see Davidic covenant and Judah-king networks)

8:3–8[4–9]~Gen 1:16, 26, 28 (B) (What are mortals?)

15:1–5*~Deut 16:2, 6, 11, 15, 16 (C) (Who may sojourn in your tent?) (* see assembly network)

22:1[2]~Deut 31:6, 8 (C) (Why have you forsaken me?)

24:3–4*~Deut 16:2, 6, 11, 15, 16 (C) (Who may stand in his holy place?) (* see assembly network)

40:6[7]>/<Lev 1–6 (C) (sacrifice and offering you do not desire)

51:16–17[18–19]>/<Lev 5:1–6:7[5:1–26] (C); ~1:4 (B) (you do not delight in sacrifice)

60 superscription[60:2]~2 Sam 8:12b–13+1 Kgs 11:15–16 (B) (striking down an enemy in the Valley of Salt)

72:8~Zech 9:10 (B) (rule to ends of the earth)

72:9>/<Isa 49:23; Mic 7:17 (lick the dust)

72:10–11*~1 Kgs 4:21*[5:1] (B)+Gen 10:4, 7 (C) (all kings bring tribute and serve) (* see Abrahamic and Davidic covenant networks)

72:17*~Gen 12:3*; 18:18*; 22:18* (B) (nations bless him) (* see Abrahamic covenant network)

78~narrative compilation (B, C) (downfall of Ephraim and election of Judah)

81:9–10[10–11]~Deut 32:12, 16+5:6, 7, 9 (B) (no other gods)

81:16[17]~Deut 32:13, 14 (B) (provisions in the wilderness)

82:1–6~Exod 22:8, 9[7, 8] (C)+23:6; Lev 19:15 (C) (confronting bad judges)

86:15–17*~Exod 34:6* (C) (covenant fidelity and grace) (* see attribute formula network)

89:3–4, 19–37*[4–5, 20–38]~2 Sam 7:11–16* (B) (Davidic covenant) (* see Davidic covenant and place networks)

91:11~Exod 23:20* (B) (guarding messengers) (* see new exodus network)

95:8–11~Exod 17:7 (B)+Deut 2:14–15 (C)+12:9 (B) (rebellion at Meribah and Massah)

96:7–8, 10//29:1–2 (new version of the old call to worship)

103:7–8, 14*~Exod 33:13 (B)+34:6* (A)+Gen 2:7 (B) (attribute formula) (* see attribute formula network)

---

1. For explanation of symbols, see Symbols and Abbreviations and Introduction. For other help, see Glossary.
2. See Bibliographic Note on Lists of Potential Parallels.

104~Gen 1 (B) (hymn of creation)

105*~Torah compilation (B) (remember the beginnings of the chosen people) (* see Abrahamic covenant network)

106*~Torah, narrative, and prophets compilation (B) (confession of ancestral sin) (* see collective confession network)

109:9–15~Exod 20:5*//Deut 5:9* (C) (request for transgenerational judgment) (* see attribute formula network)

110:1*~1 Kgs 5:3, 5[17, 19]* (C) (enemies under feet of Davidic son) (* see Davidic covenant network)

110:4*~Gen 14:18–20 (B) (priest in the order of Melchizedek) (* see Davidic covenant network)

114:3, 5, 8~Ps 77:16, 19–20[17, 20–21] (B)+Josh 4:23 (C)+Deut 8:15 (B) (sea/river crossing remix)

118:19–20~24:3–4 (C) (gates of the righteous)

118:22~Isa 28:16+Zech 4:7 (C) (the rejected cornerstone)

132:6–7~1 Sam 6:1–2 (C) (his footstool in the fields of Jaar)

132:8*~Num 10:35–36 (B)+Deut 12:9* (C) (ark to the resting place) (* see place network)

132:11–12*~2 Sam 7:12–15* (B)+7:28 (C) (oath to David) (* see Davidic covenant and place networks)

132:13~Ps 78:68–69 (C)+Deut 12:9 (C) (choosing Zion)

135:5–12~Scripture compilation (B) (retrospective of Yahweh's gracious works)

136~Torah compilation (B) (covenantal loyalty retrospective)

OLD TESTAMENT USE OF PSALMS (SEE RESPECTIVE NOTES)

8:4[5]; 144:3~Job 7:17 (B) (What are humans?)

18:32–33[33–34]~Hab 3:19 (B) (treading upon the heights)

51:11[13]~1 Sam 16:14 (C) (spirit departs from Saul)

79:6–7//Jer 10:25 (calling for wrath on oppressive nations)

96:1b–10b,* 11–13b//1 Chr 16:7–36* (psalm of worship) (* see place network)

105:1–15*//1 Chr 16:7–36 (psalm of worship) (* see Abrahamic covenant network)

106:1, 47–48//1 Chr 16:7–36 (psalm of worship)

107:40//Job 12:21, 24 (pouring contempt on nobles)

119:50~Job 6:10 (B) (parody of consolation)

132:8–10*//2 Chr 6:1–42* (dedication of temple) (* see place network)

NEW TESTAMENT USE OF PSALMS

2:1–2 LXX//Acts 4:25–26 (Why do nations rage?)

2:7//Acts 13:33; Heb 1:5; 5:5 (you are my son)

2:9~Rev 2:27; cf. 12:5; 19:15 (scepter smashes)

4:4[5] LXX~Eph 4:26 (in anger do not sin)

5:9[10]//Rom 3:13 (throats open graves)

8:2[3] LXX//Matt 21:16 (from lips of children)

8:4–6[5–7] LXX//Heb 2:6–8 (What are humans?)

8:6[7]//1 Cor 15:27 (everything under feet)

10:7 LXX//Rom 3:14 (full of cursing)

14:1–3//Rom 3:10–12 (none righteous)

16:8–11//Acts 2:25–28 (not abandoned to grave)

16:10 LXX//Acts 2:31; 13:35 (holy one not decay)

18:49[50]//Rom 15:9 (praise among gentiles)

19:4[5]//Rom 10:18 (voice has gone out)

22:1[2]//Matt 27:46; Mark 15:34 (Why have you forsaken me?)

22:18[19]//Matt 27:35; John 19:24; cf. Mark 15:24 (cast lots for clothes)

22:22[23]//Heb 2:12 (I will declare your name)

24:1//1 Cor 10:26 (earth is the Lord's)

31:5[6]//Luke 23:46 (into your hands)

32:1, 2//Rom 4:7–8 (blessed are the forgiven)

34:8[9]//1 Pet 2:3 (the Lord is good)

34:12–16[13–17]//1 Pet 3:10–12 (eyes of Lord on righteous)

34:20[21]//John 19:36 (no bones broken)

35:19//John 15:25 (hated without reason)

36:1[2]//Rom 3:18 (no fear of God)

40:6–8[7–9] LXX//Heb 10:5–7 (sacrifice you did not desire)

41:9[10]//John 13:18 (shared my bread)

44:22[23]//Rom 8:36 (for your sake)

45:6, 7[7, 8]//Heb 1:8, 9 (your throne O God)

51:4[6] LXX//Rom 3:4 (may be proved right)

53:1–3[2–4]//Rom 3:10–12 (none righteous)

62:12[13]~Rom 2:6; cf. Matt 16:27 (God will repay)

68:2[3]//Matt 13:35 (parables)
68:18[19]//Eph 4:8 (leading captives)
69:4[5]//John 15:25 (hated without reason)
69:9a[10a]//John 2:17 (zeal for your house)
69:9b[10b]//Rom 15:3 (insults fall on me)
69:22, 23[23, 24] LXX//Rom 11:9, 10 (table became a trap)
69:25[26]//Acts 1:20 (his place deserted)
78:2//Matt 13:35 (open mouth in parables)
78:24, 25~John 6:31 (bread of heaven)
82:6//John 10:34 (you are gods)
86:9~Rev 15:4 (nations will come)
89:20[21]~Acts 13:22 (I have found David)
91:11, 12//Matt 4:6; Luke 4:10–11 (guarding angels)
94:11//1 Cor 3:20 (thoughts of wise are futile)
95:7–11//Heb 3:7–11, 15; 4:3, 5, 7 (do not harden your hearts)
98:2~Rev 15:4 (righteousness revealed)
102:25–27 LXX//Heb 1:10–12 (they wear out like a garment)
104:4//Heb 1:7 (his messengers)
104:12~Matt 13:32; Mark 4:32; Luke 13:19 (birds among branches)
109:8//Acts 1:20 (another takes his place)
110:1//Matt 22:44; 26:64; Mark 12:36; 14:62; Luke 20:42–43; 22:69; Acts 2:34–35; Heb 1:13 (sit at right hand)
110:4//Heb 5:6; 7:17, 21 (priest forever)
111:2, 3~Rev 15:3, 4 (great are his deeds)
112:9//2 Cor 9:9 (scattered gifts freely)
116:10 LXX~2 Cor 4:13 (I believed)
117:1//Rom 15:11 (praise the Lord, gentiles)
118:6, 7//Heb 13:6 (What can mortals do?)
118:22, 23//Matt 21:42; Mark 12:10–11; Luke 20:17; Acts 4:11; 1 Pet 2:7 (rejected stone)
118:25, 26//Matt 21:9; 23:39; Mark 11:9, 10; Luke 13:35; 19:38; John 12:13 (blessed is he who comes)
132:11~Acts 2:30 (one of yours on your throne)
135:14~Heb 10:30 (judge his people)
140:3[4] LXX//Rom 3:13 (poison on lips)

HERMENEUTICAL PROFILE OF THE USE OF SCRIPTURE IN PSALMS

Exegetical Conventions in Psalms

The use of scriptural traditions in the Psalter differs from other scriptural venues. The differences that affect scriptural interpretation include the Psalter's transcendent qualities, concise expression, lyrical diffusion, and divine discourses within psalms.

The transcendent qualities of Hebrew poetry cause it to function at a different register than prose, which affects its scriptural exegesis. Biblical poetry comes in many forms. In the broadest sense, prophets offer a downward poetry "Thus says Yahweh" perspective, while wisdom poetry features horizonal outlooks. Within the variety of poems in the Psalter, many point upward. At other times the psalmist speaks of Yahweh in third person and calls upon the congregation to worship. All Hebrew poetry breaks free of many shackles common in other genres. The psalms enjoy special transcendence as songs and prayers spoken in direct discourse without a frame narrative.[3] All of this makes confident identification of scriptural allusion more challenging.

Concise expression in biblical Hebrew poetry means any words that can be left

3. Even the headings of individual psalms remain as external apparatus to the psalms themselves. The individual psalms retain their individual autonomy when considering the Psalter as a book. On headings and approaching the Psalter as a book as these relate to exegetical allusions, see Psalms Filters.

out are.[4] The poetic tendency for economic expression trims out some of the literary signals of allusion. The already difficult task of identifying scriptural allusion increases in the poetry of individual psalms. Likewise, poetic expression diminishes direct verbal correspondence in allusions. These are not bad things. They contribute to what makes Psalms extraordinary. The work of scriptural interpretation needs to be calibrated to more subtle signals of allusions as well as reduced expectations for many outcomes.

Lyrical diffusion refers to the broad dissemination of scriptural expressions. Once a scriptural expression gets used in a psalm, all other uses of that expression may come from lyrical diffusion rather than the original donor context. Yahweh as a compassionate and gracious God from the attribute formula can illustrate the point (see list with attribute formula network). How can an interpreter know if the use of "compassionate and gracious" in a psalm has become part of the culture of worship or if it is supposed to allude to the narrative of Yahweh's revelation in Exod 34? The situation requires patience and the necessary evidence.

Lyrical diffusion of common scriptural traditions takes place more rapidly in the psalms than other biblical poetic genres. The lyrical diffusion of prophetic traditions works similarly but within a narrower range than the Psalter (see Hermeneutical Profile of the Use of Scripture in Isaiah). The wide range of forms, genres, themes, and style vary from one psalm to the next. While the named prophets function as the organizing principle of their integrated prophetic collections, each psalm starts something new, irrespective of how the Psalter works as a "book."

Maybe everyone knows how easily songs, refrains, and poetic lines can attach themselves to new contexts.[5] The lyrics of a song can immediately transport listeners and readers to other places and times where these things have been heard, recited, or sung. To turn it around, lyrical discourse has a way of absorbing into itself new connotations during any performance. In this way lyrical diffusion of individual psalms may cross-pollinate scriptural allusions.

Several scholars have investigated divine discourses as prophetic elements within individual psalms. Though their approaches differ, they interact with many of the same psalms.[6] Gillingham's general, straightforward approach offers the most promise. She investigates the prophetic function of psalms by using "first-person divine speech as the

---

4. Hebrew poetry typically leaves out disambiguating literary signals like accusative markers and anything else that is not essential. On poetic "terseness," see Berlin, *Dynamics*, 5–7, 16.

5. See examples in Tanner, "Allusion or Illusion," 33. Also see Goldingay, *Psalms*, 2:619.

6. Gillingham regards divine speech in three functions: integrated liturgical (selected verses in 2; 50; 75; 81; 82; 95), citations of earlier oracles (2:6; 89:3–4, 19–37[4–5, 20–38]; 110:1, 4; 132:11–12, 14–18), and rhetorical device of the psalmist (12:5[6]; 91:14–16) ("New Wine," 380). Jacobson studies the functions of "God quotations" in the Psalms including a focus on the Davidic monarchy (selected verses in 2; 89; 110; 132), admonishment (50; 75; 81; 95), before petitions (60//108; 82), and assurance (12; 46; 91) (*"Many Are Saying"*, 82, n. 1; 98–122). Hilber compares the divine discourse in Psalms to Assyrian psalms and prophecies to try to legitimize royal power (2; 89; 110; 132), offer worship instruction (50; 68; 81; 95; 132), and respond to prayers and laments (12; 60; 75; 83; 91; 132) (*Cultic Prophecy*, 219–21).

sole criterion."[7] In several cases the embedded divine speech repackages divine revelation from elsewhere in Scripture. Several other aspects of voicing parts of psalms as embedded divine discourse relate to interpretation of Scripture, like divine confrontation of Israel's judges in Ps 82. Attending to divine discourse can help in evaluating interpretive interventions in the Psalter.

To summarize the points above, the rich, vibrant qualities of the psalms naturally create challenges in detecting scriptural allusions and evaluating possible exegetical interventions.

Implications of Scriptural Exegesis in Psalms

The nature of the Psalter as a collection of individual psalms make it desirable to offer some overall implications of scriptural exegesis in the Psalter by way of preview. This can help evaluation of individual psalms along the way.

The wide array of historical, social, and religious situations among the psalmists rules out the kind of specific inferences that can be made regarding the use of scriptural traditions in narrative or prophetic scrolls. As such, the observations here apply to many individual psalms collected together.

The psalmists make heavy use of scriptural traditions. Non-exegetical use of scriptural traditions, like broad allusions and drawing upon lyrical diffusion, comprise the vast majority of the psalmists' use of scriptural traditions. These remain extremely important even if they fall outside a study of exegetical use of scriptural traditions like this one. The manifold broad connections without interpretive intervention in the Psalter help account for strong continuity between Torah, prophets, narratives, and wisdom more generally. The psalms give voice to lyrical connections between many scriptural traditions. Additional thoughts on the importance of the Psalter's extensive non-exegetical use of scriptural traditions can be found in the Filters. The remainder of the discussion here focuses on implications stemming from exegetical interventions by the psalmists.

The Psalter suggests a few specific recurring areas of exegetical concern, even with psalms coming from many different times and situations. Before handling these, some things that do not require exegetical intervention in the Psalter should be noted. When psalmists engage wisdom, worship, and personal suffering, their use of scriptural traditions tends to be more at the level of shared genre traits. This amounts to broad allusions of scriptural traditions and use of stock phrases found in kindred scriptural traditions. There are too many variables to account for the lesser prominence of exegesis in these more lyrical genres. The contrast between the psalmists' lack of exegetical intervention when reusing wisdom, worship, and lament versus the psalmists' interpretive allusions with other scriptural traditions can be registered even without explaining it.

What problems motivate psalmists to the exegetical use of scriptural traditions? Most

7. See Gillingham, "New Wine," 380.

cases fit within one of five problems. First, the Davidic promises attract four psalms that feature scriptural exegesis. The exilic context of Ps 89 responds to the pressing need to interpret the covenantal promises. Exilic realities place the Davidic promises under pressure, requiring scriptural exegesis. Psalms 2, 110, and 132 engage less urgent problems—election and worship—but with equally compelling reasons to reinterpret the covenant.

The psalms that reinterpret the Davidic promise each use divine oracles to present scriptural interpretation. These four psalms make up a notable subset of the eleven cases of divine oracles embedded in the Psalter. Of the other seven cases of first-person divine discourse only three include scriptural exegesis (81:5c–17[6c–17]; 82:2–4, 6–7; 95:7c–11).[8] The psalmists' use of embedded divine discourse needs to be kept separate from New Testament occasions when selected psalms get revoiced as spoken by Messiah. New Testament writers may just as easily revoice psalms without embedded divine discourse (69:9 in Rom 15:3 versus Ps 2:7 in Heb 1:5).[9]

Psalm 72 presupposes the Davidic promise but neither directly engages it nor includes a first-person divine oracle. The psalm seems to make numerous allusions to Genesis, including an important exegetical advance by identifying the Abrahamic covenant with the ideal Davidic rule.

Second, interpretive allusions in the historical retrospective psalms attend to scriptural narrative traditions that the psalmists' congregations need to remember. The preamble to Ps 78 underscores the importance of retelling the downfall of Ephraim's ancestors. Not until the end does the psalm disclose its purpose to shed light on the election of Zion and the Davidic rule. Psalm 105 reaches back to the Hebrew ancestors to unify the postexilic congregation within the ancient covenant of Abraham. Psalm 106 puts together a confession of the sins of the ancestors for the exilic congregation to participate in a collective repentance, as called for in Lev 26, to reactivate Yahweh's covenantal memory. Psalms 135 and 136 lift up for worshipers the ancient works of Yahweh. In every one of these cases the psalmists interpret scriptural traditions to serve the worship needs of their congregations.

Besides the long retrospective psalms, other psalmists use more targeted interpretive allusions. Psalms 8 and 104 each probe ways that creation traditions can instruct congregants in worship that is infused with humility and joy. Psalms 81 and 95 demonstrate how the exodus and wilderness traditions can answer congregational needs to turn back to God and worship. These psalmists went beyond appropriating narrative traditions as lyrical ornamentation. The serious needs of their congregants prompted exegetical advances. New situations and their attendant problems call for continuity of identity according to Scripture.

---

8. The other four cases of divine oracles do not include scriptural exegetical allusions. Psalm 12:5[6] may echo Deut 15:9–11 (based on the common word pair "poor" and "needy," see Filters). Psalm 50:5–23 questions the function of sacrifice broadly (vv. 8–13), with 50:14 affirming the value of voluntary versus only obligatory sacrifice. Though this broadly leans toward Pss 40 and 51, the issue is not framed exegetically in Ps 50 (see notes on Pss 40:6[7]; 51:16–17[18–19]). Psalm 75:2–5, 10[3–6, 11] houses a divine word of warning to the arrogant. Psalm 91:14–16 ends with a divine word of assurance.

9. See Moyise, *Paul and Scripture*, 99–100; Bates, *Birth of the Trinity*, 65–69; Pate, "Who Is Speaking?" 731–45.

Third, as one might expect, many of the psalmists' interpretive allusions relate to matters of worship. Less expected are the sorts of worship issues the psalmists address and how they do so. Psalms 15 and 24 deal with the relationship of obedience to legal instruction and worship. Psalms 40 and 51 question the bases of sacrifice and worship. The psalmists do not ferret out finer points of legal standards for exegesis but focus on the meta-concepts of legal instruction and sacrifice. Although they use different kinds of exegetical strategies, these psalmists seem of one mind in emphasizing the underlying realities of obedience and devotion that stand as prerequisites of meaningful worship.

Psalms 96 and 118 turn to specific scriptural traditions to answer the challenges of particular moments. Since Ps 96 stands as something of a worship invitation to the other, the old-time call to worship of Ps 29 becomes its resource. Ps 96 includes bold interpretive adjustments in the light of the special syncretistic tendencies of the other. Psalm 118 features an interpretive parable of the rejected cornerstone that serves as something of a figural model for restoration of worship.

Fourth, extreme cases of injustice seem to be the prompts for the daring exegetical interventions housed in Pss 82 and 109. The difficult nature of both of these psalms requires caution. These psalms demonstrate the importance of turning to authoritative traditions to face crises of unrighteousness. As in the previous point, the interpretive allusions do not get at subtle details of scriptural legal instructions. These scriptural interpretations are born under the pressure of extreme injustice rather than calm dispassionate speculation.

Fifth, several different kinds of situations gave rise to the need to work out the scriptural testimonies to the good presence of God. Psalm 22 opens by poetically turning the assurance formula on its head. The promise never to leave or forsake invites the question that lingers from Ps 22 to Golgotha.

While many psalms use the attribute formula amid its common appearance in the lyrical diffusion, Ps 103 features more developed exegetical allusion to it. Psalm 91 presents a brief but important interpretive allusion to the ancient promise to send along a guarding messenger. Underneath these interpretive moves lives a conviction that the scriptural testimonies to the ancient redeeming work of Yahweh applies in analogous ways to the psalmists' congregation.

Before concluding this consideration of the use of scriptural traditions in Psalms, one outlier should be noted. The important exegetical allusions in Ps 1 stand apart from the need-based exegesis collected under the preceding five heads. The psalmist does not speak because of an emergency or a problem. The psalmist uses broad third-person stereotypes familiar in biblical wisdom, e.g., the wicked and the righteous. But Ps 1 offers a programmatic picture of the life of the blessed person seemingly based on exegesis of the great commandment.

In sum, while the psalmists engage scriptural traditions nearly constantly, certain kinds of situations prompted exegetical use of scriptural traditions. The incremental advancement of revelation embodied in the psalmists' interpretive scriptural allusions points to a significant dynamic. These advancements of revelation answer pressing needs, sometimes collective and sometimes personal. This applies even to the several cases of interpretive allusions within the psalmists' use of direct divine speech. The situational scriptural exegesis in many psalms tends toward helping the troubled congregation.

USE OF SCRIPTURE

1:1~Deut 6:7* (C) (walk, stand, sit) (* see concealing revelation network).
1:2–3~Josh 1:8 (B)+Jer 17:7–8 (B) (like a tree by water). Psalm 1 uses classic wisdom stereotypes to contrast "the wicked" against their counterparts. But instead of naming the counterpart immediately, the psalmist describes "the righteous." The "blessed" or "happy" (אַשְׁרֵי) person's actions are not like the wicked but akin to the one who meditates on Torah all the time.[10]

The Hebrew term for "impress" in Deut 6:7 seems to have the sense of "repeat" or "teach by repetition."[11] The parallel passage uses a common word for "teach" (Deut 11:19). The idea of teach by repeatedly "talking about them" draws a close connection to the sense of "meditate" by recitation or murmuring in Ps 1:2 (6:7; 11:19).[12] The correspondence between *sit, walk along the road, get up/stand* in Deut 6:7 and Ps 1:1 offers a significant verbal and thematic parallel. The classic Judaic scholar Ibn Ezra compares the two contexts this way:

> Now the text of the *Šĕma'* [Deut 6:4–9] refers to four physical states, namely, "when you sit" and its opposite "when you walk" (i.e. mobility as against immobility), and "when you lie down" and its opposite "when you rise up." Here in the Psalms passage [1:1] "sits" is equivalent to "when you sit," "walks" matches "when you walk" and "stands" also tallies with "rising." No mention is here made of "lying down" since man is generally asleep when in this position.[13]

Ibn Ezra connects the "all the time" sense of teaching the next generation to the mention of "day and night" in Ps 1:2.[14] Compare the Mosaic instruction and the opening of the Psalter (italics signify verbal parallels, and broken underlining signifies similarity):

---

10. The allusions in Ps 1:1 and 1:2–3 to Deut 6:7 and Josh 1:8 means that "Torah" in Ps 1:2 refers to the Mosaic Torah not the Psalter (see LeFebvre, "'On His Law,'" 440–44; Botha, "Intertextuality," 60–67; André, "'Walk,'" 327; contra Childs, *Introduction*, 513; Wilson, *Editing*, 206–7).

11. The term "impress" (שנן Piel) is only used in Deut 6:7 in Scripture. The root *sh-n-n* likely has the sense of "repeat" ("II שׁנן," *HALOT* 2:1606–7). A similar term is used in the Masada manuscript of Sir 42:15 in Hebrew, namely, "let me recall" or "teach by repetition" (אשננה) (for the Hebrew text of Sir 42:15 Mas1h, see Reymond, "New Readings," 341; for definition see Tigay, *Deuteronomy*, 358–59, n. 25). Reymond connects the term with Deut 6:7, making a cohortative possible in Sir 42:15 Mas1h, "let me teach" (Reymond, *Innovations*, 61, n. 107; also see Skelton, "Singers," 244, n. 9).

12. See Weinfeld, *Deuteronomy 1–11*, 333.

13. Quoted from Reif, "Ibn Ezra on Psalm I 1–2," 234 (all caps converted to words in quotation marks).

14. See ibid.

> Impress [שׁנן] them on your children. Talk about them when you *sit* at home and when you *walk along the road*, when you lie down and when you get up [קום]. (Deut 6:7)

> Teach [למד Piel] them to your children, talking about them when you *sit* at home and when you *walk along the road*, when you lie down and when you get up [קום]. (11:19)

> Blessed is the one who does not *walk along the road* with the wicked or stand [עמד] in the way that sinners take or *sit* in the company of mockers . . . but . . . who meditates on his torah day and night. (Ps 1:1, 2b†)

The psalmist does not initially describe the blessed person but the wicked counterpart. The polar opposite of one who talks of Torah all the time is one who walks, sits, and stands with the wicked, sinners, and mockers—a lifestyle contrary to the great commandment.

The psalmist goes on to allude to the call to meditate on Torah of Josh 1 as well as including a parallel to the one who trusts Yahweh of Jer 17 (cf. Ps 84:12[13]). Although the direction of relationship, whether direct or indirect, between Jer 17 and Ps 1 cannot be determined, the extended simile of the tree by water and other contextual similarities support a relationship.[15] Jeremiah contrasts two different stereotypical persons: those who trust in mortals and those who trust in Yahweh. One fares no better than a dying shrub in the desert; the other flourishes like a tree by waters. The psalmist uses this simile to embody the "prosperity" of torah study. Only Josh 1 and Ps 1 use "meditate" in reference to torah, making relationship likely. Other psalms speak of meditating on God and his works (Pss 63:6[7]; 77:12[13]). The psalmist's exegetical advances include "delighting" in Torah and spelling out a rich simile to define "prosperity" (1:2, 3). In this way the psalmist describes the "righteous" person but waits to use this term of the blessed person until the last verse (1:6) (emphases refer to verbal parallels).

> Keep this book of the **torah** always on your lips; **meditate** on it **day and night**, so that you may be careful to do everything written in it. Then you will be prosperous and successful. (Josh 1:8)

> But blessed [בָּרוּךְ] is the one who trusts in Yahweh, whose confidence is in him. *That person will be like a tree planted by the water* that sends out its roots by the stream. It does not fear when heat comes; *its leaves* are always green. It has no worries in a year of drought and never fails to bear *fruit*. (Jer 17:7–8†)

---

15. The shared literary markers of Ps 1:2–3 and Jer 17:7–8 suggest a relationship even with conventional contrasts between struggling and vibrant trees. Cf. the fourth chapter of the Instruction of Amen-em-Opet (*ANET*, 422).

> But whose delight is in the torah of Yahweh, and who **meditates** on his **torah day and night.** [3] *That person is like a tree planted by* streams of *water*, which yields its *fruit* in season and *its leaf* does not wither—whatever they do prospers . . . for Yahweh watches over the way of the righteous. (Ps 1:2–3, 6a†)

In sum, the psalmist defines the way of the life of the righteous in contrast to the wicked based on a blend of scriptural allusions. The righteous are blessed because they devote all of their time to God's will revealed in Torah.

2:6–7*~2 Sam 7:14–15* (B) (divine begetting of the king) (* see Davidic covenant and place networks).

2:8–9*~Gen 49:10* (C)+Num 24:17–19* (C) (the scepter against the nations) (* see Davidic covenant and Judah-king networks). The psalmist brilliantly revoices the Davidic covenant as direct discourse between Yahweh and his son at his coronation (Ps 2:7). The term "begotten" does not work literally since the newly adopted son hears and repeats the divine declaration.[16] A counterpart appears elsewhere: "He [the Davidic king] will call out to me [Yahweh], 'You are my father' . . . and I will appoint him my firstborn" (Ps 89:26–27[27–28]).[17]

The dynamic enactment of the Davidic covenant at the king's coronation reverts the use of "rod" of punishment back to "scepter" of rule (see note on 2 Sam 7:14–15; cf. Gen 49:10). The psalmist splices the coronation into possible loose allusions to the blessing of Judah and the fourth oracle of Balaam whereby he symbolizes fear-inspiring rule (Ps 2:8–10; Gen 49:10; Num 24:17–19).[18] The possible use of the ancient expectations for a ruler of Judah/from Jacob establishes the Davidic ruler as the one who enforces Yahweh's rule upon the nations (Ps 2:11–12). The fulfillment of these ancient expectations turns the tables upon the raging nations who gather against Yahweh's messiah (2:1–2). Notice how the ancient expectations recover another symbolic function for the scepter compared to Nathan's version of the Davidic covenant (bold signifies verbal parallels, and italics and broken underlining signify similarities):

> **The scepter** [שֵׁבֶט] shall not turn aside from Judah, nor the ruler's staff from between his feet, until that which belongs to him comes, and the obedience of the peoples is his. (Gen 49:10 lit.)

> I see him but not now, I behold him but not near, a star come out of Jacob, and **a scepter** [שֵׁבֶט] rises from Israel and smashes the borders/foreheads of Moab, the territory/skulls

16. See Goldingay, *Psalms*, 1:100. Also see Tigay, "Adoption," 2:298–301; Knobloch, "Adoption," *ABD* 1:76–79.

17. See Goldingay, *Psalms*, 1:100–1.

18. The oracles of Balaam are linked to the blessing of Judah by quotation (Gen 49:9//Num 24:9; cf. note on Num 24:9).

of the people of Sheth. Edom becomes a possession, even Seir a possession of its enemies, and Israel acts powerfully. Then a ruler comes from Jacob and **causes to perish** the survivors of the city. (Num 24:17–19 lit.)

[Yahweh says] When your days are fulfilled and you lie down with your ancestors I will raise up your seed after you who will come from your body, and I will establish his kingdom.... *I will be a father to him, and he will be* ***a son*** *to me,* when he does wrong I will punish him with **the rod** [שֵׁבֶט] of mortals and with wounds inflicted by humans. (2 Sam 7:12, 14 lit.)

[The Lord of heaven says] "I have installed my king on Zion, my holy mountain." [The new king says] I shall recount the decree of Yahweh: *He said to me "You are my* ***son.*** *Today I have begotten you.* Ask me, and I will give the nations as your inheritance, and the ends of the earth as your possession. You shall break them with **a scepter** [שֵׁבֶט] of iron, you shall shatter them like a potter's vessel." Now, kings be wise! be warned rulers of the earth! Serve Yahweh with fear, and rejoice with trembling. Kiss (the feet) of **the son** or he shall become angry and you **will perish** in the way, for his wrath is quickly kindled. Graced are all who seek refuge in him (Ps 2:6–12 lit.).[19]

In sum, limited verbal correspondence, while typical of lyrical recasting, eliminates high confidence in direct intentional dependence upon the blessing of Judah and Balaam's oracle. The psalmist uses exegetical allusion of the Davidic promise to contextualize the Davidic king within royal Torah-like expectations.

8:3–8[4–9]~Gen 1:16, 26, 28 (B) (What are mortals?). The first six creation days of Gen 1 build to a climax—the creation of humans. The vast celestial lights get relativized to their purpose for earth dwellers: "Let there be lights in the vault of the sky *to separate the day from the night,* and let them serve as signs *to mark sacred times, and days and years*" (Gen 1:14, emphasis mine). The psalmist gazes at the nighttime heavens and inverts the function of creation. He wonders about the insignificance of the human race in the light of the enormity of the celestial expanse. The psalmist frames the need for humility with a profound question, "What are mortals?" (Ps 8:4, lit.).[20] The question seems rhetorical. Rhetorical questions are not real questions—they make a point. In spite of the rhetorical sense of the two-part question, the psalmist goes on to answer it by affirming the role of humans within the creational order by allusion to the sixth creation day (bold and italics signify verbal parallels, underlining signifies similarities, and broken underlining signifies interpretation):

19. For the suggestion that "kiss the feet" is based on an Akkadian cognate, see "I נשׁק," Piel *HALOT* 1:731.

20. For other uses of this question see Ps 144:3 in Filters and note on Job 7:17–18.

> Then **God** said, "Let us make mankind in our image, in our likeness, so that they may rule over the *fish in the sea* and the birds *in the sky*, over the livestock and all the wild *animals*, and over all the creatures that move along the ground." (Gen 1:26)

> When I consider your heavens, the work of your fingers, the moon and the stars, which you have set in place, [4] what is mankind that you are mindful of them, human beings that you care for them? [5] You have made them a little lower than **God** and crowned them with glory and honor. [6] You made them rulers over the works of your hands; you put everything under their feet: [7] all flocks and herds, and the *animals* of the wild, [8] the birds *in the sky*, and *the fish in the sea*, all that swim the paths of the seas. (Ps 8:3–8[4–9], v. 5[6] lit.)

Although the verbal parallels are somewhat limited, similar contextual details suggest relationship. The specifics, such as naming the moon in Ps 8:3[4] when it goes unnamed in Gen 1 and the psalmist's use of a rhetorical question, presume allusion to something known. These details suggest Gen 1 as donor context and Ps 8 as receptor.

Before getting to the interpretation, the term the psalmist uses in Ps 8:5[6] requires attention. The psalmist speaks of being created in God's own image as "a little lower than God" (Gen 1:26; Ps 8:5[6] lit.). The Septuagint euphemistically glosses the term for "God" (*elohim* אֱלֹהִים) as "celestial delegates" (*angelous* ἀγγέλους).[21] The Scriptures include the deity using first-person plural pronouns four times. In each case celestial delegates are present (Gen 1:26 with Job 38:7; Gen 3:22, 24; 11:7 with Deut 32:8 4QDeut^{j}/4Q37/LXX [see note ad loc.]; and Isa 6:2, 8). In that sense it is entirely reasonable that the deity addresses the celestial court and says, "Let us make mankind in our image" (Gen 1:26). This fits the dramatic shift from the tenfold repetition of all lower creatures and plant life reproducing "after their kind" (לְ + מִין + וֹ/הוּ/הֶם/ ָה) in third person (1:11, 12[2x], 21[2x], 24[2x], 25[3x]).[22] Then he makes humans according to the image of God in first person (1:26). Humans in turn reproduce after his image (see note on Gen 5:1–3). If the deity addresses the celestial court concerning his intentions, he creates the humans himself, third-person masculine singular—"God created [ms] the human in his [ms] image, in the image of God he created [ms] him, male and female he created [ms] them" (1:27 lit.).[23] Genesis 1:27 uses the special term "create" three times in the singular and uses the third-person singular pronominal suffix "in *his* image." Since the Septuagintal translators show a tendency toward euphemistic glosses, it seems better to regard their use of "celestial delegates" for "God" in Ps 8:5[6] as a euphemism. The advance of revelation comes when the author to the Hebrews, who seems to use the Septuagint exclusively, strings

21. For a different view, namely that the psalmist addresses Yahweh as "you" through the psalm, so his use of *elohim* must be celestial delegates as the LXX takes it, see Sarna, *Psalms*, 63. In spite of the merits of Sarna's point, it does not work. The psalmist addresses the deity in the third person "Yahweh our Lord" twice in the context of the second-person address (Ps 8:1, 9[2, 10]).

22. On this shift see van Wolde, "Text as Eloquent Guide," 149.

23. Also observed by Levine and Brettler, *Bible With and Without Jesus*, 91.

Septuagintal Ps 8:5 together with a constellation of other contexts, affirming Messiah's place "above" the celestial delegates except "for a little while" when he condescends to go below them (Heb 2:7, 9).[24] In sum of this point, the evidence suggests: the psalmist uses *elohim* from Gen 1 in its sense as "God"; the Septuagintal translators use "celestial delegates" as a euphemism; and the author to the Hebrews takes advantage of the Septuagint's translation to advance revelation concerning Messiah.

The psalmist's exegesis pivots on how he both flips over the creational order to affirm human frailty (Ps 8:5[6]) and simultaneously affirms the place of humans according to the same account of the creation days; that is, below God and above the lesser creatures. The creation days of Genesis famously begin by repeating God as the subject four times with four verbs on day one: "God said . . . God saw . . . God separated . . . God called" (Gen 1:3–5 lit.). The creation days go on to feature God explicitly spelled out as the subject of thirty active verbs across six days: (day 1) God said, saw, separated, called (1:3–5); (2) God said, made, called (1:6–8); (3) God said, called, saw, said, saw (1:9–13); (4) God said, made, set, saw (1:14–19); (5) God said, created, saw, blessed (1:20–23); (6) God said, made, saw (1:24–25), God said on high (1:26), God created, created, created, blessed, said, saw (1:27–31). The psalmist does not only speak about Yahweh but also to him. The psalmist uses four verbs in the second person to emphasize what Yahweh did: "You made lower . . . you crowned . . . you made them rulers . . . you put" (Ps 8:5–6[6–7]). By using a rhythm similar to that found in Gen 1, the psalmist accomplishes several things. He underlines the humility that comes by looking at the nighttime celestial lights and recognizes the incongruity of humans as the lords of creation. He also demonstrates that the very unlikelihood of human lordship over creation glorifies the name of Yahweh by the threefold repetition of "what?"/"how"! (מָה) for four exclamations/rhetorical questions at the beginning, middle, and end of the psalm.[25] "*How* [מָה] majestic is your name in all the earth! . . . *What* [מָה] are mortals that you remember them? [*What*] is the human race that you attend to it? . . . *How* [מָה] majestic is your name in all the earth! (8:1, 4, 9 lit.[2, 5, 10], emphasis mine).[26] The psalmist answers all four rhetorical questions/exclamations with a single string of affirmations: "You made lower . . . you crowned . . . you made them rulers . . . you put" (8:5–6[6–7]).

15:1–5*~Deut 16:2, 6, 11, 15, 16 (C) (Who may sojourn in your tent?) (* see assembly network). See note on Ps 24:3–4.

22:1[2]~Deut 31:6, 8 (C) (Why have you forsaken me?). The use of a single common term like "forsake" may indicate allusion to the prominent divine promise to "never leave you and never forsake you" that Moses delivered to Joshua (Deut 31:6, 8; Ps 22:1[2]).

---

24. See Ps 2:7; 2 Sam 7:14; Deut 32:43; Pss 104:4; 45:6, 7; 102:25–28[26–28]; 110:1; and 8:4–6[5–7] in Heb 1:5–13; 2:5–8.

25. See Tigay, "What Is Man?" 171, n. 26. On the close relation between *mah* (מָה) as question and exclamation, see GKC §148a–c.

26. The ellipsis ("gapping") of the interrogative particle "what?" (מָה) in the B line of Ps 8:4[5] meets all four poetic requirements: coordinate lines; syntactic correspondence and same order of A and B lines; the gapped element must be identical; and the ellipsis occurs in B line (see Miller, "Ellipsis," 42–43).

Elsewhere the combination of terms "never leave and never forsake" with a divine subject appears twice and in both cases almost certainly alludes to the promise in Deut 31 (Josh 1:5; 1 Chr 28:20). This evidence, along with headlining Ps 22 with a reversal of the promise, makes allusion possible.

In Exod 23 Yahweh promises to send his delegate ahead of the people (Exod 23:20, 23, 27, 28). After the rebellion with the calf he threatens to only send the delegate but not go with the people himself (33:2–3). Moses pleads with Yahweh and he commits himself to going with his people (33:14). The declaration of the divine presence with Joshua in Deut 31 alludes to these events within the context of Torah. The promise to be with Joshua does not get treated like a personal time-bound commitment but winds up representing a general promise to his people. "Yahweh will not reject his people; *he will never forsake* his inheritance" (Ps 94:14, emphasis mine). Variations on the promise to "not forsake" appear in many scriptural contexts—a reason that allusion can only be a possibility here.[27]

Scriptural statements to the effect that Yahweh has abandoned his people appear rarely in Scripture and usually with an immediate turnaround. "But Zion said, '*Yahweh has forsaken me*, the Lord has forgotten me.' Can a mother forget the baby at her breast and have no compassion on the child she has borne? Though she may forget, *I will not forget you!*" (Isa 49:14–15, emphasis mine; cf. 54:7; 62:4, 12). In another case the psalmist puts words in his enemies' mouths in hopes that God will deliver the psalmist: "They say, 'God has forsaken him'" (Ps 71:11).

Scriptural testimony of divine faithfulness to be with his people make the fronting of a contrary interrogation in Ps 22 effective. Part of the background in Exodus can be compared (italics signify verbal agreement, and bold signifies verbal contrast):

> Yahweh replied, "My Presence *will go with you*, and I will give you rest." (Exod 33:14)

> Be strong and courageous. Do not be afraid or terrified because of them, for Yahweh your God *goes with you*; he will never leave you **nor forsake you**. . . . Yahweh himself *goes* before you and will be with you; he will never leave you **nor forsake you**. Do not be afraid; do not be discouraged. (Deut 31:6, 8)

> My God, my God, why **have you forsaken me?** Why are you so far from saving me, so far from my cries of anguish? (Ps 22:1[2])[28]

The psalmist's question could be rhetorical and accusatory.[29] Taken on its own in a straightforward sense it sounds like bad theology or lack of faith. Perhaps the sentiment

27. See Gen 28:15; Josh 1:5; 1 Kgs 8:57; Pss 16:10; 27:9–10; 37:33; 38:21[22]; 71:9, 18; 119:8; Isa 41:17; 42:16.

28. For a discussion of the parallel language in Ps 22:1b[2b]; 38:8[9]; Job 3:24 (literally, "my roaring"), see Tanner, "Allusion or Illusion," 27–28.

29. Goldingay says the "rhetorical question" implies "You should not have abandoned me" (*Psalms*, 1:325).

could be based on the idea that "Yahweh . . . will not forsake *his faithful ones*" (37:28, emphasis mine). The psalmist could be confident in his fidelity to Yahweh and express shock that he has been abandoned when he needs God most. The psalmists of Ps 44 accuse God of rejecting them to exile in spite of the fact that they had remained faithful to the covenant (44:17–19[18–20]). The psalmists go so far as to claim that their faithfulness includes both their actions and the intents of their hearts, and that God knows it (44:21[22]). In that case the psalmists do not know what is going on other than to say "because of you" (44:22[23]). The sense of anguished bewilderment seems to fit with the line of complaint in Ps 22. "My God, I cry out by day, *but you do not answer*, by night, but I find no rest" (22:2[3], emphasis mine).

The psalmist's stunning reversal of the great and enduring promise that Yahweh will never forsake puts to words the suffering of the Lord as he dies (Mark 15:34//Ps 22:1[2]). The reuse of the prayerful question at Golgotha stands as a centerpiece in the evangelist's account, built around allusions to other parts of Ps 22 and other Scriptures (Mark 15:24, 29//Ps 22:18, 7[19, 8]).

24:3–4*~Deut 16:2, 6, 11, 15, 16 (C) (Who may stand in his holy place?) (* see assembly network). The so-called entrance liturgies of Pss 15:1–5 and 24:3–6 suggest a real or poetic function in relation to the pilgrimage festivals when Israel came to worship "at the place" Yahweh will choose for Passover, Weeks, and Tabernacles (Deut 16:1–17; cf. Exod 34:22–24).[30] The first question of Ps 15 connotes the sense of pilgrimage: "Who *may sojourn* in your tent?" (Ps 15:1, emphasis mine). Deuteronomy 16 spells out when and where but casts a wide net around all of Israel's adult males. The psalmist's exegetical advance targets something else that needs to be acknowledged about who may worship. The concrete verbal connection with Deut 16 amounts to a single common term, "place" (מָקוֹם), making the potential allusion much more thematic (24:3). The key aspect of the potential allusion comes in the question and the interpretive intervention in the answer (italics signify verbal parallel, and broken underlining signifies potential interpretive intervention):

> Three times a year all your men must appear before Yahweh your God at the *place* [מָקוֹם] he will choose: at the Festival of Unleavened Bread, the Festival of Weeks and the Festival of Tabernacles. No one should appear before Yahweh empty-handed. (Deut 16:16)[31]

> Yahweh, who may sojourn in your sacred tent? Who may dwell on your holy mountain? (Ps 15:1 lit.)

30. See Sarna, *Psalms*, 103.

31. The phrase "at the place Yahweh will choose" appears repeatedly in the instructions for the pilgrimage festivals (Deut 16:2, 6, 7, 11, 15, 16) and a few related contexts (12:14, 18; 14:23; 15:20; 31:11). See note on 1 Kgs 8:15–21.

> Who may ascend the mountain of Yahweh? Who may stand in his holy *place* [מָקוֹם]? The one who has clean hands and a pure heart, who does not trust in an idol or swear by a false god. (24:3–4)[32]

For a moment attention will be given to the specific question in Ps 24:3b, "Who may stand in his *holy* place?" (emphasis mine). Holiness versus commonness differs from ritual purity versus impurity and righteousness versus sin. A right standing and ritual purity are prerequisites of relative holiness. Categorical holiness—set apart as Israel, Levite, or priest—remains even when relative holiness has been damaged by ritual impurity or sin, requiring a purification or reparation offering.[33] The answer to the question in Ps 24:4 gets at morality and fidelity to Yahweh. The question-and-answer format suggests the person in moral rebellion or unfaithfulness to God may not stand in God's holy place (24:3, 4). The emphasis in this case falls on the prerequisite of righteousness, broadly speaking.[34]

Psalm 118 includes lines that embody the sense of the moment the sojourning worshiper gains access to the courts of Yahweh.

> Open for me *the gates of the righteous*; I will enter and give thanks to Yahweh. This is *the gate of Yahweh through which the righteous may enter.* (118:19–20, emphasis mine)

In sum, the psalmist's exegetical advance comes in the form of a question-and-answer format. A central prerequisite for temple worship attaches closely to the righteous character of the worshiper. The psalm confronts the worshiper with the real issue for coming before Yahweh by means of a question: Who may stand in his holy place?

40:6[7]>/<Lev 1–6 (C) (sacrifice and offering you do not desire). The psalmist makes the bold claim that Yahweh does not want sacrifices and offerings. This sweeping interpretive statement on its surface refers to both the voluntary and required offering that open Leviticus. Leviticus repeatedly says the sacrifices make a "pleasing [נִיחֹחַ] aroma" before Yahweh (Lev 1:9, 13, 17; 2:2, 9, 12; 3:5, 16; 4:31; 6:15[8], etc.). The psalmist's different key expression "do not delight/desire" (חפץ) aligns him with the prophets who argue down the same line (1 Sam 15:22; Isa 1:11; Hos 6:6; also see Table A3 in Amos Filters; note on Ps 51:16–17[18–19]).[35] Like the prophets, the psalmist seems to speak in hyperbole.[36] Offerings were never intended to replace but to signify humble devotion to God. Sacrifices are not of value in themselves but symbolize the worshiper's devotion and repentance, depending on the kind of offering. The psalmist builds on this general

32. The expression "clean hands" (נְקִי כַפַּיִם) uses different language but a similar idea with "cleanness of my hands" (כְּבֹר יָדַי) in Ps 18:20[21]//2 Sam 22:21; Ps 18:24[25].

33. See Schnittjer, *Torah Story*, 329–30.

34. Psalm 15 goes in a similar direction by listing ten characteristics of who may sojourn in the tent (Ps 15:2–5).

35. See Kirkpatrick, *Psalms Book I*, 211.

36. See Goldingay, *Psalms*, 1:573; Longman, *Psalms*, 188.

point by affirming an internalization of torah, which, of course, includes offerings and worship. Compare a representative offering instruction (bold signifies verbal parallel, italics signify a wide range of voluntary and required offerings, and broken underlining signifies different terms for approval).

> If the offering is a **burnt offering** from the herd, you are to offer a male without defect. . . . It is a **burnt offering**, a food offering, an aroma pleasing [נִיחֹחַ] to Yahweh. (Lev 1:3a, 9b)

> *Sacrifice and offering* you did not desire [חפץ]—but my ears you have opened—***burnt offerings** and sin offerings* you did not require. Then I said, "Here I am, I have come . . . "I desire [חפץ] to do your will, my God; your law is within my heart." (Ps 40:6–7a, 8[7–8a, 9])

The psalmist's connection between obeying God's torah in his "innermost parts" (lit.) rather than sacrifice may have suggested the connection between this context and the new covenant—"I will put my torah in their minds and write it on their hearts" (Jer 31:33)—in Heb 10 (Ps 40:6–8[7–9] and Jer 31:33 in Heb 10:5–7, 16).

51:16–17[18–19]>/<Lev 5:1–6:7[5:1–26]) (C); ~1:4 (B) (you do not delight in sacrifice). In the spirit of the prophets, the psalmist claims God does not "desire" (חפץ) sacrifice or burnt offerings (51:16; 1 Sam 15:22; Isa 1:11; Hos 6:6; cf. Ps 69:30–31[31–32]; also see Table A3 in Amos Filters; note on Ps 40:6[7]). This blanket statement in one sense speaks in general to the sacrificial system (cf. 51:19[21]; Lev 1–7); but since the psalmist has been confessing sin, he would most naturally be referring to the reparation offering (Lev 5:14–6:7[5:14–26]). The superscription of Ps 51 invites association with David's pair of capital offenses subject to the death penalty not remediated by sacrifice (Exod 21:12; Lev 20:10). In spite of these tensions, the focus on cleansing from sin against God overlaps most fully with the reparation offering.

The psalmist's advancement comes by redefining sacrifice in terms of "a broken spirit and contrite heart" (Ps 51:17[19]; cf. 34:18[19]; Isa 57:15; 66:2).[37] Sacrifice was never effectual of itself but, in the case of the reparation offering, serves as a physical symbol of repentance and confession. The reparation offering signifies remorse and repentance when a person "realizes guilt" and "confesses" sin (Lev 5:5; 6:4[5:5, 23]; Num 5:7).[38] The psalmist succinctly cuts through the symbol to the humble and repentant human will itself. The psalmist uses specific language of the burnt offering (Lev 1:4) to deny that God takes pleasure in it (Ps 51:16[18]). Numbers 5:6–7a here serves as representative of the

---

37. Contra van Wolde who sees the sin itself as crushing the "spirit" and "heart" and does not acknowledge the place of confession in expressing self-humbling ("Prayer," 358).

38. The Hith of "confess" appears almost exclusively of personal or collective confession of guilt (Lev 5:5; 16:21; 26:40; Num 5:7; Dan 9:4, 20; Ezra 10:1; Neh 1:6; 9:2, 3; with one exception, 2 Chr 30:22, but see vv. 19–20); see "II ידה," *HALOT* 1:389. On "realize guilt" (אָשָׁם), see Milgrom, "Sacrifices and Offerings," *IDBSup*, 768–69; idem, *Cult and Conscience*, 119–21.

principle of the instructions repeated numerous times, as listed in the previous footnote (bold signifies verbal parallels, italics signify interpretive advance):

> You are to lay your hand on the head of **the burnt offering**, and it **will be accepted** [רצה Nif] on your behalf to make atonement for you. (Lev 1:4)

> Say to the Israelites: "Any man or woman who wrongs another in any way and so is unfaithful to Yahweh *is guilty* and *must confess* the sin they have committed." (Num 5:6–7a)

> You do not delight [חפץ] in sacrifice, or I would bring it; you do not **take pleasure** [רצה Q] in **burnt offerings.** My sacrifice, O God, is *a broken spirit; a broken and contrite heart you*, God, will not despise. (Ps 51:16–17[18–19])

Sacrifice without a contrite heart is worthless. But the psalm continues to demonstrate that the sacrificial symbols have not been abolished. The psalmist says, "*Then you will delight* [חפץ] *in the sacrifices* of the righteous, in burnt offerings offered whole; then bulls will be offered on your altar" (Ps 51:19[21], emphasis mine).

In sum, the psalmist looks past the expiatory sacrifice as symbol and foregrounds the repentant heart itself. Yet the psalmist does not thereby do away with sacrifices but "advances toward a 'new' theology of sacrifice."[39] The emphatic stress on the sacrifice as a function of true humility makes an incremental advance of revelation by means of a psalm to God. The psalmist does not work from new cloth, but his exegesis makes a step from Torah instruction toward when symbols give way to the realities themselves in Messiah's teaching (John 4:24).

60 superscription[60:2]~2 Sam 8:12b–13+1 Kgs 11:15–16 (B) (striking down an enemy in the Valley of Salt).[40] The historical superscription of Ps 60 shares details with the summaries of David's conquests in Samuel and Kings (2 Sam 8:12b–13; 1 Kgs 11:15–16; cf. 1 Chr 18:12). While all three contexts speak of striking down an enemy in the Valley of Salt, two say they were Edomites (Ps 60 superscription; 1 Kgs 11:15–16; cf. 1 Chr 18:12) and the other Aram (2 Sam 8:13).[41] These contexts focus on different subjects of the striking down: David (8:13) and Joab (1 Kgs 11:15–16; Ps 60 superscription), as well as Abishai (1 Chr 18:12).

Psalm 60 itself creates an interesting dialogue with 2 Sam 8, which speaks only of victory. Psalm 60:1–3, 9–11[3–5, 11–13] calls upon God from a context of defeat which

39. Hossfeld and Zenger, *Psalms 2*, 22.

40. Note the doublet, Pss 60:5–12[7–14]//108:6–13[7–14].

41. Second Samuel 8:13 MT says "Aram" but NIV, NRSV, JPSB, etc., follow LXX, Syriac, and a few masoretic MSS and read "Edom" (see *BHS* apparatus). Although this emendation harmonizes the problem, the more difficult MT reading is more likely original.

the psalmist turns toward hope in the psalm's closing lines (60:12[14]; cf. v. 4[6]).[42] The reference to defeating Moab, Edom, and Philistia in Ps 60:8[10] looks ahead to their defeat based upon God's word beforehand, when "God has spoken in his sanctuary" (60:6[8]).

The derogatory reference to Moab as "washbasin" in Ps 60:8[10] has sometimes been taken in a more derogatory sense. The term may connote "Moab being used as God's urinal" or as a place "to wash God's filthy feet after battle."[43] This strong, insulting way of referring to Moab accords with the slaughter of two-thirds of the Moabites who surrender (2 Sam 8:2).

In sum, the brief summaries of David's victories in 2 Sam 8 and the notices in 1 Kgs 11:15–16 and 1 Chr 18:12 point to selective details of a more extensive campaign. The superscription of Ps 60 helps bring some of the challenges into line with the psalmist's faith.

72:8~Zech 9:10 (B) (rule to ends of the earth).

72:9>/<Isa 49:23; Mic 7:17 (lick the dust).

72:10–11*~1 Kgs 4:21*[5:1] (B)+Gen 10:4, 7 (C) (all kings bring tribute and serve) (* see Abrahamic and Davidic covenant networks).

72:17*~Gen 12:3*; 18:18*; 22:18* (B) (nations bless him) (* see Abrahamic covenant network). The first psalm of Solomon everywhere presupposes the Davidic covenant without citing it. The psalm also seems to be dominated by echoes of Genesis, though most of these have been mediated by alluding to other scriptural contexts that allude to Genesis more or less directly (see Table P1).

TABLE P1: PSALM 72 AND SECONDARY ECHOES IN GENESIS‡

Psalm 72	Allusions	Secondary Echoes of Genesis
v. 8, rule ends of earth	Zech 9:10 (cf. 9:9, king coming on a donkey)	15:18, land to the Euphrates River (cf. 49:11, ruler riding on a donkey)
v. 9, lick the dust	Isa 49:23; Mic 7:17	3:14, eat dust
vv. 10–11, tribute from kings of Tarshish, distant shores, Sheba, Seba	1 Kgs 4:21[5:1]; Gen 10:4, 5, 7	49:10c, that which belongs to him = tribute[a] 10:2, 6, descendants of Japhet and Ham (who serve the Shem king)
v. 17	Gen 12:3; 18:18; 22:18	n/a

‡ This table is loosely based on the table in Schnittjer, *Torah Story*, 186.

[a] On the sense of Gen 49:10c, see Schnittjer, "Blessing of Judah," 16–17, n. 3.

The most important clue to the Genesis echoes comes with the strong allusion to the Abrahamic covenant in Ps 72:17. The other possible secondary Genesis echoes each stem from the coming king fulfilling the international expectations of the promises to

42. See discussion of possible collation of the details in Childs, "Psalm Titles," 146–47.

43. Gillingham, "'Moab Is My Washpot,'" 66.

Abraham (see Table G1 in Genesis Filters). Notice how the psalm collates together several derivative prophetic expectations with the Abrahamic promise (all emphases signify verbal parallels except broken underlining which signifies exegetical intervention):

> He will proclaim peace to the nations. His rule will extend *from sea to sea and from the River to the ends of the earth.* (Zech 9:10b)
>
> **Kings** . . . and their queens . . . **will bow down before** you with their faces to the ground; they will **lick the dust** at your feet. Then you will know that I am Yahweh; those who hope in me will not be disappointed. (Isa 49:23)
>
> They [the nations] **will lick dust** like a snake, like creatures that crawl on the ground. They will come trembling out of their dens; they will turn in fear to Yahweh our God and will be afraid of you. (Mic 7:17)
>
> And Solomon ruled over all the kingdoms from the Euphrates River to the land of the Philistines, as far as the border of Egypt. These countries brought **tribute** and were **serving** Solomon all his life. (1 Kgs 4:21†[5:1])
>
> The sons of Japhet: . . . Tarshish . . . From these the peoples of distant shores spread out into their territories by their clans within their nations, each with its own language. . . . The sons of Ham . . . Seba . . . Sheba. (Gen 10:2, 4, 5, 6, 7 lit.)
>
> I will bless those who bless you, and whoever curses you I will curse; and all peoples on earth *will be blessed through* you. (12:3; cf. 18:18; 22:18)
>
> May he rule *from sea to sea and from the River to the ends of the earth.* [9] May the desert tribes bow before him and his enemies **lick the dust.** [10] May the kings of Tarshish and of distant shores bring **tribute** to him. May the kings of Sheba and Seba present him gifts. [11] May all **kings bow down to him** and all nations **serve** him. . . . [15] Long may he live! May gold from Sheba be given him. May people ever pray for him and bless him all day long. . . . [17] May his name endure forever; may it continue as long as the sun. Then *all nations will be blessed through* him, and they will call him blessed. (Ps 72:9–11, 15, 17)

The major exegetical advancement of Ps 72 pivots on identifying the accomplishment of the Davidic covenant as essentially identical to fulfilling the Abrahamic covenant. This creates a need to briefly consider the sense of the loaded term "bless" relative to its syntactical function. The verb "bless" in the grammatical stems used in the expressions of the Abrahamic covenant could connote a passive or reflexive sense as illustrated in different modern committee translations of the present context (emphasis mine).

[passive] May his name endure forever; may it continue as long as the sun. Then all nations *will be blessed through him*, and they will call him blessed. (72:17 NIV)

[reflexive] May his name be eternal; while the sun lasts, may his name endure; let men *invoke his blessedness upon themselves*; let all nations count him happy. (72:17 JPSB)

The various occurrences of the Abrahamic blessing in Genesis feature Nif or Hith stems for the key uses of "bless" (Nif, Gen 12:3b; Nif, 18:18; Hith, 22:18; Nif, 28:14). Both stems can carry either a passive or reflexive sense: "will be blessed" or "bless themselves."[44]

The context of Gen 12:1–3 offers help. The syntactical sense of "bless" in Gen 12:3b depends on the immediately preceding context. The middle clause of Gen 12:3 starts with a disjunctive *vav* and stands apart by its use of an imperfect verb serving as a parenthetical thought—"But, whoever curses you I will curse." The syntax may be summarized:

cohortatives: "I will make . . . I will bless . . . I will make great . . . I will bless" (Gen 12:2, 3a);
disjunctive parenthetical clause with imperfect: "but . . . I will curse" (12:3b);
concluding vav-consecutive purpose of the preceding set of cohortatives: "then, they will be blessed" (12:3c).[45]

Since Yahweh "will bless" Abraham (v. 2b) and "will bless" those who bless him (v. 3a), the natural sense of the final verb concluding the preceding series of cohortative verbs is passive—to paraphrase: "they will be blessed by Yahweh's blessing upon them" (12:3c paraphrase mine). Yahweh blesses Abraham and blesses those who bless Abraham. Putting this together produces the following sense with key verbs emphasized:

I will make you into a great nation,
and *I will bless* you;
I will make your name great and you will be a blessing.
┌--- *I will bless* those who bless you,
¦ but whoever curses you *I will curse*;
└--- thus, all peoples on earth *will be blessed* through you (12:2–3 lit.).

The psalmist seems to pick up on this sense and connects those who are blessed as those who bless, now not Abraham, but the son of the king (Ps 72:1, 17). Notice the exegetical intervention in isolation (marked with broken underlining): "I will bless those

44. *IBHS* §§23.4h, n. 27; 23.6.4a; GKC §§51c–f; 54e–g.

45. Based on Miller, "Syntax," 473–74. For a different view, reading the Nif of Gen 12:3; 18:18; 28:14 as reflexive on the analogy of the formula in 48:20 (Piel), see "ברך," Nif *HALOT* 1:160; Chisholm, *From Exegesis*, 15, 18.

who bless you" (Gen 12:3a) and "all nations will be blessed through him, and they will call him blessed" (Ps 72:17cd).[46] Elsewhere the connection between the ancestral promises also gets identified with the expectation of the Judah-king (see note on Num 24:9).

In sum, the psalmist presents the idealized Genesis-shaped kingdom of the Davidic son as fulfillment of the Abrahamic covenant. The identification together of the two covenants advances revelation.

78~narrative compilation (B, C) (downfall of Ephraim and election of Judah).[47] Psalm 78 stands as the first of several long retrospectives in the Psalter (Pss 78; 105; 106; 135; 136; see Table Josh1 for comparative overview). The retrospective portion of the psalm has been called "poetic refraction" of history following a spatial more than temporal sequence: Egypt (78:12), wilderness (vv. 14–41), Egypt (vv. 42–53), Shiloh (v. 60), Zion (v. 68).[48] Note the broad retrospective comparison of Ps 78 (stylized brackets signify alternate sequence):

	narratives	**Psalm 78**
divine instruction	{Exod 20//Deut 5; Deut 6:7, 20–25}	5–8
Ephraim defeated	{1 Sam 4?; 2 Kgs 17?}	9–10
wonders in Egypt	Exod 7–12	12
sea crossing	Exod 14–15	13
wilderness provisions and rebellions	Exod 15–17; Num 11–12; 20	14–41
cosmic terrors in Egypt forgotten	{Exod 7–12}	42–51
departure and sea crossing	{Exod 13–15}	52–53
conquest and settlement	Josh 1–12; 13–21	54–55
rebellion	Judg 1–21	56–58
Shiloh abandoned	1 Sam 4	59–66
election of Judah, Zion, David	Exod 15:17; 2 Sam 7; 1 Kgs 5–8	67–72

Though the psalm enjoys Deuteronomistic undercurrents, its narrative interpretation speaks of the people and God exclusively in the third person and only mentions one individual by name, David (78:70).[49] The psalmist memorably depicts the Lord

46. Note the use of "bless/happy" (אשר) in Ps 72:17d: "I will bless [אֲבָרְכָה Piel] those who bless you [מְבָרְכֶיךָ Piel]" (Gen 12:3a) and "all nations will be blessed [וְיִתְבָּרְכוּ Hith] through him, and they will call him blessed [יְאַשְּׁרוּהוּ Piel]" (Ps 72:17cd).

47. Many of the broad allusions of the retrospective of Ps 78 listed in the comparison table are very general. Some of the verbal parallels of Ps 78 suggest interpretive allusion at the B level, such as the cosmic terrors against Egypt, Ps 78:44–51~Exod 7–12; making false images, Ps 78:58–59~Exod 20:4a, 5a//Deut 5:8a, 9a. Other verbal parallels suggest possible allusion at the C level, such as reference to the mountain and sanctuary, Ps 78:54, 68–69~Exod 15:17.

48. See Hossfeld and Zenger, *Psalms 2*, 286.

49. See ibid., 286, 292, 300. The references to Jacob and Israel in Ps 78:5 refer to the people collectively.

like a warrior waking after being overcome with wine following his dispatching of the Northern Kingdom and its shrine at Shiloh (v. 65; cf. v. 60; Jer 7:12). The purpose of the retrospective of the rebellion and downfall of Ephraim amounts to affirming the election of Judah, Zion, and David (Ps 78:68, 70).[50] According to several lines of evidence, Ps 78 appears to be broadly dependent on scriptural traditions now housed in Torah and the Deuteronomistic narrative, most importantly quasi-marking (78:2–3) and presupposing contextual details such as the ark narrative (78:59–64; cf. 1 Sam 4).[51] For the present purposes a few of the more important interpretive interventions can be noted.[52]

The psalmist uses narrative traditions to affirm faithfulness to God and to challenge his audience to obey legal instruction. All of this comes back to the "decree" and "command" God established in Israel (Ps 78:5). The psalmist speaks of teaching children from one generation to the next to obey the commandments of Torah (78:5–7). The transgenerational connection of the narrative traditions as bound up together with divine instructions runs very close to the sense of Deut 6:20–25 (cf. Deut 6:7; 11:19). The rebellion of the people repeatedly gets tied to forgetting (Ps 78:11; cf. v. 7), not believing (78:22, 32, cf. v. 8), remembering but not believing (78:35–37), not remembering (78:42), and not obeying (78:56). The root problem of Ephraim amounts to a disconnect between divine instruction, wonders, provisions, and a people who quickly forget. The psalmist's conception of legal instruction and narrative bound together matches the shape of Torah.

Though biblical narratives often appear in chronological sequence, they frequently feature dischronologized sequence for ideological and teaching purposes (e.g., Exod 33:7–11; see Glossary). The narrative sequence of Ps 78 also features dischronologized elements. The psalmist starts with the giving of torah and locates the cosmic terrors against Egypt after an account of the wilderness temptations. The psalmist presents seven divine cosmic terrors against Egypt, arranged differently than elsewhere: blood (Ps 78:44; Exod 7:14–25), flies (Ps 78:45a; Exod 8:20–24[16–20]), frogs (Ps 78:45b; Exod 8:1–7[7:26–8:3]), locusts (Ps 78:46; Exod 10:3–15), hail (Ps 78:47–48; Exod 9:22–26), pestilence (Ps 78:49–50; Exod 9:1–12), and death of firstborn (Ps 78:51; Exod 12:29).[53] The function of rehearsing the cosmic terrors turns on what Israel "did not remember" (Ps 78:42; cf. 106:7). The failure of Israel to remember the great works of God stands exactly opposite to the point of the retrospective psalm itself—"Then they would put their trust in God and would *not forget his deeds* but would keep his commands" (78:7, emphasis mine).

The psalmist frames settlement and election in terms of a "mountain" and "sanctuary" in verses 54 and 68–69. This language may evoke the expectation set out in the Song of the Sea: "You will bring them in and plant them on *the mountain* of your inheritance—the

50. See Clifford, "In Zion and David," 137.

51. See Leonard, "Identifying Inner-Biblical Allusions," 257–64.

52. For a list of (mostly non-exegetical) allusions in Psalm 78, see Kirkpatrick, *Psalms Books II and III*, 464–78.

53. On the verbal parallels of the plagues in Hebrew between Exodus and Ps 78 with an excavative agenda, see Leonard, "Identifying Inner-Biblical Allusions," 247–48.

place, Yahweh, you made for your dwelling, *the sanctuary*, Lord, your hands *established*" (Exod 15:17, emphasis signifies language used in Ps 78:54, 68–69).[54]

The psalmist's evidence for the election of Zion comes from the ark abandoning Shiloh and the rebellion and downfall of Ephraim. The psalmist does not bother with a positive argument. Instead, the rejection of Shiloh by broad allusion to the ark narrative reveals the divine choice of Judah (78:59–64, 67–68).[55] The psalmist explains that the problem with Israel stems from their transgression of the second commandment (emphases signify verbal parallels of roots):

> You shall not make for yourself an *image*. . . . You shall not bow down to them or worship them; for I, Yahweh your God, am a *jealous* God. (Exod 20:4a, 5a//Deut 5:8a, 9a)

> They angered him with their high places; they aroused his *jealousy* with their *images*.
> When God heard them, he was furious; he rejected Israel completely. (Ps 78:58–59†)

In sum, Ps 78 houses a narrative interpretation of the election of Zion. The psalm itself embodies narrative traditions of Ephraim's rebellion to offer instruction from one generation to the next. For the psalmist, not remembering scriptural narratives directly correlates to disobedience of divine instruction (78:7).

81:9–10[10–11]~Deut 32:12, 16+5:6, 7, 9 (B) (no other gods).

81:16[17]~Deut 32:13, 14 (B) (provisions in the wilderness). Psalm 81, set at the Festival of Tabernacles, houses direct discourse from Yahweh (Ps 81:6–16[7–17]).[56] The divine speech features both prophetic and liturgical qualities.[57] The psalmist draws heavily on the Song of Moses and the first two commandments using distinct language, making allusion highly likely (81:9–10, 16[10–11, 17]; Deut 5:6–9; 32:12–16). Perhaps the use of divine "jealousy" in Deut 5:9 and 32:16 serves as a catchword to suggest this interpretive blend. The psalmist poetically recasts these authoritative traditions as divine direct discourse. The instructional function of the psalmist's use of scriptural traditions comes as a warning. Tabernacles offers extended time to celebrate redemption and includes public Torah reading at least every seven years (Deut 31:10–13; Neh 8:17–18). This psalm offers an interpretive scriptural meditation for Tabernacles.

The psalmist's major exegetical advance turns on the use of the distinctive expression "stubborn heart." This favorite expression of Jeremiah only appears twice elsewhere, including here.[58] In a preview of Israel's rebellion, only one transgression gets singled out to

54. See Schniedewind, *Society*, 68.

55. See Leonard, "Psalmist as Historiographer," 20–21. For a very speculative "narrative tracking" comparison of Psalm 78 and 1 Sam 4–6, see idem, "Identifying Subtle Allusions," 106–8 (see "narrative tracking" in Glossary).

56. On blowing the trumpet at Tabernacles, see Lev 23:24, 39; Ps 81:3[4] (Kirkpatrick, *Psalms Books II and III*, 489).

57. See Gillingham, "New Wine," 377. Also see Jacobson, *"Many Are Saying"*, 113–14.

58. See Deut 29:19[18]; Jer 3:17; 7:24; 9:14[13]; 11:8; 13:10; 16:12; 18:12; 23:17; Ps 81:12[13] (Kirkpatrick, *Psalms Books II and III*, 493).

exemplify all of it: "When a person hears the words of this oath and blesses themselves in their heart, thinking, 'I will enjoy peace even while I walk according to *my stubborn heart*'" (Deut 29:19a[18a] lit., emphasis mine). The arrogant presumption represents a complete misunderstanding of covenantal election. The chosen person uses election to excuse rebellion. The psalmist borrows the idea of a stubborn heart that leads to disaster but emphasizes Yahweh's sovereignty to allow this conceited revolt (emphases signify verbal parallels):

> *I am Yahweh your God*, who brought you out *of Egypt*, out of the land of slavery. 7 You shall have no other gods before me. . . . 9 You shall not bow down to them or worship them; for I, Yahweh your God, am a jealous God, punishing the children for the sin of the parents to the third and fourth generation of those who hate me. (Deut 5:6–7, 9//Exod 20:2–5)

> When a person hears the words of this oath and blesses themselves in their heart, thinking, "I will enjoy peace even while I walk according to my stubborn heart." (Deut 29:19a[18a] lit., emphasis mine)

> Yahweh alone led him; no **foreign god** was with him. 13 He made him ride on the heights of the land and **fed** him with the fruit of the fields. He nourished him with **honey** from the rock . . . 14 and **the finest** kernels **of wheat**. You drank the foaming blood of the grape. . . . 16 They made him jealous with **strange gods** and angered him with their detestable idols. (Deut 32:12–13a, 14b, 16†)

> You shall have no **strange god** among you; you shall not bow down to a **foreign god**. 10 *I am Yahweh your God*, who brought you up out *of Egypt*. Open wide your mouth and I will fill it. 11 But my people would not listen to me; Israel would not submit to me. 12 So I gave them over to their stubborn hearts to follow their own devices. . . . 15 Those who hate Yahweh would cringe before him, and their punishment would last forever. 16 But you **would be fed** with **the finest of wheat**; with **honey** from the rock I would satisfy you. (Ps 81:9–12, 15–16[10–13, 16–17], v. 9 lit.)

Working backwards the psalmist closes by mentioning the delicacies divinely provided in the wilderness. This aptly highlights the sort of thing that Tabernacles celebrates. Yet the psalmist uses this as a punchline to accuse the worshiping community. He warns that those who hate Yahweh have been given over to their stubborn hearts and thus turn the wilderness delicacies from a gift to a presumption of Israel who does not listen. Even the inversion of Tabernacles by self-serving stubborn hearts can only be possible when Yahweh "gives them over" to it (81:12[13]).

In sum, the psalmist draws upon the Song of Moses and the Ten Commandments to present scriptural instruction suitable for Tabernacles. The warning ironically undercuts all bases for pride by reinforcing that Israel cannot even rebel except by divine permission.

82:1–6~Exod 22:8, 9[7, 8] (C)+23:6; Lev 19:15 (C) (confronting bad judges). The use of the Hebrew term *elohim* (אֱלֹהִים), usually translated God/god or gods depending on the context, provides the point of departure for an exegetical use of scriptural traditions in Ps 82. The term *elohim* can also be used of celestial delegates (Deut 32:8; Ps 29:1; possibly 95:3; 97:7) or humans (1 Sam 2:25 KJV; Ps 45:7[8]; cf. Gen 23:6 KJV, NIV, NRSV). Since the term can be used of celestial delegates, Ps 82 has been prone to interpretation as a court scene in heaven.[59] The death of the *elohim* in Ps 82:7 does not fit with anything known of celestial delegates elsewhere in Scripture, though it could be an obscure poetic analogy.[60] When used of the deity, the term "God"/*elohim* takes singular verbs because it is a singular noun.[61] The term *elohim* can also be used of celestial delegates (Deut 32:8; Ps 29:1; possibly 95:3; 97:7) or humans (1 Sam 2:25 KJV; Ps 45:7[8]; cf. Gen 23:6 KJV, NIV, NRSV). The similarity to "Do you rulers [*'elem* אֵלֶם] indeed speak justly? Do you judge people with equity?" (Ps 58:2[1]) may also be considered as referring to human versus celestial judges.[62] The contested use of the term *elohim* in Ps 82 does not allow identification of scriptural allusion to be more than a possibility.

If Ps 82 alludes to Torah standards for justice at human civil courts, then *elohim* would mean the same thing in the psalm as it does in Exod 22:8, 9[7, 8]. Vannoy presents a convincing case that *elohim* in Exod 21:6 could refer to God himself but that the term refers to human judges in Exod 22:9[8], and thus also 22:8[7].[63] The plural verb "they declare guilty" provides the most important piece of evidence to affirm that *elohim* refers to (human) "judges" (Exod 22:9[8]).[64] Other contexts corroborate this evidence. When Moses's father-in-law asked about his judicial decisions, Moses said, "Because the people come to me *to seek God's will*" (18:15, emphasis mine). Moses explains to the next generation that human judges represent the deity's will: "Do not show partiality in judging... *for judgment belongs to God*" (Deut 1:17, emphasis mine; cf. 10:17–18). In that sense

59. On *elohim* of Ps 82 as celestial delegates, see Sarna, *Psalms*, 175; as humans, see Kirkpatrick, *Psalms Books II and III*, 494–96. Also see Hossfeld and Zenger, *Psalms 2*, 329–32; Zakovitch, "Psalm 82," 213–28; Lynch, "Mapping Monotheism," 52, n. 15.

60. McClellan's view that condemning the gods to mortality in Ps 82:7 makes way for Yahweh's takeover of the divine council ("Gods-Complaint," 845) requires distinguishing between El Elyon and Yahweh in Deut 32:8–9. This does not work if Deut 32:8 refers to the events in Gen 11:7–8. It also does not fit with the next Asaph psalm which identifies Yahweh as Elyon/Most High (Ps 83:18[19]).

61. Other singular terms that use a plural-sounding form include "master" (*ba'al*) and "lord" (*adon*) (e.g., Gen 39:8 of Potiphar; Exod 21:29 of the owner). The singular terms God/god, master, lord can take the plural form as a social convention of respect, much like capitalizing the first letter of words in modern English. The plural-sounding form of *elohim* has nothing to do with plurality of a divine being, since it can be used of any individual god, such as Chemosh, the patron deity of the Moabites (Judg 11:24).

62. NIV of Ps 58:1[2] uses "rulers" based on re-vocalizing *e'lem* (אֵלֶם) as *e'lim* (אֵלִם); for "gods" (cf. NRSV). Other suggestions include emending the text to "rams" (אֵילִים) being metaphorical of rulers (*BHS* n. a; NET nt.).

63. Vannoy, "Use of *hā'elōhI`m*," 225–41, esp. 233–34, 239–40. Vannoy works out some of the loose ends in Gordon, "אלהים," 139–44; Fensham, "New Light," 160–61. Trotter's impressive genre argument is undermined because he does not take into account the plural verb in Exodus 22:9[8] ("Death," 229). Elsewhere Trotter points out the similarity of Kirta's failure to provide justice for the vulnerable as the basis for his death "like a mortal" (235) which strengthens the suggestion here of judgment against unjust judges in Psalm 82 (cf. Coogan and Smith, *Stories*, 90).

64. The plural "they declare guilty" in Exod 22:9[8] MT is preferred over "he declares guilty" (SP), since SP tends to harmonize difficulties (see *BHS* apparatus; no variants in SP apparatus).

human judges of Israel can be referred to as *elohim*—"ministers of divine judgment."

The psalmist takes advantage of the semantic range of *elohim* for his exegetical moves. The psalmist's list of terms for the socially challenged makes his secondary allusion non-specific.[65] Some of the terms do not even appear in Torah. The psalmist's language most overlaps with Exod 23:6 and Lev 19:15, which can serve as representative of the Torah standards for the general point being made here. Whether the psalm originally referred to the deity as Yahweh or God—often discussed of psalms like this in the so-called Elohistic psalter (Pss 42–83)—does not relate to the received version of the psalm. The psalmist's exegetical advances develop boldly by speaking of "God" (*elohim*) and "ministers of divine justice" (*elohim*) side by side. God even uses the term as a sarcastic wordplay to demonstrate both that the ministers of divine justice do not live up to their designation as "gods" and that they will die like any other human (82:6, 7). Notice how the psalmist frames Ps 82:2–7 as divine discourse and 82:8 as the psalmist's concluding remark, basically agreeing with Abraham in Gen 18:25—the judge of all the earth shall act justly (emphases signify verbal parallels):

> In all cases of illegal possession of an ox, a donkey, a sheep, a garment, or any other lost property about which somebody says, "This is mine," both parties are to bring their cases before **the judges** [*elohim*]. The one whom **the judges** [*elohim*] declare guilty [3mp] must pay back double to the other. (Exod 22:9[8])
>
> Do not deny *justice* to your poor people in their lawsuits. (23:6)
>
> Do not *pervert justice*; do not *show partiality* to the weak or favoritism to the great, but *judge* your neighbor fairly. (Lev 19:15†)
>
> A psalm of Asaph.
>
> God [*elohim*] presides in the assembly of God [*el*]; he renders judgment among **the ministers of divine justice** [*elohim*].
>
> [2] "How long will you *judge perversely* and *show partiality* to the wicked? [3] Defend the weak and the fatherless; uphold the cause of the poor and the oppressed. [4] Rescue the weak and the poor, deliver them from the hand of the wicked. [5] They know nothing, they understand nothing. They walk about in darkness, all the foundations of the earth are shaken. [6] I say, 'You are "**gods** [*elohim*]," you are all "sons of the Most High."' [7] But you will die like mortals, you will fall like every other ruler."
>
> [8] Rise up, God [*elohim*], *judge* the earth, for all the nations are your inheritance. (Ps 82:1–8 lit.)

65. Psalm 82:3, "weak" (דַּל) (Exod 23:3; Lev 19:15; Pss 41:2[3]; 72:13; 113:7; often used in wisdom contexts), "orphan" (יָתוֹם) (with widow in Exod 22:22[21]; with widow and residing foreigner in Deut 24:17, 19, 20, 21), "poor" (רוּשׁ) (not in Torah, used mainly in wisdom contexts), "afflicted" (עָנִי) (Exod 22:24[23]; Lev 19:10; 23:22; Deut 15:11 24:12; but not in contexts of civil justice proper); and Ps 82:4, "needy" (אֶבְיוֹן) (Exod 23:6; cf. Pss 72:13; 109:31). Also note Ps 82:2 use of "injustice" (עָוֶל) (Lev 19:15).

In sum, the psalmist seems to take advantage of the use of *elohim* for ministers of divine justice in the tradition found in Exod 22:9[8]. While the term aptly expresses the high calling of God to dispense justice, it also allows the psalmist to ridicule bad judges. The psalmist closes by calling upon God himself to bring justice upon the earth.

86:15–17*~Exod 34:6* (C) (covenant fidelity and grace) (* see attribute formula network). The attribute formula in Exod 34:6 and Ps 86 share identical language, especially in 86:15 and to a lesser extent in 86:5 and a single term in 86:13. The lyrical diffusion of commonly used elements makes it impossible to know if the psalmist works with the narrative of revelation to Moses after the golden calf or uses a widely known expression of worship (see list in attribute formula network). The important interpretive move of the psalmist, irrespective of the source of the allusion, stems from the individualization of a collective covenantal revelation (italics signify verbal parallels, and broken underlining signifies personalization):[66]

> And he passed in front of Moses, proclaiming, "Yahweh, Yahweh, *the compassionate and gracious God, slow to anger, abounding in love and faithfulness.*" (Exod 34:6)

> But you, Lord, are *the compassionate and gracious God, slow to anger, abounding in love and faithfulness.* Turn to me and *be gracious* to me, show your strength to your servant, and save the son of your maidservant. Give me a sign of your goodness . . . for you Yahweh, have helped me and *comforted* me. (Ps 86:15–16, 17a, c; v. 16 lit.)

The psalmist detects that the attribute formula applies beyond the collective context. The psalmist calls upon God to "work" a sign (Ps 86:17), which may connect to the great wonders he has "worked" (86:10). The psalmist goes further and claims that he is not a purchased slave but the offspring of a maidservant, a member of the household (86:16; cf. 116:16).[67] The psalmist's use of this imagery demonstrates that even the lowliest members of Yahweh's household may seek his favor.

89:3–4, 19–37*[4–5, 20–38]~2 Sam 7:11–16* (B) (Davidic covenant) (* see Davidic covenant and place networks). Psalm 89 cites divine discourse in verses 3–4 and 19–37[89:4–5, 20–38].[68] These prophetic inserts represent reworking of Nathan's oracle housed in 2 Sam 7, especially verses 11–16. Though the psalmist does not mark the first citation (Ps 89:3–4[5–6]), he explicitly marks the second with, "Once you spoke in a vision, to your faithful people *you said*" (89:19[20], emphasis mine). It needs to be noted that the psalmist frames the Davidic covenant as "to your faithful people," plural. Though Ps 89 uses the first-person singular (e.g., "remember how fleeting is my life" [89:47(48)]), the overall perspective is decidedly collective with "from generation to generation" (89:1, 4

66. See Kim, "Exodus 34.6," 40–41; Hossfeld and Zenger, *Psalms 2*, 375; Rendtorff, *Canonical Hebrew Bible*, 626.
67. See Hossfeld and Zenger, *Psalms 2*, 370, 375, for both of these observations.
68. See Gillingham, "New Wine," 374; Jacobson, *"Many Are Saying"*, 101–3; Hossfeld and Zenger, *Psalms 2*, 404.

lit.[2, 5]) and "forever" (89:1, 2, 4, 28, 36, 37[2, 3, 5, 29, 37, 38]).[69] The primary exegetical advances of the psalm relate to labeling the Davidic promise, clarifying its irrevocability, expanding upon the fatherhood of Yahweh, and raising painful exilic questions.

The psalmist repeatedly emphasizes the enduring character of the Davidic promise by attaching language of permanence to "covenant" (89:3, 28, 34, 39[4, 29, 35, 40]) and "oath" (89:3, 35, 49[4, 36, 50]). Both covenant and oath appear in parallel lines and serve as shorthand labels to identify the promise to David (89:3[4]). The psalmist thereby develops a covenantal lexicon to affirm the divine commitment to the covenant: "faithfulness" (noun and verb from אמן) (89:1, 2, 24, 28, 33, 37, 49[2, 3, 25, 29, 34, 38, 50]); "forever" (89:1, 2, 4, 28, 36, 37[2, 3, 5, 29, 37, 38]); "all generations" (89:1, 4[2, 5]); and "covenantal loyalty" (חֶסֶד) (89:1, 2, 14, 24, 28, 33, 49[2, 3, 15, 25, 29, 34, 50]; cf. v. 19[20]). Part of the purpose for giving attention to the celestial court relates to testifying to the "faithfulness" of Yahweh (89:5, 8, 14[6, 9, 15]). The cosmic lights testify to the enduring covenant with David forever, "like the sun" and "like the moon" (89:36, 37[37, 38]). Along the same lines, Jeremiah uses these figures to symbolize the permanence of the new covenant (Jer 31:35–37; cf. 33:20, 22).

The most direct interpretive allusion to Nathan's oracle emphasizes that disobedience does not invalidate the covenant (bold and italics signify verbal parallels, and broken underlining signifies interpretive advances):

> I will be his father, and he will be my *son*. When he does wrong, I will punish him *with a rod* wielded by men, *with floggings* inflicted by human hands. **But my love** will never be taken away **from him**, as I took it away from Saul, whom I removed from before you. Your house and your kingdom will endure **forever** before me; your throne will be established **forever.** (2 Sam 7:14–16)

> I will maintain **my love** to him **forever**, and my covenant with him will never fail. I will establish his line forever, his throne as long as the heavens endure. If his *sons* forsake my torah and do not follow my statutes, if they violate my decrees and fail to keep my commands, I will punish their sin *with the rod*, their iniquity *with flogging*; **but** I will not take **my love from him**, nor will I ever betray my faithfulness. (Ps 89:28–33[29–34])

The psalmist makes explicit the collective sense to the Davidic dynasty. He also expands upon the covenant obligations in terms of obedience to the legal instruction of Torah. The older binary contrast between "conditional" and "unconditional" fails to get at the scriptural presentation of an irrevocable covenant with obligations.[70] The term

69. See Schnittjer, "Bad Ending," 53. See similar explanation in Hossfeld and Zenger, *Psalms 2*, 404. The point here involves the collective perspective of the lament in Ps 89 not the collective messiah reading of the psalm. See Krusche, "Collective Anointed?" 87–105.

70. Indebted to Gordon Johnston for this observation, see citation in Schnittjer, "Blessing of Judah," 25–26, n. 22.

"unconditional" does not adequately express the real issues of the permanence and irrevocability of a conditionalized covenant. Broken obligations, defined by the psalmist as Torah (dis)obedience, lead to exile even while the covenant continues to promise restoration.[71]

The psalmist revoices covenantal adoption language as direct discourse of the Davidic ruler—note the counterpart in Ps 2:7—and spells out implications (italics signify verbal parallel):[72]

> I will be his *father*, and he will be my son. When he does wrong, I will punish him with a rod wielded by men, with floggings inflicted by human hands. (2 Sam 7:14)

> He will call out to me, "You are my *Father*, my God, the Rock my Savior." And I will appoint him to be my firstborn, the most exalted of the kings of the earth. (Ps 89:26–27[27–28])

Like Deut 8:5, Nathan's oracle affirms Yahweh's fatherhood by the punishment of his wayward son (see note on 2 Sam 7:14–15). The psalmist foregrounds the "birthright" of the royal sonship of Yahweh (Ps 89:27[28]).

The closing section of the psalm raises complaints because of the incongruity between the promises of the Davidic covenant and reality. The psalmist's complaints get boiled down to questions. These questions call upon Yahweh with the implied hope of renewing his covenant with the collective people with whom he made it (89:19[20]). The psalmist asks, "*How long, Yahweh?* Will you hide yourself forever? How long will your wrath burn like fire?" (89:46[47], emphasis mine). And, "*Lord, where is your former great love,* which in your faithfulness you swore to David?" (89:49[50], emphasis mine). These questions linger in the Psalter. In certain respects they get answered by psalms that assert "Yahweh rules/is king" (93:1; 96:10; 97:1; 99:1) and in other respects by Pss 110 and 132.[73] But in reality these questions continue to linger, awaiting an answer from Nazareth.

91:11~Exod 23:20* (B) (guarding messengers) (* see new exodus network). Psalm 91:11 shares verbal and conceptual elements with Exod 23:20, making allusion likely.[74] The psalmist recontextualizes and institutionalizes an ancient promise, so to speak, suggesting much broader protective services from the guarding celestial delegates (italics signify verbal parallels):

---

71. The psalmist's view corresponds to the prophets. In the twilight of the Davidic rule, Jeremiah can speak of the enduring hope for David (Jer 23:5, 6); a point that is reemphasized even after the fall of the Davidic rule (33:14–21; cf. note ad loc.). The exile does not stop the expectation for Davidic rule by Ezekiel and Zechariah (Ezek 34:23–31; 37:24–28; Zech 9:9; cf. notes ad loc.).

72. See Sarna, "Psalm 89," 38.

73. For the idea of a hovering question, see Bullock, "Double-tracking," 482.

74. Kirkpatrick suggests several other possible parallels between Ps 91 and Exod 23, but with only thematic not verbal connections (*Psalms Books IV and V*, 554).

> See, I am sending an *angel* ahead of *you to guard you along the way* and to bring you to the place I have prepared. (Exod 23:20)

> For he will command his *angels* concerning *you to guard you in all* your *ways*; they will lift you up in their hands, so that you will not strike your foot against a stone. You will tread on the lion and the cobra; you will trample the great lion and the serpent. (Ps 91:11–13)

The psalmist addresses much of his message of hope and protection to "you" singular (91:3, 4, 7, 8, 9, 10). He finally reveals the identity of his auditor as one who "desires" or "loves" Yahweh (91:14). In this way the psalmist reinterprets the promise to send a celestial delegate to protect the people through the wilderness and into the land of promise. The psalmist deduces from the ancient promise that Yahweh protects individuals who love him.

95:8–11~Exod 17:7 (B)+Deut 2:14–15 (C)+12:9 (B) (rebellion at Meribah and Massah). Psalm 95:8–11 presents a "God quotation" with prophetic qualities.[75] The psalmist prophetically revoices several narrative traditions related to the ancient rebellion at Meribah and Massah and poetically marks the retrospectives as direct discourse of Yahweh: "Today, if only you would hear his voice" (Ps 95:7). The psalmist reworks narrative traditions of Torah to speak directly in a prophetic manner to the congregation. The use of "today," though not unique to Deuteronomy, matches a favorite rhetorical device therein (too many references to list, though Deut 12:8 or 27:9–10 fits this context; not used in this sense in Numbers).[76] The term "if" underscores the urgent contingency of the presentation of a divine message that requires response.

The rebellion at Meribah and Massah gets interpreted in several scriptural narratives, making identification of a specific donor context only probable in the first of three pieces of an interpretive blend (cf. Exod 17:1–7; Num 20:2–13; 27:14; Deut 9:2). After naming the notorious incident, Yahweh makes three interpretive advances, each of which may be associated with specific donor contexts that the psalmist puts to use to challenge the congregation. First, after Yahweh repeatedly "tested" Israel, producing a series of failures (Exod 15:25; 16:4), the people "test" their God at Meribah and Massah (17:2, 7).[77] Second, only in Ps 95:10 does Yahweh appear as subject of the verb "loathe" or "detest." This verb offers a fitting way to describe the divine hand against Israel for thirty-eight years (Deut 2:15).[78] Third, the psalmist speaks of not entering "rest" as judgment against the wilderness rebellions. This suggests an allusion to Deut 12:9.

The definitive judgment against the older generation culminated at Kadesh, sentencing them to forty years in the wilderness (Num 14; Deut 1:19–45). Yet the notorious quarrel

75. See Jacobson, *"Many Are Saying"*, 109; Gillingham, "New Wine," 378.
76. Hossfeld suggests Deut 27:9–10 (Hossfeld and Zenger, *Psalms 2*, 461).
77. See Schnittjer, *Torah Story*, 243, Table 14–A.
78. On the use of the verb "detest" (קוט) with Yahweh as subject, see Hossfeld and Zenger, *Psalms 2*, 461.

with Yahweh at Meribah and Massah exemplifies Israel's "wandering heart" (Ps 95:10), which could also be described as a "hard heart" with a term once used of the pharaoh's heart (95:8; cf. Exod 7:3). Notice the psalmist's interpretive deductions to motivate the congregation to hear Yahweh's voice from the scriptural traditions of rebellion (italics and bold signify verbal parallels, and broken underlining signifies selected interpretive elements):

> And he called the place *Massah* and *Meribah* because the Israelites quarreled and because they *tested* Yahweh saying, "Is Yahweh among us or not?" (Exod 17:7)

> Thirty-eight years passed from the time we left Kadesh Barnea until we crossed the Zered Valley. By then, that entire generation of fighting men had perished from the camp, as Yahweh **had declared on oath** to them. Yahweh's hand was against them until he had completely eliminated them from the camp. (Deut 2:14–15†)

> You are not to do as we do here **today**, everyone doing as they see fit, since you have not yet **entered the rest** and the inheritance Yahweh your God is giving you. (12:8–9†)

> **Today**, if only you would hear his voice: "Do not harden your hearts as you did at *Meribah*, as you did that day at *Massah* in the wilderness, where your ancestors *tested* me; they tried me, though they had seen what I did. For forty years I loathed that generation; I said, 'They are a people whose hearts go astray, and they have not known my ways.' So I **declared on oath** in my anger, 'They shall never **enter** my **rest.**'" (Ps 95:8–11, v. 10 lit.)

In sum, the rebellion of Israel in Torah remains immediately relevant to the congregation, today. The psalmist prophetically revoices scriptural narrative traditions as direct address from Yahweh. The congregation stands as the very people who need to listen and to respond according to what Yahweh has accomplished.

96:7–8, 10//29:1–2 (new version of the old call to worship). The central panel of Ps 96 calls the families or tribes of the peoples to worship Yahweh. And, except for the divine name, the psalm lacks almost all hints of the national covenant. In that sense Ps 96 embodies Yahweh's universal mission. The psalm opens by addressing "all the earth." But this inclusive address pushes against the subset addressed by the psalmist to declare Yahweh's glory "among the nations" and "among the peoples" (Ps 96:3). Elsewhere the "families of the peoples" and "all the earth" denote the same referents (96:7a, 9b).

The "new song," like other biblical new songs, shares many familiar elements that could be drawn from the second half of Isaiah or other psalms. Goldingay quips that the psalmists never call the congregation to "oldies." He suggests that the song may be new to the others called to worship Yahweh.[79] The nature of many shared elements of

79. See Goldingay, *Psalms*, 3:103.

Ps 96 and Isaiah and other psalms point toward remixes from the lyrical diffusion (see Hermeneutical Profile of the Use of Scripture in Psalms). Yet the middle of the psalm features verbatim quotation with interpretation.

The psalmist repurposes the old call to worship from the opening of Ps 29. If Ps 29 itself repurposes Canaanite traditions, these get "repaired" in Ps 96. The old call to worship addresses the "celestial beings," or literally the "sons of God," using an old form of the term for the deity.[80] The psalmist replaces "celestial beings" with "families of the peoples" (96:7). Similar expressions appear infrequently elsewhere in contexts with similar ideology—"families of the nations" (22:27[28]) and "families of the lands" (Ezek 20:32).[81] The psalmist calls for others to pilgrimage to Yahweh's sanctuary to worship him (Ps 96:6). This suggests an important reason to change the old call to worship. The euphemistic move strongly indicates Ps 29:1–2 as donor text and Ps 96:7–9 as receptor text. The swapping out of celestial beings for families of peoples goes beyond a euphemistic move. The psalmist already needs to explain in pejorative terms that their gods are worthless (96:5).[82] That means that changing the old call to worship can assist the other toward monotheistic apprehension of Yahweh (italics signify verbatim parallels, and broken underlining signifies interpretative elements):

> *Bestow upon Yahweh* celestial beings,
> *Bestow upon Yahweh glory and strength,*
> *Bestow upon Yahweh the glory of his name.*
> *Bow down to Yahweh in holy splendor.* (29:1–2 lit.)[83]
>
> *Bestow upon Yahweh* families of peoples,
> *Bestow upon Yahweh glory and strength,*
> *Bestow upon Yahweh the glory of his name.*
> Bring an offering and come into his courts.
> *Bow down to Yahweh in holy splendor,*
> Tremble before him all the earth. (96:7–9 lit.)

Psalm 96 domesticates the old call to worship by calling upon terrestrial others to give Yahweh glory (97:7). Psalm 29 depicted the entire cosmos within Yahweh's temple—apparently referring to creation as "temple"—declaring his "glory" (29:9). The psalmist of Ps 96 identifies "all the earth" with the "families of peoples" who come into his courts

80. On the form of the term for deity in Ps 29:1, "sons of God" (בְּנֵי אֵלִים), see beginning of "V אֵל" *HALOT* 1:48.

81. See Hossfeld and Zenger, *Psalms 2*, 465.

82. On "worthless idols" in Ps 96:5, see "אֱלִיל," *HALOT* 1:55–56.

83. The more sophisticated term for "give" (יהב) seems to have the same semantic function as its more common counterpart (נתן). Though many modern committee translations gloss the term by "ascribe" (NIV, NRSV), the sense of "recognize" does not adequately get at "give." The use of "bestow" here follows Goldingay's suggestion (*Psalms*, 3:105).

with gifts. They need to bow down in reverence and trembling before Yahweh in the courts of his temple. In these ways the psalmist boldly guides right response of the other both theologically and with respect to worship.

103:7–8*, 14~Exod 33:13 (B)+34:6* (A)+Gen 2:7 (B) (attribute formula) (* see attribute formula network). The attribute formula appears frequently in Scripture, so it normally resists decisions of allusion to the narrative context in Exod 34 versus a common tradition from lyrical diffusion (see list in attribute formula network). Since Ps 103:7 makes verbal allusion to the narrative context, it indicates Exodus as donor context. The psalmist names Moses, which functions as quasi-marking for a verbatim allusion to the attribute formula. The psalmist uses the attribute formula as a starting point for an exegetical expansion centered around forgiveness. The psalmist comes to a resting place by alluding to the narrative of forming humans by hand in Gen 2. Though Yahweh does not keep anger and removes transgression far away, he "knows" how humans are formed and "remembers" they are dust (Ps 103:14; cf. Gen 2:7; 3:19). Notice the extensive interpretive emphasis the psalmist applies to forgiveness (emphases signify verbal parallels):

> Then Yahweh God **formed** a man from the **dust** of the ground and breathed into his nostrils the breath of life, and the man became a living being. (Gen 2:7)
>
> If you are pleased with me, <u>make known</u> to me your <u>ways</u> so I may know you and continue to find favor with you. Remember that this nation is your people. (Exod 33:13†)
>
> And he passed in front of Moses, proclaiming, "*Yahweh*, Yahweh, the *compassionate and gracious* God, *slow to anger, abounding in love* and faithfulness." (34:6)
>
> He <u>made known</u> his <u>ways</u> to Moses, his deeds to the people of Israel: [8] *Yahweh* is *compassionate and gracious, slow to anger, abounding in love.* [9] He will not always accuse, nor will he harbor his anger forever; [10] he does not treat us as our sins deserve or repay us according to our iniquities. [11] For as high as the heavens are above the earth, so great is his love for those who fear him; [12] as far as the east is from the west, so far has he removed our transgressions from us. [13] As a father has compassion on his children, so Yahweh has compassion on those who fear him; [14] for he knows how we **are formed**, he remembers that we are **dust.** (Ps 103:7–14)

The psalmist uses a series of analogies to depict Yahweh's handling of sin—the separation of heavens and earth, the distance between east and west, and the simile of a father's compassion for his children (103:11, 12, 13). The latter analogy runs along the lines of Moses's comments to the younger generation preparing to enter the land of promise: "Know then in your heart that *as a man disciplines his son*, so Yahweh your God disciplines you" (Deut 8:5, emphasis mine); and again, "There [in the wilderness] you saw how Yahweh your God carried you, *as a father carries his son*, all the way you went until you reached this place" (1:31, emphasis mine). Just as the fatherhood of Yahweh for his people naturally leads to punishment, the very same relationship turns to acts of compassion.

The attribute formula in Exodus continues and speaks of punishing the guilty across the generations, even spelling out "*upon the children, and the children's children*" (Exod 34:7, emphasis mine). The psalmist does not speak to punishment but echoes the reverse side of the transgenerational faithfulness of Yahweh. The psalmist emphasizes Yahweh's constant covenantal loyalty and his righteousness "*to the children's children*" (Ps 103:17, emphasis signifies verbal parallels with Exod 34:7).

In sum, the psalmist puts together a collective message but packaged for the individual congregant (first- and second-person singulars at the beginning and ending). The psalm offers a message badly needed: the extraordinary mercy of Yahweh. The psalm appropriately enjoins twice at the opening and once at the closing, "Bless Yahweh, O my soul" (103:1, 2, 22, lit.).

104~Gen 1 (B) (hymn of creation). Psalm 104 does not conform to day-by-day outlines that try to line it up with the creation days of Gen 1. Such efforts place humans in days three and four, cultivating the land and working under the sun (Ps 104:14, 23).[84] Instead, the psalmist uses the spatial categories or realms of Gen 1 to offer a wisdom tour of completed and populated creation in an idyllic state—without sinners (see below).[85] The framework of the creation days in Gen 1 consists of two sets of three days each—forming the realms on days one, two, three and filling them on days four, five, six. The wisdom tour of Ps 104 takes a vertical and then a horizontal turn. The psalmist starts in the heavens, descends to the earth, and then goes out to sea (see Table P2).

TABLE P2: COMPARING THE STRUCTURES OF GENESIS 1 AND PSALM 104

Genesis 1—Temporal Framework		**Psalm 104—Spatial Framework**
FORMING	FILLING	
day 1 light and darkness	day 4 celestial lights	**heavens** (vv. 2–4)
day 2 waters above and below	day 5 fish and birds	**seas** (vv. 25–26)
day 3 land and vegetation	day 6 land animals and humans	**earth** (vv. 5–23)

84. For a "creation days" diagram of Ps 104, see Averbeck, "Psalms 103 and 104," 142; and see Leonard, "Identifying Subtle Allusions," 100–4. Averbeck also suggests Ps 104 follows a similar sequence compared with the ancient Egyptian Great Hymn to Aten for polemical reasons (parallels listed, 144–45). Lynch rejects this suggestion based on generic evidence ("Monotheism," 343). McCarthy's view that Ps 104 and other biblical poems deal nonpolemically with Israel's relationship with Yahweh according to scriptural traditions better fits the tone and shape of the psalm ("'Creation,'" 405).

85. These wisdom and spatial approaches to Ps 104 are indebted to Berlin, "Wisdom of Creation," 71–83.

Psalm 104 offers nothing like a verse-by-verse interpretation of Gen 1. For the present purposes three major interpretive emphases can be noted. First, Yahweh provides for all creatures. He bounds the waters that provide for land and creatures (104:6–12). He makes vegetation grow to provide nourishment and shelter (104:13–18). But his gifts do more than merely sustain life. Wine gladdens human hearts and oil makes faces shine (104:15). The psalmist presents the cosmic lights as part of the terrestrial realm. The moon of evening and sun of morning, following the days of Gen 1, provide for nocturnal creatures and the human workforce (104:19–23). The psalmist's tour of earth does not focus on the fallenness of creation but on Yahweh's goodness.

Second, like Gen 1, the psalmist attends to the great sea serpents in a special way. Genesis 1:1–2:4 uses the term "create" seven times: three times in the summative narrative frame (Gen 1:1; 2:3, 4), three times to create the humans male and female (1:27), and one time of the great sea serpents (1:21). Even the great sea serpents have been created by God, like all other living beings. For the present purpose it matters little to decide if the great sea monster of Ps 104 refers to whales or multi-headed, fire-breathing poetic creatures, like those found elsewhere in Scripture (Ps 74:14; Job 41:18–21). The psalmist follows the lead of Gen 1:21 by using a creation verb associated with the creation narratives, but not "create." The psalmist uses the term in Gen 2 associated with a potter who personally "forms" humans and animals from the ground (Gen 2:7, 8, 19).[86] Rahab and Leviathan are the two named sea serpents in Scripture (Isa 27:1; 51:9; cf. Ps 89:10[11]).[87] The psalmist says Yahweh "formed" Leviathan "to play" out in the shipping lanes (Ps 104:26). Again, the psalmist's well-chosen verb—"to sport"(NRSV), "to frolic" (NIV), "to play" (KJV)—gets at more than a merely functional creation. The great sea monster embodies the *ethos* of merriment on the seas in contrast to the fearsome description of Leviathan in Job 41. The psalmist's tour of the heavens, earth, and seas idealizes creation as though the human rebellion never was.

Third, the wisdom-shaped creation of Ps 104 brings glory to Yahweh. The purpose of the psalm frames its opening and closing: "Bless Yahweh, O my soul" (104:1, 35 lit.). The psalm includes two key verses that serve as the exegetical endgame of the creational tour.

> How many are your works, Yahweh! *In wisdom you made them all*; the earth is full of your creatures. . . . *May the glory of Yahweh* endure forever; *may Yahweh rejoice* in his works. (104:24, 31, emphasis mine)

Yahweh made all creatures by wisdom. The psalmist thereby shines a light on the source of glory and joy. He speaks an invitation (jussive) toward Yahweh in the third person. And, in all of this, the psalmist waits until the very end to mention "the sinner"

---

86. Also the psalmist uses the special Gen 1 verb "create" (ברא) with Gen 1 and 2 nouns: "Then you send your *Spirit*, they *are created*, and you renew *the face of the ground*" (Ps 104:30, emphasis marks Gen 1 and 2 words).

87. See "תַּנִּין," sec. B *HALOT* 2:1764.

and "the wicked." They vanish and are no more (104:35). The idealized view of creation requires the absence of the sinner.

In sum, the psalmist offers an exegetical, wisdom-shaped, joyful creational tour. The psalmist banishes sin by means of a lyrical presentation of the potential of what Yahweh has made by wisdom for his glory. This joyful poetic view serves to call upon every congregant to say, "Bless Yahweh, O my soul."

105*~Torah compilation (B) (remember the beginnings of the chosen people) (* see Abrahamic covenant network).[88] The psalmist of Ps 105 puts together a long retrospective focusing on the ancestral covenant, divine protection of the Hebrew ancestors, and deliverance from Egypt. Based on a couple of postexilic linguistic elements, namely the function of "to establish a covenant" and "prophet" (Ps 105:10, 15), Emanuel regards Torah as the donor context for Ps 105.[89] Though not without problems, this evidence provides a working approach that will be followed here. The majority of narrative elements in the psalm broadly allude to scriptural traditions in alignment with Torah without exegetical enhancements. For the present purpose a broad overview can be collated into a table followed by targeted interaction with exegetical elements. Note the broad retrospective comparison of Ps 105 (stylized brackets signify non-sequential references; see Table Josh1 for comparative overview):

	narratives	**Psalm 105**
covenant of land with Hebrew ancestors	Gen 15:18–21; 17:8[a]	8–11
sojourning of Hebrew ancestors	12–35	12–15
famine in land	42	16
slavery of Joseph	{37; 39}	17–18
Joseph made lord	{41}	19–22
Israel came to Egypt	46	23
Israel fruitful	Exod 1:7	24
turning against Israel	1:8–22; 2:23–25	25
eight cosmic terrors against land of Ham	7–12	26–36
plundering Egypt and departing	12:33–36	37–38
cloud	13:21–22	39
sea crossing	14	—

(cont.)

88. In addition to many broad allusions (see comparative table), the retrospective of Ps 105 features several probable interpretive allusions, including two quasi-marked allusions: land promise, Ps 105:11; cf. Gen 17:8 and protecting messiahs and prophets, Ps 105:15; cf. Gen 20:6–7. Both of these allusions include quasi-marking which demonstrates intentionality of allusion for author and audience—"saying" (לֵמאֹר) (Ps 105:10[11]); "he rebuked kings" (וַיּוֹכַח . . . מְלָכִים) (105:14).

89. See Emanuel, "Elevation of God," 55.

	narratives	**Psalm 105**
quail, bread of heaven, water	16:1–17:7	40–41
departure with joy and shouting	{14:8; 15:1–21}[b]	42–43
revelation at the mountain	19–20	—
wilderness	Num 1–36	—
conquest and settlement	Josh 1–12	44
to obey precepts and instruction	{Gen 26:5}[c]	45

[a] Like Ps 105:11, two contexts of Genesis use the words "give," "land," and "Canaan/Canaanite" together (Gen 15:18–21; 17:8). The divine promise of land comes up extensively in Genesis (12:1, 7; 13:14–15, 17; 15:7, 13, 16; 22:17; 26:2–5; 28:13–15; 35:12; 46:3–4). List of Abrahamic land texts from Clines, *Theme*, 37–38.

[b] Part of the rationale for redemption in Ps 105:42 is the Abrahamic promise in accord with Exod 2:24.

[c] Genesis 26:5 refers to Abraham "*keeping* commands, *precepts*, and *torah*," and Ps 105:45 "*keeping precepts* and *torah*" (emphasis signifies verbal parallels). Thus, the use of "judgments" in Ps 105:5, while it could encompass Mosaic torah, it could also correspond to divine revelation to the Hebrew ancestors.

Third-person poetry dominates Ps 105 except for two brief citations of direct discourse of Yahweh (Ps 105:11, 15; see footnote and start of note on Ps 105). After referring to the "everlasting covenant" twice (vv. 8, 10), the psalmist quotes Yahweh speaking a key element of the promise for the purposes of the psalm. These two quasi-marked allusions to Genesis affirm Ps 105 as the receptor context. The first citation in verse 11 comes very close to a divine revelation to Abraham in Gen 17—one of only two places where Genesis uses together the terms "give," "land," and "Canaan" (see note a in table above; Table G1 in Genesis Filters). Notice the quasi-marking of the allusion (italics signify verbal parallels, and broken underlining signifies marking):

> *The* whole *land of Canaan*, where you now reside as a foreigner, *I will give* as an everlasting possession to you and your descendants after you; and I will be their God. (Gen 17:8)

> Saying, "To you *I will give the land of Canaan* as the portion you will inherit." (Ps 105:11 lit.)

The term "portion" occurs rarely of the tribal lands and not at all in Torah in that sense (Josh 17:5, 14; 19:9; Ezek 47:13).[90] Genesis only uses "inherit(ance)" of the land of promise one time to refer to Joseph's double portion through Ephraim and Manasseh (Gen 48:6). The psalmist only refers to the land of promise one time as the destiny of the redeemed community (Ps 105:44).

The other citation of Yahweh in direct discourse represents exegetical expansion by the psalmist (v. 15). The psalmist seems to refer broadly to Abimelek's dream, in which

90. See "II חֶבֶל," no. 3 *HALOT* 1:286.

God uses the term "prophet" for the first time in Scripture. The psalmist presents this direct divine discourse quasi-marked, signaling it by a shift to first-person pronouns after a verb of speech (emphases signify verbal parallels, and broken underlining signifies quasi-marking):[91]

> Then God said to him in the dream, "Yes, I know you did this with a clear conscience, and so I have kept you from sinning against me. That is why I did not let you *touch* her. Now return the man's wife, for he is a *prophet*, and he will pray for you and you will live. But if you do not return her, you may be sure that you and all who belong to you will die." (Gen 20:6–7)

> He allowed no one to oppress them; for their sake he rebuked kings: "Do not *touch* my anointed ones; do my *prophets* no harm." (Ps 105:14–15)

Aaron becomes the first recognized "messiah" in Scripture (Lev 8:12). The concept of publicly anointing with oil those divinely appointed for service offers enough flexibility for the psalmist to associate the concept with the Hebrew ancestors.[92] The rareness of "prophet" in Genesis (only Gen 20:6) and the prohibition against touching my anointed ones in Ps 105:15 suggests the referents are Abraham and Sarah. Abraham is a prophet (Gen 20:6) and Sarah is the mother of many kings (17:16). In that way the psalmist may be poetically referring to Abraham and Sarah as "anointed ones." The repetitive chiastic structure of Ps 105:15 closely associates the verbs and nouns of the A and B lines, strengthening an allusion to a specific donor context.[93] The plurality of "kings," "prophets," and "messiahs" in Ps 105:14–15 applies to all of the Hebrew patriarchs and matriarchs delivered from other threats, even if the language of the divine quotation evokes references to Sarah (mother of anointed ones) and Abraham (prophet) in the dreamed threat against Abimelek (king).

The fetters of Joseph may be the most notable gap-filling addition of Ps 105 not found in the Torah narratives. "They bruised his [Joseph's] feet with shackles, his neck was put in irons" in Ps 105:18 does not echo anything similar in Genesis. The language does not overlap with bruising the heel in Gen 3:15. The term for "shackles" only appears in Pss 105:18 and 149:8. The psalmist's poetic embellishment of Joseph's bondage may figurally associate his experiences with the exiles of Judah.[94] Berlin suggests several possible

---

91. In spite of a verb of speech and shift to first person discourse, the addressees plural are "kings" (Ps 105:14). This pluralization seems to generalize the incident with Abimelek in Gen 20 as representative. For that reason the phrase "for their sake he rebuked kings" (וַיּוֹכַח עֲלֵיהֶם מְלָכִים) (105:14) is considered quasi-marked instead of marked.

92. On gender-inclusive use of masculine nouns (or adjectival substantive in the case of "messiah"), see GKC §122a.

93. "(a) Do not touch (b) my anointed ones; (b) and my prophets (a) do not harm" (אַל־תִּגְּעוּ בִמְשִׁיחָי וְלִנְבִיאַי אַל־תָּרֵעוּ) (Ps 105:15 lit.).

94. See Allen, *Psalms 101–150*, 43; Won, *Remembering*, 112–13.

connections between the extra Joseph imagery and exile, such as, "Free yourself from the chains on your neck, Daughter Zion, now a captive" (Isa 52:2).[95]

The account of ten cosmic terrors of Exodus suggests strong literary character in its arrangement—three sets of three, then one more.[96] Elsewhere Ps 78 rehearses seven divine judgments against Egypt that Ephraim "did not remember" (Ps 78:42). Psalm 105 presents eight of the horrific signs against "the land of Ham" following the sequence of Exodus with one exception, darkness first (105:28). The psalmist peppers the cosmic terror list with references to "their land" (105:27, 30, 32, 35, 36) referring back to the "land of Ham" (105:23, 27). This constant repetition emphasizes that the chosen people of the Hebrew ancestors "sojourned" somewhere else (105:23). Living in "their land" negatively points toward the land Yahweh gave Israel (105:11, 44).

The purpose of the psalmist's long retrospective relates to the series of imperatives in the opening verses directed to the congregation, whom he identifies as "the seed of Abraham" (105:6).[97] The psalmist calls his audience to praise, call out, make known (v. 1), sing, make music, praise (v. 2), praise, rejoice (v. 3), seek, seek (v. 4), and remember (v. 5).[98] Remarkably, the long list of terms does not appear in the retrospective itself. Two of the more important examples are illustrative. The emphasized nouns in "He brought out his people with *rejoicing*, his chosen ones with *shouts of joy*" (105:43) do not share common roots with any of the series of verbs, or their objects when applicable, just listed in the psalm's opening. The only exception concerns one of the objects the psalmist calls the seed of Abraham to remember, namely, "the signs" Moses and Aaron performed in the land of Ham: "Remember the wonders he has done, his *signs*, and the judgments he pronounced" (105:5†, emphasis mine; cf. v. 27). The distinctness of the language in the opening of Ps 105 suggests that the entire redemptive storyline of the ancestral election, sojourning, and redemption—all of it together—represents the singularity of his everlasting covenant with Abraham, Isaac, and Jacob (105:8, 10).

The only use of the terms "commands," "precepts," and "torah" in Genesis appears in the oracle to Isaac. The connection between Abraham's obedience to commands, precepts, and torah and the promise of the land sets up the psalmist's closing unrealized retrospection, which is that the chosen seed might keep the precepts and the torah (italics signify verbal parallels):

> [Yahweh explains to Isaac] I . . . *will give* them all these *lands*, and through your offspring all nations on earth will be blessed because Abraham obeyed me and did everything I required of him, keeping my commands, my *precepts* and my *torah*. (Gen 26:5†)

---

95. See Berlin, "Interpreting Torah," 29–30.

96. See Schnittjer, *Torah Story*, 228–30, esp. Table 13-D and 13-E.

97. Emanuel also identifies the purpose of the psalmist's use of Scripture with the psalm's opening, but he restricts his attention to the first two verses and comes to different conclusions ("Elevation of God," 64).

98. On the two different but synonymous terms for seeking (דרשׁ, בקשׁ) often used in worship contexts, see discussion with Table C2 in Chronicles.

> He *gave* them *the lands* of the nations, and they fell heir to what others had toiled for—
> that they [the ancestors] might *keep* his *precepts* and observe his *torah.* (Ps 105:44–45)

Though for Israel the precepts and torah included the revelation at the mountain, the psalmist carefully uses language that can connect the congregation with the obedience of Abraham. But there is more.

The psalmist casts the call to remember noted above as inclusive of divine acts and legal revelation. Notice how the psalmist uses the term "judgment" in a semantically open manner to envelop all that follows in the retrospective—everlasting covenant, sojourning, redemption, and opportunity to reenter the land and obey the precepts and torah. "Remember the wonders he has done, his miracles, and *the judgments he pronounced*" (105:5, emphasis mine). The "judgments he pronounced" in this context denote the everlasting covenant and all that means—protection during sojourning, redemption, restoration of land, and precepts and torah.

In sum, the psalmist carefully uses language in the opening of the psalm to unify the entire redeeming work of Yahweh within the everlasting covenant to Abraham. He calls the congregation, the seed of Abraham, to remember the judgments he pronounced in such a way as to inextricably bind together the entire Torah narrative and instructional tradition. The ancient ancestral sojourning contributes hope to the identity of the people sojourning as exiles in the empire.

106*~Torah, narrative, and prophets compilation (B) (confession of ancestral sin) (* see collective confession network). The nature of many of the parallels suggests Ps 106 as receptor. The clearest examples include integrating "reckoning of righteous" (Gen 15:6) into a Phinehas allusion (Num 25) in Ps 106:31 and bringing together details from the priestly and Deuteronomic accounts of the rebellion at Meribah in 106:32–33 (cf. Num 20:1–13; Deut 1:37; 3:26; 4:21). These make sense with the Torah traditions as donor contexts but not with Ps 106 as donor context. It would be unreasonable to argue that the narrators of Numbers and Deuteronomy independently borrowed discrete and nonoverlapping elements tightly interwoven together in Ps 106. The same kind of observations can be made of the psalmist's use of distinctive elements from the prophets, most notably from Ezekiel, as discussed below. In short, close verbal parallels of distinctive language from many contexts require dependence and make it seem like the psalmist of Ps 106 freely drew together from Torah and prophets much like the canonical versions. This evidence becomes even more important because of the use of Ps 106 in 1 Chr 16, which presupposes the closing benediction to Book IV of the Psalter, revoiced as narrative (Ps 106:48; 1 Chr 16:35–36).[99] The much-contested relationship between Leviticus and Ezekiel needs to be settled elsewhere, but the rest can be summarized working backwards. Chronicles in its present form dates no earlier than six generations after Zerubbabel

99. This observation is not new, see Kirkpatrick, *Psalms Books IV and V*, 634.

(1 Chr 3:18–24), about 400 BCE (see note on 2 Chr 36:22–23). Psalms 96, 105, and 106 including the benediction of Book IV, all from Book IV of the Psalter, serve as donor contexts and 1 Chr 16 as receptor context. Psalm 106 features the evidence necessary to determine with a high degree of probability that it is a receptor context for elements of Genesis, Exodus, Numbers, Deuteronomy, and Ezekiel. Although this evidence does not nail down absolute dating, it helps confirm the relative priority of cases with the evidence necessary to determine direction of dependence.

Psalm 106 features a prayer of confession shaped by Leviticus and 1 Kgs 8 (see esp. Ps 106:6, 45–46). The presence of Deuteronomistic ideology complements Lev 26 through the psalm, though the important repentance language of Deut 30 gets mediated by the prayer of Solomon (1 Kgs 8:47; Ps 106:6). As such, Ps 106 should be associated with the small constellation of prayers shaped by Lev 26 and Deut 30, including Ezra 9:6–15; Neh 1:5–11; Dan 9:4–19; Septuagintal Esth 14:3–19; and Bar 1:15–3:8.[100] The most important common denominator of these prayers can be identified as collective confession. In Lev 26:40–45 and Deut 30:2–5 collective confession activates Yahweh to remember the ancient covenant and restore his people. Notice how the psalmist sets up and concludes his long retrospective by echoing Solomon and Leviticus (emphases signify verbal parallels):

> But if they will confess their sins and the sins of their **ancestors**. . . . But for their sake I will **remember the covenant** with their ancestors whom I brought out of Egypt in the sight of the nations to be their God. I am Yahweh. (Lev 26:40a, 45; cf. v. 42)

> *Hear the cry* and the prayer that your servant is praying in your presence this day. . . . If they have a change of heart in the land where they are held captive, and repent and plead with you in the land of their captors and say, "We have sinned, we have done wrong, we have acted wickedly," . . . *cause their captors to show them mercy.* (1 Kgs 8:28b, 47, 50b)

> We have sinned, even as our **ancestors** did; we have done wrong and acted wickedly. . . . Yet he took note of their distress when he *heard* their *cry* for their sake he **remembered** his **covenant** and out of his great love he relented. He *caused all who held them captive to show them mercy.* (Ps 106:6, 44–46)

Psalm 106 provides a collective confession for exiles to repent and activate Yahweh's covenantal mercy. This purpose drives the exegetical advances of the retrospective housed in Ps 106:7–46. The psalmist's lead-in further connects by a call to corporate worship (106:1–3) that underlines the place of individual responsibility in calling upon Yahweh to remember (106:4–5).

---

100. See Schnittjer, "Bad Ending," 52.

For the present purposes a broad overview of the retrospective is presented in a table followed by an examination of a few important exegetical advances. Note the broad retrospective comparison of Ps 106 including verbal parallels in most cases (see Table Josh1 for comparative overview with other retrospectives):

	allusions	**Psalm 106‡**
Opening purpose frame: collective confession	1 Kgs 8:47//2 Chr 6:37[a]	6
Sea crossing		
rebellion at the sea	Exod 14:11–12	7
salvation for his name's sake	Ezek 20:9	8
rebuke the sea	Isa 50:2; 63:13	9–10
waters cover enemies	Exod 14:28	11
they believe and sing	Exod 14:31; 15:1, 11, 21	12
Wilderness temptations		
they forgot in the wilderness	Num 11:4, 6; Exod 17:2, 7	13–15
jealous of Moses and Aaron	Num 16:3–7	16
earth swallows Dathan and Abiram	Deut 11:6[b]	17
wicked incinerated	Num 16:26, 35	18
Golden calf		
worship calf at Horeb	Exod 32:1–6	19
exchanged glory	Jer 2:11; Hos 4:7	20
forgot great things in Egypt and at the sea	Exod 7–12, 14	21–22
Moses stood in the breach	Deut 9:25–26[c]	23
Rebellion at Kadesh		
despise land and not believe	Num 14:31+Deut 1:32	24
grumbled in their tents	Deut 1:27	25
he swore to scatter them	Ezek 20:23[d]	26–27
Rebellion at Shittim		
attach themselves to Baal of Peor	Num 25:2–3	28
provoked Yahweh to send plague	Num 25:4–5[e]	29
Phinehas intervenes	Num 25:7–8	30
Phinehas reckoned righteous forever	Gen 15:6+Num 25:12–13	31

(cont.)

	allusions	Psalm 106[‡]
Rebellion at Meribah		
Moses sins during rebellion at Meribah	Num 20:1–13+Deut 1:37; 3:26; 4:21	32–33
Rebellion in the land		
they did not destroy peoples	Judg 1:21, 27, 29–31; 2:2[f]	34
mingled and became ensnared	Judg 3:5–6[g]	35–36
child sacrifice to demons and blood pollutes land	Deut 12:31+32:17+Num 35:33–34[h]	37–38
prostituted themselves	Exod 34:16; Deut 31:16	39
Exile		
Yahweh angry and gave into hand of enemies	Judg 2:14, 20; 3:8; 10:7	40–42
many deliverances then brought low	Judg 3–16[i]	43
he hears their cry	1 Kgs 8:28[j]	44
he remembers the covenant	Lev 26:42, 45[k]	45
he causes captors to show mercy	1 Kgs 8:50[a]	46
Closing frame: gather us from the nations	Ezek 36:23, 24[l]	47

[‡] Many parallels of Ps 106 are from Kirkpatrick, *Psalms Books IV and V*, 624–34.

[a] Solomon's prayer of 1 Kgs 8:47 itself echoes Lev 26:40 (with close language, cf. Jer 14:20; Dan 9:5).

[b] Psalm 106:17 seems to follow Deut 11:6 without mention of Korah (Num 16:30–33), which corresponds to Num 26:9–11.

[c] Psalm 106:23 seems to allude to the version of Moses's intercession in Deut 9:25–26, which also uses the term "destroy" (שחת) (cf. Exod 32:10).

[d] Psalm 106:26 uses "raised the hand" (lit.) as in Ezek 20:23 (vs. "swore" [שבע] Deut 1:34). In Ezek 20:23 the prophet uses the Leviticus term for "scatter" (זרה) (Lev 26:33), which appears in Ps 106:27. Boda notes that "scattering" (זרה *Piel*) "when used in reference to a nation is always used for the exile of that nation," thus linking exile to the wilderness generation (*Severe Mercy*, 440–41).

[e] Psalm 106:29 tells of the plague at Baal Peor in Num 25:4–5 but uses a characteristic Deuteronomy term "provoke" (כעס) (cf. Deut 4:25; 9:18; 31:29; 32:16, 19, 21, 27).

[f] Psalm 106:34 refers to failure of the people to drive out the nations of Canaan as noted repeatedly in Judg 1. This failure relates to the commands in Exod 23:32–33; 34:12–13; Deut 7:1–2. But Ps 106:34 uses the term "destroy" (שמד); elsewhere with this sense only in Deut 7:24.

[g] Psalm 106:35–36 presents the situation summarized in Judg 3:5–6 but uses the term "snare" appearing in Exod 23:33; 34:12; Deut 7:16; Josh 23:13; Judg 2:3; 8:27. For other terminology from Judges in Ps 106, see Swale, "Structure," 404–7.

[h] The term for "demons" only appears in Deut 32:17 and Ps 106:37 making allusion probable (see "שֵׁד," *HALOT* 2:1418). Psalm 106:37–38 infers the child sacrifice produced the "innocent blood" that "polluted" the land. But Ps 106:38 more closely echoes the murderous blood "poured out" to "pollute" land in Num 35:33–34. The expression "innocent blood" does not get used of child sacrifice per se, but is a Deuteronomistic expression for injustice (Deut 19:10; 21:8; 27:25; 2 Kgs 21:16; 24:4; cf. Ezek 24:7; 36:8). The unusual term for "pollute" (חנף) is only applied to land in Num 35:33; Jer 3:1; and Ps 106:38 (cf. normal cultic language in Lev 18:25).

[i] Psalm 106:43 uses distinct language but similar ideas found in Lev 26:39; Ezek 24:23; 33:10.

[j] Psalm 106:44 uses the term "distress" that appears in 1 Kgs 8:28.

[k] Psalm 106:45 uses "remember" the covenant, strongly echoing Lev 26:42, 45, but blends in the terms "relents," which echoes Exod 32:14, and "great covenantal loyalty," which echoes Exod 34:6.

[l] Psalm 106:47 strongly echoes the language and sense of Ezek 36:23, 24, but also uses the term "praise" (תְּהִלָּה) from Ps 106:12, which echoes Exod 15:11. For other catchwords on this set of connections see below.

The psalmist turns to Ezekiel to offer interpretation of the sea crossing. The psalmist rehearses the rebellion of the people at the sea to emphasize how quickly they had forgotten the works of Yahweh (Ps 106:7; cf. Exod 14:11–12). Ezekiel 20 explains how Yahweh delivered the people from Egypt even while they refused to turn from idolatry (Ezek 20:7–8; also see Table Ezk2). Ezekiel 20:9 provides two theological rationales for salvation at the sea even in the face of Israel's rebellion (italics signify verbal parallels):

> But *for the sake of* my *name*, I brought them out of Egypt. I did it to keep my name from being profaned in the eyes of the nations among whom they lived and in whose sight I *had made* myself *known* to the Israelites. (Ezek 20:9)

> Yet he saved them *for* his *name's sake*, to *make* his mighty power *known*. (Ps 106:8)

The psalmist borrows both of Ezekiel's rationales. Yahweh did not deliver Israel because they deserved it. He saved them for the sake of his own name and to reveal his mighty power to his people. These reasons serve the ends of the psalmist's retrospective calling his audience to repent.

The sequence of the retrospective does not follow the order of events in the Torah narratives. The most notable alternate arrangements include the rebellion with the calf (Ps 106:19–23) and Moses's sin at Meribah (106:32–33). The former features the psalmist's distinctive description of Moses who "stood in the breach" to intercede for the people (106:23). This connects with Phinehas who "stood up and interceded" during the debacle at Baal Peor (106:30) (see below).

The psalmist often closely works out interpretive blending of synoptic parallels. He does not seek to harmonize (see on Moses's sin below). Instead, the psalmist seems to take advantage of variations to craft his poetic prayer. In the case of the rebellion at Kadesh the psalmist blends Numbers's quickly narrated public rebellion with Deuteronomy's methodical individual defiance (see note on Deut 1:19–45) (emphases signify verbal parallels, and broken underlining signifies ironic allusion):

> In this wilderness your corpses shall fall—all who were counted in the census from twenty years and upward, who grumbled [לון] against me. Not one of you will come into the land which I lifted up my hand for you to reside in it . . . the land which you rejected. But you, your corpses shall fall in this wilderness. (Num 14:29, 30a, 31b, 32 lit.)

> **You grumbled to yourselves** [רגן] **in your tents** and said, "Yahweh hates us. He brought us out of Egypt to give us into the hand of the Amorites to destroy us." . . . But in spite of this word [of Moses's encouragement] *you did not believe* in Yahweh your God. (Deut 1:27, 32 lit.)

> They rejected the pleasant land, *they did not believe* in his word. **They grumbled to themselves [רגן] in their tents** and they did not obey the voice of Yahweh. So he lifted up his hand against them that he would make them fall in the wilderness. (Ps 106:24–26 lit.)

Just as the psalmist introduces the psalm with collective and individual emphases, so too he works with the accounts of rebellion in both Numbers and Deuteronomy to focus on overlapping personal and corporate responsibility in ancient Israel.[101]

After summarizing the rebellion at Baal Peor, the psalmist interprets the significance of what Phinehas did. The use of the verbs "stood and intervened" partially echoes the description the psalmist earlier coined to describe Moses's prayerful intercession, "stood in the breach" (106:23, 31). In this way Moses and Phinehas represent two ways of interceding for others. The mediatorial roles offer important motivation for a prayer of confession the psalmist provides for his audience to offer on behalf of themselves and their ancestors (106:6). The psalmist's use of a well-known phrase from Genesis to characterize Phinehas's zealous actions seems even more startling (emphases signify verbal parallels):

> Abram believed Yahweh, and he **credited it to him as righteousness.** (Gen 15:6)

> *Phinehas* son of Eleazar, the son of Aaron, the priest, has turned my anger away from the Israelites. Since he was as zealous for my honor among them as I am, I did not put an end to them in my zeal. . . . He and his descendants will have a covenant of an *endless* priesthood, because he was zealous for the honor of his God and made atonement for the Israelites. (Num 25:11, 13†)

> So he said he would destroy them—had not Moses, his chosen one, stood in the breach [פֶּרֶץ] before him to keep his wrath from destroying them. (Ps 106:23)

> They aroused Yahweh's anger by their wicked deeds, and a plague broke out [פרץ] among them. But *Phinehas* stood up and intervened, and the plague was checked. This was **credited to him as righteousness** for *endless* generations to come. (106:29–31)

The psalmist uses the verbal form of "break out" (פרץ) to describe the plague at Baal Peor in order to make a connotative parallel between Moses who "stood in the breach" (פֶּרֶץ, noun) and Phinehas who "stood up and intervened" in the plague that was "breaking out" (106:23, 29, 30). The phrase "credited to him as righteousness" appears only in Gen 15:6 and Ps 106:31, making allusion as certain as possible. The psalmist's connection attaches a rationale to the everlasting covenant (Num 25:13) based on Phinehas's

101. See Schnittjer, "Kadesh Infidelity," 116–17.

act of faithful intervention (Ps 106:31; cf. Gen 15:6). Though the fall of Jerusalem has suspended the enactment of the Davidic covenant, the psalmist affirms that the priestly covenant remains intact.[102]

The rebellion at Meribah seems to be placed at the end of the wilderness journeys in this retrospective to climactically emphasize the sin of Moses. The situation with the sin of Moses in Torah creates challenges. The narrators of Numbers and Deuteronomy repeatedly blame Moses for his sin while Moses repeatedly blames the people (see note on Deut 1:19–45). The psalmist does not harmonize these details but unflinchingly places them side by side, even strengthening the case against Moses (bold and underlining signify verbal parallels, and italics and broken underlining signify similarity):

> But Yahweh said to Moses and Aaron, "Because you did not trust in me enough to honor me as holy in the sight of the Israelites, you will not bring this community into the land I give them." (Num 20:12)
>
> [Yahweh said] for when the community rebelled at **the waters** in the Desert of Zin, both of you disobeyed my command to honor me as holy before their eyes. (27:14a)
>
> [Moses said] *Because of* you Yahweh became angry with me also and said, "You shall not enter it, either." . . . But because of you Yahweh was angry with me and would not listen to me. "That is enough," Yahweh said. "Do not speak to me anymore about this matter." . . . Yahweh was angry with me *because of* you, and he solemnly swore that I would not cross the Jordan and enter the good land Yahweh your God is giving you as your inheritance. (Deut 1:37; 3:26; 4:21)
>
> [Yahweh said] This is because both of you broke faith with me in the presence of the Israelites at **the waters of Meribah** Kadesh in the Desert of Zin and because you did not uphold my holiness among the Israelites. (32:51)
>
> They provoked him to anger by **the waters of Meribah**, so it went badly for Moses *because of* them, for they made his spirit bitter, and he spoke rashly with his own mouth. (Ps 106:32–33 lit.)[103]

The psalmist seeks to blame everyone for their rebellion—the people and Moses. The psalmist notes that Moses can rightly cast blame on the people, since the narrator of Numbers interchanges "the people contended [ריב] with Moses" and "the people of Israel contended [ריב] with Yahweh" (Num 20:3, 13), both of which play off the name Meribah

102. For both of these points, see Hossfeld and Zenger, *Psalms 3*, 91.

103. "Speak rashly" (בטא) is in Piel in Ps 106:33 with a negative connotation akin to when this root is in its noun form in Num 30:7, 9 (see "בָּטָא," "מִבְטָא," BDB 104, 105).

(מְרִיבָה). But the psalmist quickly affirms and even strengthens Moses's responsibility: "he spoke rashly with his own mouth" (Ps 106:33 lit.). The psalmist sympathizes with Moses to a point but then makes clear he spoke wrongly of his own accord. In short, the psalmist brings together in one place the apparent incongruity without letting anyone off the hook.[104]

As noted above, the psalmist had used language from Ezek 20:9 to describe the sea crossing at the beginning of the retrospective to show how Yahweh's deliverance would "make known" his "mighty acts" (Ps 106:8; cf. v. 2). The psalmist goes on to show how Israel believed and "sang his praise," echoing "sing" in Exod 15:1, 21 and "praise" (תְּהִלָּה) in 15:11 (106:12). These catchwords help explain why the psalmist closes the psalm as he does with another allusion to Ezekiel, all to answer the question posed in Ps 106:2 (bold and italics signify verbal parallels with Ezekiel, and broken underlining signifies catchwords in Ps 106):[105]

> I will show **the holiness of** my great **name**, which has been profaned among the nations, the name you have profaned among them. Then the nations will know that I am Yahweh, declares Sovereign Yahweh, when I am proved **holy** through you before their eyes. For I will take you out of *the nations*; I *will gather* you from all the countries and bring you back into your own land. (Ezek 36:23–24)

> Who can proclaim the mighty acts [גְּבוּרָה] of Yahweh or fully declare his praise [תְּהִלָּה]? (Ps 106:2)

> Yet he saved them for his name's sake, to make his mighty acts [גְּבוּרָה] known. (106:8†; cf. Ezek 20:9 with Ps 106:8 above)

> Save us, Yahweh our God, and *gather* us from *the nations*, that we may give thanks to your **holy name** and glory in your praise [תְּהִלָּה]. (Ps 106:47)

The opening question asks, "Who can proclaim the mighty acts of Yahweh or fully declare his praise?" (106:2). The psalmist offers two answers. Israel did when Yahweh delivered them at the sea and the psalmist's congregation will when they call upon Yahweh to deliver them from the nations (106:12, 47).

In sum, the psalmist's burden starts and ends with motivating the congregation to confess their sin and that of their ancestors to activate the covenantal promises. But

---

104. See the discussion of Deut 1:37; 3:26; and 4:21 in the note on Deut 1:19–45. And see Schnittjer, "Kadesh Infidelity," 117.

105. Westermann suggests that Ezekiel's importance to the psalmists of Psalms 78 and 106, relates, in part, to tracing Israel's rebellion from its earliest history in the retrospectives of Ezek 16, 20, 23 (*Praise and Lament*, 241).

confession and effective intercession do not come easy. The psalmist uses Moses and Phinehas as models of intercession for moments when Israel was under pressure. These brief models of rightful response stand amid a collective confession of the sin that led to exile. The hoped-for gathering from the nations will make known Yahweh's mighty acts to the nations and to Israel.

109:9–15~Exod 20:5*//Deut 5:9* (C) (request for transgenerational judgment) (* see attribute formula network). Several Scriptures seek to explain the threat of transgenerational judgment in the second commandment and its derivative appearance in the attribute formula (Exod 20:5//Deut 5:9; Exod 34:7; see notes on Exod 34:14–16; Deut 7:9–10). Psalm 109 houses a much-debated cursing that calls upon God to apply terrible judgments to a person's children and parents (Ps 109:9–14). Among the so-called imprecatory psalms, Ps 109 stands out for its vicious desires.

The view of Ps 109 taken here regards Ps 109:6–19 as the psalmist laying before God the ill words being spoken against him. The difficulty stems from the ill words being unmarked, which some modern committee translations "fix" by adding "They say" in 109:6 and putting quotation marks around 106:6–19 (see NRSV, REB, NEB). Although "They say" does not appear in the Hebrew text of 109:6, the syntax switches from plural referents in 106:1–5, 20–31 to singular in 109:6–19. This grammatical shift matches Fox's third criterion for identifying unmarked quotations.[106] In addition, the latter part of the psalm refers back to the quoted charges to show that they falsely represent the accused (cf. 109:22 with v. 16; 109:29 with v. 18). Elsewhere Scripture tells of Hezekiah bringing a letter against him before Yahweh (2 Kgs 19:14, 16//Isa 37:14, 17).[107] This evidence suggests that Ps 109:6–19 represents malicious words against the accused cited at length in his pleas before God.[108] The psalmist's own appeal against his accusers runs along the lines of Deut 19:19 (Ps 109:20).

The strenuous request to apply the accused's judgment to his parents and children seems to play off the transgenerational threat of judgment, whether or not it is a quotation, as suggested above. The speaker of Ps 109:6–19 extends the transgenerational judgment upward to include the accused's parents (Ps 109:14–15, contra Deut 24:16). The other surprise amounts to calling upon God to turn away from his normal practice of caring for widows and orphans (Ps 109:10–13, contra Deut 24:17–18; cf. Exod 22:22–24[21–23]). Note the extensive requests for evil upon those typically protected by scriptural legal standards (italics signify verbal parallels):

---

106. See Fox, "Identification of Quotations," 423, 431. Fox remains on the fence regarding the identification of Ps 109:6–19 as a quotation (423–24). For further discussion of identifying unmarked quotations, see note on Job 21:19.

107. These arguments are from Booij, "Psalm 109:6–19," 91–106, esp. 92–94, 105–6. For a similar line of argument that see verses 6–19 as evidence quoted in a case against the accused, see Jenkins, "Quotation in Psalm 109," 115–35.

108. For an opposing view, see Fishbane, who does not regard Ps 109:6–19 as a quotation. He takes the "vindictive appeal" as playing off the retributive side of the attribute formula to give "vibrancy to notions of deferred and vicarious punishment" (*Biblical Interpretation*, 347–48).

> You shall not bow down to them or worship them; for I, Yahweh your God, am a jealous God, punishing *the children* for *the iniquity* of the parents to the third and fourth generation of those who hate me. (Exod 20:5//Deut 5:9†)

> And he passed in front of Moses, proclaiming, "Yahweh, Yahweh, the compassionate and *merciful* God, slow to anger, abounding in love and faithfulness, maintaining *kindness* to thousands, and forgiving wickedness, rebellion and sin. Yet he does not leave the guilty unpunished; he punishes *the children* and their children for *the iniquity* of the parents to the third and fourth generation." (Exod 34:6–7†)

> May *his children* be fatherless and his wife a widow. [10] May *his children* be wandering beggars; may they be driven from their ruined homes. [11] May a creditor seize all he has; may strangers plunder the fruits of his labor. [12] May no one extend *kindness* to him or *show mercy* on his fatherless children. [13] May his descendants be cut off, their names blotted out from the next generation. [14] May *the iniquity* of his fathers be remembered before Yahweh; may the sin of his mother never be blotted out. [15] May their sins always remain before Yahweh, that he may blot out their name from the earth. (Ps 109:9–15, v. 12†)

The need to stand in the place of God and advise the deity on what can only be a divine prerogative—the condemnation of sinners—seems like the most pernicious element of the ill wishes. The ill-wisher transcends the human place. The specific realities of the divine transgenerational threat in the second commandment and the attribute formula remain sealed up in the hiddenness of divine counsel. The Hebrew Bible affirms exactly the opposite views of the ill-wisher, expressing Yahweh's protection for the other and enemies (e.g., Exod 23:4–5; Lev 19:33–34; Prov 24:17–18; 25:21). In many places the New Testament carries forward the scriptural *ethos* of mercy to the other and the enemy (e.g., Matt 5:43–48; Luke 10:25–37; Rom 12:14–21).

In sum, nothing about Ps 109 is easy. The view here regards the interpretative allusion of the accuser as an example of wrongful exegesis that presumes to take the place belonging to God alone. The counterarguments of the accused in the latter part of Ps 109 show that the would-be advisor of divine retribution badly misses the mark.

110:1*~1 Kgs 5:3, 5[17, 19]* (C) (enemies under feet of Davidic son) (* see Davidic covenant network). The present discussion does not sort through or engage the many competing interpretations of Ps 110:1 in the commentaries and other studies.[109] This note only addresses a possible parallel to the scriptural tradition in 1 Kgs 5:3, 5[17, 19] and matters that bear directly upon it.

---

109. For overview of numerous interpretations see Hossfeld and Zenger, *Psalms 3*, 143–45.

Psalm 110:1 features a divine oracle marked as direct discourse, namely, "Yahweh says to my lord" (Ps 110:1). This may infer that the psalmist serves in a prophetic capacity presenting immediate revelation or that the psalmist cites revelation from a prophet. For example, David and Solomon refer to the Davidic promise mediated by the prophet Nathan as though it was directly mediated to David (emphases mine).

> [Solomon] . . . *as Yahweh told my father David, when he said,* "Your son whom I will put on the throne in your place will build the temple for my Name." (1 Kgs 5:5[19])

> David said to Solomon: "My son, I had it in my heart to build a house for the Name of Yahweh my God. [8] But *this word of Yahweh came to me*: 'You have shed much blood and have fought many wars. You are not to build a house for my Name, because you have shed much blood on the earth in my sight. [9] But you will have a son who will be a man of peace and rest, and I will give him rest from all his enemies on every side. His name will be Solomon, and I will grant Israel peace and quiet during his reign.'" (1 Chr 22:7–9)

> [David] *But God said to me,* "You are not to build a house for my Name, because you are a warrior and have shed blood." . . . *He said to me*: "Solomon your son is the one who will build my house and my courts, for I have chosen him to be my son, and I will be his father." (28:3, 6)

These contexts speak of the promise without reference to the prophetic mediator Nathan who delivered Yahweh's message to David (see 2 Sam 7:4, 17//1 Chr 17:3, 15). In the case of David's presentation of the message to Solomon, he frames it in a manner syntactically similar to the way prophetic oracles are ascribed to the prophets in biblical prophetic collections. Compare what David says: "*the word of Yahweh was* upon me, *saying*" (1 Chr 22:8 lit.) with "*the word of Yahweh was* to Jonah . . . *saying*" (Jonah 1:1 lit.) and also with "*the word of Yahweh* that *was* to Joel" (Joel 1:1 lit.; cf. Jer 1:2; Mic 1:1; Zeph 1:1) (emphases mark verbal parallels and syntactical similarities).[110] In addition, other psalms present poetic adaptation of the Davidic promise as direct discourse to a royal figure (Ps 2:7; cf. 2 Sam 7:14) or to David (Ps 132:11–12; cf. 2 Sam 7:12–14). In sum of this point, the psalmist of Ps 110:1 did not need to be the prophet himself. The psalmist could present an oracle mediated by a prophet as direct discourse from Yahweh.

The potential parallel between Ps 110:1 and Solomon's communication to Hiram relates to similar imagery and themes (bold marks verbal parallels).[111]

---

110. Note: "the word of Yahweh was upon me, saying" (וַיְהִי עָלַי דְּבַר־יהוה לֵאמֹר) (1 Chr 22:8 lit.); "the word of Yahweh that was to Joel" (דְּבַר־יהוה אֲשֶׁר הָיָה אֶל־יוֹאֵל) (Joel 1:1 lit.); "the word of Yahweh was to Jonah . . . saying" (וַיְהִי דְּבַר־יהוה אֶל־יוֹנָה . . . לֵמאֹר) (Jonah 1:1 lit.).

111. Parallel imagery in 1 Kgs 5:3[17] and Ps 110:1 suggested by Gray, *I & II Kings*, 151; Cogan, *1 Kings*, 226.

> You know that because of the wars waged against my father David from all sides, he could not build a temple for the Name of Yahweh his God **until Yahweh** put his enemies under his **feet**. . . . I intend, therefore, to build a temple for the Name of Yahweh my God, as Yahweh told my father David, when he said, "Your son whom I will put on the throne in your place will build the temple for my Name." (1 Kgs 5:3, 5[17, 19])[112]

> **Yahweh** says to my lord: "Sit at my right hand **until** I make your enemies a footstool for your **feet**." (Ps 110:1)

The mention of a footstool for a king in Scripture only appears in Ps 110:1 as elsewhere it refers to the ark or Jerusalem (as a footstool of Yahweh).[113] The potential parallel between 1 Kgs 5:3 and Ps 110:1 pivots on the possible overlap between opponents underfoot and enemies as a footstool.

Ancient visual depictions of enthroned kings with feet on a footstool appear frequently.[114] The mention of enemies underfoot in Scripture refers to their abject submission (cf. Josh 10:24). In ancient inscriptions and iconography these two ideas can appear together such as in a victory of the Assyrian king Tukulti-Ninurta I (1243–1207 BCE): "With the support of the gods Ashur, Enlil and Shamash, the great gods, my lords, (and) with the aid of the goddess Ishtar, mistress of heaven (and) underworld, (who) marches at the fore of my army . . . I captured Kashtiliash, king of the Kassites, (and) *trod with my feet upon his lordly neck as though it were a footstool*."[115]

If Ps 110:1 offers a poetic interpretation of part of the Davidic promise akin to Solomon's paraphrase of it in 1 Kgs 5:3, 5[17, 19], how would this bear on Ps 110? The lord of the psalmist would take his place at the right hand of Yahweh "until" or "while" Yahweh places his enemies under his submission.[116] In this sense, Solomon as a king of a peaceful rule who sits upon the throne of the kingdom of Yahweh would align in certain respects with the lord of the psalmist of Ps 110 (see 1 Kgs 5:4, 12[18, 26]; 1 Chr 28:5; 29:23). The two coronation ceremonies mentioned by the Chronicler allow for a brief co-regency (1 Chr 29:22). The association of Solomon's name (שְׁלֹמֹה) with "peace" (*shalom* שָׁלוֹם) and Melchizedek as a king-priest of Salem (שָׁלֵם) would provide connecting

112. The term "enemies" does not appear in 1 Kgs 5:3[17] though NIV and other modern committee translations supply it from the pronoun "them."

113. See Isa 66:1; Ps 99:5; 132:7; Lam 2:1; 1 Chr 28:2 ("הֲדֹם," *HALOT* 1:239).

114. See images of ancient enthroned kings with feet on a footstool in ancient Egypt, Phoenicia, Mesopotamia, and Persia in *ANEP*, nos. 332, 371, 415, 417, 456, 458, 463. Also see ancient enthroned gods and goddesses with feet on a footstool, e.g., in Phoenicia and Ugarit in nos. 477 and 493. Note that the image of the Phoenician king 'Ahirom of Byblos (no. 456) dates to ca. 1000 BCE (contemporary with David and Solomon) and depicts him sitting on a throne in the form of a winged sphinx/cherub with his feet on a footstool (see inscription *COS* 2.55:181).

115. *ARI* 1:108 (no. 716), emphasis mine. For an image of enemies upon a royal footstool see *ANEP*, no. 4 and see commentary on p. 249.

116. The preposition *'ad* (עַד) in Ps 110:1 is normally taken as "until" but Zenger interprets it as "while" or "as long as"—"Sit at my right, *while* (עַד) I lay down your enemies as a footstool for your feet" (Hossfeld and Zenger, *Psalm 3*, 141, 148, emphasis mine).

thematic undertones to the oracles in verses 1 and 4. The rule of the psalmist's lord comes from victory granted by Yahweh (Ps 110:2–3, 5).

In sum, Ps 110:1 may be a loose interpretive allusion to the Davidic promise akin to Solomon's interpretation of it. If so, it would emphasize the rule of the Davidic king as based on Yahweh's faithfulness. The interpretive implications need not be worked out any further here since the potential allusion is based on several moving parts.

110:4*~Gen 14:18–20 (B) (priest in the order of Melchizedek) (* see Davidic covenant network). Psalm 110 features two prophetic citations of the divine will in verses 1 and 4.[117] Psalm 110:1 contains the only use of the prophetic formula "Yahweh utters" (נְאֻם יהוה).[118] The second oracle alludes to the ancient priest of El Elyon or the Most High God who ministered in Salem in the days of Abraham (Gen 14:18–20):

> Yahweh has sworn and will not change his mind: "You are a priest forever, in the order of Melchizedek." (Ps 110:4)

The sense of "not change his mind," literally "will not relent," means this oracle does not fit the profile of the divine consideration of killing Israel at Mount Sinai, where he did "relent" or "change his mind" (Exod 32:14). The point here does not require discussing theories of the impassibility of the divine being. The oracle affirms that the commitment to the psalmist's lord shall be forever akin to Nathan's oracle to David. In that case, Nathan contrasted the enduring promise regarding David's seed with Saul, whose house was removed (see note on 2 Sam 7:14–15).

The phrase "in the order of" (עַל־דִּבְרָתִי) in Ps 110:4 does not identify Melchizedek with the lord of the psalmist but uses the ancient king of Salem as a type or figural model.[119] The use of the language of analogy makes this a forward-looking type or expectational figural pattern (see Glossary). Making reference to Melchizedek nicely sidesteps part of the problem of civil rulers of Judah not in the Aaronic priesthood of Israel. Elsewhere the Scriptures tell of David performing sacrifices both for celebration and confession at a prophet's command and setting up his own sons as priests in the context of listing Zadok (2 Sam 6:17–18; 8:17, 18; 24:18, 25). Yet Uzziah went too far in usurping priestly activities, resulting in direct divine intervention (2 Chr 26:16–21). The mention of an ancient royal priest of Salem brings together in Ps 110:4 a divinely appointed civil ruler and priest in the very place Yahweh had chosen for his name to dwell.[120]

---

117. See Gillingham, "New Wine," 374–75; Jacobson, *"Many Are Saying"*, 105–6. Hilber, *Cultic Prophecy*, 76–86.

118. The use of "transgression utters" in Ps 36:1 should be regarded as a sarcastic parody (with NRSV, JPSB, contra NIV); thus following LXX "his heart" vs. "my heart" MT (with *BHS* apparatus Ps 36:1, n. c).

119. On the analogical function of "according to" (עַל) in relation to a norm, see *IBHS* §11.2.13e, 18. On the unusual construct form "order *of*" with *hireq yod* (דִּבְרָתִי), see *IBHS* §8.2e, 6.

120. See Hossfeld and Zenger, *Psalms 3*, 150. Allen goes further than the evidence at hand by conjecturing a setting for the psalm to celebrate David's ascension to the Jebusite throne (*Psalms 101–150*, 86–87).

114:3, 5, 8~Ps 77:16, 19–20[17, 20–21] (B)+Josh 4:23 (C)+Deut 8:15 (B) (sea/river crossing remix). Psalm 114 features highly stylized, creative, allusive poetry. The distinctive poetic imagery and rare language suggest an allusion to Ps 77 and Deut 8:15, and a possible dependence on Josh 4:23. The split up and distribute (see Glossary) kind of interpretive intervention suggests Ps 114 is the receptor context (see "hard rock" Deut 8:15 with Ps 114:8 below).

Attention here can only be devoted to two significant interpretive interventions in Ps 114:3, 5, 8.[121] First, the psalmist combines earlier interpretive suggestions. After crossing the Jordan River Joshua reflects on the event and places it side by side with the sea crossing some forty years earlier (Josh 4:23). The psalmist picks up this idea and collapses the entire wilderness experience into a single poetic event (Ps 114:3). The psalmist of Ps 77 had personified the waters speaking of their fear (77:16[17]). The psalmist speaks of Yahweh leading the people but not leaving his footprints on the path through the sea (77:19–20[20–21]). It seems that the psalmist of Ps 114 combines these ideas. He suggests to his readers that the God of Jacob caused the personified waters and mountains to flee before him (114:5–8).

Second, the psalmist adds a new element that the personified waters and hills saw causing their fear and flight: the one who provides water in the desert (114:8). This addition fits well in a diaspora and/or postexilic context to encourage a second exodus by a God who provides for his people. The context of this allusion to Deut 8:15 speaks against enjoying the benefits of settlement in the land and forgetting who provides these gifts. It may also contribute to what the psalmist wants to accomplish. The anxiety of success gets framed as: "You may say to yourself, 'My power and the strength of my hands have produced this wealth for me'" (Deut 8:17). The psalmist's brilliant combination of the personification of the sea, river, and hills to show what they see explains that they fear the one who provides water from desert rocks (Ps 114:8).

The narrative of the sea crossing speaks of splitting and congealing the waters and of the river crossing "cutting off" the waters (Exod 14:21; 15:8; Josh 4:7). The personified sea and river of Ps 114 run away with fright (emphases signify verbal parallels):

> He led you through the vast and dreadful wilderness, that thirsty and waterless land, with its venomous snakes and scorpions. He brought you *water* out of *hard* *<u>rock</u>* [מִצּוּר הַחַלָּמִישׁ]. (Deut 8:15)

> The waters **saw** you, **God**, the waters **saw** you and writhed; the very depths were convulsed. . . . Your path led through **the sea**, your way through the mighty waters, though your footprints were not seen. You led your people like a flock by the hand of Moses and Aaron. (Ps 77:16, 19–20[17, 20–21])

121. Other possible echoes include mimicking of style in Ps 114:4 of 29:6; and poetic theophany contexts like Ps 18:15[16]; and Hab 3:8. Cf. the imagery of Ps 107:35 and 114:8.

> **The sea looked** and fled, the Jordan turned back.... Why was it, **sea**, that you fled? Why, Jordan, did you turn back?... Tremble, earth, at the presence of the Lord, at the presence of the **God** of Jacob, who turned the rock [צוּר] into a pool of *water*, the *hard rock* [חַלָּמִישׁ] into springs of *water*. (Ps 114:3, 5, 7–8†)

To clarify, Deut 8:15 uses a combination term, literally "rocky hard rock" (מִצּוּר הַחַלָּמִישׁ), that the psalmist splits between the A and B lines of Ps 114:8. The term "hard rock" or "flinty rock" occurs only five times in Scripture, making allusion highly likely.[122]

In sum, the psalmist of Ps 114 combines and enhances traditional narrative and poetic elements to provide a new interpretive psalm. The psalm simultaneously heightens the redeeming power of the God of Jacob and emphasizes his work as provider even from hard, flinty rock in the desert.

118:19–20~24:3–4 (C) (gates of the righteous). See note on Ps 24:3–4.

118:22~Isa 28:16+Zech 4:7 (C) (the rejected cornerstone). Psalm 118:22 features a parable in which a stone earlier rejected by the rebuilders of the temple now becomes used for the top of the corner.[123] The psalmist may use this particular imagery to evoke the language of Isa 28:16 and Zech 4:7.[124] The many scriptural traditions that appear in Ps 118 suggest it is the receptor context (e.g., see Filters; emphases signify verbal parallels):

> So this is what Sovereign Yahweh says: "See, I lay a stone in Zion, a tested stone, a precious *cornerstone* [פִּנָּה] for a sure foundation; the one who relies on it will never be stricken with panic." (Isa 28:16)

> What are you, mighty mountain? Before Zerubbabel you will become level ground. Then he will bring out **the top** stone [הָאֶבֶן הָרֹאשָׁה] to shouts of "God bless it! God bless it!" (Zech 4:7 lit.)

> The stone the builders rejected has become **the top of** *the corner* [לְרֹאשׁ פִּנָּה]. Yahweh has done this, and it is marvelous in our eyes. This is the day in which Yahweh has acted, let us rejoice and be glad in him. (Ps 118:22–24 lit.)[125]

Psalm 118:23 credits Yahweh with having done "this." The demonstrative pronoun "this" in its feminine form would naturally refer back to the rejected stone (f) that became the top stone of the corner (f) in 118:22. The demonstrative pronoun "this" in

---

122. See "חַלָּמִישׁ," *HALOT* 1:321.

123. See Hossfeld and Zenger, *Psalms 3*, 241–42; Goldingay, *Psalms*, 3:361–62; Allen, *Psalms 101–150*, 121, n. 22a; Cahill, "Not a Cornerstone!" 345–57.

124. So Zenger in Hossfeld and Zenger, *Psalms 3*, 242.

125. The syntax does not fit the traditional "This is the day which the Lord hath made" (Ps 118:24 KJV). "This (is) the day" (זֶה הַיּוֹם) better serves as the setting than the object of the verb (see ibid., 230, n. s; Berlin, "Psalm 118:24," 567–68; Goldingay, *Psalms*, 3:354, n. 13; Allen, *Psalms 101–150*, 121, n. 24a).

its masculine form in 118:24 refers to the day (m) on which Yahweh did this work. The call to rejoice then refers to either rejoicing in "it," the day, or "him," Yahweh—either of which celebrate the surprising work of Yahweh with the rejected stone.

132:6–7~1 Sam 6:1–2 (C) (his footstool in the fields of Jaar).

132:8*~Num 10:35–36 (B)+Deut 12:9* (C) (ark to the resting place) (* see place network).

132:11–12*~2 Sam 7:12–15* (B)+7:28 (C) (oath to David) (* see Davidic covenant and place networks).

132:13~Ps 78:68–69 (C)+Deut 12:9 (C) (choosing Zion). Psalm 132 houses two direct discourses from Yahweh, one concerning his promise to David and the other his choice of Zion (Ps 132:11–12, 13–18). Though the language differs in Ps 132, it seems that both oracles relate to earlier materials.[126] The psalmist seems to draw upon several scriptural traditions.

Psalm 132:6–7 shifts from first-person singular to first-person plural to rehearse going to "his footstool" in the fields of Jaar referred to elsewhere as Kiriath Jearim. The psalmist refers to hearing of it in Ephrathah and going to it in the fields of Jaar (132:6). Ephrathah gets associated with Bethlehem in Gen 35:19, which naturally leads to "solutions" here like Ephrathah as the district in which Bethlehem and Kiriath Jearim are situated.[127] The important issue in Ps 132:6 relates to the collective decision to seek out the footstool (cf. 1 Sam 6:1–2). Psalm 132 speaks both of David's own initiative in verses 1–5 and of the people's collaboration to pursue worship in verses 6–7.[128] The Chronicler builds upon the psalmist's presentation of a collective effort in his version of securing the ark (see note on 1 Chr 13:5–14; and synoptic layout in note on 11:1–3). As such, the scriptural traditions of the ark coming to Jerusalem provide good examples of incremental advancement of revelation by interpretation.

The psalmist uses language from the Torah's ark processional ("Rise up"), but instead of focusing on setting out, the emphasis falls on coming to rest (Ps 132:8). The loaded term "resting place" seems to play a larger role in the psalm since the second oracle gets at the divine election of Zion. As such, the reference to "resting place" (מְנוּחָה) has a secondary echo of the place Yahweh would choose in Deut 12:9 (cf. 1 Kgs 8:56). The term "rest" (נוח) in Num 10:36 comes from the same root as "resting place," creating something of a catchword (emphases signify verbal parallels at the level of shared roots):

> Whenever *the ark* set out, Moses said, "*Rise up, Yahweh!* May your enemies be scattered; may your foes flee before you." Whenever it came *to rest*, he said, "Return, Yahweh, to the countless thousands of Israel. (Num 10:35–36)

126. Gillingham highlights the difficulties in deciding if they are citations ("New Wine," 375).

127. See Keil and Delitzsch, *Psalms*, 312–13; "אֶפְרָתָה," n. 3 BDB 68. See other textual issues in Allen, *Psalms 101–150*, 202, n. 6a–c. For a more detailed discussion of Ephrathah see note on Mic 5:2[1].

128. See Hossfeld and Zenger, *Psalms 3*, 461.

> Since you have not yet reached *the resting place* and the inheritance Yahweh your God is giving you . . . (Deut 12:9)

> *Rise up, Yahweh,* and come to your *resting place,* you and *the ark* of your might. (Ps 132:8†)

The psalm begins with David "swearing" a vow to Yahweh and includes Yahweh "swearing" an oath to David (Ps 132:2, 11). The term translated "sure oath" may come from David's description of the promise in his prayer after Nathan delivered the oracle (2 Sam 7:28; cf. Ps 89:35[36]). The version of the Davidic oath in Ps 132:11–12 may be loosely based on Nathan's version, but it especially gets at the obligations upon the heirs. Commentators suggest the psalmist may emphasize Yahweh "teaching" the Davidic heirs based broadly on teaching elsewhere in the psalms (Pss 25:4–5, 9, 12; 119:12, 26, 64).[129] Notice how the psalmist's version of the covenant compares to Nathan's oracle (bold signifies verbal parallels, italics signify similar elements, and broken underlining signifies counterpart views of the covenantal requirements):

> [Nathan] When your days are over and you rest with your ancestors, I will raise up *your offspring* to succeed you, your own flesh and blood, and I will establish his kingdom. He is the one who will build a house for my Name, and I will establish **the throne** of his kingdom *forever.* I will be his father, and he will be my son. When he does wrong, I will punish him with a rod wielded by men, with floggings inflicted by human hands. (2 Sam 7:12–14)

> [David] Sovereign Yahweh, you are God! Your covenant is **trustworthy** [אֱמֶת], and you have promised these good things to your servant. (7:28)

> Yahweh swore to David a **trustworthy oath** [אֱמֶת] he will not revoke: "*Of the fruit of your body* I will place on your **throne.** If your sons keep my covenant and the statutes I teach them, then their sons will sit on your **throne** *for ever and ever.*" (Ps 132:11–12, v. 11 lit.)

Psalm 132 retains the irrevocable element of the Davidic promise from Nathan's oracle (see note on 2 Sam 7:14–15). Whereas Nathan and the psalmist of Ps 89 emphasize the effects of disobeying covenantal obligations, the psalmist of Ps 132 stresses the royal son obeying what Yahweh teaches.

At the dedication of the temple, Solomon's prayer speaks of the city Yahweh had chosen (1 Kgs 8:44). The second divine oracle in Ps 132 refers to choosing Zion with language akin to the end of Ps 78. The term "resting place" of Deut 12 once again finds

129. See ibid., 464; Goldingay, *Psalms,* 3:554.

its way into the psalm. This repetition helps focus on Zion as the focal point of the ark, Davidic rule, and now the rule of Yahweh (emphases signify verbal parallels):

> Since you have not yet reached **the resting place** and the inheritance Yahweh your God is giving you . . . (Deut 12:9)
>
> But *he chose* the tribe of Judah, Mount *Zion*, which he loved. (Ps 78:68)
>
> For Yahweh has *chosen Zion*, he has desired it for his dwelling, saying, "This is my **resting place** for ever and ever; here I will sit enthroned, for I have desired it." (Ps 132:13–14)

The emotional term "desire" appears twice in the opening of this oracle (132:13, 14).[130] The oracle goes on to repeat some of the language from the psalm's frame poetry. Earlier "*your* [Yahweh's] priests," may be clothed in righteousness and now "*her* [Zion's] priests" may be clothed in salvation (132:9, 16). This shift in pronouns, like the repetition of "desire," helps signify the importance of Zion as a place of worship for the psalmist's audience.

135:5–12~Scripture compilation (B) (retrospective of Yahweh's gracious works). Each part of Ps 135 resembles Scriptures elsewhere. The opening and closing seem to depend on other psalms and Torah (Ps 135:1 with 113:1; 135:13//Exod 3:15b; Ps 135:14// Deut 32:36a; Ps 135:15–18//115:4–8; 135:19–20 with 115:9–11 and 118:2–5; see Filters for these). The middle section of Ps 135 presents a retrospective also highly dependent on other scriptural traditions. The nature of the evidence in the psalm overall in comparison to the parallel contexts suggests Ps 135 is the receptor context. Note the broad comparison with verbal parallels in a quotation-paraphrase format marked in bold (see Table Josh1 for comparative overview):

	scriptural traditions	**Psalm 135**
election of people	**Deut 7:6**	**4**
great above all gods	**Ps 96:4**	**5**
does what he pleases in all creation	**Ps 115:3+Exod 20:4b**	**6**
weather maker	**Jer 10:13**	**7**
smiting the firstborn of Egypt	**Exod 12:12**; cf. v. 29	**8**
signs and wonders against Egypt	Deut 6:22; 34:11	9
smiting Sihon and Og	Num 21:24, 35; Deut 2:33; 3:3	10–11
giving their land as an inheritance	**Deut 4:38**	**12**

130. See Allen, *Psalms 101–150*, 203, n. 13b.

As the table above indicates, the psalmist mostly follows selected source texts with re-edited paraphrastic quotations. The selection and combinations of scriptural traditions, as well as what has been excluded, may be considered exegetical in some sense. However, the present discussion focuses only on Ps 135:10–11, which represents the least verbal dependence on the donor contexts or, stated positively, the most exegesis.

After following a variety of donor contexts with close verbal paraphrase, why did the psalmist shift to interpretive paraphrase to present the conquest against the Transjordanian peoples? Two suggestions present themselves. First, the psalmist retained a focus on the storyline of Torah by using the defeat of Sihon and Og to represent settlement of the land of promise. This fits with the function of the defeat of Sihon and Og as explicit forward-looking types—"And Yahweh will do to them *according to* (כַּאֲשֶׁר) what he did to Sihon and Og" (Deut 31:4 lit., emphasis mine).[131] The psalmist often secured poetic interpretations of the Torah storyline from elsewhere—Pss 96:4, 115:3, and Jer 10:13 (see table above). A focus on the power of Yahweh in the storyline leading up to entry in the land well suits the Second Temple situation with many in diaspora. Even those who returned to actively participate in the restoration can be all too aware that their settlement and its Jerusalem shrine are part of the empire. The psalmist selects a segment of the redemptive storyline before the establishment of the Hebrew kingdom. The power of Yahweh calls for praise and blessing before the Davidic kingdom.

Second, Torah does not speak of Yahweh smiting Sihon and Og. The psalmist retells the defeat of the Transjordanian kings by using the language of the last great terror against the Egyptians.[132] Many commentators explain that the psalmist of Ps 135 borrows this material from Ps 136.[133] This may be, but even so the evidence suggests that the psalmist of Ps 135 reworks the material in the light of the Torah contexts—this includes "re-activating" the participles of Ps 136 to finite verb forms akin to the respective Torah contexts.[134] The psalmist connects the two acts of smiting by attaching the relative pronoun (שֶׁ), thus, "who-smote."[135] The psalmist boldly swaps out the subjects of the verbs, using the great definitive terror against the Egyptians as paradigmatic of the conquest and settlement of the land (italics signify verbal parallels, and bold signifies changes):

131. Thank you to Bryan Murawski for this observation.

132. As observed by Goldingay, *Psalms*, 3:582.

133. See Emanuel, *Bards to Exegetes*, 204–8, explaining how, in his view, Ps 135 uses 136. Zenger goes further suggesting that Ps 135 was created to fit between Pss 134 and 136 (Hossfeld and Zenger, *Psalms 3*, 494).

134. Compare "smite" (נכה) ptc. plus attached preposition "to" (לְ) in Ps 136:10, 17 (לְמַכֵּה) with "smite" pf. plus attached relative pronoun "who" (שֶׁ) in 135:8, 10 (שֶׁהִכָּה), and note "smite" wcp in Exod 12:12 and wci in Num 21:24, 35; Deut 2:33; 3:3. Also note "smite" pf. in Exod 12:29 and Ps 135:8, 10. The attached (שֶׁ) and the freestanding relative pronoun (אֲשֶׁר) "who/which/that" function identically (GKC §155a, n. 1).

135. See Emanuel, *Bards to Exegetes*, 186.

On that same night **I** will pass through Egypt and *strike down* [נכה wcp] every *firstborn* of the land *of Egypt, of people and animals*, and I will bring judgment on all the gods of Egypt. I am Yahweh. . . . At midnight **Yahweh** *struck down* [נכה pf] all *the firstborn* in *Egypt*. (Exod 12:12†; 29a)

Yahweh our God delivered him over to us and **we** *struck him* [Sihon] *down* [נכה wci], together with his sons and his whole army. . . . So Yahweh our God also gave into our hands *Og king of Bashan* and all his army. **We** *struck them down* [נכה wci], leaving no survivors. (Deut 2:33; 3:3; cf. Num 21:24, 35)

[Give thanks] to **him** who *struck down* [נכה ptc. + לְ] great kings . . . and killed mighty kings . . . *Sihon king of the Amorites* . . . and *Og king of Bashan*. (Ps 136:17–20, A lines only)

He *struck down* [נכה pf. + שֶׁ] *the firstborn of Egypt, of people and animals*. . . . **He** *struck down* [נכה pf. + שֶׁ] many nations and killed mighty kings—*Sihon king of the Amorites, Og king of Bashan*, and all the kings of Canaan. (Ps 135:8†, 10, 11)

The part of Exod 12:12 not quoted in Ps 135 helps explain how the pieces of the psalm fit together. Yahweh claims that striking down the firstborn of Egypt demonstrates his judgment upon their gods (Exod 12:12; cf. Num 33:4). This matches the sentiment of the psalmist's earlier paraphrase of Ps 96:4, "I know that Yahweh is great, that our Lord is greater than all gods" (Ps 135:5). After completing the retrospective, the psalmist claims Yahweh will vindicate his people and show compassion upon them (135:14). The psalmist follows this by re-presenting the taunts against idolatry from Ps 115:4–8 (135:15–18).[136] For the psalmist, Yahweh's smiting the firstborn of Egypt served as the paradigmatic evidence of his greatness over and against the idols of the nations. The psalmist exegetically re-presents the conquest of the Transjordan to demonstrate that Israel's history consistently bears witness to the greatness of their God over the nations who worship other gods.

In sum, Ps 135 appropriates and repurposes numerous scriptural traditions to glorify Yahweh above all gods. The psalm offers a badly needed apologetic to praise God in the midst of the challenges of life in the empire.

136~Torah compilation (B) (covenantal loyalty retrospective). Psalm 136 uniquely features identical B lines in every verse with the rich term "covenantal loyalty" (*hesed* חֶסֶד), variously rendered as "love" (NIV), "steadfast love" (NRSV), "mercy" (KJV).[137]

---

136. On the function of scriptural parodies against false gods, see Schnittjer, "Idolatry in Isaiah."

137. Koehler and Baumgartner suggest faithfulness and goodness, "II חֶסֶד," *HALOT* 1:336–37. In the Psalter, *hesed* (חֶסֶד) is often collocated with and/or parallel to "faithfulness" (אֱמוּנָה) (Pss 36: 5[6]; 40:11; 88:11[12]; 89:1, 2, 24,

The subordinating particle "for" (כִּי) introduces the B lines as an interpretation assigning the reason for Yahweh's character—"*because* his covenantal loyalty endures forever" (lit.).[138] Meanwhile the A lines in verses 4 through 22 present Yahweh's character as revealed in successive historical events with third-person referents as a rationale for the collective imperatives to "give thanks!" to Yahweh (136:1, 2, 3) and the God of heaven (136:26). Verses 23 and 24 identify the psalmist's congregation as "us" in first-person plural—those whom Yahweh remembered in low estate and freed from enemies. In sum, in Ps 136 the A lines feature an ABCcba format driven by verb forms.

(A) A threefold imperative to profess gratitude to Yahweh (vv. 1–3)
  (B) the deity's character as creator (vv. 4–9)
    (C) the deity's character as redeemer of Israel (vv. 10–22)
    (c) the deity's rescuer of "us" (vv. 23–24)
  (b) the deity's provider for "all flesh" (v. 25)
(a) An imperative to profess gratitude to the God of the heavens (v. 26)

The B lines of Ps 136 brilliantly affirm Yahweh's enduring covenantal loyalty inclusive of all his character as revealed in his works. The psalmist promotes Yahweh as ever-loyal to his people. His loyalty appears not just all the time, but all his acts reveal Yahweh as omni-loyal to his people, or better, omni-*hesed* to his people.

The psalmist's major set of exegetical interventions to present Yahweh as omni-*hesed* to his people come in the form of scriptural historical allusions. Note the broad retrospective comparison of Ps 136 with verbal parallels in a quotation-paraphrase format marked in bold (see Table Josh1 for comparative overview with other retrospectives):

	scriptural traditions	Psalm 136 A lines
God of gods, Lord of lords	**Deut 10:17**[a]	2, 3
who alone does great wonders	Ps 89:5[6]	4
who made the heavens by understanding	**Prov 3:19**	5
who spread out the earth upon the waters	Isa 44:24; Ps 24:2	6
who made great lights	**Gen 1:16,** 18	7–9
who struck down firstborn of Egypt	**Exod 12:29**	10
. . . and brought out Israel	Exod 7:5[b]	11

(cont.)

33, 49[2, 3, 25, 34, 50]; 92:3; 98:3; 100:5), "righteous" (צדק) (33:5; 36:10[11]; 103:17), "good" (טוֹב) (23:6; 25:7; 86:5; 109:21), "truthful/faithful" (אֱמֶת) (25:10; 40:11[12]; 57:3, 10[4, 11]; 61:7[8]; 108:4[5]; 115:1; 117:2; 138:2), "compassion" (רַחֲמִים) (40:11[12]; 51:1; 69:16[17]; 103:4; 145:8), and combinations of these and kindred terms.

138. See GKC §158a, b; Allen, *Psalms 101–150*, 229, n. 1a.

	scriptural traditions	**Psalm 136 A lines**
. . . by mighty hand and outstretched arm	**Deut 4:34**[c]	12
who divided the sea	Exod 14:21–22, 27[d]	13–15
who led his people through the wilderness	Deut 8:2	16
who struck down great kings	Num 21:24, 35; Deut 2:33; 3:3; 4:38	17–22[e]

[a] For lesser possible echoes of Deut 10–11 in Ps 136 see Brettler, "Psalm 136," 378–80, 389–91.

[b] Cf. Exod 12:17, 51; Deut 4:20, 37; 5:6, 15; 6:12, 21, 23, etc.

[c] Cf. Ezek 20:33, 34.

[d] Psalm 136:13 is the only context to use this term for "divide" (גזר) the sea; Exod 14:21 and other contexts use "split" (בקע) (see Goldingay, *Psalms*, 3:593).

[e] The defeats of Sihon and Og (Ps 136:19, 20) rightly serve as an explicit forward-looking type of the power of Yahweh. Note: "And Yahweh will do to them *according to* (כַּאֲשֶׁר) what he did to Sihon and Og" (Deut 31:4 lit., emphasis mine).

Several of the psalmist's interpretive choices give pause. The psalmist characterizes creation according to "understanding" (Ps 136:5; cf. Prov 3:19). Many have noted that Gen 1 intentionally does not name the sun and moon but refers to them as great lights (Gen 1:16).[139] The psalmist shows dependence on the narrative of the creation days by verbal parallel but refers to the great lights as sun and moon (Ps 136:8, 9; cf. 8:3[4]). The psalm does not include the settlement or kingdom but stops at the end of the Transjordan conquest of Torah and then turns immediately to post-captivity (136:23, 24). The focus on Yahweh's loyalty up to the settlement of the Transjordan before securing land and granting kingship offers much hope to Israel in the exilic diaspora or in a sub-province of the empire. All of these interpretive moves stand at the periphery of the psalmist's major interpretive advancement.

The exegetical genius of Ps 136 stems from doing one thing. The psalmist coordinates the retrospective A lines so that they together contribute to a singular proclamation. The psalmist treats the retrospective not as a series of events that tell a story, but as a series of events that bear witness to the character of Yahweh. The retrospective in the A lines of Ps 136:4–22 features a series of participles instead of active verbs to express each of several acts of Yahweh. By avoiding active verbs to describe the primary actions, the psalmist deflects attention from the outcomes of the actions. Focus turns to Yahweh's character which gives rise to the acts. The psalmist does not say "he made X" with an active verb but "who made X" with a particle and its attached subordinating preposition.

The psalmist uses syntax to subordinate all of the acts of Yahweh that reveal his character under one umbrella description.[140] The threefold imperative in verses 1, 2, 3—"Profess gratitude!"—bears down on the umbrella description: "to him who alone

139. See Emanuel, *Bards to Exegetes*, 217, n. 13.

140. For a symmetrical approach, see Bazak, "Geometric-Figurative Structure," 129–38. The approach here follows the psalm's syntax and, esp. at Ps 136:17–22, acknowledges an "irregular" stanza, which Bazak seeks to avoid (135).

does *great wonders*" (Ps 136:4a lit., emphasis mine).[141] Everything else in the retrospective fits within the "great wonders" by means of syntax. The broad point being made here does not require a full explanation of poetic syntax (see note in Table P3 for overview). The psalmist subordinates by several grammatical strategies seven divine actions under the umbrella "great wonders" in 136:4. The indentations in Table P3 graphically demonstrate the psalmist's syntactical subordination.

TABLE P3: GRAPHIC DISPLAY BY INDENTATION OF SYNTACTICAL SUBORDINATION IN PSALM 136‡

- v. 4, **"who alone does** (ptc. + לְ) **great wonders"**
- v. 5, "who made (ptc. + לְ) heavens by understanding"
- v. 6, "who spread out (ptc. + לְ) earth"
- v. 7, "who made (ptc. + לְ) great lights"
    - v. 8, "(DDO אֶת) the sun"
    - v. 9, "(DDO אֶת) the moon and stars"
- v. 10, "who struck down (ptc. + לְ) Egypt by their firstborn"
    - v. 11, "then he brought out (wci) Israel"
    - v. 12, "with (בְּ) a mighty hand and with (בְּ) an outstretched arm"
- v. 13, "who divided (ptc. + לְ) the reed sea apart"
    - v. 14, "and caused Israel to cross (pf.) through the middle of it"
    - v. 15, "and overthrew (pf.) Pharaoh and his army"
- v. 16, "who led (ptc. + לְ) his people in the wilderness"
- v. 17, "who struck down (ptc. + לְ) great kings"
    - v. 18, "and so he killed (wci) mighty kings"
        - v. 19, "namely (לְ) Sihon"
        - v. 20, "namely (לְ) Og"
    - v. 21, "and gave (pf.) their land as an inheritance"
        - v. 22, "an inheritance to (לְ) Israel"

‡ The participles with attached subordinating prepositions (ptc. + לְ) place the seven main acts under the umbrella of the "great wonders" in Ps 136:4 (136:5, 6, 7, 10, 13, 16, 17). The psalmist then uses several other syntactical strategies to subordinate the outcomes of the main acts under them: accusative markers (vv. 8, 9); active verbs with conjunctions (vv. 11, 14, 15, 18); and subordinating prepositions (vv. 12, 19, 20, 22). Translation in table lit.

The A lines together point to the one thing Ps 136 gets at, repeated twenty-six times in the B lines: "*because* his covenantal loyalty endures forever."

In sum, Ps 136 treats all of Yahweh's great acts of creation and redemption as evidence of his enduring covenantal loyalty. The psalmist thereby proposes why his people need to profess gratitude. Yahweh's covenantal loyalty to his people is the common denominator to everything he has accomplished.

---

141. See Hossfeld and Zenger, *Psalms 3*, 503, note a.

FILTERS

The Psalter brims full of scriptural echoes. The vast majority are either non-allusive, since they are part of the lyrical diffusion, or they are so broad as to be non-exegetical. The filtered-out examples need to be limited to a few of the more concrete kinds of non-exegetical connections.[142] These lists are not comprehensive or complete. The purposes of the lists include illustrating some of the other kinds of connective relationships in the Psalter by way of contrast to exegetical allusions.

Superscriptions

Of the approximately one hundred psalms with superscriptions, twelve include historical notations referring to scriptural narratives concerning David (Pss 3, 18, 34, 51, 52, 54, 56, 57, 59, 60, 63, 142).[143] Although a few of these psalms share a word or two with the narrative contexts to which the superscriptions refer, shared language does not seem to play much of a role. Instead, the twelve psalms with historical superscriptions seem to share general similarities with their respective narrative contexts (see Table P4 and its note).[144] In short, the relationship between these twelve psalms and their respective narrative contexts is not genetic or exegetical. The headings with historical settings create dialogues, of sorts, by providing David's thoughts, emotions, and prayers, often in difficult circumstances. Only the historical superscription of Ps 60 features exegetical intervention in the superscription itself (see note ad loc.).

Table P4 marks the twelve historical headings by bold amid all of the headings to illustrate their similarities and their differences. This evidence supports the non-exegetical function, of almost all of the headings, as part of the Psalter's literary and liturgical apparatus.

Besides Moses, David, and Solomon, all other persons named in the superscriptions of psalms appear in lists of Davidic singers in Chronicles: Asaph (1 Chr 6:39; 15:17, 19; cf. Ezra 2:41//Neh 7:44); sons of Korah (1 Chr 6:37; 15:17); Heman the Ezrahite (6:33; 15:17, 19; cf. 1 Kgs 4:31[5:11]); Ethan the Ezrahite (1 Chr 15:17, 19; cf. 1 Kgs 4:31[5:11]) (see Table P4).

---

142. For parallels with Psalms, see Ḥakham, *Psalms*, 1:XXXVIII–XL; Kirkpatrick, *Psalms Book I*, passim; idem, *Books II and III*, passim; idem, *Books IV and V*, passim; Kohlenberger, *Comparative Psalter*, passim (on lower portion of LXX pages). For a comparison of numerous phrases in Pss 91–100 and Isaiah see Elliott, "Excursus upon Psalms XCI—C," 506–12; and between Pss 146–150 and other Scriptures, Brodersen, *The End*, 35–41, 93–98, 137–42, 179–86, 234–41.

143. Childs mentions thirteen but then he excludes the superscription of Ps 7 because it does not use "when" (בְּ) but "concerning" (עַל), which everywhere else among Psalms superscriptions refers to how the psalm should be rendered; e.g., Ps 8 (see Childs, "Psalm Titles," 138). Childs repeats thirteen elsewhere (*Introduction*, 512).

144. See Childs, "Psalm Titles," 143–47. Also see Ḥakham, *Psalms*, 1:XLI.

TABLE P4: HEADINGS OF THE PSALMS‡

Book I

1—

2—

3 A psalm of David. **When he fled from his son Absalom.**

4 For the director of music. With stringed instruments. A psalm of David.

5 For the director of music. For pipes. A psalm of David.

6 For the director of music. With stringed instruments. According to *sheminith.* A psalm of David.

7 A *shiggaion* of David, which he sang to Yahweh concerning Cush, a Benjamite.

8 For the director of music. According to *gittith.* A psalm of David.

9 For the director of music. To the tune of "The Death of the Son." A psalm of David.

10—

11 For the director of music. Of David.

12 For the director of music. According to *sheminith.* A psalm of David.

13 For the director of music. A psalm of David.

14 For the director of music. Of David.

15 A psalm of David.

16 A *miktam* of David.

17 A prayer of David.

18 For the director of music. Of David the servant of Yahweh. **He sang to Yahweh the words of this song when Yahweh delivered him from the hand of all his enemies and from the hand of Saul.** He said:

19 For the director of music. A psalm of David.

20 For the director of music. A psalm of David.

21 For the director of music. A psalm of David.

22 For the director of music. To the tune of "The Doe of the Morning." A psalm of David.

23 A psalm of David.

24 Of David. A psalm.

25 Of David.

26 Of David.

27 Of David.

28 Of David.

29 A psalm of David.

30 A psalm. A song. For the dedication of the temple. Of David.

31 For the director of music. A psalm of David.

32 Of David. A *maskil.*

33—

34 Of David. **When he pretended to be insane before Abimelek, who drove him away, and he left.**

35 Of David.

36 For the director of music. Of David the servant of Yahweh.

37 Of David.

38 A psalm of David. A petition.

39 For the director of music. For Jeduthun. A psalm of David.

40 For the director of music. Of David. A psalm.

41 For the director of music. A psalm of David.

Book II

42 For the director of music. A *maskil* of the Sons of Korah.

43—

44 For the director of music. Of the Sons of Korah. A *maskil.*

45 For the director of music. To the tune of "Lilies." Of the Sons of Korah. A *maskil.* A wedding song.

46 For the director of music. Of the Sons of Korah. According to *alamoth.* A song.

53 For the director of music. According to *mahalath.* A *maskil* of David.

54 For the director of music. With stringed instruments. A *maskil* of David. **When the Ziphites had gone to Saul and said, "Is not David hiding among us?"**

55 For the director of music. With stringed instruments. A *maskil* of David.

60 For the director of music. To the tune of "The Lily of the Covenant." A *miktam* of David. For teaching. **When he fought Aram Naharaim and Aram Zobah, and when Joab returned and struck down twelve thousand Edomites in the Valley of Salt.**

61 For the director of music. With stringed instruments. Of David.

(cont.)

Book II *(cont.)*

47 For the director of music. Of the Sons of Korah. A psalm.
48 A song. A psalm of the Sons of Korah.
49 For the director of music. Of the Sons of Korah. A psalm.
50 A psalm of Asaph.
51 For the director of music. A psalm of David. **When the prophet Nathan came to him after David had committed adultery with Bathsheba.**
52 For the director of music. A *maskil* of David. **When Doeg the Edomite had gone to Saul and told him: "David has gone to the house of Ahimelek."**
56 For the director of music. To the tune of "A Dove on Distant Oaks." Of David. A *miktam*. **When the Philistines had seized him in Gath.**
57 For the director of music. To the tune of "Do Not Destroy." Of David. A *miktam*. **When he had fled from Saul into the cave.**
58 For the director of music. To the tune of "Do Not Destroy." Of David. A *miktam*.
59 For the director of music. To the tune of "Do Not Destroy." Of David. A *miktam*. **When Saul had sent men to watch David's house in order to kill him.**
62 For the director of music. For Jeduthun. A psalm of David.
63 A psalm of David. **When he was in the Desert of Judah.**
64 For the director of music. A psalm of David.
65 For the director of music. A psalm of David. A song.
66 For the director of music. A song. A psalm.
67 For the director of music. With stringed instruments. A psalm. A song.
68 For the director of music. Of David. A psalm. A song.
69 For the director of music. To the tune of "Lilies." Of David.
70 For the director of music. Of David. A petition.
71—
72 Of Solomon.

Book III

73 A psalm of Asaph.
74 A *maskil* of Asaph.
75 For the director of music. To the tune of "Do Not Destroy." A psalm of Asaph. A song.
76 For the director of music. With stringed instruments. A psalm of Asaph. A song.
77 For the director of music. For Jeduthun. Of Asaph. A psalm.
78 A *maskil* of Asaph.
79 A psalm of Asaph.
80 For the director of music. To the tune of "The Lilies of the Covenant." Of Asaph. A psalm.
81 For the director of music. According to *gittith*. Of Asaph.
82 A psalm of Asaph.
83 A song. A psalm of Asaph.
84 For the director of music. According to *gittith*. Of the Sons of Korah. A psalm.
85 For the director of music. Of the Sons of Korah. A psalm.
86 A prayer of David.
87 Of the Sons of Korah. A psalm. A song.
88 A song. A psalm of the Sons of Korah. For the director of music. According to *mahalath leannoth*. A *maskil* of Heman the Ezrahite.
89 A *maskil* of Ethan the Ezrahite.

Book IV

90 A prayer of Moses the man of God.
91—
92 A psalm. A song. For the Sabbath day.
93—
94—
95—
96—
97—
98 A psalm.
99—
100 A psalm. For giving grateful praise.
101 Of David. A psalm.
102 A prayer of an afflicted person who has grown weak and pours out a lament before Yahweh.
103 Of David.
104—
105—
106—

Book V

107—
108 A song. A psalm of David.
109 For the director of music. Of David. A psalm.
110 Of David. A psalm.
111—
112—
113—
114—
115—
116—
117—
118—
119-
120 A song of ascents.
121 A song of ascents.
122 A song of ascents. Of David.
123 A song of ascents.
124 A song of ascents. Of David.
125 A song of ascents.
126 A song of ascents.
127 A song of ascents. Of Solomon.
128 A song of ascents.
129 A song of ascents.
130 A song of ascents.
131 A song of ascents. Of David.
132 A song of ascents.
133 A song of ascents. Of David.
134 A song of ascents.
135—
136—
137—
138 Of David.
139 For the director of music. Of David. A psalm.
140 For the director of music. A psalm of David.
141 A psalm of David.
142 A *maskil* of David. **When he was in the cave. A prayer.**
143 A psalm of David.
144 Of David.
145 A psalm of praise. Of David.
146—
147—
148—
149—
150—

‡ Bold marks superscriptions with historical notations related to events in the David narratives, namely, Pss 3 (2 Sam 16:14; 17:22; cf. Ps 3:6); 18 (unknown setting, cf. 2 Sam 22); 34 ("fear" 1 Sam 21:12; Ps 34:5); 51 (2 Sam 12:13; cf. note on 1 Sam 16:14); 52 (1 Sam 21:7); 54 (1 Sam 23:15, 19); 56 (1 Sam 21:11); 57 (1 Sam 22:1; 24:3); 59 (1 Sam 19:11); 60 (2 Sam 8:5, 13–14+1 Kgs 11:15); 63 (unknown setting); and 142 (1 Sam 22:1; 24:3). Many of these connections are based on Childs, "Psalm Titles," 143–47.

Connection by Placement and/or Editing

Non-exegetical external connections in the Psalter include catchwords and catchphrases created by arrangement of psalms within the Psalter. The sequence of the psalms and how they function as a book has been studied intensely. While summarizing these competing approaches falls outside the present study, it needs to be noted that many studies rely upon thematic and verbal relations between individual psalms. These kinds of linkages connect psalms in non-exegetical ways.

The sub-group of psalms preferring to use God (*elohim*) versus Yahweh, the so-called Elohistic Psalter, has been subjected to various excavative conjectures (Pss 42–83).[145]

145. Older excavative diachronic explanations of the so-called Elohistic Psalter tend to coordinate these with the use of *elohim* versus Yahweh in theoretical sources of the Pentateuch. More recently, Joffe proposes a special ancient significance to the number 42 that explains how the so-called Elohistic Psalter begins with Ps 42, includes 42 psalms (Pss 42–83), and features the divine name about 42 times ("Answer to the Meaning of Life," 223–35). Burnett has sifted through Joffe's proposal and expanded its supporting logic ("Forty-Two Songs," 81–101). The gist of the conjecture relates to the number 42 as associated with ancient curses and the divine name, especially in postbiblical and rabbinic literature. Joffe and Burnett each add several more speculations that cannot be taken up here. Joffe says *BHS* attests "Yahweh" (יהוה) 44 times, but she does not list them. She suggests that with textual fluidity between the divine name (*Yahweh*) and "Lord" (*adonai*) the number originally may have been 42 (224, n. 4). Joffe does not mention the three uses of the short form of the divine name Yah (יָהּ) in these psalms. Burnett found 45 uses of the divine name but does not list them, and he only noticed two of the three uses of the shortened form of the divine name ("Forty-Two Songs," 90, n. 32). The evidence does not support conjectures based on the number 42. Here is a list of Yahweh (יהוה) 45x, and Yah (יָהּ) 3x in the so-called Elohistic Psalter: Pss 42:8[9]; 46:7, 8, 11[8, 9, 12]; 47:2, 5[3, 6]; 48:1, 8[2, 9]; 50:1; 54:6[8];

Many paired or grouped psalms feature connectors, such as beginning and ending with "Bless Yahweh, O my soul" (Pss 103:1, 2, 22; 104:1, 35). Several competing theories have been applied to the pilgrimage collection to explain the rationale of the language these psalms share with the high priestly prayer (120–134; Num 6:23–27).[146] The last five psalms each begin and end with "Praise Yah!" (*halelu-yah* הַלְלוּ־יָהּ) (Pss 146:1, 10; 147:1, 20; 148:1, 14; 149:1, 9; 150:1, 6).[147] Perhaps the most-discussed shaping relates to the so-called seams between the five books of the Psalter (esp. Pss 2, 72, 89).[148] Many other subcollections and series within the Psalter are rightly debated.[149]

Most psalms share something in common with the psalms immediately before and after them. For example, the use of "blessed" in Pss 1 and 2 likely signals some kind of "external" arranging or redacting work (1:1; 2:12). Psalm 2 tells of installing a king upon the "holy mountain," and Ps 3 speaks of Yahweh answering the psalmist from the "holy mountain" (2:6; 3:4[5]). The morning in Ps 3 and evening in Ps 4 include numerous verbal connectors (3:5[6]; 4:8).[150] The same kinds of connectors run between adjacent psalms in nearly every case, suggesting they are not coincidental.[151]

The Psalter's Books I and IV close almost identically: "Praise be to Yahweh, the God of Israel, from everlasting to everlasting. Amen and Amen/let all the people say 'Amen.' Praise Yah" (ברוך יהוה אלהי ישׂראל מהעלום ועד העולם אמן ואמן/ואמר כל העם אמן הללו יה, 41:13[14]; 106:48). Books II, III, and V close similarly: "Praise be to his glorious name forever; may the whole earth be filled with his glory. Amen and Amen" (וברוך שם כבודו לעולם וימלא כבודו את כל הארץ אמן ואמן) (72:19); "Praise be to Yahweh forever! Amen and Amen" (ברוך יהוה לעולם אמן ואמן) (89:52[53]); "Let everything that has breath praise Yah. Praise Yah" (כל הנשמה תהלל יה הללו יה) (150:6).

These kinds of catchwords and catchphrases merit close attention for how the Psalter functions as a book or an arranged or semi-arranged anthology. But these connections—external to the psalms themselves—are not exegetical interventions by the psalmists. They are theologically relevant insofar as they represent intentionality—by arranger(s) and/or editor(s) and/or redactor(s)—even while they fall outside the narrow limits of the present study. The Psalter's editorial apparatus may operate akin to constellations (see Glossary).

55:16, 22[17, 23]; 56:10[11]; 58:6[7]; 59:3, 5, 8[4, 6, 9]; 64:10[11]; 68:4 (יָהּ), 16, 18 (יָהּ), 20, 26[5, 17, 19, 21, 27]; 69:6, 13, 16, 31, 33[7, 14, 17, 32, 34]; 70:1, 5[2, 6]; 71:1, 5, 16; 72:18; 73:28; 74:18; 75:8[9]; 76:11[12]; 77:11[12] (יָהּ); 78:4, 21; 79:5; 80:4, 19[5, 20]; 81:10, 15[11, 16]; 83:16, 18[17, 19] (see Accordance; BibleWorks; but Even-Shoshan's entry on the divine name is not organized in a way that allows for convenient comparison of the evidence).

146. On the exaggerated significance of the similarities by Liebreich ("Songs of Ascents," 33–36), see the pushback in Hossfeld and Zenger, *Psalms 3*, 291–92; Fishbane, *Biblical Interpretation*, 331.

147. See Brodersen, *The End*, 3. Brodersen's work offers thoroughgoing analysis of connections in Pss 146–150 with measured results.

148. See Wilson, "Royal Psalms at the 'Seams,'" 85–94; idem, "Shape," 128–42.

149. Many of the subcollections detected by scholars relate to the persons named in the superscriptions. The evidence of variations in the superscriptions of the Psalter from Qumran and the Septuagint remains a challenge to how subcollections of psalms contribute to Psalms as a book. See Willgren Davage, "Davidic Superscriptions," 67–86.

150. See list in Goldingay, *Psalms*, 1:117.

151. See "Relationship to Neighboring Psalms" for each one in Hossfeld and Zenger, *Psalms 2*; idem, *Psalms 3*; Eng, "Semitic Catchwords," 250–52.

Doublets and Composite Psalms

Several psalms recycle other psalms in part or in whole. Repurposed psalms often feature light re-editing. For the purposes of the present study only substantive alterations count as exegesis (e.g., see note on Ps 96:7–8). The following represent seemingly non-exegetical reuse of psalms.

Reuse of entire psalms include: 18//2 Sam 22;[152] 14//53; 40:14–18//70; 108:1–5[2–6]//57:7–11[8–12];[153] 108:6–13[7–14]//60:5–12[7–14] (see note on Ps 60 superscription).

Re-presentation of parts of psalms include: 8:1//8:9[10]; 18:4a[5a]//116:3a (cf. 2 Sam 22:5); 33:18b//147:11b; 36:6//57:10[11]; 42:5[6]//11[12]//43:5 (perhaps common refrain of two-part psalm); 45:7[8]//11[12]; 49:12[13]//20[21]; 54:3[5]//86:14;[154] 56:4b+11a[5b+12a]//118:6; 56:13[14]//116:8a, 9; 57:5[6]//11[12]//108:5[6]; 59:6[7]//14[15]; 59:9–10[10–11]//17[18]; 62:1, 2[2, 3]//5a, 6[6a, 7]; 77:1a[2a]//142:1a[2a] (cf. 3:4a[5a]); 80:3[4]//7[8] (cf. 80:14[15]); 96:7–8//29:1–2; 96:10//93:1; 96:13//98:9; 107:6//13//19//28; 113:1//135:1 (Seidel's theory); 115:4–8//135:15–18 (on taunts against idols see note on Jer 10:1–16 in Jeremiah Filters and see last entry of Table I1 in Isaiah); 115:15//134:3; 121:2//124:8; 130:7a//131:3a; 144:8//11b.[155]

Psalm 115:9–11 uses three categories: Israel, house of Aaron, and those who fear Yahweh. The reference to "those who fear Yahweh" could be the most devout remnant, including Israel and the house of Aaron, or possibly God-fearing gentiles.[156] Psalm 118:2–5 reuses the same three categories in a different way. Psalm 135:19–20 uses the same three and also inserts "house of Levi" between house of Aaron and those who fear Yahweh.

Non-Exegetical Broad Allusions and Shared Themes

Book I: **12:5[6]**>/<Deut 15:9–11, when the "poor" and "needy" (אביון, עני) groan, Yahweh will rise up (cf. Exod 22:21–24[20–23]; on the term "groan" (אנקה) in similar contexts see 79:11; 102:20[21]; Mal 2:13);[157] **16:5**>/<Num 18:20; Deut 12:12; 14:27, 29; 18:1, priests and Levites have "no portion" (חלק), so Yahweh is their portion; **17:8**>/<Deut 32:8, 10, both "keep as apple of eye" (נצר/שמר צאישון עין) and "shadow of your wings/spreads its wings" (צל כנפיך/פרש כנפיו); **18:28[29]**//2 Sam 22:29>/<2 Sam

152. Most of the ostensive intentional changes between 2 Sam 22 and Ps 18, whichever is "more original," do not rise to the level of exegetical intervention. For a detailed explanation of all variants see Chisholm, "Exegetical and Theological Study," 61–102, followed by a categorization of the variants, 102–6. The four variants that may be exegetically motivated with 2 Sam 22 as the donor and Psalm 18 as the receptor context relate to "increasing the intimacy in the relationship between the implied author and the deity" (Young, "Psalm 18 and 2 Sam 22," 67; for an annotated list of these changes, see 55–56). Chisholm comes to a different conclusion. He acknowledges the complex nature of the evidence, with both 2 Sam 22 and Ps 18 preserving more original readings as well as interpretive interventions ("Exegetical and Theological Study," 107, 110).

153. Note use of "Lord" versus "Yahweh" in Pss 57:9[10]//108:3[4], with the former in the so-called Elohistic Psalter.

154. Though nearly every line of Ps 86 resembles expressions used elsewhere in the Psalter, Goldingay suggests it does not reflect direct dependence but represents being "soaked in the Scriptures," analogous to John's Apocalypse (*Psalms 42–89*, 2:619). See the discussion of lyrical diffusion in Hermeneutical Profile of the Use of Scripture in Psalms.

155. For parallels of Ps 97 with other psalms see Gray, "Parallel Passages," 225.

156. See Kirkpatrick, *Psalms Books IV and V*, 685.

157. Psalm 12:5[6] features embedded divine discourse for this broad allusion (see Gillingham, "New Wine," 379).

21:17, David as "lamp" (נר); **18:50[51]**//2 Sam 22:51>/<2 Sam 7:15, Yahweh's "covenantal loyalty" (חסד) to Davidic "messiah"/"seed" (cf. Isa 55:3; Ps 89:49[50]; 2 Chr 6:42); **20:7[8]**>/<Deut 17:16, king not trust "horses" (סוסים) (cf. 33:17; 147:10);[158] **22**>/<"servant songs" of Isa esp. 52:13–53:12—many single Hebrew word parallels;[159] **24:1–2**>/<Exod 9:29, "the earth is Yahweh's" (ליהוה הארץ); **27:12**>/<Exod 20:16+23:1, "false witness . . . malicious" (עדי שקר . . . חמס) (cf. Deut 19:16; Ps 35:11); **29:10**>/<Gen 6–9, Yahweh sits over (or since) "the flood" (מבול) (term for "flood" is only used in Genesis and Ps 29:10); **33:6, 9**>/<Gen 1, creation by divine decree—"He spoke and it came to be" (הוא אמר ויהי) (Ps 33:9), "and he said X and there was X" (ויאמר . . . ויהי . . .) (e.g., Gen 1:3); **34:6, 15, 17[7, 16, 18]**>/<Exod 22:23[22], Yahweh hears when they "call out" or "cry out" (קרא/צעק) (cf. Ps 34:17[18]); **35:11**>/<Exod 23:1; Deut 19:16, "malicious witnesses" (עדי חמס); **36:8[9]; 46:4[5]**>/<Ezek 47:1–12; Joel 3:18[4:18]; Zech 14:8, "stream/river/living water" from temple/Jerusalem (נהר/נחל/מים חיים); **39:12[13]**>/<Lev 25:23, living with Yahweh as "a residing foreigner" (גר) (cf. 1 Chr 29:15); **41:1[2]**>/<Exod 22:21–24[20–23]; Deut 15:7–10; 24:15, 17–22, the psalmist says "Blessed are those who have regard for the weak," suggesting they are helping those for whom Yahweh has special regard.

Book II: **42:1**>/<Joel 1:20, "as a deer longs . . . my soul longs for you/animals of the field long for you" (כאיל תערג . . . נפשי תערג אליך/בהמות שדה תערוג אליך) (cf. another parallel in Ps 42:3, 10[4, 11]; Joel 2:17); **42:7[8]**>/<Jonah 2:3[4], "all your waves and breakers swept over me" (כל משבריך וגליך עלי עברו); **44:2[3]**>/<Josh 1–12, "you drove out the nations"; **44:22[23]**>/<Isa 53:7; Jer 12:3, "like sheep/a lamb to be slaughtered" (כצאן טבחה/כשה לטבח/כצאן לטבחה) (cf. Ps 44:11[12]); **45:11, 17[12, 8]**>/<Gen 49:8, "peoples will praise you/your brothers will praise you" (עמים יהודך/יודוך אחיך);[160] **46:6[7]**>/<Amos 9:5, "earth melts" (תמוג ארץ); **53:1[2]**>/<1 Samuel 25, "the fool" (נָבָל) is identical to Nabal (נָבָל), whose tragic story falls between references to Doeg (1 Sam 21:7; 22:18; Ps 52 superscription) and the Ziphites (1 Sam 23:19; 26:1; Ps 54 superscription);[161] **60:7[9]//108:8[9]**>/<Gen 49:10, the phrase "Judah my ruler's staff" (יְהוּדָה מְחֹקְקִי) lit. "staff of decree" (etymology from חק based on Gen 49:10 "ruler's staff between his feet"); **66:6**>/<Exod 14:22+Josh 3:16–17, "sea to dry ground" and river/Jordan "crossed over" (ים יבשה/עבר); **67:1[2]**>/<Num 6:24–25, "may God be gracious to us and bless us, may he shine his face upon us/Yahweh bless you. . . . Yahweh shine his face upon you and be gracious to you" (אלהים יחננו ויברכנו יאר פניו אתנו/יברכך יהוה . . . יאר יהוה פניו אליך ויחנך); **68:1[2]**//Num 10:35, "May God arise, may his enemies be scattered; may his foes flee before him/Rise up, Yahweh! May your enemies be

---

158. See Craigie and Tate, *Psalms 1–50*, 187.

159. See list and discussion of comparisons of Ps 22 and Isaiah's so-called servant songs by many scholars in Lyons, "Psalm 22," 642. Lyons goes on to suggest potential thematic relations between Ps 22 and Isa 40–66 (643–51).

160. In addition to the rarity of "praise" (ידה) used of a human, Postell lists six other similarities between the blessing of Judah (Gen 49:8–12) and Ps 45, but they are all common terms ("Literary," 161–62).

161. Suggested by Kidner, *Psalms 1–72*, 1:196 cited in Goldingay, *Psalms*, 2:151; cf. 2:158, n. 8.

scattered; may your foes flee before you” (יקום אלהים יפוצו אויביו וינוסו משׂנאיו מפניו/קומה יהוה ויפצו איביך וינסו משׂנאיך מפניך); **68:7[8]**>/<Exod 13:21, “when God went out before your people”/“Yahweh went ahead of them” (אלהים בצאתך לפני עמך/יהוה הלך לפניהם); **68:8[9]**>/<Exod 19:16–18+Judg 5:5, revelation at “Sinai” (סיני) “before God, the One of Sinai, before God, the God of Israel”/“before Yahweh, the One of Sinai, before Yahweh, the God of Israel” (מפני אלהים זה סיני מפני אלהים אלהי ישׂראל/מפני יהוה זה סיני מפני יהוה אלהי ישׂראל) (cf. Ps 68:12, 13[13, 14]~Judg 5:30, 16); **68:16[17]**>/<Exod 15:17, “mountain . . . of his/your dwelling” (הר . . . לשבתו/לשבתך); **68:17[18]**>/<Deut 33:2, “Lord/Yahweh (came) from Sinai” (מסיני [א]אדני/יהוה ב);[162] **69:33[34]**>/< Exod 22:23[22], Yahweh “hears” (שׁמע) the needy; **72:4**>/<Jer 22:16, “may he judge *the afflicted* of the people and deliver the children of *the needy*”/“he [Josiah] defended the cause of *the afflicted* and *needy*” (ישפט עניי עם יושיע לבני אביון/דן דין עני ואביון) (cf. Ps 72:12; and “judge” 72:4; 1 Kgs 3:9);[163] **72:12**>/<Job 29:12, “for he will deliver the needy *who cry out, the afflicted who have no one to help*”/“for I rescued *the afflicted who cried out*, and the fatherless *who had no one to help them*” (כי יציל אביון משוע ואין עזר לו/כי אמלט עני משוע ויתום ולא עזר לו);[164] **72:15**>/<1 Kgs 10:1, 2, “gold of Sheba/queen of Sheba . . . very much gold” (מזהב שבא/מלכת שבא . . . זהב רב מאד).[165]

Book III: **73:26**>/<Num 18:20; Deut 12:12; 14:27, 29; 18:1, priests and Levites have “no portion” (חלק) so Yahweh is their portion—Asaph is of the temple singers (cf. Ps 73 superscription; 1 Chr 25:2, 6, 9); **74:4–7**>/<2 Kgs 25:9–10, destruction of the temple; **74:13–15**>/<Exod 14:21–22, opened the sea as if a dragon (cf. Isa 27:1; 51:9–10; Ps 89:10[11]; 104:26);[166] **74:16, 17**>/<Gen 8:22, “day . . . night . . . summer and winter” (יום . . . לילה . . . קיץ וחרף); 77:**8, 9[9, 10]**>/<Exod 34:6, “has his *covenantal loyalty* ceased? . . . Has *God* forgotten *to be gracious* . . . his *compassion*?/*a God compassionate* and *gracious* . . . abounding in *covenantal loyalty*” (האפס חסדו . . . השכח חנות אל . . . רחמו/אל רחום וחנון . . . רב חסד); **77:15[16]**>/<Exod 6:6, “redeem with an outstretched arm” (גאל זרוע); **79:1**>/<Isa 52:1, “the nations came into your inheritance, they ritually defiled your holy temple/holy city, the ritually defiled shall not enter you again” (באו גוים בנחלתך טמאו את היכל קדשך/עיר הקדש כי לא יוסיף יבא בך עוד וטמא) (cf. Lam 1:10); **79:2**>/<Deut 28:26, “the dead bodies of your servants as food for the birds of the heavens/your dead bodies will be food for all the birds of the heavens” (נבלת עבדיך מאכל לעוף השמים/והיתה נבלתך למאכל לכל עוף השמים); **79:10; 115:2**>/<Joel 2:17, “why should the nations/they say among the peoples ‘Where is their God?’” (למה יאמרו הגוים/בעמים

162. Instead of בם סיני Ps 68:17[18] MT, the translation attaches *mem* to Sinai and emends *bet* to בא (with *BHS* n. b).

163. See Briggs, *Psalms*, 2:132.

164. See Kirkpatrick, *Psalms Books II and III*, 417.

165. Mays suggests the themes of the justice and gold of Sheba in Ps 72 allude to the narrative of Solomon in 1 Kgs 3:3–14; 10:10 (*Psalms*, 238). She gave 120 talents of gold = 9,000 pounds = 4.5 tons (1 Kgs10:10).

166. The multiple heads of the dragon in Scripture are only mentioned in Ps 74:14 (cf. Gibson, *Canaanite Myths*, 50). On Ps 74:12–17 as an allusion to creation, see Chau, “Poetry of Creation,” 74–76.

(איה אלהיהם/איה־נא אלהיהם); **80:8–13**>/<Isa 5:1–7; 27:2–6; Jer 2:21; 12:10–11; Ezek 17:1–10; 19:10–14, allegory of the people as a vine; **80:17**>/<110:1, "the man at your right hand/sit at my right hand" (איש ימינך/שב לימיני) (cf. contexts); **81:3[4]**>/<Lev 23:24, 39, blow the trumpet for the Festival of Tabernacles; **81:5[6]**>/<Exod 11:4, "when the going out of him upon the land of Egypt/I am going out in the midst of Egypt" (בצאתו על ארץ מצרים/אני יוצא בתוך מצרים); **81:7[8]**>/<Exod 17:7; Num 20:13, "waters of Meribah/ Meribah" (מי מריבה) (cf. Deut 33:8; Ps 106:32); **83:9a, 11[10a, 12]**>/<Judg 7:25; 8:21, defeat like Midian and Oreb and Zeeb, Zebah and Zelmunna (cf. Isa 9:4[3]; 10:26); **83:9b[10b]**>/<Judg 4:12–16; 5:20–21, defeat like Sisera and Canaanites; **83:13–15[14–16]**>/<Isa 17:13–14, Beentjes evaluates a case of repeated terms, four of which are inverted in what could be a complex example of Seidel's theory: "Although the peoples roar like the roar of surging waters, when he rebukes them they flee far away, *pursued before the wind* like chaff on *the hills, like tumbleweed* before a gale" (Isa 17:13†) and "Make them *like tumbleweed*, my God, like chaff *before the wind*. As fire consumes the forest or a flame sets *the mountains* ablaze, so *pursue* them with your tempest and terrify them with your storm" (Ps 83:13–15[14–16], verbal parallels marked);[167] **86:8**>/<Exod 15:11, "among the gods there is none like you, Lord/who among the gods is like you Yahweh" (אין כמוך באלהים אדני/מי כמכה מאלם יהוה) (cf. 2 Sam 7:22; 1 Kgs 8:23);[168] **89:8[9]**>/<Exod 15:11, "Yahweh God of hosts, who is like you?" (יהוה אלהי צבאות מי־כמוך) and "Who is like you among the gods O Yahweh?" (מי־כמכה באלם יהוה).[169]

Book IV: **90:3**>/<Gen 3:19, "you turn humans to crushed matter (dust)/to dust you will return" (תשב אנוש עד דכא/אל עפר תשוב) (cf. 2:17; Eccl 12:7); **90:13**>/<Exod 32:12, "turn . . . and have compassion" (שובה/שב . . . והנחם)—the parallel of two common terms, even with imperative of "have compassion" only these two times, is insufficient for an allusion, though interpreters combine this with the "of Moses" superscription of the psalm;[170] **94:1**>/<Nah 1:2, "an avenging God is Yahweh, avenging God shine forth/ Yahweh . . . is an avenging God, Yahweh takes vengeance . . . Yahweh takes vengeance" (אל נקמות יהוה אל נקמות הופיע/אל . . . נקם יהוה נקם יהוה . . . נקם יהוה) (cf. Deut 32:35); **95:4–5**>/<Gen 1, creation (cf. similar language Ps 24:1–2; 89:11[12]); **96:1**>/<Isa 42:10, "sing to Yahweh a new song, sing to Yahweh all the earth/sing to Yahweh a new song, his praise from the end of the earth" (שירו ליהוה שיר חדש שירו ליהוה כל הארץ/שירו ליהוה שיר חדש תהלתו מקצה הארץ) (cf. Ps 98:1; 149:1); **99:5//99:9**, "exalt Yahweh our God and bow down at his footstool/holy mountain" (רוממו יהוה אלהינו והשתחוו להדם רגליו/להר קדשו)—while the parallel here suggests the footstool is the holy mountain (Zion) in the postexilic period and so also perhaps Lam 2:1, elsewhere "footstool" refers to the ark

167. See Beentjes, "Discovering a New Path," 34 (who mentions two additional terms that do not follow the pattern).
168. See Goldingay, *Psalms 42–89*, 2:624.
169. Observed by Morales, *Exodus*, 57.
170. See Anderson and Freedman, *Amos*, 649; Tanner, *Psalms*, 90–101.

(Ps 132:7; 1 Chr 28:2) and the earth (Isa 66:1);[171] **99:6–8**>/<intercessory roles of Moses (Exod 32:11; 33:7–11; 34:9; Deut 9:18–19), Aaron (Num 16:22), and Samuel (1 Sam 7:9; 12:18, 23) (cf. Jer 15:1).[172]

Book V: **107:6//13//19//28**>/<Exod 22:23[22]; Josh 24:7, they "cried/cry out" to Yahweh and he delivers/hears (צעק); **111:4**>/<Exod 34:6, "gracious and compassionate is Yahweh/Yahweh is a compassionate and gracious God" (חנון ורחום יהוה/יהוה אל רחום וחנון) (cf. "faithful" Ps 111:7; Exod 34:6);[173] **111:10a**>/<Prov 9:10, "The fear of Yahweh is the beginning of wisdom" (ראשית חכמה יראת יהוה/תחלת חכמה יראת יהוה) (the psalmist selected an alternate term for beginning [ראשית] to suit the needs of his acrostic); **112:4b**>/<Exod 34:6, "(those who are) gracious and compassionate and righteous/Yahweh is a compassionate and gracious God" (חנון ורחום וצדיק/יהוה אל רחום וחנון);[174] **113:7–8a**//1 Sam 2:8, "He raises the poor from the dust and lifts the needy from the ash heap, he seats them with princes" (מקימי/מקים מעפר דל מאשפת ירים אביון להושיבי/להושיב עם נדיבים) (cf. 1 Sam 2:5 with Ps 113:9, where the somewhat rare term for "infertile [woman]" [עקר] has children);[175] **118:14**//Exod 15:2a, "Yah is my strength and defense, he has become my salvation" (עזי וזמרה יה ויהי לי לישועה) (nearly identical to Isa 12:2b and see Ps 118:21; also cf. Exod 15:6 with Ps 118:15b).[176]

Psalm 119 sometimes uses phrases from elsewhere in the psalms but swaps out references to God for torah: "I have set *Yahweh* before me" (Ps 16:8), "I have set *your rules* (before me)" (119:30); "do not hide *your face* from me" (27:9), "do not hide *your commandments* from me" (119:19); "my soul clings to *you*" (63:8[9]), "I cling to *your decrees*" (119:31); "I trust in *Yahweh*" (31:6[7]), "I trust in *your word*" (119:42); "all of you who hope in *Yahweh*" (31:24[25]), I have put my hope in *your rules*" (119:43).[177] This interchange of objects of devotion emphasizes the striking importance of torah.[178]

Psalm 119 refers to torah (or Torah) in general in nearly all of its 176 verses, using ten synonyms, with "torah" being the umbrella term appearing in Ps 119:1 as "torah of Yahweh." The terms include: "torah" (תורה, 25x), "statute" (חק, 22x), "commandment" (מצוה, 22x), "judgment" (משפט, 23x), "testimony" (עדת, 23x), "word" (דבר, 22x), "word" (אמר, 19x), "precept" (פקד, 21x), "way" (דרך, 2x), and "path" (ארח, 1x). The first eight are the primary synonyms, and the first five occur in 1 Kgs 2:3–4, with written Torah as

171. See "הָדֹם," *HALOT* 1:239.

172. The phrase "Moses and Aaron were among his priests" in Ps 99:6 is difficult because Moses was not a priest even while he functioned in intercessory priestly roles at times. See Goldingay, *Psalms*, 3:130.

173. If Ps 111:4 directly alludes to Exod 34:6, then it follows Seidel's theory. See attribute formula network.

174. If Ps 112:4 directly alludes to Exod 34:6, then it follows Seidel's theory. See attribute formula network.

175. The binding final ***hireq yod*** (construct) on "raises up" (מְקִימִי) in Ps 113:7 also appears on ptcs. in 113:5, 6, 9; 114:8; 123:1 and may be an ornamental device of late poetic style (GKC §90m; Hurvitz, "Originals and Imitations," 115–21). The ***hireq yod*** on the inf. const. "to seat" (לְהוֹשִׁיבִי) probably should be read as "to seat him" (לְהוֹשִׁיבוֹ) with Ps 113:8 LXX (so *BHS* note a; GKC §90n).

176. For other connectors between Ps 118 and Isaiah, see Hossfeld and Zenger, *Psalm 3*, 235.

177. These are some of the examples provided by Tigay, "Torah Scroll," 329.

178. See Finsterbusch, "Yahweh's Torah," 128, n. 45.

the main term there.[179] The sum of the psalm's expressions can refer to written torah (or Torah) but does not refer strictly to legal instruction. In fact, the psalmist does not talk about the specifics of Torah but refers to it in a way that overlaps with wisdom, though not entirely.[180] Psalm 119 does not mention creation, covenant, Moses, exodus, land of promise, people of Israel, temple, sacrifice, or messiah.[181] Zenger argues that the use of "word" in Ps 119 expands the sense beyond legal traditions and infers a somewhat prophetic quality of divine revelation.[182] The psalmist does not speak from a static vantage point about torah but can speak as one who has been obedient (119:10–11) and who returns to the testimonies (119:59).[183] In sum, Ps 119 makes broad but emphatic allusion to torah as divine revelation.

124:1>/<Gen 31:42, "if Yahweh had not been on our side/if the God of my father . . . had not been on my side" (לולי יהוה שהיה לנו/לולי אלהי אבי . . . היה לי); **126:2, 3**>/<Joel 2:20, 21, "Yahweh has done great things" (הגדיל יהוה לעשות) (see Nonrecurring Doublets in Joel Filters; cf. say among the nations Joel 2:17; Ps 126:2); **127:2**>/<2 Sam 12:25, "the one he loves" (ידידו) similar to Solomon's other name Jedidiah/Beloved of Yah (ידידיה);[184] **129:6**>/<Isa 37:27, "like grass on the roof, withers/scorched before it can grow" (כחציר גגות שקדמת שלף יבש/חציר גגות ושדמה לפני קמה); **133:2**>/<Lev 8:12, simile of the anointing of Aaron; **135:13**//Exod 3:15b, "Your name Yahweh forever, your renown, Yahweh, through all generations/Yahweh . . . This is my name forever, and this is my memorial for all generations" (יהוה שמך לעולם יהוה זכרך לדר ודר/יהוה . . . זה שמי לעולם וזה זכרי לדר דר); **135:14**//Deut 32:36a, "For Yahweh will vindicate his people, and have compassion upon his servants" (כי ידין יהוה עמו ועל עבדיו יתנחם);[185] **143:3**//Lam 3:6, "he makes me dwell in the darkness/in darkness he makes me dwell like those long dead" (הושיבני במחשכים/במחשכים הושיבני כמתי עולם) (Seidel's theory); **144:3**>/<8:5; Job 7:17, "what are human beings?"; **144:5–7**>/<18:9, 14, 16[10, 15, 17]//2 Sam 10, 15, 17, excerpts of thanks for past deliverances in prayer of David repackaged a new prayer for deliverance; **144:9**>/<33:2–3, new song on a ten-stringed lyre (Seidel's theory); **144:10**>/<18 superscription//2 Sam 22:1, deliverance of David; **144:15b**>/<33:12a, "blessed is the people/nation whose God is Yahweh" (אשרי העם שיהוה אלהיו/אשרי הגוי אשר יהוה אלהיו); **145:8**//Exod 34:6, "Yahweh is gracious and compassionate, slow to anger and abounding in covenantal loyalty/Yahweh, Yahweh is a compassionate and gracious God, slow to anger and abounding in covenantal loyalty and

---

179. See Hossfeld and Zenger, *Psalms 3*, 258; Freedman, *Psalm 119*, 35.

180. See Levenson, "Sources of Torah," 566–67.

181. See ibid., 564; Freedman, *Psalm 119*, 90–91.

182. See Hossfeld and Zenger, *Psalms 3*, 260. Zenger's comment that Ps 119 is "*evangelium*" (gospel) not "*lex*" (law) does not help.

183. Finsterbusch suggests Ps 119 gives voice to "several individuals" ("Yahweh's Torah," 132). Whether or not this is the case, she demonstrates that the psalm speaks from different situations (128–30).

184. Some wonder if "the one he loves" (Ps 127:2) relates to the superscription "of Solomon" (see Kirkpatrick, *Psalms Books IV and V*, 751). For a series of other links between Ps 127 and Solomon, see Hossfeld and Zenger, *Psalms 3*, 385.

185. On Ps 135:14//Deut 32:36a, see Bendavid, *Parallels*, 195 [Hebrew].

faithfulness" (חנון ורחום יהוה ארך אפים וגדל חסד/יהוה יהוה אל רחום וחנון ארך אפים ורב חסד ואמת);[186] **146:2**>/<104:33, "I will praise/sing to Yahweh all my life, I will sing praise to my God as long as I live" (אהללה יהוה/אשירה ליהוה בחיי אזמרה לאלהי בעודי); **146:6**//Exod 20:11, "maker/Yahweh made heavens and earth, the sea and all that is in them" (עשה שמים וארץ את הים ואת כל אשר בם/עשה יהוה את השמים ואת הארץ את הים ואת כל אשר בם); **146:7**>/<Deut 10:18, "he upholds the cause . . . and gives/to give food" (עשה משפט . . . נתן/לתת לחם) (cf. orphan, widow, and residing foreigner in Ps 146:9).

Shared Stock Phrases and Other Similarities[187]

Rule of the deity: >/<2:4; 59:8[9], "The One enthroned in heaven laughs; the Lord scoffs at them/But you laugh at them, Yahweh; you scoff at all those nations" (יושב בשמים ישחק אדני ילעג למו/ואתה יהוה תשחק למו תלעג לכל גוים) (cf. 37:13); >/<9:7[8]; 29:10; 102:12[13]; Lam 5:19, "Yahweh sits/reigns forever" (יהוה ישב עולם) (cf. Ps 10:16); >/<10:16; 24:10; 29:10; 93:1; 96:10//1 Chr 16:31; Pss 97:1; 99:1 "Yahweh reigns/is king" (יהוה מלך) (cf. 95:3); >/<11:4; Hab 2:20, "Yahweh is in his holy temple" (יהוה בהיכל קדשו) (cf. "your holy temple," Pss 5:7[8]; 79:1; 138:2; Jonah 2:4, 7[5, 8]; Mic 1:2); >/<15:1; 27:5, 6; 61:4[5], "in his/your tent" (באהלך/באהלו); >/<18:6[7]//2 Sam 22:7; 1 Kgs 8:27, 30; Pss 29:9; 78:69, Yahweh's temple on high; >/<50:6; 58:11[12]; 72:1; 75:7[8]; 82:1, 8, "God judges/is judge" (אלהים שפט) (cf. Isa 33:22, "Yahweh is our judge"); >/<89:14[15]; 97:2, "righteousness and justice are the foundation of your/his throne" (צדק ומשפט מכון כסאך/כסאו); >/<90:2; 103:17, "from everlasting unto everlasting" (מעולם עד עולם); >/<94:2; Gen 18:25, "judge of (all) the earth" (שפט הארץ/כל הארץ); >/<102:12[13]; Lam 5:19, "you Yahweh sit enthroned forever" (ואתה יהוה לעולם תשב) (cf. Ps 29:10); >/<136:26; Gen 24:3, 7; Jonah 1:9; Ezra 1:2//2 Chr 36:23; Neh 1:4, 5; 2:4, 20, "God of heaven" (אל/אלהי השמים).

Honoring the deity: >/<13:6; 27:6; 33:3; 96:1; 98:1; 104:33; 105:2; 149:1; Exod 15:2; Judg 5:3; 1 Chr 16:9, "(I will) sing to Yahweh/him" (שיר ליהוה/לו) and Pss 68:32[33]; 144:9, "sing to God" (שיר לאלהים); >/<19:1–4; Ps 148:3–4, heavens and earth praise the divine being; >/<19:7[8]; 93:5, "your/the decrees (of Yahweh) are (very) trustworthy" (עדות יהוה נאמנה/עדתיך נאמנו מאד); >/<23:1; Gen 49:24; Isa 40:11; Jer 31:10, "Yahweh is my shepherd/the shepherd/like a shepherd" (יהוה רעי/רעה/כרעה) (cf. Pss 28:9; 74:1; 80:1; 95:7; 100:3; Ezek 34; Mic 7:14);[188] >/<35:27; 40:16[17]; Mal 1:5, "great is Yahweh" (יגדל יהוה) (cf. Ps 70:4[5], "God is great" [יגדל אלהים]);[189] >/<96:4//1 Chr 16:25; Pss 48:2; 145:3, "great is Yahweh and greatly to be praised" (גדול יהוה ומהלל מאד); >/<100:5;

---

186. If Ps 145:8 alludes directly to Exod 34:6 it reflects Seidel's theory. Bullock suggests the attribute formula of Exod 34:6 is not native to Pss 86, 103, and 145 but was inserted by an editor attempting to create thematic coherence in Books III, IV, and V of the Psalter ("Covenant Renewal," 33). The present study treats the allusions to Exod 34:6 in Pss 86 and 103 as exegetical (see notes ad loc.) but 145:8 as a non-exegetical broad allusion.

187. For discussion of additional parallel expressions between Psalms and other Scripture contexts with an excavative agenda, see Cheyne, *Origins*, 461–84.

188. See Mays, *Psalms*, 117–18.

189. Note the shift from Yahweh to God in Ps 70:4[5], which is a synoptic parallel to 40:16[17]. See note on the so-called Elohistic Psalter of Psalms 43–83 in Psalms Filters.

106:1//1 Chr 16:34; 136:1–26; Jer 33:11; Ezra 3:11; 2 Chr 5:13; 7:3, "for Yahweh is good, his covenantal mercy endures forever" (כי טוב יהוה לעולם חסדו); >/<102:27[28], "you remain the same" lit. "you are he" (אתה הוא) may echo "I am he" (אני הוא) (Deut 32:39; Isa 41:4; 43:10, 13, 25; 46:4; 48:12; 51:12; 52:6); >/<103:1, 2, 22; 104:1, 35, "Bless Yahweh, O my soul" (ברכי נפשי את יהוה); >/<113:2; Job 1:21, "blessed be the name of Yahweh" (יהי שם יהוה מברך).

Worship: >/<22:25[26]; 50:14; 56:12[13]; 61:5, 8[6, 9]; 65:1[2]; 66:13; 76:11[2]; 116:14, 18; Num 30:2; Deut 23:21[22]; Job 22:27 (Eliphaz); Eccl 5:4, 5[3, 4], "fulfill vows" (נדר שלם); >/<28:2; 134:2, "lift up my/your hands to the (your inner) sanctuary" (שאו ידכם קדש/נשאי ידי דביר קדשך); >/<30:4[5]; 97:12, "praise his holy name" (הודו לזכר קדשו); >/<33:2; 105:1//1 Chr 16:8; Ps 106:1//1 Chr 16:34; Pss 118:1, 29; 136:1; Isa 12:4; 2 Chr 20:21, "give praise to Yahweh" (הודו ליהוה); >/<37:4; Isa 58:14; Job 22:26; 27:10, "take delight in Yahweh/God" (התענג על יהוה/אלוה); >/<92:1[2]; 147:1, "it is good to praise . . . and to make music/it is good to make music . . . sing" (טוב להדות . . . ולזמר/טוב זמרה . . . נעים); >/<98:4; Isa 52:9, "burst forth in joyous song" (פצחו ורננו) (cf. 14:7; 44:23; 49:13; 54:1; 55:12); >/<Pss 104:35; 105:45; 106:48; 111:1; 112:1; 113:1, 9; 115:18; 116:19; 117:2; 135:1, 3, 21; 146:1, 10; 147:1, 20; 148:1, 14; 149:1, 9; 150:1, 6, "Praise Yah" (*halelu-yah* הללו יה);[190] >/<113:3; 135:1; 148:5, 13, "the name of Yahweh be praised/praise the name of Yahweh" (מהלל שם יהוה/הללו את שם יהוה); >/<118:2; 124:1; 129:1, "let Israel say" (יאמר נא ישראל); >/<122:1; Isa 2:3; Mic 4:2, "let us go to the house of Yahweh/let us go up . . . to the house of the God of Jacob" (בית יהוה נלך/נעלה . . . אל בית אלהי יעקב) (cf. Jer 31:6).

Merciful divine acts: >/<3:3[4]; 27:6, "lifts up my head" (רום ראשי); >/<4:6[7]; Num 6:25, "lift up upon us the light of your face Yahweh/Yahweh make his face to shine on you" (נסה עלינו אור פניך יהוה/יאר יהוה פניו אליך);[191] >/<5:11[12]; 91:4, "spread your protection over them/he will cover them (under his wings)" (לך תסך עלימו/יסך) (cf. 17:8; 36:7[8]; Ruth 2:12); >/<16:11; 17:7; 18:35[36]; 48:10[11]; 60:5[7]//108:6[7]; 63:8[9]; 110:1; Jer 22:24, "my/your [Yahweh's] right hand" (ימיני/ימינך); >/<17:8; 36:7[8]; 57:1[2] 61:4[5]; 63:7[8], "shadow of your wings" (בצל כנפיך) (cf. 61:4[5]; 91:4); >/<18:2[3]; 31:2[3]; 71:3, "rock" and "fortress" (צור, מצודה); >/<121:4; Isa 5:27, "not slumber nor sleep" (לא ינום ולא יישן).

Power of deity: >/<18:15[16]//2 Sam 22:16; Exod 15:8; Job 4:9, "blast/breath of his/your nostrils" (רוח אפיו/אפיך) (cf. Lam 4:20); >/<147:4; Isa 40:26, "he calls" each star "by name"; >/<95:6; 100:3; Isa 51:13, "Yahweh/he is our/your maker" (יהוה/הוא עשׂנו/עשׂך) (cf. 44:2); >/<97:5; Mic 1:4, "the mountains melt like wax/the mountains melt . . . like wax" (הרים כדונג נמסו/ונמסו ההרים . . . כדונג); >/<115:15; 121:2; 124:8; 134:3; 146:6, "maker of heaven and earth" (עשׂה שמים וארץ).

---

190. On the function in the Psalter of *hallelu-yah,* see Hossfeld and Zenger, *Psalms 3,* 39–41.

191. Echoes of the priestly blessing (Num 6:25) in Ps 4:6[7] signify it as "widely diffused throughout the culture" (Fishbane, *Biblical Interpretation,* 331). Goldingay misrepresents Fishbane on this point (*Psalms,* 1:123).

Zion: >/<9:14[15]; Lam 2:1, 4, 8, 10, 13, 18; 4:22, "daughter Zion" (בת ציון) (1x in Psalms; many times elsewhere esp. Lamentations); >/<46:4; 48:1, 8[2, 9], "city of God/our God" (עיר אלהים/אלהינו); >/<48:11[12]; 97:8, "(Mount) Zion rejoices (and) the daughters of Judah because of your judgments" (הר ציון תגלנה בנות יהודה למען משפטיך); >/<76:2[3]; Lam 2:6, Zion as "lair" (סך) (cf. Jer 25:38; roars from Zion, Joel 3:16[4:16]; Amos 1:2); >/<125:5; 128:6, "peace upon Jerusalem" (שלום על ישראל) (cf. 122:6, 7, 8).

Hope of the righteous: >/<5:5[6]; Deut 7:24; 11:25; Josh 1:5, they "cannot stand" before you (לא־יתיצב איש לפניך/לפניכם/לא־יתיצבו . . . לנגד עיניך);[192] >/<15:5; 112:6; 125:1, "not be moved forever" (לא ימוט לעולם); >/<17:5; 38:16[17]; 66:9; 94:18; 121:3; Deut 32:35, "feet/foot will (not) slip" (בל נמוטו פעמי/תמוט רגלם) (cf. Ps 18:36[37]//2 Sam 22:37; Ps 37:31); >/<18:47[48]//2 Sam 22:48; Ps 47:3[4], "subdues peoples under me/our feet" (ידבר עמים תחתי/תחתינו . . . רגלינו) (cf. 45:5[6]); >/<25:2, 20; 31:1[2]; 31:17[18]; 71:1, "do not let me be put to shame" (אל אבושה); >/<33:13; 80:14[15]; 102:19[20]; Isa 63:15; Job 28:24, "look down from heaven" (משמים הביט); >/<34:20[21]; Exod 12:46, "bones . . . not broken" (עצמות . . . לא שבר) (cf. Ps 51:8; Isa 38:13);[193] >/<37:9, 11, 22, 29, 34; Isa 60:21, those who hope in Yahweh/the meek/the blessed/the righteous "inherit the land" (יירשו ארץ/לרשת ארץ); >/<44:3[4]; Josh 24:12; 1 Sam 24:12, "not by (your/their) sword" (לא בחרב); >/<51:9[11]; 109:14; Jer 18:23; Neh 4:5[3:37], "blot out my iniquity/do not blot out [their] iniquity" (עונתי מחה/אל תמחה עון); >/<52:8[10]; Hos 14:6[7]; Job 15:33, "like an olive tree" (כזית); >/<57:4[5]; 59:7[8]; 64:3[4], "tongue/mouth (as) sword" (לשון חרב/כחרב/פה) (cf. 140:3[4]); >/<58:10[11]; 68:23[24], "dip feet in blood/wade feet in blood" (פעם רחץ בדם/מחץ רגלים בדם); >/<72:5; 89:36–37[37–38], rule as long as "sun" (שמש) and "moon" (ירח); >/<85:8[9]; Hab 2:1, "I will hear/see what he will speak" (אשמעה/לראות מה ידבר); >/<94:14; 1 Sam 12:22, "for Yahweh will not reject his people" (כי לא יטש יהוה עמו); >/<112:9; 1 Sam 2:10, "his horn is lifted/lift the horn" (קרנו תרום/ירם קרן) (cf. 2 Sam 2:1); >/<128:5; 134:3, "may Yahweh bless you from Zion" (יברכך יהוה מציון).

Identity of the righteous: >/<74:1; 79:13; Jer 23:1; Ezek 34:31, "sheep of your/my pasture" (צאן מרעתך/מרעיתי) (cf. Ps 95:7); >/<37:31; Isa 51:7; Jer 31:33; Job 22:22 (Eliphaz), "torah in heart" (תורה ל/בלב/לבב) (cf. Zech 7:12; Pss 40:8[9]; 119:70; Prov 3:1); >/<112:1; 128:1, "blessed is the one/all who fear/s Yahweh" (אשרי איש ירא את יהוה/אשרי כל ירא יהוה).

Commitment of upright: >/<25:11; 79:9; 109:21; 143:11; 1 Kgs 8:41//2 Chr 6:32; Jer 14:7, 21, "for your name's sake" (למען שמך); >/<26:2; 139:23; Job 23:10, "test me" (בחנני); >/<26:6; 73:13; Gen 20:6, "(wash) hands in innocence" (רחץ בנקיון כף); >/<27:11; 86:11, "teach me your way Yahweh" (הורני יהוה דרכך); >/<31:14[15]; Isa 25:1, "Yahweh . . . you are my God" (יהוה . . . אלהי אתה); >/<33:5; 45:7[8]; 146:8, "love the

---

192. This shared language observed by Firth, *Stranger*, 18.

193. Though Ps 34:20[21] probably does not allude to the Passover lamb, the catchwords "bones not broken" can suggest a connotative blend between "the righteous" and the lamb for John 19:36 (see Kirkpatrick, *Psalms Book I*, 175).

righteous" (אהב צדק); >/<44:1[2]; 78:3, "our ancestors have told us" (אבותינו ספרו לנו); >/<44:22[23]; 69:7[8], "for your sake" (כי עליך); >/<69:7[8]; Jer 15:15, "I suffer reproach for your sake" (נשׂא עליך חרפה);[194] >/<79:13; 95:7; 100:3, "we are your/the/his people and the sheep of your/his pasture (and sheep of his hand)" (אנחנו עמך וצאן מרעיתך/אנחנו עם מרעיתו וצאן ידו/אנחנו עמו וצאן מרעיתו) (cf. 74:1); >/<94:12; Job 5:17 (Eliphaz), "blessed is the strong person/person whom Yah disciplines/God corrects" (אשרי הגבר/אנוש אשר תיסרנו יה/יוכחנו אלוה); >/<131:1; Job 42:3, "things too wonderful for me" (נפלאות ממני).

In trouble: >/<88:8[9]; Job 19:13, "my associates/brothers far from me" (רחק מידעי ממני/אחי מעלי רחק) (cf. Ps 88:18[19]; Job 19:19); >/<94:6; Deut 24:17, 19, 20, 21, "widow, orphan, residing foreigner"; >/<124:3; Prov 1:12, "they would have swallowed us alive/let's swallow them alive like Sheol" (חיים בלעונו /נבלעם כשאול חיים) (cf. Ps 69:15 also with 124:3; and see Jer 51:34).

Psalmists' cries: >/<6:3[4]; 74:10; 80:4[5]; 82:2; 90:13; 94:3, "How long?!" (עד מתי) (cf. many times outside Psalms); >/<6:7[8]; 31:9[10], "my eyes grow weak with sorrow" (עששה בכעס עיני); >/<27:9; 10:2[3], "do not hide your face from me" (אל תסתר פניך ממני); >/<31:2[3]; 71:2; 102:2[3], "turn your ear to me" (הטה אלי אזנך); >/<38:9[10]; Jer 16:17, "not hidden" from the deity (לא סתר) (cf. Job 13:20); >/<42:3[4]; 80:5[6], "tears are bread/bread of tears" (דמעתי לחם/לחם דמעה) (cf. 102:9[10]); >/<42:4[5]; 1 Sam 1:15, "pour out soul" (שפך נפש) (cf. Ps 62:8[9]; Lam 2:19, "pour out heart" [שפך לבב]); >/<43:1; 74:22; 119:154, "defend my/your cause" (ריבה ריבי/ריבך); >/<69:17[18]; 102:2[3]; 143:7, "answer me quickly" (מהר ענני); >/<79:11; 102:20[21], "groans of the prisoners" (אנקת אסיר); >/<88:14[15]; Job 13:24, "why do you hide your face (from me)" (למה יסתיר פניך ממני) (cf. Deut 32:20); >/<102:1[2]; 18:6[7], "let my cry come before you/him" (שועתי אליך/לפניו תבוא).

Restoration: >/<14:7//53:6[7]; Jer 30:3; Hos 6:11; Amos 9:14, "restore his/my people" (שבות עמו/עמי); >/<32:5; 85:2[3], "you forgive the iniquity of my sin/of your people" (נשׂאת עון חטאתי/עמך); >/<126:2; Job 8:21 (Bildad), "our mouths will be filled with laughter/he will fill your mouth with laughter" (ימלא שׂחוק פינו/ימלה שׂחוק פיך).

Human limitations: >/<37:2; 90:5; 103:15; 129:6, "like new grass" that withers, etc. (כחציר) (cf. Isa 40:6–8; Ps 102:26[27]); >/<39:5, 11[6, 12]; 62:9; 144:4, "(all) humans are vapor" (אדם הבל) (cf. Ps 94:11; Eccl 2:21, 26; 3:19; 6:11, 12; 11:8); >/<103:15; Isa 40:6; Job 14:2, "like a flower" that withers, etc. (כציץ) (cf. simile at Ps 37:2, etc.).

Taunts: >/<42:3, 10[4, 11]; 79:10; Joel 2:17, "where is your/their God" (איה אלהיך/אלהיהם); >/<94:7; Jer 12:4, "they say Yah/he does not see" (ויאמרו לא יראה יה/אמרו לא יראה); >/<115:3–8; Isa 40:18–20; 41:7, 22–24, 28–29; 42:17; 43:9; 44:9–20; 45:16, 20; 46:1–2, 6–7; 48:5, 14; Jer 10:1–6, taunt against idolatry (see Jeremiah Filters on Jer 10:1–16).

---

194. See Parke-Taylor, *Formation*, 33.

Warnings against the sinful: >/<4:4[5]; 36:4[5]; Mic 2:1, (do not) sin/plot evil "upon his/your/their bed" (על משכבותכם/ו/תם); >/<14:1, 3//53:1, 3[2, 4]; Eccl 7:20, "there is none who does good" (אין עשה טוב); >/<36:1[2]; 2 Chr 20:29, "(no) dread of God" (אין פחד אלהים); >/<34:15; 37:27; Prov 13:19; 16:6, 17, "depart from evil" (סור מרע); >/<38:20[21]; 109:5; Gen 44:4; 1 Sam 25:21; Prov 17:13, "repay/give/return evil for good" (שלם/שים/שוב רעה תחת טובה); >/<101:5; Prov 21:4, "haughty eyes and a proud heart" (גבה/רום עינים ורחב לבב).

Judgment: >/<9:5[6]; 109:13; Exod 17:14; Deut 9:14; 25:6; 29:20; 2 Kgs 14:27, "blot out name/memory" (מחה שם/זכר) (cf. "memory perished," Isa 26:14; Ps 9:6[7]; Job 18:17); >/<11:6; Job 18:15 (Bildad), judgment by "burning sulfur" against the wicked (גפרית), against the cities of the plain (Gen 19:24), against Edom (Isa 34:9), against Israel (Deut 29:23[22]; Isa 30:33), against Gog (Ezek 38:22); >/<21:9[10]; Mal 4:1[3:19], Yahweh burns them "like a furnace" (כתנור) (cf. Isa 31:9);[195] >/<37:15; 46:9[10], "breaks the bow" (קשת שבר) (cf. 76:3[4]); >/<48:6[7]; Isa 13:8; 42:14; Jer 6:24; 30:6; 49:24; 50:43; Mic 4:9, 10, "writhe like a woman in labor/like a woman in labor" (חיל כיולדה/כיולדה); >/<50:7; 81:8[9], "listen, my people . . . and I will testify against you" (שמע עמי ואעידה בך);[196] >/<69:3[4]; 119:82, 123; Lev 26:16; Deut 28:32; 1 Sam 2:33; Jer 14:6; Job 11:20 (Zophar); 17:5; 31:16; Lam 2:11; 4:17, "eyes fail" (כלה עינים); >/<69:28[29]; Exod 32:32–33, "blot out of the book" (מחה מספר) (cf. Exod 17:14; Isa 4:3; Ps 139:16); >/<75:8[9]; Isa 51:17, 22; Jer 25:15, 17, 28; 49:12; 51:7, divine "cup" of judgment (כוס) (cf. Ps 11:6); >/<79:12; Gen 4:15, "sevenfold" vengeance (שבעתים) (contra forgive seventy-sevenfold, Matt 18:22);[197] >/<137:9; 2 Kgs 8:12; Isa 13:16; Hos 13:16; Nah 3:10, children dashed to pieces.

Nature: >/<18:7[8]; Deut 32:22, "foundations of the mountains" (מוסדי הרים) (2 Sam 22:8 "foundations of the heavens" [מוסדות השמים]); >/<50:1; 113:3; Mal 1:11, "from the rising of the sun to where it sets" (ממזרח שמש ועד מבואו) (cf. Isa 45:6); >/<74:17; 104:9, "boundaries" of creation (גבול) (cf. Deut 32:8; Jer 5:22; Job 38:8, 10); >/<77:18[19]; 97:4, "(his) lightning lights up the world" (האירו ברקים/ברקיו תבל); >/<88:6[7]; Lam 3:55, "lowest pit" (בור תחתיות) ("lowest part of earth" is common, cf. Pss 63:9[10]; 139:15; etc.); >/<88:6[7]; 107:10, 14; Job 10:21; 12:22, "from dark depths" (מחשך/חשך צלמות) (cf. 28:3); >/<96:11; 98:7, "let the sea roar and all that is in it" (ירעם הים ומלאו); >/<104:9; Jer 5:22; Job 38:10–11; Prov 8:29, "boundary" for the sea (גבול); >/<135:7b//Jer 10:13b, "he sends lightning with the rain and brings out the wind from his storehouses" (ברקים למטר עשה יצא רוח מאצרתיו) (cf. Deut 28:12; Ps 33:7; Job 38:22).

195. See Longman, *Psalms*, 127.

196. See Jacobson, "*Many Are Saying*," 108.

197. See Kirkpatrick, *Psalms Books II and III*, 482.

Chapter 26

JOB

SYMBOLS[1]

// verbal parallels (A level)
/~/ synoptic parallel (A level)
~ B, probable interpretive allusion; C, possible; D, probably not
+ interpretive blend
>/< more or less similar (see Filters)
* part of interpretive network (see Networks)

USE OF SCRIPTURE IN JOB[2]

6:10~Ps 119:50 (B) (parody of consolation)
7:17~Ps 8:4[5] (B) (What are humans?)
9:12~Isa 45:9 (C) (What are you doing?)
12:21, 24//Ps 107:40 (pouring contempt on nobles)
19:6–8~Lam 3:6–9 (B) (calling out not answered)
21:19~Deut 5:9* (B)+7:10* (B) (transgenerational retribution) (* see attribute formula network)

OLD TESTAMENT USE OF JOB

n/a

NEW TESTAMENT USE OF JOB

5:13//1 Cor 3:19 (wise in their craftiness)
41:11[3]~Rom 11:35 (Who should he repay?)

HERMENEUTICAL PROFILE OF THE USE OF SCRIPTURE IN JOB

Job sometimes evokes scriptural traditions. The increasing attention given by scholars to the scriptural use of Scripture partially accounts for shifting perspectives in many studies of Job. Older views of parallels between Job and other Scriptures often considered Job as the donor context. Closer attention to the typical ways scriptural parallels function in Job calls this into question. In Job, parody comprises the norm for scriptural parallels that likely indicate intentional relationship. Since parodies require known donor contexts to parody, Job more and more seems like the receptor context of the parallels. The main burden here relates to the challenges of interpreting parody. It will help to first note that diachronic study of Hebrew offers insight, albeit very little.

1. For explanation of symbols, see Symbols and Abbreviations and Introduction. For other help, see Glossary.
2. See Bibliographic Note on Lists of Potential Parallels.

Linguistic studies based on comparative textual evidence only work well on scriptural narrative shifts in syntax between Standard and Late Biblical Hebrew. The nature of poetic syntax does not offer the necessary evidence. The narrative frame of Job 1–2 and 42:7–16 features elements that suggest it is Late Biblical Hebrew.[3] But the small sample size can do no more than make a late date possible.

Job often evokes scriptural traditions in ways less than straightforward. Study of Job's use of scriptural traditions has resulted in numerous bold and far-reaching claims. Many of these mixed results stem from the unruly ways parody gets handled. Parody as a starting point naturally unshackles interpretive conclusions from more straightforward approaches. Dell's study identifies Job's intentional "misuse" of generic forms as parody.[4] Kynes's study on the function of parody in the Hebrew Bible makes an important distinction concerning targets that goes a long way to explaining how it works.[5]

Kynes summarizes four characteristics of the common definition of parody: (1) it alludes to a "precursor"; (2) it is antithetical to its target in some way; (3) it intends to subvert the authority of the original; and (4) it involves humor (282). Kynes accepts the first two elements of the common definition but rightly demonstrates that the third and fourth elements do not adequately speak to the range of parodies in Scripture. He notes that sometimes parody "targets" the precursor (the donor context) and sometimes a social or moral outlook (287). The target may not be the precursor scriptural context but problematic interpretations of it. Kynes also observes that parodies do not always use humor (290). Kynes puts these elements together and comes to four basic parody functions:

> (1) a humorous parody may target and ridicule the precursor to which it alludes;
> (2) a serious parody may target and reject the precursor;
> (3) a humorous parody may respect the precursor and target its (mis)interpreters;
> (4) a serious parody may reaffirm the precursor and target its (mis)interpreters (292).

Kynes aligns these four functions of parody with four possible scriptural examples: (1) Song of Songs 7:1–10 may target and ridicule the ancient Near Eastern love poem genre (*waṣf*) by going backwards from foot to head and exaggerating her unbecoming features (295–97); (2) Psalm 29 may target and reject the Canaanite praise of the storm deity while exalting Yahweh (298–300); (3) the Jonah narrative respects Exodus but targets and ridicules misapplications of prophetic teachings (300–3); (4) Job 7:17–18 reaffirms Ps 8:5[6] while targeting God not upholding retributive standards the way Job

3. See Hurvitz, "Date," 17–34, esp. syntactical evidence, 24–30. For a competing view, see Young, "Is the Prose," 606–29; for sharp critique of Young's approach, see Joosten's review of *Linguistic Dating*, 535–42. Longman's comment that linguistic arguments point in different directions errs by lumping together studies of the poetry of Job and the prose of Job (*Job*, 26, n. 9). The point here only relates to narrative.

4. See Dell, *Book of Job*, esp. 147–48, also see 109–57.

5. See Kynes, "Beat Your Parodies Into Swords," 276–310. Citation hereafter will be made parenthetically.

thinks he should (303–6). In each case, Kynes allows for several interpretive possibilities of these four biblical examples.

It is easy to agree with Kynes that not all parodies are created equal. His fourfold typology helps demonstrate that parodies do not always target with ridicule the contexts to which they allude (whether or not all of his four scriptural examples above work). A parody may affirm the donor context while ridiculing misinterpretations and misapplications of it. The present study works with Kynes's proposal, especially by identifying the target of parodies. This set of distinctions offers helpful upgrades over approaches that flatten all parodies into indiscriminate subversive ridicule—one size does not fit all.

Another element can help with considering Job's use of scriptural traditions, namely, individual versus collective suffering. The instructional qualities of the book allow Job to function, as Toews observes, "as a model of the righteous person in exile."[6] Toews's observation helps get at how Job works in exile and diaspora irrespective of when it was written.

From the eve of the fall of Jerusalem, the problem of collective retribution emerges repeatedly in Scripture. Habakkuk struggles to make sense of Yahweh's silence when the wicked Chaldeans threaten "those more righteous than themselves" (Hab 1:13). Both Jeremiah in Jerusalem and Ezekiel in exile answer those who say: "The parents have eaten sour grapes, and the children's teeth are set on edge" (Jer 31:29; Ezek 18:2). A group of psalmists claims that exilic catastrophe "came upon us, though we had not forgotten you" (Ps 44:17[18]). The psalmists mean what they say, even though Kings and the prophets never mention a group of righteous persons. The psalmists go so far as to say their faithfulness includes their actions and their hearts (44:18[19]), and God knows it (44:21[22]). These struggles with exilic judgment suggest seeds sown in a struggle to understand that had grown into a sharp debate over divine retribution.

The use of scriptural traditions in the book of Job, especially the parodies of interpretations of scriptural traditions, goes a long way to challenging faulty views of retribution.[7] Job and his friends debate the issues of justice and retribution at length. Struggles with scriptural interpretation regarding retribution do not get solved by simply quoting favorite verses. The collective suffering of God's people forces an unwelcome paradigm change on how to interpret scriptural teaching on retribution. Scriptural exegetical parodies can pull inadequate and superficial interpretation out into the open.

The handful of verifiable exegetical uses of scriptural traditions in Job signal it as the receptor context (see notes below). Job's use of Lamentations requires that the authorship of Job be set in the exilic period or later, though the narrative may be set in ancient times from the author's perspective.

---

6. Toews, "Genesis 1–4," 49.

7. For a complementary view, namely, the potential function of Elihu as saying some of the right things in the wrong way see Lynch, "Bursting," 348, 363.

An exilic or postexilic setting goes a long way to explaining the kinds of retributive distortions that had infiltrated scriptural interpretation. The realities of the exilic disaster, protracted oppression within the empire, and a stalled and failing restoration all push against simplistic and overly optimistic scriptural interpretation. How should Scripture be handled within a reality that does not easily line up with the enduring promises to Abraham and David? What happens if Isaiah's hopes for a new exodus get read literally amid postexilic suffering and struggles that never seem to end?

Part of the answer to the kinds of faulty retributive theology in the air appears in the debates of Job. The personal suffering of a righteous person among wise, friendly counselors provides an opportunity to offer instruction to help suffering individuals and collectives. Many people who suffer know what it feels like to get well-meaning advice peppered with distortions of Scripture. The use of scriptural traditions in Job aims at this old and predictable problem. Parody offers one effective tool for halting misinterpretations of Scripture at the very time people need help. Job does not parody scriptural traditions to ridicule and subvert them. The use of scriptural traditions in Job offers exegetical help to those who suffer.

USE OF SCRIPTURE

6:10~Ps 119:50 (B) (parody of consolation). The only two places the noun "consolation" appears in Scripture are Ps 119:50 and Job 6:10, making a relationship more likely than not in their similar contexts.[8] If the two passages represent a relationship, the nature of parody makes it unlikely that the psalmist would allude to dark sarcasm in an attempt to extol the virtues of Torah (bold signifies verbal parallels).[9]

> **My consolation** in my suffering is this: Your **word** preserves my life. (Ps 119:50†)

> [Job] Oh, that I might have my request, that God would grant what I hope for, that God would be willing to crush me, to let loose his hand and cut off my life! Then I would still have **my consolation**—my joy in unrelenting pain—that I had not denied **the words** of the Holy One. (Job 6:8–10†)

Job's parody targets misuse of the view that God can give "consolation in suffering" by his word which preserves life (Ps 119:50). Job sarcastically seeks to display his "joy in unrelenting pain" by dying for something he did not do before he denies the words of God (Job 6:10). Job does not target the psalm itself in his parody but parodies the psalm to target his wrongful suffering according to retributive standards (see Hermeneutical Profile

8. See "*נֶחָמָה," *HALOT* 1:689.
9. See Kynes, "Intertextuality," 207.

of the Use of Scripture in Job). The gap between his righteous life and his suffering may be served by a parody of "sweet words" turning "painful" (Ps 119:103; Job 6:25).[10] In this case, Job's parody of the psalm targets the badly mistaken retributive views of his friends.[11]

The larger function of Job's scriptural interpretive parodies needs to be kept in mind. Interpretive variations in Job display the kinds of retributive scriptural arguments that do not adequately explain individual or collective suffering. The use of scriptural traditions in the debate means to challenge the readership to turn away from distortions of Scripture in the face of suffering.

7:17~Ps 8:4[5] (B) (What are humans?). In the mid-nineteenth century Delitzsch proposed that Job's questions beginning with "What are humans?" are "in some degree a parody" on Ps 8. Driver starts his comments on Job 7:17–18 with "A bitter parody of Ps 8."[12] In the recent days of high interest in the scriptural use of Scripture, Job 7:17 and Ps 8:4[5] may attract more attention than all other scriptural parallels in Job combined.[13] The parallel in Ps 144:3 complicates things by raising the possibility that the whole idea may be commonplace. Van Leeuwen makes a good case for the conventional syntax and even notes an ancient extrabiblical parallel in the Lachish letters: "*Who is* your servant, a dog, *that* my lord *remembers* his servant?" (late 580s BCE, emphasis mine).[14] Van Leeuwen presents much evidence to support his formidable argument. Nonetheless, the other passing but significant possible parallels to Ps 8 in Job, when taken together, suggest a relationship between Job and Ps 8. Job says: "He has stripped me of my *honor* and removed *the crown* from my head" (Job 19:9), which seems a parallel to Ps 8:5[6] (see below).[15] The evidence suggests that a parallel between Job 7:17 and Ps 8:4[5] is very likely (bold and italics signify verbal parallels, and broken underlining signifies synonym):

> *What is mankind that you* are mindful of them, human beings **that you care [פקד] for them**? [5] You have made them a little lower than the angels and crowned them with glory and honor. [6] You made them rulers over the works of your hands; you put everything under their feet. (Ps 8:4–6[5–7])

10. Kynes suggests a possible allusion based on consonance between "How sweet [מלץ] are your *words* to my taste, sweeter than honey to my mouth!" (119:103) and "How painful [מרץ] are honest *words*! But what do your arguments prove?" (Job 6:25) (ibid.).

11. See Longman, *Job*, 142.

12. Keil and Delitzsch, *Job*, 124; Driver and Gray, *Job*, 72.

13. See, e.g., Mettinger, "Intertextuality," 266–68; Fishbane, "Book of Job," 86–98; Yu, "Ridiculous God," 84–102.

14. Van Leeuwen, "Psalm 8.5 and Job 7.17–18," 210. Compare the text of Lachish letter 2.3–5, with Aḥituv's suggested pointing (*Echoes*, 60): מִי עַבְדְּךָ כֶּלֶב כִּי זָכַר אֲדֹנִי אֶת [עַ]בְדּה (see translation above). Both Van Leeuwen and Aḥituv also note similar questions in the Amarna letters (fourteenth century BCE). The exact question, however, "Who is your servant, a dog? . . ." seems to be a more narrow idiom of self-abasement appearing repeatedly in the Lachish letters, including 5.3–5; 5.3–4; 6.2–3, as well as a similar formulation in 2 Kgs 8:13—"What is you servant, a dog? . . ." (lit.) (מָה עַבְדְּךָ הַכֶּלֶב) (see Dobbs-Allsopp et al., *Hebrew Inscriptions*, 307). The use of "dog" in this commonplace figure of speech takes the edge off Van Leeuwen's comparison, which only relates to similar syntax.

15. See Kynes, "Beat Your Parodies," 306.

> Yahweh, *what are* human beings *that* you care for them, mere mortals that you think of them? [4] They are like a breath; their days are like a fleeting shadow. (144:3, 4)

> [Job] *What is mankind that you* make so much of them, that you give them so much attention, [18] **that you examine** [פקד] **them** every morning and test them every moment? [19] Will you never look away from me, or let me alone even for an instant? [20] If I have sinned, what have I done to you, you who sees everything we do? Why have you made me your target? Have I become a burden to you? (Job 7:17–20)

Psalm 144:3 uses a similar rhetorical question as 8:4[5] but then gives an answer in 144:4 out of step with Ps 8. The psalmist uses the familiar question as a surprising lead-in for emphasizing the brevity of human life. This shift opens the way for the psalmist to offer a prayer for help that rings the notes of the song of David (144:5–7; 18:9, 14, 16[10, 15, 17]//2 Sam 22:10, 15, 17). The psalmist goes on to evoke other scriptural traditions as well (see Psalms Filters). Psalm 144 seems to borrow several scriptural traditions to produce a new prayer by blending some classics.

Job parodies Ps 8, starting with its famous question. Job's parody does not target the psalm but his own situation before God in the light of the affirmation in Ps 8 of a cosmos shaped according to Gen 1 (on the targeting of parody, see Hermeneutical Profile of the Use of Scripture in Job). The target of Job's parody comes out more clearly when Eliphaz follows suit and evokes the same question from Ps 8 to affirm his flawed view of retribution. Eliphaz asks: "*What is mankind, that* they could be pure, or those born of woman, that they could be righteous?" (Job 15:14, emphasis signifies verbal parallel with Ps 8:4[5] see above). The disagreement between Eliphaz and Job shows that Job does not subvert Ps 8 but uses it sarcastically against God because of his righteous suffering.[16] As noted above, Job uses Ps 8 as a standard because he does not enjoy the "honor" and "crown" of the human lot in the interpretation of Gen 1 by Ps 8 (Job 19:9).

In sum, Job alludes to Ps 8:4[5] in a parody targeting how God has been treating him (Job 7:17–18). Eliphaz also alludes to the same question to wrongly affirm that retribution works as it should upon Job (15:14). Job returns to Ps 8 and endorses its standards in his complaint against God (19:9). All of this demonstrates ways that the use of scriptural traditions in the debates in Job challenge the book's readership to rethink and modify their faulty views of retribution.

Psalm 8 includes the evidence necessary to suggest Gen 1 is the donor and the psalm is the receptor context (see note on Ps 8:3–8[4–9]). The use of parody in Job 7 provides strong evidence that Ps 8 is known to Job's friend and the book's readers. This sequence puts on display an example of incremental advances of revelation by interpretation.

16. These observations follow Kynes, "Reading Job,"137–39.

9:12~Isa 45:9 (C) (What are you doing?). In the first cycle of exchanges, Job uses two short questions that also appear in Isaiah (emphases signify verbal parallels):

> Yes, and from ancient days I am he. No one can deliver out of my hand. When I act, **who can reverse it?** (Isa 43:13)

> Woe to those who quarrel with their Maker, those who are nothing but potsherds among the potsherds on the ground. Does the clay say to the potter, *"What are you doing?"* Does your work say, "The potter has no hands"? (45:9†)

> [Job] If he snatches away, **who can reverse him?** Who can say to him, *"What are you doing?"* (Job 9:12†)

Since Job is responding to Bildad, it should be noted that in Bildad's third speech he uses language found in Isa 45:7, 8 (Job 25:2, 4). More importantly, the only two occurrences of "he makes peace" (עֹשֶׂה שָׁלוֹם) in the Hebrew Bible appear in Isa 45:7 and Job 25:2.[17] This increases the possibility that the shared phrases may be related intentionally. If they are related, Kynes does well to explain the unlikelihood of Isaiah drawing upon Job's negative use of these questions as a source to lift up the redeeming work of Yahweh. Thus, if they are related, it follows that Job is dependent on Isaiah.

If Job uses Isaiah, he takes words upholding divine sovereignty and presents them in an unflattering manner, suggesting God is an unpredictable tyrant. All of this fits the function of Job to instigate a searching inquiry on problematic views of retribution.

12:21, 24//Ps 107:40 (pouring contempt on nobles). The entire verse of Ps 107:40 also appears in two parts in Job 12. The exact match virtually requires a relationship, whether direct or indirect (emphases signify verbatim parallel):[18]

> *He who pours contempt on nobles* **made them wander in a trackless waste.** (Ps 107:40)

> [Job] *He pours contempt on nobles* and disarms the mighty. [22] He reveals the deep things of darkness and brings utter darkness into the light. [23] He makes nations great, and destroys them; he enlarges nations, and disperses them. [24] He deprives the leaders of the earth of their reason; **he makes them wander in a trackless waste.** (Job 12:21–24)

Kynes notes a couple of other places where Eliphaz also uses shorter snippets that parallel Ps 107 (Ps 107:42; Job 5:16; 22:19). Kynes remarks that Eliphaz speaks more in

---

17. For all these observations, see Kynes, "Job and Isaiah 40–55," 101–2.

18. This parallel is suggested by Kynes, *My Psalm*, 81. The only difference is the plene spelling of "pour out" (שׁוֹפֵךְ) in Job 12:21 versus the defective spelling (שֹׁפֵךְ) in Ps 107:40.

line with Ps 107 than Job.[19] The evidence of the distribution of the parallels in Job and the negative way Job uses the shared language strongly suggest Ps 107 as the donor and Job as the receptor context.[20]

The context of Ps 107 alternates between the blessing and judgment of Yahweh. In contrast, Job complains against God (Job 12:13–16). Job presents a list of human leaders that God humiliates (12:17–20). At this point Job uses an exact quotation from Ps 107:40 and inserts doom and gloom between the A and B lines (see above). Job's "deliberate reworking" blocks out "the positive aspects of reversal of fortune" from the psalm.[21] This does not fit with the context of the psalm, which goes on: "*But he lifted the needy out of affliction* and increased their families and flocks" (Ps 107:41, emphasis mine). Earlier Eliphaz had similarly said: "so the poor have hope" (Job 5:16). Perhaps in response, Job lifts Ps 107:40 out of context and interprets it against the grain as if to target Eliphaz's inadequate argument by his parody (see Hermeneutical Profile of the Use of Scripture in Job). The larger context of Job needs to be kept in mind. The debate between Job and his friends puts on display a variety of faulty scriptural interpretations. Highlighting invalid interpretation with parody can help readers repair their own misuse of Scripture.

19:6–8~Lam 3:6–9 (B) (calling out not answered). In Lam 3:1, a "man" (גֶּבֶר) begins to tell of his suffering from Yahweh. The same term used of Job invites comparison (Job 3:3; 34:7).[22] One portion of Job's remarks in Job 19 substantially overlaps the language of the man (italics signify verbal parallels, and bold signifies verbal parallels at the level of shared and/or related roots):[23]

> He has made me dwell in **darkness** [מַחְשַׁךְ] like those long dead. *He has walled* [גדר] me in so I cannot escape; he has weighed me down with chains. Even when **I cry out** or *call* for help, he shuts out my prayer. *He has blocked* [גדר] my way with blocks of stone; he has made my paths **crooked** [עוה]. (Lam 3:6–9†)

> Then know that God **has wronged** [עות] me and drawn his net around me. Though **I cry**, "Violence!" I get no response; though *I call* for help, there is no justice. *He has blocked* [גדר] my way so I cannot pass; he has shrouded my paths in **darkness** [חֹשֶׁךְ]. (Job 19:6–8)

When taken together many potential parallels from each chapter of Lamentations are concentrated in Job 19. This suggests Lamentations is the donor and Job the receptor

19. See ibid., 85–86.
20. See ibid., 96–97.
21. Clines, *Job 1–20*, 908.
22. See a list of similarities in Berlin, *Lamentations*, 85.
23. This is indebted to Kynes, "Debating Suffering," forthcoming. The root עות derives from עוה ("עות," HALOT 1:804).

context.[24] If Job depends on Lamentations, the kinds of shifts between Lamentations and Job at the mechanical level resemble the kinds of verbal alterations between Job and his friends when they allude to one another.[25] The major difference pivots on the male figure of Lamentations crying out for the sins of the people. Job uses this language ironically to speak against God, since he claims not to deserve his suffering.[26] The use of irony helps corroborate Job as receptor text.

The shared language and different circumstances create a vantage point for the readers of Job to evaluate the protracted suffering of the people in the wake of exile. The overall context of Job pushes against the kind of simplistic regard for retribution so often on the lips of Job's friends. But it also calls into question the validity of Job's complaints if he was guilty like the male figure of Lam 3. The gap between Job and the male figure of Lamentations becomes extremely important for the ironic parabolic quality of Job with respect to the collective suffering of exiles and those of the postexilic period.

21:19~Deut 5:9* (B)+7:10* (B) (transgenerational retribution) (* see attribute formula network). Many modern committee translations sense that the statement in Job 21:19a should be marked as a quotation and so add the italicized words not in the Hebrew: "*It is said*, 'God stores up the punishment of the wicked for their children'" (NIV, so too NRSV, JPSB, etc.). The appearance of unmarked citations of scriptural traditions and of other speeches in Job to which a speaker responds tends to be the norm.[27] Job, without marking it as a citation, parallels the scriptural tradition of transgenerational retribution. Hints of the common view of transgenerational judgment can be seen in earlier speeches (Job 5:4; 18:12; 20:10, 26).[28]

Gordis recognizes an implied citation formula at the head of Job 21:19, but he goes further than NIV, regarding it as "you say," meaning Job's friends say: "God stores up iniquity for his children."[29] Fox worries that identifying an unmarked passage as a quotation opens limitless opportunity to make the kinds of adjustments and harmonizations found in the targums.[30] Fox carefully investigates Gordis's study of unmarked quotations and responds with three criteria: (1) another subject is present besides the primary speaker, so the reader can determine the quoted speaker; (2) the citation is marked by a verb of speech; (3) the citation's shift to the quoted voice is signaled by a grammatical change in number and/or person.[31] In the case of Job 21:19, Fox disagrees with Gordis, saying Job does not quote his friends.[32] Likewise Clines points out that Job's friends did not argue that children pay

24. See Kynes, "Debating Suffering," forthcoming. Kynes goes on to discuss potential parallels between Lamentations and other contexts of Job. See many potential parallels listed in Aitken, "Inevitability," 208–9.

25. See Kynes, "Debating Suffering," forthcoming.

26. See Berlin, *Lamentations*, 85.

27. See Dell, *Book of Job*, 123.

28. References from Pyeon, *You Have Not*, 22. Pyeon does not discuss here an allusion to anything outside of Job.

29. See Gordis, "Quotations," 213.

30. Fox, "Identification of Quotations," 418.

31. See ibid., 423.

32. See ibid., 429.

for wrong *in place of* their parents but as *an additional* judgment for parental guilt.[33] But Fox goes too far in the other direction by saying that 21:19a "expresses Job's opinion."[34] The verbal parallel with the threat of retribution in Deut 7:10 suggests Job cites it in sarcastic parody, in line with his complaints running through Job 21. In sum, Gordis rightly recognizes Job 21:19a as a quotation but wrongly identifies Job's friends as the source. Job's complaints against injustice set up a loose sarcastic citation of Deuteronomy that affirms swift retribution.

In the present context, Job complains that the wicked live long, prosper, and their prosperity descends to their children (21:7–13). The modern committee translations rightly recognize the first half of Job 21:19 as a citation. Then Job offers a call for God to skip the delay and give people what they deserve (emphases signify verbal parallels):

> You shall not bow down to them or worship them; for I, Yahweh your God [אֱלֹהִים], am a jealous *God* [אֵל], punishing the *children* for the sin of the parents to the third and fourth generation of <u>those who hate</u> me. (Deut 5:9; cf. Exod 20:5)

> But <u>those who hate</u> him he **will repay** to their face by destruction; he will not be slow **to repay** to their face <u>those who hate</u> him. (Deut 7:10)

> [Job] "*God* [אֱלוֹהַּ] stores up their punishment for their *children*." **Let** him **repay** them, so that they themselves will know it. (Job 21:19 lit.)

The terms for "God" in Deuteronomy and Job all match their contextual norms. The commonplace language overlapping the second commandment and Job 21:19a can only register a possible relationship, but the use of "repay" probably alludes to the twofold use in Deut 7:10. Deuteronomy 7:9–10 enjoys strong evidence of its dependence on the second commandment (see note ad loc.). This makes it highly likely that it serves as the donor context and Job as the receptor context. Also, since Deut 7:9–10 presents an overt interpretive allusion to the second commandment, it raises the likelihood from possible to probable that Job 21:19a also broadly alludes to the same.

The two halves of Job 21:19 need to be handled one at a time then put together. Job 21:19a parodies the transgressional threat of the second commandment. Job alludes to the threat ironically since he has been going on about the good life of the wicked and their children (21:7–18). In Job's parody God "hides" or "stores up" but never uses the punishment against the next generation of the wicked.[35] The parody in Job 21:19a does not subvert the transgenerational threat in Scripture but targets God for not administering

33. See Clines, *Job 21–37*, 529.

34. Fox, "Identification of Quotation," 429.

35. See "צפן," Qal 1.d *HALOT* 2:1049.

judgment upon the wicked according to Job's own observations (on the target of parody, see Hermeneutical Profile of the Use of Scripture in Job).

Job 21:19b parodies Deut 7:10. The exegetical enhancement of the donor context insists that Yahweh's fidelity—"He is a faithful God" (Deut 7:9)—undergirds his repaying each generation what it deserves. The function of the chiastic structure allows the exegesis therein to be stated twice for emphasis: "(a) repaying (b) those who hate him to their faces . . . (b) those who hate him to their faces (a) he will repay them" (7:10 lit.). Job's parody of this scriptural exegetical advance does not seek to overthrow it by ridicule. Job's parody again targets the gap between the life of ease enjoyed by the wicked and the divine commitment to repay people what they deserve. Job stands in judgment of God for an unjust society that Job has seen for himself.

The two halves of Job 21:19 need to be put back together. The overall sequence of the allusions implies that God should not store up judgment for the next generation but instead should give individuals what they deserve. Both parts of this rest on ironic parodies of scriptural contexts that affirm Yahweh's fidelity to punish the guilty themselves. All of Job's parodic exegesis pivots on his confidence that the prosperity of the wicked that he has observed represents God's own view of reality. In short, Job presumes that he can judge as well as God what people deserve.

Job's presumption offers a critical challenge to those whose retributive theology does not work. The readership may too easily agree with Job's criticism thinking they too have observed the prosperity of the wicked and their children. Job's parody of the scriptural tradition of transgenerational threat speaks against all who think that they, like Job, know just as well as God himself what needs to be done. Scriptural exegesis in Job seeks to push back against arrogant questioning of Yahweh's faithfulness, especially in retributive justice. This is a central goal of the book. The effectiveness of Job's sophisticated exegesis rests on readers who can easily nod in agreement with Job. They have seen it too. Such agreement sets up readers to listen with Job when Yahweh speaks from the whirlwind.

FILTERS

The rich poetry in Job by its nature does not fit with direct verbatim citations of Scripture. The poetry tends to evoke, not quote, scriptural traditions (See Hermeneutical Profile of the Use of Scripture in Psalms). Besides the few uses of scriptural traditions with verifiable evidence treated in the notes, Job often uses scriptural language. Scholars' work on Job's use of scriptural traditions has begun to discover some of the donor contexts. The examples collected in the following filters merely represent a much wider use of scriptural language and non-exegetical broad allusions in Job.[36]

---

36. For lists of potential parallels between Job and other Scriptures, see Cheyne, *Job and Solomon*, 84–88; Dell, *Book of Job*, 125–35 (Dell compares forms not verbal parallels per se but many are somewhat related Scriptures.); Ḥakham, *Job*, XVIII–XXXIII; Hartley, *Job*, 11–15; Kwon, *Scribal Culture*, 71–105; Kynes, *Obituary for "Wisdom Literature,"* 161–65,

Non-Exegetical Broad Allusions and Shared Themes

Possible allusions to **Genesis** include: "Are you the first man ever born?" (Job 15:7 [Eliphaz]>/<Gen 2), and: "Surely you know how it has been from of old, ever since mankind was placed on the earth" (Job 20:3 [Zophar]>/<Gen 3).[37] The sarcasm of these remarks means they do not carry straightforward sense. Yet, if they are allusions, they do not offer interpretive insight into Genesis per se but criticism and debate over retribution and human sinfulness in the friends' debate with Job.

Near the opening of Job's first speech he says of his birth: "That day—let there be darkness" (יְהִי חֹשֶׁךְ), which may reverse the imagery of the first creation day when God said, "Let there be light" (יְהִי אוֹר) (Job 3:4 lit.; **Gen 1:3**). From this starting point an attempt has been made to align aspects of Job's speech with the other creation days, but most suggestions lack convincing verbal parallels or do not line up with the creation days.[38] Even without any further echoes of Gen 1, the statement "let there be darkness" efficiently sets out Job's view of the day he was born.

Shepherd suggests that the celestial accuser's idiomatic phrase needs to be translated literally to get its sense—"His bone and his flesh" (אֶל־עַצְמוֹ וְאֶל־בְּשָׂרוֹ) (Job 2:5). As such, it would not refer to Job's body but to Job's wife by allusion to the human's declaration "bone of my bone and flesh of my flesh" (עֶצֶם מֵעֲצָמַי וּבָשָׂר מִבְּשָׂרִי) (**Gen 2:23**).[39] If Shepherd is correct, it shifts the sense of Job 2:7–10 from the normal views to the satan wanting to strike Job's wife.

Job seems to use **Ps 104**, but verbal parallels do not go beyond shared terms or individual phrases. Elihu says, "If it were his intention and he *withdrew* his *spirit* and breath, all humanity would *perish* together and mankind would *return* to the *dust*" (Job 34:14–15), apparently alluding to: "When you hide your face, they are terrified; when you *withdraw* their *spirit*, they *perish* and *return* to the *dust*. When you send your *Spirit*, they are created, and you renew the face of the ground" (Ps 104:29–30†, emphases signify parallels). This is one of the ways Elihu broadly refers to Ps 104 as a counter to Job's more general possible references to the psalm.[40] Rather than making exegetical allusion, the speakers in Job wrestle with the theology of Ps 104.[41] In comparing the use of Ps 104 to the common view that Job 7:17–18 reverses in some way Ps 8:5–7, Frevel says, "[O]ne may wonder whether the book of Job argues really *against* the psalms or, whether it forms a scripturally based sapiential discourse that *uses* Scripture to solve its 'problems.'"[42]

The so-called confessions of Jeremiah (Jer 11:18–23; 12:1–6; 15:10–21; 17:14–18;

173; Pfeiffer, "Dual Origin," 202–5; Pyeon, *You Have Not*, esp. 34–40, 84–93, also see 111–16, 135–38, 150–52, 170–73, 186–88, 204–6.

37. Also cf. Job 31:35. These suggestions come from Oeming, "To Be Adam," 19–29.

38. See Fishbane, "Jeremiah IV 23–26 and Job III 3–13," 154; Pyeon, *You Have Not*, 88–92.

39. See Shepherd, "'Strike His Bone,'" 81–97.

40. So Frevel, "Telling the Secrets," 161; on Job's and Elihu's lesser lexical parallels with Ps 104, see 159–63; and on the divine lexical parallels, see 163–64.

41. See ibid., 164–65.

42. Ibid., 167, emphasis original.

18:18–23; 20:7–18) and the lament in **Job 3** share many similarities.[43] Compare: "Cursed be the day I was born! May the day my mother bore me not be blessed!" (Jer 20:14) with "and cursed the day of his birth. . . . May the day of my birth perish" (Job 3:1b, 3a); and "Cursed be the man who brought my father the news, who made him very glad, saying, 'A child is born to you—a son!'" (Jer 20:15) with "and the night that said, 'A boy is conceived!'" (Job 3:3b). If these, and many other similarities, point to a relationship, what is the significance? As opposed to parody, Dell regards Job 3 as reuse of common forms from a known tradition with essentially the same sense. She uses these observations to show how diachronic and synchronic approaches can enrich each other.[44] If the similarities between Jeremiah's and Job's laments stem in part from shared genre, with or without dependence, then their relationship may be considerably broader than figural or exegetical reworking.

Job's lament in **Job 3** may use figural imagery suggestive of the catastrophe of Judah. The imagery seems to be drawn from several scriptural contexts and themes. Burnight notes that the setting of Jeremiah's lament is the pending Babylonian invasion.[45] He goes on to compare Job's lament with language and themes of Israel's suffering. The most notable comparisons relate to the language of Job 3:5. The only places the combination of "gloom" and "utter darkness" appear with "claim" or "redeem" (גאל) are Ps 107 and Job 3:5a. And besides Job 3:5b, the only other contexts that use language akin to "may a cloud settle upon it" (lit.) refer to the tabernacle (Exod 40:35 and Num 9–10). Job inverts the collective redemption functions of this language. For Job, not God but darkness "claims" and "settles." In the following comparison Exod 40:35 stands for the set of related contexts (emphases signify verbal parallels at the level of shared roots):[46]

> Moses could not enter the tent of meeting because the <u>cloud had settled on it</u>, and the glory of Yahweh filled the tabernacle. (Exod 40:35)
>
> Let the *redeemed* [גאל] of Yahweh tell their story—those he *redeemed* [גאל] from the hand of the foe. . . . Some sat in *darkness*, in *utter darkness*, prisoners suffering in iron chains. . . . He brought them out of *darkness*, the *utter darkness*, and broke away their chains. (Ps 107:2, 10, 14)
>
> May *darkness* and *utter darkness claim* [גאל] it once more; may a <u>cloud settle upon it</u>; may blackness overwhelm it. (Job 3:5†)

---

43. For a list of similarities between Job and Jeremiah, see Cheyne, *Job and Solomon*, 86; Pyeon, *You Have Not*, 85–87.

44. See Dell, "'Cursed be the Day,'" 116–17. For the comparisons of Jer 20:14, 15 with Job 3:1, 3, see 108–9; for many other Jeremiah and Job parallels, see 110–15.

45. See Burnight, "'Reversal,'" 30–31.

46. These observations follow ibid., 31–35.

Job continues to use other imagery in 3:18 often associated with the collective suffering of Egyptian bondage and Babylonian captors—"Slave driver" (Exod 3:7; 5:6, 10, 13, 14; Isa 14:2, 4) and "oppressors" (Isa 14:17; cf. Ps 107:10). The only two contexts to speak of "way hidden" appear in Job 3:23 and Isa 40:27. Burnight warns that this shared imagery, and more like it, should not be used to transform Job into an allegory. At the same time, the readership of Job would know the scriptural traditions of collective suffering.[47] In sum, the lament in Job 3 does not feature exegesis of a particular scriptural context but seems infused with parabolic undercurrents of collective suffering and disillusionment based on scriptural language.

Eliphaz's presumptuous comments in **Job 5:17–18** echo sentiments housed in Proverbs and Deuteronomy. Though these contexts share some language, overlap involves common tradition (emphases signify verbal parallels):[48]

> See now that I myself am he! There is no god besides me. I put to death and I bring to life, I have wounded and I will <u>heal</u>, and no one can deliver out of my hand. (Deut 32:39)

> My son, *do not despise* Yahweh's *discipline*, and do not resent his *rebuke*, because Yahweh disciplines those he loves, as a father the son he delights in. (Prov 3:11–12)

> [Eliphaz says] "Blessed is the one whom God *rebukes*; so *do not despise* the *discipline* of the Almighty. For he wounds, but he also binds up; he injures, but his hands also <u>heal</u>." (Job 5:17–18†)

Job 9:4 uses the expression "mighty strength" (אַמִּיץ כֹּחַ) as part of the lead-in, the same expression used in Isa 40:26 to refer to God who calls forth the celestial lights by name.[49]

Job 9:8 shares a phrase with Isaiah emphasizing the monotheistic creational power of God:

> This is what Yahweh says—your Redeemer, who formed you in the womb: I am Yahweh, the Maker of all things, *who alone stretches out the heavens*, who spreads out the earth. (Isa 44:24)

> *He alone stretches out the heavens* and treads on the waves of the sea. (Job 9:8)

The unique shared feature is "he alone" since the phrase "stretches out the heavens" is a commonplace stock phrase in Scripture.[50] The larger function of Job's string of affirmations of God's great power relate to Job's own terrible situation before God.

47. For these several observations, see ibid., 35–36, 38, 41.
48. As observed and discussed in Crenshaw, "Divine Discipline," 180–81, 187.
49. See Brinks, "Job and Deutero Isaiah," 412; Kwon, *Scribal Culture*, 60–62.
50. See list in Kwon, *Scribal Culture*, 63.

Job 9:9 and **38:31–32** could allude to Amos 5:8 since the constellations Pleiades and Orion do not appear anywhere else in Scripture.[51]

The description of his origin in **Job 10:8–12** shares some imagery with part of Ps 139. But overlapping imagery appears elsewhere in Ps 119 (italics signify verbal parallels):[52]

> Your hands *made me* [עשׂה] and formed me; give me understanding to learn your commands. (Ps 119:73)

> For you created my inmost being; *you knit me together* in my mother's womb. I praise you because I am fearfully and wonderfully made; your works are wonderful, I know that full well. My *frame* [עֶצֶם] was not hidden from you when *I was made* [עשׂה] in the secret place, when I was woven together in the depths of the earth. Your eyes saw my unformed body; all the days ordained for me were written in your book before one of them came to be. (139:13–16)

> [Job says] Your hands shaped me and *made me* [עשׂה]. Will you now turn and destroy me? Remember that you *molded me* [עשׂה] like clay. Will you now turn me to dust again? Did you not pour me out like milk and curdle me like cheese, clothe me with skin and flesh and *knit me together* with *bones* [עֶצֶם] and sinews? You *gave* [עשׂה] me life and showed me kindness, and in your providence watched over my spirit. (Job 10:8–12)

Though Job 10:8–12 shares some striking thematic matters with Ps 139, the verbal parallels are limited to a few terms, especially the exceedingly common term "make" (עשׂה). The brief, similar line in Ps 139 demonstrates how these common creational ideas likely appear coincidentally in each of these contexts, drawn from commonplace expressions.

Psalm 119:69 and Job use the rare term "smear" (טָפַל) with "deception" as an object in a manner that may reflect a broad relationship (**Job 13:4**).[53] If this parallel reflects a relationship, it would seem Job parodies the language from the psalm to target the wrongful words of his friends against him. The use of Ps 119 elsewhere in Job increases the likelihood of broad allusion here (see note on Job 6:10).

The declaration of innocence in **Job 31** has been compared to the Ten Commandments, though the Sabbath command is missing.[54] Comparisons between the prohibitions against adultery (Job 31:1, 7–10) and idolatry (31:24–28) as well as honoring parents (31:18) and others overlap thematically, but not with extensive verbal parallels.

51. See Marlow, "Creation Themes," 145–47. For other possible parallels, see Cheyne, *Job and Solomon*, 87.

52. These parallels are based on Kynes, *My Psalm*, 102–3. Kynes evaluates the parallel as the poet of Job alluding to Ps 139, based on many other lesser similarities in associated contexts in Job (see 101–21).

53. This parallel is suggested by Kynes, "Intertextuality," 208.

54. See Witte, "Does the Torah Keep Its Promise?" 57.

Possible allusions to the Song of Moses include: "Sing O heavens with him, bow down to him all you celestial beings" (Deut 32:43a 4QDeut$^{q/4Q44}$ lit.; cf. LXX) with "while the morning stars sang together and all the celestial beings shouted for joy" (**Job 38:7** lit.);[55] and "no one can deliver out of my hand" (Deut 32:39) with "that no one can rescue me from your hand" (**Job 10:7b**).[56]

The closing includes Job's statement to God, "I know that you can do all things; no purpose of yours can be thwarted" (**Job 42:2**), which may allude to Yahweh's comments to the celestial delegates, "then nothing they plan to do will be impossible for them" (Gen 11:6b). Reading this as a straightforward allusion suggests Job praises God, but regarding it as parody amounts to Job mocking God.[57] These contrasting readings demonstrate the importance of identifying the target of parody (see Hermeneutical Profile of the Use of Scripture in Job).

Shared Stock Phrases and Other Similarities

The present purposes only allow for an extremely small set of examples of non-allusive common scriptural expressions in Job: >/<**1:21**; Ps 113:2, "blessed be the name of Yahweh" (יהי שם יהוה מברך); >/<**5:17a** (Eliphaz); Ps 94:12, "blessed is the strong person/person who Yah disciplines/God corrects" (אשרי הגבר/אנוש אשר תיסרנו יה/יוכחנו אלוה) (note "correct" in Ps 94:12 is parallel with a term with the root for "discipline" in Job 5:17b); >/<**13:24**; Ps 88:14[15], "why do you hide your face (from me)" (למה יסתיר פניך ממני) (cf. Deut 32:20); >/<**19:13**; Ps 88:8[9], "my associates/brothers far from me" (רחק מידעי ממני/אחי מעלי רחק) (cf. Ps 88:18[19]; Job 19:19); >/<**22:22** (Eliphaz); Isa 51:7; Jer 31:33; Ps 37:31, "torah in heart" (תורה ל/בלב/לבב) (cf. Zech 7:12; Pss 40:8[9]; 119:70; Prov 3:1); >/<**27:10** (Job); Isa 58:14; Ps 37:4, "take delight in Yahweh/God" (התענג על יהוה/אלוה); >/<**27:14–15**; Ezek 5:12; 6:12, death by sword, famine, pestilence;[58] >/<**42:3**; Ps 131:1, "things too wonderful for me" (נפלאות ממני); >/<**42:10**; Deut 30:3; Jer 29:14; 30:3, 18; 31:23; 32:44; 33:7, 11, 26, etc., "restore the fortunes" (שוב שבות)—the phrase used individually of Job normally applies to collective restoration.

---

55. The fragment of Deut 32:43 in 4QDeut$^{q/4Q44}$ reads: "Sing, O heavens, with him, bow down to him all you celestial beings" (הרנינו שמים עמו וחשתחוו לו כל אלהים, *BQS* 1:242). The textual problems in Deut 32:43 are very difficult—see helpful discussion and layout in Tigay, *Deuteronomy*, 516–18. The same sort of euphemistic alteration appears in Deut 32:8 (4QDeut$^{j/4Q37}$) supported by LXX, which favors following it in that case (see McCarthy, *BHQ*, 140*–41*), and suggests preference of 4QDeut$^{q/4Q44}$ with adjustments for 32:43 (McCarthy, *BHQ*, 152*–53*). Compare: "when the morning stars sang together and the celestial beings shouted for joy" (בְּרָן־יַחַד כּוֹכְבֵי בֹקֶר וַיָּרִיעוּ כָּל־בְּנֵי אֱלֹהִים, Job 38:7 MT lit.).

56. These examples are from Greenstein, "Parody," 70, 73. Greenstein also suggests parallels: Deut 32:13b–14a with Job 29:6 (71–72); Deut 37:7b with Job 8:10a (72); and others.

57. For these competing views, see Fishbane, "Book of Job," 91; Perdue, *Wisdom in Revolt*, 234; versus Greenstein, "Problem of Evil," 359.

58. Joyce, "'Even if Noah,'" 126. See many other thematic parallels (Job uses different expressions) in Ezekiel and Jeremiah in discussion of Ezek 5:1–4, 12 and following in Ezek Filters.

Chapter 27

PROVERBS

SYMBOLS[1]

// verbal parallels (A level)
/~/ synoptic parallel (A level)
~ B, probable interpretive allusion; C, possible; D, probably not
+ interpretive blend
>/< more or less similar (see Filters)
* part of interpretive network (see Networks near end of volume)

USE OF SCRIPTURE IN PROVERBS[2]

3:1–3, 21–24; 6:20–23; 7:1–3~Deut 6:6–9* (B) (instructing the next generation) (* see concealing revelation network)

30:5–6~Deut 4:2 (C) (do not add to his words)

OLD TESTAMENT USE OF PROVERBS (SEE RESPECTIVE NOTE)

3:19~Ps 136:5 (B) (made the heavens by understanding in covenantal loyalty retrospective)

NEW TESTAMENT USE OF PROVERBS

3:11, 12 LXX//Heb 12:5–6 (the Lord's discipline)

3:34 LXX//Jas 4:6; 1 Pet 5:5 (opposes the proud)

4:26//Heb 12:13 (level paths)

11:31 LXX~1 Pet 4:18 (how much harder for the sinner)

24:12~Rom 2:6 (he will repay)

25:21, 22 LXX//Rom 12:20 (feed hungry enemy)

26:11//2 Pet 2:22 (dog returns to vomit)

HERMENEUTICAL PROFILE OF THE USE OF SCRIPTURE IN PROVERBS

The Proverbs scroll houses a different kind of scriptural discourse. Wisdom sentences comprise most of the book's seven collections—2–5 (Prov 10–29).[3] The present discussion

1. For explanation of symbols, see Symbols and Abbreviations and Introduction. For other help, see Glossary.

2. See Bibliographic Note on Lists of Potential Parallels.

3. Proverbs houses seven collections each with its own heading: (1) "the proverbs of Solomon son of David, king of Israel" (1:1–9:18); (2) "the proverbs of Solomon" (10:1–22:16); (3) "the thirty sayings of the wise" (22:17–24:22); (4) "these are also sayings of the wise" (24:23–34); (5) "these are more proverbs of Solomon, copied by the men of Hezekiah king of Judah" (25:1–29:27); (6) "the sayings of Agur the son of Jakeh—an oracle" (30:1–33); (7) "the sayings of king Lemuel—an oracle his mother taught him" (31:1–31).

needs to begin somewhat differently than others in this study by considering why Proverbs does not feature much by way of direct scriptural exegesis.

In Proverbs, wisdom functions both as the object of the sage's teaching and as a teacher herself when personified. Brown says that wisdom

> traverses the domains of human intercourse that lie outside the domain of the cult: from the family to the larger corporate, particularly urban, environment defined by marketplaces, crossroads, and city gates (Prov 1:20–21; 8:2–3). But nowhere does she gain entrance to the Temple (contra Sir 24:8–11). Nowhere does she play a definitive role in the history of salvation (contra Wis 10:1–21). Corporate history and cult are not her primary domains.[4]

Fox claims that "Proverbs shows no interest in Yahweh's revealed Torah." And he remarks that Proverbs does not "show much interest in prophetic revelation." Fox acknowledges that Proverbs does not oppose Torah, cultic regulations, or prophetic revelation, but he emphasizes that "Torah is not part of his message" and "Proverbs pays virtually no attention to these [other biblical] media."[5]

These commonplace generalizations that speak about where wisdom does not fit need to be qualified. Von Rad acknowledges differences with wisdom as a genre, epitomized by the sentence-wisdom of Proverbs, but he pushes back against isolating wisdom. Von Rad claims "there is no 'wisdom and cult' problem."[6] Proverbs and priestly writings may be focused differently but not antithetically. The sage can call upon the apprentice to honor Yahweh with firstfruits or warn of the temptress who speaks of sacrifices and vows in "pick-up lines" for illicit relations (Prov 3:9; 7:14). Von Rad notes the differences between wisdom and historical narratives but affirms their shared tendencies to apprehend the divine within a "secular" context.[7] Von Rad attests the different functions of wisdom and prophets but stresses that they share the same presuppositions.[8] The point at hand, simply put, is that Proverbs as the embodiment of one brand of wisdom does not lack overt scriptural interpretive allusions because of any theological distance or antithesis to other Scriptures.[9]

The lack of direct scriptural exegesis in Proverbs seems to stem, in large part, from its discourse function. The wisdom sentences advise the youthful generation on how to live.

---

4. Brown, "'Come O Children,'" 101.

5. Fox, *Proverbs 10–31*, 946–47. Kynes's interaction alerted me to Fox's comments (*Obituary for "Wisdom Literature,"* 220).

6. Von Rad, *Wisdom*, 188.

7. See ibid., 98, 291.

8. See ibid., 62, 309.

9. For many examples of echoes of psalms and prophets in Proverbs, see Ansberry, "Proverbs," *DNTUOT*, forthcoming. Kynes argues that categorizing Job, Proverbs, and Ecclesiastes as "Wisdom Literature" has unduly quarantined them from the rest of the Hebrew Bible of which they are a part ("The 'Wisdom Literature' Category," 1–24; idem, *Obituary for "Wisdom Literature,"* 102–4).

The speaker embodies the older generation as king, mother, father, and wisdom speaking counsel. The applicational teaching of the wisdom sentences transmits scriptural instructions indirectly.

The single overt scriptural interpretive allusion in Proverbs gets directly at the connection between wisdom and Torah.[10] The importance of establishing this connection underlies the fourfold appearance of the exegetical intervention that identifies the teaching responsibility of the great commandment with the wise counsel of Proverbs. Immediately following the command to love Yahweh, parents are told to instruct children everywhere all the time (Deut 6:4–9; cf. 11:18–20). If Torah repeatedly commands the older generation to instruct the up-and-coming generation, Proverbs features what they say. Proverbs does not only command teaching. It is teaching. In Deuteronomy, Moses tells parents to teach their children. In Proverbs, parents teach. The parent's or teacher's speech may or may not be overtly marked. After situating wisdom, she may speak directly to "you" plural—her apprentices (Prov 8:4). More often the wise instruction begins unmarked: "My child, do not forget my torah" (3:1 lit.).

In sum, Proverbs includes little in the way of direct, overt scriptural exegesis. The applicational function of Proverbs largely determines its way of teaching. At the same time, the opening section of Proverbs repeatedly identifies the wisdom of Proverbs with the torah-teaching commission of the great commandment.

USE OF SCRIPTURE

3:1–3, 21–24; 6:20–23; 7:1–3~Deut 6:6–9* (B) (instructing the next generation) (* see concealing revelation network). The great commandment continues on to call upon Israel to "repeat" the commandments to the up-and-coming generation constantly (Deut 6:6–9). In place of "repeat" the parallel passage says "teach" the younger generation all the time (6:7; 11:19; see note on Ps 1:1–3). If the first collection in Proverbs demonstrates how the proverbs work, the fourfold parallel to the great commandment stands as its recurring centerpiece (Prov 3:1–3, 21–24; 6:20–23; 7:1–3). The verbal parallels and their contextual shape make allusion highly likely for at least three of four, though Prov 3:21–24 features less shared language.

Proverbs twice uses the memorable phrase "write them on the tablet of your heart" (3:3; 7:3). The absence of this phrase in Deuteronomy suggests Proverbs is the receptor context since skipping it seems less likely. The term "tablets" appears frequently in Exodus and Deuteronomy to refer to the stone tablets inscribed with the Ten Commandments on the mountain, twice.[11] The brilliant expression captures the endgame of reshaping the hearts of the next generation according to the divine revelation at the mountain.

10. Ansberry argues that Proverbs as a whole seeks to apply Deuteronomic ideals and values for courtly instruction (*Be Wise*, 188–89).

11. See Exod 24:12; 31:18; 32:15, 16, 19; 34:1, 4, 29; Deut 4:13; 5:22; 9:9–11, 15, 17; 10:1, 3 ("לוּחַ," no. 1 *HALOT* 1:523).

The imagery of writing torah on the heart of the younger generation also evokes one of the striking images of the new covenant (Jer 31:33).

The most important exegetical intervention in Prov 3:1–3 and its parallels relates to the shift in perspective. In Deuteronomy Moses instructs the older generation to teach the commands to the younger generation (Deut 6:7; 11:19). In Proverbs the sage speaks directly to "the son" according to the great command (Prov 3:1, 21; 6:20; 7:1). The fourfold exegetical allusions do not talk about instruction; they put it into practice.[12] Table Pr1 presents the verbal parallels in the main set of interpretive allusions.

TABLE PR1: PARENTAL TORAH TO THE NEXT GENERATION‡[a]

Deuteronomy 6†	**Proverbs†**			
[6] These **commandments** that I give you today are to be on **your hearts**.	[3:1] My son, do not forget my torah, but guard my **commands** in **your heart**,	[3:21] My son, do not let wisdom and understanding out of your sight, keep sound judgment and discretion;	[6:20] My son, guard your father's **command** and do not forsake your mother's torah.	[7:1] My son, keep my words and store up my **commands** within you. [2] Keep my **commands** and you will live; keep my torahs as the apple of your eye.
[7] Impress them on your children. Talk about them when you sit at home and when you walk along the way, when you lie down and when you get up.	[2] for they will prolong your life many years and bring you peace and prosperity.	{[23] Then you will walk on your way in safety, and your foot will not stumble. [24] When you lie down, you will not be afraid; when you lie down, your sleep will be sweet.}	{[22] When you walk, they will guide you; when you lie down, they will watch over you; when you awake, they will speak to you. [23] For this **command** is a lamp, this torah is a light, and correction and instruction are the way to life.}	
[8] Tie them as symbols on your hands and bind them on your foreheads. [9] Write them on the doorframes of your houses and on your gates.	[3] Let love and faithfulness never leave you; tie them around your neck, write them on the tablet of your heart.	{[22] they will be life for you, an ornament to grace your neck.}	{[21] Tie them always on **your heart**; fasten them around your neck.}	[3] Tie them on your fingers; write them on the tablet of your heart.

‡ Table developed independently (cf. Schnittjer, *Torah Story*, 491). For a similar observation regarding Deut 6:4–8 and Prov 6:20–22, see Fishbane, "Torah and Tradition," 284. Shipper expands on Fishbane's observation and develops a similar table but only regards three of the four contexts of Proverbs treated here ("When Wisdom," 59). Delitzsch makes a general comparison between the Shema of Deut 6:4–9 and Prov 1–9 and mentions the similarities between Prov 6:22 and Deut 6:7; 11:19 as well as Prov 7:3 and Deut 6:9 (Keil and Delitizsch, *Proverbs*, 34, 149, 157).

[a] Emphases signify verbal parallels between Deuteronomy and Proverbs. Stylized brackets signify alteration of sequence.

12. Similarly, Ansberry says the parental instructions of Proverbs make concrete the Mosaic command to teach children in Deuteronomy 6:7 ("Proverbs," *DNTUOT*, forthcoming).

The term "son" in Proverbs connotes both familial relationship and a sense of student or apprentice. In Prov 6 the sage puts in parallel "your father's commands" and "your mother's torah" (Prov 6:20). By placing both parents in third person it provides semantic space for the sage to be regarded as a wise teacher from the older generation, or elsewhere in Proverbs even Woman Wisdom herself. The responsibility for instructing the up-and-coming generation functions both collectively and individually.

The use of "torah" in Prov 3:1, 6:20, and 7:1 does not denote the Torah scroll of Moses or the legal collections therein. Torah in Proverbs stands for wise instruction housed in the collections of sentences in Proverbs. By calling the sages' wisdom "torah," the way opens for postbiblical interpretation to make the move of identifying wisdom and Torah (e.g., Sir 24:23–29; Bar 4:1). At the same time, the tendency toward a broad semantic sense of torah closer to divine revelation than the Torah scroll of Moses appears already in Ps 119. The fourfold use of the great commandment in Prov 3:1–3, 21–24, 6:20–23, 7:1–3 invites conceiving of wisdom and Torah as overlapping circles in a Venn diagram.

The contexts of the fourfold exegetical applications of the great commandment demonstrate priorities for the needed perpetual instruction. The instructions following Prov 3:1–3 emphasize trusting Yahweh (3:5), humility and fearing Yahweh (v. 7), honoring Yahweh by contributions including firstfruits (v. 9), and seeking wisdom as a tree of life (v. 18). Proverbs 3:21–24 leads into submitting to Yahweh (v. 26), generosity (v. 27), and prohibition against malice (v. 29). Proverbs 6:20–23 sets up a warning against lust and seduction (6:24–35). Proverbs 7:1–3 introduces embracing wisdom to avoid the temptress (7:4–27). The opening chapters of Proverbs repeatedly warn against circumstances that could lead to adultery (2:16–22; 5:1–23; 6:24–35; 7:4–27). Overall, these instructions emphasize devoutness to Yahweh and the dangers of temptation. These teachings do not exhaust the instructions of Proverbs but give voice to how the older generation instructs the younger in torah.

The imagery of "lamp" and its parallel with "light" in the A and B lines of Prov 6:23 set up a warning. Notice the correspondence of this pair of terms in a verse of Ps 119, which uses a different term for "path" often paired with "way" elsewhere (italics signify verbal parallels, and broken underlining signifies synonyms):[13]

> Your word is *a lamp* for my feet, *a light* on my path. (Ps 119:105)

> For this command is *a lamp*, this torah is *a light*, and correction and instruction are the way to life, keeping you from your neighbor's wife, from the smooth talk of a wayward woman. (Prov 6:23–24)

13. Elsewhere "path" (נְתִיבָה) is usually paired with "way" (דֶּרֶךְ), see Isa 42:16; 43:16; 59:8; Jer 6:16; 18:15; Hos 2:8; Job 24:13; Prov 1:15; 3:17; 8:20; Lam 3:9 (Even-Shoshan, 788, "נְתִיבָה," nos. 1, 6, 9, 11, 12, 14, 16, 17, 18, 19, 21).

Psalm 119 progresses in sets of eight verses, each beginning with the next letter of the Hebrew alphabet. The *mem* unit in verses 97–104 twice warns against the evil or false way (Ps 119:101, 104). Psalm 119:105 leads off the *nun* unit with the memorable comparison of "your word is a lamp for my feet." The overall emphasis of the ten key torah terms of Ps 119 connote divine revelation more than a specific body of scriptural traditions like the Torah (see Psalm Filters on Ps 119). The set of interpretive allusions to the great commandment in the first collection of Proverbs, including Prov 6:20–23, tends more specifically toward applicational use of the commands of Torah. If Psalm 119 talks about torah, Proverbs shows how the older generation mediates torah to the up and coming generation. Proverbs 6:23 leads directly into a warning against temptation from the "evil woman" (Prov 6:24 MT) or "neighbor's wife" (6:24 LXX).[14] The comparison between Ps 119:105 and Prov 6:23–24 helps highlight the dominant moral focus of the instructions for the younger generation in Proverbs.

In sum, four times the opening collection of Proverbs interpretively alludes to the mandate to constantly instruct the next generation with the commands of Torah. These allusions mimic in a variety of ways the style, rhythm, and key terms from the great commandment's mandate. The allusions establish what sort of wisdom parents should teach. The fourfold allusion programmatically suggests that wisdom for the younger generation seeks to inculcate broadly applied Torah instruction.

30:5–6~Deut 4:2 (C) (do not add to his words). Agur uses a phrase (Prov 30:5) that runs parallel to part of one of the obedience formulas in Deuteronomy (often referred to as the canon formula; cf. Recurring Traditions in Deuteronomy Filters). If Agur draws on Deuteronomy here, the sense of his allusion depends on the interpretive conclusions of his much-contested riddle (30:3–4) and other contextual difficulties. The present purpose does not include a solution to all this, simply a very brief summary of selected proposals (italics signify verbal parallel):

> See that you do all I command you; *do not add* to it or take away from it. (Deut 12:32 [13:1]; cf. 4:2)

> Every word of God is flawless; he is a shield to those who take refuge in him. *Do not add* to his words, or he will rebuke you and prove you a liar. (Prov 30:5–6)

Fox suggests "his words" may refer to the Deuteronomic collection (Deut 12–26), Deuteronomy, or the Pentateuch, but not the prophets since that collection "cannot be

14. Proverbs 6:24 MT warns against the "evil woman" (רָע) (preferred by *BHQ*), while LXX warns against "the neighbor's wife" (ὑπάνδρου perhaps from רֵעַ). Either of these fit with the broader set of warnings against temptation in Prov 1–9. But "neighbor's wife" with LXX is preferred on the analogy of Prov 6:29 (see *BHS* Prov 6:24, n. b) versus Fox's proposal for emendation to an unattested "your neighbor's wife" (רֵעֶךָ) on the analogy of "his neighbor's wife" (רֵעֵהוּ) in 6:29 (see note on 6:24 in Fox *Proverbs: Eclectic Edition*, 137).

described simply as 'God's word.'"[15] Fox's point about the prophets does not align too well with Neh 9:30 or Isa 40:8, though these references to God's word by the prophets seem general and not about a "written collection." More to the point, Fox reads Agur as using the phrase from Deut 4:2//12:32[13:1] in a straightforward manner, circumscribing divine revelation in an unspecified written collection.

Shipper suggests that Agur refers to the central passages of Deuteronomy but "turns the Deuteronomistic idea upside down." Agur claims wisdom cannot be learned (Prov 30:3) which, for Shipper, means the divine will in Deuteronomy cannot be taught but only learned by immediate revelation requiring prayer.[16]

O'Dowd sees Agur's allusion to the so-called canon formula as referring to the law or, with contextual adjustments, "a wisdom that is faithful to the law." This conclusion comes as part of a view concerning Agur's style of shortening allusions, like the short form of the "canon formula" in Prov 30:6. O'Dowd suggests a large number of other allusions, mostly by single word parallels, to wide-ranging scriptural traditions in 30:1–9.[17]

In sum, the array of conflicting interpretations reflects the difficulties of Agur's oracle. Agur may allude in Prov 30:6 to the obedience (canon) formula that appears in Deuteronomy. If so, what he has in mind by "God's word" and how the allusion fits into the context of his oracle need to be decided as part of determining how he uses Scripture. No suggestions are offered here. The slim evidence of parallel only allows allusion as a possibility.

FILTERS

Proverbs shares language and features some parallels with other Scriptures that do not constitute exegetical allusion. Proverbs also includes many parallel and partially parallel proverbs. The following filters collect non-exegetical scriptural parallels in Proverbs. These representative lists are not comprehensive or complete.[18]

Non-Exegetical Broad Allusions and Shared Themes

On occasion Proverbs makes reference to worship practices, very broadly echoing the concerns of **Leviticus** and **Numbers**. These include: sacrifice (Prov 7:14; 15:8; 21:3, 27); vows (7:14; 20:25; 31:2); casting lots (16:33); prayer (15:29; 28:9); and firstfruits offering (3:9).[19]

In several places Proverbs's wisdom sentences echo legal instructions, especially from **Deuteronomy**: "Yahweh detests dishonest scales, but accurate weights find favor with

15. Fox, *Proverbs 10–31*, 858.

16. See further details in Shipper, "'Teach Them,'" 30; idem, "When Wisdom Is Not Enough," 70–75.

17. See O'Dowd, "Poetic Allusions," 103–19, esp. 115–19; citation from 119.

18. For other lists of parallels between Proverbs and other Scriptures, see Ansberry, "Proverbs," *DNTUOT*, forthcoming; Crenshaw, "Proverbs," in *ABD* 5:519; the essays in Dell and Kynes, *Reading Proverbs Intertextually*; Kynes, *Obituary for "Wisdom Literature,"* 230–31, 235, 237; Weinfeld, *Deuteronomic School*, 362–63. For parallels within Proverbs, see Snell, *Twice-Told Proverbs*, 35–59.

19. Many of the echoes of worship references come from Kynes, *Obituary for "Wisdom Literature,"* 231.

him" (Prov 11:1; 16:11; 20:23; Deut 25:13–16; cf. Lev 19:35–36; Amos 8:5); "A truthful witness saves lives, but a false witness is deceitful" (Prov 14:25; cf. 19:28; Deut 19:15–20); "The wicked accept bribes in secret to pervert the course of justice" (Prov 15:27; cf. 17:23; Exod 23:8; Deut 16:19; 27:25); "Whoever pursues righteousness and love finds life, prosperity and honor" (Prov 21:21; Deut 16:20); "Do not move an ancient boundary stone set up by your ancestors" (Prov 22:28; Deut 19:14; 27:17), which Prov 23:10–11 extends in a Deuteronomic manner to protect orphans: "Do not move an ancient boundary stone or encroach on the fields *of the fatherless*, for their Defender is strong; he will take up their case against you" (emphasis mine); and "Do not slander a servant to their master, or they will curse you, and you will pay for it" (Prov 30:10; cf. Deut 23:15–16[16–17]).

While Proverbs shares many ethical concerns with the **prophets**, it also critiques empty worship (Prov 15:8, 29; 21:3, 27; 28:9; and see Table A3 in Amos Filters).

One of the most fundamental aspects of the teaching sentences on **fear of Yahweh** appears four times in Proverbs with similar elements and three times elsewhere (italics signify verbal parallels, and broken underlining signifies similarities):[20]

> *The fear of Yahweh* is the beginning of knowledge, but fools despise *wisdom* and instruction. (Prov 1:7)
>
> *The fear of Yahweh* is the beginning of *wisdom*, and knowledge of the Holy One is understanding. (9:10)
>
> *Wisdom's* instruction is to *fear Yahweh*, and humility comes before honor. (15:33)
>
> Charm is deceptive, and beauty is fleeting; but a woman *who fears Yahweh* is to be praised. (31:30)
>
> *The fear of Yahweh* is the beginning of *wisdom*; all who follow his precepts have good understanding. To him belongs eternal praise. (Ps 111:10)
>
> And he said to the human race, "*The fear of* the Lord—that is *wisdom*, and to shun evil is understanding." (Job 28:28)
>
> Now all has been heard; here is the conclusion of the matter: *Fear* God and keep his commandments, for this is the duty of all mankind. (Eccl 12:13)

The manifold repetition of the mantra establishing the fear of Yahweh as the on-ramp to wisdom suggests its centrality.

20. Five of these are suggested by von Rad, *Wisdom*, 65–66 (Prov 1:7; 9:10; 15:33; Ps 111:10; Job 28:28).

Proverbs identifies wisdom as a "tree of life" (עץ חיים), echoing Gen 2 and 3 (Gen 2:9; 3:22, 24; **Prov 3:18**).[21] Elsewhere the expression "tree of life" represents the fruit of righteousness, a desire fulfilled, and a gentle tongue (Prov 11:30; 13:12; 15:4). The series of prepositional phrases in the same sequence "by wisdom," "by understanding," and "by knowledge" appear in building contexts in **Proverbs 3:19–20** (creation), Exodus 31:3; 35:31 (tabernacle), and 1 Kings 7:14 (temple).[22]

Proverbs 6 features parallels, including some verbal parallels, to several of the Ten Commandments: honoring father and mother (6:20; cf. Exod 20:12//Deut 5:16), not coveting neighbor's wife (6:25–29; cf. Exod 20:17; Deut 5:21), not stealing (6:30–31; cf. Exod 20:15//Deut 5:19), not committing adultery (6:32; cf. Exod 20:14//Deut 5:18).[23]

Proverbs 8:22–31 presents wisdom in the context of creation. One segment includes a partial parallel with a creational aside in Jeremiah's taunt against idolatry (Jer 10:1–16).[24]

> But God made *the world* by his power; *he established the world* by his *wisdom* and stretched out *the heavens* by his understanding. (10:12//51:15 lit.)

> Before he made the earth or its fields or any of the dust of *the world*. I [*wisdom*] was there when *he established the heavens* in place, when he marked out the horizon on the face of the deep. (Prov 8:26–27 lit.; cf. 3:19)

Proverbs 8:22 gets interpreted christologically early (Justin, *Dialogue*, LXI, ca. 160 CE). The NIV does well to get at the semantic ambiguity of the verb: "Yahweh *brought me forth* as the first of his works" (8:22, emphasis mine).[25]

The fifth collection of proverbs collected by Hezekiah's men (**Prov 25–29**) includes a few verbal parallels with the Hezekiah narrative of Kings ("trust" and "day of trouble" in 25:19; cf. 2 Kgs 18:5; 19:3).[26]

The excellent woman of **Prov 31:10–31** thematically bridges Woman Wisdom and Ruth. The alphabetic acrostic begins with a rhetorical question: "An excellent woman who can find?" (Prov 31:10a lit.). In this case, any interpreter may doubt that the woman of excellence from A to Z (*aleph* to *tav*) should be regarded as an actual person. She embodies the ideals of Woman Wisdom known in the first collection of Proverbs.

Although rhetorical questions make points rather than asking real questions, the

---

21. See Yoder, "Wisdom Is the Tree of Life," 11–19; for other echoes of Gen 2 and 3, see Hurowitz, "Paradise," 55–62.

22. See Van Leeuwen, "Cosmos," 79, 84–85, 87–89; Ansbery, "Proverbs," *DNTUOT*, forthcoming. Note Prov 3:19–20 and Exod 31:2; 35:31 use a different preposition "with" (בְּ) than 1 Kgs 7:14 (אֵת).

23. As observed by Fishbane, "Torah and Tradition," 284; Shipper, "'Teach Them,'" 26. For other parallels between Proverbs and the Ten Commandments, see Longman, *Proverbs*, 81.

24. On the parallel between Jer 10:12//51:15 and Prov 8:26–27, see Parke-Taylor, *Formation*, 180, n. 58.

25. The term with the sense of "acquire" in an economic sense or "create" is used 83x, of which 4x carry the sense of "beget" or "bring into the world" (Gen 4:1 [wordplay consonance with Cain]; Deut 32:6; Ps 139:13; Prov 8:22), 2x "create" (Gen 14:19, 22), and the rest "acquire" (Lipiński, "קָנָה," *TDOT* 13:59).

26. For these and other similarities, see Carasik, "Who Were," 294–98.

Scriptures answer the question. An excellent woman who can find? Boaz, of course. The book of Ruth does not disappoint. It features numerous verbal and thematic similarities. For example, the narrator describes Boaz as an "excellent man," and he affirms that everyone knows Ruth as an "excellent woman" (Ruth 2:1; 3:11; cf. 4:11).[27] The expression "excellent woman" appears three times in Scripture, Prov 12:4, 31:10, and Ruth 3:11.[28] One of the traditional canonical arrangements highlights this connection by placing Ruth directly after Proverbs.[29] The relations between Woman Wisdom, the excellent woman, and Ruth represent thematic and verbal similarities, not exegetical allusions (see Table Pr2).

TABLE PR2: THE EXCELLENT WOMAN AS BRIDGE BETWEEN WOMAN WISDOM AND RUTH‡

Woman Wisdom (Proverbs 1–9)	Excellent Woman (Proverbs 31)	Ruth
for wisdom is more precious than rubies, and nothing you desire can compare with her (8:11).	A wife of noble character who can find? She is worth far more than rubies (31:10).	you are a woman of noble character (3:11b).
The beginning of wisdom is this: Acquire wisdom. Though it cost all you have, acquire understanding (4:7†).		I have also acquired Ruth the Moabite (4:10).
	She opens her arms to the poor and extends her hands to the needy (31:20).	She carried it back to town, and her mother-in-law saw how much she had gathered. Ruth also brought out and gave her what she had left (2:18).
	Her husband is respected at the town gate, where he takes his seat among the elders of the land (31:23†).	Boaz went up to the town gate and sat down. . . . Boaz took ten of the elders of the town and said, "Sit here," and they did so (4:1–2).
	Honor her for all that her hands have done, and let her works bring her praise at the city gate (31:31).	All the people at the city gate know that you are a woman of noble character (3:11†).

‡ Emphases signify verbal parallels. This table was developed independently based on class materials. For a detailed comparison of the virtues of wisdom in Proverbs and Ruth, see Dell, "Didactic Intertextuality," 107–13.

27. Contra Quick, "Ruth," 47–66. Quick argues that the Ruth narrative intentionally evokes personified wisdom language in Proverbs to subvert it. She builds her case around such things as Ruth playing the part of the Strange Woman of Proverbs by, says Quick, her illicit nocturnal sexuality in Ruth 3 (62). Quick misconstrues the function of "foreign" (נָכְרִיָּה) in Ruth 2:10 by comparing Ruth to the immoral Strange Woman of Proverbs but she fails to notice the legal allusions of the context (56). For an alternate view see note on Ruth 2:8.

28. For "excellent woman" (אֵשֶׁת חַיִל), see collocations in "I חַיִל," Even-Shoshan, 365 (nos. 34, 35, 38).

29. One of the Tanak (Torah, Prophets, Writings) arrangements places Ruth after Proverbs. Campbell suggests that this sequence intentionally highlights the thematic similarity between Ruth 3:11 and Prov 31:10, 31 (*Ruth*, 34).

Doublets

Proverbs features many doublets, near doublets, and half-verse doublets.[30] A full listing in parallel columns in Hebrew and English with shared language marked can be found elsewhere.[31] This widespread phenomenon—especially in the first five collections of Proverbs (see footnote in Hermeneutical Profile of the Use of Scripture in Proverbs)—does not constitute exegetical use of scriptural traditions in line with the purposes of the present study. If proverb repetitions develop their counterparts within and between the collections, they do so *within* the book of Proverbs. In that sense proverb doublets could be considered literary, not exegetical. Setting aside these concerns temporarily for the sake of evaluation, it may be asked: What sort of exegesis is evidenced by proverb doublets?

Heim's thoroughgoing study of proverb doublet exegesis essentially interprets one side of doublets against their counterparts.[32] A doublet from the beginning and end of the second collection can illustrate (italics signify exact verbal parallels):

A wise son brings joy to a *father, but a foolish* son is a grief to *his mother.* (Prov 10:1 lit.)

A wise son brings joy to his *father, but a foolish* man despises *his mother.* (15:20)[33]

The A lines are nearly identical with Prov 10:1 referring to "a father" versus 15:20 the son's own father. The B lines differ considerably: son versus man and noun phrase versus phrase with participle. Heim deduces that 10:1 seeks to motivate an adolescent to act wisely to bring joy to his parents. Since the foolish man of 15:20 seems independent of the parents, Heim suggests this proverb also encourages a younger person to avoid this kind of breach. He goes on to flesh out these proposals by adjacent elements to each proverb—laziness (10:4), diligence (15:19), and so on.[34] Heim treats mother and father in 10:1 and 15:20 as representing parents in general.

30. The following come from Snell, *Twice-Told Proverbs*, 35–44. Identical or nearly identical: Prov 9:4//16; 14:12//16:25; 18:8//26:22; 20:16//27:13; 21:9//25:24; 22:3//27:12. One dissimilar word: 2:1//7:1; 2:16//7:5; 5:7//7:24; 6:10–11//24:33–34; 19:5//9; 23:18//24:14b. Two dissimilar words: 1:8//6:20; 1:25//30; 2:2//5:1; 3:2//9:11; 4:20//5:1; 10:1//15:20; 11:1//20:23; 12:11//28:19; 13:14//14:27;19:1//28:6; 19:24//26:15. Three dissimilar words (single backslash indicates lesser similarities here only): 3:15/8:11; 6:24/7:5; 8:35/18:22; 10:2/11:4; 10:28/11:7; 15:13/17:22; 16:2/21:2; 22:13/26:13; 26:12/29:20. Four or more dissimilar words: 2:3/8:1; 2:16/6:24; 11:14/15:22; 12:13/29:6; 12:23/13:16/15:2; 15:16/16:8; 19:25/21:11; 21:9/25:24; 22:2/29:13; 26:1/8. Half-verses repeated: 4:4b//7:2a; 5:7a//7:24a//8:32a; 6:15b//29:1b; 6:19a//14:5b; 10:6b//11b; 10:8b//10b; 10:15a//18:11a; 10:29b//21:15b; 11:14b//24:6b; 13:9b//24:20b; 15:33b//18:12b; 17:3a//27:21a; 17:15b//20:10b; 22:28a//23:10a; 23:3a//6b; 26:7b//9b. Beyond this, the dissimilarities become too significant to list here (see 44–59). For other lists of doublets in Proverbs, see Keil and Delitzsch, *Proverbs*, 24–26; Driver, *Introduction*, 397–404. On catchwords in adjacent proverbs see Eng, "Semitic Catchwords," 252–53.

31. See Snell, *Twice-Told Proverbs*, 35–59. Snell's purposes are excavative. For sharp criticism of the excavative diachronic aims of Snell, see Fox's review, 153–57. The most valuable outcomes of Snell's work for the study of Proverbs, but not exegetical allusions, may be the parallels listed in the previous footnote.

32. See Heim, *Poetic Imagination*, 32–33.

33. Proverbs 15:20 *BHS* n. a shows that the B line assimilated to "a foolish son" with 10:1 in LXX and some Hebrew manuscripts. Like *BHQ*, Fox's eclectic text of 10:1 and 15:20 follow MT, which is preferred (*Proverbs: Eclectic Edition*, 172, 236).

34. See Heim, *Poetic Imagination*, 208–13.

Heim does not note that everywhere in Proverbs the father/mother pairs and collocations function synonymously except Prov 10:1 and 15:20, with father this *but* mother that—there is something different going on in these two verses.[35] Heim does not pursue the idea that disjointed proverbs may function like riddles that invite gap-filling.[36] For example, Heim does not explain why the wise son's own father is not joyful in 10:1a—is he dead?—or why the foolish son does not or cannot actively cause grief to his own mother in 10:1b (lacking a verb)—is he is dead?, since folly leads to death (5:5; 9:18).[37] The point at hand, however, does not relate to this or that interpretive issue of any pair of partially duplicate proverbs, but whether 10:1 or 15:20 exegetes its counterpart.

Sneed suggests proverb repetitions offer exegesis. Sneed rejects Heim's model because interpreting two proverbs against each other becomes circular reasoning. And then he uses Heim's model as one extreme for two choices: proverb doublets must be interpreted in the light of their counterparts versus ignoring similarities and interpreting each proverb on its own. Sneed selects a middle path, namely, that duplicate and partially duplicate proverbs do not determine meaning, but "they are suggestive."[38] This does not sound like exegesis *within* Scripture or *by* the author of one or both of the doublet counterparts (or even an editor of Proverbs). Sneed describes something that an interpreter of the Bible can do with proverb doublets, but this is not scriptural exegesis of Scripture.[39]

The problem may be more fundamental than the approaches noted above. Fox makes the point that no hypothesis for proverb doublets actually explains the phenomenon. He lists numerous proposals with criticisms of each: clichés that get repeated; numerology may have led editors to repeat proverbs to properly tally a collection; important proverbs get repeated for emphasis; structuring device; and so on. Fox goes on to suggest that while not all doublets may do the same thing, some may feature older and newer proverbs since development of wisdom is part of wisdom.[40]

In sum, two issues stand against treating proverb doublets and half-doublets as exegetical. Doublets are not exegetical but "literary" according to the standards of wisdom emphases of the Proverbs scroll. And, criteria for sorting out exegetical doublets from other sorts of doublets appears to push against the nature of sentence proverbs altogether. Proverb doublets should be studied but for reasons other than the scriptural exegesis of Scripture.

35. Compare Prov 1:8; 4:3; 6:20; 19:26; 20:20; 23:22, 25; 28:24; 30:11, 17. See Even-Shoshan, 79–80, nos. 7, 8, 47, 82–84, 87, 120, 180, 181, with two exceptions, 10:1; 15:20 (117, 118) and two uses of "mother" without "father," 29:15; 31:1 (119, 121).

36. See Fox, *Proverbs 10–31*, 494–98; Yoder, review of *Proverbs 10–31*. Also see Crenshaw, "Riddles," *ABD* 5:722.

37. Note Prov 10:1b uses a verbless clause "but a foolish son (is) a grief to his mother" (lit.) versus the active verb in the A line of 10:1a or the ptc. in the B line of 15:20b "a foolish man *despises* [ptc.] his mother" (lit.) (the counterpart element of the proverb in 10:1b).

38. See Sneed, "Twice-Told Proverbs as Inner-Biblical Exegesis," 96–97.

39. Note the misleading title of Sneed's essay in the previous footnote. His essay affirms doublets as "inner-biblical exegesis" even though it ultimately describes what exegetes of Scripture can do with doublets in Proverbs.

40. See Fox, *Proverbs 10–31*, 487–89. Yona alternatively proposes that some repetitions of proverbs fit the profile of "expanded repetitions"—e.g., 10:1; 15:20; 29:3, and 16:9; 20:24 ("Exegetical and Stylistic," 156, 162, 164).

Chapter 28

RUTH

SYMBOLS[1]

- ~ B, probable interpretive allusion; C, possible; D, probably not
- \+ interpretive blend
- * part of interconnected network (see Networks near end of volume)

USE OF SCRIPTURE IN RUTH[2]

2:8*~Lev 19:9–10*; Deut 24:19*+23:3–6*[4–7] (B) (Moabitess granted residing foreigner gleaning privileges) (* see assembly network)

4:5–6~Num 27:4, 7; 36:4+Lev 25:23–26*+Deut 25:5–10+23:3–6*[4–7] (B) (legal blend of laws of inheritance, responsibility of near relative, levirate marriage, and the assembly) (* see assembly and release statute networks)

4:17, 22*~Deut 23:3–8*[4–9]+2 Sam 7* (B) (Moabitess matriarch of David) (* see assembly and Davidic covenant networks)

OLD TESTAMENT USE OF RUTH (SEE RESPECTIVE NOTE)

4:18–22~1 Chr 2:3–17 (B) (genealogies of Judah through family of David)

NEW TESTAMENT USE OF RUTH

4:17~Matt 1:5 (genealogy)

HERMENEUTICAL PROFILE OF THE USE OF SCRIPTURE IN RUTH

Ruth features connecting devices as well as several bold exegetical advances. The heading of the book acts as a guide that invites juxtaposing the Ruth story with episodes of the Deuteronomistic narrative in the days of the judges (see Filters). Ruth offers a sharp covenantal counterpoint over and against the unsavory days when everyone did what was right in their own eyes. Other, more subtle connecting devices shine the light of the excellent woman and Woman Wisdom on the title character of Ruth (see Table Pr2 in Proverbs Filters). These connecting elements do not include exegesis in themselves per se. They serve as do-it-yourself invitationals for readerly comparisons of Ruth with lawlessness, covenant, and wisdom.

1. For explanation of symbols, see Symbols and Abbreviations and Introduction. For other help, see Glossary.
2. See Bibliographic Note on Lists of Potential Parallels.

The Ruth narrative also features legal exegesis of a series of thorny laws. The Ruth narrative centers around two interpretive blends of overlapping legal instructions. Boaz works out a difficult exegetical blend out in the fields in Ruth 2. Two laws rub against each other in determining the identity of those to whom they apply: the law of gleaning (Lev 19:9–10; Deut 24:19) and the law of the assembly (Deut 23:3–6[4–7]).

Boaz needs to divine if a Moabitess could be allowed the rights of a residing foreigner. In the background stands the distinction between two kinds of others found throughout Scripture.[3] The legal drama Boaz works at concerns whether a Moabitess like Ruth can transfer from the category of excluded other to included other.

In a series of studies, scholars have been investigating the overlapping and competing legal instructions in play at the city gate in Ruth 4.[4] In spite of many advances coming from the study of the scriptural use of Scriptures, things would not quite fit together. Then Embry's observation of the mention of Jubilee in the law of female inheritance in Num 36 helped to bring the pieces together with a satisfying click.[5] Notice the several legal instructions in play at the city gate in Ruth 4:

- the law of female inheritance (Num 27:1–11; 36:1–13)
- the law of the financially responsible near relative (Lev 25:23–26)
- the law of levirate marriage (Deut 25:5–10)
- (possibly) the law of the assembly (Deut 23:3–6[4–7])

The common denominator in the first three of these legal instructions concerns inheritance. When studying Torah in a classroom, legal instructions can be handled one at a time. The scene at the city gate in Ruth 4 infuses the legal interpretation with the messy details of handling three laws on inheritance plus the law of the assembly all at once. This scenario provides Ruth's audience a way to understand how to work out scriptural interpretation in complicated life situations.

The modern reader who wanders into Ruth might not consider the exegetical drama. Much of Ruth comes off like the storyline of a quaint, low-budget holiday evening drama. The widow who loses everything comes home with her young beautiful daughter-in-law, at once available and unavailable because she comes from among the other. Perhaps ancient Hebrews also would have thought the story a quaint period piece. The narrator does not let on that the story takes place in olden days until the middle of the case at the city gate when she says, "Now in earlier times in Israel" regarding a long forgotten custom

---

3. On two kinds of others in Scripture, see Tables I4 in note on Isa 52:1 and Ezk4 in note on Ezek 44:9–16.

4. See Beattie, "Ruth," 251–67 (1974); Goulder, "Ruth," 307–19 (1993); Braulik, "Ruth," 1–20 (1999); Berman, "Ancient Hermeneutics," 22–38 (2007); Fischer, "Ruth," 140–49 (2007); Berlin, "Legal Fiction," 3–18 (2010); Chan and Venter, "Midrash," 1–6 (2010); Kelly, "Ethics," 155–66 (2013); Chavel, *Oracular Law*, 250–56 (2014); Jackson, "Ruth," 75–111 (2015).

5. Embry, "Legalities," 31–44 (2016).

(Ruth 4:7).[6] Based upon the storyteller's need to explain the custom, the legal contexts will be taken as donor contexts and Ruth as receptor context. All of the quaintness flies away when the story hits the surprise in its very last word—"David" (4:17). Instantly all the stakes get raised to the highest levels as those in the know scramble back to study the fine print of the legal exegesis. Ruth's otherness suddenly becomes important far beyond romantic quests. David's place in Israel and the hopes of the promise Yahweh made to him hang in the balance of Boaz's legal exegesis out in the field and at the city gate.

The narrative insists at this point that a Moabite can assimilate into the assembly of Yahweh across three generations the same as any Egyptian or Edomite. By revealing a Moabitess as one of David's matriarchs, the narrator invites her readership to an exegetical decision regarding the law of the assembly with the Davidic covenant on the line. To insist on interpreting the law of the assembly as excluding Ammonites and Moabites on ethnic or genealogical bases removes David from the assembly of Yahweh and all that that means. But the Ruth story does the opposite. If David looks back four generations to the days when everyone did what was right in their own eyes, he could see his paternal great-grandparents as a sharp counterpoint. Boaz and Ruth represent a marriage of persons of valor. The Moabitess of valor herself turns out to be one of the matriarchs of the anointed king of Israel.

Ruth moves revelation forward by narrative exegesis of legal instruction in a complementary fashion to other scriptural advances. Elsewhere Isaiah promotes a place in temple worship for eunuchs and foreigners who join themselves to Yahweh that is better than that of sons and daughters; Ezekiel looks for a day when residing foreigners will inherit the land of promise among the tribes; the restoration narrated in Ezra-Nehemiah welcomes others who turn from the pollutions of the peoples of the lands to the Torah.[7] The prophets occasionally speak of future hope for Moab (Isa 16:4; Jer 48:47). The Ruth story looks back and finds help for Israel from a socially challenged Moabitess.

Two very minor points should be mentioned. The narrative implies a female *persona* for the storyteller. The third-person plural subject can be understood as "they" feminine or "they" masculine. Only an ancient female speaker would refer to the women—"They said" (fem)—as "the whole town" (1:19).[8] The common term "kinsman-redeemer" carries too much typological baggage and is sometimes subjected to wild typological comparisons to Christian doctrines, almost allegorizing the story by some lay teachers. The present study will use "financially responsible near relative" or the like to avoid overloading the story with figural connotations.

---

6. As observed by Levinson, "Human Voice," 44; idem, "'You Must Not Add,'" 22–23. Contra Levinson's revised view that the custom is a literary fiction (*Legal Revision*, 40–45, esp. 45). The exilic or postexilic date of Ruth is corroborated by elements of LBH including several Aramaisms (see Jones, *Reading Ruth*, 124–26) and cases of a finite verb with an attached article—"the one who returned" (הַשָּׁבָה) in Ruth 1:22; 2:6; 4:3 (GKC §138i, k; Williams §§91, n. 139; 539b; *IBHS* §19.7c; Joüon §145d; contra conjectural emendations from pf to ptc without evidence in *IBHS* §19.7d; Joüon §145e).

7. See Isa 56:1–8; Ezek 47:22–23; Ezra 6:21; Neh 10:30[31] and notes ad loc.

8. Thank you to Michael Carasik for this observation.

USE OF SCRIPTURE

2:8*~Lev 19:9–10*; Deut 24:19*+23:3–6*[4–7] (B) (Moabitess granted residing foreigner gleaning privileges) (* see assembly network). After being informed of the Moabitess's identity, Boaz interpretively deduces she enjoys a standing with rights to glean (Ruth 2:8). Boaz's deduction rests on several moving parts that need to be noted individually then put together.

The symmetrical precision of Ruth includes using several key terms seven or fourteen times. The term "Moab" appears seven times (Ruth 1:1, 2, 6[2x], 22; 2:6; 4:3). Narration and embedded speech together refer to Ruth as a Moabitess seven times (1:4, 22; 2:2, 6, 21; 4:5, 10).[9] As if to underline the point the overseer tells Boaz "She is *the Moabite* who came back *from Moab* with Naomi" (2:6, emphasis mine). Ruth's identity as Moabitess invokes the law of the assembly, which forbids Moabites from entry into the assembly of Yahweh and forbids seeking their welfare.[10] The entire context seems relevant as well as part of its own allusion to Numbers (bold and italics signify verbal parallels at the level of roots, and broken underlining signifies emphasis of issue at stake in Ruth):

> I will bless those who bless you, and **whoever curses you** [קלל] I *will curse* [ארר]; and all peoples on earth will be blessed through you. (Gen 12:3)
>
> [Balaam] May those who bless you be blessed and those *who curse* [ארר] you *be cursed!* [ארר]. (Num 24:9b)
>
> No Ammonite or Moabite or any of their descendants may enter the assembly of Yahweh, not even in the tenth generation. For they did not come to meet you with bread and water on your way when you came out of Egypt, and they hired Balaam son of Beor from Pethor in Aram Naharaim to pronounce a **curse on you** [קלל]. However, Yahweh your God would not listen to Balaam but turned **the curse** [קלל] into a blessing for you, because Yahweh your God loves you. Do not seek their welfare or benefit as long as you live. (Deut 23:3–6[4–7], v. 6[7] lit.)

The rationale for the law does not stem from genealogical or ethnic concerns. The law alludes to Moab's treachery in not only refusing hospitality but in also seeking out a mercenary prophet to damn Israel (23:4–5[5–6]). The context of the legal instruction goes on to explain that Edomites and Egyptians may enter the assembly of Yahweh in three generations (23:7–8[8–9]). The distinction between these two kinds of others,

---

9. For both of these, see Even-Shoshan, 629.

10. NIV says, "Do not seek a treaty of friendship with them" (Deut 23:6a[7a]) but NRSV says more literally, "You shall never promote their welfare or their prosperity" (cf. לֹא־תִדְרֹשׁ שְׁלֹמָם וְטֹבָתָם).

those excluded like Ammonites and Moabites versus those included like Egyptians and Edomites, needs to be read with other teachings on two kinds of others in Torah and elsewhere. The regulation for Passover excluded uncircumcised others from participation and required circumcised others to participate (Exod 12:43–49). The prophets maintain a similar distinction. Isaiah and Ezekiel exclude the uncircumcised from the temple and include other residing foreigners and foreigners within the covenantal community (Isa 52:1; 56:1–7; Ezek 14:1–11; 44:9–16; 47:22–23). The restoration assembly likewise excluded some others (Ezra 9–10; Neh 13:1–3) while including repentant others (Ezra 6:21; Neh 10:28[29]). All of these contexts distinguish two kinds of others: excluded (uncircumcised, Ammonite and Moabite, those who follow practice of the peoples of the lands) and included (circumcised, Egyptians and Edomites, covenant-keepers) (see Tables I4 in note on Isa 52:1 and Ezk6 in note on Ezek 44:9–16).

Ten generations would effectively be never, since no one could live to see it (Neh 13:1; cf. Deut 23:3, 6[4, 7]). Three generations make room to determine the integrity of a commitment to enter the assembly. If the commitment were marked by circumcision, as in Exod 12—not mentioned in Deut 23—then the passive nature of the circumcision of a child requires raising the child according to the covenant and when the grown child circumcises the third generation, the assimilation would be validated. Jeremiah 9:25–26[24–25] refers to Egyptians, Edomites, Ammonites, and Moabites (the four peoples of the law of the assembly), as well as Israelites, practicing circumcision. Thus, circumcision would be an insufficient sign of committing to the covenant of Israel's God in these cases.[11]

Scriptural exegetical advances erase gender as an issue relative to excluded others (see note on Deut 7:1–5). The restoration assembly excluded males and females alike according to Deuteronomy's ruling (Ezra 9:12; Neh 10:30[31]; 13:25). Suggestions that the law of the assembly only applies to males rest on anachronism.

Boaz does not treat Ruth as an excluded other but an included other. To unpack Boaz's interpretive decision requires noting the different terms in his exchange with Ruth. The term "foreigner" (נָכְרִי) often refers to excluded others while "residing foreigner" (גֵּר) to the protected class of included others.[12] Note the artful consonance of "notice" (*nkr* נכר) drawing additional emphasis to Ruth's self-perception as "foreigner" (*nkry* נָכְרִי) versus Boaz's informal legal decision to grant Ruth gleaning rights as a residing foreigner widow (bold and italics signify verbal parallels, and broken underlining signifies contrasting identifications of Ruth):

11. See Orian, "Numbers," 114.

12. See Siquans, "Foreignness," 449–50. Siquans makes an excellent point that Boaz treats Ruth as a "residing foreigner" (גֵּר) though Boaz did not use the term. She overstates one aspect of Ruth's complex identity by saying as a woman without a man she had no legal status (446). In the case of vows, a widow's word counts like any man's (Num 30:9[10]), and in the case of inheritance a female may inherit like a male, with qualifications (27:8; cf. 36:1–12).

> When you *reap the harvest* of your land, do not *reap* to the very edges of your *field* or *gather* **the gleanings** of your *harvest*. . . . Leave them for the poor and the residing foreigner [גֵּר]. I am Yahweh your God. (Lev 19:9–10†)

> When you are *harvesting* in your *field* and you overlook a sheaf, do not go back to get it. Leave it for the residing foreigner [גֵּר], the fatherless and the widow, so that Yahweh your God may bless you in all the work of your hands. (Deut 24:19†)

> So Boaz said to Ruth, "My daughter, listen to me. Don't go and **glean** in another *field* and don't go away from here. Stay here with the women who work for me. Watch *the field* where the men are *harvesting*, and follow along after the women." . . . At this, she bowed down with her face to the ground. She asked him, "Why have I found such favor in your eyes that you notice me [*nkr* נכר]—a foreigner [*nkry* נָכְרִי]?" (Ruth 2:8–10)

Though Boaz conceivably could have simply ignored the law of the assembly and its prohibition against seeking the welfare of Moabites (Deut 23:6[7]), the context suggests otherwise. Boaz's prayer language to Ruth offers the clue.

> Boaz replied, "*I've been told* all about what you have done for your mother-in-law since the death of your husband—how you left your father and mother and your homeland and came to live with a people you did not know before. May Yahweh repay you for what you have done. May you be richly rewarded by Yahweh, the God of Israel, *under whose wings you have come to take refuge.*" (Ruth 2:11–12, emphasis mine)

Boaz's comments go beyond the idea that Ruth shows hospitability in getting grain for Naomi, in contrast to the inhospitality of the Ammonites and Moabites in the wilderness (Deut 23:4[5]).[13] Boaz refers back to something that she had already done, namely, Ruth's oath: "Your people, my people. Your God, my God" (Ruth 1:16 lit.). The narrator previously hinted at Ruth's commitment by using the loaded term "she clung to her" (1:14).[14] The contrast of Orpah returning to her people and her god underlines Ruth's leaving Moab and its god for the God of Israel and his people (1:15). Ruth 1 represents one of the contexts that gives birth to notions of conversion and proselytes, but these terms are anachronistic here. Setting aside labels, notice that Boaz grounds his informal legal decision on Ruth's commitment of coming "under the wings of Yahweh" (2:12).[15] The narrator revisits this language when Ruth proposes marriage to Boaz with "spread your wing over me," referring to the wing-like robes of Boaz (3:9). The term "uncover

13. Contra Fischer, "Book of Ruth," 145; Braulik, "Book of Ruth," 10–11.
14. See the contextual similarity of leaving and *cleaving* in Gen 2:24. Also see Grätz, "Second," 282.
15. Compare the use of Yahweh's wings in Ps 5:11[12]; 17:8; 36:7[8].

the wing" can refer to conjugal relations (Deut 22:30[23:1]; cf. Ezek 16:8), which helps explain why Boaz regards "cover me with your wing" as a metonymy for a marriage proposal from the young widow (Ruth 3:10–11). To connect these images: Boaz's covenantal, maternal zoomorphic reference to Ruth under Yahweh's wings just as easily transposes to a different covenantal metaphor of marriage. Boaz's conclusion that Ruth should enjoy the rights of gleaning like any other residing foreigner starts with her prior covenantal commitment to take Yahweh as her God and Israel as her people—till death us do part, so to speak (1:16–17).[16]

One final element of this interpretive blend needs to be addressed. The law of the assembly is classified as apodictic law, not case law. The narrator of Ruth does not help readers here. She leaves Boaz's thought process up to readers to work out. At one level, the law of the assembly gives a narrative rationale for each of the excluded and included others: Ammon and Moab excluded by virtue of inhospitality and seeking to damn Israel, Egypt included because Israel lived as residing foreigners among them, and Edom included because of brotherhood (Deut 23:4–5, 7[5–6, 8]). This symbolic identity could work in a similar fashion as Israel does for Paul. Just as not all Israel is Israel, not all Moabites are Moabites (Rom 9:6).[17] Elsewhere, other interpretations of the law of the assembly consistently do *not* read Ammon and Moab literally, that is, ethnically or genealogically (Isa 52:1; Lam 1:10; Neh 13:1–3, see notes ad loc.). For Boaz, Ruth's birthplace had been eclipsed by how she committed to live and die. She committed herself to Yahweh, who had taken her under his wings. This may be the sort of thing Boaz deduced, but he may have come by a different path.

Torah speaks of seventy peoples (Gen 10). The law of the assembly deals with five: Israel, two excluded, and two included peoples. The narrow specification requires treating Ammon, Moab, Egypt, and Edom symbolically to allow for applying the law of the assembly to someone from any of the other sixty-five peoples. With respect to the law of the assembly, others not from the four named peoples could be treated like excluded or included others (as in 1 Kgs 11:1; cf. note ad loc). Stated directly, the very specificity of the law of the assembly naming only four peoples made this apodictic law function like a case law. For all other peoples needed to be sorted out into one of the two categories. Whether this was on his mind or not, Boaz treated a Moabitess like she did not fit her own "case."

Again, the narrator does not explain or reveal Boaz's thoughts. Instead, she demonstrates that Boaz works out an interpretive blend with the laws of gleaning and the law of the assembly. Boaz's exegetical deduction pivots on the inherent permeability of included

---

16. Ruth actually says that she will remain with Naomi even after death: "Where you die, I die, and there I will be buried. May Yahweh do to me and more, *if even death separates you and me*" (Ruth 1:17 lit., emphasis mine). Ruth's oath signifies her commitment to Naomi forever. Campbell regards Ruth's oath as inclusive of burial with her Israelite family—gathered to one's ancestors (*Ruth*, 74–75).

17. See Schnittjer, *Torah Story*, 512. On the sense of "not all Israel is Israel" see Bruno, Compton, and McFadden, *Biblical Theology*, 122–26.

and excluded classes of the other. For Boaz, a Moabitess could enjoy covenantal protection of Yahweh and thereby enjoy gleaning rights of a residing foreigner.

4:5–6~Num 27:4, 7; 36:4+Lev 25:23–26*+Deut 25:5–10+23:3–6*[4–7] (B) (legal blend of laws of inheritance, responsibility of near relative, levirate marriage, and the assembly) (* see assembly and release statute networks). The interpretive blend of four overlapping legal instructions at the city gate stands as the climactic exegetical nexus of Ruth. The textual issues in Ruth 4:5 complicate matters. The way forward needs to be in two steps: briefly assessing how each of the four laws bears on the case provisionally using Ruth 4:5 NIV, then putting the four together and running the options on the textual difficulties in 4:5.

The regulation of Jubilee includes protection of the rights of landowners who fall into poverty. The regulation commends a near relative to take financial responsibility for the land by purchasing it until the landowner can afford to buy it back or until its automatic return at Jubilee, whichever comes first (Lev 25:23–26). But this law bumps into the law of female inheritance.

The term "name" not only functions as a leading word in Ruth but a catchword in a couple of the laws in question. "Name" appears fourteen times in Ruth (1:2[3x], 4[2x]; 2:1, 19; 4:5, 10[2x], 11, 14, 17[2x]).[18] The logic of the request of Zelophehad's daughters includes preventing the "name" of the dead from disappearing even without a male heir (Num 27:4). Yahweh grants their request, yet the tribe of Manasseh petitioned that their lands not be married away with female heiresses—causing the lands to be unrecoverable at Jubilee (36:4). Yahweh adjusts his adjustment so that daughters could inherit but thereby must marry within the tribe (36:5–9). Embry explains that if female heiresses marry outside the tribe, they would eliminate the role of financially responsible near relatives to buy the land temporarily and return the land at Jubilee. Thus Ruth, as heiress of the land, must marry before a financially responsible near relative could temporarily purchase the land according to the intersection of Jubilee and female inheritance regulations (36:4).[19]

The logic of the law of levirate marriage overlaps in part because it also turns on sustaining the "name of the dead" (Deut 25:6, 7). The legal responsibilities of an *optional* levirate marriage include conditions. The premise of the law relates to brothers living together (25:5). But whatever the premise limits, the law is optional anyway, leading to a public shaming ceremony involving a sandal (25:9–10).[20]

The law of the assembly as it pertains to Ruth as a Moabitess also might be in play at the gate. The financially responsible near relative backs out after he hears about marrying Ruth. Her Moabite background may or may not be the reason—that turns on the textual issues in Ruth 4:5 (see below).

18. See Even-Shoshan, 1161–64 (nos. 25, 26, 153–57, 241–44, 605, 694, 728).

19. See Embry, "Legalities," 41.

20. On the non-obligation of levirate marriage in this case, see Block, *Ruth*, 216.

Excerpts from several of the relevant laws have been marked in Ruth 4 to illustrate how they interrelate within Boaz's masterful handling of the interpretive blending of the legal challenge. Boaz provides an exegetical solution once again within a complex life situation (italics signify verbal parallels, and underlining and broken underlining signify legal interrelations):

> If one of your fellow Israelites becomes poor and sells some of their property, their nearest relative is to come and *redeem* what they have sold. (Lev 25:25)

> [Zelophehad's daughters] Why should our father's name disappear from his clan because he had no son? Give us property among our father's relatives. (Num 27:4)

> [Family heads of Manasseh said] "When the Year of Jubilee for the Israelites comes, their inheritance will be added to that of the tribe into which they marry, and their property will be taken from the tribal inheritance of our ancestors." Then at Yahweh's command Moses gave this order to the Israelites: "What the tribe of the descendants of Joseph is saying is right. This is what Yahweh commands for Zelophehad's daughters: They may marry anyone they please as long as they marry within their father's tribal clan." (36:4–6)

> If brothers are living together and one of them dies without a son, his widow must not marry outside the family. Her husband's brother shall take her and marry her and fulfill the duty of a brother-in-law to her. The first son she bears shall carry on the name of the dead brother so that his name will not be blotted out from Israel. (Deut 25:5–6)

> Then he [Boaz] said to the *guardian-redeemer*, "Naomi, who has come back from Moab, is selling the piece of land that belonged to our relative Elimelek. [4] I thought I should bring the matter to your attention and suggest that you buy it in the presence of these seated here and in the presence of the elders of my people. If you will *redeem it*, do so **[Lev 25:23–26]**. But if you will not, tell me, so I will know. For no one has the right to do it except you, and I am next in line." "I will *redeem* it," he said. [5] Then Boaz said, "On the day you buy the land from Naomi, you also acquire Ruth the Moabite **[Deut 23:3–6 (4–7)]**, the dead man's widow **[Num 36:4–6]**, in order to maintain the name of the dead with his property" **[Num 27:4+Deut 25:6]** [6] At this, the *guardian-redeemer* said, "Then I cannot *redeem* it because I might endanger my own estate. You *redeem* it yourself. I cannot do it." (Ruth 4:3–6)

To summarize the interpretive blend itself, the series of laws underlying the case at the city gate overlap like circles of a Venn diagram. The linchpin law relates the need for the marriage of the female heiress of the land before a redemption purchase because of Jubilee (Num 36:4). The marriage, in this case, simultaneously enacts the laws of female inheritance and levirate marriage to sustain the name of the dead. In this way, the marriage of Ruth the Moabitess and heiress of the estate had to be decided before the unnamed man could fulfill his role as financially responsible next of kin. However, when he hears of the requirement of marrying Ruth the Moabitess, he backs out based on the optional clause of refusal in the levirate marriage law.

Two interrelated issues remain: the textual problems in Ruth 4:5 and the reason the unnamed financially responsible near relative said yes but then backed out. The nature of the issues requires presenting options depending on how the textual difficulty turns out. All of this needs to be handled patiently and provisionally because of the intertwined difficulties of every element.

The first textual difficulty regards the letter *mem* as either the short form of the word "from" (Ruth) or a grammatically inert enclitic *mem* representing an archaic speaking style in some of the speeches of Naomi and Boaz.[21] The enclitic *mem* would be something like the nonfunctional final vowels in a modern-day quaint merchant's sign "Ye Olde Shoppe." The sense of these possibilities are: "When you acquire the property from Naomi *and from* Ruth the Moabite" (Ruth 4:5 JPSB, emphasis mine) versus "On the day you buy the land from Naomi, *X* [I or you, see below] *acquire Ruth the Moabite* (4:5† NIV).[22] The present discussion shall treat it as the semantically unproductive archaic enclitic *mem*. But since the B line of the verse includes "the wife of the dead," neither decision controls the outcome of the more important second textual issue of the second use of the verb "acquire."

The verb in the Masoretic Text itself seems to be "I acquire" Ruth, but the Masoretes included the preferred synagogue reading in the margin "you acquire" Ruth.[23] The Septuagint glossed the term as "you acquire," but the reason for this may or may not be a difference in the consonantal parent text before the translators.[24] The Septuagintal translators may have understood the *yod* on the end of a second-person masculine verb as

21. If the *mem* is "from" (וּמֵאֵת = אֵת + מִן + וּ) then the phrase "and from Ruth" (וּמֵאֵת רוּת) finishes the first half of the verse. If it is an enclitic *mem*, then the phrase fronts the second half of the verse with "and Ruth the Moabitess" in apposition to "the wife of the dead," thus "and Ruth the Moabitess the wife of the dead [I or you] acquire to raise up the name of the dead on his inheritance" (Ruth 4:5b lit.; on the subject of the verb "acquire" see below).

22. See Gordon, "Waw Conversive," 90; *IBHS* §39.2a, n. 2. Ruth 4:5 meets Cohen's three criteria for enclitic-*mem*: (1) problematic grammar/syntax of MT; (2) can revocalize without emendation; and (3) additional textual witness to *mem* (here see LXX) (Cohen, "Enclitic-mem," 238–39). For other options, see de Waard, *BHQ*, 55*–56*.

23. The *ketiv*—if read as Q pf. 1cs—says "I acquire" (קָנִיתִי), and *qere* says "you acquire" (קָנִיתָה) (Ruth 4:5 *BHQ*).

24. See Ruth 4:5 *BHK* n. b that rightly marks the LXX with a question mark. *BHS* removes the question mark from n. b and proposes an unattested form "acquiring" (קְנֵה inf. const.) by backreading LXX as "you to acquire" (κτήσασθαί σε inf. aorist). *BHQ* moves in new direction by conjecturing that the parent text of the LXX translators matched the *qere* emendation "you acquire" (קָנִיתָה). *BHK* best handles the evidence concerning LXX, which may have regarded the *yod* on the end of a 2ms (קניתי) as an inert archaism akin to the archaic grammatically inert *yods* on the end of 2fs verbs in Naomi's speech in Ruth 3:3, 4 (see *ketiv/qere* ad loc.). The limitation of these and other potential archaisms to speeches of Naomi and Boaz suggests they could be dialect markers or period piece coloring by the narrator—i.e., Naomi and Boaz speaking in an olden manner (cf. similar in *IBHS* §31.7.1, n. 51; Noonan, *Advances*, 204). See other examples in GKC §44h. For an explanation of why these potential archaisms only appear at the end of second-person verb chains in 3:3, 4, see Holmstedt, *Handbook*, 152–53.

a syntactically inert dialect marker or archaic style of speech on the analogy of the same in Naomi's use of second-person feminine verbs elsewhere (see footnote). That is, the older generation of Bethlehem—represented by Boaz and Naomi—may have spoken in an olden style or with a traditional regional accent marked by final *yods*. In short, the Septuagintal evidence does not necessarily point to a different consonantal text than the Masoretic Text. The present approach, therefore, favors the consonantal text of the Masoretic Text without emendation, which, of itself, does not solve the interpretive difficulty. Based on this decision the verb could be "I acquire" (*ketiv*) or "you acquire" (*ketiv*, counting final *yod* as an inert archaism, see footnote). Compare the two options in modern translations:

> Boaz continued: "On the day you take over the field from Naomi, *I take over the widow, Ruth the Moabite,* so as to perpetuate the name of the dead man on his holding." (4:5 REB, emphasis mine)

> Then Boaz said, "On the day you buy the land from Naomi, *you also acquire Ruth the Moabite, the dead man's widow,* in order to maintain the name of the dead with his property." (4:5 NIV, emphasis mine)

The logic of the unnamed financially responsible near relative's motives for saying yes then backing out needs to be played out with both options "I acquire" and "you acquire" because the decision about the verb could go either way based on the evidence.

If Boaz says "*you* acquire Ruth" (emphasis mine), the unnamed financially responsible near relative may have realized he did not possess the financial resources to care for two widows and potentially an offspring without putting his own children's inheritance at risk. Or, if he hears Boaz say "you acquire Ruth *the Moabitess*" (emphasis mine), he may have been opposed to the match based on a literal ethnic or genealogical interpretation of the law of the assembly—"*you shall never promote their* [Moabites'] *welfare* or their prosperity as long as you live" (Deut 23:6[7] NRSV, emphasis mine). In this case, he may protect the inheritance of his own children by strict obedience of legal instruction. Or, if Boaz says "I acquire Ruth," the unnamed financially responsible near relative may realize that helping Naomi would only be temporary and not add the field to his own estate because Boaz and Ruth would likely produce an heir to recover the property in short order via the law of redemption (Lev 25:25).

In the case of all options, the logic of Boaz, that the field cannot be redeemed until the marriage of Ruth has been decided, stems from the legal revision in Num 36:4 explicitly tied to Jubilee regulations. And the overlapping levirate marriage law of Deut 25:5–10 gives the unnamed financially responsible near relative an out from a marriage to the widow for any reason—financial limitations, her Moabite background, or anything else.

Each of the above scenarios fits with two final observations. First, Boaz for a second time acts as a valiant exegete of Torah in accord with the commendations by the narrator and Naomi (2:1; 3:18). Second, the leading word "name" ironically shines a light on the man with no name who backed out of purchasing the field to preserve his own estate. The narrative preserves the name of the dead, but the name of the financially responsible near relative gets blotted out. The narrator helps by eliminating the man's name from Boaz's lips when he says, "Come over here and sit down, *So-and-so*!" (4:1 JPSB, emphasis mine).[25]

4:17*, 22~Deut 23:3–8*[4–9]+2 Sam 7* (B) (Moabitess matriarch of David) (* see assembly and Davidic covenant networks). The final word of the narrative proper—"David"—raises the stakes exponentially of Boaz's exegetical and marital decisions regarding the Moabitess (see notes on Ruth 2:8; 4:5–6). The narrator brilliantly withholds the larger significance of Boaz's exegetical decisions until getting to a surprise ending. Ruth turns out to be the fourth-generation matriarch of David. The genealogy from Judah to David stands as a postscript, as opposed to the normal prologue position, in order to preserve the element of surprise (4:18–22; cf., e.g., introductory genealogies in Gen 11:10–30; Ezra 7:1–5; 1 Chr 1–9; Matt 1:1–17).

The revelation that David himself is the great-grandson of Ruth forces a juxtaposition between the law of the assembly and the Davidic covenant (Deut 23:3–8[4–9]; 2 Sam 7).[26] Those who would interpret the law of the assembly to exclude ethnic or genealogical Ammonites and Moabites then need to exclude the offspring of Boaz and Ruth from Israel, including the Davidic line and the covenantal promises to David. The interpretation that the law of the assembly only applies to excluding Ammonite and Moabite males anachronistically contradicts the often-repeated biblical emphasis that wrongful marriages apply to males and females alike (1 Kgs 11:1–2; Ezra 9:1, 12; Neh 13:25; cf. Deut 7:3; Neh 10:30[31]; m. Yebam. 8:3; b. Yebam. 77a). Or, to turn it around, the narrator of Ruth ends with a surprise that directs her audience back to Boaz's exegetical decisions to affirm them. Boaz interprets that the law of the assembly uses the Ammonite and Moabite treachery against Israel to typify excluded others. Ruth does not fit that profile since she embraces her identity in the people of Israel and submission to Yahweh (Ruth 1:16; 2:11–12). The narrator goes one step further and makes explicit that David hails from Boaz and Ruth. The promise of Yahweh to David validates Boaz's exegesis of the law of the assembly.

Moreover, for Boaz, not all Moabites are Moabites, and they can be granted gleaning rights as residing foreigners (2:8). For the narrator, Ruth's marriage to Boaz puts in motion full assimilation into Israel. Ruth's great-great grandson is none other than David, king of Israel, whom Yahweh affirms as his specially chosen king by means of Nathan's covenant (4:17, 22; 2 Sam 7). Another biblical genealogy of Judah emphasizes the same thing and more by including Tamar (guilty of incest and adultery), Rahab (Canaanite prostitute), Ruth (Moabitess), and Uriah's wife (victim or adulteress) (Matt 1:3, 5, 6).

---

25. The idiomatic expression "so-and-so" (פְּלֹנִי אַלְמֹנִי) is used to intentionally avoid saying a name, see "פְּלֹנִי," BDB 811–12; and NET note on Ruth 4:5.

26. Jones wonders if the law of the assembly "exposes the Davidic dynasty to the charge of illegitimacy" but then dismisses this issue without discussion (*Reading Ruth*, 107).

FILTERS

Ruth occasionally makes broad allusions to scriptural traditions.[27] Like everything else in this carefully crafted short narrative, these allusions seem thoroughly intentional. They have been filtered out because they are broad and non-exegetical.

Ruth 1:1 situates the book with Judges in three ways. First, the opening line "in the days when judges ruled" places the narrative within the historical framework of the days of the judges (Ruth 1:1). Second, the setting in Bethlehem broadly connects with the two epilogues of Judges that are also associated with Bethlehem (Judg 17:7; 19:1–2). Third, the background narrative frame "and there was a man from Bethlehem" (Ruth 1:1) invites association with the other "and there was a man" stories embedded at the end of Judges and beginning of Samuel (17:1, 7; 19:1; 1 Sam 1:1; 9:1). These elements do not feature exegesis of themselves, but they invite the interpretation of the narrative in the light of these other contexts.

Ruth 3:11 shares language with the acrostic of the excellent woman in Prov 31:10–31, inviting consideration of Ruth in light of personified wisdom (see Table Pr2 in Proverbs Filters). Some scholars suggest the parallel between Ruth 3:11 and Prov 31:10 (cf. v. 31) could signal Second Temple redactional activity to create sequencing relationships among the Writings.[28] Others regard the parallel as initiating "dialogue among texts" but not suggesting particular arrangement(s) of books.[29]

In **Ruth 3:16** Naomi asks, "Who are you my daughter [מִי־אַתְּ בִּתִּי]?" (lit.) with verbal and syntactical parallels to Isaac's question, "Who are you my son [מִי אַתָּה בְּנִי]?" (Gen 27:18 lit.). Jones discusses whether this is a purposeful allusion, and, if so, whether the deceptive subtext of Jacob's dealing with Isaac bleeds over into Ruth 3.[30]

Ruth 4:11 refers to Leah and Rachel's baby contest in a positive light since it built up the house of Israel (Gen 29:31–30:24).

Ruth 4:12 uses the house of Perez son of Tamar as a positive simile for the marriage of Boaz and Ruth. This obscure allusion may refer to a tradition about Perez unrecorded in Scripture. If it refers to a scriptural tradition, it could be deducing the younger-over-the-older pattern in Genesis (Isaac over Ishmael, Jacob over Esau, Ephraim over Manasseh). In this light Perez exits the womb even before his older brother (Gen 38:29).

The mention of Jesse and David in **Ruth 4:17, 22** broadly evokes the anointing of David when still in his father's household (1 Sam 16). And reference to David broadly alludes to the second king of Israel, the Davidic covenant, the Davidic kings of Judah, and even Psalms.

---

27. Less convincing are genre and thematic similarities—many forced or contrived—between the relations of Lot and his daughters (Gen 19:30–38), Judah and Tamar (38), and Ruth and Boaz (Ruth 3) observed by Fisch, "Ruth," 430–31, and Ruth's marriage compared to that of Isaac and Rebekah and Jacob and Rachel as noted by Finlay, "Genres," 167–69.

28. See Stone, "Search for Order," 182–83. Stone seems to have in mind the arrangement of the scrolls in the temple (and the synagogues?) later reflected in the codices (177–78).

29. See Eskenazi, "Response," 319–20. Also see Childs, *Introduction*, 501–3.

30. See Jones, "'Who Are You?'" 658–64.

Chapter 29

SONG OF SONGS

USE OF SCRIPTURE IN SONG
n/a

OLD TESTAMENT USE OF SONG
n/a

NEW TESTAMENT USE OF SONG
n/a

FILTERS[1]

Song of Songs shares language, imagery, and themes with other Scriptures. Song of Songs does not appear to house exegetical use of scriptural traditions. The vast majority of similarities do not even constitute broad allusion to other Scriptures. Much discussed similarities like "seal" in Song 8:6 and Gen 38:18, Jer 22:24, and Hag 2:23 may represent cross-references but not interpretive allusions. The following provides a few examples of filtered elements for the sake of illustration.

Broad Similarities to Other Scriptures

The prophets use sensual and marital themes of Yahweh's relationship with his people, such as betrothal and marriage (Hos 2:19–20[21–22]); love of a youthful bride (Jer 2:2); marital relations (before infidelity) (Ezek 16:8–14); divorce (Isa 50:1); reunion (54:5–8). Isaiah says, "*As a young man marries a young woman*, so will your Builder marry you; *as a bridegroom rejoices over his bride*, so will your God rejoice over you" (62:5, emphasis mine). The frequent use of marital imagery makes it "inevitable" that Song of Songs would be interpreted allegorically, parabolically, and typologically as referring to the relationship of God and his people.[2]

Fishbane notes the similar language but different functions of type-scenes of yearning

1. See Bibliographic Note on Lists of Potential Parallels.
2. These Scriptures and this observation come from Fishbane, *Song*, xx.

for a lover in Song 3:1–4 and Prov 7:10–20. The maiden longs for her beloved on her bed and goes out to find him (Song 3:1, 2). When she finds him, she seizes (אחז) him and takes him to the room where her mother conceived her (3:4). The temptress comes out dressed as a prostitute and seizes (חזק) the young man and kisses him (Prov 7:10, 13). The temptress goes out and finds him and lures him to come to her bed (7:15–20).[3]

Schellenberg suggests purposeful parallels between the young man's pursuit of Woman Wisdom in Proverbs and the pursuit of the beloved in Song of Songs. Elements like referring to the maiden and wisdom as "my sister," for Schellenberg, suggest intentionality (7:4; Song 4:9–10, 12; 5:1–2). At the same time similarities between the temptress and the maiden—"Well," "streaming," and "spring" of water (Prov 5:15, 16; Song 4:12, 15)—also suggest intentional echoing. The description of the maiden includes "Your lips drip sweetness as the honeycomb" (Song 4:11†) and of the temptress includes "For the lips of the adulterous woman drip honey" (Prov 5:3). In Schellenberg's view, Proverbs seeks to domesticate and warn against the kind of erotic and sensual passions presented in Song of Songs.[4]

The comparisons between the sensual contexts of Prov 5–9 and Song of Songs seem to relate more to subject matter than interpretive allusion. The parallels are general even if some of the imagery was borrowed, whichever direction.

Carr suggests parallels of relational imagery in Hosea as dependent on Song of Songs. The signs of dependence, for Carr, include references to a mother's conception (Song 3:4; Hos 2:5[7]), giving of different gifts (Song 5:1; Hos 2:5[7]), seeking and not finding lover/other lovers (Song 3:1–3; Hos 2:7[9]), sitting in beloved's tree-like shade as Israel will sit in the shade of trees in the restoration (Song 2:3; Hos 14:7[8]), as well as several single word parallels, some less common and others more common, terms like "scent" (Song 2:13; Hos 14:6[7]), "lily" (Song 2:1, 2, 16; 4:5; 5:13; 6:2–3; 7:2[3]; Hos 14:5[6]), "vine" (Song 2:13; 6:11; 7:8, 12[9, 13]; Hos 14:7[8]), "wine" (Song 2:4; Hos 14:7[8]), "fruit" (Song 2:3; 4:13, 16; 8:11; Hos 14:8[9]), and a few other general similarities.[5] All of these similarities seem to be general coincidences. Examining the context of seeking and not finding reveals Israel as an adulteress looking for any other lover and, upon failure, deciding to return to her husband (Hos 2:7[9]), versus the maiden seeking her lover with singular intent (Song 3:1–3). The appearance of the term "find" in Hos 2:7[9] and Song 3:2 looks more like coincidence of a common word in unrelated contexts. Yet this fits Carr's extrapolation that Hosea did not quote Song of Songs but that its love poetry mixed together with other ancient Near Eastern love poetry and serves as a "fund of literary-Scriptural tropes in his mind." Carr suggests Hosea's dependence on this mental fund of imagery when he uses relational themes.[6] Whatever the merits of

3. See ibid., xxix. Also see Kingsmill, "Song," 315–17; Murphy, *Song*, 69.
4. See Schellenberg, "'May Her Breasts Satisfy,'" esp. 256–57, 259–61.
5. See Carr, *Formation*, 435.
6. See ibid., 436.

Carr's theory may be, his view of "dependence" amounts to shared culture and excludes exegetical allusion.[7]

Davis suggests the maiden's description of the beloved as "whom my soul loves" (שֶׁאָהֲבָה נַפְשִׁי) (Song 3:4) may allude to the great commandment "*Love* Yahweh your God with all your heart and with all your *soul* and with all your strength" (Deut 6:5, parallels emphasized).[8] Carr suggests that the great commandment depends on Song of Songs, mixed with other love imagery akin to Hosea's conjectured use of Song of Songs (see above). The use of the love imagery in the great commandment depicts a "wifelike devotion."[9] In suggesting Deuteronomy's dependence on Song of Songs, Carr does not discuss the attached relative pronoun "whom-" (־שֶׁ) of LBH in the phrase "*whom* my soul loves" (Song 3:4), a linguistic feature that makes even dependence by indirect cultural diffusion unlikely.[10]

Strollo identifies eleven shared or similar terms in Lam 4:1–10 and Song 5:10–16, many of which appear in the same sequence. The descriptive parallels, for Strollo, suggest comparison between daughter Zion and the maiden's beloved. Whereas his head is purest gold, Zion's gold has lost its luster (Song 5:11; Lam 4:1). Strollo discusses numerous broad, shared descriptive terms and other rare terms shared by the two contexts.[11] The general nature of the similarities suggests they may be coincidence.

Though Ps 45 features some similar language and themes with Song of Songs, the two compositions have different focuses.[12]

The most excellent song, the song of songs, is the song of Solomon (Song 1:1).[13] The association with the son of David provides possibilities for reading into Song of Songs themes from the Davidic covenant (2 Sam 7).[14] Kingsmill suggests the term "my beloved" (*dodi* דּוֹדִי), which resembles David's name (דָּוִד), in all its forms occurs thirty-three times in Song of Songs, corresponding to the number of years David ruled in Jerusalem (1 Kgs 2:11). For Kingsmill, this confirms a messianic interpretation of the beloved and the wisdom function of Song of Songs as an allegory.[15] These latter associations seem coincidental.

Connections within Song

Three times the refrain warns the daughters of Jerusalem to wait to awaken. The first two match verbatim and the third features a shortened form of the refrain with mild

7. Also note similar broad comparisons of the song of the vineyard in Isa 5:1–7 and vineyard imagery in Song 8:11–12 (ibid., 437–38).

8. See Davis, *Proverbs*, 245, 255.

9. Carr, *Formation*, 437.

10. See GKC §36; *IBHS* §19.2c.

11. See Strollo, "Value," 196–201, esp. table, 197.

12. See Murphy, *Song*, 67.

13. For the superlative sense see GKC §133i.

14. See Campbell, "Song of David's Son," esp. 26–32.

15. See Kingsmill, "Song," 332.

variation (Song 2:7//3:5; 8:4). These repetitions go a long way toward heightening two occasions in Song of Songs (4:16; 8:5) that call for awakening (italics and bold signify verbal parallels):

> *Daughters of Jerusalem, I charge you* by the gazelles and by the does of the field: *Do not* **arouse** *or* **awaken** *love until it so desires.* (2:7//3:5)
>
> **Awake**, north wind, and come, south wind! Blow on my garden, that its fragrance may spread everywhere. Let my beloved come into his garden and taste its choice fruits. (4:16)
>
> *Daughters of Jerusalem, I charge you: Do not* **arouse** *or* **awaken** *love until it so desires.* (8:4)
>
> Who is this coming up from the wilderness leaning on her beloved? Under the apple tree I **roused** you; there your mother conceived you, there she who was in labor gave you birth. (8:5)

The theme of seeking and not finding recurs within Song of Songs along with other parallels (3:1–2; 5:6, 8). This fits with the theme of finding (3:4).

The maiden observes her beloved leaping across mountains like a gazelle or a young stag (2:8, 9; cf. v. 17). The closing of the book presents a younger version of the maiden calling for her beloved to be like a gazelle or a young stag upon spice-laden mountains (8:14).

Chapter 30

ECCLESIASTES

SYMBOLS[1]

- ~ B, probable interpretive allusion; C, possible; D, probably not
- + interpretive blend
- >/< more or less similar (see Filters)
- * part of interconnected network (see Networks near end of volume)

USE OF SCRIPTURE IN ECCLESIASTES[2]

5:4–6[3–5]~Deut 23:21–23[22–24] (B) (on vows)

11:9~Num 15:39 (C) (following the ways of heart and eyes)

12:7~3:20–21 (B)+Gen 2:7 (C)+3:19 (B) (return dust to the earth and spirit to God)

OLD TESTAMENT USE OF ECCLESIASTES

n/a

NEW TESTAMENT USE OF ECCLESIASTES

7:20~Rom 3:10 (none righteous)

HERMENEUTICAL PROFILE OF THE USE OF SCRIPTURE IN ECCLESIASTES

The manifold interconnections within Ecclesiastes relate to the literary structure of the book. These interconnections cannot be pursued here since the present concern narrowly relates to potential uses of other scriptural traditions.

Qoheleth interacts broadly with outside scriptural themes, including recurring engagement with several of life's most difficult incongruities.[3] Yet Qoheleth rarely quotes or even overtly alludes to scriptural traditions found elsewhere. Study of Qoheleth's use of Scripture finds potential allusions "more subtle and limited in scope" than those appearing in broadly compatible scriptural literature like Job.[4] One helpful suggestion

1. For explanation of symbols, see Symbols and Abbreviations and Introduction. For other help, see Glossary.
2. See Bibliographic Note on Lists of Potential Parallels.
3. Qoheleth (קֹהֶלֶת) refers to one who leads or speaks to an assembly—"Teacher" or "Preacher."
4. Dell and Kynes, "Introduction," *Reading Ecclesiastes Intertextually*, xvii.

is to regard the use of Scripture in Ecclesiastes as "theological criticism."[5] This sensible proposal helps lower expectations from scriptural exegesis to theological criticism by Qoheleth (see Filters).

The few cases of Qoheleth's exegetical use of scriptural traditions need to be approached within the framework of the book. Sorting out the much-contested relationship between the frame narrative and Qoheleth's teaching cannot be investigated here (third-person frame, Eccl 1:1–2; 7:27; 12:8–12). The dialogical character of the book along with its use of rhetorical perspectives and irony all bear on Qoheleth's use of scriptural traditions. Patience and settling for provisional outcomes can help with evaluation of potential interpretive allusions in Ecclesiastes.

USE OF SCRIPTURE

5:4–6[3–5]~Deut 23:21–23[22–24] (B) (on vows). The context warns against foolish sacrifices and careless prayers (5:1–2[4:17–5:1]). Qoheleth goes on to present a parallel to the law of vows in Deuteronomy as part of continued warning against foolish worship. The shared language, syntax, and contextual parallels make allusion highly likely. The wisdom flavor of Deuteronomy has been the basis for suggestions that Ecclesiastes is the donor context.[6] But the reduced attention to direct divine intervention and expansive wisdom emphases in Ecclesiastes point in the other direction. Most importantly, Deuteronomy's distinctive use of the particle *ki* (כִּי) for "if" to structure legal instructions gets replaced in later syntax, including the use of Deut 23:21[22] by Eccl 5:4[3] by "when" (כַּאֲשֶׁר) and in the Temple Scroll by retaining the particle *ki* followed immediately by "if" (וכי אם) (11QT/11Q19 53:11 in *DSSSE* 2:1272).[7] This linguistic evidence strongly suggests Deuteronomy is the donor and Ecclesiastes the receptor context.

Qoheleth's interpretive allusion rearranges the order of the instruction compared to Deuteronomy:[8]

Deuteronomy	Ecclesiastes
(a) If vow, pay quickly (Deut 23:21a[22a])	(a) If vow, pay quickly (Eccl 5:4a[3a])
(b) Yahweh shall demand it (Deut 23:21b[22b])	(c) Better not to vow (5:5[4])
(c) If no vow, not guilty (23:22[23])	(d) Fulfill vow (5:4b[3b])
(d) Fulfill vow (23:23a[24a])	(b) Do not protest the messenger's request for payment of vow (5:6[5])

5. See Anderson, "Curse," 99.

6. See Weinfeld, *Deuteronomic School*, 270.

7. On Deuteronomy's innovative use of "if" (כִּי) in legal syntax, see Levinson and Zahn, "Revelation," 318–19; Levinson, *More Perfect Torah*, 10, 24–26. On the syntactical revision of Deut 32:21[22] by Eccl 5:4[3] and 11QT/11Q19 53:11, see "Revelation," 325–27; *More Perfect Torah*, 32–34. Schultz observes that Qoheleth uses "when" (כַּאֲשֶׁר) elsewhere for legal formulation (Eccl 5:1[4:17]) ("'Fear God,'" 337; idem, "Reuse," 123).

8. Three of these four parallels follow Levinson, "'Better That,'" 3. For a different view of the parallel for "fulfill your vow" (Eccl 5:4b[3b]) in Deut 23, see Schultz, "'Fear God,'" 338; idem, "Reuse," 125. Also see Bendavid, *Parallels*, 194 [Hebrew].

Some of Qoheleth's more subtle adjustments include use of the negative jussive particle "not" (אַל) (Eccl 5:4[3]) instead of the indicative "not" (לֹא) (Deut 23:21[22]) and elimination of the divine name (Eccl 5:4[3]; Deut 23:21[22]).[9] Compare the differences in the interpretive allusion that reveal characteristic tendencies of Deuteronomy and Qoheleth (bold signifies verbal parallels, underlining signifies verbal similarities, and stylized underlining signifies broad similarities):

> If [כִּי] **you make a vow to** Yahweh your God, do not [לֹא] **delay to pay it, for** Yahweh your God will certainly demand it of you and you will be guilty of sin. [22] But if you refrain from making a vow, you will not be guilty. [23] Whatever your lips utter you must be sure to do, because you made your vow freely to Yahweh your God with your own mouth. (Deut 23:21–23†[22–24])

> When [כַּאֲשֶׁר] **you make a vow to** God, do not [אַל] **delay to pay it. For** he has no pleasure in fools; fulfill your vow. [5] It is better not to make a vow than to make one and not fulfill it. [6] Do not let your mouth lead you into sin. And do not protest to the temple messenger, "My vow was a mistake." Why should God be angry at what you say and destroy the work of your hands? (Eccl 5:4–6†[3–6])

Qoheleth appears to rework Deuteronomy's allowance for not making a vow (Deut 5:22[23]).[10] Qoheleth converts the allowance into a standard "better than" format that he employs elsewhere (Eccl 5:5[4]).[11] But like Deuteronomy, Qoheleth insists that vows be fulfilled (5:4b[3b]). Both Deuteronomy and Qoheleth try to reason with their readers. Deuteronomy emphasizes that the worshiper freely made the vow and therefore must keep it (Deut 23:23[24]). Qoheleth stresses the negative consequences of failing to honor a vow (Eccl 5:6[5]).

Both Deuteronomy and Ecclesiastes refer to failing to honor a vow as sin (Deut 23:21[22]; Eccl 5:6[5]). Qoheleth goes further than Deuteronomy's argument that the vow was made freely. While Deuteronomy emphasizes that "*Yahweh your God* will certainly demand it of you" (Deut 23:21[22], emphasis mine), Qoheleth makes the circumstance concrete by identifying the "messenger," apparently of the temple where vows are fulfilled, saying, "And do not protest to *the temple messenger*" (Eccl 5:6[5], emphasis mine; NIV adds "temple").[12] Qoheleth pushes back against excuses to the messenger and

9. These observations are made by Levinson, "'Better That,'" 32.

10. Levinson notes the oddity of using "if" (*ki* כִּי) to mark a subordinate conditional clause in Deut 23:22[23] instead of "if" (*im* אִם), which only happens in one other place (cf. Deut 15:12–13). Based on this syntactical anomaly, Levinson regards the allowance not to vow in Deut 23:22[23] as a later scribal insertion to soften the law ("'Better That,'" 33–36; idem, *More Perfect Torah*, 47–50, 69–74). The comparisons here follow the MT.

11. For "better than" format, see Eccl 2:24; 3:22; 4:3, 6, 9, 13; 6:9; 7:1, 2, 3, 5, 8, 10; 9:4, 16, 18.

12. Ecclesiastes 5:6[5] LXX uses "God" not "messenger" (MT). Fox observes that the implication is identical since Deut 23:21[22] says God himself demands payment of the vow (*Ecclesiastes*, 34). The targum retains "messenger" (Qoh 5:6[5] *ArBib*). Schultz notes that Deuteronomy typically suggests direct intervention from Yahweh ("'Fear God,'" 338;

suggests a likely excuse the fool might offer, using the cultic legal term for "unintentional sin"—"It was a mistake" (Eccl 5:6[5]//Num 15:25; cf. Lev 4:2, 22, 27; 5:15, 18).[13] Like Deuteronomy, Qoheleth insists unfulfilled vows invite divine judgment.

The advancement of revelation by Qoheleth can be placed within its historical development. Qoheleth stands in continuity with Deuteronomy concerning the need to honor vows or face judgment for sin. Elsewhere Torah includes regulations to protect men from "rash vows" made by daughters and wives (Num 30:5, 8[6, 9]). Qoheleth takes aim at fools of all genders who make hasty utterances before God (Eccl 5:1, 2[4:17; 5:1]; cf. Prov 20:25). Qoheleth makes this adjustment within the framework of wisdom for worship.

The Mishnah's tractate on vows suggests the late Second Temple period shows broad popularity of vows because the tractate initiates significant adjustments, such as conditions for annulling vows (m. Ned. 3:1; cf. 2:1, 5).[14] Judaic legal interpreters recognize that the bases for annulling vows had been extrapolated extensively—the rules "hover in the air and have naught to support them" (m. Ḥag. 1:8). Messiah's own new revelation pushes hard against the increasingly complicated rationales for legitimate vows. He takes the next step from Deuteronomy's advisement that not vowing is no sin and from Qoheleth's warnings against hasty vows. Messiah insists upon integrity in all claims—"Let your word be 'Yes, yes' or 'No, no'" (Matt 5:37 NRSV; cf. 5:33–36; 23:16–22).

In sum, Qoheleth advances revealed instruction concerning vows by means of exegetical wisdom. He stresses the need to avoid the folly of hasty words by males and females. Qoheleth stands in continuity with Deuteronomy by insisting that vows must be fulfilled. He advances the instruction in Deuteronomy by denying excuses based on claims of unintentional cultic sins. Qoheleth's exegesis of Deuteronomy's law of vows provides a helpful example of incremental advancement of revelation.

11:9~Num 15:39 (C) (following the ways of heart and eyes). The law of the tassels may connect to the failure of the scouting expedition by means of wordplay and catchword: "scout" (*tur* תּוּר) and "tassel" (*tsitsit* צִיצִת) (Num 13:2, 25; 14:34; 15:39) and "whoring/whore after" (14:33; 15:39).[15] Kynes suggests Qoheleth has this background in mind when he re-contextualizes part of the law. Compare the very limited parallels (bold signifies verbal parallels):

Speak to the Israelites and say to them: "Throughout the generations to come you are to make tassels on the corners of your garments, with a blue cord on each tassel. [39] You will

idem, "Reuse," 124). Others suggest Eccl 5:6[5] moves onto a new topic (Krüger, *Qoheleth*, 109). This suggestion does not adequately account for the continued parallel with the donor context (see b in side-by-side layout of Deut 23:21–23[22–24] and Eccl 5:4–6[3–5] above).

13. The term for "unintentional sin" occurs rarely outside of priestly contexts of Torah (Josh 20:3, 9; Eccl 5:6[5]; 10:5) (see "שְׁגָגָה," *HALOT* 2:1412–13). On the parallel "that it was a mistake" (הִוא/כִּי שְׁגָגָה הִיא) only in Num 15:25//Eccl 5:6[5], see Kynes, "Follow Your Heart," 22–24.

14. Levinson observes an opposite trend away from vows among Qumran sectarian texts and Philo (*More Perfect Torah*, 54).

15. Suggested by Milgrom, *Numbers*, 127, and adopted by Kynes, "Follow Your Heart," 20.

> have these tassels to look at and so you will remember all the commands of Yahweh, that you may obey them and not prostitute yourselves by chasing after the lusts of **your** own **hearts** and **eyes.** [40] Then you will remember to obey all my commands and will be consecrated to your God." (Num 15:38–40)

> You who are young, be happy while you are young, and let your heart give you joy in the days of your youth. Follow the ways of **your heart** and whatever **your eyes** see, but know that for all these things God will bring you into judgment. (Eccl 11:9)

In Kynes's view, the problem for Israel stems from their failure to act on the good things the eyes of the scouts had seen in the land of promise.[16] This suggestion at first appears to knock out the apparent contradiction by affirming that sometimes God's people need to follow their hearts. This seems to help, but it does not get past the sense of the shared language in the law of the tassels, if it does allude to it. The term "prostitute yourself" carries an inherently negative and even immoral connotation in scriptural use. To infer the prohibition in Num 15:39 "not *prostitute yourselves* by chasing after the lusts of your own hearts and eyes" could be treated positively in Eccl 11:9 as securing joy by following "the ways of your heart . . . whatever your eyes see" requires too much (emphasis mine). To say Qohelet interprets Num 15:39 against the sense of the command does not fit with his warnings against foolish vows (Eccl 5:1–6[4:17–5:5], see note ad loc.).

The parallel itself seems rather thin, with two shared common terms appearing together elsewhere with second-person suffixes eleven times in Scripture, and more without second-person suffixes.[17] Whether Eccl 11:9 alludes to Num 15:39 or not, the traditional solutions should be kept in mind. Without the allusion, the call to follow heart and eyes picks up the repeated mantra of Qoheleth within the positive frame of reference of the good gifts of life (Eccl 3:12–13; 5:18–19[17–18]; 8:15; 9:7–10).[18] With the allusion, traditional Judaic scholars like Ibn Ezra and Rashi regard the invitation as Qoheleth's sarcastic taunt "Go ahead and sin, and see what happens to you!"[19]

In sum, Qoheleth's possible allusion to the law of the tassels remains difficult. No solutions work well.

12:7~3:20–21 (B)+Gen 2:7 (C)+3:19 (B) (return dust to the earth and spirit to God). Near the end of the book, Qoheleth transcends the previous limitations he had bemoaned and speaks of the human spirit returning to God at death (Eccl 12:7). The language of return from whence it came plays out against the natural cycles of water and wind that return from whence they came (1:6, 7).[20] In Qoheleth's interior monologue,

16. See Kynes, "Follow Your Heart," 21.
17. So ibid., 18, n. 13.
18. See Krüger, *Qoheleth*, 196.
19. As paraphrased by Fox, *Ecclesiastes*, 75.
20. For other uses of this language in Ecclesiastes, see Clemens, "Law," 8, nn. 5, 6.

he recognizes the limitations of human experience, equalizing animal and human life by death (3:18–20). In this context he asks a rhetorical question, implying a negative answer: "*Who knows if* the human spirit *rises upward* and if the spirit of the animal goes down into the earth?" (3:21, emphasis mine). Qoheleth's revelation that the human spirit returns to God plays off these earlier uses of the same language. Ecclesiastes 12:7 shares significant language with Gen 3:19. The shared language suggests an allusion. Based upon the late syntax noted elsewhere, Genesis likely serves as the donor and Ecclesiastes as the receptor context (see note on Eccl 5:4–6[3–5]). Notice how Eccl 3:18–21 provides context for the allusion to Genesis in Eccl 12:7 (bold and italics signify verbal parallels between Genesis and Ecclesiastes, and broken underlining signifies verbal parallels within Ecclesiastes):

> Then Yahweh *God* formed a man from **the dust** of the ground and breathed into his nostrils the breath of life, and the man became a living being. (Gen 2:7; cf. v. 19)
>
> By the sweat of your brow you will eat your food until **you return** to the ground, since from it you were taken; **for dust** you are and to **dust** you **will return.** (3:19)
>
> I also said to myself, "As for humans, God tests them so that they may see that they are like the animals. [19]... As one dies, so dies the other. All have the same breath [רוּחַ]. . . . [20] All go to the same place; all come from **dust**, and to **dust** all **return.** [21] Who knows if the human spirit [רוּחַ] rises upward and if the spirit [רוּחַ] of the animal goes down into the earth?" (Eccl 3:18–21)
>
> And **the dust returns** to the ground it came from, and the spirit [רוּחַ] **returns** to *God* who gave it. (12:7)

The limitation of human experience spelled out in Eccl 3:21 makes it difficult to interpret the sense of Qoheleth's statement in 12:7. Does Qoheleth enjoy confidence in the spirit going (up?) to God in 12:7? Does Qoheleth's question in 3:21 speak from human limitation in spite of his different convictions spelled out in 12:7? The nature of Ecclesiastes, of course, promotes these very kinds of questions and discussion.

A narrow focus on Eccl 12:7 reveals that it offers exegetical expansion over and against Gen 3:19, which simply gets at human mortality. Moreover, in light of Qoheleth's inner musing on a different post-life fate for humans versus for animals, 12:7 suggests a basic difference with humans, in contrast to other beings. The key difference between humans and animals in 12:7 does not rest on the fact that humans were formed by the hand of God in Gen 2:7. The same applies to the animals (Gen 2:19). Instead, the different, larger reality of the human spirit, for Qoheleth, needs to be something more. Scripture readers may offer that creation in the image of God sets humans apart from other created beings. That may be so, but Qoheleth does not explain. He leaves it to his students to work it out.

One emphasis that seems to point to a larger reality for humans than one limited to this life is Qoheleth's repeated references to God bringing humans to justice (Eccl 3:17; 11:9; cf. 12:14).[21]

In sum, Qoheleth alludes to Genesis in describing human death as returning to dust. Qoheleth makes these allusions in a way that provokes investigation of his teachings for hints of something more. This includes his subtle inference that the human spirit differs from animals by returning to God.

FILTERS

Ecclesiastes stands apart from other Scriptures linguistically as much as it broadly engages scriptural themes found elsewhere.[22] The present purpose relates to summarizing some of the ways Ecclesiastes broadly overlaps with other Scripture in non-exegetical ways.[23]

Many suggest Ecclesiastes relies on themes of **Gen 1–11**. The case of Eccl 3:19–20 and 12:7 contains evidence to support this claim (see note on Eccl 12:7). But some proposals for the reliance of Ecclesiastes upon Gen 1–11 are far-reaching. Dell critically evaluates many of the substantial studies and questions several of the more extravagant claims.[24] Qoheleth's favorite leading word "vanity, vapor, ephemeral" (הֶבֶל) is identical to the name of Abel (הֶבֶל) in Gen 4. Dell pushes back against the extensive allegorical use of Ecclesiastes and Gen 4 (6–7). Dell observes that many of the claims about the creational context of Eccl 1 ignore the lack of cyclical shaping of creation in Genesis (7). She notes that comparisons between the "royal experiment" for Qoheleth to create paradise in Eccl 2:4–6 and the garden of Genesis often exaggerate the significance of shared very common language (7–8). Dell also goes after studies that have dealt with toil in Ecclesiastes based on the curse of human toil in Gen 3. She suggests that these comparisons sometimes amount to little more than a shared motif (8). Dell grants the allusion of Eccl 3:19–20 and 12:7 to Gen 2:7 and 3:19 (9–10, 13). She sees the suggestion that Eccl 8:11 quotes Gen 8:21 from the flood narrative as lacking necessary parallels. The association, if there is one, seems more like an echo (10). Dell also challenges claims that Qoheleth designs his description around the fall of humans in Genesis. She takes note that the similarities tend to be broad thematic echoes and not quotations or allusions (10–11). Overall, Dell concludes that the evidence of Ecclesiastes considered cumulatively suggests echoes and some thematic similarities. She thinks Anderson's proposal of "theological criticism" has the promise of avoiding some of the extravagant uses of parallels that push beyond

21. See discussion in Schultz, "'Fear God,'" 332–33.

22. For a list of unique, and often seemingly late, expressions in Ecclesiastes, see Driver, *Introduction*, 474–75.

23. For additional general similarities between Ecclesiastes and other Scriptures, see Kynes, *Obituary for "Wisdom Literature,"* 194–203; Schoors, "(Mis)use of Intertextuality," 45–59.

24. See Dell, "Exploring," 3–14. Hereafter cited parenthetically. The studies Dell interacts with include Anderson, "Curse," 99–113; Clemens, "Law," 5–8; Forman, "Koheleth's Use of Genesis," 256–63; the commentaries; and numerous others.

the evidence (12). The sense of "theological criticism" versus interpretive allusion seems more fitting since it only demands general thematic similarity versus verifiable allusion for exegesis. For example, the basis for finding that the so-called seize the day (*carpe diem*) contexts of Ecclesiastes allude to Gen 2 comes down to the shared use of exceedingly common terms: "human" (אָדָם), "good" (טוֹב), "eat" (אכל), "God" (אֱלֹהִים), and "woman" (אִשָּׁה).[25] This evidence falls short of demonstrating allusion. In sum, Dell's criticism of excesses in interpreting the significance of Qoheleth's possible use of Gen 1–11 offers a helpful corrective.

Schultz puts Qoheleth in dialogue with **Isaiah** in places where the two share vocabulary, expressions, and motifs. The similarities include general comparisons based on the social locations of the powerful and the lowly. Schultz challenges claims of a parallel between new and old in Eccl 1:9–11 and in Isa 40–66 since they have very different referents and agendas.[26] Schultz sees only a broad allusion based on shared features of woe, leaders, feasting and drinking, and an inappropriately early time of day in Eccl 10:16–17 and Isa 5:11–12, 22–23. The general nature of the similarities does not suggest a direction of dependence.[27]

Schultz interacts with similarities and differences between **Job** and Ecclesiastes. The parallels include a shared unique expression for coming out of the womb naked (emphasis signifies verbal parallels):

> *Naked* I *came from* my *mother's womb*, and naked I will depart. Yahweh gave and Yahweh has taken away; may the name of Yahweh be praised. (Job 1:21)

> Everyone *comes naked from* their *mother's womb*, and as everyone comes, so they depart. They take nothing from their toil that they can carry in their hands. (Eccl 5:15[14])

The evidence does not suggest direction of dependence. Schultz observes that Job credits his misfortunes to Yahweh even though the Sabeans and Chaldeans committed some of the acts. In a broadly similar manner, Qoheleth attributes all life and possessions to God (5:18–19[17–18]).[28] Schultz reviews other, lesser similarities between Job and Ecclesiastes (Job 3:16 with Eccl 6:3–5; Job 9:12 with Eccl 8:4). Schultz concludes that, based on the criteria of shared verbal and syntactical correspondences, Job and Ecclesiastes have few formal parallels.[29]

Ecclesiastes features shared forms and content with **Proverbs**. This includes features like "better than" wisdom sentences with similar themes (Eccl 4:6; cf. Prov 15:16–17;

---

25. As proposed by Meek, "Fear God," 26, see esp. Table 1.

26. Summarized from Schultz, "Qoheleth and Isaiah," 57–69, esp. 59, 61–63. For additional comparisons of Isaiah and Ecclesiastes with negative results see Schultz, "Was Qohelet?," 199–214.

27. See Schultz, "Qoheleth and Isaiah," 59.

28. See Schultz, "Job and Ecclesiastes," 193–95.

29. See ibid., 195–97, 201.

16:8, 19; 17:1; 28:6). Ecclesiastes parallels the content of Proverbs by speaking of digging a pit, but Qoheleth uses different words (Eccl 10:8a; cf. Prov 26:27a). In sum, the similarities between Ecclesiastes and Proverbs appear at the level of genre, theme, and style, but not interpretive allusion.[30]

Qoheleth makes a broad allusion to temple worship. Ecclesiastes 5:1–2[4:17–5:1] does not refer to restraining speech in general interpersonal relations as suggested elsewhere (Prov 17:27, 28; 18:2; 29:20; cf. 10:18, 19; 11:12; 16:23; 18:13; 21:23). The encouragement "to listen rather than to offer the sacrifice of fools" implies that in the house of God there is something to hear, such as singing or Scripture reading.[31]

30. These observations are based on Saur, "Qohelet as a Reader of Proverbs," 129–38; parallel examples from 134–35.
31. These observations are based on Krüger, *Qohelet*, 107–8.

Chapter 31

LAMENTATIONS

SYMBOLS[1]

- ~ B, probable interpretive allusion; C, possible; D, probably not
- \+ interpretive blend
- >/< more or less similar (see Filters)
- * part of interconnected network (see Networks)

USE OF SCRIPTURE IN LAMENTATIONS[2]

1:10*~Deut 23:3*[4] (B) (enemy entering into Lady Jerusalem's holy place) (* see assembly network)

3:22–23*~Exod 34:6* (B)+Num 18:20 (C) (new every morning) (* see attribute formula network)

3:48–49~Jer 14:17 (B) (weeping for the daughter of my people)

5:7*~Lev 26:39 (B)+Jer 14:20 (B) (bearing the ancestors' iniquities) (* see personal responsibility network)

OLD TESTAMENT USE OF LAMENTATIONS (SEE RESPECTIVE NOTES)

1:2, 9, 16, 17, 21~Isa 40:1 (B) (comfort Jerusalem)

1:10*~Isa 52:1b (B) (uncircumcised and defiled will not enter you again) (* see assembly network)

2:10~Isa 52:2 (C) (down in dust)

3:6–9~Job 19:6–8 (B) (calling out not answered)

4:15~Isa 52:11–12 (B) (Depart! Depart! Do not touch) (* see temple vessels network)

NEW TESTAMENT USE OF LAMENTATIONS

n/a

HERMENEUTICAL PROFILE OF THE USE OF SCRIPTURE IN LAMENTATIONS

Lamentation's exegetical allusions to Torah and Jeremiah consist of short phrases thoroughly repurposed. But the poet of Lamentations does not replace the original significance of the donor contexts. The allusion to the law of the assembly requires continuity with the force of the law to give extra punch to the violent rape imagery (Lam 1:10; cf. Deut 23:3[4]). The male figure's exegetical allusion to the attribute formula infuses each new morning with the hopeful renewal of Yahweh's faithfulness (Lam 3:22–23;

1. For explanation of symbols, see Symbols and Abbreviations and Introduction. For other help, see Glossary.
2. See Bibliographic Note on Lists of Potential Parallels.

cf. Exod 34:6). The poet's allusion to bearing the guilt of the ancestors in Lev 26 stops short of the solution that anyone can see comes in the very next verse (Lam 5:7). The significance of each of these dramatic exegetical interventions requires sustained continuity with the larger donor contexts.

The several allusions to Jer 14 in Lamentations establish an important point of connection. The segment of Jeremiah these allusions come from stands as something of a turning point. Boda focuses on Jer 14 as a turning point in the evolving of corporate penitential prayer, looking ahead to Ezra 9; Neh 1; 9; Dan 9; and Ps 106.[3] This may be so, but to it needs to be added that Jer 14 is the springboard for the apex of lament embodied in Lamentations. These two views of Jer 14 share in common the repeated divine advice to stop praying, for he is done listening (Jer 14:11; 15:1; cf. 7:16; 11:14). Yahweh's resistance to the prophet's advocacy for the people provides a crucial backdrop for the exegetical advancements of Lamentations. Nowhere does this come out more clearly than the poet's several exegetical allusions to Jer 14. The underlying concern of the tears (Lam 3:48–49) and ancestral guilt (5:7) gets expressed by transforming the prophet's question—"Have you rejected Judah completely?" (Jer 14:19a)—into a terrible hypothetical statement: "*unless* you have utterly rejected us" (Lam 5:22, emphasis mine).

The exegetical engagement of Lamentations with Jer 14 does not point to despair. Instead, the larger function of Lamentations pivots on memorializing the moment of daughter Zion's angst in the aftermath of judgment. The reality of renewing mercies reawakens with each new day (3:22–23). But the necessity of memorializing grief-stricken daughter Zion—captured in the durative "now" of Lamentations—cannot, and should not, be swept aside by ending Lamentations in the middle. It ends at the end, where the poet once more evokes Jer 14, when Yahweh said he was done listening. The gracious renewal spoken of by the male figure in Lam 3 awaits those who join the poet's "us" in Lam 5:22. Lamentations 3 and 5 ceaselessly juxtapose hope and anguish. Daughter Zion's agony remains the place to call upon Yahweh to "remember!" and to "take us back!" (5:1, 21 JPSB).

Many additional elements need to be kept in mind from standard studies of Lamentations that cannot be taken up here: single alphabetical acrostics in Lam 1, 2, 4; triple acrostic in Lam 3; the interchanging of third-person and first-person grammatical forms; and the positive elements of hope housed in Lam 3 even while the book begins and ends on desperate notes. In addition, the pervasive evidence of nonrecurring doublets in all five chapters suggests a high degree of coherence in Lamentations.[4] In short, the poet of Lamentations interpretively alludes to scriptural traditions in close accord to the larger aims of the book.

---

3. See Boda, "From Complaint," 195–97.

4. See Marcus, "Non-recurring," 177–95. And see discussion of a similar phenomenon in Joel Filters.

USE OF SCRIPTURE

1:10*~Deut 23:3*[4] (B) (enemy entering into Lady Jerusalem's holy place) (* see assembly network). The poet uses female figural imagery to connote the rape of Lady Zion. The flexibility of female imagery can seamlessly move between Jerusalem as widow (Lam 1:1), prostitute (1:8), virgin daughter (1:15), grieving mother (1:16, 18), and menstruant (1:17). The poet uses personified Jerusalem as wife to evoke imagery of her brutal rape in Lam 1:10. In this case "her holy place" simultaneously evokes the temple and the secret place of intimacy reserved exclusively for her spouse.[5] The poet depicts Jerusalem as violated, desolate, and shamed.

The shared language with the law of the assembly makes a relationship likely.[6] The context includes the evidence necessary to determine with high probability the direction of dependence. The poet marks the legal instruction with "you commanded," denoting the law as the donor context and Lamentations as the receptor context (bold signifies verbal parallels, italics signify marking, and broken underlining signifies exegetical intervention):

> **No** Ammonite or Moabite **shall enter the assembly** of Yahweh, even to the tenth generation **they shall not enter into the assembly** of Yahweh, forever. (Deut 23:3[4] lit.)

> The enemy laid hands on all her treasures. She saw nations **enter** her holy place—those *you have commanded*, **they shall not enter** your **assembly.** (Lam 1:10 lit.)

The most important interpretive move stems from the poet abstracting enemy nations from Ammon and Moab—here applied to the Chaldeans.[7] The poet does not interpret Moab and Ammon as denoting ethnic or genealogical identity. The poet does not leverage a strong reading against the grain of the law of the assembly but makes this exegetical deduction from its context. Notice the rationale for law:

> For they *did not come to meet you with bread and water* on your way when you came out of Egypt, and they hired Balaam son of Beor from Pethor in Aram Naharaim *to pronounce a curse* on you. (Deut 23:4[5], emphasis mine)

The rationale for the command has nothing to do with ethnicity or genealogical identity. Ammon and Moab refer to enemies of the people of God, those who refuse

5. Mintz, "Rhetoric," 4. Mintz says, "The force of this image of violation is founded on the correspondence [of] body || Temple and genitals || Inner Sanctuary" (4).

6. So also Gordis, *Lamentations*, 156. The similar imagery in Ezek 7:21–22 appears to be coincidental and without verbal parallel except for the very common term "enter" (בוא).

7. See Berlin, *Lamentations*, 55; Tigay, *Deuteronomy*, 478.

hospitality and seek to damn Israel. The narrative of Num 22–24 stands as the primary donor context for the rationale of the prohibition against Ammon and Moab's entry into the assembly (see the note on Deut 23:4–5[5–6]). Moreover, of the seventy nations listed in Gen 10, the law of the assembly names four—two who may not enter (Ammon, Moab) and two who may enter (Edom, Egypt). Even though the rhetorical shape of the law of the assembly is apodictic, the specificity naturally causes the two excluded others and the two included others to function symbolically for those from the other sixty-five peoples (not counting Israel).[8]

The poet of Lamentations follows the lead of Deuteronomy and interprets Ammon and Moab as signifying enemies of the people of God. In that sense the poet's bold exegetical advance stems from deep continuity with the rationale of the law of the assembly itself. The symbolic interpretation of excluded others in the law of the assembly appears elsewhere in Scripture (Neh 13:1–3; see note ad loc.). Finally, the humiliation of Lady Jerusalem relates to Yahweh's promise concerning the return (see note on Isa 52:1).

In sum, the poet of Lamentations depicts the looting of the temple as violation of that special place of Yahweh's exclusive rights. The poet naturally alludes to the violent intruders according to the law of the assembly. Those who plunder the temple become archetypical examples of those forever forbidden from the assembly of Yahweh.

3:22–23*~Exod 34:6* (B)+Num 18:20 (C) (new every morning) (* see attribute formula network). The suffering male figure in Lam 3 makes a remarkable proclamation of Yahweh's covenantal fidelity (Lam 3:22–23). The pronouncement sets out a dialectic within Lamentations between profound grief and acknowledgement of Yahweh's unwavering compassion. The male figure's commentary on Yahweh's covenantal loyalty in Lam 3:22–23 complements but does not duplicate the acknowledgement of Yahweh's everlasting rule in 5:19. The latter statement regards Yahweh's sovereign transcendence unmarred by the suffering and grief of his people. The statement of confidence by the male figure in the middle of Lamentations gets at Yahweh's enduring mercy for his people in the midst of suffering.

The male figure's proclamation seems to allude to the attribute formula itself since it uses three of its key roots—here translated love, compassions, and faithfulness (3:22–23; cf. Exod 34:6). Although the attribute formula gets paraphrased and reproduced widely in the lyrical diffusion of Scripture, those including roots for "faithfulness" (אמת) only appear in Exod 34:6 and Ps 86:15 among the primary exemplars (see Table Joel 1; cf. Deut 7:9). This evidence strengthens the possibility of direct dependence. The male figure of Lam 3 connects the attribute formula allusion with a broad allusion to Yahweh as his portion. The basis of this widely diffused image grows out of the situation of priests and Levites who do not have land "allotments" or "shares"; thus Yahweh serves as their share (Num 18:20; Deut 10:9; 12:12; 14:27, 29; 18:1). The idea of Yahweh as share gets repeated

8. For further discussion of this line of interpretation see end of note on Ruth 2:8.

often in the Psalter (Pss 16:5; 73:26; 142:5[6]; and very close parallel in 119:57).[9] For the present purpose, a passage in Num 18 regarding the priestly share can stand for the set of contexts (emphases signify verbal parallels at the level of shared roots):

> And he passed in front of Moses, proclaiming, "Yahweh, Yahweh, the **compassionate** [רחום] and gracious God, slow to anger, abounding in **love** [חֶסֶד] and **faithfulness** [אֱמֶת]." (Exod 34:6)

> Yahweh said to Aaron, "You will have no inheritance in their land, nor will you have any *share* among them; I am your *share* and your inheritance among the Israelites." (Num 18:20)

> Yet this I call to mind and therefore I have hope: [22] Because of Yahweh's **love** [חֶסֶד] we are not consumed, for his **compassions** [רַחֲמִים] never fail. [23] They are new every morning; great is your **faithfulness** [אֱמוּנָה]. [24] I say to myself, "Yahweh is my *share*; therefore I will wait for him." (Lam 3:21–24†)

The importance of the attribute formula extends to its context. Israel had flagrantly violated the first two commandments with the golden calf. The people faced a real threat of the absence of the divine presence. Yahweh initially planned to leave the people in the hands of a celestial delegate to avoid striking down the rebels by his wrath (Exod 33:1–3). By Moses's pleading, Yahweh consented to forgive the people and sustain them with his ongoing presence. Yahweh's proclamation of the attribute formula signifies renewal of hope grounded in unfailing divine fidelity. The male figure's exegetical allusion loads each new morning with the hopeful connotations of the attribute formula.

The use of the daily inevitability of new mornings demonstrates the versatility of the use of cosmic realities. In support of the new covenant's dependability Jeremiah evokes the sun and moon giving light day and night in order to show the enduring permanence of Yahweh's covenantal promise (Jer 31:35–37). The male figure of Lam 3 refers to the same basic cosmic structure but not merely to speak to the enduring qualities of Yahweh's attributes. Instead, he emphasizes the daily routine of Yahweh's compassions in the "now." The male figure's confidence renews every day. As the day breaks the enduring covenantal loyalty of Yahweh renews once again.

The broad allusion to Yahweh as the share of the male figure does not need to be interpreted literally as though he were a priest. This misses the point. In the aftermath of Jerusalem's destruction no one of Judah has a "share" any longer. The people of Judah are all homeless. Every person of Judah can see a new day break and renew confidence once again in Yahweh, who alone remains the enduring portion of his people. Like the male figure and the priests of days gone by when the temple stood in Jerusalem, every captive

9. See Keil and Delitzsch, *Lamentations*, 414.

formerly from Judah can find hope in the daily renewing compassions of Yahweh who is their share.

3:48–49~Jer 14:17 (B) (weeping for the daughter of my people). The elusive identity of the male figure has been compared to many people but especially Jeremiah in his intermittent confessions (Jer 11–20).[10] Setting aside his identity, the deeper issue turns on the exegetical intervention as he explains his weeping over the brutal wound suffered by "the daughter of my people." Since the poet of Lamentations elsewhere makes verifiable allusions to Jer 14:19 and 14:20, it strengthens the likelihood of Jer 14:17 as the donor context and Lam 3:48–49 as the receptor in this case also (see note on Lam 5:7). The primary comparison can be illuminated by representative development of these running themes in both contexts (emphasis signifies verbal parallels at the level of roots; brackets signify the exegetical development):

> They dress *the wound of the daughter of my people* as though it were not serious. "Peace, peace," they say, when there is no peace. (Jer 6:14//8:11†)
>
> Since *the daughter of my people is wounded*, I am *wounded*; I mourn, and horror grips me. Is there no balm in Gilead? Is there no physician there? Why then is there no healing for *the daughter of my people*? (8:21–22†; cf. 30:17)
>
> [Speak this word to them: "**Let my eyes flow down** with tears night and day **without ceasing**; for the virgin *daughter of my people*, has suffered a grievous *wound*, a crushing injury." (14:17†)]
>
> Have you rejected Judah completely? Do you despise Zion? Why have you injured us so that we cannot be healed? We hoped for peace but no good has come, for a time of healing but there is only terror. (14:19)
>
> What can I say for you? With what can I compare you, *daughter* Jerusalem? To what can I liken you, that I may comfort you, virgin *daughter* Zion? Your *wound* is as deep as the sea. Who can heal you? (Lam 2:13†)
>
> [Streams **flow down from my eyes** because the *daughter of my people is wounded*. My eyes will flow **without ceasing**, without relief. (Lam 3:48–49†)]

10. The male figure of Lam 3 shares many similarities with Jeremiah in his suffering: "laughingstock . . . all day long" (Lam 3:14; Jer 20:7); "sit alone" (Lam 3:28; Jer 15:17); in pit (Lam 3:53–55; Jer 38); they "plot" against him (Lam 3:61; Jer 18:20–22); lawsuit language (Lam 3:58; Jer 11:20; 15:10; 20:12); bronze chains/wall (Lam 3:7; Jer 1:18; 15:20); weeping (Lam 3:48–49; Jer 8:21–9:1[8:23]; 9:17; 13:17; 14:17). This list is adapted from Bezzel, "'Man of Constant Sorrow,'" 257–58; and a comparison of Jer 14:17 and Lam 3:48–49 (258). Other details in Lam 3 may be used to compare the male figure and Job, see list in Berlin, *Lamentations*, 85. For other proposed identifications of the male figure of Lam 3, see ibid., 84.

Jeremiah's congregation did not heed his warnings. They succumbed to the peace prophets (Jer 6:14//8:11) and did not join the weeping (14:17). Jeremiah conversely felt the wound for himself (8:21).[11] He voices rhetorical questions that hang suspended in the air: "Is there no balm in Gilead? . . . Why then is there no healing for the daughter of my people?" (8:22; cf. 14:19). The male figure of Lamentations answers within the timeless grief of the aftermath of the catastrophe: "Streams flow down from my eyes because the daughter of my people is wounded . . . without ceasing, without relief" (Lam 3:48–49). Since the prophet could not convince the people to mourn for their sin, the male figure mourns in the durative moment of the grief of Lamentations.[12] The male figure responds in accord with Jeremiah's sermons. This response sets up the comfort from another prophet, Isaiah (see note on Isa 40:1).

5:7*~Lev 26:39+Jer 14:20 (B) (bearing the ancestors' iniquities) (* see personal responsibility network). Even before Jerusalem fell, Jeremiah and Ezekiel each dealt with the troubling proverb: "The parents have eaten sour grapes, and the children's teeth are set on edge" (Jer 31:29; Ezek 18:2). In both of those cases the contexts allude to the civil court law that limits punishment to the individual versus the children or parents of the accused—a law that uses the term "sin" (חֵטְא) (Deut 24:16; see notes on Jer 31:30; Ezek 18:1–4). In a similar spirit the poet of Lamentations speaks of bearing the ancestors' "sin" but also "iniquities" (עָוֹן) (Lam 5:7). This language parallels Lev 26:39. Jeremiah also alludes to Lev 26, but focuses more on the confession in 26:40 (Jer 14:20). The shared language along with related contexts suggest that both Jeremiah and Lamentations have a relationship with Lev 26.[13] Since Ezekiel likewise features striking evidence that it depends on holiness contexts including Lev 25 and 26, Lev 26 may be regarded as the donor and Lamentations as the receptor context with adequate confidence (see Hermeneutical Profile of the Use of Scripture in Ezekiel). In addition, the striking parallel between the question in Jer 14:19 and the hypothetical phrase in the final verse of Lamentations suggest the poet of Lamentations had an eye on the context of Jer 14 (italics signify verbal parallel):[14]

> Have *you utterly rejected* [מאס מאס] Judah? Do you despise Zion? Why have you afflicted us so that we cannot be healed? (Jer 14:19†)

> Unless *you have utterly rejected* [מאס מאס] us and are angry with us beyond measure. (Lam 5:22)

11. But contrast the personal use of wound imagery in Jer 15:18.

12. See Balentine, "Poetry of Exile," 346.

13. For additional evidence that Jeremiah depends on Lev 26, see Boda, "From Complaint," esp. 196, n. 46.

14. Only Jer 14:19 and Lam 5:22 use "utterly reject" (מאס inf. abs. + מאס pf.). The verb "reject" (מאס) appears twice together in finite verbal forms in 1 Sam 8:7; 15:23, 26; Hos 4:6, and in finite form and ptc. in Jer 6:30.

The striking difference in Lam 5:7 amounts to an allusion to Lev 26 but no confession. Elsewhere, to be sure, daughter Zion openly confesses her transgressions (Lam 1:22). But a foreboding sense of judgment, not relief, pervades Lam 5. The marked contrast between the hopefulness of Lam 3 and the bleak outlook of Lam 5 drives overall interpretations of the book. In that sense the absence of acknowledging personal responsibility does not get at the point of Lam 5:7. Instead, the blanket statement of paying for someone else's guilt retains a focus entirely on judgment up to Lev 26:39 without yet looking ahead hopefully to Yahweh's everlasting rule and restoration (cf. Lam 5:19, 21). In marked contrast, Jeremiah rings the notes of Lev 26:40 and the following context. Compare how Jeremiah and the poet of Lamentations interpretively allude to Lev 26 in different ways (bold signifies verbal parallels to Lev 26:39, italics to 26:40, 40, 42; and broken underlining signifies synonymous concepts):

> Those of you who are left will waste away in the lands of their enemies because of their iniquities; also because of **their ancestors' iniquities** they will waste away. [40] But if they will confess their iniquities and *the iniquities* of their *ancestors*. . . . [42] I will remember my covenant. (Lev 26:39, 40a, 42a lit.)
>
> We acknowledge our wickedness, Yahweh, and *the iniquity* of our *ancestors*; we have indeed sinned against you. (Jer 14:20)
>
> Our **ancestors** sinned and are no more, and we bear **their iniquities.** (Lam 5:7 lit.)

The refusal to move past judgment toward solution begins to get at the crucial function of the book of Lamentations. The catastrophe of exile, including the loss of sovereign rule, forced migrations, extensive destruction, and all that these mean, gets treated in different ways in Scripture. If the Deuteronomistic narrative frames exile historically as the culmination of rebellion against the covenant, Lamentations gets at the grief of the moment.[15] Lamentations does not look back at "before" or look ahead to "after." Lamentations memorializes the moment of daughter Zion's profound grief. Whereas prose narrative explains the past according to chronological temporality, the poet of Lamentations pauses within "durational time." Balentine explains, "Durational time is primarily the preoccupation of poets, whose figurations linger over the 'now,' loosening temporal connections that either explain the present or dispel the future."[16]

Lamentations makes allusion to the forecast of judgment in Lev 26:39, then stops. The poet of Lamentations only uses part of the teaching to emphasize paying for someone else's guilt. The poet does not go on to focus on relief of Yahweh once again remembering the covenant. The outlook of Lamentations as a whole, and Lam 5 in particular, remains

15. See Middlemas, *Templeless Age*, 28.
16. Balentine, "Poetry of Exile," 346.

affixed on the moment of daughter Zion's anguish. In this way Lamentations serves readers by memorializing the devastating moment that needs to be remembered. Lamentations 3 assures readers that hope breaks new every morning (3:22–24). But Lamentations begins and ends with an embodiment of daughter Zion's grief.

FILTERS

Lamentations features many examples of similarities to other Scriptures. The following examples do not represent a complete or comprehensive list.[17]

Broad allusions and shared language: **1:3**>/<Deut 28:65, "she finds no resting place/ there will be no rest for the soles of your feet" (לא מצאה מנוח/לא יהיה מנוח לכף רגלך);[18] **1:9**>/<Lev 15:19–24, her "ritual impurity" (טמאה) upon her skirts may use the ritual disability of menstruation as a metaphorical metonymy for moral culpability akin to Ezek 36:17;[19] **1:17**>/<Lev 15:19–24, Jerusalem as "menstruant" (נדה), that is ritually disabled (unrelated to a modern sense of disgust, etc.) used metaphorically for immorality;[20] **2:6**>/<Gen 13:10, Jerusalem/Sodom "like a garden/garden of Yahweh" (כגן/כגן יהוה);[21] **2:20**>/<Lev 26:29; Deut 28:53–57, women eating their children connotes severe famine of prolonged siege warfare (cf. Lam 4:10); **3:15**>/<Jer 9:15[14], "bitterness" (לענה) to drink (signifies exile in Jeremiah);[22] **3:30**>/<Isa 50:6, compare: "Let him offer his *cheek* [לחי] to one who would *strike* [נכה] him, and let him be filled with disgrace" (Lam 3:30) with "I offered my back to those who *beat* [נכה] me, my *cheeks* [לחי] to those who pulled out my beard; I did not hide my face from mocking and spitting" (Isa 50:6); **4:6**>/<Deut 29:23[22], punishment greater than Sodom; **4:10**>/<Lev 26:29; Deut 28:53–57, compassionate women boiling their children connotes severe famine of prolonged siege warfare (cf. Lam 2:20); **4:14**>/<Isa 59:3, "defiled with blood" (גאל בדם);[23] **4:21**>/<Isa 51:17, 22; Jer 25:15–29; 49:12; 51:7; Ezek 23:31–34; Hab 2:15–16; Ps 75:8[9], cup of divine wrath.[24]

Sommer suggests the shared language in two longer passages of Lamentations and Isaiah share a relationship of reversal, i.e., for Sommer, Isaiah's reversal of Lamentations (Lam 2:17–19 with Isa 62:6–7; Lam 2:13–19 with Isa 51:17–22). The evidence suggests possible relationship, but since the shared language gets spread across many verses the probability of intentional allusion becomes very slight.[25]

---

17. For lists of potential parallels between Lamentations and other Scriptures, see Gottwald, *Studies*, 44–46; Sommer, *A Prophet Reads Scripture*, 127–30, 271–72, n. 55; Willey, *Remember*, 125–32.

18. Observed by Berlin, *Lamentations*, 52. Also note: "for a head" Deut 28:44b lit.; cf. Lam 1:5a.

19. Berlin rejects this view in favor of sexual immorality clung to her skirts—"She is not a menstruant: she is a whore" (ibid., 55). This connotation could follow "nakedness" in Lam 1:8.

20. See ibid., 58–59.

21. As observed by ibid., 70.

22. See ibid., 91.

23. Sommer doubts a relationship between Lam 4:14 and Isa 59:3 (*A Prophet Reads Scripture*, 272, n. 55).

24. These references are from Berlin, *Lamentations*, 114.

25. See Sommer, *A Prophet Reads Scripture*, 128–29.

Chapter 32

ESTHER

USE OF SCRIPTURE IN ESTHER

n/a

OLD TESTAMENT USE OF ESTHER

n/a

NEW TESTAMENT USE OF ESTHER

n/a

FILTERS

Esther shares similarities with a number of other scriptural narratives.[1] These similarities operate at the literary, not exegetical, level. The purposes here include summarizing a few of the most important literary similarities between Esther and other Scriptures and briefly comparing a few different strategies for handling these.

The diaspora setting of the protagonists of Esther connects to the **exile narrative of Jehoiachin** in 597 BCE in Kings (italics signify parallels): "Mordechai . . . who had been *carried into exile* from *Jerusalem* by Nebuchadnezzar king of Babylon, among those taken captive with Jehoiachin king of Judah" (Esth 2:6) with "*He carried all Jerusalem into exile*: all the officers and fighting men, and all the skilled workers and artisans—a total of ten thousand. Only the poorest people of the land were left" (2 Kgs 24:14). The narrative closes with a source formula cast in the style of the citation formulas of Kings. Compare: "*Are* they *not written in the book of the annals of the kings of* Judah" (1 Kgs 14:29) and "*Are* they *not written in the book of the annals of the kings of* Media and Persia?" (Esth 10:2; for a list of the source citations in Kings see Kings Filters).

Esther can be included among the biblical foreign royal court stories, namely, Joseph, Daniel, Esther, Ezra, and Nehemiah (see Gen 40–50; Dan 1–6; Esth 1–10; Ezra 7;

1. On the similarities of Esther with other Scriptures, see Berlin, *Esther*, xxxvi–xli; Firth, "When Samuel Met Esther," 15–28; Grossman, "'Dynamic Analogies,'" 394–414; Schellekens, "Accession Days," 120, 127.

Neh 1–2). Whether the similarities between these accounts function more like extended type-scenes or a genre does not matter as much as the actual relationships between them.

Esther shares many thematic and structural similarities with the narratives of **Joseph** in the foreign court. The honors granted to Joseph and Mordechai share some resemblances (Gen 41:42–43; Esth 6:11; 8:2). Both Joseph and Esther help avoid tragedies, one natural and the other from an anti-Semitic pogrom. The narratives include numerous other broad thematic similarities. Verbal similarities include: "And though she spoke to Joseph day after day, he refused to go to bed with her or even be with her" (Gen 39:10) and "Day after day they spoke to him but he refused to comply" (Esth 3:4a). The most significant comparison between Joseph and Esther relates to divine providence. Genesis says things like "Yahweh was with him" (Gen 39:3, 21), but readers of Esther are left to imagine potential invisible divine causality in the face of striking "coincidences."[2]

The Esther and **Daniel** narratives share several elements.[3] Both have Hebrew and court names, Hadassah/Esther and Daniel/Belteshazzar (Esth 2:7; Dan 1:7). Most interesting are the contrasts. Daniel and his Hebrew friends do not partake of the royal diet but request vegetables and water (Dan 1:8–16). Daniel also prays regularly, so much so that he is eventually imprisoned for it (2:20–23; 6:10). The Esther narrative goes much further than not naming God in that it characterizes Mordechai and Esther as nonpracticing Jews. Esther does not follow Judaic standards but lives in the harem according to its standards and becomes a consort for an uncircumcised ruler. During a crisis she and Mordechai fast like Jews—religious fasting was not practiced by ancient Persians or Mesopotamians—but do not call upon the God of Israel.[4] The lack of evidence of covenantal fidelity by the protagonists heightens the "coincidences" that suggest divine mercy upon Israel. The contrast between the devoutness of Daniel and the assimilation of Esther, working hard to hide her Hebrew identity (Esth 2:10, 20), offers much theological significance in interpreting Esther. One way to see the issues in the Esther narrative is to compare it to the revised Septuagintal version, which saw the absence of the divine and lack of devoutness as deficiencies to be "repaired." Thus, it includes over fifty references to God, Scripture-filled prayers from the protagonists, and direct intervention with visions from God.[5]

In sum, comparisons with Daniel help reveal the theological strategy of the Esther narrative. In contrast to Daniel, the theology of Esther is do-it-yourself. Readers need to detect providence among glaring coincidences and see silent mercies for a people that do not seek him.

---

2. For these and other similarities between the narratives of Joseph and Esther, see Schnittjer, *Torah Story*, 187, Table 10-C; Berlin, *Esther*, xxxvii; Grossman, "'Dynamic Analogies,'" 397; Levenson, *Esther*, 16–17, 21; Hornung, "Nature," 57–64, 84.

3. For other comparisons of Daniel and Esther than those mentioned here, see Berlin, *Esther*, xl; Grossman, "'Dynamic Analogies,'" 398. For other contrasts, see Hornung, "Nature," 76–84.

4. On the lack of religious fasting in ancient Mesopotamia, see Wasserman, "Fasting," 250.

5. Especially noteworthy is the allusion to Lev 26:40–41 in Add Esth 14:6, in which Esther confesses the ancestral sins much like Dan 9:9–11; Ezra 9:6–7; Neh 1:6.

The lethal anti-Semitic edict gets sent out on the thirteenth day of the first month—ironically one day before **Passover** (Esth 3:12; cf. Exod 12:6; Lev 23:5). This connection leads to other suggestions regarding similarities between Esther and the exodus.[6]

The Esther narrative shares several connections with **Saul**. These similarities include a similar phrase: "give . . . to a neighbor who is better than she" (יתן . . . לרעותה הטובה ממנה) (Esth 1:19) with "has given to one of your neighbors—to one better than you" (נתנה לרעך הטוב ממך) (1 Sam 15:28). More substantially, Mordechai descends from Kish of Benjamin (Esth 2:5; 1 Sam 9:1–2) and Haman is an Agagite (Esth 3:1, 10; 8:3, 5; 9:24). Saul famously failed to kill Agag and utterly destroy the Amalekites (1 Sam 15:1–2, 8, 20; cf. Exod 17:14; Deut 25:17–19). The execution of Haman and his sons can be read as a reversal of Saul's failure (Esth 8:7; 9:10, 13–14). The hanging of the bodies of Saul and his three sons at Beth Shan and the impaling of seven additional sons of Saul at Gibeon have been compared to the hanging of Haman's ten sons (1 Sam 31:10–12; 2 Sam 21:6–9; Esth 9:13–14).[7]

Berger interprets these and many other potential parallels as Esther and Mordechai vindicating Benjamite leadership, in contrast to Saul's failures and in contrast to the vengeance meted out against the Saulides at David's permission.[8] Many of the comparisons seem general and/or coincidental. Additional suggested similarities between the narratives of Abigail and Esther also seem general and coincidental rather than intentional and interpretive.[9]

Firth takes a more reserved approach and suggests that numerous similarities in the Samuel and Esther narratives function to strengthen a "reversal of fortunes" theology.[10] An approach to parallels as broad allusions may add connotative connections into the receptor context. This comes close to the use of templates and extended echo-effect, which carry exegetical functions (see Table C10 in Chronicles and associated discussion). The reason they do not rise to the level of exegetical use of Scripture in Esther, in part, relates of the lack of specifically defined donor contexts. Instead, these broad allusive relationships work more like literary-thematic connections. Schellekens identifies primary and secondary type-scenes (e.g., threat to Moses and Mordechai; rise of Joseph and Mordechai).[11] Grossman refers to literary connections with other scriptural narratives by the more flexible category of "dynamic analogies," which acknowledges readerly difficulties of a receptor context using analogies from multiple donor contexts. Grossman suggests the receptor context intentionally intermixes parallels to multiple donor contexts to obstruct readers from drawing analogies to donor contexts.[12] Whether or not

6. See Berlin, *Esther*, xxxvii–xxxviii.

7. See ibid, 86; Berger, "Esther," 635.

8. See Berger, "Esther," 644. For other Esther/Saul parallels, see esp. tables, 631, 637.

9. See ibid., 641.

10. Firth, "When Samuel Met Esther," 28.

11. See Schellekens, "Accession Days," esp. tables, 120, 127—most of the similarities are general and thematic.

12. See Grossman, "'Dynamic Analogies,'" 395, 412–13.

the narrator is trying to be difficult, in many cases a fine line divides the literary from the exegetical function of potential parallels. To claim Esther exegetically appropriates Samuel narratives would require the necessary evidence in specific donor contexts with proper controls. Firth's broad theological comparisons, mentioned in the beginning of this paragraph, seem to fit the situation with potential Samuel echoes better than primary and secondary type-scenes or dynamic analogies.

The trouble during Ahasuerus's first year of rule, mentioned in Ezra 4:6, refers to another otherwise unknown event, not the threat dated after the seventh year of his rule (Esth 2:16).

Chapter 33

DANIEL

SYMBOLS[1]

// verbal parallels (A level)
~ B, probable interpretive allusion; C, possible; D, probably not
\+ interpretive blend
>/< more or less similar (see Filters)
* part of interpretive network (see Networks)

USE OF SCRIPTURE IN DANIEL[2]

1:2*~2 Kgs 24:13*+Jer 27:16* (C) (plundering temple vessels during siege of Jerusalem in Jehoiakim's rule) (* see temple vessels network)

2:28–29~Gen 41:25, 28, 32 (B) (divine revelation by dreams)

2:34–35, 45~Isa 41:15–16; 51:1 (C) (hewn rock destroys empires and becomes mighty kingdom)

9:2*~Jer 25:11; 29:10* (B) (seventy years) (* see seventy years network)

9:4–19*~Lev 26:40–41* (B) (collective confession of sin) (* see collective confession network)

9:4//Deut 7:9* (covenantal fidelity) (* see attribute formula network)

9:11, 13~Deut 29:20–21[19–20] (B) (curses written in Torah)

12:2~Isa 26:19 (B)+66:24 (B) (those who sleep in the dust awake)

12:3~Isa 52:13 (C)+53:11 (B) (lead many to righteousness)

OLD TESTAMENT USE OF DANIEL

n/a

NEW TESTAMENT USE OF DANIEL

7:13–14~Matt 24:30; 26:64; Mark 13:26; 14:62; Luke 21:27; 22:69; Rev 1:7, 13; 14:14 (son of a human)

9:27; 11:31; 12:11//Matt 24:15; Mark 13:14 (abomination)

HERMENEUTICAL PROFILE OF THE USE OF SCRIPTURE IN DANIEL

Daniel's exegetical use of scriptural traditions demonstrates familiarity with Genesis, Leviticus, Deuteronomy, Isaiah, and Jeremiah. Daniel refers to Jeremiah as a scroll and the Torah of Moses as written. Daniel includes numerous potential non-exegetical broad parallels of many other scriptural contexts (see Filters).

1. For explanation of symbols, see Symbols and Abbreviations and Introduction. For other help, see Glossary.
2. See Bibliographic Note on Lists of Potential Parallels.

An episode in the first half of Daniel features narrative shaping in relation to other Scriptures at an exegetical level—not merely literary similarity. The account of interpreting Nebuchadnezzar's dream in Dan 2 houses numerous striking similarities to Joseph's interpretation of the pharaoh's dreams in Gen 41. Figural relationships between narratives function analogically. The similarities between narratives tend to serve the differences between them that often make the point.

All figural patterning works more or less the same by using analogy. But the significance of some figural relations functions in prophetic ways in Scripture. Expectational figural relations often get labeled as typological. Since the term "typological" connotes prophetic expectation in many interpretations of Scripture, other terms may better describe nonprophetic figural relations. Running figural parallels between two contexts may be called "extended echo-effect" in the receptor context. The point of running parallels is not the similar elements themselves but the connotative baggage they carry over from the donor context. The pharaoh-like and Joseph-like elements recycled in Dan 2 offer connotative ways to interpret Nebuchadnezzar and Daniel. For more detail on how extended echo-effect works in comparison to other figural relations, see Table C10 in Chronicles with its associated discussion, as well as the Glossary.

The possible allusion to imagery from Isaiah's oracles within Nebuchadnezzar's vision features something new. The potential allusions amount to "secret messages" embedded in the vision for readers in the know. The scripturally allusive imagery has no significance for Nebuchadnezzar or his courtiers. Beyond this, Daniel does not overtly mark the allusive imagery. Daniel speaks of "mysteries revealed" with reference to the stated meaning of the vision in a way that could almost suggest the fuller significance of the potential scriptural allusions (e.g., Dan 2:30).

The most overt exegetical use of scriptural traditions appears in Dan 9. The first-person account relates to Daniel's study of Scripture and his Scripture-laden prayer. The controlling donor contexts come from Jer 25, 29, Lev 26, Deut 7, and 29. In addition, nearly every line seems to be laced with scriptural echoes. The gist of Daniel's Scripture study and prayer rests on a straightforward interpretation of exile and its end according to Moses and Jeremiah. All of this serves as a set up for a vision in response to Daniel's prayer. The vision advances revelation by massively adjusting the sense of Jeremiah's seventy years.

Notable exegetical interventions with several of Isaiah's oracles appear in the beginning of Dan 12, in addition to many lesser echoes elsewhere in Daniel's visions. The exegetical advancements of revelation concern resurrection and deliverance for some of those resurrected. Even while leaving many questions unanswered, Dan 12 presents the boldest and fullest revelation of resurrection in Israel's Scriptures. Fully appreciating the advances of revelation in Dan 12 requires investigating it in relation to its several Isaiah donor contexts. The revelation of resurrection in Daniel's vision does not come out of thin air. The vision interpretively enhances and expands upon Isaiah's oracles. This part of the vision advances revelation by means of scriptural exegesis.

Working with Daniel requires extra patience and care. Nearly everything about Daniel remains in sharp dispute, including dating, the identities of many rulers, the level of satire in the narratives and their larger functions, the genre of the visions as prophecy or apocalyptic or otherwise, the relationship between the Aramaic (Dan 2:4b–7:28) and Hebrew (1–2:4a, 8:1–12:13) sections, and many kinds of historical and literary difficulties. The present study focuses narrowly on the use of scriptural traditions in Daniel as it stands and cannot attend to other issues. The study of exegetical allusions in Daniel does not compete with but needs to take its place alongside other interpretive studies.

The use of scriptural traditions in Daniel provides a bright spot amid the many contested aspects of its interpretation. Daniel uses scriptural traditions much in line with scriptural exegesis elsewhere in Israel's Scriptures. The most provocative hermeneutical element may be the hidden messages by means of scriptural allusion in the king's vision in Dan 2. The advances of revelation relative to Jeremiah's seventy weeks and Isaiah on resurrection do not stem from interpretive ingenuity but proceed from the visionary revelations themselves. The use of scriptural traditions in Daniel challenges readers to return to Scripture and rethink exile as well as adopt greater hopes for resurrection.

USE OF SCRIPTURE

1:2*~2 Kgs 24:13*+Jer 27:16* (C) (plundering temple vessels during siege of Jerusalem in Jehoiakim's rule) (* see temple vessels network). Daniel 1:2 mentions plundering the temple vessels and placing them in the house of the gods without detail. The Chronicler also refers to seizing the temple vessels during Jehoiakim's rule but includes enough detail to deduce his interpretive blend (see note on 2 Chr 36:7, 10). Elsewhere Dan 5:2–4, 23 refers to the mistreatment of the temple vessels by the Neo-Babylonian court.

2:28–29~Gen 41:25, 28, 32 (B) (divine revelation by dreams). The narrative of Daniel interpreting the dream of Nebuchadnezzar in Dan 2 includes numerous parallels with the account of Joseph interpreting the pharaoh's dreams in Gen 41. The most thoroughgoing analysis detects eighteen parallels, of uneven value, between the two contexts.[3] Only a few of the parallels match verbally since the narrative switches from Hebrew to Aramaic at Dan 2:4. The numerous connections between the two narratives likely points to intentional shaping of the Daniel story after the Joseph story. Many of the differences between the two accounts shine a light on Daniel as "even more" compared to Joseph.[4] The most significant example of Daniel outshining Joseph turns on Nebuchadnezzar's insistence on being told both dream and its interpretation on the threat of death to the entire guild of court sages (Dan 2:5–6, 9).

3. See Rindge, "Jewish Identity," 88–90. Philpot lists seventeen similarities, derived independently since he nowhere cites Rindge ("Joseph a Type?" 688–89). Also see Lester, *Daniel Evokes Isaiah*, 47–54; Henze, "Use of Scripture," 280–83; Widder, "Court Stories," 1112–14; idem, *Daniel*, 42–44; Goldingay, *Daniel*, 183–84, 190–91.

4. See Rindge, "Jewish Identity," 90–98.

The majority of intentional similarities and differences may be considered literary, not exegetical.[5] Type-scene could help explain the relationship in broad terms but does not adequately get at the specific reading together of these two contexts in a way that extended echo-effect does (see Glossary).[6] The use of a scriptural tradition provides comparative connotation by which to measure the divine intervention on behalf of Daniel and the court sages. All of Nebuchadnezzar's pharaoh-like and Daniel's Joseph-like elements contribute to the literary development of the satirical story of the Neo-Babylonian court.

The interpretive theological enhancement amid the narrative of Nebuchadnezzar's vision comes from the narrator and Daniel testifying to God's role in revealing mysteries, both to Daniel and in the vision to Nebuchadnezzar (2:19, 27–28). Daniel even blesses God, providing theological interpretation of divine intervention by revelation (2:20–23). By contrast Joseph repeatedly acknowledges that God reveals future events to the pharaoh but does not make explicit his own dependence on God for interpretation of the dream (Gen 41:25, 28, 32). Ironically, the pharaoh acknowledges that God has shown these things to Joseph (41:38–39). Daniel interpretively deduces from the events something about God's power: "there is a God in heaven who reveals mysteries ... the revealer of mysteries showed you what is going to happen" (Dan 2:28–29). The thematic similarities to the revelatory power of God in Isaiah has been suggested as possibly echoed in Dan 2 (Isa 42:9; 45:19, 21).[7]

Several studies have interpreted the function of the similarities at the level of genre or general intention, such as "moderate resistance" versus the greater defiance of the midwives of Exod 1 or the Maccabean revolt.[8] While general comparisons get at broad issues, Widder helpfully identifies the significance of using Gen 41 in Dan 2. These contexts considered together provide a "paradigm of God's work among the nations." God waits to reveal his intentions to foreign rulers by dreams until someone is available to explain them.[9] These stories do more than lift up Joseph and Daniel above the foreign courts. The work of Joseph suggests and the interpretive enhancement of Daniel explains the theological significance. The God of heaven alone reveals mysteries.

2:34–35, 45~Isa 41:15–16; 51:1 (C) (hewn rock destroys empires and becomes mighty kingdom). The account of the king's dream in Dan 2:34–35, 45 has been proposed as thematically alluding to the chaff of Isa 41:15–16 and more specifically to the hewn rock of 51:1 by means of cognate parallels between Aramaic and Hebrew. The nature of the shared imagery joined together, if an allusion, suggests Isaiah is the donor and Daniel the receptor context. The subtlety of the parallels means this case may only be

5. See Henze, "Use of Scripture," 284.

6. On distinct parallels between Gen 41 and Dan 2, versus similarities not found in Esther or Ahiqar, see Lester, *Daniel Evokes Isaiah*, 51.

7. See Henze, "Use of Scripture," 284.

8. See Rindge, "Jewish Identity," 103–4. For a view of stronger resistance, see Newsom, *Daniel*, 15–18. Also see Willis, "Reversal," 112–17; Melvin, "There Is," 139–53.

9. Widder, "Court Stories," 1127; idem, *Daniel*, 55–56.

counted as a possible interpretive allusion (emphasis here signifies thematic similarities, not verbal parallels):[10]

> See, I will make you [Jacob] into a threshing sledge, new and sharp, with many teeth. You will thresh the mountains and crush them, and reduce the hills *to chaff.* You will winnow them, the wind will pick them up, and *a gale will blow them away.* (Isa 41:15–16a)

> Listen to me, you who pursue righteousness and who seek Yahweh: Look to **the rock** from which you were cut and to the quarry **from which you were hewn**; look to Abraham, your father, and to Sarah, who gave you birth. (51:1–2a)

> While you were watching, **a rock was cut out**, but not by human hands. It struck the statue on its feet of iron and clay and smashed them. Then the iron, the clay, the bronze, the silver and the gold were all broken to pieces and became *like chaff* on a threshing floor in the summer. *The wind swept them* away without leaving a trace. But the rock that struck the statue became a huge mountain and filled the whole earth. (Dan 2:34–35; cf. 2:45)

If this parallel is granted, the nature of the interconnectivity is different in kind from an ordinary interpretive allusion. In this case, the allusion in Daniel would function as a sort of hidden message only for those who get it. Neither Nebuchadnezzar and his courtiers nor Daniel's readership would know from anything Daniel says that the rock had been hewn from Abraham. This hidden message, if it exists, requires the readership to connect and identify the hewn rock in both contexts as descendants of Abraham and to connect the chaff imagery as well. Although this level of complexity and subtlety would normally rule out counting this as a potential allusion, the nature of a divine dream that needs to be decoded merits a different approach. Allusions by embedded hidden messages naturally would put special demands upon the readership. Responsible exegesis of subtle hidden messages needs to vigilantly resist zealous overinterpretation. Caution, interpretive controls, and cool heads are some of the ingredients for responsible exegesis of hidden messages in scriptural visions. In spite of the dangers of overinterpretation, the possible interpretive allusion identifying the "hewn rock" from Abraham offers much merit in this case.

The context of Isa 40–48 features crushing of gold, bronze, and iron to clay only to be blown away (Isa 40:19; 41:15–16, 25; 45:2).[11] The subsequent mountain that fills the entire earth may also evoke the mountain of Yahweh's temple in the vision of Isa 2:2

10. This potential allusion requires regarding "hew" (Aramaic גזר) in Dan 2:34, 45 as a cognate parallel to "hew" (Hebrew חצב) in Isa 51:1, as suggested by Lester, *Daniel Evokes Isaiah*, 109.

11. See Goldingay, *Daniel*, 201–2.

(Dan 2:35).[12] The point of the potential allusions is to offer a fuller hidden message to readers in the know. Daniel explains generally to Nebuchadnezzar and his court that "the God of heaven will set up a kingdom that will never be destroyed, nor will it be left to *another people*" (2:44, emphasis mine). But readers who know Israel's Scriptures can detect that the "God of heaven" refers to Yahweh and "another people" to the descendants of Jacob.

In sum, the similarities between imagery in Nebuchadnezzar's dream and Isaiah may energize Daniel to offer a hidden message for scriptural readers. The dream and its interpretation simultaneously cloak the covenantal significance from the emperor and his court.

9:2*~Jer 25:11; 29:10* (B) (seventy years) (* see seventy years network).
9:4–19*~Lev 26:40–41* (B) (collective confession of sin) (* see collective confession network).
9:4//Deut 7:9* (covenantal fidelity) (* see attribute formula network).
9:11, 13~Deut 29:20–21[19–20] (B) (curses written in Torah). When Daniel studies Jeremiah, he learns that the seventy years of Jerusalem's desolation have been completed —or so he deduces by plain-sense interpretation (Dan 9:2). Daniel prays a scriptural allusion-rich prayer to confess the collective sin of Israel, including that of their ancestors and Daniel himself in the spirit of Lev 26:40–41 (Dan 9:14–19). Daniel's prayer shares many similarities with other scriptural prayers shaped by Lev 26 (Ezra 9:6–15; Neh 1:5–11; cf. Neh 9; Ps 106; Add Esth 14:3–19; Bar 1:15–3:8).[13] Within the prayer, Daniel refers to the covenantal preview of Deut 29, overtly marking it twice as written in the Torah of Moses (Dan 9:11, 13). The explicit marking of Jeremiah and Deuteronomy strongly favor Dan 9 as the receptor of these and other donor contexts.

The scriptural echoes of Daniel's prayer include several key roots found in the interpretation of the attribute formula in Deut 7:9—"Love," "covenantal loyalty," and "faithfulness"—as well as "compassion," which appears in the covenant formula itself (9:4, 9, 13, 18; cf. Exod 34:6; Deut 7:9).[14] The parallels include the verbatim quotation of "who keeps his covenant of love with those who love him and keep his commandments" (Deut 7:9//Dan 9:4). The divine name Yahweh only appears in this single context of Daniel (Dan 9:2, 4, 8, 10, 13, 14, 20).[15] The suggestive undercurrents of Yahweh's forgiveness of Israel in the past fit well with Daniel's confession and request for mercy.

Daniel focuses on the seventy years of Jeremiah in terms of Jerusalem. In that sense it fits more with the letter in Jer 29 (italics signify verbal parallels):

> This whole country will become a desolate wasteland, and these nations will serve the king of Babylon *seventy years.* (Jer 25:11)

12. The echo of Isa 2:2–3; 11:9 is suggested by ibid., 202.
13. See Schnittjer, "Bad Ending," 52–53.
14. On several key terms in Dan 9, see Goldingay, *Daniel*, 466–67, 476–77.
15. See Scheetz, *Canonical Intertextuality*, 108.

> This is what Yahweh says: "When *seventy years* are completed for Babylon, I will come to you and fulfill my good promise to bring you back to this place." (29:10)

> In the first year of Darius son of Xerxes (a Mede by descent) . . . in the first year of his reign, I, Daniel, understood from the Scriptures, according to the word of Yahweh given to Jeremiah the prophet, that the desolation of Jerusalem would last *seventy years*. (Dan 9:1a, 2)

Like Daniel, Chronicles also interpretively blends Jeremiah's seventy years with the covenantal template of the end of exile in Lev 26. While the Chronicler, looking backward, deduces seventy missed Sabbath years (7x70), the celestial interpretation given to Daniel looks at the seventy years themselves as sevens (7x70) (see note on 2 Chr 36:21).[16] These important overlapping elements should not obscure other significant differences between these two contexts.

Leviticus 26:40 seems to be the centerpiece of Daniel's prayer.[17] The syntactical and verbal parallel between "confess" from Lev 26:40 somewhat frames the prayer by appearing in Dan 9:4, 20. Other uses of the reflexive stem of "confess" include Ezra 10:1; Neh 1:6; and 9:2, 3.[18] Daniel repeatedly uses the language of Lev 26:40, including "ancestors" (אָבֹת, Dan 9:6, 8, 16), "iniquity" (עָוֺן, 9:13, 16), and the root for "infidelity" (מעל, 9:7[2x]). Even more importantly, Daniel continuously invokes first-person plural confessional language to speak inclusively of Israel both corporately and across time.

Twice Daniel refers to the written Torah of Moses (9:11, 13). He refers to Torah in relation to the "curses" against rebels. The language of written curses verbally parallels the preview of Israel's rebellion in Deut 29, where the word "curse" written in a scroll appears more than anywhere else (Deut 29:12, 14, 19, 20, 21[11, 13, 18, 19, 20]; cf. 30:7).[19] Perhaps "curse" functions as a catchword for Daniel since it appears in Jeremiah's letter (Jer 29:18). Compare a representative sampling of Daniel's use of Lev 26 and Deut 29 with the citation of 7:9 (emphases signify verbal parallels):

> But if they **will confess** their **iniquities** and **the iniquities** of their **ancestors**—their **unfaithfulness** and their hostility toward me . . . (Lev 26:40†)

> Know therefore that Yahweh your God is God; he is the faithful God, <u>who keeps his covenant of love with those who love him and keep his commandments</u> for a thousand generations. (Deut 7:9†)

16. On other uses of the seventy years in Scripture, see Schnittjer, "Individual versus Collective," 126–29.
17. For additional examples of Lev 26 in Dan 9, see Fishbane, *Biblical Interpretation*, 488–89.
18. See Hith uses of "II ידה," *HALOT* 1:389.
19. See "אָלָה," *HALOT* 1:51. Also see Scheetz, *Canonical Intertextuality*, 139.

> Yahweh will never be willing to forgive them; his wrath and zeal will burn against them. All *the curses* written in this book will fall on them, and Yahweh will blot out their names from under heaven. Yahweh will single them out from all the tribes of Israel for disaster, according to all *the curses* of the covenant *written in* this Book of *the Torah.* (Deut 29:20–21[19–20])

> I prayed to Yahweh my God and **confessed**: "Lord, the great and awesome God, who keeps his covenant of love with those who love him and keep his commandments, we have sinned and **committed iniquities**. We have been wicked and have rebelled; we have turned away from your commands and laws. We have not listened to your servants the prophets, who spoke in your name to our kings, our princes and our **ancestors**, and to all the people of the land. Lord, you are righteous, but this day we are covered with shame—the people of Judah and the inhabitants of Jerusalem and all Israel, both near and far, in all the countries where you have scattered us because of our **unfaithfulness** to you. . . . All Israel has transgressed your torah and turned away, refusing to obey you. Therefore *the curses* and sworn judgments *written in the Torah* of Moses, the servant of God, have been poured out on us, because we have sinned against you." (Dan 9:4–7, 11†)

Daniel's interpretive prayer expressly interacts with written Scripture from Jeremiah and Moses (9:2, 11). Daniel recognizes the continuity of the judgment spoken in the prophets: "just as it is written in the Torah of Moses, all this disaster has come on us" (9:13). Daniel's prayer follows along the lines of the anticipated covenantal response at the end of exile in Lev 26:40–41. All of this shows a relatively straightforward interpretation of the contexts read together by interpretive blend.

Daniel's baseline intercessory interpretation sets in sharp relief the celestial visitor's surprising advancement of revelation. The seventy years of Jeremiah refer to seventy weeks of years (9:24–27). Elsewhere Daniel comments on his dismay and confusion about the interpretation of visions (7:28; 8:27). In the case of the challenging seventy sevens interpretation Daniel offers no comment. Solving this interpretive crux goes beyond the present purposes. The point at hand gets at Daniel's representative interpretation of exile by Torah and prophets together that requires significant adjustment in light of the progressive revelation of the divine will. The celestial interpretation does not replace the seventy years or get cast as something entirely new, but it is a new interpretive revelation that unfolds out of Torah and prophets in the form of vision. The celestial interpretative vision functions by a different center of gravity than the scriptural scrolls Daniel has been reading. The kinds of vision interpretations running through Daniel suggest caution for working out an interpretation of the interpretative vision of the seventy sevens.

12:2~Isa 26:19 (B)+66:24 (B) (those who sleep in the dust awake).

12:3~Isa 52:13 (C)+53:11 (B) (lead many to righteousness). Verbal parallels point to a probable relationship between Isa 26:19 and Dan 12:2, and between Isa 53:11 and

Dan 12:3. Daniel 12:2 and 12:3 also may include secondary parallels to Isa 66:24 and 52:13 respectively. The term "contempt(ible)" only appears in Isa 66:24 and Dan 12:2, making a relationship likely.[20] The root for "act wisely" appears an active verb in the causative stem in Isa 52:13 and as a participle in the causative stem in Dan 12:3. The proximity to the probable parallel in Isa 53:11 slightly increases the possibility of intentional parallel. Bringing together widely separate contexts of itself somewhat favors Isa 26:19 and 66:24 as donor and Dan 12 as receptor context. This direction of dependence will be followed here.

The interpretive blend of Isa 26:19 and 66:24 in Dan 12:2 develops theological concepts found elsewhere in Scripture. The use of "dust" for death and the banishment from the "tree of life" by which one may live forever in Gen 3:19, 22 demonstrate the broader context of Isaiah's oracles and Daniel's vision.[21] Daniel's vision joins together specific elements of resurrection from Isaiah. The interpretive advancement of Daniel includes resurrection to everlasting life *and* to everlasting contempt (verbal parallels of both roots and stems are signified by bold, parallel roots are signified by italics, and the same term is signified by underlining):

> But your dead *will live*, Yahweh; their bodies will rise—let those who dwell in **the dust wake up** and shout for joy—your dew is like the dew of the morning; the earth will give birth to her dead. (Isa 26:19)
>
> And they will go out and look on the dead bodies of those who rebelled against me; the worms that eat them will not die, the fire that burns them will not be quenched, and they <u>will be contemptable</u> to all mankind. (66:24†)
>
> Multitudes who sleep in **the dust** of the earth **will awake**: some to everlasting *life*, others to shame and everlasting <u>contempt.</u> (Dan 12:2)

The opening of Dan 12:2 says literally "multitudes *from*." The sense of this phrase needs to be considered to see whether it speaks of a general resurrection or something more limited. The term "from" could be used in an inclusive sense of "*away from* sleeping in the dust" leading into the verb "they will awake," or it could have a partitive sense of "multitudes *from among* those who sleep."[22] Those who will be delivered in Dan 12:1 at first seem to be "multitudes" in 12:2 (favoring partitive sense of "from"). But those resurrected exceed those delivered and include others raised to everlasting contempt. With the

20. See "דֵּרָאוֹן," *HALOT* 1:230; Ginsberg, "Oldest," 403–4; Collins, *Daniel*, 392–93; Lester, *Daniel Evokes Isaiah*, 100; Henze, "Use of Scripture," 298.

21. See Baldwin, *Daniel*, 226.

22. On "from" (מִן) in "*Multitudes from/of* those who sleep" (וְרַבִּים מִיְּשֵׁנֵי, Dan 12:2) as separation/away from, see GKC §119v, or for partitive sense, §119w, n. 2. See further discussion in Hartman and Di Lella, *Daniel*, 307–8.

multitudes made up of two classes in 12:2, it seems at least to include both those who are wise in Dan 11:33, 35 and those who join them insincerely in 11:34—thus, at least a more general resurrection beyond those who will be delivered in 12:1 (also including Daniel himself in 12:13). In either case, the twofold resurrection to everlasting life and contempt in Daniel's vision lends itself naturally to further advancement of a general resurrection in the New Testament (John 5:29; Acts 24:15; Rev 20:4–5; 21:12–13).

Isaiah 26:19 uses the term "awake" metaphorically to speak of rising from "the dead." The vision of Daniel extends the imagery to speak of death as "sleep" (Dan 12:2). In this way the vision of Daniel looks ahead to physical resurrection. The vision also expands the expectation for resurrection beyond a hope for the oppressed, whether Isa 26:19 refers to political or bodily resurrection. Isaiah 26:19 refers only positively to arising to rejoice.[23] The vision of Daniel goes beyond this and supplies a duality of those arising to judgment by using the language of perpetual contempt outside the new Jerusalem in Isa 66:24.[24] Daniel's vision interprets the prophecies of Isaiah by other prophecies of Isaiah.

The distinction between the many purified and refined who understand versus the wicked who will not understand in Dan 12:10 stems from the development of the resurrection in 12:3. This sense of understanding helps explain the interpretive intervention in Dan 12:3.

Reference to those who are wise in Dan 12:3 goes back to those killed earlier in the vision (11:33, 35; cf. 12:10). Daniel 12:3 includes two parallel lines with the second expanding the first. Those who act wisely in the first line are those who lead many to righteousness in the second line. The causative stem translated here as "make righteous" connotes teaching by the wise. Later, in Second Temple sectarian writings the term gets used in a similar sense: "*leading to righteousness* [צדק Hif] with one's brother, so that their steps become steady in the path of God" (CD 20:18 lit., emphasis mine).[25] In a similar way, those who act wisely "shine" by means of "leading many to righteousness" (Dan 12:3). The donor context uses the term in a different sense. The meaning of the verb "righteous" (צדק) in the causative stem has a legal sense of "acquit, pronounce righteous" in several cases, including Isa 53:11, where it is used in an unusual manner (see note on Isa 53:10).[26] The vision of Daniel identifies the work of leading to righteousness by those who are wise as teaching or enlightening, in keeping with its imagery (see below).[27] Note how the vision of Daniel develops the sense of the donor contexts in its new context (bold signifies verbal parallels at the level of root and stem, and broken underlining signifies similar imagery).

---

23. See Schmitz, "Grammar," 148. Schmitz also proposes taking the final yod of "corpse" (נְבֵלָתִי) as a gentilic to maintain the MT reading (146–47). And, based on similarities between shades (רְפָאִים) in Isa 26:14 with Ugaritic shades (*rapa'ūma*), McAffee demonstrates why 26:19 refers to individual bodily resurrection ("Rephaim," 92, 94).

24. See Lester, *Daniel Evokes Isaiah*, 100.

25. See ibid., 97. Translation of CD 20:18 from *DSSSE* 1:578.

26. For the legal sense of "pronounce righteous," see Exod 23:7; Deut 25:1; 1 Kgs 8:32//2 Chr 6:23; Prov 17:15; Isa 5:23 (so Isa 53:11 NET note).

27. See Lester, *Daniel Evokes Isaiah*, 97.

See, my servant **will act wisely** [שׂכל Hif]; he will be raised and lifted up and highly exalted. (Isa 52:13)

Out of the suffering of his soul he shall see [light],[28] he shall be satisfied, by his knowledge my righteous servant **shall make many righteous** [צדק Hif], and their iniquities he shall bear. (53:11 lit.)

Those who are wise [שׂכל Hif] will shine like the brightness of the heavens, and **those who lead many to righteousness** [צדק Hif], like the stars for ever and ever. (Dan 12:3)

The vision of Daniel does not advance the sense of "lead to righteousness" against the grain of the work of the servant in Isa 53. Already Isa 57:14–19 shows that the servant's suffering in Isa 53 serves as a model for the restoration (see note on Isa 53:10). The vision of Daniel applies this sense narrowly in this context to the educational, enlightening work of those who are wise, also perhaps drawn from Isa 52:13, which refers to the servant.

Collins stresses the "elevation" of the righteous to join the angelic host, whom he identifies with the stars in Dan 12:3 and 1 Enoch 104:2.[29] He suggests this idea aligns with a Hellenistic belief in astral immortality as early as the fifth century BCE whereby the dead turn into stars.[30] Hartman and Di Lella criticize the late date of the parables of Enoch (ca. 270 CE) and also that Collins wrongly "lumps together" the many resurrected in 12:2 with the many faithful in 12:3.[31] Both the A and B lines of Dan 12:3 use "like" or "as" to mark simile not identity. Those who are wise shall shine "like" the brightness of the expanse and lead in righteousness "like" the stars. The same distinction continues when Messiah says those who rise from the dead are "like" celestial delegates with respect to not marrying (Mark 12:25). In sum, the stellar lights provide a simile of the way those who are wise shine in leading many to righteousness.

The NIV and many other modern committee translations and scholars follow the Septuagint and Qumran Isaiah scrolls, which include "light" in Isa 53:11. The evidence is equivocal (see bracket in Isa 53:11 cited above and associated footnote). Whatever the original reading, the version of Isa 53:11 that serves as the donor context for Dan 12:3

---

28. The NIV and NRSV follow LXX and 1QIsa[a] in Isa 53:11a, including the word "light" (אוֹר) not in MT, "After he has suffered, he will see *the light*" (NIV). Two other Qumran Isaiah scrolls also include "light" (1QIsa[b] and 1QIsa[d] [partially] *BQS* 2:531, 535), but all of these and LXX could be traceable to one common parent text. Although the general rule prefers the shorter reading, the longer reading should be considered here (so Childs, *Isaiah*, 409, n. h). Oswalt favors the originality of "sees the light" and notes that the similarity of the terms "see" (ראה) and "light" (אור) could account for its dropping out (*Isaiah*, 586, n. 12). Another factor strengthens Oswalt's suggestion: since the change either way happened early (parent text of LXX and DSS vs. proto-MT), if the change happened before the plene marking of vowels, the terms could be even closer (ראה/רא, אור/אר).

29. See Collins, "Apocalyptic Eschatology," 34.

30. See Collins, *Daniel*, 394.

31. See Hartman and Di Lella, *Daniel*, 310.

seems also to include "light." The vision works from light to the stunning similes of celestial radiance and stars (Dan 12:3).

In sum, Dan 12:2, 3 advances revelation by expanding two interpretive blends of oracles of Isaiah. The vision of Daniel expects a resurrection of two classes, those to everlasting life and those to everlasting contempt. The vision also expands upon the work of the suffering servant as model for the restoration in Isaiah. In Daniel's vision those who are wise lead many to righteousness by enlightenment or teaching.

FILTERS

Many have suggested potential scriptural echoes in Daniel.[32] The present purpose is limited to listing a few of the more pronounced non-exegetical echoes, broad allusions, and other similarities. This listing is not comprehensive or complete.

Note: **2:36–40; 7:1–3**>/<Zech 1:18–21[2:1–4], the four symbols of kingdoms in Daniel may broadly relate to the four horns in Zechariah;[33] **3:25–27**>/<Isa 43:2, walk through fire and not be burned;[34] **7:7–8**>/<Isa 10:12; 37:23 ruler acts arrogantly toward God;[35] **8:10**>/<Isa 14:13–15, horn and intention of king of Babylon to rise up and cause fall of cosmic host of the heavens;[36] **8:19**>/<Isa 10:5, 25, end/time of "wrath" (זעם);[37] **9:26**>/<Isa 10:22–23; 28:22–23, "flood," "destruction and what is decreed" (שטף, כלה ונחרץ);[38] **11:10, 40**>/<Isa 8:8, military invasion "like a flood sweeping over" (שטף ועבר) (cf. Dan 11:22, 26);[39] **11:27, 35**>/<Hab 2:3, "for yet an end at the appointed time/until the time of the end, for it will come at the appointed time/to the appointed time . . . an end" (כי עוד קץ למועד/עד עת קץ כי עוד למועד/למועד . . . לקץ) (cf. "for still the vision" [כי עוד חזון] Hab 2:3a//Dan 10:14a);[40] **11:30**>/<Num 24:24, "ships from Kittim will come against him/ships will come from Kittim" (וצים מיד כתים/ובאו בו ציים כתים);[41] **11:36**>/<Isa 10:25, "wrath is completed" (כלה זעם).[42]

32. For other potential parallels between Daniel and other Scriptures, see Henze, "Use of Scripture," 279–307; Lester, *Daniel Evokes Isaiah*, 31–59, et passim; Scheetz, *Concept*, 129–46. For additional lesser echoes, see Lester, *Daniel Evokes Isaiah*, 107–64; Fishbane, *Biblical Interpretation*, 493–95.

33. See Koch, "Is Daniel," 125; Boda, *Zechariah*, 157.

34. For a view of these passages as an interpretive allusion see Lester, *Daniel Evokes Isaiah*, 116–23.

35. See ibid., 148–49.

36. See ibid., 149–50.

37. Lester uses the broad similarity between "wrath" in Isa 10 and similar themes in Dan 8–12 to suggest Isa 10 is the donor context (ibid., 137–40).

38. For the view that Daniel uses "direct quotation" and ironically develops Isaiah's language, see ibid., 70–72. Part of the problem with the supposed allusion stems from Lester trying to decide which Isaiah context Daniel may have in mind. What Lester sees as ironic use seems more like two different and unrelated uses of common prophetic stock phrases for military destruction.

39. Speaking of military invasion using flood imagery is common in ancient Near Eastern contexts and also employed in Scripture (e.g., *ARAB* 1:284, 285). For a different view, see Lester, *Daniel Evokes Isaiah*, 145–47.

40. See Fishbane, *Biblical Interpretation*, 492; Henze, "Use of Scripture," 297.

41. See Ginsberg, "Oldest," 401; Fishbane, *Biblical Interpretation*, 491; Henze, "Use of Scripture," 296.

42. See Lester, *Daniel Evokes Isaiah*, 65–68.

Nebuchadnezzar's blessing of the Most High has thematic similarities to selected contexts of Psalms and Isaiah (similarities marked).[43]

Your kingdom is an everlasting kingdom, and your dominion endures through all generations (Ps 145:13a). Before him all the nations are as nothing; they are regarded by him as worthless and less than nothing (Isa 40:17). Our God is in heaven; **he does whatever pleases him** (Ps 115:3). For Yahweh Almighty has purposed, and who can thwart him? His hand is stretched out, and who can turn it back? (Isa 14:27).	At the end of that time, I, Nebuchadnezzar, raised my eyes toward heaven, and my sanity was restored. Then I praised the Most High; I honored and glorified him who lives forever. His dominion is an eternal dominion; his kingdom endures from generation to generation. [35] All the peoples of the earth are regarded as nothing. **He does as he pleases** with the powers of heaven and the peoples of the earth. No one can hold back his hand or say to him: "What have you done?" (Dan 4:34–35[31–32]).

The elements of the visions of Daniel have been compared to similar elements, such as the vision in Isa 6.[44] The visions also have been compared to the night visions of Zech 1–6.[45]

The explanation of the seventy sevens shares some language with the oracle against the prince of Tyre in Ezek 28, such as "leader" (נגיד) (Dan 9:25; Ezek 28:2), "ruin" (שחת) and "desolation" (שמם) (Dan 9:26, 27; Ezek 28:8, 17, 19).[46]

43. These similarities are suggested by Baldwin, *Daniel*, 128.
44. See Nicol, "Isaiah's Vision," 501–4, esp. table on 504 (no. 4 is the weakest on his table).
45. See Koch, "Is Daniel," 125.
46. See Goldingay, *Daniel*, 488.

Chapter 34

EZRA-NEHEMIAH

SYMBOLS[1]

// verbal parallels (A level)
/~/ synoptic parallel (A level)
~ B, probable interpretive allusion; C, possible; D, probably not
+ interpretive blend
>/< more or less similar (see Filters)
* part of interpretive network (see Networks near end of volume)

USE OF SCRIPTURE IN EZRA-NEHEMIAH[2]

Ezra 1:1–3a//2 Chr 36:22–23~Jer 25:11; 29:10+Isa 44:28; 45:1 (B) (edict of Cyrus)
1:5~Hag 1:14 (B) (stir up the spirit)
1:6~1:4 (A)+Exod 12:35, 36 (C) (contributions from neighbors)
1:7, 11*~Jer 27:22* (B) (vessels of temple returned) (* see temple vessels network)
2:1–3:1/~/Neh 7:6–8:1 (list of returning exiles)
3:4~Lev 23:37+Num 29:18+Deut 16:13 (B) (observing Tabernacles as it is written)
6:3–5/~/1:2–4/~/5:13–15 (three versions of Cyrus's edict)
6:18~Deut 12:13–14+1 Chr 23–26 (C) (worship personnel serve at Jerusalem)
8:3–14/~/2:3–20//Neh 7:8–24 (list of laity families)
9:1–2*~Exod 34:11/Deut 7:1*+Deut 23:3–8*[4–9] (B) (mingling the holy seed) (* see assembly and devoting networks)
9:11–12~Lev 18:27 (C)+Deut 7:3* (B)+23:6*[7] (B) (pollution by intermarriage with the other) (* see assembly and devoting networks)
10:10–11, 19~Lev 5:15 (B)+Exod 34:16*/Deut 7:3* (C) (reparation offering and mass divorce) (* see assembly and devoting networks)
Neh 1:8–9*~Lev 26:40*+Deut 30:3+1 Kgs 8:29 (C) (Yahweh scatters his unfaithful people) (* see collective confession network)
4:5[3:37]~Jer 18:23 (B) (do not forgive them)
5:1, 4, 7, 8, 11*~Exod 22:25–27*[24–26]+Lev 25:42, 46*+Deut 24:10* (C) (reforming predatory loans) (* see release statute network)
6:13~Deut 18:22 (D) (do not fear false prophets)
7:6–8:1/~/Ezra 2:1–3:1 (discovering the list of returning exiles)
8:1–3~Deut 31:11–13 (C) (pre-Tabernacles Torah reading)
8:7, 8*~Deut 33:10* (C) (Levitical instruction) (* see teachers network)
8:14–16~Lev 23:40 (B) (making temporary shelters for Tabernacles)
9:6–37*~Scripture compilation (B) (Levitical intercessors' panoramic retrospective) (* see Abrahamic covenant and Sabbath networks)
10:30–39*[31–40]~selected legal standards of Torah (B) (solemn oath of the restoration assembly) (* see assembly and Sabbath networks)
11:25–30~Josh 15:20–41 (B) (restoration of villages of Judah)
13:1–3*//Deut 23:3–6*[4–7] (responding to the law of the assembly) (* see assembly network)
13:15, 17–18*~Jer 17:21–27*+Num 32:8, 14 (B) (Sabbath breaking by merchandizing) (* see Sabbath network)

1. For explanation of symbols, see Symbols and Abbreviations and Introduction. For other help, see Glossary.
2. See Bibliographic Note on Lists of Potential Parallels.

13:23–27*~Deut 23:3*[4]+1 Kgs 11:1–4* (B) (confronting apostasy husbands) (* see assembly and devoting networks)

OLD TESTAMENT USE OF EZRA-NEHEMIAH (SEE RESPECTIVE NOTE)

Neh 11:3–19/~/1 Chr 9:2–18 (C) (inhabitants of Jerusalem)

NEW TESTAMENT USE OF EZRA-NEHEMIAH

n/a

HERMENEUTICAL PROFILE OF THE USE OF SCRIPTURE IN EZRA-NEHEMIAH

The frequent and overt use of scriptural traditions in Ezra-Nehemiah requires attention to a couple of special issues in this profile. The main overview of scriptural interpretive tendencies in Ezra-Nehemiah comes first and lays the groundwork for the series of exegetical notes in this chapter. Two other sections in the introductory hermeneutical profile get at more involved and much-contested issues of overt marking of Torah citations and legal standards of Torah.

Exegetical Conventions in Ezra-Nehemiah

Ezra-Nehemiah displays a full range of scriptural interpretation. The narrators even take note of Ezra's own scriptural prowess as "a teacher well versed in the Torah of Moses, which Yahweh, the God of Israel, had given" (Ezra 7:6). The narrators' emphasis here on the divine granting of Torah plays an important part in the interpretation of scriptural traditions throughout the narrative. Ezra-Nehemiah begins by explicitly emphasizing the restoration as activated by Yahweh in accord with Jeremiah's prophetic word (1:1). Ezra-Nehemiah ends with Nehemiah's vigorous efforts to stem the tide of rebellion that had taken over Jerusalem. In between the bright beginning and bitter ending, Ezra-Nehemiah exhibits regular and overt attention to scriptural exegesis in the restoration.

Before getting at the main interpretive tendencies of Ezra-Nehemiah, a few aspects of this unique scriptural narrative need to be noted.[3] Several of the materials in the lists in Neh 11–12 could not have been completed before the rise of the Hellenistic Empire, especially the line of priests going down to Jaddua, who may be the same one known from when Alexander the Great took over many Near Eastern lands in 330 BCE (Neh 12:11–12).[4] As such, the normal default in this chapter for scriptural parallels will be

3. For detailed attention to the shape and function of Ezra-Neh, see Schnittjer, *Ezra-Nehemiah*, forthcoming.

4. For more on the date of Ezra-Nehemiah, see note on 2 Chr 36:22–23.

Ezra-Nehemiah as the receptor context and the scriptural parallels as donor contexts, unless stated otherwise.

Japhet's study of the comparative evidence demonstrates that Chronicles and Ezra-Nehemiah are separate books written by separate authors.[5] This became an important change of direction from the longtime treatment of the Chronicler as author of Ezra-Nehemiah, which badly skewed interpretation. The present study treats Ezra-Nehemiah as a single scroll.[6] Since substantial evidence demonstrates 1 Esdras is derivative of Chronicles and Ezra-Nehemiah, it does not relate to the present study.[7]

The present work refers to the authors or editors of Ezra-Nehemiah as narrators plural to acknowledge collaborative authorship. The special nature of Ezra-Nehemiah may be partially explained by approximately 600 verses of ostensive sources and less than 90 verses of editorial framing.[8] The heavy use of sources such as lists, letters, imperial edicts, a work report, written communal vows, and first-person narratives, in part, accounts for shifts between Hebrew and Aramaic more than once and numerous shifts between third- and first-person grammatical forms. The book reads as though the narrators elected to tell the story by literary artifacts with minimal editorial intervention. All of this bears on the kinds of scriptural interpretation housed in Ezra-Nehemiah.

In broad terms, the use of scriptural traditions in Ezra-Nehemiah can be grouped into four classes: narrative typology, deduced covenantal identity, intercessory interpretation, and legal exegesis. First, the account of the return in Ezra 1 seems to be shaped according to the exodus. In addition, Nehemiah's reflections on the list of originally returning exiles infuses this event with quasi-typological function within Neh 7–8.

Second, the recurring struggles of the returned exiles center on the identity of the restoration assembly. The most notable examples are several mass divorces of wrongful spouses in sensational attempts to get right with God (Ezra 10; Neh 9:2; 13:1–3; cf. 13:23–29). The exegetical bases for these mass divorces include interpretive blends mostly of legal contexts of Torah. If one side of restoration identity stems from excluding some others based on scriptural interpretation, the other side of assembly identity includes welcoming a different set of others into the assembly also based on scriptural interpretation (Ezra 6:21; Neh 10:28[29]).

Third, the several longer prayers housed in Ezra-Nehemiah each feature profuse scriptural interpretation. The specific concerns and scriptural allusion donor contexts differ in the prayers in Ezra 9, Neh 1, and 9. These three prayers each turn to Scripture with a collective confession angle. Scriptural narratives play a critical role in all three of these long prayers.

---

5. See Japhet, "Supposed Common Authorship," 330–71.
6. For detailed discussion of this issue, see Schnittjer, "Bad Ending," 36–38.
7. See Bird, *1 Esdras*, 9–10; Japhet, "1 Esdras," 194.
8. See Schnittjer, "Bad Ending," 36, n. 11.

Fourth, Ezra-Nehemiah features legal exegesis in several places. In addition to brief interpretive interventions with legal texts like Ezra 3:4, a lengthy community vow exegetically works through a series of legal instructions (Neh 10). The series of interpretive legal enhancements in the vow play a central role in the narrative as a whole. When Nehemiah tours Jerusalem in his second term as governor, he discovers that the people have broken every part of their exceptional vow (13:4–31). The vow along with the explicit failure to fulfill it underlines the stalled restoration. Ezra-Nehemiah begins with Yahweh faithfully accomplishing his word and ends with the people in full revolt against their own interpretive commitment to scriptural instruction. The familiar habitual rebellion of Israel makes it seem like the exile and return never happened.

The legal standards of Torah continue to apply to the people of the restoration as covenant standards even after the exile. But the legal standards of Torah no longer function as criminal law. Nehemiah fully expects Yahwistic Judeans to honor the Sabbath, but he does not seek capital punishment for Sabbath violations. This shift in legal standards from criminal law to religious standards does not stem from the rise of New Testament ideology (see note on Neh 13:15, 17–18). Many centuries before the coming of Messiah, legal standards of Torah already begin to operate as informing religious standards of the covenantal people. The shift concurs with the fall of the Davidic kingdom. The legal standards of Torah remain in force for compliance by the devout even though they no longer function as civil law. The shift in the operation of Torah's legal standards pivots on the shift from theocratic rule to life in the empire. This advancement of revelation within the Old Testament itself has not been adequately appreciated when determining the relationship of the Old and New Testaments within the Christian Bible.

In sum, scriptural interpretation enjoys a central role in Ezra-Nehemiah. The different kinds of scriptural exegesis require close attention to their own dynamics. The use of scriptural traditions in working out the covenantal identity of the restoration assembly and the legal exegesis of the people comprise the two most challenging sorts of scriptural interpretation in Ezra-Nehemiah. Attention to donor contexts, the narrative framing of the receptor context, and the rhetorical function of the citations themselves go a long way toward interpreting Ezra-Nehemiah's use of scriptural traditions.

The incremental advancement of revelation by scriptural exegesis includes mechanisms to reveal the depth of the problem of the returned exiles. The exile and restoration did not work. Yahweh would need to bring about redemption some other way.

Overt Marking of Citations in Ezra-Nehemiah

The student new to Old Testament studies may wish to skip this section and return at a later time as needed.

Ezra-Nehemiah explicitly marks Scripture citations in several places. The use of "as it is written" (כַּכָּתוּב) to refer to instructions creates challenges since the citations themselves are not direct verbatim quotations of Torah. Many cited contexts seem to make adjustments in the application of the instructions known from Torah (see list in Table EN2).

As part of his argument that Ezra's law book is different from the Pentateuch, Shaver says "as it is written" refers to direct quotation and cannot refer to interpretation or paraphrase.[9] By contrast, Spawn examines the function of "as it is written" and other citation formulas in nonlegal and legal materials in the entire Hebrew Scriptures and finds consistent, albeit varied, syntactical structures.[10] For the present purposes, Spawn's full syntactical typology of exegetical citation formulas needs to be set aside. Attention here needs to be limited to a couple of elements that apply to the citations in Ezra-Nehemiah.

Spawn claims that every use of "as it is written" serves as a somewhat formal exegetical device. The citation formulas distinguish legal discourse referents by immediate proximity to the citation formulas themselves versus interpretations slightly more distant from citation formulas. According to Spawn, allusion to the legal referent is always immediately adjacent to "as it is written" with exegetical elements further away.[11] Exegetical citations featuring "found written" in Ezra-Nehemiah govern relative clause(s) beginning with "that."[12] Table EN1 presents Spawn's findings for exegetical citation formulas in Ezra-Nehemiah in an oversimplified format for the present purpose.

According to Spawn, the results of his studies demonstrate that legal exegesis citation formulas refer to pentateuchal contexts, in contrast to Shaver who, says Spawn, has not correctly identified the referents of the citation formulas.[13] Spawn claims that legal exegesis had stable, even precise, citation conventions in the postexilic period. He does not see the citation formulas as introducing direct quotations, but allusions.

Most of the examples of citation formulas in Table EN1 have some verbal correspondence to the suggested parallels in Torah (Ezra 3:4; Neh 8:14, 15; 10:34, 36[35, 37]; 13:1). The exceptions are Ezra 3:2, which is said to refer to several texts, and 6:18, which is a special case since Jerusalem was not captured until the time of David. In all of these cases Spawn spells out the syntactical elements of these legal citations.

By way of contrast, Fishbane regards the citation formula as referring to the larger context.[14] Williamson challenges Fishbane's view and explains in more general terms that the legal citation formula "as it is written" refers to the immediately contiguous phrase.[15] At issue, then, is first, distinguishing the scriptural allusion itself from exegetical intervention (so Spawn and Williamson versus Fishbane), and second, distinguishing between adjacent scriptural allusion only versus the context introduced by a citation formula as direct quotation (so Williamson and Spawn versus Shaver).

---

9. See Shaver, *Torah*, 9–10.
10. See Spawn, *"As It Is Written"*, 249–50.
11. See Spawn, "Sources," 939.
12. E.g., "It was found written . . . that . . . and that" (מצא כָּתוּב . . . אֲשֶׁר . . . וַאֲשֶׁר).
13. Spawn, *"As It Is Written"*, 255.
14. See Fishbane, *Biblical Interpretation*, 107–11, et passim.
15. See Williamson, "History," 28.

TABLE EN1: EXEGETICAL CITATION FORMULAS IN EZRA-NEHEMIAH‡

bold	citation formula with "as, according to," i.e., "as it is written," "according to the pronouncement"
italics	exegetical legal referent governed by citation formula with "as, according to"
underlining	citation formula "found written"
broken underlining	exegetical legal referent governed by citation formula with "found written"
non-grayed-out BH/Bibl. Aram.	bold/italics/underlined text, and only relative particle of broken underlined text

Ezra 3:2 And they built the altar of the God of Israel *to offer up burnt offerings on it*, **according to what is written** in the Torah of Moses the man of God.	וַיִּבְנוּ אֶת־מִזְבַּח אֱלֹהֵי יִשְׂרָאֵל **לְהַעֲלוֹת עָלָיו עֹלוֹת כַּכָּתוּב** בְּתוֹרַת מֹשֶׁה אִישׁ־הָאֱלֹהִים	broad paraphrastic allusion to Deut 27:6 and related texts
3:4 *And they observed the Festival of Tabernacles* **as it is written**, with *burnt offerings day by day by number* **according to the pronouncement** of each day upon its day.	**וַיַּעֲשׂוּ אֶת־חַג הַסֻּכּוֹת כַּכָּתוּב וְעֹלַת יוֹם בְּיוֹם בְּמִסְפָּר כְּמִשְׁפַּט** דְּבַר־יוֹם בְּיוֹמוֹ	first citation formula alludes to Num 29:12–38 and Deut 16:13–15; second alludes to Num 29:12–38 (7x)
6:18 And they established the priests by their divisions and the Levites by their sections for the work of God *in Jerusalem*, **as it is written** in the book of Moses	וַהֲקִימוּ כָהֲנַיָּא בִּפְלֻגָּתְהוֹן וְלֵוָיֵא בְּמַחְלְקָתְהוֹן עַל־עֲבִידַת **בִּירוּשְׁלֶם כִּכְתָב** סְפַר אֱלָהָא דִּי מֹשֶׁה	citation formula governs allusion to Deut 12:13–14 (cf. 12:5, 18; 31:11)
Neh 8:14 And they found it written in the Torah, which Yahweh had commanded by the hand of Moses, that (אֲשֶׁר) the people of Israel should live in booths during the festival of the seventh month [15] and that (אֲשֶׁר) they should announce and proclaim in all their towns and in Jerusalem, saying, "Go out to the hills and bring branches of olive, wild olive, myrtle, palm, and other leafy trees *to make booths*," **as it is written**.	**וַיִּמְצְאוּ כָּתוּב** בַּתּוֹרָה אֲשֶׁר צִוָּה יהוה בְּיַד־מֹשֶׁה **אֲשֶׁר** יֵשְׁבוּ בְנֵי־יִשְׂרָאֵל בַּסֻּכּוֹת בֶּחָג בַּחֹדֶשׁ הַשְּׁבִיעִי׃ **וַאֲשֶׁר** יַשְׁמִיעוּ וְיַעֲבִירוּ קוֹל בְּכָל־עָרֵיהֶם וּבִירוּשָׁלִַם לֵאמֹר צְאוּ הָהָר וְהָבִיאוּ עֲלֵי־זַיִת וַעֲלֵי־עֵץ שֶׁמֶן וַעֲלֵי הֲדַס וַעֲלֵי תְמָרִים וַעֲלֵי עֵץ עָבֹת **לַעֲשֹׂת סֻכֹּת כַּכָּתוּב׃**	first citation formula governs two exegetical relative clauses, the one of which alludes to Lev 23:42 and the other to 23:40; second citation formula governs exegetical allusion to Lev 23:42
10:34[35] We have cast lots among the priests, the Levites, and the people, for the wood offering, to bring it into the house of our God, by ancestral houses, at appointed times, year by year, *to burn on the altar of Yahweh our God*, **as it is written** in the Torah.	וְהַגּוֹרָלוֹת הִפַּלְנוּ עַל־קֻרְבַּן הָעֵצִים הַכֹּהֲנִים הַלְוִיִּם וְהָעָם לְהָבִיא לְבֵית אֱלֹהֵינוּ לְבֵית־אֲבֹתֵינוּ לְעִתִּים מְזֻמָּנִים שָׁנָה בְשָׁנָה **לְבַעֵר עַל־מִזְבַּח יהוה אֱלֹהֵינוּ כַּכָּתוּב** בַּתּוֹרָה	citation formula governs to infinitive clause allusion to Lev 6:8–13[1–6]
10:36[37] *The firstborn of our sons and of our livestock*, **as it is written** in the Torah, and the firstborn of our cattle and of our flocks, to bring to the house of our God, to the priests who minister in the house of our God.	**וְאֶת־בְּכֹרוֹת בָּנֵינוּ וּבְהֶמְתֵּינוּ כַּכָּתוּב** בַּתּוֹרָה וְאֶת־בְּכוֹרֵי בְקָרֵינוּ וְצֹאנֵינוּ לְהָבִיא לְבֵית אֱלֹהֵינוּ לַכֹּהֲנִים הַמְשָׁרְתִים בְּבֵית אֱלֹהֵינוּ	citation formula governs preceding phrase which alludes to Num 18:15, 17
13:1 On that day the scroll of Moses was read in the ears of the people. And was found written in it that no Ammonite or Moabite should ever enter the assembly of God.	בַּיּוֹם הַהוּא נִקְרָא בְּסֵפֶר מֹשֶׁה בְּאָזְנֵי הָעָם **וְנִמְצָא כָּתוּב** בּוֹ **אֲשֶׁר** לֹא־יָבוֹא עַמֹּנִי וּמֹאָבִי בִּקְהַל הָאֱלֹהִים עַד־עוֹלָם	citation formula governs relative clause paraphrase of Deut 23:3–6[4–7]

‡ Scripture in table lit. The table summarizes graphically Spawn *"As It Is Written"*, 99–101, 102–3, 105, 107–8, 118, 120; see Spawn for further detail.

Relative to Ezra-Nehemiah, Williamson's view of citation formulas offers the clearest outcomes of the view he and Spawn espouse: only the word or phrase immediately adjacent to the citation formula is denoted by the citation formula, and citation formulas distinguish between cited texts and interpretations.[16]

Based on the preceding summary, several adjustments and complaints need to be registered. One, the use of "like, as, according to" (כְּ) is the major element in "*as* it is written" (כַּכָּתוּב), signaling agreement, likeness, or accord.[17] In Ezra 10:3, Shekeniah refers to the application of Ezra's interpretive blend of 9:11–12 to the dissolution of the marriages in question as "*according to* Torah" (כַּתּוֹרָה). Spawn sees this as the author's way of smearing Shekaniah with "shoddy" exegesis.[18] Spawn's reading goes against the sense of the text. Ezra himself affirms and enforces Shekaniah's exegetical application (10:10–11; cf. v. 3), and the author regards Ezra as a Torah expert (7:6, 10). Japhet concludes: "When Shecaniah describes these procedures as 'according to the Torah,' he does not have in mind the literal wording of the Torah but *the interpretation of its precepts*."[19]

The citation formula "as it is written" may not signal quotation per se but "congruence" with the authoritative tradition.[20] In a similar vein, Williamson notes that the relative marker "that" (אֲשֶׁר) in "found written *that*" in Neh 8:14 and 13:1 causes the citation to function in an indirect manner.[21] Acknowledgement that "as, according to" and "that" function as literary signals of interpretive citation and/or indirect discourse helps make sense of the way citation formulas actually work. The nature of many of the citation formulas signifies *agreement* or *accord* between interpretive intervention and the cited scriptural tradition itself.

In sum of this point, the sense of "as" in "*as* it is written" and related citation formulas connotes agreement or accord with scriptural tradition, including interpretive intervention, and not necessarily verbatim quotation or even direct verbal parallel.

Two, the debate on citation formulas described above seems to have things somewhat turned around. The real issue of citation formulas turns on the canonical consciousness or authority of the overtly cited Torah contexts. Citation formulas do not distinguish between direct quotation, interpretive paraphrase, and loose interpretive allusion. The citation formula "and I found written in it" (וָאֶמְצָא כָּתוּב בּוֹ) in Neh 7:5 introduces a source that, for Nehemiah, is nonscriptural. The representations of divine will by literary conventions of direct discourse in Ezra 9:11 ("Which you commanded by the hand of your servants the prophets, saying [לֵאמֹר]") and in Neh 1:8 ("The word that you commanded by Moses your servant, saying [לֵאמֹר]") (both in prayers) each introduce loose interpretive paraphrases of scriptural legal contexts. That is, citation formulas of various kinds do not of themselves

16. See ibid., 28, 29.
17. See *IBHS* §11.2.9a, b; *GBHS* §4.1.9 a, b; Williams §§255, 257; Joüon §133g; GKC §118s.
18. See Spawn, *"As It Is Written"*, 222, 223, 227, 235.
19. Japhet, "What May Be Learned," 559, emphasis mine.
20. See Grätz "Second Temple," 274. Contra Collins, "Use of Torah," 47.
21. See Williamson, "History," 30.

indicate intentional distinction between direct verbatim quotation, paraphrase, and interpretive allusion. Instead, citation formulas indicate self-consciousness of the authority of the cited sources. The point of marked versus unmarked uses of scriptural traditions in Ezra-Nehemiah relates to explicitly introducing divine authority into cited contexts.

Three, many unmarked uses of legal exegesis function virtually the same as marked uses. A good example may be the unmarked allusions to Torah in the solemn oath of the people (Neh 10:30, 31, 32–33, 35[31, 32, 33–34, 36]) side by side with two marked citations (10:34, 36[35, 37]), all of which work in the same way. Marking allusion or quotation by citation formulas is not determinative of the nature, kind, or degree of exegetical phenomena.

In sum, much confusion regarding the citation formula has come from superimposing modern and/or foreign expectations instead of inductively evaluating how citation formulas function in relation to donor contexts. The use of citation formulas to mark verbatim and loose quotations, paraphrases, or interpretations of Scripture indicates the authority of the cited context. The use of "as" in "*as* it is written" and the use of "that" in "found written *that*," and the like, point to an overt acknowledgement of accord or agreement between donor context and interpretive allusion.

Torah in Ezra-Nehemiah

The student new to Old Testament studies may want to skip this section and return later as needed.

The identity of Torah in Ezra-Nehemiah is sharply contested.[22] Proposals include: The Pentateuch (traditional view), and also Wellhausen says, "there is no doubt that the law of Ezra was the whole Pentateuch" and regards Ezra as editor not author of the Pentateuch;[23] select legal parts of the Pentateuch, especially priestly or Deuteronomic collections;[24] compilation of law collections of the Pentateuch;[25] a different version of the Pentateuch that includes other laws not in the traditional Pentateuch;[26] another law collection which is not the Pentateuch or part of it.[27] Theories of the identity of Torah pivot on evaluation of legal citations in Ezra-Nehemiah.

LeFebvre illustrates a commonplace problem of distorting the stated purpose of the use of scriptural legal traditions in Neh 10. In spite of initially noting that Neh 10 houses a covenant drawn up by the people, he repeatedly reverts to referring to it as Ezra's interpretation of Torah.[28] By failing to take account of the first-person plural frame narrative of the collective solemn oath (Neh 10:30, 31, 32, 34, 35, 36, 37, 39[31, 32, 33, 35, 36, 37,

22. This discussion is indebted to Blenkinsopp, *Ezra-Nehemiah*, 152–57; Williamson, *Ezra, Nehemiah*, xxxvii–xxxix; Duggan, *Covenant Renewal*, 19–21.

23. Wellhausen, *Prolegomena*, 408; and see 409, n. 1.

24. See Koch, "Ezra," 10–81; Klein, "Ezra-Nehemiah, Book of," *ABD* 2:737–38.

25. See von Rad, *Old Testament Theology*, 1:88–89.

26. See Shaver, *Torah*, 128. Also see critique in Ben Zvi, review, 718–20.

27. Houtman, "Ezra," 111; Pakkala, "Quotations," 214.

28. See LeFebvre, *Collections*, 114, 115, 116, 119, 121.

38, 40]; cf. Table EN16), LeFebvre misconstrues the purpose of the solemn oath and, thus, how it uses Torah. The solemn oath of the people does not pretend to either cite Torah verbatim or offer a literal interpretation of it. The people commit themselves to surpass Torah regulations. They vow to obedience above Torah standards (see Table EN17). Only ignoring the first-person plural series of promises and reading against the sense of the solemn oath in Neh 10 can offer support to some of the theories listed above. Attention to the text itself eliminates many strained interpretations of how the restoration community used Torah (see note on Neh 10:30–39[31–40]).

The study of Ezra-Nehemiah's use of Torah in the present work has detected allusion to all of the major legal collections of Torah, freely blending them together.[29] This finding corresponds with the blended use of Deuteronomistic and priestly legal traditions in Chronicles.[30] Stated positively, the evidence in Ezra-Nehemiah points toward something like the Torah as we know it rather than any of the alternative scenarios. Based on an analysis of Neh 9, Japhet comes to the same conclusion: "The author of the prayer was working with the complete text of the Pentateuch on his desk."[31]

Identifying the kinds of Torah exegesis, broadly speaking, appearing in Ezra-Nehemiah can help with difficult contexts. Clines developed a typology of kinds of legal exegesis inductively based upon the solemn oath in Neh 10. The approach here reduces Clines's five types to three since these categories only have a general function and every case must be settled individually.[32] Kinds of legal exegesis:

Type x: Creation of supplemental prescription to facilitate an existing law or new command extrapolated from an existing law.
Type y: Revision and/or adjustments to existing law or its supplemental prescription.
Type z: Integration of potentially competing interpretations of prescriptions.

Clines goes on to make several deductions about pentateuchal law based on this typology: pentateuchal law is a relatively closed system but open to reapplication; pentateuchal laws may need supplemental instructions in order to work in new contexts; pentateuchal law is essentially harmonious with apparent tensions typically solved by addition rather than compromise.[33] To these should be added that legal exegesis in Ezra-Nehemiah sometimes accords with prophetic preaching and historical precedents of Israel attested in scriptural narratives.

The kinds of legal interpretations in Neh 10 are broad enough to assist with understanding the function of other uses of scriptural legal traditions in Ezra-Nehemiah

29. See esp. notes on Ezra 3:4; 9:1–2, 11–12; 10:10–11; Neh 5:2, 4, 7, 8, 11; 8:14–16; 10:30–39[31–40]; 13:1–3.
30. See Knoppers and Harvey, "Pentateuch," 134; also see Bautch, "Holy Seed," 536.
31. Japhet, "What May Be Learned," 552.
32. See Clines, "Nehemiah 10," 112–13.
33. This has been paraphrased from ibid., 113. See evaluation of Clines's proposals in Williamson, "History," 27–31.

and elsewhere in the Hebrew Scriptures. Table EN2 collates broad generalizations of numerous examples of legal exegesis to illustrate the sorts of legal exegesis common in Ezra-Nehemiah.

TABLE EN2: BROAD FUNCTION OF REPRESENTATIVE LEGAL EXEGESIS IN EZRA-NEHEMIAH

	Legal allusion(s)	Type(s)
Ezra 3:2, renewed altar for offerings	Exod 29:38–42; cf. 27:1–8; Num 28:3–8	y
3:4, Tabernacles and burnt offerings by number	Lev 23:37; Num 29:12–38; Deut 16:13–15	z
6:18, worship personnel by division serve in Jerusalem	Deut 12:14–15; cf. 1 Chr 23–24	x and z
9:1–2,[a] prohibition against intermarriage with others	Exod 34:15–16; Deut 7:3–4; 23:3–8[4–9]; cf. Exod 19:6; Deut 7:6	y and z
9:11–12,[a] pollution via detestable practice because of intermarriages	Exod 34:15–16; Deut 7:3–4; 23:3–8[4–9]; cf. Lev 18:26, 27	y and z
10:10–11,[a] separation from others by dissolving marriages	Lev 5:15	x and y
Neh 1:8–9, rationale for return	Lev 26:33, 40; Deut 30:2–4; Deut 12:5, 11, 14, 26; 1 Kgs 8:29–30	z
8:1–3, pre-Tabernacle Torah reading	Deut 31:10–13	y
8:10, Tabernacles as a time of joy and sharing	Deut 16:14, 15	x
8:14–15, make and dwell in temporary booths using available branches	Lev 23:40–43	x and y
10:30[31], prohibition against intermarriage with others	Exod 34:15–16; Deut 7:3–4; cf. Lev 18:26, 27	y and z
10:31a[32a], prohibition against purchases on the Sabbath	Exod 34:21; 35:3; cf. Amos 8:5; Jer 17:19–27	x and z
10:31b[32b], cancel debts in seventh year	Deut 15:1–3; cf. Neh 5:1–13	z
10:32[33], annual one-third shekel for service of house of God	Exod 30:11–16; cf. 38:25	y
10:34[35], rotating responsibility to supply wood to sustain perpetual worship fire	Lev 6:12–13[5–6]	x
10:35–36[36–37], bring first fruits from crops and trees, and firstborn compensation	Num 18:11–20; Exod 23:19; 34:26; Num 28:26; Ezek 44:30	y and z
13:1–3, separation from others by dissolving marriages	Deut 23:3–6[4–7]	y

[a] The applied legal exegesis of Ezra 9:1–2, 11–12; 10:2–3, 10–11 is an interrelated set which should be read together (see notes ad loc. and Figure EN12 for connections).

In sum, Ezra-Nehemiah freely moves between the legal standards in all parts of Torah. The evidence suggests that the Torah known and used in Ezra-Nehemiah is virtually identical to the canonical Torah. Ezra-Nehemiah incrementally advances revelation by means of several strategies of legal exegesis, including supplemental legal standards, revision of legal standards of Torah, and integration of potential tensions between interpretations of Torah's legal standards.

USE OF SCRIPTURE

Ezra 1:1–3a//2 Chr 36:22–23~Jer 25:11; 29:10+Isa 44:28; 45:1 (B) (edict of Cyrus). On Ezra 1:1–3a itself see note on 2 Chr 36:22–23—they are treated comparatively. On Ezra 1:1–4 and the other versions of Cyrus's edict in Ezra-Nehemiah see note on Ezra 6:3–5.

1:5~Hag 1:14 (B) (stir up the spirit). The narratives of the restoration speak of divine stirring of Cyrus's spirit to motivate an administrative ruling to rebuild the temple (Ezra 1:1). The divine stirring of a ruler's heart to motivate sacred building projects reflects imagery found in ancient monuments.[34] The biblical prophets and narrators use this traditional motif to reveal Yahweh's otherwise invisible role in rebuilding his temple.

The restoration narratives mention Jeremiah in reference to the seventy years but use the language of "stirring up" (עור) the spirit by means of an interpretive allusion from Isa 45:13 (1:1//2 Chron 36:22; cf. Jer 51:11). Haggai 1:14 shares the same language with Isa 45:13 and applies it to Zerubbabel, Joshua, and the restoration community. The narrators of Ezra-Nehemiah make an interpretative allusion to Hag 1:14 and apply it to the divine initiation of their mission. The interpretive intervention retrojects the divine stirring of rebooting the mission by Haggai's preaching in 520 BCE and applies it to the original response to Cyrus's edict in 539 (bold signifies verbal parallels):

> Then Zerubbabel son of Shealtiel, Joshua son of Jozadak, the high priest, and the whole remnant of the people obeyed the voice of Yahweh their God and the message of the prophet Haggai, because Yahweh their God had sent him. And the people feared Yahweh. Then Haggai, Yahweh's messenger, gave this message of Yahweh to the people: "I am with you," declares Yahweh. So Yahweh **stirred up [עור] the spirit of** Zerubbabel son of Shealtiel, governor of Judah, and **the spirit of** Joshua son of Jozadak, the high priest, and **the spirit of the whole** remnant of the people.

34. The foundational cylinders of the Borsippa ziggurat called E-ur-me-imin-anki ("House that controls the seven *Mes* of heaven and underworld") records Nebuchadnezzar's declaration: "My great lord Marduk *stirred my heart* to rebuild it" (from George, "A Stele of Nebuchadnezzar II," 169, emphasis mine).

They came and began to work on the house of Yahweh Almighty, their God. (Hag 1:12–14)

Then the family heads of Judah and Benjamin, and the priests and Levites—**everyone whose spirit** God **had stirred** [עור]—prepared to go up and build the house of Yahweh in Jerusalem. (Ezra 1:5†)

Though these events stand apart by almost two decades, Yahweh uses the preaching of his prophet to again stir spirits to complete the project he began by fulfilling the word of the prophets through the emperor's edict. The restoration narrators explicitly note the combination of the imperial directives and prophetic preaching to decisively activate the rebuilding of the Second Temple (5:1–2; 6:4). This makes explicit the divine role in bringing about the return and restoration.

1:6~1:4 (A)+Exod 12:35, 36 (C) (contributions from neighbors). The edict of Cyrus calls upon people who live with the remnant to give to them for the temple (Ezra 1:4). The narrators repeat this language to show the effect of the edict (1:6). The addition of the term "vessels of" or "articles of" does not come from the edict but hints at the imagery of the exodus when the Israelites asked the Egyptians for "articles of silver and gold" (Exod 12:35; cf. Ps 105:37). In spite of the subtlety, the narrators appear to be typologically shaping the return after the exodus (emphases signify verbal parallels).

The Israelites did as Moses instructed and asked the Egyptians for **articles of silver and gold** and for clothing. Yahweh had made the Egyptians favorably disposed toward the people, and they gave them what they asked for; so they plundered the Egyptians. (Exod 12:35–36)

[Cyrus] And in any locality where survivors may now be living, the people are to provide them *with silver and gold, with goods and livestock,* and with *freewill offerings* for the temple of God in Jerusalem. (Ezra 1:4)

All their neighbors assisted them *with* **articles of *silver and gold***, *with goods and livestock*, and with valuable gifts, in addition to all *the freewill offerings.* (1:6)

The possible typological shaping of the return narrative offers one of the places to suspect a trace of the prophets. Since by definition traces lack evidence (see Glossary), it is impossible to prove. Isaiah's expectation for return as a second exodus offers good reason for the narrators to shape the story by the original exodus, without citing the prophetic contexts that make the suggestion (e.g., Isa 11:15–16).

1:7, 11*~Jer 27:22* (B) (vessels of temple returned) (* see temple vessels network).

The seizing of the temple vessels by the Neo-Babylonians and their return appears frequently in the Hebrew Bible.[35] The vessels were pillaged in three stages, with some destroyed (see 2 Chr 36:7, 10, 18, and note ad loc.). The narrators of Ezra-Nehemiah confirm Cyrus's role in releasing the temple vessels to be sent back to Jerusalem, including a partial inventory list embedded in the narrative (Ezra 1:9–11). Ezra 1:7, 11 interpretively alludes to Jer 27:22 especially by using the term "brought up" in its causal stem. The return of the temple vessels aligns with the series of prophetic fulfillments in Ezra 1 designed to testify to Yahweh's faithfulness in the restoration. Also note a shared phrase with Dan 1 (emphases signify verbal parallels):

> "**The articles** that are left in **the house of Yahweh**. . . . 'They will be taken to Babylon and there they will remain until the day I come for them,' declares Yahweh. 'Then I **will bring** them **up** and restore them to this place.'" (Jer 27:21b, 22†)

> And the Lord delivered Jehoiakim king of Judah into his hand, along with some of the articles from the temple of God. These he carried off to the temple of his god in Babylonia and put in the treasure *house of his god*. (Dan 1:2)

> Moreover, King Cyrus brought out **the articles** belonging to **the house of Yahweh**, which Nebuchadnezzar had carried away from Jerusalem and had placed in *the house of his god*. . . . Sheshbazzar **brought up** all these along with the exiles when they came up from Babylon to Jerusalem. (Ezra 1:7, 11b†)

2:1–3:1/~/Neh 7:6–8:1 (list of returning exiles). The synoptic lists of returning exiles in Ezra 2 and Neh 7 are related one to the other and very likely not from a common source since they share material that includes the narrative immediately after the lists themselves (see below). The nature of the details deflects attempts to explain direction of dependence.[36]

Lists in Scripture include special challenges relative to textual issues. Ancient scribal conventions sometimes include copyists' efforts to both copy and improve. The scribal "improvements" lead to many variants in the case of lists of numbers and names in a non-standardized spelling environment. A close comparison of the synoptic lists in Ezra 2 and Neh 7 has been housed in Table EN3 to serve as the basis for discussion of interpretive issues. Bold text in the table signifies variations in Hebrew and underlining signify shifts in arrangement.

---

35. On temple vessels, see 2 Kgs 20:17; 24:13; 25:13–15; Isa 39:6; 52:11–12; Jer 27:16, 21–22; 28:3, 6; 52:18–20; Dan 1:2; 5:2–4, 23; Ezra 1:7–11; 2 Chr 36:7, 10, 18; cf. Bar 1:8, 9. Also see temple vessels network.

36. But see Williamson's argument that Ezra 2 derives from Nehemiah 7 as part of composing Ezra 1–6 as a prologue for the rest of the book ("Composition," 1–30).

TABLE EN3: VERSE BY VERSE COMPARISON OF THE LIST IN EZRA 2 AND NEHEMIAH 7[‡]

Ezra[a]	**Nehemiah**[b]
[2:1] **Now** these are the people of the province who came from the captivity of the exiles whom Nebuchadnezzar king of Babylon had taken captive to Babylon; they returned to Jerusalem and Judah, each to their own town,	[7:6] These are the people of the province who came from the captivity of the exiles whom Nebuchadnezzar king of Babylon had taken captive to Babylon; they returned to Jerusalem and **to** Judah, each to their own town.
[2] **who** came with Zerubbabel, Jeshua, Nehemiah, **Seraiah, Reelaiah**, Mordecai, Bilshan, **Mispar**, Bigvai, **Rehum**, and Baanah. The number of the people of Israel:	[7] **They** came with Zerubbabel, Jeshua, Nehemiah, **Azariah, Raamiah**, **Nahamani,** Mordecai, Bilshan, **Mispereth**, Bigvai, **Nehum**, and Baanah. The number of the people of Israel:
[3] descendants of Parosh 2,172;	[8] descendants of Parosh 2,172;
[4] descendants of Shephatiah 372;	[9] descendants of Shephatiah 372;
[5] descendants of Arah **775**;	[10] descendants of Arah **652**;
[6] descendants of Pahath-moab (through descendants of Jeshua, Joab) 2,81**2**;	[11] descendants of Pahath-moab (through descendants of Jeshua **and** Joab) 2,81**8**;
[7] descendants of Elam 1,254;	[12] descendants of Elam 1,254;
[8] descendants of Zattu **945**;	[13] descendants of Zattu **845**;
[9] descendants of Zaccai 760;	[14] descendants of Zaccai 760;
[10] descendants of **Bani** 64**2**;	[15] descendants of **Binnui** 64**8**;
[11] descendants of Bebai 62**3**;	[16] descendants of Bebai 62**8**;
[12] descendants of Azgad **1,2**22;	[17] descendants of Azgad **3,3**22;
[13] descendants of Adonikam 66**6**;	[18] descendants of Adonikam 66**7**;
[14] descendants of Bigvai 2,0**56**;	[19] descendants of Bigvai 2,0**67**;
[15] descendants of Adin **454**;	[20] descendants of Adin **655**;
[16] descendants of Ater (through Hezekiah) 98;	[21] descendants of Ater (through Hezekiah) 98;
	[22] descendants of Hashum 328; [//Ezra 2:19]
[17] descendants of Bezai 32**3**;	[23] descendants of Bezai 32**4**;
[18] descendants of **Jorah** 112;	[24] descendants of **Hariph** 112;
[19] descendants of Hashum 223;	
[20] descendants of **Gibbar** 95;	[25] descendants of **Gibeon** 95;
[21] **descendants** of Beth-lehem **123**;	[26] **people** of Beth-lehem **and** Netophah **188**
[22] **people** of Netophah **56**;	
[23] people of Anathoth 128;	[27] people of Anathoth 128;
[24] **descendants** of Azmaveth 42;	[28] **people** of **Beth-**Azmaveth 42;
[25] **descendants** of Kiriath Jearim, Chephirah, and Beeroth 743;	[29] **people** of Kiriath Jearim, Chephirah, and Beeroth 743;

(cont.)

Ezra[a]	**Nehemiah**[b]
26 **descendants** of Ramah and Geba 621;	30 **people** of Ramah and Geba 621;
27 people of Michmas 122;	31 people of Michmas 122;
28 people of Beth-el and Ai **2**23;	32 people of Beth-el and Ai **1**23;
29 **descendants** of Nebo 52;	33 **people** of **the other** Nebo 52;
30 **descendants of Magbish 156**;	
31 descendants of the other Elam 1,254;	34 descendants of the other Elam 1,254;
32 descendants of Harim 320;	35 descendants of Harim 320;
33 descendants of Lod, Hadid, and Ono 725;	
34 descendants of Jericho 345;	36 descendants of Jericho 345;
	37 descendants of Lod, Hadid, and Ono 721; {//Ezra 2:33}
35 descendants of Senaah 3,**6**30.	38 descendants of Senaah 3,**9**30.
36 The priests: the descendants of Jedaiah (through the house of Jeshua) 973;	39 The priests: the descendants of Jedaiah (through the house of Jeshua) 973;
37 descendants of Immer 1,052;	40 descendants of Immer 1,052;
38 descendants of Pashhur 1,247;	41 descendants of Pashhur 1,247;
39 descendants of Harim 1,017.	42 descendants of Harim 1,017.
40 The Levites: the descendants of Jeshua **and** Kadmiel (through the descendants of **Hodaviah**) 74.	43 The Levites: the descendants of Jeshua (**through** Kadmiel through the descendants of **Hodevah**) 74.
41 The singers: the descendants of Asaph 1**2**8.	44 The singers: the descendants of Asaph 1**4**8.
42 The **descendants of the** gatekeepers: of Shallum, of Ater, of Talmon, of Akkub, of Hatita, and of Shobai, in all 13**9**.	45 The gatekeepers: of Shallum, of Ater, of Talmon, of Akkub, of Hatita, and of Shobai, in all 13**8**.
43 The Nethinim: the descendants of Ziha, Hasupha, Tabbaoth,	46 The Nethinim: the descendants of Ziha, Hasupha, Tabbaoth,
44 descendants of Keros, descendants of **Siaha**, descendants of Padon,	47 descendants of Keros, descendants of **Sia**, descendants of Padon,
45 descendants of Lebanah, descendants of **Hagabah, descendants of Akkub**,	48 descendants of Lebanah, descendants of **Hagabah**,
46 **descendants of Hagab**, descendants of Shalmai, descendants of Hanan,	descendants of Salmai, 49 descendants of Hanan,
47 descendants of Giddel, descendants of Gahar, descendants of Reaiah,	descendants of Giddel, descendants of Gahar, 50 descendants of Reaiah,
48 descendants of Rezin, descendants of Nekoda, descendants of Gazzam,	descendants of Rezin, descendants of Nekoda, 51 descendants of Gazzam,
49 descendants of Uzza, descendants of Paseah, descendants of Besai,	descendants of Uzza, descendants of Paseah, 52 descendants of Besai,

Ezra[a]	**Nehemiah**[b]
50 **descendants of Asnah**, descendants of Meunim, descendants of **Nephisim**,	descendants of Meunim, descendants of **Nephushesim**,
51 descendants of Bakbuk, descendants of Hakupha, descendants of Harhur,	53 descendants of Bakbuk, descendants of Hakupha, descendants of Harhur,
52 descendants of **Bazluth**, descendants of Mehida, descendants of Harsha,	54 descendants of **Bazlith**, descendants of Mehida, descendants of Harsha,
53 descendants of Barkos, descendants of Sisera, descendants of Temah,	55 descendants of Barkos, descendants of Sisera, descendants of Temah,
54 descendants of Neziah, and descendants of Hatipha.	56 descendants of Neziah, and descendants of Hatipha.
55 The descendants of the servants of Solomon: descendants of Sotai, descendants of **Hassophereth**, descendants of **Peruda**,	57 The descendants of the servants of Solomon: descendants of Sotai, descendants of **Sophereth**, descendants of **Perida**,
56 descendants of Jaalah, descendants of Darkon, descendants of Giddel,	58 descendants of Jaalah, descendants of Darkon, descendants of Giddel,
57 descendants of Shephatiah, descendants of Hattil, descendants of Pochereth-hazzebaim, and descendants of **Ami**.	59 descendants of Shephatiah, descendants of Hattil, descendants of Pochereth-hazzebaim, and descendants of **Amon**.
58 All the Nethinim and the descendants of the servants of Solomon 392.	60 All the Nethinim and the descendants of the servants of Solomon 392.
59 These came up from Tel-melah, Tel-harsha, Cherub, **Addan**, Immer, but they could not tell whether the house of their ancestors or their offspring were from Israel:	61 These came up from Tel-melah, Tel-harsha, Cherub, **Addon, and** Immer, but they could not tell whether the house of their ancestors or their offspring were from Israel:
60 the descendants of Delaiah, descendants of Tobiah, and descendants of Nekoda 6**5**2.	62 the descendants of Delaiah, descendants of Tobiah, and descendants of Nekoda 6**4**2.
61 Also, of **the descendants of** the priests: the descendants of Hobaiah, descendants of Hakkoz, and descendants of Barzillai (who had married one of the daughters of Barzillai the Gileadite, and was called by their name).	63 Also, of the priests: the descendants of Hobaiah, descendants of Hakkoz, and descendants of Barzillai (who had married one of the daughters of Barzillai the Gileadite, and was called by their name).
62 These searched for their document, "the register," but **they** were not found, so they were ritually defiled and excluded from the priesthood.	64 These searched for their document, "the register," but **it** was not found, so they were ritually defiled and excluded from the priesthood.
63 The governor told them that they were not allowed to eat of the most holy food, until consulting of **a** priest by the Urim and Thummim.	65 The governor told them that they were not allowed to eat of the most holy food, until consulting of **the** priest by the Urim and Thummim.
64 The whole assembly together was 42,360,	66 The whole assembly together was 42,360,

(cont.)

Ezra[a]	**Nehemiah**[b]
65 besides their male and female slaves, of whom there were 7,337, and they had 2**00** male and female singers,	67 besides their male and female slaves, of whom there were 7,337, and they had 2**45** male and female singers,
66 736 horses, 245 mules,	(68a [LXX] **736 horses, 245 mules,**)
67 435 camels **of theirs**, and 6,720 donkeys.	68b[69a] 435 camels, and 6,720 donkeys.
	70[69b] **Now some of the heads of the families gave to the work. The governor gave to the treasury 1,000 darics of gold, 50 bowls, 530 priestly garments.**
68 When some of the heads of the families **came to the house of Yahweh in Jerusalem, they made freewill offerings for the house of God, to set it up on its site.**	71[70] And some of the heads of the families
69 **As they were able** they gave to the treasury of the work **61**,000 darics of gold, **5,000** minas of silver,	gave to the treasury of the work **20**,000 darics of gold and **2,200** minas of silver.
and **100** priestly garments.	72[71] And what the rest of the people gave was 20,000 darics of gold, 2,000 minas of silver, and **67** priestly garments.
70 The priests, the Levites, <u>and some of the people, and the singers, and the gatekeepers,</u>[c] and the Nethinim settled **in their towns**, and all Israel in their towns.	73[72] The priests and the Levites <u>and the gatekeepers</u>, and the singers, <u>and some of the people,</u>[c] and the Nethinim, and all Israel settled in their towns.

‡ Table uses lit. translation. Underlining marks shifts in sequence. Bold type marks all differences except plene spelling, masoretic accents, and additional conjunctive *vavs* within numbers. The comparisons in the table are based on *BHS/BHQ* along with Bendavid, *Parallels*, 165–67 [Hebrew], as well as checking the work with the convenient listings in Yamauchi, "Ezra and Nehemiah," 509–13; Steinmann, *Ezra and Nehemiah*, 489–97. Since the numbers in Ezra 2//Neh 7 are written as words in Hebrew, some of the differences are more like minor spelling variants rather than numerical issues per se (e.g., Hebrew text of Ezra 2:6, 10//Neh 7:11, 15).

[a] Like all biblical lists **Ezra 2** includes many textual issues of which only a few of the more important ones can be listed here: **2:2** On Seriah (שְׂרָיָה) here see n. b on Neh 7:7 below. Many favor inserting Nahamani between Reelaiah and Mordechai as in the counterpart list in Neh 7:7 and supported by 1 Esdras (e.g., *BHS*; Williamson, *Ezra, Nehemiah*, 24, n. 2b, 32; Ryle, *Ezra and Nehemiah*, 18). However, 1 Esd 5 is derivative and the name is not included in LXX (though it appears in LXX variants, which are likely later attempts to harmonize text, see *BHS*; *BHQ*). Interpreters prefer the addition here because it brings the number to twelve, which helps typological associations with the twelve tribes of Israel (Ryle, 18; Williamson, 32). Clever suggestions, ancient and modern, to improve typological correspondence should be avoided. MT is preferred. **2:25** Read as Kiriath Jearim (קִרְיַת יְעָרִים) with LXX, ancient versions, and Neh 7:29 (see Tov, *Textual Criticism*, 221; *BHS/BHQ* apparatus). **2:46** Read Shalmai (שַׁלְמַי) with *qere*, LXX, ancient versions, and Neh 7:48 (see *BHS/BHQ* apparatus). **2:50** Read Meunim (מְעוּנִים) with *qere*, masoretic MSS, LXX, and Neh 7:52 (see Marcus, *BHQ*, 41*; Knoppers, "City," 322, n. 59). **2:69** 61,000 follows lit. "six myriads and a thousand" (שֵׁשׁ־רִבֹּאות וָאֶלֶף) (GKC §97g). The Persian loanword "drachma" (BH דַּרְכְּמוֹן) seems to function synonymously with "drachma" (Bibl. Aram. אֲדַרְכֹּן) in Ezra 8:27 and refers to minted coins that are unknown before the Persian empire (*CLLBH* 93, n. b; Schniedewind, *Social History*, 158).

[b] **Nehemiah 7** includes many textual issues of which only a few of the more important can be listed here: **7:7** For an orthographic explanation of variant between Seriah (שְׂרָיָה) in Ezra 2:2 and Neh 11:11 and Azariah (עֲזַרְיָה) here, see Tov, *Textual Criticism*, 232. **7:15** Here Bennui (so also LXX and Vulg.) but Ezra 2:10 reads Bani (so also Syriac) (see *BHS*, *BHQ*) (cf. Ezra 10:29, 34–36 with 10:38–42). **7:67** Whereas Ezra 2:65 reads "200 male and female singers" and 2:66 says "245 mules" Neh 7:67, 68 reads "245 male and female singers" but does not list horses and mules. The "45" may have been shifted based on "200" (מָאתָיִם) in Ezra 2:65, 66 (so Marcus, *BHQ*, 47*). Since LXX of Neh 7:68 includes "736 horses, 245 mules," this should be supplied (missing from MT).

[c] The transposition of "some of the people" and "gatekeepers" in Ezra 2:70//Neh 7:73[72] could be a case of Seidel's theory.

The approach here will examine more mechanical difficulties first and then briefly discuss exegetical issues. One of the more difficult issues in comparing the synoptic lists of Ezra 2 and Neh 7 pivots on the different numbers. English Bible readers need to remember that the numbers in these lists are not numerals but come in the form of the Hebrew words for the numbers spelled out. For example, Ezra 2:11 says "six hundred and twenty-three" (שֵׁשׁ מֵאוֹת עֶשְׂרִים וּשְׁלֹשָׁה) and Neh 7:16 says "six hundred and twenty-eight" (שֵׁשׁ מֵאוֹת עֶשְׂרִים וּשְׁמֹנָה) which is the difference between two different words, or actually two consonants between the words for "three" (שלשה) and "eight" (שמנה). Thus, some differences are actually spelling, not numerical, differences. In any case, the subtotals in Ezra 2 do not match the grand total, and neither of these match their counterparts in Neh 7 (see Table EN4).

TABLE EN4: SUMMARY OF NUMBERING OF RETURNED REMNANT IN EZRA 2‡

Subtotals in Ezra 2		**Totals in text**	
laity	24,144		
priests	4,289		
Levites, singers, gatekeepers	341	total in Ezra 2:64	42,360
Nethinim and Solomon's slaves	392		
unregistered	652		
sum of sub-totals	29,818		
Sum of subtotals in Neh 7	31,089	total in Neh 7:66	42,360

‡ Table based on Ryle, *Ezra and Nehemiah*, 19–20; Steinmann, *Ezra and Nehemiah*, 175.

To "solve" this discrepancy, a plus is added in the apocryphal version, "All those of Israel, twelve or more years of age" (1 Esd 5:41). Against this unlikely ancient repair, modern interpreters suggest that the grand total may have included women, since they are included in the "assembly" elsewhere (Ezra 10:1; Neh 8:2; 10:28[29]).[37] Another suggestion is that the list does not refer to a single caravan but rather all who returned between 538 and 520, thus also explaining the list's mention of hometowns of Judah.[38] Many other unlikely suggestions from silence do not need to be listed here. The more likely suggestions are also the simplest: scribal corruptions or that the sublists only cover part of the return.[39] Without evidence there is little need to adjudicate the guesswork.

Another nagging issue comes from the same names sometimes appearing in lists but separated by nearly a century (Ezra 2, 538 BCE; 10:18–44, BCE 458; Neh 10, BCE 445). This issue turns out to be more apparent than real. Many of the names refer to ancestral heads of clans—something like modern family names. This accounts for their relationship to geographical names associated with the families and their continued use over a long period of time. Tables EN5 and EN6 collate names appearing in Ezra 2//Neh 7 and reappearing in other lists in Ezra-Nehemiah.

37. See Williamson, *Ezra, Nehemiah*, 37–38.
38. See Williamson, "Ezra and Nehemiah," 59.
39. See Ryle, *Ezra and Nehemiah*, 20, 33–34.

TABLE EN5: LAITY FAMILIES OF ORIGINAL RETURN APPEARING IN OTHER LISTS‡

Family	Original return	Ezra's return	Apostasy marriages	Covenant of recommitment
Parosh	Ezra 2:3//Neh 7:8	Ezra 8:3	Ezra 10:25	Neh 10:14[15]
Shephatiah	2:4//7:9	8:8		
Arah	2:5//7:10			
Pahath-moab	2:6//7:11	8:4	10:30	10:14[15]
Elam	2:7//7:12	8:7	10:26	10:14[15]
Zattu	2:8//7:13	(8:5)[a]	10:27	10:14[15]
Zaccai	2:9//7:14			
Bani	2:10//7:15	(8:10)[a]	10:29, 34–42	10:14[15]
Bebai	2:11//7:16	8:11	10:28	10:15[16]
Azgad	2:12//7:17	8:12		10:15[16]
Adonikam	2:13//7:18	8:13		
Bigvai	2:14//7:19	8:14		10:16[17]
Adin	2:15//7:20	8:6		10:16[17]
Ater/Hezekiah	2:16//7:21			10:17[18]
Bezai	2:17//7:23			10:18[19]
Jorah/Hariph	2:18//7:24			10:19[20]
Hashum	2:19//7:22		10:33	10:18[19]
Gibbar	2:20			

‡ The table is adapted from Steinmann, *Ezra and Nehemiah*, 170.

[a] Zattu is not in Ezra 8:5 MT but appears in LXX; Bani is not in Ezra 8:10 MT but appears in LXX.

TABLE EN6: POTENTIAL OVERLAP BETWEEN PRIESTS OF ORIGINAL RETURN WITH OTHER PRIESTLY LISTS‡

Ezra 2:36–39//Neh 7:39–42	**Ezra 10:18–22**	**Neh 12:1–7**	**1 Chr 24:7–18**
Those who came up from captivity with Zerubbabel and Jeshua	Priestly families of those who repented from apostasy marriages	Priests and the Levites who came up with Zerubbabel son of Shealtiel, and Jeshua	Twenty-four priestly divisions
Jedaiah (through the house of Jeshua) descendants of **Immer** [possible alternate name of Amariah (Ryle, 294)] descendants of **Pashhur** [Pashhur listed with Malchijah in Neh 11:12; 1 Chr 9:12 (Ryle, 26; cf. Jer 21:1; 38:1)] descendants of **Harim**	Jeshua son of Jozadak and his brothers: Maaseiah, Eliezer, Jarib, and Gedaliah. Of descendants of **Immer**: Hanani and Zebadiah. Of descendants of **Harim**: Elijah, Shemaiah, Jehiel, and Uzziah. Of the descendants of Pashhur: Elioenai, Maaseiah, Ishmael, Nethanel, Jozabad, and Elasah	Seraiah, Jeremiah, Ezra, **Amariah**, Malluch, Hattush, Shecaniah, **Rehum** [=Harim (Ryle, 294)], Meremoth, Iddo, Ginnethoi, Abijah, Mijamin, Maadiah, Bilgah, Shemaiah, Joiarib, **Jedaiah**, Sallu, Amok, Hilkiah, **Jedaiah**	Jehoiarib, **Jedaiah**, **Harim**, Seorim, **Malchijah**, Mijamin, Hakkoz, Abijah, Jeshua, Shecaniah, Eliashib, Jakim, Huppah, Jeshebeab, Bilgah, **Immer**, Hezir, Happizzez, Pethahiah, Jehezkel, Jachin, Gamul, Delaiah, Maaziah

‡ The table is adapted from Steinmann, *Ezra and Nehemiah*, 170. Parallels are signified by bold.

Having briefly noted some of the mechanical challenges of the synoptic lists in Ezra 2 and Neh 7, attention needs to briefly turn to the narrative function of Ezra 2 and Neh 7. The approach here relates to contrasting respective functions of the same list housed in two contexts.

The primary purpose of the list in Ezra 2, shared with Neh 7, is a testimony to the literal fulfillment of the promise of return. The list goes so far as to bracket out those who could not prove their lineage (Ezra 2:59//Neh 7:61). The narrators use the list to demonstrate an actual continuity between the citizens of the First and Second Commonwealths. Elsewhere Ezra-Nehemiah bases standing in the assembly on covenant fidelity (Ezra 6:21; 9–10; Neh 9:2; 10:28[29]). In this way Ezra-Nehemiah emphasizes both literal fulfillment and identity of Israel based on covenantal faithfulness.

Part of the purpose of the list distinct to Ezra 2 relates to the geographical distribution of the returned exiles in Judah. The register begins in Jerusalem (Ezra 2:3–20) and moves outward (2:21–35).[40] Map EN7 graphically demonstrates the pattern.

MAP EN7: REGISTER BEGINS WITH JERUSALEM (EZRA 2:3–20) AND MOVES OUTWARD (2:21–35)

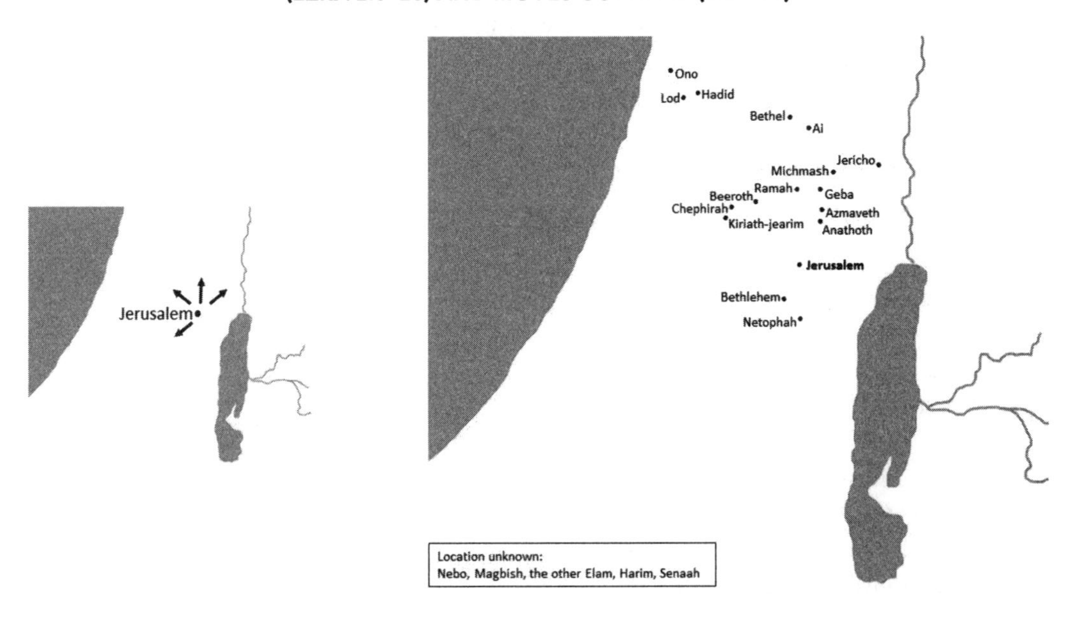

The leading purpose of the same list in Neh 7 is evidenced by Nehemiah's first-person remarks about it. Nehemiah comments about the way God put in his mind to make some lists in his own day when he found the list of the originally returning exiles (Neh 7:5). Whether or not some of the lists in Neh 11–12 come from his decision to make lists

40. See Ryle, *Ezra and Nehemiah*, 21.

cannot be deduced from the evidence. More importantly, in Neh 7–8 these interpretive comments effectively create a typological pattern of the first returning exiles *within* the book of Ezra-Nehemiah itself.

Elsewhere in Scripture, acts of God serve as figural patterns of later events. For example, the exodus gets repackaged figurally to load theological connotations on the "new exodus" in Isaiah (see note on Isa 11:15–16). Nehemiah's comments on the ninety-three-year-old list set up a type/antitype comparison within the very same scroll (7:5). Just as the list in Ezra 2 precedes a Tabernacles celebration in Ezra 3, so too Nehemiah's reuse of the same list precedes a Tabernacles celebration in Neh 8. Nehemiah's comments cause a self-conscious figural connection between two different restoration generations, namely, the first returning exiles and those who rebuilt the walls of Jerusalem. The overall effect amounts to a continuity of the works of God across the entire disparate events of restoration.

The list in Ezra 2 closes out the return subtly modeled on the exodus. This fulfillment of the type may be called an actualization. Nehemiah's reflections on the list of retuning exiles activate the typologically generative character of the first returning exiles themselves (7:5). In this way the return from exile represented in the list of Ezra 2//Neh 7 becomes both actualization and new type. The natural symbolic function of God's work in the first return triggers these figural relations with no need for heavy-handed editorialization (see Table EN8).

TABLE EN8: INITIAL RETURN FROM CAPTIVITY AS ACTUALIZATION AND TYPE

First Commonwealth		initial return		second temple assembly
• exodus • tabernacles in the wilderness	←	• list of returning exiles of the First Commonwealth (Ezra 2:1–70)	←	• reading the list of the first returning exiles (Neh 7:5–73[72])
• Solomon's temple dedicated in the seventh month at tabernacles		• restoration of worship in the seventh month at tabernacles (3:1–6)		• studying Torah in the seventh month preceding tabernacles (8:1–18)
[type]		**[actualization and type]**		**[actualization]**

In addition to the synoptic lists themselves, both contexts retain an identical narrative segue from the lists. Ezra 2:70–3:1 leads into an account of a celebration of Tabernacles in 538 BCE during the days of Zerubbabel and Joshua. Nehemiah 7:73[72]–8:1 leads into another celebration of Tabernacles ninety-three years later in 445 during the days of Nehemiah and Ezra. Stated differently, the narrators use the list and its narrative off-ramp to lead into two different accounts of Tabernacles at two different times.[41]

41. The parallels running past the ends of the two lists to introduce the subsequent narratives demonstrate clearly, says Williamson, that one must be dependent on the other ("Composition," 2). He lists four reasons why he thinks Ezra 2 is based on Neh 7: (1) "the seventh month" of Neh 7:73[72] is integral to the context of 8:2 since it also lists the same month, while the date in Ezra 3:1 "is left completely in the air"; (2) the differences between Ezra 2:68–69 are more easily

This shared narrative function accounts for significant continuity within a difficult book (see Table EN9).

TABLE EN9: ENDINGS OF PARALLEL LISTS OF EZRA 2 AND NEHEMIAH 7 LEADING INTO NARRATIVES‡

Ezra	Nehemiah
[70] The priests, the Levites, <u>and some of the people</u>, and the singers, <u>and the gatekeepers</u>, and the Nethinim settled **in their towns**, and all Israel in their towns.	[73[72]] The priests and the Levites <u>and the gatekeepers</u>, and the singers, <u>and some of the people</u>, and the Nethinim, and all Israel settled in their towns.
	When the seventh month arrived, and the Israelites were in the towns,
[3:1] When the seventh month arrived, and the Israelites were in the towns, the people gathered as one person **in Jerusalem**.	[8:1] **all** the people gathered as one person **in the plaza before the Water Gate. And they told Ezra the scribe to bring the book of Torah of Moses which Yahweh had commanded Israel.**

‡ Bold signifies differences, and underlining signifies rearranged materials (Seidel's theory).

3:4~Lev 23:37+Num 29:18+Deut 16:13 (B) (observing Tabernacles as it is written). The narrators explicitly mark a composite verbal quotation joining together elements from the Tabernacles regulations from Leviticus, Numbers, and Deuteronomy (Ezra 3:4). The legal blend integrates elements from three Torah contexts on Tabernacles (see Table EN2). Notice how the narrators bring these elements together (emphases signify verbal parallels):[42]

> These are Yahweh's appointed festivals, which you are to proclaim as sacred assemblies for bringing food offerings to Yahweh—**the burnt offerings** and grain offerings, sacrifices and drink offerings **prescribed for each day.** (Lev 23:37†)

> Offer . . . *according to the number specified.* (Num 29:18, 21, 24, 27, 30, 33, 37)

explained as a summary of Neh 7:71–73[70–72]; (3) the date in Ezra 3:1 is an anomaly in Ezra 1–6 with (almost) all others stating the year of a king; and (4) the language of Ezra 2:68 matches the language of 1:5 and 3:8 suggesting that this verse was accidentally omitted in the transmission of the parallel in Neh 7 (see 2–3). While all of these reasons are tenuous (the second being the most viable), the first and third reasons (which overlap) overreach. Williamson admits that the year is not included in the date formula of Ezra 6:19 because, he says, it is clear, but this is parallel to a fact he denies in 3:1 (3). Against Williamson, the situations between Ezra 6:19 and 3:1 are entirely analogous. Just as 6:19–22 narrates a feast (Passover) presumably in the same year, so too 3:4–5 narrates a worship celebration (Tabernacles) also presumably in the same year. Williamson's opposite treatment of these two analogous contexts illustrates where evidence ends and personal preferences informed by interpretive sensibilities begin. Williamson's larger argument for the redaction of Ezra 1–6 does well to explain the shape of the materials in spite of not adequately explaining Ezra 3:1//Neh 7:73b–8:1a. The approach here focuses narrowly on the exegetical-narrative function of these intentionally parallel narrative segues.

42. On the conflation of these legal texts in Ezra 3:4, see Berman, "Legal Blend," 106.

> Celebrate the Festival of Tabernacles for seven days after you have gathered the produce of your threshing floor and your winepress. (Deut 16:13)

> Then as it is written, they celebrated the Festival of Tabernacles *according to the number specified* of **burnt offerings prescribed for each day.** (Ezra 3:4 lit.)

By freely drawing together elements from several widely separated contexts, this case of exegetical allusion suggests the Torah of the restoration narrative is virtually identical to received version known today. The narrative significance of celebrating Tabernacles with respect to setting up the altar includes Solomon's dedication of the first temple at Tabernacles (1 Kgs 8:2; 2 Chr 5:3; see Table EN8).

6:3–5/~/1:2–4/~/5:13–15 (three versions of Cyrus's edict). Three versions of the edict of Cyrus appear in Ezra-Nehemiah (Ezra 1:2–4; 5:13–15; 6:3–5). Determining whether these synoptic versions relate directly or indirectly requires attention to numerous details. The vast majority of Ezra-Nehemiah is made up of source materials with light editorial connections (see Hermeneutical Profile of the Use of Scripture in Ezra-Nehemiah). Within such an environment, the narrators apparently felt no need to harmonize the details or wording of three versions of Cyrus's edict. The differences reflect the natural adaptations of the versions for their contexts. This aligns with the manifold synoptic contexts housed in Deuteronomy, Chronicles, the Gospels, and elsewhere in Scripture.[43] The versions of Cyrus's edict function on much the same kind of analogy (see Table EN10).

The first-person singular version of the edict of Cyrus in Ezra 1:2–4 emphasizes Yahweh's sovereignty and encourages his people to return and rebuild the temple. He also invites people near the returning remnant to give generously to this mission. The return of the temple vessels by Cyrus's authority does not get included in the decree but as narrative, along with an inventory (Ezra 1:9–11).

In an official letter, Tattenai, Shethar-Bozenai, and their associates report what Zerubbabel and his associates told them (5:13–15). The multiple framings amount to a paraphrase of a paraphrase, which reduces the edict itself to building the house of God (5:3). The letter also mentions the temple vessels but as an associated event, not part of the edict itself (5:14–15).

Darius produces a formal decree based upon the research of his scribes. The decree casts the edict of Cyrus as an utterance of his will ("Let the house be built") without first-person singular comments on his motives as in Ezra 1:2 (6:3). Darius's version emphasizes the dimensions of the temple, perhaps to avoid an overrun by those footing the costs (cf. 6:4, 8).[44]

---

43. On synoptic contexts, see Hermeneutical Profile of the Use of Torah in Deuteronomy (including a list in footnotes therein) and Hermeneutical Profile of the Use of Scripture in Chronicles.

44. See Blenkinsopp, *Ezra-Nehemiah*, 125.

TABLE EN10: THREE VERSIONS OF THE EDICT OF CYRUS IN EZRA-NEHEMIAH[‡]

As told by narrators of Ezra-Nehemiah in a narrative in 1:2–4	As told by Zerubbabel, Jeshua, and company in report by Tattenai, Shethar-Bozenai, and their associates in 5:13–15	As told by Darius, presumably *via* a scribe and/or other courtiers, in a formal decree in 6:3–5
[1:2] Thus says Cyrus king **of Persia**: "**Yahweh**, the God **of heaven, has given me all the kingdoms of the earth**, and he has charged me to build him a house at Jerusalem in Judah.	[5:13] However, in the first year of Cyrus the king **of Babylon**, Cyrus the king made a decree to build this house of God.	[6:3] In the first year of Cyrus the king, Cyrus the king gave a decree regarding the house of God in Jerusalem, "Let the house be built **a place for sacrificing sacrifices and foundations be laid height 60 cubits breadth 60 cubits 6:4 three courses of rolling stone, and one layer of timber, and the expenses will be given from the house of the king.**
[1:3] **Any of those among you who are of his people, may their God be with them, may they go up to Jerusalem in Judah, and may they rebuild the house of Yahweh, the God of Israel, he is the God who is in Jerusalem.**	—	—
[1:4] **And may all of the remnant in every place they sojourn, be assisted by the people of their place with silver and gold, with goods and with animals, along with freewill offerings for the house of God in Jerusalem."**	—	—
([1:7] King Cyrus brought out the vessels of the house of Yahweh that Nebuchadnezzar had brought out from Jerusalem and had placed in the house of his gods.)	([5:14] And also, the gold and silver vessels of the house of God, which Nebuchadnezzar took out of the temple in Jerusalem and brought them into the temple of Babylon, Cyrus the king took these out from the temple of Babylon, and they gave to Sheshbazzar his name, whom he appointed governor.)	[6:5] and also the vessels of the house of God, the gold and silver ones, which Nebuchadnezzar took from the temple in Jerusalem and to the temple in Babylon,
([1:8] **Cyrus king of Persia had them brought out by the hand of Mithredath the treasurer,** and he counted them out to Sheshbazzar the prince of Judah.)	([5:15] And he said to him, "These vessels carry; go and bring them down to the temple in Jerusalem, and let the house of God be built on its place.")	let them be returned and go back to the temple in Jerusalem, to its place, and you set down in the house of God."[a]

‡ The table collates parallel elements in a general sense. Bold signifies distinct thematic elements relative to the counterparts, and underlining signifies shared but modified elements. Translation in table lit. Remember Ezra 1:1–4:7 is Hebrew and 4:8–6:18 is Aramaic.

a Ezra 6:5 MT says "which Nebuchadnezzar took from the temple in Jerusalem, and *he* brought (וְהֵיבֵל) to Babylon" (NIV†), while 4QEzra/4Q117 adjusts and says "and *they* brought to Babylon" (והיבלו) (*BQS* 3:777). A similar grammatical number issue appears in 6:1 of 4QEzra/4Q117.

The decree of Darius includes the return of the temple vessels as part of the edict of Cyrus itself, again framed as an utterance of his will, "let them be returned" (6:5).[45]

Ancients decide how to voice narratives and embedded sources.[46] The Scriptures contain examples of revoicing from direct discourse to narration (e.g., 2 Kgs 22:4; 2 Chr 34:9). The case of the versions of the edict of Cyrus in Ezra-Nehemiah may fit these general conventions, but each of the three versions gets framed differently. While Darius's decree could cite the edict of Cyrus verbatim from the archives of Ecbatana, the detailed dimensions of the shrine suggest a paraphrase crafted for the specific situation (Ezra 6:2, 3).[47]

In sum, the three versions of the edict of Cyrus and its associated narratives in Ezra agree in terms of the emperor's commission of rebuilding the temple and returning the vessels. The nature of the case makes it possible that all three paraphrase and frame the edict in the light of their narrative purposes. Whether one or two depend on each other or if one, two, or three depend on common or related sources cannot be decided based on available evidence. The function of the three versions of the edict of Cyrus in Ezra-Nehemiah closely relates to the narrators' repeated emphasis on Yahweh's providential acts for the return, rebuilding of the temple, and restoration.

6:18~Deut 12:13–14 (C)+1 Chr 23–26 (C) (worship personnel serve at Jerusalem). The narrators mark the service of the priests and Levites by their divisions at Jerusalem as in accordance with the scroll of Moses (Ezra 6:18). The marking creates a challenge since David had set up the priestly and Levitical divisions when he prepared for Solomon to build the temple (1 Chr 23–26; cf. 2 Chr 35:2–5). Spawn argues that the citation formula here only refers to the phrase closest to it, namely, "the service of God at Jerusalem."[48] While not entirely satisfying, this may work here in light of the frequent interpretive blending of scriptural contexts in Ezra-Nehemiah (see Marking in Hermeneutical Profile of the Use of Scripture in Ezra-Nehemiah). Notice that the underlined phrase signifies a potential broad allusion to David's appointments appearing in 1 Chr 23–26, bold signifies the shared preposition with Deuteronomy, italics signify potential paraphrase, and broken underlying signifies a citation formula:

> Be careful not to sacrifice your burnt offerings anywhere you please. Offer them only **at** *the place Yahweh will choose* in one of your tribes, and there observe everything I command you. (Deut 12:13–14)

45. Ezra 6:3 uses "let it be built" (בנה Hithpeel impf.) with a jussive sense, and 6:5 "be returned" (תוב Haphel impf.) passive (Jerusalmi, *Aramaic Sections*, 31) in context also carries the jussive sense "let them be returned."

46. See Aristotle, *Poetics*, 1458b, 18–21, as discussed in Hermeneutical Profile of the Use of Torah in Deuteronomy and Hermeneutical Profile of the Use of Scripture in Chronicles.

47. On several interpretive difficulties of the dimensions in Ezra 6:3, see Ryle, *Ezra & Nehemiah*, 76.

48. Spawn, "Sources," 940.

And they installed the priests in their divisions and the Levites in their groups for the service of God **at** *Jerusalem*, according to what is written in the Book of Moses. (Ezra 6:18)

8:3–14/~/2:3–20//Neh 7:8–24 (list of laity families). See Table EN5 in note on Ezra 2.

9:1–2*~Exod 34:11/Deut 7:1*+Deut 23:3–8*[4–9] (B) (mingling the holy seed) (* see assembly and devoting networks).

9:11–12~Lev 18:27 (C)+Deut 7:3* (B)+23:6*[7] (B) (pollution by intermarriage with the other) (* see assembly and devoting networks).[49]

10:10–11, 19~Lev 5:15 (B)+Exod 34:16*/Deut 7:3* (C) (reparation offering and mass divorce) (* see assembly and devoting networks). The several interrelated, scriptural interpretive blends in Ezra 9–10 need to be discussed together because within the narrative context they build upon one another. Upon reaching the last in the series, the interrelated exegetical logic can be traced back. The verbal and contextual parallels between Ezra 9:1–2 and Deut 7:1+23:3–8[4–9] offer strong evidence of intentional relationship with Torah as donor. The same can be said of the use of Deut 7:3+23:6[7] in Ezra 9:11–12. The allusion to the reparation offering of Lev 5:14–6:7[5:14–26] in Ezra 10:10–11, 19 is somewhat broader. Since within Torah as it stands, Deut 7:1–5 interprets the genetically related prohibition against intermarriage in Exod 34:11–16, it likely functions in the undercurrents of Ezra 9–10. The clue that Ezra has Deut 7 in mind rather than Exod 34 is his reference against intermarriage of both genders, made explicit in Deut 7:3 versus Exod 34:16, which only warns against wrong daughters-in-law (Ezra 9:12). At the same time, the leadership only mentions wrongful wives, which could indicate they have Exod 34:11–16 in mind (9:2). The close interpretive relationship between the prohibitions against intermarriage may mean that whichever is in focus retains its counterpart in the background. The expression "holy seed" in Ezra 9:2 may echo "holy people" in Deut 7:6 based on its proximity to the prohibition against intermarriage. The only other use of the exact expression "holy seed" appears in Isa 6:13 but with a different sense.

A large number of studies take for granted that Ezra is a racist and that the events of Ezra 9–10 end in misogynist mistreatment of women and children stemming from elitist, rigid sectarian religious ideology. While many modern studies agree that Ezra is a bad guy with bad theology and bad exegesis and that the narrative is about bad things, sharp disagreement and confusion surround many unresolved issues.[50] The limitations of the present study only allow interaction with issues directly related to the use of Scripture.

---

49. Bendavid also notes the verbal parallels between Ezra 9:12b//Deut 23:6[7] (*Parallels*, 194 [Hebrew]).

50. Against Ezra and/or the use of Scripture in Ezra 9–10, see Janzen, *Witch-hunts*, 44–46; Becking, "Continuity," 271; idem, "Identity," 33; Hays, "Silence," esp. 60, 67, 79; Allen and Laniak, *Ezra, Nehemiah, Esther*, 11; Smith-Christopher, "Mixed Marriage Crisis," 244. For more restrained, somewhat anachronistic inferences, see Blenkinsopp, "Development of Jewish Sectarianism," 394–95; Smith-Christopher, *Biblical Theology*, 160 (where he refers to Ezra as an "Amish elder").

Since the details get somewhat involved and the conclusions herein stand apart from the dominant current norms, it may help to summarize outcomes up front. First, the identity of the restoration assembly is primarily based on faith and secondarily based on physical descent. Only the criterion of faith comes up in Ezra 9:1–2, while Ezra 2 emphasizes genealogical identity. In Ezra 9–10 the divorces are symbols of repentance from covenantal infidelity in the form of apostasy marriages. The problematic otherness of the others is refusal to submit to covenantal standards, framed as detestable practices akin to those of traditional ancient peoples listed in Torah. Elsewhere in Ezra-Nehemiah the Yahwistic Judeans welcome others into the worshiping assembly (Ezra 6:21; Neh 10:28[29]). Remarkably, some of the included others who enter into the assembly themselves divorce excluded others (Neh 9:2), and they also make a vow not to seek intermarriage with excluded others (10:30[31]). In biblical shorthand, Israel signifies God's covenantal people, but not all Israel is Israel (Rom 9:6). In a similar way, throughout the Hebrew Bible not all Canaanites are Canaanites and not all Moabites are Moabites (see notes on Josh 6:17; Ruth 2:8).[51]

Second, Ezra 9–10 is not a success story but the beginning of the end of the narrative of the failure of the restoration.[52] The high points in the rebellion against God's will in Ezra-Nehemiah are seen in the pattern established by Ezra 9–10. The people collectively enact a series of mass divorces. The ineffectiveness of the sensational mass divorces shines a bright light on the people's hardened rebellion. They are no different than their ancestors. Having summarized the conclusions by way of preview, the evidence needs to be evaluated.

In **Ezra 9:1–2** the leadership approaches Ezra and explains the infidelity of the restoration assembly. Ezra himself tacitly agrees with the report as seen in his prayer. The leaders categorize the problem as an us-and-them scenario. They designate the other vaguely as "the peoples of the lands," which refers to anyone outside the returned exiles—enemies; foreign immigrants; the remnant of the Northern Kingdom of Israel who migrated to Judah; descendants of the former northern Israelite kingdom intermarried with foreigners forcibly migrated to the land by the Assyrians; and even Judeans of the First Commonwealth who were never exiled. The leaders refrain from designating the ethnicity or genealogical identity of the other. The open-ended term "peoples of the lands" naturally includes anyone not in the assembly of Yahwistic Judeans.[53] The leaders go on to explain the problem with the other.

The leaders use a simile based on combining no longer functioning names of "nations" from lists of others in scriptural prohibitions. The simile works by the standard term

51. See Schnittjer, *Torah Story*, 506–12. On the identity of Israel in Rom 9:6, see Bruno, Compton, and McFadden, *Biblical Theology*, 122–26.

52. See Schnittjer, "Bad Ending," 32–56.

53. So Shepherd, "Ezra," 40. On "people of the land" as a relative term, see Nicholson, "Meaning," 60–66. For a view that the term has a fixed meaning of landed aristocrats, see Fried, "The *'am hā'āreṣ*," 125–28; and against Fried's argument see Williamson, "Welcome Home," 116; Giffone, *"Sit at My Right Hand,"* 97–98. Competing views work with the same texts (Gen 23:7, 12–13; 42:6; Exod 5:5; Lev 4:27; 2 Kgs 11:14, 17, 18, 19, 20; 15:5; 16:15; 21:24; 25:3).

"like" or "as" to set up an analogy.[54] Notice the overlap between the prohibitions against intermarriage and the law of the assembly in the leadership's analogy (bold, italics, and underlining signify verbal parallels; broken underlining signifies similarities; and wavy underlining signifies a literary signal of simile):[55]

> Obey what I command you today. I will drive out before you the *Amorites*, *Canaanites*, *Hittites*, *Perizzites*, Hivites and *Jebusites*. Be careful not to make a treaty with those who live in the land where you are going, or they will be a snare among you.... And when you choose some of their daughters as wives for your sons and those daughters prostitute themselves to their gods, they will lead your sons to do the same. (Exod 34:11–12, 16)

> When Yahweh your God brings you into the land you are entering to possess and drives out before you many nations—the *Hittites*, Girgashites, *Amorites*, *Canaanites*, *Perizzites*, Hivites and *Jebusites*, seven nations larger and stronger than you.... Do not intermarry with them. Do not give your daughters to their sons or take their daughters for your sons.... For you are a people holy to Yahweh your God. (Deut 7:1, 3, 6a)

> No **Ammonite** or **Moabite** or any of their descendants may enter the assembly of Yahweh, not even in the tenth generation.... Do not despise an Edomite, for the Edomites are related to you. Do not despise an **Egyptian**, because you resided as foreigners in their country. The third generation of children born to them may enter the assembly of Yahweh. (23:3, 7–8[4, 8–9])

> After these things had been done, the leaders came to me and said, "The people of Israel, including the priests and the Levites, have not kept themselves separate from the peoples of the lands with their detestable practices, like those of the *Canaanites*, *Hittites*, *Perizzites*, *Jebusites*, **Ammonites**, **Moabites**, **Egyptians** and *Amorites*. [2] They have taken some of their daughters as wives for themselves and their sons, and have mingled the holy race with the peoples around them. And the leaders and officials have led the way in this unfaithfulness." (Ezra 9:1–2†)[56]

54. The preposition "like" or "as" (כְּ) is a literary signal of analogy or similitude not identity. "Like/as" serves to compare different elements one according to the other (GKC §118s; Joüon §133g).

55. For a comparison of all scriptural lists of nations of Canaan see Murawski, "'To Study the Law,'" 291.

56. *BHS* suggests emending Ezra 9:1 from "the Amorites" (וְהָאֱמֹרִי) as in MT, LXX, Vulg., Peshitta to "the Edomites" (וְהָאֱדֹמִי) with masoretic variants, Aquila (contra *BHQ*). The attractive element in this suggestion is internal evidence, namely, completing the quartet of peoples from the law of the assembly (Moabite, Ammonite, Egyptian, Edomite, see Deut 23:3–8[4–9]), which appears in the allusion of 1 Kgs 11:1. In spite of this advantage, the external evidence favors the MT. Meanwhile, the preposition "of" (לְ) is used at the head of the list to communicate a genitive sense to the entire string of nations, "from the peoples of the lands whose abhorrent practices are like those *of* the Canaanites, etc." (מֵעַמֵּי הָאֲרָצוֹת כְּתוֹעֲבֹתֵיהֶם לַכְּנַעֲנִי; cf. GKC §131n). LXX says "of" by putting Canaan in dative but then awkwardly lists the other nations in nominative, like several other lists of names elsewhere in Ezra-Nehemiah (Wooden, "Interlinearity," 134, also 119).

The problem spoken of by the leadership has nothing to do with the ethnicity or genealogical identity of the wrongful marital matches. The other participates in detestable practices *like* the ancient nations of Canaan. The detestable practices of the others generate the anxieties of the leaders. The term "detestable practices" denotes a wide array of immoral, unjust, and cultic misdeeds in Deuteronomy.[57] In Leviticus the detestable practices of the nations of Canaan pollute the personified land, which then vomits them out (Lev 18:24–30). Just as the term "detestable practices" refers to a broad range of misdeeds, so too the simile in Ezra 9:1 refers to such practices by three classes of others: nations of Canaan, permanently excluded others (Ammonites, Moabites), and others permitted in three generations (Egyptians). Although it may seem strange to include together the excluded and allowed others from the law of the assembly, the Deuteronomist's charge against Solomon's wrongful wives also begins with Egyptian, Moabite, Ammonite, and Edomite (1 Kgs 11:1; Deut 23:3, 7–8[4, 8–9]; cf. notes ad loc.).

Alternate viewpoints often begin with racial elements. The dominant view of late presumes the peoples of the lands are ethnically-racially-biologically-genealogically other.[58] Fried surveys several ancient cultures that forbade "interracial" marriages like descendants of Genghis Khan in China in the mid-fifth century BCE, and other cultures roughly contemporary with Ezra in traditional dating. She argues that like these roughly contemporary cultures, Ezra and the Jerusalem establishment ban intermarriage "in order to maintain power and authority and to prevent it from diffusing to other groups."[59] Reducing this event to a racist power grab misconstrues its function within the book of Ezra-Nehemiah.

The ethnic and genealogical views work from the listing of ancient nations in Ezra 9:1 and focus on the intermingling of the "holy seed" in 9:2. This line of interpretation also notes the importance of the genealogical record in Ezra 2. In the immediate context, the ethnic and genealogical interpretations need to be read against the sense of the text.[60] But the leaders do not name the ethnicities or races of the problematic others. They use an inherently flexible broad relative expression "peoples of the lands" in binary opposite to the restoration assembly—us versus other (Ezra 9:1). The leaders fill in the semantic space of the others with a simile relating to unspecified detestable practices. The detestable practices are the sort that can be inferred from the ancient people groups listed in the legal prohibitions against intermarriage and the law of the assembly (Deut 7:1, 3; 23:3, 7–8[4, 8–9]). The issue presented by the leaders in Ezra 9:1 is practices not ethnicity.

---

57. "Detestable practices" include, e.g., child sacrifice (Deut 12:31), consuming ritually impure animals (14:3), blemished sacrifices (17:1), cross-dressing (22:5), giving the earnings of prostitution to the temple (23:18[19]), and dishonest measures (25:16). See "תּוֹעֵבָה," II.2.c *HALOT* 2:1703.

58. See, e.g., Hayes, *Gentile Impurities*, 19–44; Hensel, "Ethnic Fiction," 137; Becking, "Identity," 31; Johnson, *Holy Seed*, 15, 20–24; Knoppers, "'Married Into Moab,'" 172; Carroll, "Myth," 83, 91; Klingbeil, "'Not So Happily Ever After,'" 51–53; Shepherd, "Ezra," 40–41.

59. Fried, Ezra, 371, and see 368–74.

60. Even the NRSV and ESV remove the simile from Ezra 9:1, reading against the sense of the text to infer the leaders make a racial complaint. The simile is retained in more literal renderings of this context, such as that of NIV and JPSB. KJV retains but softens the simile.

In the larger context the restoration assembly welcomes others who turn away from detestable practices and toward the Torah of Moses (Ezra 6:21; Neh 10:28[29]). The returning exiles even include the names of those who joined the return without valid genealogical records (Ezra 2:59–60). At the next mass divorce, some of those who take an oath to avoid wrongful marital matches, in that case to abstain from arranging wrongful marriages for their children, are themselves former others who turned in submission to Torah (Neh 9:2; 10:28, 30[29, 31]). This evidence points to covenantal faithfulness as the primary criterion for entry into the restoration assembly and genealogical identity as a secondary criterion. Yet the secondary criterion plays no part in the complaint of the leaders in Ezra 9:1–2.

The larger context, along with taking the leaders' simile in a straightforward manner, suggests the wrongful marriages are apostasy marriages. Persons among the priests, Levites, and laity of the restoration assembly have entered into marital covenants with others who have not and do not turn from detestable practices to covenantal faithfulness.

In sum, the leaders approach Ezra because of the widespread problem of apostasy marriages. They explain the problem using a simile that includes an interpretive blend of detestable practices like those of forbidden others in the Torah's prohibitions against intermarriage and the law of the assembly.

Ezra 9:11–12 appears within Ezra's prayer of confession shaped by Lev 26 (Ezra 9:5–15). Ezra's public prayer, along with his physical postures (torn garment, kneeling, weeping, throwing himself to the ground), indicate the assembled persons likely benefit by his exegetical confession to Yahweh. Though his prayer features numerous scriptural echoes, at its midpoint Ezra overtly marks commands that God gave through the prophets (9:11). Ezra proceeds to make an allusive interpretive blend of two commands in Deuteronomy—the law of the assembly and the prohibition against intermarriages (9:12; cf. Deut 7:3; 23:6[7]). The reference to Torah of Moses as from "the prophets" stands apart from the norm of referring to "Torah" in various other ways in Ezra-Nehemiah. Ezra also mentions the pollution of the land by its peoples, extending the verbal parallels with Lev 18:24–30 (represented below by Lev 18:27). In short, Ezra both affirms and reiterates the interpretive blend the leadership has made (Ezra 9:1–2, 11–12). Note the interpretive blending by Ezra (underlining, italics, and bold signify verbal parallels, and broken underlining signifies marking):

> For all these <u>detestable practices</u> were done by the people who lived in <u>the land</u> before you, and the <u>land</u> <u>became defiled.</u> (Lev 18:27)[61]

> Do not intermarry with them [nations of Canaan]. *Do not give your daughters to their sons or* take *their daughters for your sons.* (Deut 7:3)

61. Leviticus 18:27 uses a somewhat unique phrase "men of the land" (אַנְשֵׁי־הָאָרֶץ) versus "peoples of the lands" (עַמֵּי הָאֲרָצוֹת) in Ezra 9:11. Milgrom suggests the expression "men of the land" is used in order to avoid confusion with the phrase "people of the land," which refers to Israel in the priestly texts (*Leviticus 17–22*, 1581).

> **Do not seek a treaty of friendship with them** [Ammonite and Moabite] as long as you live to **forever.** (Deut 23:6†[7])

> [Ezra] But now, our God, what can we say after this? For we have forsaken the commands [11] you gave through your servants the prophets when you said: "The land you are entering to possess is a land polluted by the corruption of its peoples. By their detestable practices they have filled it with their defilement from one end to the other. [12] Therefore, *do not give your daughters* in marriage *to their sons or* take *their daughters for your sons.* **Do not seek a treaty of friendship with them** to **forever**, that you may be strong and eat the good things of the land and leave it to your children as an everlasting inheritance." (Ezra 9:10–12†)

The function of the paraphrastic interpretive blend in Ezra's prayer includes the risk the rebels have taken. The restoration stands in jeopardy by their ritually polluting the land after the same manner as their ancestors. Ezra's prayer also connects "defilement" with "guilt" (9:6, 13, 15). One of the persons listening to Ezra's prayer made an unprecedented applicational deduction. Shekaniah proposed a mass divorce (10:3). Ezra made everyone swear to do as Shekaniah said (10:5). These two elements set up the twofold solution: mass divorces of the wrongful spouses of the apostasy marriages and "guilt offering" for the assembly (10:19).

By way of comparison with Ezra's prayer, Paul and Timothy strenuously prohibit marriage to unbelievers for their largely gentile congregation (2 Cor 6:14–18). Unlike Shekaniah, Paul and Sosthenes suggest that believers in marriages with unbelievers need not divorce since God might use it as a witness to the gospel (1 Cor 7:12–14, 16).[62] Paul and Sosthenes advocate a passive role for the believing spouse while allowing divorce initiated by the unconverted spouse (7:15). Paul and Sosthenes make explicit that these teachings are suggestions rather than commands of Messiah (7:12). These teachings help identify prescriptive norms versus the descriptive narration within Ezra-Nehemiah.

Within the larger narrative, the mass divorce of Ezra 10 does not work. Twelve years later the people find themselves in need of another mass divorce to get right with God (Neh 9:2). If Neh 13:1–3 refers to a separate incident from these two, then there is yet another ineffective mass divorce. In any case, twelve years after the mass divorce of 9:2, Nehemiah discovers that apostasy marriages have taken over Jerusalem once again (13:23–29). The function of apostasy marriages and the series of ineffective mass divorces serves as the leading symbol of the restoration assembly's addiction to covenant-breaking. Shekaniah's idea of a mass divorce remains an enduring testimony to the restoration assembly's commitment to repent. It also puts their failure into sharp relief.

Ezra 10:10–11, 19 explains that the guilt or reparation offering accompanies the mass divorce. The guilt offering serves two basic purposes. In the case of wronging one's fellow,

62. See Saysell, *"According to the Law,"* 154–58.

the sacrifice accompanies restitution plus twenty percent and confession to receive God's forgiveness (Lev 5:14–6:7[5:14–26]). And, what seems to be going on in Ezra 10:19, the reparation offering along with repentance are required after unintentionally transgressing Yahweh's "holy things" (5:15) or unintentionally sinning against the commandments (5:17). A difficulty arises because this offering is not explicitly associated with wrongful marriages in Leviticus.

Since the reparation offering does not include instructions that directly link it to wrongful marriages, the connection that the restoration assembly has in mind needs to be uncovered from the context. Jacob Milgrom notes the risk of doom for the entire nation because of "infidelity" (מַעַל) against devoted things in the case of Achan (Josh 7:1).[63] In a similar manner Ezra connects the outcome of the people's "infidelity" to "guilt" (Ezra 10:10) and the threat that this poses to the restoration (9:6, 7, 13, 15).

The guilt offering may only apply to the priests, since it appears in Ezra 10:19 within the section devoted to the priests who participated in apostasy marriages (10:18–22). Since the priests uniquely bear the burden of holiness, then in this case they would need to give guilt offerings for their work in the sanctuary (Num 18:2, 5). Earlier Ezra had emphasized that the apostasy marriages cause ritual impurity (Ezra 9:11), but this would relate to the purification offering (Lev 5:2, 3), not the guilt offering (5:15, 17). If the laity also gave guilt offerings in Ezra 10:19, they must have considered their infidelity to desacralize their standing as a "holy seed" according to the leadership (Ezra 9:2).[64] Although the guilt offering applying only to the priests seems more likely, the context does not clearly spell out who gave them.

Having worked through the evidence of several interrelated exegetical allusions in Ezra 9–10, the apostasy marriage view argued here needs to be compared to the dominant genealogical purity view. These two views look at the exegetical basis of the guilt offering differently (10:19). Christine Hayes presents one of the most significant arguments for the genealogical purity view.

It is easy to agree with the main drift of Hayes's presentation of Torah standards on gentiles. According to Torah, gentiles are not inherently impure. Residing foreigners (גֵּרִים), among whom Hayes counts Rahab the Canaanite prostitute and her family, are required to participate within Israelite worship (Num 15:25–29).[65] According to Torah, Israel cannot contract ritual impurity by contact, commerce, or social interaction with non-Israelites (22). Torah prohibitions against intermarriage are based on moral danger not ethnic difference, and thus the boundary is permeable (23, 26). Objections might be raised concerning Hayes's explanation of some sexual sins in Torah. Hayes regards

63. See Milgrom, "Concept of *Ma'al*," 245–47. This applies only in a general sense not supporting excavative diachronic concerns, contra Boda, *Praying the Tradition*, 57–61.

64. So Milgrom, "Sacrifices," in *IDBSup*, 768.

65. See Hayes, *Gentile Impurities*, 21. Hayes will be cited parenthetically in this context. Elsewhere Hayes acknowledges the possibility of the apostasy marriage view of Ezra 9:1 ("Intermarriage," 12, n. 25). Instead of pursuing the apostasy marriage view, Hayes anachronistically reads the genealogical view back onto Ezra 9:1–2 from Jubilees and 4Q394/4QMMT (21, 29, 34–35).

sexual offences as different in kind from other acts of immorality because they cause permanent defilement (Num 5; Deut 24:1–4), even if a person has been degraded against her own will (Gen 34). This observation is part of explaining Ezra's prohibition against intermarriage (24). Nevertheless, Hayes works out her interpretation of genealogical purity in Ezra-Nehemiah on a different basis.

Hayes connects the reparation offering to transgressing holiness by means of marriages to those lacking genealogical purity. Hayes's view requires Ezra's exegetical intervention to regard laity as analogous to high priests. In order to show laity as analogous to high priests she compares the purification of the priesthood by means of expulsion in Neh 13:28 (27). Hayes uses the details of Neh 13:28–30 to explain the thought in Ezra 9:1–2. She says: "Israel's holy status is analogous to the holy status of the priests in that both were separated from a larger group. And *just as the priest's holy seed is preserved by means of certain marriage restrictions, so also marriage restrictions are needed to preserve the holy seed of the ordinary Israelite.* Thus, Ezra promotes an apparently universal ban on intermarriage for the novel reason that marital union with a Gentile profanes (i.e., renders nonholy) the holy seed of even ordinary Israelites" (28, emphasis mine). The primary shortcoming of this analogy between the high priest and the laity is lack of evidence.[66]

For the apostasy marriage view, Ezra makes the connection in a different way. Ezra claims the wrongful marriages represent "infidelity" (מַעַל) causing "guilt." Notice the uses of the terms for infidelity and guilt in the following contexts (bold and italics signify verbal parallels at the level of roots, and broken underlining signifies interpretive deduction):

> When anyone **is unfaithful** [תִמְעֹל מַעַל] to Yahweh by sinning unintentionally in regard to any of Yahweh's holy things, they are to bring to Yahweh as a penalty a ram from the flock, one without defect and of the proper value in silver, according to the sanctuary shekel. It is a *guilt offering* [אָשָׁם]. (Lev 5:15)

> Then Ezra the priest stood up and said to them, "You **have been unfaithful** [מְעַלְתֶּם]; you have married foreign women, adding to Israel's *guilt* [אַשְׁמָה]. [11] Now honor Yahweh, the God of your ancestors, and do his will. Separate yourselves from the peoples around you and from your foreign wives." . . . (They all gave their hands in pledge to put away their wives, and for their *guilt* [אָשֵׁם] they each presented a ram from the flock as a *guilt offering* [אַשְׁמָה]). (Ezra 10:10–11, 19)

To summarize, both the genealogical purity and apostasy marriage views agree on the prohibition against wrongful marriages and the guilt offering. They get connected differently—racial basis versus unfaithfulness—as summarized in Figure EN11.

66. Also see other criticism by Rausche, "Relevance or Purity," 472.

FIGURE EN11: EXEGETICAL BASES OF GENEALOGICAL PURITY VERSUS APOSTASY MARRIAGE VIEWS‡

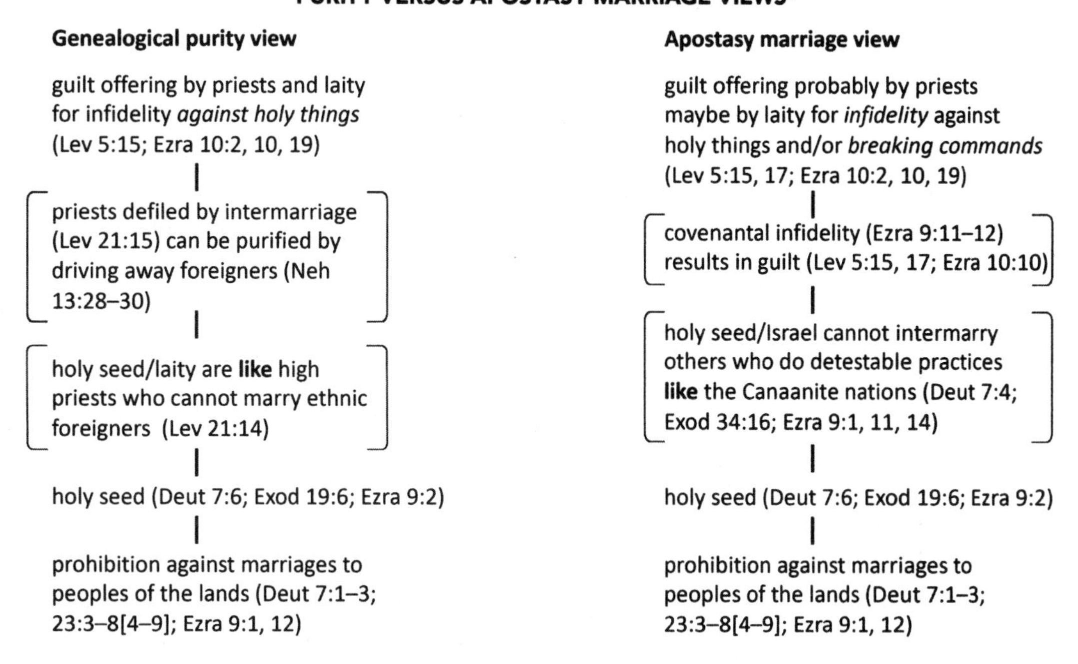

Genealogical purity view
guilt offering by priests and laity for infidelity against holy things (Lev 5:15; Ezra 10:2, 10, 19)
priests defiled by intermarriage (Lev 21:15) can be purified by driving away foreigners (Neh 13:28–30)
holy seed/laity are like high priests who cannot marry ethnic foreigners (Lev 21:14)
holy seed (Deut 7:6; Exod 19:6; Ezra 9:2)
prohibition against marriages to peoples of the lands (Deut 7:1–3; 23:3–8[4–9]; Ezra 9:1, 12)
Apostasy marriage view
guilt offering probably by priests maybe by laity for infidelity against holy things and/or breaking commands (Lev 5:15, 17; Ezra 10:2, 10, 19)
covenantal infidelity (Ezra 9:11–12) results in guilt (Lev 5:15, 17; Ezra 10:10)
holy seed/Israel cannot intermarry others who do detestable practices like the Canaanite nations (Deut 7:4; Exod 34:16; Ezra 9:1, 11, 14)
holy seed (Deut 7:6; Exod 19:6; Ezra 9:2)
prohibition against marriages to peoples of the lands (Deut 7:1–3; 23:3–8[4–9]; Ezra 9:1, 12)

‡ The parenthetical items in the figure represent interpretive deductions.

At this point the logic of the interrelated series of scriptural interpretations in Ezra 9–10 can be connected. Since the series of scriptural interpretations build upon one another, the connecting logic can best be seen by working backwards (see Figure EN12).

FIGURE EN12: BUILDING SERIES OF INTERPRETIVE BLENDS REGARDING WRONGFUL MATCHES IN EZRA 9–10

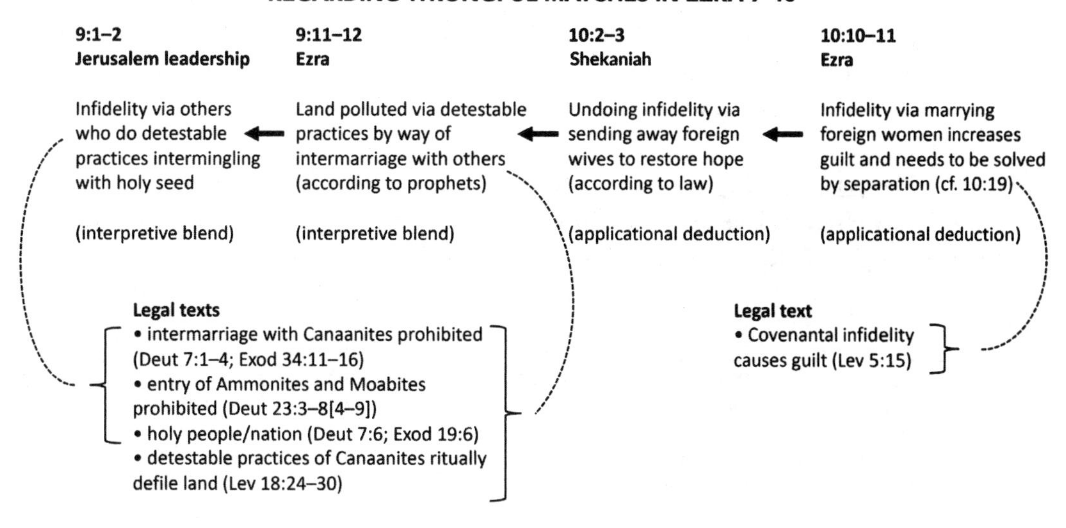

Infidelity via marrying foreign women increases guilt and needs to be solved by separation (cf. 10:19)

• intermarriage with Canaanites prohibited (Deut 7:1–4; Exod 34:11–16)

To summarize in reverse, Ezra affirms Shekaniah's deduction that dissolving the apostasy marriages can help Israel get right with God (Ezra 10:11). Ezra asserts again that apostasy marriages cause guilt (10:10; cf. 9:6, 7, 13, 15). After hearing Ezra's prayer, Shekaniah deduces that undoing the apostasy marriages can fix the problem (10:2–3). After hearing the leadership's indictment against the apostasy marriages, Ezra connects this infidelity with the dangers of defiling the land and incurring divine wrath (9:11–12). The leadership presents the debacle of the restoration assembly marrying others who engage in detestable practices like those of the ancient prohibited peoples (9:1–2).

Neh 1:8–9*~Lev 26:40*+Deut 30:3+1 Kgs 8:29 (C) (Yahweh scatters his unfaithful people) (* see collective confession network). Nehemiah's prayer practically overflows with fleeting scriptural echoes, especially of the prayer of Solomon and Deuteronomistic expressions associated with exile.[67] Nehemiah's prayer, shaped by Deut 30 and Lev 26, fits well with others that use first-person plural confession perspectives (Dan 9:4–19; Ezra 9:6–16).[68] Nehemiah 1:8 uses a quasi-marking device, "saying," which functions similarly to quotation marks in modern conventions. Rather than marking a direct quotation, it marks an interpretive blend, basically paraphrasing key elements from Lev 26 and Deut 30 regarding repentance activating a return from exile. The term "infidelity" in Torah is only associated with exile in Lev 26.[69] But instead of using the Leviticus term for "scatter" (זרה), Nehemiah uses the root for "scatter" (פוץ) favored by Deuteronomy. Notice the way Nehemiah interweaves these possible allusions (bold, italics, and underlining signify verbal parallels; and broken underlining signifies marking):

> But if they will confess their sins and the sins of their ancestors—their **unfaithfulness** [מעל] by which they were unfaithful [מעל] toward me . . .(Lev 26:40†)

> Then Yahweh your God will restore your fortunes and have compassion on you and *gather* you again from all the nations where he *scattered* [פוץ] you. Even if you have been banished to the most distant land under the heavens, *from there* Yahweh your God *will gather* you and bring you back. (Deut 30:3–4)

> May your eyes be open toward this temple night and day, this place of which you said, "My Name shall be there," so that you will hear the prayer your servant prays toward this place. (1 Kgs 8:29)

67. Cf. **Neh 1:5** with Deut 7:9, 21; 10:17; 1 Kgs 8:23//2 Chr 6:14; **Neh 1:6–7** with 1 Kgs 8:28–29, 47; Lev 26:40–45; cf. 2 Chr 6:20, 40; 7:15; **Neh 1:9** with Deut 30:2, 4; 1 Kgs 8:29; cf. Deut 12:5, 11, 14, 26; **Neh 1:10** with Deut 9:26, 29; cf. 7:8; Exod 32:11.

68. See Schnittjer, "Bad Ending," 52.

69. So Milgrom, "Concept of *Ma'al*," 239, n. 16.

> Let your ear be attentive and your eyes open to hear the prayer your servant is praying. . . . Remember the instruction you gave your servant Moses, saying, "If you **are unfaithful** [מעל], I *will scatter* [פוץ] you among the nations, [9] but if you return to me and obey my commands, then even if your exiled people are at the farthest horizon, I will *gather* them *from there* and bring them to the place I have chosen as a dwelling for my Name." (Neh 1:6a, 8–9)

If Nehemiah alludes to Lev 26:40 and/or Deut 30:3–4, his prayer fits with their criteria for activating return. But Nehemiah prays in 445 BCE, ninety-three years after the return and seventy years after the completion of the Second Temple. Since the majority of Judeans remain in captivity, the exile lingers even when Nehemiah's pressing concern relates to the shameful condition of Jerusalem with its walls in ruins. The undercurrents of protracted exile signal that return and temple worship do not completely fulfill the expectations of Moses and the prophets. In a small way, Nehemiah's prayer anticipates the bold redefinition of exile in the prayer of Neh 9.

The other important function of the prayer in Neh 1 amounts to its contrast to the series of one-line prayers Nehemiah uses with great frequency in his second term as governor (5:19; 13:14, 22, 29, 31).[70] Like Neh 1:8, the one-liners feature a call for God to "remember." Unlike 1:8, where Nehemiah repents and confesses sin, the other prayers ask God to remember Nehemiah's good deeds (5:19; 13:14, 22). In this opening prayer Nehemiah looks better than he does in any of his one-line prayers. Nehemiah's repeated echoing of this prayer as the restoration falls apart helps to underscore the disappointing ending of Ezra-Nehemiah. Although God faithfully answers his servant who calls upon him, the people of God turn back quickly to the rebellions of their ancestors.

4:5[3:37]~Jer 18:23 (B) (do not forgive them). The language of Nehemiah's vicious prayer against his opponents shares key terms with one of Jeremiah's imprecatory prayers, suggesting probable allusion (Jer 18:23; Neh 4:5[3:37]). The main difference in the parallel section itself comes down to the passive versus the active verb stems (bold signifies verbal parallel, and italics signify verbal parallel with different syntax):

> **Do not cover their iniquity** or *blot out* [מחה Hif] **their sin from before you.** (Jer 18:23b)

> **Do not cover their iniquity**, and *do not let* **their sin** *be blotted out* [מחה Nif] **from before you.** (Neh 4:5a[3:37a])

Steinmann compares this prayer to similar language in Jeremiah's bitter petition against his opponents in Jer 18:23. Steinmann does well to carefully compare the shared

70. See Schnittjer, "Bad Ending," 49–55.

language between Jeremiah and Nehemiah, even suggesting a chiastic enhancement.[71] Steinmann fails to observe the difference in contexts, which changes the function of the prayer in Nehemiah's case, making the two prayers more like apples and oranges.

Jeremiah's opponents conspire against him but are part of the temple-going community, not outsiders (Jer 18:18).[72] The different opponents need not affect Steinmann's comparison narrowly considered. More significantly, Jeremiah did not begin with prayers of condemnation but seeks his opponents' favor before God. The prophet confesses: "Remember that I stood before you and spoke in their behalf to turn your wrath away from them" (18:20). Since Jeremiah started by seeking mercy for his opponents, Nehemiah's situation is not the same. The words are similar but the situations incompatible. Calvin cautions against imitating Jeremiah in this prayer since he regards the prophet's knowledge of condemnation as oracular.[73]

Steinmann regards Nehemiah's prayer as a model for Christians to imitate. He claims that praying for God's vengeance in line with Deut 32:35 and Rom 12:19 is a virtue, as opposed to taking matters into one's own hands.[74] In order to suggest the use of Deut 32:35 in Rom 12:19 is like the prayer in Neh 4:5a[3:37a], Steinmann needs to lift Paul's citation out of context. Steinmann's comparison can only work by suppressing: "Bless those who persecute you" (Rom 12:14), "Do not repay anyone evil for evil" (12:17), and "Overcome evil with good" (12:21).

The real problem comes when Steinmann says, "We too should follow Nehemiah's example, which is part of Jesus' teaching on prayer: we should pray, 'May your will be done' (Mt 6:10)."[75] That is the end of the section and Steinmann provides no further nuance. This conclusion seems like a flat contradiction of Messiah's teaching to pray for one's enemies only a few verses earlier. Steinmann is correct that Messiah calls for his followers to seek God's will and not their own in his model for prayer (Matt 6:9–13), but he is incorrect to say that Messiah's followers should pray against their enemies. When Messiah says, "Love your enemies and pray for those who persecute you" (5:44), he does not call upon his followers to pray for their damnation. The context speaks of the Father bringing sun and rain on the just and unjust alike.

The larger context of Ezra-Nehemiah does not function as a success story. Elsewhere the narrators do not redact out Nehemiah's confession of oppressing the poorest Judeans. He admits that his predatory loans were the sort that caused them to sell their children into slavery (Neh 5:10). To take a tragic narrative as a prescriptive norm could lead to promoting false application.

---

71. See Steinmann, *Ezra and Nehemiah*, 444.
72. See Allen, *Jeremiah*, 220.
73. Calvin, *Jeremiah*, 2:427–29 (on 18:23).
74. See Steinmann, *Ezra and Nehemiah*, 444.
75. Ibid., 445.

5:1, 4, 7, 8, 11*~Exod 22:25–27*[24–26]+Lev 25:42, 46*+Deut 24:10* (C) (reforming predatory loans) (* see release statute network). Numerous challenges surround the interpretation of Neh 5, especially in terms of sorting out which scriptural legal contexts might be in question. Torah's laws regulating loans and debt slavery themselves interrelate in ways that remain much contested (see notes on Lev 25:35–43; Deut 15:1–11, 12–18). The verbal parallels constitute the most important evidence for determining potential allusions in this context (see Table EN13).

TABLE EN13: POSSIBLE INTERPRETIVE BLEND OF LEGAL REGULATIONS IN NEH 5:1–13‡

Nehemiah 5	Torah
There was a great **outcry** of the people (5:1; cf. 5:6)	And when he **cries out** to me (Exod 22:27[26])
"We have **borrowed silver**" (5:4)	If you **lend silver** (Exod 22:25[24])
"You are pressing claims on loans **each against his fellow**" (5:7)[a]	When you make a loan to your neighbor of any kind, you shall not go into his house to seize his pledge (Deut 24:10) But with regard to your fellow Israelites, **each with his fellow**, you shall not rule **over him** ruthlessly (Lev 25:46)
"We have bought back our Jewish brothers **who had been sold** to gentiles as far as we were able. But you yourselves even **are selling** your own brothers so that **they may be sold** to us" (5:8)	For they are my slaves whom I brought out from the land of Egypt, **they shall not be sold at a slave sale** (Lev 25:42)
"**Give back to them** immediately their fields . . . you have been exacting from them" (5:11)	If you take a pledge . . . **return it to him** at sunset (Exod 22:26[25]; cf. Deut 24:13)

‡ This table is indebted to Berman, "Legal Blend," 108–10; Gross, "Is There Any?" 271–74. Translation lit., and emphases signifies verbal parallel.

[a] The sense of "debt, interest, loan" (מַשָּׁא), which only appears in Neh 5:7, 10; 10:32, is much contested: "charging interest" (NIV, NRSV), "seizing collateral" (NET), "pressing claims on loans" (JPS). Ancient versions (LXX, Vulg., Syriac, and also *BHS*) read as a related term "laying burdens on" (מַשָּׁא . . . נְשִׂאִים, presumably from the root נשא) instead of "pressing claims on loans/charging interest." The related term for "collateral, debt" (מַשָּׁאָה) appears in Deut 24:10; Prov 22:26. MT preferred since it represents the more difficult reading. The difficulty cannot be resolved by the etymological and semantic maneuvers of the ancient versions mentioned earlier in this note. The sense of the term seems to align with the term "pressing claims" (נשא) in Neh 5:11 (Neh 5:7 NET nt.).

The potential parallels amount to brief shared phrases and similar ideas. The complaint of the people in Neh 5:1–5 is not against the injustice of the lending practices or high taxes per se but rather focuses on the problem of starvation. The brief echoes suggest the first-person narration may have shaped the language according to traditional legal protections in lending to the poor (Neh 1:1–5; cf. Exod 22:25, 27[24, 26]).

The most provocative statement by the starving protesters relates to their children being the same flesh and blood as the lenders (Neh 5:5). Nehemiah 5 stands as an undated episode. But its place within the collective wall-building effort gives their complaint extra punch (Neh 2–4, 6). The wall-building project required a major effort where Judeans of all classes came together for a common cause for fifty-two days. During the project the poor and well-to-do worked side by side. Whether the crisis of Neh 5 dates during this building project or from later in Nehemiah's first term as governor, its location within the wall-building narrative heightens the idea of the Judean elites oppressing their own people.

Nehemiah blasts the Judean elites with echoes of protections against debt slavery in Torah contexts that advance the legal instructions of Exodus (Neh 5:7, 8; cf. Lev 25:42, 46; Deut 24:10). Nehemiah goes on to confess his own role in predatory loans against the poorest of Judeans (Neh 5:10). Nehemiah's personal changes strengthen his attempt to persuade the other elites to participate in social reforms. It is not clear how much time elapsed between Nehemiah's initial outburst (5:7) and the follow-up assembly (5:8). In between, Nehemiah made changes himself to stop oppressing the most vulnerable Judeans in order to seek similar reforms from the other elites. He charges the elites to return the fields in the kind of language Exodus uses about a garment taken in pledge (5:11; cf. Exod 22:26[25]).

In sum, the entire context of the social crisis and reform breathes with legal echoes. Nehemiah does not engage a particular legal context but makes social reforms against the sort of predatory loans he and other elites had been using to oppress the poorest Judeans.

6:13~Deut 18:22 (D) (do not fear false prophets). Shepherd proposes that Neh 6:13 alludes to Deut 18:22 based on the protagonist saying he will not "fear" the (false) prophet.[76] But the two contexts use different terms for fear. Besides the lack of verbal parallel, the suggestion creates problems. Nehemiah, as a member of the laity, should not enter the temple itself. Shepherd notes that Nehemiah sees no issue entering into the outer temple area to toss out Tobiah's things (Neh 13:8).[77] But this proposal does not adequately handle the suggested closing of the doors of the temple in Neh 6:11 implying sanctuary within the temple itself, in contrast to the temple's outer courts and chambers in 13:8.[78]

7:6–8:1/~/Ezra 2:1–3:1 (discovering the list of returning exiles). See note on Ezra 2.

8:1–3~Deut 31:11–13 (C) (pre-Tabernacles Torah reading).

8:7, 8*~Deut 33:10* (C) (Levitical instruction) (* see teachers network). Every seventh year at the Festival of Tabernacles required Torah reading to all Israel including men, women, children, and residing foreigners (Deut 31:11–13). The Festival of Tabernacles begins on the fifteenth day of the seventh month (Lev 23:39). Ezra reads Torah every day during Tabernacles (Neh 8:18). Two weeks before Tabernacles at the Festival of Trumpets, the people themselves—not Ezra or the leadership—request Torah reading (8:1).[79] The men, women, and children participate by means of attentive listening (8:3).

76. See Shepherd, "Prophetaphobia," 243–49; idem, "Ezra," 75–79.

77. See Shepherd, "Prophetaphobia," 246.

78. See Williamson, *Ezra, Nehemiah*, 258–59.

79. The term "the people" occurs fourteen times in 8:1–16, nine of which being "all the people" (8:1, 3, 5[3x], 6, 7[2x], 9[3x], 11, 12, 16; Eskenazi notes most of the occurrences in 8:1–12, see *In an Age of Prose*, 97).

The context also includes Torah study. The Levites held responsibility for teaching legal instruction (Deut 33:10; cf. 2 Chr 17:9; 35:5). During the public Torah reading, the Levites "explain" the reading (Neh 8:7). The narration emphasizes that their explanation includes "interpretation" of the Torah so that the people "understand the explanation" (8:8).[80] The only other two uses of "interpret" appear in two precedent-setting cases in which Yahweh himself gives the legal precedent for the blasphemer and the Sabbath breaker (Lev 24:12; Num 15:34). An Aramaic form of interpret appears in Ezra 4:18 with the sense of read "distinctly" or "translate."[81] Later tradition regards the Levites as translating from the Hebrew of the Torah scroll to the Aramaic that the people spoke. Since the Levites "explained," it set a precedent for targums to include translation with interpretive expansions intermingled.

On the next day the priests, Levites, and family heads came together for Torah study with Ezra the priest (Neh 8:13). This enhances the priestly responsibility for teaching distinctions between holy versus common and ritually pure versus ritually impure along with the statutes (Lev 10:10–11). The roughly contemporary prophet Malachi affirms similarly: "For the lips of a priest *ought to preserve knowledge*, because he is the messenger of Yahweh Almighty and *people seek instruction from his mouth*" (Mal 2:7, emphasis mine).

The several Torah study enhancements housed in Neh 8 focus on laity as active Torah seekers (Neh 8:1–3), Levites as Torah interpreters (8:7–8), and priests as Torah teachers (8:13). These enhancements do not easily line up to particular donor contexts and so must be regarded as possible interpretations of the texts listed above. Scripture study here emerges as the norm for the gathered assembly to learn the will of God in Torah.

8:14–16~Lev 23:40 (B) (making temporary shelters for Tabernacles). The narrative records the people studying Torah and discovering that they should live in booths during Tabernacles (Neh 8:14). Based upon this discovery they made a proclamation including a scriptural allusion within it marked by "as it is written" (8:15). But the proclamation features an interpretive paraphrase rather than direct quotation. The sense of "as" here and elsewhere in Ezra-Nehemiah refers to interpretive advancements in accord with legal instruction of Torah (see Marking in Hermeneutical Profile of the Use of Scripture in Ezra-Nehemiah). Note the interpretive allusions in the proclamation (bold signifies verbal parallels, and broken underlining signifies marking):

> On the first day you are to take branches from luxuriant trees—from **palms**, willows and other **leafy trees**—and rejoice before Yahweh your God for seven days. . . . Live in **temporary shelters** for seven days. (Lev 23:40, 42a)

80. The term "explain" (בין Hif) literally connotes "cause to discern" (Neh 8:7) and so the people "discern" (בין Q) (8:8).

81. See Aramaic "פרשׁ," *HALOT* 2:1960; and see Hebrew "פָּרָשָׁה," *TWOT* 2:740. Since the term connotes "separate" Fishbane suggests they read out section by section (*Biblical Interpretation*, 109, n. 11).

> They should proclaim this word and spread it throughout their towns and in Jerusalem, saying, "Go out into the hill country and bring back branches from olive and wild olive trees, and from myrtles, **palms** and **leafy trees**, to make **temporary shelters**"—as it is written. (Neh 8:15†)

9:6–37*~Scripture compilation (B) (Levitical intercessors' panoramic retrospective) (* on 9:7–8 see Abrahamic covenant network; on 9:14 see Sabbath network). Nehemiah 9 features the longest and fullest summative retrospective in the Christian Bible (for comparison with others see Table Josh1). The twenty-fourth day of the seventh month began with the second mass divorce by the restoration assembly (Neh 9:2). The people then participated in their eleventh day of Scripture study during the seventh month. These eleven days of collective Scripture study produce concrete outcomes: living in shelters during Tabernacle (8:16–17); the Levitical prayer (9:6–37); and the solemn oath (9:38–10:39[10:1–40]) (see Table EN15).

The Levitical prayer includes extensive scriptural interpretive allusions. The scriptural exegesis serves the purposes of the prayer and the other agendas of the assembly's acts of devotion on the twenty-fourth day of the seventh month.

The primary goals of the prayer itself stem from redefining the exilic identity of the restoration assembly in order to take a collective solemn oath. The exiles returned ninety-three years before Nehemiah's mission to rebuild the walls (538 BCE return; 445 BCE walls). In spite of all that God had done to faithfully accomplish his word (Neh 9:32, 33), the assembly defines itself as "slaves" (9:36). The slavery does not stem from exile or captivity but vassalage and taxation to the empire (9:32). At one time the restoration assembly defined its identity according to captivity (Ezra 4:1, 3). Now that they have been living in their homeland for generations, the exile no longer adequately gets at who they are. Exile and residual diaspora now becomes a subset of slavery. They are back with temple, Torah, and shame-erasing city walls. For all this, the restoration assembly defines itself as slaves of the empire. The prayer of confession and its scriptural exegesis seek to redefine the identity of the exiles in terms of slaves in need of a renewal of divine fidelity. And, importantly, all of this bears on the solemn oath (Neh 9:38–10:39[10:1–40]).

Taken together, the second mass divorce (9:2) and the prayer (9:6–37) lead to the solemn oath. The purpose of the prayer pushes the slavery of the restoration assembly (9:36) up against Yahweh's covenant fidelity to Abraham (9:7). The Levitical prayer does not include a request per se but a confession of guilt and a statement of their oppression as slaves. The solemn oath, likewise, does not include a request. The unstated but hoped for outcome of the mass divorce, prayer, and solemn oath can only be indirectly inferred from the prayer. Perhaps they hoped the mass divorce, prayer of confession, and solemn oath would move Yahweh to redeem his people from their slavery within their homeland.

The present purposes can be served by listing the main donor contexts and highlighting the pivotal exegetical allusions relative to the goals of the prayer (namely 9:7–8, 9, 17).

The primary allusions appear among many stereotypical expressions of liturgical diffusion (see discussion of the broader associated concept of lyrical diffusion in Hermeneutical Profile of the Use of Scripture in Isaiah and Hermeneutical Profile of the Use of Scripture in Psalms).[82] Note the broad retrospective comparison of Neh 9 and probable donor contexts with interpretive allusions signified by bold—each with verbal parallels (stylized brackets signify changes from narrative sequence):

	donor texts	**Nehemiah 9**
creation[a]	Exod 20:11	6
covenant with Abraham	**Gen 12:4; 15:6, 18**	7–8
crying out at the sea	{**Exod 3:7**} cf. 14:10	9
signs against Egypt	Exod 7–12	10
sea crossing	Exod 14–15	11
cloud to lead	Exod 13:21, 22; Num 10:34	12
revelation at the mountain	Exod 19–20	13–14
provisions in wilderness	{Exod 16:4; Num 20:8; Deut 8:3}	15
rebellion in wilderness	**Num 14:4+Exod 34:6**	16–17
golden calf	{**Exod 32:4**}	18
sustaining people in wilderness	**Deut 8:4; 29:5[4]**	21
conquest of Transjordan	Num 21:21–35; Deut 2:24–3:11	22–23
conquest of Canaan	**Deut 9:3; 6:11**	24, 25
cycles of rebellion and deliverance[b]	**Lev 18:5**; cf. Ezek 20:11, 13, 21	29

[a] Echoes in **Neh 9:6** include: God alone, cf. 2 Kgs 19:15, 19; Deut 4:35; Isa 44:6; 45:22; Ps 83:18[19]; maker of heavens and their host, Gen 2:1; "the heavens, the heavens of heavens," Deut 10:14; 1 Kgs 8:27//2 Chr 6:18; the celestial host worships you, cf. Pss 29:1; 103:21; 148:2; Job 38:7.

[b] Echoes in Neh 9:26–32 include: **Neh 9:26**, kill prophets, Jer 25:4–5; Zech 1:4; cf. 1 Kgs 18:4; Jer 26:20–23; 2 Chr 24:20–22; Matt 5:12; 23:34–35; Luke 13:34; prophetic instruction, Ezra 9:11; Neh 9:30, 32; **9:27, 28**, 1 Kgs 8:30, 32, 34, 36, 39, 43, 45, 49 (cf. Neh 1:11); Neh 9:9//Exod 34:6; **9:29**, Lev 18:5; Ezek 20:11; **9:31**, mercies 2x, 9:17, 19, 27, 28; **9:32**, covenant, 9:7, 8; Assyrian vassalage, 2 Kgs 15:19; 16:7.

Nehemiah 9:7–8 interpretively blends together key elements of the Abraham narrative. The theocentric shift generates important adjustments. The Levitical intercessors make Yahweh the subject of all active verbs and Abraham the direct or indirect object.

---

82. The most important studies of exegesis in Neh 9 are Anderson, "Formation"; Newman, *Praying by the Book*; and Duggan, *Covenant Renewal*. Other studies that offer benefits for exegetical study of Neh 9 in spite of excavative agendas include Boda, *Praying the Tradition*; Bautch, *Developments*. Ryle's still may be the most helpful commentary for Scripture use in Neh 9 (*Ezra and Nehemiah*, 253–67). The list of parallels here is indebted to all of these (see esp. citations in footnotes below).

The Levitical intercessors do not tell Abraham's story but explain what Yahweh did for and with him. In Genesis Abraham "went," but in the prayer Yahweh "chose and brought him out" (Gen 12:4; Neh 9:7). In Genesis Abraham "believed," but in the prayer Yahweh "found his heart faithful" (Gen 15:6; Neh 9:8). And most importantly, in Genesis Abraham's faith was reckoned as his "righteousness," but in the prayer the election and covenant with Abraham signify Yahweh as "righteous" (Gen 15:6; Neh 9:8).[83] Notice the series of shifts from a focus on Abraham's story to Yahweh's covenantal fidelity (bold and italics signify verbal parallels, and stylized underlining signifies interpretive elements):[84]

So Abram went, as Yahweh had told him. (Gen 12:4a)

Abram believed Yahweh, and he credited it to him as **righteousness**. (15:6)

On that day Yahweh *made a covenant* with Abram and said, "*To your descendants* I *give* this *land*." (15:18a)

You are Yahweh God, who chose **Abram** and brought him out of Ur of the Chaldeans and named him Abraham. [8] You found his heart **faithful** to you, and you *made a covenant* with him *to give to his descendants* the *land* of the Canaanites, Hittites, Amorites, Perizzites, Jebusites and Girgashites. You have kept your promise because you are **righteous**. (Neh 9:7–8)

The Levitical intercessors transform the narrative of Abraham's obedience into a story of Yahweh's faithfulness. This exegetical enhancement already anticipates the concluding high point of the prayer. Yahweh, who chose Abraham and made a covenant with him, "keeps the covenant by his loyal love" (9:32 lit.). Just as Yahweh kept his word to Abraham "because *you are righteous*" (9:8, emphasis mine), so too the entire retrospective can be summarized as "*you are righteous*" (9:33 lit., emphasis mine).

The Levitical intercessors' interpretive intervention with "believe/faithful" may be even more important relative to the purpose of the prayer. The issue does not relate to the shift from active to passive—"He believed" (אמן Hif) in Gen 15:6 to his heart "was faithful" (אמן Nif) in Neh 9:8 (on this move see above). The prayer comes immediately before the people making a solemn oath (9:38[10:1]). The rare term "solemn oath" (אֲמָנָה)—appearing two times, both in Nehemiah—comes from the same root (אמן). The implication seems to be that the restoration assembly might be found faithful in their promised devotion and like Abraham enjoy Yahweh's covenantal blessing.

Nehemiah 9:9 illustrates the way the Levitical intercessors interpreted by means of

83. Contra Rendtorff who says in Genesis 15:6 Abraham acknowledges God's righteousness (*Canonical Hebrew Bible*, 27). Shepherd altered me to Rendtorff's discussion (*Text in the Middle*, 38).

84. See Anderson, "Formation," 147; Newman, *Praying by the Book*, 70–71; Duggan, *Covenant Renewal*, 203–4.

interchanging Yahweh's actions from one part of the narrative to another. The prayer takes the language of Yahweh at the bush and applies it to Israel in peril at the sea (emphases signify verbal parallels):[85]

> Yahweh said, "I **have indeed seen the suffering** of my people **in Egypt**. I <u>have heard them crying out</u> because of their slave drivers, and I am concerned about their suffering." (Exod 3:7; cf. 2:24–25)

> You **saw the suffering** of our ancestors **in Egypt**; <u>you heard their cry</u> at the Red Sea. (Neh 9:9)

The Levitical intercessors do not treat the historical events themselves as interchangeable. They detect behind the great acts of redemption a fundamental continuity of divine character. For this reason they infer Yahweh's compassion in a kindred circumstance of Israel. The larger point of the retrospective pivots on the hope that Yahweh may respond once again to the crisis of empire oppression upon the restoration assembly.

Nehemiah 9:17 features an interpretive blend with a bold exegetical intervention. In the account of the rebellion at Kadesh in Numbers, the people collectively decided to return to Egypt (Num 14:4). The Levitical intercessors use a reverse metonymy and change out Egypt for "slavery" (Neh 9:17).[86] The idea of appointing a leader to return to slavery sounds outrageous. The people feared the prospects of invading Canaan and looked to the known trouble of Egypt as the lesser of two evils. The Levitical intercessors do not read against the text, since returning to Egypt infers going back into slavery. Note the inversion of compassionate and gracious in line with Seidel's theory—and compare Table Joel1 (bold and italics signify verbal parallels, and broken underlining signifies interpretive intervention):

> And he passed in front of Moses, proclaiming, "Yahweh, Yahweh, *the compassionate and gracious God, slow to anger, abounding in love* and faithfulness." (Exod 34:6)

> And they said to each other, "We **should appoint a leader** and **return** to Egypt." (Num 14:4†)

> They became stiff-necked and in their rebellion **appointed a leader** in order to **return** to their slavery. But you are a forgiving God, *gracious and compassionate, slow to anger and abounding in love*. Therefore you did not desert them. (Neh 9:17b)

85. The correspondence of the noun form of their "cries" (from the root זעק, Neh 9:9; Exod 3:7) and the verb form "they cried out" (צעק) from Exod 14:10 makes the connection work. *Tsade* and *zayin* are interchangeable with the root spelled two ways because of phonetic similarity (see "זעק," and "צעק," *HALOT* 1:277; 2:1042).

86. See Anderson, "Formation," 170–71; Bautch, *Developments*, 124, n. 71.

The Levitical intercessor's interpretive move uncovers that rebellion against Yahweh's will amounts to a desire for enslavement. The very thing the restoration assembly desires is relief from their own slavery (9:36). Their solemn oath signifies their attempt to align themselves with Abraham's faith versus Israel's rebellion (9:38[10:1]).

The prayer of Neh 9 bridges between the wilderness, conquest, and the present by means of cyclical shaping in the style of Judges (apostasy, disaster, prayer for deliverance, divine response, relief).[87] The first two cycles in Neh 9:26–29 follow the Deuteronomistic template. The third cycle in 9:29–31 breaks the pattern by interspersing a series of new elements as illustrated in Table EN14.

TABLE EN14: CYCLES OF APOSTASY-JUDGMENT-DELIVERANCE IN NEH 9:26–31

	apostasy	disaster	prayer for deliverance	divine response	relief
Judges	2:11	2:14–16	[3:9, 15, etc.]	2:16	2:18
Nehemiah (a)	9:26	9:27a	9:27b	9:27c	9:27d–28a
(b)	9:28b	9:28c	9:28d	9:28e	9:28f
(c)	9:29b	9:30b			
	↑ prophetic warning 9:29a	↑ delay and warning 9:30a	↑ not forsaken 9:31		

One of the elements added into the third cycle seems like a quasi-paraphrase from holiness contexts (emphasis signifies verbal parallels):[88]

> You shall keep my statutes and my judgments *which the person who does them shall live by them,* I am Yahweh. (Lev 18:5 lit.)

> I gave them my statutes and my judgments, I made them known, *which the person who does them shall live by them.* (Ezek 20:11 lit.; cf. 20:13, 21)

> They sinned against your judgments, *which a person who does them will live by them.* (Neh 9:29 lit.)

In sum, the long interpretive retrospective in the prayer of Neh 9 redefines the exile as a subset of the larger problem of slavery to empire. The Levitical intercessors confess

87. See Blenkinsopp, *Ezra-Nehemiah*, 306.

88. See Boda, *Praying the Tradition*, 177; Duggan, *Covenant Renewal*, 219.

Israel's rebellion as none other than a quest for slavery. While the prayer seeks to redefine the identity of the restoration in terms of slavery, this only gets at a penultimate goal. The larger issues all turn on providing a theological rationale for the solemn oath (9:38[10:1]). The Levitical intercessors hope that as Yahweh found Abraham faithful and acted in righteousness, so too he is righteous and may find the assembly faithful in their solemn oath. The prayer explains the significance of their solemn oath to seek Yahweh's compassion, grace, and covenantal loyalty.

10:30–39*[31–40]~selected legal standards of Torah (B) (solemn oath of the restoration assembly) (* on Neh 10:30[31] see assembly network; on 10:31[32] see Sabbath network). No example of scriptural exegetical intervention features more boldness than the solemn oath of the restoration assembly. The most dramatic aspects of their exegetical program may be the use of first-person plural and their set of promises above Torah standards. For all the research poured into Neh 10, these two watershed issues have not received adequate attention.

Getting at these two watershed issues requires understanding how the solemn oath fits into the larger immediate context of Neh 8–10 (a comparison of Neh 10 and 13 is presented below). All of Neh 8, 9, and 10 moves toward the high point of the solemn oath itself. This is why the restoration assembly studies Scripture collectively for eleven days, participates in another mass divorce, and offers the great retrospective prayer of confession. The most efficient way of bringing the context to bear on the solemn oath may be to take note of the outcomes of the eleven days of Scripture study by the restoration assembly (see Table EN15).

TABLE EN15: ELEVEN DAYS OF SCRIPTURE STUDY

	Seventh month	
Attending to Scripture	day 1	Active auditing and learning of Torah by the assembly (Neh 8:1–8)
	day 2	Study of Torah by heads of families and temple personnel (8:13)
	days 15–22	Active auditing of Torah by the assembly (8:18)
	day 24	Active auditing of Torah by the assembly (9:3)
Outcomes of Scripture study	days 15–22	Enhancement of Tabernacles celebration by a living parable (8:14–17)
	day 24	Mass divorce (9:2), confession (9:3), and retrospective prayer led by Levitical intercessors (9:6–37)
	day 24	Collective solemn oath by laity and temple personnel (9:38–10:39[10:1–40])

The first half of Table EN15 illustrates the collective effort of the people to study Torah. The outcomes in the second half of the table may suggest what they studied together for eleven days (see notes above ad loc.). The earlier activities of the twenty-fourth day—mass divorce to dissolve apostasy marriages (Neh 9:2), confession (9:3), and confession by means of Levitical retrospective (9:6–37)—together set the stage for the solemn oath. Members of the priests, Levites, and laity—including both Israel and others who had joined them—signed the oath (10:1–27[2–28]).

The use of the first-person plural in Neh 10:30–39[31–40] establishes one of the solemn vow's primary interpretive advances. The use of "we" in Neh 9:38[10:1] builds directly on the series of first-person plurals in 9:32–37, especially "*We* have acted wickedly.... *We* are slaves.... *We* are slaves on it [the land].... *We* are in great distress" in 9:33, 36, 37.[89] That the series of first-person plurals continues a long string with the end of the Levitical prayer helps establish continuity but does not get to the real exegetical importance of this move.

The dramatic effect of the first-person plural shape of the solemn oath comes into sharp relief when it gets compared to other legal collections. If the legal collections of Torah include both similar laws and similar forms in comparison to other ancient Near Eastern legal collections, Neh 10 features something else altogether.[90] In Torah, the Ten Commandments repeatedly say, "Thou shalt not X; Thou shalt not Y." The use of second- and third-person case laws—"If you Y; If a person Z"—dominates the other legal collections of Torah. By contrast, "We shall (not) X" has been peppered throughout the solemn oath (see Table EN16). Just as Torah reading comes from a request of the people (8:1), so too the legal standards come from voluntary commitment of the restoration assembly (see first footnote in note on Neh 8:7, 8).

TABLE EN16: FIRST-PERSON PLURAL LEGAL EXEGESIS IN NEHEMIAH 10

commands of Torah	solemn oath of Nehemiah 10[a]
Thou shalt not.... (apodictic)	**We** shall not give our daughters....
If **you** ... **you** shall/shall not.... (casuistic)	**We** shall not buy from them on the Sabbath....
If **a person** ... **a person** shall/shall not.... (casuistic)	**We** shall forgo in the seventh year....
	We shall not neglect the house of our God.

[a] "We shall (not)...." (10:30, 31, 32, 34, 35, 36, 37, 39[31, 32, 33, 35, 36, 37, 38, 40]).

The other remarkable exegetical feature amounts to the common denominator of the entire set of promises: Each promise stands at a level of commitment to obedience above Torah regulations. They do not seek to find the easy way of mere compliance. The commitment of the restoration assembly provides a gold standard for intentions to serve Yahweh. Other examples in Scripture do not run parallel. The self-imposed collective commitment of the people seems something very different from Josiah's legislated reforms—top down mandated compliance. Perhaps the early days of the Way in Jerusalem

89. See Glatt-Gilad, "Reflections," 393; Eskenazi, "Nehemiah 9–10," 3.5.
90. See Weinfeld, "Origin," esp. 68, 73.

in the early chapters of Acts runs partially parallel. In Neh 10, readers are struck by the fact that after eleven days of Torah study initiated by the people themselves, they make promises to obey Yahweh's will at a standard higher than required.

For the present purposes, the Torah enhancements of the solemn oath have been collated into Table EN17. A few examples of these will then be summarized to illustrate the basic exegetical agenda of the restoration assembly.

TABLE EN17: TORAH UPGRADE IN NEHEMIAH 10—ZEALOUS COMMITMENTS ABOVE TORAH STANDARDS

	Torah	Nehemiah 10
Abstain from marriage to others	Exod 34:14–16; Deut 7:2–4, prohibitions of marriage to others	even others converted to Torah obedience (10:28[29]; cf. 9:2) commit to not arrange marriages for their children with others (10:30[31])
Honor the Sabbath day and Sabbath year	Exod 34:21, "rest" even during harvest Exod 35:3, not kindle a fire at your home Lev 25, release debt slaves every fifty years Exod 23:11, fallow land every seven years Deut 15:1, 2, release debts every seven years	not merchandizing (10:31[32]); fallow land and release debts every seven years (10:31[32])
Shrine contribution	Exod 30:11–16, one-time 1/2 shekel to build tabernacle	annual 1/3 shekel temple contribution ("tax") (10:32–33[33–34])
Wood contribution	Lev 6:12–13[5–6], priests keep fire of tabernacle burning continually	set rotation among laity to provide wood for altar (10:34[35])
First fruits and tithes	Deut 14:22–29; 26:12, give tithes during pilgrimage festival every third year	give firstfruits and tithes annually at local Levitical collection locations rather than delay until pilgrimages (10:35–39[36–40])

Nehemiah 10:30[31] sets out the first exegetical legal enhancement of the solemn oath to get at the Achilles heel of the restoration—apostasy marriages. The oath follows Deut 7:3 in the sense of affirming that the prohibition against apostasy marriages applies equally to both genders (see note on Deut 7:1–5). The restoration assembly continues to use the flexible relative expression "peoples of the land" to refer to the other, as elsewhere in Ezra-Nehemiah (see note on Ezra 9:1–2). Notice how closely the basic structure and syntax follow the version of the prohibition in Deuteronomy (bold signifies verbal parallels):

> Do not intermarry with them. **Do not give** your **daughters to** their sons **or take their daughters for** your **sons.** (Deut 7:3)

We promise **not to give** our **daughters** in marriage **to** the peoples around us **or take their daughters for** our **sons.** (Neh 10:30[31])

The major exegetical difference derives from the context. The "we" in Neh 10:30[31] includes others from the peoples of the lands who have joined the restoration assembly and commit themselves not to seek marital matches from the peoples of the land. These former others join together with the seed of Israel, some of whom had just dissolved their apostasy marriages that very morning (Neh 9:2). The term "separate" (בדל) is in the same reflexive verb stem (Nif) used of other mass divorces in Ezra-Nehemiah (Ezra 10:11, 16; cf. Neh 13:3 [Hif]; Ezra 9:1).[91] And, very importantly, this is identical to the language of the others who repent and join the restoration community (Neh 10:28[29]):

The seed of Israel separated themselves [בדל Nif] *from all foreigners* [בְּנֵי נֵכָר]. They stood in their places and confessed their sins and the sins of their ancestors. (9:2 lit., emphasis mine)

The rest of the people—priests, Levites, gatekeepers, musicians, temple servants and *all who separated themselves* [בדל Nif] *from the peoples of the lands* for the sake of the Torah of God, together with their wives and all their sons and daughters who are able to understand—all these now join their fellows. (10:28–29a[29–30a] lit., emphasis mine)

The former others commit to not intermarrying with excluded others. Such a commitment by Israel and others joined to the restoration assembly establishes an exegetical enhancement of the prohibition. This shared commitment by Israel and the others who have joined with them also provides additional evidence in support of the apostasy marriage view over and against the genealogical purity view regarding wrongful marriages (see set of notes on Ezra 9–10).

Views opposed to the more open stance of Ezra-Nehemiah toward welcoming others (Ezra 6:21; Neh 10:28[29]) go back to the Second Temple period. To avoid the implications of the context, 1 Esdras reads Ezra 6:21 against the sense of the text by eliminating the conjunction "and" (*vav*) between the returned exiles and the others.[92] The redactor of 1 Esdras omits anything that could allow others into fellowship with those returned from exile[93] (italics signify shared language, and bold signifies eliminated *vav*):

91. Contra Duggan, *Covenant Renewal*, 151 who suggests "separate" (Hif) is required for dismissing foreigners. See "separate" (Nif reflexive) in Ezra 10:11, 16, which cannot work for Duggan's argument.

92. "And" (וְ) in MT = "and" (καὶ) in LXX of Ezra 6:21.

93. See Bird, *1 Esdras*, 229; Japhet, "1 Esdras," 212.

> And the sons of Israel *who had returned from captivity* ate it, *all those who had been separated from* the abominations of the nations of the land, as they were seeking the Lord. (1 Esd 7:13 NETS)

> The sons of Israel, *the ones who returned from exile,* **and** *all the ones who separated themselves.* (Ezra 6:21 lit.)

Popular views of the late Second Temple era were much more exclusive than Ezra 6:21, Neh 10:28[29], or Exod 12:43–49, excluding both kinds of others: "resident sojourners" and "foreigners" (see Pss. Sol. 17:28 [first century BCE]).[94] Even more stringent opposition to admitting outsiders is reflected among sectarians of the era (e.g., 4QFlor/4Q174 I, 3–5). Many of the ancient separatist sectarians along with their modern interpreters may find "continuity" between the exclusivity of the restoration assembly and the sectarians.[95] But the evidence in Ezra-Nehemiah favors the restoration assembly as welcoming others who turned from the pollutions of the peoples of the land and to the Torah of God (Ezra 6:21; Neh 10:28[31]).

The restoration assembly struggled with apostasy marriages as much as anything. The extremes of the protracted economic depression, combined with the poverty of the returned captives, made "marrying out" very attractive. Ancient people wanted to help their children. Arranging marriages with established others remained a persistent temptation for parents who wanted something better for their children. Like moderns, ancients do the worst things for the best reasons.

In sum of this point, the solemn oath stands in continuity with Torah and prophets, maintaining two kinds of others—excluded others and included others. The first commitment of the oath shares a basic continuity with Deut 7:3 in banning apostasy marriages for both genders. The exegetical enhancement of Neh 10:30[31] comes from others who have joined the restoration assembly in denouncing marital matches to excluded others for their children.

Nehemiah 10:31a[32a] presents an enhancement above Torah standards for Sabbath rest. In spite of repeated rehearsals of Sabbath-keeping in Torah, only two contexts define what rest includes. Exodus 34:21 explains that even the pressures of plowing and harvest do not supersede Sabbath rest. Exodus 35:3 prohibits kindling fires for domestic purposes on the Sabbath. This pair of enhancements explains rest in reference to the workplace and the home. Nowhere does Torah speak to how Sabbath-keeping relates to the marketplace.

---

94. On two kinds of others, see Tables I4 in note on Isa 52:1 and Ezk6 in note on Ezek 44:9–16.

95. It is easy to believe that the separatist sectarians of the late Second Temple era thought of themselves akin to the restoration assembly in Ezra-Nehemiah. But it can only be anachronistic to read back separatist sectarian ideology onto the restoration assembly of Ezra-Nehemiah when they welcomed outsiders who turned from the pollutions of the peoples of the land to the Torah of God (Ezra 6:21; Neh 10:28[31]). Contra Harrington, "Intermarriage in Qumran Texts," 251–29; Blenkinsopp, *Judaism*, 222–27.

The exegetical enhancement of the solemn oath lays out their commitment to honor the Sabbath by refraining from buying. They may have had in mind Amos 8:5, which speaks against merchandizing on the Sabbath, or Jer 17:19–27 since Nehemiah alludes to this context (Neh 13:18).

Nehemiah 10:31b[32b] enhances regulation of the fallow land of the Sabbath year by connecting it with release of debt. These stand in close proximity in the Jubilee standards (Lev 25:1–7, 35–38). The solemn oath connects the language of fallow land in the covenant collection with debt release in the torah collection. The catchword "release" may have suggested this connection to the architects of the solemn oath (emphases signify verbal parallels at the level of shared roots):

> In the seventh year *you shall release* [שׁמט] you shall leave it [the land] uncultivated [נטשׁ]. (Exod 23:11)

> At the end of seven years you *shall make release* [שְׁמִטָּה]. . . . Every creditor *shall release* [שׁמט] **any debt** [מַשָּׁא]. (Deut 15:1, 2; cf. 15:3)

> We will forego the produce [נטשׁ] of the seventh year and **every debt** [מַשֵּׁה]. (Neh 10:31[32])

Deuteronomy associates release from debt every seven years with the Festival of Tabernacles in the same context that calls for Scripture reading every seven years at Tabernacles (Deut 31:10–13). The larger context of eleven days of Scripture reading in the seventh month, including eight days during Tabernacles itself, offers an interesting possible connection (see Table EN15). The commitment to debt release and fallow land here also offers an important area of comparison to the social reforms of Neh 5.

Nehemiah 10:34[35] explains how the restoration assembly cast lots to make a rotation for supplying wood to the house of God. Since Torah does not speak of this, the overt marking by "as it is written in the Torah" sparks trenchant debate (see Marking in Hermeneutical Profile of the Use of Scripture in Ezra-Nehemiah). The issue to get at here concerns the enhancements above Torah standards in this part of the solemn oath. Torah requires the priests to keep the fire of the shrine burning continually (Lev 6:12–13[5–6]). The instruction does not explain any kind of apparatus to supply the needed fuel for an ever-burning fire. The enhancements above Torah standards everywhere in the solemn oath fit here as well. The restoration assembly voluntarily commits to supply the needed wood for worship by means of a shared rotation.

Nehemiah 10:35–39[36–40] gathers together from Torah widely dispersed instructions for giving, but the advances focus on the when and how of the giving.[96] Deuteronomy

96. Cf. Exod 23:16–17; Num 18:14–18; Deut 15:19–23; also see Exod 13:2, 12–15; Lev 27:26–27.

makes provision to bring the firstfruits and tithes every third year to the place Yahweh chooses (Deut 14:12; 26:12). The restoration assembly upgrades the instructions in two ways. First, they commit to an annual giving of tithes and firstfruits (Neh 10:35[36]). Second, they devise a system whereby Levites go town by town collecting tithes to transport to the house of God (10:37[38]). Compare selected allusions paraphrased and overtly marked as agreeing with Torah (italics, bold, and underlining signify verbal parallels; wavy underlining signifies marking; and broken underlining signifies interpretive intervention):

> You are to give over to Yahweh the first offspring of every womb. All the firstborn males of your livestock belong to Yahweh. [13] Redeem with a lamb every firstborn donkey, but if you do not redeem it, break its neck. Redeem every firstborn among your sons. (Exod 13:12–13)

> *Bring* the best of *the firstfruits of your soil* to *the house of Yahweh* your God. (23:19a)

> Take some of the **firstfruits** of all that you produce from **the soil** of the land Yahweh your God is giving you and put them in a basket. Then go to the place Yahweh your God will choose as a dwelling for his Name. . . . When you have finished setting aside a tenth of all your produce in the third year, the year of the **tithe**, you shall give it to the Levite, the foreigner, the fatherless and the widow, so that they may eat in your towns and be satisfied. (Deut 26:2, 12; cf. 14:22–29)

> We also assume responsibility for *bringing* to *the house of Yahweh* each year *the firstfruits of our soil* and of every fruit tree. [36] As it is also written in the Torah, we will bring the firstborn of our sons and of our livestock, of our herds and of our flocks to the house of our God, to the priests ministering there. [37] Moreover, we will bring to the storerooms of the house of our God, to the priests, the **first** of our ground meal, of our grain offerings, of the fruit of all our trees and of our new wine and olive oil. And we will bring a **tithe** of our produce from **the soil** to the Levites, for it is the Levites who collect **the tithes** in all the towns where we work. (Neh 10:35–37†[36–38])

The preceding examples illustrate the common denominator of the series of exegetical enhancements in the solemn oath. In each case the solemn oath works out ways that the restoration assembly voluntarily dedicates themselves to obedience above and beyond what Torah calls for.

In sum of the interpretive interventions of the solemn oath, after eleven days of collective Scripture study, the people took it upon themselves to make a series of commitments in writing. They determined several ways they would go above the standards of Torah in their covenantal devotion. No one made them do this. They say again and again,

"We shall not" and "We shall." The theological rationale for the unprecedented interpretive adjustments to a more stringent obedience needs to be derived by inference from the prayer in Neh 9 (see note ad loc.). The suggestion here revolves around the problem of their slavery to the empire and the hope that Yahweh will find the restoration assembly faithful as he found Abraham faithful long ago.

Before moving on, one critical, messy detail needs to be noted. The larger function of the solemn oath in Ezra-Nehemiah turns on its coordinated relationship with the ending of the book. When Nehemiah returns to Jerusalem twelve years later for his second term as governor, he discovers that the people had broken every aspect of their solemn oath (Neh 13:4–31).[97] The carefully coordinated first-person narrative in Neh 13 almost reads like he had a copy of the solemn oath on hand as a checklist. Note the evidence of breaking the solemn oath: neglecting the portions for the Levites (Neh 13:10; cf. 10:37[38]), not honoring the Sabbath (13:15; cf. 10:31[32]), apostasy marriages (13:23–24, 28; cf. 10:30[31]), neglecting the wood tribute (13:31; cf. 10:34[35]), and neglecting firstfruits contributions for the priests (13:31; cf. 10:35[36]).

The highwater mark of the restoration is embodied in the solemn oath of Neh 10. The collective voluntary dedication to obedience above the level of necessity remains an enduring testimony to what eleven days of collective Scripture study can accomplish. The completeness of the failure in Neh 13 provides a proportionately inverse sobering testimony. While the restoration failed miserably, their Scripture study, confession, prayer, and especially their solemn oath invite the people of God to consider what it means to reform their ways.

11:25–30~Josh 15:20–41 (B) (restoration of villages of Judah). Nehemiah 11:25–30 presents an abridged list of villages based on Josh 15:20–41.[98] While Josh 15:20–41 contains seventy-one village names, at least ten of those in Neh 11:25–30 appear in identical order, making coincidence almost impossible: Moladah, Beth Pelet, Hazar Shual, Beersheba, Ziklag, En Rimmon, Zorah, Zanoah, Adullam, and Azekah (it could be eleven or twelve depending on how to handle Jeshua and Mekonah). The first village on the list, Kiriath Arba (Hebron), is referred to separately in Josh 14:15 and in a different part of a list in 15:54.

The reader aware of the parallels may deduce the "ideal character" of the list in Neh 11:25–30 by comparing it backward.[99] Or, the list could evoke utopian hope by looking forward.[100] The offhand comments of Zechariah show that the southern area around

97. See Schnittjer, "Bad Ending," 41–45.

98. As observed by von Rad, *Das Geschichtsbild des Chronistischen Werks*, 22–25. Lipschits says all but Kiriath Arba are in the "same order" ("Literary," 437) but then heavily qualifies this point (438, n. 59). Von Rad more broadly notes that the list is "slavishly" followed (23).

99. Von Rad suggests the *idealeren Charakter* (ideal character) of the list (*Das Geschichtsbild des Chronistischen Werks*, 23).

100. See Williamson, *Ezra, Nehemiah*, 350.

Beersheba was not part of the province of Yehud (Judah) by 518 BCE (Zech 7:7).[101] Over seventy years later the villages of the southern Negev remain under the control of Edom-Arabia, where Nehemiah's enemy Geshem was governor (Neh 2:19; 6:1–7). During the days narrated in Ezra-Nehemiah, the returned exiles only resettle the regions close to Jerusalem. Compare the locations to the far south from the list of villages in Neh 11:25–30 (see Map EN18).

MAP EN18: JUDEAN VILLAGES OF NEH 11:25–30‡

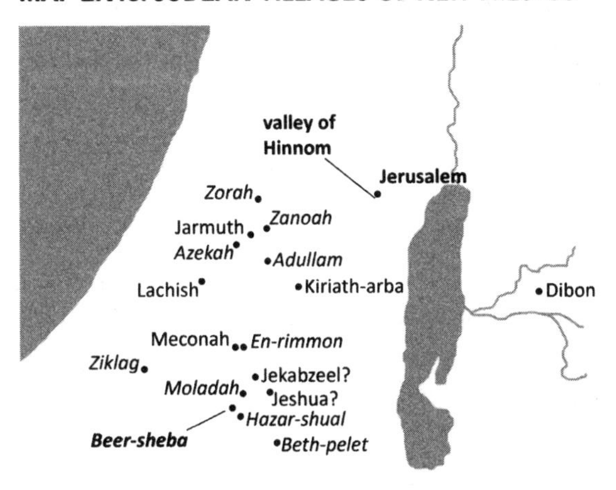

‡ The italicized villages on the map are those appearing both in Josh 15:20–41 and Neh 11:25–30 in identical sequence. Jerusalem is not on the list but is included for orientation.

The use of the verb "encamp" in Neh 11:30 may connote an idealized association with the original settlement of the land—"*they encamped* from Beersheba to the valley of Hinnom" (11:30 lit., emphasis mine; cf. e.g., Josh 5:10).[102] The only other use of the term in Ezra-Nehemiah describes when the people gathered as Ezra's caravan prepared to leave Babylon (Ezra 8:15).

In sum, the evidence suggests that the list in Neh 11:25–30 is idealized and modeled on Josh 15:20–41. The incongruity between the ancient list of Judah's villages from the days of settlement and the compact lands of Judah around Jerusalem in the restoration invites readers to lift their vision to what Judah could be.

13:1-3*//Deut 23:3–6*[4–7] (responding to the law of the assembly) (* see assembly network). The heading on Neh 13:1 makes it difficult to know where the episode fits chronologically—"On that day the Book of Moses was read aloud in the hearing of the people." If this vignette corresponds to one of the two mass divorces narrated previously, it may belong among the eleven days of Scripture reading mentioned in Neh 8 leading up

101. See von Rad, *Das Geschichtsbild des Chronistischen Werks*, 22.

102. On encampment as idealized coloring of wilderness days, see Williamson *Ezra, Nehemiah*, 353.

to the mass divorce in 9:2 (see Table EN15). But since the episode appears immediately before Nehemiah's second term twelve years later (Neh 13:4–31), it becomes unclear if it refers to a third mass divorce. The focus on the exegetical interventions in Neh 13:1–3 are not affected whether the event is the same or different than one of the previous mass divorces (cf. Ezra 9–10; Neh 9:2).

The narrative frame overtly marks the first part of the law of the assembly, thereby affirming Deuteronomy as the donor and Ezra-Nehemiah as the receptor context. The citation features interpretive abbreviation along with a report of how the restoration assembly applied the law (bold and underlining signify verbal parallels at the level of roots, italics signify paraphrase, and broken underlining signifies marking):

> **An Ammonite or a Moabite shall not enter the assembly of** *Yahweh, even to the tenth generation, their descendants shall not enter* **the assembly of** *Yahweh.* [4] *Because* **they did not meet** *you* **with bread and water** on your way coming out of Egypt, **but they hired against** *you* **Balaam** son of Beor from Pethor of Mesopotamia **to curse** *you.* [5] But Yahweh your God was not willing to listen to Balaam but *Yahweh your God* **turned the curse into a blessing** for you, for Yahweh your God loves you. [6] You shall not seek their welfare or their good all of your days forever. (Deut 23:3–6 lit.[4–7])

> On that day the scroll of Moses was read in the ears of the people and in it was found written that **an Ammonite or a Moabite shall not** *ever* **enter the assembly of** *God,* [2] *because* **they did not meet** *the Israelites* **with bread and water, but hired against** *them* **Balaam to curse** *them*—but *our God* **turned the curse into a blessing.** [3] When the people heard the Torah, they separated from Israel all those of mixed ancestry. (Neh 13:1–3 lit.)

Several exegetical inferences need to be summarized. First, the allusion uses the generic term "God" instead of the covenantal name Yahweh.

Second, the reference to "the tenth generation" in Deut 23:3[4] gets interpreted as "forever" when this language moves from 23:6[7] to Neh 13:1. This makes sense if the expression is a hyperbole and basically means never.

Third, as in Ezra 9:1, the sense of the law of the assembly has been interpreted as assimilation into the assembly of God by means of intermarriage. And, just as in Ezra 10:3, 11, so too in Neh 13:3 the fix comes in the form of mass divorce.

Fourth, they did not interpret "Moabite" and "Ammonite" literally according to genealogical purity, ethnicity, or race. They did not separate out Ammonites and Moabites, but any persons of "mixed ancestry." The term "mixed ancestry" appears in a handful of contexts referring to peoples mixed together in Babylon (Jer 50:37), mixture of mercenary troops in Egypt (25:20; Ezek 30:5), the "mixed multitude" that came out of Egypt with

Israel (Exod 12:38), and the people expelled from the postexilic assembly (Neh 13:3).[103] The uses of terms that can denote ethnic or racial senses causes much of the interpretive difficulty in Ezra-Nehemiah. In Neh 9:2 the assembly separated themselves from "foreigners," a term that usually would connote ethnic and/or genealogical otherness.[104] In that case, it did not include all "the peoples of the lands," since many of them participated in the solemn oath with Israel that same day promising that they would not arrange marriages for their children with "the peoples of the land" (Neh 10:28, 30[29, 31]; cf. note ad loc.). Ezra-Nehemiah often uses terms that could connote genealogical and/or ethnic senses in religious ways. The narrative also repeatedly affirms that the restoration assembly welcomes others to join them (Ezra 2:59–60; 6:21; Neh 10:28[29]).

Relative to Neh 13:1, the people did not interpret Ammonite and Moabite literally but may have interpreted these excluded others relative to covenant infidelity as elsewhere (Ezra 9:1). In this case, then, "mixed ancestry" carries religious connotations in Neh 13:3. This line of interpretation fits with the analogical function of Ammonites and Moabites in Ezra 9:1, especially by means of the verb "mixed" in Ezra 9:2 from the same root as "mixed ancestry" in Neh 13:1 (see note on Ezra 9:1–2).[105] Or, if "mixed ancestry" denotes ethnic/genealogical otherness in Neh 13:3, it stands apart from the other mass divorces based on apostasy (covenantal infidelity) in Ezra 9–10 and Neh 9:2. If Neh 13:1–3 is read within Ezra-Nehemiah as a whole, the evidence favors divorce for religious/faith reasons. If Neh 13:1–3 is read on its own, the evidence favors divorce for ethnic/genealogical reasons. In either case, Neh 13:1–3 does not interpret Ammonite and Moabite in the law of the assembly literally but symbolically as referring to the excluded other (for a similar reading cf. note on Lam 1:10).

Fifth, the allusion to God's unfailing covenant embedded in the narrative tradition of the law of the assembly is retained despite the abridgment (Deut 23:5–6[6–7]//Neh 13:2). The allusion to the covenant fidelity of God to the Hebrew ancestors provides the overarching connection between the redemptive narrative and the legal tradition. Notice how this connects with similar pronouncements across Torah (emphases signify verbal parallels):[106]

> [Yahweh says] I **will bless those who bless** you but the one who <u>curses</u> [קלל] you *I will curse* [ארר]. (Gen 12:3 lit.)

> [Isaac says] *May those who curse* [ארר] you *be cursed* [ארר] and **those who bless** you **be blessed.** (27:29 lit.)

---

103. See "I עֵרֶב," BDB 786; "II עֵרֶב," *HALOT* 1:878.

104. On uses of "foreigner" (בְּנֵי נֵכָר), see "נֵכָר," *HALOT* 1:700.

105. The verb "to mix" (*'rv* ערב) in Ezra 9:2 comes from the same root as the noun "mixed ancestry" (*'erev* עֵרֶב) in Neh 13:3.

106. See additional connections in Schnittjer, "Blessing of Judah," 21–22.

[Balaam says] **May those who bless** you **be blessed** *and those who curse* [ארר] *you be cursed* [ארר]. (Num 24:9 lit.)

[Moses says] Yahweh your **God turned** the curse [קלל] into a **blessing** for you, for Yahweh your God loves you. (Deut 23:5[6] lit.)

[Torah says] Our **God turned** the curse [קלל] into a **blessing.** (Neh 13:2 lit.)

Grammatically and syntactically, the parallels between Gen 27:29 and Num 24:9 and those between Deut 23:5[6] and Neh 13:2 are close, and the shared ideology among the series of parallels is not subtle. Several exchanges between Balak and Balaam draw out the theological point of God's sovereign will embodied in the covenantal language. Balaam says, for example, "How can I curse whom God has not cursed?" (Num 23:8; cf. 23:11, 20, 25, 27; 24:1, 9, 10). The important point in the Balaam narrative, carried over into the law of the assembly and the exegetical paraphrase of Neh 13:2, pivots on the reason for the rejection of Ammon and Moab. Their rejection has nothing to do with genealogical or ethnic otherness. God curses them because of his covenantal fidelity to the Hebrew ancestors to whom he promised to curse those who cursed them. The redemptive narrative of Torah provides the covenantal bases of the law of the assembly in Deuteronomy and Neh 13:2.

In sum, the restoration assembly turns to the law of the assembly once again (Neh 13:1–3; cf. Ezra 9:1). They interpret the first half of the law of the assembly as a prohibition against intermarriage. They interpret the use of Ammonites and Moabites in Deut 23:3–6[4–7] as symbolically referring to excluded others from any people. The people respond by means of a mass divorce once again, in spite of its earlier ineffectiveness. Placing accounts of mass divorce in Ezra 9–10, Neh 9:2, and Neh 13:1–3 trains readers to see their ineffectiveness as well as Israel's addiction to apostasy marriages. This sets the table for the widespread rebellion Nehemiah discovers on his return to Jerusalem in Neh 13:4–31.

13:15, 17–18*~Jer 17:21–27*+Num 32:8, 14 (B) (Sabbath breaking by merchandizing) (* see Sabbath network). Nehemiah's tour of Jerusalem during his second term as governor, about twelve years after rebuilding the city walls, uncovered total failure with respect to the terms of the solemn oath many of the restoration assembly had signed (Neh 13:4–31; cf. 9:38–10:39[10:1–40]). In Neh 10:31[32], they promise to honor a standard above what Torah spells out, namely, they would not sell merchandise on the Sabbath. In Neh 13:15 he discovers Judeans loading their animals to sell products on the Sabbath. The reference to bringing "burdens" of merchandise to Jerusalem on the Sabbath (13:15) alludes to an interpretive enhancement of Sabbath law by Jeremiah. The prophet uses the term "burden" repeatedly in his condemnation of Jerusalem for Sabbath violations (Jer 17:21, 22, 24, 27). Nehemiah goes on to make his case against defiling the Sabbath to

Judah's elites, framing it by allusion to Moses's condemnation against the Transjordanian tribes in Num 32. The importance of Moses's analogy to the rebellion of the older generation at Kadesh relates to the grave threat that the Transjordanian tribes brought upon all Israel. Nehemiah regards Sabbath breaking in the same light (bold and underlining signifies verbal parallels, italics signify similar concepts without verbal parallel, and broken underlining signifies marking):[107]

> [Moses said] Our ancestors did the same thing when I sent them from Kadesh Barnea to see the land.... And, behold, you have risen in place of your ancestors, a brood of sinners, to add more wrathful anger of Yahweh upon Israel. (Num 32:8, 14 lit.)

> [Jeremiah said] Thus says Yahweh: "Take care for your lives and do not carry **a burden on the Sabbath day** or **bring** it through the gates of **Jerusalem**. And you shall not **bring a burden** out of your houses on the Sabbath day, and any other work you shall not do, but you shall keep the Sabbath day holy, as I have commanded your ancestors.... If you do not obey me to keep the Sabbath day holy, and not carry **a burden** and come in through the gates of **Jerusalem on the Sabbath day**, *then I will kindle a fire against its gates, and it will devour the palaces of Jerusalem and it will not be quenched.*" (Jer 17:21, 22, 27 lit.)

> [Nehemiah wrote] In those days I saw in Judah people... bringing in heaps of grain and loading them on donkeys, and also wine, grapes, figs, and all kinds of **burdens**, which they **were bringing** into **Jerusalem on the Sabbath day**. So I warned them at that time against selling food.... I rebuked the nobles of Judah and said to them, "What is this evil thing that you are doing, profaning the Sabbath day? Did not our ancestors do the same, *and our God brought upon us all this evil, and upon this city?* Now you are adding more wrath upon Israel by profaning the Sabbath." (Neh 13:15, 17–18 lit.)

Nehemiah's interpretive allusion to the expansion of Sabbath regulations in Jer 17 indicates the authority of the prophet to advance revelation. Torah only offers two examples of work excluded by Sabbath rest: abstaining from agricultural labor even during the important times of planting and reaping, and prohibition against kindling fires at home (Exod 34:21; 35:3; cf. notes ad loc.). Whatever it means to rest, it needed to be extrapolated from these two cases—at work and at home. Jeremiah expanded the Sabbath prohibitions to include carrying burdens into the city (Jer 17:21–27; cf. note ad loc.; Amos 8:5). The solemn oath and Nehemiah interpret Jeremiah's interpretive advancement as related to merchandizing on the Sabbath (Neh 10:31[32]; 13:15).

107. These comparisons and associated discussion are loosely based on Schnittjer, "Bad Ending," 42–43. Also see Achenbach, "Sermon," 880–81; Jassen, *Scripture and Law*, 190–94; Fishbane, *Biblical Interpretation*, 133–34.

The manner in which Nehemiah handled the punishment for the violation of Sabbath breaking offers important insight into how scriptural legal instructions function in the postexilic period. In Torah, Sabbath breaking constituted a capital offense (Exod 31:14–15; 35:2; Num 15:35, 36). It is presented as a "crime."[108] As governor of Jerusalem, Nehemiah represented the highest local civil authority in Jerusalem in addition to his role as cupbearer to the emperor, making Nehemiah one of the most trusted officials in Persia. Nehemiah does not seek the death penalty for the Judean Sabbath breakers. The only action he takes against the Judeans is to try to persuade the local aristocrats of the threat of divine judgment for Sabbath breaking in the marketplace (Neh 13:17–18). With respect to the non-Judean merchants, he orders the city gates closed, using some of his own personal militia to enforce his orders (13:19). When he discovers the non-Judean merchants outside the city on the Sabbath, Nehemiah threatens to arrest them (13:20). If Sabbath breaking operates as a criminal offense in Torah, things are different in the restoration within a province of the empire. Nehemiah does not treat Sabbath breaking as a criminal offense but as a religious standard. The legal standards of Torah transcend the fall of the Hebrew kingdoms as covenantal regulations—the legal instructions continue to apply to the Yahwistic Judeans. But covenantal legal instructions no longer function as civil law. This change in the function of Torah's criminal law did not begin with New Testament faith but with Judah's loss of sovereignty to enforce its theocratic standards.[109] Within the empire, Mosaic covenantal instructions function as religious standards for practicing Israel.

In sum, Nehemiah's exegetical allusions to Sabbath breaking affirm the authority of the prophets to advance Mosaic law. Nehemiah's application of Sabbath instructions as a civil ruler of the empire demonstrates that Mosaic instructions do not function as criminal law. Within the empire, the Mosaic instructions work as covenantal religious standards for a faith community. Adherence to Torah's legal instructions defines religious identity within the restoration assembly.

13:23–27*~Deut 23:3*[4]+1 Kgs 11:1–4* (B) (confronting apostasy husbands) (* see assembly and devoting networks). During Nehemiah's tour of rebellious Jerusalem in his second term as governor, he discovered that apostasy marriages had again become widespread (Neh 13:23–27). The most important narrative developments in this scriptural-allusion-laden context pivot on what has changed. Previous infidelities of this sort in the restoration led to a series of spectacular mass divorces (Ezra 9–10; Neh 9:2; 13:1–3). At the close of Ezra-Nehemiah, the rebellion ramps up and the response dwindles to Nehemiah's individual efforts to stem the tide. Nehemiah's personal commitments are not in question. He violently beats, physically abuses, and verbally castigates those participating in apostasy marriages. He compares their actions to ancient infidelities

108. On the public nature of crime in a society, see in Greenberg, "Crimes and Punishments," *IDB* 1:733–34.
109. Contra Wellum, "Progressive," 231–32.

of Solomon. The lack of collective response and the now familiar propensity for the same infidelities reveal a failing restoration because of the assembly's hardened addiction to covenant-breaking.

Nehemiah observes men of Judah married to women of Ashdod, Ammon, and Moab (Neh 13:23).[110] These three names of defunct people groups more likely refer symbolically to scriptural traditions than genealogical identities, just as they do elsewhere (Ezra 9:1–2; Neh 13:1–3; see notes ad loc.). The mention of Ammon and Moab once again alludes to the excluded others in the law of the assembly (Deut 23:3[4]). The reference to Ashdodite women seems much more subtle. A possible connection comes in the form of the rare pejorative term "one born of an illicit union," appearing twice in Scripture—one of which immediately precedes the prohibition against Ammonites and Moabites within the law of the assembly.[111]

> No *one born of a forbidden marriage* [מַמְזֵר] nor any of their descendants may enter the assembly of Yahweh, not even in the tenth generation. No Ammonite or Moabite or any of their descendants may enter the assembly of Yahweh. (23:2, 3a[3, 4a])

> *A mongrel people* [מַמְזֵר] will occupy Ashdod, and I will put an end to the pride of the Philistines. (Zech 9:6)

The reference to the people of Ashdod as "a mongrel people," and the same term in Scripture only used to spell out others forbidden to enter the assembly of Yahweh alongside Ammonites and Moabites, may be the reason Nehemiah mentions this triad of others together.

Nehemiah presents as evidence of apostasy marriages the fact that the children could not speak the language of Judah but only the language of Ashdod or the language of another people (Neh 13:24).[112] Though choice of language may not be significant in most cases, Nehemiah becomes enraged, cursing and pummeling the hapless apostates (13:25).[113] Nehemiah interprets the Judeans as "marrying out" rather than the women of Moab, Ammon, and Ashdod "marrying in." If the parents were instructing their children in Torah at home, on the road, evening and morning (Deut 6:7), then they would need to

110. Because of a lack of "and" (וְ) before "Ammonite Moabite" in Neh 13:23, some have taken this as a scribal gloss (Kottsieper, "'They Did Not Care,'" 97). One problem with leveraging grammatical difficulties into alleged scribal glosses is providing evidence or criteria for sorting out authorial scribal shaping from copyist scribal "improvements." The lack of external evidence suggests the more difficult MT is preferred (see *BHS*/*BHQ*).

111. The distasteful term *mamzer* (מַמְזֵר) in Deut 23:2[3] gets translated as "one from a prostitute" (LXX/NETS; from *porne* πόρνη), "one misbegotten" (JPSB), and "those born of an illicit union" (NRSV), and in Zech 9:6 as "bastard" (KJV), "mongrel" (NIV, NRSV), or "half-breed" (*HALOT* 1:595).

112. The lack of the phrase "the language of various peoples" in LXX leads many to see it as a later scribal gloss (see Kottsieper, "'They Did Not Care,'" 97; Klein, "Ezra & Nehemiah," 3:848). Though possible, this evidence is inadequate to support emendation here, so MT preferred (see *BHS*/*BHQ*).

113. The term "smite" (נכה) connotes to hit with the intent to harm, thus "flogged" (Neh 13:25 JPSB).

speak the language of Judah. Others who submit to the covenant were welcome to join the restoration assembly (Ezra 6:21; Neh 10:28[29]). Nehemiah's evidence that these were apostasy marriages comes in the form of the children speaking the language of Ashdod. The interpretative allusion of Nehemiah relates to detecting the meaning of a marriage by how couples raise their children—according to the covenant or according to the ways of others such as Ashdodites.

Nehemiah interprets the law of the assembly of Deut 23:3[4] as a prohibition against apostasy marriage, as elsewhere in Ezra-Nehemiah (Neh 13:25; cf. Ezra 9:1; Neh 13:1–3). He calls upon the men in apostasy marriages to make an oath that they will not seek marriage matches for their Ashdodite-speaking children from among others. Nehemiah uses language from the solemn oath that addresses both sons and daughters (Neh 13:25; cf. 10:30[31]; Deut 7:3).

Nehemiah condemns the men caught in apostasy marriages by comparing the situation to Solomon's notorious, manifold treaty marriages that imported false worship in the form of high places all around Jerusalem (Neh 13:26). One of the additional connections comes in the form of the mention of all four of the representative others of the law of the assembly—excluded Ammonites and Moabites as well as allowable Edomites and Egyptians—as the first four in the list of Solomon's treaty marriages (1 Kgs 11:1). The verbal parallels between Neh 13:25 and 1 Kgs 11:1–4 are minimal despite the overt allusion. One of the more important elements that gets carried over silently from the Deuteronomist's interpretive intervention relates to the causative verb stem (Hif) transposed onto alternate verbs. In telling the story of Solomon's downfall, the Deuteronomist interpretively blends elements from the prohibitions against intermarriage in Exod 34:16 and Deut 7:3. Like Exod 34:16 and Deut 7:4, the writer uses the causative verb stem (Hif) to explain how the treaty wives "turned away" Solomon's heart (see note on 1 Kgs 11:2–4). Nehemiah provides no hint of an echo of the prohibition against apostasy marriages in Torah. Instead, Nehemiah applies the Deuteronomist's exegetical advancement. For Nehemiah, the women who led Solomon astray serve as a paradigm for the infidelity of the restoration assembly (bold signifies verbal parallels, italics signify syntactic parallel stems of different verbs, and broken underlining signifies catchwords in Neh 13:23):

> **King Solomon**, however, loved many **foreign women** besides Pharaoh's daughter—Moabites, Ammonites, Edomites, Sidonians and Hittites . . . and his wives *led him astray*. As Solomon grew old, his wives *turned* his heart after other gods, and his heart was not fully devoted to Yahweh his God, as the heart of David his father had been. (1 Kgs 11:1, 3b, 4)

Was it not because of marriages like these that **Solomon king** of Israel sinned? Among the many nations there was no king like him. He was loved by his God, and God made him king over all Israel, but even he was *led into sin* by **foreign women**. [27] Must we hear

> now that you too are doing all this terrible wickedness and are being unfaithful to our God by marrying **foreign women**? (Neh 13:26–27)[114]

In sum, Neh 13:23–27 features numerous brief interpretive allusions that serve to diagnose the failure of the restoration with its latest round of apostasy marriages. Only Nehemiah speaks and only Nehemiah acts in terms of violent attacks. If he made any progress with the Judean husbands in apostasy marriages, Nehemiah does not say so. The most important exegetical advance is Nehemiah's observation that apostasy marriages also bring harm to Israel's next generation who, in this case, speak nothing but Ashdodite.

FILTERS

The connections within Ezra-Nehemiah to itself are massive, which may seem surprising in light of the high use of source texts and limited editorialization. Connections within this narrative are literary, not interpretive allusions, and cannot be listed here.[115]

Most of the scriptural allusions in Ezra-Nehemiah feature exegesis (see notes in Use of Scripture above) with a much smaller number of broad non-exegetical allusions. This seems to be unique among all the books of the Hebrew Bible.[116]

Non-Exegetical Broad Allusions and Shared Themes

Note: **Ezra 3:2–3** refers to building an altar (" according to what is written in the Torah of Moses") on which they offer morning and evening sacrifices (cf. Exod 29:38–42; Num 28:3–8); **3:5**, new moon offerings (Num 28:11–15); **3:8**, beginning to build Solomon's Temple second month (cf. 2 Chr 3:2). **3:10**, temple foundation (cf. Isa 44:28; Hag 2:18; Zech 4:9); **3:11**, "He is good; his love toward Israel endures forever" (2 Chr 7:6; Jer 33:11; cf. Pss 100:5; 106:1; 107:1; 118:1; 136); **4:14**, covenant of salt (cf. Lev 2:13; Num 18:19; 2 Chr 13:5); **5:11**, reference to building Solomon's temple (cf. 1 Kgs 6–8; 2 Chr 3–6); **5:12**, allusion to destruction of the temple (cf. 2 Kgs 24–25; Jer 52); **6:12**, Darius's echo of the God who established his name in his house in Jerusalem (cf. Deut 12:5, 11; 1 Kgs 9:3);[117] **6:18**, division of priests and Levites (cf. 1 Chr 23–26); **6:20**, purification of priests and Levites (cf. 2 Chr 30:15); **7:14**, seven advisors to the Persian

---

114. The final clause of Neh 13:26 speaks in a forceful personal way by fronting the direct object "him" with the emphatic use of conjunctive particle "Even him!" (גַּם־אוֹתוֹ) (see GKC §153). The next line in 13:27 also fronts the pronominal suffix "you" (pl.) before the interrogative marker (הֲ)—a rare construction signaling emphasis (GKC §100n; cf. Job 34:31; Jer 22:15b). These are literary signals of shrill tone and emphasis: "Even him! . . . And you?!"

115. For a list of ways of referring to deity in Ezra-Nehemiah, see Driver, *Introduction*, 553. For an annotated list of linguistic features of Ezra-Nehemiah, see Japhet, "Supposed Common Authorship," 366–71.

116. For additional potential scriptural parallels with Ezra-Nehemiah, see Eskenazi, *In an Age of Prose*, passim; Klein, "Ezra & Nehemiah," passim; Murawski, "'To Study the Law,'" passim; Slotki, *Daniel, Ezra, Nehemiah*, passim; Smith, "Influence," 345–64.

117. For a comparison of the Hebrew of Deut 12:11 and the Aramaic of Ezra 6:12, see Murawski, "'To Study the Law,'" 90–93. On why a Persian king might use a phrase that evokes Scripture, see 95–96.

crown (cf. Esth 1:14); **10:11**, Ezra refers to a thanksgiving offering (תּוֹדָה, often translated "confession," cf. NRSV), which is very difficult to assimilate in this context that includes a guilt offering. The thanksgiving offering fits better at the wall celebration (Neh 12:27). The situation in Ps 50:14–15, 23 is not analogous to Ezra 10:11.[118]

Note: **Neh 4:14[8]**, do not fear; the Lord is "great and fear-inspiring" (Deut 7:21); **8:2**, first day of seventh month—Festival of Trumpets (cf. Lev 23:24; Num 29:1); **8:9**, the Levites urge the people not to weep, apparently based on Tabernacles as a time for joy (cf. Deut 16:14, 15); **8:10**, sharing food during festival (cf. Esth 9:19, 22); **12:45–46**, marks the service of the Levites by "according to the commands of David and his son Solomon" (2 Chr 8:14–15; cf. 1 Chr 23–28; Table C20 in Chronicles); **12:47**, provisions for the Levites and priests (cf. Num 18:21, 28); **13:29**, covenant of the priests in relation to intermarriage with a non-kinsperson may allude to Lev 21:13–15 (on covenant with priesthood cf. Num 25:12–13; Deut 33:8–11; Mal 1:7, 12; 2:4–8).

118. See Boda, "Words," 295.

Chapter 35

CHRONICLES

SYMBOLS[1]

- // verbal parallels (A level)
- /~/ synoptic parallel (A level)
- ~ B, probable interpretive allusion; C, possible; D, probably not
- >/< more or less similar (see Filters)
- + interpretive blend
- * part of interconnected network (see Networks)
- minus elements of Samuel/Kings excluded from Chronicles
- plus non-synoptic contexts of Chronicles

USE OF SCRIPTURE IN CHRONICLES[2]

The nature of Chronicles makes it a special case. Plus and minus contexts, versus synoptic passages parallel to Samuel and Kings, are indented and listed as a help since both bear on the Chronicler's use of Scripture. Only references in bold represent notes on potential exegetical parallels.

1 Chr 1:1–27~Gen 5:3–32+10:2–4, 6–8, 13–18, 22–29+11:10–29 (B) (genealogies Adam to Abraham)

1:28–33~Gen 25:12–18 (B) (families of Ishmael and Keturah's sons)

1:34–54~Gen 36:1–43 (B) (genealogies and kings of ancient Edom)

2:1–2~Gen 35:22–26 (B) (sons of Israel)

2:3–17~Gen 38:1–7, 29–30+46:12+1 Kgs 4:31[5:11]+Josh 7:1+Ruth 4:18–22+2 Sam 2:18+17:27 (B) (genealogies of Judah through family of David)

plus, 2:18–55 (other genealogies of Judah)

3:1–9~2 Sam 3:2–5+5:5, 13–16 (B)+11:3; 12:24 (C) (sons born to David in Jerusalem)

plus, 3:10–16 (kings of Davidic dynasty)

plus, 3:17–24 (Davidic line in exile and postexile)

plus, 4:1–23 (tribe of Judah)

4:17~Exod 2:7 (D) (daughter of the pharaoh marries into Judah)

4:24–31~Gen 46:10; Josh 19:1–5 (C) (early tribe of Simeon)

plus 4:32–43 (tribe of Simeon)

5:1–2~Gen 49:3–4 (B)+48:13–20 (C)+49:8–12* (C) (Reuben's incest) (* see Judah-king network)

5:3~Gen 46:8–9 (C) (sons of Reuben)

plus, 5:4–10 (tribe of Reuben)

plus, 5:11–17 (tribe of Gad)

plus, 5:18–26 (historical fragments and exile of Transjordanian tribes)

6:1–4[5:27–30]~Gen 46:11+Exod 6:16–25 (C) (line of Levi)

plus, 6:5–15[5:31–41] (line of Aaron)

6:16–19[6:1–4]~Num 3:17–20 (C) (lines of Gershon, Kohath, and Merari of Levi)

plus, 6:20–30[5–15] (Levite lines of Gershon, Kohath, and Merari)

6:27–28[12–13]~1 Sam 1:1; 8:1 (C) (Elkanah, Samuel, and his sons in the line of Kohath)

plus, 6:31–48[16–33] (Davidic singers)

plus, 6:49–53[34–38] (line of Aaron)

6:54–60[39–45]~Josh 21:1–4, 10–19 (B);

6:61–65[46–50]~Josh 21:5–9 (B);

1. For explanation of symbols, see Symbols and Abbreviations and Introduction. For other help, see Glossary.
2. See Bibliographic Note on Lists of Potential Parallels.

6:66–81[51–66]~Josh 21:20–39 (B) (Levitical cities)
plus, 7:1–5 (tribe of Issachar)
plus, 7:6–12 (tribe of Benjamin)
plus, 7:13 (family of Naphtali)
plus, 7:14–15 (early tribe of Manasseh to Zelophehad's daughters)
plus, 7:16–19 (tribe of Manasseh)
plus, 7:20–29 (tribe of Ephraim)
plus, 7:30–40 (tribe of Asher)
plus, 8:1–28 (tribe of Benjamin)
plus, 8:29–40 (Benjamite line of Saul)
9:2–18~Neh 11:3–19 (C) (first returned exiles)
plus, 9:19–34 (Levitical gatekeepers)
plus, 9:35–44 (line of Saul)
10:1–14/~/1 Sam 31:1–13+28:3–25 (B)+Deut 18:11 (C) (death of Saul)
minus, 2 Sam 1:1–16 (death of Saul reported to David)
minus, 2 Sam 1:17–27 (David's lament for Saul and Jonathan)
minus, 2 Sam 2:1–7 (David rules over Judah)
minus, 2 Sam 2:8–3:1 (contending between houses of David and Saul)
minus, 2 Sam 3:6–21 (Abner seeks treaty with David)
minus, 2 Sam 3:22–39 (Joab murders Abner)
minus, 2 Sam 4:1–12 (murder of Ish-Bosheth)
11:1–3/~/2 Sam 5:1–3 (A)+1 Sam 16:1–13 (C) (David made king over all Israel)
minus, 2 Sam 5:4–5 (chronological note concerning David's rule)
11:4–9/~/2 Sam 5:6–10 (David captures Jerusalem)
11:10–47/~/2 Sam 23:8–39 (David's mighty men)
11:18–19~Deut 12:16, 23–25; 15:23 (C) (water represents the blood of life)
12:1–22~1 Sam 22:1–2; 27:6 (C) (tribal militia gathered to David)
plus, 12:23–41 (war chiefs of David at Hebron)
plus, 13:1–4 (David and all Israel decide to get the ark)
13:5–14/~/2 Sam 6:1–11 (A)+Ps 132:6–7 (C) (all Israel to get the ark)
14:1–2/~/2 Sam 5:11–12 (Hiram acknowledges David)
14:3–7/~/2 Sam 5:13–16 (sons of David born at Jerusalem)
14:8–17/~/2 Sam 5:17–25 (David defeats Philistines)
plus, 15:1–24 (David arranges Levites in preparation for getting the ark)
15:1, 3*~Deut 12:5, 11, 14, 18, 21, 26*; 14:23, 24, 25, etc. (C) (place for the ark) (* see place network)
15:13–15~Num 4:4–15; 7:9 (B) (Levites carry the ark on their shoulders)
15:25–16:6/~/2 Sam 6:12–19 (David and all Israel accompany the Levites in bringing the ark)
16:7–36*//Pss 105:1–15*+96:1b–10b*, 11–13b+106:1, 47–48 (A)+Deut 12:5* (B) (psalm of worship) (* see Abrahamic covenant and place networks)
plus, 16:37–42 (Levites appointed for ark and Zadok and priestly family for tabernacle at Gibeon)
16:39–40~Exod 29:38–42; Num 28:3–8 (B)+1 Sam 7:1–2 (C); 1 Kgs 3:4 (B) (sacrifices at tabernacle at Gibeon)
16:43/~/2 Sam 6:19–20a (returning home and David's blessing)
minus, 2 Sam 6:20b–23 (Michal's contempt)
17:1–15*, 16–27/~/2 Sam 7:1–17*, 18–29 (Davidic covenant and David's prayer) (* see Davidic covenant, Judah-king, and place networks)
18:1–13/~/2 Sam 8:1–14* (David establishes a regional empire) (* see Judah-king network)
18:14–17/~/2 Sam 8:15–18/~/20:23–26 (David's leading officers)
minus, 2 Sam 9:1–13 (David's loyalty to Mephibosheth son of Jonathan)
19:1–19/~/2 Sam 10:1–19 (defeat of Ammonites and Arameans)
20:1–3/~/2 Sam 11:1; 12:26a, 30–31 (defeat of Rabbah)
minus, 2 Sam 11:2–12:25 (David's sin with Bathsheba and murder of Uriah)
minus, 2 Sam 12:27–29 (Joab sends for David)
minus, 2 Sam 13:1–19:44 (sibling trouble and Absalom's revolt)
minus, 2 Sam 20:1–22 (Sheba's revolt)
minus, 2 Sam 21:1–14 (Gibeonites slaughter Saul's family)
minus, 2 Sam 21:15–17 (Abishai kills Ishbi-Benob a warrior of Philistia)
20:4–8/~/2 Sam 21:18–22 (killing the giants of Gath)
minus, 2 Sam 22//Ps 18 (song of David)
minus, 2 Sam 23:1–7 (last words of David)

21:1–30/~/2 Sam 24:1–25 (David's sin of the census)
21:1/~/2 Sam 24:1+Num 22:22 (C) (inciting David)
21:16/~/2 Sam 24:17+Num 22:31 (B) (sword drawn)
21:26/~/2 Sam 24:25+Lev 9:24 (B) (fire from Yahweh)
minus, 1 Kgs 1:1–2:9 (Adonijah and Solomon vying for throne in the last days of David)
plus, 22:1–29:25 (David prepares for temple)
22:5–19*~Josh 1:5–9 (C)+2 Sam 7:13–14* (C)+1 Kgs 2:1–4 (D)+5:3–5[17–19] (C) (David privately charges Solomon to build the temple) (* see place network)
23:25–30*~Deut 12:9–10+Num 1:49–50; 3:6–9+4:2–4, 23, 30, 35, 39, 43, 47; 8:24 (C) (Levites serve at the temple beginning at age twenty) (* see teachers network)
28:2–3*//22:8–9~Deut 12:10–11* (B)+2 Sam 7:11* (C)+1 Kgs 5:3–5[17–19] (B) (David's rule lacks rest to build temple) (* see Davidic covenant and place networks)
28:4–6*~Gen 49:8–12* (B)+2 Sam 6:21 (C)+7:13–14* (B) (election of Solomon based on choosing Judah) (* see Davidic covenant, Judah-king, and place networks)
28:7~2 Sam 7:14–15* (B) (irrevocable Davidic covenant and its obligations) (* see Davidic covenant and place networks)
28:19~Exod 25:9, 40 (B) (the plan of the temple revealed)
29:6~Exod 25:2 (C) (free will contribution to the shrine)
29:25~Josh 3:7; 4:14 (C) (Yahweh exalts Solomon)
29:27–30/~/1 Kgs 2:10–11 (death of David)
minus, 1 Kgs 2:12–46 (Solomon establishes his rule)
2 Chr 1:1–13/~/1 Kgs 3:1–15; 4:1a (revelation to Solomon at Gibeon)
plus, 1:3–5 (tabernacle at Gibeon)[3]
minus, 1 Kgs 3:16–28 (Solomon judges wisely)
minus, 1 Kgs 4:1–34[4:1–5:14] (Solomon's officials and prosperous rule)
1:14–17//9:25–28/~/1 Kgs 10:26–29 (Solomon's international horse trade)
2:1–18[1:18–2:17]/~/1 Kgs 5:1–18[5:15–32]+7:13–14; 8:27; 10:9 (A) (Solomon's treaty with Hiram)
3:1–2/~/1 Kgs 6:1+1 Chr 21:25–26+Gen 22:2 (B) (building the temple in Solomon's fourth year)
3:3–14~1 Kgs 6:2–38 (C) (Solomon builds the temple)
minus, 1 Kgs 7:1–12 (Solomon builds a palace and a great court)
3:15–5:1/~/1 Kgs 7:15–51 (Hiram-abi's work on temple accessories)
5:2–14/~/1 Kgs 8:1–11 (Solomon brings the ark into the temple)
6:1–42*/~/1 Kgs 8:12–53* (A)+Deut 12:5* (A)+Ps 132:8–10* (A)+Isa 55:3 (C) (dedication of temple) (* see Davidic covenant and place networks)
minus, 1 Kgs 8:54b–61 (Solomon blesses the congregation)
7:1–3//1 Kgs 8:54a+1 Chr 21:26 (A)//Lev 9:24 (B)+2 Chr 5:13–14 (A)//Exod 40:34–35 (B) (fire falls from heaven)
7:4–10/~/1 Kgs 8:62–66 (dedicate altar and celebrate Tabernacles)
7:11–22*/~/1 Kgs 9:1–9 (A)+Deut 12:5* (B)+Lev 26:41* (B) (second revelation to Solomon) (* see collective confession and place networks)
8:1–11, 17–18/~/1 Kgs 9:10–24, 26–27 (other settlements, projects, and treaties)
8:12–15/~/1 Kgs 9:25+Deut 16:16 (B) (Solomon's worship)
9:1–12/~/1 Kgs 10:1–13 (queen of Sheba visits Solomon)
9:13–24/~/1 Kgs 10:14–29 (prosperity of Solomon)
9:25–28*//1:14–17/~/1 Kgs 10:26–29+4:21*[5:1] (Solomon's international horse trade) (* see Abrahamic covenant network)
minus, 1 Kgs 11:1–40 (Solomon's apostasy and adversaries)
9:29–31/~/1 Kgs 11:41–43 (death of Solomon)
10:1–11:4/~/1 Kgs 12:1–24 (Rehoboam's folly and the revolt)
minus, 1 Kgs 12:25–33 (Jeroboam's golden calves)
minus, 1 Kgs 13:1–34 (man of God from Judah in Bethel to warn Jeroboam)
minus, 1 Kgs 14:1–20 (Ahijah's prophecy against Jeroboam)
plus, 11:5–23 (rule of Rehoboam)
11:15~1 Kgs 12:28–33 (B)+Lev 17:7* (C) (Jeroboam's aberrant renegade worship) (* see place network)

3. On the tabernacle at Gibeon, see note on 1 Chr 16:39–40.

12:1–16/~/1 Kgs 14:21–31 (Shishak attacks Jerusalem)

13:1–23/~/1 Kgs 15:1–8 (rule of Abijah)

13:5~1 Chr 17:14//2 Sam 7:16 (C)+Num 18:19 (B) (Abijah affirms permanent Davidic rule over Israel)

13:6–9>/<11:15; 10:10–11; 11:13–14 (Abijah enhances Jeroboam's apostasies)

13:10–11>/<Exod 40:22–29; Lev 24:1–9; Num 3:10–13 (daily temple worship by descendants of Aaron and Levites)

14:1–16:14/~/1 Kgs 15:9–24 (rule of Asa)

15:2~Jer 29:13–14 (D) (Azariah speaks of seeking and finding Yahweh)

15:6~Zech 11:6 (D) (threat of crushing)

15:7~Jer 31:16 (D) (your work shall be rewarded)

16:9~Zech 4:10+1 Sam 13:13 (D) (eyes of Yahweh range through the earth)

minus, 1 Kgs 15:25–32 (rule of Nadab of Israel)

minus, 1 Kgs 15:33–16:7 (rule of Baasah of Israel)

minus, 1 Kgs 16:8–14 (rule of Elah of Israel)

minus, 1 Kgs 16:15–20 (rule of Zimri of Israel)

minus, 1 Kgs 16:21–28 (rule of Omri of Israel)

minus, 1 Kgs 16:29–34 (rule of Ahab of Israel)

minus, 1 Kgs 17:1–24 (Elijah and the drought)

minus, 1 Kgs 18:1–46 (Elijah and the contest on Mount Carmel)

minus, 1 Kgs 19:1–18 (Elijah at Horeb)

minus, 1 Kgs 19:19–21 (call of Elisha)

minus, 1 Kgs 20:1–43 (Ahab defeats Ben-Hadad of Aram)

minus, 1 Kgs 21:1–29 (Ahab and Naboth's vineyard)

plus, 17:1–19 (establishing the rule of Jehoshaphat)

17:1–21:1/~/1 Kgs 22:1–34, 41–51 (rule of Jehoshaphat)

18:1–19:3/~/1 Kgs 22:2–40 (alliance of Jehoshaphat and Ahab against Aram)

plus, 19:1–3 (the seer Jehu rebukes Jehoshaphat)

plus, 19:4–11 (Jehoshaphat establishes judges)

19:5–7, 8–11~Deut 1:17+16:18–19+17:8–11 (C) (judges accountable to Yahweh in lower and upper courts)

plus, 20:1–30 (Jehoshaphat's victory over Moab and Ammon)

20:15, 17~1 Sam 17:47+Exod 14:13 (B) (Jehaziel declares divine victory over Moab, Ammon, and Edom)

20:20–21~Isa 7:9 (B) (Jehoshaphat calls for faith and appoints lay singers)

minus, 1 Kgs 22:52–2 Kgs 1:18 (rule of Ahaziah of Israel)

minus, 2 Kgs 2:1–18 (Elijah taken up to heaven)

minus, 2 Kgs 2:19–25 (Elisha heals waters and initiates killer bears)

minus, 2 Kgs 3:1–3 (rule of Jehoram of Israel)

minus, 2 Kgs 3:4–27 (revolt of Moab)

minus, 2 Kgs 4:1–6:23 (miraculous signs of Elisha)

minus, 2 Kgs 6:24–7:20 (famine and the siege of Samaria)

minus, 2 Kgs 8:1–6 (Shunammite's land restored)

minus, 2 Kgs 8:7–15 (Elisha foresees Hazael's rule over Aram)

20:31–21:1/~/1 Kgs 22:41–51 (rule of Jehoshaphat)

21:2–20/~/2 Kgs 8:16–24 (rule of Jehoram of Judah)

21:13~Exod 34:16 (C) (Jehoram causes Judah to whore after other gods)

21:18–19~2 Sam 7:12 (D) (bowels came out)

22:1–9/~/2 Kgs 8:25–29 (rule of Ahaziah of Judah)

minus, 2 Kgs 9:1–13 (Jehu anointed king of Israel)

minus, 2 Kgs 9:14–26 (Jehu kills Joram)

minus, 2 Kgs 9:30–37 (death of Jezebel)

minus, 2 Kgs 10:1–17 (Jehu destroys the house of Ahab)

minus, 2 Kgs 10:18–36 (servants of Baal killed)

22:10–23:21/~/2 Kgs 11:1–20 (Athaliah usurps rule)

24:1–27/~/2 Kgs 12:1–22 (rule of Joash of Judah)

24:15~Gen 35:29 (C) (Jehoiada was old and full of years)

minus, 2 Kgs 13:1–9 (rule of Jehoahaz of Israel)

minus, 2 Kgs 13:10–25 (rule of Jehoash of Israel and death of Elisha)

25:1–26:2/~/2 Kgs 14:1–22 (rule of Amaziah)

minus, 2 Kgs 14:23–29 (rule of Jeroboam II)

26:3–23/~/2 Kgs 15:1–7 (rule of Uzziah/Azariah)

26:18*~Lev 10:1, 10–11* (C) (priestly instruction on holy versus common) (* see teachers network)

minus, 2 Kgs 15:8–12 (rule of Zechariah of Israel)

minus, 2 Kgs 15:13–16 (rule of Shallum of Israel)

minus, 2 Kgs 15:17–22 (rule of Menahem of Israel)

minus, 2 Kgs 15:23–26 (rule of Pekahiah of Israel)

minus, 2 Kgs 15:27–31 (rule of Pekah of Israel)

27:1–9/~/2 Kgs 15:32–38 (rule of Jotham)

28:1–27/~/2 Kgs 16:1–20 (rule of Ahaz)

minus, 2 Kgs 17:1–41 (fall of Samaria and exile of Israel)
28:3//2 Kgs 16:3 (A)+Jer 19:5–6 (B) (child sacrifice in the Valley of Ben Hinnom)
29:1–2/~/2 Kgs 18:1–8 (opening frame of rule of Hezekiah)
minus, 2 Kgs 18:9–12 (fall of Samaria)
plus, 29:3–36 (Hezekiah restores temple)
29:7~Lev 24:1–4 (B) (lamps of house of Yahweh)
29:11~Num 18:1–7 (C) (divine election of priests and Levites)
29:18~Lev 24:5–9* (B) (table and rows of bread in temple) (* see Sabbath network)
29:25–30~1 Chr 23–26 (B)+selected Psalms superscriptions (C) (authorizing use of psalms for worship)
plus, 30:1–31:1 (Hezekiah invites Israel to celebrate Passover with Judah)
30:2–3~Num 9:9–11 (B) (shifting Passover observance to second month)
30:16~Num 18:1–7+Lev 1:5 (C) (Levites bring blood from slaughter to priests)
30:18–20~Num 9:10 (C)+2 Chr 7:14 (B) (unlawful Passover participants forgiven)
plus, 31:2–21 (Hezekiah provides for priests)
31:3~Deut 16:16–17+Num 28–29 (C) (bring offerings to temple for all worship)
32:1–23~2 Kgs 18:13–19:37 (A) (Sennacherib invades Judah)
32:7–8~Deut 31:6 (D)+2 Kgs 6:16 (C) (encouragement of greater multitude with use)
32:24–26, 31~2 Kgs 20:1–11, 12–19/~/Isa 38:1–20; 39:1–8 (C)+Deut 8:2 (B) (Hezekiah's illness and receiving Babylonian representatives)
plus, 32:27–30 (wealth of Hezekiah)
32:32–33/~/2 Kgs 20:20–21 (death of Hezekiah)
33:1–20/~/2 Kgs 21:1–18 (A)+25:7 (C) (rule of Manasseh)
33:6//2 Kgs 21:6 (A)+Jer 19:5–6 (B) (child sacrifice in the Valley of Ben Hinnom)
33:21–25/~/2 Kgs 21:19–26 (A)+21:3–5 (C) (rule of Amon and revival of Manasseh's cultic rebellion)
34:1–35:27/~/2 Kgs 22:1–23:30 (rule of Josiah)
34:3–7, 33/~/2 Kgs 23:4–20 (cultic reforms of Jerusalem, Judah, and the land of Israel set in Josiah's twelfth and eighteenth years)
34:8–19/~/2 Kgs 22:3–23:3 (Torah discovered in temple)
minus, 2 Kgs 23:4–20 (Josiah's reforms)
34:20–32/~/2 Kgs 22:3–23:3 (Huldah's prophecy)
35:1–19/~/2 Kgs 23:21–23 (Josiah keeps the Passover)
35:3–4*~1 Chr 23:25–26 (B) (new Levitical responsibilities) (* see teachers network)
35:5–6, 11~Num 18:3–4, 6+Ezek 44:11–12 (C) (Levites perform sacrifices with laity in outer court)
35:12~Lev 3:3–5, 9–11, 14–16 (B) (set aside Yahweh's portion of the sacrifices)
35:13~Exod 12:9+Deut 16:7 (B) (Passover meal fire roasted and boiled)
35:16~Num 28:16–25 (C) (Josiah prescribed Passover sacrifices)
minus, 2 Kgs 23:24–27 (evaluation and judgment against Judah)
35:20–27/~/2 Kgs 23:28–30 (A)+1 Kgs 22:30, 34–35// 2 Chr 18:29, 33–34 (B) (death of Josiah)
35:25~Jer 22:10–12 (D) (Jeremiah's lament for Josiah)
36:1–4/~/2 Kgs 23:31–35 (rule of Jehoahaz)
36:5–8/~/2 Kgs 23:36–24:7 (rule of Jehoiakim)
36:7, 10*~2 Kgs 24:13*+Jer 27:16–22* (B) (removal of temple vessels when Jehoiakim and Jehoiachin are taken captive) (* see temple vessels network)
36:9–10/~/2 Kgs 24:8–17 (Jehoiachin and Babylonian captivity)
36:11–17/~/2 Kgs 24:18–20 (rule of Zedekiah)
minus, 2 Kgs 25:1–7 (fall of Jerusalem)
36:18–20/~/2 Kgs 25:8–21//Jer 52:12–30 (exile of Judah)
minus, 2 Kgs 25:22–26 (remnant flees to Egypt)
minus, 2 Kgs 25:27–30 (Jehoiachin released)
36:21*~Jer 25:11*; 29:10*+Lev 26:34–35 (B) (Jeremiah's seventy years) (* see seventy years network)
36:22–23*//Ezra 1:1–3a* (A)~Jer 25:11*; 29:10* (B)+Isa 44:28*; 45:1 (B)+45:13* (C) (edict of Cyrus) (* see seventy years network)

OLD TESTAMENT USE OF CHRONICLES[4]

n/a

4. On the relationship of 1 Chr 9:2–18 and Neh 11:3–19, see note on 1 Chr 9:2–18.

NEW TESTAMENT USE OF CHRONICLES

1 Chr 17:13~Heb 1:5 (I have become your father)
2 Chr 28:15~Luke 10:30–35 (good Samaritan)
36:15–16+Isa 5:1–2+Ps 118:22–23~Mark 12:1–11; Matt 21:33–44; Luke 20:9–18 (humiliating the messengers)

HERMENEUTICAL PROFILE OF THE USE OF SCRIPTURE IN CHRONICLES

Chronicles houses extensive scriptural interpretation. As such, the present hermeneutical profile provides guidance focused on overall exegetical conventions, section by section exegetical conventions, and implications of scriptural exegesis in Chronicles. This hermeneutical profile offers guidance for the large number of notes on the use of Scripture in Chronicles below. The notes will frequently refer back to tables, figures, and other elements in this hermeneutical profile.

Overall Exegetical Conventions in Chronicles

Introduction. Chronicles houses a bold new version of an old story. The older, authoritative version of the Davidic kingdom story had been around for a long time, and the Chronicler counts on his readers knowing it well when he surprises them with exegetical interventions again and again.[5] If Chronicles reflects the character of its author, he may be considered rigidly conservative and yet courageous or even adventurous in relation to his narration and theology. The discouraged, shamed, and stubborn community of the Second Temple badly needed a new version of the story of the kingdom and its temple. Chronicles delivers unbending conviction in proper temple worship and unbounded hope in Yahweh's renewing mercy, both grounded in a revised version of the great narrative traditions of the Davidic kingdom.

The array of the Chronicler's use of scriptural traditions includes guidance from Torah, prophets, and psalms, which play vital roles in a comprehensively repurposed version of the narrative of the rise and fall of the Davidic kingdom with special attention to the temple. If the burden of the Deuteronomistic narrative—the Deuteronomy-flavored serial narrative of Joshua-Judges-Samuel-Kings—centered on the inevitability of the fall of Jerusalem, the Chronicler's new story seeks to awaken hope and enliven renewed worship.

The present study works with Chronicles as a separate book by a separate author than Ezra-Nehemiah.[6] Questions of the common portion of the edict of Cyrus used in the last verses of Chronicles and the first verses of Ezra-Nehemiah and the list of postexilic inhabitants of Judah both depend on the dating of these books, along with other difficulties

5. The Chronicler presumes readers know of Michal in her cameo appearance (1 Chr 15:29). For many other examples, see McKenzie, "Chronicler as Redactor," 82–85; Williamson, "Mirror," 20 (right column). This evidence eliminates Fishbane's objections against Chronicles as exegetical narrative (*Biblical Interpretation*, 380–82).

6. See Japhet, "Supposed Common Authorship," 330–71; Williamson, *Israel*, 37–59.

(see notes on 1 Chr 9:2–18 and 2 Chr 36:22–23). The canonical form of Chronicles dates no earlier than the six generations after Zerubbabel, based on the list in 1 Chr 3:17–24, who played a vital role in the building of the Second Temple (520–515 BCE).[7] This places Chronicles, at the earliest, in the late fifth or early fourth century BCE—midway through the dominion of the Persian Empire—after the production of the majority of biblical writings. Thus, Chronicles will be regarded as the receptor context in cases of scriptural allusion, unless noted otherwise.

Chronicles offers interpreters an unparalleled opportunity to apprehend how scriptural narratives work. More than that, the Chronicler likely uses Samuel and Kings as sources. Having some of the likely sources and the Chronicler's product gives interpreters a chance to try to think with him. Due caution recognizes the possibility that some synoptic contexts may come from the Deuteronomist and Chronicler working with common sources. The instability of the transmission of Samuel and Kings—seen in the major differences in the Septuagint and the evidence for Hebrew texts akin to both protomasoretic and Septuagint versions at Qumran—also argues for patience and restraint.[8]

Not every variation between Chronicles and its scriptural sources may be exegetically motivated. Consideration of differences made for stylistic reasons falls outside the present study.[9] Shifts between Standard and Late Biblical Hebrew cannot be taken up here unless they bear directly and materially on exegesis of Scripture.[10] Making allowances for non-exegetical variations—shared sources, textual variations, linguistic developments—along with disciplined commitment to evidence for exegetical conclusions is necessary for responsible analysis of the Chronicler's theological interpretation of scriptural traditions.

The hermeneutical profile of scriptural exegesis in Chronicles needs to be pursued "globally" and "regionally." Several fundamental issues relate to the entire book. These need to be ever kept in mind everywhere. Yet, the Chronicler tackles each section of the narrative according to different interpretive rhythms. Whether these shifts in interpretive approach spring naturally from the scriptural sources or from the demands of his agenda does not need to be sorted out here. The next two subsections get at issues of the use of scriptural traditions relative to the entire book of Chronicles. Then the next section, with its several subsections, seeks to explain the hermeneutical rhythms of each major section of Chronicles as these relate to the Chronicler's exegesis of scriptural traditions.

Interpretive Mechanics (Entire Book). The Chronicler appears to expect his readership to evaluate the new story in light of authoritative scriptural traditions. With due caution, as noted above, analysis of the use of scriptural traditions in Chronicles needs

7. For fuller interaction with problems of dating, including the textual problem of 1 Chr 3:21, see note on 2 Chr 36:22–23.

8. See McKenzie, *Chronicler's Use*, 33–81, esp. 72; Lemke, "Synoptic Problem," 349–63; Williams, "Choosing," 193–202, esp. 202. Others suggest the Chronicler may have worked with an earlier or different version of Samuel (Nihan, "Textual Fluidity," 189–94) and/or Kings (Halpern and Vanderhooft, "Editions of Kings," 236–38).

9. For a helpful collection of stylistic differences, see Sugimoto, "Chronicler's Techniques," 36–42.

10. For a definition and citations on LBH, see Hermeneutical Profile of the Use of Scripture in Jeremiah.

to begin with comparison. The approach of many modern interpreters can be listed as questions: What's the same? What's deleted? What's new? What's changed? And, for all of these, why? These general comparisons provide a helpful modern starting point. Use of the ancient observations of Aristotle regarding parallel or synoptic narratives offers more specific interpretive advantages and will be used in this study.

While Aristotle's *Poetics* (ca. 335 BCE) primarily interacts with poetic fiction, he maintains that the same principles apply to the art of historical narration.[11] Aristotle intermittently focuses on multiple versions of the same plot. His helpful observations can be boiled down to three ways to evaluate synoptic differences:

- **Selectivity.** Authors decide which portion of the plot to dramatize (1456a, 6–9).
- **Arrangement.** Authors organize the sequence of events—chronological versus dischronological, jump cuts, and so on—and determine their focus—biographical, thematic, and so on (1459a, 32–34).
- **Voicing.** Authors decide how to voice narratives including action versus narrative comment versus embedded discourse. Aristotle notes that sometimes even adjusting one word can shift the significance of the entire context (1458b, 18–21).

Attending to the kinds of synoptic differences Aristotle observes can strengthen responsible theological interpretation of Chronicles and other scriptural synoptic narratives.

Chronicles contains hundreds of exegetical decisions to (de)select, (re)arrange, and (re)voice in its use of scriptural traditions. Responsible exegesis of the Chronicler's use of scriptural traditions requires the patience to consider each exegetical decision on its own merits, as well as collating many similar exegetical maneuvers together to identify major interpretive trends.

Ideological Function of the New Version of the Kingdom and Temple Story (Entire Book). The extensive use of scriptural traditions in Chronicles shines a light on its ideology in contradistinction to its donor texts. While the Chronicler's ideological emphases may be summarized in terms of several themes, the purpose needs to be spelled out first. The ending of a narrative may be considered its destiny and helps reveal its purpose.

The Chronicler shapes his scriptural sources and other sources into a version of the grand story, featuring a series of recurring renewals.[12] The basic sequence includes widespread rebellion followed by renewal. The period of backsliding centers on neglect

11. See *Poetics*, 1451b, 27–30. The discussion of Aristotle and synoptic interpretation here, and with a little more detail in Hermeneutical Profile of the Use of Torah in Deuteronomy, is condensed from Schnittjer, "Kadesh Infidelity," 104. For a list of synoptic contexts in Scripture, see footnote in Hermeneutical Profile of the Use of Torah in Deuteronomy.

12. See Schnittjer, "Individual versus Collective Retribution," 131–32.

of worship of and devotion to the God of Israel. The Chronicler demonstrates failure to serve Yahweh by concrete symbols of worship—ark, temple, ritual festivals, idolatry, and the city of Jerusalem itself. The pattern of renewal begins with obedient devotion to Yahweh. Figure C1 depicts the most significant examples of renewal.

FIGURE C1: RECURRING RENEWAL IN CHRONICLES‡

‡ See 1 Chr 13:1–8; 15:25–16:3; 2 Chr 29–31; 33:12–13; 36:22–23.

The ending of Chronicles situates readers between exile and accomplishment of an overt, divinely ordained imperial edict for Yahweh's people to rebuild the temple. The shared pattern in the case of David-Solomon, Hezekiah, and later Manasseh involves obedient commitment to Yahweh through temple worship signifying the purpose of the edict of Cyrus. The triggers vary from renewal to renewal offering a plurality of models for starting points, even if sincere, wholehearted worship remains the endgame.

The reference to the edict of Cyrus accomplishing the word of Yahweh through Jeremiah, along with allusion to Lev 26, provides a clue for the needed response of God's people—repentance and devotion to worship (2 Chr 36:21–23). Zedekiah embodies the collective will of the people—all Israel in his day and across the history of the Judean kingdom—when he defies the word of Yahweh by Jeremiah, refusing to "humble himself" (36:12). This defiance embodies the culmination of long rebellion punctuated by judgments. Zedekiah's refusal to listen to Jeremiah as well as the edict of Cyrus fulfilling the word of Jeremiah signals how the Chronicler expects his readership to start renewal by humbling themselves and committing themselves to temple worship. This makes Manasseh's unlikely change of heart to become like David, Solomon, and Hezekiah an ideal model for the similar transformation of readers from defiant exiles to humble worshipers. If the worst-case scenario Manasseh can get right with Yahweh during his own Babylonian captivity, the exiles of Judah have real hope.

The importance of the interrelationship between repentance and worship of Yahweh as driving aspects of the Chronicler's ideology needs to be connected backwards across the book. Notice how the language of "humbling oneself," "turning," "persistent sending," "payment," and "remedy" interconnect and set up ending upon the Chronicler's use of Leviticus and Jeremiah (emphases signify verbal parallels):[13]

> If then their uncircumcised heart **humble itself** [כנע Nif], and then they pay for their iniquity. (Lev 26:41b lit.)

13. See ibid., 118–19.

> Yahweh *has been sending* to you all of his servants the prophets, *persistently sending* [הַשְׁכֵּם וְשָׁלֹחַ], but you have not listened and you have not inclined your ear to listen. (Jer 25:4 lit.)

> Yahweh said to Solomon, "And if my people who are called by my name **humble themselves** [כנע Nif] and pray and seek my face and <u>turn</u> [שׁוב] from their wicked ways, then I will hear from the heavens and I will forgive their sin and I <u>will heal</u> [רפא] their land." (2 Chr 7:14 lit.)

> [Zedekiah] did not **humble himself** [כנע Nif] before Jeremiah the prophet from the mouth of Yahweh. . . . And he stiffened his neck and he strengthened his heart from <u>turning</u> [שׁוב] to Yahweh the God of Israel. . . . Moreover, all of the leaders of the priests and the people increased infidelity according to all of the offenses of the nations. And they polluted the house of Yahweh which he had made holy in Jerusalem. And Yahweh the God of their ancestors *sent* to them by the hand of his messengers, *persistently sending* [הַשְׁכֵּם וְשָׁלוֹחַ], because he took pity on his people and on his dwelling place. And they ridiculed the messengers of God, despising his words, mocking his prophets, until the wrath of Yahweh rose up against his people, until there was no <u>remedy</u> [רפא]. (2 Chr 36:12, 13b, 15, 16 lit.)

While the language of "humbling oneself" and "turning" concretely demonstrate how the Chronicler shapes his storyline by exegesis of scriptural traditions, the basic concept runs deeper than these verbal parallels.[14] The Chronicler includes one sin of David—one—in what may be the nexus narrative of the Chronicler's ideology of worship.[15] David's repentance receives divine sanction by fire falling on his sacrifice from on high, thus inaugurating the threshing floor of Ornan (Araunah) as the place God has chosen for worship (1 Chr 21:26). The Chronicler rearranges his source materials so that the acquisition of the place of David's repentance—the future temple mount—fronts the most massive plus of the entire story (see Figure C7). David prepares for Solomon to build the temple (1 Chr 22–29). Where? David repents on Ornan's threshing floor, that is, Mount Moriah where Abraham almost sacrificed Isaac (2 Chr 3:1; cf. Gen 22:2). These interpretive allusions promote the Chronicler's central ideological agenda by means of deep continuity. The purpose of the Chronicler's new version of the story comes out in both the major patterns and the smallest details of his use of scriptural traditions.

The Chronicler frequently uses scriptural traditions as he promotes several leading themes. Awareness of the Chronicler's theological angle helps interpreters detect many of his repeated exegetical maneuvers (see Table C2).[16]

---

14. For a more narrowly focused narrative pattern based on key words including "humble oneself," see Glatt-Gilad, "Periodization in Chronicles," esp. 252–57.

15. For a similar observation see Bodner and Johnson, "David," 132.

16. The basic theological emphases of Chronicles are widely acknowledged (e.g., Klein, "Chronicles, Book of 1–2,"

TABLE C2: DOMINANT THEMES IN CHRONICLES

- David–Solomon
- all Israel
- temple-worship-priests-Levites-Jerusalem ---------- (wisdom friendly)
- retribution ----------
- authoritative instruction

While careful inductive study of the Chronicler's use of scriptural traditions affirms these widely acknowledged themes, a few exceptions and adjustments can help avoid excesses. The main body of Chronicles features David and Solomon. In some ways the rest of the book leads up to and moves on from these royal patrons of the temple. Though speaking of David and Solomon as "idealized" in Chronicles remains commonplace, it overstates the case. Whereas the Deuteronomist makes an apologetic for the inevitability of the fall of the kingdom and seems to blame everyone, the Chronicler selects details of "public" David and Solomon, especially as they pertain to worship. David sins in Chronicles. Other shortcomings include: David fails to bring the ark to Jerusalem on his first attempt; he is disallowed to build the temple; Solomon's greatness is diminished by granting David nearly all the credit for the temple and omitting many achievements (his wisdom, administration, building projects).[17] While David and Solomon dominate Chronicles, speaking of idealization oversells the wrongs points.

Elements related to individuals in Samuel or Kings often get "democratized" in Chronicles, evidenced by the frequent insertions of "all Israel."[18] In many cases of the Chronistic handling of David, Solomon, and Israel, the real issues turn on temple and worship. Lynch goes so far as to claim that "[f]or Chronicles, the temple defined Israel's collective purpose."[19]

In many respects the Chronicler emphasizes strict justice with explicit notations of rewards or punishments delivered immediately.[20] Discussions of the Chronicler's retribution sometimes exaggerate this emphasis, not adequately handling his more complex treatment of several kings.[21] The Chronicler treats five kings—one out of every four—in a complex manner that does not fit with interpretive strategies that seek to flatten retributional patterns in Chronicles.[22] One major element not adequately factored into many

ABD 1:999–1001). "Authoritative instruction" is one theme in Table C2 that has not received adequate attention. See helpful discussions in Schniedewind, "Chronicler as Interpreter," 158–80; Glatt-Gilad, "Chronicles as Consensus Literature," 73–75. On "wisdom," see below.

17. See Japhet, *Ideology*, 368–81; Knoppers, "Changing History," 112*–13*.

18. See Japhet, *I & II Chronicles*, 47.

19. Lynch, *Monotheism*, 265.

20. See Dillard, *2 Chronicles*, 76–81.

21. See esp. Wellhausen's sarcastic disparagement of divine retribution as articulated by the prophets of Chronicles (*Prolegomena*, 203–10). For helpful cautions against exaggerating retribution in Chronicles, see Rudolph, "Problems," 405–6.

22. See notes ad loc. on Rehoboam (2 Chr 12:1–16), Jehoshaphat (18:1–19:3), Ahaziah (22:1–9), Amaziah (25:1–26:2), and Hezekiah (32:24–26, 31).

discussions of Chronistic[23] "retribution theology" relates to the deferred judgment of exile. The Chronicler uses scriptural traditions to "do the math," explaining the seventy years of exile as deferred judgment for rebellion across the entire First Commonwealth (see note on 2 Chr 36:21).

The Chronicler's worship and retribution lexicon and theological outlook overlap in certain respects with aspects of biblical wisdom. Sorting this out requires attention to shared language but also larger theological themes. Most of the distinctive terminology of biblical wisdom finds little place in Chronicles.[24] The Chronicler even decides not to use the most direct statements of wisdom in Kings.[25]

The wisdom sentences of Proverbs constantly draw attention to the relationship between actions and consequences mostly with "secular" retribution in view, though the sage refers to Yahweh on occasion:[26]

> Be sure of this: The wicked will not go unpunished, but those who are righteous will go free. (Prov 11:21)

> The wicked are overthrown and are no more, but the house of the righteous stands firm. (12:7)

On the surface the proverbial ideals of just ends seem quite akin to the Chronicler's ideology of divine retribution. But these general similarities regarding retributive justice need to be aligned with the positive side of seeking Yahweh. Chronicles, like Proverbs, repeatedly emphasizes "seeking."[27] But the importance of seeking Yahweh could be mediated just as easily through Deuteronomy or Psalms (bold signifies verbal parallels):

> But if from there [exile] you **seek** [בקשׁ] Yahweh your God, you will find him if you **seek** [דרשׁ] him with all your heart and with all your soul. (Deut 4:29; cf. 12:30)

---

23. As noted in the Glossary, in this study "Chronistic" refers to Chronicles but not Ezra-Nehemiah, and "Deuteronomistic" refers to Joshua-Judges-Samuel-Kings but not Deuteronomy.

24. For example, "wisdom/wise" only appears in 2 Chr 1:10–12; 2:12; 9:3, 5, 6, 7, 22, 23; or applied to skilled craftsmen for temple building in 1 Chr 22:15; 28:21; 2 Chr 2:12, 13.

25. See 1 Kgs 3:16–28; 4:29–34[5:9–14].

26. See von Rad, *Wisdom*, 129, with additional examples. Von Rad does not discuss wisdom in Chronicles. Also see Longman, *Proverbs*, 82–86; idem, *Fear of the Lord*, 179–80, 184–86, 188–90.

27. The general observations of Chronicles and wisdom literature using "seek" come from Toews, "Wisdom Contribution of Chronicles." For a list regarding "seek" (דרשׁ, בקשׁ) and related ideals, see "Selections from the Chronistic lexicon of (in)fidelity" in Chronicles Filters. The Chronicler uses synonymous terms for "seek" interchangeably (דרשׁ, בקשׁ), even while strongly preferring *d-r-sh* (דרשׁ). Chronicles uses the collocation of "seek Yahweh" more than anywhere else in the Bible (Even-Shoshan, 276–77). Proverbs frequently speaks of "seeking" (בקשׁ) wisdom (Prov 2:4; 14:6), good (11:27), knowledge (15:14; 18:15), love (17:9), Yahweh (28:5), and negative counterparts for folly (cf. 17:11, 19; 18:1; 21:6; 23:35; 29:10); but it uses "seek" (דרשׁ) only one time (11:27). For competing approaches to the one taken here, see Blenkinsopp, "Wisdom in the Chronicler's Work," 19–30; Oeming, "Wisdom as Central," 125*–41*.

> **Seek** [דרשׁ] Yahweh and his strength; **seek** [בקשׁ] his face always. (Ps 105:4// 1 Chr 16:11†)

> [Amaziah said] Yahweh is with you when you are with him. If you **seek him** [דרשׁ], he will be found by you, but if you forsake him, he will forsake you. (2 Chr 15:2b)

The shared outlook between Deuteronomy and Proverbs runs deep.[28] Moses can speak of obedience to the commands as "wisdom," and Solomon can speak of wise teaching as "torah" (Deut 4:6; Prov 3:1).[29] The shared retributive ideology of Chronicles, Deuteronomy, Proverbs, and other scriptural contexts may be something more like overlapping circles in a Venn diagram. The present study does not regard wisdom per se as central to Chronicles but recognizes worship and retribution in Chronicles as wisdom friendly (see Table C2).

Authoritative instruction refers to scriptural traditions of Torah, prophets, and psalms, as well as David and prophetic figures that appear in Chronicles. The relationship of the Chronicler's Torah to the final scriptural form has been sharply contested. Part of the debate turns on many contexts that seem paraphrased, interpreted, or extrapolated in relation to the wording that appears in Torah. Chronicles sometimes overtly marks citations of Torah akin to marking in Ezra-Nehemiah (see Marking in Hermeneutical Profile of the Use of Scripture in Ezra-Nehemiah). Affirmation of citations as "according to" Torah or the like refers to agreement and concord not verbatim quotation.[30]

One particular authoritative instruction looms large in the Chronistic reshaping of the David and Solomon stories, namely, the instruction for central worship (Deut 12:2–28). The Chronicler often exegetically strengthens the narrative, relative to Yahweh's election of the place for his name, beginning with David's and Israel's re-acquisition of the ark in 1 Chr 15 and continuing through the second theophany to Solomon in 2 Chr 7 (see discussion of Deut 12 in notes along the way and see place network). The Chronicler did not draw this emphasis out of thin air but enhances exegetical advancements within the Deuteronomistic narrative he retells. Solomon's address to Israel at the completion of the temple includes an interpretive blend of the election of the place Yahweh chose and Yahweh's choice of David (see note on 1 Kgs 8:16–21). In this way exegetical advances of

28. See shared emphases in Weinfeld, *Deuteronomic School*, 244–81, 362–63, irrespective of his unlikely excavative agenda. And see Longman, *Proverbs*, 80–81, who says wisdom and law are not related like "brothers" but "close cousins."

29. Also note the Second Temple identification of personified Woman Wisdom as Torah (Bar 4:1; Sir 24:23).

30. The preposition "according to" (כְּ) appears in each of these: "according to the commandment of Moses" (כְּמִצְוַת מֹשֶׁה) (2 Chr 8:13), "according to the Torah of Moses" (כְּתוֹרַת מֹשֶׁה) (30:16), "according to the word of Yahweh" (כִּדְבַר יהוה) (1 Chr 11:3, 10; 15:15; 2 Chr 35:6), and "as it is written" (כַּכָּתוּב) (23:18; 25:4; 30:5, 18; 31:3; 35:12, 26). See Schniedewind, "Chronicler as Interpreter," 166–67. The use of "like, as, according to" (כְּ) is the major element in "*as* it is written" (כַּכָּתוּב), signaling likeness or agreement (see GKC §118s; *IBHS* §11.2.9a, b).

authoritative instructions in the older Samuel-Kings narrative give rise to further exegetical advances of the very same instructions in Chronicles.

In sum, the list of theological emphases in Table C2 offers a general starting place for figuring out how the Chronicler uses scriptural traditions in individual contexts. Cautious flexibility with things that do not seem to fit also helps with responsible exegesis of Chronicles', use of scriptural traditions.

Section by Section Exegetical Conventions in Chronicles

The Chronicler presents a new version of an old story in four parts that each operate by different exegetical rhythms (see Table C3).

TABLE C3: THE BROAD STRUCTURE OF CHRONICLES

I. Universal origin for ancestry of all Israel as context for the Davidic kingdom (1 Chr 1–9)
II. David establishes Jerusalem as home of the ark and future location of the temple of Yahweh for all Israel (10–29)
III. Solomon builds the temple for the worship of Yahweh (2 Chr 1–9)
IV. The temple of Yahweh in the hands of the Davidic kings until its destruction and the captivity of its constituents (10–36)

I, Ancestry, 1 Chronicles 1–9—exegetical tendencies. Chronicles opens with a series of genealogies many of which come from other scriptural contexts.[31] While vertical or linear genealogies tend to establish claims of power, status, office, inheritance, or the like, horizontal or segmented genealogies present branches to situate internal and/or external social relations, political function, and so on.[32] Genealogies may stress equality (e.g., among the tribes of all Israel) or inequality (e.g., favored or shamed tribes).[33] The study of the scriptural use of Scripture naturally stresses theological implications of repurposing genealogies in new settings.

The Chronicler aligns his genealogies with biblical traditions to maintain a kind of conservative continuity. The Chronicler quickly takes readers from Adam to Israel to David (1 Chr 1:1; 2:1, 15). The Chronicler puts Judah first and Levi in the center and treats both more extensively than any other tribe, all of which fits with his agenda (see Table C2). The Chronicler enumerates all twelve tribes by counting the half-tribe of Manasseh of the Transjordan separately from the other half (5:23–26; 7:14–19). The Chronicler's lists move geographically from Judah south, then north through the Transjordanian tribes, then, after Levi, the remaining Galilee and hill country tribes (see Figure C4).

31. Less than half of Chronistic genealogies come from scriptural sources (Knoppers, "Greek Historiography," 633).

32. See Wilson, "Old Testament Genealogies," 179; Walton, "Genealogies," 314–16; Chavalas, "Genealogical History," 126–27.

33. See Wilson, "Genealogy, Genealogies," *ABD* 2:932.

FIGURE C4: THE ARRANGEMENT OF THE CHRONICLER'S LISTS OF THE TWELVE TRIBES OF ISRAEL

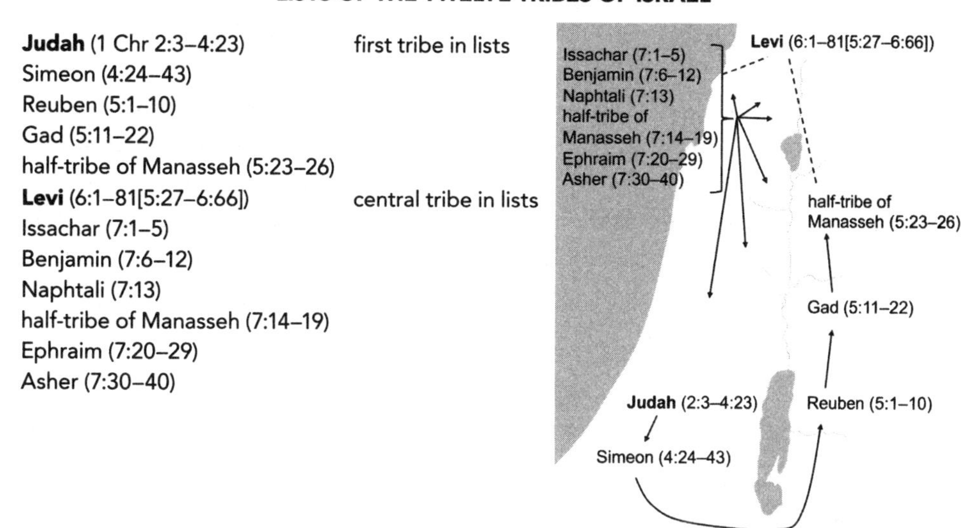

To summarize, the Chronicler uses genealogical scriptural traditions in ways that reinforce the ideology of his narrative. These include the priority of Davidic rule, the centrality of the temple and its worship personnel, and the inclusiveness of all Israel. But all these things could be accomplished—are accomplished—by the narrative itself without genealogies and, as Janzen argues, even short genealogies could strengthen such tendencies.

The massive genealogical prologue of Chronicles does something more. The many gaps eliminate using the lists for formal pedigree but could honor ordinary individuals alongside ancients of name. Ancients who could afford it used monuments to memorialize their names, like Jacob's beloved Rachel (Gen 35:20), Saul (1 Sam 15:12), and Absalom (2 Sam 18:18). The genealogies of Chronicles may offer a sort of "textual monument," inviting any individual, like the named preexilic dead, to appreciate their role in seeking Yahweh at his temple.[34]

The nature of lists, names, and fluid spelling, along with ancient scribal conventions, account for manifold textual challenges in biblical lists, including the genealogies in Chronicles. Explaining the textual issues of Chronicles and its biblical sources needs to be left to technical commentaries and specialized studies. The notes on 1 Chr 1–9 below are sharply restricted to prominent cases of exegetical intervention.

---

34. See Janzen, "Monument," 45–66. Janzen demonstrates that gaps in the genealogies do not allow them to function as proofs of pedigree. No father is listed for Manasseh (1 Chr 5:23; 7:14), Ephraim (7:20), Jahdai and others listed with the tribe of Judah (2:47; 4:8–20), and several in the tribe of Benjamin (53). The lists do not reach to the citizens of the late Persian period—only Judah runs to six generations beyond Zerubbabel (3:17–24). The point of inadequacy for establishing formal pedigree is well taken for proving "ethnicity" or "nobility" (50–55). But scriptural genealogies with gaps can be used literarily and symbolically to corroborate personal standing, like the stylized schematic genealogy of Messiah in Matt 1:1–17. In any event, Janzen makes a strong case for the equalizing effect of naming ordinary ancient individuals alongside notable ancestors who sire nations or royal and worship figures (64, 65, 66).

II, David, 1 Chronicles 10–29—exegetical tendencies (see Table C3). Three examples of the Chronicler's selectivity and rearrangement of the David traditions offer insight into his interpretive agenda in this section of his narrative. First, the Chronicler selectively uses the David traditions, beginning with 2 Sam 5 when David captures Jerusalem and becomes king of all Israel. The Deuteronomist portrayed "private" David and his troubles to emphasize divine providence in his rise to kingship, his sinfulness, and many attendant complications. For example, David's great sin with or against Uriah's wife explains the background of the queen mother of Solomon and keeps a focus on the rebellious path to exile. The Chronicler excludes all these matters even while he includes massive inserts on David's role in appointing worship leadership and preparing for the temple in Jerusalem (see Table C5).

TABLE C5: MAJOR CHANGES IN THE DAVID STORY FROM SAMUEL–KINGS TO CHRONICLES

"Personal" and troubled David excluded in Chronicles	"Public" and worship planning David added in Chronicles
• Private anointing (1 Sam 16:1–13) • Narrative of defeat of Philistine champion from Gath (17) • Evolving relationships with Saul, Jonathan, and Michal (16:14–23; 18–19) • Troubles as fugitive head of band of soldiers outside the bounds of Israel (20–31) • David mourns death of Saul and Jonathan (2 Sam 1) • David's anointing as king of Judah and civil war (2–4) • David's loyalty to Mephibosheth (9) • David and Uriah (11:2–12:25) • Trouble in David's household and failed revolution of Absalom (13–19) • Revolt of Sheba (20:1–22) • Gibeonites avenged (21:1–14) • David's song (22) and last words (23:1–7) • Adonijah's failed coup (1 Kgs 1:1–27)	• The tribes come to David before his anointing as king of all Israel (1 Chr 12) • David establishes ark and worship in Jerusalem (15–16) • David prepares for the temple (22–29)
Approximate excluded chapters, 33	**Approximate added chapters, 11**

Second, the Chronicler rearranges scriptural episodes and integrates them with his other source materials. The Chronicler may have in mind David's oath to find a place for Yahweh in Ps 132:2–5—the only psalm to mention the ark—for his rearrangement of the ark tradition.[35] Table C6 illustrates the sequential rearrangement of episodes in 1 Chronicles from David's anointing to the Davidic covenant. The rearrangement includes placing the first attempt of David to move the ark as his first act after taking Jerusalem (1 Chr 13:5–14). It needs to be remembered that 2 Sam 5–6 does not represent

35. See Knoppers, *I Chronicles 10–29*, 590–91.

"chronological sequence." Both the Deuteronomist and Chronicler use narrative sequence for theological ends, with only partial overlap. The Deuteronomist dischronologizes David's taking of Jerusalem as his first act after being anointed king over all Israel.[36] The Chronicler retains the fronting of the capture of Jerusalem and then sequentially prioritizes moving the ark, effectively aligning David's actions with Ps 132:2–5.[37]

FIGURE C6: SEQUENTIALLY PRIORITIZING WORSHIP IN 1 CHRONICLES 11–17

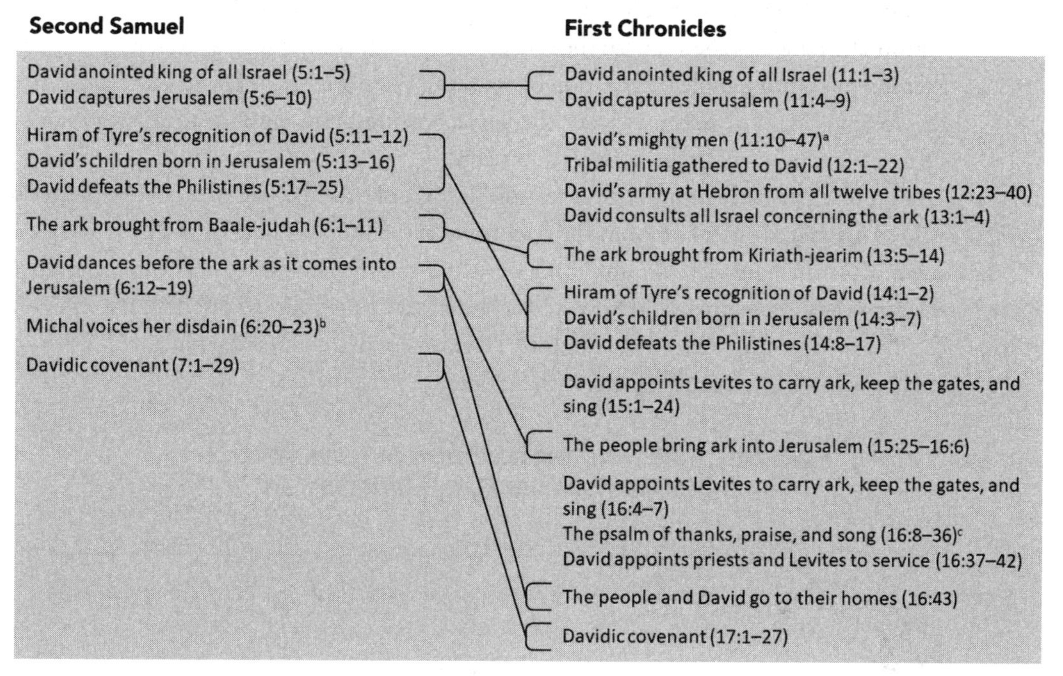

[a] 1 Chr 11:10–47/~/2 Sam 23:8–39.

[b] Only Michal's interior disdaining of David is carried over 2 Sam 6:16/~/1 Chr 15:29.

[c] 1 Chr 16:8–36//Pss 105:1–15; 96:1b–10b, 11–13b; 106:1, 47–48.

Second Samuel
First Chronicles
David anointed king of all Israel (5:1–5)
David captures Jerusalem (5:6–10)
Hiram of Tyre's recognition of David (5:11–12)
David's children born in Jerusalem (5:13–16)
David defeats the Philistines (5:17–25)
The ark brought from Baale-judah (6:1–11)
David dances before the ark as it comes into Jerusalem (6:12–19)
Michal voices her disdain (6:20–23)[b]
Davidic covenant (7:1–29)
David anointed king of all Israel (11:1–3)
David captures Jerusalem (11:4–9)
David's mighty men (11:10–47)[a]
Tribal militia gathered to David (12:1–22)
David's army at Hebron from all twelve tribes (12:23–40)
David consults all Israel concerning the ark (13:1–4)
The ark brought from Kiriath-jearim (13:5–14)
Hiram of Tyre's recognition of David (14:1–2)
David's children born in Jerusalem (14:3–7)
David defeats the Philistines (14:8–17)
David appoints Levites to carry ark, keep the gates, and sing (15:1–24)
The people bring ark into Jerusalem (15:25–16:6)
David appoints Levites to carry ark, keep the gates, and sing (16:4–7)
The psalm of thanks, praise, and song (16:8–36)[c]
David appoints priests and Levites to service (16:37–42)
The people and David go to their homes (16:43)
Davidic covenant (17:1–27)

Third, the Chronicler relocates and repurposes materials from the epilogue of Samuel. Observing the shift in function of these elements provides insight into the Chronicler's handling of scriptural traditions concerning David. In Samuel, the list of David's mighty men directly precedes the last episode. The notable placement of Uriah at the end of the list where he cannot be missed invites readerly reconsideration of one of David's worst moments (2 Sam 23:39). By juxtaposing Uriah the Hittite with the final episode, readers

36. 2 Sam 5:17 implies that the anointing of David over all Israel instigates the battle with the Philistines, an event that would stand chronologically prior to David taking Jerusalem, which in turn needs to precede bringing the ark to Jerusalem. See McCarter, *II Samuel*, 175.

37. Elsewhere the Chronicler shapes his narrative with a plus from Ps 132:1, 8–10/~/2 Chr 6:41–42, demonstrating that the psalm may be on his mind in rearranging 1 Chr 13:5–14 even without citing Ps 132:2–5.

consider the sin with the census in light of his previous sin, now made worse because of Uriah's long devotion to David.

The Chronicler separates the list of David's associates from the sin of the census and places it at the head of his political consolidation around Jerusalem (1 Chr 11:10–47). The list of David's loyal men leads into a much larger solidarity between David and the tribes of Israel (12). Together they get the ark and achieve political rest. The Chronicler also adds several names to the list, effectively displacing Uriah from the final position—he is still there but not in a prominent position (11:41; also see note on 3:1–9). The Chronicler relocates the sin with the census, along with adding several enhancements, so that it segues into temple preparation by marking the site of ideal David-like repentance for worship (21). The narrative loads theological connotation onto the threshing floor of Ornan—(re)location, (re)location, (re)location.

Figure C7 visually summarizes the possible logic of the Chronicler as he interpretively shaped his macro-storyline from the traditions in 2 Samuel. The Chronicler fronts two appendices of 2 Samuel to set up the major sections of the David story. The list of mighty men now heads a segment of David and all Israel securing political rest, and the sin with the census now provides an on-ramp to David's extensive worship initiatives. Both of these reach proximate fulfillment with Solomon.

FIGURE C7: SHIFTING THE FUNCTION OF NARRATIVE UNITS FROM SAMUEL TO CHRONICLES‡

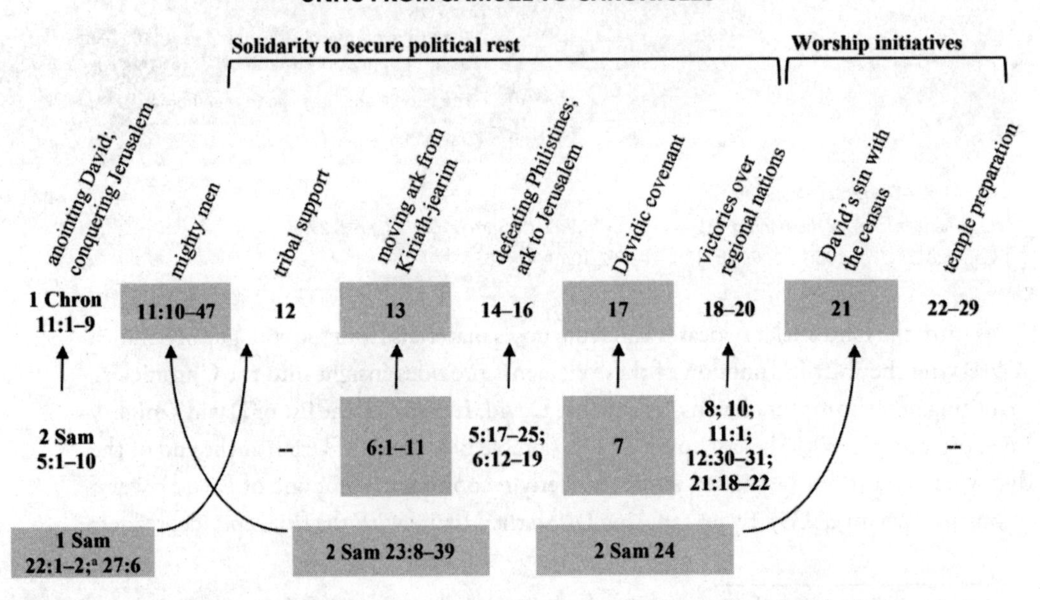

‡ This figure is adapted from my unpublished classroom workshop notes. See partially overlapping independent observations in Schniedewind, "Chronicler as Interpreter," 164.

[a] On 1 Sam 22:1–2 with 1 Chr 12, see Japhet, *I & II Chronicles*, 257, 263.

Macrolevel selection and rearrangements of source materials from Samuel offer insight into the Chronicler's exegetical agenda in his use of scriptural traditions. The broad shifts signal the kind of repurposing also evident in more detailed shifts within smaller units of the Chronistic version of David. All of this stands as part of the new version of the story the Chronicler produces to resituate the identity of his audience.

III, Solomon, 2 Chronicles 1–9—exegetical tendencies (see Table C3). Of the four major sections, the Chronicler's treatment of Solomon follows most closely the Deuteronomistic version. While the normal kinds of selection and enhancements can be noted along the way, broad shaping includes chiastic rearrangement and figural patterns.

First, the Chronistic version of the Solomon story features several adjustments and rearrangements of scriptural traditions to produce a broad chiastic structure. Though interpreters often overplay the middle section of chiastic structuring of dynamic narratives, the central panel of a descriptive narrative like Chronistic Solomon does get featured by this literary arrangement. The central panel relates to the dedication of the temple. The other interpretive outcomes of chiastic arrangement relate to symmetry and repetition. Table C8 illustrates the broad shape of the Deuteronomistic and Chronistic versions of Solomon.

TABLE C8: CHIASTIC RESHAPING OF SOLOMON IN CHRONICLES‡

1 Kings	2 Chronicles[a]
(A) David's last days and the coronation of Solomon (1–2)	
(B) Solomon's accomplishments (3–10)	(A) Solomon's wealth and wisdom (1:1–17)
• First revelation to Solomon (3:1–15)	(B) Recognition by gentiles (2:1–16)
• Wisdom (3:16–28)	(C) Temple construction featuring gentile labor (2:17–5:1)
• Wealth (4)	
• Building temple (5–6)	(D) Temple dedication (5:2–7:22)
• Building palace (7:1–12)	(C) Other construction featuring gentile labor (8:1–16)
• Temple furnishings (7:13–51)	
• Dedication of temple (8)	(B) Recognition by gentiles (8:17–9:12)
• Second revelation to Solomon (9:1–9)	(A) Solomon's wealth and wisdom (9:13–28)
• Solomon's wealth and fame (9:10–10:29)	
(C) Solomon's downfall (11)	

‡ The broad chiastic outline of 2 Chr 1–9 is based on the much more detailed outlines of Dillard, "Literary Structure," 87–88; idem, "Chronicler's Solomon," 299–300; also see Kalimi, *Reshaping*, 223–27. For a different side-by-side layout of 1 Kgs 1–11 and 2 Chr 1–9 that does not observe the somewhat symmetrical framing repetitions already present in 1 Kgs 3–10, see Spawn, "Sacred Song," 53.

[a] Also see the unit-by-unit synoptic comparison in the note on 2 Chr 1:1–13.

Although 1 Kgs 1–11 does not feature tight symmetrical repetitions, building the temple and its dedication have been framed by the two revelations (1 Kgs 3:1–15; 9:1–9), accounts of wisdom and wealth (3:16–4:34; 9:10–10:29), and references to commerce with Hiram (5:1–18[15–32]; 9:11–14; 10:11–12) (see Table C8).[38] The Chronicler more fully works out preexisting repetitions into framing symmetries by cloning and reusing several narratives (on cloning see Glossary). The Chronicler's intentional bracketing repetitions can be seen in his use of Solomon's international horse trading in 2 Chr 1:14–17 and 9:25–28 (only once in 1 Kgs 10:26–29); Hiram's preview of the queen of Sheba's declaration of Solomon's rule as a consequence of Yahweh's love in 2 Chr 2:11[10] and 9:8 (only once in 1 Kgs 10:9); and the twofold account of the theophany at the temple dedication in 2 Chr 5:13–14 and 7:1–3 (only once in 1 Kgs 8:10–11).[39]

Second, the Chronicler reshapes the Solomon narrative figurally. The Deuteronomist echoes significant traditional details portraying David's instruction of Solomon akin to Moses and Joshua (1 Kgs 2:1–4; Deut 31:7–8, 23; Josh 1:6–9), and the glory coming into the tabernacle and temple (1 Kgs 8:10–11; Exod 40:34–35). The Chronicler expands on David's instruction of Solomon with many similar allusions contextualized into the Davidic covenant to build the temple (1 Chr 22:6–16; 28:20–21) and, as noted above, presents the theophany at the temple dedication in a twofold manner (2 Chr 5:13–14; 7:1–3).[40] The Chronicler expands and adjusts his presentation of the role of the artisan Huram-Abi to intentionally echo the ancient tabernacle artisans Bezalel and Oholiab (Exod 31:1–6; 35:30–36:2; 38:22–23; 2 Chr 2:12–14[11–31]; versus 1 Kgs 7:13–14).[41] For comparative discussion of other figural reworkings, see Table C10.

IV, Temple in the Hands of the Davidic Kings, 2 Chronicles 10–36—exegetical tendencies (see Table C3). After Solomon, the Chronicler exegetically revises scriptural traditions to accent the relative (in)fidelity of the line of the kings of Judah, especially with reference to their patronage of the temple. The emphasis on retribution in 2 Chr 10–36 becomes pronounced (see Table C2 and associated discussion). Though Kings often makes explicit divine blessing and punishment, the reworking of this material in Chronicles makes it seem like the Deuteronomist allowed for numerous loose ends. In many cases the new materials inserted into Chronicles offer causal relationships, sometimes providing acts of sin or righteousness as causes to set up judgment or blessing and at other times providing effects to preexisting causes for the same reasons. The general trend toward spelling out retribution in Chronicles can be clarified by attention

38. For more detailed views of the reversals in 1 Kgs 1–11, see Parker, "Repetition," 24–25, and diagram, 27; Frisch, "Structure," 9–13.

39. See Dillard, "Literary Structure," 88–89.

40. On the commissioning of Joshua/Solomon typology, see Williamson, "Accession of Solomon," 352–56.

41. See Dillard, "Chronicler's Solomon," 297–98.

to the exclusion of the Northern Kingdom of Israel, the function of prophetic figures, the use and revision of royal formulas, and the heavy-handed use of literary patterns and templates.

First, Chronicles excludes the Northern Kingdom of Israel. In between Solomon and Hezekiah, Kings interweaves accounts of the kings of the northern and southern Hebrew kingdoms along with many colorful stories of prophets of the Northern Kingdom and a small number of more reserved prophets of Judah. The constant shifting between north and south in Kings demonstrates a commitment to all Israel, even while favoring Judah. The deletion of the Northern Kingdom and its many prophets of God does not signal a diminishment in either one of these commitments by the Chronicler. Chronicles excludes the Northern Kingdom as illegitimate in order to parade the Davidic rulers as the kingly line of all Israel.

Second, the Chronicler adds several messages by prophetic figures that interrelate in many cases with scriptural exegesis. The Chronicler's interpretive agenda does not come out in subtle shifts in prophetic function but through the prophet's messages. As Knoppers quips, "The medium is not the message; the message is the message."[42] The prophetic messages of Chronicles line up with the criteria of Deuteronomy. The message of a prophet must accord with reality (Deut 18:22). This relates especially to prophetic claims about divine intervention in history. The challenges of prophetic threats and warnings, which evoke repentance and adjust the contingent judgment, make up a normal sort of difficulty in identifying true prophets—the ironic problem of prophetic success. Stated differently, prophetic warnings always seem to have an implied "unless you repent" contingency clause.[43] The prophet's message needs to accord with Torah (13:1–5[2–6]). A prophet who performs signs but speaks against Torah must be rejected as a false prophet (13:3[4]; cf. Matt 7:21–23; 2 Thess 2:9).

The historical and instructional functions of prophetic messages—according to reality and according to Torah—offer a way to distinguish the exegetical function of the prophets' use of scriptural traditions in Chronicles. The historical and instructional emphases of prophetic messages get at different kinds of interpretation even if they overlap. Interpretation of divine intervention in historical events focuses on God's sovereignty, and interpretation of scriptural traditions focuses on human responsibility. The different kinds of prophetic messages in Chronicles often feature literary signals of exegesis such as "because," "so that," "by this," and the like. Table C9 provides broad organization of the overlapping and interrelated exegetical functions of prophetic messages.

---

42. Knoppers, "Democratizing Revelation?" 400. The discussion here is indebted to 392–404; idem, "To Him You Must Listen," 165–74; and is adapted from Schnittjer, "Individual versus Collective Retribution," 121–24.

43. See, e.g., Jer 26:18–19 for Micah not being considered a false prophet even when Jerusalem was spared, contrary to his prophecy.

TABLE C9: EXEGETICAL FUNCTION OF PROPHETIC MESSAGES IN NON-SYNOPTIC CONTEXTS OF CHRONICLES‡

	Historical—exegesis of divine intervention (Deut 18:22 oriented)	**Historical and Instructional** (Deut 13:2[3] and 18:22 oriented)	**Instructional**—exegesis of human responsibility (Deut 13:2[3] oriented)
direct discourse	**2 Chr 16:7–9**, Hanani[a] **20:14–17**, Jahaziel[b] **20:37**, Eliezer[c] **21:12–15**, Elijah[de] **25:15, 16**, prophet[f] **28:9–11**, Oded[ef]	**2 Chr 12:5, 7**, Shemaiah[h] **15:1–7**, Azariah[fi] **19:2–3**, Jehu[gj] **25:7–9**, man of God[b] **35:21**, Necho[k]	**1 Chr 12:18[19]**, Amasai[j] **2 Chr 24:20**, Zechariah[j]
summary allusion[m]		**36:21**, Jeremiah[l]	**36:12**, Jeremiah[l] **36:15**, messengers[l]

‡ This table is based on Schnittjer, "Individual versus Collective Retribution," 132, Table A. Besides the non-synoptic prophetic messages, Chronicles also includes five synoptic prophetic speeches, by Nathan (1 Chr 17:1–15/~/2 Sam 7:1–17), Gad (1 Chr 21:9–12, 18/~/2 Sam 24:11–13, 18), Shemaiah (2 Chr 11:2–4/~/1 Kgs 12:22–24), Micaiah (2 Chr 18:12–27/~/1 Kgs 22:13–28), and Huldah (2 Chr 34:22–28/~/2 Kgs 22:14–20) (see Klein, *1 Chronicles*, 19).

• Literary signals of historical contingency and/or explanation: [a] "because" (עַל־כֵּן); [b] no literary signals; [c] "because" (כְּ); [d] "because" (תַּחַת אֲשֶׁר); [e] "behold" (הִנֵּה); [f] "because, so that" (כִּי); [g] "on account of this" (בְּזֹאת).

• Literary signals of instructional motivation (parenesis) and/or explanation: [h] "so" (וְ); [i] "if" (אִם); [j] "because" (כִּי); [k] syntactical jussive; [l] no embedded direct discourse.

[m] On the textual problem related to the other Zechariah, see note on 2 Chr 26:5 (if a prophetic figure, he fits in the summary allusion row in instructional column).

Many Chronistic prophets allude to scriptural traditions. Prophetic authority maintains a decisive place in the Chronicler's understanding of divine intervention within historical contingency. A couple examples can illustrate (emphasis mine):[44]

> Jehoshaphat stood and said, "Listen to me, Judah and people of Jerusalem! Have faith in Yahweh your God and you will be upheld; *have faith in his prophets and you will be successful.*" (2 Chr 20:20)

> They abandoned the temple of Yahweh, the God of their ancestors, and worshiped Asherah poles and idols. Because of their guilt, God's anger came on Judah and Jerusalem. *Although Yahweh sent prophets to the people to bring them back to him, and though they testified against them*, they would not listen. (24:18–19; cf. 36:15–16)

The Chronicler frequently features prophetic messages with explicit acknowledgements of fulfillment, or implicitly expected fulfillment, most of which do not have a synoptic parallel in Kings.[45] The consistent pattern of divine utterance and fulfillment may be considered a function of putting divine retribution on display.

44. See Macy, "Sources of Chronicles," 48.

45. For explicit acknowledgement of fulfillment, see 2 Chr 10:15/~/1 Kgs 12:15; 2 Chr 12:5–8, 12; 24:20–25;

Third, the Chronicler frequently shapes his narrative units by means of recycling literary patterns. For the present purposes, the functions of narrative templates shall be exaggerated to illustrate the Chronicler's habits. In reality, the functions of paradigmatic shaping, extended echo-effect, and typological patterning overlap like circles in a Venn diagram. **Paradigmatic shaping** refers to narrative sequencing of characterization—good days then bad days, and the like. Kings presents all kings as morally static—evil or righteous—except Solomon, who turned away in his old age (1 Kgs 11:4).[46] Chronicles features many kings who begin one way and end another. **Extended echo-effect** denotes imagery, events, and/or persons modeled after others in order to transfer connotations (see Glossary). The exegetical effects of imitating these patterns may be thought of in terms of simile, Y is *like* X, implying the X-like qualities or actions of Y. In common with other authors before him, the Chronicler sometimes self-consciously uses the preposition "like" (כְּ) to mark (dis)similarity; for example, Amon "did not humble himself before Yahweh *like* Manasseh his father humbled himself" (2 Chr 33:23 lit., emphasis mine). More often in Chronicles, extended echo-effect is not formally marked as simile. **Typological or figural patterns** connote expectations looking forward and proximate fulfillments looking backwards (see Glossary).[47] Though narrative types are commonplace, here they refer to direct and indirect expectations of divinely established institutions. The exegetical bases of several typological fulfillments in Chronicles are summarized in Figure C17 and compared to other kinds of narrative templates in Table C10. In Chronicles, all expectational typological elements relate to the accounts of David and Solomon.

Table C10 presents representative examples of using narrative templates in Chronicles. The primary purpose of this table is to place side by side several different kinds of functions (right-hand column)—theological and homiletical—to serve as a resource for context-by-context evaluation of scriptural interpretation in 2 Chr 10–36.

Fourth, the Chronicler reveals his interpretive agenda in how he shifts the function of the royal formulaic structure of Kings on occasion. Ancient scribal conventions often use standard formulaic framing to structure royal records.[48] Kings uses a series of formulas somewhat methodically to arrange and tell the story of the rise and fall of the Hebrew kingdoms (see Kings Filters); Chronicles largely follows this scheme in the case of the kings of Judah, though with more variety according to contextual agenda. Table C11 provides the basic and generalized royal formulas of Kings and Chronicles suitable for the present purposes.

25:15–16, 20; 36:22; cf. 1 Chr 11:3, 10; 2 Chr 35:21–24 (Macy, "Sources of Chronicles," 50–51). For implicit fulfillment, see 1 Chr 14:10–12, 14–17/~/2 Sam 5:19–21, 23–25; 1 Chr 21:9–16/~/2 Sam 24:11–15; 2 Chr 15:1–9; 18/~/1 Kings 22; 2 Chr 20:14–17, 20, 37; 21:12–19; 24:20; 25:7–13; 34:22–25 (ibid., 51–52; Knoppers, "Democratizing Revelation?" 403).

46. See Begg, "Death of Josiah," 2, n. 3.

47. For a collation of many types and Chronistic fulfillments, see Boda, "Legitimizing the Temple," 313–18.

48. A streamlined royal formulaic structure houses the ancient Edomite king list in Genesis: A son of B became king of Edom; his city was named C; when A died, X son of Y from Z succeeded him as king (Gen 36:31–43). The last part matches the formulaic closing in Kings. See Bin-Nun, "Formulas from Royal Records," 429.

TABLE C10: FUNCTIONS OF THE USE OF NARRATIVE TEMPLATES IN CHRONICLES

		function
paradigmatic shaping	good, then bad:[a] Rehoboam (2 Chr 12:1–2); Asa (16:1–2, 7); Jehoshaphat (18:1–2; 19:2–3); Joash (24:17–18); Amaziah (25:14); Uzziah (26:16)	retributive apologetic/moral warning
	good, then bad, then good: Hezekiah (32:25–26)	unclear
	bad then good: Manasseh (33:12–13)	invitation to repentance
	very good but bad ending: Josiah (35:22)	warning against dismissing prophetic message
	multigenerational bad then good: Saul–David; Ahaz–Hezekiah; prophets' auditors (36:15–16)—(hopefully) Cyrus's auditors (36:22–23)	invitation to seek Yahweh
	early purging reforms, then prophetic word leading to public reforms by mandate:[b] Asa (14:3–4; 15:1–7; 15:8–15); Jehoshaphat (17:6–9; 19:2–3, 4–11); Josiah (34:3–4, 22–28, 34:31–35:19)	invitation to obey prophetic admonition
extended echo-effect	celestial delegate opposes David like Balaam (1 Chr 21:1, 12, 16, 30; cf. Num 22:31)	explanation of divine judgment
	Manasseh taken captive like Zedekiah (2 Chr 33:12; cf. 2 Kgs 25:7)	context for repentance
	Manasseh's cultic reforms like Chronistic Jotham and Deuteronomistic Josiah (2 Chr 33:14–16; cf. 27:3; 2 Kgs 23:4–7, 8, 12)	effects of humbling self
	Josiah dies like Ahab (2 Chr 35:22–24; cf. 18:29, 33–34//1 Kgs 22:30, 34–35)	effects of rebelling against prophetic word
typological patterning	**PRESENT IN KINGS AND EXPANDED IN CHRONICLES:**	
	David instructs Solomon like Moses instructs Joshua (1 Chr 22:6–16; 28:20–21; cf. Deut 31:7–8, 23; Josh 1:6–9; 1 Kgs 2:1–4)	proximate fulfillment of divinely sanctioned institutions
	glory coming into the tabernacle and temple (repeated 2x in Chronicles) (2 Chr 5:13–14; 7:1–3; cf. Exod 40:34–35; 1 Kgs 8:10–11)[c]	"
	UNIQUE TO CHRONICLES:	
	David acquires plans for shrine by revelation like Moses (1 Chr 28:19; cf. Exod 25:9, 40)	"
	Huram-Abi like Bezalel and Oholiab (2 Chr 2:12–14[11–13]; cf. Exod 31:1–6; 35:30–36:2; 38:22–23)[d]	"
	temple built on location of revelation to David, namely, Mount Moriah (2 Chr 3:1; cf. Gen 22:2; 1 Chr 21:26–28)	"
	divine consecration of sacrifice at temple dedication by fire like David's sacrifice of confession, in turn, like tabernacle dedication (2 Chr 7:3; cf. Lev 9:24; 1 Chr 21:26)	"

[a] Examples of good, then bad are from Begg, "Death of Josiah," 2; Dillard, "Reign of Asa," 210.

[b] Chronicles portrays Asa, Jehoshaphat, and Josiah as enacting limited early reforms purging false worship (Jehoshaphat also promotes Torah education, 2 Chr 17:7–9) then in response to prophetic messages enacting mandated collective reforms of extensive proportions. Asa assembled Judah and Benjamin and the other tribes residing with them and they together forced commitment to seek Yahweh (15:8–15). Jehoshaphat brings (causative form of verb, שוב Hif, 19:4) constituents from Beersheba to Ephraim and enacts judicial reforms from Torah. Josiah appoints/enforces 3x (causative form of verb, עמד Hif, 34:32, 33; 35:2) pledge and worship in accord with David and Torah. The observation of early lesser reforms, then prophetic word leading to more extensive reforms in the case of Asa, Jehoshaphat, and Josiah, is indebted to Glatt-Gilad, "Role of Huldah's Prophecy," 22–28 (though the present study differs with Glatt-Gilad on many specifics).

[c] See Dillard, "Literary Structure," 88–89.

[d] See Dillard, "Chronicler's Solomon," 297–98.

TABLE C11: STANDARD ROYAL FORMULAS IN KINGS AND CHRONICLES[‡]

Opening frame	• synchronism with northern counterpart (Kings only)[a] • age at accession (Judah only)[b] • length of reign[c] • name of mother of kings (Judah only)[d]
Evaluation	• editorial on king's fidelity (did what was evil/good in eyes of Yahweh)[e] • comparison to David (Judah) or Jeroboam (Israel)
Closing frame[f]	• summation along with source citation[g] • sometimes a supplementary notation • king's death and description of burial[h] • notice of successor

[‡] The table is indebted to Macy, "Sources of Chronicles," 115–50; Halpern and Vanderhooft, "Editions of Kings," 179–244; Glatt-Gilad, "Regnal Formulae as a Historiographic Device," 184–209.

[a] For the Chronistic references where they are missing, see Sugimoto, "Chronicler's Techniques," 56. The only exception is synchronism between Abijah of Judah and Jeroboam of Israel (2 Chr 13:1//1 Kgs 15:1). See Glatt-Gilad, "Regnal Formulae," 187–88.

[b] Chronicles follows Kings in all ages of kings at accession, except two, which both result from textual problems: Ahaziah cannot be forty-two (2 Chr 22:2) but twenty-two (2 Kgs 8:26), since his father Jehoram died at age forty (2 Kgs 8:17; 2 Chr 21:5); and Jehoiachin was not eight years old (2 Chr 36:9) but eighteen (2 Kgs 24:8), since he was already married (24:15) (see Glatt-Gilad, "Regnal Formulae," 188; *BHS* apparatus 2 Chr 22:2; 36:9).

[c] Chronicles follows the length of rule in Kings except in two cases: the additional ten days in Jehoiachin's rule, perhaps a secondary corruption related to the textual issue mentioned in the previous note (see Williamson, *1 and 2 Chronicles*, 414); and the length of Asa's rule, which may have been excluded along with the queen-mother notice (see Glatt-Gilad, "Regnal Formulae," 189).

[d] For a detailed comparative table of queen mothers in formulas, see Halpern and Vanderhooft, "Editions of Kings," 198.

[e] The evaluative statements, which are repetitive and stereotypical in Kings, are frequently adjusted by the Chronicler in relation to his contextual agenda (see Macy, "Sources of Chronicles," 126–27, and for lists 131–34; Glatt-Gilad, "Regnal Formulae," 191–92, with examples).

[f] The Chronicler sometimes adjusts the context immediately preceding the concluding formula as a sort of "tone setter" (see Glatt-Gilad, "Regnal Formulae," 194).

[g] The basic concluding summation in Kings reads, lit., "now the rest of the events [and all] which he had accomplished" (ויתר דברי [וכל] אשר עשה). Kings often embellishes concluding summations; cf. Solomon (1 Kgs 11:41); Asa (15:23); Jehoshaphat (22:46); Hezekiah (2 Kgs 20:20); Manasseh (21:17). The concluding formulas vary in Chronicles (see Glatt-Gilad, "Regnal Formulae," 196). Though Kings consistently cites the source of the kings of Judah as "the scroll of the events of the kings of Judah" (see list of references in Kings Filters), the Chronicler never refers to this source by this name (for variations see Chronicles Filters). The placement of the citation formula in Chronicles follows Kings with "slavish adherence" except in the case of Josiah (Williamson, "Reliving the Death of Josiah," 10).

[h] Japhet says, "[T]he Chronicler viewed a person's burial as a theologically meaningful event, the last opportunity for recompense according to his deeds" (*I & II Chronicles*, 909). See the detailed comparison of death and burial formulas in Halpern and Vanderhooft, "Editions of Kings," 189–90. In Kings, beginning with Hezekiah, the phrase "with his ancestors in the city of David" is no longer used. In Chronicles, Hezekiah and Josiah get minor upgrades in their burial reports (see Glatt-Gilad, "Regnal Formulae," 205).

The heavy-handed voiceover editorial evaluation in Kings seeks to determine the meaning of the historical details of the kings on the front end—for example, "he did evil in the eyes of Yahweh." Since this does not leave judgment up to readers, the Chronicler adjusts some of these by omissions, disclaimers, and other modifications. The formulaic closing summation provides the other most notable place for adjustments in the narrative interpretation of the individual kings. The variations between Kings and Chronicles in the evaluation formulas provide explicit evidence of intentional narrative reshaping.

The Chronicler cites both political and prophetic sources, and in a few cases of "double attribution," both a political and prophetic source.[49] The Chronicler maintains a pattern of referring to prophetic sources for kings who submit to the prophetic word, or at least do not reject it, versus referring only to political sources for kings who reject prophetic authority.[50]

In sum of the preceding two sections, the critical concerns of interpretive mechanics and ideology constantly need to be kept in mind everywhere in Chronicles. Meanwhile, the interpretive rhythms of the narrative differ from one section to the next. Many notes refer back to specific tables, figures, and the associated discussion above in the Hermeneutical Profile of the Use of Scripture in Chronicles.

Implications of Scriptural Exegesis in Chronicles

Chronicles houses more scriptural exegesis than any scroll in the Christian Bible by a wide margin. The extent of scriptural exegesis in Chronicles makes it desirable to spell out selected implications of Chronistic exegesis to guide the case by case evaluation below. These will be organized by implications of Chronistic exegesis overall and then implications of Chronistic exegesis from each of the four main sections of the book (see Table C3).

Overall, the Chronicler reinterprets the story of Yahweh worship by means of the royal patronage of the Davidic kingdom according to scriptural traditions. The Chronicler interprets many Deuteronomistic narratives in light of allusions to scriptural prophets and psalms, but especially Torah.

The use of Scripture in Chronicles as a whole has sometimes been misrepresented by emphasizing too narrow of a point. Commonplace caricatures in the literature speak of a rigid commitment to harmonize. The parade examples are preparing the Passover meal and Goliath (see notes on 1 Chr 20:4–8; 2 Chr 35:13). Even if the point is granted, this does not adequately explain a legion of bold and dramatic Chronistic exegetical advancements. Instead, examples of Chronistic harmonization demonstrate a commitment to the authority of scriptural traditions. Though the Chronicler can be a bold exegete, the evidence demonstrates his repeated honoring of scriptural traditions.

Many of the Chronicler's boldest exegetical maneuvers upon the narratives of Samuel and Kings come from interpretive blends with Torah, prophets, and psalms. But the Chronicler also frequently takes cues from the Deuteronomistic narrative itself. Just as the narrative of David capturing Jerusalem is dischronologically fronted in Samuel immediately after he is anointed king of all Israel (2 Sam 5:6–10), so too the Chronicler fronts conquering Jerusalem and prioritizes getting the ark to the city (see note on 1 Ch 13:5–14; Figure C6). The Chronicler enhances dischronological prioritization of Davidic worship in line with Ps 132 (see notes on 16:7–36; 2 Chr 6:1–42).

49. See 2 Chr 20:34; 32:32; 33:18–19; 35:26–27 (see Glatt-Gilad, "Regnal Formulae," 200).

50. For prophetic source citations, see 1 Chr 29:29; 2 Chr 9:29; 12:15; 13:22; 20:34; 26:22; 32:32; 33:19; for only political citations, see 2 Chr 16:11; 24:27; 25:26; 28:26; 36:8; for an exception, see 27:7 (see ibid.).

The theologically loaded poems of the Deuteronomistic narrative in Judg 5; 1 Sam 2; 2 Sam 1; 22; 23; and 2 Kgs 19 offer important models for the function of the Psalms medley in 1 Chronicles 16. The Chronicler enhances pre-existing parallels in the semi-symmetrical account of Solomon in Kings by cloning and rearranging several vignettes (see note on 2 Chr 1:14–17; Table C8). The Chronicler even takes advantage of stereotyping in Kings in transformative ways. Chronistic Josiah dies like Deuteronomistic Ahab, and Chronistic Manasseh reforms like Deuteronomistic Josiah (see notes on 2 Chr 33:1–20; 35:20–27; Table C10). In this way the Chronicler demonstrates that even the best king can fall like the worst while the worst can turn to ways of the best. In these and other cases, the Chronicler boldly advances Deuteronomistic traditions according to other Deuteronomistic traditions.

In sum of the entire book, the Chronicler does not interpret scriptural traditions to contradict or subvert them. He exegetes scriptural traditions according to scriptural traditions. As much as anywhere else in the Hebrew Scriptures, the Chronicler demonstrates that authoritative traditions and exegetical advances are not polar opposites. Effective exegetical advancements can only work within and in continuity with the authoritative scriptural traditions they advance. Speaking of Chronicles as supplementing or complementing Samuel and Kings does not explain what is going on. Chronicles embodies the advancement of revelation by honoring and celebrating the Deuteronomistic narrative even while reapplying the story for constituents facing new challenges.

The most important exegetical accomplishment of **opening the book (1 Chr 1–9)** with nine chapters of genealogies and lists may be the form itself. The Chronicler begins by evoking the entire book of Genesis by means of its genealogies lightly annotated but no narratives (see notes on 1 Chr 1; Tables C12 and C13). The subsequent sets of lightly annotated genealogical lists repeatedly reinforce the major Chronistic thrusts of the narrative by how it repurposes traditional scriptural genealogies with other source materials. The genealogical prologue of Chronicles demonstrates the importance of David's line in relation to the entire human race and all Israel. The centrality of the priests and Levites in the genealogies signal their indispensable roles in helping Israel seek Yahweh in temple worship. But foreshadowing theological outcomes by genealogical exegesis is secondary to the lists themselves.

The genealogies testify to a profound continuity from the beginning. The genealogies effectively memorize ordinary ancient persons by naming them side by side with those who are well known. The discouraged constituents of Chronicles need to find their place in the great work of God. The Chronicler shows not tells how regular people join with Davidic kings and Levitical worship personnel to seek Yahweh.

The Chronicler persistently reshapes Deuteronomistic traditions by means of allusive narration. In one sense figural recapitulation of storied elements is all the same—one story echoes another. But a granular set of distinctions seems to be the only good way to identify differences between how **the Chronicler treats David and Solomon (1 Chr 10–2 Chr 9)** versus the other Davidic kings. The sorts of figural narrative templates in Chronicles can be called paradigmatic shaping, extended echo-effect, and typological patterning (see Table C10; Figure C17; Glossary). Expectational typological patterning only appears in the Chronistic retelling of David and Solomon.

The Chronicler anchors typological patterning of the David and Solomon stories by a series of Torah contexts, especially those associated with the tabernacle. A couple of these appear in a less-developed form in Kings: David instructs Solomon like Moses instructs Joshua, and the glory fills the temple as it did the tabernacle (1 Kgs 2:1–4; 8:10–11). Besides enhancing these typological allusions, Chronicles features revelation of plans for the temple to David echoing Moses on the mountain, fire from Yahweh identifying Davidic repentance on Mount Moriah forming an allusive intersection of tabernacle and Abraham's faithfulness, and Huram-Abi working on the temple in tabernacle-like ways (see notes on 1 Chr 21:26; 28:19; 2 Chr 2:1–18[1:18–2:17]; 3:1–2). These retrospective typological patterns together serve the protracted fulfillment of establishing worship in the place of Yahweh's choosing.

More than any other Scripture, the Chronicler methodically reshapes the stories of David and Solomon around the incremental fulfillment of Yahweh choosing a place for his name to dwell anticipated in Deut 12:5–14 (see Chronicles references in place network). Though the central place of worship of divine choosing seems in the background everywhere, it moves to the foreground in Nathan's revelation of the covenant to David. A modern might think selecting a place is cut and dry. But the Chronicler understands what is at stake. The necessary conditions for establishing the place for worship involves a profound reshaping of the First Commonwealth—Chronicles narrates this set of changes. The changes involve reformatting a place for the ark to rest, Levitical identity, and securing the political and financial means to build a house of worship for Yahweh (e.g., see notes on 1 Chr 15:1, 3; 16:7–36; 23:25–30; 28:2–3).

The exclamation point of reshaping the Davidic and Solomonic narratives around Deut 12 comes at the dedication of the temple. Selections of psalms once again intrude and fire again falls from heaven (see notes on 2 Chr 6:1–42; 7:1–3). The Chronicler reinterprets the second theophany to Solomon in line with Deut 12 and reveals that choosing the place for worship changes things. The Chronicler's exegetical advances of divine revelation segues between the incremental steps involved in choosing the place of worship in the narratives of David and Solomon to what this means for the kingdom and beyond.

The Chronicler retells the story of the second theophany with a brief but exegetically loaded insert. Yahweh borrows part of Solomon's prayer of dedication and infuses it with exegetical enhancements. Solomon had called upon Yahweh to hear prayers and respond to repentance by forgiveness (1 Kgs 8:35–39//2 Chr 6:26–30). Yahweh exegetically advances this request by inserting loaded imagery and language based on Lev 26: "if my people, who are called by my name, *will humble themselves* and pray *and seek my face and turn from their wicked ways*, then I will hear from heaven, and *I will forgive their sin and will heal their land*" (2 Chr 7:14, emphasis mine). In many respects this exegetically enhanced revelation sets the course for the remainder of the Chronistic story.

Many interpreters have rightly detected the Chronistic enrichment of retributive equilibrium in **the story of the Davidic kingdom (2 Chr 10–36)**. Many new elements reinforce the Chronicler's retribution-friendly reshaping. But the Chronicler treats five kings—about a quarter of them—in a more complex way which needs to be taken seriously.[51] Prioritizing retribution does not eliminate the messy details of life in the kingdom as told by the Chronicler.

Although the Chronicler leaves aside typological patterning, in 2 Chr 10–36 he makes heavy use of paradigmatic shaping and extended echo-effect to re-present the story of the kingdom of Jerusalem (see Table C10; Glossary). In place of static good or evil characters in Kings, the Chronicler often re-narrates with scriptural elements playing a role in turning points from good to evil or vice versa. The Chronicler's use of extended echo-effect produces some of the most sensational exegetical outcomes to instruct readers. The transformation of Manasseh by "humbling himself" while in Babylonian captivity and other extended echoes demonstrate that no one, not even the worst of kings, is beyond hope (33:12; see note ad loc.). The Chronicler provides an ideal counterpoint by using unlikely extended echoes from the death of notorious Ahab to warn readers that no one, not even Josiah, can ever get beyond the need for humble obedience of Yahweh's will (see note on 35:20–27). These exegetical messages stem from interpreting one scriptural narrative in the light of another.

Perhaps nothing demonstrates the power of Chronistic exegetical advancements more than the prayer of Hezekiah. The context of Hezekiah's Passover already includes collectively taking advantage of the divinely sanctioned provision of legal adjustments originally designed for individuals to worship at an alternate time (see Num 9:9–14; note on 2 Chr 30:2–3). With the entire Passover celebration already in the alternate timing, still many participants knowingly violate standards for ritual purity. Hezekiah prays in light of the programmatic revelation to Solomon in 2 Chr 7:14 and Yahweh forgives. The Chronicler uses extended echo-effect to shape the entire context (see note on 30:18–20; Table C23). Yahweh forgives even intentional violations committed within plan B worship. These exegetical advances seem like the opposite extreme from accusations of the Chronicler's rigid need for harmonization to the letter of the law in preparing Passover meals (35:13). Both aspects of the Chronistic use of scriptural traditions need to be kept

51. See notes on Rehoboam (2 Chr 12:1–16), Jehoshaphat (18:1–19:3), Ahaziah (22:1–9), Amaziah (25:1–26:2), and Hezekiah (32:24–26, 31).

in view. Yes, Torah binds Israel to obedience. And, yes, Yahweh forgives repentant souls who seek his mercy.

In sum, Chronicles begins with Adam and ends with the edict of Cyrus. Both of these and the entire story in between feature manifold daring, sometimes subtle, sometimes complex scriptural interpretations. The voluminous exegetical advances of the Chronicler's new version of an old story offer instruction and hope to a people of Yahweh under pressure from the empire.

USE OF SCRIPTURE

1 Chr 1:1–27~Gen 5:3–32+10:2–4, 6–8, 13–18, 22–29+11:10–29 (B) (genealogies Adam to Abraham).

1:28–33~Gen 25:12–18 (B) (families of Ishmael and Keturah's sons).

1:34–54~Gen 36:1–43 (B) (genealogies and kings of ancient Edom).

2:1–2~Gen 35:22–26 (B) (sons of Israel). The genealogies from Genesis at the beginning of Chronicles need to be handled together. The Chronicler learns from Genesis how to do things with genealogies, including using annotation and, at times, symmetry to list generations. Genesis consistently presents segmented before linear genealogies, using the unfavored to set up the elect.[52] Table C12 highlights the placement and role of many of the long genealogies of Genesis.

TABLE C12: LONG GENEALOGIES IN GENESIS

creation, garden, and murder narratives (Gen 1:1–4:16)
genealogical branch Adam through Cain to Lamech (4:17–26)
linear genealogy of ten generations Adam through Seth to Noah (5)
sons of God, flood, and hangover cursing narratives (6–9)
schematic segmented genealogical branches of Noah's three sons (10)
tower narrative (11:1–9)
linear genealogy of ten generations Shem to Terah (11:10–26)
Abraham narratives (11:27–25:11)
genealogical branch of Ismael (25:12–18)
Jacob narratives (25:19–35:29)
genealogical branch of Esau and Edomite king list (36)
sons of Jacob narratives (37–50)

The Chronicler strips out the narratives and genealogical annotations of Genesis and presents a selection of its main horizontally branching and vertically descending genealogies to begin his prologue (see Table C13).

52. See Wenham, *Genesis 1–15*, 97.

TABLE C13: GENESIS-SHAPED GENEALOGIES OF 1 CHRONICLES 1

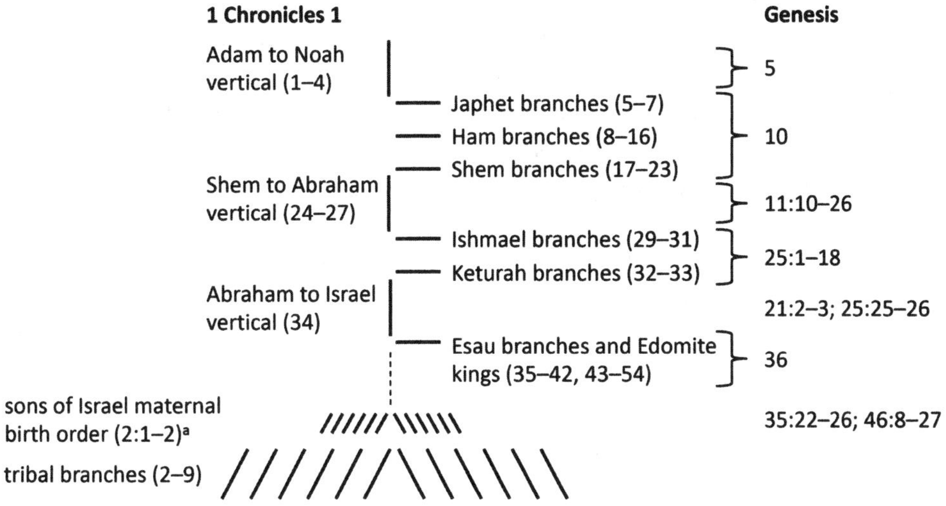

1 Chronicles 1		Genesis
Adam to Noah vertical (1–4)		5
	Japhet branches (5–7)	
	Ham branches (8–16)	10
	Shem branches (17–23)	
Shem to Abraham vertical (24–27)		11:10–26
	Ishmael branches (29–31)	25:1–18
	Keturah branches (32–33)	
Abraham to Israel vertical (34)		21:2–3; 25:25–26
	Esau branches and Edomite kings (35–42, 43–54)	36
sons of Israel maternal birth order (2:1–2)[a]	/////\\\\\	35:22–26; 46:8–27
tribal branches (2–9)	//////\\\\\\	

[a] The twelve literal male offspring of Jacob are listed in strictly genealogical terms in only a few places: (1) Gen 29:31–30:24; 35:16–20; (2) 35:23–26; (3) 46:8–27; (4) 1 Chr 2:1–2 (see Wilson, *Genealogy and History*, 183–84). Even in these cases they are listed in different orders. For other tribal lists see 184, n. 99.

Significantly, the Chronicler opens his book with Adam. In some sense the following narrative concerns the human race. If the first word serves as the title or synopsis, then Chronicles is the "Adam-book."[53] The effect of re-presenting a Genesis-shaped international setting for Israel includes both the universal function of the Davidic kingdom of Yahweh and its temple as well as fundamental continuity with the scriptural metanarrative. As Adam heads the peoples, Israel heads the people (1 Chr 1:1; 2:1).

2:3–17~Gen 38:1–7, 29–30+46:12+1 Kgs 4:31[5:11]+Josh 7:1+Ruth 4:18–22+2 Sam 2:18+17:27 (B) (genealogies of Judah through family of David). The most important points regarding the Chronistic presentation of the tribe of Judah are location and amount of attention. The Chronicler fronts Judah in accord with Torah. When the ancestor Judah temporarily broke the vicious cycles of sibling rivalry and restored the beloved son to Israel, he not only earned the blessing but also began to be placed at the head of the brotherhood (Gen 46:28). The tribe of Judah camps in first position on the east of the tabernacle (Num 2:3), worships first (7:12–17), marches first (10:14), and receives the first allotment in the land proper after crossing the Jordan (Josh 14–15).[54] The implications of God opening or closing every womb in Genesis and fruitfully multiplying his people in Egypt quietly undergirds divine blessing upon Judah in outsizing the other tribes (Exod 1:7; Num 1:26–27; 26:22). The Chronicler apparently fronts Judah and offers extensive

53. Willi, "Innovation aus Tradition," 410.

54. See Schnittjer, *Torah Story*, 385–88.

attention because of divine election to rule and build the temple (1 Chr 28:4). Among the clans of Judah, the Chronicler prioritizes the line that leads to David. In this way Chronicles moves from Adam and the Hebrew ancestors among the ancient nations to arrive at David by 1 Chr 2:15.

Chronicles cobbles together genealogies from Genesis, Ruth, and Samuel to trace out the line of Judah to David. The genealogies are peppered with annotations from Genesis, Joshua, and Kings. The Chronicler highlights Judah's intermarriage to a Canaanite, the wickedness of his eldest son, and his accidental incestuous relationship with his daughter-in-law (2:3–4; Gen 38:2, 7, 29–30). The Chronicler paraphrases Josh 7:1 on the wrongful taking of the devoted plunder (*herem*), including a wordplay on Achan's name (עָכָן), saying "Achar/Troubler [עָכָר] brought trouble [עוֹכֵר] on Israel by infidelity with the devoted things" (1 Chr 2:7 lit.).[55] The Chronicler seems to borrow language from the end of the narrative: "Joshua said, 'Why have you brought this *trouble* [עכר] on us? Yahweh will *bring trouble* [עכר] on you today.' Then all Israel stoned him, and after they had stoned the rest, they burned them" (Josh 7:25, emphasis mine).

These several annotations do not glorify or idealize Judah (see Table C2). The purpose seems exactly the opposite. Yahweh elected the royal line from a tribe that badly needed forgiveness and mercy (see note on 1 Chr 3:1–9). The inclusion of Tamar (2:4) and Bathsheba (3:5) in the Chronistic genealogy of Judah likely gets expanded by Matthew, who adds Rahab and Ruth, using their sinful and outsider/other circumstances to similar effect (Matt 1:3, 5, 6).

The ancestors of the tribe of Judah include the ancient sages Ethan and Heman and others referred to elsewhere in Scripture (2:6; 1 Kgs 4:31[5:11]). These seem to be different than Ethan and Heman of the Levites (1 Chr 6:33, 44[18, 29]; 15:17, 19; 25:1, 4; 2 Chr 5:12; Pss 88 superscription; 89 superscription).[56]

3:1–9~2 Sam 3:2–5+5:5, 13–16 (B)+11:3; 12:24 (C) (sons born to David in Jerusalem). The Chronicler's treatment of David's family acknowledges his tenure as ruler for seven and a half years in Hebron, though he suppresses that David ruled only Judah at that point (1 Chr 3:4//2 Sam 5:5). This subtle set of adjustments demonstrates that the Chronicler does not seek to idealize David, just as he does not want to divide up all Israel. The Chronicler even inserts Bathsheba, not included in the source context, as the mother of four sons, including Solomon (1 Chr 3:5//2 Sam 5:13–14).[57] The Chronicler also names Bathsheba's father Ammiel/Eliam, who is only known from the narrative of David's adultery or rape.[58] Though the Chronicler deletes the entire affair from his narrative he goes out of his way to allude to it here (see note on 1 Chr 20:1–3). The Chronicler

55. See Knoppers, *I Chronicles 1–9*, 304.

56. See ibid., 303.

57. Compare Bathshua (בַּת־שׁוּעַ) in 1 Chr 3:5 with Bathsheba (בַּת־שֶׁבַע) in 2 Sam 12:24.

58. The name Ammiel (עַמִּיאֵל) in 1 Chr 3:5 is interchangeable with Eliam (אֱלִיעָם) in 2 Sam 11:3—the parts merely reversed—having the sense of "God is my father's brother" ("אֱלִיעָם," "עַמִּיאֵל," *HALOT* 1:56, 844; BDB 45).

adds an annotation naming Tamar as the sister of David's sons, which makes important allusion to David's troubled family (1 Chr 3:9; cf. 2 Sam 13:1). In sum, many of the Chronicler's interpretive adjustments do not fit with overgeneralized accusations of his idealization of David and Solomon (see Table C2). The Chronicler does not shy away from his agenda, but it is more complex than whitewashing the Davidic rule. Just as the Chronicler goes out of his way to include allusions to sinful acts in the ancestry of the tribe of Judah, he does so too in the family of David himself (see note on 1 Chr 2:3–17).

4:17~Exod 2:7 (D) (daughter of the pharaoh marries into Judah). In spite of naming a daughter Miriam, this context refers to a rare case of marriage between Egyptian royalty and an Israelite.[59]

4:24–31~Gen 46:10; Josh 19:1–5 (C) (early tribe of Simeon). The list in Chronicles shares parallels with early lists of Simeon (1 Chr 4:24, 28–31; Gen 46:10; Josh 19:2–5; cf. Exod 6:15). After a list of names of the tribe of Simeon, a short note says, "These were their towns until the reign of David" (1 Chr 4:31). Whether it refers to David's census or his taking control of the region is not clear. Whatever its sense, Chronicles continues to see a distinguishable identity of the tribe of Simeon through the entire First Commonwealth (4:41; 2 Chr 34:6).[60]

5:1–2~Gen 49:3–4 (B)+48:13–20 (C)+49:8–12* (C) (Reuben's incest) (* see Judah-king network). The Chronicler explains why the firstborn of Israel was passed over. He paraphrases Jacob regarding the sin of Reuben with his late stepmother's slave/concubine of his father. His sin caused the traditional inheritance of the firstborn to be given to others—he "defiled the bed" of his father (1 Chr 5:1//Gen 49:4 lit.; cf. 35:22). While an allusion to Genesis seems certain for the Chronicler's interpretation of Judah and Joseph, identifying a specific donor context can only be a possibility. The Chronicler deduces that Joseph received the birthright, a double portion, in light of siring the heads of two tribes, Manasseh and Ephraim (Gen 48:13–20). He also deduces that leadership comes to Judah based on the blessing from Jacob (49:8–12). Like the Chronicler himself, David also uses the term "leader" when referring to the divine election of Judah (1 Chr 5:2; 28:4). An earlier set of episodes in Genesis demonstrates that the elements of inheritance, birthright (wealth), and blessing (power) could be parceled out separately (Gen 25:31–34; 27:27–29). The Chronicler succinctly interprets the primary dramatic outcome of Gen 37–50 as a sibling quest for birthright and blessing.

5:3~Gen 46:8–9 (C) (sons of Reuben). The first part of the list of Reubenites overlaps with several in Torah (1 Chr 5:3; Gen 46:8–9; cf. Exod 6:14; Num 26:5–11). On the arrangement of the two and a half Transjordanian tribes in the genealogies, see Figure C4. The solidarity of the Transjordanian tribes in rebellion is a common theme (Num 32:6–15; Josh 22:10–12). Their immoral character comes through in Judges whenever

59. See Japhet, *I & II Chronicles*, 115.
60. See Knoppers, *I Chronicles 1–9*, 366.

the storyline crosses over to their wild side of the Jordan River. The Chronicler explains the exile of the Transjordanian tribes under Pul/Tiglath-pileser with common stock phrases of infidelity and exilic resettlements (1 Chr 5:25–26; cf. e.g., Exod 34:15; 2 Kgs 15:29; 17:6–8; 18:11). The forced migrations of the Transjordanian tribes represents one of ten such exiles in scriptural contexts in the days of the fall of Samaria and Jerusalem.[61]

6:1–4[5:27–30]~Gen 46:11+Exod 6:16–25 (C) (line of Levi).

6:16–19[6:1–4]~Num 3:17–20 (C) (lines of Gershon, Kohath, and Merari of Levi). The early parts of the genealogical lists of priests and Levites overlap with records found in Torah. The possible Chronistic relationship with these may be indirect, mediated through more extensive lists in other source(s). The importance of the Levitical genealogical records to the Chronicler is apparent by their detail and central position among the lists (see Figure C4). The structure of the Chronistic genealogical Levitical lists relates to the use of scriptural traditions in a couple of senses—linear and segmented. The linear lists of Aaron's line present a continuous record of high priests from redemption to exile (6:3–15[5:29–41]). Zadok stands at the midpoint of the twenty-five generations from Kohath son of Levi to Jehozadak, with twelve generations listed before and after him (6:8[34]).[62] The symmetry in the list reinforces the importance placed on the Zadokite line of priests elsewhere in Chronicles and Ezekiel. A secondary accomplishment of situating Zadok as the central generation of Israel's history is to chronologically centralize David (see 15:11; 16:39; 24:3, 31 etc.; also see end of note on 2 Chr 26:21).[63] The segmented lists featuring the family lines of Gershon, Kohath, and Merari anticipate the structure David uses to arrange the institution of temple worship (see Figure C16).

6:27–28[12–13]~1 Sam 1:1; 8:1 (C) (Elkanah, Samuel, and his sons in the line of Kohath). The inclusion of Elkanah, Samuel, Joel, and Abijah in the line of Kohath sparks dispute. In a context sharply disparaging the Chronistic genealogies, Wellhausen remarks sarcastically that Samuel "must of course have been of Levitical descent, because his mother consecrated him to the service of the sanctuary."[64] The discrepancy comes from the introduction of Elkanah as of the line of Zuph, an Ephraimite (1 Sam 1:1). Though being a "Zuphite from the hill country of Ephraim" also refers to living in the land of Zuph (1:1; 9:5), one of Elkanah's ancestors is called Zuph (1 Chr 6:20[35] *qere*). Elsewhere the Deuteronomist, cited by the Chronicler in this context, speaks of families of Kohath living in cities of refuge in Ephraim (Josh 21:5, 20; 1 Chr 6:66[51]). In addi-

61. Ten exiles: (1) 2 Chr 28:5, 8; cf. 28:15 (ca. 734 BCE); (2) 28:17; cf. 2 Kgs 16:6 (ca. 733); (3) 1 Chr 5:26 (ca. 733); (4) 2 Kgs 15:29 (ca. 733); (5) 17:3–6 (ca. 722); (6) 18:13; Isa 36:1; 2 Chr 32:1 (701); (7) Dan 1:1–2 (605); (8) 2 Kgs 24:10–13; Jer 24:1; 27:21–22; 52:28 (597); (9) 2 Kgs 25; Jer 39:1–2; 52:29; 2 Chr 36:17–20 (586); (10) Jer 52:30 (582).

62. See Knoppers, "Priestly Genealogies," 125.

63. See Glatt-Gilad, "Genealogy as a Window," 76, 78.

64. Wellhausen, *Prolegomena*, 220.

tion, priestly families often recycle the same names to honor ancestors, as seen in 1 Chr 6 and throughout the Second Temple period.[65] Elkanah is the name of one of Korah's sons from the tribe of Levi (Exod 6:24; cf. 1 Chr 6:22[7]). The combination of these suggestive elements and lack of direct evidence explains the long debate. One purpose for the segmented Levitical genealogies may be to support the legitimacy of the Levitical singers appointed by David, including Heman son of Joel son of Samuel son of Elkanah (6:33[18]; 15:15–17; 16:41–42; 25:1, 5, 6; 2 Chr 35:15).[66]

6:54–60[39–45]~Josh 21:1–4, 10–19 (B); **6:61–65[46–50]**~Josh 21:5–9 (B); **6:66–81[51–66]**~Josh 21:20–39 (B) (Levitical cities). Joshua and Eleazer oversaw the allotment of the cities of refuge to the Levitical clans (Josh 21:1). The allotments were arranged by the Levitical clans of Kohath, Gerson, and Merari (21:4–8). The Chronicler adopts much of this traditional ancient allotment as part of his presentation of the genealogical background of the Levitical families appointed by David for temple worship. In spite of many complex textual issues in the masoretic and Greek versions of Josh 21, it is not likely to be derivative of Chronicles.[67]

9:2–18~Neh 11:3–19 (C) (first returned exiles). The penultimate lists of the first section of Chronicles concern those who returned from exile (1 Chr 9:2). First Chronicles 9:2–18 seems to have some kind of relationship to Neh 11:3–19, but probably indirect. The several witnesses to this list abound with challenges: 1 Chr 9:2–18 MT and LXX, and Neh 11:3–19 MT and LXX. Evaluating the evidence of these witnesses eliminates theories of 1 Chr 9:2–18 proto-MT as directly derivative of Neh 3–19 proto-MT and vice versa. Gary Knoppers's comparative study collates the complicated textual details and offers a reasonable possibility that may be summarized as Neh 11:3–19 and 1 Chr 9:2–18 are each based on a common source—the following diagram graphically summarizes Knoppers's findings.[68]

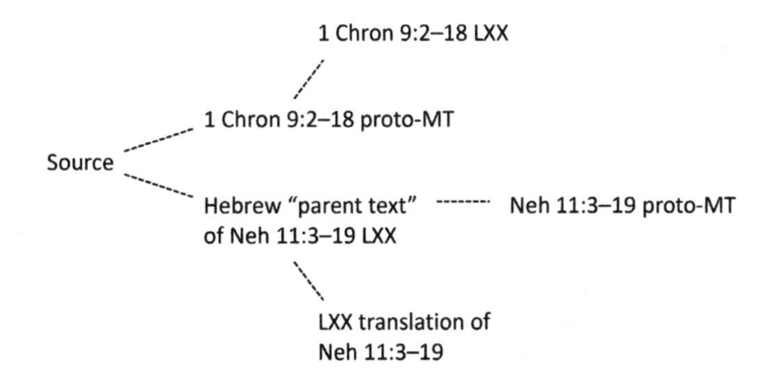

65. See VanderKam, *Joshua to Caiaphas*, 491–93.

66. See Japhet, *I & II Chronicles*, 156.

67. On the complex issues of Josh 21:1–42 and 1 Chon 6:54–60[39–45], see Knoppers, *I Chronicles 1–9*, 442–48.

68. For detailed explanation, see Knoppers, "Sources, Revisions, and Editions," 141–68. For unconvincing criticism of Knoppers's study, and an alternative, that does not get at the details, see Klein, *1 Chronicles*, 263–64.

The mention of Israel refers to laity represented by Judah and Benjamin (Neh 11:4) versus Judah, Benjamin, Ephraim, and Manasseh (1 Chr 9:3). Nehemiah 11 sets the list after a lottery by which "winners" must repopulate Jerusalem with a tithe of returned exiles (Neh 11:1–2). The newly recruited residents of Jerusalem included people from Judah and Benjamin (11:4–8), civil leaders (11:9), priests (11:10–14), Levites (11:15–18), and gatekeepers (11:19). This is followed by a series of lists of other resettlements in Judah and Benjamin (11:20–35).

Chronicles sets up the broadly corresponding list by explaining the infidelity of Judah that caused the exile (1 Chr 9:1). The Chronicler juxtaposes a list of worship personnel for the tent of meeting from the days of Phinehas (9:19–34) immediately after the list of returned laity and worship personnel (9:2–18). The set of responsibilities for the tent of meeting broadly corresponds to David's appointments for temple worship personnel narrated elsewhere (23:28–32). The shared elements between the worship personnel who return from exile, the days of the tent of meeting, and the first temple appear to be the reason for the use of this list in Chronicles (see Table C14). The Chronicler establishes continuity by showing, not telling. Whatever the exile changed, it did not alter the continuing need to worship as in the days of old.

TABLE C14: LEVITICAL RESPONSIBILITIES IN THE DAYS OF PHINEHAS AND DAVID

	return from exile	**days of Phinehas**	**days of David**
priests as chiefs over Levites	1 Chr 9:10–12	1 Chr 9:19	—
"work of the service"[a] of tabernacle/ temple	9:13	9:20	1 Chr 23:24
gatekeepers	9:17–18	9:21–27	— (cf. 26:1–32)
"service utensils"[b]	—	9:28	23:26
"holy" vessels/areas[b]	—	9:29	23:28
rows of bread[b]	—	9:32	23:29
Levitical singers[c]	—	9:33	23:30–31

[a] "The work of the service" refers to worship responsibilities in the tent of meeting/tabernacle (Exod 30:16; 36;1, 3; Num 3:7, 8; 8:24; 18:21, 23; see Knoppers, "Hierodules, Priests, or Janitors?" 56). In Torah and Chronicles much of this work is placed on the Levites, but in 1 Chr 9:13 it is the work of the priests (Knoppers, *I Chronicles 1–9*, 504).

[b] Levitical work of the service would include service utensils, holy vessels and holy areas, and rows of bread for the Sabbath.

[c] Based on David's ordinances after the Levites no longer need to transport the ark and tabernacle, singing and music would become part of their work of the service (see note on 1 Chr 23:25–30).

10:1–14/~/1 Sam 31:1–13+28:3–25 (B)+Deut 18:11 (C) (death of Saul). Chronicles begins the narrative proper with the death of Saul. Beginning with Saul serves two important functions in Chronicles. First, Saul is the first king of Israel. Chronicles treats all the kings of Israel from Saul to Zedekiah. The Chronicler does not narrate the Northern Kingdom of Israel when it secedes, only the Davidic kingdom of all Israel in Jerusalem. Second, Saul provides a negative foil against which David seeks the worship of Yahweh (see Figure C1). After Saul's death, the Chronicler jump cuts to the anointing of David as king over all Israel and David's capture of Jerusalem (1 Chr 11). David's persistent trouble with civil unrest, though essential to Samuel, falls outside the storyline of Chronicles. Note a synoptic comparison of the death of Saul and its aftermath:

	Samuel	**1 Chronicles**
death of Saul in battle	1 Sam 31:1–7	10:1–7
dishonoring Saul's corpse	31:8–13	10:8–12
theological rationale for Saul's death	—	10:13–14
death of Saul reported to David	2 Sam 1:1–16	—
lament for Saul and Jonathan	1:17–27	—
David returns to Judah	2:1–7	—
contending between Benjamin and David	2:8–3:1	—
children born at Hebron[a]	3:2–5	{3:1–4}
Abner's treaty with David	3:6–21	—
Joab murders Abner	3:22–39	—
murder of Ish-Bosheth	4:1–12	—

[a] The chronological note of David ruling Judah for seven-and-a-half years at Hebron and thirty-three years over Israel from Jerusalem appears with the birth of his sons at Hebron in 1 Chr 3:4, but with his anointing by all Israel in 2 Sam 5:5.

The basic narrative of the death of Saul in Chronicles follows Samuel. The Chronicler makes a few significant interpretive enhancements. He summarizes the downfall of Saul's entire household in the account of the battle with the Philistines (1 Chr 10:6). The drawn-out civil war is not denied (3:1–4). But the civil unrest and several lingering issues with Saul's house get edited out (2 Sam 1–4; 9; 21:1–14). The Chronicler only retains the narrative of a single member of Saul's house for one fleeting scene. Michal represents Saul's house by disdaining David for dancing before the ark of Yahweh (1 Chr 15:29; see note on 15:25–16:6).

The Deuteronomist traces the humiliation of Saul's decapitated body. The Chronicler focuses on his head (underlining signifies verbal parallels, and italics signify variation):[69]

69. The variation between Ashtoreths/their gods and the variations in 1 Sam 31:12//1 Chr 10:12 may reflect differences in the respective parent texts rather than interpretive interventions (see Nihan, "Textual Fluidity," 200).

> They put his armor in the temple of *the Ashtoreths* and hung up his *body on the wall of Beth Shan.* (1 Sam 31:10†)

> They put his armor in the temple of *their gods* and hung up his *head in the temple of Dagon.* (1 Chr 10:10)

Like Michal, so too with Saul's head as a trophy in Dagon's temple, the Chronicler seems to be relying on readers supplying the relevant context from Samuel.[70] The previously decapitated cult statue of Dagon, repeatedly humbled before the ark of Israel's God, now has the head of Israel's king before him (1 Sam 5:4).[71] The shameful fate of Saul sets up a contrast when David's first act is to recover the ark ignored in Saul's day—a Chronistic plus (1 Chr 13:3; see note on 13:5–14). The decapitation of Israel's giant also may be reminiscent of Philistine payback for taking the head of the champion from Gath to Jerusalem (1 Sam 17:54).[72]

A Chronistic evaluative plus equates Saul's infidelity with his failure to seek Yahweh (1 Chr 10:13–14). The Chronicler uses some of his favorite terms to show what not to do. "Saul's infidelity [מַעַל, noun] by which he acted unfaithfully [מעל, verb] against Yahweh" are defined by him "seeking" (דרש) ghosts, but he did not "seek [דרש] after Yahweh" (10:13, 14 lit.; see discussion after Table C2). The Chronicler creatively uses a wordplay on Saul's name (*sha'ul*, שָׁאוּל) and the prohibition against "asking [*sho'el*, שֹׁאֵל] ghosts" (Deut 18:11; 1 Chr 10:13 lit.).[73] The Chronicler marks this allusion as "according to the word of Yahweh" to make sure readers get the connection. Though Leviticus prohibits consulting ghosts, it says "Do not turn to ghosts," while Deuteronomy forbids both "asking" and "seeking" (Lev 19:31; 20:6; Deut 18:11). All of this needs to be compared to the Chronistic allusion to Saul's infidelity in Samuel to appreciate the full import of this blatant interpretive intervention with subtle implications (verbal parallels signified by bold and italics; and marking signified by broken underlining):

> There shall not be found ... **one who asks** [שאל] *ghosts* or familiar spirits, or **seeks** [דרש] the dead. (Deut 18:10a, 11 lit.)

> Saul **asked** [שאל] of Yahweh, but Yahweh did not answer him by dreams or Urim or prophets. Saul then said to his attendants, "Seek out [בקש] for me a woman who consults *ghosts*, so I may go and **seek** [דרש] of her." His attendants said, "Behold, a woman who consults *ghosts* is in Endor." (1 Sam 28:6–7 lit.)

70. McKenzie explains that the Chronicler counted on readers of Chronicles knowing of the account of Michal from Samuel to make sense of his account ("Chronicler as Redactor," 82; cf. 82–85 for many kindred examples).

71. See Williamson, *1 and 2 Chronicles*, 94.

72. See ibid.

73. See Ackroyd, "Chronicler as Exegete," 8.

> Saul died because he was unfaithful to Yahweh; he did not keep the word of Yahweh and even **asked** [שׁאל] *a ghost* to **seek guidance** [דרשׁ], and did not **seek guidance** [דרשׁ] of Yahweh. So Yahweh put him to death and turned the kingdom over to David son of Jesse. (1 Chr 10:13–14 lit.)

The Chronicler's choice of this particular infidelity to typify the problem with Saul gets at the critical issue of integrity of devotion. Saul did "ask" Yahweh but he did not "seek" him (1 Sam 28:6). He "seeks" ghosts (28:7).[74] Saul, whose name plays on the verb "ask," embodies the problem of asking even while not seeking. David and Israel explicitly state Saul's failure to seek and they learn in steps to seek Yahweh in worship according to Torah (1 Chr 13:3; 15:13; 16:11). The kingdom cannot be held by a mere asker. The Chronicler uses Saul to offer a counterpoint over and against those who seek Yahweh.

11:1–3/~/2 Sam 5:1–3 (A)+1 Sam 16:1–13 (C) (David made king over all Israel). The Chronicler makes an important interpretive intervention by beginning his treatment of David when he became king over all Israel. This decision sets apart his interests from those of the Deuteronomist. The treatment of David in Samuel includes a long, difficult period beginning with David's anointing through his years as fugitive from Israel and then in civil war with Benjamin (see Table C5). The dramatic events of David's protracted rise to power, including many personal situations, serve the Samuel narrative well. Chronicles excludes nearly all of this in the interests of getting at the story of David's public life as the original royal patron of the temple. For the Chronicler that story begins with the anointing of David as king over all Israel. This also may explain why the Chronicler moves the chronological notation of the different phases of David's rule (1 Chr 3:4; cf. 2 Sam 5:4–5).

The Chronicler's version of the anointing mostly runs parallel to the version in Samuel with minor adjustments (2 Sam 5:1–3//1 Chr 11:1–3). The Chronicler adds a notation loosely based on the story of Samuel's anointing of David—"The elders of Israel . . . anointed David king over Israel, *as Yahweh had promised through Samuel*" (1 Chr 11:3, emphasis marks plus, possibly alluding to 1 Sam 16:1–13).

The Chronicler continues the solidarity of all Israel from 1 Chronicles 11:1–3 into the act of conquering Jerusalem. Whereas the Samuel narrative reports, "the king [David] *and his men* marched to Jerusalem," Chronicles says, "David *and all the Israelites* marched to Jerusalem" (2 Sam 5:6; 1 Chr 11:4, emphasis mine).[75] Jerusalem may be the city of David, but the Chronicler wants his constituents to know that Jerusalem belongs to all Israel.

The anointing of David as king of all Israel opens a section treating David's consolidation of the kingdom over all Israel with Jerusalem as the new capital. Note a synoptic comparison of David's rise to power:

---

74. Elsewhere Saul is well known for his phony devotion (e.g., 1 Sam 15).

75. See Bodner and Johnson, "David," 131.

	2 Samuel	1 Chronicles
David anointed king over all Israel	5:1–3[a]	11:1–3
chronological notation of David's rule	5:4–5	—
David conquers Jerusalem	5:6–10	11:4–9
connecting summary	—	11:10
David's mighty men	{23:8–39}[b]	11:11–47
tribal militia gathered to David	—	12:1–23
decision of David and all Israel to retrieve ark	—	13:1–4
initial attempt to bring ark	{6:1–11}[c]	13:5–14
Hiram recognizes David's rule	5:11–12	14:1–2
children born in Jerusalem	5:13–16	14:3–7; cf. 3:5–8
David defeats Philistines	5:17–25	14:8–17

[a] See Table C5 for a long list of excluded materials in 1 Samuel and 2 Samuel leading up to David's rule over all Israel.

[b] See Figure C7 on the placement of 2 Sam 23:8–39/~/1 Chr 11:10–47.

[c] See Figure C6 on the placement of 2 Sam 6:1–11/~/1 Chr 13:5–14.

11:4–9/~/2 Sam 5:6–10 (David captures Jerusalem). The basic story of the capture of Jerusalem runs parallel in Samuel and Chronicles. The Chronicler excludes the Jebusites' taunt and the obscure notation regarding disabled persons and replaces the latter with a contest to become military commander (normal font signifies verbatim parallels, italics signify minus, and bold signifies plus):

> The Jebusites said to David, "You will not get in here; *even the blind and the lame can ward you off." They thought, "David cannot get in here."* Nevertheless, David captured the fortress of Zion—which is the City of David. *On that day* David had said, "Whoever attacks the Jebusites *will have to use the water shaft to reach those 'lame and blind' who are David's enemies." That is why they say, "The 'blind and lame' will not enter the palace."* (2 Sam 5:6b–8†)

> [The Jebusites] said to David, "You will not get in here." Nevertheless, David captured the fortress of Zion—which is the City of David. David had said, "Whoever **leads** the attack on the Jebusites **will become commander-in-chief." Joab son of Zeruiah went up first, and so he received the command.** (1 Chr 11:5–6)

The attention to Joab's appointment based on merit complements a Chronistic plus on Joab's leadership in restoring Jerusalem (11:8). Military prowess and building up Jerusalem connote worthy actions in Chronicles.

11:10–47/~/2 Sam 23:8–39 (David's mighty men). The Chronicler relocates the list of David's mighty men from an appendix of Samuel to the head of his presentation of David's rule. The Chronicler continues to demonstrate the importance of identifying the constituents of the narrative, in line with the long series of genealogies at the head of the book. The Chronicler uses the list of the prestigious heroic companions of David as an on-ramp to describe a larger commitment of the tribes of Israel in the next chapter. The Chronicler broadens the function of the mighty men by adding a new introduction. "These were the chiefs of David's mighty warriors—*they, together with all Israel,* gave his kingship strong support to extend it over the whole land, as Yahweh had promised" (1 Chr 11:10, emphasis mine).

The list of mighty men in Samuel ends with Uriah the Hittite—in a place he cannot be missed—to remind readers of David's great sin before telling the story of David's sin with the census (2 Sam 23:39).[76] The placement of Uriah in the Samuel list heightens David's sin of rape or adultery to a new level, for readers now learn that Uriah was more than a soldier but one of the named companion heroes. David's sin and repentance, in sharp contrast to Saul, play a central role in Samuel. The magnification of David's sin by identifying Uriah prepares readers for another great sin of David, but with repentance even before the prophet arrives (2 Sam 24:10–12; cf. 12:13). The Chronicler both deletes the account of David's adultery or rape and murder and uses the important story of David's sin with the census in another way (see Figure C7). The Chronicler does not delete Uriah but adds over a dozen additional names to the list of mighty men immediately after him, effectively burying him in the list (1 Chr 11:41–47). Since Uriah is no longer last on the list, he no longer serves to make a point of emphasis regarding the gravity of David's treachery. This is easy to see by comparing the end of the lists of 2 Sam 23 and 1 Chr 11. It needs to be remembered, however, that elsewhere the Chronicler retained notice of Bathsheba (see note on 1 Chr 3:1–9).

11:18–19~Deut 12:16, 23–25; 15:23 (C) (water represents the blood of life). The Chronicler's account of pouring out water includes an interpretive explanation beginning with "because" not included in the counterpart of Samuel.[77] The interpretive addition clarifies David's inference of treating the water like blood since they had risked their lives. David poured out water symbolizing the life-blood of his warriors just like animal blood (italics signify verbal parallels, and broken underlining signifies an interpretive addition):

> But be sure you do not eat *the blood*, because *the blood* is *the life* [נֶפֶשׁ], and you must not eat *the life* [נֶפֶשׁ] with the meat. You must not eat *the blood*; pour it out on the ground like *water*. (Deut 12:23–24; cf. v. 16; 15:23; Gen 9:4; Lev 17:10–14)

76. For a similar observation, see Firth, "Foreigners," 243–44, 248.

77. On the explanatory function of "because" (כִּי), see GKC, §158b. Since the plus in 1 Chr 11:19 ("Because they risked their lives to bring it back") appears in 2 Sam 23:17 LXX, it may have been in its parent text but lost in transmission by the scribe's eye jumping to the repetition of "by their lives" (בנפשותם) (so Knoppers, *I Chronicles 10–29*, 528; McCarter, *II Samuel*, 491). If this emendation is correct, the interpretive gloss derives from Samuel, not Chronicles. Also see Knoppers, *I Chronicles 10–29*, 550.

> So the Three broke through the Philistine lines, drew *water* from the well near the gate of Bethlehem and carried it back to David. But he refused to drink it; instead, he poured it out to Yahweh. "God forbid that I should do this!" he said. "Should I drink ***the blood*** of these men who went at the risk of their *lives* [נֶפֶשׁ]?" Because they risked their *lives* [נֶפֶשׁ] to bring it back, David would not drink it. (1 Chr 11:18–19a)

12:1–22~1 Sam 22:1–2; 27:6 (C) (tribal militia gathered to David). Samuel makes a few comments about those who join David during his long tenure as a fugitive from Israel. David stayed at the cave of Adullam (1 Sam 22:1) and at Ziklag, gifted to him by the Philistine ruler Achish (27:6). During this time, family members and persons in distress or in debt joined up with David (22:1–2). The Chronicler massively expands the migration of loyal warriors who came to Ziklag to join David to include men from Saul's own Benjamite military entourage (1 Chr 12:1–2), as well as men from Gad (12:8), Benjamin and Judah (12:16), and Manasseh (12:19). Part of the Chronicler's agenda relates to the broad representation from the tribes of Israel aligned with David. The Chronicler also seeks to show solidarity between David and Israel even while Saul ruled (see Table C2 and Figure C7).

13:5–14/~/2 Sam 6:1–11 (A)+Ps 132:6–7 (C) (all Israel to get the ark). The Chronicler fronts the first part of the ark's journey to Jerusalem, in contrast to Samuel where this episode appears later. The rearrangement of narrative sequence promotes David's prioritization of worship, perhaps suggested by Ps 132:2–5 (see explanation of Figure C6). While the synoptic accounts feature only minor differences, the Chronicler inserts an addition at the front end for exegetical reasons.[78]

The new Chronistic opening strenuously emphasizes the solidarity of all Israel together with David in order to prioritize its emphasis on worship. The interpretive expansion contrasts declension in the days of Saul to renewal under David. The expansion makes explicit comprehensive participation of laity and worship personnel across the land of promise from south to north at its largest extent (see Figure C1 and Table C2; cf. 1 Kgs 8:65–66; 2 Chr 7:8). The Chronicler does not invent these details to reinforce his ideological agenda but may adapt them from Ps 132, the only psalm to refer explicitly to the ark. The psalmist includes a shift from first-person singular to first-person plural at exactly the point they seek the ark (Ps 132:6–7; see note ad loc.). The Chronicler elsewhere uses Ps 132, which supports his use of it here (see note on 2 Chr 6:1–42). Note the extensive expansion (underlining signifies synoptic parallels, bold signifies plus of renewal, italics signify plus of comprehensive solidarity, and broken underlining signifies first-person plural verbs):

---

78. Other differences represent minor stylistic and/or narrative adjustments. Likewise, suggesting the addition of "hand" and/or replacing "steadied" (wci) in 2 Sam 6:6 with "to steady" (inf. const.) in 1 Chr 13:9 to shift from action to intention seems like overreading of minor text-critical differences (see Lemke, "Synoptic Problem," 350–51).

David again brought together all the able young men of Israel—thirty thousand. (2 Sam 6:1)

We heard it in Ephrathah, we came upon it in the fields of Jaar: "Let us go to his dwelling place, let us worship at his footstool." (Ps 132:6–7)

David conferred with each of his officers, the commanders of thousands and commanders of hundreds. He then said to the whole assembly of Israel, "If it seems good to you and if it is the will of Yahweh our God, *let us send word far and wide to the rest of our people throughout the territories of Israel, and also to the priests and Levites who are with them* in their towns and pasturelands, to come and join us. Let us bring the ark of our God back to us, **for we did not inquire of it during the reign of Saul**." *The whole assembly agreed to do this,* because it seemed right to all the people. So David *assembled all Israel, from the Shihor River in Egypt to Lebo Hamath,* to bring the ark of God from Kiriath Jearim. (1 Chr 13:1–5)

14:8–17/~/2 Sam 5:17–25 (David defeats Philistines). The synoptic versions of David's victories over the Philistines run very much along the same lines. A few extremely minor differences may show the agenda of the Chronicler, like adding "all" to "all Israel," but only two differences require attention here. First, the variation on how the religious images were handled probably reflects exegetical shaping rather than stylistic adjustment.[79] Consider the motives for the adjustment (plain font signifies verbally identical and italics signify variations):

The Philistines had abandoned their *idols* there, and David *and his men carried them off.* (2 Sam 5:21†)[80]

The Philistines had abandoned their *gods* there, and David *gave orders to burn them in the fire.* (1 Chr 14:12)

79. Contra Lemke, "Synoptic Problem," 351–52. Lemke cites LXX readings of 2 Sam 5:21 akin to the last phrase in 1 Chr 14:12 MT and suggests the Chronicler simply followed the version he had. The witnesses to the Septuagint (LXX^{LM}), however, actually contain additions to the MT of 2 Sam 5:21 or to a briefer version of proto-Samuel, that is, they are double readings (see LXX Cambridge, apparatus on 2 Sam 5:21 [II, 1, 123]). Also see Knoppers, *I Chronicles 10–29*, 597, 601 (and personal correspondence from Knoppers). The general testimony of the Qumran witnesses does not support Lemke's suggestion in this case. Ulrich says, "None of the 4Q[Sam and] C[hronicles] agreements either betrays characteristics commonly associated with the Chronicler's specific interests (Levitical, genealogical, cultic, etc.) or displays new types of variations from M[asoretic text of Samuel] due to the fact that C[hronicles] now provides a parallel" (*Qumran Text of Samuel*, 163).

80. MT reads "their idols" but LXX "their gods" (2 Sam 5:21), which may have been in the Chronicler's version of this source (see Klein, *1 Chronicles*, 338, n. 16).

If working from a common source, it is possible to imagine the Deuteronomist ends the account ominously with the men carrying off the idols. Or, more likely, the Chronicler may be fleshing out the details to affirm David as a reformer, burning polytheistic icons along the lines of Deut 7:5, 25 or 12:3. Second, the Chronicler adds a brief note, as he often does, exposing theological significance: "So David's fame spread throughout every land, and Yahweh made all the nations fear him" (1 Chr 14:17; cf. v. 2).[81] The Chronicler explains a universal based on a particular.

15:1, 3*~Deut 12:5, 11, 14, 18, 21, 26;* 14:23, 24, 25, etc. (C) (place for the ark) (* see place network). The Chronicler may use the term "place" to refer to the ark in Jerusalem to broadly allude to the place Yahweh would choose for his name to dwell, mentioned repeatedly starting in Deut 12, and a central concern in Chronicles (1 Chr 15:1, 3). The term is too common for more than a possibility (but see note on 1 Chr 16:7–36, esp. on 16:11).

The Chronicler's plus on David's Levitical appointments stands at the head of a series of units culminating in the divine covenant with David for his "house" to make a "house" for Yahweh in Jerusalem. Note a synoptic comparison of David's initial efforts to relocate Yahweh worship to Jerusalem (cf. Figure C6):

	2 Samuel	**1 Chronicles**	**Psalms**
Levites appointed to carry ark	—	15:1–24	
ark's procession to Jerusalem	6:12–19a	15:25–16:3	
Levites appointed before the ark	—	16:4–7	
psalm of praise	—	16:8–22	105:1–15[a]
"	—	16:23–33	96:1b–10b, 11–13b[b]
"	—	16:34–36	106:1, 47–48[c]
Levities and priest before ark	—	16:37–42	
returning to households	6:19b–20a	16:43	
Michal confronts David	6:20b–23	—	
Davidic covenant	7:1–17	17:1–15	
David's prayer	7:18–29	17:16–27	

[a] **Psalm 105:1**; cf. Isa 12:4.

[b] **Psalms 96:4**; cf. 48:1[2]; **96:7–8**//29:1b–2; **96:10**>/<10:16; 29:10; 93:1; 97:1; 99:1; **96:11**//98:7.

[c] **Psalms 106:1**>/<100:5; 107:1; Ezra 3:11; 2 Chr 5:13; 7:3, 6; 20:21; **Pss 106:48**>/<41:13[14]; 72:18; 89:52.

81. See Wright, "Founding Father," 49, 51, 52.

15:13–15~Num 4:4–15; 7:9 (B) (Levites carry the ark on their shoulders). David explains the tragedy of the initial attempt to bring the ark. He says Yahweh "broke out" against them (1 Chr 15:13; cf. 13:11; 14:11) because they did not "*seek him* in the prescribed way" (15:13 lit., emphasis mine; cf. 13:3).[82] David's allusion to Yahweh breaking out refers to the synoptic story of the death of Uzzah (13:11//2 Sam 6:8), but the absence of seeking the ark of God in the days of Saul is a Chronistic plus (1 Chr 13:3). The Chronicler explicitly marks the Levites carrying the ark "with poles upon their shoulders, *as Moses had commanded in accordance with the word of Yahweh*" (15:15, emphasis mine). When the tribes gifted a dozen oxen and half a dozen ox carts to the worship personnel, Moses excluded the Levitical clan of Kohath because they had to carry the holy worship items by poles "on their shoulders," which would include the ark (Num 7:9; cf. 4:4–15). The Chronicler's exegetical interventions include demonstrating the need to seek God according to Torah. He also emphasizes the twilight of the work of the Levites as tabernacle porters since the ark would soon get a permanent home in the temple (they are not mentioned in 2 Sam 6:13 but they are in 1 Chr 15:26–27).

15:25–16:6/~/2 Sam 6:12–19 (David and all Israel accompany the Levites in bringing the ark). The basic account of procession of the ark to Jerusalem is similar in Samuel and Chronicles, even if the latter significantly develops the worship elements (see synoptic table in note on 1 Chr 15:1, 3). Though some details in 1 Chr 15:26–27 may be due to instability in textual traditions, the addition of Levitical worship likely comes from the Chronicler.[83]

The Chronicler leaves Michal in the story (1 Chr 15:29//2 Sam 6:16) even though he deleted her elsewhere (e.g., 1 Sam 18:20–21, 28–29; 19:11–17; 2 Sam 6:20–23). Giving Michal this cameo appearance only makes sense if the Chronicler's readers know of the Samuel narrative that contextualizes her.[84] The Chronicler may have retained Michal here so she could represent Saul's family as a contrastive foil over and against David's worship (see Figure C1).[85] "As the ark of the covenant of Yahweh was entering the city of David, *Michal daughter of Saul* watched from a window. And when she saw King David dancing and celebrating, *she despised him in her heart*" (1 Chr 15:29, emphasis mine).

1 Chronicles 16:4–6 adds a plus which includes David's appointment of Levites to a ministry of praise and music before the ark in Jerusalem. This appointment may have initially related to the one-time worship celebration of bringing the ark to Jerusalem. However, David retains Levitical worship personnel with the ark perpetually since they no longer needed to transport the tabernacle (16:37–38).

---

82. Schniedewind goes too far in saying the Chronicler transformed the "tradition" (מִשְׁפָּט) of Num 4:10+7:9 to associate it with Mosaic Torah ("Chronicler as Interpreter," 176–77). The term "tradition," or better, "judgment/rule" (מִשְׁפָּט), is used many times of commands in Exodus, Leviticus, and Numbers, both without and with the attached preposition "according to" (כְּ) as in 1 Chr 15:13.

83. See Lemke, "Synoptic Problem," 352–54; Klein, *1 Chronicles*, 346, n. 27; 353.

84. See McKenzie, "Chronicler as Redactor," 82.

85. See Wilson, "Emperor," 134–35, 139.

16:7–36*//Ps 105:1–15*+96:1b–10b,* 11–13b+106:1, 47–48 (A)+Deut 12:5* (B) (psalm of worship) (* see Abrahamic covenant and place networks). The Chronicler produces a psalm compilation to provide lyrical theological interpretation of the entry of the ark into Jerusalem (see the synoptic comparison in the note on 1 Chr 15:1, 3).[86] The historical moment of the initial fulfillment of Yahweh's choice of the place his name would dwell for worship required a song. The Chronicler's medley brought together excerpts from Pss 105, 96, and 106.[87] In this case, the Chronicler appropriated and blended preexisting lyrical exegetical traditions in these psalms to provide an interpretative hymn (see Figure C6). Lyrical exegesis of Scripture transcends the literary limitations of narrative and prophetic prose discourses (the Chronicler's normal exegetical vehicles) to give appropriate voice to the momentous initial fulfillment of the divine choice of Jerusalem as the place for the temple (Deut 12:5–12).

There are several possible reasons the Chronicler selected to use excerpts from these particular scriptural traditions that might explain how the compilation functions in its new narrative home. Psalm 105 opens with several worship themes corresponding to the Chronicler's agenda. The psalmist's call to worship segues into a lyrical retrospective of the Hebrew ancestors (Ps 105:1–4//1 Chr 16:8–11 and Ps 105:5–15//1 Chr 16:12–22). The psalmist grounds a call to worship in remembrance of Yahweh's fidelity to the ancestors. Worship based on continuity with the ancestral covenant provides the Chronicler a way to connect ancient election with even more ancient election. Elsewhere the Chronicler finds other ways to connect the ancient stories of founding worship in Jerusalem on even more ancient scriptural traditions (see notes on 1 Chr 21:26; 2 Chr 3:1). Here the Davidic celebration of this place for worship stands in deep continuity with the sojourning Hebrew ancestors (Ps 105:15//1 Chr 16:22).

The exact language of the psalmist's call to worship in Ps 105 may have attracted the Chronicler. Two favorite worship terms for "seek" get used with a term for "strength," which refers to the ark in another psalm cited elsewhere in Chronicles (Ps 132:8//2 Chr 6:41).[88] Moreover, the term for strength looks like a catchword that may have suggested Ps 96. All these potential choices revolve around the language of the Torah expectation for Yahweh to choose this place—especially note the Chronicler's replacement of "sanctuary" from Ps 96:6 with "place" to match Deut 12:5 (emphases signify verbal parallels):

86. Older views tended to regard the Chronicler as a hack who mishandled poetry (Keil and Delitzsch, *Psalms 84–150*, 1:90–91). More recently, several studies build upon each other in appreciating the Chronicler's use of psalms to establish continuity. See, e.g., Butler, "A Forgotten Passage," 142–50; Hill, "Patchwork Poetry or Reasoned Verse?," 97–101; Shipp, "'Remember,'" 29–39; and Throntveit, "Songs in a New Key," 153–70. On the significance of using the closing benediction of Book IV of the Psalter (Ps 106:36), see note on Ps 106.

87. These three psalms themselves each draw heavily on other earlier narrative and lyrical scriptural traditions. See overview in note on 1 Chr 15:1, 3, synoptic comparison, nn. a, b, c. Also see notes on Pss 96:7–8, 10; 105; 106.

88. See Knoppers, *I Chronicles 10–29*, 646. On "seek," see discussion proximate to Table C2 and see Filters. Also, both Chronistic contexts use other shared key terms drawn from these Psalms, "remember" (1 Chr 16:12//Ps 105:5; 2 Chr 6:42//Ps 132:1) and "anointed one(s)" (1 Chr 16:22//Ps 105:15; 2 Chr 6:42//Ps 132:10).

> But *you are to seek* [דרשׁ] the dwelling place [מָקוֹם] Yahweh your God will choose from among all your tribes to put his Name there for his dwelling. To there you must go. (Deut 12:5†)

> *Seek* [דרשׁ] Yahweh and his **strength** [עֹז]; seek [בקשׁ] his face always. (1 Chr 16:11†// Ps 105:4)

> Splendor and majesty are before him; **strength** [עֹז] and glory are in his sanctuary [בְּמִקְדָּשׁוֹ]. (Ps 96:6)[89]

> Splendor and majesty are before him; **strength** [עֹז] and joy are in his dwelling place [מָקוֹם]. (1 Chr 16:27)[90]

> Now arise, Yahweh God, and come to your resting place, you and the ark of your **strength** [עֹז]. (2 Chr 6:41†//Ps 132:8)

The Chronicler's interpretive advance of Ps 96:6 by inserting the term "place" to connect with Deut 12:5 demonstrates the significance of what David had done. David brought the ark into Jerusalem, which initiated the long-awaited choice of the place where Yahweh's name would dwell. The Chronicler's community needs to worship like David at the very place Yahweh chose: "Seek Yahweh and his *strength*. . . . *Strength* and joy are in his dwelling place" (1 Chr 16:11†, 27, emphasis mine; on "strength" used of ark in Ps 132:8 see above).

The Chronicler makes a daring choice in how he uses Ps 96. The psalm lacks all hint of covenant, election, redemption, or any other reference to Israel—save the name Yahweh, which the psalmist uses eleven times. The psalmist calls his unnamed and invisible audience to a universal mission: declaring Yahweh's glory and kingship among the nations throughout all the earth, in order that they might worship him and pay him tribute. The universality of Yahweh's kingdom, even among the nations, is not the full extent of the interpretive advancement.

The Chronicler boldly splices the international call to worship Yahweh as ruler in Ps 96 (cf. Ps 96:10) within the covenantal framework of Israel's ancestral narrative.[91] The

89. Lynch correctly observes that "his sanctuary" (בְּמִקְדָּשׁוֹ) in Ps 96:6 did not yet fit the context of 1 Chr 16 because the temple is yet to be built (*Monotheism*, 161–62). However, Lynch does not take into account the significance of the term "place" (מָקוֹם) in light of the Chronicler's long-running agenda to reshape his narrative in relation to Yahweh's election of a "place" for his name in Deut 12 (see place network for overview).

90. The phrase "and joy in his place" (וְחֶדְוָה בִּמְקֹמוֹ) in 1 Chr 16:27 probably migrated into four manuscripts of Ps 96:6 (see *BHS* apparatus on Ps 96:6). It is less likely that "joy" (חֶדְוָה) was in the Chronicler's version of Ps 96:6 in place of "splendor of" (תִּפְאֶרֶת) (see 1 Chr 16:27 *BHS* n. a; Klein, *1 Chronicles*, 359, n. 13). Still, the use of "strength" and "splendor" as pair words referring to the ark in Ps 78:61 offers good reason for the Chronicler to retain "splendor" if it did appear in his version of Ps 96:6.

91. Nielsen, "Whose Song of Praise?," 334–35.

Chronicler affixes this universal call to worship (1 Chr 16:23–26, 28–31) onto the opening of Ps 105, which, according to Knoppers, "is the only explicit reference in Chronicles to Israel's election" (16:13, 15–18).[92] The Chronicler then sets the psalm medley, with its covenant with Israel having universal scope, into the founding of Jerusalem as the city of God by David (16:7, 37–38). By blending the two psalms, the resultant Chronistic psalm calls Israel and the nations to join together as a worshiping congregation of Yahweh whose place is in Jerusalem (see Table C15):

TABLE C15: CALLING THE CONGREGATION OF ISRAEL AND THE NATIONS TO WORSHIP‡

Give praise to Yahweh, proclaim his name; make known among the nations what he has done. . . . Glory in his holy name; let the hearts of those who seek Yahweh *rejoice*. Seek Yahweh and his **strength**; seek his face always. Remember the wonders he has done, his miracles, and the judgments [מִשְׁפָּטִים] he pronounced, you his servants, the descendants of Israel, his chosen ones, the children of Jacob. . . .	Composite psalm addresses the congregation of Israel by Ps 105
Splendor and majesty are before him; **strength** and joy are in his dwelling place. Ascribe to Yahweh, all you families of nations, ascribe to Yahweh glory and **strength**. Ascribe to Yahweh the glory due his name; bring an offering and come before him. Worship Yahweh in the splendor of his holiness. . . . Let the heavens *rejoice*, let the earth be glad; let them say among the nations, "Yahweh reigns!" . . . for he comes to judge [לִשְׁפּוֹט] the earth (1 Chr 16:8, 10, 11†, 12, 28, 29, 31, 33b).	Composite psalm addresses the international congregation by Ps 96

‡ In the table illustrating parallels within 1 Chr 16, bold, italics, and underlining signify verbal parallels; broken underlining signifies related roots; and wavy underlining signifies different subconstituencies of the congregation. Note the psalms adapted by the Chronicler: 1 Chr 16:8–22//Ps 105:1–15; 1 Chr 16:23–33//Ps 96:1b–10b, 11–13b; 1 Chr 16:34–36//Ps 106:1, 47–48.

After bringing together Israel and the nations within an invitation for one worshiping congregation, the Chronicler breaks the spell with the song's conclusion. He takes the first and last part of Ps 106 to end the song with "us" and "them" in opposition. "Cry out, 'Save *us*, God *our* Savior; gather *us* and deliver *us* from the nations'" (16:35, emphasis mine; cf. vv. 34–36//Ps 106:1, 47–48). The lyrical compilation at one time calls upon the nations to worship alongside Israel even as Israel calls upon God for deliverance from the nations. As elsewhere so here, the Chronicler's inclusive exclusivity binds Israel by Yahweh's enduring fidelity and calls faithful others to join the congregation even while hostile others remain.[93] Elsewhere in Chronicles the faithful others versus hostile others denotes the remnant tribes of the former Northern Kingdom of Israel (see note on 2 Chr 10:1–11:4).

16:39–40~Exod 29:38–42; Num 28:3–8 (B)+1 Sam 7:1–2 (C); 1 Kgs 3:4 (B) (sacrifices at tabernacle at Gibeon). The Chronicler broadly refers to the regulations for

92. Knoppers, *I Chronicles 10–29*, 646.

93. On two kinds of others elsewhere, see Tables I4 in note on Isa 52:1 and Ezk6 in note on Ezek 44:9–16.

morning and evening sacrifices, marking the allusion with "in accordance with everything written in the Torah of Yahweh" (1 Chr 16:40; cf. Exod 29:38–42; Num 28:3–8). David divides the priests, with Asaph and company to worship before the ark and Zadok and company to perform sacrifices at the tabernacle, where the altar remained. The Chronicler apparently deduces that the tabernacle had been relocated to Gibeon based on two factors. First, Solomon worshiped at "the great high place" where Yahweh appeared to him (1 Kgs 3:4–5 lit.). The theophany resulted in blessing, not judgment, which, for the Chronicler, may have set this great high place apart from the other high places where the Deuteronomist speaks negatively of Solomon's sacrifices (3:3). The narrative verb form of 1 Kgs 3:4 could signify either that the high place at Gibeon was among those mentioned in 3:3 (logical consequence, "and so he went") or a different one (temporal succession, "and then he went").[94] The Chronicler may favor the latter because, second, Gibeon was "the great one" among the quartet of towns where the ark had been residing, namely, "*Gibeon*, Kephirah, Beeroth and *Kiriath Jearim*" (Josh 9:17, emphasis mine; cf. 10:2).[95] If the ark had been at Kiriath Jearim (1 Sam 7:1–2; 1 Chr 13:5) and if Solomon was blessed at the great high place at Gibeon, then the Chronicler may have deduced that the tabernacle and its worship apparatus had been relocated to the chief town of the quartet where the ark had resided. One might sharply object that even though Gibeon and Kiriath Jearim were sister cities, it seems strange to have the ark at one and the tabernacle at the other. The Chronicler did not harmonize away this tension but left it unexplained. The Chronicler adds a deductive plus using background commentary (non-wci, here pf. with other literary signals) versus narrative verb forms (wci) and citing no source (bold signifies verbal parallels, italics signify additions, broken underlining signifies narrative verb forms [wci] in the foreground, and wavy underlining signifies background comment verb forms [pf.]—background comment indented):[96]

---

94. On the functions of *vayyiqtol* forms (wci), see GKC §111i.

95. The archeological and scriptural evidence combined do not help but provide only circumstantial evidence to make broad speculations about Gibeon, e.g., Arnold, "Gibeon," *ABD* 2:1010–12; Edelman, "Gibeon," 164.

96. Narrative foreground is governed by *vayyitqtol*/wci forms and narrative background is governed by non-*vayyiqtol*/wci forms, in this case *qatal*/perfect forms. On foregrounding/backgrounding in narrative, see van Wolde, "Linguistic Motivation," 35, n. 28; 39–40; Chisholm, *Interpreting the Historical Books*, 37–39; Heller, *Narrative Structure*, 54–62. The Chronistic plus in 2 Chr 1:3b–5a is a long, compound background element marked as a whole by "for" (כִּי, v. 3b). This background unit includes its own deep background—background of the background—in Moses's time marked by "which" (אֲשֶׁר, v. 3c) along with further background to the background marked by "for" (כִּי, v. 4b) and disjunctive *vav* (וְ, v. 5a). For these background discourse elements see Patton, "Working," 54–55, 59–60. (Patton fails to adequately handle the disjunctive *vav* as a background marker, 59–60. However, he treats *vav*+noun in Jonah 1:5 [p. 115] as background, which is a similar construction to *vav*+noun ["but the altar" וּמִזְבַּח] of the background of the background in 2 Chr 1:5a.) In the case of 2 Chr 1:3–5, the foreground action of v. 3a resumes with the next narrative verb (wci) in v. 5b: "And Solomon and the whole assembly *went* [wci] to the high place at Gibeon, [long compound background unit initiated by "for" (כִּי) in vv. 3b–5a] . . . so Solomon and the assembly *inquired* [wci] of him there" (2 Chr 1:3a, 5b, emphasis mine). On the resumptive function of wci forms after a background unit see Patton, "Working," 86.

Then the king **went** to **Gibeon** to offer sacrifices, for that was **the** most important **high place**, and **Solomon** **offered** **a thousand burnt offerings on** that altar. (1 Kgs 3:4 lit.)

And Solomon *and the whole assembly* **went** to **the high place** at **Gibeon**,
for God's tent of meeting was there, which Moses Yahweh's servant had made in the wilderness. Now David had brought up the ark of God from Kiriath Jearim to the place he had prepared for it, because he had pitched a tent for it in Jerusalem. But the bronze altar that Bezalel son of Uri, the son of Hur, had made was in Gibeon in front of the tabernacle of Yahweh.
So Solomon and the assembly inquired of him there. **Solomon** *went up to the bronze altar before Yahweh in the tent of meeting and* **offered** **a thousand burnt offerings on** it. (2 Chr 1:3–6)

While the Chronicler does not smooth out the tension of tabernacle and ark at different sister towns, he makes a small adjustment elsewhere corresponding to his tabernacle deduction. The older version of the Davidic covenant says, "I was going around in tent and in tabernacle" (2 Sam 7:6 lit.), but the Chronistic version says, "I was [going] *from* tent **to tent** and *from* tabernacle" (1 Chr 17:5 lit., italics signify revision and bold signifies addition).[97] If the donor text uses tent and tabernacle as a quasi-poetic pair to refer to the tabernacle by its two names, tent of meeting and tabernacle, the Chronicler may align it with his tabernacle locale deduction (1 Chr 16:39; 2 Chr 1:3–6).[98]

16:43/~/2 Sam 6:19–20a (returning home and David's blessing). The Chronicler retains the transition but deletes Michal (see note on 1 Chr 15:25–16:6).

17:1–15*, 16–27/~/2 Sam 7:1–17*, 18–29 (Davidic covenant and David's prayer) (* see Davidic covenant, Judah-king, and place networks). The Chronicler's version of Nathan delivering the covenant to David and David's prayer of response closely follows the version appearing in 2 Sam 7. Most of the light editing amounts to stylistic changes, some of which merely relate to tendencies of Late Biblical Hebrew (see Hermeneutical Profile of the Use of Scripture in Jeremiah). For the present purposes, only exegetical interventions need to be discussed.

The Chronicler deleted the phrase marked with italics: "After the king was settled in his palace *and Yahweh had given him rest from all his enemies around him*" (2 Sam 7:1//1 Chr 17:1). The deleted phrase echoes the language of Deut 12:10, which gets partly

97. The emendation preferring symmetry ("from tent to tent and from tabernacle to tabernacle") does not help since the ark did move from tent to tent and from tabernacle, but not to tabernacle (contra Avioz, "Nathan's Prophecy," 543).

98. The "tabernacle" is only mentioned outside Torah in Josh 22:19, 29; 2 Sam 7:6//1 Chr 17:5 and "tent of meeting" only in Josh 18:1; 19:51; 1 Sam 2:22; 1 Kgs 8:4//2 Chr 5:5. The shrine is referred to as "temple" (הֵיכַל) (1 Sam 1:9; 3:3), which leads some to think of it as a "more permanent structure" at Shiloh (Klein, *2 Chronicles*, 22). Though the Shiloh shrine could be called "tent of meeting" (2:22) or "temple" (1:9; 3:3), its destruction served as a sign of warning against Solomon's temple in twilight of the First Commonwealth (Jer 7:12–14; 26:6).

fulfilled in 1 Chr 18–20.[99] Removing this phrase from 1 Chr 17:1 smooths out the larger context, though the Chronicler still avoids the loaded term "rest" until 2 Chr 6:41, when the ark enters the temple (see notes on 1 Kgs 5:1–5[15–19]; 2 Chr 6:1–42; and 7:11–22). Note the revised promise of victory (italics signify variation):[100]

> I will also *give you rest from* all your enemies. (2 Sam 7:11)

> I will also *subdue* all your enemies. (1 Chr 17:10)

For the minor but apparently intentional interpretive adjustment of "from going around in tent and tabernacle" (2 Sam 7:6 lit.) to "from tent *to tent* and *from* tabernacle" (1 Chr 17:5 lit., emphasis mine), see the end of the note on 1 Chr 16:39–40.

The Chronicler deletes the threat to punish David's heir (signified by bold) primarily because elsewhere he removes the accounts of all Solomon's wrongdoing (though see discussion at Table C2). In addition to excising Saul's name and few minor adjustments (signified by italics), note a minor change with major effects by switching pronouns on house and kingdom (signified by underlining):

> I will be his father, and he will be my son. **When he does wrong, I will punish him with a rod wielded by men, with floggings inflicted by human hands.** But my love will never be taken away from him, as I took it away from *Saul*, whom **I removed** from before you. Your house and your kingdom *will endure* forever before me; your throne will be established forever. (2 Sam 7:14–16)[101]

> I will be his father, and he will be my son. I will never take my love away from him, as I took it away from *your predecessor. I will set him* over my house and my kingdom forever; *his* throne will be established forever. (1 Chr 17:13–14)

In Samuel, the house of David = the dynasty and house of Yahweh = the temple. In Chronicles "my house and my kingdom" collapse temple and dynasty together. Yahweh declares the Davidic son shall be "my son" and so he shall rule over "my kingdom." Unlike Samuel, the seer who saw a categorical choice between a human and divine king (1 Sam 8:6), the Chronicler directly identifies the Davidic ruler of the kingdom of Yahweh: "So Solomon sat on *the throne of Yahweh as king* in place of his father David" (1 Chr 29:23, emphasis mine; cf. 28:5).[102]

---

99. See Knoppers, "Changing History," 100*, 108*–12*.

100. See Schniedewind, "Chronicler as Interpreter," 171; Willis, "'Rest All Around,'" 143.

101. Second Samuel 7:16 MT says "before you" but NIV rightly emends to "before me" with LXX and a few Hebrew MSS (*BHS*). Second Samuel 7:16 LXX says "his throne," which may match the Chronicler's source text (Klein, *1 Chronicles*, 373, n. 30).

102. See Selman, "Kingdom of God in the Old Testament," 170–71.

In spite of the difficulties with "this torah of humankind" (2 Sam 7:19 lit.) and "you regard me as a distinguished person" (1 Chr 17:17 lit.), both accounts emphasize David's gratitude.[103]

The final line of the Chronistic version of David's prayer affirms his confidence by streamlining from "you . . . have spoken, and with your blessing the house of your servant will be blessed forever" (2 Sam 7:29) to using an active verb for bless, "*you have blessed* it, and it will be blessed forever" (1 Chr 17:17, emphasis mine).[104]

18:1–13/~/2 Sam 8:1–14* (David establishes a regional empire) (* see Judah-king network). First Chronicles 18–20 presents selected narratives of David's military exploits which appear across 2 Sam 8–21. Note a synoptic comparison of David's establishment of a regional empire (also see Figure C7):

	2 Samuel	**1 Chronicles**
campaigns against regional kingdoms	8:1–14	18:1–13
officials[a]	8:15–18	18:14–17
loyalty to Mephibosheth	9:1–13	—
warfare against Ammonites and Arameans	10:1–19	19:1–19
David remains in Jerusalem	11:1	20:1a
David and Bathsheba	11:1–27	—
Nathan confronts David	12:1–25	—
defeat of Rabbah	12:26–31	20:1b–3
Amnon and Tamar	13:1–22	—
Absalom's revolt	13:23–19:44	—
Sheba's revolt	20:1–22	—
officials[a]	20:23–26	—
Gibeonites avenged	21:1–14	—
Abishai's valor	21:15–17	—
defeating Rephaites	21:18–22	20:4–8
song of David	22:1–51; cf. Ps 18	—
last words	23:1–7	—
mighty men	23:8–39	{11:10–47}[b]

[a] The list is reused in a rearranged order in 2 Sam 8:16–18//20:23–25. The Chronicler uses the first list including its frame narrative (2 Sam 8:15//1 Chr 18:14).

[b] See Figure C7 on the placement of 2 Sam 23:8–39/~/1 Chr 11:10–47.

103. See discussion of textual issues in McCarter, *II Samuel*, 233; Knoppers, *I Chronicles 10–29*, 678–79.
104. See Williamson, *1 and 2 Chronicles*, 137.

Most of the variations in 1 Chr 18 seem minor.[105] Only those featuring exegetical intervention are mentioned here. First, the Chronicler excludes the execution of two-thirds of his Moabite prisoners of war (2 Sam 8:2//1 Chr 18:2). The absent gruesome details of forcing the Moabites to lie on the ground and be measured with a cord before execution broadly correspond with a memorable oracle of judgment (Isa 25:10–12).

Second, the Chronicler clarifies that Abishai (1 Chr 18:12) is the principle agent of David's celebrated military slaughter of eighteen thousand Edomites in the valley of salt (2 Sam 8:13). The superscription of Ps 60 alternatively shifts identification of the primary agent of the slaughter to Joab and features variation of other details (see note ad loc.).

18:14–17/~/2 Sam 8:15–18/~/20:23–26 (David's leading officers). The most important difference in the three lists is the clarification of David's sons as civil officials in Chronicles while they are referred to as priests in the proto-masoretic version of Samuel (2 Sam 8:18; 1 Chr 18:17). Wenham suggests the parent text read "administrators" (סכנים), which suffered scribal corruption to "priests" (כהנים), especially based on similarities of the letters *samek* (𐤎) and *he* (𐤄) in paleo-Hebrew script.[106] Then, the Chronicler updated an obsolete term to "chief officers" (הָרִאשֹׁנִים). Elsewhere the Chronicler accepts David's ritual performances without adjustments suggesting he may not object to worship functions by his sons (1 Chr 21:26; cf. 15:27; 16:2–3).[107] The textual instability and multiple maneuvers of Wenham's suggestion exclude anything more than possibilities.

19:1–19/~/2 Sam 10:1–19 (defeat of Ammonites and Arameans). The Chronistic version of David's victories over the Ammonites and Arameans closely follows the Deuteronomistic version. Characteristic Chronistic adjustments include giving greater detail to military accounts and what seems like hyperbolic increase of already large numbers (2 Sam 10:6, 18; 1 Chr 19:6, 7, 18; on hyperbolic numbers see note on 2 Chr 13:1–23).

20:1–3/~/2 Sam 11:1; 12:26a, 30–31 (defeat of Rabbah). The contrast between the Deuteronomistic account of David's rape or adultery, murder, and eventual repentance and the Chronistic account of taking Rabbah epitomizes, in some ways, the leading agendas of the two narratives. The nearly identical details themselves support extremely different narrative goals. The defeat of Rabbah functions as a frame narrative and a prop in the story of David's great sins (2 Sam 11:1, 11, 15; 12:26a, 30–31). The military frame

105. Though a Chronistic plus notes that the bronze plundered by David from two obscure towns provided the raw materials for Solomon to make the bronze sea and other bronze elements of the temple (1 Chr 18:8), the LXX agrees with the fuller text of Chronicles, suggesting omission by scribal corruption in the MT of 2 Sam 8:8. See 2 Sam 8:8 LXX; and for other evidence of a fuller Hebrew text akin to LXX in 4QSam[a/4Q51] of 2 Sam 8:7, see *BQS* 1:299–300; Lemke, "Synoptic Problem," 355, n. 20; Knoppers, *I Chronicles 10–29*, 691–92.

106. Paleo-Hebrew font by Kris J. Udd.

107. So Wenham, "Were David's Sons Priests?" 79–82. Wenham does not list 1 Chr 21:26 though it offers stronger support than the references he cites. Also see Klein, *1 Chronicles*, 388, n. 31; Knoppers, *I Chronicles 10–29*, 706.

narrative alone survives the Chronicler's redactional cuts (1 Chr 20:1–3). David's sin in all its detail is important within the Deuteronomistic explanation of the inevitability of the fall of Jerusalem. David's covenant violations underline the coming judgment. In addition, the signature difference between Saul and David (1 Sam 13:14) relate to how they respond when confronted by a prophet—one resists, the other repents (1 Sam 15:15, 20–21, 24–25, 30; 2 Sam 12:13; cf. Ps 51 superscription). By retaining only the frame narrative, the Chronicler presents a significant military victory in the establishment of David's regional empire and the accumulation of plunder for Solomon's building projects, especially the temple (1 Chr 18:8; cf. 22:3–4, 14; 29:2–5). The Chronicler does not erase David's sin. Anyone who has heard the lead-in "In the spring, at the time when kings go off to war. . . . But David remained in Jerusalem" (2 Sam 11:1//1 Chr 20:1) remembers what David did. Elsewhere the Chronicler goes out of his way to make allusion to Bathsheba from the context of 2 Sam 11–12 (see note on 1 Chr 3:1–9). The Chronistic version of the defeat of Rabbah speaks to what David did for Jerusalem.

20:4–8/~/2 Sam 21:18–22 (killing the giants of Gath). The primary difference relates to who killed the champion named Goliath. Interpretive attempts to handle 2 Sam 21:19 by identifying David as Elhanan or positing two Goliaths magnify rather than solve the problem. If the Hebrew texts of both 2 Sam 21:19 and 1 Chr 20:5 have been preserved without scribal corruption, then it would seem that the Chronicler adjusted the identity of the person whom Elhanan killed to harmonize the details (1 Chr 20:5)—David killed Goliath (1 Sam 17:4, 48–51) and Elhanan killed his brother (2 Sam 21:19).[108] But the evidence does not fit this conclusion. Elhanan of Bethlehem is known elsewhere (23:24//1 Chr 11:26). The Chronistic account of "Elhanan killed . . . Lahmi" (lit., וַיַּךְ אֶלְחָנָן . . . אֶת־לַחְמִי) may represent a scribal corruption from "Elhanan . . . of Bethlehem killed" (lit., וַיַּךְ אֶלְחָנָן . . . בֵּית־הַלַּחְמִי) (1 Chr 20:5 NET note). And, a scribe may have mistaken "brother of Goliath" (אֲחִי גָּלְיָת) for "Goliath" and an accusative marker (אֵת גָּלְיָת) (2 Sam 21:19 NET note).[109] The point at hand affirms the transmitted text of Chronicles as more likely intact than Samuel in this case, even while speculation on two-step textual scribal corruptions eliminates confidence. Thus, it is more likely that the Chronicler did not harmonize the details.

21:1–30/~/2 Sam 24:1–25 (David's sin of the census). The Chronicler relocates the sin of the census from its place in the appendices of Samuel to the head of a massive Chronistic insert related to David's preparations for the temple (see Figure C7). Note a synoptic comparison of David's preparations for the temple:[110]

---

108. So Knoppers, *I Chronicles 10–29*, 736 (based on a conjectured parent text of Chronicles less corrupt than Samuel).

109. See detailed discussion of the evidence in Ozolins, "Killing Goliath?" Klein presents many of the same details as the NET text notes cited above but interprets them as intentional adjustments by the Chronicle (see *1 Chronicles*, 412). For a different scenario of textual variations with almost equal merit, see Keil and Delitzsch, *1 and 2 Samuel*, 466.

110. It is difficult to align 1 Kings 1:1–2:9 with 1 Chronicles 22–29. The less than ideal placement in the synoptic comparison is based on two observations. First, note the resumptive repetition "full of days" (שְׂבַע יָמִים) (1 Chr 23:1;

	2 Samuel/1 Kings	1 Chronicles
David's sin with the census	2 Sam 24:1–25	21:1–27
threshing floor to be place for house of Yahweh	—	21:28–22:1
consultation with Solomon to build temple	—	22:2–23:1
Abishag attends to David	1 Kgs 1:1–4	—
Adonijah attempt to seize rulership	1:5–27	—
Solomon anointed	1:28–53	—
David's charge to Solomon	2:1–9	—
Levitical divisions	—	23:2–32
priestly divisions	—	24:1–19
remaining Levites	—	24:20–31
musicians	—	25:1–31
gatekeepers	—	26:1–19
officers of the treasury and others	—	26:20–32
military divisions	—	27:1–15
tribal leaders	—	27:16–24
royal officials	—	27:25–34
public proclamation of Solomon to build temple	—	28:1–21
donations toward temple	—	29:1–9
David's prayer	—	29:10–19
ceremony for Solomon's second coronation[a]	—	29:20–25
death of David	2:10–11	29:26–30

[a] Note the identification of the ceremony as the "second" coronation (1 Chr 29:22).

The sin of the census provides the lone exception to the Chronicler's strategy of redacting out David's transgressions. This exception undermines the commonplace conjecture of idealizing David (see discussion at Table C2). Why keep one sin story? The story of David's sin of the census represents central concerns of Chronicles. David's repentance epitomizes rightful temple worship. Moreover, David's purchase of the threshing floor (1 Chr 21:24–25), the future home of the temple (22:1), provides an on-ramp to collate David's many efforts to prepare for building the temple (22–29). The importance of this episode suggests why it houses extensive editing.

29:28). Second, the Chronicler makes explicit that the assembly for and coronation of Solomon in 1 Chr 28–29 is a "second" (שֵׁנִית) coronation ceremony (29:22). This seems to be the Chronicler's way of acknowledging the hasty first coronation in 1 Kings 1 that he skipped over. This second observation is from Peterson, "Did?," 557, 560–61.

The present discussion focuses on prominent exegetical interventions (with those related to 21:1, 16, 26 treated separately below). First, the Chronicler includes the term "guilt" (אַשְׁמָה) from his constellation of retributive terms (21:3; cf. "iniquity" 21:8//2 Sam 24:10). David's transgression leads to collective culpability, which matches other uses of this term in pluses of Chronicles (1 Chr 21:3; 2 Chr 24:18; 28:13). Second, Chronicles includes larger numbers than Samuel as part of its hyperbolic literary tendency (1 Chr 21:5, 21; see note on 2 Chr 13:1–23). Third, the Chronicler explains that the census excludes Levi and Benjamin. The omission of Benjamin seems to be deduced from the geographical data of Samuel not carried over into Chronicles (2 Sam 24:5–8). The exclusion of Levi fits strong Chronistic emphasis and invites a brief interpretive gloss: "But Joab did not include Levi and Benjamin in the numbering, *because the king's command was repulsive to him*" (1 Chr 21:6, emphasis mine). Perhaps Joab's reaction relates to Levi being excluded from the general military census (Num 1:47–49; 2:33). Fourth, in a pair of pluses, David twice insists on paying "full price" for the threshing floor (1 Chr 21:22, 24). This exact phrase only appears elsewhere in Abraham's purchase of a burial plot for Sarah.[111] Both Abraham and David desire to legally own the respective properties beyond any dispute.

21:1/~/2 Sam 24:1+Num 22:22 (C) (inciting David).
21:16/~/2 Sam 24:17+Num 22:31 (B) (sword drawn). The Chronicler famously adjusts the expressed identity of the one provoking David. The exact exegetical intervention of the Chronicler depends on if "an adversary," *satan* (שָׂטָן), refers to a human or celestial adversary, and, in the case of the latter, if it lacks an article because it functions as the proper name Satan (bold signifies exact verbal parallels, normal and wavy underlining signify parallel roots, and broken underlining signifies synonymous expressions):

> But God was very angry when he went, and the angel of Yahweh stood in the road to oppose him. Balaam was riding on his donkey, and his two servants were with him. (Num 22:22)

> Again the anger of Yahweh burned against **Israel, and he incited David** against them, saying, "Go and take a census **of Israel** and Judah." (2 Sam 24:1)

> Satan rose up against **Israel and he incited David** to take a census **of Israel.** (1 Chr 21:1†)

Elsewhere Yahweh raised up human adversaries (*satans*) against Solomon (1 Kgs 11:14, 23, 25); or, more generally, the term refers to human opposers (1 Sam 29:4; 2 Sam 19:22[23]). The term *the satan*, with the definite article, also refers to the celestial adversary (Zech 3:1, 2; Job 1:6, etc.; cf. Jub 17:16).[112] In another context the Chronicler

111. For the same point, along with several less convincing parallels, see Amit, "Threshing Floor," 139.
112. See Even-Shoshan, 1133; "שָׂטָן," *HALOT* 2:1317.

uses a tradition in which Yahweh judges by means of sinister celestial delegates (2 Chr 18:18–21//1 Kgs 22:19–22).[113] In the present context, if the census is a military census, it could support *a satan* as a human military adversary (1 Chr 21:2–3).[114]

Several similarities with the celestial delegate in the Balaam story suggest the Chronicler may have blended extended echoes to exegetically reshape the account in order to explain the divine judgment (see Table C10). The following verbal and thematic similarities in the Balaam story and David's sin with the census in Samuel include several general connections that may have invited the Chronicler's exegetical interventions: the deity's anger was kindled (Num 22:22; 2 Sam 24:1); the delegate of Yahweh administers judgment (Num 22:22; 2 Sam 24:16); the revelation of the celestial delegate prompts confession, "I have sinned" (Num 22:34; 2 Sam 24:17).[115] The celestial delegate's sword provides the most dramatic element of reshaping of divine judgment, appearing repeatedly within Chronistic pluses (1 Chr 21:12, 16, 27). If the Chronicler's source text included the sword, as does the fragment from the Dead Sea Scrolls of Samuel, it may have invited the use of Balaam's encounter as a catchword (bold and underlining signify verbal parallels, and italics and broken underlining signify thematic similarities):[116]

> Then Yahweh opened Balaam's **eyes, and he saw the angel of Yahweh** standing in the road **with a sword drawn in his hand.** So he bowed low *and fell facedown.* (Num 22:31†)

> [Dav]id lifted up [his eyes and saw the angel of Yahweh standing between] earth and h[ea]v[e]n, with a drawn sword in his hand extende[d] [over Jerusalem. Then the elders,] cloth[ed in s]ackcloth, [fell faced]own. (2 Sam 24:16 4QSam[a/4Q51] lit.)

> David lifted up his **eyes and saw the angel of Yahweh** standing between heaven and earth**, with a drawn sword in his hand** extended over Jerusalem. Then David and the elders, clothed in sackcloth, *fell facedown.*(1 Chr 21:16†)[117]

In sum, the evidence related to 1 Chr 21:1 itself leaves the human versus celestial identity of the adversary undecided. The verbal correspondence between Num 22:31 and 1 Chr 21:16 favors exegetical allusion by the latter. The use of "sword" in 4QSam[a/4Q51] of 2 Sam 24:16 strengthens the likelihood of the Chronicler's exegetical allusion to the Balaam narrative.

21:26/~/2 Sam 24:25 (A)+Lev 9:24 (B) (fire from Yahweh). David's repentance embodies paradigmatic worship on the future site of the temple. Yahweh responds with

113. Page, "Satan: God's Servant," 455.

114. So Japhet, *I & II Chronicles*, 373–75.

115. See Stokes, "The Devil," 101.

116. For these comparisons, see ibid., 103; Klein, *1 Chronicles*, 415–16, n. 30; and, 4QSam[a/4Q51], 164, 1–3 as reconstructed in *BQS* 1:322.

117. Though "fell facedown" in 1 Chr 21:16 is merely similar to Num 22:31 and 4QSam[a/4Q51] 164, 3, it verbally corresponds to Lev 9:23. Nevertheless, it is a common expression (see note on 1 Chr 21:26).

fire from heaven in a manner resembling the institution of tabernacle worship (italics and bold signify verbal parallels):[118]

> **Fire** came out from the presence of Yahweh and consumed **the burnt offering** and the fat portions **on the altar**. And when all the people saw it, they shouted for joy and fell facedown. (Lev 9:24)
>
> *David built an altar to Yahweh there and sacrificed burnt offerings and fellowship offerings*. Then *Yahweh* responded to his prayer in behalf of the land, and the plague on Israel was stopped. (2 Sam 24:25†)
>
> *David built an altar to Yahweh there and sacrificed burnt offerings and fellowship offerings*. He called on Yahweh, and *Yahweh* answered him with **fire** from heaven **on the altar of burnt offering.** (1 Chr 21:26)

When Solomon dedicates the temple, fire comes down from heaven to consume the burnt offerings (2 Chr 7:1–3; see note ad loc.). The Chronicler establishes concrete continuity between the temple and David's model of what temple worship should look like. These both enjoy even more ancient continuity with the dedication of the tabernacle. Elsewhere the Chronicler uses additional layers of ancient continuity for the exact same place of worship (see Table C10; Figure C17; note on 2 Chr 3:1). When David brought the ark to Jerusalem, it signaled Yahweh's choice of the city (see note on 1 Chr 16:7–36). Now Yahweh's election of the place for his name to dwell acquires a more specific location along with divine confirmation (Deut 12:5; 1 Chr 22:1).

22:5–19*~Josh 1:5–9 (C)+2 Sam 7:13–14* (C)+1 Kgs 2:1–4 (D)+5:3–5[17–19] (C) (David privately charges Solomon to build the temple) (* see place network). Though thematically similar to 1 Kgs 2:1–4, the language of 1 Chr 22 is different, and the emphasis falls on building the temple.[119] David's charge reflects a loose blending of several contexts to explain Solomon's mission to build the temple. David deduces that since his son must be a person of rest and peace to build the temple, his own constant warfare must explain his temple-building disability (1 Kgs 5:3–5[17–19]; see note ad loc.). David uses the distinctive language of "shedding much blood" (1 Chr 22:8; cf. note on 28:2–3). David connects this to the oracle from Nathan by means of Yahweh's fatherhood to Solomon (17:13; 22:10; cf. 2 Sam 7:14). David repeatedly evokes the

118. Contra Barnes, "Midrashic Element," 427, who links it to 1 Kgs 18:38. Other suggestions include Judg 6:21 (see Sugimoto, "Chronicler's Techniques," 64). Sugimoto attributes this view to Williamson (64, n. 59), but Williamson affirms something similar to the view presented here (*1 and 2 Chronicles*, 105).

119. See Williamson, *1 and 2 Chronicles*, 153–54. Elsewhere he overstates these differences: idem, "Accession of Solomon," 354.

commissioning of Joshua with "be strong and courageous" and promised "success" (Josh 1:6–9; 1 Chr 22:11, 13).

The highly ironic nature of David's interpretive deductions should not be missed. The prerequisite of securing rest by subjugating regional kingdoms as well as securing plunder and tribute to finance building projects requires warfare that simultaneously eliminates eligibility to build the temple (1 Chr 26:26–27). The focus on the qualification of "peace" (*shalom*) can be heard in the throne name Solomon (*shelomoh*), embedded in David's paraphrase of the covenant (22:9).[120] No one person could ever build the temple. A war-king gains dominion and wealth and is thereby disqualified. A peace-king builds the temple using the provisions of the war-king. Building a temple for Yahweh turns out to be an inherently multigenerational project.

23:25–30*~Deut 12:9–10+Num 1:49–50; 3:6–9+4:2–4, 23, 30, 35, 39, 43, 47; 8:24 (C) (Levites serve at the temple beginning at age twenty) (* see teachers network). The Levitical responsibilities include noninterpretive broad allusions to several worship standards such as assisting priests and showbread (1 Chr 23:28–29; cf. Exod 25:30; Lev 24:5–9; Num 3:6–8; 8:19, 22; 18:6). The ministry of singing represents a Davidic advancement (1 Chr 23:30). The Torah speaks of Levites serving from ages thirty to fifty (Num 4:2–4, 23, 30, 35, 39, 43, 47) and twenty-five to fifty (8:24). Evidence is not available to explain this discrepancy.[121] David initiated a census of Levites thirty years old and older (1 Chr 23:3). But he offers an important exegetical advance, changing the beginning age of Levitical service to twenty (23:24, 27; cf. Ezra 3:8). The same age range gets applied to priests also (2 Chr 31:17). David's pronouncements turn on the new state of rest for Israel. The Levites' role changes forever since they no longer need to transport the portable shrine and ark. David's exegetical deduction comes from the fulfillment of the divine choice of a place for his name to dwell when his people come to rest (1 Chr 23:25–26; Deut 12:9–10).[122] David seems to have in mind his own transfer of the ark to Jerusalem (1 Chr 16:1). In the next generation, the Levites have one final delivery of the ark and tabernacle to the temple (2 Chr 5:4–5; cf. 35:2). The new situation opens the way for a new range of Levitical worship responsibilities. David appoints Levites to temple service, including assisting the priests, gatekeepers, treasurers, and especially music (1 Chr 23–26).[123] Divine affirmation of David's advances comes by casting lots (24:31; 25:8, 9; 26:13, 14; cf. 24:5, 7). David set apart the Levites for different areas of temple service according to their clans akin to Torah (see Exod 6:16–20; Num 3:17–20, 38; Figure C16).

---

120. See Braun, "Solomonic Apologetic," 507, 513.

121. See Brin, "Onward/Upward," 165–69.

122. See Japhet, *I & II Chronicles*, 418–19.

123. On Levites as temple gatekeepers, see 1 Chr 9:16–32; 15:18, 23–24; 26:1–19; 2 Chr 8:14; 23:4–11, 19; 34:12–13; 35:15.

FIGURE C16: NEW LEVITICAL RESPONSIBILITIES BY ANCIENT CLANS‡

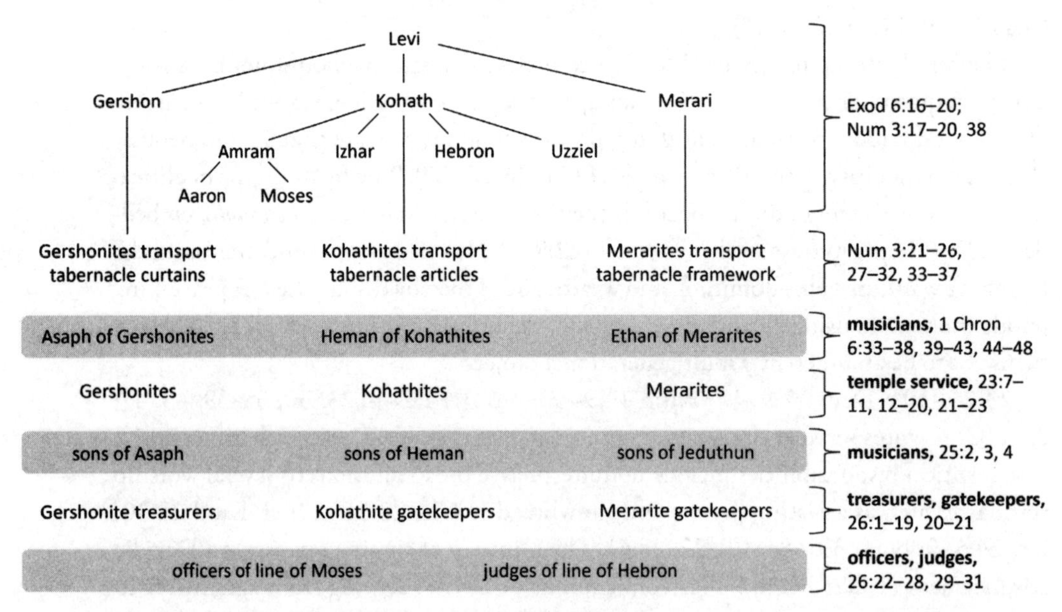

‡ This table only presents English Bible verse references.

FIGURE C17: EXEGETICAL BASES FOR DAVID'S WORSHIP INITIATIVES IN CHRONICLES

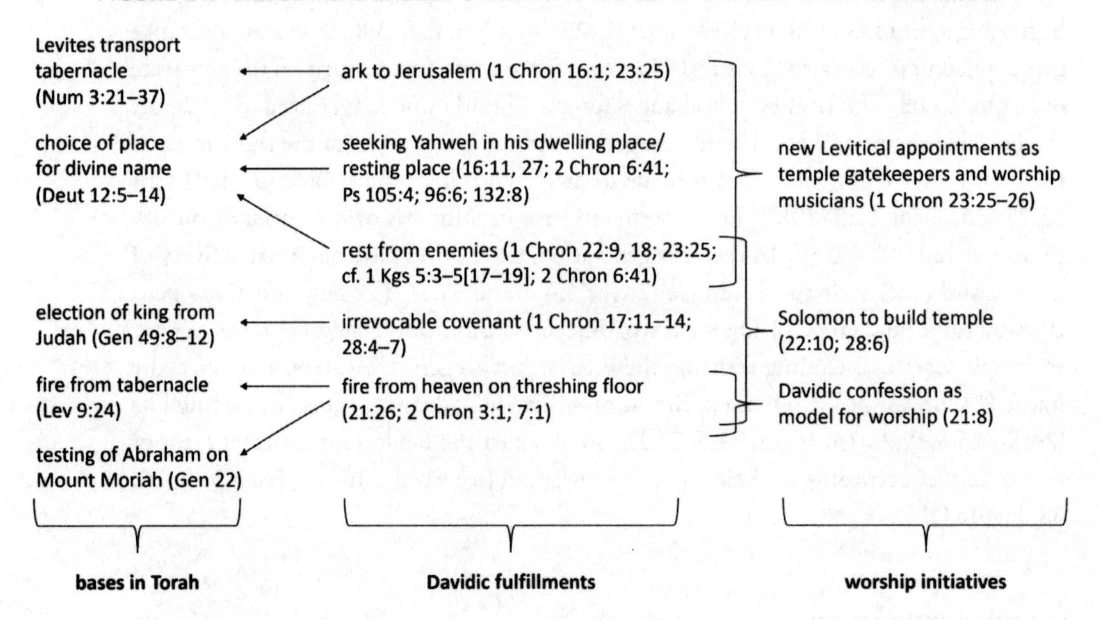

In sum, the sweeping and profound advances in worship set in motion by David in Chronicles rest on a series of exegetical deductions using a constellation of scriptural traditions. The Chronicler reshapes narratives appearing in Samuel and Kings according to numerous Torah contexts (e.g., Gen 22:1–19; 49:8–12; Lev 9:24; Num 3:21–37; Deut 12:5–14). If Chronicles answers the needs of a postexilic worshiping constituency of Judah, it does so according to the guiding testimony of Torah. The interpretive advances provide an important way to maintain continuity with ancient worship traditions established in the wilderness (see note on 1 Chr 9:2–18). Figure C17 broadly summarizes prominent exegetical bases for worship advances collated in the Chronistic David narrative (see notes ad loc.).

28:2–3*//22:8–9~Deut 12:10–11* (B)+2 Sam 7:11* (C)+1 Kgs 5:3–5[17–19] (B) (David's rule lacks rest to build temple) (* see Davidic covenant and place networks). **28:4–6***~Gen 49:8–12 (B)+2 Sam 6:21 (C)+7:13–14* (B) (election of Solomon based on choosing Judah) (* see Davidic covenant, Judah-king, and place networks). **28:7**~2 Sam 7:14–15* (B) (irrevocable Davidic covenant and its obligations) (* see Davidic covenant and place networks). The several uses of scriptural traditions in David's speech in 1 Chr 28 can be treated together as overlapping elements of a major exegetical initiative. David's public address to the great assembly (1 Chr 28:1) echoes many of the themes he had shared privately with Solomon (22:7–16; 28:2–10, 20–21). The public address goes further, bursting with the favorite scriptural stock phrases associated with Chronistic David: ark/temple as footstool of Yahweh (28:2; cf. Isa 66:1; Pss 99:5; 132:7; Lam 2:1); obedience to the covenantal instructions to remain in the land (28:8; cf. 22:12–13; Lev 18:26–28; 26:14–15, 33; Deut 4:25–27; 30:16–18; etc.); seeking and finding Yahweh (28:9; cf. 2 Chr 12:5; 15:2; 24:20; 28:6; Jer 29:13–14; Isa 55:6; and esp. Deut 4:29; see note on 2 Chr 15:2); be strong and courageous, do not be afraid or discouraged (28:10, 20//22:13; cf. Deut 1:21; 31:7, 23; Josh 1:6, 7, 9, 18; 8:1). The Scripture-laden speech should not overwhelm key allusions to control texts upon which David's exegetical advances pivot.[124]

First, like so many other elements in the Chronistic reshaping of the Deuteronomistic narrative, David here builds upon elements found within the older account.[125] David claims that Yahweh prevented him from building the temple because he had "shed blood" (28:3; cf. 22:8; see note on 22:5–19). David as war-time king precludes the rest and peace required to build the temple. David's logic accords with Solomon's commentary to Hiram about "rest" (1 Kgs 5:3–5[17–19]; see note ad loc.), just as David had earlier explained to Solomon the need for "peace" (1 Chr 22:8–9). David and Solomon apparently come to their interpretative deductions by leveraging Nathan's oracle against the place of rest spoken by Moses (all formatted text signifies verbal parallels at the level of shared roots, with wavy underlining signifying interpretive deductions):

124. Luke, too, "uses diction and even shapes his stories in order to evoke Scriptural precedents" (Johnson, *Septuagintal Midrash*, 13). Also see Hays, *Reading Backwards*, 58–59; idem, *Echoes of Scripture in the Gospels*, 193–94.

125. See von Rad, "Rest," in *From Genesis*, 84–85; Braun, "Chosen Temple Builder," 583–85.

[Moses] *He will give you rest from all your enemies* on every side so that you will live in safety. Then to the place Yahweh your God will choose as a dwelling for his Name—there you are to bring everything I command you: your burnt offerings and sacrifices, your tithes and special gifts, and all the choice possessions you have vowed to Yahweh. (Deut 12:10b–11†)

[Nathan] *I will also give you rest from all your enemies.* (2 Sam 7:11b)

[Solomon] You know that because of the wars waged against my father David on every side, **he could not build a temple for the Name of Yahweh** his God until Yahweh put his enemies under his feet. But now Yahweh my God *has given me rest* on every side, and there is no adversary or disaster. I intend, therefore, to build a temple for the Name of Yahweh my God. (1 Kgs 5:3–5a[17–19a]; v. 3[17] NIV supplies "enemies")

[David to Solomon in private] But this word of Yahweh came to me: "You have shed much blood and have fought many wars. **You are not to build a house for my Name,** because you have shed much blood on the earth in my sight. But you will have a son who will be a man of peace and *rest,* and I *will give him rest from all his enemies* on every side. His name will be Solomon, and I will grant Israel peace and quiet during his reign." (1 Chr 22:8–9)

[David to public assembly] I had it in my heart to build a house as *a place of rest* for the ark of the covenant of Yahweh, for the footstool of our God, and I made plans to build it. But God said to me, "You are **not to build a house for my Name,** because you are a warrior and have shed blood." (28:2b–3)

Second, David connects the divine selection of Solomon to build the temple to ancestral expectations stemming from the divine choice of Judah as leader of Israel (28:4).[126] David seems to be looking at Judah within the Genesis narrative along the lines of a reading appearing as a Chronistic narrative comment (5:2). The Chronicler sorts out the birthright going to Joseph (apparently a double portion because of two tribes, Gen 48:13–20) and rule to Judah (apparently by the blessing, 49:8–12). Both the Chronicler and David use the identical telltale term "leader" (נָגִיד), revealing that they share a particular interpretation of Genesis.[127] This connection suggests that the Chronicler detects Nathan's interpretive allusion to the blessing of Judah

126. For more detailed interaction with 1 Chr 28:4, see Schnittjer, "Blessing of Judah," 32–34.

127. "Leader" is not a loaded term, and not overly common or uncommon ("נָגִיד," *HALOT* 1:667–68). The point here rests on the similar distinctive connection to the Judah narrative in 1 Chr 5:2; 28:4.

(see note on 2 Sam 7:14–16). David's interpretive advance connects the choice of Judah's line through Solomon as a single divine plan by repetition of the verb "choose." The term "choose" does not appear in Nathan's oracle to David in either Samuel or Chronicles. But David taunts Michal that Yahweh *chose* him to *lead* Israel in a context the Chronicler did not include in his story (2 Sam 6:21). In his public address, David retrojects building the temple as part of the package of the ancient election of Judah. He combines the choice of himself to rule and Solomon to build and deduces the inclusion of royal temple patronage as part of the destiny set in motion by the ancient promise to Judah. David realizes these are not unrelated events but part of God's singular will. This exegetical blend provides strong evidence of the advancement of revelation of the divine will, since elsewhere Yahweh specifically notes that he had not requested a temple—it is David's idea (7:7//1 Chr 17:6). Stated differently, Chronistic David makes a retrospective connection since the temple is not something for which Yahweh had been asking. Notice David's important connections (bold, italics, and underlining signify verbal parallels):

> David said to Michal, "It was before Yahweh, who *chose* me rather than your father or anyone from his house when he appointed me **leader** over Yahweh's people Israel—I will celebrate before Yahweh." (2 Sam 6:21†)
>
> [Nathan] He is the one who will build a house for my Name, and I will establish the throne of his kingdom forever. I will be his father, and he will be my son. (7:13–14a// 1 Chr 17:12–13a)
>
> [Chronicler] Though **Judah** was the strongest of his brothers and **a leader** came from him, the rights of the firstborn belonged to Joseph. (1 Chr 5:2†)
>
> [David] Yet Yahweh, the God of Israel, *chose* me from my whole family to be king over Israel forever. *He chose* **Judah as leader**, and from the tribe of Judah my family, and from my father's sons he was pleased to make me king over all Israel. Of all my sons—and Yahweh has given me many—*he has chosen* my son Solomon to sit on the throne of the kingdom of Yahweh over Israel. He said to me: "Solomon your son is the one who will build my house and my courts, for *I have chosen* him to be my son, and I will be his father." (28:4–6†)

Third, David reinforces the permanence of the divine covenant with his house, as well as its obligations (28:7). A long debate has repeatedly reworked concerns about whether the covenant to David is conditional or unconditional. The term "unconditional" itself, meaning continuance no matter what, seems to be a significant source of the debate.

In short: How can an unconditional covenant carry conditions? Recent studies on Hittite covenants suggest a way that avoids the impasse.[128] The Davidic covenant is permanent and irrevocable even while it carries obligations. These two different kinds of qualities of the covenant help explain why later prophets without blinking could speak of discarding to exile the king and kingdom (e.g., Jer 22:24–27, 30; 24:8–10) even while expecting restoration (23:5–6). David affirms the permanence of the covenant and its obligations upon the king, building off Nathan's promise and warning which David and Yahweh repeat to Solomon privately (2 Sam 7:14; 1 Kgs 2:3–4; 3:14; 8:61; 9:4–5). David publicly paraphrases the divine message: "*I will establish his kingdom forever if he is unswerving in carrying out my commands and laws,* as is being done at this time" (1 Chr 28:7, emphasis mine).

28:19~Exod 25:9, 40 (B) (the plan of the temple revealed). David spells out his "plan" (1 Chr 28:11, 12) for the temple and all its furnishings and worship personnel (28:11–18). He concludes by explaining in broad, cryptic terms the source of his written temple plans.[129] David says Yahweh "enabled me to understand," using the causative stem of the verb (28:19). Elsewhere the verb can refer to acquiring insight by study (e.g., Neh 8:13) or revelation (e.g., 9:20; Dan 9:22).[130] This speaks of more than simply casting lots, to determine the order of service, while David observes (1 Chr 24:31). David infers some kind of undisclosed revelatory experience by the expression "the hand of Yahweh was upon me" (28:19). By the revelatory experience David understood the "figure" or "pattern" of the temple and its worship guilds. The term for figure or pattern is used in the sense of the written plans David gave Solomon (28:11, 12). The term alludes to the revelation of the "pattern" of the tabernacle to Moses upon the mountain, where it also functions as an object of a causative verb stem (Exod 25:9, 40). David's remarks establish the revelation of the pattern of the tabernacle to Moses as a retrospective type of David's written plans for the temple (see Table C10; bold signifies verbal parallel):

> [Yahweh to Moses] Make this tabernacle and all its furnishings exactly like **the pattern** I will show you [Hif]. (Exod 25:9; cf. v. 40)
>
> [David] All this I have in writing as a result of Yahweh's hand on me, and he enabled me to understand [Hif] all the details of **the pattern.** (1 Chr 28:19†)

---

128. See Johnston, "'Unconditional' and 'Conditional'"; idem, "Davidic Covenant in the Light of Intertextual Analysis"; idem, "Davidic Covenant in Light of Ancient Near Eastern Royal Grants"; idem, in Bateman, et al., *Jesus the Messiah*, esp. 68–74; Gentry, "Rethinking," 285; Gentry and Wellum, *Kingdom Through Covenant*, 397.

129. Elsewhere David's establishment of the orders of worship personnel is said to be in writing, possibly referring to the traditions in 1 Chr 23–26 (2 Chr 35:4).

130. See "שׂכל," Hif *HALOT* 2:1328–29.

29:6~Exod 25:2 (C) (free will contribution to the shrine). The allusive use of "willingly give," though in different stems in 1 Chr 29:6 (Hith) and Exod 25:2 (Q), seems likely based on the more explicit figural allusion in this context (see note on 1 Chr 28:19). Both contexts run thematically parallel, which strengthens the typology for donating to worship expenses (29:1–9; cf. Exod 25:1–9).

29:25~Josh 3:7; 4:14 (C) (Yahweh exalts Solomon). The Chronicler offers narrative comments on magnifying Solomon's rule that may allude to Joshua. The potential allusion plus several stock phrases—be strong and courageous, never leave nor forsake (see notes on 1 Chr 22:5–19; 28:7)—carry forward the general retrospective figural shaping of the transition from David to Solomon along the lines of Moses to Joshua (emphasis signifies verbal parallels):[131]

> And Yahweh said to Joshua, "Today I will begin to *exalt you in the eyes of all Israel,* so they may know that I am with you as I was with Moses." (Josh 3:7)

> Yahweh *highly exalted* Solomon *in the sight of all Israel* and bestowed on him royal splendor such as no king over Israel ever had before. (1 Chr 29:25)

29:27–30/~/1 Kgs 2:10–11 (death of David). The Chronicler greatly expands the concluding formula for David's rule even while not using the description of his burial (see Table C11). The triple prophetic source citation provides the most notable addition (1 Chr 29:29). Elsewhere only the concluding formula for Solomon's rule features triple sources (2 Chr 9:29).[132]

2 Chr 1:1–13/~/1 Kgs 3:1–15; 4:1a (revelation to Solomon at Gibeon). The Chronistic story of the theophany at Gibeon features substantial editing of its counterpart in Kings even while following the basic drift. The major differences are the tabernacle at Gibeon—this was treated in some detail in the note on 1 Chr 16:39–40 (see ad loc.)—and the larger context of theophany in the narrative of Solomon. The Chronistic narrative of the transition from David to Solomon differs substantially from the political intrigue of 1 Kgs 1–2. The Chronicler acknowledges the differences by mentioning the ceremony of 1 Chr 29 as a second coronation (29:22).[133] The Chronicler presents extensive detail concerning David's plans for the temple beginning in a meeting with his son (1 Chr 22). After David died, a descriptive narrative of Solomon features an enhanced symmetrical framing arrangement (see Table C8). Note a synoptic comparison to organize the following notes that discuss the use of scriptural traditions through the Chronistic presentation of Solomon's rule:

---

131. See Williamson, "Accession of Solomon," 355; cf. list of parallels, 353; Dillard, "Chronicler's Solomon," 293.
132. See Glatt-Gilad, "Regnal Formulae," 207.
133. As observed by Peterson, "Did?," 557, 560–61. See synoptic comparison in note on 1 Chr 21:1–30.

	1 Kings	Chronicles
political turmoil and coronation[a]	1:1–2:9	—
death of David	2:10–11	1 Chr 29:26–30
Solomon consolidates royal power	2:13–46a	—
Solomon's rule established[b]	2:12, 46b	2 Chr 1:1
treaty marriage to the pharaoh's daughter[c]	3:1–2	—
theophany at Gibeon	3:3–15	1:2–13
international horse trading[d]	—	1:14–17
a discerning judgment	3:16–28	—
Solomon's officials	4:1–19	—
prosperity of kingdom	4:20–28[4:20–5:8]	—
Solomon's wisdom	4:29–34[5:9–14]	—
arrangements with Hiram[e]	5:1–18[15–32]	2:1–18[1:18–2:17]
building the temple	6:1–38	3:1–14
building Solomon's palace	7:1–12	—
Huram of Tyre bronze craftsperson[e]	7:13–14	—
Huram's work on pillars and furniture	7:15–51	3:15–5:1
ark brought to temple	8:1–11	5:2–14
dedication of temple[f]	8:12–66	6:1–7:10
second theophany to Solomon	9:1–9	7:11–22
other settlements, projects, and treaties	9:10–28	8:1–18
visit by queen of Sheba	10:1–13	9:1–12
wealth of and tribute to Solomon	10:14–25	9:13–24
international horse trading[d]	10:26–29; 4:21[5:1]	9:25–28
Solomon's treaty marriages	11:1–13	—
political trouble	11:14–25	—
Ahijah prophesies to Jeroboam	11:26–40	—
death of Solomon	11:41–43	9:29–31

[a] For more detail, see the synoptic comparison in the note on 1 Chr 21:1–30.

[b] The resumptive repetition in 1 Kgs 2:12, 46 encloses Solomon's handling of political intrigue and settling scores for David after his coronation. The single use of the summary functions as a heading of Solomon's rule in 2 Chr 1–9.

[c] The Chronicler mentions the daughter of the pharaoh moving from Jerusalem (see note on 2 Chr 8:11). The Deuteronomist explains Gezer as the dowry of the daughter of the pharaoh (1 Kgs 9:16, 24).

[d] Second Chronicles 1:14–17 paraphrases international horse trading from 9:25–28/~/1 Kgs 10:26–29 (see Tables C8 and C18). For two other clones see nn. e and f.

[e] The Chronicler integrates a couple of other Deuteronomistic traditions into the context of arrangements with Hiram (see synoptic parallels in note of 2 Chr 2:1–18[1:18–2:17]).

[f] The Chronicler provides a twofold repetition of the theophany when the ark enters the temple, 1 Kgs 8:10–11//2 Chr 5:13–14//7:1–3 (see Table C8). The repetition of the theophany is immediately preceded by a psalm excerpt not appearing in Kings, 2 Chr 6:41–42//Ps 132:8–10, 1.

The synoptic comparison should give one pause before overemphasizing the alleged Chronistic "idealization" of Solomon. While the Chronicler excludes Solomon's marital and political troubles (1 Kgs 11:1–40), he also excludes the lengthy descriptions of his wisdom and prosperity (3:1–4:34[5:14]). These shifts point in the direction of Chronicles emphasizing public royal actions that bear on temple patronage (see qualifications at Table C2).

1:14–17//9:25–28/~/1 Kgs 10:26–29 (Solomon's international horse trade). The Chronicler clones a narrative notation of international horse trade and uses it along with other cloned narrative notations to enhance mirror imaging in his presentation of Solomon (see Table C8 and associated discussion). The Chronistic version of Solomon's international horse trade significantly shifts its function (2 Chr 1:14–17//9:25–28). The Deuteronomist uses this set of details as a subtle prologue to the rebellion of Solomon by evoking royal prohibitions from Deut 17:16–17 (1 Kgs 10:26–28; see note ad loc.). The Chronicler both eliminates Solomon's treaty marriages from the following unit and splices covenantal imagery from elsewhere into the horse trade, which spins it positively (minus 1 Kgs 11:1–13 and insert 4:21[5:1] in 1 Chr 9:25–28). Chronicles draws on imagery of the ancestral promises appearing in Kings to show proximate fulfillment in Solomon's kingdom (2 Chr 9:26; 1 Kgs 4:24[5:1]; cf. Gen 15:18). The Kings' citation inverts its elements according to convention (see Seidel's theory; bold and underlining signify verbal parallels, and italics signify conventional similarities inferring identity):[134]

> On that day Yahweh made a covenant with Abram and said, "To your descendants I give this land, from *the river of* **Egypt** to **the** great **river**, the Euphrates." (Gen 15:18†)

> And Solomon ruled over all the kingdoms from **the river** to the land of the Philistines, as far as *the border of* **Egypt**. These countries brought tribute and were Solomon's subjects all his life. (1 Kgs 4:21[5:1]†)

> He [Solomon] ruled over all the kings from **the river** to the land of the Philistines, as far as the border of Egypt. (2 Chr 9:26)

The positive Chronistic international horse trading gets cloned to serve as a frame to the entire presentation of Solomon (1:14–17//9:25–28). The Chronicler may have read 1 Kgs 10:28 "as celebrating the wide range of Solomon's commercial activities," in line with the preceding context in 10:23–25 "not as offering an exact description of his trading ventures."[135] In any case, he converts "Solomon's horses were imported from Egypt *and from Kue*" to "Solomon's horses were imported from Egypt *and from all other*

134. "The river" refers to the Euphrates River. And, the border of Egypt likely refers to the wadi of Egypt at its northern border.

135. Schley, "1 Kings 10:26–29," 599.

countries" (1 Kgs 10:28; 2 Chr 9:28, emphases mine). Figure C18 summarizes the several moving parts of this repurposed narrative:

FIGURE C18: REPURPOSED INTERNATIONAL HORSE TRADE IN CHRONICLES

		Violating Royal Limits		Royal Prosperity of Covenantal Proportions		Fronted Royal Prosperity Clone
Deut 17:16, prohibition against too many horses	←	1 Kgs 10:26, many chariots and horsemen	←	2 Chr 9:25	←	2 Chr 1:14
Gen 15:18, extent of promised land		— ← 1 Kgs 4:21[5:1]	←	9:26		—
Deut 17:17, prohibition against too much silver	←	10:27, much silver	←	9:27	←	1:15
17:16, prohibition against importing horses from Egypt	←	10:28, importing horses from Egypt	←	9:28	←	1:16
		10:29, export of horses and chariots		—	←	1:17
donor contexts		rebellion by prosperity		unrivaled prosperity		

By eliminating the description of Solomon's multitude of treaty wives, the Chronicler mutes overt echo of the prohibition against royal excess (cf. Deut 17:17; 1 Kgs 11:1–3). He then splices an echo of the extent of the promised land from river to river (2 Chr 9:26// Gen 15:18 via 1 Kgs 4:21; see Figure C18). The rehabilitated Chronistic notation on international horse trade is cloned and set against the promise of unmatched prosperity in the first theophany at Gibeon (2 Chr 1:2–13). This Chronistic juxtaposition implies that horse trading (1:14–17) fulfills the paraphrased promise: "And I will also give you wealth, possessions and honor, such as no king who was before you ever had and none after you will have" (1:12). The Chronicler repurposes Solomon's international horse trade from serving as supporting evidence of rebellious excess in 1 Kgs 10 to supporting evidence of divine blessing in 2 Chr 1 and 9.

In sum, the dramatic shift of the function of the account of international horse trading highlights the deeply ironic problems of Solomon's complex role in Kings and Chronicles. It also suggests the broad license of scriptural narrators to probe the subtle undercurrents of scriptural traditions. The Chronicler recognizes the blessings of God even underneath Solomon's abuses of these gifts.

2:1–18[1:18–2:17]/~/1 Kgs 5:1–18[5:15–32]+7:13–14; 8:27; 10:9 (A) (Solomon's treaty with Hiram).[136] The heavy editing of the same basic storyline suggests the importance of Solomon's interactions with Hiram to the Chronicler. On the surface, 2 Chr 2 basically follows 1 Kgs 5. Yet a verse-by-verse synoptic comparison shows that the Chronicler not only inserted cloned elements repeated from 1 Kgs 7, 8, and 10 but also rearranged elements from 1 Kgs 5 in two places, one of which is also a clone (stylized brackets signify variation of sequence):

2 Chronicles 2	1 Kings	2 Chronicles 2	1 Kings	2 Chronicles 2	1 Kings
1	—	6	{8:27}	15	—
2	{5:15–16}	7	—	—	5:8
—	5:1	8	5:6	16	5:9
3	5:2	9–10	{5:10–11}	—	5:12–14
—	5:3–4	11	{10:9}	17	—
4	5:5	12	5:7	18	5:15–16
5	—	13–14	{7:13–14}	—	5:17–18

The Chronicler cloned the concluding list of conscripted laborers for the temple project (2 Chr 2:18//1 Kgs 5:15–16) and fronted the derivative replica to serve as *inclusio* around the correspondence between Solomon and Hiram (2 Chr 2:2, 18). The most important revisions of Solomon's message to Hiram in 2 Chr 2:3–10 are a plus and corresponding minus concerning David's building projects, and a plus concerning the temple. In 1 Kgs 5:3–5 Solomon rehearses to Hiram David's military activity, which prevented him from building the temple and passing the task on to Solomon (cf. note on 1 Kgs 5:1–5[15–19]). The Chronicler already re-presented this in David's speeches to Solomon and the assembly and so omits it here (1 Chr 22:7–10; 28:2–3, 6). Instead, Solomon begins by making an analogy between Hiram giving building supplies to David as a model for providing the same for Solomon (2 Chr 2:3). This plus corresponds to other elements wherein Solomon matches David, such as fire falling upon sacrifice (1 Chr 21:26; 2 Chr 7:3). The Chronicler shapes Solomon and his days to be David-like. The Chronistic version of Solomon's message to Hiram also includes a long plus concerning the ritual functions of the temple (2 Chr 2:4). Solomon says, "our God is *greater than all other gods*," echoing the sentiment of the father-in-law of Moses, "Yahweh is *greater than all other gods*" (2:5; Exod 18:11, emphasis mine).[137] The long plus concludes with a paraphrased cloned statement of Solomon's on the inadequacy of the temple and even the

136. For convenience, only English Bible verse references of 1 Kgs 5 and 2 Chr 2 are used in this note.
137. Indebted to Knoppers, "Foreign Monarch Speaks," 54, n. 9.

heavens to contain Yahweh (2 Chr 2:6 based on 6:18//1 Kgs 8:27). The theological significance of this repetition needs to be underlined. Chronistic Solomon speaks of Yahweh transcending the temple even while emphasizing the importance of the temple. More than that, Solomon explains Yahweh's transcendence to a foreign king. Hiram learns that the God who is worshiped in the temple of Jerusalem cannot be bounded by the heavens themselves. The God of David and Solomon transcends earthly shrines.

Hiram begins his message in Chronicles with a plus, acknowledging Yahweh's love of Israel as the basis for Solomon's rule akin to the sentiment of the queen of Sheba (2 Chr 2:11).[138] Both of these foreign sovereigns put to words the basis of Solomon's divine election (italics signify verbal parallels):

> [Queen of Sheba] Praise be to Yahweh your God, who has delighted in you and placed you on the throne of Israel. *Because Yahweh loves* Israel forever, he has made you *king* to maintain justice and righteousness. (1 Kgs 10:9†//2 Chr 9:8)

> Hiram king of Tyre replied by letter to Solomon: "*Because Yahweh loves* his people, he has made you their *king*." (2 Chr 2:11)

The Chronicler presents Hiram's message in a manner that echoes Exodus in order to emphasize a retrospective typology of the building of the tabernacle. Chronistic King Hiram clarifies that the mother of the skilled craftsperson he sends, Huram-Abi, hails from the tribe of Dan (2:14) rather than Naphtali (1 Kgs 7:14).[139] As noted in the verse-by-verse synoptic comparison above, this detail gets spliced in from another context. This demonstrates the Chronicler going out of his way to establish the tabernacle construction/temple construction typology. The Chronicler may have emphasized this typology based on the description of Huram in Kings, which echoes those divinely enabled to work on the tabernacle in Exodus. The Chronicler's typology conflates the descriptions of Bezalel and Oholiab (bold and underlining signify verbal parallels, and italics and wavy underlining signify parallel at the level of roots):

> See, I have chosen Bezalel son of Uri, the son of Hur, of the tribe of Judah, and I have <u>filled</u> him with the Spirit of God, <u>with *skill*</u> [חָכְמָה], with understanding, <u>with *knowledge*</u> and with all kinds of works—to make artistic designs **for work in gold, silver and bronze**, to cut and set **stones**, to work in **wood**, and to engage in all kinds of crafts. Moreover, I have appointed Oholiab son of Ahisamak, of the tribe of <u>Dan</u>, to help him. Also I have given ability to all the skilled workers to make everything I have commanded you. (Exod 31:2–6†; cf. 35:30–32)

138. See Dillard, "Literary Structure," 89, who notes this relative to the mirror imaging pattern. See Table C8.

139. For several ways to harmonize this detail, but without evidence, see Dillard, "Chronicler's Solomon," 298, n. 18.

> With him was Oholiab son of Ahisamak, of the tribe of Dan—an engraver and designer, and an embroiderer in blue, purple and scarlet yarn and fine linen. (38:23)

> Huram was filled with skill [חָכְמָה], with understanding and with knowledge to do all kinds of bronze work. He came to King Solomon and did all the work assigned to him. (1 Kgs 7:14b†)

> I am sending you Huram-Abi, a man of *great skill* [חָכָם], whose mother was from Dan and whose father was from Tyre. He is *knowledgeable* **to work in gold and silver, bronze** and iron, **stone** and **wood**, and with purple and blue and crimson yarn and fine linen. He is experienced in all kinds of engraving and can execute any design given to him. He will work with your skilled workers and with those of my lord, David your father. (2 Chr 2:13–14†)[140]

Chronistic Hiram shapes Huram-Abi's background and skill set in a manner that helps the readership of Chronicles appreciate the retrospective typology of divine assistance in building the tabernacle and the temple.[141] Hiram comes off as "a pious outsider" who takes Israel's "traditions seriously enough to augment the work-order placed by Israel's king."[142] The typologically enhanced account of the acquisition of temple materials emerges from a foreign king who "takes the time to immerse himself in Israelite tradition and more specifically in the study of Torah."[143] Hiram's contribution makes the temple more "tabernacle-like" than Solomon had imagined.[144]

3:1–2/~/1 Kgs 6:1 (A)+1 Chr 21:25–26+Gen 22:2 (B) (building the temple in Solomon's fourth year). The opening section describing temple construction in Chronicles shares a parallel dating formula with Kings (italics signify verbal parallel, and stylized underlining signifies distinctive ideological shaping):

> In the four hundred and eightieth year after the Israelites came out of Egypt, *in the fourth year of Solomon's reign* over Israel, in the month of Ziv, the *second month*, he *built the temple of Yahweh*. (1 Kgs 6:1†)

> Then *Solomon* began to *build the temple of Yahweh* in Jerusalem on Mount Moriah, where Yahweh had appeared to his father David. It was on the threshing floor of

140. The inversion of "blue and purple" (Exod 38:23) to "purple and blue" (2 Chr 2:14) may be an example of Seidel's theory.

141. For more detailed discussion of the Oholiab/Huram-Abi typology, with different handling of some details, see Dillard, "Chronicler's Solomon," 296–98; also see Knoppers, "Foreign Monarch Speaks," 52–60. Typological correspondences in Chronicles are limited to proximate fulfillments of temple worship associated with David and Solomon (see Table C10; Figure C17). On retrospective versus forward-looking types, see Glossary.

142. Knoppers, "Foreign Monarch Speaks," 60.

143. Ibid., 62, n. 32.

144. See ibid., 50.

> Araunah the Jebusite, the place provided by David. He began *building* on the second day of the *second month in the fourth year of* his *reign.* (2 Chr 3:1–2)

The Deuteronomist and the Chronicler elaborate on different details to emphasize continuity between building the temple and ancient scriptural traditions. The Deuteronomist uses dating to situate the temple in continuity with redemption from Egypt, whether 480 years is literal or schematic.[145] The Chronicler ignores the timing and focuses on the location. Solomon built the temple on the threshing floor where David offered an archetypical sacrifice of repentance (1 Chr 21:25–26). But he goes even further by identifying the threshing floor as Mount Moriah, the very place where Abraham demonstrated obedience to Yahweh by nearly sacrificing Isaac (Gen 22:1–19). The economic Chronistic detail invites the Second Temple reading community to join Abraham, David, and Solomon in obedient and humble worship. The Chronicler's emphasis on location versus timing fits with his strong commitment to the temple established in the place of divine choosing (see Deut 12:5–14).

3:3–14~1 Kgs 6:2–38 (C) (Solomon builds the temple). Although the descriptions of building the temple in 1 Kgs 6 and 2 Chr 3 share verbal parallels in a few places (1 Kgs 6:2, 3, 20, 23, 24 and 2 Chr 3:3, 4, 8, 10, 11), the substantially different presentation of details make independent literary sources a real possibility in this context.[146]

3:15–5:1/~/1 Kgs 7:15–51 (Huram-Abi's work on temple accessories). The Chronicler largely follows Kings in explaining Huram-Abi's extensive work on the temple and its furnishings. This description functions as something of a proximate fulfillment of the retrospective tabernacle typology suggested by Hiram in 2 Chr 2:12–14 (see note ad loc.). While the tabernacle featured one lampstand (Exod 25:31–40; 37:17–24), Kings and Chronicles both report ten lampstands made for Solomon's temple (1 Kgs 7:49; 2 Chr 4:7). The Chronicler's twofold marking of the lampstands "as prescribed" refers to them as made of gold rather than providing the number of lampstands (2 Chr 4:7, 20).[147]

5:2–14/~/1 Kgs 8:1–11 (Solomon brings the ark into the temple). The Chronistic account of bringing the ark into the temple closely follows Kings. Both Kings and Chronicles maintain retrospective typology with the glory filling the tabernacle in Exodus (see Table C10). The Chronicler exegetically advances the account by inserting a long plus concerning the divisions of the priests and the Levitical musicians in accord with David's appointments in 1 Chr 23–26 (italics and bold signify verbal parallels):

---

145. Some interpreters see 480 years as connoting about a dozen generations (12x40) in line with the scriptural tradition of using round numbers symbolically. Reading the number in 1 Kgs 6:1 literally is a cornerstone of the so-called early date of the exodus. See discussion in Schnittjer, *Torah Story*, 226–27.

146. See Macy, "Sources of Chronicles," 31.

147. See Schniedewind, "Chronicler as Interpreter," 175.

> Then **the cloud** covered the tent of meeting, and the glory of **Yahweh filled** the tabernacle. Moses **could not** enter the tent of meeting because **the cloud** had settled on it, **and the glory of Yahweh filled the** tabernacle. (Exod 40:34–35)
>
> *The priests then withdrew from the Holy Place,* **the cloud filled the temple of Yahweh. And the priests could not perform their service because of the cloud, for the glory of Yahweh filled the temple of** Yahweh. (1 Kgs 8:10–11†)
>
> *The priests then withdrew from the Holy Place.* All the priests who were there had consecrated themselves, regardless of their divisions. All the Levites who were musicians—Asaph, Heman, Jeduthun and their sons and relatives—stood on the east side of the altar, dressed in fine linen and playing cymbals, harps and lyres. They were accompanied by 120 priests sounding trumpets. The trumpeters and musicians joined in unison to give praise and thanks to Yahweh. Accompanied by trumpets, cymbals and other instruments, the singers raised their voices in praise to Yahweh and sang: "He is good; his love endures forever." Then **the temple of Yahweh** was **filled** with **the cloud, and the priests could not perform their service because of the cloud, for the glory of Yahweh filled the temple of** God. (2 Chr 5:11–14)

Although Moses was unsurpassed in his ability to withstand the presence of the glory, even he was driven from the tabernacle when the glory filled it. The same kind of intensity of divine glory drives the priests from the temple's holy place when the ark comes to rest there. The Chronicler's interpretive intervention relates to the Levitical musical praise as the cloud filled the entire temple, represented by the liturgical stock phrase "He is good; his love endures forever" (5:13).[148] The Levitical praise and manifestation of the glory relate in a temporal, not causal, manner.[149] The laity of Israel use the same stock phrase in the repeated clone account of the glory filling the temple unique to Chronicles (7:3; see note ad loc.).

6:1–42*/~/1 Kgs 8:12–53* (A)+Deut 12:5* (A)+Ps 132:8–10* (A)+Isa 55:3 (C) (dedication of temple) (* see Davidic covenant and place networks). Solomon's prayer of dedication of the temple in Chronicles, in the main, closely follows Kings. Differences of varying degree of import may be noted briefly. First, the brief plus "But now I have chosen Jerusalem for my Name to be there" (2 Chr 6:6) makes explicit the Chronicler's favorite Torah fulfillment (Deut 12:5; see discussion in note on 2 Chr 7:11–22 below).

Second, the platform in 2 Chr 6:13 may not be a plus but rather an accidental scribal omission after 1 Kgs 8:22. A copyist scribe's eye may have jumped from "and spread out his hands" (ויפרש כפיו) to the identical phrase in the parent text of 2 Chr 6:12 and 6:13.[150]

148. See Pss 100:5; 106:1; 107:1; Ezra 3:11; 1 Chr 16:34; 2 Chr 5:13; 7:3, 6; 20:21.

149. See Spawn, "Sacred Song," 62.

150. See Lemke, "Synoptic Problem," 358.

Third, though the Chronistic version of the foreigner (s) uses a plural verb for pray (2 Chr 6:32) versus a singular verb for pray (1 Kgs 8:42), too much should not be made of this difference.[151] The Deuteronomistic version uses foreigner (s) as subject of both "hear" (p) and "pray" (s) in this context (8:42).[152]

Fourth, the most important change is the Chronistic addition of excerpts of Ps 132 directly after the prayer. The unmarked use of the psalm allows it to close Solomon's prayer. The Chronicler uses psalms exclusively in relation to the moving of the ark to Jerusalem and to the temple (1 Chr 16:8–36; 2 Chr 6:41–42).[153] Psalm 132 is the only psalm to explicitly speak of "the ark" (Ps 132:8). The liturgical excerpt concludes with echoes of Ps 132:1 possibly blended with Isa 55:3 (emphases signify verbal parallels):

> A song of ascents. Yahweh, <u>remember</u> David and all his self-denial. . . . [congregation:] *"Arise, Yahweh, and come to your resting place, you and the ark of your might. May your priests be clothed* with your righteousness; may *your faithful people* sing for joy." For the sake of <u>your servant</u> David, *do not reject your anointed one.* (Ps 132:1, 8–10)

> Give ear and come to me; listen, that you may live. I will make an everlasting covenant with you, **faithful love** promised **to David.** (Isa 55:3†)

> Now *arise, Yahweh* God, *and come to your resting place, you and the ark of your might. May your priests,* Yahweh God, *be clothed* with salvation, may *your faithful people* rejoice in your goodness. Yahweh God, *do not reject your anointed one.* <u>Remember</u> **the faithful love to David** <u>your servant.</u> (2 Chr 6:41–42†)

Subtleties of the use of Ps 132 require attention. Sometimes "faithful love" (*hesed*) in Isa 55:3 and 2 Chr 6:42 is read as subjective genitive, namely, "mercies of David" with Neh 13:14, 2 Chr 32:32, and 35:26.[154] The reference to the covenant in Isa 55:3, however, suggests regarding the phrase here as an objective genitive, hence, "mercies to David."[155] On another note, while Ps 132 begins by calling upon Yahweh to remember David, this has been relocated in Chronicles to a final position, which has been misconstrued as a "radical shift." Klein seems to make too much of the order of elements in the allu-

---

151. Contra Klein, *2 Chronicles*, 85, n. 53; 96. Klein sees this in sharp contrast to foreigners in Ezra 4:1–4; 9:1–3; Neh 9:2; 10:28[29]; 13:1–3, 23–27.

152. The LXX of 1 Kgs 8:42 lacks "for they will hear of your great name and your mighty hand and your outstretched arm." For variations in select manuscripts, see the apparatus of 1 Kgs 8:42 LXX Cambridge.

153. See Berlin, "Psalms in Chronicles," 28*. This excludes the liturgical stock phrase in 1 Chr 16:34; 2 Chr 5:13; 7:3, 6; 20:21. Berlin goes on to deduce that the Chronicler only uses psalms for formal temple liturgy to emphasize their authoritative function as divinely-inspired (30*).

154. See Japhet, *I & II Chronicles*, 604–5.

155. Williamson, "'Mercies of David,'" 33, 48–49; but on Williamson's switch to a view of subjective genitive, see Lynch, *Monotheism*, 231, n. 73; and see Gentry, "Rethinking," 279–82, 292–98. Also see Acts 13:34.

sion when he says, "The Chronicler's reuse of citations from Ps 132 puts the presence of Yahweh and the ark in the first position, the welfare of priests and people in second position, and the king in the third position."[156] The more relevant issue, in terms of observing what the Chronicler is doing, relates to the narrative sequence in this context. The Chronicler immediately follows the call to remember covenantal loyalty to David with fire falling from heaven demonstrating an answer to the prayer. The rearrangement of Ps 132 helps highlight the divine affirmation of the temple, the worshiping congregation, and his messiah.

The Chronicler's choice of these excerpts from Ps 132 may reflect a connection with Deut 12:9–12 by means of the catchword "resting place" (מְנוּחָה).[157] The glory fills the temple when the ark comes to its resting place and the Levites begin to worship with song. All of this triggers the sign of fire falling from heaven in 2 Chr 7:1.

7:1–3//1 Kgs 8:54a+1 Chr 21:26 (A)//Lev 9:24 (B)+2 Chr 5:13–14 (A)//Exod 40:34–35 (B) (fire falls from heaven). The Chronistic version of the moment of temple dedication includes the account of fire falling from heaven and brings it together with a cloned narrative offering a flashback of the moment the glory filled the temple (2 Chr 7:1–2; cf. 5:13–14). All of this prompts the congregation to spontaneous worship, repeating the stock liturgical refrain of the Levites (7:3; cf. 5:13). These allusive events in this context are not parallel to Kings. The twofold near allusions—fire falling and glory filling—carry within them deeper allusions to great moments of tabernacle completion and dedication. When Moses finished the tabernacle, the glory filled it (Exod 40:34–35). When Moses and Aaron blessed the people at the tabernacle dedication, fire from Yahweh came out upon the burnt offering (Lev 9:24). These figural allusions provide additional continuities for David's sacrifice of repentance on the threshing floor (1 Chr 21:26) and the ark set to rest in the temple (2 Chr 5:14). The Chronicler uses these double figural allusions to bind together the completion of the temple with signature continuities to these major events of Yahweh's redemptive mercies.[158] The importance of this moment of fulfillment of selection of the place for the divine name to rest (Deut 12:5–12; 2 Chr 6:41–42; 7:12) explains the Chronicler's magnification by exegetical allusions (emphases signify verbal parallels):

When Solomon finished praying . . . (1 Kgs 8:54†)

Fire came out from the presence of Yahweh and **consumed the burnt offering** and the fat portions **on the altar**. And when all the people saw it, they shouted for joy and fell facedown. (Lev 9:24)

156. Klein, *2 Chronicles*, 98.

157. See ibid.

158. See Tables C8 and C10; notes on 1 Chr 21:26; 2 Chr 3:1–2; and 5:12–14.

> David built an altar to Yahweh there and sacrificed burnt offerings and fellowship offerings. He called on Yahweh, and Yahweh answered him with **fire** from heaven **on the altar of burnt offering.** (1 Chr 21:26)

> Then the cloud covered the tent of meeting, and *the glory of Yahweh filled* the tabernacle. Moses could not enter the tent of meeting because the cloud had settled on it, and *the glory of Yahweh filled* the tabernacle. (Exod 40:34–35)

> The trumpeters and musicians joined in unison to give praise and give thanks to Yahweh. Accompanied by trumpets, cymbals and other instruments, the singers raised their voices in praise to Yahweh and sang: "He is good; his love endures forever." Then the temple of Yahweh was filled with the cloud, and the priests could not perform their service because of the cloud, for *the glory of Yahweh filled the temple* of God. (2 Chr 5:13–14†; cf. 1 Kgs 8:10–11)

> When Solomon finished praying, **fire** came down from heaven and **consumed the burnt offering** and the sacrifices, and *the glory of Yahweh filled the temple.* The priests could not enter the temple of Yahweh because *the glory of Yahweh filled* it. When all the Israelites saw the **fire** coming down and *the glory of Yahweh* above the temple, they knelt on the pavement with their faces to the ground, and they worshiped and gave thanks to Yahweh, saying, "He is good; his love endures forever." (2 Chr 7:1–3)[159]

7:4–10/~/1 Kgs 8:62–66 (dedicate altar and celebrate Tabernacles). The dedication of the altar and Festival of Tabernacles in Chronicles largely adhere to Kings, with a couple of exceptions (1 Kgs 8:62–66; 2 Chr 7:4–10). The Chronicler inserts a brief note on musical worship by priests and Levites using the instruments of David (2 Chr 7:6). The worship includes an abbreviated version of the liturgical stock phrase "for his covenantal loyalty endures forever" (7:6 lit.; cf. 5:13). Chronicles smooths out the chronological details of the event. Kings says Solomon sent the people home on the eighth day (1 Kgs 8:66). The Chronicler clarifies fourteen days: seven to dedicate the temple and seven for Tabernacles, then he dismissed them on the twenty-third day of the seventh month (2 Chr 7:9–10).

7:11–22*/~/1 Kgs 9:1–9 (A)+Deut 12:5* (B)+Lev 26:41* (B) (second revelation to Solomon) (* see collective confession and place networks). The Deuteronomist explicitly orients the second theophany to Solomon in relation to the previous one with "Yahweh appeared to him *a second time, as he had appeared to him at Gibeon*" (1 Kgs 9:2, emphasis mine). The Chronicler removes this phrase and uses a softer echo with both visions set at night (2 Chr 1:7; 7:12). The second revelation opens with a reference

159. Klein suggests the reference to "pavement" in 2 Chr 7:3 may echo the description of the outer court of Ezekiel's temple in Ezek 40:17–18; 42:3 (*2 Chronicles*, 106).

to choosing the temple, effectively aligning it with the preceding narrative of fulfillment as well as echoing the expectation for choosing this place. The many allusions to Deut 12 beginning in 1 Chr 15:1 and culminating in the present context provides evidence to suggest allusion—see place network (bold signifies verbal parallels, underlining signifies Chronistic additions, and strike-through signifies omitted Deuteronomistic narrative):

> But you are to seek **the place** Yahweh your God **will choose** from among all your tribes to put his Name there for his dwelling. To that place you must go. (Deut 12:5; cf. 11)

> Yahweh appeared to Solomon ~~a second time, as he had appeared to him at Gibeon~~. Yahweh said to him: "I have heard the prayer ~~and plea you have made before me; I have consecrated this temple, which you have built, by putting my Name there forever. My eyes and my heart will always be there.~~" (1 Kgs 9:2–3†)

> Yahweh appeared to Solomon at night and said: "I have heard your prayer and **have chosen this place** for myself as a temple for sacrifices. (2 Chr 7:12†)

Yahweh goes on in the nocturnal theophany to paraphrase Solomon's prayer of dedication and to advance revelation by interpretive allusion. Namely, Yahweh aligns Solomon's prayer with repentance as a turning point from condemnation to restoration, using the loaded term for self-humbling from Lev 26 (emphases signify verbal parallels):[160]

> But if they will confess their sins and the sins of their ancestors—their unfaithfulness and their hostility toward me, which made me hostile toward them so that I sent them into the land of their enemies—then when their uncircumcised hearts **are humbled** [כנע] and they pay for their sin . . . (Lev 26:40–41)

> [Solomon] When the heavens are shut up and there is no rain because your people have sinned against you, and when they pray toward this place and give praise to your name and turn from their sin because you have afflicted them [6:26], [27] then hear from heaven and forgive [סלח] the sin of your servants, your people Israel. Teach them the right way to live, and send rain on the land you gave your people for an inheritance. . . . [30] Then *hear from heaven*, your dwelling place. Forgive [סלח], and deal with everyone according to all they do, since you know their hearts (for you alone know the human heart). . . . [40] *Now*, my God, *may your eyes be open and your ears attentive to the prayers offered in this place.* (2 Chr 6:26–27, 30, 40//1 Kgs 8:35–36, 39, 52; cf. 2 Chr 6:20//1 Kgs 8:29)

160. Also note the shift from "rest" from enemies (2 Sam 7:11) to "subdue" (כנע Hif) enemies (1 Chr 17:10).

> [Yahweh] When I shut up the heavens so that there is no rain, or command locusts to devour the land or send a plague among my people, [14] if my people, who are called by my name, **will humble themselves** [כנע] and pray and seek my face and turn from their wicked ways, then I *will hear from heaven*, and I will forgive [סלח] their sin and will heal their land. [15] *Now* my *eyes will be open and my ears attentive to the prayers offered in this place.* (2 Chr 7:13–15)

After Yahweh's interpretive paraphrase of Solomon in 2 Chr 7:13–15, the remainder of the night vision closely follows its counterpart in Kings with mild stylistic adjustments (7:16–22//1 Kgs 9:3b–9). The Chronistic plus in 7:13–15 sets out the broad retributive paradigm that shapes most of 2 Chr 10–36 (see Table C2). Rebellion triggers divine judgment, and repentance triggers forgiveness and healing.

Solomon's prayer in Kings which emphasizes covenant obedience and his exhortation to the people is not carried over to Chronicles (1 Kgs 8:55–61). Kings also lacks reference to forgiveness in the second theophany (9:3b–9).[161] The shift to Yahweh opening the second theophany by emphasizing programmatic self-humbling and forgiveness defines worship as repentance and the purpose for seeking Yahweh (2 Chr 7:14). The Chronicler does not hereby reduce retribution to a mechanistic phenomenon. He constantly depicts Yahweh as a "personal subject" holding Israel to account.[162] Perhaps more important is the evidence of five complex cases among the kings of Judah recounted in 2 Chr 10–36, namely, Rehoboam (2 Chr 12:1–16), Jehoshaphat (18:1–19:3), Ahaziah (22:1–9), Amaziah (25:1–26:2), and Hezekiah (32:24–26, 31). An especially good example of interrupting retribution by repentance and pardon is Hezekiah's prayer (see note on 2 Chr 30:18–20).

8:1–11, 17–18/~/1 Kgs 9:10–24, 26–27 (other settlements, projects, and treaties). The materials collated in 2 Chr 8 may be part of the enhanced chiastic presentation of Solomon (Table C8).[163] Chronicles refers to three elements that reinterpret details in Kings and/or emphases elsewhere in Chronicles, namely, Hiram gifting cities to Solomon (2 Chr 8:2), Solomon's military conquests (8:3), and the relocation of the pharaoh's daughter (8:11).

The Deuteronomist speaks of Solomon giving twenty towns to Hiram as payment for temple contributions (1 Kgs 9:11–15). The Chronicler says, "Solomon rebuilt *the villages that Hiram had given him*, and settled Israelites in them" (2 Chr 8:2, emphasis mine). The stark difference has provoked extensive debate. A common solution regards the Chronicler's reversal as falsification based on embarrassment.[164] This approach does

161. See Kelly, "'Retribution' Revisited," 216.
162. See long list of references in ibid., 213, n. 25.
163. See Dillard, *2 Chronicles*, 61.
164. See Wellhausen, *Prolegomena*, 187, and many others.

not fit the evidence since elsewhere Solomon pays Hiram without embarrassing the Chronicler (2:10).[165] If the source of Kings and/or Chronicles was not corrupt, then, others suggest, Hiram may have returned the cities that did not please him.[166] The lack of evidence does not permit confident conclusions.

Chronistic Solomon, the man of peace, enjoyed rest from enemies (1 Chr 22:9) yet engaged in military campaign against Hamath Zobah (2 Chr 8:3). It is unclear why Zobah, a region north of Damascus, has been joined to Hamath.[167] Elsewhere the Chronicler adds Hamath to Zobah in David's conquests as far north as the Euphrates River (1 Chr 18:3; cf. 2 Sam 8:3). The obscure reference in 2 Chr 8:3 has attracted speculative textual emendations.[168] The context speaks of building projects as far north as Tadmor in upper Syria (8:4), which fits with the broad extent of the kingdom of David and Solomon mentioned elsewhere (7:8; cf. 1 Kgs 4:24[5:4]).[169] Rezon, Solomon's adversary from Zobah who went to Damascus (1 Kgs 11:23–25), originally served under Hadadezer, whom David defeated (1 Chr 13:5; 18:3//2 Sam 8:3). However the details get parsed out, the Chronicler would have an interest in featuring Solomon enjoying rule over the full expanse of the promised land (2 Chr 9:26; see Map C19).

MAP C19: PLACES POSSIBLY ASSOCIATED WITH SOLOMON IN 2 CHR 8:3, 4‡

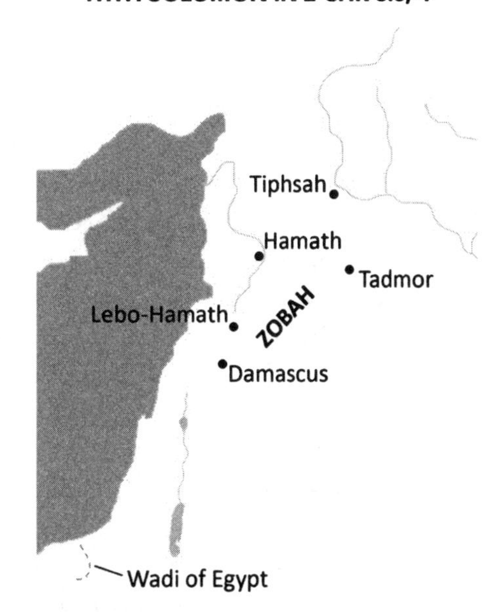

‡ Lebo Hamath and the Wadi of Egypt are mentioned in 2 Chr 7:8; Tiphsah in 1 Kgs 4:24[5:4] (cf. 2 Kgs 15:16).

Kings interacts with Solomon's treaty marriage to the daughter of the pharaoh in several places (1 Kgs 3:1; 7:8; 9:16, 24; 11:1). Chronicles only mentions her in 2 Chr 8:11, demonstrating once again the expectation of readerly familiarity with the traditional storyline. Chronicles does not mention Solomon's quasi-alliance with the pharaoh to establish a place for her in Gezer as her dowry or "wedding gift" (1 Kgs 9:16 NIV).[170] The Chronicler adds Solomon's own rationale, which puts her relocation in a new light (italics signify verbal parallel, bold signifies syntactical variation, and broken underlining signifies rationale):

165. See Williamson, *1 and 2 Chronicles*, 228.

166. See Dillard, *2 Chronicles*, 63.

167. See Japhet, *I & II Chronicles*, 622.

168. See Williamson, *1 and 2 Chronicles*, 229.

169. Although *ketiv* of 1 Kgs 9:18 says "Tamor," the *qere*, MT manuscripts, and some ancient versions say "Tadmor" in agreement with 2 Chr 9:4 (*BHS* apparatus). See Dillard, *2 Chronicles*, 64; Japhet, *I & II Chronicles*, 622–23.

170. Lemke wonders if the Chronicler's source lacked the explanatory gloss in 1 Kgs 9:16 ("Synoptic Problem," 358). The notation is often put in parentheses (1 Kgs 9:16 NIV, NRSV, etc.). For how regarding Gezer as a dowry may have influenced the adjustments in 1 Kgs 9 LXX, see Gooding, "Septuagint's Version," 328.

After Pharaoh's daughter ***had come up*** *from the City of David to* ***her*** *palace Solomon had built for her,* he constructed the terraces. (1 Kgs 9:24†)

Solomon ***brought*** *Pharaoh's daughter* ***up*** *from the City of David to* ***the*** *palace he had built for her,* for he said, "My wife must not live in the palace of David king of Israel, because the places the ark of Yahweh has entered are holy." (2 Chr 8:11)

The Chronistic version includes two exegetical interventions: the shift in subject and verbal stem from "she had come up" (Q) to "he brought up" (Hif) and the rationale clause marked by "because" or "for."[171] Her separate residence does not get explained as motivated by the father-in-law but by Solomon's desire to move her out of the city that had become holy by the residence of the ark. Solomon must have in mind a new condition of holiness by means of the installation of the ark into the temple (5:7), since the ark had been in the tent of David in Jerusalem all along (1 Chr 16:1).[172] Elsewhere the timing of building the palace for the daughter of the pharaoh aligns with building the terraces of Jerusalem after completing the temple (1 Kgs 9:15, 17, 24; 11:27). Solomon interpreted the formal installation of the ark in the temple as triggering a new situation for Jerusalem. Perhaps the manifestation of the cloud and glory signified the new holy state of Jerusalem fulfilling its role as the chosen place where the name dwells (2 Chr 5:13–14; 6:10–11; 7:2; cf. Deut 12:5–14). Or, perhaps Yahweh's statement in the second theophany that he had "made holy" the temple led to Solomon's deduction (7:16 lit.). Isaiah looks ahead to a time when "the holy city" would no longer suffer entry by "uncircumcised and defiled" (Isa 52:1). Isaiah's expectation reverses the wrongful entry of "the nations" into the temple and expands the realm of holiness to the entire city (cf. Lam 1:10). If Solomon, like Isaiah, extrapolates from the holiness of the temple to the city, his view does not rise to the extremity of Ezekiel's vision, which finally locates the city outside the temple district (Ezek 48:10, 15; see Map Ezk8). Whatever the reason, Solomon deduces that his Egyptian treaty wife is no longer fit to live in Jerusalem.[173]

8:12–15/~/1 Kgs 9:25 (A)+Deut 16:16 (B) (Solomon's worship). Kings speaks of Solomon regularly participating in the three pilgrimage festivals (1 Kgs 9:25). The Chronicler responds by naming the three festivals from Torah and adding two others (Deut 16:16; 2 Chr 8:13).[174] Then he inserts a statement about Solomon maintaining the worship personnel established by David (8:14–15). The long Chronistic insert concludes with an expansion of "so he finished the house" (1 Kgs 9:25) to state Solomon's

171. On the explanatory force of "for/because" (כִּי), see GKC §158b.

172. Compare the logic when the tabernacle moved into the encampment—see note on Num 5:1–4.

173. For a different view comparing 2 Chr 8:11 with Neh 13:23–27 but against Ezra 9:1–2, see Jonker, "'My Wife,'" 43–46.

174. See Rendtorff, "Chronicles and the Priestly Torah," 260–61.

full involvement in all phases of building the temple (2 Chr 8:16).[175] The Chronicler's exegetical expansions, then, amount to an apologetic for Solomon's commitments to worship at the temple beyond the limited statement in Kings (bold and italics signify verbal parallels, underlining signifies parallels at the level of roots, and broken underlining signifies marking):

> **Three times a year** all your men must appear before Yahweh your God at the place he will choose: at **the Festival of Unleavened Bread, the Festival of Weeks and the Festival of Tabernacles**. No one should appear before Yahweh empty-handed. (Deut 16:16)

> **Three times a year** *Solomon sacrificed burnt offerings* and fellowship offerings on the altar he had built for Yahweh, burning incense before Yahweh along with them. So he finished the house. (1 Kgs 9:25 lit.)

> On the altar of Yahweh that he had built in front of the portico, *Solomon sacrificed burnt offerings* to Yahweh, [13] according to the daily requirement for offerings commanded by Moses for the Sabbaths, the New Moons and appointed gatherings **three times a year—the Festival of Unleavened Bread, the Festival of Weeks and the Festival of Tabernacles.** [14] In keeping with the ordinance of his father David, he appointed the divisions of the priests for their duties, and the Levites to lead the praise and to assist the priests according to each day's requirement. He also appointed the gatekeepers by divisions for the various gates, because this was what David the man of God had ordered. [15] They did not deviate from the king's commands to the priests or to the Levites in any matter, including that of the treasuries. [16] All Solomon's work was carried out, from the day the foundation of the temple of Yahweh was laid until its completion. The house of Yahweh was finished. (2 Chr 8:12–16†)

The Chronicler demonstrates something like canonical consciousness by marking the worship regulations "as commanded by Moses" (8:13). He goes on to mark both the standards for priests and Levites and mark separately the gatekeepers (8:14). The Davidic standards for the courses of priests, Levites, and gatekeepers are housed in 1 Chr 23–26. The Chronicler uses various formulaic expressions as he routinely marks these standards, self-conscious of their authority (see Table C20; cf. Marking in Hermeneutical Profile of the Use of Scripture in Ezra-Nehemiah). The same kind of reference appears twice in Neh 12.

---

175. Instead of "complete" (שָׁלֵם) 2 Chr 8:16 MT, the parent text of the LXX read "Solomon" (שְׁלֹמֹה) with associated adjustments (*BHS*).

TABLE C20: SCRIPTURAL MARKING OF DAVIDIC STANDARDS FOR WORSHIP PERSONNEL‡

	marked by (lit.):	referring to:
1 Chr 6:32[17]	"according to the ordinance for them" (כְּמִשְׁפָּטָם)	1 Chr 23–26
9:22	"they had been assigned by David and Samuel the seer" (הֵמָּה יִסַּד דָּוִיד וּשְׁמוּאֵל הָרֹאֶה)	26:1–19
2 Chr 8:14, 15	"according to the ordinance of his father David" (כְּמִשְׁפַּט דָּוִיד־אָבִיו)	23:6–24:31; 26:1–19; cf. 26:20–32
23:18	"to whom David had made assignment" (אֲשֶׁר חָלַק דָּוִיד), "as David had ordered" (עַל יְדֵי דָוִיד)	23:26–24:19; 26:1–19
29:25	"as prescribed by David" (בְּמִצְוַת דָּוִיד)	23–26
35:4	"according to the instructions written by David king of Israel and his son Solomon" (בִּכְתָב דָּוִיד מֶלֶךְ יִשְׂרָאֵל וּבְמִכְתַּב שְׁלֹמֹה בְנוֹ)[a]	23:6–32
35:15	"as prescribed by David" (כְּמִצְוַת דָּוִיד)	25
Neh 12:24	"as prescribed by David the man of God" (בְּמִצְוַת דָּוִיד אִישׁ־הָאֱלֹהִים)	23:6–32
12:45	"as prescribed by David and his son Solomon" (כְּמִצְוַת דָּוִיד שְׁלֹמֹה בְנוֹ)	23–26

‡ The table is based on Wright, "Legacy of David," 234–36.

[a] Elsewhere David refers to the written plans for the temple (1 Chr 28:19).

9:1–12/~/1 Kgs 10:1–13 (queen of Sheba visits Solomon). The accounts of the visit of the queen of Sheba in Kings and Chronicles closely correspond. The most significant Chronistic exegetical adjustments relate to the way the queen defines the realm of Solomon's rule. In the older scriptural tradition, she says that Yahweh placed you on "the throne of Israel" (1 Kgs 10:9). In Chronicles she says that Solomon sits on "his throne to rule for Yahweh your God" (2 Chr 9:8). The queen's view of Solomon ruling the kingdom of Yahweh echoes the sentiments of David and the Chronicler himself (1 Chr 28:5; 29:23).

9:13–24/~/1 Kgs 10:14–29 (prosperity of Solomon). The Deuteronomistic and Chronistic accounts explain Solomon's wealth along the same lines.

9:25–28*//1:14–17/~/1 Kgs 10:26–29+4:21*[5:1] (Solomon's international horse trade) (* see Abrahamic covenant network). See note on 1 Chr 1:14–17.

9:29–31/~/1 Kgs 11:41–43 (death of Solomon). The authors of Kings and Chronicles both cite their sources, here and in general, yet refer to the sources differently. Because the sources did not survive, evaluating the source citations can only get at general issues. In this case, the Deuteronomist alludes to his selective use of traditions associated with Solomon by mentioning other elements not used in "the scroll of the accounts of

Solomon" (1 Kgs 11:41 lit.) while the Chronicler refers to "the accounts of Nathan the prophet, and concerning the prophecy of Ahijah the Shilonite, and in the visions of Iddo the visionary concerning Jeroboam son of Nebat" (2 Chr 9:29 lit.). Some interpreters regard the Chronicler's sources as homiletical historical collections or collections akin to the biblical prophetic books, and others think these are references to Samuel and Kings. In the latter case the prophets were contemporaries of the king whose reign is described (cf. 1 Chr 29:29).[176]

10:1–11:4/~/1 Kgs 12:1–24 (Rehoboam's folly and the revolt). The account of the assembly at Shechem itself runs very close in Kings and Chronicles, even with substantial synoptic differences in the larger contexts.

	1 Kings	2 Chronicles
Solomon's treaty marriages	11:1–13	—
political trouble	11:14–25	—
Ahijah prophesies to Jeroboam	11:26–40	—
death of Solomon	11:41–43	9:29–31
Rehoboam's folly	12:1–24	10:1–11:4
Jeroboam's calves	12:25–33	—
man of God warns Jeroboam at Bethel	13:1–34	—
Ahijah's oracle against Jeroboam	14:1–20	—
Rehoboam builds fortresses	—	11:5–12
northern Israelites emigrate to Judah	—	11:13–17
Rehoboam's household	—	11:18–23
Shishak attacks Judah	14:21–31	12:1–16

The omissions of Solomon's downfall and his perennial adversaries (1 Kgs 11) recontextualize the place of the assembly at Shechem. One view sees Rehoboam "victimized" by Jeroboam, who arbitrarily usurps control over much of the kingdom. Part of this claim rests on the Chronicler's omission of Ahijah's prophecy to Jeroboam (11:26–40).[177] Though it is easy to agree that the Chronicler expanded the blameworthiness of Jeroboam (see note on 2 Chr 11:15), he retains an allusion to Ahijah's prophecy and its fulfillment because he is revising that story, not contradicting it (2 Chr 10:16).

Another view suggests the Chronicler made a series of more subtle edits in the assembly at Shechem to strengthen blame on Rehoboam's folly for the schism, like the deletion of

176. See Dillard, *2 Chronicles*, 74. Dillard wonders if Iddo is the unnamed prophet of Bethel in 1 Kgs 13.

177. See Knoppers, "Rehoboam in Chronicles," 434, 440.

the verb "saw." Compare: "Because the king did not listen to them. . . ." (10:16 lit.) versus "When they saw that the that the king refused to listen to them. . . ." (1 Kgs 12:16 lit.).[178] Though the lack of the verb "saw" in the MT and LXX supports the syntactic shift, the supposed theological motivation seems overdrawn. "All Israel" remains the subject of the seditious speech in both cases. In sum, in the absence of the downfall of Solomon in Chronicles, some interpreters seem to overread the new version looking for a new culprit. Rather, the Chronistic enhancements strengthen culpability against both Rehoboam and Jeroboam for cultic transgressions (see below). The schism itself seems to exist as one of the givens, for which readers should consult the traditional story.

The Chronicler makes two shifts in how to think of those who seceded with Jeroboam versus the citizens of Israel who remained with Rehoboam. The Chronicler deletes the delimitation "Only the tribe of Judah remained loyal to the house of David" (1 Kgs 12:20). He also made a subtle enhancement of Yahweh's revelation to Shemaiah the man of God to emphasize the identity of Israel living in the tribal land of Judah and Benjamin as all Israel (strike through signifies deletion, italics signify addition, and bold signifies change):

> Say to Rehoboam son of Solomon king of Judah, and to all **the house** of Judah and Benjamin, ~~and to the rest of the people.~~ (1 Kgs 12:23†)
>
> Say to Rehoboam son of Solomon king of Judah and to all **Israel** *in* Judah and Benjamin . . . (2 Chr 11:3)

Whereas "all the house of Judah and Benjamin" denotes the tribal constituents, "all Israel in Benjamin and Judah" converts Judah and Benjamin to the locations wherein "all Israel" may be identified.[179] The Chronicler's exegetical adjustment in 2 Chr 11:3 anticipates his additions in 11:13 and 11:16, namely, the priests and Levites from all Israel and persons from every tribe of Israel emigrate to Judah and Benjamin. All of these turn from Jeroboam's golden calves to worship Yahweh at the temple.

There are no "ten lost tribes" in Chronicles. Instead, the self-imposed relocation of the laity of every tribe and the worship personnel from across Israel means that hereafter "Benjamin and Judah" refers to "all Israel" and vice versa.[180] The Chronicler confirms his intentional shift in the semantic function of Judah and Benjamin by unpacking the other tribes in 15:9.[181] Even with this important resignification of "all Israel" at the schism,

178. The translation of 2 Chr 10:16 is from Cudworth, "Division of Israel's Kingdom," 506. Virtually every modern committee translation restores the verb "saw" (ראה) to 2 Chr 10:16 from 1 Kgs 12:16, e.g., "And when all Israel saw . . ." (2 Chr 10:16 NIV). Though *BHS* suggests this emendation, the verb is missing from MT and LXX.

179. See Cudworth, "Division of Israel's Kingdom," 507–8.

180. The shift of semantic function relates to the citizens who came to Benjamin and Judah from all Israel to worship at the temple—Yahweh seekers (2 Chr 11:3, 16). The "land of Judah and Benjamin" continues to refer to the local environs of Jerusalem and does not include the hill country of Ephraim (see 2 Chr 15:9; 34:9).

181. See Klein, *2 Chronicles*, 176. For additional evidence, see Sugimoto, "Chronicler's Techniques," 58.

the outreach program of Hezekiah to the northern tribes after the fall of Samaria brings the remnant of worshiping Israel into the congregation as occasional pilgrims (30:11, 18; see Table C21). The assimilation of "all Israel" into Benjamin and Judah undermines attempts to say the Chronicler only counted Judah, Benjamin, and Levi as all Israel.[182] The Chronicler revised the details of the story to clarify that the temple-going community in Judah and Benjamin is all Israel in the sense of representing Yahweh seekers from every tribe.

TABLE C21: TRIBAL DEFECTIONS INTO THE TEMPLE WORSHIPING CONSTITUENCY AT THE RISE AND FALL OF THE NORTHERN KINGDOM

Self-imposed emigration into Judah and Benjamin in days of Rehoboam	Time of rival Northern Kingdom of Israel (2 Chr 12–28)	**Pilgrimage invitational to remnant in days of Hezekiah**
• priests and Levites formerly from all Israel (2 Chr 11:14) • Yahweh seekers from all Israel (11:16; cf. v. 3)		• people of Asher, Manasseh, Zebulun, and Issachar (30:11, 18)

11:15~1 Kgs 12:28–33 (B)+Lev 17:7* (C) (Jeroboam's aberrant renegade worship) (* see place network). The Deuteronomist famously associated the shrines at Bethel and Dan with the original sin of Israel at the mountain (see note on 1 Kgs 12:28–33). The Deuteronomist persistently drew attention to the sin of royal patronage for the cultic calves by comparing each northern king with Jeroboam, even when the crown shifted to other families more than half a dozen times. The Chronicler excludes the story in the same way he passes by all details of the Northern Kingdom not directly related to the Davidic kingdom. But the Chronicler alludes to Jeroboam's calves to explain the motives of the priests and Levites and members of every tribe of Israel who seek Yahweh to pursue asylum in Judah and Jerusalem (2 Chr 11:13–16). The Chronicler's exegetical allusion makes explicit the purpose of Jeroboam's rejection of priests and Levites living throughout the Northern Kingdom. Instead of explaining that Jeroboam's calves function as part of worshiping the God of Israel, the Chronicler associates them with high places for worship of goat demons. The rare use of the term for goat demons in Scripture may indicate an

182. For a different view, see Giffone, *"Sit at My Right Hand,"* 185, 189. Though Giffone lists 2 Chr 11:3, 13, 16, and 15:9 in a handful of places (188, 195, 237, 238, 245), he neither acknowledges nor explains the Chronicler's shift in semantic function of all Israel in Judah and Benjamin. Instead, Giffone detects the Chronicler's purpose of "reaching out" to postexilic Benjamites by including them prominently (204, 213–28). But the Chronicler refers to all Israel *in* Judah and Benjamin (11:3; cf. 15:9), namely, *all Yahweh seekers* of Israel (11:16). This point is corroborated by the evidence presented in Williamson, *Israel*, 102–111, 126–31, esp. 110, 111. These Chronistic emphases stand at some distance from treating Benjamin as merely denoting a place and/or an ethnic or racial identity. In spite of this serious problem, Giffone's larger argument correctly identifies an upgrade in the treatment of Benjamin in Chronicles versus a more negative treatment in the Deuteronomistic narrative. Also see Willi, "Innovation aus Tradition," 411–12.

intentional interpretive blend.[183] The sense of the illicit sexual language "prostitute themselves" in Lev 17:7 accords with the Chronicler's agenda of highlighting the inherent and categorical infidelity of the northern shrines (emphases signify parallel language):

> They must no longer offer any of **their sacrifices** to the **goat idols** to whom they prostitute themselves. (Lev 17:7a)
>
> Jeroboam *made high places* and appointed *priests* from all sorts of people, even though they were not *Levites*. (1 Kgs 12:31†)
>
> Levites even abandoned their pasturelands and property and came to Judah and Jerusalem, because *Jeroboam* and his sons had rejected them as *priests* of Yahweh when he appointed his own *priests* for the *high places* and for the **goat** and calf **idols** *he had made*. Those from every tribe of Israel who set their hearts on seeking Yahweh, the God of Israel, followed the *Levites* to Jerusalem to **offer sacrifices** to Yahweh, the God of their ancestors. (2 Chr 11:14–16; cf. 13:8–9)

The context of the prohibition against sacrificing to goat demons includes discontinuing worship of Yahweh in other places in favor of exclusive tabernacle worship (Lev 17:4, 9). The Chronicler explains how Jeroboam exactly reverses the law by sending people back to false worship. Jeroboam's intentional rejection of priests and Levites as worship personnel in favor of others explains their motive for leaving their appointed lands throughout Israel (Num 35:1–8; Josh 21:6–8, 20–42).

12:1–16/~/1 Kgs 14:21–31 (Shishak attacks Jerusalem). The Chronicler significantly shifts the traditional story of Shishak's invasion (for comparative synopsis see note on 2 Chr 10:1–11:4). The Deuteronomistic version places the formulaic evaluation before the account in its standard position to explain in advance the theological character of Rehoboam. The Deuteronomist uniquely characterizes Yahweh's anger against Rehoboam as based on jealousy, alluding to the demand for monotheistic fidelity in the Ten Commandments (1 Kgs 14:22; cf. Exod 20:5//Deut 5:9). This allusion sets the stage for rehearsing Judah's worship of other gods, cultic male prostitutes, and other immoralities of the nations of Canaan (1 Kgs 14:23–24). The Chronicler relocates the theological evaluation to the end of Rehoboam's account and reconfigures it dramatically (see Table C11). The shifts in subject as well as absence of loyal devotion point to the Chronicler's complex handling of Rehoboam:

> Judah *did evil* in the eyes of Yahweh. By the sins they committed they stirred up his jealous anger more than those who were before them had done. (1 Kgs 14:22)

---

183. This root only appears in Lev 17:7; Isa 13:21; 34:14; and 2 Chr 11:15, see "III שָׂעִיר," *HALOT* 2:1341.

He *did evil* because he had not set his heart on seeking Yahweh. (1 Chr 12:14)

Rehoboam's shift from good to bad pivots on turning away from Torah (see Table C10). The Chronicler's retributive agenda includes the addition of a divine intervention and instructional oracle of the prophet Shemaiah (see Table C9). If readers think the categorical language of Solomon's prayer somehow puts divine intervention "on demand," the outcome of the Shishak debacle begins to school readers in the complexities of Yahweh's gracious sovereignty. This text needs to be quoted at length, including the fulfillment the Chronicler adds, because it does not easily fit with commentators who stereotype the Chronicler's retributive theology as mechanistic and categorical (bold signifies verbal parallels and broken underlining signifies complex outcomes).

> If my people, who are called by my name, will **humble themselves** [כנע Nif] and pray and seek my face and turn from their wicked ways, then I will hear from heaven, and I will forgive their sin and will heal their land. (2 Chr 7:14, non-synoptic addition)

> Then the prophet Shemaiah came to Rehoboam and to the leaders of Judah who had assembled in Jerusalem for fear of Shishak, and he said to them, "This is what Yahweh says, 'You have abandoned me; therefore, I now abandon you to Shishak.'" [6] The leaders of Israel and the king **humbled themselves** [כנע Nif] and said, "Yahweh is just." [7] When Yahweh saw that they **humbled themselves** [כנע Nif], this word of Yahweh came to Shemaiah: "Since they have **humbled themselves** [כנע Nif], I will not destroy them but will soon give them deliverance. My wrath will not be poured out on Jerusalem through Shishak. [8] They will, however, become subject to him, so that they may learn the difference between serving me and serving the kings of other lands." . . . Because Rehoboam **humbled himself** [כנע Nif], Yahweh's anger turned from him, and he was not totally destroyed. Indeed, there was some good in Judah. (12:5–8, 12, non-synoptic additions)

While the Deuteronomist handles Rehoboam's rule in a one-sided way—evil days and judgment from Shishak—the Chronicler provides a more complicated interpretation. The abject humiliation of Lev 26:40–41 and 2 Chr 7:14 may activate forgiveness and partial restoration, but the conflicted and somewhat unfaithful people may face partial retribution. The programmatic prayer of 2 Chr 7:14 does not work like a light switch which can be turned off and on. The partial divine deliverance and partial subjection to Shishak together comprise a full measure of Yahweh's mercy. Shemaiah explains the instructional purpose of the vassalage as evidence of fulfillment of the people's prayer: "so that they may know" (12:8 lit.).[184]

184. The imperfect with simple *vav* may signify purpose in a final clause, "so that they may know" (וְיֵדְעוּ), see GKC §107q.

In sum, the Chronicler's theological disambiguation of historical events largely follows the fault lines of infidelity of worship and failure to trust God. But clarity does not always mean categorical outcomes. The Chronicler presents ups and downs of the rule of Rehoboam as a mixture of positive and negative, all of which together embodies the faithfulness of Yahweh. The evaluation formula of Rehoboam provides an overview of the more complex treatment housed in the Chronicler's version of his story (emphasis signifies Chronistic pluses):[185]

> Judah did evil in the eyes of Yahweh. (1 Kgs 14:22a)

> King Rehoboam *established himself firmly in Jerusalem and continued as king*. . . . He did evil *because he had not set his heart on seeking Yahweh*. (2 Chr 12:13–14)

13:1–23/~/1 Kgs 15:1–8 (rule of Abijah). The Chronistic expansions of Abijah's rule can be compared to the Deuteronomistic version dominated by stereotypical summary (see Table C11).[186] Note a synoptic comparison of Abijah's rule:

	1 Kings	**2 Chronicles**
formulaic opening frame	15:1–2	13:1–2a
negative comparison to David	15:3–5	—
summary reference to wars with Jeroboam	15:6	13:2b
Abijah's speech to Jeroboam and his forces	—	13:3–12
Abijah defeats Jeroboam	—	13:13–20
Abijah's strength and household	—	13:21
closing frame	15:7–8	13:22–14:1

Further evidence would be needed to sort out the sharp difference between the positive Chronistic expansion and the negative stereotypical contrast with David in the traditional version (1 Kgs 15:3–5; 2 Chr 13:3–21). The single line "There was war between Abijah and Jeroboam throughout Abijah's lifetime" (1 Kgs 15:6) provides an on-ramp for the detailed account of Abijah's victory over Israel (2 Chr 13:3–20).[187]

The excessively large numbers constitute a recurring remarkable feature in Chronistic interpretive additions. Abijah and his 400,000 troops fought against Jeroboam's 800,000 (13:3). God delivered the larger army into the hands of the smaller army, who killed

185. See Glatt-Gilad, "Regnal Formulae," 193.

186. Against arguments based on the differences between Abijah (אֲבִיָּה) (2 Chr 13:1) and Abijam (אֲבִיָּם) (1 Kgs 15:1), see Lemke, "Synoptic Problem," 359–60.

187. See Glatt-Gilad, "Regnal Formulae," 201.

500,000 soldiers (13:17). The death toll for this one battle exceeds by a large margin that of the United States military during World War II (1939–1946).[188] The recurring motif is seen in Asa's 580,000 (14:8), Jehoshaphat's 1,160,000 (17:14–19), Amaziah's 300,000 troops (25:5–6), and others. Some suggest the word commonly translated "thousand" (אֶלֶף) should be understood as "unit" or a similar term. Others note the common ancient Near East use of hyperbole and suggest biblical numbers use even larger hyperbole to glorify Israel's God.[189] Literary hyperbole seems to fit more readily in satirical historical narratives—Judges, Daniel, Esther, and the like—even while calibrating different degrees of satirical coloring remains subjective. But accounting for the function of hyperbole in historical narratives that routinely cite archival sources, like Kings and Chronicles, seems less clear. The widespread use of hyperbole in typically first-person ancient Near Eastern historical royal propaganda inscriptions offers a helpful partial analogue. The third-person prophetic-critical narrative style of Kings and Chronicles creates sharp differences over and against ancient royal inscriptions, which undermines a simplistic one-to-one analogy of the function of "parallel" literary elements. No satisfactory interpretation explains the tendency for exceptionally large numbers in Chronicles.

13:5~1 Chr 17:14//2 Sam 7:16 (C)+Num 18:19 (B) (Abijah affirms permanent Davidic rule over Israel).

13:6–9>/<11:15; 10:10–11; 11:13–14 (Abijah enhances Jeroboam's apostasies).

13:10–11>/<Exod 40:22–29; Lev 24:1–9; Num 3:10–13 (daily temple worship by descendants of Aaron and Levites). Abijah taunts Jeroboam and his forces with a series of broad allusions to several scriptural traditions listed above. Some of his claims seem like they may be overstated. Intentional distortion seems to be used in derision instead of diplomacy at times when trying to instigate battle or surrender (cf. Judg 11:24–25; 2 Kgs 18:19–25, 27–35). In any case, the most likely allusion is an interpretive blend featuring the irrevocable covenant with David housed in the covenantal language of the election of Aaron in Num 18. A covenant of salt metaphorically suggests an enduring commitment. Abijah clothes the permanent Davidic rule over all Israel with priestly idiom (emphases signify verbal parallels):[190]

> Whatever is set aside from the holy offerings the Israelites present to Yahweh **I give to you and your sons** and daughters as your perpetual share. It is *an everlasting covenant of salt* before Yahweh for both you and your offspring. (Num 18:19)

> I will set him over my house and my kingdom forever; his throne will be established forever. (1 Chr 17:14; cf. 2 Sam 7:16)

188. See Dillard, *2 Chronicles*, 106.

189. See ibid., 106–7, 120, 199; Fouts, "Another Look," 205–11; idem, "Incredible Numbers," 283–99; idem, "Hyperbolic Interpretation," 377–87. Also see second note on 2 Chr 28:1–27.

190. See Japhet, *I & II Chronicles*, 691.

> Don't you know that Yahweh, the God of Israel, **has given** the kingdom of Israel to David **and his descendants** *forever by a covenant of salt*? (2 Chr 13:5)

14:1–16:14/~/1 Kgs 15:9–24 (rule of Asa). Chronicles uses nearly all of the traditions in Kings regarding Asa, along with several expansions. Note a synoptic comparison of Asa's rule:

	1 Kings	2 Chronicles
formulaic opening frame	15:9–10	—
evaluation formula	15:11	14:2
summary statement of purging idolatry	15:12	14:3
reforms and fortifications	—	14:4–7
defeat of Cushites and looting Gerar	—	14:8–15
prophetic message of Azariah	—	15:1–7
cultic reforms and covenant renewal	—	15:8–15
deposes Maakah queen grandmother	15:13	15:16
positive evaluation in spite of high places	15:14	15:17
dedicated treasures brought to temple	15:15	15:18
treaty with Ben-hadad	15:16–22	15:19–16:6
prophetic message of Hanani	—	16:7–10
closing formula	15:23	16:11–12
death and burial	15:24	16:13–14

Chronicles closely follows most of the parallel Asa episodes. With a few exceptions, the Chronicler shifts the function of shared materials by inserting new materials. First, Asa's fortification and battle against the Cushites (2 Chr 14:4–15) fleshes out a summary statement: "As for all the other events of Asa's reign, all his achievements, all he did and the cities he built, are they not written in the book of the annals of the kings of Judah?" (1 Kgs 15:23).[191] Second, the message of Azariah sets up a series of cultic reforms to provide a basis for positive evaluation in spite of remaining high places (2 Chr 15:1–15; 1 Kgs 15:23). The addition seems to represent the Chronicler's desire to provide narrative rationale to support theological evaluation. Third, Hanani spoke against Asa's treaty with Ben-Hadad (16:7–10). The Deuteronomist often presents military collaboration with foreign nations without offering moral commentary. The Chronicler repairs this interpretive gap by supplying Hanani's prophetic message. These several expansions provide a basis to sustain the Chronicler's retributive standards—including a paradigmatic shift from good to bad

191. Concerning the extremely large military force in 2 Chr 14:8, see note on 13:1–23.

(see Table C10). The addition of this unwelcome prophetic message in Chronicles may "override" a potentially positive initiative from Asa's plunder in the Deuteronomistic version (1 Kgs 15:22/~/2 Chr 16:6).[192] Fourth, the Chronicler adds a chronological reference that organizes Asa's rule into two theological periods (16:1). The first section of Chronistic Asa presents thirty-four years of faithfulness followed by seven years of unfaithfulness.[193]

As part of the closing frame, the Deuteronomist mentions Asa's diseased feet.[194] The Chronicler expands upon it both chronologically and with details of the king's infidelity in seeking medical help without seeking help from Yahweh (2 Chr 16:12). These exegetical interventions punctuate Asa's backsliding in his final seven years. The extensive reworking only leaves behind minimal verbal parallel from the parent text, signified by italics:

> In his old age, however, *his feet* became *diseased*. (1 Kgs 15:23b)

> In the thirty-ninth year of his reign Asa was afflicted in *his feet*. Though his *disease* was severe, even in his *illness* he did not seek help from Yahweh, but only from the physicians. (2 Chr 16:12†)

The substantial Chronistic plus provides details of Asa's burial that seem positive versus the brief Deuteronomistic note (italics signify verbal parallels and broken underlining signifies pluses).

> *Then Asa rested with his ancestors* and *was buried* with them *in the city* of his father *David*. (1 Kgs 15:24a)

> Then in the forty-first year of his reign *Asa* died *and rested with his ancestors*. They *buried* him in the tomb that he had cut out for himself *in the City of David*. They laid him on a bier covered with spices and various blended perfumes, and they made a huge fire in his honor. (2 Chr 16:13–14)

The funeral fire can be deduced as an honor in contrast to the lack of a fire for Jehoram (16:4; 21:19; cf. Jer 34:5). The unique comparisons of a fire to honor Asa and no fire for Jehoram is interesting since one king died with diseased feet and the other with diseased bowels.[195]

15:2~Jer 29:13–14 (D) (Azariah speaks of seeking and finding Yahweh).[196] The similarities of "seek" and "forsake" Yahweh and associated concepts in 1 Chr 28:9; 2 Chr 12:5;

192. See Glatt-Gilad, "Regnal Formulae," 195.

193. See Knoppers, "'Yhwh Is Not with Israel,'" 605.

194. Schipper suggests that the Deuteronomist subtly infers that Asa's diseased feet was judgment for not exempting anyone from military service ("Deuteronomy 24:5," 647–48; cf. Deut 24:5; 1 Kgs 15:22).

195. See Japhet, *I & II Chronicles*, 739; Klein, *2 Chronicles*, 243.

196. This potential parallel is suggested by von Rad, "Levitical Sermon," in *From Genesis*, 235 n. 5, 265.

15:2; 24:20; 28:6; and in the prophets (Jer 29:13–14; Isa 55:6) seem more like widely disseminated stock phrases related to Deut 4:29 than interpretive allusion.

15:6~Zech 11:6 (D) (threat of crushing).[197]

15:7~Jer 31:16 (D) (your work shall be rewarded).[198] The short phrase "for your works shall be rewarded" (lit.) appears nearly identical in Jer 31:16 and 2 Chr 15:7 with only a shift from second-person singular to second-person plural. The general nature of the shared language makes the parallel seem coincidental or a stock phrase.

16:9~Zech 4:10+1 Sam 13:13 (D) (eyes of Yahweh range through the earth).[199] The phrase with close verbal parallels "the eyes of Yahweh range throughout the earth" does not share other contextual elements (2 Chr 16:9; Zech 4:10). As such, it seems more like a shared figure of speech. Another shared common single term "you have acted foolishly" seems like a coincidence (2 Chr 16:9; 1 Sam 13:13).

17:1–21:1/~/1 Kgs 22:1–34, 41–51 (rule of Jehoshaphat). This section of Chronicles excludes massive sections of Kings devoted to northern Israelite kings and episodes of Elijah and Elisha (see list of minuses at opening of chapter). Note a comparative synopsis of the rule of Jehoshaphat:

	1 Kings	**2 Chronicles**
Jehoshaphat's rule established	—	17:1–19
Micaiah prophesies defeat	22:1–40	18:1–34
Jehu rebukes Jehoshaphat	—	19:1–3
Jehoshaphat establishes judges	—	19:4–11
Jehoshaphat's victory over Moab and Ammon	—	20:1–30
formulaic framework of Jehoshaphat's rule	22:41–51	20:31–21:1

The comparative synopsis reveals that the Chronicler's primary reinterpretation of Jehoshaphat's rule comes from selecting additional episodes that shift the function of the two, largely parallel synoptic sections. The primary motivation for the Jehoshaphat pluses relates to the Chronistic theology of retribution. The narrative shape of Chronistic Jehoshaphat mainly follows the template of Chronistic Asa—reforms, building initiatives, and large militia (2 Chr 14:2–8; 17:1–19), battle report (14:9–15; 18:1–19:3), reforms (15:1–19; 19:4–11), battle report (16:1–9; 20:1–30), formulaic summary of transgression and death (16:10–14; 20:31–21:1).[200] The sequence of Asa's battle reports (fidelity/victory, then infidelity/defeat) gets reversed in Jehoshaphat, in addition

197. This potential parallel is suggested by Japhet, *Ideology*, 143, n. 538.

198. This potential parallel is suggested by von Rad, "Levitical Sermon," in *From Genesis*, 235 n. 5, 265 ([*sic*] Jer 35:15).

199. These potential parallels are suggested by ibid., 234; Keil and Delitzsch, *Isaiah*, 18.

200. See Dillard, "The Chronicler's Jehoshaphat," 18–19. On the excessively large army in 2 Chr 17:14–19, see note on 13:1–23.

to a shift to mostly generalized chronological references in the latter—"Third year" (17:7), "after some years" (18:2), none (19:4), and "after this" (20:1, 35).[201] The following notes unfold some of the Chronicler's interpretive interventions within the account of Jehoshaphat.

18:1–19:3/~/1 Kgs 22:2–40 (alliance of Jehoshaphat and Ahab against Aram). The Chronicler reworks Jehoshaphat's alliance with Ahab by framing it with a new beginning and ending and making mild adjustments within the episode. Note a synoptic comparison of the alliance with Ahab (also see the broader synoptic comparison in the note on 2 Chr 17:1–21:1):

	Kings	**2 Chronicles**
Jehoshaphat's rule established	—(cf. 2 Kgs 8:18)	18:1
alliance of Jehoshaphat and Ahab established	1 Kgs 22:2–4	18:2–3
prophets predict victory	22:5–6	18:4–5
Micaiah initially predicts victory	22:7–15	18:6–14
Micaiah predicts defeat	22:16–17	18:15–18
Micaiah's parabolic celestial vision	22:18–28	18:17–27
Aram defeats alliance	22:29–34	18:28–35
death and burial of Ahab	22:36–40	—
Jehoshaphat returns in peace	—	19:1
Jehu rebukes Jehoshaphat	—	19:2–3

The resultant version offers a complex depiction of Jehoshaphat true to the Chronistic agenda that can be observed in four ways. First, starting off with the marriage treaty explains Jehoshaphat's covenantal affirmation—"I am as you are, and my people as your people" (2 Chr 18:3//1 Kgs 22:4). If the Deuteronomist subtly impugned Jehoshaphat's loyalty to God by his alliance with the most wicked Israelite king (1 Kgs 16:30–33), the Chronicler demonstrated the basis of the alliance was a marriage treaty (2 Chr 18:1).

Second, Micaiah son of Imlah addresses Ahab in the singular in Kings but speaks to Jehoshaphat and Ahab in the plural in Chronicles (1 Kgs 22:15, 19, 25, 26; 2 Chr 18:14, 18, 25, 26). This shift does not seem theological but simply the result of converting this from an episode of Ahab's rule in Kings to a part of the rule of Jehoshaphat in Chronicles.

Third, the Chronicler adds a theological comment in a key part of the battle to make explicit divine intervention (bold signifies a plus):

201. See Williamson, *1 and 2 Chronicles*, 278.

> When the chariot commanders saw Jehoshaphat, they thought, "This is the king of Israel." So they turned to attack him, but Jehoshaphat cried out, **and Yahweh helped him. God drew them away from him.** (2 Chr 18:31; cf. 1 Kgs 22:32)

Fourth, the Chronicler adds the message of Jehu the seer to outline the complex treatment of Jehoshaphat. Jehu condemns Jehoshaphat's alliance with Ahab after the fact (2 Chr 19:2). If an alliance with the Northern Kingdom of Israel can be regarded as neutral in Kings, the Chronicler treats such alliances as infidelity to Yahweh and the same as allying with any other foreign nation.[202] Nevertheless, Jehu speaks a tempered positive evaluation of Jehoshaphat based on his cultic reforms (19:3). This prophetic message leads to a second stage of expanded reforms by Jehoshaphat (19:4–11) that resemble the prophetically activated second reforms by Asa and Josiah (15:1–19; cf. note on 17:1–21:1; Table C10).

19:5–7, 8–11~Deut 1:17+16:18–19+17:8–11 (C) (judges accountable to Yahweh in lower and upper courts). The Chronistic version of Jehoshaphat includes an account of setting up lower and upper courts. The establishment of the judicial court relates to royal, cultic, and prophetic instructions in Deut 16–18, and antecedents in Torah. The cases decided in the lower courts of the cities require sufficient evidence—"Testimony of two or three witnesses" (Deut 17:6). Appeal to the higher court is at the discretion of the court (17:8). The present concern targets the possible interpretive blend in Jehoshaphat's establishment of local lower criminal courts and a centralized higher judicial court in Jerusalem.

First, the Chronicler introduces the court system by speaking of Jehoshaphat bringing the people back to God, including the whole land from Beersheba to the hill country of Ephraim (2 Chr 19:4). The reference to the hill country of Ephraim, which stood under control of the Northern Kingdom of Israel, may seem surprising but fits with the Chronicler's treatment of Judah as inclusive of all Israel.

Second, Jehoshaphat commissions local judges to the lower courts of Judah in direct discourse (2 Chr 19:6–7). Jehoshaphat's charge sounds more like Deut 16:19 than 1:16–17, but these contexts enjoy much kinship.

Third, Jehoshaphat goes on to charge the higher court, again, presented as direct discourse (19:9–11). Jehoshaphat's exegetical interaction with Deut 17:8–12 especially includes explanation of the theological character that needs to infuse the instructional function of the higher court. Whereas Deuteronomy speaks of Levitical priests in the higher court of Jerusalem (Deut 17:9), Jehoshaphat populates it with Levites, priests, and lay leaders (2 Chr 19:8). While Jehoshaphat had called the judiciary of the lower courts to serve in dread-fear (פַּחַד) of Yahweh (19:7), he speaks to the higher court of fearing (ירא) Yahweh with characteristic wisdom idiom.[203] The instructional mission of the judges of the higher court in Jerusalem should be motivated by fear of Yahweh and faithful integrity (19:9). The Chronicler's Jehoshaphat underscores the point that the work of

202. See Knoppers, "'Yhwh Is Not with Israel,'" 621–22.

203. See Job 28:28; Prov 1:7; 9:10; 31:30; Eccl 12:13. Also see discussion of "wisdom friendly" with Table C2.

judges goes beyond legal rulings and includes Torah instruction in accord with its possible donor context (19:10; cf. Deut 17:10).

Fourth, Jehoshaphat's expansive legal enhancements include a hierarchy for the upper court: chief priest and chief lay leader of Judah as final arbiter over religious and civil cases respectively, with Levitical judges serving under them (2 Chr 19:11). Note several possible exegetical allusions (bold signifies verbal parallels and partial verbal parallels, and stylized underlining signifies exegetical interventions and expansions):

> Do not show partiality in judging; hear both small and great alike. Do not be afraid of anyone, **for judgment belongs to God**. Bring me any case too hard for you, and I will hear it. (Deut 1:17)
>
> Appoint **judges** and officials for each of your tribes in **every** town Yahweh your God is giving you, and they shall judge the people fairly. [19] **Do not** pervert justice or **show partiality. Do not accept a bribe**, for a bribe blinds the eyes of the wise and twists the words of the innocent. (16:18–19)
>
> If cases come before your courts that are too difficult for you to judge—**whether bloodshed**, lawsuits or assaults—take them to the place Yahweh your God will choose. [9] Go to the Levitical priests and to the judge who is in office at that time. Inquire of them and they will give you the verdict. [10] You must act according to the decisions they give you at the place Yahweh will choose. Be careful to do everything they instruct you to do. [11] Act according to whatever they teach you and the decisions they give you. Do not turn aside from what they tell you, to the right or to the left. (17:8–11)
>
> He appointed **judges** in the land, in **each** of the fortified cities of Judah. [6] He told them, "Consider carefully what you do, because you are not judging for mere mortals but **you are judging for Yahweh**, who is with you whenever you give a verdict. [7] Now let the fear of Yahweh be on you. Judge carefully, for with Yahweh our God there is **no** injustice or **partiality** or **bribery**." [8] In Jerusalem also, Jehoshaphat appointed some of the Levites, priests and heads of Israelite families to administer the law of Yahweh and to settle disputes. And they lived in Jerusalem. [9] He gave them these orders: "You must serve faithfully and wholeheartedly in the fear of Yahweh. [10] In every case that comes before you from your people who live in the cities—**whether bloodshed** or other concerns of the law, commands, decrees or regulations—you are to warn them not to sin against Yahweh; otherwise his wrath will come on you and your people. Do this, and you will not sin. [11] "Amariah the chief priest will be over you in any matter concerning Yahweh, and Zebadiah son of Ishmael, the leader of the tribe of Judah, will be over you in any matter concerning the king, and the Levites will serve as officials before you. Act with courage, and may Yahweh be with those who do well." (2 Chr 19:5–11†)

20:15, 17~1 Sam 17:47+Exod 14:13 (B) (Jehaziel declares divine victory over Moab, Ammon, and Edom).[204] Torah called for the priest to address the army before battle and encourage them (Deut 20:2–4). Jehaziel the Levite fills this role inspired by the Spirit (2 Chr 20:14). Jehaziel offers a prophetic message to Judah—aimed at divine intervention not instruction of human responsibility (see Table C9)—featuring close similarities to famous pre-battle speeches by Moses and David. Though the messages of the three speeches focus on general theological principles using ordinary language, the similar setting suggests interpretive allusion. The battle scene itself provides further interpretive intervention with the Levites' praise and worship of Yahweh before the battle (20:19–20). By contrast in the donor context Moses cried out to God in spite of soothing Israel (Exod 14:15). After the victory at the sea, Moses leads in a song of praise (15:1–18). Note the interpretive blend (bold and underlining signify verbal parallels, italics signify parallels of synonyms, and broken underlining signifies general verbal parallels):

> Moses answered the people, "Do not be afraid. Stand firm [הִתְיַצְּבוּ] and you will see the deliverance Yahweh will bring you today. The Egyptians you see today you will never see again. Yahweh will fight for you; you need only to be still." (14:13–14)

> [David taunts the champion of Gath] All those gathered here will know that it is not by sword or spear that Yahweh saves; **for the battle** is *Yahweh's*, and he will give all of you into our hands. (1 Sam 17:47)

> He [Jehaziel] said: "Listen, King Jehoshaphat and all who live in Judah and Jerusalem! This is what Yahweh says to you: 'Do not be afraid or discouraged because of this vast army. **For the battle** is not yours, *but God's*. . . . You will not have to fight this battle. Take up your positions; stand firm [הִתְיַצְּבוּ עִמְדוּ] and see the deliverance Yahweh will give you, Judah and Jerusalem. Do not be afraid; do not be discouraged. Go out to face them tomorrow, and Yahweh will be with you.'" (2 Chr 20:15, 17)

Jehaziel does not include Exod 14:14 in his interpretive blend—"Yahweh will fight for you; you need only to be still"—yet it may be an undercurrent in the Chronicler's mind. The actual battle features Judah praising Yahweh and singing, and the Moabites, Ammonites, and Edomites killing each other and leaving behind the spoils of war for Jehoshaphat (2 Chr 20:23–25).

---

204. These potential parallels are suggested by von Rad, "Levitical Sermon," in *From Genesis,* 237; also see Driver, "Speeches," 291.

20:20–21~Isa 7:9 (B) (Jehoshaphat calls for faith and appoints lay singers).[205] After the Levites praise Yahweh, Jehoshaphat calls the people of Judah and Jerusalem to trust Yahweh in language resembling Isaiah's exhortation to Ahaz (2 Chr 20:20; Isa 7:9). Though the language seems rather generic, the relative rarity of "prove to be reliable" in this form suggests an interpretive allusion.[206] Jehoshaphat promotes a striking interpretive enhancement by adding objects of faith, calling upon them to trust Yahweh and trust his prophets. The encouragement to trust prophetic messages points to the crucial role of the prophets in the Chronicler's ideology. The Chronicler narrates the continued democratization of leadership: just as the Levite Jehaziel addresses the people before the battle rather than the priest, so too Jehoshaphat appoints lay singers in place of Levites (2 Chr 20:14, 21). More than this, Jehoshaphat consults the people before appointing lay leaders (20:21). Note exegetical interventions (bold signifies verbal parallel, and italics signify verbatim parallel):

> If **you do** not **have faith** [אמן Hif], **you will** not **be upheld** [אמן Nif]. (Isa 7:9b lit.)

> *Give thanks to Yahweh,* for he is good; *for his love endures forever.* (1 Chr 16:34†; cf. Ps 106:1)[207]

> Early in the morning they left for the Desert of Tekoa. As they set out, Jehoshaphat stood and said, "Listen to me, Judah and people of Jerusalem! **Have faith** [אמן Hif] in Yahweh your God and **you will be upheld** [אמן Nif]; **have faith** [אמן Hif] in his prophets and you will be successful." After consulting the people, Jehoshaphat appointed men to sing to Yahweh and to praise him for the splendor of his holiness as they went out at the head of the army, saying: "*Give thanks to Yahweh, for his love endures forever.*" (2 Chr 20:20–21)

20:31–21:1/~/1 Kgs 22:41–51 (rule of Jehoshaphat). The Chronicler closes his treatment of Jehoshaphat by selective adjustments to the formulaic presentation in Kings. Note a comparative synopsis of the rule of Jehoshaphat (see the broad synoptic comparison in the note on 2 Chr 17:1–21:1):

---

205. Potential parallel of Isa 7:9 and 2 Chr 20:20 is suggested by von Rad, "Levitical Sermon," in *From Genesis,* 237. Also see Williamson *1 and 2 Chronicles,* 299.

206. The verb "prove to be reliable" (אמן) in Nif impf. only appears seven or eight times (depending on a textual issue). Note similar syntactical logic with Hif impf., then Nif impf. in Isa 7:9b; and Hif impv., then Nif impf., then Hif impv. in 2 Chr 20:20 (see "אמן," *TDOT* 1:294, 297, 306–7).

207. See 1 Chr 16:34; Pss 100:5; 106:1; 136:1; cf. 136:2–26; Jer 33:11; Ezra 3:11; 2 Chr 5:13; 7:3.

	1 Kings	2 Chronicles
formulaic opening frame	22:41–42	20:31
comparison to Asa, evaluation formula	22:43a[43]	20:32
summation	22:43b[44]	20:33
Jehoshaphat's treaty with king of Israel (Ahab)	22:44[45]	—
source citation	22:45[46]	20:34
extermination of cultic male prostitutes	22:46[47]	—
deputy ruling Edom	22:47[48]	—
Jehoshaphat's treaty with Ahaziah	—	20:35
gold ships made and lost	22:48–49[49–50]	20:36, 37b
Eliezer's prophetic judgment	—	20:37
death, burial, and succession formulas	22:50[51]	21:1

Several of the changes to the formulaic presentation of the rule of Jehoshaphat correspond with the Chronicler's tendencies. First, the Chronicler retains the comparison of Jehoshaphat to his father Asa, perhaps in relation to modeling Jehoshaphat on the template of Asa's rule (1 Kgs 22:43//2 Chr 20:32).[208] Second, the reasons for excluding notes on getting rid of cultic male prostitutes and the political rule of Edom are not evident (1 Kgs 22:46, 47[47, 48]).[209] Third, the additions of notes on Jehoshaphat's treaty with Ahaziah and Eliezer's prophetic judgment provide a retributive rationale for the loss of Jehoshaphat's gold ships (2 Chr 20:35, 37). Eliezer does not offer any instruction or motivation in his prophetic message but simply a straightforward historical exegesis of divine intervention (see Table C9).

21:2–20/~/2 Kgs 8:16–24 (rule of Jehoram of Judah). The Chronicler selectively expands the depiction of Jehoram as a wicked ruler in Kings. In addition to this main note, also see separate notes on 2 Chr 21:13 and 21:18–19. Note the comparative synopsis of the rule of Jehoram of Judah:

	2 Kings	2 Chronicles
synchronism with Northern Kingdom	8:16	—
Jehoram kills fraternal rivals and others	—	21:2–4
age at accession and length of rule	8:17	21:5
evaluation formula	8:18–19	21:6–7
rebellion of Edom and Libnah	8:20–22	21:8–10

208. See parallels in the note on 2 Chr 17:1–21:1. Also see Dillard, *2 Chronicles*, 159.
209. See Glatt-Gilad, "Regnal Formula," 202.

	2 Kings	2 Chronicles
infidelity at high places	—	21:11
letter of Elijah	—	21:12–15
uprising of Philistines and Arabians	—	21:16–17
death by intestinal disease	—	21:18–19
source citation	8:23	—
burial formula	8:24	21:20

The Chronistic expansions effectively reshape Jehoram's rule in accordance with retribution theology. First, with little explanation the Chronicler narrates Jehoram's slaughter of his sibling rivals and other officials (2 Chr 21:2–4). The slaughter offers parallels between Jehoram and his treaty-wife Athaliah, daughter of Ahab, which fits the Ahab-like evaluation the Chronicler carried over (2 Kgs 8:18//2 Chr 21:6; 2 Kgs 11:1//2 Chr 22:10).[210] Second, the Chronicler adds a brief explanation to the loss of rule over Edom and Libnah—"Because Jehoram had forsaken Yahweh, the God of his ancestors" (2 Chr 21:10). This exegetical expansion makes explicit divine causality of political troubles. Whether or not Jehoram is a good political ruler does not enter the equation. Third, the Chronicler includes notice of the high places of Judah, which lead the people to infidelity (21:11). All of these items give rise to a letter from Elijah and judgment upon Jehoram's house.

The prophet Elijah of the Northern Kingdom of Israel does not appear in Chronicles. The letter he sends to Jehoram does not include instructional warning or motivation, only historical exegesis of divine judgment (21:12–15; see Table C9). The content of the letter formally ties in with the surrounding narrative and explains it. Elijah gives voice to the divine retribution signified by the details of Jehoram's rule (see Table C22):

TABLE C22: ELIJAH'S LETTER EXPLAINS HISTORICAL CAUSES AND EFFECTS

c = cause e = effect

Letter	Links to Narrative
Jehoram received a letter from Elijah the prophet, which said: "This is what Yahweh, the God of your father David, says: 'You have not followed the ways of your father Jehoshaphat or of Asa king of Judah. [13] *But you have followed the ways of the kings of Israel,* and you have led Judah and the people of Jerusalem to prostitute themselves, *just as the house of Ahab did.* You have also murdered your own brothers, members of your own family, men who were better than you. [14] So now Yahweh is about to strike your people, your sons, your wives and everything that is yours, with a heavy blow. [15] You yourself will be very **ill with a lingering disease of the bowels, until the disease causes your bowels to come out**." (2 Chr 21:12–15).	*21:6* (c) 21:11 (c) 21:4 (c) 21:17 (e) **21:18–19** (e)

210. See Begg, "Constructing a Monster," 40.

The divine judgment signaled in Elijah's letter also explains the alteration of closing formulas (see Table C11). The lack of a source citation formula may silently support the adjustment in the burial formula compared with Kings (see the synoptic comparison above). In place of a standard burial notice, the Chronicler adjusts to "*He passed away, to no one's regret, and they* buried *him* in the City of David, *but not in the tombs of the kings*" (2 Chr 21:20, italics signify shifts from 2 Kgs 8:24). These adjustments in the closing frame interpret Jehoram's severe and shameful judgment as being cut off from his family. The absence of mourning and exclusion from burial with the royal family are appropriate for one who murders his own brothers (21:13).[211]

21:13~Exod 34:16 (C) (Jehoram causes Judah to whore after other gods). The causative stem of "to prostitute" (זנה Hif)—"cause to whore after"—only occurs in the narrow sense of cause to whore after other gods in Exod 34:16 and 2 Chr 21:11, 13 (see note on Exod 34:11–16). The idea of infidelity against God using the *Qal* stem of "to prostitute" is common enough.[212] The causative stem of the verb appears in its literal sense in one place that commands parents not to peddle carnal knowledge of their daughters (Lev 19:29). The prohibition against treaty marriages warns parents of spouses from the nations of Canaan "causing your children to whore after their gods" (Exod 34:16 lit.). Since Jehoshaphat arranged a treaty marriage for Jehoram, in one sense Judah as a whole intermarried with Israel, who here functions like any other nation of Canaan because of idolatry. Just like the prohibited treaty spouse, Jehoram caused the inhabitants of Jerusalem to whore by making high places throughout Judah (2 Chr 21:11, 13). The intermarriage of Jehoram to Ahab's daughter aligns him with Ahab, whose arranged marriage with Jezebel incited him to lead Israel into additional infidelities (1 Kgs 16:31–33). The unflattering depiction of Jehoram as a merchant of prostitution serves as a basis for the horrific intestinal disease of Elijah's predicted retribution (2 Chr 21:13, 18–19).

21:18–19~2 Sam 7:12 (D) (bowels came out). The suggestion that "internal organs" refers to reproductive organ versus bowels understands Jehoram's judgment as a negative echo of part of Nathan's oracle.[213] Compare "I will raise up your seed after you who *will come out of your own organs/insides* [יֵצֵא מִמֵּעֶיךָ]" and "*his* [Jehoram's] *organs came out* [יָצְאוּ מֵעָיו]" (2 Sam 7:12 lit.; 2 Chr 21:19 lit., emphases mine).[214] The proposal fails

211. See Zimran, "'Covenant Made with David,'" 309, 316.

212. See, e.g., Jer 3:1, 3, 6, 8; Ezek 16:15, 16, 17; 23:3, 5. Hosea 4:10, 18 and 5:3 use Hif of "to prostitute" (זנה) reflexively in the sense of "to prostitute themselves." The only uses of "cause (someone else) to whore" (זנה Hif) are Lev 19:29; Exod 34:16; and 2 Chr 21:11, 13 ("I זנה," Hif no. 1 *HALOT* 1:275). The root *znh* (זנה) as noun, participle, or other verb forms refers to illicit sexual persons and actions, such as harlot, act as harlot, fornication, fornicate, adulterous sexual infidelity (BDB 275–76; *CDCH* 101–2). As a verb, *znh* normally takes human female subjects. Erlandsson oversteps by saying "Because the woman is subordinate to the man, she is always the subject of *zānāh*" (*TDOT* 4:100), without noting the rare exceptions in Exod 34:16 (Hif) and Num 25:1 (Q). When masculine, *znh* typically refers metaphorically to covenantal infidelity (see *NIDOTTE* 1:1123 [nos. 2, 4, 5]; *TWOT* 1:246; *TDOT* 4:101–4).

213. Zimran, "'Covenant Made with David,'" 318–19.

214. The sematic range of "organ(s)" allows for reference to entrails, reproductive organ, or other organs depending on context, see "*מֵעֶה," *HALOT* 1:609–10.

both because Jehoram sires sons (2 Chr 22:1) and because the Chronicler uses a different expression in the Davidic promise—"He will be from your sons" (1 Chr 17:11).

22:1–9/~/2 Kgs 8:24–29 (rule of Ahaziah of Judah). The Chronicler selectively and significantly abbreviates the tumultuous coup of Jehu, isolating a short account of the rule of Ahaziah. Note the comparative synopsis of the rule of Ahaziah of Judah:

	2 Kings	**2 Chronicles**
citizens of Jerusalem coronate Ahaziah	—	22:1
formulaic opening frame	8:25; cf. 9:29	22:2
evaluation, comparison to Ahab	8:27	22:3–4
alliance with Joram of Israel[a]	8:28	22:5
Ahaziah visits Joram during his recovery	8:29; cf. 9:15–16	22:6
Jehu anointed king of Israel	9:1–13	—
Jehu assassinates Joram	9:14–26	—
Jehu kills Ahaziah	9:27	22:7–9
death of Jezebel	9:30–37	—
Jehu eliminates house of Ahab	10:1–17	—
Jehu purges Baal worship	10:18–36	—

[a] Joram of Israel is also known as Jehoram; the same inversion occurs for Jehoram of Judah. This likely results from close relations of the royal families of Israel and Judah at this time through intermarriage. The approach here, for convenience, refers to Joram/Jehoram of Israel as Joram and Jehoram/Joram of Judah as Jehoram.

As with Jehoram so too with Ahaziah the Chronicler retains the Deuteronomistic comparison with Ahab. The Chronicler adjusts the narrative commentary from the parent text explaining that Ahaziah followed the council of the queen mother Athaliah, the daughter of Ahab and Jezebel (2 Chr 22:3–4). Like Jehoshaphat, Ahaziah makes a military alliance with Israel to battle Aram (22:5). The Chronicler treats alliances with the Northern Kingdom of Israel as the same kind of infidelity to Yahweh as alliances with any other foreign nation.[215] On the human plane Ahaziah may seem like he was in the wrong place at the wrong time, visiting his royal relative in Israel recovering from battle wounds (22:6, 8). But the Chronicler embeds his own commentary to make explicit the divine causality for retribution, thus eliminating coincidence (exegetical interventions signified by italics):

> Through Ahaziah's visit to Joram, *God brought about Ahaziah's downfall.* When Ahaziah arrived, he went out with Joram to meet Jehu son of Nimshi, *whom Yahweh had anointed to destroy the house of Ahab.* (22:7)

---

215. See Knoppers, "'Yhwh Is Not with Israel,'" 603, 621–22.

The Deuteronomistic and Chronistic accounts of killing Ahaziah differ sharply (22:9; 2 Kgs 9:27). The available evidence does not provide a sufficient basis to sort out the differences.[216] The present concern relates to the Chronicler's interpretive retelling. The standard death and burial formulas are not carried over (2 Kgs 9:28–29), perhaps since Ahaziah died in "exile" like Jehoahaz and Jehoiakim (cf. 2 Chr 36:4, 8).[217] Those involved with Ahaziah's death go to the trouble of burying his corpse on the basis of Jehoshaphat's devotion to Yahweh (22:9). These details point to subtle and complex concepts of retribution by the Chronicler. Interpretive conclusions in this case need to remain soft based on the kind of evidence available.

22:10–23:21/~/2 Kgs 11:1–20 (Athaliah usurps rule). The Chronistic version of Athaliah's tenure largely follows Kings but with many small adjustments and additions according to its standard theological emphases. Note the comparative synopsis of Athaliah:

	2 Kings	**2 Chronicles**
Athaliah seeks to exterminate Davidic line	11:1	22:10
Jehosheba hides Joash	11:2–3	22:11–12
setting for covenant in seventh year	11:4	23:1
gathering Levites and Israelite heads throughout Judah	—	23:2–3
plot to overthrow Athaliah	11:5–8	23:4–7
coronation of Joash	11:9–12	23:8–11
execution of Athaliah	11:13–16	23:12–15
covenantal reforms	11:17–18a	23:16–17
summary statement of reforms at temple	11:18b	23:18a
restoration of temple personnel	—	23:18b–19
Joash enthroned	—	23:20–21

The Chronicler provides several noteworthy exegetical interventions by small expansions to the parent text. First, the Chronicler establishes the rationale for the collaboration of the heads of the revolution against Athaliah by explaining that Jehosheba daughter of Jehoram married Jehoiada the priest (2 Chr 22:11). Second, the Chronicler omits reference to assistance from the Carites in the revolution (23:11; 2 Kgs 11:4). This omission repairs the Deuteronomistic implication of Carites at the temple (2 Kgs 11:6–7).[218]

216. Dillard does well to take the edge off by relieving tensions without forced harmonization (*2 Chronicles*, 172–73).

217. See ibid., 173.

218. The Carites typically have been associated with Carians of Aegean background, though this has been debated. See Burney, *Notes*, 309. Carites (כָּרִי) appear in the *ketiv* of 2 Sam 20:23, while Cherethites (כְּרֵתִי) in the *qere* of 2 Sam 20:23 also appear in 8:18. Also see Cogan and Tadmor, *II Kings*, 126; McCarter, *II Samuel*, 256.

Third, an addition in Chronicles speaks of recruiting Levites and heads of Israelite clans throughout Judah (2 Chr 23:2). These recruits both emphasize the solidarity of all Israel typical of Chronicles and also ensure that only Levites and priests tend to the situation in the temple (italics signify what the Chronicler omits, and bold signifies what he adds):

> *(A)nd you who are in the other two companies [Carites and guards] that normally go off Sabbath duty are* all to guard *the temple of* Yahweh *for the king.* Station yourselves around the king. . . . (2 Kgs 11:7–8a†)

> **No one is to enter the temple of Yahweh except the priests and Levites on duty; they may enter because they are consecrated, but** all **the others are** to observe Yahweh's guard. **The Levites are to** station themselves around the king. . . . (2 Chr 23:6–7a†; cf. v. 8)

Fourth, the Chronicler explicitly triple-marks the authoritative traditions with which his narrative enhancements accord—demonstrating convincingly his exegetical intentions. The Chronicler's reference to the Levitical priests' sacrificing continues what he stated earlier (1 Chr 6:48–49). He also twice marks the authority of David to make enduring assignments for the Levites (see 1 Chr 23–26). The addition in 2 Chr 23:19 of a reference to the function of temple gatekeepers to prevent entry by those who are ritually impure (טָמֵא) invites comparison to the moral and social standards spelled out in the temple entry psalms (Pss 15:1–5; 24:3–4; cf. 118:19–21; Isa 33:14–16).[219] The Chronicler marks traditions to present Jehoiada's organization of temple personnel as a restoration of the continuity of worship (standard underlining signifies adjustment from parent text of 2 Kgs 11:18, italics signify additions, bold signifies broad allusion and marking traditions in 1 Chr 6, and broken underlining signifies marking of authoritative traditions):

> Their fellow Levites were assigned to all the other duties of the tabernacle, the house of God. [49] But **Aaron and his descendants were the ones who presented offerings** on the altar of burnt offering and on the altar of incense in connection with all that was done in the Most Holy Place, making atonement for Israel, **in accordance with all that Moses the servant of God had commanded.** (1 Chr 6:48–49)

> Then <u>Jehoiada</u> placed the oversight of the temple of Yahweh *in the hands of the Levitical priests, to whom <u>David had made assignments</u> in the temple,* ***to present the burnt offerings*** *of Yahweh <u>as written in the Law of Moses</u>, with rejoicing and singing, <u>as David had ordered</u>.* [19] *He also stationed gatekeepers at the gates of Yahweh's temple so that no one who was in any way unclean* [טָמֵא] *might enter.* (2 Chr 23:18–19)

219. See Isa 52:1 (and note ad loc.) for the expectation of the ritually impure (טָמֵא) being excluded from entry into Zion.

Exegetical intervention by excessive marking demonstrates that the Chronicler does not seek liberation from historic institutions but instead seeks to strengthen continuity with scriptural traditions.

24:1–27/~/2 Kgs 12:1–22 (rule of Joash of Judah). The basic storyline of Joash in Chronicles follows Kings but with many alterations according to Chronistic theological emphases. Note a synoptic comparison of the rule of Joash (stylized brackets signify different sequence):

	2 Kings	**2 Chronicles**
formulaic opening frame	11:21–12:1	24:1
evaluation formula	12:2	24:2
high places remain	12:3	—
Jehoiada secures wives for Joash	—	24:3
collection for temple restoration	12:4–8	24:4–6
retrospective on Athaliah's defilement of temple articles	—	24:7
temple collection chest	12:9–11	24:8–12
temple repairs from collections	12:12–13	24:13–24
notes on collections	12:14–16	—
death and burial notice of Jehoiada	—	24:15–17
infidelity to Yahweh	—	24:18–19
Zechariah's message and illegal execution	—	24:20–22
Aram defeats Judah	12:17–18	24:23–25a
conspiracy to assassinate Joash	12:20	24:25b
death and burial formula	{12:21b}	24:25c
list of conspirators	{12:21a}	24:26
source citation and successor	{12:19, 21c}	24:27

Among the many adjustments made in retelling Joash's story, several illustrate the leading Chronistic exegetical interventions. First, though the Chronicler excludes the notation on the people's syncretistic infidelity early in Joash's rule (2 Kgs 12:3), he includes a similar indictment after Jehoiada dies (2 Chr 24:18). This shift in sequence better conforms to the shared evaluation formula that "Joash did what was right in the eyes of Yahweh all the years of Jehoiada the priest" (24:2//2 Kgs 12:2). The rearrangement of good years then bad years fits with other examples of the Chronicler's reshaping royal narratives (see Table C10).

Second, the Chronicler notes that Jehoiada secured wives for Joash, acting as a surrogate father (2 Chr 24:3). Jehoiada's important role in leading an uprising against Athaliah and guiding Joash in faithfulness begins to explain the exceptional death and burial notation regarding Jehoiada, akin to those of kings (24:15, see note ad loc.).

Third, while the Chronicler's version of the collection and repairs on the temple in many ways runs parallel to Kings, he makes an important addition. The Chronicler embeds a broad allusion to Moses's one-time half-shekel collection to build the tabernacle (24:9; Exod 30:11–16). Embedding it in a context referring to the temple's free-will collection chest shifts the significance by getting at the need for ongoing upkeep and repairs of the temple. Predictably, by the later Second Temple period both the temple's free-will chest and the annual half-shekel tax stood side by side (Matt 17:24; Mark 12:41).

Fourth, following Jehoiada's death the people turned to idolatry, which incites Yahweh to send prophets to no avail (2 Chr 24:18–19; cf. 2 Kgs 12:3). The ineffective ministry of the prophets anticipates a similar summary in 2 Chr 36:15–16, which itself echoes Jer 25:3–4 (see note on 2 Chr 36:15–16; cf. Mark 12:2–5).

Fifth, Zechariah son of Jehoiada functions as a temporarily inspired prophetic figure to bring an instructional word against the backslidden people. Zechariah's message—"Because you have forsaken Yahweh, he has forsaken you" (2 Chr 24:20)—echoes one of the Chronicler's prophetic stock phrases. Although Zechariah only offers prophetic instruction, not historical causality, the Chronicler's narrative frame creates a retributive cause-effect sequence of sin and judgment. Prophetic Torah exegesis even broadly expressed often conforms to the retributional emphasis of Chronicles (see Table C9). The Chronicler adds an account of Joash conspiring to kill Zechariah for his message. Though the conspiracy is in the third-person plural, the Chronicler places the illegal execution upon Joash (24:21). Zechariah's dying words call for Yahweh to judge the murder (24:22).

Sixth, the Chronicler adds explicit narrative commentary to the account of the battle with the Arameans to close out the retributive cause and effect from Judah's backsliding and the message of Zechariah (italics signify retributive causality):

> Although the Aramean army had come with only a few men, Yahweh delivered into their hands a much larger army. *Because Judah had forsaken Yahweh*, the God of their ancestors, judgment was executed on Joash. When the Arameans withdrew, they left Joash severely wounded. His officials conspired against him *for murdering the son of Jehoiada the priest*, and they killed him in his bed. (24:24–25a)

Seventh, Chronicles offers an exceptional closing supplementary notation after the burial formula (24:25b), leading into the source citation that speaks to many prophetic oracles against him (24:27).[220] This Chronistic plus may refer back to the Chronicler's own mention of prophetic intervention that includes Zechariah (24:19–20).[221] The Chronicler for the second time uses the term *midrash* (מִדְרַשׁ) to refer to the written source of his narrative additions (24:27; cf. 13:22). The term itself connotes study, interpretation, and exegesis and may refer to prophetic annotations or commentary, but it should not be stretched to the sense of postbiblical Judaic genre of midrash as imaginative narrative embellishments.[222]

24:15~Gen 35:29 (C) (Jehoiada was old and full of years). The formulaic death and burial notation regarding Jehoiada resembles that of the kings (2 Chr 24:15–17). The summary comment at the opening reminds one of the Hebrew ancestors—with the exception of Jacob, who considered himself inferior living only 147 years (see Gen 47:9; 49:33) (italics signify verbal parallels at the level of roots):[223]

> Abraham lived a hundred and seventy-five years. Then Abraham breathed his last and *died* at a good old age, *old and full* of years; and he was gathered to his people. (Gen 25:7–8†)

> Isaac lived a hundred and eighty years. Then he breathed his last and *died* and was gathered to his people, *old and full of days.* (35:28–29a†)

> Now Jehoiada was *old and full of days,* and *he died* at the age of a hundred and thirty. (2 Chr 24:15†)

In addition to the Chronicler mimicking the death notice of the Hebrew ancestors is Jehoiada's age of 130 years. The apparent hyperbole exceeds both Moses's 120 and Aaron's 123 years (Deut 34:7; Num 33:39). One reading of the difficult sense of Gen 6:3 sees 120 years as the outer limit of human mortal potential, though the psalmist's seventy or eighty seems more realistic as an ancient norm (Ps 90:10). In any case, Jehoiada's death and burial notice—buried with the kings in the city of David (2 Chr 24:16)—provides an extraordinary commendation of the priest's exemplary service.

25:1–26:2/~/2 Kgs 14:1–22 (rule of Amaziah). The Chronistic version of Amaziah's rule basically follows the Deuteronomistic parent version but with several additions effectively reshaping it according to the Chronicler's retribution theology. Note a synoptic comparison of the rule of Amaziah:

---

220. See Table C11 and the synoptic comparison in the note on 2 Chr 24:1–27 for rearrangement of the formulaic closing frame.

221. See Glatt-Gilad, "Regnal Formulae," 197, 208.

222. See cautions in Dillard, *2 Chronicles*, 110.

223. See Schnittjer, *Torah Story*, 182–83.

	2 Kings	2 Chronicles
synchronism with Northern Kingdom	14:1	—
formulaic opening frame	14:2	25:1
evaluation formula	14:3	25:2
revenge upon his father's assassins with limitations	14:5–6	25:3–4
Amaziah musters an army and hires mercenaries	—	25:5–6
man of God prophesies against using mercenaries	—	25:7–10
defeat of Edomites	14:7	25:11
Judah slaughters prisoners of war	—	25:12
dismissed mercenaries raid towns of Judah	—	25:13
Amaziah worships Edomite gods taken as plunder	—	25:14
prophetic message against Amaziah	—	25:15–16
political taunts between Judah and Israel	14:8–11a	25:17–19
narrative commentary on divine causality	—	25:20
Israel defeats Judah and plunders temple and palace	14:11b–14	25:21–24
formulaic closing frame of Jehoash of Israel	14:15–16	—
summation and source citation of Amaziah	14:17–18	25:25–26
formulaic description of death, burial, and successor	14:19–22	25:27–26:2

A single-verse account of Judah's battle with Edom stands as a synoptic centerpiece of the Chronistic exegetical expansions of Amaziah's rule (2 Kgs 14:7; 2 Chr 25:11). The theologically laden Chronistic additions either lead up to or result from the victory over the Edomites. After mustering an army from Judah and Benjamin, Amaziah hires an exceptionally large mercenary contingent from Ephraim—together 300,000 soldiers (2 Chr 25:5–6).[224] Before the battle an unnamed man of God threatens defeat by divine intervention if Amaziah uses the mercenary soldiers from Ephraim (25:7–8). Amaziah pushes back because of the nonrefundable one-hundred talents of silver already paid to the mercenaries. The man of God assures the king Yahweh can give more than this (25:9). Amaziah consents and dismisses the mercenaries of Ephraim, inciting their anger (25:10). This detailed exchange leading up to the battle features prophetic warning regarding divine causality with historical circumstance (see Table C9). The threatened retribution makes clear that Judah may not form an alliance with Ephraim. The importance of prohibiting foreign alliances even includes an implied financial negotiation. All of these details set up the narrative outcomes according to the Chronicler's standard manner of connecting causes and effects, but with a twist.

224. On overly large military forces, see note on 2 Chr 13:1–23.

After the battle itself, the army of Judah kills 10,000 prisoners of war by casting them off a cliff, described in graphic detail (25:12). The twist comes in a report of the dismissed Ephraimite mercenaries looting and pillaging across the towns of Judah simultaneously to the defeat of the Edomites (25:13). If the cause-effect of retribution is lined up rigidly, it could imply: (cause) hiring foreign/Ephraimite mercenaries → (effect) plundering of Judah, and (cause) not relying on foreign/Ephraimite alliance → (effect) categorical victory over Edom.[225] These possible relations could be tweaked, but the point at hand has nothing to do with overspecifying causality. The point turns on the complex outcomes—"Retribution is . . . no barren unalterable principle."[226] Even while the Chronicler's conscious attention to retribution appears in the man of God's message, he retains the messy details of the unintended consequences of walking back bad choices. But that is not all.

Amaziah himself brings back the Edomite gods as spoils of war and worships them (25:14). This new infidelity provokes Yahweh to send an anonymous prophet to rebuke him for Torah violation and threaten judgment by both Torah exegesis and historical exegesis (25:15–16; see Table C9). Within Chronicles, Amaziah treats the foreign gods in the opposite manner of David, who burned them (1 Chr 14:12). While Torah speaks of destroying all idolatrous elements and everything else in the land of promise (Deut 7:5; 12:3), all plunder of defeated distant enemies may be taken (20:14). When the man of God had promised, "Yahweh can give you more than that," he did not mean false gods to worship (2 Chr 25:9). Whatever Amaziah's rationale, the anonymous prophet spoke to his folly of worshiping the very gods who could not deliver the Edomites (25:15; cf. Isa 44:17, 20). The bitter exchange between the anonymous prophet and Amaziah in the Chronistic plus of 25:15–16 functions as a cause to the synoptic parallel of defeat by Jehoash of Israel, which becomes retributive effect (2 Chr 25:17–24//2 Kgs 14:8–14). Within this very close parallel the Chronicler adds his own commentary in two reason clauses—marked by "for, because" (כִּי)[227]—to make his exegesis explicit (emphasis signifies Chronistic pluses).

> Amaziah, however, would not listen [to Jehoash king of Israel], *for* [כִּי] *God so worked that he might deliver them into the hands of Jehoash, because* [כִּי] *they sought the gods of Edom.* (2 Chr 25:20)

The Chronicler makes a loose temporal addition to make explicit that political intrigue against Amaziah fits within a retributive scheme which had started with his backsliding (italics signify Chronistic plus, normal font signifies identical to 2 Kgs 14:19).

225. For another view of causes and effects in 2 Chr 25:6–13, see Klein, "Chronicler's Theological Rewriting," 242.
226. Rudolph, "Problems of the Books of Chronicles," 405.
227. See GKC §158b; *IBHS* §38.4.a.

> *From the time that Amaziah turned away from following Yahweh*, they conspired against him in Jerusalem and he fled to Lachish, but they sent men after him to Lachish and killed him there. (2 Chr 25:27)

The cause of the deadly intrigue stands apart chronologically from the retribution by at least fifteen years (25:25), again, complicating matters over and against immediate retribution and the good times then bad times (and vice versa) paradigmatic shaping of Asa, Jehoshaphat, Joash, and Uzziah (see Table C10).

In sum, the Chronicler's exegetical re-presentation of Amaziah's rule features several additions that place explicit retributive theological shape on the narrative. Yet, the Chronicler includes some of the messy details of reality that make the overall narrative interpretation of Amaziah complex.

26:3–23/~/2 Kgs 15:1–7 (rule of Uzziah/Azariah). The Chronicler adds details of Uzziah's accomplishments and presumption to the Deuteronomistic version. These Chronistic additions exegetically recast the narrative according to the theology of retribution and sanctity of temple worship. Note a synoptic comparison of the rule of Uzziah:

	2 Kings	**2 Chronicles**
synchronism with Northern Kingdom	15:1	—
formulaic opening frame	15:2	26:3
formulaic evaluation	15:3	26:4
failure to remove high places	15:4	—
building projects and regional renown	—	26:5–10
military and defense accomplishments	—	26:11–15
Uzziah's presumption	—	26:16–20
Uzziah's leprosy	15:5	26:21
source citation	15:6	26:22
death, burial, and succession notation	15:7	26:23

The brief account of Uzziah in Kings includes only the basic standard royal formulaic structure and a single-verse note about his skin condition.[228] The short account fits with six others in 2 Kgs 15. The Chronistic version follows much of it verbatim but includes several inserts that flesh out its standard retributive narrative design.

First, the Chronicler paradigmatically divides Uzziah's rule into two periods: seeking Yahweh during the days of Zechariah then a time of pride and downfall (2 Chr 26:5;

228. Kings calls him Azariah and Chronicles Uzziah; the latter will be used here for convenience.

26:16). After presenting the rule of Amaziah in a more complex manner, the two-part rule of Uzziah aligns with the Chronicler's paradigmatic recasting of Asa, Jehoshaphat, and Joash (see Table C10).

Second, the Chronicler explains the influence of a mentor, Zechariah, under whose tutelage Uzziah sought Yahweh (26:5). While the language differs, this positive relationship echoes Jehoiada's mentorship of Joash (24:2). A small textual difficulty puts the character of Zechariah's instruction in question—whether it was wisdom "in the fear of God" or prophetic insight "in the visions of God."[229]

Third, the summary of military and political prowess (26:6–8), building initiatives and wealth (26:9–10), and military power and defense initiatives (26:11–15) together provide tangible evidence of divine blessing for devotion to Yahweh. The cause (seeking Yahweh [26:5]) and effect (blessed rule [26:6–15]) constitute typical Chronistic concrete marks of blessing for doing right in the eyes of Yahweh (26:4//2 Kgs 15:3).

Fourth, the extensive God-given success ironically and predictably leads Uzziah to pride and downfall (2 Chr 26:16).

Fifth, the priestly confrontation of the king for arrogantly entering the temple to perform rituals set apart for priests conforms to previous affirmations of this distinction in Chronicles. Though the priests do not cite Torah to Uzziah, the earlier contexts expressly mention what Moses had commanded and what is written in Torah (1 Chr 6:49; 16:37–40; see separate note on 2 Chr 26:18).

Sixth, the Chronicler slightly rewords the divine affliction of skin disease (traditionally "leprosy") from the narrative shape of the parent text to a narrator's comment to show the immediate judgment for Uzziah's arrogance. Notice the change in verb form (from foreground narrative form [wci] to background commenting form [non-wci, in this case pf.]) and insertion of literary signal of explanation (italics signify verbal parallel, and bold signifies exegetical advance):[230]

> *Yahweh afflicted* [וַיְנַגַּע] *the king with skin disease until the day he died.* (2 Kgs 15:5a lit.)

> When Azariah the chief priest and all the other priests looked at him, they saw that he had skin disease on his forehead, so they hurried him out. Indeed, he himself was eager to leave, **because** [כִּי] *Yahweh had afflicted him* [נִגְּעוֹ]. *King* Uzziah had *skin disease until the day he died.* (2 Chr 26:20–21a lit.)

229. KJV and JPSB of 2 Chr 26:5 follow MT "in the visions of God" (בִּרְאֹת הָאֱלֹהִים) from "to see" (ראה), a synonym of "vision" (חזה)—seer/visionary. NIV and NRSV follow other Hebrew MSS, LXX, and other ancient versions "in the fear of God" (ביראת) from "to fear" (ירא). See *BHS*.

230. The wci form may be called "narrative tense" (GKC, §111a) here as "and so he afflicted" (וַיְנַגַּע, 2 Kgs 15:5). The use of pf. form verbs offers background comments (see Heller, *Narrative Structure*, 52–54), here as "had afflicted him" (נִגְּעוֹ, 2 Chr 26:20). For a detailed discussion of verb forms of narrative foreground/background and associated syntactical markers, see footnote in note on 1 Chr 16:39–40. On the explanatory function of "because" (כִּי), see GKC, §158b.

Seventh, the Chronicler expands the rationale for Uzziah's burial location. For non-violent deaths, Kings uses several standard formulas, such as "he was buried in the city of David" (1 Kgs 2:10; 11:43), "he was buried with his ancestors in the city of David" (14:31; 15:24; 22:50[51]; 2 Kgs 8:24; 15:38; 16:20), and "they buried him in the city of David" (1 Kgs 15:8; 2 Kgs 15:7), the last of which includes Uzziah (see Table K1 in Kings Filters). The adjustment of the burial formula indicates Uzziah was interred separately from the other kings.[231] The Chronicler includes the rationale of those who buried him as Uzziah's skin disease (bold signifies verbatim citation, and italics signify addition):

> Azariah [Uzziah] **lay down with his ancestors and they buried him with his ancestors** in the city of David. (2 Kgs 15:7a lit.)

> Uzziah **lay down with his ancestors, and they buried him with his ancestors** *in the burial field of the kings because they said, "He had skin disease."* (2 Chr 26:23a lit.)

The isolation of Uzziah to a separate house while he was inflicted with skin disease in his life gets carried into his death by way of his separate entombment (26:21, 23). Leviticus 13:45–46 seems like a nearly inaudible undercurrent (trace) in which a person with skin disease remains alone outside the camp calling out "Ritually impure! Ritually impure!"

In sum, the Chronicler substantially expands the brief narrative of Uzziah in Kings according to his standard theological emphases. The Chronistic version spells out tangible evidence of success for devotion to Yahweh. Notably, the Chronicler provides dramatic backstory for the traditional comment on Uzziah's skin disease in Kings. In Chronicles, the immediate divine judgment against Uzziah for acting arrogantly and trespassing into the temple realm clings to him through his entire life and even into his burial.

26:18*~Lev 10:1, 10–11* (C) (priestly instruction on holy versus common) (* see teachers network). In the aftermath of Yahweh killing Nadab and Abihu for "unauthorized fire" in their censers—whatever that means—he took the opportunity to present a series of lasting ordinances for the sons of Aaron (Lev 10:1). The prohibition against serving at tabernacle intoxicated serves the purpose of ensuring clear-headed instruction of the laity regarding worship distinctions (10:9). When Uzziah walks into the temple with censer in hand to burn incense, priestly teachers offer him a crash course on worship distinctions with mild verbal parallels to Lev 10. While the terms for censer in Lev 10:1 and 2 Chr 26:19 differ, some of the language for burning incense and other thematic similarities suggest the possibility of interpretive allusion (bold signifies loose verbal similarities).

231. See discussion in Glatt-Gilad, "Regnal Formulae," 204, n. 80.

> This is . . . so that you [priests] can distinguish between **the holy** [הַקֹּדֶשׁ] and the common, between the unclean and the clean, and so you can teach the Israelites all the decrees Yahweh has given them through Moses. (Lev 10:10–11)

> They [priests] confronted King Uzziah and said, "It is not right for you, Uzziah, to burn incense to Yahweh. That is for the priests, the descendants of Aaron, **who have been made holy** [הַמְקֻדָּשִׁים] to burn incense. Leave the sanctuary, for you have been unfaithful; and you will not be honored by Yahweh God." [19] Uzziah, who had a censer in his hand ready to burn incense, became angry. While he was raging at the priests in their presence before the incense altar in Yahweh's temple, leprosy broke out on his forehead. (2 Chr 26:18–19†)

27:1–9/~/2 Kgs 15:32–38 (rule of Jotham). The Chronistic version of the rule of Jotham basically follows its synoptic counterpart with a few additions along the lines of emphasis on retribution. Note a synoptic comparison of the rule of Jotham:

	2 Kings	2 Chronicles
synchronism with Northern Kingdom	15:32	—
formulaic opening frame	15:33	27:1
formulaic evaluation	15:34	27:2a
notation on syncretistic practices of people	15:35a	27:2b
notation of rebuilding upper gate of temple	15:35b	27:3a
other building initiatives	—	27:3b–4
Jotham's regional dominion	—	27:5–6
summation and source citation	15:36	27:7
initial trouble from Israel and Aram	15:37	—
chronological note	—	27:8
death, burial, and succession notation	15:38	27:9

In recasting the comparison of Jotham and his father, the Chronicler needed to add an editorial adjustment because of the expansions in his version of Uzziah: "He did what was right in the eyes of Yahweh, just as his father Uzziah, *except he did not enter the temple of Yahweh*" (2 Chr 27:2a†, emphasis signifies Chronistic expansion). While Kings mentions the people's continued worship at open-air shrines (2 Kgs 15:35a), Chronicles softens the language to "the people, however, continued their corrupt practices" (2 Chr 27:2b). In addition to these and other minor editorial adjustments of the formulaic closing, the Chronicler adds an expansive reading of Jotham's building projects in Judah and his dominion over Ammon (27:3b–5). He also adds a theological comment, making blessing explicit, in the addition: "Jotham grew powerful because he walked steadfastly before Yahweh his God" (27:6). These minor adjustments align the brief presentation of Jotham's rule with the theological shape running across the Chronistic version of the Davidic kingdom.

28:1–27/~/2 Kgs 16:1–20 (rule of Ahaz). The Chronicler generally follows the formulaic narrative structure of Ahaz's rule in Kings but makes several changes and adds new elements. Note a synoptic comparison of the rule of Ahaz:

	2 Kings	2 Chronicles
synchronism with Northern Kingdom	16:1	—
formulaic opening frame and evaluation	16:2	28:1
list of infidelities	16:3–4	28:2–4
invasion of Aram-Israel alliance	16:5–6	—
defeat and exile to Aram-Israel alliance	—	28:5–8
Oded's prophetic message	—	28:9–11
good Samarians send Judean captives to Jericho[a]	—	28:12–15
Ahaz seeks help from Tiglath-pileser	16:7	28:16
losses to Edom, Philistia, and Assyria	—	28:17–20
tribute to Assyria from temple and palace	16:8	28:21
Ahaz's infidelity with the gods of Aram	16:9–16	28:22–23
temple treasures stripped and open air worship established	16:17–18	28:24–25
formulaic closing summation and source citations	16:19	28:26
death, burial, and succession notation	16:20	28:27

[a] "Samarians" refers to ancient peoples of Samaria versus "Samaritans" as Second Temple sectarians.

Many of the Chronicler's alterations to the rule of Ahaz accord with the kinds of changes he made to the line of Davidic kings up to this point. But some of the recasting of Ahaz goes further, including several distinct elements. The new kinds of exegetical interventions seem to bring Ahaz's infidelity to an all-time low point thus far. The Chronistic enhancement of Ahaz's declension, in part, sets up the dramatic reforms of Hezekiah. The infidelity-renewal pattern in the reigns of Ahaz and Hezekiah constitute part of the major narrative strategy of Chronicles's reinterpretation of the kingdom as presented in Kings (see Figure C1).

The Chronicler portrays Ahaz as the embodiment of infidelity: child sacrifice, exile to Aram and Ephraim (and Edom), Oded's prophetic message to Ephraim, the return of captives to Jericho, seeking help from the wrong places, and neglecting temple for false worship. First, the Chronicler expands the list of infidelities in the evaluation formula from Kings to include child sacrifice (see separate note on 2 Chr 28:3).

Second, the Chronicler inserts notations regarding the exile of Judeans to Damascus, Samaria, and Edom (28:5, 8, 17). For the Chronicler these military defeats and forced migrations signify Yahweh's judgment "because Judah had forsaken Yahweh, the God of their ancestors" (28:6). In this context "forsaking Yahweh" refers to syncretistic worship of regional deities (28:2–4).[232] Often biblical studies literature speaks of two exiles—Israel in 722 BCE and Judah in 586 BCE. These two exiles correspond to the fall of Samaria/Ephraim/Northern Kingdom of Israel and destruction of temple and fall of Jerusalem/Judah and, as such, function something like a shorthand for major political turning points. The Scriptures mention ten separate forced migrations—six in the period of the Assyrian crisis and four in the period of the Neo-Babylonian crisis.[233] There may be more, but these ten accounts point to protracted periods of forced migration associated with extinguishing the last vestiges of (puppet) political sovereignty of Samaria and Judah respectively. The Chronicler speaks of 200,000 Judean exiles to Samaria (28:8). This extremely large number comes close to Sennacherib's claim (201,105), when he performed forced migrations from many towns across Judah in 701—though this is usually taken as an extreme exaggeration according to the norms of Assyrian royal inscription propaganda.[234] The brief mention of forced migration of Judeans to Edom expands beyond the comment on their relocating to Elath after the Arameans defeated Judah there (28:17; 2 Kgs 16:6).[235] Elsewhere Scripture associates Edom with slave trade as well as eager spectatorship of Jerusalem's defeat by other predator nations.[236] In sum, the Chronicler presents forced migration as symptomatic of Yahweh's retribution against Judah's infidelity in worshiping other gods.

Third, Oded's prophetic message and Ephraim's response provide a remarkable exception to several Chronistic norms, which points to a complex reinterpretation of scriptural traditions (2 Chr 28:9–11). After the revolt of Jeroboam the only northern tribespersons to enjoy relationship with Yahweh were those who emigrated to Judah (11:14, 16; see note on 11:3). Thereafter the Chronicler treats the Northern Kingdom of Israel like any other foreign enemy (see notes on 18:1–19:3 and 22:1–9). Oded interprets the military defeat of Judah and their forced migration to Samaria as signs of divine wrath against

232. The Chronicler uses "Baals" (בְּעָלִים) to denote idols, much like one might refer to adhesive bandage strips or facial tissues by referring to popular brand names that replace the category. Referring to idols as "Baals" is commonplace in Scripture, see Judg 2:11; 3:7; 1 Sam 7:4; 12:10; 1 Kgs 18:18; Jer 2:23; 9:14[13]; Hos 2:13, 17[15, 19]; 11:2; 2 Chr 17:3; 24:7; 28:2; 33:3. Sometimes the use of Baals may refer to local versions (Judg 8:33; 10:6, 10; and maybe 2 Chr 34:4). See "בַּעַל," B.1.b *HALOT* 1:143.

233. For a list of ten exiles recorded in Scripture, see footnote in note on 1 Chr 5:3.

234. See *ANET*, 287–88. Cogan estimates c. 120,000 forced migrants (*Raging Torrent*, 120). On numerical hyperbole, see note on 2 Chr 13:1–23.

235. The Chronicler's revision works with either "of Aram" and "for Aram" MT or "of Edom" and "for Edom" in 2 Kgs 16:6 *BHS* apparatus.

236. See Amos 1:6, 9; Obad 11–14; Ps 137:7; cf. Ezek 25:12; 35:5, 12; Lam 4:22.

Judah and Israel respectively. Israel stands under "guilt" (אַשְׁמָה) here (28:10, 13) much the same way that Judah does elsewhere in Chronicles (1 Chr 21:3; 2 Chr 24:18; 33:23).[237] The reference to Ephraim as "fellow Israelites," here and in the sequel of the days of Hezekiah, highlights the Chronicler's emphasis upon the possibility of repenting and getting right with God for any of his people, even those of northern Israel (see esp. 28:8, 11; 30:7, 9). The message of Oded, focused as it is on historical exegesis, demonstrates within Chronistic narration that covenantal relationship with Yahweh may be restored even by a long wayward people like Ephraim (see Table C9). The leaders of Ephraim respond to Oded's message and talk the soldiers into liberating the Judean captives and returning the plunder (28:12–14).

Fourth, the named Ephraimite leaders act as good Samarians, providing for the needs of the Judean captives and returning them via donkey transit to Jericho (28:15). Messiah seems to appropriate and modify details of the Chronistic account of the good Samarians in his most famous parable (Luke 10:25–37). The language and structure of the Chronistic good Samarians LXX aligns in several respects with the good Samaritan.[238] Both the good Samarians and good Samaritan use their own resources to anoint and provide donkey transit to Jericho. Messiah uses his parable to cause the Torah scholar to interpret Lev 19:18b in a way that semantically stretches the "neighbor" (רֵעַ/πλησίον) (Lev 19:18b; Luke 10:36).[239] Based on the good Samaritan modeled on the good Samarians to leverage Lev 19:18b, Spencer works hard to see 2 Chr 28:15 alluding to Lev 19:18b. Even with his best evidence of a Qumran sectarian writing using "brother" (אָח) for "neighbor" (רֵעַ) to paraphrase Lev 19:18b, the lack of "love" (אהב) or any other similarity rules out an allusion.[240] It seems more likely to see Messiah's exegetical advances as beginning with a recovery of a parallel within Lev 19 itself and then going even further (bold signifies verbal parallel, and italics signify different referents):

> **Love** *your neighbor* [רֵעַ] **as yourself.** (Lev 19:18b)
>
> The *foreigner residing* [גֵּר] among you must be treated as your native-born. **Love** them **as yourself.** (19:34)

Messiah's exegetical advancement includes stretching the semantic function of "neighbor" (רֵעַ) even beyond "residing foreigner" (גֵּר) by associating the neighbor not

237. See "אַשְׁמָה," *HALOT* 1:96.

238. The contexts feature thematic similarities such as anointing and transporting by donkey, as well as numerous verbal parallels: wound (πληγή), 2 Chr 28:5 LXX; Luke 10:30; "strip off/put on," (ἐνδύω/ἐνδύω), 2 Chr 28:15 LXX; Luke 10:30; "Jericho" (Ἰεριχώ), 2 Chr 28:15 LXX; Luke 10:35 (see Spencer, "2 Chronicles 28:5–15," 320–21).

239. The LXX uses πλησίον for רֵעַ in the vast majority of cases, see Muraoka, *Greek ≈ Hebrew/Aramaic Index*, 97.

240. See Spencer, "2 Chronicles 28:5–15," 335–37. Though 4Q266/CD 6.20–21 does use "brother" (אָח) for "neighbor" (רֵעַ), the next line uses "residing foreigner" (גֵּר), which shows the sectarians are here reading Lev 19:18 in light of 19:34.

with a residing foreigner but a loathed Samaritan acting in accordance with 2 Chr 28:15 (compare note on Lev 19:18b, 33–34). Kalimi suggests that the Chronicler uses this story to portray Ahaz as "even worse" than the Northern Kingdom of Israel.[241] Kalimi deduces this by what the Samaritan of Messiah's parable might say about the Samarians of 2 Chr 28. The proposals of Spencer and Kalimi, though thoughtful, overread the parable of the good Samaritan itself as a quasi-allegory of the good Samarians versus Ahaz in 2 Chr 28. In short, the parable of the good Samaritan is loosely based on the repentant act of the good Samarians, but the parabolic riddle has been placed in a different context with a different purpose. Messiah extends the command to love neighbors as an important part of progressive revelation. The purpose of the good Samarians in 2 Chr 28, in part, turns on putting Ahaz in a bad light. The Samarians respond to Oded's threats with repentance and mercy, while Ahaz follows his own agenda seeking help from the Assyrian king and Aramean gods (2 Chr 28:16, 23).

Fifth, the Chronicler revises Ahaz's infidelities to demonstrate that he sought help in all the wrong places (28:16–23). The use of the leading word "help" (עזר) five times ties together the path of Ahaz from bad to worse (28:15, 16, 21, 23[2x]; all five appear only in Chronicles, not in Kings). In place of Deuteronomistic Ahaz making a covenant of vassalage with Tiglath-pileser—"I am your slave and your son" (2 Kgs 16:7 lit.)—Chronistic Ahaz simply seeks his "help" (2 Chr 28:16). The Chronicler's softening of the initial inquiry from overt vassalage uncovers the purpose of securing help and allows him to develop Ahaz's downfall with some irony.[242] The Chronicler does not bother to remind readers of the problem of seeking help from foreign alliances, perhaps since it has already come up repeatedly (16:7–9; 20:35–37; 25:7–8). The man of God spoke to Amaziah in a way that puts on display how the Chronicler handles Ahaz's extreme misstep (underlining and bold signify verbal parallels, and italics signify rationale clauses):

> But a man of God came to him [Amaziah] and said, "Your Majesty, these troops from Israel must not march with you, *for* [כִּי] *Yahweh is not with Israel*—not with any of the people of Ephraim. Even if you go and fight courageously in battle, God will <u>cause your downfall</u> before the enemy, *for* [כִּי] *God has the power* ***to help*** [לעזר] *or <u>to cause a downfall</u>* [לכשל]." (25:7–8†)[243]
>
> At that time King Ahaz sent to the kings of Assyria ***for help*** [לעזר]. (28:16)

241. See Kalimi, "Robbers on the Road," 52.

242. On the Chroniclers sarcasm in this context, see Williamson, *1 and 2 Chronicles*, 348.

243. Compare "to" (לְ) with inf. const. of purpose (GKC §114g), which functions as counterpart to causal "for" (כִּי) (§158b). Also, in Chronicles "downfall" (כשל) only appears in these non-synoptic passages (2 Chr 25:8; 28:15, 23).

> He offered sacrifices to the gods of Damascus, who had defeated him; for he thought, "*Since* [כִּי] *the gods of the kings of Aram* ***have helped*** *them* [עזר], *I will sacrifice to them so* ***they will help*** *me* [עזר]." But they were his <u>downfall</u> [כשל] and of all Israel. (28:23†)[244]

When Ahaz seeks *help* from Assyria, the Edomites take captives (28:17); the Philistines capture Judean towns (28:18); Tiglath-pileser gives him trouble instead of *help* (28:20); so Ahaz gives Tiglath-pileser tribute from temple and palace, which does not *help* (28:21); then Ahaz turns to the gods of Damascus for *help* (28:23). As the Chronicler says, Ahaz becomes "most unfaithful" and becomes "even more unfaithful to Yahweh" (28:19, 22).

Sixth, the Chronicler explains that not only did Ahaz take furnishings from the temple (28:24; 2 Kgs 16:12–18) but closed the temple altogether (2 Chr 28:24). In place of temple worship, Ahaz set up various open-air shrines and "aroused the anger of Yahweh" (28:25). The closing of the temple helps the Chronicler's declension-renewal paradigmatic alignment: Ahaz closing the temple doors (28:24) versus Hezekiah reopening the temple doors (29:3; see Figure C1).

Seventh, the Chronicler makes an adjustment to the burial formula. The Chronicler clarifies that Ahaz was "not placed in the tombs of the kings of Israel" (28:27; cf. 2 Kgs 16:20). Although Ahaz did not have a skin disease like Uzziah, he is buried elsewhere (2 Chr 26:23; 28:27).

In sum, the Chronicler uses divine judgment in terms of exile along with closing of the temple as symptomatic of the extreme declension in Ahaz's day. He enhances Ahaz's infidelity by contrasting him with even the people of Ephraim, who are responsive to God's prophetic message in this case. This time of rebellion anticipates the renewal of Hezekiah.

28:3//2 Kgs 16:3 (A)+Jer 19:5–6 (B) (child sacrifice in the Valley of Ben Hinnom). Kings twice uses the opaque phrase "he passed his son through the fire" of the notoriously wicked kings Ahaz and Manasseh (2 Kgs 16:3; 21:6 lit.). The phrase could be interpreted as a euphemism for child sacrifice or taken more literally as some kind of fire ritual, which does not cause the child permanent harm. The Chronicler closes the gap, inferring child sacrifice by locating the ritual in the Valley of Ben Hinnom, famously renamed "valley of slaughter" by Jeremiah due to child sacrifices to false gods (Jer 7:31–32; 19:5–6, quasi-doublet). Note how the exegetical blending makes explicit the grievous sin of Ahab (italics signify near verbatim parallels, bold signifies verbal parallels at the level of roots, and underlining signifies synonyms):

> *He* [Ahaz] *followed the ways of the kings of Israel and even made his son* [בְּנוֹ] pass through [עבר] *the fire, engaging in the detestable practices of the nations Yahweh had driven out before the Israelites.* (2 Kgs 16:3†)

---

244. Though too subtle to build on, it is worth noting the Samarians put the "downfallen" (כשל Q) on donkeys in light of the "downfall" (כשל Hif) of Ahaz (28:15, 23).

They have built the high places of Topheth **in the Valley of Ben Hinnom** to burn [סרף] **their sons** and daughters [אֶת־בְּנֵיהֶם וְאֶת־בְּנֹתֵיהֶם] **in the fire**—something I did not command, nor did it enter my mind. (Jer 7:31)

They have built the high places of **Baal** to burn [סרף] **their children** [בְּנֵיהֶם] **in the fire** as offerings to Baal—something I did not command or mention, nor did it enter my mind. So beware, the days are coming, declares Yahweh, when people will no longer call this place Topheth or **the Valley of Ben Hinnom**, but the Valley of Slaughter. (19:5–6)

He [Ahaz] *followed the ways of the kings of Israel* and also made idols for worshiping the **Baals.** [3] He burned sacrifices **in the Valley of Ben Hinnom** and he burned [בער] ***his children*** [בָּנָיו] ***in the fire***, *engaging in the detestable practices of the nations Yahweh had driven out before the Israelites.* (2 Chr 28:2–3†)

Lemke claims the shift from "his son" (בנו) in 2 Kgs 16:3 to "his sons" (בניו) in 2 Chr 28:3 is merely a defective to plene shift in accord with hundreds of such spelling updates.[245] Full or plene spellings are a sign of Late Biblical Hebrew and characteristic of Chronicles in general.[246] However, all other synoptic uses of "his son" (בנו) in Chronicles match Samuel/Kings, as do the few cases of "his sons" (בניו). The only exceptions are 2 Chr 28:3 and 33:6, which adjust the child sacrifices of Ahaz and Manasseh in an identical way by blending the context with interpretative allusion of Jer 19:5–6 (and/or 7:31). There is good reason to consider the pluralization to "his sons" in these two cases as intentional, requiring reconsideration of Lemke's pushback.[247] This textual issue—whether Ahaz and Manasseh each burned one or multiple children in sacrifice to other gods—does not bear on the larger point being made here.

One of the elements that makes splicing a paraphrase of Jer 19:5–6 into 2 Chr 28:2–3 probable versus possible is the proximate additional connection with Manasseh's sins in Kings (2 Kgs 21:6; cf. 2 Chr 33:6). Both Jeremiah and Kings speak of the "innocent blood" with which Manasseh "filled" Jerusalem (Jer 19:4; 2 Kgs 21:16).[248] Psalm 106:37–38 uses similar language for falling into child sacrifice and may serve as an undercurrent to the Chronicler's ideology since he worked with other parts of Ps 106 elsewhere (Ps 106:1, 47–48//1 Chr 16:34–36).

In sum, the Chronicler's exegetical intervention amounts to replacing a euphemism for child sacrifice with Jeremiah's stronger literal condemnation.

29:1–2/~/2 Kgs 18:1–8 (opening frame of rule of Hezekiah). Chronicles features extensive new materials on the rule of Hezekiah, reshaping the story of this important

245. See Lemke, "Synoptic Problem," 360; *BHS* apparatus.

246. See Anderson and Forbes, *Spelling*, 312–18.

247. The majority of Lemke's examples are correct, as footnotes through this chapter affirm ("Synoptic Problem").

248. Also note the use of "burned incense" (קטר) in Jer 19:4; 2 Chr 28:3, 4.

king in many ways. Most of the new materials are non-synoptic and are not treated here. But the Chronicler uses the opening frame that appears in Kings before inserting new materials, which invites broad contrast between the Deuteronomistic and Chronistic versions of Hezekiah (2 Kgs 18:1–3; 2 Chr 29:1–2). Isaiah also uses the story of Hezekiah that appears in Kings and can therefore be compared as well (see note on Isa 36–39). Note a synoptic comparison of the rule of Hezekiah:

	2 Kings	Isaiah	2 Chronicles
synchronism with Northern Kingdom	18:1	—	—
formulaic opening frame and evaluation	18:2–3	—	29:1–2
faithful reforms of Hezekiah	18:4–8	—	—
fall of Samaria	18:9–12	—	—
temple restored	—	—	29:3–36
Israel to celebrate Passover with Judah	—	—	30:1–31:1
provisions for priests	—	—	31:2–21
troubles of Hezekiah[a]	18:13–20:21	36:1–39:8	32:1–33

[a] See the detailed comparison in the synoptic comparison in the note on 2 Chr 32:1–23.

Kings presents Hezekiah as the most faithful Davidic king, making use of faith as a leading word (2 Kgs 18:5). The narrative of Hezekiah's rule ends by blaming his selfishness for the eventual fall of the kingdom (20:16–18). The disappointing conclusion to a faithful rule aligns with the central Deuteronomistic theme of the inevitability of the fall of Jerusalem. In many ways the story of Hezekiah's faithfulness in Isaiah serves as a contrast to the unfaithfulness of Ahaz (Isa 7:3; 36:2). Isaiah follows Kings and presents the ending of Hezekiah's rule as an anticipation of the Babylonian exile but looks past this to the return from exile as a new exodus and return (40–55).

The Chronicler's major exegetical advancement consists of centering Hezekiah's faithful reforms on temple worship. He contrasts Hezekiah as reopening the temple his father Ahaz had closed (2 Chr 28:24; 29:3). The Chronicler literarily but not exegetically reshaped Hezekiah in several ways to be like Solomon (see Filters). Chronistic Hezekiah in many ways epitomizes Chronistic emphases. He restores temple worship and reaches out to bring the remnant of the northern tribes back into their rightful place in temple worship (30:1–11). The Chronicler includes a greatly abbreviated version of Sennacherib's invasion and an extremely brief acknowledgement of hosting the Babylonian envoys (32:1–30, 31). In sum, the Chronicler reshapes Hezekiah to serve as a high point of worship renewal after the low point of Ahaz's rebellion (see Figure C1).

29:7~Lev 24:1–4 (B) (lamps of house of Yahweh). The Chronicler alludes to the commandment to keep the "lamps" of the worship shrine lit perpetually (Lev 24:1–4). The allusion is probable since 2 Chr 29:18 refers to the next instruction regarding bread (24:5–9; see note on 2 Chr 29:18). The violation of the command gets tied to the closing of the temple by Ahaz (2 Chr 28:24). Though the narrative only makes broad allusion to the commands for perpetually maintaining light and bread before Yahweh, the Chronicler applies these to his interpretation of divine judgment and reforms in the days of Ahaz and Hezekiah (Lev 24:1–4, 5–9; 2 Chr 29:7, 18). An important exegetical advancement in Chronicles results from applying this priestly infraction to the "infidelity" (מעל) of the worshiping community at large (29:5). The Chronicler makes direct causal connection between failing to maintain the commands for light before the divine presence and judgment by captivity, presumably by Damascus, Samaria, and Edom (29:9; cf. 28:5, 8, 17). This connection hints not too subtly at the desecration of the temple as a basis for the Babylonian exile (cf. 36:14).

29:11~Num 18:1–7 (C) (divine election of priests and Levites). Hezekiah acknowledges that the priests and Levites serve by divine election and ties that to their responsibility on behalf of Israel (2 Chr 29:11). The most explicit statement of priestly and Levitical responsibility appears in legal instruction placed directly after Korah's rebellion and the reaffirmation of the election of Aaron (Num 18:1–7; on Levites cf. 3:11–13; 4:1–3). Hezekiah's use of the term "choose" (בחר) may also echo the dramatic narrative (16:5, 7; 17:5[20]). Hezekiah makes only a broad allusion but leverages the command to explain the collective responsibility and basis for judgment by exile (2 Chr 29:9; cf. 28:8). The exegetical function here does not relate to details of the command itself or its associated narrative but to the cause-effect of retribution contingent upon (dis)obedience.

29:18~Lev 24:5–9* (B) (table and rows of bread in temple) (* see Sabbath network). The brief reference to the command for "rows of bread on the table" in the temple likely alludes to the instruction in Lev 24:5–9 (2 Chr 29:18). This allusion extends the implications for the command for perpetual lights referenced in Hezekiah's charge (29:7, see note). The Chronicler mentions the bread elsewhere (1 Chr 9:32; 2 Chr 2:4).

29:25–30~1 Chr 23–26 (B)+selected psalms superscriptions (C) (authorizing use of psalms for worship). The Chronicler explicitly marks the Levitical leadership in worship according to the authority of David (2 Chr 29:25; 1 Chr 23–26; see esp. 25:1; cf. Table C20). Chronicles advances authority by including Hezekiah's command to use the psalms of David and Asaph as a worship curriculum. The headings on the canonical psalms reflect this tradition with over seventy psalms "of David" and about a dozen psalms "of Asaph" (Pss 50; 73–83).[249]

30:2–3~Num 9:9–11 (B) (shifting Passover observance for the defiled to second month). Hezekiah collectively applies the standard command for ritually impaired individuals to reschedule Passover by decreeing a shift to the second month for all Israel (2 Chr 30:2–3; cf. Num 9:9–11). The pragmatic basis of Hezekiah's decision to adjust the worship calendar

---

249. On the association with David of almost all persons named in headings of Psalter, see Table P4 and immediately preceding paragraph in Psalms Filters.

stems from the need to reform, including ritual purification, and reinitiate temple worship after it had been closed (2 Chr 28:24; 29:3, 5–6, 15). Since Yahweh had set the precedent for adjusting the date of Passover for individual situations of ritual impurity and personal travel schedule, the collective decision of Hezekiah seems a small exegetical advancement compared to celebrating Passover while still ritually impure (see note on 30:18–20).

30:16~Num 18:1–7 (C)+Lev 1:5 (C) (Levites bring blood from slaughter to priests). The Chronicler marks as based on Torah the exchange of sacrificial blood between Levites who slaughter and priests (2 Chr 30:16).[250] The Chronicler here narrates the insertion of the Levites between laity who slaughter and priests who offer sacrifice and dash blood on the altar (Lev 1:5; 9:9, 12, 18; 17:6; Num 18:1–7). The Levites serve priests in part by preserving the inner sanctuary for the priests who alone bear the burden of holiness (Num 18:1–7; cf. Ezek 44:11, 15–16). The cooperation between priests and Levites throughout Chronicles supports tiered holiness with Levites as go-betweens for laity and priests.

30:18–20~Num 9:10 (C)+2 Chr 7:14 (B) (unlawful Passover participants forgiven). The Chronicler repeatedly and explicitly marks the accord of Hezekiah's worship with Torah, prophets, and David (2 Chr 29:15, 25; 30:12; 16; 31:3, 21; cf. Table C20). The Chronicler double marks the northern tribes breaking the law—"Contrary to *what was written* . . . not clean *according to the rules* of the sanctuary" (30:18, 19, emphasis mine). Hezekiah calls upon Yahweh to pardon the Torah violators who seek Yahweh by celebrating Passover even while ritually impaired (30:18–20). The Chronicler places the "healing" by Yahweh as part of direct narration. Torah requires Passover participation and requires ceremonial purity (Num 9:10; cf. Lev 7:19–21; 15:31). The Chronicler intentionally locates this narrative situation outside the bounds of Torah regulations. He exegetically advances past a seemingly categorical impasse by allusion to Yahweh's second revelation to Solomon (bold signifies verbal parallels, italics signify synonyms, and broken underlining signifies marking Torah):

> If my people, who are called by my name, will humble themselves and **pray** and *seek* my face and turn from their wicked ways, then **I will hear** from heaven, and I will *forgive* their sin and **will heal** their land. (2 Chr 7:14)

> Although most of the many people who came from Ephraim, Manasseh, Issachar and Zebulun had not purified themselves, yet they ate the Passover, contrary to what was written. But Hezekiah **prayed** for them, saying, "May Yahweh, who is good, *pardon* everyone [19] who sets their heart on *seeking* God—Yahweh, the God of their ancestors—even if they are not clean according to the rules of the sanctuary." [20] And Yahweh **heard** Hezekiah and **healed** the people. (30:18–20)

250. On difficulties when marked citations offer interpretations beyond the source text, see Fishbane, *Biblical Interpretation*, 533; Schniedewind, "Chronicler as Interpreter," 176. Also see Marking in Hermeneutical Profile of the Use of Scripture in Ezra-Nehemiah.

In a context dominated by the letter of legal instructions—"According to Torah" and the like—Yahweh's pardon of Torah violators surprises.[251] The exegetical advancement is based on Yahweh's own revelation to Solomon. The allusion to the theophany includes vertical context within it since the donor text—1 Chr 7:14—features an interpretive blend of, especially, Lev 26:40–41 and 2 Chr 6:27, 30 (see note on 7:11–22; on vertical context see Glossary). In the receptor text of Hezekiah's Passover, Yahweh pardons based on his earlier exegetical advancement of revelation to Solomon. In many places the prophets condemn phony worship—external practices without corresponding inward realities incite divine wrath (see Table A3 in Amos Filters). The Chronicler here offers a counterpart in which Yahweh forgives Torah violators who seek him.

The use of the paradigmatic revelation to Solomon extends across the entire context (30:6, 9, 11, 18, 19, 20). The Chronicler echoes four terms of human worship and three terms of divine restoration from 2 Chr 7:14 in the account of Hezekiah's Passover.[252] Three of four worship terms and two of three restoration terms match verbally and the other two correspond to synonyms (see Table C23):

TABLE C23: EXTENDED ECHO–EFFECT OF THE SECOND SOLOMONIC THEOPHANY IN HEZEKIAH'S PASSOVER

	Revelation to Solomon (2 Chr 7:14)	Passover of Hezekiah (2 Chr 30)
Human worship	humble themselves (כנע)	humbled themselves (כנע) (30:11)
	pray (פלל)	prayer (פלל) (30:18)
	seek (בקש)	seek (דרש)[a] (30:19)
	turn (שוב)	return (שוב) (30:6, 9)
Divine restoration	will hear (שמע)	hear (שמע) (30:20)
	will forgive (סלח)	pardon (כפר)[b] (30:18)
	will heal (רפא)	heal (רפא) (30:20)

[a] On the nearly identical function of "seek" (בקשׁ) and "seek" (דרשׁ) in Chronicles see the discussion following Table C2.

[b] On the sense of "atone" in 2 Chr 30:18 as forgive and exempt from punishment, see *Piel* no. 3 "כפר," *HALOT* 1:494.

The Chronicler does not promote relationship with Yahweh predicated upon ceremonial procedures. Worship intentions—humility, prayer, turning from sin, seeking Yahweh—"override" ceremonial regulations by Yahweh's own revelatory authority.[253] The worship elements define the kind of relationship Yahweh desires with or without ceremonial correctness. The Chronicler's exegetical advances lay the groundwork for forgiveness and redemptive relationship taken up in many ways in the New Testament.

251. Rudolph, "Problems," 407; Williamson, *1 and 2 Chronicles*, 370; Mabie, "1 and 2 Chronicles," 4:293.

252. See Williamson, *1 and 2 Chronicles*, 368, 370.

253. Ibid., 370. Also see Klein, *2 Chronicles*, 438.

31:3~Deut 16:16–17 (C)+Num 28–29 (C) (bring offerings to temple for all worship). The Chronicler makes broad allusion to Torah contexts but seems to interpret these by extrapolating the priority of bringing offerings to each worship event. The Chronicler marks Hezekiah's contribution with a Chronistic stock phrase of the worship calendar (italics signify stock phrase [see Filters], and broken underlining signifies marking Torah):

> The king contributed from his own possessions for the morning and evening burnt offerings and for the burnt offerings *on the Sabbaths, at the New Moons and at the appointed festivals* as written in the Torah of Yahweh. (2 Chr 31:3)

The Chronistic stock phrase preceded by additional contributions connotes the comprehensive list of worship in Num 28–29: daily (Num 28:3–8), Sabbath (28:9–10), new moons (28:11–15), Passover (28:16–25), Weeks (28:26–31), Trumpets (29:1–6), Day of Atonement (29:7–11), Tabernacles (29:12–38). The expanded stock phrase including all temple worship implies that each one is an opportunity for contribution. The Chronicler extrapolates from a Torah precedent by the people bringing firstfruits associated with Weeks and tithes associated with Tabernacles (2 Chr 31:5, 6). Deuteronomy houses legal exegesis based on the covenant collection (Exod 23:14–17) and affirms that Passover, Weeks, and Tabernacles form a set relative to offerings: "*No one should appear before Yahweh empty-handed.* Each of you must bring a gift in proportion to the way Yahweh your God has blessed you" (Deut 16:16–17, emphasis mine; see note ad loc.). Based on Deuteronomy's explicit principle of offerings for all three pilgrimage festivals, the Chronicler further extrapolates, making offerings part of the entire worship calendar.[254]

32:1–23~2 Kgs 18:13–19:37 (A) (Sennacherib invades Judah). Though 2 Chr 29:1–2 adapts the opening formula of the rule of Hezekiah in Kings, the two accounts treat different events except for a triple synoptic element shared by 2 Chr 32 (see the synoptic table in note on 2 Chr 29:1–2). Note a synoptic comparison of the troubles of Hezekiah:

	2 Kings	Isaiah	2 Chronicles
invasion of Assyria	18:13	36:1	32:1
submission and tribute to Assyria	18:14–16	—	—
preparation for siege	—	{22:9–11}	32:2–5
Hezekiah encourages the troops	—	—	32:6–8
Sennacherib invades Judah	18:17–19:37	36:2–37:38	32:9–23
Hezekiah's illness[a]	20:1–11	38:1–8, {21–22}	32:24–26

(cont.)

254. See Rendtorff, "Chronicles," 260–63.

	2 Kings	Isaiah	2 Chronicles
song of Hezekiah	—	38:9–20	—
wealth of Hezekiah	—	—	32:27–30
visitation of Babylonian envoys	20:12–19	39:1–8	32:31
death of Hezekiah	20:20–21	—	32:32–33

[a] On the rearrangement of 2 Kgs 20:1–13//Isa 38:1–39:2, see note on Isa 38:21–22.

The Chronicler greatly condenses, while following in the main, the Deuteronomistic account of Sennacherib's invasion. In one place the Chronicler narrates, with similarities to the valley of vision oracle, preparations for siege by frustrating the water supply outside the city and strengthening the city walls (2 Chr 32:3–5; Isa 22:9–11). If Isaiah speaks of Hezekiah and if the Chronicler alludes to this oracle, they make different points. Isaiah accuses the king of not looking to the one who "made it" and "planned it" (22:11). The Chronicler relates Hezekiah's faithfulness in direct discourse (2 Chr 32:7–8). The two accounts accord regarding material details, even while Hezekiah functions differently, according to their respective emphases.[255] Isaiah 36–39//2 Kings 18–20 present Hezekiah as faithful during the invasion and self-serving when hosting Babylonian representatives. The Chronistic story of temple patronage and worship by Davidic kings emphasizes Hezekiah's fidelity to God. These differences relate to what Aristotle refers to as plot selectivity (see Hermeneutical Profile of the Use of Scripture in Chronicles).

Though much discussion surrounds the apparently composite nature of the military drama in Kings, the rationale from the abbreviated Chronistic account seems to support a long-running emphasis on retribution. The Chronistic additions provide detail of Hezekiah's word of encouragement to his officers (32:6–8). This account accents the fortitude of Hezekiah while Kings stresses his anxieties.

Both Kings and Chronicles mention Hezekiah crying out in prayer (2 Kgs 19:15; 2 Chr 32:20). While Kings embeds the prayer and Isaiah's response in the narrative (2 Kgs 19:15–19, 20–32), the Chronicler merely mentions Hezekiah and Isaiah crying out together followed immediately by a celestial messenger of death dispatched against the Assyrian army—asked and answered in rapid succession (2 Chr 32:20–21). Like Kings, Chronicles jump cuts from the deliverance from the invasion in 701 BCE to the death of Sennacherib twenty years later in 681 (32:21b; 2 Kgs 19:37).[256]

32:24–26, 31~2 Kgs 20:1–11, 12–19/~/Isa 38:1–20; 39:1–8 (C)+Deut 8:2 (B) (Hezekiah's illness and receiving Babylonian representatives). In contrast to the lengthy presentation of Hezekiah's sickness, miraculous recovery, and hosting the dignitaries in Kings and Isaiah, the Chronicler handles these events in a few verses. Although

255. See Childs, *Isaiah and the Assyrian Crisis*, 106, 110.
256. See Kalimi, "Literary-Chronological Proximity," 335.

Chronistic Hezekiah enjoys more favorable commentary, importantly, he is accused of pride—"His heart became high" (2 Chr 32:25 lit.).

In Chronicles Hezekiah's illness and proud heart (32:24, 25–26) and visitors (32:31) frame a brief accounting of his wealth (32:27–30). The description of his affluence and related building projects seems to be part of the literary shaping of Hezekiah along the lines of Solomon (9:13–14; 32:27–29; see Filters). These praises wrap up with "He succeeded in everything he undertook" (32:30). The critical issue at hand relates to the exegetical interventions in vv. 25–26. Compare the shared language with Deut 8:2 (bold signifies verbal parallel, italics signify shift in pronouns, and stylized underlining signifies potential interpretation in Chronicles):

> Remember how Yahweh your God led you all the way in the wilderness these forty years, to humble and **test *you* in order to know** what **was in *your* heart**, whether or not you would keep his commands. (Deut 8:2)

> [Isaiah said] "And some of your descendants, your own flesh and blood who will be born to you, will be taken away, and they will become eunuchs in the palace of the king of Babylon." "The word of Yahweh you have spoken is good," Hezekiah replied. For he thought, "Will there not be peace and security in my lifetime?" (2 Kgs 20:18–19// Isa 39:7–8)

> But Hezekiah's heart was proud and he did not respond to the kindness shown him; therefore Yahweh's wrath was on him and on Judah and Jerusalem. Then Hezekiah repented of the pride of his heart, as did the people of Jerusalem; therefore Yahweh's wrath did not come on them during the days of Hezekiah. . . . But when envoys were sent by the rulers of Babylon to ask him about the miraculous sign that had occurred in the land, God left him **to test *him*** and **to know** everything that **was in *his* heart.** (2 Chr 32:25–26, 31)

The extreme vagueness of Hezekiah's pride of heart and the wrath of Yahweh, both used twice, is the remarkable feature of the Chronicler's theological commentary (32:25–26).[257] In the parent text 2 Kgs 20//Isa 39, Hezekiah's pride seems to refer to showing off the treasures of Jerusalem to his guests. But the Chronicler comes back to this event after overviewing Hezekiah's Solomon-like wealth (2 Chr 32:31). The deliverance from the "wrath of Yahweh" (32:25) initially seems like it refers to deliverance from Sennacherib, but, again, this has already been wrapped up (32:22). In both 2 Kgs 20:19 and Isa 39:8 Hezekiah's outward profession that the word of judgment is "good" gets juxtaposed with some irony against his interior speech favoring his own peace but not looking to the next

257. See Japhet, *I & II Chronicles*, 993–94.

generation.[258] In Kings, readers wonder if he trained his son in Torah as called for in Deut 6:7 and if Hezekiah's fifteen bonus years included siring the wicked Manasseh coronated at age twelve (2 Kgs 21:1). In Isaiah, the exile lives between Isa 39 and 40 immediately after Hezekiah accepts judgment on his posterity with his mouth and peace for himself in his heart. But, as marked with wavy underlining above, readers wonder if the Chronicler regards Hezekiah's verbal submission—Yahweh's word is "good" (2 Kgs 20:19//Isa 39:8)—as a "confession" (כנע). The Chronicler uses the language of deferred judgment—"Therefore Yahweh's wrath did not come on them during the days of Hezekiah" (2 Chr 32:26).[259] Although the Chronicler regularly settles retributive accounts during the rule of each ruler, the exception in the case of Hezekiah, taken over from Kings, anticipates the deferred judgment of the entire Davidic kingdom in the seventy years of Jeremiah (36:21; cf. 34:27–28).[260]

Another element suggests the complexity of the Chronicler's subtle interpretation of Hezekiah, namely, the allusive use of the forty years of wilderness temptation as heart testing (Deut 8:2). Predictably, commentators say Hezekiah passed or failed the test, often citing other contexts.[261] In the Chronicler's own context, the twofold use of pride "of his heart" in 2 Chr 32:25, 26 and the divine testing of all that was "in his heart" in v. 31 suggests he failed, then repented, securing peace in his own day even after failing like Israel had in the wilderness. This suggestion is strengthened if 32:25–26 and 32:31 frame the summary of Hezekiah's wealth as suggested above. Irrespective of how to land on these subtleties, the combination of subtlety and complexity characterizes the Chronicler's commentary on Hezekiah.

32:32–33/~/2 Kgs 20:20–21 (death of Hezekiah). The Chronicler mildly expands the death-and-burial formula of Hezekiah to align it with the extensive presentation of worship reforms introduced to turn around the kingdom after the severe decline during the rule of Ahaz. The Chronicler adds the term "his acts of devotion" (2 Chr 32:32), which may connect with his earlier addition "acts of faithfulness" (32:1).[262] Both of these theologically loaded terms could serve as shorthand for his strenuous efforts toward renewed worship of Yahweh, including Hezekiah's initiatives to regather the remnant of the Northern Kingdom of Israel.

33:1–20/~/2 Kgs 21:1–18 (A)+25:7 (C) (rule of Manasseh). The Chronicler significantly adjusts the presentation of Manasseh. Note a synoptic comparison of the rule of Manasseh:

---

258. On "and he said" (ויאמר) as short for "and he said in his heart" (ויאמר בלבו), see Carasik, *Theologies*, 203; also see Steiner, "'He Said, He Said,'" 485–91.

259. See Ackroyd, "Chronicler as Exegete," 11.

260. See Schnittjer, "Individual versus Collective Retribution," 131.

261. See Japhet, *I & II Chronicles*, 996 (passed, citing Job 1:21; 2:10); Mabie, "1 and 2 Chronicles," 4:306 (failed, citing Isa 39:3–7).

262. See Glatt-Gilad, "Regnal Formulae," 197–98. On "covenantal loyalties" (2 Chr 32:32) as "godly actions," see "II חֶסֶד," 3.a *HALOT* 1:337, on "fidelity" (32:1) as "acts of faithfulness," see "אֱמֶת," no. 3 *HALOT* 1:69.

	2 Kings	2 Chronicles
opening formula	21:1	33:1
evaluation formula	21:2	33:2
list of rebellions	21:3–9	33:3–9
prophetic warning	21:10–16	—
Babylonian captivity of Manasseh	—	33:10–11
repentance and return of Manasseh	—	33:12–13
restoration and reformation of Jerusalem and temple	—	33:14–17
formulaic source citation	21:17	33:18
synopsis of source materials of seers	—	33:19
death and burial formula[a]	21:18	33:20

[a] The absence of buried "in the garden" (בְּגַן) in 2 Chr 33:20 MT versus LXX and 2 Kgs 21:18 may be a textual corruption (see *BHS*; Dillard, *2 Chronicles*, 264; Japhet, *I & II Chronicles*, 1012–13).

The Chronistic re-presentation of Manasseh features dramatic exegetical intervention. The Chronicler's motivations may include seeking to balance the narrative retribution scales in light of Manasseh's lengthy fifty-five-year reign. The paradigmatic shape of the account of Manasseh in Chronicles—rebellious earlier Manasseh and repentant later Manasseh—recounts in one rule the full arch from decline to restoration, elsewhere handled in multi-generational sequence: Saul then David-Solomon, Ahaz then Hezekiah, and exiles then expected return under the edict of Cyrus (see Figure C1, Table C10). But in contrast with the Deuteronomistic narrative, the Chronistic enhancements become even more forceful.

While the Deuteronomist places the roots of exilic doom within the story of Hezekiah (2 Kgs 20:18), the categorical and unremitting rebellion of Manasseh garners strong condemnation. The narrator unflatteringly compares his Baal and Asherah worship with Ahab, not carried over into Chronicles (21:3; cf. 2 Chr 33:3). Kings also features prophetic condemnation assuring the doom of Jerusalem for the sin of Manasseh, also not carried over into Chronicles (2 Kgs 21:10–16). The Deuteronomist goes even further, repeating the fall of Judah because of the sin of Manasseh between Josiah's reform and death and again when narrating Nebuchadnezzar's 597 siege of Jerusalem (23:26–27; 24:3–4). The Deuteronomist blames Manasseh in line with Jeremiah's claims that even the combined efforts of the most successful intercessors—Moses and Samuel—would not stop judgment against Jerusalem for what Manasseh did many years before (Jer 15:1, 4). Appreciating what the Chronicler does here requires keeping in view these categorical traditional condemnations of Manasseh.

By the Chronicler's day Manasseh had long carried the blame for exile. The Chronicler includes the details of Manasseh's confinement in Babylon, which makes him a powerful retrospective type of Judean exiles. The Chronicler may have strengthened this by including imagery from Zedekiah's Babylonian captivity in the description of Manasseh's imprisonment (2 Kgs 25:7; 2 Chr 33:11).[263] Simply put, if even Manasseh can repent while a captive in Babylon, there is hope for anyone. Manasseh offers the Chronicler's constituency reason to think it matters if they humbly turn to Yahweh. The Chronicler uses the language of Yahweh's revelation to Solomon, which alludes to the exilic turning point anticipated in Leviticus, to interpret Manasseh's repentance (bold and underlining signify verbal parallels, italics signify thematical similarity, and broken underlining signifies important incidental similarities):

> But if they will confess their sins and the sins of their ancestors—their unfaithfulness and their hostility toward me, which made me hostile toward them so that I sent them into the land of their enemies—then when their uncircumcised hearts **are humbled** [כנע] and they pay for their sin, I will remember my covenant with Jacob and my covenant with Isaac and my covenant with Abraham, *and I will remember the* ***land.*** (Lev 26:40–42)

> They killed the sons of Zedekiah before his eyes. Then they put out his eyes, bound him with bronze shackles and brought him to Babylon. (2 Kgs 25:7†)

> If my people, who are called by my name, will **humble themselves** [כנע] and pray and seek my face and turn from their wicked ways, then **I will hear** from heaven, and I will forgive their sin *and will heal their* ***land.*** (2 Chr 7:14)

> So Yahweh brought against them the army commanders of the king of Assyria, who took Manasseh prisoner, put a hook in his nose, bound him with bronze shackles and took him to Babylon. In his distress he sought the favor of Yahweh his God and **humbled himself** [כנע] greatly before the God of his ancestors. And when he prayed to him, Yahweh was moved by his entreaty and **listened** to his plea; so he brought him back to Jerusalem and to his kingdom. Then Manasseh knew that Yahweh is God. (33:12–13)[264]

Upon his return to Jerusalem, Manasseh launches a series of restoration initiatives (33:14–17) which loosely resemble those of Chronistic Jotham (27:3) and Deuteronomistic Josiah (2 Kgs 23:4–7, 8, 12).[265] Though verbal parallels do not support formal extended echo-effect, Chronistic Manasseh's cultic reforms align in general terms with those of Josiah.

263. See Schniedewind, "Source Citations of Manasseh," 452.
264. The exact phrase "that Yahweh is God" is used with "know" in Deut 4:35, 39; 1 Kgs 8:60; 2 Chr 33:13.
265. For Manasseh in Kings as an inverted type-scene for Josiah, see Halpern and Vanderhooft, "Editions of Kings," 240.

The Chronicler may have expected pushback against his bold presentation of Manasseh. Many generations had learned of Manasseh's particular culpability for the fall of Jerusalem from Jeremiah and Kings, as discussed above. If the Chronicler realizes his portrayal stands at odds with what everyone knows about Manasseh, he may go out of his way to explain his source. Whereas Kings uses a fairly standard source citation (21:17), Chronicles mentions two sources for his prayer along with other highlights from his sources. The twofold use of "his prayer" may indicate a repetitive resumption indicating the insertion of his additional supplemental source.[266] An attempt to answer probable objections may explain the over-the-top detail in this longest of all Chronistic source citations (pluses signified by italics, and bold signifies a potential repetitive resumption):

> The other events of Manasseh's reign, and all he did, including the sin he committed, are they not written in the book of the annals of the kings of Judah? (2 Kgs 21:17†)

> The other events of Manasseh's reign, *including **his prayer** to his God and the words the seers spoke to him in the name of Yahweh, the God of Israel,* are in the annals of the kings of Israel. ***His prayer** and how God was moved by his entreaty, as well as all his sins and unfaithfulness, and the sites where he built high places and set up Asherah poles and idols before he humbled himself—all these are written in the records of the seers.* (2 Chr 33:18–19†)

The Chronicler's exegetical interventions in his account of Manasseh require pausing to underline the significance in two directions. On one hand, what would it mean if the Deuteronomist had access to source(s) referring to Manasseh's repentance? Such a bold selectivity to suppress this event and blame Manasseh for the fall of Jerusalem would reinforce his agenda relation to Jeremiah's condemnation mentioned above. On the other hand, the Chronicler's presentation of Manasseh stands with the repentance of the Assyrian king in Jonah 3 or Nebuchadnezzar in Dan 4. It would be like learning of a hitherto unknown religious conversion experience and turnaround of a long-dead, bloodthirsty modern-day political dictator—something not in the standard history textbooks. The bold and different presentations of Manasseh in Kings and Chronicles each provide crucial elements in their overall interpretations of the Davidic kingdom.

33:6//2 Kgs 21:6 (A)+Jer 19:5–6 (B) (child sacrifice in the Valley of Ben Hinnom). See note on 2 Chr 28:3.

33:21–25/~/2 Kgs 21:19–26+21:3–5 (C) (rule of Amon and revival of Manasseh's cultic rebellion). Chronicles's version of Amon's rule closely follows Kings's highly formulaic account, with significant adjustments in describing his rebellion. Note a synoptic comparison of the rule of Amon:

266. See Schniedewind, "Source Citations of Manasseh," 456–57.

	2 Kings	2 Chronicles
formulaic opening	21:19	33:21
expanded evaluation formula	21:20–22	33:22–23
death by uprising of people of the land	21:23–24	33:24–25
source citation and burial	21:25–26	—

The primary adjustments in the Chronistic account of Amon seem to be necessary in light of the sensational recasting of Manasseh. Since Manasseh had repented, the Chronicler needs to clarify the specific manner in which Amon followed after and differed from his father. This also helps explain what Josiah needed to clean up since Manasseh's reforms had just been effected. For these reasons the Chronicler briefly presents Amon as an anti-reformer without elaboration, pointing readers back to the sins of his father. This naturally sets up a concise account of Josiah's revival against the same kinds of infidelities (2 Chr 34:3–7). Notice the Chronicler's use of one of his characteristic terms, "humbled himself," most recently used of Manasseh in 33:12 (verbal parallels signified by italics, and pluses signified by bold):

> *He did evil in the eyes of Yahweh, as his father Manasseh had done.* He followed completely the ways of his father, worshiping the idols *his father* had worshiped, and bowing down to them. He forsook Yahweh, the God of his ancestors, and *did not* walk in obedience to *Yahweh*. (2 Kgs 21:20–22†)

> *He did evil in the eyes of Yahweh, as his father Manasseh had done.* Amon worshiped and offered sacrifices to all the idols Manasseh *his father* had made. **But unlike his father Manasseh, he** *did not* **humble himself before** *Yahweh*; **Amon increased his guilt.** (2 Chr 33:22–23†)

34:1–35:27/~/2 Kgs 22:1–23:30 (rule of Josiah). Chronicles largely follows Kings in the presentation of Josiah. The Chronicler's three most important exegetical interventions include Josiah's early reforms before the discovery of the Torah scroll, the expansion of the Passover celebration in the eighteenth year, and the addition of Necho's prophecy. The first two of these are part of the Chronistic paradigmatic shaping of Josiah's rule with early purging reforms. In response to finding Torah and Huldah's prophecy, Josiah mandated sweeping collective worship reforms—a similar pattern to Asa and Jehoshaphat.[267] The Chronicler's series of scriptural interpretations relating to Josiah will be taken up in a series of shorter notes for convenience. To set these up note a synoptic comparison of the rule of Josiah:

---

267. See Glatt-Gilad, "Role of Huldah's Prophecy," 22–28. See also Table C10.

	2 Kings	2 Chronicles
formulaic opening[a]	22:1	34:1
formulaic evaluation and comparison to David	22:2	34:2
cultic reforms in Judah and Israel (12th year)	—	34:3–7 (condensed)
discovery of Torah scroll (18th year)	22:3–13	34:8–21
Huldah's prophecy	22:14–20	34:22–28
king initiates pledge of the people	23:1–3	34:29–32
cultic reforms in temple, Jerusalem, and Judah	23:4–14	—
cultic reforms in Bethel and towns of Samaria	23:15–20	34:33 (condensed)
Passover celebration	23:21–23	35:1–19 (expanded)
summation of reforms	23:24–26	—
residual wrath from Manasseh's rebellion	23:26–27	—
death and burial[b]	23:28–30a	35:20–27 (expanded and rearranged)

[a] Chronicles does not include the queen mother, 2 Kgs 22:1 versus 2 Chr 34:1 (see Table C11).

[b] See the detailed synoptic comparison of Josiah's death in the note on 2 Chr 35:20–27.

34:3–7, 33/~/2 Kgs 23:4–20 (cultic reforms of Jerusalem, Judah, and the land of Israel set in Josiah's twelfth and eighteenth years). The Deuteronomist loosely organizes the extensive account of Josiah's cultic reforms geographically.

- Cultic reforms of the temple, Jerusalem, and throughout Judah (2 Kgs 23:4–14)
- Cultic reforms at Bethel (23:15–18)
- Cultic reforms in the towns of Samaria (23:19–20)

While the first part of the account jumps around, the reforms span across Judah from Geba to Beersheba (23:8) before focusing on Bethel and the villages of Samaria. The Chronicler offers a highly condensed version of the reforms from Kings but basically begins at Judah and Jerusalem and then proceeds to northern reforms. The Chronicler divides his treatment and uses it to frame the account of Josiah's reforms in the twelfth and eighteenth years of his rule (2 Chr 34:3–7, 33; see dotted lines in synoptic table above). In a similar move, the Chronicler splits the brief comments on celebrating Passover in Kings to frame his own extensive account (35:1, 18–19; cf. 2 Kgs 23:21–23). The Chronicler uses several tribal names to refer to the breadth of Josiah's cultic reforms including, strangely, Simeon (see Map C24). Perhaps from Simeon in the south to as far north as Naphtali is the Chronicler's way of emphasizing the extent of the early reforms in contrast to the later reforms across Benjamin and Judah—Geba to Beersheba—in Kings (2 Chr 34:6; 2 Kgs 23:8).

MAP C24: PLACES ASSOCIATED WITH THE REFORMS OF JOSIAH

The timing of Deuteronomistic Josiah's cultic reforms emphasizes the discovery of the Torah scroll in his eighteenth year followed by reforms in a cause-and-effect structure: Torah discovered (2 Kgs 22:8), Josiah tears his clothes (22:11), inviting prophecy (22:13), Josiah compels citizens into a covenant (23:1–3), cultic reforms (23:4–20), and celebrating an extraordinary Passover (23:21–23). By contrast, in his youth, Chronistic Josiah began seeking the God of David in the eighth year of his rule (2 Chr 34:3). Then the apparently unprompted cultic reforms of Josiah's twelfth year serve as a cause (34:3–7) and the discovery of the Torah in the eighteenth year during temple renovations an effect (34:14). Without the sources, and not knowing if the Chronicler had access to the sources of Kings, judgment of which version (or both) dischronologizes events or selectively uses different elements cannot be determined. In any case, both Kings and Chronicles present highly theological dramatizations, with the Chronicler's version stressing a retributive structure.

34:8–19/~/2 Kgs 22:3–23:3 (Torah discovered in temple). Chronicles closely follows Kings in the account of the discovery of the Torah scroll in the temple. Two theological interpretive interventions and one mechanical interpretive intervention can be noted. First, the Chronicler revoices the account from direct discourse to narrative and expands the temple repair collection from "the people" to "from the people of Manasseh, Ephraim and the entire remnant of Israel and from all the people of Judah and Benjamin and the inhabitants of Jerusalem" (2 Chr 34:9; cf. 2 Kgs 22:4). This matches significant Chronistic emphases on comprehensive participation. Second, Chronicles expands the explanation of the temple repairs itself, detailing the supervision of the project by Levites, who usually serve as worship musicians, scribes, and gatekeepers (2 Chr 34:12–13). Again, this expansion corresponds to the pervasive Chronistic enhancement of attention to the Levitical temple personnel. Third, the Chronicler explains specifically how the scroll was found in the temple. The description of Hilkiah the high priest finding the scroll uses a temporal phrase "*when they were bringing out* the silver" (34:14 lit., emphasis mine).[268]

34:20–32/~/2 Kgs 22:3–23:3 (Huldah's prophecy). The Chronicler's interpretive interventions in Huldah's prophecy, though minor, concur with his agenda elsewhere. Whereas Deuteronomistic Josiah seeks Yahweh's will for himself and "the people" (2 Kgs 22:13), Chronistic Josiah seeks it on behalf of himself and "the remnant in Israel and Judah" (2 Chr 34:21). The use of "remnant" here denotes the previous Chronistic expansion—"Manasseh, Ephraim and the entire remnant of Israel and from all the people

268. The preposition "at" (בְּ) can be attached to an inf. const. with the sense of "at that time, when" (GKC, §164g).

of Judah and Benjamin and the inhabitants of Jerusalem" (34:9). When Huldah uses one of the Chronicler's favorite worship terms—"humble yourself"—he has her say it again to explain the theological significance of Josiah tearing his clothes earlier when he heard the Torah scroll. The connection between Torah and humble response helps underline the Chronicler's preoccupation with explicit citation of scriptural traditions in the account of Josiah's Passover as an outcome of the prophecy (see note on 35:1–19; italics signify verbal parallels, bold signifies expansion, and broken underlining signifies a shared key term):

> *Because your heart was responsive and you humbled yourself before* Yahweh *when you heard what* I have *spoken against this place and its people*—that they would become a curse and be laid waste—*and because you tore your robes and wept in my presence, I also have heard you, declares Yahweh.* (2 Kgs 22:19)

> *Because your heart was responsive and you humbled yourself before* God *when you heard what* he *spoke against this place and its people, and because* **you humbled yourself before me** and *tore your robes and wept in my presence, I have heard you, declares Yahweh.* (2 Chr 34:27)

The Chronicler may have signaled his swap of "Levites" for "prophets" in the list of those that accompanied Josiah to the temple by inverting "the least until the greatest" to "the greatest to the least" according to Seidel's theory (italics signify verbal parallels, bold signifies differences, and broken underlining signifies rearrangement):

> *He went up to the temple of Yahweh with the people of Judah,* **all** *the inhabitants of Jerusalem, the priests and the* **prophets**—*all the people from the least to the greatest.* (2 Kgs 23:2a†)

> *He went up to the temple of Yahweh with the people of Judah, the inhabitants of Jerusalem, the priests and the* **Levites**—*all the people from the greatest to the least.* (2 Chr 34:30a†)

That the Chronicler mentions the prophetic function of the Levitical musicians elsewhere (1 Chr 25:1), along with his interest in drawing attention to the Levites, seems a more economical explanation of this shift than a subtle reference to Jeremiah.[269] When the Chronicler wants to refer to Jeremiah he uses his name (2 Chr 35:25; 36:12, 21).

35:1–19/~/2 Kgs 23:21–23 (Josiah keeps the Passover). The Chronicler dramatically expands the short account of Josiah's Passover in Kings. The references to celebrating Passover in the opening and closing carried over from his source function almost like a repetitive resumption to house the insertion of new material in between (2 Chr 35:1//

269. Contra Leuchter, "'The Prophets,'" 35, 37, 40, 44; but on Seidel's theory in 2 Chr 34:30, see 33–34.

2 Kgs 23:21; 2 Chr 35:18–19//2 Kgs 23:22–23). This expansion features numerous marked elements demonstrating the Chronicler's self-conscious attempt to develop continuities between scriptural traditions and Josiah's Passover. The variety of overtly marked elements includes "according to the instructions written by David king of Israel and by his son Solomon" (2 Chr 35:4), "doing what Yahweh commanded through Moses" (35:6), "as the king had ordered" (35:10), "as it is written in the Book of Moses" (35:12), "as prescribed" (35:13), "prescribed by David" (35:15), and "as King Josiah had ordered" (35:16). The Chronicler's over-the-top marking draws attention to his heavy-handed use of authoratative traditions in this context. The next series of notes briefly evaluates the marked allusions of Josiah's Passover.

35:3–4*~1 Chr 23:25–26 (B) (new Levitical responsibilities) (* see teachers network). The marked allusion refers to the "written scrolls" of David and Solomon concerning the new role of the Levites. The written scroll may refer to the source the Chronicler used for the extensive lists of the Levites in 1 Chr 23–27. More to the point, the establishment of the temple as a permanent resting place for the ark called for a change of perspective on the Levites from shrine porters to singers, gatekeepers, sacrificial assistants, and teachers. Josiah's comment that the ark "is not to be carried about on your shoulders" offers a loose paraphrase of David's rationale for reassigning the responsibilities, namely, "the Levites no longer need to carry the tabernacle or any of the articles used in its service" (2 Chr 35:3; cf. 1 Chr 23:26). Based on Josiah's pronouncement, the variously tasked Levitical families served in the Passover as "prescribed by David" and "as king Josiah had ordered" (2 Chr 35:15, 16). According to the Chronicler, Josiah addressed his remarks to the Levites "who instructed all Israel" (35:3). The exact form of this expression appears once elsewhere of the Levites who explain Torah to the congregation after Ezra's Scripture reading (Neh 8:9). Though priests had responsibility to teach on matters of worship—holiness and ritual purity (Lev 10:10–11; Ezek 44:23; Hag 2:11–13)—Levites shouldered broader scriptural teaching responsibilities (2 Chr 17:7–9; cf. Deut 33:10).

35:5–6, 11~Num 18:3–4, 6 (C)+Ezek 44:11–12 (C) (Levites perform sacrifices with laity in outer court). The responsibility for sacrificial offerings at the tabernacle originally belonged to the laity themselves (Lev 1:5). The wilderness rebellions against Moses and Aaron resulted in the death of more than 250 leaders and thousands of the congregation (Num 16:35, 49[16:35; 17:14]). The upshot includes new legislation that places the burden of divine holiness on the priests and gives the Levites responsibility to prevent laity from approaching the holy inner sanctum of the tabernacle (Num 18:3–4, 6; cf. vv. 22–23). In the vision of the new temple, Ezekiel depicts the Levites performing the sacrifices with the laity in the outer court as they prevent them from entering the inner sanctum (see note on Ezek 44:9–16; outer sacrifice table in Figure Ezk 4). In Chronicles Josiah commissions the Levites to perform Passover sacrifices with the laity (2 Chr 35:5–6). He builds this possible exegetical intervention on the authority of David and Solomon when the permanent place of worship precluded the former responsibilities of the Levites (35:4) and affirms its accord with Mosaic legal instructions (35:6). The expansion of Levitical responsibilities establishes a positive function of assisting laity with the sacrifices of worship, which complements their preventative role of protecting laity from the holiness of the inner sanctum.

Josiah affirms the expanded role of the Levites with sacrifices. This implies an additional connection when they give the blood to the priests, which gets picked up in the narrative (35:11). At the tabernacle entrance priests took the blood from the sacrifices performed by laity and transported it inside to splash against the altar (Lev 1:5; 17:6). Priests need to be present at the sacrifices by the Levites on behalf of the laity in order to get the blood, for only priests may enter the inner sanctum. The priest's role represents conformity to the standard of priests alone bearing the burden of holiness (Num 18:1–2, 5). The priests taking the blood limits Josiah's interpretive expansion to new responsibilities for Levites. The expanded role of the Levites to assist laity by performing their sacrificial slaughter at temple (2 Chr 35:6; cf. Ezek 44:11–12) does not help with the irregularity of Levites supplementing priests performing these sacrifices during Hezekiah's Passover (2 Chr 29:34).

35:12~Lev 3:3–5, 9–11, 14–16 (B) (set aside Yahweh's portion of the sacrifices). The Chronicler marks the proper handling of the massive quantity of sacrifices by "as it is written in the book of Moses" to refer to what "they set aside" (סור Hif) (2 Chr 35:12). The burnt offerings they set aside seem to be a metonymy for the part of the sacrifices which are "set aside" (סור Hif) for Yahweh (Lev 3:4, 9, 10, 15), namely, the (hind) legs, kidneys, lobe of the liver, and the suet fat (חֵלֶב) encasing them (3:3–5, 9–11, 14–16). The context makes explicit that the priests sacrificed the offerings and "fat portions" (חֵלֶב) all day (2 Chr 35:14).

Spawn emphasizes a contrast between Josiah's Passover by the letter of the law as opposed to the irregularities of Hezekiah's Passover primarily on the basis of the citation formulas. The Chronicler describes Josiah's Passover "as it is written" (35:12) but Hezekiah's Passover "contrary to what was written" (30:18, cf. v. 5).[270] Spawn's claim requires reading directly against the sense of the text, since the problem led Hezekiah to seek pardon which "Yahweh heard . . . and healed the people" (30:20). The Chronicler contrasts the Passovers of Hezekiah and Josiah not as "negative" versus "faithful" but as great ("there had been nothing like this" since Solomon, 30:26) versus even greater ("none of the kings of Israel had ever celebrated such a Passover as did Josiah" since Samuel, 35:18).

35:13~ Exod 12:9+Deut 16:7 (B) (Passover meal fire roasted and boiled). Instructions on preparing the Passover meal speak of "fire roasted" (צְלִי אֵשׁ) as opposed to eating the meat raw or boiled in water (Exod 12:9), but elsewhere the generic word for "cook"

270. See Spawn, *"As It Is Written,"* 114–16. For the opposite view—Hezekiah's good and Josiah's wrongful Passover—see Mitchell, "Ironic Death," 427–31. Both of these views read against the sense of the text.

or "boil" (בשל) describes Passover preparations (Deut 16:7). Since the clarifying terms "water" and "fire" do not appear in Deut 16:7, many modern translations say "roast" (KJV, NIV) or "cook" (NRSV, JPSB), even though they use "boil" to translate the term elsewhere. The Chronicler uses both expressions: "roasted ... over fire" (וַיְבַשְּׁלוּ . . . בָּאֵשׁ) and "boiled ... in pots" (בִּשְּׁלוּ בַּסִּירוֹת).

> They *roasted* the Passover animals *over the fire* **as prescribed**, and *boiled* the holy offerings in pots, caldrons and pans and served them quickly to all the people. (2 Chr 35:13; marking signified by bold, and Torah allusions signified by italics)

The tension between "not cooked/boiled (אַל . . . בשל) in water" but "fire roasted" in Exod 12:9 and "cook/boil (בשל)" in Deut 16:7 may explain a harmonistic expansion in the ancient Greek translation. The Septuagint inserts "roast/bake," so it says "You shall boil *and roast*" (Deut 16:7 LXX, italics signify plus).[271]

The Chronicler marks numerous elements of Josiah's Passover, including cooking procedures, to demonstrate the celebration as the epitome of Torah obedience (see note on 35:1–19). The attention to roasting over fire and boiling "as prescribed" points to the authority of Torah for the Chronicler. The need to harmonize also demonstrates that Deuteronomy does not replace or simply override Exodus.

35:16~Num 28:16–25 (C) (Josiah prescribed Passover sacrifices). The Chronicler explicitly marks the entire Passover by Josiah's royal order (2 Chr 35:16). This refers to what Josiah said in 2 Chr 35:5–6. The intervening narrative details many ways the Passover celebration accords with specific legal standards for worship, including a few exegetical allusions as noted—Levites perform sacrifices for laity (35:5–6, 11), they set aside Yahweh's fat portions (vv. 12, 14), they roasted and boiled the Passover meal (v. 13). In addition to the overall reference to "the entire service" (v. 16), the Chronicler adds one further allusion: "the offering of burnt offerings on the altar of Yahweh" (v. 16) namely, the enumerated sacrificial regulations of Passover as explained in Num 28:16–25.[272]

35:20–27/~/2 Kgs 23:28–30 (A) +1 Kgs 22:30, 34–35//2 Chr 18:29, 33–34 (B) (death of Josiah). The death of Josiah presents significant challenges in both Kings and Chronicles. In Kings, the citation formula appears before an exceptionally abrupt and vague account of Josiah's death at Megiddo (2 Kgs 23:28–29). In Chronicles, the pagan ruler Necho acts as God's own prophetic messenger to Josiah, who does not listen, is wounded at Megiddo, and dies upon his return to Jerusalem (2 Chr 35:20–24).[273] Every detail associated with Josiah's death acts as a lightning rod for wide-ranging excavative

271. See Wevers, *Notes on the Greek Text of Deuteronomy*, 269.

272. See Japhet, *I & II Chronicles*, 1052.

273. On Necho and prophetic messengers, see Table C9 and associated discussion. Dillard compares Necho to the Rabshakeh in 2 Kgs 18:19–25 (*2 Chronicles*, 289), but the taunt framework suggests they are different kinds of things. Talshir proposes that the exchange between Joash and Amaziah (2 Kgs 14:8–10//2 Chr 25:17–20) provides a prototype for the meeting of Josiah and Necho ("Three Deaths," 232), but the similarities are very broad.

studies seeking to solve historical challenges. The narrow aims of the present study require focusing on the Chronicler's daring use of scriptural traditions in this context. Note a synoptic comparison of the death of Josiah:

	2 Kings	**2 Chronicles**
source citation	23:28	—
meeting Necho	23:29a	35:20
Necho's prophecy	—	35:21
Josiah disguised himself and is wounded in battle	—	35:22–23
death and burial of Josiah	23:29b–30a	35:24
Jeremiah's laments for Josiah	—	35:25
expanded source citation	—	35:26–27

The Deuteronomist broadly locates Necho's military destination at the Euphrates River to serve in an alliance with the king of Assyria (2 Kgs 23:29). The Chronicler more precisely notes Necho's plans to go to Carchemish (2 Chr 35:20). It has been suggested that the Chronicler deduced this from the prologue to Jeremiah's oracle against Egypt that refers to the defeat of Necho at Carchemish (Jer 46:2).[274] But Josiah died in 609 BCE because of confronting Necho at Megiddo, a stop in his transit to participate as vassal of Assyria in a successful campaign at Carchemish against the Chaldeans. Three months later on Necho's journey back to Egypt, he deposed Jehoahaz taking him to Egypt and setting up Jehoiakim as king (2 Kgs 23:33–35; 2 Chr 36:1–4). In Jehoiakim's fourth year (605 BCE) Necho participated in another battle at Carchemish, though unsuccessfully, against the Chaldeans commanded by Nebuchadnezzar (Jer 46:2 LXX and MT).[275] If the Chronicler worked with Kings and Jeremiah as sources, as it seems, then he would have known these two campaigns stood four years apart. The Chronicler's source of the location of the campaign in 609 is unknown.

The Chronicler expands the account of the death of Josiah using imagery from the death of Ahab. In an unusual move, Kings briefly recounts the death of Josiah after the source citation. "King Josiah marched out to meet him in battle, but Necho faced him and killed him at Megiddo" (2 Kgs 23:29b). The Chronicler inserts distinctive language into his expansive revisions, using language from Ahab's death as Ahab-like overtones in Josiah's death (bold and underlining signify verbal parallels, and italics signify similarities):[276]

274. See Talshir, "Three Deaths," 214.

275. See Allen, *Jeremiah*, 461. In spite of the complaints discussed in McKane, *Jeremiah*, 2:1111–12, the evidence supports the language of Jer 26:2 LXX=46:2 MT (see apparatus in LXX Göttingen and *BHS*).

276. See Welch, "Death of Josiah," 255; Williamson, "Death of Josiah," 246; Talshir, "Three Deaths," 219; Delamarter, "Death of Josiah," 34–35[34, "Jehoshaphat" *sic*]; Jarick, "Two Ahabs," 315. This insight is also indebted to John Biegel.

> The king of Israel [Ahab] said to Jehoshaphat, "I will enter the battle **in disguise**, but you wear your royal robes." So the king of Israel **disguised himself** and went into battle. . . . *But someone drew his bow at random and hit the king of Israel between the breastplate and the scale armor.* The king told the chariot driver, "*Wheel around and get me out of the fighting.* **I've been wounded**." All day long the battle raged, and the king of Israel propped himself up in <u>his chariot</u> facing the Arameans until evening. Then at sunset <u>he died.</u> (2 Chr 18:29, 33–34//1 Kgs 22:30, 34–35)

> Josiah, however, would not turn away from him, but **disguised himself** to engage him in battle. He would not listen to what Necho had said at God's command but went to fight him on the plain of Megiddo. *Archers shot King Josiah*, and he told his officers, "*Take me away*; **I am *badly* wounded**." So they took him out of <u>his chariot</u>, put him in <u>his other chariot</u> and brought him to Jerusalem, where <u>he died</u>. (2 Chr 35:22–24a)

The uncommon reflexive use of the verb for "disguise himself" only appears in three places outside of the context of the deaths of Ahab and Josiah, including Saul disguising himself to consult the medium.[277] The Chronicler's use of Ahab imagery offers suggestive exegetical connotations by extended echo-effect (see Table C10).

The bold narrative shift of Josiah's death needs to be seen in the context of this section of Chronicles. The Chronicler re-presents Manasseh, one of the most wayward kings, using cultic reform imagery broadly similar to that of one of the best kings—Josiah (33:14–16). In like manner, the Chronicler reshapes the death of Josiah, one of the most devout kings, according to the figural pattern of one of the worst kings of a competing kingdom—Ahab (35:22–24). These unlikely figural inversions stand as conceptual counterparts. If there is hope for the likes of Manasseh, there is hope for anyone. If even Josiah is not safe against arrogance and swift judgment, no one is safe.

Williamson suggests that the Chronicler's emphasis on Josiah's death in Jerusalem is intended to repair the damage of the nonfulfillment of Huldah's prophecy. Mitchell counters that such a move does not make sense if dying in Jerusalem (יְרוּשָׁלַםִ) ironically puns on Huldah's expectation of burial in "peace" (*shalom*, שָׁלוֹם)—which does not literally fulfill the prophecy (34:28; 35:24).[278] These proposals do not adequately account for the inherent contingency of prophecy, which cuts both ways. A short time after Josiah's death, during the beginning of Jehoiakim's reign, defenders of Jeremiah argued that God relents from prophetic threats if his people repent—citing Micah as an

277. See "חפשׂ," Hith no. 2 *HALOT* 1:341. See also 1 Sam 28:8; Job 30:18; Prov 28:12; Coggins, "Kings and Disguises," 55–62. Based on rather thin evidence from variant readings in the ancient versions, Joosten proposes the rare term may have the sense of "to arm oneself" (חפשׂ Hith) ("Language," 62).

278. See Williamson, "Death of Josiah," 246; Mitchell, "Ironic Death," 422–23. For a different problematic proposal based on ironic fulfillment (died "in peace" not battle), see Halpern, "Why Manasseh Is Blamed," 501–5. The traditional limitation of fulfillment to one phrase—"Your eyes will not see all the disaster I am going to bring on this place" (2 Chr 34:28//2 Kgs 22:20) (498)—does not correspond to the sense of the oracle.

example (Jer 26:17–19; cf. Mic 3:12). Such alterations do not undercut the legitimacy of prophetic messages. In an analogous way, perhaps an expectation of a peaceful death can be thwarted by rejecting God's word—Josiah "would not listen to what Necho had said at God's command" (2 Chr 35:22).[279] As noted above, no one, including Josiah the devout cultic reformer and Yahweh-seeker, may rebel against the word of God and get away with it. The Chronicler underlines his bold exegetical intervention by emphasizing that the word comes from the enemy king Necho.

35:25~Jer 22:10–12 (D) (Jeremiah's lament for Josiah). This proposal does not work since Jeremiah says, "Do *not* weep for the dead king [Josiah]" (Jer 22:10, emphasis mine).[280]

36:1–4/~/2 Kgs 23:31–35 (rule of Jehoahaz). The Chronicler abbreviates the already brief account of Jehoahaz but retains the basic set of historical details. Note a synoptic comparison of the rule of Jehoahaz:

	2 Kings	2 Chronicles
coronation of Jehoahaz by people of the land	23:30b	36:1
formulaic age at accession and length of reign	23:31a	36:2
queen mother	23:31b	—
evaluation of infidelity	23:32	—
Jehoahaz captive to Egypt and Jehoiakim enthroned	23:33–34	36:3–4
death of Jehoahaz and taxes for tribute by Jehoiakim	23:34c–35	—

36:5–8/~/2 Kgs 23:36–24:7 (rule of Jehoiakim). The Chronicler abridges the traditional account of Jehoiakim as it stands in Kings. Although the treatment of the last few kings of Judah often leads to speculation regarding the ending of the Chronicler's version of Kings, or lack thereof, the adjustments here fit well with his other edits. For example, the Deuteronomist rehearsed the damning effects of Manasseh's sin amid his treatment of Jehoiakim (2 Kgs 24:2–4; cf. 21:10–16; 23:26–27; Jer 15:4), but the Chronicler deletes these elements since Manasseh turned back to God in his version (2 Chr 33:12–13). Also, the captivity of Jehoiakim, unique to Chronicles, accords with his omission of a death notice (36:6; Table C11). Note a synoptic comparison of the rule of Jehoiakim:

	2 Kings	2 Chronicles
formulaic age at accession and length of reign	23:36a	36:5a
queen mother	23:36b	—
formulaic evaluation	23:37	36:5b

(cont.)

279. The rebellion of Josiah sets this case apart from Jeremiah's cautions regarding peace prophets (Jer 28:9).
280. Contra Talshir, "Three Deaths," 234.

	2 Kings	2 Chronicles
attack of Nebuchadnezzar	24:1a	36:6a
three year vassalage and rebellion	24:1b	—
military judgment due to prophecy against Manasseh	24:2–4	—
taking king and vessels of temple to Babylon	—	36:6b–7
formulaic closing summation and source citations	24:5	36:8a[a]
abbreviated death notice	24:6a	—
notice of successor	24:6b	36:8b
notice of Egyptian campaigns curtailed	24:7	—

[a] The phrase "the detestable things he did and all that was found against him" (MT of 2 Chr 36:8a) is lacking in LXX, which follows 2 Kgs 24:5 (see *BHS*; Glatt-Gilad, "Regnal Formulae," 198). However, 2 Chr 36:1–8 seems to generally follow 2 Kings (see Macy, "Sources of Chronicles," 138).

36:7, 10*~2 Kgs 24:13*+Jer 27:16–22* (B) (removal of temple vessels when Jehoiakim and Jehoiachin are taken captive) (* see temple vessels network). The Scriptures attend to the temple vessels in several contexts, demonstrating their importance.[281] The Chronicler speaks of the temple vessels removed to Babylon by Nebuchadnezzar in three stages: (1) when he bound Jehoiakim for captivity he took "some of the vessels" (2 Chr 36:7 lit.); (2) when he brought Jehoiachin into exile he took "vessels of value" (36:10 lit.); and (3) when he took Zedekiah captive he carried away "all the vessels great and small" (36:18 lit.). The first two stages seem to result from an interpretive blend of references to Nebuchadnezzar plundering the temple vessels in Jeremiah and 2 Kings (bold signifies verbal parallels, italics and underlining signify interpretive deductions):[282]

> As Yahweh had declared, Nebuchadnezzar removed <u>all the treasures</u> **from the house of Yahweh** and from the royal palace, and cut up <u>the gold **articles**</u> that Solomon king of Israel had made for the temple of Yahweh. (2 Kgs 24:13†)

> Then I [Jeremiah] said to the priests and all these people, "This is what Yahweh says: Do not listen to the prophets who say, 'Very soon now **the articles from Yahweh's house** will be brought back from Babylon.' They are prophesying lies to you. . . . If they are prophets and have the word of Yahweh, let them plead with Yahweh Almighty *that the articles remaining in the house of Yahweh* and in the palace of the king of Judah and in Jerusalem not be taken to Babylon." (Jer 27:16, 18; cf. 28:3, 6)

281. See 2 Kgs 20:17; 24:13; 25:13–15; Isa 39:6; 52:11; Jer 27:16, 21–22; 28:3, 6; 52:18–20; Dan 1:2; 5:2–4, 23; Ezra 1:7; 5:13–15; 6:5; 2 Chr 36:7, 10, 18; cf. Bar 1:8, 9.

282. See Kalimi and Purvis, "Jehoiachin and the Vessels," 452. Contra Warhurst, who claims the Chronicler "clearly alludes" to Dan 1:2 but does not adequately explain the evidence from Jer 27, including the verbal parallel in 2 Chr 36:7, 10 versus the loose paraphrase in Dan 1:2 ("Associative Effects," 194–98). Elsewhere Warhurst says the account in 2 Chr 36 validates Jeremiah's prophecy of the preservation of the temple vessels in Jer 27:21–22 ("Merging," 211). See note on Ezra 1:7, 11.

> Nebuchadnezzar also took to Babylon *some of* **the articles from the house of Yahweh** and put them in his temple there. (2 Chr 36:7†)

> In the spring, King Nebuchadnezzar sent for him and brought him to Babylon, together with **articles of value from the house of Yahweh**, and he made Jehoiachin's uncle, Zedekiah, king over Judah and Jerusalem. (36:10†)

The Chronicler's interpretation resolves tensions created by the hyperbole of Nebuchadnezzar taking "all" the vessels when he took "all" the people of Jerusalem into exile with Jehoiachin (2 Kgs 24:14).[283] The Deuteronomist immediately qualifies the comprehensive "all" language with "only the poorest people of the land were left" (24:14b) and explains that Nebuchadnezzar appointed Zedekiah king to rule over Jerusalem (24:17; cf. Jer 24:1). Likewise, that Nebuchadnezzar cut up "all the gold vessels" needed to be collated with Jeremiah's assurance, at about that time, that the portion of the vessels taken would be returned in Jer 27:16–22.[284] The Chronicler carefully reads these contexts together to show the temple vessels pillaged in three stages.

36:9–10/~/2 Kgs 24:8–17 (Jehoiachin and Babylonian captivity). The Chronicler sharply abridges the account of Jehoiachin but retains a summary statement of his captivity. Note a synoptic comparison of the rule of Jehoiachin:

	2 Kings	**2 Chronicles**
formulaic age at accession and length of reign[a]	24:8a	36:9a
queen mother	24:8b	—
formulaic evaluation	24:9	36:9b
siege and list of captives	24:10–12, 14–16	—
removing king and temple vessels to Babylon[b]	24:13	36:10a
appointing Zedekiah	24:17	36:10b

[a] The reference to Jehoiachin as "eight" years of age (2 Chr 36:9) is likely a textual corruption since he is married (2 Kgs 24:15). The number eighteen in Hebrew is made by the words "eight-(and)-ten." The word "ten" may have drifted into his rule, adding ten days to it (see *BHS* notes a and c on 2 Chr 36:9).

[b] See note on 2 Chr 36:7, 10.

---

283. See Kalimi and Purvis, "Jehoiachin and the Vessels," 453. Dating Ezra-Nehemiah in its present form makes it implausible to say Chronicles uses it (contra 455–56; on dating Ezra-Nehemiah and Chronicles see note on 2 Chr 36:22–23).

284. Dating Jer 27 is difficult and tenuous. Jeremiah 27:1 is missing from LXX (the older edition—see Hermeneutical Profile of the Use of Scripture in Jeremiah); the plus in MT—beginning of rule of Jehoiakim—seems to be wrongly supplied from 26:1 (Allen, *Jeremiah* 303; McKane, *Jeremiah*, 2:685). A few masoretic manuscripts mention Zedekiah in 27:1 (*BHS*), followed by most modern committee translations like NIV. The details of Jer 27 seem to correspond to Jer 28, and the meeting of delegates in 27:3 fits well with Zedekiah's diplomatic visit to Babylon (51:59, and see 29:3). In this case, Jer 27 is set in ca. 593, during Zedekiah's fourth year. The relevant portion of Jer 27:1 is missing from 4QJer[c/4Q72] (*BQS* 2:574), suggesting that the plus in the MT at this point may be a later scribal gloss.

36:11–17/~/2 Kgs 24:18–20 (rule of Zedekiah). Chronicles expands attention to the infidelity of Zedekiah in comparison to the short version in Kings. Note a synoptic comparison of Zedekiah's rule:

	2 Kings	**2 Chronicles**
formulaic age at accession and length of reign	24:18a	36:11
queen mother	24:18b	—
formulaic evaluation	24:19	36:12a
summary judgment against Judah	24:20a	—
infidelity of Zedekiah and Jerusalem	24:20b	36:13–17 (expanded)

The Chronicler follows the sentiment of Jer 37:2 on Zedekiah, his court, and the people as refusing to listen to Jeremiah, but he uses the language of Yahweh to Solomon (bold and underlining signify verbal parallels, and italics signify thematic similarity):

> **He did evil in the eyes of Yahweh**, just as Jehoiakim had done. (2 Kgs 24:19)
>
> Neither he nor his attendants nor the people of the land paid any attention to *the words Yahweh had spoken through Jeremiah the prophet.* (Jer 37:2)
>
> [I]f my people, who are called by my name, will humble themselves and pray and seek my face and turn from their wicked ways, then I will hear from heaven, and I will forgive their sin and will heal their land. (2 Chr 7:14)
>
> **He did evil in the eyes of Yahweh** his God and did not humble himself before *Jeremiah the prophet, who spoke the word of Yahweh.* (36:12)

The Chronicler follows Zedekiah's refusal to submit to the prophetic word by a long, theologically pregnant, non-synoptic addition. This plus makes several points emphasizing the excessive "infidelity" of both priests and people, which "ritually pollutes" the temple (36:14).[285] The polluting infidelity provides part of the rationale for destroying the temple, apparently deduced from causes of exile in Torah (Lev 18:24–30; 26:40).

The Chronicler uses a stock phrase from Jeremiah to emphasize the transgenerational collective responsibility of God's people (2 Chr 36:15–16). The Chronicler uses

---

285. The use of "infidelity" (מעל) to describe the cause of "polluting" (טמא) the temple is a significant element in the Chronicler's explanation for the cause of Judah's downfall. See Milgrom, "Concept of *Ma'al*," 236, 247; Johnstone, *2 Chronicles 10–36*, 2:270–71; idem, "Use of Leviticus in Chronicles," 246–47.

this language to demonstrate that the exile does not function merely as the individual retribution for Zedekiah and his generation but for the cumulative guilt from rebellion across the Davidic kingdom. Conversely, based on strict, immediate retribution, Japhet contends, "Only Zedekiah and his generation are responsible for the disaster that occurred in his time."[286] But the evidence in 2 Chr 36 points in exactly the opposite direction of Japhet's widely cited contention. It is easy to agree that much of 2 Chr 10–36 emphasizes immediate retribution, notwithstanding five more complex interpretations of individual kings.[287] In spite of the Chronicler's strong interest in tying up loose ends and supplying retribution-friendly causes for judgments/blessings and effects for (dis)obedience, in this final section he uses Jeremiah twice to underscore the exile as collective judgment. The Chronicler gets at cumulative guilt and deferred punishment in two ways. First, he uses rejection of prophetic warning spoken of in Jeremiah's retrospective (36:15–16). Second, he provides a mathematical formula for Jeremiah's seventy years from Leviticus (see note on 36:21).

Anyone who reads Jeremiah will recognize a recurring phrase, "sent prophets again and again" (NIV) or "persistently sent prophets" (NRSV), rendered in similar ways in other translations. Jeremiah uses a distinct combination of "rise early" (שׁכם Hif) as an auxiliary word added to one of several verbs, including "send," "speak," "warn," and "teach." The metaphorical idea is something like getting up early in the morning sending/speaking/warning/teaching all day long, but applied to a long series of prophets. Jeremiah's frequent use of the complaint makes it seem like Yahweh has done nothing else for years other than send prophets to warn the people to turn from their sin. Though this constellation of stock phrases makes it difficult to know which context from Jeremiah the Chronicler has in mind, or if he merely makes a Jeremiah-like allusion, this language comes from Jeremiah.[288] Jeremiah 25 can represent the entire constellation of stock phrases in Jeremiah for the present purposes, since this context uses "seventy years" alluded to in 2 Chr 36:21 (bold signifies verbal parallels, underlining signifies verbal parallels at the level of roots, italics signify thematic similarity, and wavy underlining signifies interpretive rationale):

---

286. Japhet, *Ideology*, 128; and see idem, *I & II Chronicles*, 44, 1069. For critical interaction with Japhet's important view, see Schnittjer, "Individual versus Collective Retribution," 114–15, 117–18.

287. For complex Chronistic treatments of Rehoboam (2 Chr 12:1–16), Jehoshaphat (18:1–19:3), Ahaziah (22:1–9), Amaziah (25:1–26:2), and Hezekiah (32:24–26, 31), see notes ad loc.

288. On the metaphorical sense of "rising early" (שׁכם), see *IBHS* §§27.4b; 35.3.2c. The auxiliary use of "rising early" causes the associated wcp verb to refer to frequently repeated action (see GKC §112x, dd). The majority of uses of the Hif inf. abs. of "rising early" (שׁכם) combined with various verbs occurs in Jeremiah, with this one occurrence in 2 Chr 36, a couple of occurrences in Samuel, and one in Proverbs (see Even-Shoshan, 1143). Jeremiah speaks of God as subject, usually in first-person and sometimes in third-person discourse, literally as "rising early and sending" (Jer 7:25; 25:4; 26:5; 29:19; 35:15; 44:4), "rising early and speaking" (7:13; 25:3; 35:14), "rising early and warning" (11:7), and "rising early and teaching" (32:33). For a similar sentiment but different language, see Neh 9:30; 2 Chr 24:19. See Schnittjer, "Individual versus Collective Retribution," 119–20.

> And though Yahweh **has sent** all his servants the prophets to you **again and again** [הַשְׁכֵּם וְשָׁלֹחַ], you have not listened or paid any attention. They said, "Turn now, each of you, from your evil ways and your evil practices, and you can stay in the land Yahweh gave to you and your ancestors for ever and ever. Do not follow other gods to serve and worship them; do not arouse my anger with what your hands have made. Then I will not harm you. But you did not listen to me," declares Yahweh, "and you *have aroused my anger* with what your hands have made, and you have brought harm to yourselves." Therefore Yahweh Almighty says this: "Because you have not listened to my words, I will summon all the peoples of the north and my servant Nebuchadnezzar king of Babylon," declares Yahweh, "and I will bring them against this land and its inhabitants and against all the surrounding nations. I will completely destroy them and make them an object of horror and scorn, and an everlasting ruin." (Jer 25:4–9; cf. 15:5; 21:7)[289]

> [I]f my people, who are called by my name, will humble themselves and pray and seek my face and turn from their wicked ways, then I will hear from heaven, and I will forgive their sin and will heal [רפא] their land. (2 Chr 7:14)

> Yahweh, the God of their ancestors, **sent** word to them through his messengers **again and again** [הַשְׁכֵּם וְשָׁלוֹחַ], because he had pity on his people and on his dwelling place. But they mocked God's messengers, despised his words and scoffed at his prophets until *the wrath of* Yahweh *was aroused* against his people and there was no remedy [מַרְפֵּא]. (36:15–16; cf. v. 12)

The refusal to listen to the long line of prophetic messengers mentioned in Jer 25 demonstrates the callous disobedience of Jerusalem. The Chronicler affirms Yahweh's decision to defer definitive retribution based on his compassion for both his people and the temple (see the note on 2 Chr 36:21). In the coming aftermath of judgment, Jeremiah asks, "Who *will have pity* [חמל] on you, Jerusalem?" (Jer 15:5; cf. 21:7). The Chronicler retrojects the same logic, explaining the long line of prophetic delegates "because he *had pity* [חמל] on his people and on his dwelling place" (2 Chr 36:15). The Chronicler's interpretation of Zedekiah's rule does not directly quote specific oracles of Jeremiah, but after naming the prophet (36:12) he narrates the rationale for cumulative judgment coming to its fullness in Zedekiah's days by means of Jeremiah-like language.[290] The language of "no remedy" connotes illness. The only other place the Chronicler uses this language relates to the horrifying, divinely afflicted bowel disease of Jehoram (21:18; 36:16). If the Chronicler intends an echo, then the personal catastrophe of Jehoram prefigures the

289. Whereas Jer 25:4–6 LXX, and presumably its Hebrew parent text, presents a first-person retrospective, this has been revoiced to third person in the MT counterpart—both versions share language common to 2 Chr 36:15.

290. For a similar observation, see Leuchter, "Rethinking," 192; and for a list of many Jeremiah-like allusions in 2 Chr 36, see Warhurst, "Chronicler's Use of the Prophets," 176.

painful humiliation of the people.[291] The language of "no remedy" (אֵין מַרְפֵּא) makes explicit the absence of repentance that leads to "healing" (רפא) by echoing the related root in the revelation to Solomon (7:14; 36:21).[292]

36:18–20/~/2 Kgs 25:8–21//Jer 52:12–30 (exile of Judah). The Chronicler abridges his account of the exile of Judah in contrast to other scriptural traditions that appear in 2 Kgs 25, Jer 39, 52, and the Septuagintal versions of Jer 39 (=Jer 32 LXX) and 52 (see the synoptic table of all these in the note on Jer 52). The Chronicler briefly emphasizes aspects of the catastrophe—looting of the temple vessels (2 Chr 36:18; see note on 36:7, 10), burning the temple and breaking down the city walls (36:19), and carrying the remnant into exile (36:20). The Chronicler immediately follows with the mathematical rationale for judgment (36:21) and jump cuts to the edict of Cyrus (36:22–23). Note a synoptic comparison of the Deuteronomistic and Chronistic versions of the exile:

	2 Kings 25	**2 Chronicles 36**
plunder of temple vessels	—	18
temple burned	9a	19a
city walls broken down	10	19b
looting and burning important buildings	9b	19c
remnant exiled	11	—
poorest people left in Judah	12	—
temple vessels, some taken some destroyed	13–17	—
chief priests and officers executed in Riblah	18–21	—
remnant enslaved in Babylon	—	20
edict of Cyrus	—	22–23

36:21*~Jer 25:11*; 29:10*+Lev 26:34–35 (B) (Jeremiah's seventy years) (* see seventy years network). The Chronistic narration of Zedekiah's rule uses heavy-handed, Jeremiah-like allusions to pivot from individual, immediate retribution generation by generation to reveal deferred cumulative pending judgment (2 Chr 36:11–17; see note ad loc.).[293] Commitment to balancing the scales of retributive justice stands as one of the leading features of the Chronicler's presentation of the Davidic kingdom from Rehoboam up to Zedekiah. A long line of commentators since Wellhausen have affirmed the basic retributive tendencies of the Chronicler—immediate and individual.[294] The notes

291. See Begg, "Constructing a Monster," 48–49.

292. See "I מַרְפֵּא," "רפא," *HALOT* 1:637; 2:1273. Also see similar uses in Jer 3:22; 8:15//14:19; 30:17; 33:6; used ironically in 6:14//8:11; and a non-medical connotation in 19:11.

293. For extensive detail, see Schnittjer, "Individual versus Collective Retribution," 118–25.

294. See ibid., 115–16. Also see, e.g., Wellhausen, *Prolegomena*, 203–10; von Rad, *Das Geschichtsbild des Chronistischen Werks*, 11; idem, *Old Testament Theology*, 1:348–50.

above on the use of scriptural traditions in 2 Chr 10–36 affirm pervasive immediate retribution. However, a handful of complex royal accounts have been noted along the way—Rehoboam, Jehoshaphat, Ahaziah, Amaziah, and Hezekiah. These cases—one of every four kings—do not quite fit the orderly retribution evident elsewhere.[295]

Beginning more than a century before the exile, the Chronicler acknowledges deferred judgment even in moments of individual forgiveness.[296]

> Then Hezekiah repented of the pride of his heart, as did the people of Jerusalem; *therefore Yahweh's wrath did not come on them during the days of Hezekiah.* (32:26, emphasis mine)

> [Huldah said to Josiah] Now I will gather you to your ancestors, and you will be buried in peace. Your eyes will not see *all the disaster I am going to bring on this place and on those who live here.* (34:28, emphasis mine)

Both of these contexts—based on the Chronicler's interpretive adaptations of judgments by Isaiah and Huldah—anticipate the long line of prophetic figures whom kings, worship personnel, and people ignore (36:15–16).

Leviticus offers a precedent to the Chronicler's emphasis on exile as personal and collective retribution. "Those of you who are left will waste away in the lands of their enemies *because of their sins*; also *because of their ancestors' sins* they will waste away" (Lev 26:39, emphasis mine). The exile in Leviticus "occupies the middle ground between cross-generational retribution and the principle that individuals should be rewarded and punished only for their own deeds."[297] The Chronicler also condemns Zedekiah and Jerusalem of his day even in a context where he calculates the long rebellion to which the exile gives an exclamation point.

The Chronicler uses an exegetical blend based on Leviticus and Jeremiah to deduce a daring interpretation of scriptural traditions. The deferred judgment against the people of God had reached a point where they owe seventy Sabbath years (bold and italics signify verbal parallels, and underlining signifies verbal parallels at the level of roots):

> Then **the land will enjoy its sabbath years all the time that it lies** <u>desolate</u> and you are in the country of your enemies; then the land **will rest** and enjoy its sabbaths. **All the time that it lies** <u>desolate</u>**, the land will have the rest** it did not have during the sabbaths you lived in it. (Lev 26:34–35; cf. v. 43)

---

295. See notes ad loc. regarding Rehoboam (2 Chr 12:1–16), Jehoshaphat (18:1–19:3), Ahaziah (22:1–9), Amaziah (25:1–26:2), Hezekiah (32:24–26, 31).

296. Scripture references are from Kelly, *Retribution*, 102–8.

297. Tigay, *Deuteronomy*, 437.

This whole **land** will become a wasteland of desolation, and these nations will serve the king of Babylon *seventy years*. (Jer 25:11†; cf. 29:10)

The land enjoyed its sabbath rests; all the time of its desolation **it rested**, until the *seventy years* were completed in fulfillment of the word of Yahweh spoken by Jeremiah. (2 Chr 36:21)

Leviticus presents literary personifications of the land culminating in Sabbath years: the defiled land becomes sick and vomits out inhabitants (Lev 18:24–30), circumcise the fruit from the trees for three years (19:23–24), grant the land Sabbath years (25:1–7).[298] The people's neglect of Sabbath years automatically triggers exile to pay them back (26:34–39). Part of the logic comes from the idea that "*the land is mine* [Yahweh's] and you reside in my land as foreigners and strangers" (25:23, emphasis mine).[299] The Chronicler connects the neglected Sabbath years and exile to Jeremiah's seventy years.

The Chronicler may use seventy in a literal or quasi-schematic manner. Elsewhere he listed Zadok the priest contemporary with David as exactly midway between Levi and exile, with a dozen generations before and after (1 Chr 6:3–15[5:29–41]; see note on 6:1–4[5:27–30]). Knoppers suggests considering the chronological function of Zadok (contemporary with David) as the midpoint between ancestors and exile, counting each generation as forty years, thus 12 x 40 = 480 years.[300] Though speculative, this comes close to the mathematical equation of ignored Sabbath years during the kingdom in 2 Chr 36:21, namely, 490 ÷ 7 = 70 years of exile.[301]

In sum, in spite of the Chronicler's strong interest in demonstrating immediate retribution of most of Judah's kings, he handles the exile in a different manner. The Chronicler uses an interpretive blend of Lev 26:34–35 and Jer 25:11 and/or 29:10 to explain the seventy years of exile in terms of the cumulative judgment of Israel, symbolized by ignoring seventy Sabbath years. For the Chronicler, an exegetical explanation of exile points to deferred judgment and cumulative guilt.

36:22–23*//Ezra 1:1–3a*~Jer 25:11*; 29:10* (B)+Isa 44:28*; 45:1* (B)+45:13 (C) (edict of Cyrus) (* see seventy years network). The first section of Ezra-Nehemiah includes three versions of the edict of Cyrus (Ezra 1:2–4; 5:13–15; 6:3–5; laid out side by side in Table EN10 in Ezra-Nehemiah), the first of which shares near *verbatim* agreement, in both its editorial setup and opening section, with the version in the closing of Chronicles (1:1–3a//2 Chr 36:22–23). The situation creates a need to consider authorship and dating of the books in order to speak to exegetical function.

298. See Schnittjer, *Torah Story*, 344–47.

299. See Kartveit, "2 Chronicles 36.20–23," 402. The NIV's terms in Lev 25:23 "foreigners" and "strangers" refer to "residing sojourner" (תּוֹשָׁב) and "residing foreigner" (גֵּר) respectively.

300. See Knoppers, "Priestly Genealogies," 124.

301. On the ideology of exile in Chronicles, see Schnittjer, "Individual versus Collective Retribution," 125–29.

The parallel of the edict of Cyrus provided an important part of the once-dominant view that the Chronicler authored Ezra-Nehemiah. Sara Japhet's work demonstrates pervasive fundamental differences, precluding common authorship and initiating many other studies verifying her findings.[302] As noted in the opening of this chapter, the discussion here regards Chronicles and Ezra-Nehemiah as separate books by separate authors.

The virtually verbatim edict of Cyrus parallel could mean both authors draw on common or parallel source(s) or one could be directly dependent upon the other. If they draw on common or parallel source(s), then dating the books is beside the point. The nature of the indirect relationship of 1 Chr 9:2–18 and Neh 11:3–19 does not offer any help (see note on 1 Chr 9:2–18). It could be speculated that one or both contexts represents post-author scribal addition(s). Though this sounds fine in theory, it makes little sense in light of the evidence. The edict is integral and integrated into the context of both Chronicles and Ezra-Nehemiah, but in very different ways (see below).

The date of Chronicles, as it stands, could be no earlier than six generations after Zerubbabel (1 Chr 3:19–24), last referred to in Scripture shortly after the second year of Darius in 520 BCE (Hag 1:12; 2:2, 21; Zech 4:9; Ezra 5:2).[303] For the broad point being made here, Chronicles could be dated as early as 400, give or take a couple decades. Ezra-Nehemiah features contested passages that bear on dating. A list of high priests goes down to Jaddua (who may be the one by the same name when Alexander the Great conquered much of the ancient Near East in 330 [Neh 12:11–12]). The reference to Darius as "the Persian" may intend to identify him as Darius II (423–404) or III (336–330)

---

302. See Japhet, "Supposed Common Authorship," 330–71.

303. The difficulties of 1 Chr 3:21 gives rise to much speculation. *BHK* with a question mark and *BHS* with more confidence delete the entire series of "sons of" (בְּנֵי) MT—or series of "his son" (בְּנוֹ) which is presumably the Hebrew parent text of the LXX—and replace these with conjunctive *vavs* (ו) to smooth out the problem. No evidence supports this unlikely radical surgery. Knoppers follows the LXX based on its analogy to genealogical patterns elsewhere in 1 Chr 3. He reasons that the differences between *yod* (י) and *vav* (ו) in the consonantal text is slight and could be confused by a scribe. But his explanation of the extra "his son" at the end of the verse in the LXX is weak (*I Chronicles 1–9*, 322–23). If the LXX of 1 Chr 3:21 is original, it establishes a linear genealogy that runs ten generations from Zerubbabel going down to c. 320 BCE (using twenty years per generation as an average). Thus: "The sons of Zerubbabel: Meshullam and [1] Hananiah. Shelomith was their sister . . . And Hanania's sons: [2] Phalletia and [3] Isaia his son, [4] Raphaia his son, [5] Orna his son, [6] Abdia his son, [7] Sechenia his son. And Sechenia's son: [8] Samaia, and Samaia's sons: Chattous and Ioel and Mari and [9] Noadia and Saphath, six. And Noadia's sons: [10] Elithenan and Hezekia and Ezrikam, three" (1 Chr 3:19b, 21–23 LXX, enumeration of generations added). By contrast, Klein follows the MT of 1 Chr 3:21 and notes that "[t]here are no other cases where the expression 'his son' precedes the word it modifies" thus providing evidence that would eliminate the viability of the LXX of 1 Chr 3:21 (*1 Chronicles*, 121, n. 74; also see 14, 113). Williamson also notes that the MT of 1 Chr 3:21 is the more difficult reading. He combines this with the erroneous extra "his son" at the end of the verse in the LXX that suggests its corrupt status (*1 and 2 Chronicles*, 58). The MT reads: "The sons of Zerubbabel: Meshullam and [1] Hananiah. Shelomith was their sister . . . The descendants of Hananiah: Pelatiah and Jeshaiah, the sons of Rephaiah, the sons of Arnan, the sons of Obadiah, the sons of [2] Shekaniah. The descendants of Shekaniah: [3] Shemaiah and his sons, Hattush, Igal, Bariah, [4] Neariah and Shaphat—six in all. The sons of Neariah: [5] Elioenai, Hizkiah and Azrikam—three in all. [6] The sons of Elioenai: Hodaviah, Eliashib, Pelaiah, Akkub, Johanan, Delaiah and Anani—seven in all" (1 Chr 3:19b, 21–24, vv. 21, 22 lit., enumeration of generations added). While Klein and Williamson are correct to favor the MT based on this evidence, Japhet's non-decision is an attractive alternative leaving an open-ended date range for this genealogy from 460 to 320 BCE (*I & II Chronicles*, 94). The view here follows the MT suggesting that Zerubbabel's genealogy in 1 Chr 3:19–24 runs down to c. 400 BCE. Also see Murawski, "'To Study the Law,'" 37 n.14.

versus Darius I; or the reference may even be to Darius I (522–486) to distinguish him from the later ruler(s) of the same throne name (12:22). Even calling kings "the Persian" at all—like Cyrus (Ezra 1:1, etc.)—may suggest a time after the fall of the Persian empire.[304] If any one of these passages are what they seem, then Ezra-Nehemiah, as it stands, could not be compiled before the early Hellenistic period after 330. In spite of these dates for the earliest possible completion of the final forms of Ezra-Nehemiah and Chronicles, no evidence definitively demonstrates which came first. The present discussion will focus on the different functions of the parallel passages.

Chronicles uses the beginning part of the edict of Cyrus differently than Ezra-Nehemiah, ending in mid-sentence with "May he go up." The shared portion of the edict is nearly identical (regular font signifies verbatim parallels, bold signifies what is unique to Chronicles, and italics signify what is unique to Ezra-Nehemiah):[305]

> In the first year of Cyrus king of Persia, in order to fulfill the word of Yahweh spoken by Jeremiah, Yahweh moved the heart of Cyrus king of Persia to make a proclamation throughout his realm and also to put it in writing: "This is what Cyrus king of Persia says: 'Yahweh, the God of heaven, has given me all the kingdoms of the earth and he has appointed me to build a temple for him at Jerusalem in Judah. Any of his people among you, may **Yahweh** their God be with them, may he go up *to Jerusalem in Judah and build the temple of Yahweh, the God of Israel, the God who is in Jerusalem. And in any locality where survivors may now be living, the people are to provide them with silver and gold, with goods and livestock, and with freewill offerings for the temple of God in Jerusalem.*'" (2 Chr 36:22–23†//Ezra 1:1–4†)

The pair of verbs in Ezra 1:3—with the same form and nuance—"May he go up" and "may he build" preview the structure of the first unit of the book, going up from exile (Ezra 1–3) to build the temple (4–6).[306] The edict of Cyrus closes Chronicles by anticipating the last in a series of renewals (see Figure C1). Just as David and Solomon prepared for and built the first temple after the neglect of the ark by Saul, Hezekiah reopens the temple after Ahaz had closed it, and Manasseh restores proper worship after his own Babylonian captivity, so too Cyrus invites the people of Yahweh to go up and restore his temple.

The Chronicler and/or the narrator of Ezra-Nehemiah mark the prophecy of seventy years and mention "moving the heart" of the king: "in order to fulfill the word of Yahweh spoken by Jeremiah, Yahweh moved the heart [עור] of Cyrus king of Persia"

---

304. On this last point, see Ryle, *Ezra and Nehemiah*, xxiv. This does not apply to 2 Chr 36:22 because of the switch from the Neo-Babylonians in 36:17–20.

305. For very minor differences, like some full spelling in 2 Chr 36:22–23 versus defective in Ezra 1:1–3a, see Bendavid, *Parallels*, 164 [Hebrew].

306. See Lortie, "These Are the Days," 161–69. Though Lortie repeatedly identifies the verbs wrongly as impv. (161, 163, 164), in a footnote he acknowledges they are jussive forms but then (wrongly) claims they function like impv. (163, n. 5). On the permissive function of jussive verbs, see *GBHS* §3.3.1a.

(2 Chr 36:22//Ezra 1:1). While the seventy years refers to Jer 25:11 and 29:10, stirring the heart of Cyrus likely alludes to Isaiah. Isaiah names Cyrus as Yahweh's "messiah" who calls for Jerusalem to be rebuilt (Isa 44:28; 45:1). The causative stem of the verb "move the heart" or "stir up" (עור) appears in the following context: "*I will stir him up* [עור] in my righteousness: I will make all his ways straight. He will rebuild my city and set my exiles free, but not for a price or reward, says Yahweh Almighty" (45:13†, emphasis mine). The same term—"Yahweh stirred up the spirit" (lit.)—appears in other contexts referring to the returned exiles who need to rebuild the temple (Hag 1:14; cf. Ezra 1:5).

The idea of a deity stirring up a king's heart to initiate a building project occurs in an ancient Mesopotamian ziggurat building inscription on the lips of Nebuchadnezzar: "My great lord Marduk *stirred my heart* to rebuild it."[307] The traditional theological rationale of royal motivation serves as a basis to explain how Yahweh makes good on his word through the prophets. If a political analyst would interpret Cyrus's motives as prudent concessions to a group of minor subjects, the Chronicler and the narrator of Ezra-Nehemiah claim the emperor's heart is in the hands of Yahweh according to the prophets.

FILTERS

Filtering elements provide a dual function. Filters primarily prevent false positives in identifying scriptural exegesis by excluding noninterpretive and non-allusive parallels. Secondary benefits include identifying contextual tendencies to help explain other uses of Scripture. The following are merely representative, not exhaustive or complete.

Non-Exegetical Broad Allusions and Shared Themes

Thematic similarities: 2 Chr 9:23//1 Kgs 10:24>/<Prov 29:26, "seeking an audience before Solomon/a ruler" (מבקשים פני שלמה/מושל); **15:3–6**>/<Judg 2–13, time of trouble and seeking God;[308] **24:9**>/<Exod 30:11–16, one time half-shekel collection to build the tabernacle (cf. Neh 10:32–33[33–34]);[309] **29:21**>/<Lev 4:13–21, 22–26, 27–31, sin offering for congregation, ruler, and individuals (cf. Ezra 8:35); **29:22–24**>/<Lev 17:6; Num 18:17, rituals of sacrifice; **30:26**>/<2 Kgs 23:22, Chronistic Hezekiah with figural similarity to Deuteronomistic Josiah;[310] **31:11**>/<Neh 10:38–39[39–40]; 13:5, 9, 12–13, storehouses in temple complex for offerings and tithes of the people; **35:18**>/<1 Chr 6:18, 33, broad comparison between Passover of Josiah and worship in the days of Samuel.[311]

---

307. George, "Stele of Nebuchadnezzar II," 169, emphasis mine.

308. The broad allusion to a time of trouble preceding a turn to Yahweh may refer to the period of the judges, but the reference is debated (see Knoppers, "'Yhwh Is Not with Israel,'" 605–6, n. 15).

309. See Schniedewind, "Chronicler as Interpreter," 168.

310. Though Chronistic Hezekiah imagery may figurally relate to Deuteronomistic Josiah, the possible allusion is too brief to regard as exegetical. Compare examples in Table C10.

311. The days of Samuel may relate to the Chronicler's inclusion of Samuel's place in the Levitical clan of Kohath, see Dillard, *2 Chronicles*, 291.

Parallel language: >/<**1 Chr 16:41; 2 Chr 5:13; 7:3, 6; 20:21**, "for Yahweh is good, his mercy endures forever" (cf. Pss 100:5; 106:1; 107:1; Ezra 3:11); >/<**1 Chr 23:31; 2 Chr 2:4[3]; 8:13; 31:3**; Neh 10:33[34], "on Sabbaths, on new moons, and appointed times/appointed times of Yahweh our God" (לשבתות/השבתות לחדשים/לחדשות/החדשים ולמעדים/ולמועדי יהוה אלהינו); and similarly Isa 1:13, "new moon, and Sabbath, calling of convocation" (חדש ושבת קרא מקרא), 1:14, "your new moons and your appointed times" (חדשיכם ומועדיכם), Ezek 45:17, "at feasts, and at new moons, and at Sabbaths, and at every appointed time of the house of Israel" (בחגים ובחדשים ובשבתות בכל מועדי בית ישׂראל), 46:3, "on Sabbaths and on new moons" (בשׁנתות ובחדשים);[312] >/<**1 Chr 29:13**; Isa 63:14, "your glorious name" (שם תפארתך);[313] >/<**2 Chr 12:7**; Jer 42:18; 44:6, "will not/will be poured out upon" (לא/נתך חמה); >/<**15:5**; Amos 3:9, "great turmoil" (מהומות רבות); >/<**20:7**; Isa 41:8, "seed of Abraham your/my friend" (זרע אברהם אהבך/אהבי) (cf. Jas 2:23); >/<**29:17**; Jer 12:3; Pss 7:10; 17:3; Prov 17:3, "test the heart" (בחן לבב); >/<**30:7**; Zech 1:4, "do not be like your ancestors" (אל־תהיו כאבותיכם).[314]

David's prayer in 1 Chr 29:10–19 includes shared imagery with the psalmic compilation when the ark arrived in Jerusalem and David's thanksgiving after Nathan's oracle, **1 Chr 29:10–13**>/<16:24–26, praising God in psalms and prayer; **29:14**>/<17:16, humility of covenant and opportunity to give. The prayer also features numerous liturgical stock phrases, **29:12b**>/<Ps 103:19b; **29:13**>/<Isa 63:14; **29:15**>/<Ps 39:13; Job 8:9.[315]

Connections within Chronicles

Chronicles reflects a distinct style in many ways, including frequent use of favorite expressions and even characteristic terms. A small sample of these illustrate non-allusive parallels within the book itself. Recognizing these as part of Chronistic style also helps calibrate the degree of interpretive force, or lack thereof, when these serve as paraphrasing within synoptic contexts.[316]

Selections from the Chronistic lexicon of (in)fidelity.[317] The Chronicler uses a somewhat distinctive set of loaded theological terms. Here are some of the dominant ways he expresses relationship with God: >/<**1 Chr 28:9; 29:9, 19; 2 Chr 16:9; 19:9; 25:2**; 1 Kgs 8:61; 11:4; 15:3, 14//2 Chr 15:17; 2 Kgs 20:3//Isa 38:3, "wholeheartedly" (לב/לבב שלם) (cf. 1 Chr 12:39);[318] >/<**2 Chr 7:14; 12:6, 7, 12; 30:11; 32:26; 33:12, 19, 23;**

312. See Rendtorff, "Chronicles and the Priestly Torah," 260.

313. For this phrase and the next four, see Driver, "Speeches," 292, n. 1.

314. See Warhurst, "Merging," 121. Warhurst isolates numerous short snippets of prophetic language in Hezekiah's speeches in 2 Chr 29:5–11; 29:31; 30:6–9 (118–23).

315. See Driver, "Speeches," 291.

316. Older lists often misrepresent the Chronicler's style by including Ezra-Nehemiah as a continuation of his work (e.g., Driver, *Introduction*, 535–40; Curtis and Madsen, *Chronicles*, 28–36). For an important annotated list of the Chronicler's style in contradistinction to Ezra-Nehemiah, see Japhet, "Supposed Common Authorship," 357–66.

317. This list is based on research for the current project. For a fuller list of Chronistic worship expressions and extensive discussion, see Japhet, *Ideology*, ch. 2 (156–208).

318. See Driver, "Speeches," 295, n. 3.

34:27; 36:12, reflexive use of "humble oneself" (כנע Nif) (cf. esp. Lev 26:41); >/<**2 Chr 26:16; 32:25**, "his heart was proud" (גָּבַהּ לִבּוֹ); >/<**1 Chr 2:7; 5:25; 9:1; 10:13; 28:9; 2 Chr 12:2; 26:16, 18; 28:19, 22; 29:6; 29:19; 30:7; 33:19; 36:14**, "infidelity" (מעל, perhaps stemming from Lev 26:40); >/<**1 Chr 21:3; 2 Chr 24:18; 28:10, 13** (3x); **33:23**, "guilt (noun)" (אַשְׁמָה);[319] >/<**1 Chr 10:14; 16:11; 21:30; 22:19; 2 Chr 1:5; 12:14; 14:4[3]; 15:12, 13; 16:12; 17:4; 18:7; 19:3; 20:3; 22:9; 25:15; 26:5; 30:19; 31:21; 34:3, 21, 26**, "seek/seeking God/God of ancestors/Yahweh" (דרש אלהים/לאלהי אביו/ ליהוה/ביהוה/את יהוה), "seek him" (וידרשהו), "not seek Yahweh" (לא דרש ביהוה)—and synonymously, >/<**1 Chr 16:10, 11; 2 Chr 7:14; 11:16; 15:4, 15; 20:4**, "seek Yahweh" (בקש יהוה)—also, **1 Chr 15:13**, "did not seek it [ark]" (לא דרשנהו); >/<**2 Chr 12:14; 19:3; 30:19**, "he set his heart" (הכין לבו), "he did not set his heart" (לא הכין לבו), "they did not set their heart" (לא הכינו לבבם).

Other important Chronistic stock phrases: >/<2 Chr 11:1, 3, 10, 12, 23; 15:2, 8, 9; 25:5; 31:1; 34:9, "Judah and Benjamin/house of Judah and Benjamin/all Judah and Benjamin (יהודה ובנימן/בית יהודה ובנימן/כל יהודה ובנימן)," "all Israel in Benjamin and Judah" (כל ישׂראל ביהודה ובנימן), "all the land of Judah and Benjamin (כל ארץ יהודה ובנימן)";[320] >/< "land of Israel" (ארץ ישׂראל) four times—in days of David (1 Chr 22:2), Solomon (2 Chr 2:17[16]), Hezekiah (30:25), and Josiah (34:7), each when kingdom basically conformed to its traditional geographical extent;[321] >/<1 Chr 16:40; 22:12; 2 Chr 12:1; 17:9; 31:3, 4; 34:14; 35:26, "in the/Torah of Yahweh" (ב/תורת יהוה) (cf. 2 Kgs 10:31).[322]

Other thematic parallels within Chronicles: >/<1 Chr 11:11–47; 27:2–15, some of David's mighty men later enjoy ruling appointments (cf. 2 Sam 23:8–39); >/<2 Chr 24:2; 26:5, Joash and Amaziah do right/seek Yahweh all the years/days of their mentors.

Non-Exegetical Use of Templates

Not every use and/or variation of scriptural donor contexts should be construed as theologically motivated. Throughout the present treatment of Chronicles, wide latitude has been made for noninterpretive stylistic adjustments and linguistic updating. Determining the difference between interpretive use of scriptural traditions versus literary use of narrative templates seems necessary even if tentative. The following examples have been tentatively excluded as noninterpretive uses of the donor contexts as templates.

David's sacrifice at the threshing floor may have been reformatted slightly in line with Gideon's sacrifice. Several of the proposed similarities are vague, but they match pluses in the Chronistic version of the story as opposed to 2 Sam 24: threshing wheat

---

319. Elsewhere "guilt" (noun, אַשְׁמָה) only in Leviticus (many times); Ezra 9–10; Ps 69:5[6]; Amos 8:14 (see ibid., 306). Conversely, the more common verb form "be guilty" (אשם) only appears 2x in 2 Chr 19:10.

320. See Giffone, *"Sit at My Right Hand,"* 195, n. 65.

321. See Williamson, *Israel*, 123.

322. Begg, "The Death of Josiah," 6, n. 15.

(Judg 6:11; 1 Chr 21:20); hide themselves (Judg 6:11; 1 Chr 21:20); willing to give sacrifice (Judg 6:18–19; 1 Chr 21:23); supernatural fire (Judg 6:21; 1 Chr 21:26); and a few less likely alleged similarities.[323] If the literary shape of this set of adjustments in 1 Chr 21 follows Judg 6, it seems to do so merely as a literary model and not for exegetical reasons (compare Table C10).

Chronistic Hezekiah broadly conforms to the template of Deuteronomistic Solomon and slightly more to Chronistic Solomon: Passover (2 Chr 30:26); extra week of Passover celebration (1 Kgs 8:65–66/~/2 Chr 7:8–9; 30:23); organizing priests and Levites like David and Solomon (1 Chr 15:3–24; 23–26; 2 Chr 8:14–15; 29:11–14; 31:2, 11–20); great wealth (1 Kgs 10:14–15/~/2 Chr 9:13–14; 32:27–29); shields (1 Kgs 10:16–17/~/2 Chr 9:15–16; 12:9–10; 32:27); honor from gentiles (1 Kgs 9:24–25/~/2 Chr 9:23–24; 32:23); prayer at temple (re)dedication (1 Kgs 8:12–53/~/2 Chr 6:1–42; 30:19); healing promised and received (2 Chr 7:14; 30:20).[324] This extensive set of parallels seems intentional but for literary versus theological ends. Namely, the Chronicler may have used the Solomon materials as a broad template to shape the new mass of Hezekiah materials. What appears to be lacking are exegetical interventions akin to other Chronistic uses of extended echo-effect, like Manasseh's Josiah-like reforms (2 Chr 33:14–16) or Josiah's Ahab-like death (2 Chr 35:22–24; cf. 18:29, 33–34//1 Kgs 22:30, 34–35) (see Table C10 for other examples). Stated differently, in Kings Hezekiah symbolizes faithfulness like no other (2 Kgs 18:5), and yet, ironically and tragically, Isaiah blames him for the coming exile (20:16–18). Even the way the Chronicler handles these details creates challenges for the proposed Solomon-like figural sense of Hezekiah (see notes on 2 Chr 32). For the moment it can be agreed that Deuteronomistic Solomon is presented with considerable irony and Chronistic Solomon with more generosity.[325] Because of the ironies of Deuteronomistic Hezekiah and the complexities of Chronistic Hezekiah in 2 Chr 32, it is not clear how reshaping Chronistic Hezekiah after Solomon would theologically refigure him.[326] What does it mean to say Chronistic Hezekiah is Solomon-like as opposed to Deuteronomistic Hezekiah-like or Isaianic Hezekiah-like? In light of these ambiguities,

323. See Sugimoto, "Chronicler's Techniques," 64.

324. On the parallels between Chronistic Solomon and Chronistic Hezekiah see Williamson, *Israel*, 119–25; Dillard, *2 Chronicles*, 228–29. Also see Throntveit, "Relationship," 105–21. In the list here the synoptic parallels to Deuteronomistic Solomon have also been included since they run parallel except in two cases—the Chronistic pluses in 1 Chr 8:14–15 (organization of priests and Levites) and 7:14 (healing promised). The evidence of Deuteronomistic parallels for most of these Solomonic characteristics takes the edge off of the supposed significance of the typological parallels suggested by Williamson and Dillard (see below).

325. On the deep ironies of the portrayal of Solomon in Kings, impugning his character, more or less, see Hays, "Has the Narrator?" 149–74. On the more positive portrayal of Chronistic Solomon see Dillard, *2 Chronicles*, 2.

326. Someone could quibble and point out the two areas without Deuteronomistic overlap in the parallels listed above and, thus, argue Chronistic Hezekiah has been modeled after Chronistic Solomon—organizing priests and Levites and healing promised and received (see pluses at 2 Chr 7:14; 8:14–15). Such a view seems rather thin in the light of the considerable overlap with the other parallels. Moreover, it seems equally plausible that the accounts of Solomon and Hezekiah organizing the priests and Levites are meant to make them to be David-like (cf., e.g., 1 Chr 23–26). For the present purposes, Chronistic Hezekiah shall be compared to Solomon with the shared parallels listed above in both Kings and Chronicles.

the proposed Solomonic patterns in the account of Hezekiah have been filtered out as literary organization versus exegetical agenda. The studies listed in the first footnote of this paragraph take another view and offer extremely broad and unsatisfactory suggestions.

The Chronicler uses a literary *inclusio* to frame all of **1 Chr 23–29** and set it in David's closing years, >/<1 Chr 23:1; 29:28, "full of days" (שׂבע ימים).[327] Elsewhere the Chronicler uses an *inclusio*, >/<2 Chr 2:2, 18[1, 17] by cloning some of the data from 1 Kgs 5:15–16[29–30] (see table in note on 2 Chr 2:1–18[1:18–2:17]). This latter example appears to be a literary *inclusio*, not scribal repetitive resumption or exegetical intervention, suggesting caution against overreading potential indicators of scribal edits (see other examples in the discussion at Table C8).

Royal Formulaic Devices

The hermeneutical profile at the beginning of the chapter discusses the ways the Chronicler's presentation follows and differs from the formulaic structure of presenting the kings of Judah in Kings (see Table C11; also see Kings Filters). The following elements of the Chronistic closing frames, with few exceptions, seem literary rather than exegetical.[328]

Summary of rule: "from beginning to end" (הראשנים והאחרנים) (2 Chr 9:29; 12:15; 16:11; 20:34; 25:26; 26:22; 28:26; 35:27).

Source citations of kings of Judah: "they are written in the records of/scroll of/annotations of the scroll of/in the vision of. . . ." (הנם כתובים על דברי/ספר/מדרש ספר/בחזון)—(italicized references signify variations, underlining signifies prophetic source in addition to royal source, and wavy underlining signifies some kind of political source), 1 Chr 29:29 (David); *2 Chr 9:29* (Solomon); *12:15* (Rehoboam); *13:22* (Abijah); 16:11 (Asa); 20:34 (Jehoshaphat); n/a (Jehoram); 24:27 (Joash); *25:26* (Amaziah); *26:22* (Uzziah/Azariah); 27:7 (Jotham); 28:26 (Ahaz); 32:32 (Hezekiah); 33:*18*, 19 (Manasseh); n/a (Amon); 35:*26*, 27 (Josiah); 36:8 (Jehoiakim).[329]

Succession: "and X his son ruled in his place" (וימלך . . . בנו תחתיו) (1 Chr 29:28; 2 Chr 9:31; 12:16; 14:1[13:23]; 17:1; 21:1; 24:27; 26:23; 27:9; 28:27; 32:33; 33:20; 36:8; cf. 1 Chr 19:1; 2 Chr 22:1; 26:1; 33:25; 36:1).

---

327. Note a similar technique in Josh 13:1; 23:1, 2.

328. Exceptions include the double prophetic source citations for David and Solomon to highlight their importance (1 Chr 29:29; 2 Chr 9:29) and the expansive source citation for Manasseh, which seems interpretive (see note on 2 Chr 33:19).

329. Source citations indebted to Glatt-Gilad, "Regnal Formulae," 198–99; Klein, *1 Chronicles*, 39–40.

Chapter 36

TOWARD THE NEW TESTAMENT

The preceding chapters of this study evaluate scriptural exegesis within Israel's Scriptures. The present chapter seeks to identify selected implications of these findings as they bear on the New Testament. The implications will be framed by first looking back from the New Testament and then forward to the New Testament.

LOOKING BACK TO ISRAEL'S SCRIPTURES

The New Testament interprets Israel's Scriptures according to many of the ways Israel's Scriptures interpret Scripture. This proposal stands against alternative suggestions such as the New Testament interprets Scripture in a completely new way or the New Testament wholly depends on Second Temple Judaic exegesis. These differences have been overstated for the moment because the extreme form of these alternatives appears too often.

The newness of the gospel of Messiah leads some evangelical Christians to suggest getting rid of Israel's Scriptures or at least treating them as irrelevant. A minister of a large congregation says: "According to Paul, Jesus' followers are dead to the Ten Commandments. The Ten Commandments have no authority over you. None. To be clear: Thou shalt not obey the Ten Commandments."[1] That minister seeks to help the cause of the gospel by "unhitching" the old covenant.[2]

A professor at an evangelical university promotes in a somewhat more circumspect manner an attempt by some activists to frame their political agenda as "Red Letter Christians." They prioritize the teaching of Christ, especially the Sermon on the Mount. They affirm the Apostles' Creed and the inspiration of Scripture but "emphasize the 'red letters' because we believe you can only understand the rest of the Bible when you read it from the perspective provided by Christ."[3]

An introduction to the New Testament's use of Scripture, now in its second edition, features an introductory chapter on the late Second Temple interpretive context of the

1. Stanley, *Irresistible*, 136.
2. See ibid., 209, 278, 280, 315. For charitable disagreement with Stanley see Imes, *Bearing God's Name*, 2–3.
3. Campolo, *Red Letter Christians*, 23.

New Testament—the sectarian Dead Sea Scrolls, Philo, and Josephus.[4] There is no introductory chapter or substantial discussion comparing the interpretive strategies within Israel's Scriptures and the New Testament. Others go further with sectarian comparisons. Though Jesus and his followers formally may not be Essenes, it is said their ideology gave rise to some of the earliest Jesus traditions.[5]

These books provide less cause for concern than the exceedingly commonplace sharp contrast among laity and occasionally ministers of the word between the wrathful deity of Israel versus the love of Messiah.[6] Some of these distortions do not stem immediately and directly from misinterpretation of the scriptural use of Scripture. At the same time, the fundamental neglect of adequately explaining New Testament scriptural exegesis in the light of the scriptural exegesis within Israel's Scriptures stands somewhere upstream among other deficiencies.

The following discussion briefly looks back from the New Testament to exegesis within Israel's Scriptures along three lines: progressive revelation, context, and canonical consciousness. Due to space limitations, only a tiny fraction of the better studies on the New Testament use of Scripture can be engaged. These studies do not represent the extremes just mentioned. Still, the work done on the New Testament use of Scripture can benefit by greater attention to the way Israel's Scriptures interpret Scripture.

PROGRESSIVE REVELATION

The teachings, death, and resurrection of Messiah stand at the headwaters of powerful divine revelation of the gospel. But scriptural revelation cannot be "cut loose" from Messiah without theological damage. "To take Christ at all He must be taken as the centre of a movement of revelation organized around Him, and winding up the whole process of revelation."[7]

The New Testament's advancement of revelation may be categorically more and different than anything before. At the same time the entire meaning of Messiah and his people everywhere grounds itself in scriptural revelation. Just as Messiah often taunts "Have you not read?," so too Paul and Sosthenes say the death, burial, and resurrection of Messiah accords with the Scriptures.[8] The new revelation connects with revelation in Israel's Scriptures.

The comprehensive scope of revelation in Israel's Scriptures bearing witness to the

4. See Moyise, *Old Testament in the New*, 11–27 (ch. 1). See below for further discussion.

5. See Joseph, *Jesus, the Essenes*, 164. For a critique of several kindred studies, see Regev, "Were Early Christians Sectarians?" 771–93.

6. See Stanley, *Irresistible*, 223, 257. On contrasts between the wrathful deity of Old Testament versus Christ's love in New Testament by Marcion, von Harnack, and the new atheists, see Strawn, *Old Testament Is Dying*, 103–29.

7. Vos, *Biblical Theology*, 302.

8. Matthew 21:42; 22:31; 1 Cor 15:3–4. And see Seitz, "Creed," in Radner and Sumner, *Rule of Faith*, 126–35.

gospel appears in many places. Messiah tells his opponents, Moses "wrote about me."[9] He tells his followers, "Everything must be fulfilled that is written about me in the Torah of Moses, the Prophets and the Psalms."[10] The apostles likewise speak in equally comprehensive terms: "Indeed, beginning with Samuel, all the prophets who have spoken have foretold these days."[11] A sermon of Paul includes an ironic claim: "The people of Jerusalem and their rulers did not recognize Jesus, yet in condemning him they fulfilled the words of the prophets that they read every Sabbath."[12]

The "purpose" of Israel's Scriptures is to present "the history of revelation."[13] This purpose extends beyond historical narratives and encompasses all scriptural genres. Even "lyrical and didactic poetry in Israel are deployed in the service of divine revelation."[14] The author to the Hebrews opens by connecting revelation old and new: "In the past God spoke to our ancestors through the prophets at many times and in various ways, but in these last days he has spoken to us by his Son."[15] The evidence suggests that New Testament writers regard Israel's Scriptures as moving revelation forward.

Revelation grows "from century to century" leading to Messiah. As "revelation advances, Scripture increases in volume."[16] Revelation does not stand alone but proceeds by authorized exegesis.[17] Revelation progresses and culminates in the gospel of Messiah, in part, by exegesis.

In sum, the New Testament presents the revelation of God in Messiah as a culmination of his revealed works of old. The New Testament writers follow after Israel's Scriptures in advancing revelation, often by means of exegesis.

CONTEXT

Attending to context reveals that the New Testament uses Israel's Scriptures in many of the ways Israel's Scriptures use Scripture. When it comes to context, one size does not fit all. To get at this requires attention to how the New Testament approaches Israel's Scriptures in terms of horizontal, vertical, and typological contexts.

Horizontal context refers to the surrounding scriptural setting of a cited text. One side of the normal long-running debate on the New Testament use of Scripture limits the context to only the cited portion, while the other side considers the larger context, running from paragraph to chapter or even book. Many New Testament scholars favor

9. John 5:46; cf. v. 39.
10. Luke 24:44; cf. vv. 25–27.
11. Acts 3:24.
12. Acts 13:27.
13. Bavinck, *Reformed Dogmatics*, 1:444, 447.
14. Ibid., 1:393.
15. Hebrews 1:1–2a.
16. Bavinck, *Reformed Dogmatics*, 1:383.
17. See Vos, "Inaugural Address," 33. Also see Bavinck, *Reformed Dogmatics*, 1:396.

Dodd's conclusion that cited passages serve "rather as pointers to the whole context than as constituting testimonies in and for themselves."[18] Beale vigorously affirms the contextual use of all intentional allusions by New Testament writers.[19] Witherington sees variations in how New Testament writers use Scripture, though he suggests they often do so in noncontextual ways.[20]

The evidence compiled in the present study overwhelmingly favors contextual exegesis by the authors of Israel's Scriptures. Horizontal context often varies in breadth. Even ironic interpretive allusions within Israel's Scriptures that read against the sense of the donor text do so with the context in mind.[21] The vast majority of the hundreds of noncontextual scriptural parallels within Israel's Scriptures have been filtered out as non-exegetical in the preceding chapters—stock phrases, common expressions, etc.

Deciding on the debate of the breadth of horizontal contexts of scriptural donor texts used by the New Testament falls outside of the present study. If the New Testament favors more contextual use of scriptural citations, that would align it more with tendencies of exegesis within Israel's Scriptures.

Vertical context refers to cited scriptural texts that themselves feature exegesis of other Scriptures (see Figure NT1). In this case, the donor text contains *within* itself exegesis of yet another donor passage or passages. Certain favorite passages within the Hebrew Scriptures serve as donor contexts for many exegetical receptor contexts, creating veritable networks. For the moment the New Testament's use of individual vertical context needs to be considered before coming back to interpretive networks.

FIGURE NT1: AN EXAMPLE OF VERTICAL CONTEXT VIA EXEGETICAL ALLUSION‡

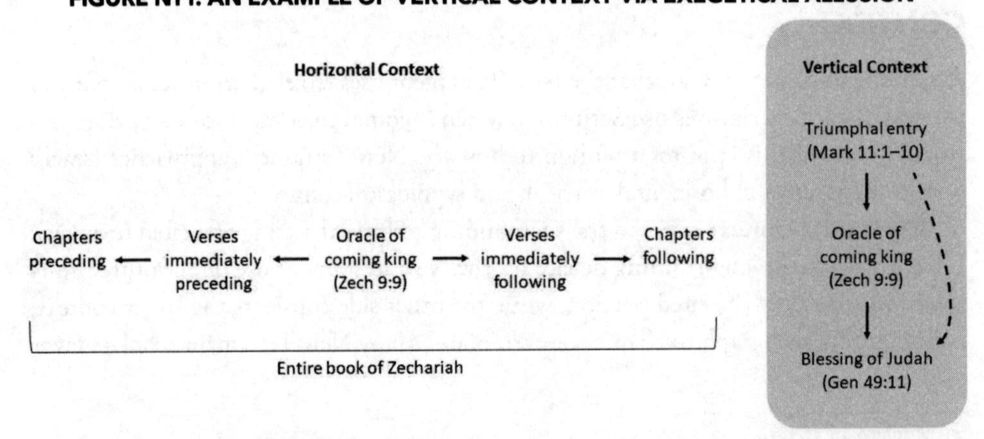

‡ From the perspective of Mark 11, the vertical context within Zech 9:9 is its interpretive allusion to Gen 49:11. Mark 11:1–10 alludes to Zech 9:9 as well as to Gen 49:11 LXX by the twofold "bound" and threefold "unbinding" (Mark 11:2, 4, 5). See Schnittjer, "Blessing," 29, n. 34.

18. Dodd, *According to the Scriptures*, 126.
19. Beale, "Cognitive Peripheral Vision," 263–93.
20. See Witherington, *Torah Old and New*, 357; idem, *Isaiah Old and New*, 353; idem, *Psalms Old and New*, 327, 330.
21. See, e.g., notes on Num 16:3, 13; Amos 2:12; 4:4, 5.

The issue at hand concerns whether New Testament scholars adequately take advantage of vertical contexts within Israel's Scriptures or if they treat donor passages exclusively in relation to their horizontal contexts. Beale maintains that the New Testament may work with an earlier scriptural text according to the way it gets developed later in the Hebrew Scriptures.[22] Beale's sensible observation needs to work in both directions.

The New Testament may use Scripture according to downward vertical context within the donor text or according to upward vertical context of its genetically related receptor text(s) within Israel's Scriptures. For example, Johnson discusses the way Jesus refers to Ps 82:6—"You are gods"—as "Law."[23] Johnson's outstanding argument on the authority of the Psalms can be strengthened at this very point by tapping into the vertical context *within* Ps 82 as a potential receptor text.[24] This evidence suggests that interpretation of New Testament exegesis of Scripture can benefit by working up or down vertical contexts of exegetically connected donor texts.

Among other things, the *Commentary on the New Testament Use of the Old Testament* edited by Beale and Carson focuses on "the use of the OT within the OT."[25] They say: "Sometimes a NT author may have in mind the earlier OT reference but may be interpreting it through the later OT development of that earlier text, and if the lens of that later text is not analyzed, then the NT use may seem strange or may not properly be understood."[26] This viewpoint is similar to what is here referred to as vertical context. In spite of the claims of the editors in the introduction, an assessment of ten representative entries in the commentary suggests a wide gap between intention and execution. Only one of the ten commentary entries evaluates Old Testament use of Old Testament as part of the context of the cited Scripture.[27] The *Commentary on the New Testament Use of the Old Testament* takes a significant step forward by pointing out the need for attention to the use of Scripture within Israel's Scriptures as it bears on the New Testament's own use

22. See Beale, *Handbook*, 98. Also see Harmon, "OT Use of the OT, Comparison to the NT," *DNTUOT*, forthcoming.

23. See John 10:34 as argued by Johnson, *Old Testament in the New*, 31–35.

24. See note on Psalm 82.

25. Beale and Carson, eds., *Commentary on the NT Use of OT*, xxiv.

26. Ibid.

27. Ten contexts were chosen before opening the *Commentary on the New Testament Use of Old Testament*. Each was selected with an attempt to avoid obscure passages and with an eye to a broad representation. Three of the passages are synoptically related to compare the work of three contributing authors. This evaluation is not comprehensive but seems fair since it relates to one of the major elements required of every entry, namely, investigation of what is here referred to as the horizontal and vertical contexts of cited Old Testament passages. The ten entries evaluated are: Matt 21:5//Zech 9:9 (Blomberg, 63–64); Matt 21:13//Isa 56:7 (67–68); Mark 11:17//Isa 56:7 (Watts, 209–10); Luke 19:46//Isa 56:7 (Pao and Schnabel, 357–38); John 10:34//Ps 82:2 (Köstenberger, 466–67); Acts 2:17–21//Joel 2:28–32[3:1–5] (Marshall, 532–36); Rom 4:3, 9, 22//Gen 15:6 (Seifrid, 622–27); 2 Cor 6:17//Isa 52:11 (Balla, 769–74); Heb 2:6–8a//Ps 8:4–6 (Guthrie, 946–47); Heb 8:8–12//Jer 31:31–34 (Guthrie, 970–72). Of these ten, only Guthrie discussed the use of Scripture in the cited Old Testament context (Gen 1:26–27 ← Ps 8 ← Heb 2:6–8b) (946–47). Three other entries of these ten listed potential related Old Testament contexts without investigating how they might advance revelation by exegesis; they are listed more like cross references (Blomberg, 64; Pao and Schnabel, 357; Seifrid, 624). Meanwhile, ten of ten of these commentary entries list and/or interact with Second Temple Judaic literature or later rabbinic potential uses of the Old Testament contexts in question. These connections can be helpful, but only if combined with evaluation of Old Testament use of Old Testament.

of Scripture. Answering this need will require a fresh approach that investigates how Old Testament use of Scripture contributes to New Testament use of Scripture.[28]

A critical evaluation of three methodologies of the New Testament use of the Old Testament considers how each goes about investigating Old Testament context.[29] By way of summary Keefer compiled a list of their eight definitions of Old Testament contexts that bear on interpreting New Testament use of Scripture:

- language of the original;
- surrounding verses of quotations;
- similar texts elsewhere in Old Testament;
- major sections of Old Testament (esp. a single book);
- Old Testament themes;
- salvation history/theology;
- historical situation of the authors;
- meaning in the minds of the authors.[30]

Scriptural interpretation by the authors of Israel's Scriptures, or what is here called vertical context, does not register within these representative approaches to New Testament use of Scripture.[31]

This whole issue of vertical context leads into a brief consideration of interpretive **networks**. Some of the most interpreted passages in Israel's Scriptures need to be considered together with their receptor contexts in terms of interpretive networks. The frequent exegetical interpretation of these Scriptures by Scriptures does not exhaust but increases the generative potential of the donor contexts. The more a scriptural tradition gets interpreted the more it offers to still later scriptural interpreters. Many networks have been laid out graphically in a chapter near the end of the present study. The issue at hand relates to the way interpretive networks affect New Testament exegesis.

Interpretive networks work in a manner even more dynamically than single-stream vertical contexts.[32] Networks tend to form around certain lightning rod passages, whether prompted from elements within the text itself, from traumatic events like exile in the situations of the biblical authors, or from a combination of internal and external prompts. Interpretive networks include multiple scriptural exegetical interventions with the same donor texts that do not always go in a single straight line one after the other.

28. Note an attempt to address this shortcoming in the form of a series of entries on the Old Testament use of Scripture in *DOTUNT*.

29. The three methodologies are Evans, "Function of the OT in the New"; Snodgrass, "Use of the OT in the New"; and Beale, *Handbook* (see Keefer, "Meaning," 73–85, esp. summary chart, 75).

30. Keefer, "Meaning," 84.

31. Though Keefer does not mention it, in three places Beale does briefly refer to the importance of Old Testament use of Scripture as it bears on New Testament use of Scripture (see *Handbook*, 47, 97, 98).

32. For an example of single-stream vertical context, see notes on Ps 96:7–8, 10; 1 Chr 16:7–36.

Some of the interpretive networks within Israel's Scriptures attract further interpretation in the New Testament. An interpretive allusion to one part of an interpretive network may be informed by another part. In the case of Messiah's mount into Jerusalem, Krause rightly asks, "Why, if the colt already resides within the imagery of Zechariah, does Mark return to Genesis?"[33] That is exactly the point. The Judah-king network creates enduring ripple effects on its constituent receptor texts. The prophetic interpretive use of the blessing of Judah does not replace the earlier expectation but actually enhances it. Blenkinsopp explains the evangelist's connection between these two scriptural contexts: "yet it would not, perhaps, be too much to say that they cannot be fully grasped except along the line—a long line—of messianic utilization and interpretation of the Judah oracle."[34] In the case of Mark 11:2–10, the exegetical interaction with the interpretive network functions exactly like many networks within Israel's Scriptures themselves.[35]

Synoptic contexts represent another kind of vertical context in cases where the donor scriptural context has gained a measure of authority. Israel's Scriptures include many legal, narrative, and lyrical synoptic contexts. The evangelists seem to take full advantage of the models of synoptic narratives within Israel's Scriptures. The New Testament narrators work along the lines of the synoptic parallel mechanics found in Deuteronomy, Isaiah, Jeremiah, and Chronicles.[36] An evaluation of the evidence of exegetical advancements by synoptic parallels within Israel's Scriptures broadly suggests continuity with the New Testament. However, synoptic studies of the New Testament sometimes confine themselves to the Gospels and tend to neglect evaluating the use of Israel's Scriptures. One scholar who writes about New Testament synoptic issues, compares the synoptic Gospels to Greco-Roman biographies to evaluate chronological re-arrangement. But he does not acknowledge analogous synoptic chronological re-arrangements that are commonplace within Israel's Scriptures (see dischronologized narratives in Glossary).[37] This lack of attention to the norms within the evangelists' Bible distorts the issue and does a disservice to student readers. While comparative evaluation of Greco-Roman biographies needs to go on, such investigation should not ignore comparable synoptic contexts within Israel's Scriptures which, by all accounts, the evangelists closely studied.

Typological contexts remain one of the most difficult areas of the New Testament's use of Israel's Scriptures. Sometimes typology gets a bad name because of its abuse, usually

33. Krause, "One Who Comes," 149.

34. Blenkinsopp, "Oracle of Judah," 56–57.

35. Discussion here based on Schnittjer, "Blessing of Judah," 35.

36. On how synoptic narratives within Israel's Scriptures work, see Hermeneutical Profile of the Use of Torah in Deuteronomy and Hermeneutical Profile of the Use of Scripture in Chronicles. For detailed interaction with competing approaches to interpreting synoptic Scriptures, see Schnittjer, "Kadesh Infidelity," 95–120, esp. 96–102.

37. Licona, *Why Are There Differences?* 190–96. Licona's neglect may be corroborated by opening the index that lists few references to the Old Testament at all (nine books: Dan, Deut, Gen, Isa, Jer, Job, Kgs, Mal, Ps), including zero references from Old Testament synoptic narratives (303–8). For a list of Old Testament synoptic narratives, see Schnittjer, "Kadesh Infidelity," 96, n. 2, plus Table 1 (96).

in the form of zealous, uncontrolled application. Many have shifted over to using the term "figural" to refer to typological interpretation. In spite of discussion in handbooks, much confusion still surrounds New Testament typological interpretation.[38]

The evidence of literary patterns in the use of Scripture within Israel's Scriptures appears to align with many figural/typological uses of Scripture in the New Testament. Reuse of patterns in the Hebrew Scriptures are not all of one sort. The key differences relate to function.

The exegetically significant intentional use of shared patterns in Israel's Scriptures includes paradigmatic shaping, extended echo-effect, and typological relations. The labels here are not important, except for the different functions they represent. These are discussed at Table C10 in the chapter on Chronicles and summarized in the Glossary. The present discussion can only illustrate a couple of possibilities of how these three relate to the New Testament.

Perhaps Messiah's recycling of the good Samarians scenario in his good Samaritan riddle provides an example of **paradigmatic shaping** in the case of a fictional story. The reuse of details from 2 Chr 28:12–15 is not of itself exegetical. Messiah's exegetical genius comes out of the way he leverages the riddle to interpret Lev 19:18, 34.[39] By contrast, the possible use of the scenario of scoffing the long line of prophets from 2 Chr 36:16 in the parable of the vine growers seems more exegetical, based on the shared details of impending doom.[40] The difference between these two parables is that the good Samaritan focuses on the ethics of individuals and the wicked vine growers on the historical threat of a collective, namely, Israel.

Extended echo-effect within books functions as part of literary development. Embedding a series of shared elements in the curse in the garden and Cain's sin, the fall of Adam and Eve and the drunkenness of Noah, and the "she's my sister" episodes in Genesis are literary, not exegetical, connections. Yet the projection of Adam-and-Eve-like connotations onto Noah works identically to the extended echo-effect when Joshua needs to remove his sandals as he stands upon holy ground.[41] That Joshua needs to remove his sandals does not make the episode at the burning bush prophetically typological. But the revelation before a mission does invite comparisons to put some Moses-like connotations onto Joshua. The difference between the two relates to literary outcomes within a book versus exegetical outcomes between books.

In sum, in both testaments of the Christian Bible many relations are literary, not exegetical. Exegetical relationship requires a donor text and exegetical outcomes in the receptor text. Also, not all analogous patterns work the same.

---

38. For helpful treatments, see Beale, *Handbook*, 13–25; France, *Jesus and the Old Testament*, 38–43.

39. See Luke 10:25–37 and see fourth item in note on 2 Chronicles 28 for details.

40. See 2 Chr 36:16+Isa 5:1–7 with Mark 12:1–12; esp. compare 2 Chr 36:16 and Mark 12:3–4.

41. Cf. Exod 3:5; Josh 5:15. For detailed side-by-side comparisons of the elements of Genesis mentioned in this paragraph see Schnittjer, *Torah Story*, 84, 105, 141.

Some New Testament scholars handle all typological contexts in the same way.[42] Treating all typological patterns in Scripture in a flat manner distorts some contexts and accounts for some of the confusion surrounding New Testament use of types.

This study has demonstrated that expectational types in Israel's Scriptures may be forward-looking or backward-looking. **Forward-looking expectational types** include explicit literary indicators: Ps 110:4 says the psalmist's lord will be "according to" Melchizedek (using the preposition *'al* עַל); Deut 18:15 records Moses expecting a prophet "like" him (using the preposition *ke* כְּ); Isa 11:16 looks forward to a new exodus that will be "like" the exodus from Egypt (using the combination preposition and relative pronoun *ka'asher* כַּאֲשֶׁר). These forward-looking prophetic types sometimes attract kindred interpretive advancements in Israel's Scriptures and the New Testament.[43] Expectational new exodus typological exegesis in Isaiah looks backward to the redemption and projects it forward to the return from exile. The typological allusion to the exodus in Ezra 1 may stem from Isaiah's many new exodus expectational contexts, even though the narrators only allude to details found in the narrative of Exodus itself.[44] As elsewhere, the use of exodus typology in Ezra-Nehemiah does not exhaust but increases the expectational function of Isaiah's forward-looking typological expectations. Mark goes a different direction and blends one of Isaiah's new exodus typological expectations with a highly ironic expectational type of the delegate who goes before the mission of settlement of the land.[45]

Other typological relations do not feature explicit expectational signals within donor contexts. These **typological relations get activated retrospectively** within Israel's Scriptures. When the divine glory descends upon the tabernacle in the wilderness, it functions as the proximate climax of redemption in Exodus.[46] The context does not include any forward-looking signals to indicate this event provides a pattern of what will come. Yahweh even said that he had not asked for a temple, which excludes the tabernacle as forward-looking toward the temple.[47] The narrator of Kings carefully presents the details of the divine glory coming into the first temple so that it becomes a fulfillment of something no one expected looking forward.[48] Perhaps the Chronicler took the glory entering the shrine as an unexpected typological fulfillment—backwards-only typological exegesis in Kings—and drew upon other narrative details to uncover other

42. Hays says figural reading is "always" retrospective ("Figural Exegesis," 34–36). In theory Bock affirms forward-looking and backward-looking typological patterns ("Single," 119–20). In practice Bock tends to treat them the same (see, e.g., Bock, *Proclamation*, 127, 221). These attempts to flatten scriptural use of figural patterns into a single approach do not fit with the evidence.

43. See, e.g., Acts 3:22–23; 7:37; Heb 7:17, 21.

44. See note on Ezra 1:6.

45. See Mark 1:2–3 with Isa 40:3 + Mal 3:1, itself ironically developing Exod 23:20–33 (see note on Mal 3:1). Also see Schnittjer, "Idolatry in Isaiah," sec. on evidence.

46. Exodus 40:34–35.

47. Second Samuel 7:7.

48. First Kings 8:10–11 (cf. note ad loc.) and compare details with Exod 40:34–35.

retrospective types: fire from heaven to consecrate site of altar, divine revelation of temple plans to David, and others.[49]

The New Testament makes heavy use of both forward-looking and backward-looking expectational typological patterns.[50] Again, the analogous literary patterns themselves work exactly like (non-expectational) extended echo-effect. Expectational typological exegesis denotes the fulfilling function of the antitype. Both direct expectational forward-looking types and indirect unexpected backward-looking types may be fulfilled. The present discussion has reserved the term "types" for expectational figural relations.[51]

In sum, the New Testament exegetically uses the Scriptures in many ways akin to scriptural exegesis within Israel's Scriptures. Though making a judgment on the debate concerning the horizontal contexts of donor texts of the New Testament's use of Scripture falls outside the present study, this study affirms the dominant contextual exegetical use of Scripture within Israel's Scriptures. Evaluating the vertical context of many donor texts appears to be a widely neglected aspect of studies of the New Testament use of Scripture. Studies of the New Testament's use of Scripture could also benefit by taking account of donor contexts within interpretive networks as well as greater attention to synoptic parallels within Israel's Scriptures. The New Testament appears to feature an identical range of interpreting forward-looking and backward-looking typological scriptural contexts as found within Israel's Scriptures, though the New Testament has greatly expanded attention to typological relations.

CANONICAL CONSCIOUSNESS

By all appearances the New Testament's use of Scripture stands in continuity with Israel's Scriptures in terms of canonical consciousness. Canonical consciousness refers to the emerging authority of the Scriptures. This authority applies to the ways donor scriptural texts work within exegetical receptor contexts.

The genre of letters of the apostles differs in many ways from that of the writings of the prophets. In spite of these differences, both forms overtly express self-consciousness regarding their own authority. The prophets do not tend to merely present the message. They constantly remind their auditors and readers of its authority with the mantra "Thus says Yahweh" and the like. Paul, Silas, and Timothy tell the congregation: "And we also thank God continually because, when you received *the word of God, which you heard from us*, you accepted it *not as a human word, but as it actually is, the word of God*, which is

49. On glory entering the temple and its clone, see 2 Chr 5:13–14; 7:1–3; on fire to consecrate altar, see Lev 9:24; 1 Chr 21:26; 2 Chr 7:3; on divine revelation of plans, see Exod 25:9, 40; 1 Chr 28:19; for other examples, see Table C10 and Figure C17 in Chronicles as well as notes on contexts of Chronicles listed in this footnote ad loc.

50. Forward-looking types include, e.g.: Isa 40:3 + Mal 3:1//Mark 1:2–3; Deut 18:15//Acts 3:22–23; Ps 110:4//Heb 7:17, 21. Backward-looking types include, e.g.: Hos 11:1//Matt 2:15; Ps 118:22–23//Mark 12:10–11; Ps 22:1//Mark 15:34.

51. In this study non-expectational analogous figural patterns are called extended echo-effect (see Glossary).

indeed at work in you who believe."[52] This kind of self-awareness helps connect scriptural authority with divine revelation.

The self-consciousness of the authority of scriptural donor contexts comes across most strongly in cases with **overt citation marking**. The marking of citations in Israel's Scriptures predictably appears more pronounced in later scriptural contexts. The especially common citation formula "as it is written" does not refer to verbatim quotation but a citation in accord with the donor context. The evidence in Ezra-Nehemiah suggests that citation formulas highlight the authority of the donor context even in cases featuring substantial exegetical enhancements. The solemn oath of Neh 10 provides an important example. Every part of the oath, with its manifold legal exegesis, includes a commitment to a higher level of obedience than the standards of Torah. The restoration assembly that made the oath uses the citation formula "as it is written in Torah" to affirm their standard of obedience in "agreement" with Torah's standards, though they repeatedly promise to do even more.[53] The remaining commitments of the solemn oath, though unmarked, feature kindred sorts of legal exegesis. The phrase "as it is written" does not so much get at exact wording like modern quotation marks but denotes agreement of the interpretive paraphrase "according to" and in continuity with the scriptural donor context.[54] Marked citations elsewhere in Israel's Scriptures work similarly to those in Ezra-Nehemiah.

Marked citations in the New Testament differ somewhat by having less of a tendency to include interpretive paraphrase. At the same time, the New Testament authors often use kindred citation formulas when leading into verbatim or paraphrastic and/or interpretive quotations.

The **quasi-fulfillment formula** in 2 Chr 36:22//Ezra 1:1 seems to provide a beta-version of the widespread use of fulfillment formulas in the Gospels, especially Matthew and John.[55] The absence of fulfillment formulas in the sectarian scrolls from Qumran reinforce this connection.[56] Biblical fulfillment formulas demonstrate narrators' self-awareness of building their stories in relation to Scripture.

Unmarked interpretive citations, quotations, and allusions abound in the Christian Bible. By nearly any standard, the manifold use of Scripture, at the level of exegesis as well as non-exegetical broad allusions and scriptural stock phrases, suggests scriptural authors were deeply invested in the study of Scripture. The tendency of scriptural authors to allude to Scripture also signifies a canonical consciousness. The many exegetical uses of Scripture evaluated in this study demonstrate an intentional commitment to advancing new revelation in continuity with authoritative scriptural traditions. The large number of non-exegetical allusions, echoes, and similarities filtered out from the exegetical uses of

---

52. First Thessalonians 2:13, emphasis mine; cf. 1 Cor 11:2; 2 Cor 13:10; 1 Thess 5:27; 2 Thess 3:6; Col 4:16.
53. See Neh 10:34, 36[35, 37].
54. See Overt Marking in Hermeneutical Profile of the Use of Scripture in Ezra-Nehemiah.
55. See, e.g., Matt 1:22; 2:15, 17; 3:3; 4:14; 8:17; 21:4; Mark 1:2; Luke 3:4; John 2:17; 12:38, 39; 19:36, 37.
56. See Moo, *Old Testament in Gospel*, 19.

Scripture in every main chapter of this study, provide evidence of devotion to scriptural study by means of what may be called unconscious and/or semi-conscious use of scriptural traditions.

New Testament hermeneutics often get **compared to scriptural exegesis within Second Temple Judaic writings**. Comparative evidence offers significant gains for scriptural interpretation. It is easy to agree that there is a need for further comparative studies of scriptural exegesis within Second Temple Judaic literature. The problem, at times, comes about when these comparisons do not take adequate account of the hermeneutical tendencies within Israel's Scriptures.

Steve Moyise lists eight "exegetical techniques" that demonstrate the similarity between the exegesis of the New Testament and Qumran sectarians: typology, allegory, catchword, quoting variant texts, altering quoted text, reading the text in an unorthodox manner, use of *haggada* legends, and traditional forms of homiletic argumentation.[57] The present concern does not require evaluating these comparisons but only the point they mean to support. In this context Moyise does not seek out if or how the authors of the New Testament and/or Qumran sectarians may independently depend on the hermeneutical tendencies of Israel's Scriptures. That is a problem. Since New Testament authors and authors of Second Temple Judaic writings make heavy use of Israel's Scriptures, they should be expected to exhibit similar hermeneutical tendencies even if they have no relation to each other. It would be strange if they did not share common hermeneutics with Israel's Scriptures.

Moyise distorts the evidence of shared tendencies by noting that the "fallen tent of David (Amos 9.11) is used in 4QFlor and Acts 15."[58] Moyise does not point out that they use Amos 9:11–12 in diametrically opposed ways. 4QFlorilegium/4Q174 makes the law of the assembly more exclusive than other Judaisms of the day by disallowing even "proselytes" or "residing foreigners" (גר).[59] Meanwhile James takes a position with Paul and Peter against the party of the Pharisees who had converted to the Way. These Pharisees who follow Messiah insist on circumcision for gentile converts.[60] James uses Amos 9:11–12 as part of his judgment that the gospel includes gentiles without a need for circumcision.[61] If the Pharisees converted to the Way represent a middling Second Temple Judaic outlook by allowing gentile converts with circumcision, then James and the authorship of 4QFlorilegium/4Q174 stand in contrast to them in opposite directions. Acts 15 and 4Q174 cite the "shelter of David" in Amos 9:11 from opposing perspectives.

57. See Moyise, *Old Testament in the New Testament*, 205–9.

58. Ibid., 205.

59. See 4Q174 1, 4. 4Q174 makes more restrictive the law of the assembly that appears in Deut 23:1–8[2–9]. Note: "This ([passage Exod 15:17–18] refers to) the house into which they shall not enter [... for] ever, namely, an Ammonite, or a Moabite, or one born of a forbidden union, or a foreigner (בן נכר), or a residing foreigner (גר), never" (4Q174 1, 3b–4a lit. from *DSSSE* 1:352). 4Q174 goes on in this context to quote Amos 9:11 in a marked citation (1, 12).

60. Acts 15:5.

61. Acts 15:16–18.

4QFlorilegium/4Q174	Pharisees	Acts 15
exclusion of all foreigners and residing foreigners ("proselytes")		inclusion of uncircumcised gentiles who turn to God

To suggest that using the same prophetic context shows a similarity between the New Testament and Qumran sectarians badly mishandles the evidence.[62] The New Testament offers accounts of the arrests of early Christian leaders, including John, Peter, and Paul, in the temple where they went to worship—something completely outside of Qumran's separatist sectarian ideology.[63]

Moreover, the use of Scripture *within* Amos 9:11–12 points in an inclusive direction.[64] The prophetic oracle looks back to "days of old" when David's "shelter" ruled over "all nations that bear my name." James uses the oracle as part of his argument for an international people of God in continuity with the invitational perspective of the prophetic oracle. In contrast, by the standard of excluding all foreigners, even those formerly included by the law of the assembly, 4QFlorilegium/4Q174 reads Amos 9:11 against the sense of the text. The use of the same scriptural context, in this case, demonstrates sharp discontinuity between sectarian ideology and New Testament teaching. James's view both accords with and advances the exegetical expectations of Amos 9:11–12.[65]

The New Testament appears to share many of its hermeneutical tendencies with those uncovered within Israel's Scriptures. More to the point, some of the New Testament's boldest theological moves work with, not against, the scriptural exegesis within Israel's Scriptures. With respect to the issue just discussed, Messiah did not stand in the court of the gentiles and make up a new interpretation of the law of the assembly. He interpretively blended Jer 7:11 and Isa 56:7, which already includes within itself exegetical advances concerning foreigners who bind themselves to Yahweh.[66] In much broader and deeper ways, the New Testament's use of Israel's Scriptures shares substantial continuity with the scriptural exegesis within Israel's Scriptures.[67] The discussion here does not stand against a measure of shared interpretive tendencies between the New Testament and sectarian writings. Rather, without adequately investigating exegesis within Israel's Scriptures, these possible shared interpretive tendencies sometimes have been wildly overstated.

New Testament scholars have been correct to investigate the exegesis of the apostles in relation to interpretive techniques of Second Temple Judaic literature. This valuable line of investigation needs to continue. The complaint raised here is that inadequate attention

---

62. See last two paragraphs of note on Amos 9:11–12 for more detail on these issues.

63. See Acts 4:3; 21:24, 33.

64. See note on Amos 9:11–12.

65. This point does not hinge on the textual difficulties with James's citation in Acts 15:16–18, however they get sorted out. For a detailed analysis of the textual issues see Glenny, "Septuagint," 1–26.

66. See note on Isa 56:1–8. See also Matt 21:13//Mark 11:17//Luke 19:46.

67. Hubbard comes to very similar conclusions based on case studies ("Reading," 125–39, esp. 134).

has been devoted to how the exegetical tendencies of the New Testament and Second Temple Judaic texts stack up against the kinds of exegesis embodied within Israel's Scriptures themselves. Some of the supposed similarities between New Testament and Second Temple exegesis may be nothing more than a coincidence since they both carry forward exegetical tendencies of Israel's Scriptures in different ways. The results of the present study demonstrate that many exegetical elements used in Second Temple Judaic contexts and the New Testament have a long history within the Hebrew Scriptures. It is necessary to first compare the use of Scripture within the Hebrew Scriptures before focusing on the much rarer, novel exegetical tendencies shared by Second Temple Judaic literature and the New Testament that are not evident within Israel's Scriptures.

Many discussions of the New Testament's reliance upon Second Temple Judaic exegetical methods refer to **the seven rules of interpretation of the ancient Judaic scholar Hillel** (active from c. 30 BCE to 10 CE). Bock, for example, lists some of Hillel's rules as part of his claim that New Testament authors depend on Judaic interpretive techniques of their day.[68] Bock does not acknowledge that all of the so-called Judaic interpretive techniques are nothing more than observations of commonplace exegetical tendencies within Israel's Scriptures.[69] Since these interpretive tendencies are not unusual but widely disseminated in the Hebrew Scriptures it not clear why the authors of the New Testament would need to consult proto-rabbinic exegetical scholarship or vice versa. It seems entirely natural that those who studied the Hebrew Bible, like the authors of the New Testament

68. See Bock, "Scripture Citing Scripture," 259–60.

69. All seven rules of interpretation of Hillel can be extrapolated, in a broad sense, from exegesis of Scripture within Israel's Scriptures: (1) Lesser to greater (*Qal vahomer*) follows the logic of "how much more" expansions in legal exegesis of Torah such as if love of residing foreigner is required, how much more one's neighbor (Lev 19:33–34 → 19:18), if tending to the animal of one's enemy is required, how much more the animal of one's fellow (Exod 23:4–5 → Deut 22:1–4); (2) Meaning deduced by analogy (*Gezerah shevah*) follows the logic of many deductions of legal exegesis of Torah such as if residing foreigners are protected from oppression because Israel once was a residing foreigner in Egypt, so too widows and orphans since they may cry out to Yahweh (Exod 22:21–23 → Deut 24:17–19; cf. Exod 3:7). If landless orphans, widows, and residing foreigners need help, so too landless Levites (Deut 14:29; 26:13); (3) Application transcends individual mandate to all kindred mandates (*Binyan av mikatuv 'ehad*), if ritually impure persons with a skin disease need to evacuate from the camp to avoid defiling the tabernacle, so too all ritually impure persons—from touching a corpse, male or female flow, and so on—are excluded from the encampment when the tabernacle moved therein (Lev 13:45–46 → Num 5:1–4); (4) Application deduced from two passages (*Binyan av mishene ketuvim*), Ahimelech seems to deduce the possibility of giving the bread of the presence to David because his men kept themselves from women to retain a "holy" state for battle (1 Sam 21:4 → Lev 24:9+Deut 23:14); (5) Particular to general, general to particular (*Kelal upherat ukelal*), if donkeys in the distinction between animals and donkeys represent ritually impure animals in general within the original Passover instruction, then this is made explicit in the wilderness (Exod 13:12–13 → Num 18:15). And if offering of firstfruits is a broad category, then it becomes particularized to include "processed" produce through the first of the dough offering based on the rationale "from the threshing floor" as processing (Exod 23:19; 34:22; Lev 23:10–11 → Num 15:18–21 → 18:12–13); (6) Similarity in content from elsewhere (*Kayoze bobemaqom 'aher*), if Moses could enter the tabernacle but had to get out when the glory came upon it, then it can be affirmed by the priests leaving the temple when the glory filled it (Exod 33:9 vs. 40:34–35 ← 1 Kgs 8:11); and (7) Meaning deduced from context (*Davar halamed me'inyano*), if celestial delegates are present to divide the peoples, then the deity's use of first person plural pronouns may come from addressing the celestial court (Gen 11:7 ← Deut 32:8 LXX/4QDeut[j]/4Q37). For Hillel's seven rules of interpretation see Tosefta, Sanhedrin, 7.11 in Danby, trans., 76–77; and for Ishmael's thirteen rules basically expanded out of Hillel's seven, along with biblical examples of each, see introduction to Sifra in Neusner, trans., 1:57–60. The scriptural example for the sixth rule here is based in part on the examples given in Ishmael's thirteenth rule in Sifra introduction.

and the Judaic scholars of late antiquity, could independently and coincidentally emulate the sorts of interpretive interventions found within Israel's Scriptures. Claims of dependence on something other than Israel's Scriptures for exegetical phenomena pervasive within Israel's Scriptures need to provide evidence of this dependence—as well as explaining why extravagant explanations of dependence are necessary for ordinary interpretive maneuvers.

When discussing how Paul and Sosthenes deduce that the law of not muzzling oxen while threshing infers the need to support gospel ministers, many commentators simply compare the teaching to methods of ancient Jewish interpreters—like the lesser to the greater—but not to the Old Testament use of Scripture.[70] Legal exegesis within Torah itself makes use of lesser to greater interpretation: if Israel must treat residing foreigners as themselves how much more their neighbors; and if persons need to tend to animals of their enemies how much more animals of their fellows.[71]

Again, it is easy to agree with the importance of studying Second Temple Judaic interpretations of Scripture as a way to help understand New Testament interpretation of Scripture. The point at hand pivots on the need to compare the exegesis of both New Testament and Second Temple Judaic interpreters to the exegesis of Scripture by the authors of Israel's Scriptures before jumping to conclusions. Lack of comparing the interpretation of Scripture by the authors of the Old and New Testaments eliminates distinguishing coincidence from dependence with respect to similar scriptural interpretive techniques by New Testament and Second Temple Judaic authors.

The much-contested claims of similarity between ***pesher* interpretation** among the sectarian writings of Qumran and interpretive tendencies in the New Testament need to be noted, though briefly. The Aramaic term derives from the root *pshr* (פשר) with a basic sense of "interpret." The term is used frequently in the Aramaic section of Daniel especially in relation to interpretation of dreams.[72] The sense of *pesher* includes both scholarship and revelatory exegesis.[73] The sectarian commentators viewed themselves as living in the last days and interpreted the mysteries of Scripture in relation to their own situation.[74] The Habakkuk Commentary quotes and interprets Habakkuk:

> "I will position myself in my fortress, and I will look out to see what he says to me . . . So that/may run/the one who reads it" [Hab 2:1–2]. *Its interpretation* [פשרו] concerns the

70. See, e.g., Blomberg, *1 Corinthians*, 304–5; Verbrugge, "1 Corinthians," 11:335–36. On "lesser to greater" in ancient Judaic interpretation see no. 1 in previous footnote. A more helpful approach is focusing on ancient Judaic interpretations of the biblical context in question, such as Beale's interaction with Second Temple Judaic handling of Deut 25:4 (*Handbook*, 68, n. 24).

71. See notes on Lev 19:18, 33–34; Deut 22:1–4.

72. See Aramaic "פשר, פְּשַׁר" *HALOT* 2:1960–61; cf. Hebrew cognate parallel "interpret" in Gen 40–41, "פתר," 2:991.

73. See Moo, *Old Testament in the Gospel*, 72–73.

74. VanderKam, *Dead Sea Scrolls Today*, 62–63.

> Teacher of Righteousness, to whom God has made known all *the mysteries* of the words of his servants, the prophets. (1QpHab 6.12–7.5, emphases mine)

This passage epitomizes the spirit of *pesharim* by pointing to the teacher of righteousness and the mysteries he made known from the Scriptures.

For the present purposes a very general comparison between select sectarian interpretive tendencies, especially *pesher*, and typological or figural interpretation in the New Testament may be made in three broad points. First, in the broadest sense Second Temple sectarian *pesharim* and New Testament figural interpretation both apply Israel's Scriptures to their own situations and view themselves as part of the latter days of scriptural fulfillment.

Second, the genre of sectarian *pesher* does not function like New Testament typological interpretation in terms of scriptural selection. Sectarian *pesharim* like 1QpHab and 4QpNah/4Q169 work through the scriptural text line by line applying elements to their own situations.[75] Since they treat the entire scriptural text the interpretative correspondences become very allegorical. By contrast New Testament figural interpretation is highly selective only making allusion to specific parts of contexts that speak to the fulfillment.[76] Moo explains the importance of selectivity. "[T]he influence has proceeded from the history [of Messiah's death] to the text [cited from the Old Testament] rather than vice versa. The relatively small number of OT passages utilized in the passion texts presumes *a strict selectivity*, conditioned by the circumstances of the passion events."[77] The selective appropriation of figural donor contexts allows New Testament authors to clothe historical narration in scriptural language. The selective use of donor contexts in New Testament figural interpretation is like the selectivity in figural interpretation of scriptural traditions within Israel's Scriptures but unlike the non-selective tendency of sectarian *pesher* interpretation.[78]

Third, scriptural figural interpretation based on shared patterns between donor and receptor contexts appears frequently in Israel's Scriptures and extensively in the New Testament, but infrequently in the sectarian literature of Qumran and rarely in rabbinic literature.[79] Typological interpretation among literature found at Qumran may be most prevalent in apocalypses like Jubilees.[80] Like the authors of Israel's Scriptures,

---

75. For a list of *pesharim* among the Qumran writings see Wold, "Old Testament Context," 117.

76. These comparisons between sectarian *pesharim* and New Testament typology indebted to Moo, *Old Testament in the Gospel*, 69–76, 363–65, 380–82, 388–92. For evaluation of allegorical interpretation in Qumran's sectarian writings see 36–40. For a diagram demonstrating the extreme selectivity of the evangelists' use of Old Testament contexts to explain the death of Messiah see chart, 352–56.

77. Ibid., 380, emphasis mine.

78. For examples of selectivity in Old Testament typological interpretation, see third section of Table C10 in chapter on Chronicles.

79. For examples of typological patterns in the Old and New Testaments see Baker, *Two Testaments*, 171–72.

80. See Moo, *Old Testament in the Gospel*, 32–33.

New Testament authors widely use both forward-looking and backward-looking figural patterns.[81]

In sum of this point, the similarity between Second Temple sectarian *pesher* and New Testament figural interpretation applies only in the most general senses that both sets of authors apply Israel's Scriptures to their own situation and view themselves as within the latter days of scriptural fulfillment. An examination of the tendencies of selective use of donor contexts demonstrate New Testament figural interpretation is like that of Israel's Scriptures and unlike sectarian *pesharim*. Figural interpretation of Scripture is uncommon in Qumran literature, used with moderation in Israel's Scriptures, and used widely in the New Testament.

The evidence from **Qumran** goes beyond the sectarian scrolls and includes the **biblical scrolls**. Molly Zahn pushes back against the concept of scriptural exegesis of Scripture. She regards textual fluidity and multiple versions of Scriptures and Rewritten Scriptures at Qumran as evidence that contradicts the very idea of scriptural exegesis of Scripture. Zahn regards distinctions between "biblical" and "nonbiblical/postbiblical" exegesis as false.[82] Zahn's points make a lot of sense. Many scholars have noted similarities between the scriptural use of Scripture and Second Temple interpretive tendencies. But the evidence of the biblical scrolls does not support Zahn's claims.

The evidence in the discoveries of the ancient scriptural texts in the Judean desert, including those of Qumran, affirms two different tendencies. To oversimplify, scribal intervention may refer to intentional modifications or accidental mistakes. Scribal interventions of both kinds characterize the work of the sectarian scribes of Qumran in sharp contrast to the contemporary proto-masoretic texts found elsewhere in the Judean desert. Emmanuel Tov collates all known evidence of scribal interventions in the Judean desert biblical texts. Regarding inadvertent mistakes, Tov summarizes: "Almost all biblical scrolls (all: proto-masoretic) from sites in the Judean Desert *other than Qumran* were copied carefully, if the criterion of scribal intervention [i.e., corrections] is accepted as being valid."[83] Regarding intentional creative scribal intervention, Tov remarks: "This applies to most compositions at Qumran, but not for all milieus, *since in the texts belonging to the Masoretic family this freedom was not sanctioned* in the period under consideration."[84] Tov's evaluation of the evidence from the ancient biblical scrolls found in the Judean desert points in the opposite direction of Zahn's claims.

The broad point being made here does not require anything more than observing

81. See "typological patterns" in Glossary and see Table C10, Figure C17 in Chronicles, and associated discussions. On typology in the New Testament see Moo and Naselli, "Problem," 393–94.

82. See Zahn, "Innerbiblical Exegesis," 108–19.

83. Tov, *Scribal Practices*, 204, emphasis mine. Also see 25–26, 252–53.

84. Ibid., 25, emphasis mine. Also see Tov, *Textual Criticism*, 178–80. On scribes with "liberties" versus "copyists" who reproduced "exactly what they saw" in ancient Hittite culture of the second millennium BCE, see Taggar-Cohen, "Subtle Citation," 64–65.

the general accord between canonical consciousness signaled by the exegesis of scriptural contexts within Scripture and the evidence of copyist scribal tendencies of the proto-masoretic texts of the Judean desert, everywhere except Qumran, to carefully copy Scripture. The differences between Second Temple scribal traditions are not absolute because they overlap, but they are real. Figure NT2 roughly depicts the tendencies suggested by the evidence.

NT2: DIVERGENT SCRIBAL TENDENCIES OF THE SECOND TEMPLE SITUATION‡

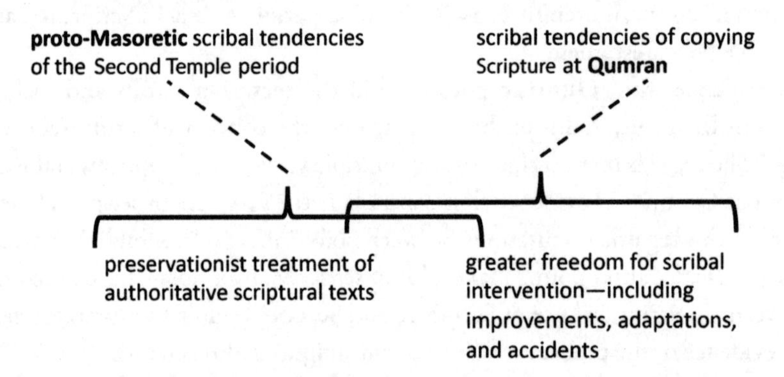

‡ These broad tendencies are deduced from evidence collated in Tov, *Scribal Practices*, 25–26, 204, 252–53; and see idem, *Textual Criticism*, 178–80.

Perhaps the most significant element of canonical consciousness comes from the observation that **Israel's Scriptures and the New Testament together comprise Christian Scripture**. New Testament authors quote, paraphrase, and interpret Israel's Scriptures.

Brevard Childs points out: "The books of the Hebrew Bible were received as Christian Scripture *in unredacted form*. There was no attempt made through alterations or interpolations to 'Christianize' the Scriptures or to bracket Old Testament books with parts of those from the New."[85] There was no need. From the beginning, Messiah and his followers interpret and teach from Israel's Scriptures. The continuity of scriptural exegesis of Scripture across the Christian Bible is a natural outcome of interpreting the same Scriptures within a shared framework of canonical consciousness. This partially explains why the New Testament writers characteristically interpret Scripture according to the exegetical tendencies utilized within the Hebrew Scriptures.

In sum of this section, overtly marked citations in the New Testament broadly affirm continuity with similar patterns within Israel's Scriptures. The similar exegetical techniques by sectarians, New Testament writers, and other Second Temple Judaic traditions of itself seems like a nonissue in many cases, since they each often appear to be

85. Childs, "Nature of the Christian Bible," in Radner and Sumner, eds., *Rule*, 116, emphasis mine.

following after exegetical tendencies within Israel's Scriptures. When the ideology itself is compared, the New Testament and the sectarians often do not share resemblance. All of these general points require qualifications. Yet scriptural exegesis within Israel's Scriptures pushes back against some overgeneralizations that have not taken adequate account of this evidence.

If the Qumran copyist scribes did not fully honor the emerging canonical status of Israel's Scriptures, they are out of step with contemporary copyist scribes of the proto-masoretic texts. The evidence from the discoveries of ancient scriptural texts in the Judean desert affirms the care of those scribes tasked with transmitting the proto-masoretic textual family. This preservationist handling of the Scriptures corroborates the diverse evidence of an emerging canonical consciousness within the Scriptures themselves. The canonical consciousness of authors throughout the Christian Scriptures helps explain their heavy investments in scriptural exegesis. The authority of their scriptural traditions makes all the difference.

LOOKING FORWARD FROM ISRAEL'S SCRIPTURES

The preceding discussion works back from the New Testament in relation to progressive revelation, context, and canonical consciousness. These same three issues need to be taken up working forward toward the New Testament.

Progressive Revelation

Yahweh reveals his sovereign will according to his great acts of creation, election, covenant, redemption, instruction, acquisition of land, rescue, kingdom, temple, judgment, and restoration. Prophets and other delegates mediate an important subset of his revelation. Scripture houses an enduring portion of the revelatory ministry of divinely sanctioned delegates. Each of these divine acts, messages delivered by delegates, and Scriptures progressively reveal the divine redemptive will. The present study focuses on a small part of scriptural revelation—scriptural exegesis of Scripture.

Scriptural exegesis within the Old Testament advances revelation. New Testament authors often exegete Scripture in accord with Old Testament interpretations of Scripture. A small sampling can illustrate a large number of continuities between exegetical advancements in both testaments of the Christian Bible. These samples need to be general and suggestive since working out interpretive advances in the New Testament contexts falls outside this study. The point at hand turns on the further exegetical advancements of Old Testament interpretations of Scripture by New Testament authors. Here are fourteen examples of a larger phenomenon.[86]

86. For more detail, see notes on Old Testament contexts listed first in the footnotes for each of the following examples.

- The commands to love thy neighbor and love the residing foreigner in the holiness collection build on treating outsiders well because Israel knows what it is like to be mistreated from their time in Egyptian bondage. Messiah pushes further the responsibility to love the other to include hateful rivals like the half-dead man that the Samaritan helps.[87]
- Moses extends the people's request for a prophet at the mountain of revelation as an expectation for a line of prophets. Peter speaks of Messiah as the fulfilment of Moses's expectation of a prophet like himself.[88]
- Joshua finds Rahab an exception to the law of devoting not because of the vow of the scouts but based on the prostitute's prior act of protecting the scouts. James deduces the activating force of the prostitute's faith and mentions it alongside the faith of Abraham.[89]
- The high priest uses his sanctioned role as teacher of the holy and ritually pure to give David and his associates the bread of the presence in a time of need. Messiah extends the priest's ruling to sanction the eating of grain with the son of a human being who is Lord of the Sabbath.[90]
- The voice of the Lord commissions Isaiah to actively harden hearts and blind eyes, strengthening the previous concealment by lack of divine enlightenment. Messiah speaks in riddles to reveal teaching to his followers even while concealing instruction from outsiders.[91]
- Isaiah uses the exodus of old as an expectational template for the return from exile. The evangelists use the new exodus of Isaiah as a mainframe for their gospel narratives.[92]
- Isaiah shares the commonplace scriptural view of two kinds of others—excluded and included—but stresses that exclusion and inclusion each pivot on covenantal (in)fidelity, not rights from birth. Messiah clears out room for others in the court of the gentiles of the temple and cites Isaiah's oracle of inclusion.[93]
- Jeremiah speaks of a new covenant written on hearts in a manner unlike the ancestors, whose hearts and eyes were not opened. The author to the Hebrews bases the new covenant on the forgiveness that comes from the definitive and singular sacrifice of Messiah.[94]
- Amos looks ahead to the restoration of the shelter of David as in days of old over

87. See Luke 10:36 with Lev 19:18, 34 and Exod 22:21[20].
88. See Acts 3:22–23 with Deut 18:15, 18, 19 and 5:25–28; Exod 20:19.
89. See Jas 2:25 with Josh 6:17 and Deut 7:2.
90. See Luke 6:3–6 with 1 Sam 21:4[5] and Lev 10:10–11.
91. See Mark 4:11–12 with Isa 6:9–10 and Deut 29:2–4[1–3]. Also see Matt 13:13–15; Luke 8:10.
92. See Matt 3:3; Mark 1:2–3; Luke 3:4–6; John 1:23 with Isa 11:15–16; 40:3–10 and Exod 23:20–33. See Schnittjer, "Idolatry in Isaiah," sec. on evidence.
93. See Mark 11:15–17 with Isa 56:1–7. Also see 52:1 and Deut 23:1–7[2–8].
94. See Heb 10:16 with Jer 31:31–34 and Deut 29:1–4[28:69–29:3]. Also see Heb 8:8–13.

the nations called by Yahweh's name. James declares God has chosen some gentiles to enter into his people by faith without circumcision.[95]

- Joel applies the hope of Jacob to everyone who calls upon the name of the Lord. Paul identifies those who declare by faith "Jesus is Lord" as the Jews and gentiles who call upon the name of the Lord.[96]
- Zechariah creates a prequel to the Judah-king arriving in his vineyard by portraying a humble ruler coming on his donkey. The narrative of the triumphal entry in Mark blends the humble king riding into Jerusalem with imagery of tying and untying associated with the blessing of Judah.[97] John goes even further when he associates the lion of Judah with the root of David and the lamb.[98]
- The psalmist recognizes with gratitude the place of humans in the cosmos based on the story of the creation days. The author of the letter to the Hebrews applies the psalmist's reflection on the place of humans to the rule of Messiah.[99]
- The psalmist recites an oath of Yahweh to David to put his descendants on the throne. Peter associates the expectation of the rule of the Davidic son with the resurrection of Messiah.[100]
- Daniel envisions resurrection of some to damnation and others to everlasting life. Messiah, Paul, and John speak of a general resurrection of the condemned and redeemed to their ends.[101]

These few examples offer a sampling of significant continuity of scriptural exegesis across the Christian Bible. To these can be added the many examples discussed earlier in this chapter.[102]

Examining scriptural exegesis in the Old and New Testaments shows many continuities. This does not mean that the exegesis of Scripture in the New Testament fully lines up with scriptural exegesis in the Hebrew Scriptures. The revelation of God in Messiah is "not the last link in a chain of events." Messiah "himself brought the fullness where before only emptiness and fragmentation existed."[103] The teaching, death, and resurrection of Messiah put all progressive revelation, including exegetical advances of revelation, in a new perspective. At the same time, exegesis of Scripture by the New Testament authors in a large number of cases aligns with the kinds of scriptural exegesis seen across Israel's Scriptures.

---

95. See Acts 15:16–18 with Amos 9:11–12 and 2 Sam 7:12.
96. See Rom 10:9–13 with Joel 2:32[3:5] and Obad 17.
97. See Mark 11:2–5 with Zech 9:9 and Gen 49:11. Also see Schnittjer, "Blessing of Judah," 27–30.
98. See Rev 5:5–6 with Gen 49:9.
99. See Heb 2:5–9 with Ps 8:4–6[5–7] and Gen 1:26–28.
100. See Acts 2:30–31 with Ps 132:11 and 2 Sam 7:12–15.
101. See John 5:29; Acts 24:15; Rev 20:11–15 with Dan 12:2 and Isa 26:19; 66:24.
102. Also see many additional examples in Harmon, "OT Use of the OT," *DNTUOT*, forthcoming; Shepherd, *Text in the Middle*, 7–166.
103. See Childs, "Prophecy and Fulfillment," 269.

Scriptural exegesis advances revelation in many ways. New Testament writers do not regard the Scriptures as containers of inert, static information. Scriptural interpretations within their Scriptures model the kinds of dynamic exegesis they likewise employ to proclaim the gospel.

Progressive revelation should not be considered a predictable, steady, step-by-step series of pronouncements that fall out of the heavens. The dynamics of revelation sometimes spring from shattering events that God's people thought could never happen, such as the destruction of Jerusalem and the captivity of king and people. These catastrophic ordeals motivate large-scale interpretations of scriptural testimony of the covenants. Questions concerning the meaning of the enduring promises to Abraham and David urgently need answers in the light of the empire's dominion. The exegetical advancements of the prophets and the prophetic voices that narrate the scriptural storyline reformat Israel's identity in the face of tragic unexpected realities.

Just as traumatic and redemptive events frequently trigger exegetical advances in Israel's Scriptures, so too in the New Testament. The game-changing revelation of God in the teaching, death, and resurrection of Messiah set in motion unprecedented exegetical advancements of Scripture.

When divine revelations come in the form of exegetical advances, they do not start all over from scratch. Exegetical advancements spring from the enduring authoritative revelation of scriptural donor contexts: new creation, new Moses, new covenant, new David, new temple. Authority and advancement do not represent opposites within scriptural exegesis of Scripture. The redemptive plan and work of Yahweh encompasses both authoritative revelation and the advancement of revelation sometimes by means of scriptural exegesis.

Context

The present study takes a book-by-book and case-by-case approach to evaluating exegesis within the array of scriptural contexts. There is nothing wrong with broad generalizations. But broad generalizations only offer value insofar as they represent detailed evaluation at the level of the nuts and bolts of scriptural exegesis.

Something comes before the hypothesis that the New Testament exegetes Scripture in many of the ways Israel's Scriptures exegete Scripture. What about Israel's Scriptures themselves? Working backward, the prophets, psalmists, narrators, and sages provide evidence of interpreting scriptural traditions in line with the way some contexts of Torah interpret other contexts of Torah. The different and varied hermeneutical profiles of scriptural exegesis book by book through Israel's Scriptures demonstrate the importance of taking every book seriously and on its own terms. Even making generous allowances for the contextual individuality of the scrolls of Israel's Scriptures, a book-by-book evaluation of scriptural exegesis shines a light on some family resemblances in interpretation and theology. A brief summary of the contextual evidence uncovered in this study can help make sense of the many aspects of scriptural exegesis within Israel's Scriptures embraced by New Testament authors.

The evaluation of scriptural exegesis of Scripture in the present study demonstrates a continuity of revelatory advancement. No book of **Torah** houses legal standards without interpretive enhancements. There is no such thing in Torah. The Ten Commandments and covenant collection enjoy interpretive allusions in the covenant renewal collection all within Exodus itself.[104] Besides numerous cases of legal exegesis, Leviticus and Numbers feature a series of precedent-setting and legal-amendment narratives in which Yahweh himself adjusts his own laws, and even adjusts his adjustments.[105] This stands against impaired views of the law as something that demands mechanical compliance without asking questions. Deuteronomy self-identifies as Torah explained, Torah set out, Torah taught, and claims to be "in addition to" the covenant at the mountain.[106]

The manifold **legal exegesis** in the main legal collections function within Torah's frame narrative. Legal exegesis represents dynamic advancements of revelation. As such, legal exegesis develops within and as an integral part of the Torah narrative. The evaluation of legal exegesis in Torah in the present study provides evidence of law in service of redemption, not the other way around. No one has a heart attack when at the very first Passover celebration in the wilderness a group of ritually impure persons appeal their exclusion. Yahweh responds by providing an alternate date one month later for people who are traveling or have temporary ceremonial impurity.[107] Yahweh not only makes a provision for female inheritance when Zelophehad leaves behind daughters only, but amends this legal adjustment when the leaders of Manasseh appeal the potential loss of tribal lands.[108] These programmatic cases provide important narrative rationale to accompany the numerous cases of legal exegesis that unfold in the holiness collection when the tabernacle is built and in the torah collection when the people need to settle in the land.[109] The major changes in the life of Israel are met with commensurate advancements in revelation by means of legal exegesis.

Torah also advances revelation by narrative-based exegesis. Especially Genesis and Deuteronomy feature interpretive allusions within narrative. One example concerns the synoptic narratives in Deuteronomy. The synoptic narratives of Deuteronomy set the course for this popular exegetical phenomenon appearing in several places but most notably in Chronicles and the Gospels. The shared exegetical traits among the synoptic narratives of the Christian Bible offer important evidence of continuity in exegetically based progressive revelation.

The present argument concerns the continuity of progressive revelation through

104. Exodus 20 (Ten Commandments), 21–23 (covenant collection), and 34:11–16 (covenant renewal collection).

105. Leviticus 24:10–23; Num 9:1–14; 15:32–36; 27:1–11; 36:1–12. See notes ad loc.

106. Deuteronomy 1:5; 4:44; 6:1; 29:1[28:69]. See Hermeneutical Profile of the Use of Torah in Deuteronomy.

107. See Num 9:1–14; and see note ad loc.

108. See Num 27:1–11; 36:1–12; and see note ad loc.

109. See Lev 17–26 (holiness collection) and Deut 12–26 (torah collection).

exegetical advancements scroll by scroll. The four-part **Deuteronomistic serial narrative** bears this out. Joshua shares continuity with Torah's legal and narrative exegesis. The stunning exception to the law of devoting in the case of Rahab stands alongside several interpretative advances within the command itself.[110] Joshua's panoramic retrospective at Shechem applies the redemptive storyline to a particular moment of danger when Israel might turn to the gods of the land.[111] A major highlight in Samuel pivots on the exegetical advancement of the blessing of Judah in the promise to David.[112] The brand new element—a temple—starts with David, not Yahweh.[113] The telling of the rise and fall of two Hebrew kingdoms features several exegetical allusions to Torah and prophets. Notable exegetical advances within Kings include Solomon's connection of election of David and Yahweh's choosing of the place for his name to dwell.[114]

Anyone who goes to the **prophets** to read detailed homilies explaining the legal intricacies of Torah will be disappointed. The prophets seem to take for granted that the problem of the people has nothing to do with lack of knowledge of or misunderstanding the laws. Amos as the earliest of the writing prophets tends to refer to laws sarcastically to taunt the bogus religiosity of his affluent target audience.[115] Another early prophet, Hosea, already refers to written torah.[116] In the main, the prophets use scriptural interpretive allusions to call Israel to repentance.

The three longest prophetic collections—Isaiah, Jeremiah, Ezekiel—use Scripture so extensively that they seem to overflow with allusive language on every column of their scrolls.[117] Simply scanning the filters of the chapters for these three prophets indicates that the exegetical uses of Scripture in the prophets only gets at a small portion of the evidence of their deep commitment to Scripture. Several of the profound exegetical advances in Isaiah and Jeremiah lay the groundwork for further development by the New Testament.[118] In many specific contexts the prophets exegetically advance revelation in ways that anticipate the teaching of Messiah and the apostles.

Psalms houses a large number of exegetical allusions to Scripture. Besides exegetical uses of Scripture, the psalmists frequently make use of the lyrical diffusion of scriptural stock phrases and expressions.[119] Since Psalms is a collection of poems by individual psalmists, it resists easy generalization. Nonetheless, numerous broad patterns emerge by considering their exegetical interventions together. Only two can be repeated here.[120]

---

110. See notes on Josh 6:17 and Deut 7:1–6.
111. Joshua 24:1–15.
112. Second Samuel 7:14–15; cf. Gen 49:10.
113. Second Samuel 7:7.
114. First Kings 5:1–5[15–19]; 8:15–21; cf. notes ad loc.
115. See, e.g., Amos 2:8, 12; 4:4, 5; 5:10, 12.
116. Hosea 8:12.
117. The same might be said for Zechariah.
118. See, e.g., interpretive allusions in Isa 6:9–10; 40:3–4; 52:11–12; 53:10; 56:1–8; Jer 31:31–34.
119. See Psalms Filters.
120. See Hermeneutical Profile of Psalms Use of Scripture for other broad patterns.

First, the divine oracles embedded in several psalms, especially four psalms of Davidic promises, along with their exegetical advances, naturally attract kindred additional exegetical advancements by the New Testament.[121] Second, most exegetical allusions in the Psalter offer responses to different kinds of problems with which the psalmists and their congregations need to deal. Stated differently, most of the exegesis of Scripture within the Psalter is situational. The situations requiring lyrical exegesis in the Psalter include things the congregation needs to remember in the form of retrospectives, worship issues, and extreme injustice.[122] Many other psalms feature exegetical interventions that do not fit into categories but make up the many one-offs of life. The heavy use of the Psalter in the New Testament, including many cases of the psalmists' exegesis of Scripture, provides a rough index of its importance toward advancing revelation in general.

The remainder of the books in **the Writings** get far less dedicated attention in the New Testament. This should not dissuade students from their importance. Notable examples of exegesis important to the New Testament's scriptural and theological interpretation, considered broadly, include the legal exegesis concerning one of David's matriarchs in Ruth, the issue of vows—a hot topic for Messiah and his opponents alike in the late Second Temple period—in Ecclesiastes, and the seventy weeks and resurrection in Daniel.[123] The narratives of Ezra-Nehemiah and Chronicles do not get much direct attention in the New Testament. Still, the extensive exegesis of Scripture in these narratives from earlier in the Second Temple context offer very important insights into the kinds of shared concerns of the late Second Temple situation during the ministries of Messiah and his apostles. The use of Scripture in the Gospels and Acts shares many hermeneutical tendencies with Ezra-Nehemiah and Chronicles from shaping narratives according to Scripture, to citation of Scripture, and even typology. Any adequate handling of the use of Scripture in New Testament narratives requires sufficient familiarity with kindred aspects of scriptural exegesis in Ezra-Nehemiah and Chronicles.

In sum, one-size-fits-all does not apply to the use of Scripture within Israel's Scriptures. Every scroll needs to be approached on its own terms. The contextual evaluation of the exegetical use of Scripture scroll by scroll bears out many shared tendencies of the exegesis of Scripture in the New Testament.

Canonical Consciousness

The very idea of scriptural exegesis implies canonical consciousness. The entire point of exegetical allusions stems from the authority of the Scriptures. Scriptural authority motivates exegesis.

121. Of the eleven psalms with divine oracles in Psalms, four relate to Davidic promises—each includes scriptural exegesis (Pss 2, 89, 110, 132). Psalms 2 and 110 get cited many times in the New Testament (see list in chapter on Psalms).

122. See notes on Pss 78, 105, 106, 135, 136 (retrospectives); Pss 15, 24, 40, 51, 96, 118 (worship issues), 82, 109 (injustice).

123. See notes on Ruth 2:8; 4:17, 22; Eccl 5:4–6[3–5]; Dan 9:2; 12:2, 3.

Authoritative divine revelation of Scripture itself functions as a tool for further revelation. Scriptural revelation shapes Israel and the authors of Scripture. The profound significance of the authority of scriptural revelation comes into view by evaluating the scriptural exegesis of Scripture. Scriptural exegesis represents only a portion of the Scriptures. But one of the reasons to attend to it is that it provides an opportunity to glimpse concrete instances of the advancement of revelation.

In one of Michael Fishbane's formative studies on scriptural exegesis within Scripture, he notes that "an incipient 'canonical consciousness'" appears in late writings of Israel's Scriptures. He says this as a way of explaining why the Chronicler sought to bring together details of cooking the Passover lamb from Exodus and Deuteronomy, roasted and boiled.[124] Fishbane, for the moment, turns to an eventual emerging sense of canonical authority to explain the Chronicler's efforts to harmonize. But toward the end of the study Fishbane takes another step. He says that "what might be termed a 'canonical consciousness' unfolded *from the beginning* in ancient Israel."[125] This adjustment comes much closer to explaining the continuity of exegesis across Scripture.

If the biblical canon points to recognizing the end of the process of producing scriptural revelation, a growing canonical consciousness was there all along. The authors of Scripture demonstrate scriptural authority by exegesis. They do not merely say something else or something new. They interpret scriptural traditions. Previous scriptural revelation plays a role in later scriptural revelation in the case of scriptural exegesis within Scripture. The word of God and its attendant authority naturally enact a fundamental continuity by means of exegetical advancements of revelation. The pervasive use of Scripture in Scripture, exegetical and non-exegetical, provides one of the strong bonds of continuity throughout the Christian Bible.

The power of scriptural exegesis includes its role in the advancement of revelation. Scriptural exegesis bears witness to the Spirit and the Word in revelation. Explaining exactly what gives rise to advancements of revelation goes beyond what can be deduced from evidence. For revelation is a gift of God.

---

124. See Fishbane, "Torah and Tradition," 283. See also Exod 12:8–11; Deut 16:7; 2 Chr 35:12–13.

125. Ibid., 289, emphasis mine. Fishbane interacts with the idea of canonical consciousness in other later studies; see, e.g., "Revelation and Tradition," 360; idem, "Law to Canon," 65–66, 85–86.

Chapter 37

NETWORKS

Anyone who scans the networks collected below will quickly recognize them as favorite contexts—favorite contexts of the biblical authors. Scriptural authors often focus on the same texts as other scriptural authors. This is not an accident.

Favorite Scriptures sometimes attract multiple exegetical allusions. Exegesis by scriptural authors does not exhaust the revelatory potential of a donor context. Instead, exegesis increases the revelatory fertility of donor contexts. Sometimes sustained exegetical interest creates an interpretive network.

A **Scripture Index of Networks** appears at the end of this chapter.[1] Here is a **list of the networks** included in this chapter following a brief explanation.

Abrahamic covenant
the assembly
attribute formula
branch
cities of the plain
concealing revelation
collective confession
Cyrus and the temple foundation
Davidic covenant
devoting (the nations of Canaan)
Judah-king
new covenant
new exodus
personal responsibility
place Yahweh chooses for his name
prophet like Moses
release statute (pledge, debt slave, interest)
Sabbath
seventy years
teachers
temple vessels

The term network seeks to get at the natural *internal* connectivity between sets of exegetically related scriptural contexts. This is different in kind from constellations that superimpose a pattern upon unrelated contexts from the outside. Earth dwellers speak of stellar constellations based on patterns between stars from the vantage point of their home planet. Examples of scriptural constellations may be seen in the catchwords at the beginning and ending of the last five psalms of the Psalter or the catchword verse strings in the New Testament (Pss 146–150; Rom 15:9–12; Heb 1:5–13).[2] By contrast, networks interconnect by exegetical allusions within the set of scriptural contexts themselves.

1. Network subjects and Scriptures are also listed in the general indices at the end of this work.
2. See "constellations" in Glossary.

Patterns do not need to be projected onto networks since their constituent Scriptures already interconnect by their own interpretive allusions.

There may be other kinds of networks. The networks collected here only include those that are exegetically connected. Several potential networks have been sorted out like "abiding presence" based on Deut 31:6, 8.[3] Many of the connections seem to be more like stock phrases than interpretive interventions. The Filters at the end of the chapters throughout this study include many favorite themes and expressions that could be studied as non-exegetical networks. Determining interpretive networks depends on a series of judgments concerning all potential constituent contexts as being exegetically related rather than broad thematic allusions and echoes. For the present purposes, "networks" refers to exegetical networks. Among the examples below, the attribute formula network refers a series of contexts exegetically related to Exod 34:6–7 amid the diffusion of broadly similar stock phrases (see note with attribute formula network). Some networks have more cohesion than others. All networks are prone to generate stock phrases and interrelated theological themes because of the manifold reuse of widely disseminated favorite contexts. (e.g., see note on new exodus network below)

The format of the present study makes detecting potential networks somewhat straightforward. The second list in every main chapter catalogs places in the Hebrew Scriptures that exegetically allude to the scroll in question. In these lists the networks jump out by having the same scriptural contexts listed repeatedly. Consider, for example, the section of the list of scriptural passages that feature interpretive parallels to the first several verses of Deut 23—the direction of dependence does not matter for the point at hand (excerpted from the chapter on Deuteronomy).

Deut 23:1–7*[2–8]~Isa 56:1–8* (B) (eunuchs and foreigners in Yahweh's house)
23:3–8*[4–9]~Ezra 9:1–2* (B) (mingling the holy seed)
23:3–6*[4–7]~Isa 52:1b* (uncircumcised and defiled will not enter you again)
23:3–6*[4–7]~Ruth 2:8* (B) (Moabitess granted residing foreigner gleaning privileges)
23:3–6*[4–7]~Ruth 4:22 (B) (Moabitess matriarch of David)
23:3–6*[4–7]//Neh 13:1–3* (responding to the law of the assembly)
23:3*[4]~Lam 1:10* (B) (enemy entering into Lady Jerusalem's holy place)
23:3*[4]~Neh 13:23–27* (B) (confronting apostasy husbands)
23:3, 7*[4, 8]~1 Kgs 11:1* (B) (women of Egypt and Edom as well as Ammon and Moab)
23:6*[7]~Ezra 9:11–12 (B) (pollution by intermarriage with the other)

* See assembly network.

3. See, e.g., Exod 33:1–3, 12–16; **Deut 31:6, 8**; Josh 1:6–9; 1 Kgs 2:1–4; Isa 7:14; etc.

Like everything else in the study of scriptural exegesis of Scripture, networks take careful, patient consideration. They should not be taken lightly. They can only be ignored at risk of misinterpretation. Networks are part of the context. Networks emanate a cumulative force over their constituent parts. The present purpose is to present networks to help facilitate study of exegetical relations across the scrolls of the Hebrew Scriptures. Also, attending to network relationships can help the study of the New Testament use of Scripture avoid taking these passages out of context.

The importance of recognizing networks includes awareness of additional interpretive connotations that may connect themselves to one or more of the exegetically associated scriptural contexts. This interpretive interconnectivity can operate as a pretext or subtext or even as interpretive momentum. An example can be seen in 1 Chr 28:4, where David goes back to the blessing of Judah even after the Davidic promise by Nathan. The exegetical allusion to the blessing of Judah in the Davidic covenant does not eliminate or replace the donor context but permanently connects it to the receptor context.[4]

Interpretive networks refer to the residual interpretive connectivity of exegetically related contexts that attract ongoing scriptural interpretive interventions. Allusions considered singularly activate interpretive connotative forces between the larger horizontal contexts of two texts.[5] The situation with the emerging canonical consciousness of the Scriptures begins to explain the ongoing power of some scriptural donor and receptor text pairs to attract further interpretive interventions to form interpretive networks. As canonical consciousness continues to increase, so too the connotative fertility of constituent scriptural contexts of networks for additional interpretive interventions. More detailed explanation of how interpretive networks function may be found elsewhere.[6]

The following interpretive networks are presented graphically, but not to scale. These graphically displayed networks are not the final destination but connections pointing back to their several constituent contexts that need to be considered individually and together. The Scriptures listed in the networks represent notes or parts of notes in the present study. Selected New Testament receptor texts are included for illustration—this sampling is not comprehensive or complete.

The length of passages purposely has been kept as small as possible. If passage size were increased, then often more connections (and more networks) could be located, but they would be more superficial.

The horizontal orientation of exegetically interconnected texts left to right is not a statement about direction of dependence, or anything else. The vertical orientation of texts also does not signify importance, or anything else. The layout of the network diagrams is simply an attempt to visually display the interpretive networks relations.

4. See Judah-king and Davidic covenant networks. Also see notes on 2 Sam 7:14–15 and 1 Chr 28:4–6. For an example of a New Testament use of network relations, see discussion of networks in chapter on Toward the New Testament.

5. See Ben-Porat, "Allusion," 107, 127. And for detailed explanation of the connotative forces of allusions upon readers who pursue the implications, including diagrams, see 105–28.

6. See Schnittjer, "Blessing of Judah," 34–37.

NETWORK SYMBOLS[7]

= A, interpretive quotation/paraphrase
– B, probable interpretive allusion
------- C, possible interpretive allusion
// parallel texts
+ interpretive blend
* part of another interpretive network
>/< more or less similar (e.g., stock phrases)

Abrahamic covenant‡

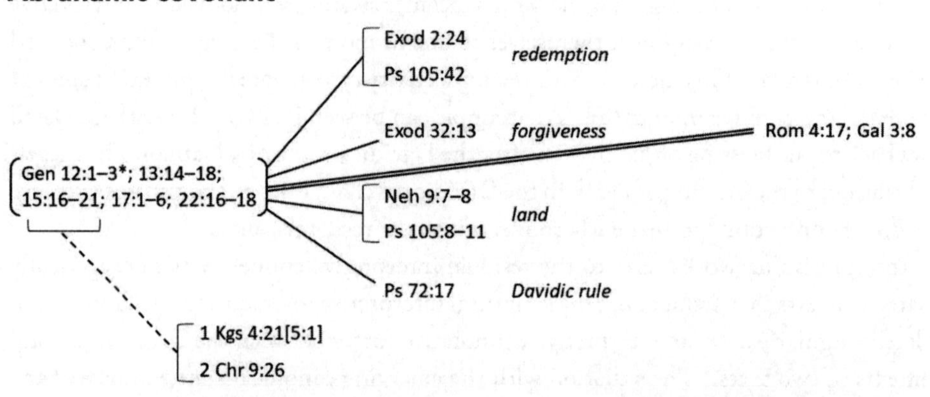

‡ See Table G1 in Genesis Filters. Torah contains a large number of allusions to the Abrahamic covenant that serve as one of its structuring devices (for a complete listing, see Clines, *Theme*, 32–47). Other brief allusions to the Abrahamic promise include his enduring status as Yahweh's friend (Isa 41:8; 2 Chr 20:7; cf. Jas 2:23). Themes closely related to this network include Abraham's faith (Gen 15:6; cf. Ps 106:31; Neh 9:7–8; Rom 4:3, 9, 22; Gal 3:6; Heb 11:8–19; Jas 2:23).

* See network: Judah-king, Gen 12:3.

the assembly

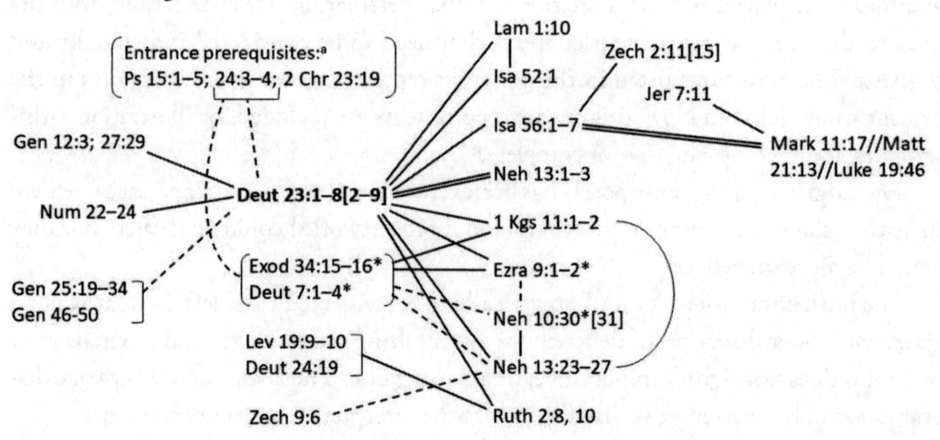

* See network: devoting, Exod 34:15–16; Deut 7:1–6; Ezra 9:1–2; Neh 10:30[31].

[a] Also see Isa 33:14–16; Jer 7:1–15; Ps 118:19–20.

7. For explanation of symbols, see Symbols and Abbreviations and Introduction. For other help, see Glossary.

attribute formula‡

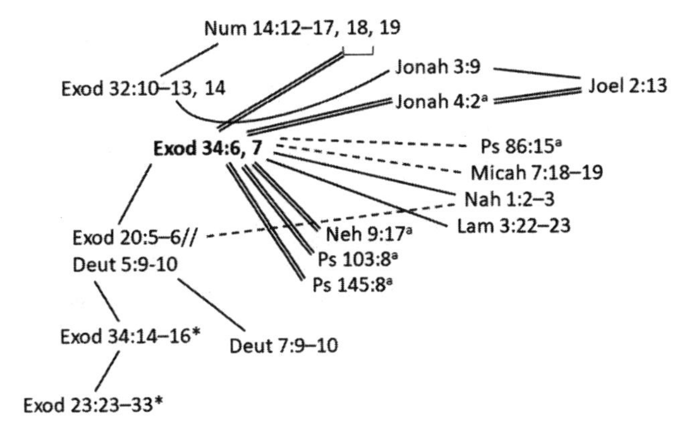

‡ See Table Joel1 for examples of Seidel's theory with key uses of attribute formula. For related shared language, see Deut 4:31; 1 Kgs 8:23//2 Chr 6:14; Dan 9:4; Neh 1:5; 9:31; 2 Chr 30:9. For brief allusions, often likely stock phrases from lyrical diffusion, see Pss 25:10; 26:3; 40:10–12[11–13]; 57:3, 10[4, 11]; 61:7[8]; 69:13[14]; 78:38; 79:8–9; 85:10–11[11–12]; 86:3, 5–6; 99:8; 109:8–13; 111:4, 7; 112:4; 115:1; 116:5; 117:2. Also see Duggan, *Covenant Renewal*, 211, nn. 95, 96; Fishbane, *Biblical Interpretation*, 347–48; Lane, "Exodus 34:6–7," 1, n. 1; Boda, *Heartbeat*, 45; Bullock, "Covenant Renewal," 20, n. 5; Bauckham, *Who?* 87.

* See networks: assembly, Exod 34:14–16; new exodus, Exod 23:23–33.

ª Alludes to Exod 34:6 only.

branch

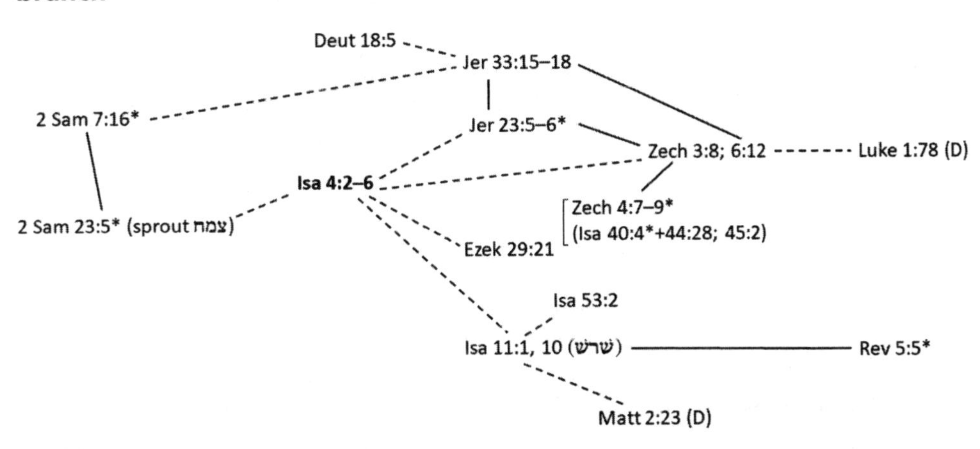

* See networks: Davidic covenant, 2 Sam 7:16; 23:5; Jer 23:5, 6; Judah-king, Rev 5:5; new exodus, Isa 40:4; Zech 4:7.

cities of the plain

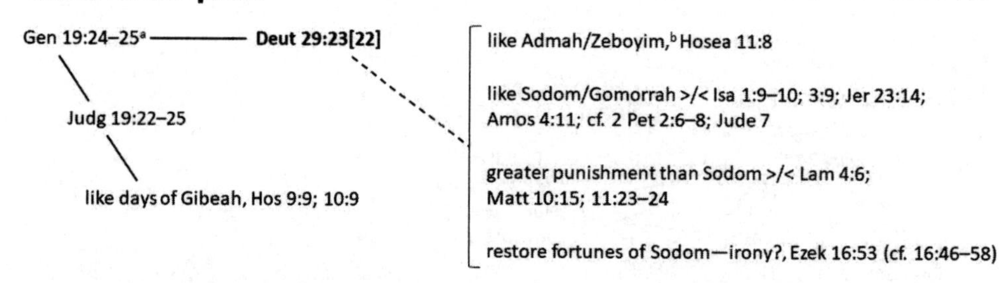

[a] The use of the cities of the plain as a symbol of judgment is assured. Whether the Torah contexts (Gen 19; Deut 29:23) continued to play a formative role seems less important than recognizing the developments within the prophetic traditions.

[b] Admah, Zeboyim, Sodom, and Gomorrah are a loose quartet of cities of the plain (Gen 14:8; cf. 10:19).

concealing revelation

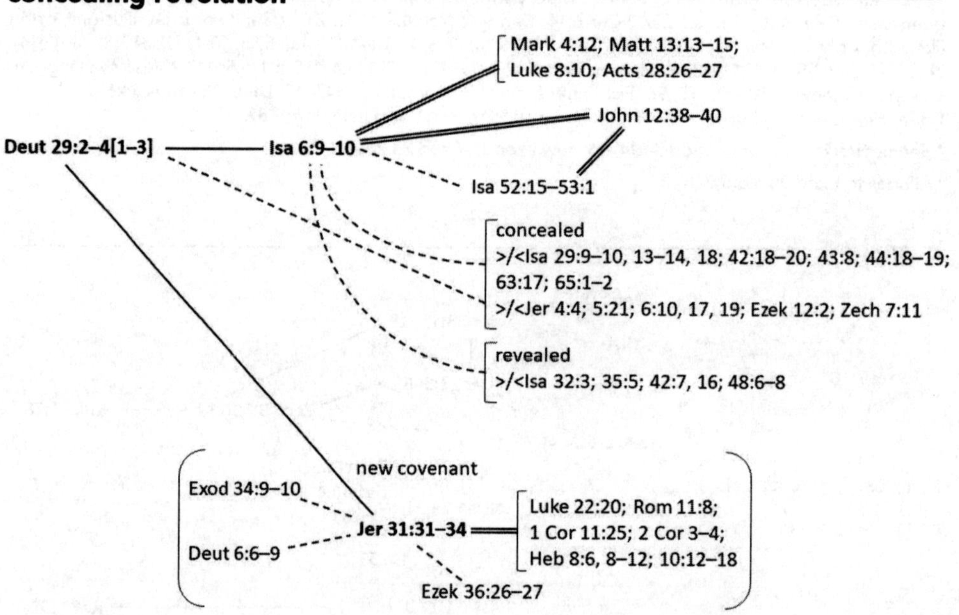

collective confession‡

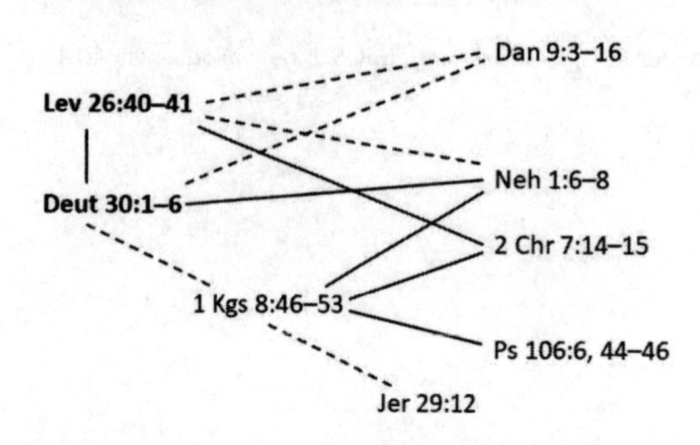

‡ See Ezra 9:6–15, esp. vv. 6–7 for a collective confession thematically related to the prayers in Neh 1:5–11 and Dan 9:3–16, but without parallel language to Lev 26:40–41 at the level of allusion. Also see Add Esth 14:3–19, esp. vv. 6, 12; Bar 1:15–3:8, esp. 3:5; 1QS/1Q7 I, 24–II, 1.

Cyrus and the temple foundation (see seventy years)

Davidic covenant

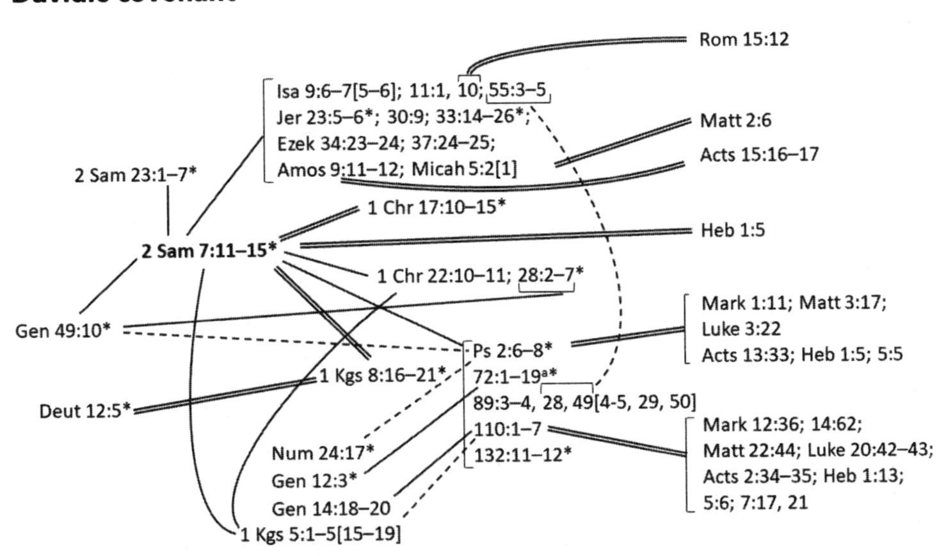

* See networks: Abrahamic covenant, Ps 72:17; branch, 2 Sam 23:5; Jer 23:5–6; 33:14–16; Judah-king, Gen 12:3; 49:10; Num 24:17; 2 Sam 7:14–15; 1 Chr 28:4; Ps 2:6–8; place, Deut 12:5; 1 Kgs 8:16–21; Ps 132; 1 Chr 17.

[a] Psalm 72 is listed here with the psalms that have explicit allusions to the Davidic promise (Pss 2; 89; 110; 132) even though its relationship to the David promise is indirect (see note ad loc.).

devoting (the nations of Canaan)

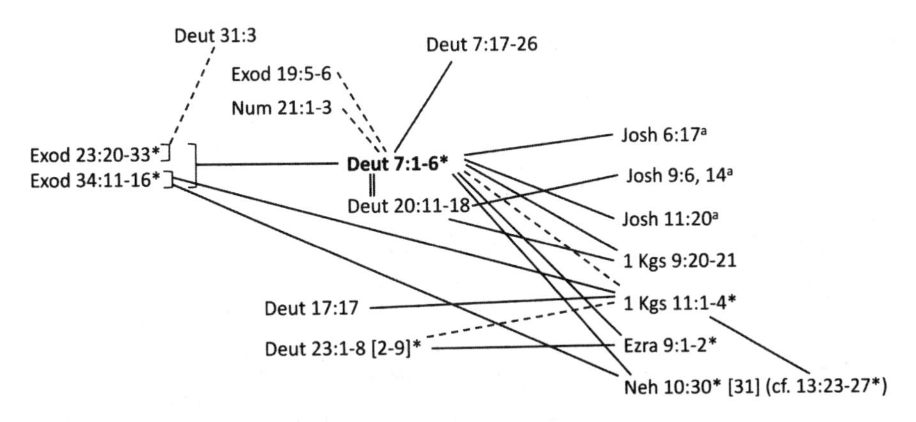

* See networks: assembly, Exod 34:11–17; Deut 7:1–6; 23:1–8[2–9]; 1 Kgs 1:1–4; Ezra 9:1–2; Neh 10:30[31]; 13:23–27; attribute formula, Exod 23:20–33; 34:11–16; new exodus, Exod 23:20–33.

[a] In addition, many contexts in Joshua and Judges make broad allusion to "devoting" the nations of Canaan (e.g., Josh 6:18–19; 7:1; 8:24–27; 10:28–43; 11:10–16; 23:9; 24:12; Judg 1:17, 19–33).

Judah-king‡

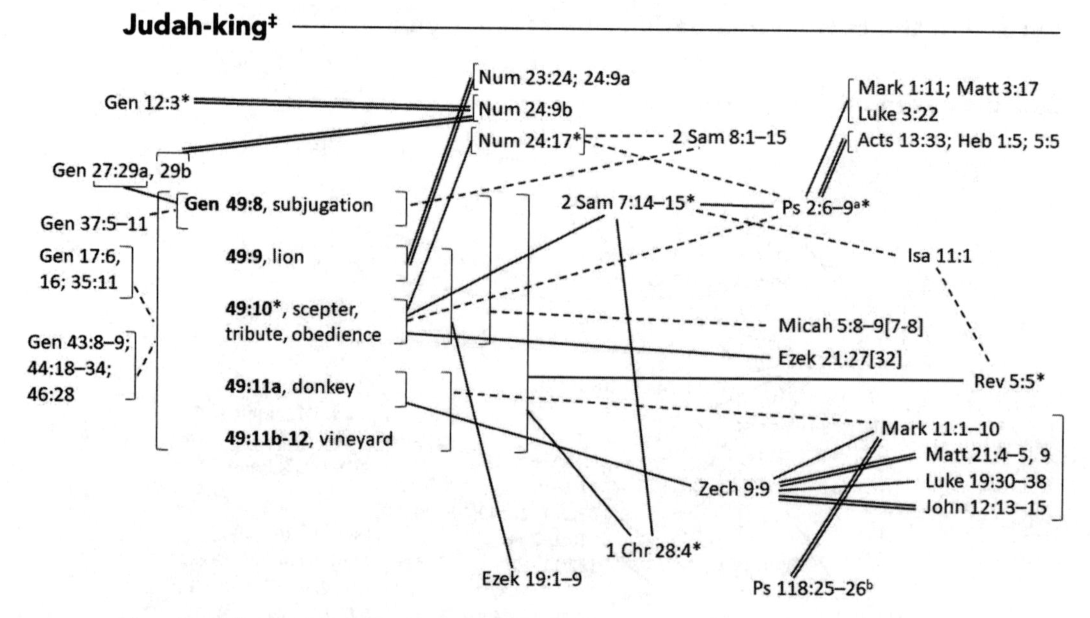

‡ Based on Schnittjer, "Blessing of Judah," 39.

* See networks: Abrahamic covenant, Gen 12:3; branch, Isa 4:2–6; 11:1; Rev 5:5; Davidic covenant, Gen 49:10; Num 24:17; 2 Sam 7:1–16; 23:1–6; Ps 2; 1 Chr 28:4.

[a] Note: Ps 2:1–2//Acts 4:25–26; cf. Rev 16:14; Ps 2:6; cf. Rev 14:1.

[b] Note: Ps 118:25–26//Matt 23:39 (cf. Matt 11:3//Luke 7:19); Ps 118:22–23//Matt 21:42 (cf. Mark 12:10–11; Luke 20:17; Acts 4:11; Eph 2:20; 1 Pet 2:4, 7).

new covenant (see concealing revelation)

new exodus‡

Mal 3:1
Mark 1:2–3//Matt 3:3//Luke 3:4–6
John 1:23
Exod 23:20–33*
Isa 40:3–10
1 Pet 1:24–25
Zech 4:7*
Isa 11:15–16
Isa 35:8–10
Isa 45:2; 52:8; 62:11

‡ The new exodus network here is restricted to explicit interpretive allusions between specific donor and receptor contexts that include exegetical outcomes. The theme is much more pervasive with all of Isaiah 40–55 manifesting new exodus connotations, largely based on some of the control texts of the interpretive network. In many ways the new exodus serves as an umbrella for several interweaved theological themes of Isaiah 40–55 (see Table I1 in Hermeneutical Profile of the Use of Scripture in Isaiah). These associated new exodus theological connotations carry over to many receptor texts of the Christian Bible for which Isaiah 40–55 serves as a donor context (see Morales, *Exodus Old and New*, 159–84, et passim; Harmon, "OT Use of OT, Comparison to the NT," *DNTUOT*, forthcoming). Nonetheless, the explicit allusions of the interpretive network are crucial control texts for the widespread new exodus theological themes in Scripture.

* See networks: attribute formula, Exod 22:20–33; branch, Zech 4:7; devoting, Exod 23:20–33.

personal responsibility statute

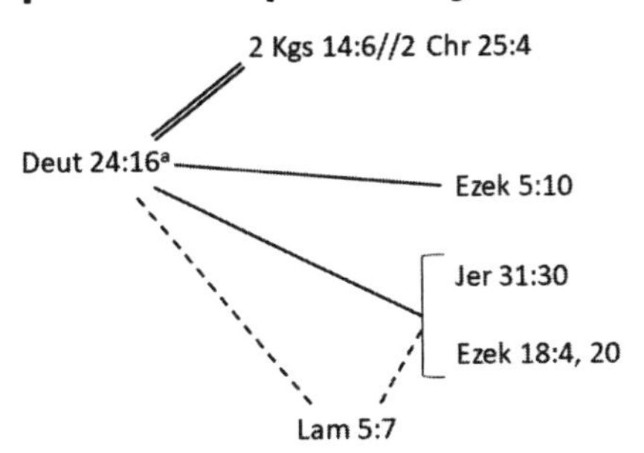

[a] Cf. Isa 14:21.

place Yahweh chooses for his name

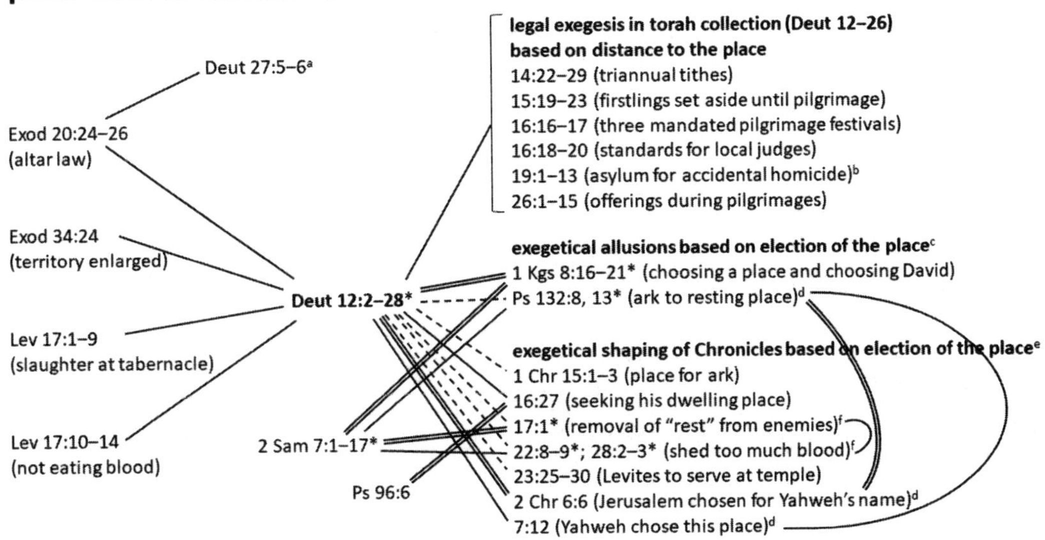

* See network: Davidic covenant, Deut 12:5; 2 Sam 7; 1 Kgs 8:16–21; Ps 132; 1 Chr 17; 22:8–9; 28:2–3.

[a] The allusion to Exod 20:25 in Deut 27:5–6 itself is not exegetical, but this allusion does relate to the exegetical advances in Deut 12 (see note on Deut 12:2–28).

[b] Note similar logic on decentralized Israel in note on Deut 19:1–13.

[c] Several passages of Scripture allude to elements of Deut 12 not directly based on choosing the place (see notes on Judg 17:6//21:25; 2 Sam 23:16–17//1 Chr 11:18–19; Hos 4:13; Ps 95:8, 11). These other allusions have not been included in this network since it focuses only on the interpretive implications of Yahweh's choosing a place for his name.

[d] Psalm 132:8–10 is cited within a Chronistic plus in 2 Chr 6:41–42 to join temple dedication (2 Chr 6:1–42), inclusive of an allusion to Deut 12:5 via Chronistic plus (6:6//Deut 12:5), to second revelation to Solomon (2 Chr 7:11–22), also inclusive of an allusion to Deut 12:5 via Chronistic plus (7:12~Deut 12:5). See notes on 2 Chr 6:1–42 and 7:11–22.

[e] All of the Chronicles contexts included here refer to Chronistic interpretive pluses (added elements not in synoptic counterparts in Samuel and Kings) or to materials unique to Chronicles (see notes ad loc).

[f] Removing the term "rest" from 1 Chr 17:1, 10 (versus 2 Sam 7:1, 11) seems to relate to the larger Chronistic strategy based on "rest" in Deut 12:10 (see note on 1 Chr 17:1–15). David appears to interpret his own restriction from building the temple as based on shedding too much blood (22:8–9; 28:3), meaning Israel did not yet enjoy "rest" from enemies (see notes on 1 Kgs 5:1–5[15–19]; 1 Chr 28:2–3; as well as Ps 110:1).

prophet like Moses

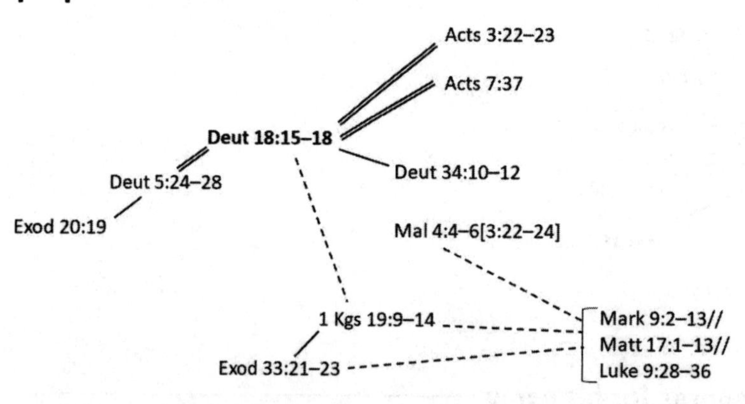

release statute (pledge, debt, slaves, interest)

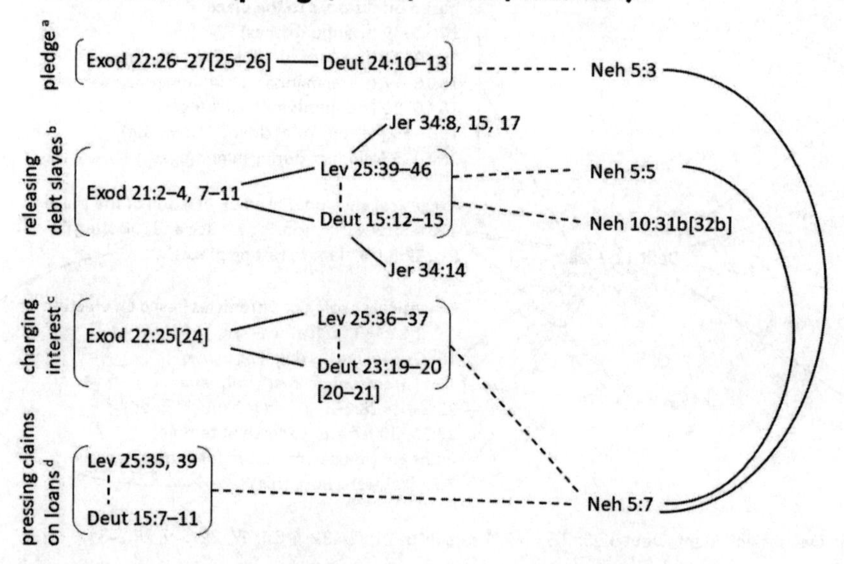

[a] On pledges, also see 2 Kgs 4:1; Isa 50:1.

[b] On debts, also see Deut 15:1–11; 23:19–20[20–21]; 24:10–13. And on release, also see Deut 31:10.

[c] On charging interest, also see Ezek 18:8, 13, 17; 22:12; Ps 15:5; Prov 28:8.

[d] Pressing claims on loans against "relatives" (lit. "brothers"). Also see Isa 58:7; Amos 2:6; Matt 18:25.

Sabbath

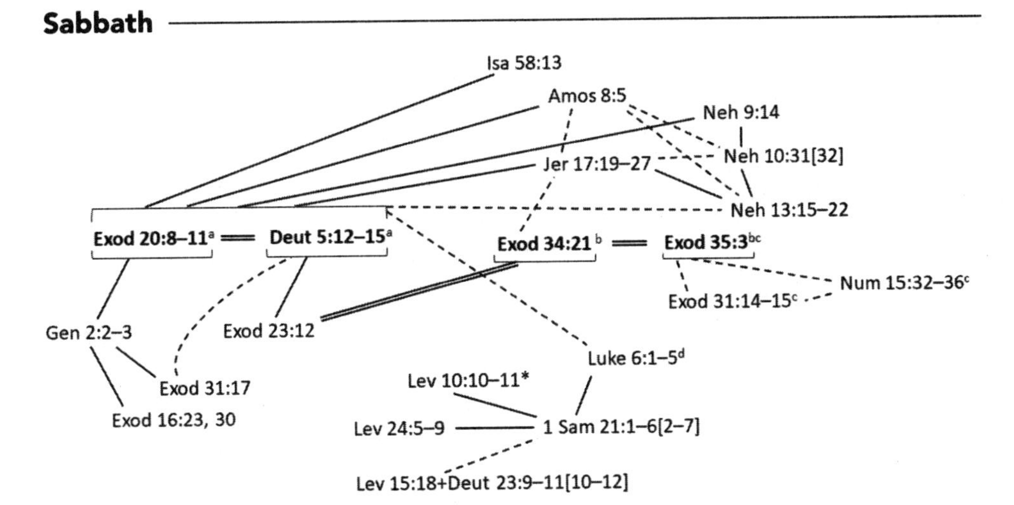

* See network: teachers, Lev 10:10–11.

[a] Also on Sabbath, see Exod 16:22–30; 31:12–17; 35:2–3; Lev 19:3b, 30; 23:3; 26:2; Num 15:32–36; 28:9–10. Sabbath as a holy day is based on an interpretive allusion to Gen 2:3 in Exod 20:11; 31:17 (cf. 16:23) and thereafter holiness mediated to other Sabbath laws by means of the fourth commandment.

[b] In Torah only two contexts qualify what counts as prohibited work (Exod 34:21; 35:2–3). Prohibitions extended to merchandising by Amos 8:5; Jer 17:21–22, 24, 27; Neh 10:31[32]; 13:15–22 (cf. m. Shab. 7:2; m. Yoma 8:6; b. Shab. 128b; contra 4Q470/CD 11:13–17).

[c] On Sabbath breaking as a capital offense, see Exod 31:14–15; 35:2; and Num 15:32–26. Also see note on Neh 13:15–18.

[d] For associated Sabbath controversies of the Lord, see Luke 6:6–11; 13:10–17; 14:1–6; cf. 4:31–39; Mark 3:1–6; John 5:1–18; 7:19–24.

seventy years

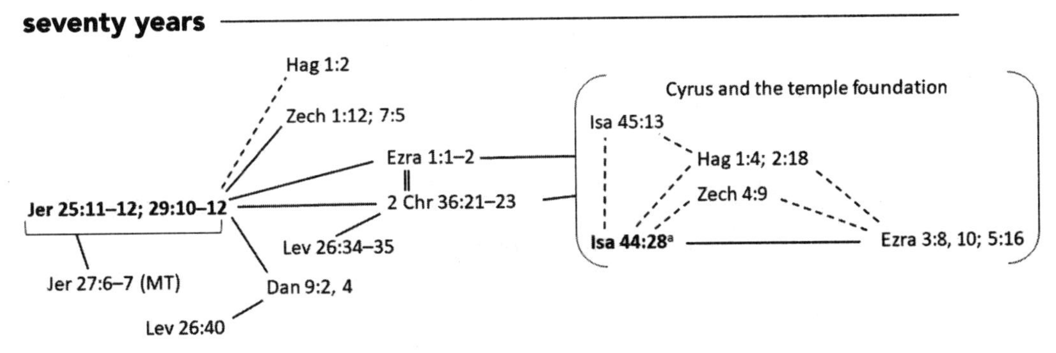

[a] See "stirred up" in Isa 41:2, 25; 45:13; 2 Chr 36:22//Ezra 1:1; cf. Hag 1:14; Ezra 1:5.

teachers

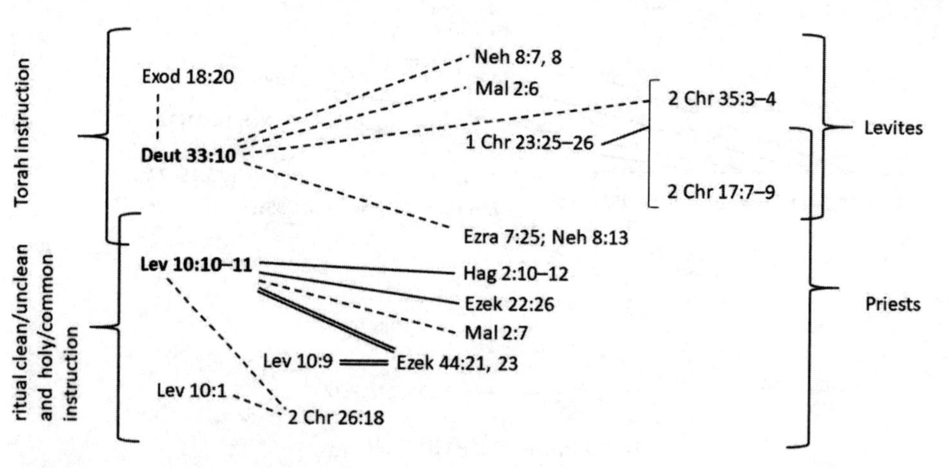

temple vessels‡

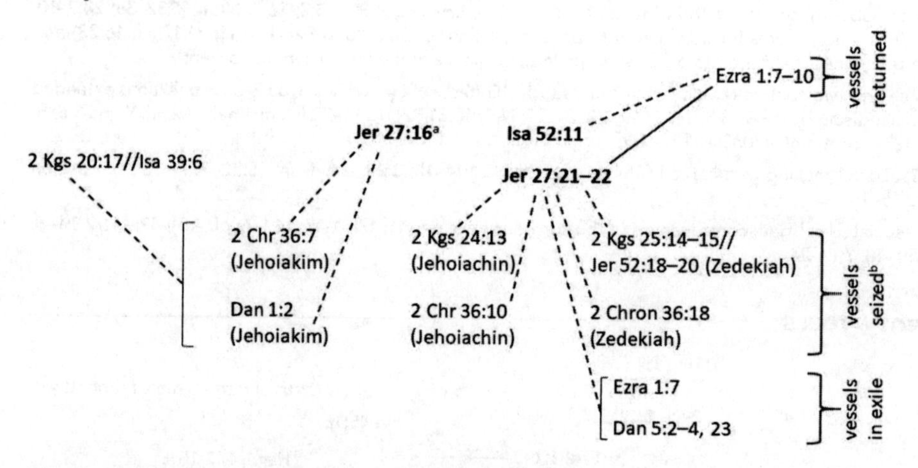

‡ On threefold looting of temple vessels see note on 2 Chr 36:7, 10.

[a] Also see Jer 28:3, 6, 15.

[b] Jehoiakim (609–598 BCE), Jehoiachin (597), Zedekiah (597–586).

SCRIPTURE INDEX OF NETWORKS

GENESIS

2:2, 3 .... Sabbath
12:1–3.......... Abrahamic covenant
12:3 .... assembly, Davidic covenant, Judah-king
13:14–18 .... Abrahamic covenant
14:18–20 .... Davidic covenant
15:16–21........ Abrahamic covenant
17:1–6.......... Abrahamic covenant
17:6, 16......... Judah-king
19:24–25 .... cities of the plain
22:16–18 .... Abrahamic covenant
25:19–34 .... assembly
27:29 .... assembly, Judah-king
35:11 .... Judah-king
43:8–9.......... Judah-king
44:18–34 .... Judah-king
46–50 .... assembly
46:28........... Judah-king
49:8–12......... Judah-king
49:10 .... Davidic covenant

EXODUS

2:24 .... Abrahamic covenant
16:23, 30........ Sabbath
18:20 .... teachers
19:5–6.......... devoting
20:5–6 .... attribute formula
20:8–11......... Sabbath
20:19 .... prophet like Moses
20:24–26 .... place
21:2–4, 7–11.... release statute
22:25[24] .... release statute
22:26–27[25–26].. release statute
23:12 .... Sabbath
23:20–33 .... attribute formula, devoting, new exodus
31:14–17........ Sabbath
32:10–13 .... attribute formula
32:13 .... Abrahamic covenant
33:21–23 .... prophet like Moses
34:6–7 .... attribute formula
34:9–10 .... concealing revelation
34:11–16........ assembly, attribute formula, devoting
34:21 .... Sabbath
34:24........... place
35:3 .... Sabbath

LEVITICUS

10:1 .... teachers
10:9 .... teachers
10:10–11 .... Sabbath, teachers
15:18 .... Sabbath
17:1–9.......... place
17:10–14........ place
19:9–10......... assembly
24:5–9.......... Sabbath
25:35, 39........ release statute
25:36–37 .... release statute
25:39–46 .... release statute
26:34–35 .... seventy years
26:40–41....... collective confession, seventy years

NUMBERS

14:12–19........ attribute formula
15:32–36 .... Sabbath
21:1–3.......... devoting
22–24 .... assembly
23:24........... Judah-king
24:9 .... Judah-king
24:17 .... Davidic covenant, Judah-king

DEUTERONOMY

5:9–10.......... attribute formula
5:12–15......... Sabbath
5:24–28 .... prophet like Moses
6:6–9........... concealing revelation
7:1–6 .... assembly, devoting
7:9–10.......... attribute formula
7:17–26......... devoting
12:2–28 .... place
12:5 .... Davidic covenant
14:22–29 .... place
15:7–11 .... release statute
15:12–15........ release statute
15:19–23........ place
16:18–20 .... place
17:17 .... devoting
18:5 .... branch
18:15–18........ prophet like Moses
19:1–13......... place
20:11–18........ devoting
23:1–8[2–9] .... assembly, devoting
23:9–11[10–12].. Sabbath
23:19–20[20–21].. release statute
24:10–13 .... release statute
24:16 .... personal responsibility
24:19 .... assembly
26:1–15......... place
27:5–6.......... place
29:2–4[1–3] .... concealing revelation
29:23[22] .... cities of the plain
30:1–6.......... collective confession
31:3 .... devoting
33:10 .... teachers
34:10–12 .... prophet like Moses

JOSHUA

6:17 .... devoting
9:6, 14.......... devoting
11:20 .... devoting

JUDGES

19:22–25 .... cities of the plain

1 SAMUEL

21:1–6[2–7]..... Sabbath

2 SAMUEL

7:1–17 .... place
7:11–15 .... Davidic covenant, Judah-king

7:16. . . . . branch
8:1–15 . . . . Judah-king
23:5 . . . . branch
23:7–8. . . . . Davidic covenant

1 KINGS

4:21[5:1] . . . . Abrahamic covenant
5:1–5[15–19]. . . . Davidic covenant
8:16–21. . . . . Davidic covenant, place
8:46–53 . . . . collective confession
9:20–21 . . . . devoting
11:1–4. . . . . assembly, devoting
19:9–14. . . . . prophet like Moses

2 KINGS

14:6 . . . . personal responsibility statute
20:17 . . . . temple vessels
24:13. . . . . temple vessels
25:14–15. . . . . . . temple vessels

ISAIAH

1:9–10. . . . . cities of the plain
3:9 . . . . cities of the plain
4:2–6. . . . . branch
6:9–10. . . . . concealing revelation
9:6–7[5–6] . . . . . Davidic covenant
11:1, 10 . . . . branch, Davidic covenant, Judah-king
11:15–16. . . . . . . new exodus
14:6 . . . . personal responsibility
29:9–18. . . . . concealing revelation
32:3 . . . . concealing revelation
35:5 . . . . concealing revelation
35:8–10. . . . . new exodus
39:6 . . . . temple vessels
40:3–10 . . . . new exodus
40:4 . . . . branch
42:7, 18–20 . . . . . concealing revelation
43:8 . . . . concealing revelation
44:18–19 . . . . . . concealing revelation
44:28. . . . . branch, seventy years
45:2 . . . . branch, new exodus
45:13 . . . . seventy years
48:6–8 . . . . concealing revelation
52:1 . . . . assembly
52:8 . . . . new exodus
52:11–12. . . . . . . temple vessels
52:15–53:1. . . . . . concealing revelation
53:2 . . . . branch
55:3–5. . . . . Davidic covenant
56:1–7. . . . . assembly
58:14 . . . . Sabbath
62:11 . . . . new exodus
63:17 . . . . concealing revelation
65:1–2. . . . . concealing revelation

JEREMIAH

4:4 . . . . concealing revelation
5:21 . . . . concealing revelation
6:10, 17, 19. . . . . concealing revelation
7:11. . . . . assembly
17:19–27. . . . . . . Sabbath
23:5–6. . . . . branch, Davidic covenant
23:14 . . . . cities of the plain
25:11–12. . . . . . . seventy years
27:6–7. . . . . seventy years
27:16, 21–22 . . . . temple vessels
29:10–12 . . . . seventy years
29:12 . . . . collective confession
30:9 . . . . Davidic covenant
31:30 . . . . personal responsibility
31:31–34. . . . . . . concealing revelation
33:14–26 . . . . . . Davidic covenant
33:15–18. . . . . . . branch
34:8–17 . . . . release statute
52:18–20 . . . . . . temple vessels

EZEKIEL

5:10 . . . . personal responsibility
12:2 . . . . concealing revelation
16:53 . . . . cities of the plain
18:4, 20. . . . . personal responsibility
19:1–9. . . . . Judah-king
21:27[32] . . . . . . Judah-king
22:26. . . . . teachers
29:21 . . . . branch
34:23–24. . . . . . . Davidic covenant
36:25–27 . . . . . . concealing revelation
37:24–25 . . . . . . Davidic covenant
44:21, 23 . . . . . . teachers

HOSEA

9:9 . . . . cities of the plain
10:9 . . . . cities of the plain
11:8 . . . . cities of the plain

JOEL

2:13 . . . . attribute formula

AMOS

4:11 . . . . cities of the plain
8:5. . . . . Sabbath
9:11, 12 . . . . Davidic covenant

JONAH

3:9 . . . . attribute formula
4:2 . . . . attribute formula

MICAH

5:2[1] . . . . Davidic covenant
5:8–9[7–8]. . . . . . Judah-king
7:18–19. . . . . attribute formula

NAHUM

1:2–3. . . . . attribute formula

HAGGAI

1:2, 4 . . . . seventy years
2:7, 10–12. . . . . . . teachers
2:18 . . . . seventy years

ZECHARIAH

1:12 . . . . seventy years
2:11[15]. . . . . assembly
3:8 . . . . branch
4:7–9 . . . . branch, new exodus, seventy years
6:12 . . . . branch
7:5. . . . . seventy years
7:11. . . . . concealing revelation
9:6 . . . . assembly
9:9 . . . . Judah-king

MALACHI

2:6 . . . . teachers
2:7. . . . . teachers
3:1. . . . . new exodus
4:4–6[3:22–24]. prophet like Moses

PSALMS

2:6–8. . . . . Davidic covenant, Judah-king
15:1–5 . . . . assembly
24:3–4 . . . . assembly
72:1–19. . . . . Davidic covenant
72:17 . . . . Abrahamic covenant
86:15 . . . . attribute formula
89:3–4[4–5] . . . . Davidic covenant
96:6 . . . . place
103:8 . . . . attribute formula
105:8–11 . . . . Abrahamic covenant
105:42. . . . . Abrahamic covenant
106:6, 44–46 . . . collective confession
110:1–7. . . . . Davidic covenant
118:25–26 . . . . . Judah-king
132:8, 13. . . . . place
132:11–12 . . . . . Davidic covenant
145:8 . . . . attribute formula

RUTH

2:8, 10 . . . . assembly

LAMENTATIONS

1:10 . . . . assembly
3:22–23 . . . . attribute formula

4:6 .... cities of the plain
5:7.............. personal responsibility

DANIEL

1:2.............. temple vessels
5:2–4, 23 .... temple vessels
9:2, 4 .... seventy years
9:3–16.......... collective confession

EZRA

1:1–2 .... seventy years
1:7–10 .... temple vessels
3:8, 10 .... seventy years
5:16 .... seventy years
7:25 .... teachers
9:1–2 .... assembly, devoting
9:6–7........... collective confession

NEHEMIAH

1:6–8........... collective confession
5:3, 5, 7 .... release statute
8:7, 8, 13 .... teachers
9:7–8 .... Abrahamic covenant
9:14 .... Sabbath
9:17 .... attribute formula
10:30[31] .... assembly, devoting
10:31[32] .... release statute, Sabbath
13:1–3.......... assembly
13:15–22 .... Sabbath
13:23–27 .... assembly, devoting

1 CHRONICLES

15:1–3.......... place
16:27 .... place
17:1............. place
17:10–15........ Davidic covenant
22:8–9.......... place
22:10–11 .... Davidic covenant
23:25–26 .... teachers
28:2–7.......... Davidic covenant
28:2–3.......... place
28:4 .... Judah-king

2 CHRONICLES

6:6 .... place
7:12 .... place
7:14–15......... collective confession
9:26 .... Abrahamic covenant
17:7–9 .... teachers
23:19 .... assembly
25:4 .... personal responsibility
26:18 .... teachers
35:3–4.......... teachers
36:7, 10, 18...... temple vessels
36:21–23 .... seventy years

MATTHEW

2:6 .... Davidic covenant
2:23 .... branch
3:3 .... new exodus
3:17 .... Davidic covenant, Judah-king
10:15 .... cities of the plain
11:23–24 .... cities of the plain
13:13–15........ concealing revelation
17:1–13......... prophet like Moses
21:4–9.......... Judah-king
21:13 .... assembly
22:44........... Davidic covenant

MARK

1:2–3........... new exodus
1:11 .... Davidic covenant, Judah-king
4:12 .... concealing revelation
9:2–13.......... prophet like Moses
11:1–10......... Judah-king
11:17 .... assembly
12:36........... Davidic covenant
14:62........... Davidic covenant

LUKE

1:78 .... branch
3:4–6........... new exodus
3:22 .... Davidic covenant, Judah-king
6:1–5 .... Sabbath
8:10 .... concealing revelation
9:28–36 .... prophet like Moses
19:30–38 .... Judah-king
19:46........... assembly
20:42–43....... Davidic covenant
22:20........... concealing revelation

JOHN

1:23 .... new exodus
12:13–15 .... Judah-king
12:38–40....... concealing revelation

ACTS

2:34–35 .... Davidic covenant
3:22–23 .... prophet like Moses
7:37 .... prophet like Moses
13:33 .... Davidic covenant, Judah-king
15:15–16........ Davidic covenant
28:26–27 .... concealing revelation

ROMANS

4:17 .... Abrahamic covenant
11:8 .... concealing revelation
15:12 .... David covenant

1 CORINTHIANS

11:25 .... concealing revelation

2 CORINTHIANS

3–4............. concealing revelation

GALATIANS

3:8 .... Abrahamic covenant

HEBREWS

1:5.............. Davidic covenant, Judah-king
1:13 .... Davidic covenant
5:5, 6 .... Davidic covenant, Judah-king
7:17, 21 .... Davidic covenant
8:6, 8–12 .... concealing revelation
10:12–18 .... concealing revelation

1 PETER

1:24–25 .... new exodus

2 PETER

2:6–8........... cities of the plain

JUDE

7 .... cities of the plain

REVELATION

5:5.............. branch, Judah-king

GLOSSARY

ALLUSION refers to *intentionally* evoking another context. Broadly speaking, scriptural allusion could include anything from direct quotation or paraphrase to loose, subtle, broad reference. Usually "quotation" is reserved for intentional sustained verbal repetition versus "allusion," which refers to intentional reference to donor context by paraphrase or with less verbal correspondence. Usually "echo" refers to a more subtle parallel than allusion. Allusion includes intentionality versus echo which may or may not be purposeful.[1] Biblical scholars often use a sliding scale from more to less parallel in receptor contexts: quotation, paraphrase, allusion, echo, trace. Quotations, paraphrases, and allusions may or may not be marked, but echoes and traces cannot be marked. In general, literary allusion may be considered "a device for the simultaneous activation of two texts."[2] The dual activating force of allusions gets at their residual effects especially within the emerging canonical consciousness of the Scriptures. The residual effects of dual activation of allusions may be seen most clearly in cases of interpretive networks (see chapter on Networks).

ASSONANCE refers to intentional relationship by means of repeated similar vowel sounds and consonance by means of repeated consonantal sounds.

ATOMIZATION refers to exegesis of scriptural content units (snippets) interpreted and reinterpreted in their own rights without respect to their contexts. Motif and/or lemmatic exegesis naturally tend toward atomization and became increasingly pronounced in Second Temple Judaic literature, the former often found in targums and the like, and the latter eventually collated in the Mishnah and its descendants and relatives. Samely explains the general relationship between atomization and midrash in proto-rabbinic context:

> These fragments or segments of Scripture are treated as if they could contain the divine author's meaning to the same degree as the whole of Scripture. Even if a verse is separated from its context, and thereby given a new topic, it is seen as retaining its power to reveal. A midrashic segment of Scripture therefore constitutes a micro-Scripture, preserving the authority and veracity of the word of God.[3]

---

1. See Irwin, "What Is an Allusion?" 294–95.

2. Ben-Porat, "Allusion," 107, 127. Ben-Porat's study explains in some detail the connotative effects on both donor and receptor contexts at large for readers who detect and pursue the interpretive implications of allusions (105–28).

3. Samely, *Forms of Rabbinic Literature*, 66. Also see Goldberg, "Rabbinic View of Scripture," 153–66.

Also see lemmatic exegesis, motif, and stock phrase.

AUTHORSHIP as it relates to biblical authors' exegetical use of scriptural traditions occurs within the context of ancient scribal culture. Ancient authorial, redactional, and editorial activities overlap like circles in a Venn diagram. The sub-activities are here artificially isolated for the sake of definition only. **Authors** refers to the agents responsible for composing texts. **Redaction** refers to collecting sources, selecting what to exclude and include, and arranging compositions.[4] Use of the term redaction in biblical studies should be kept distinct from modern use in which "redacted" sometimes refers to deleted passages in formerly classified documents released to the public, and the like. **Editing** refers to scribal interventions in re-presenting source materials. Ancient authors, of course, often acted as redactors and editors as well as producing new elements in the production of written compositions. The scribal dynamics of textual production and textual transmission can, at times, operate identically. For this reason some scholars use terms like author-scribes, editor-scribes, and copyist-scribes for clarity.[5] The watershed is the distinction between authorized scribal interventions by authors/redactors/editors in the production of a biblical text versus scribal interventions by copyists. Most intentional editorial interventions by copyist-scribes may represent attempts to "improve," but these un-authorized variations count as corruptions from the vantage point of textual criticism.[6] The study of exegetical interventions within Scripture focuses on author-intended outcomes. Since scriptural exegesis of scriptural traditions requires donor and receptor contexts, exegesis by authors naturally includes elements of redaction and editing within it.

BOILERPLATE oracles refers to the reuse of identical or nearly identical judgment sayings with the name of the people under judgment switched (see Jeremiah Filters).

CANONICAL CONSCIOUSNESS refers to the emerging awareness of scriptural authority.[7] Pushback against the "tyranny of canonical assumptions" helps moderns remember ancients did not have personal codices (books) and many other anachronisms.[8] Seeking precision leads some scholars to define "Scripture" as a precanonical ideal and "Bible" and/or "canon" as a later formal dogmatic affirmation.[9] However, adding specialized meanings to terms often used synonymously is not helpful. Canonical consciousness and/or authority are made explicit to different degrees and in different

---

4. On the place of collection and selection in redaction see basic introductory definition in Barton, "Redaction Criticism (OT)," *ABD* 5:644.

5. See Tov, *Textual Criticism*, 240, et passim.

6. The "goal" of Hebrew Bible textual criticism is sharply contested (e.g., original text, final text, canonical text, earliest attested text, pluriformity). A discussion of textual criticism falls outside of the present study. The text critical work of the present study seeks the "final text" akin to the manner defined by Waltke, "Aims," 93–108.

7. On "canonical consciousness," see Childs, *Introduction*, 60; Fishbane, "Torah and Tradition," 283, 289. This term is often used by interpreters in a general sense without carrying all of the baggage of theories of canonical criticism.

8. See Kraft, "What Is 'Bible'?" 111; idem, "Para-mania," 10–18.

9. See Sundberg, "'Old Testament': A Canon," 147. Also see, e.g., Nihan, "Textual Fluidity," 188, n. 7.

ways throughout the Hebrew Scriptures, such as the prophetic mantra "Thus says Yahweh" or "as it is written" in later books like Ezra-Nehemiah (see marked).

CATCHWORD, CATCHPHRASE refers to connecting two or more scriptural contexts by the shared word or phrase. See constellation.

CHIASTIC—see mirror imaging.

CHRONISTIC refers to Chronicles but not Ezra-Nehemiah. Chronicles and Ezra-Nehemiah are separate books written by different authors.[10]

CLONING refers to replication and reuse of the same literary element or narrative vignette. The clones may be slightly modified to accomplish specific literary and/or exegetical outcomes. Cloned narratives may serve as previews or overviews like Solomon's international horse trading (2 Chr 1:14–17; cf. note ad loc. and 9:25–28) or flashbacks like the glory entering the temple (7:1–3; cf. note ad loc. and 5:13–14). Whereas clones refer to the same event or element, boilerplates reuse the same template for something else (see boilerplates). Other kinds of re-use differ in degree and kind from clones and boilerplates, such as the use of the verbs from the message to the Edomites as a skeletal template for the firstfruits liturgy (see Deut 26:6–10; cf. note ad loc. and Num 20:15–16) or the interweaved themes of Isaiah's consolation (see Table I1 with its associated discussion in Hermeneutical Profile of the Use of Scripture in Isaiah). Doublets arguably overlap cloning as a subset of sorts with different kinds of functions like connections, cross-referencing, and emphasis or reversal in the case of nonrecurring doublets (see discussions of doublets in, e.g., Jeremiah Filters, Joel Filters, Proverbs Filters; and see examples of "the growing phrase" in Jonah Filters). For examples of cloning see, e.g., notes on Ezek 7:19; 2 Chr 2:1–8[1:18–2:27]; and Table C8 with its associated discussion in Hermeneutical Profile of the Use of Scripture in Chronicles.

CONFLATION—see interpretive blend.

CONNOTATION refers to inferences bound up together with denotations of literary signifiers (words, phrases, etc.). The prefix con- in "connotation" means something like in, with, under, and gets at the literary baggage that all discourse carries. If denotation refers to the reference of words and phrases, then connotation refers to the inferences bound up with it. Ancient Egypt and Canaan may be places (denotation), but in Lev 18:3 they become associated with the lifestyle of the citizens who call those places home (connotation). The prohibition against priests "letting their hair grow long" (Ezek 44:20) may connote something other than aesthetic or practical standards for worship personnel to look their best or keep their hair from getting burned at the altar. This prohibition does not stem from excluding Nazirite vows nor military fighting, even though those contexts may use the same root to modify long hair (Deut 32:42; Num 6:5). When high priests serve they shall not exhibit signs of mourning for

10. See Japhet, "Supposed Common Authorship," 330–71; Williamson, *Israel*, 83–86.

deceased close relatives, including keeping their hair in good order (Lev 21:10–11).[11] The original scriptural backstory associated with the prohibition—not mourning for the dead (10:6–7)—leaves behind connotative elements. In this example the *denotation* of messy hair may *connote* mourning for the dead.

CONSONANCE—see assonance.

CONSTELLATIONS intentionally situate together multiple previously separate and independent scriptural contexts. Constellations make use of juxtaposition on a larger scale. The "citing context" may use catchwords, catchphrases, thematic similarities, and/or proximate (re)location by placing elements side by side, and so forth. Interpretive constellations, like celestial constellations, superimpose relationship from another vantage point. Interpretive constellations leverage relationships among constituent cited texts from an outside vantage point versus interpretive networks that feature internal interconnectivity (see network). Constellation connectors do not generally include exegetical intervention in the constituent contexts themselves. In that sense, the multiple juxtapositions of constellations serve as do-it-yourself interpretive guidance. The point of constellations is not particular interpretive outcomes but invitation for readerly deductions. Does this mean the author/editor/redactor[12] set up predictable or inevitable conclusions for readers to "discover for themselves"? Or, does the open-endedness imply a safe area for several kinds of conclusions? These possibilities may differ from one constellation to the next, but, in any case, do not need to be decided here. Examples of constellations include the "set" of *halelu-yah* psalms at the close of the Psalter (Pss 146–150) and the "Book of the Twelve."[13] Use of interpretive constellations for messianic exegesis and the gospel appears in the New Testament (e.g., Rom 3:10–18; 15:9–12; Heb 1:5–13). See juxtaposition.

COVENANT COLLECTION refers to the legal standards housed in Exod 21–23.

COVENANT RENEWAL COLLECTION refers to the legal standards housed in Exod 34:11–26.

DENOTATION refers to the reference of literary signifiers (words, phrases, etc.). See connotation.

DEUTERONOMIC refers to the book of Deuteronomy.

DEUTERONOMISTIC NARRATIVE refers to Joshua-Judges-Samuel-Kings as a serial narrative flavored by Deuteronomy.

DIACHRONIC refers to focusing on the historical background "behind" the text versus synchronic which focuses on studying the effects "in front of" the text. That is, diachronic (through time) studies work on the author-text dialectic of production versus

11. The verb form may refer to messy or disheveled hair (Lev 21:10) while the noun may be used of long and loosely hanging hair (Num 6:5; Deut 32:42), see "פרע," Q 2.a, b and "I פֶּרַע," no. 1 *HALOT* 2:970.

12. On author, editor, and redactor, see entry on authorship.

13. See Connection by Placement and/or Editing in Psalms Filters and Parallels within the Book of the Twelve in Hosea Filters. For many examples in the Old Testament, Second Temple Judaic literature, and the New Testament see Eng, "Semitic Catchwords," 245–67.

synchronic (at one time) studies which work on the text-reader dialectic of reception. The terms diachronic and synchronic have been borrowed from linguistics and are used widely in biblical studies. These general umbrella terms include together many diverse approaches. For more explanation and a diagram see Introduction. Also see excavative.

DIRECT QUOTATION or allusion refers to citation of the donor context itself versus indirect quotation or allusion in which the interrelationship between donor and receptor contexts is mediated by a common source or shared cultural framework. See indirect relationship.

DIRECTION OF DEPENDENCE refers to which text of genetically related parallel texts uses the other. The cited context may be called the donor text and the citing text the receptor text. Determining direction of dependence requires the right kind of evidence. For extensive discussion of direction of dependence see Introduction.

DISCHRONOLOGIZED narrative refers to narrative sequence that has been rearranged in comparison to historical sequence. Dischronological narrative is very common in the Scriptures and other ancient writings. Narrative sequence is rearranged for ideological, thematic, and exegetical reasons.[14] For examples see Figures C6 and C7 in Chronicles.

DOUBLE ALLUSION—see interpretive blend.[15]

ECHO "points along a spectrum of intertextual reference, moving from the explicit to the subliminal."[16] While some scholars use echo of any parallel, many speak of allusions as author-intended parallels in contrast to echoes, which are regarded as more subtle similarities that may be intended or not. See allusion.

EDITING—see authorship.

EXCAVATIVE refers to agendas of some diachronic studies that disassemble the biblical text seeking one or more elements in its production or pre-history.[17] The term "excavative" aptly identifies approaches to biblical research that begin with the text in seeking to uncover something else. Excavative studies may seek to recover theoretical sources, theoretical editorial layers, theoretical redactors, theoretical scribal cultures, or the like, as well as theoretical life-settings and dates for these reconstructed elements that went into producing the text.

EXEGESIS is transliterated from Greek (ἐξήγησις) and can refer narrowly to explanation.[18] In line with many studies on exegesis within Scripture, the present study uses the term

---

14. As summarized by Glatt-Gilad, *Chronological Displacement*, 188. For many biblical examples see summary chart 184–85. For discussion of several dischronological narratives in Torah, see Schnittjer, *Torah Story*, 190, 246 (Table 14-B), 272–73, 373. For discussion of cases of dischronological narration in Assyrian royal inscriptions see Tadmor, "History," 13–32. Tadmor refers to several examples including Ashurnasirpal and Shalmaneser's son Tukulti-Ninurta I (cf. *ARI* 2:122–24).

15. For the term "double allusion" see Berlin, "Interpreting Torah," 27.

16. Hays, *Echoes Paul*, 23.

17. The term "excavative" to describe an agenda in biblical scholarship comes from Alter, *Narrative*, 14.

18. See use in Josephus, *Antiquities*, XI, 192.

in its broader sense when applied to the scriptural use of Scripture (e.g., of explanation, revision, expansion, development, enhancement, ironic qualification, adjustment, etc.).[19] Exegesis and interpretation are used with an identical sense.

EXTENDED ECHO-EFFECT refers to the connotative effects that derive from one context intentionally modeled after another, including multiple relations, often in the same sequence (a-b-c, a-b-c).[20] A character, event, instruction, oracle, or the like naturally gets compared as a virtual simile to its counterpart, causing connotative transfer. The shared literary sequence of details between Adam and Eve's fall and Noah's drunkenness, e.g., makes Noah "sound like" Adam and Eve, even without lining up every detail (be fruitful Gen 1:28; 9:1; garden/vineyard 2:8; 9:20; eat/drink 3:6; 9:21; naked 3:7; 9:21; fig leaf loincloths/sons cover nakedness 3:7; 9:23; knowledge of shame 3:7; 9:24; curse 3:14–19; 9:25–27). This results in connotations of Adam and Eve attaching to Noah in certain respects: Noah represents a new beginning and an immediate rebellion with a curse—these details are enhanced by their Adam-and-Eve-like qualities. Scriptural writers frequently use extended echo, which strengthens continuity (see, e.g., the "she's my sister" stories in Gen 12; 20; 26; the wilderness temptation stories in Exod 15–16; Num 11–12; 20–21; and so on). Stated differently, scriptural writers often model their contributions after scriptural traditions. Although paradigmatic shaping, extended echo, and typological patterning are three varieties of analogous relations created by intentional literary relations, they have been sorted out here because they function differently. *Paradigmatic shaping* gets more at broad formulaic narrative structure, like the cycles of the judges or the kings who go from bad to good or vice versa in Chronicles, and so forth. *Typological patterning*, especially the retrospective variety, can look identical to extended echo but functions as fulfillment akin to the explicit forward-looking typological patterns with expectation and fulfillment (see typological patterns). See comparative examples of all three with functions listed in Table C10 in Chronicles. *Type-scenes* refer to genre stereotypes like the barren woman, and so on. Whereas type-scenes are part of genre conventions within culture, extended echo-effect and typological patterning within Scripture are the products of specific, intentionally related counterpart contexts.

FIGURAL patterns—see typological patterns.

FRAME NARRATIVE refers to the controlling narrative context of quoted or embedded elements therein.[21] For example, the rebellion with the calf and its aftermath in Exod 32–34 provide the frame narrative of the covenant renewal legal collection (Exod 34:11–26). As such the covenant renewal collection makes sense within its frame narrative.

HAGGADIC—see halakic.

---

19. See Tigay, "Early Technique," 170, n. 3.
20. See Schnittjer, *Torah Story*, 17.
21. Sternberg, "Quotation-Land," 108, 131, 149.

HALAKIC interpretation focuses on legal instruction in contrast to haggadic, which deals with non-legal Scriptures, especially narrative.

HOLINESS COLLECTION refers to the legal standards housed in Lev 17–26.

HORIZONTAL CONTEXT refers to the surrounding scriptural setting of the cited text—paragraph, chapter, book (see Figure NT1 in Toward the New Testament). The unquoted context of the cited Scripture often bears on the citing context. The issue of context in the protracted debate in studies of the New Testament use of Scripture includes models of cited texts as pointers, broad reference, and peripheral vision.[22] The primary issue turns on the expectations of the citing author and how the context of the donor text bears upon receptor text. See vertical context.

INCLUSIO refers to a repeated element that frames a unit for literary reasons (a, xyz, a). The same kind of bracketing phenomenon also results from an ancient scribal technique for marking the insertion of a source or the like—see resumptive repetition.

INDIRECT RELATIONSHIP refers to Scriptures that are not directly related by one using the other but by both drawing on a common source or related sources. Ability to determine whether parallel elements derive from direct or indirect relationship or broader cultural diffusion depends on available evidence.

INNERBIBLICAL EXEGESIS refers to Scriptures that revise, adjust, or somehow interpret other scriptural traditions.[23] In spite of competing claims, responsible study of innerbiblical exegesis may be pursued both/either diachronically, when sufficient evidence indicates direction of borrowing, and/or synchronically, working with the biblical evidence itself.[24]

INTERPRETATION—see exegesis.[25]

INTERPRETIVE BLEND refers to a scriptural receptor text's interpretation of one scriptural donor text in the light of another.[26] This phenomenon is often spoken of as "conflation" of the cited texts.

INTERTEXT refers to the donor context in an innerbiblical intertextual approach. Or, in the case of broad intertextuality, every text becomes an "intertext" susceptible to the potential mutations and uses to which it may be subjected.[27] See intertextuality.

INTERTEXTUALITY is a term coined by Julia Kristeva to refer to the general theory of interrelations between media (with all media referred to as "textual"). Kristeva acknowledges the broad use of the term "intertextuality" in various kinds of literary studies: "The term *inter-textuality* denotes this transposition of one (or several) sign

22. See Beale, *Handbook*, 1–5; idem, "Cognitive Peripheral Vision," 263–93; Dodd, *According to the Scriptures*, 126; Rendall, "Wider Reference," 214–21; Turner, "Going Beyond What Is Written," 577–94.

23. The term innerbiblical exegesis was coined by Sarna, "Psalm 89," 29.

24. See Ego, "Biblical Interpretation," 53–62; Lester, "Inner-Biblical Interpretation," 444–53; contra Meek, "Intertextuality," 280–91. Hermeneutical terms often bleed over. Even Fishbane who typically speaks of inner-biblical exegesis and the like can refer to the phenomena he studies as "intertextuality" (see Fishbane, "Types of Intertextuality," 39).

25. For a view that distinguishes between interpretation and exegesis, see Berlin, "Interpreting Torah," 22–23.

26. Interpretive blend is broader and adapted from "legal blend," coined by Fishbane, *Biblical Interpretation*, 110–19, 134–136.

27. See discussion in Luz, "Intertexts in Matthew," 119–22.

system(s) into another; but since the term has often been understood in the banal sense of 'study of sources,' we prefer the term *transposition*."[28] In common use in biblical studies, "intertextuality has come to be used as a synonym for 'echo' or 'allusion.'"[29] In scholarly use, "*intertextuality* is a vague and fluid term, which can cover *any* type of relations between texts, even those unconsciously evoked by authors, as well as those not recognized by their target audience."[30] The very broadness of intertextual relations, in part, accounts for the label frequently redefined by individual scholars.

INVERTED CITATION—see Seidel's theory.

JUXTAPOSITION refers to intentionally bringing together separate and independent scriptural contexts for mutual consideration but without exegetical intervention. Juxtaposition may be thought of as a guide for do-it-yourself reading of Scripture with Scripture. Important examples include editorial superscriptions of psalms pointing to scriptural narrative contexts and placement of psalms side by side based on catchwords or the like. Juxtaposition on a larger scale may be thought of as a constellation (see above).

LATE BIBLICAL HEBREW—see Standard Biblical Hebrew.

LEMMATIC EXEGESIS refers to interpretation of a lemma—a small individual content unit (datum or *traditum*), whether a biblical word or phrase. The term lemma is commonly used in studies of legal exegesis to refer to the legal instruction, sub-unit, or individual term being interpreted. Lemmatic exegesis often leads to a focus on the content unit without respect for its biblical context (see atomization).[31]

LOCUTION refers to an utterance. Speech act theory explains locutions in broader conventions beyond "performatives" that accomplish something by the utterance itself, such as "I do" at a wedding or "not guilty" at a trial. An "illocution" refers to the *function* of a locution to suggest, order, promise, commend, deceive, and so on, versus "perlocution," which refers to the *accomplishment* of a locution. Austin offers an example: A person said "shoot her" (locution), by which the person advised/urged to shoot her (illocution), by which the person made/persuaded a person shoot her (perlocution).[32]

LYRICAL DIFFUSION refers to broad dissemination of stock phrases, refrains, stereotypical expressions, and the like that get detached from their original scriptural contexts and become part of poetic idioms common in the prophets, psalms, and/or wisdom. Lyrical diffusion in the psalms suggests a culture of worship wherein "liturgical idiom" gets picked up naturally by psalmists.[33] Lyrical diffusion deflects many cases of alleged scriptural citations. See stock phrases.

---

28. Kristeva, *Revolution*, 59–60. For a brief explanation of the historical background of Kristeva's coining intertextuality, see van Wolde, "Texts in Dialogue," 1–4.

29. Theocharous, *Lexical Dependence*, 1. For warnings, see Beale, *Handbook*, 39–40; Meek, "Intertextuality," 280–91.

30. Edenburg, "Intertextuality," 173, n. 16, emphasis original.

31. Fishbane locates the inception of lemmatic legal exegesis in late Hebrew Bible contexts like Ezra-Nehemiah (see *Biblical Interpretation*, 266).

32. See Austin, *How to Do Things with Words*, 94, 98, 100–2, 105–7.

33. The term "liturgical idiom" is coined and explained by Newman, *Praying by the Book*, 106–7.

MARKED refers to self-consciously drawing attention to the use of a source for readers/auditors versus unmarked allusions where a citing context presents cited element(s) without mentioning it(them) as such. Marking scriptural allusions varies greatly from more elaborate to simple (e.g., "as it is written"). Marking elements in receptor contexts from authoritative donor contexts suggests a measure of canonical consciousness (see above).

MASORETIC TEXT refers to the traditional Hebrew consonantal text along with the apparatus of the Tiberian Masoretes. The work of the Masoretes culminated in the tenth century CE with vocalization of the consonantal text by vowel pointing and an elaborate system of accenting. Traditionally, the older generation of the synagogue teaches the younger generation how to read the Hebrew consonantal text. The Masoretes put the traditional synagogue reading into a permanent written form.

MIDRASHIC comes from a Hebrew root with a basic sense of ask, search, explain.[34] This term can refer to Second Temple and proto-rabbinic interpretation generally, but especially to a genre of inventive haggadic literature of late antiquity. The Scripture versus midrash dialectic naturally leads to the term midrash carrying the connotation of invented postbiblical traditions. Thus, although the term midrash/midrashic of itself refers simply to interpretation, the genre known by this name creates a similar kind of semantic baggage as the myth versus history dialectic that causes "myth" to connote made up or false.

MIRROR IMAGING refers to structuring the second half of a narrative or poetic unit by echoes of the first half in reverse order (a-b-c, c-b-a), sometimes with a pivot element in the center (a-b-c-b-a). This phenomenon is often called inverted parallel, ring pattern, or chiastic after the Greek letter *chi* (χ) by connecting the parallel elements in the A and B lines of poetry.

A, a ╲ ╱ b
B, b ╱ ╲ a

Many interpreters distort this ancient convention in narratives by overstressing the central pivot. The powerful linear motion of narration moving toward endings should not be eclipsed even in infrequent cases with an emphasized central pivot.[35] Another function of mirror imaging that has not received enough attention is repetition for emphasis. Many times mirror imaging provides a conventional way to say the same thing twice. Mirror imaging is typical of ancient oral literacy contexts to help hearers retain poetry and storylines even when they may never handle the scrolls in their lifetimes and only hear them read aloud during pilgrimage festivals. Mirror imaging

34. See "דרשׁ," *HALOT* 1:233.
35. See Schnittjer, *Torah Story*, 18–19.

may have been so much a part of oral literary conventions that authors and auditors generally did not think about it. In the modern world, mirror imaging (a-b-c, c-b-a) and extended echo-effect (a-b-c, a-b-c) appear commonly in children's books to teach literacy. Even if the progressive extended echo-effect of the first half and the mirror imaging of the second half of *The Cat in the Hat* required Theodor Geisel to design it using an elaborate incrementally indented outline, the book's intended auditors can safely ignore such scaffolding.

MOTIF refers to thematic content units—subject, topic, idea, concept, or the like. A scriptural motif may transcend its original context and take on life of its own, so to speak. The motif of God as "gracious and compassionate" becomes a scriptural stock phrase (see below) and may be used apart from its narrative context (see list in attribute formula network). Determining exegetical use of a common motif requires additional literary signals. Jonah expressed anger about God as "gracious and compassionate" because he "relents" from threatened doom, grounding an allusion to Exod 34:6 to its context by allusion to 32:14 (Jonah 4:2; cf. 3:10). In Second Temple Judaic literature, motifs often became elaborate and could be joined to other motifs.[36] See atomization.

NARRATIVE TRACKING refers to one text alluding to another by mimicking narrative structure rather than verbal parallels.[37] The kinds of similarities allegedly evoked by these loose narrative similarities seem to largely fall short of exegetical interventions.

NETWORK refers to an interconnected set of interpretive allusions in several different contexts. An interpretive network may bear on the exegetical function of a cited context of the network. In contrast to an interpretive constellation that brings together unrelated texts by means of catchword or the like, an interpretive network refers to intentionally interconnected scriptural contexts. See chapter on Networks near the end of this study.

PARADIGMATIC SHAPING—see extended echo-effect.

PARALLEL PASSAGES are contexts usually with verbal correspondence, including synoptic passages and/or direct or indirect quotation or allusion and/or coincidental parallels.

PARENT TEXT refers to the text before the author scribe or copyist scribe (*Vorlage*).

PRIESTLY instruction refers to the regulations housed in Lev 1–16, 27, and kindred regulations in Numbers. Often scholars refer to priestly literature more broadly as including all of Leviticus plus the legal instructions in Numbers.

PROGRESSIVE REVELATION in Scripture features authorized incremental advancement of the divine redemptive will. Scriptural exegesis of Scripture is one small part of progressive revelation. The concept implies that revelation is not static nor comprehensive but what God has been pleased to provide at various points in his dynamic

36. See Kugel, "Beginnings," 21–22; idem, *Traditions*, 916. Kugel's book includes hundreds of examples.

37. See Leonard, "Identifying Subtle Allusions," 96–97. Leonard uses Matt 2, Ps 78, and Ps 104 as examples (97–108).

relationship with his people. Truth does not change, but it has not been granted all at once. The principle of progressive revelation leads interpreters to expect that in later Scriptures God may say more. Progressive revelation by scriptural exegesis within Scripture infers incremental organic advancements enjoying continuity and coherence within Scripture as whole.

QUOTATION refers to intentional verbal repetition of a donor text within a receptor text. While in ordinary language the function of verbal repetition is left open, in biblical hermeneutics some scholars include purpose. In this more specialized use, the term quotation can refer to author-intended verbal repetition with "an exegetical purpose."[38]

REDACTION—see authorship.

REFERENCE or **REFERENT** refers to that which is signified by the term or passage.

RESUMPTIVE REPETITION or repetitive resumption (both used often in the literature) refers to an ancient editorial technique of repeating a word or short phrase before and after inserting a source in order to show where the preceding narration or discourse resumes (a*b*, xyz, *b*cd). Sometimes words or phrases are repeated to create literary relations called *inclusios* or brackets.

REWRITTEN BIBLE (or Rewritten Scripture) refers to a postbiblical genre of exegetical works that revise and recast new versions of biblical texts, often creatively, by rearrangement, abbreviation, and expansive supplementation.[39] Authors of Rewritten Scripture produce the "same kind of text" that they are rewriting and seek to "conform to the genre expectations of their audience."[40] Rewritten Scriptures include Jubilees, Pseudo-Philo, Genesis Apocrypha, the Temple Scroll, and many other Second Temple texts (see midrashic). Commonplace references to Deuteronomy and Chronicles as Rewritten Bible/Scripture seem anachronistic and do not adequately calibrate the social locations of sectarian extremist writings. This term has become increasingly disputed and less useful.

SEIDEL'S THEORY refers to the ancient scribal practice of inverting elements in a citation (so-named for a scholar who identified it).[41] For example, Jonah accuses Yahweh of being "a gracious and compassionate God" (Jonah 4:2 lit.), making allusion to the famous revelation to Moses as "a compassionate and gracious God" (Exod 34:6 lit.). By reversing elements the author of the receptor text "attains a moment of extra attention" in the listener/reader familiar with the donor context.[42] This phenomenon has often been called Seidel's law, but since it only appears sometimes it has been downgraded to a theory in the present study.

38. See Schultz, *Search for Quotation*, 221.

39. The term "Rewritten Bible" was coined by Vermes, *Scripture and Tradition*, 95.

40. Zahn, "Genre and Rewritten Scripture," 284. See evaluation of several examples of so-called Rewritten Scripture in Shepherd, *Text in the Middle*, 166–73.

41. See Beentjes, "Inverted Quotations," 508, n. 4. For examples, see 508–20; Talmon, "Textual Study," 358–81.

42. Beentjes, "Discovering a New Path" 49.

SENSUS PLENIOR refers to "the deeper sense of the words of Scripture intended by God but not clearly intended by the human author—a sense uncovered only by further revelation or development of revelation."[43]

SEPTUAGINT refers to ancient Greek translations of the Hebrew Scriptures. After the rise of Hellenistic culture in the empire, many practicing Jews needed the Scriptures translated into Greek. The term "Septuagint" means seventy and is often abbreviated by the Roman Numeral LXX. The ancient story of the translation of Torah into Greek includes seventy-two scribes who worked individually for seventy-two days and achieved a common outcome.[44] This colorful ancient story became shorthand in antiquity to refer to ancient Greek translations of the Hebrew Scriptures beginning with the Torah in the third century BCE. The more traditional Greek translations in common use were designated LXX/Septuagint over and against other Greek translations like the trio named for their translators (Aquila, Theodotion, Symmachus). While some Septuagintal books are very loose translations, others are very literal, with Septuagintal Torah being somewhere in between.[45]

SOURCE refers to the written or oral tradition cited or used by an author, editor, or redactor. See authorship.

SPLIT-UP AND REDISTRIBUTE refers to a borrowed scriptural phrase divided into pieces that get contextualized (for example see note on Ezek 7:19).[46]

STANDARD BIBLICAL HEBREW refers to the grammar and syntax, and to a much lesser extent vocabulary, of Genesis through Kings. By contrast, Late Biblical Hebrew refers to the grammar and syntax, and to a much lesser extent vocabulary, of Esther, Daniel, Ezra-Nehemiah, and Chronicles. For the way studies of Standard and Late Biblical Hebrew inform the Transitional Biblical Hebrew of Jeremiah see Hermeneutical Profile of the Use of Scripture in Jeremiah.

STOCK PHRASES, REFRAINS, and **FORMULAS** refer to verbal repetitions, sometimes with variation, within a given scriptural book or serial narrative that are part of the literary style or structure of the book or larger tradition rather than the result of echo, allusion, quotation, or the like. Examples of stock phrases include "in those days Israel had no king" (Judg 17:6; 18:1; 19:1; 21:25) and "X did evil/right in the eyes of Yahweh" (1 Kgs 15:5, 11, 26, 34; 16:7, 19, 25, 30, etc.). While stock phrases may be used in scriptural exegesis of Scripture, the stock phrases of themselves are not exegetical. See lyrical diffusion.

SYNCHRONIC refers to the study of the Scriptures in their received form rather than diachronic, which refers to the study of the historical development of the text. See diachronic.

---

43. Brown, "*Sensus Plenior*," 460. Also see Lunde, "Introduction," 13–18.
44. See Letter of Aristeas vv. 301–7.
45. See table in Würthwein/Fischer, *Text*, 101; see also book-by-book introductions in NETS.
46. See Lyons, "Marking Innerbiblical Allusion," 247–49; Sommer, *A Prophet Reads Scripture*, 68; 237–38, n. 114, 115.

SYNOPTIC PASSAGES, literally "to see together," are two or more contexts that both refer to the same event, law, teaching, or the like. In biblical studies synoptic relations usually refer to contexts with verbal parallels and some kind of relationship, whether direct or indirect.

TANAK is an acronym referring to the three main subcollections of the scrolls housed in synagogues of late antiquity, namely, **T**orah, ***N****evi'im*/Prophets, ***K****etuvim*/Writings. The Torah includes Genesis, Exodus, Leviticus, Numbers, and Deuteronomy. The Prophets include the Former Prophets (Joshua, Judges, Samuel, and Kings) and Latter Prophets (Isaiah, Jeremiah, Ezekiel, and the Book of the Twelve). The Writings include the rest of the scrolls (Psalms, Job, Proverbs, Ruth, Song of Songs, Ecclesiastes, Lamentations, Esther, Daniel, Ezra-Nehemiah, Chronicles).[47]

TETRATEUCH, literally "four books," refers to Genesis, Exodus, Leviticus, and Numbers.

TORAH is a Hebrew loanword that in lowercase (torah) refers to instruction or teaching and in uppercase (Torah) to the first five books of the Christian Bible as a coherent serial narrative (Genesis-Exodus-Leviticus-Numbers-Deuteronomy). While torah may include laws (with a legal sense), it more broadly refers to instruction (with an educational sense).

TORAH COLLECTION refers to the legal instructions housed in Deut 12–26.

TRACES refer to the residual literary effects of deleted and/or unstated allusions or echoes. They fit at the far end of the sliding scale: quotation, paraphrase, allusion, echo, trace. The inherent absence of evidence for traces virtually eliminates speaking of them with confidence. For example, if the theme of new exodus from Isa 40–55 suggests the use of exodus imagery in a figural way in Ezra 1 to describe the return from exile, it would be a trace. Since Ezra 1 only alludes to Exodus, without citing new exodus contexts, there is no way to know if the prophetic new exodus contexts suggest the figural connection.

TRADITION, in the sense of a scriptural tradition or context, is a softer term used in recognition that the version of the scriptural tradition a scriptural author worked with may or may not be identical to the final canonical form. Referring to scriptural traditions requires no attempt to recover possible previous versions. Viable comparisons can only be made from the evidence in the received text.

TRADITUM* AND *TRADITIO refer respectively to the content of an older cited scriptural context and the later interpretation of a citing context. The text/exegesis distinction can be used to contrast *traditum* as authoritative revelation versus *traditio* as an interpretive commentary.[48] In the case of innerbiblical exegesis, a *traditio* itself becomes authoritative *traditum* to a still later *traditio*.

---

47. Other sequences of the scrolls within the Latter Prophets and Writings is not a concern here. The sequence given here follows *Biblia Hebraica*.

48. *Traditum* and *traditio* are used constantly in Fishbane's influential study (see *Biblical Interpretation*, 6–15).

TYPE-SCENE refers to the use of genre stereotypes in formulaic narration, like the barren woman scenario, and so on.[49] Type-scenes often function at the level of genre—that is, they are not exegetical of themselves, much like figures of speech, and so on. See extended echo-effect.

TYPOLOGICAL PATTERNS refer to intentional scriptural shaping to draw comparative analogies between persons, events, procedures, oracles, or a combination of these. Since the terms typology, type, and the like are often associated with prophetic fulfillment, other kinds of figural relations tend to be referred to differently, even though they are simply nonprophetic uses of analogous literary patterning. In this study distinction is made between *paradigmatic shaping* (e.g., good then bad, etc.), *extended echo-effect* (projecting connotations from donor referent to receptor referent), and *types* as prophetic and/or generally expectational figural parallels and their fulfillment or proximate fulfillment (see Table C10 and Figure C17 in Chronicles for examples). Some types are **retrospective.** This means the type is not forward-looking, but the literary relations have been retrojected from the fulfillment context, such as the glory of God filling the tabernacle/temple (1 Kgs 8:10–11; cf. Exod 40:34–35). The typological patten of the glory filling the tabernacle/temple is especially important because it is explicitly retrospective only. Yahweh makes clear that he never asked for a temple (2 Sam 7:7) which establishes the tabernacle in itself as non-expectational. Other types are **forward-looking**, marked explicitly.[50] In Deut 18:15, Moses says to expect a prophet "like" him (using the preposition *k-* כְּ). The prophet expects a new exodus in Isa 11:16 which will be "like" the exodus from Egypt (using the preposition and relative particle *ka'asher* כַּאֲשֶׁר). Psalm 110:4 says the psalmist's lord will be "according to" Melchizedek (using the preposition *'al* עַל). Typological patterns may include proximate and greater fulfillments like the return of the exiles as a new exodus or in a different and fuller way in the gospel mission of Messiah (Ezra 1; Mark 1:2–3). Overinterpretation, such as finding types where there are none, is common. Since overzealous interpretation has given types a bad name, some interpreters now use the term "figural," which means typological.[51] See extended echo-effect.

49. See Alter, "Biblical Type-Scenes," 357–60.

50. Contra Hays, who says figural reading is "always" retrospective ("Figural Exegesis," 34–36). For measured pushback against Hays' retrospective approach see Barrett, *Canon*, 35–36, n. 110.

51. Richard Hays says figural reading "is very close to what is usually meant by 'typological reading'" (in Witherington, *Isaiah*, 373). Elsewhere Hays states more directly that typological and figural interpretation are "essentially synonymous." He avoids speaking of typology in his own writings because of the stigma of its use in different ways by Roman Catholic and evangelical Protestant scholars (*Reading*, 72, n. 6). The present study uses "figural" and "typological" synonymously, but these terms do *not* mean "allegorical." In a full-length study, Collett uses "figural" as semantically identical to "allegorical." Collett admits that "allegory," in part, includes a "hermeneutic of imposition," though he says it means more than this (*Figural*, 2, n. 1). Elsewhere he seeks to include figural/allegorical within the literal sense (33). Sometimes Collette implies that figural/allegorical means "theological" (34). Collett's extensive discussion about what he means by "figural"/"allegorical," with numerous idiosyncratic qualifications, make it very difficult to be sure what he has in mind (25–57, et passim). By contrast, in the present work, forward-looking and backward-looking figural/typological patterns in Scripture rely upon organic continuity between type and antitype.

UNMARKED—see marked.

USE OF SCRIPTURE is commonly employed as a broad expression within interpretive discussions and sidesteps, sometimes purposefully, issues of authorial intention and distinctions between quotation, exegesis, and allusion.

VERBAL PARALLELS refer to the same terms even when specific grammatical forms or syntactical function has been adjusted to suit the needs of the citing context.

VERTICAL CONTEXT refers to the interconnectivity within a cited text that itself features interpretive allusion to another scriptural context. Vertical context in cited texts is common because scriptural exegesis naturally breeds scriptural exegesis. The context of the cited texts in these cases is not only the horizontal surrounding context of paragraph, chapter, book but also includes the vertical context of the interpretive allusion *within* the cited context itself. See Figure NT1 in Toward the New Testament.

WRITINGS—see Tanak.

BIBLIOGRAPHY

Aberbach, Moses, and Leivy Smolar. "Aaron, Jeroboam, and the Golden Calves." *JBL* 86 (1968): 129–40.

Abernethy, Andrew T. and Gregory Goswell. *God's Messiah in the Old Testament: Expectations of a Coming King*. Grand Rapids: Baker Academic, 2020.

Achenbach, Reinhold. "The Sermon on the Sabbath in Jeremiah 17:19–27 and the Torah." Pages 873–90 in *The Formation of the Pentateuch: Bridging the Academic Cultures of Europe, Israel, and North America*. Edited by Jan C. Gertz et al. FAT 111. Tübingen: Mohr Siebeck, 2016.

Ackroyd, Peter R. "The Chronicler as Exegete." *JSOT* 2 (1977): 2–32.

Aḥituv, Shmuel. *Echoes from the Past: Hebrew and Cognate Inscriptions from the Biblical Period*. Jerusalem: Carta, 2008.

Aitken, James K. "The Inevitability of Reading Job through Lamentations." Pages 204–15 in *Reading Job Intertextually*. Edited by Katherine Dell and Will Kynes. LHBOTS 574. New York: Bloomsbury, 2013.

Akiyama, Kengo. *The Love of Neighbor in Ancient Judaism: The Reception of Leviticus 19:18 in the Hebrew Bible, the Septuagint, the Book of Jubilees, the Dead Sea Scrolls, and the New Testament*. Leiden: Brill, 2018.

Allen, Leslie C. *The Books of Joel, Obadiah, Jonah, and Micah*. NICOT. Grand Rapids: Eerdmans, 1976.

_________. *Ezekiel 1–19*. WBC 28. 1986. Waco, TX: Word, 1986. Repr., Grand Rapids: Zondervan, 2018.

_________. *Jeremiah: A Commentary*. OTL. Louisville: Westminster John Knox, 2008.

_________. *Psalms 101–150*. Rev. ed. WBC 21. Nashville: Nelson, 2002.

_________. "The Structuring of Ezekiel's Revisionist History Lesson (Ezekiel 20:3–31)." *CBQ* 54 (1992): 448–62.

Allen, Leslie C., and Timothy S. Laniak. *Ezra, Nehemiah, Esther*. New International Biblical Commentary 9. Peabody, MA: Hendrickson, 2003.

Alter, Robert. *The Art of Biblical Narrative*. Rev. ed. New York: Basic Books, 2011.

_________. "Biblical Type-Scenes and the Use of Convention." *Critical Inquiry* 5.2 (1978): 355–68.

Amit, Yairah. "Araunah's Threshing Floor: A Lesson in Shaping Historical Memory." Pages 133–44 in *What Was Authoritative for Chronicles*. Edited by Ehud Ben Zvi and Diana Edelman. Winona Lake, IN: Eisenbrauns, 2011.

_________. "The Role of Prophecy and Prophets in the Chronicler's World." Pages 80–101 in *Prophets, Prophecy, and Prophetic Texts in Second Temple Judaism*. Edited by Michael H. Floyd and Robert D. Haak. New York: T&T Clark, 2006.

Anderson, Bernhard W. "Exodus Typology in Second Isaiah." Pages 177–95 in *Israel's Prophetic Heritage: Essays in Honor of James Muilenburg*. Edited by Bernhard W. Anderson and Walter Harrelson. New York: Harper and Brothers, 1962.

Anderson, Carl Roy. "The Formation of the Levitical Prayer in Nehemiah 9." ThD diss., Dallas Theological Seminary, 1987.

Anderson, Francis I. *Habakkuk*. AB. New York: Doubleday, 2001.

Anderson, Francis I. and A. Dean Forbes. *Spelling in the Hebrew Bible*. Biblical et Orientalia 41. Rome: Biblical Institute Press, 1986.

Anderson, Francis I. and David Noel Freedman. *Amos*. AB. New York: Doubleday, 1989.

_________. *Hosea*. AB. New York: Doubleday, 1980.

_________. *Micah*. AB. New York: Doubleday, 2000.

Anderson, William H. U. "The Curse of Work in Qoheleth: An Exposé of Genesis 3:17–19 in Ecclesiastes." *Evangelical Quarterly* 70.2 (1998): 99–113.

André, Gunnel. "'Walk,' 'Stand,' and 'Sit' in Psalm I 1–2." *VT* 32.2 (1982): 327.

Ansberry, Christopher B. *Be Wise, My Son, and Make My Heart Glad: A Exploration of the Courtly Nature of the Book of Proverbs*. BZAW 422. Berlin: De Gruyter, 2011.

Archer, Gleason L. and Gregory Chirichigno. *Old Testament Quotations in the New Testament*. Moody, 1983. Reprint, Eugene, OR: Wipf & Stock, 2005.

Aristotle, *Poetics*. Edited and translated by Stephen Halliwell. LCL 199. Cambridge: Harvard University Press, 1995.

Armerding, Carl E. "Nahum." Pages 553–601 in *Daniel–Malachi*. EBC 8. Grand Rapids: Zondervan, 2008.

Assis, Elie. "The Date and Meaning of the Book of Joel." *VT* 61.2 (2011): 163–83.

_________. "The Reproach of the Priests (Malachi 1:6–2:9) within Malachi's Conception of Covenant." Pages 271–90 in *Covenant in the Persian Period: From Genesis to Chronicles*. Edited by Richard J. Bautch and Gary N. Knoppers. Winona Lake, IN: Eisenbrauns, 2015.

Austin, J. L. *How to Do Things with Words*. Oxford: Clarendon, 1962.

Averbeck, Richard E. "The Cult in Deuteronomy and its Relationship to the Book of the Covenant and the Holiness

Code." Pages 232–60 in *Sepher Torah Mosheh: Studies in the Composition and Interpretation of Deuteronomy*. Edited by Daniel I. Block and Richard L. Schultz. Peabody, MA: Hendrickson, 2017.

_________. "The Egyptian Sojourn and Deliverance from Slavery in the Framing and Shaping of the Mosaic Law." Pages 143–75 in *"Did I Not Bring Israel Out of Egypt?": Biblical, Archaeological, and Egyptological Perspectives on the Exodus Narratives*. Edited by James K. Hoffmeier, Alan R. Millard, and Gary A. Rendsburg. Winona Lake, IN: Eisenbrauns, 2016.

_________. "The Exodus, Debt Slavery, and the Composition of the Pentateuch." Pages 26–48 in *Exploring the Composition of the Pentateuch*. Edited by L. S. Baker, Jr., et al. University Park, PA: Eisenbrauns, 2020.

_________. "Psalms 103 and 104: Hymns of Redemption and Creation." Pages 132–48 in *Interpreting the Psalms for Teaching and Preaching*. Edited by Herbert W. Bateman IV and D. Brent Sandy. St. Louis: Chalice, 2010.

Avioz, Michael. "Nathan's Prophecy in II Sam 7 and in I Chr 17: Text, Context, and Meaning." *ZAW* 116 (2004): 542–54.

Awabdy, Mark A. "Did Nadab and Abihu Draw Near before Yhwh? The Old Greek among the Witnesses of Leviticus 16:1." *CBQ* 79.4 (2017): 580–92.

_________. "Yhwh Exegetes Torah: How Ezekiel 44:7–9 Bars Foreigners form the Sanctuary." *JBL* 131.4 (2012): 685–703.

Baden, Joel S. "Literary Allusions and Assumptions about Textual Familiarity." Pages 114–30 in *Subtle Citation, Allusion, and Translation in the Hebrew Bible*. Edited by Ziony Zevit. Sheffield: Equinox, 2017.

Baker, David L. *Two Testaments, One Bible: The Theological Relationship Between the Old and New Testaments*. 3rd ed. Downers Grove, IL: IVP Academic, 2010.

Baldwin, Joyce G. *Daniel*. TOTC. Downers Grove, IL: Inter-Varsity Press, 1978.

Balentine, Samuel E. "The Prose and Poetry of Exile." Pages 345–63 in *Interpreting Exile: Displacement and Deportation in Biblical and Modern Contexts*. Edited by F. R. Ames, B. E. Kelle, and J. L. Wright. Atlanta: Society of Biblical Literature, 2011.

Bandstra, Barry. *Genesis 1–11*. BHHB. Waco, TX: Baylor University Press, 2008.

Banister, Jamie Aislinn. "Theophanies in the Minor Prophets: A Cross-Analysis of Theophanic Texts in Micah, Habakkuk, and Zechariah." PhD diss., Catholic University of America, 2013.

Barker, Joel. "From Where Does My Hope Come? Theodicy and the Character of Yhwh in Allusions to Exodus 34:6–7 in the Book of the Twelve." *JETS* 61.4 (2018): 697–715.

Barnes, E. W. "The Midrashic Element in Chronicles." *Expositor* 5.4 (1896): 426–39.

Barr, James. *The Semantics of Biblical Language*. New York: Oxford University Press, 1961.

Barrett, Matthew. *Canon, Covenant and Christology: Rethinking Jesus and the Scriptures of Israel*. Downers Grove, IL: InterVarsity Press, 2020.

_________. *God's Word Alone: The Authority of Scripture*. Grand Rapids: Zondervan, 2016.

Barter, Penelope. "The Reuse of Ezekiel 20 in the Composition of Ezekiel 36.16–32." Pages 120–37 in *Ezekiel: Current Debates and Future Directions*. Edited by William A. Tooman and Penelope Barter. FAT 112. Tübingen: Mohr Siebeck, 2017.

Barton, John. "What Is a Book?: Modern Exegesis and the Literary Conventions of Ancient Israel." Pages 1–14 in *Intertextuality in Ugarit and Israel*. Edited by Johannes C. de Moor. Leiden: Brill, 1998.

Bartor, Assnat. "Legal Texts." Pages 160–81 in *The Hebrew Bible: A Critical Companion*. Edited by John Barton. Princeton: Princeton University Press, 2016.

Bass, Derek Drummond. "Hosea's Use of Scripture: An Analysis of His Hermeneutics." PhD diss., Southern Baptist Theological Seminary, 2008.

Bateman, Herbert W., IV, Darrell Bock, and Gordon Johnston. *Jesus the Messiah: Tracing the Promise, Expectations, and Coming of Israel's King*. Grand Rapids: Kregel, 2011.

Bates, Matthew W. *The Birth of the Trinity: Jesus, God, and Spirit in New Testament and Early Christian Interpretations of the Old Testament*. New York: Oxford University Press, 2015.

Bauckham, Richard. "The Scrupulous Priest and the Good Samaritan: Jesus' Parabolic Interpretation of the Law of Moses." *NTS* 44 (1998): 475–89.

_________. *Who Is God?: Key Moments in Biblical Revelation*. Grand Rapids: Baker Academic, 2020.

Baumgartner, Walter. *Jeremiah's Poems of Lament*. Translated by David E. Orton. Sheffield: Almond Press, 1988.

Bautch, Richard J. *Developments in Genre between Post-Exilic Penitential Prayers and the Psalms of Communal Lament*. Atlanta: Society of Biblical Literature, 2003.

_________. "Holy Seed: Ezra 9–10 and the Formation of the Pentateuch." Pages 525–42 in *The Formation of the Pentateuch: Bridging the Academic Cultures of Europe, Israel, and North America*. Edited by Jan C. Gertz et al. FAT 111. Tübingen: Mohr Siebeck, 2016.

Bavinck, Herman. *Reformed Dogmatics*. Vol. 1, *Prolegomena*. Edited by John Bolt. Translated by John Vriend. Grand Rapids: Baker Academic, 2003.

Bazak, Jacob. "The Geometric-Figurative Structure of Psalm CXXXVI." *VT* 35.2 (1985): 129–38.

Beale, Greg K. "The Cognitive Peripheral Vision of Biblical Authors." *WTJ* 76 (2014): 263–93.

_________. *Handbook on the New Testament Use of the Old Testament: Exegesis and Interpretation*. Grand Rapids: Baker Academic, 2012.

Beale, Greg K., and D. A. Carson, eds. *Commentary on the New Testament Use of the Old Testament*. Grand Rapids: Baker Academic, 2007.

Beale, G. K., and Sean M. McDonough, "Revelation," Pages 1081–1161 in *Commentary on the New Testament Use of the Old Testament*. Edited by G. K. Beale and D. A. Carson. Grand Rapids: Baker Academic, 2007.

Beattie, Derek Robert George. "Book of Ruth as Evidence for Israelite Legal Practice." *VT* 24.3 (1974): 251–67.

Becking, Bob. "Continuity and Community: The Belief System of the Book of Ezra." Pages 256–75 in *The Crisis of Israelite Religion: Transformation of Religious Tradition in Exilic and Post-Exilic Times*. Edited by Bob Becking and Marjo C. A. Korpel. Leiden: Brill, 1999.

_________. "On the Identity of the 'Foreign' Women in Ezra 9–10." Pages 31–49 in *Exile and Restoration Revisited: Essays on the Babylonian and Persian Periods in Memory of Peter R. Ackroyd*. Edited by Gary N. Knoppers, Lester L. Grabbe, and Deirdre N. Fulton. New York: T&T Clark, 2009.

Beentjes, Pancratius C. "Discovering a New Path of Intertextuality: Inverted Quotations and Their Dynamics." Pages 31–49 in *Literary Structure and Rhetorical Strategies in the Hebrew Bible*. Edited by L. J. de Regt, J. de Waard, and J. P. Fokkelman. Assen: Van Gorcum, 1996.

_________. "Inverted Quotations in the Bible: A Neglected Stylistic Pattern." *Biblica* 63.4 (1982): 506–23.

Begg, Christopher T. "Constructing a Monster: The Chronicler's *Sondergut* in 2 Chronicles 21." *Australian Biblical Review* 37 (1989): 35–51.

_________. "The Death of Josiah in Chronicles: Another View." *VT* 37.1 (1987): 1–8.

Bendavid, Abba. *Parallels in the Bible*. Jerusalem: Carta, 1972 [Hebrew].

Ben-Porat, Ziva. "The Poetics of Literary Allusion." *PTL: A Journal for Descriptive Poetics and Theory of Literature* 1 (1976): 105–28.

Ben Zvi, Ehud. Review of *Torah and the Chronicler's History Work*, by Judson R. Shaver. *JBL* 110.4 (1991): 718–20.

_________. "Would Ancient Readers of the Books of Hosea or Micah be 'Competent' to Read the Book of Jeremiah?" Pages 80–98 in *Jeremiah (Dis)Placed: New Directions in Writing/Reading Jeremiah*. Edited by A. R. Pete Diamond and Louis Stulman. New York: T&T Clark, 2011.

Bergen, Robert D. *1, 2 Samuel*. NAC. Nashville: B&H, 1996.

Berger, Yitzhak. "Esther and Benjaminite Royalty: A Study in Inner-Biblical Allusion." *JBL* 129.4 (2010): 625–44.

Bergey, Ronald. "The Song of Moses (Deuteronomy 32.1–43) and Isaianic Prophecies: A Case of Early Intertextuality?" *JSOT* 28.1 (2003): 33–54.

Bergland, Kenneth. "Jeremiah 34 Originally Composed as a Legal Blend of Leviticus 25 and Deuteronomy 15." Pages 189–205 in Paradigm *Change in Pentateuchal Research*. BZAR 22. Edited by Matthias Armgardt, Benjamin Kilchör, and Markus Zehnder. Wiesbaden: Harrassowitz, 2019.

Bergren, Richard V. *The Prophets and the Law*. Cincinnati: Hebrew Union College Press, 1974.

Bergsma, John S. "The Relevance of Ezekiel and the Samaritans for Pentateuchal Composition: Converging Lines of Evidence." Pages 226–43 in *Exploring the Composition of the Pentateuch*. Edited by L. S. Baker, Jr., et al. University Park, PA: Eisenbrauns, 2020.

Berlin, Adele. *The Dynamics of Biblical Parallelism*. Rev. ed. Grand Rapids: Eerdmans, 2008.

_________. *Esther*. JPSC. Philadelphia: Jewish Publication Society, 2001.

_________. "Interpreting Torah Traditions in Psalm 105." Pages 21–36, 239–43 in *Jewish Biblical Interpretation and Cultural Exchange: Comparative Exegesis in Context*. Edited by Natalie B. Dohrmann and David Stern. Philadelphia: University of Pennsylvania Press, 2008.

_________. *Lamentations*. OTL. Louisville: Westminster John Knox, 2002.

_________. "Legal Fiction: Levirate *cum* Land Redemption in Ruth." *JAJ* 1.1 (2010): 3–18.

_________. "Psalm 118:24." *JBL* 96.4 (1977): 567–68.

_________. "Psalms in the Book of Chronicles." Pages 21*–36* in *Shai le-Sara Japhet: Studies in the Bible, its Exegesis, and its Language*. Edited by Moshe Bar-Asher et al. Jerusalem: Bialik Institute, 2007.

_________. "The Wisdom of Creation in Psalm 104." Pages 71–83 in *Seeking Out the Wisdom of the Ancients: Essays Offered to Honor Michael V. Fox on the Occasion of His Sixty-Fifth Birthday*. Edited by Ronald L. Troxel, Kelvin G. Friebel, and Dennis R. Magray. Winona Lake, IN: Eisenbrauns. 2005.

_________. *Zephaniah*. AB. New York: Doubleday, 1994.

Berman, Joshua. "Ancient Hermeneutics and the Legal Structure of the Book of Ruth." *ZAW* 119 (2007): 22–38.

_________. *Ani Maamin: Biblical Criticism, Historical Truth, and the Thirteen Principles of Faith*. Jerusalem: Maggid Books, 2020.

_________. "CTH 133 and the Hittite Provenance of Deuteronomy 13." *JBL* 130.1 (2011): 25–44.

_________. "Historicism and Its Limits: A Response to Bernard M. Levinson and Jeffrey Stackert." *JAJ* 4.3 (2013): 297–309.

_________. *Inconsistency in the Torah: Ancient Literary Convention and the Limits of Source Criticism*. New York: Oxford University Press, 2017.

_________. "The Legal Blend in Biblical Narrative (Joshua 20:1–9, Judges 6:25–31, 1 Samuel 15:2, 28:3–25, 2 Kings 4:1–7, Jeremiah 34:12–17, Nehemiah 5:1–12)." *JBL* 134.1 (2015): 105–25.

_________. "Supersessionist or Complementary?: Reassessing the Nature of Legal Revision in the Pentateuch Law Collections." *JBL* 135.2 (2016): 201–22.

Berry, Donald K. "Malachi's Dual Design: The Close of the Canon and What Comes Afterward." Pages 269–302 in *Forming Prophetic Literature: Essays on Isaiah and the Twelve in Honor of John D. W. Watts*. Edited by James W. Watts and Paul R. House. JSOTSup 235. Sheffield: Sheffield Academic, 1996.

Bertholet, Alfred. *Leviticus Erklärt*. Tübingen: Verlag Von J. C. B. Mohr (Paul Siebeck), 1901.

Bezzel, Hannes. "'Man of Constant Sorrow'—Rereading Jeremiah in Lamentations 3." Pages 253–65 in *Jeremiah (Dis)Placed: New Directions in Writing/Reading Jeremiah*. Edited by A. R. Pete Diamond and Louis Stulman. New York: T&T Clark, 2011.

Bin-Nun, Shoshana R. "Formulas from Royal Records of Israel and of Judah." *VT* 18 (1968): 414–32.

Bird, Michael. *1 Esdras: Introduction and Commentary on the Greek Text in Codex Vaticanus*. Leiden: Brill, 2012.

Blenkinsopp, Joseph. "The Development of Jewish Sectarianism from Nehemiah to the Hasidim." Pages 385–404 in *Judah and the Judeans in the Fourth Century B.C.E.* Edited by Oded Lipschits, Gary N. Knoppers, and Rainer Albertz. Winona Lake, IN: Eisenbrauns, 2007.

_________. *Ezra-Nehemiah, a Commentary*. OTL. Philadelphia: Westminster, 1988.

_________. *Isaiah 1–39*. AB. New York: Doubleday, 2000.

_________. *Isaiah 40–55*. AB. New York: Doubleday, 2002.

_________. *Isaiah 56–66*. AB. New York: Doubleday, 2003.

_________. *Judaism: The First Phase, The Place of Ezra and Nehemiah in the Origins of Judaism*. Grand Rapids: Eerdmans, 2009.

_________. "The Oracle of Judah and the Messianic Entry." *JBL* 80.1 (1961): 55–64.

_________. "Wisdom in the Chronicler's Work." Pages 19–30 in *In Search of Wisdom: Essays in Memory of John G. Gammie*. Edited by Brandon Scott and William Johnston Wiseman. Louisville: Westminster John Knox, 1993.

Bloch-Smith, Elizabeth. "The Impact of Siege Warfare on Biblical Conceptualizations of YHWH." *JBL* 137.1 (2018): 19–28.

Block, Daniel. *The Book of Ezekiel: Chapters 1–24*. NICOT. Grand Rapids: Eerdmans, 1997.

_________. *The Book of Ezekiel: Chapters 25–48*. NICOT. Grand Rapids: Eerdmans, 1998.

_________. "Echo Narrative Technique in Hebrew Literature: A Study in Judges 19." *WTJ* 52 (1990): 325–41.

_________. "In the Tradition of Moses: The Conceptual and Stylistic Imprint of Deuteronomy on the Patriarchal Narratives." Page 133–58 in *Exploring the Composition of the Pentateuch*. Edited by L. S. Baker, Jr., et al. University Park, PA: Eisenbrauns, 2020.

_________. *Obadiah*. ZECOT. Grand Rapids: Zondervan, 2017.

_________. "The Prophet of the Spirit: The Use of *Rwḥ* in the Book of Ezekiel." *JETS* 32.1 (1989); 27–49.

_________. *Ruth*. ZECOT. Grand Rapids: Zondervan, 2015.

Blomberg, Craig L. *1 Corinthians*. NIVAC. Grand Rapids: Zondervan, 1994.

_________. "'What Do These Stones Mean?': The Riddle of Deuteronomy 27." *JETS* 56.1 (2013): 17–41.

Bock, Darrell L. *Proclamation from Prophecy and Pattern: Lucan Old Testament Christology*. JSNTSup 12. Sheffield: Sheffield Academic, 1987.

_________. "Scripture Citing Scripture: Use of the Old Testament in the New" Pages 255–76 in *Interpreting the New Testament Text: Introduction to the Art and Science of Exegesis*. Edited by Darrell L. Bock and Buist M. Fanning. Wheaton: Crossway, 2006.

_________. "Single Meaning, Multiple Contexts and Referents." Pages 105–51 in *Three Views on the New Testament Use of the Old Testament*. Edited by Kenneth Berding and Jonathan Lunde. Grand Rapids: Zondervan, 2007.

Boda, Mark J. *The Book of Zechariah*. NICOT. Grand Rapids: Eerdmans, 2016.

_________. *The Development and Role of Biblical Traditions in Zechariah*. Vol. 2 of *Exploring Zechariah*. Atlanta: SBL Press, 2017.

_________. "From Complaint to Contrition: Peering through the Liturgical Window of Jer 14,1–15,4." *ZAW* 113 (2001): 186–97.

_________. *Haggai, Zechariah*. NIVAC. Grand Rapids: Zondervan, 2004.

_________. *The Heartbeat of Old Testament Theology: Three Creedal Expressions*. Grand Rapids: Baker Academic, 2017.

_________. "Legitimizing the Temple: The Chronicler's Temple Building Account." Pages 303–18 in *From the Foundations to the Crenellations: Essays on Temple Building in the Ancient Near East and Hebrew Bible*. Edited by Mark J. Boda and Jamie Novitny. Münster: Ugarit-Verlag, 2010.

_________. "Oil, Crowns, and Thrones: Prophet, Priest, and King in Zechariah 1:7–6:15." *JHebS* 3 (2001).

_________. *Praying the Tradition: The Origin and Use of Tradition in Nehemiah 9*. BZAW 277. Berlin: de Gruyter, 1999.

_________. "Recycling Heaven's Words: Receiving and Retrieving Divine Revelation in the Historiography of Judges." Pages 43–67 in *Prophets, Prophecy, and Ancient Israelite Historiography*. Edited by Mark J. Boda and Lissa M. Wray Beal. Winona Lake, IN: Eisenbrauns, 2013.

_________. *A Severe Mercy: Sin and Its Remedy in the Old Testament*. Winona Lake, IN: Eisenbrauns, 2009.

_________. "Words and Meanings: ידה in Hebrew Research." *WTJ* 57 (1995): 277–95.

Boda, Mark J., and Michael H. Floyd, eds. *Bringing Out the Treasure: Inner Biblical Allusion in Zechariah 9–14*. New York: T&T Clark, 2003.

Bodner, Keith, and Benjamin J. M. Johnson. "David: Kaleidoscope of a King." Pages 121–38 in *Characters and Characterization in the Book of Samuel*. Edited by Keith Bodner and Benjamin J. M. Johnson. LBHOTS 669. New York: T&T Clark, 2020.

Boling, Robert G. *Judges*. AB. Garden City, NJ: Doubleday, 1975.

Bolle, Menachem E. *Leviticus*. DM. 2 vols. Jerusalem: Massad Harav Kook, 1991 [Hebrew].

Booij, Thijs. "Psalm 109:6–19 as a Quotation: A Review of the Evidence." Pages 91–106 in *Give Ear to My Words: Psalms and other Poetry in and around the Hebrew Bible, Essays in Honour of Professor N. A. van Uchelen*. Edited by Janet Dyk. Amsterdam: Societas Hebraica Amstelodamensis, 1996.

Bosman, Hendrik L. "Loving the Neighbour and the Resident Alien in Leviticus 19 as Ethical Redefinition of Holiness." *OTE* 31.3 (2018): 571–90.

Botha, Phil J. "Intertextuality and the Interpretation of Psalm 1." Pages 58–76 in *Psalms and Mythology*. Edited by Dirk J. Human. LHBOTS 462. New York: T&T Clark, 2007.

Bramer, Stephen J. "The Literary Genre of the Book of Amos." *BSac* 156 (1999): 42–60.

Braulik, Georg. "The Book of Ruth as Intra-biblical Critique on the Deuteronomic Law." *Acta Theologica* 19.1 (1999): 1–20.

Braun, Roddy. "Solomon, the Chosen Temple Builder: The Significance of 1 Chronicles 22, 28, 29 for the Theology of Chronicles." *JBL* 95.4 (1976): 581–90.

_________. "Solomonic Apologetic in Chronicles." *JBL* 92.4 (1973): 503–16.

Brettler, Marc. "Psalm 136 as an Interpretive Text." *HBAI* 2 (2013): 373–95.

Briggs, Emilie Grace. *The Book of Psalms*. 2 vols. ICC. New York: Scribner's Sons, 1907.

Bright, John. "The Date of the Prose Sermons of Jeremiah." *JBL* 70 (1951): 12–35.

Brin, Gershon. "The Formulae 'From . . . and Onward/Upward' (מ . . . והלאה/ומעלה)." *JBL* 99.2 (1980): 161–71.

Brinks, C. L. "Job and Deutero Isaiah: The Use and Abuse of Traditions." *BibInt* 20 (2012): 407–20.

Brodersen, Alma. *The End of the Psalter: Psalms 146–150 in the Masoretic Text, the Dead Sea Scrolls, and the Septuagint*. Waco, TX: Baylor University Press, 2018.

Brooke, George J. *Exegesis at Qumran: 4QFlorilegium in Its Jewish Context*. JSOTSup 29. Sheffield: Sheffield Academic, 1985.

Brown, Raymond E. "The Problems of *Sensus Plenior*." *ETL* 43.3 (1967): 460–69.

Brown, William P. "'Come, O Children . . . I will Teach You the Fear of the Lord' (Psalm 34:12): Comparing Psalms and Proverbs." Pages 85–102 in *Seeking Out the Wisdom of the Ancients: Essays Offered to Honor Michael V. Fox on the Occasion of His Sixty-Fifth Birthday*. Edited by Ronald L. Troxel, Kelvin G. Friebel, and Dennis R. Magray. Winona Lake, IN: Eisenbrauns. 2005.

Brug, J. F. "Show Love to Your Neighbor." *Wisconsin Lutheran Quarterly* 92 (1995): 294–94.

Brueggemann, Walter. *Tradition for Crisis: A Study in Hosea*. Atlanta: John Knox, 1968.

Bruno, Chris, Jared Compton, and Kevin McFadden, *Biblical Theology According to the Apostles: How the Earliest Christians Told the Story of Israel*. New Studies in Biblical Theology 52. Downer Grove, IL: IVP Academic, 2020.

Bullock, C. Hassell. "Covenant Renewal and the Formula of Grace in the Psalter." *BSac* 176 (2019): 18–34.

_________. "Double-tracking in the Psalms, Book 5, as a Hermeneutical Method." *JETS* 60.3 (2017): 479–88.

Burnett, Joel S. "Forty-Two Songs for Elohim: An Ancient Near Eastern Organizing Principle in the Shaping of the Elohistic Psalter." *JSOT* 31.1 (2006): 81–101.

Burney, C. F. *Notes on the Hebrew Text of the Books of Kings*. Oxford: Clarendon, 1903.

Burnight, John. "The 'Reversal' of *Heilsgeschichte* in Job 3." Pages 30–41 in *Reading Job Intertextually*. Edited by Katharine Dell and Will Kynes. LHBOTS 574. New York: Bloomsbury, 2013.

Butler, Trent. "A Forgotten Passage from a Forgotten Era (1 Chr. XVI 8–36)." *VT* 28 (1978): 142–50.

Byargeon, Rick. "The Relationship of Micah 4:1–3 and Isaiah 2:2–4: Implications for Understanding the Prophetic Message." *Southwestern Journal of Theology* 46.1 (2003): 6–26.

Cahill, Michael. "Not a Cornerstone!: Translating Ps 118, 22 in the Jewish and Christian Scriptures." *RB* 106.3 (1999): 345–57.

Calvin, John. *Commentaries on the Book of the Prophet Jeremiah and the Lamentations*. 5 vols. Translated by John Owen. Edinburgh: Calvin Translation Society, 1851–1855.

Campbell, Edward F., Jr. *Ruth*. AB. New York: Doubleday, 1975.

Campbell, Iain D. "The Song of David's Son: Interpreting the Song of Solomon in the Light of the Davidic Covenant." *WTJ* 62 (2000): 17–32.

Campolo, Tony. *Red Letter Christians: A Citizen's Guide to Faith and Politics*. Ventura, CA: Regel, 2008.

Carasik, Michael. *Theologies of the Mind in Biblical Israel*. New York: Lang, 2006.

_________. "Who Were the 'Men of Hezekiah' (Proverbs XXV 1)?" *VT* 44.3 (1994): 289–300.

Carpenter, Eugene E. "Literary Structure and Unbelief: A Study of Deuteronomy 1:6–46." *Asbury Theological Journal* 42.1 (1987): 77–84.

Carr, David. *The Formation of the Hebrew Bible: A New Reconstruction*. New York: Oxford University Press, 2011.

_________. "Method in Determination of Direction of Dependence: An Empirical Test Case of Criteria Applied to Exodus 34,11–26 and its Parallels." Pages 107–40 in *Gottes Volk am Sinai. Untersuchungen zu Ex 32–34 und Dtn 9–10*. Edited by Matthias Köckert and Erhard Blum. Gütersloh: Gütersloher Verlaghaus, 2001.

Carroll, Robert P. "Intertextuality and the Book of Jeremiah: Animadversions on Text and Theory." Pages 55–78 in *The New Literary Criticism*. Edited by Cheryl Exum and David J. A, Clines. JSOTSup 143. Sheffield: Sheffield Academic, 1993.

_________. "The Myth of the Empty Land." Pages 79–93 in *Ideological Criticism of Biblical Texts*. Edited by David Jobling and Tina Pippin. Semeia 59. Atlanta: Scholars Press, 1992.

Cassuto, Umberto. *Biblical and Oriental Studies*. 2 vols. Translated by Israel Abrahams. Jerusalem: Magnes, 1973, 1975.

Chalmers. R. Scott. "Who Is the Real El?: A Reconstruction of the Prophet's Polemic in Hosea 12:5a." *CBQ* 68 (2006): 611–30.

Chan, Man Ki, and Pieter M. Venter, "Midrash as Exegetical Approach of Early Jewish Exegesis, With Some Examples from the Book of Ruth." *Telogiese Studies* 66.1 (2010): 1–6.

Chapman, Cynthia R. "The Breath of Life: Speech, Gender, and Authority in the Garden of Eden." *JBL* 138.2 (2019): 241–62.

Chau, Kevin. "The Poetry of Creation and Victory in the Psalms." Pages 65–83 in *Inner Biblical Allusion in the Poetry of Wisdom and Psalms*. Edited by Mark J. Boda, Kevin Chau, and Beth LaNeel Tanner. LHBOTS 659. New York: T&T Clark, 2019.

Chavalas, Mark. "Genealogical History as 'Charter': A Study of Old Babylonian Period Historiography and the Old Testament." Pages 103–28 in *Faith, Tradition, and History: Old Testament Historiography in Its Near Eastern*

Context. Edited by A. R. Millard, James K. Hoffmeier, and David W. Baker. Winona Lake, IN: Eisenbrauns, 1994.

Chavel, Simeon. "A Kingdom of Priests and its Earthen Altars in Exod 19–24." *VT* 65 (2015): 169–222.

________. *Oracular Law and Priestly Historiography in the Torah*. FAT II 71. Tübingen: Mohr Siebeck, 2014.

Cheyne, Thomas Kelly. "The Critical Study of Parallel Passages." Pages 2:241–79 in *The Prophecies of Isaiah*. 3rd ed. 2 vols. New York: Whittaker, 1884.

________. *Job and Solomon, or The Wisdom of the Old Testament*. New York: Whittaker, 1887.

________. *Micah*. CBSC. Cambridge: University Press, 1895.

________. *The Origins and Religious Contents of the Psalter*. New York: Whittaker, 1891.

Childs, Brevard S. *The Book of Exodus: A Critical, Theological Commentary*. Louisville: Westminster, 1974.

________. "Deuteronomic Formulae of the Exodus Traditions." Pages 30–39 in *Hebräische Wortforschung: Festschrift zum 80. Geburtstag von Walter Baumgartner*. Edited by G. W. Anderson et al. VTSup 16. Leiden: Brill, 1967.

________. *Introduction to the Old Testament as Scripture*. Philadelphia: Fortress, 1979.

________. *Isaiah*. OTL. Louisville: Westminster John Knox, 2001.

________. *Isaiah and the Assyrian Crisis*. London: SCM, 1967.

________. *Memory and Tradition in Israel*. London: SCM, 1962.

________. "Prophecy and Fulfillment: A Study of Contemporary Hermeneutics." *Interpretation* 12 (1958): 259–71.

________. "Psalm Titles and Midrashic Exegesis." *JSS* 16.2 (1971): 137–50.

Chisholm, Robert B., Jr. "The 'Everlasting Covenant' and the 'City of Chaos': Intentional Ambiguity and Irony in Isaiah 24." *CTR* 6.2 (1993): 237–53.

________. "An Exegetical and Theological Study of Psalm 18/2 Samuel 22." ThD diss., Dallas Theological Seminary, 1983.

________. "An Exegetical Study of Psalm 18/2 Samuel 22." Th.M. thesis, Grace Theological Seminary, Winona Lake, IN, 1978.

________. "Forgiveness and Salvation in Isaiah 53." Pages 191–210 in *The Gospel According to Isaiah 53: Encountering the Suffering Servant in Jewish and Christian Theology*. Edited by Darrell L. Bock and Mitch Glaser. Grand Rapids: Kregel, 2012.

________. *From Exegesis to Exposition: A Practical Guide to Using Biblical Hebrew*. Grand Rapids: Baker, 1998.

________. *Handbook on the Prophets*. Grand Rapids: Baker Academic, 2002.

________. *Interpreting the Historical Books: An Exegetical Handbook*. Grand Rapids: Kregel, 2006.

________. "A Theology of the Minor Prophets." Pages 397–433 in *A Biblical Theology of the Old Testament*. Edited by Roy B. Zuck. Chicago: Moody, 1991.

________. "When Prophecy Appears to Fail, Check Your Hermeneutic." *JETS* 53.3 (2010): 561–77.

Clemens, David M. "The Law of Sin and Death: Ecclesiastes and Genesis 1–3." *Themelios* 19 (1994): 5–8.

Clifford, Richard J. "In Zion and David a New Beginning: An Interpretation of Psalm 78." Pages 121–41 in *Traditions in Transformations: Turning Points in Biblical Faith*. Edited by Baruch Halpern and Jon D. Levenson. Winona Lake: IN: Eisenbrauns, 1981.

Clines, David J. A. *I, He, We, and They: A Literary Approach to Isaiah 53*. JSOTSup 1. Sheffield: Sheffield Academic, 1976.

________. *Job 1–20*. WBC. Grand Rapids: Zondervan, 1989.

________. *Job 21–37*. WBC. Grand Rapids: Zondervan, 2006.

________. "Nehemiah 10 as an Example of Early Jewish Biblical Exegesis." *JSOT* 21 (1981): 111–17.

________. *The Theme of the Pentateuch*. 2nd ed. JSOTSup 10. Sheffield: Sheffield Academic, 1997.

Clines, David J. A. and D. M. Gunn. "'You Tried to Persuade Me' and 'Violence! Outrage!' in Jeremiah XX 7–8." *VT* 28.1 (1978): 20–27

Cogan, Mordechai. *I Kings*. AB. New York: Doubleday, 2001.

________. *The Raging Torrent: Historical Inscriptions from Assyria and Babylonia Relating to Ancient Israel*. Jerusalem: Carta, 2008.

Cogan, Mordechai and Hayim Tadmor. *II Kings*. AB. Garden City, NY: Doubleday, 1988.

Coggins, Richard. "Innerbiblical Quotations in Joel." Pages 75–84 in *After the Exile: Essays in Honour of Rex Mason*. Edited by John Barton and David J. Reimer. Macon, GA: Mercer University Press, 1996.

________. "On Kings and Disguises." *JSOT* 50 (1991): 55–62.

Cohen, Chaim. "The Enclitic-mem in Biblical Hebrew: Its Existence and Initial Discovery." Pages 231–60 in *Sefer Moshe, The Moshe Weinfeld Jubilee Volume: Studies in the Bible and Ancient Near East, Qumran, and Post-Biblical Judaism*. Edited by Chaim Cohen, Avi Hurvitz, and Shalom M. Paul. Winona Lake, IN: Eisenbrauns, 2004.

Collett, Don C. *Figural Reading and the Old Testament: Theology and Practice*. Grand Rapids: Baker Academic, 2020.

Collins, John J. "Apocalyptic Eschatology as the Transcendence of Death." *CBQ* 36.1 (1974): 21–43.

________. *Daniel*. Hermeneia. Minneapolis: Augsburg Fortress, 1993.

________. "Use of Torah in the Second Temple Period." Pages 44–62 in *When Texts Are Canonized*. Edited by Timothy H. Lim. Providence, RI: Brown Judaic Studies, 2017.

Coogan, Michael D., ed. *The New Oxford Annotated Bible*. 3rd ed. New York: Oxford University Press, 2007.

Coogan, Michael D. and Mark S. Smith, eds. and trans. *Stories from Ancient Canaan*. 2nd ed. Louisville: Westminster John Knox, 2012.

Cook, Gregory D. "Naqia and Nineveh in Nahum: Ambiguity and the Prostitute Queen." *JBL* 136.4 (2017): 895–904.

Cook, Stephen L. "Innerbiblical Interpretation in Ezekiel 44 and the History of Israel." *JBL* 114.2 (1995): 193–208.

Craigie, Peter C. *Deuteronomy*. NICOT. Grand Rapids: Eerdmans, 1976.

Craigie, Peter C., and Marvin E. Tate. *Psalms 1–50*. 2nd ed. WBC. Nashville: Nelson, 2004.
Crenshaw, James L. "Divine Discipline in Job 5:17–18, Proverbs 3:11–12, and Deuteronomy 32:39, and Beyond." Pages 178–89 in *Reading Job Intertextually*. Edited by Katharine Dell and Will Kynes. LHBOTS 574. New York: Bloomsbury, 2013.
Cudworth, Troy D. "The Division of Israel's Kingdom in Chronicles: A Re-examination of the Usual Suspects." *Biblica* 95.4 (2014): 498–523.
Cundall, Arthur E. and Leon Morris. *Judges and Ruth*. TOTC 7. Downers Grove, IL: InterVarsity Press Academic, 1968.
Curtis, Edward Lewis and Albert Alonzo Madsen. *A Critical and Exegetical Commentary on the Book of Chronicles*. ICC. Edinburgh: T&T Clark, 1910.
Danby, Herbert, trans. *Tractate Sanhedrin: Mishnah and Tosefta*. New York: MacMillan, 1919.
Davidson, A. B. *Nahum, Habakkuk, Zephaniah*. CBSC. Cambridge: University Press, 1899.
Davies, G. I. "The Wilderness Itineraries and the Composition of the Pentateuch." *VT* 33.1 (1983): 1–13.
Davis, Ellen F. "Critical Traditioning: Seeking an Inner Biblical Hermeneutic." *Anglican Theological Review* 82.4 (2000): 733–51.
_________. *Proverbs, Ecclesiastes, and the Song of Songs*. Louisville: Westminster John Knox, 2000.
Dearman, J. Andrew. "Some Observations on the Exodus and Wilderness Wandering Traditions in the Books of Amos and Micah." Pages 255–67 in *"Did I Not Bring Israel Out of Egypt?": Biblical Archaeological, and Egyptological Perspectives on the Exodus Narratives*. Edited by James K. Hoffmeier, Alan R. Millard, and Gary A. Rendsburg. Winona Lake, IN: Eisenbrauns, 2016.
Delamarter, Steve. "The Death of Josiah in Scripture and Tradition: Wrestling with the Problem of Evil?" *VT* 54 (2004): 29–60.
Delitzsch, Franz. *Biblical Commentary on the Prophecies of Isaiah*. Translated by James Kennedy. 4th ed. Edinburgh: T&T Clark, 1892.
_________. *Biblical Commentary on the Psalms*. Translated by Francis Bolton. Edinburgh: T&T. Clark, 1892.
Dell, Katharine. *The Book of Job as Sceptical Literature*. BZAW 197. Berlin: de Gruyter, 1991.
_________. "'Cursed Be the Day I Was Born!': Job and Jeremiah Revisited." Pages 106–17 in *Reading Job Intertextually*. Edited by Katharine Dell and Will Kynes. LHBOTS 574. New York: Bloomsbury, 2013.
_________. "Didactic Intertextuality: Proverbial Wisdom as Illustrated in Ruth." Pages 101–14 in *Reading Proverbs Intertextually*. Edited by Katharine Dell and Will Kynes. LHBOTS 629. New York: T&T Clark, 2019.
_________. "Exploring Intertextual Links between Ecclesiastes and Genesis 1–11." Pages 3–14 in *Reading Ecclesiastes Intertextually*. Edited by Katharine Dell and Will Kynes. New York: Bloomsbury T&T Clark, 2014.
_________. "Reinventing the Wheel: The Shaping of the Book of Jonah." Pages 85–101 in *After the Exile: Essays in Honour of Rex Mason*. Edited by John Barton and David J. Reimer. Macon, GA: Mercer University Press, 1996.
Dell, Katharine, and Will Kynes, eds. *Reading Ecclesiastes Intertextually*. LHBOTS 587. New York: T&T Clark, 2014.
_________, eds. *Reading Proverbs Intertextually*. LHBOTS 629. New York: T&T Clark, 2019.
DeRouchie, Jason S. *A Call to Covenant Love: Text Grammar and Literary Structure in Deuteronomy 5–11*. Piscataway, NJ: Gorgias, 2007.
De Vries, Simon J. "The Forms of Prophetic Address in Chronicles." *HAR* 10 (1986): 15–36.
Diewert, David A. "Judah's Argument for Life as Wise Speech." Pages 61–74 in *The Way of Wisdom: Essays in Honor of Bruce K. Waltke*. Edited by J. I. Packer and Sven K. Soderlund. Grand Rapids: Zondervan, 2000.
DiFransico, Lesley. "'He Will Cast their Sins into the Depths of the Sea . . .': Exodus Allusions and the Personification of Sin in Micah 7:7–20." *VT* 67 (2017): 187–203.
Dijkstra, Meindert. "Legal Irrevocability (*lōʾ yāšûb*) in Ezekiel 7.13." *JSOT* 43 (1989): 109–16.
Dillard, Raymond B. "The Chronicler's Jehoshaphat." *Trinity Journal, NS* (1986): 17–22.
_________. "The Chronicler's Solomon." *WTJ* 43.2 (1981): 289–300.
_________. "The Literary Structure of the Chronicler's Solomon Narrative." *JSOT* 30 (1984): 85–93.
_________. "The Reign of Asa (2 Chronicles 14–16): An Example of the Chronicler's Theological Method." *JETS* 23.3 (1980): 207–18.
_________. Review of *Deuteronomy and the Deuteronomic School*, by Moshe Weinfeld. *WTJ* 36 (1974): 263–69.
_________. *2 Chronicles*. WBC. Nashville: Nelson Reference, 1987.
Dobbs-Allsopp, F. W., et al., eds. *Hebrew Inscriptions: Texts from the Biblical Period of the Monarchy with Concordance*. New Haven: Yale University Press, 2005.
Dodd, C. H. *According to the Scriptures: The Substructure of New Testament Theology*. New York: Scribner's Sons, 1953.
Domeris, William R. "Jeremiah and the Poor." Pages 45–58 in *Uprooting and Planting: Essays on Jeremiah for Leslie Allen*. Edited by John Goldingay. New York: T&T Clark, 2007.
Doolittle, William R. "On the Way to Ephrath, Beyond Migdal Eder: The Rachel Traditions in Micah 4–5." MDiv thesis, Cairn University, 2009.
Doron, Pinchas. "Motive Clauses in the Laws of Deuteronomy: Their Forms, Functions, and Contents." *HAR* 2 (1978): 61–77.
Dotan, Aron. *Biblia Hebraica Leningradensia*. Peabody, MA: Hendrickson, 2001.
Dozeman, Thomas B. "Inner-Biblical Interpretation of Yahweh's Gracious and Compassionate Character." *JBL* 108.2 (1989): 207–23.
Driver, Daniel R. *Brevard Childs, Biblical Theologian for the Church's One Bible*. Grand Rapids: Baker Academic, 2012.
Driver, S. R. *The Books of Joel and Amos*. CBSC. Cambridge: University Press, 1897.

_________. *A Critical and Exegetical Commentary on Deuteronomy*. 3rd ed. ICC. Edinburgh: T&T Clark, 1901.

_________. *An Introduction to the Literature of the Old Testament*. Rev. ed. New York: Scribner's Sons, 1913.

_________. "The Speeches in the Chronicles." *Expositor* 5th series (1896): 286–308.

Driver, S. R., and G. B. Gray. *The Book of Job*. ICC. Edinburgh: T&T Clark, 1921.

Duggan, Michael W. *The Covenant Renewal in Ezra-Nehemiah (Neh 7:72b–10:40): An Exegetical, Literary, and Theological Study*. Atlanta: Society of Biblical Literature, 2001.

Dunne, John A. "David's Tent as Temple in Amos 9:11–15: Understanding the Epilogue of Amos and Considering Implications for the Unity of the Book." *WTJ* 73 (2011): 363–74.

Edelman, Diana. "Gibeon and the Gibeonites Revisited." Pages 153–67 in *Judah and the Judeans in the Neo-Babylonian Period*. Edited by Oded Lipschits and Joseph Blenkinsopp. Winona Lake, IN: Eisenbrauns, 2013.

Edenburg, Cynthia. "Intertextuality, Literary Competence and the Question of Readership: Some Preliminary Observations." *JSOT* 35.2 (2010): 131–48.

_________. "'Overwriting and Overriding,' or What Is Not Deuteronomistic." Pages 443–60 in *Congress Volume Helsinki 2010*. Edited by Martti Nissinen. VTSup 148. Boston: Brill, 2012.

Ego, Beate. "Biblical Interpretation—Yes or No?: Some Theoretical Considerations." Pages 53–62 in *What Is Bible?* Edited by Karin Finsterbusch and Armin Lange. Leuven: Peeters, 2012.

Eichorn, Johann Gottfried. *Introduction to the Study of the Old Testament*. Translated by George Tilly Gollip. London: Spottiswoode, 1888.

Elitzur, Yehuda. *Judges*. DM. Jerusalem: Massad Harav Kook, 1976 [Hebrew].

Elliott, C. J. "Excurses upon Psalms XCI—C." Pages 4:506–12 in *Speaker's Commentary*. Vol. 4, *Job—Psalms—Proverbs—Ecclesiastes—The Song of Solomon*. Edited by F. C. Cook et al. New York: Scribner, Armstrong, and Co., 1875.

Embry, Brad. "Legalities in the Book of Ruth: A Renewed Look." *JSOT* 41.1 (2016): 31–44.

Emanuel, David. "The Elevation of God in Psalm 105." Pages 49–64 in *Inner Biblical Allusion in the Poetry of Wisdom and Psalms*. Edited by Mark J. Boda, Kevin Chau, and Beth LaNeel Tanner. LHBOTS 659. New York: T&T Clark, 2019.

_________. *From Bards to Biblical Exegetes: A Close Reading and Intertextual Analysis of Selected Exodus Psalms*. Eugene, OR: Pickwick, 2012.

Endres, John C., William R. Millar, John Barclay Burns, eds. *Chronicles and Its Synoptic Parallels in Samuel, Kings, and Related Biblical Texts*. Collegeville, MN: Liturgical Press, 1998.

Eng, Daniel K. "The Role of Semitic Catchwords on Interpreting the Epistle of James." *TynBul* 70.2 (2019): 245–67.

Enslinger, Lyle M. "Hosea 12:5a and Genesis 32:29: A Study in Inner Biblical Exegesis." *JSOT* 18 (1980): 91–99.

Erickson, Nancy. "Dressing Up: Role Playing in the *wpt-r* Ritual and a Contextualized View of the Biblical Priesthood." Paper presented for American Schools of Overseas Research, virtual meeting, 19 November 2020.

Eskenazi, Tamara Cohn. *In an Age of Prose: A Literary Approach to Ezra-Nehemiah*. Atlanta: Scholars Press, 1988.

_________. "Nehemiah 9–10: Structure and Significance." *JHebS* 3 (2000–2001).

_________. "Response." Pages 317–27 in *The Shape of the Writings*. Edited by Julius Steinberg and Timothy J. Stone. Winona Lake, IN: Eisenbrauns, 2015.

Estelle, Bryan D. *Echoes of Exodus: Tracing a Biblical Motif*. Downers Grove, IL: InterVarsity Press Academic, 2018.

Evans, Craig. "The Function of the Old Testament in the New." Pages 163–69 in *Introducing New Testament Interpretation*. Edited by Scot McKnight. Grand Rapids: Baker Books, 1989.

_________. "Jesus and the Beginnings of the Christian Canon." Pages 95–107 in *When Texts Are Canonized*. Edited by Timothy H. Lim. Providence RI: Brown Judaic Studies, 2017.

Evans, John F. *You Shall Know that I am Yahweh: An Inner-Biblical Interpretation of Ezekiel's Recognition Formula*. University Park, PA: Eisenbrauns, 2019.

Fensham, F. Charles "New Light on Exodus 21 [6] and 2 [27] from the Laws of Eshnunna." *JBL* 78.2 (1959): 160–61.

Finlay, Tim. "Genres, Intertextuality, Bible Software, and Speech Acts." Pages 153–71 in *Second Wave Intertextuality and the Hebrew Bible*. Edited by Marianne Grohmann and Hyun Chul Paul Kim. Atlanta: SBL Press, 2019.

Finsterbusch, Karin. "Yahweh's Torah and the Praying 'I' in Psalm 119." Pages 119–35 in *Wisdom and Torah: The Reception of "Torah" in the Wisdom Literature of the Second Temple Period*. Edited by Bernd Schipper and D. Andrew Teeter. Leiden: Brill, 2013.

Firth, David G. "Foreigners in David's Court." Pages 239–54 in *Characters and Characterization in the Book of Samuel*. Edited by Keith Bodner and Benjamin J. M. Johnson. LBHOTS 669. New York: T&T Clark, 2020.

_________. *Including the Stranger: Foreigners in the Former Prophets*. Downers Grove, IL: InterVarsity Press, 2019.

_________. "When Samuel Met Esther: Narrative Focalisation, Intertextuality, and Theology." *Southeastern Theological Review* 1.1 (2010): 15–28.

Fisch, Harold. "Ruth and the Structure of Covenant History." *VT* 32.4 (1982): 425–37.

Fischer, Irmraud. "The Book of Ruth as Exegetical Literature." *European Judaism* 40.2 (2007): 140–49.

Fishbane, Michael. *Biblical Interpretation in Ancient Israel*. New York: Oxford University Press, 1985.

_________. *Biblical Text and Texture: A Literary Reading of Selected Texts*. New York: Schocken Books, 1979. Repr., Oxford: Oneworld Publications, 2003.

_________. "The Book of Job and Inner-Biblical Discourse." Pages 86–98 in *The Voice from the Whirlwind:*

Interpreting the Book of Job. Edited by Leo G. Perdue and W. Clark Gilpin. Nashville: Abingdon, 1992.

———. "Form and Reformulation of the Biblical Priestly Blessing." *JAOS* 103.1 (1983): 115–21.

———. *Haftarot*. JPSC. Philadelphia: Jewish Publication Society, 2002.

———. "Jeremiah IV 23–26 and Job III 3–13: A Recovered Use of the Creation Pattern." *VT* 21.2 (1971): 151–67.

———. "Law to Canon: Some 'Ideal-Typical' Stages of Development." Pages 65–86 in *Minhah Le-Nahum: Biblical and Other Studies Presented to Nahum M. Sarna in Honour of his 70th Birthday*. Edited by Marc Brettler and Michael Fishbane. JSOTSS 154. Sheffield: Sheffield Academic Press, 1993.

———. "Revelation and Tradition: Aspects of Inner-Biblical Exegesis." *JBL* 99.3 (1980): 343–61.

———. *Song of Songs*. JPSC. Philadelphia: Jewish Publication Society, 2015.

———. "Torah and Tradition." Pages 275–300 in *Tradition and Theology in the Old Testament*. Edited by Douglas A. Knight. Philadelphia: Fortress, 1977, 275–300.

———. "Types of Biblical Intertextuality." Pages 39–44 in *Congress Volume Oslo 1998*. Edited by A. Lemaire and M. Sæbø. VTSup 80. Leiden: Brill, 2000.

———. "Varia Deuteronomica." *ZAW* 84 (1972): 349–52.

Floyd, Michael H. "The Chimerical Acrostic of Nahum 1:2–10." *JBL* 113.3 (1994): 421–37.

Ford, William. "The Challenge of the Canaanites." *TynBul* 68.2 (2017): 161–84.

Foreman, Benjamin. "Sacrifice and Centralisation in the Pentateuch: Is Exodus 20:24–26 Really at Odds with Deuteronomy?" *TynBul* 70.1 (2019): 1–21.

Forman, Charles C. "Koheleth's Use of Genesis." *JSS* 5.3 (1960): 256–63.

Fouts, David M. "Another Look at Large Numbers in Assyrian Royal Inscriptions." *JNES* 53.3 (1994): 205–11.

———. "A Defense of the Hyperbolic Interpretation of Large Numbers in the Old Testament." *JETS* 40.3 (1997): 377–87.

———. "The Incredible Numbers of the Hebrew Kings." Pages 283–99 in *Giving the Sense: Understanding and Using the Old Testament Historical Texts*. Edited by David M. Howard, Jr. and Michael A. Grisanti. Grand Rapids: Kregel, 2003.

Fox, Everette. *The Early Prophets: Joshua, Judges, Samuel, and Kings*. New York: Schoken Books, 2014.

Fox, Michael V. *Ecclesiastes*. JPSC. Philadelphia: Jewish Publication Society, 2004.

———. "The Identification of Quotations in Biblical Literature." *ZAW* 92.3 (1980): 416–31.

———. *Proverbs: An Eclectic Edition with Introduction and Textual Commentary*. Atlanta: SBL Press, 2015.

———. *Proverbs 10–31*. AYB. New Haven: Yale University Press, 2009.

———. Review of *Twice-Told Proverbs*, by Daniel C. Snell. *Critical Review of Books in Religion* 8 (1995): 153–57.

Frame, John. *Systematic Theology: An Introduction to Christian Belief*. Phillipsburg, NJ: P&R Publishing, 2013.

France, R. T. *Jesus and the Old Testament*. London: Tyndale Press, 1971.

Freedman, David Noel. *Psalm 119: The Exaltation of Torah*. Winona Lake, IN: Eisenbrauns, 1999.

Frevel, Christian. "On Untying Tangles and Tying Knots in Joshua 23–Judges 3:6: A Response to Erhard Blum, Reinhard G. Kratz, and Sarah Schultz." Pages 281–94 in *Book-Seams in the Hexateuch I: The Literary Transitions between the Books of Genesis/Exodus and Joshua/Judges*. Edited by Christoph Berner and Harald Samuel. FAT 120. Tübingen: Mohr Siebeck, 2018.

———. "Telling the Secrets of Wisdom: The Use of Psalm 104 in the Book of Job." Pages 157–68 in *Reading Job Intertextually*. Edited by Katharine Dell and Will Kynes. LHBOTS 574. New York: Bloomsbury, 2013.

Friebel, Kelvin G. "The Decrees of Yahweh That Are 'Not Good': Ezekiel 20:25–26." Pages 21–36 in *Seeking Out the Wisdom of the Ancients: Essays Offered to Honor Michael V. Fox on the Occasion of His Sixty-Fifth Birthday*. Edited by Ronald L. Troxel, Kelvin G. Friebel, and Dennis R. Magray. Winona Lake, IN: Eisenbrauns, 2005.

Fried, Lisbeth S. "The *ʿam hāʾāreṣ* in Ezra 4:4 and Persian Imperial Administration." Pages 123–45 in *Judah and Judeans in the Persian Period*. Edited by Oded Lipschits and Manfred Oeming. Winona Lake, IN: Eisenbrauns, 2006.

———. *Ezra, a Commentary*. Sheffield: Sheffield Phoenix, 2015.

Friedberg, A., and Juni Hoppe. "Deuteronomy 14.3–21: An Early Exemplar of Rewritten Scripture?" *JSOT* 45.3 (2021): 422–57.

Friedman, Richard E. *Who Wrote the Bible?* 2nd. ed. San Francisco: HarperSanFranciso, 1997.

Frisch, Amos. "Structure and Its Significance: The Narrative of Solomon's Reign (1 Kings 1–12:24)." *JSOT* 51 (1991): 3–14.

Fuad, Chelcent. "The Curious Case of the Blasphemer: Ambiguity as Literary Device in Leviticus 24:10–23." *Horizons in Biblical Theology* 41 (2019): 51–70.

Gamble, Richard C. *The Whole Counsel of God*. Vol. 2, *The Full Revelation of God*. Phillipsburg, NJ: P&R Publishing, 2018.

Ganzel, Tova. "Transformation of Pentateuchal Descriptions of Idolatry." Pages 33–49 in *Transforming Visions: Transformations of Text, Tradition, and Theology in Ezekiel*. Edited by William A. Tooman and Michael A. Lyons. Eugene, OR: Pickwick, 2010.

Gardner, Kristen H. "Hidden in Plain Sight: Intertextuality and Judges 19." Pages 53–72 in *Second Wave Intertextuality and the Hebrew Bible*. Edited by Marianne Grohmann and Hyun Chul Paul Kim. Atlanta: SBL Press, 2019.

Garr, W. Randall, and Steven E. Fassberg, eds. *A Handbook of Biblical Hebrew*. Vol. 1, *Periods, Corpora, and Reading Traditions*. Winona Lake, IN: Eisenbrauns, 2016.

Gentry, Peter J. "Rethinking the 'Sure Mercies of David' in Isaiah 55:3." *WTJ* 69 (2007): 279–304.

________. "The Septuagint and the Text of the Old Testament," *BBR* 16.2 (2006): 193–218.

________. "The Text of the Old Testament." *JETS* 52.1 (2009): 19–45.

Gentry, Peter J., and Stephen J. Wellum. *Kingdom Through Covenant: A Biblical Theological Understanding of the Covenants*. Wheaton, IL: Crossway, 2012.

George, Andrew R. "A Stele of Nebuchadnezzar II." Pages 153–69 in *Cuneiform Royal Inscriptions and Related Texts in the Schøyen Collection*. Edited by Andrew R. George. Bethesda, MD: CDL, 2011.

Gibson, J. C. L. *Canaanite Myths and Legends*. 2nd ed. New York: T&T Clark, 1978.

Gibson, Jonathan. *Covenant Continuity and Fidelity: A Study of Inner-Biblical Allusion and Exegesis in Malachi*. LHBOTS 625. New York: T&T Clark, 2016.

Giffone, Benjamin D. "Can Theological Interpretation Soften the Protestant Problem of Old Testament Textual Plurality?: Jeremiah as a Test Case." *European Journal of Theology* 29.2 (2020): 153–78.

________. "'Israel's' Only Son?: The Complexity of Benjaminite Identity between Judah and Joseph." *OTE* 32.3 (2019): 956–72.

________. *"Sit at My Right Hand": The Chronicler's Portrait of the Tribe of Benjamin in the Social Context of Yehud*. LHBOTS 628. New York: Bloomsbury T&T Clark, 2016.

Gile, Jason. "Deuteronomic Influence in the Book of Ezekiel." PhD diss., Wheaton College, 2013.

________. "Deuteronomy and Ezekiel's Theology of Exile." Pages 287–306 in *For Our God Always: Studies on the Message and Influence of Deuteronomy in Honor of Daniel I. Block*. Edited by Jason S. DeRouchie, Jason Gile, and Kenneth J. Turner. Winona Lake, IN: Eisenbrauns, 2013.

________. "Ezekiel 16 and the Song of Moses: A Prophetic Transformation?" *JBL* 130. (2011): 87–108.

Gillingham, Susan E. "'Moab Is My Washpot' (Ps 60:8 [MT 10]): Another Look at the MLF (Moabite Liberation Front)." Pages 61–72 in *Interested Readers: Essays on the Hebrew Bible in Honor of David J. A. Clines*. Edited by James K. Aitken, Jeremy M. S. Clines, and Christl M. Maier. Atlanta: Society of Biblical Literature, 2013.

________. "New Wine in Old Wineskins: Three Approaches to Prophecy and Psalmody." Pages 370–90 in *Prophecy and Prophets in Ancient Israel: Proceedings of the Oxford Old Testament Seminar*. Edited by John Day. LHBOTS 531. New York: T&T Clark, 2010.

Ginsberg, H. L. "The Oldest Interpretation of the Suffering Servant." *VT* 3.4 (1953): 400–4.

Girdlestone, Robert B. *Deuterographs: Duplicate Passages in the Old Testament*. Oxford: Clarendon, 1894.

________. *The Grammar of Prophecy: An Attempt to Discover the Method Underlying the Prophetic Scriptures*. London: Eyre and Spottiswoode, 1901.

Glanville, Mark R. *Adopting the Stranger as Kindred in Deuteronomy*. Atlanta: SBL Press, 2018.

________. "The *Gēr* (Stranger) in Deuteronomy: Family for the Displaced." *JBL* 137.3 (2018): 599–623.

Glatt-Gilad, David A. "Chronicles as Consensus Literature." Pages 67–75 in *What Was Authoritative for Chronicles?* Edited by Ehud Ben Zvi and Diana Edelman. Winona Lake, IN: Eisenbrauns, 2011.

________. *Chronological Displacement in Biblical and Related Literatures*. Atlanta: Scholars Press, 1993.

________. "Genealogy Lists as a Window to Historiographic Periodization in the Book of Chronicles." *Maarav* 21.1–2 (2014): 71–79.

________. "Reflections of the Structure and Significance of the '*ămānāh* (Neh 10,29–40)." *ZAW* 112.3 (2000): 386–95.

________. "Regnal Formulae as a Historiographic Device in the Book of Chronicles." *RB* 108.2 (2001): 184–209.

________. "The Re-Interpretation of the Edomite-Israelite Encounter in Deuteronomy II." *VT* 47.4 (1997): 441–55.

________. "The Role of Huldah's Prophecy in the Chronicler's Portrayal of Josiah's Reform." *Biblica* 77 (1996): 16–31.

________. "The Root *kn*ʿ and Historiographic Periodization in Chronicles." *CBQ* 64.2 (2002): 248–59.

Glenny, W. Edward. "The Septuagint and Apostolic Hermeneutics: Amos 9 in Acts 15." *BBR* 22.1 (2012): 1–26.

Goldberg, Arnold. "The Rabbinic View of Scripture." Pages 153–66 in *A Tribute to Geza Vermes: Essays on Jewish and Christian Literature and History*. Edited by Philip R. Davies and Richard T. White. JSOTSup 100. Sheffield: Sheffield Academic, 1990.

Goldingay, John. *Daniel*. Rev. ed. WBC. Grand Rapids: Zondervan Academic, 2019.

________. *Psalms*. 3 vols. BCOTWP. Grand Rapids: Baker Academic, 2006, 2007, 2008.

________. *The Theology of Jeremiah: The Book, the Man, the Message*. Downers Grove, IL: IVP Academic, 2021.

Gooding, D. W. "The Septuagint's Version of Solomon's Misconduct." *VT* 15.3 (1965): 325–55.

Gordis, Robert. "Quotations as a Literary Usage in Biblical, Oriental, and Rabbinic Literature." *HUCA* 22 (1949): 157–219.

________. *The Song of Songs and Lamentations*. Rev. ed. New York: Ktav, 1974.

Gordon, Cyrus H. "אלהים in Its Reputed Meaning of *Rulers, Judges*." *JBL* 54.3 (1935): 139–44.

________. "The 'Waw Conversive': From Eblaite to Hebrew." *Proceedings of the American Academy for Jewish Research* 50 (1983): 87–90.

Goswell, Gregory. "The Davidic Restoration in Jeremiah 23:1–8 and Deuteronomy 17:14–20." *BBR* 30.3 (2020): 349–66.

________. "David in the Prophecy of Amos." *VT* 61 (2011): 243–57.

Gottwald, Norman K. *Studies in the Book of Lamentations*. London: SCM, 1954.

Gough, Henry. *The New Testament Quotations, Collated with the Scriptures of the Old Testament*. London: Walton and Maberly, 1855.

Goulder, Michael D. "Ruth: A Homily of Deuteronomy 22–25." Pages 307–19 in *Of Prophets' Visions and the Wisdom of Sages: Essays in Honor of R. Norman Whybray on his Seventieth*

Birthday. Edited by Heather A. McKay and David J. A. Clines. JSOTSup 162. Sheffield: Sheffield Academic, 1993.

Grätz, Sebastian. "The Second Temple and the Legal Status of the Torah: The Hermeneutics of the Torah in the Books of Ruth and Ezra." Pages 273–87 in *The Pentateuch as Torah: New Models for Understanding Its Promulgation and Acceptance*. Edited by Gary N. Knoppers and Bernard M. Levinson. Winona Lake, IN: Eisenbrauns, 2007.

Gray, G. Buchanan. "The Parallel Passages in 'Joel' in Their Bearing on the Question of Date." *Expositor* 8 (1893): 208–25.

Gray, John. *I & II Kings, a Commentary*. 2nd ed. OTL. Philadelphia: Westminster, 1970.

Green, Douglas J. *"I Undertook Great Works": The Ideology of Domestic Achievements in West Semitic Royal Inscriptions*. FAT II 41. Tübingen: Mohr Siebeck, 2010.

Greenberg, Moshe. "The Biblical Concept of Asylum." *JBL* 78.2 (1959): 125–32.

________. "The Design and Themes of Ezekiel's Program of Restoration." *Interpretation* 38 (1984): 181–208.

________. *Ezekiel 1–20*. AB. Garden City, NY: Doubleday, 1983.

________. *Ezekiel 21–37*. AB. New York: Doubleday, 1997.

________. *The Ḫab/piru*. New Haven, CT: American Oriental Society, 1955.

________. "The Hebrew Oath Particle *Ḥay/Ḥē*." *JBL* 76.1 (1957): 34–39.

________. "Notes on the Influence of Tradition on Ezekiel." *Journal of Ancient Near Eastern Society* 22 (1993): 29–37.

________. "Some Postulates of Biblical Criminal Law." Pages 25–41 in *Studies in the Bible and Jewish Thought*. Philadelphia: Jewish Publication Society, 1995.

Greengus, Samuel. *Laws in the Bible and in Early Rabbinic Collections: The Legacy of the Ancient Near East*. Eugene, OR: Cascade, 2011.

Greenstein, Edward L. "Parody as a Challenge to Tradition: The Use of Deuteronomy 32 in the Book of Job." Pages 66–78 in *Reading Job Intertextually*. Edited by Katharine Dell and Will Kynes. LHBOTS 574. New York: Bloomsbury, 2013.

________. "The Problem of Evil in the Book of Job." Pages 333–62 in *Mishneh Todah: Studies in Deuteronomy and Its Cultural Environment in Honor of Jeffrey H. Tigay*. Edited by Nili Sacher Fox, David A. Glatt-Gilad, and Michael J. Williams. Winona Lake, IN: Eisenbrauns, 2009.

Greer, Jonathan S. "The 'Priestly Portion' in the Hebrew Bible: Its Ancient Near Eastern Context and Its Implications for the Composition of P." *JBL* 138.2 (2019): 263–84.

Grisanti, Michael. A. "Deuteronomy." Pages 457–814 in *Numbers–Ruth*. EBC 2. Grand Rapids: Zondervan, 2012.

________. "The Impact of Deuteronomy on the Deuteronomistic History." Pages 223–49 in *For Our God Always: Studies on the Message and Influence of Deuteronomy in Honor of Daniel I. Block*. Edited by Jason S. DeRouchie, Jason Gile, and Kenneth J. Turner. Winona Lake, IN: Eisenbrauns, 2013.

________. "Inspiration, Inerrancy, and the OT Canon: The Place of Textual Updating in an Inerrant View of Scripture." *JETS* 44.4 (2001): 577–98.

________. "Josiah and the Composition of Deuteronomy." Pages 110–38 in *Sepher Torah Mosheh: Studies in the Composition and Interpretation of Deuteronomy*. Edited by Daniel I. Block and Richard L. Schultz. Peabody, MA: Hendrickson, 2017.

________. Review of *The Lost World of Israelite Conquest* by John H. Walton and J. Harvey Walton, *Master's Seminary Journal* 29.2 (2018): 257–60.

Gross, Carl D. "Is There Any Interest in Nehemiah 5?" *SJOT* 11.2 (1997): 270–78.

Grossman, Jonathan. "'Dynamic Analogies' in the Book of Esther." *VT* 59 (2009): 394–414.

Grubbs, Norris C., and Curtis Scott Drumm. "What Does Theology Have to Do with the Bible?: A Call for the Expansion of the Doctrine of Inspiration." *JETS* 53.1 (2010): 65–79.

Guillaume, Philippe. "The Chronological Limits of Reshaping Social Memory in the Presence of Written Sources: The Case of Ezekiel in Late Persian and Early Hellenistic Yehud." Pages 187–96 in *History, Memory, Hebrew Scriptures: A Festschrift for Ehud Ben Zvi*. Edited by Ian Douglas Wilson and Diana V. Edelman. Winona Lake, IN: Eisenbrauns, 2015.

Guthrie, George H. "Hebrews." Pages 919–95 in *Commentary on the New Testament Use of the Old Testament*. Edited by G. K. Beale and D. A. Carson. Grand Rapids: Baker Academic, 2007.

Haag, Istvan, Stephen Llewelyn, and Jack Tsonis. "Ezekiel 16 and its use of Allegory and the Disclosure-of-Abomination Formula." *VT* 62 (2012): 198–210.

Haarmann, Volker. "'Their Burnt Offerings and their Sacrifices will be Accepted on my Altar' (Isa 56:7): Gentile Yhwh-Worshipers and their Participation in the Cult of Israel." Pages 157–71 in *The Foreigner and the Law: Perspectives from the Hebrew Bible and the Ancient Near East*. Edited by Reinhard Achenbach, Rainer Albertz, and Jakob Wöhrle. Wiesbaden: Harrassowitz, 2011.

Hahn, Scott Walker, and John Sietze Bergsma. "What Laws Were 'Not Good?: A Canonical Approach to the Theological Problem of Ezekiel 20:25–26." *JBL* 123.2 (2004): 201–18.

Ḥakham, Amos. *Exodus*. DM. 2 vols. Jerusalem: Mosad Harav Kook, 1991 [Hebrew].

________. *Job with the Jerusalem Commentary*. DM. Jerusalem: Massad Harav Kook, 2009.

________. *Psalms with the Jerusalem Commentary*. DM. 3 vols. Massad Harav Kook, 2003.

Halpern, Baruch. "Why Manasseh Is Blamed for the Babylonian Exile: The Evolution of a Biblical Tradition." *VT* 48 (1998): 473–514.

Halpern, Baruch and David S. Vanderhooft. "The Editions of Kings in the 7th–6th Centuries B.C.E." *HUCA* 62 (1991): 179–244.

Hamilton, Victor P. *Exodus: An Exegetical Commentary*. Grand Rapids: Baker Academic, 2011.

Harper, William Rainey. *Amos and Hosea*. ICC. Edinburgh: T&T Clark, 1905.

Harrington, Hannah. "Intermarriage in Qumran Texts: The Legacy of Ezra-Nehemiah." Pages 251–79 in

Mixed Marriages: Intermarriage and Group Identity in the Second Temple Period. Edited by Christian Frevel. LHBOTS 547. New York: Bloomsbury, 2011.
Hartley, John E. *The Book of Job*. NICOT. Grand Rapids: Eerdmans, 1988.
Hartman, Louis F., and Alexander A. Di Lella. *The Book of Daniel*. AB. New York: Doubleday, 1978.
Harvey, John E. *Retelling the Torah: The Deuteronomistic Historian's Use of Tetrateuchal Narratives*. New York: T&T Clark, 2004.
Hayes, Christine E. *Gentile Impurities and Jewish Identities: Intermarriage and Conversion from the Bible to the Talmud*. New York: Oxford University Press, 2002.
________. "Golden Calf Stories: The Relationship of Exodus 32 and Deuteronomy 9–10." Pages 45–93 in *The Idea of Biblical Interpretation: Essays in Honor of James L. Kugel*. Edited by Hindy Najman and Judith H. Newman. JSOTSup 83. Leiden: Brill, 2004.
________. "Intermarriage and Impurity in Ancient Jewish Sources." *HTR* 92.1 (1999): 3–36.
________. *Introduction to the Bible*. New Haven: Yale University Press, 2012.
________. *What's Divine about Divine Law?: Early Perspectives*. Princeton: Princeton University Press, 2015.
Hays, Christopher B. *The Origins of Isaiah 24–27: Josiah's Festival Scroll for the Fall of Assyria*. Cambridge: Cambridge University Press, 2019.
________. "The Silence of the Wives: Bakhtin's Monologism and Ezra 7–10." *JSOT* 33.1 (2008): 59–80.
Hays, J. Daniel. "Has the Narrator Come to Praise Solomon or Bury Him?: Narrative Subtlety in 1 Kings 1–11." *JSOT* 28.2 (2003): 149–74.
________. "Jeremiah, the Septuagint, the Dead Sea Scrolls, and Inerrancy: Just What Exactly Do We Mean by the 'Original Autographs'?" Pages 133–49 in *Evangelicals and Scripture: Tradition, Authority, and Hermeneutics*. Edited by Vincent Bacote et al. Downers Grove: InterVasity Press, 2004.
________. *The Temple and the Tabernacle: A Study of God's Dwelling Places from Genesis to Revelation*. Grand Rapids: Baker Books, 2016.
Hays, Richard B. "The Canonical Matrix of the Gospels." Pages 53–75 in *The Cambridge Companion to the Gospels*. Edited by Stephen C. Barton. Cambridge: Cambridge University Press, 2006.
________. *Echoes of Scripture in the Gospels*. Waco, TX: Baylor University Press, 2016.
________. *Echoes of Scripture in the Letters of Paul*. New Haven: Yale University Press, 1989.
________. "Figural Exegesis and the Retrospective Re-cognition of Israel's Story." *BBR* 29.1 (2019): 32–48.
________. "On the Rebound: A Response to Critiques of Echoes of Scripture in the Letters of Paul." Pages 70–96 in *Paul and the Scriptures of Israel*. Edited by Craig A. Evans and James A. Sanders. JSNTSup 83. Sheffield: Sheffield Academic, 1993.
________. *Reading Backwards: Figural Christology and the Fourfold Gospel Witness*. Waco, TX: Baylor University Press, 2014.
________. *Reading with the Grain of Scripture*. Grand Rapids: Eerdmans, 2020.
Heim, Knut Martin. *Poetic Imagination in Proverbs: Variant Repetitions and the Nature of Poetry*. Winona Lake, IN: Eisenbrauns, 2013.
Heller, Roy L. *Narrative Structure and Discourse Constellations: An Analysis of Clause Function in Biblical Hebrew Prose*. Harvard Semitic Studies 55. Winona Lake, IN: Eisenbrauns, 2004.
Hendel, Ronald and Jan Joosten. *How Old Is the Hebrew Bible?: A Linguistic, Textual, and Historical Study*. AYBRL. New Haven: Yale University Press, 2018.
Hensel, Benedikt. "Ethnic Fiction and Identity-Formation: A New Explanation for the Background of the Question of Intermarriage in Ezra-Nehemiah." Pages 133–48 in *The Bible, Qumran, and the Samaritans*. Edited by Magnar Kartveit and Gary N. Knoppers. Berlin: Walter de Gruyter, 2018.
Henze, Matthias. "The Use of Scripture in the Book of Daniel." Pages 279–307 in *A Companion to Biblical Interpretation in Early Judaism*. Edited by Matthias Henze. Grand Rapids: Eerdmans, 2012.
Hess, Richard S. *Joshua*. TOTC 6. Downers Grove: InterVarsity Press, 1996.
________. "Leviticus." Pages 563–826 in *Genesis–Leviticus*. EBC 1. Grand Rapids: Zondervan, 2008.
Hibbard, J. Todd. "Isaiah 24–27 and Trito-Isaiah: Exploring Some Connections." Pages 183–99 in *Formation and Intertextuality in Isaiah 24–27*. Edited by J. Todd Hibbard and Hyun Chul Paul Kim. Atlanta: Society of Biblical Literature, 2013.
Hilber, John W. *Cultic Prophecy in the Psalms*. BZAW 352. New York: de Gruyter, 2005.
Hill, Andrew E. *Haggai, Zechariah, and Malachi*. TOTC 28. Downers Grove: InterVarsity Press Academic, 2012.
________. *Malachi*. AB. New York: Doubleday, 1998.
________. "Malachi." Pages 5:232–45 in *Zondervan Illustrated Bible Backgrounds Commentary*. Edited by John H. Walton. 5 vols. Grand Rapids: Zondervan, 2009.
________. "Patchwork Poetry or Reasoned Verse?: Connective Structure in 1 Chronicles XVI." *VT* 33 (1983): 97–101.
Hillers, Delbert R. *Micah*. Hermeneia. Philadelphia: Fortress, 1984.
Hoffer, Vicki. "An Exegesis of Isaiah 38.21." *JSOT* 56 (1992): 69–84.
Holladay, William L. *Jeremiah 2*. Hermeneia. Minneapolis: Fortress, 1990.
Holmstedt, Robert D. *Ruth: A Handbook on the Hebrew Text*. BHHB. Waco, TX: Baylor University Press, 2010.
Hornkohl, Aaron D. *Ancient Hebrew Periodization and the Language of the Book of Jeremiah: The Case for a Sixth-Century Date of Composition*. Leiden: Brill, 2014.
________. "Biblical Hebrew: Periodization." Pages 1:315–25 in *Encyclopedia of Hebrew Language and Linguistics*. Edited by Geoffrey Khan. 4 vols. Leiden: Brill, 2013.

________. "Transitional Biblical Hebrew." Pages 31–42 in *Periods, Corpora, and Reading Traditions*. Vol. 1 of *A Handbook of Biblical Hebrew*. Edited by W. Randall Garr and Steven E. Fassberg. Winona Lake, IN: Eisenbrauns, 2016.

Hornung, Gabriel F. "The Nature and Import of the Relationship between the Joseph Story in Genesis and the Book of Esther." PhD diss., Harvard University, Cambridge, MA, 2016.

Hossfeld, Frank-Lothar. "The Gog Oracles of Ezekiel between Psalms and the Priestly Writer." Pages 194–98 in *Ezekiel: Current Debates and Future Directions*. Edited by William A. Tooman and Penelope Barter. FAT 112. Tübingen: Mohr Siebeck, 2017.

Hossfeld, Frank-Lothar and Erich Zenger. *Psalms 2: A Commentary on Psalms 51–100*. Edited by Klaus Baltzer. Translated by Linda M. Maloney. Hermeneia. Minneapolis: Fortress, 2005.

________. *Psalms 3: A Commentary on Psalms 101–150*. Edited by Klaus Baltzer. Translated by Linda M. Maloney. Hermeneia. Minneapolis: Fortress, 2001.

House, Paul R. "Examining the Narratives of Old Testament Narrative: An Exploration in Biblical Theology." *WTJ* 67 (2005):229–45.

________. *Unity of the Twelve*. Sheffield: Almond Press, 1990.

Houtman, C. "Ezra and the Law." *Old Testament Studies* 21 (1981): 91–115.

Hubbard, David Allan. *Joel and Amos*. TOTC 25. Downers Grove, IL: InterVarsity Press Academic, 1989.

Hubbard, Robert L. "Reading through the Rearview Mirror: Inner-Biblical Exegesis and the New Testament." Pages 125–39 in *Doing Theology for the Church: Essays in Honor of Klyne Snodgrass*. Edited by Rebekah A. Eklund and John E. Phelan, Jr. Eugene, OR: Wipf & Stock, 2014.

Huffmon, Herbert B. "Exodus 23:4–5: A Comparative Study." Pages 271–78 in *A Light unto My Path: Old Testament Studies in Honor of Jacob M. Myers*. Edited by Howard N. Bream, Ralph D. Heim, and Carey A. Moore. Philadelphia: Temple University Press, 1974.

Hummel, Horace D. "Enclitic *Mem* in Northwest Semitic, especially Hebrew." *JBL* 76.2 (1957): 85–104.

Hundley, Michael. "To Be or Not to Be: A Reexamination of Name Language in Deuteronomy and the Deuteronomistic History." *VT* 59 (2009): 533–55.

Hunter, Alastair. "Jonah from the Whale: Exodus Motifs in Jonah 2." Pages 142–58 in *The Elusive Prophet: The Prophet as a Historical Person, Literary Character, and Anonymous Artist*. Edited by Johannes C. de Moor. Leiden: Brill, 2001.

Hurowitz, Victor Avigdor. "Joel's Locust Plague in Light of Sargon II's Hymn to Nanaya." *JBL* 112.4 (1993): 597–603.

________. "Paradise Regained: Proverbs 3:13–20 Reconsidered." Pages 49–62 in *Sefer Moshe, The Moshe Weinfeld Jubilee Volume: Studies in the Bible and Ancient Near East, Qumran, and Post-Biblical Judaism*. Edited by Chaim Cohen, Avi Hurvitz, and Shalom M. Paul. Winona Lake, IN: Eisenbrauns, 2004.

Hurvitz, Avi. "The Date of the Prose-Tale of Job Linguistically Reconsidered." *HTR* 67.1 (1974): 17–34.

________. "Originals and Imitations in Biblical Poetry: A Comparative Examination of 1 Sam 2:1–10 and Ps 113:5–9." Pages 115–21 in *Biblical and Related Studies Presented to Samuel Iwry*. Edited by Ann Kort and Scott Morschauser. Winona Lake, IN: Eisenbrauns, 1985.

Hwang, Jerry. "'I Am Yahweh Your God from the Land of Egypt': Hosea's Use of the Exodus Tradition." Pages 243–53 in *"Did I Not Bring Israel Out of Egypt?": Biblical Archaeological, and Egyptological Perspectives on the Exodus Narratives*. Edited by James K. Hoffmeier, Alan R. Millard, and Gary A. Rendsburg. Winona Lake, IN: Eisenbrauns, 2016.

Hyatt, Philip J. "Were There an Ancient Historical Credo in Israel and an Independent Sinai Tradition?" Pages 152–70 in *Translating & Understanding the Old Testament: Essays in Honor of Herbert Gordon May*. Edited by Harry Thomas Frank and William L. Reed. Nashville: Abingdon Press, 1970.

Imes, Carmen Joy. *Bearing God's Name: Why Sinai Still Matters*. Downers Grove, IL: IVP Academic, 2019.

________. *Bearing YHWH's Name at Sinai: A Reexamination of the Name Command of the Decalogue*. University Park, PA: Eisenbrauns, 2018.

________. "Between Two Worlds: The Functional and Symbolic Significance of the High Priestly Regalia." Pages 29–62 in *Dress and Clothing in the Hebrew Bible: "For All Her Household Are Clothed in Crimson."* Edited by Antonios Finitsis. LHBOTS 679. New York: T&T Clark, 2019.

Irwin, William. "What Is an Allusion?" *Journal of Aesthetics and Art Criticism* 59.3 (2001): 287–97.

Issler, Klaus. "Lending and Interest in the OT: Examining Three Interpretations to Explain the Deuteronomy 23:19–20 Distinction in light of the Historical Usury Debate." *JETS* 59.4 (2016): 761–89.

Jackson, Bernard S. "Ruth, the Pentateuch and the Nature of Biblical Law: in Conversation with Jean Lois Ska." Pages 75–111 in *The Post-Priestly Pentateuch: New Perspectives on its Redactional Development and Theological Profiles*. Edited by Federico Giuntoli and Konrad Schmid. FAT 101. Tübingen: Mohr Siebeck, 2015.

Jacobson, Rolf A. *"Many Are Saying": The Function of Direct Discourse in the Hebrew Psalter*. JSOTSup 397. New York: T&T Clark, 2004.

Janzen, David. "A Monument and a Name: The Primary Purpose of Chronicles' Genealogies." *JSOT* 43.1 (2018): 45–66.

________. *Witch-hunts, Purity, and Social Boundaries: The Expulsion of Foreign Women in Ezra 9–10*. JSOTSup 350. Sheffield: Sheffield Academic, 2002.

Japhet, Sara. *I & II Chronicles, a Commentary*. OTL. Louisville: Westminster John Knox, 1993.

________. "1 Esdras." Pages 193–220 in *The Apocrypha*. Edited by Martin Goodman. Oxford Bible Commentary. New York: Oxford University Press, 2001.

________. *The Ideology of the Book of Chronicles and Its Place in Biblical Thought*. Translated by Anna Barber. Winona Lake, IN: Eisenbrauns, 2009.

________. "The Relationship between the Legal Corpora in the Pentateuch in Light of Manumission Laws." Pages 63–89 in *Studies in Bible*. Edited by Sara Japhet. Scripta Hierosolymitana 31. Jerusalem: Magnes, 1986.

________. "The Supposed Common Authorship of Chronicles and Ezra-Nehemiah Investigated Anew." *VT* 18 (1968): 330–71.

________. "What May Be Learned from Ezra-Nehemiah about the Composition of the Pentateuch?" Pages 543–60 in *The Formation of the Pentateuch: Bridging the Academic Cultures of Europe, Israel, and North America*. Edited by Jan C. Gertz et al. FAT 111. Tübingen: Mohr Siebeck, 2016.

Jarick, John. "The Two Ahabs of the South: Joash and Josiah." Pages 307–16 in *Let Us Go Up to Zion: Essays in Honour of H. G. M. Williamson on the Occasion of His Sixty-Fifth Birthday*. Edited by Iain Provan and Mark J. Boda. Leiden: Brill, 2011.

Jassen, Alex. *Scripture and Law in the Dead Sea Scrolls*. New York: Cambridge University Press, 2014.

Jenkins, Steffen G. "A Quotation in Psalm 109 as Defence Exhibit A." *TynBul* 71.1 (2020): 115–35.

Jeon, Yong Ho. "The Retroactive Re-evaluation Technique with Pharaoh's Daughter and the Nature of Solomon's Corruption in 1 Kings 1–12." *TynBul* 62.1 (2011): 15–40.

Jericke, Detlef. "Exodus Material in the Book of Genesis." Pages 137–56 in *Book-Seams in the Hexateuch I: The Literary Transitions between the Books of Genesis/Exodus and Joshua/Judges*. Edited by Christoph Berner and Harald Samuel. FAT 102. Tübingen: Mohr Siebeck, 2018.

Jerusalmi, Isaac. *The Aramaic Sections of Ezra and Daniel: A Philological Commentary with Frequent References to Talmudic Aramaic Parallels and a Synopsis of the Regular Verb*. Cincinnati: Hebrew Union College, 1972.

Jindo, Job Y. "Some Reflections on Interpreting Allusion: The Case of Creation Motifs in Isaiah." Pages 133–65 in *Inner Biblical Allusion in the Poetry of Wisdom and Psalms*. Edited by Mark J. Boda, Kevin Chau, and Beth LaNeel Tanner. LHBOTS 659. New York: T&T Clark, 2019.

Joffe, Laura. "The Answer to the Meaning of Life, the Universe and the Elohistic Psalter." *JSOT* 27.2 (2002): 223–35.

Johnson, Luke Timothy. *Septuagintal Midrash in the Speeches of Acts*. Milwaukee: Marquette University Press, 2002.

Johnson, S. Lewis. *The Old Testament in the New: An Argument for Biblical Inspiration*. Grand Rapids: Zondervan, 1980.

Johnson, Willa M. *The Holy Seed Has Been Defiled: The Interethnic Marriage Dilemma in Ezra 9–10*. Sheffield: Sheffield Phoenix, 2011.

Johnston, Gordon. "A Critical Evaluation of Moshe Weinfeld's Approach to the Davidic Covenant in Light of Ancient Near Eastern Royal Grants: What Did He Get Right & What Did He Get Wrong?" Paper presented at the Annual Meeting of the Evangelical Theological Society, San Francisco, 18 Nov 2011.

________. "The Nature of the Davidic Covenant in the Light of Intertextual Analysis." Paper presented at the Evangelical Theological Society. San Francisco, 16 November 2011.

________. "'Unconditional' and 'Conditional' Features of the Davidic Covenant in Light of Ancient Near Eastern Land Grant Treaties." Paper presented at the Annual Meeting of the Evangelical Theological Society. Providence, RI, 19 November 2008.

Johnstone, William. *2 Chronicles 10–36, Guilt and Atonement*. Vol. 2 of *1 and 2 Chronicles*. JSOTSup 254. Sheffield: Sheffield Academic, 1997.

________. "The Use of Leviticus in Chronicles." Pages 243–55 in *Reading Leviticus: A Conversation with Mary Douglas*. Edited by John F. A. Sawyer. JSOTSup 227. Sheffield: Sheffield Academic, 1996.

Jones, Eward Allen, III. *Reading Ruth in the Restoration Period: A Call for Inclusion*. LHBOTS 604. New York: T&T Clark, 2016.

________. "'Who Are You, My Daughter [מי את בתי]?': A Reassessment of Ruth and Naomi in Ruth 3." *CBQ* 76 (2014): 653–64.

Jonker, Louis C. "'My Wife Must Not Live in King David's Palace' (2 Chr 8:11): A Contribution to the Diachronic Study of Intermarriage Traditions in the Hebrew Bible." *JBL* 135.1 (2016): 35–47.

Joosten, Jan. "Language, Exegesis, and Creative Writing in Chronicles." *VT* 70 (2020): 55–66.

________. Review of *Linguistic Dating of Biblical Texts*, by Ian Young and Robert Rezetko, with Martin Ehrensvärd. *Bibel und Babel* 6 (2012): 535–42.

________. "The Syntax of Exodus 20:24b: Remarks on a Recent Article by Benjamin Kilchör." *Biblisch Notizen* 159 (2013): 3–8.

________. "YHWH's Farewell to Northern Israel (Micah 6,1–8)." *ZAW* 125.3 (2013): 448–62.

Joosten, Jan, Sidnie White Crawford, and Eugene Ulrich. "Sample Edition of Oxford Hebrew Bible: Deuteronomy 32:1–9, 1 Kings 11:1–8, and Jeremiah 27:1–10 (34 G)." *VT* 58 (2008): 352–66.

Joseph, Simon J. *Jesus, the Essenes, and Christian Origins: New Light on Ancient Texts and Communities*. Waco, TX: Baylor University Press, 2018.

Joyce, Paul M. "'Even if Noah, Daniel, and Job were in it . . .' (Ezekiel 14:14): The Case of Job and Ezekiel." Pages 118–28 in *Reading Job Intertextually*. Edited by Katharine Dell and Will Kynes. LHBOTS 574. New York: Bloomsbury, 2013.

Kaiser, Walter C. "Inner Biblical Exegesis as a Model for Bridging the 'Then' and 'Now' Gap: Hos 12:1–6." *JETS* 28.1 (1985): 33–46.

Kalimi, Isaac. "Literary-Chronological Proximity in the Chronicler's Historiography." *VT* 43.3 (1993): 318–38.

________. *The Reshaping of Ancient Israelite History in Chronicles*. Winona Lake, IN: Eisenbrauns, 2005.

________. "Robbers on the Road to Jericho: Luke's Story of the Good Samaritan and Its Origin in Kings/Chronicles." *ETL* 85.1 (2009): 47–53.

Kalimi, Isaac, and James D. Purvis. "King Jehoiachin and the Vessels of the Lord's House in Biblical Literature." *CBQ* 56 (1994): 449–57.

Kaminsky, Joel S. *Yet I Loved Jacob: Reclaiming the Biblical Concept of Election*. Nashville: Abingdon Press, 2007.

Kartveit, Magnar. "The Place That the Lord Your God Will Choose." *HBAI* 4.2 (2015): 205–18.

________. "2 Chronicles 36.20–23 as Literary and Theological 'Interface.'" Pages 395–403 in *The Chronicler as Author: Studies in Text and Texture*. Edited by M. Patrick Graham and Steven L. McKenzie. JSOTSup 263. Sheffield: Sheffield Academic, 1999.

Kawashima, Robert S. "The Jubilee Year and the Return of Cosmic Purity." *CBQ* 65 (2003): 370–89.

Keefer, Arthur. "The Meaning and Place of Old Testament Context in OT/NT Methodology." Pages 73–85 in *Methodology in the Use of the Old Testament in the New: Context and Criteria*. Edited by David Allen and Steve Smith. New York: T&T Clark, 2020.

Keil, C. F., and F. Delitzsch, *Commentary on the Old Testament*. Translated by James Martin et al. 10 vols. Edinburgh: T&T Clark, 1871. Repr., Peabody, MA: Hendrickson, 1989.

Kelly, Brian E. *Retribution and Eschatology in Chronicles*. JSOTSup 211. Sheffield: Sheffield Academic, 1996.

________. "'Retribution' Revisited: Covenant, Grace and Restoration." Pages 206–27 in *The Chronicler as Theologian: Essays in Honor of Ralph W. Klein*. Edited by M. Patrick Graham, Steven L. McKenzie, and Gary N. Knoppers. New York: T&T Clark, 2003.

Kelly, Joseph Ryan. "The Ethics of Inclusion: The גר and the אזרח in the Passover to Yhwh." *BBR* 23.2 (2013): 155–66.

________. "Joel, Jonah, and the Yhwh Creed: Determining the Trajectory of the Literary Influence." *JBL* 132.4 (2013): 805–26.

Kent, Charles Foster. *Israel's Historical and Biographical Narratives: From the Establishment of the Hebrew Kingdom to the End of the Maccabean Struggle*. Student's Old Testament. London: Hodder & Stoughton, 1904.

________. *Israel's Laws and Legal Precedent: From the Days of Moses to the Closing of the Legal Canon*. Student's Old Testament. New York: Hodder & Stoughton, 1907.

________. *Narratives of the Beginnings of Hebrew History: From the Creation to the Establishment of the Hebrew Kingdom*. Student's Old Testament. London: Hodder & Stoughton, 1904.

________. *The Sermons, Epistles and Apocalypses of Israel's Prophets: From the Beginning of the Assyrian Period to the End of the Maccabean Struggle*. Student's Old Testament. New York: Scribner's Sons, 1910.

________. *The Songs, Hymns, and Prayers of the Old Testament*. Student's Old Testament. London: Hodder & Stoughton, 1914.

Kent, Charles Foster, and Millar Burrows. *Proverbs and Didactic Poems*. Student's Old Testament. New York: Scribner's Sons, 1927.

Kessler, Martin. "The Scaffolding of the Book of Jeremiah." Pages 57–66 in *Reading the Book of Jeremiah: A Search for Coherence*. Edited by Martin Kessler. Winona Lake, IN: Eisenbrauns, 2004.

Kiel, Yehuda. *Genesis*. DM. 3 vols. Jerusalem: Mosad Harav Kook, 1997 [Hebrew].

________. *Joshua*. DM. Jerusalem: Massad Harav Kook, 1970 [Hebrew].

________. *Samuel*. DM. 2 vols. Jerusalem: Massad Harav Kook, 1981 [Hebrew].

Kilchör, Benjamin. "Sacred and Profane Space: The Priestly Character of Exodus 20:24–26 and Its Reception in Deuteronomy 12." *BBR* 29.4 (2019): 455–67.

________. "Wellhausen's Five Pillars for the Priority of D over P/H: Can They Still Be maintained?" Pages 101–13 in Paradigm *Change in Pentateuchal Research*. BZAR 22. Edited by Matthias Armgardt, Benjamin Kilchör, and Markus Zehnder. Wiesbaden: Harrassowitz, 2019.

Kim, Brittany and Charlie Trimm. *Understanding Old Testament Theology: Mapping the Terrain of Recent Approaches*. Grand Rapids: Zondervan Academic, 2020.

Kim, Daniel E. "The Crime of Gibeah: A Reassessment through the Lens of Deuteronomy." Unpublished conference paper, Institute for Biblical Research," San Diego, 22 November 2019.

Kim, Hee Suk. "Exodus 34.6 in Psalms 86, 103, and 145 in Relation to the Theological Perspectives of Books III, IV, and V of the Psalter." Pages 36–48 in *Inner Biblical Allusion in the Poetry of Wisdom and Psalms*. Edited by Mark J. Boda, Kevin Chau, and Beth LaNeel Tanner. LHBOTS 659. New York: T&T Clark, 2019.

Kingsmill, Edmée. "The Song of Songs: A Wisdom Book." Pages 310–35 in *Perspectives on Israelite Wisdom: Proceedings of the Oxford Old Testament Seminar*. Edited by John Jarick. LHBOTS 618. New York: Bloomsbury T&T Clark, 2016.

Kirkpatrick, A. F. *The Book of Psalms, Book I*. CBSC. Cambridge: University Press, 1897.

________. *The Book of Psalms, Books II and III*. CBSC. Cambridge: University Press, 1895.

________. *The Book of Psalms, Books IV and V*. CBSC. Cambridge: University Press, 1903.

Klein, Michael L. "Converse Translation: A Targumic Technique." *Biblica* 57.4 (1976): 515–37.

Klein, Ralph W. "The Books of Ezra & Nehemiah." Pages 661–851 in vol. 3 of *The New Interpreter's Bible Commentary*. Edited by Leander E. Keck et al. Nashville: Abingdon, 1999.

________. "The Chronicler's Theological Rewriting of the Deuteronomistic History: Amaziah, a Test Case." Pages 237–45 in *Raising Up a Faithful Exegete: Essays in Honor of Richard D. Nelson*. Edited by K. L. Noll and Brooks Schramm. Winona Lake, IN: Eisenbrauns, 2010.

________. *1 Chronicles, a Commentary*. Hermeneia. Minneapolis: Fortress, 2006.

________. *2 Chronicles, a Commentary*. Hermeneia. Minneapolis: Fortress, 2012.

Klingbeil, Gerald A. "'Not So Happily Ever After . . .': Cross-Cultural Marriages in the Time of Ezra-Nehemiah." *Maarav* 14.1 (2007): 39–75.

Koch, Klaus. "Ezra and the Origins of Judaism." *JSS* 19.2 (1974): 173–97.

________. "Is Daniel Also Among the Prophets?" *Interpretation* 34 (1985): 117–30.

Kohlenberger, John R. III. *The Comparative Psalter: Hebrew—Greek—English*. New York: Oxford University Press, 2007.

Knight, Douglas A. *Law, Power, and Justice in Ancient Israel*. Louisville: Westminster John Knox, 2011.

Knoppers, Gary N. "Changing History: Nathan's Oracle and the Structure of the Davidic Monarchy in Chronicles." Pages 99–123* in *Shai le-Sara Japhet: Studies in the Bible, its Exegesis and its Literature*. Edited by Moshe Bar-Asher et al. Jerusalem: Bialik Institute, 2007.

________. "'The City Yhwh Has Chosen': The Chronicler's Promotion of Jerusalem in Light of Recent Archaeology." Pages 307–26 in *Jerusalem in Bible and Archaeology: The First Temple Period*. Edited by Andrew G. Vaughn and Ann E. Killebrew. Atlanta: Society of Biblical Literature, 2003.

________. "Democratizing Revelation?: Prophets, Seers and Visionaries in Chronicles." Pages 391–409 in *Prophecy and Prophets in Ancient Israel: Proceedings of the Oxford Old Testament Seminar*. Edited by John Day. LHBOTS 531. New York: T&T Clark, 2010.

________. "Establishing the Rule of Law?: The Composition of Num 33,50–56 and the Relationship Among the Pentateuch, the Hexateuch, and the Deuteronomistic History." Pages 135–52 in *Das Deuteronomium zwischen Pentateuch und Deuteronomistischem Geschichtswerk*. Edited by Eckart Otto and Reinhard Achenbach. Göttingen: Vandenhoeck & Reuprecht, 2004.

________. *I Chronicles 1–9*. AB. New York: Doubleday, 2003.

________. *I Chronicles 10–29*. AB. New York: Doubleday, 2004.

________. "Greek Historiography and the Chronicler's History: A Reexamination." *JBL* 122.4 (2003): 627–50.

________. "Hierodules, Priests, or Janitors?: The Levites in Chronicles and the History of the Israelite Priesthood." *JBL* 118.1 (1999): 49–72.

________. *Jews and Samaritans: The Origins and History of Their Early Relations*. New York: Oxford University Press, 2013.

________. "'Married into Moab': The Exogamy Practiced by Judah and his Descendants in the Judahite Lineages." Pages 170–91 in *Mixed Marriages: Intermarriage and Group Identity in the Second Temple Period*. Edited by Christian Frevel. New York: Bloomsbury, 2011.

________. "Nehemiah and Sanballat: The Enemy Without or Within?" Pages 305–31 in *Judah and the Judeans in the Fourth Century B.C.E.* Edited by Oded Lipschits, Gary N. Knoppers, and Rainer Albertz. Winona Lake, IN: Eisenbrauns, 2007.

________. "Prayer and Propaganda: Solomon's Dedication of the Temple and the Deuteronomist's Program." *CBQ* 57 (1995): 229–54.

________. "Rehoboam in Chronicles: Villain or Victim?" *JBL* 109.3 (1990): 423–40.

________. "The Relationship of the Priestly Genealogies to the History of the High Priesthood in Jerusalem." Pages 109–33 in *Judah and the Judeans in the Neo-Babylonian Period*. Edited by Oded Lipschitz and Joseph Blenkinsopp. Winona Lake, IN: Eisenbrauns, 2003.

________. Review of *The Word of God in Transition: From Prophet to Exegete in the Second Temple Period,* by William M. Schniedewind. *Journal of Jewish Studies* 49.1 (1998): 133–35.

________. "Sources, Revisions, and Editions: The Lists of Jerusalem's Residents in MT and LXX Nehemiah 11 and 1 Chronicles 9." *Textus* 20 (2000): 141–68.

________. "'There Was None Like Him': Incomparability in the Book of Kings." *CBQ* 54 (1992): 411–31.

________. "'To Him You Must Listen': The Prophetic Legislation in Deuteronomy and the Reformation of Classical Tradition in Chronicles." Pages 161–94 in *Chronicling the Chronicler: The Book of Chronicles and Early Second Temple Historiography*. Edited by Paul S. Evans and Tyler F. Williams. Winona Lake, IN: Eisenbrauns, 2013.

________. *Two Nations Under God: The Deuteronomistic History of Solomon and the Dual Monarchies*. 2 vols. HSM 52. Atlanta: Scholars Press, 1993.

________. "When the Foreign Monarch Speaks About the Israelite Tabernacle." Pages 49–63 in *History, Memory, Hebrew Scriptures: A Festschrift for Ehud Ben Zvi*. Edited by Ian Douglas Wilson and Diana V. Edelman. Winona Lake, IN: Eisenbrauns, 2015.

________. "Who or What Is Israel in Trito-Isaiah?" Pages 153–65 in *Let Us Go Up to Zion: Essays in Honour of H. G. M. Williamson on the Occasion of his Sixty-Fifth Birthday*. Edited by Iain Provan and Mark Boda. VTSup 153. Leiden: Brill, 2012.

________. "'Yhwh Is Not with Israel': Alliances as a *Topos* in Chronicles." *CBQ* 58.4 (1996): 601–26.

Knoppers, Gary N., and Paul B. Harvey Jr., "The Pentateuch in Ancient Mediterranean Context: The Publication of Local Law Codes." Pages 105–41 in *The Pentateuch as Torah: New Models for Understanding Its Promulgation and Acceptance*. Edited by Gary N. Knoppers and Bernard M. Levinson. Winona Lake, IN: Eisenbrauns, 2007.

Kottsieper, Ingo. "'And They Did Not Care to Speak Yehudit': On Linguistic Change in Judah." Pages 95–124 in *Judah and the Judeans in the Fourth Century B.C.E.* Edited by Oded Lipschitz, Gary Knoppers, and Rainer Albertz. Winona Lake, IN: Eisenbrauns, 2007.

Kraft, Robert A. "Para-mania: Beside, Before, and Beyond Bible Studies." *JBL* 126.1 (2007): 5–27.

________. "What Is 'Bible'?—From the Perspective of 'Text': The Christian Connections." Pages 105–11 in *What Is Bible?* Edited by Karin Finsterbusch and Armin Lange. Leuven: Peeters, 2012.

Kratz, Reinhard G. "'The peg in the wall': Cultic Centralization Revisited." Pages 251–85 in *Law and Religion in the Eastern Mediterranean: From Antiquity to Early Islam*. Edited by Anselm C. Hagedorn and Reinhard G. Kratz. New York: Oxford University Press, 2013.

_________. "Rewriting Isaiah: The Case of Isaiah 28–31." Pages 245–66 in *Prophecy and Prophets in Ancient Israel: Proceeding of the Oxford Old Testament Seminar*. Edited by John Day. LHBOTS 531. New York: T&T Clark, 2010.

Krause, Deborah. "The One Who Comes Unbinding the Blessing of Judah: Mark 11.1–10 as a Midrash of Genesis 49.11, Zechariah 9.9, and Psalm 118.25–26." Pages 141–53 in *Early Christian Interpretation of the Scriptures of Israel*. Edited by Craig A. Evans and James A. Sanders. JSNTSup 148. Sheffield: Sheffield Academic, 1997.

Kristeva, Julia. *Revolution in Poetic Language*. Translated by Margaret Waller. New York: Columbia University Press, 1984.

Krusche, Marcel. "A Collective Anointed?: David and the People in Psalm 89." *JBL* 139.1 (2020): 87–105.

Krüger, Thomas. *Qoheleth*. Hermeneia. Minneapolis: Fortress, 2004.

Kugel, James L. "The Beginnings of Biblical Interpretation." Pages 3–23 in *A Companion to Biblical Interpretation in Early Judaism*. Edited by Matthias Henze. Grand Rapids: Eerdmans, 2012.

_________. *In Potiphar's House: The Interpretive Life of Biblical Texts*. Cambridge: Harvard University Press, 1994.

_________. Review of *Biblical Interpretation in Ancient Israel*, by Michael Fishbane. *Prooftexts* 7 (1987): 269–83.

_________. *Traditions of the Bible: A Guide to the Bible As It Was at the Start of the Common Era*. Cambridge: Harvard University Press, 1998.

Kuhrt, Amélie. *The Ancient Near East, c. 3000–330 BC*. 2 vols. New York: Routledge, 1995.

Kwon, Jiseong James. *Scribal Culture and Intertextuality: Literary and Historical Relationships between Job and Deutero-Isaiah*. FAT II 85. Tübingen: Mohr Siebeck, 2016.

Kynes, Will. "Beat Your Parodies into Swords, and Your Parodied Books into Spears: A New Paradigm for Parody in the Hebrew Bible." *BibInt* 19 (2011): 276–310.

_________. "Debating Suffering: The Voices of Lamentations Personified in Job's Dialogue." In *Reading Lamentations Intertextually*. Edited by Brittany Melton and Heath A. Thomas. LHBOTS. New York: Bloomsbury T&T Clark, forthcoming.

_________. "Follow Your Heart and Do Not Say It Was a Mistake: Qohelet's Allusions to the Story of the Spies." Pages 15–27 in *Reading Ecclesiastes Intertextually*. Edited by Katharine Dell and Will Kynes. New York: Bloomsbury T&T Clark, 2014.

_________. "Intertextuality: Method and Theory in Job and Psalm 119." Pages 201–13 in *Biblical Interpretation and Method: Essays in Honour of John Barton*. Edited by Katharine J. Dell and Paul M. Joyce. New York: Oxford University Press, 2013.

_________. "Job and Isaiah 40–55: Intertextuality in Dialogue." Pages 94–105 in *Reading Job Intertextually*. Edited by Katharine Dell and Will Kynes. LHBOTS 574. New York: Bloomsbury, 2013.

_________. *My Psalm Has Turned into Mourning: Job's Dialogue with the Psalms*. BZAW 437. Berlin: De Gruyter, 2012.

_________. *An Obituary for "Wisdom Literature": The Birth, Death, and Intertextual Reintegration of a Biblical Corpus*. New York: Oxford University Press, 2019.

_________. "Reading Job following the Psalms." Pages 131–45 in *The Shape of the Writings*. Edited by Julius Steinberg and Timothy Stone. Winona Lake, IN: Eisenbrauns, 2015.

_________. "The 'Wisdom Literature' Category: An Obituary." *JTS* 69.1 (2018): 1–24.

Lafferty, Theresa V. *The Prophetic Critique of the Priority of the Cult: A Study of Amos 5:21–24 and Isaiah 1:10–17*. Eugene, OR: Pickwick, 2012.

Lane, Nathan C., II. "Exodus 34:6–7: A Canonical Analysis." PhD diss., Baylor University, 2007.

Lang, David, ed. "Old Testament Parallels," version 1.4, in Accordance. Oaktree, 1999.

Lange, Armin. "The Book of Jeremiah in the Hebrew and Greek Texts of Ben Sira." Pages 118–61 in *Making the Biblical Text: Textual Studies in the Hebrew Bible and the Greek Bible*. Edited by Innocent Himbaza. Fribourg: Academic Press/Göttingen: Vandenhoeck & Ruprecht, 2015.

Lasine, Stuart. "Guest and Host in Judges 19: Lot's Hospitality in an Inverted World." *JSOT* 29 (1984): 37–59.

Lasserre, Guy. *Synopse des Lois du Pentateuque*. VTSup 59. Leiden: Brill, 1994.

Lee, Suk Yee. *An Intertextual Analysis of Zechariah 9–10: The Earlier Restoration Expectations of Second Zechariah*. New York: Bloomsbury T&T Clark, 2015.

LeFebvre, Michael. *Collections, Codes, and Torah: The Re-characterization of Israel's Written Law*. LBHOTS 451. New York: T&T Clark, 2006.

_________. "'On His Law He Meditates': What Is Psalm 1 Introducing?" *JSOT* 40.4 (2016): 439–50.

Lemke, Werner E. "The Synoptic Problem in the Chronicler's History." *HTR* 58 (1965): 349–63.

Leonard, Jeffery M. "Identifying Inner-Biblical Allusions: Psalm 78 as a Test Case." *JBL* 127.2 (2008): 241–65.

_________. "Identifying Subtle Allusions: The Promise of Narrative Tracking." Pages 91–113 in *Subtle Citation, Allusion, and Translation in the Hebrew Bible*. Edited by Ziony Zevit. Sheffield: Equinox, 2017.

_________. "The Psalmist as Historiographer." Pages 9–23 in *Inner Biblical Allusion in the Poetry of Wisdom and Psalms*. Edited by Mark J. Boda, Kevin Chau, and Beth LaNeel Tanner. LHBOTS 659. New York: T&T Clark, 2019.

Lester, G. Brooke. *Daniel Evokes Isaiah: Allusive Characterization of Foreign Rule in the Hebrew-Aramaic Book of Daniel*. LHBOTS 606. London: Bloomsbury T&T Clark, 2015.

_________. "Inner-Biblical Allusion." *Theological Librarianship* 2.2 (2009): 89–93.

_________. "Inner-biblical Interpretation." Pages 444–53 in *The Oxford Encyclopedia of Biblical Interpretation*. Edited by Steven L. McKenzie. New York: Oxford University Press, 2013.

Leuchter, Mark. "The Manumission Laws in Leviticus and Deuteronomy: The Jeremiah Connection." *JBL* 127.4 (2008): 635–53.

_________. "Personal Missives and National History: The Relationship between Jeremiah 29 and 36." Pages 275–93 in *Prophets, Prophecy, and Ancient Israelite Historiography*. Edited by Mark J. Boda and Lissa M. Wray Beal. Winona Lake, IN: Eisenbrauns, 2013.

_________. "'The Prophets' and 'the Levites' in Josiah's Covenant Ceremony." *ZAW* 121 (2009): 31–47.

_________. "Rethinking the 'Jeremiah' Doublet in Ezra-Nehemiah and Chronicles." Pages 183–200 in *What Was Authoritative for Chronicles*. Edited by Ehud Ben Zvi and Diana Edelman. Winona Lake, IN: Eisenbrauns, 2011.

Levine, Amy-Jill and Marc Zvi Brettler. *The Bible With and Without Jesus: How Jews and Christians Read the Same Stories*. New York: HaperOne, 2020.

Levine, Baruch A. *Leviticus*. JPSTC. Philadelphia: Jewish Publication Society, 1989.

Levenson, Jon Douglas. *Esther, a Commentary*. OTL. Louisville: Westminster John Knox, 1997.

_________. "The Sources of Torah: Psalm 119 and the Modes of Revelation in Second Temple Judaism." Pages 559–74 in *Ancient Israelite Religion: Essays in Honor of Frank Moore Cross*. Edited by Patrick D. Miller, Jr., Paul D. Hanson, and S. Dean McBride. Philadelphia: Fortress, 1987.

_________. *Theology of the Program of Restoration of Ezekiel 40–48*. Missoula, MT: Scholars Press for Harvard Semitic Museum, 1976.

Levinson, Bernard M. "'Better That You Should Not Vow Than That You Vow and Not Fulfill': Qoheleth's Use of Textual Allusion and the Transformation of Deuteronomy's Law of Vows." Pages 28–41 in *Reading Ecclesiastes Intertextually*. Edited by Katharine Dell and Will Kynes. New York: Bloomsbury T&T Clark, 2014.

_________. "The Birth of the Lemma: The Restrictive Reinterpretation of the Covenant Code's Manumission Law by the Holiness Code (Leviticus 25:44–46)." *JBL* 124.4 (2005): 617–39.

_________. *Deuteronomy and the Hermeneutics of Legal Innovation*. New York: Oxford University Press, 1997.

_________. "Esarhaddon's Succession Treaty as a Source for the Canon Formula in Deuteronomy 13:1." *JAOS* 130.3 (2010): 337–47.

_________. "The Human Voice in Divine Revelation: The Problem of Authority in Biblical Law." Pages 35–71 in *Innovations in Religious Traditions: Essays in the Interpretation of Religious Change*. Edited by M. A. Williams, C. Cox, and M. S. Jaffee. New York: Mouton de Gruyter, 1992.

_________. *Legal Revision and Religious Renewal in Ancient Israel*. New York: Cambridge University Press, 2008.

_________. *A More Perfect Torah: At the Intersection of Philology and Hermeneutics in Deuteronomy and the Temple Scroll*. Winona Lake, IN: Eisenbrauns, 2013.

_________. *"The Right Chorale": Studies in Biblical Law and Interpretation*. FAT 54. Tübingen: Mohr Siebeck, 2008. Repr., Winona Lake, IN: Eisenbrauns, 2011.

_________. "'You Must Not Add Anything to What I Command You': Paradoxes of Canon and Authorship in Ancient Israel." *Numen* 50 (2003): 1–51.

_________. "Zedekiah's Release of Slaves as the Babylonians Besiege Jerusalem: Jeremiah 34 and the Formation of the Pentateuch." Pages 313–27 in *The Fall of Jerusalem and the Rise of the Torah*. Edited by Peter Dubovský, Dominik Markl, and Jean-Pierre Sonnet. FAT 107. Tübingen: Mohr Siebeck, 2016.

Levinson, Bernard M., and Jeffrey Stackert. "Between the Covenant Code and Esarhaddon's Succession Treaty: Deuteronomy 13 and the Composition of Deuteronomy." *JAJ* 3 (2012): 123–40.

Levinson, Bernard M., and Molly M. Zahn. "Revelation Regained: The Hermeneutics of כי and אם in the Temple Scroll." *Dead Sea Discoveries* 9.3 (2002): 295–346.

Levitt Kohn, Risa. *A New Heart and a New Soul: Ezekiel, the Exile and the Torah*. JSOTSup 358. London: Sheffield Academic, 2002.

_________. "A Prophet Like Moses?: Rethinking Ezekiel's Relationship to the Torah." *ZAW* 114 (2002): 236–54.

Licona, Michael R. *Why Are There Differences in the Gospels?: What We Can Learn from Ancient Biography*. New York: Oxford University Press, 2017.

Liebreich, Leon J. "The Songs of Ascents and the Priestly Blessing." *JBL* 74.1 (1955): 33–36.

Lipschits, Oded. "Literary and Ideological Aspects of Nehemiah 11." *JBL* 121.3 (2002): 423–40.

Longman, Tremper III. *The Fear of the Lord Is Wisdom: A Theological Introduction to Wisdom in Israel*. Grand Rapids: Baker Academic, 2017.

_________. *Job*. BCOTWP. Grand Rapids: Baker Academic, 2012.

_________. *Proverbs*. BCOTWP. Grand Rapids: Baker Academic, 2006.

_________. *Psalms*. TOTC. Downers Grove, IL: InterVarsity Press Academic, 2014.

Lortie, Christopher R. "These Are the Days of the Prophets: A Literary Analysis of Ezra 1–6." *TynBul* 64.2 (2013): 161–69.

Luckenbill, Daniel David. *Historical Records of Assyria from the Earliest Times to Sargon*. Vol. 1 of *Ancient Records of Assyria and Babylonia*. Chicago: University of Chicago Press, 1926.

Lundbom, Jack R. "Haplography in the Hebrew Vorlage of LXX Jeremiah." *Hebrew Studies* 46 (2005): 301–20.

_________. *Jeremiah 1–20*. AB. New York: Doubleday, 1999.

_________. *Jeremiah 37–52*. AB. New York: Doubleday, 2004.

Lunde, Jonathan. "Introduction." Pages 7–41 in *Three Views on the New Testament Use of the Old Testament*. Edited by Kenneth Berding and Jonathan Lunde. Grand Rapids: Zondervan, 2007.

Luz, Ulrich. "Intertexts in the Gospel of Matthew." *HTR* 97.2 (2004): 119–37.

Lynch, Matthew J. "Bursting at the Seams: Phonetic Rhetoric in the Speeches of Elihu." *JSOT* 30.3 (2006): 345–64.

_________. "Mapping Monotheism: Modes of Monotheistic Rhetoric in the Hebrew Bible." *VT* 64 (2014): 47–68.

_________. *Monotheism and Institutions in the Book of Chronicles: Temple, Priesthood, and Kingship in Post-Exilic Perspective*. FAT II 64. Tübingen: Mohr Siebeck, 2014.

_________. "Monotheism in Ancient Israel." Pages 340–48 in *Behind the Scenes of the Old Testament: Cultural, Social, and Historical Contexts*. Edited by Jonathan S. Greer, John H. Wilber, and John H. Walton. Grand Rapids: Baker, 2018.

_________. "Zion's Warrior and the Nations: Isaiah 59:15b–63:6 in Isaiah's Zion Traditions." *CBQ* 70 (2008): 244–63.

Lyons, Michael A. "Extension and Allusion: The Composition of Ezekiel 34." Pages 138–52 in *Ezekiel: Current Debates and Future Directions*. Edited by William A. Tooman and Penelope Barter. FAT 112. Tübingen: Mohr Siebeck, 2017.

_________. *From Law to Prophecy: Ezekiel's Use of the Holiness Code*. New York: T&T Clark, 2009.

_________. "Marking Innerbiblical Allusion in the Book of Ezekiel." *Biblica* 88 (2007): 245–50.

_________. "Out of the (Model) City, into the Fire: The Meaning of Ezekiel 5:3–4." *JBL* 138.3 (2019): 605–23.

_________. "Persuasion and Allusion: The Rhetoric of Text-Referencing in Ezekiel." Pages 76–89 in *Text and Canon: Essays in Honor of John H. Sailhamer*. Edited by Robert L. Cole and Paul J. Kissling. Eugene, OR: Pickwick Publications, 2017.

_________. "Psalm 22 and the 'Servants' of Isaiah 54; 56–66." *CBQ* 77.4 (2015): 640–56.

_________. "Transformation of Law: Ezekiel's Use of the Holiness Code (Leviticus 17–26)." Pages 1–32 in *Transforming Visions: Transformations of Text, Tradition, and Theology in Ezekiel*. Edited by William A. Tooman and Michael A. Lyons. Eugene, OR: Pickwick, 2010.

Mabie, Frederick J. "1 and 2 Chronicles." Pages 23–336 in *1 Chronicles–Job*. EBC 4. Grand Rapids: Zondervan, 2010.

Maclear, G. F. *The Book of Joshua*. CBSC. Cambridge: University Press, 1879.

Macy, Howard Ray. "The Sources of the Book of Chronicles," PhD diss., Harvard University, Cambridge, 1975.

Mann, Thomas W. *The Book of the Former Prophets*. Eugene, OR: Cascade, 2011.

Marcus, David. "Nonrecurring Doublets in the Book of Joel." *CBQ* 56.1 (1994): 56–67.

_________. "Nonrecurring Doublets in the Book of Lamentations." *HAR* 10 (1986): 177–95.

Marlow, Hilary. "Creation Themes in Job and Amos: An Intertextual Relationship?" Pages 142–54 in *Reading Job Intertextually*. Edited by Katharine Dell and Will Kynes. LHBOTS 574. New York: Bloomsbury, 2013.

Mason, Rex. "Some Echoes of the Preaching in the Second Temple?: Tradition Elements in Zechariah 1–8." *ZAW* 96 (1984): 221–35.

Mattison, Kevin. *Rewriting and Revision as Amendment in the Laws of Deuteronomy*. FAT II 100. Tübingen: Mohr Siebeck, 2018.

Mays, James Luther. *Micah, a Commentary*. OTL. Philadelphia: Westminster, 1976.

_________. *Psalms*. IBC. Louisville: Westminster John Knox, 2011.

McCarter, P. Kyle. *I Samuel*. AB. Garden City, NY: Doubleday, 1984.

_________. *II Samuel*. AB. Garden City, NY: Doubleday, 1980.

McCarthy, Dennis J. "'Creation' Motifs in Ancient Hebrew Poetry." *CBQ* 29.3 (1967): 393–406.

_________. "II Samuel 7 and the Structure of the Deuteronomic History." *JBL* 84 (1965): 131–38.

McClellan, Daniel. "The Gods-Complaint: Psalm 82 as a Psalm of Complaint." *JBL* 137.4 (2018): 833–51.

McKane, William. *A Critical and Exegetical Commentary on Jeremiah*. ICC. 2 vols. Edinburgh: T&T Clark, 1986, 1996.

_________. Review of *The Formation of the Book of Jeremiah: Doublets and Recurring Phrases*, by Geoffrey H. Parke-Taylor. *JSS* 47.2 (2002): 326–27.

McKenzie, Steven L. "The Chronicler as Redactor." Pages 70–90 in *The Chronicler as Author: Studies in Text and Texture*. Edited by M. Patrick Graham and Steven L. McKenzie. JSOTSup 263. Sheffield: Sheffield Academic, 1999.

_________. *The Chronicler's Use of the Deuteronomistic History*. HSM 63. Atlanta: Scholars Press, 1984.

_________. "The Divided Kingdom in the Deuteronomistic History and in Scholarship on It." Pages 135–45 in *The Future of the Deuteronomistic History*. Edited by Thomas C. Römer. Leuven: Leuven University Press, 2000.

_________. "The Jacob Tradition in Hosea XII 4–5." *VT* 36.3 (1986): 312–22.

McKenzie, Tracy. "Edom's Desolation and Adam's Multiplication: Parallelism in Ezekiel 35:1–36:15." Page 90–119 in *Text and Canon: Essays in Honor of John H. Sailhamer*. Edited by Robert L. Cole and Paul J. Kissling. Eugene, OR: Pickwick Publications, 2017.

McLaughlin, John L. "Is Amos (Still) among the Wise?" *JBL* 133.2 (2014): 281–303.

_________. "Their Hearts *Were* Hardened: The Use of Isaiah 6,6–10 in the Book of Isaiah." *Biblica* 75.1 (1994): 1–25.

Meek, Russell L. "Fear God and Enjoy His Gifts: Qoheleth's Edenic Vision of Life." *CTR* 14.1 (2016): 23–34.

_________. "Intertextuality, Inner-Biblical Exegesis, and Inner-Biblical Allusion: The Ethics of a Methodology." *Biblica* 95.1 (2014): 280–91.

Melvin, David P. "There Is a God in Heaven Who Reveals Mysteries: Failed Divination and Divine Revelation in Daniel 2 and Genesis 41." *BBR* 29.2 (2019): 139–53.

Mettinger, Tryggue N. D. "Intertextuality: Allusion and Vertical Context Systems in Some Job Passages." Pages 257–80 in *Of Prophets' Visions and the Wisdom of the Sages: Essays in Honour of R. Norman Whybray on his Seventieth Birthday*. Edited by Heather A. McKay and David J. A. Clines. JSOTSup 162. Sheffield: JSOT Press, 1993.

Meyers, Carol, and Eric Meyers. *Haggai, Zechariah 1–8*. AB. New York: Doubleday, 1987.
________. *Zechariah 9–14*. AB. New York: Doubleday, 1993.
Middlemas, Jill. *The Templeless Age: An Introduction to the History, Literature, and Theology of the "Exile."* Louisville: Westminster John Knox, 2007.
Milgrom, Jacob. "The Concept of *Ma'al* in the Bible and the Ancient Near East," *JAOS* 96 (1976): 236–47.
________. "The Consecration of the Priests: A Literary Comparison of Leviticus 8 and Exodus 29." Pages 273–86 in *Ernten, was man sät: Festschrift für Klaus Koch zu seinem 65. Geburtstag*. Edited by Dwight R. Daniels, Uwe Gleßmer und Martin Rösel. Neukirchen-Vluyn: Neukirchener Verlag, 1991.
________. *Cult and Conscience: The* Asham *and the Priestly Doctrine of Repentance*. Leiden: Brill, 1976.
________. "Ezekiel and the Levites." Pages 3–12 in *Sacred History, Sacred Literature: Essays on Ancient Israel, the Bible, and Religion in Honor of R. E. Friedman on His Sixtieth Birthday*. Edited by Shawna Dolansky. Winona Lake, IN: Eisenbrauns, 2008.
________. *Leviticus 1–16*. AB. New York: Doubleday, 1991.
________. *Leviticus 17–22*. AB. New York: Doubleday, 2000.
________. *Leviticus 23–27*. AB. New York: Doubleday, 2001.
________. "Leviticus 26 and Ezekiel." Pages 57–62 in *The Quest for Context and Meaning: Studies in Biblical Intertextuality in Honor of James A. Sanders*. Edited by Craig A. Evans and Shemaryahu Talmon. Leiden: Brill, 1997.
________. *Numbers*. JPSTC. Philadelphia: Jewish Publication Society, 1990.
________. "Profane Slaughter and a Formulaic Key to the Composition of Deuteronomy." *HUCA* 47 (1976): 1–17.
________. *Studies in Levitical Terminology, I: The Encroacher and the Levite, The Term 'Aboda*. Berkeley: University of California Press, 1970.
Millard, Alan R. "A Wandering Aramean." *JNES* 39.2 (1980): 153–55.
Miller, Cynthia L. "Ellipsis Involving Negation in Biblical Hebrew." Pages 37–52 in *Seeking Out the Wisdom of the Ancients: Essays Offered to Honor Michael V. Fox on the Occasion of His Sixty-Fifth Birthday*. Edited by Ronald L. Troxel, Kelvin G. Friebel, and Dennis R. Magray. Winona Lake, IN: Eisenbrauns. 2005.
Miller, Geoffrey D. "Intertextuality in Old Testament Research." *CurBR* 9.3 (2010): 283–309.
Miller, J. Maxwell. "The Israelite Journey through (around) Moab and Moabite Toponymy." *JBL* 108.4 (1989): 577–95.
Miller, Patrick D., Jr. "Syntax and Theology in Genesis XII 3a." *VT* 34.4 (1984): 472–76.
Miller-Naudé, Cynthia L., and Ziony Zevit, eds. *Diachrony in Biblical Hebrew*. Winona Lake, IN: Eisenbrauns, 2012.
Mintz, Alan. "The Rhetoric of Lamentations and the Representation of Catastrophe." *Prooftexts* 2.1 (1982): 1–17.
Mirsky, Aharon. *Deuteronomy*. DM. Jerusalem: Mosad Harav Kook, 2001 [Hebrew].
Mirsky, Aaron, Feiwel Meltzer, and Yehudah Kiel. *Twelve*. DM. 2 vols. Jerusalem: Massad Harav Kook, 1972 [Hebrew].
Mitchell, Christine. "The Ironic Death of Josiah in 2 Chronicles." *CBQ* 68 (2006): 421–35.
________. "A Note on the Creation Formula in Zechariah 12:1–8; Isaiah 42:5–6; and Old Persian Inscriptions." *JBL* 133.2 (2014): 305–8.
Mitchell, H. G., J. M. P. Smith, J. A. Bewer, *A Critical and Exegetical Commentary on Haggai, Zechariah, Malachi, and Jonah*. ICC. New York: Scribner's Sons, 1912.
Mollo, Paola. "Did It Please God to Kill Them?: Literary Comparison between the Birth Accounts of Samson and Samuel." *Henoch* 36.1 (2014): 86–105.
Montgomery, James A. *The Book of Kings*. ICC. Edinburgh: T&T Clark, 1951.
Moo, Douglas J. *The Old Testament in the Gospel Passion Narratives*. Sheffield: Almond Press, 1983.
Moo, Douglas J., and Andrew David Naselli. "The Problem of the New Testament's Use of the Old Testament." Pages 383–406 in *The Enduring Authority of Christian Scripture*. Edited by D. A. Carson. Grand Rapids: Eerdmans, 2016.
Morales, L. Michael. *Exodus Old and New: A Biblical Theology of Redemption*. Downers Grove, IL: IVP Academic, 2020.
________. *Who Shall Ascend the Mountain of the Lord?: A Biblical Theology of the Book of Leviticus*. Downers Grove, IL: InterVarsity Press, 2015.
Moran, W. L. "Gen 49,10 and Its Use in Ez 21,32." *Biblica* 39.4 (1958): 405–25.
________. "The Literary Connection between Lv 11,13–19 and Dt 14,12–18." *CBQ* 28 (1966): 271–77.
Morrow, William S. *An Introduction to Biblical Law*. Grand Rapids: Eerdmans, 2017.
Mowinckel, Sigmund. *The Spirit and the Word: Prophecy and Tradition in Ancient Israel*. Edited by K. C. Hanson. Minneapolis: Fortress, 2002.
________. *Zur Komposition des Buches Jeremia*. Oslo: Dybwad, 1914.
Moyise, Steve. *The Old Testament in the New: An Introduction*. 2nd ed. New York: Bloomsbury, 2015.
________. *Paul and Scripture: Studying the New Testament Use of the Old Testament*. Grand Rapids: Baker Academic, 2010.
Müller, Reinhard, Juha Pakkala, and Bas ter Haar Romney. *Evidence of Editing: Growth and Change of Texts in the Hebrew Bible*. Atlanta: Society of Biblical Literature, 2014.
Muraoka, T. *A Greek ≈ Hebrew/Aramaic Two-way Index to the Septuagint*. Louvain: Peeters, 2010.
Murawski, Bryan. "'To Study the Law of the Lord': The Use of Deuteronomy in Ezra-Nehemiah." PhD diss., Westminster Theological Seminary, 2020.
________. "'Who Shall Go Up First?': Inner-biblical Interpretation in the Prologue of Judges." Paper presented at the Annual Meeting of the Evangelical Theological Society, online, 18 November 2020.

Murphy, Roland E. *The Song of Songs*. Hermeneia. Minneapolis: Fortress, 1990.

Na'aman, Nadav. "Ḫabiru and Hebrews: The Transfer of a Social Term to the Literary Sphere." *JNES* 45.4 (1986): 271–88.

Nelson, Richard. *Deuteronomy, a Commentary*. OTL. Louisville: Westminster John Knox, 2002.

Neusner, Jacob, trans. *Sifra: An Analytical Translation*. 3 vols. Atlanta: Scholars Press, 1988.

Newman, Judith H. *Praying by the Book: The Scripturalization of Prayer in Second Temple Judaism*. Atlanta: Scholars Press, 1999.

Newsom, Carol A. *Daniel, a Commentary*. OTL. Louisville: Westminster John Knox, 2014.

Nicol, George G. "Isaiah's Vision and the Visions of Daniel." *VT* 29.4 (1979): 501–4.

Nicholson, E. W. "The Meaning of the Expression עם הארץ in the Old Testament." *JSS* 10 (1965): 59–66.

_________. *Preaching to the Exiles: A Study of the Prose Traditions in the Book of Jeremiah*. New York: Schocken Books, 1970.

Niditch, Susan. "The 'Sodomite' Theme in Judges 19–20: Family, Community, and Social Disintegration." *CBQ* 44 (1982): 365–78.

Niehaus, Jeffrey. "The Central Sanctuary: Where and When?" *TynBul* 43.1 (1992): 3–30.

Nielsen, Kirsten. "Whose Song of Praise?: Reflections on the Purpose of the Psalm in 1 Chronicles 16." Pages 327–59 in *The Chronicler as Author: Studies in Text and Texture*. Edited by M. Patrick Graham and Steven L. McKenzie. JSOTSup 263. Sheffield: Sheffield Academic, 1999.

Nihan, Christophe. "Ethnicity and Identity in Isaiah 56–66." Pages 67–104 in *Judah and the Judeans in the Achaemenid Period: Negotiating Identity in an International Context*. Edited by Oded Lipschits, Gary N. Knoppers, and Manfred Oeming. Winona Lake, IN: Eisenbrauns, 2011.

_________. "Ezekiel 34–37 and Leviticus 26: A Reevaluation." Pages 153–78 in *Ezekiel: Current Debates and Future Directions*. Edited by William A. Tooman and Penelope Barter. FAT 112. Tübingen: Mohr Siebeck, 2017.

_________. "The Laws about Clean and Unclean Animals in Leviticus and Deuteronomy and Their Place in the Formation of the Pentateuch." Pages 401–32 in *The Pentateuch: International Perspectives on Current Research*. Edited by Thomas B. Dozeman, Konrad Schmidt, and Baruch J. Schwartz. FAT 78. Tübingen: Mohr Siebeck, 2011.

_________. "Textual Fluidity and Rewriting in Parallel Traditions: The Case of Samuel and Chronicles." *JAJ* 4 (2013): 186–209.

Nogalski, James. "The Day(s) of YHWH in the Book of the Twelve." Pages 192–213 in *Thematic Threads in the Book of the Twelve*. Edited by Paul L. Redditt and Aaron Schart. BZAW 325. Berlin: de Gruyter, 2003.

_________. "Intertextuality and the Twelve." Pages 102–24 in *Forming Prophetic Literature: Essays on Isaiah and the Twelve in Honor of John D. W. Watts*. Edited by James W. Watts and Paul R. House. JSOTSup 235. Sheffield: Sheffield Academic, 1996.

_________. "Joel as 'Literary Anchor' for the Book of the Twelve." Pags 91–109 in *Reading and Hearing the Book of the Twelve*. Edited by James D. Nogalski and Marvin A. Sweeney. Atlanta: Society of Biblical Literature, 2000.

_________. "The Problematic Suffixes of Amos IX 11." *VT* 43.3 (1993): 411–18.

_________. *Redactional Processes in the Book of the Twelve*. BZAW 218. Berlin: De Gruyter, 1993.

_________. "These Seventy Years: Intertextual Observations and Postulations on Jeremiah and the Twelve." Pages 247–58 in *History, Memory, Hebrew Scriptures: A Festschrift for Ehud Ben Zvi*. Edited by Ian Douglas Wilson and Diana V. Edelman. Winona Lake, IN: Eisenbrauns, 2015.

Noonan, Benjamin J. *Advances in the Study of Biblical Hebrew and Aramaic: New Insights for Reading the Old Testament*. Grand Rapids: Zondervan Academic, 2020.

_________. "Unraveling Hebrew שַׁעַטְנֵז." *JBL* 135.1 (2016): 95–101.

Noth, Martin. *The Deuteronomistic History*. JSOTSup 15. Sheffield: Sheffield Academic, 1981.

Nurmela, Risto. "The Growth of the Book of Isaiah Illustrated by Allusions in Zechariah." Pages 245–59 in *Bringing Out the Treasure: Inner Biblical Allusion in Zechariah 9–14*. Edited by Mark J. Boda and Michael H. Floyd. New York: T&T Clark International, 2003.

Nysse, Richard. "Keeping Company with Nahum: Reading the Oracles against the Nations as Scripture." *Word & World* 15.4 (1995): 412–19.

O'Connell, Robert H. *The Rhetoric of the Book of Judges*. VTSup 63. Leiden: E. J. Brill, 1996.

Oded, B. "The Table of Nations (Genesis 10)—A Socio-cultural Approach." *ZAW* 98.1 (1986): 14–31.

O'Dowd, Ryan P. "Poetic Allusions in Agur's Oracle in Proverbs 30.1–9." Pages 103–19 in *Inner Biblical Allusion in the Poetry of Wisdom and Psalms*. Edited by Mark J. Boda, Kevin Chau, and Baath LaNeel Tanner. New York: T&T Clark, 2019.

Oeming, Manfred. "To Be Adam or Not to Be Adam: The Hidden Fundamental Anthropological Discourse Revealed in an Intertextual Reading of Job and Genesis." Pages 19–29 in *Reading Job Intertextually*. Edited by Katharine Dell and Will Kynes. LHBOTS 574. New York: Bloomsbury, 2013.

_________. "Wisdom as a Central Category in the Book of the Chronicler: The Significance of the *Talio* Principle in a Sapiental Construction of History." Pages 125*–41* in *Shai le-Sara Japhet: Studies in the Bible, its Exegesis and its Literature*. Edited by Moshe Bar-Asher et al. Jerusalem: Bialik Institute, 2007.

Olive Tree Cross References: Expanded Set. Nashville: Olive Tree, n.d.

Orian, Matan. "Numbers 20:14–21 as a Reply to Deuteronomy 23:4–9." *VT* 69 (2019): 109–16.

Oswald, Wolfgang. "Genesis Materials in the Book of Exodus: Explicit Back References." Pages 157–70 in *Book-Seams in the Hexateuch I: The Literary Transitions between the Books of Genesis/Exodus and Joshua/Judges*. Edited by Christoph Berner and Harald Samuel. FAT 120. Tübingen: Mohr Siebeck, 2018.

Oswalt, John N. *Isaiah*. NIVAC. Grand Rapids: Zondervan, 2003.

Owen, H. *Critica Sacra; or, a Short Introduction to Hebrew Criticism*. London: Bowyer and Nichols, 1774.

Ozolins, Kaspars. "Killing Goliath?: Elhanan the Bethlehemite and the Text of 2 Samuel 21:19." Paper presented at Society of Biblical Literature, 1 December 2020.

Page, Sydney H. T. "Satan: God's Servant." *JETS* 50.3 (2007): 49–65.

Pakkala, Juha. "The Quotations of References of the Pentateuchal Laws in Ezra-Nehemiah." Pages 193–221 in *Changes in Scripture: Rewriting and Interpreting Authoritative Traditions in the Second Temple Period*. Edited by Hanne von Weissenberg, Juha Pakkala, and Marko Marttila. Göttingen: de Gruyter, 2011.

Parke-Taylor, Geoffrey H. *The Formation of the Book of Jeremiah: Doublets and Recurring Phrases*. Atlanta: Society of Biblical Literature, 2000.

Parker, Kim Ian. "Repetition as a Structuring Device in 1 Kings 1–11." *JSOT* 42 (1988): 19–27.

Pate, Brian. "Who Is Speaking? The Use of Isaiah 8:17–18 in Hebrews 2:13 as a Case Study for Applying the Speech of Key OT Figures to Christ." *JETS* 59.4 (2016): 731–45.

Patton, Corrine. "'I Myself Gave Them Laws that Were Not Good': Ezekiel 20 and the Exodus Traditions." *JSOT* 69 (1996): 73–90.

Patton, Matthew H. "Working with Biblical Hebrew Prose." Pages 23–144 in *Basics of Hebrew Discourse: A Guide to Working with Biblical Hebrew Prose and Poetry*. Edited by Miles V. Van Pelt. Grand Rapids: Zondervan Academic, 2019.

Paul, Shalom M. *Amos*. Hermeneia. Minneapolis: Fortress, 1991.

_________. *Studies in the Book of the Covenant in the Light of Cuneiform and Biblical Law*. Leiden: Brill, 1970.

Perdue, Leo G. *Wisdom in Revolt: Metaphorical Theology in the Book of Job*. JSOTSup 112. Sheffield: Sheffield Academic, 1991.

Petersen, David L. *Haggai and Zechariah 1–8, a Commentary*. OTL. Philadelphia: Westminster, 1984.

_________. *Late Israelite Prophecy: Studies in Deutero-Prophetic Literature and in Chronicles*. Missoula, MO: Scholars Press, 1977.

Peterson, Brian. "Did the Vassal Treaties of Esarhaddon Influence the Chronicler's Succession Narrative of Solomon?" *BBR* 28.4 (2018): 554–74.

_________. "Ezekiel's Perspective of Israel's History: Selective Revisionism?" Pages 295–314 in *Prophets, Prophecy, and Ancient Israelite Historiography*. Mark J. Boda and Lissa M. Wray Beal. Winona Lake, IN: Eisenbrauns, 2013.

Pfeiffer, Robert H. "The Dual Origin of Hebrew Monotheism." *JBL* 46.3 (1927): 193–206.

Philo, *Life of Moses II*. Edited and translated by F. H. Colson. LCL 289. Cambridge: Harvard University Press, 1935.

Philpot, Joshua M. "Was Joseph a Type of Daniel? Typological Correspondence in Genesis 37–50 and Daniel 1–6." *JETS* 61.4 (2018): 681–96.

Pitkänen, Pekka. *Central Sanctuary and Centralization of Worship in Ancient Israel*. Piscataway, NJ: Gorgias Press, 2014.

Pleins, J. David. *The Social Visions of the Hebrew Bible: A Theological Introduction*. Louisville: Westminster John Knox, 2001.

Polaski, Donald C. "Reflections on a Mosaic Covenant: The Eternal Covenant (Isaiah 24.5) and Intertextuality." *JSOT* 77 (1998): 55–73.

Postell, Seth D. "Abram as Israel, Israel as Abraham: Literary Analogy as Macro-Structural Stategy in the Torah." Pages 16–36 in *Text and Canon: Essays in Honor of John H. Sailhamer*. Edited by Robert L. Cole and Paul J. Kissling. Eugene, OR: Pickwick Publications, 2017.

_________. "A Literary, Compositional, and Intertextual Analysis of Psalm 45." *BSac* 176 (2019): 146–63.

_________. "The Old Testament in the Old Testament." Pages 93–102 in *The Moody Handbook of Messianic Prophecy: Studies and Expositions of the Messiah in the Old Testament*. Edited by Michael Rydelnik and Edwin Blum. Chicago: Moody Publishers, 2019.

_________. "Potiphar's Wife in David's Looking Glass: Reading 2 Samuel 11–12 as a Reflection Story of Genesis 39." *TynBul* 71.1 (2020): 95–113.

Propp, William H. C. *Exodus 1–18*. AB. New York: Doubleday, 1999.

_________. *Exodus 19–40*. AB. New York: Doubleday, 2006.

Pyeon, Yohan. *You Have Not Spoken What Is Right About Me: Intertextuality and the Book of Job*. New York: Lang, 2003.

Quick, Laura. "The Book of Ruth and the Limits of Proverbial Wisdom. *JBL* 139.1 (2020):47–66.

Raabe, Paul R. "King Hezekiah in Isaiah" *JBTS* 4.1 (2019): 67–81.

von Rad, Gerhard. *Deuteronomy, a Commentary*. OTL. Philadelphia: Westminster, 1966.

_________. *From Genesis to Chronicles: Explorations in Old Testament Theology*. Edited by K. C. Hanson. Translated by R. Smend. Minneapolis: Fortress, 2005.

_________. *Das Geschichtsbild des Chronistischen Werks*. Beiträge zur Wissenschaft vom Alten und Neuen Testament 3. Stuttgart: Kohlhammer, 1930.

_________. *The Message of the Prophets*. Translated by D. M. G. Stalker. New York: Harper & Row, 1967.

_________. *Moses*. 2nd ed. Translated by Stephen Neill. Eugene, OR: Cascade, 2011.

_________. *Old Testament Theology*. Translated by D. M. G. Stalker. 2 vols. New York: Harper & Row, 1965.

_________. *Studies in Deuteronomy*. Translated by David Stalker. London: SCM, 1953.

_________. *Wisdom in Israel*. Translated by James D. Martin. Nashville: Abingdon Press, 1972.

Radner, Ephraim, and George Sumner, eds. *The Rule of Faith: Scripture, Canon, and Creed in a Critical Age*. New York: Morehouse, 1998.

Rausche, Benedikt. "The Relevance of Purity in Second Temple Judaism according to Ezra-Nehemiah." Pages 457–75 in *Purity and the Forming of Religious Traditions in the Ancient Mediterranean World and Ancient Judaism*. Edited by Christian Frevel and Christophe Nihan. Leiden: Brill, 2013.

Redditt, Paul L. "The Book of Joel and Peripheral Prophecy." *CBQ* 48.2 (1986): 225–40.

_________. "Zerubbabel, Joshua, and the Night Visions of Zechariah." *CBQ* 54.2 (1992): 249–59.

Regev, Eyal. "Were the Early Christians Sectarians?" *JBL* 130.4 (2011): 771–93.

Reif, Stefan C. "Ibn Ezra on Psalm I 1–2." *VT* 34.2 (1984): 232–36.

Rendall, Robert. "Quotation in Scripture as an Index of Wider Reference." *EvQ* 36.4 (1964): 214–21.

Rendtorff, Rolf. *Canon and Theology: Overtures to an Old Testament Theology*. Minneapolis: Fortress, 1993.

_________. *The Canonical Hebrew Bible: A Theology of the Old Testament*. Translated by David E. Orton. Dorset, UK: Deo, 2005.

_________. "Chronicles and the Priestly Torah." Pages 259–66 in *Texts, Temples, and Traditions: A Tribute to Menahem Haran*. Edited by Michael V. Fox et al. Winona Lake, IN: Eisenbrauns, 1996.

_________. *The Covenant Formula: An Exegetical and Theological Investigation*. Translated by Margaret Kohl. Edinburgh: T&T Clark, 1998.

_________. "How to Read the Book of the Twelve as a Theological Unity." Pages 75–87 in *Reading and Hearing the Book of the Twelve*. Edited by James D. Nogalski and Marvin A. Sweeney. Atlanta: Society of Biblical Literature, 2000.

Renz, Thomas. "Torah in the Minor Prophets." Pages 73–94 in *Reading the Law: Studies in Honour of Gordon J. Wenham*. Edited by J. G. McConville and Karl Möller. T&T Clark, 2007.

Reymond, Eric D. *Innovations in Hebrew Poetry: Parallelism and the Poems of Sirach*. Atlanta: Society of Biblical Literature, 2004.

_________. "New Readings in the Ben Sira Masada Scroll (Mas 1h)." *Revue de Qumrân* 26.3 (2014): 327–43.

Rezetko, Robert, and Ian Young, *Historical Linguistics and Biblical Hebrew: Steps Toward an Integrated Approach*. Atlanta: Society of Biblical Literature, 2014.

Richards, Ruth. "The Influence of Hosea on Jeremiah." PhD diss., Boston University, 1927.

Richter, Sandra L. *The Deuteronomistic History and the Name Theology:* lᵉšakkē šᵉmô šām *in the Bible and the Ancient Near East*. BZAW 318. Berlin: Walter de Gruyter, 2002.

_________. "The Place of the Name." *VT* 57 (2007): 342–66.

_________. "Placing the Name, Pushing the Paradigm: A Decade with the Deuteronomistic Name Formula." Pages 64–78 in *Deuteronomy in the Pentateuch, Hexateuch, and the Deuteronomistic History*. Edited by Konrad Schmid and Raymond F. Person. FAT 56. Tübingen: Mohr Siebeck, 2012.

Rindge, Matthew S. "Jewish Identity under Foreign Rule: Daniel 2 as a Reconfiguration of Genesis 41." *JBL* 129.1 (2010): 85–104.

Robertson, O. Palmer. *The Books of Nahum, Habakkuk, and Zephaniah*. NICOT. Grand Rapids: Eerdmans, 1990.

Robinson, Bernard P. "Rahab of Canaan—and Israel." *SJOT* 23.2 (2009): 257–73.

Robson, James E. *Deuteronomy 1–11*. BHHB. Waco: Baylor University Press, 2016.

Rom-Shiloni, Dalit. "From Prophetic Words to Prophetic Literature: Challenging Paradigms That Control Our Academic Thought on Jeremiah and Ezekiel." *JBL* 138.3 (2019): 565–86.

_________. "'How can you say, 'I am not defiled . . .'?" (Jeremiah 2:20–25): Allusions to Priestly Legal Traditions in the Poetry of Jeremiah." *JBL* 133.4 (2014): 757–75.

Rooker, Mark F. "Diachronic Analysis and the Features of Late Biblical Hebrew." *BBR* 4 (1994): 135–44.

_________. "The Use of the Old Testament in the Book of Ezekiel." *Faith and Mission* 15.2 (1998): 45–52.

_________. "The Use of the Old Testament in the Book of Hosea." *CTR* 7.1 (1993): 51–66.

Ross, Jillian L. "A People Heeds Not Scripture: A Poetics of Pentateuchal Allusions in the Book of Judges." PhD diss., Trinity Evangelical Divinity School, Deerfield, IL, 2015.

Ross, William A. "Text-Critical Question Begging in Nahum 1,2–8: Re-evaluating the Evidence and Arguments." *ZAW* 127.3 (2015): 459–74.

Roth, Martha T. *Law Collections from Mesopotamia and Asia Minor*. 2nd ed. Atlanta: Society of Biblical Literature, 1997.

Rudolph, Wilhelm. "Problems of the Books of Chronicles." *VT* 4.4 (1954): 401–9.

Rüterswörden, Udo. "Concerning Deut 14." Pages 95–103 in *What Is Bible?* Edited by Karin Finsterbusch and Armin Lange. Leuven: Peeters, 2012.

Rydelnik, Michael A. "The Teacher of Righteousness: A Messianic Interpretation of Joel 2:23." *BSac* 176 (2019): 164–73.

Ryle, Herbert Edward. *The Books of Ezra and Nehemiah*. CBSC. Cambridge: University Press, 1893.

Sailhamer, John. "The Messiah and the Hebrew Bible." *JETS* 44.1 (2001): 5–23.

_________. *The Pentateuch as Narrative: A Biblical-Theological Commentary*. Grand Rapids: Zondervan, 1992.

Samely, Alexander. *Forms of Rabbinic Literature and Thought: An Introduction*. New York: Oxford University Press, 2007.

Sandy, D. Brent. *Plowshares & Pruning Hooks: Rethinking the Language of Biblical Prophecy and Apocalyptic*. Downers Grove, IL: InterVarsity Press, 2002.

Sarna, Nahum M. *Exodus*. JPSTC. Philadelphia: Jewish Publication Society, 1991.

_________. *Genesis*. JPSTC. Philadelphia: Jewish Publication Society, 1989.

_________. *On the Book of Psalms: Exploring the Prayers of Ancient Israel*. New York: Schocken Books, 1993.

_________. "Psalm 89: A Study of Inner Biblical Exegesis." Pages 29–46 in *Biblical and Other Studies*. Edited by Alexander Altmann. Cambridge: Harvard University Press, 1963.

_________. "Zedekiah's Emancipation of Slaves and the Sabbatical Year." Pages 143–49 in *Orient and Occident: Essays Presented to Cyrus H. Gordon on the Occasion of His Sixty-Fifth Birthday*. Edited by Harry A. Hoffner, Jr. Kevelaer: Butzon & Berker, 1973.

Sasson, Jack M. *Jonah*. AB. New York: Doubleday, 1990.

Saur, Markus. "Qohelet as a Reader of Proverbs." Pages 129–38 in *Reading Ecclesiastes Intertextually*. Edited by Katharine Dell and Will Kynes. New York: Bloomsbury T&T Clark, 2014.

Savran, George. "The Character as Narrator in Biblical Narrative." *Prooftexts* 5.1 (1985): 1–17.

Saysell, Csilla. *"According to the Law": Reading Ezra 9–10 as Christian Scripture*. Winona Lake, IN: Eisenbrauns, 2012.

Scalise, Pamela J. "Baruch as First Reader: Baruch's Lament in the Structure of the Book of Jeremiah." Pages 291–307 in *Uprooting and Planting: Essays on Jeremiah for Leslie Allen*. Edited by John Goldingay. New York: T&T Clark, 2007.

Schaper, Joachim. "Rereading the Law: Inner-Biblical Exegesis of Divine Oracles in Ezekiel 44 and Isaiah 56." Pages 125–44 in *Recht und Ethik im Alten Testament: Beiträge des Symposiuns 'Das Alte Testament und die Kultur der Moderne' anlässlich des 100. Geburtstegs Gerhard von Rads (1901–1971) Heidelberg, 18–21, Oktober 2001*. Edited by Bernard M. Levinson and Eckart Otto. Münster: LIT, 2004.

Scheetz, Jordan M. *The Concept of Canonical Intertextuality and the Book of Daniel*. Eugene, OR: Pickwick, 2011.

Schellekens, Jona. "Accession Days and Holidays: The Origins of the Jewish Festival of Purim." *JBL* 128.1 (2009): 115–34.

Schellenberg, Angeline Falk. "One in the Bond of War: The Unity of Deutro-Zechariah." *Didaslalia* 12.2 (2001): 101–15.

Schellenberg, Annette. "'May Her Breasts Satisfy You at All Times' (Prov 5:19): On the Erotic Passages in Proverbs and Sirach and the Question of How They Relate to the Song of Songs." *VT* 68 (2018): 252–71.

Schenker, Adrian. "The Biblical Legislation of the Release of Slaves: The Road from Exodus to Leviticus." *JSOT* 78 (1998): 23–41.

Schipper, Jeremy. "Deuteronomy 24:5 and King Asa's Foot Disease in 1 Kings 15:23." *JBL* 128.4 (2009): 643–48.

Schley, Donald D., Jr. "1 Kings 10:26–29: A Reconsideration." *JBL* 106.4 (1987): 595–601.

Schlimm, Matthew Richard. "Jealousy or Furnace Remelting?: A Response to Nissim Amzallag." *JBL* 136.3 (2017): 513–28.

Schmid, Konrad. "How to Date the Book of Jeremiah: Combining and Modifying Linguistic and Profile-based Approaches." *VT* 68.3 (2018): 444–62.

Schmitz, Philip C. "The Grammar of Resurrection in Isaiah 26:19a-c." *JBL* 122 (2003): 145–49.

Schniedewind, William M. "The Chronicler as an Interpreter of Scripture." Pages 158–80 in *The Chronicler as Author: Studies in Text and Texture*. Edited by M. Patrick Graham and Steven L. McKenzie. JSOTSup 263. Sheffield: Sheffield Academic, 1999.

_________. "Innerbiblical Exegesis." Pages 502–9 in *Dictionary of the Old Testament: Historical Books*. Edited by Bill T. Arnold and H. G. M. Williamson. Downers Grove, IL: InterVarsity Press, 2005.

_________. "Prophets and Prophecy in the Books of Chronicles." Pages 204–24 in *The Chronicler as Historian*. Edited by M. Patrick Graham, Kenneth G. Hoglund, and Steven L. McKenzie. JSOTSup 238. Sheffield: Sheffield Academic, 1997.

_________. *A Social History of Hebrew: Its Origins Through the Rabbinic Period*, AYBRL. New Haven: Yale University Press, 2013.

_________. *Society and the Promise to David: The Reception History of 2 Samuel 7:1–17*. New York: Oxford University Press, 1999.

_________. "The Source Citations of Manasseh: King Manasseh in History and Homily." *VT* 41.4 (1991): 450–61.

_________. *The Word of God in Transition: From Prophet to Exegete in the Second Temple*. JSOTSup 197. Sheffield: Sheffield Academic, 1995.

Schnittjer, Gary Edward. "The Bad Ending of Ezra-Nehemiah." *BSac* 173 (2016): 32–56.

_________. "The Blessing of Judah as Generative Expectation." *BSac* 177 (2020): 15–39.

_________. *Ezra-Nehemiah*. Baker Commentary on the Old Testament: Historical Books. Grand Rapids: Baker Academic, forthcoming.

_________. "Idolatry in Isaiah." *Credo Magazine* 8.2 (2018).

_________. "Individual versus Collective Retribution in the Chronicler's Ideology of Exile." *JBTS* 4.1 (2019): 113–32.

_________. "Kadesh Infidelity of Deuteronomy 1 and Its Synoptic Implications." *JETS* 63.1 (2020): 95–120.

_________. *The Torah Story*. Grand Rapids: Zondervan Academic, 2006.

_________. *The Torah Story Video Lectures*. Grand Rapids: Zondervan Academic, 2017.

Schoors, Antoon. "(Mis)use of Intertextuality in Qoheleth Exegesis." Pages 45–59 in *Congress Volume: Olso 1998*. Edited by André Lemaire and Magne Sæbø. VTSup 80. Leiden: Brill, 2000.

Schultz, Richard L. "'Fear God and Keep His Commandments' (Eccl 12:13): An Examination of Some Intertextual Relationships between Deuteronomy and Ecclesiastes." Pages 327–43 in *For Our God Always: Studies on the Message and Influence of Deuteronomy in Honor of Daniel I. Block*. Edited by Jason S. DeRouchie, Jason Gile, and Kenneth J. Turner. Winona Lake, IN: Eisenbrauns, 2013.

_________. "Intertextuality, Canon, and 'Undecidability': Understanding Isaiah's 'New Heavens and New Earth' (Isaiah 65:17–25)." *BBR 20*.1 (2010): 19–38.

_________. "Isaianic Intertextuality and Intratextuality as Composition-Historical Indicators: Methodological Challenges in Determining Literary Influence." Pages 33–64 in *Bind Up the Testimony: Exploration of the Genesis of the Book of Isaiah*. Edited by Daniel I. Block and Richard L. Schultz. Peabody, MA: Hendrickson, 2015.

_________. "Job and Ecclesiastes: Intertextuality and a Protesting Pair." Pages 190–203 in *Reading Job Intertextually*. Edited by Katharine Dell and Will Kynes. LHBOTS 574. New York: Bloomsbury, 2013.

_________. "Qoheleth and Isaiah in Dialogue." Pages 57–70 in *Reading Ecclesiastes Intertextually*. Edited by Katharine Dell and Will Kynes. New York: Bloomsbury T&T Clark, 2014.

_________. "The Reuse of Deuteronomy's 'Law of the Vow' in Ecclesiastes 5.3–5[4–6] as an Exemplar of Intertextuality and Reinterpretation in Ecclesiastes 4.17–5.6[5.1–7]." Pages 120–32 in *Inner Biblical Allusion in the Poetry of Wisdom and Psalms*. Edited by Mark J. Boda, Kevin Chau, and Beth LaNeel Tanner. LHBOTS 659. New York: T&T Clark, 2019.

_________. *The Search for Quotation: Verbal Parallels in the Prophets*. JSOTSup 180. Sheffield: Sheffield Academic, 1999.

_________. "The Ties that Bind: Intertextuality, the Identification of Verbal Parallels, and Reading Strategies in the Book of the Twelve." Pages 27–45 in *Thematic Threads in the Book of the Twelve*. Edited by Paul L. Redditt and Aaron Schart. New York: de Gruyter, 2003.

_________. "Was Qohelet an Eschatological or an Anti-Apocalyptic Sage?: Hebel, the Evil Day, and Divine Judgment in the Book of Ecclesiastes." Pages 199–214 in *Riddles and Revelations: Explorations into the Relationship between Wisdom and Prophecy in the Hebrew Bible*. Edited by Mark J. Boda, Russell L. Meek, and William R. Osborne. New York: T&T Clark, 2018.

Seitz, Christopher R. *Isaiah 1–39*. Interpretation. Louisville: John Knox, 1993.

Selman, Martin J. "The Kingdom of God in the Old Testament." *TynBul* 40.2 (1989): 161–83.

Seufert, Matthew. "Zechariah 1.11's Allusion to Isaiah and Jeremiah." *JSOT* 42.2 (2017): 247–63.

Sharp, Carolyn J. "'Take Another Scroll and Write': A Study of the LXX and the MT of Jeremiah's Oracles Against Egypt and Babylon." *VT* 47.4 (1997): 487–516.

Shaver, Judson R. *Torah and the Chronicler's History Work: An Inquiry into the Chronicler's References to Laws, Festivals, and Cultic Institutions in Relationship to Pentateuchal Legislation*. Atlanta: Scholars Press, 1989.

Shepherd, David J. "Commentary on Ezra." Pages 1–110 in *Ezra and Nehemiah*. Edited by David J. Shepherd and Christopher J. H. Wright. Two Horizons Old Testament Commentary. Grand Rapids: Eerdmans, 2018.

_________. "Prophetaphobia: Fear and False Prophecy in Nehemiah VI." *VT* 55.2 (2005): 232–50.

_________. "'Strike His Bone and His Flesh': Reading Job from the Beginning." *JSOT* 33.1 (2008): 81–97.

Shepherd, Michael B. *The Text in the Middle*. New York: Peter Lang, 2014.

Shipp, R. Mark. "'Remember His Covenant Forever': A Study of the Chronicler's Use of the Psalms." *Restoration Quarterly* 35 (1993): 29–39.

Shipper, Bernd U. "'Teach Them Diligently to Your Son!': The Book of Proverbs and Deuteronomy." Pages 21–34 in *Reading Proverbs Intertextually*. Edited by Katharine Dell and Will Kynes. LHBOTS 629. New York: T&T Clark, 2019.

_________. "When Wisdom Is Not Enough!: The Discourse on Wisdom and Torah and the Composition of the Book of Proverbs." Pages 55–79 in *Wisdom and Torah: The Reception of "Torah" in the Wisdom Literature of the Second Temple Period*. Edited by Bernd Schipper and D. Andrew Teeter. Leiden: Brill, 2013.

Sim, R. J. "Organization and Allusion in Ezekiel 20." Pages 95–136 in *Discourse Studies and Biblical Interpretation*. Edited by Steven E. Runge. Bellingham, WA: Logos Bible Software, 2011.

Simon, Uriel. *Jonah*. JPSBC. Philadelphia: Jewish Publication Society, 1999.

Siquans, Agnethe. "Foreignness and Poverty in the Book of Ruth: A Legal Way for a Poor Woman to Be Integrated into Israel." *JBL* 128.3 (2009): 443–52

Sjöberg, Matthew. "Inner-Biblical Interpretation in the Redaction of Jeremiah 33:14–26." Pages 175–93 in *Covenant in the Persian Period: From Genesis to Chronicles*. Edited by Richard J. Bautch and Gary N. Knoppers. Winona Lake, IN: Eisenbrauns, 2015.

Skehan, Patrick W. "Qumran and the Present State of Old Testament Text Studies: The Masoretic Text." *JBL* 78 (1959): 21–22.

Skelton, David A. "Singers of Wisdom: Hymnody and Pedagogy in Ben Sira and the Second Temple Period." PhD diss., Florida State University, 2017.

Slotki, Judah J. *Daniel, Ezra, Nehemiah*, Soncino Books of the Bible. London: Soncino, 1951.

Smelik, Klaas A. D. "The Function of Jeremiah 50 and 51 in the Book of Jeremiah." Pages 87–98 in *Reading the Book of Jeremiah: A Search for Coherence*. Edited by Martin Kessler. Winona Lake, IN: Eisenbrauns, 2004.

Smith, Gary V. "The Influence of Deuteronomy on Intercessory Prayers in Ezra and Nehemiah." Pages 345–64 in *For Our God Always: Studies on the Message and Influence of Deuteronomy in Honor of Daniel I. Block*. Edited by Jason S. DeRouchie, Jason Gile, and Kenneth J. Turner. Winona Lake, IN: Eisenbrauns, 2013.

Smith, J. M. P., W. H. Ward, and J. A. Bewer. *Micah, Zephaniah, Nahum, Habakkuk, Obadiah and Joel*. ICC. Edinburgh: T&T Clark, 1911.

Smith, Ralph L. *Micah–Malachi*. WBC. Dallas: Word Books, 1984.

Smith-Christopher, Daniel L. *A Biblical Theology of Exile*. Minneapolis: Fortress, 2002.

_________. "The Mixed Marriage Crisis in Ezra 9–10 and Nehemiah 13: A Study of the Sociology of the Post-Exilic Judean Community." Pages 243–65 in *Second Temple Studies: Vol. 2. Temple and Community in the Second*

Temple Period. Edited by Tamara C. Eskenazi and Kent H. Richards. JSOTSup 175. Sheffield: JSOT Press, 1994.

Sneed, Mark. "Twice-Told Proverbs as Inner-Biblical Exegesis." Pages 89–102 in *Reading Proverbs Intertextually*. Edited by Katharine Dell and Will Kynes. LHBOTS 629. New York: T&T Clark, 2019.

Snell, Daniel C. *Twice-Told Proverbs and the Composition of the Book of Proverbs*. Winona Lake, IN: Eisenbrauns, 1993.

Snodgrass, Klyne. "The Use of the Old Testament in the New." Pages 209–29 in *Interpreting the New Testament: Essays on Methods and Issues*. Edited by David Alan Black and David S. Dockery. Nashville: Broadman & Holman, 2001.

Sommer, Benjamin D. *A Prophet Reads Scripture: Allusion in Isaiah 40–66*. Stanford, CA: Stanford University Press, 1998.

Sonsino, Rifat. *Motive Clauses in Hebrew Laws: Biblical Forms and Near Eastern Parallels*. Chico, CA: Scholars Press, 1980.

Spawn, Kevin L. *"As It Is Written" and Other Citation Formulae in the Old Testament: Their Use, Development, Syntax, and Significance*. Berlin: de Gruyter, 2002.

_________. "Sacred Song and God's Presence in 2 Chronicles 5, the Renewal Community of Judah and Beyond." *Journal of Pentecostal Theology* 16 (2008): 51–68.

_________. "Sources, References to." Pages 934–41 in *Dictionary of the Old Testament: Historical Books*. Edited by Bill T. Arnold and H. G. M. Williamson. Downers Grove, IL: InterVarsity Press, 2005.

Spencer, F. Scott. "2 Chronicles 28:5–15 and the Parable of the Good Samaritan." *WTJ* 46.2 (1984): 317–49.

Sprinkle, Preston. "Law and Life: Leviticus 18:5 in the Literary Framework of Ezekiel." *JSOT* 31.3 (2007): 275–93.

Stackert, Jeffrey. "Distinguishing Innerbiblical Exegesis from Pentateuchal Redaction: Leviticus 26 as a Test Case." Pages 369–86 in *The Pentateuch: International Perspectives on Current Research*. Edited by Thomas B. Dozeman, Konrad Schmidt, and Baruch J. Schwartz. FAT 78. Tübingen: Mohr Siebeck, 2011.

_________. *Rewriting the Torah: Literary Revision in Deuteronomy and the Holiness Legislation*. FAT 52. Tübingen: Mohr Siebeck, 2007.

_________. "Why Does Deuteronomy Legislate Cities of Refuge?: Asylum in the Covenant Collection (Exodus 21:12–14) and Deuteronomy (19:1–13)." *JBL* 125.1 (2006): 23–49.

Stanley, Andy. *Irresistible: Reclaiming the New that Jesus Unleashed for the World*. Grand Rapids: Zondervan, 2018.

Stead, M. R. *The Intertextuality of Zechariah 1–8*. New York: T&T Clark, 2009.

_________. "The Three Shepherds: Reading Zechariah 11 in the Light of Jeremiah." Pages 149–65 in *A God of Faithfulness: Essays in Honour of J. Gordon McConville on His 60th Birthday*. Edited by Jamie A. Grant, Alison Lo, and Gordon Wenham. New York: T&T Clark, 2011.

Steiner, Richard C. "Four Inner-Biblical Interpretations of Genesis 49:10: On the Lexical and Syntactical Ambiguities of עַד as reflected in the Prophecies of Nathan, Ahijah, Ezekiel, and Zechariah." *JBL* 132.1 (2013): 33–60.

_________. "'He Said, He Said': Repetition of the Quotation Formula in the Joseph Story and Other Biblical Narratives." *JBL* 138.3 (2019): 473–95.

Steinmann, Andrew E. *Ezra and Nehemiah*. Concordia Commentary. Saint Louis: Concordia, 2010.

_________. "The Order of Amos's Oracles against the Nations: 1:3–2:16." *JBL* 111.4 (1992): 683–89.

Sternberg, Meir. "Proteus in Quotation-Land: Mimesis and the Forms of Reported Discourse." *Poetics Today* 3.2 (1982): 107–56.

Stokes, Ryan E. "The Devil Made David Do It . . . Or *Did* He? The Nature, Identity, and Literary Origins of the *Satan* in 1 Chronicles 21:1." *JBL* 128.1 (2009): 91–106.

Stone, Timothy J. "The Search for Order: The Compilational History of Ruth." Pages 175–85 in *The Shape of the Writings*. Edited by Julius Steinberg and Timothy J. Stone. Winona Lake, IN: Eisenbrauns, 2015.

Strawn, Brent A. *The Old Testament Is Dying: A Diagnosis and Recommended Treatment*. Grand Rapids: Baker Academic, 2017.

Strazicich, John. *Joel's Use of Scripture and the Scripture's Use of Joel: Appropriation and Resignification in Second Temple Judaism and Early Christianity*. Leiden: Brill, 2007.

Strine, C. A. "On the Compositional Models for Ezekiel 38–39: A Response to William Tooman's Gog of Magog." *VT* 67 (2017): 589–601.

Strollo, Megan Fullerton. "The Value of the Relationship: An Intertextual Reading of Song of Songs and Lamentations." *Review and Expositor* 114.2 (2017): 190–202.

Sugimoto, Tomotoshi. "The Chronicler's Techniques in Quoting Samuel–Kings." *Annual of the Japanese Biblical Institute* 16 (1990): 30–70.

Sumner, W. A. "Israel's Encounters with Edom, Moab, Ammon, and Og according to the Deuteronomist." *VT* 18 (1968): 216–28.

Sundberg, Albert C. "The 'Old Testament': A Christian Canon." *CBQ* 30.2 (1968): 143–55.

Swale, Matthew E. "Structure, Allusion, Theology, and Contemporary Address in Psalm 106." *BSac* 176 (2019): 400–17.

Sweeney, Marvin A. *Zephaniah*. Hermeneia. Minneapolis: Fortress, 2003.

Tadmor, Hayim. "History and Ideology in Assyrian Royal Inscriptions." Pages 13–32 in *Assyrian Royal Inscriptions: New Horizons*. Edited by Fredrick Mario Fales. Orientis Antiqvi Collectio 17. Rome: Oriental Institute, 1981.

Taggar-Cohen, Ada. "Subtle Citation, Allusion, and Translation: Evidence in Hittite Texts and Some Biblical Implications." Pages 54–72 in *Subtle Citation, Allusion, and Translation in the Hebrew Bible*. Edited by Ziony Zevit. Sheffield: Equinox, 2017.

Talmon, Shemaryahu. "The Textual Study of Bible—A New Outlook." Pages 321–400 in *Qumran and the History of the Biblical Text*. Edited by Shemaryahu Talmon and

Frank Moore Cross. Cambridge: Harvard University Press, 1975.
Talshir, Zipora. "1 Kings and 3 Kingdoms—Origin and Revision Case Study: The Sins of Solomon (1 Kgs 11)." *Textus* 21 (2002): 71–105.
_________. "The Three Deaths of Josiah and the Strata of Biblical Historiography (2 Kings XXIII 29–30; 2 Chronicles XXXV 20–5; 1 Esdras I 23–31)." *VT* 46.2 (1996): 213–36.
Tanner, Beth LaNeel. "Allusion or Illusion in the Psalms: How Do We Decide?" Pages 24–35 in *Inner Biblical Allusion in the Poetry of Wisdom and Psalms*. Edited by Mark J. Boda, Kevin Chau, and Beth LaNeel Tanner. LHBOTS 659. New York: T&T Clark, 2019.
_________. *The Book of Psalms Through the Lens of Intertextuality*. New York: Lang, 2001.
Terrien, Samuel. "Amos and Wisdom." Pages 108–15 in *Israel's Prophetic Heritage: Essays in Honor of James Muilenburg*. Edited by Bernhard W. Anderson and Walter Harrelson. New York: Harper & Brothers, 1962.
Theocharous, Myrto. *Lexical Dependence and Intertextual Allusion in the Septuagint of the Twelve Prophets: Studies in Hosea, Amos, and Micah*. LHBOTS 570. New York: Bloomsbury, 2012.
Thompson, J. A. *The Book of Jeremiah*. NICOT. Grand Rapids: Eerdmans, 1980.
Throntveit, Mark A. "The Chronicler's Speeches and Historical Reconstruction." Pages 225–45 in *The Chronicler as Historian*. Edited by M. Patrick Graham, Kenneth G. Hoglund, and Steven L. McKenzie. JSOTSup 238. Sheffield: Sheffield Academic, 1997.
_________. "The Relationship of Hezekiah to David and Solomon in the Books of Chronicles." Pages 105–21 in *The Chronicler as Theologian: Essays in Honor of Ralph W. Klein*. Edited by M. Patrick Graham, Steven L. McKenzie, and Gary N. Knoppers. New York: T&T Clark, 2003.
_________. "Songs in a New Key: The Psalmic Structure of the Chronicler's Hymn (I Chr 16:8–36)." Pages 153–70 in *A God So Near: Essays on Old Testament Theology in Honor of Patrick D. Miller*. Edited by Brent A. Strawn and Nancy R. Bowen. Winona Lake, IN: Eisenbrauns, 2003.
Tiffany, Frederick Clark. "Parenesis and Deuteronomy 5–11." PhD diss., Claremont Graduate School, 1978.
Tigay, Jeffrey H. "Adoption," *Encyclopaedia Judaica*. New York: Macmillan, 1972, 2:298–301.
_________. "Conflation as a Redactional Technique." Pages 51–95 in *Empirical Models for Biblical Criticism*. Edited by Jeffery H. Tigay. Philadelphia: University of Pennsylvania Press. Reprint; Eugene, OR: Wipf and Stock Publishers, 1985.
_________. *Deuteronomy*. JPSTC. Philadelphia: Jewish Publication Society, 1996.
_________. "Deuteronomy 4 and the Art of Homiletics in the Bible." *Proceedings of the Rabbinical Assembly* 62 (2002): 256–62.
_________. "An Early Technique of Aggadic Exegesis." Pages 169–89 in *History, Historiography and Interpretation: Studies in Biblical and Cuneiform Literatures*. Edited by H. Tadmor and M. Weinfeld. Jerusalem: Magnes, 1983.
_________. "An Empirical Basis for the Documentary Hypothesis." *JBL* 94.3 (1975): 329–42.
_________, ed. *Empirical Models for Biblical Criticism*. Philadelphia: University of Pennsylvania Press. Reprint; Eugene, OR: Wipf and Stock, 1985.
_________. "'He Begot a Son in His Likeness after His Image' (Genesis 5:3)." Pages 139–47 in *Tehillah le-Moshe: Biblical and Judaic Studies in Honor of Moshe Greenberg*. Edited by Mordechai Cogan, Barry L. Eichler, and Jeffrey H. Tigay. Winona Lake, IN: Eisenbrauns, 1997.
_________. "'Heavy of Mouth' and 'Heavy of Tongue': On Moses' Speech Difficulty." *Bulletin of the American Schools of Oriental Research* 231 (1978): 57–67.
_________. "The Significance of the End of Deuteronomy (Deuteronomy 34:10–12)." Pages 137–43 in *Texts, Temples, and Traditions: A Tribute to Menahem Haran*. Edited by Michael V. Fox et al. Winona Lake, IN: Eisenbrauns, 1996.
_________. "The Torah Scroll and God's Presence." Pages 323–40 in *Built by Wisdom, Established by Understanding: Essays on Biblical and Near Eastern Literature in Honor of Adele Berlin*. Edited by Maxine L. Grossman. Bethesda: University Press of Maryland, 2013.
_________. "What Is Man That You Have Been Mindful of Him? (on Psalm 8:4–5)." Pages 169–71 in *Love & Death in the Ancient Near East: Essays in Honor of Marvin H. Pope*. Edited by John H. Marks and Robert M. Good. Guilford, CT: Four Quarters, 1987.
Timmer, Daniel. "Possessing Edom and All the Nations over Whom YHWH's Name Is Called: Understanding ירשׁ in Amos 9:12." *BBR* 29.4 (2019): 468–87.
_________. "Where Shall Wisdom Be Found (in the Book of the Twelve)?" Pages 146–63 in *Riddles and Revelations: Explorations into the Relationship between Wisdom and Prophecy in the Hebrew Bible*. Edited by Mark J. Boda, Russell L. Meek, and William R. Osborne. New York: T&T Clark, 2018.
Todd, James M., III. "'That You May Do Them': Legal Motive Clauses and the Law's Normative Function in Ancient Israel." In a Festschrift title TBA. Nashville: B&H Academic, forthcoming.
Toews, Brian G. "Genesis 1–4: The Genesis of Old Testament Instruction." Pages 38–52 in *Biblical Theology: Retrospect and Prospect*. Edited by Scott J. Hafemann. Downers Grove, IL: InterVarsity, 2002.
_________. "The Wisdom Contribution of Chronicles in the Ketuvim." Paper presented at the Annual Meeting of the Evangelical Theological Society, Boston, 16 November 2017.
Tooman, William A. "Transformation of Israel's Hope: The Reuse of Scripture in the Gog Oracles." Pages 50–110 in *Transforming Visions: Transformations of Text, Tradition, and Theology in Ezekiel*. Edited by William A. Tooman and Michael A. Lyons. Eugene, OR: Pickwick, 2010.
Tov, Emanuel. *Hebrew Bible, Greek Bible, and Qumran*. FAT 121. Tübingen: Mohr Siebeck, 2008.

———. "Hebrew Scripture Editions: Philosophy and Praxis." Pages 281–312 in *4QMMT to Resurrection: Mélanges qumraniens en hommage à Émile Puech*. Edited by F. García Martinez, A. Steudel, and E. Tigchelaar. Leiden: Brill, 2006.

———. "The Literary History of the Book of Jeremiah in the Light of Its Textual History." Pages 211–31 in *Empirical Models for Biblical Criticism*. Edited by Jeffery H. Tigay. Philadelphia: University of Pennsylvania Press, 1985. Repr., Eugene, OR: Wipf and Stock, 2005.

———. *Scribal Practices and Approaches Reflected in the Texts Found in the Judean Desert*. Atlanta: Society of Biblical Literature, 2004.

———. *Textual Criticism of the Hebrew Bible*. 2nd ed. Minneapolis: Fortress, 2001.

———. *Textual Criticism of the Hebrew Bible*. 3rd ed. Minneapolis: Fortress, 2012.

Trimm, Charlie. "Did Yhwh Condemn the Nations When He Elected Israel?: Yhwh's Disposition toward Non-Israelites in the Torah." *JETS* 55.3 (2012): 521–36.

Trotter, James M. "Death of the אלהים in Psalm 82." *JBL* 131.2 (2012): 221–39.

Tucker, Gene M. "The Law in the Eighth-Century Prophets." Pages 201–16 in *Canon, Theology, and Old Testament Interpretation: Essays in Honor of Brevard S. Childs*. Edited by Gene M. Tucker, David L. Petersen, and Robert M. Wilson. Philadelphia: Fortress, 1988.

Tuell, Steven S. "The Book of Ezekiel as a Work in Progress: Indications from the Lament Over the King of Tyre (28.11–29)." Pages 66–91 in *Ezekiel: Current Debates and Future Directions*. Edited by William A. Tooman and Penelope Barter. FAT 112. Tübingen: Mohr Siebeck, 2017.

———. "Haggai-Zechariah: Prophecy after the Manner of Ezekiel." Pages 273–91 in *Thematic Threads in the Book of the Twelve*. Edited by Paul L. Redditt and Aaron Schart. BZAW 325. Berlin: de Gruyter, 2003.

———. "The Priesthood of the 'Foreigner': Evidence of Competing Polities in Ezekiel 44:1–14 and Isaiah 56:1–8." Pages 183–204 in *Constituting the Community: Studies on the Polity of Ancient Israel in Honor of S. Dean McBride, Jr.* Edited by John T. Strong and Steven S. Tuell. Winona Lake, IN: Eisenbrauns, 2005.

Turner, Ian. "Going Beyond What Is Written or Learning to Read?: Discovering OT/NT Broad Reference." *JETS* 61.3 (2018): 577–94.

Turpie, David McCalman. *The Old Testament in the New: A Contribution to Biblical Criticism and Interpretation*. London: Williams & Norgate, 1868.

Ulrich, Eugene C. *The Qumran Text of Samuel and Josephus*. HSM 19. Missoula, MT: Scholars Press, 1978.

VanderKam, James C. *The Dead Sea Scrolls Today*. 2nd ed. Grand Rapids: Eerdmans, 2010.

———. *From Joshua to Caiaphas: High Priests after the Exile*. Minneapolis: Fortress, 2004.

Vang, Carsten. "God's Love according to Hosea and Deuteronomy: A Prophetic Reworking of a Deuteronomic Concept?" *TynBul* 62.2 (2011): 173–94.

———. "When a Prophet Quotes Moses: On the Relationship between the Book of Hosea and Deuteronomy." Pages 277–303 in *Sepher Torah Mosheh: Studies in the Composition and Interpretation of Deuteronomy*. Edited by Daniel I. Block and Richard L. Schultz. Peabody, MA: Hendrickson, 2017.

Van Leeuwen, Raymond C. "Cosmos, Temple, House: Building and Wisdom in Mesopotamia and Israel." Pages 67–90 in *Wisdom Literature in Mesopotamia and Israel*. Edited by Richard J. Clifford. Atlanta: SBL Press, 2007.

———. "Psalm 8.5 and Job 7.17–18: A Mistaken Scholarly Commonplace?" Pages 205–15 in *The World of the Aramaeans I: Biblical Studies in Honour of Paul-Eugène Dion*. Edited by P. M. Michèle Daviau, John W. Wevers, and Michael Weigl. JSOTSup 324. Sheffield: Sheffield Academic, 2001.

Vannoy, J. Robert. "The Use of the Word *hā'ĕlōhîm* in Exodus 21:6 and 22:7, 8." Pages 225–41 in *The Law and the Prophets: Old Testament Studies Prepared in Honor of Oswald Thompson Allis*. Edited by John H. Skilton. Nutley, NJ: P & R, 1974.

Verbrugge, Verlyn D. "1 Corinthians." EBC. Grand Rapids: Zondervan, 2008.

Vermes, Geza. *Scripture and Tradition in Judaism: Haggadic Studies*. 2nd ed. Leiden: Brill, 1973.

Vogt, Peter T. "Centralization and Decentralization in Deuteronomy." Pages 118–38 in *Interpreting Deuteronomy: Issues and Approaches*. Edited by David G. Firth and Philip S. Johnston. Downers Grove, IL: InterVarsity Press Academic, 2012.

Vos, Geerhardus. *Biblical Theology: Old and New Testaments*. Grand Rapids: Eerdmans, 1948.

———. "Inaugural Address." Pages 3–40 in *Inauguration of the Rev. Geerhardus Vos, Ph.D., D.D., as Professor of Biblical Theology*. New York: Anson D. F. Randolph & Company, 1894.

Vroom, Jonathan. "A Cognitive Approach to Copying Errors: Haplography and Textual Transmission of the Hebrew Bible." *JSOT* 40.3 (2016): 259–79.

Waltke, Bruce K. "Aims of OT Textual Criticism," *WTJ* 51.1 (1989): 93–108.

Walton, John H. "Genealogies." Pages 309–16 in *Dictionary of Old Testament Historical Books*. Edited by Bill T. Arnold and H. G. M. Williamson. Downers Grove, IL: InterVarsity Press, 2005.

———. "Genesis." Pages 1:2–159 in *Zondervan Illustrated Bible Backgrounds Commentary*. Edited by John H. Walton. Grand Rapids: Zondervan, 2009.

Walton, John H., and J. Harvey Walton. *The Lost World of Israelite Conquest: Covenant, Retribution, and the Fate of the Canaanites*. Downers Grove, IL: IVP Academic, 2017.

Warhurst, Amber K. "The Associative Effects of Daniel in the Writings." Pages 187–205 in *The Shape of the Writings*. Edited by Julius Steinberg and Timothy J. Stone. Winona Lake, IN: Eisenbrauns, 2015.

———. "The Chronicler's Use of the Prophets." Pages 165–81 in *What Was Authoritative for Chronicles*. Edited by Ehud Ben Zvi and Diana Edelman. Winona Lake, IN: Eisenbrauns, 2011.

________. "Merging and Diverging: The Chronicler's Integration of Material from Kings, Isaiah, and Jeremiah in the Narratives of Hezekiah and the Fall of Judah," PhD diss., University of St Andrews, Scotland, 2011.

Warren, Nathanael James. "'The Sin of the Sanctuary' and the Referent of מקדש in Ezekiel 44." *BBR* 25.3 (2015): 311–23.

Wasserman, Nathan. "Fasting and Voluntary Not-Eating in Mesopotamian Sources." Pages 249–53 in *Libiamo ne' lieti calici: Ancient Near Eastern Studies Presented to Lucio Milano on the Occasion of his 65th Birthday by Pupils, Colleagues and Friends*. Edited by Paola Corò, et al. Münster: Ugarit-Verlag, 2016.

Watts, James W. "Text and Redaction in Jeremiah's Oracles against the Nations." *CBQ* 54 (1992): 432–47.

Way, Kenneth C. "Donkey Domain: Zechariah 9:9 and Lexical Semantics." *JBL* 129.1 (2010): 105–14.

Weinfeld, Moshe. *Deuteronomy and the Deuteronomic School*. New York: Oxford University Press, 1972. Reprint, Winona Lake, IN: Eisenbrauns, 1992.

________. *Deuteronomy 1–11*. AB. New York: Doubleday, 1991.

________. "Jeremiah and the Spiritual Metamorphosis of Israel." *ZAW* 88 (1976): 17–56.

________. "The Origin of the Apodictic Law: An Overlooked Source." *VT* 23.1 (1973): 63–75.

________. "Sabbath, Temple and the Enthronement of the Lord—The Problem of the Sitz im Leben of Genesis 1:1–2:3." Pages 501–12 in A. Caquot and M. Delcor, eds. *Mélanges bibliques et orientaux an l'honneur de M. Henri Cazelles*. Neukirchen-Vluyn: Butzon & Bercker, 1981.

Welch, Adam C. "The Death of Josiah." *ZAW* 43 (1925): 255–60.

Wellhausen, Julius. *Prolegomena to the History of Israel*. Trans. A. Menzies and J. S. Black. 1885. Reprint. Atlanta: Scholars Press, 1994.

________. *Der Text der Bücher Samuelis*. Göttingen: Vandenhoeck und Ruprecht, 1872.

Wells, Bruce. "Exodus." Pages 1:160–283 in *Zondervan Illustrated Bible Backgrounds Commentary*. Edited by John Walton. Grand Rapids: Zondervan, 2009.

________. "The Hated Wife in Deuteronomic Law." *VT* 60 (2010): 131–46.

________. "The Interpretation of Legal Traditions in Ancient Israel." *HBAI* 4 (2015): 234–66.

________. "Is It Law or Religion?: Legal Motivation in Deuteronomic and Neo-Babylonian Texts." Pages 287–309 in *Law and Religion in the Eastern Mediterranean: From Antiquity to Early Islam*. Edited by Anselm C. Hagedorn and Reinhard G. Kratz. New York: Oxford University Press, 2013.

________. *The Law of Testimony in the Pentateuchal Codes*. BZAR 4. Wiesbaden: Harrassowitz, 2004.

________. "The Quasi-Alien in Leviticus 25." Pages 135–55 in *The Foreigner and the Law: Perspectives from the Hebrew Bible and the Ancient Near East*. Edited by Reinhard Achenbach, Rainer Albertz, and Jakob Wöhrle. Wiesbaden: Harrassowitz, 2011.

Wellum, Stephen J. "Progressive Covenantalism and the Doing of Ethics." Pages 215–34 in *Progressive Covenantalism: Charting a Course between Dispensational and Covenant Theologies*. Edited by Stephen J. Wellum and Brent E. Parker. Nashville: B&H Academic, 2016.

Wenham, Gordon J. *The Book of Leviticus*. NICOT. Grand Rapids: Eerdmans, 1979.

________. "The Deuteronomic Theology of the Book of Joshua." *JBL* 90.2 (1971): 140–48.

________. *Genesis 1–15*. WBC. Nashville: Nelson Reference, 1987.

________. *Numbers*. TOTC. Downers Grove, IL: InterVarsity Press, 1981.

________. "Were David's Sons Priests?" *ZAW* 87.1 (1975): 79–82.

Westbrook, Raymond. *Law from the Tigris to the Tiber: The Writings of Raymond Westbrook*. 2 vols. Edited by Bruce Wells and Rachel Magdalene. Winona Lake, IN: Eisenbrauns, 2009.

Westbrook, Raymond, and Bruce Wells. *Everyday Law in Biblical Israel: An Introduction*. Louisville: Westminster John Knox, 2009.

Westermann, Claus. *Praise and Lament in the Psalms*. Translated by Keith R. Crim and Richard N. Soulen. Atlanta: John Knox, 1965.

Wevers, John William. *Notes on the Greek Text of Deuteronomy*. Atlanta: Scholars Press, 1995.

________. *Notes on the Greek Text of Exodus*. Atlanta: Scholars Press, 1990.

________. *Notes on the Greek Text of Genesis*. Atlanta: Scholars Press, 1993.

________. *Notes on the Greek Text of Leviticus*. Atlanta: Scholars Press, 1997.

________. *Notes on the Greek Text of Numbers*. Atlanta: Scholars Press, 1998.

Weyde, Karl William. "Inner-Biblical Interpretation: Methodological Reflections on the Relationship between Texts in the Hebrew Bible." *Svensk exegetisk årsok* 70 (2005): 287–300.

________. *Prophecy and Teaching*. BZAW 228. New York: de Gruyter, 2000.

Widder, Wendy L. "The Court Stories of Joseph (Gen 41) and Daniel (Dan 2) in Canonical Context: A Theological Paradigm for God's Work among the Nations." *OTE* 27.3 (2014): 1112–28.

________. *Daniel*. The Story of God Bible Commentary. Grand Rapids: Zondervan, 2016.

Wildberger, Hans. "Die Völkerwallfahrt zum Zion: Jes. II 1–5." *VT* 7.1 (1957): 62–81.

Willey, Patricia Tull. *Remember the Former Things: The Recollection of Previous Texts in Second Isaiah*. Atlanta: Scholars Press, 1997.

Willgren, David. "*Antwort Gottes*: Isaiah 40–55 and the Transformation of Psalmody." Pages 96–115 in *Studies in Isaiah: History, Theology, and Reception*. Edited by

Tommy Wasserman, Greger Andersson, and David Willgren. New York: Bloomsbury T&T Clark, 2017.

_________. "Why Davidic Superscriptions Do Not Demarcate Earlier Collections of Psalms." *JBL* 139.1 (2020): 67–86.

Willi, Thomas. "Innovation aus Tradition: Die chronistischen Bügerlisten Israel 1 Chr 1–9 im Focus von 1 Chr 9." Pages 405–18 in *"Sieben Augen auf einem Stein" (Sach 3,9): Studien zur Literatur des Zweiten Temples*. Edited by F. Hartenstein and M. Pietsch. Neukirchen-Vluyn: Neukirchener Verlag, 2007.

Williams, Joshua. "Choosing the Right Words: Kings, Chronicles, and the Canon." Pages 189–205 in *Text and Canon: Essays in Honor of John H. Sailhamer*. Edited by Robert L. Cole and Paul J. Kissling. Eugene, OR: Pickwick Publications, 2017.

Williamson, Hugh G. M. "The Accession of Solomon in the Books of Chronicles." *VT* 26.3 (1976): 351–61.

_________. "The Composition of Ezra i–vi." *JTS* 34.1 (1983): 1–30.

_________. "The Death of Josiah and the Continuing Development of the Deuteronomic History." *VT* 32.2 (1982): 242–48.

_________. *Ezra, Nehemiah*. WBC. Waco, TX: Word, 1985.

_________. "Ezra and Nehemiah in the Light of the Texts from Persepolis." *BBR* 1 (1991): 41–61.

_________. *1 and 2 Chronicles*. New Century Bible Commentary. Grand Rapids: Eerdmans, 1982.

_________. "Hezekiah and the Temple." Pages 47–52 in *Texts, Temples, and Traditions: A Tribute to Menahem Haran*. Edited by Michael V. Fox et al. Winona Lake, IN: Eisenbrauns, 1996.

_________. "History." Pages 25–38 in *It Is Written: Scripture Citing Scripture*. Edited by D. A. Carson and H. G. M. Williamson. Cambridge: Cambridge University Press, 1988.

_________. *Israel in the Books of Chronicles*. Cambridge: Cambridge University Press, 1977.

_________. "Mirror Images." *Expository Times* 117.1 (2005): 19–21.

_________. "Reliving the Death of Josiah: A Reply to C. T. Begg." *VT* 37.1 (1987): 9–15.

_________. "'The Sure Mercies of David': Subjective or Objective Genitive?" *JSS* 23.1 (1978): 31–49.

_________. "Welcome Home." Pages 113–23 in *The Historian and the Bible: Essays in Honour of Lester L. Grabbe*. Edited by Philip R. Davies and Diana V. Edelman. New York: T&T Clark, 2010.

Willis, Amy C. Merrill. "A Reversal of Fortunes: Daniel among the Scholars." *CurBR* 16.2 (2018): 107–30.

Willis, Timothy M. "'Rest All Around from All His Enemies' (2 Samuel 7:1b): The Occasion for David's Offer to Build the Temple." Pages 129–47 in *Raising Up a Faithful Exegete: Essays in Honor of Richard D. Nelson*. Edited by K. L. Noll and Brooks Schramm. Winona Lake, IN: Eisenbrauns, 2010.

Wilson, Gerald Henry. *Editing of the Hebrew Psalter*. Chico, CA: Scholars Press, 1985.

_________. "The Shape of the Book of Psalms." *Interpretation* 46.2 (1992): 129–42.

_________. "The Use of Royal Psalms at the 'Seams' of the Hebrew Psalter." *JSOT* 35 (1985): 85–94.

Wilson, Ian D. "The Emperor and His Clothing: David Robed and Unrobed before the Ark and Michal." Pages 125–41 in *Dress and Clothing in the Hebrew Bible: "For All Her Household Are Clothed in Crimson."* Edited by Antonios Finitsis. LHBOTS 679. New York: T&T Clark, 2019.

Wilson, Robert R. *Genealogy and History in the Biblical World*. New Haven: Yale University Press, 1977.

_________. "The Old Testament Genealogies in Recent Research." *JBL* 94 (1975): 169–89.

Witherington, Ben, III. *Isaiah Old and New: Exegesis, Intertextuality, and Hermeneutics*. Minneapolis: Fortress, 2017.

_________. *Psalms Old and New: Exegesis, Intertextuality, and Hermeneutics*. Minneapolis: Fortress, 2017.

_________. Review of *Echoes of Scripture in the Gospels*, by Richard B. Hays (20 Apr 2016) at http://www.patheos.com/blogs/bibleandculture/2016/04/20/richard-hays-echoes-of-Scripture-in-the-gospels-a-review/

_________. *Torah Old and New: Exegesis, Intertextuality, and Hermeneutics*. Minneapolis: Fortress, 2018.

Witte, Markus. "Does the Torah Keep Its Promise?: Job's Critical Intertextual Dialogue with Deuteronomy." Pages 54–65 in *Reading Job Intertextually*. Edited by Katharine Dell and Will Kynes. LHBOTS 574. New York: Bloomsbury, 2013.

Wold, Benjamin. "Old Testament Context: Insights from the Dead Sea Scrolls." Pages 115–25 in *Methodology in the Use of the Old Testament in the New: Context and Criteria*. Edited by David Allen and Steve Smith. New York: T&T Clark, 2020.

van Wolde, Ellen. "Linguistic Motivation and Biblical Exegesis." Pages 21–50 in *Narrative Syntax and the Hebrew Bible: Papers of the Tilburg Conference 1996*. Edited by Ellen van Wolde. Boston/Leiden: Brill Academic, 2002.

_________. "A Prayer for Purification: Psalm 51:12–14, 1 Pure Heart and the Verb ברא." *VT* 70 (2020): 340–60.

_________. "The Text as Eloquent Guide: Rhetorical, Linguistic, and Literary Features in Genesis 1." Pages 134–51 in *Literary Structure and Rhetorical Strategies in the Hebrew Bible*. Edited by L. J. de Regt, J. de Waard, and J. Fokkelman. Winona Lake, IN: Eisenbrauns, 1996.

_________. "Texts in Dialogue with Texts: Intertextuality in the Ruth and Tamar Narratives." *BibInt* 5.1 (1997): 1–28.

Wolff, Hans Walter. *Hosea*. Hermeneia. Philadelphia: Fortress, 1974.

_________. *Joel and Amos*. Hermeneia. Philadelphia: Fortress, 1977.

Won, Young-Sam. *Remembering the Covenants in Song: An Intertextual Study of the Abrahamic and Mosaic Covenants in Psalm 105*. Eugene, OR: Wipf & Stock, 2019.

Wooden, R. Glenn. "Interlinearity in 2 Esdras: A Test Case." Pages 119–44 in *Septuagint Research: Issues and Challenges in the Study of the Greek Jewish Scriptures*. Edited by Wolfgang Kraus and R. Glenn Wooden. Atlanta: Society of Biblical Literature, 2006.

Woods, Edward J. *Deuteronomy*, TOTC 5. Downers Grove, IL: InterVaristy, 2011.

Wray Beal, Lissa M. *1 & 2 Kings*. Apollos Old Testament Commentary. Downers Grove, IL: InterVasity Press, 2014.

_________. "The Past as Threat and Hope: Reading Joshua with Numbers." *BBR* 27.4 (2017): 461–83.

Wright, Christopher J. H. "What Happened Every Seven Years in Israel?: Old Testament Sabbatical Institutions for Land, Debts, and Slavery, Part II." *Evangelical Quarterly* 56.4 (1984): 193–201.

Wright, Jacob L., and Michael J. Chan. "King and Eunuch: Isaiah 56:1–8 in Light of Honorific Royal Burial Practices." *JBL* 131.1 (2012): 99–119.

Wright, John W. "The Founding Father: The Structure of the Chronicler's David Narrative." *JBL* 117.1 (1998): 45–59.

_________. "The Legacy of David in Chronicles: The Narrative Function of 1 Chronicles 23–27." *JBL* 110.2 (1991): 229–42.

Würthwein, Ernst. *The Text of the Old Testament: An Introduction to the* Biblia Hebraica. 3rd ed. Edited by Alexander Achilles Fischer. Translated by Erroll F. Rhodes. Grand Rapids: Eerdmans, 2014.

Yamauchi, Edwin. "Ezra and Nehemiah." Pages 337–568 in *1 Chronicles–Job*. EBC 4. Grand Rapids: Zondervan, 2010.

Yates, Gary E. "Jeremiah's Message of Judgment and Hope for God's Unfaithful 'Wife.'" *BSac* 167 (2010): 144–65.

_________. "New Exodus and No Exodus in Jeremiah 26–45: Promise and Warning to the Exiles in Babylon." *TynBul* 57.1 (2006): 1–22.

Yoder, Christine Roy. Review of *Proverbs 10–31*, AB, by Michael V. Fox. *JHebS* 12 (2012).

_________. "Wisdom Is the Tree of Life: A Study of Proverbs 3:13–20 and Genesis 2–3." Pages 11–19 in *Reading Proverbs Intertextually*. Edited by Katharine Dell and Will Kynes. LHBOTS 629. New York: T&T Clark, 2019.

Yona, Shamir. "Exegetical and Stylistic Analysis of a Number of Aphorisms in the Book of Proverbs: Mitigation of Monotony in Repetitions of Parallel Texts." Pages 155–65 in *Seeking Out the Wisdom of the Ancients: Essays Offered to Honor Michael V. Fox on the Occasion of His Sixty-Fifth Birthday*. Edited by Ronald L. Troxel, Kelvin G. Friebel, and Dennis R. Magray. Winona Lake, IN: Eisenbrauns. 2005.

Young, Ian. "Is the Prose Tale of Job in Late Biblical Hebrew?" *VT* 59 (2009): 616–29.

Young, Ian, and Robert Rezetko, with Martin Ehrensvärd. *Linguistic Dating of Biblical Texts*. Vol. 1, *An Introduction to Approaches and Problems*. Vol. 2, *A Survey of Scholarship, a New Synthesis and a Comprehensive Bibliography*. London: Equinox, 2008.

Young, Theron. "Psalm 18 and 2 Samuel 22: Two Versions of the Same Song." Pages 53–69 in *Seeking Out the Wisdom of the Ancients: Essays Offered to Honor Michael V. Fox on the Occasion of His Sixty-Fifth Birthday*. Edited by Ronald L. Troxel, Kelvin G. Friebel, and Dennis R. Magray. Winona Lake, IN: Eisenbrauns. 2005.

Yu, Charles. "A Ridiculous God: Job Uses Psalm 8.5[4] to Respond to Eliphaz." Pages 84–102 in *Inner Biblical Allusion in the Poetry of Wisdom and Psalms*. Edited by Mark J. Boda, Kevin Chau, and Beth LaNeel Tanner. LHBOTS 659. New York: T&T Clark, 2019.

Zahn, Molly M. "Genre and Rewritten Scripture: A Reassessment." *JBL* 131.2 (2012): 271–88.

_________. "Innerbiblical Exegesis: The View from beyond the Bible." Pages 107–20 in *The Formation of the Pentateuch: Bridging the Academic Cultures of Europe, Israel, and North America*. Edited by C. Gertz et al. FAT 111. Tübingen: Mohr Siebeck, 2016.

Zakovitch, Yair. "Psalm 82 and Biblical Exegesis." Pages 213–28 in *Sefer Moshe, The Moshe Weinfeld Jubilee Volume: Studies in the Bible and Ancient Near East, Qumran, and Post-Biblical Judaism*. Edited by Chaim Cohen, Avi Hurvitz, and Shalom M. Paul. Winona Lake, IN: Eisenbrauns, 2004.

_________. "Through the Looking Glass: Reflections/Inversions of Genesis Stories in the Bible." *BibInt* 1.2 (1993): 139–52.

Zalcman, Lawrence. "Intertextuality at Nahum 1,7." *ZAW* 116.4 (2004): 614–15.

Zehnder, Markus. "Building on Stone? Deuteronomy and Esarhaddon's Loyalty Oaths (Part 1): Some Preliminary Observations." *BBR* 19.3 (2009): 341–74.

_________. "Building on Stone? Deuteronomy and Esarhaddon's Loyalty Oaths (Part 2): Some Additional Observations." *BBR* 19.4 (2009): 511–35.

_________. "Leviticus 26 and Deuteronomy 28: Some Observations on Their Relationship." Pages 115–75 in Paradigm *Change in Pentateuchal Research*. BZAR 22. Edited by Matthias Armgardt, Benjamin Kilchör, and Markus Zehnder. Wiesbaden: Harrassowitz, 2019.

Zevit, Ziony. "Echoes of Texts Past" and "Afterword: A Future for Back-Referencing." Pages 1–21, 242–44 in *Subtle Citation, Allusion, and Translation in the Hebrew Bible*. Edited by Ziony Zevit. Sheffield: Equinox, 2017.

Zimmerli, Walther. *Ezekiel 1*. Hermeneia. Translated by Ronald E. Clements. Philadelphia: Fortress, 1979.

_________. *Ezekiel 2*. Hermeneia. Translated by James D. Martin. Philadelphia: Fortress, 1983.

_________. "The Message of the Prophet Ezekiel." *Interpretation* 23 (1969): 131–57.

Zimran, Yisca. "'The Covenant Made with David': The King and the Kingdom in 2 Chronicles 21." *VT* 64 (2014): 305–25.

ACKNOWLEDGMENTS

I thank the Lord for mercy and strength for this project. The opportunity for extended study of the Scriptures is a gift.

I am grateful for long and generous support from Cairn University and its administration. The provost's office has sponsored my postgraduate studies at the University of Pennsylvania and Westminster Theological Seminary, covered expenses for academic biblical studies conferences, provided frequent relief from committee assignments, as well as granting a sabbatical at a critical stage in the research for this project. The provost's office provided funding for proofreaders which helped enormously in getting the manuscript into shape. The provost's office also covered the expenses for the indexes of this project, insisting that they be done well. I am happy to thank the president and provost for supporting scholarship that serves students.

I can hardly offer enough thanks to Cairn's School of Divinity for extensive longstanding support. The School of Divinity funded a long line of teaching and research assistants, annual academic biblical studies conference expenses, annual book budget, and beneficial course schedules. I am grateful that the School of Divinity covered the costs for a special "node" that needed to be created in an "originality detection" program at a midway point in the research for this project, as explained in the Bibliographic Note on Lists of Potential Parallels. I appreciate beyond the words listed here the guidance, discussion, and fraternity of my colleagues in the School of Divinity. I am humbled by the warm reception of the research for this project I was invited to present to the Divinity School faculty.

I am happy to offer a word of thanks to Jonathan Master. During his tenure as dean of Cairn's Divinity School he spent much time in conversations with me hashing out the logistics of this project and advising me on how to handle several critical decisions. He helped me get the sabbatical noted above. His warm encouragement and extensive support for this project cleared many obstacles. Jonathan also offered pointed feedback on matters of scriptural interpretation.

Many of my colleagues have been generous with their time and expertise. Several constructive, detailed conversations and consultations in places our research overlaps or broadly relates enlarged my outlook: on Chronicles, Brian Toews; on the Septuagint and Christian interpretation, Bill Krewson; on re-visiting Abraham in Nehemiah 9 as well as new insight into the New Testament's use of Scripture, Kevin McFadden; on God himself and progressive revelation, James Dolezal; on presenting exegesis within Scripture to ministers of the word, Keith Plummer; and on many aspects of scriptural exegesis within the Old Testament, Brian Luther. Thank you for letting me press you on the details of your books and conference papers during long lunches, coffee discussions, and intrusions into busy office hours.

Special thanks go to Cai Matthews, my research assistant during several years of the formal research phase of this project. He is especially well-versed in biblical Hebrew and biblical Greek. Cai spent hundreds of hours creating color-coded, side-by-side parallel layouts in Hebrew of the list of scriptural parallels I provided for him as illustrated in the Introduction. Cai also worked under my supervision—but he did all of the grunt work—running the Old Testament through an "originality detection" program as explained in the Bibliographic Note on Lists of Potential Parallels. He, along with help from Katrina Selby, spent months sorting out the mass of undifferentiated data generated by the originality scans.

I am eager to thank research and academic assistants for enormous typing and scanning projects as well as innumerable trips to the library completed with good cheer, even for many re-dos. The help during the formal research stage of this project came from Kerenza Ryan, Carlene Glen, Briana Borowski, Katie Colabella, Courtney Bottge, and especially Katrina Selby.

I am grateful for the work of additional research assistants. I appreciate the extensive pedagogical work of Jill Printzenhoff on materials for instructors as well as brief assistance of Bobby Larew. I thank Matthew Wilson for carefully and repeatedly working through the lists at the beginning of the main chapters late in the proofreading stage.

Thank you to Cairn University's library staff. The research librarians frequently went beyond normal protocols to acquire obscure materials that I often said "I need right away" when researching this project. I am grateful for the courtesies and help while researching at the Princeton Theological Seminary Library, the Library at the Katz Center for Advanced Judaic Studies in Philadelphia, and the library at Westminster Theological Seminary.

Thanks need to be expressed for proofreading by Valeriya Kim. Her keen sense and writing aptitude saved me from many blunders and helped many elements to be expressed more clearly.

It is not possible to offer adequate gratitude to Barbara Arnold. She spent full days for an entire summer looking up every Scripture reference in this entire volume to check for mistakes. The many errors she discovered for correction are a gift to readers. She also made many valuable observations and suggestions on grammatical problems and scriptural interpretation.

Thank you to Wendy L. Widder for helpful research suggestions for Daniel's use of Scripture. Wendy also took time from her own research to offer constructive feedback on draft versions of the chapters on Proverbs and Daniel.

I am grateful to Will Kynes for permission to use a pre-publication version of his forthcoming essay entitled "Debating Suffering." Thank you to Dick Averbeck for sharing with me several conference papers and forthcoming essays on legal exegesis in Torah. I offer thanks to James Todd for providing me a pre-publication copy of his forthcoming essay on "Legal Motive Clauses." I appreciate Jillian Ross' generosity of providing me a copy of her dissertation on "Pentateuchal Allusions in Judges." I thank Daniel Kim for making available to me his conference paper "The Crime of Gibeah." Thank you to Bryan Murawski for providing a working draft and a final draft of his dissertation "Study the Law" and a copy of his conference paper on Judges 1 as well as very extensive interaction and feedback on interpretation of the use of Scripture in Ezra-Nehemiah over the past number of years. I appreciate Benj Giffone providing access to a pre-publication version of his article on Jeremiah. Thank you to Kaspars Ozolins for sharing with me his conference paper on 2 Samuel 21:19. I am grateful to the late Gary Knoppers for patient help with difficulties of 2 Sam 5:21//1 Chr 14:12 in personal correspondence. Thank you to several contributing authors of the forthcoming *Dictionary of the New Testament Use of the Old Testament* who graciously shared pre-publication versions of their entries with me: Matt Harmon, "OT Use of the OT, Comparison with the NT"; Danny Hays, "1 and 2 Samuel, Books of" and "Ezekiel, Book of"; Bob Chisholm, "Habakkuk, Book of"; and Chris Ansberry, "Proverbs, Book of." I am also indebted to Danny and Bob for discussing their research with me.

It is a pleasure to thank John Camden for taking a break in his research to produce the indexes for this project. I much appreciate the opportunity we had to spend an evening together working out the details of the indexes in an attempt to make them user-friendly, along with many other communications. John approached this mammoth, complicated indexing project with energy, an eye to detail, and constant good cheer.

I have benefitted by collegial feedback, sometimes spirited, in relation to numerous conference papers presented while researching this project. A few of these conference papers have been published in journals as noted in the bibliography.

It is with satisfaction that I express gratitude to the students in seminars and courses over the past twenty-five years into the present who engage in lively debate on all manner of concerns related to scriptural exegesis within Israel's Scriptures.

Thank you to Madison Trammel for sage insight and help in getting this project off the ground.

I offer many warm thanks to Zondervan Academic. More than two decades ago over breakfast the late Verlyn Verbrugge took up a conversation with me concerning the Old Testament use of Scripture. He later told me of his work for Zondervan and invited a proposal for a different sort of project on this subject. Although that form of the project did not come about, Verlyn graciously helped me apply some of those insights to a textbook on the Torah.

In more recent years, I appreciate the encouragement and brainstorming for this project from Nancy Erickson. It was by way of conversation with her on Zondervan's campus, in a different direction about something else, that the initial idea for the particular format of this project came into my mind. She met with me at conferences and offered much wise counsel as the idea for this project developed. Her expert editing, research suggestions, and strong command of the subject matter are invaluable. Though this project is very long and involved, Nancy grasped the broad view as well as pushing back in hundreds of cases, including very subtle matters. Nancy's PhD in the field as well as experience in the seminary classroom begin to explain how an editor can navigate subtle interpretations while always keeping the student in view. She is a sharp and generous critic. The guidance from Nancy for this project includes everything from quick replies to emails every time, many meetings, long patient discussions over minor details to benefit student readers, constructive back and forth over all manner of presentation, and abundant encouragement. Though Nancy is quite busy she always made me feel like this project is the only thing that she had to do. I here express my gratitude to Nancy.

I am grateful for the blind peer reviewers and blind academic reviewers. They detected many weak areas and suggested constructive paths forward. The places they disagreed with my arguments were especially beneficial to clarify matters.

Thank you to Matthew Miller for working on many details of marketing this project. I am grateful for the work on the interior design by Kait Lamphere, including some very nice touches. The entire staff demonstrates consistent warmth, patience, courtesy, professionalism, and support, making it a pleasure to publish with Zondervan Academic.

After these acknowledgements I need to say that any errors in this book are my responsibility.

I am pleased to dedicate this book to Nick and Jess.

It is easy to finish up here by trying to thank my wife Cheri. She put me through my graduate studies. The opportunity to devote all of my time to graduate studies, along with her encouragements through those rigors, helped make those studies of enduring value across the years including this project. Cheri made possible going back to school for postgraduate studies twice both of which were essential for this project. She offers constant support for my academic work, well aware of my enduring interest in and study of exegesis within Scripture. Cheri's gifted proofreading on this project found many things that no one else caught. She also made sure to protect the research sabbatical for this project from many kinds of intrusions. During this project she offered much advice as well as listening to me vent over issues and gush over discoveries in our daily walks. For all of these and much more I here say thank you.

INDEX OF TABLES, FIGURES, MAPS

INTRODUCTION

Figure 1: Competing Aims of Diachronic and Synchronic Studies (p. xxxv)
Figure 2: Four Models for Scriptural Interpretation of Scripture (p. xl)

GENESIS

Table G1: Expansions of the Abrahamic Covenant (p. 12)

EXODUS

Table E1: Covenant Renewal Collection and Parallel Legal Instructions (p. 27)
Table E2: Covenant Collection and Parallel Legal Instructions (p. 32)

LEVITICUS

Table L1: Collation of Debt and Service Release Standards of Torah (p. 50)

NUMBERS

Table N1: Recurring Elements in the Wilderness (p. 62)
Figure N2: Shaping Numbers after Exodus (p. 63)

DEUTERONOMY

Table D1: Narratives Retold in Deuteronomy (p. 79)
Table D2: Torah Collection of Deuteronomy 12–26 and Similar Instructions of Torah (p. 82)
Table D3: Expressed Agency in Synoptic Versions of Infidelity at Kadesh (p. 92)
Table D4: Retrospective Allusions versus Motivation in Deuteronomy 4 (p. 98)
Table D5: Economic versus Human Value in Scriptural Law versus Ancient Counterparts (p. 103)
Table D6: Comparing Dietary Regulations in Leviticus 11 and Deuteronomy 14 (p. 120)

JOSHUA

Table Josh1: Narrative Traditions in Long Scriptural Retrospectives (p. 161)

KINGS

Table K1: Sequential Comparison of the Deaths of the Kings of Israel and Judah in Kings (p. 211)

ISAIAH

Table I1: Selected Interweaved Running Themes in Isaiah 40–55 (p. 218)
Table I2: Thematic Parallels in the Field Commander's Taunts and Isaiah's Messages (p. 231)
Figure I3: Exegetical Effect of Hezekiah Narratives on Isaiah 7, 28–35 (p. 232)
Table I4: Identity Markers of Covenantal Exclusion and Inclusion (p. 240)

JEREMIAH

Table J1: Covenant Formula (p. 282)
Maps J2: Sequence of Jeremiah's Oracles Against the Nations and Geography (p. 290)
Table J3: Sequence of Jeremiah's Oracles Against the Nations and List in Jeremiah 25 (p. 291)
Table J4: Allusions to Isaiah and Torah in Jeremiah's Oracles Against Moab (p. 292)
Table J5: Cited Sources and Authorities for Pronouncements on Possession of Transjordan (p. 294)
Table J6: Parallels with Obadiah in Jeremiah's Oracles Against Edom (p. 296)

EZEKIEL

Table Ezk1: Holiness Legal Casuistic Formula in Ezekiel 14:1–11 (p. 322)
Table Ezk2: Threefold Retrospectives of Rebellion in Ezekiel 20 (p. 325)
Figure Ezk3: Relative Sizes of the Tabernacle, Solomon's Temple, and Ezekiel's Temple (p. 338)
Figure Ezk4: Ezekiel's Temple (p. 338)
Table Ezk5: Comparing Ezekiel 44 and Numbers 18 (p. 340)
Table Ezk6: Two Kinds of Others in Scripture (p. 341)
Figure Ezk7: A Typology of Persons in Ezekiel's Temple Vision (p. 341)
Map Ezk8: Apportioning of Land and Situation of Temple in Ezekiel 45–48 (p. 347)

JOEL

Table Joel1: Divine Attribute Formula in Scripture (p. 375)

AMOS

Table A1: Yahweh's Establishment of the Nations (p. 388)
Table A2: Davidic Kingdom Subjection of and Alliances with Regional Rivals (p. 389)
Table A3: Scriptural Criticism of Faithless Worship (p. 397)

ZECHARIAH

Table Z1: Zechariah 9:9 as Prequel and Mark 11:1–10 as Set-Up to Ironic Sequel (p. 453)

MALACHI

Table M1: Selected Timeline of Edom (p. 462)

PSALMS

Table P1: Psalm 72 and Secondary Echoes in Genesis (p. 489)
Table P2: Comparing the Structures of Genesis 1 and Psalm 104 (p. 505)
Table P3: Graphic Display by Indentation of Syntactical Subordination in Psalm 136 (p. 533)
Table P4: Headings of the Psalms (p. 535)

PROVERBS

Table Pr1: Parental Torah to the Next Generation (p. 569)
Table Pr2: The Excellent Woman as Bridge between Woman Wisdom and Ruth (p. 575)

EZRA-NEHEMIAH

Table EN1: Exegetical Citation Formulas in Ezra-Nehemiah (p. 635)
Table EN2: Broad Function of Representative Legal Exegesis in Ezra-Nehemiah (p. 639)
Table EN3: Verse by Verse Comparison of the List in Ezra 2 and Nehemiah 7 (p. 643)
Table EN4: Summary of Numbering of Returned Remnant in Ezra 2 (p. 647)
Table EN5: Laity Families of Original Return Appearing in Other Lists (p. 648)
Table EN6: Potential Overlap between Priests of Original Return with other Priestly Lists (p. 648)
Map EN7: Register Begins with Jerusalem (Ezra 2:3–20) and Moves Outward (2:21–35) (p. 649)
Table EN8: Initial Return from Captivity as Actualization and Type (p. 650)
Table EN9: Endings of Parallel Lists of Ezra 2 and Nehemiah 7 Leading into Narratives (p. 651)
Table EN10: Three Versions of the Edict of Cyrus in Ezra-Nehemiah (p. 653)
Figure EN11: Exegetical Bases of Genealogical Purity versus Apostasy Marriage Views (p. 663)
Figure EN12: Building Series of Interpretive Blends regarding Wrongful Matches in Ezra 9–10 (p. 663)
Table EN13: Possible Interpretive Blend of Legal Regulations in Neh 5:1–13 (p. 667)
Table EN14: Cycles of Apostasy-Judgment-Deliverance in Neh 9:26–31 (p. 674)
Table EN15: Eleven Days of Scripture Study (p. 675)
Table EN16: First-person Plural Legal Exegesis in Nehemiah 10 (p. 676)
Table EN17: Torah Upgrade in Nehemiah 10—Zealous Commitments Above Torah Standards (p. 677)
Map EN18: Judean Villages of Neh 11:25–30 (p. 683)

CHRONICLES

Figure C1: Recurring Renewal in Chronicles (p. 701)
Table C2: Dominant Themes in Chronicles (p. 703)
Table C3: The Broad Structure of Chronicles (p. 706)
Figure C4: The Arrangement of the Chronicler's Lists of the Twelve Tribes of Israel (p. 707)
Table C5: Major Changes in David Story from Samuel–Kings to Chronicles (p. 708)
Figure C6: Sequentially Prioritizing Worship in 1 Chronicles 11–17 (p. 709)
Figure C7: Shifting the Function of Narrative Units from Samuel to Chronicles (p. 710)
Table C8: Chiastic Reshaping of Solomon in Chronicles (p. 711)
Table C9: Exegetical Function of Prophetic Messages in Non-synoptic Contexts of Chronicles (p. 714)
Table C10: Functions of the Use of Narrative Templates in Chronicles (p. 716)
Table C11: Standard Royal Formulas in Kings and Chronicles (p. 717)
Table C12: Long Genealogies in Genesis (p. 722)
Table C13: Genesis-shaped Genealogies of 1 Chronicles 1 (p. 723)
Table C14: Levitical Responsibilities in the Days of Phinehas and David (p. 728)
Table C15: Calling the Congregation of Israel and the Nations to Worship (p. 740)
Figure C16: New Levitical Responsibilities by Ancient Clans (p. 752)
Figure C17: Exegetical Bases of David's Worship Initiatives in Chronicles (p. 752)
Figure C18: Repurposed International Horse Trade in Chronicles (p. 760)
Map C19: Places Possibly Associated with Solomon in 2 Chr 8:3, 4 (p. 771)
Table C20: Scriptural Marking of Davidic Standards for Worship Personnel (p. 774)
Table C21: Tribal Defections into the Temple Worshiping Constituency at the Rise and Fall of the Northern Kingdom (p. 777)
Table C22: Elijah's Letter Explains Historical Causes and Effects (p. 791)
Table C23: Extended Echo-Effect of the Second Solomonic Theophany in Hezekiah's Passover (p. 814)
Map C24: Places Associated with the Reforms of Josiah (p. 824)

TOWARD THE NEW TESTAMENT

NT1: An Example of Vertical Context via Exegetical Allusion (p. 850)
NT2: Divergent Scribal Tendencies of the Second Temple Situation (p. 864)

SCRIPTURE AND ANCIENT LITERATURE INDEX

Please note that this index only provides Scripture references based on versing in the **English Bible**.

GENESIS

. . . . 3–4, 8–10, 12, 21, 30–31, 34, 58, 68, 145, 149, 155, 161, 220, 224, 266, 269–70, 359, 362, 364–66, 434, 444, 476, 483, 489–92, 508–10, 512, 516, 540, 561, 590, 600–1, 614, 617, 672, 715, 719, 722–25, 754, 853–54, 869, 900–1

1–2 . . . . 32, 97, 149, 219

1:1–2:4 506

1–3 112

1–4 552

1:1–4:16 722

1–11 . . . . 434, 601–2

1–15 . . . . 435, 722

1 . . . . 5, 31, 149, 209, 236, 245, 269, 433–34, 481–83, 505–6, 532, 540, 542, 555, 561

1:1 . . . . 5, 221, 252–53, 309, 506

1:2 . . . . 146, 236, 351

1:3 . . . . 2, 540, 561

1:3–5 483

1:3–25 269

1:4 . . . . 31, 236

1:5 6

1:6–8 483

1:6 236

1:7 236

1:8 6

1:9–13 483

1:9 . . . . 31–32, 236

1:10 . . . . 6, 31–32, 236

1:10–11 149

1:11 482

1:12 . . . . 31, 482

1:14–19 483

1:14 . . . . 30, 236, 481

1:15 30

1:16 . . . . 30, 481, 531–32

1:18 . . . . 31, 236, 531

1:20–23 483

1:20 . . . . 7, 434

1:20–28 434

1:21 . . . . 5, 7, 31, 434, 482, 506

1:24 482

1:24–25 483

1:25 . . . . 31, 482

1:26 . . . . 6, 223, 481–83

1:26–27 851

1:26–28 . . . . 5, 80, 470, 867

1:27 . . . . 2, 5, 482, 506

1:27–28 5

1:27–31 483

1:28 . . . . 6, 31, 415, 481, 894

1:28–29 6

1:29 7

2 . . . . 504, 506, 561, 574, 602

2:1 671

2:2 . . . . 2, 20–21, 30–31

2:2–3 . . . . 21, 101–2, 883

2:3 . . . . 5, 20–22, 31, 506, 883

2:4 . . . . 5–6, 12, 80, 506

2:7 . . . . 2, 13, 236, 434, 455, 504, 506, 599–601

2:8 . . . . 470, 506, 894

2:9 . . . . 12, 574

2:16–17 xxxi

2:16 3

2:17 . . . . 3–4, 542

2:19 . . . . 506, 600

2:19–20 6

2:23 561

2:24 . . . . 2, 21, 583

3 . . . . 369, 561, 601

3:1 4

3:1–3 xxxi

3:1–5 3

3:1–6 4

3:2 4

3:3 4

3:4 4

3:5 4

3:6 . . . . 4, 12, 894

3:7 894

3:14 . . . . 252–53, 256, 414, 489

3:14–15 227

3:14–19 894

3:15 509

3:16 9

3:16–24 9

3:19 . . . . 504, 542, 599–601, 625

3:22 . . . . 223, 482, 574, 625

3:24 . . . . 482, 574

4 . . . . 455, 601

4:1 . . . . 455–56, 574

4:2 455–56

4:7 9

4:8 21

4:14 434

4:15 549

4:26 379

5 722–23

5:1 . . . . 5–6, 12

5:1–2 . . . . 5, 470

5:1–3 . . . . 3, 5–6, 482

5:2 . . . . 2, 5

5:3 6

5:3–32 722

5:24 2

6–9 . . . xxiv, 31, 227, 254, 322, 540, 722

6:3 798

6:4 63–64

6:6–7 270

6:7 434

6:9 . . . . 12, 322

7:4 434

7:11 . . . . 227, 469

7:16 12

7:22 439

8:1 52

8:2 469
8:8 434
8:20 315
8:21 ..... 315, 601
8:22 541
9:1.....6–7, 31, 894
9:1–7 .....3, 6
9:3 7
9:4 .....7, 54, 82, 116, 123, 457, 733
9:5.....7, 33–35
9:6 7
9:7..... 6–7, 31
9:8–17.....246
9:15 52
9:16 ..... 52. 227
9:20 894
9:20–25 9
9:21 ..... 9, 894
9:22 356
9:23 .....356, 894
9:24 ..... 9, 894
9:25–27 894
10 .....145, 337, 388, 434–35, 584, 607, 722–23
10:1 12
10:2–4.....722
10:2 ..... 336, 489, 490
10:3 336
10:4 ..... 337, 489–90
10:5 ..... 435, 489–90
10:6–8 722
10:6 ..... 336, 489, 490
10:7 ..... 337, 489–90
10:8–11.....418
10:10 458
10:13–18 722
10:14 .....388, 395
10:19 362
10:22–29 722
10:25 388
10:28 337
11:1–9..... xxiii, 722
11 434
11:2 458
11:3 309
11:5 12
11:6 565
11:7 ..... 144–45, 223, 482, 860
11:7–8..... 145, 496
11:7–9 ..... 387, 395, 435
11:8–9.....388
11:10 12
11:10–26 722–23
11:10–29.....722
11:10–30 589
11:27 12
11:27–32.....160–61
11:27–25:11.....722
12 ..... 149, 894
12:1–3..... 9, 12, 491, 876
12:1 ..... 2, 12, 32, 508
12:2 491
12:3 ..... 2, 68, 239, 489–92, 581, 685, 876, 879–80
12:4 671–72
12:7 ..... 2, 508
12:8 379
12:10 ..... 84, 143
12:10–20 ..... 10, 255
12:17–20.....10
12–25 357
12–35 507
13:4 379
13:6 12
13:10 612
13:10–11 388
13:14–15.....508
13:14–17 9
13:14–18 876
13:14–18 .....12, 32, 876
13:15 2
13:16 72
13:17 ..... 131–33, 508
14 183
14:8 .....362, 878
14:18–20 .....2, 523, 879
14:19 574
14:22 574
15 149
15:5 ..... 2, 9, 208
15:6 .. 2, 511, 513, 516–17, 671–72, 851
15:7 508
15:13 ..... 2, 31, 508
15:13–14.....32
15:14 2
15:16 .....10, 54, 508
15:16–21..... 12, 876
15:18 ..... 32, 149, 163, 208–9, 489, 671–72, 759–60
15:18–20.....9, 32
15:18–21.....35, 507–8
16:1–12.....183
16:2 12
16:6 185
17 ..... 32, 52, 54, 508
17:1–6.....876
17:1–16.....12
17:5.....2
17:6 178
17:7..... 32, 282
17:8 ..... 2, 32, 282, 315, 507–8
17:9–14.....9
17:13–14.....52
17:14 52
17:15–19.....183
17:16 ..... 178, 509
17:17 12
18:2–8.....323
18:10 2
18:12 12
18:12–15.....12
18:14 2
18:18 ..... 2, 84, 143–44, 489–91
18:21 12
18:25 ..... 497, 545
19 ..... 10, 149, 166, 171–72, 221, 878
19:1–3..... 172, 323
19:1–29.....221
19:5 .....165, 171–72
19:8 172
19:10 12
19:11 172–73
19:21 395
19:22–23 362
19:24 ..... 255, 549
19:24–25 878
19:25 395
19:28 255
19:29 395
19:30–37 138
19:30–38 590
19:32–35 9
19:33–38 149
20 509
20:1–18.....10
20:6 ..... 509, 547
20:6–7..... 507, 509
20:7 273
20:13 114
21:2 379
21:2–3.....723
21:6 12
21:9 12
21:10 2
21:12 2
21:33 379
22 ..... 149, 752
22:1–14.....159
22:1–19..... 753, 764
22:2 ..... 12, 702, 716, 763
22:11 ..... 32, 173
22:15–18.....9
22:16–17 2
22:16–18 ..... 12, 876
22:17 .....208–9, 254, 311, 369, 508
22:18 .....2, 489–91
23:6 496
23:7 656
23:12–13 656
23:19–20 13
24 10–11

24:1–9 . . . 11
24:1–21 . . . 11
24:3 . . . 545
24:7 . . . 2, 545
24:12–14 . . . 11
24:12–21 . . . 80
24:15 . . . 11
24:34–41 . . . 11
24:42–44 . . . 11
24:45–48 . . . 11, 80
25:1–18 . . . 723
25:2–26 . . . 364
25:7–8 . . . 12
25:12 . . . 12
25:12–18 . . . 722
25:19 . . . 12
25:19–34 . . . 876
25:19–35:29 . . . 722
25:21 . . . 12, 183
25:21–26 . . . 470
25:22 . . . 362, 364
25:23 . . . 2, 362, 364
25:25–26 . . . 461, 723
25:26 . . . 311, 362, 364
25:30 . . . 401
25:31–34 . . . 725
25–36 . . . 461
26:2–5 . . . 508
26:2–6 . . . 9
26:4 . . . 2
26:5 . . . 508
26:6–11 . . . 10
26:7 . . . xxxii
26:8 . . . 12
26:9 . . . xxxii
26:22 . . . 132
26:24 . . . 32
26:25 . . . 379
27 . . . 149
27:1 . . . 12
27:16 . . . 12, 184
27:18 . . . 590
27:27–29 . . . 725
27:29 . . 7–8, 68, 178, 685–86, 876, 880
27:36 . . . 311, 364
27:37 . . . 8
28 . . . 149
28:4 . . . 315
28:12 . . . 2
28:13 . . . 365–66
28:13–15 . . . 9, 508
28:13–19 . . . 362
28:14 . . . 491
28:15 . . . 484
28:16–17 . . . 366
28:19 . . . 366
28:20–21 . . . 69
29:1–30 . . . 369
29:14 . . . 185
29:31 . . . 151
29:31–30:24 . . . 590, 723
30:1–8 . . . 183
30:2 . . . 13
30:22 . . . 52, 184
31:19–35 . . . 10
31:32 . . . 13
31:34–35 . . . 161
31:39 . . . 41
31:42 . . . 544
32:12 . . . 311, 369
32:24 . . . 362, 364
32:24–28 . . . 364
32:26 . . . 363
32:28 . . . 208, 362, 364
32:30 . . . 99, 364
33:4 . . . 365
33:5 . . . 365
33:11 . . . 365
33:19 . . . 164
34 . . . 7, 662
34:13–29 . . . 54
35 . . . 365
35:2 . . . 162
35:2–4 . . . 365
35:3 . . . 365
35:4 . . . 162
35:7 . . . 365
35:8 . . . 173
35:9–12 . . . 9
35:9–13 . . . 365
35:10 . . . 208
35:11 . . . 7, 178, 365–66
35:11–15 . . . 362
35:12 . . . 508
35:14 . . . 365
35:14–15 . . . 364
35:15 . . . 362, 366
35:16–18 . . . 310
35:16–20 . . . 723
35:16–21 . . . 412
35:18–19 . . . 412–13
35:19 . . . 412, 526
35:20 . . . 707
35:21 . . . 412–13
35:22 . . . 7, 725
35:22–26 . . . 722–23
35:28–29 . . . 12, 798
35:29 . . . 798
36 . . . 149, 722–23
36:1 . . . 12, 401
36:1–43 . . . 722
36:7 . . . 12, 315
36:8 . . . 388
36:9 . . . 12, 401
36:15 . . . 164
36:31 . . . xx, xxviii, 359
36:31–43 . . . 715
36:42 . . . 164
37 . . . 507
37–50 . . . 722, 725
37:1 . . . 315, 880
37:2 . . . 12, 63
37:5–11 . . . 7, 880
37:10 . . . 8
37:31 . . . 12, 184
37:33 . . . 11–12
37:35 . . . 11–12
38 . . . 590
38:1–7 . . . 723
38:2 . . . 724
38:7 . . . 724
38:8 . . . 21
38:18 . . . 591
38:26 . . . 184
38:28 . . . 164
38:29 . . . 590
38:29–30 . . . 723–24
38:30 . . . 164
39 . . . 507
39:2 . . . 185
39:3 . . . 614
39:6 . . . 185
39:7 . . . 185
39:8 . . . 496
39:10 . . . 614
39:21 . . . 614
40–41 . . . 861
40–50 . . . 613
41 . . . 11, 31, 507, 618–20
41:1–4 . . . 11
41:5–8 . . . 11
41:17–21 . . . 11
41:22–24 . . . 11
41:25 . . . 619–20
41:25–27 . . . 11
41:28 . . . 619–20
41:32 . . . 619–20
41:38–39 . . . 620
41:42–43 . . . 614
41:49 . . . 311
41:54 . . . 379
42 . . . 507
42:6 . . . 656
42:7–17 . . . 11
42:7–38 . . . 80
42:18–20 . . . 11
42:21 . . . 11, 162
42:22 . . . 11
42:23–24 . . . 11
42:25–28 . . . 11, 13
42:29–31 . . . 11

42:32–34 11
42:35 .... 11, 13
42:36 11–12
42:37 11
42:38 11–12
42–43 11
43:1–7 11
43:8–9 .... 7, 880
43:8–10 11
43:13 12
43:13–14 11
43:14 12
43:17 379
43:18–23 11
43:20–22 13
44 11
44:1–5 13
44:1–13 10
44:4 549
44:8 11
44:9–10 xxxi
44:9 13
44:18–34 880
44:19–21 11
44:22 11
44:23–26 11
44:27–29 11
44:27–31 12
44:29 12
44:30–31 11
44:31 12
44:32–34 11
45–50 10
46 .... 31, 507
46:2 32
46:3–4 508
46:8–9 725
46:8–27 723
46:10 725
46:11 726
46:12 723
46:20 146
46:21 146
46:22 146
46:27 146
46:28 .... 723, 880
46:28–30 8
46–50 .... 72, 149, 255, 876
47:9 .... 12, 798
47:31 2
48:3–4 9
48:6 508
48:10 12
48:13–20 .... 725, 754
48:20 491
49 452
49:1–28 10
49:3–4 725
49:4 .... 7, 725
49:7 7
49:8 .... 3, 7–8, 178, 351, 880
49:8–9 414
49:8–10 480
49:8–12 .... 8, 351, 540, 725, 752–54
49:9 .... 68, 480, 867, 880
49:10 ... 3, 7, 181–82, 328–29, 351, 480, 489, 540, 870, 879–80
49:11 ... 208, 452–53, 489, 800, 850, 867
49:11–12 880
49:24 545
49:25 .... 13, 149, 469
49:26 149
49:29–32 13
49:33 798
50:12–14 13
50:19 13
50:24–25 164
50:24–26 .... 10, 32

EXODUS

.... 17–23, 25–26, 28–29, 31, 35, 39, 41, 43, 46–47, 49, 52, 55, 57, 61–63, 71, 73, 80–81, 101–2, 104, 106–7, 112, 115, 123–24, 132, 134–35, 155, 159, 162, 173, 184, 189, 203, 241, 249, 282, 324, 356, 369, 375, 377, 403–7, 414, 416–17, 461, 484, 493, 504–5, 510, 512, 551, 568, 668, 737, 762, 764, 855, 869, 872, 901
1 .... xxxii, 620
1:1–6 31
1:5 146
1:7 .... 31, 507, 723
1:8 .... 17, 31
1:8–22 507
1:9–18 33
1:10 32
1:11–14 31
1:13 330
1:14 330
1:22 416
1–15 173
2 33
2:2 .... 31, 185
2:3 .... xxiv, 31, 407
2:5–57 31
2:7 725
2:13 142
2:14 17
2:22 31
2:23–25 .... 32, 72, 507
2:24 .... 32, 52, 508, 876
2:24–25 673
2:25 53
3 .... 112, 892
3:4 32
3:5 .... 164, 854
3:5–10 17
3:6 .... 17, 32
3:7 .... 563, 671, 673, 860
3:8 66–67
3:11–13 108
3:12 17
3:13–16 32
3:15 .... 17, 528, 544
3:17 66–67
4 362
4:1 317
4:6 208
4:10 .... 267, 317
4:10–12 267
4:11–16 24
4:18–2 26
4:21 .... 143, 159, 184, 441
4:21–23 361–62
4:22 .... 149, 309
4:22–2 28
4:23 361–62
4:24–26 .... 32, 54
4:29–30 417
4:29–31 317
5:5 656
5:6 563
5:10 563
5:13 563
5:14 563
5–15 149
6:1–9 324
6:2–3 32
6:3–9 356
6:4 315
6:5 .... 32, 52–53, 72
6:6 .... 209, 236, 541
6:7 .... 32, 282
6:8 32
6:12 .... 52, 317
6:14 725
6:15 725
6:16–20 751–52
6:16–25 726
6:24 727
6:30 .... 52, 317
6–13 309
6–15 .... 97, 208–9, 418
7:3 .... 96, 159, 502
7:5 531
7:13 .... 159, 184
7:14–25 493
7:22 .... 159, 184
7–12 .... 184, 492, 507, 513, 671
8:1–7 493

8:6 ... 185
8:15 ... 224
8:19 ... 159, 184
8:20–24 ... 493
9:1–12 ... 493
9:12 ... 159, 184
9:16 ... 17
9:22–26 ... 493
9:29 ... 540, 671
9:35 ... 159, 184
10:1 ... 224
10:3–15 ... 493
10:20 ... 159, 184
10:27 ... 159, 184
11:4 ... 542
11:10 ... 159, 184
12 ... 43, 582
12:1–20 ... 85
12:3 ... 34
12:6 ... 615
12:8 ... 60
12:8–11 ... 872
12:9 ... 827–28
12:10 ... 34, 60
12:10–20 ... 27, 34, 54, 82, 150
12:11 ... 241–42
12:12 ... 528–30
12:15 ... 23
12:17 ... 532
12:18 ... 60
12:19 ... 43
12:29 ... 209, 493, 529, 531
12:29–39 ... 73
12:33–36 ... 507
12:35 ... 641
12:35–36 ... 641
12:36 ... 641
12:38 ... 40, 685
12:42–49 ... 85
12:43 ... 239
12:43–48 ... 240
12:43–49 ... 40, 124, 239, 582, 679
12:43–51 ... 239
12:44 ... 54
12:45 ... 341
12:46 ... 17, 60, 547
12:48 ... 42–43, 52, 54, 239
12:48–49 ... 60–61, 341
12:49 ... 43
12:51 ... 532
12–13 ... 17, 27
13–15 ... 492
13–19 ... 63
13:1–16 ... 85
13:2 ... 17, 59, 680
13:3–13 ... 27, 34, 54, 82, 150
13:4 ... 60
13:5 ... 67, 106
13:11 ... 32, 106
13:12 ... 17, 28, 33, 59, 82, 127
13:12–13 ... 26–27, 67, 681, 860
13:12–15 ... 680
13:13 ... 27–28
13:14 ... 85, 164, 173
13:19 ... 32, 164
13:21 ... 62, 541, 671
13:21–22 ... 72, 507
13:22 ... 671
14–15 ... 164, 219, 236, 492, 671
14 ... 10, 62, 507, 513
14:4 ... 159, 184
14:8 ... 159, 184, 508
14:9 ... 242
14:10 ... 671, 673
14:11–12 ... 513, 515
14:13 ... 788
14:13–14 ... 788
14:14 ... 788
14:15 ... 788
14:16 ... 32, 225, 236, 251, 407, 458
14:17 ... 159, 184
14:17–18 ... 357
14:19 ... 72, 241–42, 251
14:21 ... 208, 236, 251, 439, 524, 532
14:21–22 ... 532, 541
14:22 ... 32, 236, 407, 540
14:24 ... 143
14:27 ... 532
14:28 ... 513
14:29 ... 32, 236, 407
14:31 ... 513
15 ... 236
15:1 ... 257, 414, 416, 513, 518
15:1–18 ... 10, 62, 788
15:1–21 ... 508
15:2 ... 415, 543, 545
15:3 ... 236
15:4 ... 407, 416
15:5 ... 407, 415–16
15:6 ... 543
15:8 ... 164, 236–37, 407, 524, 546
15:10 ... 236
15:11 ... 415, 513–14, 518, 542
15:13 ... 31, 415
15:14 ... 415
15:14–16 ... 143
15:15 ... 157, 164
15:16 ... 157
15:17 ... 415, 431, 492, 494, 541
15:17–18 ... 858
15:19 ... 32, 236, 407
15:20 ... 311
15:20–21 ... 62, 417
15:21 ... 416, 513, 518
15:22 ... 407
15:23–24 ... 62
15:25 ... 62, 225, 501
15:26 ... 459
15:27 ... 62
15–16 ... 894
15–17 ... 492
15–18 ... 61
16 ... 17, 62, 149
16:2 ... 22
16:4 ... 17, 501, 671
16:18 ... 17
16:22–29 ... 20
16:22–30 ... 33, 883
16:23 ... 21–22, 883
16:26 ... 66
16:30 ... 20–21, 883
16–15 ... 309
16:1–17:7 ... 508
17:1 ... 73
17:1–7 ... 62, 108, 501
17:2 ... 225, 501, 513
17:7 ... 108, 149, 225, 501–2, 513, 542
17:8–15 ... 268
17:8–16 ... 62
17:10 ... 379
17:14 ... 84, 149, 184, 549, 615
18 ... 79, 89
18:5 ... 32
18:11 ... 761
18:13–27 ... 89
18:15 ... 496
18:17–23 ... 89
18:20 ... 884
18:20–21 ... 32
18:21 ... 89
18:24–26 ... 89
19 ... 97
19–20 ... 79, 97–98, 130, 508, 671
19–40 ... 63
19:1–2 ... 32
19:4 ... 146, 351
19:5 ... 32
19:5–6 ... 62, 879
19:6 ... 66, 224, 250, 639, 663
19:7–24 ... 97, 149
19:12 ... 17
19:13 ... 17
19:15 ... 21
19:16 ... 203, 349, 459
19:16–18 ... 541
19:18–20 ... 349
19:19 ... 459
19:22 ... 418
19:24 ... 418
20 ... xlv, 17, 149, 470, 492, 869
20:1–17 ... 97–98, 100

20:2 173
20:2–5 495
20:2–6 54
20:3 33–34
20:4 .... 23, 107, 152, 492, 494, 528
20:4–6 27
20:5 ... 20, 23–27, 107, 209, 308, 421–22, 492, 494, 519–20, 559, 778
20:5–6 .... 23, 107, 161, 310, 421, 423, 877
20:6 107
20:7 421
20:8 .... xxx, 101
20:8–11 .... 19, 22, 27, 54, 101–2, 883
20:10 .... 19, 35
20:11 .... 22, 101, 530, 545, 671, 883
20:12 .... 17, 54, 152, 184, 418, 463, 470, 574
20:13 .... 17, 271, 369
20:14 .... 17, 54, 83, 151, 271, 369, 574
20:15 .... 17, 34, 271, 369, 574
20:15–16 54
20:16 .... 17, 33–34, 83, 134, 271, 540
20:17 .... 17, 574
20:18 459
20:18–21 .... 99, 100
20:19 .... 83, 130, 866, 882
20:20 442
20:22–26 98
20:23 .... 54, 209
20:24 .... 82, 112–15, 117–19
20:24–25 .... 41, 98, 111, 113
20:24–26 .... 112, 881
20:25 .... 41, 113, 118, 152, 194, 881
20:26 .... 338, 353
21:1–11 125
21:2 .... 49, 125
21:2–6 .... 32, 48–51, 82, 126
21:2–7 49
21:2–6 .... 46, 50
21:2–11 .... 47, 49, 288
21:4 .... 50, 126
21:5–6 126
21:6 496
21:7–11 .... 32, 50–51, 82, 125
21:8 49–50
21:9 50
21:10 .... 51, 223
21:11 51
21:12 .... 23, 45, 55, 131, 153, 487
21:12–14 .... 32, 83, 131
21:13 .... 69, 133, 160
21:14 131–33
21:15 .... 23, 32, 83, 103, 134, 418
21:16 .... 23, 32, 84, 150
21:17 .... 17, 23, 32, 54, 83, 134, 152, 356, 418
21:18–19 32
21:20–21 32
21:21 23
21:22 .... 48, 84, 141
21:22–25 142
21:22–27 32
21:23–24 83
21:23–25 .... 46, 103
21:24 .... 17, 134, 141
21:24–25 .... 7, 134
21:26 46
21:26–27 103
21:28–32 .... 7, 33–34
21:29 496
21:32 459
21:33–34 .... 33, 83, 150
21:35–36 33
21–23 .... 17–18, 20, 27, 84, 97, 111, 125, 869, 892
22:1 .... 45, 55, 184
22:1–3 34
22:1–4 33
22:2 .... 103, 882
22:4 .... 45, 55, 255
22:5–15 33
22:7 .... 34, 130
22:7–8 129
22:8 .... 33, 83, 129, 496
22:9 .... 130, 496–98
22:13 41
22:16 275–76
22:16–17 .... 33, 83, 137–38
22:17 54
22:18 .... 32–33, 83, 150
22:19 .... 23, 33, 54, 153
22:20 ... 33–34, 54, 72, 82, 105, 119, 149
22:20–33 880
22:21 .... xxvi, 42–43, 152, 866
22:21–22 .... 84, 150
22:21–23 860
22:21–24 .... 33, 42, 311, 345, 539–40
22:22 497
22:22–24 519
22:23 .... 23, 141, 185, 540–41, 543
22:24 497
22:25 .... 48–50, 84, 125–26, 140, 667
22:25–27 .... 33, 46, 50, 667
22:26 .... 50, 390, 667–68
22:26–27 .... 84, 140, 395, 882
22:27 .... 50, 141, 390, 667
22:28 .... 17, 33, 44–45
22:29 .... 72, 84, 151, 326
22:29–30 .... 33, 82, 127
22:30 .... 127, 151
22:31 .... 33, 41–42, 82, 123
22–23 10
23 .... 152, 484, 500
23:1 .... 83, 134, 150, 540
23:1–3 .... 33–34, 82–83, 134
23:1–13 54
23:3 .... 135, 497
23:4 .... 83, 135
23:4–5 .... 33, 134, 520, 860
23:5 .... 83, 135
23:6 .... 135, 391, 496–97
23:6–8 .... 33–34, 54, 82–83, 134
23:6–9 311
23:7 .... 243, 626
23:8 .... 129, 153, 256, 573
23:9 .... 33, 42
23:10–11 .... 33, 55, 82, 125
23:11 .... 84, 125, 677, 680
23:12 .... 27, 29–30, 33, 54, 101–2, 275, 883
23:13 33
23:14 28
23:14–17 .... 27–28, 34, 82, 128, 815
23:15 .... 26–27, 34, 54, 60, 82, 128, 150, 344
23:16 .... 27, 34, 55, 82, 128, 150, 344
23:16–17 680
23:18 .... 27, 34–35
23:19 .... 27, 32, 34–35, 65, 82, 84, 119, 123, 124, 151, 268, 639, 681, 860
23:20 .... 35, 225, 235, 242, 251, 468, 484, 500–1
23:20–21 235
23:20–33 ... 32, 149, 855, 866, 879–80
23:21 .... 34, 235, 469
23:23 .... 28–29, 83, 106, 242, 251, 254, 468, 484
23:23–24 .... 25, 27
23:23–31 28–29
23:23–33 .... 24–25, 62, 877
23:24 .... 82, 173, 418
23:24–25 34
23:27 .... 54, 242, 251, 254, 468, 484
23:28 .... 29, 54, 160, 162, 242, 251, 468, 484
23:28–30 25
23:28–31 .... 28, 83
23:29 106
23:29–30 29
23:30 106
23:31 .... 29, 35, 106
23:32 26
23:32–33 .... 25, 27, 34, 514
23:33 .... 82, 149, 173, 258, 514
24:6 33
24:8 .... 17, 442, 459
24:10 .... 255, 349
24:10–13 33
24:11 .... 227, 254
24:12 568

24:15–18 108
24:16 349
24:17 349
24:17–18 349
24:18 62
25:1–8 35
25:1–9 757
25:2 757
25:6 30
25:9 ....35–36, 716, 756, 856
25:10–22 35
25:22 72
25:23–30 ....35, 353
25:30 ....55, 180, 751
25:31 458
25:31–39 35
25:31–40 764
25:32 458
25:40 ....17, 35–36, 716, 756, 856
25–31 ....18, 80, 337
26 338
26:1 135
26:1–6 36
26:1–11 33
26:7–14 36
26:15–25 36
26:26–29 36
26:30 35–36
26:31 ....135, 353
26:31–35 36
26:33–34 353
26:36–37 36
27:1–2 113
27:1–8 ....36, 639
27:9–19 ....36, 338
27:20 30
27:20–21 ....36, 55
28:1–4 35–36
28:5 136
28:5–14 36
28:6 135
28:12 35
28:15 135
28:15–3 36
28:17–20 354
28:29–30 35
28:30 149
28:31–35 36
28:36–38 36
28:38 ....69, 340
28:39–41 36
28:39–43 343
28:42 338
28:42–43 ....36, 353
28:43 340
29 53
29:1–37 36
29:18 315
29:25 315
29:26 54
29:27–28 72
29:35–37 353
29:38–41 73
29:38–42 ....639, 691, 740
29:38–46 36
29:41 315
29:43–44 54
29:45 ....32, 282
30:11–16 ....35, 183, 208, 639, 677, 797, 842
30:16 728
30:19–21 35
30:22–33 36
30:34–38 36
31:1–6 ....36, 712, 716
31:2 574
31:2–6 762
31:3 574
31:7–11 36
31:12–13 34
31:12–17 ....19, 22–23, 27, 29–30, 33, 101, 273, 883
31:12–18 54
31:12–27 23
31:13 ....23, 356
31:14 ....22, 102
31:14–15 ....688, 883
31:15 ....22–23, 29–30
31:16 ....23, 102
31:17 ....22–23, 883
31:18 ....108, 568
32 ....79, 108–10, 406
32:1 17
32:1–6 ....24, 513
32:1–8 62
32:4 ....27, 202–3, 671
32:5 202
32:6 17
32:7–10 108
32:8 27
32:10 514
32:10–12 64
32:10–13 ....64, 877
32:11 ....111, 543, 664
32:11–13 ....62, 109–10, 309
32:11–14 108
32:12 ....376–77, 404–6, 434, 461, 542
32:13 ....32, 52, 64, 876
32:14 ....65, 404, 514, 523, 877, 898
32:15 568
32:15–19 108
32:16 568
32:19 568
32:20 108
32:23 17
32:26–29 62
32:27 149
32:29 109
32:31–32 108–9
32:32–33 549
32:34 62
32:35 62
32–33 23
32–34 ....29, 377, 894
33:1–2 242
33:1–3 ....39, 251, 284, 608, 874
33:2–3 484
33:2 468
33:3 ....67, 468
33:7–11 ....194, 493, 543
33:9 860
33:10 254
33:11 ....72, 99, 147
33:12–16 ....309, 874
33:13 504
33:14 ....252, 484
33:17 235
33:19 17
33:21–22 203
33:21–23 882
34 ....104, 190, 200, 406, 474, 498, 504, 655, 877
34:1 568
34:1–4 ....109, 110
34:4 568
34:5 194
34:6 ....23–24, 65, 107, 375, 403–5, 415, 421–22, 498, 504, 514, 541, 543–45, 605, 607–8, 622, 671, 673, 877, 898–99
34:6–7 ....xxxiii, 20, 23–24, 64–65, 161, 203, 372, 377, 406, 414, 421, 423, 520, 874, 877
34:7 ....24, 308, 421–22, 505, 519
34:8 108
34:9 ....108, 235, 543
34:9–10 ....284–85, 878
34:10 442
34:11 ....106, 202, 655
34:11–12 657
34:11–15 663
34:11–16 ....20, 24–25, 27, 34–35, 104, 202, 655, 663, 792, 869, 879
34:11–17 879
34:11–26 ....17, 20, 28, 894
34:12 ....26, 82, 104–5, 149, 164, 173, 258, 514
34:12–13 ....34, 173, 514
34:13 ....82, 104, 418
34:14 ....20, 24–26, 421–23
34:14–16 ....421–22, 519, 677, 877

34:15 ....26, 104–5, 726
34:15–16 . 106, 164, 200, 423, 639, 876
34:16.......25–26, 105–7, 173, 200–1, 514, 655, 657, 663, 690, 792
34:17 27
34:18 ....34, 60, 82
34:18–20 ...... 26–28, 34–35, 82, 150
34:19 .... 28, 59, 82, 127
34:19–20 33
34:20................. 28, 59, 82, 128
34:21....19, 27, 29–30, 33, 35, 273–74, 639, 677, 679, 687, 883
34:22.......27, 34, 55, 65, 82, 150, 860
34:22–23 82
34:22–24 ....27–28, 34, 485
34:24........ 28–29, 112, 132–33, 881
34:25 ....27, 34–35
34:26....... 27, 34–35, 55, 82, 84, 119, 123, 124, 151, 268, 639
34:27 442
34:27–28 108
34:28....................109, 110, 203
34:28–29 208
34:29.............................568
35:1–3 .... 23, 27, 29
35:2 ....19, 22–23, 66, 688, 883
35:2–3......... 19, 29–30, 33, 66, 883
35:2–5.............................29
35:3 .....36, 66, 273–74, 639, 677, 679, 687, 883
35:4–4.............................29
35:4–9.............................35
35:8 30
35:10–19...........................36
35:13 181
35:14 30
35:28 30
35:30–32 762
35:31 574
35:30–36:2 .... 712, 716
36:1 36
36:4 321
36:8 353
36:8–13 36
36:14–19 36
36:20–30 36
36:31–34 36
36:35–36 36
36:37–38 36
37:1–9 .... 35, 110
37:10–16...................... 35, 353
37:17–24...................... 35, 764
37:25–28 36
37:29 36
38:1–2............................113
38:1–7.............................36
38:8 36
38:9–20 36
38:22–23 .... 712, 716
38:23.............................763
38:25.............................639
39 53
39:2–7.............................36
39:8–21............................36
39:22–26 36
39:27–28 343
39:28..............................36
39:28–29 353
39:29..............................36
39:30–31 36
39:33–42...........................36
39:36.............................181
39:37..............................30
39:41.............................343
40 .... 53, 72
40:10.............................353
40:17..............................72
40:21..............................36
40:22–29 781
40:23......................... 55, 180
40:33......................... 30–31
40:34..............................39
40:34–35 .....194, 353, 712, 716, 765, 767–68, 855, 860, 902
40:35.............................562
40:36–38...........................72

LEVITICUS

.... 18, 35–36, 39–44, 46–49, 51–55, 71–73, 81, 86, 104, 112, 117, 121–23, 134–35, 150–51, 177, 240, 282, 314–16, 318, 321–22, 332–34, 343–45, 348–49, 357, 396, 438, 444, 464, 486, 511–12, 514, 572, 617, 651, 658, 661, 664, 701, 730, 737, 820, 834–35, 838–39, 844, 869, 898, 901
1–6.........................340, 486
1–7.................. 39, 62, 121, 487
1–10..............................122
1–16.......................122, 898
1:2–6..............................41
1:3.......................... 55, 487
1:4.........................487–88
1:5............. 55, 339, 813, 826–27
1:7–9 55
1:9..................... 315, 486–87
1:10–13............................55
1:13 .... 315, 486
1:17 .... 315, 486
2 623
2:2 .... 315, 486
2:2–3..............................55
2:3 .... 72, 353
2:9 .... 315, 486
2:11 391
2:12 .... 315, 486
2:13 .... 72, 691
2:14 72
2:14 72
3:1–5 ....41, 55
3:3 177
3:3–5.............................827
3:4 .... 177, 827
3:5....................... 315, 486
3:6–11.............................55
3:9 .... 177, 827
3:9–11............................827
3:10 .... 177, 827
3:12–16............................55
3:14 177
3:14–16...........................827
3:15 .... 177, 827
3:16 .... 177, 315, 486
3:16–17...........................177
3:17 .... 177, 184
4:1–3 55
4:2 598
4:3 243
4:10–23 44
4:11 464
4:13 243
4:13–21...........................842
4:17 55
4:21 55
4:22..............................598
4:22–26 .... 55, 842
4:27 .... 243, 598, 656
4:27–31.................... 55, 842
4:31 .... 315, 486
4:32–35............................55
4:1–5:13 243
5–6...............................243
5:1–6:7 .... 208, 487
5:1............................... 340
5:1–6.............................243
5:1–28............................208
5:2 661
5:3 661
5:4 173
5:5...............................487
5:6 340
5:14–6:7...........243, 487, 655, 661
5:15 .... 598, 639, 655, 661–63
5:17 .... 340, 662–63
5:18 598
6:1–7 243
6:2–3..............................243
6:4 487
6:6–7.........................244–45
6:8 315
6:8–13............................635
6:12–13................ 639, 677, 680

6:14 315
6:15 486
6:15–16 55
6:16 .... 72, 353
6:26 .... 72, 353
6:27 .... 344, 439
6–7 62
7:6 72
7:6–7 353
7:13 391
7:15–20 121
7:16–18 55
7:18 .... 318, 340
7:19–21 813
7:21 357
7:24 .... 41, 353
7:25 177
7:30 72
7:32–34 .... 83, 149
7:34 .... 150, 353
8 53–54
8–10 39
8:1–36 36
8:4 53
8:9 53
8:12 .... 41, 342, 509, 544
8:13 53
8:14–15 353
8:17 .... 53, 464
8:21 .... 53, 315
8:28 315
8:29 53
8:34 53
9:6 349
9:9 813
9:12 813
9:18 813
9:23 .... 349, 749
9:24 .... 716, 749–50, 752–53, 767, 856
10 803
10:1 .... 71–72, 803, 884
10:1–2 .... 54, 122, 343
10:1–3 62
10:2 72
10:3 .... 54, 343
10:6 .... 23, 343
10:6–7 892
10:7 23
10:8 23
10:9 .... 343–44, 439, 803, 884
10:9–11 343
10:10 .... 181, 329, 343
10:10–11 .. 149, 180, 329, 343–44, 347, 439, 463–64, 669, 803–4, 826, 866, 883
10:11 343
10:11–11 884
10:13 72
10:14–15 72
10:17 .... 72, 340
11 .... 41, 119–23, 396, 457
11–15 .... 39, 59, 122, 184
11–16 62
11:1–3 120
11:1–8 458
11:1–28 119–20
11:1–47 82
11:2–3 121–22
11:4–8 120
11:9–12 120
11:10–13 357
11:13 146
11:13–19 120
11:16–19 121
11:19 121
11:20 357
11:20–23 120–21
11:23 357
11:24–25 55
11:24–28 120
11:24–45 121
11:27–28 55
11:32–40 120
11:39–40 .... 55, 318
11:40 .... 33, 82
11:41–45 120
11:44 .... 39, 55
11:44–45 122
11:45 .... 39, 282
11:46–47 120–21
12:3 54
12:6 243
12:8 39
13:3–6 55
13:18–23 233
13:20–23 55
13:25–28 55
13:45 241–42
13:45–46 .... 803, 860
13:46 208
13–14 .... 84, 141
14:4 72
15:15 243
15:15–16 180
15:16 .... 84, 139
15:18 .... 21, 51, 180, 883
15:19–24 .... 334, 612
15:26 356
15:28 184
15:30 243
15:31 813
16 .... 39, 121
16:1 .... 71–72, 122
16:1–34 55
16:21 487
16:27 464
16:29 .... 43, 123
17–26 xxxii
17 .... 41, 115–17, 119, 321–22
17–26 .... 40, 53, 111, 314, 316, 348, 355, 869, 895
17:1–9 .... 82, 111–12, 326, 881
17:1–16 321
17:2 322
17:2–4 41
17:3 .... 41, 112, 121, 322
17:3–9 .... 41, 116, 121
17:4 .... 322, 778
17:5 322
17:6 .... 315, 339, 813, 827, 842
17:7 .... 41, 149, 777–78
17:8 .... 43, 123, 322
17:9 .... 322, 778
17:10 .... 123, 322
17:10–12 116
17:10–13 184
17:10–14 .... 54, 82, 111, 457, 733, 881
17:11 7
17:11–12 117
17:12 123
17:13 .... 41, 82, 116–17, 123, 322, 329
17:13–14 116
17:14 .... 7, 117
17:15 .... 41–43, 123, 318
17:15–16 .... 33, 82
17:16 .... 322, 340
18 356
18:3 .... 328, 891
18:5 .... 39, 324–28, 671, 674
18:7 356
18:7–8 390
18:8 .... 83, 152, 153, 390–91
18:9 153
18:15 .... 181, 390–91
18:16 .... 84, 151
18:17 .... 153, 356
18:19 356
18:19–20 315
18:20 .... 54, 83, 151
18:21 .... 83, 150, 208–9
18:23 .... 33, 54, 153
18:24 54
18:24–25 54
18:24–30 .... 10, 333, 658–59, 663, 834, 839
18:25 .... 40, 308, 333, 514
18:25–29 269
18:26 .... 43, 124, 639
18:26–28 753
18:27 .... 639, 655, 659
18:28 40

18:28–29 308
18–20 355
18–26 322
19 807
19:2 .... 39–40, 55, 66
19:3 .... 33, 54, 152, 356, 883
19:4 .... 54, 152
19:5–8 55
19:7 318
19:8 .... 340, 356
19:9–10 .... 84, 150, 579, 581, 583, 876
19:10 .... 309, 497
19:11 54
19:12 33
19:13 .... 84, 141, 356
19:14 .... 152, 311
19:15 .... 33, 54, 82, 496–97
19:17 340
19:18 .... 39, 42–44, 83, 135, 377, 807–8, 854, 860–61, 866
19:19 .... xxiv, 83, 135, 343
19:20–22 .... 83, 151, 243
19:23 .... 40, 52
19:23–24 839
19:23–25 .... 40, 333
19:24 72
19:26 .... 82, 418
19:27–28 .... 82, 149
19:29 .... 84, 150, 356, 369, 792
19:30 .... 33, 54, 356, 883
19:31 .... 33, 54, 83, 150, 184, 730
19:32 54
19:33 43
19:33–34 .... xxvi, 33, 42–44, 84, 150, 520, 808, 860–61
19:34 .... 42–44, 149, 322, 344–45, 807, 854, 866
19:35–36 .... 84, 150, 395, 573
19:36 .... 369, 418
20 356
20:2 .... 124, 208–9
20:2–5 .... 83, 150
20:3 208–9
20:6 .... 184, 730
20:6–7 33
20:7–8 55
20:9 .... 32, 39, 54, 83, 134, 356
20:10 .... 54, 83, 104, 151, 487
20:11 .... 83, 356, 390
20:14 .... 153, 356
20:15 153
20:15–16 .... 33, 54
20:17 .... 153, 340
20:19 340
20:21 .... 84, 151
20:24 67
20:24–26 122
20:27 .... 33, 83, 150, 184
21:1 60
21:1–3 343
21:1–4 .... 66, 72
21:2 50
21:2–4 344
21:5 .... 82, 149, 343–44
21:7 343
21:9 84
21:10 892
21:10–11 892
21:11 .... 60, 66, 72, 344
21:13–15 .... 343–44, 692
21:14 663
21:15 663
21:18 185
21:20 151
22:2 356
22:3 .... 45, 55
22:4 440
22:8 .... 41–42, 318, 353
22:10 381
22:10–14 72
22:15 356
22:17–24 .... 83, 149
22:17–25 463
22:18 .... 250, 463
22:20 .... 83, 127
22:20–22 .... 82, 128
22:21 .... 42–43, 83, 463
22:21–22 127
22:22 127
22:23 .... 83, 463
22:25 463
22:26 50
22:27 .... 50, 151
22:28 151
22:29–30 55
22:33 282
23 54
23:3 .... 33, 54, 883
23:4–8 .... 54, 344
23:5 .... 60, 615
23:5–8 .... 27, 34, 72, 82, 150
23:7–8 72
23:9–14 .... 27, 34, 55
23:10–11 .... 65, 860
23:13 315
23:15–21 .... 27, 34, 55, 82, 150
23:17 208
23:18 315
23:20 72
23:22 .... 84, 401, 497
23:23–25 72
23:24 .... 494, 542, 692
23:24–25 54
23:26–28 72
23:26–32 55
23:29 39
23:33–4 55
23:33–36 344
23:33–43 .... 27, 34, 55, 82, 150
23:34 208
23:34–36 72
23:37 .... 639, 651
23:39 .... 494, 542, 668
23:40 .... 635, 669
23:40–43 639
23:42 .... 43, 55, 635, 669
23–27 .... 46, 48, 125, 315, 332, 345, 348
24 .... 45, 58
24:1–3 36
24:1–4 811–12
24:1–9 781
24:2–3 36
24:5–9 .... 55, 180, 353, 751, 812, 883
24:7 329
24:8 .... 180–81, 329
24:9 .... 72, 181, 860
24:10 .... 44, 142
24:10–16 45
24:10–23 .... 44, 55, 60, 62, 66, 69, 86, 869
24:11 44
24:12 .... 44, 669
24:12–13 44
24:13–23 46
24:14 44
24:15 .... 33, 45
24:15–22 44
24:16 .... 43, 45
24:17 .... 32, 45, 83
24:17–21 45
24:18 .... 33, 45, 55
24:19–20 .... 32, 46, 103
24:20 .... 39, 83, 134
24:21 .... 45, 55
24:21 .... 32–33, 83
24:22 .... 43, 45, 124
24:22–23 45
24:23 44
25 .... xxxiii, 46–49, 125–26, 289, 315, 345, 610, 677
25:1–7 .... 33, 55, 82, 333, 680, 839
25:4 .... 40, 55
25:8–24 .... 47, 69–70
25:8–55 47
25:10 .... 250, 288, 344–45
25:13 70
25:18 357
25:19 357
25:23 .... 47, 49, 333, 540, 839
25:23–26 .... 579, 585–86
25:25 .... 47, 320, 586, 588

25:25–28 309, 319–20
25:25–55 47
25:27 320
25:28 320
25:29 47, 320
25:35 47–48, 50, 882
25:35–36 48
25:35–37 84
25:35–38 48, 50, 125, 680
25:35–43 46, 667
25:35–46 288
25:36 50, 356
25:36–37 882
25:37 50, 356
25:38 50, 282
25:39 47–49, 51, 126, 882
25:39–40 49
25:39–43 49
25:39–46 32, 48, 50–51, 125, 288, 882
25:39–55 82
25:40 50, 126
25:41 49–50
25:42 47, 49, 51, 667–68
25:43 xxxii, 51, 315, 330
25:44 50
25:45 50, 344–45
25:45–46 345
25:46 xxxii, 50–51, 330, 667–68
25:47 47–48
25:47–55 32
25:48 47–48
25:50 48
25:53 xxxii, 330
26 xxvii, 52, 315, 319, 330, 332, 335, 348–50, 396, 476, 512, 605, 610–11, 618, 622–23, 659, 664, 701, 721, 769
26:1 54, 82, 357
26:2 33, 54, 356, 883
26:4 332
26:4–6 330–31
26:5 332, 369
26:6 149, 332, 369
26:6–7 254
26:12 39, 282, 332
26:12–13 283
26:13 309, 330–32
26:14 396
26:14–15 753
26:14–39 332
26:14–45 207
26:15 284
26:16 549
26:18 396
26:19 311
26:19–20 442
26:20 253
26:21 396
26:22–33 356
26:23 396
26:25 422
26:25–26 349–50
26:26 356
26:27 396
26:29 xxvii, 208, 225, 309, 318, 612
26:30 357, 397
26:30–31 319
26:31 315
26:33 315, 318, 357, 396, 514, 639, 753
26:34 333
26:34–35 40, 837–39, 883
26:34–39 839
26:36–37 255
26:39 53, 330, 514, 610–11, 838
26:39–40 330
26:40 53, 377, 487, 512, 514, 610–11, 623, 639, 664–65, 834, 844, 883
26:40–41 53, 207, 285, 309, 614, 622, 624, 769, 779, 814, 878
26:40–42 52–53, 820
26:40–45 512, 664
26:41 52, 149, 701, 768, 844
26:41–45 207
26:42 52, 514, 611
26:43 40, 333, 838
26:44 284
26:44–45 283
26:45 52, 282, 285, 512, 514
26:46 39, 299
27 67, 898
27:1–8 208
27:1–11 44
27:1–25 69
27:2 84, 151
27:4 459
27:6 59
27:9 136
27:10–11 45
27:14 517
27:16–25 46
27:21 105, 136
27:26 33, 59, 82, 127, 326
27:26–27 680
27:27 105
27:28 72, 105, 119
27:29 34, 105, 157
27:30 124
27:30–33 68, 82

NUMBERS

18, 35, 43, 57–63, 65, 68–71, 73, 81, 86, 90–92, 94–97, 109, 132–33, 139, 152, 155, 166, 169, 240, 291, 293–94, 321, 324, 357, 501, 511–12, 515–17, 572, 581, 651, 673, 737, 869, 898, 901
1–4 62
1–10 63
1–36 508
1:2–3 183
1:21 69
1:23 69
1:26–27 723
1:38 90
1:47–49 748
1:49–50 751
2:1–34 59–60
2:3 723
2:33 748
3:4 71–72
3:6–8 751
3:6–9 59, 67–68, 73, 751
3:7 728
3:8 728
3:10–13 781
3:11–13 59, 108–9, 812
3:12–13 59
3:13 33, 82, 127
3:17 67
3:17–20 726, 751–52
3:21–26 752
3:21–37 752–53
3:21–39 59–60
3:27–32 752
3:33–37 752
3:38 751–52
3:40–41 59
3:44–51 59
4:1–3 812
4:2–4 751
4:4–15 737
4:10 737
4:23 751
4:30 751
4:35 751
4:39 751
4:43 751
4:47 751
5 662
5:1–2 59
5:1–4 58–59, 66, 73, 84, 140, 772, 860
5:2 60, 73
5:3 60
5:7 487
5:11–31 268
5:13 268
5:14 268, 423
5:20 268
5:27 268
5:28 268, 422
5:29 268
5:31 340

6:2 ... 390
6:3 ... 390
6:5 ... 174, 891–92
6:6 ... 174
6:20 ... 72
6:23 ... 464
6:23–27 ... 463–64, 538
6:24 ... 464
6:24–25 ... 540
6:25 ... 464, 546
7 ... 72
7:1 ... 72
7:9 ... 737
17:12–17 ... 723
7:89 ... 99, 147
8:13 ... 72
8:16–18 ... 59, 108–9
8:17 ... 33, 82, 127
8:19 ... 59, 67–68, 73, 751
8:22 ... 751
8:24 ... 728, 751
9:1–5 ... 60
9:1–14 ... 27, 34, 44, 58, 60, 66, 69, 82, 86, 150, 869
9:6 ... 60
9:6–7 ... 60
9:7 ... 60
9:8 ... 44, 60
9:8–9 ... 60
9:9–11 ... 812
9:9–14 ... 60, 721
9:10 ... 813
9:10–12 ... 61
9:10–14 ... 60
9:11 ... 60
9:12 ... 57, 60
9:14 ... 43, 61, 123
9:15–23 ... 72
9–10 ... 562
10:11 ... 62, 149
10:14 ... 723
10:29–32 ... 62
10:34 ... 671
10:35 ... 540
10:35–36 ... 62, 84, 140, 526
10:36 ... 526
10–12 ... 61, 63
10:11–12:16 ... 149
11 ... 79, 89
11:1 ... 62
11:1–3 ... 149
11:2 ... 62
11:4 ... 100, 513
11:4–3 ... 62
11:6 ... 513
11:10–15 ... 408
11:10–30 ... 89
11:11–17 ... 86
11:14 ... 89
11:16–17 ... 89
11:17 ... 251
11:25 ... 89, 251
11:29 ... 378
11:34 ... 149
11–12 ... 492, 894
12 ... 62
12:6–8 ... 94
12:7 ... 57
12:8 ... 72, 99, 147
12:10 ... 208
12:10–15 ... 84, 141
12:15 ... 60
13 ... 174
13:1–2 ... 92
13:1–3 ... 91
13:2 ... 62, 598
13:4–16 ... 91
13:17–20 ... 91
13:21–24 ... 91
13:25 ... 62, 598
13:25–29 ... 91
13:27 ... 67
13:28 ... 91, 149, 164
13:30 ... 64, 90–92
13:31–33 ... 91
13:32 ... xxviii, 63, 333
13:32–33 ... 395
13:33 ... 58, 63, 91, 149, 164
13–14 ... 73, 79, 89–92, 94, 108, 164
13–19 ... 63
14 ... 65, 325, 501
14:1 ... 91
14:1–10 ... 62
14:2–4 ... 91
14:3 ... 369
14:4 ... 369, 671, 673
14:5 ... 91, 164, 309
14:6–9 ... 90, 92
14:6–10 ... 91
14:7–9 ... 90
14:8 ... 67
14:11 ... 178
14:11–19 ... 91
14:12–14 ... 64
14:12–17 ... 877
14:12–19 ... 65
14:13–19 ... 58, 62, 65, 92, 111
14:14 ... 64
14:16 ... 110
14:18 ... 64–65, 375, 405, 421
14:19 ... 877
14:20 ... 65
14:20–23 ... 65
14:20–25 ... 91
14:20–35 ... 62
14:22 ... 225
14:24 ... 90, 163
14:26–35 ... 91
14:29 ... 515
14:30 ... 90, 163, 325, 515
14:31 ... 91, 325, 513, 515
14:32 ... 515
14:33 ... 598
14:34 ... 149, 340, 598
14:34–35 ... 91
14:36 ... 63
14:36–38 ... 91
14:37 ... 62–63
14:38 ... 90
14:39–45 ... 91
14:41–43 ... 92
15 ... 44
15:1–31 ... 62
15:3 ... 315
15:7 ... 315
15:10 ... 315
15:13 ... 315
15:13–14 ... 43
15:14 ... 43, 315
15:14–16 ... 123, 250
15:17–20 ... 72
15:18–21 ... 65, 128, 860
15:24 ... 315
15:25 ... 598
15:25–29 ... 661
15:29 ... 43, 124
15:30 ... 43
15:32 ... 44
15:32–3 ... 66
15:32–26 ... 883
15:32–36 ... 33, 44, 58, 60, 62, 66, 69, 86, 869, 883
15:33 ... 44
15:34 ... 44, 669
15:35 ... 44, 688
15:35–36 ... 23, 46
15:36 ... 44, 688
15:37–41 ... 83, 150
15:38–40 ... 599
15:39 ... 598–99
15:41 ... 282
16 ... 73
16:1 ... 67, 73
16:1–35 ... 62
16:2 ... 357
16:3 ... 58, 66, 342, 850
16:3–7 ... 513
16:4 ... 164, 309
16:5 ... 57, 812
16:7 ... 342, 357, 812
16:9 ... 67–68

16:10 . . . 66
16:13 . . . 58, 66, 850
16:13–14 . . . 67
16:15 . . . 184
16:17 . . . 357
16:18 . . . 357
16:20–34 . . . 149
16:22 . . . 164, 309, 357, 543
16:26 . . . 513
16:30–33 . . . 514
16:31–35 . . . 342
16:35 . . . 72, 357, 513, 826
16:36–40 . . . 342
16:36–50 . . . 62
16:40 . . . 342, 357
16:41 . . . 357
16:45 . . . 164, 309
16:49 . . . 826
16–17 . . . 58, 68, 339
17:5 . . . 319–20, 812
17:8 . . . 319–20
17:8–11 . . . 342
18 . . . 58, 68, 72–73, 339–42, 608, 781
18:1 . . . 68–69, 181, 340
18:1–2 . . . 62, 342, 827
18:1–7 . . . 42, 339, 342, 812–13
18:2 . . . 661
18:2–5 . . . 59, 68, 73
18:2–6 . . . 108–9
18:2–7 . . . 339
18:3 . . . 339–40
18:3–4 . . . 340, 826
18:4 . . . 340–41, 381
18:5 . . . 181, 339–40, 342, 661, 827
18:6 . . . 67–68, 751, 826
18:7 . . . 340–42, 381
18:8–9 . . . 340
18:8–10 . . . 72
18:8–19 . . . 353
18:8–20 . . . 83, 149
18:9 . . . 136
18:11 . . . 72
18:11–20 . . . 72, 639
18:12–13 . . . 65, 84, 860
18:13 . . . 72
18:14 . . . 59, 72, 105, 119
18:14–18 . . . 680
18:15 . . . 67–68, 635, 860
18:15–16 . . . 59
18:15–18 . . . 67
18:17 . . . 315, 635, 842
18:17–18 . . . 33, 82, 127
18:17–19 . . . 59
18:19 . . . 72, 136, 691, 781
18:20 . . . 311, 340, 353, 539, 541, 607–8
18:21 . . . 692, 728
18:21–2 . . . 68
18:21–24 . . . 68, 82–83, 124, 149
18:22–23 . . . 826
18:23 . . . 339–40, 357, 728
18:24 . . . 340
18:25–29 . . . 83, 125, 150
18:25–30 . . . 68
18:26 . . . 470
18:28 . . . 692
18:30–32 . . . 83, 149
18:32 . . . 356
19 . . . 62
19:6 . . . 72
19:10 . . . 124
19:10–20 . . . 73
19:11 . . . 124
19:11–20 . . . 60
19:13 . . . 60, 334
19:18 . . . 334
19:19 . . . 334
19:20 . . . 334
20 . . . 63, 95
20–21 . . . 63, 149
20:1 . . . 62, 94
20:1–13 . . . 511, 514
20:2–13 . . . 62, 501
20:3 . . . 517
20:5 . . . 205, 412
20:6 . . . 164
20:8 . . . 671
20:12 . . . 92, 94, 97, 109, 517
20:13 . . . 108, 517, 542
20:14–17 . . . 169
20:14–21 . . . 94, 169
20:15–16 . . . 84, 143–44, 891
20:17 . . . 96
20:18 . . . 96
20:20–21 . . . 96
20:22–29 . . . 95, 108, 149
20:23–29 . . . 73
20:24–29 . . . 63
21 . . . 79, 94, 97, 169, 173
21:1–3 . . . 62, 73, 95, 268, 879
21:2 . . . 72, 106, 291
21:2–3 . . . 105
21:4 . . . 95
21:5 . . . 62
21:5–9 . . . 95
21:6 . . . 309
21:6–9 . . . 149
21:7 . . . 62
21:8–9 . . . 209
21:10 . . . 169
21:10–11 . . . 95, 169
21:10–26 . . . 165, 169
21:10–35 . . . 388
21:11 . . . 169–70
21:12 . . . 95
21:13–15 . . . 169
21:13–20 . . . 95
21:14–15 . . . 62
21:16 . . . 62
21:21–22 . . . 96, 169
21:21–35 . . . 62, 73, 95, 164, 254, 268, 671
21:22 . . . 97
21:22–23 . . . 96
21:23 . . . 96, 169
21:24 . . . 169
21:24 . . . 528–30, 532
21:24–26 . . . 96, 169
21:27–28 . . . 396
21:27–30 . . . 293–94
21:27–32 . . . 96
21:28 . . . 292
21:28–29 . . . 291, 293
21:29 . . . 169–70, 292, 294, 388
21:33–35 . . . 96
21:35 . . . 528–30, 532
22–24 . . . 62, 79, 84, 96, 138, 160, 388, 417, 607, 876
22–36 . . . 63
22:5–6 . . . 138
22:12 . . . 138
22:22 . . . 748–49
22:28–30 . . . 408
22:31 . . . 716, 748–49
22:34 . . . 749
23:8 . . . 686
23:10 . . . 72
23:11 . . . 686
23:19 . . . 72, 184
23:20 . . . 686
23:22 . . . 73
23:24 . . . 73, 880
23:25 . . . 686
23:27 . . . 686
23:30 . . . 379
24 . . . 336
24:1 . . . 686
24:3–9 . . . 10
24:7 . . . 178, 184, 336
24:7–8 . . . 268
24:8 . . . 73
24:9 . . . 68, 73, 138, 239, 480, 492, 581, 686, 880
24:10 . . . 686
24:14 . . . 336
24:15–24 . . . 10
24:17 . . . 184, 227, 292–94, 879–80
24:17–19 . . . 178, 480–81
24:18 . . . 401, 879
24:24 . . . 628
25 . . . 325, 511
25:1 . . . 792

25:1–3 . . . 62
25:1–5 . . . 164, 368
25:1–9 . . . 73
25:2 . . . 150
25:2–3 . . . 513
25:4 . . . 62
25:4–5 . . . 513–14
25:7 . . . 380
25:7–8 . . . 513
25:7–13 . . . 62
25:8–9 . . . 62
25:11 . . . 516
25:12 . . . 335
25:12–13 . . . 355, 463, 513, 692
25:13 . . . 335, 516
26 . . . 62
26:3–34 . . . 73
26:5–11 . . . 725
26:9–10 . . . 73
26:9–11 . . . 514
26:22 . . . 723
26:55 . . . 69–70
26:61 . . . 71–72
26:65 . . . 108
27:1–2 . . . 60
27:1–11 . . . 58, 60, 62, 66, 69–70, 73, 84, 86, 579, 869
27:2 . . . 70
27:3–4 . . . 60
27:4 . . . 151, 585–86
27:5 . . . 44
27:5–6 . . . 60
27:6–7 . . . 71
27:7 . . . 60, 70, 585
27:11 . . . 60
27:12 . . . 149
27:12–23 . . . 79, 152
27:14 . . . 92, 501, 517
27:17 . . . 414, 459
28:2 . . . 315
28:3–8 . . . 36, 73, 639, 691, 740, 815
28:6 . . . 315
28:8 . . . 315
28:9–10 . . . 33, 815, 883
28:11–15 . . . 73, 691, 815
28:13 . . . 315
28:16–25 . . 27, 34, 72, 82, 150, 815, 828
28:18–19 . . . 72
28:19–2 . . . 73
28:24 . . . 315
28:25 . . . 72
28:26 . . . 268, 639
28:26–31 . . . 27, 34, 82, 150, 815
28:27 . . . 315
28–29 . . . 150, 815
29:1 . . . 692
29:1–2 . . . 72
29:1–6 . . . 815
29:2 . . . 315
29:6 . . . 315
29:7–8 . . . 72
29:7–11 . . . 815
29:8 . . . 315
29:12–13 . . . 72
29:12–34 . . . 27, 34, 82, 150
29:12–38 . . . 344, 635, 639, 815
29:13 . . . 315
29:18 . . . 651
29:21 . . . 651
29:24 . . . 651
29:27 . . . 651
29:30 . . . 651
29:33 . . . 651
29:35–36 . . . 73
29:36 . . . 315
29:37 . . . 651
30 . . . 58; 69
30:2 . . . 57, 84, 546
30:3–5 . . . 73
30:5 . . . 69, 598
30:6 . . . 151
30:6–8 . . . 73, 184
30:7 . . . 517
30:8 . . . 173, 598
30:9 . . . 69, 517, 582
30:10–12 . . . 73
30:15 . . . 69, 340
31:2 . . . 423
31:3 . . . 423
31:8 . . . 164
31:16 . . . 73
31:28–30 . . . 62
32 . . . 164, 687
32:6–15 . . . 73, 138, 725
32:8 . . . 63, 686–87
32:8–14 . . . 108
32:14 . . . 63, 686–87
32:33 . . . 73
32:39 . . . 96
32:41 . . . 96
33 . . . 73, 169–70
33:3–4 . . . 73
33:4 . . . 530
33:14 . . . 73
33:35–36 . . . 95
33:38–39 . . . 63, 73
33:39 . . . 798
33:40 . . . 73
33:43–44 . . . 169
33:44 . . . 170
33:50–56 . . . 73
33:52 . . . 34, 82, 357
34 . . . 149
34:18–26 . . . 62
34:26 . . . 72
35 . . . 58, 160
35:1–8 . . . 62, 778
35:2 . . . 164
35:6 . . . 132
35:9–3 . . . 69
35:9–28 . . . 32, 83
35:9–34 . . . 62, 69, 131–33, 160
35:11 . . . 124
35:12 . . . 69, 160
35:24 . . . 69
35:24–25 . . . 133
35:25 . . . 69, 133, 160
35:28 . . . 69, 160
35:30 . . . 83, 133, 220
35:32 . . . 69
35:33 . . . 133, 514
35:33–34 . . . 357, 514
36 . . . 69, 579
36:1 . . . 70
36:1–4 . . . 70
36:1–12 . . . 58, 60, 69, 73, 86, 869
36:1–13 . . . 579
36:2 . . . 70
36:2–4 . . . 70
36:4 . . . 46, 70, 585–86, 588
36:4–6 . . . 586
36:5 . . . 70
36:5–9 . . . 70–71, 585

DEUTERONOMY

. . . xxxiii, 18, 20, 22, 24, 29, 39, 41, 44, 46–49, 51–52, 59, 78–82, 84–98, 100–5, 107–10, 112–13, 115–19, 121–28, 130, 132–36, 138, 140–53, 155, 160, 166, 170–71, 177, 185, 191, 193, 196–99, 204, 206, 249, 260–61, 270–72, 274–75, 279, 282, 306, 310, 314–16, 318, 320, 323, 326, 330, 348, 357, 359, 361, 366, 368–69, 426, 429, 434, 436, 445, 461, 466–67, 501, 511–12, 514–17, 559, 563, 568–69, 571–72, 582, 593, 596–98, 607, 617, 622, 651–52, 654, 658, 659, 664, 677, 680, 684, 686, 698, 700, 704–5, 713, 730, 786, 815, 828, 853, 869, 872, 874, 892, 899, 901
1 . . . 89–92, 94–95, 110, 174, 325, 396
1:2 . . . 149
1:3 . . . 149
1:4 . . . 95, 149
1:5 . . . 78–79, 81, 85, 105, 108, 113, 869
1:6 . . . 149
1:6–18 . . . 79
1:7 . . . 146
1:7–8 . . . 149
1:9–13 . . . 89

1:9–14 86
1:9–18 89
1:13 89
1:14 89, 100
1:14–16 89
1:15 129
1:15–16 89
1:15–17 129
1:16 391
1:16–17 89, 311
1:16–18 82
1:17 89, 130, 496, 786–87
1:18 89
1:19 93
1:19–21 91
1:19–45 79, 89, 97, 108, 501, 515, 517–18
1:20–21 90, 92
1:21 753
1:22 86, 92–93
1:22–23 91
1:23 89, 92, 100
1:25 91
1:26 93
1:26–28 91, 95, 96
1:27 93, 110, 513, 515
1:27–28 92
1:27–33 91
1:28 93, 149, 164
1:29–33 90–92
1:31 251, 505
1:32 513, 515
1:34 514
1:34–36 91
1:35 90
1:36 90, 163
1:37 90–93, 511, 514, 517–18
1:38 90, 163
1:39 90–91
1:40 91
1:41–46 91
1:42 92
1:46 94
1–11 92
1–34 63, 149
2 96, 169
2:1–7 94
2:3–4 165, 169
2:4–5 149
2:5 95, 387–88
2:6 149
2:8 95, 165, 169
2:8–12 95
2:9 95, 149, 169–70, 294–95, 387–88, 395
2:9–11 136
2:10–11 147
2:10–12 95
2:11–12 95
2:12 xx, xxviii, 95, 147, 359
2:13 165, 169
2:13–16 95
2:14–15 108, 501–2
2:14–16 149
2:15 501
2:17–23 95
2:19 95, 149, 169, 294–95, 387–88, 395
2:20 147
2:20–23 95
2:21 95, 294
2:21–22 387
2:22 95, 359
2:23 95
2:24 165, 169
2:24–25 96
2:26 165, 169
2:26–29 96–97
2:27 170
2:28–29 96, 139
2:29 170
2:30 96, 97
2:30–31 96, 169, 295
2:30–33 165, 169
2:32 96, 169
2:33 96, 169, 528–30, 532
2:33–35 96
2:33–36 169
2:34 97
2:35 97
2:36 96, 164, 169
2:36–37 96, 165, 169, 295
2:37 169
2:1–3:11 388
2:24–3:11 254, 671
2–7 130
3 100
3:1–3 96
3:2 98
3:3 528–30, 532
3:4–7 96
3:5 81, 97
3:6 96
3:7 97
3:8–20 96
3:9 96
3:10 164
3:11 96–97
3:13–14 96
3:14 96, 359
3:15 96
3:20 163
3:21 149
3:21–22 149
3:21–29 79, 152
3:22 77
3:23–28 86
3:26 92–94, 511, 514, 517–18
4 92, 98, 100, 127, 206
4:2 82, 147, 152, 274, 566, 571–72
4:3 149, 368
4:4 113, 163, 204
4:5–9 98
4:5–40 97–98
4:6 705
4:7 185
4:9 99
4:9–10 283, 285
4:10–12 97–98, 149
4:12 99
4:13–14 xviii
4:13 97–98, 149, 568
4:14 97–98, 149
4:15 97–99
4:15–16 152
4:16 357
4:16–18 357, 434
4:16–19 435
4:16–31 98
4:17 357
4:17–18 150
4:18 357, 434
4:19 150, 356
4:20 185, 255, 282, 532
4:21 92–93, 511, 514, 517–18
4:21–22 97, 150
4:24 25, 77, 108, 422
4:25 514
4:25–27 753
4:26 153
4:28 357
4:29 157, 163, 191, 704, 753, 784
4:29–30 309
4:31 877
4:32 97–98, 149
4:32–33 149
4:32–36 255
4:33 97–100
4:34 143, 147, 209, 441, 532
4:34–35 97–98, 149
4:35 77, 284, 384, 671, 820
4:36 97–100, 149
4:37 97–98, 149, 368, 532
4:38 97–98, 149, 528, 532
4:39 384, 820
4:39–40 98
4:41–43 32, 69, 83, 97, 132–33, 160
4:44 78–79, 81, 105, 108, 869
4:45–46 149
4:47–49 149
4–5 100

5 .... xxx, xlv, 78, 98, 110, 131, 152, 274, 470, 492
5:1 .... 78, 81
5:1–2 80
5:1–4 99
5:1–5 98
5:1–15 101
5:1–33 79
5:2 .... 89, 597
5:3 98
5:4 99
5:6 .... 173, 494, 532
5:6–7 495
5:6–9 494
5:6–21 .... 22, 98, 100, 110, 152, 274
5:7 .... 209, 369, 494
5:7–8 207
5:8 .... 107, 492, 494
5:8–10 .... 107, 208–9
5:9 .... 20, 24–25, 107, 108, 209, 421–22, 492, 494–95, 519–20, 558–59, 778
5:9–10 .... 107, 161, 310, 423, 877
5:10 107
5:11 421
5:12 .... xxx, 22, 101–2, 274
5:12–14 275
5:12–15 .... 27, 33, 101, 273, 883
5:13 77
5:14 101–2
5:15 .... 101–2, 143, 532
5:16 .... 77, 102, 152, 184, 463, 574
5:17 .... 77, 271, 369
5:18 .... 77, 83, 151, 271, 369, 574
5:19 .... 77, 271, 369, 574
5:20 .... 77, 134, 208, 271
5:21 .... 77, 574
5:22 568
5:22–33 98
5:23 93
5:23–29 86
5:24–26 100
5:24–28 882
5:25 130
5:25–28 .... 83, 866
5:27–28 130
5:28 .... 86, 93, 100
5:32 .... 156, 274
5–28 284
6 569
6:1 .... 78–79, 81, 105, 108, 113, 869
6:4 .... 77, 146
6:4–8 569
6:4–9 .... 478, 568–69
6:5 .... 77, 163, 191, 205, 209, 593
6:5–9 .... 79, 152
6:6–7 .... 281, 283
6:6–9 .... 99, 157, 285, 566, 568–69, 878
6:7 .... 478–79, 492–93, 568–69, 689, 818
6:7–9 169
6:9 569
6:10 .... 104, 106
6:10–11 .... 149, 160, 162
6:11 .... 366, 671
6:12 .... 149, 173, 532
6:13 .... 77, 149
6:14 .... 150, 271
6:15 .... 25, 108, 422, 434
6:16 .... 77, 108, 149, 225
6:18 149
6:20 164
6:20–24 173
6:20–25 .... 79, 85, 99, 161, 169, 492–93
6:21 532
6:21–22 149
6:22 .... 143, 528
6:22–33 99
6:23 .... 149, 532
6:24–25 149
6–2 95
6–11 .... 78, 87, 152
7 .... 97, 134, 155, 190, 200, 618, 655
7:1 .... 106, 123, 162, 188, 198, 202, 208, 254, 655, 657–58
7:1–2 .... 83, 106, 134, 198, 458, 514
7:1–3 663
7:1–4 .... 202, 663, 876
7:1–5 .... 10, 104, 582, 655, 677
7:1–6 .... 20, 24, 27, 97, 156, 870, 876, 879
7:2 .... 104–6, 157, 159, 173, 866
7:2–4 677
7:3 .... 25, 104–6, 142, 173, 200, 589, 655, 657–59, 677, 679, 690
7:3–4 .... 106, 164, 200–1, 208, 639
7:4 .... 106, 116, 157, 201, 207, 663, 690
7:4–5 155
7:5 .... 34, 82, 104, 173, 209, 418, 736, 800
7:6 .... 119, 122–23, 185, 224, 250, 282, 470, 528, 639, 655, 657, 663
7:8 .... 93, 268, 368, 461–62, 664
7:9 .... 24, 108–9, 461, 560, 607, 622–23, 664
7:9–10 .... 107, 421, 519, 559, 877
7:10 .... 108, 461, 558–60
7:12 149
7:13 .... 368, 442
7:16 .... 149, 164, 173, 258, 318, 357, 514
7:17–26 879
7:18–19 149
7:19 .... 143, 441
7:20 .... 160, 162
7:21 .... 140, 664, 692
7:24 .... 156, 514, 547
7:24–26 .... 82, 105, 209, 418
7:25 .... 104, 736
8 366
8:1 367
8:2 .... 108, 369, 532, 816–18
8:2–4 149
8:3 .... 77, 81, 671
8:4 671
8:5 .... 182, 362, 470, 500, 504
8:7–8 205
8:8 .... 205, 412
8:10 366
8:12 366
8:12–14 366
8:13 367
8:14 .... 149, 173
8:15 .... 149, 524–25
8:15–16 149
8:16–18 108
8:17 524
8:19 271
8:20 149
8–13 130
9 103
9:1 .... 108, 149
9:1–2 149
9:2 .... 79, 501
9:3 671
9:3–6 149
9:4 .... 10, 77
9:4–5 .... 109, 116
9:4–6 111
9:5 149
9:8 108
9:9 203
9:9–11 .... 108, 568
9:11 203
9:12–14 108
9:14 549
9:15 568
9:15–17 108
9:17 568
9:18 .... 203, 514
9:18–19 543
9:18–20 .... 108, 110
9:19 77
9:20 109
9:21 108
9:22 108
9:23 79
9:23–24 108
9:25–26 513–14
9:25–29 109–11
9:26 .... 255, 664
9:26–29 .... 64, 111
9:27 111

9:28 ....110–11, 461
9:29 ....255, 664
9–10 108–11
10:1 568
10:1–5 108
10:1–6 80
10:3 ....110, 568
10:4 ....110, 152
10:5 110
10:6 109
10:6–7 108
10:6–9 109
10:8–9 108–9
10:9 ....164, 311, 607
10:9–16 80
10:10 203
10:10–11 ....108, 110
10:12 ....163, 191
10:14 671
10:15 ....149, 368, 461
10:16 ....149, 309, 377
10:17 ....153, 531, 664
10:17–18 496
10:18 ....152, 271, 545
10:18–19 33
10:19 ....44, 149–50
10:20 ....149, 204
10:21 149
10:22 ....80, 149
10–11 532
11:2 ....99, 143
11:2–3 99
11:2–4 149
11:4 99
11:5 149
11:5–6 99
11:5–7 168
11:5–14 80
11:6 ....149, 514
11:7 ....99–100, 165, 167–68
11:8 494
11:9 149
11:10 149
11:13 ....152, 163, 191
11:13–14 80
11:14 ....311, 442
11:15 366
11:18 283
11:18–20 ....152, 568
11:18–21 99
11:19 ....283, 478–79, 493, 568–69
11:19–20 285
11:19–21 169
11:22 ....163, 204
11:23–25 149
11:24 ....149, 163
11:25 ....156, 547
11:26 152
11:26–28 152
11:28 271
11:29 ....104, 106
11:29–30 ....152, 160, 163
11–15 122
12 ....41, 92, 98, 102, 112–19, 121–22, 124, 127, 129, 133, 171, 193, 196, 198, 346, 360, 527, 705, 720, 736, 739, 769, 881
12:1 ....79, 113
12:1–28 113
12:2 ....207–8, 256, 310, 357, 360–61
12:2–2 111
12:2–4 ....82, 116, 118, 197
12:2–7 115
12:2–28 ....29, 111, 132, 705, 881
12:3 ....105, 197, 209, 418, 736, 800
12:3–4 209
12:5 ....115, 122, 195, 197, 635, 639, 664, 691, 736, 738–39, 750, 765, 768–69, 879, 881
12:5–6 309
12:5–7 116
12:5–12 ....738, 767
12:5–14 ....82, 720, 752–53, 764, 772
12:5–28 82
12:6 470
12:8 ....118, 165–66, 171, 501
12:8–9 ....116, 171, 502
12:8–10 118
12:8–12 115
12:9 ....256, 501, 526–28
12:9–10 751
12:9–12 767
12:10 ....193–94, 209, 742, 881
12:10–11 753–74
12:10–12 116
12:11 ....115, 197, 470, 639, 664, 691, 736, 769
12:12 ....539, 541, 607
12:13 116–18
12:13–14 ....635, 654
12:13–15 117
12:13–19 115
12:13–31 117
12:14 ....115–16, 122, 485, 639, 664, 736
12:14–15 639
12:15 ....41, 82, 116–17, 121–22
12:15–25 326
12:16 ....82, 116–17, 123, 184, 733
12:17–18 125
12:17–19 ....82, 116
12:18 ....115, 122, 485, 635, 736
12:18–19 150
12:19 125
12:20 ....112, 132–33
12:20–21 ....41, 121
12:20–22 ....82, 116
12:20–28 115
12:21 ....112, 117, 197, 736
12:21–22 122
12:23 ....7, 184
12:23–24 ....117, 123, 733
12:23–25 ....82, 116, 733
12:26 ....639, 664, 736
12:26–27 116
12:26–28 82
12:27 184
12:29 152
12:29–31 ....82, 116, 149
12:31 ....83, 150, 514, 658
12:32 ....82, 152, 274, 571–72
12–17 131
12–19 113
12–26 ....18, 78, 81, 87, 112, 122, 571, 869, 881, 901
12–28 78
12:30 704
13 119
13:1 ....82, 152
13:1–5 ....79, 82, 713
13:2 ....271, 714
13:2–6 82
13:3 ....191, 713
13:4 149
13:5 ....77, 173–74
13:6–7 149
13:6–11 82
13:7–12 82
13:8 ....318, 357
13:10 173
13:12–18 ....82, 174
13:13 ....119, 174
13:13–19 82
13:15 ....33, 72, 82, 119, 174
13:15–17 119
13:16 ....119, 174
13:17 ....33, 82, 119, 164, 174
13–14 138
14 ....41, 119–22, 124, 396
14:1–2 ....82, 122, 149
14:2 ....119, 122–23, 185, 282, 470
14:3 ....120, 658
14:3–7 458
14:3–20 82
14:3–21 ....41, 116, 119–20, 318, 457
14:4–5 ....41, 121–22
14:4–6 120
14:4–8 120
14:6–9 90
14:9–10 120
14:11 120–21
14:12 ....146, 681

14:13 . . . 121
14:13–18 . . . 120–21
14:18 . . . 121
14:19 . . . 120–21
14:20 . . . 120–21
14:21 . . . 33, 121–24
14:21a . . . 42, 82, 120
14:21b . . . 27, 34, 82, 119–20, 151
14:21c . . . 119–21
14:22–23 . . . 84
14:22–27 . . . 143
14:22–29 . . . 82, 113, 124, 677, 681, 881
14:23 . . . 197, 485, 736
14:24 . . . 90, 197, 736
14:24–25 . . . 125, 326
14:25 . . . 208, 736
14:25–26 . . . 125
14:26 . . . 227
14:27 . . . 150, 539, 541, 607
14:28 . . . 125, 391
14:28–29 . . . 84, 143
14:29 . . . 124–25, 150, 271, 366, 539, 541, 607, 860
15 . . . 102, 126, 288
15:1 . . . 50, 82, 125, 288–89, 677, 680
15:1–3 . . . 639
15:1–11 . . . 33, 49–50, 82, 125, 126, 140, 667, 882
15:1–18 . . . 113, 125
15:2 . . . 50, 125, 677, 680, 882
15:3 . . . 50, 125, 680
15:5 . . . 459
15:6 . . . 50
15:7 . . . 50
15:7–10 . . . 540
15:7–11 . . . 80, 882
15:8 . . . 50
15:9 . . . 50, 125
15:9–11 . . . 476, 539
15:10 . . . 50
15:11 . . . 77, 497
15:12 . . . xxvi, 48, 50, 126, 288–89
15:12–13 . . . 597
15:12–15 . . . 882
15:12–18 . . . 32, 49–51, 82, 125–26, 288, 667
15:13 . . . 51
15:13–14 . . . 80, 126
15:14 . . . 50
15:15 . . . 51, 87
15:16–17 . . . 126
15:17 . . . 126
15:18 . . . 51, 126
15:19 . . . 128
15:19–21 . . . 127
15:19–23 . . . 33, 82, 113, 127, 680, 881
15:20 . . . 127, 485
15:21 . . . 83, 128, 149, 463–64
15:23 . . . 733
16 . . . 485
16:1–8 . . . 27, 34, 82, 128, 150, 209, 344
16:1–17 . . . 485
16:1–18 . . . 113
16:2 . . . 128, 150, 197, 483, 485
16:3 . . . 241
16:6 . . . 128, 150, 197, 483, 485
16:7 . . . 128, 150, 485, 827–28, 872
16:9–10 . . . 309
16:9–12 . . . 27, 34, 82, 128, 143, 150
16:11 . . . 124, 128, 150, 197, 271, 483, 485
16:12 . . . 87–88
16:13 . . . 242, 651–52
16:13–15 . . . 27, 34, 82, 128, 150, 635, 639
16:13–17 . . . 344
16:14 . . . 124, 271, 639, 692
16:15 . . . 128, 150, 483, 485, 639, 692
16:16 . . . 129, 483, 485, 772–73
16:16–17 . . . 27, 34, 82, 128–29, 815, 881
16:17 . . . 129
16:18 . . . 82
16:18–2 . . . 129
16:18–19 . . . 391, 786–87
16:18–20 . . . 33, 113, 129, 881
16:19 . . . 256, 311, 573, 786
16:19–20 . . . 82
16:20 . . . 573
16:21 . . . 209
16:21–22 . . . 82
16:22 . . . 418
16–18 . . . 786
17:1 . . . 83, 149, 658
17:1–7 . . . 108
17:2 . . . 130
17:2–7 . . . 33, 83, 129
17:3 . . . 356
17:6 . . . 83, 130, 133, 220, 786
17:7 . . . 77, 149
17:8 . . . 130, 786
17:8–11 . . . 786
17:8–12 . . . 786
17:8–13 . . . 33, 83, 113, 129, 133
17:8–17 . . . 129
17:9 . . . 130, 786
17:10 . . . 787
17:14 . . . 152, 177–78, 368
17:14–20 . . . 83, 178
17:16 . . . 255, 369, 540, 760
17:16–17 . . . 199–200, 367, 759
17:17 . . . 178, 200–1, 760, 879
17:18–19 . . . 79
17:19 . . . 191
17:20 . . . 87
18 . . . 130
18:1 . . . 150, 286, 539, 541, 607
18:1–2 . . . 164
18:1–8 . . . 83, 113, 149
18:1–11 . . . 113
18:2–6 . . . 110
18:3 . . . 150
18:4 . . . 72, 84, 143
18:5 . . . 59, 286–87, 877
18:6 . . . 151
18:6–8 . . . 132
18:8 . . . 320
18:8–20 . . . 150
18:9 . . . 209
18:9–14 . . . 33, 83, 131, 150
18:10 . . . 208–9, 357, 418, 470, 730
18:11 . . . 184, 728, 730
18:14 . . . 418
18:15 . . . 77, 131, 147–48, 267, 369, 855–56, 866, 902
18:15–18 . . . 100, 130, 882
18:15–22 . . . 83, 147
18:16 . . . 149
18:16–17 . . . 86
18:18 . . . 147, 267, 369, 866
18:18–19 . . . 207
18:18–20 . . . 79
18:19 . . . 77, 866
18:19–22 . . . 147
18:20 . . . 131
18:21 . . . 285
18:22 . . . 131, 255, 278, 330, 668, 713–14
19 . . . 46, 132–33, 160
19:1 . . . 152
19:1–3 . . . 113
19:1–13 . . . 32, 69, 83, 113, 131–33, 160, 881
19:4 . . . 131
19:5 . . . 131
19:6 . . . 131
19:8 . . . 132–33
19:10 . . . 44, 88, 133, 205, 209, 514
19:11 . . . 131
19:12 . . . 131–33
19:13 . . . 69, 87–88, 133, 141, 318, 357
19:14 . . . 83, 152, 361, 573
19:15 . . . 77, 83, 133, 220, 271
19:15–20 . . . 33, 573
19:15–21 . . . 83, 113
19:16 . . . 134, 150, 540
19:18 . . . 134
19:18–21 . . . 134
19:19 . . . 77, 519
19:21 . . . 32, 77, 87, 103, 134, 318, 357
20 . . . 134, 155
20:1–20 . . . 83
20:2–4 . . . 788

20:4 140
20:5 108
20:10–14 198
20:10–15 159
20:11 198–99
20:11–18 879
20:13 149
20:14 . . . . 134, 800
20:12–14 198
20:15 . . . . xxiii, 159, 198
20:16 97
20:16–18 134
20:17 . . . . 106, 134
20:18 . . . . 106, 157
20:19 . . . . 88, 151
21:1–9 . . . . 83, 113
21:8 . . . . 271, 514
21:10–14 . . . . 83, 126
21:14 467
21:15–17 . . . . 83, 150
21:18–21 . . . . 32, 83, 103, 134–35, 220, 255
21:21 . . . . 77, 87, 134
21:22–23 83
21:23 . . . . 77, 164
22:1 135
22:1–4 . . . . 33, 83, 134, 377, 860–61
22:2 . . . . 135, 137
22:3–17 80
22:4 135
22:5 . . . . 83, 685
22:6–7 83
22:8 . . . . 33, 82–83, 150
22:9 136–37
22:9–11 . . . . 83, 135
22:11–19 xxiv
22:11 . . . . xxiv, 343
22:12 . . . . 83, 150
22:13 150
22:13–21 83
22:21 77
22:22 . . . . 87, 104
22:22–27 . . . . 83, 151
22:24 77
22:25 275–76
22:27 275–76
22:28–29 . . . . 33, 83, 137–38
22:29 138
22:30 . . . . 83, 88, 151, 152, 351, 584
23 . . . . 138, 190, 238, 247–49, 582, 596, 660, 874
23:1 . . . . 83, 88, 151, 153, 247
23:1–7 . . . . 247, 866, 874
23:1–8 . . . . 84, 239, 247, 249–50, 858, 876, 879
23:2 . . . . 138, 458, 689
23:2–6 394
23:3 . . . . xxxiii, 200–2, 238, 582, 604, 606, 658, 684, 688–90, 874
23:3–6 . . . . 79, 238–40, 249, 341, 579, 581, 585–6, 635, 639, 683–84, 686, 874
23:3–8 . . . . 202, 589, 639, 655, 657, 663, 874
23:4 . . . . 583, 606
23:4–5 . . . . 138–39, 584, 607
23:5 . . . . 239, 368, 686
23:5–6 685
23:6 . . . . xxxiii, 238, 581–82, 588, 655, 659, 684, 874
23:7 . . . . 200–2, 584, 874
23:7–8 . . . . 239–40, 341, 658
23:9 . . . . 84, 140, 150, 180–81
23:9–10 180
23:9–11 883
23:9–14 . . . . 84, 139–40
23:10 . . . . 140, 180
23:10–11 . . . . 180, 183
23:11 . . . . 82, 139
23:12 101–2
23:13 . . . . 140, 149, 356
23:14 . . . . 140, 860
23:15–16 . . . . 84, 573
23:17–18 . . . . 84, 150
23:18 . . . . 226, 658
23:19 . . . . 50, 84, 125
23:19–20 . . . . 33, 50, 84, 125, 140, 882
23:20 50
23:21 . . . . 151, 185, 546, 596–97
23:21–23 . . . . 84, 151, 596–98
23:22 . . . . 151, 596–97
23:23 596–97
23:24 366
23:24–25 84
24 . . . . 88, 142, 281
24:1 . . . . 78, 140, 269, 466–67
24:1–4 . . . . 84, 268–69, 662
24:3 . . . . 150, 467
24:4 269
24:5 . . . . 84, 783
24:6 . . . . 50, 84, 140, 204
24:7 . . . . 32, 77, 84, 150
24:8 141
24:8–9 . . . . 84, 141
24:9 87
24:10 . . . . 50, 667–68
24:10–11 . . . . 141, 280
24:10–13 . . . . 50, 84
24:12–13 . . . . 141, 280
24:12–21 80
24:12 497
24:13 . . . . 50, 667
24:14 124
24:14–15 . . . . 84, 141, 280
24:15 . . . . 141, 540
24:16 . . . . xxvii, 33, 84, 204, 279–80, 318–19, 323, 519, 610, 881
24:17 . . . . 33, 84, 124, 140, 152, 271, 390, 497, 548
24:17–18 . . . . 33, 84, 311, 345, 519
24:17–19 860
24:17–22 . . . . 280, 540
24:18 . . . . 33, 87
24:19 . . . . 124, 271, 497, 548, 579, 581, 583, 876
24:19–22 84
24:20 . . . . 124, 150, 271, 497, 548
24:21 . . . . 124, 271, 309, 401, 497, 548
24:22 87
25:1 . . . . 243, 626
25:1–3 84
25:4 . . . . 78, 84, 151, 861
25:5 . . . . 78, 151, 585
25:5–6 586
25:5–10 . . . . 21, 84, 151, 579, 585, 588
25:6 . . . . 84, 151, 549, 585–86
25:7 . . . . 78, 84, 151, 585
25:9–10 585
25:11 141
25:11–12 . . . . 84, 142
25:12 . . . . 87, 318, 357
25:13–16 . . . . 84, 150, 573
25:16 658
25:17–18 87
25:17–19 . . . . 84, 149, 615
26 . . . . 143, 147
26:1 . . . . 149, 152
26:1–5 268
26:1–11 . . . . 84, 143
26:1–15 881
26:1–16 113
26:2 . . . . 197, 681
26:4–20 80
26:5 . . . . 143, 149
26:5–8 143
26:5–9 161
26:5–10 144
26:6–8 149
26:6–10 891
26:9 . . . . 149, 273
26:11 . . . . 124, 150
26:12 . . . . 124–25, 150, 271, 366, 391, 677, 681
26:12–15 . . . . 84, 113, 143
26:13 . . . . 124–25, 150, 271, 860
26:16 191
26:17 282
26:18 . . . . 185, 272, 470
26:19 . . . . xxv, 272, 282, 436
27 113
27:1–8 79

27:1–11 86
27:1–14 .... 160, 163
27:4 .... 84, 152
27:5 .... 82, 113, 152, 163, 194
27:5–6 .... 113, 115, 118, 881
27:6 .... 41, 82, 635
27:9 282
27:9–10 501
27:9–14 79
27:11–13 152
27:14 94
27:15 .... 152, 174
27:15–26 152
27:16 .... 152, 356, 418
27:17 .... 83, 152, 361, 573
27:18 152
27:19 .... 152, 271
27:20 .... 88, 151, 152
27:21 .... 33, 153
27:22 .... 151, 153
27:23 .... 151, 153
27:24 153
27:25 .... 153, 271, 514, 573
27:26 .... 78, 153
27:15–28:68 153
28 .... 396, 427
28:1 459
28:1–14 156
28:9 .... 185, 282
28:11 253
28:12 .... 310, 549
28:14 271
28:15 153
28:20 .... 83, 470
28:22 442
28:26 .... 309, 541
28:30 .... 256, 436
28:32 549
28:33 369
28:36 357
28:39 256
28:46 143
28:48 309
28:49 .... 146, 292, 302, 311, 427
28:49–52 427
28:51 442
28:52 427
28:53 309
28:53–57 .... 208, 225, 318, 612
28:64 .... 271, 357
28:65 612
28:68 369
28:69 .... 79, 81, 85, 113
29 .... 618, 622–23
29:1 .... 79, 81, 85, 113, 282–84, 869
29:1–4 .... 281–82, 866
29:2–4 .... 224, 866, 878
29:3 441
29:3–4 149
29:4 .... 78, 224, 263, 282–84, 286, 311
29:5 671
29:5–6 149
29:7 149
29:9 156
29:11 .... 124, 164
29:12 623
29:12–13 283
29:13 .... 81, 185, 282
29:14 623
29:17 .... 318, 357
29:19 .... 397, 494–95, 623
29:20 .... 309, 423, 549, 623
29:20–21 .... 622, 624
29:21 623
29:23 .... 10, 149, 221, 255, 323, 362, 395–96, 549, 612, 878
29:23–25 309
29:24–28 309
29:26 271
29–30 .... 207, 221, 284
30 .... 512, 664
30:1–5 .... 86, 459
30:1–6 878
30:2 .... 191, 207, 664
30:2–4 639
30:2–5 512
30:3 .... 309, 311, 357, 436, 565, 664
30:3–4 664–65
30:3–6 207
30:4 664
30:5 149
30:6 .... 149, 152, 309
30:7 623
30:9 436
30:10 191
30:12 78
30:13 78
30:14 78
30:15 .... 152, 309
30:16–18 753
31 484
31:1–8 .... 79, 152
31:3 .... 149, 879
31:4 .... 149, 529, 532
31:5 149
31:5–6 156
31:6 .... 78, 140, 483–84, 874
31:7 .... 442, 753
31:7–8 .... 712, 716
31:8 .... 78, 140, 483–84, 874
31:9–11 288–89
31:10 .... 125, 289, 882
31:10–13 .... 79, 494, 639, 680
31:11 635
31:11–13 668
31:12 124
31:14 101–2
31:14–15 .... 79, 152
31:16 .... 101–2, 284, 514, 549
31:18 369
31:20 .... 284, 366
31:23 .... 79, 152, 442, 712, 716, 753
31:24–27 79
31:26 .... 110, 208, 220
31:26–27 162
31:28 .... 153, 220
31:28–30 79
31:29 514
32 .... 144, 221, 430
32:1 .... 153, 220–21, 418
32:1–43 10
32:4 .... 268, 430
32:5 78
32:6 .... 146, 149, 470, 574
32:8 .... xxiii, 144–46, 224, 294, 387–88, 395, 482, 496, 539, 549, 565, 860
32:8–9 496
32:9 .... 255, 311
32:10 .... 146, 351, 459, 539
32:10–11 .... 146, 236
32:11 .... 146, 351
32:12 .... 147, 494
32:12–16 494
32:13 .... 397, 429, 494
32:13–14 149
32:14 494–95
32:15 .... 309, 366
32:16 .... 255, 351, 494–95, 514
32:17 .... 149, 268, 271, 514
32:18 .... 185, 308, 366, 430
32:19 514
32:20 .... 272, 548, 565
32:21 .... 78, 351, 514, 596
32:22 .... 304, 549
32:27 514
32:30 .... 149, 255
32:31 430
32:32 149
32:35 .... 78, 423, 542, 547, 666
32:36 .... 78, 528, 544
32:37 .... 185, 308
32:39 .... 546, 563, 565
32:41 422–23
32:42 891–92
32:43 .... 78, 144, 351, 422–23, 483, 565
32:44–47 .... 79, 152
32:46–47 79
32:49–50 149
32:50 149
32:50–51 109
32:51–52 .... 92, 94

32:51 ... 517
33:1–29 ... 10
33:2 ... 173, 418, 431, 541
33:4 ... 149
33:8 ... 149, 225, 542
33:8–11 ... 692
33:9 ... 149
33:10 ... 149, 463, 668–69, 826, 884
33:12 ... 311
33:13 ... 149
33:16 ... 149
33:23 ... 366
33:26 ... 256
33:28 ... 193
33:29 ... 429
34:1–4 ... 149
34:4 ... 92
34:7 ... 798
34:9 ... 79, 152
34:10 ... 72, 99, 147–48, 369
34:10–12 ... 83, 100, 131, 147, 882
34:11 ... 143, 528
34:11–12 ... 147–48
34:12 ... 82, 143, 147–48

JOSHUA

... 10, 95, 134, 155, 157–58, 161–62, 164–68, 172–73, 177, 179, 184–85, 188–89, 193, 206, 260, 301, 306, 310, 346, 369, 417, 492, 507, 513, 528, 531, 698, 704, 724, 870, 879, 892, 901
1 ... 190, 479, 492
1:1 ... 156
1:1–9 ... 79, 152
1:3–4 ... 163
1:5 ... 156–57, 484, 547
1:5–9 ... 156, 190, 750
1:6 ... 156, 442, 753
1:6–9 ... 712, 716, 751, 874
1:7 ... 156, 162, 442, 753
1:7–8 ... xx, 156, 191
1:7–9 ... 157
1:8 ... 156, 162, 478–79
1:9 ... 156, 442, 753
1:10 ... 80
1:13 ... 163
1:18 ... 442, 753
1–12 ... 492, 508, 540
2 ... 157
2:1–21 ... 167
2:2–7 ... 158
2:9 ... 93, 157, 164
2:9–11 ... 158
2:10 ... 157
2:11 ... 157, 164, 256
2:12–14 ... 158
2:18 ... 164
2:21 ... 164
2:24 ... 164
3:1 ... 417
3:7 ... 757
3:13 ... 164
3:16–17 ... 540
3:17 ... 208, 439
4:1–15 ... 160
4:6 ... 164
4:7 ... 524
4:14 ... 757
4:18 ... 208, 439
4:19 ... 417
4:21 ... 164
4:23 ... 164, 524
5:1 ... 164, 256
5:10 ... 683
5:15 ... 164, 854
6 ... 157, 159
6:1–27 ... 167
6:17 ... 157–58, 160, 189, 656, 866, 870, 879
6:17–21 ... 72
6:18–19 ... 879
6:21 ... 158
6:22 ... 158
6:23 ... 158
6:25 ... 158
6:26 ... 210
7:1 ... 164, 661, 723–24, 879
7:1–2 ... 158
7:1–6 ... 157
7:2 ... 361
7:5 ... 164, 256
7:16 ... 155
7:22–24 ... 204
7:25 ... 369, 724
8:1 ... 164, 753
8:24–27 ... 879
8:26 ... 72
8:29 ... 164
8:30–35 ... 152, 160, 163
8:31 ... 113, 152, 163
8:33 ... 163
9:6 ... 159, 189, 879
9:6–7 ... xxiii, 159
9:7 ... 159
9:7–8 ... 199
9:9 ... 159
9:10 ... 164
9:14 ... 159, 189, 879
9:15 ... 199
9:16 ... 159
9:17 ... 741
9:21 ... 164
9:27 ... 164, 340
10:1 ... 72, 173
10:2 ... 741
10:10 ... 228
10:12–14 ... 431
10:13 ... 184
10:14 ... 164
10:24 ... 164, 522
10:25 ... 164
10:26 ... 164
10:28 ... 72, 105
10:28–43 ... 879
10:35 ... 105
10:37 ... 105
10:39 ... 105
10:40 ... 134
10:40–42 ... 167–68
10:42 ... 164
11:9 ... 379
11:10 ... 189
11:10–16 ... 879
11:12 ... 134
11:20 ... 134, 159–60, 879
11:21 ... 164
11:22 ... 163, 184
11:23 ... 167–68
12:5–6 ... 164
13:1 ... 164, 193, 846
13:1–7 ... 167–68
13:2 ... 164
13:2–3 ... 167
13:9 ... 164
13:11 ... 164
13:14 ... 164
13:16 ... 164
13:17 ... 161
13:18 ... 161
13:19 ... 161
13:20 ... 161
13:21 ... 164
13:21–23 ... 161
13:22 ... 164
13:33 ... 164
13–19 ... 346
14:4 ... 164
14:6 ... 164
14:9 ... 163
14:12 ... 164
14:13–15 ... 80
14:14 ... 163
14:15 ... 682
14–15 ... 723
15:13 ... 166–67
15:13–14 ... 167
15:14 ... 164, 166–67
15:15–17 ... 166
15:15–19 ... 80
15:18–19 ... 166
15:20–41 ... 682–83

15:54 .682
15:63 80, 167–68, 173, 457
16:10 80, 166–68, 199
17:3–4 .163
17:5 .508
17:12–13 .166–68
17:13 .199
17:14 .508
18:1 .742
18:3 .167–68
18:7 .164
18:12 .361
19:1–5 .725
19:2–5 .725
19:9 .167, 173, 508
19:47 .167
19:50 .163
19:51 .742
20 .32, 83, 132
20:1–9 69, 133
20:3 .598
20:4 .69, 133, 160
20:4–6 .160
20:6 .160
20:7–9 .160
20:9 .598
21 .727
21:1 .727
21:1–4 .727
21:1–42 .727
21:3 .164
21:4–8 .727
21:5 .726
21:5–9 .727
21:6–8 .778
21:10–19 .727
21:13 .160
21:20 .726
21:20–39 .727
21:20–42 .778
21:21 .160
21:27 .160
21:32 .160
21:36 .160
21:38 .160
21:43–45 .167–68
21:45 .449
22 .164
22:5 163, 191
22:10–12 .725
22:17 .164
22:19 .396, 742
22:20 .164
22:29 .742
23 .160
23:1 .164, 167–68, 193, 846
23:2 .164, 846
23:3 .164
23:6 156, 162
23:9 167–68, 879
23:9–10 .164
23:12 .173
23:12–13 164, 167–68
23:13 .173, 258, 514
23:14–15 .167–68
23:15 .449
24 160, 161, 189, 310
24:1 .160
24:1–15 177, 206
24:2 .160–61
24:2–4 .161
24:5 .417
24:5–7 .161
24:7 161, 543
24:8–10 .161
24:9–10 .160
24:10–11 .162
24:11 .162
24:11–13 .161
24:12 .160, 162, 547, 879
24:13 160, 162
24:14 162, 324
24:14–15 .160
24:15 .173
24:17 .173
24:19 25, 422
24:19–21 .162
24:23 .162
24:28–31 165, 167–68
24:29–31 .80
24:31 .167–68
24:32 10, 164

JUDGES

.10, 162, 165–68, 171–74, 179, 185, 188, 193, 206, 260, 306, 514, 590, 674, 698, 704, 725, 781, 879, 892, 901
1 .166–67, 172, 514
1:1 .166
1:1–2 .167
1:3 167, 173
1:5 .173
1:7 .46
1:8 173, 301
1:10 80, 166–67
1:10–3 .166
1:10–36 165, 193
1:11–13 .166
1:11–15 .80
1:14–15 .166
1:16 .166
1:17 167, 879
1:18–19 .167
1:19–33 .879
1:20 80, 167
1:21 .80, 167, 173, 301, 514
1:22–26 .167
1:27 80, 514
1:27–28 .166–67
1:27–29 .166
1:28 .199
1:29 80, 166–67
1:29–31 .514
1:30 166–67, 199
1:30–33 .166
1:31–32 .166–67
1:33 166–67, 199
1:34–35 .166
1:34–36 .167
1:35 .199
1:1–2:5 .165
1–21 .492
2:1 .173
2:2 173, 514
2:3 .173, 258, 514
2:4 .173
2:6–9 165, 167, 171
2:6–10 .168
2:7 .167–68
2:7–9 .80
2:10 .169
2:11 .674, 806
2:12 .173
2:14 .514
2:14–16 .674
2:16 .674
2:18 .674
2:20 .514
2:6–3:6 .165
2–13 .842
3:5–6 .514
3:6 .173
3:7 .806
3:8 .514
3:9 .674
3:15 .674
3–16 .514
4:12–16 .542
4:14 .173
5 10, 719
5:3 .545
5:4 173, 418, 439
5:4–5 .255
5:5 .541
5:8 .380
5:11 .417
5:16 .541
5:20–21 .542
5:30 .541
6 .845

6:1–22 174
6:7–10 173
6:8 173
6:10 173
6:11 845
6:13 173
6:15 184
6:18–19 845
6:21 750, 845
6:22 99
7:15–25 254
7:22 255
7:25 165, 225, 542
8:11 193
8:21 542
8:27 173, 258, 514
8:33 806
9:53–54 165, 183
10:3 96
10:6 806
10:7 514
10:10 806
10:15 185
11 169
11:14–23 388
11:15–16 169
11:15–27 165–66, 169, 294
11:17 169
11:17–27 294
11:18 169
11:19 169
11:21 169–70
11:21–22 169
11:21–24 295
11:23 169
11:24 169–70, 294, 388, 496
11:24–25 781
11:25 388
11:30 173
11:30–31 69
11:35 173
11:39 173
13:2–5 183
13:4 184
13:5 174, 183
13:7 174, 183–84
13:14 184
13:23 184
14:8–9 174
14:14 174
15:15–16 174
16:17 174, 183
16:19 174
17:3 174
17:6 165–66, 171, 881, 900
17:7 590
17:12 174
17:13 174
18 174
18:1 171, 900
18:1–10 174
18:6 174
18:27–29 167
18:30 174
18:31 174, 179, 202
19 166, 171–72
19:1 171, 900
19:1–2 590
19:10–12 173
19:12 172
19:12–16 172
19:14 172
19:18–20 172
19:22 165, 172–74
19:22–25 369
19:24 172
19:25 172–73
19:29 172
19:29–30 173, 184
20 174
20:13 174
20:16 184
20:26 173
20:27 174, 179, 202
20:45 309
20:48 174
21:2 173
21:10–11 204
21:25 165–66, 171, 900

1 SAMUEL

208, 732
1:1 590, 726
1:2–11 183
1:9 742
1:11 69
1:13 183
1:14 184
1:15 184, 548
1:19–20 183
1:21 69
1:23 69, 184–85
2 430, 719
2:1–10 10
2:2 185, 430
2:5 543
2:8 543
2:10 547
2:15–17 177–78
2:22 178, 742
2:25 184, 287, 496
2:27–28 178
2:29 178
2:30 178, 209
2:33 549
2:35 107, 209, 287
3:3 742
3:11 209
3:13 184, 209
3:17 185
3:20 185
4 492–93
4:4 185, 209, 309
4:8 184
4:10 185
4:17 184
4:18 178
4:21 178
4–6 494
5:4 730
5:4–5 436
6:1–2 526
6:6 184
7:1 192, 412
7:1–2 740–41
7:4 806
7:8–9 309
7:9 543
8:1 726
8:1–22 178
8:5 177–79, 368
8:6 368, 743
8:7 179, 610
8:20 179, 368
8:22 368
9:1 590
9:1–2 615
9:2 184–85
9:5 726
9:16 185
9:21 184, 412–13
9:1–10:16 178
10:1 255
10:2 412
10:17–27 178
10:23 184
10:26 172
11:1–15 178
11:7 172–73, 184
12 161, 189
12:1–25 178
12:3 184, 417
12:6 179
12:6–8 161
12:6–17 177, 206
12:7 417
12:8 179, 417
12:9–11 161, 179
12:10 806
12:11 179, 193
12:12 179

12:14 ... 179
12:17 ... 179
12:18 ... 543
12:18–19 ... 309
12:22 ... 185, 282, 547
12:23 ... 309, 543
13:2 ... 185
13:5 ... 361
13:13 ... 784
13:14 ... 176, 746
14:23 ... 361
14:24 ... 173
14:32 ... 184
14:36 ... 185
14:40 ... 185
14:45 ... 173
15 ... 184, 731
15:1–2 ... 615
15:2 ... 184
15:8 ... 184, 615
15:9 ... 184
15:12 ... 707
15:15 ... 746
15:19 ... 184
15:20 ... 184, 615
15:20–21 ... 746
15:22 ... 184, 397, 486–87
15:23 ... 610
15:24–25 ... 746
15:26 ... 610
15:28 ... 615
15:30 ... 746
15:32 ... 184
15:33 ... 184
16 ... 590
16:1 ... 412–13
16:1–13 ... 708, 731
16:11 ... 413
16:13 ... 412
16:14 ... 179–80, 537
16:14–23 ... 708
16:23 ... 396
17 ... 708
17:4 ... 184, 746
17:12 ... 413
17:47 ... 788
17:48–51 ... 746
17:54 ... 730
18:20–21 ... 737
18:28–29 ... 737
18–19 ... 708
19:11 ... 537
19:11–17 ... 737
19:13 ... 184
20:15 ... 434
20:26 ... 181, 184
20–31 ... 708
21:1–6 ... 883
21:4 ... 180–81, 860, 866
21:4–5 ... 140
21:4–6 ... 180
21:5 ... 181
21:6 ... 180–81
21:7 ... 537, 540
21:11 ... 537
21:12 ... 537
22:1 ... 271, 537, 734
22:1–2 ... 710, 734
22:18 ... 540
22:18–19 ... 178, 204
23:15 ... 537
23:19 ... 537, 540
24:3 ... 537
24:12 ... 423, 547
25 ... 540
25:21 ... 549
25:22 ... 173
25:33–34 ... 173
26:1 ... 540
26:19 ... 255
27:6 ... 710, 734
28:3 ... 184
28:3–25 ... 728
28:6 ... 731
28:6–7 ... 730
28:7 ... 731
28:8 ... 830
29:4 ... 748
29:9 ... 185
31:1–7 ... 729
31:1–13 ... 728
31:4 ... 185
31:5 ... 185
31:8–13 ... 729
31:10 ... 730
31:10–12 ... 615
31:12 ... 729

2 SAMUEL

... 208, 710, 732
1 ... 708, 719, 732, 736, 744
1:1–16 ... 729
1:17–27 ... 729
1:18 ... 184
1:19–27 ... 10
1–4 ... 729
2:1 ... 547
2:1–7 ... 729
2:18 ... 723
2–4 ... 708
3:2–5 ... 724, 729
3:6–21 ... 729
3:10 ... 185
3:22–39 ... 729
3:27–30 ... 208
4:1–12 ... 729
5 ... 708
5:1–3 ... 731–32
5:1–5 ... 709
5:1–10 ... 710
5:4–5 ... 731–32
5:5 ... 724, 729
5:6 ... 185, 228, 731
5:6–8 ... 732
5:6–10 ... 173, 709, 718, 732
5:8 ... 185
5:11 ... 191–92, 208, 388–89
5:11–12 ... 709, 732
5:13–14 ... 724
5:13–16 ... 709, 724, 732
5:17 ... 709
5:17–25 ... 709–10, 732, 735
5:19–21 ... 715
5:20 ... 228, 418
5:21 ... 735
5:23–25 ... 715
5–6 ... 708
5–24 ... 80
6:1 ... 735
6:1–11 ... 709–10, 732, 734
6:2 ... 185, 209, 309
6:5 ... 311
6:6 ... 734
6:8 ... 418, 737
6:12–19 ... 709–10, 737
6:13 ... 737
6:16 ... 709, 737
6:17–18 ... 523
6:19 ... 255
6:19–20 ... 736
6:20–23 ... 709, 736–37
6:21 ... 753, 755
7 ... 196, 369, 393, 492, 498, 589, 593, 710, 742, 881
7:1 ... 118, 182, 191–93, 742, 881
7:1–16 ... 880
7:1–17 ... 206, 714, 736, 742, 881
7:1–29 ... 709
7:2 ... 182
7:4 ... 521
7:5 ... 182, 208
7:6 ... 182, 195, 742–43
7:6–8 ... 195
7:7 ... 182, 192, 195, 414, 755, 855, 870, 902
7:8 ... 195, 414
7:9 ... 196
7:9–10 ... 192
7:9–13 ... 192
7:11 ... 192–93, 209, 743, 753–55, 769, 881
7:11–13 ... 118, 191

7:11–15 . . . 879
7:11–16 . . . 498
7:11–17 . . . 335
7:12 . . . 391–92, 481, 792, 867
7:12–14 . . . 521, 527
7:12–15 . . . 526, 867
7:13 . . . 182, 195–97, 210, 335
7:13–14 . . . 208, 750, 753
7:14 . . . 181–82, 190–91, 394, 481, 483, 500, 521, 750, 756
7:14–15 . . . 177, 181–82, 190, 206, 480, 500, 523, 527, 753, 870, 875, 879–80
7:14–16 . . . 208, 499, 743, 755
7:15 . . . 181, 540
7:16 . . . xx, 182, 335, 743, 781, 877
7:17 . . . 521
7:18 . . . 182
7:18–29 . . . 736
7:19 . . . 182, 744
7:22 . . . 206, 542
7:23 . . . 184–85, 196
7:24 . . . 282
7:25 . . . 182
7:26 . . . 182
7:27 . . . 182, 392
7:28 . . . 526–27
7:29 . . . 182, 190–91, 744
8 . . . 488–89, 710
8:1 . . . 389
8:1–14 . . . 388, 744
8:1–15 . . . 880
8:1–18 . . . 386
8:2 . . . 184, 389, 489, 745
8:3 . . . 208, 771
8:3–4 . . . 389
8:5 . . . 537
8:5–8 . . . 389
8:6 . . . 393
8:7 . . . 745
8:8 . . . 745
8:9–11 . . . 389
8:12–13 . . . 488
8:13 . . . 488, 745
8:13–14 . . . 537
8:14 . . . 389, 393
8:15 . . . 744
8:15–18 . . . 744–45
8:16–18 . . . 744
8:17 . . . 523
8:18 . . . 523, 745, 794
8–21 . . . 744
9 . . . 708
9:1–13 . . . 744
10 . . . 544, 710
10:1–19 . . . 744–45
10:6 . . . 745
10:18 . . . 745
10:23–25 . . . 759
10:29 . . . 760
11:1 . . . 744–46
11:1–27 . . . 744
11:1 . . . 709
11:3 . . . 724
11:4 . . . 184–85
11:11 . . . 710, 745
11:15 . . . 745
11:21 . . . 165, 183
11–12 . . . 208, 746
11:2–12:25 . . . 708
12:1–25 . . . 744
12:6 . . . 184
12:8 . . . 185
12:13 . . . 179, 537, 733, 746
12:24 . . . 724
12:25 . . . 544
12:26 . . . 745
12:26–30 . . . 386, 388–89
12:26–31 . . . 744
12:30–31 . . . 710, 745
13:1 . . . 725
13:1–22 . . . 744
13–19 . . . 708
14:6 . . . 142
14:16 . . . 255
14:17 . . . 185
15 . . . 544
15:7 . . . 185
16:5–14 . . . 208
16:8–22 . . . 736
16:12 . . . 185
16:14 . . . 537
17 . . . 544
17:11 . . . 185
17:22 . . . 537
17:23 . . . 185
17:27 . . . 723
17:27–29 . . . 208
18:13 . . . 185
18:18 . . . 707
19:8 . . . 185
19:12 . . . 185
19:13 . . . 185
19:14 . . . 185
19:16–23 . . . 208
19:22 . . . 748
19:27 . . . 185
19:31–39 . . . 208
19:38 . . . 185
20:1 . . . 185
20:1–22 . . . 708, 744
20:9–10 . . . 208
20:19 . . . 255
20:22 . . . 185
20:23 . . . 794
20:23–26 . . . 744–45
21:1–14 . . . 708, 744
21:3 . . . 255
21:6–9 . . . 615
21:8–9 . . . 204
21:15–17 . . . 744
21:17 . . . 185
21:18–22 . . . 710, 744, 746
21:19 . . . 746
22 . . . 10, 185, 431, 537, 539, 708
22:1 . . . 544
22:1–51 . . . 744
22:3 . . . 430
22:5 . . . 539
22:7 . . . 545
22:8 . . . 439, 549
22:8–14 . . . 349
22:8–16 . . . 431
22:10 . . . 555
22:10–11 . . . 256
22:11 . . . 349
22:15 . . . 555
22:16 . . . 546
22:17 . . . 539–40, 555
22:21 . . . 486
22:29 . . . 539
22:32 . . . 185
22:33 . . . 429
22:33–34 . . . 429
22:34 . . . 429, 547
22:37 . . . 547
22:43 . . . 419
22:47 . . . 430
22:48 . . . 423, 547
22:50 . . . 176
22:51 . . . 540
23 . . . 733
23:1–6 . . . 880
23:1–7 . . . 10, 708, 744, 879
23:2 . . . xviii
23:3–5 . . . 285
23:4–5 . . . 287
23:5 . . . 246–47, 335, 877
23:8–39 . . . 709–10, 732–33, 744, 844
23:16–17 . . . 881
23:17 . . . 733
23:24 . . . 746
23:39 . . . 709, 733
24 . . . 709, 844
24:1 . . . 183, 748–49
24:1–25 . . . 746–47
24:2 . . . 183, 185
24:5–8 . . . 748
24:9 . . . 183
24:10 . . . 183, 748
24:10–12 . . . 733
24:11–13 . . . 714

24:11–15 ... 715
24:13 ... 183
24:15 ... 185
24:16 ... 457, 749
24:17 ... 748–49
24:18 ... 523, 714
24:21 ... 183
24:25 ... 183, 523, 749–50

1 KINGS

1 ... 747
1:1–4 ... 747, 879
1:1–27 ... 708
1:5–27 ... 747
1:28–53 ... 747
1:33 ... 208
1:38 ... 208
1:44 ... 208
1:50 ... 133
1–2 ... 711, 757
1:1–2:9 ... 746, 758
1–11 ... 711–12
2 ... 190, 711, 775, 780, 782, 784, 790
2:1–4 ... 190, 208, 712, 716, 720, 750, 874
2:2–4 ... 191
2:3–4 ... 543, 756
2:10 ... 210–11, 803
2:10–11 ... 747, 757–58
2:11 ... 593
2:12 ... 758
2:12 ... 758
2:13–46 ... 758
2:23 ... 185
2:26 ... 287, 342
2:26–27 ... 178, 209
2:28 ... 133
2:32 ... 185
2:35 ... 209
2:44 ... 185
2:46 ... 758
3:1 ... 389, 771
3:1–2 ... 758
3:1–15 ... 711–12, 757
3:1–4:34 ... 759
3:3 ... 741
3:3–14 ... 541
3:3–15 ... 758
3:4 ... 740–41
3:4–5 ... 741
3:8 ... 369
3:9 ... 541
3:12 ... 148
3:14 ... 756
3:16–28 ... 704, 711, 758
3:16–4:34 ... 712
3–10 ... 711
3–11 ... 80
4 ... 711
4:1 ... 757
4:1–19 ... 758
4:20 ... 185
4:20–21 ... 209
4:20–28 ... 758
4:21 ... 489–90, 758–60, 774, 876
4:24 ... 459, 759, 771
4:25 ... 185, 191, 193–94, 205, 410, 412
4:29–34 ... 704, 758
4:31 ... 534, 723–24
5 ... 192, 761
5:1 ... 44, 192, 388–89, 761
5:1–5 ... 119, 188, 191–92, 743, 761, 870, 881
5:1–18 ... 712, 758, 761
5:2 ... 761
5:3 ... 164, 192, 194, 520–22, 754
5:3–4 ... 761
5:3–5 ... 202, 750, 752–54, 761
5:4 ... 193–94, 209, 522
5:5 ... 191, 193–94, 209, 520–22, 761
5:6 ... 192, 761
5:7 ... 761
5:8 ... 761
5:9 ... 761
5:10–11 ... 761
5:12 ... 192, 388–89, 522
5:12–14 ... 761
5:13 ... 198
5:15–16 ... 761, 846
5:17–18 ... 761
5–6 ... 711
5–8 ... 492
6 ... 337, 764
6:1 ... 763–64
6:1–38 ... 758
6:2 ... 338, 764
6:2–38 ... 764
6:3 ... 458, 764
6:7 ... 194
6:9 ... 438
6:15 ... 438
6:16 ... 353
6:20 ... 764
6:23 ... 764
6:24 ... 764
6:29 ... 353
6:35 ... 353
6:36 ... 194
6–8 ... 691
7 ... 761
7:1–2 ... 199
7:1–12 ... 711, 758
7:3 ... 438
7:8 ... 771
7:13–14 ... 712, 758, 761
7:13–51 ... 711
7:14 ... 574, 762–63
7:15–51 ... 758, 764
7:49 ... 764
7:50 ... 353
8 ... 189, 196–97, 206, 512, 711, 761
8:1–11 ... 758, 764
8:2 ... 652
8:4 ... 742
8:6 ... 353
8:10 ... 189, 194–95, 353
8:10–11 ... 194, 712, 716, 720, 758, 765, 768, 855, 902
8:11 ... 349, 860
8:12–53 ... 765, 845
8:12–66 ... 758
8:15 ... 195
8:15–16 ... 198
8:15–21 ... 116, 188, 195–96, 870
8:16 ... 197
8:16–21 ... 194, 705, 879, 881
8:17 ... 197
8:18 ... 197
8:19 ... 197
8:20 ... 197–98, 210
8:22 ... 765
8:22–53 ... 206
8:23 ... 206, 542, 664, 877
8:24–26 ... 206
8:25 ... 286–87
8:27 ... 207, 545, 671, 761–62
8:28 ... 512–514
8:28–29 ... 664
8:29 ... 664, 769
8:29–30 ... 639
8:30 ... 207, 545, 671
8:31–53 ... 161
8:32 ... 243, 626, 671
8:33 ... 197, 207
8:34 ... 671
8:35 ... 197, 207
8:35–36 ... 769
8:35–39 ... 720
8:36 ... 671
8:37 ... 207, 442
8:39 ... 671, 769
8:41 ... 197, 547
8:41–43 ... 207, 250
8:42 ... 197, 766
8:43 ... 197, 671
8:44 ... 197, 527
8:45 ... 671
8:46 ... 207
8:46–53 ... 878
8:47 ... 207, 512–14, 664
8:48 ... 197, 207

8:49 671
8:50 .... 207, 512, 514
8:51 .... 207, 255
8:52 769
8:53 207
8:54 767
8:55–61 770
8:56 .... 194, 256, 526
8:57 484
8:60 .... 384, 820
8:61 .... 756, 843
8:62–66 768
8:65–66 734
8:66 768
9 771
9:1–9 .... 711–12, 758, 768
9:2 .... 198, 768
9:2–3 769
9:3 691
9:3–9 770
9:4–5 756
9:7 434
9:10–24 770
9:10–28 758
9:10–10:29 711–12
9:11–14 712
9:11–15 770
9:13 388
9:15 772
9:16 .... 389, 758, 771
9:17 772
9:18 771
9:20 340
9:20–21 .... 188–89, 198–99, 202, 389, 457, 879
9:21 198
9:22 198
9:24 .... 389, 758, 771–72
9:24–25 845
9:25 772–73
9:26–27 770
9:65–66 845
9:10–10:29 711
10 760–61
10:1 541
10:1–13 .... 758, 774
10:2 541
10:9 .... 712, 761–62, 774
10:10 541
10:11–12 712
10:14–15 845
10:14–25 758
10:14–29 774
10:16–17 845
10:23–25 759
10:24 842
10:26 760
10:26–28 759
10:26–29 .... 199–200, 255, 712, 758–59, 774
10:27 760
10:28 759–60
11 .... 201, 711, 775
11:1 .... 139, 200, 202, 657–58, 690, 771, 874
11:1–2 .... 589, 876
11:1–3 760
11:1–4 .... 188–90, 199–201, 208, 688, 690, 879
11:1–8 198
11:1–13 .... 758–59, 775
11:1–40 759
11:2 200–1
11:2–4 .... 200, 690
11:3 .... 200, 690
11:4 .... 690, 715, 843
11:5 318
11:6 208
11:7 .... 202, 318
11:8 202
11:14 748
11:14–2 .... 758, 775
11:15 537
11:15–16 488–89
11:23 748
11:23–25 .... 389, 771
11:24 208
11:25 748
11:26–40 .... 758, 775
11:27 772
11:29–40 368
11:32 208
11:33 208
11:34 208
11:36 .... 185, 208
11:41 .... 210, 212, 717, 775
11:41–43 .... 758, 774
11:42 202
11:43 .... 210–12, 803
12:1–24 775
12:2 202
12:4 198
12:15 .... 368, 714
12:16 776
12:18 198
12:20 776
12:22–24 714
12:23 776
12:25–33 775
12:26–27 202
12:26–33 207
12:28 369
12:28–29 .... 189, 202–3, 207
12:28–33 777
12:31 778
12–2 80
13 775
13:1–3 .... 370, 397
13:1–34 775
13:34 434
14:1–20 775
14:6–16 368
14:9 208
14:15–16 203
14:20 210–12
14:21 .... 202, 389
14:21–31 .... 775, 778
14:22 .... 778, 780
14:23 .... 208, 256, 310, 357, 361
14:23–24 778
14:29 .... 210, 212, 613
14:31 .... 210–12, 389, 803
15:1 .... 717, 780
15:1–2 780
15:1–8 780
15:3 843
15:3–5 780
15:4 208
15:5 .... 208, 900
15:6 780
15:7 .... 210, 212
15:7–8 780
15:8 .... 210–12, 803
15:9 368
15:9–10 782
15:9–24 782
15:11 .... 208, 210, 782, 900
15:12 782
15:13 782
15:14 .... 782, 843
15:15 782
15:16–22 782
15:22 783
15:23 .... 210, 212, 717, 782–83
15:24 .... 210–12, 782–83, 803
15:26 .... 203, 900
15:27–28 210–11
15:31 210
15:34 .... 203, 900
16:2 203
16:5 210
16:6 210–12
16:7 900
16:10 210–11
16:13 203
16:14 210
16:18 .... 185, 211
16:19 .... 203, 900
16:22 211
16:25 900
16:25–26 203

16:27 210
16:28 210–12
16:30 ..... 148, 900
16:30–33 785
16:31 203
16:31–33 792
16:34 210
17–2 470
18:4 ..... 311, 671
18:18 806
18:28 380
18:31 ..... 208, 412
18:37 470
18:38 750
19:4 407
19:8 203
19:9 408
19:9–14 882
19:10 ..... 188, 311
19:11–12 203
19:11–13 ..... 189, 203–4
19:12 203
19:13 408
19:14 188
19:15 388
19:18 188
20:20 717
21:3 208
21:10 208
22 715
22:1–34 784
22:1–40 784
22:2–4 785
22:2–40 785
22:4 785
22:5–6 785
22:7–15 785
22:8 194
22:13–28 714
22:15 785
22:16–17 785
22:17 459
22:18–28 785
22:19 ..... 349, 785
22:19–22 749
22:25 785
22:26 785
22:29–34 785
22:30 ..... 716, 828, 830, 845
22:32 786
22:34–35 ..... 716, 828, 830, 845
22:35 211
22:36–40 785
22:37 210–11
22:39 210
22:40 210–12
22:41–42 790
22:41–51 ..... 784, 789
22:43 ..... 210, 790
22:44 790
22:45 ..... 210, 212, 790
22:46 ..... 717, 790
22:47 790
22:48–49 790
22:50 ..... 211–12, 790, 803
22:51 210
22:52 203

2 KINGS

1:17 210–11
1:18 210
2 ..... 790–91, 793–94, 796, 799, 801, 804–5, 819, 822–23, 831–32
2:4 191
2:5 208
2:7 208
2:8 ..... 208, 439
3:1 208
3:3 203
3:4 226
3:8 208
4:1 882
4:21 208
4:42 ..... 65, 208
5:1 208
5:5 205
5:12 208
5:27 208
6:1 208
6:12 208
6:28–29 208
7:2 469
7:3 208
7:15 208
7:19 469
8:2 208
8:9 208
8:12 ..... 397, 549
8:12–13 388
8:13 554
8:13–14 208
8:16 790
8:16–24 790
8:17 ..... 717, 790
8:18 ..... 785, 791
8:18–19 790
8:19 379
8:20–22 790
8:23 ..... 210, 212, 791
8:24 ..... 210–12, 791–92, 803
8:24–29 793
8:25 793
8:26 717
8:27 793
8:28 793
8:29 793
9:1–3 368
9:1–13 793
9:4–5 208
9:7 422
9:9 208
9:10 205
9:14–26 793
9:15–16 793
9:22 425
9:24 210–11
9:26 204
9:27 793–94
9:27–28 210–11
9:28–29 794
9:29 793
9:30–37 793
9:36 368
10:1–17 793
10:5 185
10:11 369
10:18–36 793
10:25 212
10:29 203
10:30 368
10:31 ..... 203, 844
10:34 210
10:35 210–12
11:1 ..... 791, 794
11:1–20 794
11:2 208
11:2–3 794
11:4 ..... 340, 794
11:5–8 794
11:6–7 794
11:9–12 794
11:13 208
11:13–16 794
11:14 656
11:15 208
11:16 210–11
11:17 ..... 282, 656
11:17–18 794
11:18 ..... 656, 794–95
11:19 656
11:20 656
11:21–12:1 796
12:1–22 796
12:2 796
12:3 796–97
12:4 208
12:4–8 796
12:9–11 796
12:12–13 796
12:14–16 796
12:16 208

12:17–18 .796
12:19 . 210, 212, 796
12:20 .796
12:21 .212, 796
12:21–22 . 210–11
13:2 .203
13:6 .881
13:8 .210
13:9 . 210–12
13:11 .203
13:12 .210
13:13 . 210–11
13:24 .212
14:1 .799
14:1–22 .798
14:2 .799
14:3 . 208, 210, 799
14:5–6 .799
14:6 .204
14:7 .799
14:8–10 .828
14:8–11 .799
14:8–14 .800
14:11–14 .799
14:15–16 .799
14:16 . 210–12
14:17–18 .799
14:18 .212
14:19 .800
14:19–20 . 210–11
14:19–22 .799
14:21 .212
14:24 .203
14:25 .208, 359, 389, 407
14:27 .549
14:28 .210
14:29 . 210–12
15 .801
15:1 .801
15:1–7 .801
15:2 .801
15:3 .210, 801–2
15:4 .801
15:5 .656, 801–2
15:6 . 210, 212, 801
15:7 .210–12, 801, 803
15:9 .203
15:10 . 210–11, 368
15:10–12 .368
15:12 .368
15:13–14 . 361, 368
15:13–16 .368
15:14 . 210, 212
15:16 . 369, 397, 771
15:16–21 .148
15:17–22 .368
15:18 .203
15:19 .361, 407, 671
15:19–20 .368, 370
15:21 .210
15:22 . 210, 212
15:23–26 .368
15:24 .203
15:25 . 210, 212, 369
15:26 .210
15:27–31 .368
15:28 .203
15:29 .726
15:30 . 210, 212
15:31 .210
15:32 .804
15:32–38 .804
15:33 .804
15:34 .210, 804
15:35 .804
15:36 .212, 804
15:37 .804
15:38 .210, 212, 803–4
15–17 .368
16 .225
16:1 .805
16:1–20 .805
16:2 .208, 805
16:3 . 207–9, 311, 809–10
16:3–4 .805
16:4 . 256, 310, 357, 361
16:5 .208, 225
16:5–6 . 361, 805
16:5–9 .225
16:6 .726, 806
16:7 . 671, 805, 808
16:7–9 .370
16:8 .805
16:9 .209
16:9–16 .805
16:12–18 .809
16:15 .656
16:17–18 .805
16:19 . 212, 805
16:20 .210, 212, 803, 805, 809
17 . 189, 206–7, 492
17:1–6 .368
17:3 .370
17:3–6 .726
17:4 .212
17:6–8 .726
17:7 . 207, 209
17:7–21 .207
17:8 .208
17:8–9 .207
17:10 .207, 256, 310, 357, 361
17:10–13 .109
17:12 .207
17:13 . 209, 306, 360
17:13–14 .207
17:13–15 .309
17:13–20 .206
17:15–18 .207
17:16 .203
17:16–17 .207
17:18 .209
17:19 . 207, 279
17:21–23 .203, 207
17:31 .208
17:33 .209
17:34–41 .209
17:35–39 .209
18 .189
18:1 .811
18:1–2 .229
18:1–3 .811
18:1–8 .810
18:2–3 .811
18:3 . 210, 229
18:4 .209
18:4–8 . 229, 811
18:5 . 148, 204, 230, 574, 811, 845
18:5–6 .204, 230
18:9–12 . 229, 811
18:11 .726
18:13 .229–30, 726, 815
18:13–19:37 .815
18:13–20:21 .811
18:14–16 . 229–30, 815
18:17–19:37 .229
18:19 .204, 230
18:19–25 .204–5, 781, 828
18:20 .204, 230
18:21 . 204–5, 230
18:21–32 .204
18:22 .204, 230
18:23–24 .205
18:24 .204, 230
18:27–35 .781
18:28–35 .204–5
18:30 . 204–5, 230
18:31 . 191, 205
18:32 .205
18:35 .205
18–20 . 80, 205, 225, 229–30, 816
19 .719
19:3 .574
19:10 .204, 230
19:10–13 .204–5
19:14 .519
19:15 . 185, 209, 671, 816
19:15–19 .816
19:16 .519
19:19 .671
19:20–32 .816
19:21–28 .10

19:25 209
19:35 209
19:37 212, 816
20 817
20:1–5 232
20:1–6 229
20:1–11 815–16
20:1–13 816
20:3 843
20:5 232
20:6 232–33
20:7 232–33
20:7–8 229, 232–33
20:8 232–33
20:9–11 229, 232–33
20:12–13 232–33
20:12–19 229, 816
20:16–18 811, 845
20:17 642, 832, 884
20:17–18 231, 418
20:18 819
20:18–19 817
20:19 231, 817–18
20:20 210, 212, 717
20:20–21 229, 816, 818
20:21 210, 212
21:1 818–19
21:1–18 818
21:2 209, 819
21:3 209, 819
21:3–5 821
21:3–6 207
21:3–9 819
21:6 208–9, 311, 809–10, 821
21:7 209
21:10–16 819
21:11–15 206
21:12 209
21:13 209
21:16 205, 209, 271, 311, 514, 810
21:17 210, 212, 717, 819, 821
21:18 210, 212, 819
21:19 822
21:19–26 821
21:20–22 822
21:23 210, 212
21:23–24 822
21:24 212, 656
21:25 212
21:25–26 822
21:26 210, 212
22 189, 289
22:1 823
22:2 210, 823
22:3–13 823
22:4 654, 824
22:8 824
22:11 289, 824
22:13 824
22:14–20 714, 823
22:16–19 206
22:19 289, 825
22:20 830
22–23 206
22:1–23:30 822
22:3–23:3 824
23 189
23:1–3 823–24
23:2 825
23:4–7 716, 820
23:4–14 823
23:4–20 823–24
23:5 356, 435
23:8 716, 820, 823
23:10 209
23:11 356
23:12 435, 716, 820
23:13 318, 824
23:15–18 823
23:15–20 823
23:19–20 823
23:21 209, 826
23:21–23 823–25
23:22 842
23:22–23 826
23:24–26 823
23:25 148, 205, 209
23:26 205–6, 289
23:26–27 819, 823, 831
23:27 197
23:28 210, 212, 829
23:28–29 828
23:28–30 823, 828
23:29 829
23:29–30 210, 212, 829
23:30 212, 831
23:31 831
23:31–35 831
23:32 831
23:33–34 831
23:33–35 829
23:34 212
23:34–35 831
23:36 831
23:37 831
23:36–24:7 831
24 189
24:1 832
24:2–4 831–32
24:3–4 205, 819
24:4 271, 514
24:5 210, 212, 832
24:6 210, 212, 832
24:7 832
24:8 717, 833
24:8–17 833
24:9 833
24:10–12 833
24:10–13 726
24:13 206, 289, 619, 642, 832–33, 884
24:14 301, 613, 833
24:14–16 833
24:15 212, 833
24:17 833
24:18 299, 834
24:18–20 834
24:19 299, 834
24:20 299, 834
24–25 299–301, 691
24:18–25:26 299
25 80, 299, 301–2, 726, 837
25:1 458
25:1–2 299
25:3 299, 656
25:4 299
25:4–7 299
25:5–7 301
25:7 209, 212, 716, 818, 820
25:8 300
25:8–10 450
25:8–21 837
25:9 173, 300–1, 837
25:9–10 541
25:10 300–1, 837
25:11 300–1, 837
25:11–12 301
25:12 300, 837
25:13–15 642, 832
25:13–17 300, 837
25:14–15 206, 884
25:18–21 300, 837
25:22 300
25:23–24 300
25:25 300
25:26 300
25:27–30 301

ISAIAH

xli–xlii, xlviii, 10, 147, 188–90, 205, 215–43, 245–55, 257–58, 260–62, 272, 276, 285, 291, 293–95, 303, 309–10, 316, 347, 352, 372, 375, 379, 381, 394, 410–12, 418, 424, 426, 428, 439, 444, 446–49, 451, 468–69, 474, 502–3, 530, 534, 540, 543, 553, 556, 563, 580, 582, 591, 602, 610, 612, 617–20, 622, 625–29, 641, 650, 671, 772, 789, 811, 816–18, 838, 842, 845, 853, 855, 866, 870, 891, 901
1 221
1:1 252

1:1–17 ... 397
1:2 ... 153, 218, 220–21, 235, 255, 418
1:4 ... 258, 311
1:8 ... 255
1:9 ... 214, 235
1:9–10 ... 221, 878
1:10 ... 221, 238
1:10–17 ... 218, 397
1:11 ... 243, 256, 486–87
1:13 ... 843
1:14 ... 843
1:15 ... 256, 311
1:17 ... 256, 311
1:18 ... 220
1:20 ... 222
1:21 ... 235, 351, 459
1:23 ... 255–56, 418
1:24 ... 422
1:25 ... 468, 470
1:26 ... 459
1:27 ... 258
1:28 ... 311
1:30 ... 255
1–12 ... 258
1–39 ... 217, 227, 231
2 ... 222, 372, 410
2:1 ... 222, 410
2:1–4 ... 410
2:1–5 ... 221–22, 379, 410–11, 451
2:2 ... 221–22, 247, 256, 297–98, 353, 621
2:2–3 ... 622
2:2–4 ... 451
2:3 ... 221, 223, 256, 411, 451, 546
2:3–4 ... 218
2:4 ... 221, 223, 372, 379, 451
2:5 ... 223, 410–12, 451
2:8 ... 418
2:9–11 ... 257
2:13 ... 459
2:19–21 ... 399–400
2:20 ... 258
3:6 ... 434
3:9 ... 221, 878
3:14 ... 255
3:14–15 ... 256
3:16 ... 223, 256
3:17–24 ... 223
3:24 ... 223
3:25–26 ... 223
3:16–4:1 ... 218
4:1 ... 223
4:1–4 ... 255
4:2 ... 276, 351, 394, 448
4:2–6 ... 877, 880
4:3 ... 549
4:6 ... 394
5:1–2 ... 698
5:1–7 ... 255, 542, 593, 854
5:1–10 ... 356
5:5 ... 419
5:7 ... 258
5:8 ... 256–57, 418
5:10 ... 256
5:11 ... 257
5:11–12 ... 602
5:14 ... 255, 430
5:14–26 ... 243
5:15 ... 257
5:16 ... 258
5:17 ... 256
5:18 ... 257
5:19 ... 258
5:20 ... 257, 418
5:20–26 ... 243
5:21 ... 257
5:21–22 ... 243
5:22 ... 257
5:22–23 ... 602
5:23 ... 243, 256, 258, 626
5:24 ... 258
5:25 ... 257
5:25–26 ... 244
5:26 ... 459
5:27 ... 546
6 ... 428, 629
6:1–4 ... 255, 349
6:1–13 ... 428
6:2 ... 482
6:2–3 ... 224
6:3 ... 214, 427–28
6:5 ... 254
6:8 ... 223–24, 482
6:8–10 ... 220
6:9 ... 258
6:9–10 ... 214, 220, 224, 252, 311, 866, 870, 878
6:10 ... 184, 224, 458
6:11 ... 256
6:13 ... 216, 224, 258, 655
7 ... 225, 230, 232
7:1 ... 208, 225
7:3 ... 218, 230, 255, 811
7:9 ... 789
7:11 ... 225
7:11–12 ... 230
7:12 ... 225
7:14 ... 214, 258, 874
7:18 ... 459
7:22 ... 255
8–12 ... 232
8:3 ... 218, 255
8:4–11 ... 224
8:7 ... 228
8:7–8 ... 228
8:8 ... 214, 258, 628
8:10 ... 214, 258
8:12 ... 214
8:14 ... 214, 258
8:15 ... 224, 228, 258
8:17 ... 214
8:18 ... 214, 441
8:19 ... 254
8:21–28 ... 224
8:22 ... 244
9:1–2 ... 214
9:4 ... 254, 542
9:6 ... 224, 256, 418
9:6–7 ... 256, 879
9:7 ... 258
9:9 ... 257
9:12 ... 257
9:17 ... 257
9:20 ... 225
9:21 ... 257
10 ... 628
10:2 ... 256
10:4 ... 257
10:5 ... 628
10:6 ... 419
10:9 ... 218, 256
10:12 ... 218, 256, 628
10:17 ... 258
10:20 ... 258
10:22 ... 254
10:22–23 ... 214, 628
10:23 ... 257
10:25 ... 628
10:26 ... 165, 218, 225, 542
10:28 ... 249
10:30 ... 249
10:31 ... 248
10:32 ... 256
10:33–34 ... 352
11 ... 428
11:1 ... 224, 258, 276, 351, 877, 879–80
11:1–5 ... 252
11:1–10 ... 252, 428
11:2 ... 258
11:4 ... 436
11:6–9 ... 252–54
11:8 ... 253
11:9 ... 252, 254–56, 427–28, 459, 622
11:10 ... 214, 218, 224, 256, 258, 276, 351, 877, 879
11:11 ... 419
11:12–13 ... 258
11:15 ... 251
11:15–16 ... 225, 235, 237, 241, 459, 641, 650, 866, 880

11:16 ....225–26, 468, 855, 902
12:2 543
12:4 ....257, 546, 736
12:5 257
12:6 ....257–58, 456
13–23 ....218, 232, 258, 262, 303, 390
13–27 258
13:3 436
13:6 382
13:7 256
13:8 ....255, 310, 418, 549
13:10 ....214, 256, 373, 382
13:13 ....382, 439
13:16 ....425, 549
13:19 221
13:19–22 256
13:21 ....418, 778
13:21–22 436
14 446
14:1 451
14:2 ....256, 563
14:4 563
14:7 446
14:9 255
14:12–15..........258
14:13 354
14:13–15..........628
14:14 354
14:16 439
14:17 563
14:20 254
14:21 ....254, 881
14:23 256
14:26 257
14:27 ....257, 629
15:2 418
15:2–3..........292
15:4–6..........292
15:5 ....226, 251, 292
15:7 292
15:8 251
15–16..........291, 295
16:1 ....226, 256
16:3–5..........295
16:4 ....392, 580
16:4–5..........226
16:5 ....226, 392
16:6 292–93
16:7 ....255, 292–93, 370
16:8–9..........292
16:10 292
16:11 292
16:12 226
16:13–14 226
17:2–3..........256
17:6 258
17:7..........258
17:9..........254
17:10 255
17:13 ....436, 542
17:13–14..........542
18:2 228
18:6 256
18:7 ....228, 436
19:1 256
19:2 254
19:5 250
19:10 230
19:16 257
19:16–18..........255
19:18 256
19:23 226
19:23–24 357
19:23–25 218
19:25 255
20:1–6..........218
20:3 441
21:2–4..........255
21:6–12..........255
21:8 430
21:9 214
21:11–12..........402
22:9 256
22:9–11..........815–16
22:11 816
22:13 214
22:23..........257
22:25 257
23:7 436
23:13 255
23:15 311
23:15–17..........278
23:16–18 226
23:17–18..........226
23:18 226–27
24..........227, 291
24–27 ....227, 232, 258, 262
24:2 227
24:5 227
24:13 258
24:16 254
24:17–18..........292
24:18 ....227, 311, 439
24:21 257–58
25:1 ....256, 547
25:1–12..........184
25:2 256
25:6 227
25:6–7..........256
25:8 ....214, 235, 237, 253, 258
25:9 257
25:10 227
25:10–12 ....226–27, 253, 745
25:12 ....227, 238
26:1 257
26:2 256
26:5 238
26:6–7 235
26:7–8..........235
26:14 ....549, 626
26:17 ....310, 418
26:19 ....352, 624–26, 867
26:20..........214
26:21 173
27:1 ....236–37, 257, 506, 541
27:2 257
27:2–6..........255, 542
27:9 214–15
27:10–11..........256
27:12 257
27:13 257
28–35 ....232, 258
28–66..........257
28:1 257
28:4 370
28:7 418
28:7–8..........228
28:9 228
28:10 228
28:11 ....214, 228
28:12 214
28:13..........228, 258, 311
28:14 228
28:15 228
28:16..........215, 258, 525
28:17 258
28:18 419
28:21 228–29
28:22..........257
28:22–23..........628
29:1 ....228–29, 257
29:3 228–29
29:5–8..........205, 231
29:6 459
29:8 256
29:9–10..........878
29:10 ....215, 224
29:13 ....215, 397
29:13–14 878
29:14 215
29:15 ....257, 843
29:16 ....215, 258
29:18 878
29:19 258
29:21 256
29:22 255
29:23..........258
30:1 257
30:2 ....205, 231
30:7 236–37
30:9–10 224

30:11–12 258
30:15 258
30:19 .....235, 258
30:20 .....224, 382
30:26 258
30:28 228
30:29 256
30:33 549
31:1 .....255, 257–58
31:3 .....205, 231
31:3–5 205
31:4 310
31:4–5 .....205, 231
31:6–7 258
31:8–9 .....205, 231
31:9 549
32:3 878
32:3–4 224
32:9 256
32:11 256
32:13–14 256
32:16 258
33:1 257
33:1–9 255
33:2 255
33:4 383
33:5 258
33:14 251
33:14–16 .....795, 876
33:15 .....256, 258
33:19 228
33:22 545
33:24 .....285, 340
34:3 256
34:4 .....205, 215, 412
34:5–7 402
34:5–15 .....462, 470
34:6 435
34:8 423
34:8–15 256
34:9 .....251, 549
34:13 418
34:13–15 436
34:14 778
34:16 255
35:1 255
35:4 423
35:5 .....224, 878
35:8 .....226, 235, 240
35:8–10 880
35:10 257
36–39 .....80, 205, 225, 229–30, 232, 811, 816
36:1–39:8 811
36:1 .....229–30, 726, 815
36:2 .....230–31, 811
36:4 230
36:4–10 231
36:5 230
36:6 230–31
36:7 230
36:8–9 231
36:9 230
36:13–20 231
36:15 230–31
36:18 231
36:19–20 231
36:20 231
36:2–37:38 .....229, 815
37:10 230
37:10–13 231
37:14 519
37:16 .....185, 209
37:17 519
37:22–35 218
37:23 .....258, 628
37:26 209
37:27 544
37:29 311
37:30 230
37:35 .....205, 231
37:36 256
37:38 231
38 233
38:1 233
38:1–5 232
38:1–6 229
38:1–8 815
38:1–20 816
38:3 843
38:5 233
38:5–6 232–33
38:6 234
38:7 .....230, 233–34
38:7–8 .....229, 232–33
38:9–20 .....229, 232–33, 816
38:13 547
38:20 234
38:20–21 229
38:21 232–33
38:21–22 .....225, 229, 232–34, 815–16
38:22 .....230, 232–34
38:1–39:2 816
39 817–18
39:1–2 232
39:1–8 .....229, 816
39:3–7 818
39:6 .....642, 832, 884
39:6–7 .....231, 418
39:7–8 .....231, 817
39:8 817–18
40 818
40:1 .....231, 234–35, 237–38, 241, 245, 447, 610
40:1–11 .....242, 245
40:2 .....219, 250, 255
40:3 .....215, 226, 235, 237, 242, 468, 855–56
40:3–4 .....235–36, 870
40:3–5 215
40:3–10 866
40:4 .....448–49, 877
40:5 .....222, 258
40:6 .....258, 548
40:6–8 .....215, 548
40:7–8 258
40:8 .....218, 255, 572
40:9 .....219, 256, 258, 399, 425
40:9–10 242
40:10 .....257, 469
40:11 .....252, 545
40:12 .....209, 218
40:13 215
40:17 629
40:18 309
40:18–20 .....219, 430, 548
40:19 621
40:19–20 309
40:19–22 310
40:21 .....209, 218
40:21–22 218
40:24 459
40:25 .....218, 258
40:26 .....218, 236, 546, 563
40:27 563
40:28 .....209, 218, 236
40–48 621
40–52 242
40–55 ...217–19, 231, 235, 244, 257–58, 448, 556, 811, 901
40–66 .....234, 540, 602
41:1 435
41:2 883
41:4 .....218, 546
41:5 435
41:6–7 309–10
41:7 .....219, 430, 548
41:8 .....255, 843, 876
41:8–9 219
41:9 379
41:10 258
41:13 258
41:14 .....236, 258
41:15–16 620–21
41:16 .....258, 459
41:17 484
41:20 .....218, 236, 258
41:22–24 .....219, 430, 548
41:25 .....621, 883
41:26–27 218
41:27 258

41:28–29 . . . 219, 430, 548
42:1 . . . 215, 258
42:1–4 . . . 215, 219
42:4 . . . 435
42:5 . . . 209, 218, 236, 455
42:6 . . . 379, 455
42:6–7 . . . 219
42:7 . . . 250, 459, 878
42:9 . . . 218, 620
42:10 . . . 435, 542
42:14 . . . 549
42:16 . . . 219, 226, 235, 448, 484, 570, 878
42:17 . . . 219, 430, 548
42:18–20 . . . 224, 878
42:18–21 . . . 219
43 . . . 32, 147, 219, 236, 252
43:1 . . . 236, 245, 258
43:1–2 . . . 218, 236
43:2 . . . 236–37, 251, 628
43:3 . . . 258
43:4 . . . 237
43:5–6 . . . 219
43:7 . . . 218, 236, 245
43:9 . . . 219, 430, 548
43:10 . . . 219, 546
43:12 . . . 255
43:13 . . . 546
43:14 . . . 236, 258
43:14–17 . . . 236
43:15 . . . 236, 258
43:15–17 . . . 218
43:16 . . . 226, 235, 237, 251, 570
43:18–19 . . . 252
43:19 . . . 219, 226, 235, 237
43:19–20 . . . 236
43:20 . . . 215, 418
43:21 . . . 215, 218, 236
43:24 . . . 397
43:25 . . . 546
44:1–2 . . . 219
44:2 . . . 218, 236, 245, 255, 258, 546
44:3 . . . 258, 337, 378, 384
44:6 . . . 236, 671
44:6–8 . . . 218
44:8 . . . 185, 430
44:9–14 . . . 310
44:9–20 . . . 219, 430, 548
44:12 . . . 310
44:17 . . . 800
44:18–19 . . . 878
44:20 . . . 800
44:21 . . . 218–19, 236
44:22 . . . 236
44:23 . . . 236, 546
44:24 . . . 209, 218, 236, 255, 531, 563
44:26 . . . 218–19
44:26–28 . . . 219
44:28 . . . 215, 220, 448–49, 640, 691, 839, 842, 883
45 . . . 384
45:1 . . . 640, 839, 842
45:2 . . . 621, 880
45:3 . . . 379
45:4 . . . 219, 379
45:5 . . . 384
45:5–6 . . . 218, 384
45:6 . . . 384, 470, 549
45:7 . . . 236, 556
45:7–10 . . . 218
45:8 . . . 236, 258, 556
45:9 . . . 215, 236, 258, 556
45:11 . . . 218, 236, 258
45:12 . . . 209, 218, 236
45:13 . . . 640, 839, 842, 883
45:14 . . . 218, 256, 384
45:16 . . . 219, 430, 548
45:17 . . . 384
45:18 . . . 209, 218, 236, 384
45:19 . . . 218, 620
45:20 . . . 219, 430, 548
45:21 . . . 215, 218, 384, 620
45:22 . . . 218, 384, 671
45:22–23 . . . 258
45:23 . . . 215, 218
46:1–2 . . . 219, 430, 548
46:4 . . . 236, 245, 546
46:5 . . . 218
46:6–7 . . . 219, 310, 430, 548
46:7 . . . 309
46:9 . . . 218, 384
46:10 . . . 218
46:11 . . . 236
46:12–13 . . . 219
46:13 . . . 258
47:1 . . . 238
47:2 . . . 311
47:2–3 . . . 255
47:3 . . . 311, 423
47:4 . . . 236, 258
47:6 . . . 255
47:7 . . . 215
47:8 . . . 215, 218, 436
47:10 . . . 218
48:1–2 . . . 219
48:3 . . . 218
48:5 . . . 219, 430, 548
48:6 . . . 209
48:6–8 . . . 878
48:7 . . . 209, 236
48:8 . . . 209, 224
48:10 . . . 310
48:12 . . . 546
48:13 . . . 209, 218, 236
48:14 . . . 219, 430, 548
48:16 . . . 218, 236, 258
48:17 . . . 226, 235–36, 258
48:20 . . . 219, 236
48:21 . . . 458
48:22 . . . 245, 257
49:1 . . . 255, 379
49:1–6 . . . 219
49:2 . . . 258
49:5 . . . 236, 255
49:6 . . . 215
49:7 . . . 219, 236, 258
49:8 . . . 215, 258
49:9 . . . 250, 253, 459
49:9–11 . . . 219
49:10 . . . 215
49:11 . . . 226, 235
49:13 . . . 235, 546
49:14–15 . . . 484
49:14–18 . . . 219
49:18 . . . 257
49:22 . . . 219
49:23 . . . 256, 419, 489–90
49:25 . . . 219
49:26 . . . 236, 257
50:1 . . . 268, 591, 882
50:2 . . . 258, 513
50:4–9 . . . 219
50:5–7 . . . 272
50:6 . . . 612
50:7 . . . 258
50:9 . . . 258
50:10 . . . 219
51:1 . . . 620–21
51:2 . . . 255, 379
51:3 . . . 219, 235, 255, 354, 382, 446–47
51:5 . . . 257
51:6 . . . 258
51:7 . . . 547, 565
51:8 . . . 258
51:9 . . . 237–38, 245, 251, 430, 506
51:9–10 . . . 237, 541
51:9–11 . . . 218–19, 236–38
51:10 . . . 226, 235–36, 251
51:11 . . . 219, 257, 884
51:12 . . . 235, 546
51:13 . . . 209, 236, 245, 546
51:13–14 . . . 218
51:14 . . . 219
51:16 . . . 218–19, 258
51:17 . . . 237–38, 245, 352, 549, 612
51:17–20 . . . 219
51:17–22 . . . 612
51:19 . . . 235
51:22 . . . 549, 612
51–52 . . . 425
52:1 . . . 139, 220, 237–43, 245, 249–50, 316, 340–41, 381, 541, 579,

582, 584, 607, 679, 740, 772, 795, 866, 874, 876
52:1–2 . . . . . 219, 241
52:1–10 219
52:2 . . . . . 238, 241, 510
52:3 236
52:4 255
52:5 215
52:6 . . . . . 218, 546
52:7 . . . . . 215, 424–25
52:7–8 242
52:7–10 . . . . . 242, 258
52:8 . . . . . 255, 880
52:9 . . . . . 235–36, 546
52:11 . . . 215, 217, 240–43, 440, 832, 851
52:11–12 . . . . . 219, 226, 235, 241–42, 642, 870
52:12 . . . . . 241, 258, 418
52:13 . . . . . 244, 256, 624, 627
52:15 215
52:15–53:1 878
53 243
53 . . . . . 244, 627
53:1 215
53:2 877
53:4 215
53:5 . . . . . 215, 243–45, 250
53:6 . . . . . 215, 243–44, 252, 258, 459
53:7 . . . . . 244, 272, 540
53:7–8 . . . . . 215, 272
53:9 215
53:10 . . 217, 243–46, 250, 626–27, 870
53:11 . . . . . 243–45, 624–27
53:12 . . . . . 215, 243–45
54 244
54:1 . . . . . 215, 546
54:4 245–46
54:4–8 268
54:5 . . . . . 218, 236, 258
54:5–8 591
54:6 . . . . . 246, 379, 470
54:7 484
54:8 236
54:9 246
54:10 246
54:11 235
54:13 215
54:16 . . . . . 218, 236, 458
54:17 219
55 246
55:1–2 257
55:3 . . . . . 215, 246–47, 540, 765–66
55:3–5 . . . . . 246, 879
55:5 . . . . . 247, 257–58
55:6 . . . . . 753, 784
55:11 . . . . . 218, 250, 255, 258, 285
55:12 546
55:13 250
56 248–49
56:1 . . . . . 218, 258
56:1–7 . . . . . 247, 249–50, 316, 340–41, 582, 866
56:1–8 . . . . . 139, 220, 239, 241, 247–49, 448, 451, 580, 859, 870, 874
56:2 247
56:3 . . . . . 239, 247–48, 452
56:3–7 239–40
56:4 . . . . . 247, 356
56:5 247–50
56:6 . . . . . 247, 250
56:7 . . 215, 220, 247, 249, 258, 851, 859
56:8 249
56:10 255
56:11 258
56–66 . . . . . 217, 231, 257
57:3–13 256
57:5 . . . . . 256, 310, 357
57:10 256
57:13 256
57:14 . . . . . 237, 245, 311
57:14–19 . . . . . 245, 627
57:14–21 . . . . . 244–45, 250
57:15 . . . . . 245–46, 258, 487
57:16 . . . . . 236, 245
57:17 245
57:18 245
57:19 . . . . . 236, 245
57:21 . . . . . 245, 257
58:1 . . . . . 256, 418
58:1–14 256
58:2 258
58:6 . . . . . 215, 397
58:7 882
58:8 . . . . . 241, 258
58:12 257
58:13 883
58:14 . . . . . 222, 226, 235, 546, 565
59:1 258
59:3 . . . . . 436, 612
59:7 215
59:8 . . . . . 215, 570
59:9 258
59:14 . . . . . 258, 430
59:15–17 258
59:16 257–58
59:17 422–23
59:18 422
59:20 . . . . . 215, 236
59:21 . . . . . 215, 258
60:3 256
60:4 257
60:9 257–58
60:10–14 256
60:14 258
60:16 . . . . . 236, 257
60:19–20 258
60:21 . . . . . 258, 547
61:1 . . . . . 215, 250, 258, 459
61:1–2 217
61:2 . . . . . 215, 235, 250, 422
61:3 250
61:4 . . . . . 250, 257
61:5 250
61:5–7 . . . . . 250, 256
61:6 . . . . . 215, 250
61:7 459
61:8 436
61:10–11 258
62:4 484
62:5 591
62:6–7 612
62:10 . . . . . 226, 237, 245
62:11 . . . . . 215, 257, 880
62:12 . . . . . 236, 484
63:1 . . . . . 255, 258
63:1–6 . . . . . 462, 470
63:4 423
63:5 257–58
63:7–14 . . . . . 161, 251
63:9 . . . . . 236, 251–52
63:10 251
63:11 251
63:11–12 251
63:11–14 438
63:12 251
63:12–13 237
63:13 . . . . . 251, 513
63:14 . . . . . 251–52, 843
63:15 547
63:15–19 252
63:16 . . . . . 236, 255
63:17 . . . . . 224, 252, 878
64:4 215
64:4–5 258
64:7 236
64:8 258
64:10 438
65:1 215
65:1–2 878
65:2 . . . . . 215, 255
65:4 . . . . . 318, 457
65:7 469
65:17 . . . . . 215, 221, 236
65:17–18 252–53
65:18 . . . . . 236, 245, 253
65:19 . . . . . 235, 253, 258
65:20 253
65:21 256
65:21–23 253
65:25 . . . . . 252–53, 256
66:1 . . . . . 215, 256, 522, 543, 753

66:2 .... 215, 236, 245, 257, 487
66:3 .... 397, 457
66:5 257
66:7–9..........................253
66:13..........................235
66:17..........................457
66:18..........................258
66:18–21 258
66:22.......... 221, 236, 245, 252–53
66:24..........215, 256, 624–26, 867

JEREMIAH

........xxxvi, xlviii, 139, 170, 188–90, 206, 215, 221, 226–27, 255, 257, 260–82, 284–311, 314, 323, 334–35, 347, 350, 374, 398–400, 423, 426, 434, 436, 438, 440, 444–46, 448–50, 457, 479, 494, 499–500, 552, 561–62, 574, 604–5, 608–12, 617–19, 622–24, 631, 640, 665–66, 686–87, 701–2, 714, 809–10, 818–19, 821, 825, 829–39, 841, 853, 866, 870, 900–1
1 290
1:1.......................287, 304
1:2.............................521
1:3.............................290
1:5.............................255
1:6 267
1:6–9...........................267
1:9.......................267, 311
1:10 ....270, 305
1:13 305
1:14 ....305, 309
1:15............................305
1:16 311
1:18 ....304, 609
2:2 ....267–68, 351, 591
2:2–3...........................267
2:3 268
2:5.......................268, 310
2:7....................269–70, 308
2:9 ....308, 370
2:11 ....268, 513
2:13 311
2:16 256
2:17 ....272, 311
2:19 311
2:20 ....256, 310, 357, 361
2:20–28 256
2:21 ....255, 305, 356, 542
2:22 468
2:23 ....268, 806
2:25 256
2:27 308
2:28 308
2:30 311
3 269
3:1.............262, 268–69, 514, 792
3:1–3...........................351
3:1–7...........................309
3:2 269
3:3 ....311, 792
3:6 ....256, 310, 357, 361, 792
3:6–10.....................351–52
3:6–13..........................306
3:8 792
3:9 269
3:11–12.........................269
3:12 305
3:13 ....256, 310, 357, 361
3:16–17...................281, 309
3:17 494
3:17–18.........................262
3:18 305
3:22 837
3:25 351
4:1 311
4:1–3...........................300
4:3 310
4:4 ....285, 289, 309, 377, 878
4:6 305
4:7.............................310
4:13 ....427, 430
4:14 288
4:15 305
4:16 276–77
4:19 255
4:23 146
4:23–2..........................269
4:23–25 270
4:23–26 269
4:23–28 ....262, 434
4:26 270
4:27 269–70
4:28 269–70
4:31 ....310, 418
5:7.............................311
5:9 ....304, 422
5:15 228
5:17 ....205, 412
5:19 ....309, 311
5:21 260
5:21 ....224, 285, 311, 878
5:22 549
5:24 309
5:28 ....309, 311
5:29 304
5:71–72.........................297
6:1...............299, 305, 310, 356
6:8 270
6:9 ....309, 401
6:10 ....285, 309, 311, 878
6:11 311
6:12–13.........................281
6:13 430
6:13–15.........................305
6:14 ....300, 418, 609–10, 837
6:15–18.........................300
6:16 570
6:17 ....255, 285, 310–11, 878
6:18 277
6:19 ....285, 311, 878
6:19–20.........................397
6:21 311
6:22 305
6:22–24 303–4
6:24 549
6:26 310
6:27–30.........................310
6:29 ....468, 470
6:30 610
7 ....206, 220, 271
7:1.............................270
7:1–2.....................267, 270
7:1–8:3 307–8
7:1–15 ....277, 876
7:3.............................271
7:3–15..........................270
7:4.......................271, 397
7:5.............................271
7:5–6.......................270–71
7:5–7 281
7:7.......................271, 278
7:8.......................271, 397
7:8–10..........................397
7:9.............................271
7:11...............260, 271, 859, 876
7:12 ....197, 271, 493
7:12–14.........................742
7:13 ....261, 271, 305, 835
7:14............................271
7:16..........256, 273, 304, 311, 605
7:17–18.........................397
7:18......................255, 370
7:21–23...................311, 397
7:23 282
7:24 494
7:25 ....261, 305, 835
7:29 418
7:30 304
7:31 ....208–9, 304, 311, 810
7:31–32.........................809
7:32 309
7:32–33.........................256
7:33 309
8:1.............................308
8:10 281
8:10–12.......................304–5
8:11 ....356, 609–10, 837
8:13 ....205, 412, 435
8:14 309

8:15 .... 304, 837
8:16 .... 305, 439
8:17 309
8:19 310
8:21 .... 270, 610
8:21–22 609
9:4 311
9:7 .... 310, 468, 470
9:8 422
9:10 270
9:11 256
9:12–14 309
9:14 .... 494, 806
9:15 .... 304, 612
9:17 609
9:24 260
9:25–26 .... 139, 309, 582
10 310
10:1–6 548
10:1–10 430
10:1–16 .... 309–10, 539, 548, 574
10:3 310
10:3–5 309
10:4 309
10:5 309
10:6–8 .... 267, 310
10:7 260
10:8–9 309
10:10 .... 310, 439
10:11 309
10:11–16 269
10:12 .... 309, 574
10:12–15 309
10:13 .... 305, 310, 528–29, 549
10:16 311
10:22 .... 270, 305
10:23 271
10:25 .... 271, 311
11:1–5 306
11:4 282
11:7 .... 261, 305, 835
11:7–8 .... 267, 309
11:8 494
11:9–14 306
11:13 271
11:14 .... 256, 273, 304, 311, 605
11:16 .... 289, 310
11:17 .... 271, 305
11:18–23 561
11:19 .... 244, 272
11:20 .... 272, 305, 423, 609
11:26 309
11:28 271
11–20 .... 263, 609
12:1 430
12:1–6 561
12:2 305
12:3 .... 244, 272, 459, 540, 843
12:4 .... 262, 272, 548
12:7 311
12:10 270
12:10–11 542
12:14 .... 295, 305
12:14–15 295
12:15 305
12:17 305
13:1 274
13:1–5 274
13:1–11 272
13:2 271
13:6 271
13:10 494
13:11 .... xxv, 272–73, 282
13:13 271
13:15–22 274
13:17 609
13:20 305
13:22 .... 311, 425
13:26 .... 311, 425
14 .... 605, 610
14:2 270
14:6 549
14:7 .... 273, 547
14:10 273
14:10–12 273
14:11 .... 256, 273, 304, 311, 605
14:12 .... 350, 397
14:17 609
14:19 .... 304, 605, 609–10, 837
14:20 .... 514, 609–11
14:21 547
14:22 269
15 205
15:1 .. 262, 273, 309, 311, 543, 605, 819
15:2 260
15:2 260
15:4 .... 205, 819, 831
15:5 .... 836, 843
15:8 311
15:10 .... 310, 609
15:10–21 561
15:12 305
15:13–14 .... 267, 305
15:14 .... 289, 304
15:15 548
15:16 .... 311, 349
15:17 609
15:18 610
15:20 609
16:6 418
16:10–13 309
16:12 494
16:14 281
16:14–15 262
16:15 305
16:16 .... 311, 469
16:17 .... 272, 548
16:19 310
17 .... 479, 687
17:2 .... 256, 310, 357
17:3–4 .... 267, 305
17:4 289
17:7–8 .... xxix, 478–79
17:8 .... 255, 310
17:14–18 561
17:19–27 .... xxxix, 30, 273–74, 639, 680, 883
17:21 .... 275, 686–87
17:21–22 .... xxxix, 274, 883
17:21–23 275
17:21–27 .... 395, 686–87
17:22 .... 274, 686–87
17:24 .... 274–75, 686, 883
17:27 .... 274–75, 289, 686–87, 883
18:1–6 258
18:1–12 306
18:2 665
18:7 305
18:7–8 408
18:9 305
18:12 .... 256, 494
18:15 570
18:18 666
18:18–23 562
18:20–22 .... 309, 609
18:23 .... 272, 547, 665
19:3 209
19:4 810
19:5 .... 208–9, 304
19:5–6 .... 311, 809–10, 821
19:8 .... 304, 419, 436
19:11 837
19:13 .... 271, 435
20:7 .... 275, 609
20:7–8 .... 262, 276, 408, 562
20:8 430
20:10 275
20:12 .... 305, 423, 609
20:14 .... 310, 562
20:15 562
21:1 648
21:1–10 306
21:7 .... 350, 836
21:8 309
21:9 350
21:10 .... 170, 289
21:12 289
21:13 425
21:13–14 304
21:14 289
21–52 264

22:1–5 ... 306
22:3 ... xxvi, 42
22:8–9 ... 309
22:10 ... 831
22:10–12 ... 831
22:14 ... 438
22:15 ... 691
22:16 ... 541
22:24 ... 437, 440–41, 546, 591
22:24–27 ... 756
22:30 ... 756
23 ... 332
23:1 ... 331, 458, 547
23:1–6 ... 330, 332
23:2 ... 458
23:3 ... 146
23:4–6 ... 331
23:5 ... 256, 276, 279, 287, 448, 500, 877
23:5–6 ... 286–87, 305, 351, 394, 448, 756, 877, 879
23:6 ... 311, 332, 500, 877
23:6–10 ... 352
23:7 ... 281
23:7–8 ... 262
23:8 ... 305
23:11 ... 269
23:13 ... 269
23:14 ... 221, 878
23:15 ... 304
23:17 ... 356, 494
23:19 ... 459
24 ... 350
24:1 ... 726, 833
24:2 ... 370
24:6 ... 305
24:7 ... 282, 285
24:8–10 ... 279, 756
24:10 ... 350
25 ... 290, 445, 447, 618, 835–36
25:1 ... 445
25:3 ... 261, 290, 305, 835
25:3–4 ... 209, 797
25:4 ... 261, 305, 445, 702, 835
25:4–5 ... 445, 671
25:4–6 ... 836
25:4–9 ... 836
25:5 ... 445
25:7 ... 445
25:9 ... 301, 305, 419
25:10 ... 301
25:11 ... 255, 301, 311, 438, 445–47, 450, 622, 640, 837, 839, 842
25:11–12 ... 278–79, 446, 883
25:12 ... 255, 311, 438, 445–47, 450
25:15 ... 402, 549
25:15–16 ... 352
25:15–26 ... 290–91
25:15–29 ... 277, 612
25:17 ... 295–96, 549
25:18 ... 291, 419
25:19 ... 291
25:20 ... 291, 684
25:21 ... 291, 296, 402
25:22 ... 291
25:23–24 ... 291
25:25 ... 291
25:26 ... 267, 291, 305–6
25:28 ... 277, 352, 549
25:30 ... 267, 276–77
25:36 ... 457
26:1 ... 833
26:1–2 ... 270
26:2–23 ... 311
26:3 ... 278, 408
26:4–6 ... 270, 277
26:5 ... 261, 271, 305, 835
26:6 ... 271, 742
26:17–19 ... 831
26:18 ... 278, 281
26:18–19 ... 713
26:19 ... 278
26:20–23 ... 278, 671
27 ... 278, 832–33
27:1 ... 278, 833
27:1–22 ... 306
27:3 ... 278, 833
27:6–7 ... 883
27:7 ... 255, 267, 278–79, 311, 446
27:8 ... 350
27:13 ... 350
27:16 ... 619, 642, 832, 884
27:16–22 ... 206, 832–33
27:18 ... 832
27:21 ... 642
27:21–22 ... 642, 726, 832, 884
27:22 ... 641–42
28 ... 833
28:3 ... 642, 832, 884
28:6 ... 642, 832, 884
28:8–9 ... 278
28:9 ... 285, 831
28:10 ... 309
28:11 ... 309
28:12 ... 309
28:14 ... 309
28:15 ... 884
28:16 ... 434
29 ... 422, 447, 618, 622
29:1–23 ... 306
29:3 ... 833
29:5 ... 305, 436
29:10 ... 255, 287, 311, 438, 446, 449–50, 622, 640, 837, 839, 842
29:10–11 ... 279
29:10–12 ... 278, 883
29:11–12 ... 283
29:12 ... 878
29:12–13 ... 283
29:13–14 ... 309, 753, 784
29:14 ... 311, 565
29:16–20 ... 267, 279
29:17 ... 350
29:18 ... 350, 623
29:19 ... 261, 305, 835
29:24–32 ... 306
29:28 ... 305
30:3 ... 311, 548, 565
30:6 ... 284, 549
30:9 ... 279, 879
30:10 ... 446
30:10–11 ... 305, 446
30:14 ... 284
30:17 ... 609, 837
30:18 ... 311, 565
30:22 ... 282
31:1 ... 282
31:4 ... 311
31:5 ... 305
31:6 ... 310, 546
31:8 ... 305
31:9 ... 226, 309, 470
31:10 ... 545
31:13 ... 311
31:15 ... 260
31:16 ... 784
31:18 ... 309, 470
31:20 ... 309, 470
31:21 ... 226
31:23 ... 311, 459, 565
31:28 ... 270, 305
31:29 ... 281, 552, 610
31:29–30 ... 280
31:30 ... 279–81, 323, 610, 881
31:31 ... 282, 284, 334
31:31–3 ... 281
31:31–34 ... 224, 260, 281–82, 284, 287, 334–35, 851, 866, 870, 878
31:32 ... 284
31:33 ... 215, 263, 281–82, 285, 314, 334, 487, 547, 565, 569
31:33–34 ... 285
31:34 ... 215, 263, 282, 285
31:35 ... 285, 287
31:35–36 ... 285
31:35–37 ... 269, 286–87, 499, 608
31:36 ... 285
31:37 ... 285
31:40 ... 305
32 ... 147, 161, 310, 837
32:1–2 ... 306
32:1–12 ... 291
32:4 ... 170

32:6–16 306
32:7 309
32:15 310
32:16–23 310
32:17 .... 209, 269
32:17–19 161
32:18 310
32:20–21 161
32:21 147
32:22–23 161
32:24 .... 170, 310, 350
32:24–25 161
32:25 310
32:26–44 306
32:27 269
32:29 .... 271, 289, 435
32:33 .... 261, 305, 835
32:34 304
32:35 .... 208–9, 304, 311
32:36 350
32:38 282
32:39 285
32:41 305
32:43 270
32:43–44 310
32:44 565
33:6 837
33:7 .... 311, 565
33:9 272
33:11 .... 311, 546, 565, 691, 789
33:14 .... 287, 449–50
33:14–16 .... 305, 879
33:14–18 .... 276, 286–87, 449–50
33:14–21 500
33:14–22 .... 267, 279, 286–87, 305, 448, 463
33:14–26 .... 449, 879
33:15 383
33:15–18 877
33:16 311
33:17 287
33:18–22 287
33:19–22 287
33:20 .... 269, 287
33:21 463
33:22 269
33:25 .... 269, 287
33:26 .... 311, 565
34 288–89
34:1–7 306
34:3 170
34:5 783
34:8 .... 288, 882
34:8–9 288
34:8–22 .... 288, 306
34:9 288
34:10 288
34:11 288
34:13 173
34:14 .... xxvi, 48, 288–89, 882
34:14–15 288
34:15 .... 288, 445, 882
34:16 288
34:17 .... 288–89, 350, 882
34:22 .... 270, 289
35:1–19 306
35:7 305
35:14 .... 261, 305, 835
35:15 .... 261, 305, 784, 835
35:19 287
36 289
36:23 289
36:24 289
36:25 289
36:27 289
36:32 .... 263–64, 289
37:1–10 306
37:2 834
37:10 289
37:11–16 306
37:17–21 306
38 609
38:1 648
38:2 350
38:3 170
38:6 288
38:17–18 289
38:22 288
38:23 289
39 .... 80, 301–2, 837
39:1 299
39:1–2 726
39:1–10 305
39:2 299
39:3 .... 299, 302, 306
39:4–6 299
39:4–10 302
39:4–13 .... 267, 301–2, 305
39:7 299
39:8 300
39:8 .... 289, 402
39:8–9 301
39:9 300
39:10 300
39:11–12 302
39:11–13 300
39:13 302
39:14 .... 300, 302, 306
39:14–18 302
39:15–18 .... 300, 306
39:17 170
39–44 299–301
40:1 306
40:2–12 306
40:7–10 300
41:4–18 300
42:1–22 300
42:10 305
42:17 350
42:18 843
42:22 350
43:1–7 300
43:7 256
43:8–13 300
43:13 256
44:1 256
44:1–14 306
44:4 .... 261, 305, 835
44:6 .... 270, 843
44:13 350
44:15–19 306
44:19 .... 255, 370
44:24–30 306
45:1–5 306
45:4 305
45:5 299
46 291
46:4 380
46:10 .... 305, 422–23, 435
46:20 305
46:21 304
46:24 305
46:27 446
46:27–28 .... 305, 446
46–51 .... 276, 290, 299–301, 305, 390
47 291
47:1–6 300
47:2 .... 228, 305
47:4 .... 388, 395
48 .... 291, 295
48:1–44 299
48:4–18 300
48:5 .... 261, 291–92, 295
48:29–30 292–93
48:29–47 .... 261, 291, 295, 303
48:31 292–93
48:32 292
48:33 292
48:34 292
48:34–38 292
48:34–46 295
48:36 292
48:37–38 292
48:40 .... 292, 302, 311
48:40–41 .... 295–96, 305
48:41 .... 292, 296, 310, 418
48:43–44 292
48:44 311
48:45 .... 184, 227, 292
48:45–46 293
48:45–47 299

48:46 .... 170, 292, 294, 388
48:47 .... 226, 292, 295, 297, 299, 311, 388, 580
49 .... 295–96, 398–99, 401–2
49:1–6 291
49:1–22 300
49:2 396
49:6 .... 292, 295, 297, 311, 388
49:7 .... 295–96, 398, 400
49:7–10 400
49:7–21 262
49:7–22 .... 291, 402, 462, 470
49:9–10 .... 295–96, 398, 400
49:10 400–1
49:11 .... 297, 399
49:12 .... 402, 549, 612
49:12–13 295–96
49:13 400
49:14 400
49:14–16 .... 295–96, 398–400
49:16 398–99
49:17 304
49:18 .... 221, 304, 357
49:19–21 .... 295–96, 303
49:19–22 296
49:21 439
49:22 .... 292, 296, 302, 305, 310–11, 399, 418
49:23–27 291
49:24 549
49:26 303
49:27 311
49:28–33 291
49:34–39 291
49:39 .... 292, 295, 297, 311
50 .... 290, 457
50:1–7 300
50:2 297
50:3 305
50:4 383
50:8–13 300
50:9 305
50:13 304
50:13–14 304
50:15 423
50:20 383
50:27 304
50:28 423
50:30 303
50:31 425
50:35–37 457
50:37 684
50:39 418
50:40 .... 221, 304
50:41 305
50:41–43 303–4
50:43 .... 292, 296, 310, 549
50:43–46 295–96
50:44 457
50:44–46 .... 296, 303
50:45 458
50:46 439
50–51 423
51 298–99
51:1 306
51:1–3 300
51:6 423
51:7 .... 352, 549, 612
51:11 423
51:15–19 .... 269, 304
51:16 305
51:19 311
51:25 .... 309, 425
51:29 439
51:34 .... 297, 548
51:35 297
51:36 423
51:37 419
51:41 .... 267, 306
51:44 .... 222, 297–98
51:44–50 .... 267, 297–98
51:45 260
51:48 305
51:49 298–99
51:49–53 298
51:50 298–99
51:58 .... 311, 430
51:59 833
51:64 .... 290, 299, 301
52 .... 80, 290, 299–302, 691, 837
52:1–3 299
52:1–34 .... 267, 305
52:4–16 305
52:6 457
52:12 457
52:12–14 450
52:12–30 837
52:13 289
52:15 301
52:18–20 .... 206, 642, 832, 884
52:28 .... 301, 726
52:28–30 301
52:29 726
52:30 726

EZEKIEL

.... xxxii, xlii, xlviii, 220, 240, 249, 255, 279, 281, 297, 313–26, 328–30, 332–57, 375, 378–79, 384, 444, 447–48, 453–54, 458, 500, 511–12, 515, 518, 552, 580, 582, 610, 726, 768, 772, 826, 870, 901
1:2 357
1:4 .... 349, 459
1:4–14 349
1:4–21 353
1:4–28 255
1:7 349
1:10 350
1:13 349
1:14 349
1:15–18 350
1:15–21 349
1:16 349
1:19–21 350
1:20–21 353
1:22 349
1:22–28 349
1:24 349–50
1:26 349–50
1:27 350
1:28 349
1:4–3:27 348
1–33 322
1–37 .... 336, 353
2:1 354
2:8–3:3 311
3:1–2 337
3:3 313
3:5–6 .... 52, 317–18
3:11–13 353
3:12 .... 349, 355
3:16–21 255
3:17 .... 310, 355, 430
3:20 311
3:23 349
3:25–27 355
4:2 .... xxv, 337, 343
4:4 340
4:5 340
4:6 340
4:10 357
4:12 140
4:13 .... 242, 396
4:14 .... 41, 318
4:15 318
4:16 356
4:17 330
5 350
5:1–4 349
5:2 357
5:5 337
5:8 425
5:10 .... xxvii–xxviii, 316, 318, 881
5:11 357
5:12 .... 349, 357, 565
6 350
6:1–4 352
6:1–10 353
6:2 .... 334, 352
6:3 319

6:4 357
6:4–7 319
6:6 ....319, 357
6:7 384
6:11–12 349
6:12 565
6:13 ....256, 310, 315, 357, 361
7 350
7:1 319
7:2 319
7:3 319
7:4 ....320, 357
7:6 319
7:6–7 353
7:8 ....xxv, 337
7:9 ....320, 357
7:10 ....xxvii, 319–20
7:11 320
7:13 320
7:14 320–21
7:15–16 349
7:18 419
7:19 ....311, 321, 891, 900
7:20 ....321, 357
7:21–22 606
7:24 318
8:2 350
8:3 357
8:5 357
8:10 357
8:11 357
8:12 ....355, 357
8:16–18 356
8:18 357
8–11 350
9:5 357
9:8 ....xxv, 337
9:9 355
10:1 350
10:4 349
10:5 350
10:9–13 350
10:9–22 355
10:14 350
10:15 349
10:16–17 350
10:18–19 353
10:19 355
10:20 349
11:3 354
11:4–6 354
11:7 354
11:11 354
11:18 357
11:19 ....xxv, 334, 337
11:19–20 334
11:20 ....282, 335
11:21 357
11:22–23 353
11:22–25 355
11:23 ....349, 355
12 350
12:2 878
12:6 441
12:11 441
12:14 357
12:14–16 349
12:15 357
13:10 ....356, 418
13:11 459
13:13 459
13:16 356
14 322
14:1–11 ....316, 321–22, 340, 582
14:3 321
14:3–4 311
14:4 321–22
14:4–5 321
14:5 322
14:6–8 321
14:7 ....321–22, 341
14:8 322
14:8–11 321
14:9 322
14:10 ....322, 340
14:11 ....282, 322
14:13–21 356
14:14 322
14:19 ....xxv, 337
14:19–20 353
14:20 322
14:21–23 349
15:1–8 356
16 ....161, 256, 314, 323, 350–52, 356, 518
16:1–2 350
16:1–13 351
16:2 350
16:3 351
16:3–14 ....161, 350
16:6 351
16:8 ....151, 351, 584
16:8–14 591
16:14 354
16:15 ....xxv, 337, 792
16:15–34 161
16:16 792
16:17 ....357, 792
16:19 315
16:20 ....326, 356
16:21 ....326, 356
16:26 351
16:27 356
16:32 351
16:35–43 161
16:36 ....xxv, 326, 337, 356
16:37 ....255, 311
16:38 ....xxv, 337, 356
16:39 ....255, 311
16:43 356
16:44 351
16:45 351
16:46 ....346, 878
16:49 323
16:53 ....221, 297, 311, 878
16:53–57 ....317, 323, 346, 351
16:55 297
16:58 356
16:60 355
16:63 ....323, 350–51
17:1–10 542
17:5 ....342, 357
17:17 ....xxv, 337
17:22–23 351
18 314
18:1–4 ....280–81, 323–24, 610
18:2 ....552, 610
18:4 ....xxvii, 318, 881
18:5–9 323
18:6 ....315, 321, 356
18:6–8 357
18:6–9 324
18:8 ....356, 882
18:9 326
18:10 ....xxv, 337, 356
18:10–13 323
18:11–13 357
18:13 ....356, 882
18:14–17 323
18:15–18 357
18:17 ....326, 356, 882
18:18 ....324, 356
18:19 326
18:20 ....xxvii, 318, 323–24, 881
18:20–24 353
18:21 326
18:21–32 ....330, 354
18:29–32 324
19 351
19:1 351
19:1–7 354
19:1–9 880
19:1–14 329
19:10–12 256
19:10–14 542
19:12 354
19:14 351
20 ....161, 314, 324, 328, 350, 354, 356, 515, 518
20:1–34 324
20:2–4 350

20:3 ... 325
20:4 ... 350
20:4–10 ... 161
20:5–6 ... 325
20:5–9 ... 325
20:5–10 ... 325
20:7 ... 357
20:7–8 ... 324–25, 328, 515
20:8 ... xxv, 337, 357
20:8–9 ... 325
20:9 ... 513, 515, 518
20:10 ... 325
20:10–14 ... 325
20:10–16 ... 325
20:10–17 ... 325
20:10–21 ... xxvii
20:11 ... 324–28, 350, 671, 674
20:11–12 ... 161
20:11–17 ... 325
20:12 ... 324–25, 356
20:13 ... xxv, 324–27, 325, 327, 337, 356, 671, 674
20:13–14 ... 325
20:13–26 ... 161
20:15 ... 325
20:15–16 ... 325
20:15–17 ... 325
20:16 ... 324–26, 356
20:17 ... 357
20:17–26 ... 325
20:18 ... 325–28
20:18–19 ... 325
20:18–22 ... 325
20:18–26 ... 325
20:19 ... 326
20:20 ... 324–25, 356
20:21 ... xxv, 324–28, 337, 356, 671, 674
20:21–22 ... 325
20:23 ... 357, 513–14
20:23–24 ... 325, 327
20:23–26 ... 325
20:24 ... 324–26, 356
20:25 ... 324–26, 328
20:25–26 ... 326–28
20:26 ... 325–26, 356
20:27 ... 326
20:27–29 ... 161, 325
20:28 ... 315, 325, 328
20:30 ... 357
20:30–31 ... 325
20:31 ... 326, 328, 356–57
20:32 ... 355, 357, 503
20:33 ... 532
20:33–34 ... xxv, 337
20:33–35 ... 161
20:33–42 ... 356
20:34 ... 313, 532
20:35 ... 99
20:38 ... 315
20:39 ... 397
20:40 ... 256
20:41 ... 313, 315
20:43 ... 333
20:44 ... 333
21:3 ... 425
21:7 ... 256
21:22 ... xxv, 337
21:27 ... 328, 880
21:31 ... xxv, 337, 458
21–37 ... 354
22 ... 350, 356
22:1–12 ... 350, 354
22:2 ... 350
22:3 ... xxv, 356
22:3–4 ... xxv, 337
22:6 ... xxv, 337, 356
22:6–12 ... 357
22:7 ... xxvi, 42, 344, 356
22:7–12 ... 355
22:8 ... 356
22:9 ... xxv, 337, 356
22:10 ... 321, 356
22:11 ... 356
22:12 ... xxv, 337, 356, 882
22:15 ... 315, 357
22:17–22 ... 470
22:22 ... xxv, 337
22:25 ... 329
22:26 ... 329, 343–44, 347, 356, 436, 884
22:27 ... xxv, 329, 337, 356
22:29 ... xxvi, 42, 344, 356–57
22:31 ... xxv, 329, 337, 436
23 ... 161, 314, 352, 356, 518
23:1 ... 350–51
23:3 ... 792
23:5 ... 335, 792
23:5–8 ... 161, 352
23:8 ... xxv, 337
23:9–10 ... 161
23:11–21 ... 161
23:14 ... 357
23:15 ... 255
23:17 ... 255
23:21 ... 356
23:22–35 ... 161
23:26 ... 255
23:27 ... 356
23:29 ... 255, 356
23:30 ... 347
23:31–34 ... 352, 612
23:35 ... 356
23:36 ... 350
23:37 ... 326, 356
23:38 ... 356
23:39 ... 326, 356
23:44 ... 356
23:45 ... xxv, 337, 356
24:3–14 ... 354
24:7 ... xxv, 337, 514
24:8 ... 422
24:14 ... 357
24:23 ... 330, 340, 514
24:24 ... 441
24:27 ... 355, 441
25:8 ... 355
25:11–14 ... 297
25:12 ... 357, 806
25:12–14 ... 354, 402, 462, 470
25–32 ... 390
26:3 ... 333
26:7–14 ... 255, 330
26:8 ... xxv, 337
26:20 ... 354
27 ... 336–37
27:3 ... 354
27:4 ... 354
27:10 ... 336
27:11 ... 354
27:12 ... 337
27:14 ... 336
27:15 ... 337
27:22–23 ... 337
27:25–29 ... 407
27:27 ... 354
28 ... 354, 454, 629
28:1–10 ... 354
28:2 ... 354, 629
28:3 ... 322
28:4 ... 354, 469
28:8 ... 354, 629
28:11 ... 354
28:11–19 ... 354
28:12 ... 354
28:13 ... 354
28:15 ... 436
28:17 ... 354, 629
28:19 ... 629
28:22 ... 357
28:25 ... 352
28:25–26 ... 352
28:26 ... 352–53, 357
29:1–7 ... 354
29:4 ... 311
29:7–9 ... 356
29:12 ... 357, 383
29:13–14 ... 357
29:14 ... 311
29:17–2 ... 330
29:17–20 ... 255, 330
29:20 ... 330

29:21 .... 357, 877
30:2–3 382
30:5 684
30:12 439
30:15 .... xxv, 337
30:26 357
31 352
31:9 354
31:15–17 354
31:15–18 .... 255, 352
31:16 .... 354, 439
31:18 .... 352, 354
32:1–16 354
32:17–32 354
33:7 .... 355, 430
33:10 .... 330, 514
33:10–11 330
33:10–20 .... 330, 354
33:21 332
33:24 357
33:25 .... xxv, 337, 356
33:25–26 357
33–39 332
34 .... 314–15, 330, 332, 335, 453–54, 545
34:1–31 .... 332, 453–54, 457
34:2–4 453
34:4 .... xxxii–xxxiii, 315, 330, 453
34:5 458
34:6 458
34:10 453–54
34:12 458
34:20 454
34:21 458
34:23 .... 332, 346, 454
34:23–24 .... 279, 879
34:23–28 332
34:23–31 .... 317, 330, 335, 500
34:24 282
34:24–28 332
34:25 .... 246, 332
34:26 .... 332, 469
34:27 .... 309, 332
34:28 332
34:30 .... 282, 332
34:30–31 332
34:31 547
34–37 .... 332, 335
35 402
35:1–5 297
35:1–15 .... 354, 402
35:5 .... 357, 402, 806
35:9 357
35:12 806
35:15 357
35–36 353
36 xxvii
36:1–12 319
36:1–15 353
36:5 .... 354, 357, 402
36:8 514
36:10 353
36:11 332
36:12 333
36:12–13 .... xxvii, 333
36:12–19 .... xxv, 333
36:13 333
36:16–38 354
36:17 .... 321, 333, 612
36:18 .... 333, 337, 356
36:19 .... 333, 357
36:20 313
36:22 313
36:23 514
36:23–24 518
36:24 514
36:24–28 334
36:25 334
36:26 .... xxv, 314, 334, 337
36:26–27 .... 317, 334, 878
36:27 .... xxv, 334–35, 337
36:27–28 334
36:28 282
36:35 .... 255, 354, 382
36:37 459
37 .... 314, 453–54
37:1–4 352
37:1–14 352
37:3 352
37:13 352
37:14 .... xxv, 337
37:15–27 453
37:15–28 .... 454–55, 457
37:16–17 454
37:19 454
37:23 .... 282, 355, 357
37:24 454
37:24–25 879
37:24–28 .... 279, 317, 330–32, 335, 346, 500
37:25 335
37:26 .... 246, 332, 335, 355
37:27 .... 281–82, 335
37:28 247
38:2 336
38:6 336
38:8 353
38:9 352
38:11 448
38:12 337
38:16 336
38:20 439
38:22 .... 383, 549
38:23 352
38–39 .... 336–37, 348, 352–53
38:18–39:6 458
39:2 336
39:4 353
39:10–13 354
39:11 336–37
39:15 336–37
39:17 353
39:21 352
39:22 353
39:25 .... 311, 352
39:26 352
39:27 352
39:28 353
39:29 .... xxv, 337, 377–79, 459
40:2 .... 256, 353
40:3 447
40:6–16 338
40:16 353
40:17 338
40:17–18 768
40:20–23 338
40:22 338
40:24–27 338
40:26 353
40:28–31 338
40:31 338
40:32–34 338
40:34 338
40:35–37 338
40:38–43 338
40:44 338
40:44–45 340
40:45–46 339–40
40:46 342
40:47 .... 338, 354
40:49 338
40–44 346
40–48 .... 337, 341, 346, 353
41:1–2 338
41:3–4 .... 338, 353
41:10 338
41:13 338
41:18–20 .... 338, 353
41:22 .... 338, 353
41:25–26 .... 338, 353
42:1–14 338
42:3 768
42:14 344
42:20 .... 338, 347
43:1–5 .... 338, 355
43:4 .... 353, 355
43:5 .... 349, 448
43:7–9 347
43:11 350
43:13–27 .... 338, 354
43:17 .... 338, 353

43:18–27 353
43:19 342
43–48 92
44 .... 249, 314, 339–40, 343
44:1–3 338
44:2 353
44:4 349
44:6 342
44:5–16 xxvii
44:6–16 249
44:9 .... 316, 340–41
44:9–14 339
44:9–16 ...... 239, 249, 322, 579, 582, 679, 740, 826
44:10 .... 320, 340
44:11 .... 340, 813
44:11–12 .... 339, 826–27
44:12 .... 311, 340
44:13 340
44:14 339–40
44:15 320
44:15–16 .... 339–40, 342, 813
44:17–19 343
44:17–27 343
44:17–31 339
44:19 344
44:20 .... 343–44, 891
44:21 .... 343–44, 884
44:22 343–44
44:22b 344
44:22–23 345
44:23 ...... 329, 343–44, 347, 826, 884
44:24 356
44:25 344
44:28 353
44:29–30 353
44:30 .... 65, 639
44:31 .... 41, 353
45–48 347
45:1–5 353
45:1–9 .... 347, 354
45:2 338
45:8–9 344
45:13–17 344
45:17 843
45:18–25 346
45:21–2 344
45:22 344
45:24 344
45:25 344
46:1–18 344
46:3 843
46:17 345
46:19–20 338
46:20 344
46:21–24 338
47:1–12 .... 383, 540
47:2 344
47:12 458
47:13–48:35 .... 317, 347, 448
47:13 508
47:22 345
47:22–23 ..... 316, 322, 340–41, 345, 354, 580, 582
48:1 347
48:2 347
48:3 347
48:4 347
48:5 347
48:6 347
48:7 347
48:8–22 347
48:10 .... 346–47, 772
48:13–14 340
48:15 .... 346–47, 772
48:15–20 346
48:23 347
48:24 347
48:25 347
48:26 347
48:27 347
48:35 .... 317, 346

HOSEA

.... xlviii, 172, 207, 217–19, 227–28, 246, 255, 261, 267–68, 273, 279, 282, 303, 358–70, 395, 410, 592–93, 870, 892
1:1 .... 359, 368
1:3 370
1:4 369–70
1:4–8 .... 218, 255
1:6 370
1:7 .... 207, 279, 303, 359, 362
1:9 .... 282, 369–70
1:10 .... 218, 358, 369
1:11 .... 207, 279, 303, 359, 362
2:1 358
2:2 .... 279, 359
2:5 592
2:7 .... 370, 592
2:8 .... 367, 442, 570
2:10 255
2:12 205
2:13 806
2:13–15 .... 246, 397
2:14 412
2:14–15 .... 246, 267, 351
2:15 .... 362, 369
2:17 .... 366, 806
2:18 369
2:19–20 591
2:22 359
2:23 .... 358, 370
3:1 .... 255, 293, 358, 368–70
3:5 .... 207, 279, 362, 369–70
4:1 370
4:2 369
4:4 370
4:6 .... 370, 610
4:7 .... 268, 370
4:8 340
4:9 227
4:10 .... 311, 372, 792
4:13 .... 310, 357, 360–61, 881
4:14 369
4:15 .... 207, 279, 303, 359, 361–63, 365, 370, 397
4:16 .... 366, 370
4:16–17 371
4:18 792
5:3 185
5:4 370
5:5 .... 207, 279, 303, 359, 362, 370
5:8 .... 361, 363, 365, 370, 397
5:10 ... 207, 279, 303, 311, 359, 361–62
5:11 369
5:12–14 359
5:13 361
5:14 .... 207, 279, 303, 362
5:15 370
6:1 370
6:1–3 370
6:2 358
6:4 .... 207, 279, 303, 359, 362
6:4–6 397
6:6 .... 256, 358, 486–87
6:7 369
6:8 369
6:11 ..... 207, 279, 303, 311, 359, 362, 370, 548
7:10 370
7:11 370
7:16 370
8:2 370
8:5–6 .... 370, 397
8:7–9 370
8:11 273
8:12 .... 255, 360, 870
8:13 .... 273, 369–70, 397
8:14 ...... 207, 273, 279, 303, 359, 362
9:1 .... 226, 878
9:3 .... 242, 369–70, 396
9:8 .... 310, 430
9:9 .... 172, 218, 367, 369, 878
9:10 ..... 205, 351, 368, 370, 412, 457
9:11 .... 368, 370
9:11–12 371
9:15 .... 368, 370, 397
10:1 .... 255, 356
10:5 .... 361, 363, 365, 370, 397

10:8 .... 358, 370, 397
10:9 .... 172, 218, 367, 369
10:11 .... 207, 279, 303, 309, 359, 362, 366, 418
10:11–13 370
10:12 .... 310, 383
10:13 436
10:14 425
10:15 363
11:1 ... 309, 358, 361–62, 368–69, 856
11:2 806
11:1–4 362
11:3 309
11:4 368
11:5 369–70
11:8 .... 218, 221, 323, 362, 367, 878
11:9–11 370
11:11 .... 369, 459
11:12 359
12:1 .... 359, 370
12:2 ... 207, 279, 303, 359, 362–63, 370
12:2–4 364
12:3 .... 311, 362–64
12:3–4 .... 362, 364
12:4 .... 359, 362–66
12:4–5 365–66
12:5 .... 362, 365–66
12:6 370
12:7 .... 369, 418
12:9 369
12:11 369
12:12 .... 362, 369
12:13 365
13 366
13:2 397
13:4 369
13:5 369
13:6 366–67
13:10 368
13:11 368
13:14 358
13:16 .... 397, 425, 549
14:1–9 370
14:2 370
14:4 .... 368, 370
14:5 592
14:6 .... 370, 547, 592
14:7 .... 370, 592
14:8 .... 310, 592

JOEL

.... xlix, 277, 337, 371–84, 398, 404–7, 421, 439, 460, 521, 867
1 607
1:1 521
1:2 383
1:3 382
1:4 383
1:6 373
1:7 .... 205, 412
1:8 384
1:9 374
1:10 442
1:12 .... 205, 382, 412
1:13 384
1:14 .... 374, 383
1:15 382–83
1:16 374
1:20 540
2 377
2:1 382–83
2:2 .... 256, 377, 382, 436
2:3 382
2:4 373
2:6 382
2:10 .... 256, 381–84, 439
2:11 .... 373, 381–83, 470
2:12 .... 377, 470
2:12–14 372
2:13 .... 376–77, 405, 421, 877
2:13–14 .... xxxiii, 135, 375, 379, 404–5, 421
2:14 .... 185, 377, 405–6
2:15 383
2:17 ... 374, 382, 384, 540–41, 544, 548
2:18 .... 372, 459
2:19 384
2:20 .... 383, 544
2:21 .... 383, 544
2:22 .... 205, 412
2:23 382
2:24 384
2:25 383
2:27 .... 377, 380–81, 384
2:27–28 336
2:28 .... 377, 379, 383–84, 459
2:28–29 .... xxv, 337, 375, 377–79, 381
2:28–32 .... 373, 851
2:29 .... 377, 383–84
2:30 377
2:31 .... 373, 383
2:32 .... 373, 375, 377–81, 398, 867
3:1 .... 311, 377, 383
3:1–5 373
3:2 .... 377, 383
3:3 .... 383, 402
3:4 .... 373, 377, 383
3:5 .... 373, 375, 377, 380–81
3:7 377
3:8 .... 377, 380
3:9 222
3:10 .... 372, 375, 379–80, 410
3:12 .... 377, 380, 383
3:13 .... 380, 384
3:14 383
3:15 384
3:16 .. 276, 277, 371, 375, 377, 379–81, 383–84, 439, 547
3:16–17 .... 371, 381–82
3:17 .... 375, 377–81, 384, 398, 439
3:18 .... 374, 383, 397, 458, 540
3:19 383
3:32 .... 377, 379

AMOS

.... xlii, xlix, 218–19, 223, 226, 255, 274, 276–77, 319–20, 358, 360–61, 370–71, 375, 377, 379–82, 384–97, 404, 410, 414, 455–56, 468, 542, 867, 870
1:1 389
1:2 .... 276–77, 371, 380–82, 389, 547
1:3 396
1:4 .... 311, 371, 396
1:5 395
1:6 .... 396, 399, 401–2, 806
1:7 396
1:9 .... 388, 396, 399, 401–2, 806
1:10 .... 396, 459
1:11 .... 395–96, 461
1:11–12 .... 402, 462, 470
1:12 .... 396, 402
1:13 .... 369, 396–97
1:14 396
1–2 .... 218, 290, 386, 389, 392–93
1:3–2:16 394
2:1 396
2:2 .... 294, 396
2:4 396
2:5 396
2:6 .... 390, 396, 882
2:6–8 256
2:6–16 391
2:7 390–91
2:8 .... 390–91, 395, 870
2:9 395
2:10 395
2:12 .... 390–91, 850, 870
3:1 395
3:4 418
3:8 380
3:8–9 277
3:9 843
3:12 .... 310, 418
3:14 .... 370, 397
4 396
4:1 .... 256, 397
4:1–3 .... 223, 256
4:1–5 391
4:2 311
4:4 ... 370, 391, 395, 397, 469, 850, 870

4:4–5 397
4:5 .... 391, 395, 850, 870
4:6 396
4:7 311
4:7–8 396
4:9 .... 205, 383, 396, 412, 442
4:10 395–96
4:11 .... 221, 395–96, 458, 878
4:13 .... 396–97, 418
5:5 .... 370, 397
5:6 397
5:8 564
5:8–9 396
5:10 .... 256, 391, 870
5:10–12 391
5:11 .... 256, 393, 436
5:12 .... 256, 391, 870
5:15 418
5:17–25 389
5:18 .... 257, 468
5:18–19 311
5:18–23 391
5:19 418
5:21 395
5:21–23 397
5:21–24 .... 218, 397
5:22 395
5:25 .... 311, 395
5:25–27 385
6:1 257
6:2 256
6:4 257
6:4–7 391
6:5 396
7:2 273
7:5 273
7:7–9 209
7:9 397
7:10 397
7:11 393
7:13 .... 391, 397
7:14 455–56
7:17 .... 242, 393, 395
8:2 319
8:3 320
8:4 436
8:4–6 .... 256, 391
8:5 .... 30, 274, 369, 395, 418, 573, 639, 680, 687, 883
8:5–6 395
8:6 390
8:10 .... 310, 418
8:14 844
9 .... 402, 858
9:1 .... 370, 397
9:3 .... 371, 380
9:5 540
9:5–6 396
9:7 .... 209, 388, 395
9:8 434
9:10 397
9:11 .... 385–86, 392–94, 858–59
9:11–12 .... 218, 226, 247, 369, 388–89, 391–94, 858–59, 867, 879
9:12 .... 371, 385–86, 389, 392–94, 402
9:13 .... 383, 397
9:13–15 393
9:14 .... 305, 311, 393, 548
9:15 305

OBADIAH

.... xlix, 295, 297, 371, 375, 378–80, 398–402, 436
1 399–400
1–4 .... 295–96, 400, 402
1–8 402
1–9 .... 462, 470
3 399–400
4 400
5 401
5–6 295–96
5–8 400–2
6 401
6–7 400
7–8 295–96
8 400
9 400
10 .... 383, 400, 419, 462
10–14 .... 357, 372
11 .... 383, 401–2
11–13 401
11–14 .... 399, 401, 436, 462, 806
12 .... 372, 462
12–14 401
13 402
14 401–2
15 .... 382–83, 400–1
15–21 .... 462, 470
16 .... 352, 357, 400, 402
17 .... 371, 377–82, 398, 867
18 .... 357, 401–2
21 .... 371, 402

JONAH

.... xlix, 208, 359, 372, 375–77, 403–8, 416, 421, 521, 551, 898–99
1 408
1:1 521
1:3 407
1:4 408
1:4–16 407
1:5 .... 408, 741
1:9 .... 407, 545
1:10 408
1:11 408
1:12 406
1:13 407–8
1:16 408
1:17 .... 403, 408
1–4 208
2 408
2:2 408
2:3 .... 408, 416, 540
2:4 .... 408, 545
2:5 407–8
2:6 408
2:7 .... 408, 545
2:8 408
2:10 407–8
3 821
3:7 408
3:8 408
3:9 .... 185, 372, 376–77, 404–6, 408, 877
3:10 .... 404–5, 408, 898
3–4 377
4:1 406
4:1–3 408
4:2 .... xxxiii, 372, 375–77, 404–6, 421, 877, 898–99
4:3 406–7
4:4 408
4:6 407
4:7 408
4:9 .... 406, 408
4:11 408

MICAH

.... xlix, 189–90, 205, 218–19, 222–23, 225–26, 255, 277–78, 372, 375, 379, 392, 409–19, 426, 451, 713, 830
1:1 521
1:2 .... 221, 418–19, 545
1:3 .... 173, 418
1:4 .... 418, 546
1:5 .... 278, 419
1:6 278
1:7 .... 226–27, 418
1:8 418
1:16 418
2:1 .... 418, 549
2:1–3 256
2:2 .... 256, 418
2:4 311
2:11 418
2:12 459
2:13 418
3:1 277
3:1–3 311
3:1–4 256

3:1–12 . . . 412
3:2 . . . 418
3:2–3 . . . 225
3:4 . . . 256, 311, 397
3:5 . . . 277, 418
3:8 . . . 256, 418
3:9 . . . 256
3:9–11 . . . 256
3:10 . . . 430, 436
3:11 . . . 256, 418
3:12 . . . 277–78, 416, 831
4 . . . 222, 410, 412
4:1 . . . 297, 353, 418
4:1–3 . . . 410
4:1–5 . . . 221–23, 379, 410–12, 451
4:2 . . . 451–52, 546
4:2–3 . . . 451
4:3 . . . 370, 372, 379, 411, 451
4:4 . . . 191, 205, 222–23, 410–12, 448, 451
4:4–5 . . . 218
4:5 . . . 223, 410–12, 451–52, 459
4:6 . . . 436
4:7 . . . 418, 436
4:8 . . . 412–13
4:9 . . . 255, 310, 412, 418, 549
4:10 . . . 236, 255, 310, 412–13, 418, 549
4:13 . . . 105, 418
5:2 . . . 226, 392, 409, 412–14, 526, 879
5:2–5 . . . 218
5:3 . . . 412–13
5:4 . . . 409, 412, 419
5:4–5 . . . 414
5:5 . . . 410, 418
5:6 . . . 418
5:8 . . . 278, 310, 418–19
5:8–9 . . . 414, 880
5:9 . . . 413
5:10 . . . 413
5:12 . . . 418
5:15 . . . 423
5:29 . . . 417
6:1–2 . . . 419
6:3 . . . 417
6:4 . . . 417
6:4–5 . . . 417
6:5 . . . 417
6:6–8 . . . 397
6:8 . . . 418, 436
6:11 . . . 369, 418
6:16 . . . 419
7 . . . 415
7:1 . . . 370, 419
7:2 . . . 419
7:3 . . . 418
7:6 . . . 409
7:7 . . . 415, 430
7:8–17 . . . 415
7:8–20 . . . 410, 415
7:9 . . . 419
7:10 . . . 382, 414–16, 419
7:14 . . . 414–15, 419, 545
7:15 . . . 415, 418
7:17 . . . 253, 256, 414–16, 419, 489–90
7:18 . . . 285, 415
7:18–19 . . . 372, 414–15, 877
7:18–20 . . . 218, 416
7:19 . . . 415–16

NAHUM

. . . xlix, 420–25
1 . . . 424
1:2 . . . 25, 421–24, 542
1:2–3 . . . 421–24, 877
1:2–8 . . . 424
1:3 . . . 372, 421–22, 424
1:4 . . . 424
1:5 . . . 439
1:6 . . . 424
1:7 . . . 423–24
1:8 . . . 424
1:14 . . . 422
1:15 . . . 420, 424–25
2:1 . . . 424–25
2:9 . . . 425
2:10 . . . 256, 382
2:11–12 . . . 310
2:12–13 . . . 351
2:13 . . . 41, 425
3:4 . . . 420, 425
3:5 . . . 425
3:7 . . . 425
3:10 . . . 383, 402, 425, 549
3:15–16 . . . 383

HABAKKUK

. . . xlix, 255, 311, 426–32, 552, 861
1 . . . 424, 430
1:2 . . . 430
1:3 . . . 430
1:4 . . . 430
1:5 . . . 426
1:5–11 . . . 427, 429
1:8 . . . 427, 430, 436
1:10 . . . 427
1:12 . . . 185, 430
1:13 . . . 427, 430, 432, 552
1:14–15 . . . 311, 469
1:1–2:5 . . . 430
2 . . . 428
2:1 . . . 255, 430, 547
2:1–2 . . . 861
2:3 . . . 628
2:3–4 . . . 426
2:4 . . . 426, 428
2:5 . . . 430
2:5–19 . . . 429
2:6 . . . 257, 432
2:6–19 . . . 428
2:6–20 . . . 430
2:8–9 . . . 430
2:9 . . . 257, 430, 432
2:12 . . . 257, 430, 432, 436
2:12–14 . . . 428
2:13 . . . 311, 430
2:14 . . . 255, 427–28
2:15 . . . 257, 432
2:15–16 . . . 352, 612
2:17 . . . 205
2:18 . . . 428
2:18–19 . . . 430
2:19 . . . 257, 412, 432
2:20 . . . 371, 418, 427–28, 430, 432, 456, 545
3:1–19 . . . 430
3:3 . . . 255, 431
3:3–15 . . . 429, 431–32
3:7 . . . 255
3:8 . . . 524
3:8–15 . . . 431
3:10 . . . 430
3:11 . . . 430–31, 459
3:13 . . . 430
3:15 . . . 430
3:16 . . . 255, 427, 432
3:18 . . . 430
3:19 . . . 427, 429, 547

ZEPHANIAH

. . . xlix, 255, 269, 321, 329, 374, 401, 426, 433–36
1:1 . . . 433, 521
1:2 . . . 434–35
1:2–3 . . . 269, 433–34
1:2–5 . . . 434
1:3 . . . 434–35
1:5 . . . 435
1:7 . . . 371, 382, 430, 435, 456
1:9 . . . 436
1:13 . . . 436
1:14–18 . . . 382, 401, 436
1:15 . . . 382, 436
1:18 . . . 321, 434
2:2 . . . 436
2:3 . . . 436
2:7 . . . 311
2:9 . . . 221, 436
2:11 . . . 434–35
2:13 . . . 436
2:15 . . . 419, 436
3:1–4 . . . 329

3:3 .... 329, 351, 436
3:4 .... 329, 356
3:5 436
3:7 333
3:8 .... 311, 329, 434, 436
3:9 .... 379, 434–35
3:10 436
3:11 .... 333, 436
3:12–13 333
3:13 434–36
3:14–15 .... 257, 456
3:17 436
3:19 .... 418, 434, 436
3:20 .... 311, 434, 436

HAGGAI

.... xlix, 220, 255, 437–42, 450, 457, 640
1:1 441
1:2 .... 438, 446, 450, 883
1:4 .... 438–40, 883
1:5 442
1:5–6 438
1:6 .... 438–39, 442
1:7 442
1:9 439
1:10 .... 438, 442, 457
1:10–11 311
1:11 442
1:12 .... 441, 840
1:12–14 641
1:13 442
1:14 .... 640, 842, 883
2:2 .... 441, 840
2:4 442
2:5 .... 437, 441–42
2:6 .... 437, 439, 442
2:10–12 884
2:11–13 826
2:11–14 439–40
2:14 440
2:15 440
2:17 442
2:18 .... 220, 442, 691, 883
2:18–19 .... 442, 457
2:19 .... 205, 382, 412, 442
2:20 441
2:21 .... 437, 439, 441–42, 840
2:23 .... 440–41, 591

ZECHARIAH

.... xxxvi, xlix, 215, 220, 248, 253, 255, 303, 347, 373, 438, 441–42, 444–59, 500, 628, 682, 801–2, 853, 867
1 445–47
1:3 470
1:4 .... 444–45, 671, 843
1:4–6 .... 279, 304
1:6 459
1:7 .... 441, 449
1:8 416
1:10 456
1:11 446
1:12 .... 311, 445–47, 450, 883
1:13 447
1:14 359
1:15 446
1:16 446–48
1:17 447
1:18–21 628
1:20 458
1–8 .... 440–41, 448, 459
2:1 .... 317, 347, 447–48, 453
2:4–5 448
2:5 448
2:8 459
2:10 257
2:11 .... 248, 448, 451–52, 876
2:13 .... 371, 430, 456
3 441
3:1 .... 459, 748
3:1–5 456
3:2 .... 458, 748
3:4 329
3:8 .... 394, 441, 448–50, 877
3:10 .... 410, 412, 448, 451
4:2 458
4:3 443
4:6–9 441
4:7 .... 226, 235, 448–49, 525, 880
4:7–9 .... 220, 877
4:9 .... 235, 448–50, 691, 840, 883
4:10 784
4:11 443
4:14 443
5:2 458
5:4 459
5:11 458
6 441
6:11 449–50
6:11–13 450
6:11–14 448–49
6:12 .... 394, 450, 877
6:13 449–50
6:14 449–50
6:15 459
7:1 457
7:1–7 256
7:2–3 450
7:3 450
7:3–5 470
7:5 .... 311, 446, 883
7:5–6 .... 438, 450
7:7 683
7:10 .... 311, 397, 456–57
7:11 .... 458, 878
7:12 .... 444, 456, 547, 565
7:12–13 .... 279, 304
7:13 397
8:1–8 253
8:2 459
8:3 459
8:4 459
8:4–6 438
8:4–8 451
8:6 459
8:7 459
8:8 282
8:9 .... 442, 457, 459
8:12 457
8:14 459
8:16 443
8:18–19 256
8:19 .... 450, 459
8:20 459
8:20–23 451
8:21–22 .... 448, 451–52
8:22 451
8:23 459
9:1 .... 459, 470
9:3 419
9:4 459
9:6 .... 458, 689, 876
9:7 457–58
9:9 .... 208, 443, 452–53, 489, 500, 850–51, 867, 880
9:10 .... 459, 489–90
9:11 459
9:12 459
9:14 459
9:16 459
9–14 .... 456, 459
10:2 459
10:5 419
10:8 459
10:9 459
10:10 459
10:11 .... 416, 459
10:12 459
11:1–2 459
11:1–10 453
11:3 457
11:4–16 .... 453–54, 457
11:4–17 .... 454, 457
11:6 784
11:7 454
11:7–14 454
11:10–11 454
11:12 .... 443, 459
11:13 443

11:14 454
11:14–16 454
11:16 453
12:1 .... 455, 459, 470
12:8 185
12:10 .... 310, 337, 378, 443, 459
13 448
13:1 458
13:5 .... 455–56, 458
13:7 .... 443, 457
13:9 .... 310, 468, 470
14:1–5 458
14:4 458
14:5 458
14:8 .... 383, 458, 540
14:11 458
14:16–19 .... 27, 34, 150, 256, 452, 458
14:20 458

MALACHI

.... xlii, xlix, 370, 401, 460–70, 648, 669, 853
1:1 .... 459, 470
1:2 .... 460–61, 467
1:2–3 .... 401, 461–62, 470
1:2–5 .... 297, 357, 462
1:3 .... 460, 470
1:3–4 402
1:4 467
1:4–5 462
1:5 545
1:6 .... 463–64, 467, 470
1:6–8 128
1:7 692
1:7–11 463
1:7–14 463
1:8 .... 463, 465, 467
1:9 467
1:10 .... 397, 464, 467
1:11 .... 464–65, 467, 470, 549
1:12 692
1:12–14 463
1:13 .... 463, 467
1:13–14 .... 463, 465
1:14 .... 463–65, 467, 470
1:6–2:9 463–65
2:1 465
2:2 .... 464, 467, 470
2:3 .... 397, 464
2:4 .... 463, 467
2:4–5 463
2:4–8 692
2:5 464–65
2:6 .... 436, 463, 884
2:7 .... 463, 669, 884
2:8 .... 463–64, 467
2:10 .... 466, 470
2:10–15 468
2:10–16 466
2:11 .... 466, 468
2:11–13 469
2:13 .... 466, 470, 539
2:14 .... 468, 470
2:15 466
2:16 466–67
3:1 .... 226, 382, 460, 467–70, 855–56
3:1–2 468
3:2 470
3:2–3 310
3:3 469
3:4 469
3:5 .... 397, 467, 469–70
3:7 .... 467, 470
3:8 470
3:10 .... 467, 469
3:11 .... 467, 880
3:12 467
3:13 467
3:17 .... 467, 470
4:1 .... 467, 549
4:3 467
4:4 470
4:4–6 882
4:5 .... 382, 460, 470
4:6 470

PSALMS

.... xxxv, xli, xlix, 257, 336, 424, 426, 473–75, 477–78, 482, 485–86, 489, 493–94, 496, 500, 503, 511, 514, 526, 534, 538–39, 541–42, 544–45, 547–49, 556, 560, 564, 571, 629, 671, 679, 704, 719, 736, 738, 766, 849–51, 853, 870–71, 892, 901
1 .... 477–79, 538
1:1 .... 478–79, 538
1:1–3 568
1:2 478–79
1:2–3 .... xxix, 478–80
1:3 .... 255, 479
1:3–5 483
1:4 487
1:5 472
1:6 .... 479, 480
1–61 535
2 .... xxxv, 476, 538, 871, 880
2:1 540
2:1–2 .... 472, 480, 880
2:3 472
2:4 545
2:6 .... 474, 538, 880
2:6–7 480
2:6–8 .... 472, 879
2:6–9 880
2:6–12 481
2:7 .... 256, 472–73, 476, 480, 483, 500, 521, 540
2:8–9 480
2:8–10 480
2:9 472
2:11–12 480
2:12 .... 472, 538
3 .... 534, 537–38
3:3 546
3:4 538–39
3:5 538
3:6 537
4 538
4:1 .... 542, 544
4:1–2 540
4:3 .... 473, 544
4:4 .... 472, 549
4:5 473
4:5–7 544
4:6 546
4:7 .... 473, 513
4:8 538
5:1 489–90
5:1–26 487
5:3 521
5:4–6 430
5:5 .... 472, 487, 547
5:6 473
5:7 .... 408, 545
5:9 472
5:11 .... 546, 583
6:1 542
6:2 545
6:3 548
6:6 .... 540, 545
6:7 .... 478, 545, 548
7:10 843
8 .... 482, 534, 554–55, 851
8:1 .... 482–83, 539–40
8:2 472
8:3 .... 482, 532
8:3–8 .... 224, 481–82, 555
8:4 .... 481, 483, 554–55
8:4–6 .... 472, 483, 554, 851, 867
8:5 .... 482–83, 544, 551, 554
8:5–6 483
8:5–7 561
8:6 472
8:7 541
8:8 .... 434, 540–41
8:9 .... 482–83, 539
9:5 549
9:6 549
9:7 545
9:14 547
10:2 548

10:7 472
10:16 ....545, 736
10:17–18....496
11:4 ....430, 545
11:6 ....513, 549
12:2–3....491
12:5 ....474, 476, 539
13:1 430
13:2 430
13:6 545
14 408
14:1 549
14:1–3....472
14:3 549
14:7 ....311, 548
15 ....477, 485–86, 871
15:1 ....270, 485, 545
15:1–5....483, 795, 876
15:2–5....486
15:5 ....547, 882
16:5 ....539, 608
16:8 543
16:8–11....472
16:9 311
16:10 ....472, 484
16:11 546
17:3 843
17:5....547
17:7....546
17:8 ....459, 546, 583
18 ....185, 431, 534, 537, 539, 544, 744
18:2 ....430, 546
18:4 539
18:6 ....408, 545, 548
18:7 ....439, 549
18:7–13....349
18:7–15....431
18:9 ....544, 555
18:9–10....256
18:14 ....544, 555
18:15 ....524, 546
18:16 ....544, 555
18:18 489–91
18:20 486
18:24 486
18:31 185
18:32 429
18:32–33 429
18:33 429
18:35 546
18:36 547
18:43 419
18:46 430
18:47 ....423, 547
18:49 472
19:1–4....545
19:4 472
19:7 545
19:14 430
20:7 257
21:9 549
22 ....244, 477, 484–85, 540
22:1 ....152, 472, 483–85, 856
22:2 485
22:7 485
22:12 397
22:14 256
22:18 ....472, 485
22:22....472
22:25....546
22:26....227
22:27....503
22:28....361
23:1 ....540, 545
23:6 531
24....477, 871
24:1 472
24:1–2....542
24:2 531
24:3 ....270, 485–86
24:3–4 ....483, 485–86, 525, 795, 876
24:3–6 485
24:4 486
24:7–10....257
24:10 545
25:2 547
25:4–5....527
25:7 531
25:9 527
25:10 ....531, 877
25:11 547
25:12 527
25:20 547
26:2 547
26:3 877
26:6 547
27:5 545
27:6 545–46
27:9 ....543, 548
27:9–10....484, 501
27:11 547
27:12 540
28:2 546
28:9 545
29 ....477, 503, 551
29:1 ....496, 503, 671
29:1–2....502–3, 539, 736
29:6 524
29:9 ....503, 545
29:10 ....xxiv, 540, 545, 736
30:3 408
30:4 546
31:1....547
31:2 ....546, 548
31:5 472
31:6 ....408, 543
31:9 548
31:14 ....256, 547
31:17 547
31:22....408
31:24....543
32:1 472
32:2 472
32:5 548
33:2 546
33:2–3.... 544
33:3 545
33:5 ....531, 547
33:6 540
33:7 ....310, 549
33:9 540
33:12 544
33:13 547
33:14–21 500
33:17 ....257, 540
33:18 539
33:20....499
33:22....499
34....534, 537
34:5 537
34:6....540
34:8 472
34:12–16 472
34:15....540, 549
34:17....540
34:18....487
34:20....472, 547
35:11 540
35:19 472
35:27....545
36:1 ....472, 523, 549
36:4....418, 549
36:5 530
36:6....539
36:7 ....546, 583
36:8 540
36:10 531
37:1 436
37:2 548
37:4 ....546, 565
37:9 547
37:11 ....436, 547
37:13 545
37:15 549
37:22....547
37:27....549
37:28....485
37:29....547
37:31 ....547, 565
37:33....484
37:34....547

37:35 345
38:8 484
38:9 548
38:16 547
38:20 549
38:21 484
39:5 548
39:11 548
39:13 843
40 .... 476–77, 871
40:5 243
40:6 .... 397, 476, 487
40:6–8 .... 256, 285, 472, 487
40:8 .... 285, 547
40:10–12 877
40:11 531
40:16 545
41:1 540
41:2 497
41:9 472
41:13 .... 538, 736
42 537
42:3 .... 382, 540, 548
42:4 548
42:5 539
42:7 408
42:8 537
42:10 .... 382, 540, 548
42:11 539
42–83 .... 497, 537
43:1 .... 436, 548
43:5 539
44 .... 280, 485
44:1 .... 173, 430, 548
44:3 547
44:11 .... 244, 272, 280, 459, 540
44:17 552
44:17–18 280
44:17–19 485
44:18 552
44:20 .... 255, 280
44:20–21 280
44:21 .... 485, 552
44:22 .... 244, 272, 280, 459, 472, 485, 540, 548
44:23 281
45 .... 452, 540, 593
45:4 452
45:5 547
45:6 .... 472, 483
45:7 .... 472, 483, 496, 539, 547
45:11 540
45:17 540
46:4 .... 540, 547
46:7 537
46:8 537
46:9 .... 221, 459, 549
46:11 537
47:2 .... 470, 537
47:3 547
47:5 537
47–106 536
48:1 .... 537, 547, 736
48:2 .... 221, 256, 418, 545
48:6 549
48:8 .... 221, 537, 547
48:10 546
48:11 547
49:8 540
49:12 539
49:14 459
49:20 539
50 .... 476, 812
50:1 .... 470, 537, 549
50:5–23 476
50:6 545
50:7 549
50:7–15 397
50:14 .... 408, 476, 546
50:14–15 692
50:23 .... 408, 692
51 .... 179, 476–77, 487, 534, 537, 746, 871
51:1 531
51:4 472
51:8 547
51:9 547
51:11 179–80
51:16 487
51:16–17 .... 476, 486–88
51:17 487
51:18–19 .... 256, 397
51:19 487–88
52 .... 537, 540
52:8 .... 370, 547
53:1 .... 540, 549
53:1–3 472
53:3 549
53:6 .... 311, 548
54 .... 534, 537, 540
54:3 539
54:6 537
55:16 538
55:22 538
56 .... 534, 537
56:4 539
56:10 538
56:11 539
56:12 .... 538, 546
56:13 539
57 534
57:1 546
57:3 .... 531, 877
57:4 547
57:5 539
57:7–11 539
57:9 539
57:10 .... 531, 539, 877
57:11 539
58:1 496
58:2 496
58:3 436
58:6 538
58:10 .... 422, 547
58:11 545
59 .... 534, 537
59:3 538
59:5 538
59:6 539
59:7 547
59:8 .... 538, 545
59:9–10 539
59:14 539
59:17 539
60 .... 208, 488–89, 534, 537, 539, 745
60:1–3 488
60:2 .... 439, 488
60:5 546
60:5–12 .... 488, 539
60:6 489
60:8 489
60:9–11 488
60:12 489
61:4 545–46
61:5 546
61:7 .... 531, 877
61:8 546
62:1 539
62:2 539
62:5 539
62:6 539
62:8 548
62:9 548
62:12 472
63 .... 534, 537
63:6 476
63:7 546
63:8 .... 543, 546
63:9 549
64:3 547
64:7 436
64:10 538
65:1 546
66:6 540
66:9 547
66:13 546
67:1 540
68:1 540
68:2 473
68:4 .... 256, 538
68:7 418

68:7–8 431, 541
68:8 439, 541
68:12 541
68:13 541
68:16 538, 541
68:17 541
68:17–18 349, 431
68:18 473, 538
68:20 538
68:21 431
68:22 416
68:23 547
68:26 538
68:27 413
68:32 545
69:1 408
69:2 408, 416
69:3 549
69:4 473
69:5 185, 844
69:6 538
69:7 548
69:9 423, 473, 476
69:13 538, 877
69:15 408, 416, 548
69:16 531, 538
69:17 548
69:22 473
69:23 473
69:24 311
69:25 473
69:28 549
69:30–31 487
69:31 538
69:33 538, 541
70:1 538
70:4 545
70:5 538
71:1 538, 547
71:2 548
71:3 546
71:5 538
71:9 484
71:11 484
71:16 538
71:18 484
72 68, 476, 489–90, 538, 541
72:1 491, 545
72:1–2 256
72:1–19 879
72:4 541
72:5 547
72:8 459, 489
72:9 253, 256, 414, 489
72:9–11 490
72:10–11 489
72:12 541
72:13 497
72:15 490, 541
72:17 68, 286, 489–92, 876, 879
72:18 538, 736
72:19 538
73 541
73:10 256
73:13 547
73:26 541, 608
73:28 538
73–83 812
74:1 547–48
74:2 236
74:4–7 541
74:10 548
74:12 430
74:12–17 541
74:13 506
74:13–14 257
74:14 237, 541
74:16 541
74:17 549
74:18 538
74:22 548
75:2–5 476
75:7 545
75:8 352, 538, 549, 612
75:10 476
76:2 547
76:3 221, 549
76:9 436
76:11 538, 546
77 524
77:1 539
77:8 541
77:9 541
77:11 430, 538
77:12 476, 479
77:15 236, 541
77:16 430, 524
77:16–19 430
77:18 439, 549
77:19–20 524, 541
77:20 459
78 161, 251, 310, 476, 492–94, 510, 527, 871, 898
78:2 473
78:2–3 493
78:3 548
78:3–4 382
78:4 538
78:5 492–93
78:5–6 173
78:5–7 493
78:5–8 492
78:7 493–94
78:9–10 492
78:11 493
78:12 492
78:12–13 161
78:13 164, 251, 458, 492
78:14–41 161, 492
78:15 458
78:18 225
78:21 538
78:22 493
78:24 473
78:25 473
78:32 493
78:35 236
78:35–37 493
78:38 877
78:40 251
78:41 225
78:42 493, 510
78:42–51 492
78:42–53 161, 492
78:44 493
78:44–51 492
78:45 493
78:46 383, 493
78:47–48 493
78:49–50 493
78:51 493
78:52 251, 459
78:52–53 492
78:54 492–94
78:54–55 161, 492
78:56 225, 493
78:56–58 492
78:56–66 161
78:57 370
78:58–59 492, 494
78:59–64 493–94
78:59–66 492
78:60 271, 492–93
78:61 739
78:65 493
78:67–68 494
78:67–72 161, 492
78:68 492–93, 528
78:68–69 492–94, 526
78:69 545
78:70 492–93
78:71 255
79:1 541, 545
79:1–4 352
79:2 541
79:5 256, 538
79:6–7 271
79:8–9 877
79:9 547
79:10 382, 423, 541, 548
79:11 539, 548

79:12 549
79:13 547–48
80:1 459
80:3 539
80:4 538, 548
80:5 548
80:7 539
80:8–16 255
80:10–16 356
80:14 539, 547
80:19 538
81 476, 494
81:3 494, 542
81:5 542
81:5–17 476
81:6–16 494
81:8 549
81:9 255
81:9–10 494
81:9–12 495
81:10 538
81:12 494–95
81:15 538
81:15–16 495
81:16 494
82 475–76, 496, 851, 871
82:1 545
82:1–6 496
82:1–8 497
82:2 497, 548, 851
82:2–4 476
82:2–7 497
82:3 497
82:4 497
82:6 473, 497, 851
82:6–7 476
82:7 496–97
82:8 497, 545
83:9 225, 542
83:11 225, 542
83:13–15 542
83:16 538
83:18 538
84:12 479
85:1 311
85:2 548
85:8 547
85:10–11 877
86 498, 539, 545
86:3 877
86:5 498, 531
86:5–6 877
86:8 542
86:9 473
86:10 498
86:11 547
86:13 498
86:14 539
86:15 376, 421, 498, 607, 877
86:15–16 498
86:15–17 498
86:16 498
86:17 498
87:5 221
88 724
88:6 549
88:7 416, 736
88:8 548, 565
88:11 530
88:14 548, 565
88:18 548, 565
89 161, 246, 476, 498–500, 527, 538, 724, 871, 895
89:1 498–99, 530
89:2 499, 530
89:3 499
89:3–4 474, 498, 879
89:4 498–99
89:4–5 498
89:5 499, 531
89:5–18 161
89:8 499, 542
89:9–10 237
89:10 506, 541
89:11 542
89:14 499, 545
89:19 498, 500
89:19–37 161, 474, 498
89:20 473
89:20–38 498
89:23 436
89:24 499, 530
89:26–27 480, 500
89:27 500
89:28 246–47, 499, 879
89:28–33 499
89:33 499
89:34 499
89:35 499, 527
89:36 499
89:36–37 547
89:37 499
89:38–45 161
89:39 499
89:45 419
89:46 246, 500
89:47 498
89:49 246–47, 499–500, 540, 879
89:50 246
89:52 538, 736
90:2 545
90:3 542
90:5 548
90:10 311, 798
90:13 542, 548
91 477, 500
91:3 501
91:4 501, 546
91:7 501
91:8 501
91:9 501
91:10 501
91:11 473, 500
91:11–13 501
91:12 473
91:13 418
91:14 501
91:14–16 474, 476
91–100 534
92:1 546
92:3 531
92:10 270
92:14 270
92:15 436
93:1 500, 539, 545
93:5 545
94:1 423, 542
94:2 545
94:3 548
94:6 548
94:7 548
94:11 473, 548
94:12 548, 565
94:14 185, 484, 547
94:18 547
95 476
95:3 470, 496, 545
95:4–5 542
95:6 546
95:7 501, 547–48
95:7–11 473, 476
95:8 502, 881
95:8–11 501–2
95:9 225
95:10 501–2
95:11 881
96 477, 502–3, 738–40, 871
96:1 270, 542, 545
96:1–10 709, 736, 738
96:3 502
96:4 528–30, 545
96:5 503
96:6 503, 738–39, 752, 881
96:7 502–3
96:7–8 359, 539, 736, 738, 852
96:7–9 503
96:9 502
96:10 388, 500, 539, 545, 736, 738–39, 852
96:11 549, 736
96:11–13 709, 736, 738

96:13 ... 539
97 ... 539
97:1 ... 500, 545, 736
97:2 ... 545
97:4 ... 549
97:5 ... 418, 546
97:7 ... 496, 503
97:8 ... 547
97:12 ... 546
98:1 ... 270, 542, 545
98:1–4 ... 258
98:2 ... 473
98:3 ... 531
98:4 ... 546
98:7 ... 549
98:9 ... 539
99:1 ... 500, 545, 736
99:5 ... 522, 542, 753
99:6 ... 543
99:6–8 ... 543
99:8 ... 422, 877
99:9 ... 542
100:3 ... 546, 548
100:4 ... 257
100:5 ... 531, 546, 691, 736, 765, 789, 843
101:5 ... 549
102:1 ... 548
102:2 ... 548
102:9 ... 548
102:12 ... 545
102:19 ... 547
102:20 ... 539, 548
102:25–27 ... 473
102:25–28 ... 483
102:26 ... 548
102:27 ... 546
103 ... 477, 545
103:1 ... 505, 538, 546
103:2 ... 505, 538, 546
103:4 ... 531
103:7 ... 504
103:7–14 ... 504
103:8 ... 376, 421, 877
103:11 ... 504
103:12 ... 504
103:13 ... 504
103:14 ... 504
103:15 ... 548
103:17 ... 505, 531, 545
103:19 ... 843
103:21 ... 671
103:22 ... 505, 538, 546
104 ... 476, 505–6, 561, 898
104:1 ... 506, 538, 546
104:2–4 ... 505
104:4 ... 473, 483
104:5–23 ... 505
104:6–12 ... 506
104:9 ... 549
104:12 ... 473
104:13–18 ... 506
104:14 ... 505
104:15 ... 506
104:19–23 ... 506
104:23 ... 505
104:24 ... 506
104:25–26 ... 505
104:26 ... 506, 541
104:29–30 ... 561
104:30 ... 506
104:31 ... 506
104:33 ... 545
104:35 ... 506–7, 538, 546
105 ... 161, 476, 492, 507–10, 738, 740, 871
105:1 ... 257, 510, 546, 736
105:1–4 ... 738
105:1–15 ... 709, 736, 738, 740
105:2 ... 510, 545
105:3 ... 510
105:4 ... 510–11, 705, 739
105:5 ... 508, 510–11, 738
105:5–15 ... 738
105:5–22 ... 161
105:6 ... 510
105:8 ... 508, 510
105:8–11 ... 507, 876
105:10 ... 507–8, 510
105:11 ... 507–8, 510
105:12–15 ... 507
105:14 ... 507, 509
105:14–15 ... 509
105:15 ... 507–9, 738
105:16 ... 507
105:17–18 ... 507
105:18 ... 500, 509
105:19–22 ... 507
105:23 ... 507, 510
105:24 ... 507
105:25 ... 507
105:26–36 ... 507
105:27 ... 510
105:28 ... 510
105:30 ... 510
105:32 ... 510
105:33 ... 205, 412
105:34–35 ... 383
105:35 ... 510
105:36 ... 510
105:37 ... 641
105:37–38 ... 161, 507
105:39 ... 507
105:39–43 ... 161
105:40–41 ... 508
105:42 ... 508, 876
105:42–43 ... 508
105:43 ... 510
105:44 ... 508, 510
105:44–45 ... 161
105:45 ... 508, 546
106 ... 94, 161, 476, 492, 511–14, 518, 605, 622, 738, 740, 810, 871
106:1 ... 546, 691, 709, 736, 738, 740, 765, 789, 810, 843
106:1–3 ... 512
106:1–5 ... 519
106:2 ... 518
106:4 ... 752
106:4–5 ... 512
106:6 ... 512–13, 516, 878
106:6–19 ... 519
106:7 ... 493, 513, 515
106:7–12 ... 161
106:7–46 ... 512
106:8 ... 513, 515, 518
106:9 ... 251
106:9–10 ... 513
106:10 ... 236
106:11 ... 513
106:12 ... 513–14, 518
106:13–15 ... 513
106:13–33 ... 161
106:14 ... 225
106:16 ... 513
106:17 ... 513–14
106:18 ... 513
106:19 ... 513
106:19–23 ... 515
106:20 ... 268, 513
106:20–31 ... 519
106:21–22 ... 513
106:23 ... 513–16
106:24 ... 513
106:24–26 ... 516
106:25 ... 513
106:26 ... 325, 514
106:26–27 ... 513
106:27 ... 514
106:28 ... 150, 513
106:29 ... 418, 513–14, 516
106:29–31 ... 516
106:30 ... 513, 515–16
106:31 ... 511, 513, 516–17
106:32 ... 542
106:32–33 ... 97, 511, 514–15, 517
106:33 ... 94, 517–18
106:34 ... 514
106:34–46 ... 161
106:35–36 ... 514
106:36 ... 258, 738

106:37 . . . 514
106:37–38 . . . 514, 810
106:38 . . . 269, 514
106:39 . . . 514
106:40–42 . . . 514
106:43 . . . 514
106:44 . . . 514
106:44–46 . . . 512, 878
106:45 . . . 514
106:45–46 . . . 512
106:46 . . . 514
106:47 . . . 514, 518
106:47–48 . . . 709, 736, 738, 740, 810
106:48 . . . 511, 538, 546, 736
107 . . . 556–57, 562
107:1 . . . 691, 736, 765, 843
107:2 . . . 236, 562
107:6 . . . 539
107:10 . . . 549, 562–63
107:13 . . . 539
107:14 . . . 549, 562
107:19 . . . 539
107:28 . . . 539
107:28–32 . . . 407
107:35 . . . 524
107:40 . . . 556–57
107:41 . . . 459, 557
107:42 . . . 436, 556
107–150 . . . 537
108:1–5 . . . 539
108:3 . . . 539
108:4 . . . 531
108:5 . . . 539
108:6 . . . 546
108:6–13 . . . 488, 539
109 . . . 477, 519–20, 871
109:5 . . . 549
109:6 . . . 519
109:6–19 . . . 519
109:8 . . . 473
109:8–13 . . . 877
109:9–14 . . . 519
109:9–15 . . . 520
109:10–13 . . . 519
109:13 . . . 549
109:14 . . . 547
109:14–15 . . . 519
109:20 . . . 519
109:21 . . . 531, 547
109:22 . . . 519
109:29 . . . 519
109:31 . . . 497
110 . . . 476, 500, 522–23, 871
110:1 . . . 164, 473–74, 483, 520–23, 542, 546, 881
110:1–8 . . . 879
110:2–3 . . . 523
110:4 . . . 473–74, 523, 855–56, 902
110:5 . . . 523
111:1 . . . 546
111:2 . . . 473
111:3 . . . 473
111:4 . . . 543, 877
111:7 . . . 543, 877
111:10 . . . 543, 573
112:1 . . . 546–47
112:4 . . . 543
112:4 . . . 543, 877
112:6 . . . 547
112:9 . . . 473, 547
113:1 . . . 528, 539, 546
113:2 . . . 546, 565
113:3 . . . 470, 546, 549
113:5 . . . 185, 543
113:6 . . . 543
113:7 . . . 497, 543
113:8 . . . 543
113:9 . . . 543, 546
114 . . . 524–25
114:3 . . . 524–25
114:4 . . . 524
114:5 . . . 524–25
114:5–8 . . . 524
114:7–8 . . . 525
114:8 . . . 524–25, 543
115:1 . . . 531, 877
115:2 . . . 382, 541
115:3 . . . 528–29, 629
115:3–8 . . . 309, 548
115:4–8 . . . 528, 530, 539
115:9–11 . . . 309, 528, 539
115:15 . . . 546
115:18 . . . 546
116:3 . . . 539
116:4 . . . 379
116:5 . . . 877
116:8 . . . 539
116:9 . . . 539
116:10 . . . 473
116:14 . . . 546
116:16 . . . 498
116:18 . . . 546
116:19 . . . 546
117:1 . . . 473
117:2 . . . 531, 546, 877
118 . . . 477, 486, 525, 543, 871
118:1 . . . 546, 691
118:2 . . . 546
118:2–5 . . . 528, 539
118:6 . . . 473, 539
118:7 . . . 473
118:14 . . . 543
118:15 . . . 543
118:19 . . . 256, 270
118:19–2 . . . 525
118:19–20 . . . 486, 876
118:19–21 . . . 795
118:21 . . . 543
118:22 . . . 258, 473, 525
118:22–23 . . . 698, 856, 880
118:22–24 . . . 525
118:23 . . . 473, 525
118:24 . . . 525–26
118:25 . . . 473
118:25–26 . . . 880
118:26 . . . 473
118:29 . . . 546
119 . . . 543–44, 564, 570–71
119:1 . . . 543
119:3 . . . 436
119:8 . . . 484
119:10–11 . . . 544
119:12 . . . 527
119:19 . . . 543
119:26 . . . 527
119:30 . . . 543
119:31 . . . 543
119:42 . . . 543
119:50 . . . 553
119:57 . . . 608
119:59 . . . 544
119:64 . . . 527
119:69 . . . 564
119:70 . . . 547, 565
119:73 . . . 564
119:82 . . . 549
119:97–104 . . . 571
119:101 . . . 571
119:103 . . . 554
119:104 . . . 571
119:105 . . . 570–71
119:123 . . . 549
119:154 . . . 548
119:165 . . . 311
121:2 . . . 546
121:3 . . . 547
121:4 . . . 546
122 . . . xxxv
122:1 . . . 221, 546
122:4 . . . 221
122:6 . . . 547
122:7 . . . 547
122:8 . . . 547
123:1 . . . 543
124:1 . . . 546
124:3 . . . 548
124:4–5 . . . 228
124:8 . . . 546
125:1 . . . 547
125:3 . . . 436
125:5 . . . 547

126:2 ... 544, 548
126:3 ... 544
126:4 ... 311
127 ... 544
127:2 ... 544
128:1 ... 547
128:5 ... 547
128:6 ... 547
129:1 ... 546
129:6 ... 544, 548
131:1 ... 548, 565
132 ... 190, 476, 500, 526–27, 718, 734, 766–67, 871, 879, 881
132:1 ... 709, 758, 766
132:2 ... 527
132:2–5 ... 708–9, 734
132:6 ... 412, 526
132:6–7 ... 526, 734–35
132:7 ... 522, 543, 753
132:8 ... 256, 526–27, 738–39, 752, 766, 881
132:8–10 ... 709, 758, 765–66, 881
132:9 ... 528
132:10 ... 738
132:11 ... 473, 527, 867
132:11–12 ... 474, 521, 526–27, 879
132:12 ... 191
132:13 ... 526, 528, 881
132:13–14 ... 528
132:13–18 ... 526
132:14 ... 256, 528
132:14–18 ... 474
132:16 ... 528
132:17 ... 185, 357
133:2 ... 544
134 ... 529
134:2 ... 546
134:3 ... 546–47
135 ... 161, 476, 492, 528–30, 871
135:1 ... 528, 539, 546
135:3 ... 546
135:4 ... 528
135:5 ... 528, 530
135:5–7 ... 161
135:5–12 ... 528
135:6 ... 528
135:7 ... 305, 310, 528, 549
135:8 ... 528–30
135:8–9 ... 161
135:9 ... 528
135:10 ... 161, 529
135:10–11 ... 528–29
135:11 ... 161
135:12 ... 161, 528
135:13 ... 528, 544
135:14 ... 473, 528, 530, 544
135:15–18 ... 528, 530, 539
135:19–20 ... 528, 539
135:21 ... 546
136 ... 161, 476, 492, 529–33, 691, 871
136:1 ... 531, 546, 789
136:2 ... 531
136:2–26 ... 789
136:3 ... 531
136:4 ... 531, 533
136:4–22 ... 532
136:5 ... 531–33
136:5–9 ... 161
136:6 ... 531, 533
136:7 ... 533
136:7–9 ... 531
136:8 ... 532–33
136:9 ... 532–33
136:10 ... 529, 531, 533
136:10–15 ... 161
136:11 ... 531, 533
136:12 ... 532–33
136:13 ... 532–33
136:13–15 ... 532
136:14 ... 533
136:15 ... 533
136:16 ... 161, 532–33
136:17 ... 529, 533
136:17–20 ... 530
136:17–22 ... 532
136:18 ... 161, 533
136:19 ... 532–33
136:19–20 ... 161
136:20 ... 532–33
136:22 ... 161, 533
136:23 ... 532
136:24 ... 532
136:26 ... 531, 545
137:7 ... 297, 357, 402, 806
137:8 ... 425
137:9 ... 549
138:2 ... 531, 545
139 ... 564
139:13 ... 574
139:13–16 ... 564
139:15 ... 185, 549
139:16 ... 549
139:23 ... 547
140:3 ... 473, 547
142 ... 534, 537
142:1 ... 539
142:5 ... 608
143:3 ... 544
143:7 ... 548
143:11 ... 547
144 ... 555
144:3 ... 481, 554–55
144:4 ... 548, 555
144:5–7 ... 555
144:9 ... 544–45
144:10 ... 544
145 ... 545
145:3 ... 545
145:8 ... 376, 421, 531, 544–45, 877
145:13 ... 629
146:1 ... 538, 546
146:6 ... 546
146:8 ... 547
146:9 ... 545
146:10 ... 538, 546
146–150 ... 534, 538, 873, 892
147:1 ... 538, 546
147:4 ... 546
147:6 ... 436
147:10 ... 540
147:11 ... 539
147:20 ... 538, 546
148:1 ... 538, 546
148:2 ... 671
148:3–4 ... 545
148:5 ... 546
148:13 ... 546
148:14 ... 538, 546
149:1 ... 538, 542, 545–46
149:3 ... 311
149:7 ... 423
149:8 ... 500, 509
149:9 ... 538, 546
150:1 ... 538, 546
150:6 ... 538, 546

JOB

... xlix, 269, 322, 429, 550–65, 567, 595, 602, 609, 853, 901
1:1 ... 322
1:6 ... 748
1:7 ... 456
1:8 ... 322
1:21 ... 546, 565, 602, 818
1–2 ... 456, 551
1–42 ... 322
2:2 ... 456
2:5 ... 561
2:7–10 ... 561
2:10 ... 559, 565, 818
3 ... 562–63
3:1 ... 562
3:3 ... 310, 557, 562
3:4 ... 561
3:5 ... 562
3:13 ... 556
3:16 ... 602
3:18 ... 563
3:23 ... 563
3:24 ... 484
4:7 ... 557

4:9 546
5:4 558
5:13 550
5:16 .....436, 556–57
5:17 .....548, 565
5:17–18.....563
6:8–10.....553
6:10 .....553, 564
6:25 554
6:29–30 436
7 555
7:14–15.....565
7:17.....544, 554
7:17–18 ..... 481, 551, 554–55, 561
7:17–20.....555
8:4 555
8:9 843
8:10 565
8:21 548
9:4 563
9:8 563
9:9 564
9:12 .....556, 602
10:7 565
10:8–12.....564
10:21 549
11:14 436
11:20 549
12.....556
12:13–16 557
12:17–20.....557
12:21 556
12:21–24 556
12:22.....549
12:24.....556
13:4 564
13:7 436
13:20.....548
13:24.....548, 565
14:2 548
14:13 408
15:7 561
15:14 555
15:16 436
15:33 .....370, 547
17:5.....549
17:7.....554
18:9 555
18:12 558
18:14 555
18:15 549
18:16 555
18:17 549
18:18–23 562
19 557
19:6–8.....557
19:9 554–55
19:13 .....548, 565
19:19 .....548, 565
20:3 561
20:7–18.....562
20:10 558
20:15 407
20:26.....558
21 559
21:7–13.....559
21:7–18.....559
21:19 ..... 519, 558–60
21–37.....559
22:19 556
22:22.....547, 565
22:23.....436
22:26.....546
22:27.....546
23:10 547
24:2 361
24:13 570
24:20.....436
25:2 556
25:4 556
26:6 408
27:4 436
27:10 .....546, 565
28:3 549
28:24.....547
28:28.....573, 786
29:6 565
29:12 541
30:18 830
30:22.....408
30:29.....418
31 564
31:1.....564
31:7–10.....564
31:16 549
31:18 564
31:24–28 564
31:35 561
34:14–15 561
34:31 691
36:23.....436
38:7 ..... 223, 482, 565, 671
38:8 549
38:10 549
38:10–11 549
38:22.....310, 549
38:31–32.....564
41 506
41:11 550
41:18–21.....506
41:31 416
42:2 565
42:3 .....548, 565
42:7–16.....551
42:10 .....250, 311, 459
42:16 311

PROVERBS

.... xxxv, xlix, 257, 563, 566–77, 592–93, 602–3, 704–5, 835, 901
1:1.....208
1:6 208
1:7.....573, 786
1:8.....576–77
1:11 419
1:12 548
1:15.....570
1:20–21 567
1:25 576
1:33 311
1–9..... 566, 571, 575
2:1.....576
2:2 576
2:3 576
2:4 704
2:16 576
2:16–22.....570
2:18 575
2:22 566
3:1.....547, 568–70, 705
3:1–3 .....566, 568–70
3:2 576
3:3 568
3:5.....570
3:7.....570
3:9 .....567, 570, 572
3:11 ..... 182, 566, 575
3:11–12.....563
3:12 .....182, 566
3:15 576
3:17 570
3:18 .....570, 574
3:19 .....531–32, 566, 574
3:19–20.....574
3:21 569
3:21–24..... 566, 568, 570
3:26.....570
3:27 570
3:29 570
3:34.....566
4:1–2.....575
4:2 571
4:3 577
4:4 576
4:7.....575
4:10 575
4:11 575
4:18 566
4:20 576
4:26.....566
5:1.....576

5:1–23 ... 570
5:3 ... 592
5:5 ... 566, 577
5:7 ... 576
5:15 ... 592
5:16 ... 592
5:18 ... 470
5–9 ... 592
6 ... 570, 574
6:10–11 ... 576
6:15 ... 576
6:19 ... 576
6:20 ... 569–70, 574, 576–77
6:20–23 ... 566, 568–71
6:22 ... 569
6:23 ... 570–71
6:23–24 ... 570–71
6:24 ... 571, 576
6:24–35 ... 570
6:25–29 ... 574
6:29 ... 571
6:30–31 ... 574
6:32 ... 574
7:1 ... 569–70, 576
7:1–3 ... 566, 568–70
7:2 ... 576
7:3 ... 568–69
7:4 ... 592
7:4–27 ... 570
7:5 ... 576
7:10 ... 592
7:10–20 ... 592
7:13 ... 592
7:14 ... 567, 572
7:15–20 ... 592
7:24 ... 576
8:1 ... 576
8:2–3 ... 567
8:4 ... 568
8:11 ... 575–76
8:20 ... 570
8:22 ... 574
8:22–31 ... 309, 574
8:26–27 ... 574
8:29 ... 549
8:32 ... 576
8:35 ... 576
9:1–6 ... 257
9:4 ... 576
9:8 ... 182
9:10 ... 543, 573, 786
9:11 ... 576
9:18 ... 577
10:1 ... 576–77
10:1–22:16 ... 566
10:2 ... 576
10:4 ... 576
10:6 ... 576
10:8 ... 576
10:15 ... 576
10:18 ... 603
10:19 ... 603
10:28 ... 576
10:29 ... 576
10–29 ... 566
10–31 ... 567, 572, 577
11:1 ... 369, 419, 573, 576
11:4 ... 576
11:7 ... 576
11:12 ... 603
11:14 ... 576
11:21 ... 704
11:27 ... 704
11:30 ... 574
11:31 ... 566
12:3 ... 575
12:4 ... 575
12:7 ... 704
12:11 ... 576
12:13 ... 566, 576
12:23 ... 576
13:1 ... 571–72
13:9 ... 576
13:12 ... 574
13:14 ... 576
13:16 ... 576
13:19 ... 549
14:5 ... 576
14:6 ... 704
14:12 ... 576
14:25 ... 573
14:27 ... 576
14:29 ... 421
15:2 ... 576
15:4 ... 574
15:8 ... 397, 572–73
15:12 ... 182
15:13 ... 576
15:14 ... 704
15:16 ... 576
15:16–17 ... 602
15:19 ... 576
15:20 ... 576–77
15:22 ... 576
15:27 ... 573
15:29 ... 397, 572–73
15:33 ... 573, 576
16:2 ... 576
16:6 ... 549
16:8 ... 576, 603
16:9 ... 577
16:11 ... 573
16:17 ... 549
16:19 ... 603
16:23 ... 603
16:25 ... 576
16:32 ... 421
16:33 ... 572
17:1 ... 603
17:3 ... 576, 843
17:9 ... 704
17:11 ... 704
17:13 ... 549
17:15 ... 243, 576, 626
17:19 ... 704
17:22 ... 576
17:23 ... 573
17:27 ... 603
17:28 ... 603
18:1 ... 704
18:2 ... 603
18:8 ... 576
18:11 ... 576
18:12 ... 576
18:13 ... 603
18:15 ... 704
18:22 ... 576
19:1 ... 576
19:5 ... 576
19:24 ... 576
19:25 ... 182, 576
19:26 ... 577
19:28 ... 573
20:10 ... 150, 576
20:16 ... 576
20:20 ... 356, 577
20:23 ... 369, 419, 573, 576
20:24 ... 271, 577
20:25 ... 572, 598
21:2 ... 576
21:3 ... 397, 572–73
21:4 ... 549
21:6 ... 704
21:9 ... 576
21:11 ... 576
21:15 ... 576
21:21 ... 573
21:23 ... 603
21:27 ... 397, 572–73
22:2 ... 576
22:3 ... 576
22:8 ... 436
22:13 ... 576
22:17 ... 24:22
566
22:28 ... 83, 361, 573, 576
23:3 ... 576
23:10 ... 361, 576
23:10–11 ... 83, 573
23:18 ... 576
23:22 ... 577

23:25 577
23:35 704
24:6 576
24:12 566
24:14 576
24:17 135
24:17–18 520
24:20 576
24:23–34 566
24:33–34 576
25:1 xxviii
25:1–29:27 566
25:19 574
25:21 .... 520, 566
25:21–22 135
25:22 566
25:24 576
25–29 574
26:1 576
26:7 576
26:11 566
26:12 576
26:13 576
26:15 576
26:22 576
26:27 603
27 566
27:8 412
27:12 576
27:13 576
27:18 205
27:21 576
28:5 704
28:6 .... 576, 603
28:8 .... 356, 882
28:9 .... 397, 572–73
28:12 830
28:19 576
28:24 577
29:1 576
29:3 577
29:6 576
29:10 704
29:13 576
29:15 577
29:20 .... 576, 603
29:26 842
30:1–9 572
30:1–33 566
30:3 572
30:3–4 571
30:5 571
30:5–6 .... 566, 571
30:6 572
30:10 573
30:11 .... 356, 577
30:15 396
30:17 577
30:18 396
30:21 396
30:29 396
31 575
31:1 577
31:1–31 566
31:2 572
31:10 .... 574–75, 590
31:10–31 .... 574, 590
31:20 575
31:23 575
31:30 .... 573, 786
31:31 .... 575, 590

RUTH

.... l, 166, 574–75, 578–90, 724, 871, 901
1 583
1:1 .... 581, 590
1:2 .... 581, 585
1:4 581
1:6 581
1:14 583
1:15 583
1:16 .... 583, 589
1:16–17 584
1:17 584
1:19 580
1:22 580–81
2 579
2:1 .... 575, 585, 589
2:2 581
2:4 583
2:6 580–81
2:8 .... 139, 575, 581, 589, 607, 656, 871, 874, 876
2:8–10 583
2:10 .... 575, 876
2:11–12 .... 583, 589
2:12 .... 546, 583
2:17 594
2:18 575
2:19 585
2:21 581
3 .... 575, 590
3:3 587
3:4 587
3:9 .... 151, 583
3:10–11 584
3:11 .... 575, 590
3:16 590
3:18 589
4 .... 579, 586
4:1 589
4:1–2 575
4:3 581
4:3–6 586
4:5 .... 581, 585, 587–89
4:5–6 .... 585, 589
4:7 580
4:10 .... 575, 581, 585
4:11 .... 412, 575, 590
4:12 590
4:17 .... 139, 578, 580, 589–90, 871
4:18–22 .... 589, 723
4:22 .... 139, 589–90, 871, 874

SONG OF SONGS

.... l, 10, 145–46, 565, 591–94, 901
1:1 593
1:16 310
2:1 592
2:2 592
2:3 592
2:4 592
2:5 255
2:7 594
2:8 594
2:9 594
2:13 .... 205, 412, 592
2:16 592
3:1 592
3:1–2 594
3:1–3 592
3:1–4 592
3:2 592
3:4 592–94
3:5 594
4:3 164
4:5 592
4:9–10 592
4:11 592
4:12 592
4:13 592
4:15 592
4:16 .... 592, 594
5:1 592
5:1–2 592
5:6 594
5:8 594
5:10–16 593
5:11 593
5:13 592
6:2–3 592
6:8 201
6:11 592
7:1–10 551
7:2 592
7:8 592
7:12 592
8:4 594
8:5 594
8:6 591

8:11 592
8:11–12 593
8:14 594

ECCLESIASTES

.... l, 567, 595–97, 599–603, 871, 901
1 601
1:1–2 596
1:6 599
1:7 599
1:9–11 602
2:4–6 601
2:21 548
2:24 597
2:26 548
3:12–13 599
3:14 335
3:17 601
3:18–20 600
3:18–21 600
3:19 548
3:19–20 601
3:20–21 599
3:21 600
3:22 597
4:3 597
4:6 .... 597, 602
4:9 597
4:13 597
5 597
5:1 .... 596, 598
5:1–2 .... 596, 603
5:1–6 599
5:2 598
5:4 .... 546, 596–97
5:4–6 .... 69, 84, 596–98, 600, 871
5:5 .... 546, 596–97
5:6 596–98
5:7 397
5:15 602
5:18–19 .... 599, 602
6:3–5 602
6:9 597
6:11 548
6:12 548
7:1 597
7:2 597
7:3 597
7:5 597
7:8 597
7:10 597
7:20 .... 549, 595
7:27 596
8:4 602
8:11 601
8:15 599
9:4 597
9:7–9 126
9:7–10 599
9:16 597
9:18 597
10:5 598
10:8 603
10:16–17 602
10:18 603
10:19 603
11:8 548
11:9 .... 598–99, 601
12:7 .... 542, 599–601
12:8–12 596
12:13 .... 573, 786
12:14 601

LAMENTATIONS

.... xxxv, l, 234, 241, 246, 280, 547, 552, 557–58, 604–12, 901
1 605
1:1 606
1:1–2 238
1:2 234
1:3 612
1:8 .... 311, 606, 612
1:9 .... 234, 425, 612
1:10 .... 139, 238, 240, 247, 250, 311, 541, 584, 604, 606, 685, 772, 874, 876
1:15 606
1:16 .... 234–35, 606
1:17 .... 234–35, 606, 612
1:18 606
1:21 234
1:22 611
2 605
2:1 .... 522, 542, 547, 753
2:3 357
2:4 547
2:6 .... 547, 612
2:8 .... 209, 547
2:10 .... 238, 547
2:11 549
2:13 .... 425, 547, 609
2:13–19 612
2:15 .... 354, 419
2:16 419
2:17–19 612
2:18 547
2:19 548
2:20 612
3 .... 558, 605, 607–9, 611–12
3:1 557
3:6 544
3:6–9 557
3:7 609
3:9 570
3:14 609
3:15 612
3:21–24 608
3:22–23 .... 604–5, 607, 877
3:22–24 612
3:24 311
3:28 609
3:30 612
3:48–49 .... 605, 609–10
3:53–55 609
3:55 549
3:58 609
3:61 609
4 605
4:1 593
4:1–10 593
4:6 .... 221, 323, 612, 878
4:10 612
4:11 311
4:14 612
4:15 241–42
4:17 549
4:18–19 311
4:19 402
4:20 546
4:21 612
4:21–22 402
4:22 .... 547, 806
5 611
5:1 605
5:7 .... 244, 280, 605, 609–11, 881
5:18 256
5:19 .... 545, 607, 611
5:20 256
5:20–22 246
5:21 .... 605, 611
5:22 .... 605, 610

ESTHER

.... xxxv, l, 265, 613–16, 620, 781, 900–1
1:14 692
1:19 .... 18, 615
1–10 613
2:5 615
2:6 613
2:7 614
2:10 614
2:16 616
2:20 614
2:20–23 614
3:1 615
3:4 614
3:10 615
3:12 615
6:10 614
6:11 614
8:2 614
8:3 615

8:5 . . . 615
8:7 . . . 615
8:8 . . . 18
9:10 . . . 615
9:13–14 . . . 615
9:19 . . . 692
9:22 . . . 692
9:24 . . . 615
10:2 . . . 613

DANIEL

. . . l, 265, 322, 613–14, 617–29, 781, 853, 861, 867, 900–1
1 . . . 642
1:1–2 . . . 726
1:2 . . . 619, 642, 832
1:7 . . . 614
1:8–16 . . . 614
1–6 . . . 613
2 . . . 618–20
2:1–4 . . . 628
2:3 . . . 620
2:4b–7:28 . . . 619
2:4 . . . 619
2:5–6 . . . 619
2:9 . . . 619
2:19 . . . 620
2:20–23 . . . 614, 620
2:27–28 . . . 620
2:28–29 . . . 619–20
2:30 . . . 618
2:34 . . . 621
2:34–35 . . . 620–21
2:35 . . . 622
2:44 . . . 622
2:45 . . . 620–21
3:25–27 . . . 628
4 . . . 821
4:10–17 . . . 352
4:34–35 . . . 629
5 . . . 278
5:2–4 . . . 619, 642, 832, 884
5:23 . . . 619, 642, 832, 884
6:8 . . . 18
6:10 . . . 614
6:14–15 . . . 18
7:1–3 . . . 628
7:7–8 . . . 628
7:9 . . . 623
7:13–14 . . . 617
7:28 . . . 624
8:10 . . . 628
8:19 . . . 628
8:27 . . . 624
8–12 . . . 628
9 . . . 605, 618, 622–23
9:1 . . . 623
9:2 . . . 311, 622, 624, 871, 883
9:3–16 . . . 878
9:4 . . . 487, 622–23, 877, 883
9:4–7 . . . 624
9:4–19 . . . 53, 512, 622, 664
9:5 . . . 514
9:6 . . . 623
9:7 . . . 623
9:8 . . . 622–23
9:9 . . . 622
9:9–11 . . . 614
9:10 . . . 622
9:11 . . . 622–24
9:13 . . . 622–24
9:14 . . . 622
9:14–19 . . . 622
9:16 . . . 623
9:18 . . . 622
9:20 . . . 487, 622–23
9:22 . . . 756
9:24–27 . . . 624
9:25 . . . 629
9:26 . . . 628–29
9:27 . . . 617, 629
10:14 . . . 628
11:4 . . . 628
11:10 . . . 628
11:22 . . . 628
11:26 . . . 628
11:27 . . . 628
11:30 . . . 628
11:31 . . . 617
11:33 . . . 626
11:34 . . . 626
11:35 . . . 626, 628
11:36 . . . 628
12 . . . 618, 625
12:1 . . . 625–26
12:2 . . . 624–28, 867, 871
12:3 . . . 624–28, 871
12:10 . . . 626
12:11 . . . 617
12:13 . . . 626

EZRA-NEHEMIAH

. . . xxxi, xxxiv–xxxv, l, 190, 229, 248–49, 265, 468, 580, 631–34, 636–40, 642–62, 664–66, 668–69, 671, 674, 677–80, 682–85, 688–92, 698, 704–5, 826, 833, 840–43, 855, 857, 871, 891, 896, 900–1

EZRA

1 . . . 220, 632, 642, 855, 901–2
1:1 . . . 631, 640, 841–42, 857, 883
1:1–2 . . . 883
1:1–3 . . . 640, 839
1:1–4 . . . 80, 640, 841
1:2 . . . 545, 642, 652–53
1:2–4 . . . 652–53, 839
1:3 . . . 653, 841
1:4 . . . 641, 653
1:5 . . . 640–41, 651, 842, 883
1:6 . . . 641, 855
1:7 . . . 641–42, 653, 832, 884
1:7–10 . . . 884
1:7–11 . . . 642
1:8 . . . 653
1:9–11 . . . 642, 652
1:11 . . . 642
1:11 . . . 641–42, 832
1–3 . . . 841
1:1–4:7 . . . 653
1–6 . . . 642, 651
2 . . . 80, 642, 646–47, 649–50, 655–56, 658, 668
2:1–25 . . . 643
2:1–70 . . . 650
2:1–3:1 . . . 651, 668
2:2 . . . 646
2:3 . . . 648
2:3–20 . . . 649, 655
2:4 . . . 648
2:5 . . . 648
2:6 . . . 646, 648
2:7 . . . 648
2:8 . . . 648
2:9 . . . 648
2:10 . . . 646, 648
2:11 . . . 647–48
2:12 . . . 648
2:13 . . . 648
2:14 . . . 648
2:15 . . . 648
2:16 . . . 648
2:17 . . . 648
2:18 . . . 648
2:19 . . . 643, 648
2:20 . . . 648
2:21–35 . . . 649
2:25 . . . 646
2:26–49 . . . 644
2:33 . . . 644
2:36–39 . . . 648
2:41 . . . 534
2:43–54 . . . 340
2:46 . . . 646
2:50 . . . 646
2:50–64 . . . 645
2:58 . . . 199
2:59 . . . 649
2:59–60 . . . 659, 685
2:64 . . . 647
2:65 . . . 646

2:65–70 646
2:66 646
2:68 651
2:68–69 650
2:69 646
2:70 646
2:70–3:1..........................650
3 650
3:1–6..............................650
3:1..........................650–51
3:2 .... 634–35, 639
3:2–3..............................691
3:4 .... 27, 34, 150, 633–35, 638–39, 651–52
3:4–5..............................651
3:5.................................691
3:8 ....449, 651, 691, 751, 883
3:10 .... 449, 691, 883
3:11 ...... 546, 691, 736, 765, 789, 843
4:1 ....341, 670
4:1–2............................ 440
4:1–4..............................766
4:3 670
4:4 ....341, 439
4:6 616
4:8–6:18..........................653
4:14 .... 72, 691
4:18 669
4:23–24 439
4–6.................................841
5:1–2..............................641
5:2 ....441, 840
5:3 652
5:11 691
5:12 691
5:13 653
5:13–15......... 80, 652–53, 832, 839
5:14 653
5:14–15............................652
5:14–26...................... 655, 661
5:15 653
5:16 883
6:1..................................653
6:2 654
6:3 652–54
6:3–5........... 80, 640, 652–53, 839
6:4 .... 641, 652–53
6:5 .... 653–54, 832
6:8 652
6:12 .... 197, 691
6:18 .... 634–35, 639, 654–55, 691
6:19 651
6:19–22............................651
6:20 691
6:21 ... 239, 248, 341, 451, 580, 582, 632, 649, 656, 659, 678–79, 685, 690
7 613
7:1–5 589
7:3.................................659
7:5.................................650
7:6.................... xviii, 631, 636
7:10................................636
7:12 660
7:14................................691
7:25 884
8:1..........................650–51
8:2 650
8:3 648
8:3–14..............................655
8:4 648
8:5.................................648
8:6 648
8:7.................................648
8:8 648
8:10 648
8:11 648
8:12 648
8:13 648
8:14 648
8:15 683
8:27 646
8:35 842
9 .... 605, 632, 664
9:1........ 589, 657–58, 661, 663, 678, 684–86, 690
9:1–2......... 139, 200, 249, 638–39, 655–57, 659, 661–64, 677, 685, 689, 772, 874, 876, 879
9:1–3 766
9:2 .... 655, 658, 660–61, 663, 685
9:4 257
9:5–15..............................659
9:6 ....660–61, 664
9:6–7...............................614
9:6–15.................. 512, 622, 878
9:7............................661, 664
9:8 .... 250, 257
9:10–12.............................660
9:11 .... 636, 659, 661, 663, 671
9:11–12.........636, 638–39, 655, 659, 663–64, 874
9:12 ...... 106, 582, 589, 655, 659, 663
9:13 ....660–61, 664
9:14 663
9:15 ....660–61, 664
9–10...... 582, 655–56, 661, 663, 678, 684–86, 688, 844
10 .... 468, 632, 660
10:1 .... 487, 623, 647
10:2 ....648, 663
10:2–3.................. 639, 663–64
10:3 ....257, 636, 660, 684
10:5 660
10:10 ....661, 663–64
10:10–11 ...... 636, 638–39, 655, 660, 662–63
10:11 .... 664, 678, 684, 692
10:14 648
10:16 678
10:18 441
10:18–22 ....648, 661
10:18–44 647
10:19 ....655, 660–63
10:25 648
10:26 648
10:27 648
10:28 648
10:29 646
10:30 648
10:33 648
10:34–36 646
10:38–42 646

NEHEMIAH

1 .... 605, 632, 665
1:1–2...............................728
1:1–5...............................667
1:4.................................545
1:5.................... 545, 664, 877
1:5–10...............................53
1:5–11.............207, 512, 622, 878
1:6 ....487, 614, 623, 665
1:6–7...............................664
1:6–8...............................878
1:8.......................636, 664–65
1:8–9.................. 639, 664–65
1:9.......................... 197, 664
1:10 664
1:11 671
1–2.................................614
2:4 545
2:19 683
2:20 545
2–4.................................668
4:5 .... 547, 665–66
4:13 380
4:14 692
4:16 380
4:21 380
5 ....667–68, 680
5:1.................................667
5:1–5........................438, 667
5:1–11 288
5:1–13........................639, 667
5:2 638
5:3 882
5:4 ....638, 667
5:5...........................667, 882
5:6 667
5:7................ 638, 667–68, 882
5:8 .... 638, 667–68

5:10 666–68
5:11 .... 638, 667–68
5:19 665
6 668
6:1–7 683
6:10 .... 133, 666
6:11 668
6:13 668
7 .... 80, 642, 646–47, 649–51
7:3 677
7:4 438
7:5–73 650
7:5 .... 636, 649
7:6–29 643
7:7 646
7:8 648
7:8–24 655
7:9 648
7:10 648
7:11 .... 646, 648
7:12 648
7:13 648
7:14 648
7:15 .... 646, 648
7:16 .... 647, 648
7:17 648
7:18 648
7:19 648
7:20 648
7:21 648
7:22 648
7:23 648
7:24 648
7:29 646
7:30–48 644
7:39–42 648
7:44 534
7:47–56 340
7:48 646
7:52 646
7:52–66 645
7:60 199
7:61 649
7:66 647
7:67 646
7:67–73 646
7:68 646
7:71–73 651
7:73 .... 646, 650
7–8 .... 632, 650
7:6–8:1 642
7:73–8:1 651
8 .... 650, 669, 675, 683
8:1 .... 34, 668, 676
8:1–3 .... 639, 668–69
8:1–8 675
8:1–12 668
8:1–16 668
8:2 .... 647, 692
8:3 668
8:5 668
8:7 .... 669, 676, 884
8:7–8 669
8:8 .... 669, 676, 884
8:9 .... 692, 826
8:10 .... 639, 692
8:13 .... 669, 675, 756, 884
8:13–18 150
8:14 .... 634–36, 669
8:14–15 639
8:14–16 .... 638, 669
8:14–17 675
8:14–18 27
8:15 .... 634, 669–70
8:16–17 670
8:17–18 .... 288, 494
8:18 .... 668, 675
8–10 675
9 .... 161, 216, 310, 622, 632, 638, 665, 670–71, 674–75, 682
9:2 .... 239, 249, 468, 487, 623, 632, 649, 656, 659–60, 670, 675–78, 684–86, 688, 766
9:3 .... 487, 623, 675–76
9:6 .... 161, 671
9:6–37 .... 670, 675–76
9:7 670–72
9:7–8 .... 161, 670–72, 876
9:8 671–72
9:9 670–73
9:9–11 161
9:10 671
9:11 671
9:12 .... 161, 671
9:13 883
9:13–14 .... 161, 671
9:14 .... 248, 325, 670
9:15 671
9:15–21 161
9:16–17 671
9:17 .... 376, 421, 670–71, 673, 877
9:18 671
9:19 671
9:20 756
9:21 671
9:22 161
9:22–23 671
9:23–25 161
9:24 671
9:25 671
9:26 .... 311, 671, 674
9:26–29 674
9:26–31 .... 161, 674
9:26–32 671
9:27 .... 671, 674
9:27–28 674
9:28 .... 671, 674
9:29 .... 671, 674
9:29–31 674
9:30 .... xviii, 572, 671, 835, 674
9:31 .... 671, 674, 877
9:32 670–72
9:32–35 161
9:32–37 676
9:33 .... 670, 672, 676
9:36 .... 250, 670, 674, 676
9:36–37 161
9:37 676
9:38 .... 672, 674–76
9–10 676
9:38–10:39 670
10 .... 633, 637–38, 647, 675–77, 680, 682, 857
10:1 .... 672, 674–76
10:1–27 676
10:1–38 670
10:1–40 .... 670, 675, 686
10:2–28 676
10:3 675
10:14 648
10:15 648
10:16 648
10:17 648
10:18 648
10:19 648
10:28 .... 239, 249, 340–41, 451, 582, 632, 647, 649, 656, 659, 677–79, 685, 690, 766
10:30 .... 106, 341, 580, 582, 589, 637, 639, 656, 659, 675–79, 682, 685, 690, 876, 879
10:30–39 .... 325, 340, 638, 676
10:31 .... 30, 125, 274, 288, 395, 637, 639, 675–77, 679–80, 682, 686–87, 888–83
10:32 .... 637, 639, 667, 676
10:32–33 .... 637, 677, 842
10:33 843
10:34 .... 634–35, 637, 639, 676–77, 680, 682, 857
10:35 .... 637, 676, 681–82
10:35–36 639
10:35–37 681
10:35–39 .... 677, 680
10:36 .... 634–35, 637, 676, 857
10:37 .... 82, 637, 676, 681–82
10:38 470
10:38–39 842
10:39 .... 637, 676
11 728
11:1–2 .... 438, 728

11:3 199
11:3–19.....727, 840
11:4 728
11:4–8.....728
11:9 728
11:10–14.....728
11:11 646
11:12 648
11:15–18.....728
11:19 728
11:20–35 728
11:25–30 682–83
11:30 683
11–12..... 631, 649
12.....773
12:1–7.....648
12:11–12.....631, 840
12:22.....841
12:24.....774
12:27.....692
12:36.....396
12:45.....774
12:45–46.....692
12:47.....692
13..... 675, 682, 686
13:1 ..... 582, 634–35, 683–85
13:1–3.....xxxiii, 139, 249, 582, 584, 607, 632, 638–39, 660, 683–86, 688–90, 766, 874, 876
13:2 .....685–86, 766
13:3 .....247, 468, 678, 684–85
13:4–31..... 633, 682, 684, 686
13:5 842
13:8 668
13:9 842
13:10 682
13:12–13 842
13:14 .....665, 766
13:15 .....30, 633, 682, 686–87
13:15–18..... 23, 883
13:15–22 .....248, 274, 395, 883
13:17–18.....633, 686–88
13:18 680
13:19 .....30, 688
13:20.....320, 688
13:22.....665
13:23.....458, 689–90
13:23–24 682
13:23–27 ..... 200, 249, 632, 660, 688, 691, 766, 772, 874, 876, 879
13:24.....458, 689
13:25 ..... 106, 589, 689–90
13:26–27 690–91
13:28 .....662, 682
13:28–30 662–63
13:29 .....463, 665, 692
13:31 .....665, 682, 883

1 CHRONICLES

.....708
1 719
1–9..... 589, 706–7, 719
1:1.....706, 723
1:1–4.....723
1:1–27.....722
1:2.....722
1:5–7.....723
1:8–16.....723
1:17–23.....723
1:24–27 723
1:29–31.....723
1:32–33.....723
1:34 723
1:34–54 722
1:35–42 723
1:43–54 723
2–9.....723
2:1.....706, 723
2:1–2.....722–23
2:1–9.....747
2:3–4.....724
2:3–17.....723, 725
2:3–4:23.....707
2:4 724
2:5–19.....750
2:6 724
2:7.....369, 724, 844
2:15 .....706, 724
2:47 707
2:50–51.....412
3 840
3:1–4.....729
3:1–9.....710, 724, 733, 746
3:4 ..... 724, 729, 731
3:5.....724
3:5–8.....732
3:9 725
3:17–24.....699, 707
3:18–24.....512
3:19 840
3:19–24.....840
3:21 .....699, 840
3:21–23.....840
3:21–24.....840
3:22 840
4:2 725
4:8–20.....707
4:17 ..... 417, 725
4:24.....725
4:24–43 707
4:28–31 725
4:31 725
4:41 725
5:1.....725
5:1–2.....725
5:1–10.....707
5:2 .....725, 754–55
5:3 .....725, 806
5:3–5.....750
5:11 723–24
5:11–22.....707
5:23 707
5:23–26 706–7
5:25 844
5:25–26 726
5:26 726
6 .....727, 795
6:1–4.....726, 839
6:1–81.....707
6:3 417
6:3–15.....726, 839
6:8 726
6:16–19.....726
6:18 842
6:20 726
6:22.....727
6:32 774
6:33 .....534, 724, 727, 842
6:33–38 752
6:37 534
6:39 534
6:39–43 752
6:44.....724
6:44–48.....752
6:48–49.....795
6:49.....802
6:54–60.....727
6:61–65 727
6:66.....726
6:66–81 727
7:1–5 707
7:6–12.....707
7:13 707
7:14.....707, 814, 845
7:14–19.....706–7
7:20 707
7:20–29.....707
7:30–40 707
8:14–15.....845
8:19 756
9:1.....728, 844
9:2 727
9:2–18.....699, 727–28, 753, 840
9:3 728
9:10–12.....728
9:12 648
9:13 728
9:16–32.....751
9:17–18.....728
9:19 728
9:19–34.....728
9:20 728

9:21–27 . . . 728
9:22 . . . 774
9:25–28 . . . 759
9:28 . . . 728
9:29 . . . 728
9:32 . . . 728, 812
9:33 . . . 728
10:1–7 . . . 729
10:1–14 . . . 728
10:6 . . . 729
10:8–12 . . . 729
10:10 . . . 730
10:12 . . . 729
10:13 . . . 730, 844
10:13–14 . . . 729–31
10:14 . . . 730, 844
10–29 . . . 706, 708
11 . . . 729, 733
11:1–3 . . . 526, 709, 731–32
11:1–9 . . . 710
11:3 . . . 705, 715, 731
11:4 . . . 731
11:4–9 . . . 709, 732
11:5–6 . . . 732
11:8 . . . 732
11:10 . . . 705, 715, 732–33
11:10–47 . . . 709–10, 732–33, 744
11:11–47 . . . 732, 844
11:18–19 . . . 733, 881
11:19 . . . 733
11:26 . . . 746
11:41 . . . 710
11:41–47 . . . 733
11–21 . . . 80
12 . . . 708, 710
12:1–2 . . . 734
12:1–22 . . . 709, 734
12:1–23 . . . 709, 732
12:8 . . . 734
12:14 . . . 779
12:16 . . . 734
12:18 . . . 714
12:19 . . . 734
12:23–40 . . . 709
12:39 . . . 843
13 . . . 710
13:1–4 . . . 709, 732
13:1–5 . . . 735
13:1–8 . . . 701
13:3 . . . 730–31, 737
13:5 . . . 741, 771
13:5–14 . . . 526, 708–9, 730, 732, 734
13:9 . . . 734
13:11 . . . 737
14:1–2 . . . 709, 732
14:2 . . . 736
14:3–7 . . . 709, 732
14:8–17 . . . 709, 732
14:10–12 . . . 715
14:11 . . . 418, 737
14:12 . . . 735, 800
14:14–17 . . . 715
14:17 . . . 736
14–16 . . . 710
15 . . . 198, 705
15:1 . . . 720, 736–38, 769
15:1–3 . . . 198, 881
15:1–24 . . . 709, 736
15:3 . . . 720, 736–38
15:3–24 . . . 845
15:11 . . . 726
15:13 . . . 418, 731, 737, 844
15:13–15 . . . 737
15:15 . . . 705, 737
15:15–17 . . . 727
15:17 . . . 534, 724
15:18 . . . 751
15:19 . . . 534, 724
15:23–24 . . . 751
15:25–16:3 . . . 701
15:25–16:6 . . . 709, 742
15:26–27 . . . 737
15:27 . . . 745
15:29 . . . 698, 709, 729, 737
15–16 . . . 708
16 . . . 346, 511–12, 719, 739–40
16:1 . . . 751–52, 772
16:2–3 . . . 745
16:3 . . . 255, 810
16:4–6 . . . 737
16:4–7 . . . 709, 736
16:7 . . . 740
16:7–36 . . . 718, 720, 736, 750, 852
16:8 . . . 546, 740
16:8–11 . . . 738
16:8–22 . . . 740
16:8–36 . . . 709, 766
16:9 . . . 545
16:10 . . . 740, 844
16:11 . . . 705, 731, 736, 739–40, 752, 844
16:12 . . . 738
16:12–22 . . . 738
16:13 . . . 740
16:15–18 . . . 740
16:22 . . . 738
16:23–26 . . . 740
16:23–33 . . . 736, 740
16:24–26 . . . 843
16:25 . . . 545
16:27 . . . 739, 752, 881
16:28–31 . . . 740
16:31 . . . 545
16:34 . . . 546, 765–66, 789
16:34–36 . . . 736, 740
16:35 . . . 740
16:35–36 . . . 511
16:37–38 . . . 737, 740
16:37–40 . . . 802
16:37–42 . . . 709, 736
16:39 . . . 726, 742
16:39–4 . . . 740
16:39–40 . . . 743, 757, 802
16:40 . . . 740, 844
16:41 . . . 843
16:41–42 . . . 727
16:43 . . . 709, 736, 742
17 . . . 710, 879, 881
17:1 . . . 192, 742–43, 881
17:1–15 . . . 119, 714, 736, 742, 881
17:1–27 . . . 709
17:3 . . . 521
17:5 . . . 742–43
17:6 . . . 755
17:10 . . . 743, 769, 881
17:10–15 . . . 879
17:11 . . . 793
17:11–14 . . . 752
17:13 . . . 698, 750
17:13–14 . . . 743
17:14 . . . xx, 781
17:15 . . . 521
17:16 . . . 843
17:16–27 . . . 736, 742
17:17 . . . 744
18 . . . 745
18:1–13 . . . 744
18:2 . . . 745
18:3 . . . 771
18:8 . . . 389, 745–46
18:12 . . . 488–89, 745
18:14 . . . 744
18:14–17 . . . 744–45
18:17 . . . 745
18–20 . . . 710, 743
19:1 . . . 846
19:1–19 . . . 744–45
19:6 . . . 745
19:7 . . . 745
19:18 . . . 745
20:1–3 . . . 724, 745–46
20:1 . . . 744, 746
20:4–8 . . . 718, 744, 746
20:5 . . . 746
21 . . . 710, 845
21:1 . . . 716, 748–49
21:1–3 . . . 746
21:1–14 . . . 729
21:1–27 . . . 747
21:1–30 . . . 758
21:2 . . . 749, 752

21:2–3 749
21:3 748, 807, 844
21:5 748
21:6 748
21:8 748, 752
21:9–12 714
21:9–16 715
21:12 716, 749
21:16 716, 748–49
21:18 457, 714
21:20 845
21:21 748
21:22 748
21:23 845
21:24 748
21:24–25 747
21:25–26 763–64
21:26 702, 716, 720, 738, 745, 748–50, 752, 761, 767–68, 845, 856
21:26–28 716
21:27 749
21:30 716, 844
22 750, 757
22–29 702, 708, 710, 746–47
22:1 747, 750
22:2 389, 457, 844
22:3–4 389, 746
22:5 389
22:5–19 119, 156, 190, 753, 757
22:6–16 712, 716
22:7–9 521
22:7–10 761
22:7–16 753
22:8 192, 194, 521, 750, 753
22:8–9 753–54, 881
22:9 751–52, 771
22:10 750, 752
22:10–11 879
22:11 751
22:12 844
22:12–13 753
22:13 442, 751, 753
22:14 389, 746
22:15 704
22:15–16 389, 457
22:18 752
22:19 844
23:1 746, 846
23:2–32 747
23:3 751
23:5 396
23:6–32 774
23:7–11 752
23:12–20 752
23:21–23 752
23:24 728, 751
23:25 752
23:25–3 751
23:25–26 751–52, 826, 884
23:25–30 720, 728, 881
23:26 728, 826
23:27 751
23:28 728
23:28–29 751
23:28–32 728
23:29 728
23:30 751
23:30–31 728
23:31 843
23–24 639
23–26 654, 691, 751, 756, 764, 773–74, 795, 812, 845
23–27 826
23–28 692
23–29 846
24:1–19 747
24:3 726
24:5 751
24:7 751
24:7–18 648
24:20–31 747
24:31 726, 751, 756
25 774
25:1 724, 727, 812, 825
25:1–19 752
25:1–31 747
25:2 541, 752
25:3 752
25:4 724, 752
25:5 727
25:6 541, 727
25:8 751
25:9 541, 751
25:12–18 722
25:20–21 752
26:1–19 747, 751, 774
26:1–32 728
26:13 751
26:14 751
26:20–32 747, 774
26:22–28 752
26:26–27 751
26:29–31 752
27:1–15 747
27:2–15 844
27:16–24 747
27:25–34 747
28 753
28:1 753
28:1–21 747
28:2 256, 522, 543, 753
28:2–3 119, 720, 750, 753–54, 761, 881
28:2–7 879
28:2–10 753
28:3 192, 194, 521, 753
28:4 724–25, 754, 875, 879–80
28:4–6 178, 182, 753, 875
28:4–7 752
28:5 522, 743, 774
28:6 521, 752, 761
28:7 753, 755–57
28:8 753
28:9 753, 783, 843–44
28:10 442, 753
28:11 756
28:11–18 756
28:11–19 389
28:12 756
28:15 726
28:17 726
28:19 716, 720, 756–57, 774, 856
28:20 442, 484, 753
28:20–21 712, 716, 753
28:21 704
28–29 747
29 757
29:1–9 747, 757
29:2–5 389, 746
29:6 757
29:9 843
29:10–13 843
29:10–19 747, 843
29:12 843
29:13 843
29:14 843
29:15 540
29:19 843
29:20–25 747
29:22 747, 757
29:23 522, 743, 774
29:25 757
29:26–30 747, 758
29:27–30 757
29:28 747, 846
29:29 718, 757, 775, 846

2 CHRONICLES

1 760
1:1 758
1:1–13 711, 757
1:1–17 711
1:2–13 758, 760
1:3 741
1:3–5 741
1:3–6 742
1:5 741, 844
1:5–6 742
1:7 768
1:10–12 704

1:12 760
1:14 760
1:14–17 .... 199, 208, 712, 719, 758–60, 774, 891
1:15 760
1:16 760
1:16–17 786
1:17 760
1–9 .... 80, 706, 711, 758
2 761–62
2:1 761
2:1–8 891
2:1–16 711
2:1–18 .... 720, 758, 761, 846
2:2 .... 761, 846
2:3 761
2:3–10 761
2:4 .... 761, 812, 843
2:5 761
2:6 761–62
2:7 761
2:8 761
2:9–10 761
2:9–11 815
2:10 771
2:11 .... 712, 761–62
2:11–12 794
2:12 .... 704, 761
2:12–14 .... 712, 716, 764
2:13 704
2:13–14 .... 761, 763
2:14 762–63
2:15 761
2:16 761
2:17 .... 761, 844
2:17–5:1 711
2:18 .... 761, 846
3 .... 346, 764
3:1 .... 702, 716, 738, 750, 752
3:1–2 .... 720, 763–64, 767
3:1–14 758
3:2 691
3:3 764
3:3–14 764
3:4 764
3:8 764
3:8–11 794
3:10 764
3:10–11 819
3:11 764
3:15–5:1 758
3–6 691
4:7 764
4:20 764
5:1 758–59
5:2–14 .... 758, 764
5:2–7:22 711
5:3 .... 652, 792
5:4 771
5:4–5 751
5:5 742
5:7 772
5:11–14 765
5:12 724
5:12–14 767
5:13 .... 546, 736, 765–68, 789, 843
5:13–14 .... 712, 716, 758, 767–68, 772, 856, 891
5:14 .... 349, 759, 767
6:1–4 .... 765, 831, 839
6:1–42 .... 247, 718, 720, 734, 743, 845, 881
6:1–7:10 758
6:3–23 801
6:6 .... 765, 881
6:10–11 772
6:12 765
6:13 765
6:14 .... 664, 877
6:18 .... 671, 762
6:20 .... 664, 769
6:23 .... 243, 626
6:26 769
6:26–27 769
6:26–30 720
6:27 814
6:28 442
6:30 .... 769, 814
6:32 .... 547, 766
6:37 513
6:40 .... 664, 769
6:41 .... 739, 743, 752
6:41–42 .... 709, 766–67, 881
6:42 .... 540, 738, 766
7 .... 198, 705
7:1 .... 752, 767
7:1–2 767
7:1–3 .... 712, 716, 720, 750, 758, 767–68, 856, 891
7:1–9 804
7:2 .... 349, 772
7:3 .... 546, 716, 736, 761, 765–68, 789, 843, 856
7:4–10 768
7:6 .... 691, 736, 765–66, 768, 843
7:8 .... 734, 771
7:8–9 845
7:9–10 768
7:11–22 .... 198, 207, 743, 758, 768, 814, 881
7:12 .... 767–69, 881
7:13–15 770
7:14 .... 702, 721, 770, 779, 813–14, 820, 834, 836–37, 843, 845
7:14–15 878
7:15 664
7:16 .... 197, 772
7:16–22 770
8 770
8:1–11 770
8:1–16 711
8:1–18 758
8:1–27 805
8:2 770
8:3 770–71
8:4 771
8:11 .... 758, 770–72
8:12–15 772
8:12–16 773
8:13 .... 705, 772–73, 843
8:14 .... 751, 773–74
8:14–15 .... 692, 772, 845
8:15 774
8:16 773
8:17–18 770
8:17–9:12 711
9:1–12 .... 758, 774
9:3 704
9:4 771
9:5 704
9:6 704
9:7 704
9:8 .... 712, 762, 774
9:13–2 774
9:13–14 .... 817, 845
9:13–24 758
9:13–28 711
9:15–16 845
9:22 704
9:23 .... 704, 842
9:23–24 845
9:25 760
9:25–28 .... 712, 758–59, 774, 891
9:26 .... 759–60, 771, 876
9:27 760
9:28 760
9:29 .... 718, 757, 775, 846
9:29–31 .... 758, 774–75
9:31 846
10:10–11 781
10:15 714
10:16 775–76
10:1–11:4 .... 740, 775, 778
10–36 .... 80, 706, 712, 715, 721, 770, 834–35, 838
11:1 844
11:2–4 714
11:3 .... 776–77, 806, 844
11:4 775
11:5–12 775
11:10 844

11:12 .... 380, 844
11:13 776–77
11:13–14....... 781
11:13–16....... 777
11:13–17....... 775
11:14 .... 777, 806
11:14–16....... 778
11:15 .... 775, 777–78, 781
11:16 .... 776–77, 806, 844
11:18–2....... 775
11:23 844
12:1 844
12:1–2....... 716
12:1–16....... 703, 721, 770, 775, 778, 835, 838
12:2 844
12:5 .... 714, 753, 783
12:5–8....... 714, 779
12:6 843
12:7 .... 714, 843
12:8 779
12:9–10....... 845
12:12 .... 714, 779, 843
12:13–14 780
12:14 844
12:14–16 796
12:15 .... 718, 846
12:16 846
12–28 777
13:1 .... 717, 780
13:1–23....... 745, 748, 780, 782, 784, 799, 806
13:2 780
13:3 780
13:3–12 780
13:3–20 780
13:3–21 780
13:5 .... 72, 691, 781–82, 842
13:5–14....... 718
13:6–9....... 781
13:8–9....... 778
13:9 842
13:10–11 781
13:12–13 842
13:13–20 780
13:17 781
13:21 780
13:22....... 718, 798, 846
13:22–14:1 780
14:1 846
14:2 782
14:2–8....... 784
14:3 782
14:3–4....... 716
14:4 844
14:4–7....... 782
14:4–15....... 782
14:8 .... 380, 781–82
14:8–15....... 782
14:9–15....... 784
15:1–7 .... 714, 716, 782
15:1–9....... 715
15:1–15....... 782
15:1–19....... 784, 786
15:2 .... 705, 753, 783, 844
15:3–6....... 842
15:4 844
15:7 784
15:8 844
15:8–15....... 716, 782
15:9 .... 776–77, 844
15:12 844
15:13 844
15:15 844
15:16 782
15:17 .... 782, 843
15:18 782
15:19–16:6....... 782
16:1 783
16:1–2....... 716
16:1–9....... 784
16:4 783
16:6 783
16:7 716
16:7–9....... 714, 808
16:7–10....... 782
16:9 .... 784, 843
16:10–14....... 784
16:11 .... 718, 846
16:11–12....... 782
16:12 .... 783, 844
16:13–14 782–83
17:1....... 846
17:1–19....... 784
17:1–21:1 786
17:3 806
17:4 844
17:6–9....... 716
17:7–9 .... 716, 826, 884
17:9....... 669, 844
17:14–19....... 781, 784
17:1–21:1 .... 785, 789–90
18:1 785
18:1–2....... 716
18:1–34....... 784
18:1–19:3....... 703, 721, 770, 784–85, 806, 835, 838
18:2 785
18:2–3....... 785
18:3 785
18:4–5....... 785
18:6–14....... 785
18:12–27 714
18:14 785
18:15–18....... 785
18:16 459
18:17–27....... 785
18:18 785
18:18–21....... 749
18:25 785
18:26 785
18:28–35 785
18:29 .... 716, 828, 830, 845
18:31 786
18:33–34 .... 716, 828, 830, 845
19:1 785
19:1–3....... 784
19:2 .... 44, 786
19:2–3....... 714, 716, 785
19:3 .... 786, 844
19:4 .... 716, 785–86
19:4–11....... 716, 784, 786
19:5–11....... 788
19:6–7....... 786
19:7 786
19:8 786
19:9 787–88
19:9–11....... 786
19:10 .... 787, 844
19:11 787
20:1 785
20:1–3....... 784
20:1–30....... 784
20:3 844
20:4 844
20:7 .... 843, 876
20:14 788–89
20:14–17 714–15
20:15 788
20:17 788
20:19–20 788
20:20....... 714–15, 789
20:20–21 789
20:21 .... 546, 736, 765–66, 789, 843
20:23....... 254
20:23–25 789
20:29 549
20:31 790
20:31–21:1....... 784
20:32....... 790
20:33....... 790
20:34....... 718, 790, 846
20:35....... 785, 790
20:35–37 808
20:36....... 790
20:37....... 714–15, 790
21:1 .... 790, 846
21:1–30....... 757
21:2–2....... 790
21:2–4....... 790–91
21:4 791

21:5 .... 717, 790
21:6 791
21:6–7 790
21:8–10 790
21:10 791
21:10–16 831
21:11 791–92
21:12–15 .... 714, 791
21:12–19 715
21:13 .... 790, 792
21:16–17 791
21:17 .... 717, 791, 821
21:18 836
21:18–19 790–92
21:19 .... 783, 792
21:20 791–92
22:1 .... 793, 846
22:1–9 .... 703, 721, 770, 793, 806, 835, 838
22:2 .... 717, 793
22:3–4 793
22:5 793
22:6 793
22:7 793
22:7–9 793
22:8 793
22:9 .... 794, 844
22:10 .... 791, 794
22:11 794
23:1 794
23:2 795
23:2–3 794
23:4–7 794
23:4–11 751
23:8 795
23:11 794
23:12–15 794
23:16–17 794
23:18 .... 705, 774, 794
23:18–19 794–95
23:19 .... 751, 795, 876
23:20–21 794
24:1 796
24:1–27 .... 796, 798
24:2 .... 796, 802, 844
24:3 796–97
24:4–6 796
24:7 .... 796, 806
24:8–12 796
24:9 .... 208, 797, 842
24:13–24 796
24:15 .... 717, 797–98
24:15–17 .... 796, 798
24:16 798
24:17–18 716
24:18 .... 748, 796, 807, 844
24:18–19 .... 714, 796–97
24:19 835
24:19–20 798
24:20 .... 714–15, 753, 783, 797
24:20–22 .... 311, 671, 796
24:20–25 714
24:21 797
24:25 796–97
24:26 796
24:27 .... 718, 796, 798, 846
25:1 799
25:1–2 798
25:1–26:2 .... 703, 721, 770, 798, 835, 838
25:2 .... 799, 843
25:3–4 799
25:4 .... 204, 705, 881
25:5 .... 380, 844
25:5–6 .... 781, 799
25:6–13 800
25:7–8 .... 799, 808
25:7–9 714
25:7–10 799
25:7–13 715
25:8 808
25:9 799–800
25:10 799
25:11 799
25:12 799–800
25:13 799–800
25:14 .... 716, 799–800
25:15 .... 714, 800, 844
25:15–16 .... 715, 799–800
25:16 714
25:17–19 799
25:17–20 828
25:17–24 800
25:20 .... 715, 799–800
25:21–24 799
25:22 185
25:25 801
25:25–26 799
25:26 .... 718, 846
25:27 801
26:1 846
26:3 801
26:4 801–2
26:5 .... 714, 801–2, 844
26:5–10 801
26:6–8 802
26:6–15 802
26:9–10 802
26:11–15 801–2
26:14 380
26:16 .... 716, 802, 844
26:16–20 801
26:16–21 523
26:18 .... 802–3, 844, 884
26:18–19 804
26:19 803
26:20 802
26:21 .... 726, 801, 803
26:22 .... 718, 801, 846
26:23 .... 801, 803, 809, 846
27:1 804
27:2 804
27:3 804
27:3 .... 716, 820
27:3–4 804
27:3–5 805
27:5–6 804
27:6 805
27:7 .... 718, 804, 846
27:8 804
27:9 .... 804, 846
28 .... 808, 854
28:1 805
28:1–27 781
28:2 806
28:2–3 810
28:2–4 805–6
28:3 .... 311, 326, 806, 809–10, 821
28:4 .... 256, 310, 357, 361, 810
28:5 .... 726, 806–7, 812
28:5–8 .... 361, 805
28:5–15 807
28:6 .... 753, 783, 806
28:8 .... 726, 806–7, 812
28:9–11 .... 714, 805–6
28:10 .... 807, 844
28:11 807
28:12–14 807
28:12–15 .... 805, 854
28:13 .... 748, 807, 844
28:15 .... 698, 726, 807–9
28:16 .... 805, 808
28:16–23 808
28:17 .... 726, 806, 809, 812
28:17–20 805
28:18 809
28:19 .... 809, 844
28:20 809
28:21 .... 805, 808–9
28:22 844
28:22–23 805
28:23 808–9
28:24 .... 809, 811–13
28:24–25 805
28:25 809
28:26 .... 718, 805, 846
28:27 .... 805, 809, 846
29:1–2 .... 810–11, 815
29:3 .... 809, 811, 813
29:3–36 811
29:5 812

29:5–6.....813
29:5–11.....843
29:6.....844
29:7.....811–12
29:8.....419
29:9.....812
29:11.....812
29:11–14.....845
29:15.....813
29:17.....843
29:18.....812
29:19.....844
29:21.....842
29:22–2.....842
29:25.....774, 812–13
29:25–3.....812
29:31.....843
29:34.....339, 827
29–31.....701
30.....814
30:1–11.....811
30:1–31:1.....811
30:2–3.....721, 812
30:5.....705, 827
30:6.....814
30:6–9.....843
30:7.....807, 843–44
30:9.....807, 814, 877
30:11.....777, 814, 843
30:12.....813
30:15.....691
30:16.....705, 339, 813
30:18.....705, 777, 813–14, 827
30:18–20.....721, 770, 813
30:19.....813–14, 844–45
30:19–20.....487
30:20.....814, 827, 845
30:22.....487
30:23.....845
30:25.....844
30:26.....827, 842, 845
31:1.....844
31:2.....845
31:2–21.....811
31:3.....705, 813, 815, 843–44
31:4.....844
31:5.....815
31:6.....815
31:11.....842
31:11–20.....845
31:12.....470
31:17.....751
31:21.....813, 844
32.....815, 845
32:1.....229, 726, 815, 818
32:1–23.....229, 811, 815
32:1–30.....811
32:1–33.....811
32:2–5.....815
32:3–5.....816
32:6–8.....815–16
32:7–8.....816
32:9–23.....815
32:20.....816
32:20–21.....816
32:21.....816
32:22.....817
32:23.....845
32:24.....817
32:24–26.....703, 721, 770, 815–16, 835, 838
32:25.....817–18, 844
32:25–26.....716, 817–18
32:26.....818, 838, 843
32:27.....845
32:27–29.....817, 845
32:27–30.....816–17
32:30.....817
32:31.....703, 721, 770, 811, 816–18, 835, 838
32:32.....718, 818, 846
32:32–33.....816, 818
32:33.....846
33:1.....819
33:1–2.....818
33:1–20.....719, 818
33:2.....819
33:3.....806, 819
33:3–9.....819
33:4.....197
33:6.....311, 810, 821
33:11.....820
33:12.....716, 721, 822, 843
33:12–13.....701, 716, 819–20, 831
33:13.....820
33:14–16.....716, 830, 845
33:14–17.....819–20
33:18.....819
33:18–19.....718, 821
33:19.....718, 819, 843, 846
33:20.....819, 846
33:21.....822
33:21–25.....821
33:22–23.....822
33:23.....715, 807, 843
33:24–25.....822
33:25.....846
34:1.....823
34:1–35:19.....716
34:2.....823
34:3.....824, 844
34:3–4.....716
34:3–7.....822–24
34:4.....806
34:6.....725, 823
34:7.....844
34:8–21.....823
34:9.....654, 776, 824–25, 844
34:12–13.....751, 824
34:14.....824, 844
34:20–32.....824
34:21.....824, 844
34:22–25.....715
34:22–28.....714, 716, 823
34:26.....844
34:27.....825, 844
34:27–28.....818
34:28.....830, 838
34:29–32.....823
34:30.....825
34:32.....716
34:33.....716, 823
35:1.....823, 825
35:1–19.....823, 825, 828
35:2.....716, 751
35:2–5.....654
35:3.....826
35:3–4.....826, 884
35:4.....756, 774, 826
35:5.....669
35:5–6.....339, 826, 828
35:6.....705, 826–27
35:10.....826
35:11.....826–28
35:12.....705, 826–27
35:12–13.....872
35:13.....718, 721, 826–28
35:14.....827
35:15.....727, 751, 774, 826
35:16.....826, 828
35:18.....827, 842
35:18–19.....823, 826
35:20.....829
35:20–24.....828
35:20–27.....719, 721, 823, 828
35:21.....714, 829
35:21–24.....715
35:22.....716, 831
35:22–23.....829
35:22–24.....716, 830, 845
35:24.....829–30
35:25.....825, 829, 831
35:26.....705, 766, 844
35:26–27.....718, 829
35:27.....846
36.....299–301, 832, 835–37, 839
36:1.....831, 846
36:1–4.....829
36:1–8.....832
36:2.....831
36:3–4.....831

36:4 794
36:5 831
36:5–8 831
36:6 831–32
36:7 .... 206, 619, 642, 832–33, 837, 884
36:8 .... 718, 794, 832, 846
36:9 .... 717, 833
36:10 .... 206, 619, 642, 832–33, 837, 884
36:11 .... 299, 834
36:11–17 .... 834, 837
36:12 .... 29, 701–2, 714, 825, 834, 836, 844
36:12–16 299
36:13 702
36:13–17 834
36:14 .... 812, 834, 844
36:15 .... 306, 702, 714, 836
36:15–16 .... 698, 714, 716, 797, 834–36, 838
36:16 .... 311, 702, 836, 854
36:17 299
36:17–20 .... 726, 841
36:18 .... 300, 642, 832, 837, 884
36:18–20 837
36:19 .... 300, 837
36:20 .... 300, 837
36:21 .... 301, 311, 623, 704, 714, 818, 825, 835–37, 839
36:21–23 .... 701, 883
36:22 .... 715, 841–42, 857, 883
36:22–23 .... xxxiv, 80, 301, 512, 631, 640, 699, 701, 716, 833, 837, 839, 841
36:23 545

MATTHEW

.... 17, 80, 361, 724, 857
1:1–17 .... 589, 707
1:3 .... 589, 724
1:5 .... 158, 578, 589, 724
1:6 .... 589, 724
1:22 857
1:23 214
2 898
2:6 .... 409, 879
2:15 .... 358, 361, 856–57
2:17 857
2:18 260
2:23 877
3:3 .... 215, 235, 857, 866, 880
3:17 879–80
4:4 77
4:6 473
4:7 .... 77, 225
4:10 77
4:14 857
4:15–16 214
5:12 671
5:21 .... 17, 77
5:27 .... 17, 77
5:31 78
5:33 57
5:33–36 598
5:37 598
5:38 .... 17, 39, 77
5:43 39
5:43–48 520
5:44 .... 135, 666
6:9–13 666
6:10 666
7:21–23 713
8:17 .... 215, 857
9:13 358
10:1 878
10:15 .... 323, 878
10:35–36 409
11:3 880
11:10 .... 460, 469
11:23–24 323
12:7 358
12:18–21 215
12:40 403
13:13–15 .... 214, 866, 878
13:32 473
13:35 473
15:4 .... 17, 39, 77
15:8–9 215
16:21 358
16:27 472
17:1–13 882
17:10–11 460
17:24 797
18:16 77
18:22 549
18:25 882
19:4 2
19:5 2
19:7 78
19:18 .... 17, 77
19:19 .... 17, 39, 77
21:4 857
21:4–5 880
21:5 .... 215, 443, 453, 851
21:9 .... 473, 880
21:13 .... 215, 220, 249, 260, 851, 859, 876
21:16 472
21:33–44 698
21:42 .... 473, 848, 880
22:24 78
22:31 848
22:32 17
22:37 77
22:39 39
22:44 .... 473, 879
23:16–22 598
23:34–35 671
23:35–37 311
23:39 .... 473, 880
24:15 617
24:29 .... 214–15, 373
24:30 617
24:37–41 246
26:11 77
26:31 443
26:64 .... 473, 617
27:5 185
27:10 443
27:35 472
27:46 472

MARK

.... 80, 444, 452, 853, 855, 867
1:2 .... 460, 469, 857
1:2–3 .... 215, 226, 235, 855–56, 866, 880, 902
1:4 469
1:11 879
1:15 469
1:17 469
3:1–6 883
4:11–12 866
4:12 .... 214, 878
4:32 473
7:6–7 215
7:10 .... 17, 39, 77
7:19 181
8:18 260
8:31 358
9:2–7 204
9:2–13 882
9:32 xl
9:48 215
10:4 78
10:6 2
10:7–8 2
10:19 .... 17, 77
11:1–8 443
11:1–10 .... 850, 880
11:2 850
11:2–5 867
11:2–10 853
11:4 850
11:5 850
11:9 473
11:10 473
11:15–17 866
11:17 .... 215, 220, 249, 260, 851, 859, 876
12:1–10 306

12:1–11 453, 698
12:1–12 854
12:2–5 797
12:3–4 854
12:10–11 473, 856, 880
12:19 78
12:25 627
12:26 17
12:29 77
12:30 77
12:31 39
12:32 77, 215
12:33 39, 77
12:36 xviii, 473, 879
12:41 797
13:14 617
13:24 214, 373
13:25 215
13:26 617
14:7 77
14:27 443
14:62 473, 617, 879
15:24 472, 485
15:26 453
15:29 485
15:34 472, 485

LUKE

80, 215, 753
1:7 183
1:13–20 183
1:78 877
2:23 17
2:24 39
3:4 857
3:4–6 215, 235, 866, 880
3:22 879–80
4:4 77
4:8 77
4:10–11 473
4:12 77, 225
4:18–19 215
4:19 215
6:1–5 181, 883
6:3 176
6:3–6 866
6:6–11 883
7:19 880
7:27 460, 469
8:10 214, 866, 878
9:28–36 882
10:25–37 520, 807, 854
10:27 39, 77
10:30 807
10:30–35 698
10:35 807
10:36 807, 866
11:47–51 311
13:10–17 883
13:19 473
13:34 671
13:35 473
14:1–6 883
18:20 17, 77
19:28–36 453
19:29–36 443
19:30–38 880
19:38 473
19:46 215, 220, 249, 260, 851, 859, 876
20:9–18 698
20:17 473, 880
20:28 78
20:37 17
20:42–43 473, 879
21:26 215
21:27 617
22:20 285, 878
22:37 215
22:69 473, 617
23:30 358
23:46 472
24:25–27 849
24:27 xl
24:44 849
24:44–45 xl

JOHN

80
1:21 148
1:23 215, 235, 866, 880
1:34 215
1:45 148
1:51 2
2:13–17 249
2:17 xl, 473, 857
2:22 xl
4:24 488
5:1–18 883
5:29 626, 867
5:39 849
5:46 849
6:14 148
6:31 17, 473
6:45 215
7:19–24 883
7:40 148
7:42 409
7–8 27, 34, 150
8:17 77
10:34 473, 851
12:8 77
12:13 473
12:13–15 880
12:15 443, 453
12:16 xl
12:38 215, 857
12:38–40 878
12:39 857
12:40 214
13:18 472
14:25–26 xl
15:25 472–73
16:12–14 xl
19:24 472
19:36 17, 57, 472, 547, 857
19:37 443, 857
20:9 xl
20:22 xl

ACTS

677, 871
1:20 473
2:17–21 373, 851
2:25–28 472
2:30 473
2:30–31 867
2:31 472
2:34–35 473, 879
3:13 17
3:22 77
3:22–23 855–56, 866, 882
3:22–24 148
3:23 39, 77
3:24 849
3:25 2
4:3 859
4:11 473, 880
4:25–26 472, 880
7 161
7:2–16 161
7:3 2
7:5 2
7:6–7 2
7:7 17
7:17–36 161
7:18 17
7:27–28 17
7:32 17
7:33–34 17
7:35 17
7:37 77, 148, 161, 855, 882
7:38 161
7:39–44 161
7:40 17
7:42–43 385
7:49–50 215
7:52 311
8:28 xlv
8:32–33 215
9:1–18 80

10:1–6 . . . 80
10:9–16 . . . 80
10:22 . . . 80
10:28 . . . 80
10:30–33 . . . 80
11:5–14 . . . 80
11:13–14 . . . 80
13 . . . 161, 879
13:22 . . . 176, 215, 473
13:27 . . . 849
13:33 . . . 472, 880
13:34 . . . 215, 766
13:35 . . . 472
13:41 . . . 426
13:47 . . . 215
15 . . . 858–59
15:7–11 . . . 80
15:16–17 . . . 385, 394, 879
15:16–18 . . . 858–59, 867
15:20 . . . 123, 457
15:29 . . . 123, 457
21:24 . . . 859
21:25 . . . 123, 457
21:33 . . . 859
22:3 . . . xlv
22:3–27 . . . 80
23:5 . . . 17
24:15 . . . 626, 867
26:4–20 . . . 80
28:26–27 . . . 214, 878

ROMANS

. . . xli, 215
1:17 . . . 426
1:23 . . . 268
2:6 . . . 472, 566
2:24 . . . 215, 313
3:4 . . . 472
3:10 . . . 595
3:10–12 . . . 472
3:10–18 . . . 892
3:13 . . . 472–73
3:14 . . . 472
3:15–17 . . . 215
3:18 . . . 472
4 . . . 876
4:3 . . . 2, 851
4:7–8 . . . 472
4:9 . . . 2, 851
4:17 . . . 2
4:18 . . . 2
4:22 . . . 2, 851
7:7 . . . 17, 77
8:36 . . . 472
9:6 . . . 158, 584, 656
9:7 . . . 2
9:9 . . . 2
9:12 . . . 2
9:13 . . . 460
9:15 . . . 17
9:17 . . . 17
9:20 . . . 215, 258
9:25 . . . 358
9:25–29 . . . 372
9:26 . . . 358
9:27–28 . . . 214
9:29 . . . 214
9:33 . . . 214–15
10:5 . . . 39
10:6 . . . 77–78
10:7 . . . 78
10:8 . . . 78
10:9–13 . . . 867
10:11 . . . 215
10:13 . . . 373
10:15 . . . 215, 420
10:16 . . . 215
10:18 . . . 472
10:19 . . . 78
10:20 . . . 215
10:21 . . . 215
11:2–3 . . . 204
11:3 . . . 188
11:4 . . . 188
11:8 . . . 78, 215, 224
11:9 . . . 473
11:10 . . . 473
11:26–27 . . . 215
11:27 . . . 214
11:34 . . . 215
11:35 . . . 550
12:14 . . . 666
12:14–21 . . . 520
12:17 . . . 666
12:17–21 . . . 135
12:19 . . . 78, 666
12:20 . . . 566
12:21 . . . 666
13:9 . . . 17, 39, 77
14:5 . . . 181
14:11 . . . 215
14:14 . . . 181
15:3 . . . 473, 476
15:9 . . . 176, 472
15:9–12 . . . 873, 892
15:10 . . . 78
15:11 . . . 473
15:12 . . . 214
15:21 . . . 215

1 CORINTHIANS

. . . 861
1:19 . . . 215
1:31 . . . 260
2:9 . . . 215
2:16 . . . 215
3:19 . . . 550
3:20 . . . 473
5:13 . . . 77
6:16 . . . 2
7:5 . . . 69
7:12 . . . 660
7:12–14 . . . 660
7:15 . . . 660
7:16 . . . 660
9:9 . . . 78
10:7 . . . 17
10:26 . . . 472
10:31 . . . 137
11:2 . . . 857
11:25 . . . 285, 878
14:21 . . . 214
15:3–4 . . . xlvi, 848
15:27 . . . 472
15:32 . . . 214
15:45 . . . 2
15:54 . . . 214
15:55 . . . 358

2 CORINTHIANS

3–4 . . . 285, 878
4:6 . . . 2
4:13 . . . 473
6:2 . . . 215
6:14–18 . . . 660
6:16 . . . 39
6:17 . . . 215, 313, 851
6:18 . . . 176
8:15 . . . 17
9:9 . . . 473
10:17 . . . 260
13:1 . . . 77
13:10 . . . 857

GALATIANS

3:1–22 . . . 876
3:6 . . . 2
3:8 . . . 2
3:10 . . . 78
3:11 . . . 426
3:12 . . . 39
3:13 . . . 77
3:16 . . . 2
4:27 . . . 215
4:30 . . . 2
5:14 . . . 39

EPHESIANS

2:20 . . . 880
4:8 . . . 473
4:25 . . . 443

4:26 472
5:31 2
6:2–3 17
6:3 77

PHILIPPIANS
2:10–11 215
2:15 78

COLOSSIANS
4:16 857

1 THESSALONIANS
5:27 857

2 THESSALONIANS
2:9 713
3:6 857

1 TIMOTHY
5:18 78

2 TIMOTHY
2:19 57
3:14–16 xviii
4:13 xlv

HEBREWS
.... 179, 215, 482–83, 849, 866–67
1:1–2 .... xviii, 849
1:5 .... 176, 472, 476, 698, 879–80
1:5–13 .... 483, 873, 892
1:6 78
1:7 473
1:8–9 472
1:10–12 473
1:13 .... 473, 879
2:5–8 483
2:5–9 867
2:6–8 .... 472, 851
2:7 483
2:9 483
2:12 472
2:13 214
3:5 57
3:7–11 473
3:15 473
4:3 473
4:4 2
4:5 473
4:7 473
5:5 .... 472, 879–80
5:6 .... 473, 879
6:13–14 2
6:14 2
7:1–2 2
7:17 .... 473, 855–56, 879
7:21 .... 473, 855–56, 879
8:5 17
8:6 .... 285, 878
8:8–12 .... 260, 285, 851
8:8–13 866
9:20 17
10 487
10:5–7 .... 472, 487
10:5–8 285
10:12–18 .... 285, 878
10:16 .... 487, 866
10:16–17 .... 260, 285
10:30 .... 78, 473
10:37 214
10:37–38 426
11:5 2
11:8–19 876
11:18 2
11:21 2
11:31 .... 154, 159
11:32 179
12:5–6 566
12:5–11 182
12:13 566
12:20 17
12:21 77
12:26 437
12:29 77
13:2 323
13:5 78
13:6 473

JAMES
.... 124, 159, 393–94, 858–59, 866–67
2:8 39
2:11 .... 17, 77
2:20–24 876
2:21–24 159
2:23 .... 2, 843, 876
2:25 .... 154, 159, 866
3:9–10 7
4:4 358
4:6 566

1 PETER
1:10 xviii
1:16 39
1:24–25 .... 215, 880
2:3 472
2:4 880
2:6 215
2:6–8 258
2:7 .... 473, 880
2:8 214
2:9 .... 17, 215
2:22 215
2:24 215
2:25 215
3:10–12 472
3:14 214
4:18 566
5:5 566

2 PETER
2:6–8 878
2:22 566

JUDE
7 878

REVELATION/APOCALYPSE
.... 316, 539, 713
1:7 .... 443, 617
1:13 617
2:27 472
4:1–11 255
4:5 214
4:6 214
5:5 .... 877, 880
5:5–6 867
6:12 373
6:16 358
6:17 373
7:16 215
7:17 214–15
9:7 373
9:7–8 373
10:9 313
11:4 443
12:5 472
13:10 260
14:1 880
14:8 214
14:14 617
15:3 473
15:4 .... 260, 473
16:14 880
17:2 420
18:2 214
18:4 260
18:7 215
19:15 472
20:4–5 626
20:11–15 867
21:1 215
21:4 214
21:12–13 626

JUDITH
14:10 139

ADDITIONS TO ESTHER
14:3–19 .... 512, 622, 878
14:6 614

WISDOM
10:1–21 567

SIRACH
266
8:3 142
24:8–11 567
24:23 705
24:23–29 570
42:15 478
48:10 470

BARUCH
1:8 642, 832
1:9 642, 832
1:15–3:8 512, 622, 878
4:1 570, 705

1 ESDRAS
632, 646, 678
3:1–5:3 441
4:50 462
5 646
5:41 647
7:13 678–79

1 ENOCH
104:2 627

JUBILEES
661, 899
17:16 456, 748

PSALMS OF SOLOMON
17:28 679

TESTAMENT OF THE TWELVE PATRIARCHS
xli

LETTER OF ARISTEAS
900

LAW COLLECTION OF HAMMURABI
103
§6 103
§22 103
§117 127
§193 103, 134
§195 103, 134
§196 103
§197 103
§200 103
§250 35
§251 35
§273 459

HITTITE LAWS
103
§45 135
§71 135
§79 135
§197 151

LAWS OF ESHNUNNA
§42 103
§50 135
§§53–55 35

LAWS OF UR-NAMMA
§18 103
§19 103

MIDDLE ASSYRIAN LAWS
103
§8 143
§A55 138
§A56 138

BIBLICAL TEXTS FROM THE JUDEAN DESERT
Gen 3:1 (4QGen^{k}/4Q10) 4
Lev 16:1 (11QpaleoLev^{a}/11Q1) 72
Num 36:1 (4QNum^{b}/4Q27) 70
Deut 32:8 (4QDeut^{j}/4Q37) 144–45, 224, 482, 565, 860
Deut 32:43 (4QDeut^{q}/4Q44) 565
Judg 6:7–10 (4QJudg^{a}/4Q49) 173
4QSam 735
1 Sam 1:13 (4QSam^{a}/4Q51) 183
2 Sam 8:7 (4QSam^{a}/4Q51) 745
2 Sam 24:16 (4QSam^{a}/4Q51) 749
Isaiah (1QIsa^{a}) 265
Isa 17:9 (1QIsa^{a}) 254
Isa 53:11 (1QIsa^{a}) 627
Isa 53:11 (1QIsa^{b}) 627
Isa 53:11 (1QIsa^{d}) 627
Isa 56:6 (1QIsa^{a}) 250
4QJer^{bd}/4Q71, 72^{a} 264
Jer 7:1 (4QJer^{a}/4Q70) 270
Jer 27:1 (4QJer^{c}/4Q72) 833
Jer 48:31 (2QJer/2Q13) 293
Mal 2:15 (4QXII^{a}) 466
Ezra 6:1 (4QEzra/4Q117) 653
Ezra 6:5 (4QEzra/4Q117) 653

SECTARIAN TEXTS FROM THE JUDEAN DESERT
1QpHab 6.12–7.5 861–62
1QS/1Q7 xli
1QS/1Q7 I, 24–II, 1 878
4QpNah/4Q169 862
4Q174/4QFlor 858–59
4Q174/4QFlor 1.3–5 679
4Q174/4QFlor 1.3–4 858
4Q174/4QFlor 1.4 858
4Q174/4QFlor 1.10–13 394
4Q174/4QFlor 1.12 858
4Q174/4QFlor 1.17 394
4Q266/CD 6.20–21 807
4Q266/CD 7:16 xiii, 394
4Q394/4QMMT 661
4Q470/CD 11:13–17 883
CD 20:18 626
11QT/11Q19 46:8–11 138
11QT/11Q19 53:11 596
Mas1h 478

SAMARITAN PENTATEUCH
xli
Gen 3:1 4
Gen 42:21 162
Exod 20:24 114–15
Exod 22:9 130, 496
Exod 40:33 31
Num 13:33 91
Num 24:7 336
Num 24:17 227, 294
Num 36:1 70
Deut 12:5 197
Deut 12:14 115
Deut 12:18 115
Deut 14:13 121
Deut 32:8 144

JOSEPHUS
848
Antiquities, XI, 192 893

PHILO
598, 848, 926
Moses II, §§192–245 44, 60, 66

MISHNAH
Shabbath 7:2 30, 181, 883
Yoma 8:6 181, 883
Hagigah 1:8 598
Yebamoth 8:3 589
Nedarim 2:1 598
Nedarim 2:5 598
Nedarim 3:1 69, 598
'Aboth 1:1 4
Hullin 10:1 151

BABYLONIAN TALMUD
Shabbath 128b 883
Yebamoth 77a 589
Ketuboth 39b 85

SUBJECT INDEX

Aaron, 35–36, 42, 53–54, 63, 66, 68, 71–73, 91, 94–95, 108–11, 122, 149–50, 164, 174, 180, 202–3, 320, 329, 339, 342–43, 417, 440, 464, 509–10, 513, 516–17, 524, 539, 543–44, 608, 726, 767, 781, 795, 798, 803–4, 812, 826
Abarim, 95, 149, 170
Abihu, 54, 71, 343, 803
Abijah, 648, 717, 726, 780–81, 846
Abimelek, 183, 508–9, 535
Abishai, 488, 744–45
Abner, 729
Abraham, 2, 10–12, 17, 31–32, 35, 53–54, 64, 68, 110–11, 132–33, 144, 159, 161, 173, 255, 283, 323, 357, 362, 365, 476, 490–91, 497, 508–11, 523, 553, 621, 670–72, 674–75, 682, 702, 720, 722, 748, 764, 798, 820, 843, 866, 868, 876
Abrahamic, 9, 12, 52, 64, 68, 143, 227, 286, 476, 489–92, 507–8, 670, 738, 873, 876, 879–80
Abram, 9, 143, 516, 672, 759
Absalom, 535, 707–8, 744
accusation, 66, 83, 92, 119, 256, 275, 323, 350–51, 355–56, 364, 390–91, 438, 456, 463, 721, 725
accusatory, 484
accuser, 164, 519–20, 561
accusing, 73, 151, 178, 245, 268, 275, 308, 321, 323, 325, 350, 368, 390–91, 432, 438–39, 463, 485, 495, 504, 519–20, 610, 816–17, 899
Adam, 3, 5–6, 145, 369, 561, 706, 722–24, 854, 894
Admah (also see cities of the plain), 77, 358, 362, 367, 878
adulteress, 268, 589, 592
adultery, 17, 54, 77, 83, 103–4, 151, 179, 271, 307, 351, 361, 369, 391, 536, 564, 570, 574, 589, 724, 733, 745
adversary, 192, 240, 748–49, 754, 771
Agag, 184, 336, 615
age, 28, 106, 168, 351, 647, 715, 717, 751, 783, 790, 798, 818, 831, 833–34, 898
Ahab, 148, 203, 211, 716, 719, 721, 785–86, 790–93, 809, 819, 829–30
Ahaz, 212, 225, 230, 252, 716, 789, 805, 808–12, 818–19, 841, 846
Ahaziah, 203, 211, 703, 717, 721, 770, 790, 793–94, 835, 838
Ahijah, 758, 775
Ahimelek, 176, 180–81, 536
allegory, 313, 323, 332, 337, 346, 348, 350–52, 457, 542, 563, 580, 591, 593, 601, 808, 858, 862, 902
alliance, 202, 361, 389, 392, 785–86, 793, 799–800, 805, 808, 829
allotment, 125, 163, 166, 208, 250, 322, 345–46, 354, 723, 727
allusion, xvii–xxviii, xxx–xxxii, xxxiv, xxxvi, xxxix, xliii, xlvi, l, 3–7, 9–10, 12, 17, 19, 21–22, 26, 28, 31–32, 41–42, 45, 52, 55–58, 61, 67, 70–72, 79, 81, 88, 97–98, 100–2, 108, 112–13, 115, 118–19, 130–32, 134–41, 143–47, 149, 155, 158–60, 162–66, 171–78, 180, 182–83, 185–86, 188–94, 197–201, 204, 206–7, 215–17, 219–21, 225, 227, 236, 238–39, 241, 245–47, 250–54, 258–59, 262–63, 267–72, 275–76, 280, 282–83, 287–89, 291–92, 297, 306, 308–10, 314–17, 320, 323–26, 328–29, 335–37, 339, 347–48, 350, 353, 357, 359–60, 362, 364–72, 374–75, 377–78, 380–83, 386–88, 390–92, 395–96, 401, 404, 406–7, 410, 412–15, 417–18, 427–29, 431–32, 434–35, 438–39, 441, 444–47, 450–52, 455–59, 461, 463–64, 466–67, 469, 473–85, 489, 492–94, 496–501, 504, 507–9, 511, 513–16, 518, 520, 523–25, 531, 534, 539, 541–45, 547, 551–55, 558–61, 564–65, 567–69, 571–72, 575–76, 581, 590–93, 595–97, 599–605, 607–12, 614–15, 618–22, 628, 632, 634–40, 642, 652, 654–55, 657, 659, 661, 664–65, 667–71, 680–81, 684–93, 699, 701–2, 712, 714, 718–20, 724–25, 730–31, 736–37, 740, 746, 749, 751, 753–54, 756–57, 766–67, 769, 774–75, 777–78, 781, 783, 787–89, 795, 797, 803, 807, 810–16, 818, 820, 826, 828, 832, 835–37, 842, 850, 853, 855, 857, 862, 869–71, 873–79, 881, 883, 889, 893, 896–901, 903
altar, 25, 36, 41, 98, 104–5, 111–19, 121, 127, 133, 152, 163, 171, 177, 194, 209, 248, 319, 338, 342, 353–54, 357, 360, 391, 463–66, 488, 635, 639, 652, 677, 691, 741–42, 750, 765, 767–68, 773, 795, 804, 813, 827–28, 856, 891
Amalekite, 149, 166, 184, 615
Amaziah, 204, 211, 393, 456, 703, 705, 716, 721, 770, 781, 798–802, 808, 828, 835, 838, 844
Ammon, 79, 95, 139, 149, 166, 169–70, 200, 291, 294–95, 297, 311, 387–89, 395, 435, 584, 606–7, 686, 689, 784, 788, 805, 874
Ammonite, xxxiii, 201, 238–39, 248, 581–82, 589, 606, 635, 657–58, 660, 684–85, 689, 858
Ammonites, 95, 138–39, 169, 179, 200–2, 239–40, 247, 341, 387, 394, 436, 580, 582–83, 589, 657–58, 684–86, 689–90, 744–45, 788
Amon, 212, 261, 645, 715, 821–22, 846
Amorite, 12, 169, 295
Amorites, 25, 28, 54, 67, 93, 104, 111, 158, 162, 170, 173, 199, 254, 293–95, 395, 431, 515, 530, 657, 672
Anakite, 63–64, 95, 149, 387
Anathoth, 287, 342, 643
ancestor(s)/ancestral/ancestry, xxxiii, xli, 8, 10, 12–13, 17, 29, 32, 52–53, 58, 64–65, 68, 70, 85–86, 99, 110, 119, 132–33, 138, 144, 149, 160–62, 168, 173, 177, 192, 196, 202, 208, 210, 244, 249, 262, 268, 271, 274–75, 280–81, 284, 288,

307–9, 315, 325–26, 330–31, 334, 342, 360, 407, 444–45, 461–62, 476, 481, 492, 502, 507–12, 516, 518, 527, 548, 573, 584, 586, 604–5, 610–11, 614, 622–24, 635, 645, 647, 656, 660, 662, 664–65, 673, 678, 684–87, 702, 706–7, 714, 717, 724–27, 738–39, 754, 759, 769, 778, 783, 791, 797–98, 803, 806, 813, 820, 822, 836, 838–39, 843–44, 849, 866
angel (also see celestial delegate and messenger), 25, 28, 144–45, 185, 235, 242, 251, 363–65, 446–47, 473, 501, 554, 748
anger, 24, 64–65, 93–94, 104, 110, 183, 201, 206, 245, 257, 261, 270, 298, 304, 307, 351, 368, 375–77, 403–6, 408, 415, 421–24, 446–47, 472, 481, 498, 502, 504, 514, 516–17, 520, 544, 597, 608, 610, 673, 687, 714, 748–49, 778–79, 799, 804, 809, 836, 898
animal, 4, 6–7, 17, 19, 21–22, 25, 28, 33–35, 41–42, 45–46, 55–56, 59, 67–69, 82–83, 101–2, 112, 116–17, 120–23, 127–28, 135–37, 149, 151, 177, 208, 253, 272, 275, 308–9, 318, 326, 331, 357, 397, 408, 418, 434–35, 453, 458, 464–65, 482, 505–6, 530, 540, 600–1, 653, 658, 686, 733, 828, 860–61
anointing, xxxviii, 36, 53, 179–80, 192, 342, 509, 544, 580, 590, 708–9, 718, 729, 731–32, 738, 747, 766, 793, 807
apostasy, 20, 24–26, 106, 108, 201–2, 368, 422, 441, 468, 648, 656, 659–62, 664, 674, 676–79, 682, 685–86, 688–91, 874
apple, 146, 459, 539, 569, 594
appointing, 18, 27, 32, 36, 79, 89, 128–29, 178–79, 192, 285, 296, 300, 303, 342, 368, 443, 453, 480, 500, 509, 523, 628, 635, 651, 653, 673, 708, 716, 727, 736, 751, 755, 762, 773, 778, 787, 789, 815, 833, 841, 843
appointment, 82, 368, 654, 728, 732, 736–37, 764, 844
Arad, 73, 95, 105, 449
Aramaic, xii–xiii, xvi, 92, 196, 309, 619–21, 632, 653–54, 669, 691, 807, 861
Aramean, 143–44, 797, 808
Arameans, 200, 387–88, 395, 744–45, 797, 806, 830
ark, xxiv, 31, 35, 110, 140, 147, 178, 196, 198, 208, 262, 281, 309, 493–94, 522, 526–28, 543, 701, 703, 705–6, 708–10, 718, 720, 728–30, 732, 734–39, 741–43, 750–51, 753–54, 758, 764–67, 772, 826, 841, 843–44
arm, 102, 111, 143–44, 147, 237–38, 258, 469, 532–33, 541, 766, 830
army, 230, 242, 301, 303, 349, 376, 416, 522, 530, 533, 780, 784, 788–89, 797, 799–800, 816, 820
Arnon, 169, 293, 396
aroma, 177, 315, 319, 486–87
arrogance, 109, 189, 223, 225, 231, 289, 293, 295–96, 320, 370, 399–400, 428, 461, 476, 495, 560, 802, 830
Asa, 211, 716–17, 781–84, 786, 790–91, 801–2, 822
Asaph, 492, 497, 534, 536, 541, 644, 741, 765, 812
Ashdod, 184, 458, 689–90
Asher, 166–67, 707, 777
Asherah, 25, 104–5, 209, 714, 819, 821
Ashurnasirpal, 893
assembly, xxxiii, 18, 20, 24, 45, 66, 84, 105, 124, 131, 138–39, 151, 190, 195, 200–2, 238–39, 247–50, 383, 394, 397, 440, 451–52, 454, 483, 485, 497, 578–85, 588–89, 595, 604, 606–7, 632–33, 635, 645, 647, 649, 655–61, 664, 668–70, 672–86, 688–90, 735, 741–42, 747, 753–54, 761, 775, 857–59, 873–74, 876–77, 879
assonance, 143, 434, 464, 889, 892
Assurbanipal, 337, 422
Assyria, xii, 204, 225–26, 230, 233, 235, 352, 354, 361, 370, 407, 416, 419, 459, 805, 808–9, 815, 820, 829
Assyrian, xii, xv, 103, 188–89, 204–5, 209, 219, 228, 230–32, 252, 255, 396, 412, 424, 474, 522, 656, 671, 806, 808, 816, 821, 893
asylum, 58, 69, 83–84, 124, 132–33, 149, 160, 333, 777
Athaliah, 211, 791, 793–94, 796–97
atomization, 117, 889, 896, 898
atonement, 36, 39, 55, 62, 72–73, 83, 122–23, 147, 183, 244, 488, 516, 795, 815
attribute formula, xxxiii, 20, 23–24, 28, 64–65, 105, 107, 161, 203, 372, 375–77, 403–7, 410, 414–15, 421–22, 424, 474, 477, 498, 504–5, 519–20, 545, 558, 604, 607–8, 622, 873–74, 877, 879–80, 898
authority/authoritative, xix–xx, xxx–xxxi, xxxix, xli–xlii, 3, 5, 8, 17, 21, 59, 70–71, 78, 81, 85, 88, 101, 113, 118, 129, 190, 219, 226, 262–64, 266, 274, 279, 294–95, 304, 313, 316, 359, 361, 362, 374–75, 386, 389–90, 400, 404, 438, 444–45, 477, 494, 551, 636–37, 652, 658, 687–88, 698–99, 703, 705–6, 714, 718–19, 766, 773, 795, 812, 814, 826, 828, 847, 849, 851, 853, 856–57, 865, 868, 871–72, 889–90, 897–98, 901, 905
authorship/author/authorial, xviii–xxi, xxx, xxxiv–xxxvi, xxxviii–xxxix, xliii–xliv, xlvi, 18, 80, 92, 118, 124, 167, 179, 196, 217, 220, 249, 254, 257, 264, 289, 301, 306, 372, 394, 405, 482–83, 507, 539, 552, 577, 632, 636–38, 689, 691, 698, 700, 715, 774, 839–40, 843, 849–52, 857–58, 860–67, 869, 872–73, 889–93, 895–96, 898–901, 903
Azariah, 208, 211, 643, 646, 714, 782–83, 801–2, 846
Baal, 146, 269, 271, 294, 307, 325, 351, 366–68, 434, 496, 513–16, 793, 806, 810, 819
Babylon, xii, 214, 221, 231, 262, 278–79, 287, 290–91, 296–301, 303–6, 309, 311, 354, 382, 413, 418, 423, 436, 439, 446–47, 458, 613, 622–23, 628, 642–43, 653, 683–84, 817, 819–20, 832–33, 836–37, 839
Babylonian, xii, 229, 233–34, 236, 279, 296, 299, 301–3, 424, 447, 562–63, 701, 721, 811–12, 816, 819–20, 833, 841
Balaam, 10, 58, 68, 72–73, 138–39, 160, 164, 184, 227, 268, 293–95, 336, 417, 480–81, 581, 606, 684, 686, 716, 748–49
Balak, 138, 388, 417, 686
Barak, 179, 193, 431
Baruch, 263, 289, 306
Bashan, 223, 392, 397, 459, 530
Bathsheba, 536, 724, 733, 744, 746
battle, 69, 96, 139–40, 155, 169, 171, 184, 303, 321, 362, 399, 415, 489, 709, 729, 781–82, 784–85, 788–89, 793, 797, 799–800, 808, 829–30, 860
beast, 41, 123, 278, 331–32, 349, 369, 414, 419
bed, 418, 549, 592, 614, 725, 797
Beeroth, 643, 741
Beersheba, 185, 193, 397, 682–83, 716, 786, 823

beloved, 7, 461, 592–94, 707, 723
Benjamin, 10, 12, 172, 341, 410, 412–13, 615, 641, 707, 716, 728–29, 731, 734, 748, 776–77, 799, 823–25, 844
Benjamite, 184, 361, 413, 535, 615, 734
Beor, 138–39, 581, 606, 684
bestiality, 23, 33, 54, 103, 153
Beth Aven, 361, 363, 365, 370
Beth Shan, 615, 730
Bethel, 173–74, 202–3, 207, 361, 363–66, 369–70, 396–97, 450, 644, 775, 777, 823
Bethlehem, 158, 166, 173, 409–10, 412–14, 526, 588, 590, 643, 734, 746
Bezalel, 712, 716, 742, 762
Bildad, 548–49, 556
Bilhah, 126
bird, 5–6, 83, 117, 121, 146, 149, 151, 270, 308–9, 368, 434–35, 473, 482, 505, 541
birth, xlv, 6, 30–31, 52, 54, 60–61, 94, 99, 101, 138, 142, 155, 200–1, 220, 224, 239–40, 243, 256, 275, 311, 345, 394, 410, 412–13, 455, 477, 555, 561–62, 583, 594, 621, 625, 657, 689, 724, 729, 732, 817, 858, 866
birthright, 500, 725, 754
blasphemy, 44–46, 55, 58, 60, 66, 69, 669
bless, 8, 50–51, 68, 115, 138–39, 163, 191, 449, 464, 489–92, 525, 540, 547, 581, 583, 685–86, 744
blessed, xxix, 2, 5–6, 8, 12, 21–22, 68, 101, 129, 138–39, 149, 191, 286, 472–73, 477–80, 483, 490–92, 510, 538, 544, 546–48, 562, 565, 581, 685–86, 741, 744, 767, 802, 815
blessing, xlviii, 2–3, 7–8, 10, 12–13, 58, 68, 85, 139, 149, 152, 156, 160, 163, 174–75, 177, 181–82, 188–89, 191, 193–94, 215, 231, 255–56, 279, 328, 331–32, 351, 365, 376, 380, 389, 405, 414, 434, 444, 452, 460–61, 463–66, 469, 480–81, 491, 495, 529, 540, 546, 557, 581, 583, 620, 629, 672, 684, 686, 712, 723, 725, 741–42, 744, 754, 760, 802, 805, 835, 853, 867, 870, 875
blindness, 127–29, 153, 170, 172–73, 185, 299, 301, 464, 732, 787, 866
blood, 7, 17, 41, 54, 82, 116–17, 119, 123–24, 133, 153, 177, 184, 192, 194, 196, 209, 215, 271, 281, 307, 321, 329, 333, 339, 342, 351, 354–55, 357, 369, 419, 439, 452, 457, 459, 493, 495, 514, 521, 527, 547, 612, 667, 733–34, 750, 753–54, 810, 813, 817, 827, 881
blue, 136, 598, 763
Boaz, 158, 575, 579–90
boilerplate, 262, 295, 302–4, 436, 890–91
boiling, 27, 34–35, 82, 119, 123, 178, 232–33, 500, 612, 700, 827–28, 872
bone, 17, 32, 57, 60–61, 164, 185, 308, 319, 352, 472, 547, 561, 564
Book of the Twelve Prophets: see the Twelve Prophets
border, 28, 170, 184, 208–9, 227, 294, 387, 401, 412, 480, 490, 759
boundary, 18, 35, 83, 145, 153, 240, 242, 348, 358, 361, 549, 573, 661
bow, 8, 10, 23, 25, 104, 107, 144, 215, 221, 303, 370, 414, 418, 423, 434, 459, 490, 494–95, 504, 520, 542, 549, 559, 565, 830
branch, 276, 286–87, 330–31, 351, 385, 391, 394, 441, 443, 448–50, 458, 473, 635, 639, 669–70, 706, 722, 873, 877, 879–80
bread, 17, 27, 34, 54–55, 60–61, 77, 126, 128–29, 138–39, 150, 176, 180–81, 208, 257, 349, 356, 385, 391, 401, 440, 472–73, 485, 508, 548, 581, 606, 684, 728, 773, 812, 860, 866
breastplate, 36, 354, 830
breath, 504, 538, 546, 555, 561, 600
bribe, 129, 153, 256, 355, 418, 573, 787
bride, 83, 137–38, 151, 246, 267–68, 308, 358, 362, 591
bronze, 209, 304, 349, 447, 609, 621, 742, 745, 758, 762–63, 820
brother, 9, 11, 50–51, 70, 114, 135, 152, 311, 364, 372, 383, 395, 462, 586, 590, 626, 724, 746, 807
brother-in-law, 152, 586
brothers/brotherhood, xxxi, 7–8, 63, 149, 163, 240, 288, 392, 414, 461, 470, 540, 548, 565, 584–86, 648, 667, 705, 723, 755, 791–92, 882
burial, 95, 109, 210–12, 337, 344, 347, 584, 717, 748, 757, 782–83, 785, 790–92, 794, 796–99, 801, 803–5, 809, 819, 822–23, 829–30, 848
burn, 60, 64, 104–5, 110, 119, 142, 174, 177–78, 201, 206, 263, 271, 287, 289, 300–1, 307–8, 361, 391, 457, 500, 624, 628, 635, 724, 735, 748, 800, 803–4, 810, 837, 891
burning, 114, 173, 274, 289, 349, 396, 450, 549, 677, 680, 736, 773, 803, 837, 854
burnt, 36, 41, 55, 113, 115, 248, 273, 287, 307, 397, 487–88, 635, 639, 651–52, 654, 741–42, 750, 754, 767–68, 773, 795, 815, 827–28
burying, 10, 13, 162, 308, 733, 794
bush, 114, 407, 673, 854
buying, 49–50, 126, 320–21, 345, 390, 585–88, 676, 680
Cain, 9, 455, 574, 722, 854
cake, 255, 293, 307, 370, 391
Caleb, 64, 90, 162–64, 167, 184, 412
calf, 16–17, 23, 26, 29, 39, 58, 108–11, 161, 174, 189, 202–4, 207, 251, 253, 284, 309, 349, 361, 363, 366, 369–70, 404, 406, 484, 498, 513, 515, 608, 671, 775–78, 894
camp (also see encampment), 45, 60, 63, 73, 95, 140, 158–59, 502, 803, 860
Canaan, 10–11, 26, 29, 32, 54, 97, 105–7, 116, 122, 134, 149, 155–60, 162, 164, 167–68, 188–89, 198–99, 201–2, 328, 333, 340, 508, 514, 530, 657–59, 671, 673, 778, 792, 873, 879, 891
Canaanite, 25, 28, 67, 95, 104, 106, 116, 146, 157–58, 199, 202, 294, 322, 389, 431, 435, 503, 508, 541–42, 551, 589, 656–57, 661, 672, 724
cannibalism, xxvii–xxviii, 77, 208, 225, 316, 318
canon/canonical, xix, xxxv–xxxvii, 19, 88–89, 266, 359, 441, 466, 498, 511, 571–72, 575, 622–23, 640, 672, 699, 812, 865, 872, 890, 901
canonical consciousness, xx, xxx, xli, 88, 155, 157, 190, 279, 295, 438, 444–45, 636, 773, 848, 856–57, 864–65, 871–72, 875, 889–90, 897
capital, 7, 22–23, 29–30, 34, 45–46, 54, 69, 83, 103–4, 134–35, 151, 220, 280, 462, 487, 633, 688, 731, 883
captive, xli, 83, 105, 170, 231, 250, 263, 293–94, 299, 301, 349, 362, 446, 473, 510, 512, 608, 613, 643, 679, 716, 805, 807, 809, 820, 831–33
captivity, 40, 95, 170, 188, 206, 231, 242, 250, 260, 266, 279, 294, 315, 322, 349, 643, 648, 665, 670, 679, 701, 706, 721, 812, 819–20, 831–33, 841, 868
Carchemish, 829
Carmel, 371, 380–81, 696
catchphrase, 296, 371–72, 380, 428, 537–38, 891–92

catchword, 250, 257–58, 273, 332, 334, 370–72, 391, 428, 446, 494, 514, 518, 526, 537–38, 547, 576, 585, 598, 623, 680, 690, 738, 749, 767, 858, 873, 891–92, 896, 898
cattle, 28, 33, 97, 115, 397, 635
cave, 13, 204, 536–37, 734
cedar, 72, 192, 195, 200, 438, 459
celestial, 30, 223, 256, 348–49, 354, 373, 399–400, 435, 481, 483, 503, 505, 561, 563, 565, 623–24, 628, 671, 748–49, 785, 892
celestial court, 145–46, 255, 349, 456, 482, 499, 860
celestial delegate/messenger (also see angel), 34, 72, 78, 144–45, 173, 183, 209, 225, 235, 251, 284, 359, 363–65, 323, 447–49, 460–61, 468–69, 473, 477, 482–84, 496, 500–1, 565, 608, 627, 716, 749, 816, 855, 860
census, 73, 183, 515, 710, 725, 733, 746–49, 751
ceremonial (im)purity, 42, 54, 60, 123, 180–81, 333, 813, 869
ceremony, 79, 106, 113, 152, 163, 289, 365, 585, 747, 757, 814
Chaldean, 427, 429, 458
Chaldeans, 255, 304, 424, 427–29, 552, 602, 606, 672, 829
chariot, 200, 257, 349, 353, 355, 416, 760, 785, 830
Chemosh, 106, 170, 292–95, 388, 496
cherubim, 136, 147, 185, 202, 209, 338, 349, 353
chiastic (also see mirror imaging), 8, 46, 55, 108, 116, 156, 325, 365, 408, 509, 560, 666, 711, 770, 891, 897
child, 83, 103–4, 134, 142, 150, 208–9, 220, 223, 253, 280, 310–11, 324–26, 328, 333, 356, 362, 484, 514, 562, 568, 582, 658, 805–6, 809–10, 821
children, xxvii–xxviii, 6, 10, 19, 23–26, 28, 40, 50, 65, 79, 83, 85, 99–100, 104, 107, 142, 152, 163–64, 168, 201, 204, 207, 218, 221, 249, 253–55, 257, 272, 280, 283, 297, 307–9, 316, 319, 322–23, 326–27, 331, 333, 345, 357–58, 361, 382, 401, 423, 463, 468, 470, 472, 479, 493, 495, 504–5, 519–20, 541, 543, 549, 552, 558–60, 568–69, 588, 610, 612, 655, 657, 659–60, 666–68, 677, 679, 685, 689–90, 729, 732, 740, 792, 810, 898
choice, xviii, xliv, 35, 48–49, 103, 115, 178, 183–84, 198, 228, 258, 452–54, 494, 526, 594, 689, 705, 731, 738–39, 743, 750–51, 754–55, 767
choosing, 82, 116, 125, 195, 197–98, 526–27, 720, 753, 764, 769, 870, 881
chosen, xlvii, 54, 122–23, 195, 197–98, 215, 256, 258, 286, 296, 303, 413, 440, 495, 507, 510, 516, 521, 523, 527–28, 589, 665, 702, 740, 755, 762, 765, 769, 772, 851, 867
Christ (also see Messiah), xxxvii–xxxviii, xl–xli, xliv, xlvi, 847–48
Christian, xxi, xxxvii, xl–xli, xlv–xlvi, 124, 136–37, 179, 394, 416, 580, 666, 847–48, 859
Christian Scripture/Bible, xl–xli, xlvi, 633, 670, 718, 854, 857, 864, 864–65, 867, 869, 872, 901
christological, xli, 574
Chronistic, 192, 229, 703–6, 711, 714–21, 723–24, 726, 730, 732, 734, 737–38, 740–42, 744–46, 748–49, 753–55, 757, 759–64, 766–67, 769–72, 774, 776–77, 780, 783–86, 791, 794, 796, 798–808, 811, 815–17, 819–22, 824, 835, 837, 842–46, 881, 891
circumcised/circumcision, 12, 32, 40, 43, 52, 54, 61, 124, 139, 150, 239–40, 248, 309, 333, 341, 354, 377, 582, 839, 858, 867
cities, 93, 105–6, 149, 155, 159, 200, 256, 319, 349, 361, 387, 393, 399–400, 427, 727, 741, 770–71, 782, 786–87
cities of asylum/refuge, 58, 69, 97, 132–33, 160, 726–27
cities of the plain (also see Admah, Zeboyim, Sodom, Gomorrah), 10, 149, 166, 171–72, 221, 323, 362, 369, 396, 436, 549, 873, 878
city, 69, 106, 133–34, 145, 151, 158, 160, 172–74, 195, 197–98, 205, 210, 221, 229, 232–34, 238, 243, 278, 289, 293, 301–2, 317, 330, 346–47, 350, 354–55, 381, 396, 436, 438, 444, 448, 451, 459, 481, 527, 541, 547, 567, 575, 579–80, 585–86, 646, 670, 686–88, 701, 715, 717–18, 731–32, 737, 740, 750, 772, 783, 792, 798, 803, 816, 837, 842
civil, xxvii, 33–34, 69, 79, 129–30, 134, 204, 314, 316–18, 346–47, 394, 443, 449, 465, 496–97, 523, 610, 633, 688, 708, 728–29, 731, 745, 787
clan, 47, 70, 184, 345, 413, 490, 586, 647, 724, 727, 737, 751, 795, 842
clay, 556, 564, 621
clean (also see unclean), 42, 120–21, 180, 329, 334, 343–44, 354, 395, 486, 804, 813, 822
cloak, 77, 135, 141, 204, 241, 316, 385, 390, 622
cloning/clone, 321, 712, 719, 758–61, 765, 767, 846, 856, 891
clothes, xxiv, 42, 123, 126, 129, 136–37, 223, 237–38, 242, 272–73, 289, 343, 453, 472, 528, 564, 641, 749, 766, 781, 824–25, 862, 894
cloud, 62, 65, 72, 194, 242, 394, 507, 562, 671, 765, 768, 772
command, xxx–xxxii, 2–3, 17–23, 25–27, 29–30, 35–36, 44–45, 53–55, 66, 70–71, 73, 79, 81, 85–86, 88, 101–2, 104, 106, 108, 112, 115, 118–19, 124–25, 127–28, 131, 134, 136, 141, 156–57, 160, 163–64, 173, 191, 195, 204, 207, 238, 257, 274–75, 283, 285, 307–8, 314, 320, 325, 356, 360, 376, 380, 391, 411, 416, 422, 439, 461, 493, 499, 501, 508, 510, 514, 517, 523, 564, 568–71, 586, 599, 606, 624, 635–36, 638, 651, 654, 657, 659–60, 665, 676, 687, 692, 705, 732, 737, 748, 754, 756, 762, 770, 773, 787, 792, 795, 802, 808, 810, 812, 817, 826, 829–31, 866, 870
commander, 129, 188–89, 204–5, 230–31, 369, 412, 732, 735, 785, 820
commandment, xxx, 19–26, 29, 34–35, 54, 79, 101–2, 104, 107, 161, 163, 205, 274, 285–86, 310, 369, 421–24, 463, 477, 479, 494, 519–20, 543, 559, 568, 570–71, 593, 705, 811, 883
commandments, xxx, 20, 23, 101, 107, 283, 423, 493–94, 543, 568–69, 573, 608, 622–24, 661
community(ies), xxi, xxxvii, 45–46, 66, 99–100, 122, 124, 208, 234, 240, 303, 325, 342, 346, 495, 508, 517, 582, 633, 638, 640, 666, 678, 688, 698, 739, 764, 777, 812
compassion, 24, 86, 295, 362, 404, 415–16, 421, 447, 484, 504–5, 530–31, 541–42, 544, 607–9, 622, 664, 673, 675, 836
compassionate, 20, 23–24, 64, 108, 375–76, 405, 415, 422–23, 474, 498, 504, 520, 541, 543–44, 608, 612, 673, 898–99
concubine, 126–27, 166, 172–73, 223, 725

condemnation, 91–95, 207, 221, 223, 228, 239, 256, 262–63, 274, 276, 313–14, 323, 326, 329, 350, 356, 359, 386–90, 397, 400, 404, 424–25, 433, 438, 451, 464, 520, 666, 686–87, 769, 810, 814, 819, 821
confession, 52–53, 144, 157, 179, 207, 249, 272, 275, 285, 476, 487–88, 511–13, 516, 518–19, 523, 561, 609–11, 614, 617, 622–24, 632, 659, 661, 664–66, 668, 670, 674–76, 678, 682, 692, 716, 749, 768–69, 818, 820, 873, 878
conflation, 115, 651, 762, 891, 895
congregation, xlv, 60, 66, 69, 92–95, 99–100, 133, 160, 162, 223, 227, 234, 268, 273, 438, 473, 476–78, 501–2, 510–11, 518, 531, 610, 660, 740, 766–67, 777, 826, 842, 847, 856, 871
connotation/connote, xix, xxx–xxxii, 4, 6, 9, 23, 26, 28, 34, 40, 63, 117, 124, 131, 166, 171–72, 174, 181, 190, 196, 236, 239, 241–43, 250, 278, 284, 309–10, 337, 354, 356, 370, 407, 409, 435, 469, 474, 448, 457–58, 485, 489–90, 517, 570–71, 580, 599, 606, 608, 612, 618, 620, 626, 636, 650, 669, 683, 685, 689, 710, 715, 732, 798, 815, 830, 836–37, 854, 875, 891–92, 894, 897, 902
conquest, xx, xxxiv, 34, 73–76, 79, 90, 95–98, 159–62, 166–68, 293, 301, 395, 431, 492, 508, 529–30, 532, 671, 674
consonance, 13, 223, 337, 363–64, 464, 554, 574, 582, 889, 892
constellation, 257, 372, 431, 512, 538, 564, 748, 752, 835, 873, 891–92, 896, 898
contamination, 40, 73, 120, 124, 333, 344
coronation, 441, 480, 711, 747, 757–58, 794, 831
corpse, 60, 66, 72–73, 83, 124, 172, 184, 309, 334, 352, 440, 515, 626, 729, 794, 860
corruption, 254, 264, 464, 466, 647, 660, 717, 745–46, 771, 804, 819, 833, 840, 890
cosmos, 218, 220, 285, 287, 381, 396, 433, 441, 492–93, 499, 503, 506–7, 510, 555, 608, 628, 867
country, 111, 151, 157, 159, 163, 168, 201, 205, 276, 278, 315, 331, 334, 337, 345, 387, 447, 462, 490, 518, 622, 624, 657, 670, 706, 726, 759–60, 776, 786, 838
court, xxvii, 18, 83, 129–30, 134–35, 142, 145–46, 249, 255, 278, 300–1, 338–40, 343–44, 349–50, 456, 482, 496, 499, 610, 613–14, 619–20, 622, 768, 786–87, 826, 834, 859–60, 866
courtier, xlv, 289, 618, 621, 653
courts, 18, 39–42, 81, 137, 270, 279, 338–39, 486, 496, 503–4, 521, 620, 668, 755, 786–87
courtyard, 36, 338
covenant, 9, 12, 16–20, 22–29, 32–35, 40, 42, 46–47, 49, 52–54, 64–65, 68, 72, 76–78, 81, 84–87, 97–99, 101, 104–8, 111–13, 115, 119, 123–30, 132, 135, 141–42, 147, 149–50, 152, 156, 159–61, 163, 173, 175–77, 179–82, 189–91, 195–96, 204, 206, 208, 218, 221, 224, 227, 239–40, 246–50, 262–63, 271, 274, 276, 279–89, 291, 309, 315, 317, 319, 325–26, 330–32, 334–35, 342, 349, 355, 359, 369, 376–77, 385–88, 391–94, 406, 409, 412, 421, 427, 437–38, 441–43, 448–49, 453, 459–60, 462–63, 465–66, 468–72, 476, 480, 485, 487, 489–90, 492, 498–500, 502, 507–8, 510–12, 514, 516–17, 520, 523, 526–27, 535–36, 544–45, 569, 578, 580, 582, 589–90, 593, 608, 611, 622–24, 633, 637, 649, 659, 670–72, 674, 678, 680, 685, 690–92, 708, 712, 720, 736–40, 742, 746, 751, 753–56, 759, 765–66, 770, 781–82, 792, 794, 808, 815, 820, 824, 843, 847, 865–66, 868–69, 873, 875–77, 879–81, 894
covenantal, xix, xliii, 8, 17, 19, 23, 45, 52, 58, 61, 71, 85–86, 93, 99–101, 124, 144, 155, 177, 181–82, 202, 219, 239–42, 247, 263, 268–69, 271, 282, 285, 289, 295, 314, 332, 346, 360, 368, 370, 375–76, 381, 386, 388–90, 396, 420–21, 437–38, 451, 457, 461–62, 476, 495, 498–500, 505, 512, 514, 518, 527, 530–31, 533, 540–41, 544, 546, 566, 578, 582, 584–85, 589, 607–8, 614, 617, 622–24, 632–33, 649, 656, 659, 672, 675, 681, 684–86, 688, 739, 753, 759, 767–68, 781, 785, 792, 794, 807, 818, 866
covenant collection (Exod 21–23), 17–18, 20, 27–29, 32–34, 42, 46–47, 49, 54, 84, 87, 98, 101, 111–12, 119, 123–30, 135, 141–42, 150, 152, 274, 680, 815, 869, 892
covenant renewal collection (Exod 34:11–26), 17, 19–20, 24, 26–29, 35, 87, 106, 108, 132, 150, 869, 892, 894
coveting, 17, 28–29, 77, 103–4, 112, 133, 574
creation, 3–7, 19–22, 30–32, 97–98, 101–2, 146–47, 149, 160–61, 219, 223, 236–37, 246, 252–54, 258, 262, 269–70, 285, 309–10, 396, 433–34, 455, 474, 476, 481, 483, 503, 505–7, 528, 532–33, 540–42, 544, 549, 561, 563–64, 574, 600–1, 638, 671, 722, 865, 867–68
creator, 6–7, 21, 218, 236, 252, 309, 396, 435, 443, 455, 470, 531
creature, 5–7, 117, 149, 349, 434–35, 482–83, 490, 506
crime, 19, 23, 45–46, 54, 84, 103–4, 134, 143, 174, 185, 204, 220, 255, 316, 318, 361, 386–88, 633, 688, 786
crimson, 763
crisis, 7, 219–20, 252, 255, 427, 614, 668, 673, 806
crop, 28, 128, 250, 307, 331–32, 457, 639
crown, 257, 449–50, 554–55, 692, 777
crying, 72, 253, 275, 558, 671, 673, 816
cubit, 338, 458, 653
culpability, 26, 244, 314, 324, 330, 612, 748, 776, 821
cult/cultic, 18, 84, 105, 113, 118, 130, 150, 206, 217, 243, 255, 309, 360, 391, 474, 487, 514, 523, 567, 598, 658, 716, 730, 735, 776–78, 782, 786, 790, 820–21, 823–24, 830–31
culture, xxix, xxxv, 18, 176, 216, 474, 546, 593, 863, 890, 894, 896, 900
curse, 8–9, 17, 23, 32–33, 39, 45, 54, 68, 73, 78, 85, 96, 134, 138–39, 151–53, 160, 163, 174, 182, 227, 239–40, 252–54, 414, 427, 461, 464–66, 470, 472, 490–91, 519, 537, 562, 573, 581, 601, 606, 617, 622–24, 684–86, 689, 722, 825, 854, 894
Cush, 336, 436, 535
Cushite, 388, 782
cut, 22, 25, 52, 99, 101, 104, 117, 139, 142–43, 151, 157, 192, 231, 237, 247–48, 250, 272, 319, 322, 349, 408, 487, 520, 553, 621, 700, 720, 729, 746, 762, 783, 792, 816, 830, 832–33, 837, 848

Cyrus, 301, 640–42, 652–54, 698, 701, 716, 722, 819, 837, 839–42, 873, 879
Damascus, 209, 225, 291, 303, 387–89, 771, 806, 809, 812
Darius, 441, 445, 623, 652–54, 691, 840–41
darkness, xxvii, 146, 166, 172–73, 214, 256, 270, 315, 318, 328, 351, 382, 384, 436, 468, 497, 505, 510, 544, 549, 553, 556–57, 561–62
daughter, 21–22, 45, 50, 69, 73, 101–2, 126, 137–38, 172–73, 201, 215, 275, 303, 351, 354–55, 370, 412–13, 452, 456, 466, 468, 510, 546, 583, 590, 593, 604–6, 609–12, 690, 725, 737, 758, 770–72, 791–94
daughter-in-law, 355, 361, 390, 579, 655, 724
daughters, xxv, xxvii, 9, 25, 44, 60, 70–71, 73, 104–7, 162–63, 170, 172–73, 201, 223, 249, 293–94, 308, 318, 361, 369, 378, 452, 547, 580, 585–86, 590, 593, 598, 645, 657, 659–60, 676–78, 690, 781, 792, 810, 869
David, 10, 119, 158, 166, 171–73, 176, 179–92, 194–98, 201–2, 206, 208, 210–11, 215, 218, 226, 229, 247, 271, 276, 279, 281, 285–88, 304, 317, 330–32, 335, 346, 369, 371, 385–89, 391–94, 396, 402, 412–14, 427, 429, 431, 454, 472–73, 487–89, 492–93, 499–500, 521–23, 526–27, 534–37, 540, 544, 553, 555, 566, 578, 580, 589–90, 593, 615, 634, 654, 690, 692–95, 701–3, 705–6, 708–12, 715–20, 723–37, 739–58, 761–64, 766–68, 771–74, 776, 780–83, 788, 791–92, 795, 798, 800, 803, 812–13, 823–24, 826, 839, 841, 843–46, 856, 858–60, 866–68, 870–71, 874–75, 881
Davidic, 68, 115, 118–19, 171, 175–77, 181–82, 193, 195, 197, 206, 208, 218, 227, 246–47, 276, 279, 286–88, 291, 314, 317, 330, 335, 346, 358, 385, 388–94, 409–10, 412, 414, 441, 443, 448–50, 453–54, 474, 476, 480–81, 489–90, 492, 498–500, 517, 520–23, 526–29, 534, 538, 540, 580, 589–90, 593, 633, 698, 706–8, 712–13, 718–21, 723, 725, 729, 736, 738, 742–43, 751, 753, 756, 765, 773, 777, 781, 793–94, 805, 811, 816, 818, 821, 835, 837, 867, 871, 873, 875, 877, 879–81
Day of Atonement, 39, 55, 72–73, 122–23, 815
dead, 42, 61, 73, 123, 150, 152, 174, 308, 319, 352, 408, 541, 544, 557, 577, 585–89, 625–27, 707, 730, 831, 847, 892
death, xxvii, 5, 19, 22–23, 30, 45–46, 55, 63, 65–66, 69, 71, 73, 94–95, 101, 103–5, 108–9, 111, 122, 124, 132–34, 149, 151–52, 160, 176, 178, 183, 210–12, 214, 229, 231, 236–37, 253, 277–78, 280, 308–9, 319, 323–24, 343, 354, 358, 406, 408, 487, 493, 496, 535, 563, 565, 577, 583–84, 599–601, 619, 625–26, 688, 708, 715–17, 721, 728–29, 731, 737, 747, 757–58, 774–75, 781–82, 784–85, 790–91, 793–94, 796–99, 801, 803–5, 816, 818–19, 822–23, 826–32, 844–45, 848, 862, 867–68
debt, 46–52, 125–27, 141, 223, 288, 345, 639, 667–68, 677, 680, 734, 873, 882
debt-slave, 50–51, 126, 223
debtor, 49–50
deceiving, 8, 13, 184, 204, 275, 401, 896
decree, 285, 481, 493, 540, 652–54
decrees, xxiv, 39, 79, 136, 180, 191, 285, 324–29, 331, 334–35, 343, 360, 439, 454, 499, 543, 545, 787, 804
deer, 429, 540, 547
defeat, 73, 97, 149, 164, 169, 184, 208, 225, 227, 295, 395, 400, 402, 415, 424, 431, 488–89, 529, 542, 708, 744–46, 782, 784–85, 799–800, 805–6, 829
defile, 137, 238, 240–41, 243, 250, 268–69, 308, 319, 327–28, 333, 341, 464–65, 541, 604, 612, 645, 659, 725, 772, 812, 839, 874
defilement, 60, 124, 240, 268, 315, 318, 333–34, 344, 347, 354, 356, 660, 662, 796
delegate, xxiii, 34, 72, 225, 235, 241–42, 251, 284, 359, 363–64, 447–49, 460, 468, 484, 501, 608, 716, 749, 855
deliver, 52, 106, 111, 140, 156, 204–5, 231–32, 261, 321–22, 394, 433, 484, 497, 515, 518, 541, 556, 563, 565, 740, 800
deliverance, 72, 97, 100, 157, 160, 179, 228, 233, 378–79, 381, 429, 431, 507, 518, 544, 618, 671, 674, 740, 779, 788, 816–17
delivering, 99, 104, 158, 160, 193, 199, 202, 330, 360, 393, 406, 461, 483, 509, 515, 518, 521, 527, 530, 535, 625–26, 642, 703, 780, 797, 865
demon, 41, 149, 514, 777–78
denote, xxx, 5–6, 40, 98–99, 106, 170, 196, 239, 265, 306, 333, 341, 395–96, 414, 416, 445, 502, 511, 570, 606, 636, 658, 685, 715, 740, 776–77, 806, 824, 856–57, 895
denotation, 891–92
descendants, xxxiii, 2, 12, 32, 54, 61, 64, 70–71, 96, 110–11, 139, 158, 169–70, 191, 199, 201, 222–23, 231, 238, 248, 286–87, 336, 342, 378, 384, 387, 411, 422, 435, 440, 462, 465, 489, 508, 516, 520, 581, 586, 621–22, 643–45, 648, 656–58, 672, 684, 689, 740, 759, 781–82, 795, 804, 817, 840, 867, 889
desert, 28, 91, 139, 146, 163, 225, 236, 266, 270, 406, 462, 468, 479, 490, 517, 524–25, 536, 673, 789, 863–65
destroy, 52, 64–65, 104–5, 111, 156, 160, 162, 173, 199, 201, 246, 253, 269–70, 272–73, 283, 298, 305, 319, 401, 418, 428, 434, 514–16, 564, 597, 615, 779, 793, 836
destroying, 39, 95, 170, 263, 293–94, 357, 362, 387, 401, 414, 425, 446, 457–58, 622, 642, 779, 837
destruction, 10, 34, 77, 96, 105–8, 149, 155, 158, 160, 198, 221, 228, 234, 257, 276, 323, 330, 361, 374, 382, 392–93, 398, 400, 402, 404–5, 408, 430, 447, 541, 559, 608, 611, 628, 691, 706, 742, 806, 868
Deuteronomic, 113, 119, 124, 143–44, 149, 155, 157, 206, 209, 270–71, 302, 306, 318, 326, 348, 357, 511, 568, 571–73, 596, 637, 705, 892
Deuteronomistic, 189, 206–7, 209–10, 231, 271, 287, 305–6, 346, 439, 492, 512, 514, 572, 638, 664, 674, 704, 711, 716, 719, 745–46, 758, 766, 774, 778, 780, 783, 793–94, 798, 801, 808, 811, 816, 820, 824, 837, 842, 845–46, 912, 927
Deuteronomistic History, 195–96, 915–17, 919–20, 923, 925, 927
Deuteronomistic narrative/narrator, 10, 118, 157, 188–89, 192–93, 204, 209, 260–61, 270, 282, 301,

306, 310, 318, 493, 578, 611, 698, 705, 718–19, 753, 769, 777, 819, 870, 892
devote(d), devoting, devotion (to destruction, law of devoting) (also see herem/hrm), xxiii, 24, 28, 33–34, 59, 69, 72, 82, 88, 96–97, 105–7, 119, 134, 155–60, 164, 174, 188–89, 198–201, 267–68, 353, 420, 458, 480, 524, 661, 688, 690, 724, 866, 870, 873, 876, 879–80
devotion, 61, 99, 149, 182, 241, 246–47, 362, 386, 391, 418, 435, 470, 477, 486, 543, 593, 670, 672, 681, 701, 710, 731, 778, 794, 802–3, 818, 858
diachronic, xvii, xviii–xxix, xxxiv–xxxvi, 19, 46, 80, 92, 113–14, 132, 196, 265–66, 304, 359, 374, 383, 449–50, 537, 550, 562, 576, 661, 892–93, 895, 900
diaspora, 256, 325, 524, 529, 532, 552, 613, 670
diet, 7, 41, 82, 119–23, 125, 227, 248, 318, 357, 396, 457, 614
discipline, 135, 182, 275, 563, 565–66
disease, 141, 241–42, 440, 783, 791–92, 802–3, 809, 836, 860
disobedience, 19, 108, 326, 450, 494, 499–500, 812, 835–36
divorce, 78, 84, 137–38, 140, 268–69, 466–68, 591, 632, 655–56, 659–60, 670, 675–76, 678, 683–86, 688
dog, 42, 123, 554, 566
donkey, 27–28, 30, 67, 101–3, 135–36, 174, 184, 208, 275, 443, 452–53, 489, 497, 646, 681, 687, 748, 807, 809, 860, 867
door, 12, 172–73, 267
doublet, 257, 267, 304–5, 370, 374, 377, 380–81, 383–84, 445, 488, 539, 544, 576–77, 605, 809, 891
downfall, 176, 178, 203, 324, 401–2, 425, 446, 476, 492–94, 690, 711, 729, 775–76, 793, 801–2, 808–9, 834
dream, 8, 11, 378, 508–9, 617–22, 730, 861
drink, 17, 139, 291, 296, 304, 307, 343–44, 364, 376, 390–91, 393, 436, 439, 612, 651, 734, 894
dryness, 32, 164, 208, 214, 235–36, 248, 371, 381, 407, 437, 439, 540, 720
dust, 12–13, 72, 108, 226–27, 238, 253, 256, 329, 352, 391, 409, 414, 416, 419, 423, 489–90, 504, 542–43, 561, 564, 574, 595, 599–601, 604, 617, 624–25
duty, 135, 340, 573, 586, 795
dwell, 122, 171, 193, 195–97, 250, 304–5, 346, 352, 378, 381, 485, 523, 544, 557, 625, 639, 720, 736, 738–39, 750–51, 870
dwelling, 35–36, 40, 115, 128, 178, 193, 195, 207, 277, 307, 331, 347, 381, 456, 494, 528, 541, 665, 681, 702, 735, 739–40, 754, 769, 836
dying, 3–4, 41–42, 64, 72–73, 77, 82, 100, 131–32, 168, 178, 183, 202, 204, 210, 253, 269, 276, 280, 294, 306, 318–19, 323–24, 343, 353, 406–7, 412–13, 479, 485, 497, 509, 553, 584, 586, 600, 625, 715–17, 719, 731, 757, 783, 794, 796–98, 802, 828–30
eagle, 77, 146, 292, 296, 302, 311, 351, 399–400, 426–27, 430
earth, 5–7, 12, 19, 21–22, 32, 64, 68, 101, 107, 110, 115, 117, 122–23, 145–46, 153, 157, 168, 191–92, 205, 209, 213–15, 220–21, 245–46, 252–54, 270, 277, 296, 298, 303–4, 309, 321, 328–29, 337, 371–72, 381–82, 397, 418–19, 426–28, 432, 439, 441–43, 446, 455–57, 459, 472, 481, 483, 489–91, 497–98, 500, 502–6, 510, 513, 520–21, 525, 531, 533, 538, 540–43, 545–46, 549, 556, 561, 563–64, 574, 581, 595, 599–600, 621, 625, 629, 653, 739–40, 749, 754, 784, 841
eat, xxvii–xxviii, xxxi, 3–4, 17, 25, 27, 40, 42–43, 60–61, 72, 104, 112, 117, 123, 128, 133, 139, 177, 180, 241, 253, 273, 280, 304, 307, 311, 313, 316, 318–19, 323, 331, 349, 353, 355, 366, 381, 401, 440, 453–54, 489, 600, 602, 625, 645, 660, 681, 733, 894
eating, 4, 7, 33, 40–42, 55, 60, 72, 82, 84, 116–17, 120–23, 125, 146, 174, 227, 248, 280, 309, 318, 353, 366, 396, 450, 552, 610, 612, 679, 813, 827, 866
echo, xviii, 62, 66, 72, 152–53, 174, 194, 204, 220, 246, 250, 325, 347–48, 351–52, 406, 447, 455, 463, 466, 476, 509, 512, 514, 518, 526, 546, 563, 572, 574, 592, 601, 622, 655, 665, 690–91, 712, 720, 760–61, 768–69, 792, 812, 836–37, 889, 893–94, 896, 900–1
echo-effect, 3, 9–10, 167, 172, 615, 618, 620, 715–16, 720–21, 820, 830, 845, 854, 856, 894, 898, 902
echoes, xx–xxii, xxxvii, 8, 31, 35, 72, 165–66, 173, 176, 184, 189, 203, 205, 217, 237, 241, 254, 268, 321, 350–52, 354–55, 360, 367, 376, 403–4, 406, 425–26, 431–32, 434, 436, 455–56, 469, 489, 505, 514, 516, 524, 532, 534, 561, 567, 572, 574, 601, 616, 618, 622, 628, 659, 664, 667–68, 712, 719, 721, 742, 749, 753, 762, 766, 774, 797, 802, 814, 857, 874, 889, 893, 897, 901
economy, 5, 26, 39, 46, 103–4, 129, 180, 266, 316, 321, 336, 345, 438–39, 442, 474, 574, 679, 764
Eden, 114, 252, 255, 352, 354, 374, 382
edict, 301, 615, 640–41, 652, 654, 698, 701, 722, 819, 837, 839–41
Edom, 72, 79, 94–96, 139, 144, 149, 157, 169, 200, 208, 255, 262, 291, 295–97, 303–4, 353–54, 357, 371, 383, 386–89, 392–95, 398–402, 431, 436, 461–62, 470, 481, 488–89, 549, 584, 607, 715, 722, 788, 790–91, 799–800, 805–6, 812, 874
Edomite, 143, 164, 201, 462, 536, 580, 657–58, 715, 722, 799–800
Edomites, 95, 139, 200–2, 240, 341, 400, 402, 462, 488, 535, 581–82, 657, 690, 745, 788, 799–800, 809, 891
Egypt, xxvi, 10–12, 27–28, 31, 40, 42–44, 50–51, 55–56, 59, 61–62, 64–67, 73, 85, 88, 93, 97, 100, 102, 110–11, 128, 138–39, 141, 143–44, 146–47, 149, 159, 162, 173, 179, 195–96, 198–200, 202–3, 205, 207–9, 219, 224–26, 231, 235, 237, 242, 245, 255–56, 262, 264, 267, 273, 281, 283–84, 290–91, 300, 304–5, 307, 309, 324–25, 328, 330–31, 345, 354, 357–58, 366, 369, 382–83, 387–89, 395, 406, 410, 417, 419, 437, 441, 459, 461, 490, 492–93, 495, 507, 510, 512–13, 515, 528, 530–31, 533, 542, 581, 584, 606–7, 667, 671, 673, 684, 723, 735, 759–60, 763–64, 771, 829, 831, 855, 874, 891, 902
Egyptian, 10, 17, 42–43, 45, 72, 201, 208, 235, 563, 580, 657–58, 725, 772, 832, 866
Egyptians, 53, 64–65, 110–11, 144, 184, 200, 202, 240, 331, 341, 406, 416, 461, 529, 581–82, 641, 657–58, 690, 788

Elam, 291, 295, 297, 311, 643–44, 648
elders, 160, 168, 193, 238, 251, 277–78, 321, 383, 575, 586, 731, 749
Eleazar, 70, 163, 342, 516
election, 188, 195, 197, 249–50, 252, 282, 285, 309, 320, 339, 342–43, 379, 397, 476, 492–95, 510, 526, 528, 672, 705, 724–25, 738–40, 750, 753, 755, 762, 781, 812, 865, 870
eleventh, 143, 670
Elhanan, 746
Eliezer, 648, 714, 790
Elihu, 552, 561
Elijah, 189–90, 203–4, 208, 406–7, 439, 460, 470, 648, 714, 784, 791–92
Eliphaz, 546–48, 555–57, 561, 563, 565
Elisha, 206, 784
Elkanah, 69, 184, 726–27
empire, 19, 217–19, 225–26, 247, 250, 266, 386–87, 389, 392–94, 407, 412, 416, 424, 441, 444, 511, 529–30, 532, 553, 617, 620, 631, 633, 646, 670, 673–74, 682, 688, 699, 722, 744, 746, 841, 868, 900
encampment (also see camp), 42, 58–60, 63, 66, 73, 86, 88, 94, 140, 464, 683, 772, 860
enemies, 7–8, 53, 112, 118–19, 140, 180, 192–93, 209, 238, 283, 337, 351, 383, 410, 414–16, 422–24, 429, 431, 439, 481, 484, 490, 513–14, 520–22, 526, 531, 535, 540, 606–7, 611, 656, 666, 732, 742–43, 754, 769, 771, 800, 820, 838, 861, 881
enemy, 33, 135–36, 227, 238, 254, 278, 349, 381, 384, 410, 415–16, 427, 429, 488, 520, 566, 604, 606, 683, 806, 808, 831, 860, 874
Ephraim, 163, 166–68, 307, 309, 359–60, 362, 366, 370, 454, 476, 492–94, 508, 510, 590, 707, 716, 725–26, 728, 776, 786, 799, 805–9, 813, 824
Ephraimite, 726, 800, 807
Ephrathah, 409–10, 412–14, 526, 735
Esarhaddon, 255, 278–79
Esau, 8, 96, 139, 364–65, 370–71, 387, 398, 400–2, 460–62, 470, 590, 722
eschatology, 222, 253, 276, 379, 382–83, 441, 448, 451–52, 627
ethnicity, 106, 124, 139, 155, 157, 160, 189, 239, 241–42, 248–49, 322, 340, 580–81, 588–89, 606, 656, 658, 661, 684–86, 707, 777
eunuch, xlv, 239–40, 247–48, 580, 817, 874
euphemistic/euphemism, xxxii, xlvii, 96, 144–45, 238, 242, 356, 359, 364, 366, 464, 482–83, 503, 565, 809–10
Euphrates, 12, 28, 138, 163, 208–9, 235, 489–90, 759, 771, 829
Eve, 455, 854, 894
evening, 42, 60, 123, 140, 164, 180, 436, 506, 538, 579, 689, 691, 740, 815, 830
evil, xxxi, 3–4, 17, 64, 90, 110, 135, 140, 148, 179, 210, 254, 261, 307–8, 322, 360, 397, 405, 418, 445, 453, 457, 461, 519, 549, 571, 573, 666, 687, 715, 717, 721, 778–80, 822, 834, 836, 900
excrement, 140, 318, 356, 464
exegetical advance, xvii, xli–xlii, 18, 20, 24, 29–30, 43–44, 59, 71, 81, 109, 112, 121, 133, 136, 158, 161, 177, 181–82, 194, 220, 234, 240, 243, 249, 263, 274, 282, 286, 293, 317, 324, 342–43, 362, 375, 377, 386, 406–7, 411, 415, 444, 476, 479, 485–86, 490, 494, 497, 499, 512–13, 560, 578, 582, 605, 607, 618, 690–91, 705–6, 718–22, 751, 753, 802, 807, 811–14, 853, 859, 865, 867–68, 870–72, 881
exile, xxxiv, 52–53, 161, 170, 174, 188, 207, 219, 225, 231, 234–36, 241, 248, 250, 266, 279, 295, 311, 315, 322, 324, 330, 332–33, 350, 352, 357, 393, 396, 407, 418, 424–25, 436–37, 440, 445–46, 461, 485, 500, 510, 514, 519, 552, 558, 611–13, 618–19, 623–24, 633, 650, 664–65, 670, 674, 678–79, 701, 704, 708, 726–28, 756, 794, 805–6, 809, 811–12, 818–19, 832–35, 837–39, 841, 845, 852, 855, 866, 901
exiles, 248, 250, 258, 279, 285, 301, 350, 436, 438, 442, 446–47, 451, 459, 509, 511–12, 558, 632–33, 642–43, 649–50, 656, 659, 668, 670, 678, 683, 701, 726–28, 806, 819–20, 842, 902
exilic, 217, 244, 246, 266–67, 287, 380, 392–93, 446, 449–50, 476, 499, 532, 552–53, 580, 670, 726, 819–20
exodus, 10, 28, 85, 218–20, 225–26, 231, 235, 237–38, 241–43, 245–46, 251–52, 281, 309, 325, 379, 387, 395, 431, 439, 443, 448–49, 460–61, 468–69, 476, 500, 524, 544, 553, 615, 632, 641, 650, 764, 811, 855, 866, 873, 877, 879–80, 901–2
eye, 4, 7, 17, 39, 46, 77, 134, 142–43, 146, 215, 267, 288, 318, 320, 357, 386, 459, 539, 569, 610, 733, 765, 851
eyes, xl, 4, 12, 76–78, 99, 116, 129, 147–48, 168, 171, 185, 210, 224, 257, 260, 263, 269, 283–84, 308, 311, 329–30, 380, 382, 397, 467, 472, 515, 517–18, 525, 548–49, 564, 578, 580, 583, 595, 598–99, 609–10, 629, 664–65, 717, 749, 757, 769–70, 778, 780, 784, 787, 796, 802, 804, 820, 822, 830, 834, 838, 866, 900
Ezrahite, 534, 536
fabric, 83, 136–37
face, xxv, 63–65, 99, 107–8, 110, 122–23, 138, 147, 164, 204, 242, 245, 253, 288, 298, 322, 336, 350, 364, 378, 382, 425, 434, 464–65, 477, 490, 506, 515, 540, 543, 546, 548, 554, 559–61, 565, 574, 583, 598, 612, 614, 702, 705, 721, 739–40, 749–50, 767–68, 770, 779, 788, 813, 820, 834, 836, 868
faith, 90, 92, 94, 157–59, 173, 204, 223, 230, 379, 426–27, 432, 484, 489, 517, 656, 672, 674, 685, 688, 714, 789, 811, 866–67, 876
faithful (also see fidelity), 24, 61, 107–8, 148, 155, 157, 241, 246–47, 262, 268, 280, 379, 416, 421, 459, 485, 498, 517, 531, 543, 560, 572, 623, 627, 672, 675, 682, 740, 766, 786, 811, 816, 827
faithfulness, xlii, 24, 64, 109, 122, 168, 179, 191, 230, 239, 269, 286–88, 375–76, 405, 415, 423, 438, 484–85, 493, 498–500, 504–5, 520, 523, 530, 545, 552, 560, 569, 604, 607–8, 622, 633, 642, 649, 659, 665, 670, 672–73, 720, 780, 783, 787, 797, 811, 816, 818, 845, 876
false, xxii, xxviii, 8, 17, 31, 34, 54, 67, 71, 73–75, 77, 82, 105–6, 116, 118–19, 132, 134, 148, 155, 161–62, 166, 174, 198, 207–9, 256, 262, 269, 278, 309, 315–16, 348, 354, 418, 433, 455, 465, 486, 492, 530, 540, 571, 573, 666, 668, 690, 713, 716, 778, 800, 806, 809, 842, 863, 897
fame, xxv, 196–97, 199, 272–73, 436, 711, 736

families, 12, 26, 70, 72–73, 79, 125, 128, 328, 502–3, 557, 646–48, 655, 675, 722, 726–27, 740, 777, 787, 793, 826
family, 5, 7, 47, 49–51, 59, 66, 68, 70–72, 82, 119, 128, 149, 155, 157–58, 166, 174–75, 184, 339, 342–45, 414, 441, 454, 567, 578, 584, 586, 641, 647, 661, 669, 723–26, 734, 737, 755, 791–92, 863, 865, 868
famine, 143, 273, 288–89, 299, 318, 349–50, 507, 565, 612, 696
farmer, 54, 65, 129
fast, 163, 201, 204, 240, 248, 256, 273, 376–77, 383, 443, 450–51, 614
fat, 27, 34–35, 175–78, 224, 309, 342, 454, 750, 767, 827–28
father, 2, 6–8, 32, 45, 63, 69–71, 102, 104, 135, 137–38, 143, 149, 151, 163, 176, 182, 184, 191–92, 195–96, 198, 201, 204, 210, 251, 255, 269, 283, 286, 307, 323, 355–56, 365, 385, 390–91, 394, 409, 413–14, 460, 463–64, 466, 470, 480–81, 499–500, 504–5, 520–22, 527, 544, 562–63, 568–70, 574, 576–77, 583, 586, 590, 621, 690, 698, 707, 715, 717, 724–25, 743, 750, 754–55, 763, 773–74, 783, 790–91, 797, 799, 804, 811, 822
father-in-law, 32, 62, 496, 761, 772
fatherlessness (also see orphan), 88, 124, 271, 281, 297, 307, 355, 401, 457, 497, 520, 541, 573, 583, 681
favor, 48, 64, 110, 115, 145, 155, 171, 197, 227, 245, 282–83, 314, 345, 361, 364–65, 368, 372, 392, 399, 450, 467, 498, 504, 565, 572, 583, 588, 612, 622, 625, 627, 646, 657, 666, 679, 685, 741, 749, 778, 820, 840, 849–50
feast, 29, 116, 124, 227, 257, 346, 397, 450–51, 602, 651, 843
feet, 8, 135, 163–64, 182, 192, 215, 241, 273, 288, 420, 423–25, 429, 472, 480–82, 489–90, 509, 520, 522, 540, 547, 554, 570–71, 612, 621, 754, 783
female, 2, 5, 21–22, 44, 48–51, 58, 60, 69–71, 83, 101–3, 126–27, 149, 152, 223, 275, 288, 314, 350–51, 385, 390, 425, 459, 482, 506, 579–80, 582, 585–87, 606, 646, 792, 860, 869
females, 51–52, 69–70, 107, 127, 582, 589, 598
fertility, 226, 293, 873, 875
festival, 27–28, 34, 55, 72–74, 82, 124–25, 128–29, 143, 150, 208, 288, 397, 424–25, 450, 452, 465, 485, 494, 542, 635, 651–52, 668, 677, 680, 692, 701, 768, 772–73, 815, 897
Festival of Tabernacles, 55, 129, 208, 288, 452, 485, 494, 542, 635, 652, 668, 680, 692, 768, 773
Festival of tabernacles, 27, 34
Festival of Unleavened Bread, 27, 128–29, 485, 773
Festival of Weeks, 28, 55, 128, 143, 485, 773
Festival of weeks, 27, 34
fidelity (also see faithful[ness]), 21, 24, 93, 104, 108, 167–68, 202, 224, 239–40, 248–49, 271, 276, 285, 288, 318, 332, 335, 342, 375–76, 379, 412, 420, 485–86, 498, 560, 607–8, 614, 617, 622, 649, 670, 672, 685–86, 717, 738, 740, 778, 784, 816, 818
field, 28–30, 67, 84, 125, 128, 136, 150, 188–89, 204–5, 230–31, 273, 277–78, 281, 307, 309, 331–32, 338, 412, 418, 495, 526, 540, 573–74, 579–80, 583, 588–89, 594, 667–68, 735, 803
fig, 191, 193, 205, 222, 229, 232–34, 279, 350, 370, 382, 409–12, 443, 448, 451, 687, 894
fighting, 45, 142, 156, 164, 179, 254, 502, 521, 535, 613, 754, 780, 788, 808, 830, 891
figural (also see typological), 6, 131, 188–90, 194, 204, 219–20, 241, 252, 333–34, 477, 509, 523, 562, 580, 606, 618, 650, 711–12, 715, 719, 720, 757, 767, 817, 830, 842, 845, 854–56, 862–63, 894, 901–3, 910, 916
fire, 19, 30, 54, 60, 65–66, 71–72, 76–77, 99–100, 104–5, 131, 174, 203–4, 207, 215, 221, 263, 273, 275, 292, 294, 304, 307–8, 311, 321, 326, 343, 349, 357, 396, 402, 430, 448, 458–59, 461, 468, 470, 500, 542, 625, 628, 639, 677, 680, 687, 702, 716, 720, 735, 749–50, 761, 767–68, 783, 803, 809–10, 827–28, 845, 856
firstborn, 17, 27–28, 58–59, 67–68, 73, 83, 125, 127–28, 151, 309, 326–27, 480, 493, 500, 528, 530–31, 533, 635, 639, 681, 725, 755
firstfruits, 27–28, 35, 55, 65, 68, 72, 84, 128–29, 143–44, 147, 208, 267–68, 567, 570, 572, 677, 681–82, 815, 860, 891
firstling, 33, 82, 127–28, 326
fish, 5–6, 149, 311, 403, 434–35, 482, 505
flesh, 2, 341, 379
flock, 2, 296, 409
flood, xxiv, 6, 7, 31, 52, 64, 227–29, 246, 254, 270, 322, 361, 434, 439, 469, 601, 628
folly, 577, 598, 704, 775, 800
food, 4, 12, 41, 50, 121, 126–28, 139, 150, 159, 177, 180, 223, 253, 304, 308–9, 331, 356, 396, 440, 453, 457, 464–65, 487, 541, 545, 600, 645, 651, 687, 692
fool, 173, 454, 540, 573, 576–77, 596–99, 603, 784
foot, 96, 139, 142, 163, 349, 387, 501, 547, 551, 569
footstool, 522, 526, 542–43, 735, 753–54
forbidden, 20, 52, 97, 112, 120, 136–37, 199, 202, 238, 318, 325, 394, 457–58, 567, 607, 659, 689, 858
foreign, 26, 31, 126, 201, 228, 271, 360, 387, 395, 466, 468, 495, 575, 613–14, 620, 637, 656, 662, 690–91, 762–63, 782, 786, 793, 799–800, 806, 808
foreigner(s), xxvi, 21–22, 30, 33, 35, 40, 42–48, 50, 61, 88–89, 101–2, 117, 120–21, 123–26, 129, 142, 150, 153, 201, 207, 239–40, 242, 247–50, 271, 275, 280–81, 307, 316, 322, 333, 340–41, 344–46, 355, 378, 381, 394, 451, 452, 457, 497, 508, 540, 545, 548, 578–79, 580–85, 589, 656–67, 661, 678–79, 681, 685, 688, 766, 807–8, 839, 858–61, 866, 874
foreskin, 40, 52
forest, 224, 278, 414, 419, 542
forever, xx, xxxiii, 12, 22, 64, 67, 111, 119, 163–64, 183, 191–92, 195, 221, 234, 245, 247, 249, 252–53, 286, 331, 335, 347, 415, 447, 452, 473, 490–91, 495, 499–500, 504, 506, 513, 523, 527, 531, 533, 538, 544–47, 584, 606–7, 625, 629, 660, 684, 691, 743–44, 751, 755–56, 762, 765, 768–69, 781–82, 789, 843

forgetting, 99, 246, 358, 366, 484, 493, 524, 568–69
forgive, 20, 65, 207, 283–85, 324, 406, 415, 469, 548–49, 608, 624, 665, 702, 721, 769–70, 779, 813–14, 820, 834, 836
forgiveness, 24, 32, 64–65, 204, 207, 243–44, 246, 282, 285, 404, 406–7, 415, 417, 421, 472, 504, 622, 661, 720, 724, 770, 779, 813–14, 838, 866
forgiving, 23, 406, 415, 721–22, 814
formula, xxix, xxx–xxxii, 112, 206, 210, 229, 258, 357, 380, 571, 613, 634, 636–37, 713, 715, 717, 790, 792, 794, 803, 827, 857
fornication, 73, 77, 151, 385, 390, 792
fortieth, 63
forty, 30, 62, 99, 108, 110, 149, 202–3, 395, 437, 501–2, 524, 717, 817–18, 839
foundation, 442–43, 448–49, 455, 457, 497, 525, 545, 549, 640, 653, 691, 773, 873, 879
foundling, 314, 350–51
free, xxvi, xxxi, 3–4, 42, 49–51, 103, 126–27, 151, 215, 219, 288, 300, 318, 345–46, 351, 357, 459, 473, 510–11, 531, 597, 638, 640, 652, 704, 757, 842
freedom, xxix, 4, 49, 288–89, 302, 316, 863
freewill, 55, 641, 646, 653, 797, 841
friend, xxi, 82, 147, 208, 238, 401, 552, 554–55, 557–59, 561, 564, 581, 614, 660, 843, 876
fruit, 4, 40, 52, 272, 319, 331–33, 436, 479–80, 495, 520, 527, 574, 592, 594, 639, 677, 681, 839
fulfillment, 8, 29, 44, 53, 60, 68, 163, 167, 178, 184, 193, 195, 198, 209, 253, 278, 284, 286–87, 301, 319, 330, 332, 335, 346, 351, 408, 424–25, 427, 444, 446–47, 480–81, 489–90, 492, 546, 574, 586–87, 596–98, 623, 633, 641–42, 649–50, 665, 701, 710, 714–16, 720, 738, 742, 751, 759–60, 763–65, 767, 769, 772, 775, 779, 830, 839, 841, 849, 855–57, 862–63, 866, 894, 902
Gad, 96, 707, 714, 734
garden, xxxi, 3–4, 9, 30, 114, 210, 227, 252, 352, 354, 382, 594, 601, 612, 722, 819, 854, 894
garment, 36, 53, 136–37, 150, 238, 343, 351, 376–77, 391, 439–40, 452, 467, 473, 497, 598, 646, 659, 668
gate, 160, 256, 270, 299, 302, 307, 323, 338, 366, 385, 391, 486, 575, 579–80, 585–86, 734, 804
gatekeepers, 249, 270, 644, 646–47, 651, 678, 728, 747, 751, 773, 795, 824, 826
gates, 199, 256, 270, 274–75, 307, 395, 486, 525, 567, 569, 687–88, 773, 795
Gath, 184, 536, 708, 730, 746, 788
Geba, 644, 823
Gedaliah, 300–1, 648
genealogy, 64, 106–7, 139, 155, 158, 241, 248, 322, 578, 580–81, 588–89, 606, 656, 658–59, 661–62, 678, 684–86, 689, 706–7, 719, 722–27, 733, 735, 839–40
generation, 23–26, 61, 63, 65, 73, 78, 85–86, 90–91, 93, 99–100, 107, 152, 166–69, 173, 201, 238–39, 248, 262–63, 272, 281, 285–86, 308, 314, 316, 318, 324–28, 330, 341, 345, 382, 423, 478, 493–96, 498, 501–2, 504, 514, 520, 559–60, 566–71, 581–82, 588, 606, 629, 657, 684, 687, 689, 691, 716, 726, 751, 818–19, 835, 837, 839–40, 897
generations, 3, 5, 12, 22, 63, 71, 86, 107, 177, 200, 216, 237, 280, 311, 314, 325, 328, 343, 368, 407, 423, 446, 462, 499, 505, 511, 516, 544, 580–82, 598, 623, 629, 650, 658, 670, 699, 707, 722, 726, 764, 821, 839–40
genre, xxii, xliii, 71, 219, 294–95, 390, 407, 475, 496, 551, 562, 567, 590, 603, 614, 619–20, 798, 856, 862, 894, 897, 899, 902
gentile, 124, 157, 176, 215, 248–49, 313, 394, 404, 421, 428, 457, 472–73, 539, 660–61, 667, 711, 845, 858–59, 866–67
Gershon, 726
Gezer, 167, 758, 771
ghost, 730–31
giant, 63, 95, 97, 730, 746
Gibeah, 166, 171–74, 361, 367, 369
Gibeon, 159, 228, 615, 643, 740–42, 757–58, 760, 768–69
Gibeonite, 155, 199, 340, 708, 744
Gideon, 179, 225, 844
gift(s), 69, 115, 120, 126, 128–29, 200, 216, 273, 327, 418, 436, 473, 490, 495, 504, 506, 524, 592, 599, 641, 754, 760, 771, 815, 872
Gilead, 70, 163, 369, 392, 609–10
Gilgal, 159, 370, 397, 417
Girgashites, 104, 158, 199, 657, 672
glean/gleaning(s), 84, 150, 258, 309, 401, 578–79, 581–85, 589, 874
glory, 35, 39–40, 42, 54, 100, 137, 178, 189, 194–96, 198, 203, 207, 258, 268, 328, 347, 349, 353, 355, 368, 370, 426, 428, 448, 482, 502–3, 506–7, 513, 518, 538, 554, 562, 712, 716, 720, 739–40, 764–65, 767–68, 772, 855–56, 860, 891, 902
goat, 12, 41, 119–21, 123–24, 184, 253, 777–78
gods, 10, 17, 25–26, 33–34, 104–6, 119, 150, 155, 161–62, 168–69, 173–74, 197–98, 201–3, 205, 208, 222, 226, 231, 261, 268, 271, 281, 294, 307–8, 351, 358, 360, 368–69, 411, 423, 433, 451–52, 473, 494–97, 503, 522, 528, 530–31, 542, 619, 653, 657, 690, 729–30, 735, 761, 778, 792, 799–800, 805–6, 808–10, 836, 851, 870
Gog, 336–37, 352, 375, 378, 549
gold, 26, 29, 36, 39, 43, 58, 109–11, 136, 161, 174, 189, 200, 202–4, 207, 284, 310, 321, 363, 366–68, 404, 406, 433, 458, 490, 498, 541, 593, 608, 621, 641, 646, 653, 671, 676, 762–64, 776, 790, 832–33, 841
Goliath, 718, 746
Gomer, 268, 336, 370
Gomorrah (also see cities of the plain), 221, 304–5, 362, 395, 436, 878
gospel, xxi, xl, xlvi, 220, 394, 417, 544, 660, 847–49, 858, 861, 866, 868, 892, 902
Gospel(s), xxi, xxxvii, xli, 226, 444, 652, 753, 853, 857, 861–62, 869, 871, 910, 916, 922, 924, 934
grace, xlvi, 109, 262, 378, 403, 464, 498, 569, 675
gracious, 20, 23–24, 64, 108, 185, 375–76, 405, 415, 422–23, 464–65, 474, 498, 504, 528, 540–41, 543–44, 605, 608, 673, 779, 898–99
grain, 11, 55, 58, 65, 273, 287, 376, 397, 442, 557, 583, 606, 627, 651, 681, 687, 866
grandchildren, 24, 26, 422
grandson, 174, 178, 266, 278, 440–41, 589
grape, 77, 88, 279–80, 323, 331, 401, 452, 495, 552, 610, 687
gratitude, xlvii, 144, 531–33, 744, 867
grief, 11–12, 234, 293, 343, 576–77, 607, 610–12

ground, 5–6, 8, 13, 17, 32, 66, 116–17, 120–21, 149, 164, 184, 208, 236, 241, 308, 310, 314, 331–32, 354, 391, 395, 399, 434–35, 448–49, 482, 490, 504, 506, 525, 540, 556, 561, 583, 600, 659, 681, 733, 745, 768, 838, 854
guilt, 94, 243–46, 314, 316, 324, 350, 369, 447, 487, 559, 605, 611, 660–62, 664, 670, 692, 714, 807, 822, 835, 839, 844
guilt offering (also see reparation offering), 243–46, 660–62, 692
guilty, 24, 65, 69, 130, 142, 204, 244, 267, 421, 423, 488, 496–97, 505, 520, 558, 560, 589, 596–97, 844, 896
hair, 139, 184, 242, 308, 343–44, 349, 891–92
Ham, 336, 490, 510
Hamath, 256, 389, 735, 771
Hamon, 336–37
hand, xix, xxi, 8, 29, 32, 51, 64, 93, 102, 104–5, 110–11, 119, 134, 142–44, 147–48, 156, 170, 178, 180, 195, 198, 203, 205, 216, 218, 235, 239, 241, 244–45, 253, 257, 264–65, 268, 284, 297, 306, 315, 325, 359, 362, 364, 379, 390, 414, 434, 440, 447–48, 450, 454, 462, 473, 488, 497, 501–2, 504, 514–16, 522–24, 532–33, 535, 542, 546, 548, 553, 556, 562–63, 565, 567, 577, 600, 624, 629, 635–36, 642, 653, 682, 702, 734, 746, 749, 756, 766, 800, 803–4, 817, 821, 851–52, 861, 865, 874
hands, 26, 28, 45, 106, 111, 136, 191, 193, 204, 215, 235, 238, 242, 261, 296, 303, 330–31, 349, 407, 418, 465, 472, 482, 486, 494, 499–501, 524, 527, 530, 546–47, 554, 556, 563–64, 569, 575, 583, 597, 602, 606, 608, 621, 662, 666, 706, 743, 765, 780, 788, 795, 797, 800, 836, 842
Hannah, 10, 69, 176, 183–84, 430
harvest, 19, 28, 30, 84, 88, 143, 267, 273, 309, 331, 370, 384, 583, 677, 679
hate, xlvi, 23, 25, 77, 93, 107–9, 111, 135, 151, 370, 391, 393, 397, 408, 418, 423, 460–62, 466–68, 472–73, 495, 515, 520, 559–60
head, 3, 24, 45, 102, 111, 115, 126, 151, 183, 227, 292, 376, 381, 383, 406–8, 431, 466, 477, 488, 546, 551, 554, 558, 593, 657, 708, 710, 723, 729–30, 733, 736, 746, 789
heads, 11, 70, 78–79, 112, 126, 136, 238, 257, 276, 284, 331, 391, 477, 541, 586, 621, 641, 646–47, 669, 675, 710, 723, 725, 787, 794–95
headwaters, 12, 80, 119, 224–25, 361, 395, 848
healing, 224, 229, 232–34, 243–46, 304, 453–54, 563, 609–10, 702, 721, 770, 779, 813–14, 820, 827, 834, 836–37, 845
hear, 4, 9, 50, 65, 77, 92, 100, 129–31, 135, 185, 220–21, 224, 228, 263, 273, 283–84, 296, 303, 311, 501–2, 547, 603, 664–65, 690, 702, 720–21, 766, 769–70, 779, 787, 813–14, 820, 834, 836, 897
hearing, 45, 53, 65, 69, 89, 100, 111, 131, 143–44, 147, 171, 178, 192, 204, 209, 232, 253, 289, 293, 296, 298, 303, 399–400, 408, 474, 480, 494–95, 512, 514, 540–41, 543, 573, 585, 587–88, 673, 684, 746, 751, 769, 813, 825, 827, 856
heart, xxxii, 52, 77, 79, 85–86, 96–97, 99, 139, 148, 150, 155, 159, 163, 176, 184, 191, 196, 200–1, 205, 209, 224, 245, 251, 282–85, 292–93, 296, 298, 302, 305, 314, 317–18, 320–22, 324, 334–35, 340–41, 348, 354, 357, 362, 366–67, 376–77, 399, 436, 456, 486–88, 494–95, 502, 504, 512, 521, 523, 547–49, 565, 568–69, 593, 595, 598–99, 640, 672, 690, 701–2, 704, 737, 754, 769, 779–80, 813, 817–18, 825, 838, 841–44, 869
hearts, 52–53, 77, 93, 159–60, 164, 224, 235, 252, 256, 263, 283–86, 296, 302, 307, 309, 321, 334–35, 377, 456, 470, 473, 485, 487, 495, 502, 506, 552, 568–69, 599, 740, 769, 778, 820, 866
heaven, 17, 107, 156–57, 215, 221, 253, 258, 298, 366, 437, 442–43, 455, 473, 481, 496, 508, 522, 531, 545–47, 620, 622, 624, 629, 640, 653, 720–21, 749–50, 767–70, 779, 813, 820, 834, 836, 841, 856
heavens (also see sky), 5–6, 13, 21–22, 77, 86, 93, 101, 105, 149, 153, 209, 213–15, 220–21, 227, 245, 252, 270, 277, 308–9, 371, 381–83, 418, 434, 437, 439, 441, 455, 457, 469, 481–82, 499, 504–6, 531, 533, 541, 545, 549, 563, 565–66, 574, 627–28, 664, 671, 702, 740, 762, 769–70, 868
Hebron, 167, 682, 724, 729
heifer, 72, 309, 366, 370
heir, 202, 441, 511, 585, 588, 743
herd, 28, 127–28, 366, 482, 487, 681
herem/hrm (also see devote/devoting/devotion), 34, 69, 72, 97, 105–6, 158, 198, 458, 724
Heshbon, 292–94, 396
Hezekiah, 148, 189, 204–5, 212–14, 225, 229–34, 252, 277, 519, 566, 574, 701, 703, 713, 716–17, 721, 770, 777, 805, 807, 809–19, 827, 835, 838, 841–46
high priest, 69, 72, 160, 174, 176, 344, 354, 381, 441, 448–49, 461, 463–64, 538, 640, 662, 726, 824, 840, 866, 891
highway, 225–26, 235–36, 468
hill, 163, 168, 207–9, 221–22, 236, 270, 277–78, 298, 315, 331, 358, 360–61, 378, 381, 387, 399, 411, 440–41, 449, 462–63, 466, 469–70, 524, 542, 621, 635, 670, 706, 726, 738, 776, 786
Hinnom, 256, 304, 308, 311–12, 336–37, 683, 809–10, 821
Hiram, 188, 191–94, 208, 388, 521, 712, 732, 753, 758, 761–64, 770–71
historical, xix, xxi, xxxv, xxxvii–xxxix, xli, xliv, 79–80, 139, 161, 166, 183, 226, 228, 262, 279, 292, 295, 301, 303, 310, 341, 351, 367, 374, 388–89, 410, 462, 475–76, 488, 531, 534, 537, 567, 590, 598, 619, 638, 673, 700, 713–14, 717, 738, 775, 780–81, 790–91, 797, 799–800, 807, 829, 831, 849, 852, 854, 862, 892–93, 896, 900
history, xix, xxi, xxxvii–xxxviii, 85, 100, 144, 189, 195–96, 228, 264–66, 314, 427, 450, 492, 518, 530, 567, 634, 636, 638, 646, 701, 703, 706, 713–14, 723, 726, 741–42, 796, 821, 849, 852, 860, 862, 893, 897
Hittite, 92, 103, 119, 208, 709, 733, 756, 863
Hittites, 25, 28, 67, 104, 158, 199–202, 657, 672, 690
Hivites, 25, 28, 67, 104, 158–59, 199, 254, 657
holiness, 22, 39–41, 53–54, 60, 66–68, 81, 87–88, 111, 120, 123, 125, 128, 136–37, 140–41, 151–52, 181, 240, 314–18, 321–22, 325, 334, 339–44, 347–48, 353, 355–57, 381, 428, 439, 448, 486, 517–18, 610, 661–62, 674, 740, 772, 789, 813, 826–27, 866, 869

holiness collection (Lev 17–26), xxxii–xxxiii, 40, 87, 111, 151, 314, 322, 348, 355–57, 866, 869, 895, 906
holy, xix, xxiv–xxv, xxx, 17, 19–23, 29–30, 34, 39–40, 42, 54–56, 66, 68, 72, 97, 101–2, 119–24, 136–37, 140, 164, 176, 180–81, 185, 214, 216, 224, 238, 240, 243, 245, 248–49, 252–53, 257–58, 267, 273–75, 277, 298, 329, 331, 338–39, 342–44, 346–47, 353, 355–56, 378, 381–83, 391, 398, 408, 418, 428, 430, 432, 437, 439–40, 456, 458–59, 472, 481, 485–86, 503, 517–18, 538, 541–42, 545–46, 604, 606, 645, 655, 657–58, 661–62, 669, 687, 702, 728, 737, 740, 765, 772, 781, 803–4, 826, 828, 854, 860, 866, 874, 883
Holy Spirit (see Spirit)
home, 19, 29–31, 100, 135, 172, 192, 231, 274, 283, 376, 399, 405–6, 410, 479, 569, 579, 677, 679, 687, 689, 706, 737–38, 742, 747, 768, 873, 891
homicide, 103, 132–33
honey, 66–67, 144, 174, 495, 554, 592
honor, 7, 17, 54, 77, 113–15, 136–37, 178, 196, 204, 215, 272–73, 343, 357, 422, 438, 460, 463–65, 470, 482, 516–17, 554–55, 564, 567, 570, 573–74, 597–98, 614, 629, 633, 662, 680, 682, 686, 707, 718–19, 727, 760, 783, 804, 845, 865
hope, xxxviii, 26, 89, 201, 205, 207, 218–19, 223–24, 226, 241, 246, 250, 253, 263, 267, 278, 281, 295, 297, 310, 314, 335, 350, 355, 377, 379, 382, 393, 404, 409–10, 414, 425, 436, 441, 444, 446–47, 454, 484, 489–90, 500–1, 511, 532, 543, 547, 553, 557, 580, 604–5, 608–9, 612, 619, 626, 673, 675, 682, 698, 701, 721–22, 820, 830, 867
Horeb (also see Sinai), 79, 81, 93, 109, 111, 113, 131, 149, 189, 203, 208, 283–84, 470, 696
horn, 357, 413, 547, 628
hornet, 25, 28–29, 54, 160, 162, 468
horse, 199–200, 416, 712, 758–60, 774, 891
horses, 199–200, 205, 231, 255, 257, 303, 373, 427, 430, 458, 540, 646, 759–60
house, xx, xxxviii, 38, 50, 60, 76, 103, 119, 124, 130, 139, 158, 167, 172–73, 178, 182, 185, 189, 191–92, 195–98, 208–9, 214–15, 220–21, 247–50, 268–70, 282, 285, 290, 298, 304, 307–8, 322, 332–33, 352, 360, 366–67, 383, 391, 400, 426, 431, 436, 438, 447, 467, 473, 499, 521, 523, 527, 536, 539, 546, 590–91, 603, 619, 635, 639, 641–42, 644–46, 648, 652–53, 667, 676, 680–81, 691, 696–97, 702, 704, 720, 729, 736, 743–44, 747, 754–55, 772–73, 776, 781, 791, 793, 795, 803, 811, 825, 832–33, 843–44, 858, 874
household, 10, 30, 43, 52, 61, 83, 101, 126, 141, 157–58, 161, 275, 365, 498, 590, 708, 729, 775, 780
Huldah, 714, 716, 822–25, 830, 838
human (also see mankind), 3–7, 9, 13, 21, 26, 31, 46, 52, 59, 67–71, 73, 86, 103–4, 108, 124, 142, 145–46, 149, 171, 182, 184, 191, 218, 270–71, 279, 303, 318, 335, 349, 354, 356, 364, 369, 386–88, 394, 415–16, 422–23, 434–35, 443, 455, 457, 461, 467, 472, 481–83, 487, 496–97, 499–500, 504–6, 520, 527, 540, 542, 544, 548, 550, 554–55, 557, 561, 567, 573, 580, 599–602, 617, 621, 713–14, 719, 723, 743–44, 748–49, 769, 788, 792–93, 798, 814, 856, 866–67, 900
humble, 52–53, 245, 418, 436, 444, 452, 486–87, 701–2, 715, 721, 764, 770, 779, 813–14, 817, 820, 822, 825, 834, 836, 844, 867
humbling, 52–53, 257, 289, 296, 455, 487, 701–2, 715–16, 721, 730, 769–70, 779, 814, 820–22, 825
humility, 333, 377, 436, 444, 452, 476, 481, 483, 488, 570, 573, 814, 843
husband, 4, 9, 26, 69–70, 126, 142, 158, 201, 246, 262, 268–69, 284, 466–68, 575, 583, 586, 592, 688, 691, 874
hyperbole, 202, 400, 486, 684, 781, 798, 806, 833
identity, xxxvii, xli, 19, 30, 85–86, 89, 92, 106, 122, 126, 130, 139, 143–44, 155, 162, 190, 220, 227, 238–41, 245, 249, 316, 322, 336–37, 344, 346, 394, 438, 440, 452, 476, 501, 511, 579, 581–82, 584, 589, 606, 609, 614, 619, 627, 632–33, 637, 649, 656–59, 670, 675, 688–89, 711, 720, 725, 746, 748–49, 759, 776–77, 868
idol, 153, 203, 397, 486
idolatry, 82, 105, 160–61, 207, 219, 309, 321, 324–26, 328, 333, 357, 365, 418, 422, 433–34, 457, 515, 530, 548, 564, 574, 701, 782, 792, 797, 800, 855, 866
idols, 10, 27, 104, 161, 207, 258, 298, 308–9, 315, 318–19, 321, 327, 334, 408, 428, 430, 495, 503, 530, 539, 714, 735–36, 778, 806, 810, 821–22
image, 5–7, 21, 23–26, 45, 107, 174, 220, 276, 320, 333, 352, 357, 366, 368, 383, 394, 422, 469, 482, 494, 522, 600, 606–7
impurity, 40, 42, 54, 58–60, 62, 67–68, 73, 120–23, 140, 177, 180–81, 184, 233, 241–43, 248, 318, 321, 333–34, 343, 347, 355–56, 439–40, 451, 458, 486, 612, 658, 661, 669, 795, 803, 813, 860, 869
incense, 36, 271, 307, 319, 342, 357, 465, 773, 795, 803–4, 810
incest, 123, 151, 589, 725
inclusio (also see resumptive repetition) 3, 31, 55, 122, 164, 193, 290, 391, 761, 846, 895, 899
infidelity, 26, 40, 63, 73, 77–78, 90–92, 107–8, 138, 164, 207, 248, 256, 268–69, 325, 347, 350, 360–62, 368, 388, 412, 423, 516, 591, 623, 656, 661–62, 664, 685, 688–90, 700, 702, 704, 712, 724, 726, 728, 730–31, 778, 780, 783–84, 786, 791–93, 796, 800, 805–6, 808–9, 812, 822, 831, 834, 843–44, 853, 866
inhabitant, 54, 65, 105, 157, 167, 172–73, 451, 624, 631, 698, 792, 824–25, 836, 839
inheritance, xxvii, 10, 44, 58, 60, 64, 67, 69–71, 111, 118, 151–52, 159, 162–64, 167–68, 171, 174, 185, 193, 208, 250, 255, 269, 282–83, 285, 295, 305, 333, 345–46, 353, 361, 378, 381, 384, 387, 395, 415, 462, 481, 484, 493, 497, 502, 508, 517, 527–28, 533, 541, 578–79, 582, 585–88, 608, 660, 706, 725, 769, 869
iniquity, 12, 23–25, 40, 54, 64–65, 69, 107, 164, 205, 243–45, 273, 280, 322, 330, 347, 415–16, 499, 504, 520, 547–48, 558, 604, 610–11, 623–24, 627, 665, 701, 748

injustice, 33, 256, 279–81, 354, 469, 477, 497, 514, 559, 667, 787, 871
innerbiblical, xxxiv, xxxix, 382, 577, 863, 895
innocence, 129, 153, 209, 271, 281, 307, 329, 333, 514, 547, 564, 787, 810
inspired/inspiration (also see revelation), xviii, xxvii, xxxviii, 266, 316, 766, 788, 797, 847
instruction, xix–xx, xxxviii, 5, 7, 17, 21–23, 26, 28–30, 32, 35–40, 42, 46, 53–55, 69, 71, 73, 78, 80–81, 85, 87–88, 105–6, 111, 113, 115, 119, 122, 124–26, 133, 141, 149, 155, 160, 162–63, 165, 171, 174, 188–90, 195, 221, 233, 243, 250, 268, 270, 275, 279, 285, 315–16, 320, 323, 326, 329, 334, 339, 342–43, 355–57, 359, 368, 386, 411–12, 460, 463–65, 474, 477–78, 485, 487–88, 492–95, 499, 508, 511, 544, 552–53, 568–73, 579–81, 585, 588, 596, 598, 606, 633–34, 638, 661, 665, 668–69, 671, 680–81, 688, 703, 705–6, 712–14, 716, 720, 722, 753, 774, 779, 786–88, 790–91, 797, 802–3, 812, 814, 826–27, 860, 865–66, 894–96, 898, 901
instrument, xix, 234, 243–46, 429, 535–36, 765, 768
integrity, xl, 108, 218, 322, 377, 582, 598, 731, 786
intercession, 62, 64, 109–10, 514, 516, 519
intercessor, 248, 262, 325, 670–75, 819
intermarriage, 20, 24, 105–8, 164, 190, 200, 202, 423, 639, 655–59, 661–62, 684, 686, 690, 692, 724, 792–93, 874
international, 95–96, 166, 199, 223, 380, 400, 409, 443, 451–52, 489, 712, 723, 739–40, 758–60, 774, 859, 891
intertextuality, 893, 895–96
divine intervention, 66, 71, 225, 228, 444, 523, 596, 620, 779, 785, 788, 790, 799
editorial intervention, 359, 371, 632, 890
intervention (exegetical, interpretive), xxx–xxxi, 17, 21, 71, 104–5, 123, 133–34, 136, 138, 142, 144, 156, 159, 171, 182, 198, 217, 220, 228, 230, 232–34, 242, 269, 336, 339, 364, 366, 371, 375, 398, 417, 420–21, 431, 454, 465, 467–68, 475, 485, 490–91, 517, 534, 539, 568–69, 597, 606, 609, 614, 626, 634, 636, 640, 662, 672–73, 675, 681, 690, 707, 713–14, 730–31, 745, 748, 765, 796, 798, 810, 819, 824, 826, 831, 846, 863, 892, 896
interventions (exegetical, interpretive), xviii, xxx–xxxi, xlvi, 19–20, 22, 57, 59, 81, 92, 100–1, 107, 113, 127, 190, 217, 220, 228, 254, 293, 299, 316, 353, 362, 374–75, 377, 379, 385, 399, 404, 406–7, 422, 437, 461, 475, 477, 493, 524, 531, 538–39, 605, 618, 633, 681, 684, 698, 729, 737, 742, 748–49, 772, 783, 785, 787, 789, 793–94, 796, 805, 817, 821–22, 824, 845, 852, 861, 863, 870–71, 874–75, 898
invasion, 64, 90–92, 229, 299, 337, 416, 562, 628, 778, 805, 811, 815–16
iron, 113, 163, 309, 481, 509, 562, 621, 763
irony/ironic, xxiv, xxxix, 3–4, 94, 152, 165–66, 171–74, 176, 181, 192, 204, 221, 224, 227, 255, 262–63, 270–72, 276, 278, 281–82, 285, 297, 303, 305, 309, 311, 313, 315, 317–18, 323, 325, 340, 355, 368, 370, 380, 390, 404, 407, 409–10, 412–14, 419–20, 424, 444–45, 463–64, 466, 468, 495, 515, 558–60, 589, 596, 615, 628, 713, 751, 760, 802, 808, 817, 827, 830, 837, 845, 849–50, 855, 894
Isaac, xxxii, 8, 10, 32, 53, 64, 68, 110–11, 159, 283, 365, 510, 590, 685, 702, 764, 798, 820
Ishmael, 300, 590, 722, 787, 860
Jaar, 412, 526, 735
Jacob, 2–3, 7–8, 11–13, 32, 53, 68, 72, 99, 111, 143, 146, 161, 164, 208, 222–23, 236, 256–58, 278, 283, 294, 305, 311, 331, 352, 358, 362–66, 369–70, 378–79, 381, 400, 411–12, 414, 446, 451, 460–62, 470, 480–81, 492, 510, 524–25, 546, 590, 621–22, 661, 707, 722–23, 725, 740, 798, 820, 867
Japhet, 48, 336, 435, 489–90, 632, 636, 638, 678, 691, 698, 703, 710, 717, 725, 727, 749, 751, 766, 771, 781, 783–84, 817–19, 828, 835, 840, 843, 891
Jashar, 10, 184, 431
jealousy, 20, 23–26, 104, 107–9, 321, 351, 378, 420–24, 459, 494–95, 513, 520, 559, 778
Jearim, 412, 526, 643, 646, 735, 741–42
Jebusites, 25, 28, 67, 104, 158, 167, 199, 457–58, 657, 672, 732
Jedaiah, 644, 648
Jeduthun, 535–36, 765
Jehaziel, 788–89
Jehoahaz, 203, 211–12, 368, 794, 829, 831
Jehoash, 203, 211, 368, 799–800
Jehoiachin, 188, 206, 212, 279, 301, 440–41, 613, 717, 832–33, 884
Jehoiada, 794–98, 802
Jehoiakim, 212, 263, 278, 289, 301, 440, 445, 617, 619, 642, 794, 829–34, 846, 884
Jehoram, 203, 211, 717, 783, 790–94, 836, 846
Jehoshaphat, 211, 380, 383, 703, 714, 716–17, 721, 770, 781, 784–94, 801–2, 822, 829–30, 835, 838, 846
Jehu, 203, 211–12, 368, 425, 714, 784–86, 793
Jephthah, 166, 169–71, 173, 179, 193, 294–95, 388
Jericho, 158, 210, 301, 644, 805, 807
Jeroboam, 174, 189–90, 202–3, 207, 211, 361, 368–69, 717, 758, 775–78, 780–81, 806
Jerusalem (also see Lady Jerusalem, Salem), xxxv, 124, 148, 173, 189–90, 198, 200, 202–5, 207, 209, 219, 222, 228–31, 233–35, 237–38, 241–43, 245, 250, 252–53, 256, 262, 267–68, 274–75, 277–78, 287–88, 291, 298–304, 307–9, 316–17, 323–24, 329–30, 337, 346–47, 349–50, 352, 354, 371, 377–79, 381–83, 389, 393, 399, 401–2, 409–13, 421, 424–25, 433–34, 436, 438, 443–44, 446–48, 451–53, 456, 458, 462, 517, 522, 526, 529, 540, 547, 552, 593–94, 604, 606–10, 612–13, 617, 619, 622–24, 626, 630–31, 633–35, 639, 641–43, 646, 649–51, 653–55, 658, 660, 665, 670, 676, 682–83, 686–88, 690–91, 696–98, 701–3, 706, 708–10, 713–14, 718, 721, 724, 726, 728–32, 734, 736–40, 742, 744, 746, 749–51, 758, 762–63, 765–66, 772, 776–80, 786–89, 791–93, 801, 806, 810–11, 817, 819–21, 823–25, 828, 830, 832–34, 836, 838, 841–43, 849, 853, 867–68, 874

Jesse, 158, 214, 224, 252, 258, 276, 413, 428, 590, 731
Jesus, xxxvii, 358, 666, 756, 847–49, 851, 854, 867
Jezebel, 425, 792–93
Joab, 183, 208, 488, 535, 643, 729, 732, 745, 748
Joel (son of Samuel), 726–27
Jonathan, 708, 729
Joram, 203, 211, 793
Jordan, 79, 96, 118, 160, 164, 193, 296, 303, 417, 517, 524–25, 540, 723, 726
Joseph, 8, 10–13, 17, 31–32, 63, 70–71, 149, 158, 164, 167, 335, 454, 507–10, 586, 613–15, 618–20, 725, 754–55, 848
Joshua (high priest), 441, 448–50, 640, 650
Joshua (son of Nun) 79, 90, 92, 152, 155, 156–64, 166–68, 184, 190–91, 193, 206, 324, 414, 483–84, 524, 712, 716, 720, 724, 727, 751, 757, 854, 866, 870
Jotham, 212, 716, 804–5, 820, 846
journey, 61, 69, 149, 166, 407, 517, 734, 829
joy, 248, 252, 257, 292, 298, 308, 352, 446, 456, 476, 506, 508, 510, 553, 565, 576, 599, 625, 639, 692, 739–40, 750, 766–67
Jubilee, 46–49, 50, 70, 125, 250, 289, 320–21, 345, 579, 585–86, 588, 680
Judah, xxv, 2–3, 7–8, 11–12, 68, 139, 158, 167, 173, 177, 181–82, 189, 193, 204–7, 209–12, 217, 219, 221–22, 226–27, 229, 231, 261–63, 269–70, 273, 275, 277–79, 284, 286–87, 291, 294–95, 297, 300–1, 303, 307–8, 328–29, 331, 334–35, 341, 346, 351, 358–64, 369, 381, 383, 386–88, 393, 400, 410–14, 417, 419, 424–25, 427–29, 433–35, 438, 440, 444, 447, 450, 452–54, 457, 480–81, 489, 492–94, 499, 509, 523, 528, 536, 540, 547, 562, 566, 578, 589–90, 605, 608–10, 613, 624, 640–43, 647, 649, 653, 656, 682–83, 685, 687–90, 693–98, 701, 706–8, 712–17, 723–25, 728–29, 734, 748, 753–55, 762, 770, 775–80, 782, 786–97, 799–800, 804, 806–7, 811, 815, 817, 819, 821, 823–25, 831–34, 837, 839, 841, 844, 846, 853, 867, 870, 875, 880
judge, 78, 129, 207, 222, 243–44, 305, 324, 359, 380, 388, 411, 429, 451, 454, 473, 496–97, 541, 545, 560, 740, 787, 797
judges, 32, 69, 79, 82, 86, 89, 129–30, 161, 179, 193, 362, 380, 418, 475, 496–98, 545, 578, 590, 749, 784, 786–87, 842, 894
judgment, xxii–xxiv, xxviii, xxxi, xxxvi, 3, 7, 26, 46, 65–66, 83, 89–92, 94, 96, 129, 133, 142, 146, 160, 165, 171, 174, 178, 205, 207–8, 225, 227–28, 231, 255, 258, 262, 268, 270, 272–73, 277–81, 289, 294–95, 297, 299, 303, 305, 309, 311–12, 314, 318–20, 322, 324, 326, 330, 342, 349–50, 352–56, 362, 373, 377–78, 383, 387–89, 393, 396, 399–402, 404, 407–10, 416, 421–22, 427–29, 431–34, 444, 447, 454–55, 458, 463, 465, 468–69, 496–97, 501, 511, 519, 530, 543, 549, 552, 557–60, 569, 598–99, 605, 611, 624, 626, 688, 704, 712–13, 716–17, 737, 741, 745–46, 749, 758, 770, 779, 783, 787, 790–92, 797, 800, 802–3, 806, 809, 812, 817–19, 824, 830, 832, 834–39, 856, 858, 865, 878, 890
judgments, 32, 79, 82, 278, 282, 303, 318, 349, 352, 396, 420, 436, 441, 508, 510–11, 519, 547, 624, 674, 701, 740, 835, 838, 874
justice, 7, 54, 89, 99, 129, 134–35, 153, 218, 226, 256, 258, 279, 314, 323, 385, 390–91, 393, 418, 427, 430, 496–98, 541, 545, 552, 557, 560, 573, 601, 703–4, 762, 787, 837
Kadesh, 58, 62–65, 73–74, 78–80, 89–92, 94–95, 97, 108, 111, 138, 144, 149, 166, 325, 501–2, 513, 515–18, 673, 687, 700, 853
killing, xxxii, 17, 34, 42, 45–46, 55, 58–59, 64, 67, 97, 103, 105–6, 110, 134, 164–65, 173, 183–85, 198, 204, 210, 237, 246, 257, 311, 343, 354, 362, 457, 523, 530, 533, 536, 615, 626, 671, 746, 780, 788, 790, 793–94, 797, 800–1, 803, 820, 829
king (also see kings), 17, 68–69, 72–73, 83, 87, 97, 105–6, 118, 143–44, 148, 166, 169–71, 175–80, 184–85, 188, 191–92, 199–205, 208, 210, 229–31, 233–34, 261, 263, 271, 277–79, 289, 293, 296–97, 303, 317, 331–32, 335–36, 354, 359, 368–69, 376–77, 379, 404–7, 413–14, 421–22, 430, 440, 443–44, 446–47, 452–54, 457, 465, 470–71, 480–81, 489, 491, 500, 509, 522–23, 530, 532, 538, 540, 545, 566, 568, 580, 589–90, 613, 619–20, 622, 628, 642–43, 651, 653, 690–91, 708–9, 715, 717–19, 722, 728–33, 739, 741–43, 748, 753, 755–57, 760, 762–63, 767, 772–77, 779–80, 783, 785, 787, 790–91, 793, 795, 799–800, 802, 808, 811, 815–17, 820–21, 823, 826, 829–33, 836, 839, 841–42, 867–68, 900
kingdom, xx, 66, 96, 119, 161, 176, 192, 194–95, 205, 208, 234, 250, 279, 346, 350, 352, 371, 386, 392, 394, 481, 492, 499, 522, 527, 529, 532, 617, 620, 622, 629, 633, 656, 698, 701, 703, 706, 718, 720–21, 723, 729, 731, 739, 743, 755–56, 758–59, 771, 774–75, 777, 781–82, 805, 811, 818, 820–21, 830, 835, 837, 839, 844, 865
kingdoms, xli, 96–97, 149, 164, 188–90, 205, 209, 218, 250, 278, 346, 490, 628, 653, 688, 713, 715, 744, 751, 759, 841, 870
kings (also see king), xx, xxviii, 2, 12, 73, 105, 148, 156, 200, 203–4, 206, 210–12, 278, 308, 347, 368, 481, 489–90, 500, 507, 509, 522, 529–30, 532–33, 590, 613, 624, 703, 706, 712–13, 715, 717–22, 728, 746, 759, 770, 779, 782, 784, 791–92, 797–98, 803, 805, 808–10, 816, 821, 827, 830–31, 835, 838–39, 841, 846, 894
Kir, 293, 388
Kiriath Arba, 682
Kohath, 726–27, 737, 842
Korah, 66–67, 314, 339, 342, 514, 534–36, 727, 812
Laban, 10–11, 161
labor, 21–22, 29–30, 101–2, 144, 198–99, 202, 255, 275, 296, 302–3, 310, 412–13, 418, 430, 457, 520, 549, 594, 687, 711
Lachish, 230, 554, 801
Lady Jerusalem/Lady Zion, xxxv, 238, 606–7, 874
laity, 18, 39, 41–42, 54, 66–67, 81, 122, 136–37, 250, 318, 339–41, 343, 381, 655, 659, 661–62, 668–69, 675–77, 728, 734, 765, 776, 803, 813, 826–28, 848

lamb, 27–28, 61, 67, 184, 244, 253, 272, 540, 547, 681, 867, 872
lament, 234, 275–76, 308, 329, 351, 354, 475, 499, 536, 562–63, 605, 729, 831
lamp, 185, 540, 569–71, 811
lampstand, 35–36, 448, 458, 764
land, xxvi–xxviii, 2, 6, 10, 12, 18, 25–26, 28–29, 31–32, 35, 39–43, 47, 49, 52–56, 58, 61, 64–67, 70, 73, 79, 81, 86, 88, 90–96, 98, 102–7, 111–13, 116, 118, 120–21, 125, 128–34, 138, 143–44, 146–50, 152, 155, 157–59, 161–63, 166, 168–69, 172–74, 178, 188, 193, 197–99, 202, 205, 207–8, 224–25, 242, 249, 251, 257, 261–62, 267, 269–72, 277–81, 283, 286–87, 296, 298, 303–5, 307–8, 310, 315–16, 322–23, 325, 328, 331–36, 340–41, 344–47, 352–55, 357, 359, 361, 366, 383, 387, 407, 418, 431, 434, 436–37, 439, 447, 450, 454, 459, 462, 489–90, 495, 501, 504–8, 510–18, 524, 528–30, 532–33, 542, 544, 547, 575, 580, 583, 585–88, 599, 607–8, 613, 624, 656–60, 664, 667, 672, 676–81, 683, 685, 687, 702, 721, 723, 726, 733–34, 736, 750, 753, 759–60, 769–71, 776, 779, 786–87, 800, 813, 817–18, 820, 822–23, 831, 833–34, 836, 838–39, 844, 855, 869–70
landowner (also see ownership), 49, 125, 344–45, 585
lands, xli, 49, 69–70, 95, 167, 169, 199, 202, 295, 341, 387–88, 392, 395, 446, 503, 508, 510–11, 580, 582, 585, 611, 631, 656–59, 678, 683, 685, 778–79, 838, 869
laughter, 12, 545, 548, 609
law (also see legal, prohibition), xxiii, xxvii, xxxiii, xliv, 4, 7, 18, 22–23, 28, 35, 40–41, 44–47, 49, 55–57, 60, 66, 69–71, 78–79, 81–88, 97–98, 103, 105–7, 111–13, 115–19, 121, 123, 126–27, 132–44, 147, 151–52, 155–60, 163, 177, 179, 188–91, 198–200, 202, 222–23, 238, 247–50, 262, 268–69, 275, 280, 285, 288–90, 309, 316, 319, 326, 329–30, 332, 335, 342, 348–49, 355–56, 360–61, 368–69, 386, 390–91, 394–95, 411, 417, 439, 451, 464, 466–67, 470, 478, 487, 544, 572, 579–89, 596–99, 601, 604, 606–7, 610, 633–34, 637–38, 657–60, 683--91, 705, 721, 778, 787, 795, 813, 827, 840, 851, 858–59, 861, 866, 869–70, 872, 874, 899, 901
law collections: see covenant collection, covenant renewal collection, holiness collection, torah collection
laws, xviii, xxxix, 7, 18–21, 27, 32, 35, 39–41, 44, 46–47, 49, 58, 78, 80–81, 84–87, 97, 112–13, 122, 125, 130, 133, 135, 142, 155, 191, 235, 241, 288, 321, 325–28, 331, 334–35, 390–91, 454, 578–79, 584–86, 624, 637–38, 667, 676, 756, 869–70, 883, 901
lawsuit, 135, 609
leader, 629, 673, 725, 754–55, 787
leaders, 58, 66, 70, 157, 163, 192–93, 225, 228, 251, 323, 339, 347, 357, 361, 457, 465, 556–57, 602, 656–59, 702, 728, 747, 779, 786, 789, 807, 826, 859, 869
leadership, 465, 615, 655–59, 661, 664, 668, 708, 725, 732, 789, 812
leaven, 27, 34–35, 54, 61, 128–29, 150, 385, 391, 485, 773
legal (also see law), xx, xxvi, xxxiv, xxxix, xl, xlii 3, 17–21, 26, 32–33, 35, 39–49, 54–58, 60–61, 65–66, 69–71, 88, 103–7, 112–13, 116–19, 121, 126–27, 130, 132–39, 142–43, 151, 155, 158, 162–64, 171, 174, 176, 180–81, 188–90, 194–95, 198–200, 204, 243, 254, 262, 268, 270, 275, 279–80, 288, 315, 318, 320–23, 326, 350, 357, 359, 361, 363–64, 370, 374, 385–86, 390–91, 395–96, 410, 459, 463, 477, 493, 497, 499, 511, 519, 544, 570, 572, 575, 578–83, 585–86, 588, 596, 598, 606, 626, 630–40, 651, 658, 667–69, 675–77, 685, 688, 721, 748, 787, 796–97, 812–15, 827–28, 853, 857, 860, 869–71, 892, 894–96, 898, 901
leprosy (also see skin disease), 801–2, 804
Levi, 7, 58–59, 77, 149, 163–64, 320, 460, 463, 465, 539, 706–7, 726–27, 748, 777, 839
Leviathan, 237, 257, 506
levirate, 21, 78, 84, 152, 578–79, 585, 587–88
Levite, 124, 166, 172, 174, 339, 342, 357, 381, 486, 681, 788–89
Levites, 58–59, 62, 66, 68, 73, 83, 108, 110–11, 124–25, 132, 150–51, 164, 181, 249–50, 287, 339–43, 346–47, 463–64, 539, 541, 607, 635, 641, 644, 646–48, 651, 654–55, 657, 659, 669, 676, 678, 681–82, 691–92, 719, 724, 726, 728, 735–37, 747, 751, 765, 767–68, 773, 776–78, 781, 786–89, 794–95, 812–13, 825–28, 845, 860
life, xxi, xxxii, xli, 3, 7, 13, 18–19, 21, 39–40, 46, 58, 78–80, 86, 104, 111, 117, 125, 137–38, 142, 156–57, 166, 174, 183, 232, 236, 245, 253–54, 262, 266, 308–9, 321, 325, 345, 365, 406–8, 434, 465, 477, 480, 482, 490, 498, 504, 506, 530, 545, 553–55, 559–60, 563–64, 569–70, 573–74, 579, 586, 595, 599–602, 625–26, 628, 633, 721, 731, 733, 759, 803, 867, 869, 871, 898
light, xxvii, xxxiii, xxxvii, xlii, 2, 18, 24, 30–31, 36, 40, 55, 66, 81, 86, 88, 95, 113, 115, 136, 141, 145, 155, 162, 166–68, 173, 180, 192, 207, 214–16, 222–23, 231, 238, 242, 249–50, 256, 270, 277, 289–90, 299, 307, 328, 347, 350, 363, 365, 372–73, 399–400, 411, 422, 427, 434–35, 440, 457, 461, 464–65, 468, 476–77, 481, 483, 499, 505–6, 524, 529, 531–33, 539, 546, 549, 555–56, 561, 563, 569–70, 577–78, 589–90, 600, 608, 619, 624, 627–28, 652, 654, 656, 687, 691, 699–700, 710, 718, 721, 725, 739, 742, 771, 779, 807–9, 812, 819, 822, 840, 845–46, 848, 868
lightning, 310, 349, 459, 549
lightning rod, xvii, 17, 235, 281, 828, 852
likeness, 5–7, 107, 349, 357, 482, 636, 705
linen, xxiv, 136–37, 447, 763, 765
lion, 68, 138, 174, 253, 278, 296, 303, 310, 351, 354, 373, 380, 409, 414, 418, 457, 501, 867
lioness, 68, 73, 139, 351, 414
lips, 156, 191, 215, 228, 245, 268, 308, 366, 377, 416, 465–66, 472–73, 479, 483, 558, 589, 592, 597, 669, 842
liturgy/liturgical, 84, 143–44, 147, 217, 256, 270, 365, 474, 485, 494, 534, 671, 765–68, 843, 891, 896
liturgical idiom, 216, 896
livestock, 6, 27–28, 33, 67, 164, 253, 482, 635, 641, 681, 841

living/live(s), xxvii, xlii, 2, 5–8, 10, 12, 25, 28–30, 39–40, 43, 48, 50–51, 55, 79, 86, 96, 99–102, 104, 112, 118, 129, 135, 137, 139, 143–44, 155, 157–59, 164, 168, 177, 191, 193–94, 234, 236, 238, 245–46, 248, 253, 269, 272, 275, 280–81, 283, 285–87, 296, 298, 303–5, 307, 311, 319, 321, 323–28, 331–34, 349, 352–53, 357–58, 383, 386–87, 391, 393, 399, 406–7, 418, 426, 434–36, 438–40, 452, 456–58, 461, 477, 490, 497, 504, 506, 509, 515, 540, 545, 559, 567, 569, 573, 581–86, 588, 600, 614, 625, 629, 635, 641, 657, 659–60, 669–70, 674–75, 687, 726, 733–34, 754, 766, 769, 772, 776–77, 787–88, 798, 818, 838, 841, 861

loan, 51, 77, 141, 666–68, 882

loanword, xix, xliv, 363, 646, 901

local, xlii, xlv, 82–83, 113, 119, 121–22, 125, 129–30, 146, 170, 197, 247, 326, 439, 677, 688, 776, 786, 806

locust, 373–74, 381, 383–84, 493, 770

loincloth, xxv, 272, 273, 894

Lot, 9, 170, 172, 323, 362, 387, 590

love, xxvi, xlvi, 23, 39, 42–44, 64–65, 77, 93, 107, 135, 139, 150, 152, 163, 182, 201, 240, 246, 248, 251, 267–68, 273, 308, 345, 360, 362, 368, 370, 376, 388, 405, 415, 418, 423, 436, 450, 460–62, 466, 498–501, 504, 512, 520, 528, 530, 544, 547, 551, 563, 568–69, 573, 581, 591–94, 607–8, 622–24, 666, 672–73, 684, 686, 690–91, 704, 712, 743, 762, 765–66, 768, 789, 807–8, 848, 860, 866

loyalty, 23–24, 107–8, 177, 181–82, 208, 247, 262, 360, 415, 421, 436, 499, 505, 514, 530–33, 540–41, 544, 566, 607–8, 622, 672, 675, 708, 710, 734, 744, 767–68, 776, 778, 785, 818

lust, 185, 256, 425, 570

lying, 54, 68, 125, 138, 184, 243, 253, 283, 298, 308, 331, 368–69, 391, 414, 419, 458, 478–79, 481, 493, 567, 569, 580, 745, 832, 838

lyrical (also see poetic), 71, 215–17, 219, 231, 236–38, 245, 247–51, 409–10, 474–76, 481, 507, 738, 740, 849, 853, 871

lyrical diffusion, 215–17, 254–55, 376, 403-4, 408, 410, 414, 473–75, 477, 498, 503–4, 534, 539, 607, 671, 870, 877, 896

maiden, 592–94

maidservant, 227, 498

male, 2, 5, 21–22, 40, 43, 49–50, 52, 54, 59, 61, 67–69, 101–3, 106, 126–28, 149, 151, 243, 247, 275, 288, 351, 416, 465, 482, 487, 506, 558, 582, 585, 604–5, 607–10, 646, 723, 778, 790, 860

males, 17, 27–29, 43, 51, 59, 61, 67–68, 107, 127, 134, 142, 223, 344, 485, 582, 589, 598, 681

Manasseh, 70, 96, 163, 166–67, 174, 205–7, 212, 231, 433, 508, 585–86, 590, 701, 706–7, 715–17, 719, 721, 725, 728, 734, 777, 809–10, 813, 818–24, 830–32, 841, 845–46, 869

mankind (humankind), 5–6, 257, 387, 399, 456, 482, 554–55, 561, 573, 625, 744

manna, 17, 20–21, 66

manslaughter, 32, 83, 124, 160

marriage, 20–21, 24–27, 50, 70, 78, 83–84, 104–8, 137–38, 151–52, 173, 200–2, 204, 208, 268–69, 276, 314, 344, 351, 370, 389, 394, 466–68, 578–80, 583–91, 627, 639, 645, 657–62, 664, 677–79, 689–91, 717, 725, 758–59, 771, 785, 792, 794, 833

marriages, 26, 106, 188, 198–99, 201–2, 223, 249, 422, 441, 468, 589, 636, 639, 648, 656, 658–62, 664, 676–79, 682, 685–86, 688–91, 758–59, 775, 792

Massah, 108, 149, 225, 501–2

matriarch, 12, 509, 578, 580, 589, 871, 874

measure, xxi, xxix, 5, 41, 46, 54, 103, 209, 353, 443, 447–48, 610, 620, 779, 853, 859, 897

meat, 7, 33, 42, 60, 112, 122–23, 133, 150, 178, 273, 307, 318, 354, 439–40, 454, 733, 827

meeting, 39, 41, 72, 111, 147, 178, 194, 343, 562, 728, 742, 757, 765, 768, 828–29, 833

Megiddo, 828–30

Melchizedek, 2, 522–23, 855, 902

memorial, 85, 101, 143, 358, 362, 365–66, 422, 452, 544, 605, 611–12, 707

memory, 143, 183, 226, 263–65, 268, 476, 549

menstruation, 60, 243, 315, 321, 333–34, 355–56, 606, 612

Merari, 726–27

mercenary, 340, 351, 581, 684, 799–800

mercy, xlvi, 17, 23, 86, 101, 104, 158, 160, 199, 207, 251, 262, 295, 303, 358, 365, 377, 379, 399–400, 404, 406–8, 415, 417–18, 421, 423, 447, 461, 505, 512, 514, 520, 530, 546, 607, 614, 622, 666, 698, 722, 724, 779, 808, 843

Meribah, 108–9, 149, 501–2, 511, 514–15, 517, 542

Mesha, 105–6, 170, 226

Mesopotamia(n), xli, 103, 143, 160–62, 219, 225, 235, 410, 431, 522, 614, 684, 842

messenger (celestial): see celestial delegate

messenger (human), 138, 428, 465, 470, 596–97, 640, 669, 698, 702, 714, 828, 836

messiah, 252, 394, 441, 480, 499, 507, 509, 540, 544, 593, 679, 767, 842, 853, 892

Messiah (also see Christ), xxi, xliv, xlvi, 30, 181, 220, 246, 249, 393–94, 417, 453, 457, 476, 483, 488, 598, 627, 633, 660, 666, 707, 756, 807–8, 847–49, 853–54, 858–59, 862, 864, 866–68, 870–71, 902

Micaiah, 714, 784–85

Midian, 225, 254, 542

mighty, 63–64, 98–99, 102, 110–11, 144, 147–48, 376, 427, 429, 449, 462, 469, 515, 518–19, 524–25, 530, 532–33, 556, 563, 617, 620, 709–10, 732–33, 744, 766, 844

military, 73, 84, 92, 140, 162, 166, 183, 225, 228, 238, 295, 300, 309–10, 361, 369, 383, 389, 396, 400, 402, 410, 415–16, 628, 732, 734, 744–49, 761, 770–71, 781–83, 793, 799, 801–2, 806, 816, 829, 832, 891

milk, 27, 34–35, 66–67, 82, 120–21, 123–24, 144, 151, 564

minister, xvii, xliv, 110, 240, 248, 250, 286, 342, 496–98, 635, 847–48, 861

ministry, 132, 189–90, 208, 220, 224, 250, 287, 295, 359, 368, 374–75, 406, 737, 751, 797, 865

Miriam, 62, 141, 416–17, 725

mirror imaging (also see chiastic), 8, 45, 759, 891, 897–98

mission, xxxvii, 25–26, 28, 32, 35, 106, 152, 174, 502, 640, 652, 670, 739, 750, 786, 854–55, 902

Moab, 47, 62, 79, 81, 95–96, 109, 139, 149, 157, 166, 169–70, 184, 200, 226–27, 262, 283, 291–97,

299, 311, 387–89, 392, 395–96, 435–36, 480, 489, 580–81, 583–84, 586, 606–7, 658, 686, 689, 784, 788, 874
Moabite, xxxiii, 105, 201, 238, 242, 248, 295, 575, 580–82, 585–89, 606, 635, 657–58, 660, 684–85, 689, 745, 858
Moabites, 79, 95–96, 138–39, 160, 170, 184, 200–2, 239–40, 247, 253, 293–94, 341, 387, 394, 489, 496, 580–84, 588–89, 656–58, 684–86, 689–90, 745, 788
Moabitess, 578–81, 584–85, 587–89, 874
money, 36, 48, 52
monotheism, 149, 309, 496, 503, 505, 563, 703, 739, 766, 778
month, 27, 41, 60–61, 72, 128, 208, 299, 441, 450, 457, 459, 615, 635, 650–51, 668, 670, 675, 680, 691–92, 763–64, 768, 812, 829, 869
moon, 30, 73, 149, 258, 285, 308, 382, 384, 395, 431, 482, 499, 506, 532–33, 547, 608, 691, 815, 843
Mordechai, 613–15, 646
Moriah, 702, 716, 720, 763–64
morning, 60–61, 141, 385, 391, 506, 538, 555, 565, 604, 607–8, 612, 625, 678, 689, 691, 740, 789, 815, 835
mortal, 7, 100, 182, 254, 354, 473, 479, 481, 483, 496–97, 555, 787, 798
Mosaic, 227, 281, 284–85, 326, 441, 478, 508, 569, 688, 737, 827
Moses, xx, xxx, xxxiii, xxxix, 10, 20–24, 31–32, 35–36, 39, 44–45, 47, 52–54, 57–58, 60, 62–66, 70–75, 77–79, 85–96, 98–101, 105–11, 130–32, 134, 145–49, 152, 156, 159–60, 162–64, 174, 180, 191, 193–94, 203–5, 220–21, 224, 251, 263, 267–68, 272, 274, 283–85, 295, 309, 315, 317, 329, 342–43, 351, 359–60, 366–67, 376, 378, 387, 403–6, 415–18, 423, 439, 442, 461, 463, 468, 470, 483–84, 494–96, 498, 504, 510, 513–20, 524, 526, 534, 536, 542–44, 562, 565, 568–70, 586, 608, 615, 617–18, 622–24, 631, 635–36, 641, 651, 654–55, 659, 665, 673, 683–84, 686–87, 691, 705, 712, 716, 720, 737, 741–42, 753–54, 756–57, 761, 765, 767–68, 773, 788, 795, 797–98, 802, 804, 819, 826–27, 849, 854–55, 860, 866, 868, 873, 882, 899, 902
mother, 8–9, 27, 31, 34–35, 45, 82, 102, 119–21, 123–24, 135, 146, 151, 174, 178, 202, 351, 355–56, 425, 484, 509, 520, 562, 564, 566, 568–70, 574, 576–77, 583, 592, 594, 602, 606, 708, 717, 724, 726, 762–63, 793, 823, 831, 833–34
mother-in-law, 153, 575, 583
motif, xxxviii–xxxix, xli, 277, 336, 370, 601–2, 640, 781, 889–90, 898
mount, 39, 95, 109, 114, 149, 152, 160, 163, 168, 189, 203, 221, 228, 278, 298, 371, 378, 380–81, 400, 431, 444, 452, 458, 523, 528, 547, 702, 716, 720, 763–64, 847, 853
Mount of Olives, 458
mountain, 17–18, 21, 32, 35–36, 39, 47, 58, 61, 64, 81, 85, 97–101, 108–11, 131, 137, 144, 149, 160, 188–90, 203, 213–14, 221–23, 227, 236, 247–49, 252–53, 255–56, 298, 309, 319, 325, 353, 355, 361, 377, 399, 409–12, 417, 428, 431, 443, 448–49, 451, 459, 468, 481, 485–86, 492–93, 508, 511, 525, 538, 541–42, 568, 621, 671, 720, 756, 777, 866, 869
mountains, 64, 110, 160, 203, 222, 270, 298, 319, 349, 353, 358, 360, 371, 383, 397, 401, 411, 418–19, 425, 431, 524, 542, 546, 549, 594, 621
mouth, 99, 111, 131, 147, 168, 195, 198, 204, 215, 221–22, 258, 267, 272, 284, 298, 317, 328, 350, 453, 465, 473, 484, 495, 517–18, 547–48, 554, 597, 669, 702, 818
murder, 17, 21, 23, 45–46, 55, 77, 83, 179, 271, 307, 369, 722, 729, 733, 745, 797
music, 429, 510, 535–37, 546, 728, 737, 751, 765, 768
musician, 249, 396, 678, 747, 764–65, 768, 824–25
Nadab, 54, 71, 203, 211, 343, 803
Naharaim, 139, 535, 581, 606
Nahum, 420–25
nakedness, 140, 151, 255, 338, 355–56, 612, 894
Name, 45, 115, 119, 192–93, 195–98, 210, 235, 307–8, 393, 469, 521–22, 527, 664–65, 681, 739, 754–55, 765, 769
Naomi, 581, 583–84, 586–90
Naphtali, 166–67, 762, 823
Nathan, 118, 177, 181–82, 188–95, 206, 480, 498–500, 521, 523, 527, 536, 589, 714, 720, 742, 744, 750, 753–56, 775, 792, 843, 875
nation, xxvii, 12, 64–66, 79, 144, 147, 183, 222, 224, 256, 266, 283, 285, 303–4, 308, 333, 389, 393, 411, 416, 427, 440, 447, 491, 502, 504, 514, 544, 661, 786, 792–93
nations (also see peoples), xxiii, xxv, 2, 8, 10, 12, 26–29, 34, 40, 50, 54, 65, 85–86, 97, 104–7, 111–12, 116, 122–23, 131, 133–34, 139, 144–46, 149, 155–59, 162, 164, 167–68, 177–79, 188–89, 198–99, 201–2, 207–9, 218, 220–23, 226–27, 231, 238, 240, 242, 246–50, 253, 255–59, 261–62, 268, 271, 273, 276–78, 283, 286, 290–91, 295–99, 303, 305, 309, 315, 328, 331, 333–34, 336–37, 341, 351–52, 355, 360, 362, 364, 368, 371, 380, 382–84, 386–90, 392–94, 396, 399, 402, 410–12, 414, 424–25, 430, 433–35, 443, 446–48, 451–52, 458, 461–62, 465, 471–73, 480–81, 489–92, 497, 502–3, 510–12, 514–15, 518–19, 530, 540–42, 544–45, 556, 606–7, 620, 622, 629, 656–59, 664–65, 679, 690, 702, 707, 724, 736, 739–40, 772, 778, 782, 792, 806, 809–10, 836, 839, 859, 867, 873, 879
native-born, xxvi, 40, 42–43, 45–46, 61, 123, 345–46, 807
Nazirite, 72, 173–74, 183, 385, 390–91, 891
Nebuchadnezzar, 278, 297, 300, 302, 330, 445, 613, 618–22, 629, 640, 642–43, 653, 819, 821, 829, 832–33, 836, 842
neck, 8, 27–28, 67, 414, 509–10, 522, 569, 681, 702
Necho, 714, 822, 828–31
needy, 48, 50, 77, 84, 142, 227, 256, 323, 385, 390–91, 476, 497, 539, 541, 543, 557, 575
Nehemiah (the person), xxxv, 207, 266, 438, 463, 613, 632–33, 636, 643 (a different Nehemiah), 649–50, 660, 664–66, 668, 670, 680, 683–84, 686–91
neighbor, 39–40, 42–44, 46, 50, 83–84, 102–4, 119, 130, 132, 153, 248–49, 281, 284–85, 304–5, 315, 355–56, 361, 386–88, 390, 401, 497, 570–71, 574, 615, 641, 667, 807–8, 860–61, 866

Neo-Babylonian, 133–34, 220, 255, 278, 446, 462, 619–20, 806
Neo-Babylonians, 240, 280, 446, 462, 642, 841
Nephilim, 58, 63–64
Nethinim, 644–47, 651
New Testament, xvii, xix, xxii, xxviii, xxxv, xxxvii, xxxix–xliii, xlv–xlvii, l, 9, 158, 204, 220, 266, 285, 375, 416–17, 476, 520, 626, 633, 688, 814, 847–65, 867–69, 871, 873, 875, 892, 895, 903
night, 6, 60, 65, 106, 156, 191, 209, 285, 401, 441, 449, 478–81, 485, 530, 541, 562, 608–9, 629, 664, 768–70
Nineveh, 376–77, 379, 404–7, 420–22, 424–25, 436
Noah, 3, 6–7, 9, 52, 54, 163, 246, 254, 322, 565, 722, 854, 894
noble, 383, 550, 556, 687
north, 168, 262, 278, 298, 303–5, 336, 338, 594, 706, 713, 734, 771, 823, 836
Northern Kingdom, 174, 189, 202–3, 207, 228, 279, 320, 358–59, 368, 393, 407, 493, 656, 713, 729, 740, 777, 786, 790–91, 793, 799, 801, 804–6, 808, 811, 818
oath, 13, 65, 111, 125, 133, 246, 248–49, 274, 283, 423, 462, 495, 499, 502, 526–27, 583–84, 637–38, 659, 670, 672, 674–77, 679–82, 685–87, 690, 708, 857, 867
obedience, 8, 21, 25, 34, 40, 78–79, 81–82, 85, 87, 98, 100, 104, 106, 131, 152–56, 159, 162–63, 177, 182, 184, 191, 197, 208, 250, 274–75, 307, 322, 335, 360, 394, 397, 459, 461, 477, 480, 493, 499, 508, 510–11, 516, 544, 571–72, 588, 599, 624, 638, 657, 665, 672, 676–77, 681–82, 687, 701, 705, 716, 721–22, 753, 764, 770, 822, 828, 847, 857
offering, 35–37, 39, 41, 54–55, 58, 65, 68–69, 71–73, 82, 113, 115–16, 121, 124, 127–29, 150, 152, 177–78, 180, 208, 230, 243–46, 248, 273, 287, 307, 318–19, 342–44, 353, 361, 364–65, 370, 376, 385, 391, 395, 397, 408, 417, 439–40, 463–65, 470–71, 486–88, 503, 572, 635, 639, 641, 646, 651–55, 660–62, 681, 691–92, 701, 740–42, 750, 754, 759, 767–68, 773, 781–82, 795, 810, 815, 826–28, 841–42, 860
officer, 73, 416, 613, 735, 745, 747, 816, 830, 837
official, 10, 91, 129, 133, 148, 193, 224, 299–300, 302, 308, 652, 657, 688, 744–45, 747, 758, 787, 791, 797
offspring, 2, 27, 59, 67–68, 119, 192, 245, 254, 498, 510, 527, 588–89, 645, 681, 723, 781
Oholiab, 36, 712, 716, 762–63
oil, 36, 55, 126, 301, 364, 413, 440, 442, 506, 509, 681
olive, 150, 258, 370, 443, 547, 635, 670, 681
Omri, 203, 211, 368, 696
oppression, xxvi, 31, 43–44, 50, 144, 192, 215, 219, 250, 256, 271–72, 275, 281, 307, 333, 344, 355, 369, 390–91, 457, 497, 509, 553, 626, 668, 670, 673, 860
oppressor, 256, 272, 563
oracle, xviii, 10, 58, 60, 68, 72–73, 184, 194, 204–5, 215, 218–19, 222–23, 226–27, 230–31, 247, 251–52, 254–55, 258–62, 268–70, 276–78, 285, 287, 290–91, 293–97, 299–300, 302–5, 319–21, 330, 332, 334–37, 352, 354, 358, 375, 386–88, 390, 392, 396, 399–400, 402, 410, 413–15, 420, 423–24, 430, 434–35, 439, 441–42, 444–46, 454–55, 457, 474, 476, 480–81, 498–500, 510, 521, 523, 526–28, 566, 572, 618, 625, 628–29, 745, 750, 753, 755, 775, 779, 792, 798, 816, 829–30, 836, 843, 853, 859, 866, 871, 890, 894, 902
ordinances, 324–28, 728, 803
organic (revelation/progressive revelation) (also see progressive revelation, revelation), xviii–xix, xli, 899
Oreb, 225, 542
orphan (also see fatherless), xxvi, 40, 42, 124–25, 150, 153, 280, 323, 344–45, 399–400, 497, 519, 545, 548, 573, 860
otherness, 240, 410, 580, 656, 685–86
the other(s), 26, 44, 82, 122, 188–90, 240, 249, 394, 451–52, 458, 477, 504, 520, 579, 585, 655–56, 658, 677–78, 866, 874
outsider, 121, 239, 382, 666, 679, 866
ownership (also see landowner), 32, 34, 47, 49, 126, 130, 135, 172, 197, 281, 393, 453, 496
oxen, 172–73, 184, 737, 861
palace, 118, 192, 711, 732, 742, 758, 772, 799, 805, 809, 817, 832
parallel, xviii, xx–xxix, xxxi, xxxiii, xxxv, xliii–l, 3, 5–11, 20–32, 34–35, 41–46, 48, 52–54, 59–61, 64, 66–68, 70, 73–74, 79–84, 89–91, 101–2, 104–5, 107, 109–10, 112–23, 126–29, 131–33, 135–43, 146–47, 149, 153–54, 156–60, 162, 166–69, 171–75, 177–80, 182–86, 190–91, 193–95, 197, 199–206, 221–25, 227–30, 233, 235, 237–38, 240–41, 243–44, 246–48, 251–52, 254, 257–59, 261–62, 267–68, 271–74, 276–79, 281–83, 285–86, 288–89, 291–93, 295–97, 302, 308, 310, 314–15, 317–21, 323–27, 329–34, 336, 342–43, 345, 350, 352–54, 356, 359–61, 364–71, 374, 376–83, 387, 390–92, 394, 396, 399–402, 405–6, 410–17, 421, 423–25, 427–31, 434–35, 439, 442, 445–49, 451–53, 455–57, 459, 461–64, 467–69, 478–82, 484–85, 487–88, 490, 492–95, 497–500, 502–5, 508–22, 524–32, 534, 539–40, 542, 545, 553–65, 568–76, 581–82, 586, 590, 592–94, 596–603, 606, 608–13, 615–16, 618–26, 628, 630–32, 634, 636, 640–42, 650–51, 653, 655, 657, 659, 662, 664–65, 667–69, 671–74, 676–77, 680–82, 684–87, 690–91, 700–2, 704, 714, 719, 725, 729–35, 738, 740–41, 748–50, 753, 755–59, 762–64, 766–67, 769, 771, 773, 778–79, 781–84, 787–91, 797–98, 800, 802–3, 807–9, 813, 817, 820, 822, 825, 829, 832, 834–35, 838, 840–45, 850, 853, 856, 861, 874, 876, 878, 889, 893, 895, 897–98, 901–2
paraphrase, xx, xxii, xxx–xxxi, xxxiii, 7, 41, 43, 46, 54, 138, 141, 190–91, 194, 206, 221, 227, 268, 271, 295, 305, 309, 399, 445, 461, 491, 522, 528–31, 599, 607, 634–38, 652, 654, 669, 674, 681, 684, 686, 705, 724–25, 751, 756, 758, 760–61, 769–70, 807, 810, 826, 832, 857, 864, 889, 901
parent, 6, 71–72, 115, 197, 229, 254, 264–67, 276, 280, 282, 297–98, 324, 336, 363, 394, 568, 587, 627,

729, 733, 745–46, 765, 773, 783, 793–95, 798, 802, 817, 836, 840
parents, xxvii–xxviii, 6, 9–10, 17, 23–26, 32, 39, 54, 63, 65, 77, 79, 99, 107, 134–35, 153, 162, 169, 254, 280, 316, 319, 323, 325–28, 344, 418, 423, 463, 470, 495, 519–20, 552, 559, 564, 568, 570–71, 576, 610, 679, 689, 792
parody, xxvii–xxviii, 172, 320–21, 328, 365, 391, 448, 523, 530, 550–55, 557, 559–60, 562, 564–65
Passover, 17, 26–28, 34, 40, 42–44, 54, 58, 60–61, 69, 72–73, 82, 85, 106, 124, 128, 143, 150, 209, 239, 241, 344, 485, 547, 582, 615, 651, 718, 721, 811–15, 822–28, 842, 845, 860, 869, 872
pasture, 195, 296, 303, 331–32, 457, 547–48
path, 98, 235, 237, 411, 430, 524, 543, 570, 577, 584, 626, 708, 808
Paul, xxii, xxxvii, xlv, xlvi, 34, 69, 126, 135, 137–38, 181, 204, 220, 224, 380, 387, 391–93, 396, 428, 476, 584, 660, 666, 847–49, 856, 858–59, 861, 867, 893
payment, 35, 50, 69, 124, 141, 152, 230, 243, 250, 330, 596–97, 701, 770
peace, 198, 202, 231, 244–46, 253, 257, 262, 278, 300, 304, 317, 330–32, 335, 356, 379–80, 412, 414, 418, 424–25, 428, 446, 450, 455, 463–65, 490, 495, 521–22, 547, 556, 569, 609–10, 750–51, 753–54, 771, 785, 817–18, 830–31, 838
Pekah, 203, 208, 212–13, 225, 368, 696
Pekahiah, 203, 212, 368, 696
penalty, 22–23, 46, 55, 104, 124, 135, 143, 151, 244, 487, 662, 688
Pentecost, 27, 34, 55, 150
peoples (also see nations), 8, 26, 68, 95, 116, 119, 121–23, 139, 145–46, 150, 155–56, 168, 182, 188–89, 198–99, 202, 218, 222–24, 231, 248–49, 262, 297, 299, 302–3, 318, 336–37, 341, 351–52, 382, 386–88, 392–93, 395, 399–400, 411, 414, 418–19, 425, 430, 435–36, 451, 458, 480, 490–91, 502–3, 514, 529, 540, 542, 547, 580–82, 584, 607, 629, 656–60, 662, 664, 677–79, 684–85, 689, 723, 805, 836, 860
Peor, 164, 325, 351, 368, 515–16
Perazim, 228
period, xxviii, xxxiv, 69, 99, 145, 266, 311, 322, 333, 359, 374, 446, 456, 460, 543, 552, 558, 579, 587, 598, 634, 647, 678, 688, 700, 707, 727, 731, 797, 806, 841–42, 863, 871
perishing, 292, 308, 376, 401, 405, 481, 502, 549, 561–62
Perizzites, 25, 28, 67, 104, 158, 199, 657, 672
Persia, 336–37, 522, 613, 653, 688, 841
Persian, 18, 217, 220, 455, 691, 699, 707, 840–41
personification, xxvii, 9, 13, 40, 52, 54–55, 220, 234, 236, 238, 333–34, 384, 410, 415, 524, 567, 575, 590, 606, 658, 705, 839
Pethor, 138–39, 581, 606, 684
pharaoh, 10–11, 96–97, 147–8, 155, 159, 184, 201, 224, 352, 354, 362, 416, 441, 502, 553, 618–20, 690, 725, 758, 770–72
Pharisee, 30, 858–59
Philistia, 291, 305, 388–89, 489, 805
Philistine, 167, 174–75, 184, 291, 387–88, 395, 457, 490, 536, 689, 708–9, 729–30, 732, 734–35, 759, 791, 809
Philo, 44, 60, 66, 598, 848
Phinehas, 174, 176–78, 335, 463, 511, 515–16, 519, 728
pilgrimage, 27–29, 34, 82, 112, 124–25, 128–29, 143, 150, 193, 227, 256, 326, 346, 380, 395, 409, 443, 451–52, 485, 503, 538, 677, 772, 815, 897
pit, 33, 150, 258, 292, 311, 408, 549, 603, 609
pity, 87, 142, 318–19, 357, 370, 702, 836
plague, xxxiv, 10, 65, 90–91, 161, 183, 224, 273, 278, 349–50, 383, 395, 493, 513–14, 516, 750, 770
plant, xxiv, 52, 136, 192, 305, 393, 407–8, 436, 482, 493
pledge, 48, 50, 390–91, 395, 662, 667–68, 716, 823, 873, 882
plowshares, 222, 372–73, 379–80, 409, 411
plunder, 97, 134, 174, 300, 305, 330, 402, 520, 607, 724, 746, 751, 783, 799–800, 807, 837
poem, 10, 95, 174, 244, 272, 275–76, 293, 365, 429, 431–32, 473, 505, 551, 719, 870
poet, 80, 170, 234, 238, 293–95, 396, 564, 604–7, 609–11
poetic (also see lyrical), xxiii, xlii, 145–46, 216–17, 250–51, 254, 261–62, 264, 268, 270, 273, 287, 292, 295, 304, 308, 352, 367, 399, 407–8, 410, 415, 429, 431, 474, 483, 485, 492, 496, 506–7, 509, 515, 521–22, 524–25, 529, 533, 543, 551, 700, 896–97
poetry, 10, 80, 216, 263, 292, 296, 305–6, 308, 362, 399, 429, 473–74, 508, 524, 528, 551, 560, 592, 738, 849, 897
politics, 26, 96, 131, 143, 192, 389, 402, 416, 626, 706, 710, 717–18, 720, 757–59, 775, 790–91, 799–800, 802, 806, 821, 842, 846–47
pollution, 58, 60, 72, 123, 239, 269, 333, 514, 580, 639, 655, 659–60, 679, 702, 874
polytheistic, 155, 162, 223, 736
portion, 72, 83, 87, 124, 128, 143, 150–51, 250, 311, 344, 346, 407, 459, 492, 508, 534, 539, 541, 557, 607–8, 682, 698, 700, 725, 750, 754, 767, 827–28, 833, 841, 849, 865, 870, 872
possession, 28, 59, 86, 96, 122–23, 152, 167–68, 170, 178, 185, 320, 386–87, 401–2, 470, 481, 497, 508
postexilic, xxxiii–xxxiv, 199–200, 217, 226, 253, 322, 325, 380, 392–93, 438, 454, 476, 507, 524, 543, 553, 558, 580, 634, 685, 688, 698, 753, 777
potter (pottery), 129, 215, 258, 481, 506, 556
pour, xviii, xxv, 116–17, 271, 307, 329, 336–37, 361, 364, 373, 377–79, 383–84, 428, 436, 459, 468, 514, 548, 556, 564, 624, 675, 733–34, 779, 843
poverty, 39, 47–49, 51, 88, 126, 141–42, 183, 267, 280–81, 300–1, 320, 345, 355, 386, 390–91, 393, 438, 457, 476, 497, 539, 543, 557, 575, 583, 585–86, 613, 666–68, 679, 833, 837
power, xxxii, xxxviii, xlvi, 64–65, 86, 110–11, 148, 159, 196, 239, 252, 262, 304, 309, 423, 429, 433, 437, 469, 474, 515, 524–25, 529, 532, 563, 574, 620, 658, 706, 721, 725, 731, 758, 802, 808, 872, 875, 889
praise, xxv, 8, 77, 176, 233, 245, 257, 272–73, 372, 408, 414, 436, 472–73, 510, 514, 518, 529–30, 536–38, 540, 542, 545–46, 551, 564, 573, 575, 736–37, 740, 765, 768–69, 773, 788–89

prayer, 10–11, 58, 64–65, 108–11, 189, 206–7, 215–16, 220, 232, 237, 247–50, 262, 271–73, 304, 307, 310, 325, 376, 383–84, 403, 405–8, 423, 490, 509, 512, 514–16, 527, 535–38, 544, 555, 557, 572, 583, 605, 618, 622–24, 638, 656, 659–60, 664–66, 670, 672–76, 682, 702, 720–21, 736, 742, 744, 747, 750, 765–67, 769–70, 779, 813–14, 816, 820–21, 834, 836, 843, 845
prayers, 53, 64–65, 110–11, 207, 226, 252, 256, 263, 311, 405, 473–74, 512, 534, 596, 614, 622, 632, 636, 665–66, 720, 769–70, 878
praying, 109, 161, 216, 273, 286, 512, 605, 614, 622, 661, 664–66, 671–72, 674, 721, 767–68, 896
preaching, xxxvii, 86, 189, 216, 274–75, 277, 281, 289, 358–59, 393, 407, 424, 445, 595, 638, 640–41
precept, 508, 510–11, 573, 636
pregnancy, 142, 189, 369, 397, 834
presence, 23, 39–40, 54–55, 72, 128, 130, 140–41, 156, 176, 179–81, 194, 196, 202–4, 235, 242, 251–52, 254, 281, 284, 307, 338, 353, 377, 477, 484, 512, 517, 525, 586, 608, 750, 765, 767, 804, 812, 825, 860, 866, 874
pride, 110–11, 223, 229, 257, 292–93, 323, 358, 366–67, 398–400, 495, 549, 566, 689, 801–2, 817–18, 838, 844
priest (also see high priest), 2, 66, 69–70, 137, 143, 150, 160, 163, 174, 176–78, 180–81, 227, 233, 243–44, 286, 337, 339–40, 342–44, 347, 353–54, 358, 381, 441, 448–49, 465, 472–73, 486, 516, 523, 543, 608, 640, 645, 662, 669, 736, 787–89, 794, 796–98, 802, 824, 827, 839, 866
priesthood, 17, 39, 53, 58, 66, 136, 178, 216, 250, 335, 342, 347, 464–65, 516, 523, 645, 662, 692
priestly, 18, 36–39, 53, 55–56, 62, 67, 69, 72–73, 83, 87, 122–23, 128, 130, 136–37, 140–41, 150–51, 155, 181, 209, 217, 250, 315, 318, 325, 329, 338–39, 343–44, 346, 353, 357, 394, 437, 439–40, 443, 449–50, 460–61, 463–66, 511, 517, 523, 538, 543, 546, 567, 598, 608, 637–38, 646, 648, 654, 659, 669, 726, 747, 772, 781, 802–3, 812, 839, 843, 898
priests, 18, 36–42, 53–54, 58–60, 62, 66, 68, 72–73, 81, 83, 119, 122, 125, 132, 136–37, 141, 143, 150–51, 177–78, 180–81, 194, 208, 215, 228, 249–50, 281, 286–87, 300, 308, 318, 329, 338–44, 346, 353, 381, 384, 433–34, 439–40, 449–50, 460, 463–65, 523, 528, 539, 541, 543, 607–8, 631, 635, 641, 644–47, 651, 654–55, 657, 659, 661–62, 669, 676–78, 680–82, 691–92, 702, 719, 726, 728, 735, 741, 745, 751, 764–68, 773, 776–78, 786–87, 795, 802, 804, 811–13, 825–27, 832, 834, 837, 840, 845, 860, 891
prince, 149, 317, 331–32, 335–36, 344, 349, 354, 368, 418, 543, 624, 629, 653
prisoner (prison, imprisonment), 219, 301, 548, 562, 614, 745, 799–800, 820
profane, 41, 112, 116, 121, 180, 240, 325–26, 329, 343, 356, 391, 465, 687
progressive revelation (also see organic), xvii–xix, xxxix, xli–xlii, 58–59, 61, 71, 81, 101, 181, 190, 220, 374, 417, 444, 624, 808, 848, 865, 867–69, 898–99
prohibition (also see law), 3–5, 7, 20, 24–27, 30, 33–35, 41–43, 49–51, 54–55, 60, 82–84, 105–8, 116, 119–27, 129, 137, 141, 150–52, 159, 173, 178, 181, 188, 190, 200, 202, 207, 225, 240, 273–74, 314, 316, 318, 321, 333, 343, 353, 356, 401, 422–23, 435, 457, 463, 509, 564, 570, 599, 607, 639, 655–59, 661–62, 664, 677–78, 686–87, 689–90, 730, 759–60, 778, 792, 803, 883, 891–92
promise, xlvi, 2, 12, 18, 25–26, 28–29, 32, 35, 40, 52, 58, 67–68, 72, 86, 88, 92, 95, 98, 110, 112–13, 118–19, 132–33, 144, 149–50, 162, 168, 180–82, 184, 188, 191–93, 195–98, 209, 225, 229, 232–33, 235, 246, 271, 286–87, 304–5, 315, 325, 337, 392–93, 447, 449–50, 457, 474, 476–77, 481, 483–85, 490, 499–501, 504, 507–8, 510, 521–23, 526–27, 529, 544, 564, 580, 589, 599, 601, 607–8, 623, 649, 672, 676, 678, 686, 734, 743, 755–56, 760, 793, 800, 857, 870, 875–76, 896
promised, xxv, 2, 29, 64–65, 67, 106, 111–12, 133, 163, 188, 194–96, 198, 235, 243, 252, 273, 283, 335, 468, 527, 672, 686, 731, 733, 751, 760, 766, 771, 800, 845
promised land, 335, 760, 771
promises, 12, 58, 62, 69, 181, 188, 194–95, 232, 286, 444, 476, 484, 489, 492, 500, 518, 553, 589, 638, 675–77, 759, 868, 871
property, 29, 33, 47–48, 70–71, 103–4, 136–37, 163, 256, 320, 345, 497, 586–88, 778
prophecy, 190, 216, 221, 231, 238, 245, 277–79, 288, 301, 318, 335, 337, 340, 372, 378–79, 381, 424, 434, 438, 447, 455, 474, 619, 626, 713, 775, 799, 822–25, 829–30, 832, 841
prophesying, xxv, 269, 277–78, 336, 378, 380, 391, 453, 758, 775, 784, 832
prophet, xxi, xxv, xxvii, xxx, xli, xlv, 8, 20, 58, 65, 77, 79, 82–83, 86, 88, 94, 99–100, 119, 131–32, 138, 147–48, 189–90, 203–7, 209, 216–17, 219–20, 222, 224–28, 231, 238–39, 242, 246–47, 249–50, 252, 254–55, 261–63, 267–69, 271–72, 274–81, 287, 293, 299, 302, 304, 306–11, 314–16, 318, 321, 323–24, 329–30, 334, 336, 340–41, 348–49, 351, 354–56, 358–60, 362–63, 366–75, 378, 380, 382–83, 385–88, 390–93, 395, 397, 399–400, 402, 404, 406–8, 412, 416–18, 421, 425–27, 429–30, 433–36, 439–45, 447, 450, 454–57, 460, 463, 468, 472–75, 486–87, 500, 507, 509, 511, 514, 521, 523, 536, 552, 567, 571–73, 580–82, 591, 605, 610, 612, 623–24, 636, 640–41, 659–60, 665–66, 668–69, 671, 679, 686–88, 698, 702–3, 705, 713–14, 716, 718, 730, 733, 746, 756, 775, 779, 783, 785, 789, 791, 797, 800, 813–14, 825, 831–32, 834–36, 842, 849, 854–56, 862, 866, 868, 870, 873, 882, 896, 900, 902
prophetess, 354
prophetic, xviii, xxviii, xxxviii, xlii, 71, 88, 131, 148, 153, 190, 205, 216–18, 220–21, 223, 225, 227, 229, 231, 234, 237, 246, 252, 254–55, 258–64, 266, 269–70, 273–74, 276–79, 282, 285, 288–89, 294–95,

303–4, 317, 330, 347–48, 350–52, 358–61, 368, 371–75, 377, 379–80, 385–86, 388–90, 394–99, 401, 404–5, 407, 412, 416, 418, 420, 424–26, 428–30, 437–38, 441, 443–45, 450, 453–56, 458, 460–62, 464, 468, 474–75, 490, 494, 498, 501, 521, 523, 544, 551, 567, 618, 628, 631, 638, 641–42, 671, 705, 713–14, 716–18, 738, 757, 775, 781–83, 786, 788–90, 797–99, 802, 805–6, 809, 819, 825, 828, 830–31, 834–36, 838, 843, 846, 853–55, 859, 868, 870, 878, 891, 901–2
prophets, xxxviii, xlii, xlvi, 18, 149, 163, 178, 265, 282, 302, 360, 369–72, 395, 417, 426–28, 431–32, 470, 575, 825, 836, 849, 865, 901
prosperity, 86, 156, 174, 191, 223, 412, 447–48, 479, 559–60, 569, 573, 581, 588, 758–60, 774
prostitute, 25–26, 104, 155, 157–58, 201, 226–27, 269, 323, 350, 391, 418, 425, 589, 592, 599, 606, 657, 661, 689, 778, 790–92, 866
prostitution, 77, 84, 150, 226–27, 360–61, 425, 658, 792
pruning hooks, 222, 379–80, 411
punishable, 19, 103
Pul (see Tiglath-pileser)
punishment, xxxi, 4, 7, 19, 22–25, 29–30, 33–34, 45–46, 54, 60, 65, 69, 84, 93, 103–4, 107, 109, 134–35, 138–39, 143, 151, 177, 182–84, 191, 204, 225, 237, 244–45, 255, 272–73, 280–81, 298, 304, 319–20, 330, 340, 349, 352, 364, 421–23, 446–47, 469, 480–81, 495, 499–500, 505, 519–20, 527, 558–60, 610, 612, 633, 688, 703–4, 712, 743, 814, 835, 838
purification, 39, 42, 55, 60, 72–73, 124, 139, 208, 243, 334, 342, 439, 458, 486, 661–62, 691, 813
purity, 21, 39, 59, 67, 73, 84, 107, 120–23, 127, 139–40, 177, 180–81, 183–84, 240, 242–43, 333–34, 343–44, 435, 439–40, 458, 465, 486, 555, 661–62, 669, 678, 684, 721, 813, 826, 866
purple, 136, 763
queen, xxxv, 188, 202, 210, 425, 541, 708, 712, 717, 758, 762, 774, 782, 793, 823, 831, 833–34
Qumran, xlv, 144–45, 264, 394, 538, 598, 627, 679, 699, 735, 807, 857–59, 861–65
quotation, xviii, xx–xxii, xxix, xliv, 19, 59, 112, 158, 217, 222, 227, 245, 252–54, 257, 271, 292, 305, 326, 332, 365, 370, 382, 386, 405, 410–11, 415, 417, 428, 431, 464, 474, 478, 480, 501, 503, 509, 519, 528–29, 531, 557–59, 601, 622, 628, 633–34, 636–37, 651, 664, 669, 705, 852, 857, 876, 889, 893–94, 898–901, 903
Rabbah, 396, 744–46
Rachel, 10, 52, 161, 183–84, 412–13, 590, 707
Rahab, 155, 157–60, 237, 506, 589, 661, 724, 866, 870
rain, 310–11, 332, 549, 666, 769–70
raisin, 255, 293, 370
Ramah, 260, 361, 644
rape, 83, 137–38, 179, 238, 275–76, 311, 604, 606, 724, 733, 745
Rebekah, xxxii, 10, 183, 590
rebellion, 5–6, 18, 23–24, 29, 52, 58, 63–68, 72–76, 79, 83, 89–95, 97, 99–100, 108–9, 134–35, 149, 161, 164, 174, 178, 189, 200, 207, 209, 220, 231, 243, 251, 255, 272, 280, 289, 299, 303, 310–12, 314, 317–18, 320, 323–25, 328, 330, 335, 342, 352, 357, 359–60, 366–67, 381, 391, 403–4, 406, 412, 416, 423, 427, 444, 454, 461, 464, 468–69, 484, 486, 492–95, 501–2, 506, 511, 513–18, 520, 608, 611, 623, 631, 633, 656, 660, 665, 671, 673–75, 686–88, 700–1, 704, 708, 725, 759–60, 770, 790, 809, 811–12, 819, 821, 823, 826, 831–32, 835, 838, 894
rebuilding, 250, 257, 371, 392–93, 438, 447, 640, 652–53, 670, 701, 842
redeemer, 215, 236, 255, 531
redemption, xlii, 18, 22, 27–28, 35, 39, 44, 47, 50–52, 59, 67–69, 73, 79, 85–86, 98, 101, 111, 126–27, 146, 148–49, 157, 161–62, 169, 173, 177, 179, 194, 207, 209, 219, 235–37, 240, 246, 251, 281, 309–10, 320–21, 416–17, 425, 461–62, 469, 477, 494, 508, 510–11, 525, 529, 533, 541, 556, 562, 586, 588, 633, 670, 673, 681, 685–86, 726, 739, 764, 767, 814, 855, 865, 867–70, 898
refuge, 97, 132–33, 226, 277, 371, 381, 388–89, 462, 481, 571, 583, 726–27
regional, 125, 129, 133, 202, 218–19, 226, 247, 278, 300, 385–89, 392–93, 431, 588, 744, 746, 751, 801, 804, 806
Rehoboam, 202, 703, 716, 721, 770, 775–80, 835, 837–38
reign, 203, 286, 331, 521, 623, 717, 725, 735, 754, 763–64, 775, 782–83, 819, 821, 830–31, 833–34
rejecting, xix, 86, 114, 179, 185, 226–27, 246, 283, 300, 308, 325, 327, 368, 413, 443, 472–73, 477, 484–85, 494, 505, 515–16, 525–26, 547, 551, 577, 605, 609–10, 612, 686, 713, 718, 766, 778, 831
rejection, 494, 686, 777–78, 835
rejoicing, 78, 252, 320, 456, 481, 506, 510, 525–26, 591, 626, 669, 740, 766
relationship, xix, xxiii–xxiv, xxix, xxxii, xxxviii, 6, 12, 22–26, 39, 43–45, 48, 53–54, 58, 61, 64–65, 71, 80, 85–86, 89, 100–1, 104–5, 107, 123, 130–32, 142, 145–47, 155, 166, 180, 184, 188, 192, 195, 205–6, 221–23, 225, 236, 241, 243–44, 246, 258, 261, 267–69, 272, 281–82, 285–87, 289–90, 292, 295, 303, 314, 337, 340, 361, 364, 366, 368, 370–72, 375–77, 384, 386–88, 396–99, 405–6, 410, 412, 417, 421, 424, 449, 453, 477, 479, 482, 505, 511, 534, 538–39, 550, 553–54, 556, 559, 562, 564, 570, 590–91, 596, 606, 610, 612, 614–15, 618–20, 624, 633, 647, 655, 682, 704–5, 708, 712, 724, 726–27, 802, 806–7, 814, 840, 843, 845, 854, 875, 889, 892–93, 895, 899, 901
relocation, 129, 234, 277, 290, 326, 710, 770–71, 776, 892
remembering, xxx, 21–22, 29, 32, 52–53, 64, 86–88, 96, 98, 101–2, 110–11, 141, 163, 172, 181, 184, 246, 252, 262–64, 267, 272–73, 280, 282–86, 298, 309, 358, 366, 388, 417, 470, 476, 483, 493–94, 498, 504, 507, 510–12, 514, 520, 531, 554, 564, 599, 605, 611–12, 647, 653, 665–66, 708, 733, 738, 740, 746, 766–67, 817, 820, 871, 890
remnant, 167, 204, 226, 235, 279–80, 300, 357, 371, 379, 386, 392, 402, 414–15, 418–19, 434, 457–58, 462, 539, 640–41, 652–53, 656, 740, 777, 811, 818, 824, 837

reparation offering (also see guilt offering), 208, 243–44, 486–87, 655, 660–62
repayment, 107–8, 185, 320, 364, 472, 504, 549–50, 559–60, 566, 583, 666
repentance, xlvi, 108, 217, 280, 330, 377, 379, 404, 407–8, 476, 486–88, 512, 582, 656, 661, 664–65, 701–2, 710, 713, 716, 720, 722, 733, 745–47, 749, 764, 767, 769–70, 808, 819–21, 837, 870
residing foreigner (also see sojourner), xxvi, 31, 35, 40, 42–48, 50, 52, 61, 89, 101–2, 117, 120–21, 123–26, 129, 142, 150, 153, 239–40, 275, 280, 316, 322, 333, 340–41, 344–46, 394, 497, 540, 545, 548, 578–85, 589, 668, 716, 741, 807–8, 839, 858–61, 866, 874
rest, xxi, xxxi, xlvii, 19–22, 27, 29–30, 33, 35, 40, 55, 61, 66, 101–2, 112, 118–19, 125, 145, 163, 188, 191–94, 209, 241, 245, 249, 252–53, 273–75, 392, 434, 438, 443, 446, 469, 484–85, 501–2, 511, 521, 526–27, 560, 567, 574, 581–82, 600, 612, 618, 642, 646, 677–79, 687, 703, 710, 717, 720, 724, 735, 742–43, 750–54, 765, 767, 769, 771, 775–76, 838–39, 847, 881, 901
resting, 2, 21–22, 31, 101, 118, 171, 210, 256, 504, 526–28, 612, 739, 766–67, 783, 826, 839
restoration, xxxiii, 20, 49, 86, 107, 125, 190, 199–200, 207, 219–20, 226, 231, 235, 239, 241, 243, 245–48, 250, 252–53, 255, 257, 272–74, 279, 292, 295, 297, 303, 310–12, 316, 323, 325, 335, 340, 345–46, 357–58, 365, 371, 385–86, 388–89, 391–95, 402, 413, 436, 441, 444, 447, 449–51, 454, 461, 468, 477, 500, 511–12, 529, 548, 553, 565, 580, 582, 592, 611, 627–33, 638, 640–42, 650, 652, 654, 656, 658–61, 664–65, 670, 672–86, 688–91, 723, 732, 756, 769, 776, 779, 794–96, 807, 811, 814, 819–20, 841, 857, 865, 867
resumptive repetition/repetitive resumption (also see inclusio), 122, 135, 164, 167, 193, 302, 746, 758, 821, 825, 846, 895, 899
resurrection, xxxvii, xl, 352, 358, 618–19, 625–28, 848, 867–68, 871
retribution, 161, 272, 310, 332, 519–20, 550–56, 558–61, 703–5, 712, 714, 716, 721, 748, 770, 779, 783–84, 790–94, 797–801, 804, 806, 812, 816, 818–19, 824, 835–39
return, xli, 8, 12, 54, 68, 70, 85, 140, 159, 200, 207, 219, 225, 234–38, 241, 243, 245, 257, 263, 269, 273, 279, 285, 305, 319, 345, 353, 369–70, 376–77, 383, 390, 392, 411, 414, 424–25, 436, 438, 445, 447, 451, 459, 470, 509, 542, 549, 561, 585, 592, 595, 599–600, 607, 619, 632–33, 637, 639, 641–42, 647–50, 652, 654, 659, 664–65, 667–68, 670, 673, 686, 728, 805, 811, 814, 819–20, 828, 853, 855, 866, 901–2
returning, 11, 135, 234, 411, 440, 463, 583, 599, 601, 632, 642, 649–50, 652, 654, 659, 668, 673, 736, 742, 807
Reuben, 7, 707, 725
revelation (also see inspiration, organic), xvii–xix, xxix, xxxvii, xxxix–xlii, xlvi, 2–3, 6–8, 12, 17–21, 24, 29, 39–40, 44–45, 58–59, 61, 64–65, 69, 71, 76–79, 81, 85–86, 88, 95, 97–101, 119, 121, 125, 131, 137, 140, 144, 147–49, 152, 160–62, 177, 181, 189–90, 203, 216, 219–20, 246, 252, 255, 263, 274, 279, 281–82, 285–87, 316–17, 355, 365, 374–75, 403–4, 410, 417, 427–28, 431, 444, 447, 474–75, 477–78, 482–83, 488, 492, 498, 508, 511, 521, 526, 541, 544, 555, 566–68, 570–72, 580, 589, 596, 598, 600, 617–20, 624, 628, 633, 640, 671, 687, 711, 713, 715–16, 719–21, 749, 755–57, 768–69, 776, 808, 813–14, 820, 837, 848–49, 851, 854, 856–57, 861, 865–73, 878, 880–81, 898–901
reversal, xxxvii–xxxix, 44, 61, 77, 93, 102, 149, 173, 199, 224–26, 228–29, 242, 253, 262–63, 267–70, 272, 282, 286, 289, 303, 309, 311, 313–15, 321, 325, 328, 332, 342, 345, 350, 353–54, 356, 365, 367–68, 374, 379–80, 382–83, 413, 425, 434, 440–41, 446, 450, 454, 459–61, 463–64, 466, 484–85, 505, 556–57, 561, 612, 615, 664, 673, 712, 724, 770, 772, 778, 784, 891, 897, 899
revolution, 58, 66–67, 91, 271, 300, 389, 495, 620, 633, 744, 775, 806
righteous, 50, 98, 111, 158, 184, 235, 243, 256, 270, 276, 280, 286–87, 323–24, 331, 353–54, 369, 414, 417–18, 426–27, 432, 452, 472, 477–80, 486, 488, 511, 513, 525, 531, 543, 547–48, 552–55, 595, 624, 626–27, 672, 675, 704, 715
righteousness, xlvi, 218, 226, 256, 258, 270–71, 276, 322, 324, 354, 382, 418, 436, 473, 486, 505, 516, 528, 545, 573–74, 617, 621, 624, 626–28, 672, 675, 712, 762, 766, 842, 862
rights, 50–51, 83, 138, 223, 323, 333, 340, 344–45, 387, 579, 581–82, 584–85, 589, 607, 755, 866, 889
ring, 437, 440–41, 897
rise, xxxix, xli, 73, 104, 179, 189, 203, 220, 226, 229, 294, 339, 351–52, 394, 426–27, 477–78, 532, 539, 615, 625, 627–28, 631, 633, 698, 706, 708, 715, 731, 772, 791, 835, 840, 848, 870, 872, 900
ritual, 21, 39–42, 54, 58–60, 67–68, 72–73, 84, 111, 120–22, 124–25, 127, 139–40, 177, 181, 183–84, 233–34, 238–43, 248, 250, 269, 293, 315, 318, 333–34, 341–44, 347, 355–56, 395–96, 439–40, 451, 458, 486, 541, 612, 645, 658, 660–61, 669, 701, 721, 745, 761, 795, 802, 809, 812–13, 826, 834, 842, 860, 866, 869
river, 99, 163, 209, 416, 439, 458–59, 524, 540, 726, 759–60
road, 135, 230, 237, 245, 283, 478–79, 689, 748–49
robe, 36, 151, 353, 452, 583, 825, 830
rock, 62, 185, 203–4, 225, 308, 399–400, 430, 495, 500, 524–25, 546, 617, 620–21
rod, 182, 191, 235, 320, 447, 480–81, 499–500, 527, 743, 828
royalty, xlv, 7, 17, 171, 177, 182, 198, 200–3, 207, 210, 228–29, 231, 250, 256, 276, 286, 337–38, 340, 347, 359, 368–69, 393, 449, 452, 455, 474, 481, 500, 521–23, 527, 538, 601, 613–14, 703, 707, 713, 715, 718, 724–25, 731, 747, 755–60, 777, 781, 786, 792–93, 796, 801, 806, 828, 830, 832, 838, 842, 846, 893
ruler, 7–8, 17, 45, 68, 169, 177, 182, 185, 195, 288, 298, 314, 317, 346, 375, 392–94, 409–10, 412–14, 418, 441, 448–50, 452, 454, 465,

480–81, 489, 497, 500, 523, 540, 614, 628, 640, 688, 724, 734, 739, 743, 790–91, 818, 828, 841–42, 867
rulers, 33, 79, 195–96, 208, 212, 221, 250, 301, 368, 443, 449, 481–83, 496, 523, 554, 619–20, 713, 817, 849
Sabbath, xxx, xxxix, 16–17, 19–23, 27, 29–30, 33–35, 44, 46, 49, 54–58, 60, 66, 69, 101–2, 180–81, 227, 240, 247–48, 250, 273–75, 324–27, 329, 355–56, 395, 536, 564, 633, 639, 669–70, 675, 679–80, 682, 686–88, 728, 773, 795, 812, 815, 843, 849, 866, 873, 883
Sabbath year(s), 40, 125, 301, 333, 623, 677, 680, 838–39
sackcloth, 384, 749
sacred, 25, 72, 82, 104–5, 116, 124, 151, 226–27, 346, 350, 383, 418, 481, 485, 640, 651
sacrifice, 25, 27, 34–35, 41, 55, 62, 73, 83, 104, 112–17, 121–23, 128, 137, 149–50, 159, 173, 176, 178, 208–9, 243, 245, 256, 311, 325–28, 333, 338, 356, 358, 361, 385, 391, 397, 408, 435, 464, 472, 476–77, 486–88, 514, 544, 572, 603, 653–54, 658, 661, 702, 716, 750, 761, 764, 767–68, 773, 778, 795, 805–6, 809–10, 813, 821, 826–28, 842, 844–45, 866
sacrifices, 25, 33, 39, 41, 72, 83, 104, 115–16, 119, 150–51, 177, 243, 248–50, 273, 287, 307, 311, 315, 339–40, 342, 344, 385, 460, 463–65, 486, 488, 523, 567, 596, 651, 653, 658, 691, 740–41, 754, 768–69, 778, 809–10, 822, 826–28
sage, 182, 567, 569–70, 619–20, 704, 724, 868
Salem, 522–23
salt, 72, 488, 535, 691, 745, 781–82
salvation, xix, xxxviii, 85, 144, 180, 215, 218–19, 228, 234, 252, 257–58, 379, 415, 418, 425, 427, 429, 431, 444, 513, 515, 528, 543, 567, 766, 852
Samaria, 206, 209–10, 223, 226, 229, 278, 311, 316, 323, 346, 352, 369, 410, 726, 777, 805–6, 811–12, 823
Samarian, 805, 807–9, 854
Samaritan, 115, 440, 698, 805, 807–8, 854, 866
Samaritan Pentateuch, xli, 114–15, 294, 336
Samson, 173–74, 179, 184
sanctuary, 41, 81, 132–33, 136–37, 150, 180, 238, 319, 331, 339, 342–43, 381–82, 489, 492–94, 503, 546, 661–62, 668, 726, 738–39, 804, 813
sand, 12, 185, 209, 254, 311, 369
sandal, 164, 235, 241, 390, 585, 854
Sarah, 2, 183, 509, 621, 748
sarcastic, xxxi, 4, 58, 66, 297, 311, 399–400, 410, 436, 497, 523, 553, 555, 559, 599, 703, 726, 870
satan, 456, 561, 748–49
satire, xxv, 228, 328, 365, 390–91, 404, 619–20, 781
Saul, 166, 172–73, 175–77, 179–82, 184, 368, 413–14, 499, 523, 535–36, 615, 707–8, 716, 728–31, 733–35, 737, 743, 746, 819, 830, 841
scale, xxii, 338, 347, 357, 369, 418–19, 572, 819, 830, 837, 875, 889, 892, 896, 901
scepter, 7–8, 181–82, 294, 351, 472, 480–81
scouts, xxvii, 58, 63–64, 86, 89–93, 157–58, 174, 333–34, 599, 866
scribe, 115, 250, 263–65, 359, 450, 651–53, 733, 746, 765, 824, 840, 863, 865, 898, 900
scribal, xxv, xxxv, xxxix, xl, 114, 144–45, 217, 254, 257, 260, 264–65, 292–93, 299, 332, 405, 449, 560, 563, 597, 642, 689, 707, 715, 833, 840, 846, 863–64, 890, 893, 895, 899
scribal corruption/omission, 264, 647, 745–46, 765
scriptural exegesis (exegesis of scriptural traditions), xvii–xix, xxix, xxxii, xxxiv–xxxvii, xxxix, xl, xlii–xlvi, 3, 59, 78, 88–89, 99, 100, 157, 188, 190, 217, 219, 313–14, 317, 377, 394, 444, 473, 475–76, 560, 567–68, 577, 596, 618–19, 631, 633, 670, 698–99, 702, 713, 718, 738, 842, 847–48, 851, 856, 858–61, 863–65, 867–69, 871–72, 875, 889–90, 898–900, 903
scroll, xx, xxiii, xxviii, xxxiii, xli, xlii, xlv, 73, 110, 157, 162–63, 204, 212, 216–17, 220, 257, 263–65, 289, 313, 349, 356, 363, 372, 375, 431, 458, 475, 566, 570, 577, 590, 617, 623–24, 627, 632, 635, 650, 654, 669, 684, 717–18, 774, 822–26, 846, 857, 863, 868, 870–71, 874–75, 897, 901
sea, 5–6, 21–22, 100–1, 157, 161, 164–65, 185, 209, 225, 235, 237, 245, 251, 253, 255, 297, 303, 311, 354, 369, 380, 406–8, 410, 415–16, 428, 430, 434, 439, 458–59, 482, 490, 492, 505–7, 513, 515, 518, 524–25, 532–33, 540–41, 545, 549, 563, 609, 671, 673, 745, 788
season, 30, 331–32, 480
Second Temple, xxxv, xxxviii–xxxix, xli, 69, 139, 239, 248, 393, 439, 441, 444, 448–49, 456, 460, 464–65, 529, 590, 598, 626, 636, 641, 665, 678–79, 698, 699, 705, 727, 764, 797, 805, 847, 851, 858–64, 871, 889, 892, 897–99
sectarian, xli, xlv, 114–15, 394, 598, 626, 655, 679, 805, 807, 848, 857–59, 861–65, 899
seducer, 137–38, 275
seed, xxiv, 83, 136–37, 144, 195, 216, 224, 249, 394, 422, 481, 510–11, 523, 540, 552, 655, 658, 661–62, 678, 792, 843, 874
seer, 360, 743, 774, 786, 802, 819, 821
Seidel's theory, xxv, xxx, 12, 61, 111, 221–22, 258, 272, 311, 315, 323, 329, 332, 355–56, 375, 382, 405, 411, 451, 457, 539, 542–45, 646, 651, 673, 759, 763, 825, 877, 896, 899
Seir, 96, 139, 173, 387, 431, 481
selling, xxvi, 47–52, 123, 125–27, 139, 288, 319–21, 390, 395, 455, 586, 666–67, 686–87
Sennacherib, 10, 229–31, 425, 458, 806, 811, 815–17
serpent, xxxi–xxxii, 3–5, 95, 209, 227, 237, 252–53, 297, 380, 409, 414, 416, 490, 501, 506
servant, 10–11, 21–22, 49, 101–3, 156, 163, 168, 178, 183, 191, 194–95, 215, 219, 226–27, 243–46, 272, 275, 286, 317, 331, 440–41, 448–49, 454, 498, 512, 527, 535, 540, 554, 573, 624, 627–28, 636, 664–65, 742, 744, 766, 795, 836
servants, xxv, xxxi, 47, 49–51, 64, 102, 110–11, 244, 248–49, 261, 263, 271, 275, 307, 360, 378, 445, 541, 544, 624, 636, 645, 660, 678, 702, 740, 748, 769, 836, 862
seventy nations, 146, 387–88, 584, 607
seventy sevens/weeks, 629, 871

seventy years, 52, 255, 278–79, 287, 301, 311, 402, 438, 444–48, 450, 618–19, 622–24, 640, 665, 683, 704, 818, 835, 837–39, 841–42, 873, 879, 883
sex, 51, 69, 103, 126, 180–81, 243, 262, 275, 351, 356, 390, 584, 612, 661, 778, 792
shaking, 136, 238, 382, 437, 439, 441–42
Shallum, 203, 212, 361, 368, 644, 696
Shalmaneser, 893
shame, xxv, 183, 246, 276, 298, 307, 317, 323, 350–51, 384, 391, 410, 419, 425, 455, 463, 547, 624–25, 894
Sheba, 188, 337, 489–90, 541, 708, 712, 744, 758, 762, 774
Shechem, 7, 115, 160–61, 324, 775, 870
sheep, 41, 115, 121, 128, 135, 150, 184, 215, 226, 244, 272, 280, 331–32, 413–14, 453–54, 458–59, 497, 540, 547–48
Shekaniah, 636, 660, 664, 840
shekel, 59, 137, 200, 459, 639, 662, 677
shelter, 247, 371, 385–86, 388–89, 391–94, 402, 414, 506, 858–59, 867
Shemaiah, 648, 714, 776, 779, 840
Sheol, 149, 255, 342, 430, 548
Shephatiah, 643, 645, 648
shepherd, 172, 195, 251–52, 296, 303, 314, 330–32, 369, 371, 381, 397, 414, 443, 453–54, 456–57, 545, 561, 656, 658, 668, 672, 867, 899
shepherds, 457
Shiloh, 271, 307, 492–94, 742
shine, xlii, 2, 285, 382, 384, 461, 464, 506, 540, 542, 546, 578, 619, 626–27
Shishak, 775, 778–79
shoulder, 150, 737, 826
shrine, 29, 39, 58, 69, 112, 115, 121, 125, 128, 130, 174, 183, 196–97, 202–3, 226, 321, 326, 340–41, 355, 360–61, 397, 493, 529, 654, 680, 716, 742, 751, 757, 762, 777–78, 804, 809, 811, 826, 855
sibling, 346, 723, 725, 791
siege, 208, 225, 229, 231, 233, 255, 289, 299, 310, 316, 318, 427, 458, 612, 617, 619, 815–16, 819, 833
sign, 12, 19, 22–23, 40, 52, 73, 132, 143–44, 147–48, 218, 224–25, 229–30, 232–34, 240, 255, 272, 313, 441, 448, 454, 481, 498, 510, 528, 582, 587, 592, 671, 713, 742, 767, 806, 810, 817, 891, 895
signet, 437, 440–41
Sihon, 73, 96–97, 139, 164, 169–70, 293–94, 396, 528–30, 532–33
silver, 11, 13, 125, 130, 137, 139, 174, 200, 208, 310, 321, 366–68, 433, 443, 459, 621, 641, 646, 653, 662, 667, 760, 762–63, 799, 824, 841
Simeon, 7, 167, 173, 707, 725, 823
simile, xxix, 42–43, 48, 131, 147, 172, 221, 225, 227–29, 244, 246, 250–52, 254–55, 272, 278, 296–97, 310–11, 333–34, 345, 361–62, 367–69, 383, 402, 412–14, 418, 427, 429, 479, 504, 544, 548, 590, 627, 656–59, 715, 894
sin, xxvii, xlvi, 9, 24–26, 50, 53, 64–65, 77, 85, 92, 109, 111, 116, 142, 152, 164, 178–80, 183, 189–90, 203, 208, 214, 218, 243–44, 255–56, 269, 273, 280, 283, 285–86, 319, 321, 323–24, 329, 401, 410, 415–18, 422–23, 465, 472, 479, 486–88, 495, 499, 504–5, 507, 511–12, 515, 517–20, 548–49, 555, 559, 561, 597–99, 610–11, 617, 622, 624, 665, 674, 687, 690, 702, 708, 710, 712, 721, 724–25, 733, 746–47, 749, 769–70, 777, 779, 787, 797, 809, 813–14, 819–21, 831, 834–36, 842, 854
Sinai (also see Horeb), xxxix, 39, 62, 109, 114, 149, 173, 274, 431, 523, 541
singer, 96, 338, 534, 541, 644, 646–47, 651, 727–28, 765, 768, 789, 826
singing, 216, 234, 257, 332, 416, 446, 456, 510, 513, 518, 535, 542, 545–46, 565, 603, 728, 751, 765–66, 768, 788–89, 795
sins, xxvii, 9, 26, 53, 77, 85, 179, 204, 207, 249–50, 254, 263, 273, 280, 284, 321, 324, 396, 416, 476, 504, 512, 514, 520, 558, 598, 614, 661, 664, 678, 703, 745, 769, 778, 810, 820–22, 838
sister, xxxii, 10, 153, 314, 316, 323, 352, 355, 592, 725, 741–42, 840, 854, 894
sister-in-law, 152
skin, 184, 564
skin disease, skin condition (also see leprosy), 59, 72, 84, 141, 233, 241–42, 440, 802–3, 809, 860
sky (also see heavens), 5–6, 64, 110, 270, 298, 434, 481–82
slaughtering, 41–42, 65, 82, 111–12, 116–19, 121–22, 151, 215, 244, 256, 272, 280, 301, 304, 308, 321, 326, 329, 339, 453, 489, 540, 745, 791, 799, 809–10, 813, 827
slave, xxxi, 2, 30, 32, 46, 49, 51, 101, 126–27, 151, 198–99, 240, 243, 275, 288, 399, 402, 457, 459, 464, 498, 667, 673, 725, 806, 808, 873
slavery, enslavement, xxxii, 2, 31, 47–49, 52, 125–27, 161, 173, 188, 238, 331, 345, 366, 389, 406, 425, 462, 495, 507, 647, 666–68, 670, 673–75, 682, 837
slaves, xxxi, xli, 19, 33, 35, 47–51, 67, 82, 84, 88, 101–3, 105, 125–27, 198, 223, 250, 256, 288, 331, 340, 345, 406, 445, 646–47, 667, 670, 676–77, 882
sleep, 331, 365, 390, 546, 569, 617, 624–26
smite, 132, 174, 529, 689
smiting, 209–10, 251, 528–30
snare, 25, 104, 164, 173, 258, 292, 311, 514, 657
social, 5, 18, 26, 33, 39–40, 84, 103, 124, 126, 131, 143, 181, 218, 220, 239–40, 242, 313–14, 316, 333, 344–45, 386, 390–91, 418, 444, 456, 469, 475, 496, 551, 602, 661, 668, 680, 706, 795, 899
Sodom (also see cities of the plain), 77, 214, 221, 297, 304–5, 311–12, 316, 323, 346, 362, 395, 436, 612, 878
sojourner (also see residing foreigner), 43, 50, 345, 679
sojourning, 10, 42–43, 72, 161, 315, 322, 483, 485–86, 507, 510–11, 653, 738
solidarity, 45, 93, 710, 725, 731, 734, 795
Solomon, xxviii, 119, 148, 188–202, 205–8, 211, 286–87, 337–40, 342, 346, 374, 386, 388–89, 412, 438–39, 458, 489–90, 512, 514, 521–23, 527, 534, 536–37, 541, 544, 560, 562, 564, 566, 593, 645, 647, 652, 654, 658, 664, 689–92, 701–3, 705–6, 708, 710–13, 715–17, 719–21, 724–25, 741–43, 745–48, 750–51, 753–76, 779, 811, 813–14, 817, 820, 826–27, 832, 834, 837, 841–42, 844–46, 870, 881, 891
Solomonic, 720, 751, 845–46
son, 2, 6–9, 21–22, 45, 68, 70, 101–2, 126, 134–35, 138–39, 151, 163, 168, 174, 177, 182–83, 191, 196,

202–3, 205, 212, 222, 230, 251, 256, 261, 263, 275, 278, 282, 289, 323, 336, 354, 358, 361–62, 385, 390–91, 394, 410–14, 440, 453–54, 456, 460, 463–64, 470, 472, 480–81, 491–92, 498–500, 504–5, 516, 520–22, 527, 535, 562–63, 566, 569–70, 576–77, 581, 586, 590, 593, 606, 617, 623, 640, 648, 684, 692, 715, 723–24, 726–27, 731–32, 742–43, 750, 754–55, 757, 762–63, 774–76, 785, 787, 793, 797, 808–10, 818, 826, 840, 846, 849, 866–67, 893
son-in-law, 278
song, 10, 62, 96, 185, 219, 221, 228–29, 272, 284, 294, 416, 427, 429–31, 473–74, 502, 535–37, 540, 542, 544, 546, 555, 593, 708, 738, 740, 744, 766–67, 788, 816
Song of Moses, 10, 145–46, 221, 268, 272, 351, 366, 387, 418, 494–95, 565
Song of the Sea, 10, 157, 415–16, 493
Song of David, 10, 185, 427, 429, 431, 555, 744
sons, xxv, xxvii, 6–8, 10–11, 25–28, 31, 35–36, 67, 72, 104–7, 122, 127, 144–46, 150, 163, 168, 170, 173, 176, 178–80, 191, 200–1, 210, 223, 249, 293–94, 301, 308, 318, 322, 329, 342–43, 378, 387, 413–14, 422, 452, 457, 464, 490, 497, 499, 503, 523, 527, 530, 534–36, 580, 615, 635, 657, 659–60, 677–79, 681, 690, 722, 724–27, 729, 745, 755, 765, 778, 781, 791, 793, 803, 810, 820, 840, 894
soul, 85, 148, 163, 191, 205, 209, 263, 285, 408, 505–7, 538, 540, 543, 546, 548, 593, 627, 704
source, xxi, xxvi, xxix, xxxiv–xxxv, xxxviii, xliii, xliv, xlvii, l, 66, 121, 201, 222, 225, 232, 294–95, 306, 321, 329, 398–99, 401, 410, 412, 414, 498, 506, 529, 556, 559, 613, 636, 642, 652, 691, 702, 708, 711, 717–19, 724, 726–27, 735–36, 741, 743, 749, 755–57, 771, 774, 790–92, 796–99, 801, 804–5, 813, 819, 821–22, 825–26, 829, 832, 840, 846, 890, 893, 895, 897, 899
sovereignty, xxv, 18, 28, 47, 86, 96, 101, 111, 128, 191, 241, 248–49, 253, 258–59, 271, 280, 282, 295, 307, 317, 319, 223–24, 327–28, 332, 342, 345, 355, 378, 380, 387–89, 396, 427, 429, 431, 453–54, 456, 469, 495, 518, 525, 527, 556, 607, 611, 652, 686, 688, 713, 762, 779, 806, 865
spear, 221, 303, 380, 788
spears, 222, 379–80, 411
Spirit, xix, xxv, 146, 179–80, 215, 236, 251, 306, 334–35, 337, 378–79, 383–84, 437, 441, 456, 506, 561, 762, 788, 872
spirit, xxv, xl, 4, 96, 179, 215, 235–36, 245, 251, 258, 270, 280, 313–14, 317, 324, 334, 336–37, 352, 373, 377–79, 381, 408, 437, 443, 455, 459, 466–67, 487–88, 517, 561, 564, 595, 599–601, 610, 622, 640–41, 842, 862
spouse, 25, 102–4, 423, 467, 606, 660, 792
staff, 8, 182, 225, 241, 319–20, 356, 443, 453–54, 457, 480, 540
star, 64, 110, 149, 215, 285, 294, 308, 372, 382, 384, 399, 480, 482, 533, 546, 565, 627–28, 873
statue, 357, 621, 730
statute, 46, 65, 77, 125, 141, 191, 288, 326–27, 335, 385, 390, 499, 527, 543, 578, 585, 667, 669, 674, 873, 881–82
stealing, 13, 17, 33–34, 54, 77, 104, 243, 271, 307, 369, 401, 574
stepmother, 7, 83, 151, 153, 725
stiff-necked, 275, 283, 308, 673
stone, 25, 41, 45, 104–5, 113, 152, 163, 194, 200, 208, 215, 263, 308, 334–35, 354, 357, 361, 364, 393, 416, 418, 473, 501, 525–26, 557, 568, 573, 653, 762–63
storehouse, 216, 310, 549, 842
storm, 407–8, 423, 431, 459, 542, 551
stream, 59, 221–22, 297–98, 410–11, 479, 540
strength, xxxii–xxxiii, 65, 97, 148, 205, 209, 237–38, 298, 315, 330, 389, 429, 498, 503, 524, 543, 563, 593, 705, 738–40, 780
striking, 59, 65, 73, 86, 97, 123, 134, 183–84, 204, 223, 247, 252, 277, 343, 353, 361, 375, 383, 410, 433, 437, 441, 443, 467, 488, 501, 530–33, 535, 543, 561, 564, 569, 608, 610–12, 614, 618, 621, 677, 776, 789, 791
suffering, 46, 144, 231, 243–46, 272, 280, 425, 452, 475, 485, 548, 552–55, 557–58, 562–63, 607, 609, 627–28, 673, 745, 772
sun, 30, 149, 214, 258, 285–86, 308, 356, 382, 384, 431, 465, 470, 490–91, 499, 505–6, 532–33, 547, 549, 608, 666
sunset, 140–42, 390, 667, 830
swearing, 33, 64, 110, 163, 247, 249, 283, 325, 369, 434, 462, 486, 500, 513–14, 517, 527, 660
sword, 174, 183, 222–23, 237, 273, 288–89, 298, 331, 349–50, 357, 373, 379–80, 409, 411, 457, 547, 551, 565, 748–49, 788
synchronic, xvii–xviii, xxix, xxxiv–xxxvi, 229, 359, 562, 717, 790, 799, 801, 804–5, 811, 892–93, 895, 900
synoptic, xxiii, 10–11, 31, 35, 53–54, 64, 80, 89–93, 95–96, 98, 108–10, 131, 138, 166–67, 169, 229–30, 299, 305, 515, 526, 545, 642, 647, 649–50, 652, 699–700, 711, 714, 729, 731, 734–38, 744–47, 757–59, 761–62, 765, 771, 775, 779–80, 782, 784–85, 789, 792, 796, 798–801, 804–5, 808, 810–11, 815, 818, 821–23, 829, 831, 833–834, 837, 843, 845, 851, 853, 856, 869, 881, 898, 901
tabernacle, 17–18, 22–23, 29–31, 35, 39–42, 53, 58–60, 66–68, 72–73, 113–16, 118, 121–23, 136–37, 140, 174, 181, 183, 189, 194–95, 197, 250, 335, 337–39, 344, 353, 562, 574, 677, 712, 716, 720, 723, 728, 737, 740–43, 750–51, 756–57, 762–65, 767–68, 772, 778, 795, 797, 803, 826–27, 842, 855, 860, 869, 902
tabernacles, 27, 34, 55, 494
Tabernacles, 55, 72, 82, 125, 128–29, 143, 150, 208, 288, 344, 452, 458, 485, 494–95, 542, 635, 639, 650–52, 668–69, 675, 680, 692, 768, 773, 815
tablet, 108, 110, 152, 208, 263, 496, 568–69
Tadmor (place), 771
Tamar, 589–90, 724–25, 744
Tarshish, 337, 376, 405–7, 489–90
taunt, 10, 96, 189, 204, 219, 237, 271, 276, 293–94, 297, 308–9, 385, 391, 397, 400, 430, 548, 574, 599, 732, 828, 870
teacher, 285, 382–83, 567–68, 570, 631, 862, 866
teachers, 77, 180, 329, 336, 343, 418, 433, 437, 439, 460, 463, 580, 668–69, 751, 803, 826, 873, 883–84

teaching, xix, xxi, 32, 39, 58, 79, 86, 99–100, 106, 122, 152, 180, 191, 215, 222–23, 281, 283–85, 314, 316, 329, 343–44, 411, 439, 451, 461, 478, 527, 547, 551, 566, 568–72, 574, 582, 601, 660, 769, 787, 804, 826, 835, 848, 864, 869, 898

Teman, 296, 303, 400–1, 431

temple (also see Second Temple), 30, 115, 119, 125, 130, 139, 171, 177, 182, 188–90, 192, 194–98, 202, 206–8, 210, 216, 218, 220, 222–23, 226, 230, 232–34, 238, 240–41, 247, 249–50, 270–71, 277–78, 281, 298, 300, 306–7, 313–14, 316–17, 337–42, 344, 346–47, 353, 355, 374, 381, 389, 393–94, 408, 411, 418, 428, 430, 432, 438–44, 446–52, 456–58, 464–65, 468, 486, 503–4, 521–22, 525, 527, 535, 540–41, 544–45, 574, 580, 582, 590, 597, 603–4, 606–8, 617, 619, 621, 640–42, 652–54, 658, 664–66, 668, 670, 675, 677–78, 691, 695–98, 701–8, 710–12, 714, 716, 719–20, 723–24, 726–28, 730–31, 737–39, 742–43, 745–47, 749–51, 753–59, 761–70, 772–74, 776–77, 781–82, 794–97, 799, 801–6, 809, 811–13, 815–16, 819, 823–27, 832–34, 836–37, 841–42, 845, 855–56, 859–61, 865–66, 868, 870, 873, 879, 881, 884, 891, 902

temptation, 26, 61, 73, 93, 106, 493, 513, 570–71, 592, 679, 818, 894

Ten Commandments, xxx, 20–22, 24, 34, 97–101, 131, 134, 151–52, 247, 270–71, 274, 325, 369, 442, 495, 564, 568, 574, 676, 778, 847, 869

ten lost tribes, 776–77 (cf. remnant of northern tribes, 811, 813)

tent, 31, 36–37, 39, 41, 72, 92–94, 111, 147, 168, 178, 185, 194–95, 226, 342–43, 385, 392–93, 413, 483, 485–86, 513, 515–16, 545, 562, 728, 742–43, 765, 768, 772, 858

tenth generation, xxxiii, 201, 238, 248, 581, 606, 657, 684, 689

territory, 28–29, 112, 133, 144, 163, 167, 193, 295, 361, 402, 480

test, xxiii, xlvii, 77, 108, 225, 230, 265, 501–2, 525, 547, 555, 817–18, 843

testimony, 69, 79, 99, 134, 157, 220, 247, 352, 358–59, 388, 396, 429, 431, 484, 543, 649, 660, 682, 735, 753, 868

theophany, 23, 98–99, 198, 203–4, 255, 349, 365, 429, 431–32, 459, 524, 705, 712, 720, 741, 757–58, 760, 768–70, 772, 814

threshing, 65, 84, 151, 323, 331, 384, 418, 621, 652, 702, 710, 747–48, 763–64, 767, 844–45, 860–61

throne, xx, 119, 191–92, 195–96, 198, 215, 262, 286–87, 309, 349–50, 386, 394, 472–73, 499, 521–23, 527, 545, 743, 751, 755, 762, 774, 781, 841, 867

Tiglath-pileser (Pul), 225, 228, 361, 726, 805, 808–9

tithe, 68, 84, 125, 143, 385, 391, 681, 728

tithes, 58, 68, 82, 115–16, 124–25, 128–29, 143, 208, 353, 395, 470, 677, 681, 754, 815, 842

tongue, 317, 547, 574

tooth, 24, 46, 134, 142, 280, 323, 373, 552, 610, 621

Topheth, 209, 308, 810

torah, xix–xx, 61, 78–79, 81, 110, 113, 149, 153, 156, 181, 284–85, 329, 334–35, 344, 347, 360, 410, 456, 479–80, 487, 499, 508, 511, 543–44, 547, 565, 568–71, 624, 705, 744, 870, 901

Torah, xix–xx, xxxiii–xxxv, xxxviii–xxxix, xli, xliv–xlvi, xlviii, 7–10, 12, 17–20, 22, 24–25, 27, 29, 32, 35, 39–41, 44, 46–47, 49–54, 59, 61, 63, 64, 66, 71, 78–82, 85, 87–90, 95, 99–100, 103, 105–6, 109, 112, 116–17, 122, 125, 132, 134–38, 144, 146–47, 149, 152–53, 155–58, 160–64, 170, 172–74, 177–81, 188–89, 191, 204–5, 207, 216–17, 219–21, 223–24, 226, 235–36, 239–41, 243, 248–49, 251–52, 254, 261–63, 265, 270–71, 273–74, 281–82, 284–86, 289, 291–92, 294, 313–16, 318, 324, 329, 333, 336, 339–41, 344–45, 355–56, 360, 367, 369, 374–75, 386–87, 390, 394–96, 401, 411, 417, 421–23, 428, 439–40, 444, 451, 456, 460, 465, 469–70, 475, 478–81, 484, 486, 488–89, 493–94, 496–97, 499–502, 507–11, 515, 517, 526, 528–30, 532, 543–44, 553, 564, 567–71, 574–75, 579–80, 582, 584, 588, 596–98, 604, 614, 617, 622–24, 631–40, 651–52, 655–56, 659, 661, 664, 667–70, 675–81, 684–91, 698, 705, 713, 716, 718, 720, 722–23, 725, 726, 728, 731, 737–38, 740, 742, 751, 752, 763–65, 772, 779, 786–88, 797–800, 802, 807, 813–15, 818, 822–26, 828, 834, 839, 843–44, 849–50, 854, 857, 860–61, 868–70, 872, 876, 878, 883, 890, 893–95, 897, 900–1

torah collection (Deut 12–26), 81–84, 87–88, 112, 119, 122, 125–26, 128–29, 131, 133, 135, 150–52, 680, 869, 901

town, 82, 119, 129, 144, 163, 172, 414, 575, 580, 643, 681, 741, 787

towns, 21–22, 96–97, 101–2, 119, 123, 142, 151, 159–60, 162, 164, 172, 270, 275, 304–5, 307–8, 319, 447, 635, 646, 651, 670, 681, 725, 735, 741–42, 745, 770, 799–800, 806, 809, 823

trace, xxxviii, xl, 66, 166, 220, 330, 621, 627, 641, 655, 724, 729, 803, 889, 901

trade, 125, 169, 199, 337, 399–400, 402, 712, 758–60, 774, 806, 891

traditional, xxviii, xlviii, 115, 132, 151, 239, 242–43, 263, 295, 346, 393, 410, 456, 468, 525, 575, 588, 599, 637, 640, 656, 658, 667, 712, 719, 725, 727, 771, 776, 778, 780, 802, 803, 819, 830–31, 842, 844, 858, 897, 900

transgenerational, 17, 20, 23–24, 26, 53, 107–9, 421–22, 493, 505, 519–20, 550, 558–60, 834

transgression, 5, 24, 87, 207, 243–44, 256, 272, 351, 415, 418, 420, 494, 504, 523, 611, 661–62, 747–48, 776, 784

Transjordan, 63, 70, 73–74, 79, 95–97, 118, 149, 157, 161, 164, 169, 293–95, 529–30, 532, 671, 687, 706, 725–26

travel, 28, 58, 60–63, 94–95, 149, 168, 813

treaty, 26, 119, 158–60, 188, 198–200, 202, 208, 238, 581, 657, 660, 690, 729, 758–61, 771–72, 775, 782, 785, 790, 792

tree, xxix, xxxi, 3–4, 12, 52, 77, 164, 191, 193, 205, 207–9, 222, 248, 255–56, 258, 272, 310, 352, 357, 360–61, 370, 382, 409–12, 443, 448, 451, 478–80, 547, 570, 574, 594, 625, 681

trees, 4, 40, 52, 200, 205, 307, 315, 331–33, 338, 352–53, 358, 360,

443, 446, 456, 479, 592, 635, 639, 669–70, 681, 839
tribe, 10, 58–59, 70–71, 89, 129–30, 158, 166–67, 174, 184, 197–98, 301, 320, 342, 345–47, 413–14, 508, 528, 585–86, 706–7, 723–25, 727, 732, 734, 747, 755, 762–63, 776–78, 787, 823, 869
tribes, 10, 40, 60, 63, 70, 73, 89, 115, 129, 164, 167–68, 172, 184, 195, 197, 199, 208, 221, 286, 340, 345–46, 361, 462, 490, 502, 580, 624, 646, 654, 687, 706, 708, 710, 716, 723, 725–26, 733–34, 737, 739–40, 754, 769, 776–77, 787, 811, 813
tribute, 226, 229–30, 328, 389, 489–90, 682, 739, 751, 758–59, 805, 809, 815, 831
trumpet, 72–73, 320–21, 383, 459, 494, 542, 668, 692, 815
trust, 7, 94, 204–5, 214, 225, 230–31, 255, 257, 307, 479, 486, 493, 517, 527, 540, 543, 545, 570, 574, 688, 780, 789
the Twelve Prophets/Book of the Twelve Prophets, 370–72, 380, 892, 901
twelve tribes (also see ten lost tribes), 89, 172, 184, 208, 346, 646, 706–7, 723
twilight, 60–61, 276, 407, 444, 500, 737, 742
typological (also see figural), xxxviii, 10, 114, 195, 234–37, 241, 439, 441, 448, 580, 618, 641, 646, 650, 715–16, 720–21, 845, 849, 854–56, 862–63, 894, 902–3
typology, 155, 189, 236, 238, 241, 294–95, 341, 407, 552, 591, 632, 634, 638, 641, 650, 712, 715, 757, 762–64, 853, 855, 858, 862–63, 871, 894, 902
Tyre, 77, 188, 192, 208, 226–27, 255, 278, 291, 330, 336–37, 354, 387–89, 459, 629, 758, 762–63
Ugarit, 294, 431, 626
uncircumcised, 43, 52–53, 61, 124, 139, 238–41, 243, 249–50, 309, 322, 340–41, 354, 582, 604, 614, 701, 769, 772, 820, 859, 874
unclean (also see clean), 42, 61, 68, 120, 140, 180, 215, 248, 321, 329, 343–44, 395–96, 437, 439, 795, 804
understanding, xxi, xxxvii, 85, 123, 145, 224, 239, 249, 263, 317–18, 386, 401, 427, 434, 466, 495, 497, 531–33, 552, 564, 569, 573–75, 579, 626, 638, 669, 675, 678, 714, 720, 756, 762–63, 792, 847, 861, 870
underworld, 236, 352, 354, 522, 640
unfaithful, 77, 207, 262, 272, 314, 352, 368, 467, 488, 662, 664–65, 691, 731, 779, 804, 809
unfaithfulness, 53, 94–95, 122, 201, 207, 272, 360, 486, 623–24, 657, 662, 664, 730, 769, 783, 811, 820–21
unity, 3, 9, 40, 218, 334, 370, 372, 454, 476, 511
Uriah, 185, 208, 278, 589, 708–10, 733
Urim, 149, 645, 730
Uzza, 210, 644
Uzziah, 208, 211, 523, 648, 716, 801–4, 809, 846
valley, 236, 256, 311, 380, 383, 449, 683, 745, 809, 816
vengeance, 7, 78, 204, 298, 304–5, 349, 420–24, 542, 549, 615, 666
vessels, 106, 206, 241, 243, 604, 617, 619, 641–42, 652–54, 728, 832–33, 837, 873, 884
victory, 69, 95, 105, 167, 417, 429, 431, 488, 522–23, 743, 746, 780, 784–85, 788, 799–800
vine, 191, 193, 205, 222, 351, 356, 382, 409–12, 443, 448, 451–52, 542, 592, 854
vineyard, xxiv, 67, 88, 106, 136, 150, 162, 255–56, 267, 292, 296, 393, 436, 444, 452–53, 593, 867, 894
violation, 19, 22, 29, 176, 239, 269, 274, 319, 326, 390, 470, 606–7, 633, 686, 688, 721, 746, 800, 812
violence, 103, 210–12, 276, 298, 329, 383, 430, 433, 467, 604, 607, 691
virgin, 33, 137, 172, 276, 606, 609
vision(s), xxv, xli, 219, 221–24, 247, 255, 313–14, 319–21, 337, 339, 344–48, 353, 378, 383, 399, 410, 412, 441, 444, 446–50, 458, 498, 614, 618–21, 624–29, 683, 768, 770, 772, 775, 785, 802, 816, 826, 846, 895
voice, 80, 90, 92–93, 100, 131, 147, 162, 204, 215, 236, 238, 260, 267, 270, 272, 277, 284–85, 308, 316, 349, 360, 362, 380, 400, 406, 408, 429, 434, 455, 459, 468, 472, 475, 501–2, 516, 544, 558, 570, 610, 640, 654, 700, 738, 765, 768, 791, 866, 868
vomit, 40, 54, 333, 407, 566, 658, 839
wages, 77, 141–42, 226–27, 418, 459
walk, 39, 133, 163, 191, 222–23, 268, 283, 286–87, 331, 335, 409–12, 418, 436, 451, 459, 478–79, 495, 497, 569, 628, 822
wall, 183, 298–302, 304, 338, 371, 448, 452, 609, 650, 665, 670, 686, 692, 730, 816, 837
war, 34, 46, 83–84, 97, 105–6, 134, 139–41, 147, 155, 160, 181, 192, 194, 221–23, 225, 278, 294, 310, 316, 318, 369, 380, 387, 399–400, 411–12, 415, 427, 521–22, 612, 708, 729, 731, 744–46, 750–51, 753–54, 780, 788, 799–800
warrior, 194, 296, 302, 431, 493, 521, 733–34, 754
washing, 36, 42, 123, 439, 452, 489, 547
water, xxix, 42, 73, 117, 120, 123, 138–40, 164, 180, 208, 254, 304, 334, 354, 361, 434, 458, 478–80, 508, 524–25, 540, 581, 592, 599, 606, 614, 684, 732–34, 816, 827–28
waters, 7, 32, 107, 146, 164, 228, 236–37, 251, 253, 255, 349, 407–8, 416, 428, 430, 458, 479, 505–6, 513, 517, 524, 531, 541–42, 696
wealth, 199–200, 250, 389, 524, 711–12, 725, 751, 758, 760, 774, 802, 816–18, 845
week, 19, 21, 27–28, 34, 55, 73, 82, 101, 128–29, 141, 143, 181, 309, 485, 619, 624, 668, 773, 815, 845, 871
weeping, 173, 235, 253, 292, 365, 376–77, 466, 470, 604, 609–10, 659
wheat, 28, 495, 845
whore, 200, 350, 598, 612, 792
wicked, 77, 138, 172, 174, 176, 244–45, 257, 320, 324, 369, 418, 422, 424–25, 427–28, 430–32, 434–35, 477–80, 497, 507, 513, 516, 549, 552, 558–60, 573, 624, 626, 702, 704, 721, 770, 779, 785, 790, 809, 813, 818, 820, 834, 836, 854
wickedness, 111, 172, 273, 283–85, 307, 320, 324, 354, 358, 423, 520, 611, 691, 724
widow, xxvi, 40, 42, 69, 88, 124–25, 141, 150, 152–53, 166, 215, 271, 280–81, 297, 307, 323, 344–45, 355, 384, 399–401, 457, 497, 519–20, 545, 548, 579, 582–84, 586, 588, 606, 681, 860

wife, xxxii, 10, 51, 69, 73, 103, 126, 137–38, 140, 142, 151, 183–85, 246, 268–69, 276, 315, 330, 351, 355, 358, 362, 368, 390, 466–68, 470, 509, 520, 561, 570–71, 574–75, 587, 589, 606, 708, 772
wild, 4, 6, 25, 28, 41–42, 123, 253, 256, 308–9, 331, 349, 482, 580, 635, 670, 726
wilderness, xxvii, 41, 58, 61–62, 64–65, 67, 72, 77, 86, 88, 94–96, 99–100, 111, 130, 138, 149, 161, 168, 170, 178, 184, 202, 204, 209, 215, 225, 235–36, 242, 251, 255, 267–68, 311, 314, 325, 327–28, 331–32, 339, 342–43, 350–51, 357–58, 369, 385, 394–95, 407, 458, 468, 476, 492–95, 501–2, 504, 508, 513–17, 524, 532–33, 583, 594, 671, 674, 683, 742, 753, 817–18, 826, 855, 860, 869, 894
wind, 203–4, 235–36, 310, 319, 370, 459, 542, 549, 560 (whirlwind), 594, 599, 621
windows of the heavens, 227, 469
wine, 184, 257, 292, 343–44, 380, 383, 390–91, 393, 397, 418, 436, 439–40, 442, 452, 475, 493–94, 498, 501, 506, 523, 526, 539, 592, 681, 687
wing, 146, 151, 296, 302, 349–51, 539, 546, 583–84
wisdom (also see Woman Wisdom), xxxv, 4, 71, 182, 215, 217, 257, 271, 296, 309, 322, 354, 396, 400–1, 436, 473, 475, 477–78, 497, 505–7, 543–44, 560, 565–75, 577–78, 590, 592–93, 596, 598, 601–2, 703–5, 711–12, 758–59, 786, 802, 896
wise, 11–12, 88, 129, 215, 401, 473, 481, 550, 553, 566, 568, 570, 576–77, 626–28, 704–5, 787
witness, xxxvii, 17, 34, 69, 77, 99, 134, 145, 150, 264, 270, 301, 336–37, 349, 392, 406, 530, 532, 540, 573, 587, 660, 848, 872
witnesses, 77, 83, 130, 134, 144, 153, 173, 179, 197, 208, 220, 332, 336, 540, 727, 735, 786
wives, 25–26, 83, 199–202, 249, 269, 281, 313–14, 343, 352, 598, 655, 657–58, 662, 678, 690, 760, 791, 796–97
woman, xxxi–xxxii, 2–5, 9, 13, 45, 69, 126, 137, 142–43, 180, 183, 215, 238, 255, 268, 276, 292, 296, 302–3, 310, 315, 333–34, 356, 390–91, 413, 418, 467, 488, 543, 549, 555, 567, 570–71, 573–75, 578, 582, 590–92, 602, 705, 730, 792, 894, 902
Woman Wisdom/Lady Wisdom, xxxv, 570, 574–75, 578, 592, 705
womb, 13, 27, 52, 59, 67–68, 255, 358, 362, 364, 563–64, 590, 602, 681, 723
women, xxv–xxvi, 106, 151, 178, 180, 200–1, 223, 256, 288, 307, 344, 349, 355, 369, 378, 397, 580, 583, 612, 647, 655, 662, 668, 689–91, 860, 874
wood, 66, 72, 307–8, 357, 454, 635, 639, 677, 680, 682, 762–63
wool, xxiv, 72, 136–37, 453
worker, 49, 51, 84, 136, 141–42, 240, 341, 459, 583, 613, 762–63
worship, 7, 17, 25–26, 28–29, 34, 39, 41, 54, 61, 73, 76–78, 82, 105, 107, 112–13, 115–23, 125, 127–31, 133, 136, 151, 155, 158, 161–62, 171, 173–74, 181, 193, 195–98, 202, 207–9, 216, 227, 234, 249, 256, 261, 269–70, 273, 278, 287, 307, 313–16, 339–40, 343–45, 353, 356–57, 360, 365, 379, 386, 390–91, 397, 411, 417–18, 423, 433–35, 439–40, 457, 461, 463, 465–66, 469, 471–77, 485–87, 494–95, 498, 502–4, 510, 512–13, 520, 526, 528, 530, 559, 572–73, 580, 596, 598, 603, 639, 651, 654, 661, 665, 680, 690, 694–98, 701–8, 710, 716, 718–21, 726–29, 731, 734–41, 745, 747, 749–53, 756–57, 763–64, 767–68, 770, 772–73, 776–78, 780–81, 788, 793, 795, 800–1, 803–6, 809, 811–16, 818–19, 822, 824–28, 836, 838, 841–43, 859, 871, 891, 896
worshiper, 40–41, 119, 125, 143–44, 379, 390–91, 417, 435, 476, 486, 597, 701
worshiping, 20, 24–25, 30, 41, 46, 116, 124, 162, 174, 198, 284, 308, 322, 366, 423, 435, 451–52, 495, 656, 671, 714, 723, 740–41, 753, 762, 767–68, 777, 799–800, 806, 810, 812, 822
wrath, xxv, 24, 26, 34, 39, 46, 92, 108–9, 225, 229, 246, 262, 271, 276–77, 289, 296, 305, 307–8, 311, 319–21, 329, 337, 342, 349, 352, 361–62, 368, 377, 379, 399, 421, 423–24, 428, 434, 436, 439, 446, 468, 481, 500, 516, 608, 612, 624, 628, 664, 666, 687, 702, 779, 787, 806, 814, 817–18, 823, 836, 838
yeast, 27, 34, 60, 128
yoke/yoked, xxiv, 136, 309, 331–32
youth, 9, 63, 85, 91, 99, 106, 120–21, 123–24, 137, 146, 151, 172, 178, 246, 253, 263–65, 267–68, 276, 286, 296, 303, 325, 328, 351, 358, 362, 378, 384, 391, 414, 454, 456, 468, 470, 504, 567–71, 576, 579, 584, 591–92, 594, 599, 735, 824, 897
Zadok, 342, 523, 726, 741, 839
Zadokite, 287, 340, 343, 726
zeal, 386, 391, 423, 473, 516, 624
Zeboyim (also see cities of the plain), 77, 358, 362, 367, 878
Zebulun, 166–67, 777, 813
Zechariah (ruler in Israel), 203, 211, 368
Zechariah (son of Jehoiada), 714, 796–98
Zechariah (prophet in the days of Uzziah), 801–2
Zedekiah, 188, 212, 276, 278, 288–89, 299, 301, 701–2, 716, 728, 820, 832–38, 884
Zerubbabel, xxxiv, 440–41, 443, 448–50, 454, 511, 525, 640, 643, 648, 650, 652–53, 699, 707, 840
Zilpah, 126
Zimri, 203, 211, 291, 696
Zion (also see Lady Jerusalem), 215, 218, 221–23, 226, 235, 237–39, 241–42, 253, 255–58, 276–77, 297, 303, 354, 371, 373, 377–83, 385, 389, 394, 398, 404, 409, 411–13, 418, 421, 425, 447, 451–52, 456, 459, 476, 481, 484, 492–94, 510, 525–28, 543, 546–47, 593, 605–6, 609–12, 732, 795
Zobah, 208, 389, 535, 771

AUTHOR INDEX

Aberbach, Moses, 202, 905
Abernethy, Andrew T., 393, 905
Achenbach, Reinhard, 687, 905
Ackroyd, Peter R., 730, 818, 905, 907
Aitken, James K., 558, 905, 914
Akiyama, Kengo, 43, 905
Allen, Leslie C., 221, 302, 309, 320, 325, 345, 415, 509, 523, 525–26, 528, 531, 655, 666, 829, 833, 905, 911, 928
Alter, Robert, xxxiv, 226, 293, 658, 893, 902, 905
Amit, Yairah, 748, 905
Anderson, Carl Roy, 216, 671–73, 905
Anderson, Francis I., xlix, 361, 368, 389, 415, 417, 419, 430, 542, 810, 905
Anderson, William H. U., 596, 601, 905
Anderson, Bernhard W., 236, 905, 931
André, Gunnel, 478, 905
Ansberry, Christopher B., xlix, 567–69, 572, 574, 905
Archer, Gleason L., l, 905
Aristotle, 80, 654, 700, 816, 905
Armerding, Carl E., xlix, 422, 425, 905
Assis, Elie, xlix, 374, 382, 463, 905
Austin, J. L., 896, 905
Averbeck, Richard E., 19, 49, 113, 117–18, 505, 905
Avioz, Michael, 742, 906
Awabdy, Mark A., 72, 239, 906

Baden, Joel S., xxi, 906
Baker, David L., 862, 905–6, 908–9, 911
Baldwin, Joyce G., 625, 629, 906
Balentine, Samuel E., 234, 610–11, 906
Bandstra, Barry, 5, 906
Banister, Jamie Aislinn, xlix, 415, 430, 906
Barker, Joel, 406, 906
Barnes, E. W., 750, 906
Barr, James, 275, 906
Barrett, Matthew, xix, 444, 902, 906
Barter, Penelope, 354, 906, 917, 923, 925, 932
Barton, John, 217, 890, 906, 910–11, 916, 921
Bartor, Assnat, 18, 906
Bass, Derek Drummond, xlviii, 367, 906
Bateman, Herbert W., IV, 756, 906
Bates, Matthew W., 476, 906
Bauckham, Richard, 23, 877, 906
Baumgartner, Walter, 244, 272, 275–76, 530, 906, 910
Bautch, Richard J., 638, 671, 673, 905–6, 929
Bavinck, Herman, xix, 849, 906
Bazak, Jacob, 532, 906
Beale, Greg K., xxiii, 316, 850–52, 854, 861, 895–96, 906, 915
Beattie, Derek Robert George, l, 579, 907
Becking, Bob, 655, 658, 907
Beentjes, Pancratius C., 329, 332, 355, 457, 542, 899, 907
Begg, Christopher T., 424, 715–16, 791, 837, 844, 907, 927
Ben Zvi, Ehud, 278, 419, 637, 905, 907, 914–15, 920, 922, 925, 932
Bendavid, Abba, xlviii, l, 35, 41, 55, 73, 121, 343, 376, 544, 596, 646, 655, 841, 907
Bergen, Robert D., xlviii, 185, 907
Berger, Yitzhak, 615, 907
Bergey, Ronald, 221, 907
Bergland, Kenneth, 289, 907
Bergren, Richard V., xlviii–xlix, 302, 395, 417, 907
Bergsma, John S., xlviii, 315, 325–26, 907, 915
Berlin, Adele, xlix–l, 234, 241, 435–36, 474, 505, 509–10, 525, 557–58, 579, 606, 609, 612–15, 766, 893, 895, 905, 907–8
Berman, Joshua, l, 81, 90, 119, 579, 651, 667, 907
Berry, Donald K., xlix, 469, 907
Bertholet, Alfred, 44, 907
Bewer, J. A., xlix, 407, 924, 929
Bezzel, Hannes, l, 609, 907
Bird, Michael, 632, 678, 908
Blenkinsopp, Joseph, 231, 245, 257, 637, 652, 655, 674, 679, 704, 853, 908, 912, 920
Bloch-Smith, Elizabeth, 225, 908
Block, Daniel, xlviii–xlix, 113, 124, 149, 172, 320, 322, 324–25, 328, 332, 334–37, 341, 344, 346–47, 350, 353–54, 400–1, 585, 906, 908, 914–15, 928–29, 932
Blomberg, Craig L., 851, 861, 908
Bock, Darrell L., 855, 860, 906, 908, 910
Boda, Mark J., xlix, 171, 444–46, 448–49, 453–54, 456, 458, 514, 605, 610, 628, 661, 671, 674, 692, 715, 877, 908–9, 912, 918–22, 925–26, 929, 931, 935
Bodner, Keith, 702, 731
Bodner, Keith, 702, 731, 908, 912
Boling, Robert G., 171–72, 908
Bolle, Menachem E., xlviii, 53, 348, 908
Booij, Thijs, 519, 908
Bosman, Hendrik L., 43, 908
Botha, Phil J., 478, 908
Bramer, Stephen J., xlix, 395, 908
Braulik, Georg, l, 579, 583, 908
Braun, Roddy, 751, 753, 909
Brettler, Marc, xli, 482, 532, 909, 913, 922
Briggs, Emilie Grace, 541, 909
Bright, John, xlviii, 302, 306, 909
Brin, Gershon, 172, 456, 681, 751, 787, 906, 909
Brinks, C. L., 563, 909
Brodersen, Alma, xlix, 534, 538, 909
Brooke, George J., 394, 909, 921
Brown, Raymond E., 900, 909
Brown, William P., 567, 909
Brueggemann, Walter, xlviii, 367, 909
Brug, J. F., 44, 909
Bruno, Chris, 584, 656, 909
Bullock, C. Hassell, 500, 545, 877, 909
Burnett, Joel S., 537, 909
Burney, C. F., 195, 206, 233, 794, 909

Burnight, John, 562–63, 909
Burns, John Barclay, l, 912
Burrows, Millar, 919
Butler, Trent, 738, 909
Byargeon, Rick, 222, 909

Cahill, Michael, 525, 909
Calvin, John, 297, 666, 909
Campbell, Edward F., Jr., 575, 584, 909
Campbell, Iain D., I, 593, 909
Campolo, Tony, 847, 909
Carasik, Michael, xxxii, 335, 574, 580, 818, 909
Carpenter, Eugene E., 93, 909
Carr, David, l, 302–3, 592–93, 658, 909
Carroll, Robert P., xlviii, 302–3, 658, 909
Cassuto, Umberto, xlviii, 309–10, 365, 367, 369, 909
Cathcart, Kevin J., xlix, 425, 266
Chalmers, R. Scott, 365, 909
Chan, Michael J., 247, 934
Chan, Man Ki, l, 579, 909
Chapman, Cynthia R., 4, 470, 909
Chau, Kevin, 541, 909, 912, 918–19, 921, 929, 931, 935
Chavalas, Mark, 706, 909
Chavel, Simeon, l, 44–45, 60, 66, 70, 115, 579, 910
Cheyne, Thomas Kelly, xlviii–xlix, 258, 417, 545, 560, 562, 564, 910
Childs, Brevard S., xlviii–xlix, 35, 114, 144, 178, 204, 218, 227, 230–31, 243, 258, 279, 303, 314, 316, 346, 359, 398, 441, 478, 489, 534, 537, 590, 627, 816, 864, 867, 890, 910–11, 932
Chirichigno, Gregory, l, 905
Chisholm, Robert B., Jr., xlix, 227, 243–44, 278, 330, 427–28, 430–32, 491, 539, 741, 910
Clemens, David M., 599, 601, 910
Clifford, Richard J., 493, 910, 932
Clines, David J. A., 12, 244, 275, 508, 557–59, 638, 876, 909–10, 914, 923
Cogan, Mordechai, 194, 204, 229, 521, 794, 806, 910, 931
Coggins, Richard, xlix, 382, 830, 910
Cohen, Chaim, 587, 863, 910, 917, 935
Collett, Don C., 902, 910
Collins, John J., 625, 627, 636, 910
Compton, Jared, 584, 656, 909
Coogan, Michael, xlviii, 146, 323, 496, 910
Cook, Gregory D., 425, 910, 912
Cook, Stephen L., 342, 910, 912
Craigie, Peter C., 540, 78, 910–11
Crawford, Sidnie White, 918
Crenshaw, James L., xlix, 563, 572, 577, 911
Cudworth, Troy D., 776, 911
Cundall, Arthur E., 171, 911
Curtis, Edward Lewis, l, 843, 911, 915

Danby, Herbert, 860, 911
Davidson, A. B., xlix, 435, 911
Davies, G. I., 169, 911, 914
Davis, Ellen F., l, 157, 593, 911
De Vries, Simon J., 911
DeRouchie, Jason S., 87, 911, 914–15, 928–29
Dearman, J. Andrew, 395, 417, 911
Delamarter, Steve, 829, 911
Delitzsch, Franz, xlix–l, 194, 209, 227, 245, 257, 424, 427–28, 435, 526, 554, 569, 576, 608, 738, 746, 784, 911, 919
Dell, Katharine, xlix, 407, 551, 558, 560, 562, 572, 575, 595, 601–2, 905, 909, 911, 913, 915, 918, 921–23, 925, 928–29, 934–35
Di Lella, Alexander A., 625, 627, 916
DiFransico, Lesley, 415, 911
Diewert, David A., xlviii, 11, 911
Dijkstra, Meindert, 320, 911
Dillard, Raymond B., 119, 703, 711–12, 716, 757, 762–63, 770–71, 775, 781, 784, 790, 794, 798, 819, 828, 843, 845, 911
Dodd, C. H., 850, 895, 911
Domeris, William R., 281, 911
Doolittle, William R., 412, 911
Doron, Pinchas, 911
Dotan, Aron, 911
Dozeman, Thomas B., 377, 911, 925, 930
Driver, Daniel R., xxxviii, 110, 911–12
Driver, S. R., xlviii–l, 41, 53, 84, 109–10, 121, 136, 148–49, 153, 162, 172, 185, 206, 258, 302, 348, 377, 379–80, 382, 395, 404, 407, 417, 430, 554, 576, 601, 691, 788, 843–44, 911–12
Drumm, Curtis Scott, xxviii, 915
Duggan, Michael W., 161, 376, 637, 671–72, 674, 678, 877, 912
Dunne, John A., 393, 912

Edelman, Diana, 741, 905, 912, 914–15, 920, 922, 925, 932, 934
Edenburg, Cynthia, 174, 896, 912
Ego, Beate, 895, 912
Ehrensvärd, Martin, 918, 935
Eichorn, Johann Gottfried, xlviii, 912
Elitzur, Yehuda, xlviii, 172, 912
Elliott, C. J., xlix, 534, 912
Emanuel, David, 507, 510, 529, 532, 912, 931
Embry, Brad, l, 579, 585, 912
Endres, John C., l, 912
Eng, Daniel K., 306, 538, 576, 892, 912, 93
Enslinger, Lyle M., 364–65, 912
Erickson, Nancy, 136, 912
Eskenazi, Tamara Cohn, l, 590, 668, 676, 691, 912, 929
Estelle, Bryan D., 361, 912
Evans, John F., 324, 356, 384, 912
Evans, Craig A., 358, 852, 912, 916, 921, 924
Even-Shoshan, Abraham, xxi, xxvi, 42, 43, 44, 97, 106, 142, 156, 306, 315, 345, 368–69, 379, 423, 538, 570, 575, 577, 581, 585, 704, 748, 835
Fensham, F. Charles, 496, 912
Finlay, Tim, 590, 912
Finsterbusch, Karin, 543–44, 912, 920, 927
Firth, David G., l, 156–57, 547, 613, 615–16, 733, 912, 932
Fisch, Harold, 590, 912
Fischer, Alexander Achilles, 900, 935
Fischer, Irmraud, l, 579, 583, 912
Fishbane, Michael, xxii, xxvi, xxxvii, xxxix–xli, xlviii, l, 68, 97, 105, 117–18, 149, 249, 253, 269, 274, 288, 421, 463–64, 519, 538, 546, 554, 561, 565, 569, 574, 591, 623, 628, 634, 669, 687, 698, 813, 872, 877, 890, 895–96, 901, 912–13, 921
Floyd, Michael H., xlix, 424, 456, 905, 908, 913, 925
Forbes, A. Dean, 810, 905
Ford, William, 116, 157, 913
Foreman, Benjamin, 113, 913
Forman, Charles C., 601, 913
Fouts, David M., 781, 913
Fox, Everette, 178, 913
Fox, Michael V., 519, 558–59, 567, 571–72, 576–77, 597, 599, 907, 909, 913, 915, 924, 927, 931, 934–35
Frame, John, xix, 291, 505, 913
France, R. T., 854, 913
Freedman, David Noel, xlix, 145, 361, 368, 389, 415, 417, 419, 542, 544, 905, 913
Frevel, Christian, 167, 561, 913, 916, 920, 927
Friebel, Kelvin G., 326–27, 907, 909, 913, 924, 935
Fried, Lisbeth S., 202, 656, 658, 913, 924
Friedberg, 121, 913

Friedman, Richard E., 202, 913, 924
Frisch, Amos, 712, 913
Fuad, Chelcent, 45, 913

Gamble, Richard C., xix, 913
Ganzel, Tova, 357, 913
Gardner, Kristen H., 172, 913
Gentry, Peter J., 264, 756, 766, 913
George, Andrew R., 640, 842, 914–15
Gibson, J. C. L., 146, 294, 541, 914
Gibson, Jonathan, xlix, 462–63, 466, 469–70, 914
Giffone, Benjamin D., 8, 266, 656, 777, 844, 914
Gile, Jason, xlviii, 163, 326, 348, 351, 357, 914–15, 928–29
Gillingham, Susan E., 474–75, 489, 494, 498, 501, 523, 526, 539, 914
Ginsberg, H. L., xlviii, 366–67, 625, 628, 914
Girdlestone, Robert B., xlviii, 258, 914
Glanville, Mark R., 124, 914
Glatt-Gilad, David A., 96, 676, 702–3, 716–18, 726, 757, 780, 783, 790, 798, 803, 818, 822, 832, 846, 893, 914–15
Glenny, W. Edward, 859, 914
Goldberg, Arnold, 889, 914
Goldingay, John, 267, 474, 480, 484, 486, 502–3, 525, 527, 529, 532, 538–40, 542–43, 546, 619, 621–22, 629, 911, 914, 928
Gooding, D. W., 771, 914
Gordis, Robert, 558–59, 606, 914
Gordon, Cyrus H., 496, 587, 914, 928
Gordon, Robert P., 466
Goswell, Greg, 384, 389, 393, 905, 914
Gottwald, Norman K., l, 612, 914
Gough, Henry, l, 914
Goulder, Michael D., l, 579, 914
Grätz, 583, 636, 915
Gray, John, 194, 198, 208, 521, 915
Gray, G. Buchanan, xlix, 377, 382, 404, 539, 554, 912, 915
Green, Douglas J., 106, 915
Greenberg, Moshe, xxvii, xlviii, 69, 92, 101, 103, 105, 132, 134, 204, 280–81, 318, 323–25, 348, 350–51, 354, 688, 915, 931
Greengus, Samuel, 127, 135, 138, 915
Greenstein, Edward L., 565, 915
Greer, Jonathan S., 150–51, 915, 923
Grisanti, Michael A., xxviii, 92, 105, 149, 152, 206, 274, 913, 915
Gross, Carl D., 613, 667, 915
Grossman, Jonathan, l, 613–15, 915, 931
Grubbs, Norris C., xxviii, 915
Guillaume, Philippe, 346, 915
Gunn, D. M., 275, 905, 910
Guthrie, George H., 285, 851, 915

Haag, Istvan, 350, 915
Haarmann, Volker, 249–50, 915
Hahn, Scott Walker, 325–26, 915
Hakham, Amos, xlviii–xlix, 31, 915
Halpern, Baruch, 210, 212, 699, 717, 820, 830, 910, 915
Hamilton, Victor P., 23, 915
Harper, William Rainey, 370, 395, 905, 913, 915
Harrington, Hannah, 679, 915
Hartley, John E., 560, 916
Hartman, Louis F., xlix, 625, 627, 916
Harvey, John E., xlviii, 916
Harvey, Paul B., Jr., 638, 920
Hayes, Christine E., 44, 103, 109–10, 658, 661–62, 916
Hays, Christopher B., xlviii, 227, 358, 435, 655, 916
Hays, J. Daniel, xlviii, 185, 192, 199, 266, 316, 348, 845, 916
Hays, Richard B., xxi–xxii, xxxvii, xl–xli, 361, 753, 855, 893, 902, 916, 934
Heim, Knut Martin, 576–77, 916–17
Heller, Roy L., 741, 802, 916
Hendel, Ronald, 265–66, 916
Hensel, Benedikt, 658, 916
Henze, Matthias, l, 619–20, 625, 628, 916, 921
Hess, Richard S., 41, 163, 916
Hibbard, J. Todd, 227, 258, 916
Hilber, John W., 474, 523, 916
Hill, Andrew E., xlix, 440–41, 463, 466, 469–70, 738, 916
Hillers, Delbert R., 413, 916
Hoffer, Vicki, 233, 916
Holladay, William L., xxv, xlviii, l, 268, 272, 275, 302, 304, 308–9, 311, 916
Holmstedt, Robert D., 587, 916
Hoppe, 121, 913
Hornkohl, Aaron D., 265, 916
Hornung, Gabriel F., 614, 917
Hossfeld, Frank-Lothar, 336, 378, 488, 492, 496, 498–99, 501, 503, 517, 520, 522–23, 525–26, 529, 533, 538, 543–44, 546, 917
House, Paul R., 361, 372, 907, 917
Houtman, C., 637, 917
Hubbard, David Allan, 917
Hubbard, Robert L., 859, 917
Huffmon, Herbert B., 135, 917
Hummel, Horace D., 145, 917
Hundley, Michael, 196, 917
Hunter, Alastair, xlix, 407, 917
Hurowitz, Victor Avigdor, 383, 574, 917
Hurvitz, Avi, 265, 543, 551, 910, 917, 935
Hwang, Jerry, 369, 917
Hyatt, Philip J., 144, 917

Ibn Ezra, 478, 599
Imes, Carmen Joy, 353, 393, 847, 917
Irwin, William, 889, 917
Issler, Klaus, 125, 917

Jackson, Bernard S., l, 579, 917
Jacobson, Rolf A., 474, 494, 498, 501, 523, 549, 917
Janzen, David, 655, 707, 917
Japhet, Sara, 48, 632, 636, 638, 678, 691, 698, 703, 710, 717, 725, 727, 749, 751, 766, 771, 781, 783–84, 817–19, 828, 835, 840, 843, 891, 907, 917–18, 920, 925
Jarick, John, 829, 918–19
Jassen, Alex, 687, 918
Jenkins, Steffen G., 519, 918
Jeon, Yong Ho, 200, 918
Jericke, Detlef, xlviii, 10, 31, 918
Jerusalmi, Isaac, 654, 918
Jindo, Job Y., 254, 918
Joffe, Laura, 537, 918
Johnson, Benjamin J. M., 702, 731
Johnson, Luke Timothy, 394, 753, 918
Johnson, S. Lewis, xix, 851, 918
Johnson, Willa M., 658, 918
Johnson, Benjamin J. M., 702, 731, 908, 912
Johnston, Gordon, 182, 499, 756, 906, 918
Johnston, Philip S., 932
Johnstone, William, 834, 908, 918
Jones, Edward Allen, III, l, 580, 589–90, 918
Jonker, Louis C., 772, 918
Joosten, Jan, 114, 201, 265–66, 417, 551, 830, 916, 918
Joseph, Simon J., 848, 918
Joyce, Paul M., 565, 918, 921

Kaiser, Walter C., 365, 918
Kalimi, Isaac, 711, 808, 816, 832–33, 919
Kaminsky, Joel S., 239, 919
Kartveit, Magnar, 197, 839, 916, 919
Kawashima, Robert S., 46, 919
Keefer, Arthur, 852, 919
Keil, C. F., xlix, 194, 209, 227, 257, 427–28, 435, 526, 554, 569, 576, 608, 738, 746, 784, 919

Kelly, Brian E., 770, 838, 919
Kelly, Joseph Ryan, l, 43, 376–77, 404, 406–7, 579, 919
Kent, Charles Foster, xlviii, 919
Kessler, Martin, 290, 919, 929
Kiel, Yehuda, xlviii–xlix, 9, 162, 185, 367, 401, 425, 430, 469, 919, 924
Kilchör, Benjamin, 112–15, 117, 918–19
Kim, Brittany, xix, xxxviii, 919
Kim, Daniel E., 174, 919
Kim, Hee Suk, 498, 919
Kingsmill, Edmée, l, 592–93, 919
Kirkpatrick, A. F., xlix, 486, 493–94, 496, 500, 511, 514, 534, 539, 541, 544, 547, 549, 919
Klein, Michael L., 466, 919
Klein, Ralph W., l, 637, 689, 691, 702, 714, 727, 735, 737, 739, 742–43, 745–46, 749, 766–68, 776, 783, 800, 814, 840, 846, 919, 931
Klingbeil, Gerald A., 658, 920
Knight, Douglas A., 18, 913, 920
Knoppers, Gary N., 73, 115, 148, 194, 201, 250, 638, 646, 658, 703, 706, 708, 713, 715, 724–28, 733, 735, 738, 740, 742, 744–46, 761, 763, 775, 783, 786, 793, 839–40, 842, 905, 907, 915–16, 920, 925, 929, 931
Koch, Klaus, 628–29, 637, 920, 924
Kohlenberger, John R., xlix, 534, 920
Kottsieper, Ingo, 689, 920
Kraft, Robert A., 890, 920
Kratz, Reinhard G., 113, 258, 913, 920, 933
Krause, Deborah, 853, 921
Kristeva, Julia, 895–96, 921
Krusche, Marcel, 499, 921
Krüger, Thomas, 598–99, 603, 921
Kselman, John S. xlix
Kugel, James L., xxxvii–xli, xlviii, 898, 916, 921
Kuhrt, Amélie, 278, 921
Kwon, Jiseong James, xlix, 560, 563, 921
Kynes, Will, xxix, xxxiv, xlix–l, 172, 551–58, 560, 564, 567, 572, 595, 598–99, 601, 905, 909, 911, 913, 915, 918, 921–23, 925, 928–29, 934–35

Lafferty, Theresa V., 397, 921
Lane, Nathan, II, 377, 406, 877, 921
Lang, David, xlviii, 921
Lange, Armin, 266, 912, 920–21, 927
Lasine, Stuart, 172, 921
Lasserre, Guy, xlviii, 49, 84, 121, 921
LeFebvre, Michael, 478, 637–38, 921
Lee, Suk Yee, xxiii, xlix, 456, 554, 574, 921
Lemke, Werner E., 699, 734–35, 737, 745, 765, 771, 780, 810, 921
Leonard, Jeffery M., 493–94, 505, 898, 921
Lester, G. Brooke, xxxiv, l, 619–21, 625–26, 628, 895, 907, 921, 934
Leuchter, Mark, 46, 263, 288–89, 825, 836, 922
Levenson, Jon Douglas, 544, 614, 910, 922
Levine, Amy Jill, xli, 482, 922
Levine, Baruch A., 41, 46, 121, 922
Levinson, Bernard M., xxxiv, 46, 48, 81, 116–19, 130, 289, 580, 596–98, 907, 915, 920, 922, 928
Levitt Kohn, Risa, xlviii, 315, 318, 320, 348, 357, 922
Licona, Michael R., 853, 922
Liebreich, Leon J., 538, 922
Lipschits, Oded, 682, 907, 912–13, 920, 922, 925
Llewelyn, Stephen, 350, 915
Longman, Tremper, III, 486, 549, 551, 554, 574, 704–5, 922
Lortie, Christopher R., 841, 922
Luckenbill, Daniel David, 922
Lundbom, Jack R., 264–65, 290, 922
Lunde, Jonathan, 900, 908, 922
Luz, Ulrich, 895, 922
Lynch, Matthew J., 255, 309, 496, 505, 552, 703, 739, 766, 922
Lyons, Michael A., xxix, xlviii, 244, 282, 315–16, 319–20, 329–30, 332, 335, 348–50, 355–56, 540, 900, 913, 923, 931

Mabie, Frederick J., 814, 818, 923
Maclear, G. F., 162–63, 923
Macy, Howard Ray, 311, 714–15, 717, 764, 832, 923
Madsen, Albert Alonzo, l, 843, 911
Mann, Thomas W., 62, 163, 923
Marcus, David, 374, 377, 380–81, 383, 605, 646, 923
Marlow, Hilary, 564, 923
Mason, Rex, xlix, 445, 456, 910–11, 923
Mattison, Kevin, 81, 112, 115, 118, 124, 923
Mays, James Luther, 412–13, 415, 417, 541, 545, 923
McCarter, P. Kyle, 178, 183, 709, 733, 744, 794, 923
McCarthy, Dennis J., 145, 189, 197, 505, 565, 923
McClellan, Daniel, 496, 923
McDonough, Sean M., 316, 906
McFadden, Kevin, 584, 656, 909
McKane, William, 270, 275, 297–98, 302, 304, 309, 829, 833, 923
McKenzie, Tracy, 353, 923
McKenzie, Steven L., 363, 365, 368, 698–99, 730, 737, 919, 922–23, 925, 928, 931
McLaughlin, John L., 224, 396, 923
Meek, Russell L., 602, 895–96, 923, 929, 931
Meltzer, Feiwel, xlviii–xlix, 367, 401, 425, 430, 469, 924
Melvin, David P., 620, 923
Mettinger, Tryggue N. D., 554, 923
Meyers, Carol, xlix, 441, 448, 456, 459, 924
Meyers, Eric, xlix, 441, 448, 456, 459, 924
Middlemas, Jill, 611, 924
Milgrom, Jacob, xxxiii, xlviii, 41, 46, 48, 53, 60, 65, 68–69, 72, 112, 121, 125, 136, 170, 174, 183, 208, 217, 243, 315, 332, 339–42, 345, 348, 391, 463, 487, 598, 659, 661, 664, 834, 924
Millar, William R., I, 912
Millard, Alan R., 143, 906, 909, 911, 917, 924
Miller, Cynthia L., 483, 924
Miller, Geoffrey D., xxxiv, 924
Miller, J. Maxwell, 169, 924
Miller, Patrick D., Jr., 491, 922, 924, 931
Miller-Naudé, Cynthia L., 265, 924
Mintz, Alan, 606, 924
Mirsky, Aaron, xlviii–xlix, 367, 401, 425, 430, 469, 924
Mitchell, Christine, 450, 455, 827, 830, 924
Mitchell, H. G., 450, 455, 827, 830, 924
Mollo, Paola, 184, 924
Montgomery, James A., 202, 924
Moo, Douglas J., 857, 861–63, 924
Morales, L. Michael, 10, 30, 237, 542, 924
Moran, W. L., 121, 328, 924
Morris, Leon, 171, 911
Morrow, William S., 18, 924
Mowinckel, Sigmund, 306, 924
Moyise, Steve, 220, 476, 848, 858, 924
Muraoka, T., 807, 924
Murawski, Bryan, l, 167, 529, 657, 691, 840, 924
Murphy, Roland E., l, 592–93, 925
Müller, Reinhard, 72, 291–93, 301, 924

Na'aman, Nadav, 49, 925

Naselli, Andrew David, 863, 924
Nelson, Richard, xlviii, 78, 92–93, 143, 925
Neusner, Jacob, 860, 925
Newman, Judith H., 216, 671–72, 896, 916, 925
Newsom, Carol A., 620, 925
Nicholson, E. W., 289, 656, 925
Nicol, George G., 629, 925
Niditch, Susan, 171–72, 925
Niehaus, Jeffrey, 113, 925
Nielsen, Kirsten, 739, 925
Nihan, Christophe, 121, 123, 249–50, 332, 335, 699, 729, 890, 925, 927
Nogalski, James, xlix, 370–71, 382, 392–93, 401–2, 925, 927
Noonan, Benjamin J., 136, 265, 587, 925
Noth, Martin, 189, 237, 925
Nurmela, Risto, xlix, 451, 456, 458, 925
Nysse, Richard, xlix, 425, 925

Oded, B., 435, 714, 808, 925
O'Dowd, Ryan P., 572, 925
Oeming, Manfred, 561, 704, 913, 925
Orian, Matan, 139, 582, 925
Oswald, Wolfgang, xlviii, 31, 925, 932
Oswalt, John N., 627, 926
Owen, H., xlviii, 926
Ozolins, Kaspars, 746, 926
O'Connell, Robert H., xlviii, 166, 172, 174, 925

Page, Sydney H. T., 749, 911, 926
Pakkala, Juha, 72, 291–93, 301, 637, 924, 926
Parke-Taylor, Geoffrey H., xlviii–xlix, 209, 271, 273, 293–94, 302, 304–6, 311, 400–2, 548, 574, 923, 926
Parker, Kim Ian, 712, 926
Pate, Brian, 476, 926
Patton, Corrine, 326, 926
Patton, Matthew H., 741, 926
Paul, Shalom M., xlix, 34, 126, 135, 138, 380, 387, 391–93, 395–96, 926
Perdue, Leo G., 565, 912, 926
Petersen, David L., 440, 926, 932
Peterson, Brian, 350, 747, 757, 926
Pfeiffer, Robert H., xlix, 561, 926
Philpot, Joshua M., 619, 926
Pitkänen, Pekka, 112–13, 193, 926
Pleins, J. David, xlviii, 84, 926
Polaski, Donald C., 227, 926
Postell, Seth D., 9, 68, 185, 452, 540, 926
Propp, William H. C., 23, 135, 317, 926
Purvis, James D., 832–33, 919
Pyeon, Yohan, xlix, 558, 561–62, 926

Quick, Laura, 575, 926

Raabe, Paul R., 234, 926
von Rad, Gerhard, xxxvii–xxxviii, xl–xli, xlviii, l, 87, 113, 116, 144, 194, 196, 209–10, 221, 270, 324, 567, 573, 637, 682–83, 704, 753, 783–84, 788–89, 837, 926, 928
Radner, Ephraim, 848, 864, 926
Rashi, 170, 184, 599
Rausche, Benedikt, 662, 927
Redditt, Paul L., xlix, 382, 449, 456, 925, 927, 929, 932
Regev, Eyal, 848, 927
Reif, Stefan C., 478, 927
Rendall, Robert, 895, 927
Rendtorff, Rolf, 258, 282, 284–85, 466, 498, 672, 772, 815, 843, 927
Renz, Thomas, 360, 927
Reymond, Eric D., 478, 927
Rezetko, Robert, 265–66, 918, 927, 935
Richards, Ruth, xlviii, 302, 927
Richter, Sandra L., 195–97, 927
Rindge, Matthew S., 619–20, 927
Robertson, O. Palmer, 422, 927
Robinson, Bernard P., 157, 927
Robson, James E., 92–93, 927
Romney, Bas ter Haar, 301, 924
Rooker, Mark F., xlviii, 265, 316, 329, 348, 367, 369, 927
Ross, Jillian L., xlviii, 174, 927
Ross, William A., 424, 927
Roth, Martha T., 18, 927
Rudolph, Wilhelm, 703, 800, 814, 927
Rydelnik, Michael A., 383, 927
Ryle, Herbert Edward, 646–49, 654, 671, 841, 927
Rüterswörden, Udo, 41, 121–22, 927

Sailhamer, John, 10, 923, 926–27, 934
Samely, Alexander, 889, 927
Sandy, D. Brent, 278, 906, 927
Sarna, Nahum M., xix, 23, 26, 246, 288, 412, 423, 482, 485, 496, 500, 895, 913, 927
Sasson, Jack M., 408, 928
Saur, Markus, 603, 928
Savran, George, 10–11, 928
Saysell, Csilla, 660, 928
Scalise, Pamela J., 289, 928
Schaper, Joachim, 249, 928
Scheetz, Jordan M., l, 622–23, 628, 928
Schellekens, Jona, l, 613, 615, 928
Schellenberg, Angeline Falk, 458, 928
Schellenberg, Annette, l, 592, 928
Schenker, Adrian, 48, 928
Schipper, Jeremy, 783, 912, 928–29
Schley, Donald D., Jr., 759, 928
Schlimm, Matthew Richard, 26, 928
Schmid, Konrad, 266, 287, 450, 917, 925, 927–28, 930
Schmitz, Philip C., 352, 626, 928
Schniedewind, William M., xxxiv, 265, 494, 646, 703, 705, 710, 737, 743, 764, 813, 820–21, 842, 920, 928
Schnittjer, Gary Edward, xlviii, l, 8–9, 27, 35, 40, 53, 63, 68, 78, 80, 89–92, 95, 121, 137–38, 158, 170, 177, 181–82, 219, 227, 236, 243, 255, 261, 279, 294, 306, 309, 324–25, 329, 333, 351, 446, 450, 452–53, 486, 489, 499, 501, 510, 512, 516, 518, 530, 584, 614, 622–23, 632, 656, 664–65, 682, 685, 687, 700, 713–14, 723, 754, 764, 798, 818, 835, 837, 839, 853–55, 866–67, 875, 880, 893–94, 897, 928
Schoors, Antoon, I, 601, 928
Schultz, Richard L., xxii, xxix–xxx, xlviii–xlix, 222, 245, 252–53, 257, 292, 336, 378, 380, 411, 417, 428, 469, 596–97, 601–2, 899, 906, 915, 928, 932
Seitz, Christopher R., 227, 848, 929
Selman, Martin J., 743, 929
Seufert, Matthew, 446, 929
Sharp, Carolyn J., 264, 424, 929
Shaver, Judson R., 634, 637, 907, 929
Shepherd, David J., 561, 656, 658, 668, 929
Shepherd, Michael B., xlviii, 172, 397, 672, 867, 899, 929
Shipp, R. Mark, 738, 929
Shipper, Bernd U., 569, 572, 574, 929
Sim, R. J., 324, 929
Simon, Uriel, xlix, 406–8, 911, 929
Siquans, Agnethe, 582, 929
Sjöberg, Matthew, 286–87, 450, 929
Skehan, Patrick W., 145, 929
Skelton, David A., 478, 929
Slotki, Judah J., l, 691, 929
Smelik, Klaas A. D., 106, 290, 929
Smith, Gary V., l, 691, 929
Smith, Mark S., 146, 323, 496, 910
Smith, Ralph L., 422, 929
Smith-Christopher, Daniel L., 655, 929
Smolar, Leivy, 202, 905
Sneed, Mark, 577, 930
Snell, Daniel C., l, 572, 576, 913, 930
Snodgrass, Klyne, 852, 917, 930
Sommer, Benjamin D., xxi, xlviii, l, 242, 249, 272, 287, 612, 900, 930
Sonsino, Rifat, 87–88, 930

Spawn, Kevin L., 634–36, 654, 711, 765, 827, 930
Spencer, F. Scott, 160, 807–8, 930
Sprinkle, Preston, 326, 930
Stackert, Jeffrey, 46, 52, 119, 132, 907, 922, 930
Stanley, Andy, 847–48, 930
Stead, M. R., xlix, 445, 451, 456–57, 459, 930
Steiner, Richard C., xxxii, 182, 818, 930
Steinmann, Andrew E., 387, 646–48, 665–66, 930
Sternberg, Meir, 19, 894, 930
Stokes, Ryan E., 749, 930
Stone, Timothy J., 590, 912, 930, 932
Strawn, Brent A., 848, 930–31
Strazicich, John, xlix, 379–80, 382, 930
Strine, C. A., 336, 378–79, 930
Strollo, Megan Fullerton, l, 593, 930
Sugimoto, Tomotoshi, 699, 717, 750, 776, 845, 930
Sumner, George, 848, 864, 926
Sumner, W. A., 169, 930
Sundberg, Albert C., 890, 930
Swale, Matthew E., 514, 930
Sweeney, Marvin A., 434, 925, 927, 930

Tadmor, Hayim, 204, 229, 794, 893, 910, 930–31
Taggar-Cohen, Ada, 863, 930
Talmon, Shemaryahu, 899, 924, 930
Talshir, Zipora, 201, 828–29, 831, 931
Tanner, Beth LaNeel, 474, 484, 542, 909, 912, 918–19, 921, 929, 931, 935
Tate, Marvin E., 540, 911
Terrien, Samuel, 396, 931
Theocharous, Myrto, 896, 931
Thompson, J. A., 302, 931
Throntveit, Mark A., 738, 845, 931
Tiffany, Frederick Clark, 87, 931
Tigay, Jeffrey H., xix, 6, 78, 113, 115, 122, 124, 127, 138, 140, 143–44, 151–52, 170, 224, 274, 317, 478, 480, 483, 543, 565, 606, 838, 894, 915, 931–32
Tigchelaar, Eibert, xlix, 456
Timmer, Daniel, 393, 429, 931
Todd, James M., III, 88, 931
Toews, Brian G., 552, 704, 931
Tooman, William A., xlviii, 336–37, 348, 352–53, 378, 906, 913, 917, 923, 925, 930–32
Tov, Emanuel, xlv, 197, 264, 266, 646, 863–64, 890, 931
Trimm, Charlie, xix, xxxviii, 239, 919, 932
Trotter, James M., 496, 932
Tsonis, Jack, 350, 915
Tucker, Gene M., 360, 369, 390, 932
Tuell, Steven S., 249, 354, 448, 932
Turner, Ian, 895, 915, 932
Turpie, David McCalman, l, 361, 932

Ulrich, Eugene C., 735, 918, 932

Van Leeuwen, Raymond C., 554, 574, 932
VanderKam, James C., 727, 861, 932
Vang, Carsten, xlviii, 359–60, 366–68, 932
Vannoy, J. Robert, 130, 496, 932
Venter, Pieter M., l, 579, 909
Verbrugge, Verlyn D., 861, 932
Vermes, Geza, 899, 914, 932
Vogt, Peter T., 113, 932
Vos, Geerhardus, xviii–xix, xlii, 849, 932
Vroom, Jonathan, 264–65, 932

Waltke, Bruce K., 890, 911, 932
Walton, J. Harvey, 105, 915, 932
Walton, John H., 30, 64, 105, 706, 915–16, 923, 932–33
Ward, W. H., xlix, 430, 929
Warhurst, Amber K., 299, 832, 836, 843, 932
Warren, Nathanael James, 341, 933
Wasserman, Nathan, 614, 933
Watts, James W., 291, 851, 907, 925, 933
Way, Kenneth C., 452, 933
Weinfeld, Moshe, xlviii, l, 30, 78, 93, 119, 124, 149, 178, 204, 206, 271, 281, 285, 302, 306, 478, 572, 596, 676, 705, 910–11, 917–18, 931, 933, 935
Welch, Adam C., 829, 933
Wellhausen, Julius, 112–13, 178, 637, 703, 726, 770, 837, 933
Wells, Bruce, 19, 35, 48, 81, 126, 133–34, 151, 933
Wellum, Stephen J., 688, 756, 913, 933
Wenham, Gordon J., 13, 46, 62, 155, 435, 722, 745, 927, 930, 933
Westbrook, Raymond, 126, 933
Westermann, Claus, 518, 933
Wevers, John William, 5, 23, 25, 63, 71, 78, 114, 145, 197, 336, 828, 932–33
Weyde, Karl William, xlix, 463, 469, 933
Widder, Wendy L., 619–20, 933
Wildberger, Hans, 221, 933
Willey, Patricia Tull, l, 612, 933
Willgren, David, 246, 257, 538, 933
Willi, Thomas, 229, 723, 777, 911, 934
Williams, Joshua, 229, 440, 580, 699, 934
Williamson, Hugh G. M., 229, 233–34, 634, 636–38, 642, 646–47, 650–51, 656, 668, 682–83, 698, 712, 717, 730, 744, 750, 757, 766, 771, 777, 785, 789, 808, 814, 829–30, 840, 844–45, 891, 918, 920, 928, 930, 932, 934
Willis, Amy C. Merrill, 620, 934
Willis, Timothy M., 743, 934
Wilson, Gerald Henry, 478, 538, 934
Wilson, Ian D., 737, 915, 920, 925, 934
Wilson, Robert R., 706, 723, 934
Witherington, Ben, III, xxi, 850, 902, 934
Witte, Markus, 564, 934
Wold, Benjamin, 482, 487, 741, 862, 896, 934
van Wolde, Ellen, 482, 487, 741, 896, 934
Wolff, Hans Walter, 360, 362–63, 367, 377, 379, 381–82, 384, 396, 934
Won, Young-Sam, 12, 509, 934
Wooden, R. Glenn, 657, 934
Woods, Edward J., 78, 934
Wray Beal, Lissa M., 164, 201, 908, 922, 926, 935
Wright, Christopher J. H., 49, 935
Wright, David P., 240
Wright, Jacob L., 247, 935
Wright, John W., 736, 774, 935
Würthwein, Ernst, 900, 935

Yamauchi, Edwin, 646, 935
Yates, Gary E., 276, 309, 935
Yoder, Christine Roy, 574, 577, 935
Yona, Shamir, 577, 935
Young, Ian, 265–66, 551, 918, 927, 935
Young, Theron, 539, 935
Yu, Charles, 554, 935

Zahn, Molly M., 596, 863, 899, 922, 935
Zakovitch, Yair, 10, 496, 935
Zalcman, Lawrence, 423, 935
Zehnder, Markus, 119, 315, 907, 919, 935
Zenger, Erich, 488, 492, 496, 498–99, 501, 503, 517, 520, 522–23, 525–26, 529, 533, 538, 543–44, 546, 917
Zevit, Ziony, xlvi, 216, 265, 906, 921, 924, 930, 935
Zimmerli, Walther, 319, 322, 325, 335, 337–38, 347, 350–52, 935
Zimran, Yisca, 792, 935